THE REAL PRICE OF
EVERYTHING

Rediscovering the Six Classics of Economics

THE REAL
PRICE OF
EVERYTHING

Rediscovering the Six Classics of Economics

EDITED WITH AN INTRODUCTION BY

MICHAEL LEWIS

STERLING

New York / London
www.sterlingpublishing.com

Library of Congress Cataloging-in-Publication Data Available

10 9 8 7 6 5 4 3 2 1

Published by Sterling Publishing Co., Inc.
387 Park Avenue South, New York, NY 10016
© 2007 by Michael Lewis
Distributed in Canada by Sterling Publishing
c/o Canadian Manda Group, 165 Dufferin Street
Toronto, Ontario, Canada M6K 3H6
Distributed in the United Kingdom by GMC Distribution Services
Castle Place, 166 High Street, Lewes, East Sussex, England BN7 1XU
Distributed in Australia by Capricorn Link (Australia) Pty. Ltd.
P.O. Box 704, Windsor, NSW 2756, Australia

Manufactured in the United States of America
All Rights Reserved

Sterling ISBN-13: 978-1-4027-4790-8
        ISBN-10: 1-4027-4790-X

For information about custom editions, special sales, premium and
corporate purchases, please contact Sterling Special Sales
Department at 800-805-5489 or specialsales@sterlingpublishing.com.

A Note on the Text

◆

Each text included in this book is reprinted in its entirety from an early
edition of the work, with the exception of Charles Mackay's *Memoirs of
Extraordinary Popular Delusions and the Madness of Crowds,* which is
represented by the three chapters most frequently cited by economists. In order
to ease readers' comprehension of these texts, we have updated spellings and
punctuation in most cases to make them consistent with modern American style. However, we
have not incorporated corrections and updates made to later
editions of the work except where noted.
The editors would like to thank Michael Regan and Rob McMahon for their
editorial assistance and Monica Gurevich for creating the interior design concept.

The Editors

TABLE OF CONTENTS

An Introduction by Michael Lewis

IN PRAISE OF DEAD ECONOMISTS

I should preface this introduction with an apology to its subjects. I graduated from college with just two classes in economics, and the first, beginners' macroeconomics, was such a snore that I almost didn't return for the second. But my senior year, while completely absorbed in what I took to be a more worthy course of study (art history), I discovered that, to graduate, I needed to fulfill a distribution requirement. The handiest solution was beginners' microeconomics. I enrolled pass/fail, found a seat in the back row, and yanked a baseball cap down over my eyes, prepared both for torpor and a gentleman's *D*. Economics, I was now convinced, was less a course of study than a conspiracy of the old to drain the life from the young. Macroeconomics, so far as I could tell, had sought to explain the gross national product without so much as a peep about the actual human beings who created it. No nineteen-year-old in his right mind could be interested in the gross national product, but the economics department teemed with young droids who thought that they needed to be there to get a job on Wall Street. Princeton had no business school, and the economics department had been turned into a weak substitute, a signaling device used by Wall Street employers to identify the teenagers willing to sacrifice their college educations for the sake of their investment banking careers. The whole enterprise struck me as more than a little creepy.

And so the microeconomics professor—a dry wit named Uwe Reinhardt—came as a shock. He analyzed just about everything human beings did, and he seemed to me to be basically right about everything. He explained why drug dealing was so profitable (barriers to entry created by the law) and why lawyers were overpaid (barriers to entry created by lawyers). He explained one way in which a potato differed from a steak that had never occurred to me (as their income increased, people consumed fewer, not more, potatoes) and why authors were forever falling out with their publishers. (Their interests aren't properly aligned: Publishers seek to maximize the profits from a book; authors, because they are usually paid a percentage of the gross, seek to maximize revenues.) Some of this I'm making up; the class met twenty-five years ago, and I no longer remember all the details. But I recall feeling a jolt as clearly as if it happened yesterday, the horror that such a powerful tool existed for analyzing human behavior, and exposing the hidden connections between things. I remember thinking, "If I don't find out more about this stuff, I'm doomed. Everyone but me will understand why I do what I do."

A year later, I enrolled in a master's program in economics at the London School of Economics designed for people innocent of any actual knowledge of economics. It was there, in the open stacks of the Lionel Robbins Library, that I first read most of the contents of this book. What I liked about these books is what I liked about Uwe Reindhart's course: They handed you a peculiar new lens through which to view the world. This anthology is called Value, and it has a lot to say on that subject, but its real subject is man's rare, original attempts to understand himself and his affairs. These writers aren't always right—in many places they disagree with each other—but even when they're wrong, they're interesting. Even the most spectacularly wrong of them—Malthus's argument that, because human beings reproduced faster than their means of subsistence, they faced imminent mass starvation—has exerted a spectacular influence on human thought. "I happened to read for my amusement 'Malthus on Population,'" wrote Charles Darwin, in the passage of his autobiography devoted to the origin of The Origin of Species, "and being well prepared to appreciate the struggle for existence which everywhere goes on . . . it once struck me that under these circumstances favorable variations would tend to be preserved and unfavorable ones to be destroyed. The results of this would be the formation of a new species. Here then I had at last got a theory by which to work."

John Maynard Keynes famously once said that even the most practical men lived their lives unaware they were in the thrall of the ideas of some dead economist. Here are those dead economists.

Reading these books chronologically, beginning with Adam Smith, you see how the earlier ones led to the later ones, how many of them seem to be part of the same great intellectual construction project. Or, rather, they are like a group of Russian dolls, each competing to be the big one that contains all the others. Twenty-two years after Smith published *The Wealth of Nations*, Thomas Malthus, the Eeyore of economics, sat down to explain why humanity was doomed. However, before he could lay out his argument, he needed to acknowledge that "the most important argument that I shall adduce is certainly not new. The principles on which it depends have been explained by . . . Dr. Adam Smith." The next year, 1799, a stock market mogul named David Ricardo picked up a copy of *The Wealth of Nations* and was himself provoked to think systematically about economic problems. His *Principles of Political Economy and Taxation*, published in 1817, opens by trying to define "value," which could only be done by first mentioning Adam Smith's famous distinction, between "value in use" and "value in exchange." More than a century later another stock market speculator, John Maynard Keynes, wrote *The General Theory of Employment, Interest and Money*. In it he traced the history of the idea at its center: that saving does not necessarily lead to productive investment, and so, with resources idle, government intervention might be required to maintain full employment. The first echoes of his grand theory, Keynes writes, were to be found in letters written from Thomas Malthus to David Ricardo, and in Malthus's dilations on Adam Smith. ("Adam Smith has stated," wrote Malthus, "that capitals are increased by parsimony, that every frugal man is a public benefactor, and that the increase of wealth depends upon the balance of produce above consumption. . . . That these propositions are true to a great extent is perfectly unquestionable . . . but it is quite obvious that they are not true to an indefinite extent.") "Ricardo, however, was stone deaf to what Malthus was saying," writes Keynes, as if, had Ricardo only viewed thrift with greater misgiving, Keynes wouldn't have had to work so hard to change men's minds about the inner workings of their economies. While laying the foundation, Ricardo could have sealed the crack before the castle went up.

The first thing you notice when you read these books in a gulp—or, at any rate, the first thing I noticed—is their distinctly mixed feelings toward market forces. If you are setting out to write a book that will one day be regarded as a classic work of economics, it apparently is no handicap to view markets with suspicion. Only one of these writers, David Ricardo, tends to the cloudless view that markets left to themselves lead to optimum outcomes. Four of them—Malthus, Mackay, Veblen, and Keynes—see the world through darker lenses. Malthus and Keynes explicitly set out to inform us of the urgent need to shape market forces; Mackay and Veblen seem willing to accept market insanities without feeling the need to do much more than describe them for our pleasure and edification. The most interesting case of all is Adam Smith, who probably did more than any human being for the cause of free markets, and who is, of course, identified as the founding father of classical economists. But Smith was even more than that.

One measure of the power of *The Wealth of Nations* is how much of it has become cliché, and perhaps its greatest cliché is that human beings are driven chiefly by their self-interest. "It is not of the benevolence of the butcher, the brewer, or the baker that we can expect our dinner, but from their regard to their own interest," Smith writes in one of his most cited passages. Human beings, Smith says, possess a unique ability to "truck, barter, and exchange one thing for another. . . . Nobody ever saw a dog make a fair and deliberate exchange of one bone for another with another dog." From these inherently human traits were born markets, in which people seek the highest rate of return on their resources. Markets give us the farmer growing wheat who sees a boom in the price of corn and who responds, to the benefit of all, by growing corn instead of wheat—until the price of corn falls to the point that its rate of return equals the return on wheat. Markets give us the division of labor, an almost magical source of wealth. A man who sets out by himself to make pins would be lucky to make one pin a day. Ten men who divide the pin-making trade into a series of more specialized acts can make forty-eight thousand pins a day.

All this is to be celebrated, of course. At first blush, Smith's classic is a simple paean to the benefits of commerce: between neighbors, between town and country, between nations. The Adam Smith of the early chapters of *The Wealth of Nations* appears to believe that anything that interferes with this commerce—taxes, subsidies—does more harm than good. For instance, Smith writes, there is no more useful occupation than teaching, and so in the natural order of things a great teacher would be very highly paid. "But," he writes, "the usual reward of the eminent teacher bears no proportion to that of the lawyer or physician, because the trade of the one is crowded with indigent people, who have been brought up to it at public expense; whereas those of the other two are encumbered with very few who have not been educated at their own." In paying to train teachers, the government has screwed up the market of teachers, and discouraged the most able men from performing this most valuable service.

But there is another Adam Smith who believes that self-interest is not the sole basis of human behavior, and who leans toward the need for some visible hand to take hold of the market and improve it. This is the Adam Smith who wrote in *The Theory of Moral Sentiments* of the importance of man's natural sympathy for his fellow man to regulate his selfish instincts. This Adam Smith gets less attention than the other mainly, I think, because people see in Adam Smith what they want to, but also because *The Wealth of Nations* is a very long book that most readers put down after they get what they take to be the general idea of it. The passage about the pin factory comes on page 2 of the original text, which helps to account for its fame. Somewhere around page 826 of that edition, Smith offers up a gloomier view of his pin factory, as a soul-destroying enterprise calling for government interference. "The man whose whole life is spent in performing a few simple operations," he writes, " . . . generally becomes as stupid and ignorant as it is possible for a human creature to become. The torpor of his mind renders him not only incapable of relishing or bearing a part in any rational conversation, but of conceiving any generous, noble, or tender sentiment, and consequently of forming any just judgment concerning many even of the ordinary duties of private life." And off he goes, listing the many debasements inflicted upon the soul of the ordinary worker by an efficient market economy, until he concludes that "in every improved and civilized society, this is the state into which . . . the great body of the people must necessarily fall, *unless government takes some pains to prevent it.*"

Economics, as I was eventually taught it, has no serious place for such value judgments. Economics is a science whose job it is to generate falsifiable propositions. But this isn't Adam Smith's economics; there are a great many *shoulds* in Adam Smith, and most of them concern the need to stop people from doing what they are inclined to do. The government should do something to offset the demoralizing effects of market forces; young men shouldn't be allowed to travel abroad; the rich should pay more than the poor in taxes; princes shouldn't engage in business, as they're inept at it; and on and on.

The second thing that struck me while reading these classics all at once was the rift in economics that I sensed as a college student. There are economists with a gift for observing and describing human beings, and economists with a talent for erecting systems of thought, independent of any feel for the way actual human beings behave—and both types of economists are capable of writing works now regarded as classics.

Another way to put this is that some of these writers seem to me to have greater literary powers than others. Ricardo and especially Malthus might as well be writing about Martians, and one has the sense that they might have preferred not to be writing at all, but adding, dividing, and multiplying. A typical Mathusian sentence, and sentiment: "The passion between the sexes has appeared in every age to be so nearly the same that it may always be considered, in algebraic language, as a given quantity." (Here it might be worth noting that all but one of our dead economists led unconventional romantic lives. Smith never married and lived with his mother. Ricardo eloped. Veblen preferred other professors' wives to his own. Keynes swung for the fences, from both sides of the plate. Only Malthus bothered to stay married to one woman and breed hopefully, as if the food would never run out.) On the other hand, Smith, Mackay, Veblen, and Keynes each had in him a gift for social observation that would be the envy of the modern magazine journalist. Here's Smith on what now are referred to as status goods:

> A linen shirt, for example, is, strictly speaking not a necessary of life. The Greeks and Romans lived, I suppose, very comfortably, though they had no linen. But in the present times, through the greater part of Europe, a creditable day-laborer would be ashamed to appear in public without a linen shirt, the want of which would be supposed to denote that disgraceful degree of poverty . . . .Custom, in the same manner, has rendered leather shoes a necessary of life in England. The poorest creditable person, of either sex, would be ashamed to appear in public without them. . . . In France, they are necessaries neither to men nor to women; the lowest rank of both sexes appearing there publicly, without any discredit, sometimes in wooden shoes, and sometimes barefooted.

Any commodity that is socially embarrassing to lack, Smith goes on to say, must be treated as a necessity. Everything else, for purposes of taxation, should be viewed as a luxury. And so, the economist who wishes to make the distinction must have a sixth sense for status, and for shame. Which is to say he's got to be more than just an economist.

Which brings us, in a funny way, to Thorstein Veblen—and his natural companion, Charles Mackay. In his discussion of value, Adam Smith introduced the diamond-water paradox: Why is water, necessary for man's survival, so cheap, while diamonds, trivial to man's survival, so dear? (Smith wrote before Perrier.) Because diamonds were scarce while water was plentiful, Smith explained, and left it at that, without pausing to examine the root causes of man's lust for diamonds. Veblen takes up this lust as his principal subject. *The Theory of the Leisure Class* was written in 1909, but its author might as well have just emerged from a Vanity Fair Oscar party. The book shares this with *The Wealth of Nations*: So much of it has become cliché that it's sometimes hard to see just how fresh and original it was at the time.

Adam Smith's economic theories began with an assertion about the primacy of self-interest as a motive. Veblen's contribution was to show just how perverse man's self-interest could be. He was perhaps the first, and finest, connoisseur of the nouveau riche. The key to their behavior for Veblen—indeed, the key to all human behavior in an affluent, peaceful society—was their headlong pursuit of status. "With the exception of the instinct of self-preservation," Veblen writes, "the propensity for emulation is probably the strongest and most alert and persistent of the economic motives proper. . . . The law of status is the dominant feature in the scheme of life." That is, the point of all we do—what we buy, how we work, whom we employ, how we mate, etc.—is to impress others. And in our mad rush to impress each other, we have rendered our economy essentially preposterous. Our need for display, for instance, has reached the point where "any consumer who might, Diogenes-like, insist on the elimination of all honorific or wasteful elements from his consumption, would be unable to supply his most trivial wants in the modern market." "Our dress," writes Veblen, to pull from his rack one of hundreds of similar examples, " . . . in order to serve its purpose effectually, should not only be expensive, but it should also make plain to all observers that the wearer is not engaged in any kind of productive labor."

Veblen's comic genius was to connect up our unprecedentedly wealthy and putatively civilized society with our barbaric past. In the blink of Veblen's eye, the hairy guy with the club who dragged women by the hair back to his cave becomes a hedge-fund tycoon at a raw bar. Think the trophy wife was an American creation of the 1980s? Turn to Veblen and find this: "The original reason for the seizure and appropriation of women seems to have been their usefulness as trophies." Wonder why it is that the clerk who pilfers a few hundred dollars from the till gets jail time, while the CEO who robs the company of millions remains at large? Here's Veblen: "In offenses which result in a large accession of property to the offender he does not ordinarily incur the extreme penalty or the extreme obloquy with which his offense would be visited on the ground of the naive moral code alone. The thief or swindler who has gained great wealth by his delinquency has a better chance than the small thief of escaping the rigorous penalty of the law." Want to know why spectator sports are the one reliable mechanism for turning human beings of every race and class into fanatics? Read Veblen:

> Addiction to athletic sports, not only in the way of direct participation, but also in the way of sentiment and moral support, is, in a more or less pronounced degree, a characteristic of the leisure class; and it is a trait which that class shares with the lower-class delinquents, and with such atavistic elements throughout the body of the community as are endowed with a dominant predaceous trend. Few individuals among the populations of Western civilized countries are so far devoid of the predaceous instinct as to find no diversion in contemplating athletic sports and games. . . .

Note that Veblen rarely bothers to argue his case; he's got much to observe, but nothing to prove. Every now and again he uses one of his startling observations to make some larger, seemingly logical point. For instance, having established man's need to consume conspicuously, he goes on to suggest that Malthus was wrong because people will not bring children into the world unless they can make them objects of conspicuous display. "The conspicuous consumption, and the consequent increased expense, required in the reputable maintenance of a child is very considerable and acts as a powerful deterrent," he writes. Long before the future runs out of food, it'll run out of American Girl dolls and Michael Jordan sneakers—and who among us can stand the social embarrassment of his child walking around in public so obviously deprived? However, this dead economist writes not to persuade you, but to inform you of his truth. What Freud was to the human brain, Veblen was to the marketplace: a writer of such originality and power that he has persuaded a lot of people that he must have been some kind of scientist. As with Freud and Malthus, Veblen has a phony rigor about him, yet in Veblen's hands the rigor doubles as wit. Here he is on why things once fashionable now seem absurd: "The process of developing an aesthetic nausea takes more or less time; the length of time required in any given case being inversely as the degree of intrinsic odiousness of the style in question."

"*The style in question.*" It's very much in play in these classics of economics thought. If these authors have endured, it is not because their arguments still strike us as fresh, but because their voices still strike us, in some sense, as original. Mathematics has long since become the lingua franca of economics, and symbols have replaced words. Economics has distanced itself from matters of style; economics has become weirdly detached from economists. If flair somehow creeps into a work of economics, that work is viewed with suspicion. Readers of this anthology will see that economics wasn't always this way. One of the pleasures of this anthology is the chance it gives readers to inhabit the mind of a first-rate economist, back when first-rate economists felt compelled to make their arguments in words. With words comes style. And it's a measure of how low the level of intrinsic odiousness in their styles was that to this day you can approach these books without the slightest fear of aesthetic illness.

Adam Smith (1723–1790)

AN INTRODUCTION TO HIS LIFE AND WORK

The front cover of *Time* magazine ranks as some of the most exclusive real estate in all media, a parcel well beyond the reach of most philosophers. Indeed, moral philosopher Adam Smith remains one of the few in his profession to be honored with a cover story by the popular and influential magazine. Smith also stands as the only one to pull off this feat almost two hundred years after the appearance of his most important work, *An Inquiry into the Nature and Causes of the Wealth of Nations,* the 1776 book often credited with launching free market capitalism, the Industrial Revolution, and over two centuries of unprecedented economic growth.

This 1975 media placement miracle proved the enduring vitality and immediacy of Smith's ideas and observations, even as the *Time* story's headline wondered, "Can Capitalism Survive?" The resounding "Yes" sounded by the decades that followed, with capitalism's emphatic triumph over inflation, stagnation, and communism, offered an even more impressive endorsement of the modest Scottish professor's world-conquering worldview. Still, the reasoning, rhetoric, and methods employed to gain that triumphant "Yes," raises another important question about the world's most influential economic thinker: Why do so few people read Adam Smith?

While the past three decades have inspired a new flock of free market missionaries to spread Smith's philosophy around the globe, they also proved that the vast majority of Smith's disciples seem only partially aware of his actual writings. The most vehement among them sometimes even cite Smith to denounce ideas and solutions that Smith himself advocated—solutions to problems that may in the not-so-distant future spark another deep crisis that will leave us wondering, "Can Capitalism Survive?"

Now, at the peak of his influence and popularity, Adam Smith cries out for a revival.

HIS LIFE

Adam Smith was born in Kirkcaldy, Scotland. His exact date of birth is unknown, but he was baptized on June 5, 1723, six months after the death of his father, who was controller of customs at Kirkcaldy. At the age of four, Smith was kidnapped by a band of gypsies, but was soon rescued by his uncle and returned to his mother unharmed.

Smith enrolled in the University of Glasgow at the age of fourteen, studying moral philosophy under the famous scholar Francis Hutcheson. Three years later, Smith entered Balliol College at Oxford, where he developed an extensive background in European literature. Smith left the college in 1746 as a vocal critic of Oxford's tenure process and its professors, who, he complained, had "given up altogether even the pretense of teaching."

Smith returned to Scotland and was sponsored by Lord Henry Kames to give public lectures in Edinburgh, where he expounded on topics such as "the progress of opulence" and "the obvious and simple system of natural liberty." In 1750, he met the influential Scottish philosopher David Hume, and they struck up a close friendship that would last until Hume's death in 1776. Glasgow University appointed Smith to its chair of logic in 1751, and to its chair of moral philosophy a year later (a position that was once occupied by Smith's teacher, Francis Hutcheson).

In 1759, Smith published *The Theory of Moral Sentiments,* a work inspired by his Glasgow lectures. This book, which helped establish Smith's reputation, outlined his theories on morality and its relation to feelings of sympathy. Smith left academia in 1764 to become the personal tutor to the Duke of Buccleuch, whose stepfather had been introduced to Smith by Hume. Smith and the young duke traveled extensively in France and Switzerland, where Smith was introduced to leading intellectuals, such as François Quesnay, Jean-Jacques Rousseau, Turgot, and Voltaire. Smith retired from his post as tutor to the duke with a lifetime pension and returned to Kirkcaldy to write *The Wealth of Nations,* which was published in 1776. The work was extremely well-received and made Smith famous.

Two years later, Smith was appointed as commissioner of customs in Scotland. He moved to Edinburgh to live with his mother and died there on July 17, 1790, after a bout with an unspecified illness. He had little in the way of money or material goods when he died, having apparently given away most of it in secret acts of charity.

AN OVERVIEW OF THE WORK

Most editions abridge large swaths of Adam Smith's *Wealth of Nations.* Even the book's popular title represents only a quarter of its real title, *An Inquiry into the Nature and Causes of the Wealth of Nations.* Such streamlining and efficiency can lead to greater profits for a business competing in the free market. But it inevitably misleads readers into a far less rewarding and informative experience with the book often credited with establishing free market capitalism.

Readers, of course, often find themselves urged to tackle full editions, particularly in introductions to unabridged editions of classic works such as this. But with Smith, the cajoling seems particularly apt, even vital. In *The Wealth of Nations,* Smith works diligently to present not just his ideas, but the conditions from which they emerged and the alternatives they trumped. Throughout the text, he goes to great lengths to cite processes, evidence, and real-world experiences. Extracted from those contexts, his words and ideas can become unhinged from their intentions, easily misinterpreted and then used and abused to justify competing positions.

Readers who have mastered Smith's full text will be rewarded not only with a full and accurate understanding of the theoretical foundation of modern economics and capitalism, but with an instinct for how Smith's ideas apply or can be adjusted to apply in the contemporary world. They may also gain an interesting new hobby: marveling at the parade of op-eds, political rhetoric, and economic scholarship that distort and misapply portions of Smith's work and ideas to justify arguments that Smith would have damned as foolish and dangerous.

As its complete title suggests, Adam Smith's *Inquiry into the Nature and Causes of the Wealth of Nations* offers an analytical tour of existing economic models, along with the ideas and forces that shaped them. As Machiavelli had done with political systems in his *Discourses,* Smith surveyed and rated the merits of the world's economies on how well they served the people who toiled within them. Like the infamous Italian political philosopher, Smith performed his merciless analysis to further a philanthropic and often-overlooked agenda.

Though Smith's critics often accuse him of an amoral and ruthlessly materialistic outlook, they seem even less familiar with his work than some of his misinformed disciples. Smith was no materialist, Gekkoian "greed is good" ranter, or even economist, as the field of study did not even exist during his lifetime. Adam Smith was first, foremost, and to the last a moral philosopher.

Wealth was not an end that justified any means for Smith, but a means toward a brighter future for all humanity. Smith regarded prosperity as a path to greater freedom, expression, morality, and happiness for all members of a society. After years of research and thought—and after experiencing a catastrophic decline, then revival of the Scottish economy—Smith concluded that free trade was the most just and direct route to that egalitarian brand of prosperity. He fervently believed that once adopted, free-trade policies would enrich and bind all of a nation's citizens, and ultimately extend those benefits and ties to all the peoples of all the nations of the world who also practiced free trade. Smith's words usually emerge in internal debates about an individual country's trade policies. But the *s* at the end of "Nations" in Smith's book title remains one of the most important and the most overlooked letters in his entire volume. His vision and benign intentions were global.

Smith was no utopian dreamer or idealistic madman, however. Like Machiavelli, Smith remained a dedicated pragmatist who recognized that people would never link arms and climb together to the proverbial city on the hill, goosed on by sermons or legislation or philosophy. Smith understood that people almost always act out of self-interest, and that this motivation must be harnessed to pull humanity to higher material and moral elevations. The recognition of this harmonious contradiction between self-interest and universal welfare represented the core of Smith's genius, and explains the astounding and continuing success his ideas have enjoyed in real-life applications. It also ranked as perhaps his greatest obstacle in conveying his insights.

THE STYLE OF HIS SUBSTANCE

Though composed for the average reader of the eighteenth century, Adam Smith's *Wealth of Nations* remains a challenge for the average twenty-first-century reader and even for some contemporary scholars. The Scotsman's roundabout sentence and paragraph structures can often seem like maddening detours from relevance. Oftentimes, his major points fail to appear in the sections of the book in which one would expect them to dominate, and instead pop up in faraway chapters surrounded by seemingly unrelated material. But considering that Smith's theories revolve around an apparent paradox—that the general welfare can only be furthered by individuals working to further their own self-interest—his stylistic double helixes seem appropriate, and perhaps even necessary to take readers through the full process and scope of his insights.

Those who persevere through the early pages of *The Wealth of Nations* should become acclimated to Smith's style and learn how to giant slalom along his looping syntaxes. They will also find numerous rewards. An often-playful writer and thinker, Smith delights in unique turns of phrases and a chiding, sophisticated wit.

Readers will also be heartened by certain signposts along the way—familiar terms and concepts and modes of analysis such as free trade, supply and demand, and division of labor that Smith cemented into the foundation of economic thinking, and which remain in place to this day.

SMITH'S INFLUENCE TODAY, YESTERDAY, AND TOMORROW

During Adam Smith's lifetime, the economies of Europe were, for the most part, organized for the benefit of a small number of people to the detriment of the many. Feudal lords whose realms had been established in the Dark Ages still owned much of the land. By the eighteenth century, their power and prestige were challenged and even overshadowed by an early breed of capitalists known as "mercantilists" or "merchant capitalists." But the mercantilists' own elitist, protectionist beliefs and policies proved almost as restrictive as those of the aristocratic class who oversaw feudalism.

The mercantilists emerged in the age of exploration with the opening of overseas trade routes and colonies in Asia, Africa, Australia, and the Americas. With new products and resources flooding into Europe and new markets for European products opening abroad, the merchant class of traders and guildsmen rapidly grew in number, in wealth, and in their ability to influence their nations' economic policies.

The mercantilists believed that the wealth of a nation could only grow along with its trade surplus. They successfully lobbied for policies and regulations to restrict imports, aggressively promote exports, protect leading domestic industries, and apply military force to exert control over foreign markets and vital resources that were scarce back home.

Mercantilist policies seemed logical at the time—and still do to many people. It took an astonishing, quantum intellectual leap by Adam Smith to recognize how the mercantilists were actually retarding their country's economic and cultural potential, along with those of the rest of the world. He realized that a nation, unlike a merchant, needed to focus on the gross instead of the net result of its economic activity. Smith understood that by lifting its trade restrictions and tariffs, a nation could greatly expand its economy, along with the wealth, freedom, buying power, and opportunity for self-expression enjoyed by its entire population.

It was not mere conjecture. Smith had firsthand experience on both sides of the free-trade issue. During his young adulthood, his native Scotland emerged from a long, and often catastrophic, period of economic stagnation after England lifted some trading restrictions on its neighbor to the north. The country's economy, culture, academia, and mood quickly revived into the Scottish Enlightenment (1760–1800).

Nations across Europe enjoyed a similar economic and cultural blossoming as Smith's ideas were embraced and instituted in the decades following the publication of *The Wealth of Nations*. His concepts on the division of labor also helped inspire the economic sonic booms caused by the industrial revolutions in Europe and America. His ideas on trade, regulation, and monetary policies were revived in the 1980s to help reawaken the economies of the United States and other industrial powers.

Smith also anticipated many of the problems that would result from the implementation of free-market ideas. He realized that division of labor could lead to an uneducated, underage, and dispirited workforce and advocated that governments establish public schools in every community as a preventative. Smith foresaw how his policies could tempt powerful countries to colonize and exploit weaker countries for their raw materials and labor. He advised that such efforts would not be worth the trouble, a lesson nations continue to learn from terrible experience to this day. Smith recognized the temptation for the successful to horde their money, so he lobbied for them to invest it back into productive capacities that would create more jobs and more wealth for themselves and for others. He knew all too well how the rich and powerful in his new economy could conspire themselves into monopolies and political blocs that would mimic the devastating mercantilist antics of his day. Smith railed against such practices longer and harder than he did against any other. Indeed, the very essence of Smith's philosophy and writings deplore the greed, elitism, materialism, and excesses that his critics attribute to him and that his so-called disciples use to justify their vices and confusions.

The decline in public education. An increase in monopolistic practices by large corporations. A decrease in worker wages, job security, and sense of engagement. The widening gap between the rich and poor. Upper managers hoarding profits instead of reinvesting them back into the productive capacities of the companies they lead. Wars over diminishing natural resources. Such problems present a stern challenge to the future of free market economies and humankind. The best place to find effective remedies for them may well be found in the place so few people bother to look: the complete text of Adam Smith's *Wealth of Nations*.

AN INQUIRY INTO THE NATURE AND CAUSES OF THE WEALTH OF NATIONS

BY ADAM SMITH

INTRODUCTION AND PLAN OF THE WORK

The annual labor of every nation is the fund which originally supplies it with all the necessaries and conveniences of life which it annually consumes, and which consist always either in the immediate produce of that labor, or in what is purchased with that produce from other nations.

According, therefore, as this produce, or what is purchased with it, bears a greater or smaller proportion to the number of those who are to consume it, the nation will be better or worse supplied with all the necessaries and conveniences for which it has occasion.

But this proportion must in every nation be regulated by two different circumstances: first, by the skill, dexterity, and judgment with which its labor is generally applied; and, secondly, by the proportion between the number of those who are employed in useful labor, and that of those who are not so employed. Whatever be the soil, climate, or extent of territory of any particular nation, the abundance or scantiness of its annual supply must, in that particular situation, depend upon those two circumstances.

The abundance or scantiness of this supply, too, seems to depend more upon the former of those two circumstances than upon the latter. Among the savage nations of hunters and fishers, every individual who is able to work is more or less employed in useful labor, and endeavors to provide, as well as he can, the necessaries and conveniences of life, for himself, and such of his family or tribe as are either too old, or too young, or too infirm, to go a-hunting and fishing. Such nations, however, are so miserably poor, that, from mere want, they are frequently reduced, or at least think themselves reduced, to the necessity sometimes of directly destroying, and sometimes of abandoning their infants, their old people, and those afflicted with lingering diseases, to perish with hunger, or to be devoured by wild beasts. Among civilized and thriving nations, on the contrary, though a great number of people do not labor at all, many of whom consume the produce of ten times, frequently of a hundred times, more labor than the greater part of those who work; yet the produce of the whole labor of the society is so great, that all are often abundantly supplied; and a workman, even of the lowest and poorest order, if he is frugal and industrious, may enjoy a greater share of the necessaries and conveniences of life than it is possible for any savage to acquire.

The causes of this improvement in the productive powers of labor, and the order according to which its produce is naturally distributed among the different ranks and conditions of men in the society, make the subject of the first book of this Inquiry.

Whatever be the actual state of the skill, dexterity, and judgment, with which labor is applied in any nation, the abundance or scantiness of its annual supply must depend, during the continuance of that state, upon the proportion between the number of those who are annually employed in useful labor, and that of those who are not so employed. The number of useful and productive laborers, it will hereafter appear, is everywhere in proportion to the quantity of capital stock which is employed in setting them to work, and to the particular way in which it is so employed. The second book, therefore, treats of the nature of capital stock, of the manner in which it is gradually accumulated, and of the different quantities of labor which it puts into motion, according to the different ways in which it is employed.

Nations tolerably well advanced as to skill, dexterity, and judgment, in the application of labor, have followed very different plans in the general conduct or direction of it; and those plans have not all been equally favorable to the greatness of its produce. The policy of some nations has given extraordinary encouragement to the industry of the country; that of others to the industry of towns. Scarce any nation has dealt equally and impartially with every sort of industry. Since the down-fall of the Roman empire, the policy of Europe has been more favorable to arts, manufactures, and commerce, the industry of towns, than to agriculture, the Industry of the country. The circumstances which seem to have introduced and established this policy are explained in the third book.

Though those different plans were, perhaps, first introduced by the private interests and prejudices of particular orders of men, without any regard to, or foresight of, their consequences upon the general welfare of the society; yet they have given occasion to very different theories of political economy; of which some magnify the importance of that industry which is carried on in towns, others of that which is carried on in the country. Those theories have had a considerable influence, not only upon the opinions of men of learning, but upon the public conduct of princes and sovereign states. I have endeavored, in the fourth book, to explain as fully and distinctly as I can those different theories, and the principal effects which they have produced in different ages and nations.

To explain in what has consisted the revenue of the great body of the people, or what has been the nature of those funds, which, in different ages and nations, have supplied their annual consumption, is the object of these four first books. The fifth and last book treats of the revenue of the sovereign, or commonwealth. In this book I have endeavored to show, first, what are the necessary expenses of the sovereign, or commonwealth; which of those expenses ought to be defrayed by the general contribution of the whole society, and which of them, by that of some particular part only, or of some particular members of it: secondly, what are the different methods in which the whole society may be made to contribute towards defraying the expenses incumbent on the whole society, and what are the principal advantages and inconveniences of each of those methods; and, thirdly and lastly, what are the reasons and causes which have induced almost all modern governments to mortgage some part of this revenue, or to contract debts; and what have been the effects of those debts upon the real wealth, the annual produce of the land and labor of the society.

Book I

OF THE CAUSES OF IMPROVEMENT IN THE PRODUCTIVE POWERS OF LABOR, AND OF THE ORDER ACCORDING TO WHICH ITS PRODUCE IS NATURALLY DISTRIBUTED AMONG THE DIFFERENT RANKS OF THE PEOPLE

CHAPTER I

Of the Division of Labor

The greatest improvements in the productive powers of labor, and the greater part of the skill, dexterity, and judgment, with which it is anywhere directed, or applied, seem to have been the effects of the division of labor. The effects of the division of labor, in the general business of society, will be more easily understood, by considering in what manner it operates in some particular manufactures. It is commonly supposed to be carried furthest in some very trifling ones; not perhaps that it really is carried further in them than in others of more importance: but in those trifling manufactures which are destined to supply the small wants of but a small number of people, the whole number of workmen must necessarily be small; and those employed in every different branch of the work can often be collected into the same workhouse, and placed at once under the view of the spectator.

In those great manufactures, on the contrary, which are destined to supply the great wants of the great body of the people, every different branch of the work employs so great a number of workmen, that it is impossible to collect them all into the same workhouse. We can seldom see more, at one time, than those employed in one single branch. Though in such manufactures, therefore, the work may really be divided into a much greater number of parts, than in those of a more trifling nature, the division is not near so obvious, and has accordingly been much less observed.

To take an example, therefore, from a very trifling manufacture, but one in which the division of labor has been very often taken notice of, the trade of a pin-maker: a workman not educated to this business (which the division of labor has rendered a distinct trade) nor acquainted with the use of the machinery employed in it (to the invention of which the same division of labor has probably given occasion), could scarce, perhaps, with his utmost industry, make one pin in a day, and certainly could not make twenty. But in the way in which this business is now carried on, not only the whole work is a peculiar trade, but it is divided into a number of branches, of which the greater part are likewise peculiar trades. One man draws out the wire; another straights it; a third cuts it; a fourth points it; a fifth grinds it at the top for receiving the head; to make the head requires two or three distinct operations; to put it on is a peculiar business; to whiten the pins is another; it is even a trade by itself to put them into the paper; and the important business of making a pin is, in this manner, divided into about eighteen distinct operations, which, in some manufactories, are all performed by distinct hands, though in others the same man will sometimes perform two or three of them. I have seen a small manufactory of this kind, where ten men only were employed, and where some of them consequently performed two or three distinct operations. But though they were very poor, and therefore but indifferently accommodated with the necessary machinery, they could, when they exerted themselves, make among them about twelve pounds of pins in a day. There are in a pound upwards of four thousand pins of a middling size. Those ten persons, therefore, could make among them upwards of forty-eight thousand pins in a day. Each person, therefore, making a tenth part of forty-eight thousand pins, might be considered as making four thousand eight hundred pins in a day. But if they had all wrought separately and independently, and without any of them having been educated to this peculiar business, they certainly could not each of them have made twenty, perhaps not one pin in a day; that is, certainly, not the two hundred and fortieth, perhaps not the four thousand eight hundredth, part of what they are at present capable of performing, in consequence of a proper division and combination of their different operations.

In every other art and manufacture, the effects of the division of labor are similar to what they are in this very trifling one, though, in many of them, the labor can neither be so much subdivided, nor reduced to so great a simplicity of operation. The division of labor, however, so far as it can be introduced, occasions, in every art, a proportionable increase of the productive powers of labor. The separation of different trades and employments from one another, seems to have taken place in consequence of this advantage. This separation, too, is generally carried furthest in those countries which enjoy the highest degree of industry and improvement; what is the work of one man, in a rude state of society, being generally that of several in an improved one. In every improved society, the farmer is generally nothing but a farmer; the manufacturer, nothing but a manufacturer. The labor, too, which is necessary to produce any one complete manufacture, is almost always divided among a great number of hands. How many different trades are employed in each branch of the linen and woolen manufactures, from the growers of the flax and the wool, to the bleachers and smoothers of the linen, or to the dyers and dressers of the cloth! The nature of agriculture, indeed, does not admit of so many subdivisions of labor, nor of so complete a separation of one business from another, as manufactures. It is impossible to separate so entirely the business of the grazier from that of the corn-farmer, as the trade of the carpenter is commonly separated from that of the smith. The spinner is almost always a distinct person from the weaver; but the ploughman, the harrower, the sower of the seed, and the reaper of the corn, are often the same. The occasions for those different sorts of labor returning with the different seasons of the year, it is impossible that one man should be constantly employed in any one of them. This impossibility of making so complete and entire a separation of all the different branches of labor employed in agriculture, is perhaps the reason why the improvement of the productive powers of labor, in this art, does not always keep pace with their improvement in manufactures. The most opulent nations, indeed, generally excel all their neighbors in agriculture as well as in manufactures; but they are commonly more distinguished by their superiority in the latter than in the former. Their lands are in general better cultivated, and having more labor and expense bestowed upon them, produce more in proportion to the extent and natural fertility of the ground. But this superiority of produce is seldom much more than in proportion to the superiority of labor and expense. In agriculture, the labor of the rich country is not always much more productive than that of the poor; or, at least, it is never so much more productive, as it commonly is in manufactures. The corn of the rich country, therefore, will not always, in the same degree of goodness, come cheaper to market than that of the poor. The corn of Poland, in the same degree of goodness, is as cheap as that of France, notwithstanding the superior opulence and improvement of the latter country. The corn of France is, in the corn-provinces, fully as good, and in most years nearly about the same price with the corn of England, though, in opulence and improvement, France is perhaps inferior to England. The corn-lands of England, however, are better cultivated than those of France, and the corn-lands of France are said to be much better cultivated than those of Poland. But though the poor country, notwithstanding the inferiority of its cultivation, can, in some measure, rival the rich in the cheapness and goodness of its corn, it can pretend to no such competition in its manufactures, at least if those manufactures suit the soil, climate, and situation, of the rich country. The silks of France are better and cheaper than those of England, because the silk manufacture, at least under the present high duties upon the importation of raw silk, does not so well suit the climate of England as that of France. But the hardware and the coarse woolens of England are beyond all comparison superior to those of France, and much cheaper, too, in the same degree of goodness. In Poland there are said to be scarce any manufactures of any kind, a few of those coarser household manufactures excepted, without which no country can well subsist.

This great increase in the quantity of work, which, in consequence of the division of labor, the same number of people are capable of performing, is owing to three different circumstances; first, to the increase of dexterity in every particular workman; secondly, to the saving of the time which is commonly lost in passing from one species of work to another; and, lastly, to the invention of a great number of machines which facilitate and abridge labor, and enable one man to do the work of many.

First, the improvement of the dexterity of the workmen, necessarily increases the quantity of the work he can perform; and the division of labor, by reducing every man's business to some one simple operation, and by making this operation the sole employment of his life, necessarily increases very much the dexterity of the workman. A common smith, who, though accustomed to handle the hammer, has never been used to make nails, if, upon some particular occasion, he is obliged to attempt it, will scarce, I am assured, be able to make above two or three hundred nails in a day, and those, too, very bad ones. A smith who has been accustomed to make nails, but whose sole or principal business has not been that of a nailer, can seldom, with his utmost diligence, make more than eight hundred or a thousand nails in a day. I have seen several boys, under twenty years of age, who had never exercised any other trade but that of making nails, and who, when they exerted themselves, could make, each of them, upwards of two thousand three hundred nails in a day. The making of a nail, however, is by no means one of the simplest operations. The same person blows the bellows, stirs or mends the fire as there is occasion, heats the iron, and forges every part of the nail: in forging the head, too, he is obliged to change his tools. The different operations into which the making of a pin, or of a metal button, is subdivided, are all of them much more simple, and the dexterity of the person, of whose life it has been the sole business to perform them, is usually much greater. The rapidity with which some of the operations of those manufactures are performed, exceeds what the human hand could, by those who had never seen them, he supposed capable of acquiring.

Secondly, the advantage which is gained by saving the time commonly lost in passing from one sort of work to another, is much greater than we should at first view be apt to imagine it. It is impossible to pass very quickly from one kind of work to another, that is carried on in a different place, and with quite different tools. A country weaver, who cultivates a small farm, must loose a good deal of time in passing from his loom to the field, and from the field to his loom. When the two trades can be carried on in the same workhouse, the loss of time is, no doubt, much less. It is, even in this case, however, very considerable. A man commonly saunters a little in turning his hand from one sort of employment to another. When he first begins the new work, he is seldom very keen and hearty; his mind, as they say, does not go to it, and for some time he rather trifles than applies to good purpose. The habit of sauntering, and of indolent careless application, which is naturally, or rather necessarily, acquired by every country workman who is obliged to change his work and his tools every half hour, and to apply his hand in twenty different ways almost every day of his life, renders him almost always slothful and lazy, and incapable of any vigorous application, even on the most pressing occasions. Independent, therefore, of his deficiency in point of dexterity, this cause alone must always reduce considerably the quantity of work which he is capable of performing.

Thirdly, and lastly, everybody must be sensible how much labor is facilitated and abridged by the application of proper machinery. It is unnecessary to give any example. I shall only observe, therefore, that the invention of all those machines by which labor is so much facilitated and abridged, seems to have been originally owing to the division of labor. Men are much more likely to discover easier and readier methods of attaining any object, when the whole attention of their minds is directed towards that single object, than when it is dissipated among a great variety of things. But, in consequence of the division of labor, the whole of every man's attention comes naturally to be directed towards some one very simple object. It is naturally to be expected, therefore, that some one or other of those who are employed in each particular branch of labor should soon find out easier and readier methods of performing their own particular work, whenever the nature of it admits of such improvement. A great part of the machines made use of in those manufactures in which labor is most subdivided, were originally the invention of common workmen, who, being each of them employed in some very simple operation, naturally turned their thoughts towards finding out easier and readier methods of performing it. Whoever has been much accustomed to visit such manufactures, must frequently have been shown very pretty machines, which were the inventions of such workmen, in order to facilitate and quicken their own particular part of the work. In the first fire engines {this was the current designation for steam engines}, a boy was constantly employed to open and shut alternately the communication between the boiler and the cylinder, according as the piston either ascended or descended. One of those boys, who loved to play with his companions, observed that, by tying a string from the handle of the valve which opened this communication to another part of the machine, the valve would open and shut without his assistance, and leave him at liberty to divert himself with his play-fellows. One of the greatest improvements that has been made upon this machine, since it was first invented, was in this manner the discovery of a boy who wanted to save his own labor.

All the improvements in machinery, however, have by no means been the inventions of those who had occasion to use the machines. Many improvements have been made by the ingenuity of the makers of the machines, when to make them became the business of a peculiar trade; and some by that of those who are called philosophers, or men of speculation, whose trade it is not to do any thing, but to observe every thing, and who, upon that account, are often capable of combining together the powers of the most distant and dissimilar objects in the progress of society, philosophy or speculation becomes, like every other employment, the principal or sole trade and occupation of a particular class of citizens. Like every other employment, too, it is subdivided into a great number of different branches, each of which affords occupation to a peculiar tribe or class of philosophers; and this subdivision of employment in philosophy, as well as in every other business, improve dexterity, and saves time. Each individual becomes more expert in his own peculiar branch, more work is done upon the whole, and the quantity of science is considerably increased by it.

It is the great multiplication of the productions of all the different arts, in consequence of the division of labor, which occasions, in a well-governed society, that universal opulence which extends itself to the lowest ranks of the people. Every workman has a great quantity of his own work to dispose of beyond what he himself has occasion for; and every other workman being exactly in the same situation, he is enabled to exchange a great quantity of his own goods for a great quantity or, what comes to the same thing, for the price of a great quantity of theirs. He supplies them abundantly with what they have occasion for, and they accommodate him as amply with what he has occasion for, and a general plenty diffuses itself through all the different ranks of the society.

Observe the accommodation of the most common artificer or day laborer in a civilized and thriving country, and you will perceive that the number of people, of whose industry a part, though but a small part, has been employed in procuring him this accommodation, exceeds all computation. The woolen coat, for example, which covers the day-laborer, as coarse and rough as it may appear, is the produce of the joint labor of a great multitude of workmen. The shepherd, the sorter of the wool, the wool-comber or carder, the dyer, the scribbler, the spinner, the weaver, the fuller, the dresser, with many others, must all join their different arts in order to complete even this homely production. How many merchants and carriers, besides, must have been employed in transporting the materials from some of those workmen to others who often live in a very distant part of the country? How much commerce and navigation in particular, how many ship-builders, sailors, sail-makers, rope-makers, must have been employed in order to bring together the different drugs made use of by the dyer, which often come from the remotest corners of the world? What a variety of labor, too, is necessary in order to produce the tools of the meanest of those workmen! To say nothing of such complicated machines as the ship of the sailor, the mill of the fuller, or even the loom of the weaver, let us consider only what a variety of labor is requisite in order to form that very simple machine, the shears with which the shepherd clips the wool. The miner, the builder of the furnace for smelting the ore, the feller of the timber, the burner of the charcoal to be made use of in the smelting-house, the brickmaker, the bricklayer, the workmen who attend the furnace, the millwright, the forger, the smith, must all of them join their different arts in order to produce them. Were we to examine, in the same manner, all the different parts of his dress and household furniture, the coarse linen shirt which he wears next his skin, the shoes which cover his feet, the bed which he lies on, and all the different parts which compose it, the kitchen-grate at which he prepares his victuals, the coals which he makes use of for that purpose, dug from the bowels of the earth, and brought to him, perhaps, by a long sea and a long land-carriage, all the other utensils of his kitchen, all the furniture of his table, the knives and forks, the earthen or pewter plates upon which he serves up and divides his victuals, the different hands employed in preparing his bread and his beer, the glass window which lets in the heat and the light, and keeps out the wind and the rain, with all the knowledge and art requisite for preparing that beautiful and happy invention, without which these northern parts of the world could scarce have afforded a very comfortable habitation, together with the tools of all the different workmen employed in producing those different conveniences; if we examine, I say, all these things, and consider what a variety of labor is employed about each of them, we shall be sensible that, without the assistance and co-operation of many thousands, the very meanest person in a civilized country could not be provided, even according to, what we very falsely imagine, the easy and simple manner in which he is commonly accommodated. Compared, indeed, with the more extravagant luxury of the great, his accommodation must no doubt appear extremely simple and easy; and yet it may be true, perhaps, that the accommodation of an European prince does not always so much exceed that of an industrious and frugal peasant, as the accommodation of the latter exceeds that of many an African king, the absolute masters of the lives and liberties of ten thousand naked savages.

CHAPTER II

Of the Principle Which Gives Occasion to the Division of Labor

This division of labor, from which so many advantages are derived, is not originally the effect of any human wisdom, which foresees and intends that general opulence to which it gives occasion. It is the necessary, though very slow and gradual, consequence of a certain propensity in human nature, which has in view no such extensive utility; the propensity to truck, barter, and exchange one thing for another.

Whether this propensity be one of those original principles in human nature, of which no further account can be given, or whether, as seems more probable, it be the necessary consequence of the faculties of reason and speech, it belongs not to our present subject to inquire. It is common to all men, and to be found in no other race of animals, which seem to know neither this nor any other species of contracts. Two greyhounds, in running down the same hare, have sometimes the appearance of acting in some sort of concert. Each turns her towards his companion, or endeavors to intercept her when his companion turns her towards himself. This, however, is not the effect of any contract, but of the accidental concurrence of their passions in the same object at that particular time. Nobody ever saw a dog make a fair and deliberate exchange of one bone for another with another dog. Nobody ever saw one animal, by its gestures and natural cries signify to another, this is mine, that yours; I am willing to give this for that. When an animal wants to obtain something either of a man, or of another animal, it has no other means of persuasion, but to gain the favor of those whose service it requires. A puppy fawns upon its dam, and a spaniel endeavors, by a thousand attractions, to engage the attention of its master who is at dinner, when it wants to be fed by him. Man sometimes uses the same arts with his brethren, and when he has no other means of engaging them to act according to his inclinations, endeavors by every servile and fawning attention to obtain their good will. He has not time, however, to do this upon every occasion. In civilized society he stands at all times in need of the co-operation and assistance of great multitudes, while his whole life is scarce sufficient to gain the friendship of a few persons. In almost every other race of animals, each individual, when it is grown up to maturity, is entirely independent, and in its natural state has occasion for the assistance of no other living creature. But man has almost constant occasion for the help of his brethren, and it is in vain for him to expect it from their benevolence only. He will be more likely to prevail if he can interest their self-love in his favor, and show them that it is for their own advantage to do for him what he requires of them. Whoever offers to another a bargain of any kind, proposes to do this. Give me that which I want, and you shall have this which you want, is the meaning of every such offer; and it is in this manner that we obtain from one another the far greater part of those good offices which we stand in need of.

It is not from the benevolence of the butcher, the brewer, or the baker that we expect our dinner, but from their regard to their own interest. We address ourselves, not to their humanity, but to their self-love, and never talk to them of our own necessities, but of their advantages. Nobody but a beggar chooses to depend chiefly upon the benevolence of his fellow-citizens. Even a beggar does not depend upon it entirely. The charity of well-disposed people, indeed, supplies him with the whole fund of his subsistence. But though this principle ultimately provides him with all the necessaries of life which he has occasion for, it neither does nor can provide him with them as he has occasion for them. The greater part of his occasional wants are supplied in the same manner as those of other people, by treaty, by barter, and by purchase. With the money which one man gives him he purchases food. The old clothes which another bestows upon him he exchanges for other clothes which suit him better, or for lodging, or for food, or for money, with which he can buy either food, clothes, or lodging, as he has occasion.

As it is by treaty, by barter, and by purchase, that we obtain from one another the greater part of those mutual good offices which we stand in need of, so it is this same trucking disposition which originally gives occasion to the division of labor. In a tribe of hunters or shepherds, a particular person makes bows and arrows, for example, with more readiness and dexterity than any other. He frequently exchanges them for cattle or for venison, with his companions; and he finds at last that he can, in this manner, get more cattle and venison, than if he himself went to the field to catch them. From a regard to his own interest, therefore, the making of bows and arrows grows to be his chief business, and he becomes a sort of armorer. Another excels in making the frames and covers of their little huts or moveable houses. He is accustomed to be of use in this way to his neighbors, who reward him in the same manner with cattle and with venison, till at last he finds it his interest to dedicate himself entirely to this employment, and to become a sort of house-carpenter. In the same manner a third becomes a smith or a brazier; a fourth, a tanner or dresser of hides or skins, the principal part of the clothing of savages. And thus the certainty of being able to exchange all that surplus part of the produce of his own labor, which is over and above his own consumption, for such parts of the produce of other men's labor as he may have occasion for, encourages every man to apply himself to a particular occupation, and to cultivate and bring to perfection whatever talent of genius he may possess for that particular species of business.

The difference of natural talents in different men, is, in reality, much less than we are aware of; and the very different genius which appears to distinguish men of different professions, when grown up to maturity, is not upon many occasions so much the cause, as the effect of the division of labor. The difference between the most dissimilar characters, between a philosopher and a common street porter, for example, seems to arise not so much from nature, as from habit, custom, and education. When they came into the world, and for the first six or eight years of their existence, they were, perhaps, very much alike, and neither their parents nor play-fellows could perceive any remarkable difference. About that age, or soon after, they come to be employed in very different occupations. The difference of talents comes then to be taken notice of, and widens by degrees, till at last the vanity of the philosopher is willing to acknowledge scarce any resemblance. But without the disposition to truck, barter, and exchange, every man must have procured to himself every necessary and conveniency of life which he wanted. All must have had the same duties to perform, and the same work to do, and there could have been no such difference of employment as could alone give occasion to any great difference of talents.

As it is this disposition which forms that difference of talents, so remarkable among men of different professions, so it is this same disposition which renders that difference useful. Many tribes of animals, acknowledged to be all of the same species, derive from nature a much more remarkable distinction of genius, than what, antecedent to custom and education, appears to take place among men. By nature a philosopher is not in genius and disposition half so different from a street porter, as a mastiff is from a greyhound, or a greyhound from a spaniel, or this last from a shepherd's dog. Those different tribes of animals, however, though all of the same species are of scarce any use to one another. The strength of the mastiff is not in the least supported either by the swiftness of the greyhound, or by the sagacity of the spaniel, or by the docility of the shepherd's dog. The effects of those different geniuses and talents, for want of the power or disposition to barter and exchange, cannot be brought into a common stock, and do not in the least contribute to the better accommodation and conveniency of the species. Each animal is still obliged to support and defend itself, separately and independently, and derives no sort of advantage from that variety of talents with which nature has distinguished its fellows. Among men, on the contrary, the most dissimilar geniuses are of use to one another; the different produces of their respective talents, by the general disposition to truck, barter, and exchange, being brought, as it were, into a common stock, where every man may purchase whatever part of the produce of other men's talents he has occasion for.

CHAPTER III

That the Division of Labor Is Limited by the Extent of the Market

As it is the power of exchanging that gives occasion to the division of labor, so the extent of this division must always be limited by the extent of that power, or, in other words, by the extent of the market. When the market is very small, no person can have any encouragement to dedicate himself entirely to one employment, for want of the power to exchange all that surplus part of the produce of his own labor, which is over and above his own consumption, for such parts of the produce of other men's labor as he has occasion for.

There are some sorts of industry, even of the lowest kind, which can be carried on nowhere but in a great town. A porter, for example, can find employment and subsistence in no other place. A village is by much too narrow a sphere for him; even an ordinary market-town is scarce large enough to afford him constant occupation. In the lone houses and very small villages which are scattered about in so desert a country as the highlands of Scotland, every farmer must be butcher, baker, and brewer, for his own family. In such situations we can scarce expect to find even a smith, a carpenter, or a mason, within less than twenty miles of another of the same trade. The scattered families that live at eight or ten miles distance from the nearest of them, must learn to perform themselves a great number of little pieces of work, for which, in more populous countries, they would call in the assistance of those workmen. Country workmen are almost everywhere obliged to apply themselves to all the different branches of industry that have so much affinity to one another as to be employed about the same sort of materials. A country carpenter deals in every sort of work that is made of wood; a country smith in every sort of work that is made of iron. The former is not only a carpenter, but a joiner, a cabinet-maker, and even a carver in wood, as well as a wheel-wright, a plough-wright, a cart and wagon-maker. The employments of the latter are still more various. It is impossible there should be such a trade as even that of a nailer in the remote and inland parts of the highlands of Scotland. Such a workman at the rate of a thousand nails a day, and three hundred working days in the year, will make three hundred thousand nails in the year. But in such a situation it would be impossible to dispose of one thousand, that is, of one day's work in the year.

As by means of water-carriage, a more extensive market is opened to every sort of industry than what land-carriage alone can afford it, so it is upon the seacoast, and along the banks of navigable rivers, that industry of every kind naturally begins to subdivide and improve itself, and it is frequently not till a long time after that those improvements extend themselves to the inland parts of the country. A broad-wheeled wagon, attended by two men, and drawn by eight horses, in about six weeks time, carries and brings back between London and Edinburgh near four ton weight of goods. In about the same time a ship navigated by six or eight men, and sailing between the ports of London and Leith, frequently carries and brings back two hundred ton weight of goods. Six or eight men, therefore, by the help of water-carriage, can carry and bring back, in the same time, the same quantity of goods between London and Edinburgh as fifty broad-wheeled wagons, attended by a hundred men, and drawn by four hundred horses. Upon two hundred tons of goods, therefore, carried by the cheapest land-carriage from London to Edinburgh, there must be charged the maintenance of a hundred men for three weeks, and both the maintenance and what is nearly equal to maintenance, the wear and tear of four hundred horses, as well as of fifty great wagons. Whereas, upon the same quantity of goods carried by water, there is to be charged only the maintenance of six or eight men, and the wear and tear of a ship of two hundred tons burthen, together with the value of the superior risk, or the difference of the insurance between land and water-carriage. Were there no other communication between those two places, therefore, but by land-carriage, as no goods could be transported from the one to the other, except such whose price was very considerable in proportion to their weight, they could carry on but a small part of that commerce which at present subsists between them, and consequently could give but a small part of that encouragement which they at present mutually afford to each other's industry. There could be little or no commerce of any kind between the distant parts of the world. What goods could bear the expense of land-carriage between London and Calcutta? Or if there were any so precious as to be able to support this expense, with what safety could they be transported through the territories of so many barbarous nations? Those two cities, however, at present carry on a very considerable commerce with each other, and by mutually affording a market, give a good deal of encouragement to each other's industry.

Since such, therefore, are the advantages of water-carriage, it is natural that the first improvements of art and industry should be made where this conveniency opens the whole world for a market to the produce of every sort of labor, and that they should always be much later in extending themselves into the inland parts of the country. The inland parts of the country can for a long time have no other market for the greater part of their goods, but the country which lies round about them, and separates them from the sea-coast, and the great navigable rivers. The extent of the market, therefore, must for a long time be in proportion to the riches and populousness of that country, and consequently their improvement must always be posterior to the improvement of that country. In our North American colonies, the plantations have constantly followed either the sea-coast or the banks of the navigable rivers, and have scarce anywhere extended themselves to any considerable distance from both.

The nations that, according to the best authenticated history, appear to have been first civilized, were those that dwelt round the coast of the Mediterranean sea. That sea, by far the greatest inlet that is known in the world, having no tides, nor consequently any waves, except such as are caused by the wind only, was, by the smoothness of its surface, as well as by the multitude of its islands, and the proximity of its neighboring shores, extremely favorable to the infant navigation of the world; when, from their ignorance of the compass, men were afraid to quit the view of the coast, and from the imperfection of the art of shipbuilding, to abandon themselves to the boisterous waves of the ocean. To pass beyond the pillars of Hercules, that is, to sail out of the straits of Gibraltar, was, in the ancient world, long considered as a most wonderful and dangerous exploit of navigation. It was late before even the Phoenicians and Carthaginians, the most skilful navigators and shipbuilders of those old times, attempted it; and they were, for a long time, the only nations that did attempt it.

Of all the countries on the coast of the Mediterranean sea, Egypt seems to have been the first in which either agriculture or manufactures were cultivated and improved to any considerable degree. Upper Egypt extends itself nowhere above a few miles from the Nile; and in Lower Egypt, that great river breaks itself into many different canals, which, with the assistance of a little art, seem to have afforded a communication by water-carriage, not only between all the great towns, but between all the considerable villages, and even to many farmhouses in the country, nearly in the same manner as the Rhine and the Maese do in Holland at present. The extent and easiness of this inland navigation was probably one of the principal causes of the early improvement of Egypt.

The improvements in agriculture and manufactures seem likewise to have been of very great antiquity in the provinces of Bengal, in the East Indies, and in some of the eastern provinces of China, though the great extent of this antiquity is not authenticated by any histories of whose authority we, in this part of the world, are well assured. In Bengal, the Ganges, and several other great rivers, form a great number of navigable canals, in the same manner as the Nile does in Egypt. In the eastern provinces of China, too, several great rivers form, by their different branches, a multitude of canals, and, by communicating with one another, afford an inland navigation much more extensive than that either of the Nile or the Ganges, or, perhaps, than both of them put together. It is remarkable, that neither the ancient Egyptians, nor the Indians, nor the Chinese, encouraged foreign commerce, but seem all to have derived their great opulence from this inland navigation.

All the inland parts of Africa, and all that part of Asia which lies any considerable way north of the Euxine and Caspian seas, the ancient Scythia, the modern Tartary and Siberia, seem, in all ages of the world, to have been in the same barbarous and uncivilized state in which we find them at present. The sea of Tartary is the frozen ocean, which admits of no navigation; and though some of the greatest rivers in the world run through that country, they are at too great a distance from one another to carry commerce and communication through the greater part of it. There are in Africa none of those great inlets, such as the Baltic and Adriatic seas in Europe, the Mediterranean and Euxine seas in both Europe and Asia, and the gulfs of Arabia, Persia, India, Bengal, and Siam, in Asia, to carry maritime commerce into the interior parts of that great continent; and the great rivers of Africa are at too great a distance from one another to give occasion to any considerable inland navigation. The commerce, besides, which any nation can carry on by means of a river which does not break itself into any great number of branches or canals, and which runs into another territory before it reaches the sea, can never be very considerable, because it is always in the power of the nations who possess that other territory to obstruct the communication between the upper country and the sea. The navigation of the Danube is of very little use to the different states of Bavaria, Austria, and Hungary, in comparison of what it would be, if any of them possessed the whole of its course, till it falls into the Black sea.

CHAPTER IV

Of the Origin and Use of Money

When the division of labor has been once thoroughly established, it is but a very small part of a man's wants which the produce of his own labor can supply. He supplies the far greater part of them by exchanging that surplus part of the produce of his own labor, which is over and above his own consumption, for such parts of the produce of other men's labor as he has occasion for. Every man thus lives by exchanging, or becomes, in some measure, a merchant, and the society itself grows to be what is properly a commercial society.

But when the division of labor first began to take place, this power of exchanging must frequently have been very much clogged and embarrassed in its operations. One man, we shall suppose, has more of a certain commodity than he himself has occasion for, while another has less. The former, consequently, would be glad to dispose of; and the latter to purchase, a part of this superfluity. But if this latter should chance to have nothing that the former stands in need of, no exchange can be made between them. The butcher has more meat in his shop than he himself can consume, and the brewer and the baker would each of them be willing to purchase a part of it. But they have nothing to offer in exchange, except the different productions of their respective trades, and the butcher is already provided with all the bread and beer which he has immediate occasion for. No exchange can, in this case, be made between them. He cannot be their merchant, nor they his customers; and they are all of them thus mutually less serviceable to one another. In order to avoid the inconveniency of such situations, every prudent man in every period of society, after the first establishment of the division of labor, must naturally have endeavored to manage his affairs in such a manner, as to have at all times by him, besides the peculiar produce of his own industry, a certain quantity of some one commodity or other, such as he imagined few people would be likely to refuse in exchange for the produce of their industry. Many different commodities, it is probable, were successively both thought of and employed for this purpose. In the rude ages of society, cattle are said to have been the common instrument of commerce; and, though they must have been a most inconvenient one, yet, in old times, we find things were frequently valued according to the number of cattle which had been given in exchange for them. The armor of Diomede, says Homer, cost only nine oxen; but that of Glaucus cost a hundred oxen. Salt is said to be the common instrument of commerce and exchanges in Abyssinia; a species of shells in some parts of the coast of India; dried cod at Newfoundland; tobacco in Virginia; sugar in some of our West India colonies; hides or dressed leather in some other countries; and there is at this day a village in Scotland, where it is not uncommon, I am told, for a workman to carry nails instead of money to the baker's shop or the ale-house.

In all countries, however, men seem at last to have been determined by irresistible reasons to give the preference, for this employment, to metals above every other commodity. Metals can not only be kept with as little loss as any other commodity, scarce any thing being less perishable than they are, but they can likewise, without any loss, be divided into any number of parts, as by fusion those parts can easily be re-united again; a quality which no other equally durable commodities possess, and which, more than any other quality, renders them fit to be the instruments of commerce and circulation. The man who wanted to buy salt, for example, and had nothing but cattle to give in exchange for it, must have been obliged to buy salt to the value of a whole ox, or a whole sheep, at a time. He could seldom buy less than this, because what he was to give for it could seldom be divided without loss; and if he had a mind to buy more, he must, for the same reasons, have been obliged to buy double or triple the quantity, the value, to wit, of two or three oxen, or of two or three sheep. If, on the contrary, instead of sheep or oxen, he had metals to give in exchange for it, he could easily proportion the quantity of the metal to the precise quantity of the commodity which he had immediate occasion for.

Different metals have been made use of by different nations for this purpose. Iron was the common instrument of commerce among the ancient Spartans, copper among the ancient Romans, and gold and silver among all rich and commercial nations.

Those metals seem originally to have been made use of for this purpose in rude bars, without any stamp or coinage. Thus we are told by Pliny {Plin. *Hist Nat.* lib. 33, cap. 3}, upon the authority of Timaeus, an ancient historian, that, till the time of Servius Tullius, the Romans had no coined money, but made use of unstamped bars of copper, to purchase whatever they had occasion for. These rude bars, therefore, performed at this time the function of money.

The use of metals in this rude state was attended with two very considerable inconveniences; first, with the trouble of weighing, and secondly, with that of assaying them. In the precious metals, where a small difference in the quantity makes a great difference in the value, even the business of weighing, with proper exactness, requires at least very accurate weights and scales. The weighing of gold, in particular, is an operation of some nicety. In the coarser metals, indeed, where a small error would be of little consequence, less accuracy would, no doubt, be necessary. Yet we should find it excessively troublesome if every time a poor man had occasion either to buy or sell a farthing's worth of goods, he was obliged to weigh the farthing. The operation of assaying is still more difficult, still more tedious; and, unless a part of the metal is fairly melted in the crucible, with proper dissolvents, any conclusion that can be drawn from it is extremely uncertain. Before the institution of coined money, however, unless they went through this tedious and difficult operation, people must always have been liable to the grossest frauds and impositions; and instead of a pound weight of pure silver, or pure copper, might receive, in exchange for their goods, an adulterated composition of the coarsest and cheapest materials, which had, however, in their outward appearance, been made to resemble those metals. To prevent such abuses, to facilitate exchanges, and thereby to encourage all sorts of industry and commerce, it has been found necessary, in all countries that have made any considerable advances towards improvement, to affix a public stamp upon certain quantities of such particular metals, as were in those countries commonly made use of to purchase goods. Hence the origin of coined money, and of those public offices called mints; institutions exactly of the same nature with those of the aulnagers and stamp-masters of woolen and linen cloth. All of them are equally meant to ascertain, by means of a public stamp, the quantity and uniform goodness of those different commodities when brought to market.

The first public stamps of this kind that were affixed to the current metals, seem in many cases to have been intended to ascertain, what it was both most difficult and most important to ascertain, the goodness or fineness of the metal, and to have resembled the sterling mark which is at present affixed to plate and bars of silver, or the Spanish mark which is sometimes affixed to ingots of gold, and which, being struck only upon one side of the piece, and not covering the whole surface, ascertains the fineness, but not the weight of the metal. Abraham weighs to Ephron the four hundred shekels of silver which he had agreed to pay for the field of Machpelah. They are said, however, to be the current money of the merchant, and yet are received by weight, and not by tale, in the same manner as ingots of gold and bars of silver are at present. The revenues of the ancient Saxon kings of England are said to have been paid, not in money, but in kind, that is, in victuals and provisions of all sorts. William the Conqueror introduced the custom of paying them in money. This money, however, was for a long time, received at the exchequer, by weight, and not by *tale*.

The inconveniency and difficulty of weighing those metals with exactness, gave occasion to the institution of coins, of which the stamp, covering entirely both sides of the piece, and sometimes the edges too, was supposed to ascertain not only the fineness, but the weight of the metal. Such coins, therefore, were received by tale, as at present, without the trouble of weighing.

The denominations of those coins seem originally to have expressed the weight or quantity of metal contained in them. In the time of Servius Tullius, who first coined money at Rome, the Roman *as* or *pondo* contained a Roman pound of good copper. It was divided, in the same manner as our Troyes pound, into twelve ounces, each of which contained a real ounce of good copper. The English pound sterling, in the time of Edward I contained a pound, Tower weight, of silver of a known fineness. The Tower pound seems to have been something more than the Roman pound, and something less than the Troyes pound. This last was not introduced into the mint of England till the 18th of Henry the VIII. The French *livre* contained, in the time of Charlemagne, a pound, Troyes weight, of silver of a known fineness. The *fair* of Troyes in Champaign was at that time frequented by all the nations of Europe, and the weights and measures of so famous a market were generally known and esteemed. The Scots money pound contained, from the time of Alexander the First to that of Robert Bruce, a pound of silver of the same weight and fineness with the English pound sterling. English, French, and Scots pennies, too, contained all of them originally a real pennyweight of silver, the twentieth part of an ounce, and the two hundred-and-fortieth part of a pound. The shilling, too, seems originally to have been the denomination of a weight. "When wheat is at twelve shillings the quarter," says an ancient statute of Henry III, "then wastel bread of a farthing shall weigh eleven shillings and four pence." The proportion, however, between the shilling, and either the penny on the one hand, or the pound on the other, seems not to have been so constant and uniform as that between the penny and the pound. During the first race of the kings of France, the French sou or shilling appears upon different occasions to have contained five, twelve, twenty, or forty pennies. Among the ancient Saxons, a shilling appears at one time to have contained only five pennies, and it is not improbable that it may have been as variable among them as among their neighbors, the ancient Franks. From the time of Charlemagne among the French, and from that of William the Conqueror among the English, the proportion between the pound, the shilling, and the penny, seems to have been uniformly the same as at present, though the value of each has been very different; for in every country of the world, I believe, the avarice and injustice of princes and sovereign states, abusing the confidence of their subjects, have by degrees diminished the real quantity of metal, which had been originally contained in their coins. The Roman as, in the latter ages of the republic, was reduced to the twenty-fourth part of its original value, and, instead of weighing a pound, came to weigh only half an ounce. The English pound and penny contain at present about a third only; the Scots pound and penny about a thirty-sixth; and the French pound and penny about a sixty-sixth part of their original value. By means of those operations, the princes and sovereign states which performed them were enabled, in appearance, to pay their debts and fulfill their engagements with a smaller quantity of silver than would otherwise have been requisite. It was indeed in appearance only; for their creditors were really defrauded of a part of what was due to them. All other debtors in the state were allowed the same privilege, and might pay with the same nominal sum of the new and debased coin whatever they had borrowed in the old. Such operations, therefore, have always proved favorable to the debtor, and ruinous to the creditor, and have sometimes produced a greater and more universal revolution in the fortunes of private persons, than could have been occasioned by a very great public calamity.

It is in this manner that money has become, in all civilized nations, the universal instrument of commerce, by the intervention of which goods of all kinds are bought and sold, or exchanged for one another.

What are the rules which men naturally observe, in exchanging them either for money, or for one another, I shall now proceed to examine. These rules determine what may be called the relative or exchangeable value of goods.

The word *value,* it is to be observed, has two different meanings, and sometimes expresses the utility of some particular object, and sometimes the power of purchasing other goods which the possession of that object conveys. The one may be called 'value in use'; the other, 'value in exchange.' The things which have the greatest value in use have frequently little or no value in exchange; and, on the contrary, those which have the greatest value in exchange have frequently little or no value in use. Nothing is more useful than water; but it will purchase scarce any thing; scarce any thing can be had in exchange for it. A diamond, on the contrary, has scarce any value in use; but a very great quantity of other goods may frequently be had in exchange for it.

In order to investigate the principles which regulate the exchangeable value of commodities, I shall endeavor to show.

First, what is the real measure of this exchangeable value; or wherein consists the real price of all commodities.

Secondly, what are the different parts of which this real price is composed or made up.

And, lastly, what are the different circumstances which sometimes raise some or all of these different parts of price above, and sometimes sink them below, their natural or ordinary rate; or, what are the causes which sometimes hinder the market price, that is, the actual price of commodities, from coinciding exactly with what may be called their natural price.

I shall endeavor to explain, as fully and distinctly as I can, those three subjects in the three following chapters, for which I must very earnestly entreat both the patience and attention of the reader: his patience, in order to examine a detail which may, perhaps, in some places, appear unnecessarily tedious; and his attention, in order to understand what may perhaps, after the fullest explication which I am capable of giving it, appear still in some degree obscure. I am always willing to run some hazard of being tedious, in order to be sure that I am perspicuous; and, after taking the utmost pains that I can to be perspicuous, some obscurity may still appear to remain upon a subject, in its own nature extremely abstracted.

CHAPTER V

Of the Real and Nominal Price of Commodities, or of Their Price in Labor, and Their Price in Money

Every man is rich or poor according to the degree in which he can afford to enjoy the necessaries, conveniences, and amusements of human life. But after the division of labor has once thoroughly taken place, it is but a very small part of these with which a man's own labor can supply him. The far greater part of them he must derive from the labor of other people, and he must be rich or poor according to the quantity of that labor which he can command, or which he can afford to purchase. The value of any commodity, therefore, to the person who possesses it, and who means not to use or consume it himself, but to exchange it for other commodities, is equal to the quantity of labor which it enables him to purchase or command. Labor, therefore, is the real measure of the exchangeable value of all commodities.

The real price of every thing, what every thing really costs to the man who wants to acquire it, is the toil and trouble of acquiring it. What every thing is really worth to the man who has acquired it and who wants to dispose of it, or exchange it for something else, is the toil and trouble which it can save to himself, and which it can impose upon other people. What is bought with money, or with goods, is purchased by labor, as much as what we acquire by the toil of our own body. That money, or those goods, indeed, save us this toil. They contain the value of a certain quantity of labor, which we exchange for what is supposed at the time to contain the value of an equal quantity. Labor was the first price, the original purchase money that was paid for all things. It was not by gold or by silver, but by labor, that all the wealth of the world was originally purchased; and its value, to those who possess it, and who want to exchange it for some new productions, is precisely equal to the quantity of' labor which it can enable them to purchase or command.

Wealth, as Mr. Hobbes says, is power. But the person who either acquires, or succeeds to a great fortune, does not necessarily acquire or succeed to any political power, either civil or military. His fortune may, perhaps, afford him the means of acquiring both; but the mere possession of that fortune does not necessarily convey to him either. The power which that possession immediately and directly conveys to him, is the power of purchasing a certain command over all the labor, or over all the produce of labor which is then in the market. His fortune is greater or less, precisely in proportion to the extent of this power, or to the quantity either of other men's labor, or, what is the same thing, of the produce of other men's labor, which it enables him to purchase or command. The exchangeable value of every thing must always be precisely equal to the extent of this power which it conveys to its owner.

But though labor be the real measure of the exchangeable value of all commodities, it is not that by which their value is commonly estimated. It is often difficult to ascertain the proportion between two different quantities of labor. The time spent in two different sorts of work will not always alone determine this proportion. The different degrees of hardship endured, and of ingenuity exercised, must likewise be taken into account. There may be more labor in an hour's hard work, than in two hours easy business; or in an hour's application to a trade which it cost ten years labor to learn, than in a month's industry, at an ordinary and obvious employment. But it is not easy to find any accurate measure either of hardship or ingenuity. In exchanging, indeed, the different productions of different sorts of labor for one another, some allowance is commonly made for both. It is adjusted, however, not by any accurate measure, but by the haggling and bargaining of the market, according to that sort of rough equality which, though not exact, is sufficient for carrying on the business of common life.

Every commodity, besides, is more frequently exchanged for, and thereby compared with, other commodities, than with labor. It is more natural, therefore, to estimate its exchangeable value by the quantity of some other commodity, than by that of the labor which it can produce. The greater part of people, too, understand better what is meant by a quantity of a particular commodity, than by a quantity of labor. The one is a plain palpable object; the other an abstract notion, which though it can be made sufficiently intelligible, is not altogether so natural and obvious.

But when barter ceases, and money has become the common instrument of commerce, every particular commodity is more frequently exchanged for money than for any other commodity. The butcher seldom carries his beef or his mutton to the baker or the brewer, in order to exchange them for bread or for beer; but he carries them to the market, where he exchanges them for money, and afterwards exchanges that money for bread and for beer. The quantity of money which he gets for them regulates, too, the quantity of bread and beer which he can afterwards purchase. It is more natural and obvious to him, therefore, to estimate their value by the quantity of money, the commodity for which he immediately exchanges them, than by that of bread and beer, the commodities for which he can exchange them only by the intervention of another commodity; and rather to say that his butcher's meat is worth three pence or four pence a pound, than that it is worth three or four pounds of bread, or three or four quarts of small beer. Hence it comes to pass, that the exchangeable value of every commodity is more frequently estimated by the quantity of money, than by the quantity either of labor or of any other commodity which can be had in exchange for it.

Gold and silver, however, like every other commodity, vary in their value; are sometimes cheaper and sometimes dearer, sometimes of easier and sometimes of more difficult purchase. The quantity of labor which any particular quantity of them can purchase or command, or the quantity of other goods which it will exchange for, depends always upon the fertility or barrenness of the mines which happen to be known about the time when such exchanges are made. The discovery of the abundant mines of America, reduced, in the sixteenth century, the value of gold and silver in Europe to about a third of what it had been before. As it cost less labor to bring those metals from the mine to the market, so, when they were brought thither, they could purchase or command less labor; and this revolution in their value, though perhaps the greatest, is by no means the only one of which history gives some account. But as a measure of quantity, such as the natural foot, fathom, or handful, which is continually varying in its own quantity, can never be an accurate measure of the quantity of other things; so a commodity which is itself continually varying in its own value, can never be an accurate measure of the value of other commodities. Equal quantities of labor, at all times and places, may be said to be of equal value to the laborer. In his ordinary state of health, strength, and spirits; in the ordinary degree of his skill and dexterity, he must always lay down the same portion of his ease, his liberty, and his happiness. The price which he pays must always be the same, whatever may be the quantity of goods which he receives in return for it. Of these, indeed, it may sometimes purchase a greater and sometimes a smaller quantity; but it is their value which varies, not that of the labor which purchases them. At all times and places, that is dear which it is difficult to come at, or which it costs much labor to acquire; and that cheap which is to be had easily, or with very little labor. Labor alone, therefore, never varying in its own value, is alone the ultimate and real standard by which the value of all commodities can at all times and places be estimated and compared. It is their real price; money is their nominal price only.

But though equal quantities of labor are always of equal value to the laborer, yet to the person who employs him they appear sometimes to be of greater, and sometimes of smaller value. He purchases them sometimes with a greater, and sometimes with a smaller quantity of goods, and to him the price of labor seems to vary like that of all other things. It appears to him dear in the one case, and cheap in the other. In reality, however, it is the goods which are cheap in the one case, and dear in the other.

In this popular sense, therefore, labor, like commodities, may be said to have a real and a nominal price. Its real price may be said to consist in the quantity of the necessaries and conveniences of life which are given for it; its nominal price, in the quantity of money. The laborer is rich or poor, is well or ill rewarded, in proportion to the real, not to the nominal price of his labor.

The distinction between the real and the nominal price of commodities and labor is not a matter of mere speculation, but may sometimes be of considerable use in practice. The same real price is always of the same value; but on account of the variations in the value of gold and silver, the same nominal price is sometimes of very different values. When a landed estate, therefore, is sold with a reservation of a perpetual rent, if it is intended that this rent should always be of the same value, it is of importance to the family in whose favor it is reserved, that it should not consist in a particular sum of money. Its value would in this case be liable to variations of two different kinds: first, to those which arise from the different quantities of gold and silver which are contained at different times in coin of the same denomination; and, secondly, to those which arise from the different values of equal quantities of gold and silver at different times.

Princes and sovereign states have frequently fancied that they had a temporary interest to diminish the quantity of pure metal contained in their coins; but they seldom have fancied that they had any to augment it. The quantity of metal contained in the coins, I believe of all nations, has accordingly been almost continually diminishing, and hardly ever augmenting. Such variations, therefore, tend almost always to diminish the value of a money rent.

The discovery of the mines of America diminished the value of gold and silver in Europe. This diminution, it is commonly supposed, though I apprehend without any certain proof, is still going on gradually, and is likely to continue to do so for a long time. Upon this supposition, therefore, such variations are more likely to diminish than to augment the value of a money rent, even though it should be stipulated to be paid, not in such a quantity of coined money of such a denomination (in so many pounds sterling, for example), but in so many ounces, either of pure silver, or of silver of a certain standard.

The rents which have been reserved in corn, have preserved their value much better than those which have been reserved in money, even where the denomination of the coin has not been altered. By the 18th of Elizabeth, it was enacted, that a third of the rent of all college leases should be reserved in corn, to be paid either in kind, or according to the current prices at the nearest public market. The money arising from this corn rent, though originally but a third of the whole, is, in the present times, according to Dr. Blackstone, commonly near double of what arises from the other two-thirds. The old money rents of colleges must, according to this account, have sunk almost to a fourth part of their ancient value, or are worth little more than a fourth part of the corn which they were formerly worth. But since the reign of Philip and Mary, the denomination of the English coin has undergone little or no alteration, and the same number of pounds, shillings, and pence, have contained very nearly the same quantity of pure silver. This degradation, therefore, in the value of the money rents of colleges, has arisen altogether from the degradation in the price of silver.

When the degradation in the value of silver is combined with the diminution of the quantity of it contained in the coin of the same denomination, the loss is frequently still greater. In Scotland, where the denomination of the coin has undergone much greater alterations than it ever did in England, and in France, where it has undergone still greater than it ever did in Scotland, some ancient rents, originally of considerable value, have, in this manner, been reduced almost to nothing.

Equal quantities of labor will, at distant times, be purchased more nearly with equal quantities of corn, the subsistence of the laborer, than with equal quantities of gold and silver, or, perhaps, of any other commodity. Equal quantities of corn, therefore, will, at distant times, be more nearly of the same real value, or enable the possessor to purchase or command more nearly the same quantity of the labor of other people. They will do this, I say, more nearly than equal quantities of almost any other commodity; for even equal quantities of corn will not do it exactly. The subsistence of the laborer, or the real price of labor, as I shall endeavor to show hereafter, is very different upon different occasions; more liberal in a society advancing to opulence, than in one that is standing still, and in one that is standing still, than in one that is going backwards. Every other commodity, however, will, at any particular time, purchase a greater or smaller quantity of labor, in proportion to the quantity of subsistence which it can purchase at that time. A rent, therefore, reserved in corn, is liable only to the variations in the quantity of labor which a certain quantity of corn can purchase. But a rent reserved in any other commodity is liable, not only to the variations in the quantity of labor which any particular quantity of corn can purchase, but to the variations in the quantity of corn which can be purchased by any particular quantity of that commodity.

Though the real value of a corn rent, it is to be observed, however, varies much less from century to century than that of a money rent, it varies much more from year to year. The money price of labor, as I shall endeavor to show hereafter, does not fluctuate from year to year with the money price of corn, but seems to be everywhere accommodated, not to the temporary or occasional, but to the average or ordinary price of that necessary of life. The average or ordinary price of corn, again is regulated, as I shall likewise endeavor to show hereafter, by the value of silver, by the richness or barrenness of the mines which supply the market with that metal, or by the quantity of labor which must be employed, and consequently of corn which must be consumed, in order to bring any particular quantity of silver from the mine to the market. But the value of silver, though it sometimes varies greatly from century to century, seldom varies much from year to year, but frequently continues the same, or very nearly the same, for half a century or a century together. The ordinary or average money price of corn, therefore, may, during so long a period, continue the same, or very nearly the same, too, and along with it the money price of labor, provided, at least, the society continues, in other respects, in the same, or nearly in the same, condition. In the mean time, the temporary and occasional price of corn may frequently be double one year of what it had been the year before, or fluctuate, for example, from five-and-twenty to fifty shillings the quarter. But when corn is at the latter price, not only the nominal, but the real value of a corn rent, will be double of what it is when at the former, or will command double the quantity either of labor, or of the greater part of other commodities; the money price of labor, and along with it that of most other things, continuing the same during all these fluctuations.

Labor, therefore, it appears evidently, is the only universal, as well as the only accurate, measure of value, or the only standard by which we can compare the values of different commodities, at all times, and at all places. We cannot estimate, it is allowed, the real value of different commodities from century to century by the quantities of silver which were given for them. We cannot estimate it from year to year by the quantities of corn. By the quantities of labor, we can, with the greatest accuracy, estimate it, both from century to century, and from year to year. From century to century, corn is a better measure than silver, because, from century to century, equal quantities of corn will command the same quantity of labor more nearly than equal quantities of silver. From year to year, on the contrary, silver is a better measure than corn, because equal quantities of it will more nearly command the same quantity of labor.

But though, in establishing perpetual rents, or even in letting very long leases, it may be of use to distinguish between real and nominal price; it is of none in buying and selling, the more common and ordinary transactions of human life.

At the same time and place, the real and the nominal price of all commodities are exactly in proportion to one another. The more or less money you get for any commodity, in the London market, for example, the more or less labor it will at that time and place enable you to purchase or command. At the same time and place, therefore, money is the exact measure of the real exchangeable value of all commodities. It is so, however, at the same time and place only.

Though at distant places there is no regular proportion between the real and the money price of commodities, yet the merchant who carries goods from the one to the other, has nothing to consider but the money price, or the difference between the quantity of silver for which he buys them, and that for which he is likely to sell them. Half an ounce of silver at Canton in China may command a greater quantity both of labor and of the necessaries and conveniences of life, than an ounce at London. A commodity, therefore, which sells for half an ounce of silver at Canton, may there be really dearer, of more real importance to the man who possesses it there, than a commodity which sells for an ounce at London is to the man who possesses it at London. If a London merchant, however, can buy at Canton, for half an ounce of silver, a commodity which he can afterwards sell at London for an ounce, he gains a hundred percent by the bargain, just as much as if an ounce of silver was at London exactly of the same value as at Canton. It is of no importance to him that half an ounce of silver at Canton would have given him the command of more labor, and of a greater quantity of the necessaries and conveniences of life than an ounce can do at London. An ounce at London will always give him the command of double the quantity of all these, which half an ounce could have done there, and this is precisely what he wants.

As it is the nominal or money price of goods, therefore, which finally determines the prudence or imprudence of all purchases and sales, and thereby regulates almost the whole business of common life in which price is concerned, we cannot wonder that it should have been so much more attended to than the real price.

In such a work as this, however, it may sometimes be of use to compare the different real values of a particular commodity at different times and places, or the different degrees of power over the labor of other people which it may, upon different occasions, have given to those who possessed it. We must in this case compare, not so much the different quantities of silver for which it was commonly sold, as the different quantities or labor which those different quantities of silver could have purchased. But the current prices of labor, at distant times and places, can scarce ever be known with any degree of exactness. Those of corn, though they have in few places been regularly recorded, are in general better known, and have been more frequently taken notice of by historians and other writers. We must generally, therefore, content ourselves with them, not as being always exactly in the same proportion as the current prices of labor, but as being the nearest approximation which can commonly be had to that proportion. I shall hereafter have occasion to make several comparisons of this kind.

In the progress of industry, commercial nations have found it convenient to coin several different metals into money; gold for larger payments, silver for purchases of moderate value, and copper, or some other coarse metal, for those of still smaller consideration. They have always, however, considered one of those metals as more peculiarly the measure of value than any of the other two; and this preference seems generally to have been given to the metal which they happen first to make use of as the instrument of commerce. Having once begun to use it as their standard, which they must have done when they had no other money, they have generally continued to do so even when the necessity was not the same.

The Romans are said to have had nothing but copper money till within five years before the first Punic war (Pliny, lib. xxxIII cap. 3), when they first began to coin silver. Copper, therefore, appears to have continued always the measure of value in that republic. At Rome all accounts appear to have been kept, and the value of all estates to have been computed, either in *asses* or in *sestertii*. The *as* was always the denomination of a copper coin. The word *sestertius* signifies two asses and a half. Though the sestertius, therefore, was originally a silver coin, its value was estimated in copper. At Rome, one who owed a great deal of money was said to have a great deal of other people's copper.

The northern nations who established themselves upon the ruins of the Roman empire, seem to have had silver money from the first beginning of their settlements, and not to have known either gold or copper coins for several ages thereafter. There were silver coins in England in the time of the Saxons; but there was little gold coined till the time of Edward III nor any copper till that of James I of Great Britain. In England, therefore, and for the same reason, I believe, in all other modern nations of Europe, all accounts are kept, and the value of all goods and of all estates is generally computed, in silver: and when we mean to express the amount of a person's fortune, we seldom mention the number of guineas, but the number of pounds sterling which we suppose would be given for it.

Originally, in all countries, I believe, a legal tender of payment could be made only in the coin of that metal which was peculiarly considered as the standard or measure of value. In England, gold was not considered as a legal tender for a long time after it was coined into money. The proportion between the values of gold and silver money was not fixed by any public law or proclamation, but was left to be settled by the market. If a debtor offered payment in gold, the creditor might either reject such payment altogether, or accept of it at such a valuation of the gold as he and his debtor could agree upon. Copper is not at present a legal tender, except in the change of the smaller silver coins. In this state of things, the distinction between the metal which was the standard, and that which was not the standard, was something more than a nominal distinction.

In process of time, and as people became gradually more familiar with the use of the different metals in coin, and consequently better acquainted with the proportion between their respective values, it has, in most countries, I believe, been found convenient to ascertain this proportion, and to declare by a public law, that a guinea, for example, of such a weight and fineness, should exchange for one-and-twenty shillings, or be a legal tender for a debt of that amount. In this state of things, and during the continuance of any one regulated proportion of this kind, the distinction between the metal, which is the standard, and that which is not the standard, becomes little more than a nominal distinction.

In consequence of any change, however, in this regulated proportion, this distinction becomes, or at least seems to become, something more than nominal again. If the regulated value of a guinea, for example, was either reduced to twenty, or raised to two-and-twenty shillings, all accounts being kept, and almost all obligations for debt being expressed, in silver money, the greater part of payments could in either case be made with the same quantity of silver money as before; but would require very different quantities of gold money; a greater in the one case, and a smaller in the other. Silver would appear to be more invariable in its value than gold. Silver would appear to measure the value of gold, and gold would not appear to measure the value of silver. The value of gold would seem to depend upon the quantity of silver which it would exchange for, and the value of silver would not seem to depend upon the quantity of gold which it would exchange for. This difference, however, would be altogether owing to the custom of keeping accounts, and of expressing the amount of all great and small sums rather in silver than in gold money. One of Mr. Drummond's notes for five-and-twenty or fifty guineas would, after an alteration of this kind, be still payable with five-and-twenty or fifty guineas, in the same manner as before. It would, after such an alteration, be payable with the same quantity of gold as before, but with very different quantities of silver. In the payment of such a note, gold would appear to be more invariable in its value than silver. Gold would appear to measure the value of silver, and silver would not appear to measure the value of gold. If the custom of keeping accounts, and of expressing prom-issory-notes and other obligations for money, in this manner should ever become gen-eral, gold, and not silver, would be considered as the metal which was peculiarly the standard or measure of value.

In reality, during the continuance of any one regulated proportion between the re-spective values of the different metals in coin, the value of the most precious metal reg-ulates the value of the whole coin. Twelve copper pence contain half a pound avoirdupois of copper, of not the best quality, which, before it is coined, is seldom worth seven-pence in silver. But as, by the regulation, twelve such pence are ordered to exchange for a shilling, they are in the market considered as worth a shilling, and a shilling can at any time be had for them. Even before the late reformation of the gold coin of Great Britain, the gold, that part of it at least which circulated in London and its neighborhood, was in general less degraded below its standard weight than the greater part of the silver. One-and-twenty worn and defaced shillings, however, were considered as equivalent to a guinea, which, perhaps, indeed, was worn and defaced too, but seldom so much so. The late regulations have brought the gold coin as near, perhaps, to its standard weight as it is possible to bring the current coin of any nation; and the order to receive no gold at the public offices but by weight, is likely to preserve it so, as long as that order is enforced. The silver coin still continues in the same worn and degraded state as before the refor-mation of the gold coin. In the market, however, one-and-twenty shillings of this de-graded silver coin are still considered as worth a guinea of this excellent gold coin.

The reformation of the gold coin has evidently raised the value of the silver coin which can be exchanged for it.

In the English mint, a pound weight of gold is coined into forty-four guineas and a half, which at one-and-twenty shillings the guinea, is equal to forty-six pounds fourteen shillings and sixpence. An ounce of such gold coin, therefore, is worth £3:17:10 1⁄2 in silver. In England, no duty or seignorage is paid upon the coinage, and he who carries a pound weight or an ounce weight of standard gold bullion to the mint, gets back a pound weight or an ounce weight of gold in coin, without any deduction. Three pounds sev-enteen shillings and ten pence halfpenny an ounce, therefore, is said to be the mint price of gold in England, or the quantity of gold coin which the mint gives in return for stan-dard gold bullion.

Before the reformation of the gold coin, the price of standard gold bullion in the mar-ket had, for many years, been upwards of £3:18s. sometimes £3:19s, and very frequently £4 an ounce; that sum, it is probable, in the worn and degraded gold coin, seldom con-taining more than an ounce of standard gold. Since the reformation of the gold coin, the market price of standard gold bullion seldom exceeds £3:17:7 an ounce. Before the ref-ormation of the gold coin, the market price was always more or less above the mint price.

Since that reformation, the market price has been constantly below the mint price. But that market price is the same whether it is paid in gold or in silver coin. The late reformation of the gold coin, therefore, has raised not only the value of the gold coin, but likewise that of the silver coin in proportion to gold bullion, and probably, too, in proportion to all other commodities; though the price of the greater part of other commodities being influenced by so many other causes, the rise in the value of either gold or silver coin in proportion to them may not be so distinct and sensible.

In the English mint, a pound weight of standard silver bullion is coined into sixty-two shillings, containing, in the same manner, a pound weight of standard silver. Five shillings and two pence an ounce, therefore, is said to be the mint price of silver in England, or the quantity of silver coin which the mint gives in return for standard silver bullion. Before the reformation of the gold coin, the market price of standard silver bullion was, upon different occasions, five shillings and four pence, five shillings and five pence, five shillings and sixpence, five shillings and seven pence, and very often five shillings and eight pence an ounce. Five shillings and seven pence, however, seems to have been the most common price. Since the reformation of the gold coin, the market price of standard silver bullion has fallen occasionally to five shillings and three pence, five shillings and four pence, and five shillings and five pence an ounce, which last price it has scarce ever exceeded. Though the market price of silver bullion has fallen considerably since the reformation of the gold coin, it has not fallen so low as the mint price.

In the proportion between the different metals in the English coin, as copper is rated very much above its real value, so silver is rated somewhat below it. In the market of Europe, in the French coin and in the Dutch coin, an ounce of fine gold exchanges for about fourteen ounces of fine silver. In the English coin, it exchanges for about fifteen ounces, that is, for more silver than it is worth, according to the common estimation of Europe. But as the price of copper in bars is not, even in England, raised by the high price of copper in English coin, so the price of silver in bullion is not sunk by the low rate of silver in English coin. Silver in bullion still preserves its proper proportion to gold, for the same reason that copper in bars preserves its proper proportion to silver.

Upon the reformation of the silver coin, in the reign of William III, the price of silver bullion still continued to be somewhat above the mint price. Mr. Locke imputed this high price to the permission of exporting silver bullion, and to the prohibition of exporting silver coin. This permission of exporting, he said, rendered the demand for silver bullion greater than the demand for silver coin. But the number of people who want silver coin for the common uses of buying and selling at home, is surely much greater than that of those who want silver bullion either for the use of exportation or for any other use. There subsists at present a like permission of exporting gold bullion, and a like prohibition of exporting gold coin; and yet the price of gold bullion has fallen below the mint price. But in the English coin, silver was then, in the same manner as now, under-rated in proportion to gold; and the gold coin (which at that time, too, was not supposed to require any reformation) regulated then, as well as now, the real value of the whole coin. As the reformation of the silver coin did not then reduce the price of silver bullion to the mint price, it is not very probable that a like reformation will do so now.

Were the silver coin brought back as near to its standard weight as the gold, a guinea, it is probable, would, according to the present proportion, exchange for more silver in coin than it would purchase in bullion. The silver coin containing its full standard weight, there would in this case, be a profit in melting it down, in order, first to sell the bullion for gold coin, and afterwards to exchange this gold coin for silver coin, to be melted down in the same manner. Some alteration in the present proportion seems to be the only method of preventing this inconveniency.

The inconveniency, perhaps, would be less, if silver was rated in the coin as much above its proper proportion to gold as it is at present rated below it, provided it was at the same time enacted, that silver should not be a legal tender for more than the change of a guinea, in the same manner as copper is not a legal tender for more than the change of a shilling. No creditor could, in this case, be cheated in consequence of the high valuation of silver in coin; as no creditor can at present be cheated in consequence of the high valuation of copper. The bankers only would suffer by this regulation. When a run comes upon them, they sometimes endeavor to gain time, by paying in sixpences, and they would be precluded by this regulation from this discreditable method of evading immediate payment. They would be obliged, in consequence, to keep at all times in their coffers a greater quantity of cash than at present; and though this might, no doubt, be a considerable inconveniency to them, it would, at the same time, be a considerable security to their creditors.

Three pounds seventeen shillings and ten pence halfpenny (the mint price of gold) certainly does not contain, even in our present excellent gold coin, more than an ounce of standard gold, and it may be thought, therefore, should not purchase more standard bullion. But gold in coin is more convenient than gold in bullion; and though, in England, the coinage is free, yet the gold which is carried in bullion to the mint, can seldom be returned in coin to the owner till after a delay of several weeks. In the present hurry of the mint, it could not be returned till after a delay of several months. This delay is equivalent to a small duty, and renders gold in coin somewhat more valuable than an equal quantity of gold in bullion. If, in the English coin, silver was rated according to its proper proportion to gold, the price of silver bullion would probably fall below the mint price, even without any reformation of the silver coin; the value even of the present worn and defaced silver coin being regulated by the value of the excellent gold coin for which it can be changed.

A small seignorage or duty upon the coinage of both gold and silver, would probably increase still more the superiority of those metals in coin above an equal quantity of either of them in bullion. The coinage would, in this case, increase the value of the metal coined in proportion to the extent of this small duty, for the same reason that the fashion increases the value of plate in proportion to the price of that fashion. The superiority of coin above bullion would prevent the melting down of the coin, and would discourage its exportation. If, upon any public exigency, it should become necessary to export the coin, the greater part of it would soon return again, of its own accord. Abroad, it could sell only for its weight in bullion. At home, it would buy more than that weight. There would be a profit, therefore, in bringing it home again. In France, a seignorage of about eight percent is imposed upon the coinage, and the French coin, when exported, is said to return home again, of its own accord.

The occasional fluctuations in the market price of gold and silver bullion arise from the same causes as the like fluctuations in that of all other commodities. The frequent loss of those metals from various accidents by sea and by land, the continual waste of them in gilding and plating, in lace and embroidery, in the wear and tear of coin, and in that of plate, require, in all countries which possess no mines of their own, a continual importation, in order to repair this loss and this waste. The merchant importers, like all other merchants, we may believe, endeavor, as well as they can, to suit their occasional importations to what they judge is likely to be the immediate demand. With all their attention, however, they sometimes overdo the business, and sometimes under do it. When they import more bullion than is wanted, rather than incur the risk and trouble of exporting it again, they are sometimes willing to sell a part of it for something less than the ordinary or average price. When, on the other hand, they import less than is wanted, they get something more than this price. But when, under all those occasional fluctuations, the market price either of gold or silver bullion continues for several years together steadily and constantly, either more or less above, or more or less below the mint price, we may be assured that this steady and constant, either superiority or inferiority of price, is the effect of something in the state of the coin, which, at that time, renders a certain quantity of coin either of more value or of less value than the precise quantity of bullion which it ought to contain. The constancy and steadiness of the effect supposes a proportionable constancy and steadiness in the cause.

The money of any particular country is, at any particular time and place, more or less an accurate measure or value, according as the current coin is more or less exactly agreeable to its standard, or contains more or less exactly the precise quantity of pure gold or pure silver which it ought to contain. If in England, for example, forty-four guineas and a half contained exactly a pound weight of standard gold, or eleven ounces of fine gold, and one ounce of alloy, the gold coin of England would be as accurate a measure of the actual value of goods at any particular time and place as the nature of the thing would admit. But if, by rubbing and wearing, forty-four guineas and a half generally contain less than a pound weight of standard gold, the diminution, however, being greater in some pieces than in others, the measure of value comes to be liable to the same sort of uncertainty to which all other weights and measures are commonly exposed. As it rarely happens that these are exactly agreeable to their standard, the merchant adjusts the price of his goods as well as he can, not to what those weights and measures ought to be, but to what, upon an average, he finds, by experience, they actually are. In consequence of a like disorder in the coin, the price of goods comes, in the same manner, to be adjusted, not to the quantity of pure gold or silver which the coin ought to contain, but to that which, upon an average, it is found, by experience, it actually does contain.

By the money price of goods, it is to be observed, I understand always the quantity of pure gold or silver for which they are sold, without any regard to the denomination of the coin. Six shillings and eight pence, for example, in the time of Edward I, I consider as the same money price with a pound sterling in the present times, because it contained, as nearly as we can judge, the same quantity of pure silver.

CHAPTER VI

Of the Component Parts of the Price of Commodities

In that early and rude state of society which precedes both the accumulation of stock and the appropriation of land, the proportion between the quantities of labor necessary for acquiring different objects, seems to be the only circumstance which can afford any rule for exchanging them for one another. If among a nation of hunters, for example, it usually costs twice the labor to kill a beaver which it does to kill a deer, one beaver should naturally exchange for or be worth two deer. It is natural that what is usually the produce of two days or two hours labor, should be worth double of what is usually the produce of one day's or one hour's labor.

If the one species of labor should be more severe than the other, some allowance will naturally be made for this superior hardship; and the produce of one hour's labor in the one way may frequently exchange for that of two hour's labor in the other.

Or if the one species of labor requires an uncommon degree of dexterity and ingenuity, the esteem which men have for such talents, will naturally give a value to their produce, superior to what would be due to the time employed about it. Such talents can seldom be acquired but in consequence of long application, and the superior value of their produce may frequently be no more than a reasonable compensation for the time and labor which must be spent in acquiring them. In the advanced state of society, allowances of this kind, for superior hardship and superior skill, are commonly made in the wages of labor; and something of the same kind must probably have taken place in its earliest and rudest period.

In this state of things, the whole produce of labor belongs to the laborer; and the quantity of labor commonly employed in acquiring or producing any commodity, is the only circumstance which can regulate the quantity of labor which it ought commonly to purchase, command, or exchange for.

As soon as stock has accumulated in the hands of particular persons, some of them will naturally employ it in setting to work industrious people, whom they will supply with materials and subsistence, in order to make a profit by the sale of their work, or by what their labor adds to the value of the materials. In exchanging the complete manufacture either for money, for labor, or for other goods, over and above what may be sufficient to pay the price of the materials, and the wages of the workmen, something must be given for the profits of the undertaker of the work, who hazards his stock in this adventure. The value which the workmen add to the materials, therefore, resolves itself in this case into two parts, of which the one pays their wages, the other the profits of their employer upon the whole stock of materials and wages which he advanced. He could have no interest to employ them, unless he expected from the sale of their work something more than what was sufficient to replace his stock to him; and he could have no interest to employ a great stock rather than a small one, unless his profits were to bear some proportion to the extent of his stock.

The profits of stock, it may perhaps be thought, are only a different name for the wages of a particular sort of labor, the labor of inspection and direction. They are, however, altogether different, are regulated by quite different principles, and bear no proportion to the quantity, the hardship, or the ingenuity of this supposed labor of inspection and direction. They are regulated altogether by the value of the stock employed, and are greater or smaller in proportion to the extent of this stock. Let us suppose, for example, that in some particular place, where the common annual profits of manufacturing stock are ten percent there are two different manufactures, in each of which twenty workmen are employed, at the rate of fifteen pounds a year each, or at the expense of three hundred a year in each manufactory. Let us suppose, too, that the coarse materials annually wrought up in the one cost only seven hundred pounds, while the finer materials in the other cost seven thousand. The capital annually employed in the one will, in this case, amount only to one thousand pounds; whereas that employed in the other will amount to seven thousand three hundred pounds. At the rate of ten percent therefore, the undertaker of the one will expect a yearly profit of about one hundred pounds only; while that of the other will expect about seven hundred and thirty pounds. But though their profits are so very different, their labor of inspection and direction may be either altogether or very nearly the same. In many great works, almost the whole labor of this kind is committed to some principal clerk. His wages properly express the value of this labor of inspection and direction. Though in settling them some regard is had commonly, not only to his labor and skill, but to the trust which is reposed in him, yet they never bear any regular proportion to the capital of which he oversees the management; and the owner of this capital, though he is thus discharged of almost all labor, still expects that his profit should bear a regular proportion to his capital. In the price of commodities, therefore, the profits of stock constitute a component part altogether different from the wages of labor, and regulated by quite different principles.

In this state of things, the whole produce of labor does not always belong to the laborer. He must in most cases share it with the owner of the stock which employs him. Neither is the quantity of labor commonly employed in acquiring or producing any commodity, the only circumstance which can regulate the quantity which it ought commonly to purchase, command or exchange for. An additional quantity, it is evident, must be due for the profits of the stock which advanced the wages and furnished the materials of that labor.

As soon as the land of any country has all become private property, the landlords, like all other men, love to reap where they never sowed, and demand a rent even for its natural produce. The wood of the forest, the grass of the field, and all the natural fruits of the earth, which, when land was in common, cost the laborer only the trouble of gathering them, come, even to him, to have an additional price fixed upon them. He must then pay for the license to gather them, and must give up to the landlord a portion of what his labor either collects or produces. This portion, or, what comes to the same thing, the price of this portion, constitutes the rent of land, and in the price of the greater part of commodities, makes a third component part.

The real value of all the different component parts of price, it must be observed, is measured by the quantity of labor which they can, each of them, purchase or command. Labor measures the value, not only of that part of price which resolves itself into labor, but of that which resolves itself into rent, and of that which resolves itself into profit.

In every society, the price of every commodity finally resolves itself into some one or other, or all of those three parts; and in every improved society, all the three enter, more or less, as component parts, into the price of the far greater part of commodities.

In the price of corn, for example, one part pays the rent of the landlord, another pays the wages or maintenance of the laborers and laboring cattle employed in producing it, and the third pays the profit of the farmer. These three parts seem either immediately or ultimately to make up the whole price of corn. A fourth part, it may perhaps be thought is necessary for replacing the stock of the farmer, or for compensating the wear and tear of his laboring cattle, and other instruments of husbandry. But it must be considered, that the price of any instrument of husbandry, such as a laboring horse, is itself made up of the same time parts; the rent of the land upon which he is reared, the labor of tending and rearing him, and the profits of the farmer, who advances both the rent of this land, and the wages of this labor. Though the price of the corn, therefore, may pay the price as well as the maintenance of the horse, the whole price still resolves itself, either immediately or ultimately, into the same three parts of rent, labor, and profit.

In the price of flour or meal, we must add to the price of the corn, the profits of the miller, and the wages of his servants; in the price of bread, the profits of the baker, and the wages of his servants; and in the price of both, the labor of transporting the corn from the house of the farmer to that of the miller, and from that of the miller to that of the baker, together with the profits of those who advance the wages of that labor.

The price of flax resolves itself into the same three parts as that of corn. In the price of linen we must add to this price the wages of the flax-dresser, of the spinner, of the weaver, of the bleacher, etc. together with the profits of their respective employers.

As any particular commodity comes to be more manufactured, that part of the price which resolves itself into wages and profit, comes to be greater in proportion to that which resolves itself into rent. In the progress of the manufacture, not only the number of profits increase, but every subsequent profit is greater than the foregoing; because the capital from which it is derived must always be greater. The capital which employs the weavers, for example, must be greater than that which employs the spinners; because it not only replaces that capital with its profits, but pays, besides, the wages of the weavers: and the profits must always bear some proportion to the capital.

In the most improved societies, however, there are always a few commodities of which the price resolves itself into two parts only, the wages of labor, and the profits of stock; and a still smaller number, in which it consists altogether in the wages of labor. In the price of sea-fish, for example, one part pays the labor of the fisherman, and the other the profits of the capital employed in the fishery. Rent very seldom makes any part of it, though it does sometimes, as I shall show hereafter. It is otherwise, at least through the greater part of Europe, in river fisheries. A salmon fishery pays a rent; and rent, though it cannot well be called the rent of land, makes a part of the price of a salmon, as well as wares and profit. In some parts of Scotland, a few poor people make a trade of gathering, along the sea-shore, those little variegated stones commonly known by the name of Scotch pebbles. The price which is paid to them by the stone-cutter, is altogether the wages of their labor; neither rent nor profit makes a part of it.

But the whole price of any commodity must still finally resolve itself into some one or other or all of those three parts; as whatever part of it remains after paying the rent of the land, and the price of the whole labor employed in raising, manufacturing, and bringing it to market, must necessarily be profit to somebody.

As the price or exchangeable value of every particular commodity, taken separately, resolves itself into some one or other, or all of those three parts; so that of all the commodities which compose the whole annual produce of the labor of every country, taken complexly, must resolve itself into the same three parts, and be parceled out among different inhabitants of the country, either as the wages of their labor, the profits of their stock, or the rent of their land. The whole of what is annually either collected or produced by the labor of every society, or, what comes to the same thing, the whole price of it, is in this manner originally distributed among some of its different members. Wages, profit, and rent, are the three original sources of all revenue, as well as of all exchangeable value. All other revenue is ultimately derived from some one or other of these.

Whoever derives his revenue from a fund which is his own, must draw it either from his labor, from his stock, or from his land. The revenue derived from labor is called wages; that derived from stock, by the person who manages or employs it, is called profit; that derived from it by the person who does not employ it himself, but lends it to another, is called the interest or the use of money. It is the compensation which the borrower pays to the lender, for the profit which he has an opportunity of making by the use of the money. Part of that profit naturally belongs to the borrower, who runs the risk and takes the trouble of employing it, and part to the lender, who affords him the opportunity of making this profit. The interest of money is always a derivative revenue, which, if it is not paid from the profit which is made by the use of the money, must be paid from some other source of revenue, unless perhaps the borrower is a spendthrift, who contracts a second debt in order to pay the interest of the first. The revenue which proceeds altogether from land, is called rent, and belongs to the landlord. The revenue of the farmer is derived partly from his labor, and partly from his stock. To him, land is only the instrument which enables him to earn the wages of this labor, and to make the profits of this stock. All taxes, and all the revenue which is founded upon them, all salaries, pensions, and annuities of every kind, are ultimately derived from some one or other of those three original sources of revenue, and are paid either immediately or mediately from the wages of labor, the profits of stock, or the rent of land.

When those three different sorts of revenue belong to different persons, they are readily distinguished; but when they belong to the same, they are sometimes confounded with one another, at least in common language.

A gentleman who farms a part of his own estate, after paying the expense of cultivation, should gain both the rent of the landlord and the profit of the farmer. He is apt to denominate, however, his whole gain, profit, and thus confounds rent with profit, at least in common language. The greater part of our North American and West Indian planters are in this situation. They farm, the greater part of them, their own estates: and accordingly we seldom hear of the rent of a plantation, but frequently of its profit.

Common farmers seldom employ any overseer to direct the general operations of the farm. They generally, too, work a good deal with their own hands, as ploughmen, harrowers, etc. What remains of the crop, after paying the rent, therefore, should not only replace to them their stock employed in cultivation, together with its ordinary profits, but pay them the wages which are due to them, both as laborers and overseers. Whatever remains, however, after paying the rent and keeping up the stock, is called profit. But wages evidently make a part of it. The farmer, by saving these wages, must necessarily gain them. Wages, therefore, are in this case confounded with profit.

An independent manufacturer, who has stock enough both to purchase materials, and to maintain himself till he can carry his work to market, should gain both the wages of a journeyman who works under a master, and the profit which that master makes by the sale of that journeyman's work. His whole gains, however, are commonly called profit, and wages are, in this case, too, confounded with profit.

A gardener who cultivates his own garden with his own hands, unites in his own person the three different characters, of landlord, farmer, and laborer. His produce, therefore, should pay him the rent of the first, the profit of the second, and the wages of the third. The whole, however, is commonly considered as the earnings of his labor. Both rent and profit are, in this case, confounded with wages.

As in a civilized country there are but few commodities of which the exchangeable value arises from labor only, rent and profit contributing largely to that of the far greater part of them, so the annual produce of its labor will always be sufficient to purchase or command a much greater quantity of labor than what was employed in raising, preparing, and bringing that produce to market. If the society were annually to employ all the labor which it can annually purchase, as the quantity of labor would increase greatly every year, so the produce of every succeeding year would be of vastly greater value than that of the foregoing. But there is no country in which the whole annual produce is employed in maintaining the industrious. The idle everywhere consume a great part of it; and, according to the different proportions in which it is annually divided between those two different orders of people, its ordinary or average value must either annually increase or diminish, or continue the same from one year to another.

CHAPTER VII

Of the Natural and Market Price of Commodities

There is in every society or neighborhood an ordinary or average rate, both of wages and profit, in every different employment of labor and stock. This rate is naturally regulated, as I shall show hereafter, partly by the general circumstances of the society, their riches or poverty, their advancing, stationary, or declining condition, and partly by the particular nature of each employment.

There is likewise in every society or neighborhood an ordinary or average rate of rent, which is regulated, too, as I shall show hereafter, partly by the general circumstances of the society or neighborhood in which the land is situated, and partly by the natural or improved fertility of the land.

These ordinary or average rates may be called the natural rates of wages, profit and rent, at the time and place in which they commonly prevail.

When the price of any commodity is neither more nor less than what is sufficient to pay the rent of the land, the wages of the labor, and the profits of the stock employed in raising, preparing, and bringing it to market, according to their natural rates, the commodity is then sold for what may be called its natural price.

The commodity is then sold precisely for what it is worth, or for what it really costs the person who brings it to market; for though, in common language, what is called the prime cost of any commodity does not comprehend the profit of the person who is to sell it again, yet, if he sells it at a price which does not allow him the ordinary rate of profit in his neighborhood, he is evidently a loser by the trade; since, by employing his stock in some other way, he might have made that profit. His profit, besides, is his revenue, the proper fund of his subsistence. As, while he is preparing and bringing the goods to market, he advances to his workmen their wages, or their subsistence; so he advances to himself, in the same manner, his own subsistence, which is generally suitable to the profit which he may reasonably expect from the sale of his goods. Unless they yield him this profit, therefore, they do not repay him what they may very properly be said to have really cost him.

Though the price, therefore, which leaves him this profit, is not always the lowest at which a dealer may sometimes sell his goods, it is the lowest at which he is likely to sell them for any considerable time; at least where there is perfect liberty, or where he may change his trade as often as he pleases.

The actual price at which any commodity is commonly sold, is called its market price. It may either be above, or below, or exactly the same with its natural price.

The market price of every particular commodity is regulated by the proportion between the quantity which is actually brought to market, and the demand of those who are willing to pay the natural price of the commodity, or the whole value of the rent, labor, and profit, which must be paid in order to bring it thither. Such people may be called the effectual demanders, and their demand the effectual demand; since it maybe sufficient to effectuate the bringing of the commodity to market. It is different from the absolute demand. A very poor man may be said, in some sense, to have a demand for a coach and six; he might like to have it; but his demand is not an effectual demand, as the commodity can never be brought to market in order to satisfy it.

When the quantity of any commodity which is brought to market falls short of the effectual demand, all those who are willing to pay the whole value of the rent, wages, and profit, which must be paid in order to bring it thither, cannot be supplied with the quantity which they want. Rather than want it altogether, some of them will be willing to give more. A competition will immediately begin among them, and the market price will rise more or less above the natural price, according as either the greatness of the deficiency, or the wealth and wanton luxury of the competitors, happen to animate more or less the eagerness of the competition. Among competitors of equal wealth and luxury, the same deficiency will generally occasion a more or less eager competition, according as the acquisition of the commodity happens to be of more or less importance to them. Hence the exorbitant price of the necessaries of life during the blockade of a town, or in a famine.

When the quantity brought to market exceeds the effectual demand, it cannot be all sold to those who are willing to pay the whole value of the rent, wages, and profit, which must be paid in order to bring it thither. Some part must be sold to those who are willing to pay less, and the low price which they give for it must reduce the price of the whole. The market price will sink more or less below the natural price, according as the greatness of the excess increases more or less the competition of the sellers, or according as it happens to be more or less important to them to get immediately rid of the commodity. The same excess in the importation of perishable, will occasion a much greater competition than in that of durable commodities; in the importation of oranges, for example, than in that of old iron.

When the quantity brought to market is just sufficient to supply the effectual demand, and no more, the market price naturally comes to be either exactly, or as nearly as can be judged of, the same with the natural price. The whole quantity upon hand can be disposed of for this price, and can not be disposed of for more. The competition of the different dealers obliges them all to accept of this price, but does not oblige them to accept of less.

The quantity of every commodity brought to market naturally suits itself to the effectual demand. It is the interest of all those who employ their land, labor, or stock, in bringing any commodity to market, that the quantity never should exceed the effectual demand; and it is the interest of all other people that it never should fall short of that demand.

If at any time it exceeds the effectual demand, some of the component parts of its price must be paid below their natural rate. If it is rent, the interest of the landlords will immediately prompt them to withdraw a part of their land; and if it is wages or profit, the interest of the laborers in the one case, and of their employers in the other, will prompt them to withdraw a part of their labor or stock, from this employment. The quantity brought to market will soon be no more than sufficient to supply the effectual demand. All the different parts of its price will rise to their natural rate, and the whole price to its natural price.

If, on the contrary, the quantity brought to market should at any time fall short of the effectual demand, some of the component parts of its price must rise above their natural rate. If it is rent, the interest of all other landlords will naturally prompt them to prepare more land for the raising of this commodity; if it is wages or profit, the interest of all other laborers and dealers will soon prompt them to employ more labor and stock in preparing and bringing it to market. The quantity brought thither will soon be sufficient to supply the effectual demand. All the different parts of its price will soon sink to their natural rate, and the whole price to its natural price.

The natural price, therefore, is, as it were, the central price, to which the prices of all commodities are continually gravitating. Different accidents may sometimes keep them suspended a good deal above it, and sometimes force them down even somewhat below it. But whatever may be the obstacles which hinder them from settling in this centre of repose and continuance, they are constantly tending towards it.

The whole quantity of industry annually employed in order to bring any commodity to market, naturally suits itself in this manner to the effectual demand. It naturally aims at bringing always that precise quantity thither which may be sufficient to supply, and no more than supply, that demand.

But, in some employments, the same quantity of industry will, in different years, produce very different quantities of commodities; while, in others, it will produce always the same, or very nearly the same. The same number of laborers in husbandry will, in different years, produce very different quantities of corn, wine, oil, hops, etc. But the same number of spinners or weavers will every year produce the same, or very nearly the same, quantity of linen and woolen cloth. It is only the average produce of the one species of industry which can be suited, in any respect, to the effectual demand; and as its actual produce is frequently much greater, and frequently much less, than its average produce, the quantity of the commodities brought to market will sometimes exceed a good deal, and sometimes fall short a good deal, of the effectual demand. Even though that demand, therefore, should continue always the same, their market price will be liable to great fluctuations, will sometimes fall a good deal below, and sometimes rise a good deal above, their natural price. In the other species of industry, the produce of equal quantities of labor being always the same, or very nearly the same, it can be more exactly suited to the effectual demand. While that demand continues the same, therefore, the market price of the commodities is likely to do so too, and to be either altogether, or as nearly as can be judged of, the same with the natural price. That the price of linen and woolen cloth is liable neither to such frequent, nor to such great variations, as the price of corn, every man's experience will inform him. The price of the one species of commodities varies only with the variations in the demand; that of the other varies not only with the variations in the demand, but with the much greater, and more frequent, variations in the quantity of what is brought to market, in order to supply that demand.

The occasional and temporary fluctuations in the market price of any commodity fall chiefly upon those parts of its price which resolve themselves into wages and profit. That part which resolves itself into rent is less affected by them. A rent certain in money is not in the least affected by them, either in its rate or in its value. A rent which consists either in a certain proportion, or in a certain quantity, of the rude produce, is no doubt affected in its yearly value by all the occasional and temporary fluctuations in the market price of that rude produce; but it is seldom affected by them in its yearly rate. In settling the terms of the lease, the landlord and farmer endeavor, according to their best judgment, to adjust that rate, not to the temporary and occasional, but to the average and ordinary price of the produce.

Such fluctuations affect both the value and the rate, either of wages or of profit, according as the market happens to be either overstocked or understocked with commodities or with labor, with work done, or with work to be done. A public mourning raises the price of black cloth (with which the market is almost always understocked upon such occasions), and augments the profits of the merchants who possess any considerable quantity of it. It has no effect upon the wages of the weavers. The market is understocked with commodities, not with labor, with work done, not with work to be done. It raises the wages of journeymen tailors. The market is here understocked with labor. There is an effectual demand for more labor, for more work to be done, than can be had. It sinks the price of colored silks and cloths, and thereby reduces the profits of the merchants who have any considerable quantity of them upon hand. It sinks, too, the wages of the workmen employed in preparing such commodities, for which all demand is stopped for six months, perhaps for a twelvemonth. The market is here overstocked both with commodities and with labor.

But though the market price of every particular commodity is in this manner continually gravitating, if one may say so, towards the natural price; yet sometimes particular accidents, sometimes natural causes, and sometimes particular regulations of policy, may, in many commodities, keep up the market price, for a long time together, a good deal above the natural price.

When, by an increase in the effectual demand, the market price of some particular commodity happens to rise a good deal above the natural price, those who employ their stocks in supplying that market, are generally careful to conceal this change. If it was commonly known, their great profit would tempt so many new rivals to employ their stocks in the same way, that, the effectual demand being fully supplied, the market price would soon be reduced to the natural price, and, perhaps, for some time even below it. If the market is at a great distance from the residence of those who supply it, they may sometimes be able to keep the secret for several years together, and may so long enjoy their extraordinary profits without any new rivals. Secrets of this kind, however, it must be acknowledged, can seldom be long kept; and the extraordinary profit can last very little longer than they are kept.

Secrets in manufactures are capable of being longer kept than secrets in trade. A dyer who has found the means of producing a particular color with materials which cost only half the price of those commonly made use of, may, with good management, enjoy the advantage of his discovery as long as he lives, and even leave it as a legacy to his posterity. His extraordinary gains arise from the high price which is paid for his private labor. They properly consist in the high wages of that labor. But as they are repeated upon every part of his stock, and as their whole amount bears, upon that account, a regular proportion to it, they are commonly considered as extraordinary profits of stock.

Such enhancements of the market price are evidently the effects of particular accidents, of which, however, the operation may sometimes last for many years together.

Some natural productions require such a singularity of soil and situation, that all the land in a great country, which is fit for producing them, may not be sufficient to supply the effectual demand. The whole quantity brought to market, therefore, may be disposed of to those who are willing to give more than what is sufficient to pay the rent of the land which produced them, together with the wages of the labor and the profits of the stock which were employed in preparing and bringing them to market, according to their natural rates. Such commodities may continue for whole centuries together to be sold at this high price; and that part of it which resolves itself into the rent of land, is in this case the part which is generally paid above its natural rate. The rent of the land which affords such singular and esteemed productions, like the rent of some vineyards in France of a peculiarly happy soil and situation, bears no regular proportion to the rent of other equally fertile and equally well cultivated land in its neighborhood. The wages of the labor, and the profits of the stock employed in bringing such commodities to market, on the contrary, are seldom out of their natural proportion to those of the other employments of labor and stock in their neighborhood.

Such enhancements of the market price are evidently the effect of natural causes, which may hinder the effectual demand from ever being fully supplied, and which may continue, therefore, to operate forever.

A monopoly granted either to an individual or to a trading company, has the same effect as a secret in trade or manufactures. The monopolists, by keeping the market constantly understocked by never fully supplying the effectual demand, sell their commodities much above the natural price, and raise their emoluments, whether they consist in wages or profit, greatly above their natural rate.

The price of monopoly is upon every occasion the highest which can be got. The natural price, or the price of free competition, on the contrary, is the lowest which can be taken, not upon every occasion indeed, but for any considerable time together. The one is upon every occasion the highest which can be squeezed out of the buyers, or which it is supposed they will consent to give; the other is the lowest which the sellers can commonly afford to take, and at the same time continue their business.

The exclusive privileges of corporations, statutes of apprenticeship, and all those laws which restrain in particular employments, the competition to a smaller number than might otherwise go into them, have the same tendency, though in a less degree. They are a sort of enlarged monopolies, and may frequently, for ages together, and in whole classes of employments, keep up the market price of particular commodities above the natural price, and maintain both the wages of the labor and the profits of the stock employed about them somewhat above their natural rate.

Such enhancements of the market price may last as long as the regulations of policy which give occasion to them.

The market price of any particular commodity, though it may continue long above, can seldom continue long below, its natural price. Whatever part of it was paid below the natural rate, the persons whose interest it affected would immediately feel the loss, and would immediately withdraw either so much land or no much labor, or so much stock, from being employed about it, that the quantity brought to market would soon be no more than sufficient to supply the effectual demand. Its market price, therefore, would soon rise to the natural price; this at least would be the case where there was perfect liberty.

The same statutes of apprenticeship and other corporation laws, indeed, which, when a manufacture is in prosperity, enable the workman to raise his wages a good deal above their natural rate, sometimes oblige him, when it decays, to let them down a good deal below it. As in the one case they exclude many people from his employment, so in the other they exclude him from many employments. The effect of such regulations, however, is not near so durable in sinking the workman's wages below, as in raising them above their natural rate. Their operation in the one way may endure for many centuries, but in the other it can last no longer than the lives of some of the workmen who were bred to the business in the time of its prosperity. When they are gone, the number of those who are afterwards educated to the trade will naturally suit itself to the effectual demand. The policy must be as violent as that of Indostan or ancient Egypt (where every man was bound by a principle of religion to follow the occupation of his father, and was supposed to commit the most horrid sacrilege if he changed it for another), which can in any particular employment, and for several generations together, sink either the wages of labor or the profits of stock below their natural rate.

This is all that I think necessary to be observed at present concerning the deviations, whether occasional or permanent, of the market price of commodities from the natural price.

The natural price itself varies with the natural rate of each of its component parts, of wages, profit, and rent; and in every society this rate varies according to their circumstances, according to their riches or poverty, their advancing, stationary, or declining condition. I shall, in the four following chapters, endeavor to explain, as fully and distinctly as I can, the causes of those different variations.

First, I shall endeavor to explain what are the circumstances which naturally determine the rate of wages, and in what manner those circumstances are affected by the riches or poverty, by the advancing, stationary, or declining state of the society.

Secondly, I shall endeavor to show what are the circumstances which naturally determine the rate of profit; and in what manner, too, those circumstances are affected by the like variations in the state of the society.

Though pecuniary wages and profit are very different in the different employments of labor and stock; yet a certain proportion seems commonly to take place between both the pecuniary wages in all the different employments of labor, and the pecuniary profits in all the different employments of stock. This proportion, it will appear hereafter, depends partly upon the nature of the different employments, and partly upon the different laws and policy of the society in which they are carried on. But though in many respects dependent upon the laws and policy, this proportion seems to be little affected by the riches or poverty of that society, by its advancing, stationary, or declining condition, but to remain the same, or very nearly the same, in all those different states. I shall, in the third place, endeavor to explain all the different circumstances which regulate this proportion.

In the fourth and last place, I shall endeavor to show what are the circumstances which regulate the rent of land, and which either raise or lower the real price of all the different substances which it produces.

CHAPTER VIII

Of the Wages of Labor

The produce of labor constitutes the natural recompense or wages of labor.

In that original state of things which precedes both the appropriation of land and the accumulation of stock, the whole produce of labor belongs to the laborer. He has neither landlord nor master to share with him.

Had this state continued, the wages of labor would have augmented with all those improvements in its productive powers, to which the division of labor gives occasion. All things would gradually have become cheaper. They would have been produced by a smaller quantity of labor; and as the commodities produced by equal quantities of labor would naturally in this state of things be exchanged for one another, they would have been purchased likewise with the produce of a smaller quantity.

But though all things would have become cheaper in reality, in appearance many things might have become dearer, than before, or have been exchanged for a greater quantity of other goods. Let us suppose, for example, that in the greater part of employments the productive powers of labor had been improved to tenfold, or that a day's labor could produce ten times the quantity of work which it had done originally; but that in a particular employment they had been improved only to double, or that a day's labor could produce only twice the quantity of work which it had done before. In exchanging the produce of a day's labor in the greater part of employments for that of a day's labor in this particular one, ten times the original quantity of work in them would purchase only twice the original quantity in it. Any particular quantity in it, therefore, a pound weight, for example, would appear to be five times dearer than before. In reality, however, it would be twice as cheap. Though it required five times the quantity of other goods to purchase it, it would require only half the quantity of labor either to purchase or to produce it. The acquisition, therefore, would be twice as easy as before.

But this original state of things, in which the laborer enjoyed the whole produce of his own labor, could not last beyond the first introduction of the appropriation of land and the accumulation of stock. It was at an end, therefore, long before the most considerable improvements were made in the productive powers of labor; and it would be to no purpose to trace further what might have been its effects upon the recompense or wages of labor.

As soon as land becomes private property, the landlord demands a share of almost all the produce which the laborer can either raise or collect from it. His rent makes the first deduction from the produce of the labor which is employed upon land.

It seldom happens that the person who tills the ground has wherewithal to maintain himself till he reaps the harvest. His maintenance is generally advanced to him from the stock of a master, the farmer who employs him, and who would have no interest to employ him, unless he was to share in the produce of his labor, or unless his stock was to be replaced to him with a profit. This profit makes a second deduction from the produce of the labor which is employed upon land.

The produce of almost all other labor is liable to the like deduction of profit. In all arts and manufactures, the greater part of the workmen stand in need of a master, to advance them the materials of their work, and their wages and maintenance, till it be completed. He shares in the produce of their labor, or in the value which it adds to the materials upon which it is bestowed; and in this share consists his profit.

It sometimes happens, indeed, that a single independent workman has stock sufficient both to purchase the materials of his work, and to maintain himself till it be completed. He is both master and workman, and enjoys the whole produce of his own labor, or the whole value which it adds to the materials upon which it is bestowed. It includes what are usually two distinct revenues, belonging to two distinct persons, the profits of stock, and the wages of labor.

Such cases, however, are not very frequent; and in every part of Europe twenty workmen serve under a master for one that is independent, and the wages of labor are everywhere understood to be, what they usually are, when the laborer is one person, and the owner of the stock which employs him another.

What are the common wages of labor, depends everywhere upon the contract usually made between those two parties, whose interests are by no means the same. The workmen desire to get as much, the masters to give as little, as possible. The former are disposed to combine in order to raise, the latter in order to lower, the wages of labor.

It is not, however, difficult to foresee which of the two parties must, upon all ordinary occasions, have the advantage in the dispute, and force the other into a compliance with their terms. The masters, being fewer in number, can combine much more easily: and the law, besides, authorizes, or at least does not prohibit, their combinations, while it prohibits those of the workmen. We have no acts of parliament against combining to lower the price of work, but many against combining to raise it. In all such disputes, the masters can hold out much longer. A landlord, a farmer, a master manufacturer, or merchant, though they did not employ a single workman, could generally live a year or two upon the stocks, which they have already acquired. Many workmen could not subsist a week, few could subsist a month, and scarce any a year, without employment. In the long run, the workman may be as necessary to his master as his master is to him; but the necessity is not so immediate.

We rarely hear, it has been said, of the combinations of masters, though frequently of those of workmen. But whoever imagines, upon this account, that masters rarely combine, is as ignorant of the world as of the subject. Masters are always and everywhere in a sort of tacit, but constant and uniform, combination, not to raise the wages of labor above their actual rate. To violate this combination is everywhere a most unpopular action, and a sort of reproach to a master among his neighbors and equals. We seldom, indeed, hear of this combination, because it is the usual, and, one may say, the natural state of things, which nobody ever hears of. Masters, too, sometimes enter into particular combinations to sink the wages of labor even below this rate. These are always conducted with the utmost silence and secrecy till the moment of execution; and when the workmen yield, as they sometimes do without resistance, though severely felt by them, they are never heard of by other people. Such combinations, however, are frequently resisted by a contrary defensive combination of the workmen, who sometimes, too, without any provocation of this kind, combine, of their own accord, to raise tile price of their labor. Their usual pretences are, sometimes the high price of provisions, sometimes the great profit which their masters make by their work. But whether their combinations be offensive or defensive, they are always abundantly heard of. In order to bring the point to a speedy decision, they have always recourse to the loudest clamor, and sometimes to the most shocking violence and outrage. They are desperate, and act with the folly and extravagance of desperate men, who must either starve, or frighten their masters into an immediate compliance with their demands. The masters, upon these occasions, are just as clamorous upon the other side, and never cease to call aloud for the assistance of the civil magistrate, and the rigorous execution of those laws which have been enacted with so much severity against the combination of servants, laborers, and journeymen. The workmen, accordingly, very seldom derive any advantage from the violence of those tumultuous combinations, which, partly from the interposition of the civil magistrate, partly from the superior steadiness of the masters, partly from the necessity which the greater part of the workmen are under of submitting for the sake of present subsistence, generally end in nothing but the punishment or ruin of the ringleaders.

But though, in disputes with their workmen, masters must generally have the advantage, there is, however, a certain rate, below which it seems impossible to reduce, for any considerable time, the ordinary wages even of the lowest species of labor.

A man must always live by his work, and his wages must at least be sufficient to maintain him. They must even upon most occasions be somewhat more, otherwise it would be impossible for him to bring up a family, and the race of such workmen could not last beyond the first generation. Mr. Cantillon seems, upon this account, to suppose that the lowest species of common laborers must everywhere earn at least double their own maintenance, in order that, one with another, they may be enabled to bring up two children; the labor of the wife, on account of her necessary attendance on the children, being supposed no more than sufficient to provide for herself: But one half the children born, it is computed, die before the age of manhood. The poorest laborers, therefore, according to this account, must, one with another, attempt to rear at least four children, in order that two may have an equal chance of living to that age. But the necessary maintenance of four children, it is supposed, may be nearly equal to that of one man. The labor of an able-bodied slave, the same author adds, is computed to be worth double his maintenance; and that of the meanest laborer, he thinks, cannot be worth less than that of an able-bodied slave. Thus far at least seems certain, that, in order to bring up a family, the labor of the husband and wife together must, even in the lowest species of common labor, be able to earn something more than what is precisely necessary for their own maintenance; but in what proportion, whether in that above-mentioned, or many other, I shall not take upon me to determine.

There are certain circumstances, however, which sometimes give the laborers an advantage, and enable them to raise their wages considerably above this rate, evidently the lowest which is consistent with common humanity.

When in any country the demand for those who live by wages, laborers, journeymen, servants of every kind, is continually increasing; when every year furnishes employment for a greater number than had been employed the year before, the workmen have no occasion to combine in order to raise their wages. The scarcity of hands occasions a competition among masters, who bid against one another in order to get workmen, and thus voluntarily break through the natural combination of masters not to raise wages. The demand for those who live by wages, it is evident, cannot increase but in proportion to the increase of the funds which are destined to the payment of wages. These funds are of two kinds, first, the revenue which is over and above what is necessary for the maintenance; and, secondly, the stock which is over and above what is necessary for the employment of their masters.

When the landlord, annuitant, or moneyed man, has a greater revenue than what he judges sufficient to maintain his own family, he employs either the whole or a part of the surplus in maintaining one or more menial servants. Increase this surplus, and he will naturally increase the number of those servants.

When an independent workman, such as a weaver or shoemaker, has got more stock than what is sufficient to purchase the materials of his own work, and to maintain himself till he can dispose of it, he naturally employs one or more journeymen with the surplus, in order to make a profit by their work. Increase this surplus, and he will naturally increase the number of his journeymen.

The demand for those who live by wages, therefore, necessarily increases with the increase of the revenue and stock of every country, and cannot possibly increase without it. The increase of revenue and stock is the increase of national wealth. The demand for those who live by wages, therefore, naturally increases with the increase of national wealth, and cannot possibly increase without it.

It is not the actual greatness of national wealth, but its continual increase, which occasions a rise in the wages of labor. It is not, accordingly, in the richest countries, but in the most thriving, or in those which are growing rich the fastest, that the wages of labor are highest. England is certainly, in the present times, a much richer country than any part of North America. The wages of labor, however, are much higher in North America than in any part of England. In the province of New York, common laborers earned in 1773, before the commencement of the late disturbances, three shillings and sixpence currency, equal to two shillings sterling, a day; ship-carpenters, ten shillings and sixpence currency, with a pint of rum, worth sixpence sterling, equal in all to six shillings and sixpence sterling; house-carpenters and bricklayers, eight shillings currency, equal to four shillings and sixpence sterling; journeymen tailors, five shillings currency, equal to about two shillings and ten pence sterling. These prices are all above the London price; and wages are said to be as high in the other colonies as in New York. The price of provisions is everywhere in North America much lower than in England. A dearth has never been known there. In the worst seasons they have always had a sufficiency for themselves, though less for exportation. If the money price of labor, therefore, be higher than it is anywhere in the mother-country, its real price, the real command of the necessaries and conveniences of life which it conveys to the laborer, must be higher in a still greater proportion.

But though North America is not yet so rich as England, it is much more thriving, and advancing with much greater rapidity to the further acquisition of riches. The most decisive mark of the prosperity of any country is the increase of the number of its inhabitants. In Great Britain, and most other European countries, they are not supposed to double in less than five hundred years. In the British colonies in North America, it has been found that they double in twenty or five-and-twenty years. Nor in the present times is this increase principally owing to the continual importation of new inhabitants, but to the great multiplication of the species. Those who live to old age, it is said, frequently see there from fifty to a hundred, and sometimes many more, descendants from their own body. Labor is there so well rewarded, that a numerous family of children, instead of being a burden, is a source of opulence and prosperity to the parents. The labor of each child, before it can leave their house, is computed to be worth a hundred pounds clear gain to them. A young widow with four or five young children, who, among the middling or inferior ranks of people in Europe, would have so little chance for a second husband, is there frequently courted as a sort of fortune. The value of children is the greatest of all encouragements to marriage. We cannot, therefore, wonder that the people in North America should generally marry very young. Notwithstanding the great increase occasioned by such early marriages, there is a continual complaint of the scarcity of hands in North America. The demand for laborers, the funds destined for maintaining them increase, it seems, still faster than they can find laborers to employ.

Though the wealth of a country should be very great, yet if it has been long stationary, we must not expect to find the wages of labor very high in it. The funds destined for the payment of wages, the revenue and stock of its inhabitants, may be of the greatest extent; but if they have continued for several centuries of the same, or very nearly of the same extent, the number of laborers employed every year could easily supply, and even more than supply, the number wanted the following year. There could seldom be any scarcity of hands, nor could the masters be obliged to bid against one another in order to get them. The hands, on the contrary, would, in this case, naturally multiply beyond their employment. There would be a constant scarcity of employment, and the laborers would be obliged to bid against one another in order to get it. If in such a country the wages of labor had ever been more than sufficient to maintain the laborer, and to enable him to bring up a family, the competition of the laborers and the interest of the masters would soon reduce them to the lowest rate which is consistent with common humanity. China has been long one of the richest, that is, one of the most fertile, best cultivated, most industrious, and most populous, countries in the world. It seems, however, to have been long stationary. Marco Polo, who visited it more than five hundred years ago, describes its cultivation, industry, and populousness, almost in the same terms in which they are described by travelers in the present times. It had, perhaps, even long before his time, acquired that full complement of riches which the nature of its laws and institutions permits it to acquire. The accounts of all travelers, inconsistent in many other respects, agree in the low wages of labor, and in the difficulty which a laborer finds in bringing up a family in China. If by digging the ground a whole day he can get what will purchase a small quantity of rice in the evening, he is contented. The condition of artificers is, if possible, still worse. Instead of waiting indolently in their work-houses for the calls of their customers, as in Europe, they are continually running about the streets with the tools of their respective trades, offering their services, and, as it were, begging employment. The poverty of the lower ranks of people in China far surpasses that of the most beggarly nations in Europe. In the neighborhood of Canton, many hundred, it is commonly said, many thousand families have no habitation on the land, but live constantly in little fishing-boats upon the rivers and canals. The subsistence which they find there is so scanty, that they are eager to fish up the nastiest garbage thrown overboard from any European ship. Any carrion, the carcass of a dead dog or cat, for example, though half putrid and stinking, is as welcome to them as the most wholesome food to the people of other countries. Marriage is encouraged in China, not by the profitableness of children, but by the liberty of destroying them. In all great towns, several are every night exposed in the street, or drowned like puppies in the water. The performance of this horrid office is even said to be the avowed business by which some people earn their subsistence.

China, however, though it may, perhaps, stand still, does not seem to go backwards. Its towns are nowhere deserted by their inhabitants. The lands which had once been cultivated, are nowhere neglected. The same, or very nearly the same, annual labor, must, therefore, continue to be performed, and the funds destined for maintaining it must not, consequently, be sensibly diminished. The lowest class of laborers, therefore, notwithstanding their scanty subsistence, must some way or another make shift to continue their race so far as to keep up their usual numbers.

But it would be otherwise in a country where the funds destined for the maintenance of labor were sensibly decaying. Every year the demand for servants and laborers would, in all the different classes of employments, be less than it had been the year before. Many who had been bred in the superior classes, not being able to find employment in their own business, would be glad to seek it in the lowest. The lowest class being not only overstocked with its own workmen, but with the overflowings of all the other classes, the competition for employment would be so great in it, as to reduce the wages of labor to the most miserable and scanty subsistence of the laborer. Many would not be able to find employment even upon these hard terms, but would either starve, or be driven to seek a subsistence, either by begging, or by the perpetration perhaps, of the greatest enormities. Want, famine, and mortality, would immediately prevail in that class, and from thence extend themselves to all the superior classes, till the number of inhabitants in the country was reduced to what could easily be maintained by the revenue and stock which remained in it, and which had escaped either the tyranny or calamity which had destroyed the rest. This, perhaps, is nearly the present state of Bengal, and of some other of the English settlements in the East Indies. In a fertile country, which had before been much depopulated, where subsistence, consequently, should not be very difficult, and where, notwithstanding, three or four hundred thousand people die of hunger in one year, we may be assured that the funds destined for the maintenance of the laboring poor are fast decaying. The difference between the genius of the British constitution, which protects and governs North America, and that of the mercantile company which oppresses and domineers in the East Indies, cannot, perhaps, be better illustrated than by the different state of those countries.

The liberal reward of labor, therefore, as it is the necessary effect, so it is the natural symptom of increasing national wealth. The scanty maintenance of the laboring poor, on the other hand, is the natural symptom that things are at a stand, and their starving condition, that they are going fast backwards.

In Great Britain, the wages of labor seem, in the present times, to be evidently more than what is precisely necessary to enable the laborer to bring up a family. In order to satisfy ourselves upon this point, it will not be necessary to enter into any tedious or doubtful calculation of what may be the lowest sum upon which it is possible to do this. There are many plain symptoms, that the wages of labor are nowhere in this country regulated by this lowest rate, which is consistent with common humanity.

First, in almost every part of Great Britain there is a distinction, even in the lowest species of labor, between summer and winter wages. Summer wages are always highest. But, on account of the extraordinary expense of fuel, the maintenance of a family is most expensive in winter. Wages, therefore, being highest when this expense is lowest, it seems evident that they are not regulated by what is necessary for this expense, but by the quantity and supposed value of the work. A laborer, it may be said, indeed, ought to save part of his summer wages, in order to defray his winter expense; and that, through the whole year, they do not exceed what is necessary to maintain his family through the whole year. A slave, however, or one absolutely dependent on us for immediate subsistence, would not be treated in this manner. His daily subsistence would be proportioned to his daily necessities.

Secondly, the wages of labor do not, in Great Britain, fluctuate with the price of provisions. These vary everywhere from year to year, frequently from month to month. But in many places, the money price of labor remains uniformly the same, sometimes for half a century together. If, in these places, therefore, the laboring poor can maintain their families in dear years, they must be at their ease in times of moderate plenty, and in affluence in those of extraordinary cheapness. The high price of provisions during these ten years past, has not, in many parts of the kingdom, been accompanied with any sensible rise in the money price of labor. It has, indeed, in some; owing, probably, more to the increase of the demand for labor, than to that of the price of provisions.

Thirdly, as the price of provisions varies more from year to year than the wages of labor, so, on the other hand, the wages of labor vary more from place to place than the price of provisions. The prices of bread and butchers' meat are generally the same, or very nearly the same, through the greater part of the United Kingdom. These, and most other things which are sold by retail, the way in which the laboring poor buy all things, are generally fully as cheap, or cheaper, in great towns than in the remoter parts of the country, for reasons which I shall have occasion to explain hereafter. But the wages of labor in a great town and its neighborhood, are frequently a fourth or a fifth part, twenty or five-and-twenty percent higher than at a few miles distance. Eighteen pence a day may be reckoned the common price of labor in London and its neighborhood. At a few miles distance, it falls to fourteen and fifteen pence. Ten pence may be reckoned its price in Edinburgh and its neighborhood. At a few miles distance, it falls to eight pence, the usual price of common labor through the greater part of the low country of Scotland, where it varies a good deal less than in England. Such a difference of prices, which, it seems, is not always sufficient to transport a man from one parish to another, would necessarily occasion so great a transportation of the most bulky commodities, not only from one parish to another, but from one end of the kingdom, almost from one end of the world to the other, as would soon reduce them more nearly to a level. After all that has been said of the levity and inconstancy of human nature, it appears evidently from experience, that man is, of all sorts of luggage, the most difficult to be transported. If the laboring poor, therefore, can maintain their families in those parts of the kingdom where the price of labor is lowest, they must be in affluence where it is highest.

Fourthly, the variations in the price of labor not only do not correspond, either in place or time, with those in the price of provisions, but they are frequently quite opposite.

Grain, the food of the common people, is dearer in Scotland than in England, whence Scotland receives almost every year very large supplies. But English corn must be sold dearer in Scotland, the country to which it is brought, than in England, the country from which it comes; and in proportion to its quality it cannot be sold dearer in Scotland than the Scotch corn that comes to the same market in competition with it. The quality of grain depends chiefly upon the quantity of flour or meal which it yields at the mill; and, in this respect, English grain is so much superior to the Scotch, that though often dearer in appearance, or in proportion to the measure of its bulk, it is generally cheaper in reality, or in proportion to its quality, or even to the measure of its weight. The price of labor, on the contrary, is dearer in England than in Scotland. If the laboring poor, therefore, can maintain their families in the one part of the United Kingdom, they must be in affluence in the other. Oatmeal, indeed, supplies the common people in Scotland with the greatest and the best part of their food, which is, in general, much inferior to that of their neighbors of the same rank in England. This difference, however, in the mode of their subsistence, is not the cause, but the effect, of the difference in their wages; though, by a strange misapprehension, I have frequently heard it represented as the cause. It is not because one man keeps a coach, while his neighbor walks a-foot, that the one is rich, and the other poor; but because the one is rich, he keeps a coach, and because the other is poor, he walks a-foot.

During the course of the last century, taking one year with another, grain was dearer in both parts of the United Kingdom than during that of the present. This is a matter of fact which cannot now admit of any reasonable doubt; and the proof of it is, if possible, still more decisive with regard to Scotland than with regard to England. It is in Scotland supported by the evidence of the public *fiars*, annual valuations made upon oath, according to the actual state of the markets, of all the different sorts of grain in every different county of Scotland. If such direct proof could require any collateral evidence to confirm it, I would observe, that this has likewise been the case in France, and probably in most other parts of Europe. With regard to France, there is the clearest proof. But though it is certain, that in both parts of the United Kingdom grain was somewhat dearer in the last century than in the present, it is equally certain that labor was much cheaper. If the laboring poor, therefore, could bring up their families then, they must be much more at their ease now. In the last century, the most usual day-wages of common labor through the greater part of Scotland were sixpence in summer, and five pence in winter. Three shillings a week, the same price, very nearly still continues to be paid in some parts of the Highlands and Western islands. Through the greater part of the Low country, the most usual wages of common labor are now eight pence a day; ten pence, sometimes a shilling, about Edinburgh, in the counties which border upon England, probably on account of that neighborhood, and in a few other places where there has lately been a considerable rise in the demand for labor, about Glasgow, Carron, Ayrshire, etc. In England, the improvements of agriculture, manufactures, and commerce, began much earlier than in Scotland.

The demand for labor, and consequently its price, must necessarily have increased with those improvements. In the last century, accordingly, as well as in the present, the wages of labor were higher in England than in Scotland. They have risen, too, considerably since that time, though, on account of the greater variety of wages paid there in different places, it is more difficult to ascertain how much. In 1614, the pay of a foot soldier was the same as in the present times, eight pence a day. When it was first established, it would naturally be regulated by the usual wages of common laborers, the rank of people from which foot soldiers are commonly drawn. Lord-chief-justice Hales, who wrote in the time of Charles II computes the necessary expense of a laborer's family, consisting of six persons, the father and mother, two children able to do something, and two not able, at ten shillings a week, or twenty-six pounds a year. If they cannot earn this by their labor, they must make it up, he supposes, either by begging or stealing. He appears to have enquired very carefully into this subject {See his scheme for the maintenance of the poor, in Burn's *History of the Poor Laws*.}. In 1688, Mr. Gregory King, whose skill in political arithmetic is so much extolled by Dr. Davenant, computed the ordinary income of laborers and out-servants to be fifteen pounds a year to a family, which he supposed to consist, one with another, of three and a half persons. His calculation, therefore, though different in appearance, corresponds very nearly at bottom with that of Judge Hales. Both suppose the weekly expense of such families to be about twenty-pence a head. Both the pecuniary income and expense of such families have increased considerably since that time through the greater part of the kingdom, in some places more, and in some less, though perhaps scarce anywhere so much as some exaggerated accounts of the present wages of labor have lately represented them to the public. The price of labor, it must be observed, cannot be ascertained very accurately anywhere, different prices being often paid at the same place and for the same sort of labor, not only according to the different abilities of the workman, but according to the easiness or hardness of the masters. Where wages are not regulated by law, all that we can pretend to determine is, what are the most usual; and experience seems to show that law can never regulate them properly, though it has often pretended to do so.

The real recompense of labor, the real quantity of the necessaries and conveniences of life which it can procure to the laborer, has, during the course of the present century, increased perhaps in a still greater proportion than its money price. Not only grain has become somewhat cheaper, but many other things, from which the industrious poor derive an agreeable and wholesome variety of food, have become a great deal cheaper. Potatoes, for example, do not at present, through the greater part of the kingdom, cost half the price which they used to do thirty or forty years ago. The same thing may be said of turnips, carrots, cabbages; things which were formerly never raised but by the spade, but which are now commonly raised by the plough. All sort of garden stuff, too, has become cheaper. The greater part of the apples, and even of the onions, consumed in Great Britain, were, in the last century, imported from Flanders. The great improvements in the coarser manufactories of both linen and woolen cloth furnish the laborers with cheaper and better clothing; and those in the manufactories of the coarser metals, with cheaper and better instruments of trade, as well as with many agreeable and convenient pieces of household furniture. Soap, salt, candles, leather, and fermented liquors, have, indeed, become a good deal dearer, chiefly from the taxes which have been laid upon them. The quantity of these, however, which the laboring poor are under any necessity of consuming, is so very small, that the increase in their price does not compensate the diminution in that of so many other things. The common complaint, that luxury extends itself even to the lowest ranks of the people, and that the laboring poor will not now be contented with the same food, clothing, and lodging, which satisfied them in former times, may convince us that it is not the money price of labor only, but its real recompense, which has augmented.

Is this improvement in the circumstances of the lower ranks of the people to be regarded as an advantage, or as an inconveniency, to the society? The answer seems at first abundantly plain. Servants, laborers, and workmen of different kinds, make up the far greater part of every great political society. But what improves the circumstances of the greater part, can never be regarded as any inconveniency to the whole. No society can surely be flourishing and happy, of which the far greater part of the members are poor and miserable. It is but equity, besides, that they who feed, clothe, and lodge the whole body of the people, should have such a share of the produce of their own labor as to be themselves tolerably well fed, clothed, and lodged.

Poverty, though it no doubt discourages, does not always prevent, marriage. It seems even to be favorable to generation. A half-starved Highland woman frequently bears more than twenty children, while a pampered fine lady is often incapable of bearing any, and is generally exhausted by two or three. Barrenness, so frequent among women of fashion, is very rare among those of inferior station. Luxury, in the fair sex, while it inflames, perhaps, the passion for enjoyment, seems always to weaken, and frequently to destroy altogether, the powers of generation.

But poverty, though it does not prevent the generation, is extremely unfavorable to the rearing of children. The tender plant is produced; but in so cold a soil, and so severe a climate, soon withers and dies. It is not uncommon, I have been frequently told, in the Highlands of Scotland, for a mother who has born twenty children not to have two alive. Several officers of great experience have assured me, that, so far from recruiting their regiment, they have never been able to supply it with drums and fifes, from all the soldiers' children that were born in it. A greater number of fine children, however, is seldom seen anywhere than about a barrack of soldiers. Very few of them, it seems, arrive at the age of thirteen or fourteen. In some places, one half the children die before they are four years of age, in many places before they are seven, and in almost all places before they are nine or ten. This great mortality, however will everywhere be found chiefly among the children of the common people, who cannot afford to tend them with the same care as those of better station. Though their marriages are generally more fruitful than those of people of fashion, a smaller proportion of their children arrive at maturity. In foundling hospitals, and among the children brought up by parish charities, the mortality is still greater than among those of the common people.

Every species of animals naturally multiplies in proportion to the means of their subsistence, and no species can ever multiply beyond it. But in civilized society, it is only among the inferior ranks of people that the scantiness of subsistence can set limits to the further multiplication of the human species; and it can do so in no other way than by destroying a great part of the children which their fruitful marriages produce.

The liberal reward of labor, by enabling them to provide better for their children, and consequently to bring up a greater number, naturally tends to widen and extend those limits. It deserves to be remarked, too, that it necessarily does this as nearly as possible in the proportion which the demand for labor requires. If this demand is continually increasing, the reward of labor must necessarily encourage in such a manner the marriage and multiplication of laborers, as may enable them to supply that continually increasing demand by a continually increasing population. If the reward should at any time be less than what was requisite for this purpose, the deficiency of hands would soon raise it; and if it should at any time be more, their excessive multiplication would soon lower it to this necessary rate. The market would be so much understocked with labor in the one case, and so much overstocked in the other, as would soon force back its price to that proper rate which the circumstances of the society required. It is in this manner that the demand for men, like that for any other commodity, necessarily regulates the production of men, quickens it when it goes on too slowly, and stops it when it advances too fast. It is this demand which regulates and determines the state of propagation in all the different countries of the world; in North America, in Europe, and in China; which renders it rapidly progressive in the first, slow and gradual in the second, and altogether stationary in the last.

The wear and tear of a slave, it has been said, is at the expense of his master; but that of a free servant is at his own expense. The wear and tear of the latter, however, is, in reality, as much at the expense of his master as that of the former. The wages paid to journeymen and servants of every kind must be such as may enable them, one with another to continue the race of journeymen and servants, according as the increasing, diminishing, or stationary demand of the society, may happen to require. But though the wear and tear of a free servant be equally at the expense of his master, it generally costs him much less than that of a slave. The fund destined for replacing or repairing, if I may say so, the wear and tear of the slave, is commonly managed by a negligent master or careless overseer. That destined for performing the same office with regard to the freeman is managed by the freeman himself. The disorders which generally prevail in the economy of the rich, naturally introduce themselves into the management of the former; the strict frugality and parsimonious attention of the poor as naturally establish themselves in that of the latter. Under such different management, the same purpose must require very different degrees of expense to execute it. It appears, accordingly, from the experience of all ages and nations, I believe, that the work done by freemen comes cheaper in the end than that performed by slaves. It is found to do so even at Boston, New York, and Philadelphia, where the wages of common labor are so very high.

The liberal reward of labor, therefore, as it is the effect of increasing wealth, so it is the cause of increasing population. To complain of it, is to lament over the necessary cause and effect of the greatest public prosperity.

It deserves to be remarked, perhaps, that it is in the progressive state, while the society is advancing to the further acquisition, rather than when it has acquired its full complement of riches, that the condition of the laboring poor, of the great body of the people, seems to be the happiest and the most comfortable. It is hard in the stationary, and miserable in the declining state. The progressive state is, in reality, the cheerful and the hearty state to all the different orders of the society; the stationary is dull; the declining melancholy.

The liberal reward of labor, as it encourages the propagation, so it increases the industry of the common people. The wages of labor are the encouragement of industry, which, like every other human quality, improves in proportion to the encouragement it receives. A plentiful subsistence increases the bodily strength of the laborer, and the comfortable hope of bettering his condition, and of ending his days, perhaps, in ease and plenty, animates him to exert that strength to the utmost. Where wages are high, accordingly, we shall always find the workmen more active, diligent, and expeditious, than where they are low; in England, for example, than in Scotland; in the neighborhood of great towns, than in remote country places. Some workmen, indeed, when they can earn in four days what will maintain them through the week, will be idle the other three. This, however, is by no means the case with the greater part. Workmen, on the contrary, when they are liberally paid by the piece, are very apt to overwork themselves, and to ruin their health and constitution in a few years. A carpenter in London, and in some other places, is not supposed to last in his utmost vigor above eight years. Something of the same kind happens in many other trades, in which the workmen are paid by the piece; as they generally are in manufactures, and even in country labor, wherever wages are higher than ordinary. Almost every class of artificers is subject to some peculiar infirmity occasioned by excessive application to their peculiar species of work. Ramuzzini, an eminent Italian physician, has written a particular book concerning such diseases. We do not reckon our soldiers the most industrious set of people among us; yet when soldiers have been employed in some particular sorts of work, and liberally paid by the piece, their officers have frequently been obliged to stipulate with the undertaker, that they should not be allowed to earn above a certain sum every day, according to the rate at which they were paid. Till this stipulation was made, mutual emulation, and the desire of greater gain, frequently prompted them to overwork themselves, and to hurt their health by excessive labor. Excessive application, during four days of the week, is frequently the real cause of the idleness of the other three, so much and so loudly complained of. Great labor, either of mind or body, continued for several days together is, in most men, naturally followed by a great desire of relaxation, which, if not restrained by force, or by some strong necessity, is almost irresistible. It is the call of nature, which requires to be relieved by some indulgence, sometimes of ease only, but sometimes too of dissipation and diversion. If it is not complied with, the consequences are often dangerous and sometimes fatal, and such as almost always, sooner or later, bring on the peculiar infirmity of the trade. If masters would always listen to the dictates of reason and humanity, they have frequently occasion rather to moderate, than to animate the application of many of their workmen. It will be found, I believe, in every sort of trade, that the man who works so moderately, as to be able to work constantly, not only preserves his health the longest, but, in the course of the year, executes the greatest quantity of work.

In cheap years it is pretended, workmen are generally more idle, and in dear times more industrious than ordinary. A plentiful subsistence, therefore, it has been concluded, relaxes, and a scanty one quickens their industry. That a little more plenty than ordinary may render some workmen idle, cannot be well doubted; but that it should have this effect upon the greater part, or that men in general should work better when they are ill fed, than when they are well fed, when they are disheartened than when they are in good spirits, when they are frequently sick than when they are generally in good health, seems not very probable. Years of dearth, it is to be observed, are generally among the common people years of sickness and mortality, which cannot fail to diminish the produce of their industry.

In years of plenty, servants frequently leave their masters, and trust their subsistence to what they can make by their own industry. But the same cheapness of provisions, by increasing the fund which is destined for the maintenance of servants, encourages masters, farmers especially, to employ a greater number. Farmers, upon such occasions, expect more profit from their corn by maintaining a few more laboring servants, than by selling it at a low price in the market. The demand for servants increases, while the number of those who offer to supply that demand diminishes. The price of labor, therefore, frequently rises in cheap years.

In years of scarcity, the difficulty and uncertainty of subsistence make all such people eager to return to service. But the high price of provisions, by diminishing the funds destined for the maintenance of servants, disposes masters rather to diminish than to increase the number of those they have. In dear years, too, poor independent workmen frequently consume the little stock with which they had used to supply themselves with the materials of their work, and are obliged to become journeymen for subsistence. More people want employment than easily get it; many are willing to take it upon lower terms than ordinary; and the wages of both servants and journeymen frequently sink in dear years.

Masters of all sorts, therefore, frequently make better bargains with their servants in dear than in cheap years, and find them more humble and dependent in the former than in the latter. They naturally, therefore, commend the former as more favorable to industry. Landlords and farmers, besides, two of the largest classes of masters, have another reason for being pleased with dear years. The rents of the one, and the profits of the other, depend very much upon the price of provisions. Nothing can be more absurd, however, than to imagine that men in general should work less when they work for themselves, than when they work for other people. A poor independent workman will generally be more industrious than even a journeyman who works by the piece. The one enjoys the whole produce of his own industry, the other shares it with his master. The one, in his separate independent state, is less liable to the temptations of bad company, which, in large manufactories, so frequently ruin the morals of the other. The superiority of the independent workman over those servants who are hired by the month or by the year, and whose wages and maintenance are the same, whether they do much or do little, is likely to be still greater. Cheap years tend to increase the proportion of independent workmen to journeymen and servants of all kinds, and dear years to diminish it.

A French author of great knowledge and ingenuity, Mr. Messance, receiver of the taillies in the election of St Etienne, endeavors to show that the poor do more work in cheap than in dear years, by comparing the quantity and value of the goods made upon those different occasions in three different manufactures; one of coarse woolens, carried on at Elbeuf; one of linen, and another of silk, both which extend through the whole generality of Rouen. It appears from his account, which is copied from the registers of the public offices, that the quantity and value of the goods made in all those three manufactories has generally been greater in cheap than in dear years, and that it has always been; greatest in the cheapest, and least in the dearest years. All the three seem to be stationary manufactures, or which, though their produce may vary somewhat from year to year, are, upon the whole, neither going backwards nor forwards.

The manufacture of linen in Scotland, and that of coarse woolens in the West Riding of Yorkshire, are growing manufactures, of which the produce is generally, though with some variations, increasing both in quantity and value. Upon examining, however, the accounts which have been published of their annual produce, I have not been able to observe that its variations have had any sensible connection with the dearness or cheapness of the seasons. In 1740, a year of great scarcity, both manufactures, indeed, appear to have declined very considerably. But in 1756, another year or great scarcity, the Scotch manufactures made more than ordinary advances. The Yorkshire manufacture, indeed, declined, and its produce did not rise to what it had been in 1755, till 1766, after the repeal of the American stamp act. In that and the following year, it greatly exceeded what it had ever been before, and it has continued to advance ever since.

The produce of all great manufactures for distant sale must necessarily depend, not so much upon the dearness or cheapness of the seasons in the countries where they are carried on, as upon the circumstances which affect the demand in the countries where they are consumed; upon peace or war, upon the prosperity or declension of other rival manufactures and upon the good or bad humor of their principal customers. A great part of the extraordinary work, besides, which is probably done in cheap years, never enters the public registers of manufactures. The men-servants, who leave their masters, become independent laborers. The women return to their parents, and commonly spin, in order to make clothes for themselves and their families. Even the independent workmen do not always, work for public sale, but are employed by some of their neighbors in manufactures for family use. The produce of their labor, therefore, frequently makes no figure in those public registers, of which the records are sometimes published with so much parade, and from which our merchants and manufacturers would often vainly pretend to announce the prosperity or declension of the greatest empires.

Though the variations in the price of labor not only do not always correspond with those in the price of provisions, but are frequently quite opposite, we must not, upon this account, imagine that the price of provisions has no influence upon that of labor. The money price of labor is necessarily regulated by two circumstances; the demand for labor, and the price of the necessaries and conveniences of life. The demand for labor, according as it happens to be increasing, stationary, or declining, or to require an increasing, stationary, or declining population, determines the quantities of the necessaries and conveniences of life which must be given to the laborer; and the money price of labor is determined by what is requisite for purchasing this quantity. Though the money price of labor, therefore, is sometimes high where the price of provisions is low, it would be still higher, the demand continuing the same, if the price of provisions was high.

It is because the demand for labor increases in years of sudden and extraordinary plenty, and diminishes in those of sudden and extraordinary scarcity, that the money price of labor sometimes rises in the one, and sinks in the other.

In a year of sudden and extraordinary plenty, there are funds in the hands of many of the employers of industry, sufficient to maintain and employ a greater number of industrious people than had been employed the year before; and this extraordinary number cannot always be had. Those masters, therefore, who want more workmen, bid against one another, in order to get them, which sometimes raises both the real and the money price of their labor.

The contrary of this happens in a year of sudden and extraordinary scarcity. The funds destined for employing industry are less than they had been the year before. A considerable number of people are thrown out of employment, who bid one against another, in order to get it, which sometimes lowers both the real and the money price of labor. In 1740, a year of extraordinary scarcity, many people were willing to work for bare subsistence. In the succeeding years of plenty, it was more difficult to get laborers and servants.

The scarcity of a dear year, by diminishing the demand for labor, tends to lower its price, as the high price of provisions tends to raise it. The plenty of a cheap year, on the contrary, by increasing the demand, tends to raise the price of labor, as the cheapness of provisions tends to lower it. In the ordinary variations of the prices of provisions, those two opposite causes seem to counterbalance one another, which is probably, in part, the reason why the wages of labor are everywhere so much more steady and permanent than the price of provisions.

The increase in the wages of labor necessarily increases the price of many commodities, by increasing that part of it which resolves itself into wages, and so far tends to diminish their consumption, both at home and abroad. The same cause, however, which raises the wages of labor, the increase of stock, tends to increase its productive powers, and to make a smaller quantity of labor produce a greater quantity of work. The owner of the stock which employs a great number of laborers necessarily endeavors, for his own advantage, to make such a proper division and distribution of employment, that they may be enabled to produce the greatest quantity of work possible. For the same reason, he endeavors to supply them with the best machinery which either he or they can think of. What takes place among the laborers in a particular workhouse, takes place, for the same reason, among those of a great society. The greater their number, the more they naturally divide themselves into different classes and subdivisions of employments. More heads are occupied in inventing the most proper machinery for executing the work of each, and it is, therefore, more likely to be invented. There are many commodities, therefore, which, in consequence of these improvements, come to be produced by so much less labor than before, that the increase of its price is more than compensated by the diminution of its quantity.

CHAPTER IX

Of the Profits of Stock

The rise and fall in the profits of stock depend upon the same causes with the rise and fall in the wages of labor, the increasing or declining state of the wealth of the society; but those causes affect the one and the other very differently.

The increase of stock, which raises wages, tends to lower profit. When the stocks of many rich merchants are turned into the same trade, their mutual competition naturally tends to lower its profit; and when there is a like increase of stock in all the different trades carried on in the same society, the same competition must produce the same effect in them all.

It is not easy, it has already been observed, to ascertain what are the average wages of labor, even in a particular place, and at a particular time. We can, even in this case, seldom determine more than what are the most usual wages. But even this can seldom be done with regard to the profits of stock. Profit is so very fluctuating, that the person who carries on a particular trade, cannot always tell you himself what is the average of his annual profit. It is affected, not only by every variation of price in the commodities which he deals in, but by the good or bad fortune both of his rivals and of his customers, and by a thousand other accidents, to which goods, when carried either by sea or by land, or even when stored in a warehouse, are liable. It varies, therefore, not only from year to year, but from day to day, and almost from hour to hour. To ascertain what is the average profit of all the different trades carried on in a great kingdom, must be much more difficult; and to judge of what it may have been formerly, or in remote periods of time, with any degree of precision, must be altogether impossible.

But though it may be impossible to determine, with any degree of precision, what are or were the average profits of stock, either in the present or in ancient times, some notion may be formed of them from the interest of money. It may be laid down as a maxim, that wherever a great deal can be made by the use of money, a great deal will commonly be given for the use of it; and that, wherever little can be made by it, less will commonly he given for it. Accordingly, therefore, as the usual market rate of interest varies in any country, we may be assured that the ordinary profits of stock must vary with it, must sink as it sinks, and rise as it rises. The progress of interest, therefore, may lead us to form some notion of the progress of profit.

By the 37th of Henry VIII all interest above ten percent was declared unlawful. More, it seems, had sometimes been taken before that. In the reign of Edward VI religious zeal prohibited all interest. This prohibition, however, like all others of the same kind, is said to have produced no effect, and probably rather increased than diminished the evil of usury. The statute of Henry VIII was revived by the 13th of Elizabeth, and ten percent continued to be the legal rate of interest till the 21st of James I when it was restricted to eight percent. It was reduced to six percent soon after the Restoration, and by the 12th of Queen Anne, to five percent. All these different statutory regulations seem to have been made with great propriety. They seem to have followed, and not to have gone before, the market rate of interest, or the rate at which people of good credit usually borrowed. Since the time of Queen Anne, five percent seems to have been rather above than below the market rate. Before the late war, the government borrowed at three percent; and people of good credit in the capital, and in many other parts of the kingdom, at three and a half, four, and four and a half percent.

Since the time of Henry VIII the wealth and revenue of the country have been continually advancing, and in the course of their progress, their pace seems rather to have been gradually accelerated than retarded. They seem not only to have been going on, but to have been going on faster and faster. The wages of labor have been continually increasing during the same period, and, in the greater part of the different branches of trade and manufactures, the profits of stock have been diminishing.

It generally requires a greater stock to carry on any sort of trade in a great town than in a country village. The great stocks employed in every branch of trade, and the number of rich competitors, generally reduce the rate of profit in the former below what it is in the latter. But the wages of labor are generally higher in a great town than in a country village. In a thriving town, the people who have great stocks to employ, frequently cannot get the number of workmen they want, and therefore bid against one another, in order to get as many as they can, which raises the wages of labor, and lowers the profits of stock. In the remote parts of the country, there is frequently not stock sufficient to employ all the people, who therefore bid against one another, in order to get employment, which lowers the wages of labor, and raises the profits of stock.

In Scotland, though the legal rate of interest is the same as in England, the market rate is rather higher. People of the best credit there seldom borrow under five percent. Even private bankers in Edinburgh give four percent upon their promissory-notes, of which payment, either in whole or in part may be demanded at pleasure. Private bankers in London give no interest for the money which is deposited with them. There are few trades which cannot be carried on with a smaller stock in Scotland than in England. The common rate of profit, therefore, must be somewhat greater. The wages of labor, it has already been observed, are lower in Scotland than in England. The country, too, is not only much poorer, but the steps by which it advances to a better condition, for it is evidently advancing, seem to be much slower and more tardy.

The legal rate of interest in France has not during the course of the present century, been always regulated by the market rate {See Denisart, article Taux des Interests, tom. iii, p.13}. In 1720, interest was reduced from the twentieth to the fiftieth penny, or from five to two percent. In 1724, it was raised to the thirtieth penny, or to three and a third percent. In 1725, it was again raised to the twentieth penny, or to five percent. In 1766, during the administration of Mr. Laverdy, it was reduced to the twenty-fifth penny, or to four percent. The Abbé Terray raised it afterwards to the old rate of five percent. The supposed purpose of many of those violent reductions of interest was to prepare the way for reducing that of the public debts; a purpose which has sometimes been executed. France is, perhaps, in the present times, not so rich a country as England; and though the legal rate of interest has in France frequently been lower than in England, the market rate has generally been higher; for there, as in other countries, they have several very safe and easy methods of evading the law. The profits of trade,

I have been assured by British merchants who had traded in both countries, are higher in France than in England; and it is no doubt upon this account, that many British subjects choose rather to employ their capitals in a country where trade is in disgrace, than in one where it is highly respected. The wages of labor are lower in France than in England. When you go from Scotland to England, the difference which you may remark between the dress and countenance of the common people in the one country and in the other, sufficiently indicates the difference in their condition. The contrast is still greater when you return from France. France, though no doubt a richer country than Scotland, seems not to be going forward so fast. It is a common and even a popular opinion in the country, that it is going backwards; an opinion which I apprehend, is ill-founded, even with regard to France, but which nobody can possibly entertain with regard to Scotland, who sees the country now, and who saw it twenty or thirty years ago.

The province of Holland, on the other hand, in proportion to the extent of its territory and the number of its people, is a richer country than England. The government there borrows at two percent and private people of good credit at three. The wages of labor are said to be higher in Holland than in England, and the Dutch, it is well known, trade upon lower profits than any people in Europe. The trade of Holland, it has been pretended by some people, is decaying, and it may perhaps be true that some particular branches of it are so; but these symptoms seem to indicate sufficiently that there is no general decay. When profit diminishes, merchants are very apt to complain that trade decays, though the diminution of profit is the natural effect of its prosperity, or of a greater stock being employed in it than before. During the late war, the Dutch gained the whole carrying trade of France, of which they still retain a very large share. The great property which they possess both in French and English funds, about forty millions, it is said in the latter (in which, I suspect, however, there is a considerable exaggeration), the great sums which they lend to private people, in countries where the rate of interest is higher than in their own, are circumstances which no doubt demonstrate the redundancy of their stock, or that it has increased beyond what they can employ with tolerable profit in the proper business of their own country; but they do not demonstrate that that business has decreased. As the capital of a private man, though acquired by a particular trade, may increase beyond what he can employ in it, and yet that trade continue to increase too, so may likewise the capital of a great nation.

In our North American and West Indian colonies, not only the wages of labor, but the interest of money, and consequently the profits of stock, are higher than in England. In the different colonies, both the legal and the market rate of interest run from six to eight percent. High wages of labor and high profits of stock, however, are things, perhaps, which scarce ever go together, except in the peculiar circumstances of new colonies. A new colony must always, for some time, be more understocked in proportion to the extent of its territory, and more underpeopled in proportion to the extent of its stock, than the greater part of other countries. They have more land than they have stock to cultivate. What they have, therefore, is applied to the cultivation only of what is most fertile and most favorably situated, the land near the sea-shore, and along the banks of navigable rivers. Such land, too, is frequently purchased at a price below the value even of its natural produce. Stock employed in the purchase and improvement of such lands, must yield a very large profit, and, consequently, afford to pay a very large interest. Its rapid accumulation in so profitable an employment enables the planter to increase the number of his hands faster than he can find them in a new settlement. Those whom he can find, therefore, are very liberally rewarded. As the colony increases, the profits of stock gradually diminish. When the most fertile and best situated lands have been all occupied, less profit can be made by the cultivation of what is inferior both in soil and situation, and less interest can be afforded for the stock which is so employed. In the greater part of our colonies, accordingly, both the legal and the market rate of interest have been considerably reduced during the course of the present century. As riches, improvement, and population, have increased, interest has declined. The wages of labor do not sink with the profits of stock. The demand for labor increases with the increase of stock, whatever be its profits; and after these are diminished, stock may not only continue to increase, but to increase much faster than before. It is with industrious nations, who are advancing in the acquisition of riches, as with industrious individuals. A great stock, though with small profits, generally increases faster than a small stock with great profits. Money, says the proverb, makes money. When you have got a little, it is often easy to get more. The great difficulty is to get that little. The connection between the increase of stock and that of industry, or of the demand for useful labor, has partly been explained already, but will be explained more fully hereafter, in treating of the accumulation of stock.

The acquisition of new territory, or of new branches of trade, may sometimes raise the profits of stock, and with them the interest of money, even in a country which is fast advancing in the acquisition of riches. The stock of the country, not being sufficient for the whole accession of business which such acquisitions present to the different people among whom it is divided, is applied to those particular branches only which afford the greatest profit. Part of what had before been employed in other trades, is necessarily withdrawn from them, and turned into some of the new and more profitable ones. In all those old trades, therefore, the competition comes to be less than before. The market comes to be less fully supplied with many different sorts of goods. Their price necessarily rises more or less, and yields a greater profit to those who deal in them, who can, therefore, afford to borrow at a higher interest. For some time after the conclusion of the late war, not only private people of the best credit, but some of the greatest companies in London, commonly borrowed at five percent who, before that, had not been used to pay more than four, and four and a half percent. The great accession both of territory and trade by our acquisitions in North America and the West Indies, will sufficiently account for this, without supposing any diminution in the capital stock of the society. So great an accession of new business to be carried on by the old stock, must necessarily have diminished the quantity employed in a great number of particular branches, in which the competition being less, the profits must have been greater. I shall hereafter have occasion to mention the reasons which dispose me to believe that the capital stock of Great Britain was not diminished, even by the enormous expense of the late war.

The diminution of the capital stock of the society, or of the funds destined for the maintenance of industry, however, as it lowers the wages of labor, so it raises the profits of stock, and consequently the interest of money. By the wages of labor being lowered, the owners of what stock remains in the society can bring their goods at less expense to market than before; and less stock being employed in supplying the market than before, they can sell them dearer. Their goods cost them less, and they get more for them. Their profits, therefore, being augmented at both ends, can well afford a large interest. The great fortunes so suddenly and so easily acquired in Bengal and the other British settlements in the East Indies, may satisfy us, that as the wages of labor are very low, so the profits of stock are very high in those ruined countries. The interest of money is proportionably so. In Bengal, money is frequently lent to the farmers at forty, fifty, and sixty percent and the succeeding crop is mortgaged for the payment. As the profits which can afford such an interest must eat up almost the whole rent of the landlord, so such enormous usury must in its turn eat up the greater part of those profits. Before the fall of the Roman republic, a usury of the same kind seems to have been common in the provinces, under the ruinous administration of their proconsuls. The virtuous Brutus lent money in Cyprus at eight-and-forty percent as we learn from the letters of Cicero.

In a country which had acquired that full complement of riches which the nature of its soil and climate, and its situation with respect to other countries, allowed it to acquire, which could, therefore, advance no further, and which was not going backwards, both the wages of labor and the profits of stock would probably be very low. In a country fully peopled in proportion to what either its territory could maintain, or its stock employ, the competition for employment would necessarily be so great as to reduce the wages of labor to what was barely sufficient to keep up the number of laborers, and the country being already fully peopled, that number could never be augmented. In a country fully stocked in proportion to all the business it had to transact, as great a quantity of stock would be employed in every particular branch as the nature and extent of the trade would admit. The competition, therefore, would everywhere be as great, and, consequently, the ordinary profit as low as possible.

But, perhaps, no country has ever yet arrived at this degree of opulence. China seems to have been long stationary, and had, probably, long ago acquired that full complement of riches which is consistent with the nature of its laws and institutions. But this complement may be much inferior to what, with other laws and institutions, the nature of its soil, climate, and situation, might admit of. A country which neglects or despises foreign commerce, and which admits the vessel of foreign nations into one or two of its ports only, cannot transact the same quantity of business which it might do with different laws and institutions. In a country, too, where, though the rich, or the owners of large capitals, enjoy a good deal of security, the poor, or the owners of small capitals, enjoy scarce any, but are liable, under the pretence of justice, to be pillaged and plundered at any time by the inferior mandarins, the quantity of stock employed in all the different branches of business transacted within it, can never be equal to what the nature and extent of that business might admit. In every different branch, the oppression of the poor must establish the monopoly of the rich, who, by engrossing the whole trade to themselves, will be able to make very large profits. Twelve percent accordingly, is said to be the common interest of money in China, and the ordinary profits of stock must be sufficient to afford this large interest.

A defect in the law may sometimes raise the rate of interest considerably above what the condition of the country, as to wealth or poverty, would require. When the law does not enforce the performance of contracts, it puts all borrowers nearly upon the same footing with bankrupts, or people of doubtful credit, in better regulated countries. The uncertainty of recovering his money makes the lender exact the same usurious interest which is usually required from bankrupts. Among the barbarous nations who overran the western provinces of the Roman empire, the performance of contracts was left for many ages to the faith of the contracting parties. The courts of justice of their kings seldom intermeddled in it. The high rate of interest which took place in those ancient times, may, perhaps, be partly accounted for from this cause.

When the law prohibits interest altogether, it does not prevent it. Many people must borrow, and nobody will lend without such a consideration for the use of their money as is suitable, not only to what can be made by the use of it, but to the difficulty and danger of evading the law. The high rate of interest among all Mahometan nations is accounted for by M. Montesquieu, not from their poverty, but partly from this, and partly from the difficulty of recovering the money.

The lowest ordinary rate of profit must always be something more than what is sufficient to compensate the occasional losses to which every employment of stock is exposed. It is this surplus only which is neat or clear profit. What is called gross profit comprehends frequently not only this surplus, but what is retained for compensating such extraordinary losses. The interest which the borrower can afford to pay is in proportion to the clear profit only.

The lowest ordinary rate of interest must, in the same manner, be something more than sufficient to compensate the occasional losses to which lending, even with tolerable prudence, is exposed. Were it not, mere charity or friendship could be the only motives for lending.

In a country which had acquired its full complement of riches, where, in every particular branch of business, there was the greatest quantity of stock that could be employed in it, as the ordinary rate of clear profit would be very small, so the usual market rate of interest which could be afforded out of it would be so low as to render it impossible for any but the very wealthiest people to live upon the interest of their money. All people of small or middling fortunes would be obliged to superintend themselves the employment of their own stocks. It would be necessary that almost every man should be a man of business, or engage in some sort of trade. The province of Holland seems to be approaching near to this state. It is there unfashionable not to be a man of business. Necessity makes it usual for almost every man to be so, and custom everywhere regulates fashion. As it is ridiculous not to dress, so is it, in some measure, not to be employed like other people. As a man of a civil profession seems awkward in a camp or a garrison, and is even in some danger of being despised there, so does an idle man among men of business.

The highest ordinary rate of profit may be such as, in the price of the greater part of commodities, eats up the whole of what should go to the rent of the land, and leaves only what is sufficient to pay the labor of preparing and bringing them to market, according to the lowest rate at which labor can anywhere be paid, the bare subsistence of the laborer. The workman must always have been fed in some way or other while he was about the work, but the landlord may not always have been paid. The profits of the trade which the servants of the East India Company carry on in Bengal may not, perhaps, be very far from this rate.

The proportion which the usual market rate of interest ought to bear to the ordinary rate of clear profit, necessarily varies as profit rises or falls. Double interest is in Great Britain reckoned what the merchants call a good, moderate, reasonable profit; terms which, I apprehend, mean no more than a common and usual profit. In a country where the ordinary rate of clear profit is eight or ten percent it may be reasonable that one half of it should go to interest, wherever business is carried on with borrowed money. The stock is at the risk of the borrower, who, as it were, insures it to the lender; and four or five percent may, in the greater part of trades, be both a sufficient profit upon the risk of this insurance, and a sufficient recompense for the trouble of employing the stock. But the proportion between interest and clear profit might not be the same in countries where the ordinary rate of profit was either a good deal lower, or a good deal higher. If it were a good deal lower, one half of it, perhaps, could not be afforded for interest; and more might be afforded if it were a good deal higher.

In countries which are fast advancing to riches, the low rate of profit may, in the price of many commodities, compensate the high wages of labor, and enable those countries to sell as cheap as their less thriving neighbors, among whom the wages of labor may be lower.

In reality, high profits tend much more to raise the price of work than high wages. If, in the linen manufacture, for example, the wages of the different working people, the flax-dressers, the spinners, the weavers, etc. should all of them be advanced two pence a day, it would be necessary to heighten the price of a piece of linen only by a number of topics equal to the number of people that had been employed about it, multiplied by the number of days during which they had been so employed. That part of the price of the commodity which resolved itself into the wages, would, through all the different stages of the manufacture, rise only in arithmetical proportion to this rise of wages. But if the profits of all the different employers of those working people should be raised five percent that part of the price of the commodity which resolved itself into profit would, through all the different stages of the manufacture, rise in geometrical proportion to this rise of profit. The employer of the flax dressers would, in selling his flax, require an additional five percent upon the whole value of the materials and wages which he advanced to his workmen. The employer of the spinners would require an additional five percent both upon the advanced price of the flax, and upon the wages of the spinners. And the employer of the weavers would require alike five percent both upon the advanced price of the linen-yarn, and upon the wages of the weavers. In raising the price of commodities, the rise of wages operates in the same manner as simple interest does in the accumulation of debt. The rise of profit operates like compound interest. Our merchants and master manufacturers complain much of the bad effects of high wages in raising the price, and thereby lessening the sale of their goods, both at home and abroad. They say nothing concerning the bad effects of high profits; they are silent with regard to the pernicious effects of their own gains; they complain only of those of other people.

CHAPTER X

Of Wages and Profit in the Different Employments of Labor and Stock

The whole of the advantages and disadvantages of the different employments of labor and stock, must, in the same neighborhood, be either perfectly equal, or continually tending to equality. If, in the same neighborhood, there was any employment evidently either more or less advantageous than the rest, so many people would crowd into it in the one case, and so many would desert it in the other, that its advantages would soon return to the level of other employments. This, at least, would be the case in a society where things were left to follow their natural course, where there was perfect liberty, and where every man was perfectly free both to choose what occupation he thought proper, and to change it as often as he thought proper. Every man's interest would prompt him to seek the advantageous, and to shun the disadvantageous employment.

Pecuniary wages and profit, indeed, are everywhere in Europe extremely different, according to the different employments of labor and stock. But this difference arises, partly from certain circumstances in the employments themselves, which, either really, or at least in the imagination of men, make up for a small pecuniary gain in some, and counterbalance a great one in others, and partly from the policy of Europe, which nowhere leaves things at perfect liberty.

The particular consideration of those circumstances, and of that policy, will divide this Chapter into two parts.

Part I

Inequalities Arising from the Nature of the Employments Themselves

The five following are the principal circumstances which, so far as I have been able to observe, make up for a small pecuniary gain in some employments, and counterbalance a great one in others. First, the agreeableness or disagreeableness of the employments themselves; secondly, the easiness and cheapness, or the difficulty and expense of learning them; thirdly, the constancy or inconstancy of employment in them; fourthly, the small or great trust which must be reposed in those who exercise them; and, fifthly, the probability or improbability of success in them.

First, the wages of labor vary with the ease or hardship, the cleanliness or dirtiness, the honorableness or dishonorableness, of the employment. Thus in most places, take the year round, a journeyman tailor earns less than a journeyman weaver. His work is much easier. A journeyman weaver earns less than a journeyman smith. His work is not always easier, but it is much cleanlier. A journeyman blacksmith, though an artificer, seldom earns so much in twelve hours, as a collier, who is only a laborer, does in eight. His work is not quite so dirty, is less dangerous, and is carried on in daylight, and above ground. Honor makes a great part of the reward of all honorable professions. In point of pecuniary gain, all things considered, they are generally under-recompensed, as I shall endeavor to show by and by. Disgrace has the contrary effect. The trade of a butcher is a brutal and an odious business; but it is in most places more profitable than the greater part of common trades. The most detestable of all employments, that of public executioner, is, in proportion to the quantity of work done, better paid than any common trade whatever.

Hunting and fishing, the most important employments of mankind in the rude state of society, become, in its advanced state, their most agreeable amusements, and they pursue for pleasure what they once followed from necessity. In the advanced state of society, therefore, they are all very poor people who follow as a trade, what other people pursue as a pastime. Fishermen have been so since the time of Theocritus {See Idyllium xxi}. A poacher is everywhere a very poor man in Great Britain. In countries where the rigor of the law suffers no poachers, the licensed hunter is not in a much better condition. The natural taste for those employments makes more people follow them, than can live comfortably by them; and the produce of their labor, in proportion to its quantity, comes always too cheap to market, to afford any thing but the most scanty subsistence to the laborers.

Disagreeableness and disgrace affect the profits of stock in the same manner as the wages of labor. The keeper of an inn or tavern, who is never master of his own house, and who is exposed to the brutality of every drunkard, exercises neither a very agreeable nor a very creditable business. But there is scarce any common trade in which a small stock yields so great a profit.

Secondly, the wages of labor vary with the easiness and cheapness, or the difficulty and expense, of learning the business.

When any expensive machine is erected, the extraordinary work to be performed by it before it is worn out, it must be expected, will replace the capital laid out upon it, with at least the ordinary profits. A man educated at the expense of much labor and time to any of those employments which require extraordinary dexterity and skill, may be compared to one of those expensive machines. The work which he learns to perform, it must be expected, over and above the usual wages of common labor, will replace to him the whole expense of his education, with at least the ordinary profits of an equally valuable capital. It must do this too in a reasonable time, regard being had to the very uncertain duration of human life, in the same manner as to the more certain duration of the machine.

The difference between the wages of skilled labor and those of common labor, is founded upon this principle.

The policy of Europe considers the labor of all mechanics, artificers, and manufacturers, as skilled labor; and that of all country laborers as common labor. It seems to suppose that of the former to be of a more nice and delicate nature than that of the latter. It is so perhaps in some cases; but in the greater part it is quite otherwise, as I shall endeavor to show by and by. The laws and customs of Europe, therefore, in order to qualify any person for exercising the one species of labor, impose the necessity of an apprenticeship, though with different degrees of rigor in different places. They leave the other free and open to every body. During the continuance of the apprenticeship, the whole labor of the apprentice belongs to his master. In the meantime he must, in many cases, be maintained by his parents or relations, and, in almost all cases, must be clothed by them. Some money, too, is commonly given to the master for teaching him his trade. They who cannot give money, give time, or become bound for more than the usual number of years; a consideration which, though it is not always advantageous to the master, on account of the usual idleness of apprentices, is always disadvantageous to the apprentice. In country labor, on the contrary, the laborer, while he is employed about the easier, learns the more difficult parts of his business, and his own labor maintains him through all the different stages of his employment. It is reasonable, therefore, that in Europe the wages of mechanics, artificers, and manufacturers, should be somewhat higher than those of common laborers. They are so accordingly, and their superior gains make them, in most places, be considered as a superior rank of people. This superiority, however, is generally very small: the daily or weekly earnings of journeymen in the more common sorts of manufactures, such as those of plain linen and woolen cloth, computed at an average, are, in most places, very little more than the day-wages of common laborers. Their employment, indeed, is more steady and uniform, and the superiority of their earnings, taking the whole year together, may be somewhat greater. It seems evidently, however, to be no greater than what is sufficient to compensate the superior expense of their education.

Education in the ingenious arts, and in the liberal professions, is still more tedious and expensive. The pecuniary recompense, therefore, of painters and sculptors, of lawyers and physicians, ought to be much more liberal; and it is so accordingly.

The profits of stock seem to be very little affected by the easiness or difficulty of learning the trade in which it is employed. All the different ways in which stock is commonly employed in great towns seem, in reality, to be almost equally easy and equally difficult to learn. One branch, either of foreign or domestic trade, cannot well be a much more intricate business than another.

Thirdly, the wages of labor in different occupations vary with the constancy or inconstancy of employment.

Employment is much more constant in some trades than in others. In the greater part of manufactures, a journeyman maybe pretty sure of employment almost every day in the year that he is able to work. A mason or bricklayer, on the contrary, can work neither in hard frost nor in foul weather, and his employment at all other times depends upon the occasional calls of his customers. He is liable, in consequence, to be frequently without any. What he earns, therefore, while he is employed, must not only maintain him while he is idle, but make him some compensation for those anxious and desponding moments which the thought of so precarious a situation must sometimes occasion. Where the computed earnings of the greater part of manufacturers, accordingly, are nearly upon a level with the day-wages of common laborers, those of masons and bricklayers are generally from one-half more to double those wages. Where common laborers earn four or five shillings a week, masons and bricklayers frequently earn seven and eight; where the former earn six, the latter often earn nine and ten; and where the former earn nine and ten, as in London, the latter commonly earn fifteen and eighteen. No species of skilled labor, however, seems more easy to learn than that of masons and bricklayers. Chairmen in London, during the summer season, are said sometimes to be employed as bricklayers. The high wages of those workmen, therefore, are not so much the recompense of their skill, as the compensation for the inconstancy of their employment.

A house-carpenter seems to exercise rather a nicer and a more ingenious trade than a mason. In most places, however, for it is not universally so, his day-wages are somewhat lower. His employment, though it depends much, does not depend so entirely upon the occasional calls of his customers; and it is not liable to be interrupted by the weather.

When the trades which generally afford constant employment, happen in a particular place not to do so, the wages of the workmen always rise a good deal above their ordinary proportion to those of common labor. In London, almost all journeymen artificers are liable to be called upon and dismissed by their masters from day to day, and from week to week, in the same manner as day-laborers in other places. The lowest order of artificers, journeymen tailors, accordingly, earn their half-a-crown a day, though eighteen pence may be reckoned the wages of common labor. In small towns and country villages, the wages of journeymen tailors frequently scarce equal those of common labor; but in London they are often many weeks without employment, particularly during the summer.

When the inconstancy of employment is combined with the hardship, disagreeableness, and dirtiness of the work, it sometimes raises the wages of the most common labor above those of the most skilful artificers. A collier working by the piece is supposed, at Newcastle, to earn commonly about double, and, in many parts of Scotland, about three times, the wages of common labor. His high wages arise altogether from the hardship, disagreeableness, and dirtiness of his work. His employment may, upon most occasions, be as constant as he pleases. The coal-heavers in London exercise a trade which, in hardship, dirtiness, and disagreeableness, almost equals that of colliers; and, from the unavoidable irregularity in the arrivals of coal-ships, the employment of the greater part of them is necessarily very inconstant. If colliers, therefore, commonly earn double and triple the wages of common labor, it ought not to seem unreasonable that coal-heavers should sometimes earn four and five times those wages. In the inquiry made into their condition a few years ago, it was found that, at the rate at which they were then paid, they could earn from six to ten shillings a day. Six shillings are about four times the wages of common labor in London; and, in every particular trade, the lowest common earnings may always be considered as those of the far greater number. How extravagant so ever those earnings may appear, if they were more than sufficient to compensate all the disagreeable circumstances of the business, there would soon be so great a number of competitors, as, in a trade which has no exclusive privilege, would quickly reduce them to a lower rate.

The constancy or inconstancy of employment cannot affect the ordinary profits of stock in any particular trade. Whether the stock is or is not constantly employed, depends, not upon the trade, but the trader.

Fourthly, the wages of labor vary according to the small or great trust which must be reposed in the workmen.

The wages of goldsmiths and jewelers are everywhere superior to those of many other workmen, not only of equal, but of much superior ingenuity, on account of the precious materials with which they are entrusted. We trust our health to the physician, our fortune, and sometimes our life and reputation, to the lawyer and attorney. Such confidence could not safely be reposed in people of a very mean or low condition. Their reward must be such, therefore, as may give them that rank in the society which so important a trust requires. The long time and the great expense which must be laid out in their education, when combined with this circumstance, necessarily enhance still further the price of their labor.

When a person employs only his own stock in trade, there is no trust; and the credit which he may get from other people, depends, not upon the nature of the trade, but upon their opinion of his fortune, probity, and prudence. The different rates of profit, therefore, in the different branches of trade, cannot arise from the different degrees of trust reposed in the traders.

Fifthly, the wages of labor in different employments vary according to the probability or improbability of success in them.

The probability that any particular person shall ever be qualified for the employments to which he is educated, is very different in different occupations. In the greatest part of mechanic trades success is almost certain; but very uncertain in the liberal professions. Put your son apprentice to a shoemaker, there is little doubt of his learning to make a pair of shoes; but send him to study the law, it as at least twenty to one if he ever makes such proficiency as will enable him to live by the business. In a perfectly fair lottery, those who draw the prizes ought to gain all that is lost by those who draw the blanks. In a profession, where twenty fail for one that succeeds, that one ought to gain all that should have been gained by the unsuccessful twenty. The counselor at law, who, perhaps, at near forty years of age, begins to make something by his profession,

ought to receive the retribution, not only of his own so tedious and expensive education, but of that of more than twenty others, who are never likely to make any thing by
it. How extravagant so ever the fees of counselors at law may sometimes appear, their
real retribution is never equal to this. Compute, in any particular place, what is likely
to be annually gained, and what is likely to be annually spent, by all the different workmen in any common trade, such as that of shoemakers or weavers, and you will find that
the former sum will generally exceed the latter. But make the same computation with
regard to all the counselors and students of law, in all the different Inns of Court, and
you will find that their annual gains bear but a very small proportion to their annual
expense, even though you rate the former as high, and the latter as low, as can well be
done. The lottery of the law, therefore, is very far from being a perfectly fair lottery; and
that as well as many other liberal and honorable professions, is, in point of pecuniary
gain, evidently under-recompensed.

Those professions keep their level, however, with other occupations; and, notwithstanding these discouragements, all the most generous and liberal spirits are eager to
crowd into them. Two different causes contribute to recommend them. First, the desire
of the reputation which attends upon superior excellence in any of them; and, secondly,
the natural confidence which every man has, more or less, not only in his own abilities,
but in his own good fortune.

To excel in any profession, in which but few arrive at mediocrity, it is the most decisive mark of what is called genius, or superior talents. The public admiration which attends upon such distinguished abilities makes always a part of their reward; a greater or
smaller, in proportion as it is higher or lower in degree. It makes a considerable part of
that reward in the profession of physic; a still greater, perhaps, in that of law; in poetry
and philosophy it makes almost the whole.

There are some very agreeable and beautiful talents, of which the possession commands
a certain sort of admiration, but of which the exercise, for the sake of gain, is considered,
whether from reason or prejudice, as a sort of public prostitution. The pecuniary recompense, therefore, of those who exercise them in this manner, must be sufficient, not only
to pay for the time, labor, and expense of acquiring the talents, but for the discredit which
attends the employment of them as the means of subsistence. The exorbitant rewards of
players, opera-singers, opera-dancers, etc. are founded upon those two principles; the rarity and beauty of the talents, and the discredit of employing them in this manner. It seems
absurd at first sight, that we should despise their persons, and yet reward their talents with
the most profuse liberality. While we do the one, however, we must of necessity do the
other, Should the public opinion or prejudice ever alter with regard to such occupations,
their pecuniary recompense would quickly diminish. More people would apply to them,
and the competition would quickly reduce the price of their labor. Such talents, though
far from being common, are by no means so rare as imagined. Many people possess them
in great perfection, who disdain to make this use of them; and many more are capable of
acquiring them, if any thing could be made honorably by them.

The overweening conceit which the greater part of men have of their own abilities,
is an ancient evil remarked by the philosophers and moralists of all ages. Their absurd
presumption in their own good fortune has been less taken notice of. It is, however, if

possible, still more universal. There is no man living, who, when in tolerable health and spirits, has not some share of it. The chance of gain is by every man more or less over-valued, and the chance of loss is by most men undervalued, and by scarce any man, who is in tolerable health and spirits, valued more than it is worth.

That the chance of gain is naturally overvalued, we may learn from the universal success of lotteries. The world neither ever saw, nor ever will see, a perfectly fair lottery, or one in which the whole gain compensated the whole loss; because the undertaker could make nothing by it. In the state lotteries, the tickets are really not worth the price which is paid by the original subscribers, and yet commonly sell in the market for twenty, thirty, and sometimes forty percent advance. The vain hopes of gaining some of the great prizes is the sole cause of this demand. The soberest people scarce look upon it as a folly to pay a small sum for the chance of gaining ten or twenty thousand pounds, though they know that even that small sum is perhaps twenty or thirty percent more than the chance is worth. In a lottery in which no prize exceeded twenty pounds, though in other respects it approached much nearer to a perfectly fair one than the common state lotteries, there would not be the same demand for tickets. In order to have a better chance for some of the great prizes, some people purchase several tickets; and others, small shares in a still greater number. There is not, however, a more certain proposition in mathematics, than that the more tickets you adventure upon, the more likely you are to be a loser. Adventure upon all the tickets in the lottery, and you lose for certain; and the greater the number of your tickets, the nearer you approach to this certainty.

That the chance of loss is frequently undervalued, and scarce ever valued more than it is worth, we may learn from the very moderate profit of insurers. In order to make insurance, either from fire or sea-risk, a trade at all, the common premium must be sufficient to compensate the common losses, to pay the expense of management, and to afford such a profit as might have been drawn from an equal capital employed in any common trade. The person who pays no more than this, evidently pays no more than the real value of the risk, or the lowest price at which he can reasonably expect to insure it. But though many people have made a little money by insurance, very few have made a great fortune; and, from this consideration alone, it seems evident enough that the ordinary balance of profit and loss is not more advantageous in this than in other common trades, by which so many people make fortunes. Moderate, however, as the premium of insurance commonly is, many people despise the risk too much to care to pay it. Taking the whole kingdom at an average, nineteen houses in twenty, or rather, perhaps, ninety-nine in a hundred, are not insured from fire. Sea-risk is more alarming to the greater part of people; and the proportion of ships insured to those not insured is much greater. Many sail, however, at all seasons, and even in time of war, without any insurance. This may sometimes, perhaps, be done without any imprudence. When a great company, or even a great merchant, has twenty or thirty ships at sea, they may, as it were, insure one another. The premium saved up on them all may more than compensate such losses as they are likely to meet with in the common course of chances. The neglect of insurance upon shipping, however, in the same manner as upon houses, is, in most cases, the effect of no such nice calculation, but of mere thoughtless rashness, and presumptuous contempt of the risk.

The contempt of risk, and the presumptuous hope of success, are in no period of life more active than at the age at which young people choose their professions. How little the fear of misfortune is then capable of balancing the hope of good luck, appears still more evidently in the readiness of the common people to enlist as soldiers, or to go to sea, than in the eagerness of those of better fashion to enter into what are called the liberal professions.

What a common soldier may lose is obvious enough. Without regarding the danger, however, young volunteers never enlist so readily as at the beginning of a new war; and though they have scarce any chance of preferment, they figure to themselves, in their youthful fancies, a thousand occasions of acquiring honor and distinction which never occur. These romantic hopes make the whole price of their blood. Their pay is less than that of common laborers, and, in actual service, their fatigues are much greater.

The lottery of the sea is not altogether so disadvantageous as that of the army. The son of a creditable laborer or artificer may frequently go to sea with his father's consent; but if he enlists as a soldier, it is always without it. Other people see some chance of his making something by the one trade; nobody but himself sees any of his making any thing by the other. The great admiral is less the object of public admiration than the great general; and the highest success in the sea service promises a less brilliant fortune and reputation than equal success in the land. The same difference runs through all the inferior degrees of preferment in both. By the rules of precedency, a captain in the navy ranks with a colonel in the army; but he does not rank with him in the common estimation. As the great prizes in the lottery are less, the smaller ones must be more numerous. Common sailors, therefore, more frequently get some fortune and preferment than common soldiers; and the hope of those prizes is what principally recommends the trade. Though their skill and dexterity are much superior to that of almost any artificers; and though their whole life is one continual scene of hardship and danger; yet for all this dexterity and skill, for all those hardships and dangers, while they remain in the condition of common sailors, they receive scarce any other recompense but the pleasure of exercising the one and of surmounting the other. Their wages are not greater than those of common laborers at the port which regulates the rate of seamen's wages. As they are continually going from port to port, the monthly pay of those who sail from all the different ports of Great Britain, is more nearly upon a level than that of any other workmen in those different places; and the rate of the port to and from which the greatest number sail, that is, the port of London, regulates that of all the rest. At London, the wages of the greater part of the different classes of workmen are about double those of the same classes at Edinburgh. But the sailors who sail from the port of London, seldom earn above three or four shillings a month more than those who sail from the port of Leith, and the difference is frequently not so great. In time of peace, and in the merchant-service, the London price is from a guinea to about seven-and-twenty shillings the calendar month. A common laborer in London, at the rate of nine or ten shillings a week, may earn in the calendar month from forty to five-and-forty shillings. The sailor, indeed, over and above his pay, is supplied with provisions. Their value, however, may not perhaps always exceed the difference between his pay and that of the common laborer; and though it sometimes should, the excess will not be clear gain to the sailor, because he cannot share it with his wife and family, whom he must maintain out of his wages at home.

The dangers and hairbreadth escapes of a life of adventures, instead of dishearten-ing young people, seem frequently to recommend a trade to them. A tender mother, among the inferior ranks of people, is often afraid to send her son to school at a sea-port town, lest the sight of the ships, and the conversation and adventures of the sailors, should entice him to go to sea. The distant prospect of hazards, from which we can hope to extricate ourselves by courage and address, is not disagreeable to us, and does not raise the wages of labor in any employment. It is otherwise with those in which courage and address can be of no avail. In trades which are known to be very unwhole-some, the wages of labor are always remarkably high. Unwholesomeness is a species of disagreeableness, and its effects upon the wages of labor are to be ranked under that general head.

In all the different employments of stock, the ordinary rate of profit varies more or less with the certainty or uncertainty of the returns. These are, in general, less uncertain in the inland than in the foreign trade, and in some branches of foreign trade than in oth-ers; in the trade to North America, for example, than in that to Jamaica. The ordinary rate of profit always rises more or less with the risk. It does not, however, seem to rise in proportion to it, or so as to compensate it completely. Bankruptcies are most frequent in the most hazardous trades. The most hazardous of all trades, that of a smuggler, though, when the adventure succeeds, it is likewise the most profitable, is the infallible road to bankruptcy. The presumptuous hope of success seems to act here as upon all other occasions, and to entice so many adventurers into those hazardous trades, that their competition reduces the profit below what is sufficient to compensate the risk. To compensate it completely, the common returns ought, over and above the ordinary prof-its of stock, not only to make up for all occasional losses, but to afford a surplus profit to the adventurers, of the same nature with the profit of insurers. But if the common re-turns were sufficient for all this, bankruptcies would not be more frequent in these than in other trades.

Of the five circumstances, therefore, which vary the wages of labor, two only affect the profits of stock; the agreeableness or disagreeableness of the business, and the risk or se-curity with which it is attended. In point of agreeableness or disagreeableness, there is lit-tle or no difference in the far greater part of the different employments of stock, but a great deal in those of labor; and the ordinary profit of stock, though it rises with the risk, does not always seem to rise in proportion to it. It should follow from all this, that, in the same society or neighborhood, the average and ordinary rates of profit in the differ-ent employments of stock should be more nearly upon a level than the pecuniary wages of the different sorts of labor. They are so accordingly. The difference between the earn-ings of a common laborer and those of a well employed lawyer or physician, is evidently much greater than that between the ordinary profits in any two different branches of trade. The apparent difference, besides, in the profits of different trades, is generally a de-ception arising from our not always distinguishing what ought to be considered as wages, from what ought to be considered as profit.

Apothecaries' profit is become a byword, denoting something uncommonly extrava-gant. This great apparent profit, however, is frequently no more than the reasonable wages of labor. The skill of an apothecary is a much nicer and more delicate matter than that of any artificer whatever; and the trust which is reposed in him is of much greater importance. He is the physician of the poor in all cases, and of the rich when the distress or danger is not very great. His reward, therefore, ought to be suitable to his skill and his trust; and it arises generally from the price at which he sells his drugs. But the whole drugs which the best employed apothecary in a large market-town, will sell in a year, may not perhaps cost him above thirty or forty pounds. Though he should sell them, therefore, for three or four hundred, or at a thousand percent profit, this may frequently be no more than the reasonable wages of his labor, charged, in the only way in which he can charge them, upon the price of his drugs. The greater part of the apparent profit is real wages disguised in the garb of profit.

In a small seaport town, a little grocer will make forty or fifty percent upon a stock of a single hundred pounds, while a considerable wholesale merchant in the same place will scarce make eight or ten percent upon a stock of ten thousand. The trade of the grocer may be necessary for the conveniency of the inhabitants, and the narrowness of the market may not admit the employment of a larger capital in the business. The man, however, must not only live by his trade, but live by it suitably to the qualifications which it requires. Besides possessing a little capital, he must be able to read, write, and account and must be a tolerable judge, too, of perhaps fifty or sixty different sorts of goods, their prices, qualities, and the markets where they are to be had cheapest. He must have all the knowledge, in short, that is necessary for a great merchant, which nothing hinders him from becoming but the want of a sufficient capital. Thirty or forty pounds a year cannot be considered as too great a recompense for the labor of a person so accomplished. Deduct this from the seemingly great profits of his capital, and little more will remain, perhaps, than the ordinary profits of stock. The greater part of the apparent profit is, in this case too, real wages.

The difference between the apparent profit of the retail and that of the wholesale trade, is much less in the capital than in small towns and country villages. Where ten thousand pounds can be employed in the grocery trade, the wages of the grocer's labor must be a very trifling addition to the real profits of so great a stock. The apparent profits of the wealthy retailer, therefore, are there more nearly upon a level with those of the wholesale merchant. It is upon this account that goods sold by retail are generally as cheap, and frequently much cheaper, in the capital than in small towns and country villages. Grocery goods, for example, are generally much cheaper; bread and butcher's meat frequently as cheap. It costs no more to bring grocery goods to the great town than to the country village; but it costs a great deal more to bring corn and cattle, as the greater part of them must be brought from a much greater distance. The prime cost of grocery goods, therefore, being the same in both places, they are cheapest where the least profit is charged upon them. The prime cost of bread and butcher's meat is greater in the great town than in the country village; and though the profit is less, therefore they are not always cheaper there, but often equally cheap. In such articles as bread and butcher's meat, the same cause which diminishes apparent profit, increases prime cost. The extent of the market, by giving employment to greater stocks, diminishes apparent profit; but by requiring supplies from a greater distance, it increases prime cost. This diminution of the one and increase of the other, seem, in most cases, nearly to counterbalance one another; which is probably the reason that, though the prices of corn and cattle are commonly very different in different parts of the kingdom, those of bread and butcher's meat are generally very nearly the same through the greater part of it.

Though the profits of stock, both in the wholesale and retail trade, are generally less in the capital than in small towns and country villages, yet great fortunes are frequently acquired from small beginnings in the former, and scarce ever in the latter. In small towns and country villages, on account of the narrowness of the market, trade cannot always be extended as stock extends. In such places, therefore, though the rate of a particular person's profits may be very high, the sum or amount of them can never be very great, nor consequently that of his annual accumulation. In great towns, on the contrary, trade can be extended as stock increases, and the credit of a frugal and thriving man increases much faster than his stock. His trade is extended in proportion to the amount of both; and the sum or amount of his profits is in proportion to the extent of his trade, and his annual accumulation in proportion to the amount of his profits. It seldom happens, however, that great fortunes are made, even in great towns, by any one regular, established, and well-known branch of business, but in consequence of a long life of industry, frugality, and attention. Sudden fortunes, indeed, are sometimes made in such places, by what is called the trade of speculation. The speculative merchant exercises no one regular, established, or well-known branch of business. He is a corn merchant this year, and a wine merchant the next, and a sugar, tobacco, or tea merchant the year after. He enters into every trade, when he foresees that it is likely to lie more than commonly profitable, and he quits it when he foresees that its profits are likely to return to the level of other trades. His profits and losses, therefore, can bear no regular proportion to those of any one established and well-known branch of business. A bold adventurer may sometimes acquire a considerable fortune by two or three successful speculations, but is just as likely to lose one by two or three unsuccessful ones. This trade can be carried on nowhere but in great towns. It is only in places of the most extensive commerce and correspondence that the intelligence requisite for it can be had.

The five circumstances above mentioned, though they occasion considerable inequalities in the wages of labor and profits of stock, occasion none in the whole of the advantages and disadvantages, real or imaginary, of the different employments of either. The nature of those circumstances is such, that they make up for a small pecuniary gain in some, and counterbalance a great one in others.

In order, however, that this equality may take place in the whole of their advantages or disadvantages, three things are requisite, even where there is the most perfect freedom. First the employments must be well known and long established in the neighborhood; secondly, they must be in their ordinary, or what may be called their natural state; and, thirdly, they must be the sole or principal employments of those who occupy them.

First, this equality can take place only in those employments which are well known, and have been long established in the neighborhood.

Where all other circumstances are equal, wages are generally higher in new than in old trades. When a projector attempts to establish a new manufacture, he must at first entice his workmen from other employments, by higher wages than they can either earn in their own trades, or than the nature of his work would otherwise require; and a considerable time must pass away before he can venture to reduce them to the common level. Manufactures for which the demand arises altogether from fashion and fancy, are continually changing, and seldom last long enough to be considered as old established manufactures. Those, on the contrary, for which the demand arises chiefly from use or necessity, are less liable to change, and the same form or fabric may continue in demand for whole centuries together. The wages of labor, therefore, are likely to be higher in manufactures of the former, than in those of the latter kind. Birmingham deals chiefly in manufactures of the former kind; Sheffield in those of the latter; and the wages of labor in those two different places are said to be suitable to this difference in the nature of their manufactures.

The establishment of any new manufacture, of any new branch of commerce, or of any new practice in agriculture, is always a speculation from which the projector promises himself extraordinary profits. These profits sometimes are very great, and sometimes, more frequently, perhaps, they are quite otherwise; but, in general, they bear no regular proportion to those of other old trades in the neighborhood. If the project succeeds, they are commonly at first very high. When the trade or practice becomes thoroughly established and well known, the competition reduces them to the level of other trades.

Secondly, this equality in the whole of the advantages and disadvantages of the different employments of labor and stock, can take place only in the ordinary, or what may be called the natural state of those employments.

The demand for almost every different species of labor is sometimes greater, and sometimes less than usual. In the one case, the advantages of the employment rise above, in the other they fall below the common level. The demand for country labor is greater at haytime and harvest than during the greater part of the year; and wages rise with the demand. In time of war, when forty or fifty thousand sailors are forced from the merchant service into that of the king, the demand for sailors to merchant ships necessarily rises with their scarcity; and their wages, upon such occasions, commonly rise from a guinea and seven-and-twenty shillings to forty shilling's and three pounds a month. In a decaying manufacture, on the contrary, many workmen, rather than quit their own trade, are contented with smaller wages than would otherwise be suitable to the nature of their employment.

The profits of stock vary with the price of the commodities in which it is employed. As the price of any commodity rises above the ordinary or average rate, the profits of at least some part of the stock that is employed in bringing it to market, rise above their proper level, and as it falls they sink below it. All commodities are more or less liable to variations of price, but some are much more so than others. In all commodities which are produced by human industry, the quantity of industry annually employed is necessarily regulated by the annual demand, in such a manner that the average annual produce may, as nearly as possible, be equal to the average annual consumption. In some employments, it has already been observed, the same quantity of industry will always produce the same, or very nearly the same quantity of commodities. In the linen or woolen manufactures, for example, the same number of hands will annually work up very nearly the same quantity of linen and woolen cloth. The variations in the market price of such commodities, therefore, can arise only from some accidental variation in the demand. A public mourning raises the price of black cloth. But as the demand for most sorts of plain linen and woolen cloth is pretty uniform, so is likewise the price. But there are other employments in which the same quantity of industry will not always produce the same quantity of commodities. The same quantity of industry, for example, will, in different years, produce very different quantities of corn, wine, hops, sugar tobacco, etc. The price of such commodities, therefore, varies not only with the variations of demand, but with the much greater and more frequent variations of quantity, and is consequently extremely fluctuating; but the profit of some of the dealers must necessarily fluctuate with the price of the commodities. The operations of the speculative merchant are principally employed about such commodities. He endeavors to buy them up when he foresees that their price is likely to rise, and to sell them when it is likely to fall.

Thirdly, this equality in the whole of the advantages and disadvantages of the different employments of labor and stock, can take place only in such as are the sole or principal employments of those who occupy them.

When a person derives his subsistence from one employment, which does not occupy the greater part of his time, in the intervals of his leisure he is often willing to work at another for less wages than would otherwise suit the nature of the employment.

There still subsists, in many parts of Scotland, a set of people called cottars or cottagers, though they were more frequent some years ago than they are now. They are a sort of out-servants of the landlords and farmers. The usual reward which they receive from their master is a house, a small garden for pot-herbs, as much grass as will feed a cow, and, perhaps, an acre or two of bad arable land. When their master has occasion for their labor, he gives them, besides, two pecks of oatmeal a week, worth about sixteen pence sterling. During a great part of the year, he has little or no occasion for their labor, and the cultivation of their own little possession is not sufficient to occupy the time which is left at their own disposal. When such occupiers were more numerous than they are at present, they are said to have been willing to give their spare time for a very small recompense to any body, and to have wrought for less wages than other laborers. In ancient times, they seem to have been common all over Europe. In countries ill cultivated, and worse inhabited, the greater part of landlords and farmers could not otherwise provide themselves with the extraordinary number of hands which country labor requires at certain seasons. The daily or weekly recompense which such laborers occasionally received from their masters, was evidently not the whole price of their labor. Their small tenement made a considerable part of it. This daily or weekly recompense, however, seems to have been considered as the whole of it, by many writers who have collected the prices of labor and provisions in ancient times, and who have taken pleasure in representing both as wonderfully low.

The produce of such labor comes frequently cheaper to market than would otherwise be suitable to its nature. Stockings, in many parts of Scotland, are knit much cheaper than they can anywhere be wrought upon the loom. They are the work of servants and laborers who derive the principal part of their subsistence from some other employment. More than a thousand pair of Shetland stockings are annually imported into Leith, of which the price is from five-pence to seven-pence a pair. At Lerwick, the small capital of the Shetland islands, ten pence a day, I have been assured, is a common price of common labor. In the same islands, they knit worsted stockings to the value of a guinea a pair and upwards.

The spinning of linen yarn is carried on in Scotland nearly in the same way as the knitting of stockings, by servants, who are chiefly hired for other purposes. They earn but a very scanty subsistence, who endeavor to get their livelihood by either of those trades. In most parts of Scotland, she is a good spinner who can earn twenty pence a week.

In opulent countries, the market is generally so extensive, that any one trade is sufficient to employ the whole labor and stock of those who occupy it. Instances of people living by one employment, and, at the same time, deriving some little advantage from another, occur chiefly in poor countries. The following instance, however, of something of the same kind, is to be found in the capital of a very rich one. There is no city in Europe, I believe, in which house-rent is dearer than in London, and yet I know no capital in which a furnished apartment can be hired so cheap. Lodging is not only much cheaper in London than in Paris; it is much cheaper than in Edinburgh, of the same degree of goodness; and, what may seem extraordinary, the dearness of house-rent is the cause of the cheapness of lodging. The dearness of house-rent in London arises, not only from those causes which render it dear in all great capitals, the dearness of labor, the dearness of all the materials of building, which must generally be brought from a great distance, and, above all, the dearness of ground-rent, every landlord acting the part of a monopolist, and frequently exacting a higher rent for a single acre of bad land in a town, than can be had for a hundred of the best in the country; but it arises in part from the peculiar manners and customs of the people, which oblige every master of a family to hire a whole house from top to bottom. A dwelling-house in England means every thing that is contained under the same roof. In France, Scotland, and many other parts of Europe, it frequently means no more than a single storey. A tradesman in London is obliged to hire a whole house in that part of the town where his customers live. His shop is upon the ground floor, and he and his family sleep in the garret; and he endeavors to pay a part of his house-rent by letting the two middle stories to lodgers. He expects to maintain his family by his trade, and not by his lodgers. Whereas at Paris and Edinburgh, people who let lodgings have commonly no other means of subsistence; and the price of the lodging must pay, not only the rent of the house, but the whole expense of the family.

Part II

Inequalities Occasioned by the Policy of Europe

Such are the inequalities in the whole of the advantages and disadvantages of the different employments of labor and stock, which the defect of any of the three requisites above mentioned must occasion, even where there is the most perfect liberty. But the policy of Europe, by not leaving things at perfect liberty, occasions other inequalities of much greater importance.

It does this chiefly in the three following ways. First, by restraining the competition in some employments to a smaller number than would otherwise be disposed to enter into them; secondly, by increasing it in others beyond what it naturally would be; and, thirdly, by obstructing the free circulation of labor and stock, both from employment to employment, and from place to place.

First, the policy of Europe occasions a very important inequality in the whole of the advantages and disadvantages of the different employments of labor and stock, by restraining the competition in some employments to a smaller number than might otherwise be disposed to enter into them.

The exclusive privileges of corporations are the principal means it makes use of for this purpose.

The exclusive privilege of an incorporated trade necessarily restrains the competition, in the town where it is established, to those who are free of the trade. To have served an apprenticeship in the town, under a master properly qualified, is commonly the necessary requisite for obtaining this freedom. The bye-laws of the corporation regulate sometimes the number of apprentices which any master is allowed to have, and almost always the number of years which each apprentice is obliged to serve. The intention of both regulations is to restrain the competition to a much smaller number than might otherwise be disposed to enter into the trade. The limitation of the number of apprentices restrains it directly. A long term of apprenticeship restrains it more indirectly, but as effectually, by increasing the expense of education.

In Sheffield, no master cutler can have more than one apprentice at a time, by a bye-law of the corporation. In Norfolk and Norwich, no master weaver can have more than two apprentices, under pain of forfeiting five pounds a month to the king. No master hatter can have more than two apprentices anywhere in England, or in the English plantations, under pain of forfeiting five pounds a month, half to the king, and half to him who shall sue in any court of record. Both these regulations, though they have been confirmed by a public law of the kingdom, are evidently dictated by the same corporation-spirit which enacted the bye-law of Sheffield. The silkweavers in London had scarce been incorporated a year, when they enacted a bye-law, restraining any master from having more than two apprentices at a time. It required a particular act of parliament to rescind this bye-law.

Seven years seem anciently to have been, all over Europe, the usual term established for the duration of apprenticeships in the greater part of incorporated trades. All such incorporations were anciently called *universities*, which, indeed, is the proper Latin name for any incorporation whatever. The university of smiths, the university of tailors, etc. are expressions which we commonly meet with in the old charters of ancient towns. When those particular incorporations, which are now peculiarly called universities, were first established, the term of years which it was necessary to study, in order to obtain the degree of master of arts, appears evidently to have been copied from the term of apprenticeship in common trades, of which the incorporations were much more ancient. As to have wrought seven years under a master properly qualified, was necessary, in order to entitle any person to become a master, and to have himself apprentices in a common trade; so to have studied seven years under a master properly qualified, was necessary to entitle him to become a *master, teacher,* or *doctor* (words anciently synonymous), in the liberal arts, and to have *scholars* or *apprentices* (words likewise originally synonymous) to study under him.

By the 5th year of Elizabeth, commonly called the Statute of Apprenticeship, it was enacted, that no person should, for the future, exercise any trade, craft, or mystery, at that time exercised in England, unless he had previously served to it an apprenticeship of seven years at least; and what before had been the bye-law of many particular corporations, became in England the general and public law of all trades carried on in market towns. For though the words of the statute are very general, and seem plainly to include the whole kingdom, by interpretation its operation has been limited to market towns; it having been held that, in country villages, a person may exercise several different trades, though he has not served a seven years apprenticeship to each, they being necessary for the conveniency of the inhabitants, and the number of people frequently not being sufficient to supply each with a particular set of hands.

By a strict interpretation of the words, too, the operation of this statute has been limited to those trades which were established in England before the 5th year of Elizabeth's reign, and has never been extended to such as have been introduced since that time. This limitation has given occasion to several distinctions, which, considered as rules of police, appear as foolish as can well be imagined. It has been adjudged, for example, that a coachmaker can neither himself make nor employ journeymen to make his coach-wheels, but must buy them of a master wheelwright; this latter trade having been exercised in England before the 5th year of Elizabeth. But a wheelwright, though he has never served an apprenticeship to a coachmaker, may either himself make or employ journeymen to make coaches; the trade of a coachmaker not being within the statute, because not exercised in England at the time when it was made. The manufactures of Manchester, Birmingham, and Wolverhampton, are many of them, upon this account, not within the statute, not having been exercised in England before the 5th of Elizabeth.

In France, the duration of apprenticeships is different in different towns and in different trades. In Paris, five years is the term required in a great number; but, before any person can be qualified to exercise the trade as a master, he must, in many of them, serve five years more as a journeyman. During this latter term, he is called the companion of his master, and the term itself is called his companionship.

In Scotland, there is no general law which regulates universally the duration of apprenticeships. The term is different in different corporations. Where it is long, a part of it may generally be redeemed by paying a small fine. In most towns, too, a very small fine is sufficient to purchase the freedom of any corporation. The weavers of linen and hempen cloth, the principal manufactures of the country, as well as all other artificers subservient to them, wheel-makers, reel-makers, etc. may exercise their trades in any town-corporate without paying any fine. In all towns-corporate, all persons are free to sell butcher's meat upon any lawful day of the week. Three years is, in Scotland, a common term of apprenticeship, even in some very nice trades; and, in general, I know of no country in Europe, in which corporation laws are so little oppressive.

The property which every man has in his own labor, as it is the original foundation of all other property, so it is the most sacred and inviolable. The patrimony of a poor man lies in the strength and dexterity of his hands; and to hinder him from employing this strength and dexterity in what manner he thinks proper, without injury to his neighbor, is a plain violation of this most sacred property. It is a manifest encroachment upon the just liberty, both of the workman, and of those who might be disposed to employ him. As it hinders the one from working at what he thinks proper, so it hinders the others from employing whom they think proper. To judge whether he is fit to be employed, may surely be trusted to the discretion of the employers, whose interest it so much concerns. The affected anxiety of the lawgiver, lest they should employ an improper person, is evidently as impertinent as it is oppressive.

The institution of long apprenticeships can give no security that insufficient workmanship shall not frequently be exposed to public sale. When this is done, it is generally the effect of fraud, and not of inability; and the longest apprenticeship can give no security against fraud. Quite different regulations are necessary to prevent this abuse. The sterling mark upon plate, and the stamps upon linen and woolen cloth, give the purchaser much greater security than any statute of apprenticeship. He generally looks at these, but never thinks it worth while to enquire whether the workman had served a seven years apprenticeship.

The institution of long apprenticeships has no tendency to form young people to industry. A journeyman who works by the piece is likely to be industrious, because he derives a benefit from every exertion of his industry. An apprentice is likely to be idle, and almost always is so, because he has no immediate interest to be otherwise. In the inferior employments, the sweets of labor consist altogether in the recompense of labor. They who are soonest in a condition to enjoy the sweets of it, are likely soonest to conceive a relish for it, and to acquire the early habit of industry. A young man naturally conceives an aversion to labor, when for a long time he receives no benefit from it. The boys who are put out apprentices from public charities are generally bound for more than the usual number of years, and they generally turn out very idle and worthless.

Apprenticeships were altogether unknown to the ancients. The reciprocal duties of master and apprentice make a considerable article in every modern code. The Roman law is perfectly silent with regard to them. I know no Greek or Latin word (I might venture, I believe, to assert that there is none) which expresses the idea we now annex to the word *apprentice*, a servant bound to work at a particular trade for the benefit of a master, during a term of years, upon condition that the master shall teach him that trade.

Long apprenticeships are altogether unnecessary. The arts, which are much superior to common trades, such as those of making clocks and watches, contain no such mystery as to require a long course of instruction. The first invention of such beautiful machines, indeed, and even that of some of the instruments employed in making them, must no doubt have been the work of deep thought and long time, and may justly be considered as among the happiest efforts of human ingenuity. But when both have been fairly invented, and are well understood, to explain to any young man, in the completest manner, how to apply the instruments, and how to construct the machines, cannot well require more than the lessons of a few weeks; perhaps those of a few days might be sufficient. In the common mechanic trades, those of a few days might certainly be sufficient. The dexterity of hand, indeed, even in common trades, cannot be acquired without much practice and experience. But a young man would practice with much more diligence and attention, if from the beginning he wrought as a journeyman, being paid in proportion to the little work which he could execute, and paying in his turn for the materials which he might sometimes spoil through awkwardness and inexperience. His education would generally in this way be more effectual, and always less tedious and expensive. The master, indeed, would be a loser. He would lose all the wages of the apprentice, which he now saves, for seven years together. In the end, perhaps, the apprentice himself would be a loser. In a trade so easily learnt he would have more competitors, and his wages, when he came to be a complete workman, would be much less than at present. The same increase of competition would reduce the profits of the masters, as well as the wages of workmen. The trades, the crafts, the mysteries, would all be losers. But the public would be a gainer, the work of all artificers coming in this way much cheaper to market.

It is to prevent his reduction of price, and consequently of wages and profit, by restraining that free competition which would most certainly occasion it, that all corporations, and the greater part of corporation laws have been established. In order to erect a corporation, no other authority in ancient times was requisite, in many parts of Europe, but that of the town-corporate in which it was established. In England, indeed, a charter from the king was likewise necessary. But this prerogative of the crown seems to have been reserved rather for extorting money from the subject, than for the defense of the common liberty against such oppressive monopolies. Upon paying a fine to the king, the charter seems generally to have been readily granted; and when any particular class of artificers or traders thought proper to act as a corporation, without a charter, such adulterine guilds, as they were called, were not always disfranchised upon that account, but obliged to fine annually to the king, for permission to exercise their usurped privileges {See Madox Firma Burgi p.26}. The immediate inspection of all corporations, and of the by-laws which they might think proper to enact for their own government, belonged to the town-corporate in which they were established; and whatever discipline was exercised over them, proceeded commonly, not from the king, but from that greater incorporation of which those subordinate ones were only parts or members.

The government of towns-corporate was altogether in the hands of traders and artificers, and it was the manifest interest of every particular class of them, to prevent the market from being overstocked, as they commonly express it, with their own particular species of industry; which is in reality to keep it always understocked. Each class was eager to establish regulations proper for this purpose, and, provided it was allowed to do so, was willing to consent that every other class should do the same. In consequence of such regulations, indeed, each class was obliged to buy the goods they had occasion for from every other within the town, somewhat dearer than they otherwise might have done. But, in recompense, they were enabled to sell their own just as much dearer; so that, so far it was as broad as long, as they say; and in the dealings of the different classes within the town with one another, none of them were losers by these regulations. But in their dealings with the country they were all great gainers; and in these latter dealings consist the whole trade which supports and enriches every town.

Every town draws its whole subsistence, and all the materials of its industry, from the country. It pays for these chiefly in two ways: first, by sending back to the country a part of those materials wrought up and manufactured; in which case, their price is augmented by the wages of the workmen, and the profits of their masters or immediate employers; secondly, by sending to it a part both of the rude and manufactured produce, either of other countries, or of distant parts of the same country, imported into the town; in which case, too, the original price of those goods is augmented by the wages of the carriers or sailors, and by the profits of the merchants who employ them. In what is gained upon the first of those branches of commerce, consists the advantage which the town makes by its manufactures; in what is gained upon the second, the advantage of its inland and foreign trade. The wages of the workmen, and the profits of their different employers, make up the whole of what is gained upon both. Whatever regulations, therefore, tend to increase those wages and profits beyond what they otherwise: would be, tend to enable the town to purchase, with a smaller quantity of its labor, the produce of a greater quantity of the labor of the country. They give the traders and artificers in the town an advantage over the landlords, farmers, and laborers, in the country, and break down that natural equality which would otherwise take place in the commerce which is carried on between them. The whole annual produce of the labor of the society is annually divided between those two different sets of people. By means of those regulations, a greater share of it is given to the inhabitants of the town than would otherwise fall to them, and a less to those of the country.

The price which the town really pays for the provisions and materials annually imported into it, is the quantity of manufactures and other goods annually exported from it. The dearer the latter are sold, the cheaper the former are bought. The industry of the town becomes more, and that of the country less advantageous.

That the industry which is carried on in towns is, everywhere in Europe, more advantageous than that which is carried on in the country, without entering into any very nice computations, we may satisfy ourselves by one very simple and obvious observation. In every country of Europe, we find at least a hundred people who have acquired great fortunes, from small beginnings, by trade and manufactures, the industry which properly belongs to towns, for one who has done so by that which properly belongs to the country, the raising of rude produce by the improvement and cultivation of land. Industry, therefore, must be better rewarded, the wages of labor and the profits of stock must evidently be greater, in the one situation than in the other. But stock and labor naturally seek the most advantageous employment. They naturally, therefore, resort as much as they can to the town, and desert the country.

The inhabitants of a town being collected into one place, can easily combine together. The most insignificant trades carried on in towns have, accordingly, in some place or other, been incorporated; and even where they have never been incorporated, yet the corporation-spirit, the jealousy of strangers, the aversion to take apprentices, or to communicate the secret of their trade, generally prevail in them, and often teach them, by voluntary associations and agreements, to prevent that free competition which they cannot prohibit by bye-laws. The trades which employ but a small number of hands, run most easily into such combinations. Half-a-dozen wool-combers, perhaps, are necessary to keep a thousand spinners and weavers at work. By combining not to take apprentices, they can not only engross the employment, but reduce the whole manufacture into a sort of slavery to themselves, and raise the price of their labor much above what is due to the nature of their work.

The inhabitants of the country, dispersed in distant places, cannot easily combine together. They have not only never been incorporated, but the incorporation spirit never has prevailed among them. No apprenticeship has ever been thought necessary to qualify for husbandry, the great trade of the country. After what are called the fine arts, and the liberal professions, however, there is perhaps no trade which requires so great a variety of knowledge and experience. The innumerable volumes which have been written upon it in all languages, may satisfy us, that among the wisest and most learned nations, it has never been regarded as a matter very easily understood. And from all those volumes we shall in vain attempt to collect that knowledge of its various and complicated operations which is commonly possessed even by the common farmer; how contemptuously soever the very contemptible authors of some of them may sometimes affect to speak of him. There is scarce any common mechanic trade, on the contrary, of which all the operations may not be as completely and distinctly explained in a pamphlet of a very few pages, as it is possible for words illustrated by figures to explain them. In the history of the arts, now publishing by the French Academy of Sciences, several of them are actually explained in this manner. The direction of operations, besides, which must be varied with every change of the weather, as well as with many other accidents, requires much more judgment and discretion, than that of those which are always the same, or very nearly the same.

Not only the art of the farmer, the general direction of the operations of husbandry, but many inferior branches of country labor require much more skill and experience than the greater part of mechanic trades. The man who works upon brass and iron, works with instruments, and upon materials of which the temper is always the same, or very nearly the same. But the man who ploughs the ground with a team of horses or oxen, works with instruments of which the health, strength, and temper, are very different upon different occasions. The condition of the materials which he works upon, too, is as variable as that of the instruments which he works with, and both require to be managed with much judgment and discretion. The common ploughman, though generally regarded as the pattern of stupidity and ignorance, is seldom defective in this judgment and discretion. He is less accustomed, indeed, to social intercourse, than the mechanic who lives in a town. His voice and language are more uncouth, and more difficult to be understood by those who are not used to them. His understanding, however, being accustomed to consider a greater variety of objects, is generally much superior to that of the other, whose whole attention, from morning till night, is commonly occupied in performing one or two very simple operations. How much the lower ranks of people in the country are really superior to those of the town, is well known to every man whom either business or curiosity has led to converse much with both. In China and Indostan, accordingly, both the rank and the wages of country laborers are said to be superior to those of the greater part of artificers and manufacturers. They would probably be so everywhere, if corporation laws and the corporation spirit did not prevent it.

The superiority which the industry of the towns has everywhere in Europe over that of the country, is not altogether owing to corporations and corporation laws. It is supported by many other regulations. The high duties upon foreign manufactures, and upon all goods imported by alien merchants, all tend to the same purpose. Corporation laws enable the inhabitants of towns to raise their prices, without fearing to be undersold by the free competition of their own countrymen. Those other regulations secure them equally against that of foreigners. The enhancement of price occasioned by both is everywhere finally paid by the landlords, farmers, and laborers, of the country, who have seldom opposed the establishment of such monopolies. They have commonly neither inclination nor fitness to enter into combinations; and the clamor and sophistry of merchants and manufacturers easily persuade them, that the private interest of a part, and of a subordinate part, of the society, is the general interest of the whole.

In Great Britain, the superiority of the industry of the towns over that of the country seems to have been greater formerly than in the present times. The wages of country labor approach nearer to those of manufacturing labor, and the profits of stock employed in agriculture to those of trading and manufacturing stock, than they are said to have done in the last century, or in the beginning of the present. This change may be regarded as the necessary, though very late consequence of the extraordinary encouragement given to the industry of the towns. The stocks accumulated in them come in time to be so great, that it can no longer be employed with the ancient profit in that species of industry which is peculiar to them. That industry has its limits like every other; and the increase of stock, by increasing the competition, necessarily reduces the profit. The lowering of profit in the town forces out stock to the country, where, by creating a new demand for country labor, it necessarily raises its wages. It then spreads itself, if I my say so, over the face of the land, and, by being employed in agriculture, is in part restored to the country, at the expense of which, in a great measure, it had originally been accumulated in the town. That everywhere in Europe the greatest improvements of the country have been owing to such overflowings of the stock originally accumulated in the towns, I shall endeavor to show hereafter, and at the same time to demonstrate, that though some countries have, by this course, attained to a considerable degree of opulence, it is in itself necessarily slow, uncertain, liable to be disturbed and interrupted by innumerable accidents, and, in every respect, contrary to the order of nature and of reason The interests, prejudices, laws, and customs, which have given occasion to it, I shall endeavor to explain as fully and distinctly as I can in the third and fourth books of this inquiry.

People of the same trade seldom meet together, even for merriment and diversion, but the conversation ends in a conspiracy against the public, or in some contrivance to raise prices. It is impossible, indeed, to prevent such meetings, by any law which either could be executed, or would be consistent with liberty and justice. But though the law cannot hinder people of the same trade from sometimes assembling together, it ought to do nothing to facilitate such assemblies, much less to render them necessary.

A regulation which obliges all those of the same trade in a particular town to enter their names and places of abode in a public register, facilitates such assemblies. It connects individuals who might never otherwise be known to one another, and gives every man of the trade a direction where to find every other man of it.

A regulation which enables those of the same trade to tax themselves, in order to provide for their poor, their sick, their widows and orphans, by giving them a common interest to manage, renders such assemblies necessary.

An incorporation not only renders them necessary, but makes the act of the majority binding upon the whole. In a free trade, an effectual combination cannot be established but by the unanimous consent of every single trader, and it cannot last longer than every single trader continues of the same mind. The majority of a corporation can enact a bye-law, with proper penalties, which will limit the competition more effectually and more durably than any voluntary combination whatever.

The pretence that corporations are necessary for the better government of the trade, is without any foundation. The real and effectual discipline which is exercised over a workman, is not that of his corporation, but that of his customers. It is the fear of losing their employment which restrains his frauds and corrects his negligence. An exclusive corporation necessarily weakens the force of this discipline. A particular set of workmen must then be employed, let them behave well or ill. It is upon this account that, in many large incorporated towns, no tolerable workmen are to be found, even in some of the most necessary trades. If you would have your work tolerably executed, it must be done in the suburbs, where the workmen, having no exclusive privilege, have nothing but their character to depend upon, and you must then smuggle it into the town as well as you can.

It is in this manner that the policy of Europe, by restraining the competition in some employments to a smaller number than would otherwise be disposed to enter into them, occasions a very important inequality in the whole of the advantages and disadvantages of the different employments of labor and stock.

Secondly, the policy of Europe, by increasing the competition in some employments beyond what it naturally would be, occasions another inequality, of an opposite kind, in the whole of the advantages and disadvantages of the different employments of labor and stock.

It has been considered as of so much importance that a proper number of young people should be educated for certain professions, that sometimes the public, and sometimes the piety of private founders, have established many pensions, scholarships, exhibitions, bursaries, etc. for this purpose, which draw many more people into those trades than could otherwise pretend to follow them. In all Christian countries, I believe, the education of the greater part of churchmen is paid for in this manner. Very few of them are educated altogether at their own expense. The long, tedious, and expensive education, therefore, of those who are, will not always procure them a suitable reward, the church being crowded with people, who, in order to get employment, are willing to accept of a much smaller recompense than what such an education would otherwise have entitled them to; and in this manner the competition of the poor takes away the reward of the rich. It would be indecent, no doubt, to compare either a curate or a chaplain with a journeyman in any common trade. The pay of a curate or chaplain, however, may very properly be considered as of the same nature with the wages of a journeyman. They are all three paid for their work according to the contract which they may happen to make with their respective superiors. Till after the middle of the fourteenth century, five merks, containing about as much silver as ten pounds of our present money, was in England the usual pay of a curate or a stipendiary parish priest, as we find it regulated by the decrees of several different national councils. At the same period, four pence a day, containing the same quantity of silver as a shilling of our present money, was declared to be the pay of a master mason; and three pence a day, equal to nine pence of our present money, that of a journeyman mason {See the Statue of Laborers, 25, Ed. III}. The wages of both these laborers, therefore, supposing them to have been constantly employed, were much superior to those of the curate. The wages of the master mason, supposing him to have been without employment one-third of the year, would have fully equaled them. By the 12th of Queen Anne, it is declared, "That whereas, for want of sufficient maintenance and encouragement to curates, the cures have, in several places, been meanly supplied, the bishop is, therefore, empowered to appoint, by writing under his hand and seal, a sufficient certain stipend or allowance, not exceeding fifty, and not less than, twenty pounds a year." Forty pounds a year is reckoned at present very good pay for a curate; and, notwithstanding this act of parliament, there are many curacies under twenty pounds a year. There are journeymen shoemakers in London who earn forty pounds a year, and there is scarce an industrious workman of any kind in that metropolis who does not earn more than twenty. This last sum, indeed, does not exceed what frequently earned by common laborers in many country parishes. Whenever the law has attempted to regulate the wages of workmen, it has always been rather to lower them than to raise them. But the law has, upon many occasions, attempted to raise the wages of curates, and, for the dignity of the church, to oblige the rectors of parishes to give them more than the wretched maintenance which they themselves might be willing to accept of. And, in both cases, the law seems to have been equally ineffectual, and has never either been able to raise the wages of curates, or to sink those of laborers to the degree that was intended; because it has never been able to hinder either the one from being willing to accept of less than the legal allowance, on account of the indigence of their situation and the multitude of their competitors, or the other from receiving more, on account of the contrary competition of those who expected to derive either profit or pleasure from employing them.

The great benefices and other ecclesiastical dignities support the honor of the church, notwithstanding the mean circumstances of some of its inferior members. The respect paid to the profession, too, makes some compensation even to them for the meanness of their pecuniary recompense. In England, and in all Roman catholic countries, the lottery of the church is in reality much more advantageous than is necessary. The example of the churches of Scotland, of Geneva, and of several other protestant churches, may satisfy us, that in so creditable a profession, in which education is so easily procured, the hopes of much more moderate benefices will draw a sufficient number of learned, decent, and respectable men into holy orders.

In professions in which there are no benefices, such as law and physic, if an equal proportion of people were educated at the public expense, the competition would soon be so great as to sink very much their pecuniary reward. It might then not be worth any man's while to educate his son to either of those professions at his own expense. They would be entirely abandoned to such as had been educated by those public charities, whose numbers and necessities would oblige them in general to content themselves with a very miserable recompense, to the entire degradation of the now respectable professions of law and physic.

That unprosperous race of men, commonly called men of letters, are pretty much in the situation which lawyers and physicians probably would be in, upon the foregoing supposition. In every part of Europe, the greater part of them have been educated for the church, but been hindered by different reasons from entering into holy orders. They have generally, therefore, been educated at the public expense; and their numbers are everywhere so great, as commonly to reduce the price of their labor to a very paltry recompense.

Before the invention of the art of printing, the only employment by which a man of letters could make any thing by his talents, was that of a public or private teacher, or by communicating to other people the curious and useful knowledge which he had acquired himself; and this is still surely a more honorable, a more useful, and, in general, even a more profitable employment than that other of writing for a bookseller, to which the art of printing has given occasion. The time and study, the genius, knowledge, and application requisite to qualify an eminent teacher of the sciences, are at least equal to what is necessary for the greatest practitioners in law and physic. But the usual reward of the eminent teacher bears no proportion to that of the lawyer or physician, because the trade of the one is crowded with indigent people, who have been brought up to it at the public expense; whereas those of the other two are encumbered with very few who have not been educated at their own. The usual recompense, however, of public and private teachers, small as it may appear, would undoubtedly be less than it is, if the competition of those yet more indigent men of letters, who write for bread, was not taken out of the market. Before the invention of the art of printing, a scholar and a beggar seem to have been terms very nearly synonymous. The different governors of the universities, before that time, appear to have often granted licenses to their scholars to beg.

In ancient times, before any charities of this kind had been established for the education of indigent people to the learned professions, the rewards of eminent teachers appear to have been much more considerable. Isocrates, in what is called his discourse against the sophists, reproaches the teachers of his own times with inconsistency. "They make the most magnificent promises to their scholars," says he, "and undertake to teach them to be wise, to be happy, and to be just; and, in return for so important a service, they stipulate the paltry reward of four or five minae."

"They who teach wisdom," continues he, "ought certainly to be wise themselves; but if any man were to sell such a bargain for such a price, he would be convicted of the most evident folly." He certainly does not mean here to exaggerate the reward, and we may be assured that it was not less than he represents it. Four minae were equal to thirteen pounds six shillings and eight pence; five minae to sixteen pounds thirteen shillings and four pence. Something not less than the largest of those two sums, therefore, must at that time have been usually paid to the most eminent teachers at Athens. Isocrates himself demanded ten minae, or £33:6:8 from each scholar. When he taught at Athens, he is said to have had a hundred scholars. I understand this to be the number whom he taught at one time, or who attended what we would call one course of lectures; a number which will not appear extraordinary from so great a city to so famous a teacher, who taught, too, what was at that time the most fashionable of all sciences, rhetoric. He must have made, therefore, by each course of lectures, a thousand minae, or £3335:6:8. A thousand minae, accordingly, is said by Plutarch, in another place, to have been his didactron, or usual price of teaching. Many other eminent teachers in those times appear to have acquired great fortunes. Georgias made a present to the temple of Delphi of his own statue in solid gold. We must not, I presume, suppose that it was life-size. His way of living, as well as that of Hippias and Protagoras, two other eminent teachers of those times, is represented by Plato as splendid, even to ostentation. Plato himself is said to have lived with a good deal of magnificence. Aristotle, after having been tutor to Alexander, and most munificently rewarded, as it is universally agreed, both by him and his father, Philip, thought it worth while, notwithstanding, to return to Athens, in order to resume the teaching of his school. Teachers of the sciences were probably in those times less common than they came to be in an age or two afterwards, when the competition had probably somewhat reduced both the price of their labor and the admiration for their persons. The most eminent of them, however, appear always to have enjoyed a degree of consideration much superior to any of the like profession in the present times. The Athenians sent Carneades the academic, and Diogenes the stoic, upon a solemn embassy to Rome; and though their city had then declined from its former grandeur, it was still an independent and considerable republic. Carneades, too, was a Babylonian by birth; and as there never was a people more jealous of admitting foreigners to public offices than the Athenians, their consideration for him must have been very great.

This inequality is, upon the whole, perhaps rather advantageous than hurtful to the public. It may somewhat degrade the profession of a public teacher; but the cheapness of literary education is surely an advantage which greatly overbalances this trifling inconveniency. The public, too, might derive still greater benefit from it, if the constitution of those schools and colleges, in which education is carried on, was more reasonable than it is at present through the greater part of Europe.

Thirdly, the policy of Europe, by obstructing the free circulation of labor and stock, both from employment to employment, and from place to place, occasions, in some cases, a very inconvenient inequality in the whole of the advantages and disadvantages of their different employments.

The statute of apprenticeship obstructs the free circulation of labor from one employment to another, even in the same place. The exclusive privileges of corporations obstruct it from one place to another, even in the same employment.

It frequently happens, that while high wages are given to the workmen in one manufacture, those in another are obliged to content themselves with bare subsistence. The one is in an advancing state, and has therefore a continual demand for new hands; the other is in a declining state, and the superabundance of hands is continually increasing. Those two manufactures may sometimes be in the same town, and sometimes in the same neighborhood, without being able to lend the least assistance to one another. The statute of apprenticeship may oppose it in the one case, and both that and an exclusive corporation in the other. In many different manufactures, however, the operations are so much alike, that the workmen could easily change trades with one another, if those absurd laws did not hinder them. The arts of weaving plain linen and plain silk, for example, are almost entirely the same. That of weaving plain woolen is somewhat different; but the difference is so insignificant, that either a linen or a silk weaver might become a tolerable workman in a very few days. If any of those three capital manufactures, therefore, were decaying, the workmen might find a resource in one of the other two which was in a more prosperous condition; and their wages would neither rise too high in the thriving, nor sink too low in the decaying manufacture. The linen manufacture, indeed, is in England, by a particular statute, open to everybody; but as it is not much cultivated through the greater part of the country, it can afford no general resource to the workmen of other decaying manufactures, who, wherever the statute of apprenticeship takes place, have no other choice, but either to come upon the parish, or to work as common laborers; for which, by their habits, they are much worse qualified than for any sort of manufacture that bears any resemblance to their own. They generally, therefore, choose to come upon the parish.

Whatever obstructs the free circulation of labor from one employment to another, obstructs that of stock likewise; the quantity of stock which can be employed in any branch of business depending very much upon that of the labor which can be employed in it. Corporation laws, however, give less obstruction to the free circulation of stock from one place to another, than to that of labor. It is everywhere much easier for a wealthy merchant to obtain the privilege of trading in a town-corporate, than for a poor artificer to obtain that of working in it.

The obstruction which corporation laws give to the free circulation of labor is common, I believe, to every part of Europe. That which is given to it by the poor laws is, so far as I know, peculiar to England. It consists in the difficulty which a poor man finds in obtaining a settlement, or even in being allowed to exercise his industry in any parish but that to which he belongs. It is the labor of artificers and manufacturers only of which the free circulation is obstructed by corporation laws. The difficulty of obtaining settlements obstructs even that of common labor. It may be worthwhile to give some account of the rise, progress, and present state of this disorder, the greatest, perhaps, of any in the police of England.

When, by the destruction of monasteries, the poor had been deprived of the charity of those religious houses, after some other ineffectual attempts for their relief, it was enacted, by the 43d of Elizabeth that every parish should be bound to provide for its own poor, and that overseers of the poor should be annually appointed, who, with the church-wardens, should raise, by a parish rate, competent sums for this purpose.

By this statute, the necessity of providing for their own poor was indispensably imposed upon every parish. Who were to be considered as the poor of each parish became, therefore, a question of some importance. This question, after some variation, was at last determined by the 13th and 14th of Charles II when it was enacted, that forty days undisturbed residence should gain any person a settlement in any parish; but that within that time it should be lawful for two justices of the peace, upon complaint made by the churchwardens or overseers of the poor, to remove any new inhabitant to the parish where he was last legally settled; unless he either rented a tenement of ten pounds a year, or could give such security for the discharge of the parish where he was then living, as those justices should judge sufficient.

Some frauds, it is said, were committed in consequence of this statute; parish officers sometimes bribing their own poor to go clandestinely to another parish, and, by keeping themselves concealed for forty days, to gain a settlement there, to the discharge of that to which they properly belonged. It was enacted, therefore, by the 1st of James II that the forty days undisturbed residence of any person necessary to gain a settlement, should be accounted only from the time of his delivering notice, in writing, of the place of his abode and the number of his family, to one of the churchwardens or overseers of the parish where he came to dwell.

But parish officers, it seems, were not always more honest with regard to their own than they had been with regard to other parishes, and sometimes connived at such intrusions, receiving the notice, and taking no proper steps in consequence of it. As every person in a parish, therefore, was supposed to have an interest to prevent as much as possible their being burdened by such intruders, it was further enacted by the 3rd of William III that the forty days residence should be accounted only from the publication of such notice in writing on Sunday in the church, immediately after divine service.

"After all," says Doctor Burn, "this kind of settlement, by continuing forty days after publication of notice in writing, is very seldom obtained; and the design of the acts is not so much for gaining of settlements, as for the avoiding of them by persons coming into a parish clandestinely, for the giving of notice is only putting a force upon the parish to remove. But if a person's situation is such, that it is doubtful whether he is actually removable or not, he shall, by giving of notice, compel the parish either to allow him a settlement uncontested, by suffering him to continue forty days, or by removing him to try the right."

This statute, therefore, rendered it almost impracticable for a poor man to gain a new settlement in the old way, by forty days inhabitancy. But that it might not appear to preclude altogether the common people of one parish from ever establishing themselves with security in another, it appointed four other ways by which a settlement might be gained without any notice delivered or published. The first was, by being taxed to parish rates and paying them; the second, by being elected into an annual parish office, and serving in it a year; the third, by serving an apprenticeship in the parish; the fourth, by being hired into service there for a year, and continuing in the same service during the whole of it.

Nobody can gain a settlement by either of the two first ways, but by the public deed of the whole parish, who are too well aware of the consequences to adopt any newcomer, who has nothing but his labor to support him, either by taxing him to parish rates, or by electing him into a parish office.

No married man can well gain any settlement in either of the two last ways. An apprentice is scarce ever married; and it is expressly enacted, that no married servant shall gain any settlement by being hired for a year. The principal effect of introducing settlement by service, has been to put out in a great measure the old fashion of hiring for a year; which before had been so customary in England, that even at this day, if no particular term is agreed upon, the law intends that every servant is hired for a year. But masters are not always willing to give their servants a settlement by hiring them in this manner; and servants are not always willing to be so hired, because, as every last settlement discharges all the foregoing, they might thereby lose their original settlement in the places of their nativity, the habitation of their parents and relations.

No independent workman, it is evident, whether laborer or artificer, is likely to gain any new settlement, either by apprenticeship or by service. When such a person, therefore, carried his industry to a new parish, he was liable to be removed, how healthy and industrious soever, at the caprice of any churchwarden or overseer, unless he either rented a tenement of ten pounds a year, a thing impossible for one who has nothing but his labor to live by, or could give such security for the discharge of the parish as two justices of the peace should judge sufficient. What security they shall require, indeed, is left altogether to their discretion; but they cannot well require less than thirty pounds, it having been enacted, that the purchase even of a freehold estate of less than thirty pounds value, shall not gain any person a settlement, as not being sufficient for the discharge of the parish. But this is a security which scarce any man who lives by labor can give; and much greater security is frequently demanded.

In order to restore, in some measure, that free circulation of labor which those different statutes had almost entirely taken away, the invention of certificates was fallen upon. By the 8th and 9th of William III it was enacted that if any person should bring a certificate from the parish where he was last legally settled, subscribed by the churchwardens and overseers of the poor, and allowed by two justices of the peace, that every other parish should be obliged to receive him; that he should not be removable merely upon account of his being likely to become chargeable, but only upon his becoming actually chargeable; and that then the parish which granted the certificate should be obliged to pay the expense both of his maintenance and of his removal. And in order to give the most perfect security to the parish where such certificated man should come to reside, it was further enacted by the same statute, that he should gain no settlement there by any means whatever, except either by renting a tenement of ten pounds a year, or by serving upon his own account in an annual parish office for one whole year; and consequently neither by notice nor by service, nor by apprenticeship, nor by paying parish rates. By the 12th of Queen Anne, too, it was further enacted, that neither the servants nor apprentices of such certificated man should gain any settlement in the parish where he resided under such certificate.

How far this invention has restored that free circulation of labor, which the preceding statutes had almost entirely taken away, we may learn from the following very judicious observation of Doctor Burn. "It is obvious," says he, "that there are divers good reasons for requiring certificates with persons coming to settle in any place; namely, that persons residing under them can gain no settlement, neither by apprenticeship, nor by service, nor by giving notice, nor by paying parish rates; that they can settle neither apprentices nor servants; that if they become chargeable, it is certainly known whither to remove them, and the parish shall be paid for the removal, and for their maintenance in the meantime; and that, if they fall sick, and cannot be removed, the parish which gave the certificate must maintain them; none of all which can be without a certificate. Which reasons will hold proportionably for parishes not granting certificates in ordinary cases; for it is far more than an equal chance, but that they will have the certificated persons again, and in a worse condition." The moral of this observation seems to be, that certificates ought always to be required by the parish where any poor man comes to reside, and that they ought very seldom to be granted by that which he purposes to leave. "There is somewhat of hardship in this matter of certificates," says the same very intelligent author, in his *History of the Poor Laws*, "by putting it in the power of a parish officer to imprison a man as it were for life, however inconvenient it may be for him to continue at that place where he has had the misfortune to acquire what is called a settlement, or whatever advantage he may propose himself by living elsewhere."

Though a certificate carries along with it no testimonial of good behavior, and certifies nothing but that the person belongs to the parish to which he really does belong, it is altogether discretionary in the parish officers either to grant or to refuse it. A mandamus was once moved for, says Doctor Burn, to compel the churchwardens and overseers to sign a certificate; but the Court of King's Bench rejected the motion as a very strange attempt.

The very unequal price of labor which we frequently find in England, in places at no great distance from one another, is probably owing to the obstruction which the law of settlements gives to a poor man who would carry his industry from one parish to another without a certificate. A single man, indeed who is healthy and industrious, may sometimes reside by sufferance without one; but a man with a wife and family who should attempt to do so, would, in most parishes, be sure of being removed; and, if the single man should afterwards marry, he would generally be removed likewise. The scarcity of hands in one parish, therefore, cannot always be relieved by their superabundance in another, as it is constantly in Scotland, and, I believe, in all other countries where there is no difficulty of settlement. In such countries, though wages may sometimes rise a little in the neighborhood of a great town, or wherever else there is an extraordinary demand for labor, and sink gradually as the distance from such places increases, till they fall back to the common rate of the country; yet we never meet with those sudden and unaccountable differences in the wages of neighboring places which we sometimes find in England, where it is often more difficult for a poor man to pass the artificial boundary of a parish, than an arm of the sea, or a ridge of high mountains, natural boundaries which sometimes separate very distinctly different rates of wages in other countries.

To remove a man who has committed no misdemeanor, from the parish where he chooses to reside, is an evident violation of natural liberty and justice. The common people of England, however, so jealous of their liberty, but like the common people of most other countries, never rightly understanding wherein it consists, have now, for more than a century together, suffered themselves to be exposed to this oppression without a remedy. Though men of reflection, too, have sometimes complained of the law of settlements as a public grievance; yet it has never been the object of any general popular clamor, such as that against general warrants, an abusive practice undoubtedly, but such a one as was not likely to occasion any general oppression. There is scarce a poor man in England, of forty years of age, I will venture to say, who has not, in some part of his life, felt himself most cruelly oppressed by this ill-contrived law of settlements.

I shall conclude this long chapter with observing, that though anciently it was usual to rate wages, first by general laws extending over the whole kingdom, and afterwards by particular orders of the justices of peace in every particular county, both these practices have now gone entirely into disuse. "By the experience of above four hundred years," says Doctor Burn, "it seems time to lay aside all endeavors to bring under strict regulations, what in its own nature seems incapable of minute limitation; for if all persons in the same kind of work were to receive equal wages, there would be no emulation, and no room left for industry or ingenuity."

Particular acts of parliament, however, still attempt sometimes to regulate wages in particular trades, and in particular places. Thus the 8th of George III prohibits, under heavy penalties, all master tailors in London, and five miles round it, from giving, and their workmen from accepting, more than two shillings and seven pence halfpenny a day, except in the case of a general mourning. Whenever the legislature attempts to regulate the differences between masters and their workmen, its counselors are always the masters. When the regulation, therefore, is in favor of the workmen, it is always just and equitable; but it is sometimes otherwise when in favor of the masters. Thus the law which obliges the masters in several different trades to pay their workmen in money, and not in goods, is quite just and equitable. It imposes no real hardship upon the masters. It only obliges them to pay that value in money, which they pretended to pay, but did not always really pay, in goods. This law is in favor of the workmen; but the 8th of George III is in favor of the masters. When masters combine together, in order to reduce the wages of their workmen, they commonly enter into a private bond or agreement, not to give more than a certain wage, under a certain penalty. Were the workmen to enter into a contrary combination of the same kind, not to accept of a certain wage, under a certain penalty, the law would punish them very severely; and, if it dealt impartially, it would treat the masters in the same manner. But the 8th of George III enforces by law that very regulation which masters sometimes attempt to establish by such combinations. The complaint of the workmen, that it puts the ablest and most industrious upon the same footing with an ordinary workman, seems perfectly well founded.

In ancient times, too, it was usual to attempt to regulate the profits of merchants and other dealers, by regulating the price of provisions and other goods. The assize of bread is, so far as I know, the only remnant of this ancient usage. Where there is an exclusive corporation, it may, perhaps, be proper to regulate the price of the first necessity of life;

but, where there is none, the competition will regulate it much better than any assize. The method of fixing the assize of bread, established by the 31st of George II could not be put in practice in Scotland, on account of a defect in the law, its execution depending upon the office of clerk of the market, which does not exist there. This defect was not remedied till the third of George III. The want of an assize occasioned no sensible inconveniency; and the establishment of one in the few places where it has yet taken place has produced no sensible advantage. In the greater part of the towns in Scotland, however, there is an incorporation of bakers, who claim exclusive privileges, though they are not very strictly guarded.

The proportion between the different rates, both of wages and profit, in the different employments of labor and stock, seems not to be much affected, as has already been observed, by the riches or poverty, the advancing, stationary, or declining state of the society. Such revolutions in the public welfare, though they affect the general rates both of wages and profit, must, in the end, affect them equally in all different employments. The proportion between them, therefore, must remain the same, and cannot well be altered, at least for any considerable time, by any such revolutions.

CHAPTER XI

Of the Rent of Land

Rent, considered as the price paid for the use of land, is naturally the highest which the tenant can afford to pay in the actual circumstances of the land. In adjusting the terms of the lease, the landlord endeavors to leave him no greater share of the produce than what is sufficient to keep up the stock from which he furnishes the seed, pays the labor, and purchases and maintains the cattle and other instruments of husbandry, together with the ordinary profits of farming stock in the neighborhood. This is evidently the smallest share with which the tenant can content himself, without being a loser, and the landlord seldom means to leave him any more. Whatever part of the produce, or, what is the same thing, whatever part of its price, is over and above this share, he naturally endeavors to reserve to himself as the rent of his land, which is evidently the highest the tenant can afford to pay in the actual circumstances of the land. Sometimes, indeed, the liberality, more frequently the ignorance, of the landlord, makes him accept of somewhat less than this portion; and sometimes, too, though more rarely, the ignorance of the tenant makes him undertake to pay somewhat more, or to content himself with somewhat less, than the ordinary profits of farming stock in the neighborhood. This portion, however, may still be considered as the natural rent of land, or the rent at which it is naturally meant that land should, for the most part, be let.

The rent of land, it may be thought, is frequently no more than a reasonable profit or interest for the stock laid out by the landlord upon its improvement. This, no doubt, may be partly the case upon some occasions; for it can scarce ever be more than partly the case. The landlord demands a rent even for unimproved land, and the supposed interest or profit upon the expense of improvement is generally an addition to this original rent. Those improvements, besides, are not always made by the stock of the landlord, but sometimes by that of the tenant. When the lease comes to be renewed, however, the landlord commonly demands the same augmentation of rent as if they had been all made by his own.

He sometimes demands rent for what is altogether incapable of human improvements. Kelp is a species of seaweed, which, when burnt, yields an alkaline salt, useful for making glass, soap, and for several other purposes. It grows in several parts of Great Britain, particularly in Scotland, upon such rocks only as lie within the high-water mark, which are twice every day covered with the sea, and of which the produce, therefore, was never augmented by human industry. The landlord, however, whose estate is bounded by a kelp shore of this kind, demands a rent for it as much as for his cornfields.

The sea in the neighborhood of the islands of Shetland is more than commonly abundant in fish, which makes a great part of the subsistence of their inhabitants. But, in order to profit by the produce of the water, they must have a habitation upon the neighboring land. The rent of the landlord is in proportion, not to what the farmer can make by the land, but to what he can make both by the land and the water. It is partly paid in sea fish; and one of the very few instances in which rent makes a part of the price of that commodity, is to be found in that country.

The rent of land, therefore, considered as the price paid for the use of the land, is naturally a monopoly price. It is not at all proportioned to what the landlord may have laid out upon the improvement of the land, or to what he can afford to take, but to what the farmer can afford to give.

Such parts only of the produce of land can commonly be brought to market, of which the ordinary price is sufficient to replace the stock which must be employed in bringing them thither, together with its ordinary profits. If the ordinary price is more than this, the surplus part of it will naturally go to the rent of the land. If it is not more, though the commodity may be brought to market, it can afford no rent to the landlord. Whether the price is, or is not more, depends upon the demand.

There are some parts of the produce of land, for which the demand must always be such as to afford a greater price than what is sufficient to bring them to market; and there are others for which it either may or may not be such as to afford this greater price. The former must always afford a rent to the landlord. The latter sometimes may and sometimes may not, according to different circumstances.

Rent, it is to be observed, therefore, enters into the composition of the price of commodities in a different way from wages and profit. High or low wages and profit are the causes of high or low price; high or low rent is the effect of it. It is because high or low wages and profit must be paid, in order to bring a particular commodity to market, that its price is high or low. But it is because its price is high or low, a great deal more, or very little more, or no more, than what is sufficient to pay those wages and profit, that it affords a high rent, or a low rent, or no rent at all.

The particular consideration, first, of those parts of the produce of land which always afford some rent; secondly, of those which sometimes may and sometimes may not afford rent; and, thirdly, of the variations which, in the different periods of improvement, naturally take place in the relative value of those two different sorts of rude produce, when compared both with one another and with manufactured commodities, will divide this chapter into three parts.

Part I

Of the Produce of Land Which Always Affords Rent

As men, like all other animals, naturally multiply in proportion to the means of their subsistence, food is always more or less in demand. It can always purchase or command a greater or smaller quantity of labor, and somebody can always be found who is willing to do something in order to obtain it. The quantity of labor, indeed, which it can purchase, is not always equal to what it could maintain, if managed in the most economical manner, on account of the high wages which are sometimes given to labor; but it can always purchase such a quantity of labor as it can maintain, according to the rate at which that sort of labor is commonly maintained in the neighborhood.

But land, in almost any situation, produces a greater quantity of food than what is sufficient to maintain all the labor necessary for bringing it to market, in the most liberal way in which that labor is ever maintained. The surplus, too, is always more than sufficient to replace the stock which employed that labor, together with its profits. Something, therefore, always remains for a rent to the landlord.

The most desert moors in Norway and Scotland produce some sort of pasture for cattle, of which the milk and the increase are always more than sufficient, not only to maintain all the labor necessary for tending them, and to pay the ordinary profit to the farmer or the owner of the herd or flock, but to afford some small rent to the landlord. The rent increases in proportion to the goodness of the pasture. The same extent of ground not only maintains a greater number of cattle, but as they were brought within a smaller compass, less labor becomes requisite to tend them, and to collect their produce. The landlord gains both ways; by the increase of the produce, and by the diminution of the labor which must be maintained out of it.

The rent of land not only varies with its fertility, whatever be its produce, but with its situation, whatever be its fertility. Land in the neighborhood of a town gives a greater rent than land equally fertile in a distant part of the country. Though it may cost no more labor to cultivate the one than the other, it must always cost more to bring the produce of the distant land to market. A greater quantity of labor, therefore, must be maintained out of it; and the surplus, from which are drawn both the profit of the farmer and the rent of the landlord, must be diminished. But in remote parts of the country, the rate of profit, as has already been shown, is generally higher than in the neighborhood of a large town. A smaller proportion of this diminished surplus, therefore, must belong to the landlord.

Good roads, canals, and navigable rivers, by diminishing the expense of carriage, put the remote parts of the country more nearly upon a level with those in the neighborhood of the town. They are upon that account the greatest of all improvements. They encourage the cultivation of the remote, which must always be the most extensive circle of the country. They are advantageous to the town by breaking down the monopoly of the country in its neighborhood. They are advantageous even to that part of the country. Though they introduce some rival commodities into the old market, they open many new markets to its produce. Monopoly, besides, is a great enemy to good management, which can never be universally established, but in consequence of that free and universal competition which forces every body to have recourse to it for the sake of self defense. It is not more than fifty years ago, that some of the counties in the neighborhood of London petitioned the parliament against the extension of the turnpike roads into the remoter counties. Those remoter counties, they pretended, from the cheapness of labor, would be able to sell their grass and corn cheaper in the London market than themselves, and would thereby reduce their rents, and ruin their cultivation. Their rents, however, have risen, and their cultivation has been improved since that time.

A corn field of moderate fertility produces a much greater quantity of food for man, than the best pasture of equal extent. Though its cultivation requires much more labor, yet the surplus which remains after replacing the seed and maintaining all that labor, is likewise much greater. If a pound of butcher's meat, therefore, was never supposed to be worth more than a pound of bread, this greater surplus would everywhere be of greater value and constitute a greater fund, both for the profit of the farmer and the rent of the landlord. It seems to have done so universally in the rude beginnings of agriculture.

But the relative values of those two different species of food, bread and butcher's meat, are very different in the different periods of agriculture. In its rude beginnings, the unimproved wilds, which then occupy the far greater part of the country, are all abandoned to cattle. There is more butcher's meat than bread; and bread, therefore, is the food for which there is the greatest competition, and which consequently brings the greatest price. At Buenos Ayres, we are told by Ulloa, four reals, one-and-twenty pence halfpenny sterling, was, forty or fifty years ago, the ordinary price of an ox, chosen from a herd of two or three hundred. He says nothing of the price of bread, probably because he found nothing remarkable about it. An ox there, he says, costs little more than the labor of catching him. But corn can nowhere be raised without a great deal of labor; and in a country which lies upon the river Plate, at that time the direct road from Europe to the silver mines of Potosi, the money-price of labor could be very cheap. It is otherwise when cultivation is extended over the greater part of the country. There is then more bread than butcher's meat. The competition changes its direction, and the price of butcher's meat becomes greater than the price of bread.

By the extension, besides, of cultivation, the unimproved wilds become insufficient to supply the demand for butcher's meat. A great part of the cultivated lands must be employed in rearing and fattening cattle; of which the price, therefore, must be sufficient to pay, not only the labor necessary for tending them, but the rent which the landlord, and the profit which the farmer, could have drawn from such land employed in tillage. The cattle bred upon the most uncultivated moors, when brought to the same market, are, in proportion to their weight or goodness, sold at the same price as those which are reared upon the most improved land. The proprietors of those moors profit by it, and raise the rent of their land in proportion to the price of their cattle. It is not more than a century ago, that in many parts of the Highlands of Scotland, butcher's meat was as cheap or cheaper than even bread made of oatmeal. The Union opened the market of England to the Highland cattle. Their ordinary price, at present, is about three times greater than at the beginning of the century, and the rents of many Highland estates have been tripled and quadrupled in the same time. In almost every part of Great Britain, a pound of the best butcher's meat is, in the present times, generally worth more than two pounds of the best white bread; and in plentiful years it is sometimes worth three or four pounds.

It is thus that, in the progress of improvement, the rent and profit of unimproved pasture come to be regulated in some measure by the rent and profit of what is improved, and these again by the rent and profit of corn. Corn is an annual crop; butcher's meat, a crop which requires four or five years to grow. As an acre of land, therefore, will produce a much smaller quantity of the one species of food than of the other, the inferiority of the quantity must be compensated by the superiority of the price. If it was more than compensated, more corn-land would be turned into pasture; and if it was not compensated, part of what was in pasture would be brought back into corn.

This equality, however, between the rent and profit of grass and those of corn; of the land of which the immediate produce is food for cattle, and of that of which the immediate produce is food for men, must be understood to take place only through the greater part of the improved lands of a great country. In some particular local situations it is quite otherwise, and the rent and profit of grass are much superior to what can be made by corn.

Thus, in the neighborhood of a great town, the demand for milk, and for forage to horses, frequently contribute, together with the high price of butcher's meat, to raise the value of grass above what may be called its natural proportion to that of corn. This local advantage, it is evident, cannot be communicated to the lands at a distance.

Particular circumstances have sometimes rendered some countries so populous, that the whole territory, like the lands in the neighborhood of a great town, has not been sufficient to produce both the grass and the corn necessary for the subsistence of their inhabitants. Their lands, therefore, have been principally employed in the production of grass, the more bulky commodity, and which cannot be so easily brought from a great distance; and corn, the food of the great body of the people, has been chiefly imported from foreign countries. Holland is at present in this situation; and a considerable part of ancient Italy seems to have been so during the prosperity of the Romans. To feed well, old Cato said, as we are told by Cicero, was the first and most profitable thing in the management of a private estate; to feed tolerably well, the second; and to feed ill, the third. To plough, he ranked only in the fourth place of profit and advantage. Tillage, indeed, in that part of ancient Italy which lay in the neighborhood of Rome, must have been very much discouraged by the distributions of corn which were frequently made to the people, either gratuitously, or at a very low price. This corn was brought from the conquered provinces, of which several, instead of taxes, were obliged to furnish a tenth part of their produce at a stated price, about sixpence a peck, to the republic. The low price at which this corn was distributed to the people, must necessarily have sunk the price of what could be brought to the Roman market from Latium, or the ancient territory of Rome, and must have discouraged its cultivation in that country.

In an open country, too, of which the principal produce is corn, a well-enclosed piece of grass will frequently rent higher than any cornfield in its neighborhood. It is convenient for the maintenance of the cattle employed in the cultivation of the corn; and its high rent is, in this case, not so properly paid from the value of its own produce, as from that of the corn lands which are cultivated by means of it. It is likely to fall, if ever the neighboring lands are completely enclosed. The present high rent of enclosed land in Scotland seems owing to the scarcity of enclosure, and will probably last no longer than that scarcity. The advantage of enclosure is greater for pasture than for corn. It saves the labor of guarding the cattle, which feed better, too, when they are not liable to be disturbed by their keeper or his dog.

But where there is no local advantage of this kind, the rent and profit of corn, or whatever else is the common vegetable food of the people, must naturally regulate upon the land which is fit for producing it, the rent and profit of pasture.

The use of the artificial grasses, of turnips, carrots, cabbages, and the other expedients which have been fallen upon to make an equal quantity of land feed a greater number of cattle than when in natural grass, should somewhat reduce, it might be expected, the superiority which, in an improved country, the price of butcher's meat naturally has over that of bread. It seems accordingly to have done so; and there is some reason for believing that, at least in the London market, the price of butcher's meat, in proportion to the price of bread, is a good deal lower in the present times than it was in the beginning of the last century.

In the Appendix to the life of Prince Henry, Doctor Birch has given us an account of the prices of butcher's meat as commonly paid by that prince. It is there said, that the four quarters of an ox, weighing six hundred pounds, usually cost him nine pounds ten shillings, or thereabouts; that is thirty-one shillings and eight-pence per hundred pounds weight. Prince Henry died on the 6th of November 1612, in the nineteenth year of his age.

In March 1764, there was a parliamentary inquiry into the causes of the high price of provisions at that time. It was then, among other proof to the same purpose, given in evidence by a Virginia merchant, that in March 1763, he had victualled his ships for twenty-four or twenty-five shillings the hundred weight of beef, which he considered as the ordinary price; whereas, in that dear year, he had paid twenty-seven shillings for the same weight and sort. This high price in 1764 is, however, four shillings and eight-pence cheaper than the ordinary price paid by Prince Henry; and it is the best beef only, it must be observed, which is fit to be salted for those distant voyages.

The price paid by Prince Henry amounts to 3d. 4/5ths per pound weight of the whole carcass, coarse and choice pieces taken together; and at that rate the choice pieces could not have been sold by retail for less than 41/2d. or 5d. the pound.

In the parliamentary inquiry in 1764, the witnesses stated the price of the choice pieces of the best beef to be to the consumer 4d. and 41/2d. the pound; and the coarse pieces in general to be from seven farthings to 21/2d. and 23/4d.; and this, they said, was in general one halfpenny dearer than the same sort of pieces had usually been sold in the month of March. But even this high price is still a good deal cheaper than what we can well suppose the ordinary retail price to have been in the time of Prince Henry.

During the first twelve years of the last century, the average price of the best wheat at the Windsor market was £1:18:31/2d. the quarter of nine Winchester bushels.

But in the twelve years preceding 1764 including that year, the average price of the same measure of the best wheat at the same market was £2:1:91/2d.

In the first twelve years of the last century, therefore, wheat appears to have been a good deal cheaper, and butcher's meat a good deal dearer, than in the twelve years preceding 1764, including that year.

In all great countries, the greater part of the cultivated lands are employed in producing either food for men or food for cattle. The rent and profit of these regulate the rent and profit of all other cultivated land. If any particular produce afforded less, the land would soon be turned into corn or pasture; and if any afforded more, some part of the lands in corn or pasture would soon be turned to that produce.

Those productions, indeed, which require either a greater original expense of improvement, or a greater annual expense of cultivation in order to fit the land for them, appear commonly to afford, the one a greater rent, the other a greater profit, than corn or pasture. This superiority, however, will seldom be found to amount to more than a reasonable interest or compensation for this superior expense.

In a hop garden, a fruit garden, a kitchen garden, both the rent of the landlord, and the profit of the farmer, are generally greater than in a corn or grass field. But to bring the ground into this condition requires more expense. Hence a greater rent becomes due to the landlord. It requires, too, a more attentive and skilful management. Hence a greater profit becomes due to the farmer. The crop, too, at least in the hop and fruit garden, is more precarious. Its price, therefore, besides compensating all occasional losses, must afford something like the profit of insurance. The circumstances of gardeners, generally mean, and always moderate, may satisfy us that their great ingenuity is not commonly over-recompensed. Their delightful art is practiced by so many rich people for amusement, that little advantage is to be made by those who practice it for profit; because the persons who should naturally be their best customers, supply themselves with all their most precious productions.

The advantage which the landlord derives from such improvements, seems at no time to have been greater than what was sufficient to compensate the original expense of making them. In the ancient husbandry, after the vineyard, a well-watered kitchen garden seems to have been the part of the farm which was supposed to yield the most valuable produce. But Democritus, who wrote upon husbandry about two thousand years ago, and who was regarded by the ancients as one of the fathers of the art, thought they did not act wisely who enclosed a kitchen garden. The profit, he said, would not compensate the expense of a stone wall: and bricks (he meant, I suppose, bricks baked in the sun) moldered with the rain and the winter storm, and required continual repairs. Columella, who reports this judgment of Democritus, does not controvert it, but proposes a very frugal method of inclosing with a hedge of brambles and briars, which he says he had found by experience to be both a lasting and an impenetrable fence; but which, it seems, was not commonly known in the time of Democritus. Palladius adopts the opinion of Columella, which had before been recommended by Varro. In the judgment of those ancient improvers, the produce of a kitchen garden had, it seems, been little more than sufficient to pay the extraordinary culture and the expense of watering; for in countries so near the sun, it was thought proper, in those times as in the present, to have the command of a stream of water, which could be conducted to every bed in the garden. Through the greater part of Europe, a kitchen garden is not at present supposed to deserve a better enclosure than that recommended by Columella. In Great Britain, and some other northern countries, the finer fruits cannot be brought to perfection but by the assistance of a wall. Their price, therefore, in such countries, must be sufficient to pay the expense of building and maintaining what they cannot be had without. The fruit-wall frequently surrounds the kitchen garden, which thus enjoys the benefit of an enclosure which its own produce could seldom pay for.

That the vineyard, when properly planted and brought to perfection, was the most valuable part of the farm, seems to have been an undoubted maxim in the ancient agriculture, as it is in the modern, through all the wine countries. But whether it was advantageous to plant a new vineyard, was a matter of dispute among the ancient Italian husbandmen, as we learn from Columella. He decides, like a true lover of all curious cultivation, in favor of the vineyard; and endeavors to show, by a comparison of the profit and expense, that it was a most advantageous improvement. Such comparisons, however, between the profit and expense of new projects are commonly very fallacious; and in nothing more so than in agriculture. Had the gain actually made by such plantations been commonly as great as he imagined it might have been, there could have been no dispute about it. The same point is frequently at this day a matter of controversy in the wine countries. Their writers on agriculture, indeed, the lovers and promoters of high cultivation, seem generally disposed to decide with Columella in favor of the vineyard. In France, the anxiety of the proprietors of the old vineyards to prevent the planting of any new ones, seems to favor their opinion, and to indicate a consciousness in those who must have the experience, that this species of cultivation is at present in that country more profitable than any other. It seems, at the same time, however, to indicate another opinion, that this superior profit can last no longer than the laws which at present restrain the free cultivation of the vine. In 1731, they obtained an order of council, prohibiting both the planting of new vineyards, and the renewal of these old ones, of which the cultivation had been interrupted for two years, without a particular permission from the king, to be granted only in consequence of an information from the intendant of the province, certifying that he had examined the land, and that it was incapable of any other culture. The pretense of this order was the scarcity of corn and pasture, and the superabundance of wine. But had this superabundance been real, it would, without any order of council, have effectually prevented the plantation of new vineyards, by reducing the profits of this species of cultivation below their natural proportion to those of corn and pasture. With regard to the supposed scarcity of corn occasioned by the multiplication of vineyards, corn is nowhere in France more carefully cultivated than in the wine provinces, where the land is fit for producing it: as in Burgundy, Guienne, and the Upper Languedoc. The numerous hands employed in the one species of cultivation necessarily encourage the other, by affording a ready market for its produce. To diminish the number of those who are capable of paying it, is surely a most unpromising expedient for encouraging the cultivation of corn. It is like the policy which would promote agriculture, by discouraging manufactures.

The rent and profit of those productions, therefore, which require either a greater original expense of improvement in order to fit the land for them, or a greater annual expense of cultivation, though often much superior to those of corn and pasture, yet when they do no more than compensate such extraordinary expense, are in reality regulated by the rent and profit of those common crops.

It sometimes happens, indeed, that the quantity of land which can be fitted for some particular produce, is too small to supply the effectual demand. The whole produce can be disposed of to those who are willing to give somewhat more than what is sufficient to pay the whole rent, wages, and profit, necessary for raising and bringing it to market, according to their natural rates, or according to the rates at which they are paid in the greater part of other cultivated land. The surplus part of the price which remains after defraying the whole expense of improvement and cultivation, may commonly, in this case, and in this case only, bear no regular proportion to the like surplus in corn or pasture, but may exceed it in almost any degree; and the greater part of this excess naturally goes to the rent of the landlord.

The usual and natural proportion, for example, between the rent and profit of wine, and those of corn and pasture, must be understood to take place only with regard to those vineyards which produce nothing but good common wine, such as can be raised almost anywhere, upon any light, gravelly, or sandy soil, and which has nothing to recommend it but its strength and wholesomeness. It is with such vineyards only, that the common land of the country can be brought into competition; for with those of a peculiar quality it is evident that it cannot.

The vine is more affected by the difference of soils than any other fruit tree. From some it derives a flavor which no culture or management can equal, it is supposed, upon any other. This flavor, real or imaginary, is sometimes peculiar to the produce of a few vineyards; sometimes it extends through the greater part of a small district, and sometimes through a considerable part of a large province. The whole quantity of such wines that is brought to market falls short of the effectual demand, or the demand of those who would be willing to pay the whole rent, profit, and wages, necessary for preparing and bringing them thither, according to the ordinary rate, or according to the rate at which they are paid in common vineyards. The whole quantity, therefore, can be disposed of to those who are willing to pay more, which necessarily raises their price above that of common wine. The difference is greater or less, according as the fashionableness and scarcity of the wine render the competition of the buyers more or less eager. Whatever it be, the greater part of it goes to the rent of the landlord. For though such vineyards are in general more carefully cultivated than most others, the high price of the wine seems to be, not so much the effect, as the cause of this careful cultivation. In so valuable a produce, the loss occasioned by negligence is so great, as to force even the most careless to attention. A small part of this high price, therefore, is sufficient to pay the wages of the extraordinary labor bestowed upon their cultivation, and the profits of the extraordinary stock which puts that labor into motion.

The sugar colonies possessed by the European nations in the West Indies may be compared to those precious vineyards. Their whole produce falls short of the effectual demand of Europe, and can be disposed of to those who are willing to give more than what is sufficient to pay the whole rent, profit, and wages, necessary for preparing and bringing it to market, according to the rate at which they are commonly paid by any other produce. In Cochin China, the finest white sugar generally sells for three piastres the quintal, about thirteen shillings and sixpence of our money, as we are told by Mr. Poivre {*Voyages d'un Philosophe*}, a very careful observer of the agriculture of that country. What is there called the quintal, weighs from a hundred and fifty to two hundred Paris pounds, or a hundred and seventy-five Paris pounds at a medium, which reduces the price of the hundred weight English to about eight shillings sterling; not a fourth part of what is commonly paid for the brown or muscovada sugars imported from our colonies, and not a sixth part of what is paid for the finest white sugar. The greater part of the cultivated lands in Cochin China are employed in producing corn and rice, the food of the great body of the people. The respective prices of corn, rice, and sugar are there probably in the natural proportion, or in that which naturally takes place in the different crops of the greater part of cultivated land, and which recompenses the landlord and farmer, as nearly as can be computed, according to what is usually the original expense of improvement, and the annual expense of cultivation. But in our sugar colonies, the price of sugar bears no such proportion to that of the produce of a rice or corn field either in Europe or America. It is commonly said that a sugar planter expects that the rum and the molasses should defray the whole expense of his cultivation, and that his sugar should be all clear profit. If this be true, for I pretend not to affirm it, it is as if a corn farmer expected to defray the expense of his cultivation with the chaff and the straw, and that the grain should be all clear profit. We see frequently societies of merchants in London, and other trading towns, purchase waste lands in our sugar colonies, which they expect to improve and cultivate with profit, by means of factors and agents, notwithstanding the great distance and the uncertain returns, from the defective administration of justice in those countries. Nobody will attempt to improve and cultivate in the same manner the most fertile lands of Scotland, Ireland, or the corn provinces of North America, though, from the more exact administration of justice in these countries, more regular returns might be expected.

In Virginia and Maryland, the cultivation of tobacco is preferred, as most profitable, to that of corn. Tobacco might be cultivated with advantage through the greater part of Europe; but, in almost every part of Europe, it has become a principal subject of taxation; and to collect a tax from every different farm in the country where this plant might happen to be cultivated, would be more difficult, it has been supposed, than to levy one upon its importation at the customhouse. The cultivation of tobacco has, upon this account, been most absurdly prohibited through the greater part of Europe, which necessarily gives a sort of monopoly to the countries where it is allowed; and as Virginia and Maryland produce the greatest quantity of it, they share largely, though with some competitors, in the advantage of this monopoly. The cultivation of tobacco, however, seems not to be so advantageous as that of sugar. I have never even heard of any tobacco plantation that was improved and cultivated by the capital of merchants who resided in Great Britain; and our tobacco colonies send us home no such wealthy planters as we see frequently arrive from our sugar islands. Though, from the preference given in those colonies to the cultivation of tobacco above that of corn, it would appear that the effectual demand of Europe for tobacco is not completely supplied, it probably is more nearly so than that for sugar; and though the present price of tobacco is probably more than sufficient to pay the whole rent, wages, and profit, necessary for preparing and bringing it to market, according to the rate at which they are commonly paid in corn land, it must not be so much more as the present price of sugar. Our tobacco planters, accordingly, have shown the same fear of the superabundance of tobacco, which the proprietors of the old vineyards in France have of the superabundance of wine. By act of assembly, they have restrained its cultivation to six thousand plants, supposed to yield a thousand weight of tobacco, for every negro between sixteen and sixty years of age. Such a negro, over and above this quantity of tobacco, can manage, they reckon, four acres of Indian corn. To prevent the market from being overstocked, too, they have sometimes, in plentiful years, we are told by Dr. Douglas {Douglas's *Summary*,vol. iI p. 379, 373.} (I suspect he has been ill informed), burnt a certain quantity of tobacco for every negro, in the same manner as the Dutch are said to do of spices. If such violent methods are necessary to keep up the present price of tobacco, the superior advantage of its culture over that of corn, if it still has any, will not probably be of long continuance.

It is in this manner that the rent of the cultivated land, of which the produce is human food, regulates the rent of the greater part of other cultivated land. No particular produce can long afford less, because the land would immediately be turned to another use; and if any particular produce commonly affords more, it is because the quantity of land which can be fitted for it is too small to supply the effectual demand.

In Europe, corn is the principal produce of land, which serves immediately for human food. Except in particular situations, therefore, the rent of corn land regulates in Europe that of all other cultivated land. Britain need envy neither the vineyards of France, nor the olive plantations of Italy. Except in particular situations, the value of these is regulated by that of corn, in which the fertility of Britain is not much inferior to that of either of those two countries.

If, in any country, the common and favorite vegetable food of the people should be drawn from a plant of which the most common land, with the same, or nearly the same culture, produced a much greater quantity than the most fertile does of corn; the rent of the landlord, or the surplus quantity of food which would remain to him, after paying the labor, and replacing the stock of the farmer, together with its ordinary profits, would necessarily be much greater. Whatever was the rate at which labor was commonly maintained in that country, this greater surplus could always maintain a greater quantity of it, and, consequently, enable the landlord to purchase or command a greater quantity of it. The real value of his rent, his real power and authority, his command of the necessaries and conveniences of life with which the labor of other people could supply him, would necessarily be much greater.

A rice field produces a much greater quantity of food than the most fertile corn field. Two crops in the year, from thirty to sixty bushels each, are said to be the ordinary produce of an acre. Though its cultivation, therefore, requires more labor, a much greater surplus remains after maintaining all that labor. In those rice countries, therefore, where rice is the common and favorite vegetable food of the people, and where the cultivators are chiefly maintained with it, a greater share of this greater surplus should belong to the landlord than in corn countries. In Carolina, where the planters, as in other British colonies, are generally both farmers and landlords, and where rent, consequently, is confounded with profit, the cultivation of rice is found to be more profitable than that of corn, though their fields produce only one crop in the year, and though, from the prevalence of the customs of Europe, rice is not there the common and favorite vegetable food of the people.

A good rice field is a bog at all seasons, and at one season a bog covered with water. It is unfit either for corn, or pasture, or vineyard, or, indeed, for any other vegetable produce that is very useful to men; and the lands which are fit for those purposes are not fit for rice. Even in the rice countries, therefore, the rent of rice lands cannot regulate the rent of the other cultivated land which can never be turned to that produce.

The food produced by a field of potatoes is not inferior in quantity to that produced by a field of rice, and much superior to what is produced by a field of wheat. Twelve thousand weight of potatoes from an acre of land is not a greater produce than two thousand weight of wheat. The food or solid nourishment, indeed, which can be drawn from each of those two plants, is not altogether in proportion to their weight, on account of the watery nature of potatoes. Allowing, however, half the weight of this root to go to water, a very large allowance, such an acre of potatoes will still produce six thousand weight of solid nourishment, three times the quantity produced by the acre of wheat. An acre of potatoes is cultivated with less expense than an acre of wheat; the fallow, which generally precedes the sowing of wheat, more than compensating the hoeing and other extraordinary culture which is always given to potatoes. Should this root ever become in any part of Europe, like rice in some rice countries, the common and favorite vegetable food of the people, so as to occupy the same proportion of the lands in tillage, which wheat and other sorts of grain for human food do at present, the same quantity of cultivated land would maintain a much greater number of people; and the laborers being generally fed with potatoes, a greater surplus would remain after replacing all the stock, and maintaining all the labor employed in cultivation. A greater share of this surplus, too, would belong to the landlord. Population would increase, and rents would rise much beyond what they are at present.

The land which is fit for potatoes, is fit for almost every other useful vegetable. If they occupied the same proportion of cultivated land which corn does at present, they would regulate, in the same manner, the rent of the greater part of other cultivated land.

In some parts of Lancashire, it is pretended, I have been told, that bread of oatmeal is a heartier food for laboring people than wheaten bread, and I have frequently heard the same doctrine held in Scotland. I am, however, somewhat doubtful of the truth of it. The common people in Scotland, who are fed with oatmeal, are in general neither so strong nor so handsome as the same rank of people in England, who are fed with wheaten bread. They neither work so well, nor look so well; and as there is not the same difference between the people of fashion in the two countries, experience would seem to show, that the food of the common people in Scotland is not so suitable to the human constitution as that of their neighbors of the same rank in England. But it seems to be otherwise with potatoes. The chairmen, porters, and coal-heavers in London, and those unfortunate women who live by prostitution, the strongest men and the most beautiful women perhaps in the British dominions, are said to be, the greater part of them, from the lowest rank of people in Ireland, who are generally fed with this root. No food can afford a more decisive proof of its nourishing quality, or of its being peculiarly suitable to the health of the human constitution.

It is difficult to preserve potatoes through the year, and impossible to store them like corn, for two or three years together. The fear of not being able to sell them before they rot, discourages their cultivation, and is, perhaps, the chief obstacle to their ever becoming in any great country, like bread, the principal vegetable food of all the different ranks of the people.

Part II

Of the Produce of Land, Which Sometimes Does, and Sometimes Does Not, Afford Rent.

Human food seems to be the only produce of land, which always and necessarily affords some rent to the landlord. Other sorts of produce sometimes may, and sometimes may not, according to different circumstances.

After food, clothing and lodging are the two great wants of mankind.

Land, in its original rude state, can afford the materials of clothing and lodging to a much greater number of people than it can feed. In its improved state, it can sometimes feed a greater number of people than it can supply with those materials; at least in the way in which they require them, and are willing to pay for them. In the one state, therefore, there is always a superabundance of these materials, which are frequently, upon that account, of little or no value. In the other, there is often a scarcity, which necessarily augments their value. In the one state, a great part of them is thrown away as useless and the price of what is used is considered as equal only to the labor and expense of fitting it for use, and can, therefore, afford no rent to the landlord. In the other, they are all made use of, and there is frequently a demand for more than can be had. Somebody is always willing to give more for every part of them, than what is sufficient to pay the expense of bringing them to market. Their price, therefore, can always afford some rent to the landlord.

The skins of the larger animals were the original materials of clothing. Among nations of hunters and shepherds, therefore, whose food consists chiefly in the flesh of those animals, everyman, by providing himself with food, provides himself with the materials of more clothing than he can wear. If there was no foreign commerce, the greater part of them would be thrown away as things of no value. This was probably the case among the hunting nations of North America, before their country was discovered by the Europeans, with whom they now exchange their surplus peltry, for blankets, fire-arms, and brandy, which gives it some value. In the present commercial state of the known world, the most barbarous nations, I believe, among whom land property is established, have some foreign commerce of this kind, and find among their wealthier neighbors such a demand for all the materials of clothing, which their land produces, and which can neither be wrought up nor consumed at home, as raises their price above what it costs to send them to those wealthier neighbors. It affords, therefore, some rent to the landlord. When the greater part of the Highland cattle were consumed on their own hills, the exportation of their hides made the most considerable article of the commerce of that country, and what they were exchanged for afforded some addition to the rent of the Highland estates. The wool of England, which in old times, could neither be consumed nor wrought up at home, found a market in the then wealthier and more industrious country of Flanders, and its price afforded something to the rent of the land which produced it. In countries not better cultivated than England was then, or than the Highlands of Scotland are now, and which had no foreign commerce, the materials of clothing would evidently be so superabundant, that a great part of them would be thrown away as useless, and no part could afford any rent to the landlord.

The materials of lodging cannot always be transported to so great a distance as those of clothing, and do not so readily become an object of foreign commerce. When they are superabundant in the country which produces them, it frequently happens, even in the present commercial state of the world, that they are of no value to the landlord. A good stone quarry in the neighborhood of London would afford a considerable rent. In many parts of Scotland and Wales it affords none. Barren timber for building is of great value in a populous and well-cultivated country, and the land which produces it affords a considerable rent. But in many parts of North America, the landlord would be much obliged to any body who would carry away the greater part of his large trees. In some parts of the Highlands of Scotland, the bark is the only part of the wood which, for want of roads and water-carriage, can be sent to market; the timber is left to rot upon the ground. When the materials of lodging are so superabundant, the part made use of is worth only the labor and expense of fitting it for that use. It affords no rent to the landlord, who generally grants the use of it to whoever takes the trouble of asking it. The demand of wealthier nations, however, sometimes enables him to get a rent for it. The paving of the streets of London has enabled the owners of some barren rocks on the coast of Scotland to draw a rent from what never afforded any before. The woods of Norway, and of the coasts of the Baltic, find a market in many parts of Great Britain, which they could not find at home, and thereby afford some rent to their proprietors.

Countries are populous, not in proportion to the number of people whom their produce can clothe and lodge, but in proportion to that of those whom it can feed. When food is provided, it is easy to find the necessary clothing and lodging. But though these are at hand, it may often be difficult to find food. In some parts of the British dominions, what is called a house may be built by one day's labor of one man. The simplest species of clothing, the skins of animals, require somewhat more labor to dress and prepare them for use. They do not, however, require a great deal. Among savage or barbarous nations, a hundredth, or little more than a hundredth part of the labor of the whole year, will be sufficient to provide them with such clothing and lodging as satisfy the greater part of the people. All the other ninety-nine parts are frequently no more than enough to provide them with food.

But when, by the improvement and cultivation of land, the labor of one family can provide food for two, the labor of half the society becomes sufficient to provide food for the whole. The other half, therefore, or at least the greater part of them, can be employed in providing other things, or in satisfying the other wants and fancies of mankind. Clothing and lodging, household furniture, and what is called equipage, are the principal objects of the greater part of those wants and fancies. The rich man consumes no more food than his poor neighbor. In quality it may be very different, and to select and prepare it may require more labor and art; but in quantity it is very nearly the same. But compare the spacious palace and great wardrobe of the one, with the hovel and the few rags of the other, and you will be sensible that the difference between their clothing, lodging, and household furniture, is almost as great in quantity as it is in quality. The desire of food is limited in every man by the narrow capacity of the human stomach; but the desire of the conveniences and ornaments of building, dress, equipage, and household furniture, seems to have no limit or certain boundary. Those, therefore, who have the command of more food than they themselves can consume, are always willing to exchange the surplus, or, what is the same thing, the price of it, for gratifications of this other kind. What is over and above satisfying the limited desire, is given for the amusement of those desires which cannot be satisfied, but seem to be altogether endless. The poor, in order to obtain food, exert themselves to gratify those fancies of the rich; and to obtain it more certainly, they vie with one another in the cheapness and perfection of their work. The number of workmen increases with the increasing quantity of food, or with the growing improvement and cultivation of the lands; and as the nature of their business admits of the utmost subdivisions of labor, the quantity of materials which they can work up, increases in a much greater proportion than their numbers. Hence arises a demand for every sort of material which human invention can employ, either usefully or ornamentally, in building, dress, equipage, or household furniture; for the fossils and minerals contained in the bowels of the earth, the precious metals, and the precious stones.

Food is, in this manner, not only the original source of rent, but every other part of the produce of land which afterwards affords rent, derives that part of its value from the improvement of the powers of labor in producing food, by means of the improvement and cultivation of land.

Those other parts of the produce of land, however, which afterwards afford rent, do not afford it always. Even in improved and cultivated countries, the demand for them is not always such as to afford a greater price than what is sufficient to pay the labor, and replace, together with its ordinary profits, the stock which must be employed in bringing them to market. Whether it is or is not such, depends upon different circumstances.

Whether a coalmine, for example, can afford any rent, depends partly upon its fertility, and partly upon its situation.

A mine of any kind may be said to be either fertile or barren, according as the quantity of mineral which can be brought from it by a certain quantity of labor, is greater or less than what can be brought by an equal quantity from the greater part of other mines of the same kind.

Some coalmines, advantageously situated, cannot be wrought on account of their barrenness. The produce does not pay the expense. They can afford neither profit nor rent.

There are some, of which the produce is barely sufficient to pay the labor, and replace, together with its ordinary profits, the stock employed in working them. They afford some profit to the undertaker of the work, but no rent to the landlord. They can be wrought advantageously by nobody but the landlord, who, being himself the undertaker of the work, gets the ordinary profit of the capital which he employs in it. Many coalmines in Scotland are wrought in this manner, and can be wrought in no other. The landlord will allow nobody else to work them without paying some rent, and nobody can afford to pay any.

Other coalmines in the same country, sufficiently fertile, cannot be wrought on account of their situation. A quantity of mineral, sufficient to defray the expense of working, could be brought from the mine by the ordinary, or even less than the ordinary quantity of labor: but in an inland country, thinly inhabited, and without either good roads or water-carriage, this quantity could not be sold.

Coals are a less agreeable fuel than wood: they are said too to be less wholesome. The expense of coals, therefore, at the place where they are consumed, must generally be somewhat less than that of wood.

The price of wood, again, varies with the state of agriculture, nearly in the same manner, and exactly for the same reason, as the price of cattle. In its rude beginnings, the greater part of every country is covered with wood, which is then a mere encumbrance, of no value to the landlord, who would gladly give it to any body for the cutting. As agriculture advances, the woods are partly cleared by the progress of tillage, and partly go to decay in consequence of the increased number of cattle. These, though they do not increase in the same proportion as corn, which is altogether the acquisition of human industry, yet multiply under the care and protection of men, who store up in the season of plenty what may maintain them in that of scarcity; who, through the whole year, furnish them with a greater quantity of food than uncultivated nature provides for them; and who, by destroying and extirpating their enemies, secure them in the free enjoyment of all that she provides. Numerous herds of cattle, when allowed to wander through the woods, though they do not destroy the old trees, hinder any young ones from coming up; so that, in the course of a century or two, the whole forest goes to ruin. The scarcity of wood then raises its price. It affords a good rent; and the landlord sometimes finds that he can scarce employ his best lands more advantageously than in growing barren timber, of which the greatness of the profit often compensates the lateness of the returns. This seems, in the present times, to be nearly the state of things in several parts of Great Britain, where the profit of planting is found to be equal to that of either corn or pasture. The advantage which the landlord derives from planting can nowhere exceed, at least for any considerable time, the rent which these could afford him; and in an inland country, which is highly cultivated, it will frequently not fall much short of this rent. Upon the sea-coast of a well-improved country, indeed, if coals can conveniently be had for fuel, it may sometimes be cheaper to bring barren timber for building from less cultivated foreign countries than to raise it at home. In the new town of Edinburgh, built within these few years, there is not, perhaps, a single stick of Scotch timber.

Whatever may be the price of wood, if that of coals is such that the expense of a coal fire is nearly equal to that of a wood one we may be assured, that at that place, and in these circumstances, the price of coals is as high as it can be. It seems to be so in some of the inland parts of England, particularly in Oxfordshire, where it is usual, even in the fires of the common people, to mix coals and wood together, and where the difference in the expense of those two sorts of fuel cannot, therefore, be very great. Coals, in the coal countries, are everywhere much below this highest price. If they were not, they could not bear the expense of a distant carriage, either by land or by water. A small quantity only could be sold; and the coal masters and the coal proprietors find it more for their interest to sell a great quantity at a price somewhat above the lowest, than a small quantity at the highest. The most fertile coalmine, too, regulates the price of coals at all the other mines in its neighborhood. Both the proprietor and the undertaker of the work find, the one that he can get a greater rent, the other that he can get a greater profit, by somewhat underselling all their neighbors. Their neighbors are soon obliged to sell at the same price, though they cannot so well afford it, and though it always diminishes, and sometimes takes away altogether, both their rent and their profit. Some works are abandoned altogether; others can afford no rent, and can be wrought only by the proprietor.

The lowest price at which coals can be sold for any considerable time, is, like that of all other commodities, the price which is barely sufficient to replace, together with its ordinary profits, the stock which must be employed in bringing them to market. At a coalmine for which the landlord can get no rent, but, which he must either work himself or let it alone altogether, the price of coals must generally be nearly about this price.

Rent, even where coals afford one, has generally a smaller share in their price than in that of most other parts of the rude produce of land. The rent of an estate above ground, commonly amounts to what is supposed to be a third of the gross produce; and it is generally a rent certain and independent of the occasional variations in the crop. In coalmines, a fifth of the gross produce is a very great rent, a tenth the common rent; and it is seldom a rent certain, but depends upon the occasional variations in the produce. These are so great, that in a country where thirty years purchase is considered as a moderate price for the property of a landed estate, ten years purchase is regarded as a good price for that of a coalmine.

The value of a coalmine to the proprietor, frequently depends as much upon its situation as upon its fertility. That of a metallic mine depends more upon its fertility, and less upon its situation. The coarse, and still more the precious metals, when separated from the ore, are so valuable, that they can generally bear the expense of a very long land, and of the most distant sea carriage. Their market is not confined to the countries in the neighborhood of the mine, but extends to the whole world. The copper of Japan makes an article of commerce in Europe; the iron of Spain in that of Chili and Peru. The silver of Peru finds its way, not only to Europe, but from Europe to China.

The price of coals in Westmoreland or Shropshire can have little effect on their price at Newcastle; and their price in the Lionnois can have none at all. The productions of such distant coalmines can never be brought into competition with one another. But the productions of the most distant metallic mines frequently may, and in fact commonly are. The price, therefore, of the coarse, and still more that of the precious metals, at the most fertile mines in the world, must necessarily more or less affect their price at every other in it. The price of copper in Japan must have some influence upon its price at the copper mines in Europe. The price of silver in Peru, or the quantity either of labor or of other goods which it will purchase there, must have some influence on its price, not only at the silver mines of Europe, but at those of China. After the discovery of the mines of Peru, the silver mines of Europe were, the greater part of them, abandoned. The value of silver was so much reduced, that their produce could no longer pay the expense of working them, or replace, with a profit, the food, clothes, lodging, and other necessaries which were consumed in that operation. This was the case, too, with the mines of Cuba and St. Domingo, and even with the ancient mines of Peru, after the discovery of those of Potosi.

The price of every metal, at every mine, therefore, being regulated in some measure by its price at the most fertile mine in the world that is actually wrought, it can, at the greater part of mines, do very little more than pay the expense of working, and can seldom afford a very high rent to the landlord. Rent accordingly, seems at the greater part of mines to have but a small share in the price of the coarse, and a still smaller in that of the precious metals. Labor and profit make up the greater part of both.

A sixth part of the gross produce may be reckoned the average rent of the tin mines of Cornwall, the most fertile that are known in the world, as we are told by the Rev. Mr. Borlace, vice-warden of the stannaries. Some, he says, afford more, and some do not afford so much. A sixth part of the gross produce is the rent, too, of several very fertile lead mines in Scotland.

In the silver mines of Peru, we are told by Frezier and Ulloa, the proprietor frequently exacts no other acknowledgment from the undertaker of the mine, but that he will grind the ore at his mill, paying him the ordinary multure or price of grinding. Till 1736, indeed, the tax of the king of Spain amounted to one fifth of the standard silver, which till then might be considered as the real rent of the greater part of the silver mines of Peru, the richest which have been known in the world. If there had been no tax, this fifth would naturally have belonged to the landlord, and many mines might have been wrought which could not then be wrought, because they could not afford this tax. The tax of the duke of Cornwall upon tin is supposed to amount to more than five percent or one twentieth part of the value; and whatever may be his proportion, it would naturally, too, belong to the proprietor of the mine, if tin was duty free. But if you add one twentieth to one sixth, you will find that the whole average rent of the tin mines of Cornwall, was to the whole average rent of the silver mines of Peru, as thirteen to twelve. But the silver mines of Peru are not now able to pay even this low rent; and the tax upon silver was, in 1736, reduced from one fifth to one tenth. Even this tax upon silver, too, gives more temptation to smuggling than the tax of one twentieth upon tin; and smuggling must be much easier in the precious than in the bulky commodity. The tax of the king of Spain, accordingly, is said to be very ill paid, and that of the duke of Cornwall very well. Rent, therefore, it is probable, makes a greater part of the price of tin at the most fertile tin mines than it does of silver at the most fertile silver mines in the world. After replacing the stock employed in working those different mines, together with its ordinary profits, the residue which remains to the proprietor is greater, it seems, in the coarse, than in the precious metal.

Neither are the profits of the undertakers of silver mines commonly very great in Peru. The same most respectable and well-informed authors acquaint us, that when any person undertakes to work a new mine in Peru, he is universally looked upon as a man destined to bankruptcy and ruin, and is upon that account shunned and avoided by everybody. Mining, it seems, is considered there in the same light as here, as a lottery, in which the prizes do not compensate the blanks, though the greatness of some tempts many adventurers to throw away their fortunes in such unprosperous projects.

As the sovereign, however, derives a considerable part of his revenue from the produce of silver mines, the law in Peru gives every possible encouragement to the discovery and working of new ones. Whoever discovers a new mine, is entitled to measure off two hundred and forty-six feet in length, according to what he supposes to be the direction of the vein, and half as much in breadth. He becomes proprietor of this portion of the mine, and can work it without paying any acknowledgment to the land-lord. The interest of the duke of Cornwall has given occasion to a regulation nearly of the same kind in that ancient duchy. In waste and unenclosed lands, any person who discovers a tin mine may mark out its limits to a certain extent, which is called bound-ing a mine. The bounder becomes the real proprietor of the mine, and may either work it himself, or give it in lease to another, without the consent of the owner of the land, to whom, however, a very small acknowledgment must be paid upon working it. In both regulations, the sacred rights of private property are sacrificed to the supposed interests of public revenue.

The same encouragement is given in Peru to the discovery and working of new gold mines; and in gold the king's tax amounts only to a twentieth part of the standard rental. It was once a fifth, and afterwards a tenth, as in silver; but it was found that the work could not bear even the lowest of these two taxes. If it is rare, however, say the same au-thors, Frezier and Ulloa, to find a person who has made his fortune by a silver, it is still much rarer to find one who has done so by a gold mine. This twentieth part seems to be the whole rent which is paid by the greater part of the gold mines of Chili and Peru. Gold, too, is much more liable to be smuggled than even silver; not only on account of the superior value of the metal in proportion to its bulk, but on account of the pecu-liar way in which nature produces it. Silver is very seldom found virgin, but, like most other metals, is generally mineralized with some other body, from which it is impossi-ble to separate it in such quantities as will pay for the expense, but by a very laborious and tedious operation, which cannot well be carried on but in work-houses erected for the purpose, and, therefore, exposed to the inspection of the king's officers. Gold, on the contrary, is almost always found virgin. It is sometimes found in pieces of some bulk; and, even when mixed, in small and almost insensible particles, with sand, earth, and other extraneous bodies, it can be separated from them by a very short and simple operation, which can be carried on in any private house by any body who is possessed of a small quantity of mercury. If the king's tax, therefore, is but ill paid upon silver, it is likely to be much worse paid upon gold; and rent must make a much smaller part of the price of gold than that of silver.

The lowest price at which the precious metals can be sold, or the smallest quantity of other goods for which they can be exchanged, during any considerable time, is regulated by the same principles which fix the lowest ordinary price of all other goods. The stock which must commonly be employed, the food, clothes, and lodging, which must com-monly be consumed in bringing them from the mine to the market, determine it. It must at least be sufficient to replace that stock, with the ordinary profits.

Their highest price, however, seems not to be necessarily determined by any thing but the actual scarcity or plenty of these metals themselves. It is not determined by that of any other commodity, in the same manner as the price of coals is by that of wood, be-yond which no scarcity can ever raise it. Increase the scarcity of gold to a certain degree, and the smallest bit of it may become more precious than a diamond, and exchange for a greater quantity of other goods.

The demand for those metals arises partly from their utility, and partly from their beauty. If you except iron, they are more useful than, perhaps, any other metal. As they are less liable to rust and impurity, they can more easily be kept clean; and the utensils, either of the table or the kitchen, are often, upon that account, more agreeable when made of them. A silver boiler is more cleanly than a lead, copper, or tin one; and the same quality would render a gold boiler still better than a silver one. Their principal merit, however, arises from their beauty, which renders them peculiarly fit for the ornaments of dress and furniture. No paint or dye can give so splendid a color as gilding. The merit of their beauty is greatly enhanced by their scarcity. With the greater part of rich people, the chief enjoyment of riches consists in the parade of riches; which, in their eye, is never so complete as when they appear to possess those decisive marks of opulence which nobody can possess but themselves. In their eyes, the merit of an object, which is in any degree either useful or beautiful, is greatly enhanced by its scarcity, or by the great labor which it requires to collect any considerable quantity of it; a labor which nobody can afford to pay but themselves. Such objects they are willing to purchase at a higher price than things much more beautiful and useful, but more common. These qualities of utility, beauty, and scarcity, are the original foundation of the high price of those metals, or of the great quantity of other goods for which they can everywhere be exchanged. This value was antecedent to, and independent of their being employed as coin, and was the quality which fitted them for that employment. That employment, however, by occasioning a new demand, and by diminishing the quantity which could be employed in any other way, may have afterwards contributed to keep up or increase their value.

The demand for the precious stones arises altogether from their beauty. They are of no use but as ornaments; and the merit of their beauty is greatly enhanced by their scarcity, or by the difficulty and expense of getting them from the mine. Wages and profit accordingly make up, upon most occasions, almost the whole of the high price. Rent comes in but for a very small share, frequently for no share; and the most fertile mines only afford any considerable rent. When Tavernier, a jeweler, visited the diamond mines of Golconda and Visiapour, he was informed that the sovereign of the country, for whose benefit they were wrought, had ordered all of them to be shut up except those which yielded the largest and finest stones. The other, it seems, were to the proprietor not worth the working.

As the prices, both of the precious metals and of the precious stones, is regulated all over the world by their price at the most fertile mine in it, the rent which a mine of either can afford to its proprietor is in proportion, not to its absolute, but to what may be called its relative fertility, or to its superiority over other mines of the same kind. If new mines were discovered, as much superior to those of Potosi, as they were superior to those of Europe, the value of silver might be so much degraded as to render even the mines of Potosi not worth the working. Before the discovery of the Spanish West Indies, the most fertile mines in Europe may have afforded as great a rent to their proprietors as the richest mines in Peru do at present. Though the quantity of silver was much less, it might have exchanged for an equal quantity of other goods, and the proprietor's share might have enabled him to purchase or command an equal quantity either of labor or of commodities. The value, both of the produce and of the rent, the real revenue which they afforded, both to the public and to the proprietor, might have been the same.

The most abundant mines, either of the precious metals, or of the precious stones, could add little to the wealth of the world. A produce, of which the value is principally derived from its scarcity, is necessarily degraded by its abundance. A service of plate, and the other frivolous ornaments of dress and furniture, could be purchased for a smaller quantity of commodities; and in this would consist the sole advantage which the world could derive from that abundance.

It is otherwise in estates above ground. The value, both of their produce and of their rent, is in proportion to their absolute, and not to their relative fertility. The land which produces a certain quantity of food, clothes, and lodging, can always feed, clothe, and lodge, a certain number of people; and whatever may be the proportion of the landlord, it will always give him a proportionable command of the labor of those people, and of the commodities with which that labor can supply him. The value of the most barren land is not diminished by the neighborhood of the most fertile. On the contrary, it is generally increased by it. The great number of people maintained by the fertile lands afford a market to many parts of the produce of the barren, which they could never have found among those whom their own produce could maintain.

Whatever increases the fertility of land in producing food, increases not only the value of the lands upon which the improvement is bestowed, but contributes likewise to increase that of many other lands, by creating a new demand for their produce. That abundance of food, of which, in consequence of the improvement of land, many people have the disposal beyond what they themselves can consume, is the great cause of the demand, both for the precious metals and the precious stones, as well as for every other conveniency and ornament of dress, lodging, household furniture, and equipage. Food not only constitutes the principal part of the riches of the world, but it is the abundance of food which gives the principal part of their value to many other sorts of riches. The poor inhabitants of Cuba and St. Domingo, when they were first discovered by the Spaniards, used to wear little bits of gold as ornaments in their hair and other parts of their dress. They seemed to value them as we would do any little pebbles of somewhat more than ordinary beauty, and to consider them as just worth the picking up, but not worth the refusing to any body who asked them, They gave them to their new guests at the first request, without seeming to think that they had made them any very valuable present. They were astonished to observe the rage of the Spaniards to obtain them; and had no notion that there could anywhere be a country in which many people had the disposal of so great a superfluity of food; so scanty always among themselves, that, for a very small quantity of those glittering baubles, they would willingly give as much as might maintain a whole family for many years. Could they have been made to understand this, the passion of the Spaniards would not have surprised them.

Part III

Of the Variations in the Proportion Between the Respective Values of That Sort of Produce Which Always Affords Rent, and of That Which Sometimes Does, and Sometimes Does Not, Afford Rent.

The increasing abundance of food, in consequence of the increasing improvement and cultivation, must necessarily increase the demand for every part of the produce of land which is not food, and which can be applied either to use or to ornament. In the whole progress of improvement, it might, therefore, be expected there should be only one variation in the comparative values of those two different sorts of produce. The value of that sort which sometimes does, and sometimes does not afford rent, should constantly rise in proportion to that which always affords some rent. As art and industry advance, the materials of clothing and lodging, the useful fossils and materials of the earth, the precious metals and the precious stones, should gradually come to be more and more in demand, should gradually exchange for a greater and a greater quantity of food; or, in other words, should gradually become dearer and dearer. This, accordingly, has been the case with most of these things upon most occasions, and would have been the case with all of them upon all occasions, if particular accidents had not, upon some occasions, increased the supply of some of them in a still greater proportion than the demand.

The value of a free stone quarry, for example, will necessarily increase with the increasing improvement and population of the country round about it, especially if it should be the only one in the neighborhood. But the value of a silver mine, even though there should not be another within a thousand miles of it, will not necessarily increase with the improvement of the country in which it is situated. The market for the produce of a free stone quarry can seldom extend more than a few miles round about it, and the demand must generally be in proportion to the improvement and population of that small district; but the market for the produce of a silver mine may extend over the whole known world. Unless the world in general. therefore, be advancing in improvement and population, the demand for silver might not be at all increased by the improvement even of a large country in the neighborhood of the mine. Even though the world in general were improving, yet if, in the course of its improvements, new mines should be discovered, much more fertile than any which had been known before, though the demand for silver would necessarily increase, yet the supply might increase in so much a greater proportion, that the real price of that metal might gradually fall; that is, any given quantity, a pound weight of it, for example, might gradually purchase or command a smaller and a smaller quantity of labor, or exchange for a smaller and a smaller quantity of corn, the principal part of the subsistence of the laborer.

The great market for silver is the commercial and civilized part of the world.

If, by the general progress of improvement, the demand of this market should increase, while, at the same time, the supply did not increase in the same proportion, the value of silver would gradually rise in proportion to that of corn. Any given quantity of silver would exchange for a greater and a greater quantity of corn; or, in other words, the average money price of corn would gradually become cheaper and cheaper.

If, on the contrary, the supply, by some accident, should increase, for many years together, in a greater proportion than the demand, that metal would gradually become cheaper and cheaper; or, in other words, the average money price of corn would, in spite of all improvements, gradually become dearer and dearer.

But if, on the other hand, the supply of that metal should increase nearly in the same proportion as the demand, it would continue to purchase or exchange for nearly the same quantity of corn; and the average money price of corn would, in spite of all improvements. continue very nearly the same.

These three seem to exhaust all the possible combinations of events which can happen in the progress of improvement; and during the course of the four centuries preceding the present, if we may judge by what has happened both in France and Great Britain, each of those three different combinations seems to have taken place in the European market, and nearly in the same order, too, in which I have here set them down.

Digression Concerning the Variations in the Value of Silver During the
Course of the Four Last Centuries.

First Period

In 1350, and for some time before, the average price of the quarter of wheat in England
seems not to have been estimated lower than four ounces of silver, Tower weight, equal
to about twenty shillings of our present money. From this price it seems to have fallen
gradually to two ounces of silver, equal to about ten shillings of our present money, the
price at which we find it estimated in the beginning of the sixteenth century, and at
which it seems to have continued to be estimated till about 1570.

In 1350, being the 25th of Edward III was enacted what is called the Statute of Laborers. In the preamble, it complains much of the insolence of servants, who endeavored to raise their wages upon their masters. It therefore ordains, that all servants and
laborers should, for the future, be contented with the same wages and liveries (liveries
in those times signified not only clothes, but provisions) which they had been accustomed to receive in the 20th year of the king, and the four preceding years; that, upon
this account, their livery-wheat should nowhere be estimated higher than ten pence a
bushel, and that it should always be in the option of the master to deliver them either
the wheat or the money. Ten pence a bushel, therefore, had, in the 25th of Edward III
been reckoned a very moderate price of wheat, since it required a particular statute to
oblige servants to accept of it in exchange for their usual livery of provisions; and it had
been reckoned a reasonable price ten years before that, or in the 16th year of the king,
the term to which the statute refers. But in the 16th year of Edward III ten pence contained about half an ounce of silver, Tower weight, and was nearly equal to half-a-
crown of our present money. Four ounces of silver, Tower weight, therefore, equal to
six shillings and eight pence of the money of those times, and to near twenty shillings
of that of the present, must have been reckoned a moderate price for the quarter of
eight bushels.

This statute is surely a better evidence of what was reckoned, in those times, a moderate price of grain, than the prices of some particular years, which have generally been
recorded by historians and other writers, on account of their extraordinary dearness or
cheapness, and from which, therefore, it is difficult to form any judgment concerning
what may have been the ordinary price. There are, besides, other reasons for believing
that, in the beginning of the fourteenth century, and for some time before, the common
price of wheat was not less than four ounces of silver the quarter, and that of other grain
in proportion.

In 1309, Ralph de Born, prior of St Augustine's, Canterbury, gave a feast upon his in-
stallation-day, of which William Thorn has preserved, not only the bill of fare, but the
prices of many particulars. In that feast were consumed, 1st, fifty-three quarters of wheat,
which cost nineteen pounds, or seven shillings, and two pence a quarter, equal to about
one-and-twenty shillings and sixpence of our present money; 2dly, fifty-eight quarters of
malt, which cost seventeen pounds ten shillings, or six shillings a quarter, equal to about
eighteen shillings of our present money; 3dly, twenty quarters of oats, which cost four
pounds, or four shillings a quarter, equal to about twelve shillings of our present money.

The prices of malt and oats seem here to lie higher than their ordinary proportion to the price of wheat.

These prices are not recorded, on account of their extraordinary dearness or cheapness, but are mentioned accidentally, as the prices actually paid for large quantities of grain consumed at a feast, which was famous for its magnificence.

In 1262, being the 51st of Henry III was revived an ancient statute, called the assize of bread and ale, which, the king says in the preamble, had been made in the times of his progenitors, some time kings of England. It is probably, therefore, as old at least as the time of his grandfather, Henry II and may have been as old as the Conquest. It regulates the price of bread according as the prices of wheat may happen to be, from one shilling to twenty shillings the quarter of the money of those times. But statutes of this kind are generally presumed to provide with equal care for all deviations from the middle price, for those below it, as well as for those above it. Ten shillings, therefore, containing six ounces of silver, Tower weight, and equal to about thirty shillings of our present money, must, upon this supposition, have been reckoned the middle price of the quarter of wheat when this statute was first enacted, and must have continued to be so in the 51st of Henry III. We cannot, therefore, be very wrong in supposing that the middle price was not less than one-third of the highest price at which this statute regulates the price of bread, or than six shillings and eight pence of the money of those times, containing four ounces of silver, Tower weight.

From these different facts, therefore, we seem to have some reason to conclude that, about the middle of the fourteenth century, and for a considerable time before, the average or ordinary price of the quarter of wheat was not supposed to be less than four ounces of silver, Tower weight.

From about the middle of the fourteenth to the beginning of the sixteenth century, what was reckoned the reasonable and moderate, that is, the ordinary or average price of wheat, seems to have sunk gradually to about one half of this price; so as at last to have fallen to about two ounces of silver, Tower weight, equal to about ten shillings of our present money. It continued to be estimated at this price till about 1570.

In the household book of Henry, the fifth earl of Northumberland, drawn up in 1512 there are two different estimations of wheat. In one of them it is computed at six shillings and eight pence the quarter, in the other at five shillings and eight pence only. In 1512, six shillings and eight pence contained only two ounces of silver, Tower weight, and were equal to about ten shillings of our present money.

From the 25th of Edward III to the beginning of the reign of Elizabeth, during the space of more than two hundred years, six shillings and eight pence, it appears from several different statutes, had continued to be considered as what is called the moderate and reasonable, that is, the ordinary or average price of wheat. The quantity of silver, however, contained in that nominal sum was, during the course of this period, continually diminishing in consequence of some alterations which were made in the coin. But the increase of the value of silver had, it seems, so far compensated the diminution of the quantity of it contained in the same nominal sum, that the legislature did not think it worth while to attend to this circumstance.

Thus, in 1436, it was enacted, that wheat might be exported without a license when the price was so low as six shillings and eight pence: and in 1463, it was enacted, that no wheat should be imported if the price was not above six shillings and eight pence the quarter. The legislature had imagined, that when the price was so low, there could be no inconveniency in exportation, but that when it rose higher, it became prudent to allow of importation. Six shillings and eight pence, therefore, containing about the same quantity of silver as thirteen shillings and four pence of our present money (one-third part less than the same nominal sum contained in the time of Edward III), had, in those times, been considered as what is called the moderate and reasonable price of wheat.

In 1554, by the 1st and 2nd of Philip and Mary, and in 1558, by the 1st of Elizabeth, the exportation of wheat was in the same manner prohibited, whenever the price of the quarter should exceed six shillings and eight pence, which did not then contain two penny worth more silver than the same nominal sum does at present. But it had soon been found, that to restrain the exportation of wheat till the price was so very low, was, in reality, to prohibit it altogether. In 1562, therefore, by the 5th of Elizabeth, the exportation of wheat was allowed from certain ports, whenever the price of the quarter should not exceed ten shillings, containing nearly the same quantity of silver as the like nominal sum does at present. This price had at this time, therefore, been considered as what is called the moderate and reasonable price of wheat. It agrees nearly with the estimation of the Northumberland book in 1512.

That in France the average price of grain was, in the same manner, much lower in the end of the fifteenth and beginning of the sixteenth century, than in the two centuries preceding, has been observed both by Mr. Dupré de St Maur, and by the elegant author of the *Essay on the Policy of Grain*. Its price, during the same period, had probably sunk in the same manner through the greater part of Europe.

This rise in the value of silver, in proportion to that of corn, may either have been owing altogether to the increase of the demand for that metal, in consequence of increasing improvement and cultivation, the supply, in the mean time, continuing the same as before; or, the demand continuing the same as before, it may have been owing altogether to the gradual diminution of the supply: the greater part of the mines which were then known in the world being much exhausted, and, consequently, the expense of working them much increased; or it may have been owing partly to the one, and partly to the other of those two circumstances. In the end of the fifteenth and beginning of the sixteenth centuries, the greater part of Europe was approaching towards a more settled from of government than it had enjoyed for several ages before. The increase of security would naturally increase industry and improvement; and the demand for the precious metals, as well as for every other luxury and ornament, would naturally increase with the increase of riches. A greater annual produce would require a greater quantity of coin to circulate it; and a greater number of rich people would require a greater quantity of plate and other ornaments of silver. It is natural to suppose, too, that the greater part of the mines which then supplied the European market with silver might be a good deal exhausted, and have become more expensive in the working. They had been wrought, many of them, from the time of the Romans.

It has been the opinion, however, of the greater part of those who have written upon the prices of commodities in ancient times, that, from the Conquest, perhaps from the invasion of Julius Caesar, till the discovery of the mines of America, the value of silver was continually diminishing. This opinion they seem to have been led into, partly by the observations which they had occasion to make upon the prices both of corn and of some other parts of the rude produce of land, and partly by the popular notion, that as the quantity of silver naturally increases in every country with the increase of wealth, so its value diminishes as it quantity increases.

In their observations upon the prices of corn, three different circumstances seem frequently to have misled them.

First, in ancient times, almost all rents were paid in kind; in a certain quantity of corn, cattle, poultry, etc. It sometimes happened, however, that the landlord would stipulate, that he should be at liberty to demand of the tenant, either the annual payment in kind or a certain sum of money instead of it. The price at which the payment in kind was in this manner exchanged for a certain sum of money, is in Scotland called the conversion price. As the option is always in the landlord to take either the substance or the price, it is necessary, for the safety of the tenant, that the conversion price should rather be below than above the average market price. In many places, accordingly, it is not much above one half of this price. Through the greater part of Scotland this custom still continues with regard to poultry, and in some places with regard to cattle. It might probably have continued to take place, too, with regard to corn, had not the institution of the public fiars put an end to it. These are annual valuations, according to the judgment of an assize, of the average price of all the different sorts of grain, and of all the different qualities of each, according to the actual market price in every different county. This institution rendered it sufficiently safe for the tenant, and much more convenient for the landlord, to convert, as they call it, the corn rent, rather at what should happen to be the price of the fiars of each year, than at any certain fixed price. But the writers who have collected the prices of corn in ancient times seem frequently to have mistaken what is called in Scotland the conversion price for the actual market price. Fleetwood acknowledges, upon one occasion, that he had made this mistake. As he wrote his book, however, for a particular purpose, he does not think proper to make this acknowledgment till after transcribing this conversion price fifteen times. The price is eight shillings the quarter of wheat. This sum in 1423, the year at which he begins with it, contained the same quantity of silver as sixteen shillings of our present money. But in 1562, the year at which he ends with it, it contained no more than the same nominal sum does at present.

Secondly, they have been misled by the slovenly manner in which some ancient statutes of assize had been sometimes transcribed by lazy copiers, and sometimes, perhaps, actually composed by the legislature.

The ancient statutes of assize seem to have begun always with determining what ought to be the price of bread and ale when the price of wheat and barley were at the lowest; and to have proceeded gradually to determine what it ought to be, according as the prices of those two sorts of grain should gradually rise above this lowest price. But the transcribers of those statutes seem frequently to have thought it sufficient to copy the regulation as far as the three or four first and lowest prices; saving in this manner their own labor, and judging, I suppose, that this was enough to show what proportion ought to be observed in all higher prices.

Thus, in the assize of bread and ale, of the 51st of Henry III the price of bread was regulated according to the different prices of wheat, from one shilling to twenty shillings the quarter of the money of those times. But in the manuscripts from which all the different editions of the statutes, preceding that of Mr. Ruffhead, were printed, the copiers had never transcribed this regulation beyond the price of twelve shillings. Several writers, therefore, being misled by this faulty transcription, very naturally conclude that the middle price, or six shillings the quarter, equal to about eighteen shillings of our present money, was the ordinary or average price of wheat at that time.

In the statute of Tumbrel and Pillory, enacted nearly about the same time, the price of ale is regulated according to every sixpence rise in the price of barley, from two shillings, to four shillings the quarter. That four shillings, however, was not considered as the highest price to which barley might frequently rise in those times, and that these prices were only given as an example of the proportion which ought to be observed in all other prices, whether higher or lower, we may infer from the last words of the statute: "*Et sic deinceps crescetur vel diminuetur per sex denarios.*" The expression is very slovenly, but the meaning is plain enough, "that the price of ale is in this manner to be increased or diminished according to every sixpence rise or fall in the price of barley." In the composition of this statute, the legislature itself seems to have been as negligent as the copiers were in the transcription of the other.

In an ancient manuscript of the *Regiam Majestatem*, an old Scotch law book, there is a statute of assize, in which the price of bread is regulated according to all the different prices of wheat, from ten pence to three shillings the Scotch boll, equal to about half an English quarter. Three shillings Scotch, at the time when this assize is supposed to have been enacted, were equal to about nine shillings sterling of our present money Mr. Ruddiman seems {See his Preface to Anderson's Diplomata Scotiae.} to conclude from this, that three shillings was the highest price to which wheat ever rose in those times, and that ten pence, a shilling, or at most two shillings, were the ordinary prices. Upon consulting the manuscript, however, it appears evidently, that all these prices are only set down as examples of the proportion which ought to be observed between the respective prices of wheat and bread. The last words of the statute are "*reliqua judicabis secundum praescripta, habendo respectum ad pretium bladi.*"—"You shall judge of the remaining cases, according to what is above written, having respect to the price of corn."

Thirdly, they seem to have been misled too, by the very low price at which wheat was sometimes sold in very ancient times; and to have imagined, that as its lowest price was then much lower than in later times its ordinary price must likewise have been much lower. They might have found, however, that in those ancient times its highest price was fully as much above, as its lowest price was below any thing that had ever been known in later times. Thus, in 1270, Fleetwood gives us two prices of the quarter of wheat. The one is four pounds sixteen shillings of the money of those times, equal to fourteen pounds eight shillings of that of the present; the other is six pounds eight shillings, equal to nineteen pounds four shillings of our present money. No price can be found in the end of the fifteenth, or beginning of the sixteenth century, which approaches to the extravagance of these. The price of corn, though at all times liable to variation varies most in those turbulent and disorderly societies, in which the interruption of all commerce and communication hinders the plenty of one part of the country from relieving the scarcity of another. In the disorderly state of England under the Plantagenets, who governed it from about the middle of the twelfth till towards the end of the fifteenth century, one district might be in plenty, while another, at no great distance, by having its crop destroyed, either by some accident of the seasons, or by the incursion of some neighboring baron, might be suffering all the horrors of a famine; and yet if the lands of some hostile lord were interposed between them, the one might not be able to give the least assistance to the other. Under the vigorous administration of the Tudors, who governed England during the latter part of the fifteenth, and through the whole of the sixteenth century, no baron was powerful enough to dare to disturb the public security.

The reader will find at the end of this chapter all the prices of wheat which have been collected by Fleetwood, from 1202 to 1597, both inclusive, reduced to the money of the present times, and digested, according to the order of time, into seven divisions of twelve years each. At the end of each division, too, he will find the average price of the twelve years of which it consists. In that long period of time, Fleetwood has been able to collect the prices of no more than eighty years; so that four years are wanting to make out the last twelve years. I have added, therefore, from the accounts of Eton college, the prices of 1598, 1599, 1600, and 1601. It is the only addition which I have made. The reader will see, that from the beginning of the thirteenth till after the middle of the sixteenth century, the average price of each twelve years grows gradually lower and lower; and that towards the end of the sixteenth century it begins to rise again. The prices, indeed, which Fleetwood has been able to collect, seem to have been those chiefly which were remarkable for extraordinary dearness or cheapness; and I do not pretend that any very certain conclusion can be drawn from them. So far, however, as they prove any thing at all, they confirm the account which I have been endeavoring to give. Fleetwood himself, however, seems, with most other writers, to have believed, that, during all this period, the value of silver, in consequence of its increasing abundance, was continually diminishing. The prices of corn, which he himself has collected, certainly do not agree with this opinion. They agree perfectly with that of Mr. Dupré de St Maur, and with that which I have been endeavoring to explain. Bishop Fleetwood and Mr. Dupré de St Maur are the two authors who seem to have collected, with the greatest diligence and fidelity, the prices of things in ancient times. It is some what curious that, though their opinions are so very different, their facts, so far as they relate to the price of corn at least, should coincide so very exactly.

It is not, however, so much from the low price of corn, as from that of some other parts of the rude produce of land, that the most judicious writers have inferred the great value of silver in those very ancient times. Corn, it has been said, being a sort of manufacture, was, in those rude ages, much dearer in proportion than the greater part of other commodities; it is meant, I suppose, than the greater part of unmanufactured commodities, such as cattle, poultry, game of all kinds, etc. That in those times of poverty and barbarism these were proportionably much cheaper than corn, is undoubtedly true. But this cheapness was not the effect of the high value of silver, but of the low value of those commodities. It was not because silver would in such times purchase or represent a greater quantity of labor, but because such commodities would purchase or represent a much smaller quantity than in times of more opulence and improvement. Silver must certainly be cheaper in Spanish America than in Europe; in the country where it is produced, than in the country to which it is brought, at the expense of a long carriage both by land and by sea, of a freight, and an insurance. One-and-twenty pence halfpenny sterling, however, we are told by Ulloa, was, not many years ago, at Buenos Ayres, the price of an ox chosen from a herd of three or four hundred. Sixteen shillings sterling, we are told by Mr. Byron, was the price of a good horse in the capital of Chili. In a country naturally fertile, but of which the far greater part is altogether uncultivated, cattle, poultry, game of all kinds, etc. as they can be acquired with a very small quantity of labor, so they will purchase or command but a very small quantity. The low money price for which they may be sold, is no proof that the real value of silver is there very high, but that the real value of those commodities is very low.

Labor, it must always be remembered, and not any particular commodity, or set of commodities, is the real measure of the value both of silver and of all other commodities.

But in countries almost waste, or but thinly inhabited, cattle, poultry, game of all kinds, etc. as they are the spontaneous productions of Nature, so she frequently produces them in much greater quantities than the consumption of the inhabitants requires. In such a state of things, the supply commonly exceeds the demand. In different states of society, in different states of improvement, therefore, such commodities will represent, or be equivalent, to very different quantities of labor.

In every state of society, in every stage of improvement, corn is the production of human industry. But the average produce of every sort of industry is always suited, more or less exactly, to the average consumption; the average supply to the average demand. In every different stage of improvement, besides, the raising of equal quantities of corn in the same soil and climate, will, at an average, require nearly equal quantities of labor; or, what comes to the same thing, the price of nearly equal quantities; the continual increase of the productive powers of labor, in an improved state of cultivation, being more or less counterbalanced by the continual increasing price of cattle, the principal instruments of agriculture. Upon all these accounts, therefore, we may rest assured, that equal quantities of corn will, in every state of society, in every stage of improvement, more nearly represent, or be equivalent to, equal quantities of labor, than equal quantities of any other part of the rude produce of land. Corn, accordingly, it has already been observed, is, in all the different stages of wealth and improvement, a more accurate measure of value than any other commodity or set of commodities. In all those different stages, therefore, we can judge better of the real value of silver, by comparing it with corn, than by comparing it with any other commodity or set of commodities.

Corn, besides, or whatever else is the common and favorite vegetable food of the people, constitutes, in every civilized country, the principal part of the subsistence of the laborer. In consequence of the extension of agriculture, the land of every country produces a much greater quantity of vegetable than of animal food, and the laborer everywhere lives chiefly upon the wholesome food that is cheapest and most abundant. Butcher's meat, except in the most thriving countries, or where labor is most highly rewarded, makes but an insignificant part of his subsistence; poultry makes a still smaller part of it, and game no part of it. In France, and even in Scotland, where labor is somewhat better rewarded than in France, the laboring poor seldom eat butcher's meat, except upon holidays, and other extraordinary occasions. The money price of labor, therefore, depends much more upon the average money price of corn, the subsistence of the laborer, than upon that of butcher's meat, or of any other part of the rude produce of land. The real value of gold and silver, therefore, the real quantity of labor which they can purchase or command, depends much more upon the quantity of corn which they can purchase or command, than upon that of butcher's meat, or any other part of the rude produce of land.

Such slight observations, however, upon the prices either of corn or of other commodities, would not probably have misled so many intelligent authors, had they not been influenced at the same time by the popular notion, that as the quantity of silver naturally increases in every country with the increase of wealth, so its value diminishes as its quantity increases. This notion, however, seems to be altogether groundless.

The quantity of the precious metals may increase in any country from two different causes; either, first, from the increased abundance of the mines which supply it; or, secondly, from the increased wealth of the people, from the increased produce of their annual labor. The first of these causes is no doubt necessarily connected with the diminution of the value of the precious metals; but the second is not.

When more abundant mines are discovered, a greater quantity of the precious metals is brought to market; and the quantity of the necessaries and conveniences of life for which they must be exchanged being the same as before, equal quantities of the metals must be exchanged for smaller quantities of commodities. So far, therefore, as the increase of the quantity of the precious metals in any country arises from the increased abundance of the mines, it is necessarily connected with some diminution of their value.

When, on the contrary, the wealth of any country increases, when the annual produce of its labor becomes gradually greater and greater, a greater quantity of coin becomes necessary in order to circulate a greater quantity of commodities: and the people, as they can afford it, as they have more commodities to give for it, will naturally purchase a greater and a greater quantity of plate. The quantity of their coin will increase from necessity; the quantity of their plate from vanity and ostentation, or from the same reason that the quantity of fine statues, pictures, and of every other luxury and curiosity, is likely to increase among them. But as statuaries and painters are not likely to be worse rewarded in times of wealth and prosperity, than in times of poverty and depression, so gold and silver are not likely to be worse paid for.

The price of gold and silver, when the accidental discovery of more abundant mines does not keep it down, as it naturally rises with the wealth of every country; so, whatever be the state of the mines, it is at all times naturally higher in a rich than in a poor country. Gold and silver, like all other commodities, naturally seek the market where the best price is given for them, and the best price is commonly given for every thing in the country which can best afford it. Labor, it must be remembered, is the ultimate price which is paid for every thing; and in countries where labor is equally well rewarded, the money price of labor will be in proportion to that of the subsistence of the laborer. But gold and silver will naturally exchange for a greater quantity of subsistence in a rich than in a poor country; in a country which abounds with subsistence, than in one which is but indifferently supplied with it. If the two countries are at a great distance, the difference may be very great; because, though the metals naturally fly from the worse to the better market, yet it may be difficult to transport them in such quantities as to bring their price nearly to a level in both. If the countries are near, the difference will be smaller, and may sometimes be scarce perceptible; because in this case the transportation will be easy. China is a much richer country than any part of Europe, and the difference between the price of subsistence in China and in Europe is very great. Rice in China is much cheaper than wheat is any where in Europe. England is a much richer country than Scotland, but the difference between the money price of corn in those two countries is much smaller, and is but just perceptible. In proportion to the quantity or measure, Scotch corn generally appears to be a good deal cheaper than English; but, in proportion to its quality, it is certainly somewhat dearer. Scotland receives almost every year very large supplies from England, and every commodity must commonly be somewhat dearer in the country to which it is brought than in that from which it comes. English corn, therefore, must be dearer in Scotland than in England; and yet in proportion to its quality, or to the quantity and goodness of the flour or meal which can be made from it, it cannot commonly be sold higher there than the Scotch corn which comes to market in competition with it.

The difference between the money price of labor in China and in Europe, is still greater than that between the money price of subsistence; because the real recompense of labor is higher in Europe than in China, the greater part of Europe being in an improving state, while China seems to be standing still. The money price of labor is lower in Scotland than in England, because the real recompense of labor is much lower: Scotland, though advancing to greater wealth, advances much more slowly than England. The frequency of emigration from Scotland, and the rarity of it from England, sufficiently prove that the demand for labor is very different in the two countries. The proportion between the real recompense of labor in different countries, it must be remembered, is naturally regulated, not by their actual wealth or poverty, but by their advancing, stationary, or declining condition.

Gold and silver, as they are naturally of the greatest value among the richest, so they are naturally of the least value among the poorest nations. Among savages, the poorest of all nations, they are scarce of any value.

In great towns, corn is always dearer than in remote parts of the country. This, however, is the effect, not of the real cheapness of silver, but of the real dearness of corn. It does not cost less labor to bring silver to the great town than to the remote parts of the country; but it costs a great deal more to bring corn.

In some very rich and commercial countries, such as Holland and the territory of Genoa, corn is dear for the same reason that it is dear in great towns. They do not produce enough to maintain their inhabitants. They are rich in the industry and skill of their artificers and manufacturers, in every sort of machinery which can facilitate and abridge labor; in shipping, and in all the other instruments and means of carriage and commerce: but they are poor in corn, which, as it must be brought to them from distant countries, must, by an addition to its price, pay for the carriage from those countries. It does not cost less labor to bring silver to Amsterdam than to Dantzic; but it costs a great deal more to bring corn. The real cost of silver must be nearly the same in both places; but that of corn must be very different. Diminish the real opulence either of Holland or of the territory of Genoa, while the number of their inhabitants remains the same; diminish their power of supplying themselves from distant countries; and the price of corn, instead of sinking with that diminution in the quantity of their silver, which must necessarily accompany this declension, either as its cause or as its effect, will rise to the price of a famine. When we are in want of necessaries, we must part with all superfluities, of which the value, as it rises in times of opulence and prosperity, so it sinks in times of poverty and distress. It is otherwise with necessaries. Their real price, the quantity of labor which they can purchase or command, rises in times of poverty and distress, and sinks in times of opulence and prosperity, which are always times of great abundance; for they could not otherwise be times of opulence and prosperity. Corn is a necessary, silver is only a superfluity.

Whatever, therefore, may have been the increase in the quantity of the precious metals, which, during the period between the middle of the fourteenth and that of the sixteenth century, arose from the increase of wealth and improvement, it could have no tendency to diminish their value, either in Great Britain, or in my other part of Europe. If those who have collected the prices of things in ancient times, therefore, had, during this period, no reason to infer the diminution of the value of silver from any observations which they had made upon the prices either of corn, or of other commodities, they had still less reason to infer it from any supposed increase of wealth and improvement.

Second Period

But how various so ever may have been the opinions of the learned concerning the progress of the value of silver during the first period, they are unanimous concerning it during the second.

From about 1570 to about 1640, during a period of about seventy years, the variation in the proportion between the value of silver and that of corn held a quite opposite course. Silver sunk in its real value, or would exchange for a smaller quantity of labor than before; and corn rose in its nominal price, and, instead of being commonly sold for about two ounces of silver the quarter, or about ten shillings of our present money, came to be sold for six and eight ounces of silver the quarter, or about thirty and forty shillings of our present money.

The discovery of the abundant mines of America seems to have been the sole cause of this diminution in the value of silver, in proportion to that of corn. It is accounted for, accordingly, in the same manner by every body; and there never has been any dispute, either about the fact, or about the cause of it. The greater part of Europe was, during this period, advancing in industry and improvement, and the demand for silver must consequently have been increasing; but the increase of the supply had, it seems, so far exceeded that of the demand, that the value of that metal sunk considerably. The discovery of the mines of America, it is to be observed, does not seem to have had any very sensible effect upon the prices of things in England till after 1570; though even the mines of Potosi had been discovered more than twenty years before.

From 1595 to 1620, both inclusive, the average price of the quarter of nine bushels of the best wheat, at Windsor market, appears, from the accounts of Eton college, to have been £2:1:6 9/13. From which sum, neglecting the fraction, and deducting a ninth, or 4s. 7 1/3d., the price of the quarter of eight bushels comes out to have been £1:16:10 2/3. And from this sum, neglecting likewise the fraction, and deducting a ninth, or 4s. 1 1/9d., for the difference between the price of the best wheat and that of the middle wheat, the price of the middle wheat comes out to have been about £1:12:8 8/9, or about six ounces and one-third of an ounce of silver.

From 1621 to 1636, both inclusive, the average price of the same measure of the best wheat, at the same market, appears, from the same accounts, to have been £2:10s.; from which, making the like deductions as in the foregoing case, the average price of the quarter of eight bushels of middle wheat comes out to have been £1:19:6, or about seven ounces and two-thirds of an ounce of silver.

Third Period

Between 1630 and 1640, or about 1636, the effect of the discovery of the mines of America, in reducing the value of silver, appears to have been completed, and the value of that metal seems never to have sunk lower in proportion to that of corn than it was about that time. It seems to have risen somewhat in the course of the present century, and it had probably begun to do so, even some time before the end of the last.

From 1637 to 1700, both inclusive, being the sixty-four last years of the last century the average price of the quarter of nine bushels of the best wheat, at Windsor market, appears, from the same accounts, to have been £2:11:0 1/3, which is only 1s. 0 1/3d. dearer than it had been during the sixteen years before. But, in the course of these sixty-four years, there happened two events, which must have produced a much greater scarcity of corn than what the course of the season is would otherwise have occasioned, and which, therefore, without supposing any further reduction in the value of silver, will much more than account for this very small enhancement of price.

The first of these events was the civil war, which, by discouraging tillage and interrupting commerce, must have raised the price of corn much above what the course of the seasons would otherwise have occasioned. It must have had this effect, more or less, at all the different markets in the kingdom, but particularly at those in the neighborhood of London, which require to be supplied from the greatest distance. In 1648, accordingly, the price of the best wheat, at Windsor market, appears, from the same accounts, to have been £4:5s., and, in 1649, to have been £4, the quarter of nine bushels. The excess of those two years above £2:10s. (The average price of the sixteen years preceding 1637 is £3:5s., which, divided among the sixty-four last years of the last century, will alone very nearly account for that small enhancement of price which seems to have taken place in them.) These, however, though the highest, are by no means the only high prices which seem to have been occasioned by the civil wars.

The second event was the bounty upon the exportation of corn, granted in 1688. The bounty, it has been thought by many people, by encouraging tillage, may, in a long course of years, have occasioned a greater abundance, and, consequently, a greater cheapness of corn in the home market, than what would otherwise have taken place there. How far the bounty could produce this effect at any time I shall examine hereafter: I shall only observe at present, that between 1688 and 1700, it had not time to produce any such effect. During this short period, its only effect must have been, by encouraging the exportation of the surplus produce of every year, and thereby hindering the abundance of one year from compensating the scarcity of another, to raise the price in the home market. The scarcity which prevailed in England, from 1693 to 1699, both inclusive, though no doubt principally owing to the badness of the seasons, and, therefore, extending through a considerable part of Europe, must have been somewhat enhanced by the bounty. In 1699, accordingly, the further exportation of corn was prohibited for nine months.

There was a third event which occurred in the course of the same period, and which, though it could not occasion any scarcity of corn, nor, perhaps, any augmentation in the real quantity of silver which was usually paid for it, must necessarily have occasioned some augmentation in the nominal sum. This event was the great debasement of the silver coin, by clipping and wearing. This evil had begun in the reign of Charles II and had gone on continually increasing till 1695; at which time, as we may learn from Mr. Lowndes, the current silver coin was, at an average, near five-and-twenty percent below its standard value. But the nominal sum which constitutes the market price of every commodity is necessarily regulated, not so much by the quantity of silver, which, according to the standard, ought to be contained in it, as by that which, it is found by experience, actually is contained in it. This nominal sum, therefore, is necessarily higher when the coin is much debased by clipping and wearing, than when near to its standard value.

In the course of the present century, the silver coin has not at any time been more below its standard weight than it is at present. But though very much defaced, its value has been kept up by that of the gold coin, for which it is exchanged. For though, before the late recoinage, the gold coin was a good deal defaced too, it was less so than the silver. In 1695, on the contrary, the value of the silver coin was not kept up by the gold coin; a guinea then commonly exchanging for thirty shillings of the worn and clipt silver. Before the late recoinage of the gold, the price of silver bullion was seldom higher than five shillings and seven pence an ounce, which is but five pence above the mint price. But in 1695, the common price of silver bullion was six shillings and five pence an ounce, {Lowndes's *Essay on the Silver Coin*, 68.} which is fifteen pence above the mint price. Even before the late recoinage of the gold, therefore, the coin, gold and silver together, when compared with silver bullion, was not supposed to be more than eight percent below its standard value. In 1695, on the contrary, it had been supposed to be near five-and-twenty percent below that value. But in the beginning of the present century, that is, immediately after the great recoinage in King William's time, the greater part of the current silver coin must have been still nearer to its standard weight than it is at present. In the course of the present century, too, there has been no great public calamity, such as a civil war, which could either discourage tillage, or interrupt the interior commerce of the country. And though the bounty which has taken place through the greater part of this century, must always raise the price of corn somewhat higher than it otherwise would be in the actual state of tillage; yet, as in the course of this century, the bounty has had full time to produce all the good effects commonly imputed to it to encourage tillage, and thereby to increase the quantity of corn in the home market, it may, upon the principles of a system which I shall explain and examine hereafter, be supposed to have done something to lower the price of that commodity the one way, as well as to raise it the other. It is by many people supposed to have done more. In the sixty-four years of the present century, accordingly, the average price of the quarter of nine bushels of the best wheat, at Windsor market, appears, by the accounts of Eton college, to have been £2:0:6 10/32, which is about ten shillings and six-pence, or more than five-and-twenty percent cheaper than it had been during the sixty-four last years of the last century; and about nine shillings and sixpence cheaper than it had been during the sixteen years preceding 1636, when the discovery of the abundant mines of America may be supposed to have produced its full effect; and about one shilling cheaper than it had been in the twenty-six years preceding 1620, before that discovery can well be supposed to have produced its full effect. According to this account, the average price of middle wheat, during these sixty-four first years of the present century, comes out to have been about thirty-two shillings the quarter of eight bushels.

The value of silver, therefore, seems to have risen somewhat in proportion to that of corn during the course of the present century, and it had probably begun to do so even some time before the end of the last.

In 1687, the price of the quarter of nine bushels of the best wheat, at Windsor market, was £1:5:2, the lowest price at which it had ever been from 1595.

In 1688, Mr. Gregory King, a man famous for his knowledge in matters of this kind, estimated the average price of wheat, in years of moderate plenty, to be to the grower 3s. 6d. the bushel, or eight-and-twenty shillings the quarter. The grower's price I under-stand to be the same with what is sometimes called the contract price, or the price at which a farmer contracts for a certain number of years to deliver a certain quantity of corn to a dealer. As a contract of this kind saves the farmer the expense and trouble of mar-keting, the contract price is generally lower than what is supposed to be the average mar-ket price. Mr. King had judged eight-and-twenty shillings the quarter to be at that time the ordinary contract price in years of moderate plenty. Before the scarcity occasioned by the late extraordinary course of bad seasons, it was, I have been assured, the ordinary contract price in all common years.

In 1688 was granted the parliamentary bounty upon the exportation of corn. The country gentlemen, who then composed a still greater proportion of the legislature than they do at present, had felt that the money price of corn was falling. The bounty was an expedient to raise it artificially to the high price at which it had frequently been sold in the times of Charles I and II. It was to take place, therefore, till wheat was so high as forty-eight shillings the quarter; that is, twenty shillings, or 5-7ths dearer than Mr. King had, in that very year, estimated the grower's price to be in times of moderate plenty. If his cal-culations deserve any part of the reputation which they have obtained very universally, eight-and-forty shillings the quarter was a price which, without some such expedient as the bounty, could not at that time be expected, except in years of extraordinary scarcity. But the government of King William was not then fully settled. It was in no condition to refuse anything to the country gentlemen, from whom it was, at that very time, so-liciting the first establishment of the annual land-tax.

The value of silver, therefore, in proportion to that of corn, had probably risen some-what before the end of the last century; and it seems to have continued to do so during the course of the greater part of the present, though the necessary operation of the bounty must have hindered that rise from being so sensible as it otherwise would have been in the actual state of tillage.

In plentiful years, the bounty, by occasioning an extraordinary exportation, necessarily raises the price of corn above what it otherwise would be in those years. To encourage tillage, by keeping up the price of corn, even in the most plentiful years, was the avowed end of the institution.

In years of great scarcity, indeed, the bounty has generally been suspended. It must, however, have had some effect upon the prices of many of those years. By the extraordinary exportation which it occasions in years of plenty, it must frequently hinder the plenty of one year from compensating the scarcity of another.

Both in years of plenty and in years of scarcity, therefore, the bounty raises the price of corn above what it naturally would be in the actual state of tillage. If during the sixty-four first years of the present century, therefore, the average price has been lower than during the sixty-four last years of the last century, it must, in the same state of tillage, have been much more so, had it not been for this operation of the bounty.

But, without the bounty, it may be said the state of tillage would not have been the same. What may have been the effects of this institution upon the agriculture of the country, I shall endeavor to explain hereafter, when I come to treat particularly of bounties. I shall only observe at present, that this rise in the value of silver, in proportion to that of corn, has not been peculiar to England. It has been observed to have taken place in France during the same period, and nearly in the same proportion, too, by three very faithful, diligent, and laborious collectors of the prices of corn, Mr. Dupré de St Maur, Mr. Messance, and the author of the Essay on the Police of Grain. But in France, till 1764, the exportation of grain was by law prohibited; and it is somewhat difficult to suppose, that nearly the same diminution of price which took place in one country, notwithstanding this prohibition, should, in another, be owing to the extraordinary encouragement given to exportation.

It would be more proper, perhaps, to consider this variation in the average money price of corn as the effect rather of some gradual rise in the real value of silver in the European market, than of any fall in the real average value of corn. Corn, it has already been observed, is, at distant periods of time, a more accurate measure of value than either silver or, perhaps, any other commodity. When, after the discovery of the abundant mines of America, corn rose to three and four times its former money price, this change was universally ascribed, not to any rise in the real value of corn, but to a fall in the real value of silver. If, during the sixty-four first years of the present century, therefore, the average money price of corn has fallen somewhat below what it had been during the greater part of the last century, we should, in the same manner, impute this change, not to any fall in the real value of corn, but to some rise in the real value of silver in the European market.

The high price of corn during these ten or twelve years past, indeed, has occasioned a suspicion that the real value of silver still continues to fall in the European market. This high price of corn, however, seems evidently to have been the effect of the extraordinary unfavorableness of the seasons, and ought, therefore, to be regarded, not as a permanent, but as a transitory and occasional event. The seasons, for these ten or twelve years past, have been unfavorable through the greater part of Europe; and the disorders of Poland have very much increased the scarcity in all those countries, which, in dear years, used to be supplied from that market. So long a course of bad seasons, though not a very common event, is by no means a singular one; and whoever has inquired much into the history of the prices of corn in former times, will be at no loss to recollect several other examples of the same kind. Ten years of extraordinary scarcity, besides, are not more wonderful than ten years of extraordinary plenty. The low price of corn, from 1741 to 1750, both inclusive, may very well be set in opposition to its high price during these last eight or ten years. From 1741 to 1750, the average price of the quarter of nine bushels of the best wheat, at Windsor market, it appears from the accounts of Eton College, was only £1:13:9 4/5, which is nearly 6s.3d. below the average price of the sixty-four first years of the present century. The average price of the quarter of eight bushels of middle wheat comes out, according to this account, to have been, during these ten years, only £1:6:8.

Between 1741 and 1750, however, the bounty must have hindered the price of corn from falling so low in the home market as it naturally would have done. During these ten years, the quantity of all sorts of grain exported, it appears from the customhouse books, amounted to no less than 8,029,156 quarters, one bushel. The bounty paid for this amounted to £1,514,962:17:4 1/2. In 1749, accordingly, Mr. Pelham, at that time prime minister, observed to the house of commons, that, for the three years preceding, a very extraordinary sum had been paid as bounty for the exportation of corn. He had good reason to make this observation, and in the following year he might have had still better. In that single year, the bounty paid amounted to no less than £324,176:10:6. {See *Tracts on the Corn Trade*, Tract 3,} It is unnecessary to observe how much this forced exportation must have raised the price of corn above what it otherwise would have been in the home market.

At the end of the accounts annexed to this chapter the reader will find the particular account of those ten years separated from the rest. He will find there, too, the particular account of the preceding ten years, of which the average is likewise below, though not so much below, the general average of the sixty-four first years of the century. The year 1740, however, was a year of extraordinary scarcity. These twenty years preceding 1750 may very well be set in opposition to the twenty preceding 1770. As the former were a good deal below the general average of the century, notwithstanding the intervention of one or two dear years; so the latter have been a good deal above it, notwithstanding the intervention of one or two cheap ones, of 1759, for example. If the former have not been as much below the general average as the latter have been above it, we ought probably to impute it to the bounty. The change has evidently been too sudden to be ascribed to any change in the value of silver, which is always slow and gradual. The suddenness of the effect can be accounted for only by a cause which can operate suddenly, the accidental variations of the seasons.

The money price of labor in Great Britain has, indeed, risen during the course of the present century. This, however, seems to be the effect, not so much of any diminution in the value of silver in the European market, as of an increase in the demand for labor in Great Britain, arising from the great, and almost universal prosperity of the country.

In France, a country not altogether so prosperous, the money price of labor has, since the middle of the last century, been observed to sink gradually with the average money price of corn. Both in the last century and in the present, the day wages of common labor are there said to have been pretty uniformly about the twentieth part of the average price of the septier of wheat; a measure which contains a little more than four Winchester bushels. In Great Britain, the real recompense of labor, it has already been shown, the real quantities of the necessaries and conveniences of life which are given to the laborer, has increased considerably during the course of the present century. The rise in its money price seems to have been the effect, not of any diminution of the value of silver in the general market of Europe, but of a rise in the real price of labor, in the particular market of Great Britain, owing to the peculiarly happy circumstances of the country.

For some time after the first discovery of America, silver would continue to sell at its former, or not much below its former price. The profits of mining would for some time be very great, and much above their natural rate. Those who imported that metal into Europe, however, would soon find that the whole annual importation could not be disposed of at this high price. Silver would gradually exchange for a smaller and a smaller quantity of goods. Its price would sink gradually lower and lower, till it fell to its natural price; or to what was just sufficient to pay, according to their natural rates, the wages of the labor, the profits of the stock, and the rent of the land, which must be paid in order to bring it from the mine to the market. In the greater part of the silver mines of Peru, the tax of the king of Spain, amounting to a tenth of the gross produce, eats up, it has already been observed, the whole rent of the land. This tax was originally a half; it soon afterwards fell to a third, then to a fifth, and at last to a tenth, at which late it still continues. In the greater part of the silver mines of Peru, this, it seems, is all that remains, after replacing the stock of the undertaker of the work, together with its ordinary profits; and it seems to be universally acknowledged that these profits, which were once very high, are now as low as they can well be, consistently with carrying on the works.

The tax of the king of Spain was reduced to a fifth of the registered silver in 1504 {Solorzano, vol, ii}, one-and-forty years before 1545, the date of the discovery of the mines of Potosi. In the course of ninety years, or before 1636, these mines, the most fertile in all America, had time sufficient to produce their full effect, or to reduce the value of silver in the European market as low as it could well fall, while it continued to pay this tax to the king of Spain. Ninety years is time sufficient to reduce any commodity, of which there is no monopoly, to its natural price, or to the lowest price at which, while it pays a particular tax, it can continue to be sold for any considerable time together.

The price of silver in the European market might, perhaps, have fallen still lower, and it might have become necessary either to reduce the tax upon it, not only to one-tenth, as in 1736, but to one-twentieth, in the same manner as that upon gold, or to give up working the greater part of the American mines which are now wrought. The gradual increase of the demand for silver, or the gradual enlargement of the market for the produce of the silver mines of America, is probably the cause which has prevented this from happening, and which has not only kept up the value of silver in the European market, but has perhaps even raised it somewhat higher than it was about the middle of the last century.

Since the first discovery of America, the market for the produce of its silver mines has been growing gradually more and more extensive.

First, the market of Europe has become gradually more and more extensive. Since the discovery of America, the greater part of Europe has been much improved. England, Holland, France, and Germany; even Sweden, Denmark, and Russia, have all advanced considerably, both in agriculture and in manufactures. Italy seems not to have gone backwards. The fall of Italy preceded the conquest of Peru. Since that time it seems rather to have recovered a little. Spain and Portugal, indeed, are supposed to have gone backwards. Portugal, however, is but a very small part of Europe, and the declension of Spain is not, perhaps, so great as is commonly imagined. In the beginning of the sixteenth century, Spain was a very poor country, even in comparison with France, which has been so much improved since that time. It was the well-known remark of the emperor Charles V who had traveled so frequently through both countries, that every thing abounded in France, but that every thing was wanting in Spain. The increasing produce of the agriculture and manufactures of Europe must necessarily have required a gradual increase in the quantity of silver coin to circulate it; and the increasing number of wealthy individuals must have required the like increase in the quantity of their plate and other ornaments of silver.

Secondly, America is itself a new market, for the produce of its own silver mines; and as its advances in agriculture, industry, and population, are much more rapid than those of the most thriving countries in Europe, its demand must increase much more rapidly. The English colonies are altogether a new market, which, partly for coin, and partly for plate, requires a continual augmenting supply of silver through a great continent where there never was any demand before. The greater part, too, of the Spanish and Portuguese colonies, are altogether new markets. New Granada, the Yucatan, Paraguay, and the Brazils, were, before discovered by the Europeans, inhabited by savage nations, who had neither arts nor agriculture. A considerable degree of both has now been introduced into all of them. Even Mexico and Peru, though they cannot be considered as altogether new markets, are certainly much more extensive ones than they ever were before. After all the wonderful tales which have been published concerning the splendid state of those countries in ancient times, whoever reads, with any degree of sober judgment, the history of their first discovery and conquest, will evidently discern that, in arts, agriculture, and commerce, their inhabitants were much more ignorant than the Tartars of the Ukraine are at present. Even the Peruvians, the more civilized nation of the two, though they made use of gold and silver as ornaments, had no coined money of any kind. Their whole commerce was carried on by barter, and there was accordingly scarce any division of labor among them. Those who cultivated the ground, were obliged to build their own houses, to make their own household furniture, their own clothes, shoes, and instruments of agriculture. The few artificers among them are said to have been all maintained by the sovereign, the nobles, and the priests, and were probably their servants or slaves. All the ancient arts of Mexico and Peru have never furnished one single manufacture to Europe. The Spanish armies, though they scarce ever exceeded five hundred men, and frequently did not amount to half that number, found almost everywhere great difficulty in procuring subsistence. The famines which they are said to have occasioned almost wherever they went, in countries, too, which at the same time are represented as very populous and well cultivated, sufficiently demonstrate that the story of this populousness and high cultivation is in a great measure fabulous. The Spanish colonies are under a government in many respects less favorable to agriculture, improvement, and population, than that of the English colonies. They seem, however, to be advancing in all those much more rapidly than any country in Europe. In a fertile soil and happy climate, the great abundance and cheapness of land, a circumstance common to all new colonies, is, it seems, so great an advantage, as to compensate many defects in civil government. Frezier, who visited Peru in 1713, represents Lima as containing between twenty-five and twenty-eight thousand inhabitants. Ulloa, who resided in the same country between 1740 and 1746, represents it as containing more than fifty thousand. The difference in their accounts of the populousness of several other principal towns of Chili and Peru is nearly the same; and as there seems to be no reason to doubt of the good information of either, it marks an increase which is scarce inferior to that of the English colonies. America, therefore, is a new market for the produce of its own silver mines, of which the demand must increase much more rapidly than that of the most thriving country in Europe.

Thirdly, the East Indies is another market for the produce of the silver mines of America, and a market which, from the time of the first discovery of those mines, has been continually taking off a greater and a greater quantity of silver. Since that time, the direct trade between America and the East Indies, which is carried on by means of the Acapulco ships, has been continually augmenting, and the indirect intercourse by the way of Europe has been augmenting in a still greater proportion. During the sixteenth century, the Portuguese were the only European nation who carried on any regular trade to the East Indies. In the last years of that century, the Dutch began to encroach upon this monopoly, and in a few years expelled them from their principal settlements in India. During the greater part of the last century, those two nations divided the most considerable part of the East India trade between them; the trade of the Dutch continually augmenting in a still greater proportion than that of the Portuguese declined. The English and French carried on some trade with India in the last century, but it has been greatly augmented in the course of the present. The East India trade of the Swedes and Danes began in the course of the present century. Even the Muscovites now trade regularly with China, by a sort of caravans which go over land through Siberia and Tartary to Pekin. The East India trade of all these nations, if we except that of the French, which the last war had well nigh annihilated, has been almost continually augmenting. The increasing consumptions of East India goods in Europe is, it seems, so great, as to afford a gradual increase of employment to them all. Tea, for example, was a drug very little used in Europe, before the middle of the last century. At present, the value of the tea annually imported by the English East India company, for the use of their own countrymen, amounts to more than a million and a half a year; and even this is not enough; a great deal more being constantly smuggled into the country from the ports of Holland, from Gottenburgh in Sweden, and from the coast of France, too, as long as the French East India company was in prosperity. The consumption of the porcelain of China, of the spiceries of the Moluccas, of the piece goods of Bengal, and of innumerable other articles, has increased very nearly in a like proportion. The tonnage, accordingly, of all the European shipping employed in the East India trade, at any one time during the last century, was not, perhaps, much greater than that of the English East India company before the late reduction of their shipping.

But in the East Indies, particularly in China and Indostan, the value of the precious metals, when the Europeans first began to trade to those countries, was much higher than in Europe; and it still continues to be so. In rice countries, which generally yield two, sometimes three crops in the year, each of them more plentiful than any common crop of corn, the abundance of food must be much greater than in any corn country of equal extent. Such countries are accordingly much more populous. In them, too, the rich, having a greater superabundance of food to dispose of beyond what they themselves can consume, have the means of purchasing a much greater quantity of the labor of other people. The retinue of a grandee in China or Indostan accordingly is, by all accounts, much more numerous and splendid than that of the richest subjects in Europe. The same superabundance of food, of which they have the disposal, enables them to give a greater quantity of it for all those singular and rare productions which nature furnishes but in very small quantities; such as the precious metals and the precious stones, the great objects of the competition of the rich. Though the mines, therefore, which supplied the Indian market, had been as abundant as those which supplied the European, such commodities would naturally exchange for a greater quantity of food in India than in Europe. But the mines which supplied the Indian market with the precious metals seem to have been a good deal less abundant, and those which supplied it with the precious stones a good deal more so, than the mines which supplied the European. The precious metals, therefore, would naturally exchange in India for a somewhat greater quantity of the precious stones, and for a much greater quantity of food than in Europe. The money price of diamonds, the greatest of all superfluities, would be somewhat lower, and that of food, the first of all necessaries, a great deal lower in the one country than in the other. But the real price of labor, the real quantity of the necessaries of life which is given to the laborer, it has already been observed, is lower both in China and Indostan, the two great markets of India, than it is through the greater part of Europe. The wages of the laborer will there purchase a smaller quantity of food: and as the money price of food is much lower in India than in Europe, the money price of labor is there lower upon a double account; upon account both of the small quantity of food which it will purchase, and of the low price of that food. But in countries of equal art and industry, the money price of the greater part of manufactures will be in proportion to the money price of labor; and in manufacturing art and industry, China and Indostan, though inferior, seem not to be much inferior to any part of Europe. The money price of the greater part of manufactures, therefore, will naturally be much lower in those great empires than it is anywhere in Europe. Through the greater part of Europe, too, the expense of land-carriage increases very much both the real and nominal price of most manufactures. It costs more labor, and therefore more money, to bring first the materials, and afterwards the complete manufacture to market. In China and Indostan, the extent and variety of inland navigations save the greater part of this labor, and consequently of this money, and thereby reduce still lower both the real and the nominal price of the greater part of their manufactures. Upon all these accounts, the precious metals are a commodity which it always has been, and still continues to be, extremely advantageous to carry from Europe to India. There is scarce any commodity which brings a better price there; or which, in proportion to the quantity of labor and commodities which it costs in Europe, will purchase or command a greater quantity of labor and commodities in India. It is more advantageous, too, to carry silver thither than gold; because in China, and the greater part of the other markets of India, the proportion between fine silver and fine gold is but as ten, or at most as twelve to one; whereas in Europe it is as fourteen or fifteen to one. In China, and the greater part of the other markets of India, ten, or at most twelve ounces of silver, will purchase an ounce of gold; in Europe, it requires from fourteen to fifteen ounces. In the cargoes, therefore, of the greater part of European ships which sail to India, silver has generally been one of the most valuable articles. It is the most valuable article in the Acapulco ships which sail to Manilla. The silver of the new continent seems, in this manner, to be one of the principal commodities by which the commerce between the two extremities of the old one is carried on; and it is by means of it, in a great measure, that those distant parts of the world are connected with one another.

In order to supply so very widely extended a market, the quantity of silver annually brought from the mines must not only be sufficient to support that continued increase, both of coin and of plate, which is required in all thriving countries; but to repair that continual waste and consumption of silver which takes place in all countries where that metal is used.

The continual consumption of the precious metals in coin by wearing, and in plate both by wearing and cleaning, is very sensible; and in commodities of which the use is so very widely extended, would alone require a very great annual supply. The consumption of those metals in some particular manufactures, though it may not perhaps be greater upon the whole than this gradual consumption, is, however, much more sensible, as it is much more rapid. In the manufactures of Birmingham alone, the quantity of gold and silver annually employed in gilding and plating, and thereby disqualified from ever afterwards appearing in the shape of those metals, is said to amount to more than fifty thousand pounds sterling. We may from thence form some notion how great must be the annual consumption in all the different parts of the world, either in manufactures of the same kind with those of Birmingham, or in laces, embroideries, gold and silver stuffs, the gilding of books, furniture, etc. A considerable quantity, too, must be annually lost in transporting those metals from one place to another both by sea and by land. In the greater part of the governments of Asia, besides, the almost universal custom of concealing treasures in the bowels of the earth, of which the knowledge frequently dies with the person who makes the concealment, must occasion the loss of a still greater quantity.

The quantity of gold and silver imported at both Cadiz and Lisbon (including not only what comes under register, but what may be supposed to be smuggled) amounts, according to the best accounts, to about six millions sterling a-year.

According to Mr. Meggens {Postscript to the *Universal Merchant* p. 15 and 16. This postscript was not printed till 1756, three years after the publication of the book, which has never had a second edition. The postscript is, therefore, to be found in few copies;

it corrects several errors in the book.}, the annual importation of the precious metals into Spain, at an average of six years, viz. from 1748 to 1753, both inclusive, and into Portugal, at an average of seven years, viz. from 1747 to 1753, both inclusive, amounted in silver to 1,101,107 pounds weight, and in gold to 49,940 pounds weight. The silver, at sixty-two shillings the pound troy, amounts to £3,413,431:10s. sterling. The gold, at forty-four guineas and a half the pound troy, amounts to £2,333,446:14s. sterling. Both together amount to £5,746,878:4s. sterling. The account of what was imported under register, he assures us, is exact. He gives us the detail of the particular places from which the gold and silver were brought, and of the particular quantity of each metal, which, according to the register, each of them afforded. He makes an allowance, too, for the quantity of each metal which, he supposes, may have been smuggled. The great experience of this judicious merchant renders his opinion of considerable weight.

According to the eloquent, and sometimes well-informed, author of the Philosophical and Political History of the Establishment of the Europeans in the two Indies, the annual importation of registered gold and silver into Spain, at an average of eleven years, viz. from 1754 to 1764, both inclusive, amounted to 13,984,185 3/5 piastres of ten reals. On account of what may have been smuggled, however, the whole annual importation, he supposes, may have amounted to seventeen millions of piastres, which, at 4s. 6d. the piastre, is equal to £3,825,000 sterling. He gives the detail, too, of the particular places from which the gold and silver were brought, and of the particular quantities of each metal, which according to the register, each of them afforded. He informs us, too, that if we were to judge of the quantity of gold annually imported from the Brazils to Lisbon, by the amount of the tax paid to the king of Portugal, which it seems, is one-fifth of the standard metal, we might value it at eighteen millions of cruzadoes, or forty-five millions of French livres, equal to about twenty millions sterling. On account of what may have been smuggled, however, we may safely, he says, add to this sum an eighth more, or £250,000 sterling, so that the whole will amount to £2,250,000 sterling. According to this account, therefore, the whole annual importation of the precious metals into both Spain and Portugal, mounts to about £6,075,000 sterling.

Several other very well authenticated, though manuscript accounts, I have been assured, agree in making this whole annual importation amount, at an average, to about six millions sterling; sometimes a little more, sometimes a little less.

The annual importation of the precious metals into Cadiz and Lisbon, indeed, is not equal to the whole annual produce of the mines of America. Some part is sent annually by the Acapulco ships to Manilla; some part is employed in a contraband trade, which the Spanish colonies carry on with those of other European nations; and some part, no doubt, remains in the country. The mines of America, besides, are by no means the only gold and silver mines in the world. They, are, however, by far the most abundant. The produce of all the other mines which are known is insignificant, it is acknowledged, in comparison with theirs; and the far greater part of their produce, it is likewise acknowledged, is annually imported into Cadiz and Lisbon. But the consumption of Birmingham alone, at the rate of fifty thousand pounds a-year, is equal to the hundred-and-twentieth part of this annual importation, at the rate of six millions a-year. The whole annual consumption of gold and silver, therefore, in all the different countries of the world where those metals are used, may, perhaps, be nearly equal to the whole annual produce. The remainder may be no more than sufficient to supply the increasing demand of all thriving countries. It may even have fallen so far short of this demand, as somewhat to raise the price of those metals in the European market.

The quantity of brass and iron annually brought from the mine to the market, is out of all proportion greater than that of gold and silver. We do not, however, upon this account, imagine that those coarse metals are likely to multiply beyond the demand, or to become gradually cheaper and cheaper. Why should we imagine that the precious metals are likely to do so? The coarse metals, indeed, though harder, are put to much harder uses, and, as they are of less value, less care is employed in their preservation. The precious metals, however, are not necessarily immortal any more than they, but are liable, too, to be lost, wasted, and consumed, in a great variety of ways.

The price of all metals, though liable to slow and gradual variations, varies less from year to year than that of almost any other part of the rude produce of land: and the price of the precious metals is even less liable to sudden variations than that of the coarse ones. The durableness of metals is the foundation of this extraordinary steadiness of price. The corn which was brought to market last year will be all, or almost all, consumed, long before the end of this year. But some part of the iron which was brought from the mine two or three hundred years ago, may be still in use, and, perhaps, some part of the gold which was brought from it two or three thousand years ago. The different masses of corn, which, in different years, must supply the consumption of the world, will always be nearly in proportion to the respective produce of those different years. But the proportion between the different masses of iron which may be in use in two different years, will be very little affected by any accidental difference in the produce of the iron mines of those two years; and the proportion between the masses of gold will be still less affected by any such difference in the produce of the gold mines. Though the produce of the greater part of metallic mines, therefore, varies, perhaps, still more from year to year than that of the greater part of corn fields, those variations have not the same effect upon the price of the one species of commodities as upon that of the other.

Variations in the Proportion Between the Respective Values of Gold and Silver.

Before the discovery of the mines of America, the value of fine gold to fine silver was regulated in the different mines of Europe, between the proportions of one to ten and one to twelve; that is, an ounce of fine gold was supposed to be worth from ten to twelve ounces of fine silver. About the middle of the last century, it came to be regulated, between the proportions of one to fourteen and one to fifteen; that is, an ounce of fine gold came to be supposed worth between fourteen and fifteen ounces of fine silver. Gold rose in its nominal value, or in the quantity of silver which was given for it. Both metals sunk in their real value, or in the quantity of labor which they could purchase; but silver sunk more than gold. Though both the gold and silver mines of America exceeded in fertility all those which had ever been known before, the fertility of the silver mines had, it seems, been proportionally still greater than that of the gold ones.

The great quantities of silver carried annually from Europe to India, have, in some of the English settlements, gradually reduced the value of that metal in proportion to gold. In the mint of Calcutta, an ounce of fine gold is supposed to be worth fifteen ounces of fine silver, in the same manner as in Europe. It is in the mint, perhaps, rated too high for the value which it bears in the market of Bengal. In China, the proportion of gold to silver still continues as one to ten, or one to twelve. In Japan, it is said to be as one to eight.

The proportion between the quantities of gold and silver annually imported into Europe, according to Mr. Meggens' account, is as one to twenty-two nearly; that is, for one ounce of gold there are imported a little more than twenty-two ounces of silver. The great quantity of silver sent annually to the East Indies reduces, he supposes, the quantities of those metals which remain in Europe to the proportion of one to fourteen or fifteen, the proportion of their values. The proportion between their values, he seems to think, must necessarily be the same as that between their quantities, and would therefore be as one to twenty-two, were it not for this greater exportation of silver.

But the ordinary proportion between the respective values of two commodities is not necessarily the same as that between the quantities of them which are commonly in the market. The price of an ox, reckoned at ten guineas, is about three score times the price of a lamb, reckoned at 3s. 6d. It would be absurd, however, to infer from thence, that there are commonly in the market three score lambs for one ox; and it would be just as absurd to infer, because an ounce of gold will commonly purchase from fourteen or fifteen ounces of silver, that there are commonly in the market only fourteen or fifteen ounces of silver for one ounce of gold.

The quantity of silver commonly in the market, it is probable, is much greater in proportion to that of gold, than the value of a certain quantity of gold is to that of an equal quantity of silver. The whole quantity of a cheap commodity brought to market is commonly not only greater, but of greater value, than the whole quantity of a dear one. The whole quantity of bread annually brought to market, is not only greater, but of greater value, than the whole quantity of butcher's meat; the whole quantity of butcher's meat, than the whole quantity of poultry; and the whole quantity of poultry, than the whole quantity of wild fowl. There are so many more purchasers for the cheap than for the dear commodity, that, not only a greater quantity of it, but a greater value can commonly be disposed of. The whole quantity, therefore, of the cheap commodity, must commonly be greater in proportion to the whole quantity of the dear one, than the value of a certain quantity of the dear one, is to the value of an equal quantity of the cheap one. When we compare the precious metals with one another, silver is a cheap, and gold a dear commodity. We ought naturally to expect, therefore, that there should always be in the market, not only a greater quantity, but a greater value of silver than of gold. Let any man, who has a little of both, compare his own silver with his gold plate, and he will probably find, that not only the quantity, but the value of the former, greatly exceeds that of the latter. Many people, besides, have a good deal of silver who have no gold plate, which, even with those who have it, is generally confined to watch-cases, snuff-boxes, and such like trinkets, of which the whole amount is seldom of great value. In the British coin, indeed, the value of the gold preponderates greatly, but it is not so in that of all countries.

In the coin of some countries, the value of the two metals is nearly equal. In the Scotch coin, before the union with England, the gold preponderated very little, though it did somewhat {See Ruddiman's Preface to Anderson's Diplomata, etc. Scotiae.}, as it appears by the accounts of the mint. In the coin of many countries the silver preponderates. In France, the largest sums are commonly paid in that metal, and it is there difficult to get more gold than what is necessary to carry about in your pocket. The superior value, however, of the silver plate above that of the gold, which takes place in all countries, will much more than compensate the preponderancy of the gold coin above the silver, which takes place only in some countries.

Though, in one sense of the word, silver always has been, and probably always will be, much cheaper than gold; yet, in another sense, gold may perhaps, in the present state of the Spanish market, be said to be somewhat cheaper than silver. A commodity may be said to be dear or cheap not only according to the absolute greatness or smallness of its usual price, but according as that price is more or less above the lowest for which it is possible to bring it to market for any considerable time together. This lowest price is that which barely replaces, with a moderate profit, the stock which must be employed in bringing the commodity thither. It is the price which affords nothing to the landlord, of which rent makes not any component part, but which resolves itself altogether into wages and profit. But, in the present state of the Spanish market, gold is certainly somewhat nearer to this lowest price than silver. The tax of the king of Spain upon gold is only one-twentieth part of the standard metal, or five percent.; whereas his tax upon silver amounts to one-tenth part of it, or to ten percent. In these taxes, too, it has already been observed, consists the whole rent of the greater part of the gold and silver mines of Spanish America; and that upon gold is still worse paid than that upon silver. The profits of the undertakers of gold mines, too, as they more rarely make a fortune, must, in general, be still more moderate than those of the undertakers of silver mines. The price of Spanish gold, therefore, as it affords both less rent and less profit, must, in the Spanish market, be somewhat nearer to the lowest price for which it is possible to bring it thither, than the price of Spanish silver. When all expenses are computed, the whole quantity of the one metal, it would seem, cannot, in the Spanish market, be disposed of so advantageously as the whole quantity of the other. The tax, indeed, of the king of Portugal upon the gold of the Brazils, is the same with the ancient tax of the king of Spain upon the silver of Mexico and Peru; or one-fifth part of the standard metal. It may therefore be uncertain, whether, to the general market of Europe, the whole mass of American gold comes at a price nearer to the lowest for which it is possible to bring it thither, than the whole mass of American silver.

The price of diamonds and other precious stones may, perhaps, be still nearer to the lowest price at which it is possible to bring them to market, than even the price of gold.

Though it is not very probable that any part of a tax, which is not only imposed upon one of the most proper subjects of taxation, a mere luxury and superfluity, but which affords so very important a revenue as the tax upon silver, will ever be given up as long as it is possible to pay it; yet the same impossibility of paying it, which, in 1736. made it necessary to reduce it from one-fifth to one-tenth, may in time make it necessary to reduce it still further; in the same manner as it made it necessary to reduce the tax upon gold to one-twentieth. That the silver mines of Spanish America, like all other mines, become gradually more expensive in the working, on account of the greater depths at which it is necessary to carry on the works, and of the greater expense of drawing out the water, and of supplying them with fresh air at those depths, is acknowledged by everybody who has inquired into the state of those mines.

These causes, which are equivalent to a growing scarcity of silver (for a commodity may be said to grow scarcer when it becomes more difficult and expensive to collect a certain quantity of it), must, in time, produce one or other of the three following events: The increase of the expense must either, first, be compensated altogether by a proportionable increase in the price of the metal; or, secondly, it must be compensated altogether by a proportionable diminution of the tax upon silver; or, thirdly, it must be compensated partly by the one and partly by the other of those two expedients. This third event is very possible. As gold rose in its price in proportion to silver, notwithstanding a great diminution of the tax upon gold, so silver might rise in its price in proportion to labor and commodities, notwithstanding an equal diminution of the tax upon silver.

Such successive reductions of the tax, however, though they may not prevent altogether, must certainly retard, more or less, the rise of the value of silver in the European market. In consequence of such reductions, many mines may be wrought which could not be wrought before, because they could not afford to pay the old tax; and the quantity of silver annually brought to market, must always be somewhat greater, and, therefore, the value of any given quantity somewhat less, than it otherwise would have been. In consequence of the reduction in 1736, the value of silver in the European market, though it may not at this day be lower than before that reduction, is, probably, at least ten percent lower than it would have been, had the court of Spain continued to exact the old tax.

That, notwithstanding this reduction, the value of silver has, during the course of the present century, begun to rise somewhat in the European market, the facts and arguments which have been alleged above, dispose me to believe, or more properly to suspect and conjecture; for the best opinion which I can form upon this subject, scarce, perhaps, deserves the name of belief. The rise, indeed, supposing there has been any, has hitherto been so very small, that after all that has been said, it may, perhaps, appear to many people uncertain, not only whether this event has actually taken place, but whether the contrary may not have taken place, or whether the value of silver may not still continue to fall in the European market.

It must be observed, however, that whatever may be the supposed annual importation of gold and silver, there must be a certain period at which the annual consumption of those metals will be equal to that annual importation. Their consumption must increase as their mass increases, or rather in a much greater proportion. As their mass increases, their value diminishes. They are more used, and less cared for, and their consumption consequently increases in a greater proportion than their mass. After a certain period, therefore, the annual consumption of those metals must, in this manner, become equal to their annual importation, provided that importation is not continually increasing; which, in the present times, is not supposed to be the case.

If, when the annual consumption has become equal to the annual importation, the annual importation should gradually diminish, the annual consumption may, for some time, exceed the annual importation. The mass of those metals may gradually and insensibly diminish, and their value gradually and insensibly rise, till the annual importation becoming again stationary, the annual consumption will gradually and insensibly accommodate itself to what that annual importation can maintain.

Grounds of the Suspicion that the Value of Silver Still Continues to Decrease.

The increase of the wealth of Europe, and the popular notion, that as the quantity of the precious metals naturally increases with the increase of wealth, so their value diminishes as their quantity increases, may, perhaps, dispose many people to believe that their value still continues to fall in the European market; and the still gradually increasing price of many parts of the rude produce of land may confirm them still farther in this opinion.

That that increase in the quantity of the precious metals, which arises in any country from the increase of wealth, has no tendency to diminish their value, I have endeavored to show already. Gold and silver naturally resort to a rich country, for the same reason that all sorts of luxuries and curiosities resort to it; not because they are cheaper there than in poorer countries, but because they are dearer, or because a better price is given for them. It is the superiority of price which attracts them; and as soon as that superiority ceases, they necessarily cease to go thither.

If you except corn, and such other vegetables as are raised altogether by human industry, that all other sorts of rude produce, cattle, poultry, game of all kinds, the useful fossils and minerals of the earth, etc. naturally grow dearer, as the society advances in wealth and improvement, I have endeavored to show already. Though such commodities, therefore, come to exchange for a greater quantity of silver than before, it will not from thence follow that silver has become really cheaper, or will purchase less labor than before; but that such commodities have become really dearer, or will purchase more labor than before. It is not their nominal price only, but their real price, which rises in the progress of improvement. The rise of their nominal price is the effect, not of any degradation of the value of silver, but of the rise in their real price.

Different Effects of the Progress of Improvement Upon Three Different Sorts of Rude Produce.

These different sorts of rude produce may be divided into three classes. The first comprehends those which it is scarce in the power of human industry to multiply at all. The second, those which it can multiply in proportion to the demand. The third, those in which the efficacy of industry is either limited or uncertain. In the progress of wealth and improvement, the real price of the first may rise to any degree of extravagance, and seems not to be limited by any certain boundary. That of the second, though it may rise greatly, has, however, a certain boundary, beyond which it cannot well pass for any considerable time together. That of the third, though its natural tendency is to rise in the progress of improvement, yet in the same degree of improvement it may sometimes happen even to fall, sometimes to continue the same, and sometimes to rise more or less, according as different accidents render the efforts of human industry, in multiplying this sort of rude produce, more or less successful.

First Sort. — The first sort of rude produce, of which the price rises in the progress of improvement, is that which it is scarce in the power of human industry to multiply at all. It consists in those things which nature produces only in certain quantities, and which being of a very perishable nature, it is impossible to accumulate together the produce of many different seasons. Such are the greater part of rare and singular birds and fishes, many different sorts of game, almost all wildfowl, all birds of passage in particular, as well as many other things. When wealth, and the luxury which accompanies it, increase, the demand for these is likely to increase with them, and no effort of human industry may be able to increase the supply much beyond what it was before this increase of the demand. The quantity of such commodities, therefore, remaining the same, or nearly the same, while the competition to purchase them is continually increasing, their price may rise to any degree of extravagance, and seems not to be limited by any certain boundary. If woodcocks should become so fashionable as to sell for twenty guineas apiece, no effort of human industry could increase the number of those brought to market, much beyond what it is at present. The high price paid by the Romans, in the time of their greatest grandeur, for rare birds and fishes, may in this manner easily be accounted for. These prices were not the effects of the low value of silver in those times, but of the high value of such rarities and curiosities as human industry could not multiply at pleasure. The real value of silver was higher at Rome, for sometime before, and after the fall of the republic, than it is through the greater part of Europe at present. Three sestertii equal to about sixpence sterling, was the price which the republic paid for the modius or peck of the tithe wheat of Sicily. This price, however, was probably below the average market price, the obligation to deliver their wheat at this rate being considered as a tax upon the Sicilian farmers. When the Romans, therefore, had occasion to order more corn than the tithe of wheat amounted to, they were bound by capitulation to pay for the surplus at the rate of four sestertii, or eight pence sterling the peck; and this had probably been reckoned the moderate and reasonable, that is, the ordinary or average contract price of those times; it is equal to about one-and-twenty shillings the quarter. Eight-and-twenty shillings the quarter was, before the late years of scarcity, the ordinary contract price of English wheat, which in quality is inferior to the Sicilian, and generally sells for a lower price in the European market. The value of silver, therefore, in those ancient times, must have been to its value in the present, as three to four inversely; that is, three ounces of silver would then have purchased the same quantity of labor and commodities which four ounces will do at present. When we read in Pliny, therefore, that Seius {Lib. X, c. 29.} bought a white nightingale, as a present for the empress Agrippina, at the price of six thousand sestertii, equal to about fifty pounds of our present money; and that Asinius Celer {Lib. IX, c. 17.} purchased a surmullet at the price of eight thousand sestertii, equal to about sixty-six pounds thirteen shillings and four pence of our present money; the extravagance of those prices, how much soever it may surprise us, is apt, notwithstanding, to appear to us about one third less than it really was. Their real price, the quantity of labor and subsistence which was given away for them, was about one-third more than their nominal price is apt to express to us in the present times. Seius gave for the nightingale the command of a quantity of labor and subsistence, equal to what £66:13: 4d. would purchase in the present times; and Asinius Celer gave for a surmullet the command of a quantity equal to what £88:17: 9d. would purchase. What occasioned the extravagance of those high prices was, not so much the abundance of silver, as the abundance of labor and subsistence, of which those Romans had the disposal, beyond what was necessary for their own use. The quantity of silver, of which they had the disposal, was a good deal less than what the command of the same quantity of labor and subsistence would have procured to them in the present times.

Second sort. —The second sort of rude produce, of which the price rises in the progress of improvement, is that which human industry can multiply in proportion to the demand. It consists in those useful plants and animals, which, in uncultivated countries, nature produces with such profuse abundance, that they are of little or no value, and which, as cultivation advances, are therefore forced to give place to some more profitable produce. During a long period in the progress of improvement, the quantity of these is continually diminishing, while, at the same time, the demand for them is continually increasing. Their real value, therefore, the real quantity of labor which they will purchase or command, gradually rises, till at last it gets so high as to render them as profitable a produce as any thing else which human industry can raise upon the most fertile and best cultivated land. When it has got so high, it cannot well go higher. If it did, more land and more industry would soon be employed to increase their quantity.

When the price of cattle, for example, rises so high, that it is as profitable to cultivate land in order to raise food for them as in order to raise food for man, it cannot well go higher. If it did, more corn land would soon be turned into pasture. The extension of tillage, by diminishing the quantity of wild pasture, diminishes the quantity of butcher's meat, which the country naturally produces without labor or cultivation; and, by increasing the number of those who have either corn, or, what comes to the same thing, the price of corn, to give in exchange for it, increases the demand. The price of butcher's meat, therefore, and, consequently, of cattle, must gradually rise, till it gets so high, that it becomes as profitable to employ the most fertile and best-cultivated lands in raising food for them as in raising corn. But it must always be late in the progress of improvement before tillage can be so far extended as to raise the price of cattle to this height; and, till it has got to this height, if the country is advancing at all, their price must be continually rising. There are, perhaps, some parts of Europe in which the price of cattle has not yet got to this height. It had not got to this height in any part of Scotland before the Union. Had the Scotch cattle been always confined to the market of Scotland, in a country in which the quantity of land, which can be applied to no other purpose but the feeding of cattle, is so great in proportion to what can be applied to other purposes, it is scarce possible, perhaps, that their price could ever have risen so high as to render it profitable to cultivate land for the sake of feeding them. In England, the price of cattle, it has already been observed, seems, in the neighborhood of London, to have got to this height about the beginning of the last century; but it was much later, probably, before it got through the greater part of the remoter counties, in some of which, perhaps, it may scarce yet have got to it. Of all the different substances, however, which compose this second sort of rude produce, cattle is, perhaps, that of which the price, in the progress of improvement, rises first to this height.

Till the price of cattle, indeed, has got to this height, it seems scarce possible that the greater part, even of those lands which are capable of the highest cultivation, can be completely cultivated. In all farms too distant from any town to carry manure from it, that is, in the far greater part of those of every extensive country, the quantity of well cultivated land must be in proportion to the quantity of manure which the farm itself produces; and this, again, must be in proportion to the stock of cattle which are maintained upon it. The land is manured, either by pasturing the cattle upon it, or by feeding them in the stable, and from thence carrying out their dung to it. But unless the price of the cattle be sufficient to pay both the rent and profit of cultivated land, the farmer cannot afford to pasture them upon it; and he can still less afford to feed them in the stable. It is with the produce of improved and cultivated land only that cattle can be fed in the stable; because, to collect the scanty and scattered produce of waste and unimproved lands, would require too much labor, and be too expensive. It the price of the cattle, therefore, is not sufficient to pay for the produce of improved and cultivated land, when they are allowed to pasture it, that price will be still less sufficient to pay for that produce, when it must be collected with a good deal of additional labor, and brought into the stable to them. In these circumstances, therefore, no more cattle can with profit be fed in the stable than what are necessary for tillage. But these can never afford manure enough for keeping constantly in good condition all the lands which they are capable of cultivating. What they afford, being insufficient for the whole farm, will naturally be reserved for the lands to which it can be most advantageously or conveniently applied; the most fertile, or those, perhaps, in the neighborhood of the farmyard. These, therefore, will be kept constantly in good condition, and fit for tillage. The rest will, the greater part of them, be allowed to lie waste, producing scarce anything but some miserable pasture, just sufficient to keep alive a few straggling, half-starved cattle; the farm, though much overstocked in proportion to what would be necessary for its complete cultivation, being very frequently overstocked in proportion to its actual produce. A portion of this wasteland, however, after having been pastured in this wretched manner for six or seven years together, may be ploughed up, when it will yield, perhaps, a poor crop or two of bad oats, or of some other coarse grain; and then, being entirely exhausted, it must be rested and pastured again as before, and another portion ploughed up, to be in the same manner exhausted and rested again in its turn. Such, accordingly, was the general system of management all over the low country of Scotland before the Union. The lands which were kept constantly well manured and in good condition seldom exceeded a third or fourth part of the whole farm, and sometimes did not amount to a fifth or a sixth part of it. The rest were never manured, but a certain portion of them was in its turn, notwithstanding, regularly cultivated and exhausted. Under this system of management, it is evident, even that part of the lands of Scotland which is capable of good cultivation, could produce but little in comparison of what it may be capable of producing. But how disadvantageous soever this system may appear, yet, before the Union, the low price of cattle seems to have rendered it almost unavoidable. If, notwithstanding a great rise in the price, it still continues to prevail through a considerable part of the country, it is owing in many places, no doubt, to ignorance and attachment to old customs, but, in most places, to the unavoidable obstructions which the natural course of things opposes to the immediate or speedy establishment of a better system: first, to the poverty of the tenants, to their not having yet had time to acquire a stock of cattle sufficient to cultivate their lands more completely, the same rise of price, which would render it advantageous for them to maintain a greater stock, rendering it more difficult for them to acquire it; and, secondly, to their not having yet had time to put their lands in condition to maintain this greater stock properly, supposing they were capable of acquiring it. The increase of stock and the improvement of land are two events which must go hand in hand, and of which the one can nowhere much outrun the other. Without some increase of stock, there can be scarce any improvement of land, but there can be no considerable increase of stock, but in consequence of a considerable improvement of land; because otherwise the land could not maintain it. These natural obstructions to the establishment of a better system, cannot be removed but by a long course of frugality and industry; and half a century or a century more, perhaps, must pass away before the old system, which is wearing out gradually, can be completely abolished through all the different parts of the country. Of all the commercial advantages, however, which Scotland has derived from the Union with England, this rise in the price of cattle is, perhaps, the greatest. It has not only raised the value of all highland estates, but it has, perhaps, been the principal cause of the improvement of the low country.

In all new colonies, the great quantity of wasteland, which can for many years be applied to no other purpose but the feeding of cattle, soon renders them extremely abundant; and in every thing great cheapness is the necessary consequence of great abundance. Though all the cattle of the European colonies in America were originally carried from Europe, they soon multiplied so much there, and became of so little value, that even horses were allowed to run wild in the woods, without any owner thinking it worthwhile to claim them. It must be a long time after the first establishment of such colonies, before it can become profitable to feed cattle upon the produce of cultivated land. The same causes, therefore, the want of manure, and the disproportion between the stock employed in cultivation and the land which it is destined to cultivate, are likely to introduce there a system of husbandry, not unlike that which still continues to take place in so many parts of Scotland. Mr. Kalm, the Swedish traveler, when he gives an account of the husbandry of some of the English colonies in North America, as he found it in 1749, observes, accordingly, that he can with difficulty discover there the character of the English nation, so well skilled in all the different branches of agriculture. They make scarce any manure for their cornfields, he says; but when one piece of ground has been exhausted by continual cropping, they clear and cultivate another piece of fresh land; and when that is exhausted, proceed to a third. Their cattle are allowed to wander through the woods and other uncultivated grounds, where they are half-starved; having long ago extirpated almost all the annual grasses, by cropping them too early in the spring, before they had time to form their flowers, or to shed their seeds. {Kalm's *Travels*, vol 1, pp. 343, 344.} The annual grasses were, it seems, the best natural grasses in that part of North

America; and when the Europeans first settled there, they used to grow very thick, and to rise three or four feet high. A piece of ground which, when he wrote, could not maintain one cow, would in former times, he was assured, have maintained four, each of which would have given four times the quantity of milk which that one was capable of giving. The poorness of the pasture had, in his opinion, occasioned the degradation of their cattle, which degenerated sensibly from one generation to another. They were probably not unlike that stunted breed which was common all over Scotland thirty or forty years ago, and which is now so much mended through the greater part of the low country, not so much by a change of the breed, though that expedient has been employed in some places, as by a more plentiful method of feeding them.

Though it is late, therefore, in the progress of improvement, before cattle can bring such a price as to render it profitable to cultivate land for the sake of feeding them; yet of all the different parts which compose this second sort of rude produce, they are perhaps the first which bring this price; because, till they bring it, it seems impossible that improvement can be brought near even to that degree of perfection to which it has arrived in many parts of Europe.

As cattle are among the first, so perhaps venison is among the last parts of this sort of rude produce which bring this price. The price of venison in Great Britain, how extravagant soever it may appear, is not near sufficient to compensate the expense of a deer park, as is well known to all those who have had any experience in the feeding of deer. If it was otherwise, the feeding of deer would soon become an article of common farming, in the same manner as the feeding of those small birds, called turdi, was among the ancient Romans. Varro and Columella assure us, that it was a most profitable article. The fattening of ortolans, birds of passage which arrive lean in the country, is said to be so in some parts of France. If venison continues in fashion, and the wealth and luxury of Great Britain increase as they have done for some time past, its price may very probably rise still higher than it is at present.

Between that period in the progress of improvement, which brings to its height the price of so necessary an article as cattle, and that which brings to it the price of such a superfluity as venison, there is a very long interval, in the course of which many other sorts of rude produce gradually arrive at their highest price, some sooner and some later, according to different circumstances.

Thus, in every farm, the offals of the barn and stable will maintain a certain number of poultry. These, as they are fed with what would otherwise be lost, are a mere save-all; and as they cost the farmer scarce anything, so he can afford to sell them for very little. Almost all that he gets is pure gain, and their price can scarce be so low as to discourage him from feeding this number. But in countries ill cultivated, and therefore but thinly inhabited, the poultry, which are thus raised without expense, are often fully sufficient to supply the whole demand. In this state of things, therefore, they are often as cheap as butcher's meat, or any other sort of animal food. But the whole quantity of poultry which the farm in this manner produces without expense, must always be much smaller than the whole quantity of butcher's meat which is reared upon it; and in times of wealth and luxury, what is rare, with only nearly equal merit, is always preferred to what is common. As wealth and luxury increase, therefore, in consequence of improvement and cultivation, the price of poultry gradually rises above that of butcher's meat, till at last it gets so high, that it becomes profitable to cultivate land for the sake of feeding them. When it has got to this height, it cannot well go higher. If it did, more land would soon be turned to this purpose. In several provinces of France, the feeding of poultry is considered as a very important article in rural economy, and sufficiently profitable to encourage the farmer to raise a considerable quantity of Indian corn and buckwheat for this purpose. A middling farmer will there sometimes have four hundred fowls in his yard. The feeding of poultry seems scarce yet to be generally considered as a matter of so much importance in England. They are certainly, however, dearer in England than in France, as England receives considerable supplies from France. In the progress of improvements, the period at which every particular sort of animal food is dearest, must naturally be that which immediately precedes the general practice of cultivating land for the sake of raising it. For some time before this practice becomes general, the scarcity must necessarily raise the price. After it has become general, new methods of feeding are commonly fallen upon, which enable the farmer to raise upon the same quantity of ground a much greater quantity of that particular sort of animal food. The plenty not only obliges him to sell cheaper, but, in consequence of these improvements, he can afford to sell cheaper; for if he could not afford it, the plenty would not be of long continuance. It has been probably in this manner that the introduction of clover, turnips, carrots, cabbages, etc. has contributed to sink the common price of butcher's meat in the London market, somewhat below what it was about the beginning of the last century.

The hog, that finds his food among ordure, and greedily devours many things rejected by every other useful animal, is, like poultry, originally kept as a save-all. As long as the number of such animals, which can thus be reared at little or no expense, is fully sufficient to supply the demand, this sort of butcher's meat comes to market at a much lower price than any other. But when the demand rises beyond what this quantity can supply, when it becomes necessary to raise food on purpose for feeding and fattening hogs, in the same manner as for feeding and fattening other cattle, the price necessarily rises, and becomes proportionally either higher or lower than that of other butcher's meat, according as the nature of the country, and the state of its agriculture, happen to render the feeding of hogs more or less expensive than that of other cattle. In France, according to Mr. Buffon, the price of pork is nearly equal to that of beef. In most parts of Great Britain it is at present somewhat higher.

The great rise in the price both of hogs and poultry, has, in Great Britain, been frequently imputed to the diminution of the number of cottagers and other small occupiers of land; an event which has in every part of Europe been the immediate forerunner of improvement and better cultivation, but which at the same time may have contributed to raise the price of those articles, both somewhat sooner and somewhat faster than it would otherwise have risen. As the poorest family can often maintain a cat or a dog without any expense, so the poorest occupiers of land can commonly maintain a few poultry, or a sow and a few pigs, at very little. The little offals of their own table, their whey, skimmed milk, and buttermilk, supply those animals with a part of their food, and they find the rest in the neighboring fields, without doing any sensible damage to any body. By diminishing the number of those small occupiers, therefore, the quantity of this sort of provisions, which is thus produced at little or no expense, must certainly have been a good deal diminished, and their price must consequently have been raised both sooner and faster than it would otherwise have risen. Sooner or later, however, in the progress of improvement, it must at any rate have risen to the utmost height to which it is capable of rising; or to the price which pays the labor and expense of cultivating the land which furnishes them with food, as well as these are paid upon the greater part of other cultivated land.

The business of the dairy, like the feeding of hogs and poultry, is originally carried on as a save-all. The cattle necessarily kept upon the farm produce more milk than either the rearing of their own young, or the consumption of the farmer's family requires; and they produce most at one particular season. But of all the productions of land, milk is perhaps the most perishable. In the warm season, when it is most abundant, it will scarce keep four-and-twenty hours. The farmer, by making it into fresh butter, stores a small part of it for a week; by making it into salt butter, for a year; and by making it into cheese, he stores a much greater part of it for several years. Part of all these is reserved for the use of his own family; the rest goes to market, in order to find the best price which is to be had, and which can scarce be so low is to discourage him from sending thither whatever is over and above the use of his own family. If it is very low indeed, he will be likely to manage his dairy in a very slovenly and dirty manner, and will scarce, perhaps, think it worth while to have a particular room or building on purpose for it, but will suffer the business to be carried on amidst the smoke, filth, and nastiness of his own kitchen, as was the case of almost all the farmers' dairies in Scotland thirty or forty years ago, and as is the case of many of them still. The same causes which gradually raise the price of butcher's meat, the increase of the demand, and, in consequence of the improvement of the country, the diminution of the quantity which can be fed at little or no expense, raise, in the same manner, that of the produce of the dairy, of which the price naturally connects with that of butcher's meat, or with the expense of feeding cattle. The increase of price pays for more labor, care, and cleanliness. The dairy becomes more worthy of the farmer's attention, and the quality of its produce gradually improves. The price at last gets so high, that it becomes worthwhile to employ some of the most fertile and best cultivated lands in feeding cattle merely for the purpose of the dairy; and when it has got to this height, it cannot well go higher. If it did, more land would soon be turned to this purpose. It seems to have got to this height through the greater part of England, where much good land is commonly employed in this manner. If you except the neighborhood of a few considerable towns, it seems not yet to have got to this height anywhere in Scotland, where common farmers seldom employ much good land in raising food for cattle, merely for the purpose of the dairy. The price of the produce, though it has risen very considerably within these few years, is probably still too low to admit of it. The inferiority of the quality, indeed, compared with that of the produce of English dairies, is fully equal to that of the price. But this inferiority of quality is, perhaps, rather the effect of this lowness of price, than the cause of it. Though the quality was much better, the greater part of what is brought to market could not, I apprehend, in the present circumstances of the country, be disposed of at a much better price; and the present price, it is probable, would not pay the expense of the land and labor necessary for producing a much better quality. Through the greater part of England, notwithstanding the superiority of price, the dairy is not reckoned a more profitable employment of land than the raising of corn, or the fattening of cattle, the two great objects of agriculture. Through the greater part of Scotland, therefore, it cannot yet be even so profitable.

The lands of no country, it is evident, can ever be completely cultivated and improved, till once the price of every produce, which human industry is obliged to raise upon them, has got so high as to pay for the expense of complete improvement and cultivation. In order to do this, the price of each particular produce must be sufficient, first, to pay the rent of good corn land, as it is that which regulates the rent of the greater part of other cultivated land; and, secondly, to pay the labor and expense of the farmer, as well as they are commonly paid upon good corn land; or, in other words, to replace with the ordinary profits the stock which he employs about it. This rise in the price of each particular produce must evidently be previous to the improvement and cultivation of the land which is destined for raising it. Gain is the end of all improvement; and nothing could deserve that name, of which loss was to be the necessary consequence. But loss must be the necessary consequence of improving land for the sake of a produce of which the price could never bring back the expense. If the complete improvement and cultivation of the country be, as it most certainly is, the greatest of all public advantages, this rise in the price of all those different sorts of rude produce, instead of being considered as a public calamity, ought to be regarded as the necessary forerunner and attendant of the greatest of all public advantages.

This rise, too, in the nominal or money price of all those different sorts of rude produce, has been the effect, not of any degradation in the value of silver, but of a rise in their real price. They have become worth, not only a greater quantity of silver, but a greater quantity of labor and subsistence than before. As it costs a greater quantity of labor and subsistence to bring them to market, so, when they are brought thither they represent, or are equivalent to a greater quantity.

Third Sort. — The third and last sort of rude produce, of which the price naturally rises in the progress of improvement, is that in which the efficacy of human industry, in augmenting the quantity, is either limited or uncertain. Though the real price of this sort of rude produce, therefore, naturally tends to rise in the progress of improvement, yet, according as different accidents happen to render the efforts of human industry more or less successful in augmenting the quantity, it may happen sometimes even to fall, sometimes to continue the same, in very different periods of improvement, and sometimes to rise more or less in the same period.

There are some sorts of rude produce which nature has rendered a kind of appendages to other sorts; so that the quantity of the one which any country can afford, is necessarily limited by that of the other. The quantity of wool or of rawhides, for example, which any country can afford, is necessarily limited by the number of great and small cattle that are kept in it. The state of its improvement, and the nature of its agriculture, again necessarily determine this number.

The same causes which, in the progress of improvement, gradually raise the price of butcher's meat, should have the same effect, it may be thought, upon the prices of wool and rawhides, and raise them, too, nearly in the same proportion. It probably would be so, if, in the rude beginnings of improvement, the market for the latter commodities was confined within as narrow bounds as that for the former. But the extent of their respective markets is commonly extremely different.

The market for butcher's meat is almost everywhere confined to the country which produces it. Ireland, and some part of British America, indeed, carry on a considerable trade in salt provisions; but they are, I believe, the only countries in the commercial world which do so, or which export to other countries any considerable part of their butcher's meat.

The market for wool and rawhides, on the contrary, is, in the rude beginnings of improvement, very seldom confined to the country which produces them. They can easily be transported to distant countries; wool without any preparation, and rawhides with very little; and as they are the materials of many manufactures, the industry of other countries may occasion a demand for them, though that of the country which produces them might not occasion any.

In countries ill cultivated, and therefore but thinly inhabited, the price of the wool and the hide bears always a much greater proportion to that of the whole beast, than in countries where, improvement and population being further advanced, there is more demand for butcher's meat. Mr. Hume observes, that in the Saxon times, the fleece was estimated at two-fifths of the value of the whole sheep and that this was much above the proportion of its present estimation. In some provinces of Spain, I have been assured, the sheep is frequently killed merely for the sake of the fleece and the tallow. The carcass is often left to rot upon the ground, or to be devoured by beasts and birds of prey. If this sometimes happens even in Spain, it happens almost constantly in Chili, at Buenos Ayres, and in many other parts of Spanish America, where the horned cattle are almost constantly killed merely for the sake of the hide and the tallow. This, too, used to happen almost constantly in Hispaniola, while it was infested by the buccaneers, and before the settlement, improvement, and populousness of the French plantations (which now extend round the coast of almost the whole western half of the island) had given some value to the cattle of the Spaniards, who still continue to possess, not only the eastern part of the coast, but the whole inland mountainous part of the country.

Though, in the progress of improvement and population, the price of the whole beast necessarily rises, yet the price of the carcass is likely to be much more affected by this rise than that of the wool and the hide. The market for the carcass being in the rude state of society confined always to the country which produces it, must necessarily be extended in proportion to the improvement and population of that country. But the market for the wool and the hides, even of a barbarous country, often extending to the whole commercial world, it can very seldom be enlarged in the same proportion. The state of the whole commercial world can seldom be much affected by the improvement of any particular country; and the market for such commodities may remain the same, or very nearly the same, after such improvements, as before. It should, however, in the natural course of things, rather, upon the whole, be somewhat extended in consequence of them. If the manufactures, especially, of which those commodities are the materials, should ever come to flourish in the country, the market, though it might not be much enlarged, would at least be brought much nearer to the place of growth than before; and the price of those materials might at least be increased by what had usually been the expense of transporting them to distant countries. Though it might not rise, therefore, in the same proportion as that of butcher's meat, it ought naturally to rise somewhat, and it ought certainly not to fall.

In England, however, notwithstanding the flourishing state of its woolen manufacture, the price of English wool has fallen very considerably since the time of Edward III. There are many authentic records which demonstrate that, during the reign of that prince (towards the middle of the fourteenth century, or about 1339), what was reckoned the moderate and reasonable price of the tod, or twenty-eight pounds of English wool, was not less than ten shillings of the money of those times {See Smith's *Memoirs of Wool*, vol. i e. 5, 6, 7. also vol. ii}, containing, at the rate of twenty-pence the ounce, six ounces of silver, Tower weight, equal to about thirty shillings of our present money. In the present times, one-and-twenty shillings the tod may be reckoned a good price for very good English wool. The money price of wool, therefore, in the time of Edward III was to its money price in the present times as ten to seven. The superiority of its real price was still greater. At the rate of six shillings and eight pence the quarter, ten shillings was in those ancient times the price of twelve bushels of wheat. At the rate of twenty-eight shillings the quarter, one-and-twenty shillings is in the present times the price of six bushels only. The proportion between the real price of ancient and modern times, therefore, is as twelve to six, or as two to one. In those ancient times, a tod of wool would have purchased twice the quantity of subsistence which it will purchase at present, and consequently twice the quantity of labor, if the real recompense of labor had been the same in both periods.

This degradation, both in the real and nominal value of wool, could never have happened in consequence of the natural course of things. It has accordingly been the effect of violence and artifice. First, of the absolute prohibition of exporting wool from England: secondly, of the permission of importing it from Spain, duty free: thirdly, of the prohibition of exporting it from Ireland to another country but England. In consequence of these regulations, the market for English wool, instead of being somewhat extended, in consequence of the improvement of England, has been confined to the home market, where the wool of several other countries is allowed to come into competition with it, and where that of Ireland is forced into competition with it. As the woolen manufactures, too, of Ireland, are fully as much discouraged as is consistent with justice and fair dealing, the Irish can work up but a smaller part of their own wool at home, and are therefore obliged to send a greater proportion of it to Great Britain, the only market they are allowed.

I have not been able to find any such authentic records concerning the price of raw hides in ancient times. Wool was commonly paid as a subsidy to the king, and its valuation in that subsidy ascertains, at least in some degree, what was its ordinary price. But this seems not to have been the case with rawhides. Fleetwood, however, from an account in 1425, between the prior of Burcester Oxford and one of his canons, gives us their price, at least as it was stated upon that particular occasion, viz. five ox hides at twelve shillings; five cow hides at seven shillings and three pence; thirty-six sheep skins of two years old at nine shillings; sixteen calf skins at two shillings. In 1425, twelve shillings contained about the same quantity of silver as four-and-twenty shillings of our present money. An ox hide, therefore, was in this account valued at the same quantity of silver as 4s. 4/5ths of our present money. Its nominal price was a good deal lower than at present. But at the rate of six shillings and eight pence the quarter, twelve shillings would in those times have purchased fourteen bushels and four-fifths of a bushel of wheat, which, at three and sixpence the bushel, would in the present times cost 51s. 4d. An ox hide, therefore, would in those times have purchased as much corn as ten shillings and three pence would purchase at present. Its real value was equal to ten shillings and three pence of our present money. In those ancient times, when the cattle were half starved during the greater part of the winter, we cannot suppose that they were of a very large size. An ox hide which weighs four stone of sixteen pounds of avoirdupois, is not in the present times reckoned a bad one; and in those ancient times would probably have been reckoned a very good one. But at half-a-crown the stone, which at this moment (February 1773) I understand to be the common price, such a hide would at present cost only ten shillings. Though its nominal price, therefore, is higher in the present than it was in those ancient times, its real price, the real quantity of subsistence which it will purchase or command, is rather somewhat lower. The price of cowhides, as stated in the above account, is nearly in the common proportion to that of ox hides. That of sheep-skins is a good deal above it. They had probably been sold with the wool. That of calves' skins, on the contrary, is greatly below it. In countries where the price of cattle is very low, the calves, which are not intended to be reared in order to keep up the stock, are generally killed very young, as was the case in Scotland twenty or thirty years ago. It saves the milk, which their price would not pay for. Their skins, therefore, are commonly good for little.

The price of raw hides is a good deal lower at present than it was a few years ago; owing probably to the taking off the duty upon seal skins, and to the allowing, for a limited time, the importation of rawhides from Ireland, and from the plantations, duty free, which was done in 1769. Take the whole of the present century at an average, their real price has probably been somewhat higher than it was in those ancient times. The nature of the commodity renders it not quite so proper for being transported to distant markets as wool. It suffers more by keeping. A salted hide is reckoned inferior to a fresh one, and sells for a lower price. This circumstance must necessarily have some tendency to sink the price of rawhides produced in a country which does not manufacture them, but is obliged to export them, and comparatively to raise that of those produced in a country which does manufacture them. It must have some tendency to sink their price in a barbarous, and to raise it in an improved and manufacturing country. It must have had some tendency, therefore, to sink it in ancient, and to raise it in modern times. Our tanners, besides, have not been quite so successful as our clothiers, in convincing the wisdom of the nation, that the safety of the commonwealth depends upon the prosperity of their particular manu-facture. They have accordingly been much less favored. The exportation of rawhides has, indeed, been prohibited, and declared a nuisance; but their importation from foreign countries has been subjected to a duty; and though this duty has been taken off from those of Ireland and the plantations (for the limited time of five years only), yet Ireland has not been confined to the market of Great Britain for the sale of its surplus hides, or of those which are not manufactured at home. The hides of common cattle have, but within these few years, been put among the enumerated commodities which the plantations can send nowhere but to the mother country; neither has the commerce of Ireland been in this case oppressed hitherto, in order to support the manufactures of Great Britain.

Whatever regulations tend to sink the price, either of wool or of rawhides, below what it naturally would be, must, in an improved and cultivated country, have some tendency to raise the price of butcher's meat. The price both of the great and small cattle, which are fed on improved and cultivated land, must be sufficient to pay the rent which the landlord, and the profit which the farmer, has reason to expect from improved and cultivated land. If it is not, they will soon cease to feed them. Whatever part of this price, therefore, is not paid by the wool and the hide, must be paid by the carcass. The less there is paid for the one, the more must be paid for the other. In what manner this price is to be divided upon the different parts of the beast, is indifferent to the landlords and farmers, provided it is all paid to them. In an improved and cultivated country, therefore, their interest as landlords and farmers cannot be much affected by such regulations, though their interest as consumers may, by the rise in the price of provisions. It would be quite otherwise, however, in an unimproved and uncultivated country, where the greater part of the lands could be applied to no other purpose but the feeding of cattle, and where the wool and the hide made the principal part of the value of those cattle. Their interest as landlords and farmers would in this case be very deeply affected by such regulations, and their interest as consumers very little. The fall in the price of the wool and the hide would not in this case raise the price of the carcass; because the greater part of the lands of the country being applicable to no other purpose but the feeding of cattle, the same number would still continue to be fed. The same quantity of butcher's meat would still come to market. The demand for it would be no greater than before. Its price, therefore, would be the same as before. The whole price of cattle would fall, and along with it both the rent and the profit of all those lands of which cattle was the principal produce, that is, of the greater part of the lands of the country. The perpetual prohibition of the exportation of wool, which is commonly, but very falsely, ascribed to Edward III, would, in the then circumstances of the country, have been the most destructive regulation which could well have been thought of. It would not only have reduced the actual value of the greater part of the lands in the kingdom, but by reducing the price of the most important species of small cattle, it would have retarded very much its subsequent improvement.

The wool of Scotland fell very considerably in its price in consequence of the union with England, by which it was excluded from the great market of Europe, and confined to the narrow one of Great Britain. The value of the greater part of the lands in the southern counties of Scotland, which are chiefly a sheep country, would have been very deeply affected by this event, had not the rise in the price of butcher's meat fully compensated the fall in the price of wool.

As the efficacy of human industry, in increasing the quantity either of wool or of rawhides, is limited, so far as it depends upon the produce of the country where it is exerted; so it is uncertain so far as it depends upon the produce of other countries. It so far depends not so much upon the quantity which they produce, as upon that which they do not manufacture; and upon the restraints which they may or may not think proper to impose upon the exportation of this sort of rude produce. These circumstances, as they are altogether independent of domestic industry, so they necessarily render the efficacy of its efforts more or less uncertain. In multiplying this sort of rude produce, therefore, the efficacy of human industry is not only limited, but uncertain.

In multiplying another very important sort of rude produce, the quantity of fish that is brought to market, it is likewise both limited and uncertain. It is limited by the local situation of the country, by the proximity or distance of its different provinces from the sea, by the number of its lakes and rivers, and by what may be called the fertility or barrenness of those seas, lakes, and rivers, as to this sort of rude produce. As population increases, as the annual produce of the land and labor of the country grows greater and greater, there come to be more buyers of fish; and those buyers, too, have a greater quantity and variety of other goods, or, what is the same thing, the price of a greater quantity and variety of other goods, to buy with. But it will generally be impossible to supply the great and extended market, without employing a quantity of labor greater than in proportion to what had been requisite for supplying the narrow and confined one. A market which, from requiring only one thousand, comes to require annually ten thousand ton of fish, can seldom be supplied, without employing more than ten times the quantity of labor which had before been sufficient to supply it. The fish must generally be sought for at a greater distance, larger vessels must be employed, and more expensive machinery of every kind made use of. The real price of this commodity, therefore, naturally rises in the progress of improvement. It has accordingly done so, I believe, more or less in every country.

Though the success of a particular day's fishing maybe a very uncertain matter, yet the local situation of the country being supposed, the general efficacy of industry in bringing a certain quantity of fish to market, taking the course of a year, or of several years together, it may, perhaps, be thought is certain enough; and it, no doubt, is so. As it depends more, however, upon the local situation of the country, than upon the state of its wealth and industry; as upon this account it may in different countries be the same in very different periods of improvement, and very different in the same period; its connection with the state of improvement is uncertain; and it is of this sort of uncertainty that I am here speaking.

In increasing the quantity of the different minerals and metals which are drawn from the bowels of the earth, that of the more precious ones particularly, the efficacy of human industry seems not to be limited, but to be altogether uncertain.

The quantity of the precious metals which is to be found in any country, is not limited by any thing in its local situation, such as the fertility or barrenness of its own mines. Those metals frequently abound in countries which possess no mines. Their quantity, in every particular country, seems to depend upon two different circumstances; first, upon its power of purchasing, upon the state of its industry, upon the annual produce of its land and labor, in consequence of which it can afford to employ a greater or a smaller quantity of labor and subsistence, in bringing or purchasing such superfluities as gold and silver, either from its own mines, or from those of other countries; and, secondly, upon the fertility or barrenness of the mines which may happen at any particular time to supply the commercial world with those metals. The quantity of those metals in the countries most remote from the mines, must be more or less affected by this fertility or barrenness, on account of the easy and cheap transportation of those metals, of their small bulk and great value. Their quantity in China and Indostan must have been more or less affected by the abundance of the mines of America.

So far as their quantity in any particular country depends upon the former of those two circumstances (the power of purchasing), their real price, like that of all other luxuries and superfluities, is likely to rise with the wealth and improvement of the country, and to fall with its poverty and depression. Countries which have a great quantity of labor and subsistence to spare, can afford to purchase any particular quantity of those metals at the expense of a greater quantity of labor and subsistence, than countries which have less to spare.

So far as their quantity in any particular country depends upon the latter of those two circumstances (the fertility or barrenness of the mines which happen to supply the commercial world), their real price, the real quantity of labor and subsistence which they will purchase or exchange for, will, no doubt, sink more or less in proportion to the fertility, and rise in proportion to the barrenness of those mines.

The fertility or barrenness of the mines, however, which may happen at any particular time to supply the commercial world, is a circumstance which, it is evident, may have no sort of connection with the state of industry in a particular country. It seems even to have no very necessary connection with that of the world in general. As arts and commerce, indeed, gradually spread themselves over a greater and a greater part of the earth, the search for new mines, being extended over a wider surface, may have somewhat a better chance for being successful than when confined within narrower bounds. The discovery of new mines, however, as the old ones come to be gradually exhausted, is a matter of the greatest uncertainty, and such as no human skill or industry can insure. All indications, it is acknowledged, are doubtful; and the actual discovery and successful working of a new mine can alone ascertain the reality of its value, or even of its existence. In this search there seem to be no certain limits, either to the possible success, or to the possible disappointment of human industry. In the course of a century or two, it is possible that new mines may be discovered, more fertile than any that have ever yet been known; and it is just equally possible, that the most fertile mine then known may be more barren than any that was wrought before the discovery of the mines of America. Whether the one or the other of those two events may happen to take place, is of very little importance to the real wealth and prosperity of the world, to the real value of the annual produce of the land and labor of mankind. Its nominal value, the quantity of gold and silver by which this annual produce could be expressed or represented, would, no doubt, be very different; but its real value, the real quantity of labor which it could purchase or command, would be precisely the same. A shilling might, in the one case, represent no more labor than a penny does at present; and a penny, in the other, might represent as much as a shilling does now. But in the one case, he who had a shilling in his pocket would be no richer than he who has a penny at present; and in the other, he who had a penny would be just as rich as he who has a shilling now. The cheapness and abundance of gold and silver plate would be the sole advantage which the world could derive from the one event; and the dearness and scarcity of those trifling superfluities, the only inconveniency it could suffer from the other.

Conclusion of the Digression Concerning the Variations in the Value of Silver.

The greater part of the writers who have collected the money price of things in ancient times, seem to have considered the low money price of corn, and of goods in general, or, in other words, the high value of gold and silver, as a proof, not only of the scarcity of those metals, but of the poverty and barbarism of the country at the time when it took place. This notion is connected with the system of political economy, which represents national wealth as consisting in the abundance and national poverty in the scarcity, of gold and silver; a system which I shall endeavor to explain and examine at great length in the fourth book of this Inquiry. I shall only observe at present, that the high value of the precious metals can be no proof of the poverty or barbarism of any particular country at the time when it took place. It is a proof only of the barrenness of the mines which happened at that time to supply the commercial world. A poor country, as it cannot afford to buy more, so it can as little afford to pay dearer for gold and silver than a rich one; and the value of those metals, therefore, is not likely to be higher in the former than in the latter. In China, a country much richer than any part of Europe, the value of the precious metals is much higher than in any part of Europe. As the wealth of Europe, indeed, has increased greatly since the discovery of the mines of America, so the value of gold and silver has gradually diminished. This diminution of their value, however, has not been owing to the increase of the real wealth of Europe, of the annual produce of its land and labor, but to the accidental discovery of more abundant mines than any that were known before. The increase of the quantity of gold and silver in Europe, and the increase of its manufactures and agriculture, are two events which, though they have happened nearly about the same time, yet have arisen from very different causes, and have scarce any natural connection with one another. The one has arisen from a mere accident, in which neither prudence nor policy either had or could have any share; the other, from the fall of the feudal system, and from the establishment of a government which afforded to industry the only encouragement which it requires, some tolerable security that it shall enjoy the fruits of its own labor. Poland, where the feudal system still continues to take place, is at this day as beggarly a country as it was before the discovery of America. The money price of corn, however, has risen; the real value of the precious metals has fallen in Poland, in the same manner as in other parts of Europe. Their quantity, therefore, must have increased there as in other places, and nearly in the same proportion to the annual produce of its land and labor. This increase of the quantity of those metals, however, has not, it seems, increased that annual produce, has neither improved the manufactures and agriculture of the country, nor mended the circumstances of its inhabitants. Spain and Portugal, the countries which possess the mines, are, after Poland, perhaps the two most beggarly countries in Europe. The value of the precious metals, however, must be lower in Spain and Portugal than in any other part of Europe, as they come from those countries to all other parts of Europe, loaded, not only with a freight and an insurance, but with the expense of smuggling, their exportation being either prohibited or subjected to a duty. In proportion to the annual produce of the land and labor, therefore, their quantity must be greater in those countries than in any other part of Europe; those countries, however, are poorer than the greater part of Europe. Though the feudal system has been abolished in Spain and Portugal, it has not been succeeded by a much better.

As the low value of gold and silver, therefore, is no proof of the wealth and flourishing state of the country where it takes place; so neither is their high value, or the low money price either of goods in general, or of corn in particular, any proof of its poverty and barbarism.

But though the low money price, either of goods in general, or of corn in particular, be no proof of the poverty or barbarism of the times, the low money price of some particular sorts of goods, such as cattle, poultry, game of all kinds, etc. in proportion to that of corn, is a most decisive one. It clearly demonstrates, first, their great abundance in proportion to that of corn, and, consequently, the great extent of the land which they occupied in proportion to what was occupied by corn; and, secondly, the low value of this land in proportion to that of corn land, and, consequently, the uncultivated and unimproved state of the far greater part of the lands of the country. It clearly demonstrates, that the stock and population of the country did not bear the same proportion to the extent of its territory, which they commonly do in civilized countries; and that society was at that time, and in that country, but in its infancy. From the high or low money price, either of goods in general, or of corn in particular, we can infer only, that the mines, which at that time happened to supply the commercial world with gold and silver, were fertile or barren, not that the country was rich or poor. But from the high or low money price of some sorts of goods in proportion to that of others, we can infer, with a degree of probability that approaches almost to certainty, that it was rich or poor, that the greater part of its lands were improved or unimproved, and that it was either in a more or less barbarous state, or in a more or less civilized one.

Any rise in the money price of goods which proceeded altogether from the degradation of the value of silver, would affect all sorts of goods equally, and raise their price universally, a third, or a fourth, or a fifth part higher, according as silver happened to lose a third, or a fourth, or a fifth part of its former value. But the rise in the price of provisions, which has been the subject of so much reasoning and conversation, does not affect all sorts of provisions equally. Taking the course of the present century at an average, the price of corn, it is acknowledged, even by those who account for this rise by the degradation of the value of silver, has risen much less than that of some other sorts of provisions. The rise in the price of those other sorts of provisions, therefore, cannot be owing altogether to the degradation of the value of silver. Some other causes must be taken into the account; and those which have been above assigned, will, perhaps, without having recourse to the supposed degradation of the value of silver, sufficiently explain this rise in those particular sorts of provisions, of which the price has actually risen in proportion to that of corn.

As to the price of corn itself, it has, during the sixty-four first years of the present century, and before the late extraordinary course of bad seasons, been somewhat lower than
it was during the sixty-four last years of the preceding century. This fact is attested, not
only by the accounts of Windsor market, but by the public fiars of all the different counties of Scotland, and by the accounts of several different markets in France, which have
been collected with great diligence and fidelity by Mr. Messance, and by Mr. Dupré de
St Maur. The evidence is more complete than could well have been expected in a matter which is naturally so very difficult to be ascertained.

As to the high price of corn during these last ten or twelve years, it can be sufficiently
accounted for from the badness of the seasons, without supposing any degradation in the
value of silver.

The opinion, therefore, that silver is continually sinking in its value, seems not to be
founded upon any good observations, either upon the prices of corn, or upon those of
other provisions.

The same quantity of silver, it may perhaps be said, will, in the present times, even according to the account which has been here given, purchase a much smaller quantity of
several sorts of provisions than it would have done during some part of the last century;
and to ascertain whether this change be owing to a rise in the value of those goods, or to
a fall in the value of silver, is only to establish a vain and useless distinction, which can
be of no sort of service to the man who has only a certain quantity of silver to go to market with, or a certain fixed revenue in money. I certainly do not pretend that the knowledge of this distinction will enable him to buy cheaper. It may not, however, upon that
account be altogether useless.

It may be of some use to the public, by affording an easy proof of the prosperous condition of the country. If the rise in the price of some sorts of provisions be owing altogether to a fall in the value of silver, it is owing to a circumstance, from which nothing
can be inferred but the fertility of the American mines. The real wealth of the country,
the annual produce of its land and labor, may, notwithstanding this circumstance, be either gradually declining, as in Portugal and Poland; or gradually advancing, as in most
other parts of Europe. But if this rise in the price of some sorts of provisions be owing
to a rise in the real value of the land which produces them, to its increased fertility, or,
in consequence of more extended improvement and good cultivation, to its having been
rendered fit for producing corn; it is owing to a circumstance which indicates, in the
clearest manner, the prosperous and advancing state of the country. The land constitutes
by far the greatest, the most important, and the most durable part of the wealth of every
extensive country. It may surely be of some use, or, at least, it may give some satisfaction
to the public, to have so decisive a proof of the increasing value of by far the greatest, the
most important, and the most durable part of its wealth.

It may, too, be of some use to the public, in regulating the pecuniary reward of some
of its inferior servants. If this rise in the price of some sorts of provisions be owing to a
fall in the value of silver, their pecuniary reward, provided it was not too large before,
ought certainly to be augmented in proportion to the extent of this fall. If it is not augmented, their real recompense will evidently be so much diminished. But if this rise of
price is owing to the increased value, in consequence of the improved fertility of the land

which produces such provisions, it becomes a much nicer matter to judge, either in what proportion any pecuniary reward ought to be augmented, or whether it ought to be augmented at all. The extension of improvement and cultivation, as it necessarily raises more or less, in proportion to the price of corn, that of every sort of animal food, so it as necessarily lowers that of, I believe, every sort of vegetable food. It raises the price of animal food; because a great part of the land which produces it, being rendered fit for producing corn, must afford to the landlord and farmer the rent and profit of corn land. It lowers the price of vegetable food; because, by increasing the fertility of the land, it increases its abundance. The improvements of agriculture, too, introduce many sorts of vegetable food, which requiring less land, and not more labor than corn, come much cheaper to market. Such are potatoes and maize, or what is called Indian corn, the two most important improvements which the agriculture of Europe, perhaps, which Europe itself, has received from the great extension of its commerce and navigation. Many sorts of vegetable food, besides, which in the rude state of agriculture are confined to the kitchen garden, and raised only by the spade, come, in its improved state, to be introduced into common fields, and to be raised by the plough; such as turnips, carrots, cabbages, etc. If, in the progress of improvement, therefore, the real price of one species of food necessarily rises, that of another as necessarily falls; and it becomes a matter of more nicety to judge how far the rise in the one may be compensated by the fall in the other. When the real price of butcher's meat has once got to its height (which, with regard to every sort, except perhaps that of hogs flesh, it seems to have done through a great part of England more than a century ago), any rise which can afterwards happen in that of any other sort of animal food, cannot much affect the circumstances of the inferior ranks of people. The circumstances of the poor, through a great part of England, cannot surely be so much distressed by any rise in the price of poultry, fish, wild fowl, or venison, as they must be relieved by the fall in that of potatoes.

In the present season of scarcity, the high price of corn no doubt distresses the poor. But in times of moderate plenty, when corn is at its ordinary or average price, the natural rise in the price of any other sort of rude produce cannot much affect them. They suffer more, perhaps, by the artificial rise which has been occasioned by taxes in the price of some manufactured commodities, as of salt, soap, leather, candles, malt, beer, ale, etc.

Effects of the Progress of Improvement upon the Real Price of Manufactures.

It is the natural effect of improvement, however, to diminish gradually the real price of almost all manufactures. That of the manufacturing workmanship diminishes, perhaps, in all of them without exception. In consequence of better machinery, of greater dexterity, and of a more proper division and distribution of work, all of which are the natural effects of improvement, a much smaller quantity of labor becomes requisite for executing any particular piece of work; and though, in consequence of the flourishing circumstances of the society, the real price of labor should rise very considerably, yet the great diminution of the quantity will generally much more than compensate the greatest rise which can happen in the price.

There are, indeed, a few manufactures, in which the necessary rise in the real price of the rude materials will more than compensate all the advantages which improvement can introduce into the execution of the work. In carpenters' and joiners' work, and in the coarser sort of cabinet work, the necessary rise in the real price of barren timber, in consequence of the improvement of land, will more than compensate all the advantages which can be derived from the best machinery, the greatest dexterity, and the most proper division and distribution of work.

But in all cases in which the real price of the rude material either does not rise at all, or does not rise very much, that of the manufactured commodity sinks very considerably.

This diminution of price has, in the course of the present and preceding century, been most remarkable in those manufactures of which the materials are the coarser metals. A better movement of a watch, than about the middle of the last century could have been bought for twenty pounds, may now perhaps be had for twenty shillings. In the work of cutlers and locksmiths, in all the toys which are made of the coarser metals, and in all those goods which are commonly known by the name of Birmingham and Sheffield ware, there has been, during the same period, a very great reduction of price, though not altogether so great as in watch-work. It has, however, been sufficient to astonish the workmen of every other part of Europe, who in many cases acknowledge that they can produce no work of equal goodness for double or even for triple the price. There are perhaps no manufactures, in which the division of labor can be carried further, or in which the machinery employed admits of a greater variety of improvements, than those of which the materials are the coarser metals.

In the clothing manufacture there has, during the same period, been no such sensible reduction of price. The price of superfine cloth, I have been assured, on the contrary, has, within these five-and-twenty or thirty years, risen somewhat in proportion to its quality, owing, it was said, to a considerable rise in the price of the material, which consists altogether of Spanish wool. That of the Yorkshire cloth, which is made altogether of English wool, is said, indeed, during the course of the present century, to have fallen a good deal in proportion to its quality. Quality, however, is so very disputable a matter, that I look upon all information of this kind as somewhat uncertain. In the clothing manufacture, the division of labor is nearly the same now as it was a century ago, and the machinery employed is not very different. There may, however, have been some small improvements in both, which may have occasioned some reduction of price.

But the reduction will appear much more sensible and undeniable, if we compare the price of this manufacture in the present times with what it was in a much remoter period, towards the end of the fifteenth century, when the labor was probably much less subdivided, and the machinery employed much more imperfect, than it is at present.

In 1487, being the 4th of Henry VII, it was enacted, that "whosoever shall sell by retail a broad yard of the finest scarlet grained, or of other grained cloth of the finest making, above sixteen shillings, shall forfeit forty shillings for every yard so sold." Sixteen shillings, therefore, containing about the same quantity of silver as four-and-twenty shillings of our present money, was, at that time, reckoned not an unreasonable price for a yard of the finest cloth; and as this is a sumptuary law, such cloth, it is probable, had usually been sold somewhat dearer. A guinea may be reckoned the highest price in the present times. Even though the quality of the cloths, therefore, should be supposed equal, and that of the present times is most probably much superior, yet, even upon this supposition, the money price of the finest cloth appears to have been considerably reduced since the end of the fifteenth century. But its real price has been much more reduced. Six shillings and eight pence was then, and long afterwards, reckoned the average price of a quarter of wheat. Sixteen shillings, therefore, was the price of two quarters and more than three bushels of wheat. Valuing a quarter of wheat in the present times at eight-and-twenty shillings, the real price of a yard of fine cloth must, in those times, have been equal to at least three pounds six shillings and sixpence of our present money. The man who bought it must have parted with the command of a quantity of labor and subsistence equal to what that sum would purchase in the present times.

The reduction in the real price of the coarse manufacture, though considerable, has not been so great as in that of the fine.

In 1463, being the 3rd of Edward IV it was enacted, that "no servant in husbandry nor common laborer, nor servant to any artificer inhabiting out of a city or burgh, shall use or wear in their clothing any cloth above two shillings the broad yard." In the 3rd of Edward IV, two shillings contained very nearly the same quantity of silver as four of our present money. But the Yorkshire cloth which is now sold at four shillings the yard, is probably much superior to any that was then made for the wearing of the very poorest order of common servants. Even the money price of their clothing, therefore, may, in proportion to the quality, be somewhat cheaper in the present than it was in those ancient times. The real price is certainly a good deal cheaper. Ten pence was then reckoned what is called the moderate and reasonable price of a bushel of wheat. Two shillings, therefore, was the price of two bushels and near two pecks of wheat, which in the present times, at three shillings and sixpence the bushel, would be worth eight shillings and nine pence. For a yard of this cloth the poor servant must have parted with the power of purchasing a quantity of subsistence equal to what eight shillings and nine pence would purchase in the present times. This is a sumptuary law, too, restraining the luxury and extravagance of the poor. Their clothing, therefore, had commonly been much more expensive.

The same order of people are, by the same law, prohibited from wearing hose, of which the price should exceed fourteen-pence the pair, equal to about eight-and-twenty pence of our present money. But fourteen-pence was in those times the price of a bushel and near two pecks of wheat; which in the present times, at three and sixpence the bushel, would cost five shillings and three pence. We should in the present times consider this as a very high price for a pair of stockings to a servant of the poorest and lowest order. He must however, in those times, have paid what was really equivalent to this price for them.

In the time of Edward IV the art of knitting stockings was probably not known in any part of Europe. Their hose were made of common cloth, which may have been one of the causes of their dearness. The first person that wore stockings in England is said to have been Queen Elizabeth. She received them as a present from the Spanish ambassador.

Both in the coarse and in the fine woolen manufacture, the machinery employed was much more imperfect in those ancient, than it is in the present times. It has since received three very capital improvements, besides, probably, many smaller ones, of which it may be difficult to ascertain either the number or the importance. The three capital improvements are, first, the exchange of the rock and spindle for the spinning wheel, which, with the same quantity of labor, will perform more than double the quantity of work. Secondly, the use of several very ingenious machines, which facilitate and abridge, in a still greater proportion, the winding of the worsted and woolen yarn, or the proper arrangement of the warp and woof before they are put into the loom; an operation which, previous to the invention of those machines, must have been extremely tedious and troublesome. Thirdly, the employment of the fulling-mill for thickening the cloth, instead of treading it in water. Neither wind nor water mills of any kind were known in England so early as the beginning of the sixteenth century, nor, so far as I know, in any other part of Europe north of the Alps. They had been introduced into Italy some time before.

The consideration of these circumstances may, perhaps, in some measure, explain to us why the real price both of the coarse and of the fine manufacture was so much higher in those ancient than it is in the present times. It cost a greater quantity of labor to bring the goods to market. When they were brought thither, therefore, they must have purchased, or exchanged for the price of, a greater quantity.

The coarse manufacture probably was, in those ancient times, carried on in England in the same manner as it always has been in countries where arts and manufactures are in their infancy. It was probably a household manufacture, in which every different part of the work was occasionally performed by all the different members of almost every private family, but so as to be their work only when they had nothing else to do, and not to be the principal business from which any of them derived the greater part of their subsistence. The work which is performed in this manner, it has already been observed, comes always much cheaper to market than that which is the principal or sole fund of the workman's subsistence. The fine manufacture, on the other hand, was not, in those times, carried on in England, but in the rich and commercial country of Flanders; and it was probably conducted then, in the same manner as now, by people who derived the whole, or the principal part of their subsistence from it. It was, besides, a foreign manufacture, and must have paid some duty, the ancient custom of tonnage and poundage at least, to the king. This duty, indeed, would not probably be very great. It was not then the policy of Europe to restrain, by high duties, the importation of foreign manufactures, but rather to encourage it, in order that merchants might be enabled to supply, at as easy a rate as possible, the great men with the conveniences and luxuries which they wanted, and which the industry of their own country could not afford them.

The consideration of these circumstances may, perhaps, in some measure explain to us why, in those ancient times, the real price of the coarse manufacture was, in proportion to that of the fine, so much lower than in the present times.

Conclusion of the Chapter

I shall conclude this very long chapter with observing, that every improvement in the circumstances of the society tends, either directly or indirectly, to raise the real rent of land to increase the real wealth of the landlord, his power of purchasing the labor, or the produce of the labor of other people.

The extension of improvement and cultivation tends to raise it directly. The landlord's share of the produce necessarily increases with the increase of the produce.

That rise in the real price of those parts of the rude produce of land, which is first the effect of the extended improvement and cultivation, and afterwards the cause of their being still further extended, the rise in the price of cattle, for example, tends, too, to raise the rent of land directly, and in a still greater proportion. The real value of the landlord's share, his real command of the labor of other people, not only rises with the real value of the produce, but the proportion of his share to the whole produce rises with it.

That produce, after the rise in its real price, requires no more labor to collect it than before. A smaller proportion of it will, therefore, be sufficient to replace, with the ordinary profit, the stock which employs that labor. A greater proportion of it must consequently belong to the landlord.

All those improvements in the productive powers of labor, which tend directly to reduce the rent price of manufactures, tend indirectly to raise the real rent of land. The landlord exchanges that part of his rude produce, which is over and above his own consumption, or, what comes to the same thing, the price of that part of it, for manufactured produce. Whatever reduces the real price of the latter, raises that of the former. An equal quantity of the former becomes thereby equivalent to a greater quantity of the latter; and the landlord is enabled to purchase a greater quantity of the conveniences, ornaments, or luxuries which he has occasion for.

Every increase in the real wealth of the society, every increase in the quantity of useful labor employed within it, tends indirectly to raise the real rent of land. A certain proportion of this labor naturally goes to the land. A greater number of men and cattle are employed in its cultivation, the produce increases with the increase of the stock which is thus employed in raising it, and the rent increases with the produce.

The contrary circumstances, the neglect of cultivation and improvement, the fall in the real price of any part of the rude produce of land, the rise in the real price of manufactures from the decay of manufacturing art and industry, the declension of the real wealth of the society, all tend, on the other hand, to lower the real rent of land, to reduce the real wealth of the landlord, to diminish his power of purchasing either the labor, or the produce of the labor, of other people.

The whole annual produce of the land and labor of every country, or, what comes to the same thing, the whole price of that annual produce, naturally divides itself, it has already been observed, into three parts; the rent of land, the wages of labor, and the profits of stock; and constitutes a revenue to three different orders of people; to those who live by rent, to those who live by wages, and to those who live by profit. These are the three great, original, and constituent, orders of every civilized society, from whose revenue that of every other order is ultimately derived.

The interest of the first of those three great orders, it appears from what has been just now said, is strictly and inseparably connected with the general interest of the society. Whatever either promotes or obstructs the one, necessarily promotes or obstructs the other. When the public deliberates concerning any regulation of commerce or police, the proprietors of land never can mislead it, with a view to promote the interest of their own particular order; at least, if they have any tolerable knowledge of that interest. They are, indeed, too often defective in this tolerable knowledge. They are the only one of the three orders whose revenue costs them neither labor nor care, but comes to them, as it were, of its own accord, and independent of any plan or project of their own. That indolence which is the natural effect of the ease and security of their situation, renders them too often, not only ignorant, but incapable of that application of mind, which is necessary in order to foresee and understand the consequence of any public regulation.

The interest of the second order, that of those who live by wages, is as strictly connected with the interest of the society as that of the first. The wages of the laborer, it has already been shown, are never so high as when the demand for labor is continually rising, or when the quantity employed is every year increasing considerably. When this real wealth of the society becomes stationary, his wages are soon reduced to what is barely enough to enable him to bring up a family, or to continue the race of laborers. When the society declines, they fall even below this. The order of proprietors may perhaps gain more by the prosperity of the society than that of laborers; but there is no order that suffers so cruelly from its decline. But though the interest of the laborer is strictly connected with that of the society, he is incapable either of comprehending that interest, or of understanding its connection with his own. His condition leaves him no time to receive the necessary information, and his education and habits are commonly such as to render him unfit to judge, even though he was fully informed. In the public deliberations, therefore, his voice is little heard, and less regarded; except upon particular occasions, when his clamor is animated, set on, and supported by his employers, not for his, but their own particular purposes.

His employers constitute the third order, that of those who live by profit. It is the stock that is employed for the sake of profit, which puts into motion the greater part of the useful labor of every society. The plans and projects of the employers of stock regulate and direct all the most important operation of labor, and profit is the end proposed by all those plans and projects. But the rate of profit does not, like rent and wages, rise with the prosperity, and fall with the declension of the society. On the contrary, it is naturally low in rich, and high in poor countries, and it is always highest in the countries which are going fastest to ruin. The interest of this third order, therefore, has not the same connection with the general interest of the society, as that of the other two. Merchants and master manufacturers are, in this order, the two classes of people who commonly employ the largest capitals, and who by their wealth draw to themselves the greatest share of the public consideration. As during their whole lives they are engaged in plans and projects, they have frequently more acuteness of understanding than the greater part of country gentlemen. As their thoughts, however, are commonly exercised rather about the interest of their own particular branch of business. than about that of the society, their judgment, even when given with the greatest candor (which it has not been upon every occasion), is much more to be depended upon with regard to the former of those two objects, than with regard to the latter. Their superiority over the country gentleman is, not so much in their knowledge of the public interest, as in their having a better knowledge of their own interest than he has of his. It is by this superior knowledge of their own interest that they have frequently imposed upon his generosity, and persuaded him to give up both his own interest and that of the public, from a very simple but honest conviction, that their interest, and not his, was the interest of the public.

The interest of the dealers, however, in any particular branch of trade or manufactures, is always in some respects different from, and even opposite to, that of the public. To widen the market, and to narrow the competition, is always the interest of the dealers. To widen the market may frequently be agreeable enough to the interest of the public; but to narrow the competition must always be against it, and can only serve to enable the dealers, by raising their profits above what they naturally would be, to levy, for their own benefit, an absurd tax upon the rest of their fellow-citizens. The proposal of any new law or regulation of commerce which comes from this order, ought always to be listened to with great precaution, and ought never to be adopted till after having been long and carefully examined, not only with the most scrupulous, but with the most suspicious attention. It comes from an order of men, whose interest is never exactly the same with that of the public, who have generally an interest to deceive and even to oppress the public, and who accordingly have, upon many occasions, both deceived and oppressed it.

Years XII	Price of the Quarter of Wheat each Year			Average of the different Prices of the same Year			The average Price of each Year in Money of the present Times		
	£	s.	d.	£	s.	d.	£	s.	d.
1202	0	12	0	0	0	0	1	16	0
1205	0	12	0						
	0	13	4	0	13	5	2	0	3
	0	15	0						
1223	0	12	0	0	0	0	1	16	0
1237	0	3	4	0	0	0	0	10	0
1243	0	2	0	0	0	0	0	6	0
1244	0	2	0	0	0	0	0	6	0
1246	0	16	0	0	0	0	2	8	0
1247	0	13	4	0	0	0	2	0	0
1257	1	4	0	0	0	0	3	12	0
1258	1	0	0						
	0	15	0	0	17	0	2	11	0
	0	16	0						
1270	4	16	0						
	6	8	0	5	12	0	16	16	0
1286	0	2	8						
	0	16	0	0	9	4	1	8	0
						Total	35	9	3
						Average	2	19	$1^{1}/_{4}$

Years XII	Price of the Quarter of Wheat each Year			Average of the different Prices of the same Year			The average Price of each Year in Money of the present Times		
	£	s.	d.	£	s.	d.	£	s.	d.
1287	0	3	4	0	0	0	0	10	0
1288	0	0	8						
	0	1	0						
	0	1	4						
	0	1	6						
	0	1	8	0	3	$1/4$	0	9	$3/4$
	0	2	0						
	0	3	4						
	0	9	4						
1289	0	12	0						
	0	6	0						
	0	2	0	0	10	$1^{1/2}$	1	10	$4^{1/2}$
	0	10	8						
	1	0	0						
1290	0	16	0	0	0	0	2	8	0
1294	0	16	0	0	0	0	2	8	0
1302	0	4	0	0	0	0	0	12	0
1309	0	7	2	0	0	0	1	1	6
1315	1	0	0	0	0	0	3	0	0
1316	1	0	0						
	1	10	0	1	10	6	4	11	6
	1	12	0						
	2	0	0						
1317	2	4	0						
	0	14	0						
	2	13	0	1	19	6	5	18	6
	4	0	0						
	0	6	8						
1336	0	2	0	0	0	0	0	6	0
1338	0	3	4	0	0	0	0	10	0
Total							23	4	$11^{1/4}$
Average							1	18	8

Years XII	Price of the Quarter of Wheat each Year			Average of the different Prices of the same Year			The average Price of each Year in Money of the present Times		
	£	s.	d.	£	s.	d.	£	s.	d.
1339	0	9	0	0	0	0	1	7	0
1349	0	2	0	0	0	0	0	5	2
1359	1	6	8	0	0	0	3	2	2
1361	0	2	0	0	0	0	0	4	8
1363	0	15	0	0	0	0	1	15	0
1369	1	0	0						
	1	4	0	1	2	0	2	9	4
1379	0	4	0	0	0	0	0	9	4
1387	0	2	0	0	0	0	0	4	8
1390	0	13	4						
	0	14	0	0	14	5	1	13	7
	0	16	0						
1401	0	16	0	0	0	0	1	17	6
1407	0	4	$4^3/4$						
	0	3	4	0	3	10	0	8	10
1416	0	16	0	0	0	0	1	12	0
						Total	15	9	4
						Average	1	5	$9^1/2$

Years XII	Price of the Quarter of Wheat each Year			Average of the different Prices of the same Year			The average Price of each Year in Money of the present Times		
	£	s.	d.	£	s.	d.	£	s.	d.
1423	0	8	0	0	0	0	0	16	0
1425	0	4	0	0	0	0	0	8	0
1434	1	6	8	0	0	0	2	13	4
1435	0	5	4	0	0	0	0	10	8
1439	1	0	0						
	1	6	8	1	3	4	2	6	8
1440	1	4	0	0	0	0	2	8	0
1444	0	4	4	0	4	2	0	8	4
	0	4	0						
1445	0	4	6	0	0	0	0	9	0
1447	0	8	0	0	0	0	0	16	0
1448	0	6	8	0	0	0	0	13	4
1449	0	5	0	0	0	0	0	10	0
1451	0	8	0	0	0	0	0	16	0
						Total	12	15	4
						Average	1	1	$3^1/2$

Years XII	Price of the Quarter of Wheat each Year			Average of the different Prices of the same Year			The average Price of each Year in Money of the present Times		
	£	s.	d.	£	s.	d.	£	s.	d.
1453	0	5	4	0	0	0	0	10	8
1455	0	1	2	0	0	0	0	2	4
1457	0	7	8	0	0	0	0	15	4
1459	0	5	0	0	0	0	0	10	0
1460	0	8	0	0	0	0	0	16	0
1463	0	2	0	0	1	10	0	3	8
	0	1	8						
1464	0	6	8	0	0	0	0	10	0
1486	1	4	0	0	0	0	1	17	0
1491	0	14	0	0	0	8	1	2	0
1494	0	4	0	0	0	0	0	6	0
1495	0	3	4	0	0	0	0	5	0
1497	1	0	0	0	0	0	1	11	0
						Total	8	9	0
						Average	0	14	1
1499	0	4	0	0	0	0	0	6	0
1504	0	5	8	0	0	0	0	8	6
1521	1	0	0	0	0	0	1	10	0
1551	0	8	0	0	0	0	0	2	0
1553	0	8	0	0	0	0	0	8	0
1554	0	8	0	0	0	0	0	8	0
1555	0	8	0	0	0	0	0	8	0
1556	0	8	0	0	0	0	0	8	0
1557	0	4	0						
	0	5	0	0	17	8 $1/2$	0	17	8 $1/2$
	0	8	0						
	2	13	4						
1558	0	8	0	0	0	0	0	8	0
1559	0	8	0	0	0	0	0	8	0
1560	0	8	0	0	0	0	0	8	0
						Total	6	0	2$1/2$
						Average	0	10	$1/2$

Years XII	Price of the Quarter of Wheat each Year			Average of the different Prices of the same Year			The average Price of each Year in Money of the present Times		
	£	s.	d.	£	s.	d.	£	s.	d.
1561	0	8	0	0	0	0	0	8	0
1562	0	8	0	0	0	0	0	8	0
1574	2	16	0						
	1	4	0	2	0	0	2	0	0
1587	3	4	0	0	0	0	3	4	0
1594	2	16	0	0	0	0	2	16	0
1595	2	13	0	0	0	0	2	13	0
1596	4	0	0	0	0	0	4	0	0
1597	5	4	0						
	4	0	0	4	12	0	4	12	0
1598	2	16	8	0	0	0	2	16	8
1599	1	19	2	0	0	0	1	19	2
1600	1	17	8	0	0	0	1	17	8
1601	1	14	10	0	0	0	1	14	10
						Total	28	9	4
						Average	2	7	5$\frac{1}{2}$

Prices of the Quarter of nine Bushels of the best or highest-priced Wheat at Windsor Market, on Lady Day and Michaelmas, from 1595 to 1764, both inclusive; the Price of each Year being the Medium between the highest Price of those Two Market days.

Wheat per Quarter				Wheat per Quarter			
Years	£	s.	d.	Years	£	s.	d.
1595 —	2	0	0	1621 —	1	10	4
1596 —	2	8	0	1622 —	2	18	8
1597 —	3	9	6	1623 —	2	12	0
1598 —	2	16	8	1624 —	2	8	0
1599 —	1	19	2	1625 —	2	12	0
1600 —	1	17	8	1626 —	2	9	4
1601 —	1	14	10	1627 —	1	16	0
1602 —	1	9	4	1628 —	1	8	0
1603 —	1	15	4	1629 —	2	2	0
1604 —	1	10	8	1630 —	2	15	8
1605 —	1	15	10	1631 —	3	8	0
1606 —	1	13	0	1632 —	2	13	4
1607 —	1	16	8	1633 —	2	18	0
1608 —	2	16	8	1634 —	2	16	0
1609 —	2	10	0	1635 —	2	16	0
1610 —	1	15	10	1636 —	2	16	8
1611 —	1	18	8	16)	40	0	0
1612 —	2	2	4	Average	2	10	0
1613 —	2	8	8				
1614 —	2	1	$8^{1}/_{2}$				
1615 —	1	18	8				
1616 —	2	0	4				
1617 —	2	8	8				
1618 —	2	6	8				
1619 —	1	15	4				
1620 —	1	10	4				
26)	54	0	$6^{1}/_{2}$				
Average	2	1	$6^{1}/_{2}$				

Wheat per Quarter			
Years	£	s.	d.
1637 —	2	13	0
1638 —	2	17	4
1639 —	2	4	10
1640 —	2	4	8
1641 —	2	8	0
1642 Wanting in the account. The year 1646 supplied by Bishop Fleetwood.			
	0	0	0
1643 —	0	0	0
1644 —	0	0	0
1645 —	0	0	0
1646 —	2	8	0
1647 —	3	13	8
1648 —	4	5	0
1649 —	4	0	0
1650 —	3	16	8
1651 —	3	13	4
1652 —	2	9	6
1653 —	1	15	6
1654 —	1	6	0
1655 —	1	13	4
1656 —	2	3	0
1657 —	2	6	8
1658 —	3	5	0
1659 —	3	6	0
1660 —	2	16	6
1661 —	3	10	0
1662 —	3	14	0
1663 —	2	17	0
1664 —	2	0	6
1665 —	2	9	4
1666 —	1	16	0
1667 —	1	16	0
1668 —	2	0	0
1669 —	2	4	4
1670 —	2	1	8
1671 —	2	2	0
1672 —	2	1	0
1673 —	2	6	8
1674 —	3	8	8
1675 —	3	4	8

Years	£	s.	d.
1676 —	1	18	0
1677 —	2	2	0
1678 —	2	19	0
1679 —	3	0	0
1680 —	2	5	0
1681 —	2	6	8
1682 —	2	4	0
1683 —	2	0	0
1684 —	2	4	0
1685 —	2	6	8
1686 —	1	14	0
1687 —	1	5	2
1688 —	2	6	0
1689 —	1	10	0
1690 —	1	14	8
1691 —	1	14	0
1692 —	2	6	8
1693 —	3	7	8
1694 —	3	4	0
1695 —	2	13	0
1696 —	3	11	0
1697 —	3	0	0
1698 —	3	8	4
1699 —	3	4	0
1700 —	2	0	0
60)	153	1	8
Average	2	11	$\frac{1}{3}$

Wheat per Quarter			
Years	£	s.	d.
1701 —	1	17	8
1702 —	1	9	6
1703 —	1	16	0
1704 —	2	6	6
1705 —	1	10	0
1706 —	1	6	0
1707 —	1	8	6
1708 —	2	1	6
1709 —	3	18	6
1710 —	3	18	0
1711 —	2	14	0
1712 —	2	6	4
1713 —	2	11	0
1714 —	2	10	4

1715 —	2	3	0		1757 —	3	0	0
1716 —	2	8	0		1758 —	2	10	0
1717 —	2	5	8		1759 —	1	19	10
1718 —	1	18	10		1760 —	1	16	6
1719 —	1	15	0		1761 —	1	10	3
1720 —	1	17	0		1762 —	1	19	0
1721 —	1	17	6		1763 —	2	0	9
1722 —	1	16	0		1764 —	2	6	9
1723 —	1	14	8		64)	129	13	6
1724 —	1	17	0		Average	2	0	6¾

1725 —	2	8	6
1726 —	2	6	0

Wheat per Quarter

Years	£	s.	d.
1727 —	2	2	0
1728 —	2	14	6
1731 —	1	12	10
1729 —	2	6	10
1732 —	1	6	8
1730 —	1	16	6
1733 —	1	8	4
1731 —	1	12	10
1734 —	1	18	10
1732 —	1	6	8
1735 —	2	3	0
1733 —	1	8	4
1736 —	2	0	4
1734 —	1	18	10
1737 —	1	18	0
1735 —	2	3	0
1738 —	1	15	6
1736 —	2	0	4
1739 —	1	18	6
1737 —	1	18	0
1740 —	2	10	8
1738 —	1	15	6
10)	18	12	8
1739 —	1	18	6
	1	17	3½
1740 —	2	10	8
1741 —	2	6	8

Wheat per Quarter

Years	£	s.	d.
1742 —	1	14	0
1741 —	2	6	8
1743 —	1	4	10
1742 —	1	14	0
1744 —	1	4	10
1743 —	1	4	10
1745 —	1	7	6
1744 —	1	4	10
1746 —	1	19	0
1745 —	1	7	6
1747 —	1	14	10
1746 —	1	19	0
1748 —	1	17	0
1747 —	1	14	10
1749 —	1	17	0
1748 —	1	17	0
1750 —	1	12	6
1749 —	1	17	0
10)	16	18	2
1750 —	1	12	6
	1	13	9¾
1751 —	1	18	6
1752 —	2	1	10
1753 —	2	4	8
1754 —	1	14	8
1755 —	1	13	10
1756 —	2	5	3

Book II

Of the Nature, Accumulation, and Employment of Stock

INTRODUCTION

In that rude state of society, in which there is no division of labor, in which exchanges are seldom made, and in which every man provides everything for himself, it is not necessary that any stock should be accumulated, or stored up beforehand, in order to carry on the business of the society. Every man endeavors to supply, by his own industry, his own occasional wants, as they occur. When he is hungry, he goes to the forest to hunt; when his coat is worn out, he clothes himself with the skin of the first large animal he kills: and when his hut begins to go to ruin, he repairs it, as well as he can, with the trees and the turf that are nearest it.

But when the division of labor has once been thoroughly introduced, the produce of a man's own labor can supply but a very small part of his occasional wants. The far greater part of them are supplied by the produce of other men's labor, which he purchases with the produce, or, what is the same thing, with the price of the produce, of his own. But this purchase cannot be made till such time as the produce of his own labor has not only been completed, but sold. A stock of goods of different kinds, therefore, must be stored up somewhere, sufficient to maintain him, and to supply him with the materials and tools of his work, till such time at least as both these events can be brought about. A weaver cannot apply himself entirely to his peculiar business, unless there is beforehand stored up somewhere, either in his own possession, or in that of some other person, a stock sufficient to maintain him, and to supply him with the materials and tools of his work, till he has not only completed, but sold his web. This accumulation must evidently be previous to his applying his industry for so long a time to such a peculiar business.

As the accumulation of stock must, in the nature of things, be previous to the division of labor, so labor can be more and more subdivided in proportion only as stock is previously more and more accumulated. The quantity of materials which the same number of people can work up, increases in a great proportion as labor comes to be more and more subdivided; and as the operations of each workman are gradually reduced to a greater degree of simplicity, a variety of new machines come to be invented for facilitating and abridging those operations. As the division of labor advances, therefore, in order to give constant employment to an equal number of workmen, an equal stock of provisions, and a greater stock of materials and tools than what would have been necessary in a ruder state of things, must be accumulated beforehand. But the number of workmen in every branch of business generally increases with the division of labor in that branch; or rather it is the increase of their number which enables them to class and subdivide themselves in this manner.

As the accumulation of stock is previously necessary for carrying on this great improvement in the productive powers of labor, so that accumulation naturally leads to this improvement. The person who employs his stock in maintaining labor, necessarily wishes to employ it in such a manner as to produce as great a quantity of work as possible. He endeavors, therefore, both to make among his workmen the most proper distribution of employment, and to furnish them with the best machines which he can either invent or afford to purchase. His abilities, in both these respects, are generally in proportion to the extent of his stock, or to the number of people whom it can employ. The quantity of industry, therefore, not only increases in every country with the increase of the stock which employs it, but, in consequence of that increase, the same quantity of industry produces a much greater quantity of work.

Such are in general the effects of the increase of stock upon industry and its productive powers.

In the following book, I have endeavored to explain the nature of stock, the effects of its accumulation into capital of different kinds, and the effects of the different employments of those capitals. This book is divided into five chapters. In the first chapter, I have endeavored to show what are the different parts or branches into which the stock, either of an individual, or of a great society, naturally divides itself. In the second, I have endeavored to explain the nature and operation of money, considered as a particular branch of the general stock of the society. The stock which is accumulated into a capital, may either be employed by the person to whom it belongs, or it may be lent to some other person. In the third and fourth chapters, I have endeavored to examine the manner in which it operates in both these situations. The fifth and last chapter treats of the different effects which the different employments of capital immediately produce upon the quantity, both of national industry, and of the annual produce of land and labor.

CHAPTER I

Of the Division of Stock

When the stock which a man possesses is no more than sufficient to maintain him for a few days or a few weeks, he seldom thinks of deriving any revenue from it. He consumes it as sparingly as he can, and endeavors, by his labor, to acquire something which may supply its place before it be consumed altogether. His revenue is, in this case, derived from his labor only. This is the state of the greater part of the laboring poor in all countries.

But when he possesses stock sufficient to maintain him for months or years, he naturally endeavors to derive a revenue from the greater part of it, reserving only so much for his immediate consumption as may maintain him till this revenue begins to come in. His whole stock, therefore, is distinguished into two parts. That part which he expects is to afford him this revenue is called his capital. The other is that which supplies his immediate consumption, and which consists either, first, in that portion of his whole stock which was originally reserved for this purpose; or, secondly, in his revenue, from whatever source derived, as it gradually comes in; or, thirdly, in such things as had been purchased by either of these in former years, and which are not yet entirely consumed, such as a stock of clothes, household furniture, and the like. In one or other, or all of these three articles, consists the stock which men commonly reserve for their own immediate consumption.

There are two different ways in which a capital may be employed so as to yield a revenue or profit to its employer.

First, it may be employed in raising, manufacturing, or purchasing goods, and selling them again with a profit. The capital employed in this manner yields no revenue or profit to its employer, while it either remains in his possession, or continues in the same shape. The goods of the merchant yield him no revenue or profit till he sells them for money, and the money yields him as little till it is again exchanged for goods. His capital is continually going from him in one shape, and returning to him in another; and it is only by means of such circulation, or successive changes, that it can yield him any profit. Such capitals, therefore, may very properly be called circulating capitals.

Secondly, it may be employed in the improvement of land, in the purchase of useful machines and instruments of trade, or in such like things as yield a revenue or profit without changing masters, or circulating any further. Such capitals, therefore, may very properly be called fixed capitals.

Different occupations require very different proportions between the fixed and circulating capitals employed in them.

The capital of a merchant, for example, is altogether a circulating capital. He has occasion for no machines or instruments of trade, unless his shop or warehouse be considered as such.

Some part of the capital of every master artificer or manufacturer must be fixed in the instruments of his trade. This part, however, is very small in some, and very great in others, A master tailor requires no other instruments of trade but a parcel of needles. Those of the master shoemaker are a little, though but a very little, more expensive. Those of the weaver rise a good deal above those of the shoemaker. The far greater part of the capital of all such master artificers, however, is circulated either in the wages of their workmen, or in the price of their materials, and repaid, with a profit, by the price of the work.

In other works a much greater fixed capital is required. In a great ironwork, for example, the furnace for melting the ore, the forge, the slit-mill, are instruments of trade which cannot be erected without a very great expense. In coal works, and mines of every kind, the machinery necessary, both for drawing out the water, and for other purposes, is frequently still more expensive.

That part of the capital of the farmer which is employed in the instruments of agriculture is a fixed, that which is employed in the wages and maintenance of his laboring servants is a circulating capital. He makes a profit of the one by keeping it in his own possession, and of the other by parting with it. The price or value of his laboring cattle is a fixed capital, in the same manner as that of the instruments of husbandry; their maintenance is a circulating capital, in the same manner as that of the laboring servants. The farmer makes his profit by keeping the laboring cattle, and by parting with their maintenance. Both the price and the maintenance of the cattle which are bought in and fattened, not for labor, but for sale, are a circulating capital. The farmer makes his profit by parting with them. A flock of sheep or a herd of cattle, that, in a breeding country, is brought in neither for labor nor for sale, but in order to make a profit by their wool, by their milk, and by their increase, is a fixed capital. The profit is made by keeping them. Their maintenance is a circulating capital. The profit is made by parting with it; and it comes back with both its own profit and the profit upon the whole price of the cattle, in the price of the wool, the milk, and the increase. The whole value of the seed, too, is properly a fixed capital. Though it goes backwards and forwards between the ground and the granary, it never changes masters, and therefore does not properly circulate. The farmer makes his profit, not by its sale, but by its increase.

The general stock of any country or society is the same with that of all its inhabitants or members; and, therefore, naturally divides itself into the same three portions, each of which has a distinct function or office.

The first is that portion which is reserved for immediate consumption, and of which the characteristic is, that it affords no revenue or profit. It consists in the stock of food, clothes, household furniture, etc. which have been purchased by their proper consumers, but which are not yet entirely consumed. The whole stock of mere dwelling-houses, too, subsisting at any one time in the country, make a part of this first portion. The stock that is laid out in a house, if it is to be the dwelling-house of the proprietor, ceases from that moment to serve in the function of a capital, or to afford any revenue to its owner. A dwelling-house, as such, contributes nothing to the revenue of its inhabitant; and though it is, no doubt, extremely useful to him, it is as his clothes and household furniture are useful to him, which, however, make a part of his expense, and not of his revenue. If it is to be let to a tenant for rent, as the house itself can produce nothing, the tenant must always pay the rent out of some other revenue, which he derives, either from labor, or stock, or land. Though a house, therefore, may yield a revenue to its proprietor, and thereby serve in the function of a capital to him, it cannot yield any to the public, nor serve in the function of a capital to it, and the revenue of the whole body of the people can never be in the smallest degree increased by it. Clothes and household furniture, in the same manner, sometimes yield a revenue, and thereby serve in the function of a capital to particular persons. In countries where masquerades are common, it is a trade to let or rent out masquerade dresses for a night. Upholsterers frequently let furniture by the month or by the year. Undertakers let the furniture of funerals by the day and by the week. Many people let furnished houses, and get a rent, not only for the use of the house, but for that of the furniture. The revenue, however, which is derived from such things, must always be ultimately drawn from some other source of revenue. Of all parts of the stock, either of an individual or of a society, reserved for immediate consumption, what is laid out in houses is most slowly consumed. A stock of clothes may last several years; a stock of furniture half a century or a century; but a stock of houses, well built and properly taken care of, may last many centuries. Though the period of their total consumption, however, is more distant, they are still as really a stock reserved for immediate consumption as either clothes or household furniture.

The second of the three portions into which the general stock of the society divides itself, is the fixed capital; of which the characteristic is, that it affords a revenue or profit without circulating or changing masters. It consists chiefly of the four following articles.

First, of all useful machines and instruments of trade, which facilitate and abridge labor.

Secondly, of all those profitable buildings which are the means of procuring a revenue, not only to the proprietor who lets them for a rent, but to the person who possesses them, and pays that rent for them; such as shops, warehouses, workhouses, farmhouses, with all their necessary buildings, stables, granaries, etc. These are very different from mere dwelling-houses. They are a sort of instruments of trade, and may be considered in the same light.

Thirdly, of the improvements of land, of what has been profitably laid out in clearing, draining, inclosing, manuring, and reducing it into the condition most proper for tillage and culture. An improved farm may very justly be regarded in the same light as those useful machines which facilitate and abridge labor, and by means of which an equal circulating capital can afford a much greater revenue to its employer. An improved farm is equally advantageous and more durable than any of those machines, frequently requiring no other repairs than the most profitable application of the farmer's capital employed in cultivating it.

Fourthly, of the acquired and useful abilities of all the inhabitants and members of the society. The acquisition of such talents, by the maintenance of the acquirer during his education, study, or apprenticeship, always costs a real expense, which is a capital fixed and realized, as it were, in his person. Those talents, as they make a part of his fortune, so do they likewise that of the society to which he belongs. The improved dexterity of a workman may be considered in the same light as a machine or instrument of trade which facilitates and abridges labor, and which, though it costs a certain expense, repays that expense with a profit.

The third and last of the three portions into which the general stock of the society naturally divides itself, is the circulating capital, of which the characteristic is, that it affords a revenue only by circulating or changing masters. It is composed likewise of four parts.

First, of the money, by means of which all the other three are circulated and distributed to their proper consumers.

Secondly, of the stock of provisions which are in the possession of the butcher, the grazier, the farmer, the corn merchant, the brewer, etc. and from the sale of which they expect to derive a profit.

Thirdly, of the materials, whether altogether rude, or more or less manufactured, of clothes, furniture, and building which are not yet made up into any of those three shapes, but which remain in the hands of the growers, the manufacturers, the mercers, and drapers, the timber merchants, the carpenters and joiners, the brickmakers, etc.

Fourthly, and lastly, of the work which is made up and completed, but which is still in the hands of the merchant and manufacturer, and not yet disposed of or distributed to the proper consumers; such as the finished work which we frequently find ready made in the shops of the smith, the cabinetmaker, the goldsmith, the jeweler, the china merchant, etc. The circulating capital consists, in this manner, of the provisions, materials, and finished work of all kinds that are in the hands of their respective dealers, and of the money that is necessary for circulating and distributing them to those who are finally to use or to consume them.

Of these four parts, three—provisions, materials, and finished work—are either annually or in a longer or shorter period, regularly withdrawn from it, and placed either in the fixed capital, or in the stock reserved for immediate consumption.

Every fixed capital is both originally derived from, and requires to be continually supported by, a circulating capital. All useful machines and instruments of trade are originally derived from a circulating capital, which furnishes the materials of which they are made, and the maintenance of the workmen who make them. They require, too, a capital of the same kind to keep them in constant repair.

No fixed capital can yield any revenue but by means of a circulating capital. The most useful machines and instruments of trade will produce nothing, without the circulating capital, which affords the materials they are employed upon, and the maintenance of the workmen who employ them. Land, however improved, will yield no revenue without a circulating capital, which maintains the laborers who cultivate and collect its produce.

To maintain and augment the stock which may be reserved for immediate consumption, is the sole end and purpose both of the fixed and circulating capitals. It is this stock which feeds, clothes, and lodges the people. Their riches or poverty depend upon the abundant or sparing supplies which those two capitals can afford to the stock reserved for immediate consumption.

So great a part of the circulating capital being continually withdrawn from it, in order to be placed in the other two branches of the general stock of the society, it must in its turn require continual supplies without which it would soon cease to exist. These supplies are principally drawn from three sources; the produce of land, of mines, and of fisheries. These afford continual supplies of provisions and materials, of which part is afterwards wrought up into finished work and by which are replaced the provisions, materials, and finished work, continually withdrawn from the circulating capital. From mines, too, is drawn what is necessary for maintaining and augmenting that part of it which consists in money. For though, in the ordinary course of business, this part is not, like the other three, necessarily withdrawn from it, in order to be placed in the other two branches of the general stock of the society, it must, however, like all other things, be wasted and worn out at last, and sometimes, too, be either lost or sent abroad, and must, therefore, require continual, though no doubt much smaller supplies.

Lands, mines, and fisheries, require all both a fixed and circulating capital to cultivate them; and their produce replaces, with a profit not only those capitals, but all the others in the society. Thus the farmer annually replaces to the manufacturer the provisions which he had consumed, and the materials which he had wrought up the year before; and the manufacturer replaces to the farmer the finished work which he had wasted and worn out in the same time. This is the real exchange that is annually made between those two orders of people, though it seldom happens that the rude produce of the one, and the manufactured produce of the other, are directly bartered for one another; because it seldom happens that the farmer sells his corn and his cattle, his flax and his wool, to the very same person of whom he chooses to purchase the clothes, furniture, and instruments of trade, which he wants. He sells, therefore, his rude produce for money, with which he can purchase, wherever it is to be had, the manufactured produce he has occasion for. Land even replaces, in part at least, the capitals with which fisheries and mines are cultivated. It is the produce of land which draws the fish from the waters; and it is the produce of the surface of the earth which extracts the minerals from its bowels.

The produce of land, mines, and fisheries, when their natural fertility is equal, is in proportion to the extent and proper application of the capitals employed about them. When the capitals are equal, and equally well applied, it is in proportion to their natural fertility.

In all countries where there is a tolerable security, every man of common understanding will endeavor to employ whatever stock he can command, in procuring either present enjoyment or future profit. If it is employed in procuring present enjoyment, it is a stock reserved for immediate consumption. If it is employed in procuring future profit, it must procure this profit either by staying with him, or by going from him. In the one case it is a fixed, in the other it is a circulating capital. A man must be perfectly crazy, who, where there is a tolerable security, does not employ all the stock which he commands, whether it be his own, or borrowed of other people, in some one or other of those three ways.

In those unfortunate countries, indeed, where men are continually afraid of the violence of their superiors, they frequently bury or conceal a great part of their stock, in order to have it always at hand to carry with them to some place of safety, in case of their being threatened with any of those disasters to which they consider themselves at all times exposed. This is said to be a common practice in Turkey, in Indostan, and, I believe, in most other governments of Asia. It seems to have been a common practice among our ancestors during the violence of the feudal government. Treasure-trove was, in these times, considered as no contemptible part of the revenue of the greatest sovereigns in Europe. It consisted in such treasure as was found concealed in the earth, and to which no particular person could prove any right. This was regarded, in those times, as so important an object, that it was always considered as belonging to the sovereign, and neither to the finder nor to the proprietor of the land, unless the right to it had been conveyed to the latter by an express clause in his charter. It was put upon the same footing with gold and silver mines, which, without a special clause in the charter, were never supposed to be comprehended in the general grant of the lands, though mines of lead, copper, tin, and coal were, as things of smaller consequence.

CHAPTER II

Of Money, Considered as a Particular Branch of the General Stock of the Society, or of the Expense of Maintaining the National Capital

It has been shown in the First Book, that the price of the greater part of commodities resolves itself into three parts, of which one pays the wages of the labor, another the profits of the stock, and a third the rent of the land which had been employed in producing and bringing them to market: that there are, indeed, some commodities of which the price is made up of two of those parts only, the wages of labor, and the profits of stock; and a very few in which it consists altogether in one, the wages of labor; but that the price of every commodity necessarily resolves itself into some one or other, or all, of those three parts; every part of it which goes neither to rent nor to wages, being necessarily profit to some body.

Since this is the case, it has been observed, with regard to every particular commodity, taken separately, it must be so with regard to all the commodities which compose the whole annual produce of the land and labor of every country, taken complexly. The whole price or exchangeable value of that annual produce must resolve itself into the same three parts, and be parceled out among the different inhabitants of the country, either as the wages of their labor, the profits of their stock, or the rent of their land.

But though the whole value of the annual produce of the land and labor of every country, is thus divided among, and constitutes a revenue to, its different inhabitants; yet, as in the rent of a private estate, we distinguish between the gross rent and the neat rent, so may we likewise in the revenue of all the inhabitants of a great country.

The gross rent of a private estate comprehends whatever is paid by the farmer; the neat rent, what remains free to the landlord, after deducting the expense of management, of repairs, and all other necessary charges; or what, without hurting his estate, he can afford to place in his stock reserved for immediate consumption, or to spend upon his table, equipage, the ornaments of his house and furniture, his private enjoyments and amusements. His real wealth is in proportion, not to his gross, but to his neat rent.

The gross revenue of all the inhabitants of a great country comprehends the whole annual produce of their land and labor; the neat revenue, what remains free to them, after deducting the expense of maintaining first, their fixed, and, secondly, their circulating capital, or what, without encroaching upon their capital, they can place in their stock reserved for immediate consumption, or spend upon their subsistence, conveniences, and amusements. Their real wealth, too, is in proportion, not to their gross, but to their neat revenue.

The whole expense of maintaining the fixed capital must evidently be excluded from the neat revenue of the society. Neither the materials necessary for supporting their useful machines and instruments of trade, their profitable buildings, etc. nor the produce of the labor necessary for fashioning those materials into the proper form, can ever make any part of it. The price of that labor may indeed make a part of it; as the workmen so employed may place the whole value of their wages in their stock reserved for immediate consumption. But in other sorts of labor, both the price and the produce go to this stock; the price to that of the workmen, the produce to that of other people, whose subsistence, conveniences, and amusements, are augmented by the labor of those workmen.

The intention of the fixed capital is to increase the productive powers of labor, or to enable the same number of laborers to perform a much greater quantity of work. In a farm where all the necessary buildings, fences, drains, communications, etc. are in the most perfect good order, the same number of laborers and laboring cattle will raise a much greater produce, than in one of equal extent and equally good ground, but not furnished with equal conveniences. In manufactures, the same number of hands, assisted with the best machinery, will work up a much greater quantity of goods than with more imperfect instruments of trade. The expense which is properly laid out upon a fixed capital of any kind, is always repaid with great profit, and increases the annual produce by a much greater value than that of the support which such improvements require. This support, however, still requires a certain portion of that produce. A certain quantity of materials, and the labor of a certain number of workmen, both of which might have been immediately employed to augment the food, clothing, and lodging, the subsistence and conveniences of the society, are thus diverted to another employment, highly advantageous indeed, but still different from this one. It is upon this account that all such improvements in mechanics, as enable the same number of workmen to perform an equal quantity of work with cheaper and simpler machinery than had been usual before, are always regarded as advantageous to every society. A certain quantity of materials, and the labor of a certain number of workmen, which had before been employed in supporting a more complex and expensive machinery, can afterwards be applied to augment the quantity of work which that or any other machinery is useful only for performing. The undertaker of some great manufactory, who employs a thousand a-year in the maintenance of his machinery, if he can reduce this expense to five hundred, will naturally employ the other five hundred in purchasing an additional quantity of materials, to be wrought up by an additional number of workmen. The quantity of that work, therefore, which his machinery was useful only for performing, will naturally be augmented, and with it all the advantage and convenience which the society can derive from that work.

The expense of maintaining the fixed capital in a great country, may very properly be compared to that of repairs in a private estate. The expense of repairs may frequently be necessary for supporting the produce of the estate, and consequently both the gross and the neat rent of the landlord. When by a more proper direction, however, it can be diminished without occasioning any diminution of produce, the gross rent remains at least the same as before, and the neat rent is necessarily augmented.

But though the whole expense of maintaining the fixed capital is thus necessarily excluded from the neat revenue of the society, it is not the same case with that of maintaining the circulating capital. Of the four parts of which this latter capital is composed, money, provisions, materials, and finished work, the three last, it has already been observed, are regularly withdrawn from it, and placed either in the fixed capital of the society, or in their stock reserved for immediate consumption. Whatever portion of those consumable goods is not employed in maintaining the former, goes all to the latter, and makes a part of the neat revenue of the society. The maintenance of those three parts of the circulating capital, therefore, withdraws no portion of the annual produce from the neat revenue of the society, besides what is necessary for maintaining the fixed capital.

The circulating capital of a society is in this respect different from that of an individual. That of an individual is totally excluded from making any part of his neat revenue, which must consist altogether in his profits. But though the circulating capital of every individual makes a part of that of the society to which he belongs, it is not upon that account totally excluded from making a part likewise of their neat revenue. Though the whole goods in a merchant's shop must by no means be placed in his own stock reserved for immediate consumption, they may in that of other people, who, from a revenue derived from other funds, may regularly replace their value to him, together with its profits, without occasioning any diminution either of his capital or of theirs.

Money, therefore, is the only part of the circulating capital of a society, of which the maintenance can occasion any diminution in their neat revenue.

The fixed capital, and that part of the circulating capital which consists in money, so far as they affect the revenue of the society, bear a very great resemblance to one another.

First, as those machines and instruments of trade, etc. require a certain expense, first to erect them, and afterwards to support them, both which expenses, though they make a part of the gross, are deductions from the neat revenue of the society; so the stock of money which circulates in any country must require a certain expense, first to collect it, and afterwards to support it; both which expenses, though they make a part of the gross, are, in the same manner, deductions from the neat revenue of the society. A certain quantity of very valuable materials, gold and silver, and of very curious labor, instead of augmenting the stock reserved for immediate consumption, the subsistence, conveniences, and amusements of individuals, is employed in supporting that great but expensive instrument of commerce, by means of which every individual in the society has his subsistence, conveniences, and amusements, regularly distributed to him in their proper proportions.

Secondly, as the machines and instruments of trade, etc. which compose the fixed capital either of an individual or of a society, make no part either of the gross or of the neat revenue of either; so money, by means of which the whole revenue of the society is regularly distributed among all its different members, makes itself no part of that revenue. The great wheel of circulation is altogether different from the goods which are circulated by means of it. The revenue of the society consists altogether in those goods, and not in the wheel which circulates them. In computing either the gross or the neat revenue of any society, we must always, from the whole annual circulation of money and goods, deduct the whole value of the money, of which not a single farthing can ever make any part of either.

It is the ambiguity of language only which can make this proposition appear either doubtful or paradoxical. When properly explained and understood, it is almost self-evident.

When we talk of any particular sum of money, we sometimes mean nothing but the metal pieces of which it is composed, and sometimes we include in our meaning some obscure reference to the goods which can be had in exchange for it, or to the power of purchasing which the possession of it conveys. Thus, when we say that the circulating money of England has been computed at eighteen millions, we mean only to express the amount of the metal pieces, which some writers have computed, or rather have supposed, to circulate in that country. But when we say that a man is worth fifty or a hundred pounds a-year, we mean commonly to express, not only the amount of the metal pieces which are annually paid to him, but the value of the goods which he can annually purchase or consume; we mean commonly to ascertain what is or ought to be his way of living, or the quantity and quality of the necessaries and conveniences of life in which he can with propriety indulge himself.

When, by any particular sum of money, we mean not only to express the amount of the metal pieces of which it is composed, but to include in its signification some obscure reference to the goods which can be had in exchange for them, the wealth or revenue which it in this case denotes, is equal only to one of the two values which are thus intimated somewhat ambiguously by the same word, and to the latter more properly than to the former, to the money's worth more properly than to the money.

Thus, if a guinea be the weekly pension of a particular person, he can in the course of the week purchase with it a certain quantity of subsistence, conveniences, and amusements. In proportion as this quantity is great or small, so are his real riches, his real weekly revenue. His weekly revenue is certainly not equal both to the guinea and to what can be purchased with it, but only to one or other of those two equal values, and to the latter more properly than to the former, to the guinea's worth rather than to the guinea.

If the pension of such a person was paid to him, not in gold, but in a weekly bill for a guinea, his revenue surely would not so properly consist in the piece of paper, as in what he could get for it. A guinea may be considered as a bill for a certain quantity of necessaries and conveniences upon all the tradesmen in the neighborhood The revenue of the person to whom it is paid, does not so properly consist in the piece of gold, as in what he can get for it, or in what he can exchange it for. If it could be exchanged for nothing, it would, like a bill upon a bankrupt, be of no more value than the most useless piece of paper.

Though the weekly or yearly revenue of all the different inhabitants of any country, in the same manner, may be, and in reality frequently is, paid to them in money, their real riches, however, the real weekly or yearly revenue of all of them taken together, must always be great or small, in proportion to the quantity of consumable goods which they can all of them purchase with this money. The whole revenue of all of them taken together is evidently not equal to both the money and the consumable goods, but only to one or other of those two values, and to the latter more properly than to the former.

Though we frequently, therefore, express a person's revenue by the metal pieces which are annually paid to him, it is because the amount of those pieces regulates the extent of his power of purchasing, or the value of the goods which he can annually afford to consume. We still consider his revenue as consisting in this power of purchasing or consuming, and not in the pieces which convey it.

But if this is sufficiently evident, even with regard to an individual, it is still more so with regard to a society. The amount of the metal pieces which are annually paid to an individual, is often precisely equal to his revenue, and is upon that account the shortest and best expression of its value. But the amount of the metal pieces which circulate in a society, can never be equal to the revenue of all its members. As the same guinea which pays the weekly pension of one man today, may pay that of another tomorrow, and that of a third the day thereafter, the amount of the metal pieces which annually circulate in any country, must always be of much less value than the whole money pensions annually paid with them. But the power of purchasing, or the goods which can successively be bought with the whole of those money pensions, as they are successively paid, must always be precisely of the same value with those pensions; as must likewise be the revenue of the different persons to whom they are paid. That revenue, therefore, cannot consist in those metal pieces, of which the amount is so much inferior to its value, but in the power of purchasing, in the goods which can successively be bought with them as they circulate from hand to hand.

Money, therefore, the great wheel of circulation, the great instrument of commerce, like all other instruments of trade, though it makes a part, and a very valuable part, of the capital, makes no part of the revenue of the society to which it belongs; and though the metal pieces of which it is composed, in the course of their annual circulation, distribute to every man the revenue which properly belongs to him, they make themselves no part of that revenue.

Thirdly, and lastly, the machines and instruments of trade, etc. which compose the fixed capital, bear this further resemblance to that part of the circulating capital which consists in money; that as every saving in the expense of erecting and supporting those machines, which does not diminish the introductive powers of labor, is an improvement of the neat revenue of the society; so every saving in the expense of collecting and supporting that part of the circulating capital which consists in money is an improvement of exactly the same kind.

It is sufficiently obvious, and it has partly, too, been explained already, in what manner every saving in the expense of supporting the fixed capital is an improvement of the neat revenue of the society. The whole capital of the undertaker of every work is necessarily divided between his fixed and his circulating capital. While his whole capital remains the same, the smaller the one part, the greater must necessarily be the other. It is the circulating capital which furnishes the materials and wages of labor, and puts industry into motion. Every saving, therefore, in the expense of maintaining the fixed capital, which does not diminish the productive powers of labor, must increase the fund which puts industry into motion, and consequently the annual produce of land and labor, the real revenue of every society.

The substitution of paper in the room of gold and silver money, replaces a very expensive instrument of commerce with one much less costly, and sometimes equally convenient. Circulation comes to be carried on by a new wheel, which it costs less both to erect and to maintain than the old one. But in what manner this operation is performed, and in what manner it tends to increase either the gross or the neat revenue of the society, is not altogether so obvious, and may therefore require some further explication.

There are several different sorts of paper money; but the circulating notes of banks and bankers are the species which is best known, and which seems best adapted for this purpose. When the people of any particular country have such confidence in the fortune, probity and prudence of a particular banker, as to believe that he is always ready to pay upon demand such of his promissory notes as are likely to be at any time presented to him, those notes come to have the same currency as gold and silver money, from the confidence that such money can at any time be had for them.

A particular banker lends among his customers his own promissory notes, to the extent, we shall suppose, of a hundred thousand pounds. As those notes serve all the purposes of money, his debtors pay him the same interest as if he had lent them so much money. This interest is the source of his gain. Though some of those notes are continually coming back upon him for payment, part of them continue to circulate for months and years together. Though he has generally in circulation, therefore, notes to the extent of a hundred thousand pounds, twenty thousand pounds in gold and silver may, frequently, be a sufficient provision for answering occasional demands. By this operation, therefore, twenty thousand pounds in gold and silver perform all the functions which a hundred thousand could otherwise have performed. The same exchanges may be made, the same quantity of consumable goods may be circulated and distributed to their proper consumers, by means of his promissory notes, to the value of a hundred thousand pounds, as by an equal value of gold and silver money. Eighty thousand pounds of gold and silver, therefore, can in this manner be spared from the circulation of the country; and if different operations of the the same kind should, at the same time, be carried on by many different banks and bankers, the whole circulation may thus be conducted with a fifth part only of the gold and silver which would otherwise have been requisite.

Let us suppose, for example, that the whole circulating money of some particular country amounted, at a particular time, to one million sterling, that sum being then sufficient for circulating the whole annual produce of their land and labor; let us suppose, too, that some time thereafter, different banks and bankers issued promissory notes payable to the bearer, to the extent of one million, reserving in their different coffers two hundred thousand pounds for answering occasional demands; there would remain, therefore, in circulation, eight hundred thousand pounds in gold and silver, and a million of bank notes, or eighteen hundred thousand pounds of paper and money together. But the annual produce of the land and labor of the country had before required only one million to circulate and distribute it to its proper consumers, and that annual produce cannot be immediately augmented by those operations of banking. One million, therefore, will be sufficient to circulate it after them. The goods to be bought and sold being precisely the same as before, the same quantity of money will be sufficient for buying and selling them. The channel of circulation, if I may be allowed such an expression, will remain precisely the same as before. One million we have supposed sufficient to fill that channel. Whatever, therefore, is poured into it beyond this sum, cannot run into it, but must overflow. One million eight hundred thousand pounds are poured into it. Eight hundred thousand pounds, therefore, must overflow, that sum being over and above what can be employed in the circulation of the country. But though this sum cannot be employed at home, it is too valuable to be allowed to lie idle. It will, therefore, be sent abroad, in order to seek that profitable employment which it cannot find at home. But the paper cannot go abroad; because at a distance from the banks which issue it, and from the country in which payment of it can be exacted by law, it will not be received in common payments. Gold and silver, therefore, to the amount of eight hundred thousand pounds, will be sent abroad, and the channel of home circulation will remain filled with a million of paper instead of a million of those metals which filled it before.

But though so great a quantity of gold and silver is thus sent abroad, we must not imagine that it is sent abroad for nothing, or that its proprietors make a present of it to foreign nations. They will exchange it for foreign goods of some kind or another, in order to supply the consumption either of some other foreign country, or of their own.

If they employ it in purchasing goods in one foreign country, in order to supply the consumption of another, or in what is called the carrying trade, whatever profit they make will be in addition to the neat revenue of their own country. It is like a new fund, created for carrying on a new trade; domestic business being now transacted by paper, and the gold and silver being converted into a fund for this new trade.

If they employ it in purchasing foreign goods for home consumption, they may either, first, purchase such goods as are likely to be consumed by idle people, who produce nothing, such as foreign wines, foreign silks, etc.; or, secondly, they may purchase an additional stock of materials, tools, and provisions, in order to maintain and employ an additional number of industrious people, who reproduce, with a profit, the value of their annual consumption.

So far as it is employed in the first way, it promotes prodigality, increases expense and consumption, without increasing production, or establishing any permanent fund for supporting that expense, and is in every respect hurtful to the society.

So far as it is employed in the second way, it promotes industry; and though it increases the consumption of the society, it provides a permanent fund for supporting that consumption; the people who consume reproducing, with a profit, the whole value of their annual consumption. The gross revenue of the society, the annual produce of their land and labor, is increased by the whole value which the labor of those workmen adds to the materials upon which they are employed, and their neat revenue by what remains of this value, after deducting what is necessary for supporting the tools and instruments of their trade.

That the greater part of the gold and silver which being forced abroad by those operations of banking, is employed in purchasing foreign goods for home consumption, is, and must be, employed in purchasing those of this second kind, seems not only probable, but almost unavoidable. Though some particular men may sometimes increase their expense very considerably, though their revenue does not increase at all, we maybe assured that no class or order of men ever does so; because, though the principles of common prudence do not always govern the conduct of every individual, they always influence that of the majority of every class or order. But the revenue of idle people, considered as a class or order, cannot, in the smallest degree, be increased by those operations of banking. Their expense in general, therefore, cannot be much increased by them, though that of a few individuals among them may, and in reality sometimes is. The demand of idle people, therefore, for foreign goods, being the same, or very nearly the same as before, a very small part of the money which, being forced abroad by those operations of banking, is employed in purchasing foreign goods for home consumption, is likely to be employed in purchasing those for their use. The greater part of it will naturally be destined for the employment of industry, and not for the maintenance of idleness.

When we compute the quantity of industry which the circulating capital of any society can employ, we must always have regard to those parts of it only which consist in provisions, materials, and finished work; the other, which consists in money, and which serves only to circulate those three, must always be deducted. In order to put industry into motion, three things are requisite; materials to work upon, tools to work with, and the wages or recompense for the sake of which the work is done. Money is neither a material to work upon, nor a tool to work with; and though the wages of the workman are commonly paid to him in money, his real revenue, like that of all other men, consists, not in the money, but in the money's worth; not in the metal pieces, but in what can be got for them.

The quantity of industry which any capital can employ, must evidently be equal to the number of workmen whom it can supply with materials, tools, and a maintenance suitable to the nature of the work. Money may be requisite for purchasing the materials and tools of the work, as well as the maintenance of the workmen; but the quantity of industry which the whole capital can employ, is certainly not equal both to the money which purchases, and to the materials, tools, and maintenance, which are purchased with it, but only to one or other of those two values, and to the latter more properly than to the former.

When paper is substituted in the room of gold and silver money, the quantity of the materials, tools, and maintenance, which the whole circulating capital can supply, may be increased by the whole value of gold and silver which used to be employed in purchasing them. The whole value of the great wheel of circulation and distribution is added to the goods which are circulated and distributed by means of it. The operation, in some measure, resembles that of the undertaker of some great work, who, in consequence of some improvement in mechanics, takes down his old machinery, and adds the difference between its price and that of the new to his circulating capital, to the fund from which he furnishes materials and wages to his workmen.

What is the proportion which the circulating money of any country bears to the whole value of the annual produce circulated by means of it, it is perhaps impossible to determine. It has been computed by different authors at a fifth, at a tenth, at a twentieth, and at a thirtieth, part of that value. But how small soever the proportion which the circulating money may bear to the whole value of the annual produce, as but a part, and frequently but a small part, of that produce, is ever destined for the maintenance of industry, it must always bear a very considerable proportion to that part. When, therefore, by the substitution of paper, the gold and silver necessary for circulation is reduced to, perhaps, a fifth part of the former quantity, if the value of only the greater part of the other four-fifths be added to the funds which are destined for the maintenance of industry, it must make a very considerable addition to the quantity of that industry, and, consequently, to the value of the annual produce of land and labor.

An operation of this kind has, within these five-and-twenty or thirty years, been performed in Scotland, by the erection of new banking companies in almost every considerable town, and even in some country villages. The effects of it have been precisely those above described. The business of the country is almost entirely carried on by means of the paper of those different banking companies, with which purchases and payments of all kinds are commonly made. Silver very seldom appears, except in the change of a twenty shilling bank note, and gold still seldomer. But though the conduct of all those different companies has not been unexceptionable, and has accordingly required an act of parliament to regulate it, the country, notwithstanding, has evidently derived great benefit from their trade. I have heard it asserted, that the trade of the city of Glasgow doubled in about fifteen years after the first erection of the banks there; and that the trade of Scotland has more than quadrupled since the first erection of the two public banks at Edinburgh; of which the one, called the Bank of Scotland, was established by act of parliament in 1695, and the other, called the Royal Bank, by royal charter in 1727. Whether the trade, either of Scotland in general, or of the city of Glasgow in particular, has really increased in so great a proportion, during so short a period, I do not pretend to know. If either of them has increased in this proportion, it seems to be an effect too great to be accounted for by the sole operation of this cause. That the trade and industry of Scotland, however, have increased very considerably during this period, and that the banks have contributed a good deal to this increase, cannot be doubted.

The value of the silver money which circulated in Scotland before the Union in 1707, and which, immediately after it, was brought into the Bank of Scotland, in order to be recoined, amounted to £411,117: 10: 9 sterling. No account has been got of the gold coin; but it appears from the ancient accounts of the mint of Scotland, that the value of the gold annually coined somewhat exceeded that of the silver. There were a good many people, too, upon this occasion, who, from a diffidence of repayment, did not bring their silver into the Bank of Scotland; and there was, besides, some English coin, which was not called in. The whole value of the gold and silver, therefore, which circulated in Scotland before the Union, cannot be estimated at less than a million sterling. It seems to have constituted almost the whole circulation of that country; for though the circulation of the Bank of Scotland, which had then no rival, was considerable, it seems to have made but a very small part of the whole. In the present times, the whole circulation of Scotland cannot be estimated at less than two millions, of which that part which consists in gold and silver, most probably, does not amount to half a million. But though the circulating gold and silver of Scotland have suffered so great a diminution during this period, its real riches and prosperity do not appear to have suffered any. Its agriculture, manufactures, and trade, on the contrary, the annual produce of its land and labor, have evidently been augmented.

It is chiefly by discounting bills of exchange, that is, by advancing money upon them before they are due, that the greater part of banks and bankers issue their promissory notes. They deduct always, upon whatever sum they advance, the legal interest till the bill shall become due. The payment of the bill, when it becomes due, replaces to the bank the value of what had been advanced, together with a clear profit of the interest. The banker, who advances to the merchant whose bill he discounts, not gold and silver, but his own promissory notes, has the advantage of being able to discount to a greater amount by the whole value of his promissory notes, which he finds, by experience, are commonly in circulation. He is thereby enabled to make his clear gain of interest on so much a larger sum.

The commerce of Scotland, which at present is not very great, was still more inconsiderable when the two first banking companies were established; and those companies would have had but little trade, had they confined their business to the discounting of bills of exchange. They invented, therefore, another method of issuing their promissory notes; by granting what they call cash accounts, that is, by giving credit, to the extent of a certain sum (two or three thousand pounds for example), to any individual who could procure two persons of undoubted credit and good landed estate to become surety for him, that whatever money should be advanced to him, within the sum for which the credit had been given, should be repaid upon demand, together with the legal interest. Credits of this kind are, I believe, commonly granted by banks and bankers in all different parts of the world. But the easy terms upon which the Scotch banking companies accept of repayment are, so far as I know, peculiar to them, and have perhaps been the principal cause, both of the great trade of those companies, and of the benefit which the country has received from it.

Whoever has a credit of this kind with one of those companies, and borrows a thousand pounds upon it, for example, may repay this sum piecemeal, by twenty and thirty pounds at a time, the company discounting a proportionable part of the interest of the great sum, from the day on which each of those small sums is paid in, till the whole be in this manner repaid. All merchants, therefore, and almost all men of business, find it convenient to keep such cash accounts with them, and are thereby interested to promote the trade of those companies, by readily receiving their notes in all payments, and by encouraging all those with whom they have any influence to do the same. The banks, when their customers apply to them for money, generally advance it to them in their own promissory notes. These the merchants pay away to the manufacturers for goods, the manufacturers to the farmers for materials and provisions, the farmers to their landlords for rent; the landlords repay them to the merchants for the conveniences and luxuries with which they supply them, and the merchants again return them to the banks, in order to balance their cash accounts, or to replace what they my have borrowed of them; and thus almost the whole money business of the country is transacted by means of them. Hence the great trade of those companies.

By means of those cash accounts, every merchant can, without imprudence, carry on a greater trade than he otherwise could do. If there are two merchants, one in London and the other in Edinburgh, who employ equal stocks in the same branch of trade, the Edinburgh merchant can, without imprudence, carry on a greater trade, and give employment to a greater number of people, than the London merchant. The London merchant must always keep by him a considerable sum of money, either in his own coffers, or in those of his banker, who gives him no interest for it, in order to answer the demands continually coming upon him for payment of the goods which he purchases upon credit. Let the ordinary amount of this sum be supposed five hundred pounds; the value of the goods in his warehouse must always be less, by five hundred pounds, than it would have been, had he not been obliged to keep such a sum unemployed. Let us suppose that he generally disposes of his whole stock upon hand, or of goods to the value of his whole stock upon hand, once in the year. By being obliged to keep so great a sum unemployed, he must sell in a year five hundred pounds worth less goods than he might otherwise have done. His annual profits must be less by all that he could have made by the sale of five hundred pounds worth more goods; and the number of people employed in preparing his goods for the market must be less by all those that five hundred pounds more stock could have employed. The merchant in Edinburgh, on the other hand, keeps no money unemployed for answering such occasional demands. When they actually come upon him, he satisfies them from his cash account with the bank, and gradually replaces the sum borrowed with the money or paper which comes in from the occasional sales of his goods. With the same stock, therefore, he can, without imprudence, have at all times in his warehouse a larger quantity of goods than the London merchant; and can thereby both make a greater profit himself, and give constant employment to a greater number of industrious people who prepare those goods for the market. Hence the great benefit which the country has derived from this trade.

The facility of discounting bills of exchange, it may be thought, indeed, gives the English merchants a convenience equivalent to the cash accounts of the Scotch merchants. But the Scotch merchants, it must be remembered, can discount their bills of exchange as easily as the English merchants; and have, besides, the additional convenience of their cash accounts.

The whole paper money of every kind which can easily circulate in any country, never can exceed the value of the gold and silver, of which it supplies the place, or which (the commerce being supposed the same) would circulate there, if there was no paper money. If twenty shilling notes, for example, are the lowest paper money current in Scotland, the whole of that currency which can easily circulate there, cannot exceed the sum of gold and silver which would be necessary for transacting the annual exchanges of twenty shillings value and upwards usually transacted within that country. Should the circulating paper at any time exceed that sum, as the excess could neither be sent abroad nor be employed in the circulation of the country, it must immediately return upon the banks, to be exchanged for gold and silver. Many people would immediately perceive that they had more of this paper than was necessary for transacting their business at home; and as they could not send it abroad, they would immediately demand payment for it from the banks. When this superfluous paper was converted into gold and silver, they could easily find a use for it, by sending it abroad; but they could find none while it remained in the shape of paper. There would immediately, therefore, be a run upon the banks to the whole extent of this superfluous paper, and if they showed any difficulty or backwardness in payment, to a much greater extent; the alarm which this would occasion necessarily increasing the run.

Over and above the expenses which are common to every branch of trade, such as the expense of house-rent, the wages of servants, clerks, accountants, etc. the expenses peculiar to a bank consist chiefly in two articles: first, in the expense of keeping at all times in its coffers, for answering the occasional demands of the holders of its notes, a large sum of money, of which it loses the interest; and, secondly, in the expense of replenishing those coffers as fast as they are emptied by answering such occasional demands.

A banking company which issues more paper than can be employed in the circulation of the country, and of which the excess is continually returning upon them for payment, ought to increase the quantity of gold and silver which they keep at all times in their coffers, not only in proportion to this excessive increase of their circulation, but in a much greater proportion; their notes returning upon them much faster than in proportion to the excess of their quantity. Such a company, therefore, ought to increase the first article of their expense, not only in proportion to this forced increase of their business, but in a much greater proportion.

The coffers of such a company, too, though they ought to be filled much fuller, yet must empty themselves much faster than if their business was confined within more reasonable bounds, and must require not only a more violent, but a more constant and uninterrupted exertion of expense, in order to replenish them, The coin, too, which is thus continually drawn in such large quantities from their coffers, cannot be employed in the circulation of the country. It comes in place of a paper which is over and above what can be employed in that circulation, and is, therefore, over and above what can be employed in it too. But as that coin will not be allowed to lie idle, it must, in one shape or another, be sent abroad, in order to find that profitable employment which it cannot find at home; and this continual exportation of gold and silver, by enhancing the difficulty, must necessarily enhance still farther the expense of the bank, in finding new gold and silver in order to replenish those coffers, which empty themselves so very rapidly. Such a company, therefore, must in proportion to this forced increase of their business, increase the second article of their expense still more than the first.

Let us suppose that all the paper of a particular bank, which the circulation of the country can easily absorb and employ, amounts exactly to forty thousand pounds, and that, for answering occasional demands, this bank is obliged to keep at all times in its coffers ten thousand pounds in gold and silver. Should this bank attempt to circulate forty-four thousand pounds, the four thousand pounds which are over and above what the circulation can easily absorb and employ, will return upon it almost as fast as they are issued. For answering occasional demands, therefore, this bank ought to keep at all times in its coffers, not eleven thousand pounds only, but fourteen thousand pounds. It will thus gain nothing by the interest of the four thousand pounds excessive circulation; and it will lose the whole expense of continually collecting four thousand pounds in gold and silver, which will be continually going out of its coffers as fast as they are brought into them.

Had every particular banking company always understood and attended to its own particular interest, the circulation never could have been overstocked with paper money. But every particular banking company has not always understood or attended to its own particular interest, and the circulation has frequently been overstocked with paper money.

By issuing too great a quantity of paper, of which the excess was continually returning, in order to be exchanged for gold and silver, the Bank of England was for many years together obliged to coin gold to the extent of between eight hundred thousand pounds and a million a-year; or, at an average, about eight hundred and fifty thousand pounds. For this great coinage, the bank (inconsequence of the worn and degraded state into which the gold coin had fallen a few years ago) was frequently obliged to purchase gold bullion at the high price of four pounds an ounce, which it soon after issued in coin at £3:17:10 1/2 an ounce, losing in this manner between two and a half and three percent upon the coinage of so very large a sum. Though the bank, therefore, paid no seignorage, though the government was properly at the expense of this coinage, this liberality of government did not prevent altogether the expense of the bank.

The Scotch banks, in consequence of an excess of the same kind, were all obliged to employ constantly agents at London to collect money for them, at an expense which was seldom below one and a half or two percent. This money was sent down by the wagon, and insured by the carriers at an additional expense of three quarters percent or fifteen shillings on the hundred pounds. Those agents were not always able to replenish the coffers of their employers so fast as they were emptied. In this case, the resource of the banks was, to draw upon their correspondents in London bills of exchange, to the extent of the sum which they wanted. When those correspondents afterwards drew upon them for the payment of this sum, together with the interest and commission, some of those banks, from the distress into which their excessive circulation had thrown them, had sometimes no other means of satisfying this draught, but by drawing a second set of bills, either upon the same, or upon some other correspondents in London; and the same sum, or rather bills for the same sum, would in this manner make sometimes more than two or three journeys; the debtor bank paying always the interest and commission upon the whole accumulated sum. Even those Scotch banks which never distinguished themselves by their extreme imprudence, were sometimes obliged to employ this ruinous resource.

The gold coin which was paid out, either by the Bank of England or by the Scotch banks, in exchange for that part of their paper which was over and above what could be employed in the circulation of the country, being likewise over and above what could be employed in that circulation, was sometimes sent abroad in the shape of coin, sometimes melted down and sent abroad in the shape of bullion, and sometimes melted down and sold to the Bank of England at the high price of four pounds an ounce. It was the newest, the heaviest, and the best pieces only, which were carefully picked out of the whole coin, and either sent abroad or melted down. At home, and while they remained in the shape of coin, those heavy pieces were of no more value than the light; but they were of more value abroad, or when melted down into bullion at home. The Bank of England, notwithstanding their great annual coinage, found, to their astonishment, that there was every year the same scarcity of coin as there had been the year before; and that, notwithstanding the great quantity of good and new coin which was every year issued from the bank, the state of the coin, instead of growing better and better, became every year worse and worse. Every year they found themselves under the necessity of coining nearly the same quantity of gold as they had coined the year before; and from the continual rise in the price of gold bullion, in consequence of the continual wearing and clipping of the coin, the expense of this great annual coinage became, every year, greater and greater. The Bank of England, it is to be observed, by supplying its own coffers with coin, is indirectly obliged to supply the whole kingdom, into which coin is continually flowing from those coffers in a great variety of ways. Whatever coin, therefore, was wanted to support this excessive circulation both of Scotch and English paper money, whatever vacuities this excessive circulation occasioned in the necessary coin of the kingdom, the Bank of England was obliged to supply them. The Scotch banks, no doubt, paid all of them very dearly for their own imprudence and inattention: but the Bank of England paid very dearly, not only for its own imprudence, but for the much greater imprudence of almost all the Scotch banks.

The over-trading of some bold projectors in both parts of the united kingdom, was the original cause of this excessive circulation of paper money.

What a bank can with propriety advance to a merchant or undertaker of any kind, is not either the whole capital with which he trades, or even any considerable part of that capital; but that part of it only which he would otherwise be obliged to keep by him unemployed and in ready money, for answering occasional demands. If the paper money which the bank advances never exceeds this value, it can never exceed the value of the gold and silver which would necessarily circulate in the country if there was no paper money; it can never exceed the quantity which the circulation of the country can easily absorb and employ.

When a bank discounts to a merchant a real bill of exchange, drawn by a real creditor upon a real debtor, and which, as soon as it becomes due, is really paid by that debtor; it only advances to him a part of the value which he would otherwise be obliged to keep by him unemployed and in ready money, for answering occasional demands. The payment of the bill, when it becomes due, replaces to the bank the value of what it had advanced, together with the interest. The coffers of the bank, so far as its dealings are confined to such customers, resemble a water-pond, from which, though a stream is continually running out, yet another is continually running in, fully equal to that which runs out; so that, without any further care or attention, the pond keeps always equally, or very near equally full. Little or no expense can ever be necessary for replenishing the coffers of such a bank.

A merchant, without overtrading, may frequently have occasion for a sum of ready money, even when he has no bills to discount. When a bank, besides discounting his bills, advances him likewise, upon such occasions, such sums upon his cash account, and accepts of a piecemeal repayment, as the money comes in from the occasional sale of his goods, upon the easy terms of the banking companies of Scotland; it dispenses him entirely from the necessity of keeping any part of his stock by him unemployed and in ready money for answering occasional demands. When such demands actually come upon him, he can answer them sufficiently from his cash account. The bank, however, in dealing with such customers, ought to observe with great attention, whether, in the course of some short period (of four, five, six, or eight months, for example), the sum of the repayments which it commonly receives from them, is, or is not, fully equal to that of the advances which it commonly makes to them. If, within the course of such short periods, the sum of the repayments from certain customers is, upon most occasions, fully equal to that of the advances, it may safely continue to deal with such customers. Though the stream which is in this case continually running out from its coffers may be very large, that which is continually running into them must be at least equally large, so that, without any further care or attention, those coffers are likely to be always equally or very near equally full, and scarce ever to require any extraordinary expense to replenish them. If, on the contrary, the sum of the repayments from certain other customers, falls commonly very much short of the advances which it makes to them, it cannot with any safety continue to deal with such customers, at least if they continue to deal with it in this manner. The stream which is in this case continually running out from its coffers, is necessarily much larger than that which is continually running in; so that, unless they are replenished by some great and continual effort of expense, those coffers must soon be exhausted altogether.

The banking companies of Scotland, accordingly, were for a long time very careful to require frequent and regular repayments from all their customers, and did not care to deal with any person, whatever might be his fortune or credit, who did not make, what they called, frequent and regular operations with them. By this attention, besides saving almost entirely the extraordinary expense of replenishing their coffers, they gained two other very considerable advantages.

First, by this attention they were enabled to make some tolerable judgment concerning the thriving or declining circumstances of their debtors, without being obliged to look out for any other evidence besides what their own books afforded them; men being, for the most part, either regular or irregular in their repayments, according as their circumstances are either thriving or declining. A private man who lends out his money to perhaps half a dozen or a dozen of debtors, may, either by himself or his agents, observe and inquire both constantly and carefully into the conduct and situation of each of them. But a banking company, which lends money to perhaps five hundred different people, and of which the attention is continually occupied by objects of a very different kind, can have no regular information concerning the conduct and circumstances of the greater part of its debtors, beyond what its own books afford it. In requiring frequent and regular repayments from all their customers, the banking companies of Scotland had probably this advantage in view.

Secondly, by this attention they secured themselves from the possibility of issuing more paper money than what the circulation of the country could easily absorb and employ. When they observed, that within moderate periods of time, the repayments of a particular customer were, upon most occasions, fully equal to the advances which they had made to him, they might be assured that the paper money which they had advanced to him had not, at any time, exceeded the quantity of gold and silver which he would otherwise have been obliged to keep by him for answering occasional demands; and that, consequently, the paper money, which they had circulated by his means, had not at any time exceeded the quantity of gold and silver which would have circulated in the country, had there been no paper money. The frequency, regularity, and amount of his repayments, would sufficiently demonstrate that the amount of their advances had at no time exceeded that part of his capital which he would otherwise have been obliged to keep by him unemployed, and in ready money, for answering occasional demands; that is, for the purpose of keeping the rest of his capital in constant employment. It is this part of his capital only which, within moderate periods of time, is continually returning to every dealer in the shape of money, whether paper or coin, and continually going from him in the same shape. If the advances of the bank had commonly exceeded this part of his capital, the ordinary amount of his repayments could not, within moderate periods of time, have equaled the ordinary amount of its advances. The stream which, by means of his dealings, was continually running into the coffers of the bank, could not have been equal to the stream which, by means of the same dealings was continually running out. The advances of the bank paper, by exceeding the quantity of gold and silver which, had there been no such advances, he would have been obliged to keep by him for answering occasional demands, might soon come to exceed the whole quantity of gold and silver which (the commerce being supposed the same) would have circulated in the country, had there been no paper money; and, consequently, to exceed the quantity which the circulation of the country could easily absorb and employ; and the excess of this paper money would immediately have returned upon the bank, in order to be exchanged for gold and silver. This second advantage, though equally real, was not, perhaps, so well understood by all the different banking companies in Scotland as the first.

When, partly by the convenience of discounting bills, and partly by that of cash accounts, the creditable traders of any country can be dispensed from the necessity of keeping any part of their stock by them unemployed, and in ready money, for answering occasional demands, they can reasonably expect no farther assistance from hanks and bankers, who, when they have gone thus far, cannot, consistently with their own interest and safety, go farther. A bank cannot, consistently with its own interest, advance to a trader the whole, or even the greater part of the circulating capital with which he trades; because, though that capital is continually returning to him in the shape of money, and going from him in the same shape, yet the whole of the returns is too distant from the whole of the outgoings, and the sum of his repayments could not equal the sum of his advances within such moderate periods of time as suit the convenience of a bank. Still less could a bank afford to advance him any considerable part of his fixed capital; of the capital which the undertaker of an iron forge, for example, employs in erecting his forge and smelting houses, his workhouses, and warehouses, the dwelling houses of his workmen, etc.; of the capital which the undertaker of a mine employs in sinking his shafts, in erecting engines for drawing out the water, in making roads and wagonways, etc.; of the capital which the person who undertakes to improve land employs in clearing, draining, inclosing, manuring, and ploughing waste and uncultivated fields; in building farmhouses, with all their necessary appendages of stables, granaries, etc. The returns of the fixed capital are, in almost all cases, much slower than those of the circulating capital: and such expenses, even when laid out with the greatest prudence and judgment, very seldom return to the undertaker till after a period of many years, a period by far too distant to suit the convenience of a bank. Traders and other undertakers may, no doubt with great propriety, carry on a very considerable part of their projects with borrowed money. In justice to their creditors, however, their own capital ought in this case to be sufficient to insure, if I may say so, the capital of those creditors; or to render it extremely improbable that those creditors should incur any loss, even though the success of the project should fall very much short of the expectation of the projectors. Even with this precaution, too, the money which is borrowed, and which it is meant should not be repaid till after a period of several years, ought not to be borrowed of a bank, but ought to be borrowed upon bond or mortgage, of such private people as propose to live upon the interest of their money, without taking the trouble themselves to employ the capital, and who are, upon that account, willing to lend that capital to such people of good credit as are likely to keep it for several years. A bank, indeed, which lends its money without the expense of stamped paper, or of attorneys' fees for drawing bonds and mortgages, and which accepts of repayment upon the easy terms of the banking companies of Scotland, would, no doubt, be a very convenient creditor to such traders and undertakers. But such traders and undertakers would surely be most inconvenient debtors to such a bank.

It is now more than five and twenty years since the paper money issued by the different banking companies of Scotland was fully equal, or rather was somewhat more than fully equal, to what the circulation of the country could easily absorb and employ. Those companies, therefore, had so long ago given all the assistance to the traders and other undertakers of Scotland which it is possible for banks and bankers, consistently with their own interest, to give. They had even done somewhat more. They had overtraded a little, and had brought upon themselves that loss, or at least that diminution of profit, which, in this particular business, never fails to attend the smallest degree of overtrading. Those traders and other undertakers, having got so much assistance from banks and bankers, wished to get still more. The banks, they seem to have thought, could extend their credits to whatever sum might be wanted, without incurring any other expense besides that of a few reams of paper. They complained of the contracted views and dastardly spirit of the directors of those banks, which did not, they said, extend their credits in proportion to the extension of the trade of the country; meaning, no doubt, by the extension of that trade, the extension of their own projects beyond what they could carry on either with their own capital, or with what they had credit to borrow of private people in the usual way of bond or mortgage. The banks, they seem to have thought, were in honor bound to supply the deficiency, and to provide them with all the capital which they wanted to trade with. The banks, however, were of a different opinion; and upon their refusing to extend their credits, some of those traders had recourse to an expedient which, for a time, served their purpose, though at a much greater expense, yet as effectually as the utmost extension of bank credits could have done. This expedient was no other than the well known shift of drawing and redrawing; the shift to which unfortunate traders have sometimes recourse, when they are upon the brink of bankruptcy. The practice of raising money in this manner had been long known in England; and, during the course of the late war, when the high profits of trade afforded a great temptation to overtrading, is said to have been carried on to a very great extent. From England it was brought into Scotland, where, in proportion to the very limited commerce, and to the very moderate capital of the country, it was soon carried on to a much greater extent than it ever had been in England.

The practice of drawing and redrawing is so well known to all men of business, that it may, perhaps, be thought unnecessary to give any account of it. But as this book may come into the hands of many people who are not men of business, and as the effects of this practice upon the banking trade are not, perhaps, generally understood, even by men of business themselves, I shall endeavor to explain it as distinctly as I can.

The customs of merchants, which were established when the barbarous laws of Europe did not enforce the performance of their contracts, and which, during the course of the two last centuries, have been adopted into the laws of all European nations, have given such extraordinary privileges to bills of exchange, that money is more readily advanced upon them than upon any other species of obligation; especially when they are made payable within so short a period as two or three months after their date. If, when the bill becomes due, the acceptor does not pay it as soon as it is presented, he becomes from that moment a bankrupt. The bill is protested, and returns upon the drawer, who, if he does not immediately pay it, becomes likewise a bankrupt. If, before it came to the person who presents it to the acceptor for payment, it had passed through the hands of several other persons, who had successively advanced to one another the contents of it, either in money or goods, and who, to express that each of them had in his turn received those contents, had all of them in their order indorsed, that is, written their names upon the back of the bill; each endorser becomes in his turn liable to the owner of the bill for those contents, and, if he fails to pay, he becomes too, from that moment, a bankrupt. Though the drawer, acceptor, and endorsers of the bill, should all of them be persons of doubtful credit; yet, still the shortness of the date gives some security to the owner of the bill. Though all of them may be very likely to become bankrupts, it is a chance if they all become so in so short a time. The house is crazy, says a weary traveler to himself, and will not stand very long; but it is a chance if it falls to-night, and I will venture, therefore, to sleep in it to-night.

The trader A in Edinburgh, we shall suppose, draws a bill upon B in London, payable two months after date. In reality B in London owes nothing to A in Edinburgh; but he agrees to accept of A's bill, upon condition, that before the term of payment he shall redraw upon A in Edinburgh for the same sum, together with the interest and a commission, another bill, payable likewise two months after date. B accordingly, before the expiration of the first two months, redraws this bill upon A in Edinburgh; who, again before the expiration of the second two months, draws a second bill upon B in London, payable likewise two months after date; and before the expiration of the third two months, B in London redraws upon A in Edinburgh another bill payable also two months after date. This practice has sometimes gone on, not only for several months, but for several years together, the bill always returning upon A in Edinburgh with the accumulated interest and commission of all the former bills. The interest was five percent in the year, and the commission was never less than one half percent on each draught. This commission being repeated more than six times in the year, whatever money A might raise by this expedient might necessarily have cost him something more than eight percent in the year and sometimes a great deal more, when either the price of the commission happened to rise, or when he was obliged to pay compound interest upon the interest and commission of former bills. This practice was called raising money by circulation.

In a country where the ordinary profits of stock, in the greater part of mercantile projects, are supposed to run between six and ten percent it must have been a very fortunate speculation, of which the returns could not only repay the enormous expense at which the money was thus borrowed for carrying it on, but afford, besides, a good surplus profit to the projector. Many vast and extensive projects, however, were undertaken, and for several years carried on, without any other fund to support them besides what was raised at this enormous expense. The projectors, no doubt, had in their golden dreams the most distinct vision of this great profit. Upon their awakening, however, either at the end of their projects, or when they were no longer able to carry them on, they very seldom, I believe, had the good fortune to find it.

{The method described in the text was by no means either the most common or the most expensive one in which those adventurers sometimes raised money by circulation.

It frequently happened, that A in Edinburgh would enable B in London to pay the first bill of exchange, by drawing, a few days before it became due, a second bill at three months date upon the same B in London. This bill, being payable to his own order, A sold in Edinburgh at par; and with its contents purchased bills upon London, payable at sight to the order of B, to whom he sent them by the post. Towards the end of the late war, the exchange between Edinburgh and London was frequently three percent against Edinburgh, and those bills at sight must frequently have cost A that premium. This transaction, therefore, being repeated at least four times in the year, and being loaded with a commission of at least one half percent upon each repetition, must at that period have cost A, at least, fourteen percent in the year. At other times A would enable to discharge the first bill of exchange, by drawing, a few days before it became due, a second bill at two months date, not upon B, but upon some third person, C, for example, in London. This other bill was made payable to the order of B, who, upon its being accepted by C, discounted it with some banker in London; and A enabled C to discharge it, by drawing, a few day's before it became due, a third bill likewise at two months date, sometimes upon his first correspondent B, and sometimes upon some fourth or fifth person, D or E, for example. This third bill was made payable to the order of C, who, as soon as it was accepted, discounted it in the same manner with some banker in London. Such operations being repeated at least six times in the year, and being loaded with a commission of at least one half percent upon each repetition, together with the legal interest of five percent this method of raising money, in the same manner as that described in the text, must have cost A something more than eight percent. By saving, however, the exchange between Edinburgh and London, it was less expensive than that mentioned in the foregoing part of this note; but then it required an established credit with more houses than one in London, an advantage which many of these adventurers could not always find it easy to procure.}

The bills which A in Edinburgh drew upon B in London, he regularly discounted two months before they were due, with some bank or banker in Edinburgh; and the bills which B in London redrew upon A in Edinburgh, he as regularly discounted, either with the Bank of England, or with some other banker in London. Whatever was advanced upon such circulating bills was in Edinburgh advanced in the paper of the Scotch banks; and in London, when they were discounted at the Bank of England in the paper of that bank. Though the bills upon which this paper had been advanced were all of them repaid in their turn as soon as they became due, yet the value which had been really advanced upon the first bill was never really returned to the banks which advanced it; because, before each bill became due, another bill was always drawn to somewhat a greater amount than the bill which was soon to be paid: and the discounting of this other bill was essentially necessary towards the payment of that which was soon to be due. This payment, therefore, was altogether fictitious. The stream which, by means of those circulating bills of exchange, had once been made to run out from the coffers of the banks, was never replaced by any stream which really ran into them.

The paper which was issued upon those circulating bills of exchange amounted, upon many occasions, to the whole fund destined for carrying on some vast and extensive project of agriculture, commerce, or manufactures; and not merely to that part of it which, had there been no paper money, the projector would have been obliged to keep by him unemployed, and in ready money, for answering occasional demands. The greater part of this paper was, consequently, over and above the value of the gold and silver which would have circulated in the country, had there been no paper money. It was over and above, therefore, what the circulation of the country could easily absorb and employ, and upon that account, immediately returned upon the banks, in order to be exchanged for gold and silver, which they were to find as they could. It was a capital which those projectors had very artfully contrived to draw from those banks, not only without their knowledge or deliberate consent, but for some time, perhaps, without their having the most distant suspicion that they had really advanced it.

When two people, who are continually drawing and redrawing upon one another, discount their bills always with the same banker, he must immediately discover what they are about, and see clearly that they are trading, not with any capital of their own, but with the capital which he advances to them. But this discovery is not altogether so easy when they discount their bills sometimes with one banker, and sometimes with another, and when the two same persons do not constantly draw and redraw upon one another, but occasionally run the round of a great circle of projectors, who find it for their interest to assist one another in this method of raising money and to render it, upon that account, as difficult as possible to distinguish between a real and a fictitious bill of exchange, between a bill drawn by a real creditor upon a real debtor, and a bill for which there was properly no real creditor but the bank which discounted it, nor any real debtor but the projector who made use of the money. When a banker had even made this discovery, he might sometimes make it too late, and might find that he had already discounted the bills of those projectors to so great an extent, that, by refusing to discount any more, he would necessarily make them all bankrupts; and thus by ruining them, might perhaps ruin himself. For his own interest and safety, therefore, he might find it necessary, in this very perilous situation, to go on for some time, endeavoring, however, to withdraw gradually, and, upon that account, making every day greater and greater difficulties about discounting, in order to force these projectors by degrees to have recourse, either to other bankers, or to other methods of raising money: so as that he himself might, as soon as possible, get out of the circle. The difficulties, accordingly, which the Bank of England, which the principal bankers in London, and which even the more prudent Scotch banks began, after a certain time, and when all of them had already gone too far, to make about discounting, not only alarmed, but enraged, in the highest degree, those projectors. Their own distress, of which this prudent and necessary reserve of the banks was, no doubt, the immediate occasion, they called the distress of the country; and this distress of the country, they said, was altogether owing to the ignorance, pusillanimity, and bad conduct of the banks, which did not give a sufficiently liberal aid to the spirited undertakings of those who exerted themselves in order to beautify, improve, and enrich the country. It was the duty of the banks, they seemed to think, to lend for as long a time, and to as great an extent, as they might wish to borrow. The banks, however, by refusing in this manner to give more credit to those to whom they had already given a great deal too much, took the only method by which it was now possible to save either their own credit, or the public credit of the country.

In the midst of this clamor and distress, a new bank was established in Scotland, for the express purpose of relieving the distress of the country. The design was generous; but the execution was imprudent, and the nature and causes of the distress which it meant to relieve, were not, perhaps, well understood. This bank was more liberal than any other had ever been, both in granting cash-accounts, and in discounting bills of exchange. With regard to the latter, it seems to have made scarce any distinction between real and circulating bills, but to have discounted all equally. It was the avowed principle of this bank to advance upon any reasonable security, the whole capital which was to be employed in those improvements of which the returns are the most slow and distant, such as the improvements of land. To promote such improvements was even said to be the chief of the public-spirited purposes for which it was instituted. By its liberality in granting cash-accounts, and in discounting bills of exchange, it, no doubt, issued great quantities of its bank notes. But those bank notes being, the greater part of them, over and above what the circulation of the country could easily absorb and employ, returned upon it, in order to be exchanged for gold and silver, as fast as they were issued. Its coffers were never well filled. The capital which had been subscribed to this bank, at two different subscriptions, amounted to one hundred and sixty thousand pounds, of which eighty percent only was paid up. This sum ought to have been paid in at several different installments. A great part of the proprietors, when they paid in their first installment, opened a cash account with the bank; and the directors, thinking themselves obliged to treat their own proprietors with the same liberality with which they treated all other men, allowed many of them to borrow upon this cash account what they paid in upon all their subsequent installments. Such payments, therefore, only put into one coffer what had the moment before been taken out of another. But had the coffers of this bank been filled ever so well, its excessive circulation must have emptied them faster than they could have been replenished by any other expedient but the ruinous one of drawing upon London; and when the bill became due, paying it, together with interest and commission, by another draught upon the same place. Its coffers having been filled so very ill, it is said to have been driven to this resource within a very few months after it began to do business. The estates of the proprietors of this bank were worth several millions, and, by their subscription to the original bond or contract of the bank, were really pledged for answering all its engagements. By means of the great credit which so great a pledge necessarily gave it, it was, notwithstanding its too liberal conduct, enabled to carry on business for more than two years. When it was obliged to stop, it had in the circulation about two hundred thousand pounds in bank notes. In order to support the circulation of those notes, which were continually returning upon it as fast as they were issued, it had been constantly in the practice of drawing bills of exchange upon London, of which the number and value were continually increasing, and, when it stopped, amounted to upwards of six hundred thousand pounds. This bank, therefore, had, in little more than the course of two years, advanced to different people upwards of eight hundred thousand pounds at five percent. Upon the two hundred thousand pounds which it circulated in bank notes, this five percent might perhaps be considered as a clear gain, without any other deduction besides the expense of management. But upon upwards of six hundred thousand pounds, for which it was continually drawing bills of exchange upon London, it was paying, in the way of interest and commission, upwards of eight percent and was consequently losing more than three percent upon more than three fourths of all its dealings.

The operations of this bank seem to have produced effects quite opposite to those which were intended by the particular persons who planned and directed it. They seem to have intended to support the spirited undertakings, for as such they considered them, which were at that time carrying on in different parts of the country; and, at the same time, by drawing the whole banking business to themselves, to supplant all the other Scotch banks, particularly those established at Edinburgh, whose backwardness in discounting bills of exchange had given some offence. This bank, no doubt, gave some temporary relief to those projectors, and enabled them to carry on their projects for about two years longer than they could otherwise have done. But it thereby only enabled them to get so much deeper into debt; so that, when ruin came, it fell so much the heavier both upon them and upon their creditors. The operations of this bank, therefore, instead of relieving, in reality aggravated in the long-run the distress which those projectors had brought both upon themselves and upon their country. It would have been much better for themselves, their creditors, and their country, had the greater part of them been obliged to stop two years sooner than they actually did. The temporary relief, however, which this bank afforded to those projectors, proved a real and permanent relief to the other Scotch banks. All the dealers in circulating bills of exchange, which those other banks had become so backward in discounting, had recourse to this new bank, where they were received with open arms. Those other banks, therefore, were enabled to get very easily out of that fatal circle, from which they could not otherwise have disengaged themselves without incurring a considerable loss, and perhaps, too, even some degree of discredit.

In the long-run, therefore, the operations of this bank increased the real distress of the country, which it meant to relieve; and effectually relieved, from a very great distress, those rivals whom it meant to supplant.

At the first setting out of this bank, it was the opinion of some people, that how fast soever its coffers might be emptied, it might easily replenish them, by raising money upon the securities of those to whom it had advanced its paper. Experience, I believe, soon convinced them that this method of raising money was by much too slow to answer their purpose; and that coffers which originally were so ill filled, and which emptied themselves so very fast, could be replenished by no other expedient but the ruinous one of drawing bills upon London, and when they became due, paying them by other draughts on the same place, with accumulated interest and commission. But though they had been able by this method to raise money as fast as they wanted it, yet, instead of making a profit, they must have suffered a loss of every such operation; so that in the long-run they must have ruined themselves as a mercantile company, though perhaps not so soon as by the more expensive practice of drawing and redrawing. They could still have made nothing by the interest of the paper, which, being over and above what the circulation of the country could absorb and employ, returned upon them in order to be exchanged for gold and silver, as fast as they issued it; and for the payment of which they were themselves continually obliged to borrow money. On the contrary, the whole expense of this borrowing, of employing agents to look out for people who had money to lend, of negotiating with those people, and of drawing the proper bond or assignment, must have fallen upon them, and have been so much clear loss upon the balance of their accounts. The project of replenishing their coffers in this manner may be compared to that of a man who had a water-pond from which a stream was continually running out, and into which no stream was continually running, but who proposed to keep it always equally full, by employing a number of people to go continually with buckets to a well at some miles distance, in order to bring water to replenish it.

But though this operation had proved not only practicable, but profitable to the bank, as a mercantile company; yet the country could have derived no benefit front it, but, on the contrary, must have suffered a very considerable loss by it. This operation could not augment, in the smallest degree, the quantity of money to be lent. It could only have erected this bank into a sort of general loan office for the whole country. Those who wanted to borrow must have applied to this bank, instead of applying to the private persons who had lent it their money. But a bank which lends money, perhaps to five hundred different people, the greater part of whom its directors can know very little about, is not likely to be more judicious in the choice of its debtors than a private person who lends out his money among a few people whom he knows, and in whose sober and frugal conduct he thinks he has good reason to confide. The debtors of such a bank as that whose conduct I have been giving some account of were likely, the greater part of them, to be chimerical projectors, the drawers and redrawers of circulating bills of exchange, who would employ the money in extravagant undertakings, which, with all the assistance that could be given them, they would probably never be able to complete, and which, if they should be completed, would never repay the expense which they had really cost, would never afford a fund capable of maintaining a quantity of labor equal to that which had been employed about them. The sober and frugal debtors of private persons, on the contrary, would be more likely to employ the money borrowed in sober undertakings which were proportioned to their capitals, and which, though they might have less of the grand and the marvelous, would have more of the solid and the profitable; which would repay with a large profit whatever had been laid out upon them, and which would thus afford a fund capable of maintaining a much greater quantity of labor than that which had been employed about them. The success of this operation, therefore, without increasing in the smallest degree the capital of the country, would only have transferred a great part of it from prudent and profitable to imprudent and unprofitable undertakings.

That the industry of Scotland languished for want of money to employ it, was the opinion of the famous Mr. Law. By establishing a bank of a particular kind, which he seems to have imagined might issue paper to the amount of the whole value of all the lands in the country, he proposed to remedy this want of money. The parliament of Scotland, when he first proposed his project, did not think proper to adopt it. It was afterwards adopted, with some variations, by the Duke of Orleans, at that time regent of France. The idea of the possibility of multiplying paper money to almost any extent was the real foundation of what is called the Mississippi scheme, the most extravagant project, both of banking and stock-jobbing, that perhaps the world ever saw. The different operations of this scheme are explained so fully, so clearly, and with so much order and distinctness, by Mr. Du Verney, in his Examination of the Political Reflections upon commerce and finances of Mr. Du Tot, that I shall not give any account of them. The principles upon which it was founded are explained by Mr. Law himself, in a discourse concerning money and trade, which he published in Scotland when he first proposed his project. The splendid but visionary ideas which are set forth in that and some other works upon the same principles, still continue to make an impression upon many people, and have, perhaps, in part, contributed to that excess of banking, which has of late been complained of, both in Scotland and in other places.

The Bank of England is the greatest bank of circulation in Europe. It was incorporated, in pursuance of an act of parliament, by a charter under the great seal, dated the 27th of July 1694. It at that time advanced to government the sum of £1,200,000 for an annuity of £100,000, or for £96,000 a-year, interest at the rate of eight percent and £4,000 year for the expense of management. The credit of the new government, established by the Revolution, we may believe, must have been very low, when it was obliged to borrow at so high an interest.

In 1697, the bank was allowed to enlarge its capital stock, by an engraftment of £1,001,171:10s. Its whole capital stock, therefore, amounted at this time to £2,201,171: 10s. This engraftment is said to have been for the support of public credit. In 1696, tallies had been at forty, and fifty, and sixty, percent discount, and bank notes at twenty percent. {James Postlethwaite's *History of the Public Revenue*, p.301.} During the great re-coinage of the silver, which was going on at this time, the bank had thought proper to discontinue the payment of its notes, which necessarily occasioned their discredit.

In pursuance of the 7th Anne, the bank advanced and paid into the exchequer the sum of £400,000; making in all the sum of £1,600,000, which it had advanced upon its original annuity of £96,000 interest, and £4,000 for expense of management. In 1708, therefore, the credit of government was as good as that of private persons, since it could borrow at six percent interest, the common legal and market rate of those times. In pursuance of the same act, the bank cancelled exchequer bills to the amount of £1,775,027: 17s: 10½d. at six percent interest, and was at the same time allowed to take in subscriptions for doubling its capital. In 1703, therefore, the capital of the bank amounted to £4,402,343; and it had advanced to government the sum of £3,375,027:17:10½d.

By a call of fifteen percent in 1709, there was paid in, and made stock, £656,204:1:9d.; and by another of ten percent in 1710, £501,448:12:11d. In consequence of those two calls, therefore, the bank capital amounted to £5,559,995:14:8d.

In pursuance of the 3rd George, the bank delivered up two millions of exchequer Bills to be cancelled. It had at this time, therefore, advanced to government £5,375,027:17 10d. In pursuance of the 8th George I, the bank purchased of the South-sea company, stock to the amount of £4,000,000: and in 1722, in consequence of the subscriptions which it had taken in for enabling it to make this purchase, its capital stock was increased by £3,400,000. At this time, therefore, the bank had advanced to the public £9,375,027 17s. 10d.; and its capital stock amounted only to £8,959,995:14:8d. It was upon this occasion that the sum which the bank had advanced to the public, and for which it received interest, began first to exceed its capital stock, or the sum for which it paid a dividend to the proprietors of bank stock; or, in other words, that the bank began to have an undivided capital, over and above its divided one. It has continued to have an undivided capital of the same kind ever since. In 1746, the bank had, upon different occasions, advanced to the public £11,686,800, and its divided capital had been raised by different calls and subscriptions to £10,780,000. The state of those two sums has continued to be the same ever since. In pursuance of the 4th of George III, the bank agreed to pay to government for the renewal of its charter £110,000, without interest or repayment. This sum, therefore did not increase either of those two other sums.

The dividend of the bank has varied according to the variations in the rate of the interest which it has, at different times, received for the money it had advanced to the public, as well as according to other circumstances. This rate of interest has gradually been reduced from eight to three percent. For some years past, the bank dividend has been at five and a half percent.

The stability of the Bank of England is equal to that of the British government. All that it has advanced to the public must be lost before its creditors can sustain any loss. No other banking company in England can be established by act of parliament, or can consist of more than six members. It acts, not only as an ordinary bank, but as a great engine of state. It receives and pays the greater part of the annuities which are due to the creditors of the public; it circulates exchequer bills; and it advances to government the annual amount of the land and malt taxes, which are frequently not paid up till some years thereafter. In these different operations, its duty to the public may sometimes have obliged it, without any fault of its directors, to overstock the circulation with paper money. It likewise discounts merchants' bills, and has, upon several different occasions, supported the credit of the principal houses, not only of England, but of Hamburgh and Holland. Upon one occasion, in 1763, it is said to have advanced for this purpose, in one week, about £1,600,000, a great part of it in bullion. I do not, however, pretend to warrant either the greatness of the sum, or the shortness of the time. Upon other occasions, this great company has been reduced to the necessity of paying in sixpences.

It is not by augmenting the capital of the country, but by rendering a greater part of that capital active and productive than would otherwise be so, that the most judicious operations of banking can increase the industry of the country. That part of his capital which a dealer is obliged to keep by him unemployed and in ready money, for answering occasional demands, is so much dead stock, which, so long as it remains in this situation, produces nothing, either to him or to his country. The judicious operations of banking enable him to convert this dead stock into active and productive stock; into materials to work upon; into tools to work with; and into provisions and subsistence to work for; into stock which produces something both to himself and to his country. The gold and silver money which circulates in any country, and by means of which, the produce of its land and labor is annually circulated and distributed to the proper consumers, is, in the same manner as the ready money of the dealer, all dead stock. It is a very valuable part of the capital of the country, which produces nothing to the country. The judicious operations of banking, by substituting paper in the room of a great part of this gold and silver, enable the country to convert a great part of this dead stock into active and productive stock; into stock which produces something to the country. The gold and silver money which circulates in any country may very properly be compared to a highway, which, while it circulates and carries to market all the grass and corn of the country, produces itself not a single pile of either. The judicious operations of banking, by providing, if I may be allowed so violent a metaphor, a sort of wagonway through the air, enable the country to convert, as it were, a great part of its highways into good pastures, and corn fields, and thereby to increase, very considerably, the annual produce of its land and labor. The commerce and industry of the country, however, it must be acknowledged, though they may be somewhat augmented, cannot be altogether so secure, when they are thus, as it were, suspended upon the Daedalian wings of paper money, as when they travel about upon the solid ground of gold and silver. Over and above the accidents to which they are exposed from the unskilfulness of the conductors of this paper money, they are liable to several others, from which no prudence or skill of those conductors can guard them.

An unsuccessful war, for example, in which the enemy got possession of the capital, and consequently of that treasure which supported the credit of the paper money, would occasion a much greater confusion in a country where the whole circulation was carried on by paper, than in one where the greater part of it was carried on by gold and silver. The usual instrument of commerce having lost its value, no exchanges could be made but either by barter or upon credit. All taxes having been usually paid in paper money, the prince would not have wherewithal either to pay his troops, or to furnish his magazines; and the state of the country would be much more irretrievable than if the greater part of its circulation had consisted in gold and silver. A prince, anxious to maintain his dominions at all times in the state in which he can most easily defend them, ought upon this account to guard not only against that excessive multiplication of paper money which ruins the very banks which issue it, but even against that multiplication of it which enables them to fill the greater part of the circulation of the country with it.

The circulation of every country may be considered as divided into two different branches; the circulation of the dealers with one another, and the circulation between the dealers and the consumers. Though the same pieces of money, whether paper or metal, may be employed sometimes in the one circulation and sometimes in the other; yet as both are constantly going on at the same time, each requires a certain stock of money, of one kind or another, to carry it on. The value of the goods circulated between the different dealers never can exceed the value of those circulated between the dealers and the consumers; whatever is bought by the dealers being ultimately destined to be sold to the consumers. The circulation between the dealers, as it is carried on by wholesale, requires generally a pretty large sum for every particular transaction. That between the dealers and the consumers, on the contrary, as it is generally carried on by retail, frequently requires but very small ones, a shilling, or even a halfpenny, being often sufficient. But small sums circulate much faster than large ones. A shilling changes masters more frequently than a guinea, and a halfpenny more frequently than a shilling. Though the annual purchases of all the consumers, therefore, are at least equal in value to those of all the dealers, they can generally be transacted with a much smaller quantity of money; the same pieces, by a more rapid circulation, serving as the instrument of many more purchases of the one kind than of the other.

Paper money may be so regulated as either to confine itself very much to the circulation between the different dealers, or to extend itself likewise to a great part of that between the dealers and the consumers. Where no bank notes are circulated under £10 value, as in London, paper money confines itself very much to the circulation between the dealers. When a ten pound bank note comes into the hands of a consumer, he is generally obliged to change it at the first shop where he has occasion to purchase five shillings worth of goods; so that it often returns into the hands of a dealer before the consumer has spent the fortieth part of the money. Where bank notes are issued for so small sums as 20s. as in Scotland, paper money extends itself to a considerable part of the circulation between dealers and consumers. Before the Act of parliament which put a stop to the circulation of ten and five shilling notes, it filled a still greater part of that circulation. In the currencies of North America, paper was commonly issued for so small a sum as a shilling, and filled almost the whole of that circulation. In some paper currencies of Yorkshire, it was issued even for so small a sum as a sixpence.

Where the issuing of bank notes for such very small sums is allowed, and commonly practiced, many mean people are both enabled and encouraged to become bankers. A person whose promissory note for £5, or even for 20s. would be rejected by everybody, will get it to be received without scruple when it is issued for so small a sum as a sixpence. But the frequent bankruptcies to which such beggarly bankers must be liable, may occasion a very considerable inconveniency, and sometimes even a very great calamity, to many poor people who had received their notes in payment.

It were better, perhaps, that no bank notes were issued in any part of the kingdom for a smaller sum than £5. Paper money would then, probably, confine itself, in every part of the kingdom, to the circulation between the different dealers, as much as it does at present in London, where no bank notes are issued under £10 value; £5 being, in most part of the kingdom, a sum which, though it will purchase, perhaps, little more than half the quantity of goods, is as much considered, and is as seldom spent all at once, as £10 are amidst the profuse expense of London.

Where paper money, it is to be observed, is pretty much confined to the circulation between dealers and dealers, as at London, there is always plenty of gold and silver. Where it extends itself to a considerable part of the circulation between dealers and consumers, as in Scotland, and still more in North America, it banishes gold and silver almost entirely from the country; almost all the ordinary transactions of its interior commerce being thus carried on by paper. The suppression of ten and five shilling bank notes, somewhat relieved the scarcity of gold and silver in Scotland; and the suppression of twenty shilling notes will probably relieve it still more. Those metals are said to have become more abundant in America, since the suppression of some of their paper currencies. They are said, likewise, to have been more abundant before the institution of those currencies.

Though paper money should be pretty much confined to the circulation between dealers and dealers, yet banks and bankers might still be able to give nearly the same assistance to the industry and commerce of the country, as they had done when paper money filled almost the whole circulation. The ready money which a dealer is obliged to keep by him, for answering occasional demands, is destined altogether for the circulation between himself and other dealers of whom he buys goods. He has no occasion to keep any by him for the circulation between himself and the consumers, who are his customers, and who bring ready money to him, instead of taking any from him. Though no paper money, therefore, was allowed to be issued, but for such sums as would confine it pretty much to the circulation between dealers and dealers; yet partly by discounting real bills of exchange, and partly by lending upon cash accounts, banks and bankers might still be able to relieve the greater part of those dealers from the necessity of keeping any considerable part of their stock by them unemployed, and in ready money, for answering occasional demands. They might still be able to give the utmost assistance which banks and bankers can with propriety give to traders of every kind.

To restrain private people, it may be said, from receiving in payment the promissory notes of a banker for any sum, whether great or small, when they themselves are willing to receive them; or, to restrain a banker from issuing such notes, when all his neighbors are willing to accept of them, is a manifest violation of that natural liberty, which it is the proper business of law not to infringe, but to support. Such regulations may, no doubt, be considered as in some respect a violation of natural liberty. But those exertions of the natural liberty of a few individuals, which might endanger the security of the whole society, are, and ought to be, restrained by the laws of all governments; of the most free, as well as or the most despotical. The obligation of building party walls, in order to prevent the communication of fire, is a violation of natural liberty, exactly of the same kind with the regulations of the banking trade which are here proposed.

A paper money, consisting in bank notes, issued by people of undoubted credit, payable upon demand, without any condition, and, in fact, always readily paid as soon as presented, is, in every respect, equal in value to gold and silver money, since gold and silver money can at anytime be had for it. Whatever is either bought or sold for such paper, must necessarily be bought or sold as cheap as it could have been for gold and silver.

The increase of paper money, it has been said, by augmenting the quantity, and consequently diminishing the value, of the whole currency, necessarily augments the money price of commodities. But as the quantity of gold and silver, which is taken from the currency, is always equal to the quantity of paper which is added to it, paper money does not necessarily increase the quantity of the whole currency. From the beginning of the last century to the present time, provisions never were cheaper in Scotland than in 1759, though, from the circulation of ten and five shilling bank notes, there was then more paper money in the country than at present. The proportion between the price of provisions in Scotland and that in England is the same now as before the great multiplication of banking companies in Scotland. Corn is, upon most occasions, fully as cheap in England as in France, though there is a great deal of paper money in England, and scarce any in France. In 1751 and 1752, when Mr. Hume published his Political Discourses, and soon after the great multiplication of paper money in Scotland, there was a very sensible rise in the price of provisions, owing, probably, to the badness of the seasons, and not to the multiplication of paper money.

It would be otherwise, indeed, with a paper money, consisting in promissory notes, of which the immediate payment depended, in any respect, either upon the good will of those who issued them, or upon a condition which the holder of the notes might not always have it in his power to fulfill, or of which the payment was not exigible till after a certain number of years, and which, in the mean time, bore no interest. Such a paper money would, no doubt, fall more or less below the value of gold and silver, according as the difficulty or uncertainty of obtaining immediate payment was supposed to be greater or less, or according to the greater or less distance of time at which payment was exigible.

Some years ago the different banking companies of Scotland were in the practice of inserting into their bank notes, what they called an optional clause; by which they promised payment to the bearer, either as soon as the note should be presented, or, in the option of the directors, six months after such presentment, together with the legal interest for the said six months. The directors of some of those banks sometimes took advantage of this optional clause, and sometimes threatened those who demanded gold and silver in exchange for a considerable number of their notes, that they would take advantage of it, unless such demanders would content themselves with a part of what they demanded. The promissory notes of those banking companies constituted, at that time, the far greater part of the currency of Scotland, which this uncertainty of payment necessarily degraded below value of gold and silver money. During the continuance of this abuse (which prevailed chiefly in 1762, 1763, and 1764), while the exchange between London and Carlisle was at par, that between London and Dumfries would sometimes be four percent against Dumfries, though this town is not thirty miles distant from Carlisle. But at Carlisle, bills were paid in gold and silver; whereas at Dumfries they were paid in Scotch bank notes; and the uncertainty of getting these bank notes exchanged for gold and silver coin, had thus degraded them four percent below the value of that coin. The same act of parliament which suppressed ten and five shilling bank notes, suppressed likewise this optional clause, and thereby restored the exchange between England and Scotland to its natural rate, or to what the course of trade and remittances might happen to make it.

In the paper currencies of Yorkshire, the payment of so small a sum as 6d. sometimes depended upon the condition, that the holder of the note should bring the change of a guinea to the person who issued it; a condition which the holders of such notes might frequently find it very difficult to fulfill, and which must have degraded this currency below the value of gold and silver money. An act of parliament, accordingly, declared all such clauses unlawful, and suppressed, in the same manner as in Scotland, all promissory notes, payable to the bearer, under 20s. value.

The paper currencies of North America consisted, not in bank notes payable to the bearer on demand, but in a government paper, of which the payment was not exigible till several years after it was issued; and though the colony governments paid no interest to the holders of this paper, they declared it to be, and in fact rendered it, a legal tender of payment for the full value for which it was issued. But allowing the colony security to be perfectly good, £100, payable fifteen years hence, for example, in a country where interest is at six percent, is worth little more than £40 ready money. To oblige a creditor, therefore, to accept of this as full payment for a debt of £100, actually paid down in ready money, was an act of such violent injustice, as has scarce, perhaps, been attempted by the government of any other country which pretended to be free. It bears the evident marks of having originally been, what the honest and downright Doctor Douglas assures us it was, a scheme of fraudulent debtors to cheat their creditors. The government of Pennsylvania, indeed, pretended, upon their first emission of paper money, in 1722, to render their paper of equal value with gold and silver, by enacting penalties against all those who made any difference in the price of their goods when they sold them for a colony paper, and when they sold them for gold and silver, a regulation equally tyrannical, but much less, effectual, than that which it was meant to support. A positive law may render a shilling a legal tender for a guinea, because it may direct the courts of justice to discharge the debtor who has made that tender; but no positive law can oblige a person who sells goods, and who is at liberty to sell or not to sell as he pleases, to accept of a shilling as equivalent to a guinea in the price of them. Notwithstanding any regulation of this kind, it appeared, by the course of exchange with Great Britain, that £100 sterling was occasionally considered as equivalent, in some of the colonies, to £130, and in others to so great a sum as £1100 currency; this difference in the value arising from the difference in the quantity of paper emitted in the different colonies, and in the distance and probability of the term of its final discharge and redemption.

No law, therefore, could be more equitable than the act of parliament, so unjustly complained of in the colonies, which declared, that no paper currency to be emitted there in time coming, should be a legal tender of payment.

Pennsylvania was always more moderate in its emissions of paper money than any other of our colonies. Its paper currency, accordingly, is said never to have sunk below the value of the gold and silver which was current in the colony before the first emission of its paper money. Before that emission, the colony had raised the denomination of its coin, and had, by act of assembly, ordered 5s. sterling to pass in the colonies for 6s:3d., and afterwards for 6s:8d. A pound, colony currency, therefore, even when that currency was gold and silver, was more than thirty percent below the value of £1 sterling; and when that currency was turned into paper, it was seldom much more than thirty percent below that value. The pretence for raising the denomination of the coin was to prevent the exportation of gold and silver, by making equal quantities of those metals pass for greater sums in the colony than they did in the mother country. It was found, however, that the price of all goods from the mother country rose exactly in proportion as they raised the denomination of their coin, so that their gold and silver were exported as fast as ever.

The paper of each colony being received in the payment of the provincial taxes, for the full value for which it had been issued, it necessarily derived from this use some additional value, over and above what it would have had, from the real or supposed distance of the term of its final discharge and redemption. This additional value was greater or less, according as the quantity of paper issued was more or less above what could be employed in the payment of the taxes of the particular colony which issued it. It was in all the colonies very much above what could be employed in this manner.

A prince, who should enact that a certain proportion of his taxes should be paid in a paper money of a certain kind, might thereby give a certain value to this paper money, even though the term of its final discharge and redemption should depend altogether upon the will of the prince. If the bank which issued this paper was careful to keep the quantity of it always somewhat below what could easily be employed in this manner, the demand for it might be such as to make it even bear a premium, or sell for somewhat more in the market than the quantity of gold or silver currency for which it was issued. Some people account in this manner for what is called the agio of the bank of Amsterdam, or for the superiority of bank money over current money, though this bank money, as they pretend, cannot be taken out of the bank at the will of the owner. The greater part of foreign bills of exchange must be paid in bank money, that is, by a transfer in the books of the bank; and the directors of the bank, they allege, are careful to keep the whole quantity of bank money always below what this use occasions a demand for. It is upon this account, they say, the bank money sells for a premium, or bears an agio of four or five percent above the same nominal sum of the gold and silver currency of the country. This account of the bank of Amsterdam, however, it will appear hereafter, is in a great measure chimerical.

A paper currency which falls below the value of gold and silver coin, does not thereby sink the value of those metals, or occasion equal quantities of them to exchange for a smaller quantity of goods of any other kind. The proportion between the value of gold and silver and that of goods of any other kind, depends in all cases, not upon the nature and quantity of any particular paper money, which may be current in any particular country, but upon the richness or poverty of the mines, which happen at any particular time to supply the great market of the commercial world with those metals. It depends upon the proportion between the quantity of labor which is necessary in order to bring a certain quantity of gold and silver to market, and that which is necessary in order to bring thither a certain quantity of any other sort of goods.

If bankers are restrained from issuing any circulating bank notes, or notes payable to the bearer, for less than a certain sum; and if they are subjected to the obligation of an immediate and unconditional payment of such bank notes as soon as presented, their trade may, with safety to the public, be rendered in all other respects perfectly free. The late multiplication of banking companies in both parts of the united kingdom, an event by which many people have been much alarmed, instead of diminishing, increases the security of the public. It obliges all of them to be more circumspect in their conduct, and, by not extending their currency beyond its due proportion to their cash, to guard themselves against those malicious runs, which the rivalship of so many competitors is always ready to bring upon them. It restrains the circulation of each particular company within a narrower circle, and reduces their circulating notes to a smaller number. By dividing the whole circulation into a greater number of parts, the failure of any one company, an accident which, in the course of things, must sometimes happen, becomes of less consequence to the public. This free competition, too, obliges all bankers to be more liberal in their dealings with their customers, lest their rivals should carry them away. In general, if any branch of trade, or any division of labor, be advantageous to the public, the freer and more general the competition, it will always be the more so.

CHAPTER III

Of the Accumulation of Capital, or of Productive and Unproductive Labor

There is one sort of labor which adds to the value of the subject upon which it is bestowed; there is another which has no such effect. The former as it produces a value, may be called productive, the latter, unproductive labor. {Some French authors of great learning and ingenuity have used those words in a different sense. In the last chapter of the fourth book, I shall endeavor to show that their sense is an improper one.} Thus the labor of a manufacturer adds generally to the value of the materials which he works upon, that of his own maintenance, and of his master's profit. The labor of a menial servant, on the contrary, adds to the value of nothing. Though the manufacturer has his wages advanced to him by his master, he in reality costs him no expense, the value of those wages being generally restored, together with a profit, in the improved value of the subject upon which his labor is bestowed. But the maintenance of a menial servant never is restored. A man grows rich by employing a multitude of manufacturers; he grows poor by maintaining a multitude or menial servants. The labor of the latter, however, has its value, and deserves its reward as well as that of the former. But the labor of the manufacturer fixes and realizes itself in some particular subject or vendible commodity, which lasts for some time at least after that labor is past. It is, as it were, a certain quantity of labor stocked and stored up, to be employed, if necessary, upon some other occasion. That subject, or, what is the same thing, the price of that subject, can afterwards, if necessary, put into motion a quantity of labor equal to that which had originally produced it. The labor of the menial servant, on the contrary, does not fix or realize itself in any particular subject or vendible commodity. His services generally perish in the very instant of their performance, and seldom leave any trace of value behind them, for which an equal quantity of service could afterwards be procured.

The labor of some of the most respectable orders in the society is, like that of menial servants, unproductive of any value, and does not fix or realize itself in any permanent subject, or vendible commodity, which endures after that labor is past, and for which an equal quantity of labor could afterwards be procured. The sovereign, for example, with all the officers both of justice and war who serve under him, the whole army and navy, are unproductive laborers. They are the servants of the public, and are maintained by a part of the annual produce of the industry of other people. Their service, how honorable, how useful, or how necessary soever, produces nothing for which an equal quantity of service can afterwards be procured. The protection, security, and defense, of the commonwealth, the effect of their labor this year, will not purchase its protection, security, and defense, for the year to come. In the same class must be ranked, some both of the gravest and most important, and some of the most frivolous professions; churchmen, lawyers, physicians, men of letters of all kinds; players, buffoons, musicians, opera-singers, opera-dancers, etc. The labor of the meanest of these has a certain value, regulated by the very same principles which regulate that of every other sort of labor; and that of the noblest and most useful, produces nothing which could afterwards purchase or procure an equal quantity of labor. Like the declamation of the actor, the harangue of the orator, or the tune of the musician, the work of all of them perishes in the very instant of its production.

Both productive and unproductive laborers, and those who do not labor at all, are all equally maintained by the annual produce of the land and labor of the country. This produce, how great soever, can never be infinite, but must have certain limits. According, therefore, as a smaller or greater proportion of it is in any one year employed in maintaining unproductive hands, the more in the one case, and the less in the other, will remain for the productive, and the next year's produce will be greater or smaller accordingly; the whole annual produce, if we except the spontaneous productions of the earth, being the effect of productive labor. Though the whole annual produce of the land and labor of every country is no doubt ultimately destined for supplying the consumption of its inhabitants, and for procuring a revenue to them; yet when it first comes either from the ground, or from the hands of the productive laborers, it naturally divides itself into two parts. One of them, and frequently the largest, is, in the first place, destined for replacing a capital, or for renewing the provisions, materials, and finished work, which had been withdrawn from a capital; the other for constituting a revenue either to the owner of this capital, as the profit of his stock, or to some other person, as the rent of his land. Thus, of the produce of land, one part replaces the capital of the farmer; the other pays his profit and the rent of the landlord; and thus constitutes a revenue both to the owner of this capital, as the profits of his stock, and to some other person as the rent of his land. Of the produce of a great manufactory, in the same manner, one part, and that always the largest, replaces the capital of the undertaker of the work; the other pays his profit, and thus constitutes a revenue to the owner of this capital.

That part of the annual produce of the land and labor of any country which replaces a capital, never is immediately employed to maintain any but productive hands. It pays the wages of productive labor only. That which is immediately destined for constituting a revenue, either as profit or as rent, may maintain indifferently either productive or unproductive hands.

Whatever part of his stock a man employs as a capital, he always expects it to be replaced to him with a profit. He employs it, therefore, in maintaining productive hands only; and after having served in the function of a capital to him, it constitutes a revenue to them. Whenever he employs any part of it in maintaining unproductive hands of any kind, that part is from that moment withdrawn from his capital, and placed in his stock reserved for immediate consumption.

Unproductive laborers, and those who do not labor at all, are all maintained by revenue; either, first, by that part of the annual produce which is originally destined for constituting a revenue to some particular persons, either as the rent of land, or as the profits of stock; or, secondly, by that part which, though originally destined for replacing a capital, and for maintaining productive laborers only, yet when it comes into their hands, whatever part of it is over and above their necessary subsistence, may be employed in maintaining indifferently either productive or unproductive hands. Thus, not only the great landlord or the rich merchant, but even the common workman, if his wages are considerable, may maintain a menial servant; or he may sometimes go to a play or a puppet show, and so contribute his share towards maintaining one set of unproductive laborers; or he may pay some taxes, and thus help to maintain another set, more honorable and useful, indeed, but equally unproductive. No part of the annual produce, however, which had been originally destined to replace a capital, is ever directed towards maintaining unproductive hands, till after it has put into motion its full complement of productive labor, or all that it could put into motion in the way in which it was employed. The workman must have earned his wages by work done, before he can employ any part of them in this manner. That part, too, is generally but a small one. It is his spare revenue only, of which productive laborers have seldom a great deal. They generally have some, however; and in the payment of taxes, the greatness of their number may compensate, in some measure, the smallness of their contribution. The rent of land and the profits of stock are everywhere, therefore, the principal sources from which unproductive hands derive their subsistence. These are the two sorts of revenue of which the owners have generally most to spare. They might both maintain indifferently, either productive or unproductive hands. They seem, however, to have some predilection for the latter. The expense of a great lord feeds generally more idle than industrious people. The rich merchant, though with his capital he maintains industrious people only, yet by his expense, that is, by the employment of his revenue, he feeds commonly the very same sort as the great lord.

The proportion, therefore, between the productive and unproductive hands, depends very much in every country upon the proportion between that part of the annual produce, which, as soon as it comes either from the ground, or from the hands of the productive laborers, is destined for replacing a capital, and that which is destined for constituting a revenue, either as rent or as profit. This proportion is very different in rich from what it is in poor countries.

Thus, at present, in the opulent countries of Europe, a very large, frequently the largest, portion of the produce of the land, is destined for replacing the capital of the rich and independent farmer; the other for paying his profits, and the rent of the landlord. But anciently, during the prevalence of the feudal government, a very small portion of the produce was sufficient to replace the capital employed in cultivation. It consisted commonly in a few wretched cattle, maintained altogether by the spontaneous produce of uncultivated land, and which might, therefore, be considered as a part of that spontaneous produce. It generally, too, belonged to the landlord, and was by him advanced to the occupiers of the land. All the rest of the produce properly belonged to him too, either as rent for his land, or as profit upon this paltry capital. The occupiers of land were generally bond-men, whose persons and effects were equally his property. Those who were not bond-men were tenants at will; and though the rent which they paid was often nominally little more than a quit-rent, it really amounted to the whole produce of the land. Their lord could at all times command their labor in peace and their service in war. Though they lived at a distance from his house, they were equally dependent upon him as his retainers who lived in it.

But the whole produce of the land undoubtedly belongs to him, who can dispose of the labor and service of all those whom it maintains. In the present state of Europe, the share of the landlord seldom exceeds a third, sometimes not a fourth part of the whole produce of the land. The rent of land, however, in all the improved parts of the country, has been tripled and quadrupled since those ancient times; and this third or fourth part of the annual produce is, it seems, three or four times greater than the whole had been before. In the progress of improvement, rent, though it increases in proportion to the extent, diminishes in proportion to the produce of the land.

In the opulent countries of Europe, great capitals are at present employed in trade and manufactures. In the ancient state, the little trade that was stirring, and the few homely and coarse manufactures that were carried on, required but very small capitals. These, however, must have yielded very large profits. The rate of interest was nowhere less than ten percent and their profits must have been sufficient to afford this great interest. At present, the rate of interest, in the improved parts of Europe, is nowhere higher than six percent; and in some of the most improved, it is so low as four, three, and two percent. Though that part of the revenue of the inhabitants which is derived from the profits of stock, is always much greater in rich than in poor countries, it is because the stock is much greater; in proportion to the stock, the profits are generally much less.

That part of the annual produce, therefore, which, as soon as it comes either from the ground, or from the hands of the productive laborers, is destined for replacing a capital, is not only much greater in rich than in poor countries, but bears a much greater proportion to that which is immediately destined for constituting a revenue either as rent or as profit. The funds destined for the maintenance of productive labor are not only much greater in the former than in the latter, but bear a much greater proportion to those which, though they may be employed to maintain either productive or unproductive hands, have generally a predilection for the latter.

The proportion between those different funds necessarily determines in every country the general character of the inhabitants as to industry or idleness. We are more industrious than our forefathers, because, in the present times, the funds destined for the maintenance of industry are much greater in proportion to those which are likely to be employed in the maintenance of idleness, than they were two or three centuries ago. Our ancestors were idle for want of a sufficient encouragement to industry. It is better, says the proverb, to play for nothing, than to work for nothing. In mercantile and manufacturing towns, where the inferior ranks of people are chiefly maintained by the employment of capital, they are in general industrious, sober, and thriving; as in many English, and in most Dutch towns. In those towns which are principally supported by the constant or occasional residence of a court, and in which the inferior ranks of people are chiefly maintained by the spending of revenue, they are in general idle, dissolute, and poor; as at Rome, Versailles, Compeigne, and Fontainebleau. If you except Rouen and Bourdeaux, there is little trade or industry in any of the parliament towns of France; and the inferior ranks of people, being chiefly maintained by the expense of the members of the courts of justice, and of those who come to plead before them, are in general idle and poor. The great trade of Rouen and Bourdeaux seems to be altogether the effect of their situation. Rouen is necessarily the entrepot of almost all the goods which are brought either from foreign countries, or from the maritime provinces of France, for the consumption of the great city of Paris. Bourdeaux is, in the same manner, the entrepot of the wines which grow upon the banks of the Garronne, and of the rivers which run into it, one of the richest wine countries in the world, and which seems to produce the wine fittest for exportation, or best suited to the taste of foreign nations. Such advantageous situations necessarily attract a great capital by the great employment which they afford it; and the employment of this capital is the cause of the industry of those two cities. In the other parliament towns of France, very little more capital seems to be employed than what is necessary for supplying their own consumption; that is, little more than the smallest capital which can be employed in them. The same thing may be said of Paris, Madrid, and Vienna. Of those three cities, Paris is by far the most industrious, but Paris itself is the principal market of all the manufactures established at Paris, and its own consumption is the principal object of all the trade which it carries on. London, Lisbon, and Copenhagen, are, perhaps, the only three cities in Europe, which are both the constant residence of a court, and can at the same time be considered as trading cities, or as cities which trade not only for their own consumption, but for that of other cities and countries. The situation of all the three is extremely advantageous, and naturally fits them to be the entrepots of a great part of the goods destined for the consumption of distant places. In a city where a great revenue is spent, to employ with advantage a capital for any other purpose than for supplying the consumption of that city, is probably more difficult than in one in which the inferior ranks of people have no other maintenance but what they derive from the employment of such a capital. The idleness of the greater part of the people who are maintained by the expense of revenue, corrupts, it is probable, the industry of those who ought to be maintained by the employment of capital, and renders it less advantageous to employ a capital there than in other places. There was little trade or industry in Edinburgh before the Union. When the Scotch parliament was no longer to be assembled in it, when it ceased to be the necessary residence of the principal nobility and gentry of Scotland, it became a city of some trade and industry. It still continues, however, to be the residence of the principal courts of justice in Scotland, of the boards of customs and excise, etc. A considerable revenue, therefore, still continues to be spent in it. In trade and industry, it is much inferior to Glasgow, of which the inhabitants are chiefly maintained by the employment of capital. The inhabitants of a large village, it has sometimes been observed, after having made considerable progress in manufactures, have become idle and poor, in consequence of a great lord's having taken up his residence in their neighborhood.

The proportion between capital and revenue, therefore, seems everywhere to regulate the proportion between industry and idleness. Wherever capital predominates, industry prevails; wherever revenue, idleness. Every increase or diminution of capital, therefore, naturally tends to increase or diminish the real quantity of industry, the number of productive hands, and consequently the exchangeable value of the annual produce of the land and labor of the country, the real wealth and revenue of all its inhabitants.

Capitals are increased by parsimony, and diminished by prodigality and misconduct.

Whatever a person saves from his revenue he adds to his capital, and either employs it himself in maintaining an additional number of productive hands, or enables some other person to do so, by lending it to him for an interest, that is, for a share of the profits. As the capital of an individual can be increased only by what he saves from his annual revenue or his annual gains, so the capital of a society, which is the same with that of all the individuals who compose it, can be increased only in the same manner.

Parsimony, and not industry, is the immediate cause of the increase of capital. Industry, indeed, provides the subject which parsimony accumulates; but whatever industry might acquire, if parsimony did not save and store up, the capital would never be the greater.

Parsimony, by increasing the fund which is destined for the maintenance of productive hands, tends to increase the number of those hands whose labor adds to the value of the subject upon which it is bestowed. It tends, therefore, to increase the exchangeable value of the annual produce of the land and labor of the country. It puts into motion an additional quantity of industry, which gives an additional value to the annual produce.

What is annually saved, is as regularly consumed as what is annually spent, and nearly in the same time too: but it is consumed by a different set of people. That portion of his revenue which a rich man annually spends, is, in most cases, consumed by idle guests and menial servants, who leave nothing behind them in return for their consumption. That portion which he annually saves, as, for the sake of the profit, it is immediately employed as a capital, is consumed in the same manner, and nearly in the same time too, but by a different set of people: by laborers, manufacturers, and artificers, who reproduce, with a profit, the value of their annual consumption. His revenue, we shall suppose, is paid him in money. Had he spent the whole, the food, clothing, and lodging, which the whole could have purchased, would have been distributed among the former set of people. By saving a part of it, as that part is, for the sake of the profit, immediately employed as a capital, either by himself or by some other person, the food, clothing, and lodging, which may be purchased with it, are necessarily reserved for the latter. The consumption is the same, but the consumers are different.

By what a frugal man annually saves, he not only affords maintenance to an additional number of productive hands, for that of the ensuing year, but like the founder of a public workhouse he establishes, as it were, a perpetual fund for the maintenance of an equal number in all times to come. The perpetual allotment and destination of this fund, indeed, is not always guarded by any positive law, by any trust-right or deed of mortmain. It is always guarded, however, by a very powerful principle, the plain and evident interest of every individual to whom any share of it shall ever belong. No part of it can ever afterwards be employed to maintain any but productive hands, without an evident loss to the person who thus perverts it from its proper destination.

The prodigal perverts it in this manner: By not confining his expense within his income, he encroaches upon his capital. Like him who perverts the revenues of some pious foundation to profane purposes, he pays the wages of idleness with those funds which the frugality of his forefathers had, as it were, consecrated to the maintenance of industry. By diminishing the funds destined for the employment of productive labor, he necessarily diminishes, so far as it depends upon him, the quantity of that labor which adds a value to the subject upon which it is bestowed, and, consequently, the value of the annual produce of the land and labor of the whole country, the real wealth and revenue of its inhabitants. If the prodigality of some were not compensated by the frugality of others, the conduct of every prodigal, by feeding the idle with the bread of the industrious, would tend not only to beggar himself, but to impoverish his country.

Though the expense of the prodigal should be altogether in homemade, and no part of it in foreign commodities, its effect upon the productive funds of the society would still be the same. Every year there would still be a certain quantity of food and clothing, which ought to have maintained productive, employed in maintaining unproductive hands. Every year, therefore, there would still be some diminution in what would otherwise have been the value of the annual produce of the land and labor of the country.

This expense, it may be said, indeed, not being in foreign goods, and not occasioning any exportation of gold and silver, the same quantity of money would remain in the country as before. But if the quantity of food and clothing which were thus consumed by unproductive, had been distributed among productive hands, they would have reproduced, together with a profit, the full value of their consumption. The same quantity of money would, in this case, equally have remained in the country, and there would, besides, have been a reproduction of an equal value of consumable goods. There would have been two values instead of one.

The same quantity of money, besides, can not long remain in any country in which the value of the annual produce diminishes. The sole use of money is to circulate consumable goods. By means of it, provisions, materials, and finished work, are bought and sold, and distributed to their proper consumers. The quantity of money, therefore, which can be annually employed in any country, must be determined by the value of the consumable goods annually circulated within it. These must consist, either in the immediate produce of the land and labor of the country itself, or in something which had been purchased with some part of that produce. Their value, therefore, must diminish as the value of that produce diminishes, and along with it the quantity of money which can be employed in circulating them. But the money which, by this annual diminution of produce, is annually thrown out of domestic circulation, will not be allowed to lie idle. The interest of whoever possesses it requires that it should be employed; but having no employment at home, it will, in spite of all laws and prohibitions, be sent abroad, and employed in purchasing consumable goods, which may be of some use at home. Its annual exportation will, in this manner, continue for some time to add something to the annual consumption of the country beyond the value of its own annual produce. What in the days of its prosperity had been saved from that annual produce, and employed in purchasing gold and silver, will contribute, for some little time, to support its consumption in adversity. The exportation of gold and silver is, in this case, not the cause, but the effect of its declension, and may even, for some little time, alleviate the misery of that declension.

The quantity of money, on the contrary, must in every country naturally increase as the value of the annual produce increases. The value of the consumable goods annually circulated within the society being greater, will require a greater quantity of money to circulate them. A part of the increased produce, therefore, will naturally be employed in purchasing, wherever it is to be had, the additional quantity of gold and silver necessary for circulating the rest. The increase of those metals will, in this case, be the effect, not the cause, of the public prosperity. Gold and silver are purchased everywhere in the same manner. The food, clothing, and lodging, the revenue and maintenance, of all those whose labor or stock is employed in bringing them from the mine to the market, is the price paid for them in Peru as well as in England. The country which has this price to pay, will never belong without the quantity of those metals which it has occasion for; and no country will ever long retain a quantity which it has no occasion for.

Whatever, therefore, we may imagine the real wealth and revenue of a country to consist in, whether in the value of the annual produce of its land and labor, as plain reason seems to dictate, or in the quantity of the precious metals which circulate within it, as vulgar prejudices suppose; in either view of the matter, every prodigal appears to be a public enemy, and every frugal man a public benefactor.

The effects of misconduct are often the same as those of prodigality. Every injudicious and unsuccessful project in agriculture, mines, fisheries, trade, or manufactures, tends in the same manner to diminish the funds destined for the maintenance of productive labor. In every such project, though the capital is consumed by productive hands only, yet as, by the injudicious manner in which they are employed, they do not reproduce the full value of their consumption, there must always be some diminution in what would otherwise have been the productive funds of the society.

It can seldom happen, indeed, that the circumstances of a great nation can be much affected either by the prodigality or misconduct of individuals; the profusion or imprudence of some being always more than compensated by the frugality and good conduct of others.

With regard to profusion, the principle which prompts to expense is the passion for present enjoyment; which, though sometimes violent and very difficult to be restrained, is in general only momentary and occasional. But the principle which prompts to save, is the desire of bettering our condition; a desire which, though generally calm and dispassionate, comes with us from the womb, and never leaves us till we go into the grave. In the whole interval which separates those two moments, there is scarce, perhaps, a single instance, in which any man is so perfectly and completely satisfied with his situation, as to be without any wish of alteration or improvement of any kind. An augmentation of fortune is the means by which the greater part of men propose and wish to better their condition. It is the means the most vulgar and the most obvious; and the most likely way of augmenting their fortune is to save and accumulate some part of what they acquire, either regularly and annually, or upon some extraordinary occasion. Though the principle of expense, therefore, prevails in almost all men upon some occasions, and in some men upon almost all occasions; yet in the greater part of men, taking the whole course of their life at an average, the principle of frugality seems not only to predominate, but to predominate very greatly.

With regard to misconduct, the number of prudent and successful undertakings is everywhere much greater than that of injudicious and unsuccessful ones. After all our complaints of the frequency of bankruptcies, the unhappy men who fall into this misfortune, make but a very small part of the whole number engaged in trade, and all other sorts of business; not much more, perhaps, than one in a thousand. Bankruptcy is, perhaps, the greatest and most humiliating calamity which can befall an innocent man. The greater part of men, therefore, are sufficiently careful to avoid it. Some, indeed, do not avoid it; as some do not avoid the gallows.

Great nations are never impoverished by private, though they sometimes are by public prodigality and misconduct. The whole, or almost the whole public revenue is, in most countries, employed in maintaining unproductive hands. Such are the people who compose a numerous and splendid court, a great ecclesiastical establishment, great fleets and armies, who in time of peace produce nothing, and in time of war acquire nothing which can compensate the expense of maintaining them, even while the war lasts. Such people, as they themselves produce nothing, are all maintained by the produce of other men's labor. When multiplied, therefore, to an unnecessary number, they may in a particular year consume so great a share of this produce, as not to leave a sufficiency for maintaining the productive laborers, who should reproduce it next year. The next year's produce, therefore, will be less than that of the foregoing; and if the same disorder should continue, that of the third year will be still less than that of the second. Those unproductive hands who should be maintained by a part only of the spare revenue of the people, may consume so great a share of their whole revenue, and thereby oblige so great a number to encroach upon their capitals, upon the funds destined for the maintenance of productive labor, that all the frugality and good conduct of individuals may not be able to compensate the waste and degradation of produce occasioned by this violent and forced encroachment.

This frugality and good conduct, however, is, upon most occasions, it appears from experience, sufficient to compensate, not only the private prodigality and misconduct of individuals, but the public extravagance of government. The uniform, constant, and uninterrupted effort of every man to better his condition, the principle from which public and national, as well as private opulence is originally derived, is frequently powerful enough to maintain the natural progress of things towards improvement, in spite both of the extravagance of government, and of the greatest errors of administration. Like the unknown principle of animal life, it frequently restores health and vigor to the constitution, in spite not only of the disease, but of the absurd prescriptions of the doctor.

The annual produce of the land and labor of any nation can be increased in its value by no other means, but by increasing either the number of its productive laborers, or the productive powers of those laborers who had before been employed. The number of its productive laborers, it is evident, can never be much increased, but in consequence of an increase of capital, or of the funds destined for maintaining them. The productive powers of the same number of laborers cannot be increased, but in consequence either of some addition and improvement to those machines and instruments which facilitate and abridge labor, or of more proper division and distribution of employment. In either case, an additional capital is almost always required. It is by means of an additional capital only, that the undertaker of any work can either provide his workmen with better machinery, or make a more proper distribution of employment among them. When the work to be done consists of a number of parts, to keep every man constantly employed in one way, requires a much greater capital than where every man is occasionally employed in every different part of the work. When we compare, therefore, the state of a nation at two different periods, and find that the annual produce of its land and labor is evidently greater at the latter than at the former, that its lands are better cultivated, its manufactures more numerous and more flourishing, and its trade more extensive; we may be assured that its capital must have increased during the interval between those two periods, and that more must have been added to it by the good conduct of some, than had been taken from it either by the private misconduct of others, or by the public extravagance of government. But we shall find this to have been the case of almost all nations, in all tolerably quiet and peaceable times, even of those who have not enjoyed the most prudent and parsimonious governments. To form a right judgment of it, indeed, we must compare the state of the country at periods somewhat distant from one another. The progress is frequently so gradual, that, at near periods, the improvement is not only not sensible, but, from the declension either of certain branches of industry, or of certain districts of the country, things which sometimes happen, though the country in general is in great prosperity, there frequently arises a suspicion, that the riches and industry of the whole are decaying.

The annual produce of the land and labor of England, for example, is certainly much greater than it was a little more than a century ago, at the restoration of Charles II. Though at present few people, I believe, doubt of this, yet during this period, five years have seldom passed away, in which some book or pamphlet has not been published, written, too, with such abilities as to gain some authority with the public, and pretending to demonstrate that the wealth of the nation was fast declining; that the country was depopulated, agriculture neglected, manufactures decaying, and trade undone. Nor have these publications been all party pamphlets, the wretched offspring of falsehood and venality. Many of them have been written by very candid and very intelligent people, who wrote nothing but what they believed, and for no other reason but because they believed it.

The annual produce of the land and labor of England, again, was certainly much greater at the Restoration than we can suppose it to have been about a hundred years before, at the accession of Elizabeth. At this period, too, we have all reason to believe, the country was much more advanced in improvement, than it had been about a century before, towards the close of the dissensions between the houses of York and Lancaster. Even then it was, probably, in a better condition than it had been at the Norman conquest: and at the Norman conquest, than during the confusion of the Saxon heptarchy. Even at this early period, it was certainly a more improved country than at the invasion of Julius Caesar, when its inhabitants were nearly in the same state with the savages in North America.

In each of those periods, however, there was not only much private and public profusion, many expensive and unnecessary wars, great perversion of the annual produce from maintaining productive to maintain unproductive hands; but sometimes, in the confusion of civil discord, such absolute waste and destruction of stock, as might be supposed, not only to retard, as it certainly did, the natural accumulation of riches, but to have left the country, at the end of the period, poorer than at the beginning. Thus, in the happiest and most fortunate period of them all, that which has passed since the Restoration, how many disorders and misfortunes have occurred, which, could they have been foreseen, not only the impoverishment, but the total ruin of the country would have been expected from them? The fire and the plague of London, the two Dutch wars, the disorders of the revolution, the war in Ireland, the four expensive French wars of 1688, 1701, 1742, and 1756, together with the two rebellions of 1715 and 1745. In the course of the four French wars, the nation has contracted more than £145,000,000 of debt, over and above all the other extraordinary annual expense which they occasioned; so that the whole cannot be computed at less than £200,000,000. So great a share of the annual produce of the land and labor of the country, has, since the Revolution, been employed upon different occasions, in maintaining an extraordinary number of unproductive hands. But had not those wars given this particular direction to so large a capital, the greater part of it would naturally have been employed in maintaining productive hands, whose labor would have replaced, with a profit, the whole value of their consumption. The value of the annual produce of the land and labor of the country would have been considerably increased by it every year, and every year's increase would have augmented still more that of the following year. More houses would have been built, more lands would have been improved, and those which had been improved before would have been better cultivated; more manufactures would have been established, and those which had been established before would have been more extended; and to what height the real wealth and revenue of the country might by this time have been raised, it is not perhaps very easy even to imagine.

But though the profusion of government must undoubtedly have retarded the natural progress of England towards wealth and improvement, it has not been able to stop it. The annual produce of its land and labor is undoubtedly much greater at present than it was either at the Restoration or at the Revolution. The capital, therefore, annually employed in cultivating this land, and in maintaining this labor, must likewise be much greater. In the midst of all the exactions of government, this capital has been silently and gradually accumulated by the private frugality and good conduct of individuals, by their universal, continual, and uninterrupted effort to better their own condition. It is this effort, protected by law, and allowed by liberty to exert itself in the manner that is most advantageous, which has maintained the progress of England towards opulence and improvement in almost all former times, and which, it is to be hoped, will do so in all future times. England, however, as it has never been blessed with a very parsimonious government, so parsimony has at no time been the characteristic virtue of its inhabitants. It is the highest impertinence and presumption, therefore, in kings and ministers to pretend to watch over the economy of private people, and to restrain their expense, either by sumptuary laws, or by prohibiting the importation of foreign luxuries. They are themselves always, and without any exception, the greatest spendthrifts in the society. Let them look well after their own expense, and they may safely trust private people with theirs. If their own extravagance does not ruin the state, that of the subject never will.

As frugality increases, and prodigality diminishes, the public capital, so the conduct of those whose expense just equals their revenue, without either accumulating or encroaching, neither increases nor diminishes it. Some modes of expense, however, seem to contribute more to the growth of public opulence than others.

The revenue of an individual may be spent, either in things which are consumed immediately, and in which one day's expense can neither alleviate nor support that of another; or it may be spent in things mere durable, which can therefore be accumulated, and in which every day's expense may, as he chooses, either alleviate, or support and heighten, the effect of that of the following day. A man of fortune, for example, may either spend his revenue in a profuse and sumptuous table, and in maintaining a great number of menial servants, and a multitude of dogs and horses; or, contenting himself with a frugal table, and few attendants, he may lay out the greater part of it in adorning his house or his country villa, in useful or ornamental buildings, in useful or ornamental furniture, in collecting books, statues, pictures; or in things more frivolous, jewels, baubles, ingenious trinkets of different kinds; or, what is most trifling of all, in amassing a great wardrobe of fine clothes, like the favorite and minister of a great prince who died a few years ago. Were two men of equal fortune to spend their revenue, the one chiefly in the one way, the other in the other, the magnificence of the person whose expense had been chiefly in durable commodities, would be continually increasing, every day's expense contributing something to support and heighten the effect of that of the following day; that of the other, on the contrary, would be no greater at the end of the period than at the beginning. The former too would, at the end of the period, be the richer man of the two. He would have a stock of goods of some kind or other, which, though it might not be worth all that it cost, would always be worth something. No trace or vestige of the expense of the latter would remain, and the effects of ten or twenty years' profusion would be as completely annihilated as if they had never existed.

As the one mode of expense is more favorable than the other to the opulence of an individual, so is it likewise to that of a nation. The houses, the furniture, the clothing of the rich, in a little time, become useful to the inferior and middling ranks of people. They are able to purchase them when their superiors grow weary of them; and the general accommodation of the whole people is thus gradually improved, when this mode of expense becomes universal among men of fortune. In countries which have long been rich, you will frequently find the inferior ranks of people in possession both of houses and furniture perfectly good and entire, but of which neither the one could have been built, nor the other have been made for their use. What was formerly a seat of the family of Seymour, is now an inn upon the Bath road. The marriage-bed of James I of Great Britain, which his queen brought with her from Denmark, as a present fit for a sovereign to make to a sovereign, was, a few years ago, the ornament of an alehouse at Dunfermline. In some ancient cities, which either have been long stationary, or have gone somewhat to decay, you will sometimes scarce find a single house which could have been built for its present inhabitants. If you go into those houses, too, you will frequently find many excellent, though antiquated pieces of furniture, which are still very fit for use, and which could as little have been made for them. Noble palaces, magnificent villas, great collections of books, statues, pictures, and other curiosities, are frequently both an ornament and an honor, not only to the neighborhood, but to the whole country to which they belong. Versailles is an ornament and an honor to France, Stowe and Wilton to England. Italy still continues to command some sort of veneration, by the number of monuments of this kind which it possesses, though the wealth which produced them has decayed, and though the genius which planned them seems to be extinguished, perhaps from not having the same employment.

The expense, too, which is laid out in durable commodities, is favorable not only to accumulation, but to frugality. If a person should at any time exceed in it, he can easily reform without exposing himself to the censure of the public. To reduce very much the number of his servants, to reform his table from great profusion to great frugality, to lay down his equipage after he has once set it up, are changes which cannot escape the observation of his neighbors, and which are supposed to imply some acknowledgment of preceding bad conduct. Few, therefore, of those who have once been so unfortunate as to launch out too far into this sort of expense, have afterwards the courage to reform, till ruin and bankruptcy oblige them. But if a person has, at any time, been at too great an expense in building, in furniture, in books, or pictures, no imprudence can be inferred from his changing his conduct. These are things in which further expense is frequently rendered unnecessary by former expense; and when a person stops short, he appears to do so, not because he has exceeded his fortune, but because he has satisfied his fancy.

The expense, besides, that is laid out in durable commodities, gives maintenance, commonly, to a greater number of people than that which is employed in the most profuse hospitality. Of two or three hundred weight of provisions, which may sometimes be served up at a great festival, one half, perhaps, is thrown to the dunghill, and there is always a great deal wasted and abused. But if the expense of this entertainment had been employed in setting to work masons, carpenters, upholsterers, mechanics, etc. a quantity of provisions of equal value would have been distributed among a still greater number of people, who would have bought them in pennyworths and pound weights, and not have lost or thrown away a single ounce of them. In the one way, besides, this expense maintains productive, in the other unproductive hands. In the one way, therefore, it increases, in the other it does not increase the exchangeable value of the annual produce of the land and labor of the country.

I would not, however, by all this, be understood to mean, that the one species of expense always betokens a more liberal or generous spirit than the other. When a man of fortune spends his revenue chiefly in hospitality, he shares the greater part of it with his friends and companions; but when he employs it in purchasing such durable commodities, he often spends the whole upon his own person, and gives nothing to anybody without an equivalent. The latter species of expense, therefore, especially when directed towards frivolous objects, the little ornaments of dress and furniture, jewels, trinkets, gew-gaws, frequently indicates, not only a trifling, but a base and selfish disposition. All that I mean is, that the one sort of expense, as it always occasions some accumulation of valuable commodities, as it is more favorable to private frugality, and, consequently, to the increase of the public capital, and as it maintains productive rather than unproductive hands, conduces more than the other to the growth of public opulence.

CHAPTER IV

Of Stock Lent at Interest

The stock which is lent at interest is always considered as a capital by the lender. He expects that in due time it is to be restored to him, and that, in the meantime, the borrower is to pay him a certain annual rent for the use of it. The borrower may use it either as a capital, or as a stock reserved for immediate consumption. If he uses it as a capital, he employs it in the maintenance of productive laborers, who reproduce the value, with a profit. He can, in this case, both restore the capital, and pay the interest, without alienating or encroaching upon any other source of revenue. If he uses it as a stock reserved for immediate consumption, he acts the part of a prodigal, and dissipates, in the maintenance of the idle, what was destined for the support of the industrious. He can, in this case, neither restore the capital nor pay the interest, without either alienating or encroaching upon some other source of revenue, such as the property or the rent of land.

The stock which is lent at interest is, no doubt, occasionally employed in both these ways, but in the former much more frequently than in the latter. The man who borrows in order to spend will soon be ruined, and he who lends to him will generally have occasion to repent of his folly. To borrow or to lend for such a purpose, therefore, is, in all cases, where gross usury is out of the question, contrary to the interest of both parties; and though it no doubt happens sometimes, that people do both the one and the other, yet, from the regard that all men have for their own interest, we may be assured, that it cannot happen so very frequently as we are sometimes apt to imagine. Ask any rich man of common prudence, to which of the two sorts of people he has lent the greater part of his stock, to those who he thinks will employ it profitably, or to those who will spend it idly, and he will laugh at you for proposing the question. Even among borrowers, therefore, not the people in the world most famous for frugality, the number of the frugal and industrious surpasses considerably that of the prodigal and idle.

The only people to whom stock is commonly lent, without their being expected to make any very profitable use of it, are country gentlemen, who borrow upon mortgage. Even they scarce ever borrow merely to spend. What they borrow, one may say, is commonly spent before they borrow it. They have generally consumed so great a quantity of goods, advanced to them upon credit by shopkeepers and tradesmen, that they find it necessary to borrow at interest, in order to pay the debt. The capital borrowed replaces the capitals of those shopkeepers and tradesmen which the country gentlemen could not have replaced from the rents of their estates. It is not properly borrowed in order to be spent, but in order to replace a capital which had been spent before.

Almost all loans at interest are made in money, either of paper, or of gold and silver; but what the borrower really wants, and what the lender readily supplies him with, is not the money, but the money's worth, or the goods which it can purchase. If he wants it as a stock for immediate consumption, it is those goods only which he can place in that stock. If he wants it as a capital for employing industry, it is from those goods only that the industrious can be furnished with the tools, materials, and maintenance necessary for carrying on their work. By means of the loan, the lender, as it were, assigns to the borrower his right to a certain portion of the annual produce of the land and labor of the country, to be employed as the borrower pleases.

The quantity of stock, therefore, or, as it is commonly expressed, of money, which can be lent at interest in any country, is not regulated by the value of the money, whether paper or coin, which serves as the instrument of the different loans made in that country, but by the value of that part of the annual produce, which, as soon as it comes either from the ground, or from the hands of the productive laborers, is destined, not only for replacing a capital, but such a capital as the owner does not care to be at the trouble of employing himself. As such capitals are commonly lent out and paid back in money, they constitute what is called the monied interest. It is distinct, not only from the landed, but from the trading and manufacturing interests, as in these last the owners themselves employ their own capitals. Even in the monied interest, however, the money is, as it were, but the deed of assignment, which conveys from one hand to another those capitals which the owners do not care to employ themselves. Those capitals may be greater, in almost any proportion, than the amount of the money which serves as the instrument of their conveyance; the same pieces of money successively serving for many different loans, as well as for many different purchases. A, for example, lends to W £1000, with which W immediately purchases of B £1000 worth of goods. B having no occasion for the money himself, lends the identical pieces to X, with which X immediately purchases of C another £1000 worth of goods. C, in the same manner, and for the same reason, lends them to Y, who again purchases goods with them of D. In this manner, the same pieces, either of coin or of paper, may, in the course of a few days, serve as the Instrument of three different loans, and of three different purchases, each of which is, in value, equal to the whole amount of those pieces. What the three monied men, A, B, and C, assigned to the three borrowers, W, X, and Y, is the power of making those purchases. In this power consist both the value and the use of the loans. The stock lent by the three monied men is equal to the value of the goods which can be purchased with it, and is three times greater than that of the money with which the purchases are made. Those loans, however, may be all perfectly well secured, the goods purchased by the different debtors being so employed as, in due time, to bring back, with a profit, an equal value either of coin or of paper. And as the same pieces of money can thus serve as the instrument of different loans to three, or, for the same reason, to thirty times their value, so they may likewise successively serve as the instrument of repayment.

A capital lent at interest may, in this manner, be considered as an assignment, from the lender to the borrower, of a certain considerable portion of the annual produce, upon condition that the burrower in return shall, during the continuance of the loan, annually assign to the lender a small portion, called the interest; and, at the end of it, a portion equally considerable with that which had originally been assigned to him, called the repayment. Though money, either coin or paper, serves generally as the deed of assignment, both to the smaller and to the more considerable portion, it is itself altogether different from what is assigned by it.

In proportion as that share of the annual produce which, as soon as it comes either from the ground, or from the hands of the productive laborers, is destined for replacing a capital, increases in any country, what is called the monied interest naturally increases with it. The increase of those particular capitals from which the owners wish to derive a revenue, without being at the trouble of employing them themselves, naturally accompanies the general increase of capitals; or, in other words, as stock increases, the quantity of stock to be lent at interest grows gradually greater and greater.

As the quantity of stock to be lent at interest increases, the interest, or the price which must be paid for the use of that stock, necessarily diminishes, not only from those general causes which make the market price of things commonly diminish as their quantity increases, but from other causes which are peculiar to this particular case. As capitals increase in any country, the profits which can be made by employing them necessarily diminish. It becomes gradually more and more difficult to find within the country a profitable method of employing any new capital. There arises, in consequence, a competition between different capitals, the owner of one endeavoring to get possession of that employment which is occupied by another; but, upon most occasions, he can hope to justle that other out of this employment by no other means but by dealing upon more reasonable terms. He must not only sell what he deals in somewhat cheaper, but, in order to get it to sell, he must sometimes, too, buy it dearer. The demand for productive labor, by the increase of the funds which are destined for maintaining it, grows every day greater and greater. Laborers easily find employment; but the owners of capitals find it difficult to get laborers to employ. Their competition raises the wages of labor, and sinks the profits of stock. But when the profits which can be made by the use of a capital are in this manner diminished, as it were, at both ends, the price which can be paid for the use of it, that is, the rate of interest, must necessarily be diminished with them.

Mr. Locke, Mr. Lawe, and Mr. Montesquieu, as well as many other writers, seem to have imagined that the increase of the quantity of gold and silver, in consequence of the discovery of the Spanish West Indies, was the real cause of the lowering of the rate of interest through the greater part of Europe. Those metals, they say, having become of less value themselves, the use of any particular portion of them necessarily became of less value too, and, consequently, the price which could be paid for it. This notion, which at first sight seems so plausible, has been so fully exposed by Mr. Hume, that it is, perhaps, unnecessary to say any thing more about it. The following very short and plain argument, however, may serve to explain more distinctly the fallacy which seems to have misled those gentlemen.

Before the discovery of the Spanish West Indies, ten percent seems to have been the common rate of interest through the greater part of Europe. It has since that time, in different countries, sunk to six, five, four, and three percent. Let us suppose, that in every particular country the value of silver has sunk precisely in the same proportion as the rate of interest; and that in those countries, for example, where interest has been reduced from ten to five percent the same quantity of silver can now purchase just half the quantity of goods which it could have purchased before. This supposition will not, I believe, be found anywhere agreeable to the truth; but it is the most favorable to the opinion which we are going to examine; and, even upon this supposition, it is utterly impossible that the lowering of the value of silver could have the smallest tendency to lower the rate of interest. If £100 are in those countries now of no more value than £50 were then,

£10 must now be of no more value than £5 were then. Whatever were the causes which lowered the value of the capital, the same must necessarily have lowered that of the interest, and exactly in the same proportion. The proportion between the value of the capital and that of the interest must have remained the same, though the rate had never been altered. By altering the rate, on the contrary, the proportion between those two values is necessarily altered. If £100 now are worth no more than £50 were then, £5 now can be worth no more than £2:10s. were then. By reducing the rate of interest, therefore, from ten to five percent we give for the use of a capital, which is supposed to be equal to one half of its former value, an interest which is equal to one fourth only of the value of the former interest.

Any increase in the quantity of silver, while that of the commodities circulated by means of it remained the same, could have no other effect than to diminish the value of that metal. The nominal value of all sorts of goods would be greater, but their real value would be precisely the same as before. They would be exchanged for a greater number of pieces of silver; but the quantity of labor which they could command, the number of people whom they could maintain and employ, would be precisely the same. The capital of the country would be the same, though a greater number of pieces might be requisite for conveying any equal portion of it from one hand to another. The deeds of assignment, like the conveyances of a verbose attorney, would be more cumbersome; but the thing assigned would be precisely the same as before, and could produce only the same effects. The funds for maintaining productive labor being the same, the demand for it would be the same. Its price or wages, therefore, though nominally greater, would really be the same. They would be paid in a greater number of pieces of silver, but they would purchase only the same quantity of goods. The profits of stock would be the same, both nominally and really. The wages of labor are commonly computed by the quantity of silver which is paid to the laborer. When that is increased, therefore, his wages appear to be increased, though they may sometimes be no greater than before. But the profits of stock are not computed by the number of pieces of silver with which they are paid, but by the proportion which those pieces bear to the whole capital employed. Thus, in a particular country, 5s. a-week are said to be the common wages of labor, and ten percent the common profits of stock; but the whole capital of the country being the same as before, the competition between the different capitals of individuals into which it was divided would likewise be the same. They would all trade with the same advantages and disadvantages. The common proportion between capital and profit, therefore, would be the same, and consequently the common interest of money; what can commonly be given for the use of money being necessarily regulated by what can commonly be made by the use of it.

Any increase in the quantity of commodities annually circulated within the country, while that of the money which circulated them remained the same, would, on the contrary, produce many other important effects, besides that of raising the value of the money. The capital of the country, though it might nominally be the same, would really be augmented. It might continue to be expressed by the same quantity of money, but it would command a greater quantity of labor. The quantity of productive labor which it could maintain and employ would be increased, and consequently the demand for that labor. Its wages would naturally rise with the demand, and yet might appear to sink.

They might be paid with a smaller quantity of money, but that smaller quantity might purchase a greater quantity of goods than a greater had done before. The profits of stock would be diminished, both really and in appearance. The whole capital of the country being augmented, the competition between the different capitals of which it was composed would naturally be augmented along with it. The owners of those particular capitals would be obliged to content themselves with a smaller proportion of the produce of that labor which their respective capitals employed. The interest of money, keeping pace always with the profits of stock, might, in this manner, be greatly diminished, though the value of money, or the quantity of goods which any particular sum could purchase, was greatly augmented.

In some countries the interest of money has been prohibited by law. But as something can everywhere be made by the use of money, something ought everywhere to be paid for the use of it. This regulation, instead of preventing, has been found from experience to increase the evil of usury. The debtor being obliged to pay, not only for the use of the money, but for the risk which his creditor runs by accepting a compensation for that use, he is obliged, if one may say so, to insure his creditor from the penalties of usury.

In countries where interest is permitted, the law in order to prevent the extortion of usury, generally fixes the highest rate which can be taken without incurring a penalty. This rate ought always to be somewhat above the lowest market price, or the price which is commonly paid for the use of money by those who can give the most undoubted security. If this legal rate should be fixed below the lowest market rate, the effects of this fixation must be nearly the same as those of a total prohibition of interest. The creditor will not lend his money for less than the use of it is worth, and the debtor must pay him for the risk which he runs by accepting the full value of that use. If it is fixed precisely at the lowest market price, it ruins, with honest people who respect the laws of their country, the credit of all those who cannot give the very best security, and obliges them to have recourse to exorbitant usurers. In a country such as Great Britain, where money is lent to government at three percent and to private people, upon good security, at four and four and a-half, the present legal rate, five percent is perhaps as proper as any.

The legal rate, it is to be observed, though it ought to be somewhat above, ought not to be much above the lowest market rate. If the legal rate of interest in Great Britain, for example, was fixed so high as eight or ten percent the greater part of the money which was to be lent, would be lent to prodigals and projectors, who alone would be willing to give this high interest. Sober people, who will give for the use of money no more than a part of what they are likely to make by the use of it, would not venture into the competition. A great part of the capital of the country would thus be kept out of the hands which were most likely to make a profitable and advantageous use of it, and thrown into those which were most likely to waste and destroy it. Where the legal rate of interest, on the contrary, is fixed but a very little above the lowest market rate, sober people are universally preferred, as borrowers, to prodigals and projectors. The person who lends money gets nearly as much interest from the former as he dares to take from the latter, and his money is much safer in the hands of the one set of people than in those of the other. A great part of the capital of the country is thus thrown into the hands in which it is most likely to be employed with advantage.

No law can reduce the common rate of interest below the lowest ordinary market rate at the time when that law is made. Notwithstanding the edict of 1766, by which the French king attempted to reduce the rate of interest from five to four percent, money continued to be lent in France at five percent the law being evaded in several different ways.

The ordinary market price of land, it is to be observed, depends everywhere upon the ordinary market rate of interest. The person who has a capital from which he wishes to derive a revenue, without taking the trouble to employ it himself, deliberates whether he should buy land with it, or lend it out at interest. The superior security of land, together with some other advantages which almost everywhere attend upon this species of property, will generally dispose him to content himself with a smaller revenue from land, than what he might have by lending out his money at interest. These advantages are sufficient to compensate a certain difference of revenue; but they will compensate a certain difference only; and if the rent of land should fall short of the interest of money by a greater difference, nobody would buy land, which would soon reduce its ordinary price. On the contrary, if the advantages should much more than compensate the difference, everybody would buy land, which again would soon raise its ordinary price. When interest was at ten percent land was commonly sold for ten or twelve years purchase. As interest sunk to six, five, and four percent the price of land rose to twenty, five-and-twenty, and thirty years purchase. The market rate of interest is higher in France than in England, and the common price of land is lower. In England it commonly sells at thirty, in France at twenty years purchase.

CHAPTER V

Of the Different Employment of Capitals

Though all capitals are destined for the maintenance of productive labor only, yet the quantity of that labor which equal capitals are capable of putting into motion, varies extremely according to the diversity of their employment; as does likewise the value which that employment adds to the annual produce of the land and labor of the country.

A capital may be employed in four different ways; either, first, in procuring the rude produce annually required for the use and consumption of the society; or, secondly, in manufacturing and preparing that rude produce for immediate use and consumption; or, thirdly in transporting either the rude or manufactured produce from the places where they abound to those where they are wanted; or, lastly, in dividing particular portions of either into such small parcels as suit the occasional demands of those who want them. In the first way are employed the capitals of all those who undertake improvement or cultivation of lands, mines, or fisheries; in the second, those of all master manufacturers; in the third, those of all wholesale merchants; and in the fourth, those of all retailers. It is difficult to conceive that a capital should be employed in any way which may not be classed under some one or other of those four.

Each of those four methods of employing a capital is essentially necessary, either to the existence or extension of the other three, or to the general convenience of the society.

Unless a capital was employed in furnishing rude produce to a certain degree of abundance, neither manufactures nor trade of any kind could exist.

Unless a capital was employed in manufacturing that part of the rude produce which requires a good deal of preparation before it can be fit for use and consumption, it either would never be produced, because there could be no demand for it; or if it was produced spontaneously, it would be of no value in exchange, and could add nothing to the wealth of the society.

Unless a capital was employed in transporting either the rude or manufactured produce from the places where it abounds to those where it is wanted, no more of either could be produced than was necessary for the consumption of the neighborhood. The capital of the merchant exchanges the surplus produce of one place for that of another, and thus encourages the industry, and increases the enjoyments of both.

Unless a capital was employed in breaking and dividing certain portions either of the rude or manufactured produce into such small parcels as suit the occasional demands of those who want them, every man would be obliged to purchase a greater quantity of the goods he wanted than his immediate occasions required. If there was no such trade as a butcher, for example, every man would be obliged to purchase a whole ox or a whole sheep at a time. This would generally be inconvenient to the rich, and much more so to the poor. If a poor workman was obliged to purchase a month's or six months' provisions at a time, a great part of the stock which he employs as a capital in the instruments of his trade, or in the furniture of his shop, and which yields him a revenue, he would be forced to place in that part of his stock which is reserved for immediate consumption, and which yields him no revenue. Nothing can be more convenient for such a person than to be able to purchase his subsistence from day to day, or even from hour to hour, as he wants it. He is thereby enabled to employ almost his whole stock as a capital. He is thus enabled to furnish work to a greater value; and the profit which he makes by it in this way much more than compensates the additional price which the profit of the retailer imposes upon the goods. The prejudices of some political writers against shopkeepers and tradesmen are altogether without foundation. So far is it from being necessary either to tax them, or to restrict their numbers, that they can never be multiplied so as to hurt the public, though they may so as to hurt one another. The quantity of grocery goods, for example, which can be sold in a particular town, is limited by the demand of that town and its neighborhood. The capital, therefore, which can be employed in the grocery trade, cannot exceed what is sufficient to purchase that quantity. If this capital is divided between two different grocers, their competition will tend to make both of them sell cheaper than if it were in the hands of one only; and if it were divided among twenty, their competition would be just so much the greater, and the chance of their combining together, in order to raise the price, just so much the less. Their competition might, perhaps, ruin some of themselves; but to take care of this, is the business of the parties concerned, and it may safely be trusted to their discretion. It can never hurt either the consumer or the producer; on the contrary, it must tend to make the retailers both sell cheaper and buy dearer, than if the whole trade was monopolized by one or two persons. Some of them, perhaps, may sometimes decoy a weak customer to buy what he has no occasion for. This evil, however, is of too little importance to deserve the public attention, nor would it necessarily be prevented by restricting their numbers. It is not the multitude of alehouses, to give the must suspicious example, that occasions a general disposition to drunkenness among the common people; but that disposition, arising from other causes, necessarily gives employment to a multitude of alehouses.

The persons whose capitals are employed in any of those four ways, are themselves productive laborers. Their labor, when properly directed, fixes and realizes itself in the subject or vendible commodity upon which it is bestowed, and generally adds to its price the value at least of their own maintenance and consumption. The profits of the farmer, of the manufacturer, of the merchant, and retailer, are all drawn from the price of the goods which the two first produce, and the two last buy and sell. Equal capitals, however, employed in each of those four different ways, will immediately put into motion very different quantities of productive labor; and augment, too, in very different proportions, the value of the annual produce of the land and labor of the society to which they belong.

The capital of the retailer replaces, together with its profits, that of the merchant of whom he purchases goods, and thereby enables him to continue his business. The retailer himself is the only productive laborer whom it immediately employs. In his profit consists the whole value which its employment adds to the annual produce of the land and labor of the society.

The capital of the wholesale merchant replaces, together with their profits, the capitals of the farmers and manufacturers of whom he purchases the rude and manufactured produce which he deals in, and thereby enables them to continue their respective trades. It is by this service chiefly that he contributes indirectly to support the productive labor of the society, and to increase the value of its annual produce. His capital employs, too, the sailors and carriers who transport his goods from one place to another; and it augments the price of those goods by the value, not only of his profits, but of their wages. This is all the productive labor which it immediately puts into motion, and all the value which it immediately adds to the annual produce. Its operation in both these respects is a good deal superior to that of the capital of the retailer.

Part of the capital of the master manufacturer is employed as a fixed capital in the instruments of his trade, and replaces, together with its profits, that of some other artificer of whom he purchases them. Part of his circulating capital is employed in purchasing materials, and replaces, with their profits, the capitals of the farmers and miners of whom he purchases them. But a great part of it is always, either annually, or in a much shorter period, distributed among the different workmen whom he employs. It augments the value of those materials by their wages, and by their masters' profits upon the whole stock of wages, materials, and instruments of trade employed in the business. It puts immediately into motion, therefore, a much greater quantity of productive labor, and adds a much greater value to the annual produce of the land and labor of the society, than an equal capital in the hands of any wholesale merchant.

No equal capital puts into motion a greater quantity of productive labor than that of the farmer. Not only his laboring servants, but his laboring cattle, are productive laborers. In agriculture, too, Nature labors along with man; and though her labor costs no expense, its produce has its value, as well as that of the most expensive workmen. The most important operations of agriculture seem intended, not so much to increase, though they do that too, as to direct the fertility of Nature towards the production of the plants most profitable to man. A field overgrown with briars and brambles, may frequently produce as great a quantity of vegetables as the best cultivated vineyard or cornfield. Planting and tillage frequently regulate more than they animate the active fertility of Nature; and after all their labor, a great part of the work always remains to be done by her. The laborers and laboring cattle, therefore, employed in agriculture, not only occasion, like the workmen in manufactures, the reproduction of a value equal to their own consumption, or to the capital which employs them, together with its owner's profits, but of a much greater value. Over and above the capital of the farmer, and all its profits, they regularly occasion the reproduction of the rent of the landlord. This rent may be considered as the produce of those powers of Nature, the use of which the landlord lends to the farmer. It is greater or smaller, according to the supposed extent of those powers, or, in other words, according to the supposed natural or improved fertility of the land. It is the work of Nature which remains, after deducting or compensating every thing which can be regarded as the work of man. It is seldom less than a fourth, and frequently more than a third, of the whole produce. No equal quantity of productive labor employed in manufactures, can ever occasion so great reproduction. In them Nature does nothing; man does all; and the reproduction must always be in proportion to the strength of the agents that occasion it. The capital employed in agriculture, therefore, not only puts into motion a greater quantity of productive labor than any equal capital employed in manufactures;

but in proportion, too, to the quantity of productive labor which it employs, it adds a much greater value to the annual produce of the land and labor of the country, to the real wealth and revenue of its inhabitants. Of all the ways in which a capital can be employed, it is by far the most advantageous to society.

The capitals employed in the agriculture and in the retail trade of any society, must always reside within that society. Their employment is confined almost to a precise spot, to the farm, and to the shop of the retailer. They must generally, too, though there are some exceptions to this, belong to resident members of the society.

The capital of a wholesale merchant, on the contrary, seems to have no fixed or necessary residence anywhere, but may wander about from place to place, according as it can either buy cheap or sell dear.

The capital of the manufacturer must, no doubt, reside where the manufacture is carried on; but where this shall be, is not always necessarily determined. It may frequently be at a great distance, both from the place where the materials grow, and from that where the complete manufacture is consumed. Lyons is very distant, both from the places which afford the materials of its manufactures, and from those which consume them. The people of fashion in Sicily are clothed in silks made in other countries, from the materials which their own produces. Part of the wool of Spain is manufactured in Great Britain, and some part of that cloth is afterwards sent back to Spain.

Whether the merchant whose capital exports the surplus produce of any society, be a native or a foreigner, is of very little importance. If he is a foreigner, the number of their productive laborers is necessarily less than if he had been a native, by one man only; and the value of their annual produce, by the profits of that one man. The sailors or carriers whom he employs, may still belong indifferently either to his country, or to their country, or to some third country, in the same manner as if he had been a native. The capital of a foreigner gives a value to their surplus produce equally with that of a native, by exchanging it for something for which there is a demand at home. It as effectually replaces the capital of the person who produces that surplus, and as effectually enables him to continue his business, the service by which the capital of a wholesale merchant chiefly contributes to support the productive labor, and to augment the value of the annual produce of the society to which he belongs.

It is of more consequence that the capital of the manufacturer should reside within the country. It necessarily puts into motion a greater quantity of productive labor, and adds a greater value to the annual produce of the land and labor of the society. It may, however, be very useful to the country, though it should not reside within it. The capitals of the British manufacturers who work up the flax and hemp annually imported from the coasts of the Baltic, are surely very useful to the countries which produce them. Those materials are a part of the surplus produce of those countries, which, unless it was annually exchanged for something which is in demand here, would be of no value, and would soon cease to be produced. The merchants who export it, replace the capitals of the people who produce it, and thereby encourage them to continue the production; and the British manufacturers replace the capitals of those merchants.

A particular country, in the same manner as a particular person, may frequently not have capital sufficient both to improve and cultivate all its lands, to manufacture and prepare their whole rude produce for immediate use and consumption, and to transport the surplus part either of the rude or manufactured produce to those distant markets, where it can be exchanged for something for which there is a demand at home. The inhabitants of many different parts of Great Britain have not capital sufficient to improve and cultivate all their lands. The wool of the southern counties of Scotland is, a great part of it, after a long land carriage through very bad roads, manufactured in Yorkshire, for want of a capital to manufacture it at home. There are many little manufacturing towns in Great Britain, of which the inhabitants have not capital sufficient to transport the produce of their own industry to those distant markets where there is demand and consumption for it. If there are any merchants among them, they are, properly, only the agents of wealthier merchants who reside in some of the great commercial cities.

When the capital of any country is not sufficient for all those three purposes, in proportion as a greater share of it is employed in agriculture, the greater will be the quantity of productive labor which it puts into motion within the country; as will likewise be the value which its employment adds to the annual produce of the land and labor of the society. After agriculture, the capital employed in manufactures puts into motion the greatest quantity of productive labor, and adds the greatest value to the annual produce. That which is employed in the trade of exportation has the least effect of any of the three.

The country, indeed, which has not capital sufficient for all those three purposes, has not arrived at that degree of opulence for which it seems naturally destined. To attempt, however, prematurely, and with an insufficient capital, to do all the three, is certainly not the shortest way for a society, no more than it would be for an individual, to acquire a sufficient one. The capital of all the individuals of a nation has its limits, in the same manner as that of a single individual, and is capable of executing only certain purposes. The capital of all the individuals of a nation is increased in the same manner as that of a single individual, by their continually accumulating and adding to it whatever they save out of their revenue. It is likely to increase the fastest, therefore, when it is employed in the way that affords the greatest revenue to all the inhabitants or the country, as they will thus be enabled to make the greatest savings. But the revenue of all the inhabitants of the country is necessarily in proportion to the value of the annual produce of their land and labor.

It has been the principal cause of the rapid progress of our American colonies towards wealth and greatness, that almost their whole capitals have hitherto been employed in agriculture. They have no manufactures, those household and coarser manufactures excepted, which necessarily accompany the progress of agriculture, and which are the work of the women and children in every private family. The greater part, both of the exportation and coasting trade of America, is carried on by the capitals of merchants who reside in Great Britain. Even the stores and warehouses from which goods are retailed in some provinces, particularly in Virginia and Maryland, belong many of them to merchants who reside in the mother country, and afford one of the few instances of the retail trade of a society being carried on by the capitals of those who are not resident members of it. Were the Americans, either by combination, or by any other sort of violence, to stop the importation of European manufactures, and, by thus giving a monopoly to such of their own countrymen as could manufacture the like goods, divert any considerable part of their capital into this employment, they would retard, instead of accelerating, the further increase in the value of their annual produce, and would obstruct, instead of promoting, the progress of their country towards real wealth and greatness. This would be still more the case, were they to attempt, in the same manner, to monopolize to themselves their whole exportation trade.

The course of human prosperity, indeed, seems scarce ever to have been of so long continuance as to unable any great country to acquire capital sufficient for all those three purposes; unless, perhaps, we give credit to the wonderful accounts of the wealth and cultivation of China, of those of ancient Egypt, and of the ancient state of Indostan. Even those three countries, the wealthiest, according to all accounts, that ever were in the world, are chiefly renowned for their superiority in agriculture and manufactures. They do not appear to have been eminent for foreign trade. The ancient Egyptians had a superstitious antipathy to the sea; a superstition nearly of the same kind prevails among the Indians; and the Chinese have never excelled in foreign commerce. The greater part of the surplus produce of all those three countries seems to have been always exported by foreigners, who gave in exchange for it something else, for which they found a demand there, frequently gold and silver.

It is thus that the same capital will in any country put into motion a greater or smaller quantity of productive labor, and add a greater or smaller value to the annual produce of its land and labor, according to the different proportions in which it is employed in agriculture, manufactures, and wholesale trade. The difference, too, is very great, according to the different sorts of wholesale trade in which any part of it is employed.

All wholesale trade, all buying in order to sell again by wholesale, maybe reduced to three different sorts: the home trade, the foreign trade of consumption, and the carrying trade. The home trade is employed in purchasing in one part of the same country, and selling in another, the produce of the industry of that country. It comprehends both the inland and the coasting trade. The foreign trade of consumption is employed in purchasing foreign goods for home consumption. The carrying trade is employed in transacting the commerce of foreign countries, or in carrying the surplus produce of one to another.

The capital which is employed in purchasing in one part of the country, in order to sell in another, the produce of the industry of that country, generally replaces, by every such operation, two distinct capitals, that had both been employed in the agriculture or manufactures of that country, and thereby enables them to continue that employment. When it sends out from the residence of the merchant a certain value of commodities, it generally brings hack in return at least an equal value of other commodities. When both are the produce of domestic industry, it necessarily replaces, by every such operation, two distinct capitals, which had both been employed in supporting productive labor, and thereby enables them to continue that support. The capital which sends Scotch manufactures to London, and brings back English corn and manufactures to Edinburgh, necessarily replaces, by every such operation, two British capitals, which had both been employed in the agriculture or manufactures of Great Britain.

The capital employed in purchasing foreign goods for home consumption, when this purchase is made with the produce of domestic industry, replaces, too, by every such operation, two distinct capitals; but one of them only is employed in supporting domestic industry. The capital which sends British goods to Portugal, and brings back

Portuguese goods to Great Britain, replaces, by every such operation, only one British capital. The other is a Portuguese one. Though the returns, therefore, of the foreign trade of consumption, should be as quick as those of the home trade, the capital employed in it will give but one half of the encouragement to the industry or productive labor of the country.

But the returns of the foreign trade of consumption are very seldom so quick as those of the home trade. The returns of the home trade generally come in before the end of the year, and sometimes three or four times in the year. The returns of the foreign trade of consumption seldom come in before the end of the year, and sometimes not till after two or three years. A capital, therefore, employed in the home trade, will sometimes make twelve operations, or be sent out and returned twelve times, before a capital employed in the foreign trade of consumption has made one. If the capitals are equal, therefore, the one will give four-and-twenty times more encouragement and support to the industry of the country than the other.

The foreign goods for home consumption may sometimes be purchased, not with the produce of domestic industry but with some other foreign goods. These last, however, must have been purchased, either immediately with the produce of domestic industry, or with something else that had been purchased with it; for, the case of war and conquest excepted, foreign goods can never be acquired, but in exchange for something that had been produced at home, either immediately, or after two or more different exchanges. The effects, therefore, of a capital employed in such a round-about foreign trade of consumption, are, in every respect, the same as those of one employed in the most direct trade of the same kind, except that the final returns are likely to be still more distant, as they must depend upon the returns of two or three distinct foreign trades. If the hemp and flax of Riga are purchased with the tobacco of Virginia, which had been purchased with British manufactures, the merchant must wait for the returns of two distinct foreign trades, before he can employ the same capital in repurchasing a like quantity of British manufactures. If the tobacco of Virginia had been purchased, not with British manufactures, but with the sugar and rum of Jamaica, which had been purchased with those manufactures, he must wait for the returns of three. If those two or three distinct foreign trades should happen to be carried on by two or three distinct merchants, of whom the second buys the goods imported by the first, and the third buys those imported by the second, in order to export them again, each merchant, indeed, will, in this case, receive the returns of his own capital more quickly; but the final returns of the whole capital employed in the trade will be just as slow as ever. Whether the whole capital employed in such a round about trade belong to one merchant or to three, can make no difference with regard to the country, though it may with regard to the particular merchants. Three times a greater capital must in both cases be employed, in order to exchange a certain value of British manufactures for a certain quantity of flax and hemp, than would have been necessary, had the manufactures and the flax and hemp been directly exchanged for one another. The whole capital employed, therefore, in such a round-about foreign trade of consumption, will generally give less encouragement and support to the productive labor of the country, than an equal capital employed in a more direct trade of the same kind.

Whatever be the foreign commodity with which the foreign goods for home consumption are purchased, it can occasion no essential difference, either in the nature of the trade, or in the encouragement and support which it can give to the productive labor of the country from which it is carried on. If they are purchased with the gold of Brazil, for example, or with the silver of Peru, this gold and silver, like the tobacco of Virginia, must have been purchased with something that either was the produce of the industry of the country, or that had been purchased with something else that was so. So far, therefore, as the productive labor of the country is concerned, the foreign trade of consumption, which is carried on by means of gold and silver, has all the advantages and all the inconveniences of any other equally round-about foreign trade of consumption; and will replace, just as fast, or just as slow, the capital which is immediately employed in supporting that productive labor. It seems even to have one advantage over any other equally round-about foreign trade. The transportation of those metals from one place to another, on account of their small bulk and great value, is less expensive than that of almost any other foreign goods of equal value. Their freight is much less, and their insurance not greater; and no goods, besides, are less liable to suffer by the carriage. An equal quantity of foreign goods, therefore, may frequently be purchased with a smaller quantity of the produce of domestic industry, by the intervention of gold and silver, than by that of any other foreign goods. The demand of the country may frequently, in this manner, be supplied more completely, and at a smaller expense, than in any other. Whether, by the continual exportation of those metals, a trade of this kind is likely to impoverish the country from which it is carried on in any other way, I shall have occasion to examine at great length hereafter.

That part of the capital of any country which is employed in the carrying trade, is altogether withdrawn from supporting the productive labor of that particular country, to support that of some foreign countries. Though it may replace, by every operation, two distinct capitals, yet neither of them belongs to that particular country. The capital of the Dutch merchant, which carries the corn of Poland to Portugal, and brings back the fruits and wines of Portugal to Poland, replaces by every such operation two capitals, neither of which had been employed in supporting the productive labor of Holland; but one of them in supporting that of Poland, and the other that of Portugal. The profits only return regularly to Holland, and constitute the whole addition which this trade necessarily makes to the annual produce of the land and labor of that country. When, indeed, the carrying trade of any particular country is carried on with the ships and sailors of that country, that part of the capital employed in it which pays the freight is distributed among, and puts into motion, a certain number of productive laborers of that country. Almost all nations that have had any considerable share of the carrying trade have, in fact, carried it on in this manner. The trade itself has probably derived its name from it, the people of such countries being the carriers to other countries. It does not, however, seem essential to the nature of the trade that it should be so. A Dutch merchant may, for example, employ his capital in transacting the commerce of Poland and Portugal, by carrying part of the surplus produce of the one to the other, not in Dutch, but in British bottoms. It maybe presumed, that he actually does so upon some particular occasions. It is upon this account, however, that the carrying trade has been supposed peculiarly advantageous to such a country as Great Britain, of which the defense and security depend upon the number of its sailors and shipping. But the same capital may employ as many sailors and shipping, either in the foreign trade of consumption, or even in the home trade, when carried on by coasting vessels, as it could in the carrying trade. The number of sailors and shipping which any particular capital can employ, does not depend upon the nature of the trade, but partly upon the bulk of the goods, in proportion to their value, and partly upon the distance of the ports between which they are to be carried; chiefly upon the former of those two circumstances. The coal trade from Newcastle to London, for example, employs more shipping than all the carrying trade of England, though the ports are at no great distance. To force, therefore, by extraordinary encouragements, a larger share of the capital of any country into the carrying trade, than what would naturally go to it, will not always necessarily increase the shipping of that country.

The capital, therefore, employed in the home trade of any country, will generally give encouragement and support to a greater quantity of productive labor in that country, and increase the value of its annual produce, more than an equal capital employed in the foreign trade of consumption; and the capital employed in this latter trade has, in both these respects, a still greater advantage over an equal capital employed in the carrying trade. The riches, and so far as power depends upon riches, the power of every country must always be in proportion to the value of its annual produce, the fund from which all taxes must ultimately be paid. But the great object of the political economy of every country, is to increase the riches and power of that country. It ought, therefore, to give no preference nor superior encouragement to the foreign trade of consumption above the home trade, nor to the carrying trade above either of the other two. It ought neither to force nor to allure into either of those two channels a greater share of the capital of the country, than what would naturally flow into them of its own accord.

Each of those different branches of trade, however, is not only advantageous, but necessary and unavoidable, when the course of things, without any constraint or violence, naturally introduces it.

When the produce of any particular branch of industry exceeds what the demand of the country requires, the surplus must be sent abroad, and exchanged for something for which there is a demand at home. Without such exportation, a part of the productive labor of the country must cease, and the value of its annual produce diminish. The land and labor of Great Britain produce generally more corn, woolens, and hardware, than the demand of the home market requires. The surplus part of them, therefore, must be sent abroad, and exchanged for something for which there is a demand at home. It is only by means of such exportation, that this surplus can acquired value sufficient to compensate the labor and expense of producing it. The neighborhood of the sea-coast, and the banks of all navigable rivers, are advantageous situations for industry, only because they facilitate the exportation and exchange of such surplus produce for something else which is more in demand there.

When the foreign goods which are thus purchased with the surplus produce of domestic industry exceed the demand of the home market, the surplus part of them must be sent abroad again, and exchanged for something more in demand at home. About 96,000 hogsheads of tobacco are annually purchased in Virginia and Maryland with a part of the surplus produce of British industry. But the demand of Great Britain does not require, perhaps, more than 14,000. If the remaining 82,000, therefore, could not be sent abroad, and exchanged for something more in demand at home, the importation of them must cease immediately, and with it the productive labor of all those inhabitants of Great Britain who are at present employed in preparing the goods with which these 82,000 hogsheads are annually purchased. Those goods, which are part of the produce of the land and labor of Great Britain, having no market at home, and being deprived of that which they had abroad, must cease to be produced. The most round-about foreign trade of consumption, therefore, may, upon some occasions, be as necessary for supporting the productive labor of the country, and the value of its annual produce, as the most direct.

When the capital stock of any country is increased to such a degree that it cannot be all employed in supplying the consumption, and supporting the productive labor of that particular country, the surplus part of it naturally disgorges itself into the carrying trade, and is employed in performing the same offices to other countries. The carrying trade is the natural effect and symptom of great national wealth; but it does not seem to be the natural cause of it. Those statesmen who have been disposed to favor it with particular encouragement, seem to have mistaken the effect and symptom for the cause. Holland, in proportion to the extent of the land and the number of it's inhabitants, by far the richest country in Europe, has accordingly the greatest share of the carrying trade of Europe. England, perhaps the second richest country of Europe, is likewise supposed to have a considerable share in it; though what commonly passes for the carrying trade of England will frequently, perhaps, be found to be no more than a round-about foreign trade of consumption. Such are, in a great measure, the trades which carry the goods of the East and West Indies and of America to the different European markets. Those goods are generally purchased, either immediately with the produce of British industry, or with something else which had been purchased with that produce, and the final returns of those trades are generally used or consumed in Great Britain. The trade which is carried on in British bottoms between the different ports of the Mediterranean, and some trade of the same kind carried on by British merchants between the different ports of India, make, perhaps, the principal branches of what is properly the carrying trade of Great Britain.

The extent of the home trade, and of the capital which can be employed in it, is necessarily limited by the value of the surplus produce of all those distant places within the country which have occasion to exchange their respective productions with one another; that of the foreign trade of consumption, by the value of the surplus produce of the whole country, and of what can be purchased with it; that of the carrying trade, by the value of the surplus produce of all the different countries in the world. Its possible extent, therefore, is in a manner infinite in comparison of that of the other two, and is capable of absorbing the greatest capitals.

The consideration of his own private profit is the sole motive which determines the owner of any capital to employ it either in agriculture, in manufactures, or in some particular branch of the wholesale or retail trade. The different quantities of productive labor which it may put into motion, and the different values which it may add to the annual produce of the land and labor of the society, according as it is employed in one or other of those different ways, never enter into his thoughts. In countries, therefore, where agriculture is the most profitable of all employments, and farming and improving the most direct roads to a splendid fortune, the capitals of individuals will naturally be employed in the manner most advantageous to the whole society. The profits of agriculture, however, seem to have no superiority over those of other employments in any part of Europe. Projectors, indeed, in every corner of it, have, within these few years, amused the public with most magnificent accounts of the profits to be made by the cultivation and improvement of land. Without entering into any particular discussion of their calculations, a very simple observation may satisfy us that the result of them must be false. We see, every day, the most splendid fortunes, that have been acquired in the course of a single life, by trade and manufactures, frequently from a very small capital, sometimes from no capital. A single instance of such a fortune, acquired by agriculture in the same time, and from such a capital, has not, perhaps, occurred in Europe, during the course of the present century. In all the great countries of Europe, however, much good land still remains uncultivated; and the greater part of what is cultivated, is far from being improved to the degree of which it is capable. Agriculture, therefore, is almost everywhere capable of absorbing a much greater capital than has ever yet been employed in it. What circumstances in the policy of Europe have given the trades which are carried on in towns so great an advantage over that which is carried on in the country, that private persons frequently find it more for their advantage to employ their capitals in the most distant carrying trades of Asia and America than in the improvement and cultivation of the most fertile fields in their own neighborhood, I shall endeavor to explain at full length in the two following books.

Book III

Of the Different Progress of Opulence in Different Nations

CHAPTER I

Of the Natural Progress of Opulence

The great commerce of every civilized society is that carried on between the inhabitants of the town and those of the country. It consists in the exchange of rude for manufactured produce, either immediately, or by the intervention of money, or of some sort of paper which represents money. The country supplies the town with the means of subsistence and the materials of manufacture. The town repays this supply, by sending back a part of the manufactured produce to the inhabitants of the country. The town, in which there neither is nor can be any reproduction of substances, may very properly be said to gain its whole wealth and subsistence from the country. We must not, however, upon this account, imagine that the gain of the town is the loss of the country. The gains of both are mutual and reciprocal, and the division of labor is in this, as in all other cases, advantageous to all the different persons employed in the various occupations into which it is subdivided. The inhabitants of the country purchase of the town a greater quantity of manufactured goods with the produce of a much smaller quantity of their own labor, than they must have employed had they attempted to prepare them themselves. The town affords a market for the surplus produce of the country, or what is over and above the maintenance of the cultivators; and it is there that the inhabitants of the country exchange it for something else which is in demand among them. The greater the number and revenue of the inhabitants of the town, the more extensive is the market which it affords to those of the country; and the more extensive that market, it is always the more advantageous to a great number. The corn which grows within a mile of the town, sells there for the same price with that which comes from twenty miles distance. But the price of the latter must, generally, not only pay the expense of raising it and bringing it to market, but afford, too, the ordinary profits of agriculture to the farmer. The proprietors and cultivators of the country, therefore, which lies in the neighborhood of the town, over and above the ordinary profits of agriculture, gain, in the price of what they sell, the whole value of the carriage of the like produce that is brought from more distant parts; and they save, besides, the whole value of this carriage in the price of what they buy. Compare the cultivation of the lands in the neighborhood of any considerable town, with that of those which lie at some distance from it, and you will easily satisfy yourself how much the country is benefited by the commerce of the town. Among all the absurd speculations that have been propagated concerning the balance of trade, it has never been pretended that either the country loses by its commerce with the town, or the town by that with the country which maintains it.

As subsistence is, in the nature of things, prior to convenience and luxury, so the industry which procures the former, must necessarily be prior to that which ministers to the latter. The cultivation and improvement of the country, therefore, which affords subsistence, must, necessarily, be prior to the increase of the town, which furnishes only the means of convenience and luxury. It is the surplus produce of the country only, or what is over and above the maintenance of the cultivators, that constitutes the subsistence of the town, which can therefore increase only with the increase of the surplus produce. The town, indeed, may not always derive its whole subsistence from the country in its neighborhood, or even from the territory to which it belongs, but from very distant countries; and this, though it forms no exception from the general rule, has occasioned considerable variations in the progress of opulence in different ages and nations.

That order of things which necessity imposes, in general, though not in every particular country, is in every particular country promoted by the natural inclinations of man. If human institutions had never thwarted those natural inclinations, the towns could nowhere have increased beyond what the improvement and cultivation of the territory in which they were situated could support; till such time, at least, as the whole of that territory was completely cultivated and improved. Upon equal, or nearly equal profits, most men will choose to employ their capitals, rather in the improvement and cultivation of land, than either in manufactures or in foreign trade. The man who employs his capital in land, has it more under his view and command; and his fortune is much less liable to accidents than that of the trader, who is obliged frequently to commit it, not only to the winds and the waves, but to the more uncertain elements of human folly and injustice, by giving great credits, in distant countries, to men with whose character and situation he can seldom be thoroughly acquainted. The capital of the landlord, on the contrary, which is fixed in the improvement of his land, seems to be as well secured as the nature of human affairs can admit of. The beauty of the country, besides, the pleasure of a country life, the tranquility of mind which it promises, and, wherever the injustice of human laws does not disturb it, the independency which it really affords, have charms that, more or less, attract everybody; and as to cultivate the ground was the original destination of man, so, in every stage of his existence, he seems to retain a predilection for this primitive employment.

Without the assistance of some artificers, indeed, the cultivation of land cannot be carried on, but with great inconveniency and continual interruption. Smiths, carpenters, wheelwrights and ploughwrights, masons and bricklayers, tanners, shoemakers, and tailors, are people whose service the farmer has frequent occasion for. Such artificers, too, stand occasionally in need of the assistance of one another; and as their residence is not, like that of the farmer, necessarily tied down to a precise spot, they naturally settle in the neighborhood of one another, and thus form a small town or village. The butcher, the brewer, and the baker, soon join them, together with many other artificers and retailers, necessary or useful for supplying their occasional wants, and who contribute still further to augment the town. The inhabitants of the town, and those of the country, are mutually the servants of one another. The town is a continual fair or market, to which the inhabitants of the country resort, in order to exchange their rude for manufactured produce. It is this commerce which supplies the inhabitants of the town, both with the materials of their work, and the means of their subsistence. The quantity of the finished work which they sell to the inhabitants of the country, necessarily regulates the quantity of the materials and provisions which they buy. Neither their employment nor subsistence, therefore, can augment, but in proportion to the augmentation of the demand from the country for finished work; and this demand can augment only in proportion to the extension of improvement and cultivation. Had human institutions, therefore, never disturbed the natural course of things, the progressive wealth and increase of the towns would, in every political society, be consequential, and in proportion to the improvement and cultivation of the territory or country.

In our North American colonies, where uncultivated land is still to be had upon easy terms, no manufactures for distant sale have ever yet been established in any of their towns. When an artificer has acquired a little more stock than is necessary for carrying on his own business in supplying the neighboring country, he does not, in North America, attempt to establish with it a manufacture for more distant sale, but employs it in the purchase and improvement of uncultivated land. From artificer he becomes planter; and neither the large wages nor the easy subsistence which that country affords to artificers, can bribe him rather to work for other people than for himself. He feels that an artificer is the servant of his customers, from whom he derives his subsistence; but that a planter who cultivates his own land, and derives his necessary subsistence from the labor of his own family, is really a master, and independent of all the world.

In countries, on the contrary, where there is either no uncultivated land, or none that can be had upon easy terms, every artificer who has acquired more stock than he can employ in the occasional jobs of the neighborhood, endeavors to prepare work for more distant sale. The smith erects some sort of iron, the weaver some sort of linen or woolen manufactory. Those different manufactures come, in process of time, to be gradually subdivided, and thereby improved and refined in a great variety of ways, which may easily be conceived, and which it is therefore unnecessary to explain any farther.

In seeking for employment to a capital, manufactures are, upon equal or nearly equal profits, naturally preferred to foreign commerce, for the same reason that agriculture is naturally preferred to manufactures. As the capital of the landlord or farmer is more secure than that of the manufacturer, so the capital of the manufacturer, being at all times more within his view and command, is more secure than that of the foreign merchant. In every period, indeed, of every society, the surplus part both of the rude and manufactured produce, or that for which there is no demand at home, must be sent abroad, in order to be exchanged for something for which there is some demand at home. But whether the capital which carries this surplus produce abroad be a foreign or a domestic one, is of very little importance. If the society has not acquired sufficient capital, both to cultivate all its lands, and to manufacture in the completest manner the whole of its rude produce, there is even a considerable advantage that the rude produce should be exported by a foreign capital, in order that the whole stock of the society may be employed in more useful purposes. The wealth of ancient Egypt, that of China and Indostan, sufficiently demonstrate that a nation may attain a very high degree of opulence, though the greater part of its exportation trade be carried on by foreigners. The progress of our North American and West Indian colonies, would have been much less rapid, had no capital but what belonged to themselves been employed in exporting their surplus produce.

According to the natural course of things, therefore, the greater part of the capital of every growing society is, first, directed to agriculture, afterwards to manufactures, and, last of all, to foreign commerce. This order of things is so very natural, that in every society that had any territory, it has always, I believe, been in some degree observed. Some of their lands must have been cultivated before any considerable towns could be established, and some sort of coarse industry of the manufacturing kind must have been carried on in those towns, before they could well think of employing themselves in foreign commerce.

But though this natural order of things must have taken place in some degree in every such society, it has, in all the modern states of Europe, been in many respects entirely inverted. The foreign commerce of some of their cities has introduced all their finer manufactures, or such as were fit for distant sale; and manufactures and foreign commerce together have given birth to the principal improvements of agriculture. The manners and customs which the nature of their original government introduced, and which remained after that government was greatly altered, necessarily forced them into this unnatural and retrograde order.

CHAPTER II

Of the Discouragement of Agriculture in the Ancient State of Europe, after the Fall of the Roman Empire

When the German and Scythian nations overran the western provinces of the Roman empire, the confusions which followed so great a revolution lasted for several centuries. The rapine and violence which the barbarians exercised against the ancient inhabitants, interrupted the commerce between the towns and the country. The towns were deserted, and the country was left uncultivated; and the western provinces of Europe, which had enjoyed a considerable degree of opulence under the Roman empire, sunk into the lowest state of poverty and barbarism. During the continuance of those confusions, the chiefs and principal leaders of those nations acquired, or usurped to themselves, the greater part of the lands of those countries. A great part of them was uncultivated; but no part of them, whether cultivated or uncultivated, was left without a proprietor. All of them were engrossed, and the greater part by a few great proprietors.

This original engrossing of uncultivated lands, though a great, might have been but a transitory evil. They might soon have been divided again, and broke into small parcels, either by succession or by alienation. The law of primogeniture hindered them from being divided by succession; the introduction of entails prevented their being broke into small parcels by alienation.

When land, like moveables, is considered as the means only of subsistence and enjoyment, the natural law of succession divides it, like them, among all the children of the family; of all of whom the subsistence and enjoyment may be supposed equally dear to the father. This natural law of succession, accordingly, took place among the Romans who made no more distinction between elder and younger, between male and female, in the inheritance of lands, than we do in the distribution of moveables. But when land was considered as the means, not of subsistence merely, but of power and protection, it was thought better that it should descend undivided to one. In those disorderly times, every great landlord was a sort of petty prince. His tenants were his subjects. He was their judge, and in some respects their legislator in peace and their leader in war. He made war according to his own discretion, frequently against his neighbors, and sometimes against his sovereign. The security of a landed estate, therefore, the protection which its owner could afford to those who dwelt on it, depended upon its greatness. To divide it was to ruin it, and to expose every part of it to be oppressed and swallowed up by the incursions of its neighbors. The law of primogeniture, therefore, came to take place, not immediately indeed, but in process of time, in the succession of landed estates, for the same reason that it has generally taken place in that of monarchies, though not always at their first institution. That the power, and consequently the security of the monarchy, may not be weakened by division, it must descend entire to one of the children. To which of them so important a preference shall be given, must be determined by some general rule, founded not upon the doubtful distinctions of personal merit, but upon some plain and evident difference which can admit of no dispute. Among the children of the same family there can be no indisputable difference but that of sex, and that of age. The male sex is universally preferred to the female; and when all other things are equal, the elder everywhere takes place of the younger. Hence the origin of the right of primogeniture, and of what is called lineal succession.

Laws frequently continue in force long after the circumstances which first gave occasion to them, and which could alone render them reasonable, are no more. In the present state of Europe, the proprietor of a single acre of land is as perfectly secure in his possession as the proprietor of 100,000. The right of primogeniture, however, still continues to be respected; and as of all institutions it is the fittest to support the pride of family distinctions, it is still likely to endure for many centuries. In every other respect, nothing can be more contrary to the real interest of a numerous family, than a right which, in order to enrich one, beggars all the rest of the children.

Entails are the natural consequences of the law of primogeniture. They were introduced to preserve a certain lineal succession, of which the law of primogeniture first gave the idea, and to hinder any part of the original estate from being carried out of the proposed line, either by gift, or device, or alienation; either by the folly, or by the misfortune of any of its successive owners. They were altogether unknown to the Romans. Neither their substitutions, nor *fidei commisses*, bear any resemblance to entails, though some French lawyers have thought proper to dress the modern institution in the language and garb of those ancient ones.

When great landed estates were a sort of principalities, entails might not be unreasonable. Like what are called the fundamental laws of some monarchies, they might frequently hinder the security of thousands from being endangered by the caprice or extravagance of one man. But in the present state of Europe, when small as well as great estates derive their security from the laws of their country, nothing can be more completely absurd. They are founded upon the most absurd of all suppositions, the supposition that every successive generation of men have not an equal right to the earth, and to all that it possesses; but that the property of the present generation should be restrained and regulated according to the fancy of those who died, perhaps five hundred years ago. Entails, however, are still respected, through the greater part of Europe; in those countries, particularly, in which noble birth is a necessary qualification for the enjoyment either of civil or military honors. Entails are thought necessary for maintaining this exclusive privilege of the nobility to the great offices and honors of their country; and that order having usurped one unjust advantage over the rest of their fellow-citizens, lest their poverty should render it ridiculous, it is thought reasonable that they should have another. The common law of England, indeed, is said to abhor perpetuities, and they are accordingly more restricted there than in any other European monarchy; though even England is not altogether without them. In Scotland, more than one fifth, perhaps more than one third part of the whole lands in the country, are at present supposed to be under strict entail.

Great tracts of uncultivated land were in this manner not only engrossed by particular families, but the possibility of their being divided again was as much as possible precluded forever. It seldom happens, however, that a great proprietor is a great improver.

In the disorderly times which gave birth to those barbarous institutions, the great proprietor was sufficiently employed in defending his own territories, or in extending his jurisdiction and authority over those of his neighbors. He had no leisure to attend to the cultivation and improvement of land. When the establishment of law and order afforded him this leisure, he often wanted the inclination, and almost always the requisite abilities. If the expense of his house and person either equaled or exceeded his revenue, as it did very frequently, he had no stock to employ in this manner. If he was an economist, he generally found it more profitable to employ his annual savings in new purchases than in the improvement of his old estate. To improve land with profit, like all other commercial projects, requires an exact attention to small savings and small gains, of which a man born to a great fortune, even though naturally frugal, is very seldom capable. The situation of such a person naturally disposes him to attend rather to ornament, which pleases his fancy, than to profit, for which he has so little occasion. The elegance of his dress, of his equipage, of his house and household furniture, are objects which, from his infancy, he has been accustomed to have some anxiety about. The turn of mind which this habit naturally forms, follows him when he comes to think of the improvement of land. He embellishes, perhaps, four or five hundred acres in the neighborhood of his house, at ten times the expense which the land is worth after all his improvements; and finds, that if he was to improve his whole estate in the same manner, and he has little taste for any other, he would be a bankrupt before he had finished the tenth part of it. There still remain, in both parts of the united kingdom, some great estates which have continued, without interruption, in the hands of the same family since the times of feudal anarchy. Compare the present condition of those estates with the possessions of the small proprietors in their neighborhood, and you will require no other argument to convince you how unfavorable such extensive property is to improvement.

If little improvement was to be expected from such great proprietors, still less was to be hoped for from those who occupied the land under them. In the ancient state of Europe, the occupiers of land were all tenants at will. They were all, or almost all, slaves, but their slavery was of a milder kind than that known among the ancient Greeks and Romans, or even in our West Indian colonies. They were supposed to belong more directly to the land than to their master. They could, therefore, be sold with it, but not separately. They could marry, provided it was with the consent of their master; and he could not afterwards dissolve the marriage by selling the man and wife to different persons. If he maimed or murdered any of them, he was liable to some penalty, though generally but to a small one. They were not, however, capable of acquiring property. Whatever they acquired was acquired to their master, and he could take it from them at pleasure. Whatever cultivation and improvement could be carried on by means of such slaves, was properly carried on by their master. It was at his expense. The seed, the cattle, and the instruments of husbandry, were all his. It was for his benefit. Such slaves could acquire nothing but their daily maintenance. It was properly the proprietor himself, therefore, that in this case occupied his own lands, and cultivated them by his own bondmen. This species of slavery still subsists in Russia, Poland, Hungary, Bohemia, Moravia, and other parts of Germany. It is only in the western and southwestern provinces of Europe that it has gradually been abolished altogether.

But if great improvements are seldom to be expected from great proprietors, they are least of all to be expected when they employ slaves for their workmen. The experience of all ages and nations, I believe, demonstrates that the work done by slaves, though it appears to cost only their maintenance, is in the end the dearest of any. A person who can acquire no property can have no other interest but to eat as much and to labor as little as possible. Whatever work he does beyond what is sufficient to purchase his own maintenance, can be squeezed out of him by violence only, and not by any interest of his own. In ancient Italy, how much the cultivation of corn degenerated, how unprofitable it became to the master, when it fell under the management of slaves, is remarked both by Pliny and Columella. In the time of Aristotle, it had not been much better in ancient Greece. Speaking of the ideal republic described in the laws of Plato, to maintain 5000 idle men (the number of warriors supposed necessary for its defense), together with their women and servants, would require, he says, a territory of boundless extent and fertility, like the plains of Babylon.

The pride of man makes him love to domineer, and nothing mortifies him so much as to be obliged to condescend to persuade his inferiors. Wherever the law allows it, and the nature of the work can afford it, therefore, he will generally prefer the service of slaves to that of freemen. The planting of sugar and tobacco can afford the expense of slave cultivation. The raising of corn, it seems, in the present times, cannot. In the English colonies, of which the principal produce is corn, the far greater part of the work is done by freemen. The late resolution of the Quakers in Pennsylvania, to set at liberty all their negro slaves, may satisfy us that their number cannot be very great. Had they made any considerable part of their property, such a resolution could never have been agreed to. In our sugar colonies, on the contrary, the whole work is done by slaves, and in our tobacco colonies a very great part of it. The profits of a sugar plantation in any of our West Indian colonies, are generally much greater than those of any other cultivation that is known either in Europe or America; and the profits of a tobacco plantation, though inferior to those of sugar, are superior to those of corn, as has already been observed. Both can afford the expense of slave cultivation but sugar can afford it still better than tobacco. The number of negroes, accordingly, is much greater, in proportion to that of whites, in our sugar than in our tobacco colonies.

To the slave cultivators of ancient times gradually succeeded a species of farmers, known at present in France by the name of *metayers*. They are called in Latin *Coloni Partiarii*. They have been so long in disuse in England, that at present I know no English name for them. The proprietor furnished them with the seed, cattle, and instruments of husbandry, the whole stock, in short, necessary for cultivating the farm. The produce was divided equally between the proprietor and the farmer, after setting aside what was judged necessary for keeping up the stock, which was restored to the proprietor, when the farmer either quitted or was turned out of the farm.

Land occupied by such tenants is properly cultivated at the expense of the proprietors, as much as that occupied by slaves. There is, however, one very essential difference between them. Such tenants, being freemen, are capable of acquiring property; and having a certain proportion of the produce of the land, they have a plain interest that the whole produce should be as great as possible, in order that their own proportion may be so. A slave, on the contrary, who can acquire nothing but his maintenance, consults his own ease, by making the land produce as little as possible over and above that maintenance. It is probable that it was partly upon account of this advantage, and partly upon account of the encroachments which the sovereigns, always jealous of the great lords, gradually encouraged their villains to make upon their authority, and which seem, at least, to have been such as rendered this species of servitude altogether inconvenient, that tenure in villanage gradually wore out through the greater part of Europe. The time and manner, however, in which so important a revolution was brought about, is one of the most obscure points in modern history. The church of Rome claims great merit in it; and it is certain, that so early as the twelfth century, Alexander III published a bull for the general emancipation of slaves. It seems, however, to have been rather a pious exhortation, than a law to which exact obedience was required from the faithful. Slavery continued to take place almost universally for several centuries afterwards, till it was gradually abolished by the joint operation of the two interests above mentioned; that of the proprietor on the one hand, and that of the sovereign on the other. A villain, enfranchised, and at the same time allowed to continue in possession of the land, having no stock of his own, could cultivate it only by means of what the landlord advanced to him, and must therefore have been what the French call a *metayer*.

It could never, however, be the interest even of this last species of cultivators, to lay out, in the further improvement of the land, any part of the little stock which they might save from their own share of the produce; because the landlord, who laid out nothing, was to get one half of whatever it produced. The tithe, which is but a tenth of the produce, is found to be a very great hindrance to improvement. A tax, therefore, which amounted to one half, must have been an effectual bar to it. It might be the interest of a metayer to make the land produce as much as could be brought out of it by means of the stock furnished by the proprietor; but it could never be his interest to mix any part of his own with it. In France, where five parts out of six of the whole kingdom are said to be still occupied by this species of cultivators, the proprietors complain, that their metayers take every opportunity of employing their master's cattle rather in carriage than in cultivation; because, in the one case, they get the whole profits to themselves, in the other they share them with their landlord. This species of tenants still subsists in some parts of Scotland. They are called steel-bow tenants. Those ancient English tenants, who are said by Chief-Baron Gilbert and Dr. Blackstone to have been rather bailiffs of the landlord than farmers, properly so called, were probably of the same kind.

To this species of tenantry succeeded, though by very slow degrees, farmers, properly so called, who cultivated the land with their own stock, paying a rent certain to the landlord. When such farmers have a lease for a term of years, they may sometimes find it for their interest to lay out part of their capital in the further improvement of the farm; because they may sometimes expect to recover it, with a large profit, before the expiration of the lease. The possession, even of such farmers, however, was long extremely precarious, and still is so in many parts of Europe. They could, before the expiration of their term, be legally ousted of their leases by a new purchaser; in England, even, by the fictitious action of a common recovery. If they were turned out illegally by the violence of their master, the action by which they obtained redress was extremely imperfect. It did not always reinstate them in the possession of the land, but gave them damages, which never amounted to a real loss. Even in England, the country, perhaps of Europe, where the yeomanry has always been most respected, it was not till about the 14th year of the reign of Henry VII that the action of ejectment was invented, by which the tenant recovers, not damages only, but possession, and in which his claim is not necessarily concluded by the uncertain decision of a single assize. This action has been found so effectual a remedy, that, in the modern practice, when the landlord has occasion to sue for the possession of the land, he seldom makes use of the actions which properly belong to him as a landlord, the writ of right or the writ of entry, but sues in the name of his tenant, by the writ of ejectment. In England, therefore the security of the tenant is equal to that of the proprietor. In England, besides, a lease for life of forty shillings a year value is a freehold, and entitles the lessee to a vote for a member of parliament; and as a great part of the yeomanry have freeholds of this kind, the whole order becomes respectable to their landlords, on account of the political consideration which this gives them. There is, I believe, nowhere in Europe, except in England, any instance of the tenant building upon the land of which he had no lease, and trusting that the honor of his landlord would take no advantage of so important an improvement. Those laws and customs, so favorable to the yeomanry, have perhaps contributed more to the present grandeur of England, than all their boasted regulations of commerce taken together.

The law which secures the longest leases against successors of every kind, is, so far as I know, peculiar to Great Britain. It was introduced into Scotland so early as 1449, by a law of James II. Its beneficial influence, however, has been much obstructed by entails; the heirs of entail being generally restrained from letting leases for any long term of years, frequently for more than one year. A late act of parliament has, in this respect, somewhat slackened their fetters, though they are still by much too strait. In Scotland, besides, as no leasehold gives a vote for a member of parliament, the yeomanry are upon this account less respectable to their landlords than in England.

In other parts of Europe, after it was found convenient to secure tenants both against heirs and purchasers, the term of their security was still limited to a very short period; in France, for example, to nine years from the commencement of the lease. It has in that country, indeed, been lately extended to twenty-seven, a period still too short to encourage the tenant to make the most important improvements. The proprietors of land were anciently the legislators of every part of Europe. The laws relating to land, therefore, were all calculated for what they supposed the interest of the proprietor. It was for his interest, they had imagined, that no lease granted by any of his predecessors should hinder him from enjoying, during a long term of years, the full value of his land. Avarice and injustice are always shortsighted, and they did not foresee how much this regulation must obstruct improvement, and thereby hurt, in the long run, the real interest of the landlord.

The farmers, too, besides paying the rent, were anciently, it was supposed, bound to perform a great number of services to the landlord, which were seldom either specified in the lease, or regulated by any precise rule, but by the use and wont of the manor or barony. These services, therefore, being almost entirely arbitrary, subjected the tenant to many vexations. In Scotland the abolition of all services not precisely stipulated in the lease, has, in the course of a few years, very much altered for the better the condition of the yeomanry of that country.

The public services to which the yeomanry were bound, were not less arbitrary than the private ones. To make and maintain the high roads, a servitude which still subsists, I believe, everywhere, though with different degrees of oppression in different countries, was not the only one. When the king's troops, when his household, or his officers of any kind, passed through any part of the country, the yeomanry were bound to provide them with horses, carriages, and provisions, at a price regulated by the purveyor. Great Britain is, I believe, the only monarchy in Europe where the oppression of purveyance has been entirely abolished. It still subsists in France and Germany.

The public taxes, to which they were subject, were as irregular and oppressive as the services. The ancient lords, though extremely unwilling to grant, themselves, any pecuniary aid to their sovereign, easily allowed him to *tallage*, as they called it, their tenants, and had not knowledge enough to foresee how much this must, in the end, affect their own revenue. The *taille*, as it still subsists in France. may serve as an example of those ancient tallages. It is a tax upon the supposed profits of the farmer, which they estimate by the stock that he has upon the farm. It is his interest, therefore, to appear to have as little as possible, and consequently to employ as little as possible in its cultivation, and none in its improvement. Should any stock happen to accumulate in the hands of a French farmer, the taille is almost equal to a prohibition of its ever being employed upon the land. This tax, besides, is supposed to dishonor whoever is subject to it, and to degrade him below, not only the rank of a gentleman, but that of a burgher; and whoever rents the lands of another becomes subject to it. No gentleman, nor even any burgher, who has stock, will submit to this degradation. This tax, therefore, not only hinders the stock which accumulates upon the land from being employed in its improvement, but drives away all other stock from it. The ancient tenths and fifteenths, so usual in England in former times, seem, so far as they affected the land, to have been taxes of the same nature with the taille.

Under all these discouragements, little improvement could be expected from the occupiers of land. That order of people, with all the liberty and security which law can give, must always improve under great disadvantage. The farmer, compared with the proprietor, is as a merchant who trades with burrowed money, compared with one who trades with his own. The stock of both may improve; but that of the one, with only equal good conduct, must always improve more slowly than that of the other, on account of the large share of the profits which is consumed by the interest of the loan. The lands cultivated by the farmer must, in the same manner, with only equal good conduct, be improved more slowly than those cultivated by the proprietor, on account of the large share of the produce which is consumed in the rent, and which, had the farmer been proprietor, he might have employed in the further improvement of the land. The station of a farmer, besides, is, from the nature of things, inferior to that of a proprietor. Through the greater part of Europe, the yeomanry are regarded as an inferior rank of people, even to the better sort of tradesmen and mechanics, and in all parts of Europe to the great merchants and master manufacturers. It can seldom happen, therefore, that a man of any considerable stock should quit the superior, in order to place himself in an inferior station. Even in the present state of Europe, therefore, little stock is likely to go from any other profession to the improvement of land in the way of farming. More does, perhaps, in Great Britain than in any other country, though even there the great stocks which are in some places employed in farming, have generally been acquired by fanning, the trade, perhaps, in which, of all others, stock is commonly acquired most slowly. After small proprietors, however, rich and great farmers are in every country the principal improvers. There are more such, perhaps, in England than in any other European monarchy. In the republican governments of Holland, and of Berne in Switzerland, the farmers are said to be not inferior to those of England.

The ancient policy of Europe was, over and above all this, unfavorable to the improvement and cultivation of land, whether carried on by the proprietor or by the farmer; first, by the general prohibition of the exportation of corn, without a special license, which seems to have been a very universal regulation; and, secondly, by the restraints which were laid upon the inland commerce, not only of corn, but of almost every other part of the produce of the farm, by the absurd laws against engrossers, regraters, and forestallers, and by the privileges of fairs and markets. It has already been observed in what manner the prohibition of the exportation of corn, together with some encouragement given to the importation of foreign corn, obstructed the cultivation of ancient Italy, naturally the most fertile country in Europe, and at that time the seat of the greatest empire in the world. To what degree such restraints upon the inland commerce of this commodity, joined to the general prohibition of exportation, must have discouraged the cultivation of countries less fertile, and less favorably circumstanced, it is not, perhaps, very easy to imagine.

CHAPTER III

Of the Rise and Progress of Cities and Towns, After the Fall of the Roman Empire

The inhabitants of cities and towns were, after the fall of the Roman empire, not more favored than those of the country. They consisted, indeed, of a very different order of people from the first inhabitants of the ancient republics of Greece and Italy. These last were composed chiefly of the proprietors of lands, among whom the public territory was originally divided, and who found it convenient to build their houses in the neighborhood of one another, and to surround them with a wall, for the sake of common defense. After the fall of the Roman empire, on the contrary, the proprietors of land seem generally to have lived in fortified castles on their own estates, and in the midst of their own tenants and dependants. The towns were chiefly inhabited by tradesmen and mechanics, who seem, in those days, to have been of servile, or very nearly of servile condition. The privileges which we find granted by ancient charters to the inhabitants of some of the principal towns in Europe, sufficiently show what they were before those grants. The people to whom it is granted as a privilege, that they might give away their own daughters in marriage without the consent of their lord, that upon their death their own children, and not their lord, should succeed to their goods, and that they might dispose of their own effects by will, must, before those grants, have been either altogether, or very nearly, in the same state of villanage with the occupiers of land in the country.

They seem, indeed, to have been a very poor, mean set of people, who seemed to travel about with their goods from place to place, and from fair to fair, like the hawkers and peddlers of the present times. In all the different countries of Europe then, in the same manner as in several of the Tartar governments of Asia at present, taxes used to be levied upon the persons and goods of travelers, when they passed through certain manors, when they went over certain bridges, when they carried about their goods from place to place in a fair, when they erected in it a booth or stall to sell them in. These different taxes were known in England by the names of passage, pontage, lastage, and stallage. Sometimes the king, sometimes a great lord, who had, it seems, upon some occasions, authority to do this, would grant to particular traders, to such particularly as lived in their own demesnes, a general exemption from such taxes. Such traders, though in other respects of servile, or very nearly of servile condition, were upon this account called free traders. They, in return, usually paid to their protector a sort of annual poll tax. In those days protection was seldom granted without a valuable consideration, and this tax might perhaps be considered as compensation for what their patrons might lose by their exemption from other taxes. At first, both those poll taxes and those exemptions seem to have been altogether personal, and to have affected only particular individuals, during either their lives, or the pleasure of their protectors. In the very imperfect accounts which have been published from Doomsday-book, of several of the towns of England, mention is frequently made, sometimes of the tax which particular burghers paid, each of them, either to the king, or to some other great lord, for this sort of protection, and sometimes of the general amount only of all those taxes. {see Brady's *Historical Treatise of Cities and Boroughs*, p. 3. etc.}

But how servile soever may have been originally the condition of the inhabitants of the towns, it appears evidently, that they arrived at liberty and independency much earlier than the occupiers of land in the country. That part of the king's revenue which arose from such poll taxes in any particular town, used commonly to be let in farm, during a term of years, for a rent certain, sometimes to the sheriff of the county, and sometimes to other persons. The burghers themselves frequently got credit enough to be admitted to farm the revenues of this sort which arose out of their own town, they becoming jointly and severally answerable for the whole rent. {See Madox, *Firma Burgi*, p. 18; also *History of the Exchequer*, chap. 10, sect. v, p. 223, first edition.} To let a farm in this manner, was quite agreeable to the usual economy of, I believe, the sovereigns of all the different countries of Europe, who used frequently to let whole manors to all the tenants of those manors, they becoming jointly and severally answerable for the whole rent; but in return being allowed to collect it in their own way, and to pay it into the king's exchequer by the hands of their own bailiff, and being thus altogether freed from the insolence of the king's officers; a circumstance in those days regarded as of the greatest importance.

At first, the farm of the town was probably let to the burghers, in the same manner as it had been to other farmers, for a term of years only. In process of time, however, it seems to have become the general practice to grant it to them in fee, that is forever, reserving a rent certain, never afterwards to be augmented. The payment having thus become perpetual, the exemptions, in return, for which it was made, naturally became perpetual too. Those exemptions, therefore, ceased to be personal, and could not afterwards be considered as belonging to individuals, as individuals, but as burghers of a particular burgh, which, upon this account, was called a free burgh, for the same reason that they had been called free burghers or free traders.

Along with this grant, the important privileges, above mentioned, that they might give away their own daughters in marriage, that their children should succeed to them, and that they might dispose of their own effects by will, were generally bestowed upon the burghers of the town to whom it was given. Whether such privileges had before been usually granted, along with the freedom of trade, to particular burghers, as individuals, I know not. I reckon it not improbable that they were, though I cannot produce any direct evidence of it. But however this may have been, the principal attributes of villanage and slavery being thus taken away from them, they now at least became really free, in our present sense of the word freedom.

Nor was this all. They were generally at the same time erected into a commonalty or corporation, with the privilege of having magistrates and a town council of their own, of making bye-laws for their own government, of building walls for their own defense, and of reducing all their inhabitants under a sort of military discipline, by obliging them to watch and ward; that is, as anciently understood, to guard and defend those walls against all attacks and surprises, by night as well as by day. In England they were generally exempted from suit to the hundred and county courts: and all such pleas as should arise among them, the pleas of the crown excepted, were left to the decision of their own magistrates. In other countries, much greater and more extensive jurisdictions were frequently granted to them. {See Madox, *Firma Burgi*. See also Pfeffel in the Remarkable events under Frederick II and his Successors of the House of Suabia.}

It might, probably, be necessary to grant to such towns as were admitted to farm their own revenues, some sort of compulsive jurisdiction to oblige their own citizens to make payment. In those disorderly times, it might have been extremely inconvenient to have left them to seek this sort of justice from any other tribunal. But it must seem extraordinary, that the sovereigns of all the different countries of Europe should have exchanged in this manner for a rent certain, never more to be augmented, that branch of their revenue, which was, perhaps, of all others, the most likely to be improved by the natural course of things, without either expense or attention of their own; and that they should, besides, have in this manner voluntarily erected a sort of independent republics in the heart of their own dominions.

In order to understand this, it must be remembered, that, in those days, the sovereign of perhaps no country in Europe was able to protect, through the whole extent of his dominions, the weaker part of his subjects from the oppression of the great lords. Those whom the law could not protect, and who were not strong enough to defend themselves, were obliged either to have recourse to the protection of some great lord, and in order to obtain it, to become either his slaves or vassals; or to enter into a league of mutual defense for the common protection of one another. The inhabitants of cities and burghs, considered as single individuals, had no power to defend themselves; but by entering into a league of mutual defense with their neighbors, they were capable of making no contemptible resistance. The lords despised the burghers, whom they considered not only as a different order, but as a parcel of emancipated slaves, almost of a different species from themselves. The wealth of the burghers never failed to provoke their envy and indignation, and they plundered them upon every occasion without mercy or remorse. The burghers naturally hated and feared the lords. The king hated and feared them too; but though, perhaps, he might despise, he had no reason either to hate or fear the burghers. Mutual interest, therefore, disposed them to support the king, and the king to support them against the lords. They were the enemies of his enemies, and it was his interest to render them as secure and independent of those enemies as he could. By granting them magistrates of their own, the privilege of making bye-laws for their own government, that of building walls for their own defense, and that of reducing all their inhabitants under a sort of military discipline, he gave them all the means of security and independency of the barons which it was in his power to bestow. Without the establishment of some regular government of this kind, without some authority to compel their inhabitants to act according to some certain plan or system, no voluntary league of mutual defense could either have afforded them any permanent security, or have enabled them to give the king any considerable support. By granting them the farm of their own town in fee, he took away from those whom he wished to have for his friends, and, if one may say so, for his allies, all ground of jealousy and suspicion, that he was ever afterwards to oppress them, either by raising the farm-rent of their town, or by granting it to some other farmer.

The princes who lived upon the worst terms with their barons, seem accordingly to have been the most liberal in grants of this kind to their burghs. King John of England, for example, appears to have been a most munificent benefactor to his towns. {See Madox.} Philip I of France lost all authority over his barons. Towards the end of his reign, his son Lewis, known afterwards by the name of Lewis the Fat, consulted, according to Father Daniel, with the bishops of the royal demesnes, concerning the most proper means of restraining the violence of the great lords. Their advice consisted of two different proposals. One was to erect a new order of jurisdiction, by establishing magistrates and a town council in every considerable town of his demesnes. The other was to form a new militia, by making the inhabitants of those towns, under the command of their own magistrates, march out upon proper occasions to the assistance of the king. It is from this period, according to the French antiquarians, that we are to date the institution of the magistrates and councils of cities in France. It was during the unprosperous reigns of the princes of the house of Suabia, that the greater part of the free towns of Germany received the first grants of their privileges, and that the famous Hanseatic league first became formidable. {See Pfeffel.}

The militia of the cities seems, in those times, not to have been inferior to that of the country; and as they could be more readily assembled upon any sudden occasion, they frequently had the advantage in their disputes with the neighboring lords. In countries such as Italy or Switzerland, in which, on account either of their distance from the principal seat of government, of the natural strength of the country itself, or of some other reason, the sovereign came to lose the whole of his authority; the cities generally became independent republics, and conquered all the nobility in their neighborhood; obliging them to pull down their castles in the country, and to live, like other peaceable inhabitants, in the city. This is the short history of the republic of Berne, as well as of several other cities in Switzerland. If you except Venice, for of that city the history is somewhat different, it is the history of all the considerable Italian republics, of which so great a number arose and perished between the end of the twelfth and the beginning of the sixteenth century.

In countries such as France and England, where the authority of the sovereign, though frequently very low, never was destroyed altogether, the cities had no opportunity of becoming entirely independent. They became, however, so considerable, that the sovereign could impose no tax upon them, besides the stated farm-rent of the town, without their own consent. They were, therefore, called upon to send deputies to the general assembly of the states of the kingdom, where they might join with the clergy and the barons in granting, upon urgent occasions, some extraordinary aid to the king. Being generally, too, more favorable to his power, their deputies seem sometimes to have been employed by him as a counterbalance in those assemblies to the authority of the great lords. Hence the origin of the representation of burghs in the states-general of all great monarchies in Europe.

Order and good government, and along with them the liberty and security of individuals, were in this manner established in cities, at a time when the occupiers of land in the country, were exposed to every sort of violence. But men in this defenseless state naturally content themselves with their necessary subsistence; because, to acquire more, might only tempt the injustice of their oppressors. On the contrary, when they are secure of enjoying the fruits of their industry, they naturally exert it to better their condition, and to acquire not only the necessaries, but the conveniences and elegancies of life.

That industry, therefore, which aims at something more than necessary subsistence, was established in cities long before it was commonly practiced by the occupiers of land in the country. If, in the hands of a poor cultivator, oppressed with the servitude of villanage, some little stock should accumulate, he would naturally conceal it with great care from his master, to whom it would otherwise have belonged, and take the first opportunity of running away to a town. The law was at that time so indulgent to the inhabitants of towns, and so desirous of diminishing the authority of the lords over those of the country, that if he could conceal himself there from the pursuit of his lord for a year, he was free forever. Whatever stock, therefore, accumulated in the hands of the industrious part of the inhabitants of the country, naturally took refuge in cities, as the only sanctuaries in which it could be secure to the person that acquired it.

The inhabitants of a city, it is true, must always ultimately derive their subsistence, and the whole materials and means of their industry, from the country. But those of a city, situated near either the seacoast or the banks of a navigable river, are not necessarily confined to derive them from the country in their neighborhood. They have a much wider range, and may draw them from the most remote corners of the world, either in exchange for the manufactured produce of their own industry, or by performing the office of carriers between distant countries, and exchanging the produce of one for that of another. A city might, in this manner, grow up to great wealth and splendor, while not only the country in its neighborhood, but all those to which it traded, were in poverty and wretchedness. Each of those countries, perhaps, taken singly, could afford it but a small part, either of its subsistence or of its employment; but all of them taken together, could afford it both a great subsistence and a great employment. There were, however, within the narrow circle of the commerce of those times, some countries that were opulent and industrious. Such was the Greek empire as long as it subsisted, and that of the Saracens during the reigns of the Abbasids. Such, too, was Egypt till it was conquered by the Turks, some part of the coast of Barbary, and all those provinces of Spain which were under the government of the Moors.

The cities of Italy seem to have been the first in Europe which were raised by commerce to any considerable degree of opulence. Italy lay in the centre of what was at that time the improved and civilized part of the world. The crusades, too, though, by the great waste of stock and destruction of inhabitants which they occasioned, they must necessarily have retarded the progress of the greater part of Europe, were extremely favorable to that of some Italian cities. The great armies which marched from all parts to the conquest of the Holy Land, gave extraordinary encouragement to the shipping of Venice, Genoa, and Pisa, sometimes in transporting them thither, and always in supplying them with provisions. They were the commissaries, if one may say so, of those armies; and the most destructive frenzy that ever befell the European nations, was a source of opulence to those republics.

The inhabitants of trading cities, by importing the improved manufactures and expensive luxuries of richer countries, afforded some food to the vanity of the great proprietors, who eagerly purchased them with great quantities of the rude produce of their own lands. The commerce of a great part of Europe in those times, accordingly, consisted chiefly in the exchange of their own rude, for the manufactured produce of more civilized nations.

Thus the wool of England used to be exchanged for the wines of France, and the fine cloths of Flanders, in the same manner as the corn in Poland is at this day, exchanged for the wines and brandies of France, and for the silks and velvets of France and Italy.

A taste for the finer and more improved manufactures was, in this manner, introduced by foreign commerce into countries where no such works were carried on. But when this taste became so general as to occasion a considerable demand, the merchants, in order to save the expense of carriage, naturally endeavored to establish some manufactures of the same kind in their own country. Hence the origin of the first manufactures for distant sale, that seem to have been established in the western provinces of Europe, after the fall of the Roman empire.

No large country, it must be observed, ever did or could subsist without some sort of manufactures being carried on in it; and when it is said of any such country that it has no manufactures, it must always be understood of the finer and more improved, or of such as are fit for distant sale. In every large country both the clothing and household furniture or the far greater part of the people, are the produce of their own industry. This is even more universally the case in those poor countries which are commonly said to have no manufactures, than in those rich ones that are said to abound in them. In the latter you will generally find, both in the clothes and household furniture of the lowest rank of people, a much greater proportion of foreign productions than in the former.

Those manufactures which are fit for distant sale, seem to have been introduced into different countries in two different ways.

Sometimes they have been introduced in the manner above mentioned, by the violent operation, if one may say so, of the stocks of particular merchants and undertakers, who established them in imitation of some foreign manufactures of the same kind. Such manufactures, therefore, are the offspring of foreign commerce; and such seem to have been the ancient manufactures of silks, velvets, and brocades, which flourished in Lucca during the thirteenth century. They were banished from thence by the tyranny of one of Machiavel's heroes, Castruccio Castracani. In 1310, nine hundred families were driven out of Lucca, of whom thirty-one retired to Venice, and offered to introduce there the silk manufacture. {See Sandi *Istoria civile de Vinezia*, part 2 vol. i, page 247 and 256.} Their offer was accepted, many privileges were conferred upon them, and they began the manufacture with three hundred workmen. Such, too, seem to have been the manufactures of fine cloths that anciently flourished in Flanders, and which were introduced into England in the beginning of the reign of Elizabeth, and such are the present silk manufactures of Lyons and Spitalfields. Manufactures introduced in this manner are generally employed upon foreign materials, being imitations of foreign manufactures. When the Venetian manufacture was first established, the materials were all brought from Sicily and the Levant. The more ancient manufacture of Lucca was likewise carried on with foreign materials. The cultivation of mulberry trees, and the breeding of silkworms, seem not to have been common in the northern parts of Italy before the sixteenth century. Those arts were not introduced into France till the reign of Charles IX. The manufactures of Flanders were carried on chiefly with Spanish and English wool. Spanish wool was the material, not of the first woolen manufacture of England, but of the first that was fit for distant sale. More than one half the materials of the Lyons manufacture is at this day foreign silk; when it was first established, the whole, or very nearly the whole, was so. No part of the materials of the Spitalfields manufacture is ever likely to be the produce of England. The seat of such manufactures, as they are generally introduced by the scheme and project of a few individuals, is sometimes established in a maritime city, and sometimes in an inland town, according as their interest, judgment, or caprice, happen to determine.

At other times, manufactures for distant sale grow up naturally, and as it were of their own accord, by the gradual refinement of those household and coarser manufactures which must at all times be carried on even in the poorest and rudest countries. Such manufactures are generally employed upon the materials which the country produces, and they seem frequently to have been first refined and improved in such inland countries as were not, indeed, at a very great, but at a considerable distance from the seacoast, and sometimes even from all water carriage. An inland country, naturally fertile and easily cultivated, produces a great surplus of provisions beyond what is necessary for maintaining the cultivators; and on account of the expense of land carriage, and inconveniency of river navigation, it may frequently be difficult to send this surplus abroad. Abundance, therefore, renders provisions cheap, and encourages a great number of workmen to settle in the neighborhood, who find that their industry can there procure them more of the necessaries and conveniences of life than in other places. They work up the materials of manufacture which the land produces, and exchange their finished work, or, what is the same thing, the price of it, for more materials and provisions. They give a new value to the surplus part of the rude produce, by saving the expense of carrying it to the waterside, or to some distant market; and they furnish the cultivators with something in exchange for it that is either useful or agreeable to them, upon easier terms than they could have obtained it before. The cultivators get a better price for their surplus produce, and can purchase cheaper other conveniences which they have occasion for. They are thus both encouraged and enabled to increase this surplus produce by a further improvement and better cultivation of the land; and as the fertility of the land had given birth to the manufacture, so the progress of the manufacture reacts upon the land, and increases still further its fertility. The manufacturers first supply the neighborhood, and afterwards, as their work improves and refines, more distant markets. For though neither the rude produce, nor even the coarse manufacture, could, without the greatest difficulty, support the expense of a considerable land-carriage, the refined and improved manufacture easily may. In a small bulk it frequently contains the price of a great quantity of rude produce. A piece of fine cloth, for example which weighs only eighty pounds, contains in it the price, not only of eighty pounds weight of wool, but sometimes of several thousand weight of corn, the maintenance of the different working people, and of their immediate employers. The corn which could with difficulty have been carried abroad in its own shape, is in this manner virtually exported in that of the complete manufacture, and may easily be sent to the remotest corners of the world. In this manner have grown up naturally, and, as it were, of their own accord, the manufactures of Leeds, Halifax, Sheffield, Birmingham, and Wolverhampton. Such manufactures are the offspring of agriculture. In the modern history of Europe, their extension and improvement have generally been posterior to those which were the offspring of foreign commerce. England was noted for the manufacture of fine cloths made of Spanish wool, more than a century before any of those which now flourish in the places above mentioned were fit for foreign sale. The extension and improvement of these last could not take place but in consequence of the extension and improvement of agriculture, the last and greatest effect of foreign commerce, and of the manufactures immediately introduced by it, and which I shall now proceed to explain.

CHAPTER IV

How the Commerce of Towns Contributed to the Improvement of the Country

The increase and riches of commercial and manufacturing towns contributed to the improvement and cultivation of the countries to which they belonged, in three different ways:

First, by affording a great and ready market for the rude produce of the country, they gave encouragement to its cultivation and further improvement. This benefit was not even confined to the countries in which they were situated, but extended more or less to all those with which they had any dealings. To all of them they afforded a market for some part either of their rude or manufactured produce, and, consequently, gave some encouragement to the industry and improvement of all. Their own country, however, on account of its neighborhood, necessarily derived the greatest benefit from this market. Its rude produce being charged with less carriage, the traders could pay the growers a better price for it, and yet afford it as cheap to the consumers as that of more distant countries.

Secondly, the wealth acquired by the inhabitants of cities was frequently employed in purchasing such lands as were to be sold, of which a great part would frequently be uncultivated. Merchants are commonly ambitious of becoming country gentlemen, and, when they do, they are generally the best of all improvers. A merchant is accustomed to employ his money chiefly in profitable projects; whereas a mere country gentleman is accustomed to employ it chiefly in expense. The one often sees his money go from him, and return to him again with a profit; the other, when once he parts with it, very seldom expects to see any more of it. Those different habits naturally affect their temper and disposition in every sort of business. The merchant is commonly a bold, a country gentleman a timid undertaker. The one is not afraid to lay out at once a large capital upon the improvement of his land, when he has a probable prospect of raising the value of it in proportion to the expense; the other, if he has any capital, which is not always the case, seldom ventures to employ it in this manner. If he improves at all, it is commonly not with a capital, but with what he can save out or his annual revenue. Whoever has had the fortune to live in a mercantile town, situated in an unimproved country, must have frequently observed how much more spirited the operations of merchants were in this way, than those of mere country gentlemen. The habits, besides, of order, economy, and attention, to which mercantile business naturally forms a merchant, render him much fitter to execute, with profit and success, any project of improvement.

Thirdly, and lastly, commerce and manufactures gradually introduced order and good government, and with them the liberty and security of individuals, among the inhabitants of the country, who had before lived almost in a continual state of war with their neighbors, and of servile dependency upon their superiors. This, though it has been the least observed, is by far the most important of all their effects. Mr. Hume is the only writer who, so far as I know, has hitherto taken notice of it.

In a country which has neither foreign commerce nor any of the finer manufactures, a great proprietor, having nothing for which he can exchange the greater part of the produce of his lands which is over and above the maintenance of the cultivators, consumes the whole in rustic hospitality at home. If this surplus produce is sufficient to maintain a hundred or a thousand men, he can make use of it in no other way than by maintaining a hundred or a thousand men. He is at all times, therefore, surrounded with a multitude of retainers and dependants, who, having no equivalent to give in return for their maintenance, but being fed entirely by his bounty, must obey him, for the same reason that soldiers must obey the prince who pays them. Before the extension of commerce and manufactures in Europe, the hospitality of the rich and the great, from the sovereign down to the smallest baron, exceeded every thing which, in the present times, we can easily form a notion of Westminster hall was the dining room of William Rufus, and might frequently, perhaps, not be too large for his company. It was reckoned a piece of magnificence in Thomas Becket, that he strewed the floor of his hall with clean hay or rushes in the season, in order that the knights and squires, who could not get seats, might not spoil their fine clothes when they sat down on the floor to eat their dinner. The great Earl of Warwick is said to have entertained every day, at his different manors, 30,000 people; and though the number here may have been exaggerated, it must, however, have been very great to admit of such exaggeration. A hospitality nearly of the same kind was exercised not many years ago in many different parts of the Highlands of Scotland. It seems to be common in all nations to whom commerce and manufactures are little known. I have seen, says Doctor Pocock, an Arabian chief dine in the streets of a town where he had come to sell his cattle, and invite all passengers, even common beggars, to sit down with him and partake of his banquet.

The occupiers of land were in every respect as dependent upon the great proprietor as his retainers. Even such of them as were not in a state of villanage, were tenants at will, who paid a rent in no respect equivalent to the subsistence which the land afforded them. A crown, half a crown, a sheep, a lamb, was some years ago, in the Highlands of Scotland, a common rent for lands which maintained a family. In some places it is so at this day; nor will money at present purchase a greater quantity of commodities there than in other places. In a country where the surplus produce of a large estate must be consumed upon the estate itself, it will frequently be more convenient for the proprietor, that part of it be consumed at a distance from his own house, provided they who consume it are as dependent upon him as either his retainers or his menial servants. He is thereby saved from the embarrassment of either too large a company, or too large a family. A tenant at will, who possesses land sufficient to maintain his family for little more than a quit-rent, is as dependent upon the proprietor as any servant or retainer whatever, and must obey him with as little reserve. Such a proprietor, as he feeds his servants and retainers at his own house, so he feeds his tenants at their houses. The subsistence of both is derived from his bounty, and its continuance depends upon his good pleasure.

Upon the authority which the great proprietors necessarily had, in such a state of things, over their tenants and retainers, was founded the power of the ancient barons. They necessarily became the judges in peace, and the leaders in war, of all who dwelt upon their estates. They could maintain order, and execute the law, within their respective demesnes, because each of them could there turn the whole force of all the inhabitants against the injustice of anyone. No other person had sufficient authority to do this. The king, in particular, had not. In those ancient times, he was little more than the greatest proprietor in his dominions, to whom, for the sake of common defense against their common enemies, the other great proprietors paid certain respects. To have enforced payment of a small debt within the lands of a great proprietor, where all the inhabitants were armed, and accustomed to stand by one another, would have cost the king, had he attempted it by his own authority, almost the same effort as to extinguish a civil war. He was, therefore, obliged to abandon the administration of justice, through the greater part of the country, to those who were capable of administering it; and, for the same reason, to leave the command of the country militia to those whom that militia would obey.

It is a mistake to imagine that those territorial jurisdictions took their origin from the feudal law. Not only the highest jurisdictions, both civil and criminal, but the power of levying troops, of coining money, and even that of making bye-laws for the government of their own people, were all rights possessed allodially by the great proprietors of land, several centuries before even the name of the feudal law was known in Europe. The authority and jurisdiction of the Saxon lords in England appear to have been as great before the Conquest as that of any of the Norman lords after it. But the feudal law is not supposed to have become the common law of England till after the Conquest. That the most extensive authority and jurisdictions were possessed by the great lords in France allodially, long before the feudal law was introduced into that country, is a matter of fact that admits of no doubt. That authority, and those jurisdictions, all necessarily flowed from the state of property and manners just now described. Without remounting to the remote antiquities of either the French or English monarchies, we may find, in much later times, many proofs that such effects must always flow from such causes. It is not thirty years ago since Mr. Cameron of Lochiel, a gentleman of Lochaber in Scotland, without any legal warrant whatever, not being what was then called a lord of regality, nor even a tenant in chief, but a vassal of the Duke of Argyll, and without being so much as a justice of peace, used, notwithstanding, to exercise the highest criminal jurisdictions over his own people. He is said to have done so with great equity, though without any of the formalities of justice; and it is not improbable that the state of that part of the country at that time made it necessary for him to assume this authority, in order to maintain the public peace. That gentleman, whose rent never exceeded £500 a year, carried, 800 of his own people into the rebellion with him in 1745.

The introduction of the feudal law, so far from extending, may be regarded as an attempt to moderate, the authority of the great allodial lords. It established a regular subordination, accompanied with a long train of services and duties, from the king down to the smallest proprietor. During the minority of the proprietor, the rent, together with the management of his lands, fell into the hands of his immediate superior; and, consequently, those of all great proprietors into the hands of the king, who was charged with the maintenance and education of the pupil, and who, from his authority as guardian, was supposed to have a right of disposing of him in marriage, provided it was in a manner not unsuitable to his rank. But though this institution necessarily tended to strengthen the authority of the king, and to weaken that of the great proprietors, it could not do either sufficiently for establishing order and good government among the inhabitants of the country; because it could not alter sufficiently that state of property and manners from which the disorders arose. The authority of government still continued to be, as before, too weak in the head, and too strong in the inferior members; and the excessive strength of the inferior members was the cause of the weakness of the head. After the institution of feudal subordination, the king was as incapable of restraining the violence of the great lords as before. They still continued to make war according to their own discretion, almost continually upon one another, and very frequently upon the king; and the open country still continued to be a scene of violence, rapine, and disorder.

But what all the violence of the feudal institutions could never have effected, the silent and insensible operation of foreign commerce and manufactures gradually brought about. These gradually furnished the great proprietors with something for which they could exchange the whole surplus produce of their lands, and which they could consume themselves, without sharing it either with tenants or retainers. All for ourselves, and nothing for other people, seems, in every age of the world, to have been the vile maxim of the masters of mankind. As soon, therefore, as they could find a method of consuming the whole value of their rents themselves, they had no disposition to share them with any other persons. For a pair of diamond buckles, perhaps, or for something as frivolous and useless, they exchanged the maintenance, or, what is the same thing, the price of the maintenance of 1000 men for a year, and with it the whole weight and authority which it could give them. The buckles, however, were to be all their own, and no other human creature was to have any share of them; whereas, in the more ancient method of expense, they must have shared with at least 1000 people. With the judges that were to determine the preference, this difference was perfectly decisive; and thus, for the gratification of the most childish, the meanest, and the most sordid of all vanities they gradually bartered their whole power and authority.

In a country where there is no foreign commerce, nor any of the finer manufactures, a man of £10,000 a year cannot well employ his revenue in any other way than in maintaining, perhaps, 1000 families, who are all of them necessarily at his command. In the present state of Europe, a man of £10,000 a year can spend his whole revenue, and he generally does so, without directly maintaining twenty people, or being able to command more than ten footmen, not worth the commanding. Indirectly, perhaps, he maintains as great, or even a greater number of people, than he could have done by the ancient method of expense. For though the quantity of precious productions for which he exchanges his whole revenue be very small, the number of workmen employed in collecting and preparing it must necessarily have been very great. Its great price generally arises from the wages of their labor, and the profits of all their immediate employers. By paying that price, he indirectly pays all those wages and profits, and thus indirectly contributes to the maintenance of all the workmen and their employers. He generally contributes, however, but a very small proportion to that of each; to a very few, perhaps, not a tenth, to many not a hundredth, and to some not a thousandth, or even a ten thousandth part of their whole annual maintenance. Though he contributes, therefore, to the maintenance of them all, they are all more or less independent of him, because generally they can all be maintained without him.

When the great proprietors of land spend their rents in maintaining their tenants and retainers, each of them maintains entirely all his own tenants and all his own retainers. But when they spend them in maintaining tradesmen and artificers, they may, all of them taken together, perhaps maintain as great, or, on account of the waste which attends rustic hospitality, a greater number of people than before. Each of them, however, taken singly, contributes often but a very small share to the maintenance of any individual of this greater number. Each tradesman or artificer derives his subsistence from the employment, not of one, but of a hundred or a thousand different customers. Though in some measure obliged to them all, therefore, he is not absolutely dependent upon any one of them.

The personal expense of the great proprietors having in this manner gradually increased, it was impossible that the number of their retainers should not as gradually diminish, till they were at last dismissed altogether. The same cause gradually led them to dismiss the unnecessary part of their tenants. Farms were enlarged, and the occupiers of land, notwithstanding the complaints of depopulation, reduced to the number necessary for cultivating it, according to the imperfect state of cultivation and improvement in those times. By the removal of the unnecessary mouths, and by exacting from the farmer the full value of the farm, a greater surplus, or, what is the same thing, the price of a greater surplus, was obtained for the proprietor, which the merchants and manufacturers soon furnished him with a method of spending upon his own person, in the same manner as he had done the rest. The cause continuing to operate, he was desirous to raise his rents above what his lands, in the actual state of their improvement, could afford. His tenants could agree to this upon one condition only, that they should be secured in their possession for such a term of years as might give them time to recover, with profit, whatever they should lay not in the further improvement of the land. The expensive vanity of the landlord made him willing to accept of this condition; and hence the origin of long leases.

Even a tenant at will, who pays the full value of the land, is not altogether dependent upon the landlord. The pecuniary advantages which they receive from one another are mutual and equal, and such a tenant will expose neither his life nor his fortune in the service of the proprietor. But if he has a lease for a long term of years, he is altogether independent; and his landlord must not expect from him even the most trifling service, beyond what is either expressly stipulated in the lease, or imposed upon him by the common and known law of the country.

The tenants having in this manner become independent, and the retainers being dismissed, the great proprietors were no longer capable of interrupting the regular execution of justice, or of disturbing the peace of the country. Having sold their birthright, not like Esau, for a mess of pottage in time of hunger and necessity, but, in the wantonness of plenty, for trinkets and baubles, fitter to be the playthings of children than the serious pursuits of men, they became as insignificant as any substantial burgher or tradesmen in a city. A regular government was established in the country as well as in the city, nobody having sufficient power to disturb its operations in the one, any more than in the other.

It does not, perhaps, relate to the present subject, but I cannot help remarking it, that very old families, such as have possessed some considerable estate from father to son for

many successive generations, are very rare in commercial countries. In countries which
have little commerce, on the contrary, such as Wales, or the Highlands of Scotland, they
are very common. The Arabian histories seem to be all full of genealogies; and there is a
history written by a Tartar Khan, which has been translated into several European languages, and which contains scarce any thing else; a proof that ancient families are very
common among those nations. In countries where a rich man can spend his revenue in
no other way than by maintaining as many people as it can maintain, he is apt to run
out, and his benevolence, it seems, is seldom so violent as to attempt to maintain more
than he can afford. But where he can spend the greatest revenue upon his own person,
he frequently has no bounds to his expense, because he frequently has no bounds to his
vanity, or to his affection for his own person. In commercial countries, therefore, riches,
in spite of the most violent regulations of law to prevent their dissipation, very seldom
remain long in the same family. Among simple nations, on the contrary, they frequently
do, without any regulations of law; for among nations of shepherds, such as the Tartars
and Arabs, the consumable nature of their property necessarily renders all such regulations impossible.

A revolution of the greatest importance to the public happiness, was in this manner
brought about by two different orders of people, who had not the least intention to serve
the public. To gratify the most childish vanity was the sole motive of the great proprietors. The merchants and artificers, much less ridiculous, acted merely from a view to
their own interest, and in pursuit of their own peddler principle of turning a penny wherever a penny was to be got. Neither of them had either knowledge or foresight of that
great revolution which the folly of the one, and the industry of the other, was gradually
bringing about.

It was thus, that, through the greater part of Europe, the commerce and manufactures
of cities, instead of being the effect, have been the cause and occasion of the improvement and cultivation of the country.

This order, however, being contrary to the natural course of things, is necessarily both
slow and uncertain. Compare the slow progress of those European countries of which
the wealth depends very much upon their commerce and manufactures, with the rapid
advances of our North American colonies, of which the wealth is founded altogether in
agriculture. Through the greater part of Europe, the number of inhabitants is not supposed to double in less than five hundred years. In several of our North American
colonies, it is found to double in twenty or five-and-twenty years. In Europe, the law
of primogeniture, and perpetuities of different kinds, prevent the division of great estates, and thereby hinder the multiplication of small proprietors. A small proprietor,
however, who knows every part of his little territory, views it with all the affection which
property, especially small property, naturally inspires, and who upon that account takes
pleasure, not only in cultivating, but in adorning it, is generally of all improvers the
most industrious, the most intelligent, and the most successful. The same regulations,
besides, keep so much land out of the market, that there are always more capitals to buy
than there is land to sell, so that what is sold always sells at a monopoly price. The rent
never pays the interest of the purchase-money, and is, besides, burdened with repairs and
other occasional charges, to which the interest of money is not liable. To purchase land,

is, everywhere in Europe, a most unprofitable employment of a small capital. For the sake of the superior security, indeed, a man of moderate circumstances, when he retires from business, will sometimes choose to lay out his little capital in land. A man of profession, too whose revenue is derived from another source often loves to secure his savings in the same way. But a young man, who, instead of applying to trade or to some profession, should employ a capital of two or three thousand pounds in the purchase and cultivation of a small piece of land, might indeed expect to live very happily and very independently, but must bid adieu forever to all hope of either great fortune or great illustration, which, by a different employment of his stock, he might have had the same chance of acquiring with other people. Such a person, too, though he cannot aspire at being a proprietor, will often disdain to be a farmer. The small quantity of land, therefore, which is brought to market, and the high price of what is brought thither, prevents a great number of capitals from being employed in its cultivation and improvement, which would otherwise have taken that direction. In North America, on the contrary, fifty or sixty pounds is often found a sufficient stock to begin a plantation with. The purchase and improvement of uncultivated land is there the most profitable employment of the smallest as well as of the greatest capitals, and the most direct road to all the fortune and illustration which can be required in that country. Such land, indeed, is in North America to be had almost for nothing, or at a price much below the value of the natural produce; a thing impossible in Europe, or indeed in any country where all lands have long been private property. If landed estates, however, were divided equally among all the children, upon the death of any proprietor who left a numerous family, the estate would generally be sold. So much land would come to market, that it could no longer sell at a monopoly price. The free rent of the land would go no nearer to pay the interest of the purchase-money, and a small capital might be employed in purchasing land as profitable as in any other way.

England, on account of the natural fertility of the soil, of the great extent of the sea-coast in proportion to that of the whole country, and of the many navigable rivers which run through it, and afford the convenience of water carriage to some of the most inland parts of it, is perhaps as well fitted by nature as any large country in Europe to be the seat of foreign commerce, of manufactures for distant sale, and of all the improvements which these can occasion. From the beginning of the reign of Elizabeth, too, the English legislature has been peculiarly attentive to the interest of commerce and manufactures, and in reality there is no country in Europe, Holland itself not excepted, of which the law is, upon the whole, more favorable to this sort of industry. Commerce and manufactures have accordingly been continually advancing during all this period. The cultivation and improvement of the country has, no doubt, been gradually advancing too; but it seems to have followed slowly, and at a distance, the more rapid progress of commerce and manufactures. The greater part of the country must probably have been cultivated before the reign of Elizabeth; and a very great part of it still remains uncultivated, and the cultivation of the far greater part much inferior to what it might be. The law of England, however, favors agriculture, not only indirectly, by the protection of commerce, but by several direct encouragements. Except in times of scarcity, the exportation of corn is not only free, but encouraged by a bounty. In times of moderate plenty, the importation of foreign corn is loaded with duties that amount to a prohibition. The importation of live cattle, except from Ireland, is prohibited at all times; and it is but of late that it was permitted from thence. Those who cultivate the land, therefore, have a monopoly against their countrymen for the two greatest and most important articles of land produce, bread and butcher's meat. These encouragements, although at bottom, perhaps, as I shall endeavor to show hereafter, altogether illusory, sufficiently demonstrate at least the good intention of the legislature to favor agriculture. But what is of much more importance than all of them, the yeomanry of England are rendered as secure, as independent, and as respectable, as law can make them. No country, therefore, which the right of primogeniture takes place, which pays tithes, and where perpetuities, though contrary to the spirit of the law, are admitted in some cases, can give more encouragement to agriculture than England. Such, however, notwithstanding, is the state of its cultivation. What would it have been, had the law given no direct encouragement to agriculture besides what arises indirectly from the progress of commerce, and had left the yeomanry in the same condition as in most other countries of Europe? It is now more than two hundred years since the beginning of the reign of Elizabeth, a period as long as the course of human prosperity usually endures.

France seems to have had a considerable share of foreign commerce, near a century before England was distinguished as a commercial country. The marine of France was considerable, according to the notions of the times, before the expedition of Charles VIII to Naples. The cultivation and improvement of France, however, is, upon the whole, inferior to that of England. The law of the country has never given the same direct encouragement to agriculture.

The foreign commerce of Spain and Portugal to the other parts of Europe, though chiefly carried on in foreign ships, is very considerable. That to their colonies is carried on in their own, and is much greater, on account of the great riches and extent of those colonies. But it has never introduced any considerable manufactures for distant sale into either of those countries, and the greater part of both still remains uncultivated. The foreign commerce of Portugal is of older standing than that of any great country in Europe, except Italy.

Italy is the only great country of Europe which seems to have been cultivated and improved in every part, by means of foreign commerce and manufactures for distant sale. Before the invasion of Charles VIII, Italy, according to Guicciardini, was cultivated not less in the most mountainous and barren parts of the country, than in the plainest and most fertile. The advantageous situation of the country, and the great number of independent status which at that time subsisted in it, probably contributed not a little to this general cultivation. It is not impossible, too, notwithstanding this general expression of one of the most judicious and reserved of modern historians, that Italy was not at that time better cultivated than England is at present.

The capital, however, that is acquired to any country by commerce and manufactures, is always a very precarious and uncertain possession, till some part of it has been secured and realized in the cultivation and improvement of its lands. A merchant, it has been said very properly, is not necessarily the citizen of any particular country. It is in a great measure indifferent to him from what place he carries on his trade; and a very trifling disgust will make him remove his capital, and, together with it, all the industry which it supports, from one country to another. No part of it can be said to belong to any particular country, till it has been spread, as it were, over the face of that country, either in buildings, or in the lasting improvement of lands. No vestige now remains of the great wealth said to have been possessed by the greater part of the Hanse Towns, except in the obscure histories of the thirteenth and fourteenth centuries. It is even uncertain where some of them were situated, or to what towns in Europe the Latin names given to some of them belong. But though the misfortunes of Italy, in the end of the fifteenth and beginning of the sixteenth centuries, greatly diminished the commerce and manufactures of the cities of Lombardy and Tuscany, those countries still continue to be among the most populous and best cultivated in Europe. The civil wars of Flanders, and the Spanish government which succeeded them, chased away the great commerce of Antwerp, Ghent, and Bruges. But Flanders still continues to be one of the richest, best cultivated, and most populous provinces of Europe. The ordinary revolutions of war and government easily dry up the sources of that wealth which arises from commerce only. That which arises from the more solid improvements of agriculture is much more durable, and cannot be destroyed but by those more violent convulsions occasioned by the depredations of hostile and barbarous nations continued for a century or two together; such as those that happened for some time before and after the fall of the Roman empire in the western provinces of Europe.

Book IV

Of Systems of Political Economy

Political economy, considered as a branch of the science of a statesman or legislator, proposes two distinct objects; first, to provide a plentiful revenue or subsistence for the people, or, more properly, to enable them to provide such a revenue or subsistence for themselves; and, secondly, to supply the state or commonwealth with a revenue sufficient for the public services. It proposes to enrich both the people and the sovereign.

The different progress of opulence in different ages and nations, has given occasion to two different systems of political economy, with regard to enriching the people. The one may be called the system of commerce, the other that of agriculture. I shall endeavor to explain both as fully and distinctly as I can, and shall begin with the system of commerce. It is the modern system, and is best understood in our own country and in our own times.

CHAPTER I

Of the Principle of the Commercial or Mercantile System

That wealth consists in money, or in gold and silver, is a popular notion which naturally arises from the double function of money, as the instrument of commerce, and as the measure of value. In consequence of its being the instrument of commerce, when we have money we can more readily obtain whatever else we have occasion for, than by means of any other commodity. The great affair, we always find, is to get money. When that is obtained, there is no difficulty in making any subsequent purchase. In consequence of its being the measure of value, we estimate that of all other commodities by the quantity of money which they will exchange for. We say of a rich man, that he is worth a great deal, and of a poor man, that he is worth very little money. A frugal man, or a man eager to be rich, is said to love money; and a careless, a generous, or a profuse man, is said to be indifferent about it. To grow rich is to get money; and wealth and money, in short, are, in common language, considered as in every respect synonymous.

A rich country, in the same manner as a rich man, is supposed to be a country abounding in money; and to heap up gold and silver in any country is supposed to be the readiest way to enrich it. For some time after the discovery of America, the first inquiry of the Spaniards, when they arrived upon any unknown coast, used to be, if there was any gold or silver to be found in the neighborhood? By the information which they received, they judged whether it was worthwhile to make a settlement there, or if the country was worth the conquering. Plano Carpino, a monk sent ambassador from the king of France to one of the sons of the famous Gengis Khan, says, that the Tartars used frequently to ask him, if there was plenty of sheep and oxen in the kingdom of France? Their inquiry had the same object with that of the Spaniards. They wanted to know if the country was rich enough to be worth the conquering. Among the Tartars, as among all other nations of shepherds, who are generally ignorant of the use of money, cattle are the instruments of commerce and the measures of value. Wealth, therefore, according to them, consisted in cattle, as, according to the Spaniards, it consisted in gold and silver. Of the two, the Tartar notion, perhaps, was the nearest to the truth.

Mr. Locke remarks a distinction between money and other moveable goods. All other moveable goods, he says, are of so consumable a nature, that the wealth which consists in them cannot be much depended on; and a nation which abounds in them one year may, without any exportation, but merely by their own waste and extravagance, be in great want of them the next. Money, on the contrary, is a steady friend, which, though it may travel about from hand to hand, yet if it can be kept from going out of the country, is not very liable to be wasted and consumed. Gold and silver, therefore, are, according to him, the must solid and substantial part of the moveable wealth of a nation; and to multiply those metals ought, he thinks, upon that account, to be the great object of its political economy.

Others admit, that if a nation could be separated from all the world, it would be of no consequence how much or how little money circulated in it. The consumable goods, which were circulated by means of this money, would only be exchanged for a greater or a smaller number of pieces; but the real wealth or poverty of the country, they allow, would depend altogether upon the abundance or scarcity of those consumable goods. But it is otherwise, they think, with countries which have connections with foreign nations, and which are obliged to carry on foreign wars, and to maintain fleets and armies in distant countries. This, they say, cannot be done, but by sending abroad money to pay them with; and a nation cannot send much money abroad, unless it has a good deal at home. Every such nation, therefore, must endeavor, in time of peace, to accumulate gold and silver, that when occasion requires, it may have wherewithal to carry on foreign wars.

In consequence of those popular notions, all the different nations of Europe have studied, though to little purpose, every possible means of accumulating gold and silver in their respective countries. Spain and Portugal, the proprietors of the principal mines which supply Europe with those metals, have either prohibited their exportation under the severest penalties, or subjected it to a considerable duty. The like prohibition seems anciently to have made a part of the policy of most other European nations. It is even to be found, where we should least of all expect to find it, in some old Scotch acts of Parliament, which forbid, under heavy penalties, the carrying gold or silver forth of the kingdom. The like policy anciently took place both in France and England.

When those countries became commercial, the merchants found this prohibition, upon many occasions, extremely inconvenient. They could frequently buy more advantageously with gold and silver, than with any other commodity, the foreign goods which they wanted, either to import into their own, or to carry to some other foreign country. They remonstrated, therefore, against this prohibition as hurtful to trade.

They represented, first, that the exportation of gold and silver, in order to purchase foreign goods, did not always diminish the quantity of those metals in the kingdom; that, on the contrary, it might frequently increase the quantity; because, if the consumption of foreign goods was not thereby increased in the country, those goods might be re-exported to foreign countries, and being there sold for a large profit, might bring back much more treasure than was originally sent out to purchase them. Mr. Mun compares this operation of foreign trade to the seedtime and harvest of agriculture. "If we only behold," says he, "the actions of the husbandman in the seed time, when he casteth away much good corn into the ground, we shall account him rather a madman than a husbandman. But when we consider his labors in the harvest, which is the end of his endeavors, we shall find the worth and plentiful increase of his actions."

They represented, secondly, that this prohibition could not hinder the exportation of gold and silver, which, on account of the smallness of their bulk in proportion to their value, could easily be smuggled abroad. That this exportation could only be prevented by a proper attention to what they called the balance of trade. That when the country exported to a greater value than it imported, a balance became due to it from foreign nations, which was necessarily paid to it in gold and silver, and thereby increased the quantity of those metals in the kingdom. But that when it imported to a greater value than it exported, a contrary balance became due to foreign nations, which was necessarily paid to them in the same manner, and thereby diminished that quantity: that in this case, to prohibit the exportation of those metals, could not prevent it, but only, by making it more dangerous, render it more expensive: that the exchange was thereby turned more against the country which owed the balance, than it otherwise might have been; the merchant who purchased a bill upon the foreign country being obliged to pay the banker who sold it, not only for the natural risk, trouble, and expense of sending the money thither, but for the extraordinary risk arising from the prohibition; but that the more the exchange was against any country, the more the balance of trade became necessarily against it; the money of that country becoming necessarily of so much less value, in comparison with that of the country to which the balance was due. That if the exchange between England and Holland, for example, was five percent against England, it would require 105 ounces of silver in England to purchase a bill for 100 ounces of silver in Holland: that 105 ounces of silver in England, therefore, would be worth only 100 ounces of silver in Holland, and would purchase only a proportionable quantity of Dutch goods; but that 100 ounces of silver in Holland, on the contrary, would be worth 105 ounces in England, and would purchase a proportional quantity of English goods; that the English goods which were sold to Holland would be sold so much cheaper, and the Dutch goods which were sold to England so much dearer, by the difference of the exchange: that the one would draw so much less Dutch money to England, and the other so much more English money to Holland, as this difference amounted to: and that the balance of trade, therefore, would necessarily be so much more against England, and would require a greater balance of gold and silver to be exported to Holland.

Those arguments were partly solid and partly sophistical. They were solid, so far as they asserted that the exportation of gold and silver in trade might frequently be advantageous to the country. They were solid, too, in asserting that no prohibition could prevent their exportation, when private people found any advantage in exporting them. But they were sophistical, in supposing, that either to preserve or to augment the quantity of those metals required more the attention of government, than to preserve or to augment the quantity of any other useful commodities, which the freedom of trade, without any such attention, never fails to supply in the proper quantity. They were sophistical, too, perhaps, in asserting that the high price of exchange necessarily increased what they called the unfavorable balance of trade, or occasioned the exportation of a greater quantity of gold and silver. That high price, indeed, was extremely disadvantageous to the merchants who had any money to pay in foreign countries. They paid so much dearer for the bills which their bankers granted them upon those countries. But though the risk arising from the prohibition might occasion some extraordinary expense to the bankers, it would not necessarily carry any more money out of the country. This expense would generally be all laid out in the country, in smuggling the money out of it, and could seldom occasion the exportation of a single sixpence beyond the precise sum drawn for. The high price of exchange, too, would naturally dispose the merchants to endeavor to make their exports nearly balance their imports, in order that they might have this high exchange to pay upon as small a sum as possible. The high price of exchange, besides, must necessarily have operated as a tax, in raising the price of foreign goods, and thereby diminishing their consumption. It would tend, therefore, not to increase, but to diminish, what they called the unfavorable balance of trade, and consequently the exportation of gold and silver.

Such as they were, however, those arguments convinced the people to whom they were addressed. They were addressed by merchants to parliaments and to the councils of princes, to nobles, and to country gentlemen; by those who were supposed to understand trade, to those who were conscious to them selves that they knew nothing about the matter. That foreign trade enriched the country, experience demonstrated to the nobles and country gentlemen, as well as to the merchants; but how, or in what manner, none of them well knew. The merchants knew perfectly in what manner it enriched themselves, it was their business to know it. But to know in what manner it enriched the country, was no part of their business. The subject never came into their consideration, but when they had occasion to apply to their country for some change in the laws relating to foreign trade. It then became necessary to say something about the beneficial effects of foreign trade, and the manner in which those effects were obstructed by the laws as they then stood. To the judges who were to decide the business, it appeared a most satisfactory account of the matter, when they were told that foreign trade brought money into the country, but that the laws in question hindered it from bringing so much as it otherwise would do. Those arguments, therefore, produced the wished-for effect. The prohibition of exporting gold and silver was, in France and England, confined to the coin of those respective countries. The exportation of foreign coin and of bullion was made free. In Holland, and in some other places, this liberty was extended even to the coin of the country. The attention of government was turned away from guarding against the exportation of gold and silver, to watch over the balance of trade, as the only cause which could occasion any augmentation or diminution of those metals. From one fruitless care, it was turned away to another care much more intricate, much more embarrassing, and just equally fruitless. The title of Mun's book, *England's Treasure in Foreign Trade*, became a fundamental maxim in the political economy, not of England only, but of all other commercial countries. The inland or home trade, the most important of all, the trade in which an equal capital affords the greatest revenue, and creates the greatest employment to the people of the country, was considered as subsidiary only to foreign trade. It neither brought money into the country, it was said, nor carried any out of it. The country, therefore, could never become either richer or poorer by means of it, except so far as its prosperity or decay might indirectly influence the state of foreign trade.

A country that has no mines of its own, must undoubtedly draw its gold and silver from foreign countries, in the same manner as one that has no vineyards of its own must draw its wines. It does not seem necessary, however, that the attention of government should be more turned towards the one than towards the other object. A country that has wherewithal to buy wine, will always get the wine which it has occasion for; and a country that has wherewithal to buy gold and silver, will never be in want of those metals. They are to be bought for a certain price, like all other commodities; and as they are the price of all other commodities, so all other commodities are the price of those metals. We trust, with perfect security, that the freedom of trade, without any attention of government, will always supply us with the wine which we have occasion for; and we may trust, with equal security, that it will always supply us with all the gold and silver which we can afford to purchase or to employ, either in circulating our commodities or in other uses.

The quantity of every commodity which human industry can either purchase or produce, naturally regulates itself in every country according to the effectual demand, or according to the demand of those who are willing to pay the whole rent, labor, and profits, which must be paid in order to prepare and bring it to market. But no commodities regulate themselves more easily or more exactly, according to this effectual demand, than gold and silver; because, on account of the small bulk and great value of those metals, no commodities can be more easily transported from one place to another; from the places where they are cheap, to those where they are dear; from the places where they exceed, to those where they fall short of this effectual demand. If there were in England, for example, an effectual demand for an additional quantity of gold, a packet-boat could bring from Lisbon, or from wherever else it was to be had, fifty tons of gold, which could be coined into more than five millions of guineas. But if there were an effectual demand for grain to the same value, to import it would require, at five guineas a ton, a million of tons of shipping, or a thousand ships of a thousand tons each. The navy of England would not be sufficient.

When the quantity of gold and silver imported into any country exceeds the effectual demand, no vigilance of government can prevent their exportation. All the sanguinary laws of Spain and Portugal are not able to keep their gold and silver at home. The continual importations from Peru and Brazil exceed the effectual demand of those countries, and sink the price of those metals there below that in the neighboring countries. If, on the contrary, in any particular country, their quantity fell short of the effectual demand, so as to raise their price above that of the neighboring countries, the government would have no occasion to take any pains to import them. If it were even to take pains to prevent their importation, it would not be able to effectuate it. Those metals, when the Spartans had got wherewithal to purchase them, broke through all the barriers which the laws of Lycurgus opposed to their entrance into Lacedaemon. All the sanguinary laws of the customs are not able to prevent the importation of the teas of the Dutch and

Gottenburg East India companies; because somewhat cheaper than those of the British company. A pound of tea, however, is about a hundred times the bulk of one of the highest prices, sixteen shillings, that is commonly paid for it in silver, and more than two thousand times the bulk of the same price in gold, and, consequently, just so many times more difficult to smuggle.

It is partly owing to the easy transportation of gold and silver, from the places where they abound to those where they are wanted, that the price of those metals does not fluctuate continually, like that of the greater part of other commodities, which are hindered by their bulk from shifting their situation, when the market happens to be either over or under-stocked with them. The price of those metals, indeed, is not altogether exempted from variation; but the changes to which it is liable are generally slow, gradual, and uniform. In Europe, for example, it is supposed, without much foundation, perhaps, that during the course of the present and preceding century, they have been constantly, but gradually, sinking in their value, on account of the continual importations from the Spanish West Indies. But to make any sudden change in the price of gold and silver, so as to raise or lower at once, sensibly and remarkably, the money price of all other commodities, requires such a revolution in commerce as that occasioned by the discovery of America.

If, not withstanding all this, gold and silver should at any time fall short in a country which has wherewithal to purchase them, there are more expedients for supplying their place, than that of almost any other commodity. If the materials of manufacture are wanted, industry must stop. If provisions are wanted, the people must starve. But if money is wanted, barter will supply its place, though with a good deal of inconveniency. Buying and selling upon credit, and the different dealers compensating their credits with one another, once a month, or once a year, will supply it with less inconveniency. A well-regulated paper money will supply it not only without any inconveniency, but, in some cases, with some advantages. Upon every account, therefore, the attention of government never was so unnecessarily employed, as when directed to watch over the preservation or increase of the quantity of money in any country.

No complaint, however, is more common than that of a scarcity of money. Money, like wine, must always be scarce with those who have neither wherewithal to buy it, nor credit to borrow it. Those who have either, will seldom be in want either of the money, or of the wine which they have occasion for. This complaint, however, of the scarcity of money, is not always confined to improvident spendthrifts. It is sometimes general through a whole mercantile town and the country in its neighborhood. Overtrading is the common cause of it. Sober men, whose projects have been disproportioned to their capitals, are as likely to have neither wherewithal to buy money, nor credit to borrow it, as prodigals, whose expense has been disproportioned to their revenue. Before their projects can be brought to bear, their stock is gone, and their credit with it. They run about everywhere to borrow money, and everybody tells them that they have none to lend. Even such general complaints of the scarcity of money do not always prove that the usual number of gold and silver pieces are not circulating in the country, but that many people want those pieces who have nothing to give for them. When the profits of trade happen to be greater than ordinary over-trading becomes a general error, both among great and small dealers. They do not always send more money abroad than usual, but they buy upon credit, both at home and abroad, an unusual quantity of goods, which they send to some distant market, in hopes that the returns will come in before the demand for payment. The demand comes before the returns, and they have nothing at hand with which they can either purchase money or give solid security for borrowing. It is not any scarcity of gold and silver, but the difficulty which such people find in borrowing, and which their creditor find in getting payment, that occasions the general complaint of the scarcity of money.

It would be too ridiculous to go about seriously to prove, that wealth does not consist in money, or in gold and silver; but in what money purchases, and is valuable only for purchasing. Money, no doubt, makes always a part of the national capital; but it has already been shown that it generally makes but a small part, and always the most unprofitable part of it.

It is not because wealth consists more essentially in money than in goods, that the merchant finds it generally more easy to buy goods with money, than to buy money with goods; but because money is the known and established instrument of commerce, for which every thing is readily given in exchange, but which is not always with equal readiness to be got in exchange for every thing. The greater part of goods, besides, are more perishable than money, and he may frequently sustain a much greater loss by keeping them. When his goods are upon hand, too, he is more liable to such demands for money as he may not be able to answer, than when he has got their price in his coffers. Over and above all this, his profit arises more directly from selling than from buying; and he is, upon all these accounts, generally much more anxious to exchange his goods for money than his money for goods. But though a particular merchant, with abundance of goods in his warehouse, may sometimes be ruined by not being able to sell them in time, a nation or country is not liable to the same accident, The whole capital of a merchant frequently consists in perishable goods destined for purchasing money. But it is but a very small part of the annual produce of the land and labor of a country, which can ever be destined for purchasing gold and silver from their neighbors. The far greater part is circulated and consumed among themselves; and even of the surplus which is sent abroad, the greater part is generally destined for the purchase of other foreign goods. Though gold and silver, therefore, could not be had in exchange for the goods destined to purchase them, the nation would not be ruined. It might, indeed, suffer some loss and inconvenience, and be forced upon some of those expedients which are necessary for supplying the place of money. The annual produce of its land and labor, however, would be the same, or very nearly the same as usual; because the same, or very nearly the same consumable capital would be employed in maintaining it. And though goods do not always draw money so readily as money draws goods, in the long run they draw it more necessarily than even it draws them. Goods can serve many other purposes besides purchasing money, but money can serve no other purpose besides purchasing goods. Money, therefore, necessarily runs after goods, but goods do not always or necessarily run after money. The man who buys, does not always mean to sell again, but frequently to use or to consume; whereas he who sells always means to buy again. The one may frequently have done the whole, but the other can never have done more than the one half of his business. It is not for its own sake that men desire money, but for the sake of what they can purchase with it.

Consumable commodities, it is said, are soon destroyed; whereas gold and silver are of a more durable nature, and were it not for this continual exportation, might be accumulated for ages together, to the incredible augmentation of the real wealth of the country. Nothing, therefore, it is pretended, can be more disadvantageous to any country, than the trade which consists in the exchange of such lasting for such perishable commodities. We do not, however, reckon that trade disadvantageous, which consists in the exchange of the hardware of England for the wines of France, and yet hardware is a very durable commodity, and were it not for this continual exportation, might too be accumulated for ages together, to the incredible augmentation of the pots and pans of the country. But it readily occurs, that the number of such utensils is in every country necessarily limited by the use which there is for them; that it would be absurd to have more pots and pans than were necessary for cooking the victuals usually consumed there; and that, if the quantity of victuals were to increase, the number of pots and pans would readily increase along with it; a part of the increased quantity of victuals being employed in purchasing them, or in maintaining an additional number of workmen whose business it was to make them. It should as readily occur, that the quantity of gold and silver is, in every country, limited by the use which there is for those metals; that their use consists in circulating commodities, as coin, and in affording a species of household furniture, as plate; that the quantity of coin in every country is regulated by the value of the commodities which are to be circulated by it; increase that value, and immediately a part of it will be sent abroad to purchase, wherever it is to be had, the additional quantity of coin requisite for circulating them: that the quantity of plate is regulated by the number and wealth of those private families who choose to indulge themselves in that sort of magnificence; increase the number and wealth of such families, and a part of this increased wealth will most probably be employed in purchasing, wherever it is to be found, an additional quantity of plate; that to attempt to increase the wealth of any country, either by introducing or by detaining in it an unnecessary quantity of gold and silver, is as absurd as it would be to attempt to increase the good cheer of private families, by obliging them to keep an unnecessary number of kitchen utensils. As the expense of purchasing those unnecessary utensils would diminish, instead of increasing, either the quantity or goodness of the family provisions; so the expense of purchasing an unnecessary quantity of gold and silver must, in every country, as necessarily diminish the wealth which feeds, clothes, and lodges, which maintains and employs the people. Gold and silver, whether in the shape of coin or of plate, are utensils, it must be remembered, as much as the furniture of the kitchen. Increase the use of them, increase the consumable commodities which are to be circulated, managed, and prepared by means of them, and you will infallibly increase the quantity; but if you attempt by extraordinary means to increase the quantity, you will as infallibly diminish the use, and even the quantity too, which in those metals can never be greater than what the use requires. Were they ever to be accumulated beyond this quantity, their transportation is so easy, and the loss which attends their lying idle and unemployed so great, that no law could prevent their being immediately sent out of the country.

It is not always necessary to accumulate gold and silver, in order to enable a country to carry on foreign wars, and to maintain fleets and armies in distant countries. Fleets and armies are maintained, not with gold and silver, but with consumable goods. The nation which, from the annual produce of its domestic industry, from the annual revenue arising out of its lands, and labor, and consumable stock, has wherewithal to purchase those consumable goods in distant countries, can maintain foreign wars there.

A nation may purchase the pay and provisions of an army in a distant country three different ways; by sending abroad either, first, some part of its accumulated gold and silver; or, secondly, some part of the annual produce of its manufactures; or, last of all, some part of its annual rude produce.

The gold and silver which can properly be considered as accumulated, or stored up in any country, may be distinguished into three parts; first, the circulating money; secondly, the plate of private families; and, last of all, the money which may have been collected by many years parsimony, and laid up in the treasury of the prince.

It can seldom happen that much can be spared from the circulating money of the country; because in that there can seldom be much redundancy. The value of goods annually bought and sold in any country requires a certain quantity of money to circulate and distribute them to their proper consumers, and can give employment to no more. The channel of circulation necessarily draws to itself a sum sufficient to fill it, and never admits any more. Something, however, is generally withdrawn from this channel in the case of foreign war. By the great number of people who are maintained abroad, fewer are maintained at home. Fewer goods are circulated there, and less money becomes necessary to circulate them. An extraordinary quantity of paper money of some sort or other, too, such as exchequer notes, navy bills, and bank bills, in England, is generally issued upon such occasions, and, by supplying the place of circulating gold and silver, gives an opportunity of sending a greater quantity of it abroad. All this, however, could afford but a poor resource for maintaining a foreign war, of great expense, and several years duration.

The melting down of the plate of private families has, upon every occasion, been found a still more insignificant one. The French, in the beginning of the last war, did not derive so much advantage from this expedient as to compensate the loss of the fashion.

The accumulated treasures of the prince have in former times afforded a much greater and more lasting resource. In the present times, if you except the king of Prussia, to accumulate treasure seems to be no part of the policy of European princes.

The funds which maintained the foreign wars of the present century, the most expensive perhaps which history records, seem to have had little dependency upon the exportation either of the circulating money, or of the plate of private families, or of the treasure of the prince. The last French war cost Great Britain upwards of £90,000,000, including not only the £75,000,000 of new debt that was contracted, but the additional 2s. in the pound land-tax, and what was annually borrowed of the sinking fund. More than two-thirds of this expense were laid out in distant countries; in Germany, Portugal, America, in the ports of the Mediterranean, in the East and West Indies. The kings of England had no accumulated treasure. We never heard of any extraordinary quantity of plate being melted down. The circulating gold and silver of the country had not been supposed to exceed £18,000,000. Since the late recoinage of the gold, however, it is believed to have been a good deal underrated. Let us suppose, therefore, according to the most exaggerated computation which I remember to have either seen or heard of, that, gold and silver together, it amounted to £30,000,000. Had the war been carried on by means of our money, the whole of it must, even according to this computation, have been sent out and returned again, at least twice in a period of between six and seven years. Should this be supposed, it would afford the most decisive argument, to demonstrate how unnecessary it is for government to watch over the preservation of money, since, upon this supposition, the whole money of the country must have gone from it, and returned to it again, two different times in so short a period, without any body's knowing anything of the matter. The channel of circulation, however, never appeared more empty than usual during any part of this period. Few people wanted money who had wherewithal to pay for it. The profits of foreign trade, indeed, were greater than usual during the whole war, but especially towards the end of it. This occasioned, what it always occasions, a general overtrading in all the ports of Great Britain; and this again occasioned the usual complaint of the scarcity of money, which always follows overtrading. Many people wanted it, who had neither wherewithal to buy it, nor credit to borrow it; and because the debtors found it difficult to borrow, the creditors found it difficult to get payment. Gold and silver, however, were generally to be had for their value, by those who had that value to give for them.

The enormous expense of the late war, therefore, must have been chiefly defrayed, not by the exportation of gold and silver, but by that of British commodities of some kind or other. When the government, or those who acted under them, contracted with a merchant for a remittance to some foreign country, he would naturally endeavor to pay his foreign correspondent, upon whom he granted a bill, by sending abroad rather commodities than gold and silver. If the commodities of Great Britain were not in demand in that country, he would endeavor to send them to some other country in which he could purchase a bill upon that country. The transportation of commodities, when properly suited to the market, is always attended with a considerable profit; whereas that of gold and silver is scarce ever attended with any. When those metals are sent abroad in order to purchase foreign commodities, the merchant's profit arises, not from the purchase, but from the sale of the returns. But when they are sent abroad merely to pay a debt, he gets no returns, and consequently no profit. He naturally, therefore, exerts his invention to find out a way of paying his foreign debts, rather by the exportation of commodities, than by that of gold and silver. The great quantity of British goods, exported during the course of the late war, without bringing back any returns, is accordingly remarked by the author of *The Present State of the Nation*.

Besides the three sorts of gold and silver above mentioned, there is in all great commercial countries a good deal of bullion alternately imported and exported, for the purposes of foreign trade. This bullion, as it circulates among different commercial countries, in the same manner as the national coin circulates in every country, may be considered as the money of the great mercantile republic. The national coin receives its movement and direction from the commodities circulated within the precincts of each particular country; the money in the mercantile republic, from those circulated between different countries. Both are employed in facilitating exchanges, the one between different individuals of the same, the other between those of different nations. Part of this money of the great mercantile republic may have been, and probably was, employed in carrying on the late war. In time of a general war, it is natural to suppose that a movement and direction should be impressed upon it, different from what it usually follows in profound peace, that it should circulate more about the seat of the war, and be more employed in purchasing there, and in the neighboring countries, the pay and provisions of the different armies. But whatever part of this money of the mercantile republic Great Britain may have annually employed in this manner, it must have been annually purchased, either with British commodities, or with something else that had been purchased with them; which still brings us back to commodities, to the annual produce of the land and labor of the country, as the ultimate resources which enabled us to carry on the war. It is natural, indeed, to suppose, that so great an annual expense must have been defrayed from a great annual produce. The expense of 1761, for example, amounted to more than £19,000,000. No accumulation could have supported so great an annual profusion. There is no annual produce, even of gold and silver, which could have supported it. The whole gold and silver annually imported into both Spain and Portugal, according to the best accounts, does not commonly much exceed £6,000,000 sterling, which, in some years, would scarce have paid four months expense of the late war.

The commodities most proper for being transported to distant countries, in order to purchase there either the pay and provisions of an army, or some part of the money of the mercantile republic to be employed in purchasing them, seem to be the finer and more improved manufactures; such as contain a great value in a small bulk, and can therefore be exported to a great distance at little expense. A country whose industry produces a great annual surplus of such manufactures, which are usually exported to foreign countries, may carry on for many years a very expensive foreign war, without either exporting any considerable quantity of gold and silver, or even having any such quantity to export. A considerable part of the annual surplus of its manufactures must, indeed, in this case, be exported without bringing back any returns to the country, though it does to the merchant; the government purchasing of the merchant his bills upon foreign countries, in order to purchase there the pay and provisions of an army. Some part of this surplus, however, may still continue to bring back a return. The manufacturers during the war will have a double demand upon them, and be called upon first to work up goods to be sent abroad, for paying the bills drawn upon foreign countries for the pay and provisions of the army: and, secondly, to work up such as are necessary for purchasing the common returns that had usually been consumed in the country. In the midst of the most destructive foreign war, therefore, the greater part of manufactures may frequently flourish greatly; and, on the contrary, they may decline on the return of peace. They may flourish amidst the ruin of their country, and begin to decay upon the return of its prosperity. The different state of many different branches of the British manufactures during the late war, and for some time after the peace, may serve as an illustration of what has been just now said.

No foreign war, of great expense or duration, could conveniently be carried on by the exportation of the rude produce of the soil. The expense of sending such a quantity of it into a foreign country as might purchase the pay and provisions of an army would be too great. Few countries, too, produce much more rude produce than what is sufficient for the subsistence of their own inhabitants. To send abroad any great quantity of it, therefore, would be to send abroad a part of the necessary subsistence of the people. It is otherwise with the exportation of manufactures. The maintenance of the people employed in them is kept at home, and only the surplus part of their work is exported. Mr. Hume frequently takes notice of the inability of the ancient kings of England to carry on, without interruption, any foreign war of long duration. The English in those days had nothing wherewithal to purchase the pay and provisions of their armies in foreign countries, but either the rude produce of the soil, of which no considerable part could be spared from the home consumption, or a few manufactures of the coarsest kind, of which, as well as of the rude produce, the transportation was too expensive. This inability did not arise from the want of money, but of the finer and more improved manufactures. Buying and selling was transacted by means of money in England then as well as now. The quantity of circulating money must have borne the same proportion, to the number and value of purchases and sales usually transacted at that time, which it does to those transacted at present; or, rather, it must have borne a greater proportion, because there was then no paper, which now occupies a great part of the employment of gold and silver. Among nations to whom commerce and manufactures are little known, the sovereign, upon extraordinary occasions, can seldom draw any considerable aid from his subjects, for reasons which shall be explained hereafter. It is in such countries, therefore, that he generally endeavors to accumulate a treasure, as the only resource against such emergencies. Independent of this necessity, he is, in such a situation, naturally disposed to the parsimony requisite for accumulation. In that simple state, the expense even of a sovereign is not directed by the vanity which delights in the gaudy finery of a court, but is employed in bounty to his tenants, and hospitality to his retainers. But bounty and hospitality very seldom lead to extravagance; though vanity almost always does. Every Tartar chief, accordingly, has a treasure. The treasures of Mazepa, chief of the Cossacks in the Ukraine, the famous ally of Charles XII, are said to have been very great. The French kings of the Merovingian race had all treasures. When they divided their kingdom among their different children, they divided their treasures too. The Saxon princes, and the first kings after the Conquest, seem likewise to have accumulated treasures. The first exploit of every new reign was commonly to seize the treasure of the preceding king, as the most essential measure for securing the succession. The sovereigns of improved and commercial countries are not under the same necessity of accumulating treasures, because they can generally draw from their subjects extraordinary aids upon extraordinary occasions. They are likewise less disposed to do so. They naturally, perhaps necessarily, follow the mode of the times; and their expense comes to be regulated by the same extravagant vanity which directs that of all the other great proprietors in their dominions. The insignificant pageantry of their court becomes every day more brilliant; and the expense of it not only prevents accumulation, but frequently encroaches upon the funds destined for more necessary expenses. What Dercyllidas said of the court of Persia, may be applied to that of several European princes, that he saw there much splendor, but little strength, and many servants, but few soldiers.

The importation of gold and silver is not the principal, much less the sole benefit, which a nation derives from its foreign trade. Between whatever places foreign trade is carried on, they all of them derive two distinct benefits from it. It carries out that surplus part of the produce of their land and labor for which there is no demand among them, and brings back in return for it something else for which there is a demand. It gives a value to their superfluities, by exchanging them for something else, which may satisfy a part of their wants and increase their enjoyments. By means of it, the narrowness of the home market does not hinder the division of labor in any particular branch of art or manufacture from being carried to the highest perfection. By opening a more extensive market for whatever part of the produce of their labor may exceed the home consumption, it encourages them to improve its productive power, and to augment its annual produce to the utmost, and thereby to increase the real revenue and wealth of the society. These great and important services foreign trade is continually occupied in performing to all the different countries between which it is carried on. They all derive great benefit from it, though that in which the merchant resides generally derives the greatest, as he is generally more employed in supplying the wants, and carrying out the superfluities of his own, than of any other particular country. To import the gold and silver which may be wanted into the countries which have no mines, is, no doubt a part of the business of foreign commerce. It is, however, a most insignificant part of it. A country which carried on foreign trade merely upon this account, could scarce have occasion to freight a ship in a century.

It is not by the importation of gold and silver that the discovery of America has enriched Europe. By the abundance of the American mines, those metals have become cheaper. A service of plate can now be purchased for about a third part of the corn, or a third part of the labor, which it would have cost in the fifteenth century. With the same annual expense of labor and commodities, Europe can annually purchase about three times the quantity of plate which it could have purchased at that time. But when a commodity comes to be sold for a third part of what had been its usual price, not only those who purchased it before can purchase three times their former quantity, but it is brought down to the level of a much greater number of purchasers, perhaps to more than ten, perhaps to more than twenty times the former number. So that there may be in Europe at present, not only more than three times, but more than twenty or thirty times the quantity of plate which would have been in it, even in its present state of improvement, had the discovery of the American mines never been made. So far Europe has, no doubt, gained a real convenience, though surely a very trifling one. The cheapness of gold and silver renders those metals rather less fit for the purposes of money than they were before. In order to make the same purchases, we must load ourselves with a greater quantity of them, and carry about a shilling in our pocket, where a groat would have done before. It is difficult to say which is most trifling, this inconveniency, or the opposite convenience. Neither the one nor the other could have made any very essential change in the state of Europe. The discovery of America, however, certainly made a most essential one. By opening a new and inexhaustible market to all the commodities of Europe, it gave occasion to new divisions of labor and improvements of art, which in the narrow circle of the ancient commerce could never have taken place, for want of a market to take off the greater part of their produce. The productive powers of labor were improved, and its produce increased in all the different countries of Europe, and together with it the real revenue and wealth of the inhabitants. The commodities of Europe were almost all new to America, and many of those of America were new to Europe. A new set of exchanges, therefore, began to take place, which had never been thought of before, and which should naturally have proved as advantageous to the new, as it certainly did to the old continent. The savage injustice of the Europeans rendered an event, which ought to have been beneficial to all, ruinous and destructive to several of those unfortunate countries.

The discovery of a passage to the East Indies by the Cape of Good Hope, which happened much about the same time, opened perhaps a still more extensive range to foreign commerce, than even that of America, notwithstanding the greater distance. There were but two nations in America, in any respect, superior to the savages, and these were destroyed almost as soon as discovered. The rest were mere savages. But the empires of China, Indostan, Japan, as well as several others in the East Indies, without having richer mines of gold or silver, were, in every other respect, much richer, better cultivated, and more advanced in all arts and manufactures, than either Mexico or Peru, even though we should credit, what plainly deserves no credit, the exaggerated accounts of the Spanish writers concerning the ancient state of those empires. But rich and civilized nations can always exchange to a much greater value with one another, than with savages and barbarians. Europe, however, has hitherto derived much less advantage from its commerce with the East Indies, than from that with America. The Portuguese monopolized the East India trade to themselves for about a century; and it was only indirectly, and through them, that the other nations of Europe could either send out or receive any goods from that country. When the Dutch, in the beginning of the last century, began to encroach upon them, they vested their whole East India commerce in an exclusive company. The English, French, Swedes, and Danes, have all followed their example; so that no great nation of Europe has ever yet had the benefit of a free commerce to the East Indies. No other reason need be assigned why it has never been so advantageous as the trade to America, which, between almost every nation of Europe and its own colonies, is free to all its subjects. The exclusive privileges of those East India companies, their great riches, the great favor and protection which these have procured them from their respective governments, have excited much envy against them. This envy has frequently represented their trade as altogether pernicious, on account of the great quantities of silver which it every year exports from the countries from which it is carried on. The parties concerned have replied, that their trade by this continual exportation of silver, might indeed tend to impoverish Europe in general, but not the particular country from which it was carried on; because, by the exportation of a part of the returns to other European countries, it annually brought home a much greater quantity of that metal than it carried out. Both the objection and the reply are founded in the popular notion which I have been just now examining. It is therefore unnecessary to say any thing further about either. By the annual exportation of silver to the East Indies, plate is probably somewhat dearer in Europe than it otherwise might have been; and coined silver probably purchases a larger quantity both of labor and commodities. The former of these two effects is a very small loss, the latter a very small advantage; both too insignificant to deserve any part of the public attention. The trade to the East Indies, by opening a market to the commodities of Europe, or, what comes nearly to the same thing, to the gold and silver which is purchased with those commodities, must necessarily tend to increase the annual production of European commodities, and consequently the real wealth and revenue of Europe. That it has hitherto increased them so little, is probably owing to the restraints which it everywhere labors under.

I thought it necessary, though at the hazard of being tedious, to examine at full length this popular notion, that wealth consists in money or in gold and silver. Money, in common language, as I have already observed, frequently signifies wealth; and this ambiguity of expression has rendered this popular notion so familiar to us, that even they who are convinced of its absurdity, are very apt to forget their own principles, and, in the course of their reasonings, to take it for granted as a certain and undeniable truth. Some of the best English writers upon commerce set out with observing, that the wealth of a country consists, not in its gold and silver only, but in its lands, houses, and consumable goods of all different kinds. In the course of their reasonings, however, the lands, houses, and consumable goods, seem to slip out of their memory; and the strain of their argument frequently supposes that all wealth consists in gold and silver, and that to multiply those metals is the great object of national industry and commerce.

The two principles being established, however, that wealth consisted in gold and silver, and that those metals could be brought into a country which had no mines, only by the balance of trade, or by exporting to a greater value than it imported; it necessarily became the great object of political economy to diminish as much as possible the importation of foreign goods for home consumption, and to increase as much as possible the exportation of the produce of domestic industry. Its two great engines for enriching the country, therefore, were restraints upon importation, and encouragement to exportation.

The restraints upon importation were of two kinds.

First, restraints upon the importation of such foreign goods for home consumption as could be produced at home, from whatever country they were imported.

Secondly, restraints upon the importation of goods of almost all kinds, from those particular countries with which the balance of trade was supposed to be disadvantageous.

Those different restraints consisted sometimes in high duties, and sometimes in absolute prohibitions.

Exportation was encouraged sometimes by drawbacks, sometimes by bounties, sometimes by advantageous treaties of commerce with foreign states, and sometimes by the establishment of colonies in distant countries.

Drawbacks were given upon two different occasions. When the home manufactures were subject to any duty or excise, either the whole or a part of it was frequently drawn back upon their exportation; and when foreign goods liable to a duty were imported, in order to be exported again, either the whole or a part of this duty was sometimes given back upon such exportation.

Bounties were given for the encouragement, either of some beginning manufactures, or of such sorts of industry of other kinds as were supposed to deserve particular favor.

By advantageous treaties of commerce, particular privileges were procured in some foreign state for the goods and merchants of the country, beyond what were granted to those of other countries.

By the establishment of colonies in distant countries, not only particular privileges, but a monopoly was frequently procured for the goods and merchants of the country which established them.

The two sorts of restraints upon importation above mentioned, together with these four encouragements to exportation, constitute the six principal means by which the commercial system proposes to increase the quantity of gold and silver in any country, by turning the balance of trade in its favor. I shall consider each of them in a particular chapter, and, without taking much farther notice of their supposed tendency to bring money into the country, I shall examine chiefly what are likely to be the effects of each of them upon the annual produce of its industry. According as they tend either to increase or diminish the value of this annual produce, they must evidently tend either to increase or diminish the real wealth and revenue of the country.

CHAPTER II

Of Restraints Upon Importation from Foreign Countries of Such Goods as Can Be Produced at Home

By restraining, either by high duties, or by absolute prohibitions, the importation of such goods from foreign countries as can be produced at home, the monopoly of the home market is more or less secured to the domestic industry employed in producing them. Thus the prohibition of importing either live cattle or salt provisions from foreign countries, secures to the graziers of Great Britain the monopoly of the home market for butcher's meat. The high duties upon the importation of corn, which, in times of moderate plenty, amount to a prohibition, give a like advantage to the growers of that commodity. The prohibition of the importation of foreign woolen is equally favorable to the woolen manufacturers. The silk manufacture, though altogether employed upon foreign materials, has lately obtained the same advantage. The linen manufacture has not yet obtained it, but is making great strides towards it. Many other sorts of manufactures have, in the same manner obtained in Great Britain, either altogether, or very nearly, a monopoly against their countrymen. The variety of goods, of which the importation into Great Britain is prohibited, either absolutely, or under certain circumstances, greatly exceeds what can easily be suspected by those who are not well acquainted with the laws of the customs.

That this monopoly of the home market frequently gives great encouragement to that particular species of industry which enjoys it, and frequently turns towards that employment a greater share of both the labor and stock of the society than would otherwise have gone to it, cannot be doubted. But whether it tends either to increase the general industry of the society, or to give it the most advantageous direction, is not, perhaps, altogether so evident.

The general industry of the society can never exceed what the capital of the society can employ. As the number of workmen that can be kept in employment by any particular person must bear a certain proportion to his capital, so the number of those that can be continually employed by all the members of a great society must bear a certain proportion to the whole capital of the society, and never can exceed that proportion. No regulation of commerce can increase the quantity of industry in any society beyond what its capital can maintain. It can only divert a part of it into a direction into which it might not otherwise have gone; and it is by no means certain that this artificial direction is likely to be more advantageous to the society, than that into which it would have gone of its own accord.

Every individual is continually exerting himself to find out the most advantageous employment for whatever capital he can command. It is his own advantage, indeed, and not that of the society, which he has in view. But the study of his own advantage naturally, or rather necessarily, leads him to prefer that employment which is most advantageous to the society.

First, every individual endeavors to employ his capital as near home as he can, and consequently as much as he can in the support of domestic industry, provided always that he can thereby obtain the ordinary, or not a great deal less than the ordinary profits of stock.

Thus, upon equal, or nearly equal profits, every wholesale merchant naturally prefers the home trade to the foreign trade of consumption, and the foreign trade of consumption to the carrying trade. In the home trade, his capital is never so long out of his sight as it frequently is in the foreign trade of consumption. He can know better the character and situation of the persons whom he trusts; and if he should happen to be deceived, he knows better the laws of the country from which he must seek redress. In the carrying trade, the capital of the merchant is, as it were, divided between two foreign countries, and no part of it is ever necessarily brought home, or placed under his own immediate view and command. The capital which an Amsterdam merchant employs in carrying corn from Koningsberg to Lisbon, and fruit and wine from Lisbon to Koningsberg, must generally be the one half of it at Koningsberg, and the other half at Lisbon. No part of it need ever come to Amsterdam. The natural residence of such a merchant should either be at Koningsberg or Lisbon; and it can only be some very particular circumstances which can make him prefer the residence of Amsterdam. The uneasiness, however, which he feels at being separated so far from his capital, generally determines him to bring part both of the Koningsberg goods which he destines for the market of Lisbon, and of the Lisbon goods which he destines for that of Koningsberg, to Amsterdam; and though this necessarily subjects him to a double charge of loading and unloading as well as to the payment of some duties and customs, yet, for the sake of having some part of his capital always under his own view and command, he willingly submits to this extraordinary charge; and it is in this manner that every country which has any considerable share of the carrying trade, becomes always the emporium, or general market, for the goods of all the different countries whose trade it carries on. The merchant, in order to save a second loading and unloading, endeavors always to sell in the home market, as much of the goods of all those different countries as he can; and thus, so far as he can, to convert his carrying trade into a foreign trade of consumption. A merchant, in the same manner, who is engaged in the foreign trade of consumption, when he collects goods for foreign markets, will always be glad, upon equal or nearly equal profits, to sell as great a part of them at home as he can. He saves himself the risk and trouble of exportation, when, so far as he can, he thus converts his foreign trade of consumption into a home trade. Home is in this manner the center, if I may say so, round which the capitals of the inhabitants of every country are continually circulating, and towards which they are always tending, though, by particular causes, they may sometimes be driven off and repelled from it towards more distant employments. But a capital employed in the home trade, it has already been shown, necessarily puts into motion a greater quantity of domestic industry, and gives revenue and employment to a greater number of the inhabitants of the country, than an equal capital employed in the foreign trade of consumption; and one employed in the foreign trade of consumption has the same advantage over an equal capital employed in the carrying trade. Upon equal, or only nearly equal profits, therefore, every individual naturally inclines to employ his capital in the manner in which it is likely to afford the greatest support to domestic industry, and to give revenue and employment to the greatest number of people of his own country.

Secondly, every individual who employs his capital in the support of domestic industry, necessarily endeavors so to direct that industry, that its produce may be of the greatest possible value.

The produce of industry is what it adds to the subject or materials upon which it is employed. In proportion as the value of this produce is great or small, so will likewise be the profits of the employer. But it is only for the sake of profit that any man employs a capital in the support of industry; and he will always, therefore, endeavor to employ it in the support of that industry of which the produce is likely to be of the greatest value, or to exchange for the greatest quantity either of money or of other goods.

But the annual revenue of every society is always precisely equal to the exchangeable value of the whole annual produce of its industry, or rather is precisely the same thing with that exchangeable value. As every individual, therefore, endeavors as much as he can, both to employ his capital in the support of domestic industry, and so to direct that industry that its produce maybe of the greatest value; every individual necessarily labors to render the annual revenue of the society as great as he can. He generally, indeed, neither intends to promote the public interest, nor knows how much he is promoting it. By preferring the support of domestic to that of foreign industry, he intends only his own security; and by directing that industry in such a manner as its produce may be of the greatest value, he intends only his own gain; and he is in this, as in many other cases, led by an invisible hand to promote an end which was no part of his intention. Nor is it always the worse for the society that it was no part of it. By pursuing his own interest, he frequently promotes that of the society more effectually than when he really intends to promote it. I have never known much good done by those who affected to trade for the public good. It is an affectation, indeed, not very common among merchants, and very few words need be employed in dissuading them from it.

What is the species of domestic industry which his capital can employ, and of which the produce is likely to be of the greatest value, every individual, it is evident, can in his local situation judge much better than any statesman or lawgiver can do for him. The statesman, who should attempt to direct private people in what manner they ought to employ their capitals, would not only load himself with a most unnecessary attention, but assume an authority which could safely be trusted, not only to no single person, but to no council or senate whatever, and which would nowhere be so dangerous as in the hands of a man who had folly and presumption enough to fancy himself fit to exercise it.

To give the monopoly of the home market to the produce of domestic industry, in any particular art or manufacture, is in some measure to direct private people in what manner they ought to employ their capitals, and must in almost all cases be either a useless or a hurtful regulation. If the produce of domestic can be brought there as cheap as that of foreign industry, the regulation is evidently useless. If it cannot, it must generally be hurtful. It is the maxim of every prudent master of a family, never to attempt to make at home what it will cost him more to make than to buy. The tailor does not attempt to make his own shoes, but buys them of the shoemaker. The shoemaker does not attempt to make his own clothes, but employs a tailor. The farmer attempts to make neither the one nor the other, but employs those different artificers. All of them find it for their interest to employ their whole industry in a way in which they have some advantage over their neighbors, and to purchase with a part of its produce, or, what is the same thing, with the price of a part of it, whatever else they have occasion for.

What is prudence in the conduct of every private family, can scarce be folly in that of a great kingdom. If a foreign country can supply us with a commodity cheaper than we ourselves can make it, better buy it of them with some part of the produce of our own industry, employed in a way in which we have some advantage. The general industry of the country being always in proportion to the capital which employs it, will not thereby be diminished, no more than that of the abovementioned artificers; but only left to find out the way in which it can be employed with the greatest advantage. It is certainly not employed to the greatest advantage, when it is thus directed towards an object which it can buy cheaper than it can make. The value of its annual produce is certainly more or less diminished, when it is thus turned away from producing commodities evidently of more value than the commodity which it is directed to produce. According to the supposition, that commodity could be purchased from foreign countries cheaper than it can be made at home; it could therefore have been purchased with a part only of the commodities, or, what is the same thing, with a part only of the price of the commodities, which the industry employed by an equal capital would have produced at home, had it been left to follow its natural course. The industry of the country, therefore, is thus turned away from a more to a less advantageous employment; and the exchangeable value of its annual produce, instead of being increased, according to the intention of the lawgiver, must necessarily be diminished by every such regulation.

By means of such regulations, indeed, a particular manufacture may sometimes be acquired sooner than it could have been otherwise, and after a certain time may be made at home as cheap, or cheaper, than in the foreign country. But though the industry of the society may be thus carried with advantage into a particular channel sooner than it could have been otherwise, it will by no means follow that the sum-total, either of its industry, or of its revenue, can ever be augmented by any such regulation. The industry of the society can augment only in proportion as its capital augments, and its capital can augment only in proportion to what can be gradually saved out of its revenue. But the immediate effect of every such regulation is to diminish its revenue; and what diminishes its revenue is certainly not very likely to augment its capital faster than it would have augmented of its own accord, had both capital and industry been left to find out their natural employments.

Though, for want of such regulations, the society should never acquire the proposed manufacture, it would not upon that account necessarily be the poorer in any one period of its duration. In every period of its duration its whole capital and industry might still have been employed, though upon different objects, in the manner that was most advantageous at the time. In every period its revenue might have been the greatest which its capital could afford, and both capital and revenue might have been augmented with the greatest possible rapidity.

The natural advantages which one country has over another, in producing particular commodities, are sometimes so great, that it is acknowledged by all the world to be in vain to struggle with them. By means of glasses, hot-beds, and hot-walls, very good grapes can be raised in Scotland, and very good wine, too, can be made of them, at about thirty times the expense for which at least equally good can be brought from foreign countries. Would it be a reasonable law to prohibit the importation of all foreign wines, merely to encourage the making of claret and Burgundy in Scotland? But if there would be a manifest absurdity in turning towards any employment thirty times more of the capital and industry of the country than would be necessary to purchase from foreign countries an equal quantity of the commodities wanted, there must be an absurdity, though not altogether so glaring, yet exactly of the same kind, in turning towards any such employment a thirtieth, or even a three hundredth part more of either. Whether the advantages which one country has over another be natural or acquired, is in this respect of no consequence. As long as the one country has those advantages, and the other wants them, it will always be more advantageous for the latter rather to buy of the former than to make. It is an acquired advantage only, which one artificer has over his neighbor, who exercises another trade; and yet they both find it more advantageous to buy of one another, than to make what does not belong to their particular trades.

Merchants and manufacturers are the people who derive the greatest advantage from this monopoly of the home market The prohibition of the importation of foreign cattle and of salt provisions, together with the high duties upon foreign corn, which in times of moderate plenty amount to a prohibition, are not near so advantageous to the graziers and farmers of Great Britain, as other regulations of the same kind are to its merchants and manufacturers. Manufactures, those of the finer kind especially, are more easily transported from one country to another than corn or cattle. It is in the fetching and carrying manufactures, accordingly, that foreign trade is chiefly employed. In manufactures, a very small advantage will enable foreigners to undersell our own workmen, even in the home market. It will require a very great one to enable them to do so in the rude produce of the soil. If the free importation of foreign manufactures were permitted, several of the home manufactures would probably suffer, and some of them perhaps go to ruin altogether, and a considerable part of the stock and industry at present employed in them, would be forced to find out some other employment. But the freest importation of the rude produce of the soil could have no such effect upon the agriculture of the country.

If the importation of foreign cattle, for example, were made ever so free, so few could be imported, that the grazing trade of Great Britain could be little affected by it. Live cattle are, perhaps, the only commodity of which the transportation is more expensive by sea than by land. By land they carry themselves to market. By sea, not only the cattle, but their food and their water too, must be carried at no small expense and inconveniency. The short sea between Ireland and Great Britain, indeed, renders the importation of Irish cattle more easy. But though the free importation of them, which was lately permitted only for a limited time, were rendered perpetual, it could have no considerable effect upon the interest of the graziers of Great Britain. Those parts of Great Britain which border upon the Irish sea are all grazing countries. Irish cattle could never be imported for their use, but must be drove through those very extensive countries, at no small expense and inconveniency, before they could arrive at their proper market. Fat cattle could not be drove so far. Lean cattle, therefore, could only be imported; and such importation could interfere not with the interest of the feeding or fattening countries, to which, by reducing the price of lean cattle it would rather be advantageous, but with that of the breeding countries only. The small number of Irish cattle imported since their importation was permitted, together with the good price at which lean cattle still continue to sell, seem to demonstrate, that even the breeding countries of Great Britain are never likely to be much affected by the free importation of Irish cattle. The common people of Ireland, indeed, are said to have sometimes opposed with violence the exportation of their cattle. But if the exporters had found any great advantage in continuing the trade, they could easily, when the law was on their side, have conquered this mobbish opposition.

Feeding and fattening countries, besides, must always be highly improved, whereas breeding countries are generally uncultivated. The high price of lean cattle, by augmenting the value of uncultivated land, is like a bounty against improvement. To any country which was highly improved throughout, it would be more advantageous to import its lean cattle than to breed them. The province of Holland, accordingly, is said to follow this maxim at present. The mountains of Scotland, Wales, and Northumberland, indeed, are countries not capable of much improvement, and seem destined by nature to be the breeding countries of Great Britain. The freest importation of foreign cattle could have no other effect than to hinder those breeding countries from taking advantage of the increasing population and improvement of the rest of the kingdom, from raising their price to an exorbitant height, and from laying a real tax upon all the more improved and cultivated parts of the country.

The freest importation of salt provisions, in the same manner, could have as little effect upon the interest of the graziers of Great Britain as that of live cattle. Salt provisions are not only a very bulky commodity, but when compared with fresh meat they are a commodity both of worse quality, and, as they cost more labor and expense, of higher price. They could never, therefore, come into competition with the fresh meat, though they might with the salt provisions of the country. They might be used for victualling ships for distant voyages, and such like uses, but could never make any considerable part of the food of the people. The small quantity of salt provisions imported from Ireland since their importation was rendered free, is an experimental proof that our graziers have nothing to apprehend from it. It does not appear that the price of butcher's meat has ever been sensibly affected by it.

Even the free importation of foreign corn could very little affect the interest of the farmers of Great Britain. Corn is a much more bulky commodity than butcher's meat. A pound of wheat at a penny is as dear as a pound of butcher's meat at four pence. The small quantity of foreign corn imported even in times of the greatest scarcity, may satisfy our farmers that they can have nothing to fear from the freest importation. The average quantity imported, one year with another, amounts only, according to the very well informed author of the *Tracts upon the Corn Trade*, to 23,728 quarters of all sorts of grain, and does not exceed the five hundredth and seventy-first part of the annual consumption. But as the bounty upon corn occasions a greater exportation in years of plenty, so it must, of consequence, occasion a greater importation in years of scarcity, than in the actual state of tillage would otherwise take place. By means of it, the plenty of one year does not compensate the scarcity of another; and as the average quantity exported is necessarily augmented by it, so must likewise, in the actual state of tillage, the average quantity imported. If there were no bounty, as less corn would be exported, so it is probable that, one year with another, less would be imported than at present. The corn merchants, the fetchers and carriers of corn between Great Britain and foreign countries, would have much less employment, and might suffer considerably; but the country gentlemen and farmers could suffer very little. It is in the corn merchants, accordingly, rather than the country gentlemen and farmers, that I have observed the greatest anxiety for the renewal and continuation of the bounty.

Country gentlemen and farmers are, to their great honor, of all people, the least subject to the wretched spirit of monopoly. The undertaker of a great manufactory is sometimes alarmed if another work of the same kind is established within twenty miles of him; the Dutch undertaker of the woolen manufacture at Abbeville, stipulated that no work of the same kind should be established within thirty leagues of that city. Farmers and country gentlemen, on the contrary, are generally disposed rather to promote, than to obstruct, the cultivation and improvement of their neighbors farms and estates. They have no secrets, such as those of the greater part of manufacturers, but are generally rather fond of communicating to their neighbors, and of extending as far as possible any new practice which they may have found to be advantageous. "Pius quaestus," says old Cato, "stabilissimusque, minimeque invidiosus; minimeque male cogitantes sunt, qui in eo studio occupati sunt." Country gentlemen and farmers, dispersed in different parts of the country, cannot so easily combine as merchants and manufacturers, who being collected into towns, and accustomed to that exclusive corporation spirit which prevails in them, naturally endeavor to obtain, against all their countrymen, the same exclusive privilege which they generally possess against the inhabitants of their respective towns. They accordingly seem to have been the original inventors of those restraints upon the importation of foreign goods, which secure to them the monopoly of the home market. It was probably in imitation of them, and to put themselves upon a level with those who, they found, were disposed to oppress them, that the country gentlemen and farmers of Great Britain so far forgot the generosity which is natural to their station, as to demand the exclusive privilege of supplying their countrymen with corn and butcher's meat. They did not, perhaps, take time to consider how much less their interest could be affected by the freedom of trade, than that of the people whose example they followed.

To prohibit, by a perpetual law, the importation of foreign corn and cattle, is in reality to enact, that the population and industry of the country shall, at no time, exceed what the rude produce of its own soil can maintain.

There seem, however, to be two cases, in which it will generally be advantageous to lay some burden upon foreign, for the encouragement of domestic industry.

The first is when some particular sort of industry is necessary for the defense of the country. The defense of Great Britain, for example, depends very much upon the number of its sailors and shipping. The act of navigation, therefore, very properly endeavors to give the sailors and shipping of Great Britain the monopoly of the trade of their own country, in some cases, by absolute prohibitions, and in others, by heavy burdens upon the shipping of foreign countries. The following are the principal dispositions of this act.

First, all ships, of which the owners, masters, and three-fourths of the mariners, are not British subjects, are prohibited, upon pain of forfeiting ship and cargo, from trading to the British settlements and plantations, or from being employed in the coasting trade of Great Britain.

Secondly, a great variety of the most bulky articles of importation can be brought into Great Britain only, either in such ships as are above described, or in ships of the country where those goods are produced, and of which the owners, masters, and three-fourths of the mariners, are of that particular country; and when imported even in ships of this latter kind, they are subject to double aliens duty. If imported in ships of any other country, the penalty is forfeiture of ship and goods. When this act was made, the Dutch were, what they still are, the great carriers of Europe; and by this regulation they were entirely excluded from being the carriers to Great Britain, or from importing to us the goods of any other European country.

Thirdly, a great variety of the most bulky articles of importation are prohibited from being imported, even in British ships, from any country but that in which they are produced, under pain of forfeiting ship and cargo. This regulation, too, was probably intended against the Dutch. Holland was then, as now, the great emporium for all European goods; and by this regulation, British ships were hindered from loading in Holland the goods of any other European country.

Fourthly, salt fish of all kinds, whale fins, whalebone, oil, and blubber, not caught by and cured on board British vessels, when imported into Great Britain, are subject to double aliens duty. The Dutch, as they are still the principal, were then the only fishers in Europe that attempted to supply foreign nations with fish. By this regulation, a very heavy burden was laid upon their supplying Great Britain.

When the act of navigation was made, though England and Holland were not actually at war, the most violent animosity subsisted between the two nations. It had begun during the government of the long parliament, which first framed this act, and it broke out soon after in the Dutch wars, during that of the Protector and of Charles II. It is not impossible, therefore, that some of the regulations of this famous act may have proceeded from national animosity. They are as wise, however, as if they had all been dictated by the most deliberate wisdom. National animosity, at that particular time, aimed at the very same object which the most deliberate wisdom would have recommended, the diminution of the naval power of Holland, the only naval power which could endanger the security of England.

The act of navigation is not favorable to foreign commerce, or to the growth of that opulence which can arise from it. The interest of a nation, in its commercial relations to foreign nations, is, like that of a merchant with regard to the different people with whom he deals, to buy as cheap, and to sell as dear as possible. But it will be most likely to buy cheap, when, by the most perfect freedom of trade, it encourages all nations to bring to it the goods which it has occasion to purchase; and, for the same reason, it will be most likely to sell dear, when its markets are thus filled with the greatest number of buyers. The act of navigation, it is true, lays no burden upon foreign ships that come to export the produce of British industry. Even the ancient aliens duty, which used to be paid upon all goods, exported as well as imported, has, by several subsequent acts, been taken off from the greater part of the articles of exportation. But if foreigners, either by prohibitions or high duties, are hindered from coming to sell, they cannot always afford to come to buy; because, coming without a cargo, they must lose the freight from their own country to Great Britain. By diminishing the number of sellers, therefore, we necessarily diminish that of buyers, and are thus likely not only to buy foreign goods dearer, but to sell our own cheaper, than if there was a more perfect freedom of trade. As defense, however, is of much more importance than opulence, the act of navigation is, perhaps, the wisest of all the commercial regulations of England.

The second case, in which it will generally be advantageous to lay some burden upon foreign for the encouragement of domestic industry, is when some tax is imposed at home upon the produce of the latter. In this case, it seems reasonable that an equal tax should be imposed upon the like produce of the former. This would not give the monopoly of the home market to domestic industry, nor turn towards a particular employment a greater share of the stock and labor of the country, than what would naturally go to it. It would only hinder any part of what would naturally go to it from being turned away by the tax into a less natural direction, and would leave the competition between foreign and domestic industry, after the tax, as nearly as possible upon the same footing as before it. In Great Britain, when any such tax is laid upon the produce of domestic industry, it is usual, at the same time, in order to stop the clamorous complaints of our merchants and manufacturers, that they will be undersold at home, to lay a much heavier duty upon the importation of all foreign goods of the same kind.

This second limitation of the freedom of trade, according to some people, should, upon most occasions, be extended much farther than to the precise foreign commodities which could come into competition with those which had been taxed at home. When the necessaries of life have been taxed in any country, it becomes proper, they pretend, to tax not only the like necessaries of life imported from other countries, but all sorts of foreign goods which can come into competition with any thing that is the produce of domestic industry. Subsistence, they say, becomes necessarily dearer in consequence of such taxes; and the price of labor must always rise with the price of the laborer's subsistence. Every commodity, therefore, which is the produce of domestic industry, though not immediately taxed itself, becomes dearer in consequence of such taxes, because the labor which produces it becomes so. Such taxes, therefore, are really equivalent, they say, to a tax upon every particular commodity produced at home. In order to put domestic upon the same footing with foreign industry, therefore, it becomes necessary, they think, to lay some duty upon every foreign commodity, equal to this enhancement of the price of the home commodities with which it can come into competition.

Whether taxes upon the necessaries of life, such as those in Great Britain upon soap, salt, leather, candles, etc. necessarily raise the price of labor, and consequently that of all other commodities, I shall consider hereafter, when I come to treat of taxes. Supposing, however, in the mean time, that they have this effect, and they have it undoubtedly, this general enhancement of the price of all commodities, in consequence of that labor, is a case which differs in the two following respects from that of a particular commodity, of which the price was enhanced by a particular tax immediately imposed upon it.

First, it might always be known with great exactness, how far the price of such a commodity could be enhanced by such a tax; but how far the general enhancement of the price of labor might affect that of every different commodity about which labor was employed, could never be known with any tolerable exactness. It would be impossible, therefore, to proportion, with any tolerable exactness, the tax of every foreign, to the enhancement of the price of every home commodity.

Secondly, taxes upon the necessities of life have nearly the same effect upon the circumstances of the people as a poor soil and a bad climate. Provisions are thereby rendered dearer, in the same manner as if it required extraordinary labor and expense to raise them. As, in the natural scarcity arising from soil and climate, it would be absurd to direct the people in what manner they ought to employ their capitals and industry, so is it likewise in the artificial scarcity arising from such taxes. To be left to accommodate, as well as they could, their industry to their situation, and to find out those employments in which, notwithstanding their unfavorable circumstances, they might have some advantage either in the home or in the foreign market, is what, in both cases, would evidently be most for their advantage. To lay a new tax upon them, because they are already overburdened with taxes, and because they already pay too dear for the necessaries of life, to make them likewise pay too dear for the greater part of other commodities, is certainly a most absurd way of making amends.

Such taxes, when they have grown up to a certain height, are a curse equal to the barrenness of the earth, and the inclemency of the heavens, and yet it is in the richest and most industrious countries that they have been most generally imposed. No other countries could support so great a disorder. As the strongest bodies only can live and enjoy health under an unwholesome regimen, so the nations only, that in every sort of industry have the greatest natural and acquired advantages, can subsist and prosper under such taxes. Holland is the country in Europe in which they abound most, and which, from peculiar circumstances, continues to prosper, not by means of them, as has been most absurdly supposed, but in spite of them.

As there are two cases in which it will generally be advantageous to lay some burden upon foreign for the encouragement of domestic industry, so there are two others in which it may sometimes be a matter of deliberation, in the one, how far it is proper to continue the free importation of certain foreign goods; and, in the other, how far, or in what manner, it may be proper to restore that free importation, after it has been for some time interrupted.

The case in which it may sometimes be a matter of deliberation how far it is proper to continue the free importation of certain foreign goods, is when some foreign nation restrains, by high duties or prohibitions, the importation of some of our manufactures into their country. Revenge, in this case, naturally dictates retaliation, and that we should impose the like duties and prohibitions upon the importation of some or all of their manufactures into ours. Nations, accordingly, seldom fail to retaliate in this manner. The French have been particularly forward to favor their own manufactures, by restraining the importation of such foreign goods as could come into competition with them. In this consisted a great part of the policy of Mr. Colbert, who, notwithstanding his great abilities, seems in this case to have been imposed upon by the sophistry of merchants and manufacturers, who are always demanding a monopoly against their countrymen. It is at present the opinion of the most intelligent men in France, that his operations of this kind have not been beneficial to his country. That minister, by the tariff of 1667, imposed very high duties upon a great number of foreign manufactures. Upon his refusing to moderate them in favor of the Dutch, they, in 1671, prohibited the importation of the wines, brandies, and manufactures of France. The war of 1672 seems to have been in part occasioned by this commercial dispute. The peace of Nimeguen put an end to it in 1678, by moderating some of those duties in favor of the Dutch, who in consequence took off their prohibition. It was about the same time that the French and English began mutually to oppress each other's industry, by the like duties and prohibitions, of which the French, however, seem to have set the first example, The spirit of hostility which has subsisted between the two nations ever since, has hitherto hindered them from being moderated on either side. In 1697, the English prohibited the importation of bone lace, the manufacture of Flanders. The government of that country, at that time under the dominion of Spain, prohibited, in return, the importation of English woolens. In 1700, the prohibition of importing bone lace into England was taken off; upon condition that the importation of English woolens into Flanders should be put on the same footing as before.

There may be good policy in retaliations of this kind, when there is a probability that they will procure the repeal of the high duties or prohibitions complained of. The recovery of a great foreign market will generally more than compensate the transitory inconveniency of paying dearer during a short time for some sorts of goods. To judge whether such retaliations are likely to produce such an effect, does not, perhaps, belong so much to the science of a legislator, whose deliberations ought to be governed by general principles, which are always the same, as to the skill of that insidious and crafty animal vulgarly called a statesman or politician, whose councils are directed by the momentary fluctuations of affairs. When there is no probability that any such repeal can be procured, it seems a bad method of compensating the injury done to certain classes of our people, to do another injury ourselves, not only to those classes, but to almost all the other classes of them. When our neighbors prohibit some manufacture of ours, we generally prohibit, not only the same, for that alone would seldom affect them considerably, but some other manufacture of theirs. This may, no doubt, give encouragement to some particular class of workmen among ourselves, and, by excluding some of their rivals, may enable them to raise their price in the home market. Those workmen however, who suffered by our neighbors prohibition, will not be benefited by ours. On the contrary, they, and almost all the other classes of our citizens, will thereby be obliged to pay dearer than before for certain goods. Every such law, therefore, imposes a real tax upon the whole country, not in favor of that particular class of workmen who were injured by our neighbors prohibitions, but of some other class.

The case in which it may sometimes be a matter of deliberation, how far, or in what manner, it is proper to restore the free importation of foreign goods, after it has been for some time interrupted, is when particular manufactures, by means of high duties or prohibitions upon all foreign goods which can come into competition with them, have been so far extended as to employ a great multitude of hands. Humanity may in this case require that the freedom of trade should be restored only by slow gradations, and with a good deal of reserve and circumspection. Were those high duties and prohibitions taken away all at once, cheaper foreign goods of the same kind might be poured so fast into the home market, as to deprive all at once many thousands of our people of their ordinary employment and means of subsistence. The disorder which this would occasion might no doubt be very considerable. It would in all probability, however, be much less than is commonly imagined, for the two following reasons.

First, all those manufactures of which any part is commonly exported to other European countries without a bounty, could be very little affected by the freest importation of foreign goods. Such manufactures must be sold as cheap abroad as any other foreign goods of the same quality and kind, and consequently must be sold cheaper at home. They would still, therefore, keep possession of the home market; and though a capricious man of fashion might sometimes prefer foreign wares, merely because they were foreign, to cheaper and better goods of the same kind that were made at home, this folly could, from the nature of things, extend to so few, that it could make no sensible impression upon the general employment of the people. But a great part of all the different branches of our woolen manufacture, of our tanned leather, and of our hardware, are annually exported to other European countries without any bounty, and these are the manufactures which employ the greatest number of hands. The silk, perhaps, is the manufacture which would suffer the most by this freedom of trade, and after it the linen, though the latter much less than the former.

Secondly, though a great number of people should, by thus restoring the freedom of trade, be thrown all at once out of their ordinary employment and common method of subsistence, it would by no means follow that they would thereby be deprived either of employment or subsistence. By the reduction of the army and navy at the end of the late war, more than 100,000 soldiers and seamen, a number equal to what is employed in the greatest manufactures, were all at once thrown out of their ordinary employment: but though they no doubt suffered some inconveniency, they were not thereby deprived of all employment and subsistence. The greater part of the seamen, it is probable, gradually betook themselves to the merchant service as they could find occasion, and in the meantime both they and the soldiers were absorbed in the great mass of the people, and employed in a great variety of occupations. Not only no great convulsion, but no sensible disorder, arose from so great a change in the situation of more than 100,000 men, all accustomed to the use of arms, and many of them to rapine and plunder. The number of vagrants was scarce anywhere sensibly increased by it; even the wages of labor were not reduced by it in any occupation, so far as I have been able to learn, except in that of seamen in the merchant service. But if we compare together the habits of a soldier and of any sort of manufacturer, we shall find that those of the latter do not tend so much to disqualify him from being employed in a new trade, as those of the former from being employed in any. The manufacturer has always been accustomed to look for his subsistence from his labor only; the soldier to expect it from his pay. Application and industry have been familiar to the one; idleness and dissipation to the other. But it is surely much easier to change the direction of industry from one sort of labor to another, than to turn idleness and dissipation to any. To the greater part of manufactures, besides, it has already been observed, there are other collateral manufactures of so similar a nature, that a workman can easily transfer his industry from one of them to another. The greater part of such workmen, too, are occasionally employed in country labor. The stock which employed them in a particular manufacture before, will still remain in the country, to employ an equal number of people in some other way. The capital of the country remaining the same, the demand for labor will likewise be the same, or very nearly the same, though it may be exerted in different places, and for different occupations. Soldiers and seamen, indeed, when discharged from the king's service, are at liberty to exercise any trade within any town or place of Great Britain or Ireland. Let the same natural liberty of exercising what species of industry they please, be restored to all his Majesty's subjects, in the same manner as to soldiers and seamen; that is, break down the exclusive privileges of corporations, and repeal the statute of apprenticeship, both which are really encroachments upon natural Liberty, and add to those the repeal of the law of settlements, so that a poor workman, when thrown out of employment, either in one trade or in one place, may seek for it in another trade or in another place, without the fear either of a prosecution or of a removal; and neither the public nor the individuals will suffer much more from the occasional disbanding some particular classes of manufacturers, than from that of the soldiers. Our manufacturers have no doubt great merit with their country, but they cannot have more than those who defend it with their blood, nor deserve to be treated with more delicacy.

To expect, indeed, that the freedom of trade should ever be entirely restored in Great Britain, is as absurd as to expect that an Oceana or Utopia should ever be established in it. Not only the prejudices of the public, but, what is much more unconquerable, the private interests of many individuals, irresistibly oppose it. Were the officers of the army to oppose, with the same zeal and unanimity, any reduction in the number of forces, with which master manufacturers set themselves against every law that is likely to increase the number of their rivals in the home market; were the former to animate their soldiers. In the same manner as the latter inflame their workmen, to attack with violence and outrage the proposers of any such regulation; to attempt to reduce the army would be as dangerous as it has now become to attempt to diminish, in any respect, the monopoly which our manufacturers have obtained against us. This monopoly has so much increased the number of some particular tribes of them, that, like an overgrown standing army, they have become formidable to the government, and, upon many occasions, intimidate the legislature. The member of parliament who supports every proposal for strengthening this monopoly, is sure to acquire not only the reputation of understanding trade, but great popularity and influence with an order of men whose numbers and wealth render them of great importance. If he opposes them, on the contrary, and still more, if he has authority enough to be able to thwart them, neither the most acknowledged probity, nor the highest rank, nor the greatest public services, can protect him from the most infamous abuse and detraction, from personal insults, nor sometimes from real danger, arising from the insolent outrage of furious and disappointed monopolists.

The undertaker of a great manufacture, who, by the home markets being suddenly laid open to the competition of foreigners, should be obliged to abandon his trade, would no doubt suffer very considerably. That part of his capital which had usually been employed in purchasing materials, and in paying his workmen, might, without much difficulty, perhaps, find another employment; but that part of it which was fixed in workhouses, and in the instruments of trade, could scarce be disposed of without considerable loss. The equitable regard, therefore, to his interest, requires that changes of this kind should never be introduced suddenly, but slowly, gradually, and after a very long warning. The legislature, were it possible that its deliberations could be always directed, not by the clamorous importunity of partial interests, but by an extensive view of the general good, ought, upon this very account, perhaps, to be particularly careful, neither to establish any new monopolies of this kind, nor to extend further those which are already established. Every such regulation introduces some degree of real disorder into the constitution of the state, which it will be difficult afterwards to cure without occasioning another disorder.

How far it may be proper to impose taxes upon the importation of foreign goods, in order not to prevent their importation, but to raise a revenue for government, I shall consider hereafter when I come to treat of taxes. Taxes imposed with a view to prevent, or even to diminish importation, are evidently as destructive of the revenue of the customs as of the freedom of trade.

CHAPTER III

Of the Extraordinary Restraints upon the Importation of Goods of Almost All Kinds, from Those Countries with which the Balance is Supposed to be Disadvantageous

Part I

Of the Unreasonableness of those Restraints, even upon the Principles of the Commercial System

To lay extraordinary restraints upon the importation of goods of almost all kinds, from those particular countries with which the balance of trade is supposed to be disadvantageous, is the second expedient by which the commercial system proposes to increase the quantity of gold and silver. Thus, in Great Britain, Silesia lawns may be imported for home consumption, upon paying certain duties; but French cambrics and lawns are prohibited to be imported, except into the port of London, there to be warehoused for exportation. Higher duties are imposed upon the wines of France than upon those of Portugal, or indeed of any other country. By what is called the impost 1692, a duty of five-and-twenty percent of the rate or value, was laid upon all French goods; while the goods of other nations were, the greater part of them, subjected to much lighter duties, seldom exceeding five percent. The wine, brandy, salt, and vinegar of France, were indeed excepted; these commodities being subjected to other heavy duties, either by other laws, or by particular clauses of the same law. In 1696, a second duty of twenty-five percent the first not having been thought a sufficient discouragement, was imposed upon all French goods, except brandy; together with a new duty of five-and-twenty pounds upon the ton of French wine, and another of fifteen pounds upon the ton of French vinegar. French goods have never been omitted in any of those general subsidies or duties of five percent which have been imposed upon all, or the greater part, of the goods enumerated in the book of rates. If we count the one-third and two-third subsidies as making a complete subsidy between them, there have been five of these general subsidies; so that, before the commencement of the present war, seventy-five percent may be considered as the lowest duty to which the greater part of the goods of the growth, produce, or manufacture of France, were liable. But upon the greater part of goods, those duties are equivalent to a prohibition. The French, in their turn, have, I believe, treated our goods and manufactures just as hardly; though I am not so well acquainted with the particular hardships which they have imposed upon them. Those mutual restraints have put an end to almost all fair commerce between the two nations; and smugglers are now the principal importers, either of British goods into France, or of French goods into Great Britain.

The principles which I have been examining, in the foregoing chapter, took their origin from private interest and the spirit of monopoly; those which I am going to examine in this, from national prejudice and animosity. They are, accordingly, as might well be expected, still more unreasonable. They are so, even upon the principles of the commercial system.

First, though it were certain that in the case of a free trade between France and England, for example, the balance would be in favor of France, it would by no means follow that such a trade would be disadvantageous to England, or that the general balance of its whole trade would thereby be turned more against it. If the wines of France are better and cheaper than those of Portugal, or its linens than those of Germany, it would be more advantageous for Great Britain to purchase both the wine and the foreign linen which it had occasion for of France, than of Portugal and Germany. Though the value of the annual importations from France would thereby be greatly augmented, the value of the whole annual importations would be diminished, in proportion as the French goods of the same quality were cheaper than those of the other two countries. This would be the case, even upon the supposition that the whole French goods imported were to be consumed in Great Britain.

But, secondly, a great part of them might be re-exported to other countries, where, being sold with profit, they might bring back a return, equal in value, perhaps, to the prime cost of the whole French goods imported. What has frequently been said of the East India trade, might possibly be true of the French; that though the greater part of East India goods were bought with gold and silver, the re-exportation of a part of them to other countries brought back more gold and silver to that which carried on the trade, than the prime cost of the whole amounted to. One of the most important branches of the Dutch trade at present, consists in the carriage of French goods to other European countries. Some part even of the French wine drank in Great Britain, is clandestinely imported from Holland and Zealand. If there was either a free trade between France and England, or if French goods could be imported upon paying only the same duties as those of other European nations, to be drawn back upon exportation, England might have some share of a trade which is found so advantageous to Holland.

Thirdly, and lastly, there is no certain criterion by which we can determine on which side what is called the balance between any two countries lies, or which of them exports to the greatest value. National prejudice and animosity, prompted always by the private interest of particular traders, are the principles which generally direct our judgment upon all questions concerning it. There are two criterions, however, which have frequently been appealed to upon such occasions, the customhouse books and the course of exchange. The custom-house books, I think, it is now generally acknowledged, are a very uncertain criterion, on account of the inaccuracy of the valuation at which the greater part of goods are rated in them. The course of exchange is, perhaps, almost equally so.

When the exchange between two places, such as London and Paris, is at par, it is said to be a sign that the debts due from London to Paris are compensated by those due from Paris to London. On the contrary, when a premium is paid at London for a bill upon Paris, it is said to be a sign that the debts due from London to Paris are not compensated by those due from Paris to London, but that a balance in money must be sent out from the latter place; for the risk, trouble, and expense, of exporting which, the premium is both demanded and given. But the ordinary state of debt and credit between those two cities must necessarily be regulated, it is said, by the ordinary course of their dealings with one another. When neither of them imports from the other to a greater amount than it exports to that other, the debts and credits of each may compensate one another. But when one of them imports from the other to a greater value than it exports to that other, the former necessarily becomes indebted to the latter in a greater sum than the latter becomes indebted to it: the debts and credits of each do not compensate one another, and money must be sent out from that place of which the debts overbalance the credits. The ordinary course of exchange, therefore, being an indication of the ordinary state of debt and credit between two places, must likewise be an indication of the ordinary course of their exports and imports, as these necessarily regulate that state.

But though the ordinary course of exchange shall be allowed to be a sufficient indication of the ordinary state of debt and credit between any two places, it would not from thence follow, that the balance of trade was in favor of that place which had the ordinary state of debt and credit in its favor. The ordinary state of debt and credit between any two places is not always entirely regulated by the ordinary course of their dealings with one another, but is often influenced by that of the dealings of either with many other places. If it is usual, for example, for the merchants of England to pay for the goods which they buy of Hamburg, Dantzic, Riga, etc. by bills upon Holland, the ordinary state of debt and credit between England and Holland will not be regulated entirely by the ordinary course of the dealings of those two countries with one another, but will be influenced by that of the dealings in England with those other places. England may be obliged to send out every year money to Holland, though its annual exports to that country may exceed very much the annual value of its imports from thence, and though what is called the balance of trade may be very much in favor of England.

In the way, besides, in which the par of exchange has hitherto been computed, the ordinary course of exchange can afford no sufficient indication that the ordinary state of debt and credit is in favor of that country which seems to have, or which is supposed to have, the ordinary course of exchange in its favor; or, in other words, the real exchange may be, and in fact often is, so very different from the computed one, that, from the course of the latter, no certain conclusion can, upon many occasions, be drawn concerning that of the former.

When for a sum or money paid in England, containing, according to the standard of the English mint, a certain number of ounces of pure silver, you receive a bill for a sum of money to be paid in France, containing, according to the standard of the French mint, an equal number of ounces of pure silver, exchange is said to be at par between England and France. When you pay more, you are supposed to give a premium, and exchange is said to be against England, and in favor of France. When you pay less, you are supposed to get a premium, and exchange is said to be against France, and in favor of England.

But, first, we cannot always judge of the value of the current money of different countries by the standard of their respective mints. In some it is more, in others it is less worn, clipt, and otherwise degenerated from that standard. But the value of the current coin of every country, compared with that of any other country, is in proportion, not to the quantity of pure silver which it ought to contain, but to that which it actually does contain. Before the reformation of the silver coin in King William's time, exchange between England and Holland, computed in the usual manner, according to the standard of their respective mints, was five-and twenty percent against England. But the value of the current coin of England, as we learn from Mr. Lowndes, was at that time rather more than five-and-twenty percent below its standard value. The real exchange, therefore, may even at that time have been in favor of England, notwithstanding the computed exchange was so much against it; a smaller number or ounces of pure silver, actually paid in England, may have purchased a bill for a greater number of ounces of pure silver to be paid in Holland, and the man who was supposed to give, may in reality have got the premium. The French coin was, before the late reformation of the English gold coin, much less wore than the English, and was perhaps two or three percent nearer its standard. If the computed exchange with France, therefore, was not more than two or three percent against England, the real exchange might have been in its favor. Since the reformation of the gold coin, the exchange has been constantly in favor of England, and against France.

Secondly, in some countries the expense of coinage is defrayed by the government; in others, it is defrayed by the private people, who carry their bullion to the mint, and the government even derives some revenue from the coinage. In England it is defrayed by the government; and if you carry a pound weight of standard silver to the mint, you get back sixty-two shillings, containing a pound weight of the like standard silver. In France a duty of eight percent is deducted for the coinage, which not only defrays the expense of it, but affords a small revenue to the government. In England, as the coinage costs nothing, the current coin can never be much more valuable than the quantity of bullion which it actually contains. In France, the workmanship, as you pay for it, adds to the value, in the same manner as to that of wrought plate. A sum of French money, therefore, containing an equal weight of pure silver, is more valuable than a sum of English money containing an equal weight of pure silver, and must require more bullion, or other commodities, to purchase it. Though the current coin of the two countries, therefore, were equally near the standards of their respective mints, a sum of English money could not well purchase a sum of French money containing an equal number of ounces of pure silver, nor, consequently, a bill upon France for such a sum. If, for such a bill, no more additional money was paid than what was sufficient to compensate the expense of the French coinage, the real exchange might be at par between the two countries; their debts and credits might mutually compensate one another, while the computed exchange was considerably in favor of France. If less than this was paid, the real exchange might be in favor of England, while the computed was in favor of France.

Thirdly and lastly, in some places, as at Amsterdam, Hamburg, Venice, etc. foreign bills of exchange are paid in what they call bank money; while in others, as at London, Lisbon, Antwerp, Leghorn, etc. they are paid in the common currency of the country. What is called bank money, is always of more value than the same nominal sum of common currency. A thousand guilders in the bank of Amsterdam, for example, are of more value than a thousand guilders of Amsterdam currency. The difference between them is called the agio of the bank, which at Amsterdam is generally about five percent. Supposing the current money of the two countries equally near to the standard of their respective mints, and that the one pays foreign bills in this common currency, while the other pays them in bank money, it is evident that the computed exchange may be in favor of that which pays in bank money, though the real exchange should be in favor of that which pays in current money; for the same reason that the computed exchange may be in favor of that which pays in better money, or in money nearer to its own standard, though the real exchange should be in favor of that which pays in worse. The computed exchange, before the late reformation of the gold coin, was generally against London with Amsterdam, Hamburg, Venice, and, I believe, with all other places which pay in what is called bank money. It will by no means follow, however, that the real exchange was against it. Since the reformation of the gold coin, it has been in favor of London, even with those places. The computed exchange has generally been in favor of London with Lisbon, Antwerp, Leghorn, and, if you except France, I believe with most other parts of Europe that pay in common currency; and it is not improbable that the real exchange was so too.

Digression Concerning Banks of Deposit, Particularly Concerning That of Amsterdam.

The currency of a great state, such as France or England, generally consists almost entirely of its own coin. Should this currency, therefore, be at any time worn, clipt, or otherwise degraded below its standard value, the state, by a reformation of its coin, can effectually re-establish its currency. But the currency of a small state, such as Genoa or Hamburg, can seldom consist altogether in its own coin, but must be made up, in a great measure, of the coins of all the neighboring states with which its inhabitants have a continual intercourse. Such a state, therefore, by reforming its coin, will not always be able to reform its currency. If foreign bills of exchange are paid in this currency, the uncertain value of any sum, of what is in its own nature so uncertain, must render the exchange always very much against such a state, its currency being in all foreign states necessarily valued even below what it is worth.

In order to remedy the inconvenience to which this disadvantageous exchange must have subjected their merchants, such small states, when they began to attend to the interest of trade, have frequently enacted that foreign bills of exchange of a certain value should be paid, not in common currency, but by an order upon, or by a transfer in the books of a certain bank, established upon the credit, and under the protection of the state, this bank being always obliged to pay, in good and true money, exactly according to the standard of the state. The banks of Venice, Genoa, Amsterdam, Hamburg, and Nuremberg, seem to have been all originally established with this view, though some of them may have afterwards been made subservient to other purposes. The money of such banks, being better than the common currency of the country, necessarily bore an agio, which was greater or smaller, according as the currency was supposed to be more or less degraded below the standard of the state. The agio of the bank of Hamburg, for example, which is said to be commonly about fourteen percent is the supposed difference between the good standard money of the state, and the clipt, worn, and diminished currency, poured into it from all the neighboring states.

Before 1609, the great quantity of clipt and worn foreign coin which the extensive trade of Amsterdam brought from all parts of Europe, reduced the value of its currency about nine percent below that of good money fresh from the mint. Such money no sooner appeared, than it was melted down or carried away, as it always is in such circumstances. The merchants, with plenty of currency, could not always find a sufficient quantity of good money to pay their bills of exchange; and the value of those bills, in spite of several regulations which were made to prevent it, became in a great measure uncertain.

In order to remedy these inconveniencies, a bank was established in 1609, under the guarantee of the city. This bank received both foreign coin, and the light and worn coin of the country, at its real intrinsic value in the good standard money of the country, deducting only so much as was necessary for defraying the expense of coinage and the other necessary expense of management. For the value which remained after this small deduction was made, it gave a credit in its books. This credit was called bank money, which, as it represented money exactly according to the standard of the mint, was always of the same real value, and intrinsically worth more than current money. It was at the same time enacted, that all bills drawn upon or negotiated at Amsterdam, of the value of 600 guilders and upwards, should be paid in bank money, which at once took away all uncertainty in the value of those bills. Every merchant, in consequence of this regulation, was obliged to keep an account with the bank, in order to pay his foreign bills of exchange, which necessarily occasioned a certain demand for bank money.

Bank money, over and above both its intrinsic superiority to currency, and the additional value which this demand necessarily gives it, has likewise some other advantages, It is secure from fire, robbery, and other accidents; the city of Amsterdam is bound for it; it can be paid away by a simple transfer, without the trouble of counting, or the risk of transporting it from one place to another. In consequence of those different advantages, it seems from the beginning to have borne an agio; and it is generally believed that all the money originally deposited in the bank, was allowed to remain there, nobody caring to demand payment of a debt which he could sell for a premium in the market. By demanding payment of the bank, the owner of a bank credit would lose this premium. As a shilling fresh from the mint will buy no more goods in the market than one of our common worn shillings, so the good and true money which might be brought from the coffers of the bank into those of a private person, being mixed and confounded with the common currency of the country, would be of no more value than that currency, from which it could no longer be readily distinguished. While it remained in the coffers of the bank, its superiority was known and ascertained. When it had come into those of a private person, its superiority could not well be ascertained without more trouble than perhaps the difference was worth. By being brought from the coffers of the bank, besides, it lost all the other advantages of bank money; its security, its easy and safe transferability, its use in paying foreign bills of exchange. Over and above all this, it could not be brought from those coffers, as will appear by and by, without previously paying for the keeping.

Those deposits of coin, or those deposits which the bank was bound to restore in coin, constituted the original capital of the bank, or the whole value of what was represented by what is called bank money. At present they are supposed to constitute but a very small part of it. In order to facilitate the trade in bullion, the bank has been for these many years in the practice of giving credit in its books, upon deposits of gold and silver bullion. This credit is generally about five percent below the mint price of such bullion. The bank grants at the same time what is called a recipice or receipt, entitling the person who makes the deposit, or the bearer, to take out the bullion again at any time within six months, upon transferring to the bank a quantity of bank money equal to that for which credit had been given in its books when the deposit was made, and upon paying one-fourth percent for the keeping, if the deposit was in silver; and one-half percent if it was in gold; but at the same time declaring, that in default of such payment, and upon the expiration of this term, the deposit should belong to the bank, at the price at which it had been received, or for which credit had been given in the transfer books. What is thus paid for the keeping of the deposit may be considered as a sort of warehouse rent; and why this warehouse rent should be so much dearer for gold than for silver, several different reasons have been assigned. The fineness of gold, it has been said, is more difficult to be ascertained than that of silver. Frauds are more easily practiced, and occasion a greater loss in the most precious metal. Silver, besides, being the standard metal, the state, it has been said, wishes to encourage more the making of deposits of silver than those of gold.

Deposits of bullion are most commonly made when the price is somewhat lower than ordinary, and they are taken out again when it happens to rise. In Holland the market price of bullion is generally above the mint price, for the same reason that it was so in England before the late reformation of the gold coin. The difference is said to be commonly from about six to sixteen stivers upon the mark, or eight ounces of silver, of eleven parts of fine and one part alloy. The bank price, or the credit which the bank gives for the deposits of such silver (when made in foreign coin, of which the fineness is well known and ascertained, such as Mexico dollars), is twenty-two guilders the mark: the mint price is about twenty-three guilders, and the market price is from twenty-three guilders six, to twenty-three guilders sixteen stivers, or from two to three percent above the mint price.

The following are the prices at which the bank of Amsterdam at present {September 1775} receives bullion and coin of different kinds:
SILVER

	Guilders / mark	
Mexico dollars	22	
French crowns	22	
English silver coin	22	
Mexico dollars, new coin	21	10
Ducatoons	3	0
Rix-dollars	2	8

Bar silver, containing 11-12ths fine silver, 21 Guilders / mark, and in this proportion down to 1-4th fine, on which 5 guilders are given.

	Guilders / mark
Fine bars	28

GOLD

	Guilders / mark		
Portugal coin	310		
Guineas	310		
Louis d'ors, new	310		
Ditto, old	300		
New ducats	4	19	8 per ducat

Bar or ingot gold is received in proportion to its fineness, compared with the above foreign gold coin. Upon fine bars the bank gives 340 per mark. In general, however, something more is given upon coin of a known fineness, than upon gold and silver bars, of which the fineness cannot be ascertained but by a process of melting and assaying.

The proportions between the bank price, the mint price, and the market price of gold bullion, are nearly the same. A person can generally sell his receipt for the difference between the mint price of bullion and the market price. A receipt for bullion is almost always worth something, and it very seldom happens, therefore, that anybody suffers his receipts to expire, or allows his bullion to fall to the bank at the price at which it had been received, either by not taking it out before the end of the six months, or by neglecting to pay one fourth or one half percent in order to obtain a new receipt for another six months. This, however, though it happens seldom, is said to happen sometimes, and more frequently with regard to gold than with regard to silver, on account of the higher warehouse rent which is paid for the keeping of the more precious metal.

The person who, by making a deposit of bullion, obtains both a bank credit and a receipt, pays his bills of exchange as they become due, with his bank credit; and either sells or keeps his receipt, according as he judges that the price of bullion is likely to rise or to fall. The receipt and the bank credit seldom keep long together, and there is no occasion that they should. The person who has a receipt, and who wants to take out bullion, finds always plenty of bank credits, or bank money, to buy at the ordinary price, and the person who has bank money, and wants to take out bullion, finds receipts always in equal abundance.

The owners of bank credits, and the holders of receipts, constitute two different sorts of creditors against the bank. The holder of a receipt cannot draw out the bullion for which it is granted, without reassigning to the bank a sum of bank money equal to the price at which the bullion had been received. If he has no bank money of his own, he must purchase it of those who have it. The owner of bank money cannot draw out bullion, without producing to the bank receipts for the quantity which he wants. If he has none of his own, he must buy them of those who have them. The holder of a receipt, when he purchases bank money, purchases the power of taking out a quantity of bullion, of which the mint price is five percent above the bank price. The agio of five percent therefore, which he commonly pays for it, is paid, not for an imaginary, but for a real value. The owner of bank money, when he purchases a receipt, purchases the power of taking out a quantity of bullion, of which the market price is commonly from two to three percent above the mint price. The price which he pays for it, therefore, is paid likewise for a real value. The price of the receipt, and the price of the bank money, compound or make up between them the full value or price of the bullion.

Upon deposits of the coin current in the country, the bank grant receipts likewise, as well as bank credits; but those receipts are frequently of no value and will bring no price in the market. Upon ducatoons, for example, which in the currency pass for three guilders three stivers each, the bank gives a credit of three guilders only, or five percent below their current value. It grants a receipt likewise, entitling the bearer to take out the number of ducatoons deposited at any time within six months, upon paying one fourth percent for the keeping. This receipt will frequently bring no price in the market. Three guilders, bank money, generally sell in the market for three guilders three stivers, the full value of the ducatoons, if they were taken out of the bank; and before they can be taken out, one fourth percent must be paid for the keeping, which would be mere loss to the holder of the receipt. If the agio of the bank, however, should at any time fall to three percent such receipts might bring some price in the market, and might sell for one and three-fourths percent. But the agio of the bank being now generally about five percent such receipts are frequently allowed to expire, or, as they express it, to fall to the bank. The receipts which are given for deposits of gold ducats fall to it yet more frequently, because a higher warehouse rent, or one half percent must be paid for the keeping of them, before they can be taken out again. The five percent which the bank gains, when deposits either of coin or bullion are allowed to fall to it, maybe considered as the warehouse rent for the perpetual keeping of such deposits.

The sum of bank money, for which the receipts are expired, must be very considerable. It must comprehend the whole original capital of the bank, which, it is generally supposed, has been allowed to remain there from the time it was first deposited, nobody caring either to renew his receipt, or to take out his deposit, as, for the reasons already assigned, neither the one nor the other could be done without loss. But whatever may be the amount of this sum, the proportion which it bears to the whole mass of bank money is supposed to be very small. The bank of Amsterdam has, for these many years past, been the great warehouse of Europe for bullion, for which the receipts are very seldom allowed to expire, or, as they express it, to fall to the bank. The far greater part of the bank money, or of the credits upon the books of the bank, is supposed to have been created, for these many years past, by such deposits, which the dealers in bullion are continually both making and withdrawing.

No demand can be made upon the bank, but by means of a recipice or receipt. The smaller mass of bank money, for which the receipts are expired, is mixed and confounded with the much greater mass for which they are still in force; so that, though there may be a considerable sum of bank money, for which there are no receipts, there is no specific sum or portion of it which may not at any time be demanded by one. The bank cannot be debtor to two persons for the same thing; and the owner of bank money who has no receipt, cannot demand payment of the bank till he buys one. In ordinary and quiet times, he can find no difficulty in getting one to buy at the market price, which generally corresponds with the price at which he can sell the coin or bullion it entitles him to take out of the bank.

It might be otherwise during a public calamity; an invasion, for example, such as that of the French in 1672. The owners of bank money being then all eager to draw it out of the bank, in order to have it in their own keeping, the demand for receipts might raise their price to an exorbitant height. The holders of them might form extravagant expectations, and, instead of two or three percent demand half the bank money for which credit had been given upon the deposits that the receipts had respectively been granted for. The enemy, informed of the constitution of the bank, might even buy them up, in order to prevent the carrying away of the treasure. In such emergencies, the bank, it is supposed, would break through its ordinary rule of making payment only to the holders of receipts. The holders of receipts, who had no bank money, must have received within two or three percent of the value of the deposit for which their respective receipts had been granted. The bank, therefore, it is said, would in this case make no scruple of paying, either with money or bullion, the full value of what the owners of bank money, who could get no receipts, were credited for in its books; paying, at the same time, two or three percent to such holders of receipts as had no bank money, that being the whole value which, in this state of things, could justly be supposed due to them.

Even in ordinary and quiet times, it is the interest of the holders of receipts to depress the agio, in order either to buy bank money (and consequently the bullion which their receipts would then enable them to take out of the bank) so much cheaper, or to sell their receipts to those who have bank money, and who want to take out bullion, so much dearer; the price of a receipt being generally equal to the difference between the market price of bank money and that of the coin or bullion for which the receipt had been granted. It is the interest of the owners of bank money, on the contrary, to raise the agio, in order either to sell their bank money so much dearer, or to buy a receipt so much cheaper. To prevent the stock-jobbing tricks which those opposite interests might sometimes occasion, the bank has of late years come to the resolution, to sell at all times bank money for currency at five percent agio, and to buy it in again at four percent agio. In consequence of this resolution, the agio can never either rise above five, or sink below four percent; and the proportion between the market price of bank and that of current money is kept at all times very near the proportion between their intrinsic values. Before this resolution was taken, the market price of bank money used sometimes to rise so high as nine percent agio, and sometimes to sink so low as par, according as opposite interests happened to influence the market.

The bank of Amsterdam professes to lend out no part of what is deposited with it, but for every guilder for which it gives credit in its books, to keep in its repositories the value of a guilder either in money or bullion. That it keeps in its repositories all the money or bullion for which there are receipts in force for which it is at all times liable to be called upon, and which in reality is continually going from it, and returning to it again, cannot well be doubted. But whether it does so likewise with regard to that part of its capital for which the receipts are long ago expired, for which, in ordinary and quiet times, it cannot be called upon, and which, in reality, is very likely to remain with it for ever, or as long as the states of the United Provinces subsist, may perhaps appear more uncertain. At Amsterdam, however, no point of faith is better established than that, for every guilder circulated as bank money, there is a correspondent guilder in gold or silver to be found in the treasures of the bank. The city is guarantee that it should be so. The bank is under the direction of the four reigning burgomasters who are changed every year. Each new set of burgomasters visits the treasure, compares it with the books, receives it upon oath, and delivers it over, with the same awful solemnity to the set which succeeds; and in that sober and religious country, oaths are not yet disregarded. A rotation of this kind seems alone a sufficient security against any practices which cannot be avowed. Amidst all the revolutions which faction has ever occasioned in the government of Amsterdam, the prevailing party has at no time accused their predecessors of infidelity in the administration of the bank. No accusation could have affected more deeply the reputation and fortune of the disgraced party; and if such an accusation could have been supported, we may be assured that it would have been brought. In 1672, when the French king was at Utrecht, the bank of Amsterdam paid so readily, as left no doubt of the fidelity with which it had observed its engagements. Some of the pieces which were then brought from its repositories, appeared to have been scorched with the fire which happened in the town-house soon after the bank was established. Those pieces, therefore, must have lain there from that time.

What may be the amount of the treasure in the bank, is a question which has long employed the speculations of the curious. Nothing but conjecture can be offered concerning it. It is generally reckoned, that there are about 2000 people who keep accounts with the bank; and allowing them to have, one with another, the value of £1500 sterling lying upon their respective accounts (a very large allowance), the whole quantity of bank money, and consequently of treasure in the bank, will amount to about £3,000,000 sterling, or, at eleven guilders the pound sterling, 33,000,000 of guilders; a great sum, and sufficient to carry on a very extensive circulation, but vastly below the extravagant ideas which some people have formed of this treasure.

The city of Amsterdam derives a considerable revenue from the bank. Besides what may be called the warehouse rent above mentioned, each person, upon first opening an account with the bank, pays a fee of ten guilders; and for every new account, three guilders, three stivers; for every transfer, two stivers; and if the transfer is for less than 300 guilders, six stivers, in order to discourage the multiplicity of small transactions. The person who neglects to balance his account twice in the year, forfeits twenty-five guilders. The person who orders a transfer for more than is upon his account, is obliged to pay three percent for the sum overdrawn, and his order is set aside into the bargain. The bank is supposed, too, to make a considerable profit by the sale of the foreign coin or bullion which sometimes falls to it by the expiring of receipts, and which is always kept till it can be sold with advantage. It makes a profit, likewise, by selling bank money at five percent agio, and buying it in at four. These different emoluments amount to a good deal more than what is necessary for paying the salaries of officers, and defraying the expense of management. What is paid for the keeping of bullion upon receipts, is alone supposed to amount to a neat annual revenue of between 150,000 and 200,000 guilders. Public utility, however, and not revenue, was the original object of this institution. Its object was to relieve the merchants from the inconvenience of a disadvantageous exchange. The revenue which has arisen from it was unforeseen, and may be considered as accidental. But it is now time to return from this long digression, into which I have been insensibly led, in endeavoring to explain the reasons why the exchange between the countries which pay in what is called bank money, and those which pay in common currency, should generally appear to be in favor of the former, and against the latter. The former pay in a species of money, of which the intrinsic value is always the same, and exactly agreeable to the standard of their respective mints; the latter is a species of money, of which the intrinsic value is continually varying, and is almost always more or less below that standard.

Part II

Of the Unreasonableness of those Extraordinary Restraints, upon Other Principles

In the foregoing part of this chapter, I have endeavored to show, even upon the principles of the commercial system, how unnecessary it is to lay extraordinary restraints upon the importation of goods from those countries with which the balance of trade is supposed to be disadvantageous.

Nothing, however, can be more absurd than this whole doctrine of the balance of trade, upon which, not only these restraints, but almost all the other regulations of commerce, are founded. When two places trade with one another, this doctrine supposes that, if the balance be even, neither of them either loses or gains; but if it leans in any degree to one side, that one of them loses, and the other gains, in proportion to its declension from the exact equilibrium. Both suppositions are false. A trade, which is forced by means of bounties and monopolies, may be, and commonly is, disadvantageous to the country in whose favor it is meant to be established, as I shall endeavor to show hereafter. But that trade which, without force or constraint, is naturally and regularly carried on between any two places, is always advantageous, though not always equally so, to both.

By advantage or gain, I understand, not the increase of the quantity of gold and silver, but that of the exchangeable value of the annual produce of the land and labor of the country, or the increase of the annual revenue of its inhabitants.

If the balance be even, and if the trade between the two places consist altogether in the exchange of their native commodities, they will, upon most occasions, not only both gain, but they will gain equally, or very nearly equally; each will, in this case, afford a market for a part of the surplus produce of the other; each will replace a capital which had been employed in raising and preparing for the market this part of the surplus produce of the other, and which had been distributed among, and given revenue and maintenance to, a certain number of its inhabitants. Some part of the inhabitants of each, therefore, will directly derive their revenue and maintenance from the other. As the commodities exchanged, too, are supposed to be of equal value, so the two capitals employed in the trade will, upon most occasions, be equal, or very nearly equal; and both being employed in raising the native commodities of the two countries, the revenue and maintenance which their distribution will afford to the inhabitants of each will be equal, or very nearly equal. This revenue and maintenance, thus mutually afforded, will be greater or smaller, in proportion to the extent of their dealings. If these should annually amount to £100,000, for example, or to £1,000,000, on each side, each of them will afford an annual revenue, in the one case, of £100,000, and, in the other, of £1,000,000, to the inhabitants of the other.

If their trade should be of such a nature, that one of them exported to the other nothing but native commodities, while the returns of that other consisted altogether in foreign goods; the balance, in this case, would still be supposed even, commodities being paid for with commodities. They would, in this case too, both gain, but they would not gain equally; and the inhabitants of the country which exported nothing but native commodities, would derive the greatest revenue from the trade. If England, for example, should import from France nothing but the native commodities of that country, and not having such commodities of its own as were in demand there, should annually repay them by sending thither a large quantity of foreign goods, tobacco, we shall suppose, and East India goods; this trade, though it would give some revenue to the inhabitants of both countries, would give more to those of France than to those of England. The whole French capital annually employed in it would annually be distributed among the people of France; but that part of the English capital only, which was employed in producing the English commodities with which those foreign goods were purchased, would be annually distributed among the people of England. The greater part of it would replace the capitals which had been employed in Virginia, Indostan, and China, and which had given revenue and maintenance to the inhabitants of those distant countries. If the capitals were equal, or nearly equal, therefore, this employment of the French capital would augment much more the revenue of the people of France, than that of the English capital would the revenue of the people of England. France would, in this case, carry on a direct foreign trade of consumption with England; whereas England would carry on a roundabout trade of the same kind with France. The different effects of a capital employed in the direct, and of one employed in the roundabout foreign trade of consumption, have already been fully explained.

There is not, probably, between any two countries, a trade which consists altogether in the exchange, either of native commodities on both sides, or of native commodities on one side, and of foreign goods on the other. Almost all countries exchange with one another, partly native and partly foreign goods. That country, however, in whose cargoes there is the greatest proportion of native, and the least of foreign goods, will always be the principal gainer.

If it was not with tobacco and East India goods, but with gold and silver, that England paid for the commodities annually imported from France, the balance, in this case, would be supposed uneven, commodities not being paid for with commodities, but with gold and silver. The trade, however, would in this case, as in the foregoing, give some revenue to the inhabitants of both countries, but more to those of France than to those of England. It would give some revenue to those of England. The capital which had been employed in producing the English goods that purchased this gold and silver, the capital which had been distributed among, and given revenue to, certain inhabitants of England, would thereby be replaced, and enabled to continue that employment. The whole capital of England would no more be diminished by this exportation of gold and silver, than by the exportation of an equal value of any other goods. On the contrary, it would, in most cases, be augmented. No goods are sent abroad but those for which the demand is supposed to be greater abroad than at home, and of which the returns, consequently, it is expected, will be of more value at home than the commodities exported. If the tobacco which in England is worth only £100,000, when sent to France, will purchase wine which is in England worth £110,000, the exchange will augment the capital of England by £10,000. If £100,000 of English gold, in the same manner, purchases French wine, which in England is worth £110,000, this exchange will equally augment the cap-

338 THE REAL PRICE OF EVERYTHING

ital of England by £10,000. As a merchant, who has £110,000 worth of wine in his cellar, is a richer man than he who has only £100,000 worth of tobacco in his warehouse, so is he likewise a richer man than he who has only £100,000 worth of gold in his coffers. He can put into motion a greater quantity of industry, and give revenue, maintenance, and employment, to a greater number of people, than either of the other two. But the capital of the country is equal to the capital of all its different inhabitants; and the quantity of industry which can be annually maintained in it is equal to what all those different capitals can maintain. Both the capital of the country, therefore, and the quantity of industry which can be annually maintained in it, must generally be augmented by this exchange. It would, indeed, be more advantageous for England that it could purchase the wines of France with its own hardware and broad cloth, than with either the tobacco of Virginia, or the gold and silver of Brazil and Peru. A direct foreign trade of consumption is always more advantageous than a roundabout one. But a roundabout foreign trade of consumption, which is carried on with gold and silver, does not seem to be less advantageous than any other equally roundabout one. Neither is a country which has no mines, more likely to be exhausted of gold and silver by this annual exportation of those metals, than one which does not grow tobacco by the like annual exportation of that plant. As a country which has wherewithal to buy tobacco will never be long in want of it, so neither will one be long in want of gold and silver which has wherewithal to purchase those metals.

It is a losing trade, it is said, which a workman carries on with the alehouse; and the trade which a manufacturing nation would naturally carry on with a wine country, may be considered as a trade of the same nature. I answer, that the trade with the alehouse is not necessarily a losing trade. In its own nature it is just as advantageous as any other, though, perhaps, somewhat more liable to be abused. The employment of a brewer, and even that of a retailer of fermented liquors, are as necessary divisions of labor as any other. It will generally be more advantageous for a workman to buy of the brewer the quantity he has occasion for, than to brew it himself; and if he is a poor workman, it will generally be more advantageous for him to buy it by little and little of the retailer, than a large quantity of the brewer. He may no doubt buy too much of either, as he may of any other dealers in his neighborhood; of the butcher, if he is a glutton; or of the draper, if he affects to be a beau among his companions. It is advantageous to the great body of workmen, notwithstanding, that all these trades should be free, though this freedom may be abused in all of them, and is more likely to be so, perhaps, in some than in others.

Though individuals, besides, may sometimes ruin their fortunes by an excessive consumption of fermented liquors, there seems to be no risk that a nation should do so. Though in every country there are many people who spend upon such liquors more than they can afford, there are always many more who spend less. It deserves to be remarked, too, that if we consult experience, the cheapness of wine seems to be a cause, not of drunkenness, but of sobriety. The inhabitants of the wine countries are in general the soberest people of Europe; witness the Spaniards, the Italians, and the inhabitants of the southern provinces of France. People are seldom guilty of excess in what is their daily fare. Nobody affects the character of liberality and good fellowship, by being profuse of a liquor which is as cheap as small beer. On the contrary, in the countries which, either from excessive heat or cold, produce no grapes, and where wine consequently is dear and a rarity, drunkenness is a common vice, as among the northern nations, and all those who live between the tropics, the negroes, for example on the coast of Guinea. When a French regiment comes from some of the northern provinces of France, where wine is somewhat dear, to be quartered in the southern, where it is very cheap, the soldiers, I have frequently heard it observed, are at first debauched by the cheapness and novelty of good wine; but after a few months residence, the greater part of them become as sober as the rest of the inhabitants. Were the duties upon foreign wines, and the excises upon malt, beer, and ale, to be taken away all at once, it might, in the same manner, occasion in Great Britain a pretty general and temporary drunkenness among the middling and inferior ranks of people, which would probably be soon followed by a permanent and almost universal sobriety. At present, drunkenness is by no means the vice of people of fashion, or of those who can easily afford the most expensive liquors. A gentleman drunk with ale has scarce ever been seen among us. The restraints upon the wine trade in Great Britain, besides, do not so much seem calculated to hinder the people from going, if I may say so, to the alehouse, as from going where they can buy the best and cheapest liquor. They favor the wine trade of Portugal, and discourage that of France. The Portuguese, it is said, indeed, are better customers for our manufactures than the French, and should therefore be encouraged in preference to them. As they give us their custom, it is pretended we should give them ours. The sneaking arts of underling tradesmen are thus erected into political maxims for the conduct of a great empire; for it is the most underling tradesmen only who make it a rule to employ chiefly their own customers. A great trader purchases his goods always where they are cheapest and best, without regard to any little interest of this kind.

By such maxims as these, however, nations have been taught that their interest consisted in beggaring all their neighbors. Each nation has been made to look with an invidious eye upon the prosperity of all the nations with which it trades, and to consider their gain as its own loss. Commerce, which ought naturally to be, among nations as among individuals, a bond of union and friendship, has become the most fertile source of discord and animosity. The capricious ambition of kings and ministers has not, during the present and the preceding century, been more fatal to the repose of Europe, than the impertinent jealousy of merchants and manufacturers. The violence and injustice of the rulers of mankind is an ancient evil, for which, I am afraid, the nature of human affairs can scarce admit of a remedy: but the mean rapacity, the monopolizing spirit, of merchants and manufacturers, who neither are, nor ought to be, the rulers of mankind, though it cannot, perhaps, be corrected, may very easily be prevented from disturbing the tranquility of anybody but themselves.

That it was the spirit of monopoly which originally both invented and propagated this doctrine, cannot be doubted and they who first taught it, were by no means such fools as they who believed it. In every country it always is, and must be, the interest of the great body of the people, to buy whatever they want of those who sell it cheapest. The proposition is so very manifest, that it seems ridiculous to take any pains to prove it; nor could it ever have been called in question, had not the interested sophistry of merchants and manufacturers confounded the common sense of mankind. Their interest is, in this respect, directly opposite to that of the great body of the people. As it is the interest of the freemen of a corporation to hinder the rest of the inhabitants from employing any workmen but themselves; so it is the interest of the merchants and manufacturers of every country to secure to themselves the monopoly of the home market. Hence, in Great Britain, and in most other European countries, the extraordinary duties upon almost all goods imported by alien merchants. Hence the high duties and prohibitions upon all those foreign manufactures which can come into competition with our own. Hence, too, the extraordinary restraints upon the importation of almost all sorts of goods from those countries with which the balance of trade is supposed to be disadvantageous; that is, from those against whom national animosity happens to be most violently inflamed.

The wealth of neighboring nations, however, though dangerous in war and politics, is certainly advantageous in trade. In a state of hostility, it may enable our enemies to maintain fleets and armies superior to our own; but in a state of peace and commerce it must likewise enable them to exchange with us to a greater value, and to afford a better market, either for the immediate produce of our own industry, or for whatever is purchased with that produce. As a rich man is likely to be a better customer to the industrious people in his neighborhood, than a poor, so is likewise a rich nation. A rich man, indeed, who is himself a manufacturer, is a very dangerous neighbor to all those who deal in the same way. All the rest of the neighborhood, however, by far the greatest number, profit by the good market which his expense affords them. They even profit by his underselling the poorer workmen who deal in the same way with him. The manufacturers of a rich nation, in the same manner, may no doubt be very dangerous rivals to those of their neighbors. This very competition, however, is advantageous to the great body of the people, who profit greatly, besides, by the good market which the great expense of such a nation affords them in every other way. Private people, who want to make a fortune, never think of retiring to the remote and poor provinces of the country, but resort either to the capital, or to some of the great commercial towns. They know, that where little wealth circulates, there is little to be got; but that where a great deal is in motion, some share of it may fall to them. The same maxim which would in this manner direct the common sense of one, or ten, or twenty individuals, should regulate the judgment of one, or ten, or twenty millions, and should make a whole nation regard the riches of its neighbors, as a probable cause and occasion for itself to acquire riches. A nation that would enrich itself by foreign trade, is certainly most likely to do so, when its neighbors are all rich, industrious, and commercial nations. A great nation, surrounded on all sides by wandering savages and poor barbarians, might, no doubt, acquire riches by the cultivation of its own lands, and by its own interior commerce, but not by foreign trade. It seems to have been in this manner that the ancient Egyptians and the modern Chinese acquired their great wealth. The ancient Egyptians, it is said, neglected foreign commerce, and the modern Chinese, it is known, hold it in the utmost contempt, and scarce deign to afford it the decent protection of the laws. The modern maxims of foreign commerce, by aiming at the impoverishment of all our neighbors, so far as they are capable of producing their intended effect, tend to render that very commerce insignificant and contemptible.

It is in consequence of these maxims, that the commerce between France and England has, in both countries, been subjected to so many discouragements and restraints. If those two countries, however, were to consider their real interest, without either mercantile jealousy or national animosity, the commerce of France might be more advantageous to Great Britain than that of any other country, and, for the same reason, that of Great Britain to France. France is the nearest neighbor to Great Britain. In the trade between the southern coast of England and the northern and northwestern coast of France, the returns might be expected, in the same manner as in the inland trade, four, five, or six times in the year. The capital, therefore, employed in this trade could, in each of the two countries, keep in motion four, five, or six times the quantity of industry, and afford employment and subsistence to four, five, or six times the number of people, which all equal capital could do in the greater part of the other branches of foreign trade. Between the parts of France and Great Britain most remote from one another, the returns might be expected, at least, once in the year; and even this trade would so far be at least equally advantageous, as the greater part of the other branches of our foreign European trade. It would be, at least, three times more advantageous than the boasted trade with our North American colonies, in which the returns were seldom made in less than three years, frequently not in less than four or five years. France, besides, is supposed to contain 24,000,000 of inhabitants. Our North American colonies were never supposed to contain more than 3,000,000; and France is a much richer country than North America; though, on account of the more unequal distribution of riches, there is much more poverty and beggary in the one country than in the other. France, therefore, could afford a market at least eight times more extensive, and, on account of the superior frequency of the returns, four-and-twenty times more advantageous than that which our North American colonies ever afforded. The trade of Great Britain would be just as advantageous to France, and, in proportion to the wealth, population, and proximity of the respective countries, would have the same superiority over that which France carries on with her own colonies. Such is the very great difference between that trade which the wisdom of both nations has thought proper to discourage, and that which it has favored the most.

But the very same circumstances which would have rendered an open and free commerce between the two countries so advantageous to both, have occasioned the principal obstructions to that commerce. Being neighbors, they are necessarily enemies, and the wealth and power of each becomes, upon that account, more formidable to the other; and what would increase the advantage of national friendship, serves only to inflame the violence of national animosity. They are both rich and industrious nations; and the merchants and manufacturers of each dread the competition of the skill and activity of those of the other. Mercantile jealousy is excited, and both inflames, and is itself inflamed, by the violence of national animosity, and the traders of both countries have announced, with all the passionate confidence of interested falsehood, the certain ruin of each, in consequence of that unfavorable balance of trade, which, they pretend, would be the infallible effect of an unrestrained commerce with the other.

There is no commercial country in Europe, of which the approaching ruin has not frequently been foretold by the pretended doctors of this system, from all unfavorably balance of trade. After all the anxiety, however, which they have excited about this, after all the vain attempts of almost all trading nations to turn that balance in their own favor, and against their neighbors, it does not appear that any one nation in Europe has been, in any respect, impoverished by this cause. Every town and country, on the contrary, in proportion as they have opened their ports to all nations, instead of being ruined by this free trade, as the principles of the commercial system would lead us to expect, have been enriched by it. Though there are in Europe indeed, a few towns which, in same respects, deserve the name of free ports, there is no country which does so. Holland, perhaps, approaches the nearest to this character of any, though still very remote from it; and Holland, it is acknowledged, not only derives its whole wealth, but a great part of its necessary subsistence, from foreign trade.

There is another balance, indeed, which has already been explained, very different from the balance of trade, and which, according as it happens to be either favorable or unfavorable, necessarily occasions the prosperity or decay of every nation. This is the balance of the annual produce and consumption. If the exchangeable value of the annual produce, it has already been observed, exceeds that of the annual consumption, the capital of the society must annually increase in proportion to this excess. The society in this case lives within its revenue; and what is annually saved out of its revenue, is naturally added to its capital, and employed so as to increase still further the annual produce. If the exchangeable value of the annual produce, on the contrary, fall short of the annual consumption, the capital of the society must annually decay in proportion to this deficiency. The expense of the society, in this case, exceeds its revenue, and necessarily encroaches upon its capital. Its capital, therefore, must necessarily decay, and, together with it, the exchangeable value of the annual produce of its industry.

This balance of produce and consumption is entirely different from what is called the balance of trade. It might take place in a nation which had no foreign trade, but which was entirely separated from all the world. It may take place in the whole globe of the earth, of which the wealth, population, and improvement, may be either gradually increasing or gradually decaying.

The balance of produce and consumption may be constantly in favor of a nation, though what is called the balance of trade be generally against it. A nation may import to a greater value than it exports for half a century, perhaps, together; the gold and silver which comes into it during all this time, may be all immediately sent out of it; its circulating coin may gradually decay, different sorts of paper money being substituted in its place, and even the debts, too, which it contracts in the principal nations with whom it deals, may be gradually increasing; and yet its real wealth, the exchangeable value of the annual produce of its lands and labor, may, during the same period, have been increasing in a much greater proportion. The state of our North American colonies, and of the trade which they carried on with Great Britain, before the commencement of the present disturbances, {This paragraph was written in the year 1775.} may serve as a proof that this is by no means an impossible supposition.

CHAPTER IV

Of Drawbacks

Merchants and manufacturers are not contented with the monopoly of the home market, but desire likewise the most extensive foreign sale for their goods. Their country has no jurisdiction in foreign nations, and therefore can seldom procure them any monopoly there. They are generally obliged, therefore, to content themselves with petitioning for certain encouragements to exportation.

Of these encouragements, what are called drawbacks seem to be the most reasonable. To allow the merchant to draw back upon exportation, either the whole, or a part of whatever excise or inland duty is imposed upon domestic industry, can never occasion the exportation of a greater quantity of goods than what would have been exported had no duty been imposed. Such encouragements do not tend to turn towards any particular employment a greater share of the capital of the country, than what would go to that employment of its own accord, but only to hinder the duty from driving away any part of that share to other employments. They tend not to overturn that balance which naturally establishes itself among all the various employments of the society, but to hinder it from being overturned by the duty. They tend not to destroy, but to preserve, what it is in most cases advantageous to preserve, the natural division and distribution of labor in the society.

The same thing may be said of the drawbacks upon the re-exportation of foreign goods imported, which, in Great Britain, generally amount to by much the largest part of the duty upon importation. By the second of the rules, annexed to the act of Parliament, which imposed what is now called the old subsidy, every merchant, whether English or alien, was allowed to draw back half that duty upon exportation; the English merchant, provided the exportation took place within twelve months; the alien, provided it took place within nine months. Wines, currants, and wrought silks, were the only goods which did not fall within this rule, having other and more advantageous allowances. The duties imposed by this act of parliament were, at that time, the only duties upon the importation of foreign goods. The term within which this, and all other drawbacks could be claimed, was afterwards (by 7th Geo. I. chap. 21, sect. 10.) extended to three years.

The duties which have been imposed since the old subsidy, are, the greater part of them, wholly drawn back upon exportation. This general rule, however, is liable to a great number of exceptions; and the doctrine of drawbacks has become a much less simple matter than it was at their first institution.

Upon the exportation of some foreign goods, of which it was expected that the importation would greatly exceed what was necessary for the home consumption, the whole duties are drawn back, without retaining even half the old subsidy. Before the revolt of our North American colonies, we had the monopoly of the tobacco of Maryland and Virginia. We imported about ninety-six thousand hogsheads, and the home consumption was not supposed to exceed fourteen thousand. To facilitate the great exportation which was necessary, in order to rid us of the rest, the whole duties were drawn back, provided the exportation took place within three years.

We still have, though not altogether, yet very nearly, the monopoly of the sugars of our West Indian islands. If sugars are exported within a year, therefore, all the duties upon importation are drawn back; and if exported within three years, all the duties, except half the old subsidy, which still continues to be retained upon the exportation of the greater part of goods. Though the importation of sugar exceeds a good deal what is necessary for the home consumption, the excess is inconsiderable, in comparison of what it used to be in tobacco.

Some goods, the particular objects of the jealousy of our own manufacturers, are prohibited to be imported for home consumption. They may, however, upon paying certain duties, be imported and warehoused for exportation. But upon such exportation no part of these duties is drawn back. Our manufacturers are unwilling, it seems, that even this restricted importation should be encouraged, and are afraid lest some part of these goods should be stolen out of the warehouse, and thus come into competition with their own. It is under these regulations only that we can import wrought silks, French cambrics and lawns, calicoes, painted, printed, stained, or dyed, etc.

We are unwilling even to be the carriers of French goods, and choose rather to forego a profit to ourselves than to suffer those whom we consider as our enemies to make any profit by our means. Not only half the old subsidy, but the second twenty-five percent is retained upon the exportation of all French goods.

By the fourth of the rules annexed to the old subsidy, the drawback allowed upon the exportation of all wines amounted to a great deal more than half the duties which were at that time paid upon their importation; and it seems at that time to have been the object of the legislature to give somewhat more than ordinary encouragement to the carrying trade in wine. Several of the other duties, too, which were imposed either at the same time or subsequent to the old subsidy, what is called the additional duty, the new subsidy, the one-third and two-thirds subsidies, the impost 1692, the tonnage on wine, were allowed to be wholly drawn back upon exportation. All those duties, however, except the additional duty and impost 1692, being paid down in ready money upon importation, the interest of so large a sum occasioned an expense, which made it unreasonable to expect any profitable carrying trade in this article. Only a part, therefore of the duty called the impost on wine, and no part of the twenty-five pounds the ton upon French wines, or of the duties imposed in 1745, in 1763, and in 1778, were allowed to be drawn back upon exportation. The two imposts of five percent imposed in 1779 and 1781, upon all the former duties of customs, being allowed to be wholly drawn back upon the exportation of all other goods, were likewise allowed to be drawn back upon that of wine. The last duty that has been particularly imposed upon wine, that of 1780, is allowed to be wholly drawn back; an indulgence which, when so many heavy duties are retained, most probably could never occasion the exportation of a single ton of wine. These rules took place with regard to all places of lawful exportation, except the British colonies in America.

The 15th Charles II, chap. 7, called an act for the encouragement of trade, had given Great Britain the monopoly of supplying the colonies with all the commodities of the growth or manufacture of Europe, and consequently with wines. In a country of so extensive a coast as our North American and West Indian colonies, where our authority was always so very slender, and where the inhabitants were allowed to carry out in their own ships their non-enumerated commodities, at first to all parts of Europe, and afterwards to all parts of Europe south of Cape Finisterre, it is not very probable that this monopoly could ever be much respected; and they probably at all times found means of bringing back some cargo from the countries to which they were allowed to carry out one. They seem, however, to have found some difficulty in importing European wines from the places of their growth; and they could not well import them from Great Britain, where they were loaded with many heavy duties, of which a considerable part was not drawn back upon exportation. Madeira wine, not being an European commodity, could be imported directly into America and the West Indies, countries which, in all their non-enumerated commodities, enjoyed a free trade to the island of Madeira. These circumstances had probably introduced that general taste for Madeira wine, which our officers found established in all our colonies at the commencement of the war which began in 1755, and which they brought back with them to the mother country, where that wine had not been much in fashion before. Upon the conclusion of that war, in 1763 (by the 4th Geo. III, chap. 15, sect. 12), all the duties except £3, 10s. were allowed to be drawn back upon the exportation to the colonies of all wines, except French wines, to the commerce and consumption of which national prejudice would allow no sort of encouragement. The period between the granting of this indulgence and the revolt of our North American colonies, was probably too short to admit of any considerable change in the customs of those countries.

The same act which, in the drawbacks upon all wines, except French wines, thus favored the colonies so much more than other countries, in those upon the greater part of other commodities, favored them much less. Upon the exportation of the greater part of commodities to other countries, half the old subsidy was drawn back. But this law enacted, that no part of that duty should be drawn back upon the exportation to the colonies of any commodities of the growth or manufacture either of Europe or the East Indies, except wines, white calicoes, and muslins.

Drawbacks were, perhaps, originally granted for the encouragement of the carrying trade, which, as the freight of the ship is frequently paid by foreigners in money, was supposed to be peculiarly fitted for bringing gold and silver into the country. But though the carrying trade certainly deserves no peculiar encouragement, though the motive of the institution was, perhaps, abundantly foolish, the institution itself seems reasonable enough. Such drawbacks cannot force into this trade a greater share of the capital of the country than what would have gone to it of its own accord, had there been no duties upon importation; they only prevent its being excluded altogether by those duties. The carrying trade, though it deserves no preference, ought not to be precluded, but to be left free, like all other trades. It is a necessary resource to those capitals which cannot find employment, either in the agriculture or in the manufactures of the country, either in its home trade, or in its foreign trade of consumption.

The revenue of the customs, instead of suffering, profits from such drawbacks, by that part of the duty which is retained. If the whole duties had been retained, the foreign goods upon which they are paid could seldom have been exported, nor consequently imported, for want of a market. The duties, therefore, of which a part is retained, would never have been paid.

These reasons seem sufficient to justify drawbacks, and would justify them, though the whole duties, whether upon the produce of domestic industry or upon foreign goods, were always drawn back upon exportation. The revenue of excise would, in this case indeed, suffer a little, and that of the customs a good deal more; but the natural balance of industry, the natural division and distribution of labor, which is always more or less disturbed by such duties, would be more nearly re-established by such a regulation.

These reasons, however, will justify drawbacks only upon exporting goods to those countries which are altogether foreign and independent, not to those in which our merchants and manufacturers enjoy a monopoly. A drawback, for example, upon the exportation of European goods to our American colonies, will not always occasion a greater exportation than what would have taken place without it. By means of the monopoly which our merchants and manufacturers enjoy there, the same quantity might frequently, perhaps, be sent thither, though the whole duties were retained. The drawback, therefore, may frequently be pure loss to the revenue of excise and customs, without altering the state of the trade, or rendering it in any respect more extensive. How far such drawbacks can be justified as a proper encouragement to the industry of our colonies, or how far it is advantageous to the mother country that they should be exempted from taxes which are paid by all the rest of their fellow-subjects, will appear hereafter, when I come to treat of colonies.

Drawbacks, however, it must always be understood, are useful only in those cases in which the goods, for the exportation of which they are given, are really exported to some foreign country, and not clandestinely re-imported into our own. That some drawbacks, particularly those upon tobacco, have frequently been abused in this manner, and have given occasion to many frauds, equally hurtful both to the revenue and to the fair trader, is well known.

CHAPTER V

Of Bounties

Bounties upon exportation are, in Great Britain, frequently petitioned for, and sometimes granted, to the produce of particular branches of domestic industry. By means of them, our merchants and manufacturers, it is pretended, will be enabled to sell their goods as cheap or cheaper than their rivals in the foreign market. A greater quantity, it is said, will thus be exported, and the balance of trade consequently turned more in favor of our own country. We cannot give our workmen a monopoly in the foreign, as we have done in the home market. We cannot force foreigners to buy their goods, as we have done our own countrymen. The next best expedient, it has been thought, therefore, is to pay them for buying. It is in this manner that the mercantile system proposes to enrich the whole country, and to put money into all our pockets, by means of the balance of trade.

Bounties, it is allowed, ought to be given to those branches of trade only which cannot be carried on without them. But every branch of trade in which the merchant can sell his goods for a price which replaces to him, with the ordinary profits of stock, the whole capital employed in preparing and sending them to market, can be carried on without a bounty. Every such branch is evidently upon a level with all the other branches of trade which are carried on without bounties, and cannot, therefore, require one more than they. Those trades only require bounties, in which the merchant is obliged to sell his goods for a price which does not replace to him his capital, together with the ordinary profit, or in which he is obliged to sell them for less than it really cost him to send them to market. The bounty is given in order to make up this loss, and to encourage him to continue, or, perhaps, to begin a trade, of which the expense is supposed to be greater than the returns, of which every operation eats up a part of the capital employed in it, and which is of such a nature, that if all other trades resembled it, there would soon be no capital left in the country.

The trades, it is to be observed, which are carried on by means of bounties, are the only ones which can be carried on between two nations for any considerable time together, in such a manner as that one of them shall always and regularly lose, or sell its goods for less than it really cost to send them to market. But if the bounty did not repay to the merchant what he would otherwise lose upon the price of his goods, his own interest would soon oblige him to employ his stock in another way, or to find out a trade in which the price of the goods would replace to him, with the ordinary profit, the capital employed in sending them to market. The effect of bounties, like that of all the other expedients of the mercantile system, can only be to force the trade of a country into a channel much less advantageous than that in which it would naturally run of its own accord.

The ingenious and well-informed author of the *Tracts upon the Corn Trade* has shown very clearly, that since the bounty upon the exportation of corn was first established, the price of the corn exported, valued moderately enough, has exceeded that of the corn imported, valued very high, by a much greater sum than the amount of the whole bounties which have been paid during that period. This, he imagines, upon the true principles of the mercantile system, is a clear proof that this forced corn trade is beneficial to the nation, the value of the exportation exceeding that of the importation by a much greater sum than the whole extraordinary expense which the public has been at in order to get it exported. He does not consider that this extraordinary expense, or the bounty, is the smallest part of the expense which the exportation of corn really costs the society. The capital which the farmer employed in raising it must likewise be taken into the account. Unless the price of the corn, when sold in the foreign markets, replaces not only the bounty, but this capital, together with the ordinary profits of stock, the society is a loser by the difference, or the national stock is so much diminished. But the very reason for which it has been thought necessary to grant a bounty, is the supposed insufficiency of the price to do this.

The average price of corn, it has been said, has fallen considerably since the establishment of the bounty. That the average price of corn began to fall somewhat towards the end of the last century, and has continued to do so during the course of the sixty-four first years of the present, I have already endeavored to show. But this event, supposing it to be real, as I believe it to be, must have happened in spite of the bounty, and cannot possibly have happened in consequence of it. It has happened in France, as well as in England, though in France there was not only no bounty, but, till 1764, the exportation of corn was subjected to a general prohibition. This gradual fall in the average price of grain, it is probable, therefore, is ultimately owing neither to the one regulation nor to the other, but to that gradual and insensible rise in the real value of silver, which, in the first book of this discourse, I have endeavored to show, has taken place in the general market of Europe during the course of the present century. It seems to be altogether impossible that the bounty could ever contribute to lower the price of grain.

In years of plenty, it has already been observed, the bounty, by occasioning an extraordinary exportation, necessarily keeps up the price of corn in the home market above what it would naturally fall to. To do so was the avowed purpose of the institution. In years of scarcity, though the bounty is frequently suspended, yet the great exportation which it occasions in years of plenty, must frequently hinder, more or less, the plenty of one year from relieving the scarcity of another. Both in years of plenty and in years of scarcity, therefore, the bounty necessarily tends to raise the money price of corn somewhat higher than it otherwise would be in the home market.

That in the actual state of tillage the bounty must necessarily have this tendency, will not, I apprehend, be disputed by any reasonable person. But it has been thought by many people, that it tends to encourage tillage, and that in two different ways; first, by opening a more extensive foreign market to the corn of the farmer, it tends, they imagine, to increase the demand for, and consequently the production of, that commodity; and, secondly, by securing to him a better price than he could otherwise expect in the actual state of tillage, it tends, they suppose, to encourage tillage. This double encouragement must, they imagine, in a long period of years, occasion such an increase in the production of corn, as may lower its price in the home market, much more than the bounty can raise it in the actual state which tillage may, at the end of that period, happen to be in.

I answer, that whatever extension of the foreign market can be occasioned by the bounty must, in every particular year, be altogether at the expense of the home market;

as every bushel of corn, which is exported by means of the bounty, and which would not have been exported without the bounty, would have remained in the home market to increase the consumption, and to lower the price of that commodity. The corn bounty, it is to be observed, as well as every other bounty upon exportation, imposes two different taxes upon the people; first, the tax which they are obliged to contribute, in order to pay the bounty; and, secondly, the tax which arises from the advanced price of the commodity in the home market, and which, as the whole body of the people are purchasers of corn, must, in this particular commodity, be paid by the whole body of the people. In this particular commodity, therefore, this second tax is by much the heaviest of the two. Let us suppose that, taking one year with another, the bounty of 5s. upon the exportation of the quarter of wheat raises the price of that commodity in the home market only 6d. the bushel, or 4s. the quarter higher than it otherwise would have been in the actual state of the crop. Even upon this very moderate supposition, the great body of the people, over and above contributing the tax which pays the bounty of 5s. upon every quarter of wheat exported, must pay another of 4s. upon every quarter which they themselves consume. But according to the very well informed author of the *Tracts upon the Corn Trade*, the average proportion of the corn exported to that consumed at home, is not more than that of one to thirty-one. For every 5s. therefore, which they contribute to the payment of the first tax, they must contribute £6:4s. to the payment of the second. So very heavy a tax upon the first necessary of life must either reduce the subsistence of the laboring poor, or it must occasion some augmentation in their pecuniary wages, proportional to that in the pecuniary price of their subsistence. So far as it operates in the one way, it must reduce the ability of the laboring poor to educate and bring up their children, and must, so far, tend to restrain the population of the country. So far as it operates in the other, it must reduce the ability of the employers of the poor, to employ so great a number as they otherwise might do, and must so far tend to restrain the industry of the country. The extraordinary exportation of corn, therefore occasioned by the bounty, not only in every particular year diminishes the home, just as much as it extends the foreign market and consumption, but, by restraining the population and industry of the country, its final tendency is to stint and restrain the gradual extension of the home market; and thereby, in the long-run, rather to diminish than to augment the whole market and consumption of corn.

This enhancement of the money price of corn, however, it has been thought, by rendering that commodity more profitable to the farmer, must necessarily encourage its production.

I answer that this might be the case, if the effect of the bounty was to raise the real price of corn, or to enable the farmer, with an equal quantity of it, to maintain a greater number of laborers in the same manner, whether liberal, moderate, or scanty, than other laborers are commonly maintained in his neighborhood. But neither the bounty, it is evident, nor any other human institution, can have any such effect. It is not the real, but the nominal price of corn, which can in any considerable degree be affected by the bounty. And though the tax, which that institution imposes upon the whole body of the people, may be very burdensome to those who pay it, it is of very little advantage to those who receive it.

The real effect of the bounty is not so much to raise the real value of corn, as to degrade the real value of silver; or to make an equal quantity of it exchange for a smaller quantity, not only of corn, but of all other home made commodities; for the money price of corn regulates that of all other home made commodities.

It regulates the money price of labor, which must always be such as to enable the laborer to purchase a quantity of corn sufficient to maintain him and his family, either in the liberal, moderate, or scanty manner, in which the advancing, stationary, or declining, circumstances of the society, oblige his employers to maintain him.

It regulates the money price of all the other parts of the rude produce of land, which, in every period of improvement, must bear a certain proportion to that of corn, though this proportion is different in different periods. It regulates, for example, the money price of grass and hay, of butcher's meat, of horses, and the maintenance of horses, of land carriage consequently, or of the greater part of the inland commerce of the country.

By regulating the money price of all the other parts of the rude produce of land, it regulates that of the materials of almost all manufactures; by regulating the money price of labor, it regulates that of manufacturing art and industry; and by regulating both, it regulates that of the complete manufacture. The money price of labor, and of every thing that is the produce, either of land or labor, must necessarily either rise or fall in proportion to the money price of corn.

Though in consequence of the bounty, therefore, the farmer should be enabled to sell his corn for 4s. the bushel, instead of 3s:6d. and to pay his landlord a money rent proportional to this rise in the money price of his produce; yet if, in consequence of this rise in the price of corn, 4s. will purchase no more home made goods of any other kind than 3s:6d. would have done before, neither the circumstances of the farmer, nor those of the landlord, will be much mended by this change. The farmer will not be able to cultivate much better; the landlord will not be able to live much better. In the purchase of foreign commodities, this enhancement in the price of corn may give them some little advantage. In that of homemade commodities, it can give them none at all. And almost the whole expense of the farmer, and the far greater part even of that of the landlord, is in home made commodities.

That degradation in the value of silver, which is the effect of the fertility of the mines, and which operates equally, or very nearly equally, through the greater part of the commercial world, is a matter of very little consequence to any particular country. The consequent rise of all money prices, though it does not make those who receive them really richer, does not make them really poorer. A service of plate becomes really cheaper, and every thing else remains precisely of the same real value as before.

But that degradation in the value of silver, which, being the effect either of the peculiar situation or of the political institutions of a particular country, takes place only in that country, is a matter of very great consequence, which, far from tending to make anybody really richer, tends to make everybody really poorer. The rise in the money price of all commodities, which is in this case peculiar to that country, tends to discourage more or less every sort of industry which is carried on within it, and to enable foreign nations, by furnishing almost all sorts of goods for a smaller quantity of silver than its own workmen can afford to do, to undersell them, not only in the foreign, but even in the home market.

It is the peculiar situation of Spain and Portugal, as proprietors of the mines, to be the distributors of gold and silver to all the other countries of Europe. Those metals ought naturally, therefore, to be somewhat cheaper in Spain and Portugal than in any other part of Europe. The difference, however, should be no more than the amount of the freight and insurance; and, on account of the great value and small bulk of those metals, their freight is no great matter, and their insurance is the same as that of any other goods of equal value. Spain and Portugal, therefore, could suffer very little from their peculiar situation, if they did not aggravate its disadvantages by their political institutions.

Spain by taxing, and Portugal by prohibiting, the exportation of gold and silver, load that exportation with the expense of smuggling, and raise the value of those metals in other countries so much more above what it is in their own, by the whole amount of this expense. When you dam up a stream of water, as soon as the dam is full, as much water must run over the dam-head as if there was no dam at all. The prohibition of exportation cannot detain a greater quantity of gold and silver in Spain and Portugal, than what they can afford to employ, than what the annual produce of their land and labor will allow them to employ, in coin, plate, gilding, and other ornaments of gold and silver. When they have got this quantity, the dam is full, and the whole stream which flows in afterwards must run over. The annual exportation of gold and silver from Spain and Portugal, accordingly, is, by all accounts, notwithstanding these restraints, very near equal to the whole annual importation. As the water, however, must always be deeper behind the dam-head than before it, so the quantity of gold and silver which these restraints detain in Spain and Portugal, must, in proportion to the annual produce of their land and labor, be greater than what is to be found in other countries. The higher and stronger the dam-head, the greater must be the difference in the depth of water behind and before it. The higher the tax, the higher the penalties with which the prohibition is guarded, the more vigilant and severe the police which looks after the execution of the law, the greater must be the difference in the proportion of gold and silver to the annual produce of the land and labor of Spain and Portugal, and to that of other countries. It is said, accordingly, to be very considerable, and that you frequently find there a profusion of plate in houses, where there is nothing else which would in other countries be thought suitable or correspondent to this sort of magnificence. The cheapness of gold and silver, or, what is the same thing, the dearness of all commodities, which is the necessary effect of this redundancy of the precious metals, discourages both the agriculture and manufactures of Spain and Portugal, and enables foreign nations to supply them with many sorts of rude, and with almost all sorts of manufactured produce, for a smaller quantity of gold and silver than what they themselves can either raise or make them for at home. The tax and prohibition operate in two different ways. They not only lower very much the value of the precious metals in Spain and Portugal, but by detaining there a certain quantity of those metals which would otherwise flow over other countries, they keep up their value in those other countries somewhat above what it otherwise would be, and thereby give those countries a double advantage in their commerce with Spain and Portugal. Open the floodgates, and there will presently be less water above, and more below the dam-head, and it will soon come to a level in both places. Remove the tax and the prohibition, and as the quantity of gold and silver will diminish considerably in Spain and Portugal, so it will increase somewhat in other countries; and the value of those metals, their proportion to the annual produce of land and labor, will soon come to a level, or very near to a level, in all. The loss which Spain and Portugal could sustain by this exportation of their gold and silver, would be altogether nominal and imaginary. The nominal value of their goods, and of the annual produce of their land and labor, would fall, and would be expressed or represented by a smaller quantity of silver than before; but their real value would be the same as before, and would be sufficient to maintain, command, and employ the same quantity of labor. As the nominal value of their goods would fall, the real value of what remained of their gold and silver would rise, and a smaller quantity of those metals would answer all the same purposes of commerce and circulation which had employed a greater quantity before. The gold and silver which would go abroad would not go abroad for nothing, but would bring back an equal value of goods of some kind or other. Those goods, too, would not be all matters of mere luxury and expense, to be consumed by idle people, who produce nothing in return for their consumption. As the real wealth and revenue of idle people would not be augmented by this extraordinary exportation of gold and silver, so neither would their consumption be much augmented by it. Those goods would probably, the greater part of them, and certainly some part of them, consist in materials, tools, and provisions, for the employment and maintenance of industrious people, who would reproduce, with a profit, the full value of their consumption. A part of the dead stock of the society would thus be turned into active stock, and would put into motion a greater quantity of industry than had been employed before. The annual produce of their land and labor would immediately be augmented a little, and in a few years would probably be augmented a great deal; their industry being thus relieved from one of the most oppressive burdens which it at present labors under.

The bounty upon the exportation of corn necessarily operates exactly in the same way as this absurd policy of Spain and Portugal. Whatever be the actual state of tillage, it renders our corn somewhat dearer in the home market than it otherwise would be in that state, and somewhat cheaper in the foreign; and as the average money price of corn regulates, more or less, that of all other commodities, it lowers the value of silver considerably in the one, and tends to raise it a little in the other. It enables foreigners, the Dutch in particular, not only to eat our corn cheaper than they otherwise could do, but sometimes to eat it cheaper than even our own people can do upon the same occasions; as we are assured by an excellent authority, that of Sir Matthew Decker. It hinders our own workmen from furnishing their goods for so small a quantity of silver as they otherwise might do, and enables the Dutch to furnish theirs for a smaller. It tends to render our manufactures somewhat dearer in every market, and theirs somewhat cheaper, than they otherwise would be, and consequently to give their industry a double advantage over our own.

The bounty, as it raises in the home market, not so much the real, as the nominal price of our corn; as it augments, not the quantity of labor which a certain quantity of corn can maintain and employ, but only the quantity of silver which it will exchange for; it discourages our manufactures, without rendering any considerable service, either to our farmers or country gentlemen. It puts, indeed, a little more money into the pockets of both, and it will perhaps be somewhat difficult to persuade the greater part of them that this is not rendering them a very considerable service. But if this money sinks in its value, in the quantity of labor, provisions, and home-made commodities of all different kinds which it is capable of purchasing, as much as it rises in its quantity, the service will be little more than nominal and imaginary.

There is, perhaps, but one set of men in the whole commonwealth to whom the bounty either was or could be essentially serviceable. These were the corn merchants, the exporters and importers of corn. In years of plenty, the bounty necessarily occasioned a greater exportation than would otherwise have taken place; and by hindering the plenty of the one year from relieving the scarcity of another, it occasioned in years of scarcity a greater importation than would otherwise have been necessary. It increased the business of the corn merchant in both; and in the years of scarcity, it not only enabled him to import a greater quantity, but to sell it for a better price, and consequently with a greater profit, than he could otherwise have made, if the plenty of one year had not been more or less hindered from relieving the scarcity of another. It is in this set of men, accordingly, that I have observed the greatest zeal for the continuance or renewal of the bounty.

Our country gentlemen, when they imposed the high duties upon the exportation of foreign corn, which in times of moderate plenty amount to a prohibition, and when they established the bounty, seem to have imitated the conduct of our manufacturers. By the one institution, they secured to themselves the monopoly of the home market, and by the other they endeavored to prevent that market from ever being overstocked with their commodity. By both they endeavored to raise its real value, in the same manner as our manufacturers had, by the like institutions, raised the real value of many different sorts of manufactured goods. They did not, perhaps, attend to the great and essential difference which nature has established between corn and almost every other sort of goods. When, either by the monopoly of the home market, or by a bounty upon exportation, you enable our woolen or linen manufacturers to sell their goods for somewhat a better price than they otherwise could get for them, you raise, not only the nominal, but the real price of those goods; you render them equivalent to a greater quantity of labor and subsistence; you increase not only the nominal, but the real profit, the real wealth and revenue of those manufacturers; and you enable them, either to live better themselves, or to employ a greater quantity of labor in those particular manufactures. You really encourage those manufactures, and direct towards them a greater quantity of the industry of the country than what would properly go to them of its own accord. But when, by the like institutions, you raise the nominal or money price of corn, you do not raise its real value; you do not increase the real wealth, the real revenue, either of our farmers or country gentlemen; you do not encourage the growth of corn, because you do not enable them to maintain and employ more laborers in raising it. The nature of things has stamped upon corn a real value, which cannot be altered by merely altering its money price. No bounty upon exportation, no monopoly of the home market, can raise that value. The freest competition cannot lower it. Through the world in general, that value is equal to the quantity of labor which it can maintain, and in every particular place it is equal to the quantity of labor which it can maintain in the way, whether liberal, moderate, or scanty, in which labor is commonly maintained in that place. Woolen or linen cloth are not the regulating commodities by which the real value of all other commodities must be finally measured and determined; corn is. The real value of every other commodity is finally measured and determined by the proportion which its average money price bears to the average money price of corn. The real value of corn does not vary with those variations in its average money price, which sometimes occur from one century to another; it is the real value of silver which varies with them.

Bounties upon the exportation of any homemade commodity are liable, first, to that general objection which may be made to all the different expedients of the mercantile system; the objection of forcing some part of the industry of the country into a channel less advantageous than that in which it would run of its own accord; and, secondly, to the particular objection of forcing it not only into a channel that is less advantageous, but into one that is actually disadvantageous; the trade which cannot be carried on but by means of a bounty being necessarily a losing trade. The bounty upon the exportation of corn is liable to this further objection, that it can in no respect promote the raising of that particular commodity of which it was meant to encourage the production. When our country gentlemen, therefore, demanded the establishment of the bounty, though they acted in imitation of our merchants and manufacturers, they did not act with that complete comprehension of their own interest, which commonly directs the conduct of those two other orders of people. They loaded the public revenue with a very considerable expense: they imposed a very heavy tax upon the whole body of the people; but they did not, in any sensible degree, increase the real value of their own commodity; and by lowering somewhat the real value of silver, they discouraged, in some degree, the general industry of the country, and, instead of advancing, retarded more or less the improvement of their own lands, which necessarily depend upon the general industry of the country.

To encourage the production of any commodity, a bounty upon production, one should imagine, would have a more direct operation than one upon exportation. It would, besides, impose only one tax upon the people, that which they must contribute in order to pay the bounty. Instead of raising, it would tend to lower the price of the commodity in the home market; and thereby, instead of imposing a second tax upon the people, it might, at least in part, repay them for what they had contributed to the first. Bounties upon production, however, have been very rarely granted. The prejudices established by the commercial system have taught us to believe, that national wealth arises more immediately from exportation than from production. It has been more favored, accordingly, as the more immediate means of bringing money into the country. Bounties upon production, it has been said too, have been found by experience more liable to frauds than those upon exportation. How far this is true, I know not. That bounties upon exportation have been abused, to many fraudulent purposes, is very well known. But it is not the interest of merchants and manufacturers, the great inventors of all these expedients, that the home market should be overstocked with their goods; an event which a bounty upon production might sometimes occasion. A bounty upon exportation, by enabling them to send abroad their surplus part, and to keep up the price of what remains in the home market, effectually prevents this. Of all the expedients of the mercantile system, accordingly, it is the one of which they are the fondest. I have known the different undertakers of some particular works agree privately among themselves to give a bounty out of their own pockets upon the exportation of a certain proportion of the goods which they dealt in. This expedient succeeded so well, that it more than doubled the price of their goods in the home market, notwithstanding a very considerable increase in the produce. The operation of the bounty upon corn must have been wonderfully different, if it has lowered the money price of that commodity.

Something like a bounty upon production, however, has been granted upon some particular occasions. The tonnage bounties given to the white herring and whale fisheries may, perhaps, be considered as somewhat of this nature. They tend directly, it may be supposed, to render the goods cheaper in the home market than they otherwise would be. In other respects, their effects, it must be acknowledged, are the same as those of bounties upon exportation. By means of them, a part of the capital of the country is employed in bringing goods to market, of which the price does not repay the cost, together with the ordinary profits of stock.

But though the tonnage bounties to those fisheries do not contribute to the opulence of the nation, it may, perhaps, be thought that they contribute to its defense, by augmenting the number of its sailors and shipping. This, it may be alleged, may sometimes be done by means of such bounties, at a much smaller expense than by keeping up a great standing navy, if I may use such an expression, in the same way as a standing army.

Notwithstanding these favorable allegations, however, the following considerations dispose me to believe, that in granting at least one of these bounties, the legislature has been very grossly imposed upon:

First, the herring-buss bounty seems too large.

From the commencement of the winter fishing 1771, to the end of the winter fishing 1781, the tonnage bounty upon the herring-buss fishery has been at thirty shillings the ton. During these eleven years, the whole number of barrels caught by the herring-buss fishery of Scotland amounted to 378,347. The herrings caught and cured at sea are called sea-sticks. In order to render them what are called merchantable herrings, it is necessary to repack them with an additional quantity of salt; and in this case, it is reckoned, that three barrels of sea-sticks are usually repacked into two barrels of merchantable herrings. The number of barrels of merchantable herrings, therefore, caught during these eleven years, will amount only, according to this account, to 252,231⅓. During these eleven years, the tonnage bounties paid amounted to £155,463:11s. or 8s:2¼d. upon every barrel of sea-sticks, and to 12s:3¾d. upon every barrel of merchantable herrings.

The salt with which these herrings are cured is sometimes Scotch, and sometimes foreign salt; both which are delivered, free of all excise duty, to the fish-curers. The excise duty upon Scotch salt is at present 1s:6d., that upon foreign salt 10s. the bushel. A barrel of herrings is supposed to require about one bushel and one-fourth of a bushel foreign salt. Two bushels are the supposed average of Scotch salt. If the herrings are entered for exportation, no part of this duty is paid up; if entered for home consumption, whether the herrings were cured with foreign or with Scotch salt, only one shilling the barrel is paid up. It was the old Scotch duty upon a bushel of salt, the quantity which, at a low estimation, had been supposed necessary for curing a barrel of herrings. In Scotland, foreign salt is very little used for any other purpose but the curing of fish. But from the 5th April 1771 to the 5th April 1782, the quantity of foreign salt imported amounted to 936,974 bushels, at eighty-four pounds the bushel; the quantity of Scotch salt delivered from the works to the fish-curers, to no more than 168,226, at fifty-six pounds the bushel only. It would appear, therefore, that it is principally foreign salt that is used in the fisheries. Upon every barrel of herrings exported, there is, besides, a bounty of 2s:8d. and more than two-thirds of the buss-caught herrings are exported. Put all these things together, and you will find that, during these eleven years, every barrel of buss-caught herrings, cured with Scotch salt, when exported, has cost government 1:7s:5¾d.; and, when entered for home consumption, 14s:3¾d.; and that every barrel cured with foreign salt, when exported, has cost government £1:7:5¾d.; and, when entered for home consumption, £1:3:9¾d. The price of a barrel of good merchantable herrings runs from seventeen and eighteen to four and five-and-twenty shillings; about a guinea at an average. {See the accounts at the end of this Book.}

Secondly, the bounty to the white-herring fishery is a tonnage bounty, and is proportioned to the burden of the ship, not to her diligence or success in the fishery; and it has, I am afraid, been too common for the vessels to fit out for the sole purpose of catching, not the fish but the bounty. In the year 1759, when the bounty was at fifty shillings the ton, the whole buss fishery of Scotland brought in only four barrels of sea-sticks. In that year, each barrel of sea-sticks cost government, in bounties alone, £113:15s.; each barrel of merchantable herrings £159:7:6.

Thirdly, the mode of fishing, for which this tonnage bounty in the white herring fishery has been given (by busses or decked vessels from twenty to eighty tons burden), seems not so well adapted to the situation of Scotland, as to that of Holland, from the practice of which country it appears to have been borrowed. Holland lies at a great distance from the seas to which herrings are known principally to resort, and can, therefore, carry on that fishery only in decked vessels, which can carry water and provisions sufficient for a voyage to a distant sea; but the Hebrides, or Western Islands, the islands of Shetland, and the northern and north-western coasts of Scotland, the countries in whose neighborhood the herring fishery is principally carried on, are everywhere intersected by arms of the sea, which run up a considerable way into the land, and which, in the language of the country, are called sea-lochs. It is to these sea-lochs that the herrings principally resort during the seasons in which they visit these seas; for the visits of this, and, I am assured, of many other sorts of fish, are not quite regular and constant. A boat-fishery, therefore, seems to be the mode of fishing best adapted to the peculiar situation of Scotland, the fishers carrying the herrings on shore as fast as they are taken, to be either cured or consumed fresh. But the great encouragement which a bounty of 30s. the ton gives to the buss-fishery, is necessarily a discouragement to the boat-fishery, which, having no such bounty, cannot bring its cured fish to market upon the same terms as the buss-fishery. The boat-fishery; accordingly, which, before the establishment of the buss-bounty, was very considerable, and is said to have employed a number of seamen, not inferior to what the buss-fishery employs at present, is now gone almost entirely to decay. Of the former extent, however, of this now ruined and abandoned fishery, I must acknowledge that I cannot pretend to speak with much precision. As no bounty was paid upon the outfit of the boat-fishery, no account was taken of it by the officers of the customs or salt duties.

Fourthly, in many parts of Scotland, during certain seasons of the year, herrings make no inconsiderable part of the food of the common people. A bounty which tended to lower their price in the home market, might contribute a good deal to the relief of a great number of our fellow-subjects, whose circumstances are by no means affluent. But the herring-bus bounty contributes to no such good purpose. It has ruined the boat fishery, which is by far the best adapted for the supply of the home market; and the additional bounty of 2s:8d. the barrel upon exportation, carries the greater part, more than two-thirds, of the produce of the buss-fishery abroad. Between thirty and forty years ago, before the establishment of the buss-bounty, 16s. the barrel, I have been assured, was the common price of white herrings. Between ten and fifteen years ago, before the boat-fishery was entirely ruined, the price was said to have run from seventeen to twenty shillings the barrel. For these last five years, it has, at an average, been at twenty-five shillings the barrel. This high price, however, may have been owing to the real scarcity of the herrings upon the coast of Scotland. I must observe, too, that the cask or barrel, which is usually sold with the herrings, and of which the price is included in all the foregoing prices, has, since the commencement of the American war, risen to about double its former price, or from about 3s. to about 6s. I must likewise observe, that the accounts I have received of the prices of former times, have been by no means quite uniform and consistent, and an old man of great accuracy and experience has assured me, that, more than fifty years ago, a guinea was the usual price of a barrel of good merchantable herrings; and this, I imagine, may still be looked upon as the average price. All accounts, however, I think, agree that the price has not been lowered in the home market in consequence of the buss-bounty.

When the undertakers of fisheries, after such liberal bounties have been bestowed upon them, continue to sell their commodity at the same, or even at a higher price than they were accustomed to do before, it might be expected that their profits should be very great; and it is not improbable that those of some individuals may have been so. In general, however, I have every reason to believe they have been quite otherwise. The usual effect of such bounties is, to encourage rash undertakers to adventure in a business which they do not understand; and what they lose by their own negligence and ignorance, more than compensates all that they can gain by the utmost liberality of government. In 1750, by the same act which first gave the bounty of 30s. the ton for the encouragement of the white herring fishery (the 23d Geo. II. chap. 24), a joint stock company was erected, with a capital of £500,000, to which the subscribers (over and above all other encouragements, the tonnage bounty just now mentioned, the exportation bounty of 2s:8d. the barrel, the delivery of both British and foreign salt duty free) were, during the space of fourteen years, for every hundred pounds which they subscribed and paid into the stock of the society, entitled to three pounds a year, to be paid by the receiver-general of the customs in equal half-yearly payments. Besides this great company, the residence of whose governor and directors was to be in London, it was declared lawful to erect different fishing chambers in all the different out-ports of the kingdom, provided a sum not less than £10,000 was subscribed into the capital of each, to be managed at its own risk, and for its own profit and loss. The same annuity, and the same encouragements of all kinds, were given to the trade of those inferior chambers as to that of the great company. The subscription of the great company was soon filled up, and several different fishing chambers were erected in the different out-ports of the kingdom. In spite of all these encouragements, almost all those different companies, both great and small, lost either the whole or the greater part of their capitals; scarce a vestige now remains of any of them, and the white-herring fishery is now entirely, or almost entirely, carried on by private adventurers.

If any particular manufacture was necessary, indeed, for the defense of the society, it might not always be prudent to depend upon our neighbors for the supply; and if such manufacture could not otherwise be supported at home, it might not be unreasonable that all the other branches of industry should be taxed in order to support it. The bounties upon the exportation of British made sail-cloth, and British made gunpowder, may, perhaps, both be vindicated upon this principle.

But though it can very seldom be reasonable to tax the industry of the great body of the people, in order to support that of some particular class of manufacturers; yet, in the wantonness of great prosperity, when the public enjoys a greater revenue than it knows well what to do with, to give such bounties to favorite manufactures, may, perhaps, be as natural as to incur any other idle expense. In public, as well as in private expenses, great wealth, may, perhaps, frequently be admitted as an apology for great folly. But there must surely be something more than ordinary absurdity in continuing such profusion in times of general difficulty and distress.

What is called a bounty, is sometimes no more than a drawback, and, consequently, is not liable to the same objections as what is properly a bounty. The bounty, for example, upon refined sugar exported, may be considered as a drawback of the duties upon the brown and Muscovado sugars, from which it is made; the bounty upon wrought silk exported, a drawback of the duties upon raw and thrown silk imported; the bounty upon gunpowder exported, a drawback of the duties upon brimstone and saltpeter imported. In the language of the customs, those allowances only are called drawbacks which are given upon goods exported in the same form in which they are imported. When that form has been so altered by manufacture of any kind as to come under a new denomination, they are called bounties.

Premiums given by the public to artists and manufacturers, who excel in their particular occupations, are not liable to the same objections as bounties. By encouraging extraordinary dexterity and ingenuity, they serve to keep up the emulation of the workmen actually employed in those respective occupations, and are not considerable enough to turn towards any one of them a greater share of the capital of the country than what would go to it of its own accord. Their tendency is not to overturn the natural balance of employments, but to render the work which is done in each as perfect and complete as possible. The expense of premiums, besides, is very trifling, that of bounties very great. The bounty upon corn alone has sometimes cost the public, in one year, more than £300,000.

Bounties are sometimes called premiums, as drawbacks are sometimes called bounties. But we must, in all cases, attend to the nature of the thing, without paying any regard to the word.

Digression Concerning the Corn Trade and Corn Laws

I cannot conclude this chapter concerning bounties, without observing, that the praises which have been bestowed upon the law which establishes the bounty upon the exportation of corn, and upon that system of regulations which is connected with it, are altogether unmerited. A particular examination of the nature of the corn trade, and of the principal British laws which relate to it, will sufficiently demonstrate the truth of this assertion. The great importance of this subject must justify the length of the digression.

The trade of the corn merchant is composed of four different branches, which, though they may sometimes be all carried on by the same person, are, in their own nature, four separate and distinct trades. These are, first, the trade of the inland dealer; secondly, that of the merchant-importer for home consumption; thirdly, that of the merchant-exporter of home produce for foreign consumption; and, fourthly, that of the merchant-carrier, or of the importer of corn, in order to export it again.

I. The interest of the inland dealer, and that of the great body of the people, how opposite soever they may at first appear, are, even in years of the greatest scarcity, exactly the same. It is his interest to raise the price of his corn as high as the real scarcity of the season requires, and it can never be his interest to raise it higher. By raising the price, he discourages the consumption, and puts every body more or less, but particularly the inferior ranks of people, upon thrift and good management. If, by raising it too high, he discourages the consumption so much that the supply of the season is likely to go beyond the consumption of the season, and to last for some time after the next crop begins to come in, he runs the hazard, not only of losing a considerable part of his corn by natural causes, but of being obliged to sell what remains of it for much less than what he might have had for it several months before. If, by not raising the price high enough, he discourages the consumption so little, that the supply of the season is likely to fall short of the consumption of the season, he not only loses a part of the profit which he might otherwise have made, but he exposes the people to suffer before the end of the season, instead of the hardships of a dearth, the dreadful horrors of a famine. It is the interest of the people that their daily, weekly, and monthly consumption should be proportioned as exactly as possible to the supply of the season. The interest of the inland corn dealer is the same. By supplying them, as nearly as he can judge, in this proportion, he is likely to sell all his corn for the highest price, and with the greatest profit; and his knowledge of the state of the crop, and of his daily, weekly, and monthly sales, enables him to judge, with more or less accuracy, how far they really are supplied in this manner. Without intending the interest of the people, he is necessarily led, by a regard to his own interest, to treat them, even in years of scarcity, pretty much in the same manner as the prudent master of a vessel is sometimes obliged to treat his crew. When he foresees that provisions are likely to run short, he puts them upon short allowance. Though from excess of caution he should sometimes do this without any real necessity, yet all the inconveniencies which his crew can thereby suffer are inconsiderable, in comparison of the danger, misery, and ruin, to which they might sometimes be exposed by a less provident conduct. Though, from excess of avarice, in the same manner, the inland corn merchant should sometimes raise the price of his corn somewhat higher than the scarcity of the season requires, yet all the inconveniencies which the people can suffer from this conduct, which effectually secures them from a famine in the end of the season, are inconsiderable, in comparison of what they might have been exposed to by a more liberal way of dealing in the beginning of it the corn merchant himself is likely to suffer the most by this excess of avarice; not only from the indignation which it generally excites against him, but, though he should escape the effects of this indignation, from the quantity of corn which it necessarily leaves upon his hands in the end of the season, and which, if the next season happens to prove favorable, he must always sell for a much lower price than he might otherwise have had.

Were it possible, indeed, for one great company of merchants to possess themselves of the whole crop of an extensive country, it might perhaps be their interest to deal with it, as the Dutch are said to do with the spiceries of the Moluccas, to destroy or throw away a considerable part of it, in order to keep up the price of the rest. But it is scarce possible, even by the violence of law, to establish such an extensive monopoly with regard to corn; and wherever the law leaves the trade free, it is of all commodities the least liable to be engrossed or monopolized by the forced a few large capitals, which buy up the greater part of it. Not only its value far exceeds what the capitals of a few private men are capable of purchasing; but, supposing they were capable of purchasing it, the manner in which it is produced renders this purchase altogether impracticable. As, in every civilized country, it is the commodity of which the annual consumption is the greatest; so a greater quantity of industry is annually employed in producing corn than in producing any other commodity. When it first comes from the ground, too, it is necessarily divided among a greater number of owners than any other commodity; and these owners can never be collected into one place, like a number of independent manufacturers, but are necessarily scattered through all the different corners of the country. These first owners either immediately supply the consumers in their own neighborhood, or they supply other inland dealers, who supply those consumers. The inland dealers in corn, therefore, including both the farmer and the baker, are necessarily more numerous than the dealers in any other commodity; and their dispersed situation renders it altogether impossible for them to enter into any general combination. If, in a year of scarcity, therefore, any of them should find that he had a good deal more corn upon hand than, at the current price, he could hope to dispose of before the end of the season, he would never think of keeping up this price to his own loss, and to the sole benefit of his rivals and competitors, but would immediately lower it, in order to get rid of his corn before the new crop began to come in. The same motives, the same interests, which would thus regulate the conduct of any one dealer, would regulate that of every other, and oblige them all in general to sell their corn at the price which, according to the best of their judgment, was most suitable to the scarcity or plenty of the season.

Whoever examines, with attention, the history of the dearths and famines which have afflicted any part of Europe during either the course of the present or that of the two preceding centuries, of several of which we have pretty exact accounts, will find, I believe, that a dearth never has arisen from any combination among the inland dealers in corn, nor from any other cause but a real scarcity, occasioned sometimes, perhaps, and in some particular places, by the waste of war, but in by far the greatest number of cases by the fault of the seasons; and that a famine has never arisen from any other cause but the violence of government attempting, by improper means, to remedy the inconveniencies of a dearth.

In an extensive corn country, between all the different parts of which there is a free commerce and communication, the scarcity occasioned by the most unfavorable seasons can never be so great as to produce a famine; and the scantiest crop, if managed with frugality and economy, will maintain, through the year, the same number of people that are commonly fed in a more affluent manner by one of moderate plenty. The seasons most unfavorable to the crop are those of excessive drought or excessive rain. But as corn grows equally upon high and low lands, upon grounds that are disposed to be too wet, and upon those that are disposed to be too dry, either the drought or the rain, which is hurtful to one part of the country, is favorable to another; and though, both in the wet and in the dry season, the crop is a good deal less than in one more properly tempered; yet, in both, what is lost in one part of the country is in some measure compensated by what is gained in the other. In rice countries, where the crop not only requires a very moist soil, but where, in a certain period of its growing, it must be laid under water, the effects of a drought are much more dismal. Even in such countries, however, the drought is, perhaps, scarce ever so universal as necessarily to occasion a famine, if the government would allow a free trade. The drought in Bengal, a few years ago, might probably have occasioned a very great dearth. Some improper regulations, some injudicious restraints, imposed by the servants of the East India Company upon the rice trade, contributed, perhaps, to turn that dearth into a famine.

When the government, in order to remedy the inconveniencies of a dearth, orders all the dealers to sell their corn at what it supposes a reasonable price, it either hinders them from bringing it to market, which may sometimes produce a famine even in the beginning of the season; or, if they bring it thither, it enables the people, and thereby encourages them to consume it so fast as must necessarily produce a famine before the end of the season. The unlimited, unrestrained freedom of the corn trade, as it is the only effectual preventive of the miseries of a famine, so it is the best palliative of the inconveniencies of a dearth; for the inconveniencies of a real scarcity cannot be remedied; they can only be palliated. No trade deserves more the full protection of the law, and no trade requires it so much; because no trade is so much exposed to popular odium.

In years of scarcity, the inferior ranks of people impute their distress to the avarice of the corn merchant, who becomes the object of their hatred and indignation. Instead of making profit upon such occasions, therefore, he is often in danger of being utterly ruined, and of having his magazines plundered and destroyed by their violence. It is in years of scarcity, however, when prices are high, that the corn merchant expects to make his principal profit. He is generally in contract with some farmers to furnish him, for a certain number of years, with a certain quantity of corn, at a certain price. This contract price is settled according to what is supposed to be the moderate and reasonable, that is, the ordinary or average price, which, before the late years of scarcity, was commonly about 28s. for the quarter of wheat, and for that of other grain in proportion. In years of scarcity, therefore, the corn merchant buys a great part of his corn for the ordinary price, and sells it for a much higher. That this extraordinary profit, however, is no more than sufficient to put his trade upon a fair level with other trades, and to compensate the many losses which he sustains upon other occasions, both from the perishable nature of the commodity itself, and from the frequent and unforeseen fluctuations of its price, seems evident enough, from this single circumstance, that great fortunes are as seldom made in this as in any other trade. The popular odium, however, which attends it in years of scarcity, the only years in which it can be very profitable, renders people of character and fortune averse to enter into it. It is abandoned to an inferior set of dealers; and millers, bakers, meal-men, and meal-factors, together with a number of wretched hucksters, are almost the only middle people that, in the home market, come between the grower and the consumer.

The ancient policy of Europe, instead of discountenancing this popular odium against a trade so beneficial to the public, seems, on the contrary, to have authorized and encouraged it.

By the 5th and 6th of Edward VI chap. 14, it was enacted, that whoever should buy any corn or grain, with intent to sell it again, should be reputed an unlawful engrosser, and should, for the first fault, suffer two months imprisonment, and forfeit the value of the corn; for the second, suffer six months imprisonment, and forfeit double the value; and, for the third, be set in the pillory, suffer imprisonment during the king's pleasure, and forfeit all his goods and chattels. The ancient policy of most other parts of Europe was no better than that of England.

Our ancestors seem to have imagined, that the people would buy their corn cheaper of the farmer than of the corn merchant, who, they were afraid, would require, over and above the price which he paid to the farmer, an exorbitant profit to himself. They endeavored, therefore, to annihilate his trade altogether. They even endeavored to hinder, as much as possible, any middle man of any kind from coming in between the grower and the consumer; and this was the meaning of the many restraints which they imposed upon the trade of those whom they called kidders, or carriers of corn; a trade which nobody was allowed to exercise without a license, ascertaining his qualifications as a man of probity and fair dealing. The authority of three justices of the peace was, by the statute of Edward VI necessary in order to grant this license. But even this restraint was afterwards thought insufficient, and, by a statute of Elizabeth, the privilege of granting it was confined to the quarter-sessions.

The ancient policy of Europe endeavored, in this manner, to regulate agriculture, the great trade of the country, by maxims quite different from those which it established with regard to manufactures, the great trade of the towns. By leaving a farmer no other customers but either the consumers or their immediate factors, the kidders and carriers of corn, it endeavored to force him to exercise the trade, not only of a farmer, but of a corn merchant, or corn retailer. On the contrary, it, in many cases, prohibited the manufacturer from exercising the trade of a shopkeeper, or from selling his own goods by retail. It meant, by the one law, to promote the general interest of the country, or to render corn cheap, without, perhaps, its being well understood how this was to be done. By the other, it meant to promote that of a particular order of men, the shopkeepers, who would be so much undersold by the manufacturer, it was supposed, that their trade would be ruined, if he was allowed to retail at all.

The manufacturer, however, though he had been allowed to keep a shop, and to sell his own goods by retail, could not have undersold the common shopkeeper. Whatever part of his capital he might have placed in his shop, he must have withdrawn it from his manufacture. In order to carry on his business on a level with that of other people, as he must have had the profit of a manufacturer on the one part, so he must have had that of a shopkeeper upon the other. Let us suppose, for example, that in the particular town where he lived, ten percent was the ordinary profit both of manufacturing and shopkeeping stock; he must in this case have charged upon every piece of his own goods, which he sold in his shop, a profit of twenty percent. When he carried them from his workhouse to his shop, he must have valued them at the price for which he could have sold them to a dealer or shopkeeper, who would have bought them by wholesale. If he valued them lower, he lost a part of the profit of his manufacturing capital. When, again, he sold them from his shop, unless he got the same price at which a shopkeeper would have sold them, he lost a part of the profit of his shop-keeping capital. Though he might appear, therefore, to make a double profit upon the same piece of goods, yet, as these goods made successively a part of two distinct capitals, he made but a single profit upon the whole capital employed about them; and if he made less than his profit, he was a loser, and did not employ his whole capital with the same advantage as the greater part of his neighbors.

What the manufacturer was prohibited to do, the farmer was in some measure enjoined to do; to divide his capital between two different employments; to keep one part of it in his granaries and stack-yard, for supplying the occasional demands of the market, and to employ the other in the cultivation of his land. But as he could not afford to employ the latter for less than the ordinary profits of farming stock, so he could as little afford to employ the former for less than the ordinary profits of mercantile stock. Whether the stock which really carried on the business of a corn merchant belonged to the person who was called a farmer, or to the person who was called a corn merchant, an equal profit was in both cases requisite, in order to indemnify its owner for employing it in this manner, in order to put his business on a level with other trades, and in order to hinder him from having an interest to change it as soon as possible for some other. The farmer, therefore, who was thus forced to exercise the trade of a corn merchant, could not afford to sell his corn cheaper than any other corn merchant would have been obliged to do in the case of a free competition.

The dealer who can employ his whole stock in one single branch of business, has an advantage of the same kind with the workman who can employ his whole labor in one single operation. As the latter acquires a dexterity which enables him, with the same two hands, to perform a much greater quantity of work, so the former acquires so easy and ready a method of transacting his business, of buying and disposing of his goods, that with the same capital he can transact a much greater quantity of business. As the one can commonly afford his work a good deal cheaper, so the other can commonly afford his goods somewhat cheaper, than if his stock and attention were both employed about a greater variety of objects. The greater part of manufacturers could not afford to retail their own goods so cheap as a vigilant and active shopkeeper, whose sole business it was to buy them by wholesale and to retail them again. The greater part of farmers could still less afford to retail their own corn, to supply the inhabitants of a town, at perhaps four or five miles distance from the greater part of them, so cheap as a vigilant and active corn merchant, whose sole business it was to purchase corn by wholesale, to collect it into a great magazine, and to retail it again.

The law which prohibited the manufacturer from exercising the trade of a shopkeeper, endeavored to force this division in the employment of stock to go on faster than it might otherwise have done. The law which obliged the farmer to exercise the trade of a corn merchant, endeavored to hinder it from going on so fast. Both laws were evident violations of natural liberty, and therefore unjust; and they were both, too, as impolitic as they were unjust. It is the interest of every society, that things of this kind should never either he forced or obstructed. The man who employs either his labor or his stock in a greater variety of ways than his situation renders necessary, can never hurt his neighbor by underselling him. He may hurt himself, and he generally does so. Jack-of-all-trades will never be rich, says the proverb. But the law ought always to trust people with the care of their own interest, as in their local situations they must generally be able to judge better of it than the legislature can do. The law, however, which obliged the farmer to exercise the trade of a corn merchant was by far the most pernicious of the two.

It obstructed not only that division in the employment of stock which is so advantageous to every society, but it obstructed likewise the improvement and cultivation of the land. By obliging the farmer to carry on two trades instead of one, it forced him to divide his capital into two parts, of which one only could be employed in cultivation. But if he had been at liberty to sell his whole crop to a corn merchant as fast as he could thresh it out, his whole capital might have returned immediately to the land, and have been employed in buying more cattle, and hiring more servants, in order to improve and cultivate it better. But by being obliged to sell his corn by retail, he was obliged to keep a great part of his capital in his granaries and stack-yard through the year, and could not therefore cultivate so well as with the same capital he might otherwise have done. This law, therefore, necessarily obstructed the improvement of the land, and, instead of tending to render corn cheaper, must have tended to render it scarcer, and therefore dearer, than it would otherwise have been.

After the business of the farmer, that of the corn merchant is in reality the trade which, if properly protected and encouraged, would contribute the most to the raising of corn. It would support the trade of the farmer, in the same manner as the trade of the wholesale dealer supports that of the manufacturer.

The wholesale dealer, by affording a ready market to the manufacturer, by taking his goods off his hand as fast as he can make them, and by sometimes even advancing their price to him before he has made them, enables him to keep his whole capital, and sometimes even more than his whole capital, constantly employed in manufacturing, and consequently to manufacture a much greater quantity of goods than if he was obliged to dispose of them himself to the immediate consumers, or even to the retailers. As the capital of the wholesale merchant, too, is generally sufficient to replace that of many manufacturers, this intercourse between him and them interests the owner of a large capital to support the owners of a great number of small ones, and to assist them in those losses and misfortunes which might otherwise prove ruinous to them.

An intercourse of the same kind universally established between the farmers and the corn merchants, would be attended with effects equally beneficial to the farmers. They would be enabled to keep their whole capitals, and even more than their whole capitals constantly employed in cultivation. In case of any of those accidents to which no trade is more liable than theirs, they would find in their ordinary customer, the wealthy corn merchant, a person who had both an interest to support them, and the ability to do it; and they would not, as at present, be entirely dependent upon the forbearance of their landlord, or the mercy of his steward. Were it possible, as perhaps it is not, to establish this intercourse universally, and all at once; were it possible to turn all at once the whole farming stock of the kingdom to its proper business, the cultivation of land, withdrawing it from every other employment into which any part of it may be at present diverted; and were it possible, in order to support and assist, upon occasion, the operations of this great stock, to provide all at once another stock almost equally great; it is not, perhaps, very easy to imagine how great, how extensive, and how sudden, would be the improvement which this change of circumstances would alone produce upon the whole face of the country.

The statute of Edward VI therefore, by prohibiting as much as possible any middle man from coming in between the grower and the consumer, endeavored to annihilate a trade, of which the free exercise is not only the best palliative of the inconveniencies of a dearth, but the best preventive of that calamity; after the trade of the farmer, no trade contributing so much to the growing of corn as that of the corn merchant.

The rigor of this law was afterwards softened by several subsequent statutes, which successively permitted the engrossing of corn when the price of wheat should not exceed 20s. and 24s. 32s. and 40s. the quarter. At last, by the 15th of Charles II c.7, the engrossing or buying of corn, in order to sell it again, as long as the price of wheat did not exceed 48s. the quarter, and that of other grain in proportion, was declared lawful to all persons not being forestallers, that is, not selling again in the same market within three months. All the freedom which the trade of the inland corn dealer has ever yet enjoyed was bestowed upon it by this statute. The statute of the twelfth of the present king, which repeals almost all the other ancient laws against engrossers and forestallers, does not repeal the restrictions of this particular statute, which therefore still continue in force.

This statute, however, authorizes in some measure two very absurd popular prejudices.

First, it supposes, that when the price of wheat has risen so high as 48s. the quarter, and that of other grain in proportion, corn is likely to be so engrossed as to hurt the people. But, from what has been already said, it seems evident enough, that corn can at no price be so engrossed by the inland dealers as to hurt the people; and 48s. the quarter, besides, though it may be considered as a very high price, yet, in years of scarcity, it is a price which frequently takes place immediately after harvest, when scarce any part of the new crop can be sold off, and when it is impossible even for ignorance to suppose that any part of it can be so engrossed as to hurt the people.

Secondly, it supposes that there is a certain price at which corn is likely to be forestalled, that is, bought up in order to be sold again soon after in the same market, so as to hurt the people. But if a merchant ever buys up corn, either going to a particular market, or in a particular market, in order to sell it again soon after in the same market, it must be because he judges that the market cannot be so liberally supplied through the whole season as upon that particular occasion, and that the price, therefore, must soon rise. If he judges wrong in this, and if the price does not rise, he not only loses the whole profit of the stock which he employs in this manner, but a part of the stock itself, by the expense and loss which necessarily attend the storing and keeping of corn. He hurts himself, therefore, much more essentially than he can hurt even the particular people whom he may hinder from supplying themselves upon that particular market day, because they may afterwards supply themselves just as cheap upon any other market day. If he judges right, instead of hurting the great body of the people, he renders them a most important service. By making them feel the inconveniencies of a dearth somewhat earlier than they otherwise might do, he prevents their feeling them afterwards so severely as they certainly would do, if the cheapness of price encouraged them to consume faster than suited the real scarcity of the season. When the scarcity is real, the best thing that can be done for the people is, to divide the inconvenience of it as equally as possible, through all the different months and weeks and days of the year. The interest of the corn merchant makes him study to do this as exactly as he can; and as no other person can have either the same interest, or the same knowledge, or the same abilities, to do it so exactly as he, this most important operation of commerce ought to be trusted entirely to him; or, in other words, the corn trade, so far at least as concerns the supply of the home market, ought to be left perfectly free.

The popular fear of engrossing and forestalling may be compared to the popular terrors and suspicions of witchcraft. The unfortunate wretches accused of this latter crime were not more innocent of the misfortunes imputed to them, than those who have been accused of the former. The law which put an end to all prosecutions against witchcraft, which put it out of any man's power to gratify his own malice by accusing his neighbor of that imaginary crime, seems effectually to have put an end to those fears and suspicions, by taking away the great cause which encouraged and supported them. The law which would restore entire freedom to the inland trade of corn, would probably prove as effectual to put an end to the popular fears of engrossing and forestalling.

The 15th of Charles II c. 7, however, with all its imperfections, has, perhaps, contributed more, both to the plentiful supply of the home market, and to the increase of tillage, than any other law in the statute book. It is from this law that the inland corn trade has derived all the liberty and protection which it has ever yet enjoyed; and both the supply of the home market and the interest of tillage are much more effectually promoted by the inland, than either by the importation or exportation trade.

The proportion of the average quantity of all sorts of grain imported into Great Britain to that of all sorts of grain consumed, it has been computed by the author of the *Tracts upon the Corn Trade*, does not exceed that of one to five hundred and seventy. For supplying the home market, therefore, the importance of the inland trade must be to that of the importation trade as five hundred and seventy to one.

The average quantity of all sorts of grain exported from Great Britain does not, according to the same author, exceed the one-and-thirtieth part of the annual produce. For the encouragement of tillage, therefore, by providing a market for the home produce, the importance of the inland trade must be to that of the exportation trade as thirty to one.

I have no great faith in political arithmetic, and I mean not to warrant the exactness of either of these computations. I mention them only in order to show of how much less consequence, in the opinion of the most judicious and experienced persons, the foreign trade of corn is than the home trade. The great cheapness of corn in the years immediately preceding the establishment of the bounty may, perhaps with reason, he ascribed in some measure to the operation of this statute of Charles II which had been enacted about five-and-twenty years before, and which had, therefore, full time to produce its effect.

A very few words will sufficiently explain all that I have to say concerning the other three branches of the corn trade.

II. The trade of the merchant-importer of foreign corn for home consumption, evidently contributes to the immediate supply of the home market, and must so far be immediately beneficial to the great body of the people. It tends, indeed, to lower somewhat the average money price of corn, but not to diminish its real value, or the quantity of labor which it is capable of maintaining. If importation was at all times free, our farmers and country gentlemen would probably, one year with another, get less money for their corn than they do at present, when importation is at most times in effect prohibited; but the money which they got would be of more value, would buy more goods of all other kinds, and would employ more labor. Their real wealth, their real revenue, therefore, would be the same as at present, though it might be expressed by a smaller quantity of silver, and they would neither be disabled nor discouraged from cultivating corn as much as they do at present. On the contrary, as the rise in the real value of silver, in consequence of lowering the money price of corn, lowers somewhat the money price of all other commodities, it gives the industry of the country where it takes place some advantage in all foreign markets and thereby tends to encourage and increase that industry. But the extent of the home market for corn must be in proportion to the general industry of the country where it grows, or to the number of those who produce something else, and therefore, have something else, or, what comes to the same thing, the price of something else, to give in exchange for corn. But in every country, the home market, as it is the nearest and most convenient, so is it likewise the greatest and most important market for corn. That rise in the real value of silver, therefore, which is the effect of lowering the average money price of corn, tends to enlarge the greatest and most important market for corn, and thereby to encourage, instead of discouraging its growth.

By the 22d of Charles II c. 13, the importation of wheat, whenever the price in the home market did not exceed 53s:4d. the quarter, was subjected to a duty of 16s. the quarter; and to a duty of 8s. whenever the price did not exceed £4. The former of these two prices has, for more than a century past, taken place only in times of very great scarcity; and the latter has, so far as I know, not taken place at all. Yet, till wheat has risen above this latter price, it was, by this statute, subjected to a very high duty; and, till it had risen above the former, to a duty which amounted to a prohibition. The importation of other sorts of grain was restrained at rates and by duties, in proportion to the value of the grain, almost equally high.

Before the 13th of the present king, the following were the duties payable upon the importation of the different sorts of grain:

Grain	Duties	Duties	Duties
Beans to 28s. per qr.	19s:10d. after till 40s.	16s:8d. then 12d.	
Barley to 28s.	19s:10d. -	32s. 16s. -	12d.
Malt is prohibited by the annual malt-tax bill.			
Oats to 16s.	5s:10d. after -	- -	91/2d.
Pease to 40s.	16s:0d. after -	-	91/2d.
Rye to 36s.	19s:10d. till 40s.	16s:8d. then 12d.	
Wheat to 44s.	21s:9d. till 53s:4d.	- 17s.	then 8s.
till £4, and after that about 1s:4d. Buckwheat to 32s. per qr. to pay 16s.			

These different duties were imposed, partly by the 22d of Charles II in place of the old subsidy, partly by the new subsidy, by the one-third and two-thirds subsidy, and by the subsidy 1747. Subsequent laws still further increased those duties.

The distress which, in years of scarcity, the strict execution of those laws might have brought upon the people, would probably have been very great; but, upon such occasions, its execution was generally suspended by temporary statutes, which permitted, for a limited time, the importation of foreign corn. The necessity of these temporary statutes sufficiently demonstrates the impropriety of this general one.

These restraints upon importation, though prior to the establishment of the bounty, were dictated by the same spirit, by the same principles, which afterwards enacted that regulation. How hurtful soever in themselves, these, or some other restraints upon importation, became necessary in consequence of that regulation. If, when wheat was either below 48s. the quarter, or not much above it, foreign corn could have been imported, either duty free, or upon paying only a small duty, it might have been exported again, with the benefit of the bounty, to the great loss of the public revenue, and to the entire perversion of the institution, of which the object was to extend the market for the home growth, not that for the growth of foreign countries.

III. The trade of the merchant-exporter of corn for foreign consumption, certainly does not contribute directly to the plentiful supply of the home market. It does so, however, indirectly. From whatever source this supply maybe usually drawn, whether from home growth, or from foreign importation, unless more corn is either usually grown, or usually imported into the country, than what is usually consumed in it, the supply of the home market can never be very plentiful. But unless the surplus can, in all ordinary cases, be exported, the growers will be careful never to grow more, and the importers never to import more, than what the bare consumption of the home market requires. That market will very seldom be overstocked; but it will generally be understocked; the people, whose business it is to supply it, being generally afraid lest their goods should be left upon their hands. The prohibition of exportation limits the improvement and cultivation of the country to what the supply of its own inhabitants require. The freedom of exportation enables it to extend cultivation for the supply of foreign nations.

By the 12th of Charles II c.4, the exportation of corn was permitted whenever the price of wheat did not exceed 40s. the quarter, and that of other grain in proportion. By the 15th of the same prince, this liberty was extended till the price of wheat exceeded 48s. the quarter; and by the 22d, to all higher prices. A poundage, indeed, was to be paid to the king upon such exportation; but all grain was rated so low in the book of rates, that this poundage amounted only, upon wheat to 1s., upon oats to 4d., and upon all other grain to 6d. the quarter. By the 1st of William and Mary, the act which established this bounty, this small duty was virtually taken off whenever the price of wheat did not exceed 48s. the quarter; and by the 11th and 12th of William III c. 20, it was expressly taken off at all higher prices.

The trade of the merchant-exporter was, in this manner, not only encouraged by a bounty, but rendered much more free than that of the inland dealer. By the last of these statutes, corn could be engrossed at any price for exportation; but it could not be engrossed for inland sale, except when the price did not exceed 48s. the quarter. The interest of the inland dealer, however, it has already been shown, can never be opposite to that of the great body of the people. That of the merchant-exporter may, and in fact sometimes is. If, while his own country labors under a dearth, a neighboring country should be afflicted with a famine, it might be his interest to carry corn to the latter country, in such quantities as might very much aggravate the calamities of the dearth. The plentiful supply of the home market was not the direct object of those statutes; but, under the pretence of encouraging agriculture, to raise the money price of corn as high as possible, and thereby to occasion, as much as possible, a constant dearth in the home market. By the discouragement of importation, the supply of that market; even in times of great scarcity, was confined to the home growth; and by the encouragement of exportation, when the price was so high as 48s. the quarter, that market was not, even in times of considerable scarcity, allowed to enjoy the whole of that growth. The temporary laws, prohibiting, for a limited time, the exportation of corn, and taking off, for a limited time, the duties upon its importation, expedients to which Great Britain has been obliged so frequently to have recourse, sufficiently demonstrate the impropriety of her general system. Had that system been good, she would not so frequently have been reduced to the necessity of departing from it.

Were all nations to follow the liberal system of free exportation and free importation, the different states into which a great continent was divided, would so far resemble the different provinces of a great empire. As among the different provinces of a great empire, the freedom of the inland trade appears, both from reason and experience, not only the best palliative of a dearth, but the most effectual preventive of a famine; so would the freedom of the exportation and importation trade be among the different states into which a great continent was divided. The larger the continent, the easier the communication through all the different parts of it, both by land and by water, the less would any one particular part of it ever be exposed to either of these calamities, the scarcity of any one country being more likely to be relieved by the plenty of some other. But very few countries have entirely adopted this liberal system. The freedom of the corn trade is almost everywhere more or less restrained, and in many countries is confined by such absurd regulations, as frequently aggravate the unavoidable misfortune of a dearth into the dreadful calamity of a famine. The demand of such countries for corn may frequently become so great and so urgent, that a small state in their neighborhood, which happened at the same time to be laboring under some degree of dearth, could not venture to supply them without exposing itself to the like dreadful calamity. The very bad policy of one country may thus render it, in some measure, dangerous and imprudent to establish what would otherwise be the best policy in another. The unlimited freedom of exportation, however, would be much less dangerous in great states, in which the growth being much greater, the supply could seldom be much affected by any quantity or corn that was likely to be exported. In a Swiss canton, or in some of the little states in Italy, it may, perhaps, sometimes be necessary to restrain the exportation of corn. In such great countries as France or England, it scarce ever can. To hinder, besides, the farmer from sending his goods at all times to the best market, is evidently to sacrifice the ordinary laws of justice to an idea of public utility, to a sort of reasons of state; an act or legislative authority which ought to be exercised only, which can be pardoned only, in cases of the most urgent necessity. The price at which exportation of corn is prohibited, if it is ever to be prohibited, ought always to be a very high price.

The laws concerning corn may everywhere be compared to the laws concerning religion. The people feel themselves so much interested in what relates either to their subsistence in this life, or to their happiness in a life to come, that government must yield to their prejudices, and, in order to preserve the public tranquility, establish that system which they approve of. It is upon this account, perhaps, that we so seldom find a reasonable system established with regard to either of those two capital objects.

IV. The trade of the merchant-carrier, or of the importer of foreign corn, in order to export it again, contributes to the plentiful supply of the home market. It is not, indeed, the direct purpose of his trade to sell his corn there; but he will generally be willing to do so, and even for a good deal less money than he might expect in a foreign market; because he saves in this manner the expense of loading and unloading, of freight and insurance. The inhabitants of the country which, by means of the carrying trade, becomes the magazine and storehouse for the supply of other countries, can very seldom be in want themselves. Though the carrying trade must thus contribute to reduce the average money price of corn in the home market, it would not thereby lower its real value; it would only raise somewhat the real value of silver.

The carrying trade was in effect prohibited in Great Britain, upon all ordinary occasions, by the high duties upon the importation of foreign corn, of the greater part of which there was no drawback; and upon extraordinary occasions, when a scarcity made it necessary to suspend those duties by temporary statutes, exportation was always prohibited. By this system of laws, therefore, the carrying trade was in effect prohibited.

That system of laws, therefore, which is connected with the establishment of the bounty, seems to deserve no part of the praise which has been bestowed upon it. The improvement and prosperity of Great Britain, which has been so often ascribed to those laws, may very easily be accounted for by other causes. That security which the laws in Great Britain give to every man, that he shall enjoy the fruits of his own labor, is alone sufficient to make any country flourish, notwithstanding these and twenty other absurd regulations of commerce; and this security was perfected by the Revolution, much about the same time that the bounty was established. The natural effort of every individual to better his own condition, when suffered to exert itself with freedom and security, is so powerful a principle, that it is alone, and without any assistance, not only capable of carrying on the society to wealth and prosperity, but of surmounting a hundred impertinent obstructions, with which the folly of human laws too often encumbers its operations: though the effect of those obstructions is always, more or less, either to encroach upon its freedom, or to diminish its security. In Great Britain industry is perfectly secure; and though it is far from being perfectly free, it is as free or freer than in any other part of Europe.

Though the period of the greatest prosperity and improvement of Great Britain has been posterior to that system of laws which is connected with the bounty, we must not upon that account, impute it to those laws. It has been posterior likewise to the national debt; but the national debt has most assuredly not been the cause of it.

Though the system of laws which is connected with the bounty, has exactly the same tendency with the practice of Spain and Portugal, to lower somewhat the value of the precious metals in the country where it takes place; yet Great Britain is certainly one of the richest countries in Europe, while Spain and Portugal are perhaps amongst the most beggarly. This difference of situation, however, may easily be accounted for from two different causes. First, the tax in Spain, the prohibition in Portugal of exporting gold and silver, and the vigilant police which watches over the execution of those laws, must, in two very poor countries, which between them import annually upwards of six millions sterling, operate not only more directly, but much more forcibly, in reducing the value of those metals there, than the corn laws can do in Great Britain. And, secondly, this bad policy is not in those countries counterbalanced by the general liberty and security of the people. Industry is there neither free nor secure; and the civil and ecclesiastical governments of both Spain and Portugal are such as would alone be sufficient to perpetuate their present state of poverty, even though their regulations of commerce were as wise as the greatest part of them are absurd and foolish.

The 13th of the present king, c. 43, seems to have established a new system with regard to the corn laws, in many respects better than the ancient one, but in one or two respects perhaps not quite so good.

By this statute, the high duties upon importation for home consumption are taken off, so soon as the price of middling wheat rises to 48s. the quarter; that of middling rye, pease, or beans, to 32s.; that of barley to 24s.; and that of oats to 16s.; and instead of them, a small duty is imposed of only 6d. upon the quarter of wheat, and upon that or other grain in proportion. With regard to all those different sorts of grain, but particularly with regard to wheat, the home market is thus opened to foreign supplies, at prices considerably lower than before.

By the same statute, the old bounty of 5s. upon the exportation of wheat, ceases so soon as the price rises to 44s. the quarter, instead of 48s. the price at which it ceased before; that of 2s:6d. upon the exportation of barley, ceases so soon as the price rises to 22s. instead of 24s. the price at which it ceased before; that of 2s:6d. upon the exportation of oatmeal, ceases so soon as the price rises to 14s. instead of 15s. the price at which it ceased before. The bounty upon rye is reduced from 3s:6d. to 3s. and it ceases so soon as the price rises to 28s. instead of 32s. the price at which it ceased before. If bounties are as improper as I have endeavored to prove them to be, the sooner they cease, and the lower they are, so much the better.

The same statute permits, at the lowest prices, the importation of corn in order to be exported again, duty free, provided it is in the mean time lodged in a warehouse under the joint locks of the king and the importer. This liberty, indeed, extends to no more than twenty-five of the different ports of Great Britain. They are, however, the principal ones; and there may not, perhaps, be warehouses proper for this purpose in the greater part of the others.

So far this law seems evidently an improvement upon the ancient system.

But by the same law, a bounty of 2s. the quarter is given for the exportation of oats, whenever the price does not exceed fourteen shillings. No bounty had ever been given before for the exportation of this grain, no more than for that of pease or beans.

By the same law, too, the exportation of wheat is prohibited so soon as the price rises to forty-four shillings the quarter; that of rye so soon as it rises to twenty-eight shillings; that of barley so soon as it rises to twenty-two shillings; and that of oats so soon as they rise to fourteen shillings. Those several prices seem all of them a good deal too low; and there seems to be an impropriety, besides, in prohibiting exportation altogether at those precise prices at which that bounty, which was given in order to force it, is withdrawn. The bounty ought certainly either to have been withdrawn at a much lower price, or exportation ought to have been allowed at a much higher.

So far, therefore, this law seems to be inferior to the ancient system. With all its imperfections, however, we may perhaps say of it what was said of the laws of Solon, that though not the best in itself, it is the best which the interest, prejudices, and temper of the times, would admit of. It may perhaps in due time prepare the way for a better.

CHAPTER VI

Of Treaties of Commerce

When a nation binds itself by treaty, either to permit the entry of certain goods from one foreign country which it prohibits from all others, or to exempt the goods of one country from duties to which it subjects those of all others, the country, or at least the merchants and manufacturers of the country, whose commerce is so favored, must necessarily derive great advantage from the treaty. Those merchants and manufacturers enjoy a sort of monopoly in the country which is so indulgent to them. That country becomes a market, both more extensive and more advantageous for their goods: more extensive, because the goods of other nations being either excluded or subjected to heavier duties, it takes off a greater quantity of theirs; more advantageous, because the merchants of the favored country, enjoying a sort of monopoly there, will often sell their goods for a better price than if exposed to the free competition of all other nations.

Such treaties, however, though they may be advantageous to the merchants and manufacturers of the favored, are necessarily disadvantageous to those of the favoring country. A monopoly is thus granted against them to a foreign nation; and they must frequently buy the foreign goods they have occasion for, dearer than if the free competition of other nations was admitted. That part of its own produce with which such a nation purchases foreign goods, must consequently be sold cheaper; because, when two things are exchanged for one another, the cheapness of the one is a necessary consequence, or rather is the same thing, with the dearness of the other. The exchangeable value of its annual produce, therefore, is likely to be diminished by every such treaty. This diminution, however, can scarce amount to any positive loss, but only to a lessening of the gain which it might otherwise make. Though it sells its goods cheaper than it otherwise might do, it will not probably sell them for less than they cost; nor, as in the case of bounties, for a price which will not replace the capital employed in bringing them to market, together with the ordinary profits of stock. The trade could not go on long if it did. Even the favoring country, therefore, may still gain by the trade, though less than if there was a free competition.

Some treaties of commerce, however, have been supposed advantageous, upon principles very different from these; and a commercial country has sometimes granted a monopoly of this kind, against itself, to certain goods of a foreign nation, because it expected, that in the whole commerce between them, it would annually sell more than it would buy, and that a balance in gold and silver would be annually returned to it. It is upon this principle that the treaty of commerce between England and Portugal, concluded in 1703 by Mr. Methuen, has been so much commended. The following is a literal translation of that treaty, which consists of three articles only.

374 THE REAL PRICE OF EVERYTHING

ARTICLE I

His sacred royal majesty of Portugal promises, both in his own name and that of his successors, to admit for ever hereafter, into Portugal, the woolen cloths, and the rest of the woolen manufactures of the British, as was accustomed, till they were prohibited by the law; nevertheless upon this condition:

ARTICLE II

That is to say, that her sacred royal majesty of Great Britain shall, in her own name, and that of her successors, be obliged, for ever hereafter, to admit the wines of the growth of Portugal into Britain; so that at no time, whether there shall be peace or war between the kingdoms of Britain and France, any thing more shall be demanded for these wines by the name of custom or duty, or by whatsoever other title, directly or indirectly, whether they shall be imported into Great Britain in pipes or hogsheads, or other casks, than what shall be demanded for the like quantity or measure of French wine, deducting or abating a third part of the custom or duty. But if, at any time, this deduction or abatement of customs, which is to be made as aforesaid, shall in any manner be attempted and prejudiced, it shall be just and lawful for his sacred royal majesty of Portugal, again to prohibit the woolen cloths, and the rest of the British woolen manufactures.

ARTICLE III

The most excellent lords the plenipotentiaries promise and take upon themselves, that their above named masters shall ratify this treaty; and within the space of two months the ratification shall be exchanged.

By this treaty, the crown of Portugal becomes bound to admit the English woolens upon the same footing as before the prohibition; that is, not to raise the duties which had been paid before that time. But it does not become bound to admit them upon any better terms than those of any other nation, of France or Holland, for example. The crown of Great Britain, on the contrary, becomes bound to admit the wines of Portugal, upon paying only two-thirds of the duty which is paid for those of France, the wines most likely to come into competition with them. So far this treaty, therefore, is evidently advantageous to Portugal, and disadvantageous to Great Britain.

It has been celebrated, however, as a masterpiece of the commercial policy of England. Portugal receives annually from the Brazils a greater quantity of gold than can be employed in its domestic commerce, whether in the shape of coin or of plate. The surplus is too valuable to be allowed to lie idle and locked up in coffers; and as it can find no advantageous market at home, it must, notwithstanding any prohibition, be sent abroad, and exchanged for something for which there is a more advantageous market at home. A large share of it comes annually to England, in return either for English goods, or for those of other European nations that receive their returns through England. Mr.

Barretti was informed, that the weekly packet-boat from Lisbon brings, one week with another, more than £50,000 in gold to England. The sum had probably been exaggerated. It would amount to more than £2,600,000 a year, which is more than the Brazils are supposed to afford.

Our merchants were, some years ago, out of humor with the crown of Portugal. Some privileges which had been granted them, not by treaty, but by the free grace of that crown, at the solicitation, indeed, it is probable, and in return for much greater favors, defense and protection from the crown of Great Britain, had been either infringed or revoked. The people, therefore, usually most interested in celebrating the Portugal trade, were then rather disposed to represent it as less advantageous than it had commonly been imagined. The far greater part, almost the whole, they pretended, of this annual importation of gold, was not on account of Great Britain, but of other European nations; the fruits and wines of Portugal annually imported into Great Britain nearly compensating the value of the British goods sent thither.

Let us suppose, however, that the whole was on account of Great Britain, and that it amounted to a still greater sum than Mr. Barretti seems to imagine; this trade would not, upon that account, be more advantageous than any other, in which, for the same value sent out, we received an equal value of consumable goods in return.

It is but a very small part of this importation which, it can be supposed, is employed as an annual addition, either to the plate or to the coin of the kingdom. The rest must all be sent abroad, and exchanged for consumable goods of some kind or other. But if those consumable goods were purchased directly with the produce of English industry, it would be more for the advantage of England, than first to purchase with that produce the gold of Portugal, and afterwards to purchase with that gold those consumable goods. A direct foreign trade of consumption is always more advantageous than a round-about one; and to bring the same value of foreign goods to the home market requires a much smaller capital in the one way than in the ether. If a smaller share of its industry, therefore, had been employed in producing goods fit for the Portugal market, and a greater in producing those fit for the other markets, where those consumable goods for which there is a demand in Great Britain are to be had, it would have been more for the advantage of England. To procure both the gold which it wants for its own use, and the consumable goods, would, in this way, employ a much smaller capital than at present. There would be a spare capital, therefore, to be employed for other purposes, in exciting an additional quantity of industry, and in raising a greater annual produce.

Though Britain were entirely excluded from the Portugal trade, it could find very little difficulty in procuring all the annual supplies of gold which it wants, either for the purposes of plate, or of coin, or of foreign trade. Gold, like every other commodity, is always somewhere or another to be got for its value by those who have that value to give for it. The annual surplus of gold in Portugal, besides, would still be sent abroad, and though not carried away by Great Britain, would be carried away by some other nation, which would be glad to sell it again for its price, in the same manner as Great Britain does at present. In buying gold of Portugal, indeed, we buy it at the first hand; whereas, in buying it of any other nation, except Spain, we should buy it at the second, and might pay somewhat dearer. This difference, however, would surely be too insignificant to deserve the public attention.

Almost all our gold, it is said, comes from Portugal. With other nations, the balance of trade is either against as, or not much in our favor. But we should remember, that the more gold we import from one country, the less we must necessarily import from all others. The effectual demand for gold, like that for every other commodity, is in every country limited to a certain quantity. If nine-tenths of this quantity are imported from one country, there remains a tenth only to be imported from all others. The more gold, besides, that is annually imported from some particular countries, over and above what is requisite for plate and for coin, the more must necessarily be exported to some others: and the more that most insignificant object of modern policy, the balance of trade, appears to be in our favor with some particular countries, the more it must necessarily appear to be against us with many others.

It was upon this silly notion, however, that England could not subsist without the Portugal trade, that, towards the end of the late war, France and Spain, without pretending either offence or provocation, required the king of Portugal to exclude all British ships from his ports, and, for the security of this exclusion, to receive into them French or Spanish garrisons. Had the king of Portugal submitted to those ignominious terms which his brother-in-law the king of Spain proposed to him, Britain would have been freed from a much greater inconveniency than the loss of the Portugal trade, the burden of supporting a very weak ally, so unprovided of every thing for his own defense, that the whole power of England, had it been directed to that single purpose, could scarce, perhaps, have defended him for another campaign. The loss of the Portugal trade would, no doubt, have occasioned a considerable embarrassment to the merchants at that time engaged in it, who might not, perhaps, have found out, for a year or two, any other equally advantageous method of employing their capitals; and in this would probably have consisted all the inconveniency which England could have suffered from this notable piece of commercial policy.

The great annual importation of gold and silver is neither for the purpose of plate nor of coin, but of foreign trade. A round-about foreign trade of consumption can be carried on more advantageously by means of these metals than of almost any other goods. As they are the universal instruments of commerce, they are more readily received in return for all commodities than any other goods; and, on account of their small bulk and great value, it costs less to transport them backward and forward from one place to another than almost any other sort of merchandise, and they lose less of their value by being so transported. Of all the commodities, therefore, which are bought in one foreign country, for no other purpose but to be sold or exchanged again for some other goods in another, there are none so convenient as gold and silver. In facilitating all the different round-about foreign trades of consumption which are carried on in Great Britain, consists the principal advantage of the Portugal trade; and though it is not a capital advantage, it is, no doubt, a considerable one.

That any annual addition which, it can reasonably be supposed, is made either to the plate or to the coin of the kingdom, could require but a very small annual importation of gold and silver, seems evident enough; and though we had no direct trade with Portugal, this small quantity could always, somewhere or another, be very easily got.

Though the goldsmiths trade be very considerable in Great Britain, the far greater part of the new plate which they annually sell, is made from other old plate melted down; so that the addition annually made to the whole plate of the kingdom cannot be very great, and could require but a very small annual importation.

It is the same case with the coin. Nobody imagines, I believe, that even the greater part of the annual coinage, amounting, for ten years together, before the late reformation of the gold coin, to upwards of £800,000 a year in gold, was an annual addition to the money before current in the kingdom. In a country where the expense of the coinage is defrayed by the government, the value of the coin, even when it contains its full standard weight of gold and silver, can never be much greater than that of an equal quantity of those metals uncoined, because it requires only the trouble of going to the mint, and the delay, perhaps, of a few weeks, to procure for any quantity of uncoined gold and silver an equal quantity of those metals in coin; but in every country the greater part of the current coin is almost always more or less worn, or otherwise degenerated from its standard. In Great Britain it was, before the late reformation, a good deal so, the gold being more than two percent, and the silver more than eight percent below its standard weight. But if forty-four guineas and a half, containing their full standard weight, a pound weight of gold, could purchase very little more than a pound weight of uncoined gold; forty-four guineas and a half, wanting a part of their weight, could not purchase a pound weight, and something was to be added, in order to make up the deficiency. The current price of gold bullion at market, therefore, instead of being the same with the mint price, or £46:14:6, was then about £47:14s., and sometimes about £48. When the greater part of the coin, however, was in this degenerate condition, forty-four guineas and a half, fresh from the mint, would purchase no more goods in the market than any other ordinary guineas; because, when they came into the coffers of the merchant, being confounded with other money, they could not afterwards be distinguished without more trouble than the difference was worth. Like other guineas, they were worth no more than £46:14:6. If thrown into the melting pot, however, they produced, without any sensible loss, a pound weight of standard gold, which could be sold at any time for between £47:14s. and £48, either in gold or silver, as fit for all the purposes of coin as that which had been melted down. There was an evident profit, therefore, in melting down new-coined money; and it was done so instantaneously, that no precaution of government could prevent it. The operations of the mint were, upon this account, somewhat like the web of Penelope; the work that was done in the day was undone in the night. The mint was employed, not so much in making daily additions to the coin, as in replacing the very best part of it, which was daily melted down.

Were the private people who carry their gold and silver to the mint to pay themselves for the coinage, it would add to the value of those metals, in the same manner as the fashion does to that of plate. Coined gold and silver would be more valuable than uncoined. The seignorage, if it was not exorbitant, would add to the bullion the whole value of the duty; because, the government having everywhere the exclusive privilege of coining, no coin can come to market cheaper than they think proper to afford it. If the duty was exorbitant, indeed, that is, if it was very much above the real value of the labor and expense requisite for coinage, false coiners, both at home and abroad, might be encouraged, by the great difference between the value of bullion and that of coin, to pour in so great a quantity of counterfeit money as might reduce the value of the government money. In France, however, though the seignorage is eight percent, no sensible inconveniency of this kind is found to arise from it. The dangers to which a false coiner is everywhere exposed, if he lives in the country of which he counterfeits the coin, and to which his agents or correspondents are exposed, if he lives in a foreign country, are by far too great to be incurred for the sake of a profit of six or seven percent.

The seignorage in France raises the value of the coin higher than in proportion to the quantity of pure gold which it contains. Thus, by the edict of January 1726, the mint price of fine gold of twenty-four carats was fixed at seven hundred and forty livres nine sous and one denier one-eleventh the mark of eight Paris ounces. {See Dictionnaire des Monnoies, tom. ii. article Seigneurage, p. 439, par 81. Abbot de Bazinghen, Conseiller-Commissaire en la Cour des Monnoies à Paris.} The gold coin of France, making an allowance for the remedy of the mint, contains twenty-one carats and three-fourths of fine gold, and two carats one-fourth of alloy. The mark of standard gold, therefore, is worth no more than about six hundred and seventy-one livres ten deniers. But in France this mark of standard gold is coined into thirty louis d'ors of twenty-four livres each, or into seven hundred and twenty livres. The coinage, therefore, increases the value of a mark of standard gold bullion, by the difference between six hundred and seventy-one livres ten deniers and seven hundred and twenty livres, or by forty-eight livres nineteen sous and two deniers.

A seignorage will, in many cases, take away altogether, and will in all cases diminish, the profit of melting down the new coin. This profit always arises from the difference between the quantity of bullion which the common currency ought to contain and that which it actually does contain. If this difference is less than the seignorage, there will be loss instead of profit. If it is equal to the seignorage, there will be neither profit nor loss. If it is greater than the seignorage, there will, indeed, be some profit, but less than if there was no seignorage. If, before the late reformation of the gold coin, for example, there had been a seignorage of five percent upon the coinage, there would have been a loss of three percent upon the melting down of the gold coin. If the seignorage had been two percent, there would have been neither profit nor loss. If the seignorage had been one percent, there would have been a profit but of one percent only, instead of two percent. Wherever money is received by tale, therefore, and not by weight, a seignorage is the most effectual preventive of the melting down of the coin, and, for the same reason, of its exportation. It is the best and heaviest pieces that are commonly either melted down or exported, because it is upon such that the largest profits are made.

The law for the encouragement of the coinage, by rendering it duty-free, was first enacted during the reign of Charles II for a limited time, and afterwards continued, by different prolongations, till 1769, when it was rendered perpetual. The Bank of England, in order to replenish their coffers with money, are frequently obliged to carry bullion to the mint; and it was more for their interest, they probably imagined, that the coinage should be at the expense of the government than at their own. It was probably out of complaisance to this great company, that the government agreed to render this law perpetual. Should the custom of weighing gold, however, come to be disused, as it is very likely to be on account of its inconveniency; should the gold coin of England come to be received by tale, as it was before the late recoinage this great company may, perhaps, find that they have, upon this, as upon some other occasions, mistaken their own interest not a little.

Before the late recoinage, when the gold currency of England was two percent below its standard weight, as there was no seignorage, it was two percent below the value of that quantity of standard gold bullion which it ought to have contained. When this great company, therefore, bought gold bullion in order to have it coined, they were obliged to pay for it two percent more than it was worth after the coinage. But if there had been a seignorage of two percent upon the coinage, the common gold currency, though two percent below its standard weight, would, notwithstanding, have been equal in value to the quantity of standard gold which it ought to have contained; the value of the fashion compensating in this case the diminution of the weight. They would, indeed, have had the seignorage to pay, which being two percent, their loss upon the whole transaction would have been two percent, exactly the same, but no greater than it actually was.

If the seignorage had been five percent and the gold currency only two percent below its standard weight, the bank would, in this case, have gained three percent upon the price of the bullion; but as they would have had a seignorage of five percent to pay upon the coinage, their loss upon the whole transaction would, in the same manner, have been exactly two percent.

If the seignorage had been only one percent, and the gold currency two percent below its standard weight, the bank would, in this case, have lost only one percent upon the price of the bullion; but as they would likewise have had a seignorage of one percent to pay, their loss upon the whole transaction would have been exactly two percent, in the same manner as in all other cases.

If there was a reasonable seignorage, while at the same time the coin contained its full standard weight, as it has done very nearly since the late recoinage, whatever the bank might lose by the seignorage, they would gain upon the price of the bullion; and whatever they might gain upon the price of the bullion, they would lose by the seignorage. They would neither lose nor gain, therefore, upon the whole transaction, and they would in this, as in all the foregoing cases, be exactly in the same situation as if there was no seignorage.

When the tax upon a commodity is so moderate as not to encourage smuggling, the merchant who deals in it, though he advances, does not properly pay the tax, as he gets it back in the price of the commodity. The tax is finally paid by the last purchaser or consumer. But money is a commodity, with regard to which every man is a merchant. Nobody buys it but in order to sell it again; and with regard to it there is, in ordinary cases, no last purchaser or consumer. When the tax upon coinage, therefore, is so moderate as not to encourage false coining, though every body advances the tax, nobody finally pays it; because every body gets it back in the advanced value of the coin. The government, therefore, when it defrays the expense of coinage, not only incurs some small expense, but loses some small revenue which it might get by a proper duty; and neither the bank, nor any other private persons, are in the smallest degree benefited by this useless piece of public generosity.

The directors of the bank, however, would probably be unwilling to agree to the imposition of a seignorage upon the authority of a speculation which promises them no gain, but only pretends to insure them from any loss. In the present state of the gold coin, and as long as it continues to be received by weight, they certainly would gain nothing by such a change. But if the custom of weighing the gold coin should ever go into disuse, as it is very likely to do, and if the gold coin should ever fall into the same state of degradation in which it was before the late recoinage, the gain, or more properly the savings, of the bank, inconsequence of the imposition of a seignorage, would probably be very considerable. The Bank of England is the only company which sends any considerable quantity of bullion to the mint, and the burden of the annual coinage falls entirely, or almost entirely, upon it. If this annual coinage had nothing to do but to repair the unavoidable losses and necessary wear and tear of the coin, it could seldom exceed fifty thousand, or at most a hundred thousand pounds. But when the coin is degraded below its standard weight, the annual coinage must, besides this, fill up the large vacuities which exportation and the melting pot are continually making in the current coin. It was upon this account, that during the ten or twelve years immediately preceding the late reformation of the gold coin, the annual coinage amounted, at an average, to more than £850,000. But if there had been a seignorage of four or five percent upon the gold coin, it would probably, even in the state in which things then were, have put an effectual stop to the business both of exportation and of the melting pot. The bank, instead of losing every year about two and a half percent upon the bullion which was to be coined into more than eight hundred and fifty thousand pounds, or incurring an annual loss of more than £21,250 pounds, would not probably have incurred the tenth part of that loss.

The revenue allotted by parliament for defraying the expense of the coinage is but fourteen thousand pounds a year; and the real expense which it costs the government, or the fees of the officers of the mint, do not, upon ordinary occasions, I am assured, exceed the half of that sum. The saving of so very small a sum, or even the gaining of another, which could not well be much larger, are objects too inconsiderable, it may be thought, to deserve the serious attention of government. But the saving of eighteen or twenty thousand pounds a year, in case of an event which is not improbable, which has frequently happened before, and which is very likely to happen again, is surely an object which well deserves the serious attention, even of so great a company as the bank of England.

Some of the foregoing reasonings and observations might, perhaps, have been more properly placed in those chapters of the first book which treat of the origin and use of money, and of the difference between the real and the nominal price of commodities. But as the law for the encouragement of coinage derives its origin from those vulgar prejudices which have been introduced by the mercantile system, I judged it more proper to reserve them for this chapter. Nothing could be more agreeable to the spirit of that system than a sort of bounty upon the production of money, the very thing which, it supposes, constitutes the wealth of every nation. It is one of its many admirable expedients for enriching the country.

CHAPTER VII

Of Colonies

Part I

Of the Motives for Establishing New Colonies

The interest which occasioned the first settlement of the different European colonies in America and the West Indies, was not altogether so plain and distinct as that which directed the establishment of those of ancient Greece and Rome.

All the different states of ancient Greece possessed, each of them, but a very small territory; and when the people in anyone of them multiplied beyond what that territory could easily maintain, a part of them were sent in quest of a new habitation, in some remote and distant part of the world; the warlike neighbors who surrounded them on all sides, rendering it difficult for any of them to enlarge very much its territory at home. The colonies of the Dorians resorted chiefly to Italy and Sicily, which, in the times preceding the foundation of Rome, were inhabited by barbarous and uncivilized nations; those of the Ionians and Aeolians, the two other great tribes of the Greeks, to Asia Minor and the islands of the Aegean sea, of which the inhabitants seen at that time to have been pretty much in the same state as those of Sicily and Italy. The mother city, though she considered the colony as a child, at all times entitled to great favor and assistance, and owing in return much gratitude and respect, yet considered it as an emancipated child, over whom she pretended to claim no direct authority or jurisdiction. The colony settled its own form of government, enacted its own laws, elected its own magistrates, and made peace or war with its neighbors, as an independent state, which had no occasion to wait for the approbation or consent of the mother city. Nothing can be more plain and distinct than the interest which directed every such establishment.

Rome, like most of the other ancient republics, was originally founded upon an agrarian law, which divided the public territory, in a certain proportion, among the different citizens who composed the state. The course of human affairs, by marriage, by succession, and by alienation, necessarily deranged this original division, and frequently threw the lands which had been allotted for the maintenance of many different families, into the possession of a single person. To remedy this disorder, for such it was supposed to be, a law was made, restricting the quantity of land which any citizen could possess to five hundred jugera; about 350 English acres. This law, however, though we read of its having been executed upon one or two occasions, was either neglected or evaded, and the inequality of fortunes went on continually increasing. The greater part of the citizens had no land; and without it the manners and customs of those times rendered it difficult for a freeman to maintain his independency. In the present times, though a poor man has no land of his own, if he has a little stock, he may either farm the lands of another, or he may carry on some little retail trade; and if he has no stock, he may find employment either as a country laborer, or as an artificer. But among the ancient Romans, the lands of the rich were all cultivated by slaves, who wrought under an overseer, who was likewise a slave; so that a poor freeman had little chance of being employed either as a farmer or as a laborer. All trades and manufactures, too, even the retail trade, were carried on by the slaves of the rich for the benefit of their masters, whose wealth, authority, and protection, made it difficult for a poor freeman to maintain the competition against them. The citizens, therefore, who had no land, had scarce any other means of subsistence but the bounties of the candidates at the annual elections. The tribunes, when they had a mind to animate the people against the rich and the great, put them in mind of the ancient divisions of lands, and represented that law which restricted this sort of private property as the fundamental law of the republic. The people became clamorous to get land, and the rich and the great, we may believe, were perfectly determined not to give them any part of theirs. To satisfy them in some measure, therefore, they frequently proposed to send out a new colony. But conquering Rome was, even upon such occasions, under no necessity of turning out her citizens to seek their fortune, if one may so, through the wide world, without knowing where they were to settle. She assigned them lands generally in the conquered provinces of Italy, where, being within the dominions of the republic, they could never form any independent state, but were at best but a sort of corporation, which, though it had the power of enacting bylaws for its own government, was at all times subject to the correction, jurisdiction, and legislative authority of the mother city. The sending out a colony of this kind not only gave some satisfaction to the people, but often established a sort of garrison, too, in a newly conquered province, of which the obedience might otherwise have been doubtful. A Roman colony, therefore, whether we consider the nature of the establishment itself, or the motives for making it, was altogether different from a Greek one. The words, accordingly, which in the original languages denote those different establishments, have very different meanings. The Latin word *colonia* signifies simply a plantation. The Greek word *apoixia,* on the contrary, signifies a separation of dwelling, a departure from home, a going out of the house. But though the Roman colonies were, in many respects, different from the Greek ones, the interest which prompted to establish them was equally plain and distinct. Both institutions derived their origin, either from irresistible necessity, or from clear and evident utility.

The establishment of the European colonies in America and the West Indies arose from no necessity; and though the utility which has resulted from them has been very great, it is not altogether so clear and evident. It was not understood at their first establishment, and was not the motive, either of that establishment, or of the discoveries which gave occasion to it; and the nature, extent, and limits of that utility, are not, perhaps, well understood at this day.

The Venetians, during the fourteenth and fifteenth centuries, carried on a very advantageous commerce in spiceries and other East India goods, which they distributed among the other nations of Europe. They purchased them chiefly in Egypt, at that time under the dominion of the Mamelukes, the enemies of the Turks, of whom the Venetians were the enemies; and this union of interest, assisted by the money of Venice, formed such a connection as gave the Venetians almost a monopoly of the trade.

The great profits of the Venetians tempted the avidity of the Portuguese. They had been endeavoring, during the course of the fifteenth century, to find out by sea a way to the countries from which the Moors brought them ivory and gold dust across the desert. They discovered the Madeiras, the Canaries, the Azores, the Cape de Verd islands, the coast of Guinea, that of Loango, Congo, Angola, and Benguela, and, finally, the Cape of Good Hope. They had long wished to share in the profitable traffic of the Venetians, and this last discovery opened to them a probable prospect of doing so. In 1497, Vasco de Gamo sailed from the port of Lisbon with a fleet of four ships, and, after a navigation of eleven months, arrived upon the coast of Indostan; and thus completed a course of discoveries which had been pursued with great steadiness, and with very little interruption, for near a century together.

Some years before this, while the expectations of Europe were in suspense about the projects of the Portuguese, of which the success appeared yet to be doubtful, a Genoese pilot formed the yet more daring project of sailing to the East Indies by the west. The situation of those countries was at that time very imperfectly known in Europe. The few European travelers who had been there, had magnified the distance, perhaps through simplicity and ignorance; what was really very great, appearing almost infinite to those who could not measure it; or, perhaps, in order to increase somewhat more the marvelous of their own adventures in visiting regions so immensely remote from Europe. The longer the way was by the east, Columbus very justly concluded, the shorter it would be by the west. He proposed, therefore, to take that way, as both the shortest and the surest, and he had the good fortune to convince Isabella of Castile of the probability of his project. He sailed from the port of Palos in August 1492, near five years before the expedition of Vasco de Gamo set out from Portugal; and, after a voyage of between two and three months, discovered first some of the small Bahama or Lucyan islands, and afterwards the great island of St. Domingo.

But the countries which Columbus discovered, either in this or in any of his subsequent voyages, had no resemblance to those which he had gone in quest of. Instead of the wealth, cultivation, and populousness of China and Indostan, he found, in St. Domingo, and in all the other parts of the new world which he ever visited, nothing but a country quite covered with wood, uncultivated, and inhabited only by some tribes of naked and miserable savages. He was not very willing, however, to believe that they were not the same with some of the countries described by Marco Polo, the first European who had visited, or at least had left behind him any description of China or the East Indies; and a very slight resemblance, such as that which he found between the name of Cibao, a mountain in St. Domingo, and that of Cipange, mentioned by Marco Polo, was frequently sufficient to make him return to this favorite prepossession, though contrary to the clearest evidence. In his letters to Ferdinand and Isabella, he called the countries which he had discovered the Indies. He entertained no doubt but that they were the extremity of those which had been described by Marco Polo, and that they were not very distant from the Ganges, or from the countries which had been conquered by Alexander. Even when at last convinced that they were different, he still flattered himself that those rich countries were at no great distance; and in a subsequent voyage, accordingly, went in quest of them along the coast of Terra Firma, and towards the Isthmus of Darien.

In consequence of this mistake of Columbus, the name of the Indies has stuck to those unfortunate countries ever since; and when it was at last clearly discovered that the new were altogether different from the old Indies, the former were called the West, in contradistinction to the latter, which were called the East Indies.

It was of importance to Columbus, however, that the countries which he had discovered, whatever they were, should be represented to the court of Spain as of very great consequence; and, in what constitutes the real riches of every country, the animal and vegetable productions of the soil, there was at that time nothing which could well justify such a representation of them.

The cori, something between a rat and a rabbit, and supposed by Mr. Buffon to be the same with the aperea of Brazil, was the largest viviparous quadruped in St. Domingo.

This species seems never to have been very numerous; and the dogs and cats of the Spaniards are said to have long ago almost entirely extirpated it, as well as some other tribes of a still smaller size. These, however, together with a pretty large lizard, called the ivana or iguana, constituted the principal part of the animal food which the land afforded.

The vegetable food of the inhabitants, though, from their want of industry, not very abundant, was not altogether so scanty. It consisted in Indian corn, yams, potatoes, bananas, etc., plants which were then altogether unknown in Europe, and which have never since been very much esteemed in it, or supposed to yield a sustenance equal to what is drawn from the common sorts of grain and pulse, which have been cultivated in this part of the world time out of mind.

The cotton plant, indeed, afforded the material of a very important manufacture, and was at that time, to Europeans, undoubtedly the most valuable of all the vegetable productions of those islands. But though, in the end of the fifteenth century, the muslins and other cotton goods of the East Indies were much esteemed in every part of Europe, the cotton manufacture itself was not cultivated in any part of it. Even this production, therefore, could not at that time appear in the eyes of Europeans to be of very great consequence.

Finding nothing, either in the animals or vegetables of the newly discovered countries which could justify a very advantageous representation of them, Columbus turned his view towards their minerals; and in the richness of their productions of this third kingdom, he flattered himself he had found a full compensation for the insignificancy of those of the other two. The little bits of gold with which the inhabitants ornamented their dress, and which, he was informed, they frequently found in the rivulets and torrents which fell from the mountains, were sufficient to satisfy him that those mountains abounded with the richest gold mines. St. Domingo, therefore, was represented as a country abounding with gold, and upon that account (according to the prejudices not only of the present times, but of those times), an inexhaustible source of real wealth to the crown and kingdom of Spain. When Columbus, upon his return from his first voyage, was introduced with a sort of triumphal honors to the sovereigns of Castile and Arragon, the principal productions of the countries which he had discovered were carried in solemn procession before him. The only valuable part of them consisted in some little fillets, bracelets, and other ornaments of gold, and in some bales of cotton. The rest were mere objects of vulgar wonder and curiosity; some reeds of an extraordinary size, some birds of a very beautiful plumage, and some stuffed skins of the huge alligator and manati; all of which were preceded by six or seven of the wretched natives, whose singular color and appearance added greatly to the novelty of the show.

In consequence of the representations of Columbus, the council of Castile determined to take possession of the countries of which the inhabitants were plainly incapable of defending themselves. The pious purpose of converting them to Christianity sanctified the injustice of the project. But the hope of finding treasures of gold there was the sole motive which prompted to undertake it; and to give this motive the greater weight, it was proposed by Columbus, that the half of all the gold and silver that should be found there, should belong to the crown. This proposal was approved of by the council.

As long as the whole, or the greater part of the gold which the first adventurers imported into Europe was got by so very easy a method as the plundering of the defenseless natives, it was not perhaps very difficult to pay even this heavy tax; but when the natives were once fairly stripped of all that they had, which, in St. Domingo, and in all the other countries discovered by Columbus, was done completely in six or eight years, and when, in order to find more, it had become necessary to dig for it in the mines, there was no longer any possibility of paying this tax. The rigorous exaction of it, accordingly, first occasioned, it is said, the total abandoning of the mines of St. Domingo, which have never been wrought since. It was soon reduced, therefore, to a third; then to a fifth; afterwards to a tenth; and at last to a twentieth part of the gross produce of the gold mines. The tax upon silver continued for a long time to be a fifth of the gross produce. It was reduced to a tenth only in the course of the present century. But the first adventurers do not appear to have been much interested about silver. Nothing less precious than gold seemed worthy of their attention.

All the other enterprises of the Spaniards in the New World, subsequent to those of Columbus, seem to have been prompted by the same motive. It was the sacred thirst of gold that carried Ovieda, Nicuessa, and Vasco Nugnes de Balboa, to the Isthmus of Darien; that carried Cortes to Mexico, Almagro and Pizarro to Chili and Peru. When those adventurers arrived upon any unknown coast, their first inquiry was always if there was any gold to be found there; and according to the information which they received concerning this particular, they determined either to quit the country or to settle in it.

Of all those expensive and uncertain projects, however, which bring bankruptcy upon the greater part of the people who engage in them, there is none, perhaps, more perfectly ruinous than the search after new silver and gold mines. It is, perhaps, the most disadvantageous lottery in the world, or the one in which the gain of those who draw the prizes bears the least proportion to the loss of those who draw the blanks; for though the prizes are few, and the blanks many, the common price of a ticket is the whole fortune of a very rich man. Projects of mining, instead of replacing the capital employed in them, together with the ordinary profits of stock, commonly absorb both capital and profit. They are the projects, therefore, to which, of all others, a prudent lawgiver, who desired to increase the capital of his nation, would least choose to give any extraordinary encouragement, or to turn towards them a greater share of that capital than what would go to them of its own accord. Such, in reality, is the absurd confidence which almost all men have in their own good fortune, that wherever there is the least probability of success, too great a share of it is apt to go to them of its own accord.

But though the judgment of sober reason and experience concerning such projects has always been extremely unfavorable, that of human avidity has commonly been quite otherwise. The same passion which has suggested to so many people the absurd idea of the philosopher's stone, has suggested to others the equally absurd one of immense rich mines of gold and silver. They did not consider that the value of those metals has, in all ages and nations, arisen chiefly from their scarcity, and that their scarcity has arisen from the very small quantities of them which Nature has anywhere deposited in one place, from the hard and intractable substances with which she has almost everywhere surrounded those small quantities, and consequently from the labor and expense which are everywhere necessary in order to penetrate, and get at them. They flattered themselves that veins of those metals might in many places be found, as large and as abundant as those which are commonly found of lead, or copper, or tin, or iron. The dream of Sir Walter Raleigh, concerning the golden city and country of El Dorado, may satisfy us, that even wise men are not always exempt from such strange delusions. More than a hundred years after the death of that great man, the Jesuit Gumila was still convinced of the reality of that wonderful country, and expressed, with great warmth, and, I dare say, with great sincerity, how happy he should be to carry the light of the gospel to a people who could so well reward the pious labors of their missionary.

In the countries first discovered by the Spaniards, no gold and silver mines are at present known which are supposed to be worth the working. The quantities of those metals which the first adventurers are said to have found there, had probably been very much magnified, as well as the fertility of the mines which were wrought immediately after the first discovery. What those adventurers were reported to have found, however, was sufficient to inflame the avidity of all their countrymen. Every Spaniard who sailed to America expected to find an El Dorado. Fortune, too, did upon this what she has done upon very few other occasions. She realized in some measure the extravagant hopes of her votaries; and in the discovery and conquest of Mexico and Peru (of which the one happened about thirty, and the other about forty, years after the first expedition of Columbus), she presented them with something not very unlike that profusion of the precious metals which they sought for.

A project of commerce to the East Indies, therefore, gave occasion to the first discovery of the West. A project of conquest gave occasion to all the establishments of the Spaniards in those newly discovered countries. The motive which excited them to this conquest was a project of gold and silver mines; and a course of accidents which no human wisdom could foresee, rendered this project much more successful than the undertakers had any reasonable grounds for expecting.

The first adventurers of all the other nations of Europe who attempted to make settlements in America, were animated by the like chimerical views; but they were not equally successful. It was more than a hundred years after the first settlement of the Brazils, before any silver, gold, or diamond mines, were discovered there. In the English, French, Dutch, and Danish colonies, none have ever yet been discovered, at least none that are at present supposed to be worth the working. The first English settlers in North

America, however, offered a fifth of all the gold and silver which should be found there to the king, as a motive for granting them their patents. In the patents of Sir Walter Raleigh, to the London and Plymouth companies, to the council of Plymouth, etc. this fifth was accordingly reserved to the crown. To the expectation of finding gold and silver mines, those first settlers, too, joined that of discovering a north-west passage to the East Indies. They have hitherto been disappointed in both.

Part II

Causes of the Prosperity of New Colonies

The colony of a civilized nation which takes possession either of a waste country, or of one so thinly inhabited that the natives easily give place to the new settlers, advances more rapidly to wealth and greatness than any other human society.

The colonies carry out with them a knowledge of agriculture and of other useful arts, superior to what can grow up of its own accord, in the course of many centuries, among savage and barbarous nations. They carry out with them, too, the habit of subordination, some notion of the regular government which takes place in their own country, of the system of laws which support it, and of a regular administration of justice; and they naturally establish something of the same kind in the new settlement. But among savage and barbarous nations, the natural progress of law and government is still slower than the natural progress of arts, after law and government have been so far established as is necessary for their protection. Every colonist gets more land than he can possibly cultivate. He has no rent, and scarce any taxes, to pay. No landlord shares with him in its produce, and, the share of the sovereign is commonly but a trifle. He has every motive to render as great as possible a produce which is thus to be almost entirely his own. But his land is commonly so extensive, that, with all his own industry, and with all the industry of other people whom he can get to employ, he can seldom make it produce the tenth part of what it is capable of producing. He is eager, therefore, to collect laborers from all quarters, and to reward them with the most liberal wages. But those liberal wages, joined to the plenty and cheapness of land, soon make those laborers leave him, in order to become landlords themselves, and to reward with equal liberality other laborers, who soon leave them for the same reason that they left their first master. The liberal reward of labor encourages marriage. The children, during the tender years of infancy, are well fed and properly taken care of; and when they are grown up, the value of their labor greatly overpays their maintenance. When arrived at maturity, the high price of labor, and the low price of land, enable them to establish themselves in the same manner as their fathers did before them.

In other countries, rent and profit eat up wages, and the two superior orders of people oppress the inferior one; but in new colonies, the interest of the two superior orders obliges them to treat the inferior one with more generosity and humanity, at least where that inferior one is not in a state of slavery. Waste lands, of the greatest natural fertility, are to be had for a trifle. The increase of revenue which the proprietor, who is always the undertaker, expects from their improvement, constitutes his profit, which, in these circumstances, is commonly very great; but this great profit cannot be made, without employing the labor of other people in clearing and cultivating the land; and the disproportion between the great extent of the land and the small number of the people, which commonly takes place in new colonies, makes it difficult for him to get this labor. He does not, therefore, dispute about wages, but is willing to employ labor at any price. The high wages of labor encourage population. The cheapness and plenty of good land encourage improvement, and enable the proprietor to pay those high wages. In those wages consists almost the whole price of the land; and though they are high, considered as the wages of labor, they are low, considered as the price of what is so very valuable. What encourages the progress of population and improvement, encourages that of real wealth and greatness.

The progress of many of the ancient Greek colonies towards wealth and greatness seems accordingly to have been very rapid. In the course of a century or two, several of them appear to have rivaled, and even to have surpassed, their mother cities. Syracuse and Agrigentum in Sicily, Tarentum and Locri in Italy, Ephesus and Miletus in Lesser Asia, appear, by all accounts, to have been at least equal to any of the cities of ancient Greece. Though posterior in their establishment, yet all the arts of refinement, philosophy, poetry, and eloquence, seem to have been cultivated as early, and to have been improved as highly in them as in any part of the mother country. The schools of the two oldest Greek philosophers, those of Thales and Pythagoras, were established, it is remarkable, not in ancient Greece, but the one in an Asiatic, the other in an Italian colony. All those colonies had established themselves in countries inhabited by savage and barbarous nations, who easily gave place to the new settlers. They had plenty of good land; and as they were altogether independent of the mother city, they were at liberty to manage their own affairs in the way that they judged was most suitable to their own interest.

The history of the Roman colonies is by no means so brilliant. Some of them, indeed, such as Florence, have, in the course of many ages, and after the fall of the mother city, grown up to be considerable states. But the progress of no one of them seems ever to have been very rapid. They were all established in conquered provinces, which in most cases had been fully inhabited before. The quantity of land assigned to each colonist was seldom very considerable, and, as the colony was not independent, they were not always at liberty to manage their own affairs in the way that they judged was most suitable to their own interest.

In the plenty of good land, the European colonies established in America and the West Indies resemble, and even greatly surpass, those of ancient Greece. In their dependency upon the mother state, they resemble those of ancient Rome; but their great distance from Europe has in all of them alleviated more or less the effects of this dependency. Their situation has placed them less in the view, and less in the power of their mother country. In pursuing their interest their own way, their conduct has upon many occasions been overlooked, either because not known or not understood in Europe; and upon some occasions it has been fairly suffered and submitted to, because their distance rendered it difficult to restrain it. Even the violent and arbitrary government of Spain has, upon many occasions, been obliged to recall or soften the orders which had been given for the government of her colonies, for fear of a general insurrection. The progress of all the European colonies in wealth, population, and improvement, has accordingly been very great.

The crown of Spain, by its share of the gold and silver, derived some revenue from its colonies from the moment of their first establishment. It was a revenue, too, of a nature to excite in human avidity the most extravagant expectation of still greater riches. The Spanish colonies, therefore, from the moment of their first establishment, attracted very much the attention of their mother country; while those of the other European nations were for a long time in a great measure neglected. The former did not, perhaps, thrive the better in consequence of this attention, nor the latter the worse in consequence of this neglect. In proportion to the extent of the country which they in some measure possess, the Spanish colonies are considered as less populous and thriving than those of almost any other European nation. The progress even of the Spanish colonies, however, in population and improvement, has certainly been very rapid and very great. The city of Lima, founded since the conquest, is represented by Ulloa as containing fifty thousand inhabitants near thirty years ago. Quito, which had been but a miserable hamlet of Indians, is represented by the same author as in his time equally populous. Gemel i Carreri, a pretended traveler, it is said, indeed, but who seems everywhere to have written upon extreme good information, represents the city of Mexico as containing a hundred thousand inhabitants; a number which, in spite of all the exaggerations of the Spanish writers, is probably more than five times greater than what it contained in the time of Montezuma. These numbers exceed greatly those of Boston, New York, and Philadelphia, the three greatest cities of the English colonies. Before the conquest of the Spaniards, there were no cattle fit for draught, either in Mexico or Peru. The lama was their only beast of burden, and its strength seems to have been a good deal inferior to that of a common ass. The plough was unknown among them. They were ignorant of the use of iron. They had no coined money, nor any established instrument of commerce of any kind. Their commerce was carried on by barter. A sort of wooden spade was their principal instrument of agriculture. Sharp stones served them for knives and hatchets to cut with; fish bones, and the hard sinews of certain animals, served them with needles to sew with; and these seem to have been their principal instruments of trade. In this state of things, it seems impossible that either of those empires could have been so much improved or so well cultivated as at present, when they are plentifully furnished with all sorts of European cattle, and when the use of iron, of the plough, and of many of the arts of Europe, have been introduced among them. But the populousness of every country must be in proportion to the degree of its improvement and cultivation. In spite of the cruel destruction of the natives which followed the conquest, these two great empires are probably more populous now than they ever were before; and the people are surely very different; for we must acknowledge, I apprehend, that the Spanish creoles are in many respects superior to the ancient Indians.

After the settlements of the Spaniards, that of the Portuguese in Brazil is the oldest of any European nation in America. But as for a long time after the first discovery neither gold nor silver mines were found in it, and as it afforded upon that account little or no revenue to the crown, it was for a long time in a great measure neglected; and during this state of neglect, it grew up to be a great and powerful colony. While Portugal was under the dominion of Spain, Brazil was attacked by the Dutch, who got possession of seven of the fourteen provinces into which it is divided. They expected soon to conquer the other seven, when Portugal recovered its independency by the elevation of the family of Braganza to the throne. The Dutch, then, as enemies to the Spaniards, became friends to the Portuguese, who were likewise the enemies of the Spaniards. They agreed, therefore, to leave that part of Brazil which they had not conquered to the king of Portugal, who agreed to leave that part which they had conquered to them, as a matter not worth disputing about, with such good allies. But the Dutch government soon began to oppress the Portuguese colonists, who, instead of amusing themselves with complaints, took arms against their new masters, and by their own valor and resolution, with the connivance, indeed, but without any avowed assistance from the mother country, drove them out of Brazil. The Dutch, therefore, finding it impossible to keep any part of the country to themselves, were contented that it should be entirely restored to the crown of Portugal. In this colony there are said to be more than six hundred thousand people, either Portuguese or descended from Portuguese, creoles, mulattoes, and a mixed race between Portuguese and Brazilians. No one colony in America is supposed to contain so great a number of people of European extraction.

Towards the end of the fifteenth, and during the greater part of the sixteenth century, Spain and Portugal were the two great naval powers upon the ocean; for though the commerce of Venice extended to every part of Europe, its fleet had scarce ever sailed beyond the Mediterranean. The Spaniards, in virtue of the first discovery, claimed all America as their own; and though they could not hinder so great a naval power as that of Portugal from settling in Brazil, such was at that time the terror of their name, that the greater part of the other nations of Europe were afraid to establish themselves in any other part of that great continent. The French, who attempted to settle in Florida, were all murdered by the Spaniards. But the declension of the naval power of this latter nation, in consequence of the defeat or miscarriage of what they called their invincible armada, which happened towards the end of the sixteenth century, put it out of their power to obstruct any longer the settlements of the other European nations. In the course of the seventeenth century, therefore, the English, French, Dutch, Danes, and Swedes, all the great nations who had any ports upon the ocean, attempted to make some settlements in the new world.

The Swedes established themselves in New Jersey; and the number of Swedish families still to be found there sufficiently demonstrates, that this colony was very likely to prosper, had it been protected by the mother country. But being neglected by Sweden, it was soon swallowed up by the Dutch colony of New York, which again, in 1674, fell under the dominion of the English.

The small islands of St. Thomas and Santa Cruz, are the only countries in the new world that have ever been possessed by the Danes. These little settlements, too, were under the government of an exclusive company, which had the sole right, both of purchasing the surplus produce of the colonies, and of supplying them with such goods of other countries as they wanted, and which, therefore, both in its purchases and sales, had not only the power of oppressing them, but the greatest temptation to do so. The government of an exclusive company of merchants is, perhaps, the worst of all governments for any country whatever. It was not, however, able to stop altogether the progress of these colonies, though it rendered it more slow and languid. The late king of Denmark dissolved this company, and since that time the prosperity of these colonies has been very great.

The Dutch settlements in the West, as well as those in the East Indies, were originally put under the government of an exclusive company. The progress of some of them, therefore, though it has been considerable in comparison with that of almost any country that has been long peopled and established, has been languid and slow in comparison with that of the greater part of new colonies. The colony of Surinam, though very considerable, is still inferior to the greater part of the sugar colonies of the other European nations. The colony of Nova Belgia, now divided into the two provinces of New York and New Jersey, would probably have soon become considerable too, even though it had remained under the government of the Dutch. The plenty and cheapness of good land are such powerful causes of prosperity, that the very worst government is scarce capable of checking altogether the efficacy of their operation. The great distance, too, from the mother country, would enable the colonists to evade more or less, by smuggling, the monopoly which the company enjoyed against them. At present, the company allows all Dutch ships to trade to Surinam, upon paying two and a-half percent upon the value of their cargo for a license; and only reserves to itself exclusively, the direct trade from Africa to America, which consists almost entirely in the slave trade. This relaxation in the exclusive privileges of the company, is probably the principal cause of that degree of prosperity which that colony at present enjoys. Curacoa and Eustatia, the two principal islands belonging to the Dutch, are free ports, open to the ships of all nations; and this freedom, in the midst of better colonies, whose ports are open to those of one nation only, has been the great cause of the prosperity of those two barren islands.

The French colony of Canada was, during the greater part of the last century, and some part of the present, under the government of an exclusive company. Under so unfavorable an administration, its progress was necessarily very slow, in comparison with that of other new colonies; but it became much more rapid when this company was dissolved, after the fall of what is called the Mississippi scheme. When the English got possession of this country, they found in it near double the number of inhabitants which Father Charlevoix had assigned to it between twenty and thirty years before. That Jesuit had traveled over the whole country, and had no inclination to represent it as less inconsiderable than it really was.

The French colony of St. Domingo was established by pirates and freebooters, who, for a long time, neither required the protection, nor acknowledged the authority of France; and when that race of banditti became so far citizens as to acknowledge this authority, it was for a long time necessary to exercise it with very great gentleness. During this period, the population and improvement of this colony increased very fast. Even the oppression of the exclusive company, to which it was for some time subjected with all the other colonies of France, though it no doubt retarded, had not been able to stop its progress altogether. The course of its prosperity returned as soon as it was relieved from that oppression. It is now the most important of the sugar colonies of the West Indies, and its produce is said to be greater than that of all the English sugar colonies put together. The other sugar colonies of France are in general all very thriving.

But there are no colonies of which the progress has been more rapid than that of the English in North America.

Plenty of good land, and liberty to manage their own affairs their own way, seem to be the two great causes of the prosperity of all new colonies.

In the plenty of good land, the English colonies of North America, though no doubt very abundantly provided, are, however, inferior to those of the Spaniards and Portuguese, and not superior to some of those possessed by the French before the late war. But the political institutions of the English colonies have been more favorable to the improvement and cultivation of this land, than those of the other three nations.

First, the engrossing of uncultivated land, though it has by no means been prevented altogether, has been more restrained in the English colonies than in any other. The colony law, which imposes upon every proprietor the obligation of improving and cultivating, within a limited time, a certain proportion of his lands, and which, in case of failure, declares those neglected lands grantable to any other person; though it has not perhaps been very strictly executed, has, however, had some effect.

Secondly, in Pennsylvania there is no right of primogeniture, and lands, like moveables, are divided equally among all the children of the family. In three of the provinces of New England, the oldest has only a double share, as in the Mosaical law. Though in those provinces, therefore, too great a quantity of land should sometimes be engrossed by a particular individual, it is likely, in the course of a generation or two, to be sufficiently divided again. In the other English colonies, indeed, the right of primogeniture takes place, as in the law of England. But in all the English colonies, the tenure of the lands, which are all held by free soccage, facilitates alienation; and the grantee of an extensive tract of land generally finds it for his interest to alienate, as fast as he can, the greater part of it, reserving only a small quit-rent. In the Spanish and Portuguese colonies, what is called the right of majorazzo takes place in the succession of all those great estates to which any title of honor is annexed. Such estates go all to one person, and are in effect entailed and unalienable. The French colonies, indeed, are subject to the custom of Paris, which, in the inheritance of land, is much more favorable to the younger children than the law of England. But, in the French colonies, if any part of an estate, held by the noble tenure of chivalry and homage, is alienated, it is, for a limited time, subject to the right of redemption, either by the heir of the superior, or by the heir of the family; and all the largest estates of the country are held by such noble tenures, which necessarily embarrass alienation. But, in a new colony, a great uncultivated estate is likely to be much more speedily divided by alienation than by succession. The plenty and cheapness of good land, it has already been observed, are the principal causes of the rapid prosperity of new colonies. The engrossing of land, in effect, destroys this plenty and cheapness. The engrossing of uncultivated land, besides, is the greatest obstruction to its improvement; but the labor that is employed in the improvement and cultivation of land affords the greatest and most valuable produce to the society. The produce of labor, in this case, pays not only its own wages and the profit of the stock which employs it, but the rent of the land too upon which it is employed. The labor of the English colonies, therefore, being more employed in the improvement and cultivation of land, is likely to afford a greater and more valuable produce than that of any of the other three nations, which, by the engrossing of land, is more or less diverted towards other employments.

Thirdly, the labor of the English colonists is not only likely to afford a greater and more valuable produce, but, in consequence of the moderation of their taxes, a greater proportion of this produce belongs to themselves, which they may store up and employ in putting into motion a still greater quantity of labor. The English colonists have never yet contributed any thing towards the defense of the mother country, or towards the support of its civil government. They themselves, on the contrary, have hitherto been defended almost entirely at the expense of the mother country; but the expense of fleets and armies is out of all proportion greater than the necessary expense of civil government. The expense of their own civil government has always been very moderate. It has generally been confined to what was necessary for paying competent salaries to the governor, to the judges, and to some other officers of police, and for maintaining a few of the most useful public works. The expense of the civil establishment of Massachusetts Bay, before the commencement of the present disturbances, used to be but about £18000 a year; that of New Hampshire and Rhode Island, £3500 each; that of Connecticut, £4000; that of New York and Pennsylvania, £4500 each; that of New Jersey, £1200; that of Virginia and South Carolina, £8000 each. The civil establishments of Nova Scotia and Georgia are partly supported by an annual grant of parliament; but Nova Scotia pays, besides, about £7000 a year towards the public expenses of the colony, and Georgia about £2500 a year. All the different civil establishments in North America, in short, exclusive of those of Maryland and North Carolina, of which no exact account has been got, did not, before the commencement of the present disturbances, cost the inhabitants about £64,700 a year; an ever memorable example, at how small an expense three millions of people may not only be governed but well governed. The most important part of the expense of government, indeed, that of defense and protection, has constantly fallen upon the mother country. The ceremonial, too, of the civil government in the colonies, upon the reception of a new governor, upon the opening of a new assembly, etc. though sufficiently decent, is not accompanied with any expensive pomp or parade. Their ecclesiastical government is conducted upon a plan equally frugal. Tithes are unknown among them; and their clergy, who are far from being numerous, are maintained either by moderate stipends, or by the voluntary contributions of the people. The power of Spain and Portugal, on the contrary, derives some support from the taxes levied upon their colonies. France, indeed, has never drawn any considerable revenue from its colonies, the taxes which it levies upon them being generally spent among them. But the colony government of all these three nations is conducted upon a much more extensive plan, and is accompanied with a much more expensive ceremonial. The sums spent upon the reception of a new viceroy of Peru, for example, have frequently been enormous. Such ceremonials are not only real taxes paid by the rich colonists upon those particular occasions, but they serve to introduce among them the habit of vanity and expense upon all other occasions. They are not only very grievous occasional taxes, but they contribute to establish perpetual taxes, of the same kind, still more grievous; the ruinous taxes of private luxury and extravagance. In the colonies of all those three nations, too, the ecclesiastical government is extremely oppressive. Tithes take place in all of them, and are levied with the utmost rigor in those of Spain and Portugal. All of them, besides, are oppressed with a numerous race of mendicant friars, whose beggary being not only licensed but consecrated by religion, is a most grievous tax upon the poor people, who are most carefully taught that it is a duty to give, and a very great sin to refuse them their charity. Over and above all this, the clergy are, in all of them, the greatest engrossers of land.

Fourthly, in the disposal of their surplus produce, or of what is over and above their own consumption, the English colonies have been more favored, and have been allowed a more extensive market, than those of any other European nation. Every European nation has endeavored, more or less, to monopolize to itself the commerce of its colonies, and, upon that account, has prohibited the ships of foreign nations from trading to them, and has prohibited them from importing European goods from any foreign nation. But the manner in which this monopoly has been exercised in different nations, has been very different.

Some nations have given up the whole commerce of their colonies to an exclusive company, of whom the colonists were obliged to buy all such European goods as they wanted, and to whom they were obliged to sell the whole of their surplus produce. It was the interest of the company, therefore, not only to sell the former as dear, and to buy the latter as cheap as possible, but to buy no more of the latter, even at this low price, than what they could dispose of for a very high price in Europe. It was their interest not only to degrade in all cases the value of the surplus produce of the colony, but in many cases to discourage and keep down the natural increase of its quantity. Of all the expedients that can well be contrived to stunt the natural growth of a new colony, that of an exclusive company is undoubtedly the most effectual. This, however, has been the policy of Holland, though their company, in the course of the present century, has given up in many respects the exertion of their exclusive privilege. This, too, was the policy of Denmark, till the reign of the late king. It has occasionally been the policy of France; and of late, since 1755, after it had been abandoned by all other nations on account of its absurdity, it has become the policy of Portugal, with regard at least to two of the principal provinces of Brazil, Pernambucco, and Marannon.

Other nations, without establishing an exclusive company, have confined the whole commerce of their colonies to a particular port of the mother country, from whence no ship was allowed to sail, but either in a fleet and at a particular season, or, if single, in consequence of a particular license, which in most cases was very well paid for. This policy opened, indeed, the trade of the colonies to all the natives of the mother country, provided they traded from the proper port, at the proper season, and in the proper vessels. But as all the different merchants, who joined their stocks in order to fit out those licensed vessels, would find it for their interest to act in concert, the trade which was carried on in this manner would necessarily be conducted very nearly upon the same principles as that of an exclusive company. The profit of those merchants would be almost equally exorbitant and oppressive. The colonies would be ill supplied, and would be obliged both to buy very dear, and to sell very cheap. This, however, till within these few years, had always been the policy of Spain; and the price of all European goods, accordingly, is said to have been enormous in the Spanish West Indies. At Quito, we are told by Ulloa, a pound of iron sold for about 4s:6d., and a pound of steel for about 6s:9d. sterling. But it is chiefly in order to purchase European goods that the colonies part with their own produce. The more, therefore, they pay for the one, the less they really get for the other, and the dearness of the one is the same thing with the cheapness of the other. The policy of Portugal is, in this respect, the same as the ancient policy of Spain, with regard to all its colonies, except Pernambucco and Marannon; and with regard to these it has lately adopted a still worse.

Other nations leave the trade of their colonies free to all their subjects, who may carry it on from all the different ports of the mother country, and who have occasion for no other license than the common dispatches of the custom-house. In this case the number and dispersed situation of the different traders renders it impossible for them to enter into any general combination, and their competition is sufficient to hinder them from making very exorbitant profits. Under so liberal a policy, the colonies are enabled both to sell their own produce, and to buy the goods of Europe at a reasonable price; but since the dissolution of the Plymouth company, when our colonies were but in their infancy, this has always been the policy of England. It has generally, too, been that of France, and has been uniformly so since the dissolution of what in England is commonly called their Mississippi company. The profits of the trade, therefore, which France and England carry on with their colonies, though no doubt somewhat higher than if the competition were free to all other nations, are, however, by no means exorbitant; and the price of European goods, accordingly, is not extravagantly high in the greater past of the colonies of either of those nations.

In the exportation of their own surplus produce, too, it is only with regard to certain commodities that the colonies of Great Britain are confined to the market of the mother country. These commodities having been enumerated in the act of navigation, and in some other subsequent acts, have upon that account been called enumerated commodities. The rest are called non-enumerated, and may be exported directly to other countries, provided it is in British or plantation ships, of which the owners and three fourths of the mariners are British subjects.

Among the non-enumerated commodities are some of the most important productions of America and the West Indies, grain of all sorts, lumber, salt provisions, fish, sugar, and rum.

Grain is naturally the first and principal object of the culture of all new colonies. By allowing them a very extensive market for it, the law encourages them to extend this culture much beyond the consumption of a thinly inhabited country, and thus to provide beforehand an ample subsistence for a continually increasing population.

In a country quite covered with wood, where timber consequently is of little or no value, the expense of clearing the ground is the principal obstacle to improvement. By allowing the colonies a very extensive market for their lumber, the law endeavors to facilitate improvement by raising the price of a commodity which would otherwise be of little value, and thereby enabling them to make some profit of what would otherwise be mere expense.

In a country neither half peopled nor half cultivated, cattle naturally multiply beyond the consumption of the inhabitants, and are often, upon that account, of little or no value. But it is necessary, it has already been shown, that the price of cattle should bear a certain proportion to that of corn, before the greater part of the lands of any country can be improved. By allowing to American cattle, in all shapes, dead and alive, a very extensive market, the law endeavors to raise the value of a commodity, of which the high price is so very essential to improvement. The good effects of this liberty, however, must be somewhat diminished by the 4th of George III. c. 15, which puts hides and skins among the enumerated commodities, and thereby tends to reduce the value of American cattle.

To increase the shipping and naval power of Great Britain by the extension of the fisheries of our colonies, is an object which the legislature seems to have had almost constantly in view. Those fisheries, upon this account, have had all the encouragement which freedom can give them, and they have flourished accordingly. The New England fishery, in particular, was, before the late disturbances, one of the most important, perhaps, in the world. The whale fishery which, notwithstanding an extravagant bounty, is in Great Britain carried on to so little purpose, that in the opinion of many people (which I do not, however, pretend to warrant), the whole produce does not much exceed the value of the bounties which are annually paid for it, is in New England carried on, without any bounty, to a very great extent. Fish is one of the principal articles with which the North Americans trade to Spain, Portugal, and the Mediterranean.

Sugar was originally an enumerated commodity, which could only be exported to Great Britain; but in 1751, upon a representation of the sugar-planters, its exportation was permitted to all parts of the world. The restrictions, however, with which this liberty was granted, joined to the high price of sugar in Great Britain, have rendered it in a great measure ineffectual. Great Britain and her colonies still continue to be almost the sole market for all sugar produced in the British plantations. Their consumption increases so fast, that, though in consequence of the increasing improvement of Jamaica, as well as of the ceded islands, the importation of sugar has increased very greatly within these twenty years, the exportation to foreign countries is said to be not much greater than before.

Rum is a very important article in the trade which the Americans carry on to the coast of Africa, from which they bring back negro slaves in return.

If the whole surplus produce of America, in grain of all sorts, in salt provisions, and in fish, had been put into the enumeration, and thereby forced into the market of Great Britain, it would have interfered too much with the produce of the industry of our own people. It was probably not so much from any regard to the interest of America, as from a jealousy of this interference, that those important commodities have not only been kept out of the enumeration, but that the importation into Great Britain of all grain, except rice, and of all salt provisions, has, in the ordinary state of the law, been prohibited.

The non-enumerated commodities could originally be exported to all parts of the world. Lumber and rice having been once put into the enumeration, when they were afterwards taken out of it, were confined, as to the European market, to the countries that lie south of Cape Finisterre. By the 6th of George III c. 52, all non-enumerated commodities were subjected to the like restriction. The parts of Europe which lie south of Cape Finisterre are not manufacturing countries, and we are less jealous of the colony ships carrying home from them any manufactures which could interfere with our own.

The enumerated commodities are of two sorts; first, such as are either the peculiar produce of America, or as cannot be produced, or at least are not produced in the mother country. Of this kind are molasses, coffee, cocoa-nuts, tobacco, pimento, ginger, whalefins, raw silk, cotton, wool, beaver, and other peltry of America, indigo, fustick, and other dyeing woods; secondly, such as are not the peculiar produce of America, but which are, and may be produced in the mother country, though not in such quantities as to supply the greater part of her demand, which is principally supplied from foreign countries. Of this kind are all naval stores, masts, yards, and bowsprits, tar, pitch, and turpentine, pig and bar iron, copper ore, hides and skins, pot and pearl ashes. The largest importation of commodities of the first kind could not discourage the growth, or interfere with the sale, of any part of the produce of the mother country. By confining them to the home market, our merchants, it was expected, would not only be enabled to buy them cheaper in the plantations, and consequently to sell them with a better profit at home, but to establish between the plantations and foreign countries an advantageous carrying trade, of which Great Britain was necessarily to be the center or emporium, as the European country into which those commodities were first to be imported. The importation of commodities of the second kind might be so managed too, it was supposed, as to interfere, not with the sale of those of the same kind which were produced at home, but with that of those which were imported from foreign countries; because, by means of proper duties, they might be rendered always somewhat dearer than the former, and yet a good deal cheaper than the latter. By confining such commodities to the home market, therefore, it was proposed to discourage the produce, not of Great Britain, but of some foreign countries with which the balance of trade was believed to be unfavorable to Great Britain.

The prohibition of exporting from the colonies to any other country but Great Britain, masts, yards, and bowsprits, tar, pitch, and turpentine, naturally tended to lower the price of timber in the colonies, and consequently to increase the expense of clearing their lands, the principal obstacle to their improvement. But about the beginning of the present century, in 1703, the pitch and tar company of Sweden endeavored to raise the price of their commodities to Great Britain, by prohibiting their exportation, except in their own ships, at their own price, and in such quantities as they thought proper. In order to counteract this notable piece of mercantile policy, and to render herself as much as possible independent, not only of Sweden, but of all the other northern powers, Great Britain gave a bounty upon the importation of naval stores from America; and the effect of this bounty was to raise the price of timber in America much more than the confinement to the home market could lower it; and as both regulations were enacted at the same time, their joint effect was rather to encourage than to discourage the clearing of land in America.

Though pig and bar iron, too, have been put among the enumerated commodities, yet as, when imported from America, they are exempted from considerable duties to which they are subject when imported front any other country, the one part of the regulation contributes more to encourage the erection of furnaces in America than the other to discourage it. There is no manufacture which occasions so great a consumption of wood as a furnace, or which can contribute so much to the clearing of a country overgrown with it.

The tendency of some of these regulations to raise the value of timber in America, and thereby to facilitate the clearing of the land, was neither, perhaps, intended nor understood by the legislature. Though their beneficial effects, however, have been in this respect accidental, they have not upon that account been less real.

The most perfect freedom of trade is permitted between the British colonies of America and the West Indies, both in the enumerated and in the non-enumerated commodities. Those colonies are now become so populous and thriving, that each of them finds in some of the others a great and extensive market for every part of its produce. All of them taken together, they make a great internal market for the produce of one another.

The liberality of England, however, towards the trade of her colonies, has been confined chiefly to what concerns the market for their produce, either in its rude state, or in what may be called the very first stage of manufacture. The more advanced or more refined manufactures, even of the colony produce, the merchants and manufacturers of Great Britain choose to reserve to themselves, and have prevailed upon the legislature to prevent their establishment in the colonies, sometimes by high duties, and sometimes by absolute prohibitions.

While, for example, Muscovado sugars from the British plantations pay, upon importation, only 6s:4d. the hundred weight, white sugars pay £1:1:1; and refined, either double or single, in loaves, £4:2:5 8/20ths. When those high duties were imposed, Great Britain was the sole, and she still continues to be, the principal market, to which the sugars of the British colonies could be exported. They amounted, therefore, to a prohibition, at first of claying or refining sugar for any foreign market, and at present of claying or refining it for the market which takes off, perhaps, more than nine-tenths of the whole produce. The manufacture of claying or refining sugar, accordingly, though it has flourished in all the sugar colonies of France, has been little cultivated in any of those of England, except for the market of the colonies themselves. While Grenada was in the hands of the French, there was a refinery of sugar, by claying, at least upon almost every plantation. Since it fell into those of the English, almost all works of this kind have been given up; and there are at present (October 1773), I am assured, not above two or three remaining in the island. At present, however, by an indulgence of the custom-house, clayed or refined sugar, if reduced from loaves into powder, is commonly imported as Muscovado.

While Great Britain encourages in America the manufacturing of pig and bar iron, by exempting them from duties to which the like commodities are subject when imported from any other country, she imposes an absolute prohibition upon the erection of steel furnaces and slit-mills in any of her American plantations. She will not suffer her colonies to work in those more refined manufactures, even for their own consumption; but insists upon their purchasing of her merchants and manufacturers all goods of this kind which they have occasion for.

She prohibits the exportation from one province to another by water, and even the carriage by land upon horseback, or in a cart, of hats, of wools, and woolen goods, of the produce of America; a regulation which effectually prevents the establishment of any manufacture of such commodities for distant sale, and confines the industry of her colonists in this way to such coarse and household manufactures as a private family commonly makes for its own use, or for that of some of its neighbors in the same province.

To prohibit a great people, however, from making all that they can of every part of their own produce, or from employing their stock and industry in the way that they judge most advantageous to themselves, is a manifest violation of the most sacred rights of mankind. Unjust, however, as such prohibitions may be, they have not hitherto been very hurtful to the colonies. Land is still so cheap, and, consequently, labor so dear among them, that they can import from the mother country almost all the more refined or more advanced manufactures cheaper than they could make them for themselves. Though they had not, therefore, been prohibited from establishing such manufactures, yet, in their present state of improvement, a regard to their own interest would probably have prevented them from doing so. In their present state of improvement, those prohibitions, perhaps, without cramping their industry, or restraining it from any employment to which it would have gone of its own accord, are only impertinent badges of slavery imposed upon them, without any sufficient reason, by the groundless jealousy of the merchants and manufacturers of the mother country. In a more advanced state, they might be really oppressive and insupportable.

Great Britain, too, as she confines to her own market some of the most important productions of the colonies, so, in compensation, she gives to some of them an advantage in that market, sometimes by imposing higher duties upon the like productions when imported from other countries, and sometimes by giving bounties upon their importation from the colonies. In the first way, she gives an advantage in the home market to the sugar, tobacco, and iron of her own colonies; and, in the second, to their raw silk, to their hemp and flax, to their indigo, to their naval stores, and to their building timber. This second way of encouraging the colony produce, by bounties upon importation, is, so far as I have been able to learn, peculiar to Great Britain: the first is not. Portugal does not content herself with imposing higher duties upon the importation of tobacco from any other country, but prohibits it under the severest penalties.

With regard to the importation of goods from Europe, England has likewise dealt more liberally with her colonies than any other nation.

Great Britain allows a part, almost always the half, generally a larger portion, and sometimes the whole, of the duty which is paid upon the importation of foreign goods, to be drawn back upon their exportation to any foreign country. No independent foreign country, it was easy to foresee, would receive them, if they came to it loaded with the heavy duties to which almost all foreign goods are subjected on their importation into Great Britain. Unless, therefore, some part of those duties was drawn back upon exportation, there was an end of the carrying trade; a trade so much favored by the mercantile system.

Our colonies, however, are by no means independent foreign countries; and Great Britain having assumed to herself the exclusive right of supplying them with all goods from Europe, might have forced them (in the same manner as other countries have done their colonies) to receive such goods loaded with all the same duties which they paid in the mother country. But, on the contrary, till 1763, the same drawbacks were paid upon the exportation of the greater part of foreign goods to our colonies, as to any independent foreign country. In 1763, indeed, by the 4th of George III c. 15, this indulgence was a good deal abated, and it was enacted, "That no part of the duty called the old subsidy should be drawn back for any goods of the growth, production, or manufacture of Europe or the East Indies, which should be exported from this kingdom to any British colony or plantation in America; wines, white calicoes, and muslins, excepted." Before this law, many different sorts of foreign goods might have been bought cheaper in the plantations than in the mother country, and some may still.

Of the greater part of the regulations concerning the colony trade, the merchants who carry it on, it must be observed, have been the principal advisers. We must not wonder, therefore, if, in a great part of them, their interest has been more considered than either that of the colonies or that of the mother country. In their exclusive privilege of supplying the colonies with all the goods which they wanted from Europe, and of purchasing all such parts of their surplus produce as could not interfere with any of the trades which they themselves carried on at home, the interest of the colonies was sacrificed to the interest of those merchants. In allowing the same drawbacks upon the re-exportation of the greater part of European and East India goods to the colonies, as upon their re-exportation to any independent country, the interest of the mother country was sacrificed to it, even according to the mercantile ideas of that interest. It was for the interest of the merchants to pay as little as possible for the foreign goods which they sent to the colonies, and, consequently, to get back as much as possible of the duties which they advanced upon their importation into Great Britain. They might thereby be enabled to sell in the colonies, either the same quantity of goods with a greater profit, or a greater quantity with the same profit, and, consequently, to gain something either in the one way or the other. It was likewise for the interest of the colonies to get all such goods as cheap, and in as great abundance as possible. But this might not always be for the interest of the mother country. She might frequently suffer, both in her revenue, by giving back a great part of the duties which had been paid upon the importation of such goods; and in her manufactures, by being undersold in the colony market, in consequence of the easy terms upon which foreign manufactures could be carried thither by means of those drawbacks. The progress of the linen manufacture of Great Britain, it is commonly said, has been a good deal retarded by the drawbacks upon the re-exportation of German linen to the American colonies.

But though the policy of Great Britain, with regard to the trade of her colonies, has been dictated by the same mercantile spirit as that of other nations, it has, however, upon the whole, been less illiberal and oppressive than that of any of them.

In every thing except their foreign trade, the liberty of the English colonists to manage their own affairs their own way, is complete. It is in every respect equal to that of their fellow-citizens at home, and is secured in the same manner, by an assembly of the representatives of the people, who claim the sole right of imposing taxes for the support of the colony government. The authority of this assembly overawes the executive power; and neither the meanest nor the most obnoxious colonist, as long as he obeys the law, has any thing to fear from the resentment, either of the governor, or of any other civil or military officer in the province. The colony assemblies, though, like the house of commons in England, are not always a very equal representation of the people, yet they approach more nearly to that character; and as the executive power either has not the means to corrupt them, or, on account of the support which it receives from the mother country, is not under the necessity of doing so, they are, perhaps, in general more influenced by the inclinations of their constituents. The councils, which, in the colony legislatures, correspond to the house of lords in Great Britain, are not composed of a hereditary nobility. In some of the colonies, as in three of the governments of New England, those councils are not appointed by the king, but chosen by the representatives of the people. In none of the English colonies is there any hereditary nobility. In all of them, indeed, as in all other free countries, the descendant of an old colony family is more respected than an upstart of equal merit and fortune; but he is only more respected, and he has no privileges by which he can be troublesome to his neighbors. Before the commencement of the present disturbances, the colony assemblies had not only the legislative, but a part of the executive power. In Connecticut and Rhode Island, they elected the governor. In the other colonies, they appointed the revenue officers, who collected the taxes imposed by those respective assemblies, to whom those officers were immediately responsible. There is more equality, therefore, among the English colonists than among the inhabitants of the mother country. Their manners are more republican; and their governments, those of three of the provinces of New England in particular, have hitherto been more republican too.

The absolute governments of Spain, Portugal, and France, on the contrary, take place in their colonies; and the discretionary powers which such governments commonly delegate to all their inferior officers are, on account of the great distance, naturally exercised there with more than ordinary violence. Under all absolute governments, there is more liberty in the capital than in any other part of the country. The sovereign himself can never have either interest or inclination to pervert the order of justice, or to oppress the great body of the people. In the capital, his presence overawes, more or less, all his inferior officers, who, in the remoter provinces, from whence the complaints of the people are less likely to reach him, can exercise their tyranny with much more safety. But the European colonies in America are more remote than the most distant provinces of the greatest empires which had ever been known before. The government of the English colonies is, perhaps, the only one which, since the world began, could give perfect security to the inhabitants of so very distant a province. The administration of the French colonies, however, has always been conducted with much more gentleness and moderation than that of the Spanish and Portuguese. This superiority of conduct is suitable both to the character of the French nation, and to what forms the character of every nation, the nature of their government, which, though arbitrary and violent in comparison with that of Great Britain, is legal and free in comparison with those of Spain and Portugal.

It is in the progress of the North American colonies, however, that the superiority of the English policy chiefly appears. The progress of the sugar colonies of France has been at least equal, perhaps superior, to that of the greater part of those of England; and yet the sugar colonies of England enjoy a free government, nearly of the same kind with that which takes place in her colonies of North America. But the sugar colonies of France are not discouraged, like those of England, from refining their own sugar; and what is still of greater importance, the genius of their government naturally introduces a better management of their negro slaves.

In all European colonies, the culture of the sugar-cane is carried on by negro slaves. The constitution of those who have been born in the temperate climate of Europe could not, it is supposed, support the labor of digging the ground under the burning sun of the West Indies; and the culture of the sugar-cane, as it is managed at present, is all hand labor; though, in the opinion of many, the drill plough might be introduced into it with great advantage. But, as the profit and success of the cultivation which is carried on by means of cattle, depend very much upon the good management of those cattle; so the profit and success of that which is carried on by slaves must depend equally upon the good management of those slaves; and in the good management of their slaves the French planters,

I think it is generally allowed, are superior to the English. The law, so far as it gives some weak protection to the slave against the violence of his master, is likely to be better executed in a colony where the government is in a great measure arbitrary, than in one where it is altogether free. In every country where the unfortunate law of slavery is established, the magistrate, when he protects the slave, intermeddles in some measure in the management of the private property of the master; and, in a free country, where the master is, perhaps, either a member of the colony assembly, or an elector of such a member, he dares not do this but with the greatest caution and circumspection. The respect which he is obliged to pay to the master, renders it more difficult for him to protect the slave. But in a country where the government is in a great measure arbitrary, where it is usual for the magistrate to intermeddle even in the management of the private property of individuals, and to send them, perhaps, a lettre de cachet, if they do not manage it according to his liking, it is much easier for him to give some protection to the slave; and common humanity naturally disposes him to do so. The protection of the magistrate renders the slave less contemptible in the eyes of his master, who is thereby induced to consider him with more regard, and to treat him with more gentleness. Gentle usage renders the slave not only more faithful, but more intelligent, and, therefore, upon a double account, more useful. He approaches more to the condition of a free servant, and may possess some degree of integrity and attachment to his master's interest; virtues which frequently belong to free servants, but which never can belong to a slave, who is treated as slaves commonly are in countries where the master is perfectly free and secure.

That the condition of a slave is better under an arbitrary than under a free government, is, I believe, supported by the history of all ages and nations. In the Roman history, the first time we read of the magistrate interposing to protect the slave from the violence of his master, is under the emperors. When Vidius Pollio, in the presence of Augustus, ordered one of his slaves, who had committed a slight fault, to be cut into pieces and thrown into his fish-pond, in order to feed his fishes, the emperor commanded him, with indignation, to emancipate immediately, not only that slave, but all the others that belonged to him. Under the republic no magistrate could have had authority enough to protect the slave, much less to punish the master.

The stock, it is to be observed, which has improved the sugar colonies of France, particularly the great colony of St. Domingo, has been raised almost entirely from the gradual improvement and cultivation of those colonies. It has been almost altogether the produce of the soil and of the industry of the colonists, or, what comes to the same thing, the price of that produce, gradually accumulated by good management, and employed in raising a still greater produce. But the stock which has improved and cultivated the sugar colonies of England, has, a great part of it, been sent out from England, and has by no means been altogether the produce of the soil and industry of the colonists. The prosperity of the English sugar colonies has been in a great measure owing to the great riches of England, of which a part has overflowed, if one may say so, upon these colonies. But the prosperity of the sugar colonies of France has been entirely owing to the good conduct of the colonists, which must therefore have had some superiority over that of the English; and this superiority has been remarked in nothing so much as in the good management of their slaves.

404 THE REAL PRICE OF EVERYTHING

Such have been the general outlines of the policy of the different European nations with regard to their colonies.

The policy of Europe, therefore, has very little to boast of, either in the original establishment, or, so far as concerns their internal government, in the subsequent prosperity of the colonies of America.

Folly and injustice seem to have been the principles which presided over and directed the first project of establishing those colonies; the folly of hunting after gold and silver mines, and the injustice of coveting the possession of a country whose harmless natives, far from having ever injured the people of Europe, had received the first adventurers with every mark of kindness and hospitality.

The adventurers, indeed, who formed some of the latter establishments, joined to the chimerical project of finding gold and silver mines, other motives more reasonable and more laudable; but even these motives do very little honor to the policy of Europe.

The English puritans, restrained at home, fled for freedom to America, and established there the four governments of New England. The English Catholics, treated with much greater injustice, established that of Maryland; the Quakers, that of Pennsylvania. The Portuguese Jews, persecuted by the inquisition, stripped of their fortunes, and banished to Brazil, introduced, by their example, some sort of order and industry among the transported felons and strumpets by whom that colony was originally peopled, and taught them the culture of the sugar-cane. Upon all these different occasions, it was not the wisdom and policy, but the disorder and injustice of the European governments, which peopled and cultivated America.

In effectuation some of the most important of these establishments, the different governments of Europe had as little merit as in projecting them. The conquest of Mexico was the project, not of the council of Spain, but of a governor of Cuba; and it was effectuated by the spirit of the bold adventurer to whom it was entrusted, in spite of every thing which that governor, who soon repented of having trusted such a person, could do to thwart it. The conquerors of Chile and Peru, and of almost all the other Spanish settlements upon the continent of America, carried out with them no other public encouragement, but a general permission to make settlements and conquests in the name of the king of Spain. Those adventures were all at the private risk and expense of the adventurers. The government of Spain contributed scarce any thing to any of them. That of England contributed as little towards effectuating the establishment of some of its most important colonies in North America.

When those establishments were effectuated, and had become so considerable as to attract the attention of the mother country, the first regulations which she made with regard to them, had always in view to secure to herself the monopoly of their commerce; to confine their market, and to enlarge her own at their expense, and, consequently, rather to damp and discourage, than to quicken and forward the course of their prosperity. In the different ways in which this monopoly has been exercised, consists one of the most essential differences in the policy of the different European nations with regard to their colonies. The best of them all, that of England, is only somewhat less illiberal and oppressive than that of any of the rest.

In what way, therefore, has the policy of Europe contributed either to the first estab-lishment, or to the present grandeur of the colonies of America? In one way, and in one way only, it has contributed a good deal. Magna virum mater! It bred and formed the men who were capable of achieving such great actions, and of laying the foundation of so great an empire; and there is no other quarter of the world of which the policy is ca-pable of forming, or has ever actually, and in fact, formed such men. The colonies owe to the policy of Europe the education and great views of their active and enterprising founders; and some of the greatest and most important of them, so far as concerns their internal government, owe to it scarce anything else.

Part III

Of the Advantages Which Europe Has Derived From the Discovery of America, and from That of a Passage to the East Indies by the Cape of Good Hope

Such are the advantages which the colonies of America have derived from the policy of Europe.

What are those which Europe has derived from the discovery and colonization of America?

Those advantages may be divided, first, into the general advantages which Europe, considered as one great country, has derived from those great events; and, secondly, into the particular advantages which each colonizing country has derived from the colonies which particularly belong to it, in consequence of the authority or dominion which it exercises over them.

The general advantages which Europe, considered as one great country, has derived from the discovery and colonization of America consist, first, in the increase of its enjoyments; and, secondly, in the augmentation of its industry.

The surplus produce of America imported into Europe, furnishes the inhabitants of this great continent with a variety of commodities which they could not otherwise have possessed; some for convenience and use, some for pleasure, and some for ornament; and thereby contributes to increase their enjoyments.

The discovery and colonization of America, it will readily be allowed, have contributed to augment the industry, first, of all the countries which trade to it directly, such as Spain, Portugal, France, and England; and, secondly, of all those which, without trading to it directly, send, through the medium of other countries, goods to it of their own produce, such as Austrian Flanders, and some provinces of Germany, which, through the medium of the countries before mentioned, send to it a considerable quantity of linen and other goods. All such countries have evidently gained a more extensive market for their surplus produce, and must consequently have been encouraged to increase its quantity.

But that those great events should likewise have contributed to encourage the industry of countries such as Hungary and Poland, which may never, perhaps, have sent a single commodity of their own produce to America, is not, perhaps, altogether so evident. That those events have done so, however, cannot be doubted. Some part of the produce of America is consumed in Hungary and Poland, and there is some demand there for the sugar, chocolate, and tobacco, of that new quarter of the world. But those commodities must be purchased with something which is either the produce of the industry of Hungary and Poland, or with something which had been purchased with some part of that produce. Those commodities of America are new values, new equivalents, introduced into Hungary and Poland, to be exchanged there for the surplus produce of these countries. By being carried thither, they create a new and more extensive market for that surplus produce. They raise its value, and thereby contribute to encourage its increase. Though no part of it may ever be carried to America, it may be carried to other countries, which purchase it with a part of their share of the surplus produce of America, and it may find a market by means of the circulation of that trade which was originally put into motion by the surplus produce of America.

Those great events may even have contributed to increase the enjoyments, and to augment the industry, of countries which not only never sent any commodities to America, but never received any from it. Even such countries may have received a greater abundance of other commodities from countries, of which the surplus produce had been augmented by means of the American trade. This greater abundance, as it must necessarily have increased their enjoyments, so it must likewise have augmented their industry. A greater number of new equivalents, of some kind or other, must have been presented to them to be exchanged for the surplus produce of that industry. A more extensive market must have been created for that surplus produce, so as to raise its value, and thereby encourage its increase. The mass of commodities annually thrown into the great circle of European commerce, and by its various revolutions annually distributed among all the different nations comprehended within it, must have been augmented by the whole surplus produce of America. A greater share of this greater mass, therefore, is likely to have fallen to each of those nations, to have increased their enjoyments, and augmented their industry.

The exclusive trade of the mother countries tends to diminish, or at least to keep down below what they would otherwise rise to, both the enjoyments and industry of all those nations in general, and of the American colonies in particular. It is a dead weight upon the action of one of the great springs which puts into motion a great part of the business of mankind. By rendering the colony produce dearer in all other countries, it lessens its consumption, and thereby cramps the industry of the colonies, and both the enjoyments and the industry of all other countries, which both enjoy less when they pay more for what they enjoy, and produce less when they get less for what they produce. By rendering the produce of all other countries dearer in the colonies, it cramps in the same manner the industry of all other colonies, and both the enjoyments and the industry of the colonies. It is a clog which, for the supposed benefit of some particular countries, embarrasses the pleasures and encumbers the industry of all other countries, but of the colonies more than any other. It not only excludes as much as possible all other countries from one particular market, but it confines as much as possible the colonies to one particular market; and the difference is very great between being excluded from one particular market when all others are open, and being confined to one particular market when all others are shut up. The surplus produce of the colonies, however, is the original source of all that increase of enjoyments and industry which Europe derives from the discovery and colonization of America, and the exclusive trade of the mother countries tends to render this source much less abundant than it otherwise would be.

The particular advantages which each colonizing country derives from the colonies which particularly belong to it, are of two different kinds; first, those common advantages which every empire derives from the provinces subject to its dominion; and, secondly, those peculiar advantages which are supposed to result from provinces of so very peculiar a nature as the European colonies of America.

The common advantages which every empire derives from the provinces subject to its dominion consist, first, in the military force which they furnish for its defense; and, secondly, in the revenue which they furnish for the support of its civil government. The Roman colonies furnished occasionally both the one and the other. The Greek colonies sometimes furnished a military force, but seldom any revenue. They seldom acknowledged themselves subject to the dominion of the mother city. They were generally her allies in war, but very seldom her subjects in peace.

The European colonies of America have never yet furnished any military force for the defense of the mother country. The military force has never yet been sufficient for their own defense; and in the different wars in which the mother countries have been engaged, the defense of their colonies has generally occasioned a very considerable distraction of the military force of those countries. In this respect, therefore, all the European colonies have, without exception, been a cause rather of weakness than of strength to their respective mother countries.

The colonies of Spain and Portugal only have contributed any revenue towards the defense of the mother country, or the support of her civil government. The taxes which have been levied upon those of other European nations, upon those of England in particular, have seldom been equal to the expense laid out upon them in time of peace, and never sufficient to defray that which they occasioned in time of war. Such colonies, therefore, have been a source of expense, and not of revenue, to their respective mother countries.

The advantages of such colonies to their respective mother countries, consist altogether in those peculiar advantages which are supposed to result from provinces of so very peculiar a nature as the European colonies of America; and the exclusive trade, it is acknowledged, is the sole source of all those peculiar advantages.

In consequence of this exclusive trade, all that part of the surplus produce of the English colonies, for example, which consists in what are called enumerated commodities, can be sent to no other country but England. Other countries must afterwards buy it of her. It must be cheaper, therefore, in England than it can be in any other country, and must contribute more to increase the enjoyments of England than those of any other country. It must likewise contribute more to encourage her industry. For all those parts of her own surplus produce which England exchanges for those enumerated commodities, she must get a better price than any other countries can get for the like parts of theirs, when they exchange them for the same commodities. The manufactures of England, for example, will purchase a greater quantity of the sugar and tobacco of her own colonies than the like manufactures of other countries can purchase of that sugar and tobacco. So far, therefore, as the manufactures of England and those of other countries are both to be exchanged for the sugar and tobacco of the English colonies, this superiority of price gives an encouragement to the former beyond what the latter can, in these circumstances, enjoy. The exclusive trade of the colonies, therefore, as it diminishes, or at least keeps down below what they would otherwise rise to, both the enjoyments and the industry of the countries which do not possess it, so it gives an evident advantage to the countries which do possess it over those other countries.

This advantage, however, will, perhaps, be found to be rather what may be called a relative than an absolute advantage, and to give a superiority to the country which enjoys it, rather by depressing the industry and produce of other countries, than by raising those of that particular country above what they would naturally rise to in the case of a free trade.

The tobacco of Maryland and Virginia, for example, by means of the monopoly which England enjoys of it, certainly comes cheaper to England than it can do to France to whom England commonly sells a considerable part of it. But had France and all other European countries been at all times allowed a free trade to Maryland and Virginia, the tobacco of those colonies might by this time have come cheaper than it actually does, not only to all those other countries, but likewise to England. The produce of tobacco, in consequence of a market so much more extensive than any which it has hitherto enjoyed, might, and probably would, by this time have been so much increased as to reduce the profits of a tobacco plantation to their natural level with those of a corn plantation, which it is supposed they are still somewhat above. The price of tobacco might, and probably would, by this time have fallen somewhat lower than it is at present. An equal quantity of the commodities, either of England or of those other countries, might have purchased in Maryland and Virginia a greater quantity of tobacco than it can do at present, and consequently have been sold there for so much a better price. So far as that weed, therefore, can, by its cheapness and abundance, increase the enjoyments, or augment the industry, either of England or of any other country, it would probably, in the case of a free trade, have produced both these effects in somewhat a greater degree than it can do at present. England, indeed, would not, in this case, have had any advantage over other countries. She might have bought the tobacco of her colonies somewhat cheaper, and consequently have sold some of her own commodities somewhat dearer, than she actually does; but she could neither have bought the one cheaper, nor sold the other dearer, than any other country might have done. She might, perhaps, have gained an absolute, but she would certainly have lost a relative advantage.

In order, however, to obtain this relative advantage in the colony trade, in order to execute the invidious and malignant project of excluding, as much as possible, other nations from any share in it, England, there are very probable reasons for believing, has not only sacrificed a part of the absolute advantage which she, as well as every other nation, might have derived from that trade, but has subjected herself both to an absolute and to a relative disadvantage in almost every other branch of trade.

When, by the act of navigation, England assumed to herself the monopoly of the colony trade, the foreign capitals which had before been employed in it, were necessarily withdrawn from it. The English capital, which had before carried on but a part of it, was now to carry on the whole. The capital which had before supplied the colonies with but a part of the goods which they wanted from Europe, was now all that was employed to supply them with the whole. But it could not supply them with the whole; and the goods with which it did supply them were necessarily sold very dear. The capital which had before bought but a part of the surplus produce of the colonies, was now all that was employed to buy the whole. But it could not buy the whole at any thing near the old price; and therefore, whatever it did buy, it necessarily bought very cheap. But in an employment of capital, in which the merchant sold very dear, and bought very cheap, the profit must have been very great, and much above the ordinary level of profit in other branches of trade. This superiority of profit in the colony trade could not fail to draw from other branches of trade a part of the capital which had before been employed in them. But this revulsion of capital, as it must have gradually increased the competition of capitals in the colony trade, so it must have gradually diminished that competition in all those other branches of trade; as it must have gradually lowered the profits of the one, so it must have gradually raised those of the other, till the profits of all came to a new level, different from, and somewhat higher, than that at which they had been before.

This double effect of drawing capital from all other trades, and of raising the rate of profit somewhat higher than it otherwise would have been in all trades, was not only produced by this monopoly upon its first establishment, but has continued to be produced by it ever since.

First, this monopoly has been continually drawing capital from all other trades, to be employed in that of the colonies.

Though the wealth of Great Britain has increased very much since the establishment of the act of navigation, it certainly has not increased in the same proportion as that or the colonies. But the foreign trade of every country naturally increases in proportion to its wealth, its surplus produce in proportion to its whole produce; and Great Britain having engrossed to herself almost the whole of what may be called the foreign trade of the colonies, and her capital not having increased in the same proportion as the extent of that trade, she could not carry it on without continually withdrawing from other branches of trade some part of the capital which had before been employed in them, as well as withholding from them a great deal more which would otherwise have gone to them. Since the establishment of the act of navigation, accordingly, the colony trade has been continually increasing, while many other branches of foreign trade, particularly of that to other parts of Europe, have been continually decaying. Our manufactures for foreign sale, instead of being suited, as before the act of navigation, to the neighboring market of Europe, or to the more distant one of the countries which lie round the Mediterranean sea, have the greater part of them, been accommodated to the still more distant one of the colonies; to the market in which they have the monopoly, rather than to that in which they have many competitors. The causes of decay in other branches of foreign trade, which, by Sir Matthew Decker and other writers, have been sought for in the excess and improper mode of taxation, in the high price of labor, in the increase of luxury, etc. may all be found in the overgrowth of the colony trade. The mercantile capital of Great Britain, though very great, yet not being infinite, and though greatly increased since the act of navigation, yet not being increased in the same proportion as the colony trade, that trade could not possibly be carried on without withdrawing some part of that capital from other branches of trade, nor consequently without some decay of those other branches.

England, it must be observed, was a great trading country, her mercantile capital was very great, and likely to become still greater and greater every day, not only before the act of navigation had established the monopoly of the corn trade, but before that trade was very considerable. In the Dutch war, during the government of Cromwell, her navy was superior to that of Holland; and in that which broke out in the beginning of the reign of Charles II, it was at least equal, perhaps superior to the united navies of France and Holland. Its superiority, perhaps, would scarce appear greater in the present times, at least if the Dutch navy were to bear the same proportion to the Dutch commerce now which it did then. But this great naval power could not, in either of those wars, be owing to the act of navigation. During the first of them, the plan of that act had been but just formed; and though, before the breaking out of the second, it had been fully enacted by legal authority, yet no part of it could have had time to produce any considerable effect, and least of all that part which established the exclusive trade to the colonies. Both the colonies and their trade were inconsiderable then, in comparison of what they are how. The island of Jamaica was an unwholesome desert, little inhabited, and less cultivated. New York and New Jersey were in the possession of the Dutch, the half of St. Christopher's in that of the French. The island of Antigua, the two Carolinas, Pennsylvania, Georgia, and Nova Scotia, were not planted. Virginia, Maryland, and New England were planted; and though they were very thriving colonies, yet there was not perhaps at that time, either in Europe or America, a single person who foresaw, or even suspected, the rapid progress which they have since made in wealth, population, and improvement. The island of Barbados, in short, was the only British colony of any consequence, of which the condition at that time bore any resemblance to what it is at present. The trade of the colonies, of which England, even for some time after the act of navigation, enjoyed but a part (for the act of navigation was not very strictly executed till several years after it was enacted), could not at that time be the cause of the great trade of England, nor of the great naval power which was supported by that trade. The trade which at that time supported that great naval power was the trade of Europe, and of the countries which lie round the Mediterranean sea. But the share which Great Britain at present enjoys of that trade could not support any such great naval power. Had the growing trade of the colonies been left free to all nations, whatever share of it might have fallen to Great Britain, and a very considerable share would probably have fallen to her, must have been all an addition to this great trade of which she was before in possession. In consequence of the monopoly, the increase of the colony trade has not so much occasioned an addition to the trade which Great Britain had before, as a total change in its direction.

Secondly, this monopoly has necessarily contributed to keep up the rate of profit, in all the different branches of British trade, higher than it naturally would have been, had all nations been allowed a free trade to the British colonies.

The monopoly of the colony trade, as it necessarily drew towards that trade a greater proportion of the capital of Great Britain than what would have gone to it of its own accord, so, by the expulsion of all foreign capitals, it necessarily reduced the whole quantity of capital employed in that trade below what it naturally would have been in the case of a free trade. But, by lessening the competition of capitals in that branch of trade, it necessarily raised the rate of profit in that branch. By lessening, too, the competition of British capitals in all other branches of trade, it necessarily raised the rate of British profit in all those other branches. Whatever may have been, at any particular period since the establishment of the act of navigation, the state or extent of the mercantile capital of Great Britain, the monopoly of the colony trade must, during the continuance of that state, have raised the ordinary rate of British profit higher than it otherwise would have been, both in that and in all the other branches of British trade. If, since the establishment of the act of navigation, the ordinary rate of British profit has fallen considerably, as it certainly has, it must have fallen still lower, had not the monopoly established by that act contributed to keep it up.

But whatever raises, in any country, the ordinary rate of profit higher than it otherwise would be, necessarily subjects that country both to an absolute, and to a relative disadvantage in every branch of trade of which she has not the monopoly.

It subjects her to an absolute disadvantage; because, in such branches of trade, her merchants cannot get this greater profit without selling dearer than they otherwise would do, both the goods of foreign countries which they import into their own, and the goods of their own country which they export to foreign countries. Their own country must both buy dearer and sell dearer; must both buy less, and sell less; must both enjoy less and produce less, than she otherwise would do.

It subjects her to a relative disadvantage; because, in such branches of trade, it sets other countries, which are not subject to the same absolute disadvantage, either more above her or less below her, than they otherwise would be. It enables them both to enjoy more and to produce more, in proportion to what she enjoys and produces. It renders their superiority greater, or their inferiority less, than it otherwise would be. By raising the price of her produce above what it otherwise would be, it enables the merchants of other countries to undersell her in foreign markets, and thereby to justle her out of almost all those branches of trade, of which she has not the monopoly.

Our merchants frequently complain of the high wages of British labor, as the cause of their manufactures being undersold in foreign markets; but they are silent about the high profits of stock. They complain of the extravagant gain of other people; but they say nothing of their own. The high profits of British stock, however, may contribute towards raising the price of British manufactures, in many cases, as much, and in some perhaps more, than the high wages of British labor.

It is in this manner that the capital of Great Britain, one may justly say, has partly been drawn and partly been driven from the greater part of the different branches of trade of which she has not the monopoly; from the trade of Europe, in particular, and from that of the countries which lie round the Mediterranean sea.

It has partly been drawn from those branches of trade, by the attraction of superior profit in the colony trade, in consequence of the continual increase of that trade, and of the continual insufficiency of the capital which had carried it on one year to carry it on the next.

It has partly been driven from them, by the advantage which the high rate of profit established in Great Britain gives to other countries, in all the different branches of trade of which Great Britain has not the monopoly.

As the monopoly of the colony trade has drawn from those other branches a part of the British capital, which would otherwise have been employed in them, so it has forced into them many foreign capitals which would never have gone to them, had they not been expelled from the colony trade. In those other branches of trade, it has diminished the competition of British capitals, and thereby raised the rate of British profit higher than it otherwise would have been. On the contrary, it has increased the competition of foreign capitals, and thereby sunk the rate of foreign profit lower than it otherwise would have been. Both in the one way and in the other, it must evidently have subjected Great Britain to a relative disadvantage in all those other branches of trade.

The colony trade, however, it may perhaps be said, is more advantageous to Great Britain than any other; and the monopoly, by forcing into that trade a greater proportion of the capital of Great Britain than what would otherwise have gone to it, has turned that capital into an employment, more advantageous to the country than any other which it could have found.

The most advantageous employment of any capital to the country to which it belongs, is that which maintains there the greatest quantity of productive labor, and increases the most the annual produce of the land and labor of that country. But the quantity of productive labor which any capital employed in the foreign trade of consumption can maintain, is exactly in proportion, it has been shown in the second book, to the frequency of its returns. A capital of a thousand pounds, for example, employed in a foreign trade of consumption, of which the returns are made regularly once in the year, can keep in constant employment, in the country to which it belongs, a quantity of productive labor, equal to what a thousand pounds can maintain there for a year. If the returns are made twice or thrice in the year, it can keep in constant employment a quantity of productive labor, equal to what two or three thousand pounds can maintain there for a year. A foreign trade of consumption carried on with a neighboring, is, upon that account, in general, more advantageous than one carried on with a distant country; and, for the same reason, a direct foreign trade of consumption, as it has likewise been shown in the second book, is in general more advantageous than a round-about one.

But the monopoly of the colony trade, so far as it has operated upon the employment of the capital of Great Britain, has, in all cases, forced some part of it from a foreign trade of consumption carried on with a neighboring, to one carried on with a more distant country, and in many cases from a direct foreign trade of consumption to a round-about one.

First, the monopoly of the colony trade has, in all cases, forced some part of the capital of Great Britain from a foreign trade of consumption carried on with a neighboring, to one carried on with a more distant country.

It has, in all cases, forced some part of that capital from the trade with Europe, and with the countries which lie round the Mediterranean sea, to that with the more distant regions of America and the West Indies; from which the returns are necessarily less frequent, not only on account of the greater distance, but on account of the peculiar circumstances of those countries. New colonies, it has already been observed, are always understocked. Their capital is always much less than what they could employ with great profit and advantage in the improvement and cultivation of their land. They have a constant demand, therefore, for more capital than they have of their own; and, in order to supply the deficiency of their own, they endeavor to borrow as much as they can of the mother country, to whom they are, therefore, always in debt. The most common way in which the colonies contract this debt, is not by borrowing upon bond of the rich people of the mother country, though they sometimes do this too, but by running as much in arrear to their correspondents, who supply them with goods from Europe, as those correspondents will allow them. Their annual returns frequently do not amount to more than a third, and sometimes not to so great a proportion of what they owe. The whole capital, therefore, which their correspondents advance to them, is seldom returned to Britain in less than three, and sometimes not in less than four or five years. But a British capital of a thousand pounds, for example, which is returned to Great Britain only once in five years, can keep in constant employment only one-fifth part of the British industry which it could maintain, if the whole was returned once in the year; and, instead of the quantity of industry which a thousand pounds could maintain for a year, can keep in constant employment the quantity only which two hundred pounds can maintain for a year. The planter, no doubt, by the high price which he pays for the goods from Europe, by the interest upon the bills which he grants at distant dates, and by the commission upon the renewal of those which he grants at near dates, makes up, and probably more than makes up, all the loss which his correspondent can sustain by this delay. But, though he make up the loss of his correspondent, he cannot make up that of Great Britain. In a trade of which the returns are very distant, the profit of the merchant may be as great or greater than in one in which they are very frequent and near; but the advantage of the country in which he resides, the quantity of productive labor constantly maintained there, the annual produce of the land and labor, must always be much less. That the returns of the trade to America, and still more those of that to the West Indies, are, in general, not only more distant, but more irregular and more uncertain, too, than those of the trade to any part of Europe, or even of the countries which lie round the Mediterranean sea, will readily be allowed, I imagine, by everybody who has any experience of those different branches of trade.

Secondly, the monopoly of the colony trade, has, in many cases, forced some part of the capital of Great Britain from a direct foreign trade of consumption, into a round-about one.

Among the enumerated commodities which can be sent to no other market but Great Britain, there are several of which the quantity exceeds very much the consumption of Great Britain, and of which, a part, therefore, must be exported to other countries. But this cannot be done without forcing some part of the capital of Great Britain into a round-about foreign trade of consumption. Maryland, and Virginia, for example, send annually to Great Britain upwards of ninety-six thousand hogsheads of tobacco, and the consumption of Great Britain is said not to exceed fourteen thousand. Upwards of eighty-two thousand hogsheads, therefore, must be exported to other countries, to France, to Holland, and, to the countries which lie round the Baltic and Mediterranean seas. But that part of the capital of Great Britain which brings those eighty-two thousand hogsheads to Great Britain, which re-exports them from thence to those other countries, and which brings back from those other countries to Great Britain either goods or money in return, is employed in a round-about foreign trade of consumption; and is necessarily forced into this employment, in order to dispose of this great surplus. If we would compute in how many years the whole of this capital is likely to come back to Great Britain, we must add to the distance of the American returns that of the returns from those other countries. If, in the direct foreign trade of consumption which we carry on with America, the whole capital employed frequently does not come back in less than three or four years, the whole capital employed in this round-about one is not likely to come back in less than four or five. If the one can keep in constant employment but a third or a fourth part of the domestic industry which could be maintained by a capital returned once in the year, the other can keep in constant employment but a fourth or a fifth part of that industry. At some of the outports a credit is commonly given to those foreign correspondents to whom they export them tobacco. At the port of London, indeed, it is commonly sold for ready money: the rule is weigh and pay. At the port of London, therefore, the final returns of the whole round-about trade are more distant than the returns from America, by the time only which the goods may lie unsold in the warehouse; where, however, they may sometimes lie long enough. But, had not the colonies been confined to the market of Great Britain for the sale of their tobacco, very little more of it would probably have come to us than what was necessary for the home consumption. The goods which Great Britain purchases at present for her own consumption with the great surplus of tobacco which she exports to other countries, she would, in this case, probably have purchased with the immediate produce of her own industry, or with some part of her own manufactures. That produce, those manufactures, instead of being almost entirely suited to one great market, as at present, would probably have been fitted to a great number of smaller markets. Instead of one great round-about foreign trade of consumption, Great Britain would probably have carried on a great number of small direct foreign trades of the same kind. On account of the frequency of the returns, a part, and probably but a small part, perhaps not above a third or a fourth of the capital which at present carries on this great round-about trade, might have been sufficient to carry on all those small direct ones; might have kept inconstant employment an equal quantity of British industry; and have equally supported the annual produce of the land and labor of Great Britain. All the purposes of this trade being, in this manner, answered by a much smaller capital, there would have been a large spare capital to apply to other purposes; to improve the lands, to increase the manufactures, and to extend the commerce of Great Britain; to come into competition at least with the other British capitals employed in all those different ways, to reduce the rate of profit in them all, and thereby to give to Great Britain, in all of them, a superiority over other countries, still greater than what she at present enjoys.

The monopoly of the colony trade, too, has forced some part of the capital of Great Britain from all foreign trade of consumption to a carrying trade; and, consequently from supporting more or less the industry of Great Britain, to be employed altogether in supporting partly that of the colonies, and partly that of some other countries.

The goods, for example, which are annually purchased with the great surplus of eighty-two thousand hogsheads of tobacco annually re-exported from Great Britain, are not all consumed in Great Britain. Part of them, linen from Germany and Holland, for example, is returned to the colonies for their particular consumption. But that part of the capital of Great Britain which buys the tobacco with which this linen is afterwards bought, is necessarily withdrawn from supporting the industry of Great Britain, to be employed altogether in supporting, partly that of the colonies, and partly that of the particular countries who pay for this tobacco with the produce of their own industry.

The monopoly of the colony trade, besides, by forcing towards it a much greater proportion of the capital of Great Britain than what would naturally have gone to it, seems to have broken altogether that natural balance which would otherwise have taken place among all the different branches of British industry. The industry of Great Britain, instead of being accommodated to a great number of small markets, has been principally suited to one great market. Her commerce, instead of running in a great number of small channels, has been taught to run principally in one great channel. But the whole system of her industry and commerce has thereby been rendered less secure; the whole state of her body politic less healthful than it otherwise would have been. In her present condition, Great Britain resembles one of those unwholesome bodies in which some of the vital parts are overgrown, and which, upon that account, are liable to many dangerous disorders, scarce incident to those in which all the parts are more properly proportioned. A small stop in that great blood-vessel, which has been artificially swelled beyond its natural dimensions, and through which an unnatural proportion of the industry and commerce of the country has been forced to circulate, is very likely to bring on the most dangerous disorders upon the whole body politic. The expectation of a rupture with the colonies, accordingly, has struck the people of Great Britain with more terror than they ever felt for a Spanish armada, or a French invasion. It was this terror, whether well or ill grounded, which rendered the repeal of the Stamp Act, among the merchants at least, a popular measure. In the total exclusion from the colony market, was it to last only for a few years, the greater part of our merchants used to fancy that they foresaw an entire stop to their trade; the greater part of our master manufacturers, the entire ruin of their business; and the greater part of our workmen, an end of their employment. A rupture with any of our neighbors upon the continent, though likely, too, to occasion some stop or interruption in the employments of some of all these different orders of people, is foreseen, however, without any such general emotion. The blood, of which the circulation is stopped in some of the smaller vessels, easily disgorges itself into the greater, without occasioning any dangerous disorder; but, when it is stopped in any of the greater vessels, convulsions, apoplexy, or death, are the immediate and unavoidable consequences. If but one of those overgrown manufactures, which, by means either of bounties or of the monopoly of the home and colony markets, have been artificially raised up to any unnatural height, finds some small stop or interruption in its employment, it frequently occasions a mutiny and disorder alarming to government, and embarrassing even to the deliberations of the legislature. How great, therefore, would be the disorder and confusion, it was thought, which must necessarily be occasioned by a sudden and entire stop in the employment of so great a proportion of our principal manufacturers?

Some moderate and gradual relaxation of the laws which give to Great Britain the exclusive trade to the colonies, till it is rendered in a great measure free, seems to be the only expedient which can, in all future times, deliver her from this danger; which can enable her, or even force her, to withdraw some part of her capital from this overgrown employment, and to turn it, though with less profit, towards other employments; and which, by gradually diminishing one branch of her industry, and gradually increasing all the rest, can, by degrees, restore all the different branches of it to that natural, healthful, and proper proportion, which perfect liberty necessarily establishes, and which perfect liberty can alone preserve. To open the colony trade all at once to all nations, might not only occasion some transitory inconveniency, but a great permanent loss, to the greater part of those whose industry or capital is at present engaged in it. The sudden loss of the employment, even of the ships which import the eighty-two thousand hogsheads of tobacco, which are over and above the consumption of Great Britain, might alone be felt very sensibly. Such are the unfortunate effects of all the regulations of the mercantile system. They not only introduce very dangerous disorders into the state of the body politic, but disorders which it is often difficult to remedy, without occasioning, for a time at least, still greater disorders. In what manner, therefore, the colony trade ought gradually to be opened; what are the restraints which ought first, and what are those which ought last, to be taken away; or in what manner the natural system of perfect liberty and justice ought gradually to be restored, we must leave to the wisdom of future statesmen and legislators to determine.

Five different events, unforeseen and unthought-of, have very fortunately concurred to hinder Great Britain from feeling, so sensibly as it was generally expected she would, the total exclusion which has now taken place for more than a year (from the first of December 1774) from a very important branch of the colony trade, that of the twelve associated provinces of North America. First, those colonies, in preparing themselves for their non-importation agreement, drained Great Britain completely of all the commodities which were fit for their market; secondly, the extra ordinary demand of the Spanish flota has, this year, drained Germany and the north of many commodities, linen in particular, which used to come into competition, even in the British market, with the manufactures of Great Britain; thirdly, the peace between Russia and Turkey has occasioned an extraordinary demand from the Turkey market, which, during the distress of the country, and while a Russian fleet was cruising in the Archipelago, had been very poorly supplied; fourthly, the demand of the north of Europe for the manufactures of Great Britain has been increasing from year to year, for some time past; and, fifthly, the late partition, and consequential pacification of Poland, by opening the market of that great country, have, this year, added an extraordinary demand from thence to the increasing demand of the north. These events are all, except the fourth, in their nature transitory and accidental; and the exclusion from so important a branch of the colony trade, if unfortunately it should continue much longer, may still occasion some degree of distress. This distress, however, as it will come on gradually, will be felt much less severely than if it had come on all at once; and, in the mean time, the industry and capital of the country may find a new employment and direction, so as to prevent this distress from ever rising to any considerable height.

The monopoly of the colony trade, therefore, so far as it has turned towards that trade a greater proportion of the capital of Great Britain than what would otherwise have gone to it, has in all cases turned it, from a foreign trade of consumption with a neighboring, into one with a more distant country; in many cases from a direct foreign trade of consumption into a round-about one; and, in some cases, from all foreign trade of consumption into a carrying trade. It has, in all cases, therefore, turned it from a direction in which it would have maintained a greater quantity of productive labor, into one in which it can maintain a much smaller quantity. By suiting, besides, to one particular market only, so great a part of the industry and commerce of Great Britain, it has rendered the whole state of that industry and commerce more precarious and less secure, than if their produce had been accommodated to a greater variety of markets.

We must carefully distinguish between the effects of the colony trade and those of the monopoly of that trade. The former are always and necessarily beneficial; the latter always and necessarily hurtful. But the former are so beneficial, that the colony trade, though subject to a monopoly, and, notwithstanding the hurtful effects of that monopoly, is still, upon the whole, beneficial, and greatly beneficial, though a good deal less so than it otherwise would be.

The effect of the colony trade, in its natural and free state, is to open a great though distant market, for such parts of the produce of British industry as may exceed the demand of the markets nearer home, of those of Europe, and of the countries which lie round the Mediterranean sea. In its natural and free state, the colony trade, without drawing from those markets any part of the produce which had ever been sent to them, encourages Great Britain to increase the surplus continually, by continually presenting new equivalents to be exchanged for it. In its natural and free state, the colony trade tends to increase the quantity of productive labor in Great Britain, but without altering in any respect the direction of that which had been employed there before. In the natural and free state of the colony trade, the competition of all other nations would hinder the rate of profit from rising above the common level, either in the new market, or in the new employment. The new market, without drawing any thing from the old one, would create, if one may say so, a new produce for its own supply; and that new produce would constitute a new capital for carrying on the new employment, which, in the same manner, would draw nothing from the old one.

The monopoly of the colony trade, on the contrary, by excluding the competition of other nations, and thereby raising the rate of profit, both in the new market and in the new employment, draws produce from the old market, and capital from the old employment. To augment our share of the colony trade beyond what it otherwise would be, is the avowed purpose of the monopoly. If our share of that trade were to be no greater with, than it would have been without the monopoly, there could have been no reason for establishing the monopoly. But whatever forces into a branch of trade, of which the returns are slower and more distant than those of the greater part of other trades, a greater proportion of the capital of any country, than what of its own accord would go to that branch, necessarily renders the whole quantity of productive labor annually maintained there, the whole annual produce of the land and labor of that country, less than they otherwise would be. It keeps down the revenue of the inhabitants of that country below what it would naturally rise to, and thereby diminishes their power of accumulation. It not only hinders, at all times, their capital from maintaining so great a quantity of productive labor as it would otherwise maintain, but it hinders it from increasing so fast as it would otherwise increase, and, consequently, from maintaining a still greater quantity of productive labor.

The natural good effects of the colony trade, however, more than counterbalance to Great Britain the bad effects of the monopoly; so that, monopoly and altogether, that trade, even as it is carried on at present, is not only advantageous, but greatly advantageous. The new market and the new employment which are opened by the colony trade, are of much greater extent than that portion of the old market and of the old employment which is lost by the monopoly. The new produce and the new capital which has been created, if one may say so, by the colony trade, maintain in Great Britain a greater quantity of productive labor than what can have been thrown out of employment by the revulsion of capital from other trades of which the returns are more frequent. If the colony trade, however, even as it is carried on at present, is advantageous to Great Britain, it is not by means of the monopoly, but in spite of the monopoly.

It is rather for the manufactured than for the rude produce of Europe, that the colony trade opens a new market. Agriculture is the proper business of all new colonies; a business which the cheapness of land renders more advantageous than any other. They abound, therefore, in the rude produce of land; and instead of importing it from other countries, they have generally a large surplus to export. In new colonies, agriculture either draws hands from all other employments, or keeps them from going to any other employment. There are few hands to spare for the necessary, and none for the ornamental manufactures. The greater part of the manufactures of both kinds they find it cheaper to purchase of other countries than to make for themselves. It is chiefly by encouraging the manufactures of Europe, that the colony trade indirectly encourages its agriculture. The manufacturers of Europe, to whom that trade gives employment, constitute a new market for the produce of the land, and the most advantageous of all markets; the home market for the corn and cattle, for the bread and butcher's meat of Europe, is thus greatly extended by means of the trade to America.

But that the monopoly of the trade of populous and thriving colonies is not alone sufficient to establish, or even to maintain, manufactures in any country, the examples of Spain and Portugal sufficiently demonstrate. Spain and Portugal were manufacturing countries before they had any considerable colonies. Since they had the richest and most fertile in the world, they have both ceased to be so.

In Spain and Portugal, the bad effects of the monopoly, aggravated by other causes, have, perhaps, nearly overbalanced the natural good effects of the colony trade. These causes seem to be other monopolies of different kinds: the degradation of the value of gold and silver below what it is in most other countries; the exclusion from foreign markets by improper taxes upon exportation, and the narrowing of the home market, by still more improper taxes upon the transportation of goods from one part of the country to another; but above all, that irregular and partial administration of justice which often protects the rich and powerful debtor from the pursuit of his injured creditor, and which makes the industrious part of the nation afraid to prepare goods for the consumption of those haughty and great men, to whom they dare not refuse to sell upon credit, and from whom they are altogether uncertain of repayment.

In England, on the contrary, the natural good effects of the colony trade, assisted by other causes, have in a great measure conquered the bad effects of the monopoly. These causes seem to be, the general liberty of trade, which, notwithstanding some restraints, is at least equal, perhaps superior, to what it is in any other country; the liberty of exporting, duty free, almost all sorts of goods which are the produce of domestic industry, to almost any foreign country; and what, perhaps, is of still greater importance, the unbounded liberty of transporting them from one part of our own country to any other, without being obliged to give any account to any public office, without being liable to question or examination of any kind; but, above all, that equal and impartial adminis- tration of justice, which renders the rights of the meanest British subject respectable to the greatest, and which, by securing to every man the fruits of his own industry, gives the greatest and most effectual encouragement to every sort of industry.

If the manufactures of Great Britain, however, have been advanced, as they certainly have, by the colony trade, it has not been by means of the monopoly of that trade, but in spite of the monopoly. The effect of the monopoly has been, not to augment the quantity, but to alter the quality and shape of a part of the manufactures of Great Britain, and to accommodate to a market, from which the returns are slow and distant, what would otherwise have been accommodated to one from which the returns are fre- quent and near. Its effect has consequently been, to turn a part of the capital of Great Britain from an employment in which it would have maintained a greater quantity of manufacturing industry, to one in which it maintains a much smaller, and thereby to diminish, instead of increasing, the whole quantity of manufacturing industry main- tained in Great Britain.

The monopoly of the colony trade, therefore, like all the other mean and malignant expedients of the mercantile system, depresses the industry of all other countries, but chiefly that of the colonies, without in the least increasing, but on the contrary dimin- ishing, that of the country in whose favor it is established.

The monopoly hinders the capital of that country, whatever may, at any particular time, be the extent of that capital, from maintaining so great a quantity of productive labor as it would otherwise maintain, and from affording so great a revenue to the indus- trious inhabitants as it would otherwise afford. But as capital can be increased only by savings from revenue, the monopoly, by hindering it from affording so great a revenue as it would otherwise afford, necessarily hinders it from increasing so fast as it would otherwise increase, and consequently from maintaining a still greater quantity of produc- tive labor, and affording a still greater revenue to the industrious inhabitants of that country. One great original source of revenue, therefore, the wages of labor, the monop- oly must necessarily have rendered, at all times, less abundant than it otherwise would have been.

By raising the rate of mercantile profit, the monopoly discourages the improvement of land. The profit of improvement depends upon the difference between what the land actually produces, and what, by the application of a certain capital, it can be made to pro- duce. If this difference affords a greater profit than what can be drawn from an equal cap- ital in any mercantile employment, the improvement of land will draw capital from all mercantile employments. If the profit is less, mercantile employments will draw capital from the improvement of land. Whatever, therefore, raises the rate of mercantile profit, either lessens the superiority, or increases the inferiority of the profit of improvement: and, in the one case, hinders capital from going to improvement, and in the other draws capital from it; but by discouraging improvement, the monopoly necessarily retards the natural increase of another great original source of revenue, the rent of land. By raising the rate of profit, too, the monopoly necessarily keeps up the market rate of interest higher than it otherwise would be. But the price of land, in proportion to the rent which it affords, the number of years purchase which is commonly paid for it, necessarily falls as the rate of interest rises, and rises as the rate of interest falls. The monopoly, therefore, hurts the interest of the landlord two different ways, by retarding the natural increase, first, of his rent, and, secondly, of the price which he would get for his land, in proportion to the rent which it affords.

The monopoly, indeed, raises the rate of mercantile profit and thereby augments somewhat the gain of our merchants. But as it obstructs the natural increase of capital, it tends rather to diminish than to increase the sum total of the revenue which the inhabitants of the country derive from the profits of stock; a small profit upon a great capital generally affording a greater revenue than a great profit upon a small one. The monopoly raises the rate of profit, but it hinders the sum of profit from rising so high as it otherwise would do.

All the original sources of revenue, the wages of labor, the rent of land, and the profits of stock, the monopoly renders much less abundant than they otherwise would be. To promote the little interest of one little order of men in one country, it hurts the interest of all other orders of men in that country, and of all the men in all other countries.

It is solely by raising the ordinary rate of profit, that the monopoly either has proved, or could prove, advantageous to any one particular order of men. But besides all the bad effects to the country in general, which have already been mentioned as necessarily resulting from a higher rate of profit, there is one more fatal, perhaps, than all these put together, but which, if we may judge from experience, is inseparably connected with it.

The high rate of profit seems everywhere to destroy that parsimony which, in other circumstances, is natural to the character of the merchant. When profits are high, that sober virtue seems to be superfluous, and expensive luxury to suit better the affluence of his situation. But the owners of the great mercantile capitals are necessarily the leaders and conductors of the whole industry of every nation; and their example has a much greater influence upon the manners of the whole industrious part of it than that of any other order of men. If his employer is attentive and parsimonious, the workman is very likely to be so too; but if the master is dissolute and disorderly, the servant, who shapes his work according to the pattern which his master prescribes to him, will shape his life, too, according to the example which he sets him. Accumulation is thus prevented in the hands of all those who are naturally the most disposed to accumulate; and the funds destined for the maintenance of productive labor, receive no augmentation from the revenue of those who ought naturally to augment them the most. The capital of the country, instead of increasing, gradually dwindles away, and the quantity of productive labor maintained in it grows every day less and less. Have the exorbitant profits of the merchants of Cadiz and Lisbon augmented the capital of Spain and Portugal? Have they alleviated the poverty, have they promoted the industry, of those two beggarly countries? Such has been the tone of mercantile expense in those two trading cities, that those exorbitant profits, far from augmenting the general capital of the country, seem scarce to have been sufficient to keep up the capitals upon which they were made. Foreign capitals are every day intruding themselves, if I may say so, more and more into the trade of Cadiz and Lisbon. It is to expel those foreign capitals from a trade which their own grows every day more and more insufficient for carrying on, that the Spaniards and Portuguese endeavor every day to straiten more and more the galling bands of their absurd monopoly. Compare the mercantile manners of Cadiz and Lisbon with those of Amsterdam, and you will be sensible how differently the conduct and character of merchants are affected by the high and by the low profits of stock. The merchants of London, indeed, have not yet generally become such magnificent lords as those of Cadiz and Lisbon; but neither are they in general such attentive and parsimonious burghers as those of Amsterdam. They are supposed, however, many of them, to be a good deal richer than the greater part of the former, and not quite so rich as many of the latter: but the rate of their profit is commonly much lower than that of the former, and a good deal higher than that of the latter. Light come, light go, says the proverb; and the ordinary tone of expense seems everywhere to be regulated, not so much according to the real ability of spending, as to the supposed facility of getting money to spend.

It is thus that the single advantage which the monopoly procures to a single order of men, is in many different ways hurtful to the general interest of the country.

To found a great empire for the sole purpose of raising up a people of customers, may at first sight, appear a project fit only for a nation of shopkeepers. It is, however, a project altogether unfit for a nation of shopkeepers, but extremely fit for a nation whose government is influenced by shopkeepers. Such statesmen, and such statesmen only, are capable of fancying that they will find some advantage in employing the blood and treasure of their fellow-citizens, to found and maintain such an empire. Say to a shopkeeper, Buy me a good estate, and I shall always buy my clothes at your shop, even though I should pay somewhat dearer than what I can have them for at other shops; and you will not find him very forward to embrace your proposal. But should any other person buy you such an estate, the shopkeeper will be much obliged to your benefactor if he would enjoin you to buy all your clothes at his shop. England purchased for some of her subjects, who found themselves uneasy at home, a great estate in a distant country.

The price, indeed, was very small, and instead of thirty years' purchase, the ordinary price of land in the present times, it amounted to little more than the expense of the different equipments which made the first discovery, reconnoitered the coast, and took a fictitious possession of the country. The land was good, and of great extent; and the cultivators having plenty of good ground to work upon, and being for some time at liberty to sell their produce where they pleased, became, in the course of little more than thirty or forty years (between 1620 and 1660), so numerous and thriving a people, that the shopkeepers and other traders of England wished to secure to themselves the monopoly of their custom. Without pretending, therefore, that they had paid any part, either of the original purchase money, or of the subsequent expense of improvement, they petitioned the parliament, that the cultivators of America might for the future be confined to their shop; first, for buying all the goods which they wanted from Europe; and, secondly, for selling all such parts of their own produce as those traders might find it convenient to buy. For they did not find it convenient to buy every part of it. Some parts of it imported into England, might have interfered with some of the trades which they themselves carried on at home. Those particular parts of it, therefore, they were willing that the colonists should sell where they could; the farther off the better; and upon that account proposed that their market should be confined to the countries south of Cape Finisterre. A clause in the famous act of navigation established this truly shopkeeper proposal into a law.

The maintenance of this monopoly has hitherto been the principal, or more properly, perhaps, the sole end and purpose of the dominion which Great Britain assumes over her colonies. In the exclusive trade, it is supposed, consists the great advantage of provinces, which have never yet afforded either revenue or military force for the support of the civil government, or the defense of the mother country. The monopoly is the principal badge of their dependency, and it is the sole fruit which has hitherto been gathered from that dependency. Whatever expense Great Britain has hitherto laid out in maintaining this dependency, has really been laid out in order to support this monopoly. The expense of the ordinary peace establishment of the colonies amounted, before the commencement of the present disturbances to the pay of twenty regiments of foot; to the expense of the artillery, stores, and extraordinary provisions, with which it was necessary to supply them; and to the expense of a very considerable naval force, which was constantly kept up, in order to guard from the smuggling vessels of other nations, the immense coast of North America, and that of our West Indian islands. The whole expense of this peace establishment was a charge upon the revenue of Great Britain, and was, at the same time, the smallest part of what the dominion of the colonies has cost the mother country. If we would know the amount of the whole, we must add to the annual expense of this peace establishment, the interest of the sums which, in consequence of their considering her colonies as provinces subject to her dominion, Great Britain has, upon different occasions, laid out upon their defense. We must add to it, in particular, the whole expense of the late war, and a great part of that of the war which preceded it. The late war was altogether a colony quarrel; and the whole expense of it, in whatever part of the world it might have been laid out, whether in Germany or the East Indies, ought justly to be stated to the account of the colonies. It amounted to more than ninety millions sterling, including not only the new debt which was contracted, but the two shillings in the pound additional land tax, and the sums which were every year borrowed from the sinking fund. The Spanish war which began in 1739 was principally a colony quarrel. Its principal object was to prevent the search of the colony ships, which carried on a contraband trade with the Spanish Main. This whole expense is, in reality, a bounty which has been given in order to support a monopoly. The pretended purpose of it was to encourage the manufactures, and to increase the commerce of Great Britain. But its real effect has been to raise the rate of mercantile profit, and to enable our merchants to turn into a branch of trade, of which the returns are more slow and distant than those of the greater part of other trades, a greater proportion of their capital than they otherwise would have done; two events which, if a bounty could have prevented, it might perhaps have been very well worth while to give such a bounty.

Under the present system of management, therefore, Great Britain derives nothing but loss from the dominion which she assumes over her colonies.

To propose that Great Britain should voluntarily give up all authority over her colonies, and leave them to elect their own magistrates, to enact their own laws, and to make peace and war, as they might think proper, would be to propose such a measure as never was, and never will be, adopted by any nation in the world. No nation ever voluntarily gave up the dominion of any province, how troublesome soever it might be to govern it, and how small soever the revenue which it afforded might be in proportion to the expense which it occasioned. Such sacrifices, though they might frequently be agreeable to the interest, are always mortifying to the pride of every nation; and, what is perhaps of still greater consequence, they are always contrary to the private interest of the governing part of it, who would thereby be deprived of the disposal of many places of trust and profit, of many opportunities of acquiring wealth and distinction, which the possession of the most turbulent, and, to the great body of the people, the most unprofitable province, seldom fails to afford. The most visionary enthusiasts would scarce be capable of proposing such a measure, with any serious hopes at least of its ever being adopted. If it was adopted, however, Great Britain would not only be immediately freed from the whole annual expense of the peace establishment of the colonies, but might settle with them such a treaty of commerce as would effectually secure to her a free trade, more advantageous to the great body of the people, though less so to the merchants, than the monopoly which she at present enjoys. By thus parting good friends, the natural affection of the colonies to the mother country, which, perhaps, our late dissensions have well nigh extinguished, would quickly revive. It might dispose them not only to respect, for whole centuries together, that treaty of commerce which they had concluded with us at parting, but to favor us in war as well as in trade, and instead of turbulent and factious subjects, to become our most faithful, affectionate, and generous allies; and the same sort of parental affection on the one side, and filial respect on the other, might revive between Great Britain and her colonies, which used to subsist between those of ancient Greece and the mother city from which they descended.

In order to render any province advantageous to the empire to which it belongs, it ought to afford, in time of peace, a revenue to the public, sufficient not only for defraying the whole expense of its own peace establishment, but for contributing its proportion to the support of the general government of the empire. Every province necessarily contributes, more or less, to increase the expense of that general government. If any particular province, therefore, does not contribute its share towards defraying this expense, an unequal burden must be thrown upon some other part of the empire. The extraordinary revenue, too, which every province affords to the public in time of war, ought, from parity of reason, to bear the same proportion to the extraordinary revenue of the whole empire, which its ordinary revenue does in time of peace. That neither the ordinary nor extraordinary revenue which Great Britain derives from her colonies, bears this proportion to the whole revenue of the British empire, will readily be allowed. The monopoly, it has been supposed, indeed, by increasing the private revenue of the people of Great Britain, and thereby enabling them to pay greater taxes, compensates the deficiency of the public revenue of the colonies. But this monopoly, I have endeavored to show, though a very grievous tax upon the colonies, and though it may increase the revenue of a particular order of men in Great Britain, diminishes, instead of increasing, that of the great body of the people, and consequently diminishes, instead of increasing, the ability of the great body of the people to pay taxes. The men, too, whose revenue the monopoly increases, constitute a particular order, which it is both absolutely impossible to tax beyond the proportion of other orders, and extremely impolitic even to attempt to tax beyond that proportion, as I shall endeavor to show in the following book. No particular resource, therefore, can be drawn from this particular order.

The colonies may be taxed either by their own assemblies, or by the parliament of Great Britain.

That the colony assemblies can never be so managed as to levy upon their constituents a public revenue, sufficient, not only to maintain at all times their own civil and military establishment, but to pay their proper proportion of the expense of the general government of the British empire, seems not very probable. It was a long time before even the parliament of England, though placed immediately under the eye of the sovereign, could be brought under such a system of management, or could be rendered sufficiently liberal in their grants for supporting the civil and military establishments even of their own country. It was only by distributing among the particular members of parliament a great part either of the offices, or of the disposal of the offices arising from this civil and military establishment, that such a system of management could be established, even with regard to the parliament of England. But the distance of the colony assemblies from the eye of the sovereign, their number, their dispersed situation, and their various constitutions, would render it very difficult to manage them in the same manner, even though the sovereign had the same means of doing it; and those means are wanting. It would be absolutely impossible to distribute among all the leading members of all the colony assemblies such a share, either of the offices, or of the disposal of the offices, arising from the general government of the British empire, as to dispose them to give up their popularity at home, and to tax their constituents for the support of that general government, of which almost the whole emoluments were to be divided among people who were strangers to them. The unavoidable ignorance of administration, besides, concerning the relative importance of the different members of those different assemblies, the offences which must frequently be given, the blunders which must constantly be committed, in attempting to manage them in this manner, seems to render such a system of management altogether impracticable with regard to them.

The colony assemblies, besides, cannot be supposed the proper judges of what is necessary for the defense and support of the whole empire. The care of that defense and support is not entrusted to them. It is not their business, and they have no regular means of information concerning it. The assembly of a province, like the vestry of a parish, may judge very properly concerning the affairs of its own particular district, but can have no proper means of judging concerning those of the whole empire. It cannot even judge properly concerning the proportion which its own province bears to the whole empire, or concerning the relative degree of its wealth and importance, compared with the other provinces; because those other provinces are not under the inspection and superintendence of the assembly of a particular province. What is necessary for the defense and support of the whole empire, and in what proportion each part ought to contribute, can be judged of only by that assembly which inspects and super-intends the affairs of the whole empire.

It has been proposed, accordingly, that the colonies should be taxed by requisition, the parliament of Great Britain determining the sum which each colony ought to pay, and the provincial assembly assessing and levying it in the way that suited best the circumstances of the province. What concerned the whole empire would in this way be determined by the assembly which inspects and superintends the affairs of the whole empire; and the provincial affairs of each colony might still be regulated by its own assembly. Though the colonies should, in this case, have no representatives in the British parliament, yet, if we may judge by experience, there is no probability that the parliamentary requisition would be unreasonable. The parliament of England has not, upon any occasion, shown the smallest disposition to overburden those parts of the empire which are not represented in parliament. The islands of Guernsey and Jersey, without any means of resisting the authority of parliament, are more lightly taxed than any part of Great Britain. Parliament, in attempting to exercise its supposed right, whether well or ill grounded, of taxing the colonies, has never hitherto demanded of them anything which even approached to a just proportion to what was paid by their fellow subjects at home. If the contribution of the colonies, besides, was to rise or fall in proportion to the rise or fall of the land-tax, parliament could not tax them without taxing, at the same time, its own constituents, and the colonies might, in this case, be considered as virtually represented in parliament.

Examples are not wanting of empires in which all the different provinces are not taxed, if I may be allowed the expression, in one mass; but in which the sovereign regulates the sum which each province ought to pay, and in some provinces assesses and levies it as he thinks proper; while in others he leaves it to be assessed and levied as the respective states of each province shall determine. In some provinces of France, the king not only imposes what taxes he thinks proper, but assesses and levies them in the way he thinks proper. From others he demands a certain sum, but leaves it to the states of each province to assess and levy that sum as they think proper. According to the scheme of taxing by requisition, the parliament of Great Britain would stand nearly in the same situation towards the colony assemblies, as the king of France does towards the states of those provinces which still enjoy the privilege of having states of their own, the provinces of France which are supposed to be the best governed.

But though, according to this scheme, the colonies could have no just reason to fear that their share of the public burdens should ever exceed the proper proportion to that of their fellow-citizens at home, Great Britain might have just reason to fear that it never would amount to that proper proportion. The parliament of Great Britain has not, for some time past, had the same established authority in the colonies, which the French king has in those provinces of France which still enjoy the privilege of having states of their own. The colony assemblies, if they were not very favorably disposed (and unless more skillfully managed than they ever have been hitherto, they are not very likely to be so), might still find many pretences for evading or rejecting the most reasonable requisitions of parliament. A French war breaks out, we shall suppose; ten millions must immediately be raised, in order to defend the seat of the empire. This sum must be borrowed upon the credit of some parliamentary fund mortgaged for paying the interest. Part of this fund parliament proposes to raise by a tax to be levied in Great

Britain; and part of it by a requisition to all the different colony assemblies of America and the West Indies. Would people readily advance their money upon the credit of a fund which partly depended upon the good humor of all those assemblies, far distant from the seat of the war, and sometimes, perhaps, thinking themselves not much concerned in the event of it? Upon such a fund, no more money would probably be advanced than what the tax to be levied in Great Britain might be supposed to answer for. The whole burden of the debt contracted on account of the war would in this manner fall, as it always has done hitherto, upon Great Britain; upon a part of the empire, and not upon the whole empire. Great Britain is, perhaps, since the world began, the only state which, as it has extended its empire, has only increased its expense, without once augmenting its resources. Other states have generally disburdened themselves, upon their subject and subordinate provinces, of the most considerable part of the expense of defending the empire. Great Britain has hitherto suffered her subject and subordinate provinces to disburden themselves upon her of almost this whole expense. In order to put Great Britain upon a footing of equality with her own colonies, which the law has hitherto supposed to be subject and subordinate, it seems necessary, upon the scheme of taxing them by parliamentary requisition, that parliament should have some means of rendering its requisitions immediately effectual, in case the colony assemblies should attempt to evade or reject them; and what those means are, it is not very easy to conceive, and it has not yet been explained.

Should the parliament of Great Britain, at the same time, be ever fully established in the right of taxing the colonies, even independent of the consent of their own assemblies, the importance of those assemblies would, from that moment, be at an end, and with it, that of all the leading men of British America. Men desire to have some share in the management of public affairs, chiefly on account of the importance which it gives them. Upon the power which the greater part of the leading men, the natural aristocracy of every country, have of preserving or defending their respective importance, depends the stability and duration of every system of free government. In the attacks which those leading men are continually making upon the importance of one another, and in the defense of their own, consists the whole play of domestic faction and ambition. The leading men of America, like those of all other countries, desire to preserve their own importance. They feel, or imagine, that if their assemblies, which they are fond of calling parliaments, and of considering as equal in authority to the parliament of Great Britain, should be so far degraded as to become the humble ministers and executive officers of that parliament, the greater part of their own importance would be at an end. They have rejected, therefore, the proposal of being taxed by parliamentary requisition, and, like other ambitious and high-spirited men, have rather chosen to draw the sword in defense of their own importance.

Towards the declension of the Roman republic, the allies of Rome, who had borne the principal burden of defending the state and extending the empire, demanded to be admitted to all the privileges of Roman citizens. Upon being refused, the social war broke out. During the course of that war, Rome granted those privileges to the greater part of them, one by one, and in proportion as they detached themselves from the general confederacy. The parliament of Great Britain insists upon taxing the colonies; and they refuse to be taxed by a parliament in which they are not represented. If to each colony which should detach itself from the general confederacy, Great Britain should allow such a number of representatives as suited the proportion of what it contributed to the public revenue of the empire, in consequence of its being subjected to the same taxes, and in compensation admitted to the same freedom of trade with its fellow-subjects at home; the number of its representatives to be augmented as the proportion of its contribution might afterwards augment; a new method of acquiring importance, a new and more dazzling object of ambition, would be presented to the leading men of each colony. Instead of piddling for the little prizes which are to be found in what may be called the paltry raffle of colony faction, they might then hope, from the presumption which men naturally have in their own ability and good fortune, to draw some of the great prizes which sometimes come from the wheel of the great state lottery of British politics. Unless this or some other method is fallen upon, and there seems to be none more obvious than this, of preserving the importance and of gratifying the ambition of the leading men of America, it is not very probable that they will ever voluntarily submit to us; and we ought to consider, that the blood which must be shed in forcing them to do so, is, every drop of it, the blood either of those who are, or of those whom we wish to have for our fellow citizens. They are very weak who flatter themselves that, in the state to which things have come, our colonies will be easily conquered by force alone. The persons who now govern the resolutions of what they call their continental congress, feel in themselves at this moment a degree of importance which, perhaps, the greatest subjects in Europe scarce feel. From shopkeepers, trades men, and attorneys, they are become statesmen and legislators, and are employed in contriving a new form of government for an extensive empire, which, they flatter themselves, will become, and which, indeed, seems very likely to become, one of the greatest and most formidable that ever was in the world. Five hundred different people, perhaps, who, in different ways, act immediately under the continental congress, and five hundred thousand, perhaps, who act under those five hundred, all feel, in the same manner, a proportional rise in their own importance. Almost every individual of the governing party in America fills, at present, in his own fancy, a station superior, not only to what he had ever filled before, but to what he had ever expected to fill; and unless some new object of ambition is presented either to him or to his leaders, if he has the ordinary spirit of a man, he will die in defense of that station.

It is a remark of the President Heynaut, that we now read with pleasure the account of many little transactions of the Ligue, which, when they happened, were not, perhaps, considered as very important pieces of news. But everyman then, says he, fancied himself of some importance; and the innumerable memoirs which have come down to us from those times, were the greater part of them written by people who took pleasure in recording and magnifying events, in which they flattered themselves they had been considerable actors. How obstinately the city of Paris, upon that occasion, defended itself, what a dreadful famine it supported, rather than submit to the best, and afterwards the most beloved of all the French kings, is well known. The greater part of the citizens, or those who governed the greater part of them, fought in defense of their own importance, which, they foresaw, was to be at an end whenever the ancient government should be reestablished. Our colonies, unless they can be induced to consent to a union, are very likely to defend themselves, against the best of all mother countries, as obstinately as the city of Paris did against one of the best of kings.

The idea of representation was unknown in ancient times. When the people of one state were admitted to the right of citizenship in another, they had no other means of exercising that right, but by coming in a body to vote and deliberate with the people of that other state. The admission of the greater part of the inhabitants of Italy to the privileges of Roman citizens, completely ruined the Roman republic. It was no longer possible to distinguish between who was, and who was not, a Roman citizen. No tribe could know its own members. A rabble of any kind could be introduced into the assemblies of the people, could drive out the real citizens, and decide upon the affairs of the republic, as if they themselves had been such. But though America were to send fifty or sixty new representatives to parliament, the door-keeper of the house of commons could not find any great difficulty in distinguishing between who was and who was not a member. Though the Roman constitution, therefore, was necessarily ruined by the union of Rome with the allied states of Italy, there is not the least probability that the British constitution would be hurt by the union of Great Britain with her colonies. That constitution, on the contrary, would be completed by it, and seems to be imperfect without it. The assembly which deliberates and decides concerning the affairs of every part of the empire, in order to be properly informed, ought certainly to have representatives from every part of it. That this union, however, could be easily effectuated, or that difficulties, and great difficulties, might not occur in the execution, I do not pretend. I have yet heard of none, however, which appear insurmountable. The principal, perhaps, arise, not from the nature of things, but from the prejudices and opinions of the people, both on this and on the other side of the Atlantic.

We on this side of the water are afraid lest the multitude of American representatives should overturn the balance of the constitution, and increase too much either the influence of the crown on the one hand, or the force of the democracy on the other. But if the number of American representatives were to be in proportion to the produce of American taxation, the number of people to be managed would increase exactly in proportion to the means of managing them, and the means of managing to the number of people to be managed. The monarchical and democratical parts of the constitution would, after the union, stand exactly in the same degree of relative force with regard to one another as they had done before.

The people on the other side of the water are afraid lest their distance from the seat of government might expose them to many oppressions; but their representatives in parliament, of which the number ought from the first to be considerable, would easily be able to protect them from all oppression. The distance could not much weaken the dependency of the representative upon the constituent, and the former would still feel that he owed his seat in parliament, and all the consequence which he derived from it, to the good-will of the latter. It would be the interest of the former, therefore, to cultivate that good-will, by complaining, with all the authority of a member of the legislature, of every outrage which any civil or military officer might be guilty of in those remote parts of the empire. The distance of America from the seat of government, besides, the natives of that country might flatter themselves, with some appearance of reason too, would not be of very long continuance. Such has hitherto been the rapid progress of that country in wealth, population, and improvement, that in the course of little more than a century, perhaps, the produce of the American might exceed that of the British taxation. The seat of the empire would then naturally remove itself to that part of the empire which contributed most to the general defense and support of the whole.

The discovery of America, and that of a passage to the East Indies by the Cape of Good Hope, are the two greatest and most important events recorded in the history of mankind. Their consequences have already been great; but, in the short period of between two and three centuries which has elapsed since these discoveries were made, it is impossible that the whole extent of their consequences can have been seen. What benefits or what misfortunes to mankind may hereafter result from those great events, no human wisdom can foresee. By uniting in some measure the most distant parts of the world, by enabling them to relieve one another's wants, to increase one another's enjoyments, and to encourage one another's industry, their general tendency would seem to be beneficial. To the natives, however, both of the East and West Indies, all the commercial benefits which can have resulted from those events have been sunk and lost in the dreadful misfortunes which they have occasioned. These misfortunes, however, seem to have arisen rather from accident than from any thing in the nature of those events themselves. At the particular time when these discoveries were made, the superiority of force happened to be so great on the side of the Europeans, that they were enabled to commit with impunity every sort of injustice in those remote countries. Hereafter, perhaps, the natives of those countries may grow stronger, or those of Europe may grow weaker; and the inhabitants of all the different quarters of the world may arrive at that equality of courage and force which, by inspiring mutual fear, can alone overawe the injustice of independent nations into some sort of respect for the rights of one another. But nothing seems more likely to establish this equality of force, than that mutual communication of knowledge, and of all sorts of improvements, which an extensive commerce from all countries to all countries naturally, or rather necessarily, carries along with it.

In the mean time, one of the principal effects of those discoveries has been, to raise the mercantile system to a degree of splendor and glory which it could never otherwise have attained to. It is the object of that system to enrich a great nation, rather by trade and manufactures than by the improvement and cultivation of land, rather by the industry of the towns than by that of the country. But in consequence of those discoveries, the commercial towns of Europe, instead of being the manufacturers and carriers for but a very small part of the world (that part of Europe which is washed by the Atlantic ocean, and the countries which lie round the Baltic and Mediterranean seas), have now become the manufacturers for the numerous and thriving cultivators of America, and the carriers, and in some respects the manufacturers too, for almost all the different nations of Asia, Africa, and America. Two new worlds have been opened to their industry, each of them much greater and more extensive than the old one, and the market of one of them growing still greater and greater every day.

The countries which possess the colonies of America, and which trade directly to the East Indies, enjoy indeed the whole show and splendor of this great commerce. Other countries, however, notwithstanding all the invidious restraints by which it is meant to exclude them, frequently enjoy a greater share of the real benefit of it. The colonies of Spain and Portugal, for example, give more real encouragement to the industry of other countries than to that of Spain and Portugal. In the single article of linen alone, the consumption of those colonies amounts, it is said (but I do not pretend to warrant the quantity), to more than three millions sterling a year. But this great consumption is almost entirely supplied by France, Flanders, Holland, and Germany. Spain and Portugal furnish but a small part of it. The capital which supplies the colonies with this great quantity of linen, is annually distributed among, and furnishes a revenue to, the inhabitants of those other countries. The profits of it only are spent in Spain and Portugal, where they help to support the sumptuous profusion of the merchants of Cadiz and Lisbon.

Even the regulations by which each nation endeavors to secure to itself the exclusive trade of its own colonies, are frequently more hurtful to the countries in favor of which they are established, than to those against which they are established. The unjust oppression of the industry of other countries falls back, if I may say so, upon the heads of the oppressors, and crushes their industry more than it does that of those other countries. By those regulations, for example, the merchant of Hamburg must send the linen which he destines for the American market to London, and he must bring back from thence the tobacco which he destines for the German market; because he can neither send the one directly to America, nor bring the other directly from thence. By this restraint he is probably obliged to sell the one somewhat cheaper, and to buy the other somewhat dearer, than he otherwise might have done; and his profits are probably somewhat abridged by means of it. In this trade, however, between Hamburg and London, he certainly receives the returns of his capital much more quickly than he could possibly have done in the direct trade to America, even though we should suppose, what is by no means the case, that the payments of America were as punctual as those of London. In the trade, therefore, to which those regulations confine the merchant of Hamburg, his capital can keep in constant employment a much greater quantity of German industry than he possibly could have done in the trade from which he is excluded. Though the one employment, therefore, may to him perhaps be less profitable than the other, it cannot be less advantageous to his country. It is quite otherwise with the employment into which the monopoly naturally attracts, if I may say so, the capital of the London merchant. That employment may, perhaps, be more profitable to him than the greater part of other employments; but on account of the slowness of the returns, it cannot be more advantageous to his country.

After all the unjust attempts, therefore, of every country in Europe to engross to itself the whole advantage of the trade of its own colonies, no country has yet been able to engross to itself any thing but the expense of supporting in time of peace, and of defending in time of war, the oppressive authority which it assumes over them. The inconveniencies resulting from the possession of its colonies, every country has engrossed to itself completely. The advantages resulting from their trade, it has been obliged to share with many other countries.

At first sight, no doubt, the monopoly of the great commerce of America naturally seems to be an acquisition of the highest value. To the undiscerning eye of giddy ambition it naturally presents itself, amidst the confused scramble of politics and war, as a very dazzling object to fight for. The dazzling splendor of the object, however the immense greatness of the commerce, is the very quality which renders the monopoly of it hurtful, or which makes one employment, in its own nature necessarily less advantageous to the country than the greater part of other employments, absorb a much greater proportion of the capital of the country than what would otherwise have gone to it.

The mercantile stock of every country, it has been shown in the second book, naturally seeks, if one may say so, the employment most advantageous to that country. If it is employed in the carrying trade, the country to which it belongs becomes the emporium of the goods of all the countries whose trade that stock carries on. But the owner of that stock necessarily wishes to dispose of as great a part of those goods as he can at home. He thereby saves himself the trouble, risk, and expense of exportation; and he will upon that account be glad to sell them at home, not only for a much smaller price, but with somewhat a smaller profit, than he might expect to make by sending them abroad. He naturally, therefore, endeavors as much as he can to turn his carrying trade into a foreign trade of consumption, If his stock, again, is employed in a foreign trade of consumption, he will, for the same reason, be glad to dispose of, at home, as great a part as he can of the home goods which he collects in order to export to some foreign market, and he will thus endeavor, as much as he can, to turn his foreign trade of consumption into a home trade. The mercantile stock of every country naturally courts in this manner the near, and shuns the distant employment; naturally courts the employment in which the returns are frequent, and shuns that in which they are distant and slow; naturally courts the employment in which it can maintain the greatest quantity of productive labor in the country to which it belongs, or in which its owner resides, and shuns that in which it can maintain there the smallest quantity. It naturally courts the employment which in ordinary cases is most advantageous, and shuns that which in ordinary cases is least advantageous to that country.

But if, in any one of those distant employments, which in ordinary cases are less advantageous to the country, the profit should happen to rise somewhat higher than what is sufficient to balance the natural preference which is given to nearer employments, this superiority of profit will draw stock from those nearer employments, till the profits of all return to their proper level. This superiority of profit, however, is a proof that, in the actual circumstances of the society, those distant employments are somewhat understocked in proportion to other employments, and that the stock of the society is not distributed in the properest manner among all the different employments carried on in it. It is a proof that something is either bought cheaper or sold dearer than it ought to be, and that some particular class of citizens is more or less oppressed, either by paying more, or by getting less than what is suitable to that equality which ought to take place, and which naturally does take place, among all the different classes of them. Though the same capital never will maintain the same quantity of productive labor in a distant as in a near employment, yet a distant employment maybe as necessary for the welfare of the society as a near one; the goods which the distant employment deals in being necessary, perhaps, for carrying on many of the nearer employments. But if the profits of those who deal in such goods are above their proper level, those goods will be sold dearer than they ought to be, or somewhat above their natural price, and all those engaged in the nearer employments will be more or less oppressed by this high price. Their interest, therefore, in this case, requires, that some stock should be withdrawn from those nearer employments, and turned towards that distant one, in order to reduce its profits to their proper level, and the price of the goods which it deals in to their natural price. In this extraordinary case, the public interest requires that some stock should be withdrawn from those employments which, in ordinary cases, are more advantageous, and turned towards one which, in ordinary cases, is less advantageous to the public; and, in this extraordinary case, the natural interests and inclinations of men coincide as exactly with the public interests as in all other ordinary cases, and lead them to withdraw stock from the near, and to turn it towards the distant employments.

It is thus that the private interests and passions of individuals naturally dispose them to turn their stock towards the employments which in ordinary cases, are most advantageous to the society. But if from this natural preference they should turn too much of it towards those employments, the fall of profit in them, and the rise of it in all others, immediately dispose them to alter this faulty distribution. Without any intervention of law, therefore, the private interests and passions of men naturally lead them to divide and distribute the stock of every society among all the different employments carried on in it; as nearly as possible in the proportion which is most agreeable to the interest of the whole society.

All the different regulations of the mercantile system necessarily derange more or less this natural and most advantageous distribution of stock. But those which concern the trade to America and the East Indies derange it, perhaps, more than any other; because the trade to those two great continents absorbs a greater quantity of stock than any two other branches of trade. The regulations, however, by which this derangement is effected in those two different branches of trade, are not altogether the same. Monopoly is the great engine of both; but it is a different sort of monopoly. Monopoly of one kind or another, indeed, seems to be the sole engine of the mercantile system.

In the trade to America, every nation endeavors to engross as much as possible the whole market of its own colonies, by fairly excluding all other nations from any direct trade to them. During the greater part of the sixteenth century, the Portuguese endeavored to manage the trade to the East Indies in the same manner, by claiming the sole right of sailing in the Indian seas, on account of the merit of having first found out the road to them. The Dutch still continue to exclude all other European nations from any direct trade to their spice islands. Monopolies of this kind are evidently established against all other European nations, who are thereby not only excluded from a trade to which it might be convenient for them to turn some part of their stock, but are obliged to buy the goods which that trade deals in, somewhat dearer than if they could import them themselves directly from the countries which produced them.

But since the fall of the power of Portugal, no European nation has claimed the exclusive right of sailing in the Indian seas, of which the principal ports are now open to the ships of all European nations. Except in Portugal, however, and within these few years in France, the trade to the East Indies has, in every European country, been subjected to an exclusive company. Monopolies of this kind are properly established against the very nation which erects them. The greater part of that nation are thereby not only excluded from a trade to which it might be convenient for them to turn some part of their stock, but are obliged to buy the goods which that trade deals in somewhat dearer than if it was open and free to all their countrymen. Since the establishment of the English East India company, for example, the other inhabitants of England, over and above being excluded from the trade, must have paid, in the price of the East India goods which they have consumed, not only for all the extraordinary profits which the company may have made upon those goods in consequence of their monopoly, but for all the extraordinary waste which the fraud and abuse inseparable from the management of the affairs of so great a company must necessarily have occasioned. The absurdity of this second kind of monopoly, therefore, is much more manifest than that of the first.

Both these kinds of monopolies derange more or less the natural distribution of the stock of the society; but they do not always derange it in the same way.

Monopolies of the first kind always attract to the particular trade in which they are established a greater proportion of the stock of the society than what would go to that trade of its own accord.

Monopolies of the second kind may sometimes attract stock towards the particular trade in which they are established, and sometimes repel it from that trade, according to different circumstances. In poor countries, they naturally attract towards that trade more stock than would otherwise go to it. In rich countries, they naturally repel from it a good deal of stock which would otherwise go to it.

Such poor countries as Sweden and Denmark, for example, would probably have never sent a single ship to the East Indies, had not the trade been subjected to an exclusive company. The establishment of such a company necessarily encourages adventurers. Their monopoly secures them against all competitors in the home market, and they have the same chance for foreign markets with the traders of other nations. Their monopoly shows them the certainty of a great profit upon a considerable quantity of goods, and the chance of a considerable profit upon a great quantity. Without such extraordinary encouragement, the poor traders of such poor countries would probably never have thought of hazarding their small capitals in so very distant and uncertain an adventure as the trade to the East Indies must naturally have appeared to them.

Such a rich country as Holland, on the contrary, would probably, in the case of a free trade, send many more ships to the East Indies than it actually does. The limited stock of the Dutch East India company probably repels from that trade many great mercantile capitals which would otherwise go to it. The mercantile capital of Holland is so great, that it is, as it were, continually overflowing, sometimes into the public funds of foreign countries, sometimes into loans to private traders and adventurers of foreign countries, sometimes into the most round-about foreign trades of consumption, and sometimes into the carrying trade. All near employments being completely filled up, all the capital which can be placed in them with any tolerable profit being already placed in them, the capital of Holland necessarily flows towards the most distant employments. The trade to the East Indies, if it were altogether free, would probably absorb the greater part of this redundant capital. The East Indies offer a market both for the manufactures of Europe, and for the gold and silver, as well as for the several other productions of America, greater and more extensive than both Europe and America put together.

Every derangement of the natural distribution of stock is necessarily hurtful to the society in which it takes place; whether it be by repelling from a particular trade the stock which would otherwise go to it, or by attracting towards a particular trade that which would not otherwise come to it. If, without any exclusive company, the trade of Holland to the East Indies would be greater than it actually is, that country must suffer a considerable loss, by part of its capital being excluded from the employment most convenient for that port. And, in the same manner, if, without an exclusive company, the trade of Sweden and Denmark to the East Indies would be less than it actually is, or, what perhaps is more probable, would not exist at all, those two countries must likewise suffer a considerable loss, by part of their capital being drawn into an employment which must be more or less unsuitable to their present circumstances. Better for them, perhaps, in the present circumstances, to buy East India goods of other nations, even though they should pay somewhat dearer, than to turn so great a part of their small capital to so very distant a trade, in which the returns are so very slow, in which that capital can maintain so small a quantity of productive labor at home, where productive labor is so much wanted, where so little is done, and where so much is to do.

Though without an exclusive company, therefore, a particular country should not be able to carry on any direct trade to the East Indies, it will not from thence follow, that such a company ought to be established there, but only that such a country ought not, in these circumstances, to trade directly to the East Indies. That such companies are not in general necessary for carrying on the East India trade, is sufficiently demonstrated by the experience of the Portuguese, who enjoyed almost the whole of it for more than a century together, without any exclusive company.

No private merchant, it has been said, could well have capital sufficient to maintain factors and agents in the different ports of the East Indies, in order to provide goods for the ships which he might occasionally send thither; and yet, unless he was able to do this, the difficulty of finding a cargo might frequently make his ships lose the season for returning; and the expense of so long a delay would not only eat up the whole profit of the adventure, but frequently occasion a very considerable loss. This argument, however, if it proved any thing at all, would prove that no one great branch of trade could be carried on without an exclusive company, which is contrary to the experience of all nations. There is no great branch of trade, in which the capital of any one private merchant is sufficient for carrying on all the subordinate branches which must be carried on, in order to carry on the principal one. But when a nation is ripe for any great branch of trade, some merchants naturally turn their capitals towards the principal, and some towards the subordinate branches of it; and though all the different branches of it are in this manner carried on, yet it very seldom happens that they are all carried on by the capital of one private merchant. If a nation, therefore, is ripe for the East India trade, a certain portion of its capital will naturally divide itself among all the different branches of that trade. Some of its merchants will find it for their interest to reside in the East Indies, and to employ their capitals there in providing goods for the ships which are to be sent out by other merchants who reside in Europe. The settlements which different European nations have obtained in the East Indies, if they were taken from the exclusive companies to which they at present belong, and put under the immediate protection of the sovereign, would render this residence both safe and easy, at least to the merchants of the particular nations to whom those settlements belong. If, at any particular time, that part of the capital of any country which of its own accord tended and inclined, if I may say so, towards the East India trade, was not sufficient for carrying on all those different branches of it, it would be a proof that, at that particular time, that country was not ripe for that trade, and that it would do better to buy for some time, even at a higher price, from other European nations, the East India goods it had occasion for, than to import them itself directly from the East Indies. What it might lose by the high price of those goods, could seldom be equal to the loss which it would sustain by the distraction of a large portion of its capital from other employments more necessary, or more useful, or more suitable to its circumstances and situation, than a direct trade to the East Indies.

Though the Europeans possess many considerable settlements both upon the coast of Africa and in the East Indies, they have not yet established, in either of those countries, such numerous and thriving colonies as those in the islands and continent of America. Africa, however, as well as several of the countries comprehended under the general name of the East Indies, is inhabited by barbarous nations. But those nations were by no means so weak and defenseless as the miserable and helpless Americans; and in proportion to the natural fertility of the countries which they inhabited, they were, besides, much more populous. The most barbarous nations either of Africa or of the East Indies, were shepherds; even the Hottentots were so. But the natives of every part of America, except Mexico and Peru, were only hunters and the difference is very great between the number of shepherds and that of hunters whom the same extent of equally fertile territory can maintain. In Africa and the East Indies, therefore, it was more difficult to displace the natives, and to extend the European plantations over the greater part of the lands of the original inhabitants. The genius of exclusive companies, besides, is unfavorable, it has already been observed, to the growth of new colonies, and has probably been the principal cause of the little progress which they have made in the East Indies. The Portuguese carried on the trade both to Africa and the East Indies, without any exclusive companies; and their settlements at Congo, Angola, and Benguela, on the coast of Africa, and at Goa in the East Indies though much depressed by superstition and every sort of bad government, yet bear some resemblance to the colonies of America, and are partly inhabited by Portuguese who have been established there for several generations. The Dutch settlements at the Cape of Good Hope and at Batavia, are at present the most considerable colonies which the Europeans have established, either in Africa or in the East Indies; and both those settlements are peculiarly fortunate in their situation. The Cape of Good Hope was inhabited by a race of people almost as barbarous, and quite as incapable of defending themselves, as the natives of America. It is, besides, the half-way house, if one may say so, between Europe and the East Indies, at which almost every European ship makes some stay, both in going and returning. The supplying of those ships with every sort of fresh provisions, with fruit, and sometimes with wine, affords alone a very extensive market for the surplus produce of the colonies. What the Cape of Good Hope is between Europe and every part of the East Indies, Batavia is between the principal countries of the East Indies. It lies upon the most frequented road from Indostan to China and Japan, and is nearly about mid-way upon that road. Almost all the ships too, that sail between

Europe and China, touch at Batavia; and it is, over and above all this, the center and principal mart of what is called the country trade of the East Indies; not only of that part of it which is carried on by Europeans, but of that which is carried on by the native Indians; and vessels navigated by the inhabitants of China and Japan, of Tonquin, Malacca, Cochin-China, and the island of Celebes, are frequently to be seen in its port. Such advantageous situations have enabled those two colonies to surmount all the obstacles which the oppressive genius of an exclusive company may have occasionally opposed to their growth. They have enabled Batavia to surmount the additional disadvantage of perhaps the most unwholesome climate in the world.

The English and Dutch companies, though they have established no considerable colonies, except the two above mentioned, have both made considerable conquests in the East Indies. But in the manner in which they both govern their new subjects, the natural genius of an exclusive company has shown itself most distinctly. In the spice islands, the Dutch are said to burn all the spiceries which a fertile season produces, beyond what they expect to dispose of in Europe with such a profit as they think sufficient. In the islands where they have no settlements, they give a premium to those who collect the young blossoms and green leaves of the clove and nutmeg trees, which naturally grow there, but which this savage policy has now, it is said, almost completely extirpated. Even in the islands where they have settlements, they have very much reduced, it is said, the number of those trees. If the produce even of their own islands was much greater than what suited their market, the natives, they suspect, might find means to convey some part of it to other nations; and the best way, they imagine, to secure their own monopoly, is to take care that no more shall grow than what they themselves carry to market. By different arts of oppression, they have reduced the population of several of the Moluccas nearly to the number which is sufficient to supply with fresh provisions, and other necessaries of life, their own insignificant garrisons, and such of their ships as occasionally come there for a cargo of spices. Under the government even of the Portuguese, however, those islands are said to have been tolerably well inhabited. The English company have not yet had time to establish in Bengal so perfectly destructive a system. The plan of their government, however, has had exactly the same tendency. It has not been uncommon, I am well assured, for the chief, that is, the first clerk or a factory, to order a peasant to plough up a rich field of poppies, and sow it with rice, or some other grain. The pretence was, to prevent a scarcity of provisions; but the real reason, to give the chief an opportunity of selling at a better price a large quantity of opium which he happened then to have upon hand. Upon other occasions, the order has been reversed; and a rich field of rice or other grain has been ploughed up, in order to make room for a plantation of poppies, when the chief foresaw that extraordinary profit was likely to be made by opium. The servants of the company have, upon several occasions, attempted to establish in their own favor the monopoly of some of the most important branches, not only of the foreign, but of the inland trade of the country. Had they been allowed to go on, it is impossible that they should not, at some time or another, have attempted to restrain the production of the particular articles of which they had thus usurped the monopoly, not only to the quantity which they themselves could purchase, but to that which they could expect to sell with such a profit as they might think sufficient. In the course of a century or two, the policy of the English company would, in this manner, have probably proved as completely destructive as that of the Dutch.

Nothing, however, can be more directly contrary to the real interest of those companies, considered as the sovereigns of the countries which they have conquered, than this destructive plan. In almost all countries, the revenue of the sovereign is drawn from that of the people. The greater the revenue of the people, therefore, the greater the annual produce of their land and labor, the more they can afford to the sovereign. It is his interest, therefore, to increase as much as possible that annual produce. But if this is the interest of every sovereign, it is peculiarly so of one whose revenue, like that of the sovereign of Bengal, arises chiefly from a land-rent. That rent must necessarily be in proportion to the quantity and value of the produce; and both the one and the other must depend upon the extent of the market. The quantity will always be suited, with more or less exactness, to the consumption of those who can afford to pay for it; and the price which they will pay will always be in proportion to the eagerness of their competition. It is the interest of such a sovereign, therefore, to open the most extensive market for the produce of his country, to allow the most perfect freedom of commerce, in order to increase as much as possible the number and competition of buyers; and upon this account to abolish, not only all monopolies, but all restraints upon the transportation of the home produce from one part of the country to mother, upon its exportation to foreign countries, or upon the importation of goods of any kind for which it can be exchanged. He is in this manner most likely to increase both the quantity and value of that produce, and consequently of his own share of it, or of his own revenue.

But a company of merchants, are, it seems, incapable of considering themselves as sovereigns, even after they have become such. Trade, or buying in order to sell again, they still consider as their principal business, and by a strange absurdity, regard the character of the sovereign as but an appendix to that of the merchant; as something which ought to be made subservient to it, or by means of which they may be enabled to buy cheaper in India, and thereby to sell with a better profit in Europe. They endeavor, for this purpose, to keep out as much as possible all competitors from the market of the countries which are subject to their government, and consequently to reduce, at least, some part of the surplus produce of those countries to what is barely sufficient for supplying their own demand, or to what they can expect to sell in Europe, with such a profit as they may think reasonable. Their mercantile habits draw them in this manner, almost necessarily, though perhaps insensibly, to prefer, upon all ordinary occasions, the little and transitory profit of the monopolist to the great and permanent revenue of the sovereign; and would gradually lead them to treat the countries subject to their government nearly as the Dutch treat the Moluccas. It is the interest of the East India company, considered as sovereigns, that the European goods which are carried to their Indian dominions should be sold there as cheap as possible; and that the Indian goods which are brought from thence should bring there as good a price, or should be sold there as dear as possible. But the reverse of this is their interest as merchants. As sovereigns, their interest is exactly the same with that of the country which they govern. As merchants, their interest is directly opposite to that interest.

But if the genius of such a government, even as to what concerns its direction in Europe, is in this manner essentially, and perhaps incurably faulty, that of its administration in India is still more so. That administration is necessarily composed of a council of merchants, a profession no doubt extremely respectable, but which in no country in the world carries along with it that sort of authority which naturally overawes the people, and without force commands their willing obedience. Such a council can command obedience only by the military force with which they are accompanied; and their government is, therefore, necessarily military and despotical. Their proper business, however, is that of merchants. It is to sell, upon their master's account, the European goods consigned to them, and to buy, in return, Indian goods for the European market. It is to sell the one as dear, and to buy the other as cheap as possible, and consequently to exclude, as much as possible, all rivals from the particular market where they keep their shop. The genius of the administration, therefore, so far as concerns the trade of the company, is the same as that of the direction. It tends to make government subservient to the interest of monopoly, and consequently to stunt the natural growth of some parts, at least, of the surplus produce of the country, to what is barely sufficient for answering the demand of the company.

All the members of the administration besides, trade more or less upon their own account; and it is in vain to prohibit them from doing so. Nothing can be more completely foolish than to expect that the clerk of a great counting-house, at ten thousand miles distance, and consequently almost quite out of sight, should, upon a simple order from their master, give up at once doing any sort of business upon their own account abandon for ever all hopes of making a fortune, of which they have the means in their hands; and content themselves with the moderate salaries which those masters allow them, and which, moderate as they are, can seldom be augmented, being commonly as large as the real profits of the company trade can afford. In such circumstances, to prohibit the servants of the company from trading upon their own account, can have scarce any other effect than to enable its superior servants, under pretence of executing their master's order, to oppress such of the inferior ones as have had the misfortune to fall under their displeasure. The servants naturally endeavor to establish the same monopoly in favor of their own private trade as of the public trade of the company. If they are suffered to act as they could wish, they will establish this monopoly openly and directly, by fairly prohibiting all other people from trading in the articles in which they choose to deal; and this, perhaps, is the best and least oppressive way of establishing it. But if, by an order from Europe, they are prohibited from doing this, they will, notwithstanding, endeavor to establish a monopoly of the same kind secretly and indirectly, in a way that is much more destructive to the country. They will employ the whole authority of government, and pervert the administration of Justice, in order to harass and ruin those who interfere with them in any branch of commerce, which by means of agents, either concealed, or at least not publicly avowed, they may choose to carry on. But the private trade of the servants will naturally extend to a much greater variety of articles than the public trade of the company. The public trade of the company extends no further than the trade with Europe, and comprehends a part only of the foreign trade of the country. But the private trade of the servants may extend to all the different branches both of its inland and foreign trade. The monopoly of the company can tend only to stunt the natural growth of that part of the surplus produce which, in the case of a free trade, would be exported to Europe. That of the servants tends to stunt the natural growth of every part of the produce in which they choose to deal; of what is destined for home consumption, as well as of what is destined for exportation; and consequently to degrade the cultivation of the whole country, and to reduce the number of its inhabitants. It tends to reduce the quantity of every sort of produce, even that of the necessaries of life, whenever the servants of the country choose to deal in them, to what those servants can both afford to buy and expect to sell with such a profit as pleases them.

From the nature of their situation, too, the servants must be more disposed to support with rigorous severity their own interest, against that of the country which they govern, than their masters can be to support theirs. The country belongs to their masters, who cannot avoid having some regard for the interest of what belongs to them; but it does not belong to the servants. The real interest of their masters, if they were capable of understanding it, is the same with that of the country {The interest of every proprietor of India stock, however, is by no means the same with that of the country in the government of which his vote gives him some influence. —See book v, chap. 1, part ii}; and it is from ignorance chiefly, and the meanness of mercantile prejudice, that they ever oppress it. But the real interest of the servants is by no means the same with that of the country, and the most perfect information would not necessarily put an end to their oppressions. The regulations, accordingly, which have been sent out from Europe, though they have been frequently weak, have upon most occasions been well meaning. More intelligence, and perhaps less good meaning, has sometimes appeared in those established by the servants in India. It is a very singular government in which every member of the administration wishes to get out of the country, and consequently to have done with the government, as soon as he can, and to whose interest, the day after he has left it, and carried his whole fortune with him, it is perfectly indifferent though the whole country was swallowed up by an earthquake.

I mean not, however, by any thing which I have here said, to throw any odious imputation upon the general character of the servants of the East India company, and touch less upon that of any particular persons. It is the system of government, the situation in which they are placed, that I mean to censure, not the character of those who have acted in it. They acted as their situation naturally directed, and they who have clamored the loudest against them would probably not have acted better themselves. In war and negotiation, the councils of Madras and Calcutta, have upon several occasions, conducted themselves with a resolution and decisive wisdom, which would have done honor to the senate of Rome in the best days of that republic. The members of those councils, however, had been bred to professions very different from war and politics. But their situation alone, without education, experience, or even example, seems to have formed in them all at once the great qualities which it required, and to have inspired them both with abilities and virtues which they themselves could not well know that they possessed. If upon some occasions, therefore, it has animated them to actions of magnanimity which could not well have been expected from them, we should not wonder if, upon others, it has prompted them to exploits of somewhat a different nature.

Such exclusive companies, therefore, are nuisances in every respect; always more or less inconvenient to the countries in which they are established, and destructive to those which have the misfortune to fall under their government.

CHAPTER VIII

Conclusion of the Mercantile System

Though the encouragement of exportation, and the discouragement of importation, are the two great engines by which the mercantile system proposes to enrich every country, yet, with regard to some particular commodities, it seems to follow an opposite plan: to discourage exportation, and to encourage importation. Its ultimate object, however, it pretends, is always the same, to enrich the country by an advantageous balance of trade. It discourages the exportation of the materials of manufacture, and of the instruments of trade, in order to give our own workmen an advantage, and to enable them to under-sell those of other nations in all foreign markets; and by restraining, in this manner, the exportation of a few commodities, of no great price, it proposes to occasion a much greater and more valuable exportation of others. It encourages the importation of the materials of manufacture, in order that our own people may be enabled to work them up more cheaply, and thereby prevent a greater and more valuable importation of the manufactured commodities. I do not observe, at least in our statute book, any encouragement given to the importation of the instruments of trade. When manufactures have advanced to a certain pitch of greatness, the fabrication of the instruments of trade becomes itself the object of a great number of very important manufactures. To give any particular encouragement to the importation of such instruments, would interfere too much with the interest of those manufactures. Such importation, therefore, instead of being encouraged, has frequently been prohibited. Thus the importation of wool cards, except from Ireland, or when brought in as wreck or prize goods, was prohibited by the 3rd of Edward IV; which prohibition was renewed by the 39th of Elizabeth, and has been continued and rendered perpetual by subsequent laws.

The importation of the materials of manufacture has sometimes been encouraged by an exemption from the duties to which other goods are subject, and sometimes by bounties.

The importation of sheep's wool from several different countries, of cotton wool from all countries, of undressed flax, of the greater part of dyeing drugs, of the greater part of undressed hides from Ireland, or the British colonies, of seal skins from the British Green-land fishery, of pig and bar iron from the British colonies, as well as of several other materials of manufacture, has been encouraged by an exemption from all duties, if properly entered at the custom-house. The private interest of our merchants and manufacturers may, perhaps, have extorted from the legislature these exemptions, as well as the greater part of our other commercial regulations. They are, however, perfectly just and reasonable; and if, consistently with the necessities of the state, they could be extended to all the other materials of manufacture, the public would certainly be a gainer.

The avidity of our great manufacturers, however, has in some cases extended these exemptions a good deal beyond what can justly be considered as the rude materials of their work. By the 24th George II chap. 46, a small duty of only 1d. the pound was imposed upon the importation of foreign brown linen yarn, instead of much higher duties, to which it had been subjected before, viz. of 6d. the pound upon sail yarn, of 1s.

the pound upon all French and Dutch yarn, and of £2:13:4 upon the hundred weight of all spruce or Muscovia yarn. But our manufacturers were not long satisfied with this reduction: by the 29th of the same king, chap. 15, the same law which gave a bounty upon the exportation of British and Irish linen, of which the price did not exceed 18d. the yard, even this small duty upon the importation of brown linen yarn was taken away. In the different operations, however, which are necessary for the preparation of linen yarn, a good deal more industry is employed, than in the subsequent operation of preparing linen cloth from linen yarn. To say nothing of the industry of the flax-growers and flaxdressers, three or four spinners at least are necessary in order to keep one weaver in constant employment; and more than four-fifths of the whole quantity of labor necessary for the preparation of linen cloth, is employed in that of linen yarn; but our spinners are poor people; women commonly scattered about in all different parts of the country, without support or protection. It is not by the sale of their work, but by that of the complete work of the weavers, that our great master manufacturers make their profits. As it is their interest to sell the complete manufacture as dear, so it is to buy the materials as cheap as possible. By extorting from the legislature bounties upon the exportation of their own linen, high duties upon the importation of all foreign linen, and a total prohibition of the home consumption of some sorts of French linen, they endeavor to sell their own goods as dear as possible. By encouraging the importation of foreign linen yarn, and thereby bringing it into competition with that which is made by our own people, they endeavor to buy the work of the poor spinners as cheap as possible. They are as intent to keep down the wages of their own weavers, as the earnings of the poor spinners; and it is by no means for the benefit of the workmen that they endeavor either to raise the price of the complete work, or to lower that of the rude materials. It is the industry which is carried on for the benefit of the rich and the powerful, that is principally encouraged by our mercantile system. That which is carried on for the benefit of the poor and the indigent is too often either neglected or oppressed.

Both the bounty upon the exportation of linen, and the exemption from the duty upon the importation of foreign yarn, which were granted only for fifteen years, but continued by two different prolongations, expire with the end of the session of parliament which shall immediately follow the 24th of June 1786.

The encouragement given to the importation of the materials of manufacture by bounties, has been principally confined to such as were imported from our American plantations.

The first bounties of this kind were those granted about the beginning of the present century, upon the importation of naval stores from America. Under this denomination were comprehended timber fit for masts, yards, and bowsprits; hemp, tar, pitch, and turpentine. The bounty, however, of £1 the ton upon masting-timber, and that of £6 the ton upon hemp, were extended to such as should be imported into England from Scotland. Both these bounties continued, without any variation, at the same rate, till they were severally allowed to expire; that upon hemp on the 1st of January 1741, and that upon masting-timber at the end of the session of parliament immediately following the 24th June 1781.

The bounties upon the importation of tar, pitch, and turpentine, underwent, during their continuance, several alterations. Originally, that upon tar was £4 the ton; that upon pitch the same; and that upon turpentine £3 the ton. The bounty of £4 the ton upon tar was afterwards confined to such as had been prepared in a particular manner; that upon other good, clean, and merchantable tar was reduced to £2:4s. the ton. The bounty upon pitch was likewise reduced to £1, and that upon turpentine to £1:10s. the ton.

The second bounty upon the importation of any of the materials of manufacture, according to the order of time, was that granted by the 21st George II chap. 30, upon the importation of indigo from the British plantations. When the plantation indigo was worth three-fourths of the price of the best French indigo, it was, by this act, entitled to a bounty of 6d. the pound. This bounty, which, like most others, was granted only for a limited time, was continued by several prolongations, but was reduced to 4d. the pound. It was allowed to expire with the end of the session of parliament which followed the 25th March 1781.

The third bounty of this kind was that granted (much about the time that we were beginning sometimes to court, and sometimes to quarrel with our American colonies), by the 4th George III chap. 26, upon the importation of hemp, or undressed flax, from the British plantations. This bounty was granted for twenty-one years, from the 24th June 1764 to the 24th June 1785. For the first seven years, it was to be at the rate of £8 the ton; for the second at £6; and for the third at £4. It was not extended to Scotland, of which the climate (although hemp is sometimes raised there in small quantities, and of an inferior quality) is not very fit for that produce. Such a bounty upon the importation of Scotch flax in England would have been too great a discouragement to the native produce of the southern part of the United Kingdom.

The fourth bounty of this kind was that granted by the 5th George III chap. 45, upon the importation of wood from America. It was granted for nine years from the 1st January 1766 to the 1st January 1775. During the first three years, it was to be for every hundred-and-twenty good deals, at the rate of £1, and for every load containing fifty cubic feet of other square timber, at the rate of 12s. For the second three years, it was for deals, to be at the rate of 15s., and for other squared timber at the rate of 8s.; and for the third three years, it was for deals, to be at the rate of 10s.; and for every other squared timber at the rate of 5s.

The fifth bounty of this kind was that granted by the 9th George III chap. 38, upon the importation of raw silk from the British plantations. It was granted for twenty-one years, from the 1st January 1770, to the 1st January 1791. For the first seven years, it was to be at the rate of £25 for every hundred pounds value; for the second, at £20; and for the third, at £15. The management of the silk-worm, and the preparation of silk, requires so much hand-labor, and labor is so very dear in America, that even this great bounty, I have been informed, was not likely to produce any considerable effect.

The sixth bounty of this kind was that granted by 11th George III chap. 50, for the importation of pipe, hogshead, and barrel staves and leading from the British plantations. It was granted for nine years, from 1st January 1772 to the 1st January 1781. For the first three years, it was, for a certain quantity of each, to be at the rate of £6; for the second three years at £4; and for the third three years at £2.

The seventh and last bounty of this kind was that granted by the 19th George III chap. 37, upon the importation of hemp from Ireland. It was granted in the same manner as that for the importation of hemp and undressed flax from America, for twenty-one years, from the 24th June 1779 to the 24th June 1800. The term is divided likewise into three periods, of seven years each; and in each of those periods, the rate of the Irish bounty is the same with that of the American. It does not, however, like the American bounty, extend to the importation of undressed flax. It would have been too great a discouragement to the cultivation of that plant in Great Britain. When this last bounty was granted, the British and Irish legislatures were not in much better humor with one another, than the British and American had been before. But this boon to Ireland, it is to be hoped, has been granted under more fortunate auspices than all those to America. The same commodities, upon which we thus gave bounties, when imported from America, were subjected to considerable duties when imported from any other country. The interest of our American colonies was regarded as the same with that of the mother country. Their wealth was considered as our wealth. Whatever money was sent out to them, it was said, came all back to us by the balance of trade, and we could never become a farthing the poorer by any expense which we could lay out upon them. They were our own in every respect, and it was an expense laid out upon the improvement of our own property, and for the profitable employment of our own people. It is unnecessary, I apprehend, at present to say anything further, in order to expose the folly of a system which fatal experience has now sufficiently exposed. Had our American colonies really been a part of Great Britain, those bounties might have been considered as bounties upon production, and would still have been liable to all the objections to which such bounties are liable, but to no other.

The exportation of the materials of manufacture is sometimes discouraged by absolute prohibitions, and sometimes by high duties.

Our woolen manufacturers have been more successful than any other class of workmen, in persuading the legislature that the prosperity of the nation depended upon the success and extension of their particular business. They have not only obtained a monopoly against the consumers, by an absolute prohibition of importing woolen cloths from any foreign country; but they have likewise obtained another monopoly against the sheep farmers and growers of wool, by a similar prohibition of the exportation of live sheep and wool. The severity of many of the laws which have been enacted for the security of the revenue is very justly complained of, as imposing heavy penalties upon actions which, antecedent to the statutes that declared them to be crimes, had always been understood to be innocent. But the cruelest of our revenue laws, I will venture to affirm, are mild and gentle, in comparison to some of those which the clamor of our merchants and manufacturers has extorted from the legislature, for the support of their own absurd and oppressive monopolies. Like the laws of Draco, these laws may be said to be all written in blood.

By the 8th of Elizabeth chap. 3, the exporter of sheep, lambs, or rams, was for the first offence, to forfeit all his goods for ever, to suffer a year's imprisonment, and then to have his left hand cut off in a market town, upon a market day, to be there nailed up; and for the second offence, to be adjudged a felon, and to suffer death accordingly. To prevent the breed of our sheep from being propagated in foreign countries, seems to have been the object of this law. By the 13th and 14th of Charles II chap. 18, the exportation of wool was made felony, and the exporter subjected to the same penalties and forfeitures as a felon.

For the honor of the national humanity, it is to be hoped that neither of these statutes was ever executed. The first of them, however, so far as I know, has never been directly repealed, and sergeant Hawkins seems to consider it as still in force. It may, however, perhaps be considered as virtually repealed by the 12th of Charles II chap. 32, sect. 3, which, without expressly taking away the penalties imposed by former statutes, imposes a new penalty, viz. that of 20s. for every sheep exported, or attempted to be exported, together with the forfeiture of the sheep, and of the owner's share of the sheep. The second of them was expressly repealed by the 7th and 8th of William III chap. 28, sect. 4, by which it is declared that "Whereas the statute of the 13th and 14th of king Charles II made against the exportation of wool, among other things in the said act mentioned, doth enact the same to be deemed felony, by the severity of which penalty the prosecution of offenders hath not been so effectually put in execution; be it therefore enacted, by the authority aforesaid, that so much of the said act, which relates to the making the said offence felony, be repealed and made void."

The penalties, however, which are either imposed by this milder statute, or which, though imposed by former statutes, are not repealed by this one, are still sufficiently severe. Besides the forfeiture of the goods, the exporter incurs the penalty of 3s. for every pound weight of wool, either exported or attempted to be exported, that is, about four or five times the value. Any merchant, or other person convicted of this offence, is disabled from requiring any debt or account belonging to him from any factor or other person. Let his fortune be what it will, whether he is or is not able to pay those heavy penalties, the law means to ruin him completely. But, as the morals of the great body of the people are not yet so corrupt as those of the contrivers of this statute, I have not heard that any advantage has ever been taken of this clause. If the person convicted of this offence is not able to pay the penalties within three months after judgment, he is to be transported for seven years; and if he returns before the expiration of that term, he is liable to the pains of felony, without benefit of clergy. The owner of the ship, knowing this offence, forfeits all his interest in the ship and furniture. The master and mariners, knowing this offence, forfeit all their goods and chattels, and suffer three months imprisonment. By a subsequent statute, the master suffers six months imprisonment.

In order to prevent exportation, the whole inland commerce of wool is laid under very burdensome and oppressive restrictions. It cannot be packed in any box, barrel, cask, case, chest, or any other package, but only in packs of leather or pack-cloth, on which must be marked on the outside the words *WOOL* or *YARN*, in large letters, not less than three inches long, on pain of forfeiting the same and the package, and 8s. for every pound weight, to be paid by the owner or packer. It cannot be loaded on any horse or cart, or carried by land within five miles of the coast, but between sun-rising, and sun-setting, on pain of forfeiting the same, the horses and carriages. The hundred next adjoining to the sea coast, out of, or through which the wool is carried or exported, forfeits £20, if the wool is under the value of £10; and if of greater value, then treble that value, together with treble costs, to be sued for within the year. The execution to be against any two of the inhabitants, whom the sessions must reimburse, by an assessment on the other inhabitants, as in the cases of robbery. And if any person compounds with the hundred for less than this penalty, he is to be imprisoned for five years; and any other person may prosecute. These regulations take place through the whole kingdom.

But in the particular counties of Kent and Sussex, the restrictions are still more troublesome. Every owner of wool within ten miles of the sea coast must give an account in writing, three days after shearing, to the next officer of the customs, of the number of his fleeces, and of the places where they are lodged. And before he removes any part of them, he must give the like notice of the number and weight of the fleeces, and of the name and abode of the person to whom they are sold, and of the place to which it is intended they should be carried. No person within fifteen miles of the sea, in the said counties, can buy any wool, before he enters into bond to the king, that no part of the wool which he shall so buy shall be sold by him to any other person within fifteen miles of the sea. If any wool is found carrying towards the sea side in the said counties, unless it has been entered and security given as aforesaid, it is forfeited, and the offender also forfeits 3s. for every pound weight, if any person lay any wool, not entered as aforesaid, within fifteen miles of the sea, it must be seized and forfeited; and if, after such seizure, any person shall claim the same, he must give security to the exchequer, that if he is cast upon trial he shall pay treble costs, besides all other penalties.

When such restrictions are imposed upon the inland trade, the coasting trade, we may believe, cannot be left very free. Every owner of wool, who carries, or causes to be carried, any wool to any port or place on the sea coast, in order to be from thence transported by sea to any other place or port on the coast, must first cause an entry thereof to be made at the port from whence it is intended to be conveyed, containing the weight, marks, and number, of the packages, before he brings the same within five miles of that port, on pain of forfeiting the same, and also the horses, carts, and other carriages; and also of suffering and forfeiting, as by the other laws in force against the exportation of wool. This law, however (1st of William III chap. 32), is so very indulgent as to declare, that this shall not hinder any person from carrying his wool home from the place of shearing, though it be within five miles of the sea, provided that in ten days after shearing, and before he remove the wool, he do under his hand certify to the next officer of the customs the true number of fleeces, and where it is housed; and do not remove the same, without certifying to such officer, under his hand, his intention so to do, three days before. Bond must be given that the wool to be carried coast-ways is to be landed at the particular port for which it is entered outwards; and if my part of it is landed without the presence of an officer, not only the forfeiture of the wool is incurred, as in other goods, but the usual additional penalty of 3s. for every pound weight is likewise incurred.

Our woolen manufacturers, in order to justify their demand of such extraordinary restrictions and regulations, confidently asserted, that English wool was of a peculiar quality, superior to that of any other country; that the wool of other countries could not, without some mixture of it, be wrought up into any tolerable manufacture; that fine cloth could not be made without it; that England, therefore, if the exportation of it could be totally prevented, could monopolize to herself almost the whole woolen trade of the world; and thus, having no rivals, could sell at what price she pleased, and in a short time acquire the most incredible degree of wealth by the most advantageous balance of trade. This doctrine, like most other doctrines which are confidently asserted by any considerable number of people, was, and still continues to be, most implicitly believed by a much greater number: by almost all those who are either unacquainted with the woolen trade, or who have not made particular inquiries. It is, however, so perfectly false, that English wool is in any respect necessary for the making of fine cloth, that it is altogether unfit for it. Fine cloth is made altogether of Spanish wool. English wool, cannot be even so mixed with Spanish wool, as to enter into the composition without spoiling and degrading, in some degree, the fabric of the cloth.

It has been shown in the foregoing part of this work, that the effect of these regulations has been to depress the price of English wool, not only below what it naturally would be in the present times, but very much below what it actually was in the time of Edward III. The price of Scotch wool, when, in consequence of the Union, it became subject to the same regulations, is said to have fallen about one half. It is observed by the very accurate and intelligent author of the *Memoirs of Wool*, the Reverend Mr. John Smith, that the price of the best English wool in England, is generally below what wool of a very inferior quality commonly sells for in the market of Amsterdam. To depress the price of this commodity below what may be called its natural and proper price, was the avowed purpose of those regulations; and there seems to be no doubt of their having produced the effect that was expected from them.

This reduction of price, it may perhaps be thought, by discouraging the growing of wool, must have reduced very much the annual produce of that commodity, though not below what it formerly was, yet below what, in the present state of things, it would probably have been, had it, in consequence of an open and free market, been allowed to rise to the natural and proper price. I am, however, disposed to believe, that the quantity of the annual produce cannot have been much, though it may, perhaps, have been a little affected by these regulations. The growing of wool is not the chief purpose for which the sheep farmer employs his industry and stock. He expects his profit, not so much from the price of the fleece, as from that of the carcass; and the average or ordinary price of the latter must even, in many cases, make up to him whatever deficiency there may be in the average or ordinary price of the former. It has been observed, in the foregoing part of this work, that "whatever regulations tend to sink the price, either of wool or of raw hides, below what it naturally would be, must, in an improved and cultivated country, have some tendency to raise the price of butcher's meat. The price, both of the great and small cattle which are fed on improved and cultivated land, must be sufficient to pay the rent which the landlord, and the profit which the farmer, has reason to expect from improved and cultivated land. If it is not, they will soon cease to feed them. Whatever part of this price, therefore, is not paid by the wool and the hide, must be paid by the carcass. The less there is paid for the one, the more must be paid for the other. In what manner this price is to be divided upon the different parts of the beast, is indifferent to the landlords and farmers, provided it is all paid to them. In an improved and cultivated country, therefore, their interest as landlords and farmers cannot be much affected by such regulations, though their interest as consumers may, by the rise in the price of provisions." According to this reasoning, therefore, this degradation in the price of wool is not likely, in an improved and cultivated country, to occasion any diminution in the annual produce of that commodity; except so far as, by raising the price of mutton, it may somewhat diminish the demand for, and consequently the production of, that particular species of butcher's meat. Its effect, however, even in this way, it is probable, is not very considerable.

But though its effect upon the quantity of the annual produce may not have been very considerable, its effect upon the quality, it may perhaps be thought, must necessarily have been very great. The degradation in the quality of English wool, if not below what it was in former times, yet below what it naturally would have been in the present state of improvement and cultivation, must have been, it may perhaps be supposed, very nearly in proportion to the degradation of price. As the quality depends upon the breed, upon the pasture, and upon the management and cleanliness of the sheep, during the whole progress of the growth of the fleece, the attention to these circumstances, it may naturally enough be imagined, can never be greater than in proportion to the recompense which the price of the fleece is likely to make for the labor and expense which that attention requires. It happens, however, that the goodness of the fleece depends, in a great measure, upon the health, growth, and bulk of the animal: the same attention which is necessary for the improvement of the carcass is, in some respect, sufficient for that of the fleece. Notwithstanding the degradation of price, English wool is said to have been improved considerably during the course even of the present century. The improvement, might, perhaps, have been greater if the price had been better; but the lowness of price, though it may have obstructed, yet certainly it has not altogether prevented that improvement.

The violence of these regulations, therefore, seems to have affected neither the quantity nor the quality of the annual produce of wool, so much as it might have been expected to do (though I think it probable that it may have affected the latter a good deal more than the former); and the interest of the growers of wool, though it must have been hurt in some degree, seems upon the whole, to have been much less hurt than could well have been imagined.

These considerations, however, will not justify the absolute prohibition of the exportation of wool; but they will fully justify the imposition of a considerable tax upon that exportation.

To hurt, in any degree, the interest of any one order of citizens, for no other purpose but to promote that of some other, is evidently contrary to that justice and equality of treatment which the sovereign owes to all the different orders of his subjects. But the prohibition certainly hurts, in some degree, the interest of the growers of wool, for no other purpose but to promote that of the manufacturers.

Every different order of citizens is bound to contribute to the support of the sovereign or commonwealth. A tax of five, or even of ten shillings, upon the exportation of every tod of wool, would produce a very considerable revenue to the sovereign. It would hurt the interest of the growers somewhat less than the prohibition, because it would not probably lower the price of wool quite so much. It would afford a sufficient advantage to the manufacturer, because, though he might not buy his wool altogether so cheap as under the prohibition, he would still buy it at least five or ten shillings cheaper than any foreign manufacturer could buy it, besides saving the freight and insurance which the other would be obliged to pay. It is scarce possible to devise a tax which could produce any considerable revenue to the sovereign, and at the same time occasion so little inconveniency to anybody.

The prohibition, notwithstanding all the penalties which guard it, does not prevent the exportation of wool. It is exported, it is well known, in great quantities. The great difference between the price in the home and that in the foreign market, presents such a temptation to smuggling, that all the rigor of the law cannot prevent it. This illegal exportation is advantageous to nobody but the smuggler. A legal exportation, subject to a tax, by affording a revenue to the sovereign, and thereby saving the imposition of some other, perhaps more burdensome and inconvenient taxes, might prove advantageous to all the different subjects of the state.

The exportation of fuller's earth, or fuller's clay, supposed to be necessary for preparing and cleansing the woolen manufactures, has been subjected to nearly the same penalties as the exportation of wool. Even tobacco-pipe clay, though acknowledged to be different from fuller's clay, yet, on account of their resemblance, and because fuller's clay might sometimes be exported as tobacco-pipe clay, has been laid under the same prohibitions and penalties.

By the 13th and 14th of Charles II chap. 7, the exportation, not only of raw hides, but of tanned leather, except in the shape of boots, shoes, or slippers, was prohibited; and the law gave a monopoly to our boot-makers and shoe-makers, not only against our graziers, but against our tanners. By subsequent statutes, our tanners have got themselves exempted from this monopoly, upon paying a small tax of only one shilling on the hundred weight of tanned leather, weighing one hundred and twelve pounds. They have obtained likewise the drawback of two-thirds of the excise duties imposed upon their commodity, even when exported without further manufacture. All manufactures of leather may be exported duty free; and the exporter is besides entitled to the drawback of the whole duties of excise. Our graziers still continue subject to the old monopoly. Graziers, separated from one another, and dispersed through all the different corners of the country, cannot, without great difficulty, combine together for the purpose either of imposing monopolies upon their fellow-citizens, or of exempting themselves from such as may have been imposed upon them by other people. Manufacturers of all kinds, collected together in numerous bodies in all great cities, easily can. Even the horns of cattle are prohibited to be exported; and the two insignificant trades of the horner and comb-maker enjoy, in this respect, a monopoly against the graziers.

Restraints, either by prohibitions, or by taxes, upon the exportation of goods which are partially, but not completely manufactured, are not peculiar to the manufacture of leather. As long as anything remains to be done, in order to fit any commodity for immediate use and consumption, our manufacturers think that they themselves ought to have the doing of it. Woolen yarn and worsted are prohibited to be exported, under the same penalties as wool even white cloths we subject to a duty upon exportation; and our dyers have so far obtained a monopoly against our clothiers. Our clothiers would probably have been able to defend themselves against it; but it happens that the greater part of our principal clothiers are themselves likewise dyers. Watch-cases, clock-cases, and dial-plates for clocks and watches, have been prohibited to be exported. Our clockmakers and watch-makers are, it seems, unwilling that the price of this sort of workmanship should be raised upon them by the competition of foreigners.

By some old statutes of Edward III, Henry VIII, and Edward VI the exportation of all metals was prohibited. Lead and tin were alone excepted, probably on account of the great abundance of those metals; in the exportation of which a considerable part of the trade of the kingdom in those days consisted. For the encouragement of the mining trade, the 5th of William and Mary chap. 17, exempted from this prohibition iron, copper, and mundic metal made from British ore. The exportation of all sorts of copper bars, foreign as well as British, was afterwards permitted by the 9th and 10th of William III chap. 26. The exportation of unmanufactured brass, of what is called gun-metal, bell-metal, and shroff metal, still continues to be prohibited. Brass manufactures of all sorts may be exported duty free.

The exportation of the materials of manufacture, where it is not altogether prohibited, is, in many cases, subjected to considerable duties.

By the 8th George I chap. 15, the exportation of all goods, the produce of manufacture of Great Britain, upon which any duties had been imposed by former statutes, was rendered duty free. The following goods, however, were excepted: alum, lead, lead-ore, tin, tanned leather, copperas, coals, wool, cards, white woolen cloths, lapis calaminaris, skins of all sorts, glue, coney hair or wool, hares wool, hair of all sorts, horses, and litharge of lead. If you except horses, all these are either materials of manufacture, or incomplete manufactures (which may be considered as materials for still further manufacture), or instruments of trade. This statute leaves them subject to all the old duties which had ever been imposed upon them, the old subsidy, and one percent outwards.

By the same statute, a great number of foreign drugs for dyers use are exempted from all duties upon importation. Each of them, however, is afterwards subjected to a certain duty, not indeed a very heavy one, upon exportation. Our dyers, it seems, while they thought it for their interest to encourage the importation of those drugs, by an exemption from all duties, thought it likewise for their own interest to throw some small discouragement upon their exportation. The avidity, however, which suggested this notable piece of mercantile ingenuity, most probably disappointed itself of its object. It necessarily taught the importers to be more careful than they might otherwise have been, that their importation should not exceed what was necessary for the supply of the home market. The home market was at all times likely to be more scantily supplied; the commodities were at all times likely to be somewhat dearer there than they would have been, had the exportation been rendered as free as the importation.

By the above-mentioned statute, gum senega, or gum arabic, being among the enumerated dyeing drugs, might be imported duty free. They were subjected, indeed, to a small poundage duty, amounting only to threepence in the hundred weight, upon their re-exportation. France enjoyed, at that time, an exclusive trade to the country most productive of those drugs, that which lies in the neighborhood of the Senegal; and the British market could not be easily supplied by the immediate importation of them from the place of growth. By the 25th George II therefore, gum senega was allowed to be imported (contrary to the general dispositions of the act of navigation) from any part of Europe. As the law, however, did not mean to encourage this species of trade, so contrary to the general principles of the mercantile policy of England, it imposed a duty of ten shillings the hundred weight upon such importation, and no part of this duty was to be afterwards drawn back upon its exportation. The successful war which began in 1755 gave Great Britain the same exclusive trade to those countries which France had enjoyed before. Our manufactures, as soon as the peace was made, endeavored to avail themselves of this advantage, and to establish a monopoly in their own favor both against the growers and against the importers of this commodity. By the 5th of George III therefore, chap. 37, the exportation of gum senega, from his majesty's dominions in Africa, was confined to Great Britain, and was subjected to all the same restrictions, regulations, forfeitures, and penalties, as that of the enumerated commodities of the British colonies in America and the West Indies. Its importation, indeed, was subjected to a small duty of sixpence the hundred weight; but its re-exportation was subjected to the enormous duty of one pound ten shillings the hundred weight. It was the intention of our manufacturers, that the whole produce of those countries should be imported into Great Britain; and in order that they themselves might be enabled to buy it at their own price, that no part of it should be exported again, but at such an expense as would sufficiently discourage that exportation. Their avidity, however, upon this, as well as upon many other occasions, disappointed itself of its object. This enormous duty presented such a temptation to smuggling, that great quantities of this commodity were clandestinely exported, probably to all the manufacturing countries of Europe, but particularly to Holland, not only from Great Britain, but from Africa. Upon this account, by the 14th George III chap. 10, this duty upon exportation was reduced to five shillings the hundred weight.

In the book of rates, according to which the old subsidy was levied, beaver skins were estimated at six shillings and eight pence a piece; and the different subsidies and imposts which, before the year 1722, had been laid upon their importation, amounted to one-fifth part of the rate, or to sixteen pence upon each skin; all of which, except half the old subsidy, amounting only to two pence, was drawn back upon exportation. This duty, upon the importation of so important a material of manufacture, had been thought too high; and, in the year 1722, the rate was reduced to two shillings and sixpence, which reduced the duty upon importation to sixpence, and of this only one-half was to be drawn back upon exportation. The same successful war put the country most productive of beaver under the dominion of Great Britain; and beaver skins being among the enumerated commodities, the exportation from America was consequently confined to the market of Great Britain. Our manufacturers soon bethought themselves of the advantage which they might make of this circumstance; and in the year 1764, the duty upon the importation of beaver skin was reduced to one penny, but the duty upon exportation was raised to seven pence each skin, without any drawback of the duty upon importation. By the same law, a duty of eighteen pence the pound was imposed upon the exportation of beaver wool or woumbs, without making any alteration in the duty upon the importation of that commodity, which, when imported by British, and in British shipping, amounted at that time to between four pence and five pence the piece.

Coals may be considered both as a material of manufacture, and as an instrument of trade. Heavy duties, accordingly, have been imposed upon their exportation, amounting at present (1783) to more than five shillings the ton, or more than fifteen shillings the chaldron, Newcastle measure; which is, in most cases, more than the original value of the commodity at the coal-pit, or even at the shipping port for exportation.

The exportation, however, of the instruments of trade, properly so called, is commonly restrained, not by high duties, but by absolute prohibitions. Thus, by the 7th and 8th of William III chap. 20, sect. 8, the exportation of frames or engines for knitting gloves or stockings, is prohibited, under the penalty, not only of the forfeiture of such frames or engines, so exported, or attempted to be exported, but of forty pounds, one half to the king, the other to the person who shall inform or sue for the same. In the same manner, by the 14th George III chap. 71, the exportation to foreign parts, of any utensils made use of in the cotton, linen, woolen, and silk manufactures, is prohibited under the penalty, not only of the forfeiture of such utensils, but of two hundred pounds, to be paid by the person who shall offend in this manner; and likewise of two hundred pounds, to be paid by the master of the ship, who shall knowingly suffer such utensils to be loaded on board his ship.

When such heavy penalties were imposed upon the exportation of the dead instruments of trade, it could not well be expected that the living instrument, the artificer, should be allowed to go free. Accordingly, by the 5th George I chap. 27, the person who shall be convicted of enticing any artificer, of or in any of the manufactures of Great Britain, to go into any foreign parts, in order to practice or teach his trade, is liable, for the first offence, to be fined in any sum not exceeding one hundred pounds, and to three months imprisonment, and until the fine shall be paid; and for the second offence, to be fined in any sum, at the discretion of the court, and to imprisonment for twelve months, and until the fine shall be paid. By the 23rd George II chap. 13, this penalty is increased, for the first offence, to five hundred pounds for every artificer so enticed, and to twelve months imprisonment, and until the fine shall be paid; and for the second offence, to one thousand pounds, and to two years imprisonment, and until the fine shall be paid.

By the former of these two statutes, upon proof that any person has been enticing any artificer, or that any artificer has promised or contracted to go into foreign parts, for the purposes aforesaid, such artificer may be obliged to give security, at the discretion of the court, that he shall not go beyond the seas, and may be committed to prison until he give such security.

If any artificer has gone beyond the seas, and is exercising or teaching his trade in any foreign country, upon warning being given to him by any of his majesty's ministers or consuls abroad, or by one of his majesty's secretaries of state, for the time being, if he does not, within six months after such warning, return into this realm, and from henceforth abide and inhabit continually within the same, he is from thenceforth declared incapable of taking any legacy devised to him within this kingdom, or of being executor or administrator to any person, or of taking any lands within this kingdom, by descent, devise, or purchase. He likewise forfeits to the king all his lands, goods, and chattels; is declared an alien in every respect; and is put out of the king's protection.

It is unnecessary, I imagine, to observe how contrary such regulations are to the boasted liberty of the subject, of which we affect to be so very jealous; but which, in this case, is so plainly sacrificed to the futile interests of our merchants and manufacturers.

The laudable motive of all these regulations, is to extend our own manufactures, not by their own improvement, but by the depression of those of all our neighbors, and by putting an end, as much as possible, to the troublesome competition of such odious and disagreeable rivals. Our master manufacturers think it reasonable that they themselves should have the monopoly of the ingenuity of all their countrymen. Though by restraining, in some trades, the number of apprentices which can be employed at one time, and by imposing the necessity of a long apprenticeship in all trades, they endeavor, all of them, to confine the knowledge of their respective employments to as small a number as possible; they are unwilling, however, that any part of this small number should go abroad to instruct foreigners.

Consumption is the sole end and purpose of all production; and the interest of the producer ought to be attended to, only so far as it may be necessary for promoting that of the consumer.

The maxim is so perfectly self-evident, that it would be absurd to attempt to prove it. But in the mercantile system, the interest of the consumer is almost constantly sacrificed to that of the producer; and it seems to consider production, and not consumption, as the ultimate end and object of all industry and commerce.

In the restraints upon the importation of all foreign commodities which can come into competition with those of our own growth or manufacture, the interest of the home consumer is evidently sacrificed to that of the producer. It is altogether for the benefit of the latter, that the former is obliged to pay that enhancement of price which this monopoly almost always occasions.

It is altogether for the benefit of the producer, that bounties are granted upon the exportation of some of his productions. The home consumer is obliged to pay, first the tax which is necessary for paying the bounty; and, secondly, the still greater tax which necessarily arises from the enhancement of the price of the commodity in the home market.

By the famous treaty of commerce with Portugal, the consumer is prevented by duties from purchasing of a neighboring country, a commodity which our own climate does not produce; but is obliged to purchase it of a distant country, though it is acknowledged, that the commodity of the distant country is of a worse quality than that of the near one. The home consumer is obliged to submit to this inconvenience, in order that the producer may import into the distant country some of his productions, upon more advantageous terms than he otherwise would have been allowed to do. The consumer, too, is obliged to pay whatever enhancement in the price of those very productions this forced exportation may occasion in the home market.

But in the system of laws which has been established for the management of our American and West Indian colonies, the interest of the home consumer has been sacrificed to that of the producer, with a more extravagant profusion than in all our other commercial regulations. A great empire has been established for the sole purpose of raising up a nation of customers, who should be obliged to buy, from the shops of our different producers, all the goods with which these could supply them. For the sake of that little enhancement of price which this monopoly might afford our producers, the home consumers have been burdened with the whole expense of maintaining and defending that empire. For this purpose, and for this purpose only, in the two last wars, more than two hundred millions have been spent, and a new debt of more than a hundred and seventy millions has been contracted, over and above all that had been expended for the same purpose in former wars. The interest of this debt alone is not only greater than the whole extraordinary profit which, it never could be pretended, was made by the monopoly of the colony trade, but than the whole value of that trade, or than the whole value of the goods which, at an average, have been annually exported to the colonies.

It cannot be very difficult to determine who have been the contrivers of this whole mercantile system; not the consumers, we may believe, whose interest has been entirely neglected; but the producers, whose interest has been so carefully attended to; and among this latter class, our merchants and manufacturers have been by far the principal architects. In the mercantile regulations which have been taken notice of in this chapter, the interest of our manufacturers has been most peculiarly attended to; and the interest, not so much of the consumers, as that of some other sets of producers, has been sacrificed to it.

CHAPTER IX

Of the Agricultural Systems, or of Those Systems of Political Economy which Represent the Produce of Land, as Either the Sole or the Principal Source of the Revenue and Wealth of Every Country

The agricultural systems of political economy will not require so long an explanation as that which I have thought it necessary to bestow upon the mercantile or commercial system.

That system which represents the produce of land as the sole source of the revenue and wealth of every country, has so far as I know, never been adopted by any nation, and it at present exists only in the speculations of a few men of great learning and ingenuity in France. It would not, surely, be worth while to examine at great length the errors of a system which never has done, and probably never will do, any harm in any part of the world. I shall endeavor to explain, however, as distinctly as I can, the great outlines of this very ingenious system.

Mr. Colbert, the famous minister of Louis XIV was a man of probity, of great industry, and knowledge of detail; of great experience and acuteness in the examination of public accounts; and of abilities, in short, every way fitted for introducing method and good order into the collection and expenditure of the public revenue. That minister had unfortunately embraced all the prejudices of the mercantile system, in its nature and essence a system of restraint and regulation, and such as could scarce fail to be agreeable to a laborious and plodding man of business, who had been accustomed to regulate the different departments of public offices, and to establish the necessary checks and controls for confining each to its proper sphere. The industry and commerce of a great country, he endeavored to regulate upon the same model as the departments of a public office; and instead of allowing every man to pursue his own interest his own way, upon the liberal plan of equality, liberty, and justice, he bestowed upon certain branches of industry extraordinary privileges, while he laid others under as extraordinary restraints. He was not only disposed, like other European ministers, to encourage more the industry of the towns than that of the country; but, in order to support the industry of the towns, he was willing even to depress and keep down that of the country. In order to render provisions cheap to the inhabitants of the towns, and thereby to encourage manufactures and foreign commerce, he prohibited altogether the exportation of corn, and thus excluded the inhabitants of the country from every foreign market, for by far the most important part of the produce of their industry. This prohibition, joined to the restraints imposed by the ancient provincial laws of France upon the transportation of corn from one province to another, and to the arbitrary and degrading taxes which are levied upon the cultivators in almost all the provinces, discouraged and kept down the agriculture of that country very much below the state to which it would naturally have risen in so very fertile a soil, and so very happy a climate. This state of discouragement and depression was felt more or less in every different part of the country, and many different inquiries were set on foot concerning the causes of it. One of those causes appeared to be the preference given, by the institutions of Mr. Colbert, to the industry of the towns above that of the country.

If the rod be bent too much one way, says the proverb, in order to make it straight, you must bend it as much the other. The French philosophers, who have proposed the system which represents agriculture as the sole source of the revenue and wealth of every country, seem to have adopted this proverbial maxim; and, as in the plan of Mr. Colbert, the industry of the towns was certainly overvalued in comparison with that of the country, so in their system it seems to be as certainly under-valued.

The different orders of people, who have ever been supposed to contribute in any respect towards the annual produce of the land and labor of the country, they divide into three classes. The first is the class of the proprietors of land. The second is the class of the cultivators, of farmers and country laborers, whom they honor with the peculiar appellation of the productive class. The third is the class of artificers, manufacturers, and merchants, whom they endeavor to degrade by the humiliating appellation of the barren or unproductive class.

The class of proprietors contributes to the annual produce, by the expense which they may occasionally lay out upon the improvement of the land, upon the buildings, drains, enclosures, and other ameliorations, which they may either make or maintain upon it, and by means of which the cultivators are enabled, with the same capital, to raise a greater produce, and consequently to pay a greater rent. This advanced rent may be considered as the interest or profit due to the proprietor, upon the expense or capital which he thus employs in the improvement of his land. Such expenses are in this system called ground expenses (depenses foncieres).

The cultivators or farmers contribute to the annual produce, by what are in this system called the original and annual expenses (depenses primitives, et depenses annuelles), which they lay out upon the cultivation of the land. The original expenses consist in the instruments of husbandry, in the stock of cattle, in the seed, and in the maintenance of the farmer's family, servants, and cattle, during at least a great part of the first year of his occupancy, or till he can receive some return from the land. The annual expenses consist in the seed, in the wear and tear of instruments of husbandry, and in the annual maintenance of the farmer's servants and cattle, and of his family too, so far as any part of them can be considered as servants employed in cultivation. That part of the produce of the land which remains to him after paying the rent, ought to be sufficient, first, to replace to him, within a reasonable time, at least during the term of his occupancy, the whole of his original expenses, together with the ordinary profits of stock; and, secondly, to replace to him annually the whole of his annual expenses, together likewise with the ordinary profits of stock. Those two sorts of expenses are two capitals which the farmer employs in cultivation; and unless they are regularly restored to him, together with a reasonable profit, he cannot carry on his employment upon a level with other employments; but, from a regard to his own interest, must desert it as soon as possible, and seek some other. That part of the produce of the land which is thus necessary for enabling the farmer to continue his business, ought to be considered as a fund sacred to cultivation, which, if the landlord violates, he necessarily reduces the produce of his own land, and, in a few years, not only disables the farmer from paying this racked rent, but from paying the reasonable rent which he might otherwise have got for his land. The rent which properly belongs to the landlord, is no more than the neat produce which remains after paying, in the completest manner, all the necessary expenses which must be previously laid out, in order to raise the gross or the whole produce. It is because the labor of the cultivators, over and above paying completely all those necessary expenses, affords a neat produce of this kind, that this class of people are in this system peculiarly distinguished by the honorable appellation of the productive class. Their original and annual expenses are for the same reason called, in this system, productive expenses, because, over and above replacing their own value, they occasion the annual reproduction of this neat produce.

The ground expenses, as they are called, or what the landlord lays out upon the improvement of his land, are, in this system, too, honored with the appellation of productive expenses. Till the whole of those expenses, together with the ordinary profits of stock, have been completely repaid to him by the advanced rent which he gets from his land, that advanced rent ought to be regarded as sacred and inviolable, both by the church and by the king; ought to be subject neither to tithe nor to taxation. If it is otherwise, by discouraging the improvement of land, the church discourages the future increase of her own tithes, and the king the future increase of his own taxes. As in a well ordered state of things, therefore, those ground expenses, over and above reproducing in the completest manner their own value, occasion likewise, after a certain time, a reproduction of a neat produce, they are in this system considered as productive expenses.

The ground expenses of the landlord, however, together with the original and the annual expenses of the farmer, are the only three sorts of expenses which in this system are considered as productive. All other expenses, and all other orders of people, even those who, in the common apprehensions of men, are regarded as the most productive, are, in this account of things, represented as altogether barren and unproductive.

Artificers and manufacturers, in particular, whose industry, in the common apprehensions of men, increases so much the value of the rude produce of land, are in this system represented as a class of people altogether barren and unproductive. Their labor, it is said, replaces only the stock which employs them, together with its ordinary profits. That stock consists in the materials, tools, and wages, advanced to them by their employer; and is the fund destined for their employment and maintenance. Its profits are the fund destined for the maintenance of their employer. Their employer, as he advances to them the stock of materials, tools, and wages, necessary for their employment, so he advances to himself what is necessary for his own maintenance; and this maintenance he generally proportions to the profit which he expects to make by the price of their work. Unless its price repays to him the maintenance which he advances to himself, as well as the materials, tools, and wages, which he advances to his workmen, it evidently does not repay to him the whole expense which he lays out upon it. The profits of manufacturing stock, therefore, are not, like the rent of land, a neat produce which remains after completely repaying the whole expense which must be laid out in order to obtain them. The stock of the farmer yields him a profit, as well as that of the master manufacturer; and it yields a rent likewise to another person, which that of the master manufacturer does not. The expense, therefore, laid out in employing and maintaining artificers and manufacturers, does no more than continue, if one may say so, the existence of its own value, and does not produce any new value. It is, therefore, altogether a barren and unproductive expense. The expense, on the contrary, laid out in employing farmers and country laborers, over and above continuing the existence of its own value, produces a new value the rent of the landlord. It is, therefore, a productive expense.

Mercantile stock is equally barren and unproductive with manufacturing stock. It only continues the existence of its own value, without producing any new value. Its profits are only the repayment of the maintenance which its employer advances to himself during the time that he employs it, or till he receives the returns of it. They are only the repayment of a part of the expense which must be laid out in employing it.

The labor of artificers and manufacturers never adds any thing to the value of the whole annual amount of the rude produce of the land. It adds, indeed, greatly to the value of some particular parts of it. But the consumption which, in the mean time, it occasions of other parts, is precisely equal to the value which it adds to those parts; so that the value of the whole amount is not, at any one moment of time, in the least augmented by it. The person who works the lace of a pair of fine ruffles for example, will sometimes raise the value of, perhaps, a pennyworth of flax to £30 sterling. But though, at first sight, he appears thereby to multiply the value of a part of the rude produce about seven thousand and two hundred times, he in reality adds nothing to the value of the whole annual amount of the rude produce. The working of that lace costs him, perhaps, two years labor. The £30 which he gets for it when it is finished, is no more than the repayment of the subsistence which he advances to himself during the two years that he is employed about it. The value which, by every day's, month's, or year's labor, he adds to the flax, does no more than replace the value of his own consumption during that day, month, or year. At no moment of time, therefore, does he add any thing to the value of the whole annual amount of the rude produce of the land: the portion of that produce which he is continually consuming, being always equal to the value which he is continually producing. The extreme poverty of the greater part of the persons employed in this expensive, though trifling manufacture, may satisfy us that the price of their work does not, in ordinary cases, exceed the value of their subsistence. It is otherwise with the work of farmers and country laborers. The rent of the landlord is a value which, in ordinary cases, it is continually producing over and above replacing, in the most complete manner, the whole consumption, the whole expense laid out upon the employment and maintenance both of the workmen and of their employer.

Artificers, manufacturers, and merchants, can augment the revenue and wealth of their society by parsimony only; or, as it is expressed in this system, by privation, that is, by depriving themselves of a part of the funds destined for their own subsistence. They annually reproduce nothing but those funds. Unless, therefore, they annually save some part of them, unless they annually deprive themselves of the enjoyment of some part of them, the revenue and wealth of their society can never be, in the smallest degree, augmented by means of their industry. Farmers and country laborers, on the contrary, may enjoy completely the whole funds destined for their own subsistence, and yet augment, at the same time, the revenue and wealth of their society. Over and above what is destined for their own subsistence, their industry annually affords a neat produce, of which the augmentation necessarily augments the revenue and wealth of their society. Nations, therefore, which, like France or England, consist in a great measure, of proprietors and cultivators, can be enriched by industry and enjoyment. Nations, on the contrary, which, like Holland and Hamburgh, are composed chiefly of merchants, artificers, and manufacturers, can grow rich only through parsimony and privation. As the interest of nations so differently circumstanced is very different, so is likewise the common character of the people. In those of the former kind, liberality, frankness, and good fellowship, naturally make a part of their common character; in the latter, narrowness, meanness, and a selfish disposition, averse to all social pleasure and enjoyment.

The unproductive class, that of merchants, artificers, and manufacturers, is maintained and employed altogether at the expense of the two other classes, of that of proprietors, and of that of cultivators. They furnish it both with the materials of its work, and with the fund of its subsistence, with the corn and cattle which it consumes while it is employed about that work. The proprietors and cultivators finally pay both the wages of all the workmen of the unproductive class, and the profits of all their employers. Those workmen and their employers are properly the servants of the proprietors and cultivators. They are only servants who work without doors, as menial servants work within. Both the one and the other, however, are equally maintained at the expense of the same masters. The labor of both is equally unproductive. It adds nothing to the value of the sum total of the rude produce of the land. Instead of increasing the value of that sum total, it is a charge and expense which must be paid out of it.

The unproductive class, however, is not only useful, but greatly useful, to the other two classes. By means of the industry of merchants, artificers, and manufacturers, the proprietors and cultivators can purchase both the foreign goods and the manufactured produce of their own country, which they have occasion for, with the produce of a much smaller quantity of their own labor, than what they would be obliged to employ, if they were to attempt, in an awkward and unskillful manner, either to import the one, or to make the other, for their own use. By means of the unproductive class, the cultivators are delivered from many cares, which would otherwise distract their attention from the cultivation of land. The superiority of produce, which in consequence of this undivided attention, they are enabled to raise, is fully sufficient to pay the whole expense which the maintenance and employment of the unproductive class costs either the proprietors or themselves. The industry of merchants, artificers, and manufacturers, though in its own nature altogether unproductive, yet contributes in this manner indirectly to increase the produce of the land. It increases the productive powers of productive labor, by leaving it at liberty to confine itself to its proper employment, the cultivation of land; and the plough goes frequently the easier and the better, by means of the labor of the man whose business is most remote from the plough.

It can never be the interest of the proprietors and cultivators, to restrain or to discourage, in any respect, the industry of merchants, artificers, and manufacturers. The greater the liberty which this unproductive class enjoys, the greater will be the competition in all the different trades which compose it, and the cheaper will the other two classes be supplied, both with foreign goods and with the manufactured produce of their own country.

It can never be the interest of the unproductive class to oppress the other two classes. It is the surplus produce of the land, or what remains after deducting the maintenance, first of the cultivators, and afterwards of the proprietors, that maintains and employs the unproductive class. The greater this surplus, the greater must likewise be the maintenance and employment of that class. The establishment of perfect justice, of perfect liberty, and of perfect equality, is the very simple secret which most effectually secures the highest degree of prosperity to all the three classes.

The merchants, artificers, and manufacturers of those mercantile states, which, like Holland and Hamburgh, consist chiefly of this unproductive class, are in the same manner maintained and employed altogether at the expense of the proprietors and cultivators of land. The only difference is, that those proprietors and cultivators are, the greater part of them, placed at a most inconvenient distance from the merchants, artificers, and manufacturers, whom they supply with the materials of their work and the fund of their subsistence; are the inhabitants of other countries, and the subjects of other governments.

Such mercantile states, however, are not only useful, but greatly useful, to the inhabitants of those other countries. They fill up, in some measure, a very important void; and supply the place of the merchants, artificers, and manufacturers, whom the inhabitants of those countries ought to find at home, but whom, from some defect in their policy, they do not find at home.

It can never be the interest of those landed nations, if I may call them so, to discourage or distress the industry of such mercantile states, by imposing high duties upon their trade, or upon the commodities which they furnish. Such duties, by rendering those commodities dearer, could serve only to sink the real value of the surplus produce of their own land, with which, or, what comes to the same thing, with the price of which those commodities are purchased. Such duties could only serve to discourage the increase of that surplus produce, and consequently the improvement and cultivation of their own land. The most effectual expedient, on the contrary, for raising the value of that surplus produce, for encouraging its increase, and consequently the improvement and cultivation of their own land, would be to allow the most perfect freedom to the trade of all such mercantile nations.

This perfect freedom of trade would even be the most effectual expedient for supplying them, in due time, with all the artificers, manufacturers, and merchants, whom they wanted at home; and for filling up, in the properest and most advantageous manner, that very important void which they felt there.

The continual increase of the surplus produce of their land would, in due time, create a greater capital than what would be employed with the ordinary rate of profit in the improvement and cultivation of land; and the surplus part of it would naturally turn itself to the employment of artificers and manufacturers, at home. But these artificers and manufacturers, finding at home both the materials of their work and the fund of their subsistence, might immediately, even with much less art and skill be able to work as cheap as the little artificers and manufacturers of such mercantile states, who had both to bring from a greater distance. Even though, from want of art and skill, they might not for some time be able to work as cheap, yet, finding a market at home, they might be able to sell their work there as cheap as that of the artificers and manufacturers of such mercantile states, which could not be brought to that market but from so great a distance; and as their art and skill improved, they would soon be able to sell it cheaper. The artificers and manufacturers of such mercantile states, therefore, would immediately be rivaled in the market of those landed nations, and soon after undersold and justled out of it altogether. The cheapness of the manufactures of those landed nations, in consequence of the gradual improvements of art and skill, would, in due time, extend their sale beyond the home market, and carry them to many foreign markets, from which they would, in the same manner, gradually justle out many of the manufacturers of such mercantile nations.

This continual increase, both of the rude and manufactured produce of those landed nations, would, in due time, create a greater capital than could, with the ordinary rate of profit, be employed either in agriculture or in manufactures. The surplus of this capital would naturally turn itself to foreign trade and be employed in exporting, to foreign countries, such parts of the rude and manufactured produce of its own country, as exceeded the demand of the home market. In the exportation of the produce of their own country, the merchants of a landed nation would have an advantage of the same kind over those of mercantile nations, which its artificers and manufacturers had over the artificers and manufacturers of such nations; the advantage of finding at home that cargo, and those stores and provisions, which the others were obliged to seek for at a distance. With inferior art and skill in navigation, therefore, they would be able to sell that cargo as cheap in foreign markets as the merchants of such mercantile nations; and with equal art and skill they would be able to sell it cheaper. They would soon, therefore, rival those mercantile nations in this branch of foreign trade, and, in due time, would justle them out of it altogether.

According to this liberal and generous system, therefore, the most advantageous method in which a landed nation can raise up artificers, manufacturers, and merchants of its own, is to grant the most perfect freedom of trade to the artificers, manufacturers, and merchants of all other nations. It thereby raises the value of the surplus produce of its own land, of which the continual increase gradually establishes a fund, which, in due time, necessarily raises up all the artificers, manufacturers, and merchants, whom it has occasion for.

When a landed nation on the contrary, oppresses, either by high duties or by prohibitions, the trade of foreign nations, it necessarily hurts its own interest in two different ways. First, by raising the price of all foreign goods, and of all sorts of manufactures, it necessarily sinks the real value of the surplus produce of its own land, with which, or, what comes to the same thing, with the price of which, it purchases those foreign goods and manufactures. Secondly, by giving a sort of monopoly of the home market to its own merchants, artificers, and manufacturers, it raises the rate of mercantile and manufacturing profit, in proportion to that of agricultural profit; and, consequently, either draws from agriculture a part of the capital which had before been employed in it, or hinders from going to it a part of what would otherwise have gone to it. This policy, therefore, discourages agriculture in two different ways; first, by sinking the real value of its produce, and thereby lowering the rate of its profits; and, secondly, by raising the rate of profit in all other employments. Agriculture is rendered less advantageous, and trade and manufactures more advantageous, than they otherwise would be; and every man is tempted by his own interest to turn, as much as he can, both his capital and his industry from the former to the latter employments.

Though, by this oppressive policy, a landed nation should be able to raise up artificers, manufacturers, and merchants of its own, somewhat sooner than it could do by the freedom of trade; a matter, however, which is not a little doubtful; yet it would raise them up, if one may say so, prematurely, and before it was perfectly ripe for them. By raising up too hastily one species of industry, it would depress another more valuable species of industry. By raising up too hastily a species of industry which duly replaces the stock which employs it, together with the ordinary profit, it would depress a species of industry which, over and above replacing that stock, with its profit, affords likewise a neat produce, a free rent to the landlord. It would depress productive labor, by encouraging too hastily that labor which is altogether barren and unproductive.

In what manner, according to this system, the sum total of the annual produce of the land is distributed among the three classes above mentioned, and in what manner the labor of the unproductive class does no more than replace the value of its own consumption, without increasing in any respect the value of that sum total, is represented by Mr. Quesnai, the very ingenious and profound author of this system, in some arithmetical formularies. The first of these formularies, which, by way of eminence, he peculiarly distinguishes by the name of the Economical Table, represents the manner in which he supposes this distribution takes place, in a state of the most perfect liberty, and, therefore, of the highest prosperity; in a state where the annual produce is such as to afford the greatest possible neat produce, and where each class enjoys its proper share of the whole annual produce. Some subsequent formularies represent the manner in which he supposes this distribution is made in different states of restraint and regulation; in which, either the class of proprietors, or the barren and unproductive class, is more favored than the class of cultivators; and in which either the one or the other encroaches, more or less, upon the share which ought properly to belong to this productive class. Every such encroachment, every violation of that natural distribution, which the most perfect liberty would establish, must, according to this system, necessarily degrade, more or less, from one year to another, the value and sum total of the annual produce, and must necessarily occasion a gradual declension in the real wealth and revenue of the society; a declension, of which the progress must be quicker or slower, according to the degree of this encroachment, according as that natural distribution, which the most perfect liberty would establish, is more or less violated. Those subsequent formularies represent the different degrees of declension which, according to this system, correspond to the different degrees in which this natural distribution of things is violated.

Some speculative physicians seem to have imagined that the health of the human body could be preserved only by a certain precise regimen of diet and exercise, of which every, the smallest violation, necessarily occasioned some degree of disease or disorder proportionate to the degree of the violation. Experience, however, would seem to show, that the human body frequently preserves, to all appearance at least, the most perfect state of health under a vast variety of different regimens; even under some which are generally believed to be very far from being perfectly wholesome. But the healthful state of the human body, it would seem, contains in itself some unknown principle of preservation, capable either of preventing or of correcting, in many respects, the bad effects even of a very faulty regimen. Mr. Quesnai, who was himself a physician, and a very speculative physician, seems to have entertained a notion of the same kind concerning the political body, and to have imagined that it would thrive and prosper only under a certain precise regimen, the exact regimen of perfect liberty and perfect justice. He seems not to have considered, that in the political body, the natural effort which every man is continually making to better his own condition, is a principle of preservation capable of preventing and correcting, in many respects, the bad effects of a political economy, in some degree both partial and oppressive. Such a political economy, though it no doubt retards more or less, is not always capable of stopping altogether, the natural progress of a nation towards wealth and prosperity, and still less of making it go backwards. If a nation could not prosper without the enjoyment of perfect liberty and perfect justice, there is not in the world a nation which could ever have prospered. In the political body, however, the wisdom of nature has fortunately made ample provision for remedying many of the bad effects of the folly and injustice of man; it the same manner as it has done in the natural body, for remedying those of his sloth and intemperance.

The capital error of this system, however, seems to lie in its representing the class of artificers, manufacturers, and merchants, as altogether barren and unproductive. The following observations may serve to show the impropriety of this representation.

First, this class, it is acknowledged, reproduces annually the value of its own annual consumption, and continues, at least, the existence of the stock or capital which maintains and employs it. But, upon this account alone, the denomination of barren or unproductive should seem to be very improperly applied to it. We should not call a marriage barren or unproductive, though it produced only a son and a daughter, to replace the father and mother, and though it did not increase the number of the human species, but only continued it as it was before. Farmers and country laborers, indeed, over and above the stock which maintains and employs them, reproduce annually a neat produce, a free rent to the landlord. As a marriage which affords three children is certainly more productive than one which affords only two, so the labor of farmers and country laborers is certainly more productive than that of merchants, artificers, and manufacturers. The superior produce of the one class, however, does not, render the other barren or unproductive.

Secondly, it seems, on this account, altogether improper to consider artificers, manufacturers, and merchants, in the same light as menial servants. The labor of menial servants does not continue the existence of the fund which maintains and employs them. Their maintenance and employment is altogether at the expense of their masters, and the work which they perform is not of a nature to repay that expense. That work consists in services which perish generally in the very instant of their performance, and does not fix or realize itself in any vendible commodity, which can replace the value of their wages and maintenance. The labor, on the contrary, of artificers, manufacturers, and merchants, naturally does fix and realize itself in some such vendible commodity. It is upon this account that, in the chapter in which I treat of productive and unproductive labor, I have classed artificers, manufacturers, and merchants among the productive laborers, and menial servants among the barren or unproductive.

Thirdly, it seems, upon every supposition, improper to say, that the labor of artificers, manufacturers, and merchants, does not increase the real revenue of the society. Though we should suppose, for example, as it seems to be supposed in this system, that the value of the daily, monthly, and yearly consumption of this class was exactly equal to that of its daily, monthly, and yearly production; yet it would not from thence follow, that its labor added nothing to the real revenue, to the real value of the annual produce of the land and labor of the society. An artificer, for example, who, in the first six months after harvest, executes ten pounds worth of work, though he should, in the same time, consume ten pounds worth of corn and other necessaries, yet really adds the value of ten pounds to the annual produce of the land and labor of the society. While he has been consuming a half-yearly revenue of ten pounds worth of corn and other necessaries, he has produced an equal value of work, capable of purchasing, either to himself, or to some other person, an equal half-yearly revenue. The value, therefore, of what has been consumed and produced during these six months, is equal, not to ten, but to twenty pounds. It is possible, indeed, that no more than ten pounds worth of this value may ever have existed at any one moment of time. But if the ten pounds worth of corn and other necessaries which were consumed by the artificer, had been consumed by a soldier, or by a menial servant, the value of that part of the annual produce which existed at the end of the six months, would have been ten pounds less than it actually is in consequence of the labor of the artificer. Though the value of what the artificer produces, therefore, should not, at any one moment of time, be supposed greater than the value he consumes, yet, at every moment of time, the actually existing value of goods in the market is, in consequence of what he produces, greater than it otherwise would be.

When the patrons of this system assert, that the consumption of artificers, manufacturers, and merchants, is equal to the value of what they produce, they probably mean no more than that their revenue, or the fund destined for their consumption, is equal to it. But if they had expressed themselves more accurately, and only asserted, that the revenue of this class was equal to the value of what they produced, it might readily have occurred to the reader, that what would naturally be saved out of this revenue, must necessarily increase more or less the real wealth of the society. In order, therefore, to make out something like an argument, it was necessary that they should express themselves as they have done; and this argument, even supposing things actually were as it seems to presume them to be, turns out to be a very inconclusive one.

Fourthly, farmers and country laborers can no more augment, without parsimony, the real revenue, the annual produce of the land and labor of their society, than artificers, manufacturers, and merchants. The annual produce of the land and labor of any society can be augmented only in two ways; either, first, by some improvement in the productive powers of the useful labor actually maintained within it; or, secondly, by some increase in the quantity of that labor.

The improvement in the productive powers of useful labor depends, first, upon the improvement in the ability of the workman; and, secondly, upon that of the machinery with which he works. But the labor of artificers and manufacturers, as it is capable of being more subdivided, and the labor of each workman reduced to a greater simplicity of operation, than that of farmers and country laborers; so it is likewise capable of both these sorts of improvement in a much higher degree. {See book i chap. 1.} In this respect, therefore, the class of cultivators can have no sort of advantage over that of artificers and manufacturers.

The increase in the quantity of useful labor actually employed within any society must depend altogether upon the increase of the capital which employs it; and the increase of that capital, again, must be exactly equal to the amount of the savings from the revenue, either of the particular persons who manage and direct the employment of that capital, or of some other persons, who lend it to them. If merchants, artificers, and manufacturers are, as this system seems to suppose, naturally more inclined to parsimony and saving than proprietors and cultivators, they are, so far, more likely to augment the quantity of useful labor employed within their society, and consequently to increase its real revenue, the annual produce of its land and labor.

Fifthly and lastly, though the revenue of the inhabitants of every country was supposed to consist altogether, as this system seems to suppose, in the quantity of subsistence which their industry could procure to them; yet, even upon this supposition, the revenue of a trading and manufacturing country must, other things being equal, always be much greater than that of one without trade or manufactures. By means of trade and manufactures, a greater quantity of subsistence can be annually imported into a particular country, than what its own lands, in the actual state of their cultivation, could afford. The inhabitants of a town, though they frequently possess no lands of their own, yet draw to themselves, by their industry, such a quantity of the rude produce of the lands of other people, as supplies them, not only with the materials of their work, but with the fund of their subsistence. What a town always is with regard to the country in its neighborhood, one independent state or country may frequently be with regard to other independent states or countries. It is thus that Holland draws a great part of its subsistence from other countries; live cattle from Holstein and Jutland, and corn from almost all the different countries of Europe. A small quantity of manufactured produce, purchases a great quantity of rude produce. A trading and manufacturing country, therefore, naturally purchases, with a small part of its manufactured produce, a great part of the rude produce of other countries; while, on the contrary, a country without trade and manufactures is generally obliged to purchase, at the expense of a great part of its rude produce, a very small part of the manufactured produce of other countries. The one exports what can subsist and accommodate but a very few, and imports the subsistence and accommodation of a great number. The other exports the accommodation and subsistence of a great number, and imports that of a very few only. The inhabitants of the one must always enjoy a much greater quantity of subsistence than what their own lands, in the actual state of their cultivation, could afford. The inhabitants of the other must always enjoy a much smaller quantity.

This system, however, with all its imperfections, is perhaps the nearest approximation to the truth that has yet been published upon the subject of political economy; and is upon that account, well worth the consideration of every man who wishes to examine with attention the principles of that very important science. Though in representing the labor which is employed upon land as the only productive labor, the notions which it inculcates are, perhaps, too narrow and confined; yet in representing the wealth of nations as consisting, not in the inconsumable riches of money, but in the consumable goods annually reproduced by the labor of the society, and in representing perfect liberty as the only effectual expedient for rendering this annual reproduction the greatest possible, its doctrine seems to be in every respect as just as it is generous and liberal. Its followers are very numerous; and as men are fond of paradoxes, and of appearing to understand what surpasses the comprehensions of ordinary people, the paradox which it maintains, concerning the unproductive nature of manufacturing labor, has not, perhaps, contributed a little to increase the number of its admirers. They have for some years past made a pretty considerable sect, distinguished in the French republic of letters by the name of the Economists. Their works have certainly been of some service to their country; not only by bringing into general discussion, many subjects which had never been well examined before, but by influencing, in some measure, the public administration in favor of agriculture. It has been in consequence of their representations, accordingly, that the agriculture of France has been delivered from several of the oppressions which it before labored under. The term, during which such a lease can be granted, as will be valid against every future purchaser or proprietor of the land, has been prolonged from nine to twenty-seven years. The ancient provincial restraints upon the transportation of corn from one province of the kingdom to another, have been entirely taken away; and the liberty of exporting it to all foreign countries, has been established as the common law of the kingdom in all ordinary cases. This sect, in their works, which are very numerous, and which treat not only of what is properly called Political Economy, or of the nature and causes or the wealth of nations, but of every other branch of the system of civil government, all follow implicitly, and without any sensible variation, the doctrine of Mr. Qttesnai. There is, upon this account, little variety in the greater part of their works. The most distinct and best connected account of this doctrine is to be found in a little book written by Mr. Mercier de la Riviere, sometime intendant of Martinico, entitled, *The Natural and Essential Order of Political Societies*. The admiration of this whole sect for their master, who was himself a man of the greatest modesty and simplicity, is not inferior to that of any of the ancient philosophers for the founders of their respective systems. "There have been since the world began," says a very diligent and respectable author, the Marquis de Mirabeau, "three great inventions which have principally given stability to political societies, independent of many other inventions which have enriched and adorned them. The first is the invention of writing, which alone gives human nature the power of transmitting, without alteration, its laws, its contracts, its annals, and its discoveries. The second is the invention of money, which binds together all the relations between civilized societies. The third is the economical table, the result of the other two, which completes them both by perfecting their object; the great discovery of our age, but of which our posterity will reap the benefit."

As the political economy of the nations of modern Europe has been more favorable to manufactures and foreign trade, the industry of the towns, than to agriculture, the industry of the country; so that of other nations has followed a different plan, and has been more favorable to agriculture than to manufactures and foreign trade.

The policy of China favors agriculture more than all other employments. In China, the condition of a laborer is said to be as much superior to that of an artificer, as in most parts of Europe that of an artificer is to that of a laborer. In China, the great ambition of every man is to get possession of a little bit of land, either in property or in lease; and leases are there said to be granted upon very moderate terms, and to be sufficiently secured to the lessees. The Chinese have little respect for foreign trade. Your beggarly commerce! was the language in which the Mandarins of Peking used to talk to Mr. De Lange, the Russian envoy, concerning it. {See the Journal of Mr. De Lange, in *Bell's Travels*, vol. ii. pp. 258, 276, 293.} Except with Japan, the Chinese carry on, themselves, and in their own bottoms, little or no foreign trade; and it is only into one or two ports of their kingdom that they even admit the ships of foreign nations. Foreign trade, therefore, is, in China, every way confined within a much narrower circle than that to which it would naturally extend itself, if more freedom was allowed to it, either in their own ships, or in those of foreign nations.

Manufactures, as in a small bulk they frequently contain a great value, and can upon that account be transported at less expense from one country to another than most parts of rude produce, are, in almost all countries, the principal support of foreign trade. In countries, besides, less extensive, and less favorably circumstanced for inferior commerce than China, they generally require the support of foreign trade. Without an extensive foreign market, they could not well flourish, either in countries so moderately extensive as to afford but a narrow home market, or in countries where the communication between one province and another was so difficult, as to render it impossible for the goods of any particular place to enjoy the whole of that home market which the country could afford. The perfection of manufacturing industry, it must be remembered, depends altogether upon the division of labor; and the degree to which the division of labor can be introduced into any manufacture, is necessarily regulated, it has already been shown, by the extent of the market. But the great extent of the empire of China, the vast multitude of its inhabitants, the variety of climate, and consequently of productions in its different provinces, and the easy communication by means of water-carriage between the greater part of them, render the home market of that country of so great extent, as to be alone sufficient to support very great manufactures, and to admit of very considerable subdivisions of labor. The home market of China is, perhaps, in extent, not much inferior to the market of all the different countries of Europe put together. A more extensive foreign trade, however, which to this great home market added the foreign market of all the rest of the world, especially if any considerable part of this trade was carried on in Chinese ships, could scarce fail to increase very much the manufactures of China, and to improve very much the productive powers of its manufacturing industry. By a more extensive navigation, the Chinese would naturally learn the art of using and constructing, themselves, all the different machines made use of in other countries, as well as the other improvements of art and industry which are practiced in all the different parts of the world. Upon their present plan, they have little opportunity of improving themselves by the example of any other nation, except that of the Japanese.

The policy of ancient Egypt, too, and that of the Gentoo government of Indostan, seem to have favored agriculture more than all other employments.

Both in ancient Egypt and Indostan, the whole body of the people was divided into different casts or tribes each of which was confined, from father to son, to a particular employment, or class of employments. The son of a priest was necessarily a priest; the son of a soldier, a soldier; the son of a laborer, a laborer; the son of a weaver, a weaver; the son of a tailor, a tailor, etc. In both countries, the cast of the priests holds the highest rank, and that of the soldiers the next; and in both countries the cast of the farmers and laborers was superior to the casts of merchants and manufacturers.

The government of both countries was particularly attentive to the interest of agriculture. The works constructed by the ancient sovereigns of Egypt, for the proper distribution of the waters of the Nile, were famous in antiquity, and the ruined remains of some of them are still the admiration of travelers. Those of the same kind which were constructed by the ancient sovereigns of Indostan, for the proper distribution of the waters of the Ganges, as well as of many other rivers, though they have been less celebrated, seem to have been equally great. Both countries, accordingly, though subject occasionally to dearths, have been famous for their great fertility. Though both were extremely populous, yet, in years of moderate plenty, they were both able to export great quantities of grain to their neighbors.

The ancient Egyptians had a superstitious aversion to the sea; and as the Gentoo religion does not permit its followers to light a fire, nor consequently to dress any victuals, upon the water, it, in effect, prohibits them from all distant sea voyages. Both the Egyptians and Indians must have depended almost altogether upon the navigation of other nations for the exportation of their surplus produce; and this dependency, as it must have confined the market, so it must have discouraged the increase of this surplus produce. It must have discouraged, too, the increase of the manufactured produce, more than that of the rude produce. Manufactures require a much more extensive market than the most important parts of the rude produce of the land. A single shoemaker will make more than 300 pairs of shoes in the year; and his own family will not, perhaps, wear out six pairs. Unless, therefore, he has the custom of, at least, 50 such families as his own, he cannot dispose of the whole product of his own labor. The most numerous class of artificers will seldom, in a large country, make more than one in 50, or one in a 100, of the whole number of families contained in it. But in such large countries, as France and England, the number of people employed in agriculture has, by some authors been computed at a half, by others at a third and by no author that I know of, at less that a fifth of the whole inhabitants of the country. But as the produce of the agriculture of both France and England is, the far greater part of it, consumed at home, each person employed in it must, according to these computations, require little more than the custom of one, two, or, at most, of four such families as his own, in order to dispose of the whole produce of his own labor. Agriculture, therefore, can support itself under the discouragement of a confined market much better than manufactures. In both ancient Egypt and Indostan, indeed, the confinement of the foreign market was in some measure compensated by the convenience of many inland navigations, which opened, in the most advantageous manner, the whole extent of the home market to every part of the produce of every different district of those countries. The great extent of Indostan, too, rendered the home market of that country very great, and sufficient to support a great variety of manufactures. But the small extent of ancient Egypt, which was never equal to England, must at all times, have rendered the home market of that country too narrow for supporting any great variety of manufactures. Bengal accordingly, the province of Indostan which commonly exports the greatest quantity of rice, has always been more remarkable for the exportation of a great variety of manufactures, than for that of its grain. Ancient Egypt, on the contrary, though it exported some manufactures, fine linen in particular, as well as some other goods, was always most distinguished for its great exportation of grain. It was long the granary of the Roman empire.

The sovereigns of China, of ancient Egypt, and of the different kingdoms into which Indostan has, at different times, been divided, have always derived the whole, or by far the most considerable part, of their revenue, from some sort of land tax or land rent. This land tax, or land rent, like the tithe in Europe, consisted in a certain proportion, a fifth, it is said, of the produce of the land, which was either delivered in kind, or paid in money, according to a certain valuation, and which, therefore, varied from year to year, according to all the variations of the produce. It was natural, therefore, that the sovereigns of those countries should be particularly attentive to the interests of agriculture, upon the prosperity or declension of which immediately depended the yearly increase or diminution of their own revenue.

The policy of the ancient republics of Greece, and that of Rome, though it honored agriculture more than manufactures or foreign trade, yet seems rather to have discouraged the latter employments, than to have given any direct or intentional encouragement to the former. In several of the ancient states of Greece, foreign trade was prohibited altogether; and in several others, the employments of artificers and manufacturers were considered as hurtful to the strength and agility of the human body, as rendering it incapable of those habits which their military and gymnastic exercises endeavored to form in it, and as thereby disqualifying it, more or less, for undergoing the fatigues and encountering the dangers of war. Such occupations were considered as fit only for slaves, and the free citizens of the states were prohibited from exercising them. Even in those states where no such prohibition took place, as in Rome and Athens, the great body of the people were in effect excluded from all the trades which are now commonly exercised by the lower sort of the inhabitants of towns. Such trades were, at Athens and Rome, all occupied by the slaves of the rich, who exercised them for the benefit of their masters, whose wealth, power, and protection, made it almost impossible for a poor freeman to find a market for his work, when it came into competition with that of the slaves of the rich. Slaves, however, are very seldom inventive; and all the most important improvements, either in machinery, or in the arrangement and distribution of work, which facilitate and abridge labor have been the discoveries of freemen. Should a slave propose any improvement of this kind, his master would be very apt to consider the proposal as the suggestion of laziness, and of a desire to save his own labor at the master's expense. The poor slave, instead of reward would probably meet with much abuse, perhaps with some punishment.

In the manufactures carried on by slaves, therefore, more labor must generally have been employed to execute the same quantity of work, than in those carried on by freemen. The work of the farmer must, upon that account, generally have been dearer than that of the latter. The Hungarian mines, it is remarked by Mr. Montesquieu, though not richer, have always been wrought with less expense, and therefore with more profit, than the Turkish mines in their neighborhood. The Turkish mines are wrought by slaves;

and the arms of those slaves are the only machines which the Turks have ever thought of employing. The Hungarian mines are wrought by freemen, who employ a great deal of machinery, by which they facilitate and abridge their own labor. From the very little that is known about the price of manufactures in the times of the Greeks and Romans, it would appear that those of the finer sort were excessively dear. Silk sold for its weight in gold. It was not, indeed, in those times an European manufacture; and as it was all brought from the East Indies, the distance of the carriage may in some measure account for the greatness of the price. The price, however, which a lady, it is said, would sometimes pay for a piece of very fine linen, seems to have been equally extravagant; and as linen was always either an European, or at farthest, an Egyptian manufacture, this high price can be accounted for only by the great expense of the labor which must have been employed about it, and the expense of this labor again could arise from nothing but the awkwardness of the machinery which is made use of. The price of fine woolens, too, though not quite so extravagant, seems, however, to have been much above that of the present times. Some cloths, we are told by Pliny {Plin. 1. ix.c.39.}, dyed in a particular manner, cost a hundred denarii, or £3:6s:8d. the pound weight. Others, dyed in another manner, cost a thousand denarii the pound weight, or £33:6s:8d. The Roman pound, it must be remembered, contained only twelve of our avoirdupois ounces. This high price, indeed, seems to have been principally owing to the dye. But had not the cloths themselves been much dearer than any which are made in the present times, so very expensive a dye would not probably have been bestowed upon them. The disproportion would have been too great between the value of the accessory and that of the principal. The price mentioned by the same author {Plin. 1. viii.c.48.}, of some triclinaria, a sort of woolen pillows or cushions made use of to lean upon as they reclined upon their couches at table, passes all credibility; some of them being said to have cost more than £30,000, others more than £300,000. This high price, too, is not said to have arisen from the dye. In the dress of the people of fashion of both sexes, there seems to have been much less variety, it is observed by Dr. Arbuthnot, in ancient than in modern times; and the very little variety which we find in that of the ancient statues, confirms his observation. He infers from this, that their dress must, upon the whole, have been cheaper than ours; but the conclusion does not seem to follow. When the expense of fashionable dress is very great, the variety must be very small. But when, by the improvements in the productive powers of manufacturing art and industry, the expense of any one dress comes to be very moderate, the variety will naturally be very great. The rich, not being able to distinguish themselves by the expense of any one dress, will naturally endeavor to do so by the multitude and variety of their dresses.

The greatest and most important branch of the commerce of every nation, it has already been observed, is that which is carried on between the inhabitants of the town and those of the country. The inhabitants of the town draw from the country the rude produce, which constitutes both the materials of their work and the fund of their subsistence; and they pay for this rude produce, by sending back to the country a certain portion of it manufactured and prepared for immediate use. The trade which is carried on between these two different sets of people, consists ultimately in a certain quantity of rude produce exchanged for a certain quantity of manufactured produce. The dearer the latter, therefore, the cheaper the former; and whatever tends in any country to raise the price of manufactured produce, tends to lower that of the rude produce of the land, and thereby to discourage agriculture. The smaller the quantity of manufactured produce, which any given quantity of rude produce, or, what comes to the same thing, which the price of any given quantity of rude produce, is capable of purchasing, the smaller the exchangeable value of that given quantity of rude produce; the smaller the encouragement which either the landlord has to increase its quantity by improving, or the farmer by cultivating the land. Whatever, besides, tends to diminish in any country the number of artificers and manufacturers, tends to diminish the home market, the most important of all markets, for the rude produce of the land, and thereby still further to discourage agriculture.

Those systems, therefore, which preferring agriculture to all other employments, in order to promote it, impose restraints upon manufactures and foreign trade, act contrary to the very end which they propose, and indirectly discourage that very species of industry which they mean to promote. They are so far, perhaps, more inconsistent than even the mercantile system. That system, by encouraging manufactures and foreign trade more than agriculture, turns a certain portion of the capital of the society, from supporting a more advantageous, to support a less advantageous species of industry. But still it really, and in the end, encourages that species of industry which it means to promote. Those agricultural systems, on the contrary, really, and in the end, discourage their own favorite species of industry.

It is thus that every system which endeavors, either, by extraordinary encouragements to draw towards a particular species of industry a greater share of the capital of the society than what would naturally go to it, or, by extraordinary restraints, to force from a particular species of industry some share of the capital which would otherwise be employed in it, is, in reality, subversive of the great purpose which it means to promote. It retards, instead of accelerating the progress of the society towards real wealth and greatness; and diminishes, instead of increasing, the real value of the annual produce of its land and labor.

All systems, either of preference or of restraint, therefore, being thus completely taken away, the obvious and simple system of natural liberty establishes itself of its own accord. Every man, as long as he does not violate the laws of justice, is left perfectly free to pursue his own interest his own way, and to bring both his industry and capital into competition with those of any other man, or order of men. The sovereign is completely discharged from a duty, in the attempting to perform which he must always be exposed to innumerable delusions, and for the proper performance of which, no human wisdom or knowledge could ever be sufficient; the duty of superintending the industry of private people, and of directing it towards the employments most suitable to the interests of the society. According to the system of natural liberty, the sovereign has only three duties to attend to; three duties of great importance, indeed, but plain and intelligible to common understandings: first, the duty of protecting the society from the violence and invasion of other independent societies; secondly, the duty of protecting, as far as possible, every member of the society from the injustice or oppression of every other member of it, or the duty of establishing an exact administration of justice; and, thirdly, the duty of erecting and maintaining certain public works, and certain public institutions, which it can never be for the interest of any individual, or small number of individuals to erect and maintain; because the profit could never repay the expense to any individual, or small number of individuals, though it may frequently do much more than repay it to a great society.

The proper performance of those several duties of the sovereign necessarily supposes a certain expense; and this expense again necessarily requires a certain revenue to support it. In the following book, therefore, I shall endeavor to explain, first, what are the necessary expenses of the sovereign or commonwealth; and which of those expenses ought to be defrayed by the general contribution of the whole society; and which of them, by that of some particular part only, or of some particular members of the society; secondly, what are the different methods in which the whole society may be made to contribute towards defraying the expenses incumbent on the whole society; and what are the principal advantages and inconveniencies of each of those methods; and thirdly, what are the reasons and causes which have induced almost all modern governments to mortgage some part of this revenue, or to contract debts; and what have been the effects of those debts upon the real wealth, the annual produce of the land and labor of the society. The following book, therefore, will naturally be divided into three chapters.

Appendix to Book IV

The two following accounts are subjoined, in order to illustrate and confirm what is said in the fifth chapter of the fourth book, concerning the Tonnage Bounty to the Whit-herring Fishery. The reader, I believe, may depend upon the accuracy of both accounts.

An account of Busses fitted out in Scotland for eleven Years, with the Number of empty Barrels carried out, and the Number of Barrels of Herrings caught; also the Bounty, at a Medium, on each Barrel of Sea-sticks, and on each Barrel when fully packed.

Years	Number of Busses	Empty Barrels Carried Out	Barrels of Herrings Caught	Bounty Paid on the Busses		
				£.	s.	d.
1771	29	5,948	2,832	2,885	0	0
1772	168	41,316	22,237	11,055	7	6
1773	190	42,333	42,055	12,510	8	6
1774	240	59,303	56,365	26,932	2	6
1775	275	69,144	52,879	19,315	15	0
1776	294	76,329	51,863	21,290	7	6
1777	240	62,679	43,313	17,592	2	6
1778	220	56,390	40,958	16,316	2	6
1779	206	55,194	29,367	15,287	0	0
1780	181	48,315	19,885	13,445	12	6
1781	135	33,992	16,593	9,613	15	6
Totals	2,186	550,943	378,347	165,463	14	0

Sea-sticks, 378,347   Bounty, at a medium,

for each barrel of sea-sticks,   £ 0   8   2¼

But a barrel of sea-sticks being only reckoned ⅔

of a barrel fully packed, ⅓ to be deducted,

which brings the bounty to ⅓ deducted, 126,115   £ 0   12   3¾

Barrels fully packed, 252,231

And if the herrings are exported, there is besides

a premium of   £ 0   2   8

So the bounty paid by government in money

for each barrel is   £ 0   14   11¾

But if to this, the duty of the salt usually taken credit for

as expended in curing each barrel, which at a medium, is,

of foreign, one bushel and ¼ of a bushel, at 10s.

a bushel, be added, viz   £ 0   12   6

the bounty on each barrel would amount to   £ 1   7   5¾

If the herrings are cured with British salt, it will stand thus, viz.

Bounty as before   £ 0   14   11¾

But if to this bounty, the duty on two bushels of Scotch salt, at 1s:6d. per bushel, supposed to be the quantity, at a medium, used in curing each barrel is added, viz.	£ 0	3	0
The bounty on each barrel will amount to	£ 0	17	11¾
And when buss herrings are entered for home consumption in Scotland, and pay the shilling a barrel of duty, the bounty stands thus, to wit, as before	£ 0	12	3¾
From which the shilling a barrel is to be deducted	£ 0	1	0
	£ 0	11	3¾
But to that there is to be added again, the duty of the foreign salt used curing a barrel of herring, viz	£ 0	12	6
So that the premium allowed for each barrel of herrings entered for home consumption is	£ 1	3	9¾
If the herrings are cured in British salt, it will stand as follows, viz. Bounty on each barrel brought in by the busses, as above	£ 0	12	3¾
From which deduct 1s. a barrel, paid at the time they are entered for home consumption	£ 0	1	0
	£ 0	11	3¾
But if to the bounty, the duty on two bushel of Scotch salt, at 1s:6d. per bushel supposed to be the quantity, at a medium, used in curing each barrel, is added, viz	£ 0	3	0
the premium for each barrel entered for home consumption will be	£ 1	14	3¾

Though the loss of duties upon herrings exported cannot, perhaps, properly be considered as bounty, that upon herrings entered for home consumption certainly may.

An Account of the Quantity of Foreign Salt imported into Scotland, and of Scotch Salt delivered Duty-free from the Works there, for the Fishery, from the 5th of April 1771 to the 5th of April 1782 with the Medium of both for one Year

Period	Foreign Salt Imported Bushels	Scotch Salt Delivered from the Works Bushels
From 5th of April 1771 to 5th of April 1782	936,974	168,226
Medium for one year	85,159½	15,293¼

It is to be observed, that the bushel of foreign salt weighs 48lbs., that of British weighs 56lbs. only.

Book V

Of the Revenue of the Sovereign or Commonwealth

CHAPTER I

Of the Expenses of the Sovereign or Commonwealth

Part I

Of the Expense of Defense

The first duty of the sovereign, that of protecting the society from the violence and invasion of other independent societies, can be performed only by means of a military force. But the expense both of preparing this military force in time of peace, and of employing it in time of war, is very different in the different states of society, in the different periods of improvement.

Among nations of hunters, the lowest and rudest state of society, such as we find it among the native tribes of North America, every man is a warrior, as well as a hunter. When he goes to war, either to defend his society, or to revenge the injuries which have been done to it by other societies, he maintains himself by his own labor, in the same manner as when he lives at home. His society (for in this state of things there is properly neither sovereign nor commonwealth) is at no sort of expense, either to prepare him for the field, or to maintain him while he is in it.

Among nations of shepherds, a more advanced state of society, such as we find it among the Tartars and Arabs, every man is, in the same manner, a warrior. Such nations have commonly no fixed habitation, but live either in tents, or in a sort of covered wagons, which are easily transported from place to place. The whole tribe, or nation, changes its situation according to the different seasons of the year, as well as according to other accidents. When its herds and flocks have consumed the forage of one part of the country, it removes to another, and from that to a third. In the dry season, it comes down to the banks of the rivers; in the wet season, it retires to the upper country. When such a nation goes to war, the warriors will not trust their herds and flocks to the feeble defense of their old men, their women and children; and their old men, their women and children, will not be left behind without defense, and without subsistence. The whole nation, besides, being accustomed to a wandering life, even in time of peace, easily takes the field in time of war. Whether it marches as an army, or moves about as a company of herdsmen, the way of life is nearly the same, though the object proposed by it be very different. They all go to war together, therefore, and everyone does as well as he can. Among the Tartars, even the women have been frequently known to engage in battle. If they conquer, whatever belongs to the hostile tribe is the recompense of the victory; but if they are vanquished, all is lost; and not only their herds and flocks, but their women and children become the booty of the conqueror. Even the greater part of those who survive the action are obliged to submit to him for the sake of immediate subsistence. The rest are commonly dissipated and dispersed in the desert.

The ordinary life, the ordinary exercise of a Tartar or Arab, prepares him sufficiently for war. Running, wrestling, cudgel-playing, throwing the javelin, drawing the bow, etc. are the common pastimes of those who live in the open air, and are all of them the images of war. When a Tartar or Arab actually goes to war, he is maintained by his own herds and flocks, which he carries with him, in the same manner as in peace. His chief or sovereign (for those nations have all chiefs or sovereigns) is at no sort of expense in preparing him for the field; and when he is in it, the chance of plunder is the only pay which he either expects or requires.

An army of hunters can seldom exceed two or three hundred men. The precarious subsistence which the chase affords, could seldom allow a greater number to keep together for any considerable time. An army of shepherds, on the contrary, may sometimes amount to two or three hundred thousand. As long as nothing stops their progress, as long as they can go on from one district, of which they have consumed the forage, to another, which is yet entire; there seems to be scarce any limit to the number who can march on together. A nation of hunters can never be formidable to the civilized nations in their neighborhood; a nation of shepherds may. Nothing can be more contemptible than an Indian war in North America; nothing, on the contrary, can be more dreadful than a Tartar invasion has frequently been in Asia. The judgment of Thucydides, that both Europe and Asia could not resist the Scythians united, has been verified by the experience of all ages. The inhabitants of the extensive, but defenseless plains of Scythia or Tartary, have been frequently united under the dominion of the chief of some conquering horde or clan; and the havoc and devastation of Asia have always signalized their union. The inhabitants of the inhospitable deserts of Arabia, the other great nation of shepherds, have never been united but once, under Mahomet and his immediate successors. Their union, which was more the effect of religious enthusiasm than of conquest, was signalized in the same manner. If the hunting nations of America should ever become shepherds, their neighborhood would be much more dangerous to the European colonies than it is at present.

In a yet more advanced state of society, among those nations of husbandmen who have little foreign commerce, and no other manufactures but those coarse and household ones, which almost every private family prepares for its own use, every man, in the same manner, either is a warrior, or easily becomes such. Those who live by agriculture generally pass the whole day in the open air, exposed to all the inclemencies of the seasons. The hardiness of their ordinary life prepares them for the fatigues of war, to some of which their necessary occupations bear a great analogy. The necessary occupation of a ditcher prepares him to work in the trenches, and to fortify a camp, as well as to enclose a field. The ordinary pastimes of such husbandmen are the same as those of shepherds, and are in the same manner the images of war. But as husbandmen have less leisure than shepherds, they are not so frequently employed in those pastimes. They are soldiers but soldiers not quite so much masters of their exercise. Such as they are, however, it seldom costs the sovereign or commonwealth any expense to prepare them for the field.

Agriculture, even in its rudest and lowest state, supposes a settlement, some sort of fixed habitation, which cannot be abandoned without great loss. When a nation of mere husbandmen, therefore, goes to war, the whole people cannot take the field together. The old men, the women and children, at least, must remain at home, to take care of the habitation. All the men of the military age, however, may take the field, and in small nations of this kind, have frequently done so. In every nation, the men of the military age are supposed to amount to about a fourth or a fifth part of the whole body of the people. If the campaign, too, should begin after seedtime, and end before harvest, both the husbandman and his principal laborers can be spared from the farm without much loss. He trusts that the work which must be done in the mean time, can be well enough executed by the old men, the women, and the children. He is not unwilling, therefore, to serve without pay during a short campaign; and it frequently costs the sovereign or commonwealth as little to maintain him in the field as to prepare him for it. The citizens of all the different states of ancient Greece seem to have served in this manner till after the second Persian war; and the people of Peloponnesus till after the Peloponnesian war. The Peloponnesians, Thucydides observes, generally left the field in the summer, and returned home to reap the harvest. The Roman people, under their kings, and during the first ages of the republic, served in the same manner. It was not till the siege of Veii, that they who staid at home began to contribute something towards maintaining those who went to war. In the European monarchies, which were founded upon the ruins of the Roman empire, both before, and for some time after, the establishment of what is properly called the feudal law, the great lords, with all their immediate dependents, used to serve the crown at their own expense. In the field, in the same manner as at home, they maintained themselves by their own revenue, and not by any stipend or pay which they received from the king upon that particular occasion.

In a more advanced state of society, two different causes contribute to render it altogether impossible that they who take the field should maintain themselves at their own expense. Those two causes are, the progress of manufactures, and the improvement in the art of war.

Though a husbandman should be employed in an expedition, provided it begins after seedtime, and ends before harvest, the interruption of his business will not always occasion any considerable diminution of his revenue. Without the intervention of his labor, Nature does herself the greater part of the work which remains to be done. But the moment that an artificer, a smith, a carpenter, or a weaver, for example, quits his workhouse, the sole source of his revenue is completely dried up. Nature does nothing for him; he does all for himself. When he takes the field, therefore, in defense of the public, as he has no revenue to maintain himself, he must necessarily be maintained by the public. But in a country, of which a great part of the inhabitants are artificers and manufacturers, a great part of the people who go to war must be drawn from those classes, and must, therefore, be maintained by the public as long as they are employed in its service.

When the art of war, too, has gradually grown up to be a very intricate and complicated science; when the event of war ceases to be determined, as in the first ages of society, by a single irregular skirmish or battle; but when the contest is generally spun out through several different campaigns, each of which lasts during the greater part of the year; it becomes universally necessary that the public should maintain those who serve the public in war, at least while they are employed in that service. Whatever, in time of peace, might be the ordinary occupation of those who go to war, so very tedious and expensive a service would otherwise be by far too heavy a burden upon them. After the second Persian war, accordingly, the armies of Athens seem to have been generally composed of mercenary troops, consisting, indeed, partly of citizens, but partly, too, of foreigners; and all of them equally hired and paid at the expense of the state. From the time of the siege of Veii, the armies of Rome received pay for their service during the time which they remained in the field. Under the feudal governments, the military service, both of the great lords, and of their immediate dependents, was, after a certain period, universally exchanged for a payment in money, which was employed to maintain those who served in their stead.

The number of those who can go to war, in proportion to the whole number of the people, is necessarily much smaller in a civilized than in a rude state of society. In a civilized society, as the soldiers are maintained altogether by the labor of those who are not soldiers, the number of the former can never exceed what the latter can maintain, over and above maintaining, in a manner suitable to their respective stations, both themselves and the other officers of government and law, whom they are obliged to maintain. In the little agrarian states of ancient Greece, a fourth or a fifth part of the whole body of the people considered the themselves as soldiers, and would sometimes, it is said, take the field. Among the civilized nations of modern Europe, it is commonly computed, that not more than the one hundredth part of the inhabitants of any country can be employed as soldiers, without ruin to the country which pays the expense of their service.

The expense of preparing the army for the field seems not to have become considerable in any nation, till long after that of maintaining it in the field had devolved entirely upon the sovereign or commonwealth. In all the different republics of ancient Greece, to learn his military exercises, was a necessary part of education imposed by the state upon every free citizen. In every city there seems to have been a public field, in which, under the protection of the public magistrate, the young people were taught their different exercises by different masters. In this very simple institution consisted the whole expense which any Grecian state seems ever to have been at, in preparing its citizens for war. In ancient Rome, the exercises of the Campus Martius answered the same purpose with those of the gymnasium in ancient Greece. Under the feudal governments, the many public ordinances, that the citizens of every district should practice archery, as well as several other military exercises, were intended for promoting the same purpose, but do not seem to have promoted it so well. Either from want of interest in the officers entrusted with the execution of those ordinances, or from some other cause, they appear to have been universally neglected; and in the progress of all those governments, military exercises seem to have gone gradually into disuse among the great body of the people.

In the republics of ancient Greece and Rome, during the whole period of their existence, and under the feudal governments, for a considerable time after their first establishment, the trade of a soldier was not a separate, distinct trade, which constituted the sole or principal occupation of a particular class of citizens; every subject of the state, whatever might be the ordinary trade or occupation by which he gained his livelihood, considered himself, upon all ordinary occasions, as fit likewise to exercise the trade of a soldier, and, upon many extraordinary occasions, as bound to exercise it.

The art of war, however, as it is certainly the noblest of all arts, so, in the progress of improvement, it necessarily becomes one of the most complicated among them. The state of the mechanical, as well as some other arts, with which it is necessarily connected, determines the degree of perfection to which it is capable of being carried at any particular time. But in order to carry it to this degree of perfection, it is necessary that it should become the sole or principal occupation of a particular class of citizens; and the division of labor is as necessary for the improvement of this, as of every other art. Into other arts, the division of labor is naturally introduced by the prudence of individuals, who find that they promote their private interest better by confining themselves to a particular trade, than by exercising a great number. But it is the wisdom of the state only, which can render the trade of a soldier a particular trade, separate and distinct from all others. A private citizen, who, in time of profound peace, and without any particular encouragement from the public, should spend the greater part of his time in military exercises, might, no doubt, both improve himself very much in them, and amuse himself very well; but he certainly would not promote his own interest. It is the wisdom of the state only, which can render it for his interest to give up the greater part of his time to this peculiar occupation; and states have not always had this wisdom, even when their circumstances had become such, that the preservation of their existence required that they should have it.

A shepherd has a great deal of leisure; a husbandman, in the rude state of husbandry, has some; an artificer or manufacturer has none at all. The first may, without any loss, employ a great deal of his time in martial exercises; the second may employ some part of it; but the last cannot employ a single hour in them without some loss, and his attention to his own interest naturally leads him to neglect them altogether. Those improvements in husbandry, too, which the progress of arts and manufactures necessarily introduces, leave the husbandman as little leisure as the artificer. Military exercises come to be as much neglected by the inhabitants of the country as by those of the town, and the great body of the people becomes altogether unwarlike. That wealth, at the same time, which always follows the improvements of agriculture and manufactures, and which, in reality, is no more than the accumulated produce of those improvements, provokes the invasion of all their neighbors. An industrious, and, upon that account, a wealthy nation, is of all nations the most likely to be attacked; and unless the state takes some new measure for the public defense, the natural habits of the people render them altogether incapable of defending themselves.

In these circumstances, there seems to be but two methods by which the state can make any tolerable provision for the public defense.

It may either, first, by means of a very rigorous police, and in spite of the whole bent of the interest, genius, and inclinations of the people, enforce the practice of military exercises, and oblige either all the citizens of the military age, or a certain number of them, to join in some measure the trade of a soldier to whatever other trade or profession they may happen to carry on.

Or, secondly, by maintaining and employing a certain number of citizens in the constant practice of military exercises, it may render the trade of a soldier a particular trade, separate and distinct from all others.

If the state has recourse to the first of those two expedients, its military force is said to consist in a militia; if to the second, it is said to consist in a standing army. The practice of military exercises is the sole or principal occupation of the soldiers of a standing army, and the maintenance or pay which the state affords them is the principal and ordinary fund of their subsistence. The practice of military exercises is only the occasional occupation of the soldiers of a militia, and they derive the principal and ordinary fund of their subsistence from some other occupation. In a militia, the character of the laborer, artificer, or tradesman, predominates over that of the soldier; in a standing army, that of the soldier predominates over every other character; and in this distinction seems to consist the essential difference between those two different species of military force.

Militias have been of several different kinds. In some countries, the citizens destined for defending the state seem to have been exercised only, without being, if I may say so, regimented; that is, without being divided into separate and distinct bodies of troops, each of which performed its exercises under its own proper and permanent officers. In the republics of ancient Greece and Rome, each citizen, as long as he remained at home, seems to have practiced his exercises, either separately and independently, or with such of his equals as he liked best; and not to have been attached to any particular body of troops, till he was actually called upon to take the field. In other countries, the militia has not only been exercised, but regimented. In England, in Switzerland, and, I believe, in every other country of modern Europe, where any imperfect military force of this kind has been established, every militiaman is, even in time of peace, attached to a particular body of troops, which performs its exercises under its own proper and permanent officers.

Before the invention of fire-arms, that army was superior in which the soldiers had, each individually, the greatest skill and dexterity in the use of their arms. Strength and agility of body were of the highest consequence, and commonly determined the fate of battles. But this skill and dexterity in the use of their arms could be acquired only, in the same manner as fencing is at present, by practicing, not in great bodies, but each man separately, in a particular school, under a particular master, or with his own particular equals and companions. Since the invention of fire-arms, strength and agility of body, or even extraordinary dexterity and skill in the use of arms, though they are far from being of no consequence, are, however, of less consequence. The nature of the weapon, though it by no means puts the awkward upon a level with the skillful, puts him more nearly so than he ever was before. All the dexterity and skill, it is supposed, which are necessary for using it, can be well enough acquired by practicing in great bodies.

Regularity, order, and prompt obedience to command, are qualities which, in modern armies, are of more importance towards determining the fate of battles, than the dexterity and skill of the soldiers in the use of their arms. But the noise of fire-arms, the smoke, and the invisible death to which every man feels himself every moment exposed, as soon as he comes within cannon-shot, and frequently a long time before the battle can be well said to be engaged, must render it very difficult to maintain any considerable degree of this regularity, order, and prompt obedience, even in the beginning of a modern battle. In an ancient battle, there was no noise but what arose from the human voice; there was no smoke, there was no invisible cause of wounds or death. Every man, till some mortal weapon actually did approach him, saw clearly that no such weapon was near him. In these circumstances, and among troops who had some confidence in their own skill and dexterity in the use of their arms, it must have been a good deal less difficult to preserve some degree of regularity and order, not only in the beginning, but through the whole progress of an ancient battle, and till one of the two armies was fairly defeated. But the habits of regularity, order, and prompt obedience to command, can be acquired only by troops which are exercised in great bodies.

A militia, however, in whatever manner it may be either disciplined or exercised, must always be much inferior to a well disciplined and well exercised standing army.

The soldiers who are exercised only once a week, or once a month, can never be so expert in the use of their arms, as those who are exercised every day, or every other day; and though this circumstance may not be of so much consequence in modern, as it was in ancient times, yet the acknowledged superiority of the Prussian troops, owing, it is said, very much to their superior expertness in their exercise, may satisfy us that it is, even at this day, of very considerable consequence.

The soldiers, who are bound to obey their officer only once a week, or once a month, and who are at all other times at liberty to manage their own affairs their own way, without being, in any respect, accountable to him, can never be under the same awe in his presence, can never have the same disposition to ready obedience, with those whose whole life and conduct are every day directed by him, and who every day even rise and go to bed, or at least retire to their quarters, according to his orders. In what is called discipline, or in the habit of ready obedience, a militia must always be still more inferior to a standing army, than it may sometimes be in what is called the manual exercise, or in the management and use of its arms. But, in modern war, the habit of ready and instant obedience is of much greater consequence than a considerable superiority in the management of arms.

Those militias which, like the Tartar or Arab militia, go to war under the same chieftains whom they are accustomed to obey in peace, are by far the best. In respect for their officers, in the habit of ready obedience, they approach nearest to standing armies The Highland militia, when it served under its own chieftains, had some advantage of the same kind. As the Highlanders, however, were not wandering, but stationary shepherds, as they had all a fixed habitation, and were not, in peaceable times, accustomed to follow their chieftain from place to place; so, in time of war, they were less willing to follow him to any considerable distance, or to continue for any long time in the field. When they had acquired any booty, they were eager to return home, and his authority was seldom sufficient to detain them. In point of obedience, they were always much inferior to what is reported of the Tartars and Arabs. As the Highlanders, too, from their stationary life, spend less of their time in the open air, they were always less accustomed to military exercises, and were less expert in the use of their arms than the Tartars and Arabs are said to be.

A militia of any kind, it must be observed, however, which has served for several successive campaigns in the field, becomes in every respect a standing army. The soldiers are every day exercised in the use of their arms, and, being constantly under the command of their officers, are habituated to the same prompt obedience which takes place in standing armies. What they were before they took the field, is of little importance. They necessarily become in every respect a standing army, after they have passed a few campaigns in it. Should the war in America drag out through another campaign, the American militia may become, in every respect, a match for that standing army, of which the valor appeared, in the last war at least, not inferior to that of the hardiest veterans of France and Spain.

This distinction being well understood, the history of all ages, it will be found, hears testimony to the irresistible superiority which a well-regulated standing army has over a militia.

One of the first standing armies, of which we have any distinct account in any well authenticated history, is that of Philip of Macedon. His frequent wars with the Thracians, Illyrians, Thessalians, and some of the Greek cities in the neighborhood of Macedon, gradually formed his troops, which in the beginning were probably militia, to the exact discipline of a standing army. When he was at peace, which he was very seldom, and never for any long time together, he was careful not to disband that army. It vanquished and subdued, after a long and violent struggle, indeed, the gallant and well exercised militias of the principal republics of ancient Greece; and afterwards, with very little struggle, the effeminate and ill exercised militia of the great Persian empire. The fall of the Greek republics, and of the Persian empire was the effect of the irresistible superiority which a standing arm has over every other sort of militia. It is the first great revolution in the affairs of mankind of which history has preserved any distinct and circumstantial account.

The fall of Carthage, and the consequent elevation of Rome, is the second. All the varieties in the fortune of those two famous republics may very well be accounted for from the same cause.

From the end of the first to the beginning of the second Carthaginian war, the armies of Carthage were continually in the field, and employed under three great generals, who succeeded one another in the command; Amilcar, his son-in-law Asdrubal, and his son Annibal: first in chastising their own rebellious slaves, afterwards in subduing the revolted nations of Africa; and lastly, in conquering the great kingdom of Spain. The army which Annibal led from Spain into Italy must necessarily, in those different wars, have been gradually formed to the exact discipline of a standing army. The Romans, in the meantime, though they had not been altogether at peace, yet they had not, during this period, been engaged in any war of very great consequence; and their military discipline, it is generally said, was a good deal relaxed. The Roman armies which Annibal encountered at Trebi, Thrasymenus, and Cannae, were militia opposed to a standing army. This circumstance, it is probable, contributed more than any other to determine the fate of those battles.

The standing army which Annibal left behind him in Spain had the like superiority over the militia which the Romans sent to oppose it; and, in a few years, under the command of his brother, the younger Asdrubal, expelled them almost entirely from that country.

Annibal was ill supplied from home. The Roman militia, being continually in the field, became, in the progress of the war, a well-disciplined and well-exercised standing army; and the superiority of Annibal grew every day less and less. Asdrubal judged it necessary to lead the whole, or almost the whole, of the standing army which he commanded in Spain, to the assistance of his brother in Italy. In this march, he is said to have been misled by his guides; and in a country which he did not know, was surprised and attacked, by another standing army, in every respect equal or superior to his own, and was entirely defeated.

When Asdrubal had left Spain, the great Scipio found nothing to oppose him but a militia inferior to his own. He conquered and subdued that militia, and, in the course of the war, his own militia necessarily became a well disciplined and well exercised standing army. That standing army was afterwards carried to Africa, where it found nothing but a militia to oppose it. In order to defend Carthage, it became necessary to recall the standing army of Annibal. The disheartened and frequently defeated African militia joined it, and, at the battle of Zama, composed the greater part of the troops of Annibal. The event of that day determined the fate of the two rival republics.

From the end of the second Carthaginian war till the fall of the Roman republic, the armies of Rome were in every respect standing armies. The standing army of Macedon made some resistance to their arms. In the height of their grandeur, it cost them two great wars, and three great battles, to subdue that little kingdom, of which the conquest would probably have been still more difficult, had it not been for the cowardice of its last king. The militias of all the civilized nations of the ancient world, of Greece, of Syria, and of Egypt, made but a feeble resistance to the standing armies of Rome. The militias of some barbarous nations defended themselves much better. The Scythian or Tartar militia, which Mithridates drew from the countries north of the Euxine and Caspian seas, were the most formidable enemies whom the Romans had to encounter after the second Carthaginian war. The Parthian and German militias, too, were always respectable, and upon several occasions, gained very considerable advantages over the Roman armies. In general, however, and when the Roman armies were well commanded, they appear to have been very much superior; and if the Romans did not pursue the final conquest either of Parthia or Germany, it was probably because they judged that it was not worth while to add those two barbarous countries to an empire which was already too large. The ancient Parthians appear to have been a nation of Scythian or Tartar extraction, and to have always retained a good deal of the manners of their ancestors. The ancient Germans were, like the Scythians or Tartars, a nation of wandering shepherds, who went to war under the same chiefs whom they were accustomed to follow in peace. Their militia was exactly of the same kind with that of the Scythians or Tartars, from whom, too, they were probably descended.

Many different causes contributed to relax the discipline of the Roman armies. Its extreme severity was, perhaps, one of those causes. In the days of their grandeur, when no enemy appeared capable of opposing them, their heavy amour was laid aside as unnecessarily burdensome, their laborious exercises were neglected, as unnecessarily toilsome. Under the Roman emperors, besides, the standing armies of Rome, those particularly which guarded the German and Pannonian frontiers, became dangerous to their masters, against whom they used frequently to set up their own generals. In order to render them less formidable, according to some authors, Dioclesian, according to others, Constantine, first withdrew them from the frontier, where they had always before been encamped in great bodies, generally of two or three legions each, and dispersed them in small bodies through the different provincial towns, from whence they were scarce ever removed, but when it became necessary to repel an invasion. Small bodies of soldiers, quartered in trading and manufacturing towns, and seldom removed from those quarters, became themselves trades men, artificers, and manufacturers. The civil came to predominate over the military character; and the standing armies of Rome gradually degenerated into a corrupt, neglected, and undisciplined militia, incapable of resisting the attack of the German and Scythian militias, which soon afterwards invaded the western empire. It was only by hiring the militia of some of those nations to oppose to that of others, that the emperors were for some time able to defend themselves. The fall of the western empire is the third great revolution in the affairs of mankind, of which ancient history has preserved any distinct or circumstantial account. It was brought about by the irresistible superiority which the militia of a barbarous has over that of a civilized nation; which the militia of a nation of shepherds has over that of a nation of husbandmen, artificers, and manufacturers. The victories which have been gained by militias have generally been, not over standing armies, but over other militias, in exercise and discipline inferior to themselves. Such were the victories which the Greek militia gained over that of the Persian empire; and such, too, were those which, in later times, the Swiss militia gained over that of the Austrians and Burgundians.

The military force of the German and Scythian nations, who established themselves upon ruins of the western empire, continued for some time to be of the same kind in their new settlements, as it had been in their original country. It was a militia of shepherds and husbandmen, which, in time of war, took the field under the command of the same chieftains whom it was accustomed to obey in peace. It was, therefore, tolerably well exercised, and tolerably well disciplined. As arts and industry advanced, however, the authority of the chieftains gradually decayed, and the great body of the people had less time to spare for military exercises. Both the discipline and the exercise of the feudal militia, therefore, went gradually to ruin, and standing armies were gradually introduced to supply the place of it. When the expedient of a standing army, besides, had once been adopted by one civilized nation, it became necessary that all its neighbors should follow the example. They soon found that their safety depended upon their doing so, and that their own militia was altogether incapable of resisting the attack of such an army.

The soldiers of a standing army, though they may never have seen an enemy, yet have frequently appeared to possess all the courage of veteran troops, and, the very moment that they took the field, to have been fit to face the hardiest and most experienced veterans. In 1756, when the Russian army marched into Poland, the valor of the Russian soldiers did not appear inferior to that of the Prussians, at that time supposed to be the hardiest and most experienced veterans in Europe. The Russian empire, however, had enjoyed a profound peace for near twenty years before, and could at that time have very few soldiers who had ever seen an enemy. When the Spanish war broke out in 1739,

England had enjoyed a profound peace for about eight-and-twenty years. The valor of her soldiers, however, far from being corrupted by that long peace, was never more distinguished than in the attempt upon Carthagena, the first unfortunate exploit of that unfortunate war. In a long peace, the generals, perhaps, may sometimes forget their skill; but where a well regulated standing army has been kept up, the soldiers seem never to forget their valor.

When a civilized nation depends for its defense upon a militia, it is at all times exposed to be conquered by any barbarous nation which happens to be in its neighborhood. The frequent conquests of all the civilized countries in Asia by the Tartars, sufficiently demonstrates the natural superiority which the militia of a barbarous has over that of a civilized nation. A well regulated standing army is superior to every militia. Such an army, as it can best be maintained by an opulent and civilized nation, so it can alone defend such a nation against the invasion of a poor and barbarous neighbor. It is only by means of a standing army, therefore, that the civilization of any country can be perpetuated, or even preserved, for any considerable time.

As it is only by means of a well-regulated standing army, that a civilized country can be defended, so it is only by means of it that a barbarous country can be suddenly and tolerably civilized. A standing army establishes, with an irresistible force, the law of the sovereign through the remotest provinces of the empire, and maintains some degree of regular government in countries which could not otherwise admit of any. Whoever examines with attention, the improvements which Peter the Great introduced into the Russian empire, will find that they almost all resolve themselves into the establishment of a well regulated standing army. It is the instrument which executes and maintains all his other regulations. That degree of order and internal peace, which that empire has ever since enjoyed, is altogether owing to the influence of that army.

Men of republican principles have been jealous of a standing army, as dangerous to liberty. It certainly is so, wherever the interest of the general, and that of the principal officers, are not necessarily connected with the support of the constitution of the state. The standing army of Caesar destroyed the Roman republic. The standing army of Cromwell turned the long parliament out of doors. But where the sovereign is himself the general, and the principal nobility and gentry of the country the chief officers of the army; where the military force is placed under the command of those who have the greatest interest in the support of the civil authority, because they have themselves the greatest share of that authority, a standing army can never be dangerous to liberty. On the contrary, it may, in some cases, be favorable to liberty. The security which it gives to the sovereign renders unnecessary that troublesome jealousy, which, in some modern republics, seems to watch over the minutest actions, and to be at all times ready to disturb the peace of every citizen. Where the security of the magistrate, though supported by the principal people of the country, is endangered by every popular discontent; where a small tumult is capable of bringing about in a few hours a great revolution, the whole authority of government must be employed to suppress and punish every murmur and complaint against it. To a sovereign, on the contrary, who feels himself supported, not only by the natural aristocracy of the country, but by a well regulated standing army, the rudest, the most groundless, and the most licentious remonstrances, can give little disturbance. He can safely pardon or neglect them, and his consciousness of his own superiority naturally disposes him to do so. That degree of liberty which approaches to licentiousness, can be tolerated only in countries where the sovereign is secured by a well-regulated standing army. It is in such countries only, that the public safety does not require that the sovereign should be trusted with any discretionary power, for suppressing even the impertinent wantonness of this licentious liberty.

The first duty of the sovereign, therefore, that of defending the society from the violence and injustice of other independent societies, grows gradually more and more expensive, as the society advances in civilization. The military force of the society, which originally cost the sovereign no expense, either in time of peace, or in time of war, must, in the progress of improvement, first be maintained by him in time of war, and afterwards even in time of peace.

The great change introduced into the art of war by the invention of fire-arms, has enhanced still further both the expense of exercising and disciplining any particular number of soldiers in time of peace, and that of employing them in time of war. Both their arms and their ammunition are become more expensive. A musket is a more expensive machine than a javelin or a bow and arrows; a cannon or a mortar, than a balista or a catapulta. The powder which is spent in a modern review is lost irrecoverably, and occasions a very considerable expense. The javelins and arrows which were thrown or shot in an ancient one, could easily be picked up again, and were, besides, of very little value. The cannon and the mortar are not only much dearer, but much heavier machines than the balista or catapulta; and require a greater expense, not only to prepare them for the field, but to carry them to it. As the superiority of the modern artillery, too, over that of the ancients, is very great; it has become much more difficult, and consequently much more expensive, to fortify a town, so as to resist, even for a few weeks, the attack of that superior artillery. In modern times, many different causes contribute to render the defense of the society more expensive. The unavoidable effects of the natural progress of improvement have, in this respect, been a good deal enhanced by a great revolution in the art of war, to which a mere accident, the invention of gunpowder, seems to have given occasion.

In modern war, the great expense of firearms gives an evident advantage to the nation which can best afford that expense; and, consequently, to an opulent and civilized, over a poor and barbarous nation. In ancient times, the opulent and civilized found it difficult to defend themselves against the poor and barbarous nations. In modern times, the poor and barbarous find it difficult to defend themselves against the opulent and civilized. The invention of fire-arms, an invention which at first sight appears to be so pernicious, is certainly favorable, both to the permanency and to the extension of civilization.

Part II

Of the Expense of Justice

The second duty of the sovereign, that of protecting, as far as possible, every member of the society from the injustice or oppression of every other member of it, or the duty of establishing an exact administration of justice, requires two very different degrees of expense in the different periods of society.

Among nations of hunters, as there is scarce any property, or at least none that exceeds the value of two or three days labor; so there is seldom any established magistrate, or any regular administration of justice. Men who have no property, can injure one another only in their persons or reputations. But when one man kills, wounds, beats, or defames another, though he to whom the injury is done suffers, he who does it receives no benefit. It is otherwise with the injuries to property. The benefit of the person who does the injury is often equal to the loss of him who suffers it. Envy, malice, or resentment, are the only passions which can prompt one man to injure another in his person or reputation. But the greater part of men are not very frequently under the influence of those passions; and the very worst men are so only occasionally. As their gratification, too, how agreeable soever it may be to certain characters, is not attended with any real or permanent advantage, it is, in the greater part of men, commonly restrained by prudential considerations. Men may live together in society with some tolerable degree of security, though there is no civil magistrate to protect them from the injustice of those passions. But avarice and ambition in the rich, in the poor the hatred of labor and the love of present ease and enjoyment, are the passions which prompt to invade property; passions much more steady in their operation, and much more universal in their influence. Wherever there is a great property, there is great inequality. For one very rich man, there must be at least five hundred poor, and the affluence of the few supposes the indigence of the many. The affluence of the rich excites the indignation of the poor, who are often both driven by want, and prompted by envy to invade his possessions. It is only under the shelter of the civil magistrate, that the owner of that valuable property, which is acquired by the labor of many years, or perhaps of many successive generations, can sleep a single night in security. He is at all times surrounded by unknown enemies, whom, though he never provoked, he can never appease, and from whose injustice he can be protected only by the powerful arm of the civil magistrate, continually held up to chastise it. The acquisition of valuable and extensive property, therefore, necessarily requires the establishment of civil government.

Where there is no property, or at least none that exceeds the value of two or three days labor, civil government is not so necessary.

Civil government supposes a certain subordination. But as the necessity of civil government gradually grows up with the acquisition of valuable property; so the principal causes, which naturally introduce subordination, gradually grow up with the growth of that valuable property.

The causes or circumstances which naturally introduce subordination, or which naturally and antecedent to any civil institution, give some men some superiority over the greater part of their brethren, seem to be four in number.

The first of those causes or circumstances, is the superiority of personal qualifications, of strength, beauty, and agility of body; of wisdom and virtue; of prudence, justice, fortitude, and moderation of mind. The qualifications of the body, unless supported by those of the mind, can give little authority in any period of society. He is a very strong man, who, by mere strength of body, can force two weak ones to obey him. The qualifications of the mind can alone give very great authority. They are however, invisible qualities; always disputable, and generally disputed. No society, whether barbarous or civilized, has ever found it convenient to settle the rules of precedence of rank and subordination, according to those invisible qualities; but according to something that is more plain and palpable.

The second of those causes or circumstances, is the superiority of age. An old man, provided his age is not so far advanced as to give suspicion of dotage, is everywhere more respected than a young man of equal rank, fortune, and abilities. Among nations of hunters, such as the native tribes of North America, age is the sole foundation of rank and precedence. Among them, father is the appellation of a superior; brother, of an equal; and son, of an inferior. In the most opulent and civilized nations, age regulates rank among those who are in every other respect equal; and among whom, therefore, there is nothing else to regulate it. Among brothers and among sisters, the eldest always takes place; and in the succession of the paternal estate, every thing which cannot be divided, but must go entire to one person, such as a title of honor, is in most cases given to the eldest. Age is a plain and palpable quality, which admits of no dispute.

The third of those causes or circumstances, is the superiority of fortune. The authority of riches, however, though great in every age of society, is, perhaps, greatest in the rudest ages of society, which admits of any considerable inequality of fortune. A Tartar chief, the increase of whose flocks and herds is sufficient to maintain a thousand men, cannot well employ that increase in any other way than in maintaining a thousand men. The rude state of his society does not afford him any manufactured produce any trinkets or baubles of any kind, for which he can exchange that part of his rude produce which is over and above his own consumption. The thousand men whom he thus maintains, depending entirely upon him for their subsistence, must both obey his orders in war, and submit to his jurisdiction in peace. He is necessarily both their general and their judge, and his chieftainship is the necessary effect of the superiority of his fortune. In an opulent and civilized society, a man may possess a much greater fortune, and yet not be able to command a dozen of people. Though the produce of his estate may be sufficient to maintain, and may, perhaps, actually maintain, more than a thousand people, yet, as those people pay for every thing which they get from him, as he gives scarce any thing to any body but in exchange for an equivalent, there is scarce anybody who considers himself as entirely dependent upon him, and his authority extends only over a few menial servants. The authority of fortune, however, is very great, even in an opulent and civilized society. That it is much greater than that either of age or of personal qualities, has been the constant complaint of every period of society which admitted of any considerable inequality of fortune. The first period of society, that of hunters, admits of no such inequality. Universal poverty establishes their universal equality; and the superiority, either of age or of personal qualities, are the feeble, but the sole foundations of authority and subordination. There is, therefore, little or no authority or subordination in this period of society. The second period of society, that of shepherds, admits of very great inequalities of fortune, and there is no period in which the superiority of fortune gives so great authority to those who possess it. There is no period, accordingly, in which authority and subordination are more perfectly established. The authority of an Arabian scherif is very great; that of a Tartar khan altogether despotical.

The fourth of those causes or circumstances, is the superiority of birth. Superiority of birth supposes an ancient superiority of fortune in the family of the person who claims it. All families are equally ancient; and the ancestors of the prince, though they may be better known, cannot well be more numerous than those of the beggar. Antiquity of family means everywhere the antiquity either of wealth, or of that greatness which is commonly either founded upon wealth, or accompanied with it. Upstart greatness is everywhere less respected than ancient greatness. The hatred of usurpers, the love of the family of an ancient monarch, are in a great measure founded upon the contempt which men naturally have for the former, and upon their veneration for the latter. As a military officer submits, without reluctance, to the authority of a superior by whom he has always been commanded, but cannot bear that his inferior should be set over his head; so men easily submit to a family to whom they and their ancestors have always submitted; but are fired with indignation when another family, in whom they had never acknowledged any such superiority, assumes a dominion over them.

The distinction of birth, being subsequent to the inequality of fortune, can have no place in nations of hunters, among whom all men, being equal in fortune, must likewise be very nearly equal in birth. The son of a wise and brave man may, indeed, even among them, be somewhat more respected than a man of equal merit, who has the misfortune to be the son of a fool or a coward. The difference, however will not be very great; and there never was, I believe, a great family in the world, whose illustration was entirely derived from the inheritance of wisdom and virtue.

The distinction of birth not only may, but always does, take place among nations of shepherds. Such nations are always strangers to every sort of luxury, and great wealth can scarce ever be dissipated among them by improvident profusion. There are no nations, accordingly, who abound more in families revered and honored on account of their descent from a long race of great and illustrious ancestors; because there are no nations among whom wealth is likely to continue longer in the same families.

Birth and fortune are evidently the two circumstances which principally set one man above another. They are the two great sources of personal distinction, and are, therefore, the principal causes which naturally establish authority and subordination among men. Among nations of shepherds, both those causes operate with their full force. The great shepherd or herdsman, respected on account of his great wealth, and of the great number of those who depend upon him for subsistence, and revered on account of the nobleness of his birth, and of the immemorial antiquity or his illustrious family, has a natural authority over all the inferior shepherds or herdsmen of his horde or clan. He can command the united force of a greater number of people than any of them. His military power is greater than that of any of them. In time of war, they are all of them naturally disposed to muster themselves under his banner, rather than under that of any other person; and his birth and fortune thus naturally procure to him some sort of executive power. By commanding, too, the united force of a greater number of people than any of them, he is best able to compel any one of them, who may have injured another, to compensate the wrong. He is the person, therefore, to whom all those who are too weak to defend themselves naturally look up for protection. It is to him that they naturally complain of the injuries which they imagine have been done to them; and his interposition, in such cases, is more easily submitted to, even by the person complained of, than that of any other person would be. His birth and fortune thus naturally procure him some sort of judicial authority.

It is in the age of shepherds, in the second period of society, that the inequality of fortune first begins to take place, and introduces among men a degree of authority and subordination, which could not possibly exist before. It thereby introduces some degree of that civil government which is indispensably necessary for its own preservation; and it seems to do this naturally, and even independent of the consideration of that necessity. The consideration of that necessity comes, no doubt, afterwards, to contribute very much to maintain and secure that authority and subordination. The rich, in particular, are necessarily interested to support that order of things, which can alone secure them in the possession of their own advantages. Men of inferior wealth combine to defend those of superior wealth in the possession of their property, in order that men of superior wealth may combine to defend them in the possession of theirs. All the inferior shepherds and herdsmen feel, that the security of their own herds and flocks depends upon the security of those of the great shepherd or herdsman; that the maintenance of their lesser authority depends upon that of his greater authority; and that upon their subordination to him depends his power of keeping their inferiors in subordination to them. They constitute a sort of little nobility, who feel themselves interested to defend the property, and to support the authority, of their own little sovereign, in order that he may be able to defend their property, and to support their authority. Civil government, so far as it is instituted for the security of property, is, in reality, instituted for the defense of the rich against the poor, or of those who have some property against those who have none at all.

The judicial authority of such a sovereign, however, far from being a cause of expense, was, for a long time, a source of revenue to him. The persons who applied to him for justice were always willing to pay for it, and a present never failed to accompany a petition. After the authority of the sovereign, too, was thoroughly established, the person found guilty, over and above the satisfaction which he was obliged to make to the party, was like-wise forced to pay an amercement to the sovereign. He had given trouble, he had disturbed, he had broke the peace of his lord the king, and for those offences an amercement was thought due. In the Tartar governments of Asia, in the governments of Europe which were founded by the German and Scythian nations who overturned the Roman empire, the administration of justice was a considerable source of revenue, both to the sovereign, and to all the lesser chiefs or lords who exercised under him any particular jurisdiction, either over some particular tribe or clan, or over some particular territory or district. Originally, both the sovereign and the inferior chiefs used to exercise this juris-diction in their own persons. Afterwards, they universally found it convenient to dele-gate it to some substitute, bailiff, or judge. This substitute, however, was still obliged to account to his principal or constituent for the profits of the jurisdiction. Whoever reads the instructions (They are to be found in Tyrol's *History of England*) which were given to the judges of the circuit in the time of Henry II will see clearly that those judges were a sort of itinerant factors, sent round the country for the purpose of levying certain branches of the king's revenue. In those days, the administration of justice not only afforded a cer-tain revenue to the sovereign, but, to procure this revenue, seems to have been one of the principal advantages which he proposed to obtain by the administration of justice.

This scheme of making the administration of justice subservient to the purposes of rev-enue, could scarce fail to be productive of several very gross abuses. The person who applied for justice with a large present in his hand, was likely to get something more than justice; while he who applied for it with a small one was likely to get something less. Justice, too, might frequently be delayed, in order that this present might be repeated. The amercement, besides, of the person complained of, might frequently suggest a very strong reason for finding him in the wrong, even when he had not really been so. That such abuses were far from being uncommon, the ancient history of every country in Europe bears witness.

When the sovereign or chief exercises his judicial authority in his own person, how much soever he might abuse it, it must have been scarce possible to get any redress; because there could seldom be any body powerful enough to call him to account. When he exer-cised it by a bailiff, indeed, redress might sometimes be had. If it was for his own benefit only, that the bailiff had been guilty of an act of injustice, the sovereign himself might not always be unwilling to punish him, or to oblige him to repair the wrong. But if it was for the benefit of his sovereign; if it was in order to make court to the person who appointed him, and who might prefer him, that he had committed any act of oppression; redress would, upon most occasions, be as impossible as if the sovereign had committed it him-self. In all barbarous governments, accordingly, in all those ancient governments of Europe in particular, which were founded upon the ruins of the Roman empire, the administra-tion of justice appears for a long time to have been extremely corrupt; far from being quite equal and impartial, even under the best monarchs, and altogether profligate under the worst.

Among nations of shepherds, where the sovereign or chief is only the greatest shepherd or herdsman of the horde or clan, he is maintained in the same manner as any of his vas-sals or subjects, by the increase of his own herds or flocks. Among those nations of hus-bandmen, who are but just come out of the shepherd state, and who are not much advanced beyond that state, such as the Greek tribes appear to have been about the time of the Trojan war, and our German and Scythian ancestors, when they first settled upon the ruins of the western empire; the sovereign or chief is, in the same manner, only the greatest landlord of the country, and is maintained in the same manner as any other landlord, by a revenue derived from his own private estate, or from what, in modern Eu-rope, was called the demesne of the crown. His subjects, upon ordinary occasions, con-tribute nothing to his support, except when, in order to protect them from the oppression of some of their fellow-subjects, they stand in need of his authority. The presents which they make him upon such occasions constitute the whole ordinary revenue, the whole of the emoluments which, except, perhaps, upon some very extraordinary emergencies, he derives from his dominion over them. When Agamemnon, in Homer, offers to Achilles, for his friendship, the sovereignty of seven Greek cities, the sole advantage which he mentions as likely to be derived from it was, that the people would honor him with presents. As long as such presents, as long as the emoluments of justice, or what may be called the fees of court, constituted, in this manner, the whole ordinary revenue which the sovereign derived from his sovereignty, it could not well be expected, it could not even decently be proposed, that he should give them up altogether. It might, and it frequently was proposed, that he should regulate and ascertain them. But after they had been so regulated and ascertained, how to hinder a person who was all-powerful from extending them beyond those regulations, was still very difficult, not to say impossible. During the continuance of this state of things, therefore, the corruption of justice, naturally resulting from the arbitrary and uncertain nature of those presents, scarce admitted of any effectual remedy.

But when, from different causes, chiefly from the continually increasing expense of defending the nation against the invasion of other nations, the private estate of the sovereign had become altogether insufficient for defraying the expense of the sovereignty; and when it had become necessary that the people should, for their own security, contribute towards this expense by taxes of different kinds; it seems to have been very commonly stipulated, that no present for the administration of justice should, under any pretence, be accepted either by the sovereign, or by his bailiffs and substitutes, the judges. Those presents, it seems to have been supposed, could more easily be abolished altogether, than effectually regulated and ascertained. Fixed salaries were appointed to the judges, which were supposed to compensate to them the loss of whatever might have been their share of the ancient emoluments of justice; as the taxes more than compensated to the sovereign the loss of his. Justice was then said to be administered gratis.

Justice, however, never was in reality administered gratis in any country. Lawyers and attorneys, at least, must always be paid by the parties; and if they were not, they would perform their duty still worse than they actually perform it. The fees annually paid to lawyers and attorneys, amount, in every court, to a much greater sum than the salaries of the judges. The circumstance of those salaries being paid by the crown, can nowhere much diminish the necessary expense of a law-suit. But it was not so much to diminish the expense, as to prevent the corruption of justice, that the judges were prohibited from receiving my present or fee from the parties.

The office of judge is in itself so very honorable, that men are willing to accept of it, though accompanied with very small emoluments. The inferior office of justice of peace, though attended with a good deal of trouble, and in most cases with no emoluments at all, is an object of ambition to the greater part of our country gentlemen. The salaries of all the different judges, high and low, together with the whole expense of the administration and execution of justice, even where it is not managed with very good economy, makes, in any civilized country, but a very inconsiderable part of the whole expense of government.

The whole expense of justice, too, might easily be defrayed by the fees of court; and, without exposing the administration of justice to any real hazard of corruption, the public revenue might thus be entirely discharged from a certain, though perhaps but a small encumbrance. It is difficult to regulate the fees of court effectually, where a person so powerful as the sovereign is to share in them and to derive any considerable part of his revenue from them. It is very easy, where the judge is the principal person who can reap any benefit from them. The law can very easily oblige the judge to respect the regulation though it might not always be able to make the sovereign respect it. Where the fees of court are precisely regulated and ascertained where they are paid all at once, at a certain period of every process, into the hands of a cashier or receiver, to be by him distributed in certain known proportions among the different judges after the process is decided and not till it is decided; there seems to be no more danger of corruption than when such fees are prohibited altogether. Those fees, without occasioning any considerable increase in the expense of a law-suit, might be rendered fully sufficient for defraying the whole expense of justice. But not being paid to the judges till the process was determined, they might be some incitement to the diligence of the court in examining and deciding it. In courts which consisted of a considerable number of judges, by proportioning the share of each judge to the number of hours and days which he had employed in examining the process, either in the court, or in a committee, by order of the court, those fees might give some encouragement to the diligence of each particular judge. Public services are never better performed, than when their reward comes only in consequence of their being performed, and is proportioned to the diligence employed in performing them. In the different parliaments of France, the fees of court (called epices and vacations) constitute the far greater part of the emoluments of the judges. After all deductions are made, the neat salary paid by the crown to a counselor or judge in the parliament of Thoulouse, in rank and dignity the second parliament of the kingdom, amounts only to 150 livres, about £6:11s. sterling a year. About seven years ago, that sum was in the same place the ordinary yearly wages of a common footman. The distribution of these epices, too, is according to the diligence of the judges. A diligent judge gains a comfortable, though moderate revenue, by his office; an idle one gets little more than his salary. Those parliaments are, perhaps, in many respects, not very convenient courts of justice; but they have never been accused; they seem never even to have been suspected of corruption.

The fees of court seem originally to have been the principal support of the different courts of justice in England. Each court endeavored to draw to itself as much business as it could, and was, upon that account, willing to take cognizance of many suits which were not originally intended to fall under its jurisdiction. The court of king's bench, instituted for the trial of criminal causes only, took cognizance of civil suits; the plaintiff pretending that the defendant, in not doing him justice, had been guilty of some trespass or misdemeanor. The court of exchequer, instituted for the levying of the king's revenue, and for enforcing the payment of such debts only as were due to the king, took cognizance of all other contract debts; the plaintiff alleging that he could not pay the king, because the defendant would not pay him. In consequence of such fictions, it came, in many cases, to depend altogether upon the parties, before what court they would choose to have their cause tried, and each court endeavored, by superior dispatch and impartiality, to draw to itself as many causes as it could. The present admirable constitution of the courts of justice in England was, perhaps, originally, in a great measure, formed by this emulation, which anciently took place between their respective judges: each judge endeavoring to give, in his own court, the speediest and most effectual remedy which the law would admit, for every sort of injustice. Originally, the courts of law gave damages only for breach of contract. The court of chancery, as a court of conscience, first took upon it to enforce the specific performance of agreements. When the breach of contract consisted in the non-payment of money, the damage sustained could be compensated in no other way than by ordering payment, which was equivalent to a specific performance of the agreement. In such cases, therefore, the remedy of the courts of law was sufficient. It was not so in others. When the tenant sued his lord for having unjustly ousted him of his lease, the damages which he recovered were by no means equivalent to the possession of the land. Such causes, therefore, for some time, went all to the court of chancery, to the no small loss of the courts of law. It was to draw back such causes to themselves, that the courts of law are said to have invented the artificial and fictitious writ of ejectment, the most effectual remedy for an unjust outer or dispossession of land.

A stamp-duty upon the law proceedings of each particular court, to be levied by that court, and applied towards the maintenance of the judges, and other officers belonging to it, might in the same manner, afford a revenue sufficient for defraying the expense of the administration of justice, without bringing any burden upon the general revenue of the society. The judges, indeed, might in this case, be under the temptation of multiplying unnecessarily the proceedings upon every cause, in order to increase, as much as possible, the produce of such a stamp-duty. It has been the custom in modern Europe to regulate, upon most occasions, the payment of the attorneys and clerks of court according to the number of pages which they had occasion to write; the court, however, requiring that each page should contain so many lines, and each line so many words. In order to increase their payment, the attorneys and clerks have contrived to multiply words beyond all necessity, to the corruption of the law language of, I believe, every court of justice in Europe. A like temptation might, perhaps, occasion a like corruption in the form of law proceedings.

But whether the administration of justice be so contrived as to defray its own expense, or whether the judges be maintained by fixed salaries paid to them from some other fund, it does not seem necessary that the person or persons entrusted with the executive power should be charged with the management of that fund, or with the payment of those salaries. That fund might arise from the rent of landed estates, the management of each estate being entrusted to the particular court which was to be maintained by it. That fund might arise even from the interest of a sum of money, the lending out of which might, in the same manner, be entrusted to the court which was to be maintained by it. A part, though indeed but a small part of the salary of the judges of the court of session in Scotland, arises from the interest of a sum of money. The necessary instability of such a fund seems, however, to render it an improper one for the maintenance of an institution which ought to last for ever.

The separation of the judicial from the executive power, seems originally to have arisen from the increasing business of the society, in consequence of its increasing improvement. The administration of justice became so laborious and so complicated a duty, as to require the undivided attention of the person to whom it was entrusted. The person entrusted with the executive power, not having leisure to attend to the decision of private causes himself, a deputy was appointed to decide them in his stead. In the progress of the Roman greatness, the consul was too much occupied with the political affairs of the state, to attend to the administration of justice. A praetor, therefore, was appointed to administer it in his stead. In the progress of the European monarchies, which were founded upon the ruins of the Roman empire, the sovereigns and the great lords came universally to consider the administration of justice as an office both too laborious and too ignoble for them to execute in their own persons. They universally, therefore, discharged themselves of it, by appointing a deputy, bailiff or judge.

When the judicial is united to the executive power, it is scarce possible that justice should not frequently be sacrificed to what is vulgarly called politics. The persons entrusted with the great interests of the state may even without any corrupt views, sometimes imagine it necessary to sacrifice to those interests the rights of a private man. But upon the impartial administration of justice depends the liberty of every individual, the sense which he has of his own security. In order to make every individual feel himself perfectly secure in the possession of every right which belongs to him, it is not only necessary that the judicial should be separated from the executive power, but that it should be rendered as much as possible independent of that power. The judge should not be liable to be removed from his office according to the caprice of that power. The regular payment of his salary should not depend upon the good will, or even upon the good economy of that power.

Part III

Of the Expense of Public Works and Public Institutions

The third and last duty of the sovereign or commonwealth, is that of erecting and maintaining those public institutions and those public works, which though they may be in the highest degree advantageous to a great society, are, however, of such a nature, that the profit could never repay the expense to any individual, or small number of individuals; and which it, therefore, cannot be expected that any individual, or small number of individuals, should erect or maintain. The performance of this duty requires, too, very different degrees of expense in the different periods of society.

After the public institutions and public works necessary for the defense of the society, and for the administration of justice, both of which have already been mentioned, the other works and institutions of this kind are chiefly for facilitating the commerce of the society, and those for promoting the instruction of the people. The institutions for instruction are of two kinds: those for the education of the youth, and those for the instruction of people of all ages. The consideration of the manner in which the expense of those different sorts of public works and institutions may be most properly defrayed will divide this third part of the present chapter into three different articles.

ARTICLE I

Of the Public Works and Institutions for Facilitating the Commerce of the Society

AND, FIRST, OF THOSE WHICH ARE NECESSARY FOR FACILITATING COMMERCE IN GENERAL

That the erection and maintenance of the public works which facilitate the commerce of any country, such as good roads, bridges, navigable canals, harbors, etc. must require very different degrees of expense in the different periods of society, is evident without any proof. The expense of making and maintaining the public roads of any country must evidently increase with the annual produce of the land and labor of that country, or with the quantity and weight of the goods which it becomes necessary to fetch and carry upon those roads. The strength of a bridge must be suited to the number and weight of the carriages which are likely to pass over it. The depth and the supply of water for a navigable canal must be proportioned to the number and tonnage of the lighters which are likely to carry goods upon it; the extent of a harbor, to the number of the shipping which are likely to take shelter in it.

It does not seem necessary that the expense of those public works should be defrayed from that public revenue, as it is commonly called, of which the collection and application are in most countries, assigned to the executive power. The greater part of such public works may easily be so managed, as to afford a particular revenue, sufficient for defraying their own expense without bringing any burden upon the general revenue of the society.

A highway, a bridge, a navigable canal, for example, may, in most cases, be both made and maintained by a small toll upon the carriages which make use of them; a harbor, by a moderate port-duty upon the tonnage of the shipping which load or unload in it. The coinage, another institution for facilitating commerce, in many countries, not only defrays its own expense, but affords a small revenue or a seignorage to the sovereign. The post-office, another institution for the same purpose, over and above defraying its own expense, affords, in almost all countries, a very considerable revenue to the sovereign.

When the carriages which pass over a highway or a bridge, and the lighters which sail upon a navigable canal, pay toll in proportion to their weight or their tonnage, they pay for the maintenance of those public works exactly in proportion to the wear and tear which they occasion of them. It seems scarce possible to invent a more equitable way of maintaining such works. This tax or toll, too, though it is advanced by the carrier, is finally paid by the consumer, to whom it must always be charged in the price of the goods. As the expense of carriage, however, is very much reduced by means of such public works, the goods, notwithstanding the toll, come cheaper to the consumer than they could otherwise have done, their price not being so much raised by the toll, as it is lowered by the cheapness of the carriage. The person who finally pays this tax, therefore, gains by the application more than he loses by the payment of it. His payment is exactly in proportion to his gain. It is, in reality, no more than a part of that gain which he is obliged to give up, in order to get the rest. It seems impossible to imagine a more equitable method of raising a tax.

When the toll upon carriages of luxury, upon coaches, post-chaises, etc. is made somewhat higher in proportion to their weight, than upon carriages of necessary use, such as carts, wagons, etc. the indolence and vanity of the rich is made to contribute, in a very easy manner, to the relief of the poor, by rendering cheaper the transportation of heavy goods to all the different parts of the country.

When high-roads, bridges, canals, etc. are in this manner made and supported by the commerce which is carried on by means of them, they can be made only where that commerce requires them, and, consequently, where it is proper to make them. Their expense, too, their grandeur and magnificence, must be suited to what that commerce can afford to pay. They must be made, consequently, as it is proper to make them. A magnificent high-road cannot be made through a desert country, where there is little or no commerce, or merely because it happens to lead to the country villa of the intendant of the province, or to that of some great lord, to whom the intendant finds it convenient to make his court. A great bridge cannot be thrown over a river at a place where nobody passes, or merely to embellish the view from the windows of a neighboring palace; things which sometimes happen in countries, where works of this kind are carried on by any other revenue than that which they themselves are capable of affording.

In several different parts of Europe, the toll or lock-duty upon a canal is the property of private persons, whose private interest obliges them to keep up the canal. If it is not kept in tolerable order, the navigation necessarily ceases altogether, and, along with it, the whole profit which they can make by the tolls. If those tolls were put under the management of commissioners, who had themselves no interest in them, they might be less attentive to the maintenance of the works which produced them. The canal of Languedoc cost the king of France and the province upwards of thirteen millions of livres, which (at twenty-eight livres the mark of silver, the value of French money in the end of the last century) amounted to upwards of nine hundred thousand pounds sterling. When that great work was finished, the most likely method, it was found, of keeping it in constant repair, was to make a present of the tolls to Riquet, the engineer who planned and conducted the work. Those tolls constitute, at present, a very large estate to the different branches of the family of that gentleman, who have, therefore, a great interest to keep the work in constant repair. But had those tolls been put under the management of commissioners, who had no such interest, they might perhaps, have been dissipated in ornamental and unnecessary expenses, while the most essential parts of the works were allowed to go to ruin.

The tolls for the maintenance of a highroad cannot, with any safety, be made the property of private persons. A high-road, though entirely neglected, does not become altogether impassable, though a canal does. The proprietors of the tolls upon a high-road, therefore, might neglect altogether the repair of the road, and yet continue to levy very nearly the same tolls. It is proper, therefore, that the tolls for the maintenance of such a work should be put under the management of commissioners or trustees.

In Great Britain, the abuses which the trustees have committed in the management of those tolls, have, in many cases, been very justly complained of. At many turnpikes, it has been said, the money levied is more than double of what is necessary for executing, in the completest manner, the work, which is often executed in a very slovenly manner, and sometimes not executed at all. The system of repairing the high-roads by tolls of this kind, it must be observed, is not of very long standing. We should not wonder, therefore, if it has not yet been brought to that degree of perfection of which it seems capable. If mean and improper persons are frequently appointed trustees; and if proper courts of inspection and account have not yet been established for controlling their conduct, and for reducing the tolls to what is barely sufficient for executing the work to be done by them; the recency of the institution both accounts and apologizes for those defects, of which, by the wisdom of parliament, the greater part may, in due time, be gradually remedied.

The money levied at the different turnpikes in Great Britain, is supposed to exceed so much what is necessary for repairing the roads, that the savings which, with proper economy, might be made from it, have been considered, even by some ministers, as a very great resource, which might, at some time or another, be applied to the exigencies of the state. Government, it has been said, by taking the management of the turnpikes into its own hands, and by employing the soldiers, who would work for a very small addition to their pay, could keep the roads in good order, at a much less expense than it can be done by trustees, who have no other workmen to employ, but such as derive their whole subsistence from their wages. A great revenue, half a million, perhaps {Since publishing the two first editions of this book, I have got good reasons to believe that all the turnpike tolls levied in Great Britain do not produce a neat revenue that amounts to half a million; a sum which, under the management of government, would not be sufficient to keep, in repair five of the principal roads in the kingdom}, it has been pretended, might in this manner be gained, without laying any new burden upon the people; and the turnpike roads might be made to contribute to the general expense of the state, in the same manner as the post-office does at present.

That a considerable revenue might be gained in this manner, I have no doubt, though probably not near so much as the projectors of this plan have supposed. The plan itself, however, seems liable to several very important objections.

First, if the tolls which are levied at the turnpikes should ever be considered as one of the resources for supplying the exigencies of the state, they would certainly be augmented as those exigencies were supposed to require. According to the policy of Great Britain, therefore, they would probably he augmented very fast. The facility with which a great revenue could be drawn from them, would probably encourage administration to recur very frequently to this resource. Though it may, perhaps, be more than doubtful whether half a million could by any economy be saved out of the present tolls, it can scarcely be doubted, but that a million might be saved out of them, if they were doubled; and perhaps two millions, if they were tripled. {I have now good reason to believe that all these conjectural sums are by much too large.} This great revenue, too, might be levied without the appointment of a single new officer to collect and receive it. But the turnpike tolls, being continually augmented in this manner, instead of facilitating the inland commerce of the country, as at present, would soon become a very great encumbrance upon it. The expense of transporting all heavy goods from one part of the country to another, would soon be so much increased, the market for all such goods, consequently, would soon be so much narrowed, that their production would be in a great measure discouraged, and the most important branches of the domestic industry of the country annihilated altogether.

Secondly, a tax upon carriages, in proportion to their weight, though a very equal tax when applied to the sole purpose of repairing the roads, is a very unequal one when applied to any other purpose, or to supply the common exigencies of the state. When it is applied to the sole purpose above mentioned, each carriage is supposed to pay exactly for the wear and tear which that carriage occasions of the roads. But when it is applied to any other purpose, each carriage is supposed to pay for more than that wear and tear, and contributes to the supply of some other exigency of the state. But as the turnpike toll raises the price of goods in proportion to their weight and not to their value, it is chiefly paid by the consumers of coarse and bulky, not by those of precious and light commodities. Whatever exigency of the state, therefore, this tax might be intended to supply, that exigency would be chiefly supplied at the expense of the poor, not of the rich; at the expense of those who are least able to supply it, not of those who are most able.

Thirdly, if government should at any time neglect the reparation of the high-roads, it would be still more difficult, than it is at present, to compel the proper application of any part of the turnpike tolls. A large revenue might thus be levied upon the people, without any part of it being applied to the only purpose to which a revenue levied in this manner ought ever to be applied. If the meanness and poverty of the trustees of turnpike roads render it sometimes difficult, at present, to oblige them to repair their wrong; their wealth and greatness would render it ten times more so in the case which is here supposed.

In France, the funds destined for the reparation of the high-roads are under the immediate direction of the executive power. Those funds consist, partly in a certain number of days labor, which the country people are in most parts of Europe obliged to give to the reparation of the highways; and partly in such a portion of the general revenue of the state as the king chooses to spare from his other expenses.

By the ancient law of France, as well as by that of most other parts of Europe, the labor of the country people was under the direction of a local or provincial magistracy, which had no immediate dependency upon the king's council. But, by the present practice, both the labor of the country people, and whatever other fund the king may choose to assign for the reparation of the high-roads in any particular province or generality, are entirely under the management of the intendant; an officer who is appointed and removed by the king's council who receives his orders from it, and is in constant correspondence with it. In the progress of despotism, the authority of the executive power gradually absorbs that of every other power in the state, and assumes to itself the management of every branch of revenue which is destined for any public purpose. In France, however, the great post-roads, the roads which make the communication between the principal towns of the kingdom, are in general kept in good order; and, in some provinces, are even a good deal superior to the greater part of the turnpike roads of England. But what we call the cross roads, that is, the far greater part of the roads in the country, are entirely neglected, and are in many places absolutely impassable for any heavy carriage. In some places it is even dangerous to travel on horseback, and mules are the only conveyance which can safely be trusted. The proud minister of an ostentatious court, may frequently take pleasure in executing a work of splendor and magnificence, such as a great highway, which is frequently seen by the principal nobility, whose applauses not only flatter his vanity, but even contribute to support his interest at court. But to execute a great number of little works, in which nothing that can be done can make any great appearance, or excite the smallest degree of admiration in any traveler, and which, in short, have nothing to recommend them but their extreme utility, is a business which appears, in every respect, too mean and paltry to merit the attention of so great a magistrate. Under such an administration therefore, such works are almost always entirely neglected.

In China, and in several other governments of Asia, the executive power charges itself both with the reparation of the high-roads, and with the maintenance of the navigable canals. In the instructions which are given to the governor of each province, those objects, it is said, are constantly recommended to him, and the judgment which the court forms of his conduct is very much regulated by the attention which he appears to have paid to this part of his instructions. This branch of public police, accordingly, is said to be very much attended to in all those countries, but particularly in China, where the high-roads, and still more the navigable canals, it is pretended, exceed very much every thing of the same kind which is known in Europe. The accounts of those works, however, which have been transmitted to Europe, have generally been drawn up by weak and wondering travelers; frequently by stupid and lying missionaries. If they had been examined by more intelligent eyes, and if the accounts of them had been reported by more faithful witnesses, they would not, perhaps, appear to be so wonderful. The account which Bernier gives of some works of this kind in Indostan, falls very short of what had been reported of them by other travelers, more disposed to the marvelous than he was. It may too, perhaps, be in those countries, as it is in France, where the great roads, the great communications, which are likely to be the subjects of conversation at the court and in the capital, are attended to, and all the rest neglected. In China, besides, in Indostan, and in several other governments of Asia, the revenue of the sovereign arises almost altogether from a land tax or land rent, which rises or falls with the rise and fall of the annual produce of the land. The great interest of the sovereign, therefore, his revenue, is in such countries necessarily and immediately connected with the cultivation of the land, with the greatness of its produce, and with the value of its produce. But in order to render that produce both as great and as valuable as possible, it is necessary to procure to it as extensive a market as possible, and consequently to establish the freest, the easiest, and the least expensive communication between all the different parts of the country; which can be done only by means of the best roads and the best navigable canals. But the revenue of the sovereign does not, in any part of Europe, arise chiefly from a land tax or land rent. In all the great kingdoms of Europe, perhaps, the greater part of it may ultimately depend upon the produce of the land, but that dependency is neither so immediate nor so evident. In Europe, therefore, the sovereign does not feel himself so directly called upon to promote the increase, both in quantity and value of the produce of the land, or, by maintaining good roads and canals, to provide the most extensive market for that produce. Though it should be true, therefore, what I apprehend is not a little doubtful, that in some parts of Asia this department of the public police is very properly managed by the executive power, there is not the least probability that, during the present state of things, it could be tolerably managed by that power in any part of Europe.

Even those public works, which are of such a nature that they cannot afford any revenue for maintaining themselves, but of which the convenience is nearly confined to some particular place or district, are always better maintained by a local or provincial revenue, under the management of a local and provincial administration, than by the general revenue of the state, of which the executive power must always have the management. Were the streets of London to be lighted and paved at the expense of the treasury, is there any probability that they would be so well lighted and paved as they are at present, or even at so small an expense? The expense, besides, instead of being raised by a local tax upon the inhabitants of each particular street, parish, or district in London, would, in this case, be defrayed out of the general revenue of the state, and would consequently be raised by a tax upon all the inhabitants of the kingdom, of whom the greater part derive no sort of benefit from the lighting and paving of the streets of London.

The abuses which sometimes creep into the local and provincial administration of a local and provincial revenue, how enormous soever they may appear, are in reality, however, almost always very trifling in comparison of those which commonly take place in the administration and expenditure of the revenue of a great empire. They are, besides, much more easily corrected. Under the local or provincial administration of the justices of the peace in Great Britain, the six days labor which the country people are obliged to give to the reparation of the highways, is not always, perhaps, very judiciously applied, but it is scarce ever exacted with any circumstance of cruelty or oppression. In France, under the administration of the intendants, the application is not always more judicious, and the exaction is frequently the most cruel and oppressive. Such corvees, as they are called, make one of the principal instruments of tyranny by which those officers chastise any parish or communeaute, which has had the misfortune to fall under their displeasure.

OF THE PUBLIC WORKS AND INSTITUTION WHICH ARE NECESSARY FOR FACILITATING PARTICULAR BRANCHES OF COMMERCE

The object of the public works and institutions above mentioned, is to facilitate commerce in general. But in order to facilitate some particular branches of it, particular institutions are necessary, which again require a particular and extraordinary expense.

Some particular branches of commerce which are carried on with barbarous and uncivilized nations, require extraordinary protection. An ordinary store or counting-house could give little security to the goods of the merchants who trade to the western coast of Africa. To defend them from the barbarous natives, it is necessary that the place where they are deposited should be in some measure fortified. The disorders in the government of Indostan have been supposed to render a like precaution necessary, even among that mild and gentle people; and it was under pretence of securing their persons and property from violence, that both the English and French East India companies were allowed to erect the first forts which they possessed in that country. Among other nations, whose vigorous government will suffer no strangers to possess any fortified place within their territory, it may be necessary to maintain some ambassador, minister, or consul, who may both decide, according to their own customs, the differences arising among his own countrymen, and, in their disputes with the natives, may by means of his public character, interfere with more authority and afford them a more powerful protection than they could expect from any private man. The interests of commerce have frequently made it necessary to maintain ministers in foreign countries, where the purposes either of war or alliance would not have required any. The commerce of the Turkey company first occasioned the establishment of an ordinary ambassador at Constantinople. The first English embassies to Russia arose altogether from commercial interests. The constant interference with those interests, necessarily occasioned between the subjects of the different states of Europe, has probably introduced the custom of keeping, in all neighboring countries, ambassadors or ministers constantly resident, even in the time of peace. This custom, unknown to ancient times, seems not to be older than the end of the fifteenth, or beginning of the sixteenth century; that is, than the time when commerce first began to extend itself to the greater part of the nations of Europe, and when they first began to attend to its interests.

It seems not unreasonable, that the extraordinary expense which the protection of any particular branch of commerce may occasion, should be defrayed by a moderate tax upon that particular branch; by a moderate fine, for example, to be paid by the traders when they first enter into it; or, what is more equal, by a particular duty of so much percent upon the goods which they either import into, or export out of, the particular countries with which it is carried on. The protection of trade, in general, from pirates and freebooters, is said to have given occasion to the first institution of the duties of customs. But, if it was thought reasonable to lay a general tax upon trade, in order to defray the expense of protecting trade in general, it should seem equally reasonable to lay a particular tax upon a particular branch of trade, in order to defray the extraordinary expense of protecting that branch.

The protection of trade, in general, has always been considered as essential to the defense of the commonwealth, and, upon that account, a necessary part of the duty of the executive power. The collection and application of the general duties of customs, therefore, have always been left to that power. But the protection of any particular branch of trade is a part of the general protection of trade; a part, therefore, of the duty of that power; and if nations always acted consistently, the particular duties levied for the purposes of such particular protection, should always have been left equally to its disposal. But in this respect, as well as in many others, nations have not always acted consistently; and in the greater part of the commercial states of Europe, particular companies of merchants have had the address to persuade the legislature to entrust to them the performance of this part of the duty of the sovereign, together with all the powers which are necessarily connected with it.

These companies, though they may, perhaps, have been useful for the first introduction of some branches of commerce, by making, at their own expense, an experiment which the state might not think it prudent to make, have in the long-run proved, universally, either burdensome or useless, and have either mismanaged or confined the trade.

When those companies do not trade upon a joint stock, but are obliged to admit any person, properly qualified, upon paying a certain fine, and agreeing to submit to the regulations of the company, each member trading upon his own stock, and at his own risk, they are called regulated companies. When they trade upon a joint stock, each member sharing in the common profit or loss, in proportion to his share in this stock, they are called joint-stock companies. Such companies, whether regulated or joint-stock, sometimes have, and sometimes have not, exclusive privileges.

Regulated companies resemble, in every respect, the corporation of trades, so common in the cities and towns of all the different countries of Europe; and are a sort of enlarged monopolies of the same kind. As no inhabitant of a town can exercise an incorporated trade, without first obtaining his freedom in the incorporation, so, in most cases, no subject of the state can lawfully carry on any branch of foreign trade, for which a regulated company is established, without first becoming a member of that company. The monopoly is more or less strict, according as the terms of admission are more or less difficult, and according as the directors of the company have more or less authority, or have it more or less in their power to manage in such a manner as to confine the greater part of the trade to themselves and their particular friends. In the most ancient regulated companies, the privileges of apprenticeship were the same as in other corporations, and entitled the person who had served his time to a member of the company, to become himself a member, either without paying any fine, or upon paying a much smaller one than what was exacted of other people. The usual corporation spirit, wherever the law does not restrain it, prevails in all regulated companies. When they have been allowed to act according to their natural genius, they have always, in order to confine the competition to as small a number of persons as possible, endeavored to subject the trade to many burdensome regulations. When the law has restrained them from doing this, they have become altogether useless and insignificant.

The regulated companies for foreign commerce which at present subsist in Great Britain, are the ancient merchant-adventurers company, now commonly called the Hamburgh company, the Russia company, the Eastland company, the Turkey company, and the African company.

The terms of admission into the Hamburgh company are now said to be quite easy; and the directors either have it not in their power to subject the trade to any troublesome restraint or regulations, or, at least, have not of late exercised that power. It has not always been so. About the middle of the last century, the fine for admission was fifty, and at one time one hundred pounds, and the conduct of the company was said to be extremely oppressive. In 1643, in 1645, and in 1661, the clothiers and free traders of the west of England complained of them to parliament, as of monopolists, who confined the trade, and oppressed the manufactures of the country. Though those complaints produced no act of parliament, they had probably intimidated the company so far, as to oblige them to reform their conduct. Since that time, at least, there have been no complaints against them. By the 10th and 11th of William III c. 6, the fine for admission into the Russia company was reduced to five pounds; and by the 25th of Charles II c. 7, that for admission into the Eastland company to forty shillings; while, at the same time, Sweden, Denmark, and Norway, all the countries on the north side of the Baltic, were exempted from their exclusive charter. The conduct of those companies had probably given occasion to those two acts of parliament. Before that time, Sir Josiah Child had represented both these and the Hamburgh company as extremely oppressive, and imputed to their bad management the low state of the trade, which we at that time carried on to the countries comprehended within their respective charters. But though such companies may not, in the present times, be very oppressive, they are certainly altogether useless. To be merely useless, indeed, is perhaps, the highest eulogy which can ever justly be bestowed upon a regulated company; and all the three companies above mentioned seem, in their present state, to deserve this eulogy.

The fine for admission into the Turkey company was formerly twenty-five pounds for all persons under twenty-six years of age, and fifty pounds for all persons above that age. Nobody but mere merchants could be admitted; a restriction which excluded all shopkeepers and retailers. By a bylaw, no British manufactures could be exported to Turkey but in the general ships of the company; and as those ships sailed always from the port of London, this restriction confined the trade to that expensive port, and the traders to those who lived in London and in its neighborhood. By another bylaw, no person living within twenty miles of London, and not free of the city, could be admitted a member; another restriction which, joined to the foregoing, necessarily excluded all but the freemen of London. As the time for the loading and sailing of those general ships depended altogether upon the directors, they could easily fill them with their own goods, and those of their particular friends, to the exclusion of others, who, they might pretend, had made their proposals too late. In this state of things, therefore, this company was, in every respect, a strict and oppressive monopoly. Those abuses gave occasion to the act of the 26th of George II c. 18, reducing the fine for admission to twenty pounds for all persons, without any distinction of ages, or any restriction, either to mere merchants, or to the freemen of London; and granting to all such persons the liberty of exporting, from all the ports of Great Britain, to any port in Turkey, all British goods, of which the exportation was not prohibited, upon paying both the general duties of customs, and the particular duties assessed for defraying the necessary expenses of the company; and submitting, at the same time, to the lawful authority of the British ambassador and consuls resident in Turkey, and to the bylaws of the company duly enacted. To prevent any oppression by those bylaws, it was by the same act ordained, that if any seven members of the company conceived themselves aggrieved by any bylaw which should be enacted after the passing of this act, they might appeal to the board of trade and plantations (to the authority of which a committee of the privy council has now succeeded), provided such appeal was brought within twelve months after the bylaw was enacted; and that, if any seven members conceived themselves aggrieved by any bylaw which had been enacted before the passing of this act, they might bring a like appeal, provided it was within twelve months after the day on which this act was to take place. The experience of one year, however, may not always be sufficient to discover to all the members of a great company the pernicious tendency of a particular bylaw; and if several of them should afterwards discover it, neither the board of trade, nor the committee of council, can afford them any redress. The object, besides, of the greater part of the bylaws of all regulated companies, as well as of all other corporations, is not so much to oppress those who are already members, as to discourage others from becoming so; which may be done, not only by a high fine, but by many other contrivances. The constant view of such companies is always to raise the rate of their own profit as high as they can; to keep the market, both for the goods which they export, and for those which they import, as much understocked as they can; which can be done only by restraining the competition, or by discouraging new adventurers from entering into the trade. A fine, even of twenty pounds, besides, though it may not, perhaps, be sufficient to discourage any man from entering into the Turkey trade, with an intention to continue in it, may be enough to discourage a speculative merchant from hazarding a single adventure in it. In all trades, the regular established traders, even though not incorporated, naturally combine to raise profits, which are noway so likely to be kept, at all times, down to their proper level, as by the occasional competition of speculative adventurers. The Turkey trade, though in some measure laid open by this act of parliament, is still considered by many people as very far from being altogether free. The Turkey company contribute to maintain an ambassador and two or three consuls, who, like other public ministers, ought to be maintained altogether by the state, and the trade laid open to all his majesty's subjects. The different taxes levied by the company, for this and other corporation purposes, might afford a revenue much more than sufficient to enable a state to maintain such ministers.

Regulated companies, it was observed by Sir Josiah Child, though they had frequently supported public ministers, had never maintained any forts or garrisons in the countries to which they traded; whereas joint-stock companies frequently had. And, in reality, the former seem to be much more unfit for this sort of service than the latter. First, the directors of a regulated company have no particular interest in the prosperity of the general trade of the company, for the sake of which such forts and garrisons are maintained. The decay of that general trade may even frequently contribute to the advantage of their own private trade; as, by diminishing the number of their competitors, it may enable them both to buy cheaper, and to sell dearer. The directors of a joint-stock company, on the contrary, having only their share in the profits which are made upon the common stock committed to their management, have no private trade of their own, of which the interest can be separated from that of the general trade of the company. Their private interest is connected with the prosperity of the general trade of the company, and with the maintenance of the forts and garrisons which are necessary for its defense. They are more likely, therefore, to have that continual and careful attention which that maintenance necessarily requires. Secondly, the directors of a joint-stock company have always the management of a large capital, the joint stock of the company, a part of which they may frequently employ, with propriety, in building, repairing, and maintaining such necessary forts and garrisons. But the directors of a regulated company, having the management of no common capital, have no other fund to employ in this way, but the casual revenue arising from the admission fines, and from the corporation duties imposed upon the trade of the company. Though they had the same interest, therefore, to attend to the maintenance of such forts and garrisons, they can seldom have the same ability to render that attention effectual. The maintenance of a public minister, requiring scarce any attention, and but a moderate and limited expense, is a business much more suitable both to the temper and abilities of a regulated company.

Long after the time of Sir Josiah Child, however, in 1750, a regulated company was established, the present company of merchants trading to Africa; which was expressly charged at first with the maintenance of all the British forts and garrisons that lie between Cape Blanc and the Cape of Good Hope, and afterwards with that of those only which lie between Cape Rouge and the Cape of Good Hope. The act which establishes this company (the 23rd of George II c. 51), seems to have had two distinct objects in view; first, to restrain effectually the oppressive and monopolizing spirit which is natural to the directors of a regulated company; and, secondly, to force them, as much as possible, to give an attention, which is not natural to them, towards the maintenance of forts and garrisons.

For the first of these purposes, the fine for admission is limited to forty shillings. The company is prohibited from trading in their corporate capacity, or upon a joint stock; from borrowing money upon common seal, or from laying any restraints upon the trade, which may be carried on freely from all places, and by all persons being British subjects, and paying the fine. The government is in a committee of nine persons, who meet at London, but who are chosen annually by the freemen of the company at London, Bristol, and Liverpool; three from each place. No committee-man can be continued in office for more than three years together. Any committee-man might be removed by the board of trade and plantations, now by a committee of council, after being heard in his own defense. The committee are forbid to export negroes from Africa, or to import any African goods into Great Britain. But as they are charged with the maintenance of forts and garrisons, they may, for that purpose export from Great Britain to Africa goods and stores of different kinds. Out of the moneys which they shall receive from the company, they are allowed a sum, not exceeding eight hundred pounds, for the salaries of their clerks and agents at London, Bristol, and Liverpool, the house-rent of their offices at London, and all other expenses of management, commission, and agency, in England. What remains of this sum, after defraying these different expenses, they may divide among themselves, as compensation for their trouble, in what manner they think proper. By this constitution, it might have been expected, that the spirit of monopoly would have been effectually restrained, and the first of these purposes sufficiently answered. It would seem, however, that it had not. Though by the 4th of George III c. 20, the fort of Senegal, with all its dependencies, had been invested in the company of merchants trading to Africa, yet, in the year following (by the 5th of George III c. 44), not only Senegal and its dependencies, but the whole coast, from the port of Sallee, in South Barbary, to Cape Rouge, was exempted from the jurisdiction of that company, was vested in the crown, and the trade to it declared free to all his majesty's subjects. The company had been suspected of restraining the trade and of establishing some sort of improper monopoly. It is not, however, very easy to conceive how, under the regulations of the 23d George II they could do so. In the printed debates of the house of commons, not always the most authentic records of truth, I observe, however, that they have been accused of this. The members of the committee of nine being all merchants, and the governors and factors in their different forts and settlements being all dependent upon them, it is not unlikely that the latter might have given peculiar attention to the consignments and commissions of the former, which would establish a real monopoly.

For the second of these purposes, the maintenance of the forts and garrisons, an annual sum has been allotted to them by parliament, generally about £13,000. For the proper application of this sum, the committee is obliged to account annually to the cursitor baron of exchequer; which account is afterwards to be laid before parliament. But parliament, which gives so little attention to the application of millions, is not likely to give much to that of £13,000 a year; and the cursitor baron of exchequer, from his profession and education, is not likely to be profoundly skilled in the proper expense of forts and garrisons. The captains of his majesty's navy, indeed, or any other commissioned officers, appointed by the board of admiralty, may inquire into the condition of the forts and garrisons, and report their observations to that board. But that board seems to have no direct jurisdiction over the committee, nor any authority to correct those whose conduct it may thus inquire into; and the captains of his majesty's navy, besides, are not supposed to be always deeply learned in the science of fortification. Removal from an office, which can be enjoyed only for the term of three years, and of which the lawful emoluments, even during that term, are so very small, seems to be the utmost punishment to which any committee-man is liable, for any fault, except direct malversation, or embezzlement, either of the public money, or of that of the company; and the fear of the punishment can never be a motive of sufficient weight to force a continual and careful attention to a business to which he has no other interest to attend. The committee are accused of having sent out bricks and stones from England for the reparation of Cape Coast Castle, on the coast of Guinea; a business for which parliament had several times granted an extraordinary sum of money. These bricks and stones, too, which had thus been sent upon so long a voyage, were said to have been of so bad a quality, that it was necessary to rebuild, from the foundation, the walls which had been repaired with them. The forts and garrisons which lie north of Cape Rouge, are not only maintained at the expense of the state, but are under the immediate government of the executive power; and why those which lie south of that cape, and which, too, are, in part at least, maintained at the expense of the state, should be under a different government, it seems not very easy even to imagine a good reason. The protection of the Mediterranean trade was the original purpose or pretence of the garrisons of Gibraltar and Minorca; and the maintenance and government of those garrisons have always been, very properly, committed, not to the Turkey company, but to the executive power. In the extent of its dominion consists, in a great measure, the pride and dignity of that power; and it is not very likely to fail in attention to what is necessary for the defense of that dominion. The garrisons at Gibraltar and Minorca, accordingly, have never been neglected. Though Minorca has been twice taken, and is now probably lost for ever, that disaster has never been imputed to any neglect in the executive power. I would not, however, be understood to insinuate, that either of those expensive garrisons was ever, even in the smallest degree, necessary for the purpose for which they were originally dismembered from the Spanish monarchy. That dismemberment, perhaps, never served any other real purpose than to alienate from England her natural ally the king of Spain, and to unite the two principal branches of the house of Bourbon in a much stricter and more permanent alliance than the ties of blood could ever have united them.

Joint-stock companies, established either by royal charter, or by act of parliament, are different in several respects, not only from regulated companies, but from private copartneries.

First, in a private copartnery, no partner without the consent of the company, can transfer his share to another person, or introduce a new member into the company. Each member, however, may, upon proper warning, withdraw from the copartnery, and demand payment from them of his share of the common stock. In a joint-stock company, on the contrary, no member can demand payment of his share from the company; but each member can, without their consent, transfer his share to another person, and thereby introduce a new member. The value of a share in a joint stock is always the price which it will bring in the market; and this may be either greater or less in any proportion, than the sum which its owner stands credited for in the stock of the company.

Secondly, in a private copartnery, each partner is bound for the debts contracted by the company, to the whole extent of his fortune. In a joint-stock company, on the contrary, each partner is bound only to the extent of his share.

The trade of a joint-stock company is always managed by a court of directors. This court, indeed, is frequently subject, in many respects, to the control of a general court of proprietors. But the greater part of these proprietors seldom pretend to understand any thing of the business of the company; and when the spirit of faction happens not to prevail among them, give themselves no trouble about it, but receive contentedly such half-yearly or yearly dividend as the directors think proper to make to them. This total exemption front trouble and front risk, beyond a limited sum, encourages many people to become adventurers in joint-stock companies, who would, upon no account, hazard their fortunes in any private copartnery. Such companies, therefore, commonly draw to themselves much greater stocks, than any private copartnery can boast of. The trading stock of the South Sea company at one time amounted to upwards of thirty-three millions eight hundred thousand pounds. The divided capital of the Bank of England amounts, at present, to ten millions seven hundred and eighty thousand pounds. The directors of such companies, however, being the managers rather of other people's money than of their own, it cannot well be expected that they should watch over it with the same anxious vigilance with which the partners in a private copartnery frequently watch over their own. Like the stewards of a rich man, they are apt to consider attention to small matters as not for their master's honor, and very easily give themselves a dispensation from having it. Negligence and profusion, therefore, must always prevail, more or less, in the management of the affairs of such a company. It is upon this account, that joint-stock companies for foreign trade have seldom been able to maintain the competition against private adventurers. They have, accordingly, very seldom succeeded without an exclusive privilege; and frequently have not succeeded with one. Without an exclusive privilege, they have commonly mismanaged the trade. With an exclusive privilege, they have both mismanaged and confined it.

The Royal African company, the predecessors of the present African company, had an exclusive privilege by charter; but as that charter had not been confirmed by act of parliament, the trade, in consequence of the declaration of rights, was, soon after the Revolution, laid open to all his majesty's subjects. The Hudson's Bay company are, as to their legal rights, in the same situation as the Royal African company. Their exclusive charter has not been confirmed by act of parliament. The South Sea company, as long as they continued to be a trading company, had an exclusive privilege confirmed by act of parliament; as have likewise the present united company of merchants trading to the East Indies.

The Royal African company soon found that they could not maintain the competition against private adventurers, whom, notwithstanding the declaration of rights, they continued for some time to call interlopers, and to persecute as such. In 1698, however, the private adventurers were subjected to a duty of ten percent upon almost all the different branches of their trade, to be employed by the company in the maintenance of their forts and garrisons. But, notwithstanding this heavy tax, the company were still unable to maintain the competition. Their stock and credit gradually declined. In 1712, their debts had become so great, that a particular act of parliament was thought necessary, both for their security and for that of their creditors. It was enacted, that the resolution of two-thirds of these creditors in number and value should bind the rust, both with regard to the time which should be allowed to the company for the payment of their debts, and with regard to any other agreement which it might be thought proper to make with them concerning those debts. In 1730, their affairs were in so great disorder, that they were altogether incapable of maintaining their forts and garrisons, the sole purpose and pretext of their institution. From that year till their final dissolution, the parliament judged it necessary to allow the annual sum of £10,000 for that purpose. In 1732, after having been for many years losers by the trade of carrying negroes to the West Indies, they at last resolved to give it up altogether; to sell to the private traders to America the negroes which they purchased upon the coast; all to employ their servants in a trade to the inland parts of Africa for gold dust, elephants teeth, dyeing drugs, etc. But their success in this more confined trade was not greater than in their former extensive one. Their affairs continued to go gradually to decline, till at last, being in every respect a bankrupt company, they were dissolved by act of parliament, and their forts and garrisons vested in the present regulated company of merchants trading to Africa. Before the erection of the Royal African company, there had been three other joint-stock companies successively established, one after another, for the African trade. They were all equally unsuccessful. They all, however, had exclusive charters, which, though not confirmed by act of parliament, were in those days supposed to convey a real exclusive privilege.

The Hudson's Bay company, before their misfortunes in the late war, had been much more fortunate than the Royal African company. Their necessary expense is much smaller. The whole number of people whom they maintain in their different settlements and habitations, which they have honored with the name of forts, is said not to exceed a hundred and twenty persons. This number, however, is sufficient to prepare beforehand the cargo of furs and other goods necessary for loading their ships, which, on account of the ice, can seldom remain above six or eight weeks in those seas. This advantage of having a cargo ready prepared, could not, for several years, be acquired by private adventurers; and without it there seems to be no possibility of trading to Hudson's Bay. The moderate capital of the company, which, it is said, does not exceed one hundred and ten thousand pounds, may, besides, be sufficient to enable them to engross the whole, or almost the whole trade and surplus produce, of the miserable though extensive country comprehended within their charter. No private adventurers, accordingly, have ever attempted to trade to that country in competition with them. This company, therefore, have always enjoyed an exclusive trade, in fact, though they may have no right to it in law. Over and above all this, the moderate capital of this company is said to be divided among a very small number of proprietors. But a joint-stock company, consisting of a small number of proprietors, with a moderate capital, approaches very nearly to the nature of a private copartnery, and may be capable of nearly the same degree of vigilance and attention. It is not to be wondered at, therefore, if, in consequence of these different advantages, the Hudson's Bay company had, before the late war, been able to carry on their trade with a considerable degree of success. It does not seem probable, however, that their profits ever approached to what the late Mr. Dobbs imagined them. A much more sober and judicious writer, Mr. Anderson, author of the *Historical and Chronological Deduction of Commerce*, very justly observes, that upon examining the accounts which Mr. Dobbs himself has given for several years together, of their exports and imports, and upon making proper allowances for their extraordinary risk and expense, it does not appear that their profits deserve to be envied, or that they can much, if at all, exceed the ordinary profits of trade.

The South Sea company never had any forts or garrisons to maintain, and therefore were entirely exempted from one great expense, to which other joint-stock companies for foreign trade are subject; but they had an immense capital divided among an immense number of proprietors. It was naturally to be expected, therefore, that folly, negligence, and profusion, should prevail in the whole management of their affairs. The knavery and extravagance of their stock-jobbing projects are sufficiently known, and the explication of them would be foreign to the present subject. Their mercantile projects were not much better conducted. The first trade which they engaged in, was that of supplying the Spanish West Indies with negroes, of which (in consequence of what was called the Assiento Contract granted them by the treaty of Utrecht) they had the exclusive privilege. But as it was not expected that much profit could be made by this trade, both the Portuguese and French companies, who had enjoyed it upon the same terms before them, having been ruined by it, they were allowed, as compensation, to send annually a ship of a certain burden, to trade directly to the Spanish West Indies. Of the ten voyages which this annual ship was allowed to make, they are said to have gained considerably by one, that of the *Royal Caroline*, in 1731; and to have been losers, more or less, by almost all the rest. Their ill success was imputed, by their factors and agents, to the extortion and oppression of the Spanish government; but was, perhaps, principally owing to the profusion and depredations of those very factors and agents; some of whom are said to have acquired great fortunes, even in one year. In 1734, the company petitioned the king, that they might be allowed to dispose of the trade and tonnage of their annual ship, on account of the little profit which they made by it, and to accept of such equivalent as they could obtain from the king of Spain.

In 1724, this company had undertaken the whale fishery. Of this, indeed, they had no monopoly; but as long as they carried it on, no other British subjects appear to have engaged in it. Of the eight voyages which their ships made to Greenland, they were gainers by one, and losers by all the rest. After their eighth and last voyage, when they had sold their ships, stores, and utensils, they found that their whole loss upon this branch, capital and interest included, amounted to upwards of £237,000.

In 1722, this company petitioned the parliament to be allowed to divide their immense capital of more than thirty-three millions eight hundred thousand pounds, the whole of which had been lent to government, into two equal parts; the one half, or upwards of £16,900,000, to be put upon the same footing with other government annuities, and not to be subject to the debts contracted, or losses incurred, by the directors of the company, in the prosecution of their mercantile projects; the other half to remain as before, a trading stock, and to be subject to those debts and losses. The petition was too reasonable not to be granted. In 1733, they again petitioned the parliament, that three-fourths of their trading stock might be turned into annuity stock, and only one-fourth remain as trading stock, or exposed to the hazards arising from the bad management of their directors. Both their annuity and trading stocks had, by this time, been reduced more than two millions each, by several different payments from government; so that this fourth amounted only to £3,662,784:8:6. In 1748, all the demands of the company upon the king of Spain, in consequence of the assiento contract, were, by the treaty of Aix-la-Chapelle, given up for what was supposed an equivalent. An end was put to their trade with the Spanish West Indies; the remainder of their trading stock was turned into an annuity stock; and the company ceased, in every respect, to be a trading company.

It ought to be observed, that in the trade which the South Sea company carried on by means of their annual ship, the only trade by which it ever was expected that they could make any considerable profit, they were not without competitors, either in the foreign or in the home market. At Carthagena, Porto Bello, and La Vera Cruz, they had to encounter the competition of the Spanish merchants, who brought from Cadiz to those markets European goods, of the same kind with the outward cargo of their ship; and in England they had to encounter that of the English merchants, who imported from Cadiz goods of the Spanish West Indies, of the same kind with the inward cargo. The goods, both of the Spanish and English merchants, indeed, were, perhaps, subject to higher duties. But the loss occasioned by the negligence, profusion, and malversation of the servants of the company, had probably been a tax much heavier than all those duties. That a joint-stock company should be able to carry on successfully any branch of foreign trade, when private adventurers can come into any sort of open and fair competition with them, seems contrary to all experience.

The old English East India company was established in 1600, by a charter from Queen Elizabeth. In the first twelve voyages which they fitted out for India, they appear to have traded as a regulated company, with separate stocks, though only in the general ships of the company. In 1612, they united into a joint stock. Their charter was exclusive, and, though not confirmed by act of parliament, was in those days supposed to convey a real exclusive privilege. For many years, therefore, they were not much disturbed by interlopers. Their capital, which never exceeded £744,000, and of which £50 was a share, was not so exorbitant, nor their dealings so extensive, as to afford either a pretext for gross negligence and profusion, or a cover to gross malversation. Notwithstanding some extraordinary losses, occasioned partly by the malice of the Dutch East India company, and partly by other accidents, they carried on for many years a successful trade. But in process of time, when the principles of liberty were better understood, it became every day more and more doubtful, how far a royal charter, not confirmed by act of parliament, could convey an exclusive privilege. Upon this question the decisions of the courts of justice were not uniform, but varied with the authority of government, and the humors of the times. Interlopers multiplied upon them; and towards the end of the reign of Charles II, through the whole of that of James II, and during a part of that of William III, reduced them to great distress. In 1698, a proposal was made to parliament, of advancing two millions to government, at eight percent provided the subscribers were erected into a new East India company, with exclusive privileges. The old East India company offered seven hundred thousand pounds, nearly the amount of their capital, at four percent upon the same conditions. But such was at that time the state of public credit, that it was more convenient for government to borrow two millions at eight percent than seven hundred thousand pounds at four. The proposal of the new subscribers was accepted, and a new East India company established in consequence. The old East India company, however, had a right to continue their trade till 1701. They had, at the same time, in the name of their treasurer, subscribed very artfully three hundred and fifteen thousand pounds into the stock of the new. By a negligence in the expression of the act of parliament, which vested the East India trade in the subscribers to this loan of two millions, it did not appear evident that they were all obliged to unite into a joint stock. A few private traders, whose subscriptions amounted only to seven thousand two hundred pounds, insisted upon the privilege of trading separately upon their own stocks, and at their own risks. The old East India company had a right to a separate trade upon their own stock till 1701; and they had likewise, both before and after that period, a right, like that or other private traders, to a separate trade upon the £315,000, which they had subscribed into the stock of the new company. The competition of the two companies with the private traders, and with one another, is said to have well nigh ruined both. Upon a subsequent occasion, in 1750, when a proposal was made to parliament for putting the trade under the management of a regulated company, and thereby laying it in some measure open, the East India company, in opposition to this proposal, represented, in very strong terms, what had been, at this time, the miserable effects, as they thought them, of this competition. In India, they said, it raised the price of goods so high, that they were not worth the buying; and in England, by overstocking the market, it sunk their price so low, that no profit could be made by them. That by a more plentiful supply, to the great advantage and convenience of the public, it must have reduced very much the price of India goods in the English market, cannot well be doubted; but that it should have raised very much their price in the Indian market, seems not very probable, as all the extraordinary demand which that competition could occasion must have been but as a drop of water in the immense ocean of Indian commerce. The increase of demand, besides, though in the beginning it may sometimes raise the price of goods, never fails to lower it in the long-run. It encourages production, and thereby increases the competition of the producers, who, in order to undersell one another, have recourse to new divisions or labor and new improvements of art, which might never otherwise have been thought of. The miserable effects of which the company complained, were the cheapness of consumption, and the encouragement given to production; precisely the two effects which it is the great business of political economy to promote. The competition, however, of which they gave this doleful account, had not been allowed to be of long continuance. In 1702, the two companies were, in some measure, united by an indenture tripartite, to which the queen was the third party; and in 1708, they were by act of parliament, perfectly consolidated into one company, by their present name of the United Company of Merchants trading to the East Indies. Into this act it was thought worth while to insert a clause, allowing the separate traders to continue their trade till Michaelmas 1711; but at the same time empowering the directors, upon three years notice, to redeem their little capital of seven thousand two hundred pounds, and thereby to convert the whole stock of the company into a joint stock. By the same act, the capital of the company, in consequence of a new loan to government, was augmented from two millions to three millions two hundred thousand pounds. In 1743, the company advanced another million to government. But this million being raised, not by a call upon the proprietors, but by selling annuities and contracting bond-debts, it did not augment the stock upon which the proprietors could claim a dividend. It augmented, however, their trading stock, it being equally liable with the other three millions two hundred thousand pounds, to the losses sustained, and debts contracted by the company in prosecution of their mercantile projects. From 1708, or at least from 1711, this company, being delivered from all competitors, and fully established in the monopoly of the English commerce to the East Indies, carried on a successful trade, and from their profits, made annually a moderate dividend to their proprietors. During the French war, which began in 1741, the ambition of Mr. Dupleix, the French governor of Pondicherry, involved them in the wars of the Carnatic, and in the politics of the Indian princes. After many signal successes, and equally signal losses, they at last lost Madras, at that time their principal settlement in India. It was restored to them by the treaty of Aix-la-Chapelle; and, about this time the spirit of war and conquest seems to have taken possession of their servants in India, and never since to have left them. During the French war, which began in 1755, their arms partook of the general good fortune of those of Great Britain. They defended Madras, took Pondicherry, recovered Calcutta, and acquired the revenues of a rich and extensive territory, amounting, it was then said, to upwards of three millions a year. They remained for several years in quiet possession of this revenue; but in 1767, administration laid claim to their territorial acquisitions, and the revenue arising from them, as of right belonging to the crown; and the company, in compensation for this claim, agreed to pay to government £400,000 a year. They had, before this, gradually augmented their dividend from about six to ten percent; that is, upon their capital of three millions two hundred thousand pounds, they had increased it by £128,000, or had raised it from one hundred and ninety-two thousand to three hundred and twenty thousand pounds a year. They were attempting about this time to raise it still further, to twelve and a-half percent, which would have made their annual payments to their proprietors equal to what they had agreed to pay annually to government, or to £400,000 a year. But during the two years in which their agreement with government was to take place, they were restrained from any further increase of dividend by two successive acts of parliament, of which the object was to enable them to make a speedier progress in the payment of their debts, which were at this time estimated at upwards of six or seven millions sterling. In 1769, they renewed their agreement with government for five years more, and stipulated, that during the course of that period, they should be allowed gradually to increase their dividend to twelve and a-half per cent; never increasing it, however, more than one percent in one year. This increase of dividend, therefore, when it had risen to its utmost height, could augment their annual payments, to their proprietors and government together, but by £680,000, beyond what they had been before their late territorial acquisitions. What the gross revenue of those territorial acquisitions was supposed to amount to, has already been mentioned; and by an account brought by the Cruttenden East Indiaman in 1769, the neat revenue, clear of all deductions and military charges, was stated at two millions forty-eight thousand seven hundred and forty-seven pounds. They were said, at the same time, to possess another revenue, arising partly from lands, but chiefly from the customs established at their different settlements, amounting to £439,000. The profits of their trade, too, according to the evidence of their chairman before the house of commons, amounted, at this time, to at least £400,000 a year; according to that of their accountant, to at least £500,000; according to the lowest account, at least equal to the highest dividend that was to be paid to their proprietors. So great a revenue might certainly have afforded an augmentation of £680,000 in their annual payments; and, at the same time, have left a large sinking fund, sufficient for the speedy reduction of their debt. In 1773, however, their debts, instead of being reduced, were augmented by an arrear to the treasury in the payment of the four hundred thousand pounds; by another to the custom-house for duties unpaid; by a large debt to the bank, for money borrowed; and by a fourth, for bills drawn upon them from India, and wantonly accepted, to the amount of upwards of twelve hundred thousand pounds. The distress which these accumulated claims brought upon them, obliged them not only to reduce all at once their dividend to six percent but to throw themselves upon the mercy of government, and to supplicate, first, a release from the further payment of the stipulated £400,000 a year; and, secondly, a loan of fourteen hundred thousand, to save them from immediate bankruptcy. The great increase of their fortune had, it seems, only served to furnish their servants with a pretext for greater profusion, and a cover for greater malversation, than in proportion even to that increase of fortune. The conduct of their servants in India, and the general state of their affairs both in India and in Europe, became the subject of a parliamentary inquiry: in consequence of which, several very important alterations were made in the constitution of their government, both at home and abroad. In India, their principal settlements or Madras, Bombay, and Calcutta, which had before been altogether independent of one another, were subjected to a governor-general, assisted by a council of four assessors, parliament assuming to itself the first nomination of this governor and council, who were to reside at Calcutta; that city having now become, what Madras was before, the most important of the English settlements in India. The court of the Mayor of Calcutta, originally instituted for the trial of mercantile causes, which arose in the city and neighborhood, had gradually extended its jurisdiction with the extension of the empire. It was now reduced and confined to the original purpose of its institution. Instead of it, a new supreme court of judicature was established, consisting of a chief justice and three judges, to be appointed by the crown. In Europe, the qualification necessary to entitle a proprietor to vote at their general courts was raised, from five hundred pounds, the original price of a share in the stock of the company, to a thousand pounds. In order to vote upon this qualification, too, it was declared necessary, that he should have possessed it, if acquired by his own purchase, and not by inheritance, for at least one year, instead of six months, the term requisite before. The court of twenty-four directors had before been chosen annually; but it was now enacted, that each director should, for the future, be chosen for four years; six of them, however, to go out of office by rotation every year, and not be capable of being re-chosen at the election of the six new directors for the ensuing year. In consequence of these alterations, the courts, both of the proprietors and directors, it was expected, would be likely to act with more dignity and steadiness than they had usually done before. But it seems impossible, by any alterations, to render those courts, in any respect, fit to govern, or even to share in the government of a great empire; because the greater part of their members must always have too little interest in the prosperity of that empire, to give any serious attention to what may promote it. Frequently a man of great, sometimes even a man of small fortune, is willing to purchase a thousand pounds share in India stock, merely for the influence which he expects to acquire by a vote in the court of proprietors. It gives him a share, though not in the plunder, yet in the appointment of the plunderers of India; the court of directors, though they make that appoint-

THE REAL PRICE OF EVERYTHING

ment, being necessarily more or less under the influence of the proprietors, who not only elect those directors, but sometimes over-rule the appointments of their servants in India. Provided he can enjoy this influence for a few years, and thereby provide for a certain number of his friends, he frequently cares little about the dividend, or even about the value of the stock upon which his vote is founded. About the prosperity of the great empire, in the government of which that vote gives him a share, he seldom cares at all. No other sovereigns ever were, or, from the nature of things, ever could be, so perfectly indifferent about the happiness or misery of their subjects, the improvement or waste of their dominions, the glory or disgrace of their administration, as, from irresistible moral causes, the greater part of the proprietors of such a mercantile company are, and necessarily must be. This indifference, too, was more likely to be increased than diminished by some of the new regulations which were made in consequence of the parliamentary inquiry. By a resolution of the house of commons, for example, it was declared, that when the £1,400,000 lent to the company by government, should be paid, and their bond-debts be reduced to £1,500,000, they might then, and not till then, divide eight percent upon their capital; and that whatever remained of their revenues and neat profits at home should be divided into four parts; three of them to be paid into the exchequer for the use of the public, and the fourth to be reserved as a fund, either for the further reduction of their bond-debts, or for the discharge of other contingent exigencies which the company might labor under. But if the company were bad stewards and bad sovereigns, when the whole of their neat revenue and profits belonged to themselves, and were at their own disposal, they were surely not likely to be better when three-fourths of them were to belong to other people, and the other fourth, though to be laid out for the benefit of the company, yet to be so under the inspection and with the approbation of other people.

It might be more agreeable to the company, that their own servants and dependants should have either the pleasure of wasting, or the profit of embezzling, whatever surplus might remain, after paying the proposed dividend of eight percent than that it should come into the hands of a set of people with whom those resolutions could scarce fail to set them in some measure at variance. The interest of those servants and dependants might so far predominate in the court of proprietors, as sometimes to dispose it to support the authors of depredations which had been committed in direct violation of its own authority. With the majority of proprietors, the support even of the authority of their own court might sometimes be a matter of less consequence than the support of those who had set that authority at defiance.

The regulations of 1773, accordingly, did not put an end to the disorder of the company's government in India. Notwithstanding that, during a momentary fit of good conduct, they had at one time collected into the treasury of Calcutta more than £3,000,000 sterling; notwithstanding that they had afterwards extended either their dominion or their depredations over a vast accession of some of the richest and most fertile countries in India, all was wasted and destroyed. They found themselves altogether unprepared to stop or resist the incursion of Hyder Ali; and in consequence of those disorders, the company is now (1784) in greater distress than ever; and, in order to prevent immediate bankruptcy, is once more reduced to supplicate the assistance of government. Different

plans have been proposed by the different parties in parliament for the better management of its affairs; and all those plans seem to agree in supposing, what was indeed always abundantly evident, that it is altogether unfit to govern its territorial possessions.
Even the company itself seems to be convinced of its own incapacity so far, and seems,
upon that account willing to give them up to government.

With the right of possessing forts and garrisons in distant and barbarous countries is
necessarily connected the right of making peace and war in those countries. The joint-
stock companies, which have had the one right, have constantly exercised the other, and
have frequently had it expressly conferred upon them. How unjustly, how capriciously,
how cruelly, they have commonly exercised it, is too well known from recent experience.

When a company of merchants undertake, at their own risk and expense, to establish a
new trade with some remote and barbarous nation, it may not be unreasonable to incor-
porate them into a joint-stock company, and to grant them, in case of their success, a
monopoly of the trade for a certain number of years. It is the easiest and most natural way
in which the state can recompense them for hazarding a dangerous and expensive experiment, of which the public is afterwards to reap the benefit. A temporary monopoly of this
kind may be vindicated, upon the same principles upon which a like monopoly of a new
machine is granted to its inventor, and that of a new book to its author. But upon the expiration of the term, the monopoly ought certainly to determine; the forts and garrisons, if
it was found necessary to establish any, to be taken into the hands of government, their value
to be paid to the company, and the trade to be laid open to all the subjects of the state. By
a perpetual monopoly, all the other subjects of the state are taxed very absurdly in two different ways: first, by the high price of goods, which, in the case of a free trade, they could
buy much cheaper; and, secondly, by their total exclusion from a branch of business which
it might be both convenient and profitable for many of them to carry on. It is for the most
worthless of all purposes, too, that they are taxed in this manner. It is merely to enable the
company to support the negligence, profusion, and malversation of their own servants,
whose disorderly conduct seldom allows the dividend of the company to exceed the ordinary rate of profit in trades which are altogether free, and very frequently makes a fall even
a good deal short of that rate. Without a monopoly, however, a joint-stock company, it
would appear from experience, cannot long carry on any branch of foreign trade. To buy
in one market, in order to sell with profit in another, when there are many competitors in
both; to watch over, not only the occasional variations in the demand, but the much greater
and more frequent variations in the competition, or in the supply which that demand is
likely to get from other people; and to suit with dexterity and judgment both the quantity
and quality of each assortment of goods to all these circumstances, is a species of warfare,
of which the operations are continually changing, and which can scarce ever be conducted
successfully, without such an unremitting exertion of vigilance and attention as cannot
long be expected from the directors of a joint-stock company. The East India company,
upon the redemption of their funds, and the expiration of their exclusive privilege, have a
right, by act of parliament, to continue a corporation with a joint stock, and to trade in their
corporate capacity to the East Indies, in common with the rest of their fellow subjects. But
in this situation, the superior vigilance and attention of a private adventurer would, in all
probability, soon make them weary of the trade.

An eminent French author, of great knowledge in matters of political economy, the Abbe Morellet, gives a list of fifty-five joint-stock companies for foreign trade, which have been established in different parts of Europe since the year 1600, and which, according to him, have all failed from mismanagement, notwithstanding they had exclusive privileges. He has been misinformed with regard to the history of two or three of them, which were not joint-stock companies and have not failed. But, in compensation, there have been several joint-stock companies which have failed, and which he has omitted.

The only trades which it seems possible for a joint-stock company to carry on successfully, without an exclusive privilege, are those, of which all the operations are capable of being reduced to what is called a routine, or to such a uniformity of method as admits of little or no variation. Of this kind is, first, the banking trade; secondly, the trade of insurance from fire and from sea risk, and capture in time of war; thirdly, the trade of making and maintaining a navigable cut or canal; and, fourthly, the similar trade of bringing water for the supply of a great city.

Though the principles of the banking trade may appear somewhat abstruse, the practice is capable of being reduced to strict rules. To depart upon any occasion from those rules, in consequence of some flattering speculation of extraordinary gain, is almost always extremely dangerous and frequently fatal to the banking company which attempts it. But the constitution of joint-stock companies renders them in general, more tenacious of established rules than any private copartnery. Such companies, therefore, seem extremely well fitted for this trade. The principal banking companies in Europe, accordingly, are joint-stock companies, many of which manage their trade very successfully without any exclusive privilege. The Bank of England has no other exclusive privilege, except that no other banking company in England shall consist of more than six persons. The two banks of Edinburgh are joint-stock companies, without any exclusive privilege.

The value of the risk, either from fire, or from loss by sea, or by capture, though it cannot, perhaps, be calculated very exactly, admits, however, of such a gross estimation, as renders it, in some degree, reducible to strict rule and method. The trade of insurance, therefore, may be carried on successfully by a joint-stock company, without any exclusive privilege. Neither the London Assurance, nor the Royal Exchange Assurance companies have any such privilege.

When a navigable cut or canal has been once made, the management of it becomes quite simple and easy, and it is reducible to strict rule and method. Even the making of it is so, as it may be contracted for with undertakers, at so much a mile, and so much a lock. The same thing may be said of a canal, an aqueduct, or a great pipe for bringing water to supply a great city. Such under-takings, therefore, may be, and accordingly frequently are, very successfully managed by joint-stock companies, without any exclusive privilege.

To establish a joint-stock company, however, for any undertaking, merely because such a company might be capable of managing it successfully; or, to exempt a particular set of dealers from some of the general laws which take place with regard to all their neighbors, merely because they might be capable of thriving, if they had such an exemption, would certainly not be reasonable. To render such an establishment perfectly reasonable, with the circumstance of being reducible to strict rule and method, two other circumstances ought to concur. First, it ought to appear with the clearest evidence, that the undertaking is of greater and more general utility than the greater part of common trades; and, secondly, that it requires a greater capital than can easily be collected into a private copartnery. If a moderate capital were sufficient, the great utility of the undertaking would not be a sufficient reason for establishing a joint-stock company; because, in this case, the demand for what it was to produce, would readily and easily be supplied by private adventurers. In the four trades above mentioned, both those circumstances concur.

The great and general utility of the banking trade, when prudently managed, has been fully explained in the second book of this Inquiry. But a public bank, which is to support public credit, and, upon particular emergencies, to advance to government the whole produce of a tax, to the amount, perhaps, of several millions, a year or two before it comes in, requires a greater capital than can easily be collected into any private copartnery.

The trade of insurance gives great security to the fortunes of private people, and, by dividing among a great many that loss which would ruin an individual, makes it fall light and easy upon the whole society. In order to give this security, however, it is necessary that the insurers should have a very large capital. Before the establishment of the two joint-stock companies for insurance in London, a list, it is said, was laid before the attorney-general, of one hundred and fifty private usurers, who had failed in the course of a few years.

That navigable cuts and canals, and the works which are sometimes necessary for supplying a great city with water, are of great and general utility, while, at the same time, they frequently require a greater expense than suits the fortunes of private people, is sufficiently obvious.

Except the four trades above mentioned, I have not been able to recollect any other, in which all the three circumstances requisite for rendering reasonable the establishment of a joint-stock company concur. The English copper company of London, the lead-smelting company, the glass-grinding company, have not even the pretext of any great or singular utility in the object which they pursue; nor does the pursuit of that object seem to require any expense unsuitable to the fortunes of many private men. Whether the trade which those companies carry on, is reducible to such strict rule and method as to render it fit for the management of a joint-stock company, or whether they have any reason to boast of their extraordinary profits, I do not pretend to know. The mine-adventurers company has been long ago bankrupt. A share in the stock of the British Linen company of Edinburgh sells, at present, very much below par, though less so than it did some years ago. The joint-stock companies, which are established for the public-spirited purpose of promoting some particular manufacture, over and above managing their own affairs ill, to the diminution of the general stock of the society, can, in other respects, scarce ever fail to do more harm than good. Notwithstanding the most upright intentions, the unavoidable partiality of their directors to particular branches of the manufacture, of which the undertakers mislead and impose upon them, is a real discouragement to the rest, and necessarily breaks, more or less, that natural proportion which would otherwise establish itself between judicious industry and profit, and which, to the general industry of the country, is of all encouragements the greatest and the most effectual.

ARTICLE II

Of the Expense of the Institution for the Education of Youth

The institutions for the education of the youth may, in the same manner, furnish a revenue sufficient for defraying their own expense. The fee or honorary, which the scholar pays to the master, naturally constitutes a revenue of this kind.

Even where the reward of the master does not arise altogether from this natural revenue, it still is not necessary that it should be derived from that general revenue of the society, of which the collection and application are, in most countries, assigned to the executive power. Through the greater part of Europe, accordingly, the endowment of schools and colleges makes either no charge upon that general revenue, or but a very small one. It everywhere arises chiefly from some local or provincial revenue, from the rent of some landed estate, or from the interest of some sum of money, allotted and put under the management of trustees for this particular purpose, sometimes by the sovereign himself, and sometimes by some private donor.

Have those public endowments contributed in general, to promote the end of their institution? Have they contributed to encourage the diligence, and to improve the abilities of the teachers? Have they directed the course of education towards objects more useful, both to the individual and to the public, than those to which it would naturally have gone of its own accord? It should not seem very difficult to give at least a probable answer to each of those questions.

In every profession, the exertion of the greater part of those who exercise it, is always in proportion to the necessity they are under of making that exertion. This necessity is greatest with those to whom the emoluments of their profession are the only source from which they expect their fortune, or even their ordinary revenue and subsistence. In order to acquire this fortune, or even to get this subsistence, they must, in the course of a year, execute a certain quantity of work of a known value; and, where the competition is free, the rivalship of competitors, who are all endeavoring to justle one another out of employment, obliges every man to endeavor to execute his work with a certain degree of exactness. The greatness of the objects which are to be acquired by success in some particular professions may, no doubt, sometimes animate the exertions of a few men of extraordinary spirit and ambition. Great objects, however, are evidently not necessary, in order to occasion the greatest exertions. Rivalship and emulation render excellency, even in mean professions, an object of ambition, and frequently occasion the very greatest exertions. Great objects, on the contrary, alone and unsupported by the necessity of application, have seldom been sufficient to occasion any considerable exertion. In England, success in the profession of the law leads to some very great objects of ambition; and yet how few men, born to easy fortunes, have ever in this country been eminent in that profession?

The endowments of schools and colleges have necessarily diminished, more or less, the necessity of application in the teachers. Their subsistence, so far as it arises from their salaries, is evidently derived from a fund, altogether independent of their success and reputation in their particular professions.

In some universities, the salary makes but a part, and frequently but a small part, of the emoluments of the teacher, of which the greater part arises from the honoraries or fees of his pupils. The necessity of application, though always more or less diminished, is not, in this case, entirely taken away. Reputation in his profession is still of some importance to him, and he still has some dependency upon the affection, gratitude, and favorable report of those who have attended upon his instructions; and these favorable sentiments he is likely to gain in no way so well as by deserving them, that is, by the abilities and diligence with which he discharges every part of his duty.

In other universities, the teacher is prohibited from receiving any honorary or fee from his pupils, and his salary constitutes the whole of the revenue which he derives from his office. His interest is, in this case, set as directly in opposition to his duty as it is possible to set it. It is the interest of every man to live as much at his ease as he can; and if his emoluments are to be precisely the same, whether he does or does not perform some very laborious duty, it is certainly his interest, at least as interest is vulgarly understood, either to neglect it altogether, or, if he is subject to some authority which will not suffer him to do this, to perform it in as careless and slovenly a manner as that authority will permit. If he is naturally active and a lover of labor, it is his interest to employ that activity in any way from which he can derive some advantage, rather than in the performance of his duty, from which he can derive none.

If the authority to which he is subject resides in the body corporate, the college, or university, of which he himself is a member, and in which the greater part of the other members are, like himself, persons who either are, or ought to be teachers, they are likely to make a common cause, to be all very indulgent to one another, and every man to consent that his neighbor may neglect his duty, provided he himself is allowed to neglect his own. In the university of Oxford, the greater part of the public professors have, for these many years, given up altogether even the pretence of teaching.

If the authority to which he is subject resides, not so much in the body corporate, of which he is a member, as in some other extraneous persons, in the bishop of the diocese, for example, in the governor of the province, or, perhaps, in some minister of state, it is not, indeed, in this case, very likely that he will be suffered to neglect his duty altogether. All that such superiors, however, can force him to do, is to attend upon his pupils a certain number of hours, that is, to give a certain number of lectures in the week, or in the year. What those lectures shall be, must still depend upon the diligence of the teacher; and that diligence is likely to be proportioned to the motives which he has for exerting it. An extraneous jurisdiction of this kind, besides, is liable to be exercised both ignorantly and capriciously. In its nature, it is arbitrary and discretionary; and the persons who exercise it, neither attending upon the lectures of the teacher themselves, nor perhaps understanding the sciences which it is his business to teach, are seldom capable of exercising it with judgment. From the insolence of office, too, they are frequently indifferent how they exercise it, and are very apt to censure or deprive him of his office wantonly and without any just cause. The person subject to such jurisdiction is necessarily degraded by it, and, instead of being one of the most respectable, is rendered one of the meanest and most contemptible persons in the society. It is by powerful protection only, that he can effectually guard himself against the bad usage to which he is at all times exposed; and this protection he is most likely to gain, not by ability or diligence in his profession, but by obsequiousness to the will of his superiors, and by being ready, at all times, to sacrifice to that will the rights, the interest, and the honor of the body corporate, of which he is a member. Whoever has attended for any considerable time to the administration of a French university, must have had occasion to remark the effects which naturally result from an arbitrary and extraneous jurisdiction of this kind.

Whatever forces a certain number of students to any college or university, independent of the merit or reputation of the teachers, tends more or less to diminish the necessity of that merit or reputation.

The privileges of graduates in arts, in law, physics, and divinity, when they can be obtained only by residing a certain number of years in certain universities, necessarily force a certain number of students to such universities, independent of the merit or reputation of the teachers. The privileges of graduates are a sort of statutes of apprenticeship, which have contributed to the improvement of education just as the other statutes of apprenticeship have to that of arts and manufactures.

The charitable foundations of scholarships, exhibitions, bursaries, etc. necessarily attach a certain number of students to certain colleges, independent altogether of the merit of those particular colleges. Were the students upon such charitable foundations left free to choose what college they liked best, such liberty might perhaps contribute to excite some emulation among different colleges. A regulation, on the contrary, which prohibited even the independent members of every particular college from leaving it, and going to any other, without leave first asked and obtained of that which they meant to abandon, would tend very much to extinguish that emulation.

If in each college, the tutor or teacher, who was to instruct each student in all arts and sciences, should not be voluntarily chosen by the student, but appointed by the head of the college; and if, in case of neglect, inability, or bad usage, the student should not be allowed to change him for another, without leave first asked and obtained; such a regulation would not only tend very much to extinguish all emulation among the different tutors of the same college, but to diminish very much, in all of them, the necessity of diligence and of attention to their respective pupils. Such teachers, though very well paid by their students, might be as much disposed to neglect them, as those who are not paid by them at all or who have no other recompense but their salary.

If the teacher happens to be a man of sense, it must be an unpleasant thing to him to be conscious, while he is lecturing to his students, that he is either speaking or reading nonsense, or what is very little better than nonsense. It must, too, be unpleasant to him to observe, that the greater part of his students desert his lectures; or perhaps, attend upon them with plain enough marks of neglect, contempt, and derision. If he is obliged, therefore, to give a certain number of lectures, these motives alone, without any other interest, might dispose him to take some pains to give tolerably good ones. Several different expedients, however, may be fallen upon, which will effectually blunt the edge of all those incitements to diligence. The teacher, instead of explaining to his pupils himself the science in which he proposes to instruct them, may read some book upon it; and if this book is written in a foreign and dead language, by interpreting it to them into their own, or, what would give him still less trouble, by making them interpret it to him, and by now and then making an occasional remark upon it, he may flatter himself that he is giving a lecture. The slightest degree of knowledge and application will enable him to do this, without exposing himself to contempt or derision, by saying any thing that is really foolish, absurd, or ridiculous. The discipline of the college, at the same time, may enable him to force all his pupils to the most regular attendance upon his sham lecture, and to maintain the most decent and respectful behavior during the whole time of the performance.

The discipline of colleges and universities is in general contrived, not for the benefit of the students, but for the interest, or, more properly speaking, for the ease of the masters. Its object is, in all cases, to maintain the authority of the master, and, whether he neglects or performs his duty, to oblige the students in all cases to behave to him as if he performed it with the greatest diligence and ability. It seems to presume perfect wisdom and virtue in the one order, and the greatest weakness and folly in the other. Where the masters, however, really perform their duty, there are no examples, I believe, that the greater part of the students ever neglect theirs. No discipline is ever requisite to force attendance upon lectures which are really worth the attending, as is well known wherever any such lectures are given. Force and restraint may, no doubt, be in some degree requisite, in order to oblige children, or very young boys, to attend to those parts of education, which it is thought necessary for them to acquire during that early period of life; but after twelve or thirteen years of age, provided the master does his duty, force or restraint can scarce ever be necessary to carry on any part of education. Such is the generosity of the greater part of young men, that so far from being disposed to neglect or despise the instructions of their master, provided he shows some serious intention of being of use to them, they are generally inclined to pardon a great deal of incorrectness in the performance of his duty, and sometimes even to conceal from the public a good deal of gross negligence.

Those parts of education, it is to be observed, for the teaching of which there are no public institutions, are generally the best taught. When a young man goes to a fencing or a dancing school, he does not, indeed, always learn to fence or to dance very well; but he seldom fails of learning to fence or to dance. The good effects of the riding school are not commonly so evident. The expense of a riding school is so great, that in most places it is a public institution. The three most essential parts of literary education, to read, write, and account, it still continues to be more common to acquire in private than in public schools; and it very seldom happens, that anybody fails of acquiring them to the degree in which it is necessary to acquire them.

In England, the public schools are much less corrupted than the universities. In the schools, the youth are taught, or at least may be taught, Greek and Latin; that is, everything which the masters pretend to teach, or which it is expected they should teach. In the universities, the youth neither are taught, nor always can find any proper means of being taught the sciences, which it is the business of those incorporated bodies to teach. The reward of the schoolmaster, in most cases, depends principally, in some cases almost entirely, upon the fees or honoraries of his scholars. Schools have no exclusive privileges. In order to obtain the honors of graduation, it is not necessary that a person should bring a certificate of his having studied a certain number of years at a public school. If, upon examination, he appears to understand what is taught there, no questions are asked about the place where he learnt it.

The parts of education which are commonly taught in universities, it may perhaps be said, are not very well taught. But had it not been for those institutions, they would not have been commonly taught at all; and both the individual and the public would have suffered a good deal from the want of those important parts of education.

The present universities of Europe were originally, the greater part of them, ecclesiastical corporations, instituted for the education of churchmen. They were founded by the authority of the pope; and were so entirely under his immediate protection, that their members, whether masters or students, had all of them what was then called the benefit of clergy, that is, were exempted from the civil jurisdiction of the countries in which their respective universities were situated, and were amenable only to the ecclesiastical tribunals. What was taught in the greater part of those universities was suitable to the end of their institution, either theology, or something that was merely preparatory to theology.

When Christianity was first established by law, a corrupted Latin had become the common language of all the western parts of Europe. The service of the church, accordingly, and the translation of the Bible which were read in churches, were both in that corrupted Latin; that is, in the common language of the country. After the irruption of the barbarous nations who overturned the Roman empire, Latin gradually ceased to be the language of any part of Europe. But the reverence of the people naturally preserves the established forms and ceremonies of religion long after the circumstances which first introduced and rendered them reasonable, are no more. Though Latin, therefore, was no longer understood anywhere by the great body of the people, the whole service of the church still continued to be performed in that language. Two different languages were thus established in Europe, in the same manner as in ancient Egypt: a language of the priests, and a language of the people; a sacred and a profane, a learned and an unlearned language. But it was necessary that the priests should understand something of that sacred and learned language in which they were to officiate; and the study of the Latin language therefore made, from the beginning, an essential part of university education.

It was not so with that either of the Greek or of the Hebrew language. The infallible decrees of the church had pronounced the Latin translation of the Bible, commonly called the Latin Vulgate, to have been equally dictated by divine inspiration, and therefore of equal authority with the Greek and Hebrew originals. The knowledge of those two languages, therefore, not being indispensably requisite to a churchman, the study of them did not for along time make a necessary part of the common course of university education. There are some Spanish universities, I am assured, in which the study of the Greek language has never yet made any part of that course. The first reformers found the Greek text of the New Testament, and even the Hebrew text of the Old, more favorable to their opinions than the Vulgate translation, which, as might naturally be supposed, had been gradually accommodated to support the doctrines of the Catholic Church. They set themselves, therefore, to expose the many errors of that translation, which the Roman Catholic clergy were thus put under the necessity of defending or explaining. But this could not well be done without some knowledge of the original languages, of which the study was therefore gradually introduced into the greater part of universities; both of those which embraced, and of those which rejected, the doctrines of the reformation. The Greek language was connected with every part of that classical learning, which, though at first principally cultivated by Catholics and Italians, happened to come into fashion much about the same time that the doctrines of the reformation were set on foot. In the greater part of universities, therefore, that language was taught previous to the study of philosophy, and as soon as the student had made some progress in the Latin. The Hebrew language, having no connection with classical learning, and, except the Holy Scriptures, being the language of not a single book in any esteem, the study of it did not commonly commence till after that of philosophy, and when the student had entered upon the study of theology.

Originally, the first rudiments, both of the Greek and Latin languages, were taught in universities; and in some universities they still continue to be so. In others, it is expected that the student should have previously acquired, at least, the rudiments of one or both of those languages, of which the study continues to make everywhere a very considerable part of university education.

The ancient Greek philosophy was divided into three great branches: physics, or natural philosophy; ethics, or moral philosophy; and logic. This general division seems perfectly agreeable to the nature of things.

The great phenomena of nature, the revolutions of the heavenly bodies, eclipses, comets; thunder and lightning, and other extraordinary meteors; the generation, the life, growth, and dissolution of plants and animals are objects which, as they necessarily excite the wonder, so they naturally call forth the curiosity of mankind to inquire into their causes. Superstition first attempted to satisfy this curiosity, by referring all those wonderful appearances to the immediate agency of the gods. Philosophy afterwards endeavored to account for them from more familiar causes, or from such as mankind were better acquainted with, than the agency of the gods. As those great phenomena are the first objects of human curiosity, so the science which pretends to explain them must naturally have been the first branch of philosophy that was cultivated. The first philosophers, accordingly, of whom history has preserved any account, appear to have been natural philosophers.

In every age and country of the world, men must have attended to the characters, designs, and actions of one another; and many reputable rules and maxims for the conduct of human life must have been laid down and approved of by common consent. As soon as writing came into fashion, wise men, or those who fancied themselves such, would naturally endeavor to increase the number of those established and respected maxims, and to express their own sense of what was either proper or improper conduct, sometimes in the more artificial form of apologues, like what are called the fables of Aesop; and sometimes in the more simple one of apophthegms or wise sayings, like the proverbs of Solomon, the verses of Theognis and Phocyllides, and some part of the works of Hesiod. They might continue in this manner, for a long time, merely to multiply the number of those maxims of prudence and morality, without even attempting to arrange them in any very distinct or methodical order, much less to connect them together by one or more general principles, from which they were all deducible, like effects from their natural causes. The beauty of a systematical arrangement of different observations, connected by a few common principles, was first seen in the rude essays of those ancient times towards a system of natural philosophy. Something of the same kind was afterwards attempted in morals. The maxims of common life were arranged in some methodical order, and connected together by a few common principles, in the same manner as they had attempted to arrange and connect the phenomena of nature. The science which pretends to investigate and explain those connecting principles, is what is properly called Moral Philosophy.

Different authors gave different systems, both of natural and moral philosophy. But the arguments by which they supported those different systems, far from being always demonstrations, were frequently at best but very slender probabilities, and sometimes mere sophisms, which had no other foundation but the inaccuracy and ambiguity of common language. Speculative systems, have, in all ages of the world, been adopted for reasons too frivolous to have determined the judgment of any man of common sense, in a matter of the smallest pecuniary interest. Gross sophistry has scarce ever had any influence upon the opinions of mankind, except in matters of philosophy and speculation; and in these it has frequently had the greatest. The patrons of each system of natural and moral philosophy, naturally endeavored to expose the weakness of the arguments adduced to support the systems which were opposite to their own. In examining those arguments, they were necessarily led to consider the difference between a probable and a demonstrative argument, between a fallacious and a conclusive one; and logic, or the science of the general principles of good and bad reasoning, necessarily arose out of the observations which a scrutiny of this kind gave occasion to; though, in its origin, posterior both to physics and to ethics, it was commonly taught, not indeed in all, but in the greater part of the ancient schools of philosophy, previously to either of those sciences. The student, it seems to have been thought, ought to understand well the difference between good and bad reasoning, before he was led to reason upon subjects of so great importance.

This ancient division of philosophy into three parts was, in the greater part of the universities of Europe, changed for another into five.

In the ancient philosophy, whatever was taught concerning the nature either of the human mind or of the Deity, made a part of the system of physics. Those beings, in whatever their essence might be supposed to consist, were parts of the great system of the universe, and parts, too, productive of the most important effects. Whatever human reason could either conclude or conjecture concerning them, made, as it were, two chapters, though no doubt two very important ones, of the science which pretended to give an account of the origin and revolutions of the great system of the universe. But in the universities of Europe, where philosophy was taught only as subservient to theology, it was natural to dwell longer upon these two chapters than upon any other of the science. They were gradually more and more extended, and were divided into many inferior chapters; till at last the doctrine of spirits, of which so little can be known, came to take up as much room in the system of philosophy as the doctrine of bodies, of which so much can be known. The doctrines concerning those two subjects were considered as making two distinct sciences. What are called metaphysics, or pneumatics, were set in opposition to physics, and were cultivated not only as the more sublime, but, for the purposes of a particular profession, as the more useful science of the two. The proper subject of experiment and observation, a subject in which a careful attention is capable of making so many useful discoveries, was almost entirely neglected. The subject in which, after a very few simple and almost obvious truths, the most careful attention can discover nothing but obscurity and uncertainty, and can consequently produce nothing but subtleties and sophisms, was greatly cultivated.

When those two sciences had thus been set in opposition to one another, the comparison between them naturally gave birth to a third, to what was called ontology, or the science which treated of the qualities and attributes which were common to both the subjects of the other two sciences. But if subtleties and sophisms composed the greater part of the metaphysics or pneumatics of the schools, they composed the whole of this cobweb science of ontology, which was likewise sometimes called metaphysics.

Wherein consisted the happiness and perfection of a man, considered not only as an individual, but as the member of a family, of a state, and of the great society of mankind, was the object which the ancient moral philosophy proposed to investigate. In that philosophy, the duties of human life were treated of as subservient to the happiness and perfection of human life. But when moral, as well as natural philosophy, came to be taught only as subservient to theology, the duties of human life were treated of as chiefly subservient to the happiness of a life to come. In the ancient philosophy, the perfection of virtue was represented as necessarily productive, to the person who possessed it, of the most perfect happiness in this life. In the modern philosophy, it was frequently represented as generally, or rather as almost always, inconsistent with any degree of happiness in this life; and heaven was to be earned only by penance and mortification, by the austerities and abasement of a monk, not by the liberal, generous, and spirited conduct of a man. Casuistry, and an ascetic morality, made up, in most cases, the greater part of the moral philosophy of the schools. By far the most important of all the different branches of philosophy became in this manner by far the most corrupted.

Such, therefore, was the common course of philosophical education in the greater part of the universities in Europe. Logic was taught first; ontology came in the second place; pneumatology, comprehending the doctrine concerning the nature of the human soul and of the Deity, in the third; in the fourth followed a debased system of moral philosophy, which was considered as immediately connected with the doctrines of pneumatology, with the immortality of the human soul, and with the rewards and punishments which, from the justice of the Deity, were to be expected in a life to come, a short and superficial system of physics usually concluded the course.

The alterations which the universities of Europe thus introduced into the ancient course of philosophy were all meant for the education of ecclesiastics, and to render it a more proper introduction to the study of theology. But the additional quantity of subtlety and sophistry, the casuistry and ascetic morality which those alterations introduced into it, certainly did not render it more for the education of gentlemen or men of the world, or more likely either to improve the understanding or to mend the heart.

This course of philosophy is what still continues to be taught in the greater part of the universities of Europe, with more or less diligence, according as the constitution of each particular university happens to render diligence more or less necessary to the teachers. In some of the richest and best endowed universities, the tutors content themselves with teaching a few unconnected shreds and parcels of this corrupted course; and even these they commonly teach very negligently and superficially.

The improvements which, in modern times have been made in several different branches of philosophy, have not, the greater part of them, been made in universities, though some, no doubt, have. The greater part of universities have not even been very forward to adopt those improvements after they were made; and several of those learned societies have chosen to remain, for a long time, the sanctuaries in which exploded systems and obsolete prejudices found shelter and protection, after they had been hunted out of every other corner of the world. In general, the richest and best endowed universities have been slowest in adopting those improvements, and the most averse to permit any considerable change in the established plan of education. Those improvements were more easily introduced into some of the poorer universities, in which the teachers, depending upon their reputation for the greater part of their subsistence, were obliged to pay more attention to the current opinions of the world.

But though the public schools and universities of Europe were originally intended only for the education of a particular profession, that of churchmen; and though they were not always very diligent in instructing their pupils, even in the sciences which were supposed necessary for that profession; yet they gradually drew to themselves the education of almost all other people, particularly of almost all gentlemen and men of fortune. No better method, it seems, could be fallen upon, of spending, with any advantage, the long interval between infancy and that period of life at which men begin to apply in good earnest to the real business of the world, the business which is to employ them during the remainder of their days. The greater part of what is taught in schools and universities, however, does not seem to be the most proper preparation for that business.

In England, it becomes every day more and more the custom to send young people to travel in foreign countries immediately upon their leaving school, and without sending them to any university. Our young people, it is said, generally return home much improved by their travels. A young man, who goes abroad at seventeen or eighteen, and returns home at one-and-twenty, returns three or four years older than he was when he went abroad; and at that age it is very difficult not to improve a good deal in three or four years. In the course of his travels, he generally acquires some knowledge of one or two foreign languages; a knowledge, however, which is seldom sufficient to enable him either to speak or write them with propriety. In other respects, he commonly returns home more conceited, more unprincipled, more dissipated, and more incapable of my serious application, either to study or to business, than he could well have become in so short a time had he lived at home. By traveling so very young, by spending in the most frivolous dissipation the most previous years of his life, at a distance from the inspection and control of his parents and relations, every useful habit, which the earlier parts of his education might have had some tendency to form in him, instead of being riveted and confirmed, is almost necessarily either weakened or effaced. Nothing but the discredit into which the universities are allowing themselves to fall, could ever have brought into repute so very absurd a practice as that of traveling at this early period of life. By sending his son abroad, a father delivers himself, at least for some time, from so disagreeable an object as that of a son unemployed, neglected, and going to ruin before his eyes.

Such have been the effects of some of the modern institutions for education.

Different plans and different institutions for education seem to have taken place in other ages and nations.

In the republics of ancient Greece, every free citizen was instructed, under the direction of the public magistrate, in gymnastic exercises and in music. By gymnastic exercises, it was intended to harden his body, to sharpen his courage, and to prepare him for the fatigues and dangers of war; and as the Greek militia was, by all accounts, one of the best that ever was in the world, this part of their public education must have answered completely the purpose for which it was intended. By the other part, music, it was proposed, at least by the philosophers and historians, who have given us an account of those institutions, to humanize the mind, to soften the temper, and to dispose it for performing all the social and moral duties of public and private life.

In ancient Rome, the exercises of the Campus Martius answered the same purpose as those of the gymnasium in ancient Greece, and they seem to have answered it equally well. But among the Romans there was nothing which corresponded to the musical education of the Greeks. The morals of the Romans, however, both in private and public life, seem to have been, not only equal, but, upon the whole, a good deal superior to those of the Greeks. That they were superior in private life, we have the express testimony of Polybius, and of Dionysius of Halicarnassus, two authors well acquainted with both nations; and the whole tenor of the Greek and Roman history bears witness to the superiority of the public morals of the Romans. The good temper and moderation of contending factions seem to be the most essential circumstances in the public morals of a free people. But the factions of the Greeks were almost always violent and sanguinary; whereas, till the time of the Gracchi, no blood had ever been shed in any Roman faction; and from the time of the Gracchi, the Roman republic may be considered as in reality dissolved. Notwithstanding, therefore, the very respectable authority of Plato, Aristotle, and Polybius, and notwithstanding the very ingenious reasons by which Mr. Montesquieu endeavors to support that authority, it seems probable that the musical education of the Greeks had no great effect in mending their morals, since, without any such education, those of the Romans were, upon the whole, superior. The respect of those ancient sages for the institutions of their ancestors had probably disposed them to find much political wisdom in what was, perhaps, merely an ancient custom, continued, without interruption, from the earliest period of those societies, to the times in which they had arrived at a considerable degree of refinement. Music and dancing are the great amusements of almost all barbarous nations, and the great accomplishments which are supposed to fit any man for entertaining his society. It is so at this day among the negroes on the coast of Africa. It was so among the ancient Celts, among the ancient Scandinavians, and, as we may learn from Homer, among the ancient Greeks, in the times preceding the Trojan war. When the Greek tribes had formed themselves into little republics, it was natural that the study of those accomplishments should for a long time make a part of the public and common education of the people.

The masters who instructed the young people, either in music or in military exercises, do not seem to have been paid, or even appointed by the state, either in Rome or even at Athens, the Greek republic of whose laws and customs we are the best informed. The state required that every free citizen should fit himself for defending it in war, and should upon that account, learn his military exercises. But it left him to learn them of such masters as he could find; and it seems to have advanced nothing for this purpose, but a public field or place of exercise, in which he should and perform them.

In the early ages, both of the Greek and Roman republics, the other parts of education seem to have consisted in learning to read, write, and account, according to the arithmetic of the times. These accomplishments the richer citizens seem frequently to have acquired at home, by the assistance of some domestic pedagogue, who was, generally, either a slave or a freedman; and the poorer citizens in the schools of such masters as made a trade of teaching for hire. Such parts of education, however, were abandoned altogether to the care of the parents or guardians of each individual. It does not appear that the state ever assumed any inspection or direction of them. By a law of Solon, indeed, the children were acquitted from maintaining those parents who had neglected to instruct them in some profitable trade or business.

In the progress of refinement, when philosophy and rhetoric came into fashion, the better sort of people used to send their children to the schools of philosophers and rhetoricians, in order to be instructed in these fashionable sciences. But those schools were not supported by the public. They were, for a long time, barely tolerated by it. The demand for philosophy and rhetoric was, for a long time, so small, that the first professed teachers of either could not find constant employment in any one city, but were obliged to travel about from place to place. In this manner lived Zeno of Elea, Protagoras, Gorgias, Hippias, and many others. As the demand increased, the school, both of philosophy and rhetoric, became stationary, first in Athens, and afterwards in several other cities. The state, however, seems never to have encouraged them further, than by assigning to some of them a particular place to teach in, which was sometimes done, too, by private donors. The state seems to have assigned the Academy to Plato, the Lyceum to Aristotle, and the Portico to Zeno of Citta, the founder of the Stoics. But Epicurus bequeathed his gardens to his own school. Till about the time of Marcus Antoninus, however, no teacher appears to have had any salary from the public, or to have had any other emoluments, but what arose from the honorarius or fees of his scholars. The bounty which that philosophical emperor, as we learn from Lucian, bestowed upon one of the teachers of philosophy, probably lasted no longer than his own life. There was nothing equivalent to the privileges of graduation; and to have attended any of those schools was not necessary, in order to be permitted to practice any particular trade or profession. If the opinion of their own utility could not draw scholars to them, the law neither forced anybody to go to them, nor rewarded anybody for having gone to them. The teachers had no jurisdiction over their pupils, nor any other authority besides that natural authority which superior virtue and abilities never fail to procure from young people towards those who are entrusted with any part of their education.

At Rome, the study of the civil law made a part of the education, not of the greater part of the citizens, but of some particular families. The young people, however, who wished to acquire knowledge in the law, had no public school to go to, and had no other method of studying it, than by frequenting the company of such of their relations and friends as were supposed to understand it. It is, perhaps, worth while to remark, that though the laws of the twelve tables were many of them copied from those of some ancient Greek republics, yet law never seems to have grown up to be a science in any republic of ancient Greece. In Rome it became a science very early, and gave a considerable degree of illustration to those citizens who had the reputation of understanding it. In the republics of ancient Greece, particularly in Athens, the ordinary courts of justice consisted of numerous, and therefore disorderly, bodies of people, who frequently decided almost at random, or as clamor, faction, and party-spirit, happened to determine. The ignominy of an unjust decision, when it was to be divided among five hundred, a thousand, or fifteen hundred people (for some of their courts were so very numerous), could not fall very heavy upon any individual. At Rome, on the contrary, the principal courts of justice consisted either of a single judge, or of a small number of judges, whose characters, especially as they deliberated always in public, could not fail to be very much affected by any rash or unjust decision. In doubtful cases such courts, from their anxiety to avoid blame, would naturally endeavor to shelter themselves under the example or precedent of the judges who had sat before them, either in the same or in some other court. This attention to practice and precedent, necessarily formed the Roman law into that regular and orderly system in which it has been delivered down to us; and the like attention has had the like effects upon the laws of every other country where such attention has taken place. The superiority of character in the Romans over that of the Greeks, so much remarked by Polybius and Dionysius of Halicarnassus, was probably more owing to the better constitution of their courts of justice, than to any of the circumstances to which those authors ascribe it. The Romans are said to have been particularly distinguished for their superior respect to an oath. But the people who were accustomed to make oath only before some diligent and well informed court of justice, would naturally be much more attentive to what they swore, than they who were accustomed to do the same thing before mobbish and disorderly assemblies.

The abilities, both civil and military, of the Greeks and Romans, will readily be allowed to have been at least equal to those of any modern nation. Our prejudice is perhaps rather to overrate them. But except in what related to military exercises, the state seems to have been at no pains to form those great abilities; for I cannot be induced to believe that the musical education of the Greeks could be of much consequence in forming them. Masters, however, had been found, it seems, for instructing the better sort of people among those nations, in every art and science in which the circumstances of their society rendered it necessary or convenient for them to be instructed. The demand for such instruction produced, what it always produces, the talent for giving it; and the emulation which an unrestrained competition never fails to excite, appears to have brought that talent to a very high degree of perfection. In the attention which the ancient philosophers excited, in the empire which they acquired over the opinions and principles of their auditors, in the faculty which they possessed of giving a certain tone and character to the conduct and conversation of those auditors, they appear to have been much superior to any modern teachers. In modern times, the diligence of public teachers is more or less corrupted by the circumstances which render them more or less independent of their success and reputation in their particular professions. Their salaries, too, put the private teacher, who would pretend to come into competition with them, in the same state with a merchant who attempts to trade without a bounty, in competition with those who trade with a considerable one. If he sells his goods at nearly the same price, he cannot have the same profit; and poverty and beggary at least, if not bankruptcy and ruin, will infallibly be his lot. If he attempts to sell them much dearer, he is likely to have so few customers, that his circumstances will not be much mended. The privileges of graduation, besides, are in many countries necessary, or at least extremely convenient, to most men of learned professions, that is, to the far greater part of those who have occasion for a learned education. But those privileges can be obtained only by attending the lectures of the public teachers. The most careful attendance upon the ablest instructions of any private teacher cannot always give any title to demand them. It is from these different causes that the private teacher of any of the sciences, which are commonly taught in universities, is, in modern times, generally considered as in the very lowest order of men of letters. A man of real abilities can scarce find out a more humiliating or a more unprofitable employment to turn them to. The endowments of schools and colleges have in this manner not only corrupted the diligence of public teachers, but have rendered it almost impossible to have any good private ones.

Were there no public institutions for education, no system, no science, would be taught, for which there was not some demand, or which the circumstances of the times did not render it either necessary or convenient, or at least fashionable to learn. A private teacher could never find his account in teaching either an exploded and antiquated system of a science acknowledged to be useful, or a science universally believed to be a mere useless and pedantic heap of sophistry and nonsense. Such systems, such sciences, can subsist nowhere but in those incorporated societies for education, whose prosperity and revenue are in a great measure independent of their industry. Were there no public institutions for education, a gentleman, after going through, with application and abilities, the most complete course of education which the circumstances of the times were supposed to afford, could not come into the world completely ignorant of everything which is the common subject of conversation among gentlemen and men of the world.

There are no public institutions for the education of women, and there is accordingly nothing useless, absurd, or fantastical, in the common course of their education. They are taught what their parents or guardians judge it necessary or useful for them to learn, and they are taught nothing else. Every part of their education tends evidently to some useful purpose; either to improve the natural attractions of their person, or to form their mind to reserve, to modesty, to chastity, and to economy; to render them both likely to became the mistresses of a family, and to behave properly when they have become such. In every part of her life, a woman feels some convenience or advantage from every part of her education. It seldom happens that a man, in any part of his life, derives any convenience or advantage from some of the most laborious and troublesome parts of his education.

Ought the public, therefore, to give no attention, it may be asked, to the education of the people? Or, if it ought to give any, what are the different parts of education which it ought to attend to in the different orders of the people? And in what manner ought it to attend to them?

In some cases, the state of society necessarily places the greater part of individuals in such situations as naturally form in them, without any attention of government, almost all the abilities and virtues which that state requires, or perhaps can admit of. In other cases, the state of the society does not place the greater part of individuals in such situations; and some attention of government is necessary, in order to prevent the almost entire corruption and degeneracy of the great body of the people.

In the progress of the division of labor, the employment of the far greater part of those who live by labor, that is, of the great body of the people, comes to be confined to a few very simple operations; frequently to one or two. But the understandings of the greater part of men are necessarily formed by their ordinary employments. The man whose whole life is spent in performing a few simple operations, of which the effects, too, are perhaps always the same, or very nearly the same, has no occasion to exert his understanding, or to exercise his invention, in finding out expedients for removing difficulties which never occur. He naturally loses, therefore, the habit of such exertion, and generally becomes as stupid and ignorant as it is possible for a human creature to become. The torpor of his mind renders him not only incapable of relishing or bearing a part in any rational conversation, but of conceiving any generous, noble, or tender sentiment, and consequently of forming any just judgment concerning many even of the ordinary duties of private life. Of the great and extensive interests of his country he is altogether incapable of judging; and unless very particular pains have been taken to render him otherwise, he is equally incapable of defending his country in war. The uniformity of his stationary life naturally corrupts the courage of his mind, and makes him regard, with abhorrence, the irregular, uncertain, and adventurous life of a soldier. It corrupts even the activity of his body, and renders him incapable of exerting his strength with vigor and perseverance in any other employment, than that to which he has been bred. His dexterity at his own particular trade seems, in this manner, to be acquired at the expense of his intellectual, social, and martial virtues. But in every improved and civilized society, this is the state into which the laboring poor, that is, the great body of the people, must necessarily fall, unless government takes some pains to prevent it.

It is otherwise in the barbarous societies, as they are commonly called, of hunters, of shepherds, and even of husbandmen in that rude state of husbandry which precedes the improvement of manufactures, and the extension of foreign commerce. In such societies, the varied occupations of every man oblige every man to exert his capacity, and to invent expedients for removing difficulties which are continually occurring. Invention is kept alive, and the mind is not suffered to fall into that drowsy stupidity, which, in a civilized society, seems to benumb the understanding of almost all the inferior ranks of people. In those barbarous societies, as they are called, every man, it has already been observed, is a warrior. Every man, too, is in some measure a statesman, and can form a tolerable judgment concerning the interest of the society, and the conduct of those who govern it. How far their chiefs are good judges in peace, or good leaders in war, is obvious to the observation of almost every single man among them. In such a society, indeed, no man can well acquire that improved and refined understanding which a few men sometimes possess in a more civilized state. Though in a rude society there is a good deal of variety in the occupations of every individual, there is not a great deal in those of the whole society. Every man does, or is capable of doing, almost every thing which any other man does, or is capable of being. Every man has a considerable degree of knowledge, ingenuity, and invention but scarce any man has a great degree. The degree, however, which is commonly possessed, is generally sufficient for conducting the whole simple business of the society. In a civilized state, on the contrary, though there is little variety in the occupations of the greater part of individuals, there is an almost infinite variety in those of the whole society. These varied occupations present an almost infinite variety of objects to the contemplation of those few, who, being attached to no particular occupation themselves, have leisure and inclination to examine the occupations of other people. The contemplation of so great a variety of objects necessarily exercises their minds in endless comparisons and combinations, and renders their understandings, in an extraordinary degree, both acute anti-comprehensive. Unless those few, however, happen to be placed in some very particular situations, their great abilities, though honorable to themselves, may contribute very little to the good government or happiness of their society. Notwithstanding the great abilities of those few, all the nobler parts of the human character may be, in a great measure, obliterated and extinguished in the great body of the people.

The education of the common people requires, perhaps, in a civilized and commercial society, the attention of the public, more than that of people of some rank and fortune. People of some rank and fortune are generally eighteen or nineteen years of age before they enter upon that particular business, profession, or trade, by which they propose to distinguish themselves in the world. They have, before that, full time to acquire, or at least to fit themselves for afterwards acquiring, every accomplishment which can recommend them to the public esteem, or render them worthy of it. Their parents or guardians are generally sufficiently anxious that they should be so accomplished, and are in most cases, willing enough to lay out the expense which is necessary for that purpose.

If they are not always properly educated, it is seldom from the want of expense laid out upon their education, but from the improper application of that expense. It is seldom from the want of masters, but from the negligence and incapacity of the masters who are to be had, and from the difficulty, or rather from the impossibility, which there is, in the present state of things, of finding any better. The employments, too, in which people of some rank or fortune spend the greater part of their lives, are not, like those of the common people, simple and uniform. They are almost all of them extremely complicated, and such as exercise the head more than the hands. The understandings of those who are engaged in such employments, can seldom grow torpid for want of exercise. The employments of people of some rank and fortune, besides, are seldom such as harass them from morning to night. They generally have a good deal of leisure, during which they may perfect themselves in every branch, either of useful or ornamental knowledge, of which they may have laid the foundation, or for which they may have acquired some taste in the earlier part of life.

It is otherwise with the common people. They have little time to spare for education. Their parents can scarce afford to maintain them, even in infancy. As soon as they are able to work, they must apply to some trade, by which they can earn their subsistence. That trade, too, is generally so simple and uniform, as to give little exercise to the understanding; while, at the same time, their labor is both so constant and so severe, that it leaves them little leisure and less inclination to apply to, or even to think of any thing else.

But though the common people cannot, in any civilized society, be so well instructed as people of some rank and fortune; the most essential parts of education, however, to read, write, and account, can be acquired at so early a period of life, that the greater part, even of those who are to be bred to the lowest occupations, have time to acquire them before they can be employed in those occupations. For a very small expense, the public can facilitate, can encourage and can even impose upon almost the whole body of the people, the necessity of acquiring those most essential parts of education.

The public can facilitate this acquisition, by establishing in every parish or district a little school, where children maybe taught for a reward so moderate, that even a common laborer may afford it; the master being partly, but not wholly, paid by the public; because, if he was wholly, or even principally, paid by it, he would soon learn to neglect his business. In Scotland, the establishment of such parish schools has taught almost the whole common people to read, and a very great proportion of them to write and account. In England, the establishment of charity schools has had an effect of the same kind, though not so universally, because the establishment is not so universal. If, in those little schools, the books by which the children are taught to read, were a little more instructive than they commonly are; and if, instead of a little smattering in Latin, which the children of the common people are sometimes taught there, and which can scarce ever be of any use to them, they were instructed in the elementary parts of geometry and mechanics; the literary education of this rank of people would, perhaps, be as complete as can be. There is scarce a common trade, which does not afford some opportunities of applying to it the principles of geometry and mechanics, and which would not, therefore, gradually exercise and improve the common people in those principles, the necessary introduction to the most sublime, as well as to the most useful sciences.

The public can encourage the acquisition of those most essential parts of education, by giving small premiums, and little badges of distinction, to the children of the common people who excel in them.

The public can impose upon almost the whole body of the people the necessity of acquiring the most essential parts of education, by obliging every man to undergo an examination or probation in them, before he can obtain the freedom in any corporation, or be allowed to set up any trade, either in a village or town corporate.

It was in this manner, by facilitating the acquisition of their military and gymnastic exercises, by encouraging it, and even by imposing upon the whole body of the people the necessity of learning those exercises, that the Greek and Roman republics maintained the martial spirit of their respective citizens. They facilitated the acquisition of those exercises, by appointing a certain place for learning and practicing them, and by granting to certain masters the privilege of teaching in that place. Those masters do not appear to have had either salaries or exclusive privileges of any kind. Their reward consisted altogether in what they got from their scholars; and a citizen, who had learnt his exercises in the public gymnasia, had no sort of legal advantage over one who had learnt them privately, provided the latter had learned them equally well. Those republics encouraged the acquisition of those exercises, by bestowing little premiums and badges of distinction upon those who excelled in them. To have gained a prize in the Olympic, Isthmian, or Nemaean games, gave illustration, not only to the person who gained it, but to his whole family and kindred. The obligation which every citizen was under, to serve a certain number of years, if called upon, in the armies of the republic, sufficiently imposed the necessity of learning those exercises, without which he could not be fit for that service.

That in the progress of improvement, the practice of military exercises, unless government takes proper pains to support it, goes gradually to decay, and, together with it, the martial spirit of the great body of the people, the example of modern Europe sufficiently demonstrates. But the security of every society must always depend, more or less, upon the martial spirit of the great body of the people. In the present times, indeed, that martial spirit alone, and unsupported by a well-disciplined standing army, would not, perhaps, be sufficient for the defense and security of any society. But where every citizen had the spirit of a soldier, a smaller standing army would surely be requisite. That spirit, besides, would necessarily diminish very much the dangers to liberty, whether real or imaginary, which are commonly apprehended from a standing army. As it would very much facilitate the operations of that army against a foreign invader; so it would obstruct them as much, if unfortunately they should ever be directed against the constitution of the state.

The ancient institutions of Greece and Rome seem to have been much more effectual for maintaining the martial spirit of the great body of the people, than the establishment of what are called the militias of modern times. They were much more simple. When they were once established, they executed themselves, and it required little or no attention from government to maintain them in the most perfect vigor. Whereas to maintain, even in tolerable execution, the complex regulations of any modern militia, requires the continual and painful attention of government, without which they are constantly falling into total neglect and disuse. The influence, besides, of the ancient institutions, was much more universal. By means of them, the whole body of the people was completely instructed in the use of arms; whereas it is but a very small part of them who can ever be so instructed by the regulations of any modern militia, except, perhaps, that of Switzerland. But a coward, a man incapable either of defending or of revenging himself, evidently wants one of the most essential parts of the character of a man. He is as much mutilated and deformed in his mind as another is in his body, who is either deprived of some of its most essential members, or has lost the use of them. He is evidently the more wretched and miserable of the two; because happiness and misery, which reside altogether in the mind, must necessarily depend more upon the healthful or unhealthful, the mutilated or entire state of the mind, than upon that of the body. Even though the martial spirit of the people were of no use towards the defense of the society, yet, to prevent that sort of mental mutilation, deformity, and wretchedness, which cowardice necessarily involves in it, from spreading themselves through the great body of the people, would still deserve the most serious attention of government; in the same manner as it would deserve its most serious attention to prevent a leprosy, or any other loathsome and offensive disease, though neither mortal nor dangerous, from spreading itself among them; though, perhaps, no other public good might result from such attention, besides the prevention of so great a public evil.

The same thing may be said of the gross ignorance and stupidity which, in a civilized society, seem so frequently to benumb the understandings of all the inferior ranks of people. A man without the proper use of the intellectual faculties of a man, is, if possible, more contemptible than even a coward, and seems to be mutilated and deformed in a still more essential part of the character of human nature. Though the state was to derive no advantage from the instruction of the inferior ranks of people, it would still deserve its attention that they should not be altogether uninstructed. The state, however, derives no inconsiderable advantage from their instruction. The more they are instructed, the less liable they are to the delusions of enthusiasm and superstition, which, among ignorant nations frequently occasion the most dreadful disorders. An instructed and intelligent people, besides, are always more decent and orderly than an ignorant and stupid one. They feel themselves, each individually, more respectable, and more likely to obtain the respect of their lawful superiors, and they are, therefore, more disposed to respect those superiors. They are more disposed to examine, and more capable of seeing through, the interested complaints of faction and sedition; and they are, upon that account, less apt to be misled into any wanton or unnecessary opposition to the measures of government. In free countries, where the safety of government depends very much upon the favorable judgment which the people may form of its conduct, it must surely be of the highest importance, that they should not be disposed to judge rashly or capriciously concerning it.

ARTICLE III

Of the Expense of the Institutions for the Instruction of People of All Ages

The institutions for the instruction of people of all ages, are chiefly those for religious instruction. This is a species of instruction, of which the object is not so much to render the people good citizens in this world, as to prepare them for another and a better world in the life to come. The teachers of the doctrine which contains this instruction, in the same manner as other teachers, may either depend altogether for their subsistence upon the voluntary contributions of their hearers; or they may derive it from some other fund, to which the law of their country may entitle them; such as a landed estate, a tithe or land tax, an established salary or stipend. Their exertion, their zeal and industry, are likely to be much greater in the former situation than in the latter. In this respect, the teachers of a new religion have always had a considerable advantage in attacking those ancient and established systems, of which the clergy, reposing themselves upon their benefices, had neglected to keep up the fervor of faith and devotion in the great body of the people; and having given themselves up to indolence, were become altogether incapable of making any vigorous exertion in defense even of their own establishment. The clergy of an established and well-endowed religion frequently become men of learning and elegance, who possess all the virtues of gentlemen, or which can recommend them to the esteem of gentlemen; but they are apt gradually to lose the qualities, both good and bad, which gave them authority and influence with the inferior ranks of people, and which had perhaps been the original causes of the success and establishment of their religion. Such a clergy, when attacked by a set of popular and bold, though perhaps stupid and ignorant enthusiasts, feel themselves as perfectly defenseless as the indolent, effeminate, and full fed nations of the southern parts of Asia, when they were invaded by the active, hardy, and hungry Tartars of the north. Such a clergy, upon such an emergency, have commonly no other resource than to call upon the civil magistrate to persecute, destroy, or drive out their adversaries, as disturbers of the public peace. It was thus that the Roman Catholic clergy called upon the civil magistrate to persecute the protestants, and the Church of England to persecute the dissenters; and that in general every religious sect, when it has once enjoyed, for a century or two, the security of a legal establishment, has found itself incapable of making any vigorous defense against any new sect which chose to attack its doctrine or discipline. Upon such occasions, the advantage, in point of learning and good writing, may sometimes be on the side of the established church. But the arts of popularity, all the arts of gaining proselytes, are constantly on the side of its adversaries.

In England, those arts have been long neglected by the well-endowed clergy of the established church, and are at present chiefly cultivated by the dissenters and by the Methodists. The independent provisions, however, which in many places have been made for dissenting teachers, by means of voluntary subscriptions, of trust rights, and other evasions of the law, seem very much to have abated the zeal and activity of those teachers.

They have many of them become very learned, ingenious, and respectable men; but they have in general ceased to be very popular preachers. The Methodists, without half the learning of the dissenters, are much more in vogue.

In the church of Rome the industry and zeal of the inferior clergy are kept more alive by the powerful motive of self-interest, than perhaps in any established protestant church. The parochial clergy derive many of them, a very considerable part of their subsistence from the voluntary oblations of the people; a source of revenue, which confession gives them many opportunities of improving. The mendicant orders derive their whole subsistence from such oblations. It is with them as with the hussars and light infantry of some armies; no plunder, no pay. The parochial clergy are like those teachers whose reward depends partly upon their salary, and partly upon the fees or honoraries which they get from their pupils; and these must always depend, more or less, upon their industry and reputation. The mendicant orders are like those teachers whose subsistence depends altogether upon their industry. They are obliged, therefore, to use every art which can animate the devotion of the common people. The establishment of the two great mendicant orders of St. Dominic and St. Francis, it is observed by Machiavel, revived, in the thirteenth and fourteenth centuries, the languishing faith and devotion of the Catholic church. In Roman Catholic countries, the spirit of devotion is supported altogether by the monks, and by the poorer parochial clergy. The great dignitaries of the church, with all the accomplishments of gentlemen and men of the world, and sometimes with those of men of learning, are careful to maintain the necessary discipline over their inferiors, but seldom give themselves any trouble about the instruction of the people.

"Most of the arts and professions in a state," says by far the most illustrious philosopher and historian of the present age, "are of such a nature, that, while they promote the interests of the society, they are also useful or agreeable to some individuals; and, in that case, the constant rule of the magistrate, except, perhaps, on the first introduction of any art, is, to leave the profession to itself, and trust its encouragement to the individuals who reap the benefit of it. The artisans, finding their profits to rise by the favor of their customers, increase, as much as possible, their skill and industry; and as matters are not disturbed by any injudicious tampering, the commodity is always sure to be at all times nearly proportioned to the demand.

"But there are also some callings which, though useful and even necessary in a state, bring no advantage or pleasure to any individual; and the supreme power is obliged to alter its conduct with regard to the retainers of those professions. It must give them public encouragement in order to their subsistence; and it must provide against that negligence to which they will naturally be subject, either by annexing particular honors to profession, by establishing a long subordination of ranks, and a strict dependence, or by some other expedient. The persons employed in the finances, fleets, and magistracy, are instances of this order of men.

"It may naturally be thought, at first sight, that the ecclesiastics belong to the first class, and that their encouragement, as well as that of lawyers and physicians, may safely be entrusted to the liberality of individuals, who are attached to their doctrines, and who find benefit or consolation from their spiritual ministry and assistance. Their industry and vigilance will, no doubt, be whetted by such an additional motive; and their skill in the profession, as well as their address in governing the minds of the people, must receive daily increase, from their increasing practice, study, and attention.

"But if we consider the matter more closely, we shall find that this interested diligence of the clergy is what every wise legislator will study to prevent; because, in every religion except the true, it is highly pernicious, and it has even a natural tendency to pervert the truth, by infusing into it a strong mixture of superstition, folly, and delusion. Each ghostly practitioner, in order to render himself more precious and sacred in the eyes of his retainers, will inspire them with the most violent abhorrence of all other sects, and continually endeavor, by some novelty, to excite the languid devotion of his audience. No regard will be paid to truth, morals, or decency, in the doctrines inculcated. Every tenet will be adopted that best suits the disorderly affections of the human frame. Customers will be drawn to each conventicle by new industry and address, in practicing on the passions and credulity of the populace. And, in the end, the civil magistrate will find that he has dearly paid for his intended frugality, in saving a fixed establishment for the priests; and that, in reality, the most decent and advantageous composition, which he can make with the spiritual guides, is to bribe their indolence, by assigning stated salaries to their profession, and rendering it superfluous for them to be farther active, than merely to prevent their flock from straying in quest of new pastors. And in this manner ecclesiastical establishments, though commonly they arose at first from religious views, prove in the end advantageous to the political interests of society."

But whatever may have been the good or bad effects of the independent provision of the clergy, it has, perhaps, been very seldom bestowed upon them from any view to those effects. Times of violent religious controversy have generally been times of equally violent political faction. Upon such occasions, each political party has either found it, or imagined it, for his interest, to league itself with some one or other of the contending religious sects. But this could be done only by adopting, or, at least, by favoring the tenets of that particular sect. The sect which had the good fortune to be leagued with the conquering party necessarily shared in the victory of its ally, by whose favor and protection it was soon enabled, in some degree, to silence and subdue all its adversaries.

Those adversaries had generally leagued themselves with the enemies of the conquering party, and were, therefore the enemies of that party. The clergy of this particular sect having thus become complete masters of the field, and their influence and authority with the great body of the people being in its highest vigor, they were powerful enough to overawe the chiefs and leaders of their own party, and to oblige the civil magistrate to respect their opinions and inclinations. Their first demand was generally that he should silence and subdue all their adversaries; and their second, that he should bestow an independent provision on themselves. As they had generally contributed a good deal to the victory, it seemed not unreasonable that they should have some share in the spoil.

They were weary, besides, of humoring the people, and of depending upon their caprice for a subsistence. In making this demand, therefore, they consulted their own ease and comfort, without troubling themselves about the effect which it might have, in future times, upon the influence and authority of their order. The civil magistrate, who could comply with their demand only by giving them something which he would have chosen much rather to take, or to keep to himself, was seldom very forward to grant it. Necessity, however, always forced him to submit at last, though frequently not till after many delays, evasions, and affected excuses.

But if politics had never called in the aid of religion, had the conquering party never adopted the tenets of one sect more than those of another, when it had gained the victory, it would probably have dealt equally and impartially with all the different sects, and have allowed every man to choose his own priest, and his own religion, as he thought proper. There would, and, in this case, no doubt, have been, a great multitude of religious sects. Almost every different congregation might probably have had a little sect by itself, or have entertained some peculiar tenets of its own. Each teacher, would, no doubt, have felt himself under the necessity of making the utmost exertion, and of using every art, both to preserve and to increase the number of his disciples. But as every other teacher would have felt himself under the same necessity, the success of no one teacher, or sect of teachers, could have been very great. The interested and active zeal of religious teachers can be dangerous and troublesome only where there is either but one sect tolerated in the society, or where the whole of a large society is divided into two or three great sects; the teachers of each acting by concert, and under a regular discipline and subordination. But that zeal must be altogether innocent, where the society is divided into two or three hundred, or, perhaps, into as many thousand small sects, of which no one could be considerable enough to disturb the public tranquility. The teachers of each sect, seeing themselves surrounded on all sides with more adversaries than friends, would be obliged to learn that candor and moderation which are so seldom to be found among the teachers of those great sects, whose tenets, being supported by the civil magistrate, are held in veneration by almost all the inhabitants of extensive kingdoms and empires, and who, therefore, see nothing round them but followers, disciples, and humble admirers. The teachers of each little sect, finding themselves almost alone, would be obliged to respect those of almost every other sect; and the concessions which they would mutually find in both convenient and agreeable to make one to another, might in time, probably reduce the doctrine of the greater part of them to that pure and rational religion, free from every mixture of absurdity, imposture, or fanaticism, such as wise men have, in all ages of the world, wished to see established; but such as positive law has, perhaps, never yet established, and probably never will establish in any country; because, with regard to religion, positive law always has been, and probably always will be, more or less influenced by popular superstition and enthusiasm. This plan of ecclesiastical government, or, more properly, of no ecclesiastical government, was what the sect called Independents (a sect, no doubt, of very wild enthusiasts), proposed to establish in England towards the end of the civil war. If it had been established, though of a very unphilosophical origin, it would probably, by this time, have been productive of the most philosophical good temper and moderation with regard to every sort of religious principle. It has been established in Pennsylvania, where, though the Quakers happen to be the most numerous, the law, in reality, favors no one sect more than another; and it is there said to have been productive of this philosophical good temper and moderation.

But though this equality of treatment should not be productive of this good temper and moderation in all, or even in the greater part of the religious sects of a particular country; yet, provided those sects were sufficiently numerous, and each of them conse-quently too small to disturb the public tranquility, the excessive zeal of each for its par-ticular tenets could not well be productive of any very hurtful effects, but, on the contrary, of several good ones; and if the government was perfectly decided, both to let them all alone, and to oblige them all to let alone one another, there is little danger that they would not of their own accord, subdivide themselves fast enough, so as soon to become sufficiently numerous.

In every civilized society, in every society where the distinction of ranks has once been completely established, there have been always two different schemes or systems of morality current at the same time; of which the one may be called the strict or aus-tere; the other the liberal, or, if you will, the loose system. The former is generally admired and revered by the common people; the latter is commonly more esteemed and adopted by what are called the people of fashion. The degree of disapprobation with which we ought to mark the vices of levity, the vices which are apt to arise from great prosperity, and from the excess of gaiety and good humor, seems to constitute the principal distinction between those two opposite schemes or systems. In the liberal or loose system, luxury, wanton, and even disorderly mirth, the pursuit of pleasure to some degree of intemperance, the breach of chastity, at least in one of the two sexes, etc. provided they are not accompanied with gross indecency, and do not lead to false-hood and injustice, are generally treated with a good deal of indulgence, and are eas-ily either excused or pardoned altogether. In the austere system, on the contrary, those excesses are regarded with the utmost abhorrence and detestation. The vices of levity are always ruinous to the common people, and a single week's thoughtlessness and dis-sipation is often sufficient to undo a poor workman for ever, and to drive him, through despair, upon committing the most enormous crimes. The wiser and better sort of the common people, therefore, have always the utmost abhorrence and detestation of such excesses, which their experience tells them are so immediately fatal to people of their condition. The disorder and extravagance of several years, on the contrary, will not always ruin a man of fashion; and people of that rank are very apt to consider the power of indulging in some degree of excess, as one of the advantages of their fortune; and the liberty of doing so without censure or reproach, as one of the privileges which belong to their station. In people of their own station, therefore, they regard such excesses with but a small degree of disapprobation, and censure them either very slightly or not at all.

Almost all religious sects have begun among the common people, from whom they have generally drawn their earliest, as well as their most numerous proselytes. The aus-tere system of morality has, accordingly, been adopted by those sects almost constantly, or with very few exceptions; for there have been some. It was the system by which they could best recommend themselves to that order of people, to whom they first proposed their plan of reformation upon what had been before established. Many of them, perhaps the greater part of them, have even endeavored to gain credit by refining upon this aus-tere system, and by carrying it to some degree of folly and extravagance; and this exces-sive rigor has frequently recommended them, more than any thing else, to the respect and veneration of the common people.

A man of rank and fortune is, by his station, the distinguished member of a great society, who attend to every part of his conduct, and who thereby oblige him to attend to every part of it himself. His authority and consideration depend very much upon the respect which this society bears to him. He dares not do anything which would disgrace or discredit him in it; and he is obliged to a very strict observation of that species of morals, whether liberal or austere, which the general consent of this society prescribes to persons of his rank and fortune. A man of low condition, on the contrary, is far from being a distinguished member of any great society. While he remains in a country village, his conduct may be attended to, and he may be obliged to attend to it himself. In this situation, and in this situation only, he may have what is called a character to lose. But as soon as he comes into a great city, he is sunk in obscurity and darkness. His conduct is observed and attended to by nobody; and he is, therefore, very likely to neglect it himself, and to abandon himself to every sort of low profligacy and vice. He never emerges so effectually from this obscurity, his conduct never excites so much the attention of any respectable society, as by his becoming the member of a small religious sect. He from that moment acquires a degree of consideration which he never had before. All his brother sectaries are, for the credit of the sect, interested to observe his conduct; and, if he gives occasion to any scandal, if he deviates very much from those austere morals which they almost always require of one another, to punish him by what is always a very severe punishment, even where no evil effects attend it, expulsion or excommunication from the sect. In little religious sects, accordingly, the morals of the common people have been almost always remarkably regular and orderly; generally much more so than in the established church. The morals of those little sects, indeed, have frequently been rather disagreeably rigorous and unsocial.

There are two very easy and effectual remedies, however, by whose joint operation the state might, without violence, correct whatever was unsocial or disagreeably rigorous in the morals of all the little sects into which the country was divided.

The first of those remedies is the study of science and philosophy, which the state might render almost universal among all people of middling or more than middling rank and fortune; not by giving salaries to teachers in order to make them negligent and idle, but by instituting some sort of probation, even in the higher and more difficult sciences, to be undergone by every person before he was permitted to exercise any liberal profession, or before he could be received as a candidate for any honorable office, of trust or profit. If the state imposed upon this order of men the necessity of learning, it would have no occasion to give itself any trouble about providing them with proper teachers. They would soon find better teachers for themselves, than any whom the state could provide for them. Science is the great antidote to the poison of enthusiasm and superstition; and where all the superior ranks of people were secured from it, the inferior ranks could not be much exposed to it.

The second of those remedies is the frequency and gaiety of public diversions. The state, by encouraging, that is, by giving entire liberty to all those who, from their own interest, would attempt, without scandal or indecency, to amuse and divert the people by painting, poetry, music, dancing; by all sorts of dramatic representations and exhibitions; would easily dissipate, in the greater part of them, that melancholy and gloomy humor which is almost always the nurse of popular superstition and enthusiasm. Public diversions have always been the objects of dread and hatred to all the fanatical promoters of those popular frenzies. The gaiety and good humor which those diversions inspire, were altogether inconsistent with that temper of mind which was fittest for their purpose, or which they could best work upon. Dramatic representations, besides, frequently exposing their artifices to public ridicule, and sometimes even to public execration, were, upon that account, more than all other diversions, the objects of their peculiar abhorrence.

In a country where the law favored the teachers of no one religion more than those of another, it would not be necessary that any of them should have any particular or immediate dependency upon the sovereign or executive power; or that he should have anything to do either in appointing or in dismissing them from their offices. In such a situation, he would have no occasion to give himself any concern about them, further than to keep the peace among them, in the same manner as among the rest of his subjects, that is, to hinder them from persecuting, abusing, or oppressing one another. But it is quite otherwise in countries where there is an established or governing religion. The sovereign can in this case never be secure, unless he has the means of influencing in a considerable degree the greater part of the teachers of that religion.

The clergy of every established church constitute a great incorporation. They can act in concert, and pursue their interest upon one plan, and with one spirit as much as if they were under the direction of one man; and they are frequently, too, under such direction. Their interest as an incorporated body is never the same with that of the sovereign, and is sometimes directly opposite to it. Their great interest is to maintain their authority with the people, and this authority depends upon the supposed certainty and importance of the whole doctrine which they inculcate, and upon the supposed necessity of adopting every part of it with the most implicit faith, in order to avoid eternal misery. Should the sovereign have the imprudence to appear either to deride, or doubt himself of the most trifling part of their doctrine, or from humanity, attempt to protect those who did either the one or the other, the punctilious honor of a clergy, who have no sort of dependency upon him, is immediately provoked to proscribe him as a profane person, and to employ all the terrors of religion, in order to oblige the people to transfer their allegiance to some more orthodox and obedient prince. Should he oppose any of their pretensions or usurpations, the danger is equally great. The princes who have dared in this manner to rebel against the church, over and above this crime of rebellion, have generally been charged, too, with the additional crime of heresy, notwithstanding their solemn protestations of their faith, and humble submission to every tenet which she thought proper to prescribe to them. But the authority of religion is superior to every other authority. The fears which it suggests conquer all other fears. When the authorized teachers of religion propagate through the great body of the people, doctrines subversive of the authority of the sovereign, it is by violence only, or by the force of a standing army, that he can maintain his authority. Even a standing army cannot in this case give him any lasting security; because if the soldiers are not foreigners, which can seldom be the case, but drawn from the great body of the people, which must almost always be the case, they are likely to be soon corrupted by those very doctrines. The revolutions which the turbulence of the Greek clergy was continually occasioning at Constantinople, as long as the eastern empire subsisted; the convulsions which, during the course of several centuries, the turbulence of the Roman clergy was continually occasioning in every part of Europe, sufficiently demonstrate how precarious and insecure must always be the situation of the sovereign, who has no proper means of influencing the clergy of the established and governing religion of his country.

Articles of faith, as well as all other spiritual matters, it is evident enough, are not within the proper department of a temporal sovereign, who, though he may be very well qualified for protecting, is seldom supposed to be so for instructing the people. With regard to such matters, therefore, his authority can seldom be sufficient to counterbalance the united authority of the clergy of the established church. The public tranquility, however, and his own security, may frequently depend upon the doctrines which they may think proper to propagate concerning such matters. As he can seldom directly oppose their decision, therefore, with proper weight and authority, it is necessary that he should be able to influence it; and he can influence it only by the fears and expectations which he may excite in the greater part of the individuals of the order. Those fears and expectations may consist in the fear of deprivation or other punishment, and in the expectation of further preferment.

In all Christian churches, the benefices of the clergy are a sort of freeholds, which they enjoy, not during pleasure, but during life or good behavior. If they held them by a more precarious tenure, and were liable to be turned out upon every slight disobligation either of the sovereign or of his ministers, it would perhaps be impossible for them to maintain their authority with the people, who would then consider them as mercenary dependents upon the court, in the sincerity of whose instructions they could no longer have any confidence. But should the sovereign attempt irregularly, and by violence, to deprive any number of clergymen of their freeholds, on account, perhaps, of their having propagated, with more than ordinary zeal, some factious or seditious doctrine, he would only render, by such persecution, both them and their doctrine ten times more popular, and therefore ten times more troublesome and dangerous, than they had been before. Fear is in almost all cases a wretched instrument of government, and ought in particular never to be employed against any order of men who have the smallest pretensions to independency.

To attempt to terrify them, serves only to irritate their bad humor, and to confirm them in an opposition, which more gentle usage, perhaps, might easily induce them either to soften, or to lay aside altogether. The violence which the French government usually employed in order to oblige all their parliaments, or sovereign courts of justice, to enregister any unpopular edict, very seldom succeeded. The means commonly employed, however, the imprisonment of all the refractory members, one would think, were forcible enough. The princes of the house of Stuart sometimes employed the like means in order to influence some of the members of the parliament of England, and they generally found them equally intractable. The parliament of England is now managed in another manner; and a very small experiment, which the duke of Choiseul made, about twelve years ago, upon the parliament of Paris, demonstrated sufficiently that all the parliaments of France might have been managed still more easily in the same manner. That experiment was not pursued. For though management and persuasion are always the easiest and safest instruments of government as force and violence are the worst and the most dangerous; yet such, it seems, is the natural insolence of man, that he almost always disdains to use the good instrument, except when he cannot or dare not use the bad one. The French government could and durst use force, and therefore disdained to use management and persuasion. But there is no order of men, it appears I believe, from the experience of all ages, upon whom it is so dangerous or rather so perfectly ruinous, to employ force and violence, as upon the respected clergy of an established church. The rights, the privileges, the personal liberty of every individual ecclesiastic, who is upon good terms with his own order, are, even in the most despotic governments, more respected than those of any other person of nearly equal rank and fortune. It is so in every gradation of despotism, from that of the gentle and mild government of Paris, to that of the violent and furious government of Constantinople. But though this order of men can scarce ever be forced, they may be managed as easily as any other; and the security of the sovereign, as well as the public tranquility, seems to depend very much upon the means which he has of managing them; and those means seem to consist altogether in the preferment which he has to bestow upon them.

In the ancient constitution of the Christian church, the bishop of each diocese was elected by the joint votes of the clergy and of the people of the episcopal city. The people did not long retain their right of election; and while they did retain it, they almost always acted under the influence of the clergy, who, in such spiritual matters, appeared to be their natural guides. The clergy, however, soon grew weary of the trouble of managing them, and found it easier to elect their own bishops themselves. The abbot, in the same manner, was elected by the monks of the monastery, at least in the greater part of abbacies. All the inferior ecclesiastical benefices comprehended within the diocese were collated by the bishop, who bestowed them upon such ecclesiastics as he thought proper. All church preferments were in this manner in the disposal of the church. The sovereign, though he might have some indirect influence in those elections, and though it was sometimes usual to ask both his consent to elect, and his approbation of the election, yet had no direct or sufficient means of managing the clergy. The ambition of every clergyman naturally led him to pay court, not so much to his sovereign as to his own order, from which only he could expect preferment.

Through the greater part of Europe, the pope gradually drew to himself, first the collation of almost all bishoprics and abbacies, or of what were called consistorial benefices, and afterwards, by various machinations and pretences, of the greater part of inferior benefices comprehended within each diocese, little more being left to the bishop than what was barely necessary to give him a decent authority with his own clergy. By this arrangement the condition of the sovereign was still worse than it had been before. The clergy of all the different countries of Europe were thus formed into a sort of spiritual army, dispersed in different quarters indeed, but of which all the movements and operations could now be directed by one head, and conducted upon one uniform plan. The clergy of each particular country might be considered as a particular detachment of that army, of which the operations could easily be supported and seconded by all the other detachments quartered in the different countries round about. Each detachment was not only independent of the sovereign of the country in which it was quartered, and by which it was maintained, but dependent upon a foreign sovereign, who could at any time turn its arms against the sovereign of that particular country, and support them by the arms of all the other detachments.

Those arms were the most formidable that can well be imagined. In the ancient state of Europe, before the establishment of arts and manufactures, the wealth of the clergy gave them the same sort of influence over the common people which that of the great barons gave them over their respective vassals, tenants, and retainers. In the great landed estates, which the mistaken piety both of princes and private persons had bestowed upon the church, jurisdictions were established, of the same kind with those of the great barons, and for the same reason. In those great landed estates, the clergy, or their bailiffs, could easily keep the peace, without the support or assistance either of the king or of any other person; and neither the king nor any other person could keep the peace there without the support and assistance of the clergy. The jurisdictions of the clergy, there-fore, in their particular baronies or manors, were equally independent, and equally exclusive of the authority of the king's courts, as those of the great temporal lords. The tenants of the clergy were, like those of the great barons, almost all tenants at will, entirely dependent upon their immediate lords, and, therefore, liable to be called out at pleasure, in order to fight in any quarrel in which the clergy might think proper to engage them. Over and above the rents of those estates, the clergy possessed in the tithes a very large portion of the rents of all the other estates in every kingdom of Europe. The revenues arising from both those species of rents were, the greater part of them, paid in kind, in corn, wine, cattle, poultry, etc. The quantity exceeded greatly what the clergy could themselves consume; and there were neither arts nor manufactures, for the pro-duce of which they could exchange the surplus. The clergy could derive advantage from this immense surplus in no other way than by employing it, as the great barons employed the like surplus of their revenues, in the most profuse hospitality, and in the most extensive charity. Both the hospitality and the charity of the ancient clergy, accord-ingly, are said to have been very great. They not only maintained almost the whole poor of every kingdom, but many knights and gentlemen had frequently no other means of subsistence than by traveling about from monastery to monastery, under pretence of devotion, but in reality to enjoy the hospitality of the clergy. The retainers of some par-ticular prelates were often as numerous as those of the greatest lay-lords; and the retain-ers of all the clergy taken together were, perhaps, more numerous than those of all the lay-lords. There was always much more union among the clergy than among the lay-lords. The former were under a regular discipline and subordination to the papal author-ity. The latter were under no regular discipline or subordination, but almost always equally jealous of one another, and of the king. Though the tenants and retainers of the clergy, therefore, had both together been less numerous than those of the great lay-lords, and their tenants were probably much less numerous, yet their union would have rendered them more formidable. The hospitality and charity of the clergy, too, not only gave them the command of a great temporal force, but increased very much the weight of their spiritual weapons. Those virtues procured them the highest respect and vener-ation among all the inferior ranks of people, of whom many were constantly, and almost all occasionally, fed by them.

Everything belonging or related to so popular an order, its possessions, its privileges, its doctrines, necessarily appeared sacred in the eyes of the common people; and every violation of them, whether real or pretended, the highest act of sacrilegious wickedness and profaneness. In this state of things, if the sovereign frequently found it difficult to resist the confederacy of a few of the great nobility, we cannot wonder that he should find it still more so to resist the united force of the clergy of his own dominions, supported by that of the clergy of all the neighboring dominions. In such circumstances, the wonder is, not that he was sometimes obliged to yield, but that he ever was able to resist.

The privileges of the clergy in those ancient times (which to us, who live in the present times, appear the most absurd), their total exemption from the secular jurisdiction, for example, or what in England was called the benefit of clergy, were the natural, or rather the necessary, consequences of this state of things. How dangerous must it have been for the sovereign to attempt to punish a clergyman for any crime whatever, if his order were disposed to protect him, and to represent either the proof as insufficient for convicting so holy a man, or the punishment as too severe to be inflicted upon one whose person had been rendered sacred by religion? The sovereign could, in such circumstances, do no better than leave him to be tried by the ecclesiastical courts, who, for the honor of their own order, were interested to restrain, as much as possible, every member of it from committing enormous crimes, or even from giving occasion to such gross scandal as might disgust the minds of the people.

In the state in which things were, through the greater part of Europe, during the tenth, eleventh, twelfth, and thirteenth centuries, and for some time both before and after that period, the constitution of the church of Rome may be considered as the most formidable combination that ever was formed against the authority and security of civil government, as well as against the liberty, reason, and happiness of mankind, which can flourish only where civil government is able to protect them. In that constitution, the grossest delusions of superstition were supported in such a manner by the private interests of so great a number of people, as put them out of all danger from any assault of human reason; because, though human reason might, perhaps, have been able to unveil, even to the eyes of the common people, some of the delusions of superstition, it could never have dissolved the ties of private interest. Had this constitution been attacked by no other enemies but the feeble efforts of human reason, it must have endured for ever. But that immense and well-built fabric, which all the wisdom and virtue of man could never have shaken, much less have overturned, was, by the natural course of things, first weakened, and afterwards in part destroyed; and is now likely, in the course of a few centuries more, perhaps, to crumble into ruins altogether.

The gradual improvements of arts, manufactures, and commerce, the same causes which destroyed the power of the great barons, destroyed, in the same manner, through the greater part of Europe, the whole temporal manufactures, and commerce, the clergy, like the great barons, found something for which they could exchange their rude produce, and thereby discovered the means of spending their whole revenues upon their own persons, without giving any considerable share of them to other people. Their charity became gradually less extensive, their hospitality less liberal, or less profuse. Their retainers became consequently less numerous, and, by degrees, dwindled away altogether. The clergy, too, like the great barons, wished to get a better rent from their landed estates, in order to spend it, in the same manner, upon the gratification of their own private vanity and folly. But this increase of rent could be got only by granting leases to their tenants, who thereby became, in a great measure, independent of them. The ties of interest, which bound the inferior ranks of people to the clergy, were in this manner gradually broken and dissolved. They were even broken and dissolved sooner than those which bound the same ranks of people to the great barons; because the benefices of the church being, the greater part of them, much smaller than the estates of the great barons, the possessor of each benefice was much sooner able to spend the whole of its revenue upon his own person. During the greater part of the fourteenth and fifteenth centuries, the power of the great barons was, through the greater part of Europe, in full vigor. But the temporal power of the clergy, the absolute command which they had once had over the great body of the people was very much decayed. The power of the church was, by that time, very nearly reduced, through the greater part of Europe, to what arose from their spiritual authority; and even that spiritual authority was much weakened, when it ceased to be supported by the charity and hospitality of the clergy. The inferior ranks of people no longer looked upon that order as they had done before; as the comforters of their distress, and the relievers of their indigence. On the contrary, they were provoked and disgusted by the vanity, luxury, and expense of the richer clergy, who appeared to spend upon their own pleasures what had always before been regarded as the patrimony of the poor.

In this situation of things, the sovereigns in the different states of Europe endeavored to recover the influence which they had once had in the disposal of the great benefices of the church; by procuring to the deans and chapters of each diocese the restoration of their ancient right of electing the bishop; and to the monks of each abbacy that of electing the abbot. The re-establishing this ancient order was the object of several statutes enacted in England during the course of the fourteenth century, particularly of what is called the statute of provisors; and of the pragmatic sanction, established in France in the fifteenth century. In order to render the election valid, it was necessary that the sovereign should both consent to it before hand, and afterwards approve of the person elected; and though the election was still supposed to be free, he had, however all the indirect means which his situation necessarily afforded him, of influencing the clergy in his own dominions. Other regulations, of a similar tendency, were established in other parts of Europe. But the power of the pope, in the collation of the great benefices of the church, seems, before the reformation, to have been nowhere so effectually and so universally restrained as in France and England. The concordat afterwards, in the sixteenth century, gave to the kings of France the absolute right of presenting to all the great, or what are called the consistorial, benefices of the Gallican church.

Since the establishment of the pragmatic sanction and of the concordat, the clergy of France have in general shown less respect to the decrees of the papal court, than the clergy of any other Catholic country. In all the disputes which their sovereign has had with the pope, they have almost constantly taken part with the former. This independency of the clergy of France upon the court of Rome seems to be principally founded upon the pragmatic sanction and the concordat. In the earlier periods of the monarchy, the clergy of France appear to have been as much devoted to the pope as those of any other country. When Robert, the second prince of the Capetian race, was most unjustly excommunicated by the court of Rome, his own servants, it is said, threw the victuals which came from his table to the dogs, and refused to taste any thing themselves which had been polluted by the contact of a person in his situation. They were taught to do so, it may very safely be presumed, by the clergy of his own dominions.

The claim of collating to the great benefices of the church, a claim in defense of which the court of Rome had frequently shaken, and sometimes overturned, the thrones of some of the greatest sovereigns in Christendom, was in this manner either restrained or modified, or given up altogether, in many different parts of Europe, even before the time of the reformation. As the clergy had now less influence over the people, so the state had more influence over the clergy. The clergy, therefore, had both less power, and less inclination, to disturb the state.

The authority of the church of Rome was in this state of declension, when the disputes which gave birth to the reformation began in Germany, and soon spread themselves through every part of Europe. The new doctrines were everywhere received with a high degree of popular favor. They were propagated with all that enthusiastic zeal which commonly animates the spirit of party, when it attacks established authority. The teachers of those doctrines, though perhaps, in other respects, not more learned than many of the divines who defended the established church, seem in general to have been better acquainted with ecclesiastical history, and with the origin and progress of that system of opinions upon which the authority of the church was established; and they had thereby the advantage in almost every dispute. The austerity of their manners gave them authority with the common people, who contrasted the strict regularity of their conduct with the disorderly lives of the greater part of their own clergy. They possessed, too, in a much higher degree than their adversaries, all the arts of popularity and of gaining proselytes; arts which the lofty and dignified sons of the church had long neglected, as being to them in a great measure useless. The reason of the new doctrines recommended them to some, their novelty to many; the hatred and contempt of the established clergy to a still greater number: but the zealous, passionate, and fanatical, though frequently coarse and rustic eloquence, with which they were almost everywhere inculcated, recommended them to by far the greatest number.

The success of the new doctrines was almost everywhere so great, that the princes, who at that time happened to be on bad terms with the court of Rome, were, by means of them, easily enabled, in their own dominions, to overturn the church, which having lost the respect and veneration of the inferior ranks of people, could make scarce any resistance. The court of Rome had disobliged some of the smaller princes in the northern parts of Germany, whom it had probably considered as too insignificant to be worth the managing. They universally, therefore, established the reformation in their own dominions. The tyranny of Christiern II, and of Troll archbishop of Upsal, enabled Gustavus Vasa to expel them both from Sweden. The pope favored the tyrant and the archbishop, and Gustavus Vasa found no difficulty in establishing the reformation in Sweden. Christiern II was afterwards deposed from the throne of Denmark, where his conduct had rendered him as odious as in Sweden. The pope, however, was still disposed to favor him; and Frederic of Holstein, who had mounted the throne in his stead, revenged himself, by following the example of Gustavus Vasa. The magistrates of Berne and Zurich, who had no particular quarrel with the pope, established with great ease the reformation in their respective cantons, where just before some of the clergy had, by an imposture somewhat grosser than ordinary, rendered the whole order both odious and contemptible.

In this critical situation of its affairs the papal court was at sufficient pains to cultivate the friendship of the powerful sovereigns of France and Spain, of whom the latter was at that time emperor of Germany. With their assistance, it was enabled, though not without great difficulty, and much bloodshed, either to suppress altogether, or to obstruct very much, the progress of the reformation in their dominions. It was well enough inclined, too, to be complaisant to the king of England. But from the circumstances of the times, it could not be so without giving offence to a still greater sovereign, Charles V, King of Spain and emperor of Germany. Henry VIII, accordingly, though he did not embrace himself the greater part of the doctrines of the Reformation, was yet enabled, by their general prevalence, to suppress all the monasteries, and to abolish the authority of the church of Rome in his dominions. That he should go so far, though he went no further, gave some satisfaction to the patrons of the Reformation, who, having got possession of the government in the reign of his son and successor completed, without any difficulty, the work which Henry VIII had begun.

In some countries, as in Scotland, where the government was weak, unpopular, and not very firmly established, the Reformation was strong enough to overturn, not only the church, but the state likewise, for attempting to support the church.

Among the followers of the Reformation, dispersed in all the different countries of Europe, there was no general tribunal, which, like that of the court of Rome, or an ecumenical council, could settle all disputes among them, and, with irresistible authority, prescribe to all of them the precise limits of orthodoxy. When the followers of the Reformation in one country, therefore, happened to differ from their brethren in another, as they had no common judge to appeal to, the dispute could never be decided; and many such disputes arose among them. Those concerning the government of the church, and the right of conferring ecclesiastical benefices, were perhaps the most interesting to the peace and welfare of civil society. They gave birth, accordingly, to the two principal parties or sects among the followers of the Reformation, the Lutheran and Calvinistic sects, the only sects among them, of which the doctrine and discipline have ever yet been established by law in any part of Europe.

The followers of Luther, together with what is called the Church of England, preserved more or less of the episcopal government, established subordination among the clergy, gave the sovereign the disposal of all the bishoprics, and other consistorial benefices within his dominions, and thereby rendered him the real head of the church; and without depriving the bishop of the right of collating to the smaller benefices within his diocese, they, even to those benefices, not only admitted, but favored the right of presentation, both in the sovereign and in all other lay patrons. This system of church government was, from the beginning, favorable to peace and good order, and to submission to the civil sovereign. It has never, accordingly, been the occasion of any tumult or civil commotion in any country in which it has once been established. The Church of England, in particular, has always valued herself, with great reason, upon the unexceptionable loyalty of her principles. Under such a government, the clergy naturally endeavor to recommend themselves to the sovereign, to the court, and to the nobility and gentry of the country, by whose influence they chiefly expect to obtain preferment. They pay court to those patrons, sometimes, no doubt, by the vilest flattery and assentation; but frequently, too, by cultivating all those arts which best deserve, and which are therefore most likely to gain them, the esteem of people of rank and fortune; by their knowledge in all the different branches of useful and ornamental learning, by the decent liberality of their manners, by the social good humor of their conversation, and by their avowed contempt of those absurd and hypocritical austerities which fanatics inculcate and pretend to practice, in order to draw upon themselves the veneration, and upon the greater part of men of rank and fortune, who avow that they do not practice them, the abhorrence of the common people. Such a clergy, however, while they pay their court in this manner to the higher ranks of life, are very apt to neglect altogether the means of maintaining their influence and authority with the lower. They are listened to, esteemed, and respected by their superiors; but before their inferiors they are frequently incapable of defending, effectually, and to the conviction of such hearers, their own sober and moderate doctrines, against the most ignorant enthusiast who chooses to attack them.

The followers of Zuinglius, or more properly those of Calvin, on the contrary, bestowed upon the people of each parish, whenever the church became vacant, the right of electing their own pastor; and established, at the same time, the most perfect equality among the clergy. The former part of this institution, as long as it remained in vigor, seems to have been productive of nothing but disorder and confusion, and to have tended equally to corrupt the morals both of the clergy and of the people. The latter part seems never to have had any effects but what were perfectly agreeable.

As long as the people of each parish preserved the right of electing their own pastors, they acted almost always under the influence of the clergy, and generally of the most factious and fanatical of the order. The clergy, in order to preserve their influence in those popular elections, became, or affected to become, many of them, fanatics themselves, encouraged fanaticism among the people, and gave the preference almost always to the most fanatical candidate. So small a matter as the appointment of a parish priest, occasioned almost always a violent contest, not only in one parish, but in all the neighboring parishes who seldom failed to take part in the quarrel. When the parish happened to be situated in a great city, it divided all the inhabitants into two parties; and when that city happened, either to constitute itself a little republic, or to be the head and capital of a little republic, as in the case with many of the considerable cities in Switzerland and Holland, every paltry dispute of this kind, over and above exasperating the animosity of all their other factions, threatened to leave behind it, both a new schism in the church, and a new faction in the state. In those small republics, therefore, the magistrate very soon found it necessary, for the sake of preserving the public peace, to assume to himself the right of presenting to all vacant benefices. In Scotland, the most extensive country in which this presbyterian form of church government has ever been established, the rights of patronage were in effect abolished by the act which established presbytery in the beginning of the reign of William III. That act, at least, put in the power of certain classes of people in each parish to purchase, for a very small price, the right of electing their own pastor. The constitution which this act established, was allowed to subsist for about two-and-twenty years, but was abolished by the 10th of Queen Anne, ch. 12, on account of the confusions and disorders which this more popular mode of election had almost everywhere occasioned. In so extensive a country as Scotland, however, a tumult in a remote parish was not so likely to give disturbance to government as in a smaller state. The 10th of Queen Anne restored the rights of patronage. But though, in Scotland, the law gives the benefice, without any exception to the person presented by the patron; yet the church requires sometimes (for she has not in this respect been very uniform in her decisions) a certain concurrence of the people, before she will confer upon the presentee what is called the cure of souls, or the ecclesiastical jurisdiction in the parish. She sometimes, at least, from an affected concern for the peace of the parish, delays the settlement till this concurrence can be procured. The private tampering of some of the neighboring clergy, sometimes to procure, but more frequently to prevent this concurrence, and the popular arts which they cultivate, in order to enable them upon such occasions to tamper more effectually, are perhaps the causes which principally keep up whatever remains of the old fanatical spirit, either in the clergy or in the people of Scotland.

The equality which the Presbyterian form of church government establishes among the clergy, consists, first, in the equality of authority or ecclesiastical jurisdiction; and, secondly, in the equality of benefice. In all Presbyterian churches, the equality of authority is perfect; that of benefice is not so. The difference, however, between one benefice and another, is seldom so considerable, as commonly to tempt the possessor even of the small one to pay court to his patron, by the vile arts of flattery and assentation, in order to get a better. In all the Presbyterian churches, where the rights of patronage are thoroughly established, it is by nobler and better arts, that the established clergy in general endeavor to gain the favor of their superiors; by their learning, by the irreproachable regularity of their life, and by the faithful and diligent discharge of their duty. Their patrons even frequently complain of the independency of their spirit, which they are apt to construe into ingratitude for past favors, but which, at worse, perhaps, is seldom anymore than that indifference which naturally arises from the consciousness that no further favors of the kind are ever to be expected. There is scarce, perhaps, to be found anywhere in Europe, a more learned, decent, independent, and respectable set of men, than the greater part of the Presbyterian clergy of Holland, Geneva, Switzerland, and Scotland.

Where the church benefices are all nearly equal, none of them can be very great; and this mediocrity of benefice, though it may be, no doubt, carried too far, has, however, some very agreeable effects. Nothing but exemplary morals can give dignity to a man of small fortune. The vices of levity and vanity necessarily render him ridiculous, and are, besides, almost as ruinous to him as they are to the common people. In his own conduct, therefore, he is obliged to follow that system of morals which the common people respect the most. He gains their esteem and affection, by that plan of life which his own interest and situation would lead him to follow. The common people look upon him with that kindness with which we naturally regard one who approaches somewhat to our own condition, but who, we think, ought to be in a higher. Their kindness naturally provokes his kindness. He becomes careful to instruct them, and attentive to assist and relieve them. He does not even despise the prejudices of people who are disposed to be so favorable to him, and never treats them with those contemptuous and arrogant airs, which we so often meet with in the proud dignitaries of opulent and well endowed churches. The Presbyterian clergy, accordingly, have more influence over the minds of the common people, than perhaps the clergy of any other established church. It is, accordingly, in Presbyterian countries only, that we ever find the common people converted, without persecution completely, and almost to a man, to the established church.

In countries where church benefices are, the greater part of them, very moderate, a chair in a university is generally a better establishment than a church benefice. The universities have, in this case, the picking and choosing of their members from all the churchmen of the country, who, in every country, constitute by far the most numerous class of men of letters. Where church benefices, on the contrary, are many of them very considerable, the church naturally draws from the universities the greater part of their eminent men of letters; who generally find some patron, who does himself honor by procuring them church preferment. In the former situation, we are likely to find the universities filled with the most eminent men of letters that are to be found in the country. In the latter, we are likely to find few eminent men among them, and those few among the youngest members of the society, who are likely, too, to be drained away from it, before they can have acquired experience and knowledge enough to be of much use to it. It is observed by Mr. de Voltaire, that Father Porée, a Jesuit of no great eminence in the republic of letters, was the only professor they had ever had in France, whose works were worth the reading. In a country which has produced so many eminent men of letters, it must appear somewhat singular, that scarce one of them should have been a professor in a university. The famous Cassendi was, in the beginning of his life, a professor in the university of Aix. Upon the first dawning of his genius, it was represented to him, that by going into the church he could easily find a much more quiet and comfortable subsistence, as well as a better situation for pursuing his studies; and he immediately followed the advice. The observation of Mr. de Voltaire may be applied, I believe, not only to France, but to all other Roman Catholic countries. We very rarely find in any of them an eminent man of letters, who is a professor in a university, except, perhaps, in the professions of law and physic; professions from which the church is not so likely to draw them. After the church of Rome, that of England is by far the richest and best endowed church in Christendom. In England, accordingly, the church is continually draining the universities of all their best and ablest members; and an old college tutor who is known and distinguished in Europe as an eminent man of letters, is as rarely to be found there as in any Roman Catholic country. In Geneva, on the contrary, in the protestant cantons of Switzerland, in the protestant countries of Germany, in Holland, in Scotland, in Sweden, and Denmark, the most eminent men of letters whom those countries have produced, have, not all indeed, but the far greater part of them, been professors in universities. In those countries, the universities are continually draining the church of all its most eminent men of letters.

It may, perhaps, be worth while to remark, that, if we except the poets, a few orators, and a few historians, the far greater part of the other eminent men of letters, both of

Greece and Rome, appear to have been either public or private teachers; generally either of philosophy or of rhetoric. This remark will be found to hold true, from the days of Lysias and Isocrates, of Plato and Aristotle, down to those of Plutarch and Epictetus, Suetonius, and Quintilian. To impose upon any man the necessity of teaching, year after year, in any particular branch of science seems in reality to be the most effectual method for rendering him completely master of it himself. By being obliged to go every year over the same ground, if he is good for any thing, he necessarily becomes, in a few years, well acquainted with every part of it, and if, upon any particular point, he should form too hasty an opinion one year, when he comes, in the course of his lectures to reconsider the same subject the year thereafter, he is very likely to correct it. As to be a teacher of science is certainly the natural employment of a mere man of letters; so is it likewise, perhaps, the education which is most likely to render him a man of solid learning and knowledge. The mediocrity of church benefices naturally tends to draw the greater part of men of letters in the country where it takes place, to the employment in which they can be the most useful to the public, and at the same time to give them the best education, perhaps, they are capable of receiving. It tends to render their learning both as solid as possible, and as useful as possible.

The revenue of every established church, such parts of it excepted as may arise from particular lands or manors, is a branch, it ought to be observed, of the general revenue of the state, which is thus diverted to a purpose very different from the defense of the state. The tithe, for example, is a real land tax, which puts it out of the power of the proprietors of land to contribute so largely towards the defense of the state as they otherwise might be able to do. The rent of land, however, is, according to some, the sole fund; and, according to others, the principal fund, from which, in all great monarchies, the exigencies of the state must be ultimately supplied. The more of this fund that is given to the church, the less, it is evident, can be spared to the state. It may be laid down as a certain maxim, that all other things being supposed equal, the richer the church, the poorer must necessarily be, either the sovereign on the one hand, or the people on the other; and, in all cases, the less able must the state be to defend itself. In several protestant countries, particularly in all the protestant cantons of Switzerland, the revenue which anciently belonged to the Roman Catholic church, the tithes and church lands, has been found a fund sufficient, not only to afford competent salaries to the established clergy, but to defray, with little or no addition, all the other expenses of the state. The magistrates of the powerful canton of Berne, in particular, have accumulated, out of the savings from this fund, a very large sum, supposed to amount to several millions; part or which is deposited in a public treasure, and part is placed at interest in what are called the public funds of the different indebted nations of Europe; chiefly in those of France and Great Britain. What may be the amount of the whole expense which the church, either of Berne, or of any other protestant canton, costs the state, I do not pretend to know. By a very exact account it appears, that, in 1755, the whole revenue of the clergy of the church of Scotland, including their glebe or church lands, and the rent of their manses or dwelling-houses, estimated according to a reasonable valuation, amounted only to £68,514:1:5 ½d. This very moderate revenue affords a decent subsistence to nine hundred and forty-four ministers. The whole expense of the church, including what is occasionally laid out for the building and reparation of churches, and of the manses of ministers, cannot well be supposed to exceed eighty or eighty-five thousand pounds a year. The most opulent church in Christendom does not maintain better the uniformity of faith, the fervor of devotion, the spirit of order, regularity, and austere morals, in the great body of the people, than this very poorly endowed church of Scotland. All the good effects, both civil and religious, which an established church can be supposed to produce, are produced by it as completely as by any other. The greater part of the protestant churches of Switzerland, which, in general, are not better endowed than the church of Scotland, produce those effects in a still higher degree. In the greater part of the protestant cantons, there is not a single person to be found, who does not profess himself to be of the established church. If he professes himself to be of any other, indeed, the law obliges him to leave the canton. But so severe, or, rather, indeed, so oppressive a law, could never have been executed in such free countries, had not the diligence of the clergy beforehand converted to the established church the whole body of the people, with the exception of, perhaps, a few individuals only. In some parts of Switzerland, accordingly, where, from the accidental union of a protestant and Roman Catholic country, the conversion has not been so complete, both religions are not only tolerated, but established by law.

The proper performance of every service seems to require, that its pay or recompense should be, as exactly as possible, proportioned to the nature of the service. If any service is very much underpaid, it is very apt to suffer by the meanness and incapacity of the greater part of those who are employed in it. If it is very much overpaid, it is apt to suffer, perhaps still more, by their negligence and idleness. A man of a large revenue, whatever may be his profession, thinks he ought to live like other men of large revenues; and to spend a great part of his time in festivity, in vanity, and in dissipation. But in a clergyman, this train of life not only consumes the time which ought to be employed in the duties of his function, but in the eyes of the common people, destroys almost entirely that sanctity of character, which can alone enable him to perform those duties with proper weight and authority.

Part IV

Of the Expense of Supporting the Dignity of the Sovereign

Over and above the expenses necessary for enabling the sovereign to perform his several duties, a certain expense is requisite for the support of his dignity. This expense varies, both with the different periods of improvement, and with the different forms of government.

In an opulent and improved society, where all the different orders of people are growing every day more expensive in their houses, in their furniture, in their tables, in their dress, and in their equipage; it cannot well be expected that the sovereign should alone hold out against the fashion. He naturally, therefore, or rather necessarily, becomes more expensive in all those different articles too. His dignity even seems to require that he should become so.

As, in point of dignity, a monarch is more raised above his subjects than the chief magistrate of any republic is ever supposed to be above his fellow-citizens; so a greater expense is necessary for supporting that higher dignity. We naturally expect more splendor in the court of a king, than in the mansion-house of a doge or burgo-master.

Conclusion

The expense of defending the society, and that of supporting the dignity of the chief magistrate, are both laid out for the general benefit of the whole society. It is reasonable, therefore, that they should be defrayed by the general contribution of the whole society; all the different members contributing, as nearly as possible, in proportion to their respective abilities.

The expense of the administration of justice, too, may no doubt be considered as laid out for the benefit of the whole society. There is no impropriety, therefore, in its being defrayed by the general contribution of the whole society. The persons, however, who give occasion to this expense, are those who, by their injustice in one way or another, make it necessary to seek redress or protection from the courts of justice. The persons, again, most immediately benefited by this expense, are those whom the courts of justice either restore to their rights, or maintain in their rights. The expense of the administration of justice, therefore, may very properly be defrayed by the particular contribution of one or other, or both, of those two different sets of persons, according as different occasions may require, that is, by the fees of court. It cannot be necessary to have recourse to the general contribution of the whole society, except for the conviction of those criminals who have not themselves any estate or fund sufficient for paying those fees.

Those local or provincial expenses, of which the benefit is local or provincial (what is laid out, for example, upon the police of a particular town or district), ought to be defrayed by a local or provincial revenue, and ought to be no burden upon the general revenue of the society. It is unjust that the whole society should contribute towards an expense, of which the benefit is confined to a part of the society.

The expense of maintaining good roads and communications is, no doubt, beneficial to the whole society, and may, therefore, without any injustice, be defrayed by the general contributions of the whole society. This expense, however, is most immediately and directly beneficial to those who travel or carry goods from one place to another, and to those who consume such goods. The turnpike tolls in England, and the duties called peages in other countries, lay it altogether upon those two different sets of people, and thereby discharge the general revenue of the society from a very considerable burden.

The expense of the institutions for education and religious instruction, is likewise, no doubt, beneficial to the whole society, and may, therefore, without injustice, be defrayed by the general contribution of the whole society. This expense, however, might, perhaps, with equal propriety, and even with some advantage, be defrayed altogether by those who receive the immediate benefit of such education and instruction, or by the voluntary contribution of those who think they have occasion for either the one or the other.

When the institutions, or public works, which are beneficial to the whole society, either cannot be maintained altogether, or are not maintained altogether, by the contribution of such particular members of the society as are most immediately benefited by them; the deficiency must, in most cases, be made up by the general contribution of the whole society. The general revenue of the society, over and above defraying the expense of defending the society, and of supporting the dignity of the chief magistrate, must make up for the deficiency of many particular branches of revenue. The sources of this general or public revenue, I shall endeavor to explain in the following chapter.

CHAPTER II

Of the Sources of the General or Public Revenue of the Society

The revenue which must defray, not only the expense of defending the society and of supporting the dignity of the chief magistrate, but all the other necessary expenses of government, for which the constitution of the state has not provided any particular revenue may be drawn, either, first, from some fund which peculiarly belongs to the sovereign or commonwealth, and which is independent of the revenue of the people; or, secondly, from the revenue of the people.

Part I

Of the Funds, or Sources, of Revenue, Which May Peculiarly Belong to the Sovereign or Commonwealth

The funds, or sources, of revenue, which may peculiarly belong to the sovereign or commonwealth, must consist, either in stock, or in land.

The sovereign, like, any other owner of stock, may derive a revenue from it, either by employing it himself, or by lending it. His revenue is, in the one case, profit, in the other interest.

The revenue of a Tartar or Arabian chief consists in profit. It arises principally from the milk and increase of his own herds and flocks, of which he himself superintends the management, and is the principal shepherd or herdsman of his own horde or tribe. It is, however, in this earliest and rudest state of civil government only, that profit has ever made the principal part of the public revenue of a monarchical state.

Small republics have sometimes derived a considerable revenue from the profit of mercantile projects. The republic of Hamburgh is said to do so from the profits of a public wine-cellar and apothecary's shop. {See *Memoires Concernant les Droits et Impositions en Europe*, tom. i. p. 73. This work was compiled by the order of the court, for the use of a commission employed for some years past in considering the proper means for reforming the finances of France. The account of the French taxes, which takes up three volumes in quarto, may be regarded as perfectly authentic. That of those of other European nations was compiled from such information as the French ministers at the different courts could procure. It is much shorter, and probably not quite so exact as that of the French taxes.} That state cannot be very great, of which the sovereign has leisure to carry on the trade of a wine-merchant or an apothecary. The profit of a public bank has been a source of revenue to more considerable states. It has been so, not only to Hamburgh, but to Venice and Amsterdam. A revenue of this kind has even by some people been thought not below the attention of so great an empire as that of Great Britain. Reckoning the ordinary dividend of the Bank of England at five and a-half percent, and its capital at ten millions seven hundred and eighty thousand pounds, the neat annual profit, after paying the expense of management, must amount, it is said, to five hundred and ninety-two thousand nine hundred pounds. Government, it is pretended, could borrow this capital at three percent interest, and, by taking the management of the bank into its own hands, might make a clear profit of two hundred and sixty-nine thousand five hundred pounds a year. The orderly, vigilant, and parsimonious administration of such aristocracies as those of Venice and Amsterdam, is extremely proper, it appears from experience, for the management of a mercantile project of this kind. But whether such a government us that of England, which, whatever may be its virtues, has never been famous for good economy; which, in time of peace, has generally conducted itself with the slothful and negligent profusion that is, perhaps, natural to monarchies; and, in time of war, has constantly acted with all the thoughtless extravagance that democracies are apt to fall into, could be safely trusted with the management of such a project, must at least be a good deal more doubtful.

The post-office is properly a mercantile project. The government advances the expense of establishing the different offices, and of buying or hiring the necessary horses or carriages, and is repaid, with a large profit, by the duties upon what is carried. It is, perhaps, the only mercantile project which has been successfully managed by, I believe, every sort of government. The capital to be advanced is not very considerable. There is no mystery in the business. The returns are not only certain but immediate.

Princes, however, have frequently engaged in many other mercantile projects, and have been willing, like private persons, to mend their fortunes, by becoming adventurers in the common branches of trade. They have scarce ever succeeded. The profusion with which the affairs of princes are always managed, renders it almost impossible that they should. The agents of a prince regard the wealth of their master as inexhaustible; are careless at what price they buy, are careless at what price they sell, are careless at what expense they transport his goods from one place to another. Those agents frequently live with the profusion of princes; and sometimes, too, in spite of that profusion, and by a proper method of making up their accounts, acquire the fortunes of princes. It was thus, as we are told by Machiavel, that the agents of Lorenzo of Medicis, not a prince of mean abilities, carried on his trade. The republic of Florence was several times obliged to pay the debt into which their extravagance had involved him. He found it convenient, accordingly to give up the business of merchant, the business to which his family had originally owed their fortune, and, in the latter part of his life, to employ both what remained of that fortune, and the revenue of the state, of which he had the disposal, in projects and expenses more suitable to his station.

No two characters seem more inconsistent than those of trader and sovereign. If the trading spirit of the English East India company renders them very bad sovereigns, the spirit of sovereignty seems to have rendered them equally bad traders. While they were traders only, they managed their trade successfully, and were able to pay from their profits a moderate dividend to the proprietors of their stock. Since they became sovereigns, with a revenue which, it is said, was originally more than three millions sterling, they have been obliged to beg the ordinary assistance of government, in order to avoid immediate bankruptcy. In their former situation, their servants in India considered themselves as the clerks of merchants; in their present situation, those servants consider themselves as the ministers of sovereigns.

A state may sometimes derive some part of its public revenue from the interest of money, as well as from the profits of stock. If it has amassed a treasure, it may lend a part of that treasure, either to foreign states, or to its own subjects.

The canton of Berne derives a considerable revenue by lending a part of its treasure to foreign states, that is, by placing it in the public funds of the different indebted nations of Europe, chiefly in those of France and England. The security of this revenue must depend, first, upon the security of the funds in which it is placed, or upon the good faith of the government which has the management of them; and, secondly, upon the certainty or probability of the continuance of peace with the debtor nation. In the case of a war, the very first act of hostility on the part of the debtor nation might be the forfeiture of the funds of its credit or. This policy of lending money to foreign states is, so far as I know peculiar to the canton of Berne.

The city of Hamburgh {See *Memoire Concernant les Droites et Impositions en Europe* tom. i p. 73.} has established a sort of public pawn-shop, which lends money to the subjects of the state, upon pledges, at six percent interest. This pawn-shop, or lombard, as it is called, affords a revenue, it is pretended, to the state, of a hundred and fifty thousand crowns, which, at four and sixpence the crown, amounts to £33,750 sterling.

The government of Pennsylvania, without amassing any treasure, invented a method of lending, not money, indeed, but what is equivalent to money, to its subjects. By advancing to private people, at interest, and upon land security to double the value, paper bills of credit, to be redeemed fifteen years after their date; and, in the mean time, made transferable from hand to hand, like banknotes, and declared by act of assembly to be a legal tender in all payments from one inhabitant of the province to another, it raised a moderate revenue, which went a considerable way towards defraying an annual expense of about £4,500, the whole ordinary expense of that frugal and orderly government. The success of an expedient of this kind must have depended upon three different circumstances: first, upon the demand for some other instrument of commerce, besides gold and silver money, or upon the demand for such a quantity of consumable stock as could not be had without sending abroad the greater part of their gold and silver money, in order to purchase it; secondly, upon the good credit of the government which made use of this expedient; and, thirdly, upon the moderation with which it was used, the whole value of the paper bills of credit never exceeding that of the gold and silver money which would have been necessary for carrying on their circulation, had there been no paper bills of credit. The same expedient was, upon different occasions, adopted by several other American colonies; but, from want of this moderation, it produced, in the greater part of them, much more disorder than convenience.

The unstable and perishable nature of stock and credit, however, renders them unfit to be trusted to as the principal funds of that sure, steady, and permanent revenue, which can alone give security and dignity to government. The government of no great nation, that was advanced beyond the shepherd state, seems ever to have derived the greater part of its public revenue from such sources.

Land is a fund of more stable and permanent nature; and the rent of public lands, accordingly, has been the principal source of the public revenue of many a great nation that was much advanced beyond the shepherd state. From the produce or rent of the public lands, the ancient republics of Greece and Italy derived for a long time the greater part of that revenue which defrayed the necessary expenses of the commonwealth. The rent of the crown lands constituted for a long time the greater part of the revenue of the ancient sovereigns of Europe.

War, and the preparation for war, are the two circumstances which, in modern times, occasion the greater part of the necessary expense or all great states. But in the ancient republics of Greece and Italy, every citizen was a soldier, and both served, and prepared himself for service, at his own expense. Neither of those two circumstances, therefore, could occasion any very considerable expense to the state. The rent of a very moderate landed estate might be fully sufficient for defraying all the other necessary expenses of government.

In the ancient monarchies of Europe, the manners and customs of the time sufficiently prepared the great body of the people for war; and when they took the field, they were, by the condition of their feudal tenures, to be maintained either at their own expense, or at that of their immediate lords, without bringing any new charge upon the sovereign. The other expenses of government were, the greater part of them, very moderate. The administration of justice, it has been shown, instead of being a cause of expense was a source of revenue. The labor of the country people, for three days before, and for three days after, harvest, was thought a fund sufficient for making and maintaining all the bridges, highways, and other public works, which the commerce of the country was supposed to require. In those days the principal expense of the sovereign seems to have consisted in the maintenance of his own family and household. The officers of his household, accordingly, were then the great officers of state. The lord treasurer received his rents. The lord steward and lord chamberlain looked after the expense of his family. The care of his stables was committed to the lord constable and the lord marshal. His houses were all built in the form of castles, and seem to have been the principal fortresses which he possessed. The keepers of those houses or castles might be considered as a sort of military governors. They seem to have been the only military officers whom it was necessary to maintain in time of peace. In these circumstances, the rent of a great landed estate might, upon ordinary occasions, very well defray all the necessary expenses of government.

In the present state of the greater part of the civilized monarchies of Europe, the rent of all the lands in the country, managed as they probably would be, if they all belonged to one proprietor, would scarce, perhaps, amount to the ordinary revenue which they levy upon the people even in peaceable times. The ordinary revenue of Great Britain, for example, including not only what is necessary for defraying the current expense of the year, but for paying the interest of the public debts, and for sinking a part of the capital of those debts, amounts to upwards of ten millions a year. But the land tax, at four shillings in the pound, falls short of two millions a year. This land tax, as it is called however, is supposed to be one-fifth, not only of the rent of all the land, but of that of all the houses, and of the interest of all the capital stock of Great Britain, that part of it only excepted which is either lent to the public, or employed as farming stock in the cultivation of land. A very considerable part of the produce of this tax arises from the rent of houses and the interest of capital stock. The land tax of the city of London, for example, at four shillings in the pound, amounts to £123,399:6:7; that of the city of Westminster to £63,092:1:5; that of the palaces of Whitehall and St. James's, to £30,754:6:3. A certain proportion of the land tax is, in the same manner, assessed upon all the other cities and towns corporate in the kingdom; and arises almost altogether, either from the rent of houses, or from what is supposed to be the interest of trading and capital stock. According to the estimation, therefore, by which Great Britain is rated to the land tax, the whole mass of revenue arising from the rent of all the lands, from that of all the houses, and from the interest of all the capital stock, that part of it only excepted which is either lent to the public, or employed in the cultivation of land, does not exceed ten millions sterling a year, the ordinary revenue which government levies upon the people, even in peaceable times. The estimation by which Great Britain is rated to the land tax is, no doubt, taking the whole kingdom at an average, very much below the real value; though in several particular counties and districts it is said to be nearly equal to that value. The rent of the lands alone, exclusive of that of houses and of the interest of stock, has by many people been estimated at twenty millions; an estimation made in a great measure at random, and which, I apprehend, is as likely to be above as below the truth. But if the lands of Great Britain, in the present state of their cultivation, do not afford a rent of more than twenty millions a year, they could not well afford the half, most probably not the fourth part of that rent, if they all belonged to a single proprietor, and were put under the negligent, expensive, and oppressive management of his factors and agents. The crown lands of Great Britain do not at present afford the fourth part of the rent which could probably be drawn from them if they were the property of private persons. If the crown lands were more extensive, it is probable, they would be still worse managed.

The revenue which the great body of the people derives from land is, in proportion, not to the rent, but to the produce of the land. The whole annual produce of the land of every country, if we except what is reserved for seed, is either annually consumed by the great body of the people, or exchanged for something else that is consumed by them. Whatever keeps down the produce of the land below what it would otherwise rise to, keeps down the revenue of the great body of the people, still more than it does that of the proprietors of land. The rent of land, that portion of the produce which belongs to the proprietors, is scarce anywhere in Great Britain supposed to be more than a third part of the whole produce. If the land which, in one state of cultivation, affords a revenue of ten millions sterling a year, would in another afford a rent of twenty millions; the rent being, in both cases, supposed a third part of the produce, the revenue of the proprietors would be less than it otherwise might be, by ten millions a year only; but the revenue of the great hotly of the people would be less than it otherwise might be, by thirty millions a year, deducting only what would be necessary for seed. The population of the country would be less by the number of people which thirty millions a year, deducting always the seed, could maintain, according to the particular mode of living, and expense which might take place in the different ranks of men, among whom the remainder was distributed.

Though there is not at present in Europe, any civilized state of any kind which derives the greater part of its public revenue from the rent of lands which are the property of the state; yet, in all the great monarchies of Europe, there are still many large tracts of land which belong to the crown. They are generally forest, and sometimes forests where, after traveling several miles, you will scarce find a single tree; a mere waste and loss of country, in respect both of produce and population. In every great monarchy of Europe, the sale of the crown lands would produce a very large sum of money, which, if applied to the payment of the public debts, would deliver from mortgage a much greater revenue than any which those lands have even afforded to the crown. In countries where lands, improved and cultivated very highly, and yielding, at the time of sale, as great a rent as can easily be got from them, commonly sell at thirty years purchase; the unimproved, uncultivated, and low-rented crown lands, might well be expected to sell at forty, fifty, or sixty years purchase. The crown might immediately enjoy the revenue which this great price would redeem from mortgage. In the course of a few years, it would probably enjoy another revenue. When the crown lands had become private property, they would, in the course of a few years, become well improved and well cultivated. The increase of their produce would increase the population of the country, by augmenting the revenue and consumption of the people. But the revenue which the crown derives from the duties or custom and excise, would necessarily increase with the revenue and consumption of the people.

The revenue which, in any civilized monarchy, the crown derives from the crown lands, though it appears to cost nothing to individuals, in reality costs more to the society than perhaps any other equal revenue which the crown enjoys. It would, in all cases, be for the interest of the society, to replace this revenue to the crown by some other equal revenue, and to divide the lands among the people, which could not well be done better, perhaps, than by exposing them to public sale.

Lands, for the purposes of pleasure and magnificence, parks, gardens, public walks, etc. possessions which are everywhere considered as causes of expense, not as sources of revenue, seem to be the only lands which, in a great and civilized monarchy, ought to belong to the crown.

Public stock and public lands, therefore, the two sources of revenue which may peculiarly belong to the sovereign or commonwealth, being both improper and insufficient funds for defraying the necessary expense of any great and civilized state; it remains that this expense must, the greater part of it, be defrayed by taxes of one kind or another; the people contributing a part of their own private revenue, in order to make up a public revenue to the sovereign or commonwealth.

Part II

Of Taxes

The private revenue of individuals, it has been shown in the first book of this inquiry, arises, ultimately from three different sources; rent, profit, and wages. Every tax must finally be paid from some one or other of those three different sources of revenue, or from all of them indifferently. I shall endeavor to give the best account I can, first, of those taxes which, it is intended should fall upon rent; secondly, of those which, it is intended should fall upon profit; thirdly, of those which, it is intended should fall upon wages; and fourthly, of those which, it is intended should fall indifferently upon all those three different sources of private revenue. The particular consideration of each of these four different sorts of taxes will divide the second part of the present chapter into four articles, three of which will require several other subdivisions. Many of these taxes, it will appear from the following review, are not finally paid from the fund, or source of revenue, upon which it is intended they should fall.

Before I enter upon the examination of particular taxes, it is necessary to premise the four following maxims with regard to taxes in general.

1. The subjects of every state ought to contribute towards the support of the government, as nearly as possible, in proportion to their respective abilities; that is, in proportion to the revenue which they respectively enjoy under the protection of the state. The expense of government to the individuals of a great nation, is like the expense of management to the joint tenants of a great estate, who are all obliged to contribute in proportion to their respective interests in the estate. In the observation or neglect of this maxim, consists what is called the equality or inequality of taxation. Every tax, it must be observed once for all, which falls finally upon one only of the three sorts of revenue above mentioned, is necessarily unequal, in so far as it does not affect the other two. In the following examination of different taxes, I shall seldom take much farther notice of this sort of inequality; but shall, in most cases, confine my observations to that inequality which is occasioned by a particular tax falling unequally upon that particular sort of private revenue which is affected by it.

2. The tax which each individual is bound to pay, ought to be certain and not arbitrary. The time of payment, the manner of payment, the quantity to be paid, ought all to be clear and plain to the contributor, and to every other person. Where it is otherwise, every person subject to the tax is put more or less in the power of the tax-gatherer, who can either aggravate the tax upon any obnoxious contributor, or extort, by the terror of such aggravation, some present or perquisite to himself. The uncertainty of taxation encourages the insolence, and favors the corruption, of an order of men who are naturally unpopular, even where they are neither insolent nor corrupt. The certainty of what each individual ought to pay is, in taxation, a matter of so great importance, that a very considerable degree of inequality, it appears, I believe, from the experience of all nations, is not near so great an evil as a very small degree of uncertainty.

3. Every tax ought to be levied at the time, or in the manner, in which it is most likely to be convenient for the contributor to pay it. A tax upon the rent of land or of houses, payable at the same term at which such rents are usually paid, is levied at the time when it is most likely to be convenient for the contributor to pay; or when he is most likely to have wherewithal to pay. Taxes upon such consumable goods as are articles of luxury, are all finally paid by the consumer, and generally in a manner that is very convenient for him. He pays them by little and little, as he has occasion to buy the goods. As he is at liberty too, either to buy or not to buy, as he pleases, it must be his own fault if he ever suffers any considerable inconveniency from such taxes.

4. Every tax ought to be so contrived, as both to take out and to keep out of the pockets of the people as little as possible, over and above what it brings into the public treasury of the state. A tax may either take out or keep out of the pockets of the people a great deal more than it brings into the public treasury, in the four following ways. First, the levying of it may require a great number of officers, whose salaries may eat up the greater part of the produce of the tax, and whose perquisites may impose another additional tax upon the people. Secondly, it may obstruct the industry of the people, and discourage them from applying to certain branches of business which might give maintenance and employment to great multitudes. While it obliges the people to pay, it may thus diminish, or perhaps destroy, some of the funds which might enable them more easily to do so. Thirdly, by the forfeitures and other penalties which those unfortunate individuals incur, who attempt unsuccessfully to evade the tax, it may frequently ruin them, and thereby put an end to the benefit which the community might have received from the employment of their capitals. An injudicious tax offers a great temptation to smuggling. But the penalties of smuggling must arise in proportion to the temptation. The law, contrary to all the ordinary principles of justice, first creates the temptation, and then punishes those who yield to it; and it commonly enhances the punishment, too, in proportion to the very circumstance which ought certainly to alleviate it, the temptation to commit the crime. {See *Sketches of the History of Man* p. 474, and Seq.} Fourthly, by subjecting the people to the frequent visits and the odious examination of the tax-gatherers, it may expose them to much unnecessary trouble, vexation, and oppression; and though vexation is not, strictly speaking, expense, it is certainly equivalent to the expense at which every man would be willing to redeem himself from it. It is in some one or other of these four different ways, that taxes are frequently so much more burdensome to the people than they are beneficial to the sovereign.

The evident justice and utility of the foregoing maxims have recommended them, more or less, to the attention of all nations. All nations have endeavored, to the best of their judgment, to render their taxes as equal as they could contrive; as certain, as convenient to the contributor, both the time and the mode of payment, and in proportion to the revenue which they brought to the prince, as little burdensome to the people. The following short review of some of the principal taxes which have taken place in different ages and countries, will show, that the endeavors of all nations have not in this respect been equally successful.

ARTICLE I

Taxes upon Rent—Taxes upon the Rent of Land

A tax upon the rent of land may either be imposed according to a certain canon, every district being valued at a curtain rent, which valuation is not afterwards to be altered; or it may be imposed in such a manner, as to vary with every variation in the real rent of the land, and to rise or fall with the improvement or declension of its cultivation.

A land tax which, like that of Great Britain, is assessed upon each district according to a certain invariable canon, though it should be equal at the time of its first establishment, necessarily becomes unequal in process of time, according to the unequal degrees of improvement or neglect in the cultivation of the different parts of the country. In England, the valuation, according to which the different counties and parishes were assessed to the land tax by the 4th of William and Mary, was very unequal even at its first establishment. This tax, therefore, so far offends against the first of the four maxims above mentioned. It is perfectly agreeable to the other three. It is perfectly certain. The time of payment for the tax, being the same as that for the rent, is as convenient as it can be to the contributor. Though the landlord is, in all cases, the real contributor, the tax is commonly advanced by the tenant, to whom the landlord is obliged to allow it in the payment of the rent. This tax is levied by a much smaller number of officers than any other which affords nearly the same revenue. As the tax upon each district does not rise with the rise of the rent, the sovereign does not share in the profits of the landlord's improvements. Those improvements sometimes contribute, indeed, to the discharge of the other landlords of the district. But the aggravation of the tax, which this may sometimes occasion upon a particular estate, is always so very small, that it never can discourage those improvements, nor keep down the produce of the land below what it would otherwise rise to. As it has no tendency to diminish the quantity, it can have none to raise the price of that produce. It does not obstruct the industry of the people; it subjects the landlord to no other inconveniency besides the unavoidable one of paying the tax.

The advantage, however, which the landlord has derived from the invariable constancy of the valuation, by which all the lands of Great Britain are rated to the land-tax, has been principally owing to some circumstances altogether extraneous to the nature of the tax.

It has been owing in part, to the great prosperity of almost every part of the country, the rents of almost all the estates of Great Britain having, since the time when this valuation was first established, been continually rising, and scarce any of them having fallen. The landlords, therefore, have almost all gained the difference between the tax which they would have paid, according to the present rent of their estates, and that which they actually pay according to the ancient valuation. Had the state of the country been different, had rents been gradually falling in consequence of the declension of cultivation, the landlords would almost all have lost this difference. In the state of things which has happened to take place since the revolution, the constancy of the valuation has been advantageous to the landlord and hurtful to the sovereign. In a different state of things it might have been advantageous to the sovereign and hurtful to the landlord.

As the tax is made payable in money, so the valuation of the land is expressed in money. Since the establishment of this valuation, the value of silver has been pretty uniform, and there has been no alteration in the standard of the coin, either as to weight or fineness. Had silver risen considerably in its value, as it seems to have done in the course of the two centuries which preceded the discovery of the mines of America, the constancy of the valuation might have proved very oppressive to the landlord. Had silver fallen considerably in its value, as it certainly did for about a century at least after the discovery of those mines, the same constancy of valuation would have reduced very much this branch of the revenue of the sovereign. Had any considerable alteration been made in the standard of the money, either by sinking the same quantity of silver to a lower denomination, or by raising it to a higher; had an ounce of silver, for example, instead of being coined into five shillings and two pence, been coined either into pieces which bore so low a denomination as two shillings and seven pence, or into pieces which bore so high a one as ten shillings and four pence, it would, in the one case, have hurt the revenue of the proprietor, in the other that of the sovereign.

In circumstances, therefore, somewhat different from those which have actually taken place, this constancy of valuation might have been a very great inconveniency, either to the contributors or to the commonwealth. In the course of ages, such circumstances, however, must at some time or other happen. But though empires, like all the other works of men, have all hitherto proved mortal, yet every empire aims at immortality. Every constitution, therefore, which it is meant should be as permanent as the empire itself, ought to be convenient, not in certain circumstances only, but in all circumstances; or ought to be suited, not to those circumstances which are transitory, occasional, or accidental, but to those which are necessary, and therefore always the same.

A tax upon the rent of land, which varies with every variation of the rent, or which rises and falls according to the improvement or neglect of cultivation, is recommended by that sect of men of letters in France, who call themselves the economists, as the most equitable of all taxes. All taxes, they pretend, fall ultimately upon the rent of land, and ought, therefore, to be imposed equally upon the fund which must finally pay them. That all taxes ought to fall as equally as possible upon the fund which must finally pay them, is certainly true. But without entering into the disagreeable discussion of the metaphysical arguments by which they support their very ingenious theory, it will sufficiently appear, from the following review, what are the taxes which fall finally upon the rent of the land, and what are those which fall finally upon some other fund.

In the Venetian territory, all the arable lands which are given in lease to farmers are taxed at a tenth of the rent. {Memoires Concernant les Droits, pp. 240, 241.} The leases are recorded in a public register, which is kept by the officers of revenue in each province or district. When the proprietor cultivates his own lands, they are valued according to an equitable estimation, and he is allowed a deduction of one-fifth of the tax; so that for such land he pays only eight instead of ten percent of the supposed rent.

A land-tax of this kind is certainly more equal than the land-tax of England. It might not, perhaps, be altogether so certain, and the assessment of the tax might frequently occasion a good deal more trouble to the landlord. It might, too, be a good deal more expensive in the levying.

Such a system of administration, however, might, perhaps, be contrived, as would in a great measure both prevent this uncertainty, and moderate this expense.

The landlord and tenant, for example, might jointly be obliged to record their lease in a public register. Proper penalties might be enacted against concealing or misrepresenting any of the conditions; and if part of those penalties were to be paid to either of the two parties who informed against and convicted the other of such concealment or misrepresentation, it would effectually deter them from combining together in order to defraud the public revenue. All the conditions of the lease might be sufficiently known from such a record.

Some landlords, instead of raising the rent, take a fine for the renewal of the lease. This practice is, in most cases, the expedient of a spendthrift, who, for a sum of ready money sells a future revenue of much greater value. It is, in most cases, therefore, hurtful to the landlord; it is frequently hurtful to the tenant; and it is always hurtful to the community. It frequently takes from the tenant so great a part of his capital, and thereby diminishes so much his ability to cultivate the land, that he finds it more difficult to pay a small rent than it would otherwise have been to pay a great one. Whatever diminishes his ability to cultivate, necessarily keeps down, below what it would otherwise have been, the most important part of the revenue of the community. By rendering the tax upon such fines a good deal heavier than upon the ordinary rent, this hurtful practice might be discouraged, to the no small advantage of all the different parties concerned, of the landlord, of the tenant, of the sovereign, and of the whole community.

Some leases prescribe to the tenant a certain mode of cultivation, and a certain succession of crops, during the whole continuance of the lease. This condition, which is generally the effect of the landlord's conceit of his own superior knowledge (a conceit in most cases very ill-founded), ought always to be considered as an additional rent, as a rent in service, instead of a rent in money. In order to discourage the practice, which is generally a foolish one, this species of rent might be valued rather high, and consequently taxed somewhat higher than common money-rents.

Some landlords, instead of a rent in money, require a rent in kind, in corn, cattle, poultry, wine, oil, etc.; others, again, require a rent in service. Such rents are always more hurtful to the tenant than beneficial to the landlord. They either take more, or keep more out of the pocket of the former, than they put into that of the latter. In every country where they take place, the tenants are poor and beggarly, pretty much according to the degree in which they take place. By valuing, in the same manner, such rents rather high, and consequently taxing them somewhat higher than common money-rents, a practice which is hurtful to the whole community, might, perhaps, be sufficiently discouraged.

When the landlord chose to occupy himself a part of his own lands, the rent might be valued according to an equitable arbitration of the farmers and landlords in the neighborhood, and a moderate abatement of the tax might be granted to him, in the same manner as in the Venetian territory, provided the rent of the lands which he occupied did not exceed a certain sum. It is of importance that the landlord should be encouraged to cultivate a part of his own land. His capital is generally greater than that of the tenant, and, with less skill, he can frequently raise a greater produce. The landlord can afford to try experiments, and is generally disposed to do so. His unsuccessful experiments occasion only a moderate loss to himself. His successful ones contribute to the improvement and better cultivation of the whole country. It might be of importance, however, that the abatement of the tax should encourage him to cultivate to a certain extent only. If the landlords should, the greater part of them, be tempted to farm the whole of their own lands, the country (instead of sober and industrious tenants, who are bound by their own interest to cultivate as well as their capital and skill will allow them) would be filled with idle and profligate bailiffs, whose abusive management would soon degrade the cultivation, and reduce the annual produce of the land, to the diminution, not only of the revenue of their masters, but of the most important part of that of the whole society.

Such a system of administration might, perhaps, free a tax of this kind from any degree of uncertainty, which could occasion either oppression or inconveniency to the contributor; and might, at the same time, serve to introduce into the common management of land such a plan of policy as might contribute a good deal to the general improvement and good cultivation of the country.

The expense of levying a land-tax, which varied with every variation of the rent, would, no doubt, be somewhat greater than that of levying one which was always rated according to a fixed valuation. Some additional expense would necessarily be incurred, both by the different register-offices which it would be proper to establish in the different districts of the country, and by the different valuations which might occasionally be made of the lands which the proprietor chose to occupy himself. The expense of all this, however, might be very moderate, and much below what is incurred in the levying of many other taxes, which afford a very inconsiderable revenue in comparison of what might easily be drawn from a tax of this kind.

The discouragement which a variable land-tax of this kind might give to the improvement of land, seems to be the most important objection which can be made to it. The landlord would certainly be less disposed to improve, when the sovereign, who contributed nothing to the expense, was to share in the profit of the improvement. Even this objection might, perhaps, be obviated, by allowing the landlord, before he began his improvement, to ascertain, in conjunction with the officers of revenue, the actual value of his lands, according to the equitable arbitration of a certain number of landlords and farmers in the neighborhood, equally chosen by both parties: and by rating him, according to this valuation, for such a number of years as might be fully sufficient for his complete indemnification. To draw the attention of the sovereign towards the improvement of the land, from a regard to the increase of his own revenue, is one or the principal advantages proposed by this species of land-tax. The term, therefore, allowed, for the indemnification of the landlord, ought not to be a great deal longer than what was necessary for that purpose, lest the remoteness of the interest should discourage too much this attention. It had better, however, be somewhat too long, than in any respect too short. No incitement to the attention of the sovereign can ever counterbalance the smallest discouragement to that of the landlord. The attention of the sovereign can be, at best, but a very general and vague consideration of what is likely to contribute to the better cultivation of the greater part of his dominions. The attention of the landlord is a particular and minute consideration of what is likely to be the most advantageous application of every inch of ground upon his estate. The principal attention of the sovereign ought to be, to encourage, by every means in his power, the attention both of the landlord and of the farmer, by allowing both to pursue their own interest in their own way, and according to their own judgment; by giving to both the most perfect security that they shall enjoy the full recompense of their own industry; and by procuring to both the most extensive market for every part of their produce, in consequence of establishing the easiest and safest communications, both by land and by water, through every part of his own dominions, as well as the most unbounded freedom of exportation to the dominions of all other princes.

If, by such a system of administration, a tax of this kind could be so managed as to give, not only no discouragement, but, on the contrary, some encouragement to the improvement or land, it does not appear likely to occasion any other inconveniency to the landlord, except always the unavoidable one of being obliged to pay the tax.

In all the variations of the state of the society, in the improvement and in the declension of agriculture; in all the variations in the value of silver, and in all those in the standard of the coin, a tax of this kind would, of its own accord, and without any attention of government, readily suit itself to the actual situation of things, and would be equally just and equitable in all those different changes. It would, therefore, be much more proper to be established as a perpetual and unalterable regulation, or as what is called a fundamental law of the commonwealth, than any tax which was always to be levied according to a certain valuation.

Some states, instead of the simple and obvious expedient of a register of leases, have had recourse to the laborious and expensive one of an actual survey and valuation of all the lands in the country. They have suspected, probably, that the lessor and lessee, in order to defraud the public revenue, might combine to conceal the real terms of the lease. Doomsday-book seems to have been the result of a very accurate survey of this kind.

In the ancient dominions of the king of Prussia, the land-tax is assessed according to an actual survey and valuation, which is reviewed and altered from time to time. {*Memoires Concurent les Droits*, etc. tom, i. pp. 114, 115, 116, etc.} According to that valuation, the lay proprietors pay from twenty to twenty-five percent of their revenue; ecclesiastics from forty to forty-five percent. The survey and valuation of Silesia was made by order of the present king, it is said, with great accuracy. According to that valuation, the lands belonging to the bishop of Breslaw are taxed at twenty-five percent of their rent. The other revenues of the ecclesiastics of both religions at fifty percent. The commanderies of the Teutonic order, and of that of Malta, at forty percent. Lands held by a noble tenure, at thirty-eight and one-third percent. Lands held by a base tenure, at thirty-five and one-third percent.

The survey and valuation of Bohemia is said to have been the work of more than a hundred years. It was not perfected till after the peace of 1748, by the orders of the present empress queen. {Id. tom. i. pp. 85, 84.} The survey of the duchy of Milan, which was begun in the time of Charles VI, was not perfected till after 1760 It is esteemed one of the most accurate that has ever been made. The survey of Savoy and Piedmont was executed under the orders of the late king of Sardinia. {Id. p. 280, etc.; also p. 287, etc. to 316.}

In the dominions of the king of Prussia, the revenue of the church is taxed much higher than that of lay proprietors. The revenue of the church is, the greater part of it, a burden upon the rent of land. It seldom happens that any part of it is applied towards the improvement of land; or is so employed as to contribute, in any respect, towards increasing the revenue of the great body of the people. His Prussian majesty had probably, upon that account, thought it reasonable that it should contribute a good deal more towards relieving the exigencies of the state. In some countries, the lands of the church are exempted from all taxes. In others, they are taxed more lightly than other lands. In the duchy of Milan, the lands which the church possessed before 1575, are rated to the tax at a third only or their value.

In Silesia, lands held by a noble tenure are taxed three percent higher than those held by a base tenure. The honors and privileges of different kinds annexed to the former, his Prussian majesty had probably imagined, would sufficiently compensate to the proprietor a small aggravation of the tax; while, at the same time, the humiliating inferiority of the latter would be in some measure alleviated, by being taxed somewhat more lightly. In other countries, the system of taxation, instead of alleviating, aggravates this inequality. In the dominions of the king of Sardinia, and in those provinces of France which are subject to what is called the real or predial taille, the tax falls altogether upon the lands held by a base tenure. Those held by a noble one are exempted.

A land tax assessed according to a general survey and valuation, how equal soever it may be at first, must, in the course of a very moderate period of time, become unequal. To prevent its becoming so would require the continual and painful attention of government to all the variations in the state and produce of every different farm in the country. The governments of Prussia, of Bohemia, of Sardinia, and of the duchy of Milan, actually exert an attention of this kind; an attention so unsuitable to the nature of government, that it is not likely to be of long continuance, and which, if it is continued, will probably, in the long-run, occasion much more trouble and vexation than it can possibly bring relief to the contributors.

In 1666, the generality of Montauban was assessed to the real or predial taille, according, it is said, to a very exact survey and valuation. {*Memoires Concernant les Droits*, etc. tom. ii pp. 139, etc.} By 1727, this assessment had become altogether unequal. In order to remedy this inconveniency, government has found no better expedient, than to impose upon the whole generality an additional tax of a hundred and twenty thousand livres. This additional tax is rated upon all the different districts subject to the taille according to the old assessment. But it is levied only upon those which, in the actual state of things, are by that assessment under-taxed; and it is applied to the relief of those which, by the same assessment, are over-taxed. Two districts, for example, one of which ought, in the actual state of things, to be taxed at nine hundred, the other at eleven hundred livres, are, by the old assessment, both taxed at a thousand livres. Both these districts are, by the additional tax, rated at eleven hundred livres each. But this additional tax is levied only upon the district under-charged, and it is applied altogether to the relief of that overcharged, which consequently pays only nine hundred livres. The government neither gains nor loses by the additional tax, which is applied altogether to remedy the inequalities arising from the old assessment. The application is pretty much regulated according to the discretion of the intendant of the generality, and must, therefore, be in a great measure arbitrary.

Taxes which are Proportioned, not in the Rent, but to the Produce of Land.

Taxes upon the produce of land are, in reality, taxes upon the rent; and though they may be originally advanced by the farmer, are finally paid by the landlord. When a certain portion of the produce is to be paid away for a tax, the farmer computes as well as he can, what the value of this portion is, one year with another, likely to amount to, and he makes a proportional abatement in the rent which he agrees to pay to the landlord. There is no farmer who does not compute beforehand what the church tithe, which is a land tax of this kind, is, one year with another, likely to amount to.

The tithe, and every other land tax of this kind, under the appearance of perfect equality, are very unequal taxes; a certain portion of the produce being in different situations, equivalent to a very different portion of the rent. In some very rich lands, the produce is so great, that the one half of it is fully sufficient to replace to the farmer his capital employed in cultivation, together with the ordinary profits of farming stock in the neighborhood. The other half, or, what comes to the same thing, the value of the other half, he could afford to pay as rent to the landlord, if there was no tithe. But if a tenth of the produce is taken from him in the way of tithe, he must require an abatement of the fifth part of his rent, otherwise he cannot get back his capital with the ordinary profit. In this case, the rent of the landlord, instead of amounting to a half, or five-tenths of the whole produce, will amount only to four-tenths of it. In poorer lands, on the contrary, the produce is sometimes so small, and the expense of cultivation so great, that it requires four-fifths of the whole produce, to replace to the farmer his capital with the ordinary profit. In this case, though there was no tithe, the rent of the landlord could amount to no more than one-fifth or two-tenths of the whole produce. But if the farmer pays one-tenth of the produce in the way of tithe, he must require an equal abatement of the rent of the landlord, which will thus be reduced to one-tenth only of the whole produce. Upon the rent of rich lands the tithe may sometimes be a tax of no more than one-fifth part, or four shillings in the pound; whereas upon that of poorer lands, it may sometimes be a tax of one half, or of ten shillings in the pound.

The tithe, as it is frequently a very unequal tax upon the rent, so it is always a great discouragement, both to the improvements of the landlord, and to the cultivation of the farmer. The one cannot venture to make the most important, which are generally the most expensive improvements; nor the other to raise the most valuable, which are generally, too, the most expensive crops; when the church, which lays out no part of the expense, is to share so very largely in the profit. The cultivation of madder was, for a long time, confined by the tithe to the United Provinces, which, being Presbyterian countries, and upon that account exempted from this destructive tax, enjoyed a sort of monopoly of that useful dyeing drug against the rest of Europe. The late attempts to introduce the culture of this plant into England, have been made only in consequence of the statute, which enacted that five shillings an acre should be received in lieu of all manner of tithe upon madder.

As through the greater part of Europe, the church, so in many different countries of Asia, the state, is principally supported by a land tax, proportioned not to the rent, but to the produce of the land. In China, the principal revenue of the sovereign consists in a tenth part of the produce of all the lands of the empire. This tenth part, however, is estimated so very moderately, that, in many provinces, it is said not to exceed a thirtieth part of the ordinary produce. The land tax or land rent which used to be paid to the Mahometan government of Bengal, before that country fell into the hands of the English East India company, is said to have amounted to about a fifth part of the produce. The land tax of ancient Egypt is said likewise to have amounted to a fifth part.

In Asia, this sort of land tax is said to interest the sovereign in the improvement and cultivation of land. The sovereigns of China, those of Bengal while under the Mahometan government, and those of ancient Egypt, are said, accordingly, to have been extremely attentive to the making and maintaining of good roads and navigable canals, in order to increase, as much as possible, both the quantity and value of every part of the produce of the land, by procuring to every part of it the most extensive market which their own dominions could afford. The tithe of the church is divided into such small portions that no one of its proprietors can have any interest of this kind. The parson of a parish could never find his account, in making a road or canal to a distant part of the country, in order to extend the market for the produce of his own particular parish. Such taxes, when destined for the maintenance of the state, have some advantages, which may serve in some measure to balance their inconveniency. When destined for the maintenance of the church, they are attended with nothing but inconveniency.

Taxes upon the produce of land may be levied, either in kind, or, according to a certain valuation in money.

The parson of a parish, or a gentleman of small fortune who lives upon his estate, may sometimes, perhaps find some advantage in receiving, the one his tithe, and the other his rent, in kind. The quantity to be collected, and the district within which it is to be collected, are so small, that they both can oversee, with their own eyes, the collection and disposal of every part of what is due to them. A gentleman of great fortune, who lived in the capital, would be in danger of suffering much by the neglect, and more by the fraud, of his factors and agents, if the rents of an estate in a distant province were to be paid to him in this manner. The loss of the sovereign, from the abuse and depredation of his tax-gatherers, would necessarily be much greater. The servants of the most careless private person are, perhaps, more under the eye of their master than those of the most careful prince; and a public revenue, which was paid in kind, would suffer so much from the mismanagement of the collectors, that a very small part of what was levied upon the people would ever arrive at the treasury of the prince. Some part of the public revenue of China, however, is said to be paid in this manner. The mandarins and other tax-gatherers will, no doubt, find their advantage in continuing the practice of a payment, which is so much more liable to abuse than any payment in money.

A tax upon the produce of land, which is levied in money, may be levied, either according to a valuation, which varies with all the variations of the market price; or according to a fixed valuation, a bushel of wheat, for example, being always valued at one and the same money price, whatever may be the state of the market. The produce of a tax levied in the former way will vary only according to the variations in the real produce of the land, according to the improvement or neglect of cultivation. The produce of a tax levied in the latter way will vary, not only according to the variations in the produce of the land, but according both to those in the value of the precious metals, and those in the quantity of those metals which is at different times contained in coin of the same denomination. The produce of the former will always bear the same proportion to the value of the real produce of the land. The produce of the latter may, at different times, bear very different proportions to that value.

When, instead either of a certain portion of the produce of land, or of the price of a certain portion, a certain sum of money is to be paid in full compensation for all tax or tithe; the tax becomes, in this case, exactly of the same nature with the land tax of England. It neither rises nor falls with the rent of the land. It neither encourages nor discourages improvement. The tithe in the greater part of those parishes which pay what is called a modus, in lieu of all other tithe is a tax of this kind. During the Mahometan government of Bengal, instead of the payment in kind of the fifth part of the produce, a modus, and, it is said, a very moderate one, was established in the greater part of the districts or zemindaries of the country. Some of the servants of the East India company, under pretence of restoring the public revenue to its proper value, have, in some provinces, exchanged this modus for a payment in kind. Under their management, this change is likely both to discourage cultivation, and to give new opportunities for abuse in the collection of the public revenue, which has fallen very much below what it was said to have been when it first fell under the management of the company. The servants of the company may, perhaps, have profited by the change, but at the expense, it is probable, both of their masters and of the country.

Taxes upon the Rent of Houses

The rent of a house may be distinguished into two parts, of which the one may very properly be called the building-rent; the other is commonly called the ground-rent.

The building-rent is the interest or profit of the capital expended in building the house. In order to put the trade of a builder upon a level with other trades, it is necessary that this rent should be sufficient, first, to pay him the same interest which he would have got for his capital, if he had lent it upon good security; and, secondly, to keep the house in constant repair, or, what comes to the same thing, to replace, within a certain term of years, the capital which had been employed in building it. The building-rent, or the ordinary profit of building, is, therefore, everywhere regulated by the ordinary interest of money. Where the market rate of interest is four percent the rent of a house, which, over and above paying the ground-rent, affords six or six and a-half percent upon the whole expense of building, may, perhaps, afford a sufficient profit to the builder. Where the market rate of interest is five percent it may perhaps require seven or seven and a-half percent. If, in proportion to the interest of money, the trade of the builders affords at any time much greater profit than this, it will soon draw so much capital from other trades as will reduce the profit to its proper level. If it affords at any time much less than this, other trades will soon draw so much capital from it as will again raise that profit.

Whatever part of the whole rent of a house is over and above what is sufficient for affording this reasonable profit, naturally goes to the ground-rent; and, where the owner of the ground and the owner of the building are two different persons, is, in most cases, completely paid to the former. This surplus rent is the price which the inhabitant of the house pays for some real or supposed advantage of the situation. In country houses, at a distance from any great town, where there is plenty of ground to choose upon, the ground-rent is scarce anything, or no more than what the ground which the house stands upon would pay, if employed in agriculture. In country villas, in the neighborhood of some great town, it is sometimes a good deal higher; and the peculiar convenience or beauty of situation is there frequently very well paid for. Ground-rents are generally highest in the capital, and in those particular parts of it where there happens to be the greatest demand for houses, whatever be the reason of that demand, whether for trade and business, for pleasure and society, or for mere vanity and fashion.

A tax upon house-rent, payable by the tenant, and proportioned to the whole rent of each house, could not, for any considerable time at least, affect the building-rent. If the builder did not get his reasonable profit, he would be obliged to quit the trade; which, by raising the demand for building, would, in a short time, bring back his profit to its proper level with that of other trades. Neither would such a tax fall altogether upon the ground-rent; but it would divide itself in such a manner, as to fall partly upon the inhabitant of the house, and partly upon the owner of the ground.

Let us suppose, for example, that a particular person judges that he can afford for house-rent all expense of sixty pounds a year; and let us suppose, too, that a tax of four shillings in the pound, or of one-fifth, payable by the inhabitant, is laid upon house-rent. A house of sixty pounds rent will, in that case, cost him seventy-two pounds a year, which is twelve pounds more than he thinks he can afford. He will, therefore, content himself with a worse house, or a house of fifty pounds rent, which, with the additional ten pounds that he must pay for the tax, will make up the sum of sixty pounds a year, the expense which he judges he can afford, and, in order to pay the tax, he will give up a part of the additional convenience which he might have had from a house of ten pounds a year more rent. He will give up, I say, a part of this additional convenience; for he will seldom be obliged to give up the whole, but will, in consequence of the tax, get a better house for fifty pounds a year, than he could have got if there had been no tax for as a tax of this kind, by taking away this particular competitor, must diminish the competition for houses of sixty pounds rent, so it must likewise diminish it for those of fifty pounds rent, and in the same manner for those of all other rents, except the lowest rent, for which it would for some time increase the competition. But the rents of every class of houses for which the competition was diminished, would necessarily be more or less reduced. As no part of this reduction, however, could for any considerable time at least, affect the building-rent, the whole of it must, in the long-run, necessarily fall upon the ground-rent. The final payment of this tax, therefore, would fall partly upon the inhabitant of the house, who, in order to pay his share, would be obliged to give up a part of his convenience; and partly upon the owner of the ground, who, in order to pay his share, would be obliged to give up a part of his revenue. In what proportion this final payment would be divided between them, it is not, perhaps, very easy to ascertain. The division would probably be very different in different circumstances, and a tax of this kind might, according to those different circumstances, affect very unequally, both the inhabitant of the house and the owner of the ground.

The inequality with which a tax of this kind might fall upon the owners of different ground-rents, would arise altogether from the accidental inequality of this division. But the inequality with which it might fall upon the inhabitants of different houses, would arise, not only from this, but from another cause. The proportion of the expense of house-rent to the whole expense of living, is different in the different degrees of fortune. It is, perhaps, highest in the highest degree, and it diminishes gradually through the inferior degrees, so as in general to be lowest in the lowest degree. The necessaries of life occasion the great expense of the poor. They find it difficult to get food, and the greater part of their little revenue is spent in getting it. The luxuries and vanities of life occasion the principal expense of the rich; and a magnificent house embellishes and sets off to the best advantage all the other luxuries and vanities which they possess. A tax upon house-rents, therefore, would in general fall heaviest upon the rich; and in this sort of inequality there would not, perhaps, be any thing very unreasonable. It is not very unreasonable that the rich should contribute to the public expense, not only in proportion to their revenue, but something more than in that proportion.

The rent of houses, though it in some respects resembles the rent of land, is in one respect essentially different from it. The rent of land is paid for the use of a productive subject. The land which pays it produces it. The rent of houses is paid for the use of an unproductive subject. Neither the house, nor the ground which it stands upon, produce anything. The person who pays the rent, therefore, must draw it from some other source of revenue, distinct from and independent of this subject. A tax upon the rent of houses, so far as it falls upon the inhabitants, must be drawn from the same source as the rent itself, and must be paid from their revenue, whether derived from the wages of labor, the profits of stock, or the rent of land. So far as it falls upon the inhabitants, it is one of those taxes which fall, not upon one only, but indifferently upon all the three different sources of revenue; and is, in every respect, of the same nature as a tax upon any other sort of consumable commodities. In general, there is not perhaps, any one article of expense or consumption by which the liberality or narrowness of a man's whole expense can be better judged of than by his house-rent. A proportional tax upon this particular article of expense might, perhaps, produce a more considerable revenue than any which has hitherto been drawn from it in any part of Europe. If the tax, indeed, was very high, the greater part of people would endeavor to evade it as much as they could, by contenting themselves with smaller houses, and by turning the greater part of their expense into some other channel.

The rent of houses might easily be ascertained with sufficient accuracy, by a policy of the same kind with that which would be necessary for ascertaining the ordinary rent of land. Houses not inhabited ought to pay no tax. A tax upon them would fall altogether upon the proprietor, who would thus be taxed for a subject which afforded him neither convenience nor revenue. Houses inhabited by the proprietor ought to be rated, not according to the expense which they might have cost in building, but according to the rent which an equitable arbitration might judge them likely to bring if leased to a tenant. If rated according to the expense which they might have cost in building, a tax of three or four shillings in the pound, joined with other taxes, would ruin almost all the rich and great families of this, and, I believe, of every other civilized country. Whoever will examine with attention the different town and country houses of some of the richest and greatest families in this country, will find that, at the rate of only six and a-half, or seven percent upon the original expense of building, their house-rent is nearly equal to the whole neat rent of their estates. It is the accumulated expense of several successive generations, laid out upon objects of great beauty and magnificence, indeed, but, in proportion to what they cost, of very small exchangeable value. {Since the first publication of this book, a tax nearly upon the above-mentioned principles has been imposed.}

Ground-rents are a still more proper subject of taxation than the rent of houses. A tax upon ground-rents would not raise the rent of houses; it would fall altogether upon the owner of the ground-rent, who acts always as a monopolist, and exacts the greatest rent which can be got for the use of his ground. More or less can be got for it, according as the competitors happen to be richer or poorer, or can afford to gratify their fancy for a particular spot of ground at a greater or smaller expense. In every country, the greatest number of rich competitors is in the capital, and it is there accordingly that the highest ground-rents are always to be found. As the wealth of those competitors would in no respect be increased by a tax upon ground-rents, they would not probably be disposed to pay more for the use of the ground. Whether the tax was to be advanced by the inhabitant or by the owner of the ground, would be of little importance. The more the inhabitant was obliged to pay for the tax, the less he would incline to pay for the ground; so that the final payment of the tax would fall altogether upon the owner of the ground-rent. The ground-rents of uninhabited houses ought to pay no tax.

Both ground-rents, and the ordinary rent of land, are a species of revenue which the owner, in many cases, enjoys without any care or attention of his own. Though a part of this revenue should be taken from him in order to defray the expenses of the state, no discouragement will thereby be given to any sort of industry. The annual produce of the land and labor of the society, the real wealth and revenue of the great body of the people, might be the same after such a tax as before. Ground-rents, and the ordinary rent of land, are therefore, perhaps, the species of revenue which can best bear to have a peculiar tax imposed upon them.

Ground-rents seem, in this respect, a more proper subject of peculiar taxation, than even the ordinary rent of land. The ordinary rent of land is, in many cases, owing partly, at least, to the attention and good management of the landlord. A very heavy tax might discourage, too much, this attention and good management. Ground-rents, so far as they exceed the ordinary rent of land, are altogether owing to the good government of the sovereign, which, by protecting the industry either of the whole people or of the inhabitants of some particular place, enables them to pay so much more than its real value for the ground which they build their houses upon; or to make to its owner so much more than compensation for the loss which he might sustain by this use of it. Nothing can be more reasonable, than that a fund, which owes its existence to the good government of the state, should be taxed peculiarly, or should contribute something more than the greater part of other funds, towards the support of that government.

Though, in many different countries of Europe, taxes have been imposed upon the rent of houses, I do not know of any in which ground-rents have been considered as a separate subject of taxation. The contrivers of taxes have, probably, found some difficulty in ascertaining what part of the rent ought to be considered as ground-rent, and what part ought to be considered as building-rent. It should not, however, seem very difficult to distinguish those two parts of the rent from one another.

In Great Britain the rent of houses is supposed to be taxed in the same proportion as the rent of land, by what is called the annual land tax. The valuation, according to which each different parish and district is assessed to this tax, is always the same. It was originally extremely unequal, and it still continues to be so. Through the greater part of the kingdom this tax falls still more lightly upon the rent of houses than upon that of land. In some few districts only, which were originally rated high, and in which the rents of houses have fallen considerably, the land tax of three or four shillings in the pound is said to amount to an equal proportion of the real rent of houses. Untenanted houses, though by law subject to the tax, are, in most districts, exempted from it by the favor of the assessors; and this exemption sometimes occasions some little variation in the rate of particular houses, though that of the district is always the same. Improvements of rent, by new buildings, repairs, etc. go to the discharge of the district, which occasions still further variations in the rate of particular houses.

In the province of Holland {*Memoires Concernant les Droits*, etc. p. 223}, every house is taxed at two and a-half percent of its value, without any regard, either to the rent which it actually pays, or to the circumstance of its being tenanted or untenanted. There seems to be a hardship in obliging the proprietor to pay a tax for an untenanted house, from which he can derive no revenue, especially so very heavy a tax. In Holland, where the market rate of interest does not exceed three percent, two and a-half percent upon the whole value of the house must, in most cases, amount to more than a third of the building-rent, perhaps of the whole rent. The valuation, indeed, according to which the houses are rated, though very unequal, is said to be always below the real value. When a house is rebuilt, improved, or enlarged, there is a new valuation, and the tax is rated accordingly.

The contrivers of the several taxes which in England have, at different times, been imposed upon houses, seem to have imagined that there was some great difficulty in ascertaining, with tolerable exactness, what was the real rent of every house. They have regulated their taxes, therefore, according to some more obvious circumstance, such as they had probably imagined would, in most cases, bear some proportion to the rent.

The first tax of this kind was hearth-money; or a tax of two shillings upon every hearth. In order to ascertain how many hearths were in the house, it was necessary that the tax-gatherer should enter every room in it. This odious visit rendered the tax odious. Soon after the Revolution, therefore, it was abolished as a badge of slavery.

The next tax of this kind was a tax of two shillings upon every dwelling-house inhabited. A house with ten windows to pay four shillings more. A house with twenty windows and upwards to pay eight shillings. This tax was afterwards so far altered, that houses with twenty windows, and with less than thirty, were ordered to pay ten shillings, and those with thirty windows and upwards to pay twenty shillings. The number of windows can, in most cases, be counted from the outside, and, in all cases, without entering every room in the house. The visit of the tax-gatherer, therefore, was less offensive in this tax than in the hearth-money.

This tax was afterwards repealed, and in the room of it was established the window-tax, which has undergone two several alterations and augmentations. The window tax, as it stands at present (January 1775), over and above the duty of three shillings upon every house in England, and of one shilling upon every house in Scotland, lays a duty upon every window, which in England augments gradually from two pence, the lowest rate upon houses with not more than seven windows, to two shillings, the highest rate upon houses with twenty-five windows and upwards.

The principal objection to all such taxes is their inequality; an inequality of the worst kind, as they must frequently fall much heavier upon the poor than upon the rich. A house of ten pounds rent in a country town, may sometimes have more windows than a house of five hundred pounds rent in London; and though the inhabitant of the former is likely to be a much poorer man than that of the latter, yet, so far as his contribution is regulated by the window tax, he must contribute more to the support of the state. Such taxes are, therefore, directly contrary to the first of the four maxims above mentioned. They do not seem to offend much against any of the other three.

The natural tendency of the window tax, and of all other taxes upon houses, is to lower rents. The more a man pays for the tax, the less, it is evident, he can afford to pay for the rent. Since the imposition of the window tax, however, the rents of houses have, upon the whole, risen more or less, in almost every town and village of Great Britain, with which I am acquainted. Such has been, almost everywhere, the increase of the demand for houses, that it has raised the rents more than the window tax could sink them; one of the many proofs of the great prosperity of the country, and of the increasing revenue of its inhabitants. Had it not been for the tax, rents would probably have risen still higher.

ARTICLE II

Taxes upon Profit, or upon the Revenue Arising from Stock

The revenue or profit arising from stock naturally divides itself into two parts; that which pays the interest, and which belongs to the owner of the stock; and that surplus part which is over and above what is necessary for paying the interest.

This latter part of profit is evidently a subject not taxable directly. It is the compensation, and, in most cases, it is no more than a very moderate compensation for the risk and trouble of employing the stock. The employer must have this compensation, otherwise he cannot, consistently with his own interest, continue the employment. If he was taxed directly, therefore, in proportion to the whole profit, he would be obliged either to raise the rate of his profit, or to charge the tax upon the interest of money; that is, to pay less interest. If he raised the rate of his profit in proportion to the tax, the whole tax, though it might be advanced by him, would be finally paid by one or other of two different sets of people, according to the different ways in which he might employ the stock of which he had the management. If he employed it as a farming stock, in the cultivation of land, he could raise the rate of his profit only by retaining a greater portion, or, what comes to the same thing, the price of a greater portion, of the produce of the land; and as this could be done only by a reduction of rent, the final payment of the tax would fall upon the landlord. If he employed it as a mercantile or manufacturing stock, he could raise the rate of his profit only by raising the price of his goods; in which case, the final payment of the tax would fall altogether upon the consumers of those goods. If he did not raise the rate of his profit, he would be obliged to charge the whole tax upon that part of it which was allotted for the interest of money. He could afford less interest for whatever stock he borrowed, and the whole weight of the tax would, in this case, fall ultimately upon the interest of money. So far as he could not relieve himself from the tax in the one way, he would be obliged to relieve himself in the other.

The interest of money seems, at first sight, a subject equally capable of being taxed directly as the rent of land. Like the rent of land, it is a neat produce, which remains, after completely compensating the whole risk and trouble of employing the stock. As a tax upon the rent of land cannot raise rents, because the neat produce which remains, after replacing the stock of the farmer, together with his reasonable profit, cannot be greater after the tax than before it, so, for the same reason, a tax upon the interest of money could not raise the rate of interest; the quantity of stock or money in the country, like the quantity of land, being supposed to remain the same after the tax as before it. The ordinary rate of profit, it has been shown, in the first book, is everywhere regulated by the quantity of stock to be employed, in proportion to the quantity of the employment, or of the business which must be done by it. But the quantity of the employment, or of the business to be done by stock, could neither be increased nor diminished by any tax upon the interest of money. If the quantity of the stock to be employed, therefore, was neither increased nor diminished by it, the ordinary rate of profit would necessarily remain the same. But the portion of this profit, necessary for compensating the risk and trouble of the employer, would likewise remain the same; that risk and trouble being in no respect altered. The residue, therefore, that portion which belongs to the owner of the stock, and which pays the interest of money, would necessarily remain the same too. At first sight, therefore, the interest of money seems to be a subject as fit to be taxed directly as the rent of land.

There are, however, two different circumstances, which render the interest of money a much less proper subject of direct taxation than the rent of land.

First, the quantity and value of the land which any man possesses, can never be a secret, and can always be ascertained with great exactness. But the whole amount of the capital stock which he possesses is almost always a secret, and can scarce ever be ascertained with tolerable exactness. It is liable, besides, to almost continual variations. A year seldom passes away, frequently not a month, sometimes scarce a single day, in which it does not rise or fall more or less. An inquisition into every man's private circumstances, and an inquisition which, in order to accommodate the tax to them, watched over all the fluctuations of his fortune, would be a source of such continual and endless vexation as no person could support.

Secondly, land is a subject which cannot be removed; whereas stock easily may. The proprietor of land is necessarily a citizen of the particular country in which his estate lies. The proprietor of stock is properly a citizen of the world, and is not necessarily attached to any particular country. He would be apt to abandon the country in which he was exposed to a vexatious inquisition, in order to be assessed to a burdensome tax; and would remove his stock to some other country, where he could either carry on his business, or enjoy his fortune more at his ease. By removing his stock, he would put an end to all the industry which it had maintained in the country which he left. Stock cultivates land; stock employs labor. A tax which tended to drive away stock from any particular country, would so far tend to dry up every source of revenue, both to the sovereign and to the society. Not only the profits of stock, but the rent of land, and the wages of labor, would necessarily be more or less diminished by its removal.

The nations, accordingly, who have attempted to tax the revenue arising from stock, instead of any severe inquisition of this kind, have been obliged to content themselves with some very loose, and, therefore, more or less arbitrary estimation. The extreme inequality and uncertainty of a tax assessed in this manner, can be compensated only by its extreme moderation; in consequence of which, every man finds himself rated so very much below his real revenue, that he gives himself little disturbance though his neighbor should be rated somewhat lower.

By what is called the land tax in England, it was intended that the stock should be taxed in the same proportion as land. When the tax upon land was at four shillings in the pound, or at one-fifth of the supposed rent, it was intended that stock should be taxed at one-fifth of the supposed interest. When the present annual land tax was first imposed, the legal rate of interest was six percent. Every hundred pounds stock, accordingly, was supposed to be taxed at twenty-four shillings, the fifth part of six pounds. Since the legal rate of interest has been reduced to five percent every hundred pounds stock is supposed to be taxed at twenty shillings only. The sum to be raised, by what is called the land tax, was divided between the country and the principal towns. The greater part of it was laid upon the country; and of what was laid upon the towns, the greater part was assessed upon the houses. What remained to be assessed upon the stock or trade of the towns (for the stock upon the land was not meant to be taxed) was very much below the real value of that stock or trade. Whatever inequalities, therefore, there might be in the original assessment, gave little disturbance. Every parish and district still continues to be rated for its land, its houses, and its stock, according to the original assessment; and the almost universal prosperity of the country, which, in most places, has raised very much the value of all these, has rendered those inequalities of still less importance now. The rate, too, upon each district, continuing always the same, the uncertainty of this tax, so far as it might he assessed upon the stock of any individual, has been very much diminished, as well as rendered of much less consequence. If the greater part of the lands of England are not rated to the land tax at half their actual value, the greater part of the stock of England is, perhaps, scarce rated at the fiftieth part of its actual value. In some towns, the whole land tax is assessed upon houses; as in Westminster, where stock and trade are free. It is otherwise in London.

In all countries, a severe inquisition into the circumstances of private persons has been carefully avoided.

At Hamburgh {*Memoires Concernant les Droits*, tom i, p. 74}, every inhabitant is obliged to pay to the state one fourth percent of all that he possesses; and as the wealth of the people of Hamburg consists principally in stock, this tax maybe considered as a tax upon stock. Every man assesses himself, and, in the presence of the magistrate, puts annually into the public coffer a certain sum of money, which he declares upon oath, to be one fourth percent of all that he possesses, but without declaring what it amounts to, or being liable to any examination upon that subject. This tax is generally supposed to be paid with great fidelity. In a small republic, where the people have entire confidence in their magistrates, are convinced of the necessity of the tax for the support of the state, and believe that it will be faithfully applied to that purpose, such conscientious and voluntary payment may sometimes be expected. It is not peculiar to the people of Hamburg.

The canton of Underwald, in Switzerland, is frequently ravaged by storms and inundations, and it is thereby exposed to extraordinary expenses. Upon such occasions the people assemble, and every one is said to declare with the greatest frankness what he is worth, in order to be taxed accordingly. At Zurich, the law orders, that in cases of necessity, every one should be taxed in proportion to his revenue; the amount of which he is obliged to declare upon oath. They have no suspicion, it is said, that any of their fellow citizens will deceive them. At Basil, the principal revenue of the state arises from a small custom upon goods exported. All the citizens make oath, that they will pay every three months all the taxes imposed by law. All merchants, and even all inn-keepers, are trusted with keeping themselves the account of the goods which they sell, either within or without the territory. At the end of every three months, they send this account to the treasurer, with the amount of the tax computed at the bottom of it. It is not suspected that the revenue suffers by this confidence. {*Memoires Concernant les Droits*, tom i pp. 163, 167,171.}

To oblige every citizen to declare publicly upon oath, the amount of his fortune, must not, it seems, in those Swiss cantons, be reckoned a hardship. At Hamburgh it would be reckoned the greatest. Merchants engaged in the hazardous projects of trade, all tremble at the thoughts of being obliged, at all times, to expose the real state of their circumstances. The ruin of their credit, and the miscarriage of their projects, they foresee, would too often be the consequence. A sober and parsimonious people, who are strangers to all such projects, do not feel that they have occasion for any such concealment.

In Holland, soon after the exaltation of the late prince of Orange to the stadtholdership, a tax of two percent or the fiftieth penny, as it was called, was imposed upon the whole substance of every citizen. Every citizen assessed himself, and paid his tax, in the same manner as at Hamburg, and it was in general supposed to have been paid with great fidelity. The people had at that time the greatest affection for their new government, which they had just established by a general insurrection. The tax was to be paid but once, in order to relieve the state in a particular exigency. It was, indeed, too heavy to be permanent. In a country where the market rate of interest seldom exceeds three percent, a tax of two percent amounts to thirteen shillings and four pence in the pound, upon the highest neat revenue which is commonly drawn from stock. It is a tax which very few people could pay, without encroaching more or less upon their capitals. In a particular exigency, the people may, from great public zeal, make a great effort, and give up even a part of their capital, in order to relieve the state. But it is impossible that they should continue to do so for any considerable time; and if they did, the tax would soon ruin them so completely, as to render them altogether incapable of supporting the state.

The tax upon stock, imposed by the land tax bill in England, though it is proportioned to the capital, is not intended to diminish or, take away any part of that capital. It is meant only to be a tax upon the interest of money, proportioned to that upon the rent of land; so that when the latter is at four shillings in the pound, the former may be at four shillings in the pound too. The tax at Hamburg, and the still more moderate taxes of Underwald and Zurich, are meant, in the same manner, to be taxes, not upon the capital, but upon the interest or neat revenue of stock. That of Holland was meant to be a tax upon the capital.

Taxes upon the Profit of Particular Employments

In some countries, extraordinary taxes are imposed upon the profits of stock; sometimes when employed in particular branches of trade, and sometimes when employed in agriculture.

Of the former kind, are in England the tax upon hawkers and peddlers, that upon hackney-coaches and chairs, and that which the keepers of ale-houses pay for a license to retail ale and spirituous liquors. During the late war, another tax of the same kind was proposed upon shops. The war having been undertaken, it was said, in defense of the trade of the country, the merchants, who were to profit by it, ought to contribute towards the support of it.

A tax, however, upon the profits of stock employed in any particular branch of trade, can never fall finally upon the dealers (who must in all ordinary cases have their reasonable profit, and, where the competition is free, can seldom have more than that profit), but always upon the consumers, who must be obliged to pay in the price of the goods the tax which the dealer advances; and generally with some overcharge.

A tax of this kind, when it is proportioned to the trade of the dealer, is finally paid by the consumer, and occasions no oppression to the dealer. When it is not so proportioned, but is the same upon all dealers, though in this case, too, it is finally paid by the consumer, yet it favors the great, and occasions some oppression to the small dealer. The tax of five shillings a week upon every hackney coach, and that of ten shillings a year upon every hackney chair, so far as it is advanced by the different keepers of such coaches and chairs, is exactly enough proportioned to the extent of their respective dealings. It neither favors the great, nor oppresses the smaller dealer. The tax of twenty shillings a year for a license to sell ale; of forty shillings for a license to sell spirituous liquors; and of forty shillings more for a license to sell wine, being the same upon all retailers, must necessarily give some advantage to the great, and occasion some oppression to the small dealers. The former must find it more easy to get back the tax in the price of their goods than the latter. The moderation of the tax, however, renders this inequality of less importance;

and it may to many people appear not improper to give some discouragement to the multiplication of little ale-houses. The tax upon shops, it was intended, should be the same upon all shops. It could not well have been otherwise. It would have been impossible to proportion, with tolerable exactness, the tax upon a shop to the extent of the trade carried on in it, without such an inquisition as would have been altogether insupportable in a free country. If the tax had been considerable, it would have oppressed the small, and forced almost the whole retail trade into the hands of the great dealers. The competition of the former being taken away, the latter would have enjoyed a monopoly of the trade; and, like all other monopolists, would soon have combined to raise their profits much beyond what was necessary for the payment of the tax. The final payment, instead of falling upon the shop-keeper, would have fallen upon the consumer, with a considerable overcharge to the profit of the shop-keeper. For these reasons, the project of a tax upon shops was laid aside, and in the room of it was substituted the subsidy, 1759.

What in France is called the personal taille, is perhaps, the most important tax upon the profits of stock employed in agriculture, that is levied in any part of Europe.

In the disorderly state of Europe, during the prevalence of the feudal government, the sovereign was obliged to content himself with taxing those who were too weak to refuse to pay taxes. The great lords, though willing to assist him upon particular emergencies, refused to subject themselves to any constant tax, and he was not strong enough to force them. The occupiers of land all over Europe were, the greater part of them, originally bond-men. Through the greater part of Europe, they were gradually emancipated. Some of them acquired the property of landed estates, which they held by some base or ignoble tenure, sometimes under the king, and sometimes under some other great lord, like the ancient copy-holders of England. Others, without acquiring the property, obtained leases for terms of years, of the lands which they occupied under their lord, and thus became less dependent upon him. The great lords seem to have beheld the degree of prosperity and independency, which this inferior order of men had thus come to enjoy, with a malignant and contemptuous indignation, and willingly consented that the sovereign should tax them. In some countries, this tax was confined to the lands which were held in property by an ignoble tenure; and, in this case, the taille was said to be real. The land tax established by the late king of Sardinia, and the taille in the provinces of Languedoc, Provence, Dauphine, and Britanny; in the generality of Montauban, and in the elections of Agen and Condom, as well as in some other districts of France; are taxes upon lands held in property by an ignoble tenure. In other countries, the tax was laid upon the supposed profits of all those who held, in farm or lease, lands belonging to other people, whatever might be the tenure by which the proprietor held them; and in this case, the taille was said to be personal. In the greater part of those provinces of France, which are called the countries of elections, the taille is of this kind. The real taille, as it is imposed only upon a part of the lands of the country, is necessarily an unequal, but it is not always an arbitrary tax, though it is so upon some occasions. The personal taille, as it is intended to be proportioned to the profits of a certain class of people, which can only be guessed at, is necessarily both arbitrary and unequal.

In France, the personal taille at present (1775) annually imposed upon the twenty generalities, called the countries of elections, amounts to 40,107,239 livres, 16 sous.

{*Memoires Concernant les Droits*, etc. tom ii, p. 17.} The proportion in which this sum is assessed upon those different provinces, varies from year to year, according to the reports which are made to the king's council concerning the goodness or badness of the crops, as well as other circumstances, which may either increase or diminish their respective abilities to pay. Each generality is divided into a certain number of elections; and the proportion in which the sum imposed upon the whole generality is divided among those different elections, varies likewise from year to year, according to the reports made to the council concerning their respective abilities. It seems impossible, that the council, with the best intentions, can ever proportion, with tolerable exactness, either of these two assessments to the real abilities of the province or district upon which they are respectively laid. Ignorance and misinformation must always, more or less, mislead the most upright council. The proportion which each parish ought to support of what is assessed upon the whole election, and that which each individual ought to support of what is assessed upon his particular parish, are both in the same manner varied from year to year, according as circumstances are supposed to require. These circumstances are judged of, in the one case, by the officers of the election, in the other, by those of the parish; and both the one and the other are, more or less, under the direction and influence of the intendant. Not only ignorance and misinformation, but friendship, party animosity, and private resentment, are said frequently to mislead such assessors. No man subject to such a tax, it is evident, can ever be certain, before he is assessed, of what he is to pay. He cannot even be certain after he is assessed. If any person has been taxed who ought to have been exempted, or if any person has been taxed beyond his proportion, though both must pay in the mean time, yet if they complain, and make good their complaints, the whole parish is reimposed next year, in order to reimburse them. If any of the contributors become bankrupt or insolvent, the collector is obliged to advance his tax; and the whole parish is reimposed next year, in order to reimburse the collector. If the collector himself should become bankrupt, the parish which elects him must answer for his conduct to the receiver-general of the election. But, as it might be troublesome for the receiver to prosecute the whole parish, he takes at his choice five or six of the richest contributors, and obliges them to make good what had been lost by the insolvency of the collector. The parish is afterwards reimposed, in order to reimburse those five or six. Such reimpositions are always over and above the taille of the particular year in which they are laid on.

When a tax is imposed upon the profits of stock in a particular branch of trade, the traders are all careful to bring no more goods to market than what they can sell at a price sufficient to reimburse them from advancing the tax. Some of them withdraw a part of their stocks from the trade, and the market is more sparingly supplied than before. The price of the goods rises, and the final payment of the tax falls upon the consumer. But when a tax is imposed upon the profits of stock employed in agriculture, it is not the interest of the farmers to withdraw any part of their stock from that employment. Each farmer occupies a certain quantity of land, for which he pays rent. For the proper cultivation of this land, a certain quantity of stock is necessary; and by withdrawing any part of this necessary quantity, the farmer is not likely to be more able to pay either the rent or the tax. In order to pay the tax, it can never be his interest to diminish the quantity of his produce, nor consequently to supply the market more sparingly than before. The tax, therefore, will never enable him to raise the price of his produce, so as to reimburse himself, by throwing the final payment upon the consumer. The farmer, however, must have his reasonable profit as well as every other dealer, otherwise he must give up the trade. After the imposition of a tax of this kind, he can get this reasonable profit only by paying less rent to the landlord. The more he is obliged to pay in the way of tax, the less he can afford to pay in the way of rent. A tax of this kind, imposed during the currency of a lease, may, no doubt, distress or ruin the farmer. Upon the renewal of the lease, it must always fall upon the landlord.

In the countries where the personal taille takes place, the farmer is commonly assessed in proportion to the stock which he appears to employ in cultivation. He is, upon this account, frequently afraid to have a good team of horses or oxen, but endeavors to cultivate with the meanest and most wretched instruments of husbandry that he can. Such is his distrust in the justice of his assessors, that he counterfeits poverty, and wishes to appear scarce able to pay anything, for fear of being obliged to pay too much. By this miserable policy, he does not, perhaps, always consult his own interest in the most effectual manner; and he probably loses more by the diminution of his produce, than he saves by that of his tax. Though, in consequence of this wretched cultivation, the market is, no doubt, somewhat worse supplied; yet the small rise of price which this may occasion, as it is not likely even to indemnify the farmer for the diminution of his produce, it is still less likely to enable him to pay more rent to the landlord. The public, the farmer, the landlord, all suffer more or less by this degraded cultivation. That the personal taille tends, in many different ways, to discourage cultivation, and consequently to dry up the principal source of the wealth of every great country, I have already had occasion to observe in the third book of this Inquiry.

What are called poll-taxes in the southern provinces of North America, and the West India islands, annual taxes of so much a head upon every negro, are properly taxes upon the profits of a certain species of stock employed in agriculture. As the planters, are the greater part of them, both farmers and landlords, the final payment of the tax falls upon them in their quality of landlords, without any retribution.

Taxes of so much a head upon the bondmen employed in cultivation, seem anciently to have been common all over Europe. There subsists at present a tax of this kind in the empire of Russia. It is probably upon this account that poll-taxes of all kinds have often been represented as badges of slavery. Every tax, however, is, to the person who pays it, a badge, not of slavery, but of liberty. It denotes that he is subject to government, indeed; but that, as he has some property, he cannot himself be the property of a master. A poll tax upon slaves is altogether different from a poll-tax upon freemen. The latter is paid by the persons upon whom it is imposed; the former, by a different set of persons. The latter is either altogether arbitrary, or altogether unequal, and, in most cases, is both the one and the other; the former, though in some respects unequal, different slaves being of different values, is in no respect arbitrary. Every master, who knows the number of his own slaves, knows exactly what he has to pay. Those different taxes, however, being called by the same name, have been considered as of the same nature.

The taxes which in Holland are imposed upon men and maid servants, are taxes, not upon stock, but upon expense; and so far resemble the taxes upon consumable commodities. The tax of a guinea a head for every man-servant, which has lately been imposed in Great Britain, is of the same kind. It falls heaviest upon the middling rank. A man of two hundred a year may keep a single man-servant. A man of ten thousand a year will not keep fifty. It does not affect the poor.

Taxes upon the profits of stock, in particular employments, can never affect the interest of money. Nobody will lend his money for less interest to those who exercise the taxed, than to those who exercise the untaxed employments. Taxes upon the revenue arising from stock in all employments, where the government attempts to levy them with any degree of exactness, will, in many cases, fall upon the interest of money. The vingtieme, or twentieth penny, in France, is a tax of the same kind with what is called the land tax in England, and is assessed, in the same manner, upon the revenue arising upon land, houses, and stock. So far as it affects stock, it is assessed, though not with great rigor, yet with much more exactness than that part of the land tax in England which is imposed upon the same fund. It, in many cases, falls altogether upon the interest of money. Money is frequently sunk in France, upon what are called contracts for the constitution of a rent; that is, perpetual annuities, redeemable at any time by the debtor, upon payment of the sum originally advanced, but of which this redemption is not exigible by the creditor except in particular cases. The vingtieme seems not to have raised the rate of those annuities, though it is exactly levied upon them all.

APPENDIX TO ARTICLES I AND II

Taxes upon the Capital Value of Lands, Houses, and Stock

While property remains in the possession of the same person, whatever permanent taxes may have been imposed upon it, they have never been intended to diminish or take away any part of its capital value, but only some part of the revenue arising from it. But when property changes hands, when it is transmitted either from the dead to the living, or from the living to the living, such taxes have frequently been imposed upon it as necessarily take away some part of its capital value.

The transference of all sorts of property from the dead to the living, and that of immoveable property of land and houses from the living to the living, are transactions which are in their nature either public and notorious, or such as cannot be long concealed. Such transactions, therefore, may be taxed directly. The transference of stock or moveable property, from the living to the living, by the lending of money, is frequently a secret transaction, and may always be made so. It cannot easily, therefore, be taxed directly. It has been taxed indirectly in two different ways; first, by requiring that the deed, containing the obligation to repay, should be written upon paper or parchment which had paid a certain stamp duty, otherwise not to be valid; secondly, by requiring, under the like penalty of invalidity, that it should be recorded either in a public or secret register, and by imposing certain duties upon such registration. Stamp duties, and duties of registration, have frequently been imposed likewise upon the deeds transferring property of all kinds from the dead to the living, and upon those transferring immoveable property from the living to the living; transactions which might easily have been taxed directly.

The vicesima hereditatum, or the twentieth penny of inheritances, imposed by Augustus upon the ancient Romans, was a tax upon the transference of property from the dead to the living. Dion Cassius, {Lib. 55. See also *Burman. de Vectigalibus Pop. Rom. cap. xi. and Bouchaud de L'impot du Vingtieme sur les Successions.*} the author who writes concerning it the least indistinctly, says, that it was imposed upon all successions, legacies and donations, in case of death, except upon those to the nearest relations, and to the poor.

Of the same kind is the Dutch tax upon successions. {See *Memoires Concernant les Droits*, etc. tom. i, p. 225.} Collateral successions are taxed according to the degree of relation, from five to thirty percent upon the whole value of the succession. Testamentary donations, or legacies to collaterals, are subject to the like duties. Those from husband to wife, or from wife to husband, to the fiftieth penny. The luctuosa hereditas, the mournful succession of ascendants to descendants, to the twentieth penny only. Direct successions, or those of descendants to ascendants, pay no tax. The death of a father, to such of his children as live in the same house with him, is seldom attended with any increase, and frequently with a considerable diminution of revenue; by the loss of his industry, of his office, or of some life-rent estate, of which he may have been in possession. That tax would be cruel and oppressive, which aggravated their loss, by taking from them any part of his succession. It may, however, sometimes be otherwise with those children, who, in the language of the Roman law, are said to be emancipated; in that of the Scotch law, to be forisfamiliated; that is, who have received their portion, have got families of their own, and are supported by funds separate and independent of those of their father. Whatever part of his succession might come to such children, would be a real addition to their fortune, and might, therefore, perhaps, without more inconveniency than what attends all duties of this kind, be liable to some tax.

The casualties of the feudal law were taxes upon the transference of land, both from the dead to the living, and from the living to the living. In ancient times, they constituted, in every part of Europe, one of the principal branches of the revenue of the crown.

The heir of every immediate vassal of the crown paid a certain duty, generally a year's rent, upon receiving the investiture of the estate. If the heir was a minor, the whole rents of the estate, during the continuance of the minority, devolved to the superior, without any other charge besides the maintenance of the minor, and the payment of the widow's dower, when there happened to be a dowager upon the land. When the minor came to be of age, another tax, called relief, was still due to the superior, which generally amounted likewise to a year's rent. A long minority, which, in the present times, so frequently disburdens a great estate of all its encumbrances, and restores the family to their ancient splendor, could in those times have no such effect. The waste, and not the disencumbrance of the estate, was the common effect of a long minority.

By a feudal law, the vassal could not alienate without the consent of his superior, who generally extorted a fine or composition on granting it. This fine, which was at first arbitrary, came, in many countries, to be regulated at a certain portion of the price of the land. In some countries, where the greater part of the other feudal customs have gone into disuse, this tax upon the alienation of land still continues to make a very considerable branch of the revenue of the sovereign. In the canton of Berne it is so high as a sixth part of the price of all noble fiefs, and a tenth part of that of all ignoble ones. {*Memoires Concernant les Droits*, etc. tom. i. p. 154} In the canton of Lucern, the tax upon the sale of land is not universal, and takes place only in certain districts. But if any person sells his land in order to remove out of the territory, he pays ten percent upon the whole price of the sale. {Id. p.157.} Taxes of the same kind, upon the sale either of all lands, or of lands held by certain tenures, take place in many other countries, and make a more or less considerable branch of the revenue of the sovereign.

Such transactions may be taxed indirectly, by means either of stamp duties, or of duties upon registration; and those duties either may, or may not, be proportioned to the value of the subject which is transferred.

In Great Britain, the stamp duties are higher or lower, not so much according to the value of the property transferred (an eighteen-penny or half-crown stamp being sufficient upon a bond for the largest sum of money), as according to the nature of the deed. The highest do not exceed six pounds upon every sheet of paper, or skin of parchment; and these high duties fall chiefly upon grants from the crown, and upon certain law proceedings, without any regard to the value of the subject. There are, in Great Britain, no duties on the registration of deeds or writings, except the fees of the officers who keep the register; and these are seldom more than a reasonable recompense for their labor. The crown derives no revenue from them.

In Holland {*Memoires Concernant les Droits*, etc. tom. i. pp. 223, 224, 225} there are both stamp duties and duties upon registration; which in some cases are, and in some are not, proportioned to the value of the property transferred. All testaments must be written upon stamped paper, of which the price is proportioned to the property disposed of; so that there are stamps which cost from three pence or three stivers a sheet, to three hundred florins, equal to about twenty-seven pounds ten shillings of our money. If the stamp is of an inferior price to what the testator ought to have made use of, his succession is confiscated. This is over and above all their other taxes on succession. Except bills of exchange, and some other mercantile bills, all other deeds, bonds, and contracts, are subject to a stamp duty. This duty, however, does not rise in proportion to the value of the subject. All sales of land and of houses, and all mortgages upon either, must be registered, and, upon registration, pay a duty to the state of two and a-half percent upon the amount of the price or of the mortgage. This duty is extended to the sale of all ships and vessels of more than two tons burden, whether decked or undecked. These, it seems, are considered as a sort of houses upon the water. The sale of moveables, when it is ordered by a court of justice, is subject to the like duty of two and a-half percent.

In France, there are both stamp duties and duties upon registration. The former are considered as a branch of the aids of excise, and, in the provinces where those duties take place, are levied by the excise officers. The latter are considered as a branch of the domain of the crown and are levied by a different set of officers.

Those modes of taxation by stamp duties and by duties upon registration, are of very modern invention. In the course of little more than a century, however, stamp duties have, in Europe, become almost universal, and duties upon registration extremely common. There is no art which one government sooner learns of another, than that of draining money from the pockets of the people.

Taxes upon the transference of property from the dead to the living, fall finally, as well as immediately, upon the persons to whom the property is transferred. Taxes upon the sale of land fall altogether upon the seller. The seller is almost always under the necessity of selling, and must, therefore, take such a price as he can get. The buyer is scarce ever under the necessity of buying, and will, therefore, only give such a price as he likes. He considers what the land will cost him, in tax and price together. The more he is obliged to pay in the way of tax, the less he will be disposed to give in the way of price. Such taxes, therefore, fall almost always upon a necessitous person, and must, therefore, be frequently very cruel and oppressive. Taxes upon the sale of new-built houses, where the building is sold without the ground, fall generally upon the buyer, because the builder must generally have his profit; otherwise he must give up the trade. If he advances the tax, therefore, the buyer must generally repay it to him. Taxes upon the sale of old houses, for the same reason as those upon the sale of land, fall generally upon the seller; whom, in most cases, either convenience or necessity obliges to sell. The number of new-built houses that are annually brought to market, is more or less regulated by the demand. Unless the demand is such as to afford the builder his profit, after paying all expenses, he will build no more houses. The number of old houses which happen at any time to come to market, is regulated by accidents, of which the greater part have no relation to the demand. Two or three great bankruptcies in a mercantile town, will bring many houses to sale, which must be sold for what can be got for them. Taxes upon the sale of ground-rents fall altogether upon the seller, for the same reason as those upon the sale of lands. Stamp duties, and duties upon the registration of bonds and contracts for borrowed money, fall altogether upon the borrower, and, in fact, are always paid by him. Duties of the same kind upon law proceedings fall upon the suitors. They reduce to both the capital value of the subject in dispute. The more it costs to acquire any property, the less must be the neat value of it when acquired.

All taxes upon the transference of property of every kind, so far as they diminish the capital value of that property, tend to diminish the funds destined for the maintenance of productive labor. They are all more or less unthrifty taxes that increase the revenue of the sovereign, which seldom maintains any but unproductive laborers, at the expense of the capital of the people, which maintains none but productive.

Such taxes, even when they are proportioned to the value of the property transferred, are still unequal; the frequency of transference not being always equal in property of equal value. When they are not proportioned to this value, which is the case with the greater part of the stamp duties and duties of registration, they are still more so. They are in no respect arbitrary, but are, or may be, in all cases, perfectly clear and certain. Though they sometimes fall upon the person who is not very able to pay, the time of payment is, in most cases, sufficiently convenient for him. When the payment becomes due, he must, in most cases, have the more to pay. They are levied at very little expense, and in general subject the contributors to no other inconveniency, besides always the unavoidable one of paying the tax.

In France, the stamp duties are not much complained of. Those of registration, which they call the Controle, are. They give occasion, it is pretended, to much extortion in the officers of the farmers-general who collect the tax, which is in a great measure arbitrary and uncertain. In the greater part of the libels which have been written against the present system of finances in France, the abuses of the Controle make a principal article. Uncertainty, however, does not seem to be necessarily inherent in the nature of such taxes. If the popular complaints are well founded, the abuse must arise, not so much from the nature of the tax as from the want of precision and distinctness in the words of the edicts or laws which impose it.

The registration of mortgages, and in general of all rights upon immoveable property, as it gives great security both to creditors and purchasers, is extremely advantageous to the public. That of the greater part of deeds of other kinds, is frequently inconvenient and even dangerous to individuals, without any advantage to the public. All registers which, it is acknowledged, ought to be kept secret, ought certainly never to exist. The credit of individuals ought certainly never to depend upon so very slender a security, as the probity and religion of the inferior officers of revenue. But where the fees of registration have been made a source of revenue to the sovereign, register-offices have commonly been multiplied without end, both for the deeds which ought to be registered, and for those which ought not. In France there are several different sorts of secret registers. This abuse, though not perhaps a necessary, it must be acknowledged, is a very natural effect of such taxes.

Such stamp duties as those in England upon cards and dice, upon newspapers and periodical pamphlets, etc. are properly taxes upon consumption; the final payment falls upon the persons who use or consume such commodities. Such stamp duties as those upon licenses to retail ale, wine, and spirituous liquors, though intended, perhaps, to fall upon the profits of the retailers, are likewise finally paid by the consumers of those liquors. Such taxes, though called by the same name, and levied by the same officers, and in the same manner with the stamp duties above mentioned upon the transference of property, are, however, of a quite different nature, and fall upon quite different funds.

ARTICLE III

Taxes upon the Wages of Labor

The wages of the inferior classes of work men, I have endeavored to show in the first book are everywhere necessarily regulated by two different circumstances; the demand for labor, and the ordinary or average price of provisions. The demand for labor, according as it happens to be either increasing stationary or declining; or to require an increasing, stationary, or declining population, regulates the subsistence of the laborer, and determines in what degree it shall be either liberal, moderate, or scanty. The ordinary average price of provisions determines the quantity of money which must be paid to the workman, in order to enable him, one year with another, to purchase this liberal, moderate, or scanty subsistence. While the demand for the labor and the price of provisions, therefore, remain the same, a direct tax upon the wages of labor can have no other effect, than to raise them somewhat higher than the tax. Let us suppose, for example, that, in a particular place, the demand for labor and the price of provisions were such as to render ten shillings a week the ordinary wages of labor; and that a tax of one-fifth, or four shillings in the pound, was imposed upon wages. If the demand for labor and the price of provisions remained the same, it would still be necessary that the laborer should, in that place, earn such a subsistence as could be bought only for ten shillings a week; so that, after paying the tax, he should have ten shillings a week free wages. But, in order to leave him such free wages, after paying such a tax, the price of labor must, in that place, soon rise, not to twelve shillings a week only, but to twelve and sixpence; that is, in order to enable him to pay a tax of one-fifth, his wages must necessarily soon rise, not one-fifth part only, but one-fourth. Whatever was the proportion of the tax, the wages of labor must, in all cases rise, not only in that proportion, but in a higher proportion. If the tax for example, was one-tenth, the wages of labor must necessarily soon rise, not one-tenth part only, but one-eighth.

A direct tax upon the wages of labor, therefore, though the laborer might, perhaps, pay it out of his hand, could not properly be said to be even advanced by him; at least if the demand for labor and the average price of provisions remained the same after the tax as before it. In all such cases, not only the tax, but something more than the tax, would in reality be advanced by the person who immediately employed him. The final payment would, in different cases, fall upon different persons. The rise which such a tax might occasion in the wages of manufacturing labor would be advanced by the master manufacturer, who would both be entitled and obliged to charge it, with a profit, upon the price of his goods. The final payment of this rise of wages, therefore, together with the additional profit of the master manufacturer would fall upon the consumer. The rise which such a tax might occasion in the wages of country labor would be advanced by the farmer, who, in order to maintain the same number of laborers as before, would be obliged to employ a greater capital. In order to get back this greater capital, together with the ordinary profits of stock, it would be necessary that he should retain a larger portion, or, what comes to the same thing, the price of a larger portion, of the produce of the land, and, consequently, that he should pay less rent to the landlord. The final payment of this rise of wages, therefore, would, in this case, fall upon the landlord, together with the additional profit of the farmer who had advanced it. In all cases, a direct tax upon the wages of labor must, in the long-run, occasion both a greater reduction in the rent of land, and a greater rise in the price of manufactured goods than would have followed from the proper assessment of a sum equal to the produce of the tax, partly upon the rent of land, and partly upon consumable commodities.

If direct taxes upon the wages of labor have not always occasioned a proportional rise in those wages, it is because they have generally occasioned a considerable fall in the demand of labor. The declension of industry, the decrease of employment for the poor, the diminution of the annual produce of the land and labor of the country, have generally been the effects of such taxes. In consequence of them, however, the price of labor must always be higher than it otherwise would have been in the actual state of the demand; and this enhancement of price, together with the profit of those who advance it, must always be finally paid by the landlords and consumers.

A tax upon the wages of country labor does not raise the price of the rude produce of land in proportion to the tax; for the same reason that a tax upon the farmer's profit does not raise that price in that proportion.

Absurd and destructive as such taxes are, however, they take place in many countries. In France, that part of the taille which is charged upon the industry of workmen and day-laborers in country villages, is properly a tax of this kind. Their wages are computed according to the common rate of the district in which they reside; and, that they may be as little liable as possible to any overcharge, their yearly gains are estimated at no more than two hundred working days in the year. {*Memoires Concernant les Droits*, etc. tom. ii, p. 108.} The tax of each individual is varied from year to year, according to different circumstances, of which the collector or the commissary, whom intendant appoints to assist him, are the judges. In Bohemia, in consequence of the alteration in the system of finances which was begun in 1748, a very heavy tax is imposed upon the industry of artificers. They are divided into four classes. The highest class pay a hundred florins a year, which, at two-and-twenty pence half penny a florin, amounts to £9:7:6. The second class are taxed at seventy; the third at fifty; and the fourth, comprehending artificers in villages, and the lowest class of those in towns, at twenty-five florins. {*Memoires Concernant les Droits*, etc. tom. iii, p. 87.}

The recompense of ingenious artists, and of men of liberal professions, I have endeavored to show in the first book, necessarily keeps a certain proportion to the emoluments of inferior trades. A tax upon this recompense, therefore, could have no other effect than to raise it somewhat higher than in proportion to the tax. If it did not rise in this manner, the ingenious arts and the liberal professions, being no longer upon a level with other trades, would be so much deserted, that they would soon return to that level.

The emoluments of offices are not, like those of trades and professions, regulated by the free competition of the market, and do not, therefore, always bear a just proportion to what the nature of the employment requires. They are, perhaps, in most countries, higher than it requires; the persons who have the administration of government being generally disposed to regard both themselves and their immediate dependents, rather more than enough. The emoluments of offices, therefore, can, in most cases, very well bear to be taxed. The persons, besides, who enjoy public offices, especially the more lucrative, are, in all countries, the objects of general envy; and a tax upon their emoluments, even though it should be somewhat higher than upon any other sort of revenue, is always a very popular tax. In England, for example, when, by the land-tax, every other sort of revenue was supposed to be assessed at four shillings in the pound, it was very popular to lay a real tax of five shillings and sixpence in the pound upon the salaries of offices which exceeded a hundred pounds a year; the pensions of the younger branches of the royal family, the pay of the officers of the army and navy, and a few others less obnoxious to envy, excepted. There are in England no other direct taxes upon the wages of labor.

ARTICLE IV

Taxes which It Is Intended Should Fall Indifferently upon Every Different Species of Revenue

The taxes which it is intended should fall indifferently upon every different species of revenue, are capitation taxes, and taxes upon consumable commodities. Those must be paid indifferently, from whatever revenue the contributors may possess; from the rent of their land, from the profits of their stock, or from the wages of their labor.

Capitation Taxes

Capitation taxes, if it is attempted to proportion them to the fortune or revenue of each contributor, become altogether arbitrary. The state of a man's fortune varies from day to day; and, without an inquisition, more intolerable than any tax, and renewed at least once every year, can only be guessed at. His assessment, therefore, must, in most cases, depend upon the good or bad humor of his assessors, and must, therefore, be altogether arbitrary and uncertain.

Capitation taxes, if they are proportioned, not to the supposed fortune, but to the rank of each contributor, become altogether unequal; the degrees of fortune being frequently unequal in the same degree of rank.

Such taxes, therefore, if it is attempted to render them equal, become altogether arbitrary and uncertain; and if it is attempted to render them certain and not arbitrary, become altogether unequal. Let the tax be light or heavy, uncertainty is always a great grievance. In a light tax, a considerable degree of inequality may be supported; in a heavy one, it is altogether intolerable.

In the different poll-taxes which took place in England during the reign of William III the contributors were, the greater part of them, assessed according to the degree of their rank; as dukes, marquises, earls, viscounts, barons, esquires, gentlemen, the eldest and youngest sons of peers, etc. All shop-keepers and tradesmen worth more than three hundred pounds, that is, the better sort of them, were subject to the same assessment, how great soever might be the difference in their fortunes. Their rank was more considered than their fortune. Several of those who, in the first poll-tax, were rated according to their supposed fortune were afterwards rated according to their rank. Sergeants, attorneys, and proctors at law, who, in the first poll-tax, were assessed at three shillings in the pound of their supposed income, were afterwards assessed as gentlemen. In the assessment of a tax which was not very heavy, a considerable degree of inequality had been found less insupportable than any degree of uncertainty.

In the capitation which has been levied in France without any interruption, since the beginning of the present century, the highest orders of people are rated according to their rank, by an invariable tariff; the lower orders of people, according to what is supposed to be their fortune, by an assessment which varies from year to year. The officers of the king's court, the judges, and other officers in the superior courts of justice, the officers of the troops, etc are assessed in the first manner. The inferior ranks of people in the provinces are assessed in the second. In France, the great easily submit to a considerable degree of inequality in a tax which, so far as it affects them, is not a very heavy one; but could not brook the arbitrary assessment of an intendant.

The inferior ranks of people must, in that country, suffer patiently the usage which their superiors think proper to give them.

In England, the different poll-taxes never produced the sum which had been expected from them, or which it was supposed they might have produced, had they been exactly levied. In France, the capitation always produces the sum expected from it. The mild government of England, when it assessed the different ranks of people to the poll-tax, contented itself with what that assessment happened to produce, and required no compensation for the loss which the state might sustain, either by those who could not pay, or by those who would not pay (for there were many such), and who, by the indulgent execution of the law, were not forced to pay. The more severe government of France assesses upon each generality a certain sum, which the intendant must find as he can. If any province complains of being assessed too high, it may, in the assessment of next year, obtain an abatement proportioned to the overcharge of the year before; but it must pay in the mean time. The intendant, in order to be sure of finding the sum assessed upon his generality, was empowered to assess it in a larger sum, that the failure or inability of some of the contributors might be compensated by the overcharge of the rest; and till 1765, the fixation of this surplus assessment was left altogether to his discretion. In that year, indeed, the council assumed this power to itself. In the capitation of the provinces, it is observed by the perfectly well informed author of the *Memoirs upon the Impositions* in France, the proportion which falls upon the nobility, and upon those whose privileges exempt them from the taille, is the least considerable. The largest falls upon those subject to the taille, who are assessed to the capitation at so much a pound of what they pay to that other tax.

Capitation taxes, so far as they are levied upon the lower ranks of people, are direct taxes upon the wages of labor, and are attended with all the inconveniencies of such taxes.

Capitation taxes are levied at little expense; and, where they are rigorously exacted, afford a very sure revenue to the state. It is upon this account that, in countries where the case, comfort, and security of the inferior ranks of people are little attended to, capitation taxes are very common. It is in general, however, but a small part of the public revenue, which, in a great empire, has ever been drawn from such taxes; and the greatest sum which they have ever afforded, might always have been found in some other way much more convenient to the people.

Taxes upon Consumable Commodities

The impossibility of taxing the people, in proportion to their revenue, by any capitation, seems to have given occasion to the invention of taxes upon consumable commodities.

The state not knowing how to tax, directly and proportionally, the revenue of its subjects, endeavors to tax it indirectly by taxing their expense, which, it is supposed, will, in most cases, be nearly in proportion to their revenue. Their expense is taxed, by taxing the consumable commodities upon which it is laid out.

Consumable Commodities are Either Necessaries or Luxuries

By necessaries I understand, not only the commodities which are indispensably necessary for the support of life, but whatever the custom of the country renders it indecent for creditable people, even of the lowest order, to be without. A linen shirt, for example, is, strictly speaking, not a necessary of life. The Greeks and Romans lived, I suppose, very comfortably, though they had no linen. But in the present times, through the greater part of Europe, a creditable day-laborer would be ashamed to appear in public without a linen shirt, the want of which would be supposed to denote that disgraceful degree of poverty, which, it is presumed, nobody can well fall into without extreme bad conduct. Custom, in the same manner, has rendered leather shoes a necessary of life in England. The poorest creditable person, of either sex, would be ashamed to appear in public without them. In Scotland, custom has rendered them a necessary of life to the lowest order of men; but not to the same order of women, who may, without any discredit, walk about barefooted. In France, they are necessaries neither to men nor to women; the lowest rank of both sexes appearing there publicly, without any discredit, sometimes in wooden shoes, and sometimes barefooted. Under necessaries, therefore, I comprehend, not only those things which nature, but those things which the established rules of decency have rendered necessary to the lowest rank of people. All other things I call luxuries, without meaning, by this appellation, to throw the smallest degree of reproach upon the temperate use of them. Beer and ale, for example, in Great Britain, and wine, even in the wine countries, I call luxuries. A man of any rank may, without any reproach, abstain totally from tasting such liquors. Nature does not render them necessary for the support of life; and custom nowhere renders it indecent to live without them.

As the wages of labor are everywhere regulated, partly by the demand for it, and partly by the average price of the necessary articles of subsistence; whatever raises this average price must necessarily raise those wages; so that the laborer may still be able to purchase that quantity of those necessary articles which the state of the demand for labor, whether increasing, stationary, or declining, requires that he should have. {See book i, chap. 8.} A tax upon those articles necessarily raises their price somewhat higher than the amount of the tax, because the dealer, who advances the tax, must generally get it back, with a profit. Such a tax must, therefore, occasion a rise in the wages of labor, proportional to this rise of price.

It is thus that a tax upon the necessaries of life operates exactly in the same manner as a direct tax upon the wages of labor. The laborer, though he may pay it out of his hand, cannot, for any considerable time at least, be properly said even to advance it. It must always, in the long-run, be advanced to him by his immediate employer, in the advanced state of wages. His employer, if he is a manufacturer, will charge upon the price of his goods the rise of wages, together with a profit, so that the final payment of the tax, together with this overcharge, will fall upon the consumer. If his employer is a farmer, the final payment, together with a like overcharge, will fall upon the rent of the landlord.

It is otherwise with taxes upon what I call luxuries, even upon those of the poor. The rise in the price of the taxed commodities, will not necessarily occasion any rise in the wages of labor. A tax upon tobacco, for example, though a luxury of the poor, as well as of the rich, will not raise wages. Though it is taxed in England at three times, and in France at fifteen times its original price, those high duties seem to have no effect upon the wages of labor. The same thing maybe said of the taxes upon tea and sugar, which, in England and Holland, have become luxuries of the lowest ranks of people; and of those upon chocolate, which, in Spain, is said to have become so.

The different taxes which, in Great Britain, have, in the course of the present century, been imposed upon spirituous liquors, are not supposed to have had any effect upon the wages of labor. The rise in the price of porter, occasioned by an additional tax of three shillings upon the barrel of strong beer, has not raised the wages of common labor in London. These were about eighteen pence or twenty pence a day before the tax, and they are not more now.

The high price of such commodities does not necessarily diminish the ability of the inferior ranks of people to bring up families. Upon the sober and industrious poor, taxes upon such commodities act as sumptuary laws, and dispose them either to moderate, or to refrain altogether from the use of superfluities which they can no longer easily afford. Their ability to bring up families, in consequence of this forced frugality, instead of being diminished, is frequently, perhaps, increased by the tax. It is the sober and industrious poor who generally bring up the most numerous families, and who principally supply the demand for useful labor. All the poor, indeed, are not sober and industrious; and the dissolute and disorderly might continue to indulge themselves in the use of such commodities, after this rise of price, in the same manner as before, without regarding the distress which this indulgence might bring upon their families. Such disorderly persons, however, seldom rear up numerous families, their children generally perishing from neglect, mismanagement, and the scantiness or unwholesomeness of their food. If by the strength of their constitution, they survive the hardships to which the bad conduct of their parents exposes them, yet the example of that bad conduct commonly corrupts their morals; so that, instead of being useful to society by their industry, they become public nuisances by their vices and disorders. Through the advanced price of the luxuries of the poor, therefore, might increase somewhat the distress of such disorderly families, and thereby diminish somewhat their ability to bring up children, it would not probably diminish much the useful population of the country.

Any rise in the average price of necessaries, unless it be compensated by a proportional rise in the wages of labor, must necessarily diminish, more or less, the ability of the poor to bring up numerous families, and, consequently, to supply the demand for useful labor; whatever may be the state of that demand, whether increasing, stationary, or declining; or such as requires an increasing, stationary, or declining population.

Taxes upon luxuries have no tendency to raise the price of any other commodities, except that of the commodities taxed. Taxes upon necessaries, by raising the wages of labor, necessarily tend to raise the price of all manufactures, and consequently to diminish the extent of their sale and consumption. Taxes upon luxuries are finally paid by the consumers of the commodities taxed, without any retribution. They fall indifferently upon every species of revenue, the wages of labor, the profits of stock, and the rent of land. Taxes upon necessaries, so far as they affect the laboring poor, are finally paid, partly by landlords, in the diminished rent of their lands, and partly by rich consumers, whether landlords or others, in the advanced price of manufactured goods; and always with a considerable overcharge. The advanced price of such manufactures as are real necessaries of life, and are destined for the consumption of the poor; of coarse woolens, for example, must be compensated to the poor by a farther advancement of their wages. The middling and superior ranks of people, if they understood their own interest, ought always to oppose all taxes upon the necessaries of life, as well as all taxes upon the wages of labor. The final payment of both the one and the other falls altogether upon themselves, and always with a considerable overcharge. They fall heaviest upon the landlords, who always pay in a double capacity; in that of landlords, by the reduction, of their rent; and in that of rich consumers, by the increase of their expense. The observation of Sir Matthew Decker, that certain taxes are, in the price of certain goods, sometimes repeated and accumulated four or five times, is perfectly just with regard to taxes upon the necessaries of life. In the price of leather, for example, you must pay not only for the tax upon the leather of your own shoes, but for a part of that upon those of the shoemaker and the tanner.

You must pay, too, for the tax upon the salt, upon the soap, and upon the candles which those workmen consume while employed in your service; and for the tax upon the leather, which the saltmaker, the soap-maker, and the candle-maker consume, while employed in their service.

In Great Britain, the principal taxes upon the necessaries of life, are those upon the four commodities just now mentioned, salt, leather, soap, and candles.

Salt is a very ancient and a very universal subject of taxation. It was taxed among the Romans, and it is so at present in, I believe, every part of Europe. The quantity annually consumed by any individual is so small, and may be purchased so gradually, that nobody, it seems to have been thought, could feel very sensibly even a pretty heavy tax upon it. It is in England taxed at three shillings and four pence a bushel; about three times the original price of the commodity. In some other countries, the tax is still higher. Leather is a real necessary of life. The use of linen renders soap such. In countries where the winter nights are long, candles are a necessary instrument of trade. Leather and soap are in Great Britain taxed at three halfpence a pound; candles at a penny; taxes which, upon the original price of leather, may amount to about eight or ten percent; upon that of soap, to about twenty or five-and-twenty percent; and upon that of candles to about fourteen or fifteen percent; taxes which, though lighter than that upon salt, are still very heavy. As all those four commodities are real necessaries of life, such heavy taxes upon them must increase somewhat the expense of the sober and industrious poor, and must consequently raise more or less the wages of their labor.

In a country where the winters are so cold as in Great Britain, fuel is, during that season, in the strictest sense of the word, a necessary of life, not only for the purpose of dressing victuals, but for the comfortable subsistence of many different sorts of workmen who work within doors; and coals are the cheapest of all fuel. The price of fuel has so important an influence upon that of labor, that all over Great Britain, manufactures have confined themselves principally to the coal counties; other parts of the country, on account of the high price of this necessary article, not being able to work so cheap. In some manufactures, besides, coal is a necessary instrument of trade; as in those of glass, iron, and all other metals. If a bounty could in any case be reasonable, it might perhaps be so upon the transportation of coals from those parts of the country in which they abound, to those in which they are wanted. But the legislature, instead of a bounty, has imposed a tax of three shillings and threepence a ton upon coals carried coastways; which, upon most sorts of coal, is more than sixty percent of the original price at the coal pit. Coals carried, either by land or by inland navigation, pay no duty. Where they are naturally cheap, they are consumed duty free; where they are naturally dear, they are loaded with a heavy duty.

Such taxes, though they raise the price of subsistence, and consequently the wages of labor, yet they afford a considerable revenue to government, which it might not be easy to find in any other way. There may, therefore, be good reasons for continuing them. The bounty upon the exportation of corn, so far us it tends, in the actual state of tillage, to raise the price of that necessary article, produces all the like bad effects; and instead of affording any revenue, frequently occasions a very great expense to government. The high duties upon the importation of foreign corn, which, in years of moderate plenty, amount to a prohibition; and the absolute prohibition of the importation, either of live cattle, or of salt provisions, which takes place in the ordinary state of the law, and which, on account of the scarcity, is at present suspended for a limited time with regard to Ireland and the British plantations, have all had the bad effects of taxes upon the necessaries of life, and produce no revenue to government. Nothing seems necessary for the repeal of such regulations, but to convince the public of the futility of that system in consequence of which they have been established.

Taxes upon the necessaries of life are much higher in many other countries than in Great Britain. Duties upon flour and meal when ground at the mill, and upon bread when baked at the oven, take place in many countries. In Holland the money-price of the bread consumed in towns is supposed to be doubled by means of such taxes. In lieu of a part of them, the people who live in the country, pay every year so much a head, according to the sort of bread they are supposed to consume. Those who consume wheaten bread pay three guilders fifteen stivers; about six shillings and nine pence halfpenny. Those, and some other taxes of the same kind, by raising the price of labor, are said to have ruined the greater part of the manufactures of Holland {*Memoires Concernant les Droits*, etc. pp. 210, 211}. Similar taxes, though not quite so heavy, take place in the Milanese, in the states of Genoa, in the duchy of Modena, in the duchies of Parma, Placentia, and Guastalla, and the Ecclesiastical state. A French author {Le Reformateur} of some note, has proposed to reform the finances of his country, by substituting in the room of the greater part of other taxes, this most ruinous of all taxes. There is nothing so absurd, says Cicero, which has not sometimes been asserted by some philosophers.

Taxes upon butcher's meat are still more common than those upon bread. It may indeed be doubted, whether butcher's meat is any where a necessary of life. Grain and other vegetables, with the help of milk, cheese, and butter, or oil, where butter is not to be had, it is known from experience, can, without any butcher's meat, afford the most plentiful, the most wholesome, the most nourishing, and the most invigorating diet. Decency nowhere requires that any man should eat butcher's meat, as it in most places requires that he should wear a linen shirt or a pair of leather shoes.

Consumable commodities, whether necessaries or luxuries, may be taxed in two different ways. The consumer may either pay an annual sum on account of his using or consuming goods of a certain kind; or the goods may be taxed while they remain in the hands of the dealer, and before they are delivered to the consumer. The consumable goods which last a considerable time before they are consumed altogether, are most properly taxed in the one way; those of which the consumption is either immediate or more speedy, in the other. The coach-tax and plate tax are examples of the former method of imposing; the greater part of the other duties of excise and customs, of the latter.

A coach may, with good management, last ten or twelve years. It might be taxed, once for all, before it comes out of the hands of the coach-maker. But it is certainly more convenient for the buyer to pay four pounds a year for the privilege of keeping a coach, than to pay all at once forty or forty-eight pounds additional price to the coach-maker; or a sum equivalent to what the tax is likely to cost him during the time he uses the same coach. A service of plate in the same manner, may last more than a century. It is certainly-easier for the consumer to pay five shillings a year for every hundred ounces of plate, near one percent of the value, than to redeem this long annuity at five-and-twenty or thirty years purchase, which would enhance the price at least five-and-twenty or thirty percent. The different taxes which affect houses, are certainly more conveniently paid by moderate annual payments, than by a heavy tax of equal value upon the first building or sale of the house.

It was the well-known proposal of Sir Matthew Decker, that all commodities, even those of which the consumption is either immediate or speedy, should be taxed in this manner; the dealer advancing nothing, but the consumer paying a certain annual sum for the license to consume certain goods. The object of his scheme was to promote all the different branches of foreign trade, particularly the carrying trade, by taking away all duties upon importation and exportation, and thereby enabling the merchant to employ his whole capital and credit in the purchase of goods and the freight of ships, no part of either being diverted towards the advancing of taxes. The project, however, of taxing, in this manner, goods of immediate or speedy consumption, seems liable to the four following very important objections. First, the tax would be more unequal, or not so well proportioned to the expense and consumption of the different contributors, as in the way in which it is commonly imposed. The taxes upon ale, wine, and spirituous liquors, which are advanced by the dealers, are finally paid by the different consumers, exactly in proportion to their respective consumption. But if the tax were to be paid by purchasing a license to drink those liquors, the sober would, in proportion to his consumption, be taxed much more heavily than the drunken consumer. A family which exercised great hospitality, would be taxed much more lightly than one who entertained fewer guests. Secondly, this mode of taxation, by paying for an annual, half-yearly, or quarterly license to consume certain goods, would diminish very much one of the principal conveniences of taxes upon goods of speedy consumption; the piece-meal payment. In the price of threepence halfpenny, which is at present paid for a pot of porter, the different taxes upon malt, hops, and beer, together with the extraordinary profit which the brewer charges for having advanced than, may perhaps amount to about three halfpence. If a workman can conveniently spare those three halfpence, he buys a pot of porter. If he cannot, he contents himself with a pint; and, as a penny saved is a penny got, he thus gains a farthing by his temperance. He pays the tax piece-meal, as he can afford to pay it, and when he can afford to pay it, and every act of payment is perfectly voluntary, and what he can avoid if he chooses to do so. Thirdly, such taxes would operate less as sumptuary laws.

When the license was once purchased, whether the purchaser drunk much or drunk little, his tax would be the same. Fourthly, if a workman were to pay all at once, by yearly, half-yearly, or quarterly payments, a tax equal to what he at present pays, with little or no inconveniency, upon all the different pots and pints of porter which he drinks in any such period of time, the sum might frequently distress him very much. This mode of taxation, therefore, it seems evident, could never, without the most grievous oppression, produce a revenue nearly equal to what is derived from the present mode without any oppression. In several countries, however, commodities of an immediate or very speedy consumption are taxed in this manner. In Holland, people pay so much a head for a license to drink tea. I have already mentioned a tax upon bread, which, so far as it is consumed in farm houses and country villages, is there levied in the same manner.

The duties of excise are imposed chiefly upon goods of home produce, destined for home consumption. They are imposed only upon a few sorts of goods of the most general use. There can never be any doubt, either concerning the goods which are subject to those duties, or concerning the particular duty which each species of goods is subject to. They fall almost altogether upon what I call luxuries, excepting always the four duties above mentioned, upon salt, soap, leather, candles, and perhaps that upon green glass.

The duties of customs are much more ancient than those of excise. They seem to have been called customs, as denoting customary payments, which had been in use for time immemorial. They appear to have been originally considered as taxes upon the profits of merchants. During the barbarous times of feudal anarchy, merchants, like all the other inhabitants of burghs, were considered as little better than emancipated bondmen, whose persons were despised, and whose gains were envied. The great nobility, who had consented that the king should tallage the profits of their own tenants, were not unwilling that he should tallage likewise those of an order of men whom it was much less their interest to protect. In those ignorant times, it was not understood, that the profits of merchants are a subject not taxable directly; or that the final payment of all such taxes must fall, with a considerable overcharge, upon the consumers.

The gains of alien merchants were looked upon more unfavorably than those of English merchants. It was natural, therefore, that those of the former should be taxed more heavily than those of the latter. This distinction between the duties upon aliens and those upon English merchants, which was begun from ignorance, has been continued front the spirit of monopoly, or in order to give our own merchants an advantage, both in the home and in the foreign market.

With this distinction, the ancient duties of customs were imposed equally upon all sorts of goods, necessaries as well its luxuries, goods exported as well as goods imported. Why should the dealers in one sort of goods, it seems to have been thought, be more favored than those in another? Or why should the merchant exporter be more favored than the merchant importer?

The ancient customs were divided into three branches. The first, and, perhaps, the most ancient of all those duties, was that upon wool and leather. It seems to have been chiefly or altogether an exportation duty. When the woolen manufacture came to be established in England, lest the king should lose any part of his customs upon wool by the exportation of woolen cloths, a like duty was imposed upon them. The other two branches were, first, a duty upon wine, which being imposed at so much a ton, was called a tonnage; and, secondly, a duty upon all other goods, which being imposed at so much a pound of their supposed value, was called a poundage. In the 47th year of Edward III, a duty of sixpence in the pound was imposed upon all goods exported and imported, except wools, wool-felts, leather, and wines which were subject to particular duties. In the 14th of Richard II, this duty was raised to one shilling in the pound; but, three years afterwards, it was again reduced to sixpence. It was raised to eight pence in the 2nd year of Henry IV; and, in the 4th of the same prince, to one shilling. From this time to the 9th year of William III, this duty continued at one shilling in the pound. The duties of tonnage and poundage were generally granted to the king by one and the same act of parliament, and were called the subsidy of tonnage and poundage. The subsidy of poundage having continued for so long a time at one shilling in the pound, or at five percent, a subsidy came, in the language of the customs, to denote a general duty of this kind of five percent. This subsidy, which is now called the old subsidy, still continues to be levied, according to the book of rates established by the 12th of Charles II. The method of ascertaining, by a book of rates, the value of goods subject to this duty, is said to be older than the time of James I. The new subsidy, imposed by the 9th and 10th of William III, was an additional five percent upon the greater part of goods. The one-third and the two-third subsidy made up between them another five percent of which they were proportional parts. The subsidy of 1747 made a fourth five percent upon the greater part of goods; and that of 1759, a fifth upon some particular sorts of goods. Besides those five subsidies, a great variety of other duties have occasionally been imposed upon particular sorts of goods, in order sometimes to relieve the exigencies of the state, and sometimes to regulate the trade of the country, according to the principles of the mercantile system.

That system has come gradually more and more into fashion. The old subsidy was imposed indifferently upon exportation, as well as importation. The four subsequent subsidies, as well as the other duties which have since been occasionally imposed upon particular sorts of goods, have, with a few exceptions, been laid altogether upon importation. The greater part of the ancient duties which had been imposed upon the exportation of the goods of home produce and manufacture, have either been lightened or taken away altogether. In most cases, they have been taken away. Bounties have even been given upon the exportation of some of them. Drawbacks, too, sometimes of the whole, and, in most cases, of a part of the duties which are paid upon the importation of foreign goods, have been granted upon their exportation. Only half the duties imposed by the old subsidy upon importation, are drawn back upon exportation; but the whole of those imposed by the latter subsidies and other imposts are, upon the greater parts of the goods, drawn back in the same manner. This growing favor of exportation, and discouragement of importation, have suffered only a few exceptions, which chiefly concern the materials of some manufactures. These our merchants and manufacturers are willing should come as cheap as possible to themselves, and as dear as possible to their rivals and competitors in other countries. Foreign materials are, upon this account, sometimes allowed to be imported duty-free; Spanish wool, for example, flax, and raw linen yarn. The exportation of the materials of home produce, and of those which are the particular produce of our colonies, has sometimes been prohibited, and sometimes subjected to higher duties. The exportation of English wool has been prohibited. That of beaver skins, of beaver wool, and of gum-senega, has been subjected to higher duties; Great Britain, by the conquests of Canada and Senegal, having got almost the monopoly of those commodities.

That the mercantile system has not been very favorable to the revenue of the great body of the people, to the annual produce of the land and labor of the country, I have endeavored to show in the fourth book of this Inquiry. It seems not to have been more favorable to the revenue of the sovereign; so far, at least, as that revenue depends upon the duties of customs.

In consequence of that system, the importation of several sorts of goods has been prohibited altogether. This prohibition has, in some cases, entirely prevented, and in others has very much diminished, the importation of those commodities, by reducing the importers to the necessity of smuggling. It has entirely prevented the importation of foreign woolens; and it has very much diminished that of foreign silks and velvets, In both cases, it has entirely annihilated the revenue of customs which might have been levied upon such importation.

The high duties which have been imposed upon the importation of many different sorts of foreign goods in order to discourage their consumption in Great Britain, have, in many cases, served only to encourage smuggling, and, in all cases, have reduced the revenues of the customs below what more moderate duties would have afforded. The saying of Dr. Swift, that in the arithmetic of the customs, two and two, instead of making four, make sometimes only one, holds perfectly true with regard to such heavy duties, which never could have been imposed, had not the mercantile system taught us, in many cases, to employ taxation as an instrument, not of revenue, but of monopoly.

The bounties which are sometimes given upon the exportation of home produce and manufactures, and the drawbacks which are paid upon the re-exportation of the greater part of foreign goods, have given occasion to many frauds, and to a species of smuggling, more destructive of the public revenue than any other. In order to obtain the bounty or drawback, the goods, it is well known, are sometimes shipped, and sent to sea, but soon afterwards clandestinely re-landed in some other part of the country. The defalcation of the revenue of customs occasioned by bounties and drawbacks, of which a great part are obtained fraudulently, is very great. The gross produce of the customs, in the year which ended on the 5th of January 1755, amounted to £5,068,000. The bounties which were paid out of this revenue, though in that year there was no bounty upon corn, amounted to £167,806. The drawbacks which were paid upon debentures and certificates, to £2,156,800. Bounties and drawbacks together amounted to £2,324,600. In consequence of these deductions, the revenue of the customs amounted only to £2,743,400; from which deducting £287,900 for the expense of management, in salaries and other incidents, the neat revenue of the customs for that year comes out to be £2,455,500. The expense of management, amounts, in this manner, to between five and six percent upon the gross revenue of the customs; and to something more than ten percent upon what remains of that revenue, after deducting what is paid away in bounties and drawbacks.

Heavy duties being imposed upon almost all goods imported, our merchant importers smuggle as much, and make entry of as little as they can. Our merchant exporters, on the contrary, make entry of more than they export; sometimes out of vanity, and to pass for great dealers in goods which pay no duty gain a bounty back. Our exports, in consequence of these different frauds, appear upon the custom-house books greatly to overbalance our imports, to the unspeakable comfort of those politicians, who measure the national prosperity by what they call the balance of trade.

All goods imported, unless particularly exempted, and such exemptions are not very numerous, are liable to some duties of customs. If any goods are imported, not mentioned in the book of rates, they are taxed at 4s:9%d. for every twenty shillings value, according to the oath of the importer, that is, nearly at five subsidies, or five poundage duties. The book of rates is extremely comprehensive, and enumerates a great variety of articles, many of them little used, and, therefore, not well known. It is, upon this account, frequently uncertain under what article a particular sort of goods ought to be classed, and, consequently what duty they ought to pay. Mistakes with regard to this sometimes ruin the custom-house officer, and frequently occasion much trouble, expense, and vexation to the importer. In point of perspicuity, precision, and distinctness, therefore, the duties of customs are much inferior to those of excise.

In order that the greater part of the members of any society should contribute to the public revenue, in proportion to their respective expense, it does not seem necessary that every single article of that expense should be taxed. The revenue which is levied by the duties of excise is supposed to fall as equally upon the contributors as that which is levied by the duties of customs; and the duties of excise are imposed upon a few articles only of the most general used and consumption. It has been the opinion of many people, that, by proper management, the duties of customs might likewise, without any loss to the public revenue, and with great advantage to foreign trade, be confined to a few articles only.

The foreign articles, of the most general use and consumption in Great Britain, seem at present to consist chiefly in foreign wines and brandies; in some of the productions of America and the West Indies, sugar, rum, tobacco, cocoa-nuts, etc. and in some of those of the East Indies, tea, coffee, china-ware, spiceries of all kinds, several sorts of piece-goods, etc. These different articles afford, the greater part of the perhaps, at present, revenue which is drawn from the duties of customs. The taxes which at present subsist upon foreign manufactures, if you except those upon the few contained in the foregoing enumeration, have, the greater part of them, been imposed for the purpose, not of revenue, but of monopoly, or to give our own merchants an advantage in the home market. By removing all prohibitions, and by subjecting all foreign manufactures to such moderate taxes, as it was found from experience, afforded upon each article the greatest revenue to the public, our own workmen might still have a considerable advantage in the home market; and many articles, some of which at present afford no revenue to government, and others a very inconsiderable one, might afford a very great one.

High taxes, sometimes by diminishing the consumption of the taxed commodities, and sometimes by encouraging smuggling frequently afford a smaller revenue to government than what might be drawn from more moderate taxes.

When the diminution of revenue is the effect of the diminution of consumption, there can be but one remedy, and that is the lowering of the tax.

When the diminution of revenue is the effect of the encouragement given to smuggling, it may, perhaps, be remedied in two ways; either by diminishing the temptation to smuggle, or by increasing the difficulty of smuggling. The temptation to smuggle can be diminished only by the lowering of the tax; and the difficulty of smuggling can be increased only by establishing that system of administration which is most proper for preventing it.

The excise laws, it appears, I believe, from experience, obstruct and embarrass the operations of the smuggler much more effectually than those of the customs. By introducing into the customs a system of administration as similar to that of the excise as the nature of the different duties will admit, the difficulty of smuggling might be very much increased. This alteration, it has been supposed by many people, might very easily be brought about.

The importer of commodities liable to any duties of customs, it has been said, might, at his option, be allowed either to carry them to his own private warehouse; or to lodge them in a warehouse, provided either at his own expense or at that of the public, but under the key of the custom-house officer, and never to be opened but in his presence. If the merchant carried them to his own private warehouse, the duties to be immediately paid, and never afterwards to be drawn back; and that warehouse to be at all times subject to the visit and examination of the custom-house officer, in order to ascertain how far the quantity contained in it corresponded with that for which the duty had been paid. If he carried them to the public warehouse, no duty to be paid till they were taken out for home consumption. If taken out for exportation, to be duty-free; proper security being always given that they should be so exported. The dealers in those particular commodities, either by wholesale or retail, to be at all times subject to the visit and examination of the custom-house officer; and to be obliged to justify, by proper certificates, the payment of the duty upon the whole quantity contained in their shops or warehouses. What are called the excise duties upon rum imported, are at present levied in this manner; and the same system of administration might, perhaps, be extended to all duties upon goods imported; provided always that those duties were, like the duties of excise, confined to a few sorts of goods of the most general use and consumption. If they were extended to almost all sorts of goods, as at present, public warehouses of sufficient extent could not easily be provided; and goods of a very delicate nature, or of which the preservation required much care and attention, could not safely be trusted by the merchant in any warehouse but his own.

If, by such a system of administration, smuggling to any considerable extent could be prevented, even under pretty high duties; and if every duty was occasionally either heightened or lowered according as it was most likely, either the one way or the other, to afford the greatest revenue to the state; taxation being always employed as an instrument of revenue, and never of monopoly; it seems not improbable that a revenue, at least equal to the present neat revenue of the customs, might be drawn from duties upon the importation of only a few sorts of goods of the most general use and consumption; and that the duties of customs might thus be brought to the same degree of simplicity, certainty, and precision, as those of excise. What the revenue at present loses by drawbacks upon the re-exportation of foreign goods, which are afterwards re-landed and consumed at home, would, under this system, be saved altogether. If to this saving, which would alone be very considerable, were added the abolition of all bounties upon the exportation of home produce; in all cases in which those bounties were not in reality drawbacks of some duties of excise which had before been advanced; it cannot well be doubted, but that the neat revenue of customs might, after an alteration of this kind, be fully equal to what it had ever been before.

If, by such a change of system, the public revenue suffered no loss, the trade and manufactures of the country would certainly gain a very considerable advantage. The trade in the commodities not taxed, by far the greatest number would be perfectly free, and might be carried on to and from all parts of the world with every possible advantage. Among those commodities would be comprehended all the necessaries of life, and all the materials of manufacture. So far as the free importation of the necessaries of life reduced their average money price in the home market, it would reduce the money price of labor, but without reducing in any respect its real recompense. The value of money is in proportion to the quantity of the necessaries of life which it will purchase. That of the necessaries of life is altogether independent of the quantity of money which can be had for them. The reduction in the money price of labor would necessarily be attended with a proportional one in that of all home manufactures, which would thereby gain some advantage in all foreign markets. The price of some manufactures would be reduced, in a still greater proportion, by the free importation of the raw materials. If raw silk could be imported from China and Indostan, duty-free, the silk manufacturers in England could greatly undersell those of both France and Italy. There would be no occasion to prohibit the importation of foreign silks and velvets. The cheapness of their goods would secure to our own workmen, not only the possession of a home, but a very great command of the foreign market. Even the trade in the commodities taxed, would be carried on with much more advantage than at present. If those commodities were delivered out of the public warehouse for foreign exportation, being in this case exempted from all taxes, the trade in them would be perfectly free. The carrying trade, in all sorts of goods, would, under this system, enjoy every possible advantage. If these commodities were delivered out for home consumption, the importer not being obliged to advance the tax till he had an opportunity of selling his goods, either to some dealer, or to some consumer, he could always afford to sell them cheaper than if he had been obliged to advance it at the moment of importation. Under the same taxes, the foreign trade of consumption, even in the taxed commodities, might in this manner be carried on with much more advantage than it is at present.

It was the object of the famous excise scheme of Sir Robert Walpole, to establish, with regard to wine and tobacco, a system not very unlike that which is here proposed. But though the bill which was then brought into parliament, comprehended those two commodities only, it was generally supposed to be meant as an introduction to a more extensive scheme of the same kind. Faction, combined with the interest of smuggling merchants, raised so violent, though so unjust a clamor, against that bill, that the minister thought proper to drop it; and, from a dread of exciting a clamor of the same kind, none of his successors have dared to resume the project.

The duties upon foreign luxuries, imported for home consumption, though they sometimes fall upon the poor, fall principally upon people of middling or more than middling fortune. Such are, for example, the duties upon foreign wines, upon coffee, chocolate, tea, sugar, etc.

The duties upon the cheaper luxuries of home produce, destined for home consumption, fall pretty equally upon people of all ranks, in proportion to their respective expense. The poor pay the duties upon malt, hops, beer, and ale, upon their own consumption; the rich, upon both their own consumption and that of their servants.

The whole consumption of the inferior ranks of people, or of those below the middling rank, it must be observed, is, in every country, much greater, not only in quantity, but in value, than that of the middling, and of those above the middling rank. The whole expense of the inferior is much greater titan that of the superior ranks. In the first place, almost the whole capital of every country is annually distributed among the inferior ranks of people, as the wages of productive labor. Secondly, a great part of the revenue, arising from both the rent of land and the profits of stock, is annually distributed among the same rank, in the wages and maintenance of menial servants, and other unproductive laborers. Thirdly, some part of the profits of stock belongs to the same rank, as a revenue arising from the employment of their small capitals. The amount of the profits annually made by small shopkeepers, tradesmen, and retailers of all kinds, is everywhere very considerable, and makes a very considerable portion of the annual produce. Fourthly and lastly, some part even of the rent of land belongs to the same rank; a considerable part to those who are somewhat below the middling rank, and a small part even to the lowest rank; common laborers sometimes possessing in property an acre or two of land. Though the expense of those inferior ranks of people, therefore, taking them individually, is very small, yet the whole mass of it, taking them collectively, amounts always to by much the largest portion of the whole expense of the society; what remains of the annual produce of the land and labor of the country, for the consumption of the superior ranks, being always much less, not only in quantity, but in value. The taxes upon expense, therefore, which fall chiefly upon that of the superior ranks of people, upon the smaller portion of the annual produce, are likely to be much less productive than either those which fall indifferently upon the expense of all ranks, or even those which fall chiefly upon that of the inferior ranks, than either those which fall indifferently upon the whole annual produce, or those which fall chiefly upon the larger portion of it. The excise upon the materials and manufacture of home-made fermented and spirituous liquors, is, accordingly, of all the different taxes upon expense, by far the most productive; and this branch of the excise falls very much, perhaps principally, upon the expense of the common people. In the year which ended on the 5th of July 1775, the gross produce of this branch of the excise amounted to £3,341,837:9:9.

It must always be remembered, however, that it is the luxuries, and not the necessary expense of the inferior ranks of people, that ought ever to be taxed. The final payment of any tax upon their necessary expense, would fall altogether upon the superior ranks of people; upon the smaller portion of the annual produce, and not upon the greater. Such a tax must, in all cases, either raise the wages of labor, or lessen the demand for it. It could not raise the wages of labor, without throwing the final payment of the tax upon the superior ranks of people. It could not lessen the demand for labor, without lessening the annual produce of the land and labor of the country, the fund upon which all taxes must be finally paid. Whatever might be the state to which a tax of this kind reduced the demand for labor, it must always raise wages higher than they otherwise would be in that state; and the final payment of this enhancement of wages must, in all cases, fall upon the superior ranks of people.

Fermented liquors brewed, and spirituous liquors distilled, not for sale, but for private use, are not in Great Britain liable to any duties of excise. This exemption, of which the object is to save private families from the odious visit and examination of the tax-gatherer, occasions the burden of those duties to fall frequently much lighter upon the rich than upon the poor. It is not, indeed, very common to distil for private use, though it is done sometimes. But in the country, many middling and almost all rich and great families, brew their own beer. Their strong beer, therefore, costs them eight shillings a barrel less than it costs the common brewer, who must have his profit upon the tax, as well as upon all the other expense which he advances. Such families, therefore, must drink their beer at least nine or ten shillings a barrel cheaper than any liquor of the same quality can be drank by the common people, to whom it is everywhere more convenient to buy their beer, by little and little, from the brewery or the ale-house. Malt, in the same manner, that is made for the use of a private family, is not liable to the visit or examination of the tax-gatherer but, in this case the family must compound at seven shillings and sixpence a head for the tax. Seven shillings and sixpence are equal to the excise upon ten bushels of malt; a quantity fully equal to what all the different members of any sober family, men, women, and children, are, at an average, likely to consume. But in rich and great families, where country hospitality is much practiced, the malt liquors consumed by the members of the family make but a small part of the consumption of the house. Either on account of this composition, however, or for other reasons, it is not near so common to malt as to brew for private use. It is difficult to imagine any equitable reason, why those who either brew or distil for private use should not be subject to a composition of the same kind.

A greater revenue than what is at present drawn from all the heavy taxes upon malt, beer, and ale, might be raised, it has frequently been said, by a much lighter tax upon malt; the opportunities of defrauding the revenue being much greater in a brewery than in a malt-house; and those who brew for private use being exempted from all duties or composition for duties, which is not the case with those who malt for private use.

In the porter brewery of London, a quarter of malt is commonly brewed into more than two barrels and a-half, sometimes into three barrels of porter. The different taxes upon malt amount to six shillings a quarter; those upon strong ale and beer to eight shillings a barrel. In the porter brewery, therefore, the different taxes upon malt, beer, and ale, amount to between twenty-six and thirty shillings upon the produce of a quarter of malt. In the country brewery for common country sale, a quarter of malt is seldom brewed into less than two barrels of strong, and one barrel of small beer; frequently into two barrels and a-half of strong beer. The different taxes upon small beer amount to one shilling and four pence a barrel. In the country brewery, therefore, the different taxes upon malt, beer, and ale, seldom amount to less than twenty-three shillings and four pence, frequently to twenty-six shillings, upon the produce of a quarter of malt. Taking the whole kingdom at an average, therefore, the whole amount of the duties upon malt, beer, and ale, cannot be estimated at less than twenty-four or twenty-five shillings upon the produce of a quarter of malt. But by taking off all the different duties upon beer and ale, and by trebling the malt tax, or by raising it from six to eighteen shillings upon the quarter of malt, a greater revenue, it is said, might be raised by this single tax, than what is at present drawn from all those heavier taxes.

	£.	s.	d.
In 1772, the old malt tax produced	722,023	11	11
The additional	356,776	7	9¾
In 1775, the old tax produced	561,627	3	7¾
The additional	278,650	15	3¾
In 1774, the old tax produced	624,614	17	5¾
The additional	310,745	2	8½
In 1775, the old tax produced	657,357	0	8¼
The additional	323,785	12	6¼
4)	3,835,580	12	¾
Average of these four years	958,895	3	0
In 1772, the country excise produced	1,243,120	5	3
The London brewery	408,260	7	2¾
In 1773, the country excise	1,245,808	3	3
The London brewery	405,406	17	10½
In 1774, the country excise	1,246,373	14	5½
The London brewery	320,601	18	¼
In 1775, the country excise	1,214,583	6	1¼
The London brewery	463,670	7	¼
4)	6,547,832	19	2¼
Average of these four years	1,636,958	4	9½
To which adding the average malt tax	958,895	3	¼

The whole amount of those different taxes comes out to be	2,595,835	7	10
But, by trebling the malt tax, or by raising it from six to eighteen shillings upon the quarter of malt, that single tax would produce	2,876,685	9	0
A sum which exceeds the foregoing by	280,832	1	3

Under the old malt tax, indeed, is comprehended a tax of four shillings upon the hogshead of cider, and another of ten shillings upon the barrel of mum. In 1774, the tax upon cider produced only £3,083:6:8. It probably fell somewhat short of its usual amount; all the different taxes upon cider, having, that year, produced less than ordinary. The tax upon mum, though much heavier, is still less productive, on account of the smaller consumption of that liquor. But to balance whatever may be the ordinary amount of those two taxes, there is comprehended under what is called the country excise, first, the old excise of six shillings and eight pence upon the hogshead of cider; secondly, a like tax of six shillings and eight pence upon the hogshead of verjuice; thirdly, another of eight shillings and nine pence upon the hogshead of vinegar; and, lastly, a fourth tax of eleven pence upon the gallon of mead or metheglin. The produce of those different taxes will probably much more than counterbalance that of the duties imposed, by what is called the annual malt tax, upon cider and mum.

Malt is consumed, not only in the brewery of beer and ale, but in the manufacture of low wines and spirits. If the malt tax were to be raised to eighteen shillings upon the quarter, it might be necessary to make some abatement in the different excises which are imposed upon those particular sorts of low wines and spirits, of which malt makes any part of the materials. In what are called malt spirits, it makes commonly but a third part of the materials; the other two-thirds being either raw barley, or one-third barley and one-third wheat. In the distillery of malt spirits, both the opportunity and the temptation to smuggle are much greater than either in a brewery or in a malt-house; the opportunity, on account of the smaller bulk and greater value of the commodity, and the temptation, on account of the superior height of the duties, which amounted to 3s. 10 ⅔d. upon the gallon of spirits. {Though the duties directly imposed upon proof spirits amount only to 2s. 6d, per gallon, these, added to the duties upon the low wines, from which they are distilled, amount to 3s 10⅔d. Both low wines and proof spirits are, to prevent frauds, now rated according to what they gauge in the wash.}

By increasing the duties upon malt, and reducing those upon the distillery, both the opportunities and the temptation to smuggle would be diminished, which might occasion a still further augmentation of revenue.

It has for some time past been the policy of Great Britain to discourage the consumption of spirituous liquors, on account of their supposed tendency to ruin the health and to corrupt the morals of the common people. According to this policy, the abatement of the taxes upon the distillery ought not to be so great as to reduce, in any respect, the price of those liquors. Spirituous liquors might remain as dear as ever; while, at the same time, the wholesome and invigorating liquors of beer and ale might be considerably reduced in their price. The people might thus be in part relieved from one of the burdens of which they at present complain the most; while, at the same time, the revenue might be considerably augmented.

The objections of Dr. Davenant to this alteration in the present system of excise duties, seem to be without foundation. Those objections are, that the tax, instead of dividing itself, as at present, pretty equally upon the profit of the maltster, upon that of the brewer and upon that of the retailer, would so far as it affected profit, fall altogether upon that of the maltster; that the maltster could not so easily get back the amount of the tax in the advanced price of his malt, as the brewer and retailer in the advanced price of their liquor; and that so heavy a tax upon malt might reduce the rent and profit of barley land.

No tax can ever reduce, for any considerable time, the rate of profit in any particular trade, which must always keep its level with other trades in the neighborhood. The present duties upon malt, beer, and ale, do not affect the profits of the dealers in those commodities, who all get back the tax with an additional profit, in the enhanced price of their goods. A tax, indeed, may render the goods upon which it is imposed so dear, as to diminish the consumption of them. But the consumption of malt is in malt liquors; and a tax of eighteen shillings upon the quarter of malt could not well render those liquors dearer than the different taxes, amounting to twenty-four or twenty-five shillings, do at present. Those liquors, on the contrary, would probably become cheaper, and the consumption of them would be more likely to increase than to diminish.

It is not very easy to understand why it should be more difficult for the maltster to get back eighteen shillings in the advanced price of his malt, than it is at present for the brewer to get back twenty-four or twenty-five, sometimes thirty shillings, in that of his liquor. The maltster, indeed, instead of a tax of six shillings, would be obliged to advance one of eighteen shilling upon every quarter of malt. But the brewer is at present obliged to advance a tax of twenty-four or twenty-five, sometimes thirty shillings, upon every quarter of malt which he brews. It could not be more inconvenient for the maltster to advance a lighter tax, than it is at present for the brewer to advance a heavier one. The maltster does not always keep in his granaries a stock of malt, which it will require a longer time to dispose of than the stock of beer and ale which the brewer frequently keeps in his cellars. The former, therefore, may frequently get the returns of his money as soon as the latter. But whatever inconveniency might arise to the maltster from being obliged to advance a heavier tax, it could easily be remedied, by granting him a few months longer credit than is at present commonly given to the brewer.

Nothing could reduce the rent and profit of barley land, which did not reduce the demand for barley. But a change of system, which reduced the duties upon a quarter of malt brewed into beer and ale, from twenty-four and twenty-five shillings to eighteen shillings, would be more likely to increase than diminish that demand. The rent and profit of barley land, besides, must always be nearly equal to those of other equally fertile and equally well cultivated land. If they were less, some part of the barley land would soon be turned to some other purpose; and if they were greater, more land would soon be turned to the raising of barley. When the ordinary price of any particular produce of land is at what may be called a monopoly price, a tax upon it necessarily reduces the rent and profit of the land which grows it. A tax upon the produce of those precious vineyards, of which the wine falls so much short of the effectual demand, that its price is always above the natural proportion to that of the produce of other equally fertile and equally well cultivated land, would necessarily reduce the rent and profit of those vineyards. The price of the wines being already the highest that could be got for the quantity commonly sent to market, it could not be raised higher without diminishing that quantity; and the quantity could not be diminished without still greater loss, because the lands could not be turned to any other equally valuable produce. The whole weight of the tax, therefore, would fall upon the rent and profit; properly upon the rent of the vineyard. When it has been proposed to lay any new tax upon sugar, our sugar planters have frequently complained that the whole weight of such taxes fell not upon the consumer, but upon the producer; they never having been able to raise the price of their sugar after the tax higher than it was before. The price had, it seems, before the tax, been a monopoly price; and the arguments adduced to show that sugar was an improper subject of taxation, demonstrated perhaps that it was a proper one; the gains of monopolists, whenever they can be come at, being certainly of all subjects the most proper. But the ordinary price of barley has never been a monopoly price; and the rent and profit of barley land have never been above their natural proportion to those of other equally fertile and equally well cultivated land. The different taxes which have been imposed upon malt, beer, and ale, have never lowered the price of barley; have never reduced the rent and profit of barley land. The price of malt to the brewer has constantly risen in proportion to the taxes imposed upon it; and those taxes, together with the different duties upon beer and ale, have constantly either raised the price, or, what comes to the same thing, reduced the quality of those commodities to the consumer. The final payment of those taxes has fallen constantly upon the consumer, and not upon the producer.

The only people likely to suffer by the change of system here proposed, are those who brew for their own private use. But the exemption, which this superior rank of people at present enjoy, from very heavy taxes which are paid by the poor laborer and artificer, is surely most unjust and unequal, and ought to be taken away, even though this change was never to take place. It has probably been the interest of this superior order of people, however, which has hitherto prevented a change of system that could not well fail both to increase the revenue and to relieve the people.

Besides such duties as those of custom and excise above mentioned, there are several others which affect the price of goods more unequally and more indirectly. Of this kind are the duties, which, in French, are called peages, which in old Saxon times were called the duties of passage, and which seem to have been originally established for the same purpose as our turnpike tolls, or the tolls upon our canals and navigable rivers, for the maintenance of the road or of the navigation. Those duties, when applied to such purposes, are most properly imposed according to the bulk or weight of the goods. As they were originally local and provincial duties, applicable to local and provincial purposes, the administration of them was, in most cases, entrusted to the particular town, parish, or lordship, in which they were levied; such communities being, in some way or other, supposed to be accountable for the application. The sovereign, who is altogether unaccountable, has in many countries assumed to himself the administration of those duties; and though he has in most cases enhanced very much the duty, he has in many entirely neglected the application. If the turnpike tolls of Great Britain should ever become one of the resources of government, we may learn, by the example of many other nations, what would probably be the consequence. Such tolls, no doubt, are finally paid by the consumer; but the consumer is not taxed in proportion to his expense, when he pays, not according to the value, but according to the bulk or weight of what he consumes. When such duties are imposed, not according to the bulk or weight, but according to the supposed value of the goods, they become properly a sort of inland customs or excise, which obstruct very much the most important of all branches of commerce, the interior commerce of the country.

In some small states, duties similar to those passage duties are imposed upon goods carried across the territory, either by land or by water, from one foreign country to another. These are in some countries called transit-duties. Some of the little Italian states which are situated upon the Po, and the rivers which run into it, derive some revenue from duties of this kind, which are paid altogether by foreigners, and which, perhaps, are the only duties that one state can impose upon the subjects of another, without obstruction in any respect, the industry or commerce of its own. The most important transit-duty in the world, is that levied by the king of Denmark upon all merchant ships which pass through the Sound.

Such taxes upon luxuries, as the greater part of the duties of customs and excise, though they all fall indifferently upon every different species of revenue, and are paid finally, or without any retribution, by whoever consumes the commodities upon which they are imposed; yet they do not always fall equally or proportionally upon the revenue of every individual. As every man's humor regulates the degree of his consumption, every man contributes rather according to his humor, than proportion to his revenue: the profuse contribute more, the parsimonious less, than their proper proportion. During the minority of a man of great fortune, he contributes commonly very little, by his consumption, towards the support of that state from whose protection he derives a great revenue. Those who live in another country, contribute nothing by their consumption towards the support of the government of that country, in which is situated the source of their revenue. If in this latter country there should be no land tax, nor any considerable duty upon the transference either of moveable or immoveable property, as is the case in Ireland, such absentees may derive a great revenue from the protection of a government, to the support of which they do not contribute a single shilling. This inequality is likely to be greatest in a country of which the government is, in some respects, subordinate and dependant upon that of some other. The people who possess the most extensive property in the dependant, will, in this case, generally choose to live in the governing country. Ireland is precisely in this situation; and we cannot therefore wonder, that the proposal of a tax upon absentees should be so very popular in that country. It might, perhaps, be a little difficult to ascertain either what sort, or what degree of absence, would subject a man to be taxed as an absentee, or at what precise time the tax should either begin or end. If you except, however, this very peculiar situation, any inequality in the contribution of individuals which can arise from such taxes, is much more than compensated by the very circumstance which occasions that inequality; the circumstance that every man's contribution is altogether voluntary; it being altogether in his power, either to consume, or not to consume, the commodity taxed. Where such taxes, therefore, are properly assessed, and upon proper commodities, they are paid with less grumbling than any other. When they are advanced by the merchant or manufacturer, the consumer, who finally pays them, soon comes to confound them with the price of the commodities, and almost forgets that he pays any tax.

Such taxes are, or may be, perfectly certain; or may be assessed, so as to leave no doubt concerning either what ought to be paid, or when it ought to be paid; concerning either the quantity or the time of payment. What ever uncertainty there may sometimes be, either in the duties of customs in Great Britain, or in other duties of the same kind in other countries, it cannot arise from the nature of those duties, but from the inaccurate or unskillful manner in which the law that imposes them is expressed.

Taxes upon luxuries generally are, and always may be, paid piece-meal, or in proportion as the contributors have occasion to purchase the goods upon which they are imposed. In the time and mode of payment, they are, or may be, of all taxes the most convenient. Upon the whole, such taxes, therefore, are perhaps as agreeable to the three first of the four general maxims concerning taxation, as any other. They offend in every respect against the fourth.

Such taxes, in proportion to what they bring into the public treasury of the state, always take out, or keep out, of the pockets of the people, more than almost any other taxes. They seem to do this in all the four different ways in which it is possible to do it.

First, the levying of such taxes, even when imposed in the most judicious manner, requires a great number of custom-house and excise officers, whose salaries and perquisites are a real tax upon the people, which brings nothing into the treasury of the state. This expense, however, it must be acknowledged, is more moderate in Great Britain than in most other countries. In the year which ended on the 5th of July, 1775, the gross produce of the different duties, under the management of the commissioners of excise in England, amounted to £5,507,308:18:8¼, which was levied at an expense of little more than five and a-half percent. From this gross produce, however, there must be deducted what was paid away in bounties and drawbacks upon the exportation of exciseable goods, which will reduce the neat produce below five millions. {The neat produce of that year, after deducting all expenses and allowances, amounted to £4,975,652:19:6.} The levying of the salt duty, and excise duty, but under a different management, is much more expensive. The neat revenue of the customs does not amount to two millions and a-half, which is levied at an expense of more than ten percent, in the salaries of officers and other incidents. But the perquisites of custom-house officers are everywhere much greater than their salaries; at some ports more than double or triple those salaries. If the salaries of officers, and other incidents, therefore, amount to more than ten percent upon the neat revenue of the customs, the whole expense of levying that revenue may amount, in salaries and perquisites together, to more than twenty or thirty percent. The officers of excise receive few or no perquisites; and the administration of that branch of the revenue being of more recent establishment, is in general less corrupted than that of the customs, into which length of time has introduced and authorized many abuses. By charging upon malt the whole revenue which is at present levied by the different duties upon malt and malt liquors, a saving, it is supposed, of more than £50,000, might be made in the annual expense of the excise. By confining the duties of customs to a few sorts of goods, and by levying those duties according to the excise laws, a much greater saving might probably be made in the annual expense of the customs.

Secondly, such taxes necessarily occasion some obstruction or discouragement to certain branches of industry. As they always raise the price of the commodity taxed, they so far discourage its consumption, and consequently its production. If it is a commodity of home growth or manufacture, less labor comes to be employed in raising and producing it. If it is a foreign commodity of which the tax increases in this manner the price, the commodities of the same kind which are made at home may thereby, indeed, gain some advantage in the home market, and a greater quantity of domestic industry may thereby be turned toward preparing them. But though this rise of price in a foreign commodity, may encourage domestic industry in one particular branch, it necessarily discourages that industry in almost every other. The dearer the Birmingham manufacturer buys his foreign wine, the cheaper he necessarily sells that part of his hardware with which, or, what comes to the same thing, with the price of which, he buys it. That part of his hardware, therefore, becomes of less value to him, and he has less encouragement to work at it. The dearer the consumers in one country pay for the surplus produce of another, the cheaper they necessarily sell that part of their own surplus produce with which, or, what comes to the same thing, with the price of which, they buy it. That part of their own surplus produce becomes of less value to them, and they have less encouragement to increase its quantity. All taxes upon consumable commodities, therefore, tend to reduce the quantity of productive labor below what it otherwise would be, either in preparing the commodities taxed, if they are home commodities, or in preparing those with which they are purchased, if they are foreign commodities. Such taxes, too, always alter, more or less, the natural direction of national industry, and turn it into a channel always different from, and generally less advantageous, than that in which it would have run of its own accord.

Thirdly, the hope of evading such taxes by smuggling, gives frequent occasion to forfeitures and other penalties, which entirely ruin the smuggler; a person who, though no doubt highly blamable for violating the laws of his country, is frequently incapable of violating those of natural justice, and would have been, in every respect, an excellent citizen, had not the laws of his country made that a crime which nature never meant to be so. In those corrupted governments, where there is at least a general suspicion of much unnecessary expense, and great misapplication of the public revenue, the laws which guard it are little respected. Not many people are scrupulous about smuggling, when, without perjury, they can find an easy and safe opportunity of doing so. To pretend to have any scruple about buying smuggled goods, though a manifest encouragement to the violation of the revenue laws, and to the perjury which almost always attends it, would, in most countries, be regarded as one of those pedantic pieces of hypocrisy which, instead of gaining credit with anybody, serve only to expose the person who affects to practice them to the suspicion of being a greater knave than most of his neighbors. By this indulgence of the public, the smuggler is often encouraged to continue a trade, which he is thus taught to consider as in some measure innocent; and when the severity of the revenue laws is ready to fall upon him, he is frequently disposed to defend with violence, what he has been accustomed to regard as his just property. From being at first, perhaps, rather imprudent than criminal, he at last too often becomes one of the hardiest and most determined violators of the laws of society. By the ruin of the smuggler, his capital, which had before been employed in maintaining productive labor, is absorbed either in the revenue of the state, or in that of the revenue officer; and is employed in maintaining unproductive, to the diminution of the general capital of the society, and of the useful industry which it might otherwise have maintained.

Fourthly, such taxes, by subjecting at least the dealers in the taxed commodities, to the frequent visits and odious examination of the tax-gatherers, expose them sometimes, no doubt, to some degree of oppression, and always to much trouble and vexation; and though vexation, as has already been said, is not strictly speaking expense, it is certainly equivalent to the expense at which every man would be willing to redeem himself from it. The laws of excise, though more effectual for the purpose for which they were instituted, are, in this respect, more vexatious than those of the customs. When a merchant has imported goods subject to certain duties of customs; when he has paid those duties, and lodged the goods in his warehouse; he is not, in most cases, liable to any further trouble or vexation from the custom-house officer. It is otherwise with goods subject to duties of excise. The dealers have no respite from the continual visits and examination of the excise officers. The duties of excise are, upon this account, more unpopular than those of the customs; and so are the officers who levy them. Those officers, it is pretended, though in general, perhaps, they do their duty fully as well as those of the customs; yet, as that duty obliges them to be frequently very troublesome to some of their neighbors, commonly contract a certain hardness of character, which the others frequently have not. This observation, however, may very probably be the mere suggestion of fraudulent dealers, whose smuggling is either prevented or detected by their diligence.

The inconveniencies, however, which are, perhaps, in some degree inseparable from taxes upon consumable communities, fall as light upon the people of Great Britain as upon those of any other country of which the government is nearly as expensive. Our state is not perfect, and might be mended; but it is as good, or better, than that of most of our neighbors.

In consequence of the notion, that duties upon consumable goods were taxes upon the profits of merchants, those duties have, in some countries, been repeated upon every successive sale of the goods. If the profits of the merchant-importer or merchant-manufacturer were taxed, equality seemed to require that those of all the middle buyers, who intervened between either of them and the consumer, should likewise be taxed. The famous alcavala of Spain seems to have been established upon this principle. It was at first a tax of ten percent afterwards of fourteen percent and it is at present only six percent upon the sale of every sort of property whether moveable or immoveable; and it is repeated every time the property is sold. {*Memoires Concernant les Droits*, etc. tom. i, p. 15.} The levying of this tax requires a multitude of revenue officers, sufficient to guard the transportation of goods, not only from one province to another, but from one shop to another. It subjects, not only the dealers in some sorts of goods, but those in all sorts, every farmer, every manufacturer, every merchant and shopkeeper, to the continual visit and examination of the tax-gatherers. Through the greater part of the country in which a tax of this kind is established, nothing can be produced for distant sale. The produce of every part of the country must be proportioned to the consumption of the neighborhood. It is to the alcavala, accordingly, that Ustaritz imputes the ruin of the manufactures of Spain. He might have imputed to it, likewise, the declension of agriculture, it being imposed not only upon manufactures, but upon the rude produce of the land.

In the kingdom of Naples, there is a similar tax of three percent upon the value of all contracts, and consequently upon that of all contracts of sale. It is both lighter than the Spanish tax, and the greater part of towns and parishes are allowed to pay a composition in lieu of it. They levy this composition in what manner they please, generally in a way that gives no interruption to the interior commerce of the place. The Neapolitan tax, therefore, is not near so ruinous as the Spanish one.

The uniform system of taxation, which, with a few exception of no great consequence, takes place in all the different parts of the united kingdom of Great Britain, leaves the interior commerce of the country, the inland and coasting trade, almost entirely free. The inland trade is almost perfectly free; and the greater part of goods may be carried from one end of the kingdom to the other, without requiring any permit or let-pass, without being subject to question, visit or examination, from the revenue officers. There are a few exceptions, but they are such as can give no interruption to any important branch of inland commerce of the country. Goods carried coastwise, indeed, require certificates or coast-cockets. If you except coals, however, the rest are almost all duty-free. This freedom of interior commerce, the effect of the uniformity of the system of taxation, is perhaps one of the principal causes of the prosperity of Great Britain; every great country being necessarily the best and most extensive market for the greater part of the productions of its own industry. If the same freedom in consequence of the same uniformity, could be extended to Ireland and the plantations, both the grandeur of the state, and the prosperity of every part of the empire, would probably be still greater than at present.

In France, the different revenue laws which take place in the different provinces, require a multitude of revenue officers to surround, not only the frontiers of the kingdom, but those of almost each particular province, in order either to prevent the importation of certain goods, or to subject it to the payment of certain duties, to the no small interruption of the interior commerce of the country. Some provinces are allowed to compound for the gabelle, or salt tax; others are exempted from it altogether. Some provinces are exempted from the exclusive sale of tobacco, which the farmers-general enjoy through the greater part of the kingdom. The aides, which correspond to the excise in England, are very different in different provinces. Some provinces are exempted from them, and pay a composition or equivalent. In those in which they take place, and are in farm, there are many local duties which do not extend beyond a particular town or district. The traites, which correspond to our customs, divide the kingdom into three great parts; first, the provinces subject to the tariff of 1664, which are called the provinces of the five great farms, and under which are comprehended Picardy, Normandy, and the greater part of the interior provinces of the kingdom; secondly, the provinces subject to the tariff of 1667, which are called the provinces reckoned foreign, and under which are comprehended the greater part of the frontier provinces; and, thirdly, those provinces which are said to be treated as foreign, or which, because they are allowed a free commerce with foreign countries, are, in their commerce with the other provinces of France, subjected to the same duties as other foreign countries. These are Alsace, the three bishoprics of Mentz, Toul, and Verdun, and the three cities of Dunkirk, Bayonne, and Marseilles. Both in the provinces of the five great farms (called so on account of an ancient division of the duties of customs into five great branches, each of which was originally the subject of a particular farm, though they are now all united into one), and in those which are said to be reckoned foreign, there are many local duties which do not extend beyond a particular town or district. There are some such even in the provinces which are said to be treated as foreign, particularly in the city of Marseilles. It is unnecessary to observe how much both the restraints upon the interior commerce of the country, and the number of the revenue officers, must be multiplied, in order to guard the frontiers of those different provinces and districts which are subject to such different systems of taxation.

Over and above the general restraints arising from this complicated system of revenue laws, the commerce of wine (after corn, perhaps, the most important production of France) is, in the greater part of the provinces, subject to particular restraints arising from the favor which has been shown to the vineyards of particular provinces and districts above those of others. The provinces most famous for their wines, it will be found, I believe, are those in which the trade in that article is subject to the fewest restraints of this kind. The extensive market which such provinces enjoy, encourages good management both in the cultivation of their vineyards, and in the subsequent preparation of their wines.

Such various and complicated revenue laws are not peculiar to France. The little duchy of Milan is divided into six provinces, in each of which there is a different system of taxation, with regard to several different sorts of consumable goods. The still smaller territories of the duke of Parma are divided into three or four, each of which has, in the same manner, a system of its own. Under such absurd management, nothing but the great fertility of the soil, and happiness of the climate, could preserve such countries from soon relapsing into the lowest state of poverty and barbarism.

Taxes upon consumable commodities may either he levied by an administration, of which the officers are appointed by government, and are immediately accountable to government, of which the revenue must, in this case, vary from year to year, according to the occasional variations in the produce of the tax; or they may be let in farm for a rent certain, the farmer being allowed to appoint his own officers, who, though obliged to levy the tax in the manner directed by the law, are under his immediate inspection, and are immediately accountable to him. The best and most frugal way of levying a tax can never be by farm. Over and above what is necessary for paying the stipulated rent, the salaries of the officers, and the whole expense of administration, the farmer must always draw from the produce of the tax a certain profit, proportioned at least to the advance which he makes, to the risk which he runs, to the trouble which he is at, and to the knowledge and skill which it requires to manage so very complicated a concern. Government, by establishing an administration under their own immediate inspection, of the same kind with that which the farmer establishes, might at least save this profit, which is almost always exorbitant. To farm any considerable branch of the public revenue requires either a great capital, or a great credit; circumstances which would alone restrain the competition for such an undertaking to a very small number of people. Of the few who have this capital or credit, a still smaller number have the necessary knowledge or experience; another circumstance which restrains the competition still further. The very few who are in condition to become competitors, find it more for their interest to combine together; to become copartners, instead of competitors; and, when the farm is set up to auction, to offer no rent but what is much below the real value. In countries where the public revenues are in farm, the farmers are generally the most opulent people. Their wealth would alone excite the public indignation; and the vanity which almost always accompanies such upstart fortunes, the foolish ostentation with which they commonly display that wealth, excite that indignation still more.

The farmers of the public revenue never find the laws too severe, which punish any attempt to evade the payment of a tax. They have no bowels for the contributors, who are not their subjects, and whose universal bankruptcy, if it should happen the day after the farm is expired, would not much affect their interest. In the greatest exigencies of the state, when the anxiety of the sovereign for the exact payment of his revenue is necessarily the greatest, they seldom fail to complain, that without laws more rigorous than those which actually took place, it will be impossible for them to pay even the usual rent. In those moments of public distress, their commands cannot be disputed. The revenue laws, therefore, become gradually more and more severe. The most sanguinary are always to be found in countries where the greater part of the public revenue is in farm; the mildest, in countries where it is levied under the immediate inspection of the sovereign. Even a bad sovereign feels more compassion for his people than can ever be expected from the farmers of his revenue. He knows that the permanent grandeur of his family depends upon the prosperity of his people, and he will never knowingly ruin that prosperity for the sake of any momentary interest of his own. It is otherwise with the farmers of his revenue, whose grandeur may frequently be the effect of the ruin, and not of the prosperity, of his people.

A tax is sometimes not only farmed for a certain rent, but the farmer has, besides, the monopoly of the commodity taxed. In France, the duties upon tobacco and salt are levied in this manner. In such cases, the farmer, instead of one, levies two exorbitant profits upon the people; the profit of the farmer, and the still more exorbitant one of the monopolist. Tobacco being a luxury, every man is allowed to buy or not to buy as he chooses; but salt being a necessary, every man is obliged to buy of the farmer a certain quantity of it; because, if he did not buy this quantity of the farmer, he would, it is presumed, buy it of some smuggler. The taxes upon both commodities are exorbitant. The temptation to smuggle, consequently, is to many people irresistible; while, at the same time, the rigor of the law, and the vigilance of the farmer's officers, render the yielding to the temptation almost certainly ruinous. The smuggling of salt and tobacco sends every year several hundred people to the galleys, besides a very considerable number whom it sends to the gibbet. Those taxes, levied in this manner, yield a very considerable revenue to government. In 1767, the farm of tobacco was let for twenty-two millions five hundred and forty-one thousand two hundred and seventy-eight livres a year; that of salt for thirty-six millions four hundred and ninety-two thousand four hundred and four livres. The farm, in both cases, was to commence in 1768, and to last for six years. Those who consider the blood of the people as nothing, in comparison with the revenue of the prince, may, perhaps, approve of this method of levying taxes. Similar taxes and monopolies of salt and tobacco have been established in many other countries, particularly in the Austrian and Prussian dominions, and in the greater part of the states of Italy.

In France, the greater part of the actual revenue of the crown is derived from eight different sources; the taille, the capitation, the two vingtiemes, the gabelles, the aides, the traites, the domaine, and the farm of tobacco. The live last are, in the greater part of the provinces, under farm. The three first are everywhere levied by an administration, under the immediate inspection and direction of government; and it is universally acknowledged, that in proportion to what they take out of the pockets of the people, they bring more into the treasury of the prince than the other five, of which the administration is much more wasteful and expensive.

The finances of France seem, in their present state, to admit of three very obvious reformations. First, by abolishing the taille and the capitation, and by increasing the number of the vingtiemes, so as to produce an additional revenue equal to the amount of those other taxes, the revenue of the crown might be preserved; the expense of collection might be much diminished; the vexation of the inferior ranks of people, which the taille and capitation occasion, might be entirely prevented; and the superior ranks might not be more burdened than the greater part of them are at present. The vingtieme, I have already observed, is a tax very nearly of the same kind with what is called the land tax of England. The burden of the taille, it is acknowledged, falls finally upon the proprietors of land; and as the greater part of the capitation is assessed upon those who are subject to the taille, at so much a pound of that other tax, the final payment of the greater part of it must likewise fall upon the same order of people. Though the number of the vingtiemes, therefore, was increased, so as to produce an additional revenue equal to the amount of both those taxes, the superior ranks of people might not be more burdened than they are at present; many individuals, no doubt, would, on account of the great inequalities with which the taille is commonly assessed upon the estates and tenants of different individuals. The interest and opposition of such favored subjects, are the obstacles most likely to prevent this, or any other reformation of the same kind. Secondly, by rendering the gabelle, the aides, the traites, the taxes upon tobacco, all the different customs and excises, uniform in all the different parts of the kingdom, those taxes might be levied at much less expense, and the interior commerce of the kingdom might be rendered as free as that England. Thirdly, and lastly, by subjecting all those taxes to an administration under the immediate inspection and direction or government, the exorbitant profits of the farmers-general might be added to the revenue of the state. The opposition arising from the private interest of individuals, is likely to be as effectual for preventing the two last as the first-mentioned scheme of reformation.

The French system of taxation seems, in every respect, inferior to the British. In Great Britain, ten millions sterling are annually levied upon less than eight millions of people, without its being possible to say that any particular order is oppressed. From the Collections of the Abbé Expilly, and the observations of the author of the Essay upon the Legislation and Commerce of Corn, it appears probable that France, including the provinces of Lorraine and Bar, contains about twenty-three or twenty-four millions of people; three times the number, perhaps, contained in Great Britain. The soil and climate of France are better than those of Great Britain. The country has been much longer in a state of improvement and cultivation, and is, upon that account, better stocked with all those things which it requires a long time to raise up and accumulate; such as great towns, and convenient and well-built houses, both in town and country. With these advantages, it might be expected, that in France a revenue of thirty millions might be levied for the support of the state, with as little inconvenience as a revenue of ten millions is in Great Britain. In 1765 and 1766, the whole revenue paid into the treasury of France, according to the best, though, I acknowledge, very imperfect accounts which I could get of it, usually run between 308 and 325 millions of livres; that is, it did not amount to fifteen millions sterling; not the half of what might have been expected, had the people contributed in the same proportion to their numbers as the people of Great Britain. The people of France, however, it is generally acknowledged, are much more oppressed by taxes than the people of Great Britain. France, however, is certainly the great empire in Europe, which, after that of Great Britain, enjoys the mildest and most indulgent government.

In Holland, the heavy taxes upon the necessaries of life have ruined, it is said, their principal manufacturers, and are likely to discourage, gradually, even their fisheries and their trade in ship-building. The taxes upon the necessaries of life are inconsiderable in Great Britain, and no manufacture has hitherto been ruined by them. The British taxes which bear hardest on manufactures, are some duties upon the importation of raw materials, particularly upon that of raw silk. The revenue of the States-General and of the different cities, however, is said to amount to more than five millions two hundred and fifty thousand pounds sterling; and as the inhabitants of the United Provinces cannot well be supposed to amount to more than a third part of those of Great Britain, they must, in proportion to their number, be much more heavily taxed.

After all the proper subjects of taxation have been exhausted, if the exigencies of the state still continue to require new taxes, they must be imposed upon improper ones. The taxes upon the necessaries of life, therefore, may be no impeachment of the wisdom of that republic, which, in order to acquire and to maintain its independency, has, in spite of its meat frugality, been involved in such expensive wars as have obliged it to contract great debts. The singular countries of Holland and Zealand, besides, require a considerable expense even to preserve their existence, or to prevent their being swallowed up by the sea, which must have contributed to increase considerably the load of taxes in those two provinces. The republican form of government seems to be the principal support of the present grandeur of Holland. The owners of great capitals, the great mercantile families, have generally either some direct share, or some indirect influence, in the administration of that government. For the sake of the respect and authority which they derive from this situation, they are willing to live in a country where their capital, if they employ it themselves, will bring them less profit, and if they lend it to another, less interest; and where the very moderate revenue which they can draw from it will purchase less of the necessaries and conveniences of life than in any other part of Europe. The residence of such wealthy people necessarily keeps alive, in spite of all disadvantages, a certain degree of industry in the country. Any public calamity which should destroy the republican form of government, which should throw the whole administration into the hands of nobles and of soldiers, which should annihilate altogether the importance of those wealthy merchants, would soon render it disagreeable to them to live in a country where they were no longer likely to be much respected. They would remove both their residence and their capital to some other country, and the industry and commerce of Holland would soon follow the capitals which supported them.

CHAPTER III

Of Public Debts

In that rude state of society which precedes the extension of commerce and the improvement of manufactures; when those expensive luxuries, which commerce and manufactures can alone introduce, are altogether unknown; the person who possesses a large revenue, I have endeavored to show in the third book of this Inquiry, can spend or enjoy that revenue in no other way than by maintaining nearly as many people as it can maintain. A large revenue may at all times be said to consist in the command of a large quantity of the necessaries of life. In that rude state of things, it is commonly paid in a large quantity of those necessaries, in the materials of plain food and coarse clothing, in corn and cattle, in wool and raw hides. When neither commerce nor manufactures furnish any thing for which the owner can exchange the greater part of those materials which are over and above his own consumption, he can do nothing with the surplus, but feed and clothe nearly as many people as it will feed and clothe. A hospitality in which there is no luxury, and a liberality in which there is no ostentation, occasion, in this situation of things, the principal expenses of the rich and the great. But these I have likewise endeavored to show, in the same book, are expenses by which people are not very apt to ruin themselves. There is not, perhaps, any selfish pleasure so frivolous, of which the pursuit has not sometimes ruined even sensible men. A passion for cock-fighting has ruined many. But the instances, I believe, are not very numerous, of people who have been ruined by a hospitality or liberality of this kind; though the hospitality of luxury, and the liberality of ostentation have ruined many. Among our feudal ancestors, the long time during which estates used to continue in the same family, sufficiently demonstrates the general disposition of people to live within their income. Though the rustic hospitality, constantly exercised by the great landholders, may not, to us in the present times, seem consistent with that order which we are apt to consider as inseparably connected with good economy; yet we must certainly allow them to have been at least so far frugal, as not commonly to have spent their whole income. A part of their wool and raw hides, they had generally an opportunity of selling for money. Some part of this money, perhaps, they spent in purchasing the few objects of vanity and luxury, with which the circumstances of the times could furnish them; but some part of it they seem commonly to have hoarded. They could not well, indeed, do any thing else but hoard whatever money they saved. To trade, was disgraceful to a gentleman; and to lend money at interest, which at that time was considered as usury, and prohibited bylaw, would have been still more so. In those times of violence and disorder, besides, it was convenient to have a hoard of money at hand, that in case they should be driven from their own home, they might have something of known value to carry with them to some place of safety. The same violence which made it convenient to hoard, made it equally convenient to conceal the hoard. The frequency of treasure-trove, or of treasure found, of which no owner was known, sufficiently demonstrates the frequency, in those times, both of hoarding and of concealing the hoard. Treasure-trove was then considered as an important branch of the revenue of the sovereign. All the treasure-trove of the kingdom would scarce, perhaps, in the present times, make an important branch of the revenue of a private gentleman of a good estate.

The same disposition, to save and to hoard, prevailed in the sovereign, as well as in the subjects. Among nations, to whom commerce and manufacture are little known, the sovereign, it has already been observed in the fourth book, is in a situation which naturally disposes him to the parsimony requisite for accumulation. In that situation, the expense, even of a sovereign, cannot be directed by that vanity which delights in the gaudy finery of a court. The ignorance of the times affords but few of the trinkets in which that finery consists. Standing armies are not then necessary; so that the expense, even of a sovereign, like that of any other great lord can be employed in scarce any thing but bounty to his tenants, and hospitality to his retainers. But bounty and hospitality very seldom lead to extravagance; though vanity almost always does. All the ancient sovereigns of Europe, accordingly, it has already been observed, had treasures. Every Tartar chief, in the present times, is said to have one.

In a commercial country, abounding with every sort of expensive luxury, the sovereign, in the same manner as almost all the great proprietors in his dominions, naturally spends a great part of his revenue in purchasing those luxuries. His own and the neighboring countries supply him abundantly with all the costly trinkets which compose the splendid, but insignificant, pageantry of a court. For the sake of an inferior pageantry of the same kind, his nobles dismiss their retainers, make their tenants independent, and become gradually themselves as insignificant as the greater part of the wealthy burghers in his dominions. The same frivolous passions, which influence their conduct, influence his. How can it be supposed that he should be the only rich man in his dominions who is insensible to pleasures of this kind? If he does not, what he is very likely to do, spend upon those pleasures so great a part of his revenue as to debilitate very much the defensive power of the state, it cannot well be expected that he should not spend upon them all that part of it which is over and above what is necessary for supporting that defensive power. His ordinary expense becomes equal to his ordinary revenue, and it is well if it does not frequently exceed it. The amassing of treasure can no longer be expected; and when extraordinary exigencies require extraordinary expenses, he must necessarily call upon his subjects for an extraordinary aid. The present and the late king of Prussia are the only great princes of Europe, who, since the death of Henry IV of France, in 1610, are supposed to have amassed any considerable treasure. The parsimony which leads to accumulation has become almost as rare in republican as in monarchical governments. The Italian republics, the United Provinces of the Netherlands, are all in debt. The canton of Berne is the single republic in Europe which has amassed any considerable treasure. The other Swiss republics have not. The taste for some sort of pageantry, for splendid buildings, at least, and other public ornaments, frequently prevails as much in the apparently sober senate-house of a little republic, as in the dissipated court of the greatest king.

The want of parsimony, in time of peace, imposes the necessity of contracting debt in time of war. When war comes, there is no money in the treasury, but what is necessary for carrying on the ordinary expense of the peace establishment. In war, an establishment of three or four times that expense becomes necessary for the defense of the state; and consequently, a revenue three or four times greater than the peace revenue. Supposing that the sovereign should have, what he scarce ever has, the immediate means of augmenting his revenue in proportion to the augmentation of his expense; yet still the produce of the taxes, from which this increase of revenue must be drawn, will not begin to come into the treasury, till perhaps ten or twelve months after they are imposed. But the moment in which war begins, or rather the moment in which it appears likely to begin, the army must be augmented, the fleet must be fitted out, the garrisoned towns must be put into a posture of defense; that army, that fleet, those garrisoned towns, must be furnished with arms, ammunition, and provisions. An immediate and great expense must be incurred in that moment of immediate danger, which will not wait for the gradual and slow returns of the new taxes. In this exigency, government can have no other resource but in borrowing.

The same commercial state of society which, by the operation of moral causes, brings government in this manner into the necessity of borrowing, produces in the subjects both an ability and an inclination to lend. If it commonly brings along with it the necessity of borrowing, it likewise brings with it the facility of doing so.

A country abounding with merchants and manufacturers, necessarily abounds with a set of people through whose hands, not only their own capitals, but the capitals of all those who either lend them money, or trust them with goods, pass as frequently, or more frequently, than the revenue of a private man, who, without trade or business, lives upon his income, passes through his hands. The revenue of such a man can regularly pass through his hands only once in a year. But the whole amount of the capital and credit of a merchant, who deals in a trade of which the returns are very quick, may sometimes pass through his hands two, three, or four times in a year. A country abounding with merchants and manufacturers, therefore, necessarily abounds with a set of people, who have it at all times in their power to advance, if they choose to do so, a very large sum of money to government. Hence the ability in the subjects of a commercial state to lend.

Commerce and manufactures can seldom flourish long in any state which does not enjoy a regular administration of justice; in which the people do not feel themselves secure in the possession of their property; in which the faith of contracts is not supported by law; and in which the authority of the state is not supposed to be regularly employed in enforcing the payment of debts from all those who are able to pay. Commerce and manufactures, in short, can seldom flourish in any state, in which there is not a certain degree of confidence in the justice of government. The same confidence which disposes great merchants and manufacturers upon ordinary occasions, to trust their property to the protection of a particular government, disposes them, upon extraordinary occasions, to trust that government with the use of their property. By lending money to government, they do not even for a moment diminish their ability to carry on their trade and manufactures; on the contrary, they commonly augment it. The necessities of the state render government, upon most occasions willing to borrow upon terms extremely advantageous to the lender. The security which it grants to the original creditor, is made transferable to any other creditor; and from the universal confidence in the justice of the state, generally sells in the market for more than was originally paid for it. The merchant or monied man makes money by lending money to government, and instead of diminishing, increases his trading capital. He generally considers it as a favor, therefore, when the administration admits him to a share in the first subscription for a new loan. Hence the inclination or willingness in the subjects of a commercial state to lend.

The government of such a state is very apt to repose itself upon this ability and willingness of its subjects to lend it their money on extraordinary occasions. It foresees the facility of borrowing, and therefore dispenses itself from the duty of saving.

In a rude state of society, there are no great mercantile or manufacturing capitals. The individuals, who hoard whatever money they can save, and who conceal their hoard, do so from a distrust of the justice of government; from a fear, that if it was known that they had a hoard, and where that hoard was to be found, they would quickly be plundered. In such a state of things, few people would be able, and nobody would be willing to lend their money to government on extraordinary exigencies. The sovereign feels that he must provide for such exigencies by saving, because he foresees the absolute impossibility of borrowing. This foresight increases still further his natural disposition to save.

The progress of the enormous debts which at present oppress, and will in the long-run probably ruin, all the great nations of Europe, has been pretty uniform. Nations, like private men, have generally begun to borrow upon what may be called personal credit, without assigning or mortgaging any particular fund for the payment of the debt; and when this resource has failed them, they have gone on to borrow upon assignments or mortgages of particular funds.

What is called the unfunded debt of Great Britain, is contracted in the former of those two ways. It consists partly in a debt which bears, or is supposed to bear, no interest, and which resembles the debts that a private man contracts upon account; and partly in a debt which bears interest, and which resembles what a private man contracts upon his bill or promissory-note. The debts which are due, either for extraordinary services, or for services either not provided for, or not paid at the time when they are performed; part of the extraordinaries of the army, navy, and ordnance, the arrears of subsidies to foreign princes, those of seamen's wages, etc. usually constitute a debt of the first kind. Navy and exchequer bills, which are issued sometimes in payment of a part of such debts, and sometimes for other purposes, constitute a debt of the second kind; exchequer bills bearing interest from the day on which they are issued, and navy bills six months after they are issued. The Bank of England, either by voluntarily discounting those bills at their current value, or by agreeing with government for certain considerations to circulate exchequer bills, that is, to receive them at par, paying the interest which happens to be due upon them, keeps up their value, and facilitates their circulation, and thereby frequently enables government to contract a very large debt of this kind. In France, where there is no bank, the state bills (billets d'etat {See Examen des Reflections Politiques sur les Finances.}) have sometimes sold at sixty and seventy percent discount. During the great recoinage in king William's time, when the Bank of England thought proper to put a stop to its usual transactions, exchequer bills and tallies are said to have sold from twenty-five to sixty percent discount; owing partly, no doubt, to the supposed instability of the new government established by the Revolution, but partly, too, to the want of the support of the Bank of England.

When this resource is exhausted, and it becomes necessary, in order to raise money, to assign or mortgage some particular branch of the public revenue for the payment of the debt, government has, upon different occasions, done this in two different ways. Sometimes it has made this assignment or mortgage for a short period of time only, a year, or a few years, for example; and sometimes for perpetuity. In the one case, the fund was supposed sufficient to pay, within the limited time, both principal and interest of the money borrowed. In the other, it was supposed sufficient to pay the interest only, or a perpetual annuity equivalent to the interest, government being at liberty to redeem, at any time, this annuity, upon paying back the principal sum borrowed. When money was raised in the one way, it was said to be raised by anticipation; when in the other, by perpetual funding, or, more shortly, by funding.

In Great Britain, the annual land and malt taxes are regularly anticipated every year, by virtue of a borrowing clause constantly inserted into the acts which impose them. The Bank of England generally advances at an interest, which, since the Revolution, has varied from eight to three percent, the sums of which those taxes are granted, and receives payment as their produce gradually comes in. If there is a deficiency, which there always is, it is provided for in the supplies of the ensuing year. The only considerable branch of the public revenue which yet remains unmortgaged, is thus regularly spent before it comes in. Like an improvident spendthrift, whose pressing occasions will not allow him to wait for the regular payment of his revenue, the state is in the constant practice of borrowing of its own factors and agents, and of paying interest for the use of its own money.

In the reign of King William, and during a great part of that of Queen Anne, before we had become so familiar as we are now with the practice of perpetual funding, the greater part of the new taxes were imposed but for a short period of time (for four, five, six, or seven years only), and a great part of the grants of every year consisted in loans upon anticipations of the produce of those taxes. The produce being frequently insufficient for paying, within the limited term, the principal and interest of the money borrowed, deficiencies arose; to make good which, it became necessary to prolong the term.

In 1697, by the 8th of William III, c. 20, the deficiencies of several taxes were charged upon what was then called the first general mortgage or fund, consisting of a prolongation to the first of August 1706, of several different taxes, which would have expired within a shorter term, and of which the produce was accumulated into one general fund. The deficiencies charged upon this prolonged term amounted to £5,160,459: 14: 9¼.

In 1701, those duties, with some others, were still further prolonged, for the like purposes, till the first of August 1710, and were called the second general mortgage or fund. The deficiencies charged upon it amounted to £2,055,999: 7: 11½.

In 1707, those duties were still further prolonged, as a fund for new loans, to the first of August 1712, and were called the third general mortgage or fund. The sum borrowed upon it was £983,254:11:9¼.

In 1708, those duties were all (except the old subsidy of tonnage and poundage, of which one moiety only was made a part of this fund, and a duty upon the importation of Scotch linen, which had been taken off by the articles of union) still further continued, as a fund for new loans, to the first of August 1714, and were called the fourth general mortgage or fund. The sum borrowed upon it was £925,176:9:2¼.

In 1709, those duties were all (except the old subsidy of tonnage and poundage, which was now left out of this fund altogether) still further continued, for the same purpose, to the first of August 1716, and were called the fifth general mortgage or fund. The sum borrowed upon it was £922,029:6s.

In 1710, those duties were again prolonged to the first of August 1720, and were called the sixth general mortgage or fund. The sum borrowed upon it was £1,296,552:9:11.

In 1711, the same duties (which at this time were thus subject to four different anticipations), together with several others, were continued for ever, and made a fund for paying the interest of the capital of the South-sea company, which had that year advanced to government, for paying debts, and making good deficiencies, the sum of £9,177,967:15:4d, the greatest loan which at that time had ever been made.

Before this period, the principal, so far as I have been able to observe, the only taxes, which, in order to pay the interest of a debt, had been imposed for perpetuity, were those for paying the interest of the money which had been advanced to government by the bank and East-India company, and of what it was expected would be advanced, but which was never advanced, by a projected land bank. The bank fund at this time amounted to £3,375,027:17:10½, for which was paid an annuity or interest of £206,501:15:5d. The East-India fund amounted to £3,200,000, for which was paid an annuity or interest of £160,000; the bank fund being at six percent, the East-India fund at five percent interest.

In 1715, by the 1st of George I, c. 12, the different taxes which had been mortgaged for paying the bank annuity, together with several others, which, by this act, were likewise rendered perpetual, were accumulated into one common fund, called the aggregate fund, which was charged not only with the payment of the bank annuity, but with several other annuities and burdens of different kinds. This fund was afterwards augmented by the 3rd of George I, c. 8, and by the 5th of George I, c. 3, and the different duties which were then added to it were likewise rendered perpetual.

In 1717, by the 3rd of George I, c. 7, several other taxes were rendered perpetual, and accumulated into another common fund, called the general fund, for the payment of certain annuities, amounting in the whole to £724,849:6:10½.

In consequence of those different acts, the greater part of the taxes, which before had been anticipated only for a short term of years were rendered perpetual, as a fund for paying, not the capital, but the interest only, of the money which had been borrowed upon them by different successive anticipations.

Had money never been raised but by anticipation, the course of a few years would have liberated the public revenue, without any other attention of government besides that of not overloading the fund, by charging it with more debt than it could pay within the limited term, and not of anticipating a second time before the expiration of the first anticipation. But the greater part of European governments have been incapable of those attentions. They have frequently overloaded the fund, even upon the first anticipation; and when this happened not to be the case, they have generally taken care to overload it, by anticipating a second and a third time, before the expiration of the first anticipation. The fund becoming in this manner altogether insufficient for paying both principal and interest of the money borrowed upon it, it became necessary to charge it with the interest only, or a perpetual annuity equal to the interest; and such improvident anticipations necessarily gave birth to the more ruinous practice of perpetual funding. But though this practice necessarily puts off the liberation of the public revenue from a fixed period, to one so indefinite that it is not very likely ever to arrive; yet, as a greater sum can, in all cases, be raised by this new practice than by the old one of anticipation, the former, when men have once become familiar with it, has, in the great exigencies of the state, been universally preferred to the latter. To relieve the present exigency, is always the object which principally interests those immediately concerned in the administration of public affairs. The future liberation of the public revenue they leave to the care of posterity.

During the reign of Queen Anne, the market rate of interest had fallen from six to five percent; and, in the twelfth year of her reign, five percent was declared to be the highest rate which could lawfully be taken for money borrowed upon private security. Soon after the greater part of the temporary taxes of Great Britain had been rendered perpetual, and distributed into the aggregate, South-sea, and general funds, the creditors of the public, like those of private persons, were induced to accept of five percent for the interest of their money, which occasioned a saving of one percent upon the capital of the greater part or the debts which had been thus funded for perpetuity, or of one-sixth of the greater part of the annuities which were paid out of the three great funds above mentioned. This saving left a considerable surplus in the produce of the different taxes which had been accumulated into those funds, over and above what was necessary for paying the annuities which were now charged upon them, and laid the foundation of what has since been called the sinking fund. In 1717, it amounted to £523,454:7:7. In 1727, the interest of the greater part of the public debts was still further reduced to four percent; and, in 1753 and 1757, to three and a-half, and three percent, which reductions still further augmented the sinking fund.

A sinking fund, though instituted for the payment of old, facilitates very much the contracting of new debts. It is a subsidiary fund, always at hand, to be mortgaged in aid of any other doubtful fund, upon which money is proposed to be raised in any exigency of the state. Whether the sinking fund of Great Britain has been more frequently applied to the one or to other of those two purposes, will sufficiently appear by and by.

Besides those two methods of borrowing, by anticipations and by a perpetual funding, there are two other methods, which hold a sort of middle place between them; these are, that of borrowing upon annuities for terms of years, and that of borrowing upon annuities for lives.

During the reigns of King William and Queen Anne, large sums were frequently borrowed upon annuities for terms of years, which were sometimes longer and sometimes shorter. In 1695, an act was passed for borrowing one million upon an annuity of fourteen percent, or £140,000 a year, for sixteen years. In 1691, an act was passed for borrowing a million upon annuities for lives, upon terms which, in the present times, would appear very advantageous; but the subscription was not filled up. In the following year, the deficiency was made good, by borrowing upon annuities for lives, at fourteen percent or a little more than seven years purchase. In 1695, the persons who had purchased those annuities were allowed to exchange them for others of ninety-six years, upon paying into the exchequer sixty-three pounds in the hundred; that is, the difference between fourteen percent for life, and fourteen percent for ninety-six years, was sold for sixty-three pounds, or for four and a-half years purchase. Such was the supposed instability of government, that even these terms procured few purchasers. In the reign of Queen Anne, money was, upon different occasions, borrowed both upon annuities for lives, and upon annuities for terms of thirty-two, of eighty-nine, of ninety-eight, and of ninety-nine years. In 1719, the proprietors of the annuities for thirty-two years were induced to accept, in lieu of them, South-sea stock to the amount of eleven and a-half years purchase of the annuities, together with an additional quantity of stock, equal to the arrears which happened then to be due upon them. In 1720, the greater part of the other annuities for terms of years, both long and short, were subscribed into the same fund. The long annuities, at that time, amounted to £666,821: 8:3½ a year. On the 5th of January 1775, the remainder of them, or what was not subscribed at that time, amounted only to £136,453:12:8d.

During the two wars which began in 1739 and in 1755, little money was borrowed, either upon annuities for terms of years, or upon those for lives. An annuity for ninety-eight or ninety-nine years, however, is worth nearly as much as a perpetuity, and should therefore, one might think, be a fund for borrowing nearly as much. But those who, in order to make family settlements, and to provide for remote futurity, buy into the public stocks, would not care to purchase into one of which the value was continually diminishing; and such people make a very considerable proportion, both of the proprietors and purchasers of stock. An annuity for a long term of years, therefore, though its intrinsic value may be very nearly the same with that of a perpetual annuity, will not find nearly the same number of purchasers. The subscribers to a new loan, who mean generally to sell their subscription as soon as possible, prefer greatly a perpetual annuity, redeemable by parliament, to an irredeemable annuity, for a long term of years, of only equal amount. The value of the former may be supposed always the same, or very nearly the same; and it makes, therefore, a more convenient transferable stock than the latter.

During the two last-mentioned wars, annuities, either for terms of years or for lives, were seldom granted, but as premiums to the subscribers of a new loan, over and above the redeemable annuity or interest, upon the credit of which the loan was supposed to be made. They were granted, not as the proper fund upon which the money was borrowed, but as an additional encouragement to the lender.

Annuities for lives have occasionally been granted in two different ways; either upon separate lives, or upon lots of lives, which, in French, are called tontines, from the name of their inventor. When annuities are granted upon separate lives, the death of every individual annuitant disburdens the public revenue, so far as it was affected by his annuity. When annuities are granted upon tontines, the liberation of the public revenue does not commence till the death of all the annuitants comprehended in one lot, which may sometimes consist of twenty or thirty persons, of whom the survivors succeed to the annuities of all those who die before them; the last survivor succeeding to the annuities of the whole lot. Upon the same revenue, more money can always be raised by tontines than by annuities for separate lives. An annuity, with a right of survivorship, is really worth more than an equal annuity for a separate life; and, from the confidence which every man naturally has in his own good fortune, the principle upon which is founded the success of all lotteries, such an annuity generally sells for something more than it is worth. In countries where it is usual for government to raise money by granting annuities, tontines are, upon this account, generally preferred to annuities for separate lives. The expedient which will raise most money, is almost always preferred to that which is likely to bring about, in the speediest manner, the liberation of the public revenue.

In France, a much greater proportion of the public debts consists in annuities for lives than in England. According to a memoir presented by the parliament of Bourdeaux to the king, in 1764, the whole public debt of France is estimated at twenty-four hundred millions of livres; of which the capital, for which annuities for lives had been granted, is supposed to amount to three hundred millions, the eighth part of the whole public debt. The annuities themselves are computed to amount to thirty millions a year, the fourth part of one hundred and twenty millions, the supposed interest of that whole debt. These estimations, I know very well, are not exact; but having been presented by so very respectable a body as approximations to the truth, they may, I apprehend, be considered as such. It is not the different degrees of anxiety in the two governments of France and England for the liberation of the public revenue, which occasions this difference in their respective modes of borrowing; it arises altogether from the different views and interests of the lenders.

In England, the seat of government being in the greatest mercantile city in the world, the merchants are generally the people who advance money to government. By advancing it, they do not mean to diminish, but, on the contrary, to increase their mercantile capitals; and unless they expected to sell, with some profit, their share in the subscription for a new loan, they never would subscribe. But if, by advancing their money, they were to purchase, instead of perpetual annuities, annuities for lives only, whether their own or those of other people, they would not always be so likely to sell them with a profit. Annuities upon their own lives they would always sell with loss; because no man will give for an annuity upon the life of another, whose age and state of health are nearly the same with his own, the same price which he would give for one upon his own. An annuity upon the life of a third person, indeed, is, no doubt, of equal value to the buyer and the seller; but its real value begins to diminish from the moment it is granted, and continues to do so, more and more, as long as it subsists. It can never, therefore, make so convenient a transferable stock as a perpetual annuity, of which the real value may be supposed always the same, or very nearly the same.

In France, the seat of government not being in a great mercantile city, merchants do not make so great a proportion of the people who advance money to government. The people concerned in the finances, the farmers-general, the receivers of the taxes which are not in farm, the court-bankers, etc. make the greater part of those who advance their money in all public exigencies. Such people are commonly men of mean birth, but of great wealth, and frequently of great pride. They are too proud to marry their equals, and women of quality disdain to marry them. They frequently resolve, therefore, to live bachelors; and having neither any families of their own, nor much regard for those of their relations, whom they are not always very fond of acknowledging, they desire only to live in splendor during their own time, and are not unwilling that their fortune should end with themselves. The number of rich people, besides, who are either averse to marry, or whose condition of life renders it either improper or inconvenient for them to do so, is much greater in France than in England. To such people, who have little or no care for posterity, nothing can be more convenient than to exchange their capital for a revenue, which is to last just as long, and no longer, than they wish it to do.

The ordinary expense of the greater part of modern governments, in time of peace, being equal, or nearly equal, to their ordinary revenue, when war comes, they are both unwilling and unable to increase their revenue in proportion to the increase of their expense. They are unwilling, for fear of offending the people, who, by so great and so sudden an increase of taxes, would soon be disgusted with the war; and they are unable, from not well knowing what taxes would be sufficient to produce the revenue wanted. The facility of borrowing delivers them from the embarrassment which this fear and inability would otherwise occasion. By means of borrowing, they are enabled, with a very moderate increase of taxes, to raise, from year to year, money sufficient for carrying on the war; and by the practice of perpetual funding, they are enabled, with the smallest possible increase of taxes, to raise annually the largest possible sum of money. In great empires, the people who live in the capital, and in the provinces remote from the scene of action, feel, many of them, scarce any inconveniency from the war, but enjoy, at their ease, the amusement of reading in the newspapers the exploits of their own fleets and armies. To them this amusement compensates the small difference between the taxes which they pay on account of the war, and those which they had been accustomed to pay in time of peace. They are commonly dissatisfied with the return of peace, which puts an end to their amusement, and to a thousand visionary hopes of conquest and national glory, from a longer continuance of the war.

The return of peace, indeed, seldom relieves them from the greater part of the taxes imposed during the war. These are mortgaged for the interest of the debt contracted, in order to carry it on. If, over and above paying the interest of this debt, and defraying the ordinary expense of government, the old revenue, together with the new taxes, produce some surplus revenue, it may, perhaps, be converted into a sinking fund for paying off the debt. But, in the first place, this sinking fund, even supposing it should be applied to no other purpose, is generally altogether inadequate for paying, in the course of any period during which it can reasonably be expected that peace should continue, the whole debt contracted during the war; and, in the second place, this fund is almost always applied to other purposes.

The new taxes were imposed for the sole purpose of paying the interest of the money borrowed upon them. If they produce more, it is generally something which was neither intended nor expected, and is, therefore, seldom very considerable. Sinking funds have generally arisen, not so much from any surplus of the taxes which was over and above what was necessary for paying the interest or annuity originally charged upon them, as from a subsequent reduction of that interest; that of Holland in 1655, and that of the ecclesiastical state in 1685, were both formed in this manner. Hence the usual insufficiency of such funds.

During the most profound peace, various events occur, which require an extraordinary expense; and government finds it always more convenient to defray this expense by misapplying the sinking fund, than by imposing a new tax. Every new tax is immediately felt more or less by the people. It occasions always some murmur, and meets with some opposition. The more taxes may have been multiplied, the higher they may have been raised upon every different subject of taxation; the more loudly the people complain of every new tax, the more difficult it becomes, too, either to find out new subjects of taxation, or to raise much higher the taxes already imposed upon the old. A momentary suspension of the payment of debt is not immediately felt by the people, and occasions neither murmur nor complaint. To borrow of the sinking fund is always an obvious and easy expedient for getting out of the present difficulty. The more the public debts may have been accumulated, the more necessary it may have become to study to reduce them; the more dangerous, the more ruinous it may be to misapply any part of the sinking fund; the less likely is the public debt to be reduced to any considerable degree, the more likely, the more certainly, is the sinking fund to be misapplied towards defraying all the extraordinary expenses which occur in time of peace. When a nation is already overburdened with taxes, nothing but the necessities of a new war, nothing but either the animosity of national vengeance, or the anxiety for national security, can induce the people to submit, with tolerable patience, to a new tax. Hence the usual misapplication of the sinking fund.

In Great Britain, from the time that we had first recourse to the ruinous expedient of perpetual funding, the reduction of the public debt, in time of peace, has never borne any proportion to its accumulation in time of war. It was in the war which began in 1668, and was concluded by the Treaty of Ryswick, in 1697, that the foundation of the present enormous debt of Great Britain was first laid.

On the 31st of December 1697, the public debts of Great Britain, funded and unfunded, amounted to £21,515,742:13:8½. A great part of those debts had been contracted upon short anticipations, and some part upon annuities for lives; so that, before the 31st of December 1701, in less than four years, there had partly been paid off; and partly reverted to the public, the sum of £5,121,041:12:0¾d; a greater reduction of the public debt than has ever since been brought about in so short a period of time. The remaining debt, therefore, amounted only to £16,394,701:1:7¼d.

In the war which began in 1702, and which was concluded by the Treaty of Utrecht, the public debts were still more accumulated. On the 31st of December 1714, they amounted to £53,681,076:5:6½. The subscription into the South-sea fund, of the short and long annuities, increased the capital of the public debt; so that, on the 31st of December 1722, it amounted to £55,282,978:1:3 ⅚. The reduction of the debt began in 1723, and went on so slowly, that, on the 31st of December 1739, during seventeen years of profound peace, the whole sum paid off was no more than £8,328,554:17:11³⁄₁₂, the capital of the public debt, at that time, amounting to £46,954,623:3:4 ⁷⁄₁₂.

The Spanish war, which began in 1739, and the French war which followed it, occasioned a further increase of the debt, which, on the 31st of December 1748, after the war had been concluded by the treaty of Aix-la-Chapelle, amounted to £78,293,313:1:10¾. The most profound peace, of seventeen years continuance, had taken no more than £8,328,354, 17:11³⁄₁₂ from it. A war, of less than nine years continuance, added £31,338,689:18: 6 ⅙ to it. {See James Postlethwaite's *History of the Public Revenue.*}

During the administration of Mr. Pelham, the interest of the public debt was reduced, or at least measures were taken for reducing it, from four to three percent; the sinking fund was increased, and some part of the public debt was paid off. In 1755, before the breaking out of the late war, the funded debt of Great Britain amounted to £72,289,675. On the 5th of January 1763, at the conclusion of the peace, the funded debt amounted debt to £122,603,336:8:2¼. The unfunded debt has been stated at £13,927,589:2:2. But the expense occasioned by the war did not end with the conclusion of the peace; so that, though on the 5th of January 1764, the funded debt was increased (partly by a new loan, and partly by funding a part of the unfunded debt) to £129,586,789:10:1¾, there still remained (according to the very well informed author of *Considerations on the Trade and Finances of Great Britain*) an unfunded debt, which was brought to account in that and the following year, of £9,975,017: 12:2 15/44d. In 1764, therefore, the public debt of Great Britain, funded and unfunded together, amounted, according to this author, to £139,561,807:2:4. The annuities for lives, too, which had been granted as premiums to the subscribers to the new loans in 1757, estimated at fourteen years purchase, were valued at £472,500; and the annuities for long terms of years, granted as premiums likewise, in 1761 and 1762, estimated at twenty-seven and a half years purchase, were valued at £6,826,875. During a peace of about seven years continuance, the prudent and truly patriotic administration of Mr. Pelham was not able to pay off an old debt of six millions. During a war of nearly the same continuance, a new debt of more than seventy-five millions was contracted.

On the 5th of January 1775, the funded debt of Great Britain amounted to £124,996,086, 1:6¼d. The unfunded, exclusive of a large civil-list debt, to £4,150,236:3:11 7/8. Both together, to £129,146,322:5:6. According to this account, the whole debt paid off, during eleven years of profound peace, amounted only to £10,415,476:16:9 7/8. Even this small reduction of debt, however, has not been all made from the savings out of the ordinary revenue of the state. Several extraneous sums, altogether independent of that ordinary revenue, have contributed towards it. Amongst these we may reckon an additional shilling in the pound land tax, for three years; the two millions received from the East-India company, as indemnification for their territorial acquisitions; and the one hundred and ten thousand pounds received from the bank for the renewal of their charter. To these must be added several other sums, which, as they arose out of the late war, ought perhaps to be considered as deductions from the expenses of it. The principal are,

The produce of French prizes	£690,449	18	9
Composition for French prisoners	670,000	0	0
What has been received from the sale of the ceded islands . . .	95,500	0	0
Total	£1,455,949	18	9

If we add to this sum the balance of the earl of Chatham's and Mr. Calcraft's accounts, and other army savings of the same kind, together with what has been received from the bank, the East-India company, and the additional shilling in the pound land tax, the whole must be a good deal more than five millions. The debt, therefore, which, since the peace, has been paid out of the savings from the ordinary revenue of the state, has not, one year with another, amounted to half a million a year. The sinking fund has, no doubt, been considerably augmented since the peace, by the debt which had been paid off, by the reduction of the redeemable four per cents to three per cents, and by the annuities for lives which have fallen in; and, if peace were to continue, a million, perhaps, might now be annually spared out of it towards the discharge of the debt. Another million, accordingly, was paid in the course of last year; but at the same time, a large civil-list debt was left unpaid, and we are now involved in a new war, which, in its progress, may prove as expensive as any of our former wars. {It has proved more expensive than any one of our former wars, and has involved us in an additional debt of more than one hundred millions. During a profound peace of eleven years, little more than ten millions of debt was paid; during a war of seven years, more than one hundred millions was contracted.} The new debt which will probably be contracted before the end of the next campaign, may, perhaps, be nearly equal to all the old debt which has been paid off from the savings out of the ordinary revenue of the state. It would be altogether chimerical, therefore, to expect that the public debt should ever be completely discharged, by any savings which are likely to be made from that ordinary revenue as it stands at present.

The public funds of the different indebted nations of Europe, particularly those of England, have, by one author, been represented as the accumulation of a great capital, superadded to the other capital of the country, by means of which its trade is extended, its manufactures are multiplied, and its lands cultivated and improved, much beyond what they could have been by means of that other capital only. He does not consider that the capital which the first creditors of the public advanced to government, was, from the moment in which he advanced it, a certain portion of the annual produce, turned away from serving in the function of a capital, to serve in that of a revenue; from maintaining productive laborers, to maintain unproductive ones, and to be spent and wasted, generally in the course of the year, without even the hope of any future reproduction. In return for the capital which they advanced, they obtained, indeed, an annuity of the public funds, in most cases, of more than equal value. This annuity, no doubt, replaced to them their capital, and enabled them to carry on their trade and business to the same, or, perhaps, to a greater extent than before; that is, they were enabled, either to borrow of other people a new capital, upon the credit of this annuity or, by selling it, to get from other people a new capital of their own, equal, or superior, to that which they had advanced to government. This new capital, however, which they in this manner either bought or borrowed of other people, must have existed in the country before, and must have been employed, as all capitals are, in maintaining productive labor. When it came into the hands of those who had advanced their money to government, though it was, in some respects, a new capital to them, it was not so to the country, but was only a capital withdrawn from certain employments, in order to be turned towards others. Though it replaced to them what they had advanced to government, it did not replace it to the country. Had they not advanced this capital to government, there would have been in the country two capitals, two portions of the annual produce, instead of one, employed in maintaining productive labor.

When, for defraying the expense of government, a revenue is raised within the year, from the produce of free or unmortgaged taxes, a certain portion of the revenue of private people is only turned away from maintaining one species of unproductive labor, towards maintaining another. Some part of what they pay in those taxes, might, no doubt, have been accumulated into capital, and consequently employed in maintaining productive labor; but the greater part would probably have been spent, and consequently employed in maintaining unproductive labor. The public expense, however, when defrayed in this manner, no doubt hinders, more or less, the further accumulation of new capital; but it does not necessarily occasion the destruction of any actually-existing capital.

When the public expense is defrayed by funding, it is defrayed by the annual destruction of some capital which had before existed in the country; by the perversion of some portion of the annual produce which had before been destined for the maintenance of productive labor, towards that of unproductive labor. As in this case, however, the taxes are lighter than they would have been, had a revenue sufficient for defraying the same expense been raised within the year; the private revenue of individuals is necessarily less burdened, and consequently their ability to save and accumulate some part of that revenue into capital, is a good deal less impaired. If the method of funding destroys more old capital, it, at the same time, hinders less the accumulation or acquisition of new capital, than that of defraying the public expense by a revenue raised within the year. Under the system of funding, the frugality and industry of private people can more easily repair the breaches which the waste and extravagance of government may occasionally make in the general capital of the society.

It is only during the continuance of war, however, that the system of funding has this advantage over the other system. Were the expense of war to be defrayed always by a revenue raised within the year, the taxes from which that extraordinary revenue was drawn would last no longer than the war. The ability of private people to accumulate, though less during the war, would have been greater during the peace, than under the system of funding. War would not necessarily have occasioned the destruction of any old capitals, and peace would have occasioned the accumulation of many more new. Wars would, in general, be more speedily concluded, and less wantonly undertaken. The people feeling, during continuance of war, the complete burden of it, would soon grow weary of it; and government, in order to humor them, would not be under the necessity of carrying it on longer than it was necessary to do so. The foresight of the heavy and unavoidable burdens of war would hinder the people from wantonly calling for it when there was no real or solid interest to fight for. The seasons during which the ability of private people to accumulate was somewhat impaired, would occur more rarely, and be of shorter continuance. Those, on the contrary, during which that ability was in the highest vigor would be of much longer duration than they can well be under the system of funding.

When funding, besides, has made a certain progress, the multiplication of taxes which it brings along with it, sometimes impairs as much the ability of private people to accumulate, even in time of peace, as the other system would in time of war. The peace revenue of Great Britain amounts at present to more than ten millions a year. If free and unmortgaged, it might be sufficient, with proper management, and without contracting a shilling of new debt, to carry on the most vigorous war. The private revenue of the inhabitants of Great Britain is at present as much encumbered in time of peace, their ability to accumulate is as much impaired, as it would have been in the time of the most expensive war, had the pernicious system of funding never been adopted.

In the payment of the interest of the public debt, it has been said, it is the right hand which pays the left. The money does not go out of the country. It is only a part of the revenue of one set of the inhabitants which is transferred to another; and the nation is not a farthing the poorer. This apology is founded altogether in the sophistry of the mercantile system; and, after the long examination which I have already bestowed upon that system, it may, perhaps, be unnecessary to say anything further about it. It supposes, besides, that the whole public debt is owing to the inhabitants of the country, which happens not to be true; the Dutch, as well as several other foreign nations, having a very considerable share in our public funds. But though the whole debt were owing to the inhabitants of the country, it would not, upon that account, be less pernicious.

Land and capital stock are the two original sources of all revenue, both private and public. Capital stock pays the wages of productive labor, whether employed in agriculture, manufactures, or commerce. The management of those two original sources of revenue belongs to two different sets of people; the proprietors of land, and the owners or employers of capital stock.

The proprietor of land is interested, for the sake of his own revenue, to keep his estate in as good condition as he can, by building and repairing his tenants houses, by making and maintaining the necessary drains and enclosures, and all those other expensive improvements which it properly belongs to the landlord to make and maintain. But, by different land taxes, the revenue of the landlord may be so much diminished, and, by different duties upon the necessaries and conveniences of life, that diminished revenue may be rendered of so little real value, that he may find himself altogether unable to make or maintain those expensive improvements. When the landlord, however, ceases to do his part, it is altogether impossible that the tenant should continue to do his. As the distress of the landlord increases, the agriculture of the country must necessarily decline.

When, by different taxes upon the necessaries and conveniences of life, the owners and employers of capital stock find, that whatever revenue they derive from it, will not, in a particular country, purchase the same quantity of those necessaries and conveniences which an equal revenue would in almost any other, they will be disposed to remove to some other. And when, in order to raise those taxes, all or the greater part of merchants and manufacturers, that is, all or the greater part of the employers of great capitals, come to be continually exposed to the mortifying and vexatious visits of the tax-gatherers, this disposition to remove will soon be changed into an actual removing. The industry of the country will necessarily fall with the removal of the capital which supported it, and the ruin of trade and manufactures will follow the declension of agriculture.

To transfer from the owners of those two great sources of revenue, land, and capital stock, from the persons immediately interested in the good condition of every particular portion of land, and in the good management of every particular portion of capital stock, to another set of persons (the creditors of the public, who have no such particular interest), the greater part of the revenue arising from either, must, in the long-run, occasion both the neglect of land, and the waste or removal of capital stock. A creditor of the public has, no doubt, a general interest in the prosperity of the agriculture, manufactures, and commerce of the country; and consequently in the good condition of its land, and in the good management of its capital stock. Should there be any general failure or declension in any of these things, the produce of the different taxes might no longer be sufficient to pay him the annuity or interest which is due to him. But a creditor of the public, considered merely as such, has no interest in the good condition of any particular portion of land, or in the good management of any particular portion of capital stock. As a creditor of the public, he has no knowledge of any such particular portion. He has no inspection of it. He can have no care about it. Its ruin may in some cases be unknown to him, and cannot directly affect him.

The practice of funding has gradually enfeebled every state which has adopted it. The Italian republics seem to have begun it. Genoa and Venice, the only two remaining which can pretend to an independent existence, have both been enfeebled by it. Spain seems to have learned the practice from the Italian republics, and (its taxes being probably less judicious than theirs) it has, in proportion to its natural strength, been still more enfeebled. The debts of Spain are of very old standing. It was deeply in debt before the end of the sixteenth century, about a hundred years before England owed a shilling. France, notwithstanding all its natural resources, languishes under an oppressive load of the same kind. The republic of the United Provinces is as much enfeebled by its debts as either Genoa or Venice. Is it likely that, in Great Britain alone, a practice, which has brought either weakness or dissolution into every other country, should prove altogether innocent?

The system of taxation established in those different countries, it may be said, is inferior to that of England. I believe it is so. But it ought to be remembered, that when the wisest government has exhausted all the proper subjects of taxation, it must, in cases of urgent necessity, have recourse to improper ones. The wise republic of Holland has, upon some occasions, been obliged to have recourse to taxes as inconvenient as the greater part of those of Spain. Another war, begun before any considerable liberation of the public revenue had been brought about, and growing in its progress as expensive as the last war, may, from irresistible necessity, render the British system of taxation as oppressive as that of Holland, or even as that of Spain. To the honor of our present system of taxation, indeed, it has hitherto given so little embarrassment to industry, that, during the course even of the most expensive wars, the frugality and good conduct of individuals seem to have been able, by saving and accumulation, to repair all the breaches which the waste and extravagance of government had made in the general capital of the society. At the conclusion of the late war, the most expensive that Great Britain ever waged, her agriculture was as flourishing, her manufacturers as numerous and as fully employed, and her commerce as extensive, as they had ever been before. The capital, therefore, which supported all those different branches of industry, must have been equal to what it had ever been before. Since the peace, agriculture has been still further improved; the rents of houses have risen in every town and village of the country, a proof of the increasing wealth and revenue of the people; and the annual amount of the greater part of the old taxes, of the principal branches of the excise and customs, in particular, has been continually increasing, an equally clear proof of an increasing consumption, and consequently of an increasing produce, which could alone support that consumption. Great Britain seems to support with ease, a burden which, half a century ago, nobody believed her capable of supporting. Let us not, however, upon this account, rashly conclude that she is capable of supporting any burden; nor even be too confident that she could support, without great distress, a burden a little greater than what has already been laid upon her.

When national debts have once been accumulated to a certain degree, there is scarce, I believe, a single instance of their having been fairly and completely paid. The liberation of the public revenue, if it has ever been brought about at all, has always been brought about by a bankruptcy; sometimes by an avowed one, though frequently by a pretended payment.

The raising of the denomination of the coin has been the most usual expedient by which a real public bankruptcy has been disguised under the appearance of a pretended payment. If a sixpence, for example, should, either by act of parliament or royal proclamation, be raised to the denomination of a shilling, and twenty sixpences to that of a pound sterling; the person who, under the old denomination, had borrowed twenty shillings, or near four ounces of silver, would, under the new, pay with twenty sixpences, or with something less than two ounces. A national debt of about a hundred and twenty-eight millions, near the capital of the funded and unfunded debt of Great Britain, might, in this manner, be paid with about sixty-four millions of our present money. It would, indeed, be a pretended payment only, and the creditors of the public would really be defrauded of ten shillings in the pound of what was due to them. The calamity, too, would extend much further than to the creditors of the public, and those of every private person would suffer a proportional loss; and this without any advantage, but in most cases with a great additional loss, to the creditors of the public. If the creditors of the public, indeed, were generally much in debt to other people, they might in some measure compensate their loss by paying their creditors in the same coin in which the public had paid them. But in most countries, the creditors of the public are, the greater part of them, wealthy people, who stand more in the relation of creditors than in that of debtors, towards the rest of their fellow citizens. A pretended payment of this kind, therefore, instead of alleviating, aggravates, in most cases, the loss of the creditors of the public; and, without any advantage to the public, extends the calamity to a great number of other innocent people. It occasions a general and most pernicious subversion of the fortunes of private people; enriching, in most cases, the idle and profuse debtor, at the expense of the industrious and frugal creditor; and transporting a great part of the national capital from the hands which were likely to increase and improve it, to those who are likely to dissipate and destroy it. When it becomes necessary for a state to declare itself bankrupt, in the same manner as when it becomes necessary for an individual to do so, a fair, open, and avowed bankruptcy, is always the measure which is both least dishonorable to the debtor, and least hurtful to the creditor. The honor of a state is surely very poorly provided for, when, in order to cover the disgrace of a real bankruptcy, it has recourse to a juggling trick of this kind, so easily seen through, and at the same time so extremely pernicious.

Almost all states, however, ancient as well as modern, when reduced to this necessity, have, upon some occasions, played this very juggling trick. The Romans, at the end of the first Punic war, reduced the As, the coin or denomination by which they computed the value of all their other coins, from containing twelve ounces of copper, to contain only two ounces; that is, they raised two ounces of copper to a denomination which had always before expressed the value of twelve ounces. The republic was, in this manner, enabled to pay the great debts which it had contracted with the sixth part of what it really owed. So sudden and so great a bankruptcy, we should in the present times be apt to imagine, must have occasioned a very violent popular clamor. It does not appear to have occasioned any. The law which enacted it was, like all other laws relating to the coin, introduced and carried through the assembly of the people by a tribune, and was probably a very popular law. In Rome, as in all other ancient republics, the poor people were constantly in debt to the rich and the great, who, in order to secure their votes at the annual elections, used to lend them money at exorbitant interest, which, being never paid, soon accumulated into a sum too great either for the debtor to pay, or for any body else to pay for him. The debtor, for fear of a very severe execution, was obliged, without any further gratuity, to vote for the candidate whom the creditor recommended. In spite of all the laws against bribery and corruption, the bounty of the candidates, together with the occasional distributions of coin which were ordered by the senate, were the principal funds from which, during the latter times of the Roman republic, the poorer citizens derived their subsistence. To deliver themselves from this subjection to their creditors, the poorer citizens were continually calling out, either for an entire abolition of debts, or for what they called new tables; that is, for a law which should entitle them to a complete acquittance, upon paying only a certain proportion of their accumulated debts. The law which reduced the coin of all denominations to a sixth part of its former value, as it enabled them to pay their debts with a sixth part of what they really owed, was equivalent to the most advantageous new tables. In order to satisfy the people, the rich and the great were, upon several different occasions, obliged to consent to laws, both for abolishing debts, and for introducing new tables; and they probably were induced to consent to this law, partly for the same reason, and partly that, by liberating the public revenue, they might restore vigor to that government, of which they themselves had the principal direction. An operation of this kind would at once reduce a debt of £128,000,000 to £21,333,333:6:8. In the course of the second Punic war, the As was still further reduced, first, from two ounces of copper to one ounce, and afterwards from one ounce to half an ounce; that is, to the twenty-fourth part of its original value. By combining the three Roman operations into one, a debt of a hundred and twenty-eight millions of our present money, might in this manner be reduced all at once to a debt of £5,333,333:6:8. Even the enormous debt of Great Britain might in this manner soon be paid.

By means of such expedients, the coin of, I believe, all nations, has been gradually reduced more and more below its original value, and the same nominal sum has been gradually brought to contain a smaller and a smaller quantity of silver.

Nations have sometimes, for the same purpose, adulterated the standard of their coin; that is, have mixed a greater quantity of alloy in it. If in the pound weight of our silver coin, for example, instead of eighteen penny-weight, according to the present standard, there were mixed eight ounces of alloy; a pound sterling, or twenty shillings of such coin, would be worth little more than six shillings and eight pence of our present money. The quantity of silver contained in six shillings and eight pence of our present money, would thus be raised very nearly to the denomination of a pound sterling. The adulteration of the standard has exactly the same effect with what the French call an augmentation, or a direct raising of the denomination of the coin.

An augmentation, or a direct raising of the denomination of the coin, always is, and from its nature must be, an open and avowed operation. By means of it, pieces of a smaller weight and bulk are called by the same name, which had before been given to pieces of a greater weight and bulk. The adulteration of the standard, on the contrary, has generally been a concealed operation. By means of it, pieces are issued from the mint, of the same denomination, and, as nearly as could be contrived, of the same weight, bulk, and appearance, with pieces which had been current before of much greater value. When King John of France {*See Du Cange Glossary, voce Moneta*; the Benedictine Edition.}, in order to pay his debts, adulterated his coin, all the officers of his mint were sworn to secrecy. Both operations are unjust. But a simple augmentation is an injustice of open violence; whereas an adulteration is an injustice of treacherous fraud. This latter operation, therefore, as soon as it has been discovered, and it could never be concealed very long, has always excited much greater indignation than the former. The coin, after any considerable augmentation, has very seldom been brought back to its former weight; but after the greatest adulterations, it has almost always been brought back to its former fineness. It has scarce ever happened, that the fury and indignation of the people could otherwise be appeased.

In the end of the reign of Henry VIII, and in the beginning of that of Edward VI, the English coin was not only raised in its denomination, but adulterated in its standard. The like frauds were practiced in Scotland during the minority of James VI. They have occasionally been practiced in most other countries.

That the public revenue of Great Britain can never be completely liberated, or even that any considerable progress can ever be made towards that liberation, while the surplus of that revenue, or what is over and above defraying the annual expense of the peace establishment, is so very small, it seems altogether in vain to expect. That liberation, it is evident, can never be brought about, without either some very considerable augmentation of the public revenue, or some equally considerable reduction of the public expense.

A more equal land tax, a more equal tax upon the rent of houses, and such alterations in the present system of customs and excise as those which have been mentioned in the foregoing chapter, might, perhaps, without increasing the burden of the greater part of the people, but only distributing the weight of it more equally upon the whole, produce a considerable augmentation of revenue. The most sanguine projector, however, could scarce flatter himself, that any augmentation of this kind would be such as could give any reasonable hopes, either of liberating the public revenue altogether, or even of making such progress towards that liberation in time of peace, as either to prevent or to compensate the further accumulation of the public debt in the next war.

By extending the British system of taxation to all the different provinces of the empire, inhabited by people either of British or European extraction, a much greater augmentation of revenue might be expected. This, however, could scarce, perhaps, be done, consistently with the principles of the British constitution, without admitting into the British parliament, or, if you will, into the states-general of the British empire, a fair and equal representation of all those different provinces; that of each province bearing the same proportion to the produce of its taxes, as the representation of Great Britain might bear to the produce of the taxes levied upon Great Britain. The private interest of many powerful individuals, the confirmed prejudices of great bodies of people, seem, indeed, at present, to oppose to so great a change, such obstacles as it may be very difficult, perhaps altogether impossible, to surmount. Without, however, pretending to determine whether such a union be practicable or impracticable, it may not, perhaps, be improper, in a speculative work of this kind, to consider how far the British system of taxation might be applicable to all the different provinces of the empire; what revenue might be expected from it, if so applied; and in what manner a general union of this kind might be likely to affect the happiness and prosperity of the different provinces comprehended within it. Such a speculation, can, at worst, be regarded but as a new Utopia, less amusing, certainly, but no more useless and chimerical than the old one.

The land-tax, the stamp duties, and the different duties of customs and excise, constitute the four principal branches of the British taxes.

Ireland is certainly as able, and our American and West India plantations more able, to pay a land tax, than Great Britain. Where the landlord is subject neither to tithe nor poor's rate, he must certainly be more able to pay such a tax, than where he is subject to both those other burdens. The tithe, where there is no modus, and where it is levied in kind, diminishes more what would otherwise be the rent of the landlord, than a land tax which really amounted to five shillings in the pound. Such a tithe will be found, in most cases, to amount to more than a fourth part of the real rent of the land, or of what remains after replacing completely the capital of the farmer, together with his reasonable profit. If all moduses and all impropriations were taken away, the complete church tithe of Great Britain and Ireland could not well be estimated at less than six or seven millions. If there was no tithe either in Great Britain or Ireland, the landlords could afford to pay six or seven millions additional land tax, without being more burdened than a very great part of them are at present. America pays no tithe, and could, therefore, very well afford to pay a land tax. The lands in America and the West Indies, indeed, are, in general, not tenanted nor leased out to farmers. They could not, therefore, be assessed according to any rent roll. But neither were the lands of Great Britain, in the 4th of William and Mary, assessed according to any rent roll, but according to a very loose and inaccurate estimation. The lands in America might be assessed either in the same manner, or according to an equitable valuation, in consequence of an accurate survey, like that which was lately made in the Milanese, and in the dominions of Austria, Prussia, and Sardinia.

Stamp duties, it is evident, might be levied without any variation, in all countries where the forms of law process, and the deeds by which property, both real and personal, is transferred, are the same, or nearly the same.

The extension of the custom-house laws of Great Britain to Ireland and the plantations, provided it was accompanied, as in justice it ought to be, with an extension of the freedom of trade, would be in the highest degree advantageous to both. All the invidious restraints which at present oppress the trade of Ireland, the distinction between the enumerated and non-enumerated commodities of America, would be entirely at an end.

The countries north of Cape Finisterre would be as open to every part of the produce of America, as those south of that cape are to some parts of that produce at present. The trade between all the different parts of the British empire would, in consequence of this uniformity in the custom-house laws, be as free as the coasting trade of Great Britain is at present. The British empire would thus afford, within itself, an immense internal market for every part of the produce of all its different provinces. So great an extension of market would soon compensate, both to Ireland and the plantations, all that they could suffer from the increase of the duties of customs.

The excise is the only part of the British system of taxation, which would require to be varied in any respect, according as it was applied to the different provinces of the empire. It might be applied to Ireland without any variation; the produce and consumption of that kingdom being exactly of the same nature with those of Great Britain. In its application to America and the West Indies, of which the produce and consumption are so very different from those of Great Britain, some modification might be necessary, in the same manner as in its application to the cider and beer counties of England.

A fermented liquor, for example, which is called beer, but which, as it is made of molasses, bears very little resemblance to our beer, makes a considerable part of the common drink of the people in America. This liquor, as it can be kept only for a few days, cannot, like our beer, be prepared and stored up for sale in great breweries; but every private family must brew it for their own use, in the same manner as they cook their victuals. But to subject every private family to the odious visits and examination of the tax-gatherers, in the same manner as we subject the keepers of ale-houses and the brewers for public sale, would be altogether inconsistent with liberty. If, for the sake of equality, it was thought necessary to lay a tax upon this liquor, it might be taxed by taxing the material of which it is made, either at the place of manufacture, or, if the circumstances of the trade rendered such an excise improper, by laying a duty upon its importation into the colony in which it was to be consumed. Besides the duty of one penny a gallon imposed by the British parliament upon the importation of molasses into America, there is a provincial tax of this kind upon their importation into Massachusetts Bay, in ships belonging to any other colony, of eight-pence the hogshead; and another upon their importation from the northern colonies into South Carolina, of five-pence the gallon. Or, if neither of these methods was found convenient, each family might compound for its consumption of this liquor, either according to the number of persons of which it consisted, in the same manner as private families compound for the malt tax in England; or according to the different ages and sexes of those persons, in the same manner as several different taxes are levied in Holland; or, nearly as Sir Matthew Decker proposes, that all taxes upon consumable commodities should be levied in England. This mode of taxation, it has already been observed, when applied to objects of a speedy consumption, is not a very convenient one. It might be adopted, however, in cases where no better could be done.

Sugar, rum, and tobacco, are commodities which are nowhere necessaries of life, which are become objects of almost universal consumption, and which are, therefore, extremely proper subjects of taxation. If a union with the colonies were to take place, those commodities might be taxed, either before they go out of the hands of the manufacturer or grower; or, if this mode of taxation did not suit the circumstances of those persons, they might be deposited in public warehouses, both at the place of manufacture, and at all the different ports of the empire, to which they might afterwards be transported, to remain there, under the joint custody of the owner and the revenue officer, till such time as they should be delivered out, either to the consumer, to the merchant-retailer for home consumption, or to the merchant-exporter; the tax not to be advanced till such delivery. When delivered out for exportation, to go duty-free, upon proper security being given, that they should really be exported out of the empire. These are, perhaps, the principal commodities, with regard to which the union with the colonies might require some considerable change in the present system of British taxation.

What might be the amount of the revenue which this system of taxation, extended to all the different provinces of the empire, might produce, it must, no doubt, be altogether impossible to ascertain with tolerable exactness. By means of this system, there is annually levied in Great Britain, upon less than eight millions of people, more than ten millions of revenue. Ireland contains more than two millions of people, and, according to the accounts laid before the congress, the twelve associated provinces of America contain more than three. Those accounts, however, may have been exaggerated, in order, perhaps, either to encourage their own people, or to intimidate those of this country; and we shall suppose, therefore, that our North American and West Indian colonies, taken together, contain no more than three millions; or that the whole British empire, in Europe and America, contains no more than thirteen millions of inhabitants. If, upon less than eight millions of inhabitants, this system of taxation raises a revenue of more than ten millions sterling; it ought, upon thirteen millions of inhabitants, to raise a revenue of more than sixteen millions two hundred and fifty thousand pounds sterling. From this revenue, supposing that this system could produce it, must be deducted the revenue usually raised in Ireland and the plantations, for defraying the expense of the respective civil governments. The expense of the civil and military establishment of Ireland, together with the interest of the public debt, amounts, at a medium of the two years which ended March 1775, to something less than seven hundred and fifty thousand pounds a year. By a very exact account of the revenue of the principal colonies of America and the West Indies, it amounted, before the commencement of the present disturbances, to a hundred and forty-one thousand eight hundred pounds. In this account, however, the revenue of Maryland, of North Carolina, and of all our late acquisitions, both upon the continent, and in the islands, is omitted; which may, perhaps, make a difference of thirty or forty thousand pounds. For the sake of even numbers, therefore, let us suppose that the revenue necessary for supporting the civil government of Ireland and the plantations may amount to a million. There would remain, consequently, a revenue of fifteen millions two hundred and fifty thousand pounds, to be applied towards defraying the general expense of the empire, and towards paying the public debt. But if, from the present revenue of Great Britain, a million could, in peaceable times, be spared towards the payment of that debt, six millions two hundred and fifty thousand pounds could very well be spared from this improved revenue. This great sinking fund, too, might be augmented every year by the interest of the debt which had been discharged the year before; and might, in this manner, increase so very rapidly, as to be sufficient in a few years to discharge the whole debt, and thus to restore completely the at-present debilitated and languishing vigor of the empire. In the meantime, the people might be relieved from some of the most burdensome taxes; from those which are imposed either upon the necessaries of life, or upon the materials of manufacture. The laboring poor would thus be enabled to live better, to work cheaper, and to send their goods cheaper to market. The cheapness of their goods would increase the demand for them, and consequently for the labor of those who produced them. This increase in the demand for labor would both increase the numbers, and improve the circumstances of the laboring poor. Their consumption would increase, and, together with it, the revenue arising from all those articles of their consumption upon which the taxes might be allowed to remain.

The revenue arising from this system of taxation, however, might not immediately increase in proportion to the number of people who were subjected to it. Great indulgence would for some time be due to those provinces of the empire which were thus subjected to burdens to which they had not before been accustomed; and even when the same taxes came to be levied everywhere as exactly as possible, they would not everywhere produce a revenue proportioned to the numbers of the people. In a poor country, the consumption of the principal commodities subject to the duties of customs and excise, is very small; and in a thinly inhabited country, the opportunities of smuggling are very great. The consumption of malt liquors among the inferior ranks of people in Scotland is very small; and the excise upon malt, beer, and ale, produces less there than in England, in proportion to the numbers of the people and the rate of the duties, which upon malt is different, on account of a supposed difference of quality. In these particular branches of the excise, there is not, I apprehend, much more smuggling in the one country than in the other. The duties upon the distillery, and the greater part of the duties of customs, in proportion to the numbers of people in the respective countries, produce less in Scotland than in England, not only on account of the smaller consumption of the taxed commodities, but of the much greater facility of smuggling. In Ireland, the inferior ranks of people are still poorer than in Scotland, and many parts of the country are almost as thinly inhabited. In Ireland, therefore, the consumption of the taxed commodities might, in proportion to the number of the people, be still less than in Scotland, and the facility of smuggling nearly the same. In America and the West Indies, the white people, even of the lowest rank, are in much better circumstances than those of the same rank in England; and their consumption of all the luxuries in which they usually indulge themselves, is probably much greater. The blacks, indeed, who make the greater part of the inhabitants, both of the southern colonies upon the continent and of the West India islands, as they are in a state of slavery, are, no doubt, in a worse condition than the poorest people either in Scotland or Ireland. We must not, however, upon that account, imagine that they are worse fed, or that their consumption of articles which might be subjected to moderate duties, is less than that even of the lower ranks of people in England. In order that they may work well, it is the interest of their master that they should be fed well, and kept in good heart, in the same manner as it is his interest that his working cattle should be so.

The blacks, accordingly, have almost everywhere their allowance of rum, and of molasses or spruce-beer, in the same manner as the white servants; and this allowance would not probably be withdrawn, though those articles should be subjected to moderate duties. The consumption of the taxed commodities, therefore, in proportion to the number of inhabitants, would probably be as great in America and the West Indies as in any part of the British empire. The opportunities of smuggling, indeed, would be much greater; America, in proportion to the extent of the country, being much more thinly inhabited than either Scotland or Ireland. If the revenue, however, which is at present raised by the different duties upon malt and malt liquors, were to be levied by a single duty upon malt, the opportunity of smuggling in the most important branch of the excise would be almost entirely taken away; and if the duties of customs, instead of being imposed upon almost all the different articles of importation, were confined to a few of the most general use and consumption, and if the levying of those duties were subjected to the excise laws, the opportunity of smuggling, though not so entirely taken away, would be very much diminished. In consequence of those two apparently very simple and easy alterations, the duties of customs and excise might probably produce a revenue as great, in proportion to the consumption of the most thinly inhabited province, as they do at present, in proportion to that of the most populous.

The Americans, it has been said, indeed, have no gold or silver money, the interior commerce of the country being carried on by a paper currency; and the gold and silver, which occasionally come among them, being all sent to Great Britain, in return for the commodities which they receive from us. But without gold and silver, it is added, there is no possibility of paying taxes. We already get all the gold and silver which they have. How is it possible to draw from them what they have not?

The present scarcity of gold and silver money in America, is not the effect of the poverty of that country, or of the inability of the people there to purchase those metals. In a country where the wages of labor are so much higher, and the price of provisions so much lower than in England, the greater part of the people must surely have wherewithal to purchase a greater quantity, if it were either necessary or convenient for them to do so. The scarcity of those metals, therefore, must be the effect of choice, and not of necessity.

It is for transacting either domestic or foreign business, that gold or silver money is either necessary or convenient.

The domestic business of every country, it has been shown in the second book of this inquiry, may, at least in peaceable times, be transacted by means of a paper currency, with nearly the same degree of convenience as by gold and silver money. It is convenient for the Americans, who could always employ with profit, in the improvement of their lands, a greater stock than they can easily get, to save as much as possible the expense of so costly an instrument of commerce as gold and silver; and rather to employ that part of their surplus produce which would be necessary for purchasing those metals, in purchasing the instruments of trade, the materials of clothing, several parts of household furniture, and the iron work necessary for building and extending their settlements and plantations; in purchasing not dead stock, but active and productive stock. The colony governments find it for their interest to supply the people with such a quantity of paper money as is fully sufficient, and generally more than sufficient, for transacting their domestic business. Some of those governments, that of Pennsylvania, particularly, derive a revenue from lending this paper money to their subjects, at an interest of so much percent. Others, like that of Massachusetts Bay, advance, upon extraordinary emergencies, a paper money of this kind for defraying the public expense; and afterwards, when it suits the convenience of the colony, redeem it at the depreciated value to which it gradually falls. In 1747, {See Hutchinson's *History of Massachusetts Bay* vol. ii. page 436 et seq.} that colony paid in this manner the greater part of its public debts, with the tenth part of the money for which its bills had been granted. It suits the convenience of the planters, to save the expense of employing gold and silver money in their domestic transactions; and it suits the convenience of the colony governments, to supply them with a medium, which, though attended with some very considerable disadvantages, enables them to save that expense. The redundancy of paper money necessarily banishes gold and silver from the domestic transactions of the colonies, for the same reason that it has banished those metals from the greater part of the domestic transactions in Scotland; and in both countries, it is not the poverty, but the enterprising and projecting spirit of the people, their desire of employing all the stock which they can get, as active and productive stock, which has occasioned this redundancy of paper money.

In the exterior commerce which the different colonies carry on with Great Britain, gold and silver are more or less employed, exactly in proportion as they are more or less necessary. Where those metals are not necessary, they seldom appear. Where they are necessary, they are generally found.

In the commerce between Great Britain and the tobacco colonies, the British goods are generally advanced to the colonists at a pretty long credit, and are afterwards paid for in tobacco, rated at a certain price. It is more convenient for the colonists to pay in tobacco than in gold and silver. It would be more convenient for any merchant to pay for the goods which his correspondents had sold to him, in some other sort of goods which he might happen to deal in, than in money. Such a merchant would have no occasion to keep any part of his stock by him unemployed, and in ready money, for answering occasional demands. He could have, at all times, a larger quantity of goods in his shop or warehouse, and he could deal to a greater extent. But it seldom happens to be convenient for all the correspondents of a merchant to receive payment for the goods which they sell to him, in goods of some other kind which he happens to deal in. The British merchants who trade to Virginia and Maryland, happen to be a particular set of correspondents, to whom it is more convenient to receive payment for the goods which they sell to those colonies in tobacco, than in gold and silver. They expect to make a profit by the sale of the tobacco; they could make none by that of the gold and silver. Gold and silver, therefore, very seldom appear in the commerce between Great Britain and the tobacco colonies. Maryland and Virginia have as little occasion for those metals in their foreign, as in their domestic commerce. They are said, accordingly, to have less gold and silver money than any other colonies in America. They are reckoned, however, as thriving, and consequently as rich, as any of their neighbors.

In the northern colonies, Pennsylvania, New York, New Jersey, the four governments of New England, etc. the value of their own produce which they export to Great Britain is not equal to that of the manufactures which they import for their own use, and for that of some of the other colonies, to which they are the carriers. A balance, therefore, must be paid to the mother-country in gold and silver and this balance they generally find.

In the sugar colonies, the value of the produce annually exported to Great Britain is much greater than that of all the goods imported from thence. If the sugar and rum annually sent to the mother-country were paid for in those colonies, Great Britain would be obliged to send out, every year, a very large balance in money; and the trade to the West Indies would, by a certain species of politicians, be considered as extremely disadvantageous. But it so happens, that many of the principal proprietors of the sugar plantations reside in Great Britain. Their rents are remitted to them in sugar and rum, the produce of their estates. The sugar and rum which the West India merchants purchase in those colonies upon their own account, are not equal in value to the goods which they annually sell there. A balance, therefore, must necessarily be paid to them in gold and silver, and this balance, too, is generally found.

The difficulty and irregularity of payment from the different colonies to Great Britain, have not been at all in proportion to the greatness or smallness of the balances which were respectively due from them. Payments have, in general, been more regular from the northern than from the tobacco colonies, though the former have generally paid a pretty large balance in money, while the latter have either paid no balance, or a much smaller one. The difficulty of getting payment from our different sugar colonies has been greater or less in proportion, not so much to the extent of the balances respectively due from them, as to the quantity of uncultivated land which they contained; that is, to the greater or smaller temptation which the planters have been under of over-trading, or of undertaking the settlement and plantation of greater quantities of waste land than suited the extent of their capitals. The returns from the great island of Jamaica, where there is still much uncultivated land, have, upon this account, been, in general, more irregular and uncertain than those from the smaller islands of Barbados, Antigua, and St. Christopher's, which have, for these many years, been completely cultivated, and have, upon that account, afforded less field for the speculations of the planter. The new acquisitions of Grenada, Tobago, St. Vincent's, and Dominica, have opened a new field for speculations of this kind; and the returns from those islands have of late been as irregular and uncertain as those from the great island of Jamaica.

It is not, therefore, the poverty of the colonies which occasions, in the greater part of them, the present scarcity of gold and silver money. Their great demand for active and productive stock makes it convenient for them to have as little dead stock as possible, and disposes them, upon that account, to content themselves with a cheaper, though less commodious instrument of commerce, than gold and silver. They are thereby enabled to convert the value of that gold and silver into the instruments of trade, into the materials of clothing, into household furniture, and into the iron work necessary for building and extending their settlements and plantations. In those branches of business which cannot be transacted without gold and silver money, it appears, that they can always find the necessary quantity of those metals; and if they frequently do not find it, their failure is generally the effect, not of their necessary poverty, but of their unnecessary and excessive enterprise. It is not because they are poor that their payments are irregular and uncertain, but because they are too eager to become excessively rich.

Though all that part of the produce of the colony taxes, which was over and above what was necessary for defraying the expense of their own civil and military establishments, were to be remitted to Great Britain in gold and silver, the colonies have abundantly wherewithal to purchase the requisite quantity of those metals. They would in this case be obliged, indeed, to exchange a part of their surplus produce, with which they now purchase active and productive stock, for dead stock. In transacting their domestic business, they would be obliged to employ a costly, instead of a cheap instrument of commerce; and the expense of purchasing this costly instrument might damp somewhat the vivacity and ardor of their excessive enterprise in the improvement of land. It might not, however, be necessary to remit any part of the American revenue in gold and silver. It might be remitted in bills drawn upon, and accepted by, particular merchants or companies in Great Britain, to whom a part of the surplus produce of America had been consigned, who would pay into the treasury the American revenue in money, after having themselves received the value of it in goods; and the whole business might frequently be transacted without exporting a single ounce of gold or silver from America.

It is not contrary to justice, that both Ireland and America should contribute towards the discharge of the public debt of Great Britain. That debt has been contracted in support of the government established by the Revolution; a government to which the Protestants of Ireland owe, not only the whole authority which they at present enjoy in their own country, but every security which they possess for their liberty, their property, and their religion; a government to which several of the colonies of America owe their present charters, and consequently their present constitution; and to which all the colonies of America owe the liberty, security, and property, which they have ever since enjoyed. That public debt has been contracted in the defense, not of Great Britain alone, but of all the different provinces of the empire. The immense debt contracted in the late war in particular, and a great part of that contracted in the war before, were both properly contracted in defense of America.

By a union with Great Britain, Ireland would gain, besides the freedom of trade, other advantages much more important, and which would much more than compensate any increase of taxes that might accompany that union. By the union with England, the middling and inferior ranks of people in Scotland gained a complete deliverance from the power of an aristocracy, which had always before oppressed them. By a union with Great Britain, the greater part of people of all ranks in Ireland would gain an equally complete deliverance from a much more oppressive aristocracy; an aristocracy not founded, like that of Scotland, in the natural and respectable distinctions of birth and fortune, but in the most odious of all distinctions, those of religious and political prejudices; distinctions which, more than any other, animate both the insolence of the oppressors, and the hatred and indignation of the oppressed, and which commonly render the inhabitants of the same country more hostile to one another than those of different countries ever are. Without a union with Great Britain, the inhabitants of Ireland are not likely, for many ages, to consider themselves as one people.

No oppressive aristocracy has ever prevailed in the colonies. Even they, however, would, in point of happiness and tranquility, gain considerably by a union with Great Britain. It would, at least, deliver them from those rancorous and virulent factions which are inseparable from small democracies, and which have so frequently divided the affections of their people, and disturbed the tranquility of their governments, in their form so nearly democratical. In the case of a total separation from Great Britain, which, unless prevented by a union of this kind, seems very likely to take place, those factions would be ten times more virulent than ever. Before the commencement of the present disturbances, the coercive power of the mother-country had always been able to restrain those factions from breaking out into any thing worse than gross brutality and insult. If that coercive power were entirely taken away, they would probably soon break out into open violence and bloodshed. In all great countries which are united under one uniform government, the spirit of party commonly prevails less in the remote provinces than in the center of the empire. The distance of those provinces from the capital, from the principal seat of the great scramble of faction and ambition, makes them enter less into the views of any of the contending parties, and renders them more indifferent and impartial spectators of the conduct of all. The spirit of party prevails less in Scotland than in England. In the case of a union, it would probably prevail less in Ireland than in Scotland; and the colonies would probably soon enjoy a degree of concord and unanimity, at present unknown in any part of the British empire. Both Ireland and the colonies, indeed, would be subjected to heavier taxes than any which they at present pay. In consequence, however, of a diligent and faithful application of the public revenue towards the discharge of the national debt, the greater part of those taxes might not be of long continuance, and the public revenue of Great Britain might soon be reduced to what was necessary for maintaining a moderate peace-establishment.

The territorial acquisitions of the East India Company, the undoubted right of the crown, that is, of the state and people of Great Britain, might be rendered another source of revenue, more abundant, perhaps, than all those already mentioned. Those countries are represented as more fertile, more extensive, and, in proportion to their extent, much richer and more populous than Great Britain. In order to draw a great revenue from them, it would not probably be necessary to introduce any new system of taxation into countries which are already sufficiently, and more than sufficiently, taxed. It might, perhaps, be more proper to lighten than to aggravate the burden of those unfortunate countries, and to endeavor to draw a revenue from them, not by imposing new taxes, but by preventing the embezzlement and misapplication of the greater part of those which they already pay.

If it should be found impracticable for Great Britain to draw any considerable augmentation of revenue from any of the resources above mentioned, the only resource which can remain to her, is a diminution of her expense. In the mode of collecting and in that of expending the public revenue, though in both there may be still room for improvement, Great Britain seems to be at least as economical as any of her neighbors. The military establishment which she maintains for her own defense in time of peace, is more moderate than that of any European state, which can pretend to rival her either in wealth or in power. None of these articles, therefore, seem to admit of any considerable reduction of expense. The expense of the peace-establishment of the colonies was, before the commencement of the present disturbances, very considerable, and is an expense which may, and, if no revenue can be drawn from them, ought certainly to be saved altogether.

This constant expense in time of peace, though very great, is insignificant in comparison with what the defense of the colonies has cost us in time of war. The last war, which was undertaken altogether on account of the colonies, cost Great Britain, it has already been observed, upwards of ninety millions. The Spanish war of 1739 was principally undertaken on their account; in which, and in the French war that was the consequence of it, Great Britain, spent upwards of forty millions; a great part of which ought justly to be charged to the colonies. In those two wars, the colonies cost Great Britain much more than double the sum which the national debt amounted to before the commencement of the first of them. Had it not been for those wars, that debt might, and probably would by this time, have been completely paid; and had it not been for the colonies, the former of those wars might not, and the latter certainly would not, have been undertaken. It was because the colonies were supposed to be provinces of the British empire, that this expense was laid out upon them. But countries which contribute neither revenue nor military force towards the support of the empire, cannot be considered as provinces. They may, perhaps, be considered as appendages, as a sort of splendid and showy equipage of the empire. But if the empire can no longer support the expense of keeping up this equipage, it ought certainly to lay it down; and if it cannot raise its revenue in proportion to its expense, it ought at least to accommodate its expense to its revenue. If the colonies, notwithstanding their refusal to submit to British taxes, are still to be considered as provinces of the British empire, their defense, in some future war, may cost Great Britain as great an expense as it ever has done in any former war. The rulers of Great Britain have, for more than a century past, amused the people with the imagination that they possessed a great empire on the west side of the Atlantic. This empire, however, has hitherto existed in imagination only. It has hitherto been, not an empire, but the project of an empire; not a gold mine, but the project of a gold mine; a project which has cost, which continues to cost, and which, if pursued in the same way as it has been hitherto, is likely to cost, immense expense, without being likely to bring any profit; for the effects of the monopoly of the colony trade, it has been shown, are to the great body of the people, mere loss instead of profit. It is surely now time that our rulers should either realize this golden dream, in which they have been indulging themselves, perhaps, as well as the people; or that they should awake from it themselves, and endeavor to awaken the people. If the project cannot be completed, it ought to be given up. If any of the provinces of the British empire cannot be made to contribute towards the support of the whole empire, it is surely time that Great Britain should free herself from the expense of defending those provinces in time of war, and of supporting any part of their civil or military establishment in time of peace; and endeavor to accommodate her future views and designs to the real mediocrity of her circumstances.

Thomas Robert Malthus (1766–1834)

INTRODUCTION

For a thinker whose theories were dismissed on moral grounds over two centuries ago and supposedly disenfranchised in the middle of the last century by advances in technology, Thomas Robert Malthus remains oddly and uncomfortably relevant.

Malthus's theories on population dynamics changed the course of economics and raised serious questions about the future course of humanity. Despite being dismissed by his generation and every generation since, those questions still loom large. Their answers will likely emerge or perhaps erupt in this generation as humanity is finally forced to confront the limits of population expansion and the role that economics plays in the process.

HIS LIFE

Thomas Robert Malthus was born in 1766 in Dorking, England into a prosperous family. The family's home was known as "The Rookery," and played host to many of the era's leading thinkers, including Hume and Rousseau, both friends of Malthus's father, Daniel, a country gentleman and intellectual.

Born with a cleft palate, a hare lip, and a speech impediment, Malthus was schooled at home until 1784, when he enrolled in Jesus College at the prestigious University of Cambridge. He studied Latin, Greek, declamation, and mathematics on his way to earning a master's degree in 1791. He was named a fellow at Jesus College and became an ordained minister of the Church of England during his time at school.

In 1796, Malthus was sent to serve a small, impoverished country parish in Albury. His tenure in Albury brought him for the first time into sustained contact with the lower class. Though his stay there was brief, it would greatly affect his views on poverty throughout his career.

Malthus applied those views in friendly arguments with his father, contesting the elder Malthus's utopian notions about humanity and the future of society. Malthus committed his ideas about poverty and the effects of population on society and economy in 1798 with the limited publication of *An Essay on the Principle of Population*. He revised the work and published an expanded version of his *Essay* in 1803, an event that won him great renown and greater infamy.

In 1804, Malthus married Harriet Eckersail and was forced to forfeit his religious position at Cambridge. The marriage, a happy one by all accounts, lasted the rest of his life and eventually produced three children.

The following year, Malthus became England's first official professor of political economy when he assumed the newly created position at the East India Company College in Haileybury. He was well-regarded by his fellow faculty members and students, who dubbed him "Pop," short for "population," still his favorite topic of discussion. Malthus did write books on a number of other topics, including *Principles of Political Economy Considered with a View to Their Practical Application and an Inquiry into the Nature and Progress of Rent* (1815).

He accumulated many honors during his lifetime, including a fellowship at the Royal Society in 1819 and a seat on the Political Economy Club with his friend David Ricardo, as well as being named as one of the ten associates of the Royal Society of Literature in 1824. In 1833, Malthus was elected to the French Academy of Moral and Political Sciences and to the Royal Academy of Berlin. The following year, he co-founded the Statistical Society of London.

Malthus died in 1834 and was buried at Bath Abbey in England.

AN ESSAY ON POPULATION

Thomas Malthus wrote extensively on a number of economic issues over the course of his long and prestigious life. But his first large-scale effort, *An Essay on the Principle of Population*, remains by far his most well-known and influential work. Indeed, it still ranks as one of the most important books on economics ever written.

First published in 1798, *Essay* examined the dynamics between population, production, and prosperity. In doing so, the work cast serious doubts about utopian notions then coming into vogue with the spread of Romanticism across Europe. Malthus's full title, *An Essay on the Principle of Population, as It Affects the Future Improvement of Society with Remarks on the Speculations of Mr. Godwin, M. Condorcet, and Other Writers*, even singled out leading Romantic theorists Marquis de Condorcet and William Godwin, a friend of Malthus's father, Daniel.

Like many learned men of their era, Godwin and the elder Malthus believed in "human perfectibility"—the notion that scientific progress would eventually elevate humanity to a state of perpetual material abundance and moral harmony. But Thomas Malthus held that population pressures would always frustrate civilization's efforts to sustain peace and widespread prosperity. Impressed by his son's reasoning and intellectual vigor, Daniel Malthus urged him to put his arguments in writing.

Others, including Benjamin Franklin, had already written about their concerns with population growth. But Malthus was the first to begin with the simple, irrefutable premise that "Population is necessarily limited by means of subsistence," and follow it to its logical and often unpleasant conclusions. In doing so, he forever changed the way people thought about population, economics, human potential, and the future.

A trained mathematician, Malthus added a simple, yet unsettling pair of mathematical formulas to the premise. He noted that food production tends to increase at a linear rate (1 to 2 to 3 to 4 to 5 to 6 to 7 to 8 to 9) but that human population, if unchecked, expands at an exponential, or doubling, rate (1 to 2 to 4 to 8 to 16 to 32 to 64 to 128 to 256). Considering the long-term implications of these two formulas (i.e., 9 < 256), Malthus concluded that, unless humanity aggressively addressed population growth, it faced imminent and recurring famine.

Mass starvation would reduce the population until it fell back in line with the food supply. But the equilibrium would not last long. The differing rates of growth between population and food supply—along with what Malthus saw as humanity's tendency to procreate beyond its capacity to feed itself—would again exert themselves and skew the situation dangerously out of balance. The result? Another famine, another population decline, another temporary equilibrium, another spurt in population growth, another famine, et cetera. Malthus believed this cycle of growth and retraction had occurred, to one degree or another, throughout human history and would continue to play an important role in the future.

Malthus contended that the population-subsistence dynamic must eventually return to equilibrium. It was just a question of which path it took to get there and who would lead the way. Society could pull it along a kinder, gentler route through rational, proactive, preventative measures to slow birth rates. But if society failed to act, nature and the darker parts of human nature would drag population numbers down swiftly and dramatically through disease, war, and famine.

Malthus spends much of *Essay* exploring the preventative or proactive checks that societies could undertake to slow population growth. But he expressed deep skepticism about whether people could exercise enough foresight and discipline for such measures to succeed.

Malthus's friends and fellow intellectuals reacted to these theories with a skepticism of their own after the first publication of his *Essay* in 1798. Malthus responded by gathering evidence to support his theories from historians and the accounts of explorers. He also became perhaps the first economic thinker to collect extensive field data, traveling through Europe for several years to gather whatever information he could find on population histories and dynamics.

THE SECOND EDITION

In 1803, Malthus presented his new evidence in a muscled up version of *An Essay on the Principle of Population*. Though he continued revising the work, ultimately producing six editions, the 1803 effort still stands as the definitive version.

In this second edition, Malthus discussed at length another possible check on population—"moral restraint." While performing research in Scandinavia, Malthus became impressed by the region's low death rates, low birth rates, and relatively stable population figures. He credited various social customs and laws that encouraged abstinence and late marriage for helping the region achieve population equilibrium without the usual brutal enforcers of war, disease, and famine.

Malthus practiced what he preached, not marrying until he was almost forty, and then fathering only three children, a small brood by the standards of his day. He felt that other members of the upper and middle classes would also limit their family sizes to sustain their higher standards of living. But based on his years working at an impoverished country parish in England, he doubted that the poor would follow suit.

Malthus believed that the lower class would always have difficulty limiting their number of offspring. And he believed that civilization would always have difficulty limiting the size of the lower class and in improving their standard of living.

Though he admired Godwin's vision of a peaceful, egalitarian world where everyone lived in peace and prosperity, Malthus believed population growth would quickly undermine any such utopia. He argued that universal equality and abundance would lead to an explosion in the birth rate, which would lead to a lower standard of living and the reemergence of a lower class.

Malthus posited that increases in population would also lead to a glut in the labor supply, driving down wages at the same time food prices were rising due to higher demands from a larger population. He believed working-class wages would ultimately always hover at the subsistence level. If they rose, workers would respond by producing more children, which would lead to a glut in the labor market, which would drive wages back down to subsistence levels. If wages fell below the subsistence level, workers would perish from want and produce less children, bringing down their numbers and leading to an increase in their wages back to subsistence levels.

Malthus advocated for universal education to help the poor, but lobbied vigorously against England's Poor Laws, which had provided Britain's underclass with government assistance for centuries. Malthus believed that such subsidies encouraged poor parents to increase the size of their families beyond their ability to support it. In addition to swelling the population, Malthus felt such government assistance artificially inflated the price of food by making more money available for its purchase. The increased price of food would force more people to seek government assistance, further perpetuating the problem.

MALTHUS'S IMPACT

Though his original *Essay* met mostly with polite skepticism and mild interest from his fellow intellectuals, Malthus found himself almost universally denounced after the publication of the revised edition. Many declaimed the work as the doom and gloom prophecies of an angry madman. The book's views on the lower class inspired many more to accuse Malthus of being a cruel, uncaring monster and elitist.

Romantic poet Percy Shelley, a leading voice of the age who would later become Godwin's son-in-law, produced a pamphlet denouncing Malthus as a "tyrant" and a "eunuch." They were curious assessments, considering Malthus's character and family circumstances, not to mention Shelley's usually genial and relatively reasonable nature. But Malthus's theories on population had that effect on people, as many others echoed Shelley's virulent anti-Malthus sentiments.

The disdain did not fade with time. Over a half-century after its publication, Karl Marx's benefactor and writing partner, Friedrich Engels, reviled Malthus's *Essay* as "the crudest, most barbarous theory that ever existed." Still, Malthus's work impressed many of the best minds of his day and in subsequent eras, leading to some vital breakthroughs in economics, politics, demography, and biological science.

In the decades and centuries that followed the publication of *Essay*, many of history's most important economic thinkers—including David Ricardo, John Stuart Mill, and John Maynard Keynes—cited Malthus as a major influence in their work. Even Marx paid tribute to Malthus as the first thinker to seriously address the plight of the lower class and employed Malthusian notions into his theory of social determinism. Perhaps most astonishingly and significantly of all, Charles Darwin revealed that he came up with his theory of natural selection and the concept of evolution while reading Malthus's *Essay*.

An Essay on the Principle of Population also made a deep impact on government policy. Under Prime Minister William Pitt the Younger, an admirer of Malthus, England scaled back its long-standing Poor Laws in 1834. Similar arguments and results resurfaced a century and a half later, when Britain and the United States began downsizing their social welfare systems in the 1980s.

Essay's most immediate impact came in 1801 when Great Britain launched its first census. The nation completed another census every ten years, a practice they continue to this day along with every other developed country in the world. The field of demographics was formally established and the results showed that England's population was indeed growing just as rapidly as Malthus predicted.

The Malthusian catastrophe of famine and mass death, however, did not occur as a result of England's population boom. Food production and the standard of living in England improved steadily and sometimes dramatically over time, while its birth rate leveled off. Most of the rest of the industrialized world has also managed to avoid famine by promoting birth control, agricultural improvements, higher standards of living, and the limitation of family size. That success has prompted many to dismiss Malthus as "wrong" and largely irrelevant. Yet the Malthusian nightmare of disease, war, and mass starvation swept across Africa during the past century, and still looms large over much of the Third World. Efforts by Western nations to banish hunger from the Third World met with initial "success," but ultimately pointed back to Malthus and the potential for failure on a larger scale.

The industrialized world escaped famine over the last two centuries in large part by greatly expanding agricultural outputs through the use of technology and new farming techniques. Fertilizers, pesticides, tractors, and other mechanized farming equipment was exported to the Third Word as part of the Green Revolution in the middle of the last century. Crop yields increased dramatically and many declared hunger extinct, along with the theories of Thomas Malthus. But the years that followed showed that the Malthusian catastrophe had only been temporarily delayed, and perhaps increased in its potential scope. While the Green Revolution's introduction of tractors and chemicals to Third World farming did increase crop outputs, it also decreased the need for human labor. A tractor and driver could do the work of one hundred laborers, which pretty much meant that every tractor introduced put ninety-nine people out of work. These unemployed streamed into Third World cities looking for work. Living at closer quarters and removed from their traditional social structures, their birth rates skyrocketed.

At the same time, the new agricultural techniques that had displaced these people, along with the increased urban populations, caused a massive spike in pollution, further straining the land's capacity to support the new, larger population. Indeed, environmental degradation caused by population growth and the technologies applied to accommodate billions of people on the earth seem to be hurtling humanity toward a global-wide Malthusian showdown with our capacity to sustain ourselves and the catastrophes that erupt when we grow beyond that capacity. The outcome could depend, in part, on people's ability to put aside their disdain and instead embrace the ideas of Thomas Malthus on managing population growth.

AN ESSAY ON THE PRINCIPLE OF POPULATION, AS IT AFFECTS THE FUTURE IMPROVEMENT OF SOCIETY WITH REMARKS ON THE SPECULATIONS OF MR. GODWIN, M. CONDORCET, AND OTHER WRITERS, SECOND EDITION

BY THOMAS ROBERT MALTHUS

Preface

The following Essay owes its origin to a conversation with a friend, on the subject of Mr. Godwin's essay on avarice and profusion, in his Enquirer. The discussion started the general question of the future improvement of society, and the Author at first sat down with an intention of merely stating his thoughts to his friend, upon paper, in a clearer manner than he thought he could do in conversation. But as the subject opened upon him, some ideas occurred, which he did not recollect to have met with before; and as he conceived that every least light, on a topic so generally interesting, might be received with candor, he determined to put his thoughts in a form for publication.

The Essay might, undoubtedly, have been rendered much more complete by a collection of a greater number of facts in elucidation of the general argument. But a long and almost total interruption from very particular business, joined to a desire (perhaps imprudent) of not delaying the publication much beyond the time that he originally proposed, prevented the Author from giving to the subject an undivided attention. He presumes, however, that the facts which he has adduced will be found to form no inconsiderable evidence for the truth of his opinion respecting the future improvement of mankind. As the Author contemplates this opinion at present, little more appears to him to be necessary than a plain statement, in addition to the most cursory view of society, to establish it.

It is an obvious truth, which has been taken notice of by many writers, that population must always be kept down to the level of the means of subsistence; but no writer that the Author recollects has inquired particularly into the means by which this level is effected: and it is a view of these means which forms, to his mind, the strongest obstacle in the way to any very great future improvement of society. He hopes it will appear that, in the discussion of this interesting subject, he is actuated solely by a love of truth, and not by any prejudices against any particular set of men, or of opinions. He professes to have read some of the speculations on the future improvement of society in a temper very different from a wish to find them visionary, but he has not acquired that command over his understanding which would enable him to believe what he wishes, without evidence, or to refuse his assent to what might be unpleasing, when accompanied with evidence.

The view which he has given of human life has a melancholy hue, but he feels conscious that he has drawn these dark tints from a conviction that they are really in the picture, and not from a jaundiced eye or an inherent spleen of disposition. The theory of mind which he has sketched in the two last chapters accounts to his own understanding in a satisfactory manner for the existence of most of the evils of life, but whether it will have the same effect upon others must be left to the judgment of his readers.

If he should succeed in drawing the attention of more able men to what he conceives to be the principal difficulty in the way to the improvement of society and should, in consequence, see this difficulty removed, even in theory, he will gladly retract his present opinions and rejoice in a conviction of his error.

7 June 1798

CHAPTER 1

Question Stated—Little Prospect of a Determination of it, From the Enmity of the Opposing Parties—The Principal Argument Against the Perfectibility of Man and of Society has never been Fairly Answered—Nature of the Difficulty Arising from Population—Outline of the Principal Argument of the Essay.

The great and unlooked for discoveries that have taken place of late years in natural philosophy, the increasing diffusion of general knowledge from the extension of the art of printing, the ardent and unshackled spirit of inquiry that prevails throughout the lettered and even unlettered world, the new and extraordinary lights that have been thrown on political subjects which dazzle and astonish the understanding, and particularly that tremendous phenomenon in the political horizon, the French Revolution, which, like a blazing comet, seems destined either to inspire with fresh life and vigor, or to scorch up and destroy the shrinking inhabitants of the earth, have all concurred to lead many able men into the opinion that we were touching on a period big with the most important changes, changes that would in some measure be decisive of the future fate of mankind.

It has been said that the great question is now at issue, whether man shall henceforth start forwards with accelerated velocity towards illimitable, and hitherto unconceived improvement, or be condemned to a perpetual oscillation between happiness and misery, and after every effort remain still at an immeasurable distance from the wished-for goal.

Yet, anxiously as every friend of mankind must look forwards to the termination of this painful suspense, and eagerly as the inquiring mind would hail every ray of light that might assist its view into futurity, it is much to be lamented that the writers on each side of this momentous question still keep far aloof from each other. Their mutual arguments do not meet with a candid examination. The question is not brought to rest on fewer points, and even in theory scarcely seems to be approaching to a decision.

The advocate for the present order of things is apt to treat the sect of speculative philosophers either as a set of artful and designing knaves who preach up ardent benevolence and draw captivating pictures of a happier state of society only the better to enable them to destroy the present establishments and to forward their own deep-laid schemes of ambition, or as wild and mad-headed enthusiasts whose silly speculations and absurd paradoxes are not worthy the attention of any reasonable man.

The advocate for the perfectibility of man, and of society, retorts on the defender of establishments a more than equal contempt. He brands him as the slave of the most miserable and narrow prejudices; or as the defender of the abuses of civil society only because he profits by them. He paints him either as a character who prostitutes his understanding to his interest, or as one whose powers of mind are not of a size to grasp any thing great and noble, who cannot see above five yards before him, and who must therefore be utterly unable to take in the views of the enlightened benefactor of mankind.

In this unamicable contest the cause of truth cannot but suffer. The really good arguments on each side of the question are not allowed to have their proper weight. Each pursues his own theory, little solicitous to correct or improve it by an attention to what is advanced by his opponents.

The friend of the present order of things condemns all political speculations in the gross. He will not even condescend to examine the grounds from which the perfectibility of society is inferred. Much less will he give himself the trouble in a fair and candid manner to attempt an exposition of their fallacy.

The speculative philosopher equally offends against the cause of truth. With eyes fixed on a happier state of society, the blessings of which he paints in the most captivating colors, he allows himself to indulge in the most bitter invectives against every present establishment, without applying his talents to consider the best and safest means of removing abuses and without seeming to be aware of the tremendous obstacles that threaten, even in theory, to oppose the progress of man towards perfection.

It is an acknowledged truth in philosophy that a just theory will always be confirmed by experiment. Yet so much friction, and so many minute circumstances occur in practice, which it is next to impossible for the most enlarged and penetrating mind to foresee, that on few subjects can any theory be pronounced just, till all the arguments against it have been maturely weighed and clearly and consistently refuted.

I have read some of the speculations on the perfectibility of man and of society with great pleasure. I have been warmed and delighted with the enchanting picture which they hold forth. I ardently wish for such happy improvements. But I see great, and, to my understanding, unconquerable difficulties in the way to them. These difficulties it is my present purpose to state, declaring, at the same time, that so far from exulting in them, as a cause of triumph over the friends of innovation, nothing would give me greater pleasure than to see them completely removed.

The most important argument that I shall adduce is certainly not new. The principles on which it depends have been explained in part by Hume, and more at large by Dr. Adam Smith. It has been advanced and applied to the present subject, though not with its proper weight, or in the most forcible point of view, by Mr. Wallace, and it may probably have been stated by many writers that I have never met with. I should certainly therefore not think of advancing it again, though I mean to place it in a point of view in some degree different from any that I have hitherto seen, if it had ever been fairly and satisfactorily answered.

The cause of this neglect on the part of the advocates for the perfectibility of mankind is not easily accounted for. I cannot doubt the talents of such men as Godwin and Condorcet. I am unwilling to doubt their candor. To my understanding, and probably to that of most others, the difficulty appears insurmountable. Yet these men of acknowledged ability and penetration scarcely deign to notice it, and hold on their course in such speculations with unabated ardor and undiminished confidence. I have certainly no right to say that they purposely shut their eyes to such arguments. I ought rather to doubt the validity of them, when neglected by such men, however forcibly their truth may strike my own mind. Yet in this respect it must be acknowledged that we are all of us too prone to err. If I saw a glass of wine repeatedly presented to a man, and he took no notice of it, I should be apt to think that he was blind or uncivil. A juster philosophy might teach me rather to think that my eyes deceived me and that the offer was not really what I conceived it to be.

In entering upon the argument I must premise that I put out of the question, at present, all mere conjectures, that is, all suppositions, the probable realization of which cannot be inferred upon any just philosophical grounds. A writer may tell me that he thinks man will ultimately become an ostrich. I cannot properly contradict him. But before he can expect to bring any reasonable person over to his opinion, he ought to show that the necks of mankind have been gradually elongating, that the lips have grown harder and more prominent, that the legs and feet are daily altering their shape, and that the hair is beginning to change into stubs of feathers. And till the probability of so wonderful a conversion can be shown, it is surely lost time and lost eloquence to expatiate on the happiness of man in such a state; to describe his powers, both of running and flying, to paint him in a condition where all narrow luxuries would be contemned, where he would be employed only in collecting the necessaries of life, and where, consequently, each man's share of labor would be light, and his portion of leisure ample.

I think I may fairly make two postulata.

First, that food is necessary to the existence of man.

Secondly, that the passion between the sexes is necessary and will remain nearly in its present state.

These two laws, ever since we have had any knowledge of mankind, appear to have been fixed laws of our nature, and, as we have not hitherto seen any alteration in them, we have no right to conclude that they will ever cease to be what they now are, without an immediate act of power in that Being who first arranged the system of the universe, and for the advantage of his creatures, still executes, according to fixed laws, all its various operations.

I do not know that any writer has supposed that on this earth man will ultimately be able to live without food. But Mr. Godwin has conjectured that the passion between the sexes may in time be extinguished. As, however, he calls this part of his work a deviation into the land of conjecture, I will not dwell longer upon it at present than to say that the best arguments for the perfectibility of man are drawn from a contemplation of the great progress that he has already made from the savage state and the difficulty of saying where he is to stop. But towards the extinction of the passion between the sexes, no progress whatever has hitherto been made. It appears to exist in as much force at present as it did two thousand or four thousand years ago. There are individual exceptions now as there always have been. But, as these exceptions do not appear to increase in number, it would surely be a very unphilosophical mode of arguing to infer, merely from the existence of an exception, that the exception would, in time, become the rule, and the rule the exception.

Assuming then my postulata as granted, I say, that the power of population is indefinitely greater than the power in the earth to produce subsistence for man.

Population, when unchecked, increases in a geometrical ratio. Subsistence increases only in an arithmetical ratio. A slight acquaintance with numbers will show the immensity of the first power in comparison of the second.

By that law of our nature which makes food necessary to the life of man, the effects of these two unequal powers must be kept equal.

This implies a strong and constantly operating check on population from the difficulty of subsistence. This difficulty must fall somewhere and must necessarily be severely felt by a large portion of mankind.

Through the animal and vegetable kingdoms, nature has scattered the seeds of life abroad with the most profuse and liberal hand. She has been comparatively sparing in the room and the nourishment necessary to rear them. The germs of existence contained in this spot of earth, with ample food, and ample room to expand in, would fill millions of worlds in the course of a few thousand years. Necessity, that imperious all pervading law of nature, restrains them within the prescribed bounds. The race of plants and the race of animals shrink under this great restrictive law. And the race of man cannot, by any efforts of reason, escape from it. Among plants and animals its effects are waste of seed, sickness, and premature death. Among mankind, misery and vice. The former, misery, is an absolutely necessary consequence of it. Vice is a highly probable consequence, and we therefore see it abundantly prevail, but it ought not, perhaps, to be called an absolutely necessary consequence. The ordeal of virtue is to resist all temptation to evil.

This natural inequality of the two powers of population and of production in the earth, and that great law of our nature which must constantly keep their effects equal, form the great difficulty that to me appears insurmountable in the way to the perfectibility of society. All other arguments are of slight and subordinate consideration in comparison of this. I see no way by which man can escape from the weight of this law which pervades all animated nature. No fancied equality, no agrarian regulations in their utmost extent, could remove the pressure of it even for a single century. And it appears, therefore, to be decisive against the possible existence of a society, all the members of which should live in ease, happiness, and comparative leisure; and feel no anxiety about providing the means of subsistence for themselves and families.

Consequently, if the premises are just, the argument is conclusive against the perfectibility of the mass of mankind.

I have thus sketched the general outline of the argument, but I will examine it more particularly, and I think it will be found that experience, the true source and foundation of all knowledge, invariably confirms its truth.

CHAPTER 2

The Different Ratio in which Population and Food Increase—The Necessary Effects of these Different Ratios of Increase— Oscillation Produced by them in the Condition of the Lower Classes of Society— Reasons why this Oscillation has not been so much Observed as Might be Expected—Three Propositions on which the General Argument of the Essay Depends—The Different States in which Mankind have been Known to Exist Proposed to be Examined with Reference to These Three Propositions.

I said that population, when unchecked, increased in a geometrical ratio, and subsistence for man in an arithmetical ratio.

Let us examine whether this position be just. I think it will be allowed, that no state has hitherto existed (at least that we have any account of) where the manners were so pure and simple, and the means of subsistence so abundant, that no check whatever has existed to early marriages, among the lower classes, from a fear of not providing well for their families, or among the higher classes, from a fear of lowering their condition in life. Consequently in no state that we have yet known has the power of population been left to exert itself with perfect freedom.

Whether the law of marriage be instituted or not, the dictate of nature and virtue seems to be an early attachment to one woman. Supposing a liberty of changing in the case of an unfortunate choice, this liberty would not affect population till it arose to a height greatly vicious; and we are now supposing the existence of a society where vice is scarcely known.

In a state therefore of great equality and virtue, where pure and simple manners prevailed, and where the means of subsistence were so abundant that no part of the society could have any fears about providing amply for a family, the power of population being left to exert itself unchecked, the increase of the human species would evidently be much greater than any increase that has been hitherto known.

In the United States of America, where the means of subsistence have been more ample, the manners of the people more pure, and consequently the checks to early marriages fewer, than in any of the modern states of Europe, the population has been found to double itself in twenty-five years.

This ratio of increase, though short of the utmost power of population, yet as the result of actual experience, we will take as our rule, and say, that population, when unchecked, goes on doubling itself every twenty-five years or increases in a geometrical ratio.

Let us now take any spot of earth, this Island for instance, and see in what ratio the subsistence it affords can be supposed to increase. We will begin with it under its present state of cultivation.

If I allow that by the best possible policy, by breaking up more land and by great encouragements to agriculture, the produce of this Island may be doubled in the first twenty-five years, I think it will be allowing as much as any person can well demand.

In the next twenty-five years, it is impossible to suppose that the produce could be quadrupled. It would be contrary to all our knowledge of the qualities of land. The very utmost that we can conceive, is, that the increase in the second twenty-five years might equal the present produce. Let us then take this for our rule, though certainly far beyond the truth, and allow that, by great exertion, the whole produce of the Island might be increased every twenty-five years, by a quantity of subsistence equal to what it at present produces. The most enthusiastic speculator cannot suppose a greater increase than this. In a few centuries it would make every acre of land in the Island like a garden.

Yet this ratio of increase is evidently arithmetical.

It may be fairly said, therefore, that the means of subsistence increase in an arithmetical ratio. Let us now bring the effects of these two ratios together.

The population of the Island is computed to be about seven millions, and we will suppose the present produce equal to the support of such a number. In the first twenty-five years the population would be fourteen millions, and the food being also doubled, the means of subsistence would be equal to this increase. In the next twenty-five years the population would be twenty-eight millions, and the means of subsistence only equal to the support of twenty-one millions. In the next period, the population would be fifty-six millions, and the means of subsistence just sufficient for half that number. And at the conclusion of the first century the population would be one hundred and twelve millions and the means of subsistence only equal to the support of thirty-five millions, which would leave a population of seventy-seven millions totally unprovided for.

A great emigration necessarily implies unhappiness of some kind or other in the country that is deserted. For few persons will leave their families, connections, friends, and native land, to seek a settlement in untried foreign climes, without some strong subsisting causes of uneasiness where they are, or the hope of some great advantages in the place to which they are going.

But to make the argument more general and less interrupted by the partial views of emigration, let us take the whole earth, instead of one spot, and suppose that the restraints to population were universally removed. If the subsistence for man that the earth affords was to be increased every twenty-five years by a quantity equal to what the whole world at present produces, this would allow the power of production in the earth to be absolutely unlimited, and its ratio of increase much greater than we can conceive that any possible exertions of mankind could make it.

Taking the population of the world at any number, a thousand millions, for instance, the human species would increase in the ratio of—1, 2, 4, 8, 16, 32, 64, 128, 256, 512, etc. and subsistence as—1, 2, 3, 4, 5, 6, 7, 8, 9, 10, etc. In two centuries and a quarter, the population would be to the means of subsistence as 512 to 10: in three centuries as 4096 to 13, and in two thousand years the difference would be almost incalculable, though the produce in that time would have increased to an immense extent.

No limits whatever are placed to the productions of the earth; they may increase forever and be greater than any assignable quantity, yet still the power of population being a power of a superior order, the increase of the human species can only be kept commensurate to the increase of the means of subsistence by the constant operation of the strong law of necessity acting as a check upon the greater power.

The effects of this check remain now to be considered.

Among plants and animals the view of the subject is simple. They are all impelled by a powerful instinct to the increase of their species, and this instinct is interrupted by no reasoning or doubts about providing for their offspring. Wherever therefore there is liberty, the power of increase is exerted, and the superabundant effects are repressed afterwards by want of room and nourishment, which is common to animals and plants, and among animals by becoming the prey of others.

The effects of this check on man are more complicated. Impelled to the increase of his species by an equally powerful instinct, reason interrupts his career and asks him whether he may not bring beings into the world for whom he cannot provide the means of subsistence. In a state of equality, this would be the simple question. In the present state of society, other considerations occur. Will he not lower his rank in life? Will he not subject himself to greater difficulties than he at present feels? Will he not be obliged to labor harder? And if he has a large family, will his utmost exertions enable him to support them? May he not see his offspring in rags and misery, and clamoring for bread that he cannot give them? And may he not be reduced to the grating necessity of forfeiting his independence, and of being obliged to the sparing hand of charity for support?

These considerations are calculated to prevent, and certainly do prevent, a very great number in all civilized nations from pursuing the dictate of nature in an early attachment to one woman. And this restraint almost necessarily, though not absolutely so, produces vice. Yet in all societies, even those that are most vicious, the tendency to a virtuous attachment is so strong that there is a constant effort towards an increase of population. This constant effort as constantly tends to subject the lower classes of the society to distress and to prevent any great permanent amelioration of their condition.

The way in which these effects are produced seems to be this. We will suppose the means of subsistence in any country just equal to the easy support of its inhabitants. The constant effort towards population, which is found to act even in the most vicious societies, increases the number of people before the means of subsistence are increased. The food therefore which before supported seven millions must now be divided among seven millions and a half or eight millions. The poor consequently must live much worse, and many of them be reduced to severe distress. The number of laborers also being above the proportion of the work in the market, the price of labor must tend toward a decrease, while the price of provisions would at the same time tend to rise. The laborer therefore must work harder to earn the same as he did before. During this season of distress, the discouragements to marriage, and the difficulty of rearing a family are so great that population is at a stand. In the mean time the cheapness of labor, the plenty of laborers, and the necessity of an increased industry amongst them, encourage cultivators to employ more labor upon their land, to turn up fresh soil, and to manure and improve more completely what is already in tillage, till ultimately the means of subsistence become in the same proportion to the population as at the period from which we set out. The situation of the laborer being then again tolerably comfortable, the restraints to population are in some degree loosened, and the same retrograde and progressive movements with respect to happiness are repeated.

This sort of oscillation will not be remarked by superficial observers, and it may be difficult even for the most penetrating mind to calculate its periods. Yet that in all old states some such vibration does exist, though from various transverse causes, in a much less marked, and in a much more irregular manner than I have described it, no reflecting man who considers the subject deeply can well doubt.

Many reasons occur why this oscillation has been less obvious, and less decidedly confirmed by experience, than might naturally be expected.

One principal reason is that the histories of mankind that we possess are histories only of the higher classes. We have but few accounts that can be depended upon of the manners and customs of that part of mankind where these retrograde and progressive movements chiefly take place. A satisfactory history of this kind, on one people, and of one period, would require the constant and minute attention of an observing mind during a long life. Some of the objects of inquiry would be, in what proportion to the number of adults was the number of marriages, to what extent vicious customs prevailed in consequence of the restraints upon matrimony, what was the comparative mortality among the children of the most distressed part of the community and those who lived rather more at their ease, what were the variations in the real price of labor, and what were the observable differences in the state of the lower classes of society with respect to ease and happiness, at different times during a certain period.

Such a history would tend greatly to elucidate the manner in which the constant check upon population acts and would probably prove the existence of the retrograde and progressive movements that have been mentioned, though the times of their vibrations must necessarily be rendered irregular from the operation of many interrupting causes, such as the introduction or failure of certain manufactures, a greater or less prevalent spirit of agricultural enterprise, years of plenty, or years of scarcity, wars and pestilence, poor laws, the invention of processes for shortening labor without the proportional extension of the market for the commodity, and, particularly, the difference between the nominal and real price of labor, a circumstance which has perhaps more than any other contributed to conceal this oscillation from common view.

It very rarely happens that the nominal price of labor universally falls, but we well know that it frequently remains the same, while the nominal price of provisions has been gradually increasing. This is, in effect, a real fall in the price of labor, and during this period the condition of the lower orders of the community must gradually grow worse and worse. But the farmers and capitalists are growing rich from the real cheapness of labor. Their increased capitals enable them to employ a greater number of men. Work therefore may be plentiful, and the price of labor would consequently rise. But the want of freedom in the market of labor, which occurs more or less in all communities, either from parish laws, or the more general cause of the facility of combination among the rich, and its difficulty among the poor, operates to prevent the price of labor from rising at the natural period, and keeps it down some time longer; perhaps till a year of scarcity, when the clamor is too loud and the necessity too apparent to be resisted.

The true cause of the advance in the price of labor is thus concealed, and the rich affect to grant it as an act of compassion and favor to the poor, in consideration of a year of scarcity, and, when plenty returns, indulge themselves in the most unreasonable of all complaints, that the price does not again fall, when a little rejection would show them that it must have risen long before but from an unjust conspiracy of their own.

But though the rich by unfair combinations contribute frequently to prolong a season of distress among the poor, yet no possible form of society could prevent the almost constant action of misery upon a great part of mankind, if in a state of inequality, and upon all, if all were equal.

The theory on which the truth of this position depends appears to me so extremely clear that I feel at a loss to conjecture what part of it can be denied.

That population cannot increase without the means of subsistence is a proposition so evident that it needs no illustration.

That population does invariably increase where there are the means of subsistence, the history of every people that have ever existed will abundantly prove.

And that the superior power of population cannot be checked without producing misery or vice, the ample portion of these too bitter ingredients in the cup of human life and the continuance of the physical causes that seem to have produced them bear too convincing a testimony.

But, in order more fully to ascertain the validity of these three propositions, let us examine the different states in which mankind have been known to exist. Even a cursory review will, I think, be sufficient to convince us that these propositions are incontrovertible truths.

CHAPTER 3

The Savage or Hunter State Shortly Reviewed—
The Shepherd State, or the Tribes of Barbarians
that Overran the Roman Empire—The Superiority
of the Power of Population to the Means of
Subsistence—the Cause of the Great Tide of
Northern Emigration.

In the rudest state of mankind, in which hunting is the principal occupation, and the only mode of acquiring food; the means of subsistence being scattered over a large extent of territory, the comparative population must necessarily be thin. It is said that the passion between the sexes is less ardent among the North American Indians, than among any other race of men. Yet, notwithstanding this apathy, the effort towards population, even in this people, seems to be always greater than the means to support it. This appears, from the comparatively rapid population that takes place, whenever any of the tribes happen to settle in some fertile spot, and to draw nourishment from more fruitful sources than that of hunting; and it has been frequently remarked that when an Indian family has taken up its abode near any European settlement, and adopted a more easy and civilized mode of life, that one woman has reared five, or six, or more children; though in the savage state it rarely happens that above one or two in a family grow up to maturity. The same observation has been made with regard to the Hottentots near the Cape. These facts prove the superior power of population to the means of subsistence in nations of hunters, and that this power always shows itself the moment it is left to act with freedom.

It remains to inquire whether this power can be checked, and its effects kept equal to the means of subsistence, without vice or misery.

The North American Indians, considered as a people, cannot justly be called free and equal. In all the accounts we have of them, and, indeed, of most other savage nations, the women are represented as much more completely in a state of slavery to the men than the poor are to the rich in civilized countries. One half the nation appears to act as Helots to the other half, and the misery that checks population falls chiefly, as it always must do, upon that part whose condition is lowest in the scale of society. The infancy of man in the simplest state requires considerable attention, but this necessary attention the women cannot give, condemned as they are to the inconveniences and hardships of frequent change of place and to the constant and unremitting drudgery of preparing every thing for the reception of their tyrannic lords. These exertions, sometimes during pregnancy or with children at their backs, must occasion frequent miscarriages, and prevent any but the most robust infants from growing to maturity. Add to these hardships of the women the constant war that prevails among savages, and the necessity which they frequently labor under of exposing their aged and helpless parents, and of thus violating the first feelings of nature, and the picture will not appear very free from the blot of misery. In estimating the happiness of a savage nation, we must not fix our eyes only on the warrior in the prime of life: he is one of a hundred: he is the gentleman, the man of fortune, the chances have been in his favor and many efforts have failed ere this fortunate being was produced, whose guardian genius should preserve him through the numberless dangers with which he would be surrounded from infancy to manhood. The true points of comparison between two nations seem to be the ranks in each which appear nearest to answer to each other. And in this view, I should compare the warriors in the prime of life with the gentlemen, and the women, children, and aged, with the lower classes of the community in civilized states.

May we not then fairly infer from this short review, or rather, from the accounts that may be referred to of nations of hunters, that their population is thin from the scarcity of food, that it would immediately increase if food was in greater plenty, and that, putting vice out of the question among savages, misery is the check that represses the superior power of population and keeps its effects equal to the means of subsistence. Actual observation and experience tell us that this check, with a few local and temporary exceptions, is constantly acting now upon all savage nations, and the theory indicates that it probably acted with nearly equal strength a thousand years ago, and it may not be much greater a thousand years hence.

Of the manners and habits that prevail among nations of shepherds, the next state of mankind, we are even more ignorant than of the savage state. But that these nations could not escape the general lot of misery arising from the want of subsistence, Europe, and all the fairest countries in the world, bear ample testimony. Want was the goad that drove the Scythian shepherds from their native haunts, like so many famished wolves in search of prey. Set in motion by this all powerful cause, clouds of Barbarians seemed to collect from all points of the northern hemisphere. Gathering fresh darkness and terror as they rolled on, the congregated bodies at length obscured the sun of Italy and sunk the whole world in universal night. These tremendous effects, so long and so deeply felt throughout the fairest portions of the earth, may be traced to the simple cause of the superior power of population to the means of subsistence.

It is well known that a country in pasture cannot support so many inhabitants as a country in tillage, but what renders nations of shepherds so formidable is the power which they possess of moving all together and the necessity they frequently feel of exerting this power in search of fresh pasture for their herds. A tribe that was rich in cattle had an immediate plenty of food. Even the parent stock might be devoured in a case of absolute necessity. The women lived in greater ease than among nations of hunters. The men bold in their united strength and confiding in their power of procuring pasture for their cattle by change of place, felt, probably, but few fears about providing for a family. These combined causes soon produced their natural and invariable effect, an extended population. A more frequent and rapid change of place became then necessary. A wider and more extensive territory was successively occupied. A broader desolation extended all around them. Want pinched the less fortunate members of the society, and, at length, the impossibility of supporting such a number together became too evident to be resisted.

Young scions were then pushed out from the parent-stock and instructed to explore fresh regions and to gain happier seats for themselves by their swords. "The world was all before them where to choose." Restless from present distress, flushed with the hope of fairer prospects, and animated with the spirit of hardy enterprise, these daring adventurers were likely to become formidable adversaries to all who opposed them. The peaceful inhabitants of the countries on which they rushed could not long withstand the energy of men acting under such powerful motives of exertion. And when they fell in with any tribes like their own, the contest was a struggle for existence, and they fought with a desperate courage, inspired by the rejection that death was the punishment of defeat and life the prize of victory.

In these savage contests many tribes must have been utterly exterminated. Some, probably, perished by hardship and famine. Others, whose leading star had given them a happier direction, became great and powerful tribes, and, in their turns, sent off fresh adventurers in search of still more fertile seats. The prodigious waste of human life occasioned by this perpetual struggle for room and food was more than supplied by the mighty power of population, acting, in some degree, unshackled from the consent habit of emigration. The tribes that migrated towards the South, though they won these more fruitful regions by continual battles, rapidly increased in number and power, from the increased means of subsistence. Till at length the whole territory, from the confines of China to the shores of the Baltic, was peopled by a various race of Barbarians, brave, robust, and enterprising, inured to hardship, and delighting in war. Some tribes maintained their independence. Others ranged themselves under the standard of some barbaric chieftain who led them to victory after victory, and what was of more importance, to regions abounding in corn, wine, and oil, the long wished for consummation, and great reward of their labors. An Alaric, an Attila, or a Zingis Khan, and the chiefs around them, might fight for glory, for the fame of extensive conquests, but the true cause that set in motion the great tide of northern emigration, and that continued to propel it till it rolled at different periods against China, Persia, Italy, and even Egypt, was a scarcity of food, a population extended beyond the means of supporting it.

The absolute population at any one period, in proportion to the extent of territory, could never be great, on account of the unproductive nature of some of the regions occupied; but there appears to have been a most rapid succession of human beings, and as fast as some were mowed down by the scythe of war or of famine, others rose in increased numbers to supply their place. Among these bold and improvident Barbarians, population was probably but little checked, as in modern states, from a fear of future difficulties. A prevailing hope of bettering their condition by change of place, a constant expectation of plunder, a power even, if distressed, of selling their children as slaves, added to the natural carelessness of the barbaric character, all conspired to raise a population which remained to be repressed afterwards by famine or war.

Where there is any inequality of conditions, and among nations of shepherds this soon takes place, the distress arising from a scarcity of provisions must fall hardest upon the least fortunate members of the society. This distress also must frequently have been felt by the women, exposed to casual plunder in the absence of their husbands, and subject to continual disappointments in their expected return.

But without knowing enough of the minute and intimate history of these people, to point out precisely on what part the distress for want of food chiefly fell, and to what extent it was generally felt, I think we may fairly say, from all the accounts that we have of nations of shepherds, that population invariably increased among them whenever, by emigration or any other cause, the means of subsistence were increased, and that a further population was checked, and the actual population kept equal to the means of subsistence, by misery and vice.

For, independently of any vicious customs that might have prevailed amongst them with regard to women, which always operate as checks to population, it must be acknowledged, I think, that the commission of war is vice, and the effect of it misery, and none can doubt the misery of want of food.

CHAPTER 4

State of Civilized Nations—Probability that
Europe is Much More Populous Now Than in the
Time of Julius Caesar—Best Criterion of
Population—Probable Error of Hume in One of
the Criterions that He Proposes as Assisting in an
Estimate of Population—Slow Increase of
Population at Present in Most of the States of
Europe—The Two Principal Checks to
Population—The First, or Preventive Check
Examined with Regard to England.

In examining the next state of mankind with relation to the question before us, the state of mixed pasture and tillage, in which with some variation in the proportions the most civilized nations must always remain, we shall be assisted in our review by what we daily see around us, by actual experience, by facts that come within the scope of every man's observation.

Notwithstanding the exaggerations of some old historians, there can remain no doubt in the mind of any thinking man that the population of the principal countries of Europe, France, England, Germany, Russia, Poland, Sweden, and Denmark is much greater than ever it was in former times. The obvious reason of these exaggerations is the formidable aspect that even a thinly peopled nation must have, when collected together and moving all at once in search of fresh seats. If to this tremendous appearance be added a succession at certain intervals of similar emigrations, we shall not be much surprised that the fears of the timid nations of the South represented the North as a region absolutely swarming with human beings. A nearer and juster view of the subject at present enables us to see that the inference was as absurd as if a man in this country, who was continually meeting on the road droves of cattle from Wales and the North, was immediately to conclude that these countries were the most productive of all the parts of the kingdom.

The reason that the greater part of Europe is more populous now than it was in former times, is that the industry of the inhabitants has made these countries produce a greater quantity of human subsistence. For I conceive that it may be laid down as a position not to be controverted, that, taking a sufficient extent of territory to include within it exportation and importation, and allowing some variation for the prevalence of luxury, or of frugal habits, that population constantly bears a regular proportion to the food that the earth is made to produce. In the controversy concerning the populousness of ancient and modern nations, could it be clearly ascertained that the average produce of the countries in question, taken altogether, is greater now than it was in the times of Julius Caesar, the dispute would be at once determined.

When we are assured that China is the most fertile country in the world, that almost all the land is in tillage, and that a great part of it bears two crops every year, and further, that the people live very frugally, we may infer with certainty that the population must be immense, without busying ourselves in inquiries into the manners and habits of the lower classes and the encouragements to early marriages. But these inquiries are of the utmost importance, and a minute history of the customs of the lower Chinese would be of the greatest use in ascertaining in what manner the checks to a further population operate; what are the vices, and what are the distresses that prevent an increase of numbers beyond the ability of the country to support.

Hume, in his essay on the populousness of ancient and modern nations, when he intermingles, as he says, an inquiry concerning causes with that concerning facts, does not seem to see with his usual penetration how very little some of the causes he alludes to could enable him to form any judgment of the actual population of ancient nations. If any inference can be drawn from them, perhaps it should be directly the reverse of what Hume draws, though I certainly ought to speak with great diffidence in dissenting from a man who of all others on such subjects was the least likely to be deceived by first appearances. If I find that at a certain period in ancient history, the encouragements to have a family were great, that early marriages were consequently very prevalent, and that few persons remained single, I should infer with certainty that population was rapidly increasing, but by no means that it was then actually very great, rather; indeed, the contrary, that it was then thin and that there was room and food for a much greater number. On the other hand, if I find that at this period the difficulties attending a family were very great, that, consequently, few early marriages took place, and that a great number of both sexes remained single, I infer with certainty that population was at a stand, and, probably, because the actual population was very great in proportion to the fertility of the land and that there was scarcely room and food for more. The number of footmen, housemaids, and other persons remaining unmarried in modern states, Hume allows to be rather an argument against their population. I should rather draw a contrary inference and consider it an argument of their fullness, though this inference is not certain, because there are many thinly inhabited states that are yet stationary in their population. To speak, therefore, correctly, perhaps it may be said that the number of unmarried persons in proportion to the whole number, existing at different periods, in the same or different states will enable us to judge whether population at these periods was increasing, stationary, or decreasing, but will form no criterion by which we can determine the actual population.

There is, however, a circumstance taken notice of in most of the accounts we have of China that it seems difficult to reconcile with this reasoning. It is said that early marriages very generally prevail through all the ranks of the Chinese. Yet Dr. Adam Smith supposes that population in China is stationary. These two circumstances appear to be irreconcilable. It certainly seems very little probable that the population of China is fast increasing. Every acre of land has been so long in cultivation that we can hardly conceive there is any great yearly addition to the average produce. The fact, perhaps, of the universality of early marriages may not be sufficiently ascertained. If it be supposed true, the only way of accounting for the difficulty, with our present knowledge of the subject, appears to be that the redundant population, necessarily occasioned by the prevalence of early marriages, must be repressed by occasional famines, and by the custom of exposing children, which, in times of distress, is probably more frequent than is ever acknowledged to Europeans. Relative to this barbarous practice, it is difficult to avoid remarking, that there cannot be a stronger proof of the distresses that have been felt by mankind for want of food, than the existence of a custom that thus violates the most natural principle of the human heart. It appears to have been very general among ancient nations, and certainly tended rather to increase population.

In examining the principal states of modern Europe, we shall find that though they have increased very considerably in population since they were nations of shepherds, yet that at present their progress is but slow, and instead of doubling their numbers every twenty-five years they require three or four hundred years, or more, for that purpose. Some, indeed, may be absolutely stationary, and others even retrograde. The cause of this slow progress in population cannot be traced to a decay of the passion between the sexes. We have sufficient reason to think that this natural propensity exists still in undiminished vigor. Why then do not its effects appear in a rapid increase of the human species? An intimate view of the state of society in any one country in Europe, which may serve equally for all, will enable us to answer this question, and to say that a foresight of the difficulties attending the rearing of a family acts as a preventive check, and the actual distresses of some of the lower classes, by which they are disabled from giving the proper food and attention to their children, act as a positive check to the natural increase of population.

England, as one of the most flourishing states of Europe, may be fairly taken for an example, and the observations made will apply with but little variation to any other country where the population increases slowly.

The preventive check appears to operate in some degree through all the ranks of society in England. There are some men, even in the highest rank, who are prevented from marrying by the idea of the expenses that they must retrench, and the fancied pleasures that they must deprive themselves of, on the supposition of having a family. These considerations are certainly trivial, but a preventive foresight of this kind has objects of much greater weight for its contemplation as we go lower.

A man of liberal education, but with an income only just sufficient to enable him to associate in the rank of gentlemen, must feel absolutely certain that if he marries and has a family he shall be obliged, if he mixes at all in society, to rank himself with moderate farmers and the lower class of tradesmen. The woman that a man of education would naturally make the object of his choice would be one brought up in the same tastes and sentiments with himself and used to the familiar intercourse of a society totally different from that to which she must be reduced by marriage. Can a man consent to place the object of his affection in a situation so discordant, probably, to her tastes and inclinations? Two or three steps of descent in society, particularly at this round of the ladder, where education ends and ignorance begins, will not be considered by the generality of people as a fancied and chimerical, but a real and essential evil. If society be held desirable, it surely must be free, equal, and reciprocal society, where benefits are conferred as well as received, and not such as the dependent finds with his patron or the poor with the rich.

These considerations undoubtedly prevent a great number in this rank of life from following the bent of their inclinations in an early attachment. Others, guided either by a stronger passion, or a weaker judgment, break through these restraints, and it would be hard indeed, if the gratification of so delightful a passion as virtuous love, did not, sometimes, more than counterbalance all its attendant evils. But I fear it must be owned that the more general consequences of such marriages are rather calculated to justify than to repress the forebodings of the prudent.

The sons of tradesmen and farmers are exhorted not to marry, and generally find it necessary to pursue this advice till they are settled in some business or farm that may enable them to support a family. These events may not, perhaps, occur till they are far advanced in life. The scarcity of farms is a very general complaint in England. And the competition in every kind of business is so great that it is not possible that all should be successful.

The laborer who earns eighteen pence a day and lives with some degree of comfort as a single man, will hesitate a little before he divides that pittance among four or five, which seems to be but just sufficient for one. Harder fare and harder labor he would submit to for the sake of living with the woman that he loves, but he must feel conscious, if he thinks at all, that should he have a large family, and any ill luck whatever, no degree of frugality, no possible exertion of his manual strength could preserve him from the heart-rending sensation of seeing his children starve, or of forfeiting his independence, and being obliged to the parish for their support. The love of independence is a sentiment that surely none would wish to be erased from the breast of man, though the parish law of England, it must be confessed, is a system of all others the most calculated gradually to weaken this sentiment, and in the end may eradicate it completely.

The servants who live in gentlemen's families have restraints that are yet stronger to break through in venturing upon marriage. They possess the necessaries, and even the comforts of life, almost in as great plenty as their masters. Their work is easy and their food luxurious compared with the class of laborers. And their sense of dependence is weakened by the conscious power of changing their masters, if they feel themselves offended. Thus comfortably situated at present, what are their prospects in marrying? Without knowledge or capital, either for business, or farming, and unused and therefore unable, to earn a subsistence by daily labor, their only refuge seems to be a miserable alehouse, which certainly offers no very enchanting prospect of a happy evening to their lives. By much the greater part, therefore, deterred by this uninviting view of their future situation, content themselves with remaining single where they are.

If this sketch of the state of society in England be near the truth, and I do not conceive that it is exaggerated, it will be allowed that the preventive check to population in this country operates, though with varied force, through all the classes of the community. The same observation will hold true with regard to all old states. The effects, indeed, of these restraints upon marriage are but too conspicuous in the consequent vices that are produced in almost every part of the world, vices that are continually involving both sexes in inextricable unhappiness.

CHAPTER 5

The Second, or Positive Check to Population Examined, in England—The True Cause why the Immense Sum Collected in England for the Poor does not Better Their Condition—The Powerful Tendency of the Poor Laws to Defeat Their Own Purpose—Palliative of the Distresses of the Poor Proposed—The Absolute Impossibility, from the Fixed Laws of Our Nature, that the Pressure of Want Can Ever be Completely Removed from the Lower Classes of Society—All the Checks to Population may be Resolved into Misery or Vice.

The positive check to population, by which I mean the check that represses an increase which is already begun, is confined chiefly, though not perhaps solely, to the lowest orders of society.

This check is not so obvious to common view as the other I have mentioned, and, to prove distinctly the force and extent of its operation would require, perhaps, more data than we are in possession of. But I believe it has been very generally remarked by those who have attended to bills of mortality that of the number of children who die annually, much too great a proportion belongs to those who may be supposed unable to give their offspring proper food and attention, exposed as they are occasionally to severe distress and confined, perhaps, to unwholesome habitations and hard labor. This mortality among the children of the poor has been constantly taken notice of in all towns. It certainly does not prevail in an equal degree in the country, but the subject has not hitherto received sufficient attention to enable anyone to say that there are not more deaths in proportion among the children of the poor, even in the country, than among those of the middling and higher classes. Indeed, it seems difficult to suppose that a laborer's wife who has six children, and who is sometimes in absolute want of bread, should be able always to give them the food and attention necessary to support life. The sons and daughters of peasants will not be found such rosy cherubs in real life as they are described to be in romances. It cannot fail to be remarked by those who live much in the country that the sons of laborers are very apt to be stunted in their growth, and are a long while arriving at maturity. Boys that you would guess to be fourteen or fifteen are, upon inquiry, frequently found to be eighteen or nineteen. And the lads who drive plough, which must certainly be a healthy exercise, are very rarely seen with any appearance of calves to their legs: a circumstance which can only be attributed to a want either of proper or of sufficient nourishment.

To remedy the frequent distresses of the common people, the poor laws of England have been instituted; but it is to be feared, that though they may have alleviated a little the intensity of individual misfortune, they have spread the general evil over a much larger surface. It is a subject often started in conversation and mentioned always as a matter of great surprise that, notwithstanding the immense sum that is annually collected for the poor in England, there is still so much distress among them. Some think that the money must be embezzled, others that the church-wardens and overseers consume the greater part of it in dinners. All agree that somehow or other it must be very ill-managed. In short the fact that nearly three millions are collected annually for the poor and yet that their distresses are not removed is the subject of continual astonishment. But a man who sees a little below the surface of things would be very much more astonished if the fact were otherwise than it is observed to be, or even if a collection universally of eighteen shillings in the pound, instead of four, were materially to alter it. I will state a case which I hope will elucidate my meaning.

Suppose that by a subscription of the rich the eighteen pence a day which men earn now was made up five shillings, it might be imagined, perhaps, that they would then be able to live comfortably and have a piece of meat every day for their dinners. But this would be a very false conclusion. The transfer of three shillings and six pence a day to every laborer would not increase the quantity of meat in the country. There is not at present enough for all to have a decent share. What would then be the consequence? The competition among the buyers in the market of meat would rapidly raise the price from six pence or seven pence, to two or three shillings in the pound, and the commodity would not be divided among many more than it is at present. When an article is scarce, and cannot be distributed to all, he that can show the most valid patent, that is, he that offers most money, becomes the possessor. If we can suppose the competition among the buyers of meat to continue long enough for a greater number of cattle to be reared annually, this could only be done at the expense of the corn, which would be a very disadvantageous exchange, for it is well known that the country could not then support the same population, and when subsistence is scarce in proportion to the number of people, it is of little consequence whether the lowest members of the society possess eighteen pence or five shillings. They must at all events be reduced to live upon the hardest fare and in the smallest quantity.

It will be said, perhaps, that the increased number of purchasers in every article would give a spur to productive industry and that the whole produce of the island would be increased. This might in some degree be the case. But the spur that these fancied riches would give to population would more than counterbalance it, and the increased produce would be to be divided among a more than proportionally increased number of people. All this time I am supposing that the same quantity of work would be done as before. But this would not really take place. The receipt of five shillings a day, instead of eighteen pence, would make every man fancy himself comparatively rich and able to indulge himself in many hours or days of leisure. This would give a strong and immediate check to productive industry, and, in a short time, not only the nation would be poorer, but the lower classes themselves would be much more distressed than when they received only eighteen pence a day.

A collection from the rich of eighteen shillings in the pound, even if distributed in the most judicious manner, would have a little the same effect as that resulting from the supposition I have just made, and no possible contributions or sacrifices of the rich, particularly in money, could for any time prevent the recurrence of distress among the lower members of society, whoever they were. Great changes might, indeed, be made. The rich might become poor, and some of the poor rich, but a part of the society must necessarily feel a difficulty of living, and this difficulty will naturally fall on the least fortunate members.

It may at first appear strange, but I believe it is true, that I cannot by means of money raise a poor man and enable him to live much better than he did before, without proportionally depressing others in the same class. If I retrench the quantity of food consumed in my house, and give him what I have cut off, I then benefit him, without depressing any but myself and family, who, perhaps, may be well able to bear it. If I turn up a piece of uncultivated land, and give him the produce, I then benefit both him and all the members of the society, because what he before consumed is thrown into the common stock, and probably some of the new produce with it. But if I only give him money, supposing the produce of the country to remain the same, I give him a title to a larger share of that produce than formerly, which share he cannot receive without diminishing the shares of others. It is evident that this effect, in individual instances, must be so small as to be totally imperceptible; but still it must exist, as many other effects do, which, like some of the insects that people the air, elude our grosser perceptions.

Supposing the quantity of food in any country to remain the same for many years together, it is evident that this food must be divided according to the value of each man's patent, or the sum of money that he can afford to spend on this commodity so universally in request. (Mr. Godwin calls the wealth that a man receives from his ancestors a moldy patent. It may, I think, very properly be termed a patent, but I hardly see the propriety of calling it a moldy one, as it is an article in such constant use.) It is a demonstrative truth, therefore, that the patents of one set of men could not be increased in value without diminishing the value of the patents of some other set of men. If the rich were to subscribe and give five shillings a day to five hundred thousand men without retrenching their own tables, no doubt can exist, that as these men would naturally live more at their ease and consume a greater quantity of provisions, there would be less food remaining to divide among the rest, and consequently each man's patent would be diminished in value or the same number of pieces of silver would purchase a smaller quantity of subsistence.

An increase of population without a proportional increase of food will evidently have the same effect in lowering the value of each man's patent. The food must necessarily be distributed in smaller quantities, and consequently a day's labor will purchase a smaller quantity of provisions. An increase in the price of provisions would arise either from an increase of population faster than the means of subsistence, or from a different distribution of the money of the society. The food of a country that has been long occupied, if it be increasing, increases slowly and regularly and cannot be made to answer any sudden demands, but variations in the distribution of the money of a society are not infrequently occurring, and are undoubtedly among the causes that occasion the continual variations which we observe in the price of provisions.

The poor laws of England tend to depress the general condition of the poor in these two ways. Their first obvious tendency is to increase population without increasing the food for its support. A poor man may marry with little or no prospect of being able to support a family in independence. They may be said therefore in some measure to create the poor which they maintain, and as the provisions of the country must, in consequence of the increased population, be distributed to every man in smaller proportions, it is evident that the labor of those who are not supported by parish assistance will purchase a smaller quantity of provisions than before and consequently more of them must be driven to ask for support.

Secondly, the quantity of provisions consumed in workhouses upon a part of the society that cannot in general be considered as the most valuable part diminishes the shares that would otherwise belong to more industrious and more worthy members, and thus in the same manner forces more to become dependent. If the poor in the workhouses were to live better than they now do, this new distribution of the money of the society would tend more conspicuously to depress the condition of those out of the workhouses by occasioning a rise in the price of provisions.

Fortunately for England, a spirit of independence still remains among the peasantry. The poor laws are strongly calculated to eradicate this spirit. They have succeeded in part, but had they succeeded as completely as might have been expected their pernicious tendency would not have been so long concealed.

Hard as it may appear in individual instances, dependent poverty ought to be held disgraceful. Such a stimulus seems to be absolutely necessary to promote the happiness of the great mass of mankind, and every general attempt to weaken this stimulus, however benevolent its apparent intention, will always defeat its own purpose. If men are induced to marry from a prospect of parish provision, with little or no chance of maintaining their families in independence, they are not only unjustly tempted to bring unhappiness and dependence upon themselves and children, but they are tempted, without knowing it, to injure all in the same class with themselves. A laborer who marries without being able to support a family may in some respects be considered as an enemy to all his fellow-laborers.

I feel no doubt whatever that the parish laws of England have contributed to raise the price of provisions and to lower the real price of labor. They have therefore contributed to impoverish that class of people whose only possession is their labor. It is also difficult to suppose that they have not powerfully contributed to generate that carelessness and want of frugality observable among the poor, so contrary to the disposition frequently to be remarked among petty tradesmen and small farmers. The laboring poor, to use a vulgar expression, seem always to live from hand to mouth. Their present wants employ their whole attention, and they seldom think of the future. Even when they have an opportunity of saving they seldom exercise it, but all that is beyond their present necessities goes, generally speaking, to the ale-house. The poor laws of England may therefore be said to diminish both the power and the will to save among the common people, and thus to weaken one of the strongest incentives to sobriety and industry, and consequently to happiness.

It is a general complaint among master manufacturers that high wages ruin all their workmen, but it is difficult to conceive that these men would not save a part of their high wages for the future support of their families, instead of spending it in drunkenness and dissipation, if they did not rely on parish assistance for support in case of accidents. And that the poor employed in manufactures consider this assistance as a reason why they may spend all the wages they earn and enjoy themselves while they can appears to be evident from the number of families that, upon the failure of any great manufactory, immediately fall upon the parish, when perhaps the wages earned in this manufactory while it flourished were sufficiently above the price of common country labor to have allowed them to save enough for their support till they could find some other channel for their industry.

A man who might not be deterred from going to the ale-house from the consideration that on his death, or sickness, he should leave his wife and family upon the parish might yet hesitate in thus dissipating his earnings if he were assured that, in either of these cases, his family must starve or be left to the support of casual bounty. In China, where the real as well as nominal price of labor is very low, sons are yet obliged by law to support their aged and helpless parents. Whether such a law would be advisable in this country I will not pretend to determine. But it seems at any rate highly improper, by positive institutions, which render dependent poverty so general, to weaken that disgrace, which for the best and most humane reasons ought to attach to it.

The mass of happiness among the common people cannot but be diminished when one of the strongest checks to idleness and dissipation is thus removed, and when men are thus allured to marry with little or no prospect of being able to maintain a family in independence. Every obstacle in the way of marriage must undoubtedly be considered as a species of unhappiness. But as from the laws of our nature some check to population must exist, it is better that it should be checked from a foresight of the difficulties attending a family and the fear of dependent poverty than that it should be encouraged, only to be repressed afterwards by want and sickness.

It should be remembered always that there is an essential difference between food and those wrought commodities, the raw materials of which are in great plenty. A demand for these last will not fail to create them in as great a quantity as they are wanted. The demand for food has by no means the same creative power. In a country where all the fertile spots have been seized, high offers are necessary to encourage the farmer to lay his dressing on land from which he cannot expect a profitable return for some years. And before the prospect of advantage is sufficiently great to encourage this sort of agricultural enterprise, and while the new produce is rising, great distresses may be suffered from the want of it. The demand for an increased quantity of subsistence is, with few exceptions, constant everywhere, yet we see how slowly it is answered in all those countries that have been long occupied.

The poor laws of England were undoubtedly instituted for the most benevolent purpose, but there is great reason to think that they have not succeeded in their intention. They certainly mitigate some cases of very severe distress which might otherwise occur, yet the state of the poor who are supported by parishes, considered in all its circumstances, is very far from being free from misery. But one of the principal objections to them is that for this assistance which some of the poor receive, in itself almost a doubtful blessing, the whole class of the common people of England is subjected to a set of grating, inconvenient, and tyrannical laws, totally inconsistent with the genuine spirit of the constitution. The whole business of settlements, even in its present amended state, is utterly contradictory to all ideas of freedom. The parish persecution of men whose families are likely to become chargeable, and of poor women who are near lying-in, is a most disgraceful and disgusting tyranny. And the obstructions continuity occasioned in the market of labor by these laws have a constant tendency to add to the difficulties of those who are struggling to support themselves without assistance.

These evils attendant on the poor laws are in some degree irremediable. If assistance be to be distributed to a certain class of people, a power must be given somewhere of discriminating the proper objects and of managing the concerns of the institutions that are necessary, but any great interference with the affairs of other people is a species of tyranny, and in the common course of things the exercise of this power may be expected to become grating to those who are driven to ask for support. The tyranny of justices, churchwardens, and overseers, is a common complaint among the poor, but the fault does not lie so much in these persons, who probably, before they were in power, were not worse than other people, but in the nature of all such institutions.

The evil is perhaps gone too far to be remedied, but I feel little doubt in my own mind that if the poor laws had never existed, though there might have been a few more instances of very severe distress, yet that the aggregate mass of happiness among the common people would have been much greater than it is at present.

Mr. Pitt's Poor Bill has the appearance of being framed with benevolent intentions, and the clamor raised against it was in many respects ill directed, and unreasonable. But it must be confessed that it possesses in a high degree the great and radical defect of all systems of the kind, that of tending to increase population without increasing the means for its support, and thus to depress the condition of those that are not supported by parishes, and, consequently, to create more poor.

To remove the wants of the lower classes of society is indeed an arduous task. The truth is that the pressure of distress on this part of a community is an evil so deeply seated that no human ingenuity can reach it. Were I to propose a palliative, and palliatives are all that the nature of the case will admit, it should be, in the first place, the total abolition of all the present parish-laws. This would at any rate give liberty and freedom of action to the peasantry of England, which they can hardly be said to possess at present. They would then be able to settle without interruption, wherever there was a prospect of a greater plenty of work and a higher price for labor. The market of labor would then be free, and those obstacles removed which, as things are now, often for a considerable time prevent the price from rising according to the demand.

Secondly, premiums might be given for turning up fresh land, and it possible encouragements held out to agriculture above manufactures, and to tillage above grazing. Every endeavor should be used to weaken and destroy all those institutions relating to corporations, apprenticeships, etc., which cause the labors of agriculture to be worse paid than the labors of trade and manufactures. For a country can never produce its proper quantity of food while these distinctions remain in favor of artisans. Such encouragements to agriculture would tend to furnish the market with an increasing quantity of healthy work, and at the same time, by augmenting the produce of the country, would raise the comparative price of labor and ameliorate the condition of the laborer. Being now in better circumstances, and seeing no prospect of parish assistance, he would be more able, as well as more inclined, to enter into associations for providing against the sickness of himself or family.

Lastly, for cases of extreme distress, county workhouses might be established, supported by rates upon the whole kingdom, and free for persons of all counties, and indeed of all nations. The fare should be hard, and those that were able obliged to work. It would be desirable that they should not be considered as comfortable asylums in all difficulties, but merely as places where severe distress might find some alleviation. A part of these houses might be separated, or others built for a most beneficial purpose, which has not been infrequently taken notice of, that of providing a place where any person, whether native or foreigner, might do a day's work at all times and receive the market price for it. Many cases would undoubtedly be left for the exertion of individual benevolence.

A plan of this kind, the preliminary of which should be an abolition of all the present parish laws, seems to be the best calculated to increase the mass of happiness among the common people of England. To prevent the recurrence of misery, is, alas! beyond the power of man. In the vain endeavor to attain what in the nature of things is impossible, we now sacrifice not only possible but certain benefits. We tell the common people that if they will submit to a code of tyrannical regulations, they shall never be in want. They do submit to these regulations. They perform their part of the contract, but we do not, nay cannot, perform ours, and thus the poor sacrifice the valuable blessing of liberty and receive nothing that can be called an equivalent in return.

Notwithstanding, then, the institution of the poor laws in England, I think it will be allowed that considering the state of the lower classes altogether, both in the towns and in the country, the distresses which they suffer from the want of proper and sufficient food, from hard labor and unwholesome habitations, must operate as a constant check to incipient population.

To these two great checks to population, in all long occupied countries, which I have called the preventive and the positive checks, may be added vicious customs with respect to women, great cities, unwholesome manufactures, luxury, pestilence, and war.

All these checks may be fairly resolved into misery and vice. And that these are the true causes of the slow increase of population in all the states of modern Europe, will appear sufficiently evident from the comparatively rapid increase that has invariably taken place whenever these causes have been in any considerable degree removed.

CHAPTER 6

New Colonies—Reasons for their Rapid Increase—
North American Colonies—Extraordinary Instance
of Increase in the Back Settlements—Rapidity with
which Even Old States Recover the
Ravages of War, Pestilence, Famine, or the
Convulsions of Nature.

It has been universally remarked that all new colonies settled in healthy countries, where there was plenty of room and food, have constantly increased with astonishing rapidity in their population. Some of the colonies from ancient Greece, in no very long period, more than equaled their parent states in numbers and strength. And not to dwell on remote instances, the European settlements in the new world bear ample testimony to the truth of a remark, which, indeed, has never, that I know of, been doubted. A plenty of rich land, to be had for little or nothing, is so powerful a cause of population as to overcome all other obstacles. No settlements could well have been worse managed than those of Spain in Mexico, Peru, and Quito. The tyranny, superstition, and vices of the mother-country were introduced in ample quantities among her children. Exorbitant taxes were exacted by the Crown. The most arbitrary restrictions were imposed on their trade. And the governors were not behind hand in rapacity and extortion for themselves as well as their master. Yet, under all these difficulties, the colonies made a quick progress in population. The city of Lima, founded since the conquest, is represented by Ulloa as containing fifty thousand inhabitants near fifty years ago. Quito, which had been but a hamlet of Indians, is represented by the same author as in his time equally populous. Mexico is said to contain a hundred thousand inhabitants, which, notwithstanding the exaggerations of the Spanish writers, is supposed to be five times greater than what it contained in the time of Montezuma.

In the Portuguese colony of Brazil, governed with almost equal tyranny, there were supposed to be, thirty years since, six hundred thousand inhabitants of European extraction.

The Dutch and French colonies, though under the government of exclusive companies of merchants, which, as Dr. Adam Smith says very justly, is the worst of all possible governments, still persisted in thriving under every disadvantage.

But the English North American colonies, now the powerful people of the United States of America, made by far the most rapid progress. To the plenty of good land which they possessed in common with the Spanish and Portuguese settlements, they added a greater degree of liberty and equality. Though not without some restrictions on their foreign commerce, they were allowed a perfect liberty of managing their own internal affairs. The political institutions that prevailed were favorable to the alienation and division of property. Lands that were not cultivated by the proprietor within a limited time were declared grantable to any other person. In Pennsylvania there was no right of primogeniture, and in the provinces of New England the eldest had only a double share.

There were no tithes in any of the States, and scarcely any taxes. And on account of the extreme cheapness of good land a capital could not be more advantageously employed than in agriculture, which at the same time that it supplies the greatest quantity of healthy work affords much the most valuable produce to the society.

The consequence of these favorable circumstances united was a rapidity of increase probably without parallel in history. Throughout all the northern colonies, the population was found to double itself in twenty-five years. The original number of persons who had settled in the four provinces of New England in 1643 was 21,200. (I take these figures from Dr. Price's two volumes of Observations; not having Dr. Styles's pamphlet, from which he quotes, by me.) Afterwards, it is supposed that more left them than went to them. In the year 1760, they were increased to half a million. They had therefore all along doubled their own number in twenty-five years. In New Jersey the period of doubling appeared to be twenty-two years; and in Rhode Island still less. In the back settlements, where the inhabitants applied themselves solely to agriculture, and luxury was not known, they were found to double their own number in fifteen years, a most extraordinary instance of increase. Along the seacoast, which would naturally be first inhabited, the period of doubling was about thirty-five years; and in some of the maritime towns, the population was absolutely at a stand.

(In instances of this kind the powers of the earth appear to be fully equal to answer it the demands for food that can be made upon it by man. But we should be led into an error if we were thence to suppose that population and food ever really increase in the same ratio. The one is still a geometrical and the other an arithmetical ratio, that is, one increases by multiplication, and the other by addition. Where there are few people, and a great quantity of fertile land, the power of the earth to afford a yearly increase of food may be compared to a great reservoir of water, supplied by a moderate stream. The faster population increases, the more help will be got to draw off the water, and consequently an increasing quantity will be taken every year. But the sooner, undoubtedly, will the reservoir be exhausted, and the streams only remain. When acre has been added to acre, till all the fertile land is occupied, the yearly increase of food will depend upon the amelioration of the land already in possession; and even this moderate stream will be gradually diminishing. But population, could it be supplied with food, would go on with unexhausted vigor, and the increase of one period would furnish the power of a greater increase the next, and this without any limit.)

These facts seem to show that population increases exactly in the proportion that the two great checks to it, misery and vice, are removed, and that there is not a truer criterion of the happiness and innocence of a people than the rapidity of their increase. The unwholesomeness of towns, to which some persons are necessarily driven from the nature of their trades, must be considered as a species of misery, and every the slightest check to marriage, from a prospect of the difficulty of maintaining a family, may be fairly classed under the same head. In short it is difficult to conceive any check to population which does not come under the description of some species of misery or vice.

The population of the thirteen American States before the war was reckoned at about three millions. Nobody imagines that Great Britain is less populous at present for the emigration of the small parent stock that produced these numbers. On the contrary, a certain degree of emigration is known to be favorable to the population of the mother country. It has been particularly remarked that the two Spanish provinces from which the greatest number of people emigrated to America, became in consequence more populous. Whatever was the original number of British emigrants that increased so fast in the North American Colonies, let us ask, why does not an equal number produce an equal increase in the same time in Great Britain? The great and obvious cause to be assigned is the want of room and food, or, in other words, misery, and that this is a much more powerful cause even than vice appears sufficiently evident from the rapidity with which even old states recover the desolations of war, pestilence, or the accidents of nature. They are then for a short time placed a little in the situation of new states, and the effect is always answerable to what might be expected. If the industry of the inhabitants be not destroyed by fear or tyranny, subsistence will soon increase beyond the wants of the reduced numbers, and the invariable consequence will be that population which before, perhaps, was nearly stationary, will begin immediately to increase.

The fertile province of Flanders, which has been so often the seat of the most destructive wars, after a respite of a few years, has appeared always as fruitful and as populous as ever. Even the Palatinate lifted up its head again after the execrable ravages of Louis the Fourteenth. The effects of the dreadful plague in London in 1666 were not perceptible fifteen or twenty years afterwards. The traces of the most destructive famines in China and Indostan are by all accounts very soon obliterated. It may even be doubted whether Turkey and Egypt are upon an average much less populous for the plagues that periodically lay them waste. If the number of people which they contain be less now than formerly, it is, probably, rather to be attributed to the tyranny and oppression of the government under which they groan, and the consequent discouragements to agriculture, than to the loss which they sustain by the plague. The most tremendous convulsions of nature, such as volcanic eruptions and earthquakes, if they do not happen so frequently as to drive away the inhabitants, or to destroy their spirit of industry, have but a trifling effect on the average population of any state. Naples, and the country under Vesuvius, are still very populous, notwithstanding the repeated eruptions of that mountain. And Lisbon and Lima are now, probably, nearly in the same state with regard to population as they were before the last earthquakes.

CHAPTER 7

A Probable Cause of Epidemics—Extracts from Mr. Suessmilch's Tables—Periodical Returns of Sickly Seasons to be Expected in Certain Cases— Proportion of Births to Burials for Short Periods in any Country an Inadequate Criterion of the Real Average Increase of Population—Best Criterion of a Permanent Increase of Population—Great Frugality of Living One of the Causes of the Famines of China and Indostan—Evil Tendency of One of the Clauses in Mr. Pitt's Poor Bill—Only One Proper way of Encouraging Population—Causes of the Happiness of Nations— Famine, the Last and Most Dreadful Mode by Which Nature Represses a Redundant Population—The Three Propositions Considered as Established.

By great attention to cleanliness, the plague seems at length to be completely expelled from London. But it is not improbable that among the secondary causes that produce even sickly seasons and epidemics ought to be ranked a crowded population and unwholesome and insufficient food. I have been led to this remark, by looking over some of the tables of Mr. Suessmilch, which Dr. Price has extracted in one of his notes to the postscript on the controversy respecting the population of England and Wales. They are considered as very correct, and if such tables were general, they would throw great light on the different ways by which population is repressed and prevented from increasing beyond the means of subsistence in any country. I will extract a part of the tables, with Dr. Price's remarks.

IN THE KINGDOM OF PRUSSIA, AND DUKEDOM OF LITHUANIA

Annual Averages	Births	Burials	Marriages	Proportion of Births to Marriages	Proportion of Births to Burials
10 Yrs to 1702	21,963	14,718	5,928	37 to 10	150 to 100
5 Yrs to 1716	21,602	11,984	4,968	37 to 10	180 to 100
5 Yrs to 1756	28,392	19,154	5,599	50 to 10	148 to 100

"N.B. In 1709 and 1710, a pestilence carried off 247,733 of the inhabitants of this country, and in 1736 and 1737, epidemics prevailed, which again checked its increase."

It may be remarked, that the greatest proportion of births to burials, was in the five years after the great pestilence.

DUCHY OF POMERANIA

Annual Averages	Births	Burials	Marriages	Proportion of Births to Marriages	Proportion of Births to Burials
6 yrs to 1702	6,540	4,647	1,810	36 to 10	140 to 100
6 yrs to 1708	7,455	4,208	1,875	39 to 10	177 to 100
6 yrs to 1726	8,432	5,627	2,131	39 to 10	150 to 100
6 yrs to 1756	12,767	9,281	2,957	43 to 10	137 to 100

"In this instance the inhabitants appear to have been almost doubled in fifty-six years, no very bad epidemics having once interrupted the increase, but the three years immediately following the last period (to 1759) were so sickly that the births were sunk to 10,229 and the burials raised to 15,068."

Is it not probable that in this case the number of inhabitants had increased faster than the food and the accommodations necessary to preserve them in health? The mass of the people would, upon this supposition, be obliged to live harder, and a greater number would be crowded together in one house, and it is not surely improbable that these were among the natural causes that produced the three sickly years. These causes may produce such an effect, though the country, absolutely considered, may not be extremely crowded and populous. In a country even thinly inhabited, if an increase of population take place, before more food is raised, and more houses are built, the inhabitants must be distressed in some degree for room and subsistence. Were the marriages in England, for the next eight or ten years, to be more prolific than usual, or even were a greater number of marriages than usual to take place, supposing the number of houses to remain the same, instead of five or six to a cottage, there must be seven or eight, and this, added to the necessity of harder living, would probably have a very unfavorable effect on the health of the common people.

NEUMARK OF BRANDENBURGH

Annual Averages	Births	Burials	Marriages	Proportion of Births to Marriages	Proportion of Births to Burials
5 yrs to 1701	5,433	3,483	1,436	37 to 10	155 to 100
5 yrs to 1726	7,012	4,254	1,713	40 to 10	164 to 100
5 yrs to 1756	7,978	5,567	1,891	42 to 10	143 to 100

"Epidemics prevailed for six years, from 1736, to 1741, which checked the increase."

DUKEDOM OF MAGDEBURGH

Annual Averages	Births	Burials	Marriages	Proportion of Births to Marriages	Proportion of Births to Burials
5 yrs to 1702	6,431	4,103	1,681	38 to 10	156 to 100
5 yrs to 1717	7,590	5,335	2,076	36 to 10	142 to 100
5 yrs to 1756	8,850	8,069	2,193	40 to 10	109 to 100

"The years 1738, 1740, 1750, and 1751, were particularly sickly."

For further information on this subject, I refer the reader to Mr. Suessmilch's tables. The extracts that I have made are sufficient to show the periodical, though irregular, returns of sickly seasons, and it seems highly probable that a scantiness of room and food was one of the principal causes that occasioned them.

It appears from the tables that these countries were increasing rather fast for old states, notwithstanding the occasional seasons that prevailed. Cultivation must have been improving, and marriages, consequently, encouraged. For the checks to population appear to have been rather of the positive, than of the preventive kind. When from a prospect of increasing plenty in any country, the weight that represses population is in some degree removed, it is highly probable that the motion will be continued beyond the operation of the cause that first impelled it. Or, to be more particular, when the increasing produce of a country, and the increasing demand for labor, so far ameliorate the condition of the laborer as greatly to encourage marriage, it is probable that the custom of early marriages will continue till the population of the country has gone beyond the increased produce, and sickly seasons appear to be the natural and necessary consequence. I should expect, therefore, that those countries where subsistence was increasing sufficiency at times to encourage population but not to answer all its demands, would be more subject to periodical epidemics than those where the population could more completely accommodate itself to the average produce.

An observation the converse of this will probably also be found true. In those countries that are subject to periodical sicknesses, the increase of population, or the excess of births above the burials, will be greater in the intervals of these periods than is usual, *caeteris paribus*, in the countries not so much subject to such disorders. If Turkey and Egypt have been nearly stationary in their average population for the last century, in the intervals of their periodical plagues, the births must have exceeded the burials in a greater proportion than in such countries as France and England.

The average proportion of births to burials in any country for a period of five to ten years, will hence appear to be a very inadequate criterion by which to judge of its real progress in population. This proportion certainly shows the rate of increase during those five or ten years; but we can by no means thence infer what had been the increase for the twenty years before, or what would be the increase for the twenty years after. Dr. Price observes that Sweden, Norway, Russia, and the kingdom of Naples, are increasing fast; but the extracts from registers that he has given are not for periods of sufficient extent to establish the fact. It is highly probable, however, that Sweden, Norway, and Russia, are really increasing their population, though not at the rate that the proportion of births to burials for the short periods that Dr. Price takes would seem to show. (See Dr. Price's Observations, Vol. ii, postscript to the controversy on the population of England and Wales.) For five years, ending in 1777, the proportion of births to burials in the kingdom of Naples was 144 to 100, but there is reason to suppose that this proportion would indicate an increase much greater than would be really found to have taken place in that kingdom during a period of a hundred years.

Dr. Short compared the registers of many villages and market towns in England for two periods; the first, from Queen Elizabeth to the middle of the last century, and the second, from different years at the end of the last century to the middle of the present. And from a comparison of these extracts, it appears that in the former period the births exceeded the burials in the proportion of 124 to 100, but in the latter, only in the proportion of 111 to 100. Dr. Price thinks that the registers in the former period are not to be depended upon, but, probably, in this instance they do not give incorrect proportions. At least there are many reasons for expecting to find a greater excess of births above the burials in the former period than in the latter. In the natural progress of the population of any country, more good land will, caeteris paribus, be taken into cultivation in the earlier stages of it than in the later. (I say "caeteris paribus," because the increase of the produce of any country will always very greatly depend on the spirit of industry that prevails, and the way in which it is directed. The knowledge and habits of the people, and other temporary causes, particularly the degree of civil liberty and equality existing at the time, must always have great influence in exciting and directing this spirit.) And a greater proportional yearly increase of produce will almost invariably be followed by a greater proportional increase of population. But, besides this great cause, which would naturally give the excess of births above burials greater at the end of Queen Elizabeth's reign than in the middle of the present century, I cannot help thinking that the occasional ravages of the plague in the former period must have had some tendency to increase this proportion. If an average of ten years had been taken in the intervals of the returns of this dreadful disorder, or if the years of plague had been rejected as accidental, the registers would certainly give the proportion of births to burials too high for the real average increase of the population. For some few years after the great plague in 1666, it is probable that there was a more than usual excess of births above burials, particularly if Dr. Price's opinion be founded, that England was more populous at the revolution (which happened only twenty-two years afterwards) than it is at present.

Mr. King, in 1693, stated the proportion of the births to the burials throughout the Kingdom, exclusive of London, as 115 to 100. Dr. Short makes it, in the middle of the present century, 111 to 100, including London. The proportion in France for five years, ending in 1774, was 117 to 100. If these statements are near the truth; and if there are no very great variations at particular periods in the proportions, it would appear that the population of France and England has accommodated itself very nearly to the average produce of each country. The discouragements to marriage, the consequent vicious habits, war, luxury, the silent though certain depopulation of large towns, and the close habitations, and insufficient food of many of the poor, prevent population from increasing beyond the means of subsistence; and, if I may use an expression which certainly at first appears strange, supercede the necessity of great and ravaging epidemics to repress what is redundant. Were a wasting plague to sweep off two millions in England, and six millions in France, there can be no doubt whatever that, after the inhabitants had recovered from the dreadful shock, the proportion of births to burials would be much above what it is in either country at present.

In New Jersey, the proportion of births to deaths on an average of seven years, ending in 1743, was as 300 to 100. In France and England, taking the highest proportion, it is as 117 to 100. Great and astonishing as this difference is, we ought not to be so wonder-struck at it as to attribute it to the miraculous interposition of heaven. The causes of it are not remote, latent and mysterious; but near us, round about us, and open to the investigation of every inquiring mind. It accords with the most liberal spirit of philosophy to suppose that not a stone can fall, or a plant rise, without the immediate agency of divine power. But we know from experience that these operations of what we call nature have been conducted almost invariably according to fixed laws. And since the world began, the causes of population and depopulation have probably been as constant as any of the laws of nature with which we are acquainted.

The passion between the sexes has appeared in every age to be so nearly the same that it may always be considered, in algebraic language, as a given quantity. The great law of necessity which prevents population from increasing in any country beyond the food which it can either produce or acquire, is a law so open to our view, so obvious and evident to our understandings, and so completely confirmed by the experience of every age, that we cannot for a moment doubt it. The different modes which nature takes to prevent or repress a redundant population do not appear, indeed, to us so certain and regular, but though we cannot always predict the mode we may with certainty predict the fact. If the proportion of births to deaths for a few years indicate an increase of numbers much beyond the proportional increased or acquired produce of the country, we may be perfectly certain that unless an emigration takes place, the deaths will shortly exceed the births; and that the increase that had taken place for a few years cannot be the real average increase of the population of the country. Were there no other depopulating causes, every country would, without doubt, be subject to periodical pestilences or famine.

The only true criterion of a real and permanent increase in the population of any country is the increase of the means of subsistence. But even, this criterion is subject to some slight variations which are, however, completely open to our view and observations. In some countries population appears to have been forced, that is, the people have been habituated by degrees to live almost upon the smallest possible quantity of food. There must have been periods in such counties when population increased permanently, without an increase in the means of subsistence. China seems to answer to this description. If the accounts we have of it are to be trusted, the lower classes of people are in the habit of living almost upon the smallest possible quantity of food and are glad to get any putrid offals that European laborers would rather starve than eat. The law in China which permits parents to expose their children has tended principally thus to force the population. A nation in this state must necessarily be subject to famines. Where a country is so populous in proportion to the means of subsistence that the average produce of it is but barely sufficient to support the lives of the inhabitants, any deficiency from the badness of seasons must be fatal. It is probable that the very frugal manner in which the Gentoos are in the habit of living contributes in some degree to the famines of Indostan.

In America, where the reward of labor is at present so liberal, the lower classes might retrench very considerably in a year of scarcity without materially distressing themselves. A famine therefore seems to be almost impossible. It may be expected that in the progress of the population of America, the laborers will in time be much less liberally rewarded. The numbers will in this case permanently increase without a proportional increase in the means of subsistence.

In the different states of Europe there must be some variations in the proportion between the number of inhabitants and the quantity of food consumed, arising from the different habits of living that prevail in each state. The laborers of the South of England are so accustomed to eat fine wheaten bread that they will suffer themselves to be half starved before they will submit to live like the Scotch peasants. They might perhaps in time, by the constant operation of the hard law of necessity, be reduced to live even like the Lower Chinese, and the country would then, with the same quantity of food, support a greater population. But to effect this must always be a most difficult, and, every friend to humanity will hope, an abortive attempt. Nothing is so common as to hear of encouragements that ought to be given to population. If the tendency of mankind to increase be so great as I have represented it to be, it may appear strange that this increase does not come when it is thus repeatedly called for. The true reason is that the demand for a greater population is made without preparing the funds necessary to support it. Increase the demand for agricultural labor by promoting cultivation, and with it consequently increase the produce of the country, and ameliorate the condition of the laborer, and no apprehensions whatever need be entertained of the proportional increase of population. An attempt to effect this purpose in any other way is vicious, cruel, and tyrannical, and in any state of tolerable freedom cannot therefore succeed. It may appear to be the interest of the rulers, and the rich of a state, to force population, and thereby lower the price of labor, and consequently the expense of fleets and armies, and the cost of manufactures for foreign sale; but every attempt of the kind should be carefully watched and strenuously resisted by the friends of the poor, particularly when it comes under the deceitful garb of benevolence, and is likely, on that account, to be cheerfully and cordially received by the common people.

I entirely acquit Mr. Pitt of any sinister intention in that clause of his Poor Bill which allows a shilling a week to every laborer for each child he has above three. I confess, that before the bill was brought into Parliament, and for some time after, I thought that such a regulation would be highly beneficial, but further reflection on the subject has convinced me that if its object be to better the condition of the poor, it is calculated to defeat the very purpose which it has in view. It has no tendency that I can discover to increase the produce of the country, and if. It tend to increase the population, without increasing the produce, the necessary and inevitable consequence appears to be that the same produce must be divided among a greater number, and consequently that a day's labor will purchase a smaller quantity of provisions, and the poor therefore in general must be more distressed.

I have mentioned some cases where population may permanently increase without a proportional increase in the means of subsistence. But it is evident that the variation in different states, between the food and the numbers supported by it, is restricted to a limit beyond which it cannot pass. In every country, the population of which is not absolutely decreasing, the food must be necessarily sufficient to support, and to continue, the race of laborers.

Other circumstances being the same, it may be affirmed that countries are populous according to the quantity of human food which they produce, and happy according to the liberality with which that food is divided, or the quantity which a day's labor will purchase. Corn countries are more populous than pasture countries, and rice countries more populous than corn countries. The lands in England are not suited to rice, but they would all bear potatoes; and Dr. Adam Smith observes that if potatoes were to become the favorite vegetable food of the common people, and if the same quantity of land was employed in their culture as is now employed in the culture of corn, the country would be able to support a much greater population, and would consequently in a very short time have it.

The happiness of a country does not depend, absolutely, upon its poverty or its riches, upon its youth or its age, upon its being thinly or fully inhabited, but upon the rapidity with which it is increasing, upon the degree in which the yearly increase of food approaches to the yearly increase of an unrestricted population. This approximation is always the nearest in new colonies, where the knowledge and industry of an old state operate on the fertile unappropriated land of a new one. In other cases, the youth or the age of a state is not in this respect of very great importance. It is probable that the food of Great Britain is divided in as great plenty to the inhabitants, at the present period, as it was two thousand, three thousand, or four thousand years ago. And there is reason to believe that the poor and thinly inhabited tracts of the Scotch Highlands are as much distressed by an overcharged population as the rich and populous province of Flanders.

Were a country never to be overrun by a people more advanced in arts, but left to its own natural progress in civilization; from the time that its produce might be considered as an unit, to the time that it might be considered as a million, during the lapse of many hundred years, there would not be a single period when the mass of the people could be said to be free from distress, either directly or indirectly, for want of food. In every state in Europe, since we have first had accounts of it, millions and millions of human existences have been repressed from this simple cause; though perhaps in some of these states an absolute famine has never been known.

Famine seems to be the last, the most dreadful resource of nature. The power of population is so superior to the power in the earth to produce subsistence for man, that premature death must in some shape or other visit the human race. The vices of mankind are active and able ministers of depopulation. They are the precursors in the great army of destruction; and often finish the dreadful work themselves. But should they fail in this war of extermination, sickly seasons, epidemics, pestilence, and plague, advance in terrific array, and sweep off their thousands and ten thousands. Should success be still incomplete, gigantic inevitable famine stalks in the rear, and with one mighty blow levels the population with the food of the world.

Must it not then be acknowledged by an attentive examiner of the histories of mankind, that in every age and in every state in which man has existed, or does now exist.

That the increase of population is necessarily limited by the means of subsistence.

That population does invariably increase when the means of subsistence increase. And that the superior power of population it repressed, and the actual population kept equal to the means of subsistence, by misery and vice?

CHAPTER 8

Mr. Wallace—Error of Supposing that the Difficulty Arising from Population is at a Great Distance— Mr. Condorcet's Sketch of the Progress of the Human Mind—Period when the Oscillation, Mentioned by Mr. Condorcet, Ought to be Applied to the Human Race.

To a person who draws the preceding obvious inferences, from a view of the past and present state of mankind, it cannot but be a matter of astonishment that all the writers on the perfectibility of man and of society who have noticed the argument of an over-charged population, treat it always very slightly and invariably represent the difficulties arising from it as at a great and almost immeasurable distance. Even Mr. Wallace, who thought the argument itself of so much weight as to destroy his whole system of equality, did not seem to be aware that any difficulty would occur from this cause till the whole earth had been cultivated like a garden and was incapable of any further increase of produce. Were this really the case, and were a beautiful system of equality in other respects practicable, I cannot think that our ardor in the pursuit of such a scheme ought to be damped by the contemplation of so remote a difficulty. An event at such a distance might fairly be left to providence, but the truth is that if the view of the argument given in this Essay be just the difficulty, so far from being remote, would be imminent and immediate. At every period during the progress of cultivation, from the present moment to the time when the whole earth was become like a garden, the distress for want of food would be constantly pressing on all mankind, if they were equal. Though the produce of the earth might be increasing every year, population would be increasing much faster, and the redundancy must necessarily be repressed by the periodical or constant action of misery or vice.

Mr. Condorcet's *Esquisse d'un Tableau Historique des Progres de l'Esprit Humain*, was written, it is said, under the pressure of that cruel proscription which terminated in his death. If he had no hopes of its being seen during his life and of its interesting France in his favor, it is a singular instance of the attachment of a man to principles, which every day's experience was so fatally for himself contradicting. To see the human mind in one of the most enlightened nations of the world, and after a lapse of some thousand years, debased by such a fermentation of disgusting passions, of fear, cruelty, malice, revenge, ambition, madness, and folly as would have disgraced the most savage nation in the most barbarous age must have been such a tremendous shock to his ideas of the necessary and inevitable progress of the human mind that nothing but the firmest conviction of the truth of his principles, in spite of all appearances, could have withstood.

This posthumous publication is only a sketch of a much larger work, which he proposed should be executed. It necessarily, therefore, wants that detail and application which can alone prove the truth of any theory. A few observations will be sufficient to show how completely the theory is contradicted when it is applied to the real, and not to an imaginary, state of things.

In the last division of the work, which treats of the future progress of man towards perfection, he says, that comparing, in the different civilized nations of Europe, the actual population with the extent of territory, and observing their cultivation, their industry, their divisions of labor, and their means of subsistence, we shall see that it would be impossible to preserve the same means of subsistence, and, consequently, the same population, without a number of individuals who have no other means of supplying their wants than their industry. Having allowed the necessity of such a class of men, and adverting afterwards to the precarious revenue of those families that would depend so entirely on the life and health of their chief, he says, very justly: "There exists then, a necessary cause of inequality, of dependence, and even of misery, which menaces, without ceasing, the most numerous and active class of our societies." (To save time and long quotations, I shall here give the substance of some of Mr. Condorcet's sentiments, and hope I shall not misrepresent them. But I refer the reader to the work itself, which will amuse, if it does not convince him.) The difficulty is just and well stated, and I am afraid that the mode by which he proposes it should be removed will be found inefficacious. By the application of calculations to the probabilities of life and the interest of money, he proposes that a fund should be established which should assure to the old an assistance, produced, in part, by their own former savings, and, in part, by the savings of individuals who in making the same sacrifice die before they reap the benefit of it. The same, or a similar fund, should give assistance to women and children who lose their husbands, or fathers, and afford a capital to those who were of an age to found a new family, sufficient for the proper development of their industry. These establishments, he observes, might be made in the name and under the protection of the society. Going still further, he says that, by the just application of calculations, means might be found of more completely preserving a state of equality, by preventing credit from being the exclusive privilege of great fortunes, and yet giving it a basis equally solid, and by rendering the progress of industry, and the activity of commerce, less dependent on great capitalists.

Such establishments and calculations may appear very promising upon paper, but when applied to real life they will be found to be absolutely nugatory. Mr. Condorcet allows that a class of people which maintains itself entirely by industry is necessary to every state. Why does he allow this? No other reason can well be assigned than that he conceives that the labor necessary to procure subsistence for an extended population will not be performed without the goad of necessity. If by establishments of this kind of spur to industry be removed, if the idle and the negligent are placed upon the same footing with regard to their credit, and the future support of their wives and families, as the active and industrious, can we expect to see men exert that animated activity in bettering their condition which now forms the master spring of public prosperity? If an inquisition were to be established to examine the claims of each individual and to determine whether he had or had not exerted himself to the utmost, and to grant or refuse assistance accordingly, this would be little else than a repetition upon a larger scale of the English poor laws and would be completely destructive of the true principles of liberty and equality.

696 THE REAL PRICE OF EVERYTHING

But independent of this great objection to these establishments, and supposing for a moment that they would give no check to productive industry, by far the greatest difficulty remains yet behind.

Were every man sure of a comfortable provision for his family, almost every man would have one, and were the rising generation free from the "killing frost" of misery, population must rapidly increase. Of this Mr. Condorcet seems to be fully aware himself, and after having described further improvements, he says:

> But in this process of industry and happiness, each generation will be called to more extended enjoyments, and in consequence, by the physical constitution of the human frame, to an increase in the number of individuals. Must not there arrive a period then, when these laws, equally necessary, shall counteract each other? When the increase of the number of men surpassing their means of subsistence, the necessary result must be either a continual diminution of happiness and population, a movement truly retrograde, or, at least, a kind of oscillation between good and evil? In societies arrived at this term, will not this oscillation be a constantly subsisting cause of periodical misery? Will it not mark the limit when all further amelioration will become impossible, and point out that term to the perfectibility of the human race which it may reach in the course of ages, but can never pass?

He then adds,

> There is no person who does not see how very distant such a period is from us, but shall we ever arrive at it? It is equally impossible to pronounce for or against the future realization of an event which cannot take place but at an era when the human race will have attained improvements, of which we can at present scarcely form a conception.

Mr. Condorcet's picture of what may be expected to happen when the number of men shall surpass the means of their subsistence is justly drawn. The oscillation which he describes will certainly take place and will without doubt be a constantly subsisting cause of periodical misery. The only point in which I differ from Mr. Condorcet with regard to this picture is the period when it may be applied to the human race. Mr. Condorcet thinks that it cannot possibly be applicable but at an era extremely distant. If the proportion between the natural increase of population and food which I have given be in any degree near the truth, it will appear, on the contrary, that the period when the number of men surpass their means of subsistence has long since arrived, and that this necessity oscillation, this constantly subsisting cause of periodical misery, has existed ever since we have had any histories of mankind, does exist at present, and will forever continue to exist, unless some decided change take place in the physical constitution of our nature.

Mr. Condorcet, however, goes on to say that should the period, which he conceives to be so distant, ever arrive, the human race, and the advocates for the perfectibility of man, need not be alarmed at it. He then proceeds to remove the difficulty in a manner which I profess not to understand. Having observed, that the ridiculous prejudices of superstition would by that time have ceased to throw over morals a corrupt and degrading austerity, he alludes, either to a promiscuous concubinage, which would prevent breeding, or to something else as unnatural. To remove the difficulty in this way will, surely, in the opinion of most men, be to destroy that virtue and purity of manners, which the advocates of equality, and of the perfectibility of man, profess to be the end and object of their views.

CHAPTER 9

Mr. Condorcet's Conjecture Concerning the Organic Perfectibility of Man, and the Indefinite Prolongation of Human Life—Fallacy of the Argument, which Infers an Unlimited Progress from a Partial Improvement, the Limit of which Cannot be Ascertained, Illustrated in the Breeding of Animals, and the Cultivation of Plants.

The last question which Mr. Condorcet proposes for examination is the organic perfectibility of man. He observes that if the proofs which have been already given and which, in their development will receive greater force in the work itself, are sufficient to establish the indefinite perfectibility of man upon the supposition of the same natural faculties and the same organization which he has at present, what will be the certainty, what the extent of our hope, if this organization, these natural faculties themselves, are susceptible of amelioration?

From the improvement of medicine, from the use of more wholesome food and habitations, from a manner of living which will improve the strength of the body by exercise without impairing it by excess, from the destruction of the two great causes of the degradation of man, misery, and too great riches, from the gradual removal of transmissible and contagious disorders by the improvement of physical knowledge, rendered more efficacious by the progress of reason and of social order, he infers that though man will not absolutely become immortal, yet that the duration between his birth and natural death will increase without ceasing, will have no assignable term, and may properly be expressed by the word "indefinite." He then defines this word to mean either a constant approach to an unlimited extent, without ever reaching it, or an increase. In the immensity of ages to an extent greater than any assignable quantity.

But surely the application of this term in either of these senses to the duration of human life is in the highest degree unphilosophical and totally unwarranted by any appearances in the laws of nature. Variations from different causes are essentially distinct from a regular and unretrograde increase. The average duration of human life will to a certain degree vary from healthy or unhealthy climates, from wholesome or unwholesome food, from virtuous or vicious manners, and other causes, but it may be fairly doubted whether there is really the smallest perceptible advance in the natural duration of human life since first we have had any authentic history of man. The prejudices of all ages have indeed been directly contrary to this supposition, and though I would not lay much stress upon these prejudices, they will in some measure tend to prove that there has been no marked advance in an opposite direction.

It may perhaps be said that the world is yet so young, so completely in its infancy, that it ought not to be expected that any difference should appear so soon.

If this be the case, there is at once an end of all human science. The whole train of reasonings from effects to causes will be destroyed. We may shut our eyes to the book of nature, as it will no longer be of any use to read it. The wildest and most improbable conjectures may be advanced with as much certainty as the most just and sublime theories, founded on careful and reiterated experiments. We may return again to the old mode of philosophizing and make facts bend to systems, instead of establishing systems upon facts. The grand and consistent theory of Newton will be placed upon the same footing as the wild and eccentric hypotheses of Descartes. In short, if the laws of nature are thus fickle and inconstant, if it can be affirmed and be believed that they will change, when for ages and ages they have appeared immutable, the human mind will no longer have any incitements to inquiry, but must remain fixed in inactive torpor, or amuse itself only in bewildering dreams and extravagant fancies.

The constancy of the laws of nature and of effects and causes is the foundation of all human knowledge, though far be it from me to say that the same power which framed and executes the laws of nature may not change them all "in a moment, in the twinkling of an eye."

Such a change may undoubtedly happen. All that I mean to say is that it is impossible to infer it from reasoning. If without any previous observable symptoms or indications of a change, we can infer that a change will take place, we may as well make any assertion whatever and think it as unreasonable to be contradicted in affirming that the moon will come in contact with the earth tomorrow, as in saying that the sun will rise at its usual time.

With regard to the duration of human life, there does not appear to have existed from the earliest ages of the world to the present moment the smallest permanent symptom or indication of increasing prolongation. The observable effects of climate, habit, diet, and other causes, on length of life have furnished the pretext for asserting its indefinite extension; and the sandy foundation on which the argument rests is that because the limit of human life is undefined; because you cannot mark its precise term, and say so far exactly shall it go and no further; that therefore its extent may increase forever, and be properly termed indefinite or unlimited. But the fallacy and absurdity of this argument will sufficiently appear from a slight examination of what Mr. Condorcet calls the organic perfectibility, or degeneration, of the race of plants and animals, which he says may be regarded as one of the general laws of nature.

I am told that it is a maxim among the improvers of cattle that you may breed to any degree of nicety you please, and they found this maxim upon another, which is that some of the offspring will possess the desirable qualities of the parents in a greater degree. In the famous Leicestershire breed of sheep, the object is to procure them with small heads and small legs. Proceeding upon these breeding maxims, it is evident that we might go on till the heads and legs were evanescent quantities, but this is so palpable an absurdity that we may be quite sure that the premises are not just and that there really is a limit, though we cannot see it or say exactly where it is. In this case, the point of the greatest degree of improvement, or the smallest size of the head and legs, may be said to be undefined, but this is very different from unlimited, or from indefinite, in Mr. Condorcet's acceptation of the term. Though I may not be able in the present instance to mark the limit at which further improvement will stop, I can very easily mention a point at which it will not arrive. I should not scruple to assert that were the breeding to continue forever, the head and legs of these sheep would never be so small as the head and legs of a rat.

It cannot be true, therefore, that among animals, some of the offspring will possess the desirable qualities of the parents in a greater degree, or that animals are indefinitely perfectible.

The progress of a wild plant to a beautiful garden flower is perhaps more marked and striking than anything that takes place among animals, yet even here it would be the height of absurdity to assert that the progress was unlimited or indefinite.

One of the most obvious features of the improvement is the increase of size. The flower has grown gradually larger by cultivation. If the progress were really unlimited it might be increased ad infinitum, but this is so gross an absurdity that we may be quite sure that among plants as well as among animals there is a limit to improvement, though we do not exactly know where it is. It is probable that the gardeners who contend for flower prizes have often applied stronger dressing without success. At the same time it would be highly presumptuous in any man to say that he had seen the finest carnation or anemone that could ever be made to grow. He might however assert without the smallest chance of being contradicted by a future fact, that no carnation or anemone could ever by cultivation be increased to the size of a large cabbage; and yet there are assignable quantities much greater than a cabbage. No man can say that he has seen the largest ear of wheat, or the largest oak that could ever grow; but he might easily, and with perfect certainty, name a point of magnitude at which they would not arrive. In all these cases therefore, a careful distinction should be made, between an unlimited progress, and a progress where the limit is merely undefined.

It will be said, perhaps, that the reason why plants and animals cannot increase indefinitely in size is, that they would fall by their own weight. I answer, how do we know this but from experience?—from experience of the degree of strength with which these bodies are formed. I know that a carnation, long before it reached the size of a cabbage, would not be supported by its stalk, but I only know this from my experience of the weakness and want of tenacity in the materials of a carnation stalk. There are many substances in nature of the same size that would support as large a head as a cabbage.

The reasons of the mortality of plants are at present perfectly unknown to us. No man can say why such a plant is annual, another biennial, and another endures for ages. The whole affair in all these cases, in plants, animals, and in the human race, is an affair of experience, and I only conclude that man is mortal because the invariable experience of all ages has proved the mortality of those materials of which his visible body is made: What can we reason, but from what we know?

Sound philosophy will not authorize me to alter this opinion of the mortality of man on earth, till it can be clearly proved that the human race has made, and is making, a decided progress towards an illimitable extent of life. And the chief reason why I adduced the two particular instances from animals and plants was to expose and illustrate, if I could, the fallacy of that argument which infers an unlimited progress, merely because some partial improvement has taken place, and that the limit of this improvement can not be precisely ascertained.

The capacity of improvement in plants and animals, to a certain degree, no person can possibly doubt. A clear and decided progress has already been made, and yet, I think, it appears that it would be highly absurd to say that this progress has no limits. In human life, though there are great variations from different causes, it may be doubted whether, since the world began, any organic improvement whatever in the human frame can be clearly ascertained. The foundations, therefore, on which the arguments for the organic perfectibility of man rest, are unusually weak, and can only be considered as mere conjectures. It does not, however, by any means seem impossible that by an attention to breed, a certain degree of improvement, similar to that among animals, might take place among men. Whether intellect could be communicated may be a matter of doubt: but size, strength, beauty, complexion, and perhaps even longevity are in a degree transmissible. The error does not seem to lie in supposing a small degree of improvement possible, but in not discriminating between a small improvement, the limit of which is undefined, and an improvement really unlimited. As the human race, however, could not be improved in this way, without condemning all the bad specimens to celibacy, it is not probable that an attention to breed should ever become general; indeed, I know of no well-directed attempts of this kind, except in the ancient family of the Bickerstaffs, who are said to have been very successful in whitening the skins and increasing the height of their race by prudent marriages, particularly by that very judicious cross with Maud, the milk-maid, by which some capital defects in the constitutions of the family were corrected.

It will not be necessary, I think, in order more completely to show the improbability of any approach in man towards immortality on earth, to urge the very great additional weight that an increase in the duration of life would give to the argument of population.

Many, I doubt not, will think that the attempting gravely to controvert so absurd a paradox as the immortality of man on earth, or indeed, even the perfectibility of man and society, is a waste of time and words, and that such unfounded conjectures are best answered by neglect. I profess, however, to be of a different opinion. When paradoxes of this kind are advanced by ingenious and able men, neglect has no tendency to convince them of their mistakes. Priding themselves on what they conceive to be a mark of the reach and size of their own understandings, of the extent and comprehensiveness of their views, they will look upon this neglect merely as an indication of poverty, and narrowness, in the mental exertions of their contemporaries, and only think that the world is not yet prepared to receive their sublime truths.

On the contrary, a candid investigation of these subjects, accompanied with a perfect readiness to adopt any theory warranted by sound philosophy, may have a tendency to convince them that in forming improbable and unfounded hypotheses, so far from enlarging the bounds of human science, they are contracting it, so far from promoting the improvement of the human mind, they are obstructing it; they are throwing us back again almost into the infancy of knowledge and weakening the foundations of that mode of philosophizing, under the auspices of which science has of late made such rapid advances. The present rage for wide and unrestrained speculation seems to be a kind of mental intoxication, arising, perhaps, from the great and unexpected discoveries which have been made of late years, in various branches of science. To men elate and giddy with such successes, every thing appeared to be within the grasp of human powers; and, under this illusion, they confounded subjects where no real progress could be proved with those where the progress had been marked, certain, and acknowledged. Could they be persuaded to sober themselves with a little severe and chastised thinking, they would see, that the cause of truth, and of sound philosophy, cannot but suffer by substituting wild flights and unsupported assertions for patient investigation, and well authenticated proofs.

Mr. Condorcet's book may be considered not only as a sketch of the opinions of a celebrated individual, but of many of the literary men in France at the beginning of the Revolution. As such, though merely a sketch, it seems worthy of attention.

CHAPTER 10

Mr. Godwin's System of Equality—Error of Attributing All the Vices of Mankind to Human Institutions—Mr. Godwin's First Answer to the Difficulty Arising from Population Totally Insufficient—Mr. Godwin's Beautiful System of Equality Supposed to be Realized—Its Utter Destruction Simply from the Principle of Population in so Short a Time as Thirty Years.

In reading Mr. Godwin's ingenious and able work on political justice, it is impossible not to be struck with the spirit and energy of his style, the force and precision of some of his reasonings, the ardent tone of his thoughts, and particularly with that impressive earnestness of manner which gives an air of truth to the whole. At the same time, it must be confessed that he has not proceeded in his inquiries with the caution that sound philosophy seems to require. His conclusions are often unwarranted by his premises. He fails sometimes in removing the objections which he himself brings forward. He relies too much on general and abstract propositions which will not admit of application. And his conjectures certainly far outstrip the modesty of nature.

The system of equality which Mr. Godwin proposes is, without doubt, by far the most beautiful and engaging of any that has yet appeared. An amelioration of society to be produced merely by reason and conviction wears much more the promise of permanence than any change effected and maintained by force. The unlimited exercise of private judgment is a doctrine inexpressibly grand and captivating and has a vast superiority over those systems where every individual is in a manner the slave of the public. The substitution of benevolence as the master-spring and moving principle of society, instead of self-love, is a consummation devoutly to be wished. In short, it is impossible to contemplate the whole of this fair structure without emotions of delight and admiration, accompanied with ardent longing for the period of its accomplishment. But, alas! that moment can never arrive. The whole is little better than a dream, a beautiful phantom of the imagination. These "gorgeous palaces" of happiness and immortality, these "solemn temples" of truth and virtue will dissolve, "like the baseless fabric of a vision," when we awaken to real life and contemplate the true and genuine situation of man on earth. Mr. Godwin, at the conclusion of the third chapter of his eighth book, speaking of population, says:

> There is a principle in human society, by which population is perpetually kept down to the level of the means of subsistence. Thus among the wandering tribes of America and Asia, we never find through the lapse of ages that population has so increased as to render necessary the cultivation of the earth.

This principle, which Mr. Godwin thus mentions as some mysterious and occult cause and which he does not attempt to investigate, will be found to be the grinding law of necessity, misery, and the fear of misery.

The great error under which Mr. Godwin labors throughout his whole work is the attributing almost all the vices and misery that are seen in civil society to human institutions. Political regulations and the established administration of property are with him the fruitful sources of all evil, the hotbeds of all the crimes that degrade mankind. Were this really a true state of the case, it would not seem a hopeless task to remove evil completely from the world, and reason seems to be the proper and adequate instrument for effecting so great a purpose. But the truth is, that though human institutions appear to be the obvious and obtrusive causes of much mischief to mankind, yet in reality they are light and superficial, they are mere feathers that float on the surface, in comparison with those deeper seated causes of impurity that corrupt the springs and render turbid the whole stream of human life.

Mr. Godwin, in his chapter on the benefits attendant on a system of equality, says:

> The spirit of oppression, the spirit of servility, and the spirit of fraud, these are the immediate growth of the established administration of property. They are alike hostile to intellectual improvement. The other vices of envy, malice, and revenge are their inseparable companions. In a state of society where men lived in the midst of plenty and where all shared alike the bounties of nature, these sentiments would inevitably expire. The narrow principle of selfishness would vanish. No man being obliged to guard his little store or provide with anxiety and pain for his restless wants, each would lose his individual existence in the thought of the general good. No man would be an enemy to his neighbor, for they would have no subject of contention, and, of consequence, philanthropy would resume the empire which reason assigns her. Mind would be delivered from her perpetual anxiety about corporal support, and free to expatiate in the field of thought, which is congenial to her. Each would assist the inquiries of all.

This would, indeed, be a happy state. But that it is merely an imaginary picture, with scarcely a feature near the truth, the reader, I am afraid, is already too well convinced.

Man cannot live in the midst of plenty. All cannot share alike the bounties of nature. Were there no established administration of property, every man would be obliged to guard with force his little store. Selfishness would be triumphant. The subjects of contention would be perpetual. Every individual mind would be under a constant anxiety about corporal support, and not a single intellect would be left free to expatiate in the field of thought.

How little Mr. Godwin has turned the attention of his penetrating mind to the real state of man on earth will sufficiently appear from the manner in which he endeavors to remove the difficulty of an overcharged population. He says:

> The obvious answer to this objection, is, that to reason thus is to foresee difficulties at a great distance. Three fourths of the habitable globe is now uncultivated. The parts already cultivated are capable of immeasurable improvement. Myriads of centuries of still increasing population may pass away, and the earth be still found sufficient for the subsistence of its inhabitants.

I have already pointed out the error of supposing that no distress and difficulty would arise from an overcharged population before the earth absolutely refused to produce any more. But let us imagine for a moment Mr. Godwin's beautiful system of equality realized in its utmost purity, and see how soon this difficulty might be expected to press under so perfect a form of society. A theory that will not admit of application cannot possibly be just.

Let us suppose all the causes of misery and vice in this island removed. War and contention cease. Unwholesome trades and manufactories do not exist. Crowds no longer collect together in great and pestilent cities for purposes of court intrigue, of commerce, and vicious gratifications. Simple, healthy, and rational amusements take place of drinking, gaming, and debauchery. There are no towns sufficiently large to have any prejudicial effects on the human constitution. The greater part of the happy inhabitants of this terrestrial paradise live in hamlets and farmhouses scattered over the face of the country. Every house is clean, airy, sufficiently roomy, and in a healthy situation. All men are equal. The labors of luxury are at end. And the necessary labors of agriculture are shared amicably among all. The number of persons, and the produce of the island, we suppose to be the same as at present. The spirit of benevolence, guided by impartial justice, will divide this produce among all the members of the society according to their wants. Though it would be impossible that they should all have animal food every day, yet vegetable food, with meat occasionally, would satisfy the desires of a frugal people and would be sufficient to preserve them in health, strength, and spirits.

Mr. Godwin considers marriage as a fraud and a monopoly. Let us suppose the commerce of the sexes established upon principles of the most perfect freedom. Mr. Godwin does not think himself that this freedom would lead to a promiscuous intercourse, and in this I perfectly agree with him. The love of variety is a vicious, corrupt, and unnatural taste and could not prevail in any great degree in a simple and virtuous state of society. Each man would probably select himself a partner, to whom he would adhere as long as that adherence continued to be the choice of both parties. It would be of little consequence, according to Mr. Godwin, how many children a woman had or to whom they belonged. Provisions and assistance would spontaneously flow from the quarter in which they abounded, to the quarter that was deficient. (See Bk VIII, ch. 8; in the third edition, Vol II, p. 512.) And every man would be ready to furnish instruction to the rising generation according to his capacity.

I cannot conceive a form of society so favorable upon the whole to population. The irremediableness of marriage, as it is at present constituted, undoubtedly deters many from entering into that state. An unshackled intercourse on the contrary would be a most powerful incitement to early attachments, and as we are supposing no anxiety about the future support of children to exist, I do not conceive that there would be one woman in a hundred, of twenty-three, without a family.

With these extraordinary encouragements to population, and every cause of depopulation, as we have supposed, removed, the numbers would necessarily increase faster than in any society that has ever yet been known. I have mentioned, on the authority of a pamphlet published by a Dr. Styles and referred to by Dr. Price, that the inhabitants of the back settlements of America doubled their numbers in fifteen years. England is certainly a more healthy country than the back settlements of America, and as we have supposed every house in the island to be airy and wholesome, and the encouragements to have a family greater even than with the back settlers, no probable reason can be assigned why the population should not double itself in less, if possible, than fifteen years. But to be quite sure that we do not go beyond the truth, we will only suppose the period of doubling to be twenty-five years, a ratio of increase which is well known to have taken place throughout all the Northern States of America.

There can be little doubt that the equalization of property which we have supposed, added to the circumstance of the labor of the whole community being directed chiefly to agriculture, would tend greatly to augment the produce of the country. But to answer the demands of a population increasing so rapidly, Mr. Godwin's calculation of half an hour a day for each man would certainly not be sufficient. It is probable that the half of every man's time must be employed for this purpose. Yet with such, or much greater exertions, a person who is acquainted with the nature of the soil in this country, and who reflects on the fertility of the lands already in cultivation, and the barrenness of those that are not cultivated, will be very much disposed to doubt whether the whole average produce could possibly be doubled in twenty-five years from the present period. The only chance of success would be the plowing up all the grazing countries and putting an end almost entirely to the use of animal food. Yet a part of this scheme might defeat itself. The soil of England will not produce much without dressing, and cattle seem to be necessary to make that species of manure which best suits the land. In China it is said that the soil in some of the provinces is so fertile as to produce two crops of rice in the year without dressing. None of the lands in England will answer to this description.

Difficult, however, as it might be to double the average produce of the island in twenty-five years, let us suppose it effected. At the expiration of the first period therefore, the food, though almost entirely vegetable, would be sufficient to support in health the doubled population of fourteen millions.

During the next period of doubling, where will the food be found to satisfy the importunate demands of the increasing numbers? Where is the fresh land to turn up? Where is the dressing necessary to improve that which is already in cultivation? There is no person with the smallest knowledge of land but would say that it was impossible that the average produce of the country could be increased during the second twenty-five years by a quantity equal to what it at present yields. Yet we will suppose this increase, however improbable, to take place. The exuberant strength of the argument allows of almost any concession. Even with this concession, however, there would be seven millions at the expiration of the second term unprovided for. A quantity of food equal to the frugal support of twenty-one millions, would be to be divided among twenty-eight millions.

Alas! what becomes of the picture where men lived in the midst of plenty, where no man was obliged to provide with anxiety and pain for his restless wants, where the narrow principle of selfishness did not exist, where Mind was delivered from her perpetual anxiety about corporal support and free to expatiate in the field of thought which is congenial to her. This beautiful fabric of imagination vanishes at the severe touch of truth. The spirit of benevolence, cherished and invigorated by plenty, is repressed by the chilling breath of want. The hateful passions that had vanished reappear. The mighty law of self-preservation expels all the softer and more exalted emotions of the soul. The temptations to evil are too strong for human nature to resist. The corn is plucked before it is ripe, or secreted in unfair proportions, and the whole black train of vices that belong to falsehood are immediately generated. Provisions no longer flow in for the support of the mother with a large family. The children are sickly from insufficient food. The rosy flush of health gives place to the pallid cheek and hollow eye of misery. Benevolence, yet lingering in a few bosoms, makes some faint expiring struggles, till at length self-love resumes his wonted empire and lords it triumphant over the world.

No human institutions here existed, to the perverseness of which Mr. Godwin ascribes the original sin of the worst men. (Bk VIII, ch. 3; in the third edition, Vol. II, p. 462.) No opposition had been produced by them between public and private good. No monopoly had been created of those advantages which reason directs to be left in common. No man had been goaded to the breach of order by unjust laws. Benevolence had established her reign in all hearts: and yet in so short a period as within fifty years, violence, oppression, falsehood, misery, every hateful vice, and every form of distress, which degrade and sadden the present state of society, seem to have been generated by the most imperious circumstances, by laws inherent in the nature of man, and absolutely independent of it human regulations.

If we are not yet too well convinced of the reality of this melancholy picture, let us but look for a moment into the next period of twenty-five years; and we shall see twenty-eight millions of human beings without the means of support; and before the conclusion of the first century, the population would be one hundred and twelve millions, and the food only sufficient for thirty-five millions, leaving seventy-seven millions unprovided for. In these ages want would be indeed triumphant, and rapine and murder must reign at large: and yet all this time we are supposing the produce of the earth absolutely unlimited, and the yearly increase greater than the boldest speculator can imagine.

This is undoubtedly a very different view of the difficulty arising from population from that which Mr. Godwin gives, when he says, "Myriads of centuries of still increasing population may pass away, and the earth be still found sufficient for the subsistence of its inhabitants.'

I am sufficiently aware that the redundant twenty-eight millions, or seventy-seven millions, that I have mentioned, could never have existed. It is a perfectly just observation of Mr. Godwin, that, "There is a principle in human society, by which population is perpetually kept down to the level of the means of subsistence." The sole question is, what is this principle? Is it some obscure and occult cause? Is it some mysterious interference of heaven which, at a certain period, strikes the men with impotence, and the women with barrenness? Or is it a cause, open to our researches, within our view, a cause, which has constantly been observed to operate, though with varied force, in every state in which man has been placed? Is it not a degree of misery, the necessary and inevitable result of the laws of nature, which human institutions, so far from aggravating, have tended considerably to mitigate, though they never can remove?

It may be curious to observe, in the case that we have been supposing, how some of the laws which at present govern civilized society, would be successively dictated by the most imperious necessity. As man, according to Mr. Godwin, is the creature of the impressions to which he is subject, the goadings of want could not continue long, before some violations of public or private stock would necessarily take place. As these violations increased in number and extent, the more active and comprehensive intellects of the society would soon perceive, that while population was fast increasing, the yearly produce of the country would shortly begin to diminish. The urgency of the case would suggest the necessity of some mediate measures to be taken for the general safety. Some kind of convention would then be called, and the dangerous situation of the country stated in the strongest terms. It would be observed, that while they lived in the midst of plenty, it was of little consequence who labored the least, or who possessed the least, as every man was perfectly willing and ready to supply the wants of his neighbor. But that the question was no longer whether one man should give to another that which he did not use himself, but whether he should give to his neighbor the food which was absolutely necessary to his own existence. It would be represented, that the number of those that were in want very greatly exceeded the number and means of those who should supply them; that these pressing wants, which from the state of the produce of the country could not all be gratified, had occasioned some flagrant violations of justice; that these violations had already checked the increase of food, and would, if they were not by some means or other prevented, throw the whole community in confusion; that imperious necessity seemed to dictate that a yearly increase of produce should, if possible, be obtained at all events; that in order to effect this first, great, and indispensable purpose, it would be advisable to make a more complete division of land, and to secure every man's stock against violation by the most powerful sanctions, even by death itself.

It might be urged perhaps by some objectors that, as the fertility of the land increased, and various accidents occurred, the share of some men might be much more than sufficient for their support, and that when the reign of self-love was once established, they would not distribute their surplus produce without some compensation in return. It would be observed, in answer, that this was an inconvenience greatly to be lamented; but that it was an evil which bore no comparison to the black train of distresses that would inevitably be occasioned by the insecurity of property; that the quantity of food which one man could consume was necessarily limited by the narrow capacity of the human stomach; that it was not certainly probable that he should throw away the rest; but that even if he exchanged his surplus food for the labor of others, and made them in some degree dependent on him, this would still be better than that these others should absolutely starve.

It seems highly probable, therefore, that an administration of property, not very different from that which prevails in civilized states at present, would be established, as the best, though inadequate, remedy for the evils which were pressing on the society.

The next subject that would come under discussion, intimately connected with the preceding, is the commerce between the sexes. It would be urged by those who had turned their attention to the true cause of the difficulties under which the community labored, that while every man felt secure that all his children would be well provided for by general benevolence, the powers of the earth would be absolutely inadequate to produce food for the population which would inevitably ensue; that even if the whole attention and labor of the society were directed to this sole point, and if, by the most perfect security of property, and every other encouragement that could be thought of, the greatest possible increase of produce were yearly obtained; yet still, that the increase of food would by no means keep pace with the much more rapid increase of population; that some check to population therefore was imperiously called for; that the most natural and obvious check seemed to be to make every man provide for his own children; that this would operate in some respect as a measure and guide in the increase of population, as it might be expected that no man would bring beings into the world, for whom he could not find the means of support; that where this notwithstanding was the case, it seemed necessary, for the example of others, that the disgrace and inconvenience attending such a conduct should fall upon the individual, who had thus inconsiderately plunged himself and innocent children in misery and want.

The institution of marriage, or at least, of some express or implied obligation on every man to support his own children, seems to be the natural result of these reasonings in a community under the difficulties that we have supposed.

The view of these difficulties presents us with a very natural origin of the superior disgrace which attends a breach of chastity in the woman than in the man. It could not be expected that women should have resources sufficient to support their own children. When therefore a woman was connected with a man, who had entered into no compact to maintain her children, and, aware of the inconveniences that he might bring upon himself, had deserted her, these children must necessarily fall for support upon the society, or starve. And to prevent the frequent recurrence of such an inconvenience, as it would be highly unjust to punish so natural a fault by personal restraint or infliction, the men might agree to punish it with disgrace. The offence is besides more obvious and conspicuous in the woman, and less liable to any mistake. The father of a child may not always be known, but the same uncertainty cannot easily exist with regard to the mother. Where the evidence of the offence was most complete, and the inconvenience to the society at the same time the greatest, there it was agreed that the large share of blame should fall. The obligation on every man to maintain his children, the society would enforce, if there were occasion; and the greater degree of inconvenience or labor, to which a family would necessarily subject him, added to some portion of disgrace which every human being must incur who leads another into unhappiness, might be considered as a sufficient punishment for the man.

That a woman should at present be almost driven from society for an offence which men commit nearly with impunity, seems to be undoubtedly a breach of natural justice. But the origin of the custom, as the most obvious and effectual method of preventing the frequent recurrence of a serious inconvenience to a community, appears to be natural, though not perhaps perfectly justifiable. This origin, however, is now lost in the new train of ideas which the custom has since generated. What at first might be dictated by state necessity is now supported by female delicacy, and operates with the greatest force on that part of society where, if the original intention of the custom were preserved, there is the least real occasion for it.

When these two fundamental laws of society, the security of property, and the institution of marriage, were once established, inequality of conditions must necessarily follow. Those who were born after the division of property would come into a world already possessed. If their parents, from having too large a family, could not give them sufficient for their support, what are they to do in a world where everything is appropriated? We have seen the fatal effects that would result to a society, if every man had a valid claim to an equal share of the produce of the earth. The members of a family which was grown too large for the original division of land appropriated to it could not then demand a part of the surplus produce of others, as a debt of justice. It has appeared, that from the inevitable laws of our nature some human beings must suffer from want. These are the unhappy persons who, in the great lottery of life, have drawn a blank. The number of these claimants would soon exceed the ability of the surplus produce to supply. Moral merit is a very difficult distinguishing criterion, except in extreme cases. The owners of surplus produce would in general seek some more obvious mark of distinction. And it seems both natural and just that, except upon particular occasions, their choice should fall upon those who were able, and professed themselves willing, to exert their strength in procuring a further surplus produce; and thus at once benefiting the community, and enabling these proprietors to afford assistance to greater numbers. All who were in want of food would be urged by imperious necessity to offer their labor in exchange for this article so absolutely essential to existence. The fund appropriated to the maintenance of labor would be the aggregate quantity of food possessed by the owners of land beyond their own consumption. When the demands upon this fund were great and numerous, it would naturally be divided in very small shares. Labor would be ill paid. Men would offer to work for a bare subsistence, and the rearing of families would be checked by sickness and misery. On the contrary, when this fund was increasing fast, when it was great in proportion to the number of claimants, it would be divided in much larger shares. No man would exchange his labor without receiving an ample quantity of food in return. Laborers would live in ease and comfort, and would consequently be able to rear a numerous and vigorous offspring.

On the state of this fund, the happiness, or the degree of misery, prevailing among the lower classes of people in every known state at present chiefly depends. And on this happiness, or degree of misery, depends the increase, stationariness, or decrease of population.

And thus it appears, that a society constituted according to the most beautiful form that imagination can conceive, with benevolence for its moving principle, instead of self-love, and with every evil disposition in all its members corrected by reason and not force, would, from the inevitable laws of nature, and not from any original depravity of man, in a very short period degenerate into a society constructed upon a plan not essentially different from that which prevails in every known state at present; I mean, a society divided into a class of proprietors, and a class of laborers, and with self-love the mainspring of the great machine.

In the supposition I have made, I have undoubtedly taken the increase of population smaller, and the increase of produce greater, than they really would be. No reason can be assigned why, under the circumstances I have supposed, population should not increase faster than in any known instance. If then we were to take the period of doubling at fifteen years, instead of twenty-five years, and reflect upon the labor necessary to double the produce in so short a time, even if we allow it possible, we may venture to pronounce with certainty that if Mr. Godwin's system of society was established in its utmost perfection, instead of myriads of centuries, not thirty years could elapse before its utter destruction from the simple principle of population.

I have taken no notice of emigration for obvious reasons. If such societies were instituted in other parts of Europe, these countries would be under the same difficulties with regard to population, and could admit no fresh members into their bosoms. If this beautiful society were confined to this island, it must have degenerated strangely from its original purity, and administer but a very small portion of the happiness it proposed; in short, its essential principle must be completely destroyed, before any of its members would voluntarily consent to leave it, and live under such governments as at present exist in Europe, or submit to the extreme hardships of first settlers in new regions. We well know, from repeated experience, how much misery and hardship men will undergo in their own country, before they can determine to desert it; and how often the most tempting proposals of embarking for new settlements have been rejected by people who appeared to be almost starving.

CHAPTER 11

Mr. Godwin's Conjecture Concerning the Future Extinction of the Passion Between the Sexes— Little Apparent Grounds for Such a Conjecture—Passion of Love Not Inconsistent Either with Reason or Virtue.

We have supported Mr. Godwin's system of society once completely established. But it is supposing an impossibility. The same causes in nature which would destroy it so rapidly, were it once established, would prevent the possibility of its establishment. And upon what grounds we can presume a change in these natural causes, I am utterly at a loss to conjecture. No move towards the extinction of the passion between the sexes has taken place in the five or six thousand years that the world has existed. Men in the decline of life have in all ages declaimed against a passion which they have ceased to feel, but with as little reason as success. Those who from coldness of constitutional temperament have never felt what love is, will surely be allowed to be very incompetent judges with regard to the power of this passion to contribute to the sum of pleasurable sensations in life. Those who have spent their youth in criminal excesses and have prepared for themselves, as the comforts of their age, corporeal debility and mental remorse may well inveigh against such pleasures as vain and futile, and unproductive of lasting satisfaction. But the pleasures of pure love will bear the contemplation of the most improved reason, and the most exalted virtue. Perhaps there is scarcely a man who has once experienced the genuine delight of virtuous love, however great his intellectual pleasure may have been, that does not look back to the period as the sunny spot in his whole life, where his imagination loves to bask, which he recollects and contemplates with the fondest regrets, and which he would most wish to live over again. The superiority of intellectual to sensual pleasures consists rather in their filling up more time, in their having a larger range, and in their being less liable to satiety, than in their being more real and essential.

Intemperance in every enjoyment defeats its own purpose. A walk in the finest day through the most beautiful country, if pursued too far, ends in pain and fatigue. The most wholesome and invigorating food, eaten with an unrestrained appetite, produces weakness instead of strength. Even intellectual pleasures, though certainly less liable than others to satiety, pursued with too little intermission, debilitate the body, and impair the vigor of the mind. To argue against the reality of these pleasures from their abuse seems to be hardly just. Morality, according to Mr. Godwin, is a calculation of consequences, or, as Archdeacon Paley very justly expresses it, the will of God, as collected from general expediency. According to either of these definitions, a sensual pleasure not attended with the probability of unhappy consequences does not offend against the laws of morality, and if it be pursued with such a degree of temperance as to leave the most ample room for intellectual attainments, it must undoubtedly add to the sum of pleasurable sensations in life. Virtuous love, exalted by friendship, seems to be that sort of mixture of sensual and intellectual enjoyment particularly suited to the nature of man, and most powerfully calculated to awaken the sympathies of the soul, and produce the most exquisite gratifications.

Mr. Godwin says, in order to show the evident inferiority of the pleasures of sense, "Strip the commerce of the sexes of all its attendant circumstances, and it would be generally despised" (Bk. I, ch. 5; in the third edition, Vol. I, pp. 71-72). He might as well say to a man who admired trees: strip them of their spreading branches and lovely foliage, and what beauty can you see in a bare pole? But it was the tree with the branches and foliage, and not without them, that excited admiration. One feature of an object may be as distinct, and excite as different emotions, from the aggregate as any two things the most remote, as a beautiful woman, and a map of Madagascar. It is "the symmetry of person, the vivacity, the voluptuous softness of temper, the affectionate kindness of feelings, the imagination and the wit" of a woman that excite the passion of love, and not the mere distinction of her being female. Urged by the passion of love, men have been driven into acts highly prejudicial to the general interests of society, but probably they would have found no difficulty in resisting the temptation, had it appeared in the form of a woman with no other attractions whatever but her sex. To strip sensual pleasures of all their adjuncts, in order to prove their inferiority, is to deprive a magnet of some of its most essential causes of attraction, and then to say that it is weak and inefficient.

In the pursuit of every enjoyment, whether sensual or intellectual, reason, that faculty which enables us to calculate consequences, is the proper corrective and guide. It is probable therefore that improved reason will always tend to prevent the abuse of sensual pleasures, though it by no means follows that it will extinguish them.

I have endeavored to expose the fallacy of that argument which infers an unlimited progress from a partial improvement, the limits of which cannot be exactly ascertained. It has appeared, I think, that there are many instances in which a decided progress has been observed, where yet it would be a gross absurdity to suppose that progress indefinite. But towards the extinction of the passion between the sexes, no observable progress whatever has hitherto been made. To suppose such an extinction, therefore, is merely to offer an unfounded conjecture, unsupported by any philosophical probabilities.

It is a truth, which history I am afraid makes too clear, that some men of the highest mental powers have been addicted not only to a moderate, but even to an immoderate indulgence in the pleasures of sensual love. But allowing, as I should be inclined to do, notwithstanding numerous instances to the contrary, that great intellectual exertions tend to diminish the empire of this passion over man, it is evident that the mass of mankind must be improved more highly than the brightest ornaments of the species at present before any difference can take place sufficient sensibly to affect population. I would by no means suppose that the mass of mankind has reached its term of improvement, but the principal argument of this essay tends to place in a strong point of view the improbability that the lower classes of people in any country should ever be sufficiently free from want and labor to obtain any high degree of intellectual improvement.

CHAPTER 12

Mr. Godwin's Conjecture Concerning the Indefinite Prolongation of Human Life—Improper Inference Drawn from the Effects of Mental Stimulants on the Human frame, Illustrated in Various Instances—Conjectures not Founded on Any Indications in the Past Not to be Considered as Philosophical Conjectures—Mr. Godwin's and Mr. Condorcet's Conjecture Respecting the Approach of Man Towards Immortality on Earth, a Curious Instance of the Inconsistency of Skepticism.

Mr. Godwin's conjecture respecting the future approach of man towards immortality on earth seems to be rather oddly placed in a chapter which professes to remove the objection to his system of equality from the principle of population. Unless he supposes the passion between the sexes to decrease faster than the duration of life increases, the earth would be more encumbered than ever. But leaving this difficulty to Mr. Godwin, let us examine a few of the appearances from which the probable immortality of man is inferred.

To prove the power of the mind over the body, Mr. Godwin observes, "How often do we find a piece of good news dissipating a distemper? How common is the remark that those accidents which are to the indolent a source of disease are forgotten and extirpated in the busy and active? I walk twenty miles in an indolent and half determined temper and am extremely fatigued. I walk twenty miles full of ardor, and with a motive that engrosses my soul, and I come in as fresh and as alert as when I began my journey. Emotion excited by some unexpected word, by a letter that is delivered to us, occasions the most extraordinary revolutions in our frame, accelerates the circulation, causes the heart to palpitate, the tongue to refuse its office, and has been known to occasion death by extreme anguish or extreme joy. There is nothing indeed of which the physician is more aware than of the power of the mind in assisting or reading convalescence."

The instances here mentioned are chiefly instances of the effects of mental stimulants on the bodily frame. No person has ever for a moment doubted the near, though mysterious, connection of mind and body. But it is arguing totally without knowledge of the nature of stimulants to suppose, either that they can be applied continually with equal strength, or if they could be so applied, for a time, that they would not exhaust and wear out the subject. In some of the cases here noticed, the strength of the stimulus depends upon its novelty and unexpectedness. Such a stimulus cannot, from its nature, be repeated often with the same effect, as it would by repetition lose that property which gives it its strength.

In the other cases, the argument is from a small and partial effect, to a great and general effect, which will in numberless instances be found to be a very fallacious mode of reasoning. The busy and active man may in some degree counteract, or what is perhaps nearer the truth, may disregard those slight disorders of frame which fix the attention of a man who has nothing else to think of; but this does not tend to prove that activity of mind will enable a man to disregard a high fever, the smallpox, or the plague.

The man who walks twenty miles with a motive that engrosses his soul does not attend to his slight fatigue of body when he comes in; but double his motive, and set him to walk another twenty miles, quadruple it, and let him start a third time, and so on; and the length of his walk will ultimately depend upon muscle and not mind. Powell, for a motive of ten guineas, would have walked further probably than Mr. Godwin, for a motive of half a million. A motive of uncommon power acting upon a frame of moderate strength would, perhaps, make the man kill himself by his exertions, but it would not make him walk a hundred miles in twenty-four hours. This statement of the case shows the fallacy of supposing that the person was really not at all tired in his first walk of twenty miles, because he did not appear to be so, or, perhaps, scarcely felt any fatigue himself. The mind cannot fix its attention strongly on more than one object at once. The twenty thousand pounds so engrossed his thoughts that he did not attend to any slight soreness of foot, or stiffness of limb. But had he been really as fresh and as alert, as when he first set off, he would be able to go the second twenty miles with as much ease as the first, and so on, the third, &c. Which leads to a palpable absurdity. When a horse of spirit is nearly half tired, by the stimulus of the spur, added to the proper management of the bit, he may be put so much upon his mettle, that he would appear to a standerby, as fresh and as high spirited as if he had not gone a mile. Nay, probably, the horse himself, while in the heat and passion occasioned by this stimulus, would not feel any fatigue; but it would be strangely contrary to all reason and experience, to argue from such an appearance that, if the stimulus were continued, the horse would never be tired. The cry of a pack of hounds will make some horses, after a journey of forty miles on the road, appear as fresh, and as lively, as when they first set out. Were they then to be hunted, no perceptible abatement would at first be felt by their riders in their strength and spirits, but towards the end of a hard day, the previous fatigue would have its full weight and effect, and make them tire sooner. When I have taken a long walk with my gun, and met with no success, I have frequently returned home feeling a considerable degree of uncomfortableness from fatigue. Another day, perhaps, going over nearly the same extent of ground with a good deal of sport, I have come home fresh, and alert. The difference in the sensation of fatigue upon coming in, on the different days, may have been very striking, but on the following mornings I have found no such difference. I have not perceived that I was less stiff in my limbs, or less footsore, on the morning after the day of the sport, than on the other morning.

In all these cases, stimulants upon the mind seem to act rather by taking off the attention from the bodily fatigue, than by really and truly counteracting it. If the energy of my mind had really counteracted the fatigue of my body, why should I feel tired the next morning? if the stimulus of the hounds had as completely overcome the fatigue of the journey in reality, as it did in appearance, why should the horse be tired sooner than if he had not gone the forty miles? I happen to have a very bad fit of the toothache at the time I am writing this. In the eagerness of composition, I every now and then, for a moment or two, forget it. Yet I cannot help thinking that the process, which causes the pain, is still going forwards, and that the nerves which carry the information of it to the brain are even during these moments demanding attention and room for their appropriate vibrations. The multiplicity of vibrations of another kind may perhaps prevent their admission, or overcome them for a time when admitted, till a shoot of extraordinary energy puts all other vibration to the rout, destroys the vividness of my argumentative conceptions, and rides triumphant in the brain. In this case, as in the others, the mind seems to have little or no power in counteracting or curing the disorder, but merely possesses a power, if strongly excited, of fixing its attention on other subjects.

I do not, however, mean to say that a sound and vigorous mind has no tendency whatever to keep the body in a similar state. So close and intimate is the union of mind and body that it would be highly extraordinary if they did not mutually assist each other's functions. But, perhaps, upon a comparison, the body has more effect upon the mind than the mind upon the body. The first object of the mind is to act as purveyor to the wants of the body. When these wants are completely satisfied, an active mind is indeed apt to wander further, to range over the fields of science, or sport in the regions of. Imagination, to fancy that it has "shuffled off this mortal coil," and is seeking its kindred element. But all these efforts are like the vain exertions of the hare in the fable. The slowly moving tortoise, the body, never fails to overtake the mind, however widely and extensively it may have ranged, and the brightest and most energetic intellects, unwillingly as they may attend to the first or second summons, must ultimately yield the empire of the brain to the calls of hunger, or sink with the exhausted body in sleep.

It seems as if one might say with certainty that if a medicine could be found to immortalize the body there would be no fear of its [not] being accompanied by the immortality of the mind. But the immortality of the mind by no means seems to infer the immortality of the body. On the contrary, the greatest conceivable energy of mind would probably exhaust and destroy the strength of the body. A temperate vigor of mind appears to be favorable to health, but very great intellectual exertions tend rather, as has been often observed, to wear out the scabbard. Most of the instances which Mr. Godwin has brought to prove the power of the mind over the body, and the consequent probability of the immortality of man, are of this latter description, and could such stimulants be continually applied, instead of tending to immortalize, they would tend very rapidly to destroy the human frame.

The probable increase of the voluntary power of man over his animal frame comes next under Mr. Godwin's consideration, and he concludes by saying, that the voluntary power of some men, in this respect, is found to extend to various articles in which other men are impotent. But this is reasoning against an almost universal rule from a few exceptions; and these exceptions seem to be rather tricks, than powers that may be exerted to any good purpose. I have never heard of any man who could regulate his pulse in a fever, and doubt much, if any of the persons here alluded to have made the smallest perceptible progress in the regular correction of the disorders of their frames and the consequent prolongation of their lives.

Mr. Godwin says, "Nothing can be more unphilosophical than to conclude, that, because a certain species of power is beyond the train of our present observation, that it is beyond the limits of the human mind." I own my ideas of philosophy are in this respect widely different from Mr. Godwin's. The only distinction that I see, between a philosophical conjecture, and the assertions of the Prophet Mr. Brothers, is, that one is founded upon indications arising from the train of our present observations, and the other has no foundation at all. I expect that great discoveries are yet to take place in all the branches of human science, particularly in physics; but the moment we leave past experience as the foundation of our conjectures concerning the future, and, still more, if our conjectures absolutely contradict past experience, we are thrown upon a wide field of uncertainty, and any one supposition is then just as good as another. If a person were to tell me that men would ultimately have eyes and hands behind them as well as before them, I should admit the usefulness of the addition, but should give as a reason for my disbelief of it, that I saw no indications whatever in the past from which I could infer the smallest probability of such a change. If this be not allowed a valid objection, all conjectures are alike, and all equally philosophical. I own it appears to me that in the train of our present observations, there are no more genuine indications that man will become immortal upon earth than that he will have four eyes and four hands, or that trees will grow horizontally instead of perpendicularly.

It will be said, perhaps, that many discoveries have already taken place in the world that were totally unforeseen and unexpected. This I grant to be true; but if a person had predicted these discoveries without being guided by any analogies or indications from past facts, he would deserve the name of seer or prophet, but not of philosopher. The wonder that some of our modern discoveries would excite in the savage inhabitants of Europe in the times of Theseus and Achilles, proves but little. Persons almost entirely unacquainted with the powers of a machine cannot be expected to guess at its effects. I am far from saying, that we are at present by any means fully acquainted with the powers of the human mind; but we certainly know more of this instrument than was known four thousand years ago; and therefore, though not to be called competent judges, we are certainly much better able than savages to say what is, or is not, within its grasp. A watch would strike a savage with as much surprise as a perpetual motion; yet one is to us a most familiar piece of mechanism, and the other has constantly eluded the efforts of the most acute intellects. In many instances we are now able to perceive the causes, which prevent an unlimited improvement in those inventions, which seemed to promise fairly for it at first. The original improvers of telescopes would probably think, that as long as the size of the specula and the length of the tubes could be increased, the powers and advantages of the instrument would increase; but experience has since taught us, that the smallness of the field, the deficiency of light, and the circumstance of the atmosphere being magnified, prevent the beneficial results that were to be expected from telescopes of extraordinary size and power. In many parts of knowledge, man has been almost constantly making some progress; in other parts, his efforts have been invariably baffled. The savage would not probably be able to guess at the causes of this mighty difference. Our further experience has given us some little insight into these causes, and has therefore enabled us better to judge, if not of what we are to expect in future, at least of what we are not to expect, which, though negative, is a very useful piece of information.

As the necessity of sleep seems rather to depend upon the body than the mind, it does not appear how the improvement of the mind can tend very greatly to supersede this "conspicuous infirmity." A man who by great excitements on his mind is able to pass two or three nights without sleep, proportionally exhausts the vigor of his body, and this diminution of health and strength will soon disturb the operations of his understanding, so that by these great efforts he appears to have made no real progress whatever in superseding the necessity of this species of rest.

There is certainly a sufficiently marked difference in the various characters of which we have some knowledge, relative to the energies of their minds, their benevolent pursuits, etc., to enable us to judge whether the operations of intellect have any decided effect in prolonging the duration of human life. It is certain that no decided effect of this kind has yet been observed. Though no attention of any kind has ever produced such an effect as could be construed into the smallest semblance of an approach towards immortality, yet of the two, a certain attention to the body seems to have more effect in this respect than an attention to the mind. The man who takes his temperate meals and his bodily exercise, with scrupulous regularity, will generally be found more healthy than the man who, very deeply engaged in intellectual pursuits, often forgets for a time these bodily cravings. The citizen who has retired, and whose ideas, perhaps, scarcely soar above or extend beyond his little garden, puddling all the morning about his borders of box, will, perhaps, live as long as the philosopher whose range of intellect is the most extensive, and whose views are the clearest of any of his contemporaries. It has been positively observed by those who have attended to the bills of mortality that women live longer upon an average than men, and, though I would not by any means say that their intellectual faculties are inferior, yet, I think, it must be allowed that, from their different education, there are not so many women as men, who are excited to vigorous mental exertion.

As in these and similar instances, or to take a larger range, as in the great diversity of characters that have existed during some thousand years, no decided difference has been observed in the duration of human life from the operation of intellect, the mortality of man on earth seems to be as completely established, and exactly upon the same grounds, as any one, the most constant, of the laws of nature. An immediate act of power in the Creator of the Universe might, indeed, change one or all of these laws, either suddenly or gradually, but without some indications of such a change, and such indications do not exist, it. Is just as unphilosophical to suppose that the life of man may be prolonged beyond any assignable limits, as to suppose that the attraction of the earth will gradually be changed into repulsion and that stones will ultimately rise instead of fall or that the earth will fly off at a certain period to some more genial and warmer sun.

The conclusion of this chapter presents us, undoubtedly, with a very beautiful and desirable picture, but like some of the landscapes drawn from fancy and not imagined with truth, it fails of that interest in the heart which nature and probability can alone give.

I cannot quit this subject without taking notice of these conjectures of Mr. Godwin and Mr. Condorcet concerning the indefinite prolongation of human life, as a very curious instance of the longing of the soul after immortality. Both these gentlemen have rejected the light of revelation which absolutely promises eternal life in another state. They have also rejected the light of natural religion, which to the ablest intellects in all ages has indicated the future existence of the soul. Yet so congenial is the idea of immortality to the mind of man that they cannot consent entirely to throw it out of their systems. After all their fastidious skepticisms concerning the only probable mode of immortality, they introduce a species of immortality of their own, not only completely contradictory to every law of philosophical probability, but in itself in the highest degree narrow, partial, and unjust. They suppose that all the great, virtuous, and exalted minds that have ever existed or that may exist for some thousands, perhaps millions of years, will be sunk in annihilation, and that only a few beings, not greater in number than can exist at once upon the earth, will be ultimately crowned with immortality. Had such a tenet been advanced as a tenet of revelation I am very sure that all the enemies of religion, and probably Mr. Godwin and Mr. Condorcet among the rest, would have exhausted the whole force of their ridicule upon it, as the most puerile, the most absurd, the poorest, the most pitiful, the most iniquitously unjust, and, consequently, the most unworthy of the Deity that the superstitious folly of man could invent.

What a strange and curious proof do these conjectures exhibit of the inconsistency of skepticism! For it should be observed, that there is a very striking and essential difference between believing an assertion which absolutely contradicts the most uniform experience, and an assertion which contradicts nothing, but is merely beyond the power of our present observation and knowledge. So diversified are the natural objects around us, so many instances of mighty power daily offer themselves to our view, that we may fairly presume, that there are many forms and operations of nature which we have not yet observed, or which, perhaps, we are not capable of observing with our present confined inlets of knowledge. The resurrection of a spiritual body from a natural body does not appear in itself a more wonderful instance of power than the germination of a blade of wheat from the grain, or of an oak from an acorn. Could we conceive an intelligent being, so placed as to be conversant only with inanimate or full grown objects, and never to have witnessed the process of vegetation and growth; and were another being to show him two little pieces of matter, a grain of wheat, and an acorn, to desire him to examine them, to analyze them if he pleased, and endeavor to find out their properties and essences; and then to tell him, that however trifling these little bits of matter might appear to him, that they possessed such curious powers of selection, combination, arrangement, and almost of creation, that upon being put into the ground, they would choose, amongst all the dirt and moisture that surrounded them, those parts which best suited their purpose, that they would collect and arrange these parts with wonderful taste, judgment, and execution, and would rise up into beautiful forms, scarcely in any respect analogous to the little bits of matter which were first placed in the earth. I feel very little doubt that the imaginary being which I have supposed would hesitate more, would require better authority, and stronger proofs, before he believed these strange assertions, than if he had been told, that a being of mighty power, who had been the cause of all that he saw around him, and of that existence of which he himself was conscious, would, by a great act of power upon the death and corruption of human creatures, raise up the essence of thought in an incorporeal, or at least invisible form, to give it a happier existence in another state.

The only difference, with regard to our own apprehensions, that is not in favor of the latter assertion is that the first miracle we have repeatedly seen, and the last miracle we have not seen. I admit the full weight of this prodigious difference, but surely no man can hesitate a moment in saying that, putting Revelation out of the question, the resurrection of a spiritual body from a natural body, which may be merely one among the many operations of nature which we cannot see, is an event indefinitely more probable than the immortality of man on earth, which is not only an event of which no symptoms or indications have yet appeared, but is a positive contradiction to one of the most constant of the laws of nature that has ever come within the observation of man.

When we extend our view beyond this life, it is evident that we can have no other guides than authority, or conjecture, and perhaps, indeed, an obscure and undefined feeling. What I say here, therefore, does not appear to me in any respect to contradict what I said before, when I observed that it was unphilosophical to expect any specific event that was not indicated by some kind of analogy in the past. In ranging beyond the bourne from which no traveler returns, we must necessarily quit this rule; but with regard to events that may be expected to happen on earth, we can seldom quit it consistently with true philosophy. Analogy has, however, as I conceive, great latitude. For instance, man has discovered many of the laws of nature: analogy seems to indicate that he will discover many more; but no analogy seems to indicate that he will discover a sixth sense, or a new species of power in the human mind, entirely beyond the train of our present observations.

The powers of selection, combination, and transmutation, which every seed shows, are truly miraculous. Who can imagine that these wonderful faculties are contained in these little bits of matter? To me it appears much more philosophical to suppose that the mighty God of nature is present in full energy in all these operations. To this all powerful Being, it would be equally easy to raise an oak without an acorn as with one. The preparatory process of putting seeds into the ground is merely ordained for the use of man, as one among the various other excitements necessary to awaken matter into mind. It is an idea that will be found consistent, equally with the natural phenomena around us, with the various events of human life, and with the successive revelations of God to man, to suppose that the world is a mighty process for the creation and formation of mind.

Many vessels will necessarily come out of this great furnace in wrong shapes. These will be broken and thrown aside as useless; while those vessels whose forms are full of truth, grace, and loveliness, will be wafted into happier situations, nearer the presence of the mighty maker.

I ought perhaps again to make an apology to my readers for dwelling so long upon a conjecture which many, I know, will think too absurd and improbable to require the least discussion. But if it be as improbable and as contrary to the genuine spirit of philosophy as I own I think it is, why should it not be shown to be so in a candid examination? A conjecture, however improbable on the first view of it, advanced by able and ingenious men, seems at least to deserve investigation. For my own part I feel no disinclination whatever to give that degree of credit to the opinion of the probable immortality of man on earth, which the appearances that can be brought in support of it deserve. Before we decide upon the utter improbability of such an event, it is but fair impartially to examine these appearances; and from such an examination I think we may conclude, that we have rather less reason for supposing that the life of man may be indefinitely prolonged, than that trees may be made to grow indefinitely high, or potatoes indefinitely large. Though Mr. Godwin advances the idea of the indefinite prolongation of human life merely as a conjecture, yet as he has produced some appearances, which in his conception favor the supposition, he must certainly intend that these appearances should be examined and this is all that I have meant to do.

CHAPTER 13

Error of Mr. Godwin is Considering Man Too Much in the Light of a being Merely Rational—In the Compound being, Man, the Passions will Always Act as Disturbing Forces in the Decisions of the Understanding—Reasonings of Mr. Godwin on the Subject of Coercion—Some Truths of a Nature not to be Communicated from One Man to Another.

In the chapter which I have been examining, Mr. Godwin professes to consider the objection to his system of equality from the principle of population. It has appeared, I think clearly, that he is greatly erroneous in his statement of the distance of this difficulty, and that instead of myriads of centuries, it is really not thirty years, or even thirty days, distant from us. The supposition of the approach of man to immortality on earth is certainly not of a kind to soften the difficulty. The only argument, therefore, in the chapter which has any tendency to remove the objection is the conjecture concerning the extinction of the passion between the sexes, but as this is a mere conjecture, unsupported by the smallest shadow of proof, the force of the objection may be fairly said to remain unimpaired, and it is undoubtedly of sufficient weight of itself completely to overturn Mr. Godwin's whole system of equality. I will, however, make one or two observations on a few of the prominent parts of Mr. Godwin's reasonings which will contribute to place in a still clearer point of view the little hope that we can reasonably entertain of those vast improvements in the nature of man and of society which he holds up to our admiring gaze in his Political Justice.

Mr. Godwin considers man too much in the light of a being merely intellectual. This error, at least such I conceive it to be, pervades his whole work and mixes itself with all his reasonings. The voluntary actions of men may originate in their opinions, but these opinions will be very differently modified in creatures compounded of a rational faculty and corporal propensities from what they would be in beings wholly intellectual. Mr. Godwin, in proving that sound reasoning and truth are capable of being adequately communicated, examines the proposition first practically, and then adds, "Such is the appearance which this proposition assumes, when examined in a loose and practical view. In strict consideration it will not admit of debate. Man is a rational being, etc." (Bk. I, ch. 5; in the third edition Vol. I, p. 88). So far from calling this a strict consideration of the subject, I own I should call it the loosest, and most erroneous, way possible, of considering it. It is the calculating the velocity of a falling body in vacuo, and persisting in it, that it would be the same through whatever resisting mediums it might fall. This was not Newton's mode of philosophizing. Very few general propositions are just in application to a particular subject. The moon is not kept in her orbit round the earth, nor the earth in her orbit round the sun, by a force that varies merely in the inverse ratio of the squares of the distances. To make the general theory just in application to the revolutions of these bodies, it was necessary to calculate accurately the disturbing force of the sun upon the moon, and of the moon upon the earth; and till these disturbing forces were properly estimated, actual observations on the motions of these bodies would have proved that the theory was not accurately true.

I am willing to allow that every voluntary act is preceded by a decision of the mind, but it is strangely opposite to what I should conceive to be the just theory upon the subject, and a palpable contradiction to all experience, to say that the corporal propensities of man do not act very powerfully, as disturbing forces, in these decisions. The question, therefore, does not merely depend upon whether a man may be made to understand a distinct proposition or be convinced by an unanswerable argument. A truth may be brought home to his conviction as a rational being, though he may determine to act contrary to it, as a compound being. The cravings of hunger, the love of liquor, the desire of possessing a beautiful woman, will urge men to actions, of the fatal consequences of which, to the general interests of society, they are perfectly well convinced, even at the very time they commit them. Remove their bodily cravings, and they would not hesitate a moment in determining against such actions. Ask them their opinion of the same conduct in another person, and they would immediately reprobate it. But in their own case, and under all the circumstances of their situation with these bodily cravings, the decision of the compound being is different from the conviction of the rational being.

If this be the just view of the subject, and both theory and experience unite to prove that it is, almost all Mr. Godwin's reasonings on the subject of coercion in his seventh chapter, will appear to be founded on error. He spends some time in placing in a ridiculous point of view the attempt to convince a man's understanding and to clear up a doubtful proposition in his mind, by blows. Undoubtedly it is both ridiculous and barbarous, and so is cock-fighting, but one has little more to do with the real object of human punishments than the other. One frequent (indeed much too frequent) mode of punishment is death. Mr. Godwin will hardly think this intended for conviction, at least it does not appear how the individual or the society could reap much future benefit from an understanding enlightened in this manner.

The principal objects which human punishments have in view are undoubtedly restraint and example; restraint, or removal, of an individual member whose vicious habits are likely to be prejudicial to the society; and example, which by expressing the sense of the community with regard to a particular crime, and by associating more nearly and visibly crime and punishment, holds out a moral motive to dissuade others from the commission of it.

Restraint, Mr. Godwin thinks, may be permitted as a temporary expedient, though he reprobates solitary imprisonment, which has certainly been the most successful, and, indeed, almost the only attempt towards the moral amelioration of offenders. He talks of the selfish passions that are fostered by solitude and of the virtues generated in society. But surely these virtues are not generated in the society of a prison. Were the offender confined to the society of able and virtuous men he would probably be more improved than in solitude. But is this practicable? Mr. Godwin's ingenuity is more frequently employed in finding out evils than in suggesting practical remedies.

Punishment, for example, is totally reprobated. By endeavoring to make examples too impressive and terrible, nations have, indeed, been led into the most barbarous cruelties, but the abuse of any practice is not a good argument against its use. The indefatigable pains taken in this country to find out a murder, and the certainty of its punishment, has powerfully contributed to generate that sentiment which is frequent in the mouths of the common people, that a murder will sooner or later come to light; and the habitual horror in which murder is in consequence held will make a man, in the agony of passion, throw down his knife for fear he should be tempted to use it in the gratification of his revenge. In Italy, where murderers, by flying to a sanctuary, are allowed more frequently to escape, the crime has never been held in the same detestation and has consequently been more frequent. No man, who is at all aware of the operation of moral motives, can doubt for a moment, that if every murder in Italy had been invariably punished, the use of the stiletto in transports of passion would have been comparatively but little known.

That human laws either do, or can, proportion the punishment accurately to the offence, no person will have the folly to assert. From the inscrutability of motives the thing is absolutely impossible, but this imperfection, though it may be called a species of injustice, is no valid argument against human laws. It is the lot of man, that he will frequently have to choose between two evils; and it is a sufficient reason for the adoption of any institution, that it is the best mode that suggests itself of preventing greater evils. A continual endeavor should undoubtedly prevail to make these institutions as perfect as the nature of them will admit. But nothing is so easy as to find fault with human institutions; nothing so difficult as to suggest adequate practical improvements. It is to be lamented, that more men of talents employ their time in the former occupation than in the tatter.

The frequency of crime among men, who, as the common saying is, know better, sufficiently proves, that some truths may be brought home to the conviction of the mind without always producing the proper effect upon the conduct. There are other truths of a nature that perhaps never can be adequately communicated from one man to another. The superiority of the pleasures of intellect to those of sense, Mr. Godwin considers as a fundamental truth. Taking all circumstances into consideration, I should be disposed to agree with him; but how am I to communicate this truth to a person who has scarcely ever felt intellectual pleasure? I may as well attempt to explain the nature and beauty of colors to a blind man. If I am ever so laborious, patient, and clear, and have the most repeated opportunities of expostulation, any real progress toward the accomplishment of my purpose seems absolutely hopeless. There is no common measure between us. I cannot proceed step by step. It is a truth of a nature absolutely incapable of demonstration. All that I can say is, that the wisest and best men in all ages had agreed in giving the preference, very greatly, to the pleasures of intellect; and that my own experience completely confirmed the truth of their decisions; that I had found sensual pleasures vain, transient, and continually attended with tedium and disgust; but that intellectual pleasures appeared to me ever fresh and young, filled up all my hours satisfactorily, gave a new zest to life, and diffused a lasting serenity over my mind. If he believe me, it can only be from respect and veneration for my authority. It is credulity, and not conviction. I have not said any thing, nor can any thing be said, of a nature to produce real conviction. The affair is not an affair of reasoning, but of experience. He would probably observe in reply, what you say may be very true with regard to yourself and many other good men, but for my own part I feel very differently upon the subject. I have very frequently taken up a book and almost as frequently gone to sleep over it; but when I pass an evening with a gay party, or a pretty woman, I feel alive, and in spirits, and truly enjoy my existence.

Under such circumstances, reasoning and arguments are not instruments from which success can be expected. At some future time perhaps, real satiety of sensual pleasures, or some accidental impressions that awakened the energies of his mind, might effect that, in a month, which the most patient and able expostulations might be incapable of effecting in forty years.

CHAPTER 14

Mr. Godwin's Five Propositions Respecting Political Truth, on which His Whole Work Hinges, not Established—Reasons We have for Supposing, from the Distress Occasioned by the Principle of Population, that the Vices and Moral Weakness of Man can Never be wholly Eradicated— Perfectibility, in the Sense in which Mr. Godwin Uses the Term, not Applicable to Man—Nature of the Real Perfectibility of Man Illustrated.

If the reasonings of the preceding chapter are just, the corollaries respecting political truth, which Mr. Godwin draws from the proposition, that the voluntary actions of men originate in their opinions, will not appear to be clearly established. These corollaries are, "Sound reasoning and truth, when adequately communicated, must always be victorious over error: Sound reasoning and truth are capable of being so communicated: Truth is omnipotent: The vices and moral weakness of man are not invincible: Man is perfectible, or in other words, susceptible of perpetual improvement."

The first three propositions may be considered a complete syllogism. If by adequately communicated, be meant such a conviction as to produce an adequate effect upon the conduct, the major may be allowed and the minor denied. The consequent, or the omnipotence of truth, of course falls to the ground. If by "adequately communicated" be meant merely the conviction of the rational faculty, the major must be denied, the minor will be only true in cases capable of demonstration, and the consequent equally falls. The fourth proposition Mr. Godwin calls the preceding proposition, with a slight variation in the statement. If so, it must accompany the preceding proposition in its fall. But it may be worth while to inquire, with reference to the principal argument of this essay, into the particular reasons which we have for supposing that the vices and moral weakness of man can never be wholly overcome in this world.

Man, according to Mr. Godwin, is a creature formed what he is by the successive impressions which he has received, from the first moment that the germ from which he sprung was animated. Could he be placed in a situation, where he was subject to no evil impressions whatever, though it might be doubted whether in such a situation virtue could exist, vice would certainly be banished. The great bent of Mr. Godwin's work on Political Justice, if I understand it rightly, is to show that the greater part of the vices and weaknesses of men proceed from the injustice of their political and social institutions, and that if these were removed and the understandings of men more enlightened, there would be little or no temptation in the world to evil. As it has been clearly proved, however, (at least as I think) that this is entirely a false conception, and that, independent of any political or social institutions whatever, the greater part of mankind, from the fixed and unalterable laws of nature, must ever be subject to the evil temptations arising from want, besides other passions, it follows from Mr. Godwin's definition of man that such impressions, and combinations of impressions, cannot be afloat in the world without generating a variety of bad men. According to Mr. Godwin's own conception of the formation of character, it is surely as improbable that under such circumstances all men will be virtuous as that sixes will come up a hundred times following upon the dice. The great variety of combinations upon the dice in a repeated succession of throws appears to me not inaptly to represent the great variety of character that must necessarily exist in the world, supposing every individual to be formed what he is by that combination of impressions which he has received since his first existence. And this comparison will, in some measure, show the absurdity of supposing, that exceptions will ever become general rules; that extraordinary and unusual combinations will be frequent; or that the individual instances of great virtue which had appeared in all ages of the world will ever prevail universally.

I am aware that Mr. Godwin might say that the comparison is in one respect inaccurate, that in the case of the dice, the preceding causes, or rather the chances respecting the preceding causes, were always the same, and that, therefore, I could have no good reason for supposing that a greater number of sixes would come up in the next hundred times of throwing than in the preceding same number of throws. But, that man had in some sort a power of influencing those causes that formed character, and that every good and virtuous man that was produced, by the influence which he must necessarily have, rather increased the probability that another such virtuous character would be generated, whereas the coming up of sixes upon the dice once, would certainly not increase the probability of their coming up a second time. I admit this objection to the accuracy of the comparison, but it is only partially valid. Repeated experience has assured us, that the influence of the most virtuous character will rarely prevail against very strong temptations to evil. It will undoubtedly affect some, but it will fail with a much greater number. Had Mr. Godwin succeeded in his attempt to prove that these temptations to evil could by the exertions of man be removed, I would give up the comparison; or at least allow, that a man might be so far enlightened with regard to the mode of shaking his elbow, that he would be able to throw sixes every time. But as long as a great number of those impressions which form character, like the nice motions of the arm, remain absolutely independent of the will of man, though it would be the height of folly and presumption to attempt to calculate the relative proportions of virtue and vice at the future periods of the world, it may be safely asserted that the vices and moral weakness of mankind, taken in the mass, are invincible.

The fifth proposition is the general deduction from the four former and will consequently fall, as the foundations which support it have given way. In the sense in which Mr. Godwin understands the term "perfectible," the perfectibility of man cannot be asserted, unless the preceding propositions could have been clearly established. There is, however, one sense, which the term will bear, in which it is, perhaps, just. It may be said with truth that man is always susceptible of improvement, or that there never has been, or will be, a period of his history, in which he can be said to have reached his possible acme of perfection. Yet it does not by any means follow from this, that our efforts to improve man will always succeed, or even that he will ever make, in the greatest number of ages, any extraordinary strides towards perfection. The only inference that can be drawn is that the precise limit of his improvement cannot possibly be known. And I cannot help again reminding the reader of a distinction which, it appears to me, ought particularly to be attended to in the present question: I mean, the essential difference there is between an unlimited improvement and an improvement the limit of which cannot be ascertained. The former is an improvement not applicable to man under the present laws of his nature. The latter, undoubtedly, is applicable.

The real perfectibility of man may be illustrated, as I have mentioned before, by the perfectibility of a plant. The object of the enterprising florist is, as I conceive, to unite size, symmetry, and beauty of color. It would surely be presumptuous in the most successful improver to affirm, that he possessed a carnation in which these qualities existed in the greatest possible state of perfection. However beautiful his flower may be, other care, other soil, or other suns, might produce one still more beautiful.

Yet, although he may be aware of the absurdity of supposing that he has reached perfection, and though he may know by what means he attained that degree of beauty in the flower which he at present possesses, yet he cannot be sure that by pursuing similar means, rather increased in strength, he will obtain a more beautiful blossom. By endeavoring to improve one quality, he may impair the beauty of another. The richer mould which he would employ to increase the size of his plant would probably burst the calyx, and destroy at once its symmetry. In a similar manner, the forcing manure used to bring about the French Revolution, and to give a greater freedom and energy to the human mind, has burst the calyx of humanity, the restraining bond of all society; and, however large the separate petals have grown, however strongly, or even beautifully, a few of them have been marked, the whole is at present a loose, deformed, disjointed mass, without union, symmetry, or harmony of coloring.

Were it of consequence to improve pinks and carnations, though we could have no hope of raising them as large as cabbages, we might undoubtedly expect, by successive efforts, to obtain more beautiful specimens than we at present possess. No person can deny the importance of improving the happiness of the human species. Every the least advance in this respect is highly valuable. But an experiment with the human race is not like an experiment upon inanimate objects. The bursting of a flower may be a trifle. Another will soon succeed it. But the bursting of the bonds of society is such a separation of parts as cannot take place without giving the most acute pain to thousands: and a long time may elapse, and much misery may be endured, before the wound grows up again.

As the five propositions which I have been examining may be considered as the corner stones of Mr. Godwin's fanciful structure, and, indeed, as expressing the aim and bent of his whole work, however excellent much of his detached reasoning may be, he must be considered as having failed in the great object of his undertaking. Besides the difficulties arising from the compound nature of man, which he has by no means sufficiently smoothed, the principal argument against the perfectibility of man and society remains whole and unimpaired from any thing that he has advanced. And as far as I can trust my own judgment, this argument appears to be conclusive, not only against the perfectibility of man, in the enlarged sense in which Mr. Godwin understands the term, but against any very marked and striking change for the better, in the form and structure of general society; by which I mean any great and decided amelioration of the condition of the lower classes of mankind, the most numerous, and, consequently, in a general view of the subject, the most important part of the human race. Were I to live a thousand years, and the laws of nature to remain the same, I should little fear, or rather little hope, a contradiction from experience in asserting that no possible sacrifices or exertions of the rich, in a country which had been long inhabited, could for any time place the lower classes of the community in a situation equal, with regard to circumstances, to the situation of the common people about thirty years ago in the northern States of America.

The lower classes of people in Europe may at some future period be much better instructed than they are at present; they may be taught to employ the little spare time they have in many better ways than at the ale-house; they may live under better and more equal laws than they have ever hitherto done, perhaps, in any country; and I even conceive it possible, though not probable that they may have more leisure; but it is not in the nature of things that they can be awarded such a quantity of money or subsistence as will allow them all to marry early, in the full confidence that they shall be able to provide with ease for a numerous family.

CHAPTER 15

Models too Perfect may Sometimes Rather Impede than Promote Improvement—Mr. Godwin's Essay on "Avarice and Profusion"—Impossibility of Dividing the Necessary Labor of a Society Amicably Among All—Invectives Against Labor May Produce Present Evil, with Little or no Chance of Producing Future Good—An Accession to the Mass of Agricultural Labor must Always be an Advantage to the Laborer.

Mr. Godwin in the preface to his Enquirer, drops a few expressions which seem to hint at some change in his opinions since he wrote the Political Justice; and as this is a work now of some years standing, I should certainly think that I had been arguing against opinions which the author had himself seen reason to alter, but that in some of the essays of the Enquirer, Mr. Godwin's peculiar mode of thinking appears in as striking a light as ever.

It has been frequently observed that though we cannot hope to reach perfection in any thing, yet that it must always be advantageous to us to place before our eyes the most perfect models. This observation has a plausible appearance, but is very far from being generally true. I even doubt its truth in one of the most obvious exemplifications that would occur. I doubt whether a very young painter would receive so much benefit, from an attempt to copy a highly finished and perfect picture, as from copying one where the outlines were more strongly marked and the manner of laying on the colors was more easily discoverable. But in cases where the perfection of the model is a perfection of a different and superior nature from that towards which we should naturally advance, we shall not always fail in making any progress towards it, but we shall in all probability impede the progress which we might have expected to make had we not fixed our eyes upon so perfect a model. A highly intellectual being, exempt from the infirm calls of hunger or sleep, is undoubtedly a much more perfect existence than man, but were man to attempt to copy such a model, he would not only fail in making any advances towards it; but by unwisely straining to imitate what was inimitable, he would probably destroy the little intellect which he was endeavoring to improve.

The form and structure of society which Mr. Godwin describes is as essentially distinct from any forms of society which have hitherto prevailed in the world as a being that can live without food or sleep is from a man. By improving society in its present form, we are making no more advances towards such a state of things as he pictures than we should make approaches towards a line, with regard to which we were walking parallel. The question, therefore, is whether, by looking to such a form of society as our polar star, we are likely to advance or retard the improvement of the human species? Mr. Godwin appears to me to have decided this question against himself in his essay on "Avarice and Profusion" in the Enquirer.

Dr. Adam Smith has very justly observed that nations as well as individuals grow rich by parsimony and poor by profusion, and that, therefore, every frugal man was a friend and every spendthrift an enemy to his country. The reason he gives is that what is saved from revenue is always added to stock, and is therefore taken from the maintenance of labor that is generally unproductive and employed in the maintenance of labor that realizes itself in valuable commodities. No observation can be more evidently just. The subject of Mr. Godwin's essay is a little similar in its first appearance, but in essence is as distinct as possible. He considers the mischief of profusion as an acknowledged truth, and therefore makes his comparison between the avaricious man, and the man who spends his income. But the avaricious man of Mr. Godwin is totally a distinct character, at least with regard to his effect upon the prosperity of the state, from the frugal man of Dr. Adam Smith. The frugal man in order to make more money saves from his income and adds to his capital, and this capital he either employs himself in the maintenance of productive labor, or he lends it to some other person who will probably employ it in this way. He benefits the state because he adds to its general capital, and because wealth employed as capital not only sets in motion more labor than when spent as income, but the labor is besides of a more valuable kind. But the avaricious man of Mr. Godwin locks up his wealth in a chest and sets in motion no labor of any kind, either productive or unproductive. This is so essential a difference that Mr. Godwin's decision in his essay appears at once as evidently false as Dr. Adam Smith's position is evidently true. It could not, indeed, but occur to Mr. Godwin that some present inconvenience might arise to the poor from thus locking up the funds destined for the maintenance of labor. The only way, therefore, he had of weakening this objection was to compare the two characters chiefly with regard to their tendency to accelerate the approach of that happy state of cultivated equality, on which he says we ought always to fix our eyes as our polar star.

I think it has been proved in the former parts of this essay that such a state of society is absolutely impracticable. What consequences then are we to expect from looking to such a point as our guide and polar star in the great sea of political discovery? Reason would teach us to expect no other than winds perpetually adverse, constant but fruitless toil, frequent shipwreck, and certain misery. We shall not only fail in making the smallest real approach towards such a perfect form of society; but by wasting our strength of mind and body, in a direction in which it is impossible to proceed, and by the frequent distress which we must necessarily occasion by our repeated failures, we shall evidently impede that degree of improvement in society, which is really attainable.

It has appeared that a society constituted according to Mr. Godwin's system must, from the inevitable laws of our nature, degenerate into a class of proprietors and a class of laborers, and that the substitution of benevolence for self-love as the moving principle of society, instead of producing the happy effects that might be expected from so fair a name, would cause the same pressure of want to be felt by the whole of society, which is now felt only by a part. It is to the established administration of property and to the apparently narrow principle of self-love that we are indebted for all the noblest exertions of human genius, all the finer and more delicate emotions of the soul, foreverything, indeed, that distinguishes the civilized from the savage state; and no sufficient change has as yet taken place in the nature of civilized man to enable us to say that he either is, or ever will be, in a state when he may safely throw down the ladder by which he has risen to this eminence.

If in every society that has advanced beyond the savage state, a class of proprietors and a class of laborers must necessarily exist, it is evident that, as labor is the only property of the class of laborers, every thing that tends to diminish the value of this property must tend to diminish the possession of this part of society. The only way that a poor man has of supporting himself in independence is by the exertion of his bodily strength. This is the only commodity he has to give in exchange for the necessaries of life. It would hardly appear then that you benefit him by narrowing the market for this commodity, by decreasing the demand for labor, and lessening the value of the only property that he possesses.

It should be observed that the principal argument of this Essay only goes to prove the necessity of a class of proprietors, and a class of laborers, but by no means infers that the present great inequality of property is either necessary or useful to society. On the contrary, it must certainly be considered as an evil, and every institution that promotes it is essentially bad and impolitic. But whether a government could with advantage to society actively interfere to repress inequality of fortunes may be a matter of doubt. Perhaps the generous system of perfect liberty adopted by Dr. Adam Smith and the French economists would be ill exchanged for any system of restraint.

Mr. Godwin would perhaps say that the whole system of barter and exchange is a vile and iniquitous traffic. If you would essentially relieve the poor man, you should take a part of his labor upon yourself, or give him your money, without exacting so severe a return for it. In answer to the first method proposed, it may be observed, that even if the rich could be persuaded to assist the poor in this way, the value of the assistance would be comparatively trifling. The rich, though they think themselves of great importance, bear but a small proportion in point of numbers to the poor, and would, therefore, relieve them but of a small part of their burdens by taking a share. Were all those that are employed in the labors of luxuries added to the number of those employed in producing necessaries, and could these necessary labors be amicably divided among all, each man's share might indeed be comparatively light; but desirable as such an amicable division would undoubtedly be, I cannot conceive any practical principle according to which it could take place. It has been shown, that the spirit of benevolence, guided by the strict impartial justice that Mr. Godwin describes, would, if vigorously acted upon, depress in want and misery the whole human race. Let us examine what would be the consequence, if the proprietor were to retain a decent share for himself, but to give the rest away to the poor, without exacting a task from them in return. Not to mention the idleness and the vice that such a proceeding, if general, would probably create in the present state of society, and the great risk there would be, of diminishing the produce of land, as well as the labors of luxury, another objection yet remains.

Mr. Godwin seems to have but little respect for practical principles; but I own it appears to me, that he is a much greater benefactor to mankind, who points out how an inferior good may be attained, than he who merely expatiates on the deformity of the present state of society, and the beauty of a different state, without pointing out a practical method, that might be immediately applied, of accelerating our advances from the one, to the other.

It has appeared that from the principle of population more will always be in want than can be adequately supplied. The surplus of the rich man might be sufficient for three, but four will be desirous to obtain it. He cannot make this selection of three out of the four without conferring a great favor on those that are the objects of his choice. These persons must consider themselves as under a great obligation to him and as dependent upon him for their support. The rich man would feel his power and the poor man his dependence, and the evil effects of these two impressions on the human heart are well known. Though I perfectly agree with Mr. Godwin therefore in the evil of hard labor, yet I still think it a less evil, and less calculated to debase the human mind, than dependence, and every history of man that we have ever read places in a strong point of view the danger to which that mind is exposed which is entrusted with constant power.

In the present state of things, and particularly when labor is in request, the man who does a day's work for me confers full as great an obligation upon me as I do upon him. I possess what he wants, he possesses what I want. We make an amicable exchange. The poor man walks erect in conscious independence; and the mind of his employer is not vitiated by a sense of power.

Three or four hundred years ago there was undoubtedly much less labor in England, in proportion to the population, than at present, but there was much more dependence, and we probably should not now enjoy our present degree of civil liberty if the poor, by the introduction of manufactures, had not been enabled to give something in exchange for the provisions of the great Lords, instead of being dependent upon their bounty. Even the greatest enemies of trade and manufactures, and I do not reckon myself a very determined friend to them, must allow that when they were introduced into England, liberty came in their train.

Nothing that has been said tends in the most remote degree to undervalue the principle of benevolence. It is one of the noblest and most Godlike qualities of the human heart, generated, perhaps, slowly and gradually from self-love, and afterwards intended to act as a general law, whose kind office it should be, to soften the partial deformities, to correct the asperities, and to smooth the wrinkles of its parent: and this seems to be the analog of all nature. Perhaps there is no one general law of nature that will not appear, to us at least, to produce partial evil; and we frequently observe at the same time, some bountiful provision which, acting as another general law, corrects the inequalities of the first.

The proper office of benevolence is to soften the partial evils arising from self-love, but it can never be substituted in its place. If no man were to allow himself to act till he had completely determined that the action he was about to perform was more conducive than any other to the general good, the most enlightened minds would hesitate in perplexity and amazement; and the unenlightened would be continually committing the grossest mistakes.

As Mr. Godwin, therefore, has not laid down any practical principle according to which the necessary labors of agriculture might be amicably shared among the whole class of laborers, by general invectives against employing the poor he appears to pursue an unattainable good through much present evil. For if every man who employs the poor ought to be considered as their enemy, and as adding to the weight of their oppressions, and if the miser is for this reason to be preferred to the man who spends his income, it follows that any number of men who now spend their incomes might, to the advantage of society, be converted into misers. Suppose then that a hundred thousand persons who now employ ten men each were to lock up their wealth from general use, it is evident, that a million of working men of different kinds would be completely thrown out of all employment. The extensive misery that such an event would produce in the present state of society Mr. Godwin himself could hardly refuse to acknowledge, and I question whether he might not find some difficulty in proving that a conduct of this kind tended more than the conduct of those who spend their incomes to "place human beings in the condition in which they ought to be placed." But Mr. Godwin says that the miser really locks up nothing, that the point has not been rightly understood, and that the true development and definition of the nature of wealth have not been applied to illustrate it.

Having defined therefore wealth, very justly, to be the commodities raised and fostered by human labor, he observes that the miser locks up neither corn, nor oxen, nor clothes, nor houses. Undoubtedly he does not really lock up these articles, but he locks up the power of producing them, which is virtually the same. These things are certainly used and consumed by his contemporaries, as truly, and to as great an extent, as if he were a beggar; but not to as great an extent as if he had employed his wealth in turning up more land, in breeding more oxen, in employing more tailors, and in building more houses. But supposing, for a moment, that the conduct of the miser did not tend to check any really useful produce, how are all those who are thrown out of employment to obtain patents which they may show in order to be awarded a proper share of the food and raiment produced by the society? This is the unconquerable difficulty.

I am perfectly willing to concede to Mr. Godwin that there is much more labor in the world than is really necessary, and that, if the lower classes of society could agree among themselves never to work more than six or seven hours in the day, the commodities essential to human happiness might still be produced in as great abundance as at present. But it is almost impossible to conceive that such an agreement could be adhered to. From the principle of population, some would necessarily be more in want than others. Those that had large families would naturally be desirous of exchanging two hours more of their labor for an ampler quantity of subsistence. How are they to be prevented from making this exchange? It would be a violation of the first and most sacred property that a man possesses to attempt, by positive institutions, to interfere with his command over his own labor.

Till Mr. Godwin, therefore, can point out some practical plan according to which the necessary labor in a society might be equitably divided, his invectives against labor, if they were attended to, would certainly produce much present evil without approximating us to that state of cultivated equality to which he looks forward as his polar star, and which, he seems to think, should at present be our guide in determining the nature and tendency of human actions. A mariner guided by such a polar star is in danger of shipwreck.

Perhaps there is no possible way in which wealth could in general be employed so beneficially to a state, and particularly to the lower orders of it, as by improving and rendering productive that land which to a farmer would not answer the expense of cultivation.

Had Mr. Godwin exerted his energetic eloquence in painting the superior worth and usefulness of the character who employed the poor in this way, to him who employed them in narrow luxuries, every enlightened man must have applauded his efforts. The increasing demand for agricultural labor must always tend to better the condition of the poor; and if the accession of work be of this kind, so far is it from being true that the poor would be obliged to work ten hours for the same price that they before worked eight, that the very reverse would be the fact; and a laborer might then support his wife and family as well by the labor of six hours as he could before by the labor of eight.

The labor created by luxuries, though useful in distributing the produce of the country, without vitiating the proprietor by power, or debasing the laborer by dependence, has not, indeed, the same beneficial effects on the state of the poor. A great accession of work from manufacturers, though it may raise the price of labor even more than an increasing demand for agricultural labor, yet, as in this case the quantity of food in the country may not be proportionally increasing, the advantage to the poor will be but temporary, as the price of provisions must necessarily rise in proportion to the price of labor. Relative to this subject, I cannot avoid venturing a few remarks on a part of Dr. Adam Smith's *Wealth of Nations*, speaking at the same time with that diffidence which I ought certainly to feel in differing from a person so justly celebrated in the political world.

CHAPTER 16

Probable Error of Dr. Adam Smith in Representing
Every Increase of the Revenue or Stock of a
Society as an Increase in the Funds for the
Maintenance of Labor—Instances Where an
Increase of Wealth can have no Tendency to Better
the Condition of the Laboring Poor—England has
Increased in Riches without a Proportional
Increase in the Funds for the Maintenance of
Labor—The State of the Poor in China would not
be Improved by an Increase
of Wealth from Manufactures.

The professed object of Dr. Adam Smith's inquiry is the nature and causes of the wealth of nations. There is another inquiry, however, perhaps still more interesting, which he occasionally mixes with it; I mean an inquiry into the causes which affect the happiness of nations or the happiness and comfort of the lower orders of society, which is the most numerous class in every nation. I am sufficiency aware of the near connection of these two subjects, and that the causes which tend to increase the wealth of a state tend also, generally speaking, to increase the happiness of the lower classes of the people. But perhaps Dr. Adam Smith has considered these two inquiries as still more nearly connected than they really are; at least, he has not stopped to take notice of those instances where the wealth of a society may increase (according to his definition of "wealth") without having any tendency to increase the comforts of the laboring part of it. I do not mean to enter into a philosophical discussion of what constitutes the proper happiness of man, but shall merely consider two universally acknowledged ingredients, health, and the command of the necessaries and conveniences of life.

Little or no doubt can exist that the comforts of the laboring poor depend upon the increase of the funds destined for the maintenance of labor, and will be very exactly in proportion to the rapidity of this increase. The demand for labor which such increase would occasion, by creating a competition in the market, must necessarily raise the value of labor, and, till the additional number of hands required were reared, the increased funds would be distributed to the same number of persons as before the increase, and therefore every laborer would live comparatively at his ease. But perhaps Dr. Adam Smith errs in representing every increase of the revenue or stock of a society as an increase of these funds. Such surplus stock or revenue will, indeed, always be considered by the individual possessing it as an additional fund from which he may maintain more labor: but it will not be a real and effectual fund for the maintenance of an additional number of laborers, unless the whole, or at least a great part of this increase of the stock or revenue of the society, be convertible into a proportional quantity of provisions; and it will not be so convertible where the increase has arisen merely from the produce of labor, and not from the produce of land. A distinction will in this case occur, between the number of hands which the stock of the society could employ, and the number which its territory can maintain.

To explain myself by an instance, Dr. Adam Smith defines the wealth of a nation to consist in the annual produce of its land and labor. This definition evidently includes manufactured produce, as well as the produce of the land. Now supposing a nation for a course of years was to add what it saved from its yearly revenue to its manufacturing capital solely, and not to its capital employed upon land, it is evident that it might grow richer according to the above definition, without a power of supporting a greater number of laborers, and, therefore, without an increase in the real funds for the maintenance of labor. There would, notwithstanding, be a demand for labor from the power which each manufacturer would possess, or at least think he possessed, of extending his old stock in trade or of setting up fresh works. This demand would of course raise the price of labor, but if the yearly stock of provisions in the country was not increasing, this rise would soon turn out to be merely nominal, as the price of provisions must necessarily rise with it. The demand for manufacturing laborers might, indeed, entice many from agriculture and thus tend to diminish the annual produce of the land, but we will suppose any effect of this kind to be compensated by improvements in the instruments of agriculture, and the quantity of provisions therefore to remain the same. Improvements in manufacturing machinery would of course take place, and this circumstance, added to the greater number of hands employed in manufactures, would cause the annual produce of the labor of the country to be upon the whole greatly increased. The wealth therefore of the country would be increasing annually, according to the definition, and might not, perhaps, be increasing very slowly.

The question is whether wealth, increasing in this way, has any tendency to better the condition of the laboring poor. It is a self-evident proposition that any general rise in the price of labor, the stock of provisions remaining the same, can only be a nominal rise, as it must very shortly be followed by a proportional rise in the price of provisions. The increase in the price of labor, therefore, which we have supposed, would have little or no effect in giving the laboring poor a greater command over the necessaries and conveniences of life. In this respect they would be nearly in the same state as before. In one other respect they would be in a worse state. A greater proportion of them would be employed in manufactures, and fewer, consequently, in agriculture. And this exchange of professions will be allowed, I think, by all, to be very unfavorable in respect of health, one essential ingredient of happiness, besides the greater uncertainty of manufacturing labor, arising from the capricious taste of man, the accidents of war, and other causes.

It may be said, perhaps, that such an instance as I have supposed could not occur, because the rise in the price of provisions would immediately turn some additional capital into the channel of agriculture. But this is an event which may take place very slowly, as it should be remarked that a rise in the price of labor had preceded the rise of provisions, and would, therefore, impede the good effects upon agriculture, which the increased value of the produce of the land might otherwise have occasioned.

It might also be said, that the additional capital of the nation would enable it to import provisions sufficient for the maintenance of those whom its stock could employ. A small country with a large navy, and great inland accommodations for carriage, such as Holland, may, indeed, import and distribute an effectual quantity of provisions; but the price of provisions must be very high to make such an importation and distribution answer in large countries less advantageously circumstanced in this respect.

An instance, accurately such as I have supposed, may not, perhaps, ever have occurred, but I have little doubt that instances nearly approximating to it may be found without any very laborious search. Indeed I am strongly inclined to think that England herself, since the Revolution, affords a very striking elucidation of the argument in question.

The commerce of this country, internal as well as external, has certainly been rapidly advancing during the last century. The exchangeable value in the market of Europe of the annual produce of its land and labor has, without doubt, increased very considerably. But, upon examination, it will be found that the increase has been chiefly in the produce of labor and not in the produce of land, and therefore, though the wealth of the nation has been advancing with a quick pace, the effectual funds for the maintenance of labor have been increasing very slowly, and the result is such as might be expected. The increasing wealth of the nation has had little or no tendency to better the condition of the laboring poor. They have not, I believe, a greater command of the necessaries and conveniences of life, and a much greater proportion of them than at the period of the Revolution is employed in manufactures and crowded together in close and unwholesome rooms.

Could we believe the statement of Dr. Price that the population of England has decreased since the Revolution, it would even appear that the effectual funds for the maintenance of labor had been declining during the progress of wealth in other respects. For I conceive that it may be laid down as a general rule that if the effectual funds for the maintenance of labor are increasing, that is, if the territory can maintain as well as the stock employ a greater number of laborers, this additional number will quickly spring up, even in spite of such wars as Dr. Price enumerates. And, consequently, if the population of any country has been stationary, or declining, we may safely infer, that, however it may have advanced in manufacturing wealth, its effectual funds for the maintenance of labor cannot have increased.

It is difficult, however, to conceive that the population of England has been declining since the Revolution, though every testimony concurs to prove that its increase, if it has increased, has been very slow. In the controversy which the question has occasioned, Dr. Price undoubtedly appears to be much more completely master of his subject, and to possess more accurate information, than his opponents. Judging simply from this controversy, I think one should say that Dr. Price's point is nearer being proved than Mr. Howlett's. Truth, probably, lies between the two statements, but this supposition makes the increase of population since the Revolution to have been very slow in comparison with the increase of wealth.

That the produce of the land has been decreasing, or even that it has been absolutely stationary during the last century, few will be disposed to believe. The enclosure of commons and waste lands certainly tends to increase the food of the country, but it has been asserted with confidence that the enclosure of common fields has frequently had a contrary effect, and that large tracts of land which formerly produced great quantities of corn, by being converted into pasture both employ fewer hands and feed fewer mouths than before their enclosure. It is, indeed, an acknowledged truth, that pasture land produces a smaller quantity of human subsistence than corn land of the same natural fertility, and could it be clearly ascertained that from the increased demand for butchers' meat of the best quality, and its increased price in consequence, a greater quantity of good land has annually been employed in grazing, the diminution of human subsistence, which this circumstance would occasion, might have counterbalanced the advantages derived from the enclosure of waste lands, and the general improvements in husbandry.

It scarcely need be remarked that the high price of butchers' meat at present, and its low price formerly, were not caused by the scarcity in the one case or the plenty in the other, but by the different expense sustained at the different periods, in preparing cattle for the market. It is, however, possible, that there might have been more cattle a hundred years ago in the country than at present; but no doubt can be entertained, that there is much more meat of a superior quality brought to market at present than ever there was. When the price of butchers' meat was very low, cattle were reared chiefly upon waste lands; and except for some of the principal markets, were probably killed with but little other fatting. The veal that is sold so cheap in some distant counties at present bears little other resemblance than the name, to that which is bought in London. Formerly, the price of butchers, meat would not pay for rearing, and scarcely for feeding, cattle on land that would answer in tillage; but the present price will not only pay for fatting cattle on the very best land, but will even allow of the rearing many, on land that would bear good crops of corn. The same number of cattle, or even the same weight of cattle at the different periods when killed, will have consumed (if I may be allowed the expression) very different quantities of human substance. A fatted beast may in some respects be considered, in the language of the French economists, as an unproductive laborer: he has added nothing to the value of the raw produce that he has consumed. The present system of grating, undoubtedly tends more than the former system to diminish the quantity of human subsistence in the country, in proportion to the general fertility of the land.

I would not by any means be understood to say that the former system either could or ought to have continued. The increasing price of butchers' meat is a natural and inevitable consequence of the general progress of cultivation; but I cannot help thinking, that the present great demand for butchers' meat of the best quality, and the quantity of good land that is in consequence annually employed to produce it, together with the great number of horses at present kept for pleasure, are the chief causes that have prevented the quantity of human food in the country from keeping pace with the generally increased fertility of the soil; and a change of custom in these respects would, I have little doubt, have a very sensible effect on the quantity of subsistence in the country, and consequently on its population.

The employment of much of the most fertile land in grating, the improvements in agricultural instruments, the increase of large farms, and particularly the diminution of the number of cottages throughout the kingdom, all concur to prove, that there are not probably so many persons employed in agricultural labor now as at the period of the

Revolution. Whatever increase of population, therefore, has taken place, must be employed almost wholly in manufactures, and it is well known that the failure of some of these manufactures, merely from the caprice of fashion, such as the adoption of muslins instead of silks, or of shoe-strings and covered buttons, instead of buckles and metal buttons, combined with the restraints in the market of labor arising from corporation and parish laws, have frequently driven thousands on charity for support. The great increase of the poor rates is, indeed, of itself a strong evidence that the poor have not a greater command of the necessaries and conveniences of life, and if to the consideration, that their condition in this respect is rather worse than better, be added the circumstance, that a much greater proportion of them is employed in large manufactories, unfavorable both to health and virtue, it must be acknowledged, that the increase of wealth of late years has had no tendency to increase the happiness of the laboring poor.

That every increase of the stock or revenue of a nation cannot be considered as an increase of the real funds for the maintenance of labor and, therefore, cannot have the same good effect upon the condition of the poor, will appear in a strong light if the argument be applied to China.

Dr. Adam Smith observes that China has probably long been as rich as the nature of her laws and institutions will admit, but that with other laws and institutions, and if foreign commerce were had in honor, she might still be much richer. The question is, would such an increase of wealth be an increase of the real funds for the maintenance of labor, and consequently tend to place the lower classes of people in China in a state of greater plenty?

It is evident, that if trade and foreign commerce were held in great honor in China, from the plenty of laborers, and the cheapness of labor, she might work up manufactures for foreign sale to an immense amount. It is equally evident that from the great bulk of provisions and the amazing extent of her inland territory she could not in return import such a quantity as would be any sensible addition to the annual stock of subsistence in the country. Her immense amount of manufactures, therefore, she would exchange, chiefly, for luxuries collected from all parts of the world. At present, it appears, that no labor whatever is spared in the production of food. The country is rather over-people in proportion to what its stock can employ, and labor is, therefore, so abundant, that no pains are taken to abridge it. The consequence of this is, probably, the greatest production of food that the soil can possibly afford, for it will be generally observed, that processes for abridging labor, though they may enable a farmer to bring a certain quantity of grain cheaper to market, tend rather to diminish than increase the whole produce; and in agriculture, therefore, may, in some respects, be considered rather as private than public advantages.

An immense capital could not be employed in China in preparing manufactures for foreign trade without taking off so many laborers from agriculture as to alter this state of things, and in some degree to diminish the produce of the country. The demand for manufacturing laborers would naturally raise the price of labor, but as the quantity of subsistence would not be increased, the price of provisions would keep pace with it, or even more than keep pace with it if the quantity of provisions were really decreasing. The country would be evidently advancing in wealth, the exchangeable value of the annual produce of its land and labor would be annually augmented, yet the real funds for the maintenance of labor would be stationary, or even declining, and, consequently, the increasing wealth of the nation would rather tend to depress than to raise the condition of the poor. With regard to the command over the necessaries and comforts of life, they would be in the same or rather worse state than before; and a great part of them would have exchanged the healthy labors of agriculture for the unhealthy occupations of manufacturing industry.

The argument, perhaps, appears clearer when applied to China, because it is generally allowed that the wealth of China has been long stationary. With regard to any other country it might be always a matter of dispute at which of the two periods, compared, wealth was increasing the fastest, as it is upon the rapidity of the increase of wealth at any particular period that Dr. Adam Smith says the condition of the poor depends. It is evident, however, that two nations might increase exactly with the same rapidity in the exchangeable value of the annual produce of their land and labor, yet if one had applied itself chiefly to agriculture, and the other chiefly to commerce, the funds for the maintenance of labor, and consequently the effect of the increase of wealth in each nation, would be extremely different. In that which had applied itself chiefly to agriculture, the poor would live in great plenty, and population would rapidly increase. In that which had applied itself chiefly to commerce, the poor would be comparatively but little benefited and consequently population would increase slowly.

CHAPTER 17

Question of the Proper Definition of the Wealth of a State—Reason Given by the French Economists for Considering all Manufacturers as Unproductive Laborers, not the True Reason—The Labor of Artificers and Manufacturers Sufficiently Productive to Individuals, though not to the State—A Remarkable Passage in Dr. Price's Two Volumes of Observations—Error of Dr. Price in Attributing the Happiness and Rapid Population of America, Chiefly, to its Peculiar State of Civilization—No Advantage can be Expected from Shutting Our Eyes to the Difficulties in the Way to the Improvement of Society.

A question seems naturally to arise here whether the exchangeable value of the annual produce of the land and labor be the proper definition of the wealth of a country, or whether the gross produce of the land, according to the French economists, may not be a more accurate definition. Certain it is that every increase of wealth, according to the definition of the economists, will be an increase of the funds for the maintenance of labor, and consequently will always tend to ameliorate the condition of the laboring poor, though an increase of wealth, according to Dr. Adam Smith's definition, will by no means invariably have the same tendency. And yet it may not follow from this consideration that Dr. Adam Smith's definition is not just. It seems in many respects improper to exclude the clothing and lodging of a whole people from any part of their revenue. Much of it may, indeed, be of very trivial and unimportant value in comparison with the food of the country, yet still it may be fairly considered as a part of its revenue; and, therefore, the only point in which I should differ from Dr. Adam Smith is where he seems to consider every increase of the revenue or stock of a society as an increase of the funds for the maintenance of labor, and consequently as tending always to ameliorate the condition of the poor.

The fine silks and cottons, the laces, and other ornamental luxuries of a rich country, may contribute very considerably to augment the exchangeable value of its annual produce; yet they contribute but in a very small degree to augment the mass of happiness in the society, and it appears to me that it is with some view to the real utility of the produce that we ought to estimate the productiveness or unproductiveness of different sorts of labor. The French economists consider all labor employed in manufactures as unproductive. Comparing it with the labor employed upon land, I should be perfectly disposed to agree with them, but not exactly for the reasons which they give.

They say that labor employed upon land is productive because the produce, over and above completely paying the laborer and the farmer, affords a clear rent to the landlord, and that the labor employed upon a piece of lace is unproductive because it merely replaces the provisions that the workman had consumed, and the stock of his employer, without affording any clear rent whatever. But supposing the value of the wrought lace to be such as that, besides paying in the most complete manner the workman and his employer, it could afford a clear rent to a third person, it appears to me that, in comparison with the labor employed upon land, it would be still as unproductive as ever. Though, according to the reasoning used by the French economists, the man employed in the manufacture of lace would, in this case, seem to be a productive laborer. Yet according to their definition of the wealth of a state, he ought not to be considered in that light. He will have added nothing to the gross produce of the land: he has consumed a portion of this gross produce, and has left a bit of lace in return; and though he may sell this bit of lace for three times the quantity of provisions that he consumed whilst he was making it, and thus be a very productive laborer with regard to himself, yet he cannot be considered as having added by his labor to any essential part of the riches of the state. The clear rent, therefore, that a certain produce can afford, after paying the expenses of procuring it, does not appear to be the sole criterion, by which to judge of the productiveness or unproductiveness to a state of any particular species of labor.

Suppose that two hundred thousand men, who are now employed in producing manufactures that only tend to gratify the vanity of a few rich people, were to be employed upon some barren and uncultivated lands, and to produce only half the quantity of food that they themselves consumed; they would be still more productive laborers with regard to the state than they were before, though their labor, so far from affording a rent to a third person, would but half replace the provisions used in obtaining the produce. In their former employment they consumed a certain portion of the food of the country and left in return some silks and laces. In their latter employment they consumed the same quantity of food and left in return provision for a hundred thousand men. There can be little doubt which of the two legacies would be the most really beneficial to the country, and it will, I think, be allowed that the wealth which supported the two hundred thousand men while they were producing silks and laces would have been more usefully employed in supporting them while they were producing the additional quantity of food.

A capital employed upon land may be unproductive to the individual that employs it and yet be highly productive to the society. A capital employed in trade, on the contrary, may be highly productive to the individual, and yet be almost totally unproductive to the society: and this is the reason why I should call manufacturing labor unproductive, in comparison of that which is employed in agriculture, and not for the reason given by the French economists. It is, indeed, almost impossible to see the great fortunes that are made in trade, and the liberality with which so many merchants live, and yet agree in the statement of the economists, that manufacturers can only grow rich by depriving themselves of the funds destined for their support. In many branches of trade the profits are so great as would allow of a clear rent to a third person; but as there is no third person in the case, and as all the profits centre in the master manufacturer, or merchant, he seems to have a fair chance of growing rich, without much privation; and we consequently see large fortunes acquired in trade by persons who have not been remarked for their parsimony.

Daily experience proves that the labor employed in trade and manufactures is suffi- ciently productive to individuals, but it certainly is not productive in the same degree to the state. Every accession to the food of a country tends to the immediate benefit of the whole society; but the fortunes made in trade tend but in a remote and uncertain manner to the same end, and in some respects have even a contrary tendency. The home trade of consumption is by far the most important trade of every nation. China is the richest country in the world, without any other. Putting then, for a moment, foreign trade out of the question, the man who, by an ingenious manufacture, obtains a dou- ble portion out of the old stock of provisions, will certainly not to be so useful to the state as the man who, by his labor, adds a single share to the former stock. The consumable commodities of silks, laces, trinkets, and expensive furniture, are undoubtedly a part of the revenue of the society; but they are the revenue only of the rich, and not of the so- ciety in general. An increase in this part of the revenue of a state, cannot, therefore, be considered of the same importance as an increase of food, which forms the principal rev- enue of the great mass of the people.

Foreign commerce adds to the wealth of a state, according to Dr. Adam Smith's def- inition, though not according to the definition of the economists. Its principal use, and the reason, probably, that it has in general been held in such high estimation is that it adds greatly to the external power of a nation or to its power of commanding the labor of other countries; but it will be found, upon a near examination, to contribute but lit- tle to the increase of the internal funds for the maintenance of labor, and consequently but little to the happiness of the greatest part of society. In the natural progress of a state towards riches, manufactures, and foreign commerce would follow, in their order, the high cultivation of the soil. In Europe, this natural order of things has been in- verted, and the soil has been cultivated from the redundancy of manufacturing capital, instead of manufactures rising from the redundancy of capital employed upon land. The superior encouragement that has been given to the industry of the towns, and the consequent higher price that is paid for the labor of artificers than for the labor of those employed in husbandry, are probably the reasons why so much soil in Europe remains uncultivated. Had a different policy been pursued throughout Europe, it might un- doubtedly have been much more populous than at present, and yet not be more encum- bered by its population.

I cannot quit this curious subject of the difficulty arising from population, a subject that appears to me to deserve a minute investigation and able discussion much beyond my power to give it, without taking notice of an extraordinary passage in Dr. Price's two volumes of Observations. Having given some tables on the probabilities of life, in towns and in the country, he says (Vol. II, p. 243):

> From this comparison, it appears with how much truth great cities have been called the graves of mankind. It must also convince all who consider it, that ac- cording to the observation, at the end of the fourth essay, in the former volume, it is by no means strictly proper to consider our diseases as the original intention of nature. They are, without doubt, in general our own creation. Were there a

country where the inhabitants led lives entirely natural and virtuous, few of them would die without measuring out the whole period of present existence allotted to them; pain and distemper would be unknown among them, and death would come upon them like a sleep, in consequence of no other cause than gradual and unavoidable decay.

I own that I felt myself obliged to draw a very opposite conclusion from the facts advanced in Dr. Price's two volumes. I had for some time been aware that population and food increased in different ratios, and a vague opinion had been floating in my mind that they could only be kept equal by some species of misery or vice, but the perusal of Dr. Price's two volumes of Observations, after that opinion had been conceived, raised it at once to conviction. With so many facts in his view to prove the extraordinary rapidity with which population increases when unchecked, and with such a body of evidence before him to elucidate even the manner by which the general laws of nature repress a redundant population, it is perfectly inconceivable to me how he could write the passage that I have quoted. He was a strenuous advocate for early marriages, as the best preservative against vicious manners. He had no fanciful conceptions about the extinction of the passion between the sexes, like Mr. Godwin, nor did he ever think of eluding the difficulty in the ways hinted at by Mr. Condorcet. He frequently talks of giving the prolific powers of nature room to exert themselves. Yet with these ideas, that his understanding could escape from the obvious and necessary inference that an unchecked population would increase, beyond comparison, faster than the earth, by the best directed exertions of man, could produce food for its support, appears to me as astonishing as if he had resisted the conclusion of one of the plainest propositions of Euclid.

Dr. Price, speaking of the different stages of the civilized state, says, "The first, or simple stages of civilization, are those which favor most the increase and the happiness of mankind." He then instances the American colonies, as being at that time in the first and happiest of the states that he had described, and as affording a very striking proof of the effects of the different stages of civilization on population. But he does not seem to be aware that the happiness of the Americans depended much less upon their peculiar degree of civilization than upon the peculiarity of their situation, as new colonies, upon their having a great plenty of fertile uncultivated land. In parts of Norway, Denmark, or Sweden, or in this country, two or three hundred years ago, he might have found perhaps nearly the same degree of civilization, but by no means the same happiness or the same increase of population. He quotes himself a statute of Henry the Eighth, complaining of the decay of tillage, and the enhanced price of provisions, "whereby a marvelous number of people were rendered incapable of maintaining themselves and families." The superior degree of civil liberty which prevailed in America contributed, without doubt, its share to promote the industry, happiness, and population of these states, but even civil liberty, all powerful as it is, will not create fresh land. The Americans may be said, perhaps, to enjoy a greater degree of civil liberty, now they are an independent people, than while they were in subjection in England, but we may be perfectly sure that population will not long continue to increase with the same rapidity as it did then.

A person who contemplated the happy state of the lower classes of people in America twenty years ago would naturally wish to retain them forever in that state, and might think, perhaps, that by preventing the introduction of manufactures and luxury he might effect his purpose, but he might as reasonably expect to prevent a wife or mistress from growing old by never exposing her to the sun or air. The situation of new colonies, well governed, is a bloom of youth that no efforts can arrest. There are, indeed, many modes of treatment in the political, as well as animal, body, that contribute to accelerate or retard the approaches of age, but there can be no chance of success, in any mode that could be devised, for keeping either of them in perpetual youth. By encouraging the industry of the towns more than the industry of the country, Europe may be said, perhaps, to have brought on a premature old age. A different policy in this respect would infuse fresh life and vigor into every state. While from the law of primogeniture, and other European customs, land bears a monopoly price, a capital can never be employed in it with much advantage to the individual; and, therefore, it is not probable that the soil should be properly cultivated. And, though in every civilized state a class of proprietors and a class of laborers must exist, yet one permanent advantage would always result from a nearer equalization of property. The greater the number of proprietors, the smaller must be the number of laborers: a greater part of society would be in the happy state of possessing property: and a smaller part in the unhappy state of possessing no other property than their labor. But the best directed exertions, though they may alleviate, can never remove the pressure of want, and it will be difficult for any person who contemplates the genuine situation of man on earth, and the general laws of nature, to suppose it possible that any, the most enlightened, efforts could place mankind in a state where "few would die without measuring out the whole period of present existence allotted to them; where pain and distemper would be unknown among them; and death would come upon them like a sleep, in consequence of no other cause than gradual and unavoidable decay."

It is, undoubtedly, a most disheartening reflection that the great obstacle in the way to any extraordinary improvement in society is of a nature that we can never hope to overcome. The perpetual tendency in the race of man to increase beyond the means of subsistence is one of the general laws of animated nature which we can have no reason to expect will change. Yet, discouraging as the contemplation of this difficulty must be to those whose exertions are laudably directed to the improvement of the human species, it is evident that no possible good can arise from any endeavors to slur it over or keep it in the background. On the contrary, the most baleful mischiefs may be expected from the unmanly conduct of not daring to face truth because it is unpleasing. Independently of what relates to this great obstacle, sufficient yet remains to be done for mankind to animate us to the most unremitted exertion. But if we proceed without a thorough knowledge and accurate comprehension of the nature, extent, and magnitude of the difficulties we have to encounter, or if we unwisely direct our efforts towards an object in which we cannot hope for success, we shall not only exhaust our strength in fruitless exertions and remain at as great a distance as ever from the summit of our wishes, but we shall be perpetually crushed by the recoil of this rock of Sisyphus.

CHAPTER 18

The Constant Pressure of Distress on Man, from the Principle of Population, Seems to Direct our Hopes to the Future—State of Trial Inconsistent with our Ideas of the Foreknowledge of God—The World, Probably, a Mighty Process for Awakening Matter into Mind—Theory of the Formation of Mind—Excitements from the Wants of the Body— Excitements from the Operation of General Laws—Excitements from the Difficulties of Life Arising from the Principle of Population.

The view of human life which results from the contemplation of the constant pressure of distress on man from the difficulty of subsistence, by showing the little expectation that he can reasonably entertain of perfectibility on earth, seems strongly to point his hopes to the future. And the temptations to which he must necessarily be exposed, from the operation of those laws of nature which we have been examining, would seem to represent the world in the light in which it has been frequently considered, as a state of trial and school of virtue preparatory to a superior state of happiness. But I hope I shall be pardoned if I attempt to give a view in some degree different of the situation of man on earth, which appears to me to be more consistent with the various phenomena of nature which we observe around us and more consonant to our ideas of the power, goodness, and foreknowledge of the Deity.

It cannot be considered as an unimproving exercise of the human mind to endeavor to "vindicate the ways of God to man" if we proceed with a proper distrust of our own understandings and a just sense of our insufficiency to comprehend the reason of all we see, if we hail every ray of light with gratitude, and, when no light appears, think that the darkness is from within and not from without, and bow with humble deference to the supreme wisdom of him whose "thoughts are above our thoughts" "as the heavens are high above the earth."

In all our feeble attempts, however, to "find out the Almighty to perfection" it seems absolutely necessary that we should reason from nature up to nature's God and not presume to reason from God to nature. The moment we allow ourselves to ask why some things are not otherwise, instead of endeavoring to account for them as they are, we shall never know where to stop, we shall be led into the grossest and most childish absurdities, all progress in the knowledge of the ways of Providence must necessarily be at an end, and the study will even cease to be an improving exercise of the human mind. Infinite power is so vast and incomprehensible an idea that the mind of man must necessarily be bewildered in the contemplation of it. With the crude and puerile conceptions which we sometimes form of this attribute of the Deity, we might imagine that God could call into being myriads and myriads of existences, all free from pain and imperfection, all eminent in goodness and wisdom, all capable of the highest enjoyments, and unnumbered as the points throughout infinite space. But when from these vain and extravagant dreams of fancy, we turn our eyes to the book of nature, where alone we can read God as he is, we see a constant succession of sentient beings, rising apparently from so many specks of matter, going through a long and sometimes painful process in this world, but many of them attaining, ere the termination of it, such high qualities and powers as seem to indicate their fitness for some superior state. Ought we not then to correct our crude and puerile ideas of infinite Power from the contemplation of what we actually see existing? Can we judge of the Creator but from his creation? And, unless we wish to exalt the power of God at the expense of his goodness, ought we not to conclude that even to the great Creator, almighty as he is, a certain process may be necessary, a certain time (or at least what appears to us as time) may be requisite, in order to form beings with those exalted qualities of mind which will fit them for his high purposes?

A state of trial seems to imply a previously formed existence that does not agree with the appearance of man in infancy and indicates something like suspicion and want of foreknowledge, inconsistent with those ideas which we wish to cherish of the Supreme Being. I should be inclined, therefore, as I have hinted before, to consider the world and this life as the mighty process of God, not for the trial, but for the creation and formation of mind, a process necessary to awaken inert, chaotic matter into spirit, to sublimate the dust of the earth into soul, to elicit an ethereal spark from the clod of clay. And in this view of the subject, the various impressions and excitements which man receives through life may be considered as the forming hand of his Creator, acting by general laws, and awakening his sluggish existence, by the animating touches of the Divinity, into a capacity of superior enjoyment. The original sin of man is the torpor and corruption of the chaotic matter in which he may be said to be born.

It could answer no good purpose to enter into the question whether mind be a distinct substance from matter, or only a finer form of it. The question is, perhaps, after all, a question merely of words. Mind is as essentially mind, whether formed from matter or any other substance. We know from experience that soul and body are most intimately united, and every appearance seems to indicate that they grow from infancy together. It would be a supposition attended with very little probability to believe that a complete and full formed spirit existed in every infant, but that it was clogged and impeded in its operations during the first twenty years of life by the weakness, or hebetude, of the organs in which it was enclosed. As we shall all be disposed to agree that God is the creator of mind as well as of body, and as they both seem to be forming and unfolding themselves at the same time, it cannot appear inconsistent either with reason or revelation, if it appear to be consistent with phenomena of nature, to suppose that God is constantly occupied in forming mind out of matter and that the various impressions that man receives through life is the process for that purpose. The employment is surely worthy of the highest attributes of the Deity.

This view of the state of man on earth will not seem to be unattended with probability, if, judging from the little experience we have of the nature of mind, it shall appear upon investigation that the phenomena around us, and the various events of human life, seem peculiarly calculated to promote this great end, and especially if, upon this supposition, we can account, even to our own narrow understandings, for many of those roughnesses and inequalities in life which querulous man too frequently makes the subject of his complaint against the God of nature.

The first great awakeners of the mind seem to be the wants of the body. (It was my intention to have entered at some length into this subject as a kind of second part to the Essay. A long interruption, from particular business, has obliged me to lay aside this intention, at least for the present. I shall now, therefore, only give a sketch of a few of the leading circumstances that appear to me to favor the general supposition that I have advanced.) They are the first stimulants that rouse the brain of infant man into sentient activity, and such seems to be the sluggishness of original matter that unless by a peculiar course of excitements other wants, equally powerful, are generated, these stimulants seem, even afterwards, to be necessary to continue that activity which they first awakened. The savage would slumber forever under his tree unless he were roused from his torpor by the cravings of hunger or the pinchings of cold, and the exertions that he makes to avoid these evils, by procuring food, and building himself a covering, are the exercises which form and keep in motion his faculties, which otherwise would sink into listless inactivity. From all that experience has taught us concerning the structure of the human mind, if those stimulants to exertion which arise from the wants of the body were removed from the mass of mankind, we have much more reason to think that they would be sunk to the level of brutes, from a deficiency of excitements, than that they would be raised to the rank of philosophers by the possession of leisure. In those countries where nature is the most redundant in spontaneous produce the inhabitants will not be found the most remarkable for acuteness of intellect. Necessity has been with great truth called the mother of invention. Some of the noblest exertions of the human mind have been set in motion by the necessity of satisfying the wants of the body. Want has not unfrequently given wings to the imagination of the poet, pointed the flowing periods of the historian, and added acuteness to the researches of the philosopher, and though there are undoubtedly many minds at present so far improved by the various excitements of knowledge, or of social sympathy, that they would not relapse into listlessness if their bodily stimulants were removed, yet it can scarcely be doubted that these stimulants could not be withdrawn from the mass of mankind without producing a general and fatal torpor, destructive of all the germs of future improvement.

Locke, if I recollect, says that the endeavor to avoid pain rather than the pursuit of pleasure is the great stimulus to action in life: and that in looking to any particular pleasure, we shall not be roused into action in order to obtain it, till the contemplation of it has continued so long as to amount to a sensation of pain or uneasiness under the absence of it. To avoid evil and to pursue good seem to be the great duty and business of man, and this world appears to be peculiarly calculated to afford opportunity of the most unremitted exertion of this kind, and it is by this exertion, by these stimulants, that mind is formed. If Locke's idea be just, and there is great reason to think that it is, evil seems to be necessary to create exertion, and exertion seems evidently necessary to create mind.

The necessity of food for the support of life gives rise, probably, to a greater quantity of exertion than any other want, bodily or mental. The Supreme Being has ordained that the earth shall not produce good in great quantities till much preparatory labor and ingenuity has been exercised upon its surface. There is no conceivable connection to our comprehensions, between the seed and the plant or tree that rises from it. The Supreme Creator might, undoubtedly, raise up plants of all kinds, for the use of his creatures, without the assistance of those little bits of matter, which we call seed, or even without the assisting labor and attention of man. The processes of plowing and clearing the ground, of collecting and sowing seeds, are not surely for the assistance of God in his creation, but are made previously necessary to the enjoyment of the blessings of life, in order to rouse man into action, and form his mind to reason.

To furnish the most unremitted excitements of this kind, and to urge man to further the gracious designs of Providence by the full cultivation of the earth, it has been ordained that population should increase much faster than food. This general law (as it has appeared in the former parts of this Essay) undoubtedly produces much partial evil, but a little reflection may, perhaps, satisfy us, that it produces a great overbalance of good. Strong excitements seem necessary to create exertion, and to direct this exertion, and form the reasoning faculty, it seems absolutely necessary, that the Supreme Being should act always according to general laws. The constancy of the laws of nature, or the certainty with which we may expect the same effects from the same causes, is the foundation of the faculty of reason. If in the ordinary course of things, the finger of God were frequently visible, or to speak more correctly, if God were frequently to change his purpose (for the finger of God is, indeed, visible in every blade of grass that we see), a general and fatal torpor of the human faculties would probably ensue; even the bodily wants of mankind would cease to stimulate them to exertion, could they not reasonably expect that if their efforts were well directed they would be crowned with success. The constancy of the laws of nature is the foundation of the industry and foresight of the husbandman, the indefatigable ingenuity of the artificer, the skilful researches of the physician and anatomist, and the watchful observation and patient investigation of the natural philosopher. To this constancy we owe all the greatest and noblest efforts of intellect. To this constancy we owe the immortal mind of a Newton.

As the reasons, therefore, for the constancy of the laws of nature seem, even to our understandings, obvious and striking; if we return to the principle of population and consider man as he really is, inert, sluggish, and averse from labor, unless compelled by necessity (and it is surely the height of folly to talk of man, according to our crude fancies of what he might be), we may pronounce with certainty that the world would not have been peopled, but for the superiority of the power of population to the means of subsistence. Strong and constantly operative as this stimulus is on man to urge him to the cultivation of the earth, if we still see that cultivation proceeds very slowly, we may fairly conclude that a less stimulus would have been insufficient. Even under the operation of this constant excitement, savages will inhabit countries of the greatest natural fertility for a long period before they betake themselves to pasturage or agriculture. Had population and food increased in the same ratio, it is probable that man might never have emerged from the savage state. But supposing the earth once well peopled, an Alexander, a Julius Caesar, a Tamberlane, or a bloody revolution might irrecoverably thin the human race, and defeat the great designs of the Creator. The ravages of a contagious disorder would be felt for ages; and an earthquake might unpeople a region forever. The principle, according to which population increases, prevents the vices of mankind, or the accidents of nature, the partial evils arising from general laws, from obstructing the high purpose of the creation. It keeps the inhabitants of the earth always fully up to the level of the means of subsistence; and is constantly acting upon man as a powerful stimulus, urging him to the further cultivation of the earth, and to enable it, consequently, to support a more extended population. But it is impossible that this law can operate, and produce the effects apparently intended by the Supreme Being, without occasioning partial evil. Unless the principle of population were to be altered according to the circumstances of each separate country (which would not only be contrary to our universal experience, with regard to the laws of nature, but would contradict even our own reason, which sees the absolute necessity of general laws for the formation of intellect), it is evident that the same principle which, seconded by industry, will people a fertile region in a few years must produce distress in countries that have been long inhabited.

It seems, however, every way probable that even the acknowledged difficulties occasioned by the law of population tend rather to promote than impede the general purpose of Providence. They excite universal exertion and contribute to that infinite variety of situations, and consequently of impressions, which seems upon the whole favorable to the growth of mind. It is probable, that too great or too little excitement, extreme poverty, or too great riches may be alike unfavorable in this respect. The middle regions of society seem to be best suited to intellectual improvement, but it is contrary to the analogy of all nature to expect that the whole of society can be a middle region. The temperate zones of the earth seem to be the most favorable to the mental and corporal energies of man, but all cannot be temperate zones. A world, warmed and enlightened but by one sun, must from the laws of matter have some parts chilled by perpetual frosts and others scorched by perpetual heats. Every piece of matter lying on a surface must have an upper and an under side, all the particles cannot be in the middle. The most valuable parts of an oak, to a timber merchant, are not either the roots or the branches, but these are absolutely necessary to the existence of the middle part, or stem, which is the object in request. The timber merchant could not possibly expect to make an oak grow without roots or branches, but if he could find out a mode of cultivation which would cause more of the substance to go to stem, and less to root and branch, he would be right to exert himself in bringing such a system into general use.

In the same manner, though we cannot possibly expect to exclude riches and poverty from society, yet if we could find out a mode of government by which the numbers in the extreme regions would be lessened and the numbers in the middle regions increased, it would be undoubtedly our duty to adopt it. It is not, however, improbable that as in the oak, the roots and branches could not be diminished very greatly without weakening the vigorous circulation of the sap in the stem, so in society the extreme parts could not be diminished beyond a certain degree without lessening that animated exertion throughout the middle parts, which is the very cause that they are the most favorable to the growth of intellect. If no man could hope to rise or fear to fall, in society, if industry did not bring with it its reward and idleness its punishment, the middle parts would not certainly be what they now are. In reasoning upon this subject, it is evident that we ought to consider chiefly the mass of mankind and not individual instances. There are undoubtedly many minds, and there ought to be many, according to the chances out of so great a mass, that, having been vivified early by a peculiar course of excitements, would not need the constant action of narrow motives to continue them in activity. But if we were to review the various useful discoveries, the valuable writings, and other laudable exertions of mankind, I believe we should find that more were to be attributed to the narrow motives that operate upon the many than to the apparently more enlarged motives that operate upon the few.

Leisure is, without doubt, highly valuable to man, but taking man as he is, the probability seems to be that in the greater number of instances it will produce evil rather than good. It has been not infrequently remarked that talents are more common among younger brothers than among elder brothers, but it can scarcely be imagined that younger brothers are, upon an average, born with a greater original susceptibility of parts. The difference, if there really is any observable difference, can only arise from their different situations. Exertion and activity are in general absolutely necessary in one case and are only optional in the other.

That the difficulties of life contribute to generate talents, every day's experience must convince us. The exertions that men find it necessary to make, in order to support themselves or families, frequently awaken faculties that might otherwise have lain forever dormant, and it has been commonly remarked that new and extraordinary situations generally create minds adequate to grapple with the difficulties in which they are involved.

CHAPTER 19

The Sorrows of Life Necessary to Soften and Humanize the Heart—The Excitement of Social Sympathy Often Produce Characters of a Higher Order than the Mere Possessors of Talents—Moral Evil Probably Necessary to the Production of Moral Excellence—Excitements from Intellectual Wants Continually Kept up by the Infinite Variety of Nature, and the Obscurity that Involves Metaphysical Subjects—The Difficulties in Revelation to be Accounted for upon this Principle—The Degree of Evidence which the Scriptures Contain, Probably, Best Suited to the Improvements of the Human Faculties, and the Moral Amelioration of Mankind—The Idea that Mind is Created by Excitements Seems to Account for the Existence of Natural and Moral Evil.

The sorrows and distresses of life form another class of excitements, which seem to be necessary, by a peculiar train of impressions, to soften and humanize the heart, to awaken social sympathy, to generate all the Christian virtues, and to afford scope for the ample exertion of benevolence. The general tendency of a uniform course of prosperity is rather to degrade than exalt the character. The heart that has never known sorrow itself will seldom be feelingly alive to the pains and pleasures, the wants and wishes, of its fellow beings. It will seldom be overflowing with that warmth of brotherly love, those kind and amiable affections, which dignify the human character even more than the possession of the highest talents. Talents, indeed, though undoubtedly a very prominent and fine feature of mind, can by no means be considered as constituting the whole of it. There are many minds which have not been exposed to those excitements that usually form talents, that have yet been vivified to a high degree by the excitements of social sympathy. In every rank of life, in the lowest as frequently as in the highest, characters are to be found overflowing with the milk of human kindness, breathing love towards God and man, and, though without those peculiar powers of mind called talents, evidently holding a higher rank in the scale of beings than many who possess them. Evangelical charity, meekness, piety, and all that class of virtues distinguished particularly by the name of Christian virtues do not seem necessarily to include abilities; yet a soul possessed of these amiable qualities, a soul awakened and vivified by these delightful sympathies, seems to hold a nearer commerce with the skies than mere acuteness of intellect.

The greatest talents have been frequently misapplied and have produced evil proportionate to the extent of their powers. Both reason and revelation seem to assure us that such minds will be condemned to eternal death, but while on earth, these vicious instruments performed their part in the great mass of impressions, by the disgust and abhorrence which they excited. It seems highly probable that moral evil is absolutely necessary to the production of moral excellence. A being with only good placed in view may be justly said to be impelled by a blind necessity. The pursuit of good in this case can be no indication of virtuous propensities. It might be said, perhaps, that infinite Wisdom cannot want such an indication as outward action, but would foreknow with certainly whether the being would choose good or evil. This might be a plausible argument against a state of trial, but will not hold against the supposition that mind in this world is in a state of formation. Upon this idea, the being that has seen moral evil and has felt disapprobation and disgust at it is essentially different from the being that has seen only good. They are pieces of clay that have received distinct impressions: they must, therefore, necessarily be in different shapes; or, even if we allow them both to have the same lovely form of virtue, it must be acknowledged that one has undergone the further process, necessary to give firmness and durability to its substance, while the other is still exposed to injury, and liable to be broken by every accidental impulse. An ardent love and admiration of virtue seems to imply the existence of something opposite to it, and it seems highly probable that the same beauty of form and substance, the same perfection of character, could not be generated without the impressions of disapprobation which arise from the spectacle of moral evil.

When the mind has been awakened into activity by the passions, and the wants of the body, intellectual wants arise; and the desire of knowledge, and the impatience under ignorance, form a new and important class of excitements. Every part of nature seems peculiarly calculated to furnish stimulants to mental exertion of this kind, and to offer inexhaustible food for the most unremitted inquiry. Our mortal Bard says of Cleopatra:

Custom cannot stale
Her infinite variety.

The expression, when applied to any one object, may be considered as a poetical amplification, but it is accurately true when applied to nature. Infinite variety seems, indeed, eminently her characteristic feature. The shades that are here and there blended in the picture give spirit, life, and prominence to her exuberant beauties, and those roughnesses and inequalities, those inferior parts that support the superior, though they sometimes offend the fastidious microscopic eye of short-sighted man, contribute to the symmetry, grace, and fair proportion of the whole.

The infinite variety of the forms and operations of nature, besides tending immediately to awaken and improve the mind by the variety of impressions that it creates, opens other fertile sources of improvement by offering so wide and extensive a field for investigation and research. Uniform, undiversified perfection could not possess the same awakening powers. When we endeavor then to contemplate the system of the universe, when we think of the stars as the suns of other systems scattered throughout infinite space, when we reflect that we do not probably see a millionth part of those bright orbs that are beaming light and life to unnumbered worlds, when our minds, unable to grasp the immeasurable conception, sink, lost and confounded, in admiration at the mighty incomprehensible power of the Creator, let us not querulously complain that all climates are not equally genial, that perpetual spring does not reign throughout the year, that it

God's creatures do not possess the same advantages, that clouds and tempests sometimes darken the natural world and vice and misery the moral world, and that all the works of the creation are not formed with equal perfection. Both reason and experience seem to indicate to us that the infinite variety of nature (and variety cannot exist without inferior parts, or apparent blemishes) is admirably adapted to further the high purpose of the creation and to produce the greatest possible quantity of good.

The obscurity that involves all metaphysical subjects appears to me, in the same manner, peculiarly calculated to add to that class of excitements which arise from the thirst of knowledge. It is probable that man, while on earth, will never be able to attain complete satisfaction on these subjects; but this is by no means a reason that he should not engage in them. The darkness that surrounds these interesting topics of human curiosity may be intended to furnish endless motives to intellectual activity and exertion. The constant effort to dispel this darkness, even if it fail of success, invigorates and improves the thinking faculty. If the subjects of human inquiry were once exhausted, mind would probably stagnate; but the infinitely diversified forms and operations of nature, together with the endless food for speculation which metaphysical subjects offer, prevent the possibility that such a period should ever arrive.

It is by no means one of the wisest sayings of Solomon that "there is no new thing under the sun." On the contrary, it is probable that were the present system to continue for millions of years, continual additions would be making to the mass of human knowledge, and yet, perhaps, it may be a matter of doubt whether what may be called the capacity of mind be in any marked and decided manner increasing. A Socrates, a Plato, or an Aristotle, however confessedly inferior in knowledge to the philosophers of the present day, do not appear to have been much below them in intellectual capacity. Intellect rises from a speck, continues in vigor only for a certain period, and will not perhaps admit while on earth of above a certain number of impressions. These impressions may, indeed, be infinitely modified, and from these various modifications, added probably to a difference in the susceptibility of the original germs, arise the endless diversity of character that we see in the world; but reason and experience seem both to assure us that the capacity of individual minds does not increase in proportion to the mass of existing knowledge. (It is probable that no two grains of wheat are exactly alike. Soil undoubtedly makes the principal difference in the blades that spring up, but probably not all. It seems natural to suppose some sort of difference in the original germs that are afterwards awakened into thought, and the extraordinary difference of susceptibility in very young children seems to confirm the supposition.)

The finest minds seem to be formed rather by efforts at original thinking, by endeavors to form new combinations, and to discover new truths, than by passively receiving the impressions of other men's ideas. Could we suppose the period arrived, when there was not further hope of future discoveries, and the only employment of mind was to acquire pre-existing knowledge, without any efforts to form new and original combinations, though the mass of human knowledge were a thousand times greater than it is at present, yet it is evident that one of the noblest stimulants to mental exertion would have ceased; the finest feature of intellect would be lost; everything allied to genius would be at an end; and it appears to be impossible, that, under such circumstances, any individuals could possess the same intellectual energies as were possessed by a Locke, a Newton, or a Shakespeare, or even by a Socrates, a Plato, an Aristotle, or a Homer.

If a revelation from heaven of which no person could feel the smallest doubt were to dispel the mists that now hang over metaphysical subjects, were to explain the nature and structure of mind, the affections and essences of all substances, the mode in which the Supreme Being operates in the works of the creation, and the whole plan and scheme of the Universe, such an accession of knowledge so obtained, instead of giving additional vigor and activity to the human mind, would in all probability tend to repress future exertion and to damp the soaring wings of intellect.

For this reason I have never considered the doubts and difficulties that involve some parts of the sacred writings as any ardent against their divine original. The Supreme Being might, undoubtedly, have accompanied his revelations to man by such a succession of miracles, and of such a nature, as would have produced universal overpowering conviction and have put an end at once to all hesitation and discussion. But weak as our reason is to comprehend the plans of the great Creator, it is yet sufficiently strong to see the most striking objections to such a revelation. From the little we know of the structure of the human understanding, we must be convinced that an overpowering conviction of this kind, instead of tending to the improvement and moral amelioration of man, would act like the touch of a torpedo on all intellectual exertion and would almost put an end to the existence of virtue. If the scriptural denunciations of eternal punishment were brought home with the same certainty to every man's mind as that the night will follow the day, this one vast and gloomy idea would take such full possession of the human faculties as to leave no room for any other conceptions, the external actions of men would be all nearly alike, virtuous conduct would be no indication of virtuous disposition, vice and virtue would be blended together in one common mass, and though the all-seeing eye of God might distinguish them they must necessarily make the same impressions on man, who can judge only from external appearances. Under such a dispensation, it is difficult to conceive how human beings could be formed to a detestation of moral evil, and a love and admiration of God, and of moral excellence.

Our ideas of virtue and vice are not, perhaps, very accurate and well-defined; but few, I think, would call an action really virtuous which was performed simply and solely from the dread of a very great punishment or the expectation of a very great reward. The fear of the Lord is very justly said to be the beginning of wisdom, but the end of wisdom is the love of the Lord and the admiration of moral good. The denunciations of future punishment contained in the scriptures seem to be well calculated to arrest the progress of the vicious and awaken the attention of the careless, but we see from repeated experience that they are not accompanied with evidence of such a nature as to overpower the human will and to make men lead virtuous lives with vicious dispositions, merely from a dread of hereafter. A genuine faith, by which I mean a faith that shows itself in it the virtues of a truly Christian life, may generally be considered as an indication of an amiable and virtuous disposition, operated upon more by love than by pure unmixed fear.

When we reflect on the temptations to which man must necessarily be exposed in this world, from the structure of his frame, and the operation of the laws of nature, and the consequent moral certainty that many vessels will come out of this mighty creative furnace in wrong shapes, it is perfectly impossible to conceive that any of these creatures of God's hand can be condemned to eternal suffering. Could we once admit such an idea, it our natural conceptions of goodness and justice would be completely overthrown, and we could no longer look up to God as a merciful and righteous Being. But the doctrine of life and Mortality which was brought to light by the gospel, the doctrine that the end of righteousness is everlasting life, but that the wages of sin are death, is in every respect just and merciful, and worthy of the great Creator. Nothing can appear more consonant to our reason than that those beings which come out of the creative process of the world in lovely and beautiful forms should be crowned with immortality, while those which come out misshapen, those whose minds are not suited to a purer and happier state of existence, should perish and be condemned to mix again with their original clay. Eternal condemnation of this kind may be considered as a species of eternal punishment, and it is not wonderful that it should be represented, sometimes, under images of suffering. But life and death, salvation and destruction, are more frequently opposed to each other in the New Testament than happiness and misery. The Supreme Being would appear to us in a very different view if we were to consider him as pursuing the creatures that had offended him with eternal hate and torture, instead of merely condemning to their original insensibility those beings that, by the operation of general laws, had not been formed with qualities suited to a purer state of happiness.

Life is, generally speaking, a blessing independent of a future state. It is a gift which the vicious would not always be ready to throw away, even if they had no fear of death. The partial pain, therefore, that is inflicted by the supreme Creator, while he is forming numberless beings to a capacity of the highest enjoyments, is but as the dust of the balance in comparison of the happiness that is communicated, and we have every reason to think that there is no more evil in the world than what is absolutely necessary as one of the ingredients in the mighty process.

The striking necessity of general laws for the formation of intellect will not in any respect be contradicted by one or two exceptions, and these evidently not intended for partial purposes, but calculated to operate upon a great part of mankind, and through many ages. Upon the idea that I have given of the formation of mind, the infringement of the general law of nature, by a divine revelation, will appear in the light of the immediate hand of God mixing new ingredients in the mighty mass, suited to the particular state of the process, and calculated to give rise to a new and powerful train of impressions, tending to purify, exalt, and improve the human mind. The miracles that accompanied these revelations when they had once excited the attention of mankind, and rendered it a matter of most interesting discussion, whether the doctrine was from God or man, had performed their part, had answered the purpose of the Creator, and these communications of the divine will were afterwards left to make their way by their own intrinsic excellence; and, by operating as moral motives, gradually to influence and improve, and not to overpower and stagnate the faculties of man.

It would be, undoubtedly, presumptuous to say that the Supreme Being could not possibly have effected his purpose in any other way than that which he has chosen, but as the revelation of the divine will which we possess is attended with some doubts and difficulties, and as our reason points out to us the strongest objections to a revelation which would force immediate, implicit, universal belief, we have surely just cause to think that these doubts and difficulties are no argument against the divine origin of the scriptures, and that the species of evidence which they possess is best suited to the improvement of the human faculties and the moral amelioration of mankind.

The idea that the impressions and excitements of this world are the instruments with which the Supreme Being forms matter into mind, and that the necessity of constant exertion to avoid evil and to pursue good is the principal spring of these impressions and excitements, seems to smooth many of the difficulties that occur in a contemplation of human life, and appears to me to give a satisfactory reason for the existence of natural and moral evil, and, consequently, for that part of both, and it certainly is not a very small part, which arises from the principle of population. But, though, upon this supposition, it seems highly improbable that evil should ever be removed from the world; yet it is evident that this impression would not answer the apparent purpose of the Creator; it would not act so powerfully as an excitement to exertion, if the quantity of it did not diminish or increase with the activity or the indolence of man. The continual variations in the weight and in the distribution of this pressure keep alive a constant expectation of throwing it off.

"Hope springs eternal in the Human breast, Man never is, but always to be blest."

Evil exists in the world not to create despair but activity. We are not patiently to submit to it, but to exert ourselves to avoid it. It is not only the interest but the duty of every individual to use his utmost efforts to remove evil from himself and from as large a circle as he can influence, and the more he exercises himself in this duty, the more wisely he directs his efforts, and the more successful these efforts are; the more he will probably improve and exalt his own mind, and the more completely does he appear to fulfill the will of his Creator.

David Ricardo
(1772–1823)

AN INTRODUCTION TO HIS LIFE AND WORK

Adam Smith provided the blueprint, but classical economics still stands, in large part, as the house that David Ricardo built. Ricardo admired Smith's grand vision and solid frame. But he recognized the need to adjust the floor plan, accommodate the flow between rooms, and equip the place with its basic mathematical wiring and plumbing. Classical economics may have been possible without his work, but it might not have survived inspection or the test of time without his vital contributions.

Ricardo's influence extends well beyond the classical period or free market ideology. His thoughtful, systematic approach informed and inspired the efforts of economic thinkers across the ideological spectrum for years to come. He imbued the field of economics itself with a scientific respectability and processes for future thinkers to employ in adding additions.

HIS LIFE

David Ricardo came to economics as a second career in middle age, bolstered by a résumé that made him especially suited for the field. While most economists come to their profession through studying theory and models, Ricardo learned from the ground up. He was born in 1772 in London, England, to Jewish parents shortly after they had relocated from Holland. The third of seventeen children, Ricardo received little formal education before going to work with his father on the London Stock Exchange at the age of fourteen, where he learned market dynamics firsthand. He also displayed a precocious grasp of making money, gaining a reputation as one of England's leading stock traders and analysts by the age when most contemporary economics students are still working toward their undergraduate degrees.

Ricardo would have likely remained on the exchange and taken over his father's practice. However, his personal life suffered several crosses in the years ahead that roiled his life, but turned out to be fortuitous events for the evolution of economic theory. At twenty-one, Ricardo married a Quaker woman named Priscilla Wilkinson, causing his family to essentially banish him from their lives. Still, Ricardo refused to break off the marriage and became a Unitarian. The split with his family also forced Ricardo out of the stock exchange and into his own business as a securities trader.

Ricardo proved equally shrewd in his new line of work and quickly amassed an impressive fortune.

The second stage of David Ricardo's education began when his wife became chronically ill. He had probably given little consideration to the larger theoretical questions behind his life's work until the age of twenty-seven, when he accompanied his ailing wife to a vacation resort in Bath, England. There he happened upon a copy of Adam Smith's *Wealth of Nations* and read it to pass the time while his wife convalesced in the resort's spa.

Adam Smith's words and ideas struck a chord and the gregarious Ricardo began discussing them with friends when he returned to London. That circle of friends eventually grew to include political economist and population theorist Thomas Malthus, utilitarian philosopher and political activist Jeramy Bentham, and economist James Mill. Interacting with these thinkers and others helped Ricardo further develop his own theoretical ideas, just as his years on the floor of the London Stock Exchange informed his professional practices and free market instincts.

Still, it would be another ten years before Mill talked Ricardo into committing his positions to writing. Ricardo's long apprenticeship as an economic thinker then entered a new phase, as he tested his ideas in the theater of public debate. At the age of thirty-seven, Ricardo published articles about monetary policy and the controversy over whether England should return to the gold standard. In the course of the debate, Ricardo essentially established what came to be understood as the classical approach to monetary theory.

Ricardo ended his business career in 1814 at the age of forty-one a very wealthy man, and retired to a large English country estate at Gatacomb Park. In retirement, Ricardo dedicated much of his time to thinking about, discussing, and writing on economic theory. His position on monetary policy, his view on Say's Law, and his disbelief in the potential for supply gluts inspired Thomas Malthus, by then a famous economic thinker, to begin corresponding with Ricardo. Though they often disagreed about the fundamental questions of economics, they became friends and continued their debate through letters and interactions at the Political Economy Club, which Malthus had founded. In 1815, they both published works outlining the concept of "the law of diminishing returns" within a few weeks of each other, showing how important their interactions had become for their respective evolutions as economic thinkers. The following year Ricardo produced *Proposals for an Economical and Secure Currency*.

In 1817, Ricardo put all his years of practical experience, debate, and theoretical musing into *On the Principles of Political Economy and Taxation*. It is still considered his finest work and one of the most important books on economics ever written. Two years later, Ricardo became representative for the Irish borough of Portarlington in the English Parliament, where he served as a leading advocate for free trade and the abolition of protectionist laws. He died at home in Gatacomb Park in 1823.

AN OVERVIEW OF THE WORK

In the preface of *On the Principles of Political Economy and Taxation*, Ricardo paid tribute to Adam Smith, Jean-Baptiste Say, Thomas Malthus, and several other economic thinkers, then declared that he would spend the rest of the book essentially correcting their mistakes. He identified the book's focus as what he considered the principal problem of political economy: distribution of wealth. As he wrote in a letter to Malthus:

> Political Economy, you think, is an enquiry into the nature and causes of wealth—I think it should rather be called an enquiry into the laws which determine the division of produce of industry amongst the classes that concur in its formation. No law can be laid down respecting quantity, but a tolerably correct one can be laid down respecting proportions. Every day I am more satisfied that the former enquiry is vain and delusive, and the latter the only true object of the science.

Ricardo makes it equally clear in the opening pages of *On the Principles of Political Economy and Taxation* that he considers the analysis of this distribution process and all economic processes to be matters of science, reducible to a system of interrelated formulas and equations. Though largely accepted today, this systematic approach to economics was not a popular one in Ricardo's time.

Ricardo recognized all the intersections between the various players in an economy and how sophisticated his system of analysis would have to be to account for how all this complex interplay. Ricardo's sophisticated view of economic forces and how they perpetually impact one another can make his ideas difficult to summarize or separate from one another. He does not look at economics in terms of laws and conditions so much as processes that continually adjust to ever-changing conditions.

As a result, Ricardo is often employed to further positions he did not see as permanent or even valid. For instance, he is often cited as an advocate of the so-called Iron Law of Wages, which postulates that labor wages will always hover near subsistence level due to population pressures and other factors. Though he recognized the challenges the working class faced and believed that profits depended, in large part, on cheap labor, he still saw reason to be optimistic on wages.

> Notwithstanding the tendency of wages to conform to their natural rate, their market rate may, in an improving society, for an indefinite period, be constantly above it; for no sooner may the impulse, which an increased capital gives to a new demand for labor, be obeyed, than another increase of capital may produce the same effect; and thus, if the increase of capital be gradual and constant, the demand for labor may give a continued stimulus to an increase of people.

His outlook on the matter was certainly not as sunny as Adam Smith's. But Ricardo, as always, based his view on objective analysis:

> It has been calculated, that under favorable circumstances population may be doubled in twenty-five years; but under the same favorable circumstances, the whole capital of a country might possibly be doubled in a shorter period. In that case, wages during the whole period would have a tendency to rise, because the demand for labor would increase still faster than the supply.

Though his sentence structures and vocabulary may seem a little stuffy to modern readers, David Ricardo wrote in a relatively straightforward style appropriate to someone who felt he was only communicating the objective facts. He was no missionary preaching on behalf of a cherished theory or ideology, just someone reporting what he had come to know after years of firsthand experience and analysis.

Still, perhaps the simplest, most important and enduring idea that Ricardo put forth in *On the Principles of Political Economy and Taxation* remains widely misunderstood—even as it has assumed a more and more prominent position in our era's political debates. Though others had suggested it before, Ricardo presented the concept of "comparative advantage" so thoroughly in *On the Principles of Political Economy and Taxation* that it immediately became one of the foundations of international trade and economic theory, and remains so to this day. Comparative advantage differs from the trade idea of "absolute advantage" put forth by Adam Smith in *Wealth of Nations.*

> If a foreign country can supply us with a commodity cheaper than we ourselves can make it, better buy it of them with some part of the produce of our own industry, employed in a way in which we have some advantage.

Ricardo takes the idea one step further, making a logical, mathematical case for international trade even if a country possesses only a "comparative advantage" in the transaction. To demonstrate his point, Ricardo cites a trade scenario between Portugal and England:

> To produce the wine in Portugal, might require only the labor of 80 men for one year, and to produce the cloth in the same country, might require the labor of 90 men for the same time. It would therefore be advantageous for her to export wine in exchange for cloth. This exchange might even take place, notwithstanding that the commodity imported by Portugal could be produced there with less labor than in England. Though she could make the cloth with the labor of 90 men, she would import it from a country where it required the labor of 100 men to produce it, because it would be advantageous to her rather to employ her capital in the production of wine, for which she would obtain more cloth from England, than she could produce by diverting a portion of her capital from the cultivation of vines to the manufacture of cloth.

While the idea of comparative advantage seems simple for trained economists to comprehend and apply—and remains part of the foundation of international trade theory and practice—it still eludes the grasp of many people, including leading politicians and intellectuals. The general public's inability to master this relatively simple principle and economists' inability to explain it to them points to one of the many reasons why more economists need to thoroughly read Ricardo to appreciate the full context and mechanics of his reasoning.

RICARDO'S IMPACT

Ricardo's vigorous, systematic approach to economics forever changed the way economics was studied, regarded, researched, and advanced. His system dominated the field for most of the nineteenth century. Though he stood at the other end of the ideological spectrum, Karl Marx employed Ricardo in much of his theorizing. The marginalists in the 1870s claimed to have undermined Ricardo's system of analysis, but a century later his methodologies began to reemerge and his reputation was restored.

While the complexity of modern economic modeling may make much of Ricardo's methodology seem outdated, they all flow from the same intention and toward the same end. Economics became a science and the free market system emerged and sustained itself as the dominant form of political economy in large part because of the efforts of David Ricardo.

PRINCIPLES OF POLITICAL ECONOMY BY DAVID RICARDO

CHAPTER I

On Value

SECTION I

The value of a commodity, or the quantity of any other commodity for which it will exchange, depends on the relative quantity of labor which is necessary for its production, and not on the greater or less compensation which is paid for that labor.

It has been observed by Adam Smith that "the word Value has two different meanings, and sometimes expresses the utility of some particular object, and sometimes the power of purchasing other goods which the possession of that object conveys. The one may be called *value in use;* the other *value in exchange.* The things," he continues, "which have the greatest value in use, have frequently little or no value in exchange; and, on the contrary, those which have the greatest value in exchange, have little or no value in use." Water and air are abundantly useful; they are indeed indispensable to existence, yet, under ordinary circumstances, nothing can be obtained in exchange for them. Gold, on the contrary, though of little use compared with air or water, will exchange for a great quantity of other goods.

Utility then is not the measure of exchangeable value, although it is absolutely essential to it. If a commodity were in no way useful—in other words, if it could in no way contribute to our gratification—it would be destitute of exchangeable value, however scarce it might be, or whatever quantity of labor might be necessary to procure it.

Possessing utility, commodities derive their exchangeable value from two sources: from their scarcity, and from the quantity of labor required to obtain them.

There are some commodities, the value of which is determined by their scarcity alone. No labor can increase the quantity of such goods, and therefore their value cannot be lowered by an increased supply. Some rare statues and pictures, scarce books and coins, wines of a peculiar quality, which can be made only from grapes grown on a particular soil, of which there is a very limited quantity, are all of this description. Their value is wholly independent of the quantity of labor originally necessary to produce them, and varies with the varying wealth and inclinations of those who are desirous to possess them.

These commodities, however, form a very small part of the mass of commodities daily exchanged in the market. By far the greatest part of those goods which are the objects of desire are procured by labor; and they may be multiplied, not in one country alone, but in many, almost without any assignable limit, if we are disposed to bestow the labor necessary to obtain them.

In speaking, then, of commodities, of their exchangeable value, and of the laws which regulate their relative prices, we mean always such commodities only as can be increased in quantity by the exertion of human industry, and on the production of which competition operates without restraint.

In the early stages of society, the exchangeable value of these commodities, or the rule which determines how much of one shall be given in exchange for another, depends almost exclusively on the comparative quantity of labor expended on each.

"The real price of everything," says Adam Smith, "what everything really costs to the man who wants to acquire it, is the toil and trouble of acquiring it. What everything is really worth to the man who has acquired it, and who wants to dispose of it, or exchange it for something else, is the toil and trouble which it can save to himself, and which it can impose upon other people." "Labor was the first price—the original purchase-money that was paid for all things." Again, "in that early and rude state of society which precedes both the accumulation of stock and the appropriation of land, the proportion between the quantities of labor necessary for acquiring different objects seems to be the only circumstance which can afford any rule for exchanging them for one another. If, among a nation of hunters, for example, it usually cost twice the labor to kill a beaver which it does to kill a deer, one beaver should naturally exchange for, or be worth, two deer. It is natural that what is usually the produce of two days' or two hours' labor should be worth double of what is usually the produce of one day's or one hour's labour."[1]

That this is really the foundation of the exchangeable value of all things, excepting those which cannot be increased by human industry, is a doctrine of the utmost importance in political economy; for from no source do so many errors, and so much difference of opinion in that science proceed, as from the vague ideas which are attached to the word value.

If the quantity of labor realized in commodities regulate their exchangeable value, every increase of the quantity of labor must augment the value of that commodity on which it is exercised, as every diminution must lower it.

Adam Smith, who so accurately defined the original source of exchangeable value, and who was bound in consistency to maintain that all things became more or less valuable in proportion as more or less labor was bestowed on their production, has himself erected another standard measure of value, and speaks of things being more or less valuable in proportion as they will exchange for more or less of this standard measure. Sometimes he speaks of corn, at other times of labor, as a standard measure; not the quantity of labor bestowed on the production of any object, but the quantity which it can command in the market: as if these were two equivalent expressions, and as if, because a man's labor had become doubly efficient, and he could therefore produce twice the quantity of a commodity, he would necessarily receive twice the former quantity in exchange for it.

If this indeed were true, if the reward of the laborer were always in proportion to what he produced, the quantity of labor bestowed on a commodity, and the quantity of labor which that commodity would purchase, would be equal, and either might accurately measure the variations of other things; but they are not equal; the first is under many circumstances an invariable standard, indicating correctly the variations of other things;

the latter is subject to as many fluctuations as the commodities compared with it. Adam Smith, after most ably showing the insufficiency of a variable medium, such as gold and silver, for the purpose of determining the varying value of other things, has himself, by fixing on corn or labor, chosen a medium no less variable.

Gold and silver are no doubt subject to fluctuations from the discovery of new and more abundant mines; but such discoveries are rare, and their effects, though powerful, are limited to periods of comparatively short duration. They are subject also to fluctuation from improvements in the skill and machinery with which the mines may be worked; as in consequence of such improvements a greater quantity may be obtained with the same labor. They are further subject to fluctuation from the decreasing produce of the mines, after they have yielded a supply to the world for a succession of ages. But from which of these sources of fluctuation is corn exempted? Does not that also vary, on one hand, from improvements in agriculture, from improved machinery and implements used in husbandry, as well as from the discovery of new tracts of fertile land, which in other countries may be taken into cultivation, and which will affect the value of corn in every market where importation is free? Is it not on the other hand subject to be enhanced in value from prohibitions of importation, from increasing population and wealth, and the greater difficulty of obtaining the increased supplies, on account of the additional quantity of labor which the cultivation of inferior land requires? Is not the value of labor equally variable; being not only affected, as all other things are, by the proportion between the supply and demand, which uniformly varies with every change in the condition of the community, but also by the varying price of food and other necessaries, on which the wages of labor are expended?

In the same country double the quantity of labor may be required to produce a given quantity of food and necessaries at one time that may be necessary at another and a distant time; yet the laborer's reward may possibly be very little diminished. If the laborer's wages at the former period were a certain quantity of food and necessaries, he probably could not have subsisted if that quantity had been reduced. Food and necessaries in this case will have risen 100 percent, if estimated by the *quantity* of labor necessary to their production, while they will scarcely have increased in value if measured by the *quantity* of labor for which they will *exchange*.

The same remark may be made respecting two or more countries. In America and Poland, on the land last taken into cultivation, a year's labor of any given number of men will produce much more corn than on land similarly circumstanced in England. Now, supposing all other necessaries to be equally cheap in those three countries, would it not be a great mistake to conclude that the quantity of corn awarded to the laborer would in each country be in proportion to the facility of production?

If the shoes and clothing of the laborer could, by improvements in machinery, be produced by one-fourth of the labor now necessary to their production, they would probably fall 75 percent; but so far is it from being true that the laborer would thereby be enabled permanently to consume four coats, or four pair of shoes, instead of one, that it is probable his wages would in no long time be adjusted by the effects of competition, and the stimulus to population, to the new value of the necessaries on which they were expended. If these improvements extended to all the objects of the laborer's consumption, we should find him probably, at the end of a very few years, in possession of only a small, if any, addition to his enjoyments, although the exchangeable value of those commodities, compared with any other commodity, in the manufacture of which no such improvement were made, had sustained a very considerable reduction; and though they were the produce of a very considerably diminished quantity of labor.

It cannot then be correct to say with Adam Smith, "that as labor may sometimes *purchase* a greater and sometimes a smaller quantity of goods, it is their value which varies, not that of the labor which purchases them;" and therefore, "that labor, *alone never varying in its own value,* is alone the ultimate and real standard by which the value of all commodities can at all times and places be estimated and compared;"—but it is correct to say, as Adam Smith had previously said, "that the proportion between the quantities of labor necessary for acquiring different objects seems to be the only circumstance which can afford any rule for exchanging them for one another; "or in other words that it is the comparative quantity of commodities which labor will produce that determines their present or past relative value, and not the comparative quantities of commodities which are given to the laborer in exchange for his labor.

Two commodities vary in relative value, and we wish to know in which the variation has really taken place. If we compare the present value of one with shoes, stockings, hats, iron, sugar, and all other commodities, we find that it will exchange for precisely the same quantity of all these things as before. If we compare the other with the same commodities, we find it has varied with respect to them all: we may then with great probability infer that the variation has been in this commodity, and not in the commodities with which we have compared it. If on examining still more particularly into all the circumstances connected with the production of these various commodities, we find that precisely the same quantity of labor and capital are necessary to the production of the shoes, stockings, hats, iron, sugar, etc.; but that the same quantity as before is not necessary to produce the single commodity whose relative value is altered, probability is changed into certainty, and we are sure that the variation is in the single commodity: we then discover also the cause of its variation.

If I found that an ounce of gold would exchange for a less quantity of all the commodities above enumerated and many others; and if, moreover, I found that by the discovery of a new and more fertile mine, or by the employment of machinery to great advantage, a given quantity of gold could be obtained with a less quantity of labor, I should be justified in saying that the cause of the alteration in the Value of gold relatively to other commodities was the greater facility of its production, or the smaller quantity of labor necessary to obtain it. In like manner, if labor fell very considerably in value, relatively to all other things, and if I found that its fall was in consequence of an abundant supply, encouraged by the great facility with which corn, and the other necessaries of the laborer, were produced, it would, I apprehend, be correct for me to say that corn and necessaries had fallen in value in consequence of less quantity of labor being necessary to produce them, and that this facility of providing for the support of the laborer had been followed by a fall in the value of labor. No, say Adam Smith and Mr. Malthus, in the case of the gold you were correct in calling its variation a fall of its value, because corn and labor had not then varied; and as gold would command a less quantity of them, as well as of all other things, than before, it was correct to say that all things had remained stationary and that gold only had varied; but when corn and labor fall, things which we have selected to be our standard measure of value, notwithstanding all the variations to which we acknowledge they are subject, it would be highly improper to say so; the correct language will be to say that corn and labor have remained stationary, and all other things have risen in value.

Now it is against this language that I protest. I find that precisely, as in the case of the gold, the cause of the variation between corn and other things is the smaller quantity of labor necessary to produce it, and therefore, by all just reasoning, I am bound to call the variation of corn and labor a fall in their value, and not a rise in the value of the things with which they are compared. If I have to hire a laborer for a week, and instead of ten shillings I pay him eight, no variation having taken place in the value of money, the laborer can probably obtain more food and necessaries with his eight shillings than he before obtained for ten: but this is owing, not to a rise in the real value of his wages, as stated by Adam Smith, and more recently by Mr. Malthus, but to a fall in the value of the things on which his wages are expended, things perfectly distinct; and yet for calling this a fall in the real value of wages, I am told that I adopt new and unusual language, not reconcilable with the true principles of the science. To me it appears that the unusual and, indeed, inconsistent language is that used by my opponents.

Suppose a laborer to be paid a bushel of corn for a week's work when the price of corn is 80s. per quarter, and that he is paid a bushel and a quarter when the price falls to 40s. Suppose, too, that he consumes half a bushel of corn a week in his own family, and exchanges the remainder for other things, such as fuel, soap, candles, tea, sugar, salt, etc. etc.; if the three-fourths of a bushel which will remain to him, in one case, cannot procure him as much of the above commodities as half a bushel did in the other, which it will not, will labor have risen or fallen in value? Risen, Adam Smith must say, because his standard is corn, and the laborer receives more corn for a week's labor. Fallen, must the same Adam Smith say, "because the value of a thing depends on the power of purchasing other goods which the possession of that object conveys," and labor has a less power of purchasing such other goods.

SECTION II

Labor of different qualities differently rewarded. This no cause of variation in the relative value of commodities.

In speaking, however, of labor, as being the foundation of all value, and the relative quantity of labor as almost exclusively determining the relative value of commodities, I must not be supposed to be inattentive to the different qualities of labor, and the difficulty of comparing an hour's or a day's labor in one employment with the same duration of labor in another. The estimation in which different qualities of labor are held comes soon to be adjusted in the market with sufficient precision for all practical purposes, and depends much on the comparative skill of the laborer and intensity of the labor performed. The scale, when once formed, is liable to little variation. If a day's labor of a working jeweler be more valuable than a day's labor of a common laborer, it has long ago been adjusted and placed in its proper position in the scale of value.[2]

In comparing, therefore, the value of the same commodity at different periods of time, the consideration of the comparative skill and intensity of labor required for that particular commodity needs scarcely to be attended to, as it operates equally at both periods. One description of labor at one time is compared with the same description of labor at another; if a tenth, a fifth, or a fourth has been added or taken away, an effect proportioned to the cause will be produced on the relative value of the commodity.

If a piece of cloth be now of the value of two pieces of linen, and if, in ten years hence, the ordinary value of a piece of cloth should be four pieces of linen, we may safely conclude that either more labor is required to make the cloth, or less to make the linen, or that both causes have operated.

As the inquiry to which I wish to draw the reader's attention relates to the effect of the variations in the relative value of commodities, and not in their absolute value, it will be of little importance to examine into the comparative degree of estimation in which the different kinds of human labor are held. We may fairly conclude that whatever inequality there might originally have been in them, whatever the ingenuity, skill, or time necessary for the acquirement of one species of manual dexterity more than another, it continues nearly the same from one generation to another; or at least that the variation is very inconsiderable from year to year, and therefore can have little effect, for short periods, on the relative value of commodities.

"The proportion between the different rates both of wages and profit in the different employments of labor and stock seems not to be much affected, as has already been observed, by the riches or poverty, the advancing, stationary, or declining state of the society. Such revolutions in the public welfare, though they affect the general rates both of wages and profit, must in the end affect them equally in all different employments. The proportion between them therefore must remain the same, and cannot well be altered, at least for any considerable time, by any such revolutions."[3]

SECTION III

Not only the labor applied immediately to commodities affect their value, but the labor also which is bestowed on the implements, tools, and buildings, with which such labor is assisted.

Even in that early state to which Adam Smith refers, some capital, though possibly made and accumulated by the hunter himself, would be necessary to enable him to kill his game. Without some weapon, neither the beaver nor the deer could be destroyed, and therefore the value of these animals would be regulated, not solely by the time and labor necessary to their destruction, but also by the time and labor necessary for providing the hunter's capital, the weapon, by the aid of which their destruction was effected.

Suppose the weapon necessary to kill the beaver was constructed with much more labor than that necessary to kill the deer, on account of the greater difficulty of approaching near to the former animal, and the consequent necessity of its being more true to its mark; one beaver would naturally be of more value than two deer, and precisely for this reason, that more labor would, on the whole, be necessary to its destruction. Or suppose that the same quantity of labor was necessary to make both weapons, but that they were of very unequal durability; of the durable implement only a small portion of its value would be transferred to the commodity, a much greater portion of the value of the less durable implement would be realized in the commodity which it contributed to produce.

All the implements necessary to kill the beaver and deer might belong to one class of men, and the labor employed in their destruction might be furnished by another class; still, their comparative prices would be in proportion to the actual labor bestowed, both on the formation of the capital and on the destruction of the animals. Under different circumstances of plenty or scarcity of capital, as compared with labor, under different circumstances of plenty or scarcity of the food and necessaries essential to the support of men, those who furnished an equal value of capital for either one employment or for the other might have a half, a fourth, or an eighth of the produce obtained, the remainder being paid as wages to those who furnished the labor; yet this division could not affect the relative value of these commodities, since whether the profits of capital were greater or less, whether they were 50, 20, or 10 percent, or whether the wages of labor were high or low, they would operate equally on both employments.

If we suppose the occupations of the society extended, that some provide canoes and tackle necessary for fishing, others the seed and rude machinery first used in agriculture, still the same principle would hold true, that the exchangeable value of the commodities produced would be in proportion to the labor bestowed on their production; not on their immediate production only, but on all those implements or machines required to give effect to the particular labor to which they were applied.

If we look to a state of society in which greater improvements have been made, and in which arts and commerce flourish, we shall still find that commodities vary in value conformably with this principle: in estimating the exchangeable value of stockings, for example, we shall find that their value, comparatively with other things, depends on the total quantity of labor necessary to manufacture them and bring them to market. First, there is the labor necessary to cultivate the land on which the raw cotton is grown; secondly, the labor of conveying the cotton to the country where the stockings are to be manufactured, which includes a portion of the labor bestowed in building the ship in which it is conveyed, and which is charged in the freight of the goods; thirdly, the labor of the spinner and weaver; fourthly, a portion of the labor of the engineer, smith, and carpenter, who erected the buildings and machinery, by the help of which they are made; fifthly, the labor of the retail dealer, and of many others, whom it is unnecessary further to particularize. The aggregate sum of these various kinds of labor determines the quantity of other things for which these stocking will exchange, while the same consideration of the various quantities of labor which have been bestowed on those other things will equally govern the portion of them which will be given for the stockings.

To convince ourselves that this is the real foundation of exchangeable value, let us suppose any improvement to be made in the means of abridging labor in any one of the various processes through which the raw cotton must pass before the manufactured stockings come to the market to be exchanged for other things, and observe the effects which will follow. If fewer men were required to cultivate the raw cotton, or if fewer sailors were employed in navigating, or shipwrights in constructing the ship, in which it was conveyed to us; if fewer hands were employed in raising the buildings and machinery, or if these, when raised, were rendered more efficient, the stockings would inevitably fall in value, and consequently command less of other things. They would fall, because a less quantity of labor was necessary to their production, and would therefore exchange for a smaller quantity of those things in which no such abridgment of labor had been made.

Economy in the use of labor never fails to reduce the relative value of a commodity, whether the saving be in the labor necessary to the manufacture of the commodity itself, or in that necessary to the formation of the capital by the aid of which it is produced. In either case the price of stockings would fall, whether there were fewer men employed as bleachers, spinners, and weavers, persons immediately necessary to their manufacture; or as sailors, carriers, engineers, and smiths, persons more indirectly concerned. In the one case, the whole saving of labor would fall on the stockings, because that portion of labor was wholly confined to the stockings; in the other, a portion only would fall on the stockings, the remainder being applied to all those other commodities, to the production of which the buildings, machinery, and carriage were subservient.

Suppose that, in the early stages of society, the bows and arrows of the hunter were of equal value, and of equal durability, with the canoe and implements of the fisherman, both being the produce of the same quantity of labor. Under such circumstances the value of the deer, the produce of the hunter's day's labor, would be exactly equal to the value of the fish, the produce of the fisherman's day's labor. The comparative value of the fish and the game would be entirely regulated by the quantity of labor realized in each, whatever might be the quantity of production or however high or low general wages or profits might be. If, for example, the canoes and implements of the fisherman were of the value of £100, and were calculated to last for ten years, and he employed ten men, whose annual labor cost £100, and who in one day obtained by their labor twenty salmon: If the weapons employed by the hunter were also of £100 value, and calculated to last ten years, and if he also employed ten men, whose annual labor cost £100, and who in one day procured him ten deer; then the natural price of a deer would be two salmon, whether the proportion of the whole produce bestowed on the men who obtained it were large or small. The proportion which might be paid for wages is of the utmost importance in the question of profits; for it must at once be seen that profits would be high or low exactly in proportion as wages were low or high; but it could not in the least affect the relative value of fish and game, as wages would be high or low at the same time in both occupations. If the hunter urged the plea of his paying a large proportion, or the value of a large proportion of his game for wages, as an inducement to the fisherman to give him more fish in exchange for his game, the latter would state that he was equally affected by the same cause; and therefore, under all variations of wages and profits, under all the effects of accumulation of capital, as long as they continued by a day's labor to obtain respectively the same quantity of fish and the same quantity of game, the natural rate of exchange would be one deer for two salmon.

If with the same quantity of labor a less quantity of fish or a greater quantity of game were obtained, the value of fish would rise in comparison with that of game. If, on the contrary, with the same quantity of labor a less quantity of game or a greater quantity of fish was obtained, game would rise in comparison with fish.

If there were any other commodity which was invariable in its value, we should be able to ascertain, by comparing the value of fish and game with this commodity, how much of the variation was to be attributed to a cause which affected the value of fish, and how much to a cause which affected the value of game.

Suppose money to be that commodity. If a salmon were worth £1 and a deer £2, one deer would be worth two salmon. But a deer might become of the value of three salmon, for more labor might be required to obtain the deer, or less to get the salmon, or both these causes might operate at the same time. If we had this invariable standard, we might easily ascertain in what degree either of these causes operated. If salmon continued to sell for £1, whilst deer rose to £3, we might conclude that more labor was required to obtain the deer. If deer continued at the same price of £2 and salmon sold for 13s. 4d., we might then be sure that less labor was required to obtain the salmon; and if deer rose to £2 10s. and salmon fell to 16s. 8d., we should be convinced that both causes had operated in producing the alteration of the relative value of these commodities.

No alteration in the wages of labor could produce any alteration in the relative value of these commodities; for suppose them to rise, no greater quantity of labor would be required in any of these occupations but it would be paid for at a higher price, and the same reasons which should make the hunter and fisherman endeavor to raise the value of their game and fish would cause the owner of the mine to raise the value of his gold. This inducement acting with the same force on all these three occupations, and the relative situation of those engaged in them being the same before and after the rise of wages, the relative value of game, fish, and gold would continue unaltered. Wages might rise twenty percent, and profits consequently fall in a greater or less proportion, without occasioning the least alteration in the relative value of these commodities.

Now suppose that, with the same labor and fixed capital, more fish could be produced, but no more gold or game, the relative value of fish would fall in comparison with gold or game. If, instead of twenty salmon, twenty-five were the produce of one day's labor, the price of a salmon would be sixteen shillings instead of a pound, and two salmon and a half, instead of two salmon, would be given in exchange for one deer, but the price of deer would continue at £2 as before. In the same manner, if fewer fish could be obtained with the same capital and labor, fish would rise in comparative value. Fish then would rise or fall in exchangeable value, only because more or less labor was required to obtain a given quantity; and it never could rise or fall beyond the proportion of the increased or diminished quantity of labor required.

If we had then an invariable standard, by which we could measure the variation in other commodities, we should find that the utmost limit to which they could permanently rise, if produced under the circumstances supposed, was proportioned to the additional quantity of labor required for their production; and that unless more labor were required for their production they could not rise in any degree whatever. A rise of wages would not raise them in money value, nor relatively to any other commodities, the production of which required no additional quantity of labor, which employed the same proportion of fixed and circulating capital, and fixed capital of the same durability. If more or less labor were required in the production of the other commodity, we have already stated that this will immediately occasion an alteration in its relative value, but such alteration is owing to the altered quantity of requisite labor, and not to the rise of wages.

SECTION IV

The principle that the quantity of labor bestowed on the production of commodities regulates their relative value considerably modified by the employment of machinery and other fixed and durable capital.

In the former section we have supposed the implements and weapons necessary to kill the deer and salmon to be equally durable, and to be the result of the same quantity of labor, and we have seen that the variations in the relative value of deer and salmon depended solely on the varying quantities of labor necessary to obtain them, but in every state of society, the tools, implements, buildings, and machinery employed in different trades may be of various degrees of durability, and may require different portions of labor to produce them. The proportions, too, in which the capital that is to support labor, and the capital that is invested in tools, machinery, and buildings, may be variously combined. This difference in the degree of durability of fixed capital, and this variety in the proportions in which the two sorts of capital may be combined, introduce another cause, besides the greater or less quantity of labor necessary to produce commodities, for the variations in their relative value—this cause is the rise or fall in the value of labor.

The food and clothing consumed by the laborer, the buildings in which he works, the implements with which his labor is assisted, are all of a perishable nature. There is, however, a vast difference in the time for which these different capitals will endure: a steam-engine will last longer than a ship, a ship than the clothing of the laborer, and the clothing of the laborer longer than the food which he consumes.

According as capital is rapidly perishable, and requires to be frequently reproduced, or is of slow consumption, it is classed under the heads of circulating or of fixed capital.[4] A brewer whose buildings and machinery are valuable and durable is said to employ a large portion of fixed capital: on the contrary, a shoemaker, whose capital is chiefly employed in the payment of wages, which are expended on food and clothing, commodities more perishable than buildings and machinery, is said to employ a large proportion of his capital as circulating capital.

It is also to be observed that the circulating capital may circulate, or be returned to its employer, in very unequal times. The wheat bought by a farmer to sow is comparatively a fixed capital to the wheat purchased by a baker to make into loaves. One leaves it in the ground and can obtain no return for a year; the other can get it ground into flour, sell it as bread to his customers, and have his capital free to renew the same or commence any other employment in a week.

Two trades then may employ the same amount of capital; but it may be very differently divided with respect to the portion which is fixed and that which is circulating.

In one trade very little capital may be employed as circulating capital, that is to say, in the support of labor—it may be principally invested in machinery, implements, buildings, etc., capital of a comparatively fixed and durable character. In another trade the same amount of capital may be used, but it may be chiefly employed in the support of labor, and very little may be invested in implements, machines, and buildings. A rise in the wages of labor cannot fail to affect unequally commodities produced under such different circumstances.

Again, two manufacturers may employ the same amount of fixed and the same amount of circulating capital; but the durability of their fixed capitals may be very unequal. One may have steam-engines of the value of £10,000, the other, ships of the same value.

If men employed no machinery in production but labor only, and were all the same length of time before they brought their commodities to market, the exchangeable value of their goods would be precisely in proportion to the quantity of labor employed.

If they employed fixed capital of the same value and of the same durability, then, too, the value of the commodities produced would be the same, and they would vary with the greater or less quantity of labor employed on their production.

But although commodities produced under similar circumstances would not vary with respect to each other from any cause but an addition or diminution of the quantity of labor necessary to produce one or other of them, yet, compared with others not produced with the same proportionate quantity of fixed capital, they would vary from the other cause also which I have before mentioned, namely, a rise in the value of labor, although neither more nor less labor were employed in the production of either of them. Barley and oats would continue to bear the same relation to each other under any variation of wages. Cotton goods and cloth would do the same, if they also were produced under circumstances precisely similar to each other, but yet with a rise or fall of wages barley might be more or less valuable compared with cotton goods and oats compared with cloth.

Suppose two men employ one hundred men each for a year in the construction of two machines, and another man employs the same number of men in cultivating corn, each of the machines at the end of the year will be of the same value as the corn, for they will each be produced by the same quantity of labor. Suppose one of the owners of one of the machines to employ it, with the assistance of one hundred men, the following year in making cloth, and the owner of the other machine to employ his also, with the assistance likewise of one hundred men, in making cotton goods, while the farmer continues to employ one hundred men as before in the cultivation of corn. During the second year they will all have employed the same quantity of labor, but the goods and machine together of the clothier, and also of the cotton manufacturer, will be the result of the labor of two hundred men employed for a year; or, rather, of the labor of one hundred men for two years; whereas the corn will be produced by the labor of one hundred men for one year, consequently if the corn be of the value of £500, the machine and cloth of the clothier together ought to be of the value of £1000, and the machine and cotton goods of the cotton manufacturer ought to be also of twice the value of the corn. But they will be of more than twice the value of the corn, for the profit on the clothier's and cotton manufacturer's capital for the first year has been added to their capitals, while that of the farmer has been expended and enjoyed. On account then of the different degrees of durability of their capitals, or, which is the same thing, on account of the time which must elapse before one set of commodities can be brought to market, they will be valuable, not exactly in proportion to the quantity of labor bestowed on them—they will not be as two to one, but something more, to compensate for the greater length of time which must elapse before the most valuable can be brought to market.

Suppose that for the labor of each workman £50 per annum were paid, or that £5000 capital were employed and profits were 10 percent, the value of each of the machines as well as of the corn, at the end of the first year, would be £5500. The second year the manufacturers and farmers will again employ £5000 each in the support of labor, and will therefore again sell their goods for £5500; but the men using the machines, to be on a par with the farmer, must not only obtain £5500 for the equal capitals of £5000 employed on labor, but they must obtain a further sum of £550 for the profit on £5500, which they have invested in machinery, and consequently their goods must sell for £6050. Here, then, are capitalists employing precisely the same quantity of labor annually on the production of their commodities, and yet the goods they produce differ in value on account of the different quantities of fixed capital, or accumulated labor, employed by each respectively. The cloth and cotton goods are of the same value, because they are the produce of equal quantities of labor and equal quantities of fixed capital; but corn is not of the same value as these commodities, because it is produced, as far as regards fixed capital, under different circumstances.

But how will their relative value be affected by a rise in the value of labor? It is evident that the relative values of cloth and cotton goods will undergo no change, for what affects one must equally affect the other under the circumstances supposed; neither will the relative values of wheat and barley undergo any change, for they are produced under the same circumstances as far as fixed and circulating capital are concerned; but the relative value of corn to cloth, or to cotton goods, must be altered by a rise of labor.

There can be no rise in the value of labor without a fall of profits. If the corn is to be divided between the farmer and the laborer, the larger the proportion that is given to the latter the less will remain for the former. So, if cloth or cotton goods be divided between the workman and his employer, the larger the proportion given to the former the less remains for the latter. Suppose then, that owing to a rise of wages, profits fall from 10 to 9 percent, instead of adding £550 to the common price of their goods (to £5500) for the profits on their fixed capital, the manufacturers would add only 9 percent, on that sum, or £495, consequently the price would be £5995 instead of £6050. As the corn would continue to sell for £5500 the manufactured goods in which more fixed capital was employed would fall relatively to corn or to any other goods in which a less portion of fixed capital entered. The degree of alteration in the relative value of goods, on account of a rise or fall of labor, would depend on the proportion which the fixed capital bore to the whole capital employed. All commodities which are produced by very valuable machinery, or in very valuable buildings, or which require a great length of time before they can be brought to market, would fall in relative value, while all those which were chiefly produced by labor, or which would be speedily brought to market, would rise in relative value.

The reader, however, should remark that this cause of the variation of commodities is comparatively slight in its effects. With such a rise of wages as should occasion a fall of

1 percent, in profits, goods produced under the circumstances I have supposed vary in relative value only 1 percent; they fall with so great a fall of profits from £6050 to £5995. The greatest effects which could be produced on the relative prices of these goods from a rise of wages could not exceed 6 or 7 percent; for profits could not, probably, under any circumstances, admit of a greater general and permanent depression than to that amount.

Not so with the other great cause of the variation in the value of commodities, namely, the increase or diminution in the quantity of labor necessary to produce them. If to produce the corn, eighty, instead of one hundred men, should be required, the value of the corn would fall 20 percent, or from £5500 to £4400. If to produce the cloth, the labor of eighty instead of one hundred men would suffice, cloth would fall from £6050 to £4950. An alteration in the permanent rate of profits, to any great amount, is the effect of causes which do not operate but in the course of years, whereas alterations in the quantity of labor necessary to produce commodities are of daily occurrence. Every improvement in machinery, in tools, in buildings, in raising the raw material, saves labor, and enables us to produce the commodity to which the improvement is applied with more facility, and consequently its value alters. In estimating, then, the causes of the variations in the value of commodities, although it would be wrong wholly to omit the consideration of the effect produced by a rise or fall of labor, it would be equally incorrect to attach much importance to it; and consequently, in the subsequent part of this work, though I shall occasionally refer to this cause of variation, I shall consider all the great variations which take place in the relative value of commodities to be produced by the greater or less quantity of labor which may be required from time to time to produce them.

It is hardly necessary to say that commodities which have the same quantity of labor bestowed on their production will differ in exchangeable value if they cannot be brought to market in the same time.

Suppose I employ twenty men at an expense of £1000 for a year in the production of a commodity, and at the end of the year I employ twenty men again for another year, at a further expense of £1000 in finishing or perfecting the same commodity, and that I bring it to market at the end of two years, if profits be 10 percent, my commodity must sell for £2310; for I have employed £1000 capital for one year, and £2100 capital for one year more. Another man employs precisely the same quantity of labor, but he employs it all in the first year; he employs forty men at an expense of £2000, and at the end of the first year he sells it with 10 percent, profit, or for £2200. Here, then, are two commodities having precisely the same quantity of labor bestowed on them, one of which sells for £2310—the other for £2200.

This case appears to differ from the last, but is, in fact, the same. In both cases the superior price of one commodity is owing to the greater length of time which must elapse before it can be brought to market. In the former case the machinery and cloth were more than double the value of the corn, although only double the quantity of labor was bestowed on them. In the second case, one commodity is more valuable than the other, although no more labor was employed on its production. The difference in value arises in both cases from the profits being accumulated as capital, and is only a just compensation for the time that the profits were withheld.

It appears, then, that the division of capital into different proportions of fixed and circulating capital, employed in different trades, introduces a considerable modification to the rule, which is of universal application when labor is almost exclusively employed in production; namely, that commodities never vary in value unless a greater or less quantity of labor be bestowed on their production, it being shown in this section that, without any variation in the quantity of labor, the rise of its value merely will occasion a fall in the exchangeable value of those goods in the production of which fixed capital is employed; the larger the amount of fixed capital, the greater will be the fall.

SECTION V

The principle that value does not vary with the rise or fall of wages, modified also by the unequal durability of capital, and by the unequal rapidity with which it is returned to its employer.

In the last section we have supposed that, of two equal capitals, in two different occupations, the proportions of fixed and circulating capitals were unequal; now let us suppose them to be in the same proportion, but of unequal durability. In proportion as fixed capital is less durable it approaches to the nature of circulating capital. It will be consumed and its value reproduced in a shorter time, in order to preserve the capital of the manufacturer. We have just seen that in proportion as fixed capital preponderates in a manufacture, when wages rise the value of commodities produced in that manufacture is relatively lower than that of commodities produced in manufactures where circulating capital preponderates. In proportion to the less durability of fixed capital, and its approach to the nature of circulating capital, the same effect will be produced by the same cause.

If fixed capital be not of a durable nature it will require a great quantity of labor annually to keep it in its original state of efficiency; but the labor so bestowed may be considered as really expended on the commodity manufactured, which must bear a value in proportion to such labor. If I had a machine worth £20,000 which with very little labor was efficient to the production of commodities, and if the wear and tear of such machine were of trifling amount, and the general rate of profit 10 percent, I should not require much more than £2000 to be added to the price of the goods, on account of the employment of my machine; but if the wear and tear of the machine were great, if the quantity of labor requisite to keep it in an efficient state were that of fifty men annually, I should require an additional price for my goods equal to that which would be obtained by any other manufacturer who employed fifty men in the production of other goods, and who used no machinery at all.

But a rise in the wages of labor would not equally affect commodities produced with machinery quickly consumed, and commodities produced with machinery slowly consumed. In the production of the one, a great deal of labor would be continually transferred to the commodity produced—in the other very little would be so transferred. Every rise of wages, therefore, or, which is the same thing, every fall of profits, would lower the relative value of those commodities which were produced with a capital of a durable nature, and would proportionally elevate those which were produced with capital more perishable. A fall of wages would have precisely the contrary effect.

I have already said that fixed capital is of various degrees of durability—suppose now a machine which could in any particular trade be employed to do the work of one hundred men for a year, and that it would last only for one year. Suppose, too, the machine to cost £5000, and the wages annually paid to one hundred men to be £5000, it is evident that it would be a matter of indifference to the manufacturer whether he bought the machine or employed the men. But suppose labor to rise, and consequently the wages of one hundred men for a year to amount to £5500, it is obvious that the manufacturer would now no longer hesitate, it would be for his interest to buy the machine and get his work done for £5000. But will not the machine rise in price, will not that also be worth £5500 in consequence of the rise of labor? It would rise in price if there were no stock employed on its construction, and no profits to be paid to the maker of it. If, for example, the machine were the produce of the labor of one hundred men, working one year upon it with wages of £50 each, and its price were consequently £5000; should those wages rise to £55, its price would be £5500, but this cannot be the case; less than one hundred men are employed or it could not be sold for £5000, for out of the £5000 must be paid the profits of stock which employed the men. Suppose then that only eighty-five men were employed at an expense of £50 each, or £4250 per annum, and that the £750 which the sale of the machine would produce over and above the wages advanced to the men constituted the profits of the engineer's stock. When wages rose 10 percent, he would be obliged to employ an additional capital of £425, and would therefore employ £4675 instead of £4250, on which capital he would only get a profit of £325 if he continued to sell his machine for £5000; but this is precisely the case of all manufacturers and capitalists; the rise of wages affects them all. If therefore the maker of the machine should raise the price of it in consequence of a rise of wages, an unusual quantity of capital would be employed in the construction of such machines, till their price afforded only the common rate of profits.[5] We see then that machines would not rise in price in consequence of a rise of wages.

The manufacturer, however, who in a general rise of wages can have recourse to a machine which shall not increase the charge of production on his commodity, would enjoy peculiar advantages if he could continue to charge the same price for his goods; but he, as we have already seen, would be obliged to lower the price of his commodities, or capital would flow to his trade till his profits had sunk to the general level. Thus then is the public benefited by machinery: these mute agents are always the produce of much less labor than that which they displace, even when they are of the same money value. Through their influence an increase in the price of provisions which raises wages will affect fewer persons; it will reach, as in the above instance, eighty-five men instead of a hundred, and the saving which is the consequence shows itself in the reduced price of the commodity manufactured. Neither machines, nor the commodities made by them, rise in real value, but all commodities made by machines fall, and fall in proportion to their durability.

It will be seen then, that in the early stages of society, before much machinery or durable capital is used, the commodities produced by equal capitals will be nearly of equal value, and will rise or fall only relatively to each other on account of more or less labor being required for their production; but after the introduction of these expensive and durable instruments, the commodities produced by the employment of equal capitals will be of very unequal value, and although they will still be liable to rise or fall relatively to each other, as more or less labor becomes necessary to their production, they will be subject to another, though a minor variation, also from the rise or fall of wages and profits. Since goods which sell for £5000 may be the produce of a capital equal in amount to that from which are produced other goods which sell for £10,000, the profits on their manufacture will be the same; but those profits would be unequal if the prices of the goods did not vary with a rise or fall in the rate of profits.

It appears, too, that in proportion to the durability of capital employed in any kind of production the relative prices of those commodities on which such durable capital is employed will vary inversely as wages; they will fall as wages rise, and rise as wages fall; and, on the contrary, those which are produced chiefly by labor with less fixed capital, or with fixed capital of a less durable character than the medium in which price is estimated, will rise as wages rise, and fall as wages fall.

SECTION VI

On an invariable measure of value

When commodities varied in relative value it would be desirable to have the means of ascertaining which of them fell and which rose in real value, and this could be effected only by comparing them one after another with some invariable standard measure of value, which should itself be subject to none of the fluctuations to which other commodities are exposed. Of such a measure it is impossible to be possessed, because there is no commodity which is not itself exposed to the same variations as the things the value of which is to be ascertained; that is, there is none which is not subject to require more or less labor for its production. But if this cause of variation in the value of a medium could be removed—if it were possible that in the production of our money, for instance, the same quantity of labor should at all times be required, still it would not be a perfect standard or invariable measure of value, because, as I have already endeavored to explain, it would be subject to relative variations from a rise or fall of wages, on account of the different proportions of fixed capital which might be necessary to produce it, and to produce those other commodities whose alteration of value we wished to ascertain. It might be subject to variations, too, from the same cause, on account of the different degrees of durability of the fixed capital employed on it, and the commodities to be compared with it—or the time necessary to bring the one to market might be longer or shorter than the time necessary to bring the other commodities to market, the variations of which were to be determined; all which circumstances disqualify any commodity that can be thought of from being a perfectly accurate measure of value.

If, for example, we were to fix on gold as a standard, it is evident that it is but a commodity obtained under the same contingencies as every other commodity, and requiring labor and fixed capital to produce it. Like every other commodity, improvements in the saving of labor might be applied to its production, and consequently it might fall in relative value to other things merely on account of the greater facility of producing it.

If we suppose this cause of variation to be removed, and the same quantity of labor to be always required to obtain the same quantity of gold, still gold would not be a perfect measure of value, by which we could accurately ascertain the variations in all other things, because it would not be produced with precisely the same combinations of fixed and circulating capital as all other things; nor with fixed capital of the same durability; nor would it require precisely the same length of time before it could be brought to market. It would be a perfect measure of value for all things produced under the same circumstances precisely as itself, but for no others. If, for example, it were produced under the same circumstances as we have supposed necessary to produce cloth and cotton goods, it would be a perfect measure of value for those things, but not so for corn, for coals, and other commodities produced with either a less or a greater proportion of fixed capital, because, as we have shown, every alteration in the permanent rate of profits would have some effect on the relative value of all these goods, independently of any alteration in the quantity of labor employed on their production. If gold were produced under the same circumstances as corn, even if they never changed, it would not, for the same reasons, be at all times a perfect measure of the value of cloth and cotton goods. Neither gold, then, nor any other commodity, can ever be a perfect measure of value for all things; but I have already remarked that the effect on the relative prices of things, from a variation in profits, is comparatively slight; that by far the most important effects are produced by the varying quantities of labor required for production; and therefore, if we suppose this important cause of variation removed from the production of gold, we shall probably possess as near an approximation to a standard measure of value as can be theoretically conceived. May not gold be considered as a commodity produced with such proportions of the two kinds of capital as approach nearest to the average quantity employed in the production of most commodities? May not these proportions be so nearly equally distant from the two extremes, the one where little fixed capital is used, the other where little labor is employed, as to form a just mean between them?

If, then, I may suppose myself to be possessed of a standard so nearly approaching to an invariable one, the advantage is that I shall be enabled to speak of the variations of other things without embarrassing myself on every occasion with the consideration of the possible alteration in the value of the medium in which price and value are estimated.

To facilitate, then, the object of this inquiry, although I fully allow that money made of gold is subject to most of the variations of other things, I shall suppose it to be invariable, and therefore all alterations in price to be occasioned by some alteration in the value of the commodity of which I may be speaking.

Before I quit this subject, it may be proper to observe that Adam Smith, and all the writers who have followed him, have, without one exception that I know of, maintained that a rise in the price of labor would be uniformly followed by a rise in the price of all commodities. I hope I have succeeded in showing that there are no grounds for such an opinion, and that only those commodities would rise which had less fixed capital employed upon them than the medium in which price was estimated, and that all those which had more would positively fall in price when wages rose. On the contrary, if wages fell, those commodities only would fall which had a less proportion of fixed capital employed on them than the medium in which price was estimated; all those which had more would positively rise in price.

It is necessary for me also to remark that I have not said, because one commodity has so much labor bestowed upon it as will cost £1000, and another so much as will cost £2000, that therefore one would be of the value of £1000, and the other of the value of £2000; but I have said that their value will be to each other as two to one, and that in those proportions they will be exchanged. It is of no importance to the truth of this doctrine whether one of these commodities sells for £1100 and the other for £2200, or one for £1500 and the other for £3000; into that question I do not at present inquire; I affirm only that their relative values will be governed by the relative quantities of labor bestowed on their production.[6]

SECTION VII

Different effects from the alteration in the value of money, the medium in which PRICE is always expressed, or from the alteration in the value of the commodities which money purchases.

Although I shall, as I have already explained, have occasion to consider money as invariable in value, for the purpose of more distinctly pointing out the causes of relative variations in the value of other things, it may be useful to notice the different effects which will follow from the prices of goods being altered by the causes to which I have already adverted, namely, the different quantities of labor required to produce them, and their being altered by a variation in the value of money itself.

Money being a variable commodity, the rise of money-wages will be frequently occasioned by a fall in the value of money. A rise of wages from this cause will, indeed, be invariably accompanied by a rise in the price of commodities; but in such cases it will be found that labor and all commodities have not varied in regard to each other, and that the variation has been confined to money.

Money, from its being a commodity obtained from a foreign country, from its being the general medium of exchange between all civilized countries, and from its being also distributed among those countries in proportions which are ever changing with every improvement in commerce and machinery, and with every increasing difficulty of obtaining food and necessaries for an increasing population, is subject to incessant variations. In stating the principles which regulate exchangeable value and price, we should carefully distinguish between those variations which belong to the commodity itself, and those which are occasioned by a variation in the medium in which value is estimated or price expressed.

A rise in wages, from an alteration in the value of money, produces a general effect on price, and for that reason it produces no real effect whatever on profits. On the contrary, a rise of wages, from the circumstance of the laborer being more liberally rewarded, or from a difficulty of procuring the necessaries on which wages are expended, does not, except in some instances, produce the effect of raising price, but has a great effect in lowering profits. In the one case, no greater proportion of the annual labor of the country is devoted to the support of the laborers; in the other case, a larger portion is so devoted.

It is according to the division of the whole produce of the land of any particular farm, between the three classes, of landlord, capitalist, and laborer, that we are to judge of the rise or fall of rent, profit, and wages, and not according to the value at which that produce may be estimated in a medium which is confessedly variable.

It is not by the absolute quantity of produce obtained by either class that we can correctly judge the rate of profit, rent, and wages, but by the quantity of labor required to obtain that produce. By improvements in machinery and agriculture the whole produce may be doubled; but if wages, rent, and profit be also doubled, these three will bear the same proportions to one another as before, and neither could be said to have relatively varied. But if wages partook not of the whole of this increase; if they, instead of being doubled, were only increased one-half; if rent, instead of being doubled, were only increased three-fourths, and the remaining increase went to profit, it would, I apprehend, be correct for me to say that rent and wages had fallen while profits had risen; for if we had an invariable standard by which to measure the value of this produce we should find that a less value had fallen to the class of laborers and landlords, and a greater to the class of capitalists, than had been given before. We might find, for example, that though the absolute quantity of commodities had been doubled, they were the produce of precisely the former quantity of labor. Of every hundred hats, coats, and quarters of corn produced, if

The laborers had before	25
The landlords	25
And the capitalists	50
	100:

And if, after these commodities were double the quantity, of every 100

The labourers had only	22
The landlords	22
And the capitalists	56
	100:

In that case I should say that wages and rent had fallen and profits risen; though, in consequence of the abundance of commodities, the quantity paid to the laborer and landlord would have increased in the proportion of 25 to 44. Wages are to be estimated by their real value, viz., by the quantity of labor and capital employed in producing them, and not by their nominal value either in coats, hats, money, or corn. Under the circumstances I have just supposed, commodities would have fallen to half their former value, and if money had not varied, to half their former price also. If then in this medium, which had not varied in value, the wages of the laborer should be found to have fallen, it will not the less be a real fall because they might furnish him with a greater quantity of cheap commodities than his former wages.

The variation in the value of money, however great, makes no difference in the *rate* of profits; for suppose the goods of the manufacturer to rise from £1000 to £2000, or 100 percent, if his capital, on which the variations of money have as much effect as on the value of produce, if his machinery, buildings, and stock in trade rise also a 100 percent, his rate of profits will be the same, and he will have the same quantity, and no more, of the produce of the labor of the country at his command.

If, with a capital of a given value, he can, by economy in labor, double the quantity of produce, and it fall to half its former price, it will bear the same proportion to the capital that produced it which it did before, and consequently profits will still be at the same rate.

If, at the same time that he doubles the quantity of produce by the employment of the same capital, the value of money is by any accident lowered one half, the produce will sell for twice the money value that it did before; but the capital employed to produce it will also be of twice its former money value; and therefore in this case, too, the value of the produce will bear the same proportion to the value of the capital as it did before; and although the produce be doubled, rent, wages, and profits will only vary as the proportions vary, in which this double produce may be divided among the three classes that share it.

Chapter II

On Rent

It remains however to be considered whether the appropriation of land, and the consequent creation of rent, will occasion any variation in the relative value of commodities independently of the quantity of labor necessary to production. In order to understand this part of the subject we must inquire into the nature of rent, and the laws by which its rise or fall is regulated.

Rent is that portion of the produce of the earth which is paid to the landlord for the use of the original and indestructible powers of the soil. It is often, however, confounded with the interest and profit of capital, and, in popular language, the term is applied to whatever is annually paid by a farmer to his landlord. If, of two adjoining farms of the same extent, and of the same natural fertility, one had all the conveniences of farming buildings, and, besides, were properly drained and manured, and advantageously divided by hedges, fences, and walls, while the other had none of these advantages, more remuneration would naturally be paid for the use of one than for the use of the other; yet in both cases this remuneration would be called rent. But it is evident that a portion only of the money annually to be paid for the improved farm would be given for the original and indestructible powers of the soil; the other portion would be paid for the use of the capital which had been employed in ameliorating the quality of the land, and in erecting such buildings as were necessary to secure and preserve the produce. Adam Smith sometimes speaks of rent in the strict sense to which I am desirous of confining it, but more often in the popular sense in which the term is usually employed. He tells us that the demand for timber, and its consequent high price, in the more southern countries of Europe caused a rent to be paid for forests in Norway which could before afford no rent. Is it not, however, evident that the person who paid what he thus calls rent, paid it in consideration of the valuable commodity which was then standing on the land, and that he actually repaid himself with a profit by the sale of the timber? If, indeed, after the timber was removed, any compensation were paid to the landlord for the use of the land, for the purpose of growing timber or any other produce, with a view to future demand, such compensation might justly be called rent, because it would be paid for the productive powers of the land; but in the case stated by Adam Smith, the compensation was paid for the liberty of removing and selling the timber, and not for the liberty of growing it. He speaks also of the rent of coal mines, and of stone quarries, to which the same observation applies—that the compensation given for the mine or quarry is paid for the value of the coal or stone which can be removed from them, and has no connection with the original and indestructible powers of the land. This is a distinction of great importance in an inquiry concerning rent and profits; for it is found that the laws which regulate the progress of rent are widely different from those which regulate the progress of profits, and seldom operate in the same direction. In all improved countries, that which is annually paid to the landlord, partaking of both characters, rent and profit, is sometimes kept stationary by the effects of

DAVID RICARDO 785

opposing causes; at other times advances or recedes as one or the other of these causes preponderates. In the future pages of this work, then, whenever I speak of the rent of land, I wish to be understood as speaking of that compensation which is paid to the owner of land for the use of its original and indestructible powers.

On the first settling of a country in which there is an abundance of rich and fertile land, a very small proportion of which is required to be cultivated for the support of the actual population, or indeed can be cultivated with the capital which the population can command, there will be no rent; for no one would pay for the use of land when there was an abundant quantity not yet appropriated, and, therefore, at the disposal of whosoever might choose to cultivate it.

On the common principles of supply and demand, no rent could be paid for such land, for the reason stated why nothing is given for the use of air and water, or for any other of the gifts of nature which exist in boundless quantity. With a given quantity of materials, and with the assistance of the pressure of the atmosphere, and the elasticity of steam, engines may perform work, and abridge human labor to a very great extent; but no charge is made for the use of these natural aids, because they are inexhaustible and at every man's disposal. In the same manner, the brewer, the distiller, the dyer, make incessant use of the air and water for the production of their commodities; but as the supply is boundless, they bear no price.[7] If all land had the same properties, if it were unlimited in quantity, and uniform in quality, no charge could be made for its use, unless where it possessed peculiar advantages of situation. It is only, then, because land is not unlimited in quantity and uniform in quality, and because, in the progress of population, land of an inferior quality, or less advantageously situated, is called into cultivation, that rent is ever paid for the use of it. When, in the progress of society, land of the second degree of fertility is taken into cultivation, rent immediately commences on that of the first quality, and the amount of that rent will depend on the difference in the quality of these two portions of land.

When land of the third quality is taken into cultivation, rent immediately commences on the second, and it is regulated as before by the difference in their productive powers. At the same time, the rent of the first quality will rise, for that must always be above the rent of the second by the difference between the produce which they yield with a given quantity of capital and labor. With every step in the progress of population, which shall oblige a country to have recourse to land of a worse quality, to enable it to raise its supply of food, rent, on all the more fertile land, will rise.

Thus suppose land—No. 1, 2, 3—to yield, with an equal employment of capital and labor, a net produce of 100, 90, and 80 quarters of corn. In a new country, where there is an abundance of fertile land compared with the population, and where therefore it is only necessary to cultivate No. 1, the whole net produce will belong to the cultivator, and will be the profits of the stock which he advances. As soon as population had so far increased as to make it necessary to cultivate No. 2, from which ninety quarters only can be obtained after supporting the laborers, rent would commence on No. 1; for either there must be two rates of profit on agricultural capital, or ten quarters, or the value of ten quarters must be withdrawn from the produce of No. 1 for some other purpose. Whether the proprietor of the land, or any other person, cultivated No.1, these ten quarters would equally constitute rent; for the cultivator of No. 2 would get the same result with his capital whether he cultivated No. 1, paying ten quarters for rent, or continued to cultivate No. 2, paying no rent. In the same manner it might be shown that when No. 3 is brought into cultivation, the rent of No. 2 must be ten quarters, or the value of ten quarters, whilst the rent of No. 1 would rise to twenty quarters; for the cultivator of No. 3 would have the same profits whether he paid twenty quarters for the rent of No. 1, ten quarters for the rent of No. 2, or cultivated No. 3 free of all rent.

It often, and, indeed, commonly happens, that before No. 2, 3, 4, or 5, or the inferior lands are cultivated, capital can be employed more productively on those lands which are already in cultivation. It may perhaps be found that by doubling the original capital employed on No. 1, though the produce will not be doubled, will not be increased by 100 quarters, it may be increased by eighty-five quarters, and that this quantity exceeds what could be obtained by employing the same capital on land No. 3.

In such case, capital will be preferably employed on the old land, and will equally create a rent; for rent is always the difference between the produce obtained by the employment of two equal quantities of capital and labor. If, with a capital of £1000 a tenant obtain 100 quarters of wheat from his land, and by the employment of a second capital of £1000 he obtain a further return of eighty-five, his landlord would have the power, at the expiration of his lease, of obliging him to pay fifteen quarters or an equivalent value for additional rent; for there cannot be two rates of profit. If he is satisfied with a diminution of fifteen quarters in the return for his second £1000, it is because no employment more profitable can be found for it. The common rate of profit would be in that proportion, and if the original tenant refused, some other person would be found willing to give all which exceeded that rate of profit to the owner of the land from which he derived it.

In this case, as well as in the other, the capital last employed pays no rent. For the greater productive powers of the first £1000, fifteen quarters, is paid for rent, for the employment of the second £1000 no rent whatever is paid. If a third £1000 be employed on the same land, with a return of seventy-five quarters, rent will then be paid for the second £1000, and will be equal to the difference between the produce of these two, or ten quarters; and at the same time the rent for the first £1000 will rise from fifteen to twenty-five quarters; while the last £1000 will pay no rent whatever.

If, then, good land existed in a quantity much more abundant than the production of food for an increasing population required, or if capital could be indefinitely employed without a diminished return on the old land, there could be no rise of rent; for rent invariably proceeds from the employment of an additional quantity of labor with a proportionally less return.

The most fertile and most favorably situated land will be first cultivated, and the exchangeable value of its produce will be adjusted in the same manner as the exchangeable value of all other commodities, by the total quantity of labor necessary in various forms, from first to last, to produce it and bring it to market. When land of an inferior quality is taken into cultivation, the exchangeable value of raw produce will rise, because more labor is required to produce it.

The exchangeable value of all commodities, whether they be manufactured, or the produce of the mines, or the produce of land, is always regulated, not by the less quantity of labor that will suffice for their production under circumstances highly favorable, and exclusively enjoyed by those who have peculiar facilities of production; but by the greater quantity of labor necessarily bestowed on their production by those who have no such facilities; by those who continue to produce them under the most unfavorable circumstances; meaning—by the most unfavorable circumstances, the most unfavorable under which the quantity of produce required renders it necessary to carry on the production.

Thus, in a charitable institution, where the poor are set to work with the funds of benefactors, the general prices of the commodities, which are the produce of such work, will not be governed by the peculiar facilities afforded to these workmen, but by the common, usual, and natural difficulties which every other manufacturer will have to encounter. The manufacturer enjoying none of these facilities might indeed be driven altogether from the market if the supply afforded by these favored workmen were equal to all the wants of the community; but if he continued the trade, it would be only on condition that he should derive from it the usual and general rate of profits on stock; and that could only happen when his commodity sold for a price proportioned to the quantity of labor bestowed on its production.[8]

It is true, that on the best land, the same produce would still be obtained with the same labor as before, but its value would be enhanced in consequence of the diminished returns obtained by those who employed fresh labor and stock on the less fertile land. Notwithstanding, then, that the advantages of fertile over inferior lands are in no case lost, but only transferred from the cultivator, or consumer, to the landlord, yet, since more labor is required on the inferior lands, and since it is from such land only that we are enabled to furnish ourselves with the additional supply of raw produce, the comparative value of that produce will continue permanently above its former level, and make it exchange for more hats, cloth, shoes, etc., etc., in the production of which no such additional quantity of labor is required.

The reason, then, why raw produce rises in comparative value is because more labor is employed in the production of the last portion obtained, and not because a rent is paid to the landlord. The value of corn is regulated by the quantity of labor bestowed on its production on that quality of land, or with that portion of capital, which pays no rent. Corn is not high because a rent is paid, but a rent is paid because corn is high; and it has been justly observed that no reduction would take place in the price of corn although landlords should forego the whole of their rent. Such a measure would only enable some farmers to live like gentlemen, but would not diminish the quantity of labor necessary to raise raw produce on the least productive land in cultivation.

Nothing is more common than to hear of the advantages which the land possesses over every other source of useful produce, on account of the surplus which it yields in the form of rent. Yet when land is most abundant, when most productive, and most fertile, it yields no rent; and it is only when its powers decay, and less is yielded in return for labor, that a share of the original produce of the more fertile portions is set apart for rent. It is singular that this quality in the land, which should have been noticed as an imperfection compared with the natural agents by which manufacturers are assisted, should have been pointed out as constituting its peculiar preeminence. If air, water, the elasticity of steam, and the pressure of the atmosphere were of various qualities; if they could be appropriated, and each quality existed only in moderate abundance, they, as well as the land, would afford a rent, as the successive qualities were brought into use. With every worse quality employed, the value of the commodities in the manufacture of which they were used would rise, because equal quantities of labor would be less productive. Man would do more by the sweat of his brow and nature perform less; and the land would be no longer pre-eminent for its limited powers.

If the surplus produce which land affords in the form of rent be an advantage, it is desirable that, every year, the machinery newly constructed should be less efficient than the old, as that would undoubtedly give a greater exchangeable value to the goods manufactured, not only by that machinery but by all the other machinery in the kingdom; and a rent would be paid to all those who possessed the most productive machinery.[9]

The rise of rent is always the effect of the increasing wealth of the country, and of the difficulty of providing food for its augmented population. It is a symptom, but it is never a cause of wealth; for wealth often increases most rapidly while rent is either stationary, or even falling. Rent increases most rapidly as the disposable land decreases in its productive powers. Wealth increases most rapidly in those countries where the disposable land is most fertile, where importation is least restricted, and where, through agricultural improvements, productions can be multiplied without any increase in the proportional quantity of labor, and where consequently the progress of rent is slow.

If the high price of corn were the effect, and not the cause of rent, price would be proportionally influenced as rents were high or low, and rent would be a component part of price. But that corn which is produced by the greatest quantity of labor is the regulator of the price of corn; and rent does not and cannot enter in the least degree as a component part of its price.[10] Adam Smith, therefore, cannot be correct in supposing that the original rule which regulated the exchangeable value of commodities, namely, the comparative quantity of labor by which they were produced, can be at all altered by the appropriation of land and the payment of rent. Raw material enters into the composition of most commodities, but the value of that raw material, as well as corn, is regulated by the productiveness of the portion of capital last employed on the land and paying no rent; and therefore rent is not a component part of the price of commodities.

We have been hitherto considering the effects of the natural progress of wealth and population on rent in a country in which the land is of variously productive powers, and we have seen that with every portion of additional capital which it becomes necessary to employ on the land with a less productive return rent would rise. It follows from the same principles that any circumstances in the society which should make it unnecessary to employ the same amount of capital on the land, and which should therefore make the portion last employed more productive, would lower rent. Any great reduction in the capital of a country which should materially diminish the funds destined for the maintenance of labor, would naturally have this effect. Population regulates itself by the funds which are to employ it, and therefore always increases or diminishes with the increase or diminution of capital. Every reduction of capital is therefore necessarily followed by a less effective demand for corn, by a fall of price, and by diminished cultivation. In the reverse order to that in which the accumulation of capital raises rent will the diminution of it lower rent. Land of a less unproductive quality will be in succession relinquished, the exchangeable value of produce will fall, and land of a superior quality will be the land last cultivated, and that which will then pay no rent.

The same effects may, however, be produced when the wealth and population of a country are increased, if that increase is accompanied by such marked improvements in agriculture as shall have the same effect of diminishing the necessity of cultivating the poorer lands, or of expending the same amount of capital on the cultivation of the more fertile portions.

If a million of quarters of corn be necessary for the support of a given population, and it be raised on land of the qualities of No. 1, 2, 3; and if an improvement be afterwards discovered by which it can be raised on No. 1 and 2, without employing No. 3, it is evident that the immediate effect must be a fall of rent; for No. 2, instead of No. 3, will then be cultivated without paying any rent; and the rent of No. 1, instead of being the difference between the produce of No. 3 and No. 1, will be the difference only between No. 2 and 1. With the same population, and no more, there can be no demand for any additional quantity of corn; the capital and labor employed on No. 3 will be devoted to the production of other commodities desirable to the community, and can have no effect in raising rent, unless the raw material from which they are made cannot be obtained without employing capital less advantageously on the land, in which case No. 3 must again be cultivated.

It is undoubtedly true that the fall in the relative price of raw produce, in consequence of the improvement in agriculture, or rather in consequence of less labor being bestowed on its production, would naturally lead to increased accumulation; for the profits of stock would be greatly augmented. This accumulation would lead to an increased demand for labor, to higher wages, to an increased population, to a further demand for raw produce, and to an increased cultivation. It is only, however, after the increase in the population that rent would be as high as before; that is to say, after No. 3 was taken into cultivation. A considerable period would have elapsed, attended with a positive diminution of rent.

But improvements in agriculture are of two kinds: those which increase the productive powers of the land and those which enable us, by improving our machinery, to obtain its produce with less labor. They both lead to a fall in the price of raw produce; they both affect rent, but they do not affect it equally. If they did not occasion a fall in the price of raw produce they would not be improvements; for it is the essential quality of an improvement to diminish the quantity of labor before required to produce a commodity; and this diminution cannot take place without a fall of its price or relative value.

The improvements which increased the productive powers of the land are such as the more skilful rotation of crops or the better choice of manure. These improvements absolutely enable us to obtain the same produce from a smaller quantity of land. If, by the introduction of a course of turnips, I can feed my sheep besides raising my corn, the land on which the sheep were before fed becomes unnecessary, and the same quantity of raw produce is raised by the employment of a less quantity of land. If I discover a manure which will enable me to make a piece of land produce 20 percent more corn, I may withdraw at least a portion of my capital from the most unproductive part of my farm.

But, as I before observed, it is not necessary that land should be thrown out of cultivation in order to reduce rent: to produce this effect, it is sufficient that successive portions of capital are employed on the same land with different results, and that the portion which gives the least result should be withdrawn. If, by the introduction of the turnip husbandry, or by the use of a more invigorating manure, I can obtain the same produce with less capital, and without disturbing the difference between the productive powers of the successive portions of capital, I shall lower rent; for a different and more productive portion will be that which will form the standard from which every other will be reckoned. If, for example, the successive portions of capital yielded 100, 90, 80, 70; whilst I employed these four portions, my rent would be 60, or the difference between

70 and 100 = 30		100
70 and 90 = 20		90
70 and 80 = 10		80
	whilst the produce would be 340	70
60		340

and while I employed these portions, the rent would remain the same, although the produce of each should have an equal augmentation. If, instead of 100, 90, 80, 70, the produce should be increased to 125, 115, 105, 95, the rent would still be 60, or the difference between

95 and 125 = 39		125
95 and 115 = 20		115
95 and 105 = 10	whilst the produce	105
	would be increase to 440	95
60		440

But with such an increase of produce, without an increase of demand,[11] there could be no motive for employing so much capital on the land; one portion would be withdrawn, and consequently the last portion of capital would yield 105 instead of 95, and rent would fall to 30, or the difference between

105 and 125 = 20	whilst the produce will be still	125
105 and 115 = 10	adequate to the wants of the population 115	
	for it would be 345 quarters, or	105
30		345

the demand being only for 340 quarters.—But there are improvements which may lower the relative value of produce without lowering the corn rent, though they will lower the money rent of land. Such improvements do not increase the productive powers of the land, but they enable us to obtain its produce with less labor. They are rather directed to the formation of the capital applied to the land than to the cultivation of the land itself. Improvements in agricultural implements, such as the plough and the thrashing machine, economy in the use of horses employed in husbandry, and a better knowledge of the veterinary art, are of this nature. Less capital, which is the same thing as less labor, will be employed on the land; but to obtain the same produce, less land cannot be cultivated. Whether improvements of this kind, however, affect corn rent, must depend on the question whether the difference between the produce obtained by the employment of different portions of capital be increased, stationary, or diminished. If four portions of capital, 50, 60, 70, 80, be employed on the land, giving each the same results, and any improvement in the formation of such capital should enable me to withdraw 5 from each, so that they should be 45, 55, 65, and 75, no alteration would take place in the corn rent; but if the improvements were such as to enable me to make the whole saving on that portion of capital which is least productively employed, corn rent would immediately fall, because the difference between the capital most productive and the capital least productive would be diminished; and it is this difference which constitutes rent.

Without multiplying instances, I hope enough has been said to show that whatever diminishes the inequality in the produce obtained from successive portions of capital employed on the same or on new land tends to lower rent; and that whatever increases that inequality, necessarily produces an opposite effect, and tends to raise it.

In speaking of the rent of the landlord, we have rather considered it as the proportion of the produce, obtained with a given capital on any given farm, without any reference to its exchangeable value; but since the same cause, the difficulty of production, raises the exchangeable value of raw produce, and raises also the proportion of raw produce paid to the landlord for rent, it is obvious that the landlord is doubly benefited by difficulty of production. First, he obtains a greater share, and, secondly, the commodity in which he is paid is of greater value.[12]

CHAPTER III

On the Rent of Mines

The metals, like other things, are obtained by labor. Nature, indeed, produces them; but it is the labor of man which extracts them from the bowels of the earth and prepares them for our service.

Mines, as well as land, generally pay a rent to their owner; and this rent, as well as the rent of land, is the effect and never the cause of the high value of their produce.

If there were abundance of equally fertile mines, which any one might appropriate, they could yield no rent; the value of their produce would depend on the quantity of labor necessary to extract the metal from the mine and bring it to market.

But there are mines of various qualities affording very different results with equal quantities of labor. The metal produced from the poorest mine that is worked must at least have an exchangeable value, not only sufficient to procure all the clothes, food, and other necessaries consumed by those employed in working it, and bringing the produce to market, but also to afford the common and ordinary profits to him who advances the stock necessary to carry on the undertaking. The return for capital from the poorest mine paying no rent would regulate the rent of all the other more productive mines. This mine is supposed to yield the usual profits of stock. All that the other mines produce more than this will necessarily be paid to the owners for rent. Since this principle is precisely the same as that which we have already laid down respecting land, it will not be necessary further to enlarge on it.

It will be sufficient to remark that the same general rule which regulates the value of raw produce and manufactured commodities is applicable also to the metals; their value depending not on the rate of profits, nor on the rate of wages, nor on the rent paid for mines, but on the total quantity of labor necessary to obtain the metal and to bring it to market.

Like every other commodity, the value of the metals is subject to variation. Improvements may be made in the implements and machinery used in mining, which may considerably abridge labor; new and more productive mines may be discovered, in which, with the same labor, more metal may be obtained; or the facilities of bringing it to market may be increased. In either of these cases the metals would fall in value, and would therefore exchange for a less quantity of other things. On the other hand, from the increasing difficulty of obtaining the metal, occasioned by the greater depth at which the mine must be worked, and the accumulation of water, or any other contingency, its value compared with that of other things might be considerably increased.

It has therefore been justly observed that however honestly the coin of a country may conform to its standard, money made of gold and silver is still liable to fluctuations in value, not only to accidental and temporary, but to permanent and natural variations, in the same manner as other commodities.

By the discovery of America, and the rich mines in which it abounds, a very great effect was produced on the natural price of the precious metals. This effect is by many supposed not yet to have terminated. It is probable, however, that all the effects on the value of the metals resulting from the discovery of America have long ceased; and if any fall has of late years taken place in their value, it is to be attributed to improvements in the mode of working the mines.

From whatever cause it may have proceeded, the effect has been so slow and gradual that little practical inconvenience has been felt from gold and silver being the general medium in which the value of all other things is estimated. Though undoubtedly a variable measure of value, there is probably no commodity subject to fewer variations. This and the other advantages which these metals possess, such as their hardness, their malleability, their divisibility, and many more, have justly secured the preference everywhere given to them as a standard for the money of civilized countries.

If equal quantities of labor, with equal quantities of fixed capital, could at all times obtain from that mine which paid no rent equal quantities of gold, gold would be as nearly an invariable measure of value as we could in the nature of things possess. The quantity indeed would enlarge with the demand, but its value would be invariable, and it would be eminently well calculated to measure the varying value of all other things. I have already in a former part of this work considered gold as endowed with this uniformity, and in the following chapter I shall continue the supposition. In speaking therefore of varying price, the variation will be always considered as being in the commodity, and never in the medium in which it is estimated.

CHAPTER IV

On Natural and Market Price

In making labor the foundation of the value of commodities, and the comparative quantity of labor which is necessary to their production, the rule which determines the respective quantities of goods which shall be given in exchange for each other, we must not be supposed to deny the accidental and temporary deviations of the actual or market price of commodities from this, their primary and natural price.

In the ordinary course of events, there is no commodity which continues for any length of time to be supplied precisely in that degree of abundance which the wants and wishes of mankind require, and therefore there is none which is not subject to accidental and temporary variations of price.

It is only in consequence of such variations that capital is apportioned precisely, in the requisite abundance and no more, to the production of the different commodities which happen to be in demand. With the rise or fall of price, profits are elevated above, or depressed below, their general level; and capital is either encouraged to enter into, or is warned to depart from, the particular employment in which the variation has taken place.

Whilst every man is free to employ his capital where he pleases, he will naturally seek for it that employment which is most advantageous; he will naturally be dissatisfied with a profit of 10 percent, if by removing his capital he can obtain a profit of 15 percent. This restless desire on the part of all the employers of stock to quit a less profitable for a more advantageous business has a strong tendency to equalize the rate of profits of all, or to fix them in such proportions as may, in the estimation of the parties, compensate for any advantage which one may have, or may appear to have, over the other. It is perhaps very difficult to trace the steps by which this change is effected: it is probably effected by a manufacturer not absolutely changing his employment, but only lessening the quantity of capital he has in that employment. In all rich countries there is a number of men forming what is called the moneyed class; these men are engaged in no trade, but live on the interest of their money, which is employed in discounting bills, or in loans to the more industrious part of the community. The bankers too employ a large capital on the same objects. The capital so employed forms a circulating capital of a large amount, and is employed, in larger or smaller proportions, by all the different trades of a country. There is perhaps no manufacturer, however rich, who limits his business to the extent that his own funds alone will allow: he has always some portion of this floating capital, increasing or diminishing according to the activity of the demand for his commodities. When the demand for silks increases, and that for cloth diminishes, the clothier does not remove with his capital to the silk trade, but he dismisses some of his workmen, he discontinues his demand for the loan from bankers and moneyed men; while the case of the silk manufacturer is the reverse: he wishes to employ more workmen, and thus his motive for borrowing is increased; he borrows more, and thus capital is transferred from one employment to another without the necessity of a manufacturer discontinuing his usual occupation. When we look to the markets of a large town, and observe how regularly they are supplied both with home and foreign commodities, in the quantity in which they are required, under all the circumstances of varying demand, arising from the caprice of taste, or a change in the amount of population, without often producing either the effects of a glut from a too abundant supply, or an enormously high price from the supply being unequal to the demand, we must confess that the principle which apportions capital to each trade in the precise amount that it is required is more active than is generally supposed.

A capitalist, in seeking profitable employment for his funds, will naturally take into consideration all the advantages which one occupation possesses over another. He may therefore be willing to forego a part of his money profit in consideration of the security, cleanliness, ease, or any other real or fancied advantage which one employment may possess over another.

If from a consideration of these circumstances, the profits of stock should be so adjusted that in one trade they were 20, in another 25, and in another 30 percent, they would probably continue permanently with that relative difference, and with that difference only; for if any cause should elevate the profits of one of these trades 10 percent, either these profits would be temporary, and would soon again fall back to their usual station, or the profits of the others would be elevated in the same proportion.

The present time appears to be one of the exceptions to the justness of this remark. The termination of the war has so deranged the division which before existed of employments in Europe, that every capitalist has not yet found his place in the new division which has now become necessary.

Let us suppose that all commodities are at their natural price, and consequently that the profits of capital in all employments are exactly at the same rate, or differ only so much as, in the estimation of the parties, is equivalent to any real or fancied advantage which they possess or forego. Suppose now that a change of fashion should increase the demand for silks and lessen that for woolens; their natural price, the quantity of labor necessary to their production, would continue unaltered, but the market price of silks would rise and that of woolens would fall; and consequently the profits of the silk manufacturer would be above, whilst those of the woolen manufacturer would be below, the general and adjusted rate of profits. Not only the profits, but the wages of the workmen, would be affected in these employments. This increased demand for silks would, however, soon be supplied by the transference of capital and labor from the woolen to the silk manufacture; when the market prices of silks and woolens would again approach their natural prices, and then the usual profits would be obtained by the respective manufacturers of those commodities.

It is then the desire, which every capitalist has, of diverting his funds from a less to a more profitable employment that prevents the market price of commodities from continuing for any length of time either much above or much below their natural price. It is this competition which so adjusts the changeable value of commodities that, after paying the wages for the labor necessary to their production, and all other expenses required to put the capital employed in its original state of efficiency, the remaining value or overplus will in each trade be in proportion to the value of the capital employed.

In the seventh chapter of the *Wealth of Nations*, all that concerns this question is most ably treated. Having fully acknowledged the temporary effects which, in particular employments of capital, may be produced on the prices of commodities, as well as on the wages of labor, and the profits of stock, by accidental causes, without influencing the general price of commodities, wages, or profits, since these effects are equally operative in all stages of society, we will leave them entirely out of our consideration whilst we are treating of the laws which regulate natural prices, natural wages, and natural profits, effects totally independent of these accidental causes. In speaking, then, of the exchangeable value of commodities, or the power of purchasing possessed by any one commodity, I mean always that power which it would possess if not disturbed by any temporary or accidental cause, and which is its natural price.

CHAPTER V

On Wages

Labor, like all other things which are purchased and sold, and which may be increased or diminished in quantity, has its natural and its market price. The natural price of labor is that price which is necessary to enable the laborers, one with another, to subsist and to perpetuate their race, without either increase or diminution.

The power of the laborer to support himself, and the family which may be necessary to keep up the number of laborers, does not depend on the quantity of money which he may receive for wages, but on the quantity of food, necessaries, and conveniences become essential to him from habit which that money will purchase. The natural price of labor, therefore, depends on the price of the food, necessaries, and conveniences required for the support of the laborer and his family. With a rise in the price of food and necessaries, the natural price of labor will rise; with the fall in their price, the natural price of labor will fall.

With the progress of society the natural price of labor has always a tendency to rise, because one of the principal commodities by which its natural price is regulated has a tendency to become dearer from the greater difficulty of producing it. As, however, the improvements in agriculture, the discovery of new markets, whence provisions may be imported, may for a time counteract the tendency to a rise in the price of necessaries, and may even occasion their natural price to fall, so will the same causes produce the correspondent effects on the natural price of labor.

The natural price of all commodities, excepting raw produce and labor, has a tendency to fall in the progress of wealth and population; for though, on one hand, they are enhanced in real value, from the rise in the natural price of the raw material of which they are made, this is more than counterbalanced by the improvements in machinery, by the better division and distribution of labor, and by the increasing skill, both in science and art, of the producers.

The market price of labor is the price which is really paid for it, from the natural operation of the proportion of the supply to the demand; labor is dear when it is scarce and cheap when it is plentiful. However much the market price of labor may deviate from its natural price, it has, like commodities, a tendency to conform to it.

It is when the market price of labor exceeds its natural price that the condition of the laborer is flourishing and happy, that he has it in his power to command a greater proportion of the necessaries and enjoyments of life, and therefore to rear a healthy and numerous family. When, however, by the encouragement which high wages give to the increase of population, the number of laborers is increased, wages again fall to their natural price, and indeed from a reaction sometimes fall below it.

When the market price of labor is below its natural price, the condition of the laborers is most wretched: then poverty deprives them of those comforts which custom renders absolute necessaries. It is only after their privations have reduced their number, or the demand for labor has increased, that the market price of labor will rise to its natural price, and that the laborer will have the moderate comforts which the natural rate of wages will afford.

Notwithstanding the tendency of wages to conform to their natural rate, their market rate may, in an improving society, for an indefinite period, be constantly above it; for no sooner may the impulse which an increased capital gives to a new demand for labor be obeyed, than another increase of capital may produce the same effect; and thus, if the increase of capital be gradual and constant, the demand for labor may give a continued stimulus to an increase of people.

Capital is that part of the wealth of a country which is employed in production, and consists of food, clothing, tools, raw materials, machinery, etc., necessary to give effect to labor.

Capital may increase in quantity at the same time that its value rises. An addition may be made to the food and clothing of a country at the same time that more labor may be required to produce the additional quantity than before; in that case not only the quantity but the value of capital will rise.

Or capital may increase without its value increasing, and even while its value is actually diminishing; not only may an addition be made to the food and clothing of a country, but the addition may be made by the aid of machinery, without any increase, and even with an absolute diminution in the proportional quantity of labor required to produce them. The quantity of capital may increase, while neither the whole together, nor any part of it singly, will have a greater value than before, but may actually have a less.

In the first case, the natural price of labor, which always depends on the price of food, clothing, and other necessaries, will rise; in the second, it will remain stationary or fall; but in both cases the market rate of wages will rise, for in proportion to the increase of capital will be the increase in the demand for labor; in proportion to the work to be done will be the demand for those who are to do it.

In both cases, too, the market price of labor will rise above its natural price; and in both cases it will have a tendency to conform to its natural price, but in the first case this agreement will be most speedily effected. The situation of the laborer will be improved, but not much improved; for the increased price of food and necessaries will absorb a large portion of his increased wages; consequently a small supply of labor, or a trifling increase in the population, will soon reduce the market price to the then increased natural price of labor.

In the second case, the condition of the laborer will be very greatly improved; he will receive increased money wages without having to pay any increased price, and perhaps even a diminished price for the commodities which he and his family consume; and it will not be till after a great addition has been made to the population that the market price of labor will again sink to its then low and reduced natural price.

Thus, then, with every improvement of society, with every increase in its capital, the market wages of labor will rise; but the permanence of their rise will depend on the question whether the natural price of labor has also risen; and this again will depend on the rise in the natural price of those necessaries on which the wages of labor are expended.

It is not to be understood that the natural price of labor, estimated even in food and necessaries, is absolutely fixed and constant. It varies at different times in the same country, and very materially differs in different countries.[13] It essentially depends on the habits and customs of the people. An English laborer would consider his wages under their natural rate, and too scanty to support a family, if they enabled him to purchase no other food than potatoes, and to live in no better habitation than a mud cabin; yet these moderate demands of nature are often deemed sufficient in countries where "man's life is cheap" and his wants easily satisfied. Many of the conveniences now enjoyed in an English cottage would have been thought luxuries at an earlier period of our history.

From manufactured commodities always falling and raw produce always rising, with the progress of society, such a disproportion in their relative value is at length created, that in rich countries a laborer, by the sacrifice of a very small quantity only of his food, is able to provide liberally for all his other wants.

Independently of the variations in the value of money, which necessarily affect money wages, but which we have here supposed to have no operation, as we have considered money to be uniformly of the same value, it appears then that wages are subject to a rise or fall from two causes:

First, the supply and demand of laborers.

Secondly, the price of the commodities on which the wages of labor are expended.

In different stages of society, the accumulation of capital, or of the means of employing labor, is more or less rapid, and must in all cases depend on the productive powers of labor. The productive powers of labor are generally greatest when there is an abundance of fertile land: at such periods accumulation is often so rapid that laborers cannot be supplied with the same rapidity as capital.

It has been calculated that under favorable circumstances population may be doubled in twenty-five years; but under the same favorable circumstances the whole capital of a country might possibly be doubled in a shorter period. In that case, wages during the whole period would have a tendency to rise, because the demand for labor would increase still faster than the supply.

In new settlements, where the arts and knowledge of countries far advanced in refinement are introduced, it is probable that capital has a tendency to increase faster than mankind; and if the deficiency of laborers were not supplied by more populous countries, this tendency would very much raise the price of labor. In proportion as these countries become populous, and land of a worse quality is taken into cultivation, the tendency to an increase of capital diminishes; for the surplus produce remaining, after satisfying the wants of the existing population, must necessarily be in proportion to the facility of production, viz. to the smaller number of persons employed in production. Although, then, it is probable that, under the most favorable circumstances, the power of production is still greater than that of population, it will not long continue so; for the land being limited in quantity, and differing in quality, with every increased portion of capital employed on it there will be a decreased rate of production, whilst the power of population continues always the same.

In those countries where there is abundance of fertile land, but where, from the ignorance, indolence, and barbarism of the inhabitants, they are exposed to all the evils of want and famine, and where it has been said that population presses against the means of subsistence, a very different remedy should be applied from that which is necessary in long settled countries, where, from the diminishing rate of the supply of raw produce, all the evils of a crowded population are experienced. In the one case, the evil proceeds from bad government, from the insecurity of property, and from a want of education in all ranks of the people. To be made happier they require only to be better governed and instructed, as the augmentation of capital, beyond the augmentation of people, would be the inevitable result. No increase in the population can be too great, as the powers of production are still greater. In the other case, the population increases faster than the funds required for its support. Every exertion of industry, unless accompanied by a diminished rate of increase in the population, will add to the evil, for production cannot keep pace with it.

With a population pressing against the means of subsistence, the only remedies are either a reduction of people or a more rapid accumulation of capital. In rich countries, where all the fertile land is already cultivated, the latter remedy is neither very practicable nor very desirable, because its effort would be, if pushed very far, to render all classes equally poor. But in poor countries, where there are abundant means of production in store, from fertile land not yet brought into cultivation, it is the only safe and efficacious means of removing the evil, particularly as its effect would be to elevate all classes of the people.

The friends of humanity cannot but wish that in all countries the laboring classes should have a taste for comforts and enjoyments, and that they should be stimulated by all legal means in their exertions to procure them. There cannot be a better security against a superabundant population. In those countries where the laboring classes have the fewest wants, and are contented with the cheapest food, the people are exposed to the greatest vicissitudes and miseries. They have no place of refuge from calamity; they cannot seek safety in a lower station; they are already so low that they can fall no lower. On any deficiency of the chief article of their subsistence there are few substitutes of which they can avail themselves and dearth to them is attended with almost all the evils of famine.

In the natural advance of society, the wages of labor will have a tendency to fall, as far as they are regulated by supply and demand; for the supply of laborers will continue to increase at the same rate, whilst the demand for them will increase at a slower rate. If, for instance, wages were regulated by a yearly increase of capital at the rate of 2 percent, they would fall when it accumulated only at the rate of 1 1/2 percent. They would fall still lower when it increased only at the rate of 1 or 1/2 percent, and would continue to do so until the capital became stationary, when wages also would become stationary, and be only sufficient to keep up the numbers of the actual population. I say that, under these circumstances, wages would fall if they were regulated only by the supply and demand of laborers; but we must not forget that wages are also regulated by the prices of the commodities on which they are expended.

As population increases, these necessaries will be constantly rising in price, because more labor will be necessary to produce them. If, then, the money wages of labor should fall, whilst every commodity on which the wages of labor were expended rose, the laborer would be doubly affected, and would be soon totally deprived of subsistence. Instead, therefore, of the money wages of labor falling, they would rise; but they would not rise sufficiently to enable the laborer to purchase as many comforts and necessaries as he did before the rise in the price of those commodities. If his annual wages were before £24, or six quarters of corn when the price was £4 per quarter, he would probably receive only the value of five quarters when corn rose to £5 per quarter. But five quarters would cost £25; he would, therefore, receive an addition in his money wages, though with that addition he would be unable to furnish himself with the same quantity of corn and other commodities which he had before consumed in his family.

Notwithstanding, then, that the laborer would be really worse paid, yet this increase in his wages would necessarily diminish the profits of the manufacturer; for his goods would sell at no higher price, and yet the expense of producing them would be increased. This, however, will be considered in our examination into the principles which regulate profits.

It appears, then, that the same cause which raises rent, namely, the increasing difficulty of providing an additional quantity of food with the same proportional quantity of labor, will also raise wages; and therefore, if money be of an unvarying value, both rent and wages will have a tendency to rise with the progress of wealth and population.

But there is this essential difference between the rise of rent and the rise of wages. The rise in the money value of rent is accompanied by an increased share of the produce; not only is the landlord's money rent greater, but his corn rent also; he will have more corn, and each denned measure of that corn will exchange for a greater quantity of all other goods which have not been raised in value. The fate of the laborer will be less happy; he will receive more money wages, it is true, but his corn wages will be reduced; and not only his command of corn, but his general condition will be deteriorated, by his finding it more difficult to maintain the market rate of wages above their natural rate. While the price of corn rises 10 percent, wages will always rise less than 10 percent, but rent will always rise more; the condition of the laborer will generally decline, and that of the landlord will always be improved.

When wheat was at £4 per quarter, suppose the laborer's wages to be £24 per annum, or the value of six quarters of wheat, and suppose half his wages to be expended on wheat, and the other half, or £12, on other things. He would receive

£24 14s		£4 4s. 8d.		5.83 quarters
£25 10s.	when wheat	£4 10s.	or the	5.66 quarters
£26 8s.	was at	£4 16s.	value of	5.50 quarters
£27 8s. 6d.		£5 2s.10d.		5.33 quarters

He would receive these wages to enable him to live just as well, and no better, than before; for when corn was at £4 per quarter, he would expend for three quarters of corn,

at £4 per quarter	£12
and on other things	£12
	£24

When wheat was £4 4s. 8d., three quarters, which he and his family consumed, would cost him . . .	£12 14s.
other things not altered in price . . .	£12
	£24 14s.

When at £4 10s., three quarters of wheat would cost	£13 10s.
and other things	£12
	£25 10s.

When at £4 16s., three quarters of wheat	£14 8s.
other things	£12
	£26 8s.

When at £5 28s. 10d., three quarters of wheat would cost	£15 8s. 6d.
other things	£12
	£27 8s. 6d.

In proportion as corn became dear, he would receive less corn wages, but his money wages would always increase, whilst his enjoyments, on the above supposition, would be precisely the same. But as other commodities would be raised in price in proportion as raw produce entered into their composition, he would have more to pay for some of them. Although his tea, sugar, soap, candles, and house rent would probably be no dearer, he would pay more for his bacon, cheese, butter, linen shoes, and cloth; and therefore, even with the above increase of wages, his situation would be comparatively worse. But it may be said that I have been considering the effect of wages on price on the supposition that gold, or the metal from which money is made, is the produce of the country in which wages varied; and that the consequences which I have deduced agree little with the actual state of things, because gold is a metal of foreign production. The circumstance, however, of gold being a foreign production will not invalidate the truth of the argument, because it may be shown that whether it were found at home, or were imported from abroad, the effects ultimately, and, indeed, immediately, would be the same.

When wages rise it is generally because the increase of wealth and capital have occasioned a new demand for labor, which will infallibly be attended with an increased production of commodities. To circulate these additional commodities, even at the same prices as before, more money is required, more of this foreign commodity from which money is made, and which can only be obtained by importation. Whenever a commodity is required in greater abundance than before, its relative value rises comparatively with those commodities with which its purchase is made. If more hats were wanted, their price would rise, and more gold would be given for them. If more gold were required, gold would rise, and hats would fall in price, as a greater quantity of hats and of all other things would then be necessary to purchase the same quantity of gold. But in the case supposed, to say that commodities will rise because wages rise, is to affirm a positive contradiction; for we, first, say that gold will rise in relative value in consequence of demand, and, secondly, that it will fall in relative value because prices will rise, two effects which are totally incompatible with each other. To say that commodities are raised in price is the same thing as to say that money is lowered in relative value; for it is by commodities that the relative value of gold is estimated. If, then, all commodities rose in price, gold could not come from abroad to purchase those dear commodities, but it would go from home to be employed with advantage in purchasing the comparatively cheaper foreign commodities. It appears, then, that the rise of wages will not raise the prices of commodities, whether the metal from which money is made be produced at home or in a foreign country. All commodities cannot rise at the same time without an addition to the quantity of money. This addition could not be obtained at home, as we have already shown; nor could it be imported from abroad. To purchase any additional quantity of gold from abroad, commodities at home must be cheap, not dear. The importation of gold, and a rise in the price of all home-made commodities with which gold is purchased or paid for, are effects absolutely incompatible. The extensive use of paper money does not alter this question, for paper money conforms, or ought to conform, to the value of gold, and therefore its value is influenced by such causes only as influence the value of that metal.

These, then, are the laws by which wages are regulated, and by which the happiness of far the greatest part of every community is governed. Like all other contracts, wages should be left to the fair and free competition of the market, and should never be controlled by the interference of the legislature.

The clear and direct tendency of the poor laws is in direct opposition to these obvious principles: it is not, as the legislature benevolently intended, to amend the condition of the poor, but to deteriorate the condition of both poor and rich; instead of making the poor rich, they are calculated to make the rich poor; and whilst the present laws are in force, it is quite in the natural order of things that the fund for the maintenance of the poor should progressively increase till it has absorbed all the net revenue of the country, or at least so much of it as the state shall leave to us, after satisfying its own never-failing demands for the public expenditure.[14]

This pernicious tendency of these laws is no longer a mystery, since it has been fully developed by the able hand of Mr. Malthus; and every friend to the poor must ardently wish for their abolition. Unfortunately, however, they have been so long established, and the habits of the poor have been so formed upon their operation, that to eradicate them with safety from our political system requires the most cautious and skilful management. It is agreed by all who are most friendly to a repeal of these laws that, if it be desirable to prevent the most overwhelming distress to those for whose benefit they were erroneously enacted, their abolition should be effected by the most gradual steps.

It is a truth which admits not a doubt that the comforts and well-being of the poor cannot be permanently secured without some regard on their part, or some effort on the part of the legislature, to regulate the increase of their numbers, and to render less frequent among them early and improvident marriages. The operation of the system of poor laws has been directly contrary to this. They have rendered restraint superfluous, and have invited imprudence, by offering it a portion of the wages of prudence and industry.[15]

The nature of the evil points out the remedy. By gradually contracting the sphere of the poor laws; by impressing on the poor the value of independence, by teaching them that they must look not to systematic or casual charity, but to their own exertions for support, that prudence and forethought are neither unnecessary nor unprofitable virtues, we shall by degrees approach a sounder and more healthful state.

No scheme for the amendment of the poor laws merits the least attention which has not their abolition for its ultimate object; and he is the best friend of the poor, and to the cause of humanity, who can point out how this end can be attained with the most security, and at the same time with the least violence. It is not by raising in any manner different from the present the fund from which the poor are supported that the evil can be mitigated. It would not only be no improvement, but it would be an aggravation of the distress which we wish to see removed, if the fund were increased in amount or were levied according to some late proposals, as a general fund from the country at large. The present mode of its collection and application has served to mitigate its pernicious effects. Each parish raises a separate fund for the support of its own poor. Hence it becomes an object of more interest and more practicability to keep the rates low than if one general fund were raised for the relief of the poor of the whole kingdom. A parish is much more interested in an economical collection of the rate, and a sparing distribution of relief, when the whole saving will be for its own benefit, than if hundreds of other parishes were to partake of it.

It is to this cause that we must ascribe the fact of the poor laws not having yet absorbed all the net revenue of the country; it is to the rigor with which they are applied that we are indebted for their not having become overwhelmingly oppressive. If by law every human being wanting support could be sure to obtain it, and obtain it in such a degree as to make life tolerably comfortable, theory would lead us to expect that all other taxes together would be light compared with the single one of poor rates. The principle of gravitation is not more certain than the tendency of such laws to change wealth and power into misery and weakness; to call away the exertions of labor from every object, except that of providing mere subsistence; to confound all intellectual distinction; to busy the mind continually in supplying the body's wants until at last all classes should be infected with the plague of universal poverty. Happily these laws have been in operation during a period of progressive prosperity, when the funds for the maintenance of labor have regularly increased, and when an increase of population would be naturally called for. But if our progress should become slower; if we should attain the stationary state, from which I trust we are yet far distant, then will the pernicious nature of these laws become more manifest and alarming; and then, too, will their removal be obstructed by many additional difficulties.

CHAPTER VI

On Profits

The profits of stock, in different employments, having been shown to bear a proportion to each other, and to have a tendency to vary all in the same degree and in the same direction, it remains for us to consider what is the cause of the permanent variations in the rate of profit, and the consequent permanent alterations in the rate of interest.

We have seen that the price[16] of corn is regulated by the quantity of labor necessary to produce it, with that portion of capital which pays no rent. We have seen, too, that all manufactured commodities rise and fall in price in proportion as more or less labor becomes necessary to their production. Neither the farmer who cultivates that quantity of land which regulates price, nor the manufacturer who manufactures goods, sacrifice any portion of the produce for rent. The whole value of their commodities is divided into two portions only: one constitutes the profits of stock, the other the wages of labor.

Supposing corn and manufactured goods always to sell at the same price, profits would be high or low in proportion as wages were low or high. But suppose corn to rise in price because more labor is necessary to produce it; that cause will not raise the price of manufactured goods in the production of which no additional quantity of labor is required. If, then, wages continued the same, the profits of manufacturers would remain the same; but if, as is absolutely certain, wages should rise with the rise of corn, then their profits would necessarily fall.

If a manufacturer always sold his goods for the same money, for £1000, for example, his profits would depend on the price of the labor necessary to manufacture those goods. His profits would be less when wages amounted to £800 than when he paid only £600. In proportion then as wages rose, would profits fall. But if the price of raw produce would increase, it may be asked whether the farmer at least would not have the same rate of profits, although he should pay an additional sum for wages? Certainly not: for he will not only have to pay, in common with the manufacturer, an increase of wages to each laborer he employs, but he will be obliged either to pay rent, or to employ an additional number of laborers to obtain the same produce; and the rise in the price of raw produce will be proportioned only to that rent, or that additional number, and will not compensate him for the rise of wages.

If both the manufacturer and farmer employed ten men, on wages rising from £24 to £25 per annum per man, the whole sum paid by each would be £250 instead of £240. This is, however, the whole addition that would be paid by the manufacturer to obtain the same quantity of commodities; but the farmer on new land would probably be obliged to employ an additional man, and therefore to pay an additional sum of £25 for wages; and the farmer on the old land would be obliged to pay precisely the same additional sum of £25 for rent; without which additional labor, corn would not have risen nor rent have been increased. One will therefore have to pay £275 for wages alone, the other for wages and rent together; each £25 more than the manufacturer: for this latter £25 the farmer is compensated by the addition to the price of raw produce, and therefore his profits still conform to the profits of the manufacturer. As this proposition is important, I will endeavor still further to elucidate it.

We have shown that in early stages of society, both the landlord's and the laborer's share of the *value* of the produce of the earth would be but small; and that it would increase in proportion to the progress of wealth and the difficulty of procuring food. We have shown, too, that although the value of the laborer's portion will be increased by the high value of food, his real share will be diminished; whilst that of the landlord will not only be raised in value, but will also be increased in quantity.

The remaining quantity of the produce of the land, after the landlord and are paid, necessarily belongs to the farmer, and constitutes the profits of his stock. But it may be alleged, that though, as society advances, his proportion of the whole produce will be diminished, yet as it will rise in value, he, as well as the landlord and laborer, may, notwithstanding, receive a greater value.

It may be said, for example, that when corn rose from £4 to £10, the 180 quarters obtained from the best land would sell for £1800 instead of £720; and, therefore, though the landlord and laborer be proved to have a greater value for rent and wages, still the value of the farmer's profit might also be augmented. This, however, is impossible, as I shall now endeavor to show.

In the first place, the price of corn would rise only in proportion to the increased difficulty of growing it on land of a worse quality.

It has been already remarked, that if the labor of ten men will, on land of a certain quality, obtain 180 quarters of wheat, and its value be £4 per quarter, or £720; and if the labor of ten additional men will, on the same or any other land, produce only 170 quarters in addition, wheat would rise from £4 to £4 4s. 8d.; for 170:180::£4:£4 4s. 8d. In other words, as for the production of 170 quarters, the labor of ten men is necessary in the one case, and only that of 9.44 in the other, the rise would be as 9.44 to 10, or as £4 to £4 4s. 8d. In the same manner it might be shown that, if the labor of ten additional men would only produce 160 quarters, the price would further rise to £4 10s.; if 150, to £4 16s., etc., etc.

But when 180 quarters were produced on the land paying no rent,
and its price was £4 per quarter, it is sold for £720
And when 170 quarters were produced on the land paying no rent,
and the price rose to £4 4s. 8d. it still sold for 720
So 160 quarters at £4 10s. produce 720
And 150 quarters at £4 16s. produce the same sum of 720

Now, it is evident that if, out of these equal values, the farmer is at one time obliged to pay wages regulated by the price of wheat at £4, and at other times at higher prices, the rate of his profits will diminish in proportion to the rise in the price of corn.

In this case, therefore, I think it is clearly demonstrated that a rise in the price of corn, which increases the money wages of the laborer, diminishes the money value of the farmer's profits.

But the case of the farmer of the old and better land will be in no way different; he also will have increased wages to pay, and will never retain more of the value of the produce, however high may be its price, than £720 to be divided between himself and his always equal number of laborers; in proportion therefore as they get more, he must retain less.

When the price of corn was at £4, the whole 180 quarters belonged to the cultivator, and he sold it for £720. When corn rose to £4 4s. 8d., he was obliged to pay the value of ten quarters out of his 180 for rent, consequently the remaining 170 yielded him no more than £720: when it rose further to £4 10s., he paid twenty quarters, or their value, for rent and consequently only retained 160 quarters, which yielded the same sum of £720. It will be seen, then, that whatever rise may take place in the price of corn, in consequence of the necessity of employing more labor and capital to obtain a given additional quantity of produce, such rise will always be equaled in value by the additional rent or additional labor employed; so that whether corn sells for £4, £4 10s., or £5 2s. 10d. the farmer will obtain for that which remains to him, after paying rent, the same real value. Thus we see that whether the produce belonging to the farmer be 180, 170, 160, or 150 quarters, he always obtains the same sum of £720 for it; the price increasing in an inverse proportion to the quantity.

Rent, then, it appears, always falls on the consumer, and never on the farmer; for if the produce of his farm should uniformly be 180 quarters, with the rise of price he would retain the value of a less quantity for himself, and give the value of a larger quantity to his landlord; but the deduction would be such as to leave him always the same sum of £720.

It will be seen too, that, in all cases, the same sum of £720 must be divided between wages and profits. If the value of the raw produce from the land exceed this value it belongs to rent, whatever may be its amount. If there be no excess, there will be no rent. Whether wages or profits rise or fall, it is this sum of £720 from which they must both be provided. On the one hand, profits can never rise so high as to absorb so much of this £720 that enough will not be left to furnish the laborers with absolute necessaries; on the other hand, wages can never rise so high as to leave no portion of this sum for profits.

Thus in every case, agricultural as well as manufacturing profits are lowered by a rise in the price of raw produce, if it be accompanied by a rise of wages.[17] If the farmer gets no additional value for the corn which remains to him after paying rent, if the manufacturer gets no additional value for the goods which he manufactures, and if both are obliged to pay a greater value in wages, can any point be more clearly established than that profits must fall with a rise of wages?

The farmer, then, although he pays no part of his landlord's rent, that being always regulated by the price of produce, and invariably falling on the consumers, has however a very decided interest in keeping rent low, or rather in keeping the natural price of produce low. As a consumer of raw produce, and of those things into which raw produce enters as a component part, he will, in common with all other consumers, be interested in keeping the price low. But he is most materially concerned with the high price of corn as it affects wages. With every rise in the price of corn, he will have to pay, out of an equal and unvarying sum of £720, an additional sum for wages to the ten men whom he is supposed constantly to employ. We have seen, in treating on wages, that they invariably rise with the rise in the price of raw produce. On a basis assumed for the purpose of calculation, page 58, it will be seen that if when wheat is at £4 per quarter, wages should be £24 per annum,

	£	s.	d.			£	s.	d.
When wheat is at	4	4	8	wages would be		24	14	0
	4	10	0			25	10	0
	4	16	0			26	8	0
	5	2	10			27	8	6

Now, of the unvarying fund of £720 to be distributed between laborers and farmers,

	£	s.	d.		£	s.	d.		£	s.	d.
When the price of wheat is at	4	0	0	the laborers will receive	240	0	0	the farmer will receive	480	0	0
	4	4	8		247	0	0		473	0	0
	4	10	0		255	0	0		465	0	0
	4	16	0		264	0	0		456	0	0
	5	2	10		274	5	0		445	15	3

Price per qr.			Rent.	Profit.	Wages.	Total.
£	s.	d.	In Wheat.	In Wheat.	In Wheat.	
4	0	0	None.	120 qrs.	60 qrs.	
4	4	8	10 qrs.	111.7	58.3	
4	10	0	20	103.4	56.6	180
4	16	0	30	95	55	
5	2	10	40	86.7	53.3	

and, under the same circumstances, money rent, wages, and profit would be as follows:

Price per qr.			Rent.			Profit.			Wages.			Total.		
£	s.	d.	£	s.	d.	£	s.	d.	£	s.	d.	£	s.	d.
4	0	0		None.		480	0	0	240	0	0	720	0	0
4	4	8	42	7	6	473	0	0	247	0	0	762	7	6
4	10	0	90	0	0	465	0	0	255	0	0	810	0	0
4	16	0	144	0	0	456	0	0	264	0	0	864	0	0
5	2	10	205	13	4	445	15	0	274	5	0	925	13	4

And supposing that the original capital of the farmer was £3000, the profits of his stock being in the first instance £480, would be at the rate of 16 percent. When his profits fell to £473, they would be at the rate of 15.7 percent.

£465	15.5
£456	15.2
£445	14.8

But the *rate* of profits will fall still more, because the capital of the farmer, it must be recollected, consists in a great measure of raw produce, such as his corn and hay-ricks, his unthreshed wheat and barley, his horses and cows, which would all rise in price in consequence of the rise of produce. His absolute profits would fall from £480 to £445 15s.; but if, from the cause which I have just stated, his capital should rise from £3000 to £3200, the rate of his profits would, when corn was at £5 2s. 10d, be under 14 percent.

If a manufacturer had also employed £3000 in his business, he would be obliged, in consequence of the rise of wages, to increase his capital, in order to be enabled to carry on the same business. If his commodities sold before for £720 they would continue to sell at the same price; but the wages of labor, which were before £240, would rise, when corn was at £5 2s. 10d. to £274 5s. In the first case he would have a balance of £480 as profit on £3000, in the second he would have a profit only of £445 15s., on an increased capital, and therefore his profits would conform to the altered rate of those of the farmer.

There are few commodities which are not more or less affected in their price by the rise of raw produce, because some raw material from the land enters into the composition of most commodities. Cotton goods, linen, and cloth will all rise in price with the rise of wheat; but they rise on account of the greater quantity of labor expended on the raw material from which they are made, and not because more was paid by the manufacturer to the laborers whom he employed on those commodities.

In all cases, commodities rise because more labor is expended on them, and not because the labor which is expended on them is at a higher value. Articles of jewelry, of iron, of plate, and of copper, would not rise, because none of the raw produce from the surface of the earth enters into their composition.

It may be said that I have taken it for granted that money wages would rise with a rise in the price of raw produce, but that this is by no means a necessary consequence, as the laborer may be contented with fewer enjoyments. It is true that the wages of labor may previously have been at a high level, and that they may bear some reduction. If so, the fall of profits will be checked; but it is impossible to conceive that the money price of wages should fall or remain stationary with a gradually increasing price of necessaries; and therefore it may be taken for granted that, under ordinary circumstances, no permanent rise takes place in the price of necessaries without occasioning, or having been preceded by, a rise in wages.

The effects produced on profits would have been the same, or nearly the same, if there had been any rise in the price of those other necessaries, besides food, on which the wages of labor are expended. The necessity which the laborer would be under of paying an increased price for such necessaries would oblige him to demand more wages; and whatever increases wages, necessarily reduces profits. But suppose the price of silks, velvets, furniture, and any other commodities, not required by the laborer, to rise in consequence of more labor being expended on them, would not that affect profits? Certainly not: for nothing can affect profits but a rise in wages; silks and velvets are not consumed by the laborer, and therefore cannot raise wages.

It is to be understood that I am speaking of profits generally. I have already remarked that the market price of a commodity may exceed its natural or necessary price, as it may be produced in less abundance than the new demand for it requires. This, however, is but a temporary effect. The high profits on capital employed in producing that commodity will naturally attract capital to that trade; and as soon as the requisite funds are supplied, and the quantity of the commodity is duly increased, its price will fall, and the profits of the trade will conform to the general level. A fall in the general rate of profits is by no means incompatible with a partial rise of profits in particular employments. It is through the inequality of profits that capital is moved from one employment to another. Whilst, then, general profits are falling, and gradually settling at a lower level in consequence of the rise of wages, and the increasing difficulty of supplying the increasing population with necessaries, the profits of the farmer may, for an interval of some little duration, be above the former level. An extraordinary stimulus may be also given for a certain time to a particular branch of foreign and colonial trade; but the admission of this fact by no means invalidates the theory, that profits depend on high or low wages, wages on the price of necessaries, and the price of necessaries chiefly on the price of food, because all other requisites may be increased almost without limit.

It should be recollected that prices always vary in the market, and in the first instance, through the comparative state of demand and supply. Although cloth could be furnished at 40s. per yard, and give the usual profits of stock, it may rise to 60s. or 80s. from a general change of fashion, or from any other cause which should suddenly and unexpectedly increase the demand or diminish the supply of it. The makers of cloth will for a time have unusual profits, but capital will naturally flow to that manufacture, till the supply and demand are again at their fair level, when the price of cloth will again sink to 40s., its natural or necessary price. In the same manner, with every increased demand for corn, it may rise so high as to afford more than the general profits to the farmer. If there be plenty of fertile land, the price of corn will again fall to its former standard, after the requisite quantity of capital has been employed in producing it, and profits will be as before; but if there be not plenty of fertile land, if, to produce this additional quantity, more than the usual quantity of capital and labor be required, corn will not fall to its former level. Its natural price will be raised, and the farmer, instead of obtaining permanently larger profits, will find himself obliged to be satisfied with the diminished rate which is the inevitable consequence of the rise of wages, produced by the rise of necessaries.

The natural tendency of profits then is to fall; for, in the progress of society and wealth, the additional quantity of food required is obtained by the sacrifice of more and more labor. This tendency, this gravitation as it were of profits, is happily checked at repeated intervals by the improvements in machinery connected with the production of necessaries, as well as by discoveries in the science of agriculture, which enable us to relinquish a portion of labor before required, and therefore to lower the price of the prime necessary of the laborer. The rise in the price of necessaries and in the wages of labor is, however, limited; for as soon as wages should be equal (as in the case formerly stated) to £720, the whole receipts of the farmer, there must be an end of accumulation; for no capital can then yield any profit whatever, and no additional labor can be demanded, and consequently population will have reached its highest point. Long, indeed, before this period, the very low rate of profits will have arrested all accumulation, and almost the whole produce of the country, after paying the laborers, will be the property of the owners of land and the receivers of tithes and taxes.

Thus, taking the former very imperfect basis as the grounds of my calculation, it would appear that when corn was at £20 per quarter, the whole net income of the country would belong to the landlords, for then the same quantity of labor that was originally necessary to produce 180 quarters would be necessary to produce 36; since £20:£4::180:36. The farmer, then, who produced 180 quarters (if any such there were, for the old and new capital employed on the land would be so blended that it could in no way be distinguished); would sell the

	180 qrs.	at £20 per qr. or	3600
the value of	144 qrs.	{ to landlord for rent, being the difference } { between 36 and 180 qrs. }	2880
	36 qrs.		720

the value of 36 qrs. to laborers, ten in number	720

leaving nothing whatever for profit.

I have supposed that at this price of £20 the laborers would

continue to consume three quarters each per annum, or	£60
And that on the other commodities they would expend	12
	72 for each laborer.

And therefore ten laborers would cost £720 per annum.

In all these calculations I have been desirous only to elucidate the principle, and it is scarcely necessary to observe that my whole basis is assumed at random, and merely for the purpose of exemplification. The results, though different in degree, would have been the same in principle, however accurately I might have set out in stating the difference in the number of laborers necessary to obtain the successive quantities of corn required by an increasing population, the quantity consumed by the laborer's family, etc., etc. My object has been to simplify the subject, and I have therefore made no allowance for the increasing price of the other necessaries, besides food, of the laborer; an increase which would be the consequence of the increased value of the raw materials from which they are made, and which would of course further increase wages and lower profits.

I have already said that long before this state of prices was become permanent there would be no motive for accumulation; for no one accumulates but with a view to make his accumulation productive, and it is only when so employed that it operates on profits. Without a motive there could be no accumulation, and consequently such a state of prices never could take place. The farmer and manufacturer can no more live without profit than the laborer without wages. Their motive for accumulation will diminish with every diminution of profit, and will cease altogether when their profits are so low as not to afford them an adequate compensation for their trouble, and the risk which they must necessarily encounter in employing their capital productively.

I must again observe that the rate of profits would fall much more rapidly than I have estimated in my calculation; for the value of the produce being what I have stated it under the circumstances supposed, the value of the farmer's stock would be greatly increased from its necessarily consisting of many of the commodities which had risen in value. Before corn could rise from £4 to £12, his capital would probably be doubled in exchangeable value, and be worth £6000 instead of £3000. If then his profit were £180, or 6 percent, on his original capital, profits would not at that time be really at a higher *rate* than 3 percent; for £6000 at 3 percent, gives £180; and on those terms only could a new farmer with £6000 money in his pocket enter into the farming business.

Many trades would derive some advantage, more or less, from the same source. The brewer, the distiller, the clothier, the linen manufacturer, would be partly compensated for the diminution of their profits by the rise in the value of their stock of raw and finished materials; but a manufacturer of hardware, of jewelry, and of many other commodities, as well as those whose capitals uniformly consisted of money, would be subject to the whole fall in the rate of profits, without any compensation whatever.

We should also expect that, however the rate of the profits of stock might diminish in consequence of the accumulation of capital on the land, and the rise of wages, yet that the aggregate amount of profits would increase. Thus, supposing that, with repeated accumulations of £100,000, the rate of profit should fall from 20 to 19, to 18, to 17 percent, a constantly diminishing rate, we should expect that the whole amount of profits received by those successive owners of capital would be always progressive; that it would be greater when the capital was £200,000 than when £100,000; still greater when £300,000; and so on, increasing, though at a diminishing rate, with every increase of capital. This progression, however, is only true for a certain time; thus, 19 percent, on £200,000 is more than 20 on £100,000; again, 18 percent, on £300,000 is more than 19 percent, on £200,000; but after capital has accumulated to a large amount, and profits have fallen, the further accumulation diminishes the aggregate of profits. Thus, suppose the accumulation should be £1,000,000, and the profits 7 percent, the whole amount of profits will be £70,000; now if an addition of £100,000 capital be made to the million, and profits should fall to 6 percent, £66,000 or a diminution of £4000 will be received by the owners of stock, although the whole amount of stock will be increased from £1,000,000 to £1,100,000.

There can, however, be no accumulation of capital so long as stock yields any profit at all, without its yielding not only an increase of produce, but an increase of value. By employing £100,000 additional capital, no part of the former capital will be rendered less productive. The produce of the land and labor of the country must increase, and its value will be raised, not only by the value of the addition which is made to the former quantity of productions, but by the new value which is given to the whole produce of the land, by the increased difficulty of producing the last portion of it. When the accumulation of capital, however, becomes very great, notwithstanding this increased value, it will be so distributed that a less value than before will be appropriated to profits, while that which is devoted to rent and wages will be increased. Thus with successive additions of £100,000 to capital, with a fall in the rate of profits, from 20 to 19, to 18, to 17 percent, etc., the productions annually obtained will increase in quantity, and be of more than the whole additional value which the additional capital is calculated to produce. From £20,000 it will rise to more than £39,000, and then to more than £57,000, and when the capital employed is a million, as we before supposed, if £100,000 more be added to it, and the aggregate of profits is actually lower than before, more than £6000 will nevertheless be added to the revenue of the country, but it will be to the revenue of the landlords and laborers; they will obtain more than the additional produce, and will from their situation be enabled to encroach even on the former gains of the capitalist. Thus, suppose the price of corn to be £4 per quarter, and that therefore, as we before calculated, of every £720 remaining to the farmer after payment of his rent, £480 were retained by him, and £240 were paid to his laborers; when the price rose to £6 per quarter, he would be obliged to pay his laborers £300 and retain only £420 for profits: he would be obliged to pay them £300 to enable them to consume the same quantity of necessaries as before, and no more. Now if the capital employed were so large as to yield a hundred thousand times £720, or £72,000,000, the aggregate of profits would be £48,000,000 when wheat was at £4 per quarter; and if by employing a larger capital 105,000 times £720 were obtained when wheat was at £6, or £75,600,000, profits would actually fall from £48,000,000 to £44,100,000 or 105,000 times £420, and wages would rise from £24,000,000 to £31,500,000. Wages would rise because more laborers would be employed in proportion to capital; and each laborer would receive more money wages; but the condition of the laborer, as we have already shown, would be worse, in as much as he would be able to command a less quantity of the produce of the country. The only real gainers would be the landlords; they would receive higher rents, first, because produce would be of a higher value, and secondly, because they would have a greatly increased proportion of that produce.

Although a greater value is produced, a greater proportion of what remains of that value, after paying rent, is consumed by the producers, and it is this, and this alone, which regulates profits. Whilst the land yields abundantly, wages may temporarily rise, and the producers may consume more than their accustomed proportion; but the stimulus which will thus be given to population will speedily reduce the laborers to their usual consumption. But when poor lands are taken into cultivation, or when more capital and labor are expended on the old land, with a less return of produce, the effect must be permanent. A greater proportion of that part of the produce which remains to be divided, after paying rent, between the owners of stock and the laborers, will be apportioned to the latter. Each man may, and probably will, have a less absolute quantity; but as more laborers are employed in proportion to the whole produce retained by the farmer, the value of a greater proportion of the whole produce will be absorbed by wages, and consequently the value of a smaller proportion will be devoted to profits. This will necessarily be rendered permanent by the laws of nature, which have limited the productive powers of the land.

Thus we again arrive at the same conclusion which we have before attempted to establish:—that in all countries, and all times, profits depend on the quantity of labor requisite to provide necessaries for the laborers on that land or with that capital which yields no rent. The effects then of accumulation will be different in different countries, and will depend chiefly on the fertility of the land. However extensive a country may be where the land is of a poor quality, and where the importation of food is prohibited, the most moderate accumulations of capital will be attended with great reductions in the rate of profit and a rapid rise in rent; and on the contrary a small but fertile country, particularly if it freely permits the importation of food, may accumulate a large stock of capital without any great diminution in the rate of profits, or any great increase in the rent of land. In the Chapter on Wages we have endeavored to show that the money price of commodities would not be raised by a rise of wages, either on the supposition that gold, the standard of money, was the produce of this country, or that it was imported from abroad. But if it were otherwise, if the prices of commodities were permanently raised by high wages, the proposition would not be less true, which asserts that high wages invariably affect the employers of labor by depriving them of a portion of their real profits. Supposing the hatter, the hosier, and the shoemaker each paid £10 more wages in the manufacture of a particular quantity of their commodities, and that the price of hats, stockings, and shoes rose by a sum sufficient to repay the manufacturer the £10; their situation would be no better than if no such rise took place. If the hosier sold his stockings for £110 instead of £100, his profits would be precisely the same money amount as before; but as he would obtain in exchange for this equal sum, one-tenth less of hats, shoes, and every other commodity, and as he could with his former amount of savings employ fewer laborers at the increased wages, and purchase fewer raw materials at the increased prices, he would be in no better situation than if his money profits had been really diminished in amount and everything had remained at its former price. Thus, then, I have endeavored to show, first, that a rise of wages would not raise the price of commodities, but would invariably lower profits; and secondly, that if the prices of all commodities could be raised, still the effect on profits would be the same; and that, in fact, the value of the medium only in which prices and profits are estimated would be lowered.

CHAPTER VII

On Foreign Trade

No extension of foreign trade will immediately increase the amount of value in a country, although it will very powerfully contribute to increase the mass of commodities, and therefore the sum of enjoyments. As the value of all foreign goods is measured by the quantity of the produce of our land and labor which is given in exchange for them, we should have no greater value if, by the discovery of new markets, we obtained double the quantity of foreign goods in exchange for a given quantity of ours. If by the purchase of English goods to the amount of £1000 a merchant can obtain a quantity of foreign goods, which he can sell in the English market for £1200, he will obtain 20 percent, profit by such an employment of his capital; but neither his gains, nor the value of the commodities imported, will be increased or diminished by the greater or smaller quantity of foreign goods obtained. Whether, for example, he imports twenty-five or fifty pipes of wine, his interest can be no way affected if at one time the twenty-five pipes, and at another the fifty pipes, equally sell for £1200. In either case his profit will be limited to £200, or 20 percent, on his capital; and in either case the same value will be imported into England. If the fifty pipes sold for more than £1200, the profits of this individual merchant would exceed the general rate of profits, and capital would naturally flow into this advantageous trade, till the fall of the price of wine had brought everything to the former level.

It has indeed been contended that the great profits which are sometimes made by particular merchants in foreign trade will elevate the general rate of profits in the country, and that the abstraction of capital from other employments, to partake of the new and beneficial foreign commerce, will raise prices generally, and thereby increase profits. It has been said, by high authority, that less capital being necessarily devoted to the growth of corn, to the manufacture of cloth, hats, shoes, etc., while the demand continues the same, the price of these commodities will be so increased, that this farmer, hatter, clothier, and shoemaker will have an increase of profits as well as the foreign merchant.[18]

They who hold this argument agree with me that the profits of different employments have a tendency to conform to one another; to advance and recede together. Our variance consists in this: They contend that the equality of profits will be brought about by the general rise of profits; and I am of opinion that the profits of the favored trade will speedily subside to the general level.

For, first, I deny that less capital will necessarily be devoted to the growth of corn, to the manufacture of cloth, hats, shoes, etc., unless the demand for these commodities be diminished; and if so, their price will not rise. In the purchase of foreign commodities, either the same, a larger, or a less portion of the produce of the land and labor of England will be employed. If the same portion be so employed, then will the same demand exist for cloth, shoes, corn, and hats as before, and the same portion of capital will be devoted to their production. If, in consequence of the price of foreign commodities being cheaper, a less portion of the annual produce of the land and labor of England is employed in the purchase of foreign commodities, more will remain for the purchase of other things. If there be a greater demand for hats, shoes, corn, etc., than before, which there may be, the consumers of foreign commodities having an additional portion of their revenue disposable, the capital is also disposable with which the greater value of foreign commodities was before purchased; so that with the increased demand for corn, shoes, etc., there exists also the means of procuring an increased supply, and therefore neither prices nor profits can permanently rise. If more of the produce of the land and labor of England be employed in the purchase of foreign commodities, less can be employed in the purchase of other things, and therefore fewer hats, shoes, etc., will be required. At the same time that capital is liberated from the production of shoes, hats, etc., more must be employed in manufacturing those commodities with which foreign commodities are purchased; and, consequently, in all cases the demand for foreign and home commodities together, as far as regards value, is limited by the revenue and capital of the country. If one increases the other must diminish. If the quantity of wine imported in exchange for the same quantity of English commodities be doubled, the people of England can either consume double the quantity of wine that they did before, or the same quantity of wine and a greater quantity of English commodities. If my revenue had been £1000 with which I purchased annually one pipe of wine for £100, and a certain quantity of English commodities for £900; when wine fell to £50 per pipe, I might lay out the £50 saved, either in the purchase of an additional pipe of wine or in the purchase of more English commodities. If I bought more wine, and every wine-drinker did the same, the foreign trade would not be in the least disturbed; the same quantity of English commodities would be exported in exchange for wine, and we should receive double the quantity, though not double the value of wine. But if I, and others, contented ourselves with the same quantity of wine as before, fewer English commodities would be exported, and the wine-drinkers might either consume the commodities which were before exported, or any others for which they had an inclination. The capital required for their production would be supplied by the capital liberated from the foreign trade.

There are two ways in which capital may be accumulated; it may be saved either in consequence of increased revenue or of diminished consumption. If my profits are raised from £1000 to £1200, while my expenditure continues the same, I accumulate annually £200 more than I did before. If I save £200 out of my expenditure, while my profits continue the same, the same effect will be produced; £200 per annum will be added to my capital. The merchant who imported wine after profits had been raised from 20 percent, to 40 percent, instead of purchasing his English goods for £1000, must purchase them for £857 2s. 10d., still selling the wine which he imports in return for those goods for £1200; or, if he continued to purchase his English goods for £1000, must raise the price of his wine to £1400; he would thus obtain 40 instead of 20 percent, profit on his capital; but if, in consequence of the cheapness of all the commodities on which his revenue was expended, he and all other consumers could save the value of £200 out of every £1000 they before expended, they would more effectually add to the real wealth of the country; in one case, the savings would be made in consequence of an increase of revenue, in the other, in consequence of diminished expenditure.

If, by the introduction of machinery, the generality of the commodities on which revenue was expended fell 20 percent in value, I should be enabled to save as effectually as if my revenue had been raised 20 percent; but in one case the rate of profits is stationary, in the other it is raised 20 percent.—If, by the introduction of cheap foreign goods, I can save 20 percent, from my expenditure, the effect will be precisely the same as if machinery had lowered the expense of their production, but profits would not be raised.

It is not, therefore, in consequence of the extension of the market that the rate of profit is raised, although such extension may be equally efficacious in increasing the mass of commodities, and may thereby enable us to augment the funds destined for the maintenance of labor, and the materials on which labor may be employed. It is quite as important to the happiness of mankind that our enjoyments should be increased by the better distribution of labor, by each country producing those commodities for which by its situation, its climate, and its other natural or artificial advantages it is adapted, and by their exchanging them for the commodities of other countries, as that they should be augmented by a rise in the rate of profits.

It has been my endeavor to show throughout this work that the rate of profits can never be increased but by a fall in wages, and that there can be no permanent fall of wages but in consequence of a fall of the necessaries on which wages are expended. If, therefore, by the extension of foreign trade, or by improvements in machinery, the food and necessaries of the laborer can be brought to market, at a reduced price, profits will rise. If, instead of growing our own corn, or manufacturing the clothing and other necessaries of the laborer, we discover a new market from which we can supply ourselves with these commodities at a cheaper price, wages will fall and profits rise; but if the commodities obtained at a cheaper rate, by the extension of foreign commerce, or by the improvement of machinery, be exclusively the commodities consumed by the rich, no alteration will take place in the rate of profits. The rate of wages would not be affected, although wine, velvets, silks, and other expensive commodities should fall 50 percent, and consequently profits would continue unaltered.

Foreign trade, then, though highly beneficial to a country, as it increases the amount and variety of the objects on which revenue may be expended, and affords, by the abundance and cheapness of commodities, incentives to saving, and to the accumulation of capital, has no tendency to raise the profits of stock unless the commodities imported be of that description of which the wages of labor are expended.

The remarks which have been made respecting foreign trade apply equally to home trade. The rate of profits is never increased by a better distribution of labor, by the invention of machinery, by the establishment of roads and canals, or by any means of abridging labor either in the manufacture or in the conveyance of goods. These are causes which operate on price, and never fail to be highly beneficial to consumers; since they enable them, with the same labor, or with the value of the produce of the same labor, to obtain in exchange a greater quantity of the commodity to which the improvement is applied; but they have no effect whatever on profit. On the other hand, every diminution in the wages of labor raises profits, but produces no effect on the price of commodities. One is advantageous to all classes, for all classes are consumers; the other is beneficial only to producers; they gain more, but everything remains at its former price. In the first case they get the same as before; but everything on which their gains are expended is diminished in exchangeable value.

The same rule which regulates the relative value of commodities in one country does not regulate the relative value of the commodities exchanged between two or more countries.

Under a system of perfectly free commerce, each country naturally devotes its capital and labor to such employments as are most beneficial to each. This pursuit of individual advantage is admirably connected with the universal good of the whole. By stimulating industry by rewarding ingenuity and by using most efficaciously the peculiar powers bestowed by nature, it distributes labor most effectively and most economically: while, by increasing the general mass of productions, it diffuses general benefit, and binds together, by one common tie of interest and intercourse, the universal society of nations throughout the civilized world. It is this principle which determines that wine shall be made in France and Portugal, that corn shall be grown in America and Poland, and that hardware and other goods shall be manufactured in England.

In one and the same country, profits are, generally speaking, always on the same level; or differ only as the employment of capital may be more or less secure and agreeable. It is not so between different countries. If the profits of capital employed in Yorkshire should exceed those of capital employed in London, capital would speedily move from London to Yorkshire, and an equality of profits would be effected; but if in consequence of the diminished rate of production in the lands of England from the increase of capital and population wages should rise and profits fall, it would not follow that capital and population would necessarily move from England to Holland, or Spain, or Russia, where profits might be higher.

If Portugal had no commercial connection with other countries, instead of employing a great part of her capital and industry in the production of wines, with which she purchases for her own use the cloth and hardware of other countries, she would be obliged to devote a part of that capital to the manufacture of those commodities, which she would thus obtain probably inferior in quality as well as quantity.

The quantity of wine which she shall give in exchange for the cloth of England is not determined by the respective quantities of labor devoted to the production of each, as it would be if both commodities were manufactured in England, or both in Portugal.

England may be so circumstanced that to produce the cloth may require the labor of 100 men for one year; and if she attempted to make the wine, it might require the labor of 120 men for the same time. England would therefore find it her interest to import wine, and to purchase it by the exportation of cloth.

To produce the wine in Portugal might require only the labor of 80 men for one year, and to produce the cloth in the same country might require the labor of 90 men for the same time. It would therefore be advantageous for her to export wine in exchange for cloth. This exchange might even take place notwithstanding that the commodity imported by Portugal could be produced there with less labor than in England. Though she could make the cloth with the labor of 90 men, she would import it from a country where it required the labor of 100 men to produce it, because it would be advantageous to her rather to employ her capital in the production of wine, for which she would obtain more cloth from England, than she could produce by diverting a portion of her capital from the cultivation of vines to the manufacture of cloth.

Thus England would give the produce of the labor of 100 men for the produce of the labor of 80. Such an exchange could not take place between the individuals of the same country. The labor of 100 Englishmen cannot be given for that of 80 Englishmen, but the produce of the labor of 100 Englishmen may be given for the produce of the labor of 80 Portuguese, 60 Russians, or 120 East Indians. The difference in this respect, between a single country and many, is easily accounted for, by considering the difficulty with which capital moves from one country to another, to seek a more profitable employment, and the activity with which it invariably passes from one province to another in the same country.[19]

It would undoubtedly be advantageous to the capitalists of England, and to the consumers in both countries, that under such circumstances the wine and the cloth should both be made in Portugal, and therefore that the capital and labor of England employed in making cloth should be removed to Portugal for that purpose. In that case, the relative value of these commodities would be regulated by the same principle as if one were the produce of Yorkshire and the other of London: and in every other case, if capital freely flowed towards those countries where it could be most profitably employed, there could be no difference in the rate of profit, and no other difference in the real or labor price of commodities than the additional quantity of labor required to convey them to the various markets where they were to be sold.

Experience, however, shows that the fancied or real insecurity of capital, when not under the immediate control of its owner, together with the natural disinclination which every man has to quit the country of his birth and connections, and entrust himself, with all his habits fixed, to a strange government and new laws, check the emigration of capital. These feelings, which I should be sorry to see weakened, induce most men of property to be satisfied with a low rate of profits in their own country, rather than seek a more advantageous employment for their wealth in foreign nations.

Gold and silver having been chosen for the general medium of circulation, they are, by the competition of commerce, distributed in such proportions amongst the different countries of the world as to accommodate themselves to the natural traffic which would take place if no such metals existed, and the trade between countries were purely a trade of barter.

Thus, cloth cannot be imported into Portugal unless it sell there for more gold than it cost in the country from which it was imported; and wine cannot be imported into England unless it will sell for more there than it cost in Portugal. If the trade were purely a trade of barter, it could only continue whilst England could make cloth so cheap as to obtain a greater quantity of wine with a given quantity of labor by manufacturing cloth than by growing vines; and also whilst the industry of Portugal were attended by the reverse effects. Now suppose England to discover a process for making wine, so that it should become her interest rather to grow it than import it; she would naturally divert a portion of her capital from the foreign trade to the home trade; she would cease to manufacture cloth for exportation, and would grow wine for herself. The money price of these commodities would be regulated accordingly; wine would fall here while cloth continued at its former price, and in Portugal no alteration would take place in the price of either commodity. Cloth would continue for some time to be exported from this country, because its price would continue to be higher in Portugal than here; but money instead of wine would be given in exchange for it, till the accumulation of money here, and its diminution abroad, should so operate on the relative value of cloth in the two countries that it would cease to be profitable to export it. If the improvement in making wine were of a very important description, it might become profitable for the two countries to exchange employments; for England to make all the wine, and Portugal all the cloth consumed by them; but this could be effected only by a new distribution of the precious metals, which should raise the price of cloth in England and lower it in Portugal. The relative price of wine would fall in England in consequence of the real advantage from the improvement of its manufacture; that is to say, its natural price would fall; the relative price of cloth would rise there from the accumulation of money.

Thus, suppose before the improvement in making wine in England the price of wine here were £50 per pipe, and the price of a certain quantity of cloth were £45, whilst in Portugal the price of the same quantity of wine was £45, and that of the same quantity of cloth £50; wine would be exported from Portugal with a profit of £5, and cloth from England with a profit of the same amount.

Suppose that, after the improvement, wine falls to £45 in England, the cloth continuing at the same price. Every transaction in commerce is an independent transaction. Whilst a merchant can buy cloth in England for £45, and sell it with the usual profit in Portugal, he will continue to export it from England. His business is simply to purchase English cloth, and to pay for it by a bill of exchange, which he purchases with Portuguese money. It is to him of no importance what becomes of this money: he has discharged his debt by the remittance of the bill. His transaction is undoubtedly regulated by the terms on which he can obtain this bill, but they are known to him at the time; and the causes which may influence the market price of bills, or the rate of exchange, is no consideration of his.

If the markets be favorable for the exportation of wine from Portugal to England, the exporter of the wine will be a seller of a bill, which will be purchased either by the importer of the cloth, or by the person who sold him his bill; and thus, without the necessity of money passing from either country, the exporters in each country will be paid for their goods. Without having any direct transaction with each other, the money paid in Portugal by the importer of cloth will be paid to the Portuguese exporter of wine; and in England by the negotiation of the same bill the exporter of the cloth will be authorized to receive its value from the importer of wine.

But if the prices of wine were such that no wine could be exported to England, the importer of cloth would equally purchase a bill; but the price of that bill would be higher, from the knowledge which the seller of it would possess that there was no counter bill in the market by which he could ultimately settle the transactions between the two countries; he might know that the gold or silver money which he received in exchange for his bill must be actually exported to his correspondent in England, to enable him to pay the demand which he had authorized to be made upon him, and he might therefore charge in the price of his bill all the expenses to be incurred, together with his fair and usual profit.

If then this premium for a bill on England should be equal to the profit on importing cloth, the importation would of course cease; but if the premium on the bill were only

2 percent, if to be enabled to pay a debt in England of £100, £102 should be paid in Portugal, whilst cloth which cost £45 would sell for £50, cloth would be imported, bills would be bought, and money would be exported, till the diminution of money in Portugal; and its accumulation in England, had produced such a state of prices as would make it no longer profitable to continue these transactions.

But the diminution of money in one country, and its increase in another, do not operate on the price of one commodity only, but on the prices of all, and therefore the price of wine and cloth will be both raised in England and both lowered in Portugal. The price of cloth, from being £45 in one country and £50 in the other, would probably fall to £49 or £48 in Portugal, and rise to £46 or £47 in England, and not afford a sufficient profit after paying a premium for a bill to induce any merchant to import that commodity.

It is thus that the money of each country is apportioned to it in such quantities only as may be necessary to regulate a profitable trade of barter. England exported cloth in exchange for wine because, by so doing, her industry was rendered more productive to her; she had more cloth and wine than if she had manufactured both for herself; and Portugal imported cloth and exported wine because the industry of Portugal could be more beneficially employed for both countries in producing wine. Let there be more difficulty in England in producing cloth, or in Portugal in producing wine, or let there be more facility in England in producing wine, or in Portugal in producing cloth, and the trade must immediately cease.

No change whatever takes place in the circumstances of Portugal; but England finds that she can employ her labor more productively in the manufacture of wine, and instantly the trade of barter between the two countries changes. Not only is the exportation of wine from Portugal stopped, but a new distribution of the precious metals takes place, and her importation of cloth is also prevented.

Both countries would probably find it their interest to make their own wine and their own cloth; but this singular result would take place: in England, though wine would be cheaper, cloth would be elevated in price, more would be paid for it by the consumer; while in Portugal the consumers, both of cloth and of wine, would be able to purchase those commodities cheaper. In the country where the improvement was made prices would be enhanced; in that where no change had taken place, but where they had been deprived of a profitable branch of foreign trade, prices would fall.

This, however, is only a seeming advantage to Portugal, for the quantity of cloth and wine together produced in that country would be diminished, while the quantity produced in England would be increased. Money would in some degree have changed its value in the two countries; it would be lowered in England and raised in Portugal. Estimated in money, the whole revenue of Portugal would be diminished; estimated in the same medium the whole revenue of England would be increased.

Thus, then, it appears that the improvement of a manufacture in any country tends to alter the distribution of the precious metals amongst the nations of the world: it tends to increase the quantity of commodities, at the same time that it raises general prices in the country where the improvement takes place.

To simplify the question, I have been supposing the trade between two countries to be confined to two commodities—to wine and cloth; but it is well known that many and various articles enter into the list of exports and imports. By the abstraction of money from one country, and the accumulation of it in another, all commodities are affected in price, and consequently encouragement is given to the exportation of many more commodities besides money, which will therefore prevent so great an effect from taking place on the value of money in the two countries as might otherwise be expected.

Beside the improvements in arts and machinery, there are various other causes which are constantly operating on the natural course of trade, and which interfere with the equilibrium and the relative value of money. Bounties on exportation or importation, new taxes on commodities, sometimes by their direct, and at other times by their indirect operation, disturb the natural trade of barter, and produce a consequent necessity of importing or exporting money, in order that prices may be accommodated to the natural course of commerce; and this effect is produced not only in the country where the disturbing cause takes place, but, in a greater or less degree, in every country of the commercial world.

This will in some measure account for the different value of money in different countries; it will explain to us why the prices of home commodities, and those of great bulk, though of comparatively small value, are, independently of other causes, higher in those countries where manufactures flourish. Of two countries having precisely the same population, and the same quantity of land of equal fertility in cultivation, with the same knowledge too of agriculture, the prices of raw produce will be highest in that where the greater skill and the better machinery is used in the manufacture of exportable commodities. The rate of profits will probably differ but little; for wages, or the real reward of the laborer, may be the same in both; but those wages, as well as raw produce, will be rated higher in money in that country, into which, from the advantages attending their skill and machinery, an abundance of money is imported in exchange for their goods.

Of these two countries, if one had the advantage in the manufacture of goods of one quality, and the other in the manufacture of goods of another quality, there would be no decided influx of the precious metals into either; but if the advantage very heavily preponderated in favor of either, that effect would be inevitable.

In the former part of this work, we have assumed, for the purpose of argument, that money always continued of the same value; we are now endeavoring to show that, besides the ordinary variations in the value of money, and those which are common to the whole commercial world, there are also partial variations to which money is subject in particular countries; and to the fact that the value of money is never the same in any two countries, depending as it does on relative taxation, on manufacturing skill, on the advantages of climate, natural productions, and many other causes.

Although, however, money is subject to such perpetual variations, and consequently the prices of the commodities which are common to most countries are also subject to considerable difference, yet no effect will be produced on the rate of profits, either from the influx or efflux of money. Capital will not be increased because the circulating medium is augmented. If the rent paid by the farmer to his landlord, and the wages to his laborers, be 20 percent, higher in one country than another, and if at the same time the nominal value of the farmer's capital be 20 percent, more, he will receive precisely the same rate of profits, although he should sell his raw produce 20 percent, higher.

Profits, it cannot be too often repeated, depend on wages; not on nominal, but real wages; not on the number of pounds that may be annually paid to the laborer, but on the number of days' work necessary to obtain those pounds. Wages may therefore be precisely the same in two countries; they may bear, too, the same proportion to rent, and to the whole produce obtained from the land, although in one of those countries the laborer should receive ten shillings per week and in the other twelve.

In the early states of society, when manufactures have made little progress, and the produce of all countries is nearly similar, consisting of the bulky and most useful commodities, the value of money in different countries will be chiefly regulated by their distance from the mines which supply the precious metals; but as the arts and improvements of society advance, and different nations excel in particular manufactures, although distance will still enter into the calculation, the value of the precious metals will be chiefly regulated by the superiority of those manufactures.

Suppose all nations to produce corn, cattle, and coarse clothing only, and that it was by the exportation of such commodities that gold could be obtained from the countries which produced them, or from those who held them in subjection; gold would naturally be of greater exchangeable value in Poland than in England, on account of the greater expense of sending such a bulky commodity as corn the more distant voyage, and also the greater expense attending the conveying of gold to Poland. This difference in the value of gold, or, which is the same thing, this difference in the price of corn in the two countries, would exist, although the facilities of producing corn in England should far exceed those of Poland, from the greater fertility of the land and the superiority in the skill and implements of the laborer.

If, however, Poland should be the first to improve her manufactures, if she should succeed in making a commodity which was generally desirable, including great value in little bulk, or if she should be exclusively blessed with some natural production, generally desirable, and not possessed by other countries, she would obtain an additional quantity of gold in exchange for this commodity, which would operate on the price of her corn, cattle, and coarse clothing. The disadvantage of distance would probably be more than compensated by the advantage of having an exportable commodity of great value, and money would be permanently of lower value in Poland than in England. If, on the contrary, the advantage of skill and machinery were possessed by England, another reason would be added to that which before existed why gold should be less valuable in England than in Poland, and why corn, cattle, and clothing should be at a higher price in the former country.

These I believe to be the only two causes which regulate the comparative value of money in the different countries of the world; for although taxation occasions a disturbance of the equilibrium of money, it does so by depriving the country in which it is imposed of some of the advantages attending skill, industry, and climate.

It has been my endeavor carefully to distinguish between a low value of money and a high value of corn, or any other commodity with which money may be compared. These have been generally considered as meaning the same thing; but it is evident that when corn rises from five to ten shillings a bushel, it may be owing either to a fall in the value of money or to a rise in the value of corn. Thus we have seen that, from the necessity of having recourse successively to land of a worse and worse quality, in order to feed an increasing population, corn must rise in relative value to other things. If therefore money continue permanently of the same value, corn will exchange for more of such money, that is to say, it will rise in price. The same rise in the price of corn will be produced by such improvement of machinery in manufactures as shall enable us to manufacture commodities with peculiar advantages: for the influx of money will be the consequence; it will fall in value, and therefore exchange for less corn. But the effects resulting from a high price of corn when produced by the rise in the value of corn, and when caused by a fall in the value of money, are totally different. In both cases the money price of wages will rise, but if it be in consequence of the fall in the value of money, not only wages and corn, but all other commodities will rise. If the manufacturer has more to pay for wages he will receive more for his manufactured goods, and the rate of profits will remain unaffected. But when the rise in the price of corn is the effect of the difficulty of production, profits will fall; for the manufacturer will be obliged to pay more wages, and will not be enabled to remunerate himself by raising the price of his manufactured commodity.

Any improvement in the facility of working the mines, by which the precious metals may be produced with a less quantity of labor, will sink the value of money generally. It will then exchange for fewer commodities in all countries; but when any particular country excels in manufactures, so as to occasion an influx of money towards it, the value of money will be lower, and the prices of corn and labor will be relatively higher in that country than in any other.

This higher value of money will not be indicated by the exchange; bills may continue to be negotiated at par, although the prices of corn and labor should be 10, 20, or 30 percent higher in one country than another. Under the circumstances supposed, such a difference of prices is the natural order of things, and the exchange can only be at par when a sufficient quantity of money is introduced into the country excelling in manufactures, so as to raise the price of its corn and labor. If foreign countries should prohibit the exportation of money, and could successfully enforce obedience to such a law, they might indeed prevent the rise in the prices of the corn and labor of the manufacturing country; for such rise can only take place after the influx of the precious metals, supposing paper money not to be used; but they could not prevent the exchange from being very unfavorable to them. If England were the manufacturing country, and it were possible to prevent the importation of money, the exchange with France, Holland, and Spain might be 5, 10, or 20 percent, against those countries.

Whenever the current of money is forcibly stopped, and when money is prevented from settling at its just level, there are no limits to the possible variations of the exchange. The effects are similar to those which follow when a paper money, not exchangeable for specie at the will of the holder, is forced into circulation. Such a currency is necessarily confined to the country where it is issued: it cannot, when too abundant, diffuse itself generally amongst other countries. The level of circulation is destroyed, and the exchange will inevitably be unfavorable to the country where it is excessive in quantity: just so would be the effects of a metallic circulation if by forcible means, by laws which could not be evaded, money should be detained in a country, when the stream of trade gave it an impetus towards other countries.

When each country has precisely the quantity of money which it ought to have, money will not indeed be of the same value in each, for with respect to many commodities it may differ 5, 10, or even 20 percent, but the exchange will be at par. One hundred pounds in England, or the silver which is in £100, will purchase a bill of £100, or an equal quantity of silver in France, Spain, or Holland.

In speaking of the exchange and the comparative value of money in different countries, we must not in the least refer to the value of money estimated in commodities in either country. The exchange is never ascertained by estimating the comparative value of money in corn, cloth, or any commodity whatever, but by estimating the value of the currency of one country in the currency of another.

It may also be ascertained by comparing it with some standard common to both countries. If a bill on England for £100 will purchase the same quantity of goods in France or Spain that a bill on Hamburg for the same sum will do, the exchange between Hamburg and England is at par; but if a bill on England for £130 will purchase no more than a bill on Hamburg for £100, the exchange is 30 percent, against England.

In England £100 may purchase a bill, or the right of receiving £101 in Holland, £102 in France, and £105 in Spain. The exchange with England is, in that case, said to be 1 percent, against Holland, 2 percent, against France, and 5 percent against Spain. It indicates that the level of currency is higher than it should be in those countries, and the comparative value of their currencies, and that of England, would be immediately restored to par by extracting from theirs or by adding to that of England.

Those who maintain that our currency was depreciated during the last ten years, when the exchange varied from 20 to 30 percent, against this country, have never contended, as they have been accused of doing, that money could not be more valuable in one country than another as compared with various commodities; but they did contend that £130 could not be detained in England unless it was depreciated, when it was of no more value, estimated in the money of Hamburg or of Holland, than the bullion in £100.

By sending 130 good English pounds sterling to Hamburg, even at an expense of £5, I should be possessed there of £125; what then could make me consent to give £130 for a bill which would give me £100 in Hamburg, but that my pounds were not good pounds sterling?—they were deteriorated, were degraded in intrinsic value below the pounds sterling of Hamburg, and if actually sent there, at an expense of £5, would sell only for £100. With metallic pounds sterling, it is not denied that my £130 would procure me £125 in Hamburg, but with paper pounds sterling I can only obtain £100; and yet it was maintained that £130 in paper was of equal value with £130 in silver or gold.

Some indeed more reasonably maintained that £130 in paper was not of equal value with £130 in metallic money; but they said that it was the metallic money which had changed its value and not the paper money. They wished to confine the meaning of the word depreciation to an actual fall of value, and not to a comparative difference between the value of money and the standard by which by law it is regulated. One hundred pounds of English money was formerly of equal value with and could purchase £100 of Hamburg money: in any other country a bill of £100 on England, or on Hamburg, could purchase precisely the same quantity of commodities. To obtain the same things, I was lately obliged to give £130 English money, when Hamburg could obtain them for

£100 Hamburg money. If English money was of the same value then as before, Hamburg money must have risen in value. But where is the proof of this? How is it to be ascertained whether English money has fallen or Hamburg money has risen? there is no standard by which this can be determined. It is a plea which admits of no proof, and can neither be positively affirmed nor positively contradicted. The nations of the world must have been early convinced that there was no standard of value in nature to which they might unerringly refer, and therefore chose a medium which on the whole appeared to them less variable than any other commodity.

To this standard we must conform till the law is changed, and till some other commodity is discovered by the use of which we shall obtain a more perfect standard than that which we have established. While gold is exclusively the standard in this country money will be depreciated when a pound sterling is not of equal value with 5 dwts. and 3 grs. of standard gold, and that whether gold rises or falls in general value.

CHAPTER VIII

On Taxes

Taxes are a portion of the produce of the land and labor of a country placed at the disposal of the government; and are always ultimately paid either from the capital or from the revenue of the country.

We have already shown how the capital of a country is either fixed or circulating, according as it is of a more or of a less durable nature. It is difficult to define strictly where the distinction between circulating and fixed capital begins; for there are almost infinite degrees in the durability of capital. The food of a country is consumed and reproduced at least once in every year, the clothing of the laborer is probably not consumed and reproduced in less than two years; whilst his house and furniture are calculated to endure for a period of ten or twenty years.

When the annual productions of a country more than replace its annual consumption, it is said to increase its capital; when its annual consumption is not at least replaced by its annual production, it is said to diminish its capital. Capital may therefore be increased by an increased production, or by a diminished unproductive consumption.

If the consumption of the government when increased by the levy of additional taxes be met either by an increased production or by a diminished consumption on the part of the people, the taxes will fall upon revenue, and the national capital will remain unimpaired; but if there be no increased production or diminished unproductive consumption on the part of the people, the taxes will necessarily fall on capital, that is to say, they will impair the fund allotted to productive consumption.[20]

In proportion as the capital of a country is diminished, its productions will be necessarily diminished; and, therefore, if the same unproductive expenditure on the part of the people and of the government continue, with a constantly diminishing annual reproduction, the resources of the people and the state will fall away with increasing rapidity, and distress and ruin will follow.

Notwithstanding the immense expenditure of the English government during the last twenty years, there can be little doubt but that the increased production on the part of the people has more than compensated for it. The national capital has not merely been unimpaired, it has been greatly increased, and the annual revenue of the people, even after the payment of their taxes, is probably greater at the present time than at any former period of our history.

For the proof of this, we might refer to the increase of population—to the extension of agriculture—to the increase of shipping and manufactures—to the building of docks—to the opening of numerous canals, as well as to many other expensive undertakings; all denoting an increase both of capital and of annual production.

Still, however, it is certain that, but for taxation, this increase of capital would have been much greater. There are no taxes which have not a tendency to lessen the power to accumulate. All taxes must either fall on capital or revenue. If they encroach on capital, they must proportionally diminish that fund by whose extent the extent of the productive industry of the country must always be regulated; and if they fall on revenue, they must either lessen accumulation, or force the contributors to save the amount of the tax, by making a corresponding diminution of their former unproductive consumption of the necessaries and luxuries of life. Some taxes will produce these effects in a much greater degree than others; but the great evil of taxation is to be found, not so much in any selection of its objects, as in the general amount of its effects taken collectively.

Taxes are not necessarily taxes on capital because they are laid on capital; nor on income because they are laid on income. If from my income of £1000 per annum I am required to pay £100, it will really be a tax on my income should I be content with the expenditure of the remaining £900; but it will be a tax on capital if I continue to spend £1000.

The capital from which my income of £1000 is derived may be of the value of £10,000; a tax of one percent, on such capital would be £100; but my capital would be unaffected if, after paying this tax, I in like manner contented myself with the expenditure of £900.

The desire which every man has to keep his station in life, and to maintain his wealth at the height which it has once attained, occasions most taxes, whether laid on capital or on income, to be paid from income; and, therefore, as taxation proceeds, or as government increases its expenditure, the annual enjoyments of the people must be diminished, unless they are enabled proportionally to increase their capitals and income. It should be the policy of governments to encourage a disposition to do this in the people, and never to lay such taxes as will inevitably fall on capital; since, by so doing, they impair the funds the maintenance of labor, and thereby diminish the future production of the country.

In England this policy has been neglected in taxing the probates of wills, in the legacy duty, and in all taxes affecting the transference of property from the dead to the living. If a legacy of £1000 be subject to a tax of £100, the legatee considers his legacy as only £900 and feels no particular motive to save the £100 duty from his expenditure, and thus the capital of the country is diminished; but if he had really received £1000, and had been required to pay £100 as a tax on income, on wine, on horses, or on servants, he would probably have diminished, or rather not increased his expenditure by that sum, and the capital of the country would have been unimpaired.

"Taxes upon the transference of property from the dead to the living," says Adam Smith, "fall finally, as well as immediately, upon the persons to whom the property is transferred. Taxes on the sale of land fall altogether upon the seller. The seller is almost always under the necessity of selling, and must, therefore, take such a price as he can get. The buyer is scarce ever under the necessity of buying, and will, therefore, only give such a price as he likes. He considers what the land will cost him in tax and price together. The more he is obliged to pay in the way of tax, the less he will be disposed to give in the way of price. Such taxes, therefore, fall almost always upon a necessitous person, and must, therefore, be very cruel and oppressive," "Stamp duties, and duties upon the registration of bonds and contracts for borrowed money, fall altogether upon the borrower, and in fact are always paid by him. Duties of the same kind upon law proceedings fall upon the suitors. They reduce to both the capital value of the subject in dispute. The more it costs to acquire any property, the less must be the net value of it when acquired. All taxes upon the transference of property of every kind, so far as they diminish the capital value of that property, tend to diminish the funds destined for the maintenance of labor. They are all more or less unthrifty taxes that increase the revenue of the sovereign, which seldom maintains any but unproductive laborers, at the expense of the capital of the people, which maintains none but productive."

But this is not the only objection to taxes on the transference of property; they prevent the national capital from being distributed in the way most beneficial to the community. For the general prosperity there cannot be too much facility given to the conveyance and exchange of all kinds of property, as it is by such means that capital of every species is likely to find its way into the hands of those who will best employ it in increasing the productions of the country. "Why," asks M. Say, "does an individual wish to sell his land? It is because he has another employment in view in which his funds will be more productive. Why does another wish to purchase this same land? It is to employ a capital which brings him in too little, which was unemployed, or the use of which he thinks susceptible of improvement. This exchange will increase the general income, since it increases the income of these parties. But if the charges are so exorbitant as to prevent the exchange, they are an obstacle to this increase of the general income." Those taxes, however, are easily collected; and this by many may be thought to afford some compensation for their injurious effects.

CHAPTER IX

Taxes on Raw Produce

Having in a former part of this work established, I hope satisfactorily, the principle that the price of corn is regulated by the cost of its production on that land exclusively, or rather with that capital exclusively, which pays no rent, it will follow that whatever may increase the cost of production will increase the price; whatever may reduce it will lower the price. The necessity of cultivating poorer land, or of obtaining a less return with a given additional capital on land already in cultivation, will inevitably raise the exchangeable value of raw produce. The discovery of machinery, which will enable the cultivator to obtain his corn at a less cost of production, will necessarily lower its exchangeable value. Any tax which may be imposed on the cultivator, whether in the shape of land-tax, tithes, or a tax on the produce when obtained, will increase the cost of production, and will therefore raise the price of raw produce.

If the price of raw produce did not rise so as to compensate the cultivator for the tax, he would naturally quit a trade where his profits were reduced below the general level of profits; this would occasion a diminution of supply, until the unabated demand should have produced such a rise in the price of raw produce as to make the cultivation of it equally profitable with the investment of capital in any other trade.

A rise of price is the only means by which he could pay the tax, and continue to derive the usual and general profits from this employment of his capital. He could not deduct the tax from his rent, and oblige his landlord to pay it, for he pays no rent. He would not deduct it from his profits, for there is no reason why he should continue in an employment which yields small profits, when all other employments are yielding greater. There can then be no question but that he will have the power of raising the price of raw produce by a sum equal to the tax.

A tax on raw produce would not be paid by the landlord; it would not be paid by the farmer; but it would be paid, in an increased price, by the consumer.

Rent, it should be remembered, is the difference between the produce obtained by equal portions of labor and capital employed on land of the same or different qualities. It should be remembered, too, that the money rent of land, and the corn rent of land, do not vary in the same proportion.

In the case of a tax on raw produce, of a land-tax, or tithes, the corn rent of land will vary, while the money rent will remain as before.

If, as we have before supposed, the land in cultivation were of three qualities, and that with an equal amount of capital,

180	qrs. of corn were obtained from land No.	1
170	from	2
160	from	3

the rent of No. 1 would be 20 quarters, the difference between that of No. 3 and No. 1; and of No. 2, 10 quarters, the difference between that of No. 3 and No. 2; while No. 3 would pay no rent whatever.

Now, if the price of corn were £4 per quarter, the money rent of No. 1 would be £80, and that of No. 2, £40.

Suppose a tax of 8s. per quarter to be imposed on corn; then the price would rise to £4 8s.; and if the landlords obtained the same corn rent as before, the rent of No. 1 would be £88 and that of No. 2, £44. But they would not obtain the same corn rent; the tax would fall heavier on No. 1 than on No. 2, and on No. 2 than on No. 3, because it would be levied on a greater quantity of corn. It is the difficulty of production on No. 3 which regulates price; and corn rises to £4 8s., that the profits of the capital employed on No. 3 may be on a level with the general profits of stock.

The produce and tax on the three qualities of land will be as follows:

No. 1, yielding	180	qrs. at £4 8s. per qr.	£792
Deduct the value of	16.3	or 8s. per qr. on 180 qrs.	72
Net corn produce	163.7	Net money produce	£720
No. 2ᵗ yielding	170	qrs. at £4 8s. per qr.	£748
Deduct the value of	15.4	qrs. at £4 8s. or 8s. per qr. on 170 qrs.	68
Net corn produce,	154.6	Net money produce	£680
No. 3, yielding	160	qrs. at £4 8s.	£704
Deduct the value of	14.5	qrs at £4 8s. or 8s. per qr. on 160	64
Net corn produce	145.5	Net money produce	£640

The money rent of No. 1 would continue to be £80, or the difference between £640 and £720; and that of No. 2, £40, or the difference between £640 and £680, precisely the same as before; but the corn rent will be reduced from 20 quarters on No. 1, to 18.2 quarters, the difference between 145.5 and 163.7 quarters, and that on No. 2 from 10 to 9.12 quarters, the difference between 145.5 and 154.6 quarters.

A tax on corn, then, would fall on the consumers of corn, and would raise its value, as compared with all other commodities, in a degree proportioned to the tax. In proportion as raw produce entered into the composition of other commodities would their value also be raised, unless the tax were countervailed by other causes. They would in fact be indirectly taxed, and their value would rise in proportion to the tax.

A tax, however, on raw produce, and on the necessaries of the laborer, would have another effect—it would raise wages. From the effect of the principle of population on the increase of mankind, wages of the lowest kind never continue much above that rate which nature and habit demand for the support of the laborers. This class is never able to bear any considerable proportion of taxation; and, consequently, if they had to pay 8s. per quarter in addition for wheat, and in some smaller proportion for other necessaries, they would not be able to subsist on the same wages as before, and to keep up the race of laborers. Wages would inevitably and necessarily rise; and, in proportion as they rose, profits would fall. Government would receive a tax of 8s. per quarter on all the corn consumed in the country, a part of which would be paid directly by the consumers of corn; the other part would be paid indirectly by those who employed labor, and would affect profits in the same manner as if wages had been raised from the increased demand for labor compared with the supply, or from an increasing difficulty of obtaining the food and necessaries required by the laborer.

In as far as the tax might affect consumers it would be an equal tax, but in as far as it would affect profits it would be a partial tax; for it would neither operate on the landlord nor on the stockholder, since they would continue to receive, the one the same money rent, the other the same money dividends as before. A tax on the produce of the land then would operate as follows:

1st, It would raise the price of raw produce by a sum equal to the tax, and would therefore fall on each consumer in proportion to his consumption.

2nd, It would raise the wages of labor, and lower profits.

It may then be objected against such a tax,

1st, That by raising the wages of labor, and lowering profits, it is an unequal tax, as affects the income of the farmer, trader, and manufacturer, and leaves untaxed the income of the landlord, stockholder, and others enjoying fixed incomes.

2nd, That there would be a considerable interval between the rise in the price of corn and the rise of wages, during which much distress would be experienced by the laborer.

3rd, That raising wages and lowering profits is a discouragement to accumulation, and acts in the same way as a natural poverty of soil.

4th, That by raising the price of raw produce, the prices of all commodities into which raw produce enters would be raised, and that therefore we should not meet the foreign manufacturer on equal terms in the general market.

With respect to the first objection, that by raising the wages of labor and lowering profits, it acts unequally, as it affects the income of the farmer, trader, and manufacturer, and leaves untaxed the income of the landlord, stockholder, and others enjoying fixed incomes—it may be answered that if the operation of the tax be unequal it is for the legislature to make it equal, by taxing directly the rent of land and the dividends from stock. By so doing, all the objects of an income tax would be obtained without the inconvenience of having recourse to the obnoxious measure of prying into every man's concerns, and arming commissioners with powers repugnant to the habits and feelings of a free country.

With respect to the second objection, that there would be a considerable interval between the rise of the price of corn and the rise of wages, during which much distress would be experienced by the lower classes—I answer that under different circumstances, wages follow the price of raw produce with very different degrees of celerity; that in some cases no effect whatever is produced on wages by a rise of corn; in others, the rise of wages precedes the rise in the price of corn; again, in some the effect on wages is slow, and in others rapid.

Those who maintain that it is the price of necessaries which regulates the price of labor, always allowing for the particular state of progression in which the society may be, seem to have conceded too readily that a rise or fall in the price of necessaries will be very slowly succeeded by a rise or fall of wages. A high price of provisions may arise from very different causes, and may accordingly produce very different effects. It may arise from

1st, A deficient supply.

2nd, From a gradually increasing demand, which may be ultimately attended with an increased cost of production.

3rd, From a fall in the value of money.

4th, From taxes on necessaries.

These four causes have not been sufficiently distinguished and separated by those who have inquired into the influence of a high price of necessaries on wages. We will examine them severally.

A bad harvest will produce a high price of provisions, and the high price is the only means by which the consumption is compelled to conform to the state of the supply. If all the purchasers of corn were rich, the price might rise to any degree, but the result would remain unaltered; the price would at last be so high, that the least rich would be obliged to forego the use of a part of the quantity which they usually consumed, as by diminished consumption alone the demand could be brought down to the limits of the supply. Under such circumstances no policy can be more absurd than that of forcibly regulating money wages by the price of food, as is frequently done, by misapplication of the poor laws. Such a measure affords no real relief to the laborer, because its effect is to raise still higher the price of corn, and at last he must be obliged to limit his consumption in proportion to the limited supply. In the natural course of affairs a deficient supply from bad seasons, without any pernicious and unwise interference, would not be followed by a rise of wages. The raising of wages is merely nominal to those who receive them; it increases the competition in the corn market, and its ultimate effect is to raise the profits of the growers and dealers in corn. The wages of labor are really regulated by the proportion between the supply and demand of necessaries, and the supply and demand of labor; and money is merely the medium, or measure, in which wages are expressed. In this case, then, the distress of the laborer is unavoidable, and no legislation can afford a remedy, except by the importation of additional food or by adopting the most useful substitutes.

When a high price of corn is the effect of an increasing demand, it is always preceded by an increase of wages, for demand cannot increase without an increase of means in the people to pay for that which they desire. An accumulation of capital naturally produces an increased competition among the employers of labor, and a consequent rise in its price. The increased wages are not always immediately expended on food, but are first made to contribute to the other enjoyments of the laborer. His improved condition, however, induces and enables him to marry, and then the demand for food for the support of his family naturally supersedes that of those other enjoyments on which his wages were temporarily expended. Corn rises, then, because the demand for it increases, because there are those in the society who have improved means of paying for it; and the profits of the farmer will be raised above the general level of profits, till the requisite quantity of capital has been employed on its production. Whether, after this has taken place, corn shall again fall to its former price, or shall continue permanently higher, will depend on the quality of the land from which the increased quantity of corn has been supplied. If it be obtained from land of the same fertility as that which was last in cultivation, and with no greater cost of labor, the price will fall to its former state; if from poorer land, it will continue permanently higher. The high wages in the first instance proceeded from an increase in the demand for labor: in as much as it encouraged marriage, and supported children, it produced the effect of increasing the supply of labor. But when the supply is obtained, wages will again fall to their former price, if corn has fallen to its former price: to a higher than the former price, if the increased supply of corn has been produced from land of an inferior quality. A high price is by no means incompatible with an abundant supply: the price is permanently high, not because the quantity is deficient, but because there has been an increased cost in producing it. It generally happens, indeed, that when a stimulus has been given to population, an effect is produced beyond what the case requires; the population may be, and generally is, so much increased as, notwithstanding the increased demand for labor, to bear a greater proportion to the funds for maintaining laborers than before the increase of capital.   In this case a reaction will take place, wages will be below their natural level, and will continue so, till the usual proportion between the supply and demand has been restored. In this case, then, the rise in the price of corn is preceded by a rise of wages, and therefore entails no distress on the laborer.

A fall in the value of money, in consequence of an influx of the precious metals from the mines, or from the abuse of the privileges of banking, is another cause for the rise of the price of food; but it will make no alteration in the quantity produced. It leaves undisturbed too the number of laborers, as well as the demand for them; for there will be neither an increase nor a diminution of capital. The quantity of necessaries to be allotted to the laborer depends on the comparative demand and supply of necessaries, with the comparative demand and supply of labor; money being only the medium in which the quantity is expressed; and as neither of these is altered, the real reward of the laborer will not alter. Money wages will rise, but they will only enable him to furnish himself with the same quantity of necessaries as before. Those who dispute this principle are bound to show why an increase of money should not have the same effect in raising the price of labor, the quantity of which has not been increased, as they acknowledge it would have on the price of shoes, of hats, and of corn, if the quantity of those commodities were not increased. The relative market value of hats and shoes is regulated by the demand and supply of hats, compared with the demand and supply of shoes, and money is but the medium in which their value is expressed. If shoes be doubled in price, hats will also be doubled in price, and they will retain the same comparative value. So if corn and all the necessaries of the laborer be doubled in price, labor will be doubled in price also; and while there is no interruption to the usual demand and supply of necessaries and of labor, there can be no reason why they should not preserve their relative value.

Neither a fall in the value of money, nor a tax on raw produce, though each will raise the price, will *necessarily* interfere with the quantity of raw produce, or with the number of people, who are both able to purchase and willing to consume it. It is very easy to perceive why, when the capital of a country increases irregularly, wages should rise, whilst the price of corn remains stationary, or rises in a less proportion; and why, when the capital of a country diminishes, wages should fall whilst corn remains stationary, or falls in a much less proportion, and this Taxes on Raw Produce too for a considerable time; the reason is, because labor is a commodity which cannot be increased and diminished at pleasure. If there are too few hats in the market for the demand the price will rise, but only for a short time; for in the course of one year, by employing more capital in that trade, any reasonable addition may be made to the quantity of hats, and therefore their market price cannot long very much exceed their natural price; but it is not so with men; you cannot increase their number in one or two years when there is an increase of capital, nor can you rapidly diminish their number when capital is in a retrograde state; and, therefore, the number of hands increasing or diminishing slowly, whilst the funds for the maintenance of labor increase or diminish rapidly, there must be a considerable interval before the price of labor is exactly regulated by the price of corn and necessaries; but in the case of a fall in the value of money, or of a tax on corn, there is not necessarily any excess in the supply of labor, nor any abatement of demand, and therefore there can be no reason why the laborer should sustain a real diminution of wages.

A tax on corn does not necessarily diminish the quantity of corn, it only raises its money price; it does not necessarily diminish the demand compared with the supply of labor; why then should it diminish the portion paid to the laborer? Suppose it true that it did diminish the quantity given to the laborer, in other words, that it did not raise his money wages in the same proportion as the tax raised the price of the corn which he consumed; would not the supply of corn exceed the demand?—would it not fall in price? And would not the laborer thus obtain his usual portion? In such case, indeed, capital would be withdrawn from agriculture; for if the price were not increased by the whole amount of the tax, agricultural profits would be lower than the general level of profits, and capital would seek a more advantageous employment. In regard, then, to a tax on raw produce, which is the point under discussion, it appears to me that no interval which could bear oppressively on the laborer would elapse between the rise in the price of raw produce and the rise in the wages of the laborer; and that therefore no other inconvenience would be suffered by this class than that which they would suffer from any other mode of taxation, namely, the risk that the tax might infringe on the funds destined for the maintenance of labor, and might therefore check or abate the demand for it.

With respect to the third objection against taxes on raw produce, namely, that the raising wages, and lowering profits, is a discouragement to accumulation, and acts in the same way as a natural poverty of soil; I have endeavored to show in another part of this work that savings may be as effectually made from expenditure as from production; from a reduction in the value of commodities as from a rise in the rate of profits. By increasing my profits from £1000 to £1200, whilst prices continue the same, my power of increasing my capital by savings is increased, but it is not increased so much as it would be if my profits continued as before, whilst commodities were so lowered in price that £800 would procure me as much as £1000 purchased before.

Now the sum required by the tax must be raised, and the question simply is, whether the same amount shall be taken from individuals by diminishing their profits, or by raising the prices of the commodities on which their profits will be expanded.

Taxation under every form presents but a choice of evils; if it do not act on profit, or other sources of income, it must act on expenditure; and provided the burthen be equally borne, and do not repress reproduction, it is indifferent on which it is laid. Taxes on production, or on the profits of stock, whether applied immediately to profits or indirectly by taxing the land or its produce, have this advantage over other taxes; that, provided all other income be taxed, no class of the community can escape them, and each contributes according to his means.

From taxes on expenditure a miser may escape; he may have an income of £10,000 per annum, and expend only £300; but from taxes on profits, whether direct or indirect, he cannot escape; he will contribute to them either by giving up a part, or the value of a part, of his produce; or by the advanced prices of the necessaries essential to production he will be unable to continue to accumulate at the same rate. He may, indeed, have an income of the same value but he will not have the same command of labor, nor of an equal quantity of materials on which such labor can be exercised.

If a country is insulated from all others, having no commerce with any of its neighbors, it can in no way shift any portion of its taxes from itself. A portion of the produce of its land and labor will be devoted to the service of the state; and I cannot but think that, unless it presses unequally on that class which accumulates and saves, it will be of little importance whether the taxes be levied on profits, on agricultural, or on Taxes on Raw Produce manufactured commodities. If my revenue be £1000 per annum, and I must pay taxes to the amount of £100, it is of little importance whether I pay it from my revenue, leaving myself only £900, or pay £100 in addition for my agricultural commodities, or for my manufactured goods. If £100 is my fair proportion of the expenses of the country, the virtue of taxation consists in making sure that I shall pay that £100, neither more nor less; and that cannot be effected in any manner so securely as by taxes on wages, profits, or raw produce.

The fourth and last objection which remains to be noticed is: That by raising the price of raw produce, the prices of all commodities into which raw produce enters will be raised, and that, therefore, we shall not meet the foreign manufacturer on equal terms in the general market.

In the first place, corn and *all* home commodities could not be materially raised in price without an influx of the precious metals; for the same quantity of money could not circulate the same quantity of commodities at high as at low prices, and the precious metals never could be purchased with dear commodities. When more gold is required, *it* must be obtained by giving more and not fewer commodities in exchange for it. Neither could the want of money be supplied by paper, for it is not paper that regulates the value of gold as a commodity, but gold that regulates the value of paper. Unless, then, the value of gold could be lowered, no paper could be added to the circulation without being depreciated. And that the value of gold could not be lowered appears clear when we consider that the value of gold as a commodity must be regulated by the quantity of goods which must be given to foreigners in exchange for it. When gold is cheap, commodities are dear; and when gold is dear, commodities are cheap, and fail in price. Now as no cause is shown why foreigners should sell their gold cheaper than usual, it does not appear probable that there would be any influx of gold. Without such an influx there can be no increase of quantity, no fall in its value, no rise in the general price of goods.[21]

The probable effect of a tax on raw produce would be to raise the price of raw produce, and of all commodities in which raw produce entered, but not in any degree proportioned to the tax; while other commodities in which no raw produce entered, such as articles made of the metals and the earths, would fall in price: so that the same quantity of money as before would be adequate to the whole circulation.

A tax which should have the effect of raising the price of all home productions would not discourage exportation, except during a very limited time. If they were raised in price at home, they could not indeed immediately be profitably exported, because they would be subject to a burthen here from which abroad they were free. The tax would produce the same effect as an alteration in the value of money, which was not general and common to all countries, but confined to a single one. If England were that country, she might not be able to sell, but she would be able to buy, because importable commodities would not be raised in price. Under these circumstances nothing but money could be exported in return for foreign commodities, but this is a trade which could not long continue; a nation cannot be exhausted of its money, for after a certain quantity has left it, the value of the remainder will rise, and such a price of commodities will be the consequence that they will again be capable of being profitably exported. When money had risen, therefore, we should no longer export it in return for goods, but we should export those manufactures which had first been raised in price by the rise in the price of the raw produce from which they were made, and then again lowered by the exportation of money.

But it may be objected that when money so rose in value it would rise with respect to foreign as well as home commodities, and therefore that all encouragement to import foreign goods would cease. Thus, suppose we imported goods which cost £100 abroad, and which sold for £120 here, we should cease to import them when the value of money had so risen in England that they would only sell for £100 here: this, however, could never happen. The motive which determines us to import a commodity is the discovery of its relative cheapness abroad: it is the comparison of its price abroad with its price at home. If a country exports hats, and imports cloth, it does so because it can obtain more cloth by making hats and exchanging them for cloth than if it made the cloth itself. If the rise of raw produce occasions any increased cost of production in making hats, it would occasion also an increased cost in making cloth. If, therefore, both commodities were made at home, they would both rise. One, however, being a commodity which we import, would not rise, neither would it fall when the value of money Taxes on Raw Produce rose; for by not falling it would regain its natural relation to the exported commodity. The rise of raw produce makes a hat rise from 30s. to 33s., or 10 percent; the same cause, if we manufactured cloth, would make it rise from 20s. to 22s. per yard. This rise does not destroy the relation between cloth and hats; a hat was, and continues to be, worth one yard and a half of cloth. But if we import cloth, its price will continue uniformly at 20s. per yard, unaffected first by the fall, and then by the rise in the value of money; whilst hats, which had risen from 30s. to 33s., will again fall from 33s. to 30s., at which point the relation between cloth and hats will be restored.

To simplify the consideration of this subject, I have been supposing that a rise in the value of raw materials would affect, in an equal proportion, all home commodities; that if the effect on one were to raise it 10 percent, it would raise all 10 percent; but as the value of commodities is very differently made up of raw material and labor; as some commodities, for instance, all those made from the metals, would be unaffected by the rise of raw produce from the surface of the earth, it is evident that there would be the greatest variety in the effects produced on the value of commodities by a tax on raw produce. As far as this effect was produced, it would stimulate or retard the exportation of particular commodities, and would undoubtedly be attended with the same inconvenience that attends the taxing of commodities; it would destroy the natural relation between the value of each. Thus the natural price of a hat, instead of being the same as a yard and a half of cloth, might only be of the value of a yard and a quarter, or it might be of the value of a yard and three quarters, and therefore rather a different direction might be given to foreign trade. All these inconveniences would probably not interfere with the value of the exports and imports; they would only prevent the very best distribution of the capital of the whole world, which is never so well regulated as when every commodity is freely allowed to settle at its natural price, unfettered by artificial restraints.

Although, then, the rise in the price of most of our own commodities would for a time check exportation generally, and might permanently prevent the exportation of a few commodities, it could not materially interfere with foreign trade, and would not place us under any comparative disadvantage as far as regarded competition in foreign markets.

CHAPTER X

Taxes on Rent

A tax on rent would affect rent only; it would fall wholly on landlords, and could not be shifted to any class of consumers. The landlord could not raise his rent, because he would leave unaltered the difference between the produce obtained from the least productive land in cultivation, and that obtained from land of every other quality. Three sorts of land, No. 1, 2, and 3, are in cultivation, and yield respectively, with the same labor, 180, 170, and 160 quarters of wheat; but No. 3 pays no rent, and is therefore untaxed: the rent then of No. 2 cannot be made to exceed the value of ten, nor No. 1 of twenty quarters. Such a tax could not raise the price of raw produce, because, as the cultivator of No. 3 pays neither rent nor tax, he would in no way be enabled to raise the price of the commodity produced. A tax on rent would not discourage the cultivation of fresh land, for such land pays no rent, and would be untaxed. If No. 4 were taken into cultivation, and yielded 150 quarters, no tax would be paid for such land; but it would create a rent of ten quarters on No. 3, which would then commence paying the tax.

A tax on rent, as rent is constituted, would discourage cultivation, because it would be a tax on the profits of the landlord. The term rent of land, as I have elsewhere observed, is applied to the whole amount of the value paid by the farmer to his landlord, a part only of which is strictly rent. The buildings and fixtures, and other expenses paid for by the landlord, form strictly a part of the stock of the farm, and must have been furnished by the tenant, if not provided by the landlord. Rent is the sum paid to the landlord for the use of the land, and for the use of the land only. The further sum that is paid to him under the name of rent is for the use of the buildings, etc., and is really the profits of the landlord's stock. In taxing rent, as no distinction would be made between that part paid for the use of the land, and that paid for the use of the landlord's stock, a portion of the tax would fall on the landlord's profits, and would, therefore, discourage cultivation, unless the price of raw produce rose. On that land, for the use of which no rent was paid, a compensation under that name might be given to the landlord for the use of his buildings. These buildings would not be erected, nor would raw produce be grown on such land, till the price at which it sold would not only pay for all the usual outgoings, but also this additional one of the tax. This part of the tax does not fall on the landlord, nor on the farmer, but on the consumer of raw produce.

There can be little doubt but that if a tax were laid on rent, landlords would soon find a way to discriminate between that which is paid to them for the use of the land, and that which is paid for the use of the buildings, and the improvements which are made by the landlord's stock. The latter would either be called the rent of house and buildings, or on all new land taken into cultivation such buildings would be erected and improvements would be made by the tenant and not by the landlord. The landlord's capital might indeed be really employed for that purpose; it might be nominally expended by the tenant, the landlord furnishing him with the means, either in the shape of a loan, or in the purchase of an annuity for the duration of the lease. Whether distinguished or not, there is a real difference between the nature of the compensations which the landlord receives for these different objects; and it is quite certain that a tax on the real rent of land falls wholly on the landlord, but that a tax on that remuneration which the landlord receives for the use of this stock expended on the farm, falls, in a progressive country, on the consumer of raw produce. If a tax were laid on rent, and no means of separating the remuneration now paid by the tenant to the landlord under the name of rent were adopted, the tax, as far as it regarded the rent on the buildings and other fixtures, would never fall for any length of time on the landlord, but on the consumer. The capital expended on these buildings, etc., must afford the usual profit of stock; but it would cease to afford this profit on the land last cultivated if the expenses of those buildings, etc., did not fall on the tenant; and if they did, the tenant would then cease to make his usual profits of stock, unless he could charge them on the consumer.

CHAPTER XI

Tithes

Tithes are a tax on the gross produce of the land, and, like taxes on raw produce, fall wholly on the consumer. They differ from a tax on rent, inasmuch as they affect land which such a tax would not reach; and raise the price of raw produce which that tax would not alter. Lands of the worst quality, as well as of the best, pay tithes, and exactly in proportion to the quantity of produce obtained from them; tithes are therefore an equal tax.

If land of the last quality, or that which pays no rent, and which regulates the price of corn, yield a sufficient quantity to give the farmer the usual profits of stock, when the price of wheat is £4 per quarter, the price must rise to £4 8s. before the same profits can be obtained after the tithes are imposed, because for every quarter of wheat the cultivator must pay eight shillings to the church, and if he does not obtain the same profits, there is no reason why he should not quit his employment, when he can get them in other trades.

The only difference between tithes and taxes on raw produce is that one is a variable money tax, the other a fixed money tax. In a stationary state of society; where there is neither increased nor diminished facility of producing corn, they will be precisely the same in their effects; for, in such a state, corn will be at an invariable price, and the tax will therefore be also invariable. In either a retrograde state, or in a state in which great improvements are made in agriculture, and where consequently raw produce will fall in value comparatively with other things, tithes will be a lighter tax than a permanent money tax; for if the price of corn should fall from £4 to £3, the tax would fall from eight to six shillings. In a progressive state of society, yet without any marked improvements in agriculture, the price of corn would rise, and tithes would be a heavier tax than a permanent money tax. If corn rose from £4 to £5, the tithes on the same land would advance from eight to ten shillings.

Neither tithes nor a money tax will affect the money rent of landlords, but both will materially affect corn rents. We have already observed how a money tax operates on corn rents, and it is equally evident that a similar effect would be produced by tithes. If the lands, No. 1, 2, 3, respectively produced 180, 170, and 160 quarters, the rents might be on No. 1, twenty quarters, and on No. 2, ten quarters; but they would no longer preserve that proportion after the payment of tithes; for if a tenth be taken from each, the remaining produce will be 162, 153, 154, and consequently the corn rent of No. 1 will be reduced to eighteen, and that of No. 2 to nine quarters. But the price of corn would rise from £4 to £4 8s. 102/3 d.; for 144 quarters are to £4 as 160 quarters to £4. 8s. 102/3 d. and consequently the money rent would continue unaltered; for on No. 1 it would be £80[22], and on No. 2, £40.[23]

The chief objection against tithes is that they are not a permanent and fixed tax, but increase in value in proportion as the difficulty of producing corn increases. If those difficulties should make the price of corn £4, the tax is 8s., if they should increase it to £5, the tax is 10s.; and at £6 it is 12s. They not only rise in value, but they increase in amount: thus, when No. 1 was cultivated, the tax was only levied on 180 quarters; when No. 2 was cultivated, it was levied on 180 + 170, or 350 quarters; and when No. 3 was cultivated, on 180 + 170 + 160 = 510 quarters. Not only is the amount of tax increased from 100,000 quarters to 200,000 quarters when the produce is increased from one to two millions of quarters; but, owing to the increased labor necessary to produce the second million, the relative value of raw produce is so advanced that the 200,000 quarters may be, though only twice in quantity, yet in value three times that of the 100,000 quarters which were paid before.

If an equal value were raised for the church by any other means, increasing in the same manner as tithes increase, proportionally with the difficulty of cultivation, the effect would be the same; and therefore it is a mistake to suppose that, because they are raised on the land, they discourage cultivation more than an equal amount would do if raised in any other manner. The church would in both cases be constantly obtaining an increased portion of the net produce of the land and labor of the country. In an improving state of society, the net produce of land is always diminishing in proportion to its gross produce; but it is from the net income of a country that all taxes are ultimately paid, either in a progressive or in a stationary country. A tax increasing with the gross income, and falling on the net income, must necessarily be a very burdensome and a very intolerable tax. Tithes are a tenth of the gross and not of the net produce of the land, and therefore as society improves in wealth, they must, though the same proportion of the gross produce, become a larger and larger proportion of the net produce.

Tithes, however, may be considered as injurious to landlords, in as much as they act as a bounty on importation, by taxing the growth of home corn while the importation of foreign corn remains unfettered. And if, in order to relieve the landlords from the effects of the diminished demand for land which such a bounty must encourage, imported corn were also taxed, in an equal degree with corn grown at home, and the produce paid to the state, no measure could be more fair and equitable; since whatever were paid to the state by this tax would go to diminish the other taxes which the expenses of government make necessary; but if such a tax were devoted only to increase the fund paid to the church, it might indeed on the whole increase the general mass of production, but it would diminish the portion of that mass allotted to the productive classes.

If the trade of cloth were left perfectly free, our manufacturers might be able to sell cloth cheaper than we could import it. If a tax were laid on the home[1] manufacturer, and not on the importer of cloth, capital might be injuriously driven from the manufacture of cloth to the manufacture of some other commodity, as cloth might then be imported cheaper than it could be made at home. If imported cloth should also be taxed, cloth would again be manufactured at home. The consumer first bought cloth at home because it was cheaper than foreign cloth; he then bought foreign cloth because it was cheaper untaxed than home cloth taxed: he lastly bought it again at home because it was cheaper when both home and foreign cloth were taxed. It is in the last case that he pays the greatest price for his cloth; but all his additional payment is gained by the state. In the second case, he pays more than in the first, but all he pays in addition is not received by the state, it is an increased price caused by difficulty of production, which is incurred because the easiest means of production are taken away from us by being fettered with a tax.

CHAPTER XII

Land-Tax

A land-tax, levied in proportion to the rent of land, and varying with every variation of rent, is in effect a tax on rent; and as such a tax will not apply to that land which yields no rent, nor to the produce of that capital which is employed on the land with a view to profit merely, and which never pays rent; it will not in any way affect the price of raw produce, but will fall wholly on the landlords. In no respect would such a tax differ from a tax on rent. But if a land-tax be imposed on all cultivated land, however moderate that tax may be, it will be a tax on produce, and will therefore raise the price of produce. If No. 3 be the land last cultivated, although it should pay no rent, it cannot, after the tax, be cultivated, and afford the general rate of profit, unless the price of produce rise to meet the tax. Either capital will be withheld from that employment, until the price of corn shall have risen, in consequence of demand, sufficiently to afford the usual profit; or if already employed on such land, it will quit it, to seek a more advantageous employment. The tax cannot be removed to the landlord, for by the supposition he receives no rent. Such a tax may be proportioned to the quality of the land and the abundance of its produce, and then it differs in no respect from tithes; or it may be a fixed tax per acre on all land cultivated, whatever its quality may be.

A land-tax of this latter description would be a very unequal tax, and would be contrary to one of the four maxims with regard to taxes in general, to which, according to Adam Smith, all taxes should conform. The four maxims are as follows:

1. "The subjects of every state ought to contribute towards the support of the government, as nearly as possible in proportion to their respective abilities.

2. "The tax which each individual is bound to pay ought to be certain, and not arbitrary.

3. "Every tax ought to be levied at the time or in the manner in which it is most likely to be convenient for the contributor to pay it.

4. "Every tax ought to be so contrived as both to take out and to keep out of the pockets of the people as little as possible, over and above what it brings into the public treasury of the state."

An equal land-tax, imposed indiscriminately and without any regard to the distinction of its quality, on all land cultivated, will raise the price of corn in proportion to the tax paid by the cultivator of the land of the worst quality. Lands of different quality, with the employment of the same capital, will yield very different quantities of raw produce. If on the land which yields a thousand quarters of corn with a given capital a tax of £100 be laid, corn will rise 2s. per quarter to compensate the farmer for the tax. But with the same capital on land of a better quality, 2000 quarters may be produced, which at 2s., a quarter advance would give £200; the tax, however, bearing equally on both lands will be £100 on the better as well as on the inferior, and consequently the consumer of corn will be taxed, not only to pay the exigencies of the state, but also to give to the cultivator of the better land £100 per annum during the period of his lease, and afterwards to raise the rent of the landlord to that amount. A tax of this description, then, would be contrary to the fourth maxim of Adam Smith—it would take out and keep out of the pockets of the people more than what it brought into the treasury of the state. The taille in France, before the Revolution, was a tax of this description; those lands only were taxed which were held by an ignoble tenure, the price of raw produce rose in proportion to the tax, and therefore they whose lands were not taxed were benefited by the increase of their rent. Taxes on raw produce, as well as tithes, are free from this objection: they raise the price of raw produce, but they take from each quality of land a contribution in proportion to its actual produce, and not in proportion to the produce of that which is the least productive.

From the peculiar view which Adam Smith took of rent, from his not having observed that much capital is expended in every country on the land for which no rent is paid, he concluded that all taxes on the land, whether they were laid on the land itself in the form of land-tax or tithes, or on the produce of the land, or were taken from the profits of the farmer, were all invariably paid by the landlord, and that he was in all cases the real contributor, although the tax was, in general, nominally advanced by the tenant. "Taxes upon the produce of the land," he says, "are in reality taxes upon the rent; and though they may be originally advanced by the farmer, are finally paid by the landlord. When a certain portion of the produce is to be paid away for a tax, the farmer computes as well as he can what the value of this portion is, one year with another, likely to amount to, and he makes a proportionable abatement in the rent which he agrees to pay to the landlord. There is no farmer who does not compute beforehand what the church-tithe, which is a land-tax of this kind, is, one year with another, likely to amount to." It is undoubtedly true that the farmer does calculate his probable outgoings of all descriptions when agreeing with his landlord for the rent of his farm; and if, for the tithe paid to the church, or for the tax on the produce of the land, he were not compensated by a rise in the relative value of the produce of his farm, he would naturally endeavor to deduct them from his rent. But this is precisely the question in dispute: whether he will eventually deduct them from his rent, or be compensated by a higher price of produce. For the reasons which have been already given, I cannot have the least doubt but that they would raise the price of produce, and consequently that Adam Smith has taken an incorrect view of this important question.

Dr. Smith's view of this subject is probably the reason why he has described "the tithe, and every other land-tax of this kind, under the appearance of perfect equality, as very unequal taxes; a certain portion of the produce being in different situations equivalent to a very different portion of the rent." I have endeavored to show that such taxes do not fall with unequal weight on the different classes of farmers or landlords, as they are both compensated by the rise of raw produce, and only contribute to the tax in proportion as they are consumers of raw produce. In as much indeed as wages, and through wages, the rate of profits are affected, landlords, instead of contributing their full share to such a tax, are the class peculiarly exempted. It is the profits of stock from which that portion of the tax is derived which falls on those laborers, who, from the insufficiency of their funds, are incapable of paying taxes; this portion is exclusively borne by all those whose income is derived from the employment of stock, and therefore it in no degree affects landlords.

It is not to be inferred from this view of tithes, and taxes on the land and its produce, that they do not discourage cultivation. Everything which raises the exchangeable value of commodities of any kind which are in very general demand tends to discourage both cultivation and production; but this is an evil inseparable from all taxation, and is not confined to the particular taxes of which we are now speaking.

This may be considered, indeed, as the unavoidable disadvantage attending all taxes received and expended by the state. Every new tax becomes a new charge on production, and raises natural price. A portion of the labor of the country which was before at the disposal of the contributor to the tax is placed at the disposal of the state, and cannot therefore be employed productively. This portion may become so large that sufficient surplus produce may not be left to stimulate the exertions of those who usually augment by their savings the capital of the state. Taxation has happily never yet in any free country been carried so far as constantly from year to year to diminish its capital. Such a state of taxation could not be long endured; or if endured, it would be constantly absorbing so much of the annual produce of the country as to occasion the most extensive scene of misery, famine, and depopulation.

"A land-tax," says Adam Smith, "which, like that of Great Britain, is assessed upon each district according to a certain invariable canon, though it should be equal at the time of its first establishment, necessarily becomes unequal in process of time, according to the unequal degrees of improvement or neglect in the cultivation of the different parts of the country. In England the valuation according to which the different counties and parishes were assessed to the land-tax by the 4th William and Mary was very unequal, even at its first establishment. This tax, therefore, so far offends against the first of the four maxims above mentioned. It is perfectly agreeable to the other three. It is perfectly certain. The time of payment for the tax being the same as that for the rent, is as convenient as it can be to the contributor. Though the landlord is in all cases the real contributor, the tax is commonly advanced by the tenant, to whom the landlord is obliged to allow it in the payment of the rent."

If the tax be shifted by the tenant not on the landlord but on the consumer, then if it be not unequal at first, it can never become so; for the price of produce has been at once raised in proportion to the tax, and will afterwards vary no more on that account. It may offend, if unequal, as I have attempted to show that it will, against the fourth maxim above mentioned, but it will not offend against the first. It may take more out of the pockets of the people than it brings into the public treasury of the state, but it will not fall unequally on any particular class of contributors. M. Say appears to me to have mistaken the nature and effects of the English land-tax, when he says, "Many persons attribute to this fixed valuation the great prosperity of English agriculture." That it has very much contributed to it there can be no doubt. But what should we say to a government which, addressing itself to a small trader, should hold this language: 'With a small capital you are carrying on a limited trade, and your direct contribution is in consequence very small. Borrow and accumulate capital; extend your trade, so that it may procure you immense profits; yet you shall never pay a greater contribution. Moreover, when your successors shall inherit your profits, and shall have further increased them, they shall not be valued higher to them than they are to you; and your successors shall not bear a greater portion of the public burdens.'

"Without doubt this would be a great encouragement given to manufacturers and trade; but would it be just? Could not their advancement be obtained at any other price? In England itself, has not manufacturing and commercial industry made even greater progress, since the same period, without being distinguished with so much partiality? A landlord by his assiduity, economy, and skill increases his annual revenue by 5000 francs. If the state claim of him the fifth part of his augmented income, will there not remain 4000 francs of increase to stimulate his further exertions?"

M. Say supposes, "A landlord by his assiduity, economy, and skill to increase his annual revenue by 5000 francs;" but a landlord has no means of employing his assiduity, economy, and skill on his land unless he farms it himself; and then it is in quality of capitalist and farmer that he makes the improvement, and not in quality of landlord. It is not conceivable that he could so augment the produce of his farm by any *peculiar* skill on his part, without first increasing the quantity of capital employed upon it. If he increased the capital, his larger revenue might bear the same proportion to his increased capital, as the revenue of all other farmers to their capitals.

If M. Say's suggestion were followed, and the state were to claim the fifth part of the augmented income of the farmer, it would be a partial tax on farmers, acting on their profits, and not affecting the profits of those in other employments. The tax would be paid by all lands, by those which yielded scantily as well as by those which yielded abundantly; and on some lands there could be no compensation for it by deduction from rent, for no rent is paid. A partial tax on profits never falls on the trade on which it is laid, for the trader will either quit his employment or remunerate himself for the tax. Now, those who pay no rent could be recompensed only by a rise in the price of produce, and thus would M. Say's proposed tax fall on the consumer, and not either on the landlord or farmer.

If the proposed tax were increased in proportion to the increased quantity or value of the gross produce obtained from the land, it would differ in nothing from tithes, and would equally be transferred to the consumer. Whether then it fell on the gross or on the net produce of land, it would be equally a tax on consumption, and would only affect the landlord and farmer in the same way as other taxes on raw produce.

If no tax whatever had been laid on the land, and the same sum had been raised by any other means, agriculture would have flourished at least as well as it has done; for it is impossible that any tax on land can be an *encouragement* to agriculture; a moderate tax may not, and probably does not, greatly prevent, but it cannot encourage production. The English government has held no such language as M. Say has supposed. It did not promise to exempt the agricultural class and their successors from all future taxation, and to raise the further supplies which the state might require from the other classes of society; it said only, "in this mode we will no further burthen the land; but we retain to ourselves the most perfect liberty of making you pay, under some other form, your full quota to the future exigencies of the state."

Speaking of taxes in kind, or a tax of a certain proportion of the produce, which is precisely the same as tithes, M. Say says, "This mode of taxation appears to be the most equitable; there is, however, none which is less so: it totally leaves out of consideration the advances made by the producer; it is proportioned by the gross, and not to the net revenue. Two agriculturists cultivate different kinds of raw produce: one cultivates corn on middling land, his expenses amounting annually on an average to 8000 francs; the raw produce from his lands sells for 12,000 francs; he has then a net revenue of 4000 francs.

"His neighbor has pasture or wood land, which brings in every year a like sum of 12,000 francs, but his expenses amount only to 2000 francs. He has therefore on an average a net revenue of 10,000 francs.

"A law ordains that a twelfth of the produce of all the fruits of the earth be levied in kind, whatever they may be. From the first is taken, in consequence of this law, corn of the value of 1000 francs; and from the second, hay, cattle, or wood, of the same value of 1000 francs. What has happened? From the one, a quarter of his net income, 4000 francs, has been taken; from the other, whose income was 10,000 francs, a tenth only has been taken. Income is the net profit which remains after replacing the capital exactly in its former state. Has a merchant an income equal to all the sales which he makes in the course of a year; certainly not; his income only amounts to the excess of his sales above his advances, and it is on this excess only that taxes on income should fall."

M. Say's error in the above passage lies in supposing that because the value of the produce of one of these two farms, after reinstating the capital, is greater than the value of the produce of the other, on that account the net income of the cultivators will differ by the same amount. The net income of the landlords and tenants together of the wood land may be much greater than the net income of the landlords and tenants of the corn land; but it is on account of the difference of rent, and not on account of the difference in the rate of profit. M. Say has wholly omitted the consideration of the different amount of rent which these cultivators would have to pay. There cannot be two rates of profit in the same employment, and therefore when the value of produce is in different proportions to capital, it is the rent which will differ, and not the profit. Upon what pretence would one man, with a capital of 2000 francs, be allowed to obtain a net profit of 10,000 francs from its employment, whilst another, with a capital of 8000 francs, would only obtain 4000 francs? Let M. Say make a due allowance for rent; let him further allow for the effect which such a tax would have on the prices of these different kinds of raw produce, and he will then perceive that it is not an unequal tax, and, further, that the producers themselves will no otherwise contribute to it than any other class of consumers.

CHAPTER XIII

Taxes on Gold

The rise in the price of commodities, in consequence of taxation or of difficulty of production, will in all cases ultimately ensue; but the duration of the interval before the market price will conform to the natural price must depend on the nature of the commodity, and on the facility with which it can be reduced in quantity. If the quantity of the commodity taxed could not be diminished, if the capital of the farmer or of the hatter, for instance, could not be withdrawn to other employments, it would be of no consequence that their profits were reduced below the general level by means of a tax; unless the demand for their commodities should increase, they would never be able to elevate the market price of corn and of hats up to their increased natural price. Their threats to leave their employments, and remove their capitals to more favored trades, would be treated as an idle menace which could not be carried into effect; and consequently the price would not be raised by diminished production. Commodities, however, of all descriptions, can be reduced in quantity, and capital can be removed from trades which are less profitable to those which are more so, but with different degrees of rapidity. In proportion as the supply of a particular commodity can be more easily reduced, without inconvenience to the producer, the price of it will more quickly rise after the difficulty of its production has been increased by taxation, or by any other means. Corn being a commodity indispensably necessary to every one, little effect will be produced on the demand for it in consequence of a tax, and therefore the supply would not probably be long excessive, even if the producers had great difficulty in removing their capitals from the land. For this reason, the price of corn will speedily be raised by taxation, and the farmer will be enabled to transfer the tax from himself to the consumer.

If the mines which supply us with gold were in this country, and if gold were taxed, it could not rise in relative value to other things till its quantity were reduced. This would be more particularly the case if gold were used exclusively for money.

It is true that the least productive mines, those which paid no rent, could no longer be worked; as they could not afford the general rate of profits till the relative value of gold rose by a sum equal to the tax. The quantity of gold, and, therefore, the quantity of money, would be slowly reduced: it would be a little diminished in one year, a little more in another, and finally its value would be raised in proportion to the tax; but, in the interval, the proprietors or holders, as they would pay the tax, would be the sufferers, and not those who used money. If out of every 1000 quarters of wheat in the country, and every 1000 produced in future; government should exact 100 quarters as a tax, the remaining 900 quarters would exchange for the same quantity of other commodities that 1000 did before; but if the same thing took place with respect to gold, if of every £1000 money now in the country, or in future to be brought into it, government could exact £100 as a tax, the remaining £900 would purchase very little more than £900 purchased before. The tax would fall upon him whose property consisted of money, and would continue to do so till its quantity were reduced in proportion to the increased cost of its production caused by the tax.

This, perhaps, would be more particularly the case with respect to a metal used for money than any other commodity; because the demand for money is not for a definite quantity, as is the demand for clothes, or for food. The demand for money is regulated entirely by its value, and its value by its quantity. If gold were of double the value, half the quantity would perform the same functions in circulation, and if it were of half the value, double the quantity would be required. If the market value of corn be increased one-tenth by taxation, or by difficulty of production, it is doubtful whether any effect whatever would be produced on the quantity consumed, because every man's want is for a definite quantity, and, therefore, if he has the means of purchasing, he will continue to consume as before: but for money, the demand is exactly proportioned to its value. No man could consume twice the quantity of corn which is usually necessary for his support, but every man purchasing and selling only the same quantity of goods may be obliged to employ twice, thrice, or any number of times the same quantity of money.

The argument which I have just been using applies only to those states of society in which the precious metals are used for money, and where paper credit is not established. The metal gold, like all other commodities, has its value in the market ultimately regulated by the comparative facility or difficulty of producing it; and although, from its durable nature, and from the difficulty of reducing its quantity, it does not readily bend to variations in its market value, yet that difficulty is much increased from the circumstance of its being used as money. If the quantity of gold in the market for the purpose of commerce only were 10,000 ounces, and the consumption in our manufactures were 2000 ounces annually, it might be raised one-fourth or 25 percent, in its value in one year by withholding the annual supply; but if, in consequence of its being used as money, the quantity employed were 100,000 ounces, it would not be raised one-fourth in value in less than ten years. As money made of paper may be readily reduced in quantity, its value, though its standard were gold, would be increased as rapidly as that of the metal itself would be increased, if the metal, by forming a very small part of the circulation, had a very slight connection with money.

If gold were the produce of one country only, and it were used universally for money, a very considerable tax might be imposed on it, which would not fall on any country, except in proportion as they used it in manufactures and for utensils; upon that portion which was used for money, though a large tax might be received, nobody would pay it. This is a quality peculiar to money. All other commodities of which there exists a limited quantity, and which cannot be increased by competition, are dependent for their value on the tastes, the caprice, and the power of purchasers; but money is a commodity which no country has any wish or necessity to increase: no more advantage results from using twenty millions than from using ten millions of currency. A country might have a monopoly of silk, or of wine, and yet the prices of silks and wine might fall, because from caprice, or fashion, or taste, cloth and brandy might be preferred and substituted; the same effect might in a degree take place with gold, as far as its use is confined to manufactures: but while money is the general medium of exchange, the demand for it is never a matter of choice, but always of necessity: you must take it in exchange for your goods, and, therefore, there are no limits to the quantity which may be forced on you by foreign trade if it fall in value; and no reduction to which you must not submit if it rise. You may, indeed, substitute paper money, but by this you do not and cannot lessen the quantity of money, for that is regulated by the value of the standard for which it is exchangeable; it is only by the rise of the price of commodities that you can prevent them from being exported from a country where they are purchased with little money, to a country where they can be sold for more, and this rise can only be effected by an importation of metallic money from abroad, or by the creation or addition of paper money at home. If, then, the King of Spain, supposing him to be in exclusive possession of the mines, and gold alone to be used for money, were to lay a considerable tax on gold, he would very much raise its natural value; and as its market value in Europe is ultimately regulated by its natural value in Spanish America, more commodities would be given by Europe for a given quantity of gold. But the same quantity of gold would not be produced in America, as its value would only be increased in proportion to the diminution of quantity consequent on its increased cost of production. No more goods, then, would be obtained in America in exchange for all their gold exported than before; and it may be asked where then would be the benefit to Spain and her colonies? The benefit would be this, that if less gold were produced, less capital would be employed in producing it; the same value of goods from Europe would be imported by the employment of the smaller capital that was before obtained by the employment of the larger; and, therefore, all the productions obtained by the employment of the capital withdrawn from the mines would be a benefit which Spain would derive from the imposition of the tax, and which she could not obtain in such abundance, or with such certainty, by possessing the monopoly of any other commodity whatever. From such a tax, as far as money was concerned, the nations of Europe would suffer no injury whatever; they would have the same quantity of goods, and consequently the same means of enjoyment as before, but these goods would be circulated with a less quantity, because a more valuable money.

If in consequence of the tax only one-tenth of the present quantity of gold were obtained from the mines, that tenth would be of equal value with the ten tenths now produced. But the King of Spain is not exclusively in possession of the mines of the precious metals; and if he were, his advantage from their possession, and the power of taxation, would be very much reduced by the limitation of demand and consumption in Europe, in consequence of the universal substitution, in a greater or less degree, of paper money. The agreement of the market and natural prices of all commodities depends at all times on the facility with which the supply can be increased or diminished. In the case of gold, houses, and labor, as well as many other things, this effect cannot, under some circumstances, be speedily produced. But it is different with those commodities which are consumed and reproduced from year to year, such as hats, shoes, corn, and cloth; they may be reduced, if necessary, and the interval cannot be long before the supply is contracted in proportion to the increased charge of producing them.

A tax on raw produce from the surface of the earth will, as we have seen, fall on the consumer, and will in no way affect rent; unless by diminishing the funds for the maintenance of labor it lowers wages, reduces the population, and diminishes the demand for corn. But a tax on the produce of gold mines must, by enhancing the value of that metal, necessarily reduce the demand for it, and must therefore necessarily displace capital from the employment to which it was applied. Notwithstanding, then, that Spain would derive all the benefits which I have stated from a tax on gold, the proprietors of those mines from which capital was withdrawn would lose all their rent. This would be a loss to individuals, but not a national loss; rent being not a creation, but merely a transfer of wealth: the King of Spain, and the proprietors of the mines which continued to be worked, would together receive, not only all that the liberated capital produced, but all that the other proprietors lost.

Suppose the mines of the 1st, 2nd, and 3rd quality to be worked, and to produce respectively 100, 80, and 70 pounds weight of gold, and therefore the rent of No. 1 to be thirty pounds, and that of No. 2 ten pounds. Suppose, now, the tax to be seventy pounds of gold per annum on each mine worked; and consequently that No. 1 alone could be profitably worked, it is evident that all rent would immediately disappear. Before the imposition of the tax, out of the 100 pounds produced on No. 1, a rent was paid of thirty pounds, and the worker of the mine retained seventy, a sum equal to the produce of the least productive mine. The value, then, of what remains to the capitalist of the mine No, 1 must be the same as before, or he would not obtain the common profits of stock; and, consequently, after paying seventy out of his 100 pounds for tax, the value of the remaining thirty must be as great as the value of seventy was before, and therefore the value of the whole hundred as great as 233 pounds before. Its value might be higher, but it could not be lower, or even this mine would cease to be worked. Being a monopolized commodity, it could exceed its natural value, and then it would pay a rent equal to that excess; but no funds would be employed in the mine if it were below this value. In return for one-third of the labor and capital employed in the mines, Spain would obtain as much gold as would exchange for the same, or very nearly the same, quantity of commodities as before. She would be richer by the produce of the two-thirds liberated from the mines. If the value of the 100 pounds of gold should be equal to that of the 250 pounds extracted before, the King of Spain's portion, his seventy pounds would be equal to 175 at the former value: a small part of the king's tax only would fall on his own subjects, the greater part being obtained by the better distribution of capital.

The account of Spain would stand thus:

Formerly produced: Gold, 250 pounds, of the value of (suppose)	10,000 yards of cloth.
Now produced: By the two capitalists who quitted the mines, the same value as 140 pounds of gold formerly exchanged for; equal to	5600 yards of cloth.
By the capitalist who works the mine, No. 1, thirty pounds of gold, increased in value, as 1 to 21/2 and therefore now of the value of	3000 yards of cloth.
Tax to the king, seventy pounds, increased also in value as 1 to 21/2, and therefore now of the value of	7000 yards of cloth.
	15,600

Of the 7000 received by the king, the people of Spain would contribute only 1400, and 5600 would be pure gain, effected by the liberated capital.

If the tax, instead of being a fixed sum per mine worked, were a certain portion of its produce, the quantity would not be immediately reduced in consequence. If a half, a fourth, or a third of each mine were taken for the tax, it would nevertheless be the interest of the proprietors to make their mines yield as abundantly as before; but if the quantity were not reduced, but only a part of it transferred from the proprietor to the king, its value would not rise; the tax would fall on the people of the colonies, and no advantage would be gained. A tax of this kind would have the effect that Adam Smith supposes taxes on raw produce would have on the rent of land—it would fall entirely on the rent of the mine. If pushed a little further, indeed, the tax would not only absorb the whole rent, but would deprive the worker of the mine of the common profits of stock, and he would consequently withdraw his capital from the production of gold. If still further extended, the rent of still better mines would be absorbed, and capital would be further withdrawn; and thus the quantity would be continually reduced, and its value raised, and the same effects would take place as we have already pointed out; a part of the tax would be paid by the people of the Spanish colonies, and the other part would be a new creation of produce, by increasing the power of the instrument used as a medium of exchange.

Taxes on gold are of two kinds, one on the actual quantity of gold in circulation, the other on the quantity that is annually produced from the mines. Both have a tendency to reduce the quantity and to raise the value of gold; but by neither will its value be raised till the quantity is reduced, and therefore such taxes will fall for a time, until the supply is diminished, on the proprietors of money, but ultimately that part which will permanently fall on the community will be paid by the owner of the mine in the reduction of rent, and by the purchasers of that portion of gold which is used as a commodity contributing to the enjoyments of mankind, and not set apart exclusively for a circulating medium.

CHAPTER XIV

Taxes on Houses

There are also other commodities besides gold which cannot be speedily reduced in quantity; any tax on which will therefore fall on the proprietor if the increase of price should lessen the demand.

Taxes on houses are of this description; though laid on the occupier, they will frequently fall by a diminution of rent on the landlord. The produce of the land is consumed and reproduced from year to year, and so are many other commodities; as they may therefore be speedily brought to a level with the demand, they cannot long exceed their natural price. But as a tax on houses may be considered in the light of an additional rent paid by the tenant, its tendency will be to diminish the demand for houses of the same annual rent without diminishing their supply. Rent will therefore fall, and a part of the tax that will be paid indirectly by the landlord.

"The rent of a house," says Adam Smith, "may be distinguished into two parts, of which the one may very properly be called the building rent, the other is commonly called the ground rent. The building rent is the interest or profit of the capital expended in building the house. In order to put the trade of a builder upon a level with other trades, it is necessary that this rent should be sufficient first to pay the same interest which he would have got for his capital if he had lent it upon good security; and, secondly, to keep the house in constant repair, or, what comes to the same thing, to replace within a certain term of years the capital which had been employed in building it." "If, in proportion to the interest of money, the trade of the builder affords at any time a much greater profit than this, it will soon draw so much capital from other trades as will reduce the profit to its proper level. If it affords at any time much less than this, other trades will soon draw so much capital from it as will again raise that profit. Whatever part of the whole rent of a house is over and above what is sufficient for affording this reasonable profit, naturally goes to the ground rent; and where the owner of the ground, and the owner of the building, are two different persons, it is in most cases completely paid to the former. In country houses, at a distance from any great town, where there is a plentiful choice of ground, the ground rent is scarcely anything, or no more than what the space upon which the house stands would pay employed in agriculture. In country villas, in the neighborhood of some great town, it is sometimes a good deal higher, and the peculiar conveniency, or beauty of situation, is there frequently very highly paid for. Ground rents are generally highest in the capital, and in those particular parts of it where there happens to be the greatest demand for houses, whatever be the reason for that demand, whether for trade and business, for pleasure and society, or for mere vanity and fashion." A tax on the rent of houses may either fall on the occupier, on the ground landlord, or on the building landlord. In ordinary cases it may be presumed that the whole tax would be paid, both immediately and finally, by the occupier.

If the tax be moderate, and the circumstances of the country such that it is either stationary or advancing, there would be little motive for the occupier of a house to content

himself with one of a worse description. But if the tax be high, or any other circumstances should diminish the demand for houses, the landlord's income would fall, for the
occupier would be partly compensated for the tax by a diminution of rent. It is, however,
difficult to say in what proportions that part of the tax, which was saved by the occupier
by a fall of rent, would fall on the building rent and the ground rent. It is probable that,
in the first instance, both would be affected; but as houses are, though slowly, yet certainly perishable, and as no more would be built till the profits of the builder were restored to the general level, building rent would, after an interval, be restored to its natural
price. As the builder receives rent only whilst the building endures, he could pay no part
of the tax, under the most disastrous circumstances, for any longer period.

The payment of this tax, then, would ultimately fall on the occupier and ground landlord, but, "in what proportion this final payment would be divided between them," says
Adam Smith, "it is not perhaps very easy to ascertain. The division would probably be
very different in different circumstances, and a tax of this kind might, according to those
different circumstances, affect very unequally both the inhabitant of the house and the
owner of the ground."[24]

Adam Smith considers ground rents as peculiarly fit subjects for taxation. "Both
ground rents and the ordinary rent of land," he says, "are a species of revenue, which the
owner in many cases enjoys without any care or attention of his own. Though a part of
this revenue should be taken from him, in order to defray the expenses of the state, no
discouragement will thereby be given to any sort of industry. The annual produce of the
land and labor of the society, the real wealth and revenue of the great body of the people, might be the same after such a tax as before. Ground rents and the ordinary rent of
land are, therefore, perhaps, the species of revenue which can best bear to have a peculiar tax imposed upon them." It must be admitted that the effects of these taxes would
be such as Adam Smith has described; but it would surely be very unjust to tax exclusively
the revenue of any particular class of a community. The burdens of the state should be
borne by all in proportion to their means: this is one of the four maxims mentioned by
Adam Smith which should govern all taxation. Rent often belongs to those who, after
many years of toil, have realized their gains and expended their fortunes in the purchase
of land or houses; and it certainly would be an infringement of that principle which
should ever be held sacred, the security of property, to subject it to unequal taxation. It
is to be lamented that the duty by stamps, with which the transfer of landed property is
loaded, materially impedes the conveyance of it into those hands where it would probably be made most productive. And if it be considered that land, regarded as a fit subject for exclusive taxation, would not only be reduced in price, to compensate for the risk
of that taxation, but in proportion to the indefinite nature and uncertain value of the risk
would become a fit subject for speculations, partaking more of the nature of gambling
than of sober trade, it will appear probable that the hands into which land would in that
case be most apt to fall would be the hands of those who possess more of the qualities of
the gambler than of the qualities of the sober-minded proprietor, who is likely to employ
his land to the greatest advantage.

CHAPTER XV

Taxes on Profits

Taxes on those commodities which are generally denominated luxuries fall on those only who make use of them. A tax on wine is paid by the consumer of wine. A tax on pleasure horses, or on coaches, is paid by those who provide for themselves such enjoyments, and in exact proportion as they provide them. But taxes on necessaries do not affect the consumers of necessaries in proportion to the quantity that may be consumed by them, but often in a much higher proportion. A tax on corn, we have observed, not only affects a manufacturer in the proportion that he and his family may consume corn, but it alters the rate of profits of stock, and therefore also affects his income. Whatever raises the wages of labor, lowers the profits of stock; therefore every tax on any commodity consumed by the laborer has a tendency to lower the rate of profits.

A tax on hats will raise the price of hats; a tax on shoes, the price of shoes; if this were not the case, the tax would be finally paid by the manufacturer; his profits would be reduced below the general level, and he would quit his trade. A partial tax on profits will raise the price of the commodity on which it falls: a tax, for example, on the profits of the hatter would raise the price of hats; for if his profits were taxed, and not those of any other trade, his profits, unless he raised the price of his hats, would be below the general rate of profits, and he would quit his employment for another.

In the same manner, a tax on the profits of the fanner would raise the price of corn; a tax on the profits of the clothier, the price of cloth; and if a tax in proportion to profits were laid on all trades, every commodity would be raised in price. But if the mine which supplied us with the standard of our money were in this country, and the profits of the miner were also taxed, the price of no commodity would rise, each man would give an equal proportion of his income, and everything would be as before.

If money be not taxed, and therefore be permitted to preserve its value, whilst everything else is taxed and is raised in value, the hatter, the fanner, and clothier, each employing the same capitals, and obtaining the same profits, will pay the same amount of tax. If the tax be £100, the hats, the cloth, and the corn will each be increased in value £100. If the hatter gains by his hats £1100, instead of £1000, he will pay £100 to government for the tax; and therefore will still have £1000 to lay out on goods for his own consumption. But as the cloth, corn, and all other commodities will be raised in price from the same cause, he will not obtain more for his £1000 than he before obtained for £910, and thus will he contribute by his diminished expenditure to the exigencies of the state; he will, by the payment of the tax, have placed a portion of the produce of the land and labor of the country at the disposal of government, instead of using that portion himself. If, instead of expending his £1000, he adds it to his capital, he will find in the rise of wages, and in the increased cost of the raw material and machinery, that his saving of £1000 does not amount to more than a saving of £910 amounted to before.

If money be taxed, or if by any other cause its value be altered, and all commodities remain precisely at the same price as before, the profits of the manufacturer and farmer will also be the same as before, they will continue to be £1000; and as they will each have to pay £100 to government, they will retain only £900, which will give them a less command over the produce of the land and labor of the country, whether they expend it in productive or unproductive labor. Precisely what they lose, government will gain. In the first case, the contributor to the tax would, for £1000, have as great a quantity of goods as he before had for £910; in the second, he would have only as much as he before had for £900, for the price of goods would remain unaltered, and he would have only £900 to expend. This proceeds from the difference in the amount of the tax; in the first case, it is only an eleventh of his income; in the second, it is a tenth; money in the two cases being of a different value.

But although, if money be not taxed, and do not alter in value, all commodities will rise in price, they will not rise in the same proportion; they will not after the tax bear the same relative value to each other which they did before the tax. In a former part of this work we discussed the effects of the division of capital into fixed and circulating, or rather into durable and perishable capital, on the prices of commodities. We showed that two manufacturers might employ precisely the same amount of capital, and might derive from it precisely the same amount of profits, but that they would sell their commodities for very different sums of money, according as the capitals they employed were rapidly, or slowly, consumed and reproduced. The one might sell his goods for £4000, the other for £10,000, and they might both employ £10,000 of capital, and obtain 20 percent, profit, or £2000. The capital of one might consist, for example, of £2000 circulating capital, to be reproduced, and £8000 fixed, in buildings and machinery; the capital of the other, on the contrary, might consist of £8000 of circulating, and of only £2000 fixed capital in machinery and buildings. Now, if each of these persons were to be taxed 10 percent, on his income, or £200, the one to make his business yield him the general rate of profit must raise his goods from £10,000 to £10,200; the other would also be obliged to raise the price of his goods from £4000 to £4200. Before the tax, the goods sold by one of these manufacturers were 2 1/2 times more valuable than the goods of the other; after the tax they will be 2.42 times more valuable: the one kind will have risen two percent: the other five percent: consequently a tax upon income, whilst money continued unaltered in value, would alter the relative prices and value of commodities. This would be true also if the tax, instead of being laid on the profits, were laid on the commodities themselves: provided they were taxed in proportion to the value of the capital employed on their production, they would rise equally, whatever might be their value, and therefore they would not preserve the same proportion as before. A commodity which rose from ten to eleven thousand pounds would not bear the same relation as before to another which rose from £2000 to £3000. If, under these circumstances, money rose in value, from whatever cause it might proceed, it would not affect the prices of commodities in the same proportion. The same cause which would lower the price of one from £10,200 to £10,000 or less than two percent, would lower the price of the other from £4200 to £4000 or 4 3/4 percent. If they fell in any different proportion, profits would not be equal; for to make them equal, when the price of the first commodity was £10,000, the price of the second should be £4000; and when the price of the first was £10,200, the price of the other should be £4200.

The consideration of this fact will lead to the understanding of a very important principle, which, I believe, has never been adverted to. It is this : that in a country where no taxation subsists, the alteration in the value of money arising from scarcity or abundance will operate in an equal proportion on the prices of all commodities; that if a commodity of £1000 value rise to £1200, or fall to £800, a commodity of £10,000 value will rise to £12,000 or fall to £8000; but in a country where prices are artificially raised by taxation, the abundance of money from an influx, or the exportation and consequent scarcity of it from foreign demand, will not operate in the same proportion on the prices of all commodities; some it will raise or lower 5, 6, or 12 percent, others 3, 4, or 7 percent. If a country were not taxed, and money should fall in value, its abundance in every market would produce similar effects in each. If meat rose 20 percent, bread, beer, shoes, labor, and every commodity would also rise 20 percent; it is necessary they should do so, to secure to each trade the same rate of profits. But this is no longer true when any of these commodities is taxed; if, in that case, they should all rise in proportion to the fall in the value of money, profits would be rendered unequal; in the case of the commodities taxed, profits would be raised above the general level, and capital would be removed from one employment to another, till an equilibrium of profits was restored, which could only be after the relative prices were altered.

Will not this principle account for the different effects, which it was remarked were produced on the prices of commodities from the altered value of money during the bank-restriction? It was objected to those who contended that the currency was at that period depreciated, from the too great abundance of the paper circulation, that, if that were the fact, all commodities ought to have risen in the same proportion; but it was found that many had varied considerably more than others, and thence it was inferred that the rise of prices was owing to something affecting the value of commodities, and not to any alteration in the value of the currency. It appears, however, as we have just seen, that in a country where commodities are taxed, they will not all vary in price in the same proportion, either in consequence of a rise or of a fall in the value of currency.

If the profits of all trades were taxed, excepting the profits of the farmer, all goods would rise in money value, excepting raw produce. The farmer would have the same corn income as before, and would sell his corn also for the same money price; but as he would be obliged to pay an additional price for all the commodities, except corn, which he consumed, it would be to him a tax on expenditure. Nor would he be relieved from this tax by an alteration in the value of money, for an alteration in the value of money might sink all the taxed commodities to their former price, but the untaxed one would sink below its former level; and, therefore, though the farmer would purchase his commodities at the same price as before, he would have less money with which to purchase them.

The landlord, too, would be precisely in the same situation; he would have the same corn, and the same money-rent as before, if all commodities rose in price and money remained at the same value; and he would have the same corn, but a less money-rent, if all commodities remained at the same price: so that in either case, though his income were not directly taxed, he would indirectly contribute towards the money raised.

But suppose the profits of the farmer to be also taxed, he then would be in the same situation as other traders: his raw produce would rise, so that he would have the same money revenue, after paying the tax, but he would pay an additional price for all the commodities he consumed, raw produce included.

His landlord, however, would be differently situated; he would be benefited by the tax on his tenant's profits, as he would be compensated for the additional price at which he would purchase his manufactured commodities, if they rose in price; and he would have the same money revenue, if, in consequence of a rise in the value of money, commodities sold at their former price. A tax on the profits of the farmer is not a tax proportioned to the gross produce of the land, but to its net produce, after the payment of rent, wages, and all other charges. As the cultivators of the different kinds of land, No. 1, 2, and 3, employ precisely the same capitals, they will get precisely the same profits, whatever may be the quantity of gross produce which one may obtain more than the other; and consequently they will be all taxed alike. Suppose the gross produce of the land of the quality of No. 1 to be 180 qrs., that of No. 2, 170 qrs., and of No. 3, 160, and each to be taxed 10 quarters, the difference between the produce of No. 1, No. 2, and No. 3, after paying the tax, will be the same as before; for if No. 1 be reduced to 170, No. 2 to 160, and No. 3 to 150 qrs., the difference between 3 and 1 will be as before, 20 qrs.; and of No. 3 and No. 2, 10 qrs. If, after the tax, the prices of corn and of every other commodity should remain the same as before, money rent, as well as corn rent, would continue unaltered; but if the price of corn and every other commodity should rise in consequence of the tax, money rent will also rise in the same proportion. If the price of corn were £4 per quarter, the rent of No. 1 would be £80, and that of No. 2, £40; but if corn rose five percent, or to £4 4s., rent would also rise five percent, for twenty quarters of corn would then be worth £84, and ten quarters £42; so that in every case the landlord will be unaffected by such a tax. A tax on the profits of stock always leaves corn rent unaltered, and therefore money rent varies with the price of corn; but a tax on raw produce, or tithes, never leaves corn rent unaltered, but generally leaves money rent the same as before. In another part of this work I have observed that if a land-tax of the same money amount were laid on every kind of land in cultivation, without any allowance for difference of fertility, it would be very unequal in its operation, as it would be a profit to the landlord of the more fertile lands. It would raise the price of corn in proportion to the burden borne by the farmer of the worst land; but this additional price being obtained for the greater quantity of produce yielded by the better land, farmers of such land would be benefited during their leases, and afterwards the advantage would go to the landlord in the form of an increase of rent. The effect of an equal tax on the *profits* of the farmer is precisely the same; it raises the money rent of the landlords if money retains the same value; but as the profits of all other trades are taxed as well as those of the farmer, and consequently the prices of all goods, as well as corn, are raised, the landlord loses as much by the increased money price of the goods and corn on which his rent is expended, as he gains by the rise of his rent. If money should rise in value, and all things should, after a tax on the profits of stock, fall to their former prices, rent also would be the same as before. The landlord would receive the same money rent, and would obtain all the commodities on which it was expended at their former price; so that under all circumstances he would continue untaxed.[25]

This circumstance is curious. By taxing the profits of the farmer you do not burthen him more than if you exempted his profits from the tax, and the landlord has a decided interest that his tenants' profits should be taxed, as it is only on that condition that he himself continues really untaxed.

A tax on the profits of capital would also affect the stockholder, if all commodities were to rise in proportion to the tax although his dividends continued untaxed; but if, from the alteration in the value of money, all commodities were to sink to their former price, the stock-holder would pay nothing towards the tax; he would purchase all his commodities at the same price, but would still receive the same money dividend.

If it be agreed that by taxing the profits of one manufacturer only, the price of his goods would rise, to put him on an equality with all other manufacturers; and that by taxing the profits of two manufacturers the prices of two descriptions of goods must rise, I do not see how it can be disputed that by taxing the profits of ail manufacturers the prices of all goods would rise, provided the mine which supplied us with money were in this country and continued untaxed. But as money, or the standard of money, is a commodity imported from abroad, the prices of all goods could not rise; for such an effect could not take place without an additional quantity of money,[26] which could not be obtained in exchange for dear goods, as was shown in Chapter V. If, however, such a rise could take place, it could not be permanent, for it would have a powerful influence on foreign trade. In return for commodities imported, those dear goods could not be exported, and therefore we should for a time continue to buy, although we ceased to sell; and should export money, or bullion, till the relative prices of commodities were nearly the same as before. It appears to me absolutely certain that a well regulated tax on profits would ultimately restore commodities, both of home and foreign manufacture, to the same money price which they bore before the tax was imposed.

As taxes on raw produce, tithes, taxes on wages, and on the necessaries of the laborer will, by raising wages, lower profits, they will all, though not in an equal degree, be attended with the same effects.

The discovery of machinery, which materially improves home manufactures, always tends to raise the relative value of money, and therefore to encourage its importation. All taxation, all increased impediments, either to the manufacturer or the grower of commodities, tend, on the contrary, to lower the relative value of money, and therefore to encourage its exportation.

CHAPTER XVI

Taxes on Wages

Taxes on wages will raise wages, and therefore will diminish the rate of the profits of stock. We have already seen that a tax on necessaries will raise their prices, and will be followed by a rise of wages. The only difference between a tax on necessaries and a tax on wages is, that the former will necessarily be accompanied by a rise in the price of necessaries, but the latter will not; towards a tax on wages, consequently, neither the stockholder, the landlord, nor any other class but the employers of labor will contribute. A tax on wages is wholly a tax on profits; a tax on necessaries is partly a tax on profits and partly a tax on rich consumers. The ultimate effects which will result from such taxes, then, are precisely the same as those which result from a direct tax on profits.

"The wages of the inferior classes of workmen," says Adam Smith, "I have endeavored to show in the first book, are everywhere necessarily regulated by two different circumstances—the demand for labor and the ordinary or average price of provisions. The demand for labor, according as it happens to be either increasing, stationary, or declining, or to require an increasing, stationary, or declining population, regulates the subsistence of the laborer, and determines in what degree it shall be either liberal, moderate, or scanty. The *ordinary or average* price of provisions determines the quantity of money which must be paid to the workmen, in order to enable him, one year with another, to purchase this liberal, moderate, or scanty subsistence. While the demand for labor and the price of provisions, therefore, remain the same, a direct tax upon the wages of labor can have no other effect than to raise them somewhat higher than the tax."

To the proposition, as it is here advanced by Dr. Smith, Mr. Buchanan offers two objections. First, he denies that the money wages of labor are regulated by the price of provisions; and secondly, he denies that a tax on the wages of labor would raise the price of labor. On the first point Mr. Buchanan's argument is as follows, page 59: "The wages of labor, it has already been remarked, consist not in money, but in what money purchases, namely, provisions and other necessaries; and the allowance of the laborer out of the common stock will always be in proportion to the supply. Where provisions are *cheap and abundant,* his share will be the larger; and where they are *scarce and dear,* it will be the less. His wages will always give him his just share, and they cannot give him more. It is an opinion, indeed, adopted by Dr. Smith and most other writers, that the money price of labor is regulated by the money price of provisions, and that, when provisions rise in price, wages rise in proportion. But it is clear that the price of labor has no necessary connection with the price of food, since it depends entirely on the supply of laborers compared with the demand. Besides, it is to be observed that the high price of provisions is a certain indication of a deficient supply, and arises in the natural course of things for the purpose of retarding the consumption. A smaller supply of food, shared among the same number of consumers, will evidently leave a smaller portion to each, and the laborer must bear his share of the common want. To distribute this burden equally, and to prevent the laborer from consuming subsistence so freely as before, the price rises. But wages, it seems, must rise along with it, that he may still use the same quantity of a scarcer commodity; and thus nature is represented as counteracting her own purposes; first, raising the price of food to diminish the consumption, and afterwards raising wages to give the laborer the same supply as before."

In this argument of Mr. Buchanan, there appears to me to be a great mixture of truth and error. Because a high price of provisions is sometimes occasioned by a deficient supply, Mr. Buchanan assumes it as a certain indication of deficient supply. He attributes to one cause exclusively that which may arise from many. It is undoubtedly true that, in the case of a deficient supply, a smaller quantity will be shared among the same number of consumers, and a smaller portion will fall to each. To distribute this privation equally, and to prevent the laborer from consuming subsistence so freely as before, the price rises. It must, therefore, be conceded to Mr. Buchanan that any rise in the price of provisions occasioned by a deficient supply will not necessarily raise the money wages of labor as the consumption must be retarded, which can only be effected by diminishing the power of the consumers to purchase. But, because the price of provisions is raised by a deficient supply, we are by no means warranted in concluding, as Mr. Buchanan appears to do, that there may not be an abundant supply with a high price; not a high price with regard to money only, but with regard to all other things.

The natural price of commodities, which always ultimately governs their market price, depends on the facility of production; but the quantity produced is not in proportion to that facility. Although the lands which are now taken into cultivation are much inferior to the lands in cultivation three centuries ago, and therefore the difficulty of production is increased, who can entertain any doubt but that the quantity produced now very far exceeds the quantity then produced? Not only is a high price compatible with an increased supply, but it rarely fails to accompany it. If, then, in consequence of taxation, or of difficulty of production, the price of provisions be raised and the quantity be not diminished, the money wages of labor will rise; for, as Mr. Buchanan has justly observed, "The wages of labor consist not in money, but in what money purchases, namely, provisions and other necessaries; and the allowance of the laborer out of the common stock will always be in proportion to the supply."

With respect to the second point, whether a tax on the wages of labor would raise the price of labor, Mr. Buchanan says, "After the laborer has received the fair recompense of his labor, how can he have recourse on his employer for what he is afterwards compelled to pay away in taxes? There is no law or principle in human affairs to warrant such a conclusion. After the laborer has received his wages, they are in his own keeping, and he must, as far as he is able, bear the burden of whatever exactions he may ever afterwards be exposed to: for he has clearly no way of compelling those to reimburse him who have already paid him the fair price of his work." Mr. Buchanan has quoted, with great approbation, the following able passage from Mr. Malthus's work on population, which appears to me completely to answer his objection. "The price of labor, when left to find its natural level, is a most important political barometer, expressing the relation between the supply of provisions and the demand for them, between the quantity to be consumed and the number of consumers; and, taken on the average, independently of accidental circumstances, it further expresses, clearly, the wants of the society respecting population;

that is, whatever may be the number of children to a marriage necessary to maintain exactly the present population, the price of labor will be just sufficient to support this number, or be above it, or below it, according to the state of the real funds for the maintenance of labor, whether stationary, progressive, or retrograde. Instead, however, of considering it in this light, we consider it as something which we may raise or depress at pleasure, something which depends principally on his majesty's justices of the peace. When an advance in the price of provisions already expresses that the demand is too great for the supply, in order to put the laborer in the same condition as before, we raise the price of labor, that is, we increase the demand, and are then much surprised that the price of provisions continues rising. In this, we act much in the same manner as if, when the quicksilver in the common weatherglass stood at *stormy,* we were to raise it by some forcible pressure to settled fair, and then be greatly astonished that it continued raining."

"The price of labor will express dearly the wants of the society respecting population;" it will be just sufficient to support the population, which at that time the state of the funds for the maintenance of laborers requires. If the laborer's wages were before only adequate to supply the requisite population, they will, after the tax, be inadequate to that supply, for he will not have the same funds to expend on his family. Labor will therefore rise, because the demand continues, and it is only by raising the price that the supply is not checked.

Nothing is more common than to see hats or malt rise when taxed; they rise because the requisite supply would not be afforded if they did not rise: so with labor, when wages are taxed, its price rises, because, if it did not, the requisite population would not be kept up. Does not Mr. Buchanan allow all that is contended for, when he says that "were he (the laborer) indeed reduced to a bare allowance of necessaries, he would then suffer no further abatement of his wages, as he could not on such conditions continue his race?" Suppose the circumstances of the country to be such that the lowest laborers are not only called upon to continue their race, but to increase it; their wages would be regulated accordingly. Can they multiply in the degree required if a tax takes from them a part of their wages, and reduces them to bare necessaries?

It is undoubtedly true that a taxed commodity will not rise in proportion to the tax if the demand for it diminish, and if the quantity cannot be reduced. If metallic money were in general use, its value would not for a considerable time be increased by a tax, in proportion to the amount of the tax, because at a higher price the demand would be diminished and the quantity would not he diminished; and unquestionably the same cause frequently influences the wages of labor; the number of laborers cannot be rapidly increased or diminished in proportion to the increase or diminution of the fund which is to employ them; but in the case supposed, there is no necessary diminution of demand for labor, and if diminished, the demand does not abate in proportion to the tax. Mr. Buchanan forgets that the fund raised by the tax is employed by government in maintaining laborers, unproductive indeed, but still laborers. If labor were not to rise when wages are taxed, there would be a great increase in the competition for labor, because the owners of capital, who would have nothing to pay towards such a tax, would have the same funds for employing labor; whilst the government who received the tax would have an additional fund for the same purpose. Government and the people thus become competitors, and the consequence of their competition is a rise in the price of labor. The same number of men only will be employed, but they will be employed at additional wages.

If the tax had been laid at once on the people of capital, their fund for the maintenance of labor would have been diminished in the very same degree that the fund of government for that purpose had been increased; and therefore there would have been no rise in wages; for though there would be the same demand, there would not be the same competition. If when the tax were levied government at once exported the produce of it as a subsidy to a foreign state, and if therefore these funds were devoted to the maintenance of foreign and not of English laborers, such as soldiers, sailors, etc., etc.; then, indeed, there would be a diminished demand for labor, and wages might not increase although they were taxed; but the same thing would happen if the tax had been laid on consumable commodities, on the profits of stock, or if in any other manner the same sum had been raised to supply this subsidy: less labor could be employed at home. In one case wages are prevented from rising, in the other they must absolutely fall. But suppose the amount of a tax on wages were, after being raised on the laborers, paid gratuitously to their employers, it would increase their money fund for the maintenance of labor, but it would not increase either commodities or labor. It would consequently increase the competition amongst the employers of labor, and the tax would be ultimately attended with no loss either to master or laborer. The master would pay an increased price for labor; the addition which the laborer received would be paid as a tax to government, and would be again returned to the masters. It must, however, not be forgotten that the produce of taxes is generally wastefully expended, they are always obtained at the expense of the people's comforts and enjoyments, and commonly either diminish capital or retard its accumulation. By diminishing capital they tend to diminish the real fund destined for the maintenance of labor; and therefore to diminish the real demand for it. Taxes, then, generally, as far as they impair the real capital of the country, diminish the demand for labor, and therefore it is a probable, but not a necessary nor a peculiar consequence of a tax on wages, that though wages would rise, they would not rise by a sum precisely equal to the tax.

Adam Smith, as we have seen, has fully allowed that the effect of a tax on wages would be to raise wages by a sum at least equal to the tax, and would be finally, if not immediately, paid by the employer of labor. Thus far we fully agree; but we essentially differ in our views of the subsequent operation of such a tax.

"A direct tax upon the wages of labor, therefore," says Adam Smith, though the laborer might perhaps pay it out of his hand, could not properly be said to be even advanced by him; at least if the demand for labor and the average price of provisions remained the same after the tax as before it. In all such cases, not only the tax but something more than the tax would in reality be advanced by the person who immediately employed him. The final payment would in different cases fall upon different persons. The rise which such a tax might occasion in the wages of manufacturing labor would be advanced by the master manufacturer, *who would be entitled and obliged to charge it with a profit upon the price of his goods*. The rise which such a tax might occasion in country labor would be advanced by the farmer, who, in order to maintain the same number of laborers as before, would be obliged to employ a greater capital. In order to get back this greater capital, *together with the ordinary profits of stock,* it would be necessary that he should retain a larger portion, or what comes to the same thing, the price of a larger portion, of the produce of the land, and consequently that he should pay less rent to the landlord. The final payment of this rise of wages would in this case fall upon the landlord, *together with the additional profits of the farmer who had advanced it.* In all cases, a direct tax upon the wages of labor must, in the long run, occasion both a greater reduction in the rent of land and a greater rise in the price of manufactured goods than would have followed from the proper assessment of a sum equal to the produce of the tax partly upon the rent of land and partly upon consumable commodities." Vol. iii. p. 337. In this passage it is asserted that the additional wages paid by farmers will ultimately fall on the landlords, who will receive a diminished rent; but that the additional wages paid by manufacturers will occasion a rise in the price of manufactured goods, and will therefore fall on the consumers of those commodities.

Now, suppose a society to consist of landlords, manufacturers, farmers, and laborers, the laborers, it is agreed, would be recompensed for the tax;—but by whom?—who would pay that portion which did not fall on the landlords?—the manufacturers could pay no part of it; for if the price of their commodities should rise in proportion to the additional wages they paid, they would be in a better situation after than before the tax. If the clothier, the hatter, the shoemaker, etc., should be each able to raise the price of their goods 10 percent—supposing 10 percent, to recompense them completely for the additional wages they paid—if, as Adam Smith says, "they would be entitled and obliged to charge the additional wages *with a profit* upon the price of their goods," they could each consume as much as before of each other's goods, and therefore they would pay nothing towards the tax. If the clothier paid more for his hats and shoes, he would receive more for his cloth, and if the hatter paid more for his cloth and shoes, he would receive more for his hats. All manufactured commodities, then, would be bought by them with as much advantage as before, and inasmuch as corn would not be raised in price, which is Dr. Smith's supposition, whilst they had an additional sum to lay out upon its purchase, they would be benefited but not injured by such a tax.

If, then, neither the laborers nor the manufacturers would contribute towards such a tax; if the farmers would be also recompensed by a fall of rent, landlords alone must not only bear its whole weight, but they must also contribute to the increased gains of the manufacturers. To do this, however, they should consume all the manufactured commodities in the country, for the additional price charged on the whole mass is little more than the tax originally imposed on the laborers in manufactures.

Now, it will not be disputed that the clothier, the hatter, and all other manufacturers are consumers of each other's goods; it will not be disputed that laborers of all descriptions consume soap, cloth, shoes, candles, and various other commodities; it is therefore impossible that the whole weight of these taxes should fall on landlords only.

But if the laborers pay no part of the tax, and yet manufactured commodities rise in price, wages must rise, not only to compensate them for the tax, but for the increased price of manufactured necessaries, which, as far as it affects agricultural labor, will be a new cause for the fall of rent; and, as far as it affects manufacturing labor, for a further rise in the price of goods. This rise in the price of goods will again operate on wages, and the action and re-action, first of wages on goods, and then of goods on wages, will be extended without any assignable limits. The arguments by which this theory is supported lead to such absurd conclusions that it may at once be seen that the principle is wholly indefensible.

All the effects which are produced on the profits of stock and the wages of labor by a rise of rent and a rise of necessaries, in the natural progress of society and increasing difficulty of production, will equally follow from a rise of wages in consequence of taxation; and, therefore, the enjoyments of the laborer, as well as those of his employers, will be curtailed by the tax; and not by this tax particularly, but by every other which should raise an equal amount, as they would all tend to diminish the fund destined for the maintenance of labor.

The error of Adam Smith proceeds in the first place from supposing that all taxes paid by the farmer must necessarily fall on the landlord in the shape of a deduction from rent. On this subject I have explained myself most fully, and I trust that it has been shown, to the satisfaction of the reader, that since much capital is employed on the land which pays no rent, and since it is the result obtained by this capital which regulates the price of raw produce, no deduction can be made from rent; and, consequently, either no remuneration will be made to the farmer for a tax on wages, or if made, it must be made by an addition to the price of raw produce.

If taxes press unequally on the farmer, he will be enabled to raise the price of raw produce, to place himself on a level with those who carry on other trades; but a tax on wages, which would not affect him more than it would affect any other trade, could not be removed or compensated by a high price of raw produce; for the same reason which should induce him to raise the price of corn, namely, to remunerate himself for the tax, would induce the clothier to raise the price of cloth, the shoemaker, hatter, and upholsterer to raise the price of shoes, hats, and furniture.

If they could all raise the price of their goods so as to remunerate themselves, with a profit, for the tax: as they are all consumers of each other's commodities, it is obvious that the tax could never be paid; for who would be the contributors if all were compensated?

I hope, then, that I have succeeded in showing that any tax which shall have the effect of raising wages will be paid by a diminution of profits, and, therefore, that a tax on wages is in fact a tax on profits.

This principle of the division of the produce of labor and capital between wages and profits, which I have attempted to establish, appears to me so certain, that excepting in the immediate effects, I should think it of little importance whether the profits of stock or the wages of labor, were taxed. By taxing the profits of stock you would probably alter the rate at which the funds for the maintenance of labor increase, and wages would be disproportioned to the state of that fund, by being too high. By taxing wages, the reward paid to the laborer would also be disproportioned to the state of that fund, by being too low. In the one case by a fall, and in the other by a rise in money wages, the natural equilibrium between profits and wages would be restored. A tax on wages, then, does not fall on the landlord, but it falls on the profits of stock: it does not "entitle and oblige the master manufacturer to charge it with a profit on the prices of his goods," for he will be unable to increase their price, and therefore he must himself wholly and without compensation pay such a tax.[27]

If the effect of taxes on wages be such as I have described, they do not merit the censure cast upon them by Dr. Smith. He observes of such taxes, "These, and some other taxes of the same kind, by raising the price of labor, are said to have ruined the greater part of the manufactures of Holland. Similar taxes, though not quite so heavy, take place in the Milanese, in the states of Genoa, in the duchy of Modena, in the duchies of Parma, Placentia, and Guastalla, and in the ecclesiastical states. A French author of some note has proposed to reform the finances of his country by substituting in the room of other taxes this most ruinous of all taxes. 'There is nothing so absurd,' says Cicero, 'which has not sometimes been asserted by some philosophers.'" And in another place he says: "Taxes upon necessaries, by raising the wages of labor, necessarily tend to raise the price of all manufactures, and consequently to diminish the extent of their sale and consumption." They would not merit this censure, even if Dr. Smith's principle were correct, that such taxes would enhance the prices of manufactured commodities; for such an effect could be only temporary, and would subject us to no disadvantage in our foreign trade. If any cause should raise the price of a few manufactured commodities, it would prevent or check their exportation; but if the same cause operated generally on all, the effect would be merely nominal, and would neither interfere with their relative value, nor in any degree diminish the stimulus to a trade of barter, which all commerce, both foreign and domestic, really is.

I have already attempted to show that when any cause raises the prices of all commodities the effects are nearly similar to a fall in the value of money. If money falls in value all commodities rise in price; and if the effect is confined to one country, it will affect its foreign commerce in the same way as a high price of commodities caused by general taxation; and, therefore, in examining the effects of a low value of money confined to one country, we are also examining the effects of a high price of commodities confined to one country. Indeed, Adam Smith was fully aware of the resemblance between these two cases, and consistently maintained that the low value of money, or, as he calls it, of silver in Spain, in consequence of the prohibition against its exportation, was very highly prejudicial to the manufactures and foreign commerce of Spain. "But that degradation in the value of silver, which being the effect either of the peculiar situation, or of the political institutions of a particular country, takes place only in that country, is a matter of very great consequence, which, far from tending to make anybody really richer, tends to make everybody really poorer. *The rise in the money price of all commodities, which is in this case peculiar to that country,* tends to discourage more or less every sort of industry which is carried on within it, and to enable foreign nations, by furnishing almost all sorts of goods for a smaller quantity of silver than its own workmen can afford to do, to undersell them not only in the foreign but even in the home market." Vol. ii. p. 278.

One, and I think the only one, of the disadvantages of a low value of silver in a country, proceeding from a forced abundance, has been ably explained by Dr. Smith. If the trade in gold and silver were free, "the gold and silver which would go abroad would not go abroad for nothing, but would bring back an equal value of goods of some kind or another. Those goods, too, would not be all matters of mere luxury and expense to be consumed by idle people, who produce nothing in return for their consumption. As the real wealth and revenue of idle people would not be augmented by this extraordinary exportation of gold and silver, so would neither their consumption be augmented by it. Those goods would—probably the greater part of them, and certainly some part of them—consist in materials, tools, and provisions, for the employment and maintenance of industrious people, who would reproduce with a profit the full value of their consumption. A part of the dead stock of the society would thus be turned into active stock, and would put into motion a greater quantity of industry than had been employed before."

By not allowing a free trade in the precious metals when the prices of commodities are raised, either by taxation, or by the influx of the precious metals, you prevent a part of the dead stock of the society from being turned into active stock—you prevent a greater quantity of industry from being employed. But this is the whole amount of the evil—an evil never felt by those countries where the exportation of silver is either allowed or connived at.

The exchanges between countries are at par only whilst they have precisely that quantity of currency which, in the actual situation of things, they should have to carry on the circulation of their commodities. If the trade in the precious metals were perfectly free, and money could be exported without any expense whatever, the exchanges could be no otherwise in every country than at par. If the trade in the precious metals were perfectly free—if they were generally used in circulation, even with the expenses of transporting them, the exchange could never in any of them deviate more from par than by these expenses. These principles, I believe, are now nowhere disputed. If a country used paper money not exchangeable for specie, and, therefore, not regulated by any fixed standard, the exchanges in that country might deviate from par in the same proportion as its money might be multiplied beyond that quantity which would have been allotted to it by general commerce, if the trade in money had been free, and the precious metals had been used, either for money, or for the standard of money.

If by the general operations of commerce, 10 millions of pounds sterling, of a known weight and fineness of bullion, should be the portion of England, and 10 millions of paper pounds were substituted, no effect would be produced on the exchange; but if by the abuse of the power of issuing paper money, 11 millions of pounds should be employed in the circulation, the exchange would be 9 percent, against England; if 12 millions were employed, the exchange would be 16 percent; and if 20 millions, the exchange would be 50 percent, against England. To produce this effect it is not, however, necessary that paper money should be employed: any cause which retains in circulation a greater quantity of pounds than would have circulated if commerce had been free, and the precious metals of a known weight and fineness had been used, either for money or for the standard of money, would exactly produce the same effects. Suppose that by clipping the money each pound did not contain the quantity of gold or silver which by law it should contain, a greater number of such pounds might be employed in the circulation than if they were not clipped. If from each pound one-tenth were taken away, 11 millions of such pounds might be used instead of 10; if two-tenths were taken away, 12 millions might be employed; and if one-half were taken away, 20 millions might not be found superfluous. If the latter sum were used instead of 10 millions, every commodity in England would be raised to double its former price, and the exchange would be 50 percent, against England; but this would occasion no disturbance in foreign commerce, nor discourage the manufacture of any one commodity. If, for example, cloth rose in England from £20 to £40 per piece, we should just as freely export it after as before the rise, for a compensation of 50 percent, would be made to the foreign purchaser in the exchange; so that with £20 of his money, he could purchase a bill which would enable him to pay a debt of £40 in England. In the same manner, if he exported a commodity which cost £20 at home, and which sold in England for £40, he would only receive £20, for £40 in England would only purchase a bill for £20 on a foreign country. The same effects would follow from whatever cause 20 millions could be forced to perform the business of circulation in England if 10 millions only were necessary. If so absurd a law as the prohibition of the exportation of the precious metals could be enforced, and the consequence of such prohibition were to force 11 millions of good pounds, fresh from the mint, instead of 10, into circulation, the exchange would be 9 percent, against England; if 12 millions, 16 percent; and if 20 millions, 50 percent against England. But no discouragement would be given to the manufactures of England; if home commodities sold at a high price in England, so would foreign commodities; and whether they were high or low would be of little importance to the foreign exporter and importer, whilst he would, on the one hand, be obliged to allow a compensation in the exchange when his commodities sold at a dear rate, and would receive the same compensation when he was obliged to purchase English commodities at a high price. The sole disadvantage, then, which could happen to a country from retaining, by prohibitory laws, a greater quantity of gold and silver in circulation than would otherwise remain there, would be the loss which it would sustain from employing a portion of its capital unproductively instead of employing it productively. In the form of money, this capital is productive of no profit; in the form of materials, machinery, and food, for which it might be exchanged, it would be productive of revenue, and would add to the wealth and the resources of the state. Thus, then, I hope, I have satisfactorily proved that a comparatively low price of the precious metals, in consequence of taxation, or in other words, a generally high price of commodities, would be of no disadvantage to a state, as a part of the metals would be exported, which, by raising their value, would again lower the prices of commodities. And further, that if they were not exported, if by prohibitory laws they could be retained in a country, the effect on the exchange would counterbalance the effect of high prices. If, then, taxes on necessaries and on wages would not raise the prices of all commodities on which labor was expended, they cannot be condemned on such grounds; and moreover, even if the opinion given by Adam Smith, that they would have such an effect, were well founded, they would be in no degree injurious on that account. They would be objectionable for no other reason than those which might be justly urged against taxes of any other description.

The landlords, as such, would be exempted from the burden of the tax; but as far as they directly employed labor in the expenditure of their revenues, by supporting gardeners, menial servants, etc., they would be subject to its operation.

It is undoubtedly true that "taxes upon luxuries have no tendency to raise the price of any other commodities, except that of the commodities taxed," but it is not true "that taxes upon necessaries, by raising the wages of labor, necessarily tend to raise the price of all manufactures." It is true that "taxes upon luxuries are finally paid by the consumers of the commodities taxed, without any retribution. They fall indifferently upon every species of revenue, the wages of labor, the profits of stock, and the rent of land;" but it is not true "that taxes upon necessaries, *so far as they affect the laboring poor,* are finally paid partly by landlords in the diminished rent of their lands, and partly by rich consumers, whether landlords or others, in the advanced price of manufactured goods;" for, *so far as these taxes affect the laboring poor,* they will be almost wholly paid by the diminished profits of stock, a small part only being paid by the laborers themselves in the diminished demand for labor, which taxation of every kind has a tendency to produce.

It is from Dr. Smith's erroneous view of the effect of those taxes that he has been led to the conclusion that "the middling and superior ranks of people, if they understood their own interest, ought always to oppose all taxes upon the necessaries of life, as well as all direct taxes upon the wages of labor." This conclusion follows from his reasoning, "that the final payment of both one and the other falls altogether upon themselves, and always with a considerable overcharge. They fall heaviest upon the landlords,[28] who always pay in a double capacity; in that of landlords by the reduction of their rent, and in that of rich consumers by the increase of their expense. The observation of Sir Matthew Decker, that certain taxes are, in the price of certain goods, sometimes repeated and accumulated four or five times, is perfectly just with regard to taxes upon the necessaries of life. In the price of leather, for example, you must pay, not only for the tax upon the leather of your own shoes, but for a part of that upon those of the shoemaker and the tanner. You must pay, too, for the tax upon the salt, upon the soap, and upon the candles which those workmen consume while employed in your service, and for the tax upon the leather which the salt-maker, the soap-maker, and the candle-maker consume while employed in their service."

Now as Dr. Smith does not contend that the tanner, the salt-maker, the soap-maker, and the candle-maker will either of them be benefited by the tax on leather, salt, soap, and candles; and as it is certain that government will receive no more than the tax imposed, it is impossible to conceive that more can be paid by the public upon whomsoever the tax may fall. The rich consumers may, and indeed will, pay for the poor consumer, but they will pay no more than the whole amount of the tax; and it is not in the nature of things that "the tax should be repeated and accumulated four or five times."

A system of taxation may be defective; more may be raised from the people than what finds its way into the coffers of the state, as a part, in consequence of its effect on prices, may possibly be received by those who are benefited by the peculiar mode in which taxes are laid. Such taxes are pernicious, and should not be encouraged; for it may be laid down as a principle, that when taxes operate justly, they conform to the first of Dr. Smith's maxims, and raise from the people as little as possible beyond what enters into the public treasury of the state. M. Say says, "others offer plans of finance, and propose means for filling the coffers of the sovereign, without any charge to his subjects. But unless a plan of finance is of the nature of a commercial undertaking, it cannot give to government more than it takes away either from individuals or from government itself, under some other form. Something cannot be made out of nothing by the stroke of a wand. In whatever way an operation may be disguised, whatever forms we may constrain a value to take, whatever metamorphosis we may make it undergo, we can only have a value by creating it, or by taking it from others. The very best of all plans of finance is to spend little, and the best of all taxes is that which is the least in amount."

Dr. Smith uniformly, and I think justly, contends that the laboring classes cannot materially contribute to the burdens of the state. A tax on necessaries, or on wages, will therefore be shifted from the poor to the rich: if then the meaning of Dr. Smith is, "that certain taxes are in the price of certain goods sometimes repeated, and accumulated four or five times," for the purpose only of accomplishing this end, namely, the transference of the tax from the poor to the rich, they cannot be liable to censure on that account.

Suppose the just share of the taxes of a rich consumer to be £100, and that he would pay it directly if the tax were laid on income, on wine, or on any other luxury, he would suffer no injury if, by the taxation of necessaries, he should be only called upon for the payment of £25, as far as his own consumption of necessaries and that of his family was concerned; but should be required to repeat this tax three times, by paying an additional price for other commodities to remunerate the laborers, or their employers, for the tax which they have been called upon to advance. Even in that case the reasoning is inconclusive: for if there be no more paid than what is required by government, of what importance can it be to the rich consumer whether he pay the tax directly, by paying an increased price for an object of luxury, or indirectly, by paying an increased price for the necessaries and other commodities he consumes? If more be not paid by the people than what is received by government, the rich consumer will only pay his equitable share; if more is paid, Adam Smith should have stated by whom it is received; but his whole argument is founded in error, for the prices of commodities would not be raised by such taxes.

M. Say does not appear to me to have consistently adhered to the obvious principle which I have quoted from his able work; for in the next page, speaking of taxation, he says, "When it is pushed too far, it produces this lamentable effect, it deprives the contributor of a portion of his riches, without enriching the state. This is what we may comprehend if we consider that every man's power of consuming, whether productively or not, is limited by his income. He cannot then be deprived of a part of his income without being obliged proportionally to reduce his consumption. Hence arises a diminution of demand for those goods which he no longer consumes, and particularly for those on which the tax is imposed. From this diminution of demand there results a diminution of production, and consequently of taxable commodities. The contributor then will lose a portion of his enjoyments; the producer a portion of his profits; and the treasury a portion of its receipts."

M. Say instances the tax on salt in France previous to the revolution; which, he says, diminished the production of salt by one half. If, however, less salt was consumed, less capital was employed in producing it; and, therefore, though the producer would obtain less profit on the production of salt, he would obtain more on the production of other things. If a tax, however burdensome it may be, falls on revenue, and not on capital, it does not diminish demand, it only alters the nature of it. It enables government to consume as much of the produce of the land and labor of the country as was before consumed by the individuals who contribute to the tax, an evil sufficiently great without overcharging it. If my income is £1000 per annum, and I am called upon for £100 per annum for a tax, I shall only be able to demand nine-tenths of the quantity of goods which I before consumed, but I enable government to demand the other tenth. If the commodity taxed be corn, it is not necessary that my demand for corn should diminish, as I may prefer to pay £100 per annum more for my corn, and to the same amount abate in my demand for wine, furniture, or any other luxury.[29] Less capital will consequently be employed in the wine or upholstery trade, but more will be employed in manufacturing those commodities, on which the taxes levied by government will be expended.

M. Say says that M. Turgot, by reducing the market dues on fish *(les droits d'entrée et de halle sur la marée)* in Paris one half, did not diminish the amount of their produce, and that consequently the consumption of fish must have doubled. He infers from this that the profits of the fishermen and those engaged in the trade must also have doubled, and that the income of the country must have increased by the whole amount of these increased profits; and by giving a stimulus to accumulation, must have increased the resources of the state.[30]

Without calling in question the policy which dictated this alteration of the tax, I have my doubts whether it gave any great stimulus to accumulation. If the profits of the fishermen and others engaged in the trade were doubled in consequence of more fish being consumed, capital and labor must have been withdrawn from other occupations to engage them in this particular trade. But in those occupations capital and labor were productive of profits, which must have been given up when they were withdrawn. The ability of the country to accumulate was only increased by the difference between the profits obtained in the business in which the capital was newly engaged, and those obtained in that from which it was withdrawn.

Whether taxes be taken from revenue or capital they diminish the taxable commodities of the state. If I cease to expend £100 on wine, because by paying a tax of that amount I have enabled government to expend £100 instead of expending it myself, one hundred pounds' worth of goods are necessarily withdrawn from the list of taxable commodities. If the revenue of the individuals of a country be 10 millions, they will have at least 10 millions' worth of taxable commodities. If, by taxing some, one million be transferred to the disposal of government, their revenue will still be nominally 10 millions, but they will remain with only nine millions' worth of taxable commodities. There are no circumstances under which taxation does not abridge the enjoyments of those on whom the taxes ultimately fall, and no means by which those enjoyments can again be extended but the accumulation of new revenue.

Taxation can never be so equally applied as to operate in the same proportion on the value of all commodities, and still to preserve them at the same relative value. It frequently operates very differently from the intention of the legislature by its indirect effects. We have already seen that the effect of a direct tax on corn and raw produce is, if money be also produced in the country, to raise the price of all commodities in proportion as raw produce enters into their composition, and thereby to destroy the natural relation which previously existed between them. Another indirect effect is that it raises wages and lowers the rate of profits; and we have also seen, in another part of this work, that the effect of a rise of wages and a fall of profits is to lower the money prices of those commodities which are produced in a greater degree by the employment of fixed capital.

That a commodity, when taxed, can no longer be so profitably exported is so well understood that a drawback is frequently allowed on its exportation, and a duty laid on its importation. If these drawbacks and duties be accurately laid, not only on the commodities themselves, but on all which they may indirectly affect, then, indeed, there will be no disturbance in the value of the precious metals. Since we could as readily export a commodity after being taxed as before, and since no peculiar facility would be given to importation, the precious metals would not, more than before, enter into the list of exportable commodities.

Of all commodities none axe perhaps so proper for taxation as those which, either by the aid of nature or art, are produced with peculiar facility. With respect to foreign countries, such commodities may be classed under the head of those which are not regulated in their price by the quantity of labor bestowed, but rather by the caprice, the tastes, and the power of the purchasers. If England had more productive tin mines than other countries, or if, from superior machinery or fuel, she had peculiar facilities in manufacturing cotton goods, the prices of tin and cotton goods would still in England be regulated by the comparative quantity of labor and capital required to produce them, and the competition of our merchants would make them very little dearer to the foreign consumer. Our advantage in the production of these commodities might be so decided that probably they could bear a very great additional price in the foreign market without very materially diminishing their consumption. This price they never could attain, whilst competition was free at home, by any other means but by a tax on their exportation. This tax would fall wholly on foreign consumers, and part of the expenses of the government of England would be defrayed by a tax on the land and labor of other countries. The tax on tea, which at present is paid by the people of England, and goes to aid the expenses of the government of England, might, if laid in China on the exportation of the tea, be diverted to the payment of the expenses of the government of China.

Taxes on luxuries have some advantage over taxes on necessaries. They are generally paid from income, and therefore do not diminish the productive capital of the country. If wine were much raised in price in consequence of taxation, it is probable that a man would rather forego the enjoyments of wine than make any important encroachments on his capital to be enabled to purchase it. They are so identified with price that the contributor is hardly aware that he is paying a tax. But they have also their disadvantages. First, they never reach capital, and on some extraordinary occasions it may be expedient that even capital should contribute towards the public exigencies; and, secondly, there is no certainty as to the amount of the tax, for it may not reach even income. A man intent on saving will exempt himself from a tax on wine by giving up the use of it. The income of the country may be undiminished, and yet the state may be unable to raise a shilling by the tax.

Whatever habit has rendered delightful will be relinquished with reluctance, and will continue to be consumed notwithstanding a very heavy tax; but this reluctance has its limits, and experience every day demonstrates that an increase in the nominal amount of taxation often diminishes the produce. One man will continue to drink the same quantity of wine, though the price of every bottle should be raised three shillings, who would yet relinquish the use of wine rather than pay four. Another will be content to pay four, yet refuse to pay five shillings. The same may be said of other taxes on luxuries: many would pay a tax of £5 for the enjoyment which a horse affords, who would not pay £10 or £20. It is not because they cannot pay more that they give up the use of wine and of horses, but because they will not pay more. Every man has some standard in his own mind by which he estimates the value of his enjoyments, but that standard is as various as the human character. A country whose financial situation has become extremely artificial, by the mischievous policy of accumulating a large national debt, and a consequently enormous taxation, is particularly exposed to the inconvenience attendant on this mode of raising taxes. After visiting with a tax the whole round of luxuries; after laying horses, carriages, wine, servants, and all the other enjoyments of the rich under contribution; a minister is induced to have recourse to more direct taxes, such as income and property taxes, neglecting the golden maxim of M. Say, "that the very best of all plans of finance is to spend little, and the best of all taxes is that which is the least in amount."

CHAPTER XVII

Taxes on Other Commodities than Raw Produce

On the same principle that a tax on corn would raise the price of corn, a tax on any other commodity would raise the price of that commodity. If the commodity did not rise by a sum equal to the tax, it would not give the same profit to the producer which he had before, and he would remove his capital to some other employment.

The taxing of all commodities, whether they be necessaries or luxuries, will, while money remains at an unaltered value, raise their prices by a sum at least equal to the tax.[31] A tax on the manufactured necessaries of the laborer would have the same effect on wages as a tax on corn, which differs from other necessaries only by being the first and most important on the list; and it would produce precisely the same effects on the profits of stock and foreign trade. But a tax on luxuries would have no other effect than to raise their price. It would fall wholly on the consumer, and could neither increase wages nor lower profits.

Taxes which are levied on a country for the purpose of supporting war, or for the ordinary expenses of the state, and which are chiefly devoted to the support of unproductive laborers, are taken from the productive industry of the country; and every saving which can be made from such expenses will be generally added to the income, if not to the capital of the contributors. When, for the expenses of a year's war, twenty millions are raised by means or a loan, it is the twenty millions which are withdrawn from the productive capital of the nation. The million per annum which is raised by taxes to pay the interest of this loan is merely transferred from those who pay it to those who receive it, from the contributor to the tax to the national creditor. The real expense is the twenty millions, and not the interest which must be paid for it.[32] Whether the interest be or be not paid, the country will neither be richer nor poorer. Government might at once have required the twenty millions in the shape of taxes; in which case it would not have been necessary to raise annual taxes to the amount of a million. This, however, would not have changed the nature of the transaction. An individual, instead of being called upon to pay £100 per annum, might have been obliged to pay £2000 once for all. It might also have suited his convenience rather to borrow this £2000, and to pay £100 per annum for interest to the lender, than to spare the larger sum from his own funds. In one case, it is a private transaction between A and B, in the other government guarantees to B the payment of interest to be equally paid by A. If the transaction had been of a private nature, no public record would be kept of it, and it would be a matter of comparative indifference to the country whether A faithfully performed his contract to B or unjustly retained the £100 per annum in his own possession. The country would have a general interest in the faithful performance of a contract, but with respect to the national wealth it would have no other interest than whether A or B would make this £100 most productive; but on this question it would neither have the right nor the ability to decide. It might be possible that, if A retained it for his own use, he might squander it unprofitably, and if it were paid to B he might add it to his capital and employ it productively. And the converse would also be possible; B might squander it, and A might employ it productively. With a view to wealth only, it might be equally or more desirable that A should or should not pay it; but the claims of justice and good faith, a greater utility, are not to be compelled to yield to those of a less; and accordingly, if the state were called upon to interfere, the courts of justice would oblige A to perform his contract. A debt guaranteed by the nation differs in no respect from the above transaction. Justice and good faith demand that the interest of the national debt should continue to be paid, and that those who have advanced their capitals for the general benefit should not be required to forego their equitable claims on the plea of expediency.

But independently of this consideration, it is by no means certain that political utility would gain anything by the sacrifice of political integrity; it does by no means follow that the party exonerated from the payment of the interest of the national debt would employ it more productively than those to whom indisputably it is due. By canceling the national debt, one man's income might be raised from £1000 to £1500, but another man's would be lowered from £1500 to £1000. These two men's incomes now amount to £2500; they would amount to no more then. If it be the object of government to raise taxes, there would be precisely the same taxable capital and income in one case as in the other. It is not, then, by the payment of the interest on the national debt that a country is distressed, nor is it by the exoneration from payment that it can be relieved. It is only by saving from income, and retrenching in expenditure, that the national capital can be increased; and neither the income would be increased nor the expenditure diminished by the annihilation of the national debt. It is by the profuse expenditure of government and of individuals, and by loans, that the country is impoverished; every measure, therefore, which is calculated to promote public and private economy will relieve the public distress; but it is error and delusion to suppose that a real national difficulty can be removed by shifting it from the shoulders of one class of the community, who justly ought to bear it, to the shoulders of another class, who, upon every principle of equity, ought to bear no more than their share.

From what I have said, it must not be inferred that I consider the system of borrowing as the best calculated to defray the extraordinary expenses of the state. It is a system which tends to make us less thrifty—to blind us to our real situation. If the expenses of a war be 40 millions per annum, and the share which a man would have to contribute towards that annual expense were £100, he would endeavor, on being at once called upon for his portion, to save speedily the £100 from his income. By the system of loans, he is called upon to pay only the interest of this £100, or £5 per annum, and considers that he does enough by saving this £5 from his expenditure, and then deludes himself with the belief that he is as rich as before. The whole nation, by reasoning and acting in this manner, save only the interest of 40 millions, or two millions; and thus not only lose all the interest or profit which 40 millions of capital, employed productively, would afford, but also 38 millions, the difference between their savings and expenditure. If, as I before observed, each man had to make his own loan, and contribute his full proportion to the exigencies of the state, as soon as the war ceased taxation would cease, and we should immediately fall into a natural state of prices. Out of his private funds, A might have to pay to B interest for the money he borrowed of him during the war to enable him to pay his quota of the expense; but with this the nation would have no concern.

A country which has accumulated a large debt is placed in a most artificial situation; and although the amount of taxes, and the increased price of labor, may not, and I believe does not, place it under any other disadvantage with respect to foreign countries, except the unavoidable one of paying those taxes, yet it becomes the interest of every contributor to withdraw his shoulder from the burthen, and to shift this payment from himself to another; and the temptation to remove himself and his capital to another country, where he will be exempted from such burdens, becomes at last irresistible, and overcomes the natural reluctance which every man feels to quit the place of his birth and the scene of his early associations. A country which has involved itself in the difficulties attending this artificial system would act wisely by ransoming itself from them at the sacrifice of any portion of its property which might be necessary to redeem its debt. That which is wise in an individual is wise also in a nation. A man who has £10,000, paying him an income of £500, out of which he has to pay £100 per annum towards the interest of the debt, is really worth only £8000, and would be equally rich, whether he continued to pay £100 per annum, or at once, and for only once, sacrificed £2000. But where, it is asked, would be the purchaser of the property which he must sell to obtain this £2000? The answer is plain: the national creditor, who is to receive this £2000, will want an investment for his money, and will be disposed either to lend it to the landholder, or manufacturer, or to purchase from them a part of the property of which they have to dispose. To such a payment the stockholders themselves would largely contribute. This scheme has been often recommended, but we have, I fear, neither wisdom enough, nor virtue enough, to adopt it. It must, however, be admitted, that during peace, our unceasing efforts should be directed towards paying off that part of the debt which has been contracted during war; and that no temptation of relief, no desire of escape from present, and I hope temporary, distresses should induce us to relax in our attention to that great object.

No sinking fund can be efficient for the purpose of diminishing the debt if it be not derived from the excess of the public revenue over the public expenditure. It is to be regretted that the sinking fund in this country is only such in name; for there is no excess of revenue above expenditure. It ought, by economy, to be made what it is professed to be, a really efficient fund for the payment of the debt. If, on the breaking out of any future war, we shall not have very considerably reduced our debt, one of two things must happen, either the whole expenses of that war must be defrayed by taxes raised from year to year, or we must, at the end of that war, if not before, submit to a national bankruptcy; not that we shall be unable to bear any large additions to the debt; it would be difficult to set limits to the powers of a great nation; but assuredly there are limits to the price, which in the form of perpetual taxation, individuals will submit to pay for the privilege merely of living in their native country.[33]

When a commodity is at a monopoly price it is at the very highest price at which the consumers are willing to purchase it. Commodities are only at a monopoly price when by no possible device their quantity can be augmented; and when, therefore, the competition is wholly on one side—amongst the buyers. The monopoly price of one period may be much lower or higher than the monopoly price of another, because the competition amongst the purchasers must depend on their wealth, and their tastes and caprices.

Those peculiar wines which are produced in very limited quantity, and those works of art which, from their excellence or rarity, have acquired a fanciful value, will be exchanged for a very different quantity of the produce of ordinary labor, according as the society is rich or poor, as it possesses an abundance or scarcity of such produce, or as it may be in a rude or polished state. The exchangeable value therefore of a commodity which is at a monopoly price is nowhere regulated by the cost of production.

Raw produce is not at a monopoly price, because the market price of barley and wheat is as much regulated by their cost of production as the market price of cloth and linen. The only difference is this, that one portion of the capital employed in agriculture regulates the price of corn, namely, that portion which pays no rent; whereas, in the production of manufactured commodities, every portion of capital is employed with the same results; and as no portion pays rent, every portion is equally a regulator of price: corn, and other raw produce, can be augmented, too, in quantity, by the employment of more capital on the land, and therefore they are not at a monopoly price. There is competition among the sellers, as well as amongst the buyers. This is not the case in the production of those rare wines, and those valuable specimens of art, of which we have been speaking; their quantity cannot be increased, and their price is limited only by the extent of the power and will of the purchasers. The rent of these vineyards may be raised beyond any moderately assignable limits, because no other land being able to produce such wines, none can be brought into competition with them.

The corn and raw produce of a country may, indeed, for a time, sell at a monopoly price; but they can do so permanently only when no more capital can be profitably employed on the lands, and when, therefore, their produce cannot be increased. At such time, every portion of land in cultivation, and every portion of capital employed on the land, will yield a rent, differing, indeed, in proportion to the difference in the return. At such a time, too, any tax which may be imposed on the farmer will fall on rent, and not on the consumer. He cannot raise the price of his corn, because, by the supposition, it is already at the highest price at which the purchasers will or can buy it. He will not be satisfied with a lower rate of profits than that obtained by other capitalists, and, therefore, his only alternative will be to obtain a reduction of rent or to quit his employment.

Mr. Buchanan considers corn and raw produce as at a monopoly price, because they yield a rent: all commodities which yield a rent, he supposes, must be at a monopoly price; and thence he infers that all taxes on raw produce would fall on the landlord, and not on the consumer. "The price of corn," he says, "which always affords a rent, being in no respect influenced by the expenses of its production, those expenses must be paid out of the rent; and when they rise or fall, therefore, the consequence is not a higher or lower price, but a higher or a lower rent. In this view, all taxes on farm servants, horses, or the implements of agriculture are in reality land-taxes—the burden falling on the farmer during the currency of his lease, and on the landlord when the lease comes to be renewed. In like manner, all those improved implements of husbandry which save expense to the farmer, such as machines for thrashing and reaping, whatever gives him easier access to the market, such as good roads, canals, and bridges, though they lessen the original cost of corn, do not lessen its market price. Whatever is saved by those improvements, therefore, belongs to the landlord as part of his rent."

It is evident that if we yield to Mr. Buchanan the basis on which his argument is built, namely, that the price of corn always yields a rent, all the consequences which he contends for would follow of course. Taxes on the farmer would then fall, not on the consumer, but on rent; and all improvements in husbandry would increase rent: but I hope I have made it sufficiently clear that, until a country is cultivated in every part, and up to the highest degree, there is always a portion of capital employed on the land which yields no rent, and that it is this portion of capital, the result of which, as in manufactures, is divided between profits and wages, that regulates the price of corn. The price of corn, then, which does not afford a rent, being influenced by the expenses of its production, those expenses cannot be paid out of rent. The consequence, therefore, of those expenses increasing, is a higher price, and not a lower rent.[34]

It is remarkable that both Adam Smith and Mr. Buchanan, who entirely agree that taxes on raw produce, a land-tax, and tithes, all fall on the rent of land, and not on the consumers of raw produce, should nevertheless admit that taxes on malt would fall on the consumer of beer, and not on the rent of the landlord. Adam Smith's argument is so able a statement of the view which I take of the subject of the tax on malt, and every other tax on raw produce, that I cannot refrain from offering it to the attention of the reader.

"The rent and profits of barley land must always be nearly equal to those of other equally fertile and equally well cultivated land. If they were less, some part of the barley land would soon be turned to some other purpose; and if they were greater, more land would soon be turned to the raising of barley. When the ordinary price of any particular produce of land is at what may be called a monopoly price, a tax upon it necessarily reduces the rent and profit[35] of the land which grows it. A tax upon the produce of those precious vineyards, of which the wine falls so much short of the effectual demand that its price is always above the natural proportion to that of other equally fertile and equally well cultivated land, would necessarily reduce the rent and profit[35] of those vineyards. The price of the wines being already the highest that could be got for the quantity commonly sent to market, it could not be raised higher without diminishing that quantity; and the quantity could not be diminished without still greater loss, because the lands could not be turned to any other equally valuable produce. The whole weight of the tax, therefore, would fall upon the rent and profit;[35] properly upon the *rent* of the vineyard." "But the ordinary price of barley has never been a monopoly price; and the rent and profits of barley land have never been above their natural proportion to those of other equally fertile and equally well cultivated land. The different taxes which have been imposed upon malt, beer, and ale have never lowered the price of barley; have never reduced the rent and profit[35] of barley land. The price of malt to the brewer has constantly risen in proportion to the taxes imposed upon it; and those taxes, together with the different duties upon beer and ale, have constantly either raised the price, or, what comes to the same thing, reduced the quality of those commodities to the consumer. The final payment of those taxes has fallen constantly upon the consumer and not upon the producer." On this passage Mr. Buchanan remarks, "A duty on malt never could reduce the price of barley, because, unless as much could be made of barley by malting it as by selling it unmalted, the quantity required would not be brought to market. It is clear, therefore, that the price of malt must rise in proportion to the tax imposed on it, as the demand could not otherwise be supplied. The price of barley, however, is just as much a monopoly price as that of sugar; they both yield a rent, and the market price of both has equally lost all connection with the original cost."

It appears, then, to be the opinion of Mr. Buchanan, that a tax on malt would raise the price of malt, but that a tax on the barley from which malt is made would not raise the price of barley; and, therefore, if malt is taxed, the tax will be paid by the consumer; if barley is taxed, it will be paid by the landlord, as he will receive a diminished rent. According to Mr. Buchanan, then, barley is at a monopoly price at the highest price which the purchasers are willing to give for it; but malt made of barley is not at a monopoly price, and consequently it can be raised in proportion to the taxes that may be imposed upon it. This opinion of Mr. Buchanan of the effects of a tax on malt appears to me to be in direct contradiction to the opinion he has given of a similar tax, a tax on bread. "A tax on bread will be ultimately paid, not by a rise of price, but by a reduction of rent."[36] If a tax on malt would raise the price of beer, a tax on bread must raise the price of bread.

The following argument of M. Say is founded on the same views as Mr. Buchanan's: "The quantity of wine or corn which a piece of land will produce will remain nearly the same, whatever may be the tax with which it is charged. The tax may take away a half, or even three-fourths of its net produce, or of its rent, if you please, yet the land would nevertheless be cultivated for the half or the quarter not absorbed by the tax. The rent, that is to say, the landlord's share, would merely be somewhat lower. The reason of this will be perceived if we consider that, in the case supposed, the quantity of produce obtained from the land and sent to market will remain nevertheless the same. On the other hand, the motives on which the demand for the produce is founded continue also the same.

"Now, if the quantity of produce supplied, and the quantity demanded, necessarily continue the same, notwithstanding the establishment or the increase of the tax, the price of that produce will not vary; and if the price do not vary, the consumer will not pay the smallest portion of this tax.

"Will it be said that the farmer, he who furnishes labor and capital, will, jointly with the landlord, bear the burden of this tax? certainly not; because the circumstance of the tax has not diminished the number of farms to be let, nor increased the number of farmers. Since, in this instance also, the supply and demand remain the same, the rent of farms must also remain the same. The example of the manufacturer of salt, who can only make the consumers pay a portion of the tax, and that of the landlord, who cannot reimburse himself in the smallest degree, prove the error of those who maintain, in opposition to the economists, that all taxes fall ultimately on the consumer."—Vol. ii. p. 338.

If the tax "took away half, or even three-fourths of the net produce of the land," and the price of produce did not rise, how could those farmers obtain the usual profits of stock who paid very moderate rents, having that quality of land which required a much larger proportion of labor to obtain a given result than land of a more fertile quality? If the whole rent were remitted, they would still obtain lower profits than those in other trades, and would therefore not continue to cultivate their land, unless they could raise the price of its produce. If the tax fell on the farmers, there would be fewer farmers disposed to hire farms; if it fell on the landlord, many farms would not be let at all, for they would afford no rent. But from what fund would those pay the tax who produce corn without paying any rent? It is quite clear that the tax must fall on the consumer. How would such land as M. Say describes in the following passage pay a tax of one-half or three-fourths of its produce?

"We see in Scotland poor lands thus cultivated by the proprietor, and which could be cultivated by no other person. Thus, too, we see in the interior provinces of the United States vast and fertile lands, the revenue of which, alone, would not be sufficient for the maintenance of the proprietor. These lands are cultivated nevertheless, but it must be by the proprietor himself, or, in other words, he must add to the rent, which is little or nothing, the profits of his capital and industry, to enable him to live in competence. It is well known that land, though cultivated, yields no revenue to the landlord when no farmer will be willing to pay a rent for it: which is a proof that such land will give only the profits of the capital, and of the industry necessary for its cultivation."—Say, Vol. ii. p. 127.

CHAPTER XVIII

Poor Rates

We have seen that taxes on raw produce, and on the profits of the farmer, will fall on the consumer of raw produce; since, unless he had the power of remunerating himself by an increase of price, the tax would reduce his profits below the general level of profits, and would urge him to remove his capital to some other trade. We have seen, too, that he could not, by deducting it from his rent, transfer the tax to his landlord; because that farmer who paid no rent would, equally with the cultivator of better land, be subject to the tax, whether it were laid on raw produce or on the profits of the farmer. I have also attempted to show that if a tax were general, and affected equally all profits, whether manufacturing or agricultural, it would not operate either on the price of goods or raw produce, but would be immediately, as well as ultimately, paid by the producers. A tax on rent, it has been observed, would fall on the landlord only, and could not by any means be made to devolve on the tenant.

The poor rate is a tax which partakes of the nature of all these taxes, and, under different circumstances, falls on the consumer of raw produce and goods, on the profits of stock, and on the rent of land. It is a tax which falls with peculiar weight on the profits of the farmer, and therefore may be considered as affecting the price of raw produce. According to the degree in which it bears on manufacturing and agricultural profits equally, it will be a general tax on the profits of stock, and will occasion no alteration in the price of raw produce and manufactures. In proportion to the farmer's inability to remunerate himself, by raising the price of raw produce for that portion of the tax which peculiarly affects him, it will be a tax on rent and will be paid by the landlord. To know, then, the operation of the poor rate at any particular time, we must ascertain whether at that time it affects in an equal or an unequal degree the profits of the farmer and manufacturer; and also whether the circumstances be such as to afford to the farmer the power of raising the price of raw produce.

The poor rates are professed to be levied on the farmer in proportion to his rent; and, accordingly, the farmer who paid a very small rent, or no rent at all, should pay little or no tax. If this were true, poor rates, as far as they are paid by the agricultural class, would entirely fall on the landlord, and could not be shifted to the consumer of raw produce. But I believe that it is not true; the poor rate is not levied according to the rent which a farmer actually pays to his landlord; it is proportioned to the annual value of his land, whether that annual value be given to it by the capital of the landlord or of the tenant.

If two farmers rented land of two different qualities in the same parish, the one paying a rent of £100 per annum for 50 acres of the most fertile land, and the other the same sum of £100 for 1000 acres of the least fertile land, they would pay the same amount of poor rates, if neither of them attempted to improve the land; but if the farmer of the poor land, presuming on a very long lease, should be induced, at a great expense, to improve the productive powers of his land, by manuring, draining, fencing, etc., he would contribute to the poor rates, not in proportion to the actual rent paid to the landlord, but to the actual annual value of the land. The rate might equal or exceed the rent; but whether it did or not, no part of this rate would be paid by the landlord. It would have been previously calculated upon by the tenant; and if the price of produce were not sufficient to compensate him for all his expenses, together with this additional charge for poor rates, his improvements would not have been undertaken. It is evident, then, that the tax in this case is paid by the consumer; for if there had been no rate, the same improvements would have been undertaken, and the usual and general rate of profits would have been obtained on the stock employed with a lower price of corn.

Nor would it make the slightest difference in this question if the landlord had made these improvements himself, and had in consequence raised his rent from £100 to £500; the rate would be equally charged to the consumer; for whether the landlord should expend a large sum of money on his land would depend on the rent, or what is called rent, which he would receive as a remuneration for it; and this again would depend on the price of corn, or other raw produce, being sufficiently high, not only to cover this additional rent, but also the rate to which the land would be subject. If at the same time all manufacturing capital contributed to the poor rates in the same proportion as the capital expended by the farmer or landlord in improving the land, then it would no longer be a partial tax on the profits of the farmer's or landlord's capital, but a tax on the capital of all producers; and, therefore, it could no longer be shifted either on the consumer of raw produce or on the landlord. The farmer's profits would feel the effect of the rate no more than those of the manufacturer; and the former could not, any more than the latter, plead it as a reason for an advance in the price of his commodity. It is not the absolute but the relative fall of profits which prevents capital from being employed in any particular trade: it is the difference of profit which sends capital from one employment to another.

It must be acknowledged, however, that in the actual state of the poor rates, a much larger amount falls on the farmer than on the manufacturer, in proportion to their respective profits; the farmer being rated according to the actual productions which he obtains, the manufacturer only according to the value of the buildings in which he works, without any regard to the value of the machinery, labor, or stock which he may employ. From this circumstance it follows that the farmer will be enabled to raise the price of his produce by this whole difference. For since the tax falls unequally, and peculiarly on his profits, he would have less motive to devote his capital to the land than to employ it in some other trade, were not the price of raw produce raised. If, on the contrary, the rate had fallen with greater weight on the manufacturer than on the farmer, he would have been enabled to raise the price of his goods by the amount of the difference, for the same reason that the farmer under similar circumstances could raise the price of raw produce. In a society, therefore, which is extending its agriculture, when poor rates fall with peculiar weight on the land, they will be paid partly by the employers of capital in a diminution of the profits of stock, and partly by the consumer of raw produce in its increased price. In such a state of things, the tax may, under some circumstances, be even advantageous rather than injurious to landlords; for if the tax paid by the cultivator of the worst land be higher in proportion to the quantity of produce obtained than that paid by the farmers of the more fertile lands, the rise in the price of corn, which will extend to all corn, will more than compensate the latter for the tax. This advantage will remain with them during the continuance of their leases, but it will afterwards be transferred to their landlords. This, then, would be the effect of poor rates in an advancing society; but in a stationary, or in a retrograde country, so far as capital could not be withdrawn from the land, if a further rate were levied for the support of the poor, that part of it which fell on agriculture would be paid, during the current leases, by the farmers; but, at the expiration of those leases it would almost wholly fall on the landlords. The farmer, who, during his former lease, had expended his capital in improving his land, if it were still in his own lands, would be rated for this new tax according to the new value which the land had acquired by its improvement, and this amount he would be obliged to pay during his lease, although his profits might thereby be reduced below the general rate of profits; for the capital which he has expended may be so incorporated with the land that it cannot be removed from it.

If, indeed, he or his landlord (should it have been expended by him) were able to re-move this capital, and thereby reduce the annual value of the land, the rate would pro-portionally fall; and as the produce would at the same time be diminished, its price would rise; he would be compensated for the tax by charging it to the consumer, and no part would fall on rent; but this is impossible, at least with respect to some propor-tion of the capital, and consequently in that proportion the tax will be paid by the farmers during their leases, and by landlords at their expiration. This additional tax, if it fell with peculiar severity on manufacturers, which it does not, would, under such circumstances, be added to the price of their goods; for there can be no reason why their profits should be reduced below the general rate of profits when their capitals might be easily removed to agriculture.[37]

CHAPTER XIX

On Sudden Changes in the Channels of Trade

A great manufacturing country is peculiarly exposed to temporary reverses and contingencies, produced by the removal of capital from one employment to another. The demands for the produce of agriculture are uniform; they are not under the influence of fashion, prejudice, or caprice. To sustain life, food is necessary, and the demand for food must continue in all ages and in all countries. It is different with manufactures; the demand for any particular manufactured commodity is subject, not only to the wants, but to the tastes and caprice of the purchasers. A new tax, too, may destroy the comparative advantage which a country before possessed in the manufacture of a particular commodity; or the effects of war may so raise the freight and insurance on its conveyance, that it can no longer enter into competition with the home manufacture of the country to which it was before exported. In all such cases, considerable distress, and no doubt some loss, will be experienced by those who are engaged in the manufacture of such commodities; and it will be felt, not only at the time of the change, but through the whole interval during which they are removing their capitals, and the labor which they can command, from one employment to another.

Nor will distress be experienced in that country alone where such difficulties originate, but in the countries to which its commodities were before exported. No country can long import, unless it also exports, or can long export unless it also imports. If, then, any circumstance should occur which should permanently prevent a country from importing the usual amount of foreign commodities, it will necessarily diminish the manufacture of some of those commodities which were usually exported; and although the total value of the productions of the country will probably be but little altered, since the same capital will be employed, yet they will not be equally abundant and cheap; and considerable distress will be experienced through the change of employments. If, by the employment of £10,000 in the manufacture of cotton goods for exportation, we imported annually 3000 pair of silk stockings of the value of £2000, and by the interruption of foreign trade we should be obliged to withdraw this capital from the manufacture of cotton, and employ it ourselves in the manufacture of stockings, we should still obtain stockings of the value of £2000, provided no part of the capital were destroyed; but instead of having 3000 pair, we might only have 2500. In the removal of the capital from the cotton to the stocking trade, much distress might be experienced, but it would not considerably impair the value of the national property, although it might lessen the quantity of our annual productions.[38]

The commencement of war after a long peace, or of peace after a long war, generally produces considerable distress in trade. It changes in a great degree the nature of the employments to which the respective capitals of countries were before devoted; and during the interval while they are settling in the situations which new circumstances have made the most beneficial, much fixed capital is unemployed, perhaps wholly lost, and laborers are without full employment. The duration of this distress will be longer or shorter according to the strength of that disinclination which most men feel to abandon that employment of their capital to which they have long been accustomed. It is often protracted, too, by the restrictions and prohibitions to which the absurd jealousies which prevail between the different states of the commercial commonwealth give rise.

The distress which proceeds from a revulsion of trade is often mistaken for that which accompanies a diminution of the national capital and a retrograde state of society; and it would perhaps be difficult to point out any marks by which they may be accurately distinguished.

When, however, such distress immediately accompanies a change from war to peace, our knowledge of the existence of such a cause will make it reasonable to believe that the funds for the maintenance of labor have rather been diverted from their usual channel than materially impaired, and that, after temporary suffering;, the nation will again advance in prosperity. It must be remembered, too, that the retrograde condition is always an unnatural state of society. Man from youth grows to manhood, then decays, and dies; but this is not the progress of nations. When arrived to a state of the greatest vigor, their further advance may indeed be arrested, but their natural tendency is to continue for ages to sustain undiminished their wealth and their population.

In rich and powerful countries, where large capitals are invested in machinery, more distress will be experienced from a revulsion in trade than in poorer countries where there is proportionally a much smaller amount of fixed, and a much larger amount of circulating capital, and where consequently more work is done by the labor of men. It is not so difficult to withdraw a circulating as a fixed capital from any employment in which it may be engaged. It is often impossible to divert the machinery which may have been erected for one manufacture to the purposes of another; but the clothing, the food, and the lodging of the laborer in one employment may be devoted to the support of the laborer in another; or the same laborer may receive the same food, clothing, and lodging, whilst his employment is changed. This, however, is an evil to which a rich nation must submit; and it would not be more reasonable to complain of it than it would be in a rich merchant to lament that his ship was exposed to the dangers of the sea, whilst his poor neighbor's cottage was safe from all such hazard.

From contingencies of this kind, though in an inferior degree, even agriculture is not exempted. War, which, in a commercial country, interrupts the commerce of states, frequently prevents the exportation of corn from countries where it can be produced with little cost to others not so favorably situated. Under such circumstances an unusual quantity of capital is drawn to agriculture, and the country which before imported becomes independent of foreign aid. At the termination of the war, the obstacles to importation are removed, and a competition destructive to the home-grower commences, from which he is unable to withdraw without the sacrifice of a great part of his capital. The best policy of the state would be to lay a tax, decreasing in amount from time to time, on the importation of foreign corn, for a limited number of years, in order to afford to the home-grower an opportunity to withdraw his capital gradually from the land.[39] In so doing, the country might not be making the most advantageous distribution of its capital, but the temporary tax to which it was subjected would be for the advantage of a particular class, the distribution of whose capital was highly useful in procuring a supply of food when importation was stopped. If such exertions in a period of emergency were followed by a risk of ruin on the termination of the difficulty, capital would shun such an employment. Besides the usual profits of stock, farmers would expect to be compensated for the risk which they incurred of a sudden influx of corn; and, therefore, the price to the consumer, at the seasons when he most required a supply, would be enhanced, not only by the superior cost of growing corn at home, but also by the insurance which he would have to pay in the price for the peculiar risk to which this employment of capital was exposed. Notwithstanding, then, that it would be more productive of wealth to the country, at whatever sacrifice of capital it might be done, to allow the importation of cheap corn, it would, perhaps, be advisable to charge it with a duty for a few years.

In examining the question of rent, we found that, with every increase in the supply of corn, and with the consequent fall of its price, capital would be withdrawn from the poorer land, and land of a better description, which would then pay no rent, would become the standard by which the natural price of corn would be regulated. At £4 per quarter, land of an inferior quality, which may be designated by No. 6, might be cultivated; at £3 10s., No. 5; at £3, No. 4, and so on. If corn, in consequence of permanent abundance, fell to £3 10s., the capital employed on No. 6 would cease to be employed; for it was only when corn was at £4 that it could obtain the general profits, even without paying rent: it would, therefore, be withdrawn to manufacture those commodities with which all the corn grown on No. 6 would be purchased and imported. In this employment it would necessarily be more productive to its owner, or it would not be withdrawn from the other; for if he could not obtain more corn by purchasing it with a commodity which he manufactured than he got from the land for which he paid no rent, its price could not be under £4.

It has, however, been said, that capital cannot be withdrawn from the land; that it takes the form of expenses which cannot be recovered, such as manuring, fencing, draining, etc., which are necessarily inseparable from the land. This is in some degree true; but that capital which consists of cattle, sheep, hay and corn ricks, carts, etc., may be withdrawn; and it always becomes a matter of calculation whether these shall continue to be employed on the land, notwithstanding the low price of corn, or whether they shall be sold, and their value transferred to another employment.

Suppose, however, the fact to be as stated, and that no part of the capital could be withdrawn;[40] the farmer would continue to raise corn, and precisely the same quantity, too, at whatever price it might sell; for it could not be his interest to produce less, and if he did not so employ his capital, he would obtain from it no return whatever. Corn would not be imported, because he would sell it lower than £3 10s. rather than not sell it at all, and by the supposition the importer could not sell it under that price. Although, then, the farmers, who cultivated land of this quality, would undoubtedly be injured by the fall in the exchangeable value of the commodity which they produced—how would the country be affected? We should have precisely the same quantity of every commodity produced, but raw produce and corn would sell at a much cheaper price. The capital of a country consists of its commodities, and as these would be the same as before, reproduction would go on at the same rate. This low price of corn would, however, only afford the usual profits of stock to the land No. 5, which would then pay no rent, and the rent of all better land would fall: wages would also fall, and profits would rise.

However low the price of corn might fall, if capital could not be removed from the land, and the demand did not increase, no importation would take place, for the same quantity as before would be produced at home. Although there would be a different division of the produce, and some classes would be benefited and others injured, the aggregate of production would be precisely the same, and the nation collectively would neither be richer nor poorer.

But there is this advantage always resulting from a relatively low price of corn—that the division of the actual production is more likely to increase the fund for the maintenance of labor, inasmuch as more will be allotted, under the name of profit, to the productive class—a less, under the name rent, to the unproductive class.

This is true, even if the capital cannot be withdrawn from the land, and must be employed there, or not be employed at all; but if great part of the capital can be withdrawn, as it evidently could, it will be only withdrawn when it will yield more to the owner by being withdrawn than by being suffered to remain where it was; it will only be withdrawn then, when it can elsewhere be employed more productively both for the owner and the public. He consents to sink that part of his capital which cannot be separated from the land, because with that part which he can take away he can obtain a greater value, and a greater quantity of raw produce, than by not sinking this part of the capital. His case is precisely similar to that of a man who has erected machinery in his manufactory at a great expense, machinery which is afterwards so much improved upon by more modern inventions that the commodities manufactured by him very much sink in value. It would be entirely a matter of calculation with him whether he should abandon the old machinery, and erect the more perfect, losing all the value of the old, or continue to avail himself of its comparatively feeble powers. Who, under such circumstances, would exhort him to forego the use of the better machinery, because it would deteriorate or annihilate the value of the old? Yet, this is the argument of those who would wish us to prohibit the importation of corn, because it will deteriorate or annihilate that part of the capital of the farmer which is for ever sunk in land. They do not see that the end of all commerce is to increase production, and that, by increasing production, though you may occasion partial loss, you increase the general happiness. To be consistent, they should endeavor to arrest all improvements in agriculture and manufactures, and all inventions of machinery; for, though these contribute to general abundance, and therefore to the general happiness, they never fail, at the moment of their introduction, to deteriorate or annihilate the value of a part of the existing capital of farmers and manufacturers.[41]

Agriculture, like all the other trades, and particularly in a commercial country, is subject to a reaction, which, in an opposite direction, succeeds the action of a strong stimulus. Thus, when war interrupts the importation of corn, its consequent high price attracts capital to the land, from the large profits which such an employment of it affords; this will probably cause more capital to be employed, and more raw produce to be brought to market than the demands of the country require. In such case, the price of corn will fall from the effects of a glut, and much agricultural distress will be produced, till the average supply is brought to a level with the average demand.

CHAPTER XX

Value and Riches, Their Distinctive Properties

"A man is rich or poor," says Adam Smith, "according to the degree in which he can afford to enjoy the necessaries, conveniences, and amusements of human life."

Value, then, essentially differs from riches, for value depends not on abundance, but on the difficulty or facility of production. The labor of a million of men in manufactures will always produce the same value, but will not always produce the same riches. By the invention of machinery, by improvements in skill, by a better division of labor, or by the discovery of new markets, where more advantageous exchanges may be made, a million of men may produce double or treble the amount of riches, of "necessaries, conveniences, and amusements," in one state of society that they could produce in another, but they will not on that account add anything to value; for everything rises or falls in value "in proportion to the facility or difficulty of producing it, or, in other words, in proportion to the quantity of labor employed on its production. Suppose, with a given capital, the labor of a certain number of men produced 1000 pair of stockings, and that by inventions in machinery the same number of men can produce 2000 pair, or that they can continue to produce 1000 pair, and can produce besides 500 hats; then the value of the 2000 pair of stockings, or of the 1000 pair of stockings and 500 hats, will be neither more nor less than that of the 1000 pair of stockings before the introduction of machinery; for they will be the produce of the same quantity of labor. But the value of the general mass of commodities will nevertheless be diminished; for, although the value of the increased quantity produced in consequence of the improvement will be the same exactly as the value would have been of the less quantity that would have been produced, had no improvement taken place, an effect is also produced on the portion of goods still unconsumed, which were manufactured previously to the improvement; the value of those goods will be reduced, inasmuch as they must fall to the level, quantity for quantity, of the goods produced under all the advantages of the improvement:

and the society will, notwithstanding the increased quantity of commodities, notwithstanding its augmented riches, and its augmented means of enjoyment, have a less amount of value. By constantly increasing the facility of production, we constantly diminish the value of some of the commodities before produced, though by the same means we not only add to the national riches, but also to the power of future production. Many of the errors in political economy have arisen from errors on this subject, from considering an increase of riches, and an increase of value, as meaning the same thing, and from unfounded notions as to what constituted a standard measure of value. One man considers money as a standard of value, and a nation grows richer or poorer, according to him, in proportion as its commodities of all kinds can exchange for more or less money. Others represent money as a very convenient medium for the purpose of barter, but not as a proper measure by which to estimate the value of other things; the real measure of value according to them is corn,[42] and a country is rich or poor according as its commodities will exchange for more or less corn.[43] There are others again who consider a country rich or poor according to the quantity of labor that it can purchase. But why should gold, or corn, or labor, be the standard measure of value, more than coals or iron?—more than cloth, soap, candles, and the other necessities of the laborer?—why, in short, should any commodity, or all commodities together, be the standard, when such a standard is itself subject to fluctuations in value? Corn, as well as gold, may from difficulty or facility of production vary 10, 20, or 30 percent, relatively to other things; why should we always say that it is those other things which have varied, and not the corn? That commodity is alone invariable which at all times requires the same sacrifice of toil and labor to produce it. Of such a commodity we have no knowledge, but we may hypothetically argue and speak about it as if we had; and may improve our knowledge of the science by showing distinctly the absolute inapplicability of all the standards which have been hitherto adopted. But supposing either of these to be a correct standard of value, still it would not be a standard of riches, for riches do not depend on value. A man is rich or poor according to the abundance of necessaries and luxuries which he can command; and whether the exchangeable value of these for money, for corn, or for labor be high or low, they will equally contribute to the enjoyment of their possessor. It is through confounding the ideas of value and wealth, or riches, that it has been asserted that by diminishing the quantity of commodities, that is to say, of the necessaries, conveniences, and enjoyments of human life, riches may be increased. If value were the measure of riches, this could not be denied, because by scarcity the value of commodities is raised; but if Adam Smith be correct, if riches consist in necessaries and enjoyments, then they cannot be increased by a diminution of quantity.

It is true that the man in possession of a scarce commodity is richer, if by means of it he can command more of the necessaries and enjoyments of human life; but as the general stock out of which each man's riches are drawn is diminished in quantity by all that any individual takes from it, other men's shares must necessarily be reduced in proportion as this favored individual is able to appropriate a greater quantity to himself.

Let water become scarce, says Lord Lauderdale, and be exclusively possessed by an individual, and you will increase his riches, because water will then have value; and if wealth be the aggregate of individual riches, you will by the same means also increase wealth. You undoubtedly will increase the riches of this individual, but inasmuch as the farmer must sell a part of his corn, the shoemaker a part of his shoes, and all men give up a portion of their possessions for the sole purpose of supplying themselves with water, which they before had for nothing, they are poorer by the whole quantity of commodities which they are obliged to devote to this purpose, and the proprietor of water is benefited precisely by the amount of their loss. The same quantity of water, and the same quantity of commodities, are enjoyed by the whole society, but they are differently distributed. This is, however, supposing rather a monopoly of water than a scarcity of it. If it should be scarce, then the riches of the country and of individuals would be actually diminished, inasmuch as it would be deprived of a portion of one of its enjoyments. The farmer would not only have less corn to exchange for the other commodities which might be necessary or desirable to him, but he, and every other individual, would be abridged in the enjoyment of one of the most essential of their comforts. Not only would there be a different distribution of riches, but an actual loss of wealth.

It may be said, then, of two countries possessing precisely the same quantity of all the necessaries and comforts of life, that they are equally rich, but the value of their respective riches would depend on the comparative facility or difficulty with which they were produced. For if an improved piece of machinery should enable us to make two pair of stockings instead of one, without additional labor, double the quantity would be given in exchange for a yard of cloth. If a similar improvement be made in the manufacture of cloth, stockings and cloth will exchange in the same proportions as before, but they will both have fallen in value; for in exchanging them for hats, for gold, or other commodities in general, twice the former quantity must be given. Extend the improvement to the production of gold, and every other commodity, and they will all regain their former proportions. There will be double the quantity of commodities annually produced in the country, and therefore the wealth of the country will be doubled, but this wealth will not have increased in value.

Although Adam Smith has given the correct description of riches which I have more than once noticed, he afterwards explains them differently, and says, "that a man must be rich or poor according to the quantity of labor which he can afford to purchase." Now, this description differs essentially from the other, and is certainly incorrect; for suppose the mines were to become more productive, so that gold and silver fell in value, from the greater facility of their production; or that velvets were to be manufactured with so much less labor than before, that they fell to half their former value; the riches of all those who purchased those commodities would be increased; one man might increase the quantity of his plate, another might buy double the quantity of velvet; but with the possession of this additional plate and velvet, they could employ no more labor than before; because, as the exchangeable value of velvet and of plate would be lowered, they must part with proportionally more of these species of riches to purchase a day's labor. Riches, then, cannot be estimated by the quantity of labor which they can purchase.

From what has been said, it will be seen that the wealth of a country may be increased in two ways: it may be increased by employing a greater portion of revenue in the maintenance of productive labor, which will not only add to the quantity, but to the value of the mass of commodities; or it may be increased, without employing any additional quantity of labor, by making the same quantity more productive, which will add to the abundance, but not to the value of commodities.

In the first case, a country would not only become rich, but the value of its riches would increase. It would become rich by parsimony—by diminishing its expenditure on objects of luxury and enjoyment, and employing those savings in reproduction.

In the second case, there will not necessarily be either any diminished expenditure on luxuries and enjoyments, or any increased quantity of productive labor employed, but, with the same labor, more would be produced; wealth would increase, but not value. Of these two modes of increasing wealth, the last must be preferred, since it produces the same effect without the privation and diminution of enjoyments which can never fail to accompany the first mode. Capital is that part of the wealth of a country which is employed with a view to future production, and may be increased in the same manner as wealth. An additional capital will be equally efficacious in the production of future wealth, whether it be obtained from improvements in skill and machinery, or from using more revenue reproductively; for wealth always depends on the quantity of commodities produced, without any regard to the facility with which the instruments employed in production may have been procured. A certain quantity of clothes and provisions will maintain and employ the same number of men, and will therefore procure the same quantity of work to be done, whether they be produced by the labor of 100 or 200 men; but they will be of twice the value if 200 have been employed on their production.

M. Say, notwithstanding the corrections he has made in the fourth and last edition of his work, *Traité d'Economie Politique,* appears to me to have been singularly unfortunate in his definition of riches and value. He considers these two terms as synonymous, and that a man is rich in proportion as he increases the value of his possessions, and is enabled to command an abundance of commodities. "The value of incomes is then increased," he observes, "if they can procure, it does not signify by what means, a greater quantity of products." According to M. Say, if the difficulty of producing cloth were to double, and consequently cloth was to exchange for double the quantity of the commodities for which it is exchanged before, it would be doubled in value, to which I give my fullest assent; but if there were any peculiar facility in producing the commodities, and no increased difficulty in producing cloth, and cloth should in consequence exchange as before for double the quantity of commodities, M. Say would still say that cloth had doubled in value, whereas, according to my view of the subject, he should say, that cloth retained its former value, and those particular commodities had fallen to half their former value. Must not M. Say be inconsistent with himself when he says that, by facility of production, two sacks of corn may be produced by the same means that one was produced before, and that each sack will therefore fall to half its former value, and yet maintain that the clothier who exchanges his cloth for two sacks of corn will obtain double the value he before obtained, when he could only get one sack in exchange for his cloth. If two sacks be of the value that one was of before, he evidently obtains the same value and no more—he gets, indeed, double the quantity of riches—double the quantity of utility—double the quantity of what Adam Smith calls value in use, but not double the quantity of value, and therefore M. Say cannot be right in considering value, riches, and utility to be synonymous. Indeed, there are many parts of M. Say's work to which I can confidently refer in support of the doctrine which I maintain respecting the essential difference between value and riches, although it must be confessed that there are also various other passages in which a contrary doctrine is maintained. These passages I cannot reconcile, and I point them out by putting them in opposition to each other, that M. Say may, if he should do me the honor to notice these observations in any future edition of his work, give such explanations of his views as may remove the difficulty which many others, as well as myself, feel in our endeavors to expound them.

1. In the exchange of two products, we only in fact exchange the productive services which have served to create them. (p. 504)

2. There is no real dearness but that which arises from the cost of production. A thing really dear, is that which cost, much in producing. (p. 457)

3. The value of all the productive services that must be consumed to create a product, constitute the cost of production of that product. (p. 505)

4. It is utility which determines the demand for a commodity, but it is the cost of its production which limits the extent of its demand. When its utility does not elevate its value to the level of the cost of production, the thing is not worth what it cost; it is a proof that the productive services might be employed to create a commodity of a superior value. The possessors of productive funds, that is to say, those who have the disposal of labor, of capital or land, are perpetually occupied in comparing the cost of production with the value of the things produced, or which comes to the same thing, in comparing the value of different commodities with each other; because the cost of production is nothing else but the value of productive services, consumed in forming a production; and the value of a productive service is nothing else than the value of the commodity, which is the result. The value of a commodity, the value of a productive service, the value of the cost of production are all, then, similar values when every thing is left to its natural course.

5. The value of incomes is then increased, if they can procure (it does not signify by what means,) a greater quantity of product.

6. Price is the measure of the value of things, and their value is the measure of their utility. (Vol. 2, p. 4)

7. Exchanges made freely, show at the time, in the place, and in the state of society in which we are, the value which men attach to the things exchanged. (p. 466)

8. To produce, is to create value, by giving or increasing the utility of a thing, and thereby establishing a demand for it, which is the first cause of its value. (Vol. 2, p. 487)

9. Utility being created, constitutes a product. The exchangeable value which results, is only the measure of this utility, the measure of the production which has taken place. (p. 490)

10. The utility which people of a particular country find in a product can no otherwise be appreciated than by the price which they give for it. (p. 502)

11. This price is the measure of the utility, which it has in the judgment of men; of the satisfaction which they derive from consuming it, because they would not prefer consuming this utility, if for the price which it cost they could acquire a utility which would give them more satisfaction. (p. 506)

12. The quantity of all other commodities which a person can immediately obtain in exchange for the commodity of which he wishes to dispose, is at all times a value not to be disputed. (Vol. 2, p. 4)

If there is no real dearness but that which arises from cost of production (*see* 2.), how can a commodity be said to rise in value (*see* 5.), if its cost of production be not increased? and merely because it will exchange for more of a cheap commodity—for more of a commodity the cost of production of which has diminished? When I give 2000 times more cloth for a pound of gold than I give for a pound of iron, does it prove that I attach 2000 times more utility to gold than I do to iron? certainly not; it proves only as admitted by M. Say (*see* 4.), that the cost of production of gold is 2000 times greater than the cost of production of iron. If the cost of production of the two metals were the same, I should give the same price for them; but if utility were the measure of value, it is probable I should give more for the iron. It is the competition of the producers "who are perpetually employed in comparing the cost of production with the value of the thing produced," (*see* 4.) which regulates the value of different commodities. If, then, I give one shilling for a loaf, and 21 shillings for a guinea, it is no proof that this in my estimation is the comparative measure of their utility.

In No. 4, M. Say maintains, with scarcely any variation, the doctrine which I hold concerning value. In his productive services he includes the services rendered by land, capital, and labor; in mine I include only capital and labor, and wholly exclude land. Our difference proceeds from the different view which we take of rent: I always consider it as the result of a partial monopoly, never really regulating price, but rather as the effect of it. If all rent were relinquished by landlords, I am of opinion that the commodities produced on the land would be no cheaper, because there is always a portion of the same commodities produced on land for which no rent is or can be paid, as the surplus produce is only sufficient to pay the profits of stock.

To conclude, although no one is more disposed than I am to estimate highly the advantage which results to all classes of consumers from the real abundance and cheapness of commodities, I cannot agree with M. Say in estimating the value of a commodity by the abundance of other commodities for which it will exchange; I am of the opinion of a very distinguished writer, M. Destutt de Tracy, who says that, "To measure any one thing is to compare it with a determinate quantity of that same thing which we take for a standard of comparison, for unity. To measure, then, to ascertain a length, a weight, a value, is to find how many times they contain meters, grams, francs, in a word, unities of the same description." A franc is not a measure of value for any thing, but for a quantity of the same metal of which francs are made, unless francs, and the thing to be measured, can be referred to some other measure which is common to both. This, I think, they can be, for they are both the result of labor; and, therefore, labor is a common measure, by which their real as well as their relative value may be estimated. This also, I am happy to say, appears to be M. Destutt de Tracy's opinion.[44] He says, "As it is certain that our physical and moral faculties are alone our original riches, the employment of those faculties, labor of some kind, is our only original treasure, and that it is always from this employment that all those things are created which we call riches, those which are the most necessary as well as those which are the most purely agreeable. It is certain too, that all those things only represent the labor which has created them, and if they have a value, or even two distinct values, they can only derive them from that of the labor from which they emanate."

M. Say, in speaking of the excellences and imperfections of the great work of Adam Smith, imputes to him, as an error, that "he attributes to the labor of man alone the power of producing value. A more correct analysis shows us that value is owing to the action of labor, or rather the industry of man, combined with the action of those agents which nature supplies, and with that of capital. His ignorance of this principle prevented him from establishing the true theory of the influence of machinery in the production of riches."

In contradiction to the opinion of Adam Smith, M. Say, in the fourth chapter, speaks of the value which is given to commodities by natural agents, such as the sun, the air, the pressure of the atmosphere, etc., which are sometimes substituted for the labor of man, and sometimes concur with him in producing.[45] But these natural agents, though they add greatly to *value in use,* never add exchangeable value, of which M. Say is speaking, to a commodity: as soon as by the aid of machinery, or by the knowledge of natural philosophy, you oblige natural agents to do the work which was before done by man, the exchangeable value of such work falls accordingly. If ten men turned a corn mill, and it be discovered that by the assistance of wind, or of water, the labor of these ten men may be spared, the flour which is the produce partly of the work performed by the mill, would immediately fall in value, in proportion to the quantity of labor saved; and the society would be richer by the commodities which the labor of the ten men could produce, the funds destined for their maintenance being in no degree impaired. M. Say constantly overlooks the essential difference that there is between value in use and value in exchange.

M. Say accuses Dr. Smith of having overlooked the value which is given to commodities by natural agents, and by machinery, because he considered that the value of all things was derived from the labor of man; but it does not appear to me that this charge is made out; for Adam Smith nowhere undervalues the services which these natural agents and machinery perform for us, but he very justly distinguishes the nature of the value which they add to commodities—they are serviceable to us, by increasing the abundance of productions, by making men richer, by adding to value in use; but as they perform their work gratuitously, as nothing is paid for the use of air, of heat, and of water, the assistance which they afford us adds nothing to value in exchange.

CHAPTER XXI

Effects of Accumulation on Profits and Interest

From the account which has been given of the profits of stock, it will appear that no accumulation of capital will permanently lower profits unless there be some permanent cause for the rise of wages. If the funds for the maintenance of labor were doubled, trebled, or quadrupled, there would not long be any difficulty in procuring the requisite number of hands to be employed by those funds; but owing to the increasing difficulty of making constant additions to the food of the country, funds of the same value would probably not maintain the same quantity of labor. If the necessaries of the workman could be constantly increased with the same facility, there could be no permanent alteration in the rate of profit or wages, to whatever amount capital might be accumulated. Adam Smith, however, uniformly ascribes the fall of profits to the accumulation of capital, and to the competition which will result from it, without ever adverting to the increasing difficulty of providing food for the additional number of laborers which the additional capital will employ. "The increase of stock," he says, "which raises wages, tends to lower profit. When the stocks of many rich merchants are turned into the same trade, their mutual competition naturally tends to lower its profit; and when there is a like increase of stock in all the different trades carried on in the same society, the same competition must produce the same effect in all." Adam Smith speaks here of a rise of wages, but it is of a temporary rise, proceeding from increased funds before the population is increased; and he does not appear to see that at the same time that capital is increased the work to be effected by capital is increased in the same proportion. M. Say has, however, most satisfactorily shown that there is no amount of capital which may not be employed in a country, because a demand is only limited by production. No man produces but with a view to consume or sell, and he never sells but with an intention to purchase some other commodity, which may be immediately useful to him, or which may contribute to future production. By producing, then, he necessarily becomes either the consumer of his own goods, or the purchaser and consumer of the goods of some other person. It is not to be supposed that he should, for any length of time, be ill-informed of the commodities which he can most advantageously produce, to attain the object which he has in view, namely, the possession of other goods; and, therefore, it is not probable that he will continually produce a commodity for which there is no demand.[46]

There cannot, then, be accumulated in a country any amount of capital which cannot be employed productively until wages rise so high in consequence of the rise of necessaries, and so little consequently remains for the profits of stock, that the motive for accumulation ceases.[47] While the profits of stock are high, men will have a motive to accumulate. Whilst a man has any wished-for gratification unsupplied, he will have a demand for more commodities; and it will be an effectual demand while he has any new value to offer in exchange for them. If ten thousand pounds were given to a man having £100,000 per annum, he would not lock it up in a chest, but would either increase his expenses by £10,000, employ it himself productively, or lend it to some other person for that purpose; in either case, demand would be increased, although it would be for different objects. If he increased his expenses, his effectual demand might probably be for buildings, furniture, or some such enjoyment. If he employed his £10,000 productively, his effectual demand would be for food, clothing, and raw material, which might set new laborers to work; but still it would be demand.[48]

Productions are always bought by productions, or by services; money is only the medium by which the exchange is effected. Too much of a particular commodity may be produced, of which there may be such a glut in the market as not to repay the capital expended on it; but this cannot be the case with respect to all commodities; the demand for corn is limited by the mouths which are to eat it, for shoes and coats by the persons who are to wear them; but though a community, or a part of a community, may have as much corn, and as many hats and shoes as it is able, or may wish to consume, the same cannot be said of every commodity produced by nature or by art. Some would consume more wine if they had the ability to procure it. Others, having enough of wine, would wish to increase the quantity or improve the quality of their furniture. Others might wish to ornament their grounds, or to enlarge their houses. The wish to do all or some of these is implanted in every man's breast; nothing is required but the means, and nothing can afford the means but an increase of production. If I had food and necessaries at my disposal, I should not be long in want of workmen who would put me in possession of some of the objects most useful or most desirable to me.

Whether these increased productions and the consequent demand which they occasion shall or shall not lower profits, depends solely on the rise of wages; and the rise of wages, excepting for a limited period, on the facility of producing the food and necessaries of the laborer. I say excepting for a limited period, because no point is better established, than that the supply of laborers will always ultimately be in proportion to the means of supporting them.

There is only one case, and that will be temporary, in which the accumulation of capital with a low price of food may be attended with a fall of profits; and that is when the funds for the maintenance of labor increase much more rapidly than population;—wages will then be high and profits low. If every man were to forego the use of luxuries , and be intent only on accumulation, a quantity of necessaries might be produced for which there could not be any immediate consumption. Of commodities so limited in number there might undoubtedly be a universal glut, and consequently there might neither be demand for an additional quantity of such commodities nor profits on the employment of more capital. If men ceased to consume, they would cease to produce. This admission does not impugn the general principle. In such a country as England, for example, it is difficult to suppose that there can be any disposition to devote the whole capital and labor of the country to the production of necessaries only.

When merchants engage their capitals in foreign trade, or in the carrying trade, it is always from choice and never from necessity: it is because in that trade their profits will be somewhat greater than in the home trade.

Adam Smith has justly observed "that the desire of food is limited in every man by the narrow capacity of the human stomach, but the desire of the conveniences and ornaments of building, dress, equipage, and household furniture seems to have no limit or certain boundary." Nature, then, has necessarily limited the amount of capital which can at any one time be profitably engaged in agriculture, but she has placed no limits to the amount of capital that may be employed in procuring "the conveniences and ornaments" of life. To procure these gratifications in the greatest abundance is the object in view, and it is only because foreign trade, or the carrying trade, will accomplish it better, that men engage in them in preference to manufacturing the commodities required, or a substitute for them, at home. If, however, from peculiar circumstances, we were precluded from engaging capital in foreign trade, or in the carrying trade, we should, though with less advantage, employ it at home; and while there is no limit to the desire of "conveniences, ornaments of building, dress, equipage, and household furniture," there can be no limit to the capital that may be employed in procuring them, except that which bounds our power to maintain the workmen who are to produce them.

Adam Smith, however, speaks of the carrying trade as one not of choice, but of necessity; as if the capital engaged in it would be inert if not so employed, as if the capital in the home trade could overflow if not confined to a limited amount. He says, "when the capital stock of any country is increased to such a degree *that it cannot be all employed in supplying the consumption, and supporting the productive labor of that particular country,* the surplus part of it naturally disgorges itself into the carrying trade, and is employed in performing the same offices to other countries."

"About ninety-six thousand hogsheads of tobacco are annually purchased with a part of the surplus produce of British industry. But the demand of Great Britain does not require, perhaps, more than fourteen thousand. If the remaining eighty-two thousand, therefore, could not be sent abroad *and exchanged for something more in demand at home,* the importation of them would cease immediately, *and with it the productive labor of all the inhabitants of Great Britain who are at present employed in preparing the goods with which these eighty-two thousand hogsheads are annually purchased.*" But could not this portion of the productive labor of Great Britain be employed in preparing some other sort of goods, with which something more in demand at home might be purchased? And if it could not, might we not employ this productive labor, though with less advantage, in making those goods in demand at home, or at least some substitute for them? If we wanted velvets, might we not attempt to make velvets; and if we could not succeed, might we not make more cloth, or some other object desirable to us?

We manufacture commodities, and with them buy goods abroad, because we can obtain a greater quantity than we could make at home. Deprive us of this trade, and we immediately manufacture again for ourselves. But this opinion of Adam Smith is at variance with all his general doctrines on this subject. "If a foreign country can supply us with a commodity cheaper than we ourselves can make it, better buy it of them with some part of the produce of our own industry, employed in a way in which we have some advantage. *The general industry of the country, being always in proportion to the capital which employs it,* will not thereby be diminished, but only left to find out the way in which it can be employed with the greatest advantage."

Again. "Those, therefore, who have the command of more food than they themselves can consume, are always willing to exchange the surplus, or, what is the same thing, the price of it, for gratifications of another kind. What is over and above satisfying the limited desire is given for the amusement of those desires which cannot be satisfied, but seem to be altogether endless. The poor, in order to obtain food, exert themselves to gratify those fancies of the rich; and to obtain it more certainly, they vie with one another in the cheapness and perfection of their work. The number of workmen increases with the increasing quantity of food, or with the growing improvement and cultivation of the lands; and as the nature of their business admits of the utmost subdivisions of labors, the quantity of materials which they can work up increases in a much greater proportion than their numbers. Hence arises a demand for every sort of material which human invention can employ, either usefully or ornamentally, in building, dress, equipage, or household furniture; for the fossils and minerals contained in the bowels of the earth, the precious metals, and the precious stones."

It follows, then, from these admissions, that there is no limit to demand—no limit to the employment of capital while it yields any profit, and that, however abundant capital may become, there is no other adequate reason for a fall of profit but a rise of wages, and further, it may be added that the only adequate and permanent cause for the rise of wages is the increasing difficulty of providing food and necessaries for the increasing number of workmen.

Adam Smith has justly observed that it is extremely difficult to determine the rate of the profits of stock. "Profit is so fluctuating that even in a particular trade, and much more in trades in general, it would be difficult to state the average rate of it. To judge of what it may have been formerly, or in remote periods of time, with any degree of precision, must be altogether impossible." Yet since it is evident that much will be given for the use of money when much can be made by it, he suggests that "the market rate of interest will lead us to form some notion of the rate of profits, and the history of the progress of interest afford us that of the progress of profits." Undoubtedly, if the market rate of interest could be accurately known for any considerable period, we should have a tolerably correct criterion by which to estimate the progress of profits.

But in all countries, from mistaken notions of policy, the state has interfered to prevent a fair and free market rate of interest by imposing heavy and ruinous penalties on all those who shall take more than the rate fixed by law. In all countries probably these laws are evaded, but records give us little information on this head, and point out rather the legal and fixed rate than the market rate of interest. During the present war, Exchequer and Navy Bills have been frequently at so high a discount as to afford the purchasers of them 7, 8 percent, or a greater rate of interest for their money. Loans have been raised by government at an interest exceeding 6 percent, and individuals have been frequently obliged, by indirect means, to pay more than 10 percent, for the interest of money; yet during this same period the legal rate of interest has been uniformly at 5 percent. Little dependence for information, then., can be placed on that which is the fixed and legal rate of interest, when we find it may differ so considerably from the market rate. Adam Smith informs us that from the 37th of Henry VIII to 21st of James I, 10 percent, continued to be the legal rate of interest. Soon after the restoration, it was reduced to 6 percent, and by the 12th of Anne, to 5 percent. He thinks the legal rate followed, and did not precede, the market rate of interest. Before the American war, government borrowed at 3 percent, and the people of credit in the capital and in many other parts of the kingdom at 31/2, 4, and 41/2 percent.

The rate of interest, though ultimately and permanently governed by the rate of profit, is, however, subject to temporary variations from other causes. With every fluctuation in the quantity and value of money, the prices of commodities naturally vary. They vary also, as we have already shown, from the alteration in the proportion of supply to demand, although there should not be either greater facility or difficulty of production. When the market prices of goods fall from an abundant supply, from a diminished demand, or from a rise in the value of money, a manufacturer naturally accumulates an unusual quantity of finished goods, being unwilling to sell them at very depressed prices. To meet his ordinary payments, for which he used to depend on the sale of his goods, he now endeavors to borrow on credit, and is often obliged to give an increased rate of interest. This, however, is but of temporary duration; for either the manufacturer's expectations were well grounded, and the market price of his commodities rises, or he discovers that there is a permanently diminished demand, and he no longer resists the course of affairs: prices fall, and money and interest regain their real value. If, by the discovery of a new mine, by the abuses of banking, or by any other cause, the quantity of money be greatly increased, its ultimate effect is to raise the prices of commodities in proportion to the increased quantity of money; but there is probably always an interval during which some effect is produced on the rate of interest.

The price of funded property is not a steady criterion by which to judge of the rate of interest. In time of war, the stock market is so loaded by the continual loans of government that the price of stock has not time to settle at its fair level before a new operation of funding takes place, or it is affected by anticipation of political events. In time of peace, on the contrary, the operations of the sinking fund, the unwillingness which a particular class of persons feel to divert their funds to any other employment than that to which they have been accustomed, which they think secure, and in which their dividends are paid with the utmost regularity, elevates the price of stock, and consequently depresses the rate of interest on these securities below the general market rate. It is observable, too, that for different securities government pays very different rates of interest. Whilst £100 capital in 5 percent stock is selling for £95, an exchequer bill of £100 will be sometimes selling for £100 5s., for which exchequer bill no more interest will be annually paid than £4 11s. 3d.: one of these securities pays to a purchaser, at the above prices, an interest of more than 51/4 percent, the other but little more than 41/4; a certain quantity of these exchequer bills is required as a safe and marketable investment for bankers; if they were increased much beyond this demand they would probably be as much depreciated as the 5 percent stock. A stock paying 3 percent per annum will always sell at a proportionally greater price than stock paying 5 percent, for the capital debt of neither can be discharged but at par, or £100 money for £100 stock. The market rate of interest may fall to 4 percent, and government would then pay the holder of 5 percent stock at par, unless he consented to take 4 percent, on some diminished rate of interest under 5 percent: they would have no advantage from so paying the holder of 3 percent, stock till the market rate of interest had fallen below 3 percent, per annum. To pay the interest on the national debt large sums of money are withdrawn from circulation four times in the year for a few days. These demands for money being only temporary seldom affect prices; they are generally surmounted by the payment of a large rate of interest.[49]

CHAPTER XXII

Bounties on Exportation, and Prohibitions of Importation

A bounty on the exportation of corn tends to lower its price to the foreign consumer, but it has no permanent effect on its price in the home market.

Suppose that to afford the usual and general profits of stock, the price of corn should in England be £4 per quarter; it could not then be exported to foreign countries where it sold for £3 15s., per quarter. But if a bounty of 10s. per quarter were given on exportation, it could be sold in the foreign market at £3 10s., and consequently the same profit would be afforded to the corn grower whether he sold it at £3 10s. in the foreign, or at £4 in the home market.

A bounty then, which should lower the price of British corn in the foreign country below the cost of producing corn in that country, would naturally extend the demand for British and diminish the demand for their own corn. This extension of demand for British corn could not fail to raise its price for a time in the home market, and during that time to prevent also its falling so low in the foreign market as the bounty has a tendency to effect. But the causes which would thus operate on the market price of corn in England would produce no effect whatever on its natural price, or its real cost of production. To grow corn would neither require more labor nor more capital, and, consequently, if the profits of the farmer's stock were before only equal to the profits of the stock of other traders, they will, after the rise of price, be considerably above them. By raising the profits of the farmer's stock, the bounty will operate as an encouragement to agriculture, and capital will be withdrawn from manufactures to be employed on the land till the enlarged demand for the foreign market has been supplied, when the price of corn will again fall in the home market to its natural and necessary price, and profits will be again at their ordinary and accustomed level. The increased supply of grain operating on the foreign market will also lower its price in the country to which it is exported, and will thereby restrict the profits of the exporter to the lowest rate at which he can afford to trade.

The ultimate effect then of a bounty on the exportation of corn is not to raise or to lower the price in the home market, but to lower the price of corn to the foreign consumer—to the whole extent of the bounty, if the price of corn had not before been lower in the foreign than in the home market—and in a less degree if the price in the home had been above the price in the foreign market.

A writer in the fifth volume of the *Edinburgh Review*, on the subject of a bounty on the exportation of corn, has very clearly pointed out its effects on the foreign and home demand. He has also justly remarked that it would not fail to give encouragement to agriculture in the exporting country; but he appears to have imbibed the common error which has misled Dr. Smith, and, I believe, most other writers on this subject. He supposes, because the price of corn ultimately regulates wages, that therefore it will regulate the price of all other commodities. He says that the bounty, "by raising the profits of farming, will operate as an encouragement to husbandry; by raising the price of corn to the consumers at home it will diminish for the time their power of purchasing this necessary of life, and thus abridge their real wealth. It is evident, however, that this last effect must be temporary: the wages of the laboring consumers had been adjusted before by competition, and the same principle will adjust them again to the same rate, by raising the money price of labor, *and through that, of other commodities, to the money price of corn.* The bounty upon exportation, therefore, will ultimately raise the money price of corn in the home market; not directly, however, but through the medium of an extended demand in the foreign market, and a consequent enhancement of the real price at home: *and this rise of the money price, when it has once been communicated to other commodities, will of course become fixed."*

If, however, I have succeeded in showing that it is not the rise in the money wages of labor which raises the price of commodities, but that such rise always affects profits, it will follow that the prices of commodities would not rise in consequence of a bounty.

But a temporary rise in the price of corn, produced by an increased demand from abroad, would have no effect on the money price of labor. The rise of corn is occasioned by a competition for that supply which was before exclusively appropriated to the home market. By raising profits, additional capital is employed in agriculture, and the increased supply is obtained; but till it be obtained, the high price is absolutely necessary to proportion the consumption to the supply, which would be counteracted by a rise of wages. The rise of corn is the consequence of its scarcity, and is the means by which the demand of the home purchasers is diminished. If wages were increased, the competition would increase, and a further rise of the price of corn would become necessary. In this account of the effects of a bounty nothing has been supposed to occur to raise the natural price of corn, by which its market price is ultimately governed; for it has not been supposed that any additional labor would be required on the land to insure a given production, and this alone can raise its natural price. If the natural price of cloth were 20s. per yard, a great increase in the foreign demand might raise the price to 25s., or more, but the profits which would then be made by the clothier would not fail to attract capital in that direction, and although the demand should be doubled, trebled, or quadrupled, the supply would ultimately be obtained, and cloth would fall to its natural price of 20s. So, in the supply of corn, although we should export 200,000, 300,000, or 800,000 quarters annually, it would ultimately be produced at its natural price, which never varies, unless a different quantity of labor becomes necessary to production.

Perhaps in no part of Adam Smith's justly celebrated work are his conclusions more liable to objection than in the chapter on bounties. In the first place, he speaks of corn as of a commodity of which the production cannot be increased in consequence of a bounty on exportation; he supposes invariably that it acts only on the quantity actually produced, and is no stimulus to farther production. "In years of plenty," he says, "by occasioning an extraordinary exportation, it necessarily keeps up the price of corn in the home market above what it would naturally fall to. In years of scarcity, though the bounty is frequently suspended, yet the great exportation which it occasions in years of plenty must frequently hinder, more or less, the plenty of one year from relieving the scarcity of another. Both in the years of plenty and in years of scarcity, therefore, the bounty necessarily tends to raise the money price of corn somewhat higher than it otherwise would be in the home market."[50]

Adam Smith appears to have been fully aware that the correctness of his argument entirely depended on the fact whether the increase "of the money price of corn, by rendering that commodity more profitable to the farmer, would not necessarily encourage its production."

"I answer," he says, "that this might be the case if the effect of the bounty was to raise the real price of corn, or to enable the farmer, with an equal quantity of it, to maintain a greater number of laborers in the same manner, whether liberal, moderate, or scanty, as other laborers are commonly maintained in his neighborhood."

If nothing were consumed by the laborer but corn, and if the portion which he received was the very lowest which his sustenance required, there might be some ground for supposing that the quantity paid to the laborer could, under no circumstances, be reduced—but the money wages of labor sometimes do not rise at all, and never rise in proportion to the rise, in the money price of corn, because corn, though an important part, is only a part of the consumption of the laborer. If half his wages were expended on corn, and the other half on soap, candles, fuel, tea, sugar, clothing, etc., commodities on which no rise is supposed to take place, it is evident that he would be quite as well paid with a bushel and a half of wheat when it was 16s., a bushel, as he was with two bushels when the price was 8s. per bushel; or with 24s. in money as he was before with 16s. His wages would rise only 50 percent, though corn rose 100 percent; and, consequently, there would be sufficient motive to divert more capital to the land if profits on other trades continued the same as before. But such a rise of wages would also induce manufacturers to withdraw their capitals from manufactures to employ them on the land; for, whilst the farmer increased the price of his commodity 100 percent, and his wages only 50 percent, the manufacturer would be obliged also to raise wages 50 percent, whilst he had no compensation whatever in the rise of his manufactured commodity for this increased charge of production; capital would consequently flow from manufactures to agriculture, till the supply would again lower the price of corn to 8s. per bushel and wages to 16s. per week; when the manufacturer would obtain the same profits as the farmer, and the tide of capital would cease to set in either direction. This is, in fact, the mode in which the cultivation of corn is always extended, and the increased wants of the market supplied. The funds for the maintenance of labor increase, and wages are raised. The comfortable situation of the laborer induces him to marry—population increases, and the demand for corn raises its price relatively to other things—more capital is profitably employed on agriculture, and continues to flow towards it, till the supply is equal to the demand, when the price again falls, and agricultural and manufacturing profits are again brought to a level.

But whether wages were stationary after the rise in the price of corn, or advanced moderately or enormously, is of no importance to this question, for wages are paid by the manufacturer as well as by the farmer, and, therefore, in this respect they must be equally affected by a rise in the price of corn. But they are unequally affected in their profits, inasmuch as the farmer sells his commodity at an advanced price, while the manufacturer sells his for the same price as before. It is, however, the inequality of profit which is always the inducement to remove capital from one employment to another; and, therefore, more corn would be produced, and fewer commodities manufactured. Manufactures would not rise, because fewer would be manufactured, for a supply of them would be obtained in exchange for the exported corn.

A bounty, if it raises the price of corn, either raises it in comparison with the price of other commodities or it does not. If the affirmative be true, it is impossible to deny the greater profits of the farmer, and the temptation to the removal of capital till its price is again lowered by an abundant supply. If it does not raise it in comparison with other commodities, where is the injury to the home consumer beyond the inconvenience of paying the tax? If the manufacturer pays a greater price for his corn, he is compensated by the greater price at which he sells his commodity, with which his corn is ultimately purchased.

The error of Adam Smith proceeds precisely from the same source as that of the writer in the *Edinburgh Review*; for they both think "that the money price of corn regulates that of all other home-made commodities."[51] "It regulates," says Adam Smith, "the money price of labor, which must always be such as to enable the laborer to purchase a quantity of corn sufficient to maintain him and his family, either in the liberal, moderate, or scanty manner, in which the advancing, stationary, or declining circumstances of the society oblige his employers to maintain him. By regulating the money price of all the other parts of the rude produce of land, it regulates that of the materials of almost all manufactures. By regulating the money price of labor, it regulates that of manufacturing art and industry; and by regulating both, it regulates that of the complete manufacture. *The money price of labor, and of everything that is the produce either of land or labor, must necessarily rise or fall in proportion to the money price of corn.*"

This opinion of Adam Smith I have before attempted to refute. In considering a rise in the price of commodities as a necessary consequence of a rise in the price of corn, he reasons as though there were no other fund from which the increased charge could be paid. He has wholly neglected the consideration of profits, the diminution of which forms that fund, without raising the price of commodities. If this opinion of Dr. Smith were well founded, profits could never really fall, whatever accumulation of capital there might be. If, when wages rose, the farmer could raise the price of his corn, and the clothier, the hatter, the shoemaker, and every other manufacturer could also raise the price of their goods in proportion to the advance, although estimated in money they might be all raised, they would continue to bear the same value relatively to each other. Each of these trades could command the same quantity as before of the goods of the others, which, since it is goods, and not money, which constitute wealth, is the only circumstance that could be of importance to them; and the whole rise in the price of raw produce and of goods would be injurious to no other persons but to those whose property consisted of gold and silver, or whose annual income was paid in a contributed quantity of those metals, whether in the form of bullion or of money. Suppose the use of money to be wholly laid aside, and all trade to be carried on by barter. Under such circumstances, could corn rise in exchangeable value with other things? If it could, then it is not true that the value of corn regulates the value of all other commodities; for to do that, it should not vary in relative value to them. If it could not, then it must be maintained that whether corn be obtained on rich or on poor land, with much labor or with little, with the aid of machinery or without, it would always exchange for an equal quantity of all other commodities.

I cannot, however, but remark that though Adam Smith's general doctrines correspond with this which I have just quoted, yet in one part of his work he appears to have given a correct account of the nature of value. "The proportion between the value of gold and silver, and that of goods of any other kind, depends in all cases," he says, *"upon the proportion between the quantity of labor which is necessary in order to bring a certain quantity of gold and silver to market, and that which is necessary to bring thither a certain quantity of any other sort of goods."* Does he not here fully acknowledge, that if any increase takes place in the quantity of labor required to bring one sort of goods to market, whilst no such increase takes place in bringing another sort thither, the first sort will rise in relative value? If no more labor than before be required to bring either cloth or gold to market, they will not vary in relative value, but if more labor be required to bring corn and shoes to market, will not corn and shoes rise in value relatively to cloth and money made of gold?

Adam Smith again considers that the effect of the bounty is to cause a partial degradation in the value of money. "That degradation," says he, "in the value of silver which is the effect of the fertility of the mines, and which operates equally, or very nearly equally, through the greater part of the commercial world, is a matter of very little consequence to any particular country. The consequent rise of all money prices, though it does not make those who receive them really richer, does not make them really poorer. A service of plate becomes really cheaper, and everything else remains precisely of the same real value as before." This observation is most correct.

"But that degradation in the value of silver, which, being the effect either of the peculiar situation or of the political institutions of a particular country, takes place only in that country, is a matter of very great consequence, which, far from tending to make anybody really richer, tends to make everybody really poorer. The rise in the money price of all commodities, which is in this case peculiar to that country, tends to discourage more or less every sort of industry which is carried on within it, and to enable foreign nations, by furnishing almost all sorts of goods for a smaller quantity of silver than its own workmen can afford to do, to undersell them, not only in the foreign, but even in the home market."

I have elsewhere attempted to show that a partial degradation in the value of money, which shall affect both agricultural produce and manufactured commodities, cannot possibly be permanent. To say that money is partially degraded, in this sense, is to say that all commodities are at a high price; but while gold and silver are at liberty to make purchases in the cheapest market, they will be exported for the cheaper goods of other countries, and the reduction of their quantity will increase their value at home; commodities will regain their usual level, and those fitted for foreign markets will be exported as before.

A bounty, therefore, cannot, I think, be objected to on this ground.

If, then, a bounty raises the price of corn in comparison with all other things, the farmer will be benefited, and more land will be cultivated; but if the bounty do not raise the value of corn relatively to other things then no other inconvenience will attend it than that of paying the bounty; one which I neither wish to conceal nor underrate.

Dr. Smith states, that "by establishing high duties on the importation, and bounties on the exportation of corn, the country gentlemen seemed to have imitated the conduct of the manufacturers." By the same means, both had endeavored to raise the value of their commodities. "They did not, perhaps, attend to the great and essential difference which nature has established between corn and almost every other sort of goods. When by either of the above means you enable our manufacturers to sell their goods for somewhat a better price than they otherwise could get for them, you raise not only the nominal, but the real price of those goods. You increase not only the nominal, but the real profit, the real wealth and revenue of those manufacturers—you really encourage those manufacturers. But when, by the like institutions, you raise the nominal or money price of corn, you do not raise its real value, you do not increase the real wealth of our farmers or country gentlemen, you do not encourage the growth of corn. The nature of things has stamped upon corn a real value which cannot be altered by merely altering its money price. Through the world in general that value is equal to the quantity of labor which it can maintain."

I have already attempted to show that the market price of corn would, under an increased demand from the effects of a bounty, exceed its natural price, till the requisite additional supply was obtained, and that then it would again fall to its natural price. But the natural price of corn is not so fixed as the natural price of commodities; because, with any great additional demand for corn, land of a worse quality must be taken into cultivation, on which more labor will be required to produce a given quantity, and the natural price of corn will be raised. By a continued bounty, therefore, on the exportation of corn, there would be created a tendency to a permanent rise in the price of corn, and this, as I have shown elsewhere,[52] never fails to raise rent. Country gentlemen, then, have not only a temporary but a permanent interest in prohibitions of the importation of corn, and in bounties on its exportation; but manufacturers have no permanent interest in establishing high duties on the importation, and bounties on the exportation of commodities; their interest is wholly temporary.

A bounty on the exportation of manufactures will, undoubtedly, as Dr. Smith contends, raise for a time the market price of manufactures, but it will not raise their natural price. The labor of 200 men will produce double the quantity of these goods that 100 could produce before; and, consequently, when the requisite quantity of capital was employed in supplying the requisite quantity of manufactures, they would again fall to their natural price, and all advantage from a high market price would cease. It is, then, only during the interval after the rise in the market price of commodities, and till the additional supply is obtained, that the manufacturers will enjoy high profits; for as soon as prices had subsided, their profits would sink to the general level.

Instead of agreeing, therefore, with Adam Smith, that the country gentlemen had not so great an interest in prohibiting the importation of corn, as the manufacturer had in prohibiting the importation of manufactured goods, I contend, that they have a much superior interest; for their advantage is permanent, while that of the manufacturer is only temporary. Dr. Smith observes that nature has established a great and essential difference between corn and other goods, but the proper inference from that circumstance is directly the reverse of that which he draws from it; for it is on account of this difference that rent is created, and that country gentlemen have an interest in the rise of the natural price of corn. Instead of comparing the interest of the manufacturer with the interest of the country gentleman, Dr. Smith should have compared it with the interest of the farmer, which is very distinct from that of his landlord. Manufacturers have no interest in the rise of the natural price of their commodities, nor have farmers any interest in the rise of the natural price of corn, or other raw produce, though both these classes are benefited while the market price of their productions exceeds their natural price. On the contrary, landlords have a most decided interest in the rise of the natural price of corn; for the rise of rent is the inevitable consequence of the difficulty of producing raw produce, without which its natural price could not rise. Now, as bounties on exportation and prohibitions of the importation of corn increase the demand, and drive us to the cultivation of poorer lands, they necessarily occasion an increased difficulty of production.

The sole effect of high duties on the importation, either of manufactures or of corn, or of a bounty on their exportation, is to divert a portion of capital to an employment which it would not naturally seek. It causes a pernicious distribution of the general funds of the society—it bribes a manufacturer to commence or continue in a comparatively less profitable employment. It is the worst species of taxation, for it does not give to the foreign country all that it takes away from the home country, the balance of loss being made up by the less advantageous distribution of the general capital. Thus, if the price of corn is in England £4, and in France £3 15s., a bounty of 10s. will ultimately reduce it to £3 10s. in France, and maintain it at the same price of £4 in England. For every quarter exported, England pays a tax of 10s. For every quarter imported into France, France gains only 5s., so that the value of 5s. per quarter is absolutely lost to the world by such a distribution of its funds, as to cause diminished production, probably not of corn, but of some other object of necessity or enjoyment.

Mr. Buchanan appears to have seen the fallacy of Dr. Smith's arguments respecting bounties, and on the last passage which I have quoted very judiciously remarks: "In asserting that nature has stamped a real value on corn, which cannot be altered by merely altering its money price. Dr. Smith confounds its value in use with its value in exchange. A bushel of wheat will not feed more people during scarcity than during plenty; but a bushel of wheat will exchange for a greater quantity of luxuries and conveniences when it is scarce? than when it is abundant; and the landed proprietors, who have a surplus of food to dispose of, will therefore, in times of scarcity, be richer men; they will exchange their surplus for a greater value of other enjoyments than when corn is in greater plenty. It is vain to argue, therefore, that if the bounty occasions a forced exportation of corn, it will not also occasion a real rise of price." The whole of Mr. Buchanan's arguments on this part of the subject of bounties appear to me to be perfectly clear and satisfactory.

Mr. Buchanan, however, has not, I think, any more than Dr. Smith or the writer in the Edin*burgh Review,* correct opinions as to the influence of a rise in the price of labor on manufactured commodities. From his peculiar views, which I have elsewhere noticed, he thinks that the price of labor has no connection with the price of corn, and, therefore, that the real value of corn might and would rise without affecting the price of labor; but if labor were affected, he would maintain with Adam Smith and the writer in the *Edinburgh Review* that the price of manufactured commodities would also rise; and then I do not see how he would distinguish such a rise of corn from a fall in the value of money, or how he could come to any other conclusion than that of Dr. Smith. In a note to page

276, vol. i. of the *Wealth of Nations,* Mr. Buchanan observes, "but the price of corn does not regulate the money price of all the other parts of the rude produce of land. It regulates the price of neither metals, nor of various other useful substances, such as coals, wood, stones, etc.; *and as it does not regulate the price of labor, it does not regulate the price of manufactures;* so that the bounty, in so far as it raises the price of corn, is undoubtedly a real benefit to the farmer. It is not on this ground, therefore, that its policy must be argued. Its encouragement to agriculture, by raising the price of corn, must be admitted; and the question then comes to be whether agriculture ought to be thus encouraged?"— It is then, according to Mr. Buchanan, a real benefit to the farmer, because it does not raise the price of labor; but if it did, it would raise the price of all things in proportion, and then it would afford no particular encouragement to agriculture.

It must, however, be conceded that the tendency of a bounty on the exportation of any commodity is to lower in a small degree the value of money. Whatever facilitates exportation tends to accumulate money in a country; and, on the contrary, whatever impedes exportation tends to diminish it. The general effect of taxation, by raising the prices of the commodities taxed, tends to diminish exportation, and, therefore, to check the influx of money; and, on the same principle, a bounty encourages the influx of money. This is more fully explained in the general observations on taxation.

The injurious effects of the mercantile system have been fully exposed by Dr. Smith; the whole aim of that system was to raise the price of commodities in the home market by prohibiting foreign competition; but this system was no more injurious to the agricultural classes than to any other part of the community. By forcing capital into channels where it would not otherwise flow, it diminished the whole amount of commodities produced. The price, though permanently higher, was not sustained by scarcity, but by difficulty of production; and therefore, though the sellers of such commodities sold them for a higher price, they did not sell them, after the requisite quantity of capital was employed in producing them, at higher profits.[53]

The manufacturers themselves, as consumers, had to pay an additional price for such commodities, and, therefore, it cannot be correctly said that "the enhancement of price occasioned by both (corporation laws and high duties on the importations of foreign commodities) is everywhere finally paid by the landlords, farmers, and laborers of the country."

It is the more necessary to make this remark as in the present day the authority of Adam Smith is quoted by country gentlemen for imposing similar high duties on the importation of foreign corn. Because the cost of production, and, therefore, the prices of various manufactured commodities, are raised to the consumer by one error in legislation, the country has been called upon, on the plea of justice, quietly to submit to fresh exactions. Because we all pay an additional price for our linen, muslin, and cottons, it is thought just that we should pay also an additional price for our corn. Because, in the general distribution of the labor of the world, we have prevented the greatest amount of productions from being obtained by our portion of that labor in manufactured commodities, we should further punish ourselves by diminishing the productive powers of the general labor in the supply of raw produce. It would be much wiser to acknowledge the errors which a mistaken policy has induced us to adopt and immediately to commence a gradual recurrence to the sound principles of a universally free trade.[54]

"I have already had occasion to remark," observes M. Say, "in speaking of what is improperly called the balance of trade, that if it suits a merchant better to export the precious metals to a foreign country than any other goods, it is also the interest of the state that he should export them, because the state only gains or loses through the channel of its citizens; and in what concerns foreign trade, that which best suits the individual best suits also the state; therefore, by opposing obstacles to the exportation which individuals would be inclined to make of the precious metals, nothing more is done than to force them to substitute some other commodity less profitable to themselves and to the state. It must, however, be remarked that I say only *in what concerns foreign trade;* because the profits which merchants make by their dealings with their countrymen, as well as those which are made in the exclusive commerce with colonies, are not entirely gains for the state. In the trade between individuals of the same country there is no other gain but the value of a utility produced; *que la valeur d'une utilite produite"* [55] Vol. i. p. 401. I cannot see the distinction here made between the profits of the home and foreign trade. The object of all trade is to increase productions. If, for the purchase of a pipe of wine, I had it in my power to export bullion which was bought with the value of the produce of 100 days' labor, but government, by prohibiting the exportation of bullion, should oblige me to purchase my wine with a commodity bought with the value of the produce of 105 days' labor, the produce of five days' labor is lost to me, and, through me, to the state. But if these transactions took place between individuals in different provinces of the same country, the same advantage would accrue both to the individual, and, through him, to the country, if he were unfettered in his choice of the commodities with which he made his purchases, and the same disadvantage if he were obliged by government to purchase with the least beneficial commodity. If a manufacturer could work up with the same capital more iron where coals are plentiful than he could where coals are scarce, the country would be benefited by the difference. But if coals were nowhere plentiful, and he imported iron, and could get this additional quantity by the manufacture of a commodity with the same capital and labor, he would, in like manner, benefit his country by the additional quantity of iron. In the sixth chapter of this work I have endeavored to show that all trade, whether foreign or domestic, is beneficial, by increasing the quantity and not by increasing the value of productions. We shall have no greater value whether we carry on the most beneficial home and foreign trade, or, in consequence of being fettered by prohibitory laws, we are obliged to content ourselves with the least advantageous. The rate of profits and the value produced will be the same. The advantage always resolves itself into that which M. Say appears to confine to the home trade; in both cases there is no other gain but that of the value of a *utilité produite.*

CHAPTER XXIII

On Bounties on Productions

It may not be uninstructive to consider the effects of a bounty on the *production* of raw produce and other commodities, with a view to observe the application of the principles which I have been endeavoring to establish with regard to the profits of stock, the division of the annual produce of the land and labor, and the relative prices of manufactures and raw produce. In the first place, let us suppose that a tax was imposed on all commodities for the purpose of raising a fund to be employed by government in giving a bounty on the *production* of corn. As no part of such a tax would be expended by government, and as all that was received from one class of the people would be returned to another, the nation collectively would be neither richer nor poorer from such a tax and bounty. It would be readily allowed that the tax on commodities by which the fund was created would raise the price of the commodities taxed; all the consumers of those commodities, therefore, would contribute towards that fund; in other words, their natural or necessary price being raised, so would, too, their market price. But for the same reason that the natural price of those commodities would be raised, the natural price of corn would be lowered; before the bounty was paid on production, the farmers obtained as great a price for their corn as was necessary to repay them their rent and their expenses, and afford them the general rate of profits; after the bounty, they would receive more than that rate, unless the price of corn fell by a sum at least equal to the bounty. The effect, then, of the tax and bounty would be to raise the price of commodities in a degree equal to the tax levied on them, and to lower the price of corn by a sum equal to the bounty paid. It will be observed, too, that no permanent alteration could be made in the distribution of capital between agriculture and manufactures, because, as there would be no alteration either in the amount of capital or population, there would be precisely the same demand for bread and manufactures. The profits of the farmer would be no higher than the general level after the fall in the price of corn; nor would the profits of the manufacturer be lower after the rise of manufactured goods; the bounty, then, would not occasion any more capital to be employed on the land in the production of corn, nor any less in the manufacture of goods. But how would the interest of the landlord be affected? On the same principles that a tax on raw produce would lower the corn rent of land, leaving the money rent unaltered, a bounty on production, which is directly the contrary of a tax, would raise corn rent, leaving the money rent unaltered.[56] With the same money rent the landlord would have a greater price to pay for his manufactured goods, and a less price for his corn; he would probably, therefore, be neither richer nor poorer.

Now, whether such a measure would have any operation on the wages of labor would depend on the question whether the laborer, in purchasing commodities, would pay as much towards the tax as he would receive from the effects of the bounty in the low price of his food. If these two quantities were equal, wages would continue unaltered; but if the commodities taxed were not those consumed by the laborer, his wages would fall, and his employer would be benefited by the difference. But this is no real advantage to his employer; it would indeed operate to increase the rate of his profits, as every fall of wages must do; but in proportion as the laborer contributed less to the fund from which the bounty was paid, and which, let it be remembered, must be raised, his employer must contribute more; in other words, he would contribute as much to the tax by his expenditure as he would receive in the effects of the bounty and the higher rate of profits together. He obtains a higher rate of profits to requite him for his payment, not only of his own quota of the tax, but of his laborer's also; the remuneration which he receives for his laborer's quota appears in diminished wages, or, which is the same thing, in increased profits; the remuneration for his own appears in the diminution in the price of the corn which he consumes, arising from the bounty.

Here it will be proper to remark the different effects produced on profits from an alteration in the real labor, or natural value of corn, and an alteration in the relative value of corn, from taxation and from bounties. If corn is lowered in price by an alteration in its labor price, not only will the rate of the profits of stock be altered, but the condition of the capitalist will be improved. With greater profits, he will have no more to pay for the objects on which those profits are expended; which does not happen, as we have just seen, when the fall is occasioned artificially by a bounty. In the real fall in the value of corn, arising from less labor being required to produce one of the most important objects of man's consumption, labor is rendered more productive. With the same capital the same labor is employed, and an increase of productions is the result; not only then will the rate of profits be increased, but the condition of him who obtains them will be improved; not only will each capitalist have a greater money revenue, if he employs the same money capital, but also when that money is expended it will procure him a greater sum of commodities; his enjoyments will be augmented. In the case of the bounty, to balance the advantage which he derives from the fall of one commodity, he has the disadvantage of paying a price more than proportionally high for another; he receives an increased rate of profits in order to enable him to pay this higher price; so that his real situation, though not deteriorated, is in no way improved: though he gets a higher rate of profits, he has no greater command of the produce of the land and labor of the country. When the fall in the value of corn is brought about by natural causes, it is not counteracted by the rise of other commodities; on the contrary, they fall from the raw material falling from which they are made: but when the fall in corn is occasioned by artificial means, it is always counteracted by a real rise in the value of some other commodity, so that if corn be bought cheaper, other commodities are bought dearer.

This, then, is a further proof that no particular disadvantage arises from taxes on necessaries, on account of their raising wages and lowering the rate of profits. Profits are indeed lowered, but only to the amount of the laborer's portion of the tax, which must at all events be paid either by his employer or by the consumer of the produce of the laborer's work. Whether you deduct £50 per annum from the employer's revenue, or add £50 to the prices of the commodities which he consumes, can be of no other consequence to him or to the community than as it may equally affect all other classes. If it be added to the prices of the commodity, a miser may avoid the tax by not consuming; if it be indirectly deducted from every man's revenue, he cannot avoid paying his fair proportion of the public burdens.

A bounty on the production of corn, then, would produce no real effect on the annual produce of the land and labor of the country, although it would make corn relatively cheap and manufactures relatively dear. But suppose now that a contrary measure should be adopted—that a tax should be raised on corn for the purpose of affording a fund for a bounty on the production of commodities.

In such case, it is evident that corn would be dear and commodities cheap; labor would continue at the same price if the laborer were as much benefited by the cheapness of commodities as he was injured by the dearness of corn; but if he were not, wages would rise and profits would fall, while money rent would continue the same as before; profits would fall, because, as we have just explained, that would be the mode in which the laborer's share of the tax would be paid by the employers of labor. By the increase of wages the laborer would be compensated for the tax which he would pay in the increased price of corn; by not expending any part of his wages on the manufactured commodities he would receive no part of the bounty; the bounty would be all received by the employers, and the tax would be partly paid by the employed; a remuneration would be made to the laborers, in the shape of wages, for this increased burden laid upon them, and thus the rate of profits would be reduced. In this case, too, there would be a complicated measure producing no national result whatever.

In considering this question we have purposely left out of our consideration the effect of such a measure on foreign trade; we have rather been supposing the case of an insulated country having no commercial connection with other countries. We have seen that, as the demand of the country for corn and commodities would be the same, whatever direction the bounty might take, there would be no temptation to remove capital from one employment to another; but this would no longer be the case if there were foreign commerce, and that commerce were free. By altering the relative value of commodities and corn, by producing so powerful an effect on their natural prices, we should be applying a strong stimulus to the exportation of those commodities whose natural prices were lowered, and an equal stimulus to the importation of those commodities whose natural prices were raised, and thus such a financial measure might entirely alter the natural distribution of employments, to the advantage indeed of the foreign countries, but ruinously to that in which so absurd a policy was adopted.

CHAPTER XXIV

Doctrine of Adam Smith Concerning the Rent of Land

"Such parts only of the produce of land," says Adam Smith, "can commonly be brought to market of which the ordinary price is sufficient to replace the stock which must be employed in bringing them thither, together with its ordinary profits. If the ordinary price is more than this, the surplus part of it will naturally go to the rent of land. *If it is not more, though the commodity can be brought to market, it can afford no rent to the landlord.* Whether the price is, or is not more, depends upon the demand."

This passage would naturally lead the reader to conclude that its author could not have mistaken the nature of rent, and that he must have seen that the quality of land which the exigencies of society might require to be taken into cultivation would depend on *"the ordinary price of its produce"* whether it were *"sufficient to replace the stock which must be employed in cultivating it, together with its ordinary profits."*

But he had adopted the notion that "there were some parts of the produce of land for which the demand must always be such as to afford a greater price than what is sufficient to bring them to market;" and he considered food as one of those parts.

He says that "land, in almost any situation, produces a greater quantity of food than what is sufficient to maintain all the labor necessary for bringing it to market, in the most liberal way in which that labor is ever maintained. The surplus, too, is always more than sufficient to replace the stock which employed that labor, together with its profits. Something, therefore, always remains for a rent to the landlord."

But what proof does he give of this?—no other than the assertion that "the most desert moors in Norway and Scotland produce some sort of pasture for cattle, of which the milk and the increase are always more than sufficient, not only to maintain all the labor necessary for tending them, and to pay the ordinary profit to the farmer, or owner of the herd or flock, but to afford some small rent to the landlord." Now, of this I may be permitted to entertain a doubt; I believe that as yet in every country, from the rudest to the most refined, there is land of such a quality that it cannot yield a produce more than sufficiently valuable to replace the stock employed upon it, together with the profits ordinary and usual in that country. In America we all know that this is the case, and yet no one maintains that the principles which regulate rent are different in that country and in Europe. But if it were true that England had so far advanced in cultivation that at this time there were no lands remaining which did not afford a rent, it would be equally true that there formerly must have been such lands; and that whether there be or not is of no importance to this question, for it is the same thing if there be any capital employed in Great Britain on land which yields only the return of stock with its ordinary profits, whether it be employed on old or on new land. If a farmer agrees for land on a lease of seven or fourteen years, he may propose to employ on it a capital of £10,000, knowing that at the existing price of grain and raw produce he can replace that part of his stock which he is obliged to expend, pay his rent, and obtain the general rate of profit. He will not employ £11,000, unless the last £1000 can be employed so productively as to afford him the usual profits of stock. In his calculation, whether he shall employ it or not, he considers only whether the price of raw produce is sufficient to replace his expenses and profits, for he knows that he shall have no additional rent to pay. Even at the expiration of his lease his rent will not be raised; for if his landlord should require rent, because this additional £1000 was employed, he would withdraw it; since, by employing it, he gets, by the supposition, only the ordinary and usual profits which he may obtain by any other employment of stock; and, therefore, he cannot afford to pay rent for it, unless the price of raw produce should further rise, or, which is the same thing, unless the usual and general rate of profits should fall.

If the comprehensive mind of Adam Smith had been directed to this fact, he would not have maintained that rent forms one of the component parts of the price of raw produce; for price is everywhere regulated by the return obtained by this last portion of capital, for which no rent whatever is paid. If he had adverted to this principle, he would have made no distinction between the law which regulates the rent of mines and the rent of land.

"Whether a coal mine, for example," he says, "can afford any rent depends partly upon its fertility and partly upon its situation. A mine of any kind may be said to be either fertile or barren according as the quantity of mineral which can be brought from it by a certain quantity of labor is greater or less than what can be brought by an equal quantity from the greater part of other mines of the same kind. Some coal mines, advantageously situated, cannot be wrought on account of their barrenness. The produce does not pay the expense. They can afford neither profit nor rent. There are some of which the produce is barely sufficient to pay the labor and replace, together with its ordinary profits, the stock employed in working them. They afford some profit to the undertaker of the work, but no rent to the landlord. They can be wrought advantageously by nobody but the landlord, who being himself the undertaker of the work, gets the ordinary profit of the capital which he employs in it. Many coal mines in Scotland are wrought in this manner, and can be wrought in no other. The landlord will allow nobody else to work them without paying some rent, and nobody can afford to pay any.

"Other coal mines in the same country, sufficiently fertile, cannot be wrought on account of their situation. A quantity of mineral sufficient to defray the expense of working could be brought from the mine by the ordinary, or even less than the ordinary, quantity of labor; but in an inland country, thinly inhabited, and without either good roads or water-carriage, this quantity could not be sold." The whole principle of rent is here admirably and perspicuously explained, but every word is as applicable to land as it is to mines; yet he affirms that "it is otherwise in estates above ground. The proportion, both of their produce and of their rent, is in proportion to their absolute, and not to their relative, fertility." But, suppose that there were no land which did not afford a rent; then the amount of rent on the worst land would be in proportion to the excess of the value of the produce above the expenditure of capital and the ordinary profits of stock: the same principle would govern the rent of land of a somewhat better quality, or more favorably situated, and, therefore, the rent of this land would exceed the rent of that inferior to it by the superior advantages which it possessed; the same might be said of that of the third quality, and so on to the very best. Is it not, then, as certain that it is the relative fertility of the land which determines the portion of the produce which shall be paid for the rent of land as it is that the relative fertility of mines determines the portion of their produce which shall be paid for the rent of mines?

After Adam Smith has declared that there are some mines which can only be worked by the owners, as they will afford only sufficient to defray the expense of working, together with the ordinary profits of the capital employed, we should expect that he would admit that it was these particular mines which regulated the price of the produce from all mines. If the old mines are insufficient to supply the quantity of coal required, the price of coal will rise, and will continue rising till the owner of a new and inferior mine finds that he can obtain the usual profits of stock by working his mine. If his mine be tolerably fertile, the rise will not be great before it becomes his interest so to employ his capital; but if it be not tolerably fertile, it is evident that the price must continue to rise till it will afford him the means of paying his expenses, and obtaining the ordinary profits of stock. It appears, then, that it is always the least fertile mine which regulates the price of coal. Adam Smith, however, is of a different opinion: he observes that "the most fertile coal mine, too, regulates the price of coals at all the other mines in its neighborhood. Both the proprietor and the undertaker of the work find, the one that he can get a greater rent, the other that he can get a greater profit, by somewhat underselling all their neighbors. Their neighbors are soon obliged to sell at the same price, though they cannot so well afford it, and though it always diminishes, and sometimes takes away altogether, both their rent and their profit. Some works are abandoned altogether; others can afford no rent, and can be wrought only by the proprietor." If the demand for coal should be diminished, or if by new processes the quantity should be increased, the price would fall, and some mines would be abandoned; but in every case, the price must be sufficient to pay the expenses and profit of that mine which is worked without being charged with rent. It is, therefore, the least fertile mine which regulates price. Indeed, it is so stated in another place by Adam Smith himself, for he says, "The lowest price at which coals can be sold for any considerable time is like that of all other commodities, the price which is barely sufficient to replace, together with its ordinary profits, the stock which must be employed in bringing them to market. At a coal mine for which the landlord can get no rent, but which he must either work himself, or let it alone all altogether, the price of coals must generally be nearly about this price."

But the same circumstance, namely, the abundance and consequent cheapness of coals, from whatever cause it may arise, which would make it necessary to abandon those mines on which there was no rent, or a very moderate one, would, if there were the same abundance and consequent cheapness of raw produce, render it necessary to abandon the cultivation of those lands for which either no rent was paid or a very moderate one. If, for example, potatoes should become the general and common food of the people, as rice is in some countries, one-fourth or one-half of the land now in cultivation would probably be immediately abandoned; for if, as Adam Smith says, "an acre of potatoes will produce six thousand weight of solid nourishment, three times the quantity produced by the acre of wheat," there could not be for a considerable time such a multiplication of people as to consume the quantity that might be raised on the land before employed for the cultivation of wheat; much land would consequently be abandoned, and rent would fall; and it would not be till the population had been doubled or trebled that the same quantity of land could be in cultivation and the rent paid for it as high as before.

Neither would any greater proportion of the gross produce be paid to the landlord whether it consisted of potatoes, which would feed three hundred people, or of wheat, which would feed only one hundred; because, though the expenses of production would be very much diminished if the laborer's wages were chiefly regulated by the price of potatoes, and not by the price of wheat, and though, therefore, the proportion of the whole gross produce, after paying the laborers, would be greatly increased, yet no part of that additional proportion would go to rent, but the whole invariably to profits—profits being at all times raised as wages fall, and lowered as wages rise. Whether wheat or potatoes were cultivated, rent would be governed by the same principle—it would be always equal to the difference between the quantities of produce obtained with equal capitals, either on the same land or on land of different qualities; and, therefore, while lands of the same quality were cultivated, and there was no alteration in their relative fertility or advantages, rent would always bear the same proportion to the gross produce.

Adam Smith, however, maintains that the proportion which falls to the landlord would be increased by a diminished cost of production, and, therefore, that he would receive a larger share as well as a larger quantity from an abundant than from a scanty produce. "A rice field," he says, "produces a much greater quantity of food than the most fertile corn field. Two crops in the year, from thirty to sixty bushels each, are said to be the ordinary produce of an acre. Though its cultivation, therefore, requires more labor, a much greater surplus remains after maintaining all that labor. In those rice countries, therefore, where rice is the common and favorite vegetable food of the people, and where the cultivators are chiefly maintained with it, *a greater share of this greater surplus should belong to the landlord than in corn countries.*"

Mr. Buchanan also remarks that "it is quite clear that if any other produce, which the land yielded more abundantly than corn, were to become the common food of the people, the rent of the landlord would be improved in proportion to its greater abundance."

If potatoes were to become the common food of the people, there would be a long interval during which the landlords would suffer an enormous deduction of rent. They would not probably receive nearly so much of the sustenance of man as they now receive, while that sustenance would fall to a third of its present value. But all manufactured commodities, on which a part of the landlord's rent is expended, would suffer no other fall than that which proceeded from the fall in the raw material of which they were made, and which would arise only from the greater fertility of the land which might then be devoted to its production.

When, from the progress of population, land of the same quality as before should be taken into cultivation, the landlord would have not only the same proportion of the produce as before, but that proportion would also be of the same value as before. Rent, then, would be the same as before; profits, however, would be much higher, because the price of food, and consequently wages, would be much lower. High profits are favorable to the accumulation of capital. The demand for labor would further increase, and landlords would be permanently benefited by the increased demand for land.

Indeed, the very same lands might be cultivated much higher when such an abundance of food could be produced from them, and, consequently, they would, in the progress of society, admit of much higher rents, and would sustain a much greater population than before. This could not fail to be highly beneficial to landlords, and is consistent with the principle which this inquiry, I think, will not fail to establish—that all extraordinary profits are in their nature but of limited duration, as the whole surplus produce of the soil, after deducting from it only such moderate profits as are sufficient to encourage accumulation, must finally rest with the landlord.

With so low a price of labor as such an abundant produce would cause, not only would the lands already in cultivation yield a much greater quantity of produce, but they would admit of a great additional capital being employed on them, and a greater value to be drawn from them, and, at the same time, lands of a very inferior quality could be cultivated with high profits, to the great advantage of landlords, as well as to the whole class of consumers. The machine which produced the most important article of consumption would be improved, and would be well paid for according as its services were demanded. All the advantages would, in the first instance, be enjoyed by laborers, capitalists, and consumers; but, with the progress of population, they would be gradually transferred to the proprietors of the soil.

Independently of these improvements, in which the community have an immediate and the landlords a remote interest, the interest of the landlord is always opposed to that of the consumer and manufacturer. Corn can be permanently at an advanced price only because additional labor is necessary to produce it; because its cost of production is increased. The same cause invariably raises rent, it is therefore for the interest of the landlord that the cost attending the production of corn should be increased. This, however, is not the interest of the consumer; to him it is desirable that corn should be low relatively to money and commodities, for it is always with commodities or money that corn is purchased. Neither is it the interest of the manufacturer that corn should be at a high price, for the high price of corn will occasion high wages, but will not raise the price of his commodity. Not only, then, must more of his commodity, or, which comes to the same thing, the value of more of his commodity, be given in exchange for the corn which he himself consumes, but more must be given, or the value of more, for wages to his workmen, for which he will receive no remuneration. All classes, therefore, except the landlords, will be injured by the increase in the price of corn. The dealings between the landlord and the public are not like dealings in trade, whereby both the seller and buyer may equally be said to gain, but the loss is wholly on one side, and the gain wholly on the other; and if corn could by importation be procured cheaper, the loss in consequence of not importing is far greater on one side than the gain is on the other.

Adam Smith never makes any distinction between a low value of money and a high value of corn, and therefore infers that the interest of the landlord is not opposed to that of the rest of the community. In the first case, money is low relatively to all commodities; in the other, corn is high relatively to all. In the first, corn and commodities continue at the same relative values; in the second, corn is higher relatively to commodities as well as money.

The following observation of Adam Smith is applicable to a low value of money, but it is totally inapplicable to a high value of corn. "If importation (of corn) was at all times free, our farmers and country gentlemen would probably, one year with another, get less money for their corn than they do at present when importation is at most times in effect prohibited; but the money which they got would be of more value, *would buy more goods of all other kinds,* and would employ more labor. Their real wealth, their real revenue, therefore, would be the same as at present, though it might be expressed by a smaller quantity of silver; and they would neither be disabled nor discouraged from cultivating corn as much as they do at present. On the contrary, as the rise in the real value of silver, in consequence of lowering the money price of corn, lowers somewhat the money price of all other commodities, it gives the industry of the country where it takes place some advantage in all foreign markets, and thereby tends to encourage and increase that industry. But the extent of the home market for corn must be in proportion to the general industry of the country where it grows, or to the number of those who produce something else to give in exchange for corn. But in every country the home market, as it is the nearest and most convenient, so is it likewise the greatest and most important market for corn. That rise in the real value of silver, therefore, which is the effect of lowering the average money price of corn, tends to enlarge the greatest and most important market for corn, and thereby to encourage instead of discouraging its growth."

A high or low money price of corn, arising from the abundance and cheapness of gold and silver, is of no importance to the landlord, as every sort of produce would be equally affected just as Adam Smith describes; but a relatively high price of corn is at all times greatly beneficial to the landlord; for, first, it gives him a greater quantity of corn for rent; and, secondly, for every equal measure of corn he will have a command, not only over a greater quantity of money, but over a greater quantity of every commodity which money can purchase.

CHAPTER XXV

On Colonial Trade

Adam Smith, in his observations on colonial trade, has shown most satisfactorily the advantages of a free trade, and the injustice suffered by colonies in being prevented by their mother countries from selling their produce at the dearest market and buying their manufactures and stores at the cheapest. He has shown that, by permitting every country freely to exchange the produce of its industry when and where it pleases, the best distribution of the labor of the world will be effected, and the greatest abundance of the necessaries and enjoyments of human life will be secured.

He has attempted also to show that this freedom of commerce, which undoubtedly promotes the interest of the whole, promotes also that of each particular country; and that the narrow policy adopted in the countries of Europe respecting their colonies is not less injurious to the mother countries themselves than to the colonies whose interests are sacrificed.

"The monopoly of the colony trade," he says, "like all the other mean and malignant expedients of the mercantile system, depresses the industry of all other countries, but chiefly that of the colonies, without in the least increasing, but, on the contrary, diminishing that of the country in whose favor it is established."

This part of his subject, however, is not treated in so clear and convincing a manner as that in which he shows the injustice of this system towards the colony.

It may, I think, be doubted whether a mother country may not sometimes be benefited by the restraints to which she subjects her colonial possessions. Who can doubt, for example, that if England were the colony of France, the latter country would be benefited by a heavy bounty paid by England on the exportation of corn, cloth, or any other commodities? In examining the question of bounties, on the supposition of corn being at £4 per quarter in this country, we saw that with a bounty of 10s. per quarter on exportation in England, corn would have been reduced to £3 10s. in France. Now, if corn had previously been at £3 15s. per quarter in France, the French consumers would have been benefited by 5s. per quarter on all imported corn; if the natural price of corn in France were before £4, they would have gained the whole bounty of 10s. per quarter. France would thus be benefited by the loss sustained by England: she would not gain a part only of what England lost, but the whole.

It may, however, be said that a bounty on exportation is a measure of internal policy, and could not easily be imposed by the mother country. If it would suit the interests of Jamaica and Holland to make an exchange of the commodities which they respectively produce, without the intervention of England, it is quite certain that by their being prevented from so doing the interests of Holland and Jamaica would suffer; but if Jamaica is obliged to send her goods to England, and there exchange them for Dutch goods, an English capital, or English agency, will be employed in a trade in which it would not otherwise be engaged. It is allured thither by a bounty, not paid by England, but by Holland and Jamaica.

That the loss sustained through a disadvantageous distribution of labor in two countries may be beneficial to one of them, while the other is made to suffer more than the loss actually belonging to such a distribution, has been stated by Adam Smith himself; which, if true, will at once prove that a measure which may be greatly hurtful to a colony may be partially beneficial to the mother country.

Speaking of treaties of commerce, he says, "When a nation binds itself by treaty, either to permit the entry of certain goods from one foreign country which it prohibits from all others, or to exempt the goods of one country from duties to which it subjects those of all others, the country, or at least the merchants and manufacturers of the country, whose commerce is so favored, must necessarily derive great advantage from the treaty. Those merchants and manufacturers enjoy a sort of monopoly in the country which is so indulgent to them. That country becomes a market both more extensive and more advantageous for their goods; more extensive, because the goods of other nations, being either excluded or subjected to heavier duties, it takes off a greater quantity of them; more advantageous, because the merchants of the favored country, enjoying a sort of monopoly there, will often sell their goods for a better price than if exposed to the free competition of all other nations."

Let the two nations between which the commercial treaty is made be the mother country and her colony, and Adam Smith, it is evident, admits that a mother country may be benefited by oppressing her colony. It may, however, be again remarked, that unless the monopoly of the foreign market be in the hands of an exclusive company, no more will be paid for commodities by foreign purchasers than by home purchasers; the price which they will both pay will not differ greatly from their natural price in the country where they are produced. England, for example, will, under ordinary circumstances, always be able to buy French goods at the natural price of those goods in France, and France would have an equal privilege of buying English goods at their natural price in England. But at these prices goods would be bought without a treaty. Of what advantage or disadvantage, then, is the treaty to either party?

The disadvantage of the treaty to the importing country would be this: it would bind her to purchase a commodity, from England, for example, at the natural price of that commodity in England, when she might perhaps have bought it at the much lower natural price of some other country. It occasions then a disadvantageous distribution of the general capital, which falls chiefly on the country bound by its treaty to buy in the least productive market; but it gives no advantage to the seller on account of any supposed monopoly, for he is prevented by the competition of his own countrymen from selling his goods above their natural price; at which he would sell them, whether he exported them to France, Spain, or the West Indies, or sold them for home consumption.

In what, then, does the advantage of the stipulation in the treaty consist? It consists in this: these particular goods could not have been made in England for exportation, but for the privilege which she alone had of serving this particular market; for the competition of that country, where the natural price was lower, would have deprived her of all chance of selling those commodities. This, however, would have been of little importance if England were quite secure that she could sell to the same amount any other goods which she might fabricate, either in the French market or with equal advantage in any other. The object which England has in view is, for example, to buy a quantity of French wines of the value of £5000—she desires, then, to sell goods somewhere by which she may get £5000 for this purpose. If France gives her a monopoly of the cloth market she will readily export cloth for this purpose; but if the trade is free, the competition of other countries may prevent the natural price of cloth in England from being sufficiently low to enable her to get £5000 by the sale of cloth, and to obtain the usual profits by such an employment of her stock. The industry of England must be employed, then, on some other commodity; but there may be none of her productions which, at the existing value of money, she can afford to sell at the natural price of other countries. What is the consequence? The wine drinkers of England are still willing to give £5000 for their wine, and consequently £5000 in money is exported to France for that purpose. By this exportation of money, its value is raised in England and lowered in other countries; and with it the *natural price* of all commodities produced by British industry is also lowered. The advance in the value of money is the same thing as the decline in the price of commodities. To obtain £5000, British commodities may now be exported; for at their reduced natural price they may now enter into competition with the goods of other countries. More goods are sold, however, at the low prices to obtain the £5000 required, which, when obtained, will not procure the same quantity of wine; because, whilst the diminution of money in England has lowered the natural price of goods there, the increase of money in France has raised the natural price of goods and wine in France. Less wine, then, will be imported into England, in exchange for its commodities, when the trade is perfectly free than when she is peculiarly favored by commercial treaties. The *rate* of profits, however, will not have varied; money will have altered in relative value in the two countries, and the advantage gained by France will be the obtaining a greater quantity of English, in exchange for a given quantity of French, goods, while the loss sustained by England will consist in obtaining a smaller quantity of French goods in exchange for a given quantity of those of England.

Foreign trade, then, whether fettered, encouraged, or free, will always continue, whatever may be the comparative difficulty of production in different countries; but it can only be regulated by altering the natural price, not the natural value, at which commodities can be produced in those countries, and that is effected by altering the distribution of the precious metals. This explanation confirms the opinion which I have elsewhere given, that there is not a tax, a bounty, or a prohibition on the importation or exportation of commodities which does not occasion a different distribution of the precious metals, and which does not, therefore, everywhere alter both the natural and the market price of commodities.

It is evident, then, that the trade with a colony may be so regulated that it shall at the same time be less beneficial to the colony, and more beneficial to the mother country, than a perfectly free trade. As it is disadvantageous to a single consumer to be restricted in his dealings to one particular shop, so is it disadvantageous for a nation of consumers to be obliged to purchase of one particular country. If the shop or the country afforded the goods required the cheapest, they would be secure of selling them without any such exclusive privilege; and if they did not sell cheaper, the general interest would require that they should not be encouraged to continue a trade which they could not carry on at an equal advantage with others. The shop, or the selling country, might lose by the change of employments, but the general benefit is never so fully secured as by the most productive distribution of the general capital; that is to say, by a universally free trade.

An increase in the cost of production of a commodity, if it be an article of the first necessity, will not necessarily diminish its consumption; for although the general power of the purchasers to consume is diminished by the rise of any one commodity, yet they may relinquish the consumption of some other commodity whose cost of production has not risen. In that case, the quantity supplied, and the quantity demanded, will be the same as before; the cost of production only will have increased, and yet the price will rise, and must rise, to place the profits of the producer of the enhanced commodity on a level with the profits derived from other trades.

M. Say acknowledges that the cost of production is the foundation of price, and yet in various parts of his book he maintains that price is regulated by the proportion which demand bears to supply. The real and ultimate regulator of the relative value of any two commodities is the cost of their production, and not the respective quantities which may be produced, nor the competition amongst the purchasers.

According to Adam Smith, the colony trade, by being one in which British capital only can be employed, has raised the rate of profits of all other trades; and as, in his opinion, high profits, as well as high wages, raise the prices of commodities, the monopoly of the colony trade has been, he thinks, injurious to the mother country; as it has diminished her power of selling manufactured commodities as cheap as other countries. He says that "in consequence of the monopoly, the increase of the colony trade has not so much occasioned an addition to the trade which Great Britain had before as a total change in its direction. Secondly, this monopoly has necessarily contributed to keep up the rate of profit in all the different branches of British trade higher than it naturally would have been had all nations been allowed a free trade to the British colonies." "But whatever raises in any country the ordinary rate of profit higher than it otherwise would be, necessarily subjects that country both to an absolute and to a relative disadvantage in every branch of trade of which she has not the monopoly. It subjects her to an absolute disadvantage, because in such branches of trade her merchants cannot get this greater profit without selling dearer than they otherwise would do both the goods of foreign countries which they import into their own and the goods of their own country which they export to foreign countries. Their own country must both buy dearer and sell dearer; must both buy less and sell less; must both enjoy less and produce less than she otherwise would do.

"Our merchants frequently complain of the high wages of British labor as the cause of their manufactures being undersold in foreign markets; but they are silent about the high profits of stock. They complain of the extravagant gain of other people, but they say nothing of their own. The high profits of British stock, however, may contribute towards raising the price of British manufacture in many cases as much, and in some perhaps more, than the high wages of British labor."

I allow that the monopoly of the colony trade will change, and often prejudicially, the direction of capital; but from what I have already said on the subject of profits, it will be seen that any change from one foreign trade to another, or from home to foreign trade, cannot, in my opinion, affect the rate of profits. The injury suffered will be what I have just described; there will be a worse distribution of the general capital and industry, and, therefore, less will be produced. The natural price of commodities will be raised, and therefore, though the consumer will be able to purchase to the same money value, he will obtain a less quantity of commodities. It will be seen, too, that if it even had the effect of raising profits, it would not occasion the least alteration in prices; prices being regulated neither by wages nor profits.

And does not Adam Smith agree in this opinion, when he says that "the prices of commodities, or the value of gold and silver as compared with commodities, depends upon the proportion between the *quantity of labor* which is necessary in order to bring a certain quantity of gold and silver to market, and that which is necessary to bring thither a certain quantity of any other sort of goods?" That quantity will not be affected, whether profits be high or low, or wages low or high. How then can prices be raised by high profits?

CHAPTER XXVI

On Gross and Net Revenue

Adam Smith constantly magnifies the advantages which a country derives from a large gross, rather than a large net income. "In proportion as a greater share of the capital of a country is employed in agriculture," he says, "the greater will be the quantity of productive labor which it puts into motion within the country; as will likewise be the value which its employment adds to the annual produce of the land and labor of the society. After agriculture, the capital employed in manufactures puts into motion the greatest quantity of productive labor, and adds the greatest value to the annual produce. That which is employed in the trade of exportation has the least effect of any of the three."[57]

Granting, for a moment, that this were true, what would be the advantage resulting to a country from the employment of a great quantity of productive labor, if, whether it employed that quantity or a smaller, its net rent and profits together would be the same. The whole produce of the land and labor of every country is divided into three portions: of these, one portion is devoted to wages, another to profits, and the other to rent. It is from the two last portions only that any deductions can be made for taxes or for savings; the former, if moderate, constituting always the necessary expenses of production.[58] To an individual with a capital of £20,000, whose profits were £2000 per annum, it would be a matter quite indifferent whether his capital would employ a hundred or a thousand men, whether the commodity produced sold for £10,000 or for £20,000, provided, in all cases, his profits were not diminished below £2000. Is not the real interest of the nation similar? Provided its net real income, its rent and profits be the same, it is of no importance whether the nation consists of ten or of twelve millions of inhabitants. Its power of supporting fleets and armies, and all species of unproductive labor, must be in proportion to its net, and not in proportion to its gross, income. If five millions of men could produce as much food and clothing as was necessary for ten millions, food and clothing for five millions would be the net revenue. Would it be of any advantage to the country that, to produce this same net revenue, seven millions of men should be required, that is to say, that seven millions should be employed to produce food and clothing sufficient for twelve millions? The food and clothing of five millions would be still the net revenue. The employing a greater number of men would enable us neither to add a man to our army and navy, nor to contribute one guinea more in taxes.

It is not on the grounds of any supposed advantage accruing from a large population, or of the happiness that may be enjoyed by a greater number of human beings, that Adam Smith supports the preference of that employment of capital which gives motion to the greatest quantity of industry, but expressly on the ground of its increasing the power of the country[59] for he says that "the riches and, so far as power depends upon riches, the power of every country must always be in proportion to the value of its annual produce, the fund from which all taxes must ultimately be paid." It must, however, be obvious that the power of paying taxes is in proportion to the net, and not in proportion to the gross, revenue.

In the distribution of employments amongst all countries, the capital of poorer nations will be naturally employed in those pursuits wherein a great quantity of labor is supported at home, because in such countries the food and necessaries for an increasing population can be most easily procured. In rich countries, on the contrary, where food is dear, capital will naturally flow, when trade is free, into those occupations wherein the least quantity of labor is required to be maintained at home: such as the carrying trade, the distant foreign trade, and trades where expensive machinery is required; to trades where profits are in proportion to the capital, and not in proportion to the quantity of labor employed.[60]

Although I admit that, from the nature of rent, a given capital employed in agriculture, on any but the land last cultivated, puts in motion a greater quantity of labor than an equal capital employed in manufactures and trade, yet I cannot admit that there is any difference in the quantity of labor employed by a capital engaged in the home trade and an equal capital engaged in the foreign trade.

"The capital which sends Scotch manufactures to London, and brings back English corn and manufactures to Edinburgh," says Adam Smith, "necessarily replaces, by every such operation, two British capitals which had both been employed in the agriculture or manufactures of Great Britain.

"The capital employed in purchasing foreign goods for home consumption, when this purchase is made with the produce of domestic industry, replaces, too, by every such operation, two distinct capitals; but one of them only is employed in supporting domestic industry. The capital which sends British goods to Portugal, and brings back Portuguese goods to Great Britain, replaces, by every such operation, only one British capital, the other is a Portuguese one. Though the returns, therefore, of the foreign trade of consumption should be as quick as the home trade, the capital employed in it will give but one half the encouragement to the industry or productive labor of the country."

This argument appears to me to be fallacious; for though two capitals, one Portuguese and one English, be employed, as Dr. Smith supposes, still a capital will be employed in the foreign trade double of what would be employed in the home trade. Suppose that Scotland employs a capital of a thousand pounds in making linen, which she exchanges for the produce of a similar capital employed in making silks in England, two thousand pounds and a proportional quantity of labor will be employed by the two countries. Suppose now that England discovers that she can import more linen from Germany for the silks which she before exported to Scotland, and that Scotland discovers that she can obtain more silks from France in return for her linen than she before obtained from England, will not England and Scotland immediately cease trading with each other, and will not the home trade of consumption be changed for a foreign trade of consumption? But although two additional capitals will enter into this trade, the capital of Germany and that of France, will not the same amount of Scotch and of English capital continue to be employed, and will it not give motion to the same quantity of industry as when it was engaged in the home trade?

CHAPTER XXVII

On Currency and Banks

So much has already been written on currency that of those who give their attention to such subjects none but the prejudiced are ignorant of its true principles. I shall, therefore, take only a brief survey of some of the general laws which regulate its quantity and value.

Gold and silver, like all other commodities, are valuable only in proportion to the quantity of labor necessary to produce them and bring them to market. Gold is about fifteen times dearer than silver, not because there is a greater demand for it, nor because the supply of silver is fifteen times greater than that of gold, but solely because fifteen times the quantity of labor is necessary to procure a given quantity of it.

The quantity of money that can be employed in a country must depend on its value: if gold alone were employed for the circulation of commodities, a quantity would be required one fifteenth only of what would be necessary if silver were made use of for the same purpose.

A circulation can never be so abundant as to overflow; for by diminishing its value in the same proportion you will increase its quantity, and by increasing its value, diminish its quantity.

While the state coins money, and charges no seignorage, money will be of the same value as any other piece of the same metal of equal weight and fineness; but if the state charges a seignorage for coinage, the coined piece of money will generally exceed the value of the uncoined piece of metal by the whole seignorage charged, because it will require a greater quantity of labor, or, which is the same thing, the value of the produce of a greater quantity of labor, to procure it.

While the state alone coins, there can be no limit to this charge of seignorage; for by limiting the quantity of coin, it can be raised to any conceivable value.

It is on this principle that paper money circulates: the whole charge for paper money may be considered as seignorage. Though it has no intrinsic value, yet, by limiting its quantity, its value in exchange is as great as an equal denomination of coin, or of bullion in that coin. On the same principle, too, namely, by a limitation of its quantity, a debased coin would circulate at the value it should bear if it were of the legal weight and fineness, and not at the value of the quantity of metal which it actually contained. In the history of the British coinage we find, accordingly, that the currency was never depreciated in the same proportion that it was debased; the reason of which was, that it never was increased in quantity in proportion to its diminished intrinsic value.[61]

There is no point more important in issuing paper money than to be fully impressed with the effects which follow from the principle of limitation of quantity. It will scarcely be believed fifty years hence that bank directors and ministers gravely contended in our times, both in Parliament and before committees of Parliament, that the issues of notes by the Bank of England, unchecked by any power in the holders of such notes to demand in exchange either specie or bullion, had not, nor could have, any effect on the prices of commodities, bullion, or foreign exchanges.

After the establishment of banks, the state has not the sole power of coming or issuing money. The currency may as effectually be increased by paper as by coin; so that if a state were to debase its money, and limit its quantity, it could not support its value, because the banks would have an equal power of adding to the whole quantity of circulation.

On these principles, it will be seen that it is not necessary that paper money should be payable in specie to secure its value; it is only necessary that its quantity should be regulated according to the value of the metal which is declared to be the standard. If the standard were gold of a given weight and fineness, paper might be increased with every fall in the value of gold, or, which is the same thing in its effects, with every rise in the price of goods.

"By issuing too great a quantity of paper," says Dr. Smith, "of which the excess was continually returning in order to be exchanged for gold and silver, the Bank of England was, for many years together, obliged to coin gold to the extent of between eight hundred thousand pounds and a million a year, or, at an average, about eight hundred and fifty thousand pounds. For this great coinage, the Bank, in consequence of the worn and degraded state into which the gold coin had fallen a few years ago, was frequently obliged to purchase bullion at the high price of four pounds an ounce, which it soon after issued in coin at £3 17s. 101/2d. an ounce, losing in this manner between two and a half and three percent, upon the coinage of so very large a sum. Though the Bank, therefore, paid no seignorage, though the government was properly at the expense of the coinage, this liberality of government did not prevent altogether the expense of the Bank."

On the principle above stated, it appears to me most clear that by not re-issuing the paper thus brought in, the value of the whole currency, of the degraded as well as the new gold coin, would have been raised, when all demands on the Bank would have ceased.

Mr. Buchanan, however, is not of this opinion, for he says "that the great expense to which the Bank was at this time exposed was occasioned, not as Dr. Smith seems to imagine, by an imprudent issue of paper, but by the debased state of the currency and the consequent high price of bullion. The Bank, it will be observed, having no other way of procuring guineas but by sending bullion to the Mint to be coined, was always forced to issue new coined guineas in exchange for its returned notes; and when the currency was generally deficient in weight, and the price of bullion high in proportion, it became profitable to draw these heavy guineas from the bank in exchange for its paper; to convert them into bullion, and to sell them with a profit for Bank paper, to be again returned to the Bank for a new supply of guineas, which were again melted and sold. To this drain of specie the Bank must always be exposed while the currency is deficient in weight, as both an easy and a certain profit then arises from the constant interchange of paper for specie. It may be remarked, however, that to whatever inconvenience and expense the Bank was then exposed by the drain of its specie, it never was imagined necessary to rescind the obligation to pay money for its notes."

Mr. Buchanan evidently thinks that the whole currency must necessarily be brought down to the level of the value of the debased pieces; but surely, by a diminution of the quantity of the currency, the whole that remains can be elevated to the value of the best pieces.

Dr. Smith appears to have forgotten his own principle in his argument on colony currency. Instead of ascribing the depreciation of that paper to its too great abundance, he asks whether, allowing the colony security to be perfectly good, a hundred pounds, payable fifteen years hence, would be equally valuable with a hundred pounds to be paid immediately? I answer yes, if it be not too abundant.

Experience, however, shows that neither a state nor a bank ever have had the unrestricted power of issuing paper money without abusing that power; in all states, therefore, the issue of paper money ought to be under some check and control; and none seems so proper for that purpose as that of subjecting the issuers of paper money to the obligation of paying their notes either in gold coin or bullion.

["To secure the public[62] against any other variations in the value of currency than those to which the standard itself is subject, and, at the same time, to carry on the circulation with a medium the least expensive, is to attain the most perfect state to which a currency can be brought, and we should possess all these advantages by subjecting the Bank to the delivery of uncoined gold or silver at the Mint standard and price, in exchange for their notes, instead of the delivery of guineas; by which means paper would never fall below the value of bullion without being followed by a reduction of its quantity. To prevent the rise of paper above the value of bullion, the Bank should be also obliged to give their paper in exchange for standard gold at the price of £3 17s. per ounce. Not to give too much trouble to the Bank, the quantity of gold to be demanded in exchange for paper at the Mint price of £3 17s. 101/2d., or the quantity to be sold to the Bank at £3 17s., should never be less than twenty ounces. In other words, the Bank should be obliged to purchase any quantity of gold that was offered them, not less than twenty ounces, at £3 17s.[63] per ounce, and to sell any quantity that might be demanded at £3 17s. 101/2d. While they have the power of regulating the quantity of their paper there is no possible inconvenience that could result to them from such a regulation.

"The most perfect liberty should be given, at the same time, to export or import every description of bullion. These transactions in bullion would be very few in number, if the Bank regulated their loans and issues of paper by the criterion which I have so often mentioned, namely, the price of standard bullion, without attending to the absolute quantity of paper in circulation.

"The object which I have in view would be in a great measure attained if the Bank were obliged to deliver uncoined bullion, in exchange for their notes, at the Mint price and standard, though they were not under the necessity of purchasing any quantity of bullion offered them at the prices to be fixed, particularly if the Mint were to continue open to the public for the coinage of money; for that regulation is merely suggested to prevent the value of money from varying from the value of bullion more than the trifling difference between the prices at which the Bank should buy and sell, and which would be an approximation to that uniformity in its value which is acknowledged to be so desirable.

"If the Bank capriciously limited the quantity of their paper they would raise its value, and gold might appear to fall below the limits at which I propose the Bank should purchase. Gold, in that case, might be carried to the Mint, and the money returned from thence, being added to the circulation, would have the effect of lowering its value, and making it again conform to the standard; but it would neither be done so safely, so economically, nor so expeditiously as by the means which I have proposed, against which the Bank can have no objection to offer, as it is for their interest to furnish the circulation with paper rather than oblige others to furnish it with coin.

"Under such a system, and with a currency so regulated, the bank would never be liable to any embarrassments whatever, excepting on those extraordinary occasions when a general panic seizes the country, and when every one is desirous of possessing the precious metals as the most convenient mode of realizing or concealing his property. Against such panics banks have no security *on any system;* from their very nature they are subject to them, as at no time can there be in a bank, or in a country, so much specie or bullion as the moneyed individuals of such country have a right to demand. Should every man withdraw his balance from his banker on the same day, many times the quantity of bank notes now in circulation would be insufficient to answer such a demand. A panic of this kind was the cause of the crisis in 1797; and not, as has been supposed, the large advances which the Bank had then made to government. Neither the Bank nor government were at that time to blame; it was the contagion of the unfounded fears of the timid part of the community which occasioned the run on the Bank, and it would equally have taken place if they had not made any advances to government and had possessed twice their present capital. If the Bank had continued paying in cash, probably the panic would have subsided before their coin had been exhausted.

"With the known opinion of the Bank directors as to the rule for issuing paper money, they may be said to have exercised their powers without any great indiscretion. It is evident that they have followed their own principle with extreme caution. In the present state of the law, they have the power, without any control whatever, of increasing or reducing the circulation in any degree they may think proper; a power which should neither be entrusted to the state itself, nor to anybody in it, as there can be no security for the uniformity in the value of the currency when its augmentation or diminution depends solely on the will of the issuers. That the Bank have the power of reducing the circulation to the very narrowest limits will not be denied, even by those who agree in opinion with the directors that they have not the power of adding indefinitely to its quantity. Though I am fully assured that it is both against the interest and the wish of the Bank to exercise this power to the detriment of the public, yet, when I contemplate the evil consequences which might ensue from a sudden and great reduction of the circulation, as well as from a great addition to it, I cannot but deprecate the facility with which the state has armed the Bank with so formidable a prerogative.

"The inconvenience to which country banks were subjected before the restriction on cash payments must at times have been very great. At all periods of alarm, or of expected alarm, they must have been under the necessity of providing themselves with guineas, that they might be prepared for every exigency which might occur. Guineas, on these occasions, were obtained at the Bank in exchange for the larger notes, and were conveyed by some confidential agent, at expense and risk, to the country bank. After performing the offices to which they were destined, they found their way again to London, and in all probability were again lodged in the Bank, provided they had not suffered such a loss of weight as to reduce them below the legal standard.

"If the plan now proposed of paying bank notes in bullion be adopted, it would be necessary either to extend the same privilege to country banks, or to make bank notes a legal tender, in which latter case there would be no alteration in the law respecting country banks, as they would be required, precisely as they now are, to pay their notes when demanded in Bank of England notes.

"The saving which would take place from not submitting the guineas to the loss of weight from the friction which they must undergo in their repeated journeys, as well as of the expenses of conveyance, would be considerable; but by far the greatest advantage would result from the permanent supply of the country as well as of the London circulation, as far as the smaller payments are concerned, being provided in the very cheap medium paper, instead of the very valuable medium, gold; thereby enabling the country to derive all the profit which may be obtained by the productive employment of a capital to that amount. We should surely not be justified in rejecting so decided a benefit unless some specific inconvenience could be pointed out as likely to follow from adopting the cheaper medium."]

A currency is in its most perfect state when it consists wholly of paper money, but of paper money of an equal value with the gold which it professes to represent. The use of paper instead of gold substitutes the cheapest in place of the most expensive medium, and enables the country, without loss to any individual, to exchange all the gold which it before used for this purpose for raw materials, utensils, and food; by the use of which both its wealth and its enjoyments are increased.

In a national point of view, it is of no importance whether the issuers of this well regulated paper money be the government or a bank, it will, on the whole, be equally productive of riches whether it be issued by one or by the other; but it is not so with respect to the interest of individuals. In a country where the market rate of interest is 7 percent, and where the state requires for a particular expense £70,000 per annum, it is a question of importance to the individuals of that country whether they must be taxed to pay this £70,000 per annum, or whether they could raise it without taxes. Suppose that a million of money should be required to fit out an expedition. If the state issued a million of paper and displaced a million of coin, the expedition would be fitted out without any charge to the people; but if a bank issued a million of paper, and lent it to government at 7 percent, thereby displacing a million of coin, the country would be charged with a continual tax of £70,000 per annum: the people would pay the tax, the bank would receive it, and the society would in either case be as wealthy as before; the expedition would have been really fitted out by the improvement of our system, by rendering capital of the value of a million productive in the form of commodities instead of letting it remain unproductive in the form of coin; but the advantage would always be in favor of the issuers of paper; and as the state represents the people, the people would have saved the tax if they, and not the bank, had issued this million.

I have already observed that if there were perfect security that the power of issuing paper money would not be abused, it would be of no importance with respect to the riches of the country collectively by whom it was issued; and I have now shown that the public would have a direct interest that the issuers should be the state, and not a company of merchants or bankers. The danger, however, is that this power would be more likely to be abused if in the hands of government than if in the hands of a banking company. A company would, it is said, be more under the control of law, and although it might be their interest to extend their issues beyond the bounds of discretion, they would be limited and checked by the power which individuals would have of calling for bullion or specie. It is argued that the same check would not be long respected if government had the privilege of issuing money; that they would be too apt to consider present convenience rather than future security, and might, therefore, on the alleged grounds of expediency, be too much inclined to remove the checks by which the amount of their issues was controlled.

Under an arbitrary government this objection would have great force; but in a free country, with an enlightened legislature, the power of issuing paper money, under the requisite checks of convertibility at the will of the holder, might be safely lodged in the hands of commissioners appointed for that special purpose, and they might be made totally independent of the control of ministers.

The sinking fund is managed by commissioners responsible only to Parliament, and the investment of the money entrusted to their charge proceeds with the utmost regularity; what reason can there be to doubt that the issues of paper money might be regulated with equal fidelity, if placed under similar management?

It may be said that although the advantage accruing to the State, and, therefore, to the public, from issuing paper money is sufficiently manifest, as it would exchange a portion of the national debt, on which interest is paid by the public, into a debt bearing no interest: yet it would be disadvantageous to commerce, as it would preclude the merchants from borrowing money and getting their bills discounted, the method in which bank paper is partly issued.

This, however, is to suppose that money could not be borrowed if the Bank did not lend it, and that the market rate of interest and profit depends on the amount of the issues of money and on the channel through which it is issued. But as a country would have no deficiency of cloth, of wine, or any other commodity, if they had the means of paying for it, in the same manner neither would there be any deficiency of money to be lent if the borrowers offered good security and were willing to pay the market rate of interest for it.

In another part of this work I have endeavored to show that the real value of a commodity is regulated, not by the accidental advantages which may be enjoyed by some of its producers, but by the real difficulties encountered by that producer who is least favored. It is so with respect to the interest for money; it is not regulated by the rate at which the bank will lend, whether it be 5, 4, or 3 percent, but by the rate of profits which can be made by the employment of capital, and which is totally independent of the quantity or of the value of money. Whether a bank lent one million, ten million, or a hundred millions, they would not permanently alter the market rate of interest; they would alter only the value of the money which they thus issued. In one case, ten or twenty times more money might be required to carry on the same business than what might be required in the other. The applications to the bank for money, then, depend on the comparison between the rate of profits that may be made by the employment of it and, the rate at which they are willing to lend it. If they charge less than the market rate of interest, there is no amount of money which they might not lend; if they charge more than that rate none but spendthrifts and prodigals would be found to borrow of them. We accordingly find that when the market rate of interest exceeds the rate of 5 percent, at which the Bank uniformly lend, the discount office is besieged with applicants for money; and, on the contrary, when the market rate is even temporarily under 5 percent, the clerks of that office have no employment.

The reason, then, why for the last twenty years the Bank is said to have given so much aid to commerce, by assisting the merchants with money, is because they have, during that whole period, lent money below the market rate of interest; below that rate at which the merchants could have borrowed elsewhere; but I confess that to me this seems rather an objection to their establishment than an argument in favor of it.

What should we say of an establishment which should regularly supply half the clothiers with wool under the market price? Of what benefit would it be to the community? It would not extend our trade, because the wool would equally have been bought if they had charged the market price for it. It would not lower the price of cloth to the consumer, because the price, as I have said before, would be regulated by the cost of its production to those who were the least favored. Its sole effect, then, would be to swell the profits of a part of the clothiers beyond the general and common rate of profits. The establishment would be deprived of its fair profits, and another part of the community would be in the same degree benefited. Now, this is precisely the effect of our banking establishments; a rate of interest is fixed by the law below that at which it can be borrowed in the market, and at this rate the Bank are required to lend or not to lend at all. From the nature of their establishment, they have large funds which they can only dispose of in this way; and a part of the traders of the country are unfairly, and, for the country, unprofitably benefited, by being enabled to supply themselves with an instrument of trade at a less charge than those who must be influenced only by a market price.

The whole business which the whole community can carry on depends on the quantity of its capital, that is, of its raw material, machinery, food, vessels, etc., employed in production. After a well-regulated paper money is established, these can neither be increased nor diminished by the operations of banking. If, then, the state were to issue the paper money of the country, although it should never discount a bill, or lend one shilling to the public, there would be no alteration in the amount of trade; for we should have the same quantity of raw materials, of machinery, food, and ships; and it is probable, too, that the same amount of money might be lent, not always at 5 percent, indeed, a rate fixed by law, when that might be under the market rate, but at 6, 7, or 8 percent, the result of the fair competition in the market between the lenders and the borrowers.

Adam Smith speaks of the advantages derived by merchants from the superiority of the Scotch mode of affording accommodation to trade over the English mode, by means of cash accounts. These cash accounts are credits given by the Scotch banker to his customers, in addition to the bills which he discounts for them; but as the banker, in proportion as he advances money and sends it into circulation in one way, is debarred from issuing so much in the other, it is difficult to perceive in what the advantage consists. If the whole circulation will bear only one million of paper, one million only will be circulated; and it can be of no real importance either to the banker or merchant whether the whole be issued in discounting bills, or a part be so issued, and the remainder be issued by means of these cash accounts.

It may perhaps be necessary to say a few words on the subject of the two metals, gold and silver, which are employed in currency, particularly as this question appears to perplex, in many people's minds, the plain and simple principles of currency. "In England," says Dr. Smith, "gold was not considered as a legal tender for a long time after it was coined into money. The proportion between the values of gold and silver money was not fixed by any public law or proclamation, but was left to be settled by the market. If a debtor offered payment in gold, the creditor might either reject such payment altogether, or accept of it at such a valuation of the gold as he and his debtor could agree upon."

In this state of things it is evident that a guinea might sometimes pass for 22s. or more, and sometimes for 18s. or less, depending entirely on the alteration in the relative market value of gold and silver. All the variations, too, in the value of gold, as well as in the value of silver, would be rated in the gold coin—it would appear as if silver was invariable, and as if gold only was subject to rise and fall. Thus, although a guinea passed for 22s instead of 18s, gold might not have varied in value; the variation might have been wholly confined to the silver, and therefore 22s. might have been of no more value than 18s. were before. And, on the contrary, the whole variation might have been in the gold; a guinea which was worth 18s. might have risen to the value of 22s.

If, now, we suppose this silver currency to be debased by clipping, and also increased in quantity, a guinea might pass for 30s.; for the silver in 30s. of such debased money might be of no more value than the gold in one guinea. By restoring the silver currency to its Mint value, silver money would rise; but it would appear as if gold fell, for a guinea would probably be of no more value than 21 of such good shillings.

If now gold be also made a legal tender, and every debtor be at liberty to discharge a debt by the payment of 420 shillings, or twenty guineas for every £21 that he owes, he will pay in one or the other according as he can most cheaply discharge his debt. If with five quarters of wheat he can procure as much gold bullion as the Mint will coin into twenty guineas, and for the same wheat as much silver bullion as the Mint will coin for him into 430 shillings, he will prefer paying in silver, because he would be a gainer of ten shillings by so paying his debt. But if, on the contrary, he could obtain with this wheat as much gold as would be coined into twenty guineas and a half, and as much silver only as would coin into 420 shillings, he would naturally prefer paying his debt in gold. If the quantity of gold which he could procure could be coined only into twenty guineas, and the quantity of silver into 420 shillings, it would be a matter of perfect indifference to him in which money, silver or gold, it was that he paid his debt. It is not, then, a matter of chance; it is not because gold is better fitted for carrying on the circulation of a rich country that gold is ever preferred for the purpose of paying debts, but simply because it is the interest of the debtor so to pay them.

During a long period previous to 1797, the year of the restriction on the Bank payments in coin, gold was so cheap, compared with silver, that it suited the Bank of England, and all other debtors, to purchase gold in the market, and not silver, for the purpose of carrying it to the Mint to be coined, as they could in that coined metal more cheaply discharge their debts. The silver currency was, during a great part of this period, very much debased; but it existed in a degree of scarcity, and therefore, on the principle which I have before explained, it never sunk in its current value. Though so debased, it was still the interest of debtors to pay in the gold coin. If, indeed, the quantity of this debased silver coin had been enormously great, or if the Mint had issued such debased pieces, it might have been the interest of debtors to pay in this debased money; but its quantity was limited, and it sustained its value, and, therefore, gold was in practice the real standard of currency.

That it was so is nowhere denied; but it has been contended that it was made so by the law, which declared that silver should not be a legal tender for any debt exceeding £25, unless by weight, according to the Mint standard.

But this law did not prevent any debtor from paying his debt, however large its amount, in silver currency fresh from the Mint; that the debtor did not pay in this metal was not a matter of chance nor a matter of compulsion, but wholly the effect of choice; it did not suit him to take silver to the Mint, it did suit him to take gold thither. It is probable that if the quantity of this debased silver in circulation had been enormously great, and also a legal tender, that a guinea would have been again worth thirty shillings; but it would have been the debased shilling that would have fallen in value, and not the guinea that had risen.

It appears, then, that whilst each of the two metals was equally a legal tender for debts of any amount, we were subject to a constant change in the principal standard measure of value. It would sometimes be gold, sometimes silver, depending entirely on the variations in the relative value of the two metals; and at such times the metal which was not the standard would be melted and withdrawn from circulation, as its value would be greater in bullion than in coin. This was an inconvenience which it was highly desirable should be remedied; but so slow is the progress of improvement that, although it had been unanswerably demonstrated by Mr. Locke, and had been noticed by all writers on the subject of money since his day, a better system was never adopted till the session of Parliament 1816, when it was enacted that gold only should be a legal tender for any sum exceeding forty shillings.

Dr. Smith does not appear to have been quite aware of the effect of employing two metals as currency, and both a legal tender for debts of any amount; for he says that "in reality, during the continuance of any one regulated proportion between the respective values of the different metals in coin, the value of the most precious metal regulates the value of the whole coin." Because gold was in his day the medium in which it suited debtors to pay their debts, he thought that it had some inherent quality by which it did then, and always would, regulate the value of silver coin.

On the reformation of the gold coin in 1774, a new guinea fresh from the Mint would exchange for only twenty-one debased shillings; but in the reign of King William, when the silver coin was in precisely the same condition, a guinea also new and fresh from the Mint would exchange for thirty shillings. On this Mr. Buchanan observes, "here, then, is a most singular fact, of which the common theories of currency offer no account; the guinea exchanging at one time for thirty shillings, its intrinsic worth in a debased silver currency, and afterwards the same guinea exchanged for only twenty-one of those debased shillings. It is clear that some great change must have intervened in the state of the currency between these two different periods, of which Dr. Smith's hypothesis offers no explanation."

It appears to me that the difficulty may be very simply solved by referring this different state of the value of the guinea at the two periods mentioned to the different quantities of debased silver currency in circulation. In King William's reign gold was not a legal
tender; it passed only at a conventional value. All the large payments were probably made
in silver, particularly as paper currency and the operations of banking were then little understood. The quantity of this debased silver money exceeded the quantity of silver
money which would have been maintained in circulation if nothing but undebased
money had been in use; and, consequently, it was depreciated as well as debased. But in
the succeeding period, when gold was a legal tender, when bank notes also were used in
effecting payments, the quantity of debased silver money did not exceed the quantity of
silver coin fresh from the Mint which would have circulated if there had been no debased
silver money; hence, though the money was debased it was not depreciated. Mr.
Buchanan's explanation is somewhat different; he thinks that a subsidiary currency is
not liable to depreciation, but that the main currency is. In King William's reign silver
was the main currency, and hence was liable to depreciation. In 1774 it was a subsidiary
currency, and, therefore, maintained its value. Depreciation, however, does not depend
on a currency being the subsidiary or the main currency, it depends wholly on its being
in excess of quantity.[64]

To a moderate seignorage on the coinage of money there cannot be much objection,
particularly on that currency which is to effect the smaller payments. Money is generally
enhanced in value to the full amount of the seignorage, and, therefore, it is a tax which
in no way affects those who pay it, while the quantity of money is not in excess. It must,
however, be remarked that in a country where a paper currency is established, although
the issuers of such paper should be liable to pay it in specie on the demand of the holder,
still, both their notes and the coin might be depreciated to the full amount of the seignorage on that coin, which is alone the legal tender, before the check, which limits the circulation of paper, would operate. If the seignorage of gold coin were 5 percent for
instance, the currency, by an abundant issue of bank notes, might be really depreciated
5 percent before it would be the interest of the holders to demand coin for the purpose
of melting it into bullion; a depreciation to which we should never be exposed if either
there was no seignorage on the gold coin or, if a seignorage were allowed, the holders of
bank notes might demand bullion, and not coin, in exchange for them, at the Mint price
of £3 17s. 10d. Unless, then, the Bank should be obliged to pay their notes in bullion
or coin, at the will of the holder, the late law which allows a seignorage of 6 percent, or
four pence per oz., on the silver coin, but which directs that gold shall be coined by the
Mint without any charge whatever, is perhaps the most proper, as it will most effectually prevent any unnecessary variation of the currency.

CHAPTER XXVIII

On the Comparative Value of Gold, Corn, and Labor in Rich and Poor Countries

"Gold and silver, like all other commodities," says Adam Smith, "naturally seek the market where the best price is given for them; and the best price is commonly given for everything in the country which can best afford it. Labor, it must be remembered, is the ultimate price which is paid for everything; and in countries where labor is equally well rewarded, the money price of labor will be in proportion to that of the subsistence of the laborer. But gold and silver will naturally exchange for a greater quantity of subsistence in a rich than in a poor country; in a country which abounds with subsistence, than in one which is but indifferently supplied with it."

But corn is a commodity, as well as gold, silver, and other things; if all commodities, therefore, have a high exchangeable value in a rich country, corn must not be excepted; and hence we might correctly say that corn exchanged for a great deal of money because it was dear, and that money, too, exchanged for a great deal of corn because that also was dear; which is to assert that corn is dear and cheap at the same time. No point in political economy can be better established than that a rich country is prevented from increasing in population, in the same ratio as a poor country, by the progressive difficulty of providing food. That difficulty must necessarily raise the relative price of food and give encouragement to its importation. How then can money, or gold and silver, exchange for more corn in rich, than in poor, countries? It is only in rich countries, where corn is dear, that landholders induce the legislature to prohibit the importation of corn. Who ever heard of a law to prevent the importation of raw produce in America or Poland?— Nature has effectually precluded its importation by the comparative facility of its production in those countries.

How, then, can it be true that, "if you except corn, and such other vegetables as are raised altogether by human industry, all other sorts of rude produce—cattle, poultry, game of all kinds, the useful fossils and minerals of the earth, etc., naturally grow dearer as the society advances." Why should corn and vegetables alone be excepted? Dr. Smith's error, throughout his whole work, lies in supposing that the value of corn is constant; that though the value of all other things may, the value of corn never can, be raised. Corn, according to him, is always of the same value, because it will always feed the same number of people. In the same manner, it might be said that cloth is always of the same value, because it will always make the same number of coats. What can value have to do with the power of feeding and clothing?

Corn, like every other commodity, has in every country its natural price, viz. that price which is necessary to its production, and without which it could not be cultivated: it is this price which governs its market price, and which determines the expediency of exporting it to foreign countries. If the importation of corn were prohibited in England, its natural price might rise to £6 per quarter in England, whilst it was only at half that price in France. If at this time the prohibition of importation were removed, corn would fall in the English market, not to a price between £6 and £3, but ultimately and permanently to the natural price of France, the price at which it could be furnished to the English market and afford the usual and ordinary profits of stock in France; and it would remain at this price whether England consumed a hundred thousand or a million of quarters. If the demand of England were for the latter quantity, it is probable that, owing to the necessity under which France would be of having recourse to land of a worse quality, to furnish this large supply, the natural price would rise in France; and this would of course affect also the price of corn in England. All that I contend for is, that it is the natural price of commodities in the exporting country which ultimately regulates the prices at which they shall be sold, if they are not the objects of monopoly in the importing country.

But Dr. Smith, who has so ably supported the doctrine of the natural price of commodities ultimately regulating their market price, has supposed a case in which he thinks that the market price would not be regulated either by the natural price of the exporting or of the importing country. "Diminish the real opulence either of Holland or the territory of Genoa," he says, "while the number of their inhabitants remains the same; diminish their power of supplying themselves from distant countries, and the price of corn, instead of sinking with that diminution in the quantity of their silver which must necessarily accompany this declension, either as its cause or as its effect, will rise to the price of a famine."

To me it appears that the very reverse would take place: the diminished power of the Dutch or Genoese to purchase generally might depress the price of corn for a time below its natural price in the country from which it was exported, as well as in the countries in which it was imported; but it is quite impossible that it could ever raise it above that price. It is only by increasing the opulence of the Dutch and Genoese that you could increase the demand, and raise the price of corn above its former price; and that would take place only for a very limited time, unless new difficulties should arise in obtaining the supply.

Dr. Smith further observes on this subject: "When we are in want of necessaries we must part with all superfluities, of which the value, as it rises in times of opulence and prosperity, so it sinks in times of poverty and distress." This is undoubtedly true; but he continues, "it is otherwise with necessaries. Their real price, the quantity of labor which they can purchase or command, rises in times of poverty and distress, and sinks in times of opulence and prosperity, which are always times of great abundance, for they could not otherwise be times of opulence and prosperity. Corn is a necessary, silver is only a superfluity."

Two propositions are here advanced which have no connection with each other; one, that under the circumstances supposed, corn would command more labor, which is not disputed; the other, that corn would sell at a higher money price, that it would exchange for more silver; this I contend to be erroneous. It might be true if corn were at the same time scarce—if the usual supply had not been furnished. But in this case it is abundant; it is not pretended that a less quantity than usual is imported, or that more is required. To purchase corn, the Dutch or Genoese want money, and to obtain this money they are obliged to sell their superfluities. It is the market value and price of these superfluities which falls, and money appears to rise as compared with them. But this will not tend to increase the demand for corn, nor to lower the value of money, the only two causes which can raise the price of corn. Money, from a want of credit, and from other causes, may be in great demand, and consequently dear, comparatively with corn; but on no just principle can it be maintained that under such circumstances money would be cheap and, therefore, that the price of corn would rise.

When we speak of the high or low value of gold, silver, or any other commodity in different countries, we should always mention some medium in which we are estimating them, or no idea can be attached to the proposition. Thus, when gold is said to be dearer in England than in Spain, if no commodity is mentioned, what notion does the assertion convey? If corn, olives, oil, wine, and wool be at a cheaper price in Spain than in England, estimated in those commodities gold is dearer in Spain. If, again, hardware, sugar, cloth, etc., be at a lower price in England than in Spain, then, estimated in those commodities, gold is dearer in England. Thus gold appears dearer or cheaper in Spain as the fancy of the observer may fix on the medium by which he estimates its value. Adam Smith, having stamped corn and labor as a universal measure of value, would naturally estimate the comparative value of gold by the quantity of those two objects for which it would exchange: and, accordingly, when he speaks of the comparative value of gold in two countries, I understand him to mean its value estimated in corn and labor.

But we have seen that, estimated in corn, gold may be of very different value in two countries. I have endeavored to show that it will be low in rich countries and high in poor countries; Adam Smith is of a different opinion: he thinks that the value of gold, estimated in corn, is highest in rich countries. But without further examining which of these opinions is correct, either of them is sufficient to show that gold will not necessarily be lower in those countries which are in possession of the mines, though this is a proposition maintained by Adam Smith. Suppose England to be possessed of the mines, and Adam Smith's opinion, that gold is of the greatest value in rich countries, to be correct: although gold would naturally flow from England to all other countries in exchange for their goods it would not follow that gold was necessarily lower in England, as compared with corn and labor, than in those countries. In another place, however, Adam Smith speaks of the precious metals being necessarily lower in Spain and Portugal than in other parts of Europe, because those countries happen to be almost the exclusive possessors of the mines which produce them. "Poland, where the feudal system still continues to take place, is at this day as beggarly a country as it was before the discovery of America. *The money price of corn, however, has risen;* the real value of the precious metals has fallen in Poland in the same manner as in other parts of Europe. Their quantity, therefore, must have increased there as in other places, *and nearly in the same proportion to the annual produce of the land and labor.* This increase of the quantity of those metals, however, has not, it seems, increased that annual produce; has neither improved the manufactures and agriculture of the country, nor mended the circumstances of its inhabitants. Spain and Portugal, the countries which possess the mines, are, after Poland, perhaps the two most beggarly countries in Europe. The value of the precious metals, however, *must be lower in Spain and Portugal* than in any other parts of Europe, loaded not only with a freight and insurance, but with the expense of smuggling, their exportation being either prohibited or subjected to a duty. *In proportion to the annual produce of the land and labor, therefore, their quantity must be greater in* those countries than in any other part of Europe: those countries, however, are poorer than the greater part of Europe. Though the feudal system has been abolished in Spain and Portugal, it has not been succeeded by a much better."

Dr. Smith's argument appears to me to be this: Gold, when estimated in corn, is cheaper in Spain than in other countries, and the proof of this is not that corn is given by other countries to Spain for gold, but that cloth, sugar, hardware, are by those countries given in exchange for that metal.

CHAPTER XXIX

Taxes Paid by the Producer

M. Say greatly magnifies the inconveniences which result if a tax on a manufactured commodity is levied at an early, rather than at a late, period of its manufacture. The manufacturers, he observes, through whose hands the commodity may successively pass, must employ greater funds in consequence of having to advance the tax, which is often attended with considerable difficulty to a manufacturer of very limited capital and credit. To this observation no objection can be made.

Another inconvenience on which he dwells is that, in consequence of the advance of the tax, the profits on the advance also must be charged to the consumer, and that this additional tax is one from which the treasury derives no advantage.

In this latter objection I cannot agree with M. Say. The state, we will suppose, wants to raise *immediately* £1000, and levies it on a manufacturer, who will not for a twelvemonth be able to charge it to the consumer on his finished commodity. In consequence of such delay, he is obliged to charge for his commodity an additional price, not only of £1000, the amount of the tax, but probably of £1100, £100 being for interest on the £1000 advanced. But in return for this additional £100 paid by the consumer, he has a real benefit, inasmuch as his payment of the tax which government required immediately, and which he must finally pay, has been postponed for a year; an opportunity, therefore, has been afforded to him of lending to the manufacturer who had occasion for it the £1000, at 10 percent, or at any other rate of interest which might be agreed upon. Eleven hundred pounds, payable at the end of one year, when money is at 10 percent interest, is of no more value than £1000 to be paid immediately. If government delayed receiving the tax for one year till the manufacture of the commodity was completed, it would perhaps be obliged to issue an exchequer bill bearing interest, and it would pay as much for interest as the consumer would save in price, excepting, indeed, that portion of the price which the manufacturer might be enabled, in consequence of the tax, to add to his own real gains.   If for the interest of the exchequer bill government would pay 5 percent, a tax of £50 is saved by not issuing it. If the manufacturer borrowed the additional capital at 5 percent, and charged the consumer 10 percent, he also will have gained 5 percent, on his advance, over and above his usual profits, so that the manufacturer and government together gain or save precisely the sum which the consumer pays.

M. Simonde, in his excellent work, *De la Richesse Commerciale,* following the same line of argument as M. Say, has calculated that a tax of 4000 francs, paid originally by a manufacturer, whose profits were at the moderate rate of 10 percent, would, if the commodity manufactured only passed through the hands of five different persons, be raised to the consumer to the sum of 6734 francs. This calculation proceeds on the supposition that he who first advanced the tax would receive from the next manufacturer 4400 francs, and he again from the next, 4840 francs; so that at each step 10 percent, on its value would be added to it. This is to suppose that the value of the tax would be accumulating at compound interest; not at the rate of 10 percent, per annum, but at an absolute rate of 10 percent at every step of its progress. This opinion of M. de Simonde would be correct if five years elapsed between the first advance of the tax and the sale of the taxed commodity to the consumer; but if one year only elapsed, a remuneration of 400 francs, instead of 2734, would give a profit at the rate of 10 percent per annum to all who had contributed to the advance of the tax, whether the commodity had passed through the hands of five manufacturers or fifty.

CHAPTER XXX

On the Influence of Demand and Supply on Prices

It is the cost of production which must ultimately regulate the price of commodities, and not, as has been often said, the proportion between the supply and demand: the proportion between supply and demand may, indeed, for a time, affect the market value of a commodity, until it is supplied in greater or less abundance, according as the demand may have increased or diminished; but this effect will be only of temporary duration.

Diminish the cost of production of hats, and their price will ultimately fall to their new natural price, although the demand should be doubled, trebled, or quadrupled. Diminish the cost of subsistence of men, by diminishing the natural price of the food and clothing by which life is sustained, and wages will ultimately fall, notwithstanding that the demand for laborers may very greatly increase.

The opinion that the price of commodities depends solely on the proportion of supply to demand, or demand to supply, has become almost an axiom in political economy, and has been the source of much error in that science. It is this opinion which has made Mr. Buchanan maintain that wages are not influenced by a rise or fall in the price of provisions, but solely by the demand and supply of labor; and that a tax on the wages of labor would not raise wages, because it would not alter the proportion of the demand of laborers to the supply.

The demand for a commodity cannot be said to increase if no additional quantity of it be purchased or consumed; and yet under such circumstances its money value may rise. Thus, if the value of money were to fall, the price of every commodity would rise, for each of the competitors would be willing to spend more money than before on its purchase; but though its price rose 10 or 20 percent, if no more were bought than before, it would not, I apprehend, be admissible to say that the variation in the price of the commodity was caused by the increased demand for it. Its natural price, its money cost of production, would be really altered by the altered value of money; and without any increase of demand, the price of the commodity would be naturally adjusted to that new value.

"We have seen," says M. Say, "that the cost of production determines the lowest price to which things can fall: the price below which they cannot remain for any length of time, because production would then be either entirely stopped or diminished." Vol. ii, p. 26.

He afterwards says that the demand for gold having increased in a still greater proportion than the supply, since the discovery of the mines, "its price in goods, instead of falling in the proportion of ten to one, fell only in the proportion of four to one; " that is to say, instead of falling in proportion as its natural price had fallen, fell in proportion as the supply exceeded the demand.[65]— *"The value of every commodity rises always in a direct ratio to the demand, and in an inverse ratio to the supply."*

The same opinion is expressed by the Earl of Lauderdale.

"With respect to the variations in value, of which everything valuable is susceptible, if we could for a moment suppose that any substance possessed intrinsic and fixed value, so as to render an assumed quantity of it constantly, under all circumstances, of an equal value, then the degree of value of all things, ascertained by such a fixed standard, would vary according to the proportion *betwixt the quantity of them* and the demand for them, and every commodity would, of course, be subject to a variation in its value, from four different circumstances:

1. "It would be subject to an increase of its value, from a diminution of its quantity.

2. "To a diminution of its value, from an augmentation of its quantity.

3. "It might suffer an augmentation in its value, from the circumstance of an increased demand.

4. "Its value might be diminished by a failure of demand.

"As it will, however, clearly appear that no commodity can possess fixed and intrinsic value, so as to qualify it for a measure of the value of other commodities, mankind are induced to select, as a practical measure of value, that which appears the least liable to any of these four sources of variations, *which are the sole causes of alteration of value.*

"When, in common language, therefore, we express the value of any commodity, it may vary at one period from what it is at another, in consequence of eight different contingencies:

1. "From the four circumstances above stated, in relation to the commodity of which we mean to express the value.

2. "From the same four circumstances, in relation to the commodity we have adopted as a measure of value."[66]

This is true of monopolized commodities, and, indeed, of the market price of all other commodities for a limited period. If the demand for hats should be doubled, the price would immediately rise, but that rise would be only temporary, unless the cost of production of hats or their natural price were raised. If the natural price of bread should fall 50 percent, from some great discovery in the science of agriculture, the demand would not greatly increase, for no man would desire more than would satisfy his wants, and as the demand would not increase, neither would the supply; for a commodity is not supplied merely because it can be produced, but because there is a demand for it. Here, then, we have a case where the supply and demand have scarcely varied, or, if they have increased, they have increased in the same proportion; and yet the price of bread will have fallen 50 percent, at a time, too, when the value of money had continued invariable.

Commodities which are monopolized, either by an individual or by a company, vary according to the law which Lord Lauderdale has laid down: they fall in proportion as the sellers augment their quantity, and rise in proportion to the eagerness of the buyers to purchase them; their price has no necessary connection with their natural value: but the prices of commodities which are subject to competition, and whose quantity may be increased in any moderate degree, will ultimately depend, not on the state of demand and supply, but on the increased or diminished cost of their production.

CHAPTER XXXI

On Machinery

In the present chapter I shall enter into some inquiry respecting the influence of machinery on the interests of the different classes of society, a subject of great importance, and one which appears never to have been investigated in a manner to lead to any certain or satisfactory results. It is more incumbent on me to declare my opinion on this question, because they have, on further reflection, undergone a considerable change; and although I am not aware that I have ever published anything respecting machinery which it is necessary for me to retract, yet I have in other ways given my support to doctrines which I now think erroneous; it therefore becomes a duty in me to submit my present views to examination, with my reasons for entertaining them.

Ever since I first turned my attention to questions of political economy, I have been of opinion that such an application of machinery to any branch of production as should have the effect of saving labor was a general good, accompanied only with that portion of inconvenience which in most cases attends the removal of capital and labor from one employment to another. It appeared to me that, provided the landlords had the same money rents, they would be benefited by the reduction in the prices of some of the commodities on which those rents were expended, and which reduction of price could not fail to be the consequence of the employment of machinery. The capitalist, I thought, was eventually benefited precisely in the same manner. He, indeed, who made the discovery of the machine, or who first usefully applied it, would enjoy an additional advantage by making great profits for a time; but, in proportion as the machine came into general use, the price of the commodity produced would, from the effects of competition, sink to its cost of production, when the capitalist would get the same money profits as before, and he would only participate in the general advantage as a consumer, by being enabled, with the same money revenue, to command an additional quantity of comforts and enjoyments. The class of laborers also, I thought, was equally benefited by the use of machinery, as they would have the means of buying more commodities with the same money wages, and I thought that no reduction of wages would take place because the capitalist would have the power of demanding and employing the same quantity of labor as before, although he might be under the necessity of employing it in the production of a new or, at any rate, of a different commodity. If, by improved machinery, with the employment of the same quantity of labor, the quantity of stockings could be quadrupled, and the demand for stockings were only doubled, some laborers would necessarily be discharged from the stocking trade; but as the capital which employed them was still in being, and as it was the interest of those who had it to employ it productively, it appeared to me that it would be employed on the production of some other commodity useful to the society, for which there could not fail to be a demand; for I was, and am, deeply impressed with the truth of the observation of Adam Smith, that "the desire for food is limited in every man by the narrow capacity of the human stomach, but the desire of the conveniences and ornaments of building, dress, equipage, and household furniture, seems to have no limit or certain boundary." As, then, it appeared to me that there would be the same demand for labor as before, and that wages would be no lower, I thought that the laboring class would, equally with the other classes, participate in the advantage, from the general cheapness of commodities arising from the use of machinery.

These were my opinions, and they continue unaltered, as far as regards the landlord and the capitalist; but I am convinced that the substitution of machinery for human labor is often very injurious to the interests of the class of laborers.

My mistake arose from the supposition that whenever the net income of a society increased, its gross income would also increase; I now, however, see reason to be satisfied that the one fund, from which landlords and capitalists derive their revenue, may increase, while the other, that upon which the laboring class mainly depend, may diminish, and therefore it follows, if I am right, that the same cause which may increase the net revenue of the country may at the same time render the population redundant, and deteriorate the condition of the laborer.

A capitalist, we will suppose, employs a capital of the value of £20,000, and that he carries on the joint business of a farmer and a manufacturer of necessaries. We will further suppose that £7000 of this capital is invested in fixed capital, viz. in buildings, implements, etc., etc., and that the remaining £13,000 is employed as circulating capital in the support of labor. Let us suppose, too, that profits are 10 percent, and consequently that the capitalist's capital is every year put into its original state of efficiency and yields a profit of £2000.

Each year the capitalist begins his operations by having food and necessaries in his possession of the value of £13,000, all of which he sells in the course of the year to his own workmen for that sum of money, and, during the same period, he pays them the like amount of money for wages: at the end of the year they replace in his possession food and necessaries of the value of £15,000, £2000 of which he consumes himself, or disposes of as may best suit his pleasure and gratification. As far as these products are concerned, the gross produce for that year is £15,000, and the net produce £2000.

Suppose, now, that the following year the capitalist employs half his men in constructing a machine, and the other half in producing food and necessaries as usual. During that year he would pay the sum of £13,000 in wages as usual, and would sell food and necessaries to the same amount to his workmen; but what would be the case the following year?

While the machine was being made, only one-half of the usual quantity of food and necessaries would be obtained, and they would be only one-half the value of the quantity which was produced before. The machine would be worth £7500, and the food and necessaries £7500, and, therefore, the capital of the capitalist would be as great as before; for he would have, besides these two values, his fixed capital worth £7000, making in the whole £20,000 capital, and £2000 profit. After deducting this latter sum for his own expenses, he would have a no greater circulating capital than £5500 with which to carry on his subsequent operations; and, therefore, his means of employing labor would be reduced in the proportion of £13,000 to £5500, and, consequently, all the labor which was before employed by £7500 would become redundant.

The reduced quantity of labor which the capitalist can employ, must, indeed, with the assistance of the machine, and after deductions for its repairs, produce a value equal to £7500, it must replace the circulating capital with a profit of £2000 on the whole capital; but if this be done, if the net income be not diminished, of what importance is it to the capitalist whether the gross income be of the value of £3000, of £10,000, or of £15,000?

In this case, then, although the net produce will not be diminished in value, although its power of purchasing commodities may be greatly increased, the gross produce will have fallen from a value of £15,000 to a value of £7500; and as the power of supporting a population, and employing labor, depends always on the gross produce of a nation, and not on its net produce, there will necessarily be a diminution in the demand for labor, population will become redundant, and the situation of the laboring classes will be that of distress and poverty.

As, however, the power of saving from revenue to add to capital must depend on the efficiency of the net revenue, to satisfy the wants of the capitalist, it could not fail to follow from the reduction in the price of commodities consequent on the introduction of machinery that with the same wants he would have increased means of saving—increased facility of transferring revenue into capital. But with every increase of capital he would employ more laborers; and, therefore, a portion of the people thrown out of work in the first instance would be subsequently employed; and if the increased production, in consequence of the employment of the machine, was so great as to afford, in the shape of net produce, as great a quantity of food and necessaries as existed before in the form of gross produce, there would be the same ability to employ the whole population, and, therefore, there would not necessarily be any redundancy of people.

All I wish to prove is that the discovery and use of machinery may be attended with a diminution of gross produce; and whenever that is the case, it will be injurious to the laboring class, as some of their number will be thrown out of employment, and population will become redundant compared with the funds which are to employ it.

The case which I have supposed is the most simple that I could select; but it would make no difference in the result if we supposed that the machinery was applied to the trade of any manufacturer—that of a clothier, for example, or of a cotton manufacturer. If, in the trade of a clothier, less cloth would be produced after the introduction of machinery, for a part of that quantity which is disposed of for the purpose of paying a large body of workmen would not be required by their employer. In consequence of using the machine, it would be necessary for him to reproduce a value only equal to the value consumed, together with the profits on the whole capital. £7500 might do this as effectually as £15,000 did before, the case differing in no respect from the former instance. It may be said, however, that the demand for cloth would be as great as before, and it may be asked from whence would this supply come? But by whom would the cloth be demanded? By the farmers and the other producers of necessaries, who employed their capitals in producing these necessaries as a means of obtaining cloth: they gave corn and necessaries to the clothier for cloth, and he bestowed them on his workmen for the cloth which their work afforded him.

This trade would now cease; the clothier would not want the food and clothing, having fewer men to employ and having less cloth to dispose of. The farmers and others, who only produced necessaries as means to an end, could no longer obtain cloth by such an application of their capitals, and, therefore, they would either themselves employ their capitals in producing cloth, or would lend them to others, in order that the commodity really wanted might be furnished; and that for which no one had the means of paying, or for which there was no demand, might cease to be produced. This, then, leads us to the same result; the demand for labor would diminish, and the commodities necessary to the support of labor would not be produced in the same abundance.

If these views be correct, it follows, first, that the discovery and useful application of machinery always leads to the increase of the net produce of the country, although it may not, and will not, after an inconsiderable interval, increase the value of that net produce.

Secondly, that an increase of the net produce of a country is compatible with a diminution of the gross produce, and that the motives for employing machinery are always sufficient to ensure its employment if it will increase the net produce, although it may, and frequently must, diminish both the quantity of the gross produce and its value.

Thirdly, that the opinion entertained by the laboring class, that the employment of machinery is frequently detrimental to their interests, is not founded on prejudice and error, but is conformable to the correct principles of political economy.

Fourthly, that if the improved means of production, in consequence of the use of machinery, should increase the net produce of a country in a degree so great as not to diminish the gross produce (I mean always quantity of commodities, and not value), then the situation of all classes will be improved. The landlord and capitalist will benefit, not by an increase of rent and profit, but by the advantages resulting from the expenditure of the same rent and profit on commodities very considerably reduced in value, while the situation of the laboring classes will also be considerably improved: First, from the increased demand for menial servants; secondly, from the stimulus to savings from revenue which such an abundant net produce will afford; and, thirdly, from the low price of all articles of consumption on which their wages will be expended.

Independently of the consideration of the discovery and use of machinery, to which our attention has been just directed, the laboring class have no small interest in the manner in which the net income of the country is expended, although it should, in all cases, be expended for the gratification and enjoyments of those who are fairly entitled to it.

If a landlord, or a capitalist, expends his revenue in the manner of an ancient baron, in the support of a great number of retainers, or menial servants, he will give employment to much more labor than if he expended it on fine clothes or costly furniture, on carriages, on horses, or in the purchase of any other luxuries.

In both cases the net revenue would be the same, and so would be the gross revenue, but the former would be realized in different commodities. If my revenue were £10,000, the same quantity nearly of productive labor would be employed whether I realized it in fine clothes and costly furniture, etc., etc., or in a quantity of food and clothing of the same value. If, however, I realized my revenue in the first set of commodities, no more labor would be *consequently* employed: I should enjoy my furniture and my clothes, and there would be an end of them; but if I realized my revenue in food and clothing, and my desire was to employ menial servants, all those whom I could so employ with my revenue of £10,000, or with the food and clothing which it would purchase, would be to be added to the former demand for laborers, and this addition would take place only because I chose this mode of expending my revenue. As the laborers, then, are interested in the demand for labor, they must naturally desire that as much of the revenue as possible should be diverted from expenditure on luxuries to be expended in the support of menial servants.

In the same manner, a country engaged in war, and which is under the necessity of maintaining large fleets and armies, employs a great many more men than will be employed when the war terminates, and the annual expenses which it brings with it, cease.

If I were not called upon for a tax of £500 during the war, and which is expended on men in the situations of soldiers and sailors, I might probably expend that portion of my income on furniture, clothes, books, etc., etc., and whether it was expended in the one way or in the other, there would be the same quantity of labor employed in production; for the food and clothing of the soldier and sailor would require the same amount of industry to produce it as the more luxurious commodities; but in the case of the war, there would be the additional demand for men as soldiers and sailors; and, consequently, a war which is supported out of the revenue, and not from the capital of a country, is favorable to the increase of population.

At the termination of the war, when part of my revenue reverts to me, and is employed as before in the purchase of wine, furniture, or other luxuries, the population which it before supported, and which the war called into existence, will become redundant, and by its effect on the rest of the population, and its competition with it for employment, will sink the value of wages, and very materially deteriorate the condition of the laboring classes.

There is one other case that should be noticed of the possibility of an increase in the amount of the net revenue of a country, and even of its gross revenue, with a diminution of demand for labor, and that is when the labor of horses is substituted for that of man. If I employed one hundred men on my farm, and if I found that the food bestowed on fifty of those men could be diverted to the support of horses, and afford me a greater return of raw produce, after allowing for the interest of the capital which the purchase of the horses would absorb, it would be advantageous to me to substitute the horses for the men, and I should accordingly do so; but this would not be for the interest of the men, and unless the income I obtained was so much increased as to enable me to employ the men as well as the horses, it is evident that the population would become redundant and the laborer's condition would sink in the general scale. It is evident he could not, under any circumstances, be employed in agriculture; but if the produce of the land were increased by the substitution of horses for men, he might be employed in manufactures, or as a menial servant.

The statements, which I have made, will not, I hope, lead to the inference that machinery should not be encouraged. To elucidate the principle, I have been supposing that improved machinery is suddenly discovered and extensively used; but the truth is that these discoveries are gradual, and rather operate in determining the employment of the capital which is saved and accumulated than in diverting capital from its actual employment.

With every increase of capital and population food will generally rise, on account of its being more difficult to produce. The consequence of a rise of food will be a rise of wages, and every rise of wages will have a tendency to determine the saved capital in a greater proportion than before to the employment of machinery. Machinery and labor are in constant competition, and the former can frequently not be employed until labor rises.

In America and many other countries, where the food of man is easily provided, there is not nearly such great temptation to employ machinery as in England, where food is high and costs much labor for its production. The same cause that raises labor does not raise the value of machines, and, therefore, with every augmentation of capital, a greater proportion of it is employed on machinery. The demand for labor will continue to increase with an increase of capital, but not in proportion to its increase; the ratio will necessarily be a diminishing ratio.[1]

I have before observed, too, that the increase of net incomes, estimated in commodities, which is always the consequence of improved machinery, will lead to new savings and accumulations. These savings, it must be remembered, are annual, and must soon create a fund much greater than the gross revenue originally lost by the discovery of the machine, when the demand for labor will be as great as before, and the situation of the people will be still further improved by the increased savings which the increased net revenue will still enable them to make.

The employment of machinery could never be safely discouraged in a state, for if a capital is not allowed to get the greatest net revenue that the use of machinery will afford here, it will be carried abroad, and this must be a much more serious discouragement to the demand for labor than the most extensive employment of machinery; for while a capital is employed in this country it must create a demand for some labor; machinery cannot be worked without the assistance of men, it cannot be made but with the contribution of their labor. By investing part of a capital in improved machinery there will be a diminution in the progressive demand for labor; by exporting it to another country the demand will be wholly annihilated.

The prices of commodities, too, are regulated by their cost of production. By employing improved machinery, the cost of production of commodities is reduced, and, consequently, you can afford to sell them in foreign markets at a cheaper price. If, however, you were to reject the use of machinery, while all other countries encouraged it, you would be obliged to export your money, in exchange for foreign goods, till you sunk the natural prices of your goods to the prices of other countries. In making your exchanges with those countries you might give a commodity which cost two days' labor here for a commodity which cost one abroad, and this disadvantageous exchange would be the consequence of your own act, for the commodity which you export, and which cost you two days' labor, would have cost you only one if you had not rejected the use of machinery, the services of which your neighbors had more wisely appropriated to themselves.

CHAPTER XXXII

Mr. Malthus's Opinions on Rent

Although the nature of rent has in the former pages of this work been treated on at some length, yet I consider myself bound to notice some opinions on the subject which appear to me erroneous, and which are the more important as they are found in the writings of one to whom, of all men of the present day, some branches of economical science are the most indebted. Of Mr. Malthus's *Essay on Population* I am happy in the opportunity here afforded me of expressing my admiration. The assaults of the opponents of this great work have only served to prove its strength; and I am persuaded that its just reputation will spread with the cultivation of that science of which it is so eminent an ornament. Mr. Malthus, too, has satisfactorily explained the principles of rent, and showed that it rises or falls in proportion to the relative advantages, either of fertility or situation, of the different lands in cultivation, and has thereby thrown much light on many difficult points connected with the subject of rent, which were before either unknown or very imperfectly understood; yet he appears to me to have fallen into some errors which his authority makes it the more necessary, whilst his characteristic candor renders it less unpleasing, to notice. One of these errors lies in supposing rent to be a clear gain and a new creation of riches.

I do not assent to all the opinions of Mr. Buchanan concerning rent; but with those expressed in the following passage, quoted from his work by Mr. Malthus, I fully agree, and therefore I must dissent from Mr. Malthus's comment on them.

"In this view it (rent) can form no general addition to the stock of the community, as the neat surplus in question is nothing more than a revenue transferred from one class to another; and from the mere circumstance of its thus changing hands, it is clear that no fund can arise out of which to pay taxes. The revenue which pays for the produce of the land exists already in the hands of those who purchase that produce; and if the price of subsistence were lower, it would still remain in their hands, where it would be just as available for taxation as when, by a higher price, it is transferred to the landed proprietor."

After various observations on the difference between raw produce and manufactured commodities, Mr. Malthus asks, "Is it possible, then, with M. de Sismondi, to regard rent as the sole produce of labor, which has a value purely nominal, and the mere result of that augmentation of price which a seller obtains in consequence of a peculiar privilege; or, with Mr. Buchanan, to consider it as no addition to the national wealth, but merely a transfer of value, advantageous only to the landlords, and proportionally injurious to the consumers?"[68]

I have already expressed my opinion on this subject in treating of rent, and have now only further to add, that rent is a creation of value, as I understand that word, but not a creation of wealth. If the price of corn, from the difficulty of producing any portion of it, should rise from £4 to £5 per quarter, a million of quarters will be of the value of £5,000,000 instead of £4,000,000, and as this corn will exchange not only for more money, but for more of every other commodity, the possessors will have a greater amount of value; and as no one else will, in consequence, have a less, the society altogether will be possessed of greater value, and, in that sense, rent is a creation of value. But this value is so far nominal that it adds nothing to the wealth, that is to say, the necessaries, conveniences, and enjoyments of the society. We should have precisely the same quantity and no more of commodities, and the same million quarters of corn as before; but the effect of its being rated at £5 per quarter instead of £4 would be to transfer a portion of the value of the corn and commodities from their former possessors to the landlords. Rent, then, is a creation of value, but not a creation of wealth; it adds nothing to the resources of a country; it does not enable it to maintain fleets and armies; for the country would have a greater disposable fund if its land were of a better quality, and it could employ the same capital without generating a rent.

It must then be admitted that Mr. Sismondi and Mr. Buchanan, for both their opinions are substantially the same, were correct when they considered rent as a value purely nominal, and as forming no addition to the national wealth, but merely as a transfer of value, advantageous only to the landlords and proportionally injurious to the consumer.

In another part of Mr. Malthus's *Inquiry* he observes, "that the immediate cause of rent is obviously the excess of price above the cost of production at which raw produce sells in the market;" and, in another place, he says, "that the causes of the high price of raw produce may be stated to be three:—

"First, and mainly, that quality of the earth by which it can be made to yield a greater portion of the necessaries of life than is required for the maintenance of the persons employed on the land.

"Secondly, that quality peculiar to the necessaries of life, of being able to create their own demand, or to raise up a number of demanders in proportion to the quantity of necessaries produced.

"And thirdly, the comparative scarcity of the most fertile land." In speaking of the high price of corn, Mr. Malthus evidently does not mean the price per quarter or per bushel, but rather the excess of price for which the whole produce will sell above the cost of its production, including always in the term "cost of its production" profits as well as wages. One hundred and fifty quarters of corn at £3 10s. per quarter would yield a larger rent to the landlord than 100 quarters at £4, provided the cost of production were in both cases the same.

High price, if the expression be used in this sense, cannot then be called a cause of rent; it cannot be said "that the immediate cause of rent is obviously the excess of price above the cost of production, at which raw produce sells in the market," for that excess is itself rent. Rent, Mr. Malthus has defined to be "that portion of the value of the whole produce which remains to the owner of the land after all the outgoings belonging to its cultivation, of whatever kind, have been paid, including the profits of the capital employed, estimated according to the usual and ordinary rate of the profits of agricultural stock at the time being." Now, whatever sum this excess may sell for, is money rent; it is what Mr. Malthus means by "the excess of price above the cost of production at which raw produce sells in the market;" and, therefore, in an inquiry into the causes which may elevate the price of raw produce, compared with the cost of production, we are inquiring into the causes which may elevate rent.

In reference to the first cause which Mr. Malthus has assigned for the rise of rent, namely, "that quality of the earth by which it can be made to yield a greater portion of the necessaries on life than is required for the maintenance of the persons employed on the land," he makes the following observations: "We still want to know why the consumption and supply are such as to make the price so greatly exceed the cost of production, and the main cause is evidently the *fertility* of the earth in producing the necessaries of life. Diminish this plenty, diminish the fertility of the soil, and the excess will diminish; diminish it still further, and it will disappear." True, the excess of necessaries will diminish and disappear, but that is not the question. The question is, whether the excess of their price above the cost of their production will diminish and disappear, for it is on this that money rent depends. Is Mr. Malthus warranted in his inference, that because the excess of quantity will diminish and disappear, therefore "the cause of the *high price* of the necessaries of life above the cost of production is to be found in their abundance, rather than in their scarcity, and is not only essentially different from the high price occasioned by artificial monopolies, but from the high price of those peculiar products of the earth, not connected with food, which may be called natural and necessary monopolies?"

Are there no circumstances under which the fertility of the land and the plenty of its produce may be diminished without occasioning a diminished excess of its price above the cost of production, that is to say, a diminished rent? If there are, Mr. Malthus's proposition is much too universal; for he appears to me to state it as a general principle, true under all circumstances, that rent will rise with the increased fertility of the land, and will fall with its diminished fertility.

Mr. Malthus would undoubtedly be right if, of any given farm, in proportion as the land yielded abundantly, a greater share of the whole produce were paid to the landlord; but the contrary is the fact; when no other but the most fertile land is in cultivation, the landlord has the smallest proportion of the whole produce, as well as the smallest value, and it is only when inferior lands are required to feed an augmenting population that both the landlord's share of the whole produce and the value he receives progressively increase.

Suppose that the demand is for a million of quarters of corn, and that they are the produce of the land actually in cultivation. Now, suppose the fertility of all the land to be so diminished that the very same lands will yield only 900,000 quarters. The demand being for a million of quarters, the price of corn would rise, and recourse must necessarily be had to land of an inferior quality sooner than if the superior land had continued to produce a million of quarters. But it is this necessity of taking inferior land into cultivation which is the cause of the rise of rent, and will elevate it, although the quantity of corn received by the landlord be reduced in quantity. Rent, it must be remembered, is not in proportion to the absolute fertility of the land in cultivation, but in proportion to its relative fertility. Whatever cause may drive capital to inferior land must elevate rent on the superior land; the cause of rent being, as stated by Mr. Malthus in his third proposition, "the comparative scarcity of the most fertile land." The price of corn will naturally rise with the difficulty of producing the last portions of it, and the value of the whole quantity produced on a particular farm will be increased, although its quantity be diminished; but as the cost of production will not increase on the more fertile land, as wages and profits taken together will continue always of the same value,[69] it is evident that the excess of price above the cost of production, or, in other words, rent, must rise with the diminished fertility of the land, unless it is counteracted by a great reduction of capital, population, and demand. It does not appear, then, that Mr. Malthus's proposition is correct: rent does not immediately and necessarily rise or fall with the increased or diminished fertility of the land; but its increased fertility renders it capable of paying at some future time an augmented rent. Land possessed of very little fertility can never bear any rent; land of moderate fertility may be made, as population increases, to bear a moderate rent; and land of great fertility a high rent; but it is one thing to be able to bear a high rent, and another thing actually to pay it. Rent may be lower in a country where lands are exceedingly fertile than in a country where they yield a moderate return, it being in proportion rather to relative than absolute fertility—to the value of the produce, and not to its abundance.[70]

Mr. Malthus supposes that the rent on land yielding those peculiar products of the earth which may be called natural and necessary monopolies is regulated by a principle essentially different format which regulates the rent of land that yields the necessaries of life. He thinks that it is the scarcity of the products of the first which is the cause of a high rent, but that it is the abundance of the latter which produces the same effect.

This distinction does not appear to me to be well founded; for you would as surely raise the rent of land yielding scarce wines, as the rent of corn land, by increasing the abundance of its produce, if, at the same time, the demand for this peculiar commodity increased; and without a similar increase of demand, an abundant supply of corn would lower instead of raise the rent of corn land. Whatever the nature of the land may be, high rent must depend on the high price of the produce; but, given the high price, rent must be high in proportion to abundance and not to scarcity.

We are under no necessity of producing permanently any greater quantity of a commodity than that which is demanded. If by accident any greater quantity were produced it would fall below its natural price, and therefore would not pay the cost of production, including in that cost the usual and ordinary profits of stock: thus the supply would be checked till it conformed to the demand, and the market price rose to the natural price.

Mr. Malthus appears to me to be too much inclined to think that population is only increased by the previous provision of food—"that it is food that creates its own demand"—that it is by first providing food that encouragement is given to marriage, instead of considering that the general progress of population is affected by the increase of capital, the consequent demand for labor, and the rise of wages; and that the production of food is but the effect of that demand.

It is by giving the workmen more money, or any other commodity in which wages are paid, and which has not fallen in value, that his situation is improved. The increase of population and the increase of food will generally be the effect, but not the necessary effect, of high wages. The amended condition of the laborer, in consequence of the increased value which is paid him, does not necessarily oblige him to marry and take upon himself the charge of a family—he will, in all probability, employ a portion of his increased wages in furnishing himself abundantly with food and necessaries—but with the remainder he may, if it please him, purchase any commodities that may contribute to his enjoyments—chairs, tables, and hardware; or better clothes, sugar, and tobacco. His increased wages, then, will be attended with no other effect than an increased demand for some of those commodities; and as the race of laborers will not be materially increased, his wages will continue permanently high. But although this might be the consequence of high wages, yet so great are the delights of domestic society, that, in practice, it is invariably found that an increase of population follows the amended condition of the laborer; and it is only because it does so, that, with the trifling exception already mentioned, a new and increased demand arises for food. This demand, then, is the effect of an increase of capital and population, but not the cause—it is only because the expenditure of the people takes this direction, that the market price of necessaries exceeds the natural price, and that the quantity of food required is produced; and it is because the number of people is increased that wages again fall.

What motive can a farmer have to produce more corn than is actually demanded, when the consequence would be a depression of its market price below its natural price, and consequently a privation to him of a portion of his profits, by reducing them below the general rate? "If," says Mr. Malthus, "the necessaries of life, the most important products of land, had not the property of creating an increase of demand proportioned to their increased quantity, such increased quantity would occasion a fall in their exchangeable value.[71] However abundant might be the produce of the country, its population might remain stationary; and this abundance without a proportionate demand, and with a very high corn price of labor, which would naturally take place under these circumstances, might reduce the price of raw produce, like the price of manufactures, to the cost of production."

Might reduce the price of raw produce to the cost of production. Is it ever for any length of time either above or below this price? Does not Mr. Malthus himself state it never to be so? "I hope," he says, "to be excused for dwelling a little, and presenting to the reader, in various forms, the doctrine that corn, in reference to the quantity *actually produced,* is sold at its necessary price like manufactures, because I consider it as a truth of the highest importance, which has been overlooked by the economists, by Adam Smith, and all those writers, who have represented raw produce as selling always at a monopoly price.

"Every extensive country may thus be considered as possessing a gradation of machines for the production of corn and raw-materials, including in this gradation not only all the various qualities of poor land, of which every territory has generally an abundance, but the inferior machinery, which may be said to be employed when good land is further and further forced for additional produce. As the price of raw produce continues to rise, these inferior machines are successively called into action; and as the price of raw produce continues to fall, they are successively thrown out of action. The illustration here used serves to show at once *the necessity of the actual price of corn to the actual produce,* and the different effect which would attend a great reduction in the price of any particular manufacture, and a great reduction in the price of raw produce."[72]

How are these passages to be reconciled to that which affirms, that if the necessaries of life had not the property of creating an increase of demand proportioned to their increased quantity, the abundant quantity produced would then, and then only, reduce the price of raw produce to the cost of production? If corn is never under its natural price, it is never more abundant than the actual population require it to be for their own consumption; no store can be laid up for the consumption of others; it can never, then, by its cheapness and abundance, be a stimulus to population. In proportion as corn can be produced cheaply, the increased wages of the laborers will have more power to maintain families. In America population increases rapidly because food can be produced at a cheap price, and not because an abundant supply has been previously provided. In Europe population increases comparatively slowly, because food cannot be produced at a cheap value. In the usual and ordinary course of things the demand for all commodities precedes their supply. By saying that corn would, like manufactures, sink to its price of production, if it could not raise up demanders, Mr. Malthus cannot mean that all rent would be absorbed; for he has himself justly remarked that if all rent were given up by the landlords corn would not fall in price; rent being the effect and not the cause of high price, and there being always one quality of land in cultivation which pays no rent whatever, the corn from which replaces by its price only wages and profits.

In the following passage, Mr. Malthus has given an able exposition of the causes of the rise in the price of raw produce in rich and progressive countries, in every word of which I concur; but it appears to me to be at variance with some of the propositions maintained by him in his essay on rent. "I have no hesitation in stating that, independently of the irregularities in the currency of a country, and other temporary and accidental circumstances, the cause of the high comparative money price of corn is its high comparative *real price*, or the greater quantity of capital and labor which must be employed to produce it; and that the reasons why the real price of corn is higher, and continually rising in countries which are already rich and still advancing in prosperity and population, is to be found in the necessity of resorting constantly to poorer land, to machines which require a greater expenditure to work them, and which consequently occasion each fresh addition to the raw produce of the country to be purchased at a greater cost; in short, it is to be found in the important truth that corn in a progressive country is sold at a price necessary to yield the actual supply; and that, as this supply becomes more and more difficult, the price rises in proportion."

The real price of a commodity is here properly stated to depend on the greater or less quantity of labor and capital (that is, accumulated labor) which must be employed to produce it. Real price does not, as some have contended, depend on money value; nor, as others have said, on value relatively to corn, labor, or any other commodity taken singly, or to all commodities collectively; but, as Mr. Malthus justly says, "on the greater (or less) quantity of capital and labor which must be employed to produce it."

Among the causes of the rise of rent, Mr. Malthus mentions, "such an increase of population as will lower the wages of labor." But if, as the wages of labor fall, the profits of stock rise, and they be together always of the same value,[73] no fall of wages can raise rent, for it will neither diminish the portion nor the value of the portion of the produce which will be allotted to the farmer and laborer together; and, therefore, will not leave a larger portion nor a larger value for the landlord. In proportion as less is appropriated for wages, more will be appropriated for profits, and vice versa. This division will be settled by the farmer and his laborers without any interference of the landlord; and, indeed, it is a matter in which he can have no interest, otherwise than as one division may be more favorable than another, to new accumulations, and to a further demand for land. If wages fell, profits, and not rent, would rise. If wages rose, profits, and not rent, would fall. The rise of rent and wages, and the fall of profits, are generally the inevitable effects of the same cause—the increasing demand for food, the increased quantity of labor required to produce it, and its consequently high price. If the landlord were to forego this whole rent, the laborers would not be in the least benefited. If it were possible for the laborers to give up their whole wages, the landlords would derive no advantage from such a circumstance; but in both cases the farmers would receive and retain all which they relinquish. It has been my endeavor to show in this work that a fall of wages would have no other effect than to raise profits. Every rise of profits is favorable to the accumulation of capital, and to the further increase of population, and therefore would, in all probability, ultimately lead to an increase of rent.

Another cause of the rise of rent, according to Mr. Malthus, is "such agricultural improvements or such increase of exertions as will diminish the number of laborers necessary to produce a given effect." To this passage I have the same objection that I had against that which speaks of the increased fertility of land being the cause of an immediate rise of rent. Both the improvement in agriculture, and the superior fertility, will give to the land a capability of bearing at some future period a higher rent, because with the same price of food there will be a great additional quantity; but till the increase of population be in the same proportion, the additional quantity of food would not be required, and, therefore, rents would be lowered and not raised. The quantity that could under the then existing circumstances be consumed could be furnished either with fewer hands, or with a less quantity of land, the price of raw produce would fall, and capital would be withdrawn from the land.[74] Nothing can raise rent but a demand for new land of an inferior quality, or some cause which shall occasion an alteration in the relative fertility of the land already under cultivation.[75] Improvements in agriculture, and in the division of labor, are common to all land; they increase the absolute quantity of raw produce obtained from each, but probably do not much disturb the relative proportions which before existed between them.

Mr. Malthus has justly commented on the error of Dr. Smith's argument, that corn is of so peculiar a nature that its production cannot be encouraged by the same means that the production of all other commodities is encouraged. He observes, "It is by no means intended to deny the powerful influence of the price of corn upon the price of labor, on an average of a considerable number of years; but that this influence is not such as to prevent the movement of capital to or from the land, which is the precise point in question, will be made sufficiently evident by a short inquiry into the manner in which labor is paid and brought into the market, and by a consideration of the consequences to which the assumption of Adam Smith's proposition would inevitably lead."[76]

Mr. Malthus then proceeds to show that demand and high price will as effectually encourage the production of raw produce as the demand and high price of any other commodity will encourage its production. In this view it will be seen, from what I have said of the effects of bounties, that I entirely concur. I have noticed the passage from Mr. Malthus's *Observations on the Corn Laws,* for the purpose of showing in what a different sense the term real price is used here, and in his other pamphlet, entitled *Grounds of an Opinion*, etc. In this passage Mr. Malthus tells us that "it is clearly an increase of real price alone which can encourage the production of corn," and, by real price, he evidently means the increase in its value relatively to all other things, or, in other words, the rise in its market above its natural price, or the cost of its production. If by real price this is what is meant, although I do not admit the propriety of thus naming it, Mr. Malthus's opinion is undoubtedly correct; it is the rise in the market price of corn which alone encourages its production; for it may be laid down as a principle uniformly true that the only great encouragement to the increased production of a commodity is its market value exceeding its natural or necessary value.

But this is not the meaning which Mr. Malthus, on other occasions, attaches to the term real price. In the essay on rent Mr. Malthus says, by "the real growing price of corn I mean the real *quantity* of labor and capital *which has been employed* to produce the last additions which have been made to the national produce." In another part he states "the cause of the high comparative real price of corn to be the greater *quantity* of capital and labor which must be *employed* to produce it."[77] Suppose that, in the foregoing passage, we were to substitute this definition of real price, would it not then run thus?— "It is clearly the increase in the quantity of labor and capital which must be employed to produce corn, which alone can encourage its production." This would be to say, that it is clearly the rise in the natural or necessary price of corn which encourages its production—a proposition which could not be maintained. It is not the price at which corn can be produced that has any influence on the quantity produced, but the price at which it can be sold. It is in proportion to the degree of the difference of its price above or below the cost of production that capital is attracted to or repelled from the land. If that excess be such as to give to capital so employed a greater than the general profit of stock, capital will go to the land; if less, it will be withdrawn from it.

It is not, then, by an alteration in the real price of corn that its production is encouraged, but by an alteration in its market price. It is not "because a greater quantity of capital and labor must be employed to produce it (Mr. Malthus's just definition of real price) that more capital and labor are attracted to the land, but because the market price rises above this, its real price, and, notwithstanding the increased charge, makes the cultivation of land the more profitable employment of capital."

Nothing can be more just than the following observations of Mr. Malthus on Adam Smith's standard of value. "Adam Smith was evidently led into this train of argument from his habit of considering *labor as the standard measure of value* and corn as the measure of labor. But that corn is a very inaccurate measure of labor the history of our own country will amply demonstrate; where labor, compared with corn, will be found to have experienced very great and striking variations, not only from year to year, but from century to century, and for ten, twenty, and thirty years together. *And that neither labor nor any other commodity can be an accurate measure of real value in exchange* is now considered as one of the most incontrovertible doctrines of political economy, and, indeed, follows from the very definition of value in exchange."

If neither corn nor labor are accurate measures of real value in exchange, which they clearly are not, what other commodity is?—certainly none. If, then, the expression, real price of commodities, have any meaning, it must be that which Mr. Malthus has stated in the essay on rent—it must be measured by the proportionate quantity of capital and labor necessary to produce them.

In Mr. Malthus's *Inquiry into the Nature of Rent,* he says, "that, independently of irregularities in the currency of a country, and other temporary and accidental circumstances, the cause of the high comparative money price of corn is its high comparative real price, *or the greater quantity of capital and labor which must be employed to produce it.*"[78]

This, I apprehend, is the correct account of all permanent variations in price, whether of corn or of any other commodity. A commodity can only permanently rise in price either because a greater quantity of capital and labor must be employed to produce it, or because money has fallen in value; and, on the contrary, it can only fall in price, either because a less quantity of capital and labor may be employed to produce it, or because money has risen in value.

A variation arising from the latter of these alternatives, an altered value of money, is common at once to all commodities; but a variation arising from the former cause is confined to the particular commodity requiring more or less labor in its production. By allowing the free importation of corn, or by improvements in agriculture, raw produce would fall; but the price of no other commodity would be affected, except in proportion to the fall in the real value, or cost of production, of the raw produce which entered into its composition.

Mr. Malthus, having acknowledged this principle, cannot, I think, consistently maintain that the whole money value of all the commodities in the country must sink exactly in proportion to the fall in the price of corn. If the corn consumed in the country were of the value of 10 millions per annum, and the manufactured and foreign commodities consumed were of the value of 20 millions, making altogether 30 millions, it would not be admissible to infer that the annual expenditure was reduced to 15 millions because corn had fallen 50 percent, or from 10 to 5 millions.

The value of the raw produce which entered into the composition of these manufactures might not, for example, exceed 20 percent of their whole value, and, therefore, the fall in the value of manufactured commodities, instead of being from 20 to 10 millions, would be only from 20 to 18 millions; and after the fall in the price of corn of 50 percent, the whole amount of the annual expenditure, instead of falling from 30 to 15 millions, would fall from 30 to 23 millions.[79]

This, I say, would be their value if you supposed it possible that with such a cheap price of corn no more corn and commodities would be consumed; but as all those who had employed capital in the production of corn on those lands which would no longer be cultivated could employ it in the production of manufactured goods, and only a part of those manufactured goods would be given in exchange for foreign corn, as on any other supposition no advantage would be gained by importation and low prices, we should have the additional value of all that quantity of manufactured goods which were so produced and not exported to add to the above value, so that the real diminution, even in money value, of all the commodities in the country, corn included, would be equal only to the loss of the landlords, by the reduction of their rents, while the quantity of objects of enjoyment would be greatly increased.

Instead of thus considering the effect of a fall in the value of raw produce, as Mr. Malthus was bound to do by his previous admission, he considers it as precisely the same thing as a rise of 100 percent, in the value of money, and, therefore, argues as if all commodities would sink to half their former price.

"During the twenty years beginning with 1794," he says, "and ending with 1813, the average price of British corn per quarter was about 83 shillings; during the ten years ending with 1813, 92 shillings; and during the last five years of the twenty, 108 shillings. In the course of these twenty years, the government borrowed near 500 millions of real capital; for which, on a rough average, exclusive of the sinking fund, it engaged to pay about 5 percent. But if corn should fall to 50 shillings a quarter, and other commodities in proportion, instead of an interest of about 5 percent, the government would really pay an interest of 7, 8, 9, and, for the last 200 millions, 10 percent.

"To this extraordinary generosity towards the stockholders I should be disposed to make no kind of objection, if it were not necessary to consider by whom it is to be paid; and a moment's reflection will show us that it can only be paid by the industrious classes of society and the landlords, that is, by all those whose nominal income will vary with the variations in the measure of value. The nominal revenues of this part of the society, compared with the average of the last five years, will be diminished one half, and out of this nominally reduced income they will have to pay the same nominal amount of taxes."[80]

In the first place, I think I have already shown that even the value of the gross income of the whole country will not be diminished in the proportion for which Mr. Malthus here contends; it would not follow that because corn fell 50 percent, each man's gross income would be reduced 50 percent, in value; [81] his net income might be actually increased in value.

In the second place, I think the reader will agree with me that the increased charge, if admitted, would not fall exclusively "on the landlords and the industrious classes of society;" the stockholder, by his expenditure, contributes his share to the support of the public burdens in the same way as the other classes of society. If, then, money became really more valuable, although he would receive a greater value, he would also pay a greater value in taxes, and, therefore, it cannot be true that the whole addition to the real value of the interest would be paid by "the landlords and the industrious classes."

The whole argument, however, of Mr. Malthus, is built on an infirm basis: it supposes, because the gross income of the country is diminished, that, therefore, the net income must also be diminished in the same proportion. It has been one of the objects of this work to show that, with every fall in the real value of necessaries, the wages of labor would fall, and that the profits of stock would rise; in other words, that of any given annual value a less portion would be paid to the laboring class, and a larger portion to those whose funds employed this class. Suppose the value of the commodities produced in a particular manufacture to be £1000, and to be divided between tie master and his laborers in the proportion of £800 to laborers and £200 to the master; if the value of these commodities should fall to £900, and £100 be saved from the wages of labor, in consequence of the fall of necessaries, the net income of the master would be in no degree impaired, and, therefore, he could with just as much facility pay the same amount of taxes after as before the reduction of price.[82]

It is of importance to distinguish clearly between gross revenue and net revenue, for it is from the net revenue of a society that all taxes must be paid. Suppose that all the commodities in the country, all the corn, raw produce, manufactured goods, etc., which could be brought to market in the course of the year, were of the value of 20 millions, and that in order to obtain this value the labor of a certain number of men was necessary, and that the absolute necessaries of these laborers required an expenditure of 10 millions; I should say that the gross revenue of such society was 20 millions, and its net revenue 10 millions. It does not follow from this supposition that the laborers should receive only 10 millions for their labor; they might receive 12, 14, or 15 millions, and in that case they would have 2, 4, or 5 millions of the net income. The rest would be divided between landlords and capitalists; but the whole net income would not exceed 10 millions. Suppose such a society paid 2 millions in taxes, its net income would be reduced to 8 millions.

Suppose now money to become more valuable by one-tenth, all commodities would fall, and the price of labor would fall, because the absolute necessaries of the laborer formed a part of those commodities, consequently the gross income would be reduced to 18 millions and the net income to 9 millions. If the taxes fell in the same proportion, and, instead of 2 millions, £1,800,000 only were raised, the net income would be further reduced to £7,200,000, precisely of the same value as the 8 millions were before, and therefore the society would neither be losers nor gainers by such an event. But suppose that after the rise of money, 2 millions were raised for taxes as before, the society would be poorer by £200,000 per annum, their taxes would be really raised one-ninth. To alter the money value of commodities, by altering the value of money, and yet to raise the same money amount by taxes, is then undoubtedly to increase the burdens of society.

But suppose of the 10 millions net revenue the landlords received five millions as rent, and that by facility of production, or by the importation of corn, the necessary cost of that article in labor was reduced 1 million, rent would fall 1 million, and the prices of the mass of commodities would also fall to the same amount, but the net revenue would be just as great as before; the gross income would, it is true, be only 19 millions, and the necessary expenditure to obtain it 9 millions, but the net income would be 10 millions.

Now, suppose 2 millions raised in taxes on this diminished gross income, would the society altogether be richer or poorer? Richer, certainly; for after the payment of their taxes, they would have, as before, a clear income of 8 millions to bestow on the purchase of commodities, which had increased in quantity, and fallen in price, in the proportion of 20 to 19; not only then could the same taxation be endured, but greater, and yet the mass of the people be better provided with conveniences and necessaries.

If the net income of the society, after paying the same money taxation, be as great as before, and the class of landholders lose 1 million from a fall of rent, the other productive classes must have increased money incomes, notwithstanding the fall of prices. The capitalist will then be doubly benefited; the corn and butcher's meat consumed by himself and his family will be reduced in price; and the wages of his menial servants, of his gardeners, and laborers of all descriptions, will be also lowered. His horses and cattle will cost less, and be supported at a less expense. All the commodities in which raw produce enters as a principal part of their value will fall. This aggregate amount of savings, made on the expenditure of income, at the same time that his money income is increased, will then be doubly beneficial to him, and will enable him not only to add to his enjoyments, but to bear additional taxes, if they should be required: his additional consumption of taxed commodities will much more than make up for the diminished demand of land-lords, consequent on the reduction of their rents. The same observations apply to farm-ers and traders of every description.

But it may be said that the capitalist's income will not be increased; that the million deducted from the landlord's rent will be paid in additional wages to laborers! Be it so; this will make no difference in the argument: the situation of the society will be im-proved, and they will be able to bear the same money burdens with greater facility than before; it will only prove what is still more desirable, that the situation of an-other class, and by far the most important class in society, is the one which is chiefly benefited by the new distribution. All that they receive more than 9 millions forms part of the net income of the country, and it cannot be expended without adding to its revenue, its happiness, or its power. Distribute, then, the net income as you please. Give a little more to one class and a little less to another, yet you do not thereby di-minish it; a greater amount of commodities will be still produced with the same labor, although the amount of the gross money value of such commodities will be dimin-ished; but the net money income of the country, that fund from which taxes are paid and enjoyments procured, would be much more adequate than before to maintain the actual population, to afford it enjoyments and luxuries, and to support any given amount of taxation.

That the stockholder is benefited by a great fall in the value of corn cannot be doubted; but if no one else be injured, that is no reason why corn should be made dear; for the gains of the stockholder are national gains, and increase, as all other gains do, the real wealth and power of the country. If they are unjustly benefited, let the degree in which they are so be accurately ascertained, and then it is for the legislature to devise a remedy; but no policy can be more unwise than to shut ourselves out from the great advantages arising from cheap corn, and abundant productions, merely because the stockholder would have an undue proportion of the increase.

To regulate the dividends on stock by the money value of corn has never yet been at-tempted. If justice and good faith required such a regulation, a great debt is due to the old stockholders; for they have been receiving the same money dividends for more than a century, although corn has, perhaps, been doubled or trebled in price.[83]

But it is a great mistake to suppose that the situation of the stockholder will be more improved than that of the farmer, the manufacturer, and the other capitalists of the coun-try; it will, in fact, be less improved.

The stockholder will undoubtedly receive the same money dividend, while not only the price of raw produce and labor fell, but the prices of many other things into which raw produce entered as a component part. This, however, is an advantage, as I have just stated, which he would enjoy in common with all other persons who had the same money incomes to expend:—his money income would not be increased; that of the farmer, manufacturer, and other employers of labor would, and consequently they would be doubly benefited.

It may be said that, although it may be true that capitalists would be benefited by a rise of profits, in consequence of a fall of wages, yet that their incomes would be diminished by the fall in the money value of their commodities. What is to lower them? Not any alteration in the value of money for nothing has been supposed to occur to alter the value of money. Not any diminution in the quantity of labor necessary to produce their commodities, for no such cause has operated, and if it did operate, would not lower money profits, though it might lower money prices. But the raw produce of which commodities are made is supposed to have fallen in price, and, therefore, commodities will fall on that account. True, they will fall, but their fall will not be attended with any diminution in the money income of the producer. If he sells his commodity for less money, it is only because one of the materials from which it is made has fallen in value. If the clothier sell his cloth for £900 instead of £1000, his income will not be less, if the wool from which it is made has declined £100 in value.

Mr. Malthus says, "It is true that the last additions to the agricultural produce of an improving country are not attended with a large proportion of rent; and it is precisely this circumstance that may make it answer to a rich country to import some of its corn, if it can be secure of obtaining an equable supply. But in all cases the importation of foreign corn must fail to answer nationally if it is not so much cheaper than the corn that can be grown at home as to equal both the profits and the rent of the grain which it displaces."—*Grounds,* etc., p. 36.

In this observation Mr. Malthus is quite correct; but imported corn must be always so much cheaper than the corn that can be grown at home, "as to equal both the profits and the rent of the grain which it displaces." If it were not, no advantage to any one could be obtained by importing it.

As rent is the effect of the high price of corn, the loss of rent is the effect of a low price. Foreign corn never enters into competition with such home corn as affords a rent; the fall of price invariably affects the landlord till the whole of his rent is absorbed;—if it fall still more, the price will not afford even the common profits of stock; capital will then quit the land for some other employment, and the corn which was before grown upon it will then, and not till then, be imported. From the loss of rent there will be a loss of value, of estimated money value, but there will be a gain of wealth. The amount of the raw produce and other productions together will be increased; from the greater facility with which they are produced they will, though augmented in quality, be diminished in value.

Two men employ equal capitals—one in agriculture, the other in manufactures. That in agriculture produces a net annual value of £1200, of which £1000 is retained for profit and £200 is paid for rent; the other in manufactures produces only an annual value of £1000. Suppose that, by importation, the same quantity of corn which cost £1200 can be obtained for commodities which cost £950, and that, in consequence, the capital employed in agriculture is diverted to manufactures, where it can produce a value of £1000, the net revenue of the country will be of less value, it will be reduced from £2200 to £2000; but there will not only be the same quantity of commodities and corn for its own consumption, but also as much addition to that quantity as £50 would purchase, the difference between the value at which its manufactures were sold to the foreign country and the value of the corn which was purchased from it.

Now this is precisely the question respecting the advantage of importing or growing corn; it never can be imported till the quantity obtained from abroad by the employment of a given capital exceeds the quantity which the same capital will enable us to grow at home—exceeds not only that quantity which falls to the share of the farmer, but also that which is paid as rent to the landlord.

Mr. Malthus says, "It has been justly observed by Adam Smith that no equal quantity of productive labor employed in manufactures can ever occasion so great a reproduction as in agriculture." If Adam Smith speaks of value, he is correct; but if he speaks of riches, which is the important point, he is mistaken; for he has himself defined riches to consist of the necessaries, conveniences, and enjoyments of human life. One set of necessaries and conveniences admits of no comparison with another set; value in use cannot be measured by any known standard; it is differently estimated by different persons.

Notes

¹ Book I, chap. 5

² "But though labor be the real measure of the exchangeable value of all commodities, it is not that by which their value is commonly estimated. It is often difficult to ascertain the proportion between two different quantities of labor. The time spent in two different sorts of work will not always alone determine this proportion. The different degrees of hardship endured, and of ingenuity exercised, must likewise be taken into account. There may be more labor in an hour's hard work than in two hours' easy business; or in an hour's application to a trade, which it costs ten years' labor to learn, than in a month's industry at an ordinary and obvious employment. But it is not easy to find any accurate measure, either of hardship or ingenuity. In exchanging, indeed, the different productions of different sorts of labor for one another, some allowance is commonly made for both. It is adjusted, however, not by any accurate measure, but by the haggling and bargaining of the market, according to that sort of rough equality which, though not exact, is sufficient for carrying on the business of common life."

³ *Wealth of Nations*, book I, chap. 10

⁴ A division not essential, and in which the line of demarcation cannot be accurately drawn.

⁵ We here see why it is that old countries are constantly impelled to employ machinery, and new countries to employ labor. With every difficulty of providing for the maintenance of men, labor necessarily rises, and with every rise in the price of labor, new temptations are offered to the use of machinery. This difficulty of providing for the maintenance of men is in constant operation in old countries; in new ones a very great increase in the population may take place without the least rise in the wages of labor. It may be as easy to provide for the seventh, eighth, and ninth million of men as for the second, third, and fourth.

⁶ Mr. Malthus remarks on this doctrine, "We have the power indeed, arbitrarily, to call the labor which has been employed upon a commodity its real value, but in so doing we use words in a different sense from that in which they are customarily used; we confound at once the very important distinction between *cost* and *value*; and render it almost impossible to explain with clearness the main stimulus to the production of wealth, which in fact depends upon this distinction."

Mr. Malthus appears to think that it is a part of my doctrine that the cost and value of a thing should be the same; it is, if he means by cost, "cost of production" including profits. In the above passage, this is what he does not mean, and therefore he has not clearly understood me.

⁷ "The earth, as we have already seen, is not the only agent of nature which has a productive power; but it is the only one, or nearly so, that one set of men take to themselves to the exclusion of others; and of which, consequently, they can appropriate the benefits. The waters of rivers, and of the sea, by the power which they have of giving movement to our machines, carrying our boats, nourishing our fish, have also a productive power; the wind which turns our mills, and even the heat of the sun, work for us; but happily no one has yet been able to say, the 'wind and the sun are mine, and the service which they render must be paid for.'" —*Economie Politique*, par J. B. Say, vol. ii. p. 124.

⁸ Has not M. Say forgotten, in the following passage, that it is the cost of production which ultimately regulates price? "The produce of labor employed on the land has this peculiar property, that it does not become more dear by becoming scarce, because population always diminishes at the same time that food diminishes, and consequently the quantity of these products *demanded* diminishes at the same time as the quantity supplied. Besides, it is not observed that corn is dearer in those places where there is plenty of uncultivated land, than in completely cultivated countries. England and France were much more imperfectly cultivated in the middle ages than they are now; they produced much less raw produce: nevertheless, from all that we can judge by a comparison with the value of other things, corn was not sold at a dearer price. If the produce was less, so was the population; the

weakness of the demand compensated the feebleness of the supply." (Vol. ii. 338) M. Say being impressed with the opinion that the price of commodities is regulated by the price of labor, and justly supposing that charitable institutions of all sorts tend to increase the population beyond what it otherwise would be, and therefore to lower wages, says, "I suspect that the cheapness of the goods which come from England is partly caused by the numerous charitable institutions which exist in that country." (Vol. ii. 277) This is a consistent opinion in one who maintains that wages regulate price.

[9] "In agriculture, too," says Adam Smith, "nature labors along with man; and though her labor costs no expense, its produce has its value, as well as that of the most expensive workman." The labor of nature is paid, not because she does much, but because she does little. In proportion as she becomes niggardly in her gifts she exacts a greater price for her work. Where she is munificently beneficent she always works gratis. "The laboring cattle employed in agriculture not only occasion, like the workmen in manufactures, the reproduction of a value equal to their own consumption, or to the capital which employs them, together with its owner's profits, but of a much greater value. Over and above the capital of the farmer and all its profits, they regularly occasion the reproduction of the rent of the landlord. This rent may be considered as the produce of those powers of nature, the use of which the landlord lends to the farmer. It is greater or smaller according to the supposed extent of those powers, or, in other words, according to the supposed natural or improved fertility of the land. It is the work of nature which remains, after deducting or compensating everything which can be regarded as the work of man. It is seldom less than a fourth, and frequently more than a third of the whole produce. No equal quantity of productive labor employed in manufactures can ever occasion so great a reproduction. *In them nature does nothing, man does all*; and the reproduction must always be in proportion to the strength of the agents that occasion it. The capital employed in agriculture, therefore, not only puts into motion a greater quantity of productive labor than any equal capital employed in manufactures, but in proportion, too, to the quantity of the productive labor which it employs it adds a much greater value to the annual produce of the land and labor of the country, to the real wealth and revenue of its inhabitants. Of all the ways in which a capital can be employed, it is by far the most advantageous to the society."—Book II, chap. v. p. 15.

Does nature nothing for man in manufactures? Are the powers of wind and water, which move our machinery and assist navigation, nothing? The pressure of the atmosphere and the elasticity of steam, which enable us to work the most stupendous engines—are they not the gifts of nature? To say nothing of the effects of the matter of heat in softening and melting metals, of the decomposition of the atmosphere in the process of dyeing and fermentation. There is not a manufacture which can be mentioned in which nature does not give her assistance to man, and give it, too, generously and gratuitously.

In remarking on the passage which I have copied from Adam Smith, Mr. Buchanan observes, I have endeavored to show, in the observations on productive and unproductive labor, contained in the fourth volume, that agriculture adds no more to the national stock than any other sort of industry. In dwelling on the reproduction of rent as so great an advantage to society, Dr. Smith does not reflect that rent is the effect of high price, and that what the landlord gains in this way he gains at the expense of the community at large. There is no absolute gain to the society by the reproduction of rent; it is only one class profiting at the expense of another class. The notion of agriculture yielding a produce, and a rent in consequence, because nature concurs with human industry in the process of cultivation, is a mere fancy. It is not from the produce, but from the price at which the produce is sold, that the rent is derived; and this price is got not because nature assists, in the production, but because it is the price which suits the consumption to the supply.

[10] The clearly understanding this principle is, I am persuaded, of the utmost importance to the science of political economy.

[11] I hope I am not understood as undervaluing the importance of all sorts of improvements in agriculture to landlords—their immediate effect is to lower rent; but as they give a great stimulus to population, and at the same time

enable us to cultivate poorer lands with less labor, they are ultimately of immense advantage to landlords. A period, however, must elapse during which they are positively injurious to him.

[12] To make this obvious, and to show the degrees in which corn and money rent will vary, let us suppose that the labor of ten men will, on land of a certain quality, obtain 180 quarters of wheat, and its value to be £4 per quarter, or £720; and that the labor of ten additional men will, on the same or any other land, produce only 170 quarters in addition; wheat would rise from £4 to 4s. 8d. for 170:180::£4:£4 4s. 8d.; or, as in the production of 170 quarters, the labor of 10 men is necessary in one case, and only of 9.44 in the other, the rise would be as 9.44 to 10, or as £4 to £4 4s. 8d. If 10 men be further employed, and the return be

160 the price will rise to £4 10s. 0d.

150 the price will rise to £4 16s. 0d.

140 the price will rise to £5 2s. 10d.

Now, if no rent was paid for the land which yielded 180 quarters, when corn was at £4 per quarter, the value of 10 quarters would be paid as rent when only 170 could be procured, which at £4 4s. 8d. would be £42 7s. 6d.

20 quarters when 160 were produced, which at £4 10s. 0d. would be £90 0s. 0d.

| 30 quarters | ... 150 | 4 16s. 0d. | 144 0s. 0d. |
| 40 quarters | ... 140 | 52s. 10d. | 205 13s. 4d. |

Corn rent would increase in the proportion of	and money rent in the proportion of
100	100
200	212
300	340
400	485

[13] "The shelter and the clothing which are indispensable in one country may be no way necessary in another; and a laborer in Hindostan may continue to work with perfect vigor, though receiving, as his natural wages, only such a supply of covering as would be insufficient to preserve a laborer in Russia from perishing. Even in countries situated in the same climate, different habits of living will often occasion variations in the natural price of labor as considerable as those which are produced by natural causes."—p. 68, *An Essay on the External Corn Trade* by R. Torrens, Esq.

The whole of this subject is most ably illustrated by Colonel Torrens.

[14] With Mr. Buchanan, in the following passage, if it refers to temporary states of misery, I so far agree, that "the great evil of the laborer's condition is poverty, arising either from a scarcity of food or of work; and in all countries laws without number have been enacted for his relief. But there are miseries in the social state which legislation cannot relieve; and it is useful therefore to know its limits, that we may not, by aiming at what is impracticable, miss the good which is really in our power."— Buchanan, p. 61.

[15] The progress of knowledge manifested upon this subject in the House of Commons since 1796 has happily not been very small, as may be seen by contrasting the late report of the committee on the poor laws and the following sentiments of Mr. Pitt in that year: "Let us," said he, "make relief in cases where there are a number of children a matter of right and honor, instead of a ground of opprobrium and Contempt. This will make a large family a blessing and not a curse; and this will draw a proper line of distinction between those who are able to provide for themselves by their labor, and those who, after having enriched their country with a number of children, have a claim upon its assistance for support." —Hansard's Parliamentary History, vol. xxxii. p. 710.

[16] The reader is desired to bear in mind that, for the purpose of making the subject more clear, I consider money to be invariable in value, and therefore every variation of price to be referable to an alteration in the value of the commodity.
[17] The reader is aware that we are leaving out of our consideration the accidental variations arising from bad and good seasons, or from the demand increasing or diminishing by any sudden effect on the state of population. We are speaking of the natural and constant, not of the accidental and fluctuating, price of corn.

The 180 quarters of corn would be divided in the following proportions between landlords, farmers, and laborers, with the above-named variations in the value of corn.

[18] See Adam Smith, book i. chap. 9.

[19] It will appear, then, that a country possessing very considerable advantages in machinery and skill, and which may therefore be enabled to manufacture commodities with much less labor than her neighbors, may, in return for such commodities, import a portion of the corn required for its consumption, even if its land were more fertile and corn could be grown with less labor than in the country from which it was imported. Two men can both make shoes and hats, and one is superior to the other in both employments; but in making hats he can only exceed his competitor by one-fifth or 20 percent, and in making shoes he can excel him by one-third or 33 percent;— will it not be for the interest of both that the superior man should employ himself exclusively in making shoes, and the inferior man in making hats?

[20] It must be understood that all the productions of a country are consumed; but it makes the greatest difference imaginable whether they are consumed by those who reproduce or by those who do not reproduce another value. When we say that revenue is saved and added to capital, what we mean is, that the portion of revenue, so said to be added to capital, is consumed by productive instead of unproductive laborers. There can be no greater error than in supposing that capital is increased by non-consumption. If the price of labor should rise so high that, notwithstanding the increase of capital, no more could be employed, I should say that such increase of capital would be still unproductively consumed.

[21] It may be doubted whether commodities, raised in price merely by taxation, would require any more money for their circulation. I believe they would not.

[22] 18 quarters at £4 8s. 102/3d.

[23] 9 quarters at £4 8s 102/3d.

[24] Book v. chap, ii.

[25] That the profits of the farmer only should be taxed, and not the profits of any other capitalist, would be highly beneficial to landlords. It would, in fact, be a tax on the consumers of raw produce, partly for the benefit of the state, and partly for the benefit of landlords.

[26] On further consideration, I doubt whether any more money would be required to circulate the same quantity of commodities if their prices be raised by taxation and not by difficulty of production. Suppose 100,000 quarters of corn to be sold in a certain district, and in a certain time, at £4 per quarter, and that in consequence of a direct tax of 8s. per quarter, corn rises to £4 8s., the same quantity of money, I think, and no more, would be required to circulate this corn at the increased price. If I before purchased 11 quarters at £4, and, in consequence of the tax, am obliged to reduce my consumption to 10 quarters, I shall not require more money, for in all cases I shall pay £44 for my corn. The public would, in fact, consume one-eleventh less, and this quantity would be consumed by government. The money necessary to purchase it would be derived from the 8s. per quarter, to be received from the farmers in the shape of a tax, but the amount levied would at the same time be paid to them for their corn; therefore the tax is in fact a tax in kind, and does not make it necessary that any more money should be used, or, if any, so little that the quantity may be safely neglected.

[27] M. Say appears to have imbibed the general opinion on this subject. Speaking of corn, he says, "thence it results that its price influences the price of *all* other commodities. A farmer, a manufacturer, or a merchant employs a cer-

tain number of workmen who all have occasion to consume a certain quantity of corn. If the price of corn rises, he is obliged to raise, in. an equal proportion, the price of his production." —Vol. i. p. 255.

[28] So far from this being true, they would scarcely affect the landlords and stockholder.

[29] M. Say says, "that the tax added to the price of a commodity raises its price. Every increase in the price of a commodity necessarily reduces the number of those who are able to purchase it, or at least the quantity they will consume of it." This is by no means a necessary consequence.

I do not believe that if bread were taxed the consumption of bread would be diminished, more than if cloth, wine, or soap were taxed.

[30] The following remark of the same author appears to me equally erroneous: "When a high duty is laid on cotton the production of all those goods of which cotton is the basis is diminished. If the total value added to cotton in its various manufactures, in a particular country, amounted to 100 millions of francs per annum, and the effect of the tax was to diminish the consumption one half, then the tax would deprive that country every year of 50 million of francs, in addition to the sum received by government." —Vol. ii. p. 314.

[31] It is observed by M. Say, "that a manufacturer is not enabled to make the consumer pay the whole tax levied on his commodity, because its increased price will diminish its consumption." Should this be the case, should the consumption be diminished, will not the supply also speedily be diminished? Why should the manufacturer continue in the trade if his profits are below the general level? M. Say appears here also to have forgotten the doctrine which he elsewhere supports, "that the cost of production determines the price, below which commodities cannot fall for any length of time, because production would be then either suspended or diminished." —Vol. ii. p. 26.

"The tax in this case falls then partly on the consumer, who is obliged to give more for the commodity taxed, and partly on the producer, who, after deducting the tax will receive less. The public treasury will be benefited by what the purchaser pays in addition, and also by the sacrifice which the producer is obliged to make of a part of his profits. It is the effort of gunpowder, which acts at the same time on the bullet which it projects and on the gun which it causes to recoil." —Vol. ii. p. 333.

[32] "Melon says that the debts of a nation are debts due from the right hand to the left, by which the body is not weakened. It is true that the general wealth is not diminished by the payment of the interest on arrears of the debt: The dividends are a value which passes from the hand of the contributor to the national creditor: Whether it be the national creditor or the contributor who accumulates or consumes it is, I agree, of little importance to the society; but the principal of the debt—what has become of that? It exists no more. The consumption which has followed the loan has annihilated a capital which will never yield any further revenue. The society is deprived not of the amount of interest, since that passes from one hand to the other, but of the revenue from a destroyed capital. This capital, if it had been employed productively by him who lent it to the state, would equally have yielded him an income, but that income would have been derived from a real production, and would not have been furnished from the pocket of a fellow citizen."—Say, vol. ii. p. 357. This is both conceived and expressed in the true spirit of the science.

[33] "Credit, in general, is good, as it allows capitals to leave those hands where they are not usefully employed, to pass into those where they will be made productive: it diverts a capital from an employment useful only to the capitalist, such as an investment in the public funds, to make it productive in the hands of industry. It facilitates the employments of all capitals, and leaves none unemployed."—*Economie Politique*, p. 463, vol. ii. 4th edition. This must be an oversight of M. Say. The capital of the stockholder can never be made productive—it is, in fact, no capital, If he were to sell his stock, and employ the capital he obtained for it, productively, he could only do so by detaching the capital of the buyer of his stock from a productive employment.

[34] "Manufacturing industry increases its produce in proportion to the demand, and the price falls; *but the produce of land cannot be so increased*; and a high price is still necessary to prevent the consumption from exceeding the sup-

ply." Buchanan, vol. iv. p. 40. Is it possible that Mr. Buchanan can seriously assert that the produce of the land cannot be increased if the demand increases?

[35] I wish the word "profit" had been omitted. Dr. Smith must suppose the profits of the tenants of these precious vineyards to be above the general rate of profits. If they were not, they would not pay the tax, unless they could shift it either to the landlord or consumer.

[36] Vol. iii. p. 355.

[37] In a former part of this work I have noticed the difference between rent, properly so called, and the remuneration paid to the landlord under that name for the advantages which the expenditure of his capital has procured to his tenant; but I did not perhaps sufficiently distinguish the difference which would arise from the different modes in which this capital might be applied. As a part of this capital, when once expended in the improvement of a farm, is inseparably amalgamated with the land, and tends to increase its productive powers, the remuneration paid to the landlord for its use is strictly of the nature of rent, and is subject to all the laws of rent. Whether the improvement be made at the expense of the landlord or the tenant, it will not be undertaken in the first instance unless there is a strong probability that the return will at least be equal to the profit that can be made by the disposition of any other equal capital; but when once made, the return obtained will ever after be wholly of the nature of rent, and will be subject to all the variations of rent. Some of these expenses, however, only give advantages to the land for a limited period, and do not add permanently to its productive powers: being bestowed on buildings, and other perishable improvements, they require to be constantly renewed, and therefore do not obtain for the landlord any permanent addition to his real rent.

[38] "Commerce enables us to obtain a commodity in the place where it is to be found, and to convey it to another where it is to be consumed; it therefore gives us the power of increasing the value of the commodity, by the whole difference between its price in the first of these places and its price in the second."—M. Say, p. 458, vol. ii.—True, but how is this additional value given to it? By adding to the cost of production, first, the expenses of conveyance; secondly, the profit on the advances of capital made by the merchant. The commodity is only more valuable for the same reasons that every other commodity may become more valuable, because more labor is expended on its production and conveyance before it is purchased by the consumer. This must not be mentioned as one of the advantages of commerce. When the subject is more closely examined, it will be found that the whole benefits of commerce resolve themselves into the means which it gives us of acquiring, not more valuable objects, but more useful ones.

[39] In the last volume of the supplement to the *Encyclopaedia Britannica*, article "Corn. Laws and Trade," are the following excellent suggestions and observations:— "If we shall at any future period think of retracing our steps, in order to give time to withdraw capital from the cultivation of our poor soils, and to invest it in more lucrative employments, a gradually diminishing scale of duties may be adopted. The price at which foreign grain should be admitted duty free may be made to decrease from 80s, its present limit, by 4s. or 5s. per quarter annually till it reaches 50s., when the ports could safely be thrown open, and the restrictive system be for ever abolished. When this happy event shall have taken place, it will be no longer necessary to force nature. The capital and enterprise of the country will be turned into those departments of industry in which our physical situation, national character, or political institutions fit us to excel. The corn of Poland and the raw cotton of Carolina will be exchanged for the wares of Birmingham and the muslins of Glasgow. The genuine commercial spirit, that which permanently secures the prosperity of nations, is altogether inconsistent with the dark and shallow policy of monopoly. The nations of the earth are like provinces of the same kingdom—a free and unfettered intercourse is alike productive of general and of local advantage." The whole article is well worthy of attention; it is very instructive, is ably written, and shows that the author is completely master of the subject.

[40] Whatever capital becomes fixed on the land must necessarily be the landlord's, and not the tenant's, at the expiration of the lease. Whatever compensation the landlord may receive for this capital on re-letting his land

will appear in the form of rent; but no rent will be paid if, with a given capital, more corn can be obtained from abroad than can be grown on this land at home. If the circumstances of the society should require corn to be imported, and 1000 quarters can be obtained by the employment of a given capital, and if this land, with the employment of the same capital, will yield 1100 quarters, 100 quarters will necessarily go to rent; but if 1200 can be got from abroad, then this land will go out of cultivation, for it will not then yield even the general rate of profit. But this is no disadvantage, however great the capital may have been that had been expended on the land. Such capital is spent with a view to augment the produce—that, it should be remembered, is the end; of what importance, then, can it be to the society whether half its capital be sunk in value, or even annihilated, if they obtain a great annual quantity of production?

Those who deplore the loss of capital in this case are for sacrificing the end to the means.

[41] Among the most able of the publications on the impolicy of restricting the importation of corn may be classed Major Torrens' *Essay on the External Corn Trade.* His arguments appear to me to be unanswered, and to be unanswerable.

[42] Adam Smith says, "that the difference between the real and the nominal price of commodities and labor is not a matter of mere speculation, but may sometimes be of considerable use in practice." I agree with him; but the real price of labor and commodities is no more to be ascertained by their price in goods, Adam Smith's real measure, than by their price in gold and silver, his nominal measure. The laborer is only paid a really high price for his labor when his wages will purchase the produce of a great deal of labor.

[43] In vol. i. p. 108, M. Say infers, that silver is now of the same value, as in the reign of Louis XIV, "because the same quantity of silver will buy the same quantity of corn."

[44] *Elemens d'Ideologie*, vol. iv. p. 99.—In this work M. de Tracy has given a useful and an able treatise on the general principles of Political Economy, and I am sorry to be obliged to add that he supports, by his authority, the definitions which M. Say has given of the words "value," "riches," and "utility."

[45] "The first man who knew how to soften metals by fire is not the creator of the value which that process adds to the melted metal. That value is the result of the physical action of fire added to the industry and capital of those who availed themselves of this knowledge."

From this error Smith has drawn this false result, "that the value of all productions represents the recent or former labor of man, *or, in other words, that riches are nothing else but accumulated labor; from which, by a second consequence, equally false, labor is the sole measure of riches, or of the value of productions.*"—Chap. iv. p. 31. The inferences with which M. Say concludes are his own and not Dr. Smith's; they are correct if no distinction be made between value and riches, and in this passage M. Say makes none: but though Adam Smith, who deemed riches to consist in the abundance of necessaries, convenience, and enjoyments of human life, would have allowed that machines and natural agents might very greatly add to the riches of a country, he would not have allowed that they add anything to the value of those riches.

[46] Adam Smith speaks of Holland as affording an instance of the fall of profits from the accumulation of capital, and from every employment being consequently overcharged. "The government there borrows at 2 percent, and private people of good credit at 3 percent." But it should be remembered that Holland was obliged to import almost all the corn which she consumed, and by imposing heavy taxes on the necessaries of the laborer she further raised the wages of labor. These facts will sufficiently account for the low rate of profits and interest in Holland.

[47] Is the following quite consistent with M. Say's principle? "The more disposable capitals are abundant in proportion to the extent of employment for them, the more will the rate of interest on loans of capital fall."—Vol. ii. p. 108. If capital to any extent can be employed by a country, how can it be said to be abundant, compared with the extent of employment for it?

[48] Adam Smith says that, "When the produce of any particular branch of industry exceeds what the demand of the country requires, the surplus must be sent abroad, and exchanged for something for which there is a demand

at home. *Without such exportation, a part of the productive labor of the country must cease, and the value of its annual produce diminish.* The land and labor of Great Britain produce generally more corn, woolens, and hardware than the demand of the home market requires. The surplus part of them, therefore, must be sent abroad, and exchanged for something for which there is a demand at home.   It is only by means of such exportation that this surplus can acquire a value sufficient to compensate the labor and expense of producing it." One would be led to think by the above passage that Adam Smith concluded we were under some necessity of producing a surplus of corn, woolen goods, and hardware, and that the capital which produced them could not be otherwise employed. It is, however, always a matter of choice in what way a capital shall be employed, and therefore there can never for any length of time be a surplus of any commodity; for if there were, it would fall below its natural price, and capital would be removed to some more profitable employment. No writer has more satisfactorily and ably shown than Dr. Smith the tendency of capital to move from employments in which the goods produced do not repay by their price the whole expenses, including the ordinary profits, of producing and bringing them to market.— See chap. x. book i.

[49] "All kinds of public loans," observes M. Say, "are attended with the inconvenience of withdrawing capital, or portions of capital, from productive employments, to devote them to consumption; and when they take place in a country, *the government of which does not inspire much confidence*, they have the further inconvenience of raising the interest of capital. Who would lend at 5 percent, per annum to agriculture, to manufacturers, and to commerce, when a borrower may be found ready to pay an interest of 7 or 8 percent? That sort of income which is called profit of stock would rise then at the expense of the consumer. Consumption would be reduced *by* the rise in the price of produce; and the other productive services would be less in demand, less well paid. The whole nation, capitalists excepted, would be the sufferers from such a state of things." To the question, "who would lend money to farmers, manufacturers, and merchants, at 5 percent, per annum, when another borrower, having little credit, would give 7 or 8?" I reply, that every prudent and reasonable man would. Because the rate of interest is 7 or 8 percent there where the lender runs extraordinary risk is this any reason that it should be equally high in those places where they are secured from such risks? M. Say allows that the rate of interest depends on the rate of profits; but it does not therefore follow that the rate of profits depends on the rate of interest. One is the cause, the other the effect, and it is impossible for any circumstances to make them change places.

[50] In another place he says, that "whatever extension of the foreign market can be occasioned by the bounty must, in every particular year, be altogether at the expense of the home market, as every bushel of corn which is exported by means of the bounty, and which would not have been exported without the bounty, would have remained in the home market to increase the consumption and to lower the price of that commodity. The corn bounty, it is to be observed, as well as every other bounty upon exportation, imposes two different taxes upon the people:— first, the tax which they are obliged to contribute in order to pay the bounty; and, secondly, the tax which arises from the advanced price of the commodity in the home market, and which, as the whole body of the people are purchasers of corn, must, in this particular commodity, be paid by the whole body of the people. In this particular commodity, therefore, this second tax is by much the heaviest of the two." For every five shillings, therefore, which they contribute to the payment of the first tax, they must contribute six pounds four shillings to the payment of the second. "The extraordinary exportation of corn, therefore, occasioned by the bounty, not only in every particular year diminishes the home just as much as it extends the foreign market and consumption; but, by restraining the population and industry of the country, its final tendency is to stunt and restrain the gradual extension of the home market, and thereby, in the long run, rather to diminish than to augment the whole market and consumption of corn."

[51] The same opinion is held by M. Say.—Vol. ii. p. 335.

[52] See chapter on Rent.

[53] M. Say supposes the advantage of the manufacturers at home to be more than temporary. "A government which absolutely prohibits the importation of certain foreign goods establishes a monopoly *in favor of those* who produce such commodities at home *against those* who consume them; in other words, those at home who produce them having the exclusive privilege of selling them, may elevate their price above the natural price; and the consumers at home, not being able to obtain them elsewhere, are obliged to purchase them at a higher price." —Vol. i. p. 201. But how can they permanently support the market price of their goods above the natural price, when every one of their fellow citizens is free to enter into the trade? They are guaranteed against foreign, but not against home competition. The real evil arising to the country from such monopolies, if they can be called by that name, lies not in raising the market price of such goods, but in raising their real and natural price. By increasing the cost of production, a portion of the labor of the country is less productively employed.

[54] "A freedom of trade is alone wanted to guarantee a country like Britain, abounding in all the varied products of industry, in merchandise suited to the wants of every society, from the possibility of a scarcity. The nations of the earth are not condemned to throw the dice to determine which of them shall submit to famine. There is always abundance of food in the world. To enjoy a constant plenty we have only to lay aside our prohibitions and restrictions, and cease to counteract the benevolent wisdom of Providence." —Article "Corn Laws and Trade," Supplement to *Encyclopedia Britannica*.

[55] Are not the following passages contradictory to the one above quoted? "Besides, that home trade, though less noticed (because it is in a variety of hands), is the most considerable, it is also the most profitable. The commodities exchanged in that trade are necessarily the productions of the same country." ——Vol. i. p. 84.

"The English government has not observed that the most profitable sales are those which a country makes to itself, because they cannot take place without two values being produced by the nation; the value which is sold, and the value with which the purchase is made." —Vol. i. p. 221.

I shall, in the twenty-sixth chapter, examine the soundness of this opinion.

[56] See Chapter 9, paragraphs 10–12.

[57] M. Say is of the same opinion with Adam Smith: "The most productive employment of capital, for the country in general, after that on the land, is that of manufactures and of home trade; because it puts in activity an industry of which the profits are gained in the country, while those capitals which are employed in foreign commerce make the industry and lands of all countries to be productive, without distinction.

"The employment of capital the least favorable to a nation is that of carrying the produce of one foreign country to another." —Say, vol. ii. p. 120.

[58] Perhaps this is expressed too strongly, as more is generally allotted to the laborer under the name of wages than the absolutely necessary expenses of production. In that case a part of the net produce of the country is received by the laborer, and may be saved or expended by him; or it may enable him to contribute to the defense of the country.

[59] M. Say has totally misunderstood me in supposing that I have considered as nothing the happiness of so many human beings. I think the text sufficiently shows that I was confining: my remarks to the particular grounds on which Adam Smith had rested it.

[60] "It is fortunate that the natural course of things draws capital, not to those employments where the greatest profits are made, but to those where the operation is most profitable to the community." —Vol. ii. p. 122. M. Say has not told us what those employments are which, while they are the most profitable to the individual, are not the most profitable to the state. If countries with limited capitals, but with abundance of fertile land, do not early engage in foreign trade, the reason is, because it is less profitable to individuals, and therefore also less profitable to the state.

[61] Whatever I say of gold coin is equally applicable to silver coin; but it is not necessary to mention both on every occasion.

[62] This, and the following paragraphs, to the close of the bracket, p. 244, is extracted from a pamphlet entitled *Proposals for an Economical and Secure Currency,* published by the author in the year 1816.

[63] The price of £3 17s. here mentioned is of course an arbitrary price. There might be good reason, perhaps, for fixing it either a little above or a little below.   In naming £3 17s., I wish only to elucidate the principle. The price ought to be so fixed as to make it the interest of the seller of gold rather to sell it to the Bank than to carry it to the Mint to be coined.

The same remark applies to the specified quantity of twenty ounces.

There might be good reason for making it ten or thirty.

[64] It has lately been contended in Parliament by Lord Lauderdale that, with the existing Mint regulation, the Bank could not pay their notes in specie, because the relative value of the two metals is such that it would be for the interest of all debtors to pay their debts with silver and not with gold coin, while the law gives a power to all the creditors of the Bank to demand gold in exchange for Bank notes. This gold, his lordship thinks, could be profitably exported, and if so, he contends that the Bank, to keep a supply, will be obliged to buy gold constantly at a premium and sell it at par. If every other debtor could pay in silver, Lord Lauderdale would be right; but he cannot do so if his debt exceed 40s. This, then, would limit the amount of silver coin in circulation (if government had not reserved to itself the power to stop the coinage of that metal whenever they might think it expedient); because if too much silver were coined it would sink in relative value to gold, and no man would accept it in payment for a debt exceeding 40s., unless a compensation were made for its lower value. To pay a debt of £100, 100 sovereigns, or bank notes to the amount of £100, would be necessary, but £105 in silver coin might be required if there were too much silver in circulation. There are, then, two checks against an excessive quantity of silver coin; first, the direct check which government may at any time interpose to prevent more from being coined; secondly, no motive of interest would lead any one to take silver to the Mint, if he might do so, for if it were coined, it would not pass current at its Mint but only at its market value.

[65] If, with the quantity of gold and silver which actually exists, these metals only served for the manufacture of utensils and ornaments, they would be abundant, and would be much cheaper than they are at present: in other words, in exchanging them for any other species of goods, we should be obliged to give proportionally a greater quantity of them. But as a large quantity of these metals is used for money, and as this portion is used for no other purpose, there remains less to be employed in furniture and jewelry; now this scarcity adds to their value. —Say, vol. ii. p. 316.

[66] *An Inquiry into the Nature and Origin of Public Wealth,* p. 13.

[67] "The demand for labor depends on the increasing of circulating and not of fixed capital. Were it true that the proportion between these two sorts of capital is the same at all times, and in all countries, then, indeed, it follows that the number of laborers employed is in proportion to the the wealth of the state. But such a position has not the semblance of probability. As arts are cultivated, and civilization is extended, fixed capital bears a larger and larger proportion to circulating capital. The amount of fixed capital employed in the production of a piece of British muslin is at least a hundred, probably a thousand times greater than that employed in the production of a similar piece of Indian muslin. And the proportion of circulating capital employed is a hundred or a thousand times less. It is easy to conceive that, under certain circumstances, the whole of the annual savings of an industrious people might be added to fixed capital, in which case they would have no effect in increasing the demand for labor." —Barton, *On the Condition of the Laboring Classes of Society,* page 16.

It is not easy, I think, to conceive that, under any circumstances, an increase of capital should not be followed by an increased demand for labor; the most that can be said is, that the demand will be in a diminishing ratio. Mr. Barton, in the above publication, has, I think, taken a correct view of some of the effects of an increasing amount of fixed capital on the condition of the laboring classes. His essay contains much valuable information.

68 *An Inquiry into the Nature and Progress of Rent*, p. 15.

69 See [Chapter 6, paragraphs 16–18], where I have endeavored to show that whatever facility or difficulty there may be in the production of corn, wages and profits together will be of the same value. When wages rise; it is always at the expense of profits, and when they fall, profits always rise.

70 Mr. Malthus has observed in a late publication that I have misunderstood him in this passage, as he did not mean to say that rent immediately and necessarily rises and falls with the increased or diminished fertility of the land. If so, I certainly did misunderstand him. Mr. Malthus's words are, "Diminish this plenty, diminish the fertility of the soil, and the excess (rent) will diminish; diminish it still further, and it will disappear." Mr. Malthus does not state his proposition conditionally, but absolutely. I contended against what I understood him to maintain, that a diminution of the fertility of the soil was incompatible with an increase of rent.

71 Of what increased quantity does Mr. Malthus speak? Who is to produce it? Who can have any motive to produce it before any demand exists for an additional quantity?

72 *Inquiry*, etc. "In all progressive countries the average price of corn is never higher than what is necessary to continue the average increase of produce." —*Observations*, p. 21.

"In the employment of fresh capital upon the land, to provide for the wants of an increasing population, whether this fresh capital is employed in bringing more land under the plough, or improving land already in cultivation, the main question always depends upon the expected returns of this capital; and no part of the gross profits can be diminished without diminishing the motive to this mode of employing it. Every diminution of price not fully and immediately balanced by a proportionate fall in all the necessary expenses of a farm, every tax on the land, every tax on farming stock, every tax on the necessaries of farmers, will tell in the computation; and if, after all these outgoings are allowed for, the price of the produce will not leave a fair remuneration for the capital employed, according to the general rate of profits, and a rent at least equal to the rent of the land in its former state, no sufficient motive can exist to undertake the projected improvement." —*Observations*, p. 22.

73 See p. 72.

74 See page 44, etc

75 It is not necessary to state on every occasion, but it must be always understood, that the same results will follow, as far as regards the price of raw produce and the rise of rents, whether an additional capital of a given amount be employed on new land, for which no rent is paid, or on land already in cultivation, if the produce obtained from both be precisely the same in quantity. —See p. 37.

M. Say, in his notes to the French translation of this work, has endeavored to show that there is not at any time land in cultivation which does not pay a rent, and having satisfied himself on this point, he concludes that he has overturned all the conclusions which result from that doctrine. He infers, for example, that I am not correct in saying that taxes on corn and other raw produce, by elevating their price, fall on the consumer, and do not fall on rent. He contends that such taxes must fall on rent. But before M. Say can establish the correctness of this inference, he must also show that there is not any capital employed on the land for which no rent is paid (see the beginning of this note, and pages 33 and 38 of the present work); now this he has not attempted to do. In no part of his notes has he refuted or even noticed that important doctrine. By his note to page 182 of the second volume of the French edition, he does not appear to be aware that it has even been advanced.

76 *Observations on the Corn Laws*, p. 4.

77 Upon showing this passage to Mr. Malthus, at the time when these papers were going to the press, he observed, "that in these two instances he had inadvertently used the term *real price*, instead of *cost of production*. It will be

seen, from what I have already said, that to me it appears that in these two instances he has used the term *real price* in its true and just acceptation, and that in the former case only it is incorrectly applied.

[78] [Chapter 1, paragraph 69].

[79] Manufactures, indeed, could not fall in any such proportion, because, under the circumstances supposed, there would be a new distribution of the precious metals among the different countries. Our cheap commodities would be exported in exchange for corn and gold, till the accumulation of gold should lower its value and raise the money price of commodities.

[80] *The Grounds of an Opinion, etc.,* p. 36.

[81] Mr. Malthus, in another part of the same work, supposes commodities to vary 25 or 20 percent, when corn varies 331/3.

[82] Of net produce and gross produce M. Say speaks as follows: "The whole value produced is the gross produce; this value, after deducting from it the cost of production, is the net produce." —Vol. ii. p. 491. There can, then, be no net produce, because the cost of production, according to M. Say, consists of rent, wages, and profits. In page 508 he says, "The value of a product, the value of a productive service, the value of the cost of production, are all, then, similar values, whenever things are left to their natural course." Take a whole from a whole and nothing remains.

[83] Mr. M'Culloch, in an able publication, has very strongly contended for the justice of making the dividends on the national debt conform to the reduced value of corn. He is in favor of a free trade in corn, but he thinks it should be accompanied by a reduction of interest to the national creditor.

Charles Mackay (1814–1889)

AN INTRODUCTION TO HIS LIFE AND WORK

Charles Mackay was a celebrated journalist and a widely popular poet whose greatest recognition came when some of his verses were set to music. During his lifetime he received many accolades, but not once was he hailed as the author of the most insightful book ever written about market psychology, as he often is today. In fact, while *Extraordinary Popular Delusions and the Madness of Crowds* was greeted with positive response upon publication more than one hundred fifty years ago, it was not considered a seminal work. Rather, it was seen as a historical recounting of various scams and schemes and the ensuing madness that played out as folks scrambled to make a quick buck. It is believed Mackay saw the book as an opportunity to warn the citizens of his time against jumping on a risky financial band wagon, rather than as an opportunity to explore the science of mass hysteria and crowd behavior. The fact that there is no genuine analysis is perhaps why the book was originally viewed more as a collection of cautionary tales rather than as an essential work of social science.

HIS LIFE

Charles Mackay was born on March 27, 1814, in Perth, Scotland, the son of a navy lieutenant. His mother died while he was an infant, so Mackay was cared for by a nurse, Grace Stuart, until he was eight years old. Stuart married Thomas Threlkeld in 1822, at which time Mackay went to live with them in Woolrich.

Mackay attended the Caledonian Asylum in London beginning in 1825, and three years later his father enrolled him in a school in Brussels where he became fluent in French, German, Spanish, and Italian. In 1830, Mackay became private secretary to William Cockerill, an ironmaster in Belgium. When not working, he showed the first signs of literary aspirations writing articles in French for the *Courier Belge* and English poems for *The Telegraph*, a local newspaper.

Returning to London in 1832, he initially supported himself by teaching Italian, before becoming an occasional contributor to The Sun and publishing his first book, *Songs and Poems*, in 1834. The following year Mackay landed his first permanent job in journalism, joining the staff of the Morning Chronicle as an assistant sub editor, where one of his colleagues was Charles Dickens. Mackay quickly established himself as an industrious and highly regarded journalist.

During his time at the *Morning Chronicle*, Mackay published *Memoirs of Extraordinary Popular Delusions* in 1841, with the promise of additional material should the original work meet with a favorable response. The substantially revised two volume set, *Extraordinary Popular Delusions and the Madness of Crowds*, was released in 1852, and to this day is still regarded as a classic study of social science and mass behavior. The first three chapters of the book, which detail the Mississippi Scheme, the South Sea Bubble, and Tulipomania, expertly warn against the dangers of market speculation.

In fall of 1844, Mackay left the *Morning Chronicle* to become editor of the *Glasgow Argus*. While in Scotland, his poems often appeared in the *Daily News*, a newspaper established by Charles Dickens. It was these poems that brought Mackay his greatest recognition when he released *Voices from the Crowd* in 1846. Many of the verses were set to music by Henry Russell and became wildly popular throughout the world—the most famous being *The Good Time Coming*.

Mackay returned to London in 1848 to work for the *Illustrated London News*, of which he was named editor in 1852. From 1851 to 1855, the magazine issued one of his songs as a weekly supplement, bringing him even greater notoriety when they were published in a singular volume.

After leaving the *Illustrated London News* in 1859, Mackay launched two ventures—The London Review (1860) and Robin Goodfellow (1861)—but both magazines failed. Mackay then went on to serve as special correspondent for the *Times* in New York from 1862 to 1865 during the civil war and is credited with revealing the Fenian conspiracy in America. Mackay spent his later years traveling and lecturing before publishing a two-volume autobiography, *Forty Years Recollections* and *Through the Long Day*, two years before he died on December 24, 1889.

Mackay was widowed twice and survived by three sons and daughter upon his death. Celebrated as a poet, song writer, journalist, and author during his life, Mackay is most well-known today for having written *Extraordinary Popular Delusions and the Madness of Crowds*.

AN OVERVIEW OF THE WORK

Regardless of its perception upon release, the measure of *Extraordinary Popular Delusions and the Madness of Crowds* has grown exponentially over time and established Mackay's reputation as an astute critic of social and financial history. Today, the book is regarded a classic text on human behavior. The book explores the mysterious allure of stock speculation, alchemy, witches, haunted houses, and the crusades, but it is the first three chapters, which detail some of the earliest stock bubbles, that enforce the merit of the book in regards to the world we live today.

Mackay uses case studies of the Mississippi Scheme, the South-Sea Bubble, and Tulipomania to showcase the power of greed and demonstrate how easily intelligent and sensible human beings can be manipulated and led astray by following pack mentality when the opportunity to get rich presents itself, no matter how dangerously it is cloaked. This seems to be the only way to explain why normally rational individuals would risk their

life savings by purchasing stock in a company that promised to change warfare by manufacturing square cannonballs or why others might sell their homes in order to purchase
a flower that looks like an onion (more on that later). In the end, the book proves how
even the sanest individuals are capable of being swept up by mass hysteria when the allure of the mighty dollar is dangled before them like a carrot on a stick.

For the modern day investor to appreciate the relevance of the book, first one needs
to see how individuals were enticed by stock market bubbles more than three hundred
and four hundred years ago. A brief snapshot of the first three chapters lends even greater
credence to the cliché that the more things change, the more they stay the same.

*"Men, it has been said, think in herds; it will be seen that they go mad in herds, while they only re-
cover their senses slowly, and one by one."* —*Charles Mackay*

The Mississippi Scheme was a financial arrangement orchestrated by Scotsman John
Law in France in 1717. In short, the plan initially centered on the development of the
territory now known as Louisiana, but then referred to as Mississippi. After Law gained
a monopoly on commercial concessions in that territory from financier Antoine Crozat,
he created the Compagnie d'Occident. Soon popular belief was that this venture was a
license to print money, so stock in the company sold feverishly. But the promise of even
greater riches arrived in 1718 and 1719, thanks to a favorable series of events. First, the
company obtained sole rights to trading tobacco from the French East India Company;
secondly, it was granted control over public debt accrued by the French government and
given the right to collect taxes. Now renamed The Mississippi Company, this reconfig-
ured company jumpstarted a financial feeding frenzy rarely seen before, as Law launched
an effective publicity campaign that exaggerated the company's prospects and encouraged
widespread stock speculation. Wealthy and poor individuals lined the streets and camped
outside of Law's residence, willing to sacrifice their savings and possessions in hopes of
buying stock. It was a scene cut straight from Roald Dahl's *Charlie and the Chocolate
Factory*, but instead of trying to secure a golden ticket, folks were trying to secure stock
shares. The demand so far outweighed supply that one woman deliberately crashed her
horse and carriage in hopes of earning Law's sympathy and attention. It worked; he sold
her a number of shares. By the tail end of 1719, shares were selling at nearly fifty times
their original value. During this time, as the price of the stock rose it was not uncommon for a person of modest means to awaken poor and go to bed rich. Yet, by the summer of 1720, confidence in the company began to falter and stock prices nose-dived and
panic set in throughout the country. Law's attempts to salvage the situation by first setting the price at a certain value, and then later deflating the price only caused greater dis-
ruption. As expected, the bubble burst and individuals and families who were caught in
the vortex of the hysteria surrounding the Mississippi Scheme were rendered penniless,
only left to wonder how they allowed themselves to be tempted by such a deadly fruit.

The South-Sea Bubble took place in England at almost the same time the Mississippi
Scheme was devastating France. The two scams share many other similar characteris-

tics, the most obvious being that once again educated and sensible people were enticed by the prospect of instant wealth, and were willing to gamble their individual and family fortunes on unfounded stock speculations.

The South-Sea Bubble sprang from the incorporation of the South Sea Company in 1711, and ended with the veritable bubble bursting nine years later. The company was originally formed when it was granted exclusive trading rights with South America and the Pacific Islands, with the hope that the treaty that would end the War of the Spanish Succession would also allow for bountiful trade. The treaty that was eventually signed allowed for restricted trade, and the initial voyage in 1716 was met with limited success. These were not exactly the results the company had hoped for, but their fortunes changed the following year when the King of England was named governor of the company. This shift in management instilled an overwhelming confidence in the public, who began clamoring to buy the stock. Once again, demand far exceeded supply and the price of the stock skyrocketed. But this is where the legacy of the South-Sea Bubble takes a different shape. Enterprising investors (to be polite) and swindlers in various guises preyed on those individuals unable to purchase South Sea stock by offering them other get-rich-quick opportunities via bubble companies. Individuals were given the chance to buy shares in a company manufacturing a perpetually spinning wheel or one carrying out an undisclosed undertaking of great advantage (no additional information was provided). Certainly it is easy to see how frivolous these opportunities were, but as money mania swept through England and every other person seemed to be striking it rich, it was nearly impossible for people to turn their backs on a potential windfall, and these nefarious companies thrived. In 1720, South-Sea stock rose from one hundred to one thousand pounds a share in August, when the stock finally reached its ceiling and selling frenzy ensued, driving the price back down to 124 by December. As the South Sea stock plummeted, so did the stock prices of all the other bubble companies that had popped up on the landscape. While a certain lucky few were able to escape with a fortune, the majority went bankrupt, only left to wonder why and what if. An investigation into this financial massacre by the House of Commons revealed numerous bookkeeping discrepancies (undoubtedly one of the earliest cases of cooking the books) and that three prominent ministers had accepted bribes in return for driving up the price of the stock. Although these events transpired more than three hundred years ago, the whole scenario sounds like something pulled from the front pages of today's *Wall Street Journal*.

"Every age has its peculiar folly: some scheme, project, or fantasy which it plunges, spurred on by the love of gain, the necessity of excitement, or the mere force of imitation." —Charles Mackay

The most celebrated and well-known financial bubble Charles Mackay documented was Tulipomania. This account is viewed with skepticism and amazement. The outrageousness and audacity of tying one's financial fortunes on a single flower seems beyond the scope of even an irrational human being, let alone an entire country. Yet the events that transpired in Holland beginning in 1634 tell a different story, as it was considered in bad taste for any person of even moderate wealth to be without a collection of tulips.

From this determination sprang a hysteria that swept through the country, as the race was on to possess the rarest tulips regardless of the price. Soon the ordinary industry of the Dutch country was neglected, as citizens from all social classes began taking part in the tulip trade. Prices for tulips reached stratospheric heights as certain rare bulbs sold for more than four thousand florins. Consider that at the time, eight fat swine cost 240 florins and one thousand pounds of cheese cost 120 florins, and you'll better understand how ridiculously overpriced these tulips were. An even better gauge of assessing the tenor of the times is the story concerning the aforementioned onion. It seems a wealthy merchant rewarded a sailor for his assistance with a particular trade with some fine red herring. The sailor in turn took an onion to accompany his meal, thinking it would not be missed from the merchant's shop. When the merchant later confronted the sailor in panic as the sailor was eating the last bite of the onion, the sailor learned that what he had eaten with his herring was no ordinary onion, but a rare and valuable tulip. Although it was the merchant who was sick to his stomach, it was the sailor who suffered most, as he was imprisoned on felony charges.

By 1636, the demand for tulips had become so widespread that markets were set up throughout the country to conduct sales on the Stock Exchange of Amsterdam. Now the game was on, as stock-jobbers treated tulips like a more traditional stock and immediately began manipulating the price. Initially prices rose in an effort to boost consumer confidence, and those who "invested" made a profit. Popular belief was that the fascination with tulips would continue, and the wealthy from around the word would embark for Holland and pay exorbitant amounts for these prized possessions. Individuals were so certain this scenario would play out that they liquidized all their assets in an effort to purchase as many tulips as possible. But, as with the previous two scenarios, reality struck with a thud. In 1637, the wisest purveyors of tulips realized the mania could not last and soon they began selling their flowers for profit and in turn the price for the bulbs quickly bottomed-out and many speculators were left in financial ruin. Panic ensued, as certain individuals were left holding contracts to purchase tulips for ten times the market rate, while others owned bulbs only worth a fraction of what they paid for them. Attempts were made to resolve these discrepancies, but ultimately the Dutch court ruled that all were stuck with the flowers they possessed at the time of the crash and no contracts need be honored, on the grounds that the debts were acquired through gambling, and not enforceable by law.

MACKAY'S RELEVANCE

Three or four hundred years ago, *Extraordinary Popular Delusions and the Madness of Crowds* would have served as a crystal ball, shedding light on the financial traumas the United States has endured over the last one hundred years. From the stock market crash of 1929, to the slumps the market withstood in the late 60s and mid 70s, to the junk bond scandal of the 1980s, the stories Mackay chronicled are a precursor to these very events. But of even greater immediate relevance is how much the Mississippi Scheme, South-Sea Bubble, and Tulipomania mirror the dot-com bubble and the disasters embroiling companies like Enron and Tyco. Obviously the mania to get rich quick is most apparent, but it's the specific details that are even more haunting. The over-inflated stock prices of tulips immediately calls to mind a dot-com company like Priceline, whose share price zoomed high before crashing back to earth—but not before company spokesman William Shattner sold his shares for considerable profit, unlike many less-fortunate investors. The many risky and less-than-solid bubble companies that sprang up around the time of the South Sea Company resemble the countless start-ups like Pets.com (which sold pet supplies online) and Kozmo.com (which promised delivery of anything in less than one hour) that littered the landscape in the late 1990s before falling under the weight of their own expectations. Likewise, the manner in which John Law and others exaggerated the potential of the Mississippi Company is eerily similar to what the key officers did at Enron—right down to the way they cost those who put their faith in the company their personal fortunes. As Mackay's book proves, we only need to look to the past to see what the future holds. So when the next stock market bubble captures the fascination of millions, rather than wonder how so many could be driven mad by greed, perhaps you'll now better understand how any individual or group is liable to be swept away by mass hysteria when the promise is great wealth. Sadly though, as Mackay deftly shows, there are no sure things when you gamble with your hard-earned money on highly speculative properties, particularly when you might not have the discipline to walk away from the table when the cards aren't turning in your favor or the dice seem to have a mind of their own.

SELECTIONS FROM MEMOIRS OF EXTRAORDINARY POPULAR DELUSIONS AND THE MADNESS OF CROWDS BY CHARLES MACKAY

CHAPTER 1

The Mississippi Scheme

Some in clandestine companies combine;
Erect new stocks to trade beyond the line;
With air and empty names beguile the town,
And raise new credits first, then cry 'em down;
Divide the empty nothing into shares,
And set the crowd together by the ears.
—Defoe.

The personal character and career of one man are so intimately connected with the great scheme of the years 1719 and 1720, that a history of the Mississippi madness can have no fitter introduction than a sketch of the life of its great author, John Law. Historians are divided in opinion as to whether they should designate him a knave or a madman. Both epithets were unsparingly applied to him in his lifetime, and while the unhappy consequences of his projects were still deeply felt. Posterity, however, has found reason to doubt the justice of the accusation, and to confess that John Law was neither knave nor madman, but one more deceived than deceiving; more sinned against than sinning. He was thoroughly acquainted with the philosophy and true principles of credit. He understood the monetary question better than any man of his day; and if his system fell with a crash so tremendous, it was not so much his fault as that of the people amongst whom he had erected it. He did not calculate upon the avaricious frenzy of a whole nation; he did not see that confidence, like mistrust, could be increased, almost ad infinitum, and that hope was as extravagant as fear. How was he to foretell that the French people, like the man in the fable, would kill, in their frantic eagerness, the fine goose he had brought to lay them so many golden eggs? His fate was like that which may be supposed to have overtaken the first adventurous boatman who rowed from Erie to Ontario. Broad and smooth was the river on which he embarked; rapid and pleasant was his progress; and who was to stay him in his career? Alas for him! the cataract was nigh. He saw, when it was too late, that the tide which wafted him so joyously along was a tide of destruction; and when he endeavored to retrace his way, he found that the current was too strong for his weak efforts to stem, and that he drew nearer every instant to the tremendous falls. Down he went over the sharp rocks, and the waters with him. He was dashed to pieces with his bark, but the waters, maddened and turned to foam by the rough descent, only boiled and bubbled for a time, and then flowed on again as smoothly as ever. Just so it was with Law and the French people. He was the boatman and they were the waters.

John Law was born at Edinburgh in the year 1671. His father was the younger son of an ancient family in Fife, and carried on the business of a goldsmith and banker. He amassed considerable wealth in his trade, sufficient to enable him to gratify the wish, so common among his countrymen, of adding a territorial designation to his name. He purchased with this view the estates of Lauriston and Randleston, on the Frith of Forth on the borders of West and Mid Lothian, and was thenceforth known as Law of Lauriston. The subject of our memoir, being the eldest son, was received into his father's counting-house at the age of fourteen, and for three years labored hard to acquire an insight into the principles of banking, as then carried on in Scotland. He had always manifested great love for the study of numbers, and his proficiency in the mathematics was considered extraordinary in one of his tender years. At the age of seventeen he was tall, strong, and well made; and his face, although deeply scarred with the small-pox, was agreeable in its expression, and full of intelligence. At this time he began to neglect his business, and becoming vain of his person, indulged in considerable extravagance of attire. He was a great favorite with the ladies, by whom he was called Beau Law, while the other sex, despising his foppery, nicknamed him Jessamy John. At the death of his father, which happened in 1688, he withdrew entirely from the desk, which had become so irksome, and being possessed of the revenues of the paternal estate of Lauriston, he proceeded to London, to see the world.

He was now very young, very vain, good-looking, tolerably rich, and quite uncontrolled. It is no wonder that, on his arrival in the capital, he should launch out into extravagance. He soon became a regular frequenter of the gaming-houses, and by pursuing a certain plan, based upon some abstruse calculation of chances, he contrived to gain considerable sums. All the gamblers envied him his luck, and many made it a point to watch his play, and stake their money on the same chances. In affairs of gallantry he was equally fortunate; ladies of the first rank smiled graciously upon the handsome Scotchman—the young, the rich, the witty, and the obliging. But all these successes only paved the way for reverses. After he had been for nine years exposed to the dangerous attractions of the gay life he was leading, he became an irrecoverable gambler. As his love of play increased in violence, it diminished in prudence. Great losses were only to be repaired by still greater ventures, and one unhappy day he lost more than he could repay without mortgaging his family estate. To that step he was driven at last. At the same time his gallantry brought him into trouble. A love affair, or slight flirtation, with a lady of the name of Villiers [Miss Elizabeth Villiers, afterwards Countess of Orkney] exposed him to the resentment of a Mr. Wilson, by whom he was challenged to fight a duel. Law accepted, and had the ill fortune to shoot his antagonist dead upon the spot. He was arrested the same day, and brought to trial for murder by the relatives of Mr. Wilson. He was afterwards found guilty, and sentenced to death. The sentence was commuted to a fine, upon the ground that the offence only amounted to manslaughter. An appeal being lodged by a brother of the deceased, Law was detained in the King's Bench, whence, by some means or other, which he never explained, he contrived to escape; and an action being instituted against the sheriffs, he was advertised in the Gazette, and a reward offered for his apprehension. He was described as "Captain John Law, a Scotchman, aged twenty-six; a very tall, black, lean man; well shaped, above six feet high, with large pock holes in his face; big nosed, and speaking broad and loud." As this was rather a caricature than a description of him, it has been supposed that it was drawn up with a view to favor his escape. He succeeded in reaching the Continent, where he traveled for three years, and devoted much of his attention to the monetary and banking affairs of the countries through which he passed. He stayed a few months in Amsterdam, and speculated to some extent in the funds. His mornings were devoted to the study of finance and the principles of trade, and his evenings to the gaming-house. It is generally believed that he returned to Edinburgh in the year 1700. It is certain that he published in that city his *Proposals and Reasons for constituting a Council of Trade*. This pamphlet did not excite much attention.

In a short time afterwards he published a project for establishing what he called a Land-bank [The wits of the day called it a sand-bank, which would wreck the vessel of the state.], the notes issued by which were never to exceed the value of the entire lands of the state, upon ordinary interest, or were to be equal in value to the land, with the right to enter into possession at a certain time. The project excited a good deal of discussion in the Scottish parliament, and a motion for the establishment of such a bank was brought forward by a neutral party, called the Squadrone, whom Law had interested in his favor. The Parliament ultimately passed a resolution to the effect, that, to establish any kind of paper credit, so as to force it to pass, was an improper expedient for the nation.

Upon the failure of this project, and of his efforts to procure a pardon for the murder of Mr. Wilson, Law withdrew to the Continent, and resumed his old habits of gaming. For fourteen years he continued to roam about, in Flanders, Holland, Germany, Hungary, Italy, and France. He soon became intimately acquainted with the extent of the trade and resources of each, and daily more confirmed in his opinion that no country could prosper without a paper currency. During the whole of this time he appears to have chiefly supported himself by successful play. At every gambling-house of note in the capitals of Europe, he was known and appreciated as one better skilled in the intricacies of chance than any other man of the day. It is stated in the *Biographie Universelle* that he was expelled, first from Venice, and afterwards from Genoa, by the magistrates, who thought him a visitor too dangerous for the youth of those cities. During his residence in Paris he rendered himself obnoxious to D'Argenson, the lieutenant-general of the police, by whom he was ordered to quit the capital. This did not take place, however, before he had made the acquaintance in the saloons, of the Duke de Vendome, the Prince de Conti, and of the gay Duke of Orleans, the latter of whom was destined afterwards to exercise so much influence over his fate. The Duke of Orleans was pleased with the vivacity and good sense of the Scottish adventurer, while the latter was no less pleased with the wit and amiability of a prince who promised to become his patron. They were often thrown into each other's society, and Law seized every opportunity to instill his financial doctrines into the mind of one whose proximity to the throne pointed him out as destined, at no very distant date, to play an important part in the government.

Shortly before the death of Louis XIV, or, as some say, in 1708, Law proposed a scheme of finance to Desmarets, the Comptroller. Louis is reported to have inquired whether the projector were a Catholic, and, on being answered in the negative, to have declined having anything to do with him. [This anecdote, which is related in the correspondence of Madame de Baviere, Duchess of Orleans, and mother of the regent, is discredited by Lord John Russell, in his "History of the principal States of Europe, from the Peace of Utrecht;" for what reason he does not inform us. There is no doubt that Law proposed his scheme to Desmarets, and that Louis refused to hear of it. The reason given for the refusal is quite consistent with the character of that bigoted and tyrannical monarch.]

It was after this repulse that he visited Italy. His mind being still occupied with schemes of finance, he proposed to Victor Amadeus, Duke of Savoy, to establish his land-bank in that country. The Duke replied that his dominions were too circumscribed for the execution of so great a project, and that he was by far too poor a potentate to be ruined. He advised him, however, to try the King of France once more; for he was sure, if he knew anything of the French character, that the people would be delighted with a plan, not only so new, but so plausible.

Louis XIV died in 1715, and the heir to the throne being an infant only seven years of age, the Duke of Orleans assumed the reins of government, as regent, during his minority. Law now found himself in a more favorable position. The tide in his affairs had come, which, taken at the flood, was to waft him on to fortune. The regent was his friend, already acquainted with his theory and pretensions, and inclined, moreover, to aid him in any efforts to restore the wounded credit of France, bowed down to the earth by the extravagance of the long reign of Louis XIV.

Hardly was that monarch laid in his grave ere the popular hatred, suppressed so long, burst forth against his memory. He who, during his life, had been flattered with an excess of adulation, to which history scarcely offers a parallel, was now cursed as a tyrant, a bigot, and a plunderer. His statues were pelted and disfigured; his effigies torn down, amid the execrations of the populace, and his name rendered synonymous with selfishness and oppression. The glory of his arms was forgotten, and nothing was remembered but his reverses, his extravagance, and his cruelty.

The finances of the country were in a state of the utmost disorder. A profuse and corrupt monarch, whose profuseness and corruption were imitated by almost every functionary, from the highest to the lowest grade, had brought France to the verge of ruin. The national debt amounted to 3000 millions of livres, the revenue to 145 millions, and the expenditure to 142 millions per annum; leaving only three millions to pay the interest upon 3000 millions. The first care of the regent was to discover a remedy for an evil of such magnitude, and a council was early summoned to take the matter into consideration. The Duke de St. Simon was of opinion that nothing could save the country from revolution but a remedy at once bold and dangerous. He advised the regent to convoke the States-General, and declare a national bankruptcy. The Duke de Noailles, a man of accommodating principles, an accomplished courtier, and totally averse from giving himself any trouble or annoyance that ingenuity could escape from, opposed the project of St. Simon with all his influence. He represented the expedient as alike dishonest and ruinous. The regent was of the same opinion, and this desperate remedy fell to the ground.

The measures ultimately adopted, though they promised fair, only aggravated the evil. The first, and most dishonest measure, was of no advantage to the state. A recoinage was ordered, by which the currency was depreciated one-fifth; those who took a thousand pieces of gold or silver to the mint received back an amount of coin of the same nominal value, but only four-fifths of the weight of metal. By this contrivance the treasury gained seventy-two millions of livres, and all the commercial operations of the country were disordered. A trifling diminution of the taxes silenced the clamors of the people, and for the slight present advantage the great prospective evil was forgotten.

A chamber of justice was next instituted, to inquire into the malversations of the loan-contractors and the farmers of the revenues. Tax collectors are never very popular in any country, but those of France at this period deserved all the odium with which they were loaded. As soon as these farmers-general, with all their hosts of subordinate agents, called *maltôtiers* [From maltote, an oppressive tax.], were called to account for their misdeeds, the most extravagant joy took possession of the nation. The Chamber of Justice, instituted chiefly for this purpose, was endowed with very extensive powers. It was composed of the presidents and councils of the parliament, the judges of the Courts of Aid and of Requests, and the officers of the Chamber of Account, under the general presidency of the minister of finance. Informers were encouraged to give evidence against the offenders by the promise of one-fifth part of the fines and confiscations. A tenth of all concealed effects belonging to the guilty was promised to such as should furnish the means of discovering them.

The promulgation of the edict constituting this court caused a degree of consternation among those principally concerned which can only be accounted for on the supposition that their peculation had been enormous. But they met with no sympathy. The proceedings against them justified their terror. The Bastile was soon unable to contain the prisoners that were sent to it, and the gaols all over the country teemed with guilty or suspected persons. An order was issued to all innkeepers and postmasters to refuse horses to such as endeavored to seek safety in flight; and all persons were forbidden, under heavy fines, to harbor them or favor their evasion. Some were condemned to the pillory, others to the gallies, and the least guilty to fine and imprisonment. One only, Samuel Bernard, a rich banker, and farmer-general of a province remote from the capital, was sentenced to death. So great had been the illegal profits of this man,—looked upon as the tyrant and oppressor of his district,—that he offered six millions of livres, or 250,000 pounds sterling, to be allowed to escape.

His bribe was refused, and he suffered the penalty of death. Others, perhaps more guilty, were more fortunate. Confiscation, owing to the concealment of their treasures by the delinquents, often produced less money than a fine. The severity of the government relaxed, and fines, under the denomination of taxes, were indiscriminately levied upon all offenders. But so corrupt was every department of the administration, that the country benefited but little by the sums which thus flowed into the treasury. Courtiers, and courtiers' wives and mistresses, came in for the chief share of the spoils. One contractor had been taxed in proportion to his wealth and guilt, at the sum of twelve millions of livres. The Count * * *, a man of some weight in the government, called upon him, and offered to procure a remission of the fine, if he would give him a hundred thousand crowns. "Vous êtes trop tard, mon ami," replied the financier; "I have already made a bargain with your wife for fifty thousand." [This anecdote is related by M. de la Hode, in his Life of Philippe of Orleans. It would have looked more authentic if he had given the names of the dishonest contractor and the still more dishonest minister. But M. de la Hode's book is liable to the same objection as most of the French memoirs of that and of subsequent periods. It is sufficient with most of them that an anecdote be ben trovato; the veto is but matter of secondary consideration.]

About a hundred and eighty millions of livres were levied in this manner, of which eighty were applied in payment of the debts contracted by the government. The remainder found its way into the pockets of the courtiers. Madame de Maintenon, writing on this subject, says, "We hear every day of some new grant of the regent; the people murmur very much at this mode of employing the money taken from the peculators." The people, who, after the first burst of their resentment is over, generally express a sympathy for the weak, were indignant that so much severity should be used to so little purpose. They did not see the justice of robbing one set of rogues to fatten another. In a few months all the more guilty had been brought to punishment, and the chamber of justice looked for victims in humbler walks of life. Charges of fraud and extortion were brought against tradesmen of good character, in consequence of the great inducements held out to common informers. They were compelled to lay open their affairs before this tribunal in order to establish their innocence. The voice of complaint resounded from every side, and at the expiration of a year the government found it advisable to discontinue further proceedings. The chamber of justice was suppressed, and a general amnesty granted to all against whom no charges had yet been preferred.

In the midst of this financial confusion Law appeared upon the scene. No man felt more deeply than the regent the deplorable state of the country, but no man could be more averse from putting his shoulders manfully to the wheel. He disliked business; he signed official documents without proper examination, and trusted to others what he should have undertaken himself. The cares inseparable from his high office were burdensome to him; he saw that something was necessary to be done, but he lacked the energy to do it, and had not virtue enough to sacrifice his case and his pleasures in the attempt. No wonder that, with this character, he listened favorably to the mighty projects, so easy of execution, of the clever adventurer whom he had formerly known, and whose talents he appreciated.

When Law presented himself at court, he was most cordially received. He offered two memorials to the regent, in which he set forth the evils that had befallen France, owing to an insufficient currency, at different times depreciated. He asserted that a metallic currency, unaided by a paper money, was wholly inadequate to the wants of a commercial country, and particularly cited the examples of Great Britain and Holland to show the advantages of paper. He used many sound arguments on the subject of credit, and proposed, as a means of restoring that of France, then at so low an ebb among the nations, that he should be allowed to set up a bank, which should have the management of the royal revenues, and issue notes, both on that and on landed security. He further proposed that this bank should be administered in the King's name, but subject to the control of commissioners, to be named by the States-General.

While these memorials were under consideration, Law translated into French his essay on money and trade, and used every means to extend through the nation his renown as a financier. He soon became talked of. The confidants of the regent spread abroad his praise, and every one expected great things of Monsieur Lass. [The French pronounced his name in this manner to avoid the ungallic sound, *aw*. After the failure of his scheme, the wags said the nation was lasse de lui, and proposed that he should in future be known by the name of Monsieur Helas!]

On the 5th of May, 1716, a royal edict was published, by which Law was authorized, in conjunction with his brother, to establish a bank, under the name of Law and Company, the notes of which should be received in payment of the taxes. The capital was fixed at six millions of livres, in twelve thousand shares of five hundred livres each, purchasable one-fourth in specie and the remainder in *billets d'état*. It was not thought expedient to grant him the whole of the privileges prayed for in his memorials until experience should have shown their safety and advantage.

Law was now on the high road to fortune. The study of thirty years was brought to guide him in the management of his bank. He made all his notes payable at sight, and in the coin current at the time they were issued. This last was a master-stroke of policy, and immediately rendered his notes more valuable than the precious metals. The latter were constantly liable to depreciation by the unwise tampering of the government. A thousand livres of silver might be worth their nominal value one day and be reduced one-sixth the next, but a note of Law's bank retained its original value. He publicly declared at the same time that a banker deserved death if he made issues without having sufficient security to answer all demands. The consequence was, that his notes advanced rapidly in public estimation, and were received at one percent more than specie. It was not long before the trade of the country felt the benefit. Languishing commerce began to lift up her head; the taxes were paid with greater regularity and less murmuring, and a degree of confidence was established that could not fail, if it continued, to become still more advantageous. In the course of a year Law's notes rose to fifteen percent premium, while the *billets d'état*, or notes issued by the government, as security for the debts contracted by the extravagant Louis XIV, were at a discount of no less than seventy-eight and a half percent. The comparison was too great in favor of Law not to attract the attention of the whole kingdom, and his credit extended itself day by day. Branches of his bank were almost simultaneously established at Lyons, Rochelle, Tours, Amiens, and Orleans.

The regent appears to have been utterly astonished at his success, and gradually to have conceived the idea, that paper, which could so aid a metallic currency, could entirely supersede it. Upon this fundamental error he afterwards acted. In the mean time, Law commenced the famous project which has handed his name down to posterity. He proposed to the regent, who could refuse him nothing, to establish a company, that should have the exclusive privilege of trading to the great river Mississippi and the province of Louisiana, on its western bank. The country was supposed to abound in the precious metals, and the company, supported by the profits of their exclusive commerce, were to be the sole farmers of the taxes, and sole coiners of money. Letters patent were issued, incorporating the company, in August 1717. The capital was divided into two hundred thousand shares of five hundred livres each, the whole of which might be paid in *billets d'état*, at their nominal value, although worth no more than 160 livres in the market.

It was now that the frenzy of speculating began to seize upon the nation. Law's bank had effected so much good, that any promises for the future which he thought proper to make were readily believed. The regent every day conferred new privileges upon the fortunate projector. The bank obtained the monopoly of the sale of tobacco; the sole right of refinage of gold and silver, and was finally erected into the Royal Bank of France. Amid the intoxication of success, both Law and the regent forgot the maxim so loudly proclaimed by the former, that a banker deserved death who made issues of paper without the necessary funds to provide for them. As soon as the bank, from a private, became a public institution, the regent caused a fabrication of notes to the amount of one thousand millions of livres. This was the first departure from sound principles, and one for which Law is not justly blamable. While the affairs of the bank were under his control, the issues had never exceeded sixty millions. Whether Law opposed the inordinate increase is not known, but as it took place as soon as the bank was made a royal establishment, it is but fair to lay the blame of the change of system upon the regent.

Law found that he lived under a despotic government, but he was not yet aware of the pernicious influence which such a government could exercise upon so delicate a framework as that of credit. He discovered it afterwards to his cost, but in the mean time suffered himself to be impelled by the regent into courses which his own reason must have disapproved. With a weakness most culpable, he lent his aid in inundating the country with paper money, which, based upon no solid foundation, was sure to fall, sooner or later. The extraordinary present fortune dazzled his eyes, and prevented him from seeing the evil day that would burst over his head, when once, from any cause or other, the alarm was sounded. The Parliament were from the first jealous of his influence as a foreigner, and had, besides, their misgivings as to the safety of his projects. As his influence extended, their animosity increased. D'Aguesseau, the Chancellor, was unceremoniously dismissed by the regent for his opposition to the vast increase of paper money, and the constant depreciation of the gold and silver coin of the realm. This only served to augment the enmity of the Parliament, and when D'Argenson, a man devoted to the interests of the regent, was appointed to the vacant chancellorship, and made at the same time minister of finance, they became more violent than ever. The first measure of the new minister caused a further depreciation of the coin. In order to extinguish the *billets d'état*, it was ordered that persons bringing to the mint four thousand livres in specie and one thousand livres in *billets d'état*, should receive back coin to the amount of five thousand livres. D'Argenson plumed himself mightily upon thus creating five thousand new and smaller livres out of the four thousand old and larger ones, being too ignorant of the true principles of trade and credit to be aware of the immense injury he was inflicting upon both.

The Parliament saw at once the impolicy and danger of such a system, and made repeated remonstrances to the regent. The latter refused to entertain their petitions, when the Parliament, by a bold, and very unusual stretch of authority, commanded that no money should be received in payment but that of the old standard. The regent summoned a *lit de justice*, and annulled the decree. The Parliament resisted, and issued another. Again the regent exercised his privilege, and annulled it, till the Parliament, stung to fiercer opposition, passed another decree, dated August 12th, 1718, by which they forbade the bank of Law to have any concern, either direct or indirect, in the administration of the revenue; and prohibited all foreigners, under heavy penalties, from interfering, either in their own names, or in that of others, in the management of the finances of the state. The Parliament considered Law to be the author of all the evil, and some of the counselors, in the virulence of their enmity, proposed that he should be brought to trial, and, if found guilty, be hung at the gates of the Palais de Justice.

Law, in great alarm, fled to the Palais Royal, and threw himself on the protection of the regent, praying that measures might be taken to reduce the Parliament to obedience. The regent had nothing so much at heart, both on that account and because of the disputes that had arisen relative to the legitimation of the Duke of Maine and the Count of Thoulouse, the sons of the late King. The Parliament was ultimately overawed by the arrest of their president and two of the counselors, who were sent to distant prisons.

Thus the first cloud upon Law's prospects blew over: freed from apprehension of personal danger, he devoted his attention to his famous Mississippi project, the shares of which were rapidly rising, in spite of the Parliament. At the commencement of the year 1719 an edict was published, granting to the Mississippi Company the exclusive privilege of trading to the East Indies, China, and the South Seas, and to all the possessions of the French East India Company, established by Colbert. The Company, in consequence of this great increase of their business, assumed, as more appropriate, the title of Company of the Indies, and created fifty thousand new shares. The prospects now held out by Law were most magnificent. He promised a yearly dividend of two hundred livres upon each share of five hundred, which, as the shares were paid for in *billets d'état,* at their nominal value, but worth only 100 livres, was at the rate of about 120 percent profit.

The public enthusiasm, which had been so long rising, could not resist a vision so splendid. At least three hundred thousand applications were made for the fifty thousand new shares, and Law's house in the Rue de Quincampoix was beset from morning to night by the eager applicants. As it was impossible to satisfy them all, it was several weeks before a list of the fortunate new stockholders could be made out, during which time the public impatience rose to a pitch of frenzy. Dukes, marquises, counts, with their duchesses, marchionesses, and countesses, waited in the streets for hours every day before Mr. Law's door to know the result. At last, to avoid the jostling of the plebeian crowd, which, to the number of thousands, filled the whole thoroughfare, they took apartments in the adjoining houses, that they might be continually near the temple whence the new Plutus was diffusing wealth. Every day the value of the old shares increased, and the fresh applications, induced by the golden dreams of the whole nation, became so numerous that it was deemed advisable to create no less than three hundred thousand new shares, at five thousand livres each, in order that the regent might take advantage of the popular enthusiasm to pay off the national debt. For this purpose, the sum of fifteen hundred millions of livres was necessary. Such was the eagerness of the nation, that thrice the sum would have been subscribed if the government had authorized it.

Law was now at the zenith of his prosperity, and the people were rapidly approaching the zenith of their infatuation. The highest and the lowest classes were alike filled with a vision of boundless wealth. There was not a person of note among the aristocracy, with the exception of the Duke of St. Simon and Marshal Villars, who was not engaged in buying or selling stock. People of every age and sex, and condition in life, speculated in the rise and fall of the Mississippi bonds. The Rue de Quincampoix was the grand resort of the jobbers, and it being a narrow, inconvenient street, accidents continually occurred in it, from the tremendous pressure of the crowd. Houses in it, worth, in ordinary times, a thousand livres of yearly rent, yielded as much as twelve or sixteen thousand. A cobbler, who had a stall in it, gained about two hundred livres a day by letting it out, and furnishing writing materials to brokers and their clients. The story goes, that a hump-backed man who stood in the street gained considerable sums by lending his hump as a writing-desk to the eager speculators! The great concourse of persons who assembled to do business brought a still greater concourse of spectators. These again drew all the thieves and immoral characters of Paris to the spot, and constant riots and disturbances took place. At nightfall, it was often found necessary to send a troop of soldiers to clear the street.

Law, finding the inconvenience of his residence, removed to the Place Vendome, whither the crowd of *agioteurs* followed him. That spacious square soon became as thronged as the Rue de Quincampoix : from morning to night it presented the appearance of a fair. Booths and tents were erected for the transaction of business and the sale of refreshments, and gamblers with their roulette tables stationed themselves in the very middle of the place, and reaped a golden, or rather a paper, harvest from the throng. The Boulevards and public gardens were forsaken; parties of pleasure took their walks in preference in the Place Vendome, which became the fashionable lounge of the idle, as well as the general rendezvous of the busy. The noise was so great all day, that the Chancellor, whose court was situated in the square, complained to the regent and the municipality, that he could not hear the advocates. Law, when applied to, expressed his willingness to aid in the removal of the nuisance, and for this purpose entered into a treaty with the Prince de Carignan for the Hôtel de Soissons, which had a garden of several acres in the rear. A bargain was concluded, by which Law became the purchaser of the hotel, at an enormous price, the Prince reserving to himself the magnificent gardens as a new source of profit. They contained some fine statues and several fountains, and were altogether laid out with much taste. As soon as Law was installed in his new abode, an edict was published, forbidding all persons to buy or sell stock anywhere but in the gardens of the Hôtel de Soissons. In the midst among the trees, about five hundred small tents and pavilions were erected, for the convenience of the stock-jobbers. Their various colors, the gay ribands and banners which floated from them, the busy crowds which passed continually in and out—the incessant hum of voices, the noise, the music, and the strange mixture of business and pleasure on the countenances of the throng, all combined to give the place an air of enchantment that quite enraptured the Parisians. The Prince de Carignan made enormous profits while the delusion lasted. Each tent was let at the rate of five hundred livres a month; and, as there were at least five hundred of them, his monthly revenue from this source alone must have amounted to 250,000 livres, or upwards of 10,000 pounds sterling.

The honest old soldier, Marshal Villars, was so vexed to see the folly which had smitten his countrymen, that he never could speak with temper on the subject. Passing one day through the Place Vendome in his carriage, the choleric gentleman was so annoyed at the infatuation of the people, that he abruptly ordered his coachman to stop, and, putting his head out of the carriage window, harangued them for full half an hour on their "disgusting avarice." This was not a very wise proceeding on his part. Hisses and shouts of laughter resounded from every side, and jokes without number were aimed at him. There being at last strong symptoms that something more tangible was flying through the air in the direction of his head, Marshal was glad to drive on. He never again repeated the experiment.

Two sober, quiet, and philosophic men of letters, M. de la Motte and the Abbé Terrason, congratulated each other, that they, at least, were free from this strange infatuation. A few days afterwards, as the worthy Abbé was coming out of the Hôtel de Soissons, whither he had gone to buy shares in the Mississippi, whom should he see but his friend La Motte entering for the same purpose. "Ha!" said the Abbé, smiling, "is that *you*?" "Yes," said La Motte, pushing past him as fast as he was able; "and can that be *you*?" The next time the two scholars met, they talked of philosophy, of science, and of religion, but neither had courage for a long time to breathe one syllable about the Mississippi. At last, when it was mentioned, they agreed that a man ought never to swear against his doing any one thing, and that there was no sort of extravagance of which even a wise man was not capable.

During this time, Law, the new Plutus, had become all at once the most important personage of the state. The ante-chambers of the regent were forsaken by the courtiers. Peers, judges, and bishops thronged to the Hôtel de Soissons; officers of the army and navy, ladies of title and fashion, and every one to whom hereditary rank or public employ gave a claim to precedence, were to be found waiting in his ante-chambers to beg for a portion of his India stock. Law was so pestered that he was unable to see one-tenth part of the applicants, and every maneuver that ingenuity could suggest was employed to gain access to him. Peers, whose dignity would have been outraged if the regent had made them wait half an hour for an interview, were content to wait six hours for the chance of seeing Monsieur Law. Enormous fees were paid to his servants, if they would merely announce their names. Ladies of rank employed the blandishments of their smiles for the same object; but many of them came day after day for a fortnight before they could obtain an audience. When Law accepted an invitation, he was sometimes so surrounded by ladies, all asking to have their names put down in his lists as shareholders in the new stock, that, in spite of his well-known and habitual gallantry, he was obliged to tear himself away par force. The most ludicrous stratagems were employed to have an opportunity of speaking to him. One lady, who had striven in vain during several days, gave up in despair all attempts to see him at his own house, but ordered her coachman to keep a strict watch whenever she was out in her carriage, and if he saw Mr. Law coming, to drive against a post, and upset her. The coachman promised obedience, and for three days the lady was driven incessantly through the town, praying inwardly for the opportunity to be overturned. At last she espied Mr. Law, and, pulling the string, called out to the coachman, "Upset us now! for God's sake, upset us now!" The coachman drove against a post, the lady screamed, the coach was overturned, and Law, who had seen the *accident*, hastened to the spot to render assistance. The cunning dame was led into the Hôtel de Soissons, where she soon thought it advisable to recover from her fright, and, after apologizing to Mr. Law, confessed her stratagem. Law smiled, and entered the lady in his books as the purchaser of a quantity of India stock. Another story is told of a Madame de Boucha, who, knowing that Mr. Law was at dinner at a certain house, proceeded thither in her carriage, and gave the alarm of fire. The company started from table, and Law among the rest; but, seeing one lady making all haste into the house towards him, while everybody else was scampering away, he suspected the trick, and ran off in another direction.

Many other anecdotes are related, which even, though they may be a little exaggerated, are nevertheless worth preserving, as showing the spirit of that singular period. [The curious reader may find an anecdote of the eagerness of the French ladies to retain Law in their company, which will make him blush or smile according as he happens to be very modest or the reverse. It is related in the Letters of Madame Charlotte Elizabeth de Baviere, Duchess of Orleans, vol. ii. p. 274.] The regent was one day mentioning, in the presence of D'Argenson, the Abbé Dubois, and some other persons, that he was desirous of deputing some lady, of the rank at least of a Duchess, to attend upon his daughter at Modena; "but," added he, "I do not exactly know where to find one." "No!" replied one, in affected surprise; "I can tell you where to find every Duchess in France: you have only to go to Mr. Law's; you will see them every one in his ante-chamber."

M. de Chirac, a celebrated physician, had bought stock at an unlucky period, and was very anxious to sell out. Stock, however continued to fall for two or three days, much to his alarm. His mind was filled with the subject, when he was suddenly called upon to attend a lady, who imagined herself unwell. He arrived, was shown up stairs, and felt the lady's pulse. "It falls! it falls! good God! it falls continually!" said he, musingly, while the lady looked up in his face, all anxiety for his opinion. "Oh! M. de Chirac," said she, starting to her feet, and ringing the bell for assistance; "I am dying! I am dying! it falls! it falls! it falls!" "What falls?" inquired the doctor, in amazement. "My pulse! my pulse!" said the lady; "I must be dying." "Calm your apprehensions, my dear Madam," said M. de Chirac; "I was speaking of the stocks. The truth is, I have been a great loser, and my mind is so disturbed, I hardly know what I have been saying."

The price of shares sometimes rose ten or twenty percent in the course of a few hours, and many persons in the humbler walks of life, who had risen poor in the morning, went to bed in affluence. An extensive holder of stock, being taken ill, sent his servant to sell two hundred and fifty shares, at eight thousand livres each, the price at which they were then quoted. The servant went, and, on his arrival in the Jardin de Soissons, found that in the interval the price had risen to ten thousand livres. The difference of two thousand livres on the two hundred and fifty shares, amounting to 500,000 livres, or 20,000 pounds sterling, he very coolly transferred to his own use, and, giving the remainder to his master, set out the same evening for another country. Law's coachman in a very short time made money enough to set up a carriage of his own, and requested permission to leave his service. Law, who esteemed the man, begged of him as a favor, that he would endeavor, before he went, to find a substitute as good as himself. The coachman consented, and in the evening brought two of his former comrades, telling Mr. Law to choose between them, and he would take the other. Cookmaids and footmen were now and then as lucky, and, in the full-blown pride of their easily-acquired wealth, made the most ridiculous mistakes. Preserving the language and manners of their old, with the finery of their new station, they afforded continual subjects for the pity of the sensible, the contempt of the sober, and the laughter of everybody. But the folly and meanness of the higher ranks of society were still more disgusting. One instance alone, related by the Duke de St. Simon, will show the unworthy avarice which infected the whole of society.

A man of the name of Andre, without character or education, had, by a series of well-timed speculations in Mississippi bonds, gained enormous wealth, in an incredibly short space of time. As St. Simon expresses it, "he had amassed mountains of gold." As he became rich, he grew ashamed of the lowness of his birth, and anxious above all things to be allied to nobility. He had a daughter, an infant only three years of age, and he opened a negotiation with the aristocratic and needy family of D'Oyse, that this child should, upon certain conditions, marry a member of that house. The Marquis d'Oyse, to his shame, consented, and promised to marry her himself on her attaining the age of twelve, if the father would pay him down the sum of a hundred thousand crowns, and twenty thousand livres every year, until the celebration of the marriage. The Marquis was himself in his thirty-third year. This scandalous bargain was duly signed and sealed, the stockjobber furthermore agreeing to settle upon his daughter, on the marriage-day, a fortune of several millions. The Duke of Brancas, the head of the family, was present throughout the negotiation, and shared in all the profits. St. Simon, who treats the matter with the levity becoming what he thought so good a joke, adds, "that people did not spare their animadversions on this beautiful marriage," and further informs us, "that the project fell to the ground some months afterwards by the overthrow of Law, and the ruin of the ambitious Monsieur Andre." It would appear, however, that the noble family never had the honesty to return the hundred thousand crowns.

Amid events like these, which, humiliating though they be, partake largely of the ludicrous, others occurred of a more serious nature. Robberies in the streets were of daily occurrence, in consequence of the immense sums, in paper, which people carried about with them. Assassinations were also frequent. One case in particular fixed the attention of the whole of France, not only on account of the enormity of the offence, but of the rank and high connections of the criminal.

The Count d'Horn, a younger brother of the Prince d'Horn, and related to the noble families of D'Aremberg, De Ligne, and De Montmorency, was a young man of dissipated character, extravagant to a degree, and unprincipled as he was extravagant. In connection with two other young men as reckless as himself, named Mille, a Piedmontese captain, and one Destampes, or Lestang, a Fleming, he formed a design to rob a very rich broker, who was known, unfortunately for himself, to carry great sums about his person. The Count pretended a desire to purchase of him a number of shares in the Company of the Indies, and for that purpose appointed to meet him in a cabaret, or low public-house, in the neighborhood of the Place Vendome. The unsuspecting broker was punctual to his appointment; so were the Count d'Horn and his two associates, whom he introduced as his particular friends. After a few moments' conversation, the Count d'Horn suddenly sprang upon his victim, and stabbéd him three times in the breast with a poniard. The man fell heavily to the ground, and, while the Count was employed in rifling his portfolio of bonds in the Mississippi and Indian schemes to the amount of one hundred thousand crowns, Mille, the Piedmontese, stabbéd the unfortunate broker again and again, to make sure of his death. But the broker did not fall without a struggle, and his cries brought the people of the *cabaret* to his assistance. Lestang, the other assassin, who had been set to keep watch at a staircase, sprang from a window and escaped; but Mille and the Count d'Horn were seized in the very act.

This crime, committed in open day, and in so public a place as a *cabaret*, filled Paris with consternation. The trial of the assassins commenced on the following day, and the evidence being so clear, they were both found guilty and condemned to be broken alive on the wheel. The noble relatives of the Count d'Horn absolutely blocked up the antechambers of the regent, praying for mercy on the misguided youth, and alleging that he was insane. The regent avoided them as long as possible, being determined that, in a case so atrocious, justice should take its course; but the importunity of these influential suitors was not to be overcome so silently, and they at last forced themselves into the presence of the regent, and prayed him to save their house the shame of a public execution. They hinted that the Princes d'Horn were allied to the illustrious family of Orleans, and added that the regent himself would be disgraced if a kinsman of his should die by the hands of a common executioner. The regent, to his credit, was proof against all their solicitations, and replied to their last argument in the words of Corneille,
    "Le crime fait la honte, et non pas l'echafaud:"
adding, that whatever shame there might be in the punishment he would very willingly share with the other relatives. Day after day they renewed their entreaties, but always with the same result. At last they thought that if they could interest the Duke de St. Simon in their layout, a man for whom the regent felt sincere esteem, they might succeed in their object. The Duke, a thorough aristocrat, was as shocked as they were, that a noble assassin should die by the same death as a plebeian felon, and represented to the regent the impolicy of making enemies of so numerous, wealthy, and powerful a family. He urged, too, that in Germany, where the family of D'Aremberg had large possessions, it was the law, that no relative of a person broken on the wheel could succeed to any public office or employ until a whole generation had passed away. For this reason he thought the punishment of the guilty Count might be transmuted into beheading, which was considered all over Europe as much less infamous. The regent was moved by this argument, and was about to consent, when Law, who felt peculiarly interested in the fate of the murdered man, confirmed him in his former resolution, to let the law take its course.

The relatives of D'Horn were now reduced to the last extremity. The Prince de Robec Montmorency, despairing of other methods, found means to penetrate into the dungeon of the criminal, and offering him a cup of poison, implored him to save them from disgrace. The Count d'Horn turned away his head, and refused to take it. Montmorency pressed him once more, and losing all patience at his continued refusal, turned on his heel, and exclaiming, "Die, then, as thou wilt, mean-spirited wretch! thou art fit only to perish by the hands of the hangman!" left him to his fate.

D'Horn himself petitioned the regent that he might be beheaded, but Law, who exercised more influence over his mind than any other person, with the exception of the notorious Abbé Dubois, his tutor, insisted that he could not in justice succumb to the self-interested views of the D'Horns. The regent had from the first been of the same opinion, and within six days after the commission of their crime, D'Horn and Mille were broken on the wheel in the Place de Greve. The other assassin, Lestang, was never apprehended.

This prompt and severe justice was highly pleasing to the populace of Paris; even M. de Quincampoix, as they called Law, came in for a share of their approbation for having induced the regent to show no favor to a patrician. But the number of robberies and assassinations did not diminish. No sympathy was shown for rich jobbers when they were plundered: the general laxity of public morals, conspicuous enough before, was rendered still more so by its rapid pervasion of the middle classes, who had hitherto remained comparatively pure, between the open vices of the class above and the hidden crimes of the class below them. The pernicious love of gambling diffused itself through society, and bore all public, and nearly all private, virtue before it.

For a time, while confidence lasted, an impetus was given to trade, which could not fail to be beneficial. In Paris, especially, the good results were felt. Strangers flocked into the capital from every part, bent, not only upon making money, but on spending it. The Duchess of Orleans, mother of the regent, computes the increase of the population during this time, from the great influx of strangers from all parts of the world, at 305,000 souls. The housekeepers were obliged to make up beds in garrets, kitchens, and even stables, for the accommodation of lodgers; and the town was so full of carriages and vehicles of every description, that they were obliged in the principal streets to drive at a foot-pace for fear of accidents. The looms of the country worked with unusual activity, to supply rich laces, silks, broad-cloth, and velvets, which being paid for in abundant paper, increased in price four-fold. Provisions shared the general advance; bread, meat, and vegetables were sold at prices greater than had ever before been known; while the wages of labor rose in exactly the same proportion. The artisan, who formerly gained fifteen sous per diem, now gained sixty. New houses were built in every direction; an illusory prosperity shone over the land, and so dazzled the eyes of the whole nation that none could see the dark cloud on the horizon, announcing the storm that was too rapidly approaching.

Law himself, the magician whose wand had wrought so surprising a change, shared, of course, in the general prosperity. His wife and daughter were courted by the highest nobility, and their alliance sought by the heirs of ducal and princely houses. He bought two splendid estates in different parts of France, and entered into a negotiation with the family of the Duke de Sully for the purchase of the Marquisate of Rosny. His religion being an obstacle to his advancement, the regent promised, if he would publicly conform to the Catholic faith, to make him comptroller-general of the finances. Law, who had no more real religion than any other professed gambler, readily agreed, and was confirmed by the Abbé de Tencin in the cathedral of Melun, in presence of a great crowd of spectators. [The following squib was circulated on the occasion:

"Foin de ton zele seraphique,
Malheureux Abbé de Tencin,
Depuis que Law est Catholique,
Tout le royaume est Capucin"
Thus, somewhat weakly and paraphrastically rendered by Justansond, in his translation of the "Memoirs of Louis XV:"—
"Tencin, a curse on thy seraphic zeal,
Which by persuasion hath contrived the means
To make the Scotchman at our altars kneel,
Since which we all are poor as Capucines!"]
On the following day he was elected honorary churchwarden of the parish of St. Roch, upon which occasion he made it a present of the sum of five hundred thousand livres. His charities, always magnificent, were not always so ostentatious. He gave away great sums privately, and no tale of real distress ever reached his ears in vain.

At this time, he was by far the most influential person of the state. The Duke of Orleans had so much confidence in his sagacity, and the success of his plans, that he always consulted him upon every matter of moment. He was by no means unduly elevated by his prosperity, but remained the same simple, affable, sensible man that he had shown himself in adversity. His gallantry, which was always delightful to the fair objects of it, was of a nature, so kind, so gentlemanly, and so respectful, that not even a lover could have taken offence at it. If upon any occasion he showed any symptoms of haughtiness, it was to the cringing nobles, who lavished their adulation upon him till it became fulsome.

He often took pleasure in seeing how long he could make them dance attendance upon him for a single favor. To such of his own countrymen as by chance visited Paris, and sought an interview with him, he was, on the contrary, all politeness and attention. When Archibald Campbell, Earl of Islay, and afterwards Duke of Argyle, called upon him in the Place Vendome, he had to pass through an ante-chamber crowded with persons of the first distinction, all anxious to see the great financier, and have their names put down as first on the list of some new subscription. Law himself was quietly sitting in his library, writing a letter to the gardener at his paternal estate of Lauriston about the planting of some cabbages! The Earl stayed for a considerable time, played a game of piquet with his countryman, and left him, charmed with his ease, good sense, and good breeding.

Among the nobles who, by means of the public credulity at this time, gained sums sufficient to repair their ruined fortunes, may be mentioned the names of the Dukes de Bourbon, de Guiche, de la Force [The Duke de la Force gained considerable sums, not only by jobbing in the stocks, but in dealing in porcelain, spices, &c. It was debated for a length of time in the Parliament of Paris whether he had not, in his quality of spice-merchant, forfeited his rank in the peerage. It was decided in the negative. A caricature of him was made, dressed as a street porter, carrying a large bale of spices on his back, with the inscription, "Admirez La Force."], de Chaulnes, and d'Antin; the Marechal d'Estrees, the Princes de Rohan, de Poix, and de Leon. The Duke de Bourbon, son of Louis XIV by Madame de Montespan, was peculiarly fortunate in his speculations in Mississippi paper. He rebuilt the royal residence of Chantilly in a style of unwonted magnificence, and, being passionately fond of horses, he erected a range of stables, which were long renowned throughout Europe, and imported a hundred and fifty of the finest racers from England, to improve the breed in France. He bought a large extent of country in Picardy, and became possessed of nearly all the valuable lands lying between the Oise and the Somme.

When fortunes such as these were gained, it is no wonder that Law should have been almost worshipped by the mercurial population. Never was monarch more flattered than he was. All the small poets and littérateurs of the day poured floods of adulation upon him. According to them he was the savior of the country, the tutelary divinity of France; wit was in all his words, goodness in all his looks, and wisdom in all his actions. So great a crowd followed his carriage whenever he went abroad, that the regent sent him a troop of horse as his permanent escort, to clear the streets before him.

It was remarked at this time, that Paris had never before been so full of objects of elegance and luxury. Statues, pictures, and tapestries were imported in great quantities from foreign countries, and found a ready market. All those pretty trifles in the way of furniture and ornament which the French excel in manufacturing, were no longer the exclusive play-things of the aristocracy, but were to be found in abundance in the houses of traders and the middle classes in general. Jewellery of the most costly description was brought to Paris as the most favorable mart. Among the rest, the famous diamond, bought by the regent, and called by his name, and which long adorned the crown of France. It was purchased for the sum of two millions of livres, under circumstances which show that the regent was not so great a gainer as some of his subjects, by the impetus which trade had received. When the diamond was first offered to him, he refused to buy it, although he desired, above all things, to possess it, alleging as his reason, that his duty to the country he governed would not allow him to spend so large a sum of the public money for a mere jewel. This valid and honorable excuse threw all the ladies of the court into alarm, and nothing was heard for some days but expressions of regret, that so rare a gem should be allowed to go out of France; no private individual being rich enough to buy it. The regent was continually importuned about it; but all in vain, until the Duke de St. Simon, who, with all his ability, was something of a twaddler, undertook the weighty business. His entreaties, being seconded by Law, the good-natured regent gave his consent, leaving to Law's ingenuity to find the means to pay for it. The owner took security for the payment of the sum of two millions of livres within a stated period, receiving, in the mean time, the interest of five percent upon that amount, and being allowed, besides, all the valuable clippings of the gem. St. Simon, in his *Memoirs*, relates, with no little complacency, his share in this transaction. After describing the diamond to be as large as a greengage, of a form nearly round, perfectly white, and without flaw, and weighing more than five hundred grains, he concludes with a chuckle, by telling the world, "that he takes great credit to himself for having induced the regent to make so illustrious a purchase." In other words, he was proud that he had induced him to sacrifice his duty, and buy a bauble for himself, at an extravagant price, out of the public money.

Thus the system continued to flourish till the commencement of the year 1720. The warnings of the Parliament, that too great a creation of paper money would, sooner or later, bring the country to bankruptcy, were disregarded. The regent, who knew nothing whatever of the philosophy of finance, thought that a system which had produced such good effects could never be carried to excess. If five hundred millions of paper had been of such advantage, five hundred millions additional would be of still greater advantage. This was the grand error of the regent, and which Law did not attempt to dispel. The extraordinary avidity of the people kept up the delusion; and the higher the price of Indian and Mississippi stock, the more *billets de banque* were issued to keep pace with it. The edifice thus reared might not inaptly be compared to the gorgeous palace erected by Potemkin, that princely barbarian of Russia, to surprise and please his imperial mistress: huge blocks of ice were piled one upon another; ionic pillars, of chastest workmanship, in ice, formed a noble portico; and a dome, of the same material, shone in the sun, which had just strength enough to gild, but not to melt it. It glittered afar, like a palace of crystals and diamonds; but there came one warm breeze from the south, and the stately building dissolved away, till none were able even to gather up the fragments. So with Law and his paper system. No sooner did the breath of popular mistrust blow steadily upon it, than it fell to ruins, and none could raise it up again.

The first slight alarm that was occasioned was early in 1720. The Prince de Conti, offended that Law should have denied him fresh shares in India stock, at his own price, sent to his bank to demand payment in specie of so enormous a quantity of notes, that three wagons were required for its transport. Law complained to the regent, and urged on his attention the mischief that would be done, if such an example found many imitators. The regent was but too well aware of it, and, sending for the Prince de Conti, ordered him, under penalty of his high displeasure, to refund to the Bank two-thirds of the specie which he had withdrawn from it. The Prince was forced to obey the despotic mandate. Happily for Law's credit, De Conti was an unpopular man: everybody condemned his meanness and cupidity, and agreed that Law had been hardly treated. It is strange, however, that so narrow an escape should not have made both Law and the regent more anxious to restrict their issues. Others were soon found who imitated, from motives of distrust, the example which had been set by De Conti in revenge. The more acute stock-jobbers imagined justly that prices could not continue to rise for ever. Bourdon and La Richardiere, renowned for their extensive operations in the funds, quietly and in small quantities at a time, converted their notes into specie, and sent it away to foreign countries. They also bought as much as they could conveniently carry of plate and expensive jewellery, and sent it secretly away to England or to Holland. Vermalet, a jobber, who sniffed the coming storm, procured gold and silver coin to the amount of nearly a million of livres, which he packed in a farmer's cart, and covered over with hay and cow-dung. He then disguised himself in the dirty smock-frock, or *blouse*, of a peasant, and drove his precious load in safety into Belgium. From thence he soon found means to transport it to Amsterdam.

Hitherto no difficulty had been experienced by any class in procuring specie for their wants. But this system could not long be carried on without causing a scarcity. The voice of complaint was heard on every side, and inquiries being instituted, the cause was soon discovered. The council debated long on the remedies to be taken, and Law, being called on for his advice, was of opinion, that an edict should be published, depreciating the value of coin five percent below that of paper. The edict was published accordingly; but, failing of its intended effect, was followed by another, in which the depreciation was increased to ten percent. The payments of the bank were at the same time restricted to one hundred livres in gold, and ten in silver. All these measures were nugatory to restore confidence in the paper, though the restriction of cash payments within limits so extremely narrow kept up the credit of the Bank.

Notwithstanding every effort to the contrary, the precious metals continued to be conveyed to England and Holland. The little coin that was left in the country was carefully treasured, or hidden until the scarcity became so great, that the operations of trade could no longer be carried on. In this emergency, Law hazarded the bold experiment of forbidding the use of specie altogether. In February 1720 an edict was published, which, instead of restoring the credit of the paper, as was intended, destroyed it irrecoverably, and drove the country to the very brink of revolution. By this famous edict it was forbidden to any person whatever to have more than five hundred livres (20 pounds sterling) of coin in his possession, under pain of a heavy fine, and confiscation of the sums found. It was also forbidden to buy up jewellery, plate, and precious stones, and informers were encouraged to make search for offenders, by the promise of one-half the amount they might discover. The whole country sent up a cry of distress at this unheard-of tyranny. The most odious persecution daily took place. The privacy of families was violated by the intrusion of informers and their agents. The most virtuous and honest were denounced for the crime of having been seen with a louis d'or in their possession. Servants betrayed their masters, one citizen became a spy upon his neighbor, and arrests and confiscations so multiplied, that the courts found a difficulty in getting through the immense increase of business thus occasioned. It was sufficient for an informer to say that he suspected any person of concealing money in his house, and immediately a search-warrant was granted. Lord Stair, the English ambassador, said, that it was now impossible to doubt of the sincerity of Law's conversion to the Catholic religion; he had established the *inquisition*, after having given abundant evidence of his faith in *transubstantiation*, by turning so much gold into paper.

Every epithet that popular hatred could suggest was showered upon the regent and the unhappy Law. Coin, to any amount above five hundred livres, was an illegal tender, and nobody would take paper if he could help it. No one knew to-day what his notes would be worth to-morrow. "Never," says Duclos, in his *Secret Memoirs of the Regency*, "was seen a more capricious government—never was a more frantic tyranny exercised by hands less firm. It is inconceivable to those who were witnesses of the horrors of those times, and who look back upon them now as on a dream, that a sudden revolution did not break out—that Law and the regent did not perish by a tragical death. They were both held in horror, but the people confined themselves to complaints; a sombre and timid despair, a stupid consternation, had seized upon all, and men's minds were too vile even to be capable of a courageous crime." It would appear that, at one time, a movement of the people was organized. Seditious writings were posted up against the walls, and were sent, in hand-bills, to the houses of the most conspicuous people. One of them, given in the *Mémoires de la Régence*, was to the following effect: "Sir and Madam,—This is to give you notice that a St. Bartholomew's Day will be enacted again on Saturday and Sunday, if affairs do not alter. You are desired not to stir out, nor you, nor your servants. God preserve you from the flames! Give notice to your neighbors. Dated Saturday, May

25th, 1720." The immense number of spies with which the city was infested rendered the people mistrustful of one another, and beyond some trifling disturbances made in the evening by an insignificant group, which was soon dispersed, the peace of the capital was not compromised.

The value of shares in the Louisiana, or Mississippi stock, had fallen very rapidly, and few indeed were found to believe the tales that had once been told of the immense wealth of that region. A last effort was therefore tried to restore the public confidence in the Mississippi project. For this purpose, a general conscription of all the poor wretches in Paris was made by order of government. Upwards of six thousand of the very refuse of the population were impressed, as if in time of war, and were provided with clothes and tools to be embarked for New Orleans, to work in the gold mines alleged to abound there.

They were paraded day after day through the streets with their pikes and shovels, and then sent off in small detachments to the out-ports to be shipped for America. Two-thirds of them never reached their destination, but dispersed themselves over the country, sold their tools for what they could get, and returned to their old course of life. In less than three weeks afterwards, one-half of them were to be found again in Paris. The maneuver, however, caused a trifling advance in Mississippi stock. Many persons of superabundant gullibility believed that operations had begun in earnest in the new Golconda, and that gold and silver ingots would again be found in France.

In a constitutional monarchy some surer means would have been found for the restoration of public credit. In England, at a subsequent period, when a similar delusion had brought on similar distress, how different were the measures taken to repair the evil; but in France, unfortunately, the remedy was left to the authors of the mischief. The arbitrary will of the regent, which endeavored to extricate the country, only plunged it deeper into the mire. All payments were ordered to be made in paper, and between the 1st of February and the end of May, notes were fabricated to the amount of upwards of 1500 millions of livres, or 60,000,000 pounds sterling. But the alarm once sounded, no art could make the people feel the slightest confidence in paper which was not exchangeable into metal. M. Lambert, the President of the Parliament of Paris, told the regent to his face that he would rather have a hundred thousand livres in gold or silver than five millions in the notes of his bank. When such was the general feeling, the superabundant issues of paper but increased the evil, by rendering still more enormous the disparity between the amount of specie and notes in circulation. Coin, which it was the object of the regent to depreciate, rose in value on every fresh attempt to diminish it. In February, it was judged advisable that the Royal Bank should be incorporated with the Company of the Indies. An edict to that effect was published and registered by the Parliament. The state remained the guarantee for the notes of the bank, and no more were to be issued without an order in council. All the profits of the bank, since the time it had been taken out of Law's hands and made a national institution, were given over by the regent to the Company of the Indies. This measure had the effect of raising for a short time the value of the Louisiana and other shares of the company, but it failed in placing public credit on any permanent basis.

A council of state was held in the beginning of May, at which Law, D'Argenson (his colleague in the administration of the finances), and all the ministers were present. It was then computed that the total amount of notes in circulation was 2600 millions of livres, while the coin in the country was not quite equal to half that amount. It was evident to the majority of the council that some plan must be adopted to equalize the currency. Some proposed that the notes should be reduced to the value of the specie, while others proposed that the nominal value of the specie should be raised till it was on an equality with the paper. Law is said to have opposed both these projects, but failing in suggesting any other, it was agreed that the notes should be depreciated one-half. On the 21st of May, an edict was accordingly issued, by which it was decreed that the shares of the Company of the Indies, and the notes of the bank, should gradually diminish in value, till at the end of a year they should only pass current for one half of their nominal worth. The Parliament refused to register the edict—the greatest outcry was excited, and the state of the country became so alarming, that, as the only means of preserving tranquillity, the council of the regency was obliged to stultify its own proceedings, by publishing within seven days another edict, restoring the notes to their original value.

On the same day (the 27th of May) the bank stopped payment in specie. Law and D'Argenson were both dismissed from the ministry. The weak, vacillating, and cowardly regent threw the blame of all the mischief upon Law, who, upon presenting himself at the Palais Royal, was refused admittance. At nightfall, however, he was sent for, and admitted into the palace by a secret door, [Duclos, *Mémoires Secrets de la Régence.*] when the regent endeavored to console him, and made all manner of excuses for the severity with which in public he had been compelled to treat him. So capricious was his conduct, that, two days afterwards, he took him publicly to the opera, where he sat in the royal box, alongside of the regent, who treated him with marked consideration in face of all the people. But such was the hatred against Law that the experiment had well nigh proved fatal to him. The mob assailed his carriage with stones just as he was entering his own door; and if the coachman had not made a sudden jerk into the court-yard, and the domestics closed the gate immediately, he would, in all probability, have been dragged out and torn to pieces. On the following day, his wife and daughter were also assailed by the mob as they were returning in their carriage from the races. When the regent was informed of these occurrences he sent Law a strong detachment of Swiss guards, who were stationed night and day in the court of his residence. The public indignation at last increased so much, that Law, finding his own house, even with this guard, insecure, took refuge in the Palais Royal, in the apartments of the regent.

The Chancellor, D'Aguesseau, who had been dismissed in 1718 for his opposition to the projects of Law, was now recalled to aid in the restoration of credit. The regent acknowledged too late, that he had treated with unjustifiable harshness and mistrust one of the ablest, and perhaps the sole honest public man of that corrupt period. He had retired ever since his disgrace to his country-house at Fresnes, where, in the midst of severe but delightful philosophic studies, he had forgotten the intrigues of an unworthy court. Law himself, and the Chevalier de Conflans, a gentleman of the regent's household, were dispatched in a post-chaise, with orders to bring the ex-chancellor to Paris along with them. D'Aguesseau consented to render what assistance he could, contrary to the advice of his friends, who did not approve that he should accept any recall to office of which Law was the bearer. On his arrival in Paris, five counselors of the Parliament were admitted to confer with the Commissary of Finance, and on the 1st of June an order was published, abolishing the law which made it criminal to amass coin to the amount of more than five hundred livres. Every one was permitted to have as much specie as he pleased. In order that the bank-notes might be withdrawn, twenty-five millions of new notes were created, on the security of the revenues of the city of Paris, at two-and-a-half percent. The bank-notes withdrawn were publicly burned in front of the Hôtel de Ville. The new notes were principally of the value of ten livres each; and on the 10th of June the bank was re-opened, with a sufficiency of silver coin to give in change for them.

These measures were productive of considerable advantage. All the population of Paris hastened to the bank, to get coin for their small notes; and silver becoming scarce, they were paid in copper. Very few complained that this was too heavy, although poor fellows might be continually seen toiling and sweating along the streets, laden with more than they could comfortably carry, in the shape of change for fifty livres. The crowds around the bank were so great, that hardly a day passed that some one was not pressed to death. On the 9th of July, the multitude was so dense and clamorous that the guards stationed at the entrance of the Mazarin Gardens closed the gate, and refused to admit any more. The crowd became incensed, and flung stones through the railings upon the soldiers. The latter, incensed in their turn, threatened to fire upon the people. At that instant one of them was hit by a stone, and, taking up his piece, he fired into the crowd. One man fell dead immediately, and another was severely wounded. It was every instant expected that a general attack would have been commenced upon the bank; but the gates of the Mazarin Gardens being opened to the crowd, who saw a whole troop of soldiers, with their bayonets fixed, ready to receive them, they contented themselves by giving vent to their indignation in groans and hisses.

Eight days afterwards the concourse of people was so tremendous, that fifteen persons were squeezed to death at the doors of the bank. The people were so indignant that they took three of the bodies on stretchers before them, and proceeded, to the number of seven or eight thousand, to the gardens of the Palais Royal, that they might show the regent the misfortunes that he and Law had brought upon the country. Law's coachman, who was sitting on the box of his master's carriage, in the court-yard of the palace, happened to have more zeal than discretion, and, not liking that the mob should abuse his master, he said, loud enough to be overheard by several persons, that they were all blackguards, and deserved to be hanged. The mob immediately set upon him, and, thinking that Law was in the carriage, broke it to pieces. The imprudent coachman narrowly escaped with his life. No further mischief was done; a body of troops making their appearance, the crowd quietly dispersed, after an assurance had been given by the regent that the three bodies they had brought to show him should be decently buried at his own expense. The Parliament was sitting at the time of this uproar, and the President took upon himself to go out and see what was the matter. On his return he informed the councilors, that Law's carriage had been broken by the mob. All the members rose simultaneously, and expressed their joy by a loud shout, while one man, more zealous in his hatred than the rest, exclaimed, "And Law himself, is *he* torn to pieces?" [The Duchess of Orleans gives a different version of this story; but whichever be the true one, the manifestation of such feeling in a legislative assembly was not very creditable. She says, that the President was so transported with joy, that he was seized with a rhyming fit, and, returning into the hall, exclaimed to the members:— "Messieurs! Messieurs! bonne nouvelle! Le carfosse de Lass est reduit en canelle!"]

Much undoubtedly depended on the credit of the Company of the Indies, which was answerable for so great a sum to the nation. It was, therefore, suggested in the council of the ministry, that any privileges which could be granted to enable it to fulfil its engagements, would be productive of the best results. With this end in view, it was proposed that the exclusive privilege of all maritime commerce should be secured to it, and an edict to that effect was published. But it was unfortunately forgotten that by such a measure all the merchants of the country would be ruined. The idea of such an immense privilege was generally scouted by the nation, and petition on petition was presented to the Parliament, that they would refuse to register the decree. They refused accordingly, and the regent, remarking that they did nothing but fan the flame of sedition, exiled them to Blois. At the intercession of D'Aguesseau, the place of banishment was changed to Pontoise, and thither accordingly the councilors repaired, determined to set the regent at defiance. They made every arrangement for rendering their temporary exile as agreeable as possible. The President gave the most elegant suppers, to which he invited all the gayest and wittiest company of Paris. Every night there was a concert and ball for the ladies. The usually grave and solemn judges and councilors joined in cards and other diversions, leading for several weeks a life of the most extravagant pleasure, for no other purpose than to show the regent of how little consequence they deemed their banishment, and that when they willed it, they could make Pontoise a pleasanter residence than Paris.

Of all the nations in the world the French are the most renowned for singing over their grievances. Of that country it has been remarked with some truth, that its whole history may be traced in its songs. When Law, by the utter failure of his best-laid plans, rendered himself obnoxious, satire of course seized hold upon him, and, while caricatures of his person appeared in all the shops, the streets resounded with songs, in which neither he nor the regent was spared. Many of these songs were far from decent; and one of them in particular counselled the application of all his notes to the most ignoble use to which paper can be applied. But the following, preserved in the letters of the Duchess of Orleans, was the best and the most popular, and was to be heard for months in all the *carrefours* of Paris. The application of the chorus is happy enough:

Aussitot que Lass arriva
Dans notre bonne ville,
Monsieur le Régent publia
Que Lass serait utile
Pour rétablir la nation.
La faridondaine! la faridondon!
Mais il nous a tous enrich,

Biribi!

A la facon de Barbari,

Mort ami!

Ce parpaillot, pour attirer
Tout l'argent de la France,
Songea d'abord à s'assurer
De notre confiance.
Il fit son abjuration.
La faridondaine! la faridondon!
Mais le fourbe s'est converti,

Biribi!

A la facon de Barbari,

Mon ami!

Lass, le fils ainé de Satan
Nous met tous à l'aumône,
Il nous a pris tout notre argent
Et n'en rend à personne.
Mais le Régent, humain et bon,
La faridondaine! la faridondon!
Nous rendra ce qu'on nous a pris,

Biribi!

A la façon de Barbari,

Mon ami!

The following smart epigram is of the same date:
    Lundi, j'achetai des actions;
    Mardi, je gagnai des millions;
    Mercredi, j'arrangeai mon ménage,
    Jeudi, je pris un équipage,
    Vendredi, je m'en fus au bal,
    Et Samedi, a l'hôpital.

Among the caricatures that were abundantly published, and that showed as plainly as graver matters, that the nation had awakened to a sense of its folly, was one, a facsimile of which is preserved in the *Mémoires de la Régence*. It was thus described by its author: "The 'Goddess of Shares,' in her triumphal car, driven by the Goddess of Folly. Those who are drawing the car are impersonations of the Mississippi, with his wooden leg, the South Sea, the Bank of England, the Company of the West of Senegal, and of various assurances. Lest the car should not roll fast enough, the agents of these companies, known by their long fox-tails and their cunning looks, turn round the spokes of the wheels, upon which are marked the names of the several stocks, and their value, sometimes high and sometimes low, according to the turns of the wheel. Upon the ground are the merchandise, day-books and ledgers of legitimate commerce, crushed under the chariot of Folly. Behind is an immense crowd of persons, of all ages, sexes, and conditions, clamoring after Fortune, and fighting with each other to get a portion of the shares which she distributes so bountifully among them. In the clouds sits a demon, blowing bubbles of soap, which are also the objects of the admiration and cupidity of the crowd, who jump upon one another's backs to reach them ere they burst. Right in the pathway of the car, and blocking up the passage, stands a large building, with three doors, through one of which it must pass, if it proceeds further, and all the crowd along with it.

Over the first door are the words, 'Hôpital des Foux,' over the second, 'Hôpital des Malades,' and over the third, 'Hôpital des Gueux.' Another caricature represented Law sitting in a large cauldron, boiling over the flames of popular madness, surrounded by an impetuous multitude, who were pouring all their gold and silver into it, and receiving gladly in exchange the bits of paper which he distributed among them by handfuls.

While this excitement lasted, Law took good care not to expose himself unguarded in the streets. Shut up in the apartments of the regent, he was secure from all attack, and, whenever he ventured abroad, it was either *incognito*, or in one of the Royal carriages, with a powerful escort. An amusing anecdote is recorded of the detestation in which he was held by the people, and the ill treatment he would have met, had he fallen into their hands. A gentleman, of the name of Boursel, was passing in his carriage down the Rue St. Antoine, when his further progress was stayed by a hackney coach that had blocked up the road. M. Boursel's servant called impatiently to the hackney coachman to get out of the way, and, on his refusal, struck him a blow on the face. A crowd was soon drawn together by the disturbance, and M. Boursel got out of the carriage to restore order. The hackney-coachman, imagining that he had now another assailant, bethought him of an expedient to rid himself of both, and called out as loudly as he was able, "Help! help! murder! murder! Here are Law and his servant going to kill me! Help! help!" At this cry, the people came out of their shops, armed with sticks and other weapons, while the mob gathered stones to inflict summary vengeance upon the supposed financier. Happily for M. Boursel and his servant, the door of the church of the Jesuits stood wide open, and, seeing the fearful odds against them, they rushed towards it with all speed. They reached the altar, pursued by the people, and would have been ill treated even there, if, finding the door open leading to the sacristy, they had not sprang through, and closed it after them.

The mob were then persuaded to leave the church by the alarmed and indignant priests; and, finding M. Boursel's carriage still in the streets, they vented their ill-will against it, and did it considerable damage.

The twenty-five millions secured on the municipal revenues of the city of Paris, bearing so low an interest as two and a half percent, were not very popular among the large holders of Mississippi stock. The conversion of the securities was, therefore, a work of considerable difficulty; for many preferred to retain the falling paper of Law's Company, in the hope that a favorable turn might take place. On the 15th of August, with a view to hasten the conversion, an edict was passed, declaring that all notes for sums between one thousand and ten thousand livres; should not pass current, except for the purchase of annuities and bank accounts, or for the payment of installments still due on the shares of the company.

In October following another edict was passed, depriving these notes of all value whatever after the month of November next ensuing. The management of the mint, the farming of the revenue, and all the other advantages and privileges of the India, or Mississippi Company, were taken from them, and they were reduced to a mere private company. This was the deathblow to the whole system, which had now got into the hands of its enemies. Law had lost all influence in the Council of Finance, and the company, being despoiled of its immunities, could no longer hold out the shadow of a prospect of being able to fulfil its engagements. All those suspected of illegal profits at the time the public delusion was at its height, were sought out and amerced in heavy fines. It was previously ordered that a list of the original proprietors should be made out, and that such persons as still retained their shares should place them in deposit with the company, and that those who had neglected to complete the shares for which they had put down their names, should now purchase them of the company, at the rate of 13,500 livres for each share of 500 livres. Rather than submit to pay this enormous sum for stock which was actually at a discount, the shareholders packed up all their portable effects, and endeavored to find a refuge in foreign countries. Orders were immediately issued to the authorities at the ports and frontiers, to apprehend all travelers who sought to leave the kingdom, and keep them in custody, until it was ascertained whether they had any plate or jewellery with them, or were concerned in the late stock-jobbing. Against such few as escaped, the punishment of death was recorded, while the most arbitrary proceedings were instituted against those who remained.

Law himself, in a moment of despair, determined to leave a country where his life was no longer secure. He at first only demanded permission to retire from Paris to one of his country-seats; a permission which the regent cheerfully granted. The latter was much affected at the unhappy turn affairs had taken, but his faith continued unmoved in the truth and efficacy of Law's financial system. His eyes were opened to his own errors, and during the few remaining years of his life, he constantly longed for an opportunity of again establishing the system upon a securer basis. At Law's last interview with the Prince, he is reported to have said—"I confess that I have committed many faults; I committed them because I am a man, and all men are liable to error; but I declare to you most solemnly that none of them proceeded from wicked or dishonest motives, and that nothing of the kind will be found in the whole course of my conduct."

Two or three days after his departure the regent sent him a very kind letter, permitting him to leave the kingdom whenever he pleased, and stating that he had ordered his passports to be made ready. He at the same time offered him any sum of money he might require. Law respectfully declined the money, and set out for Brussels in a postchaise belonging to Madame de Prie, the mistress of the Duke of Bourbon, escorted by six horse-guards. From thence he proceeded to Venice, where he remained for some months, the object of the greatest curiosity to the people, who believed him to be the possessor of enormous wealth. No opinion, however, could be more erroneous. With more generosity than could have been expected from a man who during the greatest part of his life had been a professed gambler, he had refused to enrich himself at the expense of a ruined nation. During the height of the popular frenzy for Mississippi stock, he had never doubted of the final success of his projects, in making France the richest and most powerful nation of Europe. He invested all his gains in the purchase of landed property in France—a sure proof of his own belief in the stability of his schemes. He had hoarded no plate or jewellery, and sent no money, like the dishonest jobbers, to foreign countries. His all, with the exception of one diamond, worth about five or six thousand pounds sterling, was invested in the French soil; and when he left that country, he left it almost a beggar. This fact alone ought to rescue his memory from the charge of knavery, so often and so unjustly brought against him.

As soon as his departure was known, all his estates and his valuable library were confiscated. Among the rest, an annuity of 200,000 livres, (8000 pounds sterling,) on the lives of his wife and children, which had been purchased for five millions of livres, was forfeited, notwithstanding that a special edict, drawn up for the purpose in the days of his prosperity, had expressly declared that it should never be confiscated for any cause whatever. Great discontent existed among the people that Law had been suffered to escape. The mob and the Parliament would have been pleased to have seen him hanged. The few who had not suffered by the commercial revolution, rejoiced that the *quack* had left the country; but all those (and they were by far the most numerous class) whose fortunes were implicated, regretted that his intimate knowledge of the distress of the country, and of the causes that had led to it, had not been rendered more available in discovering a remedy.

At a meeting of the Council of Finance, and the general council of the Regency, documents were laid upon the table, from which it appeared that the amount of notes in circulation was 2700 millions. The regent was called upon to explain how it happened that there was a discrepancy between the dates at which these issues were made, and those of the edicts by which they were authorized. He might have safely taken the whole blame upon himself, but he preferred that an absent man should bear a share of it, and he therefore stated that Law, upon his own authority, had issued 1200 millions of notes at different times, and that he (the regent) seeing that the thing had been irrevocably done, had screened Law, by antedating the decrees of the council, which authorized the augmentation. It would have been more to his credit if he had told the whole truth while he was about it, and acknowledged that it was mainly through his extravagance and impatience that Law had been induced to overstep the bounds of safe speculation. It was also ascertained that the national debt, on the 1st of January, 1721, amounted to upwards of $100 millions of livres, or more than 124,000,000 pounds sterling, the interest upon which was 3,196,000 pounds. A commission, or visa, was forthwith appointed to examine into all the securities of the state creditors, who were to be divided into five classes, the first four comprising those who had purchased their securities with real effects, and the latter comprising those who could give no proofs that the transactions they had entered into were real and bona fide. The securities of the latter were ordered to be destroyed, while those of the first four classes were subjected to a most rigid and jealous scrutiny. The result of the labors of the visa was a report, in which they counselled the reduction of the interest upon these securities to fifty-six millions of livres. They justified this advice by a statement of the various acts of peculation and extortion which they had discovered, and an edict to that effect was accordingly published and duly registered by the parliaments of the kingdom.

Another tribunal was afterwards established, under the title of the Chambre de l'Arsenal, which took cognizance of all the malversations committed in the financial departments of the government during the late unhappy period. A Master of Requests, named Falhonet, together with the Abbé Clement, and two clerks in their employ, had been concerned in divers acts of peculation, to the amount of upwards of a million of livres. The first two were sentenced to be beheaded, and the latter to be hanged; but their punishment was afterwards commuted into imprisonment for life in the Bastile. Numerous other acts of dishonesty were discovered, and punished by fine and imprisonment.

D'Argenson shared with Law and the regent the unpopularity which had alighted upon all those concerned in the Mississippi madness. He was dismissed from his post of Chancellor, to make room for D'Aguesseau; but he retained the title of Keeper of the Seals, and was allowed to attend the councils whenever he pleased. He thought it better, however, to withdraw from Paris, and live for a time a life of seclusion at his country-seat. But he was not formed for retirement, and becoming moody and discontented, he aggravated a disease under which he had long labored, and died in less than a twelvemonth. The populace of of Paris so detested him, that they carried their hatred even to his grave. As his funeral procession passed to the church of St. Nicholas du Chardonneret, the burying-place of his family, it was beset by a riotous mob, and his two sons, who were following as chief-mourners, were obliged to drive as fast as they were able down a by-street to escape personal violence.

As regards Law, he for some time entertained a hope that he should be recalled to France, to aid in establishing its credit upon a firmer basis. The death of the regent, in 1723, who expired suddenly, as he was sitting by the fireside conversing with his mistress, the Duchess de Phalaris, deprived him of that hope, and he was reduced to lead his former life of gambling. He was more than once obliged to pawn his diamond, the sole remnant of his vast wealth, but successful play generally enabled him to redeem it. Being persecuted by his creditors at Rome, he proceeded to Copenhagen, where he received permission from the English ministry to reside in his native country, his pardon for the murder of Mr. Wilson having been sent over to him in 1719. He was brought over in the admiral's ship, a circumstance which gave occasion for a short debate in the House of Lords. Earl Coningsby complained that a man, who had renounced both his country and his religion, should have been treated with such honor, and expressed his belief that his presence in England, at a time when the people were so bewildered by the nefarious practices of the South Sea directors, would be attended with no little danger. He gave notice of a motion on the subject; but it was allowed to drop, no other member of the House having the slightest participation in his lordship's fears. Law remained for about four years in England, and then proceeded to Venice, where he died in 1729, in very embarrassed circumstances. The following epitaph was written at the time:

"Ci gît cet Ecossais célébre,
Ce calculateur sans égal,
Qui, par les régles de l'algébre,
A mis la France à l'hôpital."

His brother, William Law, who had been concerned with him in the administration both of the Bank and the Louisiana Company, was imprisoned in the Bastile for alleged malversation, but no guilt was ever proved against him. He was liberated after fifteen months, and became the founder of a family, which is still known in France under the title of Marquises of Lauriston.

In the next chapter will be found an account of the madness which infected the people of England at the same time, and under very similar circumstances, but which, thanks to the energies and good sense of a constitutional government, was attended with results far less disastrous than those which were seen in France.

CHAPTER 2

The South-Sea Bubble

At length corruption, like a general flood,
Did deluge all, and avarice creeping on,
Spread, like a low-born mist, and hid the sun.
Statesmen and patriots plied alike the stocks,
Peeress and butler shared alike the box;
And judges jobbed, and bishops bit the town,
And mighty dukes packed cards for half-a-crown:
Britain was sunk in lucre's sordid charms.
—Pope.

The South Sea Company was originated by the celebrated Harley, Earl of Oxford, in the year 1711, with the view of restoring public credit, which had suffered by the dismissal of the Whig ministry, and of providing for the discharge of the army and navy debentures, and other parts of the floating debt, amounting to nearly ten millions sterling. A company of merchants, at that time without a name, took this debt upon themselves, and the government agreed to secure them, for a certain period, the interest of six percent. To provide for this interest, amounting to 600,000 pounds per annum, the duties upon wines, vinegar, India goods, wrought silks, tobacco, whale-fins, and some other articles, were rendered permanent. The monopoly of the trade to the South Seas was granted, and the company, being incorporated by Act of Parliament, assumed the title by which it has ever since been known. The minister took great credit to himself for his share in this transaction, and the scheme was always called by his flatterers "the Earl of Oxford's masterpiece."

Even at this early period of its history, the most visionary ideas were formed by the company and the public of the immense riches of the eastern coast of South America. Everybody had heard of the gold and silver mines of Peru and Mexico; every one believed them to be inexhaustible, and that it was only necessary to send the manufactures of England to the coast, to be repaid a hundredfold in gold and silver ingots by the natives. A report, industriously spread, that Spain was willing to concede four ports, on the coasts of Chili and Peru, for the purposes of traffic, increased the general confidence; and for many years the South Sea Company's stock was in high favor.

Philip V of Spain, however, never had any intention of admitting the English to a free trade in the ports of Spanish America. Negotiations were set on foot, but their only result was the *assiento* contract, or the privilege of supplying the colonies with Negroes for thirty years, and of sending once a year a vessel, limited both as to tonnage and value of cargo, to trade with Mexico, Peru, or Chile. The latter permission was only granted upon the hard condition, that the King of Spain should enjoy one-fourth of the profits, and a tax of five percent on the remainder. This was a great disappointment to the Earl of Oxford and his party, who were reminded much oftener than they found agreeable of the

"Parturiunt montes, nascitur ridiculus mus."

But the public confidence in the South Sea Company was not shaken. The Earl of Oxford declared, that Spain would permit two ships, in addition to the annual ship, to carry out merchandise during the first year; and a list was published, in which all the ports and harbors of these coasts were pompously set forth as open to the trade of Great Britain. The first voyage of the annual ship was not made till the year 1717, and in the following year the trade was suppressed by the rupture with Spain.

The King's speech, at the opening of the session of 1717, made pointed allusion to the state of public credit, and recommended that proper measures should be taken to reduce the national debt. The two great monetary corporations, the South Sea Company and the Bank of England, made proposals to Parliament on the 20th of May ensuing. The South Sea Company prayed that their capital stock of ten millions might be increased to twelve, by subscription or otherwise, and offered to accept five percent instead of six upon the whole amount. The Bank made proposals equally advantageous. The House debated for some time, and finally three acts were passed, called the South Sea Act, the Bank Act, and the General Fund Act. By the first, the proposals of the South Sea Company were accepted, and that body held itself ready to advance the sum of two millions towards discharging the principal and interest of the debt due by the state for the four lottery funds of the ninth and tenth years of Queen Anne. By the second act, the Bank received a lower rate of interest for the sum of 1,775,027 pounds 15 shillings due to it by the state, and agreed to deliver up to be cancelled as many Exchequer bills as amounted to two millions sterling, and to accept of an annuity of one hundred thousand pounds, being after the rate of five percent, the whole redeemable at one year's notice. They were further required to be ready to advance, in case of need, a sum not exceeding 2,500,000 pounds upon the same terms of five percent interest, redeemable by Parliament. The General Fund Act recited the various deficiencies, which were to be made good by the aids derived from the foregoing sources.

The name of the South Sea Company was thus continually before the public. Though their trade with the South American States produced little or no augmentation of their revenues, they continued to flourish as a monetary corporation. Their stock was in high request, and the directors, buoyed up with success, began to think of new means for extending their influence. The Mississippi scheme of John Law, which so dazzled and captivated the French people, inspired them with an idea that they could carry on the same game in England. The anticipated failure of his plans did not divert them from their intention. Wise in their own conceit, they imagined they could avoid his faults, carry on their schemes for ever, and stretch the cord of credit to its extremist tension, without causing it to snap asunder.

It was while Law's plan was at its greatest height of popularity, while people were crowding in thousands to the Rue Quincampoix, and ruining themselves with frantic eagerness, that the South Sea directors laid before Parliament their famous plan for paying off the national debt. Visions of boundless wealth floated before the fascinated eyes of the people in the two most celebrated countries of Europe. The English commenced their career of extravagance somewhat later than the French; but as soon as the delirium seized them, they were determined not to be outdone. Upon the 22nd of January 1720, the House of Commons resolved itself into a Committee of the whole House, to take into consideration that part of the King's speech at the opening of the session which related to the public debts, and the proposal of the South Sea Company towards the redemption and sinking of the same. The proposal set forth at great length, and under several heads, the debts of the state, amounting to 30,981,712 pounds, which the Company were anxious to take upon themselves, upon consideration of five percent per annum, secured to them until Midsummer 1727; after which time, the whole was to become redeemable at the pleasure of the legislature, and the interest to be reduced to four percent. The proposal was received with great favor; but the Bank of England had many friends in the House of Commons, who were desirous that that body should share in the advantages that were likely to accrue. On behalf of this corporation it was represented, that they had performed great and eminent services to the state, in the most difficult times, and deserved, at least, that if any advantage was to be made by public bargains of this nature, they should be preferred before a company that had never done any thing for the nation. The further consideration of the matter was accordingly postponed for five days. In the mean time, a plan was drawn up by the Governors of the Bank. The South Sea Company, afraid that the Bank might offer still more advantageous terms to the government than themselves, reconsidered their former proposal, and made some alterations in it, which they hoped would render it more acceptable. The principal change was a stipulation that the government might redeem these debts at the expiration of four years, instead of seven, as at first suggested. The Bank resolved not to be outbidden in this singular auction, and the Governors also reconsidered their first proposal, and sent in a new one.

Thus, each corporation having made two proposals, the House began to deliberate. Mr. Robert Walpole was the chief speaker in favor of the Bank, and Mr. Aislabie, the Chancellor of the Exchequer, the principal advocate on behalf of the South Sea Company. It was resolved, on the 2nd of February, that the proposals of the latter were most advantageous to the country. They were accordingly received, and leave was given to bring in a bill to that effect.

Exchange Alley was in a fever of excitement. The Company's stock, which had been at a hundred and thirty the previous day, gradually rose to three hundred, and continued to rise with the most astonishing rapidity during the whole time that the bill in its several stages was under discussion. Mr. Walpole was almost the only statesman in the House who spoke out boldly against it. He warned them, in eloquent and solemn language, of the evils that would ensue. It countenanced, he said, "the dangerous practice of stock-jobbing, and would divert the genius of the nation from trade and industry. It would hold out a dangerous lure to decoy the unwary to their ruin, by making them part with the earnings of their labor for a prospect of imaginary wealth. The great principle of the project was an evil of first-rate magnitude; it was to raise artificially the value of the stock, by exciting and keeping up a general infatuation, and by promising dividends out of funds which could never be adequate to the purpose. In a prophetic spirit he added, that if the plan succeeded, the directors would become masters of the government, form a new and absolute aristocracy in the kingdom, and control the resolutions of the legislature. If it failed, which he was convinced it would, the result would bring general discontent and ruin upon the country. Such would be the delusion, that when the evil day came, as come it would, the people would start up, as from a dream, and ask themselves if these things could have been true. All his eloquence was in vain. He was looked upon as a false prophet, or compared to the hoarse raven, croaking omens of evil. His friends, however, compared him to Cassandra, predicting evils which would only be believed when they came home to men's hearths, and stared them in the face at their own boards.

Although, in former times, the House had listened with the utmost attention to every word that fell from his lips, the benches became deserted when it was known that he would speak on the South Sea question.

The bill was two months in its progress through the House of Commons. During this time every exertion was made by the directors and their friends, and more especially by the Chairman, the noted Sir John Blunt, to raise the price of the stock. The most extravagant rumors were in circulation. Treaties between England and Spain were spoken of, whereby the latter was to grant a free trade to all her colonies; and the rich produce of the mines of Potosi-la-Paz was to be brought to England until silver should become almost as plentiful as iron. For cotton and woolen goods, with which we could supply them in abundance, the dwellers in Mexico were to empty their golden mines. The company of merchants trading to the South Seas would be the richest the world ever saw, and every hundred pounds invested in it would produce hundreds per annum to the stock-holder. At last the stock was raised by these means to near four hundred; but, after fluctuating a good deal, settled at three hundred and thirty, at which price it remained when the bill passed the Commons by a majority of 172 against 55.

In the House of Lords the bill was hurried through all its stages with unexampled rapidity. On the 4th of April it was read a first time; on the 5th, it was read a second time; on the 6th, it was committed; and on the 7th, was read a third time, and passed.

Several peers spoke warmly against the scheme; but their warnings fell upon dull, cold ears. A speculating frenzy had seized them as well as the plebeians. Lord North and Grey said the bill was unjust in its nature, and might prove fatal in its consequences, being calculated to enrich the few and impoverish the many. The Duke of Wharton followed; but, as he only retailed at second-hand the arguments so eloquently stated by Walpole in the Lower House, he was not listened to with even the same attention that had been bestowed upon Lord North and Grey. Earl Cowper followed on the same side, and compared the bill to the famous horse of the siege of Troy. Like that, it was ushered in and received with great pomp and acclamations of joy, but bore within it treachery and destruction. The Earl of Sunderland endeavored to answer all objections; and, on the question being put, there appeared only seventeen peers against, and eighty-three in favor of the project. The very same day on which it passed the Lords, it received the Royal assent, and became the law of the land.

It seemed at that time as if the whole nation had turned stock-jobbers. Exchange Alley was every day blocked up by crowds, and Cornhill was impassable for the number of carriages. Everybody came to purchase stock. "Every fool aspired to be a knave." In the words of a ballad, published at the time, and sung about the streets, ["A South Sea Ballad; or, Merry Remarks upon Exchange Alley Bubbles. To a new tune, called 'The Grand Elixir; or, the Philosopher's Stone Discovered.'"]

"Then stars and garters did appear
Among the meaner rabble;
To buy and sell, to see and hear,
The Jews and Gentiles squabble.

The greatest ladies thither came,
And plied in chariots daily,
Or pawned their jewels for a sum
To venture in the Alley."

The inordinate thirst of gain that had afflicted all ranks of society, was not to be slaked even in the South Sea. Other schemes, of the most extravagant kind, were started. The share-lists were speedily filled up, and an enormous traffic carried on in shares, while, of course, every means were resorted to, to raise them to an artificial value in the market.

Contrary to all expectation, South Sea stock fell when the bill received the Royal assent.

On the 7th of April the shares were quoted at three hundred and ten, and. on the following day, at two hundred and ninety. Already the directors had tasted the profits of their scheme, and it was not likely that they should quietly allow the stock to find its natural level, without an effort to raise it. Immediately their busy emissaries were set to work. Every person interested in the success of the project endeavored to draw a knot of listeners around him, to whom he expatiated on the treasures of the South American seas. Exchange Alley was crowded with attentive groups. One rumor alone, asserted with the utmost confidence, had an immediate effect upon the stock. It was said, that Earl Stanhope had received overtures in France from the Spanish Government to exchange Gibraltar and Port Mahon for some places on the coast of Peru, for the security and enlargement of the trade in the South Seas. Instead of one annual ship trading to those ports, and allowing the King of Spain twenty-five percent out of the profits, the Company might build and charter as many ships as they pleased, and pay no percentage whatever to any foreign potentate.

"Visions of ingots danced before their eyes,"
and stock rose rapidly. On the 12th of April, five days after the bill had become law, the directors opened their books for a subscription of a million, at the rate of 300 pounds for every 100 pounds capital. Such was the concourse of persons, of all ranks, that this first subscription was found to amount to above two millions of original stock. It was to be paid at five payments, of 60 pounds each for every 100 pounds. In a few days the stock advanced to three hundred and forty, and the subscriptions were sold for double the price of the first payment. To raise the stock still higher, it was declared, in a general court of directors, on the 21st of April, that the midsummer dividend should be ten percent, and that all subscriptions should be entitled to the same. These resolutions answering the end designed, the directors, to improve the infatuation of the monied men, opened their books for a second subscription of a million, at four hundred percent. Such was the frantic eagerness of people of every class to speculate in these funds, that in the course of a few hours no less than a million and a half was subscribed at that rate.

In the mean time, innumerable joint-stock companies started up everywhere. They soon received the name of Bubbles, the most appropriate that imagination could devise.

The populace are often most happy in the nicknames they employ. None could be more apt than that of Bubbles. Some of them lasted for a week, or a fortnight, and were no more heard of, while others could not even live out that short span of existence. Every evening produced new schemes, and every morning new projects. The highest of the aristocracy were as eager in this hot pursuit of gain as the most plodding jobber in Cornhill. The Prince of Wales became governor of one company, and is said to have cleared 40,000 pounds by his speculations. [Coxe's *Walpole,* Correspondence between Mr. Secretary Craggs and Earl Stanhope.] The Duke of Bridgewater started a scheme for the improvement of London and Westminster, and the Duke of Chandos another. There were nearly a hundred different projects, each more extravagant and deceptive than the other. To use the words of the *Political State*, they were "set on foot and promoted by crafty knaves, then pursued by multitudes of covetous fools, and at last appeared to be, in effect, what their vulgar appellation denoted them to be—bubbles and mere cheats." It was computed that near one million and a half sterling was won and lost by these unwarrantable practices, to the impoverishment of many a fool, and the enriching of many a rogue.

Some of these schemes were plausible enough, and, had they been undertaken at a time when the public mind was unexcited, might have been pursued with advantage to all concerned. But they were established merely with the view of raising the shares in the market. The projectors took the first opportunity of a rise to sell out, and next morning the scheme was at an end. Maitland, in his *History of London*, gravely informs us, that one of the projects which received great encouragement, was for the establishment of a company "to make deal-boards out of saw-dust." This is, no doubt, intended as a joke; but there is abundance of evidence to show that dozens of schemes hardly a whir more reasonable, lived their little day, ruining hundreds ere they fell. One of them was for a wheel for perpetual motion—capital, one million; another was "for encouraging the breed of horses in England, and improving of glebe and church lands, and repairing and rebuilding parsonage and vicarage houses." Why the clergy, who were so mainly interested in the latter clause, should have taken so much interest in the first, is only to be explained on the supposition that the scheme was projected by a knot of the foxhunting parsons, once so common in England. The shares of this company were rapidly subscribed for. But the most absurd and preposterous of all, and which showed, more completely than any other, the utter madness of the people, was one, started by an unknown adventurer, entitled "A company for carrying on an undertaking of great advantage, but nobody to know what it is." Were not the fact stated by scores of credible witnesses, it would be impossible to believe that any person could have been duped by such a project. The man of genius who essayed this bold and successful inroad upon public credulity, merely stated in his prospectus that the required capital was half a million, in five thousand shares of 100 pounds each, deposit 2 pounds per share. Each subscriber, paying his deposit, would be entitled to 100 pounds per annum per share. How this immense profit was to be obtained, he did not condescend to inform them at that time, but promised, that in a month full particulars should be duly announced, and a call made for the remaining 98 pounds of the subscription. Next morning, at nine o'clock, this great man opened an office in Cornhill. Crowds of people beset his door, and when he shut up at three o'clock, he found that no less than one thousand shares had been subscribed for, and the deposits paid. He was thus, in five hours, the winner of 2,000 pounds. He was philosopher enough to be contented with his venture, and set off the same evening for the Continent. He was never heard of again.

Well might Swift exclaim, comparing Change Alley to a gulf in the South Sea:

"Subscribers here by thousands float,
And jostle one another down,
Each paddling in his leaky boat,
And here they fish for gold, and drown.

Now buried in the depths below,
Now mounted up to heaven again,
They reel and stagger to and fro,
At their wit's end, like drunken men.

Meantime, secure on Garraway cliffs,
A savage race, by shipwrecks fed,
Lie waiting for the foundered skiffs,
And strip the bodies of the dead."

Another fraud that was very successful, was that of the "Globe Permits," as they were called. They were nothing more than square pieces of playing cards, on which was the impression of a seal, in wax, bearing the sign of the Globe Tavern, in the neighborhood of Exchange Alley, with the inscription of "Sail Cloth Permits." The possessors enjoyed no other advantage from them than permission to subscribe, at some future time, to a new sail-cloth manufactory, projected by one who was then known to be a man of fortune, but who was afterwards involved in the peculation and punishment of the South Sea directors. These permits sold for as much as sixty guineas in the Alley.

Persons of distinction, of both sexes, were deeply engaged in all these bubbles, those of the male sex going to taverns and coffee-houses to meet their brokers, and the ladies resorting for the same purpose to the shops of milliners and haberdashers. But it did not follow that all these people believed in the feasibility of the schemes to which they subscribed; it was enough for their purpose that their shares would, by stock-jobbing arts, be soon raised to a premium, when they got rid of them with all expedition to the really credulous. So great was the confusion of the crowd in the alley, that shares in the same bubble were known to have been sold at the same instant ten percent higher at one end of the alley than at the other. Sensible men beheld the extraordinary infatuation of the people with sorrow and alarm. There were some, both in and out of Parliament, who foresaw clearly the ruin that was impending. Mr. Walpole did not cease his gloomy forebodings. His fears were shared by all the thinking few, and impressed most forcibly upon the government. On the 11th of June, the day the Parliament rose, the King published a proclamation, declaring that all these unlawful projects should be deemed public nuisances, and prosecuted accordingly, and forbidding any broker, under a penalty of five hundred pounds, from buying or selling any shares in them. Notwithstanding this proclamation, roguish speculators still carried them on, and the deluded people still encouraged them. On the

12th of July, an order of the Lords Justices assembled in privy council was published, dismissing all the petitions that had been presented for patents and charters, and dissolving all the bubble companies. The following copy of their lordships' order, containing a list of all these nefarious projects, will not be deemed uninteresting at the present day, when there is but too much tendency in the public mind to indulge in similar practices:

"At the Council Chamber, Whitehall, the 12th day of July, 1720. Present, their Excellencies the Lords Justices in Council.

"Their Excellencies, the Lords Justices in council, taking into consideration the many inconveniences arising to the public from several projects set on foot for raising of joint stock for various purposes, and that a great many of his Majesty's subjects have been drawn in to part with their money on pretence of assurances that their petitions for patents and charters, to enable them to carry on the same, would be granted: to prevent such impositions, their Excellencies, this day, ordered the said several petitions, together with such reports from the Board of Trade, and from his Majesty's Attorney and Solicitor General, as had been obtained thereon, to be laid before them, and after mature consideration thereof, were pleased, by advice of his Majesty's Privy Council, to order that the said petitions be dismissed, which are as follow:

"1. Petition of several persons, praying letters patent for carrying on a fishing trade, by the name of the Grand Fishery of Great Britain.

"2. Petition of the Company of the Royal Fishery of England, praying letters patent for such further powers as will effectually contribute to carry on the said fishery.

"3. Petition of George James, on behalf of himself and divers persons of distinction concerned in a national fishery; praying letters patent of incorporation to enable them to carry on the same.

"4. Petition of several merchants, traders, and others, whose names are thereunto subscribed, praying to be incorporated for reviving and carrying on a whale fishery to Greenland and elsewhere.

"5. Petition of Sir John Lambert, and others thereto subscribing, on behalf of themselves and a great number of merchants, praying to be incorporated for carrying on a Greenland trade, and particularly a whale fishery in Davis's Straits.

"6. Another petition for a Greenland trade.

"7. Petition of several merchants, gentlemen, and citizens, praying to be incorporated, for buying and building of ships to let or freight.

"8. Petition of Samuel Antrim and others, praying for letters patent for sowing hemp and flax.

"9. Petition of several merchants, masters of ships, sail-makers, and manufacturers of sail-cloth, praying a charter of incorporation, to enable them to carry on and promote the said manufactory by a joint stock.

"10. Petition of Thomas Boyd, and several hundred merchants, owners and masters of ships, sailmakers, weavers, and other traders, praying a charter of incorporation, empowering them to borrow money for purchasing lands, in order to the manufacturing sail-cloth and fine Holland.

"11. Petition on behalf of several persons interested in a patent granted by the late King William and Queen Mary, for the making of linen and sail-cloth, praying that no charter may be granted to any persons whatsoever for making sail-cloth, but that the privilege now enjoyed by them may be confirmed, and likewise an additional power to carry on the cotton and cotton-silk manufactures.

"12. Petition of several citizens, merchants, and traders in London, and others, subscribers to a British stock, for a general insurance from fire in any part of England, praying to be incorporated for carrying on the said undertaking.

"13. Petition of several of his Majesty's loyal subjects of the city of London, and other parts of Great Britain, praying to be incorporated, for carrying on a general insurance from losses by fire within the kingdom of England.

"14. Petition of Thomas Burges, and others his Majesty's subjects thereto subscribing, in behalf of themselves and others, subscribers to a fund of 1,200,000 pounds, for carrying on a trade to his Majesty's German dominions, praying to be incorporated, by the name of the Harburg Company.

"15. Petition of Edward Jones, a dealer in timber, on behalf of himself and others, praying to be incorporated for the importation of timber from Germany.

"16. Petition of several merchants of London, praying a charter of incorporation for carrying on a salt-work.

"17. Petition of Captain Macphedris, of London, merchant, on behalf of himself and several merchants, clothiers, hatters, dyers, and other traders, praying a charter of incorporation, empowering them to raise a sufficient sum of money to purchase lands for planting and rearing a wood called madder, for the use of dyers.

"18. Petition of Joseph Galendo, of London, snuff-maker, praying a patent for his invention to prepare and cure Virginia tobacco for snuff in Virginia, and making it into the same in all his Majesty's dominions."

LIST OF BUBBLES.

The following Bubble Companies were by the same order declared to be illegal, and abolished accordingly:

1. For the importation of Swedish iron.

2. For supplying London with sea-coal. Capital, three millions.

3. For building and rebuilding houses throughout all England. Capital, three millions.

4. For making of muslin.

5. For carrying on and improving the British alum works.

6. For effectually settling the island of Blanco and Sal Tartagus.

7. For supplying the town of Deal with fresh water.

8. For the importation of Flanders lace.

9. For improvement of lands in Great Britain. Capital, four millions.

10. For encouraging the breed of horses in England, and improving of glebe and church lands, and for repairing and rebuilding parsonage and vicarage houses.

11. For making of iron and steel in Great Britain.

12. For improving the land in the county of Flint. Capital, one million.

13. For purchasing lands to build on. Capital, two millions.

14. For trading in hair.

15. For erecting salt-works in Holy Island. Capital, two millions.

16. For buying and selling estates, and lending money on mortgage.

17. For carrying on an undertaking of great advantage, but nobody to know what it is.

18. For paving the streets of London. Capital, two millions.

19. For furnishing funerals to any part of Great Britain.

20. For buying and selling lands and lending money at interest. Capital, five millions.

21. For carrying on the Royal Fishery of Great Britain. Capital, ten millions.

22. For assuring of seamen's wages.

23. For erecting loan-offices for the assistance and encouragement of the industrious. Capital, two millions.

24. For purchasing and improving leasable lands. Capital, four millions.

25. For importing pitch and tar, and other naval stores, from North Britain and America.

26. For the clothing, felt, and pantile trade.

27. For purchasing and improving a manor and royalty in Essex.

28. For insuring of horses. Capital, two millions.

29. For exporting the woolen manufacture, and importing copper, brass, and iron. Capital, four millions.

30. For a grand dispensary. Capital, three millions.

31. For erecting mills and purchasing lead mines. Capital, two millions.

32. For improving the art of making soap.

33. For a settlement on the island of Santa Cruz.

34. For sinking pits and smelting lead ore in Derbyshire.

35. For making glass bottles and other glass.

36. For a wheel for perpetual motion. Capital, one million.

37. For improving of gardens.

38. For insuring and increasing children's fortunes.

39. For entering and loading goods at the custom-house, and for negotiating business for merchants.

40. For carrying on a woolen manufacture in the north of England.

41. For importing walnut-trees from Virginia. Capital, two millions.

42. For making Manchester stuffs of thread and cotton.

43. For making Joppa and Castile soap.

44. For improving the wrought-iron and steel manufactures of this kingdom. Capital, four millions.

45. For dealing in lace, hollands, cambrics, lawns, &c. Capital, two millions.

46. For trading in and improving certain commodities of the produce of this kingdom, &c. Capital, three millions.

47. For supplying the London markets with cattle.

48. For making looking-glasses, coach glasses, &c. Capital, two millions.

49. For working the tin and lead mines in Cornwall and Derbyshire.

50. For making rape-oil.

51. For importing beaver fur. Capital, two millions.

52. For making pasteboard and packing-paper.

53. For importing of oils and other materials used in the woolen manufacture.

54. For improving and increasing the silk manufactures.

55. For lending money on stock, annuities, tallies, &c.

56. For paying pensions to widows and others, at a small discount. Capital, two millions.

57. For improving malt liquors. Capital, four millions.

58. For a grand American fishery.

59. For purchasing and improving the fenny lands in Lincolnshire. Capital, two millions.

60. For improving the paper manufacture of Great Britain.

61. The Bottomry Company.

62. For drying malt by hot air.

63. For carrying on a trade in the river Oronooko.

64. For the more effectual making of baize, in Colchester and other parts of Great Britain.

65. For buying of naval stores, supplying the victualling, and paying the wages of the workmen.

66. For employing poor artificers, and furnishing merchants and others with watches.

67. For improvement of tillage and the breed of cattle.

68. Another for the improvement of our breed of horses.

69. Another for a horse-insurance.

70. For carrying on the corn trade of Great Britain.

71. For insuring to all masters and mistresses the losses they may sustain by servants. Capital, three millions.

72. For erecting houses or hospitals, for taking in and maintaining illegitimate children. Capital, two millions.

73. For bleaching coarse sugars, without the use of fire or loss of substance.

74. For building turnpikes and wharfs in Great Britain.

75. For insuring from thefts and robberies.

76. For extracting silver from lead.

77. For making China and Delft ware. Capital, one million.

78. For importing tobacco, and exporting it again to Sweden and the north of Europe. Capital, four millions.

79. For making iron with pit coal.

80. For furnishing the cities of London and Westminster with hay and straw. Capital, three millions.

81. For a sail and packing cloth manufactory in Ireland.

82. For taking up ballast.

83. For buying and fitting out ships to suppress pirates.

84. For the importation of timber from Wales. Capital, two millions.

85. For rock-salt.

86. For the transmutation of quicksilver into a malleable fine metal.

Besides these bubbles, many others sprang up daily, in spite of the condemnation of the Government and the ridicule of the still sane portion of the public. The print-shops teemed with caricatures, and the newspapers with epigrams and satires, upon the prevalent folly. An ingenious card-maker published a pack of South Sea playing-cards, which are now extremely rare, each card containing, besides the usual figures, of a very small size, in one corner, a caricature of a bubble company, with appropriate verses underneath. One of the most famous bubbles was "Puckle's Machine Company," for discharging round and square cannon-balls and bullets, and making a total revolution in the art of war. Its pretensions to public favor were thus summed up, on the eight of spades:

"A rare invention to destroy the crowd
Of fools at home, instead of fools abroad.
Fear not, my friends, this terrible machine,
They're only wounded who have shares therein."

The nine of hearts was a caricature of the English Copper and Brass Company, with the following epigram:

"The headlong fool that wants to be a swopper
Of gold and silver coin for English copper,
May, in Change Alley, prove himself an ass,
And give rich metal for adulterate brass."

The eight of diamonds celebrated the Company for the Colonization of Acadia, with this doggrel:

"He that is rich and wants to fool away
A good round sum in North America,

Let him subscribe himself a headlong sharer,
And asses' ears shall honor him or bearer."

And in a similar style every card of the pack exposed some knavish scheme, and ridiculed the persons who were its dupes. It was computed that the total amount of the sums proposed for carrying on these projects was upwards of three hundred millions sterling, a sum so immense that it exceeded the value of all the lands in England at twenty years' purchase.

It is time, however, to return to the great South Sea gulf, that swallowed the fortunes of so many thousands of the avaricious and the credulous. On the 29th of May, the stock had risen as high as five hundred, and about two thirds of the government annuitants had exchanged the securities of the state for those of the South Sea Company. During the whole of the month of May the stock continued to rise, and on the 28th it was quoted at five hundred and fifty. In four days after this it took a prodigious leap, rising suddenly from five hundred and fifty to eight hundred and ninety. It was now the general opinion that the stock could rise no higher, and many persons took that opportunity of selling out, with a view of realizing their profits. Many noblemen and persons in the train of the King, and about to accompany him to Hanover, were also anxious to sell out. So many sellers, and so few buyers, appeared in the Alley on the 3rd of June, that the stock fell at once from eight hundred and ninety to six hundred and forty. The directors were alarmed, and gave their agents orders to buy. Their efforts succeeded. Towards evening confidence was restored, and the stock advanced to seven hundred and fifty. It continued at this price, with some slight fluctuation, until the company closed their books on the 22nd of June.

It would be needless and uninteresting to detail the various arts employed by the directors to keep up the price of stock. It will be sufficient to state that it finally rose to one thousand percent. It was quoted at this price in the commencement of August. The bubble was then full-blown, and began to quiver and shake, preparatory to its bursting.

Many of the government annuitants expressed dissatisfaction against the directors. They accused them of partiality in making out the lists for shares in each subscription. Further uneasiness was occasioned by its being generally known that Sir John Blunt, the chairman, and some others, had sold out. During the whole of the month of August the stock fell, and on the 2nd of September it was quoted at seven hundred only.

The state of things now became alarming. To prevent, if possible, the utter extinction of public confidence in their proceedings, the directors summoned a general court of the whole corporation, to meet in Merchant Tailors' Hall, on the 8th of September. By nine o'clock in the morning, the room was filled to suffocation; Cheapside was blocked up by a crowd unable to gain admittance, and the greatest excitement prevailed. The directors and their friends mustered in great numbers. Sir John Fellowes, the sub-governor, was called to the chair. He acquainted the assembly with the cause of their meeting, read to them the several resolutions of the court of directors, and gave them an account of their proceedings; of the taking in the redeemable and unredeemable funds, and of the subscriptions in money. Mr. Secretary Craggs then made a short speech, wherein he commended the conduct of the directors, and urged that nothing could more effectually contribute to the bringing this scheme to perfection than union among themselves. He concluded with a motion for thanking the court of directors for their prudent and skil-ful management, and for desiring them to proceed in such manner as they should think most proper for the interest and advantage of the corporation. Mr. Hungerford, who had rendered himself very conspicuous in the House of Commons for his zeal in behalf of the South Sea Company, and who was shrewdly suspected to have been a consider-able gainer by knowing the right time to sell out, was very magniloquent on this occa-sion. He said that he had seen the rise and fall, the decay and resurrection of many communities of this nature, but that, in his opinion, none had ever performed such won-derful things in so short a time as the South Sea Company. They had done more than the crown, the pulpit, or the bench could do. They had reconciled all parties in one com-mon interest; they had laid asleep, if not wholly extinguished, all the domestic jars and animosities of the nation. By the rise of their stock, monied men had vastly increased their fortunes; country-gentlemen had seen the value of their lands doubled and trebled in their hands. They had at the same time done good to the Church, not a few of the rev-erend clergy having got great sums by the project. In short, they had enriched the whole nation, and he hoped they had not forgotten themselves. There was some hissing at the latter part of this speech, which for the extravagance of its eulogy was not far removed from satire; but the directors and their friends, and all the winners in the room, ap-plauded vehemently. The Duke of Portland spoke in a similar strain, and expressed his great wonder why anybody should be dissatisfied: of course, he was a winner by his spec-ulations, and in a condition similar to that of the fat alderman in Joe Miller's Jests, who, whenever he had eaten a good dinner, folded his hands upon his paunch, and expressed his doubts whether there could be a hungry man in the world.

Several resolutions were passed at this meeting, but they had no effect upon the pub-lic. Upon the very same evening the stock fell to six hundred and forty, and on the mor-row to five hundred and forty. Day after day it continued to fall, until it was as low as four hundred. In a letter dated September 13th, from Mr. Broderick, M.P. to Lord Chan-cellor Middleton, and published in Coxe's *Walpole*, the former says,—"Various are the conjectures why the South Sea directors have suffered the cloud to break so early. I made no doubt but they would do so when they found it to their advantage. They have stretched credit so far beyond what it would bear, that specie proves insufficient to sup-port it. Their most considerable men have drawn out, securing themselves by the losses of the deluded, thoughtless numbers, whose understandings have been overruled by avarice and the hope of making mountains out of mole-hills. Thousands of families will be reduced to beggary. The consternation is inexpressible—the rage beyond description, and the case altogether so desperate that I do not see any plan or scheme so much as thought of for averting the blow, so that I cannot pretend to guess what is next to be done." Ten days afterwards, the stock still falling, he writes,—"The Company have yet come to no determination, for they are in such a wood that they know not which way to turn. By several gentlemen lately come to town, I perceive the very name of a South-Sea-man grows abominable in every country. A great many goldsmiths are already run off, and more will daily. I question whether one-third, nay, one-fourth, of them can stand it. From the very beginning, I founded my judgment of the whole affair upon the un-questionable maxim, that ten millions (which is more than our running cash) could not circulate two hundred millions, beyond which our paper credit extended. That, therefore, whenever that should become doubtful, be the cause what it would, our noble state machine must inevitably fall to the ground."

On the 12th of September, at the earnest solicitation of Mr. Secretary Craggs, several conferences were held between the directors of the South Sea and the directors of the Bank. A report which was circulated, that the latter had agreed to circulate six millions of the South Sea Company's bonds, caused the stock to rise to six hundred and seventy; but in the afternoon, as soon as the report was known to be groundless, the stock fell again to five hundred and eighty; the next day to five hundred and seventy, and so gradually to four hundred. [Gay (the poet), in that disastrous year, had a present from young Craggs of some South Sea stock, and once supposed himself to be master of twenty thousand pounds. His friends persuaded him to sell his share, but he dreamed of dignity and splendor, and could not bear to obstruct his own fortune. He was then importuned to sell as much as would purchase a hundred a year for life, "which," says Fenton, "will make you sure of a clean shirt and a shoulder of mutton every day." This counsel was rejected; the profit and principal were lost, and Gay sunk under the calamity so low that his life became in danger.—Johnson's *Lives of the Poets*.]

The ministry were seriously alarmed at the aspect of affairs. The directors could not appear in the streets without being insulted; dangerous riots were every moment apprehended. Dispatches were sent off to the King at Hanover, praying his immediate return. Mr. Walpole, who was staying at his country-seat, was sent for, that he might employ his known influence with the directors of the Bank of England to induce them to accept the proposal made by the South Sea Company for circulating a number of their bonds.

The Bank was very unwilling to mix itself up with the affairs of the Company; it dreaded being involved in calamities which it could not relieve, and received all overtures with visible reluctance. But the universal voice of the nation called upon it to come to the rescue. Every person of note in commercial politics was called in to advise in the emergency. A rough draft of a contract drawn up by Mr. Walpole was ultimately adopted as the basis of further negotiations, and the public alarm abated a little.

On the following day, the 20th of September, a general court of the South Sea Company was held at Merchant Tailors' Hall, in which resolutions were carried, empowering the directors to agree with the Bank of England, or any other persons, to circulate the Company's bonds, or make any other agreement with the Bank which they should think proper. One of the speakers, a Mr. Pulteney, said it was most surprising to see the extraordinary panic which had seized upon the people. Men were running to and fro in alarm and terror, their imaginations filled with some great calamity, the form and dimensions of which nobody knew:

"Black it stood as night—
Fierce as ten furies—terrible as hell."

At a general court of the Bank of England held two days afterwards, the governor informed them of the several meetings that had been held on the affairs of the South Sea Company, adding that the directors had not yet thought fit to come to any decision upon the matter. A resolution was then proposed, and carried without a dissentient voice, empowering the directors to agree with those of the South Sea to circulate their bonds, to what sum, and upon what terms, and for what time, they might think proper.

Thus both parties were at liberty to act as they might judge best for the public interest. Books were opened at the Bank for a subscription of three millions for the support of public credit, on the usual terms of 15 pounds percent deposit, percent premium, and 5 pounds percent interest. So great was the concourse of people in the early part of the morning, all eagerly bringing their money, that it was thought the subscription would be filled that day; but before noon, the tide turned. In spite of all that could be done to prevent it, the South Sea Company's stock fell rapidly. Their bonds were in such discredit, that a run commenced upon the most eminent goldsmiths and bankers, some of whom having lent out great sums upon South Sea stock were obliged to shut up their shops and abscond. The Sword-blade Company, who had hitherto been the chief cashiers of the South Sea Company, stopped payment. This being looked upon as but the beginning of evil, occasioned a great run upon the Bank, who were now obliged to pay out money much faster than they had received it upon the subscription in the morning. The day succeeding was a holiday (the 29th of September), and the Bank had a little breathing time. They bore up against the storm; but their former rivals, the South Sea Company, were wrecked upon it. Their stock fell to one hundred and fifty, and gradually, after various fluctuations, to one hundred and thirty-five.

The Bank, finding they were not able to restore public confidence, and stem the tide of ruin, without running the risk of being swept away with those they intended to save, declined to carry out the agreement into which they had partially entered. They were under no obligation whatever to continue; for the so called Bank contract was nothing more than the rough draught of an agreement, in which blanks had been left for several important particulars, and which contained no penalty for their secession. "And thus," to use the words of the *Parliamentary History,* "were seen, in the space of eight months, the rise, progress, and fall of that mighty fabric, which, being wound up by mysterious springs to a wonderful height, had fixed the eyes and expectations of all Europe, but whose foundation, being fraud, illusion, credulity, and infatuation, fell to the ground as soon as the artful management of its directors was discovered."

In the hey-day of its blood, during the progress of this dangerous delusion, the manners of the nation became sensibly corrupted. The Parliamentary inquiry, set on foot to discover the delinquents, disclosed scenes of infamy, disgraceful alike to the morals of the offenders and the intellects of the people among whom they had arisen. It is a deeply interesting study to investigate all the evils that were the result. Nations, like individuals, cannot become desperate gamblers with impunity. Punishment is sure to overtake them sooner or later. A celebrated writer [Smollett.] is quite wrong, when he says, "that such an era as this is the most unfavorable for a historian; that no reader of sentiment and imagination can be entertained or interested by a detail of transactions such as these, which admit of no warmth, no coloring, no embellishment; a detail of which only serves to exhibit an inanimate picture of tasteless vice and mean degeneracy." On the contrary, and Smollett might have discovered it, if he had been in the humor—the subject is capable of inspiring as much interest as even a novelist can desire. Is there no warmth in the despair of a plundered people?—no life and animation in the picture which might be drawn of the woes of hundreds of impoverished and ruined families? of the wealthy of yesterday become the beggars of to-day? of the powerful and influential changed into exiles and outcasts, and the voice of self-reproach and imprecation resounding from every corner of the land? Is it a dull or uninstructive picture to see a whole people shaking suddenly off the trammels of reason, and running wild after a golden vision, refusing obstinately to believe that it is not real, till, like a deluded hind running after an *ignis fatuus,* they are plunged into a quagmire? But in this false spirit has history too often been written. The intrigues of unworthy courtiers to gain the favor of still more unworthy kings; or the records of murderous battles and sieges have been dilated on, and told over and over again, with all the eloquence of style and all the charms of fancy; while the circumstances which have most deeply affected the morals and welfare of the people, have been passed over with but slight notice as dry and dull, and capable of neither warmth nor coloring.

During the progress of this famous bubble, England presented a singular spectacle. The public mind was in a state of unwholesome fermentation. Men were no longer satisfied with the slow but sure profits of cautious industry. The hope of boundless wealth for the morrow made them heedless and extravagant for today. A luxury, till then unheard-of, was introduced, bringing in its train a corresponding laxity of morals. The overbearing insolence of ignorant men, who had arisen to sudden wealth by successful gambling, made men of true gentility of mind and manners, blush that gold should have power to raise the unworthy in the scale of society. The haughtiness of some of these "cyphering cits," as they were termed by Sir Richard Steele, was remembered against them in the day of their adversity. In the Parliamentary inquiry, many of the directors suffered more for their insolence than for their peculation. One of them, who, in the full-blown pride of an ignorant rich man, had said that he would feed his horse upon gold, was reduced almost to bread and water for himself; every haughty look, every overbearing speech, was set down, and repaid them a hundredfold in poverty and humiliation.

The state of matters all over the country was so alarming, that George I shortened his intended stay in Hanover, and returned in all haste to England. He arrived on the 11th of November, and Parliament was summoned to meet on the 8th of December. In the mean time, public meetings were held in every considerable town of the empire, at which petitions were adopted, praying the vengeance of the Legislature upon the South Sea directors, who, by their fraudulent practices, had brought the nation to the brink of ruin. Nobody seemed to imagine that the nation itself was as culpable as the South Sea Company. Nobody blamed the credulity and avarice of the people,—the degrading lust of gain, which had swallowed up every nobler quality in the national character, or the infatuation which had made the multitude run their heads with such frantic eagerness into the net held out for them by scheming projectors. These things were never mentioned. The people were a simple, honest, hard-working people, ruined by a gang of robbers, who were to be hanged, drawn, and quartered without mercy.

This was the almost unanimous feeling of the country. The two Houses of Parliament were not more reasonable. Before the guilt of the South Sea directors was known, punishment was the only cry. The King, in his speech from the throne, expressed his hope that they would remember that all their prudence, temper, and resolution were necessary to find out and apply the proper remedy for their misfortunes. In the debate on the answer to the address, several speakers indulged in the most violent invectives against the directors of the South Sea project. The Lord Molesworth was particularly vehement. "It had been said by some, that there was no law to punish the directors of the South Sea Company, who were justly looked upon as the authors of the present misfortunes of the state. In his opinion they ought, upon this occasion, to follow the example of the ancient Romans, who, having no law against parricide, because their legislators supposed no son could be so unnaturally wicked as to embrue his hands in his father's blood, made a law to punish this heinous crime as soon as it was committed. They adjudged the guilty wretch to be sown in a sack, and thrown alive into the Tyber. He looked upon the contrivers and executors of the villainous South Sea scheme as the parricides of their country, and should be satisfied to see them tied in like manner in sacks, and thrown into the Thames." Other members spoke with as much want of temper and discretion. Mr. Walpole was more moderate. He recommended that their first care should be to restore public credit. "If the city of London were on fire, all wise men would aid in extinguishing the flames, and preventing the spread of the conflagration before they inquired after the incendiaries. Public credit had received a dangerous wound, and lay bleeding, and they ought to apply a speedy remedy to it. It was time enough to punish the assassin afterwards." On the 9th of December an address, in answer to his Majesty's speech, was agreed upon, after an amendment, which was carried without a division, that words should be added expressive of the determination of the House not only to seek a remedy for the national distresses, but to punish the authors of them.

The inquiry proceeded rapidly. The directors were ordered to lay before the House a full account of all their proceedings. Resolutions were passed to the effect that the calamity was mainly owing to the vile arts of stock-jobbers, and that nothing could tend more to the re-establishment of public credit than a law to prevent this infamous practice. Mr. Walpole then rose, and said, that "as he had previously hinted, he had spent some time upon a scheme for restoring public credit, but that, the execution of it depending upon a position which had been laid down as fundamental, he thought it proper, before he opened out his scheme, to be informed whether he might rely upon that foundation. It was, whether the subscription of public debts and encumbrances, money subscriptions, and other contracts, made with the South Sea Company should remain in the present state?" This question occasioned an animated debate. It was finally agreed, by a majority of 259 against 117, that all these contracts should remain in their present state, unless altered for the relief of the proprietors by a general court of the South Sea Company, or set aside by due course of law. On the following day Mr. Walpole laid before a committee of the whole House his scheme for the restoration of public credit, which was, in substance, to ingraft nine millions of South Sea stock into the Bank of England, and the same sum into the East India Company, upon certain conditions. The plan was favorably received by the House. After some few objections, it was ordered that proposals should be received from the two great corporations. They were both unwilling to lend their aid, and the plan met with a warm but fruitless opposition at the general courts summoned for the purpose of deliberating upon it. They, however, ultimately agreed upon the terms on which they would consent to circulate the South Sea bonds, and their report, being presented to the committee, a bill was brought in, under the superintendence of Mr. Walpole, and safely carried through both Houses of Parliament.

A bill was at the same time brought in, for restraining the South Sea directors, governor, sub-governor, treasurer, cashier, and clerks from leaving the kingdom for a twelvemonth, and for discovering their estates and effects, and preventing them from transporting or alienating the same. All the most influential members of the House supported the bill.

Mr. Shippen, seeing Mr. Secretary Craggs in his place, and believing the injurious rumors that were afloat of that minister's conduct in the South Sea business, determined to touch him to the quick. He said, he was glad to see a British House of Commons resuming its pristine vigor and spirit, and acting with so much unanimity for the public good. It was necessary to secure the persons and estates of the South Sea directors and their officers; "but," he added, looking fixedly at Mr. Craggs as he spoke, "there were other men in high station, whom, in time, he would not be afraid to name, who were no less guilty than the directors." Mr. Craggs arose in great wrath, and said, that if the innuendo were directed against him, he was ready to give satisfaction to any man who questioned him, either in the House or out of it. Loud cries of order immediately arose on every side. In the midst of the uproar Lord Molesworth got up, and expressed his wonder at the boldness of Mr. Craggs in challenging the whole House of Commons. He, Lord Molesworth, though somewhat old, past sixty, would answer Mr. Craggs whatever he had to say in the House, and he trusted there were plenty of young men beside him, who would not be afraid to look Mr. Craggs in the face, out of the House. The cries of order again resounded from every side; the members arose simultaneously; everybody seemed to be vociferating at once. The Speaker in vain called order. The confusion lasted several minutes, during which Lord Molesworth and Mr. Craggs were almost the only members who kept their seats. At last the call for Mr. Craggs became so violent that he thought proper to submit to the universal feeling of the House, and explain his unparliamentary expression. He said, that by giving satisfaction to the impugners of his conduct in that House, he did not mean that he would fight, but that he would explain his conduct. Here the matter ended, and the House proceeded to debate in what manner they should conduct their inquiry into the affairs of the South Sea Company, whether in a grand or a select committee. Ultimately, a Secret Committee of thirteen was appointed, with power to send for persons, papers, and records.

The Lords were as zealous and as hasty as the Commons. The Bishop of Rochester said the scheme had been like a pestilence. The Duke of Wharton said the House ought to show no respect of persons; that, for his part, he would give up the dearest friend he had, if he had been engaged in the project. The nation had been plundered in a most shameful and flagrant manner, and he would go as far as anybody in the punishment of the offenders. Lord Stanhope said, that every farthing possessed by the criminals, whether directors or not directors, ought to be confiscated, to make good the public losses.

During all this time the public excitement was extreme. We learn, from Coxe's *Walpole*, that the very name of a South Sea director was thought to be synonymous with every species of fraud and villany. Petitions from counties, cities, and boroughs, in all parts of the kingdom, were presented, crying for the justice due to an injured nation and the punishment of the villainous peculators. Those moderate men, who would not go to extreme lengths, even in the punishment of the guilty, were accused of being accomplices, were exposed to repeated insults and virulent invectives, and devoted, both in anonymous letters and public writings, to the speedy vengeance of an injured people. The accusations against Mr. Aislabie, Chancellor of the Exchequer, and Mr. Craggs, another member of the ministry, were so loud, that the House of Lords resolved to proceed at once into the investigation concerning them. It was ordered, on the 21st of January, that all brokers concerned in the South Sea scheme should lay before the House an account of the stock or subscriptions bought or sold by them for any of the officers of the Treasury or Exchequer, or in trust for any of them, since Michaelmas 1719. When this account was delivered, it appeared that large quantities of stock had been transferred to the use of Mr. Aislabie. Five of the South Sea directors, ineluding Mr. Edward Gibbon, the grandfather of the celebrated historian, were ordered into the custody of the black rod. Upon a motion made by Earl Stanhope, it was unanimously resolved, that the taking in or giving credit for stock without a valuable consideration actually paid or sufficiently secured; or the purchasing stock by any director or agent of the South Sea Company, for the use or benefit of any member of the administration, or any member of either House of Parliament, during such time as the South Sea Bill was yet pending in Parliament, was a notorious and dangerous corruption. Another resolution was passed a few days afterwards, to the effect that several of the directors and officers of the Company having, in a clandestine manner, sold their own stock to the Company, had been guilty of a notorious fraud and breach of trust, and had thereby mainly caused the unhappy turn of affairs that had so much affected public credit. Mr. Aislabie resigned his office as Chancellor of the Exchequer, and absented himself from Parliament until the formal inquiry into his individual guilt was brought under the consideration of the Legislature.

In the mean time, Knight, the treasurer of the Company, and who was intrusted with all the dangerous secrets of the dishonest directors, packed up his books and documents, and made his escape from the country. He embarked in disguise, in a small boat on the river, and proceeding to a vessel hired for the purpose, was safely conveyed to Calais. The Committee of Secrecy informed the House of the circumstance, when it was resolved unanimously that two addresses should be presented to the King; the first praying that he would issue a proclamation, offering a reward for the apprehension of Knight; and the second, that he would give immediate orders to stop the ports, and to take effectual care of the coasts, to prevent the said Knight, or any other officers of the South Sea Company, from escaping out of the kingdom. The ink was hardly dry upon these addresses before they were carried to the King by Mr. Methuen, deputed by the House for that purpose. The same evening a royal proclamation was issued, offering a reward of two thousand pounds for the apprehension of Knight. The Commons ordered the doors of the House to be locked, and the keys to be placed upon the table. General Ross, one of the members of the Committee of Secrecy, acquainted them that they had already discovered a train of the deepest villany and fraud that Hell had ever contrived to ruin a nation, which in due time they would lay before the House. In the mean time, in order to a further discovery, the Committee thought it highly necessary to secure the persons of some of the directors and principal South Sea officers, and to seize their papers. A motion to this effect having been made, was carried unanimously. Sir Robert Chaplin, Sir Theodore Janssen, Mr. Sawbridge, and Mr. F. Eyles, members of the House, and directors of the South Sea Company, were summoned to appear in their places, and answer for their corrupt practices. Sir Theodore Janssen and Mr. Sawbridge answered to their names, and endeavored to exculpate themselves. The House heard them patiently, and then ordered them to withdraw. A motion was then made, and carried *nemine contradicente,* that they had been guilty of a notorious breach of trust—had occasioned much loss to great numbers of his Majesty's subjects, and had highly prejudiced the public credit. It was then ordered that, for their offence, they should be expelled the House, and taken into the custody of the sergeant-at-arms. Sir Robert Chaplin and Mr. Eyles, attending in their places four days afterwards, were also expelled the House. It was resolved at the same time to address the King, to give directions to his ministers at foreign courts to make application for Knight, that he might be delivered up to the English authorities, in ease he took refuge in any of their dominions. The King at once agreed, and messengers were dispatched to all parts of the Continent the same night.

Among the directors taken into custody, was Sir John Blunt, the man whom popular opinion has generally accused of having been the original author and father of the scheme. This man, we are informed by Pope, in his epistle to Allen, Lord Bathurst, was a dissenter, of a most religious deportment, and professed to be a great believer. He constantly declaimed against the luxury and corruption of the age, the partiality of parliaments, and the misery of party spirit. He was particularly eloquent against avarice in great and noble persons. He was originally a scrivener, and afterwards became, not only a director, but the most active manager of the South Sea Company. Whether it was during his career in this capacity that he first began to declaim against the avarice of the great, we are not informed. He certainly must have seen enough of it to justify his severest anathema; but if the preacher had himself been free from the vice he condemned, his declamations would have had a better effect. He was brought up in custody to the bar of the House of Lords, and underwent a long examination. He refused to answer several important questions. He said he had been examined already by a committee of the House of Commons, and as he did not remember his answers, and might contradict himself, he refused to answer before another tribunal. This declaration, in itself an indirect proof of guilt, occasioned some commotion in the House. He was again asked peremptorily whether he had ever sold any portion of the stock to any member of the administration, or any member of either House of Parliament, to facilitate the passing of the bill. He again declined to answer. He was anxious, he said, to treat the House with all possible respect, but he thought it hard to be compelled to accuse himself. After several ineffectual attempts to refresh his memory, he was directed to withdraw. A violent discussion ensued between the friends and opponents of the ministry. It was asserted that the administration were no strangers to the convenient taciturnity of Sir John Blunt. The Duke of Wharton made a reflection upon the Earl Stanhope, which the latter warmly resented. He spoke under great excitement, and with such vehemence as to cause a sudden determination of blood to the head. He felt himself so ill that he was obliged to leave the House and retire to his chamber. He was cupped immediately, and also let blood on the following morning, but with slight relief. The fatal result was not anticipated. Towards evening he became drowsy, and turning himself on his face, expired. The sudden death of this statesman caused great grief to the nation. George I was exceedingly affected, and shut himself up for some hours in his closet, inconsolable for his loss.

Knight, the treasurer of the company, was apprehended at Tirlemont, near Liege, by one of the secretaries of Mr. Leathes, the British resident at Brussels, and lodged in the citadel of Antwerp. Repeated applications were made to the court of Austria to deliver him up, but in vain. Knight threw himself upon the protection of the states of Brabant, and demanded to be tried in that country. It was a privilege granted to the states of Brabant by one of the articles of the *Joyeuse Entrée*, that every criminal apprehended in that country should be tried in that country. The states insisted on their privilege, and refused to deliver Knight to the British authorities. The latter did not cease their solicitations; but in the mean time, Knight escaped from the citadel.

On the 16th of February the Committee of Secrecy made their first report to the House. They stated that their inquiry had been attended with numerous difficulties and embarrassments; every one they had examined had endeavored, as far as in him lay, to defeat the ends of justice. In some of the books produced before them, false and fictitious entries had been made; in others, there were entries of money, with blanks for the name of the stockholders. There were frequent erasures and alterations, and in some of the books leaves were torn out. They also found that some books of great importance had been destroyed altogether, and that some had been taken away or secreted. At the very entrance into their inquiry, they had observed that the matters referred to them were of great variety and extent. Many persons had been intrusted with various parts in the execution of the law, and under color thereof had acted in an unwarrantable manner, in disposing of the properties of many thousands of persons, amounting to many millions of money. They discovered that, before the South Sea Act was passed, there was an entry in the Company's books of the sum of 1,259,325 pounds, upon account of stock stated to have been sold to the amount of 574,500 pounds. This stock was all fictitious, and had been disposed of with a view to promote the passing of the bill. It was noted as sold at various days, and at various prices, from 150 to 325 percent. Being surprised to see so large an account disposed of, at a time when the Company were not empowered to increase their capital, the committee determined to investigate most carefully the whole transaction. The governor, sub-governor, and several directors were brought before them, and examined rigidly. They found that, at the time these entries were made, the Company was not in possession of such a quantity of stock, having in their own right only a small quantity, not exceeding thirty thousand pounds at the utmost. Pursuing the inquiry, they found that this amount of stock, was to be esteemed as taken in or holden by the Company, for the benefit of the pretended purchasers, although no mutual agreement was made for its delivery or acceptance at any certain time. No money was paid down, nor any deposit or security whatever given to the Company by the supposed purchasers; so that if the stock had fallen, as might have been expected, had the act not passed, they would have sustained no loss. If, on the contrary, the price of stock advanced (as it actually did by the success of the scheme), the difference by the advanced price was to be made good to them. Accordingly, after the passing of the act, the account of stock was made up and adjusted with Mr. Knight, and the pretended purchasers were paid the difference out of the Company's cash. This fictitious stock, which had been chiefly at the disposal of Sir John Blunt, Mr. Gibbon, and Mr. Knight, was distributed among several members of the government and their connections, by way of bribe, to facilitate the passing of the bill. To the Earl of Sunderland was assigned 50,000 pounds of this stock; to the Duchess of Kendal 10,000 pounds; to the Countess of Platen 10,000 pounds; to her two nieces 10,000 pounds; to Mr. Secretary Craggs 30,000 pounds; to Mr. Charles Stanhope (one of the Secretaries of the Treasury) 10,000 pounds; to the Swordblade Company 50,000 pounds. It also appeared that Mr. Stanhope had received the enormous sum of 250,000 pounds as the difference in the price of some stock, through the hands of Turner, Caswall, and Co., but that his name had been partly erased from their books, and altered to Stangape. Aislabie, the Chancellor of the Exchequer, had made profits still more abominable. He had an account with the same firm, who were also South Sea directors, to the amount of 794,451 pounds. He had, besides, advised the Company to make their second subscription one million and a half, instead of a million, by their own authority, and without any warrant. The third subscription had been conducted in a manner as disgraceful. Mr. Aislabie's name was down for 70,000 pounds; Mr. Craggs, senior, for 659,000 pounds; the Earl of Sunderland's for 160,000 pounds; and Mr. Stanhope for 47,000 pounds. This report was succeeded by six others, less important. At the end of the last, the committee declared that the absence of Knight, who had been principally intrusted, prevented them from carrying on their inquiries.

The first report was ordered to be printed, and taken into consideration on the next day but one succeeding. After a very angry and animated debate, a series of resolutions were agreed to, condemnatory of the conduct of the directors, of the members of the Parliament and of the administration concerned with them; and declaring that they ought, each and all, to make satisfaction out of their own estates for the injury they had done the public. Their practices were declared to be corrupt, infamous, and dangerous; and a bill was ordered to be brought in for the relief of the unhappy sufferers.

Mr. Charles Stanhope was the first person brought to account for his share in these transactions. He urged in his defense that, for some years past, he had lodged all the money he was possessed of in Mr. Knight's hands, and whatever stock Mr. Knight had taken in for him, he had paid a valuable consideration for it. As to the stock that had been bought for him by Turner, Caswall, and Co. he knew nothing about it. Whatever had been done in that matter was done without his authority, and he could not be responsible for it. Turner and Co. took the latter charge upon themselves, but it was notorious to every unbiased and unprejudiced person that Mr. Stanhope was a gainer of the 250,000 pounds which lay in the hands of that firm to his credit. He was, however, acquitted by a majority of three only. The greatest exertions were made to screen him. Lord Stanhope, the son of the Earl of Chesterfield, went round to the wavering members, using all the eloquence he was possessed of to induce them either to vote for the acquittal or to absent themselves from the house. Many weak-headed country-gentlemen were led astray by his persuasions, and the result was as already stated. The acquittal caused the greatest discontent throughout the country.

Mobs of a menacing character assembled in different parts of London; fears of riots were generally entertained, especially as the examination of a still greater delinquent was expected by many to have a similar termination. Mr. Aislabie, whose high office and deep responsibilities should have kept him honest, even had native principle been insufficient, was very justly regarded as perhaps the greatest criminal of all. His case was entered into on the day succeeding the acquittal of Mr. Stanhope. Great excitement prevailed, and the lobbies and avenues of the house were beset by crowds, impatient to know the result. The debate lasted the whole day. Mr. Aislabie found few friends: his guilt was so apparent and so heinous that nobody had courage to stand up in his favor. It was finally resolved, without a dissentient voice, that Mr. Aislabie had encouraged and promoted the destructive execution of the South Sea scheme with a view to his own exorbitant profit, and had combined with the directors in their pernicious practices to the ruin of the public trade and credit of the kingdom: that he should for his offences be ignominiously expelled from the House of Commons, and committed a close prisoner to the Tower of London; that he should be restrained from going out of the kingdom for a whole year, or till the end of the next session of Parliament; and that he should make out a correct account of all his estate, in order that it might be applied to the relief of those who had suffered by his malpractices.

This verdict caused the greatest joy. Though it was delivered at half-past twelve at night, it soon spread over the city. Several persons illuminated their houses in token of their joy. On the following day, when Mr. Aislabie was conveyed to the Tower, the mob assembled on Tower-hill with the intention of hooting and pelting him. Not succeeding in this, they kindled a large bonfire, and danced around it in the exuberance of their delight. Several bonfires were made in other places; London presented the appearance of a holiday, and people congratulated one another as if they had just escaped from some great calamity. The rage upon the acquittal of Mr. Stanhope had grown to such a height that none could tell where it would have ended, had Mr. Aislabie met with the like indulgence.

To increase the public satisfaction, Sir George Caswall, of the firm of Turner, Caswall, & Co. was expelled the House on the following day, and ordered to refund the sum of 250,000 pounds.

That part of the report of the Committee of Secrecy which related to the Earl of Sunderland was next taken into consideration. Every effort was made to clear his Lordship from the imputation. As the case against him rested chiefly on the evidence extorted from Sir John Blunt, great pains were taken to make it appear that Sir John's word was not to be believed, especially in a matter affecting the honor of a peer and privy councilor. All the friends of the ministry rallied around the Earl, it being generally reported that a verdict of guilty against him would bring a Tory ministry into power. He was eventually acquitted, by a majority of 233 against 172; but the country was convinced of his guilt. The greatest indignation was everywhere expressed, and menacing mobs again assembled in London. Happily no disturbances took place.

This was the day on which Mr. Craggs, the elder, expired. The morrow had been appointed for the consideration of his case. It was very generally believed that he had poisoned himself. It appeared, however, that grief for the loss of his son, one of the Secretaries of the Treasury, who had died five weeks previously of the small-pox, preyed much on his mind. For this son, dearly beloved, he had been amassing vast heaps of riches: he had been getting money, but not honestly; and he for whose sake he had bartered his honor and sullied his fame, was now no more. The dread of further exposure increased his trouble of mind, and ultimately brought on an apoplectic fit, in which he expired. He left a fortune of a million and a half, which was afterwards confiscated for the benefit of the sufferers by the unhappy delusion he had been so mainly instrumental in raising.

One by one the case of every director of the Company was taken into consideration. A sum amounting to two millions and fourteen thousand pounds was confiscated from their estates towards repairing the mischief they had done, each man being allowed a certain residue, in proportion to his conduct and circumstances, with which he might begin the world anew. Sir John Blunt was only allowed 5,000 pounds out of his fortune of upwards of 183,000 pounds; Sir John Fellows was allowed 10,000 pounds out of 243,000 pounds; Sir Theodore Janssen, 50,000 pounds out of 243,000 pounds; Mr. Edward Gibbon, 10,000 pounds out of 106,000 pounds.; Sir John Lambert, 5000 pounds out of 72,000 pounds. Others, less deeply involved, were treated with greater liberality. Gibbon, the historian, whose grandfather was the Mr. Edward Gibbon so severely mulcted, has given, in the *Memoirs of his Life and Writings*, an interesting account of the proceedings in Parliament at this time. He owns that he is not an unprejudiced witness; but, as all the writers from which it is possible to extract any notice of the proceedings of these disastrous years, were prejudiced on the other side, the statements of the great historian become of additional value. If only on the principle of *audi alteram partem*, his opinion is entitled to consideration. "In the year 1716," he says, "my grandfather was elected one of the directors of the South Sea Company, and his books exhibited the proof that before his acceptance of that fatal office, he had acquired an independent fortune of 60,000 pounds. But his fortune was overwhelmed in the shipwreck of the year twenty, and the labors of thirty years were blasted in a single day. Of the use or abuse of the South Sea scheme, of the guilt or innocence of my grandfather and his brother directors, I am neither a competent nor a disinterested judge. Yet the equity of modern times must condemn the violent and arbitrary proceedings, which would have disgraced the cause of justice, and rendered injustice still more odious. No sooner had the nation awakened from its golden dream, than a popular, and even a Parliamentary clamor, demanded its victims; but it was acknowledged on all sides, that the directors, however guilty, could not be touched by any known laws of the land. The intemperate notions of Lord Molesworth were not literally acted on; but a bill of pains and penalties was introduced—a retro-active statute, to punish the offences which did not exist at the time they were committed.

The Legislature restrained the persons of the directors, imposed an exorbitant security for their appearance, and marked their character with a previous note of ignominy. They were compelled to deliver, upon oath, the strict value of their estates, and were disabled from making any transfer or alienation of any part of their property. Against a bill of pains and penalties, it is the common right of every subject to be heard by his counsel at the bar. They prayed to be heard. Their prayer was refused, and their oppressors, who required no evidence, would listen to no defense. It had been at first proposed, that one eighth of their respective estates should be allowed for the future support of the directors; but it was speciously urged, that in the various shades of opulence and guilt, such a proportion would be too light for many, and for some might possibly be too heavy. The character and conduct of each man were separately weighed; but, instead of the calm solemnity of a judicial inquiry, the fortune and honor of thirty-three Englishmen were made the topics of hasty conversation, the sport of a lawless majority; and the basest member of the committee, by a malicious word, or a silent vote, might indulge his general spleen or personal animosity. Injury was aggravated by insult, and insult was embittered by pleasantry. Allowances of 20 pounds or 1 shilling were facetiously moved. A vague report that a director had formerly been concerned in another project, by which some unknown persons had lost their money, was admitted as a proof of his actual guilt.

One man was ruined because he had dropped a foolish speech, that his horses should feed upon gold; another, because he was grown so proud, that one day, at the Treasury, he had refused a civil answer to persons much above him. All were condemned, absent and unheard, in arbitrary fines and forfeitures, which swept away the greatest part of their substance. Such bold oppression can scarcely be shielded by the omnipotence of Parliament. My grandfather could not expect to be treated with more lenity than his companions. His Tory principles and connections rendered him obnoxious to the ruling powers. His name was reported in a suspicious secret. His well-known abilities could not plead the excuse of ignorance or error. In the first proceedings against the South Sea directors, Mr. Gibbon was one of the first taken into custody, and in the final sentence the measure of his fine proclaimed him eminently guilty. The total estimate, which he delivered on oath to the House of Commons, amounted to 106,543 pounds 5 shillings 6 pence, exclusive of antecedent settlements. Two different allowances of 15,000 pounds and of 10,000 pounds were moved for Mr. Gibbon; but, on the question being put, it was carried without a division for the smaller sum. On these ruins, with the skill and credit of which Parliament had not been able to despoil him, my grandfather, at a mature age, erected the edifice of a new fortune. The labors of sixteen years were amply rewarded; and I have reason to believe that the second structure was not much inferior to the first."

The next consideration of the Legislature, after the punishment of the directors, was to restore public credit. The scheme of Walpole had been found insufficient, and had fallen into disrepute. A computation was made of the whole capital stock of the South Sea Company at the end of the year 1720. It was found to amount to thirty-seven millions eight hundred thousand pounds, of which the stock allotted to all the proprietors only amounted to twenty-four millions five hundred thousand pounds. The remainder of thirteen millions three hundred thousand pounds belonged to the Company in their corporate capacity, and was the profit they had made by the national delusion. Upwards of eight millions of this were taken from the Company, and divided among the proprietors and subscribers generally, making a dividend of about 33 pounds 6 shillings 8 pence percent. This was a great relief. It was further ordered, that such persons as had borrowed money from the South Sea Company upon stock actually transferred and pledged at the time of borrowing to or for the use of the Company, should be free from all demands, upon payment of ten percent of the sums so borrowed. They had lent about eleven millions in this manner, at a time when prices were unnaturally raised; and they now received back one million one hundred thousand, when prices had sunk to their ordinary level.

But it was a long time before public credit was thoroughly restored. Enterprise, like Icarus, had soared too high, and melted the wax of her wings; like Icarus, she had fallen into a sea, and learned, while floundering in its waves, that her proper element was the solid ground. She has never since attempted so high a flight.

In times of great commercial prosperity there has been a tendency to over-speculation on several occasions since then. The success of one project generally produces others of a similar kind. Popular imitativeness will always, in a trading nation, seize hold of such successes, and drag a community too anxious for profits into an abyss from which extrication is difficult. Bubble companies, of a kind similar to those engendered by the South Sea project, lived their little day in the famous year of the panic, 1825. On that occasion, as in 1720, knavery gathered a rich harvest from cupidity, but both suffered when the day of reckoning came. The schemes of the year 1836 threatened, at one time, results as disastrous; but they were happily averted before it was too late. The South Sea project thus remains, and, it is to be hoped, always will remain, the greatest example in British history, of the infatuation of the people for commercial gambling. From the bitter experience of that period, posterity may learn how dangerous it is to let speculation riot unrestrained, and to hope for enormous profits from inadequate causes. Degrading as were the circumstances, there is wisdom to be gained from the lesson which they teach.

CHAPTER 3

The Tulipomania

Quis furor ô cives!—Lucan.

The tulip,—so named, it is said, from a Turkish word, signifying a turban,—was introduced into western Europe about the middle of the sixteenth century. Conrad Gesner, who claims the merit of having brought it into repute,—little dreaming of the extraordinary commotion it was to make in the world,—says that he first saw it in the year 1559, in a garden at Augsburg, belonging to the learned Counselor Herwart, a man very famous in his day for his collection of rare exotics. The bulbs were sent to this gentleman by a friend at Constantinople, where the flower had long been a favorite. In the course of ten or eleven years after this period, tulips were much sought after by the wealthy, especially in Holland and Germany. Rich people at Amsterdam sent for the bulbs direct to Constantinople, and paid the most extravagant prices for them. The first roots planted in England were brought from Vienna in 1600. Until the year 1634 the tulip annually increased in reputation, until it was deemed a proof of bad taste in any man of fortune to be without a collection of them. Many learned men, including Pompeius de Angelis and the celebrated Lipsius of Leyden, the author of the treatise "De Constantia," were passionately fond of tulips. The rage for possessing them soon caught the middle classes of society, and merchants and shopkeepers, even of moderate means, began to vie with each other in the rarity of these flowers and the preposterous prices they paid for them. A trader at Harlaem was known to pay one-half of his fortune for a single root—not with the design of selling it again at a profit, but to keep in his own conservatory for the admiration of his acquaintance.

One would suppose that there must have been some great virtue in this flower to have made it so valuable in the eyes of so prudent a people as the Dutch; but it has neither the beauty nor the perfume of the rose—hardly the beauty of the "sweet, sweet-pea;" neither is it as enduring as either. Cowley, it is true, is loud in its praise. He says—

"The tulip next appeared, all over gay,
But wanton, full of pride, and full of play;
The world can't show a dye but here has place;
Nay, by new mixtures, she can change her face;
Purple and gold are both beneath her care,
The richest needlework she loves to wear;
Her only study is to please the eye,
And to outshine the rest in finery."

This, though not very poetical, is the description of a poet. Beckmann, in his *History of Inventions*, paints it with more fidelity, and in prose more pleasing than Cowley's poetry. He says, "There are few plants which acquire, through accident, weakness, or disease, so many variegations as the tulip. When uncultivated, and in its natural state, it is almost of one color, has large leaves, and an extraordinarily long stem. When it has been weakened by cultivation, it becomes more agreeable in the eyes of the florist. The petals are then paler, smaller, and more diversified in hue; and the leaves acquire a softer green color. Thus this masterpiece of culture, the more beautiful it turns, grows so much the weaker, so that, with the greatest skill and most careful attention, it can scarcely be transplanted, or even kept alive."

Many persons grow insensibly attached to that which gives them a great deal of trouble, as a mother often loves her sick and ever-ailing child better than her more healthy offspring. Upon the same principle we must account for the unmerited encomia lavished upon these fragile blossoms. In 1634, the rage among the Dutch to possess them was so great that the ordinary industry of the country was neglected, and the population, even to its lowest dregs, embarked in the tulip trade. As the mania increased, prices augmented, until, in the year 1635, many persons were known to invest a fortune of 100,000 florins in the purchase of forty roots. It then became necessary to sell them by their weight in perits, a small weight less than a grain. A tulip of the species called *Admiral Liefken*, weighing 400 perits, was worth 4400 florins; an *Admiral Von der Eyk*, weighing 446 perits, was worth 1260 florins; a *Childer* of 106 perits was worth 1615 florins; a *Viceroy* of 400 perits, 3000 florins, and, most precious of all, a Semper Augustus, weighing 200 perits, was thought to be very cheap at 5500 florins. The latter was much sought after, and even an inferior bulb might command a price of 2000 florins. It is related that, at one time, early in 1636, there were only two roots of this description to be had in all Holland, and those not of the best. One was in the possession of a dealer in Amsterdam, and the other in Harlaem. So anxious were the speculators to obtain them that one person offered the fee-simple of twelve acres of building ground for the Harlaem tulip. That of Amsterdam was bought for 4600 florins, a new carriage, two grey horses, and a complete suit of harness. Munting, an industrious author of that day, who wrote a folio volume of one thousand pages upon the tulipomania, has preserved the following list of the various articles, and their value, which were delivered for one single root of the rare species called the *Viceroy*:

	florins.
Two lasts of wheat	448
Four lasts of rye	558
Four fat oxen	480
Eight fat swine	240
Twelve fat sheep	120
Two hogsheads of wine	70
Four tuns of beer	32
Two tons of butter	192
One thousand lbs. of cheese	120
A complete bed	100
A suit of clothes	80
A silver drinking cup	60
	————
	2500

People who had been absent from Holland, and whose chance it was to return when this folly was at its maximum, were sometimes led into awkward dilemmas by their ignorance. There is an amusing instance of the kind related in Blainville's *Travels*. A wealthy merchant, who prided himself not a little on his rare tulips, received upon one occasion a very valuable consignment of merchandise from the Levant. Intelligence of its arrival was brought him by a sailor, who presented himself for that purpose at the counting-house, among bales of goods of every description. The merchant, to reward him for his news, munificently made him a present of a fine red herring for his breakfast. The sailor had, it appears, a great partiality for onions, and seeing a bulb very like an onion lying upon the counter of this liberal trader, and thinking it, no doubt, very much out of its place among silks and velvets, he slyly seized an opportunity and slipped it into his pocket, as a relish for his herring. He got clear off with his prize, and proceeded to the quay to eat his breakfast. Hardly was his back turned when the merchant missed his valuable *Semper Augustus*, worth three thousand florins, or about 280 pounds sterling. The whole establishment was instantly in an uproar; search was everywhere made for the precious root, but it was not to be found. Great was the merchant's distress of mind. The search was renewed, but again without success. At last some one thought of the sailor.

The unhappy merchant sprang into the street at the bare suggestion. His alarmed household followed him. The sailor, simple soul! had not thought of concealment. He was found quietly sitting on a coil of ropes, masticating the last morsel of his "onion." Little did he dream that he had been eating a breakfast whose cost might have regaled a whole ship's crew for a twelvemonth; or, as the plundered merchant himself expressed it, "might have sumptuously feasted the Prince of Orange and the whole court of the Stadtholder." Anthony caused pearls to be dissolved in wine to drink the health of Cleopatra; Sir Richard Whittington was as foolishly magnificent in an entertainment to King Henry V; and Sir Thomas Gresham drank a diamond, dissolved in wine, to the health of Queen Elizabeth, when she opened the Royal Exchange: but the breakfast of this roguish Dutchman was as splendid as either. He had an advantage, too, over his wasteful predecessors: *their* gems did not improve the taste or the wholesomeness of *their* wine, while *his* tulip was quite delicious with his red herring. The most unfortunate part of the business for him was, that he remained in prison for some months, on a charge of felony, preferred against him by the merchant.

Another story is told of an English traveler, which is scarcely less ludicrous. This gentleman, an amateur botanist, happened to see a tulip-root lying in the conservatory of a wealthy Dutchman. Being ignorant of its quality, he took out his penknife, and peeled off its coats, with the view of making experiments upon it. When it was by this means reduced to half its original size, he cut it into two equal sections, making all the time many learned remarks on the singular appearances of the unknown bulb. Suddenly the owner pounced upon him, and, with fury in his eyes, asked him if he knew what he had been doing? "Peeling a most extraordinary onion," replied the philosopher. *"Hundert tausend duyvel,"* said the Dutchman; "it's an *Admiral Van der Eyck*." "Thank you," replied the traveler, taking out his note-book to make a memorandum of the same; "are these admirals common in your country?" "Death and the devil," said the Dutchman, seizing the astonished man of science by the collar; "come before the syndic, and you shall see." In spite of his remonstrances, the traveler was led through the streets, followed by a mob of persons.

When brought into the presence of the magistrate, he learned, to his consternation, that the root upon which he had been experimentalizing was worth four thousand florins; and, notwithstanding all he could urge in extenuation, he was lodged in prison until he found securities for the payment of this sum.

The demand for tulips of a rare species increased so much in the year 1636, that regular marts for their sale were established on the Stock Exchange of Amsterdam, in Rotterdam, Harlaem, Leyden, Alkmar, Hoorn, and other towns. Symptoms of gambling now became, for the first time, apparent. The stock-jobbers, ever on the alert for a new speculation, dealt largely in tulips, making use of all the means they so well knew how to employ, to cause fluctuations in prices. At first, as in all these gambling mania, confidence was at its height, and everybody gained. The tulip-jobbers speculated in the rise and fall of the tulip stocks, and made large profits by buying when prices fell, and selling out when they rose.

Many individuals grew suddenly rich. A golden bait hung temptingly out before the people, and, one after the other, they rushed to the tulip marts, like flies around a honey pot. Every one imagined that the passion for tulips would last for ever, and that the wealthy from every part of the world would send to Holland, and pay whatever prices were asked for them. The riches of Europe would be concentrated on the shores of the Zuyder Zee, and poverty banished from the favored clime of Holland. Nobles, citizens, farmers, mechanics, seamen, footmen, maidservants, even chimney-sweeps and old clotheswomen, dabbled in tulips. People of all grades converted their property into cash, and invested it in flowers. Houses and lands were offered for sale at ruinously low prices, or assigned in payment of bargains made at the tulip-mart. Foreigners became smitten with the same frenzy, and money poured into Holland from all directions. The prices of the necessaries of life rose again by degrees; houses and lands, horses and carriages, and luxuries of every sort, rose in value with them, and for some months Holland seemed the very antechamber of Plutus. The operations of the trade became so extensive and so intricate, that it was found necessary to draw up a code of laws for the guidance of the dealers. Notaries and clerks were also appointed, who devoted themselves exclusively to the interests of the trade. The designation of public notary was hardly known in some towns, that of tulip notary usurping its place. In the smaller towns, where there was no exchange, the principal tavern was usually selected as the "showplace," where high and low traded in tulips, and confirmed their bargains over sumptuous entertainments. These dinners were sometimes attended by two or three hundred persons, and large vases of tulips, in full bloom, were placed at regular intervals upon the tables and sideboards, for their gratification during the repast.

At last, however, the more prudent began to see that this folly could not last for ever. Rich people no longer bought the flowers to keep them in their gardens, but to sell them again at cent. percent profit. It was seen that somebody must lose fearfully in the end. As this conviction spread, prices fell, and never rose again. Confidence was destroyed, and a universal panic seized upon the dealers. *A* had agreed to purchase ten *Sempers Augustines* from *B*, at four thousand florins each, at six weeks after the signing of the contract. *B* was ready with the flowers at the appointed time; but the price had fallen to three or four hundred florins, and *A* refused either to pay the difference or receive the tulips. Defaulters were announced day after day in all the towns of Holland. Hundreds who, a few months previously, had begun to doubt that there was such a thing as poverty in the land, suddenly found themselves the possessors of a few bulbs, which nobody would buy, even though they offered them at one quarter of the sums they had paid for them. The cry of distress resounded everywhere, and each man accused his neighbor. The few who had contrived to enrich themselves hid their wealth from the knowledge of their fellow-citizens, and invested it in the English or other funds. Many who, for a brief season, had emerged from the humbler walks of life, were cast back into their original obscurity. Substantial merchants were reduced almost to beggary, and many a representative of a noble line saw the fortunes of his house ruined beyond redemption.

When the first alarm subsided, the tulip-holders in the several towns held public meetings to devise what measures were best to be taken to restore public credit. It was generally agreed, that deputies should be sent from all parts to Amsterdam, to consult with the government upon some remedy for the evil. The Government at first refused to interfere, but advised the tulip-holders to agree to some plan among themselves. Several meetings were held for this purpose; but no measure could be devised likely to give satisfaction to the deluded people, or repair even a slight portion of the mischief that had been done. The language of complaint and reproach was in everybody's mouth, and all the meetings were of the most stormy character. At last, however, after much bickering and ill-will, it was agreed, at Amsterdam, by the assembled deputies, that all contracts made in the height of the mania, or prior to the month of November 1636, should be declared null and void, and that, in those made after that date, purchasers should be freed from their engagements, on paying ten percent to the vendor. This decision gave no satisfaction. The vendors who had their tulips on hand were, of course, discontented, and those who had pledged themselves to purchase, thought themselves hardly treated. Tulips which had, at one time, been worth six thousand florins, were now to be procured for five hundred; so that the composition of ten percent was one hundred florins more than the actual value. Actions for breach of contract were threatened in all the courts of the country; but the latter refused to take cognizance of gambling transactions.

The matter was finally referred to the Provincial Council at the Hague, and it was confidently expected that the wisdom of this body would invent some measure by which credit should be restored. Expectation was on the stretch for its decision, but it never came. The members continued to deliberate week after week, and at last, after thinking about it for three months, declared that they could offer no final decision until they had more information. They advised, however, that, in the mean time, every vendor should, in the presence of witnesses, offer the tulips in natural to the purchaser for the sums agreed upon. If the latter refused to take them, they might be put up for sale by public auction, and the original contractor held responsible for the difference between the actual and the stipulated price. This was exactly the plan recommended by the deputies, and which was already shown to be of no avail. There was no court in Holland which would enforce payment. The question was raised in Amsterdam, but the judges unanimously refused to interfere, on the ground that debts contracted in gambling were no debts in law.

Thus the matter rested. To find a remedy was beyond the power of the government. Those who were unlucky enough to have had stores of tulips on hand at the time of the sudden reaction were left to bear their ruin as philosophically as they could; those who had made profits were allowed to keep them; but the commerce of the country suffered a severe shock, from which it was many years ere it recovered.

The example of the Dutch was imitated to some extent in England. In the year 1636 tulips were publicly sold in the Exchange of London, and the jobbers exerted themselves to the utmost to raise them to the fictitious value they had acquired in Amsterdam. In Paris also the jobbers strove to create a tulipomania. In both cities they only partially succeeded. However, the force of example brought the flowers into great favor, and amongst a certain class of people tulips have ever since been prized more highly than any other flowers of the field. The Dutch are still notorious for their partiality to them, and continue to pay higher prices for them than any other people. As the rich Englishman boasts of his fine race-horses or his old pictures, so does the wealthy Dutchman vaunt him of his tulips.

In England, in our day, strange as it may appear, a tulip will produce more money than an oak. If one could be found, *rara in terris*, and black as the black swan alluded to by Juvenal, its price would equal that of a dozen acres of standing corn. In Scotland, towards the close of the seventeenth century, the highest price for tulips, according to the authority of a writer in the supplement to the third edition of the *Encyclopedia Britannica*, was ten guineas. Their value appears to have diminished from that time till the year 1769, when the two most valuable species in England were the *Don Quevedo* and the *Valentinier*, the former of which was worth two guineas and the latter two guineas and a half. These prices appear to have been the minimum. In the year 1800, a common price was fifteen guineas for a single bulb. In 1835, so foolish were the fanciers, that a bulb of the species called the *Miss Fanny Kemble* was sold by public auction in London for seventy-five pounds. Still more astonishing was the price of a tulip in the possession of a gardener in the King's Road, Chelsea. In his catalogues, it was labeled at two hundred guineas! Thus a flower, which for beauty and perfume was surpassed by the abundant roses of the garden,—a nosegay of which might be purchased for a penny,—was priced at a sum which would have provided an industrious laborer and his family with food, and clothes, and lodging for six years! Should chickweed and groundsel ever come into fashion, the wealthy would, no doubt, vie with each other in adorning their gardens with them, and paying the most extravagant prices for them. In so doing, they would hardly be more foolish than the admirers of tulips. The common prices for these flowers at the present time vary from five to fifteen guineas, according to the rarity of the species.

Thorstein Veblen
(1857–1929)

AN INTRODUCTION TO HIS LIFE AND WORK

Thorstein Veblen continues to fascinate contemporary readers and academics due almost as much to his infamous life as for the famous books and essays he authored. With an appetite and aptitude for quick romance and iconoclastic misadventure more in keeping with a 1960s rock star than a Victorian Era academic, debates about Veblen focus almost as much on his lifestyle as his scholarship. Indeed, Veblen's sexual proclivities alone gained him the status of legend, even with the decades since his death raising that bar so high that few rock stars even manage to pole vault over it anymore. What other economist ever inspired the *Journal of Economic Issues* to publish a piece with a headline like, "Shameless Lothario: Thorstein Veblen as Sexual Predator and Sexual Liberator."

Fortunately, Veblen's biography has never quite overwhelmed his bibliography. A curious, cantankerous, often maddening, occasionally shocking, and thoroughly innovative thinker, Veblen advanced the study of economics by taking it a few steps back and several more to either side. This intellectual square dance broadened and deepened the perspective of economic thinking by forcing it to include sociology, psychology, theology, anthropology, and other fields of study into its theoretical accounting.

In the process, Veblen helped rescue economics from "the dismal science" dungeon Thomas Carlyle had damned it to in the mid-19th century. Veblen reinvigorated economics as a lively and engaging activity with a greater relevance to other realms of study and to people's inner, as well as material, lives.

His work also proved quite relevant to the future. Over time, Veblen turned out to be a stunningly accurate soothsayer on certain, vital aspects of the economic world. Instead of new mathematical formulations and statistical projections to predict the course of the economy, he employed his understanding of the human heart and history. Looking around today, one sees his insights about society and economy in full bloom.

HIS LIFE

Thorstein Veblen was born in 1857 in Cato, Wisconsin, a small, Norwegian immigrant farming community. The sixth of twelve children, Veblen did not learn English until his teens, when he attended Carleton College in Northfield, Minnesota. Veblen earned his

B.A. at Carleton in 1880, studying under famed neoclassical economist John Bates Clarke. After graduating, he taught at a Norwegian community school for a year before returning to his own education, this time to study at John Hopkins with Charles Sanders Pierce, founder of the pragmatist school of philosophy. In 1884, Veblen earned his Ph.D. in Moral Philosophy at Yale University, studying under William Graham Sumner, an advocate of laissez-faire economics. Veblen wrote his Yale doctoral thesis on Immanuel Kant.

Upon graduation, Veblen struggled to find work in academia. He was unemployed for six years and lived for a time at his father's farm, reading voraciously. In 1888, he married his first wife, Ellen Rolfe, niece of the president of Carleton College.

Three years later, Veblen returned to graduate school to study economics at Cornell University with James Laurence Laughlin, who helped found the Federal Reserve system. In 1892, Laughlin was appointed head of the new economics department at the University of Chicago. He gave Veblen a position as an assistant professor. While teaching at the University of Chicago, Veblen also founded and served as the managing editor for the *Journal of Political Economy.*

In 1899, Veblen wrote *The Theory of The Leisure Class.* The book, in which Veblen coined the phrase "conspicuous consumption," enjoyed a wide following. His next book, *The Theory of Business Enterprise* (1904) was more controversial and less popular. Veblen was asked to resign from the University of Chicago in 1905, due to allegations over numerous sexual improprieties with the wives of fellow faculty members. The next year, he was appointed to teach at Stanford University. He left after only three years, again due to scandals involving his personal life.

Veblen's first wife divorced him in 1911. That same year he was hired at a reduced salary by the University of Missouri-Columbia, where he remained for seven years. In 1914, Veblen married his second wife, Anne Fessenden Bradley and published *Instinct of Workmanship.* Although he disliked Missouri, he was very prolific during this time, also publishing *Imperial Germany* in 1915, *Inquiry Into the Nature of Peace* in 1917 and *The Higher Learning in America* in 1918.

After leaving the University of Missouri-Columbia, Veblen began lecturing at the New School for Social Research (later known as The New School) in Manhattan in 1919. His second wife died in 1920 after a nervous collapse. Veblen left the New School in 1926 and stopped teaching altogether. At the end of his life, he was taken in by his stepdaughter and lived with her in a cabin in the hills above Stanford until his death in 1929.

THE THEORY OF THE LEISURE CLASS

As important as it is to separate Veblen's life from his work, it may be equally important to segregate his works from one another. To embrace the full Veblen output all at once is to tempt confusion and theoretical overload. Veblen's ambitious curiosity and nose for controversy compelled him to investigate and propose new theories on topics so varied that he was perhaps the only one who recognized their organizing principle. He authored works on educational policy, sexism, Germany, sociology, Karl Marx, women's fashion and how to achieve greater business efficiency through the use of technology, among other topics.

The Theory of the Leisure Class (1899) still ranks as Veblen's most compelling and resilient work. Published in the dying days of the Gilded Age, it offers a critique of the social and economic impacts of that period's astonishing booms in wealth, opulence, and population. Perhaps every other historian, social critic, and economist viewed the age as a period of unprecedented change—but not Veblen. Surveying the era's frenzied economic activity, social and environmental upheaval, flood of new immigrants, explosions in technology and new consumer goods, plus its widening gap between the rich and poor, Veblen saw the same behavioral and economic patterns that people had exhibited since the earliest days of tribal Africa.

Veblen chose perhaps the least obvious demographic to connect modern humans to their prehistoric ancestors—the ultra rich, or, as he called them, "the leisure class." Veblen's leisure class consisted of those who enjoyed a level of wealth and social stature that essentially absolved them of productive labor. They were free to pursue lives of leisure or to perform ceremonial jobs whose main function was to remind people of their superior social status.

In ancient tribal societies and pre-Industrial Revolution Europe, these jobs consisted of priestly and upper-rank military duties. In the post-Industrial world, upper-management business people and celebrities gained the distinction, with the awards banquet, board meeting, and restructuring plan taking place of the military parade, elders council, and ritual sacrifice.

In Veblen's social and economic view, "division of labor" therefore did not serve as a means to greater efficiency like it had for Adam Smith. Instead, division of labor was another way for the elites to enforce class distinctions. The rich and powerful could not be troubled to fill blue-collar jobs or to even clean up after themselves. The working class was forced to perform all the functions that produced tangible benefits for society, while being paid a tiny fraction of what the members of the feckless leisure class earned. Even their spare time might be compromised by a second job helping maintain luxury items or homes for the rich, or aiding them in their pursuit of leisure. By dominating capital, the decision-making process, religious practices, the means of warfare, and luxury consumption, the leisure class shielded itself from the troubles and complaints of the working classes. They ensured that they would not only be more rich, powerful, and respectable than members of the masses, but also more moral.

The division of labor and compensation also led to what might be called a division of consumption. The poor would be forced to spend most of their low wages on essentials like food and shelter. The rich, on the other hand, enjoyed vast pools of disposable income. They could purchase showy, useless luxury items designed to announce their wealth and status. While the lower classes could not possibly afford to indulge in such luxuries, many were willing to die—or at least go bankrupt—trying.

Unable to rise to the level of the leisure class, members of the underclass would mimic the social elite's behavior as often as possible. In their spare time they would dabble in the trappings of an upper class existence by buying luxurious items (or their generic brand facsimiles), visiting exclusive locations, or engaging in showy acts of leisure. The more useless and expensive items you owned or pointless recreational activities you mastered, the more respectable you became. The main focus of people's economic lives, for Veblen, was more than just a "keeping up with the Jones," but a "trying to keep up with the Rockefellers or the Shaka Zulus." Far from Adam Smith's utilitarian notions of people working rationally and progressively toward improving their circumstances, Veblen believed the primary and dominant forces behind economic activity were decidedly unutilitarian—the often counter-productive lust for status that he believed had driven people since prehistoric times.

Veblen is often cited as a disciple of Marx, and he clearly borrowed heavily from Marx's concept of "commodity fetishism" and class distinctions in formulating his ideas. But Veblen reached far different conclusions about class dynamics. Amongst the aristocrats, nouveau riche, middle class, and poor, he saw not Marx's class struggle, warfare, and inevitable revolution, but envy and emulation and inevitable replication. Workers of the world could not be troubled to unite and overthrow their economic masters. They were too busy vogueing.

VEBLEN'S STYLE AND VOCABULARY

Veblen coined several new terms, including "conspicuous consumption," "pecuniary emulation," and "the ceremonial/instrumental dichotomy" to describe the activities he theorized about in *The Theory of the Leisure Class*. Indeed, the eccentric professor often seemed to communicate in a language all his own. The son of poor Norwegian immigrant farmers, Veblen did not master English until his college years. As a result, the highly stylized, ornate, and inbred language of late 19th-century academia formed his ABCs and Dick and Jane readers. Veblen's penchant for inventing new terms, along with his reliance on polysyllabic, academic verbiage can make navigating *The Theory of the Leisure Class* a challenge, particularly during passages such as this:

> Extraneous habits and proclivities encroach upon the field of action occupied by this canon, and it presently comes about that the ecclesiastical and sacerdotal structures are partially converted to other uses, in some measure alien to the purpose of the scheme of devout life as it stood in the days of the most vigorous and characteristic development of the priesthood.

Yet this absurdly turgid linguistic style seems all too appropriate for the book's subject matter and format. Though some doubt still surrounds Veblen's intentions, *The Theory of the Leisure Class* has been embraced as a satire on the useless extravagances of upper class culture. Veblen's highfalutin, sometimes confounding language and bizarre sentence structures may be seen, then, as an apt means to describe the highfalutin, confounding, bizarre excesses of the rich he portrayed.

IMPACTS

Because Veblen's *The Theory of the Leisure Class* offers social satire and criticism more than economic prescriptions, it can be difficult to gauge its impact. The book gained great popularity and renown after influential critic William Dean Howells praised it, but others were not so kind. H.L. Mencken, perhaps the most influential critic of the era, denounced Veblen's work to a degree that was extreme even by the standards of the infamously cantankerous critic. He assailed Veblen's methods of reasoning and dismissed his conclusions as obvious or patently false.

A number of people came to disagree in the coming decades. Veblen gained a hearty following in academia and among the social justice movement. Veblen's devastating take on the economic elite's attitudes toward the underclasses gave leftist thinkers and activists a new caliber of rhetorical ammunition and angle of attack. His portrait of women's objectification to the point of them being viewed as material possessions still echoes in feminist rhetoric.

Veblen also impressed a number of his fellow academics and thinkers. He lectured at Harvard and Stanford and was hired in 1906 as a full-time faculty member at the newly established University of Chicago, where he also served as managing editor of its *Journal of Political Economy*. His brilliance, however, was quickly overshadowed by his unpleasant eccentricities and sexual infidelities, and he was dismissed after less than a year.

If any residue of Veblen's theories and influence remained after his departure from the University of Chicago, it was long ago steam-blasted from the scene. A half-century after Veblen's brief tenure, the university and its *Journal of Political Economy* served as home base for the free market Chicago School of Economics. The movement launched the career of Milton Friedman, the godfather of Reaganomics, and what might be called America's second Gilded Age, beginning in the 1980s.

Still, time has validated many of Veblen's insights and bolstered his reputation. Conspicuous consumption has not just become more conspicuous in recent decades, but an increasingly important aspect of economic behavior. Advertising, which remains, in large part, a means of manipulating people into consuming conspicuously, now ranks as one of the world's leading industries. Invidious distinctions cleaved between the rich and poor rank as a growing problem to social and economic stability. Pecuniary emulation has elbowed more and more people to the brink of financial ruin due to their use of credit to purchase homes and luxury items conspicuously beyond their means. Consumer debt now looms as a major threat to the fiscal futures of tens of millions of people, but also to the world economy as a whole.

On the other hand, some unpleasant practices and social structures described by Veblen have mostly faded into the past. In particular, women have climbed a long way up from the roles of trophy wives and menial labor slaves that they were mostly limited to in Veblen's day. Through progressive action and confrontation, women have in recent decades escaped many of the limits and woes that Veblen saw them as doomed to endure in the shadow of the leisure class.

Ultimately, Veblen may gain a greater influence if other problems he described are recognized and tackled with similar vigor and skill. The first step may be reading what the brilliant, challenging and painfully insightful Thorstein Veblen had to say in *The Theory of the Leisure Class*.

THE THEORY OF THE LEISURE CLASS: AN ECONOMIC STUDY OF INSTITUTIONS BY THORSTEIN VEBLEN

CHAPTER ONE

Introductory

The institution of a leisure class is found in its best development at the higher stages of the barbarian culture; as, for instance, in feudal Europe or feudal Japan. In such communities the distinction between classes is very rigorously observed; and the feature of most striking economic significance in these class differences is the distinction maintained between the employments proper to the several classes. The upper classes are by custom exempt or excluded from industrial occupations, and are reserved for certain employments to which a degree of honor attaches. Chief among the honorable employments in any feudal community is warfare; and priestly service is commonly second to warfare. If the barbarian community is not notably warlike, the priestly office may take the precedence, with that of the warrior second. But the rule holds with but slight exceptions that, whether warriors or priests, the upper classes are exempt from industrial employments, and this exemption is the economic expression of their superior rank. Brahmin India affords a fair illustration of the industrial exemption of both these classes. In the communities belonging to the higher barbarian culture there is a considerable differentiation of sub-classes within what may be comprehensively called the leisure class; and there is a corresponding differentiation of employments between these sub-classes. The leisure class as a whole comprises the noble and the priestly classes, together with much of their retinue. The occupations of the class are correspondingly diversified; but they have the common economic characteristic of being non-industrial. These non-industrial upper-class occupations may be roughly comprised under government, warfare, religious observances, and sports.

At an earlier, but not the earliest, stage of barbarism, the leisure class is found in a less differentiated form. Neither the class distinctions nor the distinctions between leisure-class occupations are so minute and intricate. The Polynesian islanders generally show this stage of the development in good form, with the exception that, owing to the absence of large game, hunting does not hold the usual place of honor in their scheme of life. The Icelandic community in the time of the Sagas also affords a fair instance. In such a community there is a rigorous distinction between classes and between the occupations peculiar to each class. Manual labor, industry, whatever has to do directly with the everyday work of getting a livelihood, is the exclusive occupation of the inferior class. This inferior class includes slaves and other dependents, and ordinarily also all the women. If there are several grades of aristocracy, the women of high rank are commonly exempt from industrial employment, or at least from the more vulgar kinds of manual labor. The men of the upper classes are not only exempt, but by prescriptive custom they are debarred, from all industrial occupations. The range of employments open to them is rigidly defined. As on the higher plane already spoken of, these employments are government, warfare, religious observances, and sports. These four lines of activity govern the scheme of life of the upper classes, and for the highest rank—the kings or chieftains—these are the only kinds of activity that custom or the common sense of the community will allow. Indeed, where the scheme is well developed even sports are accounted doubtfully legitimate for the members of the highest rank. To the lower grades of the leisure class certain other employments are open, but they are employments that are subsidiary to one or another of these typical leisure-class occupations. Such are, for instance, the manufacture and care of arms and accoutrements and of war canoes, the dressing and handling of horses, dogs, and hawks, the preparation of sacred apparatus, etc. The lower classes are excluded from these secondary honorable employments, except from such as are plainly of an industrial character and are only remotely related to the typical leisure-class occupations.

If we go a step back of this exemplary barbarian culture, into the lower stages of barbarism, we no longer find the leisure class in fully developed form. But this lower barbarism shows the usages, motives, and circumstances out of which the institution of a leisure class has arisen, and indicates the steps of its early growth. Nomadic hunting tribes in various parts of the world illustrate these more primitive phases of the differentiation. Any one of the North American hunting tribes may be taken as a convenient illustration. These tribes can scarcely be said to have a defined leisure class. There is a differentiation of function, and there is a distinction between classes on the basis of this difference of function, but the exemption of the superior class from work has not gone far enough to make the designation "leisure class" altogether applicable. The tribes belonging on this economic level have carried the economic differentiation to the point at which a marked distinction is made between the occupations of men and women, and this distinction is of an invidious character. In nearly all these tribes the women are, by prescriptive custom, held to those employments out of which the industrial occupations proper develop at the next advance. The men are exempt from these vulgar employments and are reserved for war, hunting, sports, and devout observances. A very nice discrimination is ordinarily shown in this matter.

This division of labor coincides with the distinction between the working and the leisure class as it appears in the higher barbarian culture. As the diversification and specialization of employments proceed, the line of demarcation so drawn comes to divide the industrial from the non-industrial employments. The man's occupation as it stands at the earlier barbarian stage is not the original out of which any appreciable portion of later industry has developed. In the later development it survives only in employments that are not classed as industrial,—war, politics, sports, learning, and the priestly office. The only notable exceptions are a portion of the fishery industry and certain slight employments that are doubtfully to be classed as industry; such as the manufacture of arms, toys, and sporting goods. Virtually the whole range of industrial employments is an outgrowth of what is classed as woman's work in the primitive barbarian community.

The work of the men in the lower barbarian culture is no less indispensable to the life of the group than the work done by the women. It may even be that the men's work contributes as much to the food supply and the other necessary consumption of the group. Indeed, so obvious is this "productive" character of the men's work that in the conventional economic writings the hunter's work is taken as the type of primitive industry. But such is not the barbarian's sense of the matter. In his own eyes he is not a laborer, and he is not to be classed with the women in this respect; nor is his effort to be classed with the women's drudgery, as labor or industry, in such a sense as to admit of its being confounded with the latter. There is in all barbarian communities a profound sense of the disparity between man's and woman's work. His work may conduce to the maintenance of the group, but it is felt that it does so through an excellence and an efficacy of a kind that cannot without derogation be compared with the uneventful diligence of the women.

At a farther step backward in the cultural scale—among savage groups—the differentiation of employments is still less elaborate and the invidious distinction between classes and employments is less consistent and less rigorous. Unequivocal instances of a primitive savage culture are hard to find. Few of these groups or communities that are classed as "savage" show no traces of regression from a more advanced cultural stage. But there are groups—some of them apparently not the result of retrogression—which show the traits of primitive savagery with some fidelity. Their culture differs from that of the barbarian communities in the absence of a leisure class and the absence, in great measure, of the animus or spiritual attitude on which the institution of a leisure class rests. These communities of primitive savages in which there is no hierarchy of economic classes make up but a small and inconspicuous fraction of the human race. As good an instance of this phase of culture as may be had is afforded by the tribes of the Andamans, or by the Todas of the Nilgiri Hills. The scheme of life of these groups at the time of their earliest contact with Europeans seems to have been nearly typical, so far as regards the absence of a leisure class. As a further instance might be cited the Ainu of Yezo, and, more doubtfully, also some Bushman and Eskimo groups. Some Pueblo communities are less confidently to be included in the same class. Most, if not all, of the communities here cited may well be cases of degeneration from a higher barbarism, rather than bearers of a culture that has never risen above its present level. If so, they are for the present purpose to be taken with the allowance, but they may serve nonetheless as evidence to the same effect as if they were really "primitive" populations.

These communities that are without a defined leisure class resemble one another also in certain other features of their social structure and manner of life. They are small groups and of a simple (archaic) structure; they are commonly peaceable and sedentary; they are poor; and individual ownership is not a dominant feature of their economic system. At the same time it does not follow that these are the smallest of existing communities, or that their social structure is in all respects the least differentiated; nor does the class necessarily include all primitive communities which have no defined system of individual ownership. But it is to be noted that the class seems to include the most peaceable—perhaps all the characteristically peaceable—primitive groups of men. Indeed, the most notable trait common to members of such communities is a certain amiable inefficiency when confronted with force or fraud.

The evidence afforded by the usages and cultural traits of communities at a low stage of development indicates that the institution of a leisure class has emerged gradually during the transition from primitive savagery to barbarism; or more precisely, during the transition from a peaceable to a consistently warlike habit of life. The conditions apparently necessary to its emergence in a consistent form are: (1) the community must be of a predatory habit of life (war or the hunting of large game or both); that is to say, the men, who constitute the inchoate leisure class in these cases, must be habituated to the infliction of injury by force and stratagem; (2) subsistence must be obtainable on sufficiently easy terms to admit of the exemption of a considerable portion of the community from steady application to a routine of labor. The institution of leisure class is the outgrowth of an early discrimination between employments, according to which some employments are worthy and others unworthy. Under this ancient distinction the worthy employments are those which may be classed as exploit; unworthy are those necessary everyday employments into which no appreciable element of exploit enters.

This distinction has but little obvious significance in a modern industrial community, and it has, therefore, received but slight attention at the hands of economic writers. When viewed in the light of that modern common sense which has guided economic discussion, it seems formal and insubstantial. But it persists with great tenacity as a commonplace preconception even in modern life, as is shown, for instance, by our habitual aversion to menial employments. It is a distinction of a personal kind—of superiority and inferiority. In the earlier stages of culture, when the personal force of the individual counted more immediately and obviously in shaping the course of events, the element of exploit counted for more in the everyday scheme of life. Interest centered about this fact to a greater degree. Consequently a distinction proceeding on this ground seemed more imperative and more definitive then than is the case today. As a fact in the sequence of development, therefore, the distinction is a substantial one and rests on sufficiently valid and cogent grounds.

The ground on which a discrimination between facts is habitually made changes as the interest from which the facts are habitually viewed changes. Those features of the facts at hand are salient and substantial upon which the dominant interest of the time throws its light. Any given ground of distinction will seem insubstantial to any one who habitually apprehends the facts in question from a different point of view and values them for a different purpose. The habit of distinguishing and classifying the various purposes and directions of activity prevails of necessity always and everywhere; for it is indispensable in reaching a working theory or scheme of life. The particular point of view, or the particular characteristic that is pitched upon as definitive in the classification of the facts of life depends upon the interest from which a discrimination of the facts is sought. The grounds of discrimination, and the norm of procedure in classifying the facts, therefore, progressively change as the growth of culture proceeds; for the end for which the facts of life are apprehended changes, and the point of view consequently changes also. So that what are recognized as the salient and decisive features of a class of activities or of a social class at one stage of culture will not retain the same relative importance for the purposes of classification at any subsequent stage.

But the change of standards and points of view is gradual only, and it seldom results in the subversion or entire suppression of a standpoint once accepted. A distinction is still habitually made between industrial and non-industrial occupations; and this modern distinction is a transmuted form of the barbarian distinction between exploit and drudgery. Such employments as warfare, politics, public worship, and public merrymaking, are felt, in the popular apprehension, to differ intrinsically from the labor that has to do with elaborating the material means of life. The precise line of demarcation is not the same as it was in the early barbarian scheme, but the broad distinction has not fallen into disuse.

The tacit, commonsense distinction today is, in effect, that any effort is to be accounted industrial only so far as its ultimate purpose is the utilization of non-human things. The coercive utilization of man by man is not felt to be an industrial function; but all effort directed to enhance human life by taking advantage of the non-human environment is classed together as industrial activity. By the economists who have best retained and adapted the classical tradition, man's "power over nature" is currently postulated as the characteristic fact of industrial productivity. This industrial power over nature is taken to include man's power over the life of the beasts and over all the elemental forces. A line is in this way drawn between mankind and brute creation.

In other times and among men imbued with a different body of preconceptions this line is not drawn precisely as we draw it today. In the savage or the barbarian scheme of life it is drawn in a different place and in another way. In all communities under the barbarian culture there is an alert and pervading sense of antithesis between two comprehensive groups of phenomena, in one of which barbarian man includes himself, and in the other, his victual. There is a felt antithesis between economic and non-economic phenomena, but it is not conceived in the modern fashion; it lies not between man and brute creation, but between animate and inert things.

It may be an excess of caution at this day to explain that the barbarian notion which it is here intended to convey by the term "animate" is not the same as would be conveyed by the word "living." The term does not cover all living things, and it does cover a great many others. Such a striking natural phenomenon as a storm, a disease, a waterfall, are recognized as "animate"; while fruits and herbs, and even inconspicuous animals, such as house-flies, maggots, lemmings, sheep, are not ordinarily apprehended as "animate" except when taken collectively. As here used the term does not necessarily imply an indwelling soul or spirit. The concept includes such things as in the apprehension of the animistic savage or barbarian are formidable by virtue of a real or imputed habit of initiating action. This category comprises a large number and range of natural objects and phenomena. Such a distinction between the inert and the active is still present in the habits of thought of unreflecting persons, and it still profoundly affects the prevalent theory of human life and of natural processes; but it does not pervade our daily life to the extent or with the far-reaching practical consequences that are apparent at earlier stages of culture and belief.

To the mind of the barbarian, the elaboration and utilization of what is afforded by inert nature is activity on quite a different plane from his dealings with "animate" things and forces. The line of demarcation may be vague and shifting, but the broad distinction is sufficiently real and cogent to influence the barbarian scheme of life. To the class of things apprehended as animate, the barbarian fancy imputes an unfolding of activity directed to some end. It is this teleological unfolding of activity that constitutes any object or phenomenon an "animate" fact. Wherever the unsophisticated savage or barbarian meets with activity that is at all obtrusive, he construes it in the only terms that are ready to hand—the terms immediately given in his consciousness of his own actions. Activity is, therefore, assimilated to human action, and active objects are in so far assimilated to the human agent. Phenomena of this character—especially those whose behavior is notably formidable or baffling—have to be met in a different spirit and with proficiency of a different kind from what is required in dealing with inert things. To deal successfully with such phenomena is a work of exploit rather than of industry. It is an assertion of prowess, not of diligence.

Under the guidance of this naive discrimination between the inert and the animate, the activities of the primitive social group tend to fall into two classes, which would in modern phrase be called exploit and industry. Industry is effort that goes to create a new thing, with a new purpose given it by the fashioning hand of its maker out of passive ("brute") material; while exploit, so far as it results in an outcome useful to the agent, is the conversion to his own ends of energies previously directed to some other end by another agent. We still speak of "brute matter" with something of the barbarian's realization of a profound significance in the term.

The distinction between exploit and drudgery coincides with a difference between the sexes. The sexes differ, not only in stature and muscular force, but perhaps even more decisively in temperament, and this must early have given rise to a corresponding division of labor. The general range of activities that come under the head of exploit falls to the males as being the stouter, more massive, better capable of a sudden and violent strain, and more readily inclined to self assertion, active emulation, and aggression. The difference in mass, in physiological character, and in temperament may be slight among the members of the primitive group; it appears, in fact, to be relatively slight and inconsequential in some of the more archaic communities with which we are acquainted—as for instance the tribes of the Andamans. But so soon as a differentiation of function has well begun on the lines marked out by this difference in physique and animus, the original difference between the sexes will itself widen. A cumulative process of selective adaptation to the new distribution of employments will set in, especially if the habitat or the fauna with which the group is in contact is such as to call for a considerable exercise of the sturdier virtues. The habitual pursuit of large game requires more of the manly qualities of massiveness, agility, and ferocity, and it can therefore scarcely fail to hasten and widen the differentiation of functions between the sexes. And so soon as the group comes into hostile contact with other groups, the divergence of function will take on the developed form of a distinction between exploit and industry.

In such a predatory group of hunters it comes to be the able-bodied men's office to fight and hunt. The women do what other work there is to do—other members who are unfit for man's work being for this purpose classed with women. But the men's hunting and fighting are both of the same general character. Both are of a predatory nature; the warrior and the hunter alike reap where they have not strewn. Their aggressive assertion of force and sagacity differs obviously from the women's assiduous and uneventful shaping of materials; it is not to be accounted productive labor but rather an acquisition of substance by seizure. Such being the barbarian man's work, in its best development and widest divergence from women's work, any effort that does not involve an assertion of prowess comes to be unworthy of the man. As the tradition gains consistency, the common sense of the community erects it into a canon of conduct; so that no employment and no acquisition is morally possible to the self respecting man at this cultural stage, except such as proceeds on the basis of prowess—force or fraud. When the predatory habit of life has been settled upon the group by long habituation, it becomes the able-bodied man's accredited office in the social economy to kill, to destroy such competitors in the struggle for existence as attempt to resist or elude him, to overcome and reduce to subservience those alien forces that assert themselves refractorily in the environment. So tenaciously and with such nicety is this theoretical distinction between exploit and drudgery adhered to that in many hunting tribes the man must not bring home the game which he has killed, but must send his woman to perform that baser office.

As has already been indicated, the distinction between exploit and drudgery is an invidious distinction between employments. Those employments which are to be classed as exploit are worthy, honorable, noble; other employments, which do not contain this element of exploit, and especially those which imply subservience or submission, are unworthy, debasing, ignoble. The concept of dignity, worth, or honor, as applied either to persons or conduct, is of first-rate consequence in the development of classes and of class distinctions, and it is therefore necessary to say something of its derivation and meaning. Its psychological ground may be indicated in outline as follows.

As a matter of selective necessity, man is an agent. He is, in his own apprehension, a centre of unfolding impulsive activity—"teleological" activity. He is an agent seeking in every act the accomplishment of some concrete, objective, impersonal end. By force of his being such an agent he is possessed of a taste for effective work, and a distaste for futile effort. He has a sense of the merit of serviceability or efficiency and of the demerit of futility, waste, or incapacity. This aptitude or propensity may be called the instinct of workmanship. Wherever the circumstances or traditions of life lead to a habitual comparison of one person with another in point of efficiency, the instinct of workmanship works out in an emulative or invidious comparison of persons. The extent to which this result follows depends in some considerable degree on the temperament of the population. In any community where such an invidious comparison of persons is habitually made, visible success becomes an end sought for its own utility as a basis of esteem. Esteem is gained and dispraise is avoided by putting one's efficiency in evidence. The result is that the instinct of workmanship works out in an emulative demonstration of force.

During that primitive phase of social development, when the community is still habitually peaceable, perhaps sedentary, and without a developed system of individual ownership, the efficiency of the individual can be shown chiefly and most consistently in some employment that goes to further the life of the group. What emulation of an economic kind there is between the members of such a group will be chiefly emulation in industrial serviceability. At the same time the incentive to emulation is not strong, nor is the scope for emulation large.

When the community passes from peaceable savagery to a predatory phase of life, the conditions of emulation change. The opportunity and the incentive to emulate increase greatly in scope and urgency. The activity of the men more and more takes on the character of exploit; and an invidious comparison of one hunter or warrior with another grows continually easier and more habitual. Tangible evidences of prowess—trophies—find a place in men's habits of thought as an essential feature of the paraphernalia of life. Booty, trophies of the chase or of the raid, come to be prized as evidence of pre-eminent force. Aggression becomes the accredited form of action, and booty serves as prima facie evidence of successful aggression. As accepted at this cultural stage, the accredited, worthy form of self-assertion is contest; and useful articles or services obtained by seizure or compulsion, serve as a conventional evidence of successful contest. Therefore, by contrast, the obtaining of goods by other methods than seizure comes to be accounted unworthy of man in his best estate. The performance of productive work, or employment in personal service, falls under the same odium for the same reason. An invidious distinction in this way arises between exploit and acquisition on the other hand. Labor acquires a character of irksomeness by virtue of the indignity imputed to it.

With the primitive barbarian, before the simple content of the notion has been obscured by its own ramifications and by a secondary growth of cognate ideas, "honorable" seems to connote nothing else than assertion of superior force. "Honorable" is "formidable"; "worthy" is "prepotent." A honorific act is in the last analysis little if anything else than a recognized successful act of aggression; and where aggression means conflict with men and beasts, the activity which comes to be especially and primarily honorable is the assertion of the strong hand. The naive, archaic habit of construing all manifestations of force in terms of personality or "will power" greatly fortifies this conventional exaltation of the strong hand. Honorific epithets, in vogue among barbarian tribes as well as among peoples of a more advance culture, commonly bear the stamp of this unsophisticated sense of honor. Epithets and titles used in addressing chieftains, and in the propitiation of kings and gods, very commonly impute a propensity for overbearing violence and an irresistible devastating force to the person who is to be propitiated. This holds true to an extent also in the more civilised communities of the present day. The predilection shown in heraldic devices for the more rapacious beasts and birds of prey goes to enforce the same view.

Under this common-sense barbarian appreciation of worth or honor, the taking of life—the killing of formidable competitors, whether brute or human—is honorable in the highest degree. And this high office of slaughter, as an expression of the slayer's prepotence, casts glamour of worth over every act of slaughter and over all the tools and accessories of the act. Arms are honorable, and the use of them, even in seeking the life of the meanest creatures of the fields, becomes an honorific employment. At the same time, employment in industry becomes correspondingly odious, and, in the common-sense apprehension, the handling of the tools and implements of industry falls beneath the dignity of able-bodied men. Labor becomes irksome.

It is here assumed that in the sequence of cultural evolution primitive groups of men have passed from an initial peaceable stage to a subsequent stage at which fighting is the avowed and characteristic employment of the group. But it is not implied that there has been an abrupt transition from unbroken peace and good-will to a later or higher phase of life in which the fact of combat occurs for the first time. Neither is it implied that all peaceful industry disappears on the transition to the predatory phase of culture. Some fighting, it is safe to say, would be met with at any early stage of social development. Fights would occur with more or less frequency through sexual competition. The known habits of primitive groups, as well as the habits of the anthropoid apes, argue to that effect, and the evidence from the well-known promptings of human nature enforces the same view.

It may therefore be objected that there can have been no such initial stage of peaceable life as is here assumed. There is no point in cultural evolution prior to which fighting does not occur.

But the point in question is not as to the occurrence of combat, occasional or sporadic, or even more or less frequent and habitual; it is a question as to the occurrence of an habitual; it is a question as to the occurrence of a habitual bellicose frame of mind—a prevalent habit of judging facts and events from the point of view of the fight. The predatory phase of culture is attained only when the predatory attitude has become the habitual and accredited spiritual attitude for the members of the group; when the fight has become the dominant note in the current theory of life; when the common-sense appreciation of men and things has come to be an appreciation with a view to combat.

The substantial difference between the peaceable and the predatory phase of culture, therefore, is a spiritual difference, not a mechanical one. The change in spiritual attitude is the outgrowth of a change in the material facts of the life of the group, and it comes on gradually as the material circumstances favorable to a predatory attitude supervene. The inferior limit of the predatory culture is an industrial limit. Predation can not become the habitual, conventional resource of any group or any class until industrial methods have been developed to such a degree of efficiency as to leave a margin worth fighting for, above the subsistence of those engaged in getting a living. The transition from peace to predation therefore depends on the growth of technical knowledge and the use of tools. A predatory culture is similarly impracticable in early times, until weapons have been developed to such a point as to make man a formidable animal. The early development of tools and of weapons is of course the same fact seen from two different points of view.

The life of a given group would be characterized as peaceable so long as habitual recourse to combat has not brought the fight into the foreground in men's every day thoughts, as a dominant feature of the life of man. A group may evidently attain such a predatory attitude with a greater or less degree of completeness, so that its scheme of life and canons of conduct may be controlled to a greater or less extent by the predatory animus. The predatory phase of culture is therefore conceived to come on gradually, through a cumulative growth of predatory aptitudes habits, and traditions this growth being due to a change in the circumstances of the group's life, of such a kind as to develop and conserve those traits of human nature and those traditions and norms of conduct that make for a predatory rather than a peaceable life.

The evidence for the hypothesis that there has been such a peaceable stage of primitive culture is in great part drawn from psychology rather than from ethnology, and cannot be detailed here. It will be recited in part in a later chapter, in discussing the survival of archaic traits of human nature under the modern culture.

CHAPTER TWO

Pecuniary Emulation

In the sequence of cultural evolution the emergence of a leisure class coincides with the beginning of ownership. This is necessarily the case, for these two institutions result from the same set of economic forces. In the inchoate phase of their development they are but different aspects of the same general facts of social structure.

It is as elements of social structure—conventional facts—that leisure and ownership are matters of interest for the purpose in hand. A habitual neglect of work does not constitute a leisure class; neither does the mechanical fact of use and consumption constitute ownership. The present inquiry, therefore, is not concerned with the beginning of indolence, nor with the beginning of the appropriation of useful articles to individual consumption. The point in question is the origin and nature of a conventional leisure class on the one hand and the beginnings of individual ownership as a conventional right or equitable claim on the other hand.

The early differentiation out of which the distinction between a leisure and a working class arises is a division maintained between men's and women's work in the lower stages of barbarism. Likewise the earliest form of ownership is an ownership of the women by the able bodied men of the community. The facts may be expressed in more general terms, and truer to the import of the barbarian theory of life, by saying that it is an ownership of the woman by the man.

There was undoubtedly some appropriation of useful articles before the custom of appropriating women arose. The usages of existing archaic communities in which there is no ownership of women is warrant for such a view. In all communities the members, both male and female, habitually appropriate to their individual use a variety of useful things; but these useful things are not thought of as owned by the person who appropriates and consumes them. The habitual appropriation and consumption of certain slight personal effects goes on without raising the question of ownership; that is to say, the question of a conventional, equitable claim to extraneous things.

The ownership of women begins in the lower barbarian stages of culture, apparently with the seizure of female captives. The original reason for the seizure and appropriation of women seems to have been their usefulness as trophies. The practice of seizing women from the enemy as trophies, gave rise to a form of ownership-marriage, resulting in a household with a male head. This was followed by an extension of slavery to other captives and inferiors, besides women, and by an extension of ownership-marriage to other women than those seized from the enemy. The outcome of emulation under the circumstances of a predatory life, therefore, has been on the one hand a form of marriage resting on coercion, and on the other hand the custom of ownership. The two institutions are not distinguishable in the initial phase of their development; both arise from the desire of the successful men to put their prowess in evidence by exhibiting some durable result of their exploits. Both also minister to that propensity for mastery which pervades all predatory communities. From the ownership of women the concept of ownership extends itself to include the products of their industry, and so there arises the ownership of things as well as of persons.

In this way a consistent system of property in goods is gradually installed. And although in the latest stages of the development, the serviceability of goods for consumption has come to be the most obtrusive element of their value, still, wealth has by no means yet lost its utility as a honorific evidence of the owner's prepotence.

Wherever the institution of private property is found, even in a slightly developed form, the economic process bears the character of a struggle between men for the possession of goods. It has been customary in economic theory, and especially among those economists who adhere with least faltering to the body of modernized classical doctrines, to construe this struggle for wealth as being substantially a struggle for subsistence. Such is, no doubt, its character in large part during the earlier and less efficient phases of industry. Such is also its character in all cases where the "niggardliness of nature" is so strict as to afford but a scanty livelihood to the community in return for strenuous and unremitting application to the business of getting the means of subsistence. But in all progressing communities an advance is presently made beyond this early stage of technological development. Industrial efficiency is presently carried to such a pitch as to afford something appreciably more than a bare livelihood to those engaged in the industrial process. It has not been unusual for economic theory to speak of the further struggle for wealth on this new industrial basis as a competition for an increase of the comforts of life,—primarily for an increase of the physical comforts which the consumption of goods affords.

The end of acquisition and accumulation is conventionally held to be the consumption of the goods accumulated—whether it is consumption directly by the owner of the goods or by the household attached to him and for this purpose identified with him in theory. This is at least felt to be the economically legitimate end of acquisition, which alone it is incumbent on the theory to take account of. Such consumption may of course be conceived to serve the consumer's physical wants—his physical comfort—or his so-called higher wants—spiritual, aesthetic, intellectual, or what not; the latter class of wants being served indirectly by an expenditure of goods, after the fashion familiar to all economic readers.

But it is only when taken in a sense far removed from its naive meaning that consumption of goods can be said to afford the incentive from which accumulation invariably proceeds. The motive that lies at the root of ownership is emulation; and the same motive of emulation continues active in the further development of the institution to which it has given rise and in the development of all those features of the social structure which this institution of ownership touches. The possession of wealth confers honor; it is an invidious distinction. Nothing equally cogent can be said for the consumption of goods, nor for any other conceivable incentive to acquisition, and especially not for any incentive to accumulation of wealth.

It is of course not to be overlooked that in a community where nearly all goods are private property the necessity of earning a livelihood is a powerful and ever present incentive for the poorer members of the community. The need of subsistence and of an increase of physical comfort may for a time be the dominant motive of acquisition for those classes who are habitually employed at manual labor, whose subsistence is on a precarious footing, who possess little and ordinarily accumulate little; but it will appear in the course of the discussion that even in the case of these impecunious classes the predominance of the motive of physical want is not so decided as has sometimes been assumed. On the other hand, so far as regards those members and classes of the community who are chiefly concerned in the accumulation of wealth, the incentive of subsistence or of physical comfort never plays a considerable part. Ownership began and grew into a human institution on grounds unrelated to the subsistence minimum. The dominant incentive was from the outset the invidious distinction attaching to wealth, and, save temporarily and by exception, no other motive has usurped the primacy at any later stage of the development.

Property set out with being booty held as trophies of the successful raid. So long as the group had departed and so long as it still stood in close contact with other hostile groups, the utility of things or persons owned lay chiefly in an invidious comparison between their possessor and the enemy from whom they were taken. The habit of distinguishing between the interests of the individual and those of the group to which he belongs is apparently a later growth. Invidious comparison between the possessor of the honorific booty and his less successful neighbors within the group was no doubt present early as an element of the utility of the things possessed, though this was not at the outset the chief element of their value. The man's prowess was still primarily the group's prowess, and the possessor of the booty felt himself to be primarily the keeper of the honor of his group. This appreciation of exploit from the communal point of view is met with also at later stages of social growth, especially as regards the laurels of war.

But as soon as the custom of individual ownership begins to gain consistency, the point of view taken in making the invidious comparison on which private property rests will begin to change. Indeed, the one change is but the reflex of the other. The initial phase of ownership, the phase of acquisition by naive seizure and conversion, begins to pass into the subsequent stage of an incipient organization of industry on the basis of private property (in slaves); the horde develops into a more or less self-sufficing industrial community; possessions then come to be valued not so much as evidence of successful foray, but rather as evidence of the prepotence of the possessor of these goods over other individuals within the community. The invidious comparison now becomes primarily a comparison of the owner with the other members of the group. Property is still of the nature of trophy, but, with the cultural advance, it becomes more and more a trophy of successes scored in the game of ownership carried on between the members of the group under the quasi-peaceable methods of nomadic life.

Gradually, as industrial activity further displaced predatory activity in the community's everyday life and in men's habits of thought, accumulated property more and more replaces trophies of predatory exploit as the conventional exponent of prepotence and success. With the growth of settled industry, therefore, the possession of wealth gains in relative importance and effectiveness as a customary basis of repute and esteem. Not that esteem ceases to be awarded on the basis of other, more direct evidence of prowess; not that successful predatory aggression or warlike exploit ceases to call out the approval and admiration of the crowd, or to stir the envy of the less successful competitors; but the opportunities for gaining distinction by means of this direct manifestation of superior force grow less available both in scope and frequency. At the same time opportunities for industrial aggression, and for the accumulation of property, increase in scope and availability. And it is even more to the point that property now becomes the most easily recognized evidence of a reputable degree of success as distinguished from heroic or signal achievement. It therefore becomes the conventional basis of esteem. Its possession in some amount becomes necessary in order to any reputable standing in the community.

It becomes indispensable to accumulate, to acquire property, in order to retain one's good name. When accumulated goods have in this way once become the accepted badge of efficiency, the possession of wealth presently assumes the character of an independent and definitive basis of esteem. The possession of goods, whether acquired aggressively by one's own exertion or passively by transmission through inheritance from others, becomes a conventional basis of reputability. The possession of wealth, which was at the outset valued simply as an evidence of efficiency, becomes, in popular apprehension, itself a meritorious act. Wealth is now itself intrinsically honorable and confers honor on its possessor. By a further refinement, wealth acquired passively by transmission from ancestors or other antecedents presently becomes even more honorific than wealth acquired by the possessor's own effort; but this distinction belongs at a later stage in the evolution of the pecuniary culture and will be spoken of in its place.

Prowess and exploit may still remain the basis of award of the highest popular esteem, although the possession of wealth has become the basis of common place reputability and of a blameless social standing. The predatory instinct and the consequent approbation of predatory efficiency are deeply ingrained in the habits of thought of those peoples who have passed under the discipline of a protracted predatory culture. According to popular award, the highest honors within human reach may, even yet, be those gained by an unfolding of extraordinary predatory efficiency in war, or by a quasi-predatory efficiency in statecraft; but for the purposes of a commonplace decent standing in the community these means of repute have been replaced by the acquisition and accumulation of goods. In order to stand well in the eyes of the community, it is necessary to come up to a certain, somewhat indefinite, conventional standard of wealth; just as in the earlier predatory stage it is necessary for the barbarian man to come up to the tribe's standard of physical endurance, cunning, and skill at arms. A certain standard of wealth in the one case, and of prowess in the other, is a necessary condition of reputability, and anything in excess of this normal amount is meritorious.

Those members of the community who fall short of this, somewhat indefinite, normal degree of prowess or of property suffer in the esteem of their fellow-men; and consequently they suffer also in their own esteem, since the usual basis of self-respect is the respect accorded by one's neighbors. Only individuals with an aberrant temperament can in the long run retain their self-esteem in the face of the disesteem of their fellows. Apparent exceptions to the rule are met with, especially among people with strong religious convictions. But these apparent exceptions are scarcely real exceptions, since such persons commonly fall back on the putative approbation of some supernatural witness of their deeds.

So soon as the possession of property becomes the basis of popular esteem, therefore, it becomes also a requisite to the complacency which we call self-respect. In any community where goods are held in severalty it is necessary, in order to his own peace of mind, that an individual should possess as large a portion of goods as others with whom he is accustomed to class himself; and it is extremely gratifying to possess something more than others. But as fast as a person makes new acquisitions, and becomes accustomed to the resulting new standard of wealth, the new standard forthwith ceases to afford appreciably greater satisfaction than the earlier standard did. The tendency in any case is constantly to make the present pecuniary standard the point of departure for a fresh increase of wealth; and this in turn gives rise to a new standard of sufficiency and a new pecuniary classification of one's self as compared with one's neighbors. So far as concerns the present question, the end sought by accumulation is to rank high in comparison with the rest of the community in point of pecuniary strength. So long as the comparison is distinctly unfavorable to himself, the normal, average individual will live in chronic dissatisfaction with his present lot; and when he has reached what may be called the normal pecuniary standard of the community, or of his class in the community, this chronic dissatisfaction will give place to a restless straining to place a wider and ever-widening pecuniary interval between himself and this average standard. The invidious comparison can never become so favorable to the individual making it that he would not gladly rate himself still higher relatively to his competitors in the struggle for pecuniary reputability.

In the nature of the case, the desire for wealth can scarcely be satiated in any individual instance, and evidently a satiation of the average or general desire for wealth is out of the question. However widely, or equally, or "fairly," it may be distributed, no general increase of the community's wealth can make any approach to satiating this need, the ground of which approach to satiating this need, the ground of which is the desire of every one to excel every one else in the accumulation of goods.

If, as is sometimes assumed, the incentive to accumulation were the want of subsistence or of physical comfort, then the aggregate economic wants of a community might conceivably be satisfied at some point in the advance of industrial efficiency; but since the struggle is substantially a race for reputability on the basis of an invidious comparison, no approach to a definitive attainment is possible.

What has just been said must not be taken to mean that there are no other incentives to acquisition and accumulation than this desire to excel in pecuniary standing and so gain the esteem and envy of one's fellow-men. The desire for added comfort and security from want is present as a motive at every stage of the process of accumulation in a modern industrial community; although the standard of sufficiency in these respects is in turn greatly affected by the habit of pecuniary emulation. To a great extent this emulation shapes the methods and selects the objects of expenditure for personal comfort and decent livelihood.

Besides this, the power conferred by wealth also affords a motive to accumulation. That propensity for purposeful activity and that repugnance to all futility of effort which belong to man by virtue of his character as an agent do not desert him when he emerges from the naive communal culture where the dominant note of life is the unanalyzed and undifferentiated solidarity of the individual with the group with which his life is bound up. When he enters upon the predatory stage, where self-seeking in the narrower sense becomes the dominant note, this propensity goes with him still, as the pervasive trait that shapes his scheme of life. The propensity for achievement and the repugnance to futility remain the underlying economic motive. The propensity changes only in the form of its expression and in the proximate objects to which it directs the man's activity. Under the regime of individual ownership the most available means of visibly achieving a purpose is that afforded by the acquisition and accumulation of goods; and as the self-regarding antithesis between man and man reaches fuller consciousness, the propensity for achievement—the instinct of workmanship—tends more and more to shape itself into a straining to excel others in pecuniary achievement. Relative success, tested by an invidious pecuniary comparison with other men, becomes the conventional end of action.

The currently accepted legitimate end of effort becomes the achievement of a favorable comparison with other men; and therefore the repugnance to futility to a good extent coalesces with the incentive of emulation. It acts to accentuate the struggle for pecuniary reputability by visiting with a sharper disapproval all shortcoming and all evidence of shortcoming in point of pecuniary success. Purposeful effort comes to mean, primarily, effort directed to or resulting in a more creditable showing of accumulated wealth. Among the motives which lead men to accumulate wealth, the primacy, both in scope and intensity, therefore, continues to belong to this motive of pecuniary emulation.

In making use of the term "invidious," it may perhaps be unnecessary to remark, there is no intention to extol or depreciate, or to commend or deplore any of the phenomena which the word is used to characterize. The term is used in a technical sense as describing a comparison of persons with a view to rating and grading them in respect of relative worth or value—in an aesthetic or moral sense—and so awarding and defining the relative degrees of complacency with which they may legitimately be contemplated by themselves and by others. An invidious comparison is a process of valuation of persons in respect of worth.

CHAPTER THREE

Conspicuous Leisure

If its working were not disturbed by other economic forces or other features of the emulative process, the immediate effect of such a pecuniary struggle as has just been described in outline would be to make men industrious and frugal. This result actually follows, in some measure, so far as regards the lower classes, whose ordinary means of acquiring goods is productive labor. This is more especially true of the laboring classes in a sedentary community which is at an agricultural stage of industry, in which there is a considerable subdivision of industry, and whose laws and customs secure to these classes a more or less definite share of the product of their industry. These lower classes can in any case not avoid labor, and the imputation of labor is therefore not greatly derogatory to them, at least not within their class. Rather, since labor is their recognized and accepted mode of life, they take some emulative pride in a reputation for efficiency in their work, this being often the only line of emulation that is open to them. For those for whom acquisition and emulation is possible only within the field of productive efficiency and thrift, the struggle for pecuniary reputability will in some measure work out in an increase of diligence and parsimony. But certain secondary features of the emulative process, yet to be spoken of, come in to very materially circumscribe and modify emulation in these directions among the pecuniary inferior classes as well as among the superior class.

But it is otherwise with the superior pecuniary class, with which we are here immediately concerned. For this class also the incentive to diligence and thrift is not absent; but its action is so greatly qualified by the secondary demands of pecuniary emulation, that any inclination in this direction is practically overborne and any incentive to diligence tends to be of no effect. The most imperative of these secondary demands of emulation, as well as the one of widest scope, is the requirement of abstention from productive work. This is true in an especial degree for the barbarian stage of culture. During the predatory culture labor comes to be associated in men's habits of thought with weakness and subjection to a master. It is therefore a mark of inferiority, and therefore comes to be accounted unworthy of man in his best estate. By virtue of this tradition labor is felt to be debasing, and this tradition has never died out. On the contrary, with the advance of social differentiation it has acquired the axiomatic force due to ancient and unquestioned prescription.

In order to gain and to hold the esteem of men it is not sufficient merely to possess wealth or power. The wealth or power must be put in evidence, for esteem is awarded only on evidence. And not only does the evidence of wealth serve to impress one's importance on others and to keep their sense of his importance alive and alert, but it is of scarcely less use in building up and preserving one's self-complacency. In all but the lowest stages of culture the normally constituted man is comforted and upheld in his self-respect by "decent surroundings" and by exemption from "menial offices." Enforced departure from his habitual standard of decency, either in the paraphernalia of life or in the kind and amount of his everyday activity, is felt to be a slight upon his human dignity, even apart from all conscious consideration of the approval or disapproval of his fellows.

The archaic theoretical distinction between the base and the honorable in the manner of a man's life retains very much of its ancient force even today. So much so that there are few of the better class who are not possessed of an instinctive repugnance for the vulgar forms of labor. We have a realizing sense of ceremonial uncleanness attaching in an especial degree to the occupations which are associated in our habits of thought with menial service. It is felt by all persons of refined taste that a spiritual contamination is inseparable from certain offices that are conventionally required of servants. Vulgar surroundings, mean (that is to say, inexpensive) habitations, and vulgarly productive occupations are unhesitatingly condemned and avoided. They are incompatible with life on a satisfactory spiritual plane __ with "high thinking." From the days of the Greek philosophers to the present, a degree of leisure and of exemption from contact with such industrial processes as serve the immediate everyday purposes of human life has ever been recognized by thoughtful men as a prerequisite to a worthy or beautiful, or even a blameless, human life. In itself and in its consequences the life of leisure is beautiful and ennobling in all civilized men's eyes.

This direct, subjective value of leisure and of other evidences of wealth is no doubt in great part secondary and derivative. It is in part a reflex of the utility of leisure as a means of gaining the respect of others, and in part it is the result of a mental substitution. The performance of labor has been accepted as a conventional evidence of inferior force; therefore it comes itself, by a mental short-cut, to be regarded as intrinsically base.

During the predatory stage proper, and especially during the earlier stages of the quasi-peaceable development of industry that follows the predatory stage, a life of leisure is the readiest and most conclusive evidence of pecuniary strength, and therefore of superior force; provided always that the gentleman of leisure can live in manifest ease and comfort. At this stage wealth consists chiefly of slaves, and the benefits accruing from the possession of riches and power take the form chiefly of personal service and the immediate products of personal service. Conspicuous abstention from labor therefore becomes the conventional mark of superior pecuniary achievement and the conventional index of reputability; and conversely, since application to productive labor is a mark of poverty and subjection, it becomes inconsistent with a reputable standing in the community. Habits of industry and thrift, therefore, are not uniformly furthered by a prevailing pecuniary emulation. On the contrary, this kind of emulation indirectly discountenances participation in productive labor. Labor would unavoidably become dishonorable, as being an evidence indecorous under the ancient tradition handed down from an earlier cultural stage. The ancient tradition of the predatory culture is that productive effort is to be shunned as being unworthy of ablebodied men, and this tradition is reinforced rather than set aside in the passage from the predatory to the quasi-peaceable manner of life.

Even if the institution of a leisure class had not come in with the first emergence of individual ownership, by force of the dishonor attaching to productive employment, it would in any case have come in as one of the early consequences of ownership. And it is to be remarked that while the leisure class existed in theory from the beginning of predatory culture, the institution takes on a new and fuller meaning with the transition from the predatory to the next succeeding pecuniary stage of culture. It is from this time forth a "leisure class" in fact as well as in theory. From this point dates the institution of the leisure class in its consummate form.

During the predatory stage proper the distinction between the leisure and the laboring class is in some degree a ceremonial distinction only. The able bodied men jealously stand aloof from whatever is in their apprehension, menial drudgery; but their activity in fact contributes appreciably to the sustenance of the group. The subsequent stage of quasi-peaceable industry is usually characterized by an established chattel slavery, herds of cattle, and a servile class of herdsmen and shepherds; industry has advanced so far that the community is no longer dependent for its livelihood on the chase or on any other form of activity that can fairly be classed as exploit. From this point on, the characteristic feature of leisure class life is a conspicuous exemption from all useful employment.

The normal and characteristic occupations of the class in this mature phase of its life history are in form very much the same as in its earlier days. These occupations are government, war, sports, and devout observances. Persons unduly given to difficult theoretical niceties may hold that these occupations are still incidentally and indirectly "productive"; but it is to be noted as decisive of the question in hand that the ordinary and ostensible motive of the leisure class in engaging in these occupations is assuredly not an increase of wealth by productive effort. At this as at any other cultural stage, government and war are, at least in part, carried on for the pecuniary gain of those who engage in them; but it is gain obtained by the honorable method of seizure and conversion. These occupations are of the nature of predatory, not of productive, employment. Something similar may be said of the chase, but with a difference. As the community passes out of the hunting stage proper, hunting gradually becomes differentiated into two distinct employments. On the one hand it is a trade, carried on chiefly for gain; and from this the element of exploit is virtually absent, or it is at any rate not present in a sufficient degree to clear the pursuit of the imputation of gainful industry. On the other hand, the chase is also a sport—an exercise of the predatory impulse simply. As such it does not afford any appreciable pecuniary incentive, but it contains a more or less obvious element of exploit. It is this latter development of the chase—purged of all imputation of handicraft—that alone is meritorious and fairly belongs in the scheme of life of the developed leisure class.

Abstention from labor is not only an honorific or meritorious act, but it presently comes to be a requisite of decency. The insistence on property as the basis of reputability is very naive and very imperious during the early stages of the accumulation of wealth. Abstention from labor is the convenient evidence of wealth and is therefore the conventional mark of social standing; and this insistence on the meritoriousness of wealth leads to a more strenuous insistence on leisure. *Nota notae est nota rei ipsius.* According to well established laws of human nature, prescription presently seizes upon this conventional evidence of wealth and fixes it in men's habits of thought as something that is in itself substantially meritorious and ennobling; while productive labor at the same time and by a like process becomes in a double sense intrinsically unworthy. Prescription ends by making labor not only disreputable in the eyes of the community, but morally impossible to the noble, freeborn man, and incompatible with a worthy life.

This taboo on labor has a further consequence in the industrial differentiation of classes. As the population increases in density and the predatory group grows into a settled industrial community, the constituted authorities and the customs governing ownership gain in scope and consistency. It then presently becomes impracticable to accumulate wealth by simple seizure, and, in logical consistency, acquisition by industry is equally impossible for high minded and impecunious men. The alternative open to them is beggary or privation. Wherever the canon of conspicuous leisure has a chance undisturbed to work out its tendency, there will therefore emerge a secondary, and in a sense spurious, leisure class—abjectly poor and living in a precarious life of want and discomfort, but morally unable to stoop to gainful pursuits. The decayed gentleman and the lady who has seen better days are by no means unfamiliar phenomena even now. This pervading sense of the indignity of the slightest manual labor is familiar to all civilized peoples, as well as to peoples of a less advanced pecuniary culture. In persons of a delicate sensibility who have long been habituated to gentle manners, the sense of the shamefulness of manual labor may become so strong that, at a critical juncture, it will even set aside the instinct of self-preservation. So, for instance, we are told of certain Polynesian chiefs, who, under the stress of good form, preferred to starve rather than carry their food to their mouths with their own hands. It is true, this conduct may have been due, at least in part, to an excessive sanctity or taboo attaching to the chief's person.

The taboo would have been communicated by the contact of his hands, and so would have made anything touched by him unfit for human food. But the taboo is itself a derivative of the unworthiness or moral incompatibility of labor; so that even when construed in this sense the conduct of the Polynesian chiefs is truer to the canon of honorific leisure than would at first appear. A better illustration, or at least a more unmistakable one, is afforded by a certain king of France, who is said to have lost his life through an excess of moral stamina in the observance of good form. In the absence of the functionary whose office it was to shift his master's seat, the king sat uncomplaining before the fire and suffered his royal person to be toasted beyond recovery. But in so doing he saved his Most Christian Majesty from menial contamination.

Summum crede nefas animam praeferre pudori, Et propter vitam vivendi perdere causas.

It has already been remarked that the term "leisure," as here used, does not connote indolence or quiescence. What it connotes is non-productive consumption of time. Time is consumed non-productively (1) from a sense of the unworthiness of productive work, and (2) as an evidence of pecuniary ability to afford a life of idleness. But the whole of the life of the gentleman of leisure is not spent before the eyes of the spectators who are to be impressed with that spectacle of honorific leisure which in the ideal scheme makes up his life. For some part of the time his life is perforce withdrawn from the public eye, and of this portion which is spent in private the gentleman of leisure should, for the sake of his good name, be able to give a convincing account. He should find some means of putting in evidence the leisure that is not spent in the sight of the spectators. This can be done only indirectly, through the exhibition of some tangible, lasting results of the leisure so spent—in a manner analogous to the familiar exhibition of tangible, lasting products of the labor performed for the gentleman of leisure by handicraftsmen and servants in his employ.

The lasting evidence of productive labor is its material product—commonly some article of consumption. In the case of exploit it is similarly possible and usual to procure some tangible result that may serve for exhibition in the way of trophy or booty. At a later phase of the development it is customary to assume some badge of insignia of honor that will serve as a conventionally accepted mark of exploit, and which at the same time indicates the quantity or degree of exploit of which it is the symbol. As the population increases in density, and as human relations grow more complex and numerous, all the details of life undergo a process of elaboration and selection; and in this process of elaboration the use of trophies develops into a system of rank, titles, degrees and insignia, typical examples of which are heraldic devices, medals, and honorary decorations.

As seen from the economic point of view, leisure, considered as an employment, is closely allied in kind with the life of exploit; and the achievements which characterize a life of leisure, and which remain as its decorous criteria, have much in common with the trophies of exploit. But leisure in the narrower sense, as distinct from exploit and from any ostensibly productive employment of effort on objects which are of no intrinsic use, does not commonly leave a material product. The criteria of a past performance of leisure therefore commonly take the form of "immaterial" goods. Such immaterial evidences of past leisure are quasi-scholarly or quasi-artistic accomplishments and a knowledge of processes and incidents which do not conduce directly to the furtherance of human life.

So, for instance, in our time there is the knowledge of the dead languages and the occult sciences; of correct spelling; of syntax and prosody; of the various forms of domestic music and other household art; of the latest properties of dress, furniture, and equipage; of games, sports, and fancy-bred animals, such as dogs and race-horses. In all these branches of knowledge the initial motive from which their acquisition proceeded at the outset, and through which they first came into vogue, may have been something quite different from the wish to show that one's time had not been spent in industrial employment; but unless these accomplishments had approved themselves as serviceable evidence of an unproductive expenditure of time, they would not have survived and held their place as conventional accomplishments of the leisure class.

These accomplishments may, in some sense, be classed as branches of learning. Beside and beyond these there is a further range of social facts which shade off from the region of learning into that of physical habit and dexterity. Such are what is known as manners and breeding, polite usage, decorum, and formal and ceremonial observances generally. This class of facts are even more immediately and obtrusively presented to the observation, and they therefore more widely and more imperatively insisted on as required evidences of a reputable degree of leisure. It is worth while to remark that all that class of ceremonial observances which are classed under the general head of manners hold a more important place in the esteem of men during the stage of culture at which conspicuous leisure has the greatest vogue as a mark of reputability, than at later stages of the cultural development. The barbarian of the quasi-peaceable stage of industry is notoriously a more high-bred gentleman, in all that concerns decorum, than any but the very exquisite among the men of a later age. Indeed, it is well known, or at least it is currently believed, that manners have progressively deteriorated as society has receded from the patriarchal stage. Many a gentleman of the old school has been provoked to remark regretfully upon the under-bred manners and bearing of even the better classes in the modern industrial communities; and the decay of the ceremonial code—or as it is otherwise called, the vulgarization of life—among the industrial classes proper has become one of the chief enormities of latter-day civilization in the eyes of all persons of delicate sensibilities. The decay which the code has suffered at the hands of a busy people testifies—all depreciation apart—to the fact that decorum is a product and an exponent of leisure class life and thrives in full measure only under a regime of status.

The origin, or better the derivation, of manners is no doubt, to be sought elsewhere than in a conscious effort on the part of the well-mannered to show that much time has been spent in acquiring them. The proximate end of innovation and elaboration has been the higher effectiveness of the new departure in point of beauty or of expressiveness. In great part the ceremonial code of decorous usages owes its beginning and its growth to the desire to conciliate or to show good-will, as anthropologists and sociologists are in the habit of assuming, and this initial motive is rarely if ever absent from the conduct of well-mannered persons at any stage of the later development. Manners, we are told, are in part an elaboration of gesture, and in part they are symbolical and conventionalized survivals representing former acts of dominance or of personal service or of personal contact. In large part they are an expression of the relation of status,—a symbolic pantomime of mastery on the one hand and of subservience on the other. Wherever at the present time the predatory habit of mind, and the consequent attitude of mastery and of subservience, gives its character to the accredited scheme of life, there the importance of all punctilios of conduct is extreme, and the assiduity with which the ceremonial observance of rank and titles is attended to approaches closely to the ideal set by the barbarian of the quasi-peaceable nomadic culture. Some of the Continental countries afford good illustrations of this spiritual survival. In these communities the archaic ideal is similarly approached as regards the esteem accorded to manners as a fact of intrinsic worth.

Decorum set out with being symbol and pantomime and with having utility only as an exponent of the facts and qualities symbolized; but it presently suffered the transmutation which commonly passes over symbolical facts in human intercourse. Manners presently came, in popular apprehension, to be possessed of a substantial utility in themselves; they acquired a sacramental character, in great measure independent of the facts which they originally prefigured. Deviations from the code of decorum have become intrinsically odious to all men, and good breeding is, in everyday apprehension, not simply an adventitious mark of human excellence, but an integral feature of the worthy human soul. There are few things that so touch us with instinctive revulsion as a breach of decorum; and so far have we progressed in the direction of imputing intrinsic utility to the ceremonial observances of etiquette that few of us, if any, can dissociate an offence against etiquette from a sense of the substantial unworthiness of the offender. A breach of faith may be condoned, but a breach of decorum can not. "Manners maketh man."

Nonetheless, while manners have this intrinsic utility, in the apprehension of the performer and the beholder alike, this sense of the intrinsic rightness of decorum is only the proximate ground of the vogue of manners and breeding. Their ulterior, economic ground is to be sought in the honorific character of that leisure or non-productive employment of time and effort without which good manners are not acquired. The knowledge and habit of good form come only by long-continued use. Refined tastes, manners, habits of life are a useful evidence of gentility, because good breeding requires time, application and expense, and can therefore not be compassed by those whose time and energy are taken up with work. A knowledge of good form is prima facie evidence that that portion of the well-bred person's life which is not spent under the observation of the spectator has been worthily spent in acquiring accomplishments that are of no lucrative effect. In the last analysis the value of manners lies in the fact that they are the voucher of a life of leisure. Therefore, conversely, since leisure is the conventional means of pecuniary repute, the acquisition of some proficiency in decorum is incumbent on all who aspire to a modicum of pecuniary decency.

So much of the honorable life of leisure as is not spent in the sight of spectators can serve the purposes of reputability only in so far as it leaves a tangible, visible result that can be put in evidence and can be measured and compared with products of the same class exhibited by competing aspirants for repute. Some such effect, in the way of leisurely manners and carriage, etc., follows from simple persistent abstention from work, even where the subject does not take thought of the matter and studiously acquire an air of leisurely opulence and mastery. Especially does it seem to be true that a life of leisure in this way persisted in through several generations will leave a persistent, ascertainable effect in the conformation of the person, and still more in his habitual bearing and demeanor. But all the suggestions of a cumulative life of leisure, and all the proficiency in decorum that comes by the way of passive habituation, may be further improved upon by taking thought and assiduously acquiring the marks of honorable leisure, and then carrying the exhibition of these adventitious marks of exemption from employment out in a strenuous and systematic discipline. Plainly, this is a point at which a diligent application of effort and expenditure may materially further the attainment of a decent proficiency in the leisure-class properties. Conversely, the greater the degree of proficiency and the more patent the evidence of a high degree of habituation to observances which serve no lucrative or other directly useful purpose, the greater the consumption of time and substance impliedly involved in their acquisition, and the greater the resultant good repute. Hence under the competitive struggle for proficiency in good manners, it comes about that much pains in taken with the cultivation of habits of decorum; and hence the details of decorum develop into a comprehensive discipline, conformity to which is required of all who would be held blameless in point of repute. And hence, on the other hand, this conspicuous leisure of which decorum is a ramification grows gradually into a laborious drill in deportment and an education in taste and discrimination as to what articles of consumption are decorous and what are the decorous methods of consuming them.

In this connection it is worthy of notice that the possibility of producing pathological and other idiosyncrasies of person and manner by shrewd mimicry and a systematic drill have been turned to account in the deliberate production of a cultured class—often with a very happy effect. In this way, by the process vulgarly known as snobbery, a syncopated evolution of gentle birth and breeding is achieved in the case of a goodly number of families and lines of descent. This syncopated gentle birth gives results which, in point of serviceability as a leisure-class factor in the population, are in no wise substantially inferior to others who may have had a longer but less arduous training in the pecuniary properties.

There are, moreover, measurable degrees of conformity to the latest accredited code of the punctilios as regards decorous means and methods of consumption. Differences between one person and another in the degree of conformity to the ideal in these respects can be compared, and persons may be graded and scheduled with some accuracy and effect according to a progressive scale of manners and breeding. The award of reputability in this regard is commonly made in good faith, on the ground of conformity to accepted canons of taste in the matters concerned, and without conscious regard to the pecuniary standing or the degree of leisure practiced by any given candidate for reputability; but the canons of taste according to which the award is made are constantly under the surveillance of the law of conspicuous leisure, and are indeed constantly undergoing change and revision to bring them into closer conformity with its requirements. So that while the proximate ground of discrimination may be of another kind, still the pervading principle and abiding test of good breeding is the requirement of a substantial and patent waste of time. There may be some considerable range of variation in detail within the scope of this principle, but they are variations of form and expression, not of substance.

Much of the courtesy of everyday intercourse is of course a direct expression of consideration and kindly good-will, and this element of conduct has for the most part no need of being traced back to any underlying ground of reputability to explain either its presence or the approval with which it is regarded; but the same is not true of the code of properties. These latter are expressions of status. It is of course sufficiently plain, to any one who cares to see, that our bearing towards menials and other pecuniary dependent inferiors is the bearing of the superior member in a relation of status, though its manifestation is often greatly modified and softened from the original expression of crude dominance. Similarly, our bearing towards superiors, and in great measure towards equals, expresses a more or less conventionalized attitude of subservience. Witness the masterful presence of the high-minded gentleman or lady, which testifies to so much of dominance and independence of economic circumstances, and which at the same time appeals with such convincing force to our sense of what is right and gracious. It is among this highest leisure class, who have no superiors and few peers, that decorum finds its fullest and maturest expression; and it is this highest class also that gives decorum that definite formulation which serves as a canon of conduct for the classes beneath. And there also the code is most obviously a code of status and shows most plainly its incompatibility with all vulgarly productive work. A divine assurance and an imperious complaisance, as of one habituated to require subservience and to take no thought for the morrow, is the birthright and the criterion of the gentleman at his best; and it is in popular apprehension even more than that, for this demeanor is accepted as an intrinsic attribute of superior worth, before which the base-born commoner delights to stoop and yield.

As has been indicated in an earlier chapter, there is reason to believe that the institution of ownership has begun with the ownership of persons, primarily women. The incentives to acquiring such property have apparently been: (1) a propensity for dominance and coercion; (2) the utility of these persons as evidence of the prowess of the owner; (3) the utility of their services.

Personal service holds a peculiar place in the economic development. During the stage of quasi-peaceable industry, and especially during the earlier development of industry within the limits of this general stage, the utility of their services seems commonly to be the dominant motive to the acquisition of property in persons. Servants are valued for their services. But the dominance of this motive is not due to a decline in the absolute importance of the other two utilities possessed by servants. It is rather that the altered circumstance of life accentuate the utility of servants for this last-named purpose. Women and other slaves are highly valued, both as an evidence of wealth and as a means of accumulating wealth. Together with cattle, if the tribe is a pastoral one, they are the usual form of investment for a profit. To such an extent may female slavery give its character to the economic life under the quasi-peaceable culture that the women even comes to serve as a unit of value among peoples occupying this cultural stage—as for instance in Homeric times. Where this is the case there need be little question but that the basis of the industrial system is chattel slavery and that the women are commonly slaves. The great, pervading human relation in such a system is that of master and servant. The accepted evidence of wealth is the possession of many women, and presently also of other slaves engaged in attendance on their master's person and in producing goods for him.

A division of labor presently sets in, whereby personal service and attendance on the master becomes the special office of a portion of the servants, while those who are wholly employed in industrial occupations proper are removed more and more from all immediate relation to the person of their owner. At the same time those servants whose office is personal service, including domestic duties, come gradually to be exempted from productive industry carried on for gain.

This process of progressive exemption from the common run of industrial employment will commonly begin with the exemption of the wife, or the chief wife. After the community has advanced to settled habits of life, wife-capture from hostile tribes becomes impracticable as a customary source of supply. Where this cultural advance has been achieved, the chief wife is ordinarily of gentle blood, and the fact of her being so will hasten her exemption from vulgar employment. The manner in which the concept of gentle blood originates, as well as the place which it occupies in the development of marriage, cannot be discussed in this place. For the purpose in hand it will be sufficient to say that gentle blood is blood which has been ennobled by protracted contact with accumulated wealth or unbroken prerogative. The woman with these antecedents is preferred in marriage, both for the sake of a resulting alliance with her powerful relatives and because a superior worth is felt to inhere in blood which has been associated with many goods and great power. She will still be her husband's chattel, as she was her father's chattel before her purchase, but she is at the same time of her father's gentle blood; and hence there is a moral incongruity in her occupying herself with the debasing employments of her fellow-servants. However completely she may be subject to her master, and however inferior to the male members of the social stratum in which her birth has placed her, the principle that gentility is transmissible will act to place her above the common slave; and so soon as this principle has acquired a prescriptive authority it will act to invest her in some measure with that prerogative of leisure which is the chief mark of gentility. Furthered by this principle of transmissible gentility the wife's exemption gains in scope, if the wealth of her owner permits it, until it includes exemption from debasing menial service as well as from handicraft. As the industrial development goes on and property becomes massed in relatively fewer hands, the conventional standard of wealth of the upper class rises. The same tendency to exemption from handicraft, and in the course of time from menial domestic employments, will then assert itself as regards the other wives, if such there are, and also as regards other servants in immediate attendance upon the person of their master. The exemption comes more tardily the remoter the relation in which the servant stands to the person of the master.

If the pecuniary situation of the master permits it, the development of a special class of personal or body servants is also furthered by the very grave importance which comes to attach to this personal service. The master's person, being the embodiment of worth and honor, is of the most serious consequence. Both for his reputable standing in the community and for his self-respect, it is a matter of moment that he should have at his call efficient specialized servants, whose attendance upon his person is not diverted from this their chief office by any by-occupation. These specialized servants are useful more for show than for service actually performed. In so far as they are not kept for exhibition simply, they afford gratification to their master chiefly in allowing scope to his propensity for dominance. It is true, the care of the continually increasing household apparatus may require added labor; but since the apparatus is commonly increased in order to serve as a means of good repute rather than as a means of comfort, this qualification is not of great weight. All these lines of utility are better served by a larger number of more highly specialized servants. There results, therefore, a constantly increasing differentiation and multiplication of domestic and body servants, along with a concomitant progressive exemption of such servants from productive labor. By virtue of their serving as evidence of ability to pay, the office of such domestics regularly tends to include continually fewer duties, and their service tends in the end to become nominal only. This is especially true of those servants who are in most immediate and obvious attendance upon their master. So that the utility of these comes to consist, in great part, in their conspicuous exemption from productive labor and in the evidence which this exemption affords of their master's wealth and power.

After some considerable advance has been made in the practice of employing a special corps of servants for the performance of a conspicuous leisure in this manner, men begin to be preferred above women for services that bring them obtrusively into view. Men, especially lusty, personable fellows, such as footmen and other menials should be, are obviously more powerful and more expensive than women. They are better fitted for this work, as showing a larger waste of time and of human energy. Hence it comes about that in the economy of the leisure class the busy housewife of the early patriarchal days, with her retinue of hard-working handmaidens, presently gives place to the lady and the lackey.

In all grades and walks of life, and at any stage of the economic development, the leisure of the lady and of the lackey differs from the leisure of the gentleman in his own right in that it is an occupation of an ostensibly laborious kind. It takes the form, in large measure, of a painstaking attention to the service of the master, or to the maintenance and elaboration of the household paraphernalia; so that it is leisure only in the sense that little or no productive work is performed by this class, not in the sense that all appearance of labor is avoided by them. The duties performed by the lady, or by the household or domestic servants, are frequently arduous enough, and they are also frequently directed to ends which are considered extremely necessary to the comfort of the entire household. So far as these services conduce to the physical efficiency or comfort of the master or the rest of the household, they are to be accounted productive work. Only the residue of employment left after deduction of this effective work is to be classed as a performance of leisure.

But much of the services classed as household cares in modern everyday life, and many of the "utilities" required for a comfortable existence by civilized man, are of a ceremonial character. They are, therefore, properly to be classed as a performance of leisure in the sense in which the term is here used. They may be nonetheless imperatively necessary from the point of view of decent existence: they may be nonetheless requisite for personal comfort even, although they may be chiefly or wholly of a ceremonial character. But in so far as they partake of this character they are imperative and requisite because we have been taught to require them under pain of ceremonial uncleanness or unworthiness. We feel discomfort in their absence, but not because their absence results directly in physical discomfort; nor would a taste not trained to discriminate between the conventionally good and the conventionally bad take offence at their omission. In so far as this is true the labor spent in these services is to be classed as leisure; and when performed by others than the economically free and self-directed head of the establishment, they are to be classed as vicarious leisure.

The vicarious leisure performed by housewives and menials, under the head of household cares, may frequently develop into drudgery, especially where the competition for reputability is close and strenuous. This is frequently the case in modern life. Where this happens, the domestic service which comprises the duties of this servant class might aptly be designated as wasted effort, rather than as vicarious leisure. But the latter term has the advantage of indicating the line of derivation of these domestic offices, as well as of neatly suggesting the substantial economic ground of their utility; for these occupations are chiefly useful as a method of imputing pecuniary reputability to the master or to the household on the ground that a given amount of time and effort is conspicuously wasted in that behalf.

In this way, then, there arises a subsidiary or derivative leisure class, whose office is the performance of a vicarious leisure for the behoof of the reputability of the primary or legitimate leisure class. This vicarious leisure class is distinguished from the leisure class proper by a characteristic feature of its habitual mode of life. The leisure of the master class is, at least ostensibly, an indulgence of a proclivity for the avoidance of labor and is presumed to enhance the master's own well-being and fullness of life; but the leisure of the servant class exempt from productive labor is in some sort a performance exacted from them, and is not normally or primarily directed to their own comfort. The leisure of the servant is not his own leisure. So far as he is a servant in the full sense, and not at the same time a member of a lower order of the leisure class proper, his leisure normally passes under the guise of specialized service directed to the furtherance of his master's fullness of life. Evidence of this relation of subservience is obviously present in the servant's carriage and manner of life. The like is often true of the wife throughout the protracted economic stage during which she is still primarily a servant—that is to say, so long as the household with a male head remains in force. In order to satisfy the requirements of the leisure class scheme of life, the servant should show not only an attitude of subservience, but also the effects of special training and practice in subservience. The servant or wife should not only perform certain offices and show a servile disposition, but it is quite as imperative that they should show an acquired facility in the tactics of subservience—a trained conformity to the canons of effectual and conspicuous subservience. Even today it is this aptitude and acquired skill in the formal manifestation of the servile relation that constitutes the chief element of utility in our highly paid servants, as well as one of the chief ornaments of the well-bred housewife.

The first requisite of a good servant is that he should conspicuously know his place. It is not enough that he knows how to effect certain desired mechanical results; he must above all, know how to effect these results in due form. Domestic service might be said to be a spiritual rather than a mechanical function. Gradually there grows up an elaborate system of good form, specifically regulating the manner in which this vicarious leisure of the servant class is to be performed. Any departure from these canons of form is to be depreciated, not so much because it evinces a shortcoming in mechanical efficiency, or even that it shows an absence of the servile attitude and temperament, but because, in the last analysis, it shows the absence of special training. Special training in personal service costs time and effort, and where it is obviously present in a high degree, it argues that the servant who possesses it, neither is nor has been habitually engaged in any productive occupation. It is prima facie evidence of a vicarious leisure extending far back in the past. So that trained service has utility, not only as gratifying the master's instinctive liking for good and skilful workmanship and his propensity for conspicuous dominance over those whose lives are subservient to his own, but it has utility also as putting in evidence a much larger consumption of human service than would be shown by the mere present conspicuous leisure performed by an untrained person. It is a serious grievance if a gentleman's butler or footman performs his duties about his master's table or carriage in such unformed style as to suggest that his habitual occupation may be ploughing or sheepherding. Such bungling work would imply inability on the master's part to procure the service of specially trained servants; that is to say, it would imply inability to pay for the consumption of time, effort, and instruction required to fit a trained servant for special service under the exacting code of forms. If the performance of the servant argues lack of means on the part of his master, it defeats its chief substantial end; for the chief use of servants is the evidence they afford of the master's ability to pay.

What has just been said might be taken to imply that the offence of an under-trained servant lies in a direct suggestion of inexpensiveness or of usefulness. Such, of course, is not the case. The connection is much less immediate. What happens here is what happens generally. Whatever approves itself to us on any ground at the outset, presently comes to appeal to us as a gratifying thing in itself; it comes to rest in our habits of thought as substantially right. But in order that any specific canon of deportment shall maintain itself in favor, it must continue to have the support of, or at least not be incompatible with, the habit or aptitude which constitutes the norm of its development. The need of vicarious leisure, or conspicuous consumption of service, is a dominant incentive to the keeping of servants. So long as this remains true it may be set down without much discussion that any such departure from accepted usage as would suggest an abridged apprenticeship in service would presently be found insufferable. The requirement of an expensive vicarious leisure acts indirectly, selectively, by guiding the formation of our taste,—of our sense of what is right in these matters,—and so weeds out unconformable departures by withholding approval of them.

As the standard of wealth recognized by common consent advances, the possession and exploitation of servants as a means of showing superfluity undergoes a refinement. The possession and maintenance of slaves employed in the production of goods argues wealth and prowess, but the maintenance of servants who produce nothing argues still higher wealth and position. Under this principle there arises a class of servants, the more numerous the better, whose sole office is fatuously to wait upon the person of their owner, and so to put in evidence his ability unproductively to consume a large amount of service. There supervenes a division of labor among the servants or dependents whose life is spent in maintaining the honor of the gentleman of leisure. So that, while one group produces goods for him, another group, usually headed by the wife, or chief, consumes for him in conspicuous leisure; thereby putting in evidence his ability to sustain large pecuniary damage without impairing his superior opulence.

This somewhat idealized and diagrammatic outline of the development and nature of domestic service comes nearest being true for that cultural stage which was here been named the "quasi-peaceable" stage of industry. At this stage personal service first rises to the position of an economic institution, and it is at this stage that it occupies the largest place in the community's scheme of life. In the cultural sequence, the quasi-peaceable stage follows the predatory stage proper, the two being successive phases of barbarian life. Its characteristic feature is a formal observance of peace and order, at the same time that life at this stage still has too much of coercion and class antagonism to be called peaceable in the full sense of the word. For many purposes, and from another point of view than the economic one, it might as well be named the stage of status. The method of human relation during this stage, and the spiritual attitude of men at this level of culture, is well summed up under the term. But as a descriptive term to characterize the prevailing methods of industry, as well as to indicate the trend of industrial development at this point in economic evolution, the term "quasi-peaceable" seems preferable. So far as concerns the communities of the Western culture, this phase of economic development probably lies in the past; except for a numerically small though very conspicuous fraction of the community in whom the habits of thought peculiar to the barbarian culture have suffered but a relatively slight disintegration.

Personal service is still an element of great economic importance, especially as regards the distribution and consumption of goods; but its relative importance even in this direction is no doubt less than it once was. The best development of this vicarious leisure lies in the past rather than in the present; and its best expression in the present is to be found in the scheme of life of the upper leisure class. To this class the modern culture owes much in the way of the conservation of traditions, usages, and habits of thought which belong on a more archaic cultural plane, so far as regards their widest acceptance and their most effective development.

In the modern industrial communities the mechanical contrivances available for the comfort and convenience of everyday life are highly developed. So much so that body servants, or, indeed, domestic servants of any kind, would now scarcely be employed by anybody except on the ground of a canon of reputability carried over by tradition from earlier usage. The only exception would be servants employed to attend on the persons of the infirm and the feeble-minded. But such servants properly come under the head of trained nurses rather than under that of domestic servants, and they are, therefore, an apparent rather than a real exception to the rule.

The proximate reason for keeping domestic servants, for instance, in the moderately well-to-do household of today, is (ostensibly) that the members of the household are unable without discomfort to compass the work required by such a modern establishment. And the reason for their being unable to accomplish it is (1) that they have too many "social duties," and (2) that the work to be done is too severe and that there is too much of it. These two reasons may be restated as follows: (1) Under the mandatory code of decency, the time and effort of the members of such a household are required to be ostensibly all spent in a performance of conspicuous leisure, in the way of calls, drives, clubs, sewing-circles, sports, charity organizations, and other like social functions. Those persons whose time and energy are employed in these matters privately avow that all these observances, as well as the incidental attention to dress and other conspicuous consumption, are very irksome but altogether unavoidable. (2) Under the requirement of conspicuous consumption of goods, the apparatus of living has grown so elaborate and cumbrous, in the way of dwellings, furniture, bric-a-brac, wardrobe and meals, that the consumers of these things cannot make way with them in the required manner without help. Personal contact with the hired persons whose aid is called in to fulfill the routine of decency is commonly distasteful to the occupants of the house, but their presence is endured and paid for, in order to delegate to them a share in this onerous consumption of household goods. The presence of domestic servants, and of the special class of body servants in an eminent degree, is a concession of physical comfort to the moral need of pecuniary decency.

The largest manifestation of vicarious leisure in modern life is made up of what are called domestic duties. These duties are fast becoming a species of services performed, not so much for the individual behoof of the head of the household as for the reputability of the household taken as a corporate unit—a group of which the housewife is a member on a footing of ostensible equality. As fast as the household for which they are performed departs from its archaic basis of ownership-marriage, these household duties of course tend to fall out of the category of vicarious leisure in the original sense; except so far as they are performed by hired servants. That is to say, since vicarious leisure is possible only on a basis of status or of hired service, the disappearance of the relation of status from human intercourse at any point carries with it the disappearance of vicarious leisure so far as regards that much of life. But it is to be added, in qualification of this qualification, that so long as the household subsists, even with a divided head, this class of non-productive labor performed for the sake of the household reputability must still be classed as vicarious leisure, although in a slightly altered sense. It is now leisure performed for the quasi-personal corporate household, instead of, as formerly, for the proprietary head of the household.

CHAPTER FOUR

Conspicuous Consumption

In what has been said of the evolution of the vicarious leisure class and its differentiation from the general body of the working classes, reference has been made to a further division of labor,—that between the different servant classes. One portion of the servant class, chiefly those persons whose occupation is vicarious leisure, come to undertake a new, subsidiary range of duties—the vicarious consumption of goods. The most obvious form in which this consumption occurs is seen in the wearing of liveries and the occupation of spacious servants' quarters. Another, scarcely less obtrusive or less effective form of vicarious consumption, and a much more widely prevalent one, is the consumption of food, clothing, dwelling, and furniture by the lady and the rest of the domestic establishment.

But already at a point in economic evolution far antedating the emergence of the lady, specialized consumption of goods as an evidence of pecuniary strength had begun to work out in a more or less elaborate system. The beginning of a differentiation in consumption even antedates the appearance of anything that can fairly be called pecuniary strength. It is traceable back to the initial phase of predatory culture, and there is even a suggestion that an incipient differentiation in this respect lies back of the beginnings of the predatory life. This most primitive differentiation in the consumption of goods is like the later differentiation with which we are all so intimately familiar, in that it is largely of a ceremonial character, but unlike the latter it does not rest on a difference in accumulated wealth. The utility of consumption as an evidence of wealth is to be classed as a derivative growth. It is an adaption to a new end, by a selective process, of a distinction previously existing and well established in men's habits of thought.

In the earlier phases of the predatory culture the only economic differentiation is a broad distinction between an honorable superior class made up of the able-bodied men on the one side, and a base inferior class of laboring women on the other. According to the ideal scheme of life in force at the time it is the office of the men to consume what the women produce. Such consumption as falls to the women is merely incidental to their work; it is a means to their continued labor, and not a consumption directed to their own comfort and fullness of life. Unproductive consumption of goods is honorable, primarily as a mark of prowess and a perquisite of human dignity; secondarily it becomes substantially honorable to itself, especially the consumption of the more desirable things. The consumption of choice articles of food, and frequently also of rare articles of adornment, becomes taboo to the women and children; and if there is a base (servile) class of men, the taboo holds also for them. With a further advance in culture this taboo may change into simple custom of a more or less rigorous character; but whatever be the theoretical basis of the distinction which is maintained, whether it be a taboo or a larger conventionality, the features of the conventional scheme of consumption do not change easily. When the quasi-peaceable stage of industry is reached, with its fundamental institution of chattel slavery, the general principle, more or less rigorously applied, is that the base, industrious class should consume only what may be necessary to their subsistence. In the nature of things, luxuries and the comforts of life belong to the leisure class. Under the taboo, certain victuals, and more particularly certain beverages, are strictly reserved for the use of the superior class.

The ceremonial differentiation of the dietary is best seen in the use of intoxicating beverages and narcotics. If these articles of consumption are costly, they are felt to be noble and honorific. Therefore the base classes, primarily the women, practice an enforced continence with respect to these stimulants, except in countries where they are obtainable at a very low cost. From archaic times down through all the length of the patriarchal regime it has been the office of the women to prepare and administer these luxuries, and it has been the perquisite of the men of gentle birth and breeding to consume them. Drunkenness and the other pathological consequences of the free use of stimulants therefore tend in their turn to become honorific, as being a mark, at the second remove, of the superior status of those who are able to afford the indulgence. Infirmities induced by over-indulgence are among some peoples freely recognized as manly attributes. It has even happened that the name for certain diseased conditions of the body arising from such an origin has passed into everyday speech as a synonym for "noble" or "gentle." It is only at a relatively early stage of culture that the symptoms of expensive vice are conventionally accepted as marks of a superior status, and so tend to become virtues and command the deference of the community; but the reputability that attaches to certain expensive vices long retains so much of its force as to appreciably lessen the disapprobation visited upon the men of the wealthy or noble class for any excessive indulgence. The same invidious distinction adds force to the current disapproval of any indulgence of this kind on the part of women, minors, and inferiors. This invidious traditional distinction has not lost its force even among the more advanced peoples of today. Where the example set by the leisure class retains its imperative force in the regulation of the conventionalities, it is observable that the women still in great measure practice the same traditional continence with regard to stimulants.

This characterization of the greater continence in the use of stimulants practiced by the women of the reputable classes may seem an excessive refinement of logic at the expense of common sense. But facts within easy reach of any one who cares to know them go to say that the greater abstinence of women is in some part due to an imperative conventionality; and this conventionality is, in a general way, strongest where the patriarchal tradition—the tradition that the woman is a chattel—has retained its hold in greatest vigor. In a sense which has been greatly qualified in scope and rigor, but which has by no means lost its meaning even yet, this tradition says that the woman, being a chattel, should consume only what is necessary to her sustenance,—except so far as her further consumption contributes to the comfort or the good repute of her master. The consumption of luxuries, in the true sense, is a consumption directed to the comfort of the consumer himself, and is, therefore, a mark of the master. Any such consumption by others can take place only on a basis of sufferance. In communities where the popular habits of thought have been profoundly shaped by the patriarchal tradition we may accordingly look for survivals of the taboo on luxuries at least to the extent of a conven-

tional deprecation of their use by the unfree and dependent class. This is more particularly true as regards certain luxuries, the use of which by the dependent class would de-
tract sensibly from the comfort or pleasure of their masters, or which are held to be of
doubtful legitimacy on other grounds. In the apprehension of the great conservative
middle class of Western civilization the use of these various stimulants is obnoxious to
at least one, if not both, of these objections; and it is a fact too significant to be passed
over that it is precisely among these middle classes of the Germanic culture, with their
strong surviving sense of the patriarchal proprieties, that the women are to the greatest
extent subject to a qualified taboo on narcotics and alcoholic beverages. With many
qualifications—with more qualifications as the patriarchal tradition has gradually weakened—the general rule is felt to be right and binding that women should consume only
for the benefit of their masters. The objection of course presents itself that expenditure
on women's dress and household paraphernalia is an obvious exception to this rule; but
it will appear in the sequel that this exception is much more obvious than substantial.
During the earlier stages of economic development, consumption of goods without
stint, especially consumption of the better grades of goods,—ideally all consumption in
excess of the subsistence minimum,—pertains normally to the leisure class. This restriction tends to disappear, at least formally, after the later peaceable stage has been
reached, with private ownership of goods and an industrial system based on wage labor
or on the petty household economy. But during the earlier quasi-peaceable stage, when
so many of the traditions through which the institution of a leisure class has affected the
economic life of later times were taking form and consistency, this principle has had the
force of a conventional law. It has served as the norm to which consumption has tended
to conform, and any appreciable departure from it is to be regarded as an aberrant form,
sure to be eliminated sooner or later in the further course of development.

The quasi-peaceable gentleman of leisure, then, not only consumes of the staff of life
beyond the minimum required for subsistence and physical efficiency, but his consumption also undergoes a specialization as regards the quality of the goods consumed. He consumes freely and of the best, in food, drink, narcotics, shelter, services, ornaments,
apparel, weapons and accoutrements, amusements, amulets, and idols or divinities. In the
process of gradual amelioration which takes place in the articles of his consumption, the
motive principle and proximate aim of innovation is no doubt the higher efficiency of
the improved and more elaborate products for personal comfort and well-being. But that
does not remain the sole purpose of their consumption. The canon of reputability is at
hand and seizes upon such innovations as are, according to its standard, fit to survive.
Since the consumption of these more excellent goods is an evidence of wealth, it becomes honorific; and conversely, the failure to consume in due quantity and quality becomes a mark of inferiority and demerit.

This growth of punctilious discrimination as to qualitative excellence in eating, drinking, etc. presently affects not only the manner of life, but also the training and intellectual activity of the gentleman of leisure. He is no longer simply the successful, aggressive
male,—the man of strength, resource, and intrepidity. In order to avoid stultification he
must also cultivate his tastes, for it now becomes incumbent on him to discriminate with
some nicety between the noble and the ignoble in consumable goods. He becomes a

connoisseur in creditable viands of various degrees of merit, in manly beverages and trinkets, in seemly apparel and architecture, in weapons, games, dancers, and the narcotics. This cultivation of aesthetic faculty requires time and application, and the demands made upon the gentleman in this direction therefore tend to change his life of leisure into a more or less arduous application to the business of learning how to live a life of ostensible leisure in a becoming way. Closely related to the requirement that the gentleman must consume freely and of the right kind of goods, there is the requirement that he must know how to consume them in a seemly manner. His life of leisure must be conducted in due form. Hence arise good manners in the way pointed out in an earlier chapter. High-bred manners and ways of living are items of conformity to the norm of conspicuous leisure and conspicuous consumption.

Conspicuous consumption of valuable goods is a means of reputability to the gentleman of leisure. As wealth accumulates on his hands, his own unaided effort will not avail to sufficiently put his opulence in evidence by this method. The aid of friends and competitors is therefore brought in by resorting to the giving of valuable presents and expensive feasts and entertainments. Presents and feasts had probably another origin than that of naive ostentation, but they required their utility for this purpose very early, and they have retained that character to the present; so that their utility in this respect has now long been the substantial ground on which these usages rest. Costly entertainments, such as the potlatch or the ball, are peculiarly adapted to serve this end. The competitor with whom the entertainer wishes to institute a comparison is, by this method, made to serve as a means to the end. He consumes vicariously for his host at the same time that he is witness to the consumption of that excess of good things which his host is unable to dispose of single-handed, and he is also made to witness his host's facility in etiquette.

In the giving of costly entertainments other motives, of more genial kind, are of course also present. The custom of festive gatherings probably originated in motives of conviviality and religion; these motives are also present in the later development, but they do not continue to be the sole motives. The latter-day leisure-class festivities and entertainments may continue in some slight degree to serve the religious need and in a higher degree the needs of recreation and conviviality, but they also serve an invidious purpose; and they serve it nonetheless effectually for having a colorable non-invidious ground in these more avowable motives. But the economic effect of these social amenities is not therefore lessened, either in the vicarious consumption of goods or in the exhibition of difficult and costly achievements in etiquette.

As wealth accumulates, the leisure class develops further in function and structure, and there arises a differentiation within the class. There is a more or less elaborate system of rank and grades. This differentiation is furthered by the inheritance of wealth and the consequent inheritance of gentility. With the inheritance of gentility goes the inheritance of obligatory leisure; and gentility of a sufficient potency to entail a life of leisure may be inherited without the complement of wealth required to maintain a dignified leisure. Gentle blood may be transmitted without goods enough to afford a reputably free consumption at one's ease. Hence results a class of impecunious gentlemen of leisure, incidentally referred to already. These half-caste gentlemen of leisure fall into a system of hierarchical gradations. Those who stand near the higher and the highest grades of the wealthy leisure class, in point of birth, or in point of wealth, or both, out-rank the remoter-born and the pecuniarily weaker. These lower grades, especially the impecunious, or marginal, gentlemen of leisure, affiliate themselves by a system of de-pendence or fealty to the great ones; by so doing they gain an increment of repute, or of the means with which to lead a life of leisure, from their patron. They become his courtiers or retainers, servants; and being fed and countenanced by their patron they are indices of his rank and vicarious consumer of his superfluous wealth. Many of these af-filiated gentlemen of leisure are at the same time lesser men of substance in their own right; so that some of them are scarcely at all, others only partially, to be rated as vicari-ous consumers. So many of them, however, as make up the retainer and hangers-on of the patron may be classed as vicarious consumer without qualification. Many of these again, and also many of the other aristocracy of less degree, have in turn attached to their persons a more or less comprehensive group of vicarious consumer in the persons of their wives and children, their servants, retainers, etc.

Throughout this graduated scheme of vicarious leisure and vicarious consumption the rule holds that these offices must be performed in some such manner, or under some such circumstance or insignia, as shall point plainly to the master to whom this leisure or consumption pertains, and to whom therefore the resulting increment of good repute of right inures. The consumption and leisure executed by these persons for their mas-ter or patron represents an investment on his part with a view to an increase of good fame. As regards feasts and largesses this is obvious enough, and the imputation of re-pute to the host or patron here takes place immediately, on the ground of common no-toriety. Where leisure and consumption is performed vicariously by henchmen and retainers, imputation of the resulting repute to the patron is affected by their residing near his person so that it may be plain to all men from what source they draw. As the group whose good esteem is to be secured in this way grows larger, more patent means are required to indicate the imputation of merit for the leisure performed, and to this end uniforms, badges, and liveries come into vogue. The wearing of uniforms or liver-ies implies a considerable degree of dependence, and may even be said to be a mark of servitude, real or ostensible.

The wearers of uniforms and liveries may be roughly divided into two classes—the free and the servile, or the noble and the ignoble. The services performed by them are likewise divisible into noble and ignoble. Of course the distinction is not observed with strict con-sistency in practice; the less debasing of the base services and the less honorific of the noble functions are not infrequently merged in the same person. But the general distinc-tion is not on that account to be overlooked. What may add some perplexity is the fact that this fundamental distinction between noble and ignoble, which rests on the nature of the ostensible service performed, is traversed by a secondary distinction into honorific and humiliating, resting on the rank of the person for whom the service is performed or whose livery is worn. So, those offices which are by right the proper employment of the leisure class are noble; such as government, fighting, hunting, the care of arms and accou-trements, and the like—in short, those which may be classed as ostensibly predatory em-ployments. On the other hand, those employments which properly fall to the industrious class are ignoble; such as handicraft or other productive labor, menial services and the like. But a base service performed for a person of very high degree may become a very honorific office; as for instance the office of a Maid of Honor or of a Lady in Waiting to the Queen, or the King's Master of the Horse or his Keeper of the Hounds. The two offices last named suggest a principle of some general bearing.

Whenever, as in these cases, the menial service in question has to do directly with the primary leisure employments of fighting and hunting, it easily acquires a reflected honorific character. In this way great honor may come to attach to an employment which in its own nature belongs to the baser sort. In the later development of peaceable industry, the usage of employing an idle corps of uniformed men-at-arms gradually lapses.

Vicarious consumption by dependents bearing the insignia of their patron or master narrows down to a corps of liveried menials. In a heightened degree, therefore, the livery comes to be a badge of servitude, or rather servility. Something of a honorific character always attached to the livery of the armed retainer, but this honorific character disappears when the livery becomes the exclusive badge of the menial. The livery becomes obnoxious to nearly all who are required to wear it. We are yet so little removed from a state of effective slavery as still to be fully sensitive to the sting of any imputation of servility. This antipathy asserts itself even in the case of the liveries or uniforms which some corporations prescribe as the distinctive dress of their employees. In this country the aversion even goes the length of discrediting—in a mild and uncertain way—those government employments, military and civil, which require the wearing of a livery or uniform.

With the disappearance of servitude, the number of vicarious consumers attached to any one gentleman tends, on the whole, to decrease. The like is of course true, and perhaps in a still higher degree, of the number of dependents who perform vicarious leisure for him. In a general way, though not wholly nor consistently, these two groups coincide. The dependent who was first delegated for these duties was the wife, or the chief wife; and, as would be expected, in the later development of the institution, when the number of persons by whom these duties are customarily performed gradually narrows, the wife remains the last. In the higher grades of society a large volume of both these kinds of service is required; and here the wife is of course still assisted in the work by a more or less numerous corps of menials. But as we descend the social scale, the point is presently reached where the duties of vicarious leisure and consumption devolve upon the wife alone. In the communities of the Western culture, this point is at present found among the lower middle class.

And here occurs a curious inversion. It is a fact of common observance that in this lower middle class there is no pretense of leisure on the part of the head of the household. Through force of circumstances it has fallen into disuse. But the middle-class wife still carries on the business of vicarious leisure, for the good name of the household and its master. In descending the social scale in any modern industrial community, the primary fact—the conspicuous leisure of the master of the household—disappears at a relatively high point. The head of the middle-class household has been reduced by economic circumstances to turn his hand to gaining a livelihood by occupations which often partake largely of the character of industry, as in the case of the ordinary business man of today. But the derivative fact—the vicarious leisure and consumption rendered by the wife, and the auxiliary vicarious performance of leisure by menials—remains in vogue as a conventionality which the demands of reputability will not suffer to be slighted. It is by no means an uncommon spectacle to find a man applying himself to work with the utmost assiduity, in order that his wife may in due form render for him that degree of vicarious leisure which the common sense of the time demands.

The leisure rendered by the wife in such cases is, of course, not a simple manifestation of idleness or indolence. It almost invariably occurs disguised under some form of work or household duties or social amenities, which prove on analysis to serve little or no ulterior end beyond showing that she does not occupy herself with anything that is gainful or that is of substantial use. As has already been noticed under the head of manners, the greater part of the customary round of domestic cares to which the middle-class housewife gives her time and effort is of this character. Not that the results of her attention to household matters, of a decorative and mundificatory character, are not pleasing to the sense of men trained in middle-class proprieties; but the taste to which these effects of household adornment and tidiness appeal is a taste which has been formed under the selective guidance of a canon of propriety that demands just these evidences of wasted effort. The effects are pleasing to us chiefly because we have been taught to find them pleasing.

There goes into these domestic duties much solicitude for a proper combination of form and color, and for other ends that are to be classed as aesthetic in the proper sense of the term; and it is not denied that effects having some substantial aesthetic value are sometimes attained. Pretty much all that is here insisted on is that, as regards these amenities of life, the housewife's efforts are under the guidance of traditions that have been shaped by the law of conspicuously wasteful expenditure of time and substance. If beauty or comfort is achieved—and it is a more or less fortuitous circumstance if they are—they must be achieved by means and methods that commend themselves to the great economic law of wasted effort. The more reputable, "presentable" portion of middle-class household paraphernalia are, on the one hand, items of conspicuous consumption, and on the other hand, apparatus for putting in evidence the vicarious leisure rendered by the housewife.

The requirement of vicarious consumption at the hands of the wife continues in force even at a lower point in the pecuniary scale than the requirement of vicarious leisure. At a point below which little if any pretense of wasted effort, in ceremonial cleanness and the like, is observable, and where there is assuredly no conscious attempt at ostensible leisure, decency still requires the wife to consume some goods conspicuously for the reputability of the household and its head. So that, as the latter-day outcome of this evolution of an archaic institution, the wife, who was at the outset the drudge and chattel of the man, both in fact and in theory—the producer of goods for him to consume—has become the ceremonial consumer of goods which he produces. But she still quite unmistakably remains his chattel in theory; for the habitual rendering of vicarious leisure and consumption is the abiding mark of the unfree servant.

This vicarious consumption practiced by the household of the middle and lower classes can not be counted as a direct expression of the leisure-class scheme of life, since the household of this pecuniary grade does not belong within the leisure class. It is rather that the leisure-class scheme of life here comes to an expression at the second remove. The leisure class stands at the head of the social structure in point of reputability; and its manner of life and its standards of worth therefore afford the norm of reputability for the community. The observance of these standards, in some degree of approximation, becomes incumbent upon all classes lower in the scale. In modern civilized communities the lines of demarcation between social classes have grown vague and transient, and wherever this happens the norm of reputability imposed by the upper class extends its coercive influence with but slight hindrance down through the social structure to the lowest strata. The result is that the members of each stratum accept as their ideal of decency the scheme of life in vogue in the next higher stratum, and bend their energies to live up to that ideal. On pain of forfeiting their good name and their self-respect in case of failure, they must conform to the accepted code, at least in appearance. The basis on which good repute in any highly organized industrial community ultimately rests is pecuniary strength; and the means of showing pecuniary strength, and so of gaining or retaining a good name, are leisure and a conspicuous consumption of goods.

Accordingly, both of these methods are in vogue as far down the scale as it remains possible; and in the lower strata in which the two methods are employed, both offices are in great part delegated to the wife and children of the household. Lower still, where any degree of leisure, even ostensible, has become impracticable for the wife, the conspicuous consumption of goods remains and is carried on by the wife and children.

The man of the household also can do something in this direction, and indeed, he commonly does; but with a still lower descent into the levels of indigence—along the margin of the slums—the man, and presently also the children, virtually cease to consume valuable goods for appearances, and the woman remains virtually the sole exponent of the household's pecuniary decency. No class of society, not even the most abjectly poor, forgoes all customary conspicuous consumption. The last items of this category of consumption are not given up except under stress of the direst necessity. Very much of squalor and discomfort will be endured before the last trinket or the last pretense of pecuniary decency is put away. There is no class and no country that has yielded so abjectly before the pressure of physical want as to deny themselves all gratification of this higher or spiritual need.

From the foregoing survey of the growth of conspicuous leisure and consumption, it appears that the utility of both alike for the purposes of reputability lies in the element of waste that is common to both. In the one case it is a waste of time and effort, in the other it is a waste of goods. Both are methods of demonstrating the possession of wealth, and the two are conventionally accepted as equivalents. The choice between them is a question of advertising expediency simply, except so far as it may be affected by other standards of propriety, springing from a different source. On grounds of expediency the preference may be given to the one or the other at different stages of the economic development. The question is, which of the two methods will most effectively reach the persons whose convictions it is desired to affect. Usage has answered this question in different ways under different circumstances.

So long as the community or social group is small enough and compact enough to be effectually reached by common notoriety alone that is to say, so long as the human environment to which the individual is required to adapt himself in respect of reputability is comprised within his sphere of personal acquaintance and neighborhood gossip—so long the one method is about as effective as the other. Each will therefore serve about equally well during the earlier stages of social growth. But when the differentiation has gone farther and it becomes necessary to reach a wider human environment, consumption begins to hold over leisure as an ordinary means of decency. This is especially true during the later, peaceable economic stage. The means of communication and the mobility of the population now expose the individual to the observation of many persons who have no other means of judging of his reputability than the display of goods (and perhaps of breeding) which he is able to make while he is under their direct observation.

The modern organization of industry works in the same direction also by another line. The exigencies of the modern industrial system frequently place individuals and households in juxtaposition between whom there is little contact in any other sense than that of juxtaposition. One's neighbors, mechanically speaking, often are socially not one's neighbors, or even acquaintances; and still their transient good opinion has a high degree of utility. The only practicable means of impressing one's pecuniary ability on these unsympathetic observers of one's everyday life is an unremitting demonstration of ability to pay. In the modern community there is also a more frequent attendance at large gatherings of people to whom one's everyday life is unknown; in such places as churches, theaters, ballrooms, hotels, parks, shops, and the like. In order to impress these transient observers, and to retain one's self-complacency under their observation, the signature of one's pecuniary strength should be written in characters which he who runs may read. It is evident, therefore, that the present trend of the development is in the direction of heightening the utility of conspicuous consumption as compared with leisure.

It is also noticeable that the serviceability of consumption as a means of repute, as well as the insistence on it as an element of decency, is at its best in those portions of the community where the human contact of the individual is widest and the mobility of the population is greatest. Conspicuous consumption claims a relatively larger portion of the income of the urban than of the rural population, and the claim is also more imperative. The result is that, in order to keep up a decent appearance, the former habitually live hand-to-mouth to a greater extent than the latter. So it comes, for instance, that the American farmer and his wife and daughters are notoriously less modish in their dress, as well as less urbane in their manners, than the city artisan's family with an equal income.

It is not that the city population is by nature much more eager for the peculiar complacency that comes of a conspicuous consumption, nor has the rural population less regard for pecuniary decency. But the provocation to this line of evidence, as well as its transient effectiveness, is more decided in the city. This method is therefore more readily resorted to, and in the struggle to outdo one another the city population push their normal standard of conspicuous consumption to a higher point, with the result that a relatively greater expenditure in this direction is required to indicate a given degree of pecuniary decency in the city. The requirement of conformity to this higher conventional standard becomes mandatory. The standard of decency is higher, class for class, and this requirement of decent appearance must be lived up to on pain of losing caste.

Consumption becomes a larger element in the standard of living in the city than in the country. Among the country population its place is to some extent taken by sav-

ings and home comforts known through the medium of neighborhood gossip sufficiently to serve the like general purpose of pecuniary repute. These home comforts
and the leisure indulged in—where the indulgence is found—are of course also in
great part to be classed as items of conspicuous consumption; and much the same is
to be said of the savings. The smaller amount of the savings laid by by the artisan class
is no doubt due, in some measure, to the fact that in the case of the artisan the savings
are a less effective means of advertisement, relative to the environment in which he is
placed, than are the savings of the people living on farms and in the small villages.
Among the latter, everybody's affairs, especially everybody's pecuniary status, are known
to everybody else. Considered by itself simply—taken in the first degree—this added
provocation to which the artisan and the urban laboring classes are exposed may not
very seriously decrease the amount of savings; but in its cumulative action, through
raising the standard of decent expenditure, its deterrent effect on the tendency to save
cannot but be very great.

A felicitous illustration of the manner in which this canon of reputability works out
its results is seen in the practice of dram-drinking, "treating," and smoking in public
places, which is customary among the laborers and handicraftsmen of the towns, and
among the lower middle class of the urban population generally journeymen printers
may be named as a class among whom this form of conspicuous consumption has a
great vogue, and among whom it carries with it certain well-marked consequences that
are often deprecated. The peculiar habits of the class in this respect are commonly set
down to some kind of an ill-defined moral deficiency with which this class is credited,
or to a morally deleterious influence which their occupation is supposed to exert, in
some unascertainable way, upon the men employed in it. The state of the case for the
men who work in the composition and press rooms of the common run of printing-
houses may be summed up as follows. Skill acquired in any printing-house or any city
is easily turned to account in almost any other house or city; that is to say, the inertia
due to special training is slight. Also, this occupation requires more than the average of
intelligence and general information, and the men employed in it are therefore ordinarily more ready than many others to take advantage of any slight variation in the demand for their labor from one place to another. The inertia due to the home feeling is
consequently also slight. At the same time the wages in the trade are high enough to
make movement from place to place relatively easy. The result is a great mobility of the
labor employed in printing; perhaps greater than in any other equally well-defined and
considerable body of workmen. These men are constantly thrown in contact with new
groups of acquaintances, with whom the relations established are transient or ephemeral,
but whose good opinion is valued nonetheless for the time being. The human proclivity to ostentation, reinforced by sentiments of good-fellowship, leads them to spend
freely in those directions which will best serve these needs. Here as elsewhere prescription seizes upon the custom as soon as it gains a vogue, and incorporates it in the accredited standard of decency. The next step is to make this standard of decency the
point of departure for a new move in advance in the same direction—for there is no
merit in simple spiritless conformity to a standard of dissipation that is lived up to as a
matter of course by everyone in the trade.

The greater prevalence of dissipation among printers than among the average of workmen is accordingly attributable, at least in some measure, to the greater ease of movement and the more transient character of acquaintance and human contact in this trade. But the substantial ground of this high requirement in dissipation is in the last analysis no other than that same propensity for a manifestation of dominance and pecuniary decency which makes the French peasant-proprietor parsimonious and frugal, and induces the American millionaire to found colleges, hospitals and museums. If the canon of conspicuous consumption were not offset to a considerable extent by other features of human nature, alien to it, any saving should logically be impossible for a population situated as the artisan and laboring classes of the cities are at present, however high their wages or their income might be.

But there are other standards of repute and other, more or less imperative, canons of conduct, besides wealth and its manifestation, and some of these come in to accentuate or to qualify the broad, fundamental canon of conspicuous waste. Under the simple test of effectiveness for advertising, we should expect to find leisure and the conspicuous consumption of goods dividing the field of pecuniary emulation pretty evenly between them at the outset. Leisure might then be expected gradually to yield ground and tend to obsolescence as the economic development goes forward, and the community increases in size; while the conspicuous consumption of goods should gradually gain in importance, both absolutely and relatively, until it had absorbed all the available product, leaving nothing over beyond a bare livelihood. But the actual course of development has been somewhat different from this ideal scheme. Leisure held the first place at the start, and came to hold a rank very much above wasteful consumption of goods, both as a direct exponent of wealth and as an element in the standard of decency, during the quasi-peaceable culture. From that point onward, consumption has gained ground, until, at present, it unquestionably holds the primacy, though it is still far from absorbing the entire margin of production above the subsistence minimum.

The early ascendancy of leisure as a means of reputability is traceable to the archaic distinction between noble and ignoble employments. Leisure is honorable and becomes imperative partly because it shows exemption from ignoble labor. The archaic differentiation into noble and ignoble classes is based on an invidious distinction between employments as honorific or debasing; and this traditional distinction grows into an imperative canon of decency during the early quasi-peaceable stage. Its ascendancy is furthered by the fact that leisure is still fully as effective an evidence of wealth as consumption. Indeed, so effective is it in the relatively small and stable human environment to which the individual is exposed at that cultural stage, that, with the aid of the archaic tradition which deprecates all productive labor, it gives rise to a large impecunious leisure class, and it even tends to limit the production of the community's industry to the subsistence minimum. This extreme inhibition of industry is avoided because slave labor, working under a compulsion more vigorous than that of reputability, is forced to turn out a product in excess of the subsistence minimum of the working class.

The subsequent relative decline in the use of conspicuous leisure as a basis of repute is due partly to an increasing relative effectiveness of consumption as an evidence of wealth; but in part it is traceable to another force, alien, and in some degree antagonistic, to the usage of conspicuous waste.

This alien factor is the instinct of workmanship. Other circumstances permitting, that instinct disposes men to look with favor upon productive efficiency and on whatever is of human use. It disposes them to deprecate waste of substance or effort. The instinct of workmanship is present in all men, and asserts itself even under very adverse circumstances. So that however wasteful a given expenditure may be in reality, it must at least have some colorable excuse in the way of an ostensible purpose. The manner in which, under special circumstances, the instinct eventuates in a taste for exploit and an invidious discrimination between noble and ignoble classes has been indicated in an earlier chapter. In so far as it comes into conflict with the law of conspicuous waste, the instinct of workmanship expresses itself not so much in insistence on substantial usefulness as in an abiding sense of the odiousness and aesthetic impossibility of what is obviously futile. Being of the nature of an instinctive affection, its guidance touches chiefly and immediately the obvious and apparent violations of its requirements. It is only less promptly and with less constraining force that it reaches such substantial violations of its requirements as are appreciated only upon reflection.

So long as all labor continues to be performed exclusively or usually by slaves, the baseness of all productive effort is too constantly and deterrently present in the mind of men to allow the instinct of workmanship seriously to take effect in the direction of industrial usefulness; but when the quasi-peaceable stage (with slavery and status) passes into the peaceable stage of industry (with wage labor and cash payment) the instinct comes more effectively into play. It then begins aggressively to shape men's views of what is meritorious, and asserts itself at least as an auxiliary canon of self-complacency. All extraneous considerations apart, those persons (adult) are but a vanishing minority today who harbor no inclination to the accomplishment of some end, or who are not impelled of their own motion to shape some object or fact or relation for human use. The propensity may in large measure be overborne by the more immediately constraining incentive to a reputable leisure and an avoidance of indecorous usefulness, and it may therefore work itself out in make-believe only; as for instance in "social duties," and in quasi-artistic or quasi-scholarly accomplishments, in the care and decoration of the house, in sewing-circle activity or dress reform, in proficiency at dress, cards, yachting, golf, and various sports. But the fact that it may under stress of circumstances eventuate in inanities no more disproves the presence of the instinct than the reality of the brooding instinct is disproved by inducing a hen to sit on a nestful of china eggs.

This latter-day uneasy reaching-out for some form of purposeful activity that shall at the same time not be indecorously productive of either individual or collective gain marks a difference of attitude between the modern leisure class and that of the quasi-peaceable stage. At the earlier stage, as was said above, the all-dominating institution of slavery and status acted resistlessly to discountenance exertion directed to other than naively predatory ends. It was still possible to find some habitual employment for the inclination to action in the way of forcible aggression or repression directed against hostile groups or against the subject classes within the group; and this sewed to relieve the pressure and draw off the energy of the leisure class without a resort to actually useful, or even ostensibly useful employments. The practice of hunting also sewed the same purpose in some degree. When the community developed into a peaceful industrial organization, and when fuller occupation of the land had reduced the opportunities for the hunt to an inconsiderable residue, the pressure of energy seeking purposeful employment was left to find an outlet in some other direction. The ignominy which attaches to useful effort also entered upon a less acute phase with the disappearance of compulsory labor; and the instinct of workmanship then came to assert itself with more persistence and consistency.

The line of least resistance has changed in some measure, and the energy which formerly found a vent in predatory activity, now in part takes the direction of some ostensibly useful end. Ostensibly purposeless leisure has come to be deprecated, especially among that large portion of the leisure class whose plebeian origin acts to set them at variance with the tradition of the *otium cum dignitate.* But that canon of reputability which discountenances all employment that is of the nature of productive effort is still at hand, and will permit nothing beyond the most transient vogue to any employment that is substantially useful or productive. The consequence is that a change has been wrought in the conspicuous leisure practiced by the leisure class; not so much in substance as in form. A reconciliation between the two conflicting requirements is effected by a resort to make-believe. Many and intricate polite observances and social duties of a ceremonial nature are developed; many organizations are founded, with some specious object of amelioration embodied in their official style and title; there is much coming and going, and a deal of talk, to the end that the talkers may not have occasion to reflect on what is the effectual economic value of their traffic. And along with the make-believe of purposeful employment, and woven inextricably into its texture, there is commonly, if not invariably, a more or less appreciable element of purposeful effort directed to some serious end.

In the narrower sphere of vicarious leisure a similar change has gone forward. Instead of simply passing her time in visible idleness, as in the best days of the patriarchal regime, the housewife of the advanced peaceable stage applies herself assiduously to household cares. The salient features of this development of domestic service have already been indicated. Throughout the entire evolution of conspicuous expenditure, whether of goods or of services or human life, runs the obvious implication that in order to effectually mend the consumer's good fame it must be an expenditure of superfluities. In order to be reputable it must be wasteful. No merit would accrue from the consumption of the bare necessaries of life, except by comparison with the abjectly poor who fall short even of the subsistence minimum; and no standard of expenditure could result from such a comparison, except the most prosaic and unattractive level of decency. A standard of life would still be possible which should admit of invidious comparison in other respects than that of opulence; as, for instance, a comparison in various directions in the manifestation of moral, physical, intellectual, or aesthetic force. Comparison in all these directions is in vogue today; and the comparison made in these respects is commonly so inextricably bound up with the pecuniary comparison as to be scarcely distinguishable from the latter. This is especially true as regards the current rating of expressions of intellectual and aesthetic force or proficiency' so that we frequently interpret as aesthetic or intellectual a difference which in substance is pecuniary only.

The use of the term "waste" is in one respect an unfortunate one. As used in the speech of everyday life the word carries an undertone of deprecation. It is here used for

want of a better term that will adequately describe the same range of motives and of phenomena, and it is not to be taken in an odious sense, as implying an illegitimate expenditure of human products or of human life. In the view of economic theory the
expenditure in question is no more and no less legitimate than any other expenditure.
It is here called "waste" because this expenditure does not serve human life or human
well-being on the whole, not because it is waste or misdirection of effort or expenditure
as viewed from the standpoint of the individual consumer who chooses it. If he chooses
it, that disposes of the question of its relative utility to him, as compared with other
forms of consumption that would not be deprecated on account of their wastefulness.
Whatever form of expenditure the consumer chooses, or whatever end he seeks in making his choice, has utility to him by virtue of his preference. As seen from the point of
view of the individual consumer, the question of wastefulness does not arise within the
scope of economic theory proper. The use of the word "waste" as a technical term, therefore, implies no deprecation of the motives or of the ends sought by the consumer under
this canon of conspicuous waste.

But it is, on other grounds, worth noting that the term "waste" in the language of
everyday life implies deprecation of what is characterized as wasteful. This common-
sense implication is itself an outcropping of the instinct of workmanship. The popular
reprobation of waste goes to say that in order to be at peace with himself the common
man must be able to see in any and all human effort and human enjoyment an enhancement of life and well-being on the whole. In order to meet with unqualified approval, any economic fact must approve itself under the test of impersonal
usefulness—usefulness as seen from the point of view of the generically human. Relative or competitive advantage of one individual in comparison with another does not
satisfy the economic conscience, and therefore competitive expenditure has not the approval of this conscience.

In strict accuracy nothing should be included under the head of conspicuous waste but
such expenditure as is incurred on the ground of an invidious pecuniary comparison. But
in order to bring any given item or element in under this head it is not necessary that it
should be recognized as waste in this sense by the person incurring the expenditure. It
frequently happens that an element of the standard of living which set out with being primarily wasteful, ends with becoming, in the apprehension of the consumer, a necessary
of life; and it may in this way become as indispensable as any other item of the consumer's habitual expenditure. As items which sometimes fall under this head, and are
therefore available as illustrations of the manner in which this principle applies, may be
cited carpets and tapestries, silver table service, waiter's services, silk hats, starched linen,
many articles of jewelry and of dress. The indispensability of these things after the habit
and the convention have been formed, however, has little to say in the classification of
expenditures as waste or not waste in the technical meaning of the word. The test to
which all expenditure must be brought in an attempt to decide that point is the question whether it serves directly to enhance human life on the whole—whether it furthers
the life process taken impersonally. For this is the basis of award of the instinct of workmanship, and that instinct is the court of final appeal in any question of economic truth
or adequacy. It is a question as to the award rendered by a dispassionate common sense.

The question is, therefore, not whether, under the existing circumstances of individual habit and social custom, a given expenditure conduces to the particular consumer's gratification or peace of mind; but whether, aside from acquired tastes and from the canons of usage and conventional decency, its result is a net gain in comfort or in the fullness of life. Customary expenditure must be classed under the head of waste in so far as the custom on which it rests is traceable to the habit of making an invidious pecuniary comparison—in so far as it is conceived that it could not have become customary and prescriptive without the backing of this principle of pecuniary reputability or relative economic success. It is obviously not necessary that a given object of expenditure should be exclusively wasteful in order to come in under the category of conspicuous waste. An article may be useful and wasteful both, and its utility to the consumer may be made up of use and waste in the most varying proportions. Consumable goods, and even productive goods, generally show the two elements in combination, as constituents of their utility; although, in a general way, the element of waste tends to predominate in articles of consumption, while the contrary is true of articles designed for productive use.

Even in articles which appear at first glance to serve for pure ostentation only, it is always possible to detect the presence of some, at least ostensible, useful purpose; and on the other hand, even in special machinery and tools contrived for some particular industrial process, as well as in the rudest appliances of human industry, the traces of conspicuous waste, or at least of the habit of ostentation, usually become evident on a close scrutiny. It would be hazardous to assert that a useful purpose is ever absent from the utility of any article or of any service, however obviously its prime purpose and chief element is conspicuous waste; and it would be only less hazardous to assert of any primarily useful product that the element of waste is in no way concerned in its value, immediately or remotely.

CHAPTER FIVE

The Pecuniary Standard of Living

For the great body of the people in any modern community, the proximate ground of expenditure in excess of what is required for physical comfort is not a conscious effort to excel in the expensiveness of their visible consumption, so much as it is a desire to live up to the conventional standard of decency in the amount and grade of goods consumed. This desire is not guided by a rigidly invariable standard, which must be lived up to, and beyond which there is no incentive to go. The standard is flexible; and especially it is indefinitely extensible, if only time is allowed for habituation to any increase in pecuniary ability and for acquiring facility in the new and larger scale of expenditure that follows such an increase. It is much more difficult to recede from a scale of expenditure once adopted than it is to extend the accustomed scale in response to an accession of wealth. Many items of customary expenditure prove on analysis to be almost purely wasteful, and they are therefore honorific only, but after they have once been incorporated into the scale of decent consumption, and so have become an integral part of one's scheme of life, it is quite as hard to give up these as it is to give up many items that conduce directly to one's physical comfort, or even that may be necessary to life and health. That is to say, the conspicuously wasteful honorific expenditure that confers spiritual well-being may become more indispensable than much of that expenditure which ministers to the "lower" wants of physical well-being or sustenance only. It is notoriously just as difficult to recede from a "high" standard of living as it is to lower a standard which is already relatively low; although in the former case the difficulty is a moral one, while in the latter it may involve a material deduction from the physical comforts of life.

But while retrogression is difficult, a fresh advance in conspicuous expenditure is relatively easy; indeed, it takes place almost as a matter of course. In the rare cases where it occurs, a failure to increase one's visible consumption when the means for an increase are at hand is felt in popular apprehension to call for explanation, and unworthy motives of miserliness are imputed to those who fall short in this respect. A prompt response to the stimulus, on the other hand, is accepted as the normal effect. This suggests that the standard of expenditure which commonly guides our efforts is not the average, ordinary expenditure already achieved; it is an ideal of consumption that lies just beyond our reach, or to reach which requires some strain. The motive is emulation—the stimulus of an invidious comparison which prompts us to outdo those with whom we are in the habit of classing ourselves. Substantially the same proposition is expressed in the commonplace remark that each class envies and emulates the class next above it in the social scale, while it rarely compares itself with those below or with those who are considerably in advance. That is to say, in other words, our standard of decency in expenditure, as in other ends of emulation, is set by the usage of those next above us in reputability; until, in this way, especially in any community where class distinctions are somewhat vague, all canons of reputability and decency, and all standards of consumption, are traced back by insensible gradations to the usages and habits of thought of the highest social and pecuniary class—the wealthy leisure class.

It is for this class to determine, in general outline, what scheme of life the community shall accept as decent or honorific; and it is their office by precept and example to set forth this scheme of social salvation in its highest, ideal form. But the higher leisure class can exercise this quasi-sacerdotal office only under certain material limitations. The class cannot at discretion effect a sudden revolution or reversal of the popular habits of thought with respect to any of these ceremonial requirements. It takes time for any change to permeate the mass and change the habitual attitude of the people; and especially it takes time to change the habits of those classes that are socially more remote from the radiant body. The process is slower where the mobility of the population is less or where the intervals between the several classes are wider and more abrupt. But if time be allowed, the scope of the discretion of the leisure class as regards questions of form and detail in the community's scheme of life is large; while as regards the substantial principles of reputability, the changes which it can effect lie within a narrow margin of tolerance. Its example and precept carries the force of prescription for all classes below it; but in working out the precepts which are handed down as governing the form and method of reputability—in shaping the usages and the spiritual attitude of the lower classes—this authoritative prescription constantly works under the selective guidance of the canon of conspicuous waste, tempered in varying degree by the instinct of workmanship. To those norms is to be added another broad principle of human nature—the predatory animus—which in point of generality and of psychological content lies between the two just named. The effect of the latter in shaping the accepted scheme of life is yet to be discussed. The canon of reputability, then, must adapt itself to the economic circumstances, the traditions, and the degree of spiritual maturity of the particular class whose scheme of life it is to regulate. It is especially to be noted that however high its authority and however true to the fundamental requirements of reputability it may have been at its inception, a specific formal observance can under no circumstances maintain itself in force if with the lapse of time or on its transmission to a lower pecuniary class it is found to run counter to the ultimate ground of decency among civilized peoples, namely, serviceability for the purpose of an invidious comparison in pecuniary success. It is evident that these canons of expenditure have much to say in determining the standard of living for any community and for any class. It is no less evident that the standard of living which prevails at any time or at any given social altitude will in its turn have much to say as to the forms which honorific expenditure will take, and as to the degree to which this "higher" need will dominate a people's consumption. In this respect the control exerted by the accepted standard of living is chiefly of a negative character; it acts almost solely to prevent recession from a scale of conspicuous expenditure that has once become habitual.

A standard of living is of the nature of habit. It is a habitual scale and method of responding to given stimuli. The difficulty in the way of receding from an accustomed standard is the difficulty of breaking a habit that has once been formed. The relative facility with which an advance in the standard is made means that the life process is a process of unfolding activity and that it will readily unfold in a new direction whenever and wherever the resistance to self-expression decreases. But when the habit of expression along such a given line of low resistance has once been formed, the discharge will seek the accustomed outlet even after a change has taken place in the environment whereby the external resistance has appreciably risen. That heightened facility of expression in a given direction which is called habit may offset a considerable increase in the resistance offered by external circumstances to the unfolding of life in the given direction. As between the various habits, or habitual modes and directions of expression, which go to make up an individual's standard of living, there is an appreciable difference in point of persistence under counteracting circumstances and in point of the degree of imperativeness with which the discharge seeks a given direction.

That is to say, in the language of current economic theory, while men are reluctant to retrench their expenditures in any direction, they are more reluctant to retrench in some directions than in others; so that while any accustomed consumption is reluctantly given up, there are certain lines of consumption which are given up with relatively extreme reluctance. The articles or forms of consumption to which the consumer clings with the greatest tenacity are commonly the so-called necessaries of life, or the subsistence minimum. The subsistence minimum is of course not a rigidly determined allowance of goods, definite and invariable in kind and quantity; but for the purpose in hand it may be taken to comprise a certain, more or less definite, aggregate of consumption required for the maintenance of life. This minimum, it may be assumed, is ordinarily given up last in case of a progressive retrenchment of expenditure. That is to say, in a general way, the most ancient and ingrained of the habits which govern the individual's life—those habits that touch his existence as an organism—are the most persistent and imperative. Beyond these come the higher wants—later-formed habits of the individual or the race—in a somewhat irregular and by no means invariable gradation. Some of these higher wants, as for instance the habitual use of certain stimulants, or the need of salvation (in the eschatological sense), or of good repute, may in some cases take precedence of the lower or more elementary wants. In general, the longer the habituation, the more unbroken the habit, and the more nearly it coincides with previous habitual forms of the life process, the more persistently will the given habit assert itself. The habit will be stronger if the particular traits of human nature which its action involves, or the particular aptitudes that find exercise in it, are traits or aptitudes that are already largely and profoundly concerned in the life process or that are intimately bound up with the life history of the particular racial stock. The varying degrees of ease with which different habits are formed by different persons, as well as the varying degrees of reluctance with which different habits are given up, goes to say that the formation of specific habits is not a matter of length of habituation simply. Inherited aptitudes and traits of temperament count for quite as much as length of habituation in deciding what range of habits will come to dominate any individual's scheme of life. And the prevalent type of transmitted aptitudes, or in other words the type of temperament belonging to the dominant ethnic element in any community, will go far to decide what will be the scope and form of expression of the community's habitual life process. How greatly the transmitted idiosyncrasies of aptitude may count in the way of a rapid and definitive formation of habit in individuals is illustrated by the extreme facility with which an all-dominating habit of alcoholism is sometimes formed; or in the similar facility and the similarly inevitable formation of a habit of devout observances in the case of persons gifted with a special aptitude in that direction. Much the same meaning attaches to that peculiar facility of habituation to a specific human environment that is called romantic love.

Men differ in respect of transmitted aptitudes, or in respect of the relative facility with which they unfold their life activity in particular directions; and the habits which coincide with or proceed upon a relatively strong specific aptitude or a relatively great specific facility of expression become of great consequence to the man's well-being. The part played by this element of aptitude in determining the relative tenacity of the several habits which constitute the standard of living goes to explain the extreme reluctance with which men give up any habitual expenditure in the way of conspicuous consumption. The aptitudes or propensities to which a habit of this kind is to be referred as its ground are those aptitudes whose exercise is comprised in emulation; and the propensity for emulation—for invidious comparison—is of ancient growth and is a pervading trait of human nature. It is easily called into vigorous activity in any new form, and it asserts itself with great insistence under any form under which it has once found habitual expression. When the individual has once formed the habit of seeking expression in a given line of honorific expenditure—when a given set of stimuli have come to be habitually responded to in activity of a given kind and direction under the guidance of these alert and deep-reaching propensities of emulation—it is with extreme reluctance that such an habitual expenditure is given up. And on the other hand, whenever an accession of pecuniary strength puts the individual in a position to unfold his life process in larger scope and with additional reach, the ancient propensities of the race will assert themselves in determining the direction which the new unfolding of life is to take. And those propensities which are already actively in the field under some related form of expression, which are aided by the pointed suggestions afforded by a current accredited scheme of life, and for the exercise of which the material means and opportunities are readily available—these will especially have much to say in shaping the form and direction in which the new accession to the individual's aggregate force will assert itself. That is to say, in concrete terms, in any community where conspicuous consumption is an element of the scheme of life, an increase in an individual's ability to pay is likely to take the form of an expenditure for some accredited line of conspicuous consumption.

With the exception of the instinct of self-preservation, the propensity for emulation is probably the strongest and most alert and persistent of the economic motives proper. In an industrial community this propensity for emulation expresses itself in pecuniary emulation; and this, so far as regards the Western civilized communities of the present, is virtually equivalent to saying that it expresses itself in some form of conspicuous waste. The need of conspicuous waste, therefore, stands ready to absorb any increase in the community's industrial efficiency or output of goods, after the most elementary physical wants have been provided for. Where this result does not follow, under modern conditions, the reason for the discrepancy is commonly to be sought in a rate of increase in the individual's wealth too rapid for the habit of expenditure to keep abreast of it; or it may be that the individual in question defers the conspicuous consumption of the increment to a later date—ordinarily with a view to heightening the spectacular effect of the aggregate expenditure contemplated. As increased industrial efficiency makes it possible to procure the means of livelihood with less labor, the energies of the industrious members of the community are bent to the compassing of a higher result in conspicuous expenditure, rather than slackened to a more comfortable pace. The strain is not lightened as industrial efficiency increases and makes a lighter strain possible, but the increment of output is turned to use to meet this want, which is indefinitely expansible, after the manner commonly imputed in economic theory to higher or spiritual wants. It is owing chiefly to the presence of this element in the standard of living that J. S. Mill was able to say that "hitherto it is questionable if all the mechanical inventions yet made have lightened the day's toil of any human being." The accepted standard of expenditure in the community or in the class to which a person belongs largely determines what his standard of living will be. It does this directly by commending itself to his common sense as right and good, through his habitually contemplating it and assimilating the scheme of life in which it belongs; but it does so also indirectly through popular insistence on conformity to the accepted scale of expenditure as a matter of propriety, under pain of disesteem and ostracism. To accept and practice the standard of living which is in vogue is both agreeable and expedient, commonly to the point of being indispensable to personal comfort and to success in life. The standard of living of any class, so far as concerns the element of conspicuous waste, is commonly as high as the earning capacity of the class will permit—with a constant tendency to go higher. The effect upon the serious activities of men is therefore to direct them with great singleness of purpose to the largest possible acquisition of wealth, and to discountenance work that brings no pecuniary gain. At the same time the effect on consumption is to concentrate it upon the lines which are most patent to the observers whose good opinion is sought; while the inclinations and aptitudes whose exercise does not involve a honorific expenditure of time or substance tend to fall into abeyance through disuse.

Through this discrimination in favor of visible consumption it has come about that the domestic life of most classes is relatively shabby, as compared with the that of that overt portion of their life that is carried on before the eyes of observers. As a secondary consequence of the same discrimination, people habitually screen their private life from observation. So far as concerns that portion of their consumption that may without blame be carried on in secret, they withdraw from all contact with their neighbors, hence the exclusiveness of people, as regards their domestic life, in most of the industrially developed communities; and hence, by remoter derivation, the habit of privacy and reserve that is so large a feature in the code of proprieties of the better class in all communities. The low birthrate of the classes upon whom the requirements of reputable expenditure fall with great urgency is likewise traceable to the exigencies of a standard of living based on conspicuous waste. The conspicuous consumption, and the consequent increased expense, required in the reputable maintenance of a child is very considerable and acts as a powerful deterrent. It is probably the most effectual of the Malthusian prudential checks.

The effect of this factor of the standard of living, both in the way of retrenchment in the obscurer elements of consumption that go to physical comfort and maintenance, and also in the paucity or absence of children, is perhaps seen at its best among the classes given to scholarly pursuits. Because of a presumed superiority and scarcity of the gifts and attainments that characterize their life, these classes are by convention subsumed under a higher social grade than their pecuniary grade should warrant. The scale of decent expenditure in their case is pitched correspondingly high, and it consequently leaves an exceptionally narrow margin disposable for the other ends of life. By force of circumstances, their habitual sense of what is good and right in these matters, as well as the expectations of the community in the way of pecuniary decency among the learned, are excessively high—as measured by the prevalent degree of opulence and earning capacity of the class, relatively to the non-scholarly classes whose social equals they nominally are. In any modern community where there is no priestly monopoly of these occupations, the people of scholarly pursuits are unavoidably thrown into contact with classes that are pecuniarily their superiors. The high standard of pecuniary decency in force among these superior classes is transfused among the scholarly classes with but little mitigation of its rigor; and as a consequence there is no class of the community that spends a larger proportion of its substance in conspicuous waste than these.

CHAPTER SIX

Pecuniary Canons of Taste

The caution has already been repeated more than once, that while the regulating norm of consumption is in large part the requirement of conspicuous waste, it must not be understood that the motive on which the consumer acts in any given case is this principle in its bald, unsophisticated form. Ordinarily his motive is a wish to conform to established usage, to avoid unfavorable notice and comment, to live up to the accepted canons of decency in the kind, amount, and grade of goods consumed, as well as in the decorous employment of his time and effort. In the common run of cases this sense of prescriptive usage is present in the motives of the consumer and exerts a direct constraining force, especially as regards consumption carried on under the eyes of observers. But a considerable element of prescriptive expensiveness is observable also in consumption that does not in any appreciable degree become known to outsiders—as, for instance, articles of underclothing, some articles of food, kitchen utensils, and other household apparatus designed for service rather than for evidence. In all such useful articles a close scrutiny will discover certain features which add to the cost and enhance the commercial value of the goods in question, but do not proportionately increase the serviceability of these articles for the material purposes which alone they ostensibly are designed to serve.

Under the selective surveillance of the law of conspicuous waste there grows up a code of accredited canons of consumption, the effect of which is to hold the consumer up to a standard of expensiveness and wastefulness in his consumption of goods and in his employment of time and effort. This growth of prescriptive usage has an immediate effect upon economic life, but it has also an indirect and remoter effect upon conduct in other respects as well. Habits of thought with respect to the expression of life in any given direction unavoidably affect the habitual view of what is good and right in life in other directions also. In the organic complex of habits of thought which make up the substance of an individual's conscious life the economic interest does not lie isolated and distinct from all other interests. Something, for instance, has already been said of its relation to the canons of reputability.

The principle of conspicuous waste guides the formation of habits of thought as to what is honest and reputable in life and in commodities. In so doing, this principle will traverse other norms of conduct which do not primarily have to do with the code of pecuniary honor, but which have, directly or incidentally, an economic significance of some magnitude. So the canon of honorific waste may, immediately or remotely, influence the sense of duty, the sense of beauty, the sense of utility, the sense of devotional or ritualistic fitness, and the scientific sense of truth.

It is scarcely necessary to go into a discussion here of the particular points at which, or the particular manner in which, the canon of honorific expenditure habitually traverses the canons of moral conduct. The matter is one which has received large attention and illustration at the hands of those whose office it is to watch and admonish with respect to any departures from the accepted code of morals. In modern communities, where the dominant economic and legal feature of the community's life is the institution of private property, one of the salient features of the code of morals is the sacredness of property. There needs no insistence or illustration to gain assent to the proposition that the habit of holding private property inviolate is traversed by the other habit of seeking wealth for the sake of the good repute to be gained through its conspicuous consumption. Most offenses against property, especially offenses of an appreciable magnitude, come under this head. It is also a matter of common notoriety and byword that in offenses which result in a large accession of property to the offender he does not ordinarily incur the extreme penalty or the extreme obloquy with which his offenses would be visited on the ground of the naive moral code alone. The thief or swindler who has gained great wealth by his delinquency has a better chance than the small thief of escaping the rigorous penalty of the law and some good repute accrues to him from his increased wealth and from his spending the irregularly acquired possessions in a seemly manner. A well-bred expenditure of his booty especially appeals with great effect to persons of a cultivated sense of the proprieties, and goes far to mitigate the sense of moral turpitude with which his dereliction is viewed by them. It may be noted also—and it is more immediately to the point—that we are all inclined to condone an offense against property in the case of a man whose motive is the worthy one of providing the means of a "decent" manner of life for his wife and children. If it is added that the wife has been "nurtured in the lap of luxury," that is accepted as an additional extenuating circumstance. That is to say, we are prone to condone such an offense where its aim is the honorific one of enabling the offender's wife to perform for him such an amount of vicarious consumption of time and substance as is demanded by the standard of pecuniary decency. In such a case the habit of approving the accustomed degree of conspicuous waste traverses the habit of deprecating violations of ownership, to the extent even of sometimes leaving the award of praise or blame uncertain. This is peculiarly true where the dereliction involves an appreciable predatory or piratical element.

This topic need scarcely be pursued further here; but the remark may not be out of place that all that considerable body of morals that clusters about the concept of an inviolable ownership is itself a psychological precipitate of the traditional meritoriousness of wealth. And it should be added that this wealth which is held sacred is valued primarily for the sake of the good repute to be got through its conspicuous consumption. The bearing of pecuniary decency upon the scientific spirit or the quest of knowledge will be taken up in some detail in a separate chapter. Also as regards the sense of devout or ritual merit and adequacy in this connection, little need be said in this place. That topic will also come up incidentally in a later chapter. Still, this usage of honorific expenditure has much to say in shaping popular tastes as to what is right and meritorious in sacred matters, and the bearing of the principle of conspicuous waste upon some of the commonplace devout observances and conceits may therefore be pointed out.

Obviously, the canon of conspicuous waste is accountable for a great portion of what may be called devout consumption; as, e.g., the consumption of sacred edifices, vestments, and other goods of the same class. Even in those modern cults to whose divinities is imputed a predilection for temples not built with hands, the sacred buildings and the other properties of the cult are constructed and decorated with some view to a reputable degree of wasteful expenditure. And it needs but little either of observation or introspection—and either will serve the turn—to assure us that the expensive splendor of the house of worship has an appreciable uplifting and mellowing effect upon the worshipper's frame of mind. It will serve to enforce the same fact if we reflect upon the sense of abject shamefulness with which any evidence of indigence or squalor about the sacred place affects all beholders. The accessories of any devout observance should be pecuniarily above reproach. This requirement is imperative, whatever latitude may be allowed with regard to these accessories in point of aesthetic or other serviceability. It may also be in place to notice that in all communities, especially in neighborhoods where the standard of pecuniary decency for dwellings is not high, the local sanctuary is more ornate, more conspicuously wasteful in its architecture and decoration, than the dwelling houses of the congregation. This is true of nearly all denominations and cults, whether Christian or Pagan, but it is true in a peculiar degree of the older and maturer cults. At the same time the sanctuary commonly contributes little if anything to the physical comfort of the members. Indeed, the sacred structure not only serves the physical well-being of the members to but a slight extent, as compared with their humbler dwelling-houses; but it is felt by all men that a right and enlightened sense of the true, the beautiful, and the good demands that in all expenditure on the sanctuary anything that might serve the comfort of the worshipper should be conspicuously absent. If any element of comfort is admitted in the fittings of the sanctuary, it should be at least scrupulously screened and masked under an ostensible austerity. In the most reputable latter-day houses of worship, where no expense is spared, the principle of austerity is carried to the length of making the fittings of the place a means of mortifying the flesh, especially in appearance. There are few persons of delicate tastes, in the matter of devout consumption to whom this austerely wasteful discomfort does not appeal as intrinsically right and good. Devout consumption is of the nature of vicarious consumption. This canon of devout austerity is based on the pecuniary reputability of conspicuously wasteful consumption, backed by the principle that vicarious consumption should conspicuously not conduce to the comfort of the vicarious consumer.

The sanctuary and its fittings have something of this austerity in all the cults in which the saint or divinity to whom the sanctuary pertains is not conceived to be present and make personal use of the property for the gratification of luxurious tastes imputed to him. The character of the sacred paraphernalia is somewhat different in this respect in those cults where the habits of life imputed to the divinity more nearly approach those of an earthly patriarchal potentate—where he is conceived to make use of these consumable goods in person. In the latter case the sanctuary and its fittings take on more of the fashion given to goods destined for the conspicuous consumption of a temporal master or owner. On the other hand, where the sacred apparatus is simply employed in the divinity's service, that is to say, where it is consumed vicariously on his account by his servants, there the sacred properties take the character suited to goods that are destined for vicarious consumption only.

In the latter case the sanctuary and the sacred apparatus are so contrived as not to enhance the comfort or fullness of life of the vicarious consumer, or at any rate not to convey the impression that the end of their consumption is the consumer's comfort. For the end of vicarious consumption is to enhance, not the fullness of life of the consumer, but the pecuniary repute of the master for whose behoof the consumption takes place. Therefore priestly vestments are notoriously expensive, ornate, and inconvenient; and in the cults where the priestly servitor of the divinity is not conceived to serve him in the capacity of consort, they are of an austere, comfortless fashion. And such it is felt that they should be.

It is not only in establishing a devout standard of decent expensiveness that the principle of waste invades the domain of the canons of ritual serviceability. It touches the ways as well as the means, and draws on vicarious leisure as well as on vicarious consumption. Priestly demeanor at its best is aloof, leisurely, perfunctory, and uncontaminated with suggestions of sensuous pleasure. This holds true, in different degrees of course, for the different cults and denominations; but in the priestly life of all anthropomorphic cults the marks of a vicarious consumption of time are visible.

The same pervading canon of vicarious leisure is also visibly present in the exterior details of devout observances and need only be pointed out in order to become obvious to all beholders. All ritual has a notable tendency to reduce itself to a rehearsal of formulas. This development of formula is most noticeable in the maturer cults, which have at the same time a more austere, ornate, and severe priestly life and garb; but it is perceptible also in the forms and methods of worship of the newer and fresher sects, whose tastes in respect of priests, vestments, and sanctuaries are less exacting. The rehearsal of the service (the term "service" carries a suggestion significant for the point in question) grows more perfunctory as the cult gains in age and consistency, and this perfunctoriness of the rehearsal is very pleasing to the correct devout taste. And with a good reason, for the fact of its being perfunctory goes to say pointedly that the master for whom it is performed is exalted above the vulgar need of actually proficuous service on the part of his servants. They are unprofitable servants, and there is an honorific implication for their master in their remaining unprofitable. It is needless to point out the close analogy at this point between the priestly office and the office of the footman. It is pleasing to our sense of what is fitting in these matters, in either case, to recognize in the obvious perfunctoriness of the service that it is a pro forma execution only. There should be no show of agility or of dexterous manipulation in the execution of the priestly office, such as might suggest a capacity for turning off the work.

In all this there is of course an obvious implication as to the temperament, tastes, propensities, and habits of life imputed to the divinity by worshippers who live under the tradition of these pecuniary canons of reputability. Through its pervading men's habits of thought, the principle of conspicuous waste has colored the worshippers' notions of the divinity and of the relation in which the human subject stands to him. It is of course in the more naive cults that this suffusion of pecuniary beauty is most patent, but it is visible throughout. All peoples, at whatever stage of culture or degree of enlightenment, are fain to eke out a sensibly scant degree of authentic formation regarding the personality and habitual surroundings of their divinities. In so calling in the aid of fancy to enrich and fill in their picture of the divinity's presence and manner of life they habitually impute to him such traits as go to make up their ideal of a worthy man. And in seeking communion with the divinity the ways and means of approach are assimilated as nearly as may be to the divine ideal that is in men's minds at the time. It is felt that the divine presence is entered with the best grace, and with the best effect, according to certain accepted methods and with the accompaniment of certain material circumstances which in popular apprehension are peculiarly consonant with the divine nature. This popularly accepted ideal of the bearing and paraphernalia adequate to such occasions of communion is, of course, to a good extent shaped by the popular apprehension of what is intrinsically worthy and beautiful in human carriage and surroundings on all occasions of dignified intercourse. It would on this account be misleading to attempt an analysis of devout demeanor by referring all evidences of the presence of a pecuniary standard of reputability back directly and baldly to the underlying norm of pecuniary emulation. So it would also be misleading to ascribe to the divinity, as popularly conceived, a jealous regard for his pecuniary standing and a habit of avoiding and condemning squalid situations and surroundings simply because they are under grade in the pecuniary respect.

And still, after all allowance has been made, it appears that the canons of pecuniary reputability do, directly or indirectly, materially affect our notions of the attributes of divinity, as well as our notions of what are the fit and adequate manner and circumstances of divine communion. It is felt that the divinity must be of a peculiarly serene and leisurely habit of life. And whenever his local habitation is pictured in poetic imagery, for edification or in appeal to the devout fancy, the devout word-painter, as a matter of course, brings out before his auditors' imagination a throne with a profusion of the insignia of opulence and power, and surrounded by a great number of servitors. In the common run of such presentations of the celestial abodes, the office of this corps of servants is a vicarious leisure, their time and efforts being in great measure taken up with an industrially unproductive rehearsal of the meritorious characteristics and exploits of the divinity; while the background of the presentation is filled with the shimmer of the precious metals and of the more expensive varieties of precious stones. It is only in the crasser expressions of devout fancy that this intrusion of pecuniary canons into the devout ideals reaches such an extreme. An extreme case occurs in the devout imagery of the Negro population of the South. Their word-painters are unable to descend to anything cheaper than gold; so that in this case the insistence on pecuniary beauty gives a startling effect in yellow—such as would be unbearable to a soberer taste. Still, there is probably no cult in which ideals of pecuniary merit have not been called in to supplement the ideals of ceremonial adequacy that guide men's conception of what is right in the matter of sacred apparatus.

Similarly it is felt—and the sentiment is acted upon—that the priestly servitors of the divinity should not engage in industrially productive work; that work of any kind—any employment which is of tangible human use—must not be carried on in the divine presence, or within the precincts of the sanctuary; that whoever comes into the presence should come cleansed of all profane industrial features in his apparel or person, and should come clad in garments of more than everyday expensiveness; that on holidays set apart in honor of or for communion with the divinity no work that is of human use should be performed by any one. Even the remoter, lay dependents should render a vicarious leisure to the extent of one day in seven. In all these deliverances of men's uninstructed sense of what is fit and proper in devout observance and in the relations of the divinity, the effectual presence of the canons of pecuniary reputability is obvious enough, whether these canons have had their effect on the devout judgment in this respect immediately or at the second remove.

These canons of reputability have had a similar, but more far-reaching and more specifically determinable, effect upon the popular sense of beauty or serviceability in consumable goods. The requirements of pecuniary decency have, to a very appreciable extent, influenced the sense of beauty and of utility in articles of use or beauty. Articles are to an extent preferred for use on account of their being conspicuously wasteful; they are felt to be serviceable somewhat in proportion as they are wasteful and ill adapted to their ostensible use.

The utility of articles valued for their beauty depends closely upon the expensiveness of the articles. A homely illustration will bring out this dependence. A hand-wrought silver spoon, of a commercial value of some ten to twenty dollars, is not ordinarily more serviceable—in the first sense of the word—than a machine-made spoon of the same material. It may not even be more serviceable than a machine-made spoon of some "base" metal, such as aluminum, the value of which may be no more than some ten to twenty cents. The former of the two utensils is, in fact, commonly a less effective contrivance for its ostensible purpose than the latter. The objection is of course ready to hand that, in taking this view of the matter, one of the chief uses, if not the chief use, of the costlier spoon is ignored; the hand-wrought spoon gratifies our taste, our sense of the beautiful, while that made by machinery out of the base metal has no useful office beyond a brute efficiency. The facts are no doubt as the objection states them, but it will be evident on rejection that the objection is after all more plausible than conclusive. It appears (1) that while the different materials of which the two spoons are made each possesses beauty and serviceability for the purpose for which it is used, the material of the hand-wrought spoon is some one hundred times more valuable than the baser metal, without very greatly excelling the latter in intrinsic beauty of grain or color, and without being in any appreciable degree superior in point of mechanical serviceability; (2) if a close inspection should show that the supposed hand-wrought spoon were in reality only a very clever citation of hand-wrought goods, but an imitation so cleverly wrought as to give the same impression of line and surface to any but a minute examination by a trained eye, the utility of the article, including the gratification which the user derives from its contemplation as an object of beauty, would immediately decline by some eighty or ninety per cent, or even more; (3) if the two spoons are, to a fairly close observer, so nearly identical in appearance that the lighter weight of the spurious article alone betrays it, this identity of form and color will scarcely add to the value of the machine-made spoon, nor appreciably enhance the gratification of the user's "sense of beauty" in contemplating it, so long as the cheaper spoon is not a novelty, and so long as it can be procured at a nominal cost. The case of the spoons is typical. The superior gratification derived from the use and contemplation of costly and supposedly beautiful products is, commonly, in great measure a gratification of our sense of costliness masquerading under the name of beauty. Our higher appreciation of the superior article is an appreciation of its superior honorific character, much more frequently than it is an unsophisticated appreciation of its beauty. The requirement of conspicuous wastefulness is not commonly present, consciously, in our canons of taste, but it is nonetheless present as a constraining norm selectively shaping and sustaining our sense of what is beautiful, and guiding our discrimination with respect to what may legitimately be approved as beautiful and what may not.

It is at this point, where the beautiful and the honorific meet and blend, that a discrimination between serviceability and wastefulness is most difficult in any concrete case. It frequently happens that an article which serves the honorific purpose of conspicuous waste is at the same time a beautiful object; and the same application of labor to which it owes its utility for the former purpose may, and often does, give beauty of form and color to the article. The question is further complicated by the fact that many objects, as, for instance, the precious stones and the metals and some other materials used for adornment and decoration, owe their utility as items of conspicuous waste to an antecedent utility as objects of beauty. Gold, for instance, has a high degree of sensuous beauty very many if not most of the highly prized works of art are intrinsically beautiful, though often with material qualification; the like is true of some stuffs used for clothing, of some landscapes, and of many other things in less degree. Except for this intrinsic beauty which they possess, these objects would scarcely have been coveted as they are, or have become monopolized objects of pride to their possessors and users. But the utility of these things to the possessor is commonly due less to their intrinsic beauty than to the honor which their possession and consumption confers, or to the obloquy which it wards off.

Apart from their serviceability in other respects, these objects are beautiful and have a utility as such; they are valuable on this account if they can be appropriated or monopolized; they are, therefore, coveted as valuable possessions, and their exclusive enjoyment gratifies the possessor's sense of pecuniary superiority at the same time that their contemplation gratifies his sense of beauty. But their beauty, in the naive sense of the word, is the occasion rather than the ground of their monopolization or of their commercial value. "Great as is the sensuous beauty of gems, their rarity and price adds an expression of distinction to them, which they would never have if they were cheap." There is, indeed, in the common run of cases under this head, relatively little incentive to the exclusive possession and use of these beautiful things, except on the ground of their honorific character as items of conspicuous waste. Most objects of this general class, with the partial exception of articles of personal adornment, would serve all other purposes than the honorific one equally well, whether owned by the person viewing them or not; and even as regards personal ornaments it is to be added that their chief purpose is to lend that to the person of their wearer (or owner) by comparison with other persons who are compelled to do without. The aesthetic serviceability of objects of beauty is not greatly nor universally heightened by possession.

The generalization for which the discussion so far affords ground is that any valuable object in order to appeal to our sense of beauty must conform to the requirements of beauty and of expensiveness both. But this is not all. Beyond this the canon of expensiveness also affects our tastes in such a way as to inextricably blend the marks of expensiveness, in our appreciation, with the beautiful features of the object, and to subsume the resultant effect under the head of an appreciation of beauty simply. The marks of expensiveness come to be accepted as beautiful features of the expensive articles. They are pleasing as being marks of honorific costliness, and the pleasure which they afford on this score blends with that afforded by the beautiful form and color of the object; so that we often declare that an article of apparel, for instance, is "perfectly lovely," when pretty much all that an analysis of the aesthetic value of the article would leave ground for is the declaration that it is pecuniarily honorific.

This blending and confusion of the elements of expensiveness and of beauty is, perhaps, best exemplified in articles of dress and of household furniture. The code of reputability in matters of dress decides what shapes, colors, materials, and general effects in human apparel are for the time to be accepted as suitable; and departures from the code are offensive to our taste, supposedly as being departures from aesthetic truth. The approval with which we look upon fashionable attire is by no means to be accounted pure make-believe. We readily, and for the most part with utter sincerity, find those things pleasing that are in vogue. Shaggy dress-stuffs and pronounced color effects, for instance, offend us at times when the vogue is goods of a high, glossy finish and neutral colors. A fancy bonnet of this year's model unquestionably appeals to our sensibilities today much more forcibly than an equally fancy bonnet of the model of last year; although when viewed in the perspective of a quarter of a century, it would, I apprehend, be a matter of the utmost difficulty to award the palm for intrinsic beauty to the one rather than to the other of these structures. So, again, it may be remarked that, considered simply in their physical juxtaposition with the human form, the high gloss of a gentleman's hat or of a patent-leather shoe has no more of intrinsic beauty than a similarly high gloss on a threadbare sleeve; and yet there is no question but that all well-bred people (in the Occidental civilized communities) instinctively and unaffectedly cleave to the one as a phenomenon of great beauty, and eschew the other as offensive to every sense to which it can appeal. It is extremely doubtful if any one could be induced to wear such a contrivance as the high hat of civilized society, except for some urgent reason based on other than aesthetic grounds.

By further habituation to an appreciative perception of the marks of expensiveness in goods, and by habitually identifying beauty with reputability, it comes about that a beautiful article which is not expensive is accounted not beautiful. In this way it has happened, for instance, that some beautiful flowers pass conventionally for offensive weeds; others that can be cultivated with relative ease are accepted and admired by the lower middle class, who can afford no more expensive luxuries of this kind; but these varieties are rejected as vulgar by those people who are better able to pay for expensive flowers and who are educated to a higher schedule of pecuniary beauty in the florist's products; while still other flowers, of no greater intrinsic beauty than these, are cultivated at great cost and call out much admiration from flower-lovers whose tastes have been matured under the critical guidance of a polite environment.

The same variation in matters of taste, from one class of society to another, is visible also as regards many other kinds of consumable goods, as, for example, is the case with furniture, houses, parks, and gardens. This diversity of views as to what is beautiful in these various classes of goods is not a diversity of the norm according to which the unsophisticated sense of the beautiful works. It is not a constitutional difference of endowments in the aesthetic respect, but rather a difference in the code of reputability which specifies what objects properly lie within the scope of honorific consumption for the class to which the critic belongs. It is a difference in the traditions of propriety with respect to the kinds of things which may, without derogation to the consumer, be consumed under the head of objects of taste and art. With a certain allowance for variations to be accounted for on other grounds, these traditions are determined, more or less rigidly, by the pecuniary plane of life of the class.

Everyday life affords many curious illustrations of the way in which the code of pecuniary beauty in articles of use varies from class to class, as well as of the way in which the conventional sense of beauty departs in its deliverances from the sense untutored by the requirements of pecuniary repute. Such a fact is the lawn, or the close-cropped yard or park, which appeals so unaffectedly to the taste of the Western peoples. It appears especially to appeal to the tastes of the well-to-do classes in those communities in which the dolicho-blond element predominates in an appreciable degree. The lawn unquestionably has an element of sensuous beauty, simply as an object of apperception, and as such no doubt it appeals pretty directly to the eye of nearly all races and all classes; but it is, perhaps, more unquestionably beautiful to the eye of the dolicho-blond than to most other varieties of men. This higher appreciation of a stretch of greensward in this ethnic element than in the other elements of the population, goes along with certain other features of the dolicho-blond temperament that indicate that this racial element had once been for a long time a pastoral people inhabiting a region with a humid climate. The close-cropped lawn is beautiful in the eyes of a people whose inherited bent it is to readily find pleasure in contemplating a well-preserved pasture or grazing land.

For the aesthetic purpose the lawn is a cow pasture; and in some cases today—where the expensiveness of the attendant circumstances bars out any imputation of thrift—the idyll of the dolicho-blond is rehabilitated in the introduction of a cow into a lawn or private ground. In such cases the cow made use of is commonly of an expensive breed. The vulgar suggestion of thrift, which is nearly inseparable from the cow, is a standing objection to the decorative use of this animal. So that in all cases, except where luxurious surroundings negate this suggestion, the use of the cow as an object of taste must be avoided. Where the predilection for some grazing animal to fill out the suggestion of the pasture is too strong to be suppressed, the cow's place is often given to some more or less inadequate substitute, such as deer, antelopes, or some such exotic beast. These substitutes, although less beautiful to the pastoral eye of Western man than the cow, are in such cases preferred because of their superior expensiveness or futility, and their consequent repute. They are not vulgarly lucrative either in fact or in suggestion.

Public parks of course fall in the same category with the lawn; they too, at their best, are imitations of the pasture. Such a park is of course best kept by grazing, and the cattle on the grass are themselves no mean addition to the beauty of the thing, as need scarcely be insisted on with anyone who has once seen a well-kept pasture. But it is worth noting, as an expression of the pecuniary element in popular taste, that such a method of keeping public grounds is seldom resorted to. The best that is done by skilled workmen under the supervision of a trained keeper is a more or less close imitation of a pasture, but the result invariably falls somewhat short of the artistic effect of grazing. But to the average popular apprehension a herd of cattle so pointedly suggests thrift and usefulness that their presence in the public pleasure ground would be intolerably cheap. This method of keeping grounds is comparatively inexpensive, therefore it is indecorous.

Of the same general bearing is another feature of public grounds. There is a studious exhibition of expensiveness coupled with a make-believe of simplicity and crude serviceability. Private grounds also show the same physiognomy wherever they are in the management or ownership of persons whose tastes have been formed under middle-class habits of life or under the upper-class traditions of no later a date than the childhood of the generation that is now passing. Grounds which conform to the instructed tastes of the latter-day upper class do not show these features in so marked a degree. The reason for this difference in tastes between the past and the incoming generation of the well-bred lies in the changing economic situation. A similar difference is perceptible in other respects, as well as in the accepted ideals of pleasure grounds. In this country as in most others, until the last half century but a very small proportion of the population were possessed of such wealth as would exempt them from thrift. Owing to imperfect means of communication, this small fraction were scattered and out of effective touch with one another. There was therefore no basis for a growth of taste in disregard of expensiveness.

The revolt of the well-bred taste against vulgar thrift was unchecked. Wherever the unsophisticated sense of beauty might show itself sporadically in an approval of inexpensive or thrifty surroundings, it would lack the "social confirmation" which nothing but a considerable body of like-minded people can give. There was, therefore, no effective upper-class opinion that would overlook evidences of possible inexpensiveness in the management of grounds; and there was consequently no appreciable divergence between the leisure-class and the lower middle-class ideal in the physiognomy of pleasure grounds. Both classes equally constructed their ideals with the fear of pecuniary disrepute before their eyes.

Today a divergence in ideals is beginning to be apparent. The portion of the leisure class that has been consistently exempt from work and from pecuniary cares for a generation or more is now large enough to form and sustain opinion in matters of taste. Increased mobility of the members has also added to the facility with which a "social confirmation" can be attained within the class. Within this select class the exemption from thrift is a matter so commonplace as to have lost much of its utility as a basis of pecuniary decency. Therefore the latter-day upper-class canons of taste do not so consistently insist on an unremitting demonstration of expensiveness and a strict exclusion of the appearance of thrift. So, a predilection for the rustic and the "natural" in parks and grounds makes its appearance on these higher social and intellectual levels. This predilection is in large part an outcropping of the instinct of workmanship; and it works out its results with varying degrees of consistency. It is seldom altogether unaffected, and at times it shades off into something not widely different from that make-believe of rusticity which has been referred to above.

A weakness for crudely serviceable contrivances that pointedly suggest immediate and wasteless use is present even in the middle-class tastes; but it is there kept well in hand under the unbroken dominance of the canon of reputable futility. Consequently it works out in a variety of ways and means for shamming serviceability—in such contrivances as rustic fences, bridges, bowers, pavilions, and the like decorative features. An expression of this affectation of serviceability, at what is perhaps its widest divergence from the first promptings of the sense of economic beauty, is afforded by the cast-iron rustic fence and trellis or by a circuitous drive laid across level ground.

The select leisure class has outgrown the use of these pseudo-serviceable variants of pecuniary beauty, at least at some points. But the taste of the more recent accessions to the leisure class proper and of the middle and lower classes still requires a pecuniary beauty to supplement the aesthetic beauty, even in those objects which are primarily admired for the beauty that belongs to them as natural growths.

The popular taste in these matters is to be seen in the prevalent high appreciation of topiary work and of the conventional flower-beds of public grounds. Perhaps as happy an illustration as may be had of this dominance of pecuniary beauty over aesthetic beauty in middle-class tastes is seen in the reconstruction of the grounds lately occupied by the Columbian Exposition. The evidence goes to show that the requirement of reputable expensiveness is still present in good vigor even where all ostensibly lavish display is avoided. The artistic effects actually wrought in this work of reconstruction diverge somewhat widely from the effect to which the same ground would have lent itself in hands not guided by pecuniary canons of taste. And even the better class of the city's population view the progress of the work with an unreserved approval which suggests that there is in this case little if any discrepancy between the tastes of the upper and the lower or middle classes of the city. The sense of beauty in the population of this representative city of the advanced pecuniary culture is very chary of any departure from its great cultural principle of conspicuous waste.

The love of nature, perhaps itself borrowed from a higher-class code of taste, sometimes expresses itself in unexpected ways under the guidance of this canon of pecuniary beauty, and leads to results that may seem incongruous to an unreflecting beholder. The well-accepted practice of planting trees in the treeless areas of this country, for instance, has been carried over as an item of honorific expenditure into the heavily wooded areas; so that it is by no means unusual for a village or a farmer in the wooded country to clear the land of its native trees and immediately replant saplings of certain introduced varieties about the farmyard or along the streets. In this way a forest growth of oak, elm, beech, butternut, hemlock, basswood, and birch is cleared off to give room for saplings of soft maple, cottonwood, and brittle willow. It is felt that the inexpensiveness of leaving the forest trees standing would derogate from the dignity that should invest an article which is intended to serve a decorative and honorific end.

The like pervading guidance of taste by pecuniary repute is traceable in the prevalent standards of beauty in animals. The part played by this canon of taste in assigning her place in the popular aesthetic scale to the cow has already been spoken of. Something to the same effect is true of the other domestic animals, so far as they are in an appreciable degree industrially useful to the community—as, for instance, barnyard fowl, hogs, cattle, sheep, goats, draught-horses. They are of the nature of productive goods, and serve a useful, often a lucrative end; therefore beauty is not readily imputed to them. The case is different with those domestic animals which ordinarily serve no industrial end; such as pigeons, parrots and other cage-birds, cats, dogs, and fast horses. These commonly are items of conspicuous consumption, and are therefore honorific in their nature and may legitimately be accounted beautiful. This class of animals are conventionally admired by the body of the upper classes, while the pecuniarily lower classes—and that select minority of the leisure class among whom the rigorous canon that abjures thrift is in a measure obsolescent—find beauty in one class of animals as in another, without drawing a hard and fast line of pecuniary demarcation between the beautiful and the ugly. In the case of those domestic animals which are honorific and are reputed beautiful, there is a subsidiary basis of merit that should be spoken of. Apart from the birds which belong in the honorific class of domestic animals, and which owe their place in this class to their non-lucrative character alone, the animals which merit particular attention are cats, dogs, and fast horses. The cat is less reputable than the other two just named, because she is less wasteful; she may even serve a useful end. At the same time the cat's temperament does not fit her for the honorific purpose. She lives with man on terms of equality, knows nothing of that relation of status which is the ancient basis of all distinctions of worth, honor, and repute, and she does not lend herself with facility to an invidious comparison between her owner and his neighbors. The exception to this last rule occurs in the case of such scarce and fanciful products as the Angora cat, which have some slight honorific value on the ground of expensiveness, and have, therefore, some special claim to beauty on pecuniary grounds.

The dog has advantages in the way of uselessness as well as in special gifts of temperament. He is often spoken of, in an eminent sense, as the friend of man, and his intelligence and fidelity are praised. The meaning of this is that the dog is man's servant and that he has the gift of an unquestioning subservience and a slave's quickness in guessing his master's mood. Coupled with these traits, which fit him well for the relation of status—and which must for the present purpose be set down as serviceable traits—the dog has some characteristics which are of a more equivocal aesthetic value. He is the filthiest of the domestic animals in his person and the nastiest in his habits. For this he makes up in a servile, fawning attitude towards his master, and a readiness to inflict damage and discomfort on all else. The dog, then, commends himself to our favor by affording play to our propensity for mastery, and as he is also an item of expense, and commonly serves no industrial purpose, he holds a well-assured place in men's regard as a thing of good repute. The dog is at the same time associated in our imagination with the chase—a meritorious employment and an expression of the honorable predatory impulse. Standing on this vantage ground, whatever beauty of form and motion and whatever commendable mental traits he may possess are conventionally acknowledged and magnified. And even those varieties of the dog which have been bred into grotesque deformity by the dog-fancier are in good faith accounted beautiful by many. These varieties of dogs—and the like is true of other fancy-bred animals—are rated and graded in aesthetic value somewhat in proportion to the degree of grotesqueness and instability of the particular fashion which the deformity takes in the given case. For the purpose in hand, this differential utility on the ground of grotesqueness and instability of structure is reducible to terms of a greater scarcity and consequent expense. The commercial value of canine monstrosities, such as the prevailing styles of pet dogs both for men's and women's use, rests on their high cost of production, and their value to their owners lies chiefly in their utility as items of conspicuous consumption. In directly, through reflection upon their honorific expensiveness, a social worth is imputed to them; and so, by an easy substitution of words and ideas, they come to be admired and reputed beautiful. Since any attention bestowed upon these animals is in no sense gainful or useful, it is also reputable; and since the habit of giving them attention is consequently not deprecated, it may grow into an habitual attachment of great tenacity and of a most benevolent character. So that in the affection bestowed on pet animals the canon of expensiveness is present more or less remotely as a norm which guides and shapes the sentiment and the selection of its object. The like is true, as will be noticed presently, with respect to affection for persons also; although the manner in which the norm acts in that case is somewhat different.

The case of the fast horse is much like that of the dog. He is on the whole expensive, or wasteful and useless—for the industrial purpose. What productive use he may possess, in the way of enhancing the well-being of the community or making the way of life easier for men, takes the form of exhibitions of force and facility of motion that gratify the popular aesthetic sense. This is of course a substantial serviceability. The horse is not endowed with the spiritual aptitude for servile dependence in the same measure as the dog; but he ministers effectually to his master's impulse to convert the "animate" forces of the environment to his own use and discretion and so express his own dominating individuality through them. The fast horse is at least potentially a race-horse, of high or low degree; and it is as such that he is peculiarly serviceable to his owner. The utility of the fast horse lies largely in his efficiency as a means of emulation; it gratifies the owner's sense of aggression and dominance to have his own horse outstrip his neighbor's. This use being not lucrative, but on the whole pretty consistently wasteful, and quite conspicuously so, it is honorific, and therefore gives the fast horse a strong presumptive position of reputability. Beyond this, the race-horse proper has also a similarly non-industrial but honorific use as a gambling instrument.

The fast horse, then, is aesthetically fortunate, in that the canon of pecuniary good repute legitimates a free appreciation of whatever beauty or serviceability he may possess. His pretensions have the countenance of the principle of conspicuous waste and the backing of the predatory aptitude for dominance and emulation. The horse is, moreover, a beautiful animal, although the race-horse is so in no peculiar degree to the uninstructed taste of those persons who belong neither in the class of race-horse fanciers nor in the class whose sense of beauty is held in abeyance by the moral constraint of the horse fancier's award. To this untutored taste the most beautiful horse seems to be a form which has suffered less radical alteration than the race-horse under the breeder's selective development of the animal. Still, when a writer or speaker—especially of those whose eloquence is most consistently commonplace—wants an illustration of animal grace and serviceability, for rhetorical use, he habitually turns to the horse; and he commonly makes it plain before he is done that what he has in mind is the race-horse.

It should be noted that in the graduated appreciation of varieties of horses and of dogs, such as one meets with among people of even moderately cultivated tastes in these matters, there is also discernible another and more direct line of influence of the leisure-class canons of reputability. In this country, for instance, leisure-class tastes are to some extent shaped on usages and habits which prevail, or which are apprehended to prevail, among the leisure class of Great Britain. In dogs this is true to a less extent than in horses. In horses, more particularly in saddle horses—which at their best serve the purpose of wasteful display simply—it will hold true in a general way that a horse is more beautiful in proportion as he is more English; the English leisure class being, for purposes of reputable usage, the upper leisure class of this country, and so the exemplar for the lower grades. This mimicry in the methods of the apperception of beauty and in the forming of judgments of taste need not result in a spurious, or at any rate not a hypocritical or affected, predilection. The predilection is as serious and as substantial an award of taste when it rests on this basis as when it rests on any other, the difference is that this taste is and as substantial an award of taste when it rests on this basis as when it rests on any other; the difference is that this taste is a taste for the reputably correct, not for the aesthetically true.

The mimicry, it should be said, extends further than to the sense of beauty in horseflesh simply. It includes trappings and horsemanship as well, so that the correct or reputably beautiful seat or posture is also decided by English usage, as well as the equestrian gait. To show how fortuitous may sometimes be the circumstances which decide what shall be becoming and what not under the pecuniary canon of beauty, it may be noted that this English seat, and the peculiarly distressing gait which has made an awkward seat necessary, are a survival from the time when the English roads were so bad with mire and mud as to be virtually impassable for a horse traveling at a more comfortable gait; so that a person of decorous tastes in horsemanship today rides a punch with docked tail, in an uncomfortable posture and at a distressing gait, because the English roads during a great part of the last century were impassable for a horse traveling at a more horselike gait, or for an animal built for moving with ease over the firm and open country to which the horse is indigenous. It is not only with respect to consumable goods—including domestic animals—that the canons of taste have been colored by the canons of pecuniary reputability. Something to the like effect is to be said for beauty in persons. In order to avoid whatever may be matter of controversy, no weight will be given in this connection to such popular predilection as there may be for the dignified (leisurely) bearing and poly presence that are by vulgar tradition associated with opulence in mature men. These traits are in some measure accepted as elements of personal beauty. But there are certain elements of feminine beauty, on the other hand, which come in under this head, and which are of so concrete and specific a character as to admit of itemized appreciation. It is more or less a rule that in communities which are at the stage of economic development at which women are valued by the upper class for their service, the ideal of female beauty is a robust, large-limbed woman. The ground of appreciation is the physique, while the conformation of the face is of secondary weight only. A well-known instance of this ideal of the early predatory culture is that of the maidens of the Homeric poems.

This ideal suffers a change in the succeeding development, when, in the conventional scheme, the office of the high-class wife comes to be a vicarious leisure simply. The ideal then includes the characteristics which are supposed to result from or to go with a life of leisure consistently enforced. The ideal accepted under these circumstances may be gathered from descriptions of beautiful women by poets and writers of the chivalric times. In the conventional scheme of those days ladies of high degree were conceived to be in perpetual tutelage, and to be scrupulously exempt from all useful work. The resulting chivalric or romantic ideal of beauty takes cognizance chiefly of the face, and dwells on its delicacy, and on the delicacy of the hands and feet, the slender figure, and especially the slender waist. In the pictured representations of the women of that time, and in modern romantic imitators of the chivalric thought and feeling, the waist is attenuated to a degree that implies extreme debility. The same ideal is still extant among a considerable portion of the population of modern industrial communities; but it is to be said that it has retained its hold most tenaciously in those modern communities which are least advanced in point of economic and civil development, and which show the most considerable survivals of status and of predatory institutions. That is to say, the chivalric ideal is best preserved in those existing communities which are substantially least modern. Survivals of this lackadaisical or romantic ideal occur freely in the tastes of the well-to-do classes of Continental countries. In modern communities which have reached the higher levels of industrial development, the upper leisure class has accumulated so great a mass of wealth as to place its women above all imputation of vulgarly productive labor. Here the status of women as vicarious consumers is beginning to lose its place in the sections of the body of the people; and as a consequence the ideal of feminine beauty is beginning to change back again from the infirmly delicate, translucent, and hazardously slender, to a woman of the archaic type that does not disown her hands and feet, nor, indeed, the other gross material facts of her person. In the course of economic development the ideal of beauty among the peoples of the Western culture has shifted from the woman of physical presence to the lady, and it is beginning to shift back again to the woman; and all in obedience to the changing conditions of pecuniary emulation. The exigencies of emulation at one time required lusty slaves; at another time they required a conspicuous performance of vicarious leisure and consequently an obvious disability; but the situation is now beginning to outgrow this last requirement, since, under the higher efficiency of modern industry, leisure in women is possible so far down the scale of reputability that it will no longer serve as a definitive mark of the highest pecuniary grade.

Apart from this general control exercised by the norm of conspicuous waste over the ideal of feminine beauty, there are one or two details which merit specific mention as showing how it may exercise an extreme constraint in detail over men's sense of beauty in women. It has already been noticed that at the stages of economic evolution at which conspicuous leisure is much regarded as a means of good repute, the ideal requires delicate and diminutive hands and feet and a slender waist. These features, together with the other, related faults of structure that commonly go with them, go to show that the person so affected is incapable of useful effort and must therefore be supported in idleness by her owner. She is useless and expensive, and she is consequently valuable as evidence of pecuniary strength. It results that at this cultural stage women take thought to alter their persons, so as to conform more nearly to the requirements of the instructed taste of the time; and under the guidance of the canon of pecuniary decency, the men find the resulting artificially induced pathological features attractive. So, for instance, the constricted waist which has had so wide and persistent a vogue in the communities of the Western culture, and so also the deformed foot of the Chinese. Both of these are mutilations of unquestioned repulsiveness to the untrained sense. It requires habituation to become reconciled to them. Yet there is no room to question their attractiveness to men into whose scheme of life they fit as honorific items sanctioned by the requirements of pecuniary reputability. They are items of pecuniary and cultural beauty which have come to do duty as elements of the ideal of womanliness.

The connection here indicated between the aesthetic value and the invidious pecuniary value of things is of course not present in the consciousness of the valuer. So far as a person, in forming a judgment of taste, takes thought and reflects that the object of beauty under consideration is wasteful and reputable, and therefore may legitimately be accounted beautiful; so far the judgment is not a bona fide judgment of taste and does not come up for consideration in this connection. The connection which is here insisted on between the reputability and the apprehended beauty of objects lies through the effect which the fact of reputability has upon the valuer's habits of thought. He is in the habit of forming judgments of value of various kinds—economic, moral, aesthetic, or reputable concerning the objects with which he has to do, and his attitude of commendation towards a given object on any other ground will affect the degree of his appreciation of the object when he comes to value it for the aesthetic purpose. This is more particularly true as regards valuation on grounds so closely related to the aesthetic ground as that of reputability. The valuation for the aesthetic purpose and for the purpose of repute are not held apart as distinctly as might be. Confusion is especially apt to arise between these two kinds of valuation, because the value of objects for repute is not habitually distinguished in speech by the use of a special descriptive term. The result is that the terms in familiar use to designate categories or elements of beauty are applied to cover this unnamed element of pecuniary merit, and the corresponding confusion of ideas follows by easy consequence. The demands of reputability in this way coalesce in the popular apprehension with the demands of the sense of beauty, and beauty which is not accompanied by the accredited marks of good repute is not accepted. But the requirements of pecuniary reputability and those of beauty in the naive sense do not in any appreciable degree coincide. The elimination from our surroundings of the pecuniarily unfit, therefore, results in a more or less thorough elimination of that considerable range of elements of beauty which do not happen to conform to the pecuniary requirement. The underlying norms of taste are of very ancient growth, probably far antedating the advent of the pecuniary institutions that are here under discussion. Consequently, by force of the past selective adaptation of men's habits of thought, it happens that the requirements of beauty, simply, are for the most part best satisfied by inexpensive contrivances and structures which in a straightforward manner suggest both the office which they are to perform and the method of serving their end. It may be in place to recall the modern psychological position. Beauty of form seems to be a question of facility of apperception. The proposition could perhaps safely be made broader than this. If abstraction is made from association, suggestion, and "expression," classed as elements of beauty, then beauty in any perceived object means that the mind readily unfolds its apperceptive activity in the directions which the object in question affords. But the directions in which activity readily unfolds or expresses itself are the directions to which long and close habituation has made the mind prone. So far as concerns the essential elements of beauty, this habituation is an habituation so close and long as to have induced not only a proclivity to the apperceptive form in question, but an adaptation of physiological structure and function as well. So far as the economic interest enters into the constitution of beauty, it enters as a suggestion or expression of adequacy to a purpose, a manifest and readily inferable subservience to the life process. This expression of economic facility or economic serviceability in any object—what may be called the economic beauty of the object—is best sewed by neat and unambiguous suggestion of its office and its efficiency for the material ends of life.

On this ground, among objects of use the simple and unadorned article is aesthetically the best. But since the pecuniary canon of reputability rejects the inexpensive in articles appropriated to individual consumption, the satisfaction of our craving for beautiful things must be sought by way of compromise. The canons of beauty must be circumvented by some contrivance which will give evidence of a reputably wasteful expenditure, at the same time that it meets the demands of our critical sense of the useful and the beautiful, or at least meets the demand of some habit which has come to do duty in place of that sense. Such an auxiliary sense of taste is the sense of novelty; and this latter is helped out in its surrogateship by the curiosity with which men view ingenious and puzzling contrivances. Hence it comes that most objects alleged to be beautiful, and doing duty as such, show considerable ingenuity of design and are calculated to puzzle the beholder—to bewilder him with irrelevant suggestions and hints of the improbable—at the same time that they give evidence of an expenditure of labor in excess of what would give them their fullest efficiency for their ostensible economic end.

This may be shown by an illustration taken from outside the range of our everyday habits and everyday contact, and so outside the range of our bias. Such are the remarkable feather mantles of Hawaii, or the well-known cawed handles of the ceremonial adzes of several Polynesian islands. These are undeniably beautiful, both in the sense that they offer a pleasing composition of form, lines, and color, and in the sense that they evince great skill and ingenuity in design and construction. At the same time the articles are manifestly ill fitted to serve any other economic purpose. But it is not always that the evolution of ingenious and puzzling contrivances under the guidance of the canon of wasted effort works out so happy a result. The result is quite as often a virtually complete suppression of all elements that would bear scrutiny as expressions of beauty, or of serviceability, and the substitution of evidences of misspent ingenuity and labor, backed by a conspicuous ineptitude; until many of the objects with which we surround ourselves in everyday life, and even many articles of everyday dress and ornament, are such as would not be tolerated except under the stress of prescriptive tradition. Illustrations of this substitution of ingenuity and expense in place of beauty and serviceability are to be seen, for instance, in domestic architecture, in domestic art or fancy work, in various articles of apparel, especially of feminine and priestly apparel.

The canon of beauty requires expression of the generic. The "novelty" due to the demands of conspicuous waste traverses this canon of beauty, in that it results in making the physiognomy of our objects of taste a congeries of idiosyncrasies; and the idiosyncrasies are, moreover, under the selective surveillance of the canon of expensiveness.

This process of selective adaptation of designs to the end of conspicuous waste, and the substitution of pecuniary beauty for aesthetic beauty, has been especially effective in the development of architecture. It would be extremely difficult to find a modern civilized residence or public building which can claim anything better than relative inoffensiveness in the eyes of anyone who will dissociate the elements of beauty from those of honorific waste. The endless variety of fronts presented by the better class of tenements and apartment houses in our cities is an endless variety of architectural distress and of suggestions of expensive discomfort. Considered as objects of beauty, the dead walls of the sides and back of these structures, left untouched by the hands of the artist, are commonly the best feature of the building.

What has been said of the influence of the law of conspicuous waste upon the canons of taste will hold true, with but a slight change of terms, of its influence upon our notions of the serviceability of goods for other ends than the aesthetic one. Goods are produced and consumed as a means to the fuller unfolding of human life; and their utility consists, in the first instance, in their efficiency as means to this end. The end is, in the first instance, the fullness of life of the individual, taken in absolute terms. But the human proclivity to emulation has seized upon the consumption of goods as a means to an invidious comparison, and has thereby invested constable goods with a secondary utility as evidence of relative ability to pay. This indirect or secondary use of consumable goods lends an honorific character to consumption and presently also to the goods which best serve the emulative end of consumption. The consumption of expensive goods is meritorious, and the goods which contain an appreciable element of cost in excess of what goes to give them serviceability for their ostensible mechanical purpose are honorific. The marks of superfluous costliness in the goods are therefore marks of worth—of high efficiency for the indirect, invidious end to be served by their consumption; and conversely, goods are humilific, and therefore unattractive, if they show too thrifty an adaptation to the mechanical end sought and do not include a margin of expensiveness on which to rest a complacent invidious comparison. This indirect utility gives much of their value to the "better" grades of goods. In order to appeal to the cultivated sense of utility, an article must contain a modicum of this indirect utility.

While men may have set out with disapproving an inexpensive manner of living because it indicated inability to spend much, and so indicated a lack of pecuniary success, they end by falling into the habit of disapproving cheap things as being intrinsically dishonorable or unworthy because they are cheap. As time has gone on, each succeeding generation has received this tradition of meritorious expenditure from the generation before it, and has in its turn further elaborated and fortified the traditional canon of pecuniary reputability in goods consumed; until we have finally reached such a degree of conviction as to the unworthiness of all inexpensive things, that we have no longer any misgivings in formulating the maxim, "Cheap and nasty."

So thoroughly has the habit of approving the expensive and disapproving the inexpensive been ingrained into our thinking that we instinctively insist upon at least some measure of wasteful expensiveness in all our consumption, even in the case of goods which are consumed in strict privacy and without the slightest thought of display. We all feel, sincerely and without misgiving, that we are the more lifted up in spirit for having, even in the privacy of our own household, eaten our daily meal by the help of hand-wrought silver utensils, from hand-painted china (often of dubious artistic value) laid on high-priced table linen. Any retrogression from the standard of living which we are accustomed to regard as worthy in this respect is felt to be a grievous violation of our human dignity. So, also, for the last dozen years candles have been a more pleasing source of light at dinner than any other. Candlelight is now softer, less distressing to well-bred eyes, than oil, gas, or electric light. The same could not have been said thirty years ago, when candles were, or recently had been, the cheapest available light for domestic use. Nor are candles even now found to give an acceptable or effective light for any other than a ceremonial illumination.

A political sage still living has summed up the conclusion of this whole matter in the dictum: "A cheap coat makes a cheap man," and there is probably no one who does not feel the convincing force of the maxim.

The habit of looking for the marks of superfluous expensiveness in goods, and of requiring that all goods should afford some utility of the indirect or invidious sort, leads to a change in the standards by which the utility of goods is gauged. The honorific element and the element of brute efficiency are not held apart in the consumer's appreciation of commodities, and the two together go to make up the unanalyzed aggregate serviceability of the goods. Under the resulting standard of serviceability, no article will pass muster on the strength of material sufficiency alone. In order to completeness and full acceptability to the consumer it must also show the honorific element. It results that the producers of articles of consumption direct their efforts to the production of goods that shall meet this demand for the honorific element. They will do this with all the more alacrity and effect, since they are themselves under the dominance of the same standard of worth in goods, and would be sincerely grieved at the sight of goods which lack the proper honorific finish. Hence it has come about that there are today no goods supplied in any trade which do not contain the honorific element in greater or less degree. Any consumer who might, Diogenes-like, insist on the elimination of all honorific or wasteful elements from his consumption, would be unable to supply his most trivial wants in the modern market. Indeed, even if he resorted to supplying his wants directly by his own efforts, he would find it difficult if not impossible to divest himself of the current habits of thought on this head; so that he could scarcely compass a supply of the necessaries of life for a day's consumption without instinctively and by oversight incorporating in his home-made product something of this honorific, quasi-decorative element of wasted labor.

It is notorious that in their selection of serviceable goods in the retail market purchasers are guided more by the finish and workmanship of the goods than by any marks of substantial serviceability. Goods, in order to sell, must have some appreciable amount of labor spent in giving them the marks of decent expensiveness, in addition to what goes to give them efficiency for the material use which they are to serve. This habit of making obvious costliness a canon of serviceability of course acts to enhance the aggregate cost of articles of consumption. It puts us on our guard against cheapness by identifying merit in some degree with cost. There is ordinarily a consistent effort on the part of the consumer to obtain goods of the required serviceability at as advantageous a bargain as may be; but the conventional requirement of obvious costliness, as a voucher and a constituent of the serviceability of the goods, leads him to reject as under grade such goods as do not contain a large element of conspicuous waste.

It is to be added that a large share of those features of consumable goods which figure in popular apprehension as marks of serviceability, and to which reference is here had as elements of conspicuous waste, commend themselves to the consumer also on other grounds than that of expensiveness alone. They usually give evidence of skill and effective workmanship, even if they do not contribute to the substantial serviceability of the goods; and it is no doubt largely on some such ground that any particular mark of honorific serviceability first comes into vogue and afterward maintains its footing as a normal constituent element of the worth of an article. A display of efficient workmanship is pleasing simply as such, even where its remoter, for the time unconsidered, outcome is futile. There is a gratification of the artistic sense in the contemplation of skillful work. But it is also to be added that no such evidence of skillful workmanship, or of ingenious and effective adaptation of means to an end, will, in the long run, enjoy the approbation of the modern civilized consumer unless it has the sanction of the Canon of conspicuous waste.

The position here taken is enforced in a felicitous manner by the place assigned in the economy of consumption to machine products. The point of material difference between machine-made goods and the hand-wrought goods which serve the same purposes is, ordinarily, that the former serve their primary purpose more adequately. They are a more perfect product—show a more perfect adaptation of means to end. This does not save them from disesteem and deprecation, for they fall short under the test of honorific waste. Hand labor is a more wasteful method of production; hence the goods turned out by this method are more serviceable for the purpose of pecuniary reputability; hence the marks of hand labor come to be honorific, and the goods which exhibit these marks take rank as of higher grade than the corresponding machine product. Commonly, if not invariably, the honorific marks of hand labor are certain imperfections and irregularities in the lines of the hand-wrought article, showing where the workman has fallen short in the execution of the design. The ground of the superiority of hand-wrought goods, therefore, is a certain margin of crudeness. This margin must never be so wide as to show bungling workmanship, since that would be evidence of low cost, nor so narrow as to suggest the ideal precision attained only by the machine, for that would be evidence of low cost.

The appreciation of those evidences of honorific crudeness to which hand-wrought goods owe their superior worth and charm in the eyes of well-bred people is a matter of nice discrimination. It requires training and the formation of right habits of thought with respect to what may be called the physiognomy of goods. Machine-made goods of daily use are often admired and preferred precisely on account of their excessive perfection by the vulgar and the underbred who have not given due thought to the punctilios of elegant consumption. The ceremonial inferiority of machine products goes to show that the perfection of skill and workmanship embodied in any costly innovations in the finish of goods is not sufficient of itself to secure them acceptance and permanent favor. The innovation must have the support of the canon of conspicuous waste.

Any feature in the physiognomy of goods, however pleasing in itself, and however well it may approve itself to the taste for effective work, will not be tolerated if it proves obnoxious to this norm of pecuniary reputability.

The ceremonial inferiority or uncleanness in consumable goods due to "commonness," or in other words to their slight cost of production, has been taken very seriously by many persons. The objection to machine products is often formulated as an objection to the commonness of such goods. What is common is within the (pecuniary) reach of many people. Its consumption is therefore not honorific, since it does not serve the purpose of a favorable invidious comparison with other consumers. Hence the consumption, or even the sight of such goods, is inseparable from an odious suggestion of the lower levels of human life, and one comes away from their contemplation with a pervading sense of meanness that is extremely distasteful and depressing to a person of sensibility. In persons whose tastes assert themselves imperiously, and who have not the gift, habit, or incentive to discriminate between the grounds of their various judgments of taste, the deliverances of the sense of the honorific coalesce with those of the sense of beauty and of the sense of serviceability—in the manner already spoken of; the resulting composite valuation serves as a judgment of the object's beauty or its serviceability, according as the valuer's bias or interest inclines him to apprehend the object in the one or the other of these aspects. It follows not infrequently that the marks of cheapness or commonness are accepted as definitive marks of artistic unfitness, and a code or schedule of aesthetic proprieties on the one hand, and of aesthetic abominations on the other, is constructed on this basis for guidance in questions of taste.

As has already been pointed out, the cheap, and therefore indecorous, articles of daily consumption in modern industrial communities are commonly machine products; and the generic feature of the physiognomy of machine-made goods as compared with the hand-wrought article is their greater perfection in workmanship and greater accuracy in the detail execution of the design. Hence it comes about that the visible imperfections of the hand-wrought goods, being honorific, are accounted marks of superiority in point of beauty, or serviceability, or both. Hence has arisen that exaltation of the defective, of which John Ruskin and William Morris were such eager spokesmen in their time; and on this ground their propaganda of crudity and wasted effort has been taken up and carried forward since their time. And hence also the propaganda for a return to handicraft and household industry. So much of the work and speculations of this group of men as fairly comes under the characterization here given would have been impossible at a time when the visibly more perfect goods were not the cheaper.

It is of course only as to the economic value of this school of aesthetic teaching that anything is intended to be said or can be said here. What is said is not to be taken in the sense of depreciation, but chiefly as a characterization of the tendency of this teaching in its effect on consumption and on the production of consumable goods.

The manner in which the bias of this growth of taste has worked itself out in production is perhaps most cogently exemplified in the book manufacture with which Morris busied himself during the later years of his life; but what holds true of the work of the Kelmscott Press in an eminent degree, holds true with but slightly abated force when applied to latter-day artistic book-making generally—as to type, paper, illustration, bind-

ing materials, and binder's work. The claims to excellence put forward by the later products of the bookmaker's industry rest in some measure on the degree of its approximation to the crudities of the time when the work of book-making was a doubtful struggle
with refractory materials carried on by means of insufficient appliances. These products,
since they require hand labor, are more expensive; they are also less convenient for use
than the books turned out with a view to serviceability alone; they therefore argue ability on the part of the purchaser to consume freely, as well as ability to waste time and effort. It is on this basis that the printers of today are returning to "old-style," and other
more or less obsolete styles of type which are less legible and give a cruder appearance to
the page than the "modern." Even a scientific periodical, with ostensibly no purpose but
the most effective presentation of matter with which its science is concerned, will concede so much to the demands of this pecuniary beauty as to publish its scientific discussions in old style type, on laid paper, and with uncut edges. But books which are not
ostensibly concerned with the effective presentation of their contents alone, of course go
farther in this direction. Here we have a somewhat cruder type, printed on hand-laid,
deckel-edged paper, with excessive margins and uncut leaves, with bindings of a painstaking crudeness and elaborate ineptitude. The Kelmscott Press reduced the matter to an absurdity—as seen from the point of view of brute serviceability alone—by issuing books
for modern use, edited with the obsolete spelling, printed in black-letter, and bound in
limp vellum fitted with thongs. As a further characteristic feature which fixes the economic place of artistic book-making, there is the fact that these more elegant books are,
at their best, printed in limited editions. A limited edition is in effect a guarantee—
somewhat crude, it is true—that this book is scarce and that it therefore is costly and
lends pecuniary distinction to its consumer.

The special attractiveness of these book-products to the book-buyer of cultivated taste
lies, of course, not in a conscious, naive recognition of their costliness and superior clum-
siness. Here, as in the parallel case of the superiority of hand-wrought articles over machine products, the conscious ground of preference is an intrinsic excellence imputed to
the costlier and more awkward article. The superior excellence imputed to the book
which imitates the products of antique and obsolete processes is conceived to be chiefly
a superior utility in the aesthetic respect; but it is not unusual to find a well-bred book-
lover insisting that the clumsier product is also more serviceable as a vehicle of printed
speech. So far as regards the superior aesthetic value of the decadent book, the chances
are that the book-lover's contention has some ground. The book is designed with an eye
single to its beauty, and the result is commonly some measure of success on the part of
the designer. What is insisted on here, however, is that the canon of taste under which
the designer works is a canon formed under the surveillance of the law of conspicuous
waste, and that this law acts selectively to eliminate any canon of taste that does not conform to its demands. That is to say, while the decadent book may be beautiful, the limits within which the designer may work are fixed by requirements of a non-aesthetic
kind. The product, if it is beautiful, must also at the same time be costly and ill adapted
to its ostensible use. This mandatory canon of taste in the case of the book-designer,
however, is not shaped entirely by the law of waste in its first form; the canon is to some
extent shaped in conformity to that secondary expression of the predatory temperament,

veneration for the archaic or obsolete, which in one of its special developments is called classicism. In aesthetic theory it might be extremely difficult, if not quite impracticable, to draw a line between the canon of classicism, or regard for the archaic, and the canon of beauty. For the aesthetic purpose such a distinction need scarcely be drawn, and indeed it need not exist. For a theory of taste the expression of an accepted ideal of archaism, on whatever basis it may have been accepted, is perhaps best rated as an element of beauty; there need be no question of its legitimation. But for the present purpose—for the purpose of determining what economic grounds are present in the accepted canons of taste and what is their significance for the distribution and consumption of goods—the distinction is not similarly beside the point. The position of machine products in the civilized scheme of consumption serves to point out the nature of the relation which subsists between the canon of conspicuous waste and the code of proprieties in consumption. Neither in matters of art and taste proper, nor as regards the current sense of the serviceability of goods, does this canon act as a principle of innovation or initiative. It does not go into the future as a creative principle which makes innovations and adds new items of consumption and new elements of cost. The principle in question is, in a certain sense, a negative rather than a positive law. It is a regulative rather than a creative principle. It very rarely initiates or originates any usage or custom directly. Its action is selective only. Conspicuous wastefulness does not directly afford ground for variation and growth, but conformity to its requirements is a condition to the survival of such innovations as may be made on other grounds. In whatever way usages and customs and methods of expenditure arise, they are all subject to the selective action of this norm of reputability; and the degree in which they conform to its requirements is a test of their fitness to survive in the competition with other similar usages and customs. Other things being equal, the more obviously wasteful usage or method stands the better chance of survival under this law. The law of conspicuous waste does not account for the origin of variations, but only for the persistence of such forms as are fit to survive under its dominance. It acts to conserve the fit, not to originate the acceptable. Its office is to prove all things and to hold fast that which is good for its purpose.

CHAPTER SEVEN

Dress as an Expression of the Pecuniary Culture

It will in place, by way of illustration, to show in some detail how the economic principles so far set forth apply to everyday facts in some one direction of the life process. For this purpose no line of consumption affords a more apt illustration than expenditure on dress. It is especially the rule of the conspicuous waste of goods that finds expression in dress, although the other, related principles of pecuniary repute are also exemplified in the same contrivances. Other methods of putting one's pecuniary standing in evidence serve their end effectually, and other methods are in vogue always and everywhere; but expenditure on dress has this advantage over most other methods, that our apparel is always in evidence and affords an indication of our pecuniary standing to all observers at the first glance. It is also true that admitted expenditure for display is more obviously present, and is, perhaps, more universally practiced in the matter of dress than in any other line of consumption. No one finds difficulty in assenting to the commonplace that the greater part of the expenditure incurred by all classes for apparel is incurred for the sake of a respectable appearance rather than for the protection of the person. And probably at no other point is the sense of shabbiness so keenly felt as it is if we fall short of the standard set by social usage in this matter of dress. It is true of dress in even a higher degree than of most other items of consumption, that people will undergo a very considerable degree of privation in the comforts or the necessaries of life in order to afford what is considered a decent amount of wasteful consumption; so that it is by no means an uncommon occurrence, in an inclement climate, for people to go ill clad in order to appear well dressed. And the commercial value of the goods used for clotting in any modern community is made up to a much larger extent of the fashionableness, the reputability of the goods than of the mechanical service which they render in clothing the person of the wearer. The need of dress is eminently a "higher" or spiritual need.

This spiritual need of dress is not wholly, nor even chiefly, a naive propensity for display of expenditure. The law of conspicuous waste guides consumption in apparel, as in other things, chiefly at the second remove, by shaping the canons of taste and decency. In the common run of cases the conscious motive of the wearer or purchaser of conspicuously wasteful apparel is the need of conforming to established usage, and of living up to the accredited standard of taste and reputability. It is not only that one must be guided by the code of proprieties in dress in order to avoid the mortification that comes of unfavorable notice and comment, though that motive in itself counts for a great deal; but besides that, the requirement of expensiveness is so ingrained into our habits of thought in matters of dress that any other than expensive apparel is instinctively odious to us. Without reflection or analysis, we feel that what is inexpensive is unworthy. "A cheap coat makes a cheap man." "Cheap and nasty" is recognized to hold true in dress with even less mitigation than in other lines of consumption. On the ground both of taste and of serviceability, an inexpensive article of apparel is held to be inferior, under the maxim "cheap and nasty." We find things beautiful, as well as serviceable, somewhat in proportion as they are costly. With few and inconsequential exceptions, we all find a costly hand-wrought article of apparel much preferable, in point of beauty and of serviceability, to a less expensive imitation of it, however cleverly the spurious article may imitate the costly original; and what offends our sensibilities in the spurious article is not that it falls short in form or color, or, indeed, in visual effect in any way. The offensive object may be so close an imitation as to defy any but the closest scrutiny; and yet so soon as the counter-feit is detected, its aesthetic value, and its commercial value as well, declines precipi-tately. Not only that, but it may be asserted with but small risk of contradiction that the aesthetic value of a detected counterfeit in dress declines somewhat in the same propor-tion as the counterfeit is cheaper than its original. It loses caste aesthetically because it falls to a lower pecuniary grade.

But the function of dress as an evidence of ability to pay does not end with simply showing that the wearer consumes valuable goods in excess of what is required for phys-ical comfort. Simple conspicuous waste of goods is effective and gratifying as far as it goes; it is good prima facie evidence of pecuniary success, and consequently prima facie evi-dence of social worth. But dress has subtler and more far-reaching possibilities than this crude, first-hand evidence of wasteful consumption only. If, in addition to showing that the wearer can afford to consume freely and uneconomically, it can also be shown in the same stroke that he or she is not under the necessity of earning a livelihood, the evidence of social worth is enhanced in a very considerable degree. Our dress, therefore, in order to serve its purpose effectually, should not only be expensive, but it should also make plain to all observers that the wearer is not engaged in any kind of productive labor. In the evolutionary process by which our system of dress has been elaborated into its pres-ent admirably perfect adaptation to its purpose, this subsidiary line of evidence has re-ceived due attention. A detailed examination of what passes in popular apprehension for elegant apparel will show that it is contrived at every point to convey the impression that the wearer does not habitually put forth any useful effort. It goes without saying that no apparel can be considered elegant, or even decent, if it shows the effect of manual labor on the part of the wearer, in the way of soil or wear. The pleasing effect of neat and spot-less garments is chiefly, if not altogether, due to their carrying the suggestion of leisure—exemption from personal contact with industrial processes of any kind. Much of the charm that invests the patent-leather shoe, the stainless linen, the lustrous cylindrical hat, and the walking-stick, which so greatly enhance the native dignity of a gentleman, comes of their pointedly suggesting that the wearer cannot when so attired bear a hand in any employment that is directly and immediately of any human use. Elegant dress serves its purpose of elegance not only in that it is expensive, but also because it is the insignia of leisure. It not only shows that the wearer is able to consume a relatively large value, but it argues at the same time that he consumes without producing.

The dress of women goes even farther than that of men in the way of demonstrating the wearer's abstinence from productive employment. It needs no argument to enforce the generalization that the more elegant styles of feminine bonnets go even farther to-wards making work impossible than does the man's high hat. The woman's shoe adds the so-called French heel to the evidence of enforced leisure afforded by its polish; because this high heel obviously makes any, even the simplest and most necessary manual work extremely difficult. The like is true even in a higher degree of the skirt and the rest of the drapery which characterizes woman's dress. The substantial reason for our tenacious attachment to the skirt is just this; it is expensive and it hampers the wearer at every turn and incapacitates her for all useful exertion. The like is true of the feminine custom of wearing the hair excessively long.

But the woman's apparel not only goes beyond that of the modern man in the degree in which it argues exemption from labor; it also adds a peculiar and highly characteristic feature which differs in kind from anything habitually practiced by the men. This feature is the class of contrivances of which the corset is the typical example. The corset is, in economic theory, substantially a mutilation, undergone for the purpose of lowering the subject's vitality and rendering her permanently and obviously unfit for work. It is true, the corset impairs the personal attractions of the wearer, but the loss suffered on that score is offset by the gain in reputability which comes of her visibly increased expensiveness and infirmity. It may broadly be set down that the womanliness of woman's apparel resolves itself, in point of substantial fact, into the more effective hindrance to useful exertion offered by the garments peculiar to women. This difference between masculine and feminine apparel is here simply pointed out as a characteristic feature. The ground of its occurrence will be discussed presently.

So far, then, we have, as the great and dominant norm of dress, the broad principle of conspicuous waste. Subsidiary to this principle, and as a corollary under it, we get as a second norm the principle of conspicuous leisure. In dress construction this norm works out in the shape of divers contrivances going to show that the wearer does not and, as far as it may conveniently be shown, can not engage in productive labor. Beyond these two principles there is a third of scarcely less constraining force, which will occur to any one who reflects at all on the subject. Dress must not only be conspicuously expensive and inconvenient, it must at the same time be up to date. No explanation at all satisfactory has hitherto been offered of the phenomenon of changing fashions. The imperative requirement of dressing in the latest accredited manner, as well as the fact that this accredited fashion constantly changes from season to season, is sufficiently familiar to every one, but the theory of this flux and change has not been worked out. We may of course say, with perfect consistency and truthfulness, that this principle of novelty is another corollary under the law of conspicuous waste. Obviously, if each garment is permitted to serve for but a brief term, and if none of last season's apparel is carried over and made further use of during the present season, the wasteful expenditure on dress is greatly increased. This is good as far as it goes, but it is negative only. Pretty much all that this consideration warrants us in saying is that the norm of conspicuous waste exercises a controlling surveillance in all matters of dress, so that any change in the fashions most conspicuous waste exercises a controlling surveillance in all matters of dress, so that any change in the fashions must conform to the requirement of wastefulness; it leaves unanswered the question as to the motive for making and accepting a change in the prevailing styles, and it also fails to explain why conformity to a given style at a given time is so imperatively necessary as we know it to be.

For a creative principle, capable of serving as motive to invention and innovation in fashions, we shall have to go back to the primitive, non-economic motive with which apparel originated—the motive of adornment. Without going into an extended discussion of how and why this motive asserts itself under the guidance of the law of expensiveness, it may be stated broadly that each successive innovation in the fashions is an effort to reach some form of display which shall be more acceptable to our sense of form and color or of effectiveness, than that which it displaces. The changing styles are the expression of a restless search for something which shall commend itself to our aesthetic sense; but as each innovation is subject to the selective action of the norm of conspicuous waste, the range within which innovation can take place is somewhat restricted. The innovation must not only be more beautiful, or perhaps oftener less offensive, than that which it displaces, but it must also come up to the accepted standard of expensiveness.

It would seem at first sight that the result of such an unremitting struggle to attain the beautiful in dress should be a gradual approach to artistic perfection. We might naturally expect that the fashions should show a well-marked trend in the direction of some one or more types of apparel eminently becoming to the human form; and we might even feel that we have substantial ground for the hope that today, after all the ingenuity and effort which have been spent on dress these many years, the fashions should have achieved a relative perfection and a relative stability, closely approximating to a permanently tenable artistic ideal. But such is not the case. It would be very hazardous indeed to assert that the styles of today are intrinsically more becoming than those of ten years ago, or than those of twenty, or fifty, or one hundred years ago. On the other hand, the assertion freely goes uncontradicted that styles in vogue two thousand years ago are more becoming than the most elaborate and painstaking constructions of today.

The explanation of the fashions just offered, then, does not fully explain, and we shall have to look farther. It is well known that certain relatively stable styles and types of costume have been worked out in various parts of the world; as, for instance, among the Japanese, Chinese, and other Oriental nations; likewise among the Greeks, Romans, and other Eastern peoples of antiquity so also, in later times, among the peasants of nearly every country of Europe. These national or popular costumes are in most cases adjudged by competent critics to be more becoming, more artistic, than the fluctuating styles of modern civilized apparel. At the same time they are also, at least usually, less obviously wasteful; that is to say, other elements than that of a display of expense are more readily detected in their structure.

These relatively stable costumes are, commonly, pretty strictly and narrowly localized, and they vary by slight and systematic gradations from place to place. They have in every case been worked out by peoples or classes which are poorer than we, and especially they belong in countries and localities and times where the population, or at least the class to which the costume in question belongs, is relatively homogeneous, stable, and immobile. That is to say, stable costumes which will bear the test of time and perspective are worked out under circumstances where the norm of conspicuous waste asserts itself less imperatively than it does in the large modern civilized cities, whose relatively mobile wealthy population today sets the pace in matters of fashion. The countries and classes which have in this way worked out stable and artistic costumes have been so placed that the pecuniary emulation among them has taken the direction of a competition in conspicuous leisure rather than in conspicuous consumption of goods. So that it will hold true in a general way that fashions are least stable and least becoming in those communities where the principle of a conspicuous waste of goods asserts itself most imperatively, as among ourselves. All this points to an antagonism between expensiveness and artistic apparel. In point of practical fact, the norm of conspicuous waste is incompatible with the requirement that dress should be beautiful or becoming. And this antagonism offers an explanation of that restless change in fashion which neither the canon of expensiveness nor that of beauty alone can account for.

The standard of reputability requires that dress should show wasteful expenditure; but all wastefulness is offensive to native taste. The psychological law has already been pointed out that all men—and women perhaps even in a higher degree—abhor futility, whether of effort or of expenditure—much as Nature was once said to abhor a vacuum. But the principle of conspicuous waste requires an obviously futile expenditure; and the resulting conspicuous expensiveness of dress is therefore intrinsically ugly. Hence we find that in all innovations in dress, each added or altered detail strives to avoid condemnation by showing some ostensible purpose, at the same time that the requirement of conspicuous waste prevents the purposefulness of these innovations from becoming anything more than a somewhat transparent pretense. Even in its freest flights, fashion rarely if ever gets away from a simulation of some ostensible use. The ostensible usefulness of the fashionable details of dress, however, is always so transparent a make-believe, and their substantial futility presently forces itself so baldly upon our attention as to become unbearable, and then we take refuge in a new style. But the new style must conform to the requirement of reputable wastefulness and futility. Its futility presently becomes as odious as that of its predecessor; and the only remedy which the law of waste allows us is to seek relief in some new construction, equally futile and equally untenable. Hence the essential ugliness and the unceasing change of fashionable attire.

Having so explained the phenomenon of shifting fashions, the next thing is to make the explanation tally with everyday facts. Among these everyday facts is the well-known liking which all men have for the styles that are in vogue at any given time. A new style comes into vogue and remains in favor for a season, and, at least so long as it is a novelty, people very generally find the new style attractive. The prevailing fashion is felt to be beautiful. This is due partly to the relief it affords in being different from what went before it, partly to its being reputable. As indicated in the last chapter, the canon of reputability to some extent shapes our tastes, so that under its guidance anything will be accepted as becoming until its novelty wears off, or until the warrant of reputability is transferred to a new and novel structure serving the same general purpose. That the alleged beauty, or "loveliness," of the styles in vogue at any given time is transient and spurious only is attested by the fact that none of the many shifting fashions will bear the test of time. When seen in the perspective of half-a-dozen years or more, the best of our fashions strike us as grotesque, if not unsightly. Our transient attachment to whatever happens to be the latest rests on other than aesthetic grounds, and lasts only until our abiding aesthetic sense has had time to assert itself and reject this latest indigestible contrivance.

The process of developing an aesthetic nausea takes more or less time; the length of time required in any given case being inversely as the degree of intrinsic odiousness of the style in question. This time relation between odiousness and instability in fashions affords ground for the inference that the more rapidly the styles succeed and displace one another, the more offensive they are to sound taste. The presumption, therefore, is that the farther the community, especially the wealthy classes of the community, develop in wealth and mobility and in the range of their human contact, the more imperatively will the law of conspicuous waste assert itself in matters of dress, the more will the sense of beauty tend to fall into abeyance or be overborne by the canon of pecuniary reputability, the more rapidly will fashions shift and change, and the more grotesque and intolerable will be the varying styles that successively come into vogue.

There remains at least one point in this theory of dress yet to be discussed. Most of what has been said applies to men's attire as well as to that of women; although in modern times it applies at nearly all points with greater force to that of women. But at one point the dress of women differs substantially from that of men. In woman's dress there is obviously greater insistence on such features as testify to the wearer's exemption from or incapacity for all vulgarly productive employment. This characteristic of woman's apparel is of interest, not only as completing the theory of dress, but also as confirming what has already been said of the economic status of women, both in the past and in the present.

As has been seen in the discussion of woman's status under the heads of Vicarious Leisure and Vicarious Consumption, it has in the course of economic development become the office of the woman to consume vicariously for the head of the household; and her apparel is contrived with this object in view. It has come about that obviously productive labor is in a peculiar degree derogatory to respectable women, and therefore special pains should be taken in the construction of women's dress, to impress upon the beholder the fact (often indeed a fiction) that the wearer does not and can not habitually engage in useful work. Propriety requires respectable women to abstain more consistently from useful effort and to make more of a show of leisure than the men of the same social classes. It grates painfully on our nerves to contemplate the necessity of any well-bred woman's earning a livelihood by useful work. It is not "woman's sphere." Her sphere is within the household, which she should "beautify," and of which she should be the "chief ornament." The male head of the household is not currently spoken of as its ornament. This feature taken in conjunction with the other fact that propriety requires more unremitting attention to expensive display in the dress and other paraphernalia of women, goes to enforce the view already implied in what has gone before. By virtue of its descent from a patriarchal past, our social system makes it the woman's function in an especial degree to put in evidence her household's ability to pay. According to the modern civilized scheme of life, the good name of the household to which she belongs should be the special care of the woman; and the system of honorific expenditure and conspicuous leisure by which this good name is chiefly sustained is therefore the woman's sphere. In the ideal scheme, as it tends to realize itself in the life of the higher pecuniary classes, this attention to conspicuous waste of substance and effort should normally be the sole economic function of the woman.

At the stage of economic development at which the women were still in the full sense the property of the men, the performance of conspicuous leisure and consumption came to be part of the services required of them. The women being not their own masters, obvious expenditure and leisure on their part would redound to the credit of their master rather than to their own credit; and therefore the more expensive and the more obviously unproductive the women of the household are, the more creditable and more effective for the purpose of reputability of the household or its head will their life be. So much so that the women have been required not only to afford evidence of a life of leisure, but even to disable themselves for useful activity.

It is at this point that the dress of men falls short of that of women, and for sufficient reason. Conspicuous waste and conspicuous leisure are reputable because they are evidence of pecuniary strength; pecuniary strength is reputable or honorific because, in the last analysis, it argues success and superior force; therefore the evidence of waste and leisure put forth by any individual in his own behalf cannot consistently take such a form or be carried to such a pitch as to argue incapacity or marked discomfort on his part; as the exhibition would in that case show not superior force, but inferiority, and so defeat its own purpose. So, then, wherever wasteful expenditure and the show of abstention from effort is normally, or on an average, carried to the extent of showing obvious discomfort or voluntarily induced physical disability. There the immediate inference is that the individual in question does not perform this wasteful expenditure and undergo this disability for her own personal gain in pecuniary repute, but in behalf of some one else to whom she stands in a relation of economic dependence; a relation which in the last analysis must, in economic theory, reduce itself to a relation of servitude.

To apply this generalization to women's dress, and put the matter in concrete terms: the high heel, the skirt, the impracticable bonnet, the corset, and the general disregard of the wearer's comfort which is an obvious feature of all civilized women's apparel, are so many items of evidence to the effect that in the modern civilized scheme of life the woman is still, in theory, the economic dependent of the man—that, perhaps in a highly idealized sense, she still is the man's chattel. The homely reason for all this conspicuous leisure and attire on the part of women lies in the fact that they are servants to whom, in the differentiation of economic functions, has been delegated the office of putting in evidence their master's ability to pay. There is a marked similarity in these respects between the apparel of women and that of domestic servants, especially liveried servants. In both there is a very elaborate show of unnecessary expensiveness, and in both cases there is also a notable disregard of the physical comfort of the wearer. But the attire of the lady goes farther in its elaborate insistence on the idleness, if not on the physical infirmity of the wearer, than does that of the domestic. And this is as it should be; for in theory, according to the ideal scheme of the pecuniary culture, the lady of the house is the chief menial of the household.

Besides servants, currently recognized as such, there is at least one other class of persons whose garb assimilates them to the class of servants and shows many of the features that go to make up the womanliness of woman's dress. This is the priestly class. Priestly vestments show, in accentuated form, all the features that have been shown to be evidence of a servile status and a vicarious life. Even more strikingly than the everyday habit of the priest, the vestments, properly so called, are ornate, grotesque, inconvenient, and, at least ostensibly, comfortless to the point of distress. The priest is at the same time expected to refrain from useful effort and, when before the public eye, to present an impassively disconsolate countenance, very much after the manner of a well-trained domestic servant. The shaven face of the priest is a further item to the same effect. This assimilation of the priestly class to the class of body servants, in demeanor and apparel, is due to the similarity of the two classes as regards economic function. In economic theory, the priest is a body servant, constructively in attendance upon the person of the divinity whose livery he wears. His livery is of a very expensive character, as it should be in order to set forth in a beseeming manner the dignity of his exalted master; but it is contrived to show that the wearing of it contributes little or nothing to the physical comfort of the wearer, for it is an item of vicarious consumption, and the repute which accrues from its consumption is to be imputed to the absent master, not to the servant.

The line of demarcation between the dress of women, priests, and servants, on the one hand, and of men, on the other hand, is not always consistently observed in practice, but it will scarcely be disputed that it is always present in a more or less definite way in the popular habits of thought. There are of course also free men, and not a few of them, who, in their blind zeal for faultless reputable attire, transgress the theoretical line between man's and woman's dress, to the extent of arraying themselves in apparel that is obviously designed to vex the mortal frame; but everyone recognizes without hesitation that such apparel for men is a departure from the normal. We are in the habit of saying that such dress is "effeminate"; and one sometimes hears the remark that such or such an exquisitely attired gentleman is as well dressed as a footman.

Certain apparent discrepancies under this theory of dress merit a more detailed examination, especially as they mark a more or less evident trend in the later and maturer development of dress. The vogue of the corset offers an apparent exception from the rule of which it has here been cited as an illustration. A closer examination, however, will show that this apparent exception is really a verification of the rule that the vogue of any given element or feature in dress rests on its utility as an evidence of pecuniary standing. It is well known that in the industrially more advanced communities the corset is employed only within certain fairly well defined social strata. The women of the poorer classes, especially of the rural population, do not habitually use it, except as a holiday luxury. Among these classes the women have to work hard, and it avails them little in the way of a pretense of leisure to so crucify the flesh in everyday life. The holiday use of the contrivance is due to imitation of a higher-class canon of decency. Upwards from this low level of indigence and manual labor, the corset was until within a generation or two nearly indispensable to a socially blameless standing for all women, including the wealthiest and most reputable. This rule held so long as there still was no large class of people wealthy enough to be above the imputation of any necessity for manual labor and at the same time large enough to form a self-sufficient, isolated social body whose mass would afford a foundation for special rules of conduct within the class, enforced by the current opinion of the class alone. But now there has grown up a large enough leisure class possessed of such wealth that any aspersion on the score of enforced manual employment would be idle and harmless calumny; and the corset has therefore in large measure fallen into disuse within this class. The exceptions under this rule of exemption from the corset are more apparent than real. They are the wealthy classes of countries with a lower industrial structure—nearer the archaic, quasi-industrial type—together with the later accessions of the wealthy classes in the more advanced industrial communities. The latter have not yet had time to divest themselves of the plebeian canons of taste and of reputability carried over from their former, lower pecuniary grade. Such survival of the corset is not infrequent among the higher social classes of those American cities, for instance, which have recently and rapidly risen into opulence. If the word be used as a technical term, without any odious implication, it may be said that the corset persists in great measure through the period of snobbery—the interval of uncertainty and of transition from a lower to the upper levels of pecuniary culture. That is to say, in all countries which have inherited the corset it continues in use wherever and so long as it serves its purpose as an evidence of honorific leisure by arguing physical disability in the wearer. The same rule of course applies to other mutilations and contrivances for decreasing the visible efficiency of the individual.

Something similar should hold true with respect to diverse items of conspicuous consumption, and indeed something of the kind does seem to hold to a slight degree of sundry features of dress, especially if such features involve a marked discomfort or appearance of discomfort to the wearer. During the past one hundred years there is a tendency perceptible, in the development of men's dress especially, to discontinue methods of expenditure and the use of symbols of leisure which must have been irksome, which may have served a good purpose in their time, but the continuation of which among the upper classes today would be a work of supererogation; as, for instance, the use of powdered wigs and of gold lace, and the practice of constantly shaving the face. There has of late years been some slight recrudescence of the shaven face in polite society, but this is probably a transient and unadvised mimicry of the fashion imposed upon body servants, and it may fairly be expected to go the way of the powdered wig of our grandfathers.

These indices and others which resemble them in point of the boldness with which they point out to all observers the habitual uselessness of those persons who employ them, have been replaced by other, more delicate methods of expressing the same fact; methods which are no less evident to the trained eyes of that smaller, select circle whose good opinion is chiefly sought. The earlier and cruder method of advertisement held its ground so long as the public to which the exhibitor had to appeal comprised large portions of the community who were not trained to detect delicate variations in the evidences of wealth and leisure. The method of advertisement undergoes a refinement when a sufficiently large wealthy class has developed, who have the leisure for acquiring skill in interpreting the subtler signs of expenditure. "Loud" dress becomes offensive to people of taste, as evincing an undue desire to reach and impress the untrained sensibilities of the vulgar. To the individual of high breeding, it is only the more honorific esteem accorded by the cultivated sense of the members of his own high class that is of material consequence. Since the wealthy leisure class has grown so large, or the contact of the leisure-class individual with members of his own class has grown so wide, as to constitute a human environment sufficient for the honorific purpose, there arises a tendency to exclude the baser elements of the population from the scheme even as spectators whose applause or mortification should be sought. The result of all this is a refinement of methods, a resort to subtler contrivances, and a spiritualization of the scheme of symbolism in dress. And as this upper leisure class sets the pace in all matters of decency, the result for the rest of society also is a gradual amelioration of the scheme of dress. As the community advances in wealth and culture, the ability to pay is put in evidence by means which require a progressively nicer discrimination in the beholder. This nicer discrimination between advertising media is in fact a very large element of the higher pecuniary culture.

CHAPTER EIGHT

Industrial Exemption and Conservatism

The life of man in society, just like the life of other species, is a struggle for existence, and therefore it is a process of selective adaptation. The evolution of social structure has been a process of natural selection of institutions. The progress which has been and is being made in human institutions and in human character may be set down, broadly, to a natural selection of the fittest habits of thought and to a process of enforced adaptation of individuals to an environment which has progressively changed with the growth of the community and with the changing institutions under which men have lived. Institutions are not only themselves the result of a selective and adaptive process which shapes the prevailing or dominant types of spiritual attitude and aptitudes; they are at the same time special methods of life and of human relations, and are therefore in their turn efficient factors of selection. So that the changing institutions in their turn make for a further selection of individuals endowed with the fittest temperament, and a further adaptation of individual temperament and habits to the changing environment through the formation of new institutions.

The forces which have shaped the development of human life and of social structure are no doubt ultimately reducible to terms of living tissue and material environment; but proximately for the purpose in hand, these forces may best be stated in terms of an environment, partly human, partly non-human, and a human subject with a more or less definite physical and intellectual constitution. Taken in the aggregate or average, this human subject is more or less variable; chiefly, no doubt, under a rule of selective conservation of favorable variations. The selection of favorable variations is perhaps in great measure a selective conservation of ethnic types. In the life history of any community whose population is made up of a mixture of divers ethnic elements, one or another of several persistent and relatively stable types of body and of temperament rises into dominance at any given point. The situation, including the institutions in force at any given time, will favor the survival and dominance of one type of character in preference to another; and the type of man so selected to continue and to further elaborate the institutions handed down from the past will in some considerable measure shape these institutions in his own likeness. But apart from selection as between relatively stable types of character and habits of mind, there is no doubt simultaneously going on a process of selective adaptation of habits of thought within the general range of aptitudes which is characteristic of the dominant ethnic type or types. There may be a variation in the fundamental character of any population by selection between relatively stable types; but there is also a variation due to adaptation in detail within the range of the type, and to selection between specific habitual views regarding any given social relation or group of relations.

For the present purpose, however, the question as to the nature of the adaptive process—whether it is chiefly a selection between stable types of temperament and character, or chiefly an adaptation of men's habits of thought to changing circumstances—

is of less importance than the fact that, by one method or another, institutions change and develop. Institutions must change with changing circumstances, since they are of the nature of an habitual method of responding to the stimuli which these changing circumstances afford. The development of these institutions is the development of society. The institutions are, in substance, prevalent habits of thought with respect to particular relations and particular functions of the individual and of the community; and the scheme of life, which is made up of the aggregate of institutions in force at a given time or at a given point in the development of any society, may, on the psychological side, be broadly characterized as a prevalent spiritual attitude or a prevalent theory of life. As regards its generic features, this spiritual attitude or theory of life is in the last analysis reducible to terms of a prevalent type of character.

The situation of today shapes the institutions of tomorrow through a selective, coercive process, by acting upon men's habitual view of things, and so altering or fortifying a point of view or a mental attitude banded down from the past. The institutions—that is to say the habits of thought—under the guidance of which men live are in this way received from an earlier time; more or less remotely earlier, but in any event they have been elaborated in and received from the past. Institutions are products of the past process, are adapted to past circumstances, and are therefore never in full accord with the requirements of the present. In the nature of the case, this process of selective adaptation can never catch up with the progressively changing situation in which the community finds itself at any given time; for the environment, the situation, the exigencies of life which enforce the adaptation and exercise the selection, change from day to day; and each successive situation of the community in its turn tends to obsolescence as soon as it has been established. When a step in the development has been taken, this step itself constitutes a change of situation which requires a new adaptation; it becomes the point of departure for a new step in the adjustment, and so on interminably.

It is to be noted then, although it may be a tedious truism, that the institutions of today—the present accepted scheme of life—do not entirely fit the situation of today. At the same time, men's present habits of thought tend to persist indefinitely, except as circumstances enforce a change. These institutions which have thus been handed down, these habits of thought, points of view, mental attitudes and aptitudes, or what not, are therefore themselves a conservative factor. This is the factor of social inertia, psychological inertia, conservatism. Social structure changes, develops, adapts itself to an altered situation, only through a change in the habits of thought of the several classes of the community, or in the last analysis, through a change in the habits of thought of the individuals which make up the community. The evolution of society is substantially a process of mental adaptation on the part of individuals under the stress of circumstances which will no longer tolerate habits of thought formed under and conforming to a different set of circumstances in the past. For the immediate purpose it need not be a question of serious importance whether this adaptive process is a process of selection and survival of persistent ethnic types or a process of individual adaptation and an inheritance of acquired traits.

Social advance, especially as seen from the point of view of economic theory, consists in a continued progressive approach to an approximately exact "adjustment of inner relations to outer relations," but this adjustment is never definitively established, since the "outer relations" are subject to constant change as a consequence of the progressive change going on in the "inner relations." But the degree of approximation may be greater or less, depending on the facility with which an adjustment is made. A readjustment of men's habits of thought to conform with the exigencies of an altered situation is in any case made only tardily and reluctantly, and only under the coercion exercised by a stipulation which has made the accredited views untenable. The readjustment of institutions and habitual views to an altered environment is made in response to pressure from without; it is of the nature of a response to stimulus. Freedom and facility of readjustment, that is to say capacity for growth in social structure, therefore depends in great measure on the degree of freedom with which the situation at any given time acts on the individual members of the community—the degree of exposure of the individual members to the constraining forces of the environment. If any portion or class of society is sheltered from the action of the environment in any essential respect, that portion of the community, or that class, will adapt its views and its scheme of life more tardily to the altered general situation; it will in so far tend to retard the process of social transformation. The wealthy leisure class is in such a sheltered position with respect to the economic forces that make for change and readjustment. And it may be said that the forces which make for a readjustment of institutions, especially in the case of a modern industrial community, are, in the last analysis, almost entirely of an economic nature.

Any community may be viewed as an industrial or economic mechanism, the structure of which is made up of what is called its economic institutions. These institutions are habitual methods of carrying on the life process of the community in contact with the material environment in which it lives. When given methods of unfolding human activity in this given environment have been elaborated in this way, the life of the community will express itself with some facility in these habitual directions. The community will make use of the forces of the environment for the purposes of its life according to methods learned in the past and embodied in these institutions. But as population increases, and as men's knowledge and skill in directing the forces of nature widen, the habitual methods of relation between the members of the group, and the habitual method of carrying on the life process of the group as a whole, no longer give the same result as before; nor are the resulting conditions of life distributed and apportioned in the same manner or with the same effect among the various members as before. If the scheme according to which the life process of the group was carried on under the earlier conditions gave approximately the highest attainable result—under the circumstances—in the way of efficiency or facility of the life process of the group; then the same scheme of life unaltered will not yield the highest result attainable in this respect under the altered conditions. Under the altered conditions of population, skill, and knowledge, the facility of life as carried on according to the traditional scheme may not be lower than under the earlier conditions; but the chances are always that it is less than might be if the scheme were altered to suit the altered conditions.

The group is made up of individuals, and the group's life is the life of individuals carried on in at least ostensible severalty. The group's accepted scheme of life is the consensus of views held by the body of these individuals as to what is right, good, expedient, and beautiful in the way of human life. In the redistribution of the conditions of life that comes of the altered method of dealing with the environment, the outcome is not an equable change in the facility of life throughout the group. The altered conditions may increase the facility of life for the group as a whole, but the redistribution will usually result in a decrease of facility or fullness of life for some members of the group. An advance in technical methods, in population, or in industrial organization will require at least some of the members of the community to change their habits of life, if they are to enter with facility and effect into the altered industrial methods; and in doing so they will be unable to live up to the received notions as to what are the right and beautiful habits of life.

Any one who is required to change his habits of life and his habitual relations to his fellow men will feel the discrepancy between the method of life required of him by the newly arisen exigencies, and the traditional scheme of life to which he is accustomed. It is the individuals placed in this position who have the liveliest incentive to reconstruct the received scheme of life and are most readily persuaded to accept new standards; and it is through the need of the means of livelihood that men are placed in such a position. The pressure exerted by the environment upon the group, and making for a readjustment of the group's scheme of life, impinges upon the members of the group in the form of pecuniary exigencies; and it is owing to this fact—that external forces are in great part translated into the form of pecuniary or economic exigencies—it is owing to this fact that we can say that the forces which count toward a readjustment of institutions in any modern industrial community are chiefly economic forces; or more specifically, these forces take the form of pecuniary pressure. Such a readjustment as is here contemplated is substantially a change in men's views as to what is good and right, and the means through which a change is wrought in men's apprehension of what is good and right is in large part the pressure of pecuniary exigencies.

Any change in men's views as to what is good and right in human life makes its way but tardily at the best. Especially is this true of any change in the direction of what is called progress; that is to say, in the direction of divergence from the archaic position—from the position which may be accounted the point of departure at any step in the social evolution of the community. Retrogression, reapproach to a standpoint to which the race has been long habituated in the past, is easier. This is especially true in case the development away from this past standpoint has not been due chiefly to a substitution of an ethnic type whose temperament is alien to the earlier standpoint. The cultural stage which lies immediately back of the present in the life history of Western civilization is what has here been called the quasi-peaceable stage. At this quasi-peaceable stage the law of status is the dominant feature in the scheme of life. There is no need of pointing out how prone the men of today are to revert to the spiritual attitude of mastery and of personal subservience which characterizes that stage. It may rather be said to be held in an uncertain abeyance by the economic exigencies of today, than to have been definitely supplanted by a habit of mind that is in full accord with these later-developed exigencies. The predatory and quasi-peaceable stages of economic evolution seem to have been of long duration in life history of all the chief ethnic elements which go to make up the populations of the Western culture. The temperament and the propensities proper to those cultural stages have, therefore, attained such a persistence as to make a speedy reversion to the broad features of the corresponding psychological constitution inevitable in the case of any class or community which is removed from the action of those forces that make for a maintenance of the later-developed habits of thought.

It is a matter of common notoriety that when individuals, or even considerable groups of men, are segregated from a higher industrial culture and exposed to a lower cultural environment, or to an economic situation of a more primitive character, they quickly show evidence of reversion toward the spiritual features which characterize the predatory type; and it seems probable that the dolicho-blond type of European man is possessed of a greater facility for such reversion to barbarism than the other ethnic elements with which that type is associated in the Western culture. Examples of such a reversion on a small scale abound in the later history of migration and colonization. Except for the fear of offending that chauvinistic patriotism which is so characteristic a feature of the predatory culture, and the presence of which is frequently the most striking mark of reversion in modern communities, the case of the American colonies might be cited as an example of such a reversion on an unusually large scale, though it was not a reversion of very large scope.

The leisure class is in great measure sheltered from the stress of those economic exigencies which prevail in any modern, highly organized industrial community. The exigencies of the struggle for the means of life are less exacting for this class than for any other; and as a consequence of this privileged position we should expect to find it one of the least responsive of the classes of society to the demands which the situation makes for a further growth of institutions and a readjustment to an altered industrial situation. The leisure class is the conservative class. The exigencies of the general economic situation of the community do not freely or directly impinge upon the members of this class. They are not required under penalty of forfeiture to change their habits of life and their theoretical views of the external world to suit the demands of an altered industrial technique, since they are not in the full sense an organic part of the industrial community. Therefore these exigencies do not readily produce, in the members of this class, that degree of uneasiness with the existing order which alone can lead any body of men to give up views and methods of life that have become habitual to them. The office of the leisure class in social evolution is to retard the movement and to conserve what is obsolescent. This proposition is by no means novel; it has long been one of the commonplaces of popular opinion.

The prevalent conviction that the wealthy class is by nature conservative has been popularly accepted without much aid from any theoretical view as to the place and relation of that class in the cultural development. When an explanation of this class conservatism is offered, it is commonly the invidious one that the wealthy class opposes innovation because it has a vested interest, of an unworthy sort, in maintaining the present conditions. The explanation here put forward imputes no unworthy motive. The opposition of the class to changes in the cultural scheme is instinctive, and does not rest primarily on an interested calculation of material advantages; it is an instinctive revulsion at any departure from the accepted way of doing and of looking at things—a revulsion common to all men and only to be overcome by stress of circumstances. All change in habits of life and of thought is irksome. The difference in this respect between the wealthy and the common run of mankind lies not so much in the motive which prompts to conservatism as in the degree of exposure to the economic forces that urge a change. The members of the wealthy class do not yield to the demand for innovation as readily as other men because they are not constrained to do so.

This conservatism of the wealthy class is so obvious a feature that it has even come to be recognized as a mark of respectability. Since conservatism is a characteristic of the wealthier and therefore more reputable portion of the community, it has acquired a certain honorific or decorative value. It has become prescriptive to such an extent that an adherence to conservative views is comprised as a matter of course in our notions of respectability; and it is imperatively incumbent on all who would lead a blameless life in point of social repute. Conservatism, being an upper-class characteristic, is decorous; and conversely, innovation, being a lower-class phenomenon, is vulgar. The first and most unreflected element in that instinctive revulsion and reprobation with which we turn from all social innovators is this sense of the essential vulgarity of the thing. So that even in cases where one recognizes the substantial merits of the case for which the innovator is spokesman—as may easily happen if the evils which he seeks to remedy are sufficiently remote in point of time or space or personal contact—still one cannot but be sensible of the fact that the innovator is a person with whom it is at least distasteful to be associated, and from whose social contact one must shrink. Innovation is bad form.

The fact that the usages, actions, and views of the well-to-do leisure class acquire the character of a prescriptive canon of conduct for the rest of society, gives added weight and reach to the conservative influence of that class. It makes it incumbent upon all reputable people to follow their lead. So that, by virtue of its high position as the avatar of good form, the wealthier class comes to exert a retarding influence upon social development far in excess of that which the simple numerical strength of the class would assign it. Its prescriptive example acts to greatly stiffen the resistance of all other classes against any innovation, and to fix men's affections upon the good institutions handed down from an earlier generation. There is a second way in which the influence of the leisure class acts in the same direction, so far as concerns hindrance to the adoption of a conventional scheme of life more in accord with the exigencies of the time. This second method of upper-class guidance is not in strict consistency to be brought under the same category as the instinctive conservatism and aversion to new modes of thought just spoken of; but it may as well be dealt with here, since it has at least this much in common with the conservative habit of mind that it acts to retard innovation and the growth of social structure. The code of proprieties, conventionalities, and usages in vogue at any given time and among any given people has more or less of the character of an organic whole; so that any appreciable change in one point of the scheme involves something of a change or readjustment at other points also, if not a reorganization all along the line.

When a change is made which immediately touches only a minor point in the scheme, the consequent derangement of the structure of conventionalities may be inconspicuous; but even in such a case it is safe to say that some derangement of the general scheme, more or less far-reaching, will follow. On the other hand, when an attempted reform involves the suppression or thorough-going remodeling of an institution of first-rate importance in the conventional scheme, it is immediately felt that a serious derangement of the entire scheme would result; it is felt that a readjustment of the structure to the new form taken on by one of its chief elements would be a painful and tedious, if not a doubtful process.

In order to realize the difficulty which such a radical change in any one feature of the conventional scheme of life would involve, it is only necessary to suggest the suppression of the monogamic family, or of the agnatic system of consanguinity, or of private property, or of the theistic faith, in any country of the Western civilization; or suppose the suppression of ancestor worship in China, or of the caste system in India, or of slavery in Africa, or the establishment of equality of the sexes in Mohammedan countries. It needs no argument to show that the derangement of the general structure of conventionalities in any of these cases would be very considerable. In order to effect such an innovation a very far-reaching alteration of men's habits of thought would be involved also at other points of the scheme than the one immediately in question. The aversion to any such innovation amounts to a shrinking from an essentially alien scheme of life.

The revulsion felt by good people at any proposed departure from the accepted methods of life is a familiar fact of everyday experience. It is not unusual to hear those persons who dispense salutary advice and admonition to the community express themselves forcibly upon the far-reaching pernicious effects which the community would suffer from such relatively slight changes as the disestablishment of the Anglican Church, an increased facility of divorce, adoption of female suffrage, prohibition of the manufacture and sale of intoxicating beverages, abolition or restriction of inheritances, etc. Any one of these innovations would, we are told, "shake the social structure to its base," "reduce society to chaos," "subvert the foundations of morality," "make life intolerable," "confound the order of nature," etc. These various locutions are, no doubt, of the nature of hyperbole; but, at the same time, like all overstatement, they are evidence of a lively sense of the gravity of the consequences which they are intended to describe. The effect of these and like innovations in deranging the accepted scheme of life is felt to be of much graver consequence than the simple alteration of an isolated item in a series of contrivances for the convenience of men in society. What is true in so obvious a degree of innovations of first-rate importance is true in a less degree of changes of a smaller immediate importance. The aversion to change is in large part an aversion to the bother of making the readjustment which any given change will necessitate; and this solidarity of the system of institutions of any given culture or of any given people strengthens the instinctive resistance offered to any change in men's habits of thought, even in matters which, taken by themselves, are of minor importance. A consequence of this increased reluctance, due to the solidarity of human institutions, is that any innovation calls for a greater expenditure of nervous energy in making the necessary readjustment than would otherwise be the case. It is not only that a change in established habits of thought is distasteful. The process of readjustment of the accepted theory of life involves a degree of mental effort—a more or less protracted and laborious effort to find and to keep one's bearings under the altered circumstances. This process requires a certain expenditure of energy, and so presumes, for its successful accomplishment, some surplus of energy beyond that absorbed in the daily struggle for subsistence. Consequently it follows that progress is hindered by underfeeding and excessive physical hardship, no less effectually than by such a luxurious life as will shut out discontent by cutting off the occasion for it. The abjectly poor, and all those persons whose energies are entirely absorbed by the struggle for daily sustenance, are conservative because they cannot afford the effort of taking thought for the day after tomorrow; just as the highly prosperous are conservative because they have small occasion to be discontented with the situation as it stands today.

From this proposition it follows that the institution of a leisure class acts to make the lower classes conservative by withdrawing from them as much as it may of the means of sustenance, and so reducing their consumption, and consequently their available energy, to such a point as to make them incapable of the effort required for the learning and adoption of new habits of thought. The accumulation of wealth at the upper end of the pecuniary scale implies privation at the lower end of the scale. It is a commonplace that, wherever it occurs, a considerable degree of privation among the body of the people is a serious obstacle to any innovation.

This direct inhibitory effect of the unequal distribution of wealth is seconded by an indirect effect tending to the same result. As has already been seen, the imperative example set by the upper class in fixing the canons of reputability fosters the practice of conspicuous consumption. The prevalence of conspicuous consumption as one of the main elements in the standard of decency among all classes is of course not traceable wholly to the example of the wealthy leisure class, but the practice and the insistence on it are no doubt strengthened by the example of the leisure class. The requirements of decency in this matter are very considerable and very imperative; so that even among classes whose pecuniary position is sufficiently strong to admit a consumption of goods considerably in excess of the subsistence minimum, the disposable surplus left over after the more imperative physical needs are satisfied is not infrequently diverted to the purpose of a conspicuous decency, rather than to added physical comfort and fullness of life. Moreover, such surplus energy as is available is also likely to be expended in the acquisition of goods for conspicuous consumption or conspicuous boarding. The result is that the requirements of pecuniary reputability tend (1) to leave but a scanty subsistence minimum available for other than conspicuous consumption, and (2) to absorb any surplus energy which may be available after the bare physical necessities of life have been provided for. The outcome of the whole is a strengthening of the general conservative attitude of the community. The institution of a leisure class hinders cultural development immediately (1) by the inertia proper to the class itself, (2) through its prescriptive example of conspicuous waste and of conservatism, and (3) indirectly through that system of unequal distribution of wealth and sustenance on which the institution itself rests. To this is to be added that the leisure class has also a material interest in leaving things as they are. Under the circumstances prevailing at any given time this class is in a privileged position, and any departure from the existing order may be expected to work to the detriment of the class rather than the reverse. The attitude of the class, simply as influenced by its class interest, should therefore be to let well-enough alone. This interested motive comes in to supplement the strong instinctive bias of the class, and so to render it even more consistently conservative than it otherwise would be.

All this, of course, has nothing to say in the way of eulogy or deprecation of the office of the leisure class as an exponent and vehicle of conservatism or reversion in social structure. The inhibition which it exercises may be salutary or the reverse. Whether it is the one or the other in any given case is a question of casuistry rather than of general theory. There may be truth in the view (as a question of policy) so often expressed by the spokesmen of the conservative element, that without some such substantial and consistent resistance to innovation as is offered by the conservative well-to-do classes, social innovation and experiment would hurry the community into untenable and intolerable situations; the only possible result of which would be discontent and disastrous reaction. All this, however, is beside the present argument.

But apart from all deprecation, and aside from all question as to the indispensability of some such check on headlong innovation, the leisure class, in the nature of things, consistently acts to retard that adjustment to the environment which is called social advance or development. The characteristic attitude of the class may be summed up in the maxim: "Whatever is, is right" whereas the law of natural selection, as applied to human institutions, gives the axiom: "Whatever is, is wrong." Not that the institutions of today are wholly wrong for the purposes of the life of today, but they are, always and in the nature of things, wrong to some extent. They are the result of a more or less inadequate adjustment of the methods of living to a situation which prevailed at some point in the past development; and they are therefore wrong by something more than the interval which separates the present situation from that of the past. "Right" and "wrong" are of course here used without conveying any rejection as to what ought or ought not to be. They are applied simply from the (morally colorless) evolutionary standpoint, and are intended to designate compatibility or incompatibility with the effective evolutionary process. The institution of a leisure class, by force or class interest and instinct, and by precept and prescriptive example, makes for the perpetuation of the existing maladjustment of institutions, and even favors a reversion to a somewhat more archaic scheme of life; a scheme which would be still farther out of adjustment with the exigencies of life under the existing situation even than the accredited, obsolescent scheme that has come down from the immediate past.

But after all has been said on the head of conservation of the good old ways, it remains true that institutions change and develop. There is a cumulative growth of customs and habits of thought; a selective adaptation of conventions and methods of life. Something is to be said of the office of the leisure class in guiding this growth as well as in retarding it; but little can be said here of its relation to institutional growth except as it touches the institutions that are primarily and immediately of an economic character. These institutions—the economic structure—may be roughly distinguished into two classes or categories, according as they serve one or the other of two divergent purposes of economic life.

To adapt the classical terminology, they are institutions of acquisition or of production; or to revert to terms already employed in a different connection in earlier chapters, they are pecuniary or industrial institutions; or in still other terms, they are institutions serving either the invidious or the non-invidious economic interest. The former category has to do with "business," the latter with industry, taking the latter word in the mechanical sense. The latter class are not often recognized as institutions, in great part because they do not immediately concern the ruling class, and are, therefore, seldom the subject of legislation or of deliberate convention. When they do receive attention they are commonly approached from the pecuniary or business side; that being the side or phase of economic life that chiefly occupies men's deliberations in our time, especially the deliberations of the upper classes. These classes have little else than a business interest in things economic, and on them at the same time it is chiefly incumbent to deliberate upon the community's affairs.

The relation of the leisure (that is, propertied non-industrial) class to the economic process is a pecuniary relation—a relation of acquisition, not of production; of exploitation, not of serviceability. Indirectly their economic office may, of course, be of the utmost importance to the economic life process; and it is by no means here intended to depreciate the economic function of the propertied class or of the captains of industry. The purpose is simply to point out what is the nature of the relation of these classes to the industrial process and to economic institutions. Their office is of a parasitic character, and their interest is to divert what substance they may to their own use, and to retain whatever is under their hand. The conventions of the business world have grown up under the selective surveillance of this principle of predation or parasitism. They are conventions of ownership; derivatives, more or less remote, of the ancient predatory culture. But these pecuniary institutions do not entirely fit the situation of today, for they have grown up under a past situation differing somewhat from the present. Even for effectiveness in the pecuniary way, therefore, they are not as apt as might be. The changed industrial life requires changed methods of acquisition; and the pecuniary classes have some interest in so adapting the pecuniary institutions as to give them the best effect for acquisition of private gain that is compatible with the continuance of the industrial process out of which this gain arises. Hence there is a more or less consistent trend in the leisure-class guidance of institutional growth, answering to the pecuniary ends which shape leisure-class economic life.

The effect of the pecuniary interest and the pecuniary habit of mind upon the growth of institutions is seen in those enactments and conventions that make for security of property, enforcement of contracts, facility of pecuniary transactions, vested interests. Of such bearing are changes affecting bankruptcy and receiverships, limited liability, banking and currency, coalitions of laborers or employers, trusts and pools. The community's institutional furniture of this kind is of immediate consequence only to the propertied classes, and in proportion as they are propertied; that is to say, in proportion as they are to be ranked with the leisure class. But indirectly these conventions of business life are of the gravest consequence for the industrial process and for the life of the community. And in guiding the institutional growth in this respect, the pecuniary classes, therefore, serve a purpose of the most serious importance to the community, not only in the conservation of the accepted social scheme, but also in shaping the industrial process proper. The immediate end of this pecuniary institutional structure and of its amelioration is the greater facility of peaceable and orderly exploitation; but its remoter effects far outrun this immediate object. Not only does the more facile conduct of business permit industry and extra-industrial life to go on with less perturbation; but the resulting elimination of disturbances and complications calling for an exercise of astute discrimination in everyday affairs acts to make the pecuniary class itself superfluous. As fast as pecuniary transactions are reduced to routine, the captain of industry can be dispensed with. This consummation, it is needless to say, lies yet in the indefinite future. The ameliorations wrought in favor of the pecuniary interest in modern institutions tend, in another field, to substitute the "soulless" joint-stock corporation for the captain, and so they make also for the dispensability, of the great leisure-class function of ownership. Indirectly, therefore, the bent given to the growth of economic institutions by the leisure-class influence is of very considerable industrial consequence.

CHAPTER NINE

The Conservation of Archaic Traits

The institution of a leisure class has an effect not only upon social structure but also upon the individual character of the members of society. So soon as a given proclivity or a given point of view has won acceptance as an authoritative standard or norm of life it will react upon the character of the members of the society which has accepted it as a norm. It will to some extent shape their habits of thought and will exercise a selective surveillance over the development of men's aptitudes and inclinations. This effect is wrought partly by a coercive, educational adaptation of the habits of all individuals, partly by a selective elimination of the unfit individuals and lines of descent. Such human material as does not lend itself to the methods of life imposed by the accepted scheme suffers more or less elimination as well as repression. The principles of pecuniary emulation and of industrial exemption have in this way been erected into canons of life, and have become coercive factors of some importance in the situation to which men have to adapt themselves.

These two broad principles of conspicuous waste and industrial exemption affect the cultural development both by guiding men's habits of thought, and so controlling the growth of institutions, and by selectively conserving certain traits of human nature that conduce to facility of life under the leisure-class scheme, and so controlling the effective temper of the community. The proximate tendency of the institution of a leisure class in shaping human character runs in the direction of spiritual survival and reversion. Its effect upon the temper of a community is of the nature of an arrested spiritual development. In the later culture especially, the institution has, on the whole, a conservative trend. This proposition is familiar enough in substance, but it may to many have the appearance of novelty in its present application. Therefore a summary review of its logical grounds may not be uncalled for, even at the risk of some tedious repetition and formulation of commonplaces.

Social evolution is a process of selective adaptation of temperament and habits of thought under the stress of the circumstances of associated life. The adaptation of habits of thought is the growth of institutions. But along with the growth of institutions has gone a change of a more substantial character. Not only have the habits of men changed with the changing exigencies of the situation, but these changing exigencies have also brought about a correlative change in human nature. The human material of society itself varies with the changing conditions of life. This variation of human nature is held by the later ethnologists to be a process of selection between several relatively stable and persistent ethnic types or ethnic elements. Men tend to revert or to breed true, more or less closely, to one or another of certain types of human nature that have in their main features been fixed in approximate conformity to a situation in the past which differed from the situation of today. There are several of these relatively stable ethnic types of mankind comprised in the populations of the Western culture. These ethnic types survive in the race inheritance today, not as rigid and invariable moulds, each of a single precise and specific pattern, but in the form of a greater or smaller number of variants. Some variation of the ethnic types has resulted under the protracted selective process to which the several types and their hybrids have been subjected during the prehistoric and historic growth of culture.

This necessary variation of the types themselves, due to a selective process of considerable duration and of a consistent trend, has not been sufficiently noticed by the writers who have discussed ethnic survival. The argument is here concerned with two main divergent variants of human nature resulting from this, relatively late, selective adaptation of the ethnic types comprised in the Western culture; the point of interest being the probable effect of the situation of today in furthering variation along one or the other of these two divergent lines.

The ethnological position may be briefly summed up; and in order to avoid any but the most indispensable detail the schedule of types and variants and the scheme of reversion and survival in which they are concerned are here presented with a diagrammatic meagerness and simplicity which would not be admissible for any other purpose. The man of our industrial communities tends to breed true to one or the other of three main ethic types; the dolichocephalic-blond, the brachycephalic-brunette, and the Mediterranean—disregarding minor and outlying elements of our culture. But within each of these main ethnic types the reversion tends to one or the other of at least two main directions of variation; the peaceable or antepredatory variant and the predatory variant. The former of these two characteristic variants is nearer to the generic type in each case, being the reversional representative of its type as it stood at the earliest stage of associated life of which there is available evidence, either archaeological or psychological. This variant is taken to represent the ancestors of existing civilized man at the peaceable, savage phase of life which preceded the predatory culture, the regime of status, and the growth of pecuniary emulation. The second or predatory variant of the types is taken to be a survival of a more recent modification of the main ethnic types and their hybrids—of these types as they were modified, mainly by a selective adaptation, under the discipline of the predatory culture and the latter emulative culture of the quasi-peaceable stage, or the pecuniary culture proper.

Under the recognized laws of heredity there may be a survival from a more or less remote past phase. In the ordinary, average, or normal case, if the type has varied, the traits of the type are transmitted approximately as they have stood in the recent past—which may be called the hereditary present. For the purpose in hand this hereditary present is represented by the later predatory and the quasi-peaceable culture.

It is to the variant of human nature which is characteristic of this recent—hereditarily still existing—predatory or quasi-predatory culture that the modern civilized man tends to breed true in the common run of cases. This proposition requires some qualification so far as concerns the descendants of the servile or repressed classes of barbarian times, but the qualification necessary is probably not so great as might at first thought appear. Taking the population as a whole, this predatory, emulative variant does not seem to have attained a high degree of consistency or stability. That is to say, the human nature inherited by modern Occidental man is not nearly uniform in respect of the range or the relative strength of the various aptitudes and propensities which go to make it up.

The man of the hereditary present is slightly archaic as judged for the purposes of the latest exigencies of associated life. And the type to which the modern man chiefly tends to revert under the law of variation is a somewhat more archaic human nature. On the other hand, to judge by the reversional traits which show themselves in individuals that vary from the prevailing predatory style of temperament, the ante-predatory variant seems to have a greater stability and greater symmetry in the distribution or relative force of its temperamental elements.

This divergence of inherited human nature, as between an earlier and a later variant of the ethnic type to which the individual tends to breed true, is traversed and obscured by a similar divergence between the two or three main ethnic types that go to make up the Occidental populations. The individuals in these communities are conceived to be, in virtually every instance, hybrids of the prevailing ethnic elements combined in the most varied proportions; with the result that they tend to take back to one or the other of the component ethnic types. These ethnic types differ in temperament in a way somewhat similar to the difference between the predatory and the antepredatory variants of the types; the dolicho-blond type showing more of the characteristics of the predatory temperament—or at least more of the violent disposition—than the brachycephalic-brunette type, and especially more than the Mediterranean. When the growth of institutions or of the effective sentiment of a given community shows a divergence from the predatory human nature, therefore, it is impossible to say with certainty that such a divergence indicates a reversion to the ante-predatory variant. It may be due to an increasing dominance of the one or the other of the "lower" ethnic elements in the population. Still, although the evidence is not as conclusive as might be desired, there are indications that the variations in the effective temperament of modern communities is not altogether due to a selection between stable ethnic types. It seems to be to some appreciable extent a selection between the predatory and the peaceable variants of the several types. This conception of contemporary human evolution is not indispensable to the discussion. The general conclusions reached by the use of these concepts of selective adaptation would remain substantially true if the earlier, Darwinian and Spencerian, terms and concepts were substituted. Under the circumstances, some latitude may be admissible in the use of terms. The word "type" is used loosely, to denote variations of temperament which the ethnologists would perhaps recognize only as trivial variants of the type rather than as distinct ethnic types. Wherever a closer discrimination seems essential to the argument, the effort to make such a closer discrimination will be evident from the context.

The ethnic types of today, then, are variants of the primitive racial types. They have suffered some alteration, and have attained some degree of fixity in their altered form, under the discipline of the barbarian culture. The man of the hereditary present is the barbarian variant, servile or aristocratic, of the ethnic elements that constitute him. But this barbarian variant has not attained the highest degree of homogeneity or of stability. The barbarian culture—the predatory and quasi-peaceable cultural stages—though of great absolute duration, has been neither protracted enough nor invariable enough in character to give an extreme fixity of type. Variations from the barbarian human nature occur with some frequency, and these cases of variation are becoming more noticeable today, because the conditions of modern life no longer act consistently to repress departures from the barbarian normal. The predatory temperament does not lead itself to all the purposes of modern life, and more especially not to modern industry.

Departures from the human nature of the hereditary present are most frequently of the nature of reversions to an earlier variant of the type. This earlier variant is represented by the temperament which characterizes the primitive phase of peaceable savagery. The circumstances of life and the ends of effort that prevailed before the advent of the barbarian culture, shaped human nature and fixed it as regards certain fundamental traits. And it is to these ancient, generic features that modern men are prone to take back in case of variation from the human nature of the hereditary present. The conditions under which men lived in the most primitive stages of associated life that can properly be called human, seem to have been of a peaceful kind; and the character—the temperament and spiritual attitude of men under these early conditions or environment and institutions seems to have been of a peaceful and unaggressive, not to say an indolent, cast. For the immediate purpose this peaceable cultural stage may be taken to mark the initial phase of social development. So far as concerns the present argument, the dominant spiritual feature of this presumptive initial phase of culture seems to have been an unreflecting, unformulated sense of group solidarity, largely expressing itself in a complacent, but by no means strenuous, sympathy with all facility of human life, and an uneasy revulsion against apprehended inhibition or futility of life. Through its ubiquitous presence in the habits of thought of the ante-predatory savage man, this pervading but uneager sense of the generically useful seems to have exercised an appreciable constraining force upon his life and upon the manner of his habitual contact with other members of the group.

The traces of this initial, undifferentiated peaceable phase of culture seem faint and doubtful if we look merely to such categorical evidence of its existence as is afforded by usages and views in vogue within the historical present, whether in civilized or in rude communities; but less dubious evidence of its existence is to be found in psychological survivals, in the way of persistent and pervading traits of human character. These traits survive perhaps in an especial degree among those ethic elements which were crowded into the background during the predatory culture. Traits that were suited to the earlier habits of life then became relatively useless in the individual struggle for existence. And those elements of the population, or those ethnic groups, which were by temperament less fitted to the predatory life were repressed and pushed into the background. On the transition to the predatory culture the character of the struggle for existence changed in some degree from a struggle of the group against a non-human environment to a struggle against a human environment. This change was accompanied by an increasing antagonism and consciousness of antagonism between the individual members of the group. The conditions of success within the group, as well as the conditions of the survival of the group, changed in some measure; and the dominant spiritual attitude for the group gradually changed, and brought a different range of aptitudes and propensities into the position of legitimate dominance in the accepted scheme of life. Among these archaic traits that are to be regarded as survivals from the peaceable cultural phase, are that instinct of race solidarity which we call conscience, including the sense of truthfulness and equity, and the instinct of workmanship, in its naive, non-invidious expression.

Under the guidance of the later biological and psychological science, human nature will have to be restated in terms of habit; and in the restatement, this, in outline, appears to be the only assignable place and ground of these traits. These habits of life are of too pervading a character to be ascribed to the influence of a late or brief discipline. The ease with which they are temporarily overborne by the special exigencies of recent and modern life argues that these habits are the surviving effects of a discipline of extremely ancient date, from the teachings of which men have frequently been constrained to depart in detail under the altered circumstances of a later time; and the almost ubiquitous fashion in which they assert themselves whenever the pressure of special exigencies is relieved, argues that the process by which the traits were fixed and incorporated into the spiritual make-up of the type must have lasted for a relatively very long time and without serious intermission. The point is not seriously affected by any question as to whether it was a process of habituation in the old-fashioned sense of the word or a process of selective adaptation of the race.

The character and exigencies of life, under that regime of status and of individual and class antithesis which covers the entire interval from the beginning of predatory culture to the present, argue that the traits of temperament here under discussion could scarcely have arisen and acquired fixity during that interval. It is entirely probable that these traits have come down from an earlier method of life, and have survived through the interval of predatory and quasi-peaceable culture in a condition of incipient, or at least imminent, desuetude, rather than that they have been brought out and fixed by this later culture. They appear to be hereditary characteristics of the race, and to have persisted in spite of the altered requirements of success under the predatory and the later pecuniary stages of culture. They seem to have persisted by force of the tenacity of transmission that belongs to a hereditary trait that is present in some degree in every member of the species, and which therefore rests on a broad basis of race continuity.

Such a generic feature is not readily eliminated, even under a process of selection so severe and protracted as that to which the traits here under discussion were subjected during the predatory and quasi-peaceable stages. These peaceable traits are in great part alien to the methods and the animus of barbarian life. The salient characteristic of the barbarian culture is an unremitting emulation and antagonism between classes and between individuals. This emulative discipline favors those individuals and lines of descent which possess the peaceable savage traits in a relatively slight degree. It therefore tends to eliminate these traits, and it has apparently weakened them, in an appreciable degree, in the populations that have been subject to it. Even where the extreme penalty for non-conformity to the barbarian type of temperament is not paid, there results at least a more or less consistent repression of the non-conforming individuals and lines of descent. Where life is largely a struggle between individuals within the group, the possession of the ancient peaceable traits in a marked degree would hamper an individual in the struggle for life.

Under any known phase of culture, other or later than the presumptive initial phase here spoken of, the gifts of good-nature, equity, and indiscriminate sympathy do not appreciably further the life of the individual. Their possession may serve to protect the individual from hard usage at the hands of a majority that insists on a modicum of these ingredients in their ideal of a normal man; but apart from their indirect and negative effect in this way, the individual fares better under the regime of competition in proportion as he has less of these gifts. Freedom from scruple, from sympathy, honesty and regard for life, may, within fairly wide limits, be said to further the success of the individual in the pecuniary culture. The highly successful men of all times have commonly been of this type; except those whose success has not been scored in terms of either wealth or power. It is only within narrow limits, and then only in a Pickwickian sense, that honesty is the best policy.

As seen from the point of view of life under modern civilized conditions in an enlightened community of the Western culture, the primitive, ante-predatory savage, whose character it has been attempted to trace in outline above, was not a great success. Even for the purposes of that hypothetical culture to which his type of human nature owes what stability it has—even for the ends of the peaceable savage group—this primitive man has quite as many and as conspicuous economic failings as he has economic virtues—as should be plain to any one whose sense of the case is not biased by leniency born of a fellow-feeling. At his best he is "a clever, good-for-nothing fellow." The shortcomings of this presumptively primitive type of character are weakness, inefficiency, lack of initiative and ingenuity, and a yielding and indolent amiability, together with a lively but inconsequential animistic sense. Along with these traits go certain others which have some value for the collective life process, in the sense that they further the facility of life in the group. These traits are truthfulness, peaceableness, good-will, and a non-emulative, non-invidious interest in men and things.

With the advent of the predatory stage of life there comes a change in the requirements of the successful human character. Men's habits of life are required to adapt themselves to new exigencies under a new scheme of human relations. The same unfolding of energy, which had previously found expression in the traits of savage life recited above, is now required to find expression along a new line of action, in a new group of habitual responses to altered stimuli. The methods which, as counted in terms of facility of life, answered measurably under the earlier conditions, are no longer adequate under the new conditions. The earlier situation was characterized by a relative absence of antagonism or differentiation of interests, the later situation by an emulation constantly increasing in relative absence of antagonism or differentiation of interests, the later situation by an emulation constantly increasing in intensity and narrowing in scope. The traits which characterize the predatory and subsequent stages of culture, and which indicate the types of man best fitted to survive under the regime of status, are (in their primary expression) ferocity, self-seeking, clannishness, and disingenuousness—a free resort to force and fraud.

Under the severe and protracted discipline of the regime of competition, the selection of ethnic types has acted to give a somewhat pronounced dominance to these traits of character, by favoring the survival of those ethnic elements which are most richly endowed in these respects. At the same time the earlier, acquired, more generic habits of the race have never ceased to have some usefulness for the purpose of the life of the collectivity and have never fallen into definitive abeyance. It may be worth while to point out that the dolicho-blond type of European man seems to owe much of its dominating influence and its masterful position in the recent culture to its possessing the character-istics of predatory man in an exceptional degree. These spiritual traits, together with a large endowment of physical energy—itself probably a result of selection between groups and between lines of descent—chiefly go to place any ethnic element in the position of a leisure or master class, especially during the earlier phases of the development of the in-stitution of a leisure class. This need not mean that precisely the same complement of ap-titudes in any individual would insure him an eminent personal success. Under the competitive regime, the conditions of success for the individual are not necessarily the same as those for a class. The success of a class or party presumes a strong element of clan-nishness, or loyalty to a chief, or adherence to a tenet; whereas the competitive individ-ual can best achieve his ends if he combines the barbarian's energy, initiative, self-seeking and disingenuousness with the savage's lack of loyalty or clannishness. It may be re-marked by the way, that the men who have scored a brilliant (Napoleonic) success on the basis of an impartial self-seeking and absence of scruple, have not uncommonly shown more of the physical characteristics of the brachycephalic-brunette than of the dolicho-blond. The greater proportion of moderately successful individuals, in a self-seeking way, however, seem, in physique, to belong to the last-named ethnic element.

The temperament induced by the predatory habit of life makes for the survival and fullness of life of the individual under a regime of emulation; at the same time it makes for the survival and success of the group if the group's life as a collectivity is also predom-inantly a life of hostile competition with other groups. But the evolution of economic life in the industrially more mature communities has now begun to take such a turn that the interest of the community no longer coincides with the emulative interests of the in-dividual. In their corporate capacity, these advanced industrial communities are ceasing to be competitors for the means of life or for the right to live—except in so far as the predatory propensities of their ruling classes keep up the tradition of war and rapine.

These communities are no longer hostile to one another by force of circumstances, other than the circumstances of tradition and temperament. Their material interests—apart, possibly, from the interests of the collective good fame—are not only no longer in-compatible, but the success of any one of the communities unquestionably furthers the fullness of life of any other community in the group, for the present and for an incalcu-lable time to come. No one of them any longer has any material interest in getting the better of any other. The same is not true in the same degree as regards individuals and their relations to one another.

The collective interests of any modern community center in industrial efficiency. The individual is serviceable for the ends of the community somewhat in proportion to his ef-ficiency in the productive employments vulgarly so called. This collective interest is best served by honesty, diligence, peacefulness, good-will, an absence of self-seeking, and a ha-bitual recognition and apprehension of causal sequence, without admixture of animistic belief and without a sense of dependence on any preternatural intervention in the course of events. Not much is to be said for the beauty, moral excellence, or general worthiness and reputability of such a prosy human nature as these traits imply; and there is little ground of enthusiasm for the manner of collective life that would result from the preva-lence of these traits in unmitigated dominance. But that is beside the point. The successful working of a modern industrial community is best secured where these traits concur, and it is attained in the degree in which the human material is characterized by their possession. Their presence in some measure is required in order to have a tolerable adjustment to the circumstances of the modern industrial situation. The complex, comprehensive, essentially peaceable, and highly organized mechanism of the modern industrial community works to the best advantage when these traits, or most of them, are present in the highest practicable degree. These traits are present in a markedly less degree in the man of the predatory type than is useful for the purposes of the modern collective life.

On the other hand, the immediate interest of the individual under the competitive regime is best served by shrewd trading and unscrupulous management. The characteristics named above as serving the interests of the community are disserviceable to the individual, rather than otherwise. The presence of these aptitudes in his make-up diverts his energies to other ends than those of pecuniary gain; and also in his pursuit of gain they lead him to seek gain by the indirect and ineffectual channels of industry, rather than by a free and unfaltering career of sharp practice. The industrial aptitudes are pretty consistently a hindrance to the individual. Under the regime of emulation the members of a modern industrial community are rivals, each of whom will best attain his individual and immediate advantage if, through an exceptional exemption from scruple, he is able serenely to overreach and injure his fellows when the chance offers.

It has already been noticed that modern economic institutions fall into two roughly distinct categories—the pecuniary and the industrial. The like is true of employments. Under the former head are employments that have to do with ownership or acquisition; under the latter head, those that have to do with workmanship or production. As was found in speaking of the growth of institutions, so with regard to employments. The economic interests of the leisure class lie in the pecuniary employments; those of the working classes lie in both classes of employments, but chiefly in the industrial. Entrance to the leisure class lies through the pecuniary employments.

These two classes of employment differ materially in respect of the aptitudes required for each; and the training which they give similarly follows two divergent lines. The discipline of the pecuniary employments acts to conserve and to cultivate certain of the predatory aptitudes and the predatory animus. It does this both by educating those individuals and classes who are occupied with these employments and by selectively repressing and eliminating those individuals and lines of descent that are unfit in this respect. So far as men's habits of thought are shaped by the competitive process of acquisition and tenure; so far as their economic functions are comprised within the range of ownership of wealth as conceived in terms of exchange value, and its management and financiering through a permutation of values; so far their experience in economic life favors the survival and accentuation of the predatory temperament and habits of thought. Under the modern, peaceable system, it is of course the peaceable range of predatory habits and aptitudes that is chiefly fostered by a life of acquisition. That is to say, the pecuniary employments give proficiency in the general line of practices comprised under fraud, rather than in those that belong under the more archaic method of forcible seizure.

These pecuniary employments, tending to conserve the predatory temperament, are the employments which have to do with ownership—the immediate function of the leisure class proper—and the subsidiary functions concerned with acquisition and accumulation. These cover the class of persons and that range of duties in the economic process which have to do with the ownership of enterprises engaged in competitive industry; especially those fundamental lines of economic management which are classed as financiering operations. To these may be added the greater part of mercantile occupations. In their best and clearest development these duties make up the economic office of the "captain of industry." The captain of industry is an astute man rather than an ingenious one, and his captaincy is a pecuniary rather than an industrial captaincy. Such administration of industry as he exercises is commonly of a permissive kind. The mechanically effective details of production and of industrial organization are delegated to subordinates of a less "practical" turn of mind—men who are possessed of a gift for workmanship rather than administrative ability. So far as regards their tendency in shaping human nature by education and selection, the common run of non-economic employments are to be classed with the pecuniary employments. Such are politics and ecclesiastical and military employments.

The pecuniary employments have also the sanction of reputability in a much higher degree than the industrial employments. In this way the leisure-class standards of good repute come in to sustain the prestige of those aptitudes that serve the invidious purpose; and the leisure-class scheme of decorous living, therefore, also furthers the survival and culture of the predatory traits. Employments fall into a hierarchical gradation of reputability. Those which have to do immediately with ownership on a large scale are the most reputable of economic employments proper. Next to these in good repute come those employments that are immediately subservient to ownership and financiering—such as banking and the law. Banking employments also carry a suggestion of large ownership, and this fact is doubtless accountable for a share of the prestige that attaches to the business. The profession of the law does not imply large ownership; but since no taint of usefulness, for other than the competitive purpose, attaches to the lawyer's trade, it grades high in the conventional scheme. The lawyer is exclusively occupied with the details of predatory fraud, either in achieving or in checkmating chicanery, and success in the profession is therefore accepted as marking a large endowment of that barbarian astuteness which has always commanded men's respect and fear. Mercantile pursuits are only half-way reputable, unless they involve a large element of ownership and a small element of usefulness. They grade high or low somewhat in proportion as they serve the higher or the lower needs; so that the business of retailing the vulgar necessaries of life descends to the level of the handicrafts and factory labor. Manual labor, or even the work of directing mechanical processes, is of course on a precarious footing as regards respectability. A qualification is necessary as regards the discipline given by the pecuniary employments. As the scale of industrial enterprise grows larger, pecuniary management comes to bear less of the character of chicanery and shrewd competition in detail. That is to say, for an ever-increasing proportion of the persons who come in contact with this phase of economic life, business reduces itself to a routine in which there is less immediate suggestion of overreaching or exploiting a competitor. The consequent exemption from predatory habits extends chiefly to subordinates employed in business. The duties of ownership and administration are virtually untouched by this qualification. The case is different as regards those individuals or classes who are immediately occupied with the technique and manual operations of production. Their daily life is not in the same degree a course of habituation to the emulative and invidious motives and maneuvers of the pecuniary side of industry. They are consistently held to the apprehension and coordination of mechanical facts and sequences, and to their appreciation and utilization for the purposes of human life. So far as concerns this portion of the population, the educative and selective action of the industrial process with which they are immediately in contact acts to adapt their habits of thought to the non-invidious purposes of the collective life. For them, therefore, it hastens the obsolescence of the distinctively predatory aptitudes and propensities carried over by heredity and tradition from the barbarian past of the race.

The educative action of the economic life of the community, therefore, is not of a uniform kind throughout all its manifestations. That range of economic activities which is concerned immediately with pecuniary competition has a tendency to conserve certain predatory traits; while those industrial occupations which have to do immediately with the production of goods have in the main the contrary tendency. But with regard to the latter class of employments it is to be noticed in qualification that the persons engaged in them are nearly all to some extent also concerned with matters of pecuniary competition (as, for instance, in the competitive fixing of wages and salaries, in the purchase of goods for consumption, etc.). Therefore the distinction here made between classes of employments is by no means a hard and fast distinction between classes of persons.

The employments of the leisure classes in modern industry are such as to keep alive certain of the predatory habits and aptitudes. So far as the members of those classes take part in the industrial process, their training tends to conserve in them the barbarian temperament. But there is something to be said on the other side. Individuals so placed as to be exempt from strain may survive and transmit their characteristics even if they differ widely from the average of the species both in physique and in spiritual make-up. The chances for a survival and transmission of atavistic traits are greatest in those classes that are most sheltered from the stress of circumstances. The leisure class is in some degree sheltered from the stress of the industrial situation, and should, therefore, afford an exceptionally great proportion of reversions to the peaceable or savage temperament. It should be possible for such aberrant or atavistic individuals to unfold their life activity on ante-predatory lines without suffering as prompt a repression or elimination as in the lower walks of life.

Something of the sort seems to be true in fact. There is, for instance, an appreciable proportion of the upper classes whose inclinations lead them into philanthropic work, and there is a considerable body of sentiment in the class going to support efforts of reform and amelioration. And much of this philanthropic and reformatory effort, moreover, bears the marks of that amiable "cleverness" and incoherence that is characteristic of the primitive savage. But it may still be doubtful whether these facts are evidence of a larger proportion of reversions in the higher than in the lower strata, even if the same inclinations were present in the impecunious classes, it would not as easily find expression there; since those classes lack the means and the time and energy to give effect to their inclinations in this respect. The prima facie evidence of the facts can scarcely go unquestioned.

In further qualification it is to be noted that the leisure class of today is recruited from those who have been successful in a pecuniary way, and who, therefore, are presumably endowed with more than an even complement of the predatory traits. Entrance into the leisure class lies through the pecuniary employments, and these employments, by selection and adaptation, act to admit to the upper levels only those lines of descent that are pecuniarily fit to survive under the predatory test. And so soon as a case of reversion to non-predatory human nature shows itself on these upper levels, it is commonly weeded out and thrown back to the lower pecuniary levels. In order to hold its place in the class, a stock must have the pecuniary temperament; otherwise its fortune would be dissipated and it would presently lose caste. Instances of this kind are sufficiently frequent. The constituency of the leisure class is kept up by a continual selective process, whereby the individuals and lines of descent that are eminently fitted for an aggressive pecuniary competition are withdrawn from the lower classes. In order to reach the upper levels the aspirant must have, not only a fair average complement of the pecuniary aptitudes, but he must have these gifts in such an eminent degree as to overcome very material difficulties that stand in the way of his ascent. Barring accidents, the nouveaux arrived are a picked body.

This process of selective admission has, of course, always been going on; ever since the fashion of pecuniary emulation set in—which is much the same as saying, ever since the institution of a leisure class was first installed. But the precise ground of selection has not always been the same, and the selective process has therefore not always given the same results. In the early barbarian, or predatory stage proper, the test of fitness was prowess, in the naive sense of the word. To gain entrance to the class, the candidate had to be gifted with clannishness, massiveness, ferocity, unscrupulousness, and tenacity of purpose. These were the qualities that counted toward the accumulation and continued tenure of wealth. The economic basis of the leisure class, then as later, was the possession of wealth; but the methods of accumulating wealth, and the gifts required for holding it, have changed in some degree since the early days of the predatory culture. In consequence of the selective process the dominant traits of the early barbarian leisure class were bold aggression, an alert sense of status, and a free resort to fraud. The members of the class held their place by tenure of prowess. In the later barbarian culture society attained settled methods of acquisition and possession under the quasi-peaceable regime of status. Simple aggression and unrestrained violence in great measure gave place to shrewd practice and chicanery, as the best approved method of accumulating wealth. A different range of aptitudes and propensities would then be conserved in the leisure class. Masterful aggression, and the correlative massiveness, together with a ruthlessly consistent sense of status, would still count among the most splendid traits of the class. These have remained in our traditions as the typical "aristocratic virtues." But with these were associated an increasing complement of the less obtrusive pecuniary virtues; such as providence, prudence, and chicanery. As time has gone on, and the modern peaceable stage of pecuniary culture has been approached, the last-named range of aptitudes and habits has gained in relative effectiveness for pecuniary ends, and they have counted for relatively more in the selective process under which admission is gained and place is held in the leisure class.

The ground of selection has changed, until the aptitudes which now qualify for admission to the class are the pecuniary aptitudes only. What remains of the predatory barbarian traits is the tenacity of purpose or consistency of aim which distinguished the successful predatory barbarian from the peaceable savage whom he supplanted. But this trait can not be said characteristically to distinguish the pecuniarily successful upper-class man from the rank and file of the industrial classes. The training and the selection to which the latter are exposed in modern industrial life give a similarly decisive weight to this trait. Tenacity of purpose may rather be said to distinguish both these classes from two others; the shiftless ne'er do-well and the lower-class delinquent. In point of natural endowment the pecuniary man compares with the delinquent in much the same way as the industrial man compares with the good-natured shiftless dependent. The ideal pecuniary man is like the ideal delinquent in his unscrupulous conversion of goods and persons to his own ends, and in a callous disregard of the feelings and wishes of others and of the remoter effects of his actions; but he is unlike him in possessing a keener sense of status, and in working more consistently and farsightedly to a remoter end. The kinship of the two types of temperament is further shown in a proclivity to "sport" and gambling, and a relish of aimless emulation. The ideal pecuniary man also shows a curious kinship with the delinquent in one of the concomitant variations of the predatory human nature. The delinquent is very commonly of a superstitious habit of mind; he is a great believer in luck, spells, divination and destiny, and in omens and shamanistic ceremony. Where circumstances are favorable, this proclivity is apt to express itself in a certain servile devotional fervor and a punctilious attention to devout observances; it may perhaps be better characterized as devoutness than as religion. At this point the temperament of the delinquent has more in common with the pecuniary and leisure classes than with the industrial man or with the class of shiftless dependents.

Life in a modern industrial community, or in other words life under the pecuniary culture, acts by a process of selection to develop and conserve a certain range of aptitudes and propensities. The present tendency of this selective process is not simply a reversion to a given, immutable ethnic type. It tends rather to a modification of human nature differing in some respects from any of the types or variants transmitted out of the past. The objective point of the evolution is not a single one. The temperament which the evolution acts to establish as normal differs from any one of the archaic variants of human nature in its greater stability of aim—greater singleness of purpose and greater persistence in effort. So far as concerns economic theory, the objective point of the selective process is on the whole single to this extent; although there are minor tendencies of considerable importance diverging from this line of development. But apart from this general trend the line of development is not single. As concerns economic theory, the development in other respects runs on two divergent lines. So far as regards the selective conservation of capacities or aptitudes in individuals, these two lines may be called the pecuniary and the industrial. As regards the conservation of propensities, spiritual attitude, or animus, the two may be called the invidious or self-regarding and the non-invidious or economical. As regards the intellectual or cognitive bent of the two directions of growth, the former may be characterized as the personal standpoint, of conation, qualitative relation, status, or worth; the latter as the impersonal standpoint, of sequence, quantitative relation, mechanical efficiency, or use.

The pecuniary employments call into action chiefly the former of these two ranges of aptitudes and propensities, and act selectively to conserve them in the population. The industrial employments, on the other hand, chiefly exercise the latter range, and act to conserve them. An exhaustive psychological analysis will show that each of these two ranges of aptitudes and propensities is but the multiform expression of a given temperamental bent. By force of the unity or singleness of the individual, the aptitudes, animus, and interests comprised in the first-named range belong together as expressions of a given variant of human nature. The like is true of the latter range. The two may be conceived as alternative directions of human life, in such a way that a given individual inclines more or less consistently to the one or the other. The tendency of the pecuniary life is, in a general way, to conserve the barbarian temperament, but with the substitution of fraud and prudence, or administrative ability, in place of that predilection for physical damage that characterizes the early barbarian. This substitution of chicanery in place of devastation takes place only in an uncertain degree. Within the pecuniary employments the selective action runs pretty consistently in this direction, but the discipline of pecuniary life, outside the competition for gain, does not work consistently to the same effect. The discipline of modern life in the consumption of time and goods does not act unequivocally to eliminate the aristocratic virtues or to foster the bourgeois virtues. The conventional scheme of decent living calls for a considerable exercise of the earlier barbarian traits. Some details of this traditional scheme of life, bearing on this point, have been noticed in earlier chapters under the head of leisure, and further details will be shown in later chapters.

From what has been said, it appears that the leisure-class life and the leisure-class scheme of life should further the conservation of the barbarian temperament; chiefly of the quasi-peaceable, or bourgeois, variant, but also in some measure of the predatory variant. In the absence of disturbing factors, therefore, it should be possible to trace a difference of temperament between the classes of society. The aristocratic and the bourgeois virtues—that is to say the destructive and pecuniary traits—should be found chiefly among the upper classes, and the industrial virtues—that is to say the peaceable traits—chiefly among the classes given to mechanical industry.

In a general and uncertain way this holds true, but the test is not so readily applied nor so conclusive as might be wished. There are several assignable reasons for its partial failure. All classes are in a measure engaged in the pecuniary struggle, and in all classes the possession of the pecuniary traits counts towards the success and survival of the individual. Wherever the pecuniary culture prevails, the selective process by which men's habits of thought are shaped, and by which the survival of rival lines of descent is decided, proceeds proximately on the basis of fitness for acquisition. Consequently, if it were not for the fact that pecuniary efficiency is on the whole incompatible with industrial efficiency, the selective action of all occupations would tend to the unmitigated dominance of the pecuniary temperament. The result would be the installation of what has been known as the "economic man," as the normal and definitive type of human nature. But the "economic man," whose only interest is the self-regarding one and whose only human trait is prudence is useless for the purposes of modern industry.

The modern industry requires an impersonal, non-invidious interest in the work in hand. Without this the elaborate processes of industry would be impossible, and would, indeed, never have been conceived. This interest in work differentiates the workman from the criminal on the one hand, and from the captain of industry on the other. Since work must be done in order to the continued life of the community, there results a qualified selection favoring the spiritual aptitude for work, within a certain range of occupations. This much, however, is to be conceded, that even within the industrial occupations the selective elimination of the pecuniary traits is an uncertain process, and that there is consequently an appreciable survival of the barbarian temperament even within these occupations. On this account there is at present no broad distinction in this respect between the leisure-class character and the character of the common run of the population.

The whole question as to a class distinction in respect to spiritual make-up is also obscured by the presence, in all classes of society, of acquired habits of life that closely simulate inherited traits and at the same time act to develop in the entire body of the population the traits which they simulate. These acquired habits, or assumed traits of character, are most commonly of an aristocratic cast. The prescriptive position of the leisure class as the exemplar of reputability has imposed many features of the leisure-class theory of life upon the lower classes; with the result that there goes on, always and throughout society, a more or less persistent cultivation of these aristocratic traits. On this ground also these traits have a better chance of survival among the body of the people than would be the case if it were not for the precept and example of the leisure class. As one channel, and an important one, through which this transfusion of aristocratic views of life, and consequently more or less archaic traits of character goes on, may be mentioned the class of domestic servants. These have their notions of what is good and beautiful shaped by contact with the master class and carry the preconceptions so acquired back among their low-born equals, and so disseminate the higher ideals abroad through the community without the loss of time which this dissemination might otherwise suffer. The saying "Like master, like man," has a greater significance than is commonly appreciated for the rapid popular acceptance of many elements of upper-class culture.

There is also a further range of facts that go to lessen class differences as regards the survival of the pecuniary virtues. The pecuniary struggle produces an underfed class, of large proportions. This underfeeding consists in a deficiency of the necessaries of life or of the necessaries of a decent expenditure. In either case the result is a closely enforced struggle for the means with which to meet the daily needs; whether it be the physical or the higher needs. The strain of self-assertion against odds takes up the whole energy of the individual; he bends his efforts to compass his own invidious ends alone, and becomes continually more narrowly self-seeking. The industrial traits in this way tend to obsolescence through disuse. Indirectly, therefore, by imposing a scheme of pecuniary decency and by withdrawing as much as may be of the means of life from the lower classes, the institution of a leisure class acts to conserve the pecuniary traits in the body of the population. The result is an assimilation of the lower classes to the type of human nature that belongs primarily to the upper classes only. It appears, therefore, that there is no wide difference in temperament between the upper and the lower classes; but it appears also that the absence of such a difference is in good part due to the prescriptive example of the leisure class and to the popular acceptance of those broad principles of conspicuous waste and pecuniary emulation on which the institution of a leisure class rests. The institution acts to lower the industrial efficiency of the community and retard the adaptation of human nature to the exigencies of modern industrial life. It affects the prevalent or effective human nature in a conservative direction, (1) by direct transmission of archaic traits, through inheritance within the class and wherever the leisure-class blood is transfused outside the class, and (2) by conserving and fortifying the traditions of the archaic regime, and so making the chances of survival of barbarian traits greater also outside the range of transfusion of leisure-class blood.

But little if anything has been done towards collecting or digesting data that are of special significance for the question of survival or elimination of traits in the modern populations. Little of a tangible character can therefore be offered in support of the view here taken, beyond a discursive review of such everyday facts as lie ready to hand. Such a recital can scarcely avoid being commonplace and tedious, but for all that it seems necessary to the completeness of the argument, even in the meager outline in which it is here attempted. A degree of indulgence may therefore fairly be bespoken for the succeeding chapters, which offer a fragmentary recital of this kind.

CHAPTER TEN

Modern Survivals of Prowess

The leisure class lives by the industrial community rather than in it. Its relations to industry are of a pecuniary rather than an industrial kind. Admission to the class is gained by exercise of the pecuniary aptitudes—aptitudes for acquisition rather than for serviceability. There is, therefore, a continued selective sifting of the human material that makes up the leisure class, and this selection proceeds on the ground of fitness for pecuniary pursuits. But the scheme of life of the class is in large part a heritage from the past, and embodies much of the habits and ideals of the earlier barbarian period. This archaic, barbarian scheme of life imposes itself also on the lower orders, with more or less mitigation. In its turn the scheme of life, of conventions, acts selectively and by education to shape the human material, and its action runs chiefly in the direction of conserving traits, habits, and ideals that belong to the early barbarian age—the age of prowess and predatory life.

The most immediate and unequivocal expression of that archaic human nature which characterizes man in the predatory stage is the fighting propensity proper. In cases where the predatory activity is a collective one, this propensity is frequently called the martial spirit, or, latterly, patriotism. It needs no insistence to find assent to the proposition that in the countries of civilized Europe the hereditary leisure class is endowed with this martial spirit in a higher degree than the middle classes. Indeed, the leisure class claims the distinction as a matter of pride, and no doubt with some grounds. War is honorable, and warlike prowess is eminently honorific in the eyes of the generality of men; and this admiration of warlike prowess is itself the best voucher of a predatory temperament in the admirer of war. The enthusiasm for war, and the predatory temper of which it is the index, prevail in the largest measure among the upper classes, especially among the hereditary leisure class. Moreover, the ostensible serious occupation of the upper class is that of government, which, in point of origin and developmental content, is also a predatory occupation.

The only class which could at all dispute with the hereditary leisure class the honor of a habitual bellicose frame of mind is that of the lower-class delinquents. In ordinary times, the large body of the industrial classes is relatively apathetic touching warlike interests. When unexcited, this body of the common people, which makes up the effective force of the industrial community, is rather averse to any other than a defensive fight; indeed, it responds a little tardily even to a provocation which makes for an attitude of defense. In the more civilized communities, or rather in the communities which have reached an advanced industrial development, the spirit of warlike aggression may be said to be obsolescent among the common people. This does not say that there is not an appreciable number of individuals among the industrial classes in whom the martial spirit asserts itself obtrusively. Nor does it say that the body of the people may not be fired with martial ardor for a time under the stimulus of some special provocation, such as is seen in operation today in more than one of the countries of Europe, and for the time in

America. But except for such seasons of temporary exaltation, and except for those individuals who are endowed with an archaic temperament of the predatory type, together with the similarly endowed body of individuals among the higher and the lowest classes, the inertness of the mass of any modern civilized community in this respect is probably so great as would make war impracticable, except against actual invasion. The habits and aptitudes of the common run of men make for an unfolding of activity in other, less picturesque directions than that of war.

This class difference in temperament may be due in part to a difference in the inheritance of acquired traits in the several classes, but it seems also, in some measure, to correspond with a difference in ethnic derivation. The class difference is in this respect visibly less in those countries whose population is relatively homogeneous, ethnically, than in the countries where there is a broader divergence between the ethnic elements that make up the several classes of the community. In the same connection it may be noted that the later accessions to the leisure class in the latter countries, in a general way, show less of the martial spirit than contemporary representatives of the aristocracy of the ancient line. These nouveaux arrived have recently emerged from the commonplace body of the population and owe their emergence into the leisure class to the exercise of traits and propensities which are not to be classed as prowess in the ancient sense.

Apart from warlike activity proper, the institution of the duel is also an expression of the same superior readiness for combat; and the duel is a leisure-class institution. The duel is in substance a more or less deliberate resort to a fight as a final settlement of a difference of opinion. In civilized communities it prevails as a normal phenomenon only where there is an hereditary leisure class, and almost exclusively among that class. The exceptions are (1) military and naval officers who are ordinarily members of the leisure class, and who are at the same time specially trained to predatory habits of mind and (2) the lower-class delinquents—who are by inheritance, or training, or both, of a similarly predatory disposition and habit. It is only the high-bred gentleman and the rowdy that normally resort to blows as the universal solvent of differences of opinion. The plain man will ordinarily fight only when excessive momentary irritation or alcoholic exaltation act to inhibit the more complex habits of response to the stimuli that make for provocation. He is then thrown back upon the simpler, less differentiated forms of the instinct of self-assertion; that is to say, he reverts temporarily and without reflection to an archaic habit of mind.

This institution of the duel as a mode of finally settling disputes and serious questions of precedence shades off into the obligatory, unprovoked private fight, as a social obligation due to one's good repute. As a leisure-class usage of this kind we have, particularly, that bizarre survival of bellicose chivalry, the German student duel. In the lower or spurious leisure class of the delinquents there is in all countries a similar, though less formal, social obligation incumbent on the rowdy to assert his manhood in unprovoked combat with his fellows. And spreading through all grades of society, a similar usage prevails among the boys of the community. The boy usually knows to nicety, from day to day, how he and his associates grade in respect of relative fighting capacity; and in the community of boys there is ordinarily no secure basis of reputability for any one who, by exception, will not or can not fight on invitation.

All this applies especially to boys above a certain somewhat vague limit of maturity. The child's temperament does not commonly answer to this description during infancy and the years of close tutelage, when the child still habitually seeks contact with its mother at every turn of its daily life. During this earlier period there is little aggression and little propensity for antagonism. The transition from this peaceable temper to the predaceous, and in extreme cases malignant, mischievousness of the boy is a gradual one, and it is accomplished with more completeness, covering a larger range of the individual's aptitudes, in some cases than in others. In the earlier stage of his growth, the child, whether boy or girl, shows less of initiative and aggressive self-assertion and less of an inclination to isolate himself and his interests from the domestic group in which he lives, and he shows more of sensitiveness to rebuke, bashfulness, timidity, and the need of friendly human contact. In the common run of cases this early temperament passes, by a gradual but somewhat rapid obsolescence of the infantile features, into the temperament of the boy proper; though there are also cases where the predaceous futures of boy life do not emerge at all, or at the most emerge in but a slight and obscure degree.

In girls the transition to the predaceous stage is seldom accomplished with the same degree of completeness as in boys; and in a relatively large proportion of cases it is scarcely undergone at all. In such cases the transition from infancy to adolescence and maturity is a gradual and unbroken process of the shifting of interest from infantile purposes and aptitudes to the purposes, functions, and relations of adult life. In the girls there is a less general prevalence of a predaceous interval in the development; and in the cases where it occurs, the predaceous and isolating attitude during the interval is commonly less accentuated.

In the male child the predaceous interval is ordinarily fairly well marked and lasts for some time, but it is commonly terminated (if at all) with the attainment of maturity. This last statement may need very material qualification. The cases are by no means rare in which the transition from the boyish to the adult temperament is not made, or is made only partially—understanding by the "adult" temperament the average temperament of those adult individuals in modern industrial life who have some serviceability for the purposes of the collective life process, and who may therefore be said to make up the effective average of the industrial community.

The ethnic composition of the European populations varies. In some cases even the lower classes are in large measure made up of the peace-disturbing dolicho-blond; while in others this ethnic element is found chiefly among the hereditary leisure class. The fighting habit seems to prevail to a less extent among the working-class boys in the latter class of populations than among the boys of the upper classes or among those of the populations first named.

If this generalization as to the temperament of the boy among the working classes should be found true on a fuller and closer scrutiny of the field, it would add force to the view that the bellicose temperament is in some appreciable degree a race characteristic; it appears to enter more largely into the make-up of the dominant, upper-class ethnic type—the dolicho-blond—of the European countries than into the subservient, lower-class types of man which are conceived to constitute the body of the population of the same communities.

The case of the boy may seem not to bear seriously on the question of the relative endowment of prowess with which the several classes of society are gifted; but it is at least of some value as going to show that this fighting impulse belongs to a more archaic temperament than that possessed by the average adult man of the industrious classes. In this, as in many other features of child life, the child reproduces, temporarily and in miniature, some of the earlier phases of the development of adult man. Under this interpretation, the boy's predilection for exploit and for isolation of his own interest is to be taken as a transient reversion to the human nature that is normal to the early barbarian culture—the predatory culture proper. In this respect, as in much else, the leisure-class and the delinquent-class character shows a persistence into adult life of traits that are normal to childhood and youth, and that are likewise normal or habitual to the earlier stages of culture. Unless the difference is traceable entirely to a fundamental difference between persistent ethnic types, the traits that distinguish the swaggering delinquent and the punctilious gentleman of leisure from the common crowd are, in some measure, marks of an arrested spiritual development. They mark an immature phase, as compared with the stage of development attained by the average of the adults in the modern industrial community. And it will appear presently that the puerile spiritual make-up of these representatives of the upper and the lowest social strata shows itself also in the presence of other archaic traits than this proclivity to ferocious exploit and isolation.

As if to leave no doubt about the essential immaturity of the fighting temperament, we have, bridging the interval between legitimate boyhood and adult manhood, the aimless and playful, but more or less systematic and elaborate, disturbances of the peace in vogue among schoolboys of a slightly higher age. In the common run of cases, these disturbances are confined to the period of adolescence. They recur with decreasing frequency and acuteness as youth merges into adult life, and so they reproduce, in a general way, in the life of the individual, the sequence by which the group has passed from the predatory to a more settled habit of life. In an appreciable number of cases the spiritual growth of the individual comes to a close before he emerges from this puerile phase; in these cases the fighting temper persists through life. Those individuals who in spiritual development eventually reach man's estate, therefore, ordinarily pass through a temporary archaic phase corresponding to the permanent spiritual level of the fighting and sporting men. Different individuals will, of course, achieve spiritual maturity and sobriety in this respect in different degrees; and those who fail of the average remain as an undissolved residue of crude humanity in the modern industrial community and as a foil for that selective process of adaptation which makes for a heightened industrial efficiency and the fullness of life of the collectivity. This arrested spiritual development may express itself not only in a direct participation by adults in youthful exploits of ferocity, but also indirectly in aiding and abetting disturbances of this kind on the part of younger persons. It thereby furthers the formation of habits of ferocity which may persist in the later life of the growing generation, and so retard any movement in the direction of a more peaceable effective temperament on the part of the community. If a person so endowed with a proclivity for exploits is in a position to guide the development of habits in the adolescent members of the community, the influence which he exerts in the direction of conservation and reversion to prowess may be very considerable. This is the significance, for instance, of the fostering care latterly bestowed by many clergymen and other pillars of society upon "boys' brigades" and similar pseudo-military organizations. The same is true of the encouragement given to the growth of "college spirit," college athletics, and the like, in the higher institutions of learning.

These manifestations of the predatory temperament are all to be classed under the head of exploit. They are partly simple and unreflected expressions of an attitude of emulative ferocity, partly activities deliberately entered upon with a view to gaining repute for prowess. Sports of all kinds are of the same general character, including prize-fights, bull-fights, athletics, shooting, angling, yachting, and games of skill, even where the element of destructive physical efficiency is not an obtrusive feature. Sports shade off from the basis of hostile combat, through skill, to cunning and chicanery, without its being possible to draw a line at any point. The ground of an addiction to sports is an archaic spiritual constitution—the possession of the predatory emulative propensity in a relatively high potency, a strong proclivity to adventuresome exploit and to the infliction of damage is especially pronounced in those employments which are in colloquial usage specifically called sportsmanship.

It is perhaps truer, or at least more evident, as regards sports than as regards the other expressions of predatory emulation already spoken of, that the temperament which inclines men to them is essentially a boyish temperament. The addiction to sports, therefore, in a peculiar degree marks an arrested development of the man's moral nature. This peculiar boyishness of temperament in sporting men immediately becomes apparent when attention is directed to the large element of make-believe that is present in all sporting activity. Sports share this character of make-believe with the games and exploits to which children, especially boys, are habitually inclined. Make-believe does not enter in the same proportion into all sports, but it is present in a very appreciable degree in all. It is apparently present in a larger measure in sportsmanship proper and in athletic contests than in set games of skill of a more sedentary character; although this rule may not be found to apply with any great uniformity. It is noticeable, for instance, that even very mild-mannered and matter-of-fact men who go out shooting are apt to carry an excess of arms and accoutrements in order to impress upon their own imagination the seriousness of their undertaking. These huntsmen are also prone to a histrionic, prancing gait and to an elaborate exaggeration of the motions, whether of stealth or of onslaught, involved in their deeds of exploit. Similarly in athletic sports there is almost invariably present a good share of rant and swagger and ostensible mystification—features which mark the histrionic nature of these employments. In all this, of course, the reminder of boyish make-believe is plain enough. The slang of athletics, by the way, is in great part made up of extremely sanguinary locutions borrowed from the terminology of warfare. Except where it is adopted as a necessary means of secret communication, the use of a special slang in any employment is probably to be accepted as evidence that the occupation in question is substantially make-believe.

A further feature in which sports differ from the duel and similar disturbances of the peace is the peculiarity that they admit of other motives being assigned for them besides the impulses of exploit and ferocity. There is probably little if any other motive present in any given case, but the fact that other reasons for indulging in sports are frequently assigned goes to say that other grounds are sometimes present in a subsidiary way. Sportsmen—hunters and anglers—are more or less in the habit of assigning a love of nature, the need of recreation, and the like, as the incentives to their favorite pastime. These motives are no doubt frequently present and make up a part of the attractiveness of the sportsman's life; but these can not be the chief incentives. These ostensible needs could be more readily and fully satisfied without the accompaniment of a systematic effort to take the life of those creatures that make up an essential feature of that "nature" that is beloved by the sportsman. It is, indeed, the most noticeable effect of the sportsman's activity to keep nature in a state of chronic desolation by killing off all living thing whose destruction he can compass.

Still, there is ground for the sportsman's claim that under the existing conventionalities his need of recreation and of contact with nature can best be satisfied by the course which he takes. Certain canons of good breeding have been imposed by the prescriptive example of a predatory leisure class in the past and have been somewhat painstakingly conserved by the usage of the latter-day representatives of that class; and these canons will not permit him, without blame, to seek contact with nature on other terms. From being an honorable employment handed down from the predatory culture as the highest form of everyday leisure, sports have come to be the only form of outdoor activity that has the full sanction of decorum. Among the proximate incentives to shooting and angling, then, may be the need of recreation and outdoor life. The remoter cause which imposes the necessity of seeking these objects under the cover of systematic slaughter is a prescription that can not be violated except at the risk of disrepute and consequent lesion to one's self-respect.

The case of other kinds of sport is somewhat similar. Of these, athletic games are the best example. Prescriptive usage with respect to what forms of activity, exercise, and recreation are permissible under the code of reputable living is of course present here also. Those who are addicted to athletic sports, or who admire them, set up the claim that these afford the best available means of recreation and of "physical culture." And prescriptive usage gives countenance to the claim. The canons of reputable living exclude from the scheme of life of the leisure class all activity that can not be classed as conspicuous leisure. And consequently they tend by prescription to exclude it also from the scheme of life of the community generally. At the same time purposeless physical exertion is tedious and distasteful beyond tolerance. As has been noticed in another connection, recourse is in such a case had to some form of activity which shall at least afford a colorable pretense of purpose, even if the object assigned be only a make-believe. Sports satisfy these requirements of substantial futility together with a colorable make-believe of purpose. In addition to this they afford scope for emulation, and are attractive also on that account. In order to be decorous, an employment must conform to the leisure-class canon of reputable waste; at the same time all activity, in order to be persisted in as a habitual, even if only partial, expression of life, must conform to the generically human canon of efficiency for some serviceable objective end. The leisure-class canon demands strict and comprehensive futility; the instinct of workmanship demands purposeful action. The leisure-class canon of decorum acts slowly and pervasively, by a selective elimination of all substantially useful or purposeful modes of action from the accredited scheme of life; the instinct of workmanship acts impulsively and may be satisfied, pro-visionally, with a proximate purpose. It is only as the apprehended ulterior futility of a given line of action enters the reflective complex of consciousness as an element essen-tially alien to the normally purposeful trend of the life process that its disquieting and deterrent effect on the consciousness of the agent is wrought.

The individual's habits of thought make an organic complex, the trend of which is necessarily in the direction of serviceability to the life process. When it is attempted to assimilate systematic waste or futility, as an end in life, into this organic complex, there presently supervenes a revulsion. But this revulsion of the organism may be avoided if the attention can be confined to the proximate, unreflected purpose of dexterous or emula-tive exertion. Sports—hunting, angling, athletic games, and the like—afford an exercise for dexterity and for the emulative ferocity and astuteness characteristic of predatory life. So long as the individual is but slightly gifted with reflection or with a sense of the ulte-rior trend of his actions so long as his life is substantially a life of naive impulsive action—so long the immediate and unreflected purposefulness of sports, in the way of an expression of dominance, will measurably satisfy his instinct of workmanship. This is especially true if his dominant impulses are the unreflecting emulative propensities of the predaceous temperament. At the same time the canons of decorum will commend sports to him as expressions of a pecuniarily blameless life. It is by meeting these two require-ments, of ulterior wastefulness and proximate purposefulness, that any given employment holds its place as a traditional and habitual mode of decorous recreation. In the sense that other forms of recreation and exercise are morally impossible to persons of good breed-ing and delicate sensibilities, then, sports are the best available means of recreation under existing circumstances.

But those members of respectable society who advocate athletic games commonly jus-tify their attitude on this head to themselves and to their neighbors on the ground that these games serve as an invaluable means of development. They not only improve the contestant's physique, but it is commonly added that they also foster a manly spirit, both in the participants and in the spectators. Football is the particular game which will prob-ably first occur to any one in this community when the question of the serviceability of athletic games is raised, as this form of athletic contest is at present uppermost in the mind of those who plead for or against games as a means of physical or moral salvation.

This typical athletic sport may, therefore, serve to illustrate the bearing of athletics upon the development of the contestant's character and physique. It has been said, not inaptly, that the relation of football to physical culture is much the same as that of the bull-fight to agriculture. Serviceability for these lusory institutions requires sedulous training or breeding. The material used, whether brute or human, is subjected to care-ful selection and discipline, in order to secure and accentuate certain aptitudes and propensities which are characteristic of the ferine state, and which tend to obsolescence under domestication.

This does not mean that the result in either case is an all around and consistent reha-bilitation of the ferine or barbarian habit of mind and body. The result is rather a one-sided return to barbarism or to the *feroe natura*—a rehabilitation and accentuation of those fer-ine traits which make for damage and desolation, without a corresponding development of the traits which would serve the individual's self-preservation and fullness of life in a ferine environment. The culture bestowed in football gives a product of exotic ferocity and cunning. It is a rehabilitation of the early barbarian temperament, together with a suppression of those details of temperament, which, as seen from the standpoint of the social and economic exigencies, are the redeeming features of the savage character.

The physical vigor acquired in the training for athletic games—so far as the training may be said to have this effect—is of advantage both to the individual and to the collectivity, in that, other things being equal, it conduces to economic serviceability. The spiritual traits which go with athletic sports are likewise economically advantageous to the individual, as contradistinguished from the interests of the collectivity. This holds true in any community where these traits are present in some degree in the population. Modern competition is in large part a process of self-assertion on the basis of these traits of predatory human nature. In the sophisticated form in which they enter into the modern, peaceable emulation, the possession of these traits in some measure is almost a necessary of life to the civilized man. But while they are indispensable to the competitive individual, they are not directly serviceable to the community. So far as regards the serviceability of the individual for the purposes of the collective life, emulative efficiency is of use only indirectly if at all. Ferocity and cunning are of no use to the community except in its hostile dealings with other communities; and they are useful to the individual only because there is so large a proportion of the same traits actively present in the human environment to which he is exposed. Any individual who enters the competitive struggle without the due endowment of these traits is at a disadvantage, somewhat as a hornless steer would find himself at a disadvantage in a drove of horned cattle.

The possession and the cultivation of the predatory traits of character may, of course, be desirable on other than economic grounds. There is a prevalent aesthetic or ethical predilection for the barbarian aptitudes, and the traits in question minister so effectively to this predilection that their serviceability in the aesthetic or ethical respect probably offsets any economic unserviceability which they may give. But for the present purpose that is beside the point. Therefore nothing is said here as to the desirability or advisability of sports on the whole, or as to their value on other than economic grounds.

In popular apprehension there is much that is admirable in the type of manhood which the life of sport fosters. There is self-reliance and good-fellowship, so termed in the somewhat loose colloquial use of the words. From a different point of view the qualities currently so characterized might be described as truculence and clannishness. The reason for the current approval and admiration of these manly qualities, as well as for their being called manly, is the same as the reason for their usefulness to the individual. The members of the community, and especially that class of the community which sets the pace in canons of taste, are endowed with this range of propensities in sufficient measure to make their absence in others felt as a shortcoming, and to make their possession in an exceptional degree appreciated as an attribute of superior merit. The traits of predatory man are by no means obsolete in the common run of modern populations. They are present and can be called out in bold relief at any time by any appeal to the sentiments in which they express themselves—unless this appeal should clash with the specific activities that make up our habitual occupations and comprise the general range of our everyday interests. The common run of the population of any industrial community is emancipated from these, economically considered, untoward propensities only in the sense that, through partial and temporary disuse, they have lapsed into the background of sub-conscious motives. With varying degrees of potency in different individuals, they remain available for the aggressive shaping of men's actions and sentiments whenever a stimulus of more than everyday intensity comes in to call them forth. And they assert themselves forcibly in any case where no occupation alien to the predatory culture has usurped the individual's everyday range of interest and sentiment. This is the case among the leisure class and among certain portions of the population which are ancillary to that class. Hence the facility with which any new accessions to the leisure class take to sports; and hence the rapid growth of sports and of the sporting sentient in any industrial community where wealth has accumulated sufficiently to exempt a considerable part of the population from work.

A homely and familiar fact may serve to show that the predaceous impulse does not prevail in the same degree in all classes. Taken simply as a feature of modern life, the habit of carrying a walking-stick may seem at best a trivial detail; but the usage has a significance for the point in question. The classes among whom the habit most prevails—the classes with whom the walking-stick is associated in popular apprehension—are the men of the leisure class proper, sporting men, and the lower-class delinquents. To these might perhaps be added the men engaged in the pecuniary employments. The same is not true of the common run of men engaged in industry and it may be noted by the way that women do not carry a stick except in case of infirmity, where it has a use of a different kind. The practice is of course in great measure a matter of polite usage; but the basis of polite usage is, in turn, the proclivities of the class which sets the pace in polite usage. The walking-stick serves the purpose of an advertisement that the bearer's hands are employed otherwise than in useful effort, and it therefore has utility as an evidence of leisure. But it is also a weapon, and it meets a felt need of barbarian man on that ground.

The handling of so tangible and primitive a means of offense is very comforting to any one who is gifted with even a moderate share of ferocity. The exigencies of the language make it impossible to avoid an apparent implication of disapproval of the aptitudes, propensities, and expressions of life here under discussion. It is, however, not intended to imply anything in the way of deprecation or commendation of any one of these phases of human character or of the life process. The various elements of the prevalent human nature are taken up from the point of view of economic theory, and the traits discussed are gauged and graded with regard to their immediate economic bearing on the facility of the collective life process. That is to say, these phenomena are here apprehended from the economic point of view and are valued with respect to their direct action in furtherance or hindrance of a more perfect adjustment of the human collectivity to the environment and to the institutional structure required by the economic situation of the collectivity for the present and for the immediate future. For these purposes the traits handed down from the predatory culture are less serviceable than might be. Although even in this connection it is not to be overlooked that the energetic aggressiveness and pertinacity of predatory man is a heritage of no mean value. The economic value—with some regard also to the social value in the narrower sense—of these aptitudes and propensities is attempted to be passed upon without reflecting on their value as seen from another point of view. When contrasted with the prosy mediocrity of the latter-day industrial scheme of life, and judged by the accredited standards of morality, and more especially by the standards of aesthetics and of poetry, these survivals from a more primitive type of manhood may have a very different value from that here assigned them. But all this being foreign to the purpose in hand, no expression of opinion on this latter head would be in place here. All that is admissible is to enter the caution that these standards of excellence, which are alien to the present purpose, must not be allowed to influence our economic appreciation of these traits of human character or of the activities which foster their growth. This applies both as regards those persons who actively participate in sports and those whose sporting experience consists in contemplation only. What is here said of the sporting propensity is likewise pertinent to sundry reflections presently to be made in this connection on what would colloquially be known as the religious life.

The last paragraph incidentally touches upon the fact that everyday speech can scarcely be employed in discussing this class of aptitudes and activities without implying deprecation or apology. The fact is significant as showing the habitual attitude of the dispassionate common man toward the propensities which express themselves in sports and in exploit generally. And this is perhaps as convenient a place as any to discuss that undertone of deprecation which runs through all the voluminous discourse in defense or in laudation of athletic sports, as well as of other activities of a predominantly predatory character. The same apologetic frame of mind is at least beginning to be observable in the spokesmen of most other institutions handed down from the barbarian phase of life. Among these archaic institutions which are felt to need apology are comprised, with others, the entire existing system of the distribution of wealth, together with the resulting class distinction of status; all or nearly all forms of consumption that come under the head of conspicuous waste; the status of women under the patriarchal system; and many features of the traditional creeds and devout observances, especially the exoteric expressions of the creed and the naive apprehension of received observances. What is to be said in this connection of the apologetic attitude taken in commending sports and the sporting character will therefore apply, with a suitable change in phraseology, to the apologies offered in behalf of these other, related elements of our social heritage.

There is a feeling—usually vague and not commonly avowed in so many words by the apologist himself, but ordinarily perceptible in the manner of his discourse—that these sports, as well as the general range of predaceous impulses and habits of thought which underlie the sporting character, do not altogether commend themselves to common sense. "As to the majority of murderers, they are very incorrect characters." This aphorism offers a valuation of the predaceous temperament, and of the disciplinary effects of its overt expression and exercise, as seen from the moralist's point of view. As such it affords an indication of what is the deliverance of the sober sense of mature men as to the degree of availability of the predatory habit of mind for the purposes of the collective life. It is felt that the presumption is against any activity which involves habituation to the predatory attitude, and that the burden of proof lies with those who speak for the rehabilitation of the predaceous temper and for the practices which strengthen it. There is a strong body of popular sentiment in favor of diversions and enterprises of the kind in question; but there is at the same time present in the community a pervading sense that this ground of sentiment wants legitimation. The required legitimation is ordinarily sought by showing that although sports are substantially of a predatory, socially disintegrating effect; although their proximate effect runs in the direction of reversion to propensities that are industrially disserviceable; yet indirectly and remotely—by some not readily comprehensible process of polar induction, or counter-irritation perhaps—sports are conceived to foster a habit of mind that is serviceable for the social or industrial purpose. That is to say, although sports are essentially of the nature of invidious exploit, it is presumed that by some remote and obscure effect they result in the growth of a temperament conducive to non-invidious work. It is commonly attempted to show all this empirically or it is rather assumed that this is the empirical generalization which must be obvious to any one who cares to see it. In conducting the proof of this thesis the treacherous ground of inference from cause to effect is somewhat shrewdly avoided, except so far as to show that the "manly virtues" spoken of above are fostered by sports. But since it is these manly virtues that are (economically) in need of legitimation, the chain of proof breaks off where it should begin. In the most general economic terms, these apologies are an effort to show that, in spite of the logic of the thing, sports do in fact further what may broadly be called workmanship. So long as he has not succeeded in persuading himself or others that this is their effect the thoughtful apologist for sports will not rest content, and commonly, it is to be admitted, he does not rest content. His discontent with his own vindication of the practice in question is ordinarily shown by his truculent tone and by the eagerness with which he heaps up asseverations in support of his position. But why are apologies needed? If there prevails a body of popular sentient in favor of sports, why is not that fact a sufficient legitimation? The protracted discipline of prowess to which the race has been subjected under the predatory and quasi-peaceable culture has transmitted to the men of today a temperament that finds gratification in these expressions of ferocity and cunning. So, why not accept these sports as legitimate expressions of a normal and wholesome human nature? What other norm is there that is to be lived up to than that given in the aggregate range of propensities that express themselves in the sentiments of this generation, including the hereditary strain of prowess? The ulterior norm to which appeal is taken is the instinct of workmanship, which is an instinct more fundamental, of more ancient prescription, than the propensity to predatory emulation. The latter is but a special development of the instinct of workmanship, a variant, relatively late and ephemeral in spite of its great absolute antiquity. The emulative predatory impulse—or the instinct of sportsmanship, as it might well be called—is essentially unstable in comparison with the primordial instinct of workmanship out of which it has been developed and differentiated. Tested by this ulterior norm of life, predatory emulation, and therefore the life of sports, falls short.

The manner and the measure in which the institution of a leisure class conduces to the conservation of sports and invidious exploit can of course not be succinctly stated. From the evidence already recited it appears that, in sentient and inclinations, the leisure class is more favorable to a warlike attitude and animus than the industrial classes. Something similar seems to be true as regards sports. But it is chiefly in its indirect effects, through the canons of decorous living, that the institution has its influence on the prevalent sentiment with respect to the sporting life. This indirect effect goes almost unequivocally in the direction of furthering a survival of the predatory temperament and habits; and this is true even with respect to those variants of the sporting life which the higher leisure-class code of proprieties proscribes; as, e.g., prize-fighting, cock-fighting, and other like vulgar expressions of the sporting temper. Whatever the latest authenticated schedule of detail proprieties may say, the accredited canons of decency sanctioned by the institution say without equivocation that emulation and waste are good and their opposites are disreputable. In the crepuscular light of the social nether spaces the details of the code are not apprehended with all the facility that might be desired, and these broad underlying canons of decency are therefore applied somewhat unreflectingly, with little question as to the scope of their competence or the exceptions that have been sanctioned in detail.

Addiction to athletic sports, not only in the way of direct participation, but also in the way of sentiment and moral support, is, in a more or less pronounced degree, a characteristic of the leisure class; and it is a trait which that class shares with the lower-class delinquents, and with such atavistic elements throughout the body of the community as are endowed with a dominant predaceous trend. Few individuals among the populations of Western civilized countries are so far devoid of the predaceous instinct as to find no diversion in contemplating athletic sports and games, but with the common run of individuals among the industrial classes the inclination to sports does not assert itself to the extent of constituting what may fairly be called a sporting habit. With these classes sports are an occasional diversion rather than a serious feature of life. This common body of the people can therefore not be said to cultivate the sporting propensity. Although it is not obsolete in the average of them, or even in any appreciable number of individuals, yet the predilection for sports in the commonplace industrial classes is of the nature of a reminiscence, more or less diverting as an occasional interest, rather than a vital and permanent interest that counts as a dominant factor in shaping the organic complex of habits of thought into which it enters. As it manifests itself in the sporting life of today, this propensity may not appear to be an economic factor of grave consequence. Taken simply by itself it does not count for a great deal in its direct effects on the industrial efficiency or the consumption of any given individual; but the prevalence and the growth of the type of human nature of which this propensity is a characteristic feature is a matter of some consequence. It affects the economic life of the collectivity both as regards the rate of economic development and as regards the character of the results attained by the development. For better or worse, the fact that the popular habits of thought are in any degree dominated by this type of character can not but greatly affect the scope, direction, standards, and ideals of the collective economic life, as well as the degree of adjustment of the collective life to the environment.

Something to a like effect is to be said of other traits that go to make up the barbarian character. For the purposes of economic theory, these further barbarian traits may be taken as concomitant variations of that predaceous temper of which prowess is an expression. In great measure they are not primarily of an economic character, nor do they have much direct economic bearing. They serve to indicate the stage of economic evolution to which the individual possessed of them is adapted. They are of importance, therefore, as extraneous tests of the degree of adaptation of the character in which they are comprised to the economic exigencies of today, but they are also to some extent important as being aptitudes which themselves go to increase or diminish the economic serviceability of the individual.

As it finds expression in the life of the barbarian, prowess manifests itself in two main directions—force and fraud. In varying degrees these two forms of expression are similarly present in modern warfare, in the pecuniary occupations, and in sports and games. Both lines of aptitudes are cultivated and strengthened by the life of sport as well as by the more serious forms of emulative life. Strategy or cunning is an element invariably present in games, as also in warlike pursuits and in the chase. In all of these employments strategy tends to develop into finesse and chicanery. Chicanery, falsehood, browbeating, hold a well-secured place in the method of procedure of any athletic contest and in games generally. The habitual employment of an umpire, and the minute technical regulations governing the limits and details of permissible fraud and strategic advantage, sufficiently attest the fact that fraudulent practices and attempts to overreach one's opponents are not adventitious features of the game. In the nature of the case habituation to sports should conduce to a fuller development of the aptitude for fraud; and the prevalence in the community of that predatory temperament which inclines men to sports connotes a prevalence of sharp practice and callous disregard of the interests of others, individually and collectively. Resort to fraud, in any guise and under any legitimation of law or custom, is an expression of a narrowly self-regarding habit of mind. It is needless to dwell at any length on the economic value of this feature of the sporting character.

In this connection it is to be noted that the most obvious characteristic of the physiognomy affected by athletic and other sporting men is that of an extreme astuteness. The gifts and exploits of Ulysses are scarcely second to those of Achilles, either in their substantial furtherance of the game or in that which they give the astute sporting man among his associates. The pantomime of astuteness is commonly the first step in that assimilation to the professional sporting man which a youth undergoes after matriculation in any reputable school, of the secondary or the higher education, as the case may be. And the physiognomy of astuteness, as a decorative feature, never ceases to receive the thoughtful attention of men whose serious interest lies in athletic games, races, or other contests of a similar emulative nature. As a further indication of their spiritual kinship, it may be pointed out that the members of the lower delinquent class usually show this physiognomy of astuteness in a marked degree, and that they very commonly show the same histrionic exaggeration of it that is often seen in the young candidate for athletic honors. This, by the way, is the most legible mark of what is vulgarly called "toughness" in youthful aspirants for a bad name.

The astute man, it may be remarked, is of no economic value to the community—unless it be for the purpose of sharp practice in dealings with other communities. His functioning is not a furtherance of the generic life process. At its best, in its direct economic bearing, it is a conversion of the economic substance of the collectivity to a growth alien to the collective life process—very much after the analogy of what in medicine would be called a benign tumor, with some tendency to transgress the uncertain line that divides the benign from the malign growths. The two barbarian traits, ferocity and astuteness, go to make up the predaceous temper or spiritual attitude. They are the expressions of a narrowly self-regarding habit of mind. Both are highly serviceable for individual expediency in a life looking to invidious success. Both also have a high aesthetic value. Both are fostered by the pecuniary culture. But both alike are of no use for the purposes of the collective life.

CHAPTER ELEVEN

The Belief in Luck

The gambling propensity is another subsidiary trait of the barbarian temperament. It is a concomitant variation of character of almost universal prevalence among sporting men and among men given to warlike and emulative activities generally. This trait also has a direct economic value. It is recognized to be a hindrance to the highest industrial efficiency of the aggregate in any community where it prevails in an appreciable degree. The gambling proclivity is doubtfully to be classed as a feature belonging exclusively to the predatory type of human nature. The chief factor in the gambling habit is the belief in luck; and this belief is apparently traceable, at least in its elements, to a stage in human evolution antedating the predatory culture. It may well have been under the predatory culture that the belief in luck was developed into the form in which it is present, as the chief element of the gambling proclivity, in the sporting temperament. It probably owes the specific form under which it occurs in the modern culture to the predatory discipline. But the belief in luck is in substance a habit of more ancient date than the predatory culture. It is one form of the artistic apprehension of things. The belief seems to be a trait carried over in substance from an earlier phase into the barbarian culture, and transmuted and transmitted through that culture to a later stage of human development under a specific form imposed by the predatory discipline. But in any case, it is to be taken as an archaic trait, inherited from a more or less remote past, more or less incompatible with the requirements of the modern industrial process, and more or less of a hindrance to the fullest efficiency of the collective economic life of the present.

While the belief in luck is the basis of the gambling habit, it is not the only element that enters into the habit of betting. Betting on the issue of contests of strength and skill proceeds on a further motive, without which the belief in luck would scarcely come in as a prominent feature of sporting life. This further motive is the desire of the anticipated winner, or the partisan of the anticipated winning side, to heighten his side's ascendancy at the cost of the loser. Not only does the stronger side score a more signal victory, and the losing side suffer a more painful and humiliating defeat, in proportion as the pecuniary gain and loss in the wager is large; although this alone is a consideration of material weight. But the wager is commonly laid also with a view, not avowed in words nor even recognized in set terms in petto, to enhancing the chances of success for the contestant on which it is laid. It is felt that substance and solicitude expended to this end can not go for naught in the issue. There is here a special manifestation of the instinct of workmanship, backed by an even more manifest sense that the animistic congruity of things must decide for a victorious outcome for the side in whose behalf the propensity inherent in events has been propitiated and fortified by so much of conative and kinetic urging. This incentive to the wager expresses itself freely under the form of backing one's favorite in any contest, and it is unmistakably a predatory feature. It is as ancillary to the predaceous impulse proper that the belief in luck expresses itself in a wager. So that it may be set down that in so far as the belief in luck comes to expression in the form of laying a wager, it is to be accounted an integral element of the predatory type of character. The belief is, in its elements, an archaic habit which belongs substantially to early, undifferentiated human nature; but when this belief is helped out by the predatory emulative impulse, and so is differentiated into the specific form of the gambling habit, it is, in this higher-developed and specific form, to be classed as a trait of the barbarian character.

The belief in luck is a sense of fortuitous necessity in the sequence of phenomena. In its various mutations and expressions, it is of very serious importance for the economic efficiency of any community in which it prevails to an appreciable extent. So much so as to warrant a more detailed discussion of its origin and content and of the bearing of its various ramifications upon economic structure and function, as well as a discussion of the relation of the leisure class to its growth, differentiation, and persistence. In the developed, integrated form in which it is most readily observed in the barbarian of the predatory culture or in the sporting man of modern communities, the belief comprises at least two distinguishable elements—which are to be taken as two different phases of the same fundamental habit of thought, or as the same psychological factor in two successive phases of its evolution. The fact that these two elements are successive phases of the same general line of growth of belief does not hinder their coexisting in the habits of thought of any given individual. The more primitive form (or the more archaic phase) is an incipient animistic belief, or an animistic sense of relations and things, that imputes a quasi-personal character to facts. To the archaic man all the obtrusive and obviously consequential objects and facts in his environment have a quasi-personal individuality. They are conceived to be possessed of volition, or rather of propensities, which enter into the complex of causes and affect events in an inscrutable manner. The sporting man's sense of luck and chance, or of fortuitous necessity, is an inarticulate or inchoate animism. It applies to objects and situations, often in a very vague way; but it is usually so far defined as to imply the possibility of propitiating, or of deceiving and cajoling, or otherwise disturbing the holding of propensities resident in the objects which constitute the apparatus and accessories of any game of skill or chance. There are few sporting men who are not in the habit of wearing charms or talismans to which more or less of efficacy is felt to belong. And the proportion is not much less of those who instinctively dread the "hoodooing" of the contestants or the apparatus engaged in any contest on which they lay a wager; or who feel that the fact of their backing a given contestant or side in the game does and ought to strengthen that side; or to whom the "mascot" which they cultivate means something more than a jest.

In its simple form the belief in luck is this instinctive sense of an inscrutable teleological propensity in objects or situations. Objects or events have a propensity to eventuate in a given end, whether this end or objective point of the sequence is conceived to be fortuitously given or deliberately sought. From this simple animism the belief shades off by insensible gradations into the second, derivative form or phase above referred to, which is a more or less articulate belief in an inscrutable preternatural agency. The preternatural agency works through the visible objects with which it is associated, but is not identified with these objects in point of individuality. The use of the term "preternatural agency" here carries no further implication as to the nature of the agency spoken of as preternatural. This is only a farther development of animistic belief. The preternatural agency is not necessarily conceived to be a personal agent in the full sense, but it is an agency which partakes of the attributes of personality to the extent of somewhat arbitrarily influencing the outcome of any enterprise, and especially of any contest. The pervading belief in the *hamingia* or *gipta (gaefa, authna)* which lends so much of color to the Icelandic sagas specifically, and to early Germanic folk-legends, is an illustration of this sense of an extra-physical propensity in the course of events.

In this expression or form of the belief the propensity is scarcely personified although to a varying extent an individuality is imputed to it; and this individuated propensity is sometimes conceived to yield to circumstances, commonly to circumstances of a spiritual or preternatural character. A well-known and striking exemplification of the belief— in a fairly advanced stage of differentiation and involving an anthropomorphic personification of the preternatural agent appealed to—is afforded by the wager of battle. Here the preternatural agent was conceived to act on request as umpire, and to shape the outcome of the contest in accordance with some stipulated ground of decision, such as the equity or legality of the respective contestants' claims. The like sense of an inscrutable but spiritually necessary tendency in events is still traceable as an obscure element in current popular belief, as shown, for instance, by the well-accredited maxim, "Thrice is he armed who knows his quarrel just,"—a maxim which retains much of its significance for the average unreflecting person even in the civilized communities of today. The modern reminiscence of the belief in the *hamingia,* or in the guidance of an unseen hand, which is traceable in the acceptance of this maxim is faint and perhaps uncertain; and it seems in any case to be blended with other psychological moments that are not clearly of an animistic character.

For the purpose in hand it is unnecessary to look more closely into the psychological process or the ethnological line of descent by which the later of these two animistic apprehensions of propensity is derived from the earlier. This question may be of the gravest importance to folk-psychology or to the theory of the evolution of creeds and cults. The same is true of the more fundamental question whether the two are related at all as successive phases in a sequence of development. Reference is here made to the existence of these questions only to remark that the interest of the present discussion does not lie in that direction. So far as concerns economic theory, these two elements or phases of the belief in luck, or in an extra-causal trend or propensity in things, are of substantially the same character. They have an economic significance as habits of thought which affect the individual's habitual view of the facts and sequences with which he comes in contact, and which thereby affect the individual's serviceability for the industrial purpose. Therefore, apart from all question of the beauty, worth, or beneficence of any animistic belief, there is place for a discussion of their economic bearing on the serviceability of the individual as an economic factor, and especially as an industrial agent.

It has already been noted in an earlier connection, that in order to have the highest serviceability in the complex industrial processes of today, the individual must be endowed with the aptitude and the habit of readily apprehending and relating facts in terms of causal sequence. Both as a whole and in its details, the industrial process is a process of quantitative causation. The "intelligence" demanded of the workman, as well as of the director of an industrial process, is little else than a degree of facility in the apprehension of and adaptation to a quantitatively determined causal sequence. This facility of apprehension and adaptation is what is lacking in stupid workmen, and the growth of this facility is the end sought in their education—so far as their education aims to enhance their industrial efficiency.

In so far as the individual's inherited aptitudes or his training incline him to account for facts and sequences in other terms than those of causation or matter-of-fact, they lower his productive efficiency or industrial usefulness. This lowering of efficiency through a penchant for animistic methods of apprehending facts is especially apparent when taken in the mass—when a given population with an animistic turn is viewed as a whole. The economic drawbacks of animism are more patent and its consequences are more far-reaching under the modern system of large industry than under any other. In the modern industrial communities, industry is, to a constantly increasing extent, being organized in a comprehensive system of organs and functions mutually conditioning one another; and therefore freedom from all bias in the causal apprehension of phenomena grows constantly more requisite to efficiency on the part of the men concerned in industry. Under a system of handicraft an advantage in dexterity, diligence, muscular force, or endurance may, in a very large measure, offset such a bias in the habits of thought of the workmen.

Similarly in agricultural industry of the traditional kind, which closely resembles handicraft in the nature of the demands made upon the workman. In both, the workman is himself the prime mover chiefly depended upon, and the natural forces engaged are in large part apprehended as inscrutable and fortuitous agencies, whose working lies beyond the workman's control or discretion. In popular apprehension there is in these forms of industry relatively little of the industrial process left to the fateful swing of a comprehensive mechanical sequence which must be comprehended in terms of causation and to which the operations of industry and the movements of the workmen must be adapted. As industrial methods develop, the virtues of the handicraftsman count for less and less as an offset to scanty intelligence or a halting acceptance of the sequence of cause and effect. The industrial organization assumes more and more of the character of a mechanism, in which it is man's office to discriminate and select what natural forces shall work out their effects in his service. The workman's part in industry changes from that of a prime mover to that of discrimination and valuation of quantitative sequences and mechanical facts. The faculty of a ready apprehension and unbiased appreciation of causes in his environment grows in relative economic importance and any element in the complex of his habits of thought which intrudes a bias at variance with this ready appreciation of matter-of-fact sequence gains proportionately in importance as a disturbing element acting to lower his industrial usefulness. Through its cumulative effect upon the habitual attitude of the population, even a slight or inconspicuous bias towards accounting for everyday facts by recourse to other ground than that of quantitative causation may work an appreciable lowering of the collective industrial efficiency of a community.

The animistic habit of mind may occur in the early, undifferentiated form of an inchoate animistic belief, or in the later and more highly integrated phase in which there is an anthropomorphic personification of the propensity imputed to facts. The industrial value of such a lively animistic sense, or of such recourse to a preternatural agency or the guidance of an unseen hand, is of course very much the same in either case. As affects the industrial serviceability of the individual, the effect is of the same kind in either case; but the extent to which this habit of thought dominates or shapes the complex of his habits of thought varies with the degree of immediacy, urgency, or exclusiveness with which the individual habitually applies the animistic or anthropomorphic formula in dealing with the facts of his environment. The animistic habit acts in all cases to blur the appreciation of causal sequence; but the earlier, less reflected, less defined animistic sense of propensity may be expected to affect the intellectual processes of the individual in a more pervasive way than the higher forms of anthropomorphism. Where the animistic habit is present in the naive form, its scope and range of application are not defined or limited. It will therefore palpably affect his thinking at every turn of the person's life— wherever he has to do with the material means of life. In the later, maturer development of animism, after it has been defined through the process of anthropomorphic elaboration, when its application has been limited in a somewhat consistent fashion to the remote and the invisible, it comes about that an increasing range of everyday facts are provisionally accounted for without recourse to the preternatural agency in which a cultivated animism expresses itself. A highly integrated, personified preternatural agency is not a convenient means of handling the trivial occurrences of life, and a habit is therefore easily fallen into of accounting for many trivial or vulgar phenomena in terms of sequence. The provisional explanation so arrived at is by neglect allowed to stand as definitive, for trivial purposes, until special provocation or perplexity recalls the individual to his allegiance. But when special exigencies arise, that is to say, when there is peculiar need of a full and free recourse to the law of cause and effect, then the individual commonly has recourse to the preternatural agency as a universal solvent, if he is possessed of an anthropomorphic belief.

The extra-causal propensity or agent has a very high utility as a recourse in perplexity, but its utility is altogether of a non-economic kind. It is especially a refuge and a fund of comfort where it has attained the degree of consistency and specialization that belongs to an anthropomorphic divinity. It has much to commend it even on other grounds than that of affording the perplexed individual a means of escape from the difficulty of accounting for phenomena in terms of causal sequence. It would scarcely be in place here to dwell on the obvious and well-accepted merits of an anthropomorphic divinity, as seen from the point of view of the aesthetic, moral, or spiritual interest, or even as seen from the less remote standpoint of political, military, or social policy. The question here concerns the less picturesque and less urgent economic value of the belief in such a preternatural agency, taken as a habit of thought which affects the industrial serviceability of the believer. And even within this narrow, economic range, the inquiry is perforce confined to the immediate bearing of this habit of thought upon the believer's workmanlike serviceability, rather than extended to include its remoter economic effects. These remoter effects are very difficult to trace. The inquiry into them is so encumbered with current preconceptions as to the degree in which life is enhanced by spiritual contact with such a divinity, that any attempt to inquire into their economic value must for the present be fruitless.

The immediate, direct effect of the animistic habit of thought upon the general frame of mind of the believer goes in the direction of lowering his effective intelligence in the respect in which intelligence is of especial consequence for modern industry. The effect follows, in varying degree, whether the preternatural agent or propensity believed in is of a higher or a lower cast. This holds true of the barbarian's and the sporting man's sense of luck and propensity, and likewise of the somewhat higher developed belief in an anthropomorphic divinity, such as is commonly possessed by the same class. It must be taken to hold true also—though with what relative degree of cogency is not easy to say— of the more adequately developed anthropomorphic cults, such as appeal to the devout civilized man. The industrial disability entailed by a popular adherence to one of the higher anthropomorphic cults may be relatively slight, but it is not to be overlooked. And even these high-class cults of the Western culture do not represent the last dissolving phase of this human sense of extra-causal propensity. Beyond these the same animistic sense shows itself also in such attenuations of anthropomorphism as the eighteenth-century appeal to an order of nature and natural rights, and in their modern representative, the ostensibly post-Darwinian concept of a meliorative trend in the process of evolution.

This animistic explanation of phenomena is a form of the fallacy which the logicians knew by the name of *ignava ratio*. For the purposes of industry or of science it counts as a blunder in the apprehension and valuation of facts. Apart from its direct industrial consequences, the animistic habit has a certain significance for economic theory on other grounds. (1) It is a fairly reliable indication of the presence, and to some extent even of the degree of potency, of certain other archaic traits that accompany it and that are of substantial economic consequence; and (2) the material consequences of that code of devout proprieties to which the animistic habit gives rise in the development of an anthropomorphic cult are of importance both (a) as affecting the community's consumption of goods and the prevalent canons of taste, as already suggested in an earlier chapter, and (b) by inducing and conserving a certain habitual recognition of the relation to a superior, and so stiffening the current sense of status and allegiance.

As regards the point last named (b), that body of habits of thought which makes up the character of any individual is in some sense an organic whole. A marked variation in a given direction at any one point carries with it, as its correlative, a concomitant variation in the habitual expression of life in other directions or other groups of activities. These various habits of thought, or habitual expressions of life, are all phases of the single life sequence of the individual; therefore a habit formed in response to a given stimulus will necessarily affect the character of the response made to other stimuli. A modification of human nature at any one point is a modification of human nature as a whole. On this ground, and perhaps to a still greater extent on obscurer grounds that can not be discussed here, there are these concomitant variations as between the different traits of human nature. So, for instance, barbarian peoples with a well-developed predatory scheme of life are commonly also possessed of a strong prevailing animistic habit, a well formed anthropomorphic cult, and a lively sense of status. On the other hand, anthropomorphism and the realizing sense of an animistic propensity in material are less obtrusively present in the life of the peoples at the cultural stages which precede and which follow the barbarian culture. The sense of status is also feebler; on the whole, in peaceable communities. It is to be remarked that a lively, but slightly specialized, animistic belief is to be found in most if not all peoples living in the ante-predatory, savage stage of culture. The primitive savage takes his animism less seriously than the barbarian or the degenerate savage. With him it eventuates in fantastic myth-making, rather than in coercive superstition. The barbarian culture shows sportsmanship, status, and anthropomorphism. There is commonly observable a like concomitance of variations in the same respects in the individual temperament of men in the civilized communities of today. Those modern representatives of the predaceous barbarian temper that make up the sporting element are commonly believers in luck; at least they have a strong sense of an animistic propensity in things, by force of which they are given to gambling. So also as regards anthropomorphism in this class. Such of them as give in their adhesion to some creed commonly attach themselves to one of the naively and consistently anthropomorphic creeds; there are relatively few sporting men who seek spiritual comfort in the less anthropomorphic cults, such as the Unitarian or the Universalist.

Closely bound up with this correlation of anthropomorphism and prowess is the fact that anthropomorphic cults act to conserve, if not to initiate, habits of mind favorable to a regime of status. As regards this point, it is quite impossible to say where the disciplinary effect of the cult ends and where the evidence of a concomitance of variations in inherited traits begins. In their finest development, the predatory temperament, the sense of status, and the anthropomorphic cult all together belong to the barbarian culture; and something of a mutual causal relation subsists between the three phenomena as they come into sight in communities on that cultural level. The way in which they recur in correlation in the habits and attitudes of individuals and classes today goes far to imply a like causal or organic relation between the same psychological phenomena considered as traits or habits of the individual. It has appeared at an earlier point in the discussion that the relation of status, as a feature of social structure, is a consequence of the predatory habit of life. As regards its line of derivation, it is substantially an elaborated expression of the predatory attitude. On the other hand, an anthropomorphic cult is a code of detailed relations of status superimposed upon the concept of a preternatural, inscrutable propensity in material things. So that, as regards the external facts of its derivation, the cult may be taken as an outgrowth of archaic man's pervading animistic sense, defined and in some degree transformed by the predatory habit of life, the result being a personified preternatural agency, which is by imputation endowed with a full complement of the habits of thought that characterize the man of the predatory culture.

The grosser psychological features in the case, which have an immediate bearing on economic theory and are consequently to be taken account of here, are therefore: (a) as has appeared in an earlier chapter, the predatory, emulative habit of mind here called prowess is but the barbarian variant of the generically human instinct of workmanship, which has fallen into this specific form under the guidance of a habit of invidious comparison of persons; (b) the relation of status is a formal expression of such an invidious comparison duly gauged and graded according to a sanctioned schedule; (c) an anthropomorphic cult, in the days of its early vigor at least, is an institution the characteristic element of which is a relation of status between the human subject as inferior and the personified preternatural agency as superior. With this in mind, there should be no difficulty in recognizing the intimate relation which subsists between these three phenomena of human nature and of human life; the relation amounts to an identity in some of their substantial elements. On the one hand, the system of status and the predatory habit of life are an expression of the instinct of workmanship as it takes form under a custom of invidious comparison; on the other hand, the anthropomorphic cult and the habit of devout observances are an expression of men's animistic sense of a propensity in material things, elaborated under the guidance of substantially the same general habit of invidious comparison. The two categories—the emulative habit of life and the habit of devout observances—are therefore to be taken as complementary elements of the barbarian type of human nature and of its modern barbarian variants. They are expressions of much the same range of aptitudes, made in response to different sets of stimuli.

CHAPTER TWELVE

Devout Observances

A discoursive rehearsal of certain incidents of modern life will show the organic relation of the anthropomorphic cults to the barbarian culture and temperament. It will likewise serve to show how the survival and efficacy of the cults and the prevalence of their schedule of devout observances are related to the institution of a leisure class and to the springs of action underlying that institution. Without any intention to commend or to deprecate the practices to be spoken of under the head of devout observances, or the spiritual and intellectual traits of which these observances are the expression, the everyday phenomena of current anthropomorphic cults may be taken up from the point of view of the interest which they have for economic theory. What can properly be spoken of here are the tangible, external features of devout observances. The moral, as well as the devotional value of the life of faith lies outside of the scope of the present inquiry. Of course no question is here entertained as to the truth or beauty of the creeds on which the cults proceed. And even their remoter economic bearing can not be taken up here; the subject is too recondite and of too grave import to find a place in so slight a sketch.

Something has been said in an earlier chapter as to the influence which pecuniary standards of value exert upon the processes of valuation carried out on other bases, not related to the pecuniary interest. The relation is not altogether one-sided. The economic standards or canons of valuation are in their turn influenced by extra-economic standards of value. Our judgments of the economic bearing of facts are to some extent shaped by the dominant presence of these weightier interests. There is a point of view, indeed, from which the economic interest is of weight only as being ancillary to these higher, non-economic interests. For the present purpose, therefore, some thought must be taken to isolate the economic interest or the economic hearing of these phenomena of anthropomorphic cults. It takes some effort to divest oneself of the more serious point of view, and to reach an economic appreciation of these facts, with as little as may be of the bias due to higher interests extraneous to economic theory. In the discussion of the sporting temperament, it has appeared that the sense of an animistic propensity in material things and events is what affords the spiritual basis of the sporting man's gambling habit. For the economic purpose, this sense of propensity is substantially the same psychological element as expresses itself, under a variety of forms, in animistic beliefs and anthropomorphic creeds. So far as concerns those tangible psychological features with which economic theory has to deal, the gambling spirit which pervades the sporting element shades off by insensible gradations into that frame of mind which finds gratification in devout observances. As seen from the point of view of economic theory, the sporting character shades off into the character of a religious devotee. Where the betting man's animistic sense is helped out by a somewhat consistent tradition, it has developed into a more or less articulate belief in a preternatural or hyperphysical agency, with something of an anthropomorphic content. And where this is the case, there is commonly a perceptible inclination to make terms with the preternatural agency by some approved method of approach and conciliation. This element of propitiation and cajoling has much in common with the crasser forms of worship—if not in historical derivation, at least in actual psychological content. It obviously shades off in unbroken continuity into what is recognized as superstitious practice and belief, and so asserts its claim to kinship with the grosser anthropomorphic cults.

The sporting or gambling temperament, then, comprises some of the substantial psychological elements that go to make a believer in creeds and an observer of devout forms, the chief point of coincidence being the belief in an inscrutable propensity or a preternatural interposition in the sequence of events. For the purpose of the gambling practice the belief in preternatural agency may be, and ordinarily is, less closely formulated, especially as regards the habits of thought and the scheme of life imputed to the preternatural agent; or, in other words, as regards his moral character and his purposes in interfering in events. With respect to the individuality or personality of the agency whose presence as luck, or chance, or hoodoo, or mascot, etc., he feels and sometimes dreads and endeavors to evade, the sporting man's views are also less specific, less integrated and differentiated. The basis of his gambling activity is, in great measure, simply an instinctive sense of the presence of a pervasive extraphysical and arbitrary force or propensity in things or situations, which is scarcely recognized as a personal agent. The betting man is not infrequently both a believer in luck, in this naive sense, and at the same time a pretty staunch adherent of some form of accepted creed. He is especially prone to accept so much of the creed as concerns the inscrutable power and the arbitrary habits of the divinity which has won his confidence. In such a case he is possessed of two, or sometimes more than two, distinguishable phases of animism. Indeed, the complete series of successive phases of animistic belief is to be found unbroken in the spiritual furniture of any sporting community. Such a chain of animistic conceptions will comprise the most elementary form of an instinctive sense of luck and chance and fortuitous necessity at one end of the series, together with the perfectly developed anthropomorphic divinity at the other end, with all intervening stages of integration. Coupled with these beliefs in preternatural agency goes an instinctive shaping of conduct to conform with the surmised requirements of the lucky chance on the one hand, and a more or less devout submission to the inscrutable decrees of the divinity on the other hand.

There is a relationship in this respect between the sporting temperament and the temperament of the delinquent classes; and the two are related to the temperament which inclines to an anthropomorphic cult. Both the delinquent and the sporting man are on the average more apt to be adherents of some accredited creed, and are also rather more inclined to devout observances, than the general average of the community. It is also noticeable that unbelieving members of these classes show more of a proclivity to become proselytes to some accredited faith than the average of unbelievers. This fact of observation is avowed by the spokesmen of sports, especially in apologizing for the more naively predatory athletic sports. Indeed, it is somewhat insistently claimed as a meritorious feature of sporting life that the habitual participants in athletic games are in some degree peculiarly given to devout practices. And it is observable that the cult to which sporting men and the predaceous delinquent classes adhere, or to which proselytes from these classes commonly attach themselves, is ordinarily not one of the so-called higher faiths, but a cult which has to do with a thoroughly anthropomorphic divinity. Archaic, predatory human nature is not satisfied with abstruse conceptions of a dissolving personality that shades off into the concept of quantitative causal sequence, such as the speculative, esoteric creeds of Christendom impute to the First Cause, Universal Intelligence, World Soul, or Spiritual Aspect. As an instance of a cult of the character which the habits of mind of the athlete and the delinquent require, may be cited that branch of the church militant known as the Salvation Army. This is to some extent recruited from the lower-class delinquents, and it appears to comprise also, among its officers especially, a larger proportion of men with a sporting record than the proportion of such men in the aggregate population of the community.

College athletics afford a case in point. It is contended by exponents of the devout element in college life—and there seems to be no ground for disputing the claim—that the desirable athletic material afforded by any student body in this country is at the same time predominantly religious; or that it is at least given to devout observances to a greater degree than the average of those students whose interest in athletics and other college sports is less. This is what might be expected on theoretical grounds. It may be remarked, by the way, that from one point of view this is felt to reflect credit on the college sporting life, on athletic games, and on those persons who occupy themselves with these matters. It happens not frequently that college sporting men devote themselves to religious propaganda, either as a vocation or as a by-occupation; and it is observable that when this happens they are likely to become propagandists of some one of the more anthropomorphic cults. In their teaching they are apt to insist chiefly on the personal relation of status which subsists between an anthropomorphic divinity and the human subject.

This intimate relation between athletics and devout observance among college men is a fact of sufficient notoriety; but it has a special feature to which attention has not been called, although it is obvious enough. The religious zeal which pervades much of the college sporting element is especially prone to express itself in an unquestioning devoutness and a naive and complacent submission to an inscrutable Providence. It therefore by preference seeks affiliation with some one of those lay religious organizations which occupy themselves with the spread of the exoteric forms of faith—as, e.g., the Young Men's Christian Association or the Young People's Society for Christian Endeavor. These lay bodies are organized to further "practical" religion; and as if to enforce the argument and firmly establish the close relationship between the sporting temperament and the archaic devoutness, these lay religious bodies commonly devote some appreciable portion of their energies to the furtherance of athletic contests and similar games of chance and skill. It might even be said that sports of this kind are apprehended to have some efficacy as a means of grace. They are apparently useful as a means of proselyting, and as a means of sustaining the devout attitude in converts once made. That is to say, the games which give exercise to the animistic sense and to the emulative propensity help to form and to conserve that habit of mind to which the more exoteric cults are congenial. Hence, in the hands of the lay organizations, these sporting activities come to do duty as a novitiate or a means of induction into that fuller unfolding of the life of spiritual status which is the privilege of the full communicant along.

That the exercise of the emulative and lower animistic proclivities are substantially useful for the devout purpose seems to be placed beyond question by the fact that the priesthood of many denominations is following the lead of the lay organizations in this respect.

Those ecclesiastical organizations especially which stand nearest the lay organizations in their insistence on practical religion have gone some way towards adopting these or analogous practices in connection with the traditional devout observances. So there are "boys' brigades," and other organizations, under clerical sanction, acting to develop the emulative proclivity and the sense of status in the youthful members of the congregation. These pseudo-military organizations tend to elaborate and accentuate the proclivity to emulation and invidious comparison, and so strengthen the native facility for discerning and approving the relation of personal mastery and subservience. And a believer is eminently a person who knows how to obey and accept chastisement with good grace. But the habits of thought which these practices foster and conserve make up but one half of the substance of the anthropomorphic cults. The other, complementary element of devout life—the animistic habit of mind—is recruited and conserved by a second range of practices organized under clerical sanction. These are the class of gambling practices of which the church bazaar or raffle may be taken as the type. As indicating the degree of legitimacy of these practices in connection with devout observances proper, it is to be remarked that these raffles, and the like trivial opportunities for gambling, seem to appeal with more effect to the common run of the members of religious organizations than they do to persons of a less devout habit of mind.

All this seems to argue, on the one hand, that the same temperament inclines people to sports as inclines them to the anthropomorphic cults, and on the other hand that the habituation to sports, perhaps especially to athletic sports, acts to develop the propensities which find satisfaction in devout observances. Conversely; it also appears that habituation to these observances favors the growth of a proclivity for athletic sports and for all games that give play to the habit of invidious comparison and of the appeal to luck. Substantially the same range of propensities finds expression in both these directions of the spiritual life. That barbarian human nature in which the predatory instinct and the animistic standpoint predominate is normally prone to both. The predatory habit of mind involves an accentuated sense of personal dignity and of the relative standing of individuals. The social structure in which the predatory habit has been the dominant factor in the shaping of institutions is a structure based on status. The pervading norm in the predatory community's scheme of life is the relation of superior and inferior, noble and base, dominant and subservient persons and classes, master and slave. The anthropomorphic cults have come down from that stage of industrial development and have been shaped by the same scheme of economic differentiation—a differentiation into consumer and producer—and they are pervaded by the same dominant principle of mastery and subservience. The cults impute to their divinity the habits of thought answering to the stage of economic differentiation at which the cults took shape. The anthropomorphic divinity is conceived to be punctilious in all questions of precedence and is prone to an assertion of mastery and an arbitrary exercise of power—an habitual resort to force as the final arbiter.

In the later and maturer formulations of the anthropomorphic creed this imputed habit of dominance on the part of a divinity of awful presence and inscrutable power is chastened into "the fatherhood of God." The spiritual attitude and the aptitudes imputed to the preternatural agent are still such as belong under the regime of status, but they now assume the patriarchal cast characteristic of the quasi-peaceable stage of culture. Still it is to be noted that even in this advanced phase of the cult the observances in which devoutness finds expression consistently aim to propitiate the divinity by extolling his greatness and glory and by professing subservience and fealty. The act of propitiation or of worship is designed to appeal to a sense of status imputed to the inscrutable power that is thus approached. The propitiatory formulas most in vogue are still such as carry or imply an invidious comparison. A loyal attachment to the person of an anthropomorphic divinity endowed with such an archaic human nature implies the like archaic propensities in the devotee. For the purposes of economic theory, the relation of fealty, whether to a physical or to an extraphysical person, is to be taken as a variant of that personal subservience which makes up so large a share of the predatory and the quasi-peaceable scheme of life.

The barbarian conception of the divinity, as a warlike chieftain inclined to an overbearing manner of government, has been greatly softened through the milder manners and the soberer habits of life that characterize those cultural phases which lie between the early predatory stage and the present. But even after this chastening of the devout fancy, and the consequent mitigation of the harsher traits of conduct and character that are currently imputed to the divinity, there still remains in the popular apprehension of the divine nature and temperament a very substantial residue of the barbarian conception. So it comes about, for instance, that in characterizing the divinity and his relations to the process of human life, speakers and writers are still able to make effective use of similes borrowed from the vocabulary of war and of the predatory manner of life, as well as of locutions which involve an invidious comparison. Figures of speech of this import are used with good effect even in addressing the less warlike modern audiences, made up of adherents of the blander variants of the creed. This effective use of barbarian epithets and terms of comparison by popular speakers argues that the modern generation has retained a lively appreciation of the dignity and merit of the barbarian virtues; and it argues also that there is a degree of congruity between the devout attitude and the predatory habit of mind. It is only on second thought, if at all, that the devout fancy of modern worshippers revolts at the imputation of ferocious and vengeful emotions and actions to the object of their adoration. It is a matter of common observation that sanguinary epithets applied to the divinity have a high aesthetic and honorific value in the popular apprehension. That is to say, suggestions which these epithets carry are very acceptable to our unreflecting apprehension.

> Mine eyes have seen the glory of the coming of the Lord:
> He is trampling out the vintage where the grapes of wrath are stored;
> He hath loosed the fateful lightning of his terrible swift sword;
> His truth is marching on.

The guiding habits of thought of a devout person move on the plane of an archaic scheme of life which has outlived much of its usefulness for the economic exigencies of the collective life of today. In so far as the economic organization fits the exigencies of the collective life of today, it has outlived the regime of status, and has no use and no place for a relation of personal subserviency. So far as concerns the economic efficiency of the community, the sentiment of personal fealty, and the general habit of mind of which that sentiment is an expression, are survivals which cumber the ground and hinder an adequate adjustment of human institutions to the existing situation. The habit of mind which best lends itself to the purposes of a peaceable, industrial community, is that matter-of-fact temper which recognizes the value of material facts simply as opaque items in the mechanical sequence. It is that frame of mind which does not instinctively impute an animistic propensity to things, nor resort to preternatural intervention as an explanation of perplexing phenomena, nor depend on an unseen hand to shape the course of events to human use. To meet the requirements of the highest economic efficiency under modern conditions, the world process must habitually be apprehended in terms of quantitative, dispassionate force and sequence.

As seen from the point of view of the later economic exigencies, devoutness is, perhaps in all cases, to be looked upon as a survival from an earlier phase of associated life—a mark of arrested spiritual development. Of course it remains true that in a community where the economic structure is still substantially a system of status; where the attitude of the average of persons in the community is consequently shaped by and adapted to the relation of personal dominance and personal subservience; or where for any other reason—of tradition or of inherited aptitude—the population as a whole is strongly inclined to devout observances; there a devout habit of mind in any individual, not in excess of the average of the community, must be taken simply as a detail of the prevalent habit of life. In this light, a devout individual in a devout community can not be called a case of reversion, since he is abreast of the average of the community. But as seen from the point of view of the modern industrial situation, exceptional devoutness—devotional zeal that rises appreciably above the average pitch of devoutness in the community—may safely be set down as in all cases an atavistic trait.

It is, of course, equally legitimate to consider these phenomena from a different point of view. They may be appreciated for a different purpose, and the characterization here offered may be turned about. In speaking from the point of view of the devotional interest, or the interest of devout taste, it may, with equal cogency, be said that the spiritual attitude bred in men by the modern industrial life is unfavorable to a free development of the life of faith. It might fairly be objected to the later development of the industrial process that its discipline tends to "materialism," to the elimination of filial piety. From the aesthetic point of view, again, something to a similar purport might be said. But, however legitimate and valuable these and the like reflections may be for their purpose, they would not be in place in the present inquiry, which is exclusively concerned with the valuation of these phenomena from the economic point of view.

The grave economic significance of the anthropomorphic habit of mind and of the addiction to devout observances must serve as apology for speaking further on a topic which it can not but be distasteful to discuss at all as an economic phenomenon in a community so devout as ours. Devout observances are of economic importance as an index of a concomitant variation of temperament, accompanying the predatory habit of mind and so indicating the presence of industrially disserviceable traits. They indicate the presence of a mental attitude which has a certain economic value of its own by virtue of its influence upon the industrial serviceability of the individual. But they are also of importance more directly, in modifying the economic activities of the community, especially as regards the distribution and consumption of goods.

The most obvious economic bearing of these observances is seen in the devout consumption of goods and services. The consumption of ceremonial paraphernalia required by any cult, in the way of shrines, temples, churches, vestments, sacrifices, sacraments, holiday attire, etc., serves no immediate material end. All this material apparatus may, therefore, without implying deprecation, be broadly characterized as items of conspicuous waste. The like is true in a general way of the personal service consumed under this head; such as priestly education, priestly service, pilgrimages, fasts, holidays, household devotions, and the like. At the same time the observances in the execution of which this consumption takes place serve to extend and protract the vogue of those habits of thought on which an anthropomorphic cult rests. That is to say, they further the habits of thought characteristic of the regime of status. They are in so far an obstruction to the most effective organization of industry under modern circumstances; and are, in the first instance, antagonistic to the development of economic institutions in the direction required by the situation of today. For the present purpose, the indirect as well as the direct effects of this consumption are of the nature of a curtailment of the community's economic efficiency. In economic theory, then, and considered in its proximate consequences, the consumption of goods and effort in the service of an anthropomorphic divinity means a lowering of the vitality of the community. What may be the remoter, indirect, moral effects of this class of consumption does not admit of a succinct answer, and it is a question which can not be taken up here.

It will be to the point, however, to note the general economic character of devout consumption, in comparison with consumption for other purposes. An indication of the range of motives and purposes from which devout consumption of goods proceeds will help toward an appreciation of the value both of this consumption itself and of the general habit of mind to which it is congenial. There is a striking parallelism, if not rather a substantial identity of motive, between the consumption which goes to the service of an anthropomorphic divinity and that which goes to the service of a gentleman of leisure chieftain or patriarch—in the upper class of society during the barbarian culture. Both in the case of the chieftain and in that of the divinity there are expensive edifices set apart for the behoof of the person served. These edifices, as well as the properties which supplement them in the service, must not be common in kind or grade; they always show a large element of conspicuous waste. It may also be noted that the devout edifices are invariably of an archaic cast in their structure and fittings. So also the servants, both of the chieftain and of the divinity, must appear in the presence clothed in garments of a special, ornate character. The characteristic economic feature of this apparel is a more than ordinarily accentuated conspicuous waste, together with the secondary feature— more accentuated in the case of the priestly servants than in that of the servants or courtiers of the barbarian potentate—that this court dress must always be in some degree of an archaic fashion. Also the garments worn by the lay members of the community when they come into the presence, should be of a more expensive kind than their everyday apparel. Here, again, the parallelism between the usage of the chieftain's audience hall and that of the sanctuary is fairly well marked. In this respect there is required a certain ceremonial "cleanness" of attire, the essential feature of which, in the economic respect, is that the garments worn on these occasions should carry as little suggestion as may be of any industrial occupation or of any habitual addiction to such employments as are of material use.

This requirement of conspicuous waste and of ceremonial cleanness from the traces of industry extends also to the apparel, and in a less degree to the food, which is consumed on sacred holidays; that is to say, on days set apart—taboo—for the divinity or for some member of the lower ranks of the preternatural leisure class. In economic theory, sacred holidays are obviously to be construed as a season of vicarious leisure performed for the divinity or saint in whose name the taboo is imposed and to whose good repute the abstention from useful effort on these days is conceived to inure. The characteristic feature of all such seasons of devout vicarious leisure is a more or less rigid taboo on all activity that is of human use. In the case of fast-days the conspicuous abstention from gainful occupations and from all pursuits that (materially) further human life is further accentuated by compulsory abstinence from such consumption as would conduce to the comfort or the fullness of life of the consumer.

It may be remarked, parenthetically, that secular holidays are of the same origin, by slightly remoter derivation. They shade off by degrees from the genuinely sacred days, through an intermediate class of semi-sacred birthdays of kings and great men who have been in some measure canonized, to the deliberately invented holiday set apart to further the good repute of some notable event or some striking fact, to which it is intended to do honor, or the good fame of which is felt to be in need of repair. The remoter refinement in the employment of vicarious leisure as a means of augmenting the good repute of a phenomenon or datum is seen at its best in its very latest application. A day of vicarious leisure has in some communities been set apart as Labor Day. This observance is designed to augment the prestige of the fact of labor, by the archaic, predatory method of a compulsory abstention from useful effort. To this datum of labor-in-general is imputed the good repute attributable to the pecuniary strength put in evidence by abstaining from labor. Sacred holidays, and holidays generally, are of the nature of a tribute levied on the body of the people. The tribute is paid in vicarious leisure, and the honorific effect which emerges is imputed to the person or the fact for whose good repute the holiday has been instituted. Such a tithe of vicarious leisure is a perquisite of all members of the preternatural leisure class and is indispensable to their good fame. *Un saint qu'on ne chôme pas* is indeed a saint fallen on evil days.

Besides this tithe of vicarious leisure levied on the laity, there are also special classes of persons—the various grades of priests and hierodules—whose time is wholly set apart for a similar service. It is not only incumbent on the priestly class to abstain from vulgar labor, especially so far as it is lucrative or is apprehended to contribute to the temporal well-being of mankind. The taboo in the case of the priestly class goes farther and adds a refinement in the form of an injunction against their seeking worldly gain even where it may be had without debasing application to industry. It is felt to be unworthy of the servant of the divinity, or rather unworthy the dignity of the divinity whose servant he is, that he should seek material gain or take thought for temporal matters. "Of all contemptible things a man who pretends to be a priest of God and is a priest to his own comforts and ambitions is the most contemptible." There is a line of discrimination, which a cultivated taste in matters of devout observance finds little difficulty in drawing, between such actions and conduct as conduce to the fullness of human life and such as conduce to the good fame of the anthropomorphic divinity; and the activity of the priestly class, in the ideal barbarian scheme, falls wholly on the hither side of this line. What falls within the range of economics falls below the proper level of solicitude of the priesthood in its best estate. Such apparent exceptions to this rule as are afforded, for instance, by some of the medieval orders of monks (the members of which actually labored to some useful end), scarcely impugn the rule. These outlying orders of the priestly class are not a sacerdotal element in the full sense of the term. And it is noticeable also that these doubtfully sacerdotal orders, which countenanced their members in earning a living, fell into disrepute through offending the sense of propriety in the communities where they existed.

The priest should not put his hand to mechanically productive work; but he should consume in large measure. But even as regards his consumption it is to be noted that it should take such forms as do not obviously conduce to his own comfort or fullness of life; it should conform to the rules governing vicarious consumption, as explained under that head in an earlier chapter. It is not ordinarily in good form for the priestly class to appear well fed or in hilarious spirits. Indeed, in many of the more elaborate cults the injunction against other than vicarious consumption by this class frequently goes so far as to enjoin mortification of the flesh. And even in those modern denominations which have been organized under the latest formulations of the creed, in a modern industrial community, it is felt that all levity and avowed zest in the enjoyment of the good things of this world is alien to the true clerical decorum. Whatever suggests that these servants of an invisible master are living a life, not of devotion to their master's good fame, but of application to their own ends, jars harshly on our sensibilities as something fundamentally and eternally wrong. They are a servant class, although, being servants of a very exalted master, they rank high in the social scale by virtue of this borrowed light. Their consumption is vicarious consumption; and since, in the advanced cults, their master has no need of material gain, their occupation is vicarious leisure in the full sense. "Whether therefore ye eat, or drink, or whatsoever ye do, do all to the glory of God." It may be added that so far as the laity is assimilated to the priesthood in the respect that they are conceived to be servants of the divinity. So far this imputed vicarious character attaches also to the layman's life. The range of application of this corollary is somewhat wide. It applies especially to such movements for the reform or rehabilitation of the religious life as are of an austere, pietistic, ascetic cast—where the human subject is conceived to hold his life by a direct servile tenure from his spiritual sovereign. That is to say, where the institution of the priesthood lapses, or where there is an exceptionally lively sense of the immediate and masterful presence of the divinity in the affairs of life, there the layman is conceived to stand in an immediate servile relation to the divinity, and his life is construed to be a performance of vicarious leisure directed to the enhancement of his master's repute. In such cases of reversion there is a return to the unmediated relation of sub-servience, as the dominant fact of the devout attitude. The emphasis is thereby thrown on an austere and discomforting vicarious leisure, to the neglect of conspicuous consumption as a means of grace.

A doubt will present itself as to the full legitimacy of this characterization of the sacerdotal scheme of life, on the ground that a considerable proportion of the modern priesthood departs from the scheme in many details. The scheme does not hold good for the clergy of those denominations which have in some measure diverged from the old established schedule of beliefs or observances. These take thought, at least ostensibly or permissively, for the temporal welfare of the laity, as well as for their own. Their manner of life, not only in the privacy of their own household, but often even before the public, does not differ in an extreme degree from that of secular-minded persons, either in its ostensible austerity or in the archaism of its apparatus. This is truest for those denominations that have wandered the farthest. To this objection it is to be said that we have here to do not with a discrepancy in the theory of sacerdotal life, but with an imperfect conformity to the scheme on the part of this body of clergy. They are but a partial and imperfect representative of the priesthood, and must not be taken as exhibiting the sacerdotal scheme of life in an authentic and competent manner. The clergy of the sects and denominations might be characterized as a half-caste priesthood, or a priesthood in process of becoming or of reconstitution. Such a priesthood may be expected to show the characteristics of the sacerdotal office only as blended and obscured with alien motives and traditions, due to the disturbing presence of other factors than those of animism and status in the purposes of the organizations to which this non-conforming fraction of the priesthood belongs.

Appeal may be taken direct to the taste of any person with a discriminating and cultivated sense of the sacerdotal proprieties, or to the prevalent sense of what constitutes clerical decorum in any community at all accustomed to think or to pass criticism on what a clergyman may or may not do without blame. Even in the most extremely secularized denominations, there is some sense of a distinction that should be observed between the sacerdotal and the lay scheme of life. There is no person of sensibility but feels that where the members of this denominational or sectarian clergy depart from traditional usage, in the direction of a less austere or less archaic demeanor and apparel, they are departing from the ideal of priestly decorum. There is probably no community and no sect within the range of the Western culture in which the bounds of permissible indulgence are not drawn appreciably closer for the incumbent of the priestly office than for the common layman. If the priest's own sense of sacerdotal propriety does not effectually impose a limit, the prevalent sense of the proprieties on the part of the community will commonly assert itself so obtrusively as to lead to his conformity or his retirement from office.

Few if any members of any body of clergy, it may be added, would avowedly seek an increase of salary for gain's sake; and if such avowal were openly made by a clergyman, it would be found obnoxious to the sense of propriety among his congregation. It may also be noted in this connection that no one but the scoffers and the very obtuse are not instinctively grieved inwardly at a jest from the pulpit; and that there are none whose respect for their pastor does not suffer through any mark of levity on his part in any conjuncture of life, except it be levity of a palpably histrionic kind—a constrained unbending of dignity. The diction proper to the sanctuary and to the priestly office should also carry little if any suggestion of effective everyday life, and should not draw upon the vocabulary of modern trade or industry. Likewise, one's sense of the proprieties is readily offended by too detailed and intimate a handling of industrial and other purely human questions at the hands of the clergy. There is a certain level of generality below which a cultivated sense of the proprieties in homiletical discourse will not permit a well-bred clergyman to decline in his discussion of temporal interests. These matters that are of human and secular consequence simply, should properly be handled with such a degree of generality and aloofness as may imply that the speaker represents a master whose interest in secular affairs goes only so far as to permissively countenance them.

It is further to be noticed that the non-conforming sects and variants whose priesthood is here under discussion, vary among themselves in the degree of their conformity to the ideal scheme of sacerdotal life. In a general way it will be found that the divergence in this respect is widest in the case of the relatively young denominations, and especially in the case of such of the newer denominations as have chiefly a lower middle-class constituency. They commonly show a large admixture of humanitarian, philanthropic, or other motives which can not be classed as expressions of the devotional attitude; such as the desire of learning or of conviviality, which enter largely into the effective interest shown by members of these organizations. The non-conforming or sectarian movements have commonly proceeded from a mixture of motives, some of which are at variance with that sense of status on which the priestly office rests. Sometimes, indeed, the motive has been in good part a revulsion against a system of status. Where this is the case the institution of the priesthood has broken down in the transition, at least partially. The spokesman of such an organization is at the outset a servant and representative of the organization, rather than a member of a special priestly class and the spokesman of a divine master. And it is only by a process of gradual specialization that, in succeeding generations, this spokesman regains the position of priest, with a full investiture of sacerdotal authority, and with its accompanying austere, archaic and vicarious manner of life. The like is true of the breakdown and reintegration of devout ritual after such a revulsion. The priestly office, the scheme of sacerdotal life, and the schedule of devout observances are rehabilitated only gradually, insensibly, and with more or less variation in details, as a persistent human sense of devout propriety reasserts its primacy in questions touching the interest in the preternatural—and it may be added, as the organization increases in wealth, and so acquires more of the point of view and the habits of thought of a leisure class.

Beyond the priestly class, and ranged in an ascending hierarchy, ordinarily comes a superhuman vicarious leisure class of saints, angels, etc.—or their equivalents in the ethnic cults. These rise in grade, one above another, according to elaborate system of status. The principle of status runs through the entire hierarchical system, both visible and invisible. The good fame of these several orders of the supernatural hierarchy also commonly requires a certain tribute of vicarious consumption and vicarious leisure. In many cases they accordingly have devoted to their service sub-orders of attendants or dependents who perform a vicarious leisure for them, after much the same fashion as was found in an earlier chapter to be true of the dependent leisure class under the patriarchal system.

It may not appear without reflection how these devout observances and the peculiarity of temperament which they imply, or the consumption of goods and services which is comprised in the cult, stand related to the leisure class of a modern community, or to the economic motives of which that class is the exponent in the modern scheme of life to this end a summary review of certain facts bearing on this relation will be useful. It appears from an earlier passage in this discussion that for the purpose of the collective life of today, especially so far as concerns the industrial efficiency of the modern community, the characteristic traits of the devout temperament are a hindrance rather than a help. It should accordingly be found that the modern industrial life tends selectively to eliminate these traits of human nature from the spiritual constitution of the classes that are immediately engaged in the industrial process. It should hold true, approximately, that devoutness is declining or tending to obsolescence among the members of what may be called the effective industrial community. At the same time it should appear that this aptitude or habit survives in appreciably greater vigor among those classes which do not immediately or primarily enter into the community's life process as an industrial factor.

It has already been pointed out that these latter classes, which live by, rather than in, the industrial process, are roughly comprised under two categories (1) the leisure class proper, which is shielded from the stress of the economic situation; and (2) the indigent classes, including the lower-class delinquents, which are unduly exposed to the stress. In the case of the former class an archaic habit of mind persists because no effectual economic pressure constrains this class to an adaptation of its habits of thought to the changing situation; while in the latter the reason for a failure to adjust their habits of thought to the altered requirements of industrial efficiency is innutrition, absence of such surplus of energy as is needed in order to make the adjustment with facility, together with a lack of opportunity to acquire and become habituated to the modern point of view. The trend of the selective process runs in much the same direction in both cases.

From the point of view which the modern industrial life inculcates, phenomena are habitually subsumed under the quantitative relation of mechanical sequence. The indigent classes not only fall short of the modicum of leisure necessary in order to appropriate and assimilate the more recent generalizations of science which this point of view involves, but they also ordinarily stand in such a relation of personal dependence or subservience to their pecuniary superiors as materially to retard their emancipation from habits of thought proper to the regime of status. The result is that these classes in some measure retain that general habit of mind the chief expression of which is a strong sense of personal status, and of which devoutness is one feature.

In the older communities of the European culture, the hereditary leisure class, together with the mass of the indigent population, are given to devout observances in an appreciably higher degree than the average of the industrious middle class, wherever a considerable class of the latter character exists. But in some of these countries, the two categories of conservative humanity named above comprise virtually the whole population. Where these two classes greatly preponderate, their bent shapes popular sentiment to such an extent as to bear down any possible divergent tendency in the inconsiderable middle class, and imposes a devout attitude upon the whole community.

This must, of course, not be construed to say that such communities or such classes as are exceptionally prone to devout observances tend to conform in any exceptional degree to the specifications of any code of morals that we may be accustomed to associate with this or that confession of faith. A large measure of the devout habit of mind need not carry with it a strict observance of the injunctions of the Decalogue or of the common law.

Indeed, it is becoming somewhat of a commonplace with observers of criminal life in European communities that the criminal and dissolute classes are, if anything, rather more devout, and more naively so, than the average of the population. It is among those who constitute the pecuniary middle class and the body of law-abiding citizens that a relative exemption from the devotional attitude is to be looked for. Those who best appreciate the merits of the higher creeds and observances would object to all this and say that the devoutness of the low-class delinquents is a spurious, or at the best a superstitious devoutness; and the point is no doubt well taken and goes directly and cogently to the purpose intended. But for the purpose of the present inquiry these extra-economic, extra-psychological distinctions must perforce be neglected, however valid and however decisive they may be for the purpose for which they are made.

What has actually taken place with regard to class emancipation from the habit of devout observance is shown by the latter-day complaint of the clergy—that the churches are losing the sympathy of the artisan classes, and are losing their hold upon them. At the same time it is currently believed that the middle class, commonly so called, is also falling away in the cordiality of its support of the church, especially so far as regards the adult male portion of that class. These are currently recognized phenomena, and it might seem that a simple reference to these facts should sufficiently substantiate the general position outlined. Such an appeal to the general phenomena of popular church attendance and church membership may be sufficiently convincing for the proposition here advanced. But it will still be to the purpose to trace in some detail the course of events and the particular forces which have wrought this change in the spiritual attitude of the more advanced industrial communities of today. It will serve to illustrate the manner in which economic causes work towards a secularization of men's habits of thought. In this respect the American community should afford an exceptionally convincing illustration, since this community has been the least trammeled by external circumstances of any equally important industrial aggregate.

After making due allowance for exceptions and sporadic departures from the normal, the situation here at the present time may be summarized quite briefly. As a general rule the classes that are low in economic efficiency, or in intelligence, or both, are peculiarly devout—as, for instance, the Negro population of the South, much of the lower-class foreign population, much of the rural population, especially in those sections which are backward in education, in the stage of development of their industry, or in respect of their industrial contact with the rest of the community. So also such fragments as we possess of a specialized or hereditary indigent class, or of a segregated criminal or dissolute class; although among these latter the devout habit of mind is apt to take the form of a naive animistic belief in luck and in the efficacy of shamanistic practices perhaps more frequently than it takes the form of a formal adherence to any accredited creed. The artisan class, on the other hand, is notoriously falling away from the accredited anthropomorphic creeds and from all devout observances. This class is in an especial degree exposed to the characteristic intellectual and spiritual stress of modern organized industry, which requires a constant recognition of the undisguised phenomena of impersonal, matter-of-fact sequence and an unreserved conformity to the law of cause and effect. This class is at the same time not underfed nor over-worked to such an extent as to leave no margin of energy for the work of adaptation.

The case of the lower or doubtful leisure class in America—the middle class commonly so called—is somewhat peculiar. It differs in respect of its devotional life from its European counterpart, but it differs in degree and method rather than in substance. The churches still have the pecuniary support of this class; although the creeds to which the class adheres with the greatest facility are relatively poor in anthropomorphic content. At the same time the effective middle-class congregation tends, in many cases, more or less remotely perhaps, to become a congregation of women and minors. There is an appreciable lack of devotional fervor among the adult males of the middle class, although to a considerable extent there survives among them a certain complacent, reputable assent to the outlines of the accredited creed under which they were born. Their everyday life is carried on in a more or less close contact with the industrial process.

This peculiar sexual differentiation, which tends to delegate devout observances to the women and their children, is due, at least in part, to the fact that the middle-class women are in great measure a (vicarious) leisure class. The same is true in a less degree of the women of the lower, artisan classes. They live under a regime of status handed down from an earlier stage of industrial development, and thereby they preserve a frame of mind and habits of thought which incline them to an archaic view of things generally. At the same time they stand in no such direct organic relation to the industrial process at large as would tend strongly to break down those habits of thought which, for the modern industrial purpose, are obsolete. That is to say, the peculiar devoutness of women is a particular expression of that conservatism which the women of civilized communities owe, in great measure, to their economic position. For the modern man the patriarchal relation of status is by no means the dominant feature of life; but for the women on the other hand, and for the upper middle-class women especially, confined as they are by prescription and by economic circumstances to their "domestic sphere," this relation is the most real and most formative factor of life. Hence a habit of mind favorable to devout observances and to the interpretation of the facts of life generally in terms of personal status. The logic, and the logical processes, of her everyday domestic life are carried over into the realm of the supernatural, and the woman finds herself at home and content in a range of ideas which to the man are in great measure alien and imbecile.

Still the men of this class are also not devoid of piety, although it is commonly not piety of an aggressive or exuberant kind. The men of the upper middle class commonly take a more complacent attitude towards devout observances than the men of the artisan class. This may perhaps be explained in part by saying that what is true of the women of the class is true to a less extent also of the men. They are to an appreciable extent a sheltered class; and the patriarchal relation of status which still persists in their conjugal life and in their habitual use of servants, may also act to conserve an archaic habit of mind and may exercise a retarding influence upon the process of secularization which their habits of thought are undergoing. The relations of the American middle-class man to the economic community, however, are usually pretty close and exacting; although it may be remarked, by the way and in qualification, that their economic activity frequently also partakes in some degree of the patriarchal or quasi-predatory character. The occupations which are in good repute among this class and which have most to do with shaping the class habits of thought, are the pecuniary occupations which have been spoken of in a similar connection in an earlier chapter. There is a good deal of the relation of arbitrary command and submission, and not a little of shrewd practice, remotely akin to predatory fraud. All this belongs on the plane of life of the predatory barbarian, to whom a devotional attitude is habitual. And in addition to this, the devout observances also commend themselves to this class on the ground of reputability. But this latter incentive to piety deserves treatment by itself and will be spoken of presently. There is no hereditary leisure class of any consequence in the American community, except in the South. This Southern leisure class is somewhat given to devout observances; more so than any class of corresponding pecuniary standing in other parts of the country. It is also well known that the creeds of the South are of a more old-fashioned cast than their counterparts in the North. Corresponding to this more archaic devotional life of the South is the lower industrial development of that section. The industrial organization of the South is at present, and especially it has been until quite recently, of a more primitive character than that of the American community taken as a whole. It approaches nearer to handicraft, in the paucity and rudeness of its mechanical appliances, and there is more of the element of mastery and subservience. It may also be noted that, owing to the peculiar economic circumstances of this section, the greater devoutness of the Southern population, both white and black, is correlated with a scheme of life which in many ways recalls the barbarian stages of industrial development. Among this population offenses of an archaic character also are and have been relatively more prevalent and are less deprecated than they are elsewhere; as, for example, duels, brawls, feuds, drunkenness, horse-racing, cock-fighting, gambling, male sexual incontinence (evidenced by the considerable number of mulattoes). There is also a livelier sense of honor—an expression of sportsmanship and a derivative of predatory life.

As regards the wealthier class of the North, the American leisure class in the best sense of the term, it is, to begin with, scarcely possible to speak of an hereditary devotional attitude. This class is of too recent growth to be possessed of a well-formed transmitted habit in this respect, or even of a special home-grown tradition. Still, it may be noted in passing that there is a perceptible tendency among this class to give in at least a nominal, and apparently something of a real, adherence to some one of the accredited creeds. Also, weddings, funerals, and the like honorific events among this class are pretty uniformly solemnized with some especial degree of religious circumstance. It is impossible to say how far this adherence to a creed is a bona fide reversion to a devout habit of mind, and how far it is to be classed as a case of protective mimicry assumed for the purpose of an outward assimilation to canons of reputability borrowed from foreign ideals. Something of a substantial devotional propensity seems to be present, to judge especially by the somewhat peculiar degree of ritualistic observance which is in process of development in the upper-class cults. There is a tendency perceptible among the upper-class worshippers to affiliate themselves with those cults which lay relatively great stress on ceremonial and on the spectacular accessories of worship; and in the churches in which an upper-class membership predominates, there is at the same time a tendency to accentuate the ritualistic, at the cost of the intellectual features in the service and in the apparatus of the devout observances. This holds true even where the church in question belongs to a denomination with a relatively slight general development of ritual and paraphernalia.

This peculiar development of the ritualistic element is no doubt due in part to a predilection for conspicuously wasteful spectacles, but it probably also in part indicates something of the devotional attitude of the worshippers. So far as the latter is true, it indicates a relatively archaic form of the devotional habit. The predominance of spectacular effects in devout observances is noticeable in all devout communities at a relatively primitive stage of culture and with a slight intellectual development. It is especially characteristic of the barbarian culture. Here there is pretty uniformly present in the devout observances a direct appeal to the emotions through all the avenues of sense. And a tendency to return to this naive, sensational method of appeal is unmistakable in the upper-class churches of today. It is perceptible in a less degree in the cults which claim the allegiance of the lower leisure class and of the middle classes. There is a reversion to the use of colored lights and brilliant spectacles, a freer use of symbols, orchestral music and incense, and one may even detect in "processionals" and "recessionals" and in richly varied genuflexional evolutions, an incipient reversion to so antique an accessory of worship as the sacred dance. This reversion to spectacular observances is not confined to the upper-class cults, although it finds its best exemplification and its highest accentuation in the higher pecuniary and social altitudes.

The cults of the lower-class devout portion of the community, such as the Southern Negroes and the backward foreign elements of the population, of course also show a strong inclination to ritual, symbolism, and spectacular effects; as might be expected from the antecedents and the cultural level of those classes. With these classes the prevalence of ritual and anthropomorphism are not so much a matter of reversion as of continued development out of the past. But the use of ritual and related features of devotion are also spreading in other directions. In the early days of the American community the prevailing denominations started out with a ritual and paraphernalia of an austere simplicity; but it is a matter familiar to every one that in the course of time these denominations have, in a varying degree, adopted much of the spectacular elements which they once renounced. In a general way, this development has gone hand in hand with the growth of the wealth and the ease of life of the worshippers and has reached its fullest expression among those classes which grade highest in wealth and repute.

The causes to which this pecuniary stratification of devoutness is due have already been indicated in a general way in speaking of class differences in habits of thought. Class differences as regards devoutness are but a special expression of a generic fact. The lax allegiance of the lower middle class, or what may broadly be called the failure of filial piety among this class, is chiefly perceptible among the town populations engaged in the mechanical industries. In a general way, one does not, at the present time, look for a blameless filial piety among those classes whose employment approaches that of the engineer and the mechanician. These mechanical employments are in a degree a modern fact. The handicraftsmen of earlier times, who served an industrial end of a character similar to that now served by the mechanician, were not similarly refractory under the discipline of devoutness. The habitual activity of the men engaged in these branches of industry has greatly changed, as regards its intellectual discipline, since the modern industrial processes have come into vogue; and the discipline to which the mechanician is exposed in his daily employment affects the methods and standards of his thinking also on topics which lie outside his everyday work. Familiarity with the highly organized and highly impersonal industrial processes of the present acts to derange the animistic habits of thought. The workman's office is becoming more and more exclusively that of discretion and supervision in a process of mechanical, dispassionate sequences. So long as the individual is the chief and typical prime mover in the process; so long as the obtrusive feature of the industrial process is the dexterity and force of the individual handicraftsman; so long the habit of interpreting phenomena in terms of personal motive and propensity suffers no such considerable and consistent derangement through facts as to lead to its elimination. But under the later developed industrial processes, when the prime movers and the contrivances through which they work are of an impersonal, non-individual character, the grounds of generalization habitually present in the workman's mind and the point of view from which he habitually apprehends phenomena is an enforced cognizance of matter-of-fact sequence. The result, so far as concerns the workman's life of faith, is a proclivity to undevout skepticism.

It appears, then, that the devout habit of mind attains its best development under a relatively archaic culture; the term "devout" being of course here used in its anthropological sense simply, and not as implying anything with respect to the spiritual attitude so characterized, beyond the fact of a proneness to devout observances. It appears also that this devout attitude marks a type of human nature which is more in consonance with the predatory mode of life than with the later-developed, more consistently and organically industrial life process of the community. It is in large measure an expression of the archaic habitual sense of personal status—the relation of mastery and subservience—and it therefore fits into the industrial scheme of the predatory and the quasi-peaceable culture, but does not fit into the industrial scheme of the present. It also appears that this habit persists with greatest tenacity among those classes in the modern communities whose everyday life is most remote from the mechanical processes of industry and which are the most conservative also in other respects; while for those classes that are habitually in immediate contact with modern industrial processes, and whose habits of thought are therefore exposed to the constraining force of technological necessities, that animistic interpretation of phenomena and that respect of persons on which devout observance proceeds are in process of obsolescence. And also—as bearing especially on the present discussion—it appears that the devout habit to some extent progressively gains in scope and elaboration among those classes in the modern communities to whom wealth and leisure accrue in the most pronounced degree. In this as in other relations, the institution of a leisure class acts to conserve, and even to rehabilitate, that archaic type of human nature and those elements of the archaic culture which the industrial evolution of society in its later stages acts to eliminate.

CHAPTER THIRTEEN

Survivals of the Non-Invidious Interests

In an increasing proportion as time goes on, the anthropomorphic cult, with its code of devout observations, suffers a progressive disintegration through the stress of economic exigencies and the decay of the system of status. As this disintegration proceeds, there come to be associated and blended with the devout attitude certain other motives and impulses that are not always of an anthropomorphic origin, nor traceable to the habit of personal subservience. Not all of these subsidiary impulses that blend with the habit of devoutness in the later devotional life are altogether congruous with the devout attitude or with the anthropomorphic apprehension of the sequence of phenomena. The origin being not the same, their action upon the scheme of devout life is also not in the same direction.

In many ways they traverse the underlying norm of subservience or vicarious life to which the code of devout observations and the ecclesiastical and sacerdotal institutions are to be traced as their substantial basis. Through the presence of these alien motives the social and industrial regime of status gradually disintegrates, and the canon of personal subservience loses the support derived from an unbroken tradition. Extraneous habits and proclivities encroach upon the field of action occupied by this canon, and it presently comes about that the ecclesiastical and sacerdotal structures are partially converted to other uses, in some measure alien to the purposes of the scheme of devout life as it stood in the days of the most vigorous and characteristic development of the priesthood.

Among these alien motives which affect the devout scheme in its later growth, may be mentioned the motives of charity and of social good-fellowship, or conviviality; or, in more general terms, the various expressions of the sense of human solidarity and sympathy. It may be added that these extraneous uses of the ecclesiastical structure contribute materially to its survival in name and form even among people who may be ready to give up the substance of it. A still more characteristic and more pervasive alien element in the motives which have gone to formally uphold the scheme of devout life is that non-reverent sense of aesthetic congruity with the environment, which is left as a residue of the latter-day act of worship after elimination of its anthropomorphic content.

This has done good service for the maintenance of the sacerdotal institution through blending with the motive of subservience. This sense of impulse of aesthetic congruity is not primarily of an economic character, but it has a considerable indirect effect in shaping the habit of mind of the individual for economic purposes in the later stages of industrial development; its most perceptible effect in this regard goes in the direction of mitigating the somewhat pronounced self-regarding bias that has been transmitted by tradition from the earlier, more competent phases of the regime of status. The economic bearing of this impulse is therefore seen to transverse that of the devout attitude; the former goes to qualify, if not eliminate, the self-regarding bias, through sublation of the antithesis or antagonism of self and not-self; while the latter, being and expression of the sense of personal subservience and mastery, goes to accentuate this antithesis and to insist upon the divergence between the self-regarding interest and the interests of the generically human life process.

This non-invidious residue of the religious life—the sense of communion with the environment, or with the generic life process—as well as the impulse of charity or of sociability, act in a pervasive way to shape men's habits of thought for the economic purpose. But the action of all this class of proclivities is somewhat vague, and their effects are difficult to trace in detail. So much seems clear, however, as that the action of this entire class of motives or aptitudes tends in a direction contrary to the underlying principles of the institution of the leisure class as already formulated. The basis of that institution, as well as of the anthropomorphic cults associated with it in the cultural development, is the habit of invidious comparison; and this habit is incongruous with the exercise of the aptitudes now in question. The substantial canons of the leisure-class scheme of life are a conspicuous waste of time and substance and a withdrawal from the industrial process; while the particular aptitudes here in question assert themselves, on the economic side, in a deprecation of waste and of a futile manner of life, and in an impulse to participation in or identification with the life process, whether it be on the economic side or in any other of its phases or aspects.

It is plain that these aptitudes and habits of life to which they give rise where circumstances favor their expression, or where they assert themselves in a dominant way, run counter to the leisure-class scheme of life; but it is not clear that life under the leisure-class scheme, as seen in the later stages of its development, tends consistently to the repression of these aptitudes or to exemption from the habits of thought in which they express themselves. The positive discipline of the leisure-class scheme of life goes pretty much all the other way. In its positive discipline, by prescription and by selective elimination, the leisure-class scheme favors the all-pervading and all-dominating primacy of the canons of waste and invidious comparison at every conjuncture of life. But in its negative effects the tendency of the leisure-class discipline is not so unequivocally true to the fundamental canons of the scheme. In its regulation of human activity for the purpose of pecuniary decency the leisure-class canon insists on withdrawal from the industrial process. That is to say, it inhibits activity in the directions in which the impecunious members of the community habitually put forth their efforts. Especially in the case of women, and more particularly as regards the upper-class and upper-middle-class women of advanced industrial communities, this inhibition goes so far as to insist on withdrawal even from the emulative process of accumulation by the quasi-predator methods of the pecuniary occupations.

The pecuniary or the leisure-class culture, which set out as an emulative variant of the impulse of workmanship, is in its latest development beginning to neutralize its own ground, by eliminating the habit of invidious comparison in respect of efficiency, or even of pecuniary standing. On the other hand, the fact that members of the leisure class, both men and women, are to some extent exempt from the necessity of finding a livelihood in a competitive struggle with their fellows, makes it possible for members of this class not only to survive, but even, within bounds, to follow their bent in case they are not gifted with the aptitudes which make for success in the competitive struggle. That is to say, in the latest and fullest development of the institution, the livelihood of members of this class does not depend on the possession and the unremitting exercise of those aptitudes are therefore greater in the higher grades of the leisure class than in the general average of a population living under the competitive system.

In an earlier chapter, in discussing the conditions of survival of archaic traits, it has appeared that the peculiar position of the leisure class affords exceptionally favorable chances for the survival of traits which characterize the type of human nature proper to an earlier and obsolete cultural stage. The class is sheltered from the stress of economic exigencies, and is in this sense withdrawn from the rude impact of forces which make for adaptation to the economic situation. The survival in the leisure class, and under the leisure-class scheme of life, of traits and types that are reminiscent of the predatory culture has already been discussed. These aptitudes and habits have an exceptionally favorable chance of survival under the leisure-class regime. Not only does the sheltered pecuniary position of the leisure class afford a situation favorable to the survival of such individuals as are not gifted with the complement of aptitudes required for serviceability in the modern industrial process; but the leisure-class canons of reputability at the same time enjoin the conspicuous exercise of certain predatory aptitudes. The employments in which the predatory aptitudes find exercise serve as an evidence of wealth, birth, and withdrawal from the industrial process. The survival of the predatory traits under the leisure-class culture is furthered both negatively, through the industrial exemption of the class, and positively, through the sanction of the leisure-class canons of decency.

With respect to the survival of traits characteristic of the ante-predatory savage culture the case is in some degree different. The sheltered position of the leisure class favors the survival also of these traits; but the exercise of the aptitudes for peace and good-will does not have the affirmative sanction of the code of proprieties. Individuals gifted with a temperament that is reminiscent of the ante-predatory culture are placed at something of an advantage within the leisure class, as compared with similarly gifted individuals outside the class, in that they are not under a pecuniary necessity to thwart these aptitudes that make for a non-competitive life; but such individuals are still exposed to something of a moral constraint which urges them to disregard these inclinations, in that the code of proprieties enjoins upon them habits of life based on the predatory aptitudes. So long as the system of status remains intact, and so long as the leisure class has other lines of non-industrial activity to take to than obvious killing of time in aimless and wasteful fatigation, so long no considerable departure from the leisure-class scheme of reputable life is to be looked for. The occurrence of non-predatory temperament with the class at that stage is to be looked upon as a case of sporadic reversion. But the reputable non-industrial outlets for the human propensity to action presently fail, through the advance of economic development, the disappearance of large game, the decline of war, the obsolescence of proprietary government, and the decay of the priestly office. When this happens, the situation begins to change. Human life must seek expression in one direction if it may not in another; and if the predatory outlet fails, relief is sought elsewhere.

As indicated above, the exemption from pecuniary stress has been carried farther in the case of the leisure-class women of the advanced industrial communities than in that of any other considerable group of persons. The women may therefore be expected to show a more pronounced reversion to a non-invidious temperament than the men. But there is also among men of the leisure class a perceptible increase in the range and scope of activities that proceed from aptitudes which are not to be classed as self-regarding, and the end of which is not an invidious distinction. So, for instance, the greater number of men who have to do with industry in the way of pecuniarily managing an enterprise take some interest and some pride in seeing that the work is well done and is industrially effective, and this even apart from the profit which may result from any improvement of this kind. The efforts of commercial clubs and manufacturers' organizations in this direction of non-invidious advancement of industrial efficiency are also well known.

The tendency to some other than an invidious purpose in life has worked out in a multitude of organizations, the purpose of which is some work of charity or of social amelioration. These organizations are often of a quasi-religious or pseudo-religious character, and are participated in by both men and women. Examples will present themselves in abundance on reflection, but for the purpose of indicating the range of the propensities in question and of characterizing them, some of the more obvious concrete cases may be cited. Such, for instance, are the agitation for temperance and similar social reforms, for prison reform, for the spread of education, for the suppression of vice, and for the avoidance of war by arbitration, disarmament, or other means; such are, in some measure, university settlements, neighborhood guilds, the various organizations typified by the Young Men's Christian Association and Young People's Society for Christian Endeavor, sewing-clubs, art clubs, and even commercial clubs; such are also, in some slight measure, the pecuniary foundations of semi-public establishments for charity, education, or amusement, whether they are endowed by wealthy individuals or by contributions collected from persons of smaller means—in so far as these establishments are not of a religious character.

It is of course not intended to say that these efforts proceed entirely from other motives than those of a self-regarding kind. What can be claimed is that other motives are present in the common run of cases, and that the perceptibly greater prevalence of effort of this kind under the circumstances of the modern industrial life than under the unbroken regime of the principle of status, indicates the presence in modern life of an effective skepticism with respect to the full legitimacy of an emulative scheme of life. It is a matter of sufficient notoriety to have become a commonplace jest that extraneous motives are commonly present among the incentives to this class of work—motives of a self-regarding kind, and especially the motive of an invidious distinction. To such an extent is this true, that many ostensible works of disinterested public spirit are no doubt initiated and carried on with a view primarily to the enhanced repute or even to the pecuniary gain, of their promoters. In the case of some considerable groups of organizations or establishments of this kind the invidious motive is apparently the dominant motive both with the initiators of the work and with their supporters. This last remark would hold true especially with respect to such works as lend distinction to their doer through large and conspicuous expenditure; as, for example, the foundation of a university or of a public library or museum; but it is also, and perhaps equally, true of the more commonplace work of participation in such organizations. These serve to authenticate the pecuniary reputability of their members, as well as gratefully to keep them in mind of their superior status by pointing the contrast between themselves and the lower-lying humanity in whom the work of amelioration is to be wrought; as, for example, the university settlement, which now has some vogue. But after all allowances and deductions have been made, there is left some remainder of motives of a non-emulative kind. The fact itself that distinction or a decent good fame is sought by this method is evidence of a prevalent sense of the legitimacy, and of the presumptive effectual presence, of a non-emulative, non-invidious interest, as a consistent factor in the habits of thought of modern communities.

In all this latter-day range of leisure-class activities that proceed on the basis of a non-invidious and non-religious interest, it is to be noted that the women participate more actively and more persistently than the men—except, of course, in the case of such works as require a large expenditure of means. The dependent pecuniary position of the women disables them for work requiring large expenditure. As regards the general range of ameliorative work, the members of the priesthood or clergy of the less naively devout sects, or the secularized denominations, are associated with the class of women. This is as the theory would have it. In other economic relations, also, this clergy stands in a somewhat equivocal position between the class of women and that of the men engaged in economic pursuits. By tradition and by the prevalent sense of the proprieties, both the clergy and the women of the well-to-do classes are placed in the position of a vicarious leisure class; with both classes the characteristic relation which goes to form the habits of thought of the class is a relation of subservience—that is to say, an economic relation conceived in personal terms; in both classes there is consequently perceptible a special proneness to construe phenomena in terms of personal relation rather than of causal sequence; both classes are so inhibited by the canons of decency from the ceremonially unclean processes of the lucrative or productive occupations as to make participation in the industrial life process of today a moral impossibility for them. The result of this ceremonial exclusion from productive effort of the vulgar sort is to draft a relatively large share of the energies of the modern feminine and priestly classes into the service of other interests than the self-regarding one. The code leaves no alternative direction in which the impulse to purposeful action may find expression. The effect of a consistent inhibition on industrially useful activity in the case of the leisure-class women shows itself in a restless assertion of the impulse to workmanship in other directions than that of business activity.

As has been noticed already, the everyday life of the well-to-do women and the clergy contains a larger element of status than that of the average of the men, especially than that of the men engaged in the modern industrial occupations proper. Hence the devout attitude survives in a better state of preservation among these classes than among the common run of men in the modern communities. Hence an appreciable share of the energy which seeks expression in a non-lucrative employment among these members of the vicarious leisure classes may be expected to eventuate in devout observances and works of piety. Hence, in part, the excess of the devout proclivity in women, spoken of in the last chapter. But it is more to the present point to note the effect of this proclivity in shaping the action and coloring the purposes of the non-lucrative movements and organizations here under discussion. Where this devout coloring is present it lowers the immediate efficiency of the organizations for any economic end to which their efforts may be directed. Many organizations, charitable and ameliorative, divide their attention between the devotional and the secular well-being of the people whose interests they aim to further. It can scarcely be doubted that if they were to give an equally serious attention and effort undividedly to the secular interests of these people, the immediate economic value of their work should be appreciably higher than it is. It might of course similarly be said, if this were the place to say it, that the immediate efficiency of these works of amelioration for the devout might be greater if it were not hampered with the secular motives and aims which are usually present.

Some deduction is to be made from the economic value of this class of non-invidious enterprise, on account of the intrusion of the devotional interest. But there are also deductions to be made on account of the presence of other alien motives which more or less broadly traverse the economic trend of this non-emulative expression of the instinct of workmanship. To such an extent is this seen to be true on a closer scrutiny, that, when all is told, it may even appear that this general class of enterprises is of an altogether dubious economic value—as measured in terms of the fullness or facility of life of the individuals or classes to whose amelioration the enterprise is directed. For instance, many of the efforts now in reputable vogue for the amelioration of the indigent population of large cities are of the nature, in great part, of a mission of culture. It is by this means sought to accelerate the rate of speed at which given elements of the upper-class culture find acceptance in the everyday scheme of life of the lower classes. The solicitude of "settlements," for example, is in part directed to enhance the industrial efficiency of the poor and to teach them the more adequate utilization of the means at hand; but it is also no less consistently directed to the inculcation, by precept and example, of certain punctilios of upper-class propriety in manners and customs. The economic substance of these proprieties will commonly be found on scrutiny to be a conspicuous waste of time and goods. Those good people who go out to humanize the poor are commonly, and advisedly, extremely scrupulous and silently insistent in matters of decorum and the decencies of life. They are commonly persons of an exemplary life and gifted with a tenacious insistence on ceremonial cleanness in the various items of their daily consumption. The cultural or civilizing efficacy of this inculcation of correct habits of thought with respect to the consumption of time and commodities is scarcely to be overrated; nor is its economic value to the individual who acquires these higher and more reputable ideals inconsiderable. Under the circumstances of the existing pecuniary culture, the reputability, and consequently the success, of the individual is in great measure dependent on his proficiency in demeanor and methods of consumption that argue habitual waste of time and goods. But as regards the ulterior economic bearing of this training in worthier methods of life, it is to be said that the effect wrought is in large part a substitution of costlier or less efficient methods of accomplishing the same material results, in relations where the material result is the fact of substantial economic value. The propaganda of culture is in great part an inculcation of new tastes, or rather of a new schedule of proprieties, which have been adapted to the upper-class scheme of life under the guidance of the leisure-class formulation of the principles of status and pecuniary decency. This new schedule of proprieties is intruded into the lower-class scheme of life from the code elaborated by an element of the population whose life lies outside the industrial process; and this intrusive schedule can scarcely be expected to fit the exigencies of life for these lower classes more adequately than the schedule already in vogue among them, and especially not more adequately than the schedule which they are themselves working out under the stress of modern industrial life.

All this of course does not question the fact that the proprieties of the substituted schedule are more decorous than those which they displace. The doubt which presents itself is simply a doubt as to the economic expediency of this work of regeneration—that is to say, the economic expediency in that immediate and material bearing in which the effects of the change can be ascertained with some degree of confidence, and as viewed from the standpoint not of the individual but of the facility of life of the collectivity. For an appreciation of the economic expediency of these enterprises of amelioration, therefore, their effective work is scarcely to be taken at its face value, even where the aim of the enterprise is primarily an economic one and where the interest on which it proceeds is in no sense self-regarding or invidious. The economic reform wrought is largely of the nature of a permutation in the methods of conspicuous waste.

But something further is to be said with respect to the character of the disinterested motives and canons of procedure in all work of this class that is affected by the habits of thought characteristic of the pecuniary culture; and this further consideration may lead to a further qualification of the conclusions already reached. As has been seen in an earlier chapter, the canons of reputability or decency under the pecuniary culture insist on habitual futility of effort as the mark of a pecuniarily blameless life. There results not only a habit of disesteem of useful occupations, but there results also what is of more decisive consequence in guiding the action of any organized body of people that lays claim to social good repute. There is a tradition which requires that one should not be vulgarly familiar with any of the processes or details that have to do with the material necessities of life. One may meritoriously show a quantitative interest in the well-being of the vulgar, through subscriptions or through work on managing committees and the like. One may, perhaps even more meritoriously, show solicitude in general and in detail for the cultural welfare of the vulgar, in the way of contrivances for elevating their tastes and affording them opportunities for spiritual amelioration. But one should not betray an intimate knowledge of the material circumstances of vulgar life, or of the habits of thought of the vulgar classes, such as would effectually direct the efforts of these organizations to a materially useful end. This reluctance to avow an unduly intimate knowledge of the lower-class conditions of life in detail of course prevails in very different degrees in different individuals; but there is commonly enough of it present collectively in any organization of the kind in question profoundly to influence its course of action. By its cumulative action in shaping the usage and precedents of any such body, this shrinking from an imputation of unseemly familiarity with vulgar life tends gradually to set aside the initial motives of the enterprise, in favor of certain guiding principles of good repute, ultimately reducible to terms of pecuniary merit. So that in an organization of long standing the initial motive of furthering the facility of life in these classes comes gradually to be an ostensible motive only, and the vulgarly effective work of the organization tends to obsolescence.

What is true of the efficiency of organizations for non-invidious work in this respect is true also as regards the work of individuals proceeding on the same motives; though it perhaps holds true with more qualification for individuals than for organized enterprises. The habit of gauging merit by the leisure-class canons of wasteful expenditure and unfamiliarity with vulgar life, whether on the side of production or of consumption, is necessarily strong in the individuals who aspire to do some work of public utility. And if the individual should forget his station and turn his efforts to vulgar effectiveness, the common sense of the community—the sense of pecuniary decency—would presently reject his work and set him right. An example of this is seen in the administration of bequests made by public-spirited men for the single purpose (at least ostensibly) of furthering the facility of human life in some particular respect. The objects for which bequests of this class are most frequently made at present are most frequently made at present are schools, libraries, hospitals, and asylums for the infirm or unfortunate. The avowed purpose of the donor in these cases is the amelioration of human life in the particular respect which is named in the bequest; but it will be found an invariable rule that in the execution of the work not a little of other motives, frequency incompatible with the initial motive, is present and determines the particular disposition eventually made of a good share of the means which have been set apart by the bequest. Certain funds, for instance, may have been set apart as a foundation for a foundling asylum or a retreat for invalids.

The diversion of expenditure to honorific waste in such cases is not uncommon enough to cause surprise or even to raise a smile. An appreciable share of the funds is spent in the construction of an edifice faced with some aesthetically objectionable but expensive stone, covered with grotesque and incongruous details, and designed, in its battlemented walls and turrets and its massive portals and strategic approaches, to suggest certain barbaric methods of warfare. The interior of the structure shows the same pervasive guidance of the canons of conspicuous waste and predatory exploit. The windows, for instance, to go no farther into detail, are placed with a view to impress their pecuniary excellence upon the chance beholder from the outside, rather than with a view to effectiveness for their ostensible end in the convenience or comfort of the beneficiaries within; and the detail of interior arrangement is required to conform itself as best it may to this alien but imperious requirement of pecuniary beauty.

In all this, of course, it is not to be presumed that the donor would have found fault, or that he would have done otherwise if he had taken control in person; it appears that in those cases where such a personal direction is exercised—where the enterprise is conducted by direct expenditure and superintendence instead of by bequest—the aims and methods of management are not different in this respect. Nor would the beneficiaries, or the outside observers whose ease or vanity are not immediately touched, be pleased with a different disposition of the funds. It would suit no one to have the enterprise conducted with a view directly to the most economical and effective use of the means at hand for the initial, material end of the foundation. All concerned, whether their interest is immediate and self-regarding, or contemplative only, agree that some considerable share of the expenditure should go to the higher or spiritual needs derived from the habit of an invidious comparison in predatory exploit and pecuniary waste. But this only goes to say that the canons of emulative and pecuniary reputability so far pervade the common sense of the community as to permit no escape or evasion, even in the case of an enterprise which ostensibly proceeds entirely on the basis of a non-invidious interest.

It may even be that the enterprise owes its honorific virtue, as a means of enhancing the donor's good repute, to the imputed presence of this non-invidious motive; but that does not hinder the invidious interest from guiding the expenditure. The effectual presence of motives of an emulative or invidious origin in non-emulative works of this kind might be shown at length and with detail, in any one of the classes of enterprise spoken of above.

Where these honorific details occur, in such cases, they commonly masquerade under designations that belong in the field of the aesthetic, ethical or economic interest. These special motives, derived from the standards and canons of the pecuniary culture, act surreptitiously to divert effort of a non-invidious kind from effective service, without disturbing the agent's sense of good intention or obtruding upon his consciousness the substantial futility of his work. Their effect might be traced through the entire range of that schedule of non-invidious, meliorative enterprise that is so considerable a feature, and especially so conspicuous a feature, in the overt scheme of life of the well-to-do. But the theoretical bearing is perhaps clear enough and may require no further illustration; especially as some detailed attention will be given to one of these lines of enterprise—the establishments for the higher learning—in another connection.

Under the circumstances of the sheltered situation in which the leisure class is placed there seems, therefore, to be something of a reversion to the range of non-invidious impulses that characterizes the ante-predatory savage culture. The reversion comprises both the sense of workmanship and the proclivity to indolence and good-fellowship. But in the modern scheme of life canons of conduct based on pecuniary or invidious merit stand in the way of a free exercise of these impulses; and the dominant presence of these canons of conduct goes far to divert such efforts as are made on the basis of the non-invidious interest to the service of that invidious interest on which the pecuniary culture rests. The canons of pecuniary decency are reducible for the present purpose to the principles of waste, futility, and ferocity. The requirements of decency are imperiously present in meliorative enterprise as in other lines of conduct, and exercise a selective surveillance over the details of conduct and management in any enterprise. By guiding and adapting the method in detail, these canons of decency go far to make all non-invidious aspiration or effort nugatory. The pervasive, impersonal, un-eager principle of futility is at hand from day to day and works obstructively to hinder the effectual expression of so much of the surviving ante-predatory aptitudes as is to be classed under the instinct of workmanship; but its presence does not preclude the transmission of those aptitudes or the continued recurrence of an impulse to find expression for them.

In the later and farther development of the pecuniary culture, the requirement of withdrawal from the industrial process in order to avoid social odium is carried so far as to comprise abstention from the emulative employments. At this advanced stage the pecuniary culture negatively favors the assertion of the non-invidious propensities by relaxing the stress laid on the merit of emulative, predatory, or pecuniary occupations, as compared with those of an industrial or productive kind. As was noticed above, the requirement of such withdrawal from all employment that is of human use applies more rigorously to the upper-class women than to any other class, unless the priesthood of certain cults might be cited as an exception, perhaps more apparent than real, to this rule.

The reason for the more extreme insistence on a futile life for this class of women than for the men of the same pecuniary and social grade lies in their being not only an upper-grade leisure class but also at the same time a vicarious leisure class. There is in their case a double ground for a consistent withdrawal from useful effort.

It has been well and repeatedly said by popular writers and speakers who reflect the common sense of intelligent people on questions of social structure and function that the position of woman in any community is the most striking index of the level of culture attained by the community, and it might be added, by any given class in the community.

This remark is perhaps truer as regards the stage of economic development than as regards development in any other respect. At the same time the position assigned to the woman in the accepted scheme of life, in any community or under any culture, is in a very great degree an expression of traditions which have been shaped by the circumstances of an earlier phase of development, and which have been but partially adapted to the existing economic circumstances, or to the existing exigencies of temperament and habits of mind by which the women living under this modern economic situation are actuated.

The fact has already been remarked upon incidentally in the course of the discussion of the growth of economic institutions generally, and in particular in speaking of vicarious leisure and of dress, that the position of women in the modern economic scheme is more widely and more consistently at variance with the promptings of the instinct of workmanship than is the position of the men of the same classes. It is also apparently true that the woman's temperament includes a larger share of this instinct that approves peace and disapproves futility. It is therefore not a fortuitous circumstance that the women of modern industrial communities show a livelier sense of the discrepancy between the accepted scheme of life and the exigencies of the economic situation.

The several phases of the "woman question" have brought out in intelligible form the extent to which the life of women in modern society, and in the polite circles especially, is regulated by a body of common sense formulated under the economic circumstances of an earlier phase of development. It is still felt that woman's life, in its civil, economic, and social bearing, is essentially and normally a vicarious life, the merit or demerit of which is, in the nature of things, to be imputed to some other individual who stands in some relation of ownership or tutelage to the woman. So, for instance, any action on the part of a woman which traverses an injunction of the accepted schedule of proprieties is felt to reflect immediately upon the honor of the man whose woman she is. There may of course be some sense of incongruity in the mind of any one passing an opinion of this kind on the woman's frailty or perversity; but the common-sense judgment of the community in such matters is, after all, delivered without much hesitation, and few men would question the legitimacy of their sense of an outraged tutelage in any case that might arise. On the other hand, relatively little discredit attaches to a woman through the evil deeds of the man with whom her life is associated.

The good and beautiful scheme of life, then—that is to say the scheme to which we are habituated—assigns to the woman a "sphere" ancillary to the activity of the man; and it is felt that any departure from the traditions of her assigned round of duties is unwomanly.

If the question is as to civil rights or the suffrage, our common sense in the matter—that is to say the logical deliverance of our general scheme of life upon the point in question—says that the woman should be represented in the body politic and before the law, not immediately in her own person, but through the mediation of the head of the household to which she belongs. It is unfeminine in her to aspire to a self-directing, self-centered life; and our common sense tells us that her direct participation in the affairs of the community, civil or industrial, is a menace to that social order which expresses our habits of thought as they have been formed under the guidance of the traditions of the pecuniary culture. "All this fume and froth of 'emancipating woman from the slavery of man' and so on, is, to use the chaste and expressive language of Elizabeth Cady Stanton inversely, 'utter rot.' The social relations of the sexes are fixed by nature. Our entire civilization—that is whatever is good in it—is based on the home." The "home" is the household with a male head. This view, but commonly expressed even more chastely, is the prevailing view of the woman's status, not only among the common run of the men of civilized communities, but among the women as well. Women have a very alert sense of what the scheme of proprieties requires, and while it is true that many of them are ill at ease under the details which the code imposes, there are few who do not recognize that the existing moral order, of necessity and by the divine right of prescription, places the woman in a position ancillary to the man. In the last analysis, according to her own sense of what is good and beautiful, the woman's life is, and in theory must be, an expression of the man's life at the second remove.

But in spite of this pervading sense of what is the good and natural place for the woman, there is also perceptible an incipient development of sentiment to the effect that this whole arrangement of tutelage and vicarious life and imputation of merit and demerit is somehow a mistake. Or, at least, that even if it may be a natural growth and a good arrangement in its time and place, and in spite of its patent aesthetic value, still it does not adequately serve the more everyday ends of life in a modern industrial community. Even that large and substantial body of well-bred, upper and middle-class women to whose dispassionate, matronly sense of the traditional proprieties this relation of status commends itself as fundamentally and eternally right—even these, whose attitude is conservative, commonly find some slight discrepancy in detail between things as they are and things as they should be in this respect. But that less manageable body of modern women who, by force of youth, education, or temperament, are in some degree out of touch with the traditions of status received from the barbarian culture, and in whom there is, perhaps, an undue reversion to the impulse of self-expression and workmanship—these are touched with a sense of grievance too vivid to leave them at rest.

In this "New-Woman" movement—as these blind and incoherent efforts to rehabilitate the woman's pre-glacial standing have been named—there are at least two elements discernible, both of which are of an economic character. These two elements or motives are expressed by the double watchword, "Emancipation" and "Work." Each of these words is recognized to stand for something in the way of a wide-spread sense of grievance. The prevalence of the sentiment is recognized even by people who do not see that there is any real ground for a grievance in the situation as it stands today. It is among the women of the well-to-do classes, in the communities which are farthest advanced in industrial development, that this sense of a grievance to be redressed is most alive and finds most frequent expression. That is to say, in other words, there is a demand, more or less serious, for emancipation from all relation of status, tutelage, or vicarious life; and the revulsion asserts itself especially among the class of women upon whom the scheme of life handed down from the regime of status imposes with least litigation a vicarious life, and in those communities whose economic development has departed farthest from the circumstances to which this traditional scheme is adapted. The demand comes from that portion of womankind which is excluded by the canons of good repute from all effectual work, and which is closely reserved for a life of leisure and conspicuous consumption.

More than one critic of this new-woman movement has misapprehended its motive. The case of the American "new woman" has lately been summed up with some warmth by a popular observer of social phenomena: "She is petted by her husband, the most devoted and hard-working of husbands in the world. ... She is the superior of her husband in education, and in almost every respect. She is surrounded by the most numerous and delicate attentions. Yet she is not satisfied. ... The Anglo-Saxon 'new woman' is the most ridiculous production of modern times, and destined to be the most ghastly failure of the century." Apart from the deprecation—perhaps well placed—which is contained in this presentment, it adds nothing but obscurity to the woman question. The grievance of the new woman is made up of those things which this typical characterization of the movement urges as reasons why she should be content. She is petted, and is permitted, or even required, to consume largely and conspicuously—vicariously for her husband or other natural guardian. She is exempted, or debarred, from vulgarly useful employment—in order to perform leisure vicariously for the good repute of her natural (pecuniary) guardian. These offices are the conventional marks of the un-free, at the same time that they are incompatible with the human impulse to purposeful activity. But the woman is endowed with her share—which there is reason to believe is more than an even share—of the instinct of workmanship, to which futility of life or of expenditure is obnoxious. She must unfold her life activity in response to the direct, unmediated stimuli of the economic environment with which she is in contact. The impulse is perhaps stronger upon the woman than upon the man to live her own life in her own way and to enter the industrial process of the community at something nearer than the second remove.

So long as the woman's place is consistently that of a drudge, she is, in the average of cases, fairly contented with her lot. She not only has something tangible and purposeful to do, but she has also no time or thought to spare for a rebellious assertion of such human propensity to self-direction as she has inherited. And after the stage of universal female drudgery is passed, and a vicarious leisure without strenuous application becomes the accredited employment of the women of the well-to-do classes, the prescriptive force of the canon of pecuniary decency, which requires the observance of ceremonial futility on their part, will long preserve high-minded women from any sentimental leaning to self-direction and a "sphere of usefulness." This is especially true during the earlier phases of the pecuniary culture, while the leisure of the leisure class is still in great measure a predatory activity, an active assertion of mastery in which there is enough of tangible purpose of an invidious kind to admit of its being taken seriously as an employment to which one may without shame put one's hand. This condition of things has obviously lasted well down into the present in some communities. It continues to hold to a different extent for different individuals, varying with the vividness of the sense of status and with the feebleness of the impulse to workmanship with which the individual is endowed. But where the economic structure of the community has so far outgrown the scheme of life based on status that the relation of personal subservience is no longer felt to be the sole "natural" human relation; there the ancient habit of purposeful activity will begin to assert itself in the less conformable individuals against the more recent, relatively superficial, relatively ephemeral habits and views which the predatory and the pecuniary culture have contributed to our scheme of life. These habits and views begin to lose their coercive force for the community or the class in question so soon as the habit of mind and the views of life due to the predatory and the quasi-peaceable discipline cease to be in fairly close accord with the later-developed economic situation. This is evident in the case of the industrious classes of modern communities; for them the leisure-class scheme of life has lost much of its binding force, especially as regards the element of status. But it is also visibly being verified in the case of the upper classes, though not in the same manner.

The habits derived from the predatory and quasi-peaceable culture are relatively ephemeral variants of certain underlying propensities and mental characteristics of the race; which it owes to the protracted discipline of the earlier, proto-anthropoid cultural stage of peaceable, relatively undifferentiated economic life carried on in contact with a relatively simple and invariable material environment. When the habits superinduced by the emulative method of life have ceased to enjoy the section of existing economic exigencies, a process of disintegration sets in whereby the habits of thought of more recent growth and of a less generic character to some extent yield the ground before the more ancient and more pervading spiritual characteristics of the race.

In a sense, then, the new-woman movement marks a reversion to a more generic type of human character, or to a less differentiated expression of human nature. It is a type of human nature which is to be characterized as proto-anthropoid, and, as regards the substance if not the form of its dominant traits, it belongs to a cultural stage that may be classed as possibly sub-human. The particular movement or evolutional feature in question of course shares this characterization with the rest of the later social development, in so far as this social development shows evidence of a reversion to the spiritual attitude that characterizes the earlier, undifferentiated stage of economic revolution. Such evidence of a general tendency to reversion from the dominance of the invidious interest is not entirely wanting, although it is neither plentiful nor unquestionably convincing. The general decay of the sense of status in modern industrial communities goes some way as evidence in this direction; and the perceptible return to a disapproval of futility in human life, and a disapproval of such activities as serve only the individual gain at the cost of the collectivity or at the cost of other social groups, is evidence to a like effect. There is a perceptible tendency to deprecate the infliction of pain, as well as to discredit all marauding enterprises, even where these expressions of the invidious interest do not tangibly work to the material detriment of the community or of the individual who passes an opinion on them. It may even be said that in the modern industrial communities the average, dispassionate sense of men says that the ideal character is a character which makes for peace, good-will, and economic efficiency, rather than for a life of self-seeking, force, fraud, and mastery.

The influence of the leisure class is not consistently for or against the rehabilitation of this proto-anthropoid human nature. So far as concerns the chance of survival of individuals endowed with an exceptionally large share of the primitive traits, the sheltered position of the class favors its members directly by withdrawing them from the pecuniary struggle; but indirectly, through the leisure-class canons of conspicuous waste of goods and effort, the institution of a leisure class lessens the chance of survival of such individuals in the entire body of the population. The decent requirements of waste absorb the surplus energy of the population in an invidious struggle and leave no margin for the non-invidious expression of life. The remoter, less tangible, spiritual effects of the discipline of decency go in the same direction and work perhaps more effectually to the same end. The canons of decent life are an elaboration of the principle of invidious comparison, and they accordingly act consistently to inhibit all non-invidious effort and to inculcate the self-regarding attitude.

CHAPTER FOURTEEN

The Higher Learning as an Expression of the Pecuniary Culture

To the end that suitable habits of thought on certain heads may be conserved in the in-coming generation, a scholastic discipline is sanctioned by the common sense of the community and incorporated into the accredited scheme of life. The habits of thought which are so formed under the guidance of teachers and scholastic traditions have an economic value—a value as affecting the serviceability of the individual—no less real than the similar economic value of the habits of thought formed without such guidance under the discipline of everyday life. Whatever characteristics of the accredited scholas-tic scheme and discipline are traceable to the predilections of the leisure class or to the guidance of the canons of pecuniary merit are to be set down to the account of that in-stitution, and whatever economic value these features of the educational scheme pos-sess are the expression in detail of the value of that institution. It will be in place, therefore, to point out any peculiar features of the educational system which are trace-able to the leisure-class scheme of life, whether as regards the aim and method of the discipline, or as regards the compass and character of the body of knowledge incul-cated. It is in learning proper, and more particularly in the higher learning, that the in-fluence of leisure-class ideals is most patent; and since the purpose here is not to make an exhaustive collation of data showing the effect of the pecuniary culture upon edu-cation, but rather to illustrate the method and trend of the leisure-class influence in education, a survey of certain salient features of the higher learning, such as may serve this purpose, is all that will be attempted.

In point of derivation and early development, learning is somewhat closely related to the devotional function of the community, particularly to the body of observances in which the service rendered the supernatural leisure class expresses itself. The service by which it is sought to conciliate supernatural agencies in the primitive cults is not an in-dustrially profitable employment of the community's time and effort. It is, therefore, in great part, to be classed as a vicarious leisure performed for the supernatural powers with whom negotiations are carried on and whose good-will the service and the professions of subservience are conceived to procure. In great part, the early learning consisted in an acquisition of knowledge and facility in the service of a supernatural agent. It was there-fore closely analogous in character to the training required for the domestic service of a temporal master. To a great extent, the knowledge acquired under the priestly teachers of the primitive community was knowledge of ritual and ceremonial; that is to say, a knowledge of the most proper, most effective, or most acceptable manner of approach-ing and of serving the preternatural agents. What was learned was how to make oneself indispensable to these powers, and so to put oneself in a position to ask, or even to re-quire, their intercession in the course of events or their abstention from interference in any given enterprise. Propitiation was the end, and this end was sought, in great part, by acquiring facility in subservience. It appears to have been only gradually that other elements than those of efficient service of the master found their way into the stock of priestly or shamanistic instruction.

The priestly servitor of the inscrutable powers that move in the external world came to stand in the position of a mediator between these powers and the common run of unrestricted humanity; for he was possessed of a knowledge of the supernatural etiquette which would admit him into the presence. And as commonly happens with mediators between the vulgar and their masters, whether the masters be natural or preternatural, he found it expedient to have the means at hand tangibly to impress upon the vulgar the fact that these inscrutable powers would do what he might ask of them. Hence, presently, a knowledge of certain natural processes which could be turned to account for spectacular effect, together with some sleight of hand, came to be an integral part of priestly lore. Knowledge of this kind passes for knowledge of the "unknowable," and it owes its serviceability for the sacerdotal purpose to its recondite character. It appears to have been from this source that learning, as an institution, arose, and its differentiation from this its parent stock of magic ritual and shamanistic fraud has been slow and tedious, and is scarcely yet complete even in the most advanced of the higher seminaries of learning.

The recondite element in learning is still, as it has been in all ages, a very attractive and effective element for the purpose of impressing, or even imposing upon, the unlearned; and the standing of the savant in the mind of the altogether unlettered is in great measure rated in terms of intimacy with the occult forces. So, for instance, as a typical case, even so late as the middle of this century, the Norwegian peasants have instinctively formulated their sense of the superior erudition of such doctors of divinity as Luther, Malanchthon, Peder Dass, and even so late a scholar in divinity as Grundtvig, in terms of the Black Art. These, together with a very comprehensive list of minor celebrities, both living and dead, have been reputed masters in all magical arts; and a high position in the ecclesiastical personnel has carried with it, in the apprehension of these good people, an implication of profound familiarity with magical practice and the occult sciences. There is a parallel fact nearer home, similarly going to show the close relationship, in popular apprehension, between erudition and the unknowable; and it will at the same time serve to illustrate, in somewhat coarse outline, the bent which leisure-class life gives to the cognitive interest. While the belief is by no means confined to the leisure class, that class today comprises a disproportionately large number of believers in occult sciences of all kinds and shades. By those whose habits of thought are not shaped by contact with modern industry, the knowledge of the unknowable is still felt to the ultimate if not the only true knowledge.

Learning, then, set out by being in some sense a by-product of the priestly vicarious leisure class; and, at least until a recent date, the higher learning has since remained in some sense a by-product or by-occupation of the priestly classes. As the body of systematized knowledge increased, there presently arose a distinction, traceable very far back in the history of education, between esoteric and exoteric knowledge, the former—so far as there is a substantial difference between the two—comprising such knowledge as is primarily of no economic or industrial effect, and the latter comprising chiefly knowledge of industrial processes and of natural phenomena which were habitually turned to account for the material purposes of life. This line of demarcation has in time become, at least in popular apprehension, the normal line between the higher learning and the lower.

It is significant, not only as an evidence of their close affiliation with the priestly craft, but also as indicating that their activity to a good extent falls under that category of conspicuous leisure known as manners and breeding, that the learned class in all primitive communities are great sticklers for form, precedent, gradations of rank, ritual, ceremonial vestments, and learned paraphernalia generally. This is of course to be expected, and it goes to say that the higher learning, in its incipient phase, is a leisure-class occupation—more specifically an occupation of the vicarious leisure class employed in the service of the supernatural leisure class. But this predilection for the paraphernalia of learning goes also to indicate a further point of contact or of continuity between the priestly office and the office of the savant. In point of derivation, learning, as well as the priestly office, is largely an outgrowth of sympathetic magic; and this magical apparatus of form and ritual therefore finds its place with the learned class of the primitive community as a matter of course. The ritual and paraphernalia have an occult efficacy for the magical purpose; so that their presence as an integral factor in the earlier phases of the development of magic and science is a matter of expediency, quite as much as of affectionate regard for symbolism simply.

This sense of the efficacy of symbolic ritual, and of sympathetic effect to be wrought through dexterous rehearsal of the traditional accessories of the act or end to be compassed, is of course present more obviously and in larger measure in magical practice than in the discipline of the sciences, even of the occult sciences. But there are, I apprehend, few persons with a cultivated sense of scholastic merit to whom the ritualistic accessories of science are altogether an idle matter. The very great tenacity with which these ritualistic paraphernalia persist through the later course of the development is evident to any one who will reflect on what has been the history of learning in our civilization. Even today there are such things in the usage of the learned community as the cap and gown, matriculation, initiation, and graduation ceremonies, and the conferring of scholastic degrees, dignities, and prerogatives in a way which suggests some sort of a scholarly apostolic succession. The usage of the priestly orders is no doubt the proximate source of all these features of learned ritual, vestments, sacramental initiation, the transmission of peculiar dignities and virtues by the imposition of hands, and the like; but their derivation is traceable back of this point, to the source from which the specialized priestly class proper came to be distinguished from the sorcerer on the one hand and from the menial servant of a temporal master on the other hand. So far as regards both their derivation and their psychological content, these usages and the conceptions on which they rest belong to a stage in cultural development no later than that of the angekok and the rain-maker. Their place in the later phases of devout observance, as well as in the higher educational system, is that of a survival from a very early animistic phase of the development of human nature.

These ritualistic features of the educational system of the present and of the recent past, it is quite safe to say, have their place primarily in the higher, liberal, and classic institutions and grades of learning, rather than in the lower, technological, or practical grades, and branches of the system. So far as they possess them, the lower and less reputable branches of the educational scheme have evidently borrowed these things from the higher grades; and their continued persistence among the practical schools, without the sanction of the continued example of the higher and classic grades, would be highly improbable, to say the least. With the lower and practical schools and scholars, the adoption and cultivation of these usages is a case of mimicry—due to a desire to conform as far as may be to the standards of scholastic reputability maintained by the upper grades and classes, who have come by these accessory features legitimately, by the right of lineal devolution.

The analysis may even be safely carried a step farther. Ritualistic survivals and reversions come out in fullest vigor and with the freest air of spontaneity among those seminaries of learning which have to do primarily with the education of the priestly and leisure classes. Accordingly it should appear, and it does pretty plainly appear, on a survey of recent developments in college and university life, that wherever schools founded for the instruction of the lower classes in the immediately useful branches of knowledge grow into institutions of the higher learning, the growth of ritualistic ceremonial and paraphernalia and of elaborate scholastic "functions" goes hand in hand with the transition of the schools in question from the field of homely practicality into the higher, classical sphere. The initial purpose of these schools, and the work with which they have chiefly had to do at the earlier of these two stages of their evolution, has been that of fitting the young of the industrious classes for work. On the higher, classical plane of learning to which they commonly tend, their dominant aim becomes the preparation of the youth of the priestly and the leisure classes—or of an incipient leisure class—for the consumption of goods, material and immaterial, according to a conventionally accepted, reputable scope and method. This happy issue has commonly been the fate of schools founded by "friends of the people" for the aid of struggling young men, and where this transition is made in good form there is commonly, if not invariably, a coincident change to a more ritualistic life in the schools.

In the school life of today, learned ritual is in a general way best at home in schools whose chief end is the cultivation of the "humanities." This correlation is shown, perhaps more neatly than anywhere else, in the life-history of the American colleges and universities of recent growth. There may be many exceptions from the rule, especially among those schools which have been founded by the typically reputable and ritualistic churches, and which, therefore, started on the conservative and classical plane or reached the classical position by a short-cut; but the general rule as regards the colleges founded in the newer American communities during the present century has been that so long as the constituency from which the colleges have drawn their pupils has been dominated by habits of industry and thrift, so long the reminiscences of the medicine-man have found but a scant and precarious acceptance in the scheme of college life. But so soon as wealth begins appreciably to accumulate in the community, and so soon as a given school begins to lean on a leisure-class constituency, there comes also a perceptibly increased insistence on scholastic ritual and on conformity to the ancient forms as regards vestments and social and scholastic solemnities. So, for instance, there has been an approximate coincidence between the growth of wealth among the constituency which supports any given college of the Middle West and the date of acceptance—first into tolerance and then into imperative vogue—of evening dress for men and of the décolleté for women, as the scholarly vestments proper to occasions of learned solemnity or to the seasons of social amenity within the college circle. Apart from the mechanical difficulty of so large a task, it would scarcely be a difficult matter to trace this correlation. The like is true of the vogue of the cap and gown.

Cap and gown have been adopted as learned insignia by many colleges of this section within the last few years; and it is safe to say that this could scarcely have occurred at a much earlier date, or until there had grown up a leisure-class sentiment of sufficient volume in the community to support a strong movement of reversion towards an archaic view as to the legitimate end of education. This particular item of learned ritual, it may be noted, would not only commend itself to the leisure-class sense of the fitness of things, as appealing to the archaic propensity for spectacular effect and the predilection for antique symbolism; but it at the same time fits into the leisure-class scheme of life as involving a notable element of conspicuous waste. The precise date at which the reversion to cap and gown took place, as well as the fact that it affected so large a number of schools at about the same time, seems to have been due in some measure to a wave of atavistic sense of conformity and reputability that passed over the community at that period.

It may not be entirely beside the point to note that in point of time this curious reversion seems to coincide with the culmination of a certain vogue of atavistic sentiment and tradition in other directions also. The wave of reversion seems to have received its initial impulse in the psychologically disintegrating effects of the Civil War. Habituation to war entails a body of predatory habits of thought, whereby clannishness in some measure replaces the sense of solidarity, and a sense of invidious distinction supplants the impulse to equitable, everyday serviceability. As an outcome of the cumulative action of these factors, the generation which follows a season of war is apt to witness a rehabilitation of the element of status, both in its social life and in its scheme of devout observances and other symbolic or ceremonial forms. Throughout the eighties, and less plainly traceable through the seventies also, there was perceptible a gradually advancing wave of sentiment favoring quasi-predatory business habits, insistence on status, anthropomorphism, and conservatism generally. The more direct and unmediated of these expressions of the barbarian temperament, such as the recrudescence of outlawry and the spectacular quasi-predatory careers of fraud run by certain "captains of industry," came to a head earlier and were appreciably on the decline by the close of the seventies. The recrudescence of anthropomorphic sentiment also seems to have passed its most acute stage before the close of the eighties. But the learned ritual and paraphernalia here spoken of are a still remoter and more recondite expression of the barbarian animistic sense; and these, therefore, gained vogue and elaboration more slowly and reached their most effective development at a still later date. There is reason to believe that the culmination is now already past. Except for the new impetus given by a new war experience, and except for the support which the growth of a wealthy class affords to all ritual, and especially to whatever ceremonial is wasteful and pointedly suggests gradations of status, it is probable that the late improvements and augmentation of scholastic insignia and ceremonial would gradually decline. But while it may be true that the cap and gown, and the more strenuous observance of scholastic proprieties which came with them, were floated in on this post-bellum tidal wave of reversion to barbarism, it is also no doubt true that such a ritualistic reversion could not have been effected in the college scheme of life until the accumulation of wealth in the hands of a propertied class had gone far enough to afford the requisite pecuniary ground for a movement which should bring the colleges of the country up to the leisure-class requirements in the higher learning. The adoption of the cap and gown is one of the striking atavistic features of modern college life, and at the same time it marks the fact that these colleges have definitely become leisure-class establishments, either in actual achievement or in aspiration.

As further evidence of the close relation between the educational system and the cultural standards of the community, it may be remarked that there is some tendency latterly to substitute the captain of industry in place of the priest, as the head of seminaries of the higher learning. The substitution is by no means complete or unequivocal. Those heads of institutions are best accepted who combine the sacerdotal office with a high degree of pecuniary efficiency. There is a similar but less pronounced tendency to entrust the work of instruction in the higher learning to men of some pecuniary qualification.

Administrative ability and skill in advertising the enterprise count for rather more than they once did, as qualifications for the work of teaching. This applies especially in those sciences that have most to do with the everyday facts of life, and it is particularly true of schools in the economically single-minded communities. This partial substitution of pecuniary for sacerdotal efficiency is a concomitant of the modern transition from conspicuous leisure to conspicuous consumption, as the chief means of reputability. The correlation of the two facts is probably clear without further elaboration.

The attitude of the schools and of the learned class towards the education of women serves to show in what manner and to what extent learning has departed from its ancient station of priestly and leisure-class prerogatives, and it indicates also what approach has been made by the truly learned to the modern, economic or industrial, matter-of-fact standpoint. The higher schools and the learned professions were until recently taboo to the women. These establishments were from the outset, and have in great measure continued to be, devoted to the education of the priestly and leisure classes.

The women, as has been shown elsewhere, were the original subservient class, and to some extent, especially so far as regards their nominal or ceremonial position, they have remained in that relation down to the present. There has prevailed a strong sense that the admission of women to the privileges of the higher learning (as to the Eleusinian mysteries) would be derogatory to the dignity of the learned craft. It is therefore only very recently, and almost solely in the industrially most advanced communities, that the higher grades of schools have been freely opened to women. And even under the urgent circumstances prevailing in the modern industrial communities, the highest and most reputable universities show an extreme reluctance in making the move. The sense of class worthiness, that is to say of status, of a honorific differentiation of the sexes according to a distinction between superior and inferior intellectual dignity, survives in a vigorous form in these corporations of the aristocracy of learning. It is felt that the woman should, in all propriety, acquire only such knowledge as may be classed under one or the other of two heads: (1) such knowledge as conduces immediately to a better performance of domestic service—the domestic sphere; (2) such accomplishments and dexterity, quasi-scholarly and quasi-artistic, as plainly come in under the head of a performance of vicarious leisure. Knowledge is felt to be unfeminine if it is knowledge which expresses the unfolding of the learner's own life, the acquisition of which proceeds on the learner's own cognitive interest, without prompting from the canons of propriety, and without reference back to a master whose comfort or good repute is to be enhanced by the employment or the exhibition of it. So, also, all knowledge which is useful as evidence of leisure, other than vicarious leisure, is scarcely feminine.

For an appreciation of the relation which these higher seminaries of learning bear to the economic life of the community, the phenomena which have been reviewed are of importance rather as indications of a general attitude than as being in themselves facts of first-rate economic consequence. They go to show what is the instinctive attitude and animus of the learned class towards the life process of an industrial community. They serve as an exponent of the stage of development, for the industrial purpose, attained by the higher learning and by the learned class, and so they afford an indication as to what may fairly be looked for from this class at points where the learning and the life of the class bear more immediately upon the economic life and efficiency of the community, and upon the adjustment of its scheme of life to the requirements of the time. What these ritualistic survivals go to indicate is a prevalence of conservatism, if not of reactionary sentiment, especially among the higher schools where the conventional learning is cultivated.

To these indications of a conservative attitude is to be added another characteristic which goes in the same direction, but which is a symptom of graver consequence than this playful inclination to trivialities of form and ritual. By far the greater number of American colleges and universities, for instance, are affiliated to some religious denomination and are somewhat given to devout observances. Their putative familiarity with scientific methods and the scientific point of view should presumably exempt the faculties of these schools from animistic habits of thought; but there is still a considerable proportion of them who profess an attachment to the anthropomorphic beliefs and observances of an earlier culture. These professions of devotional zeal are, no doubt, to a good extent expedient and perfunctory, both on the part of the schools in their corporate capacity, and on the part of the individual members of the corps of instructors; but it can not be doubted that there is after all a very appreciable element of anthropomorphic sentiment present in the higher schools. So far as this is the case it must be set down as the expression of an archaic, animistic habit of mind. This habit of mind must necessarily assert itself to some extent in the instruction offered, and to this extent its influence in shaping the habits of thought of the student makes for conservatism and reversion; it acts to hinder his development in the direction of matter-of-fact knowledge, such as best serves the ends of industry.

The college sports, which have so great a vogue in the reputable seminaries of learning today, tend in a similar direction; and, indeed, sports have much in common with the devout attitude of the colleges, both as regards their psychological basis and as regards their disciplinary effect. But this expression of the barbarian temperament is to be credited primarily to the body of students, rather than to the temper of the schools as such; except in so far as the colleges or the college officials—as sometimes happens—actively countenance and foster the growth of sports. The like is true of college fraternities as of college sports, but with a difference. The latter are chiefly an expression of the predatory impulse simply; the former are more specifically an expression of that heritage of clannishness which is so large a feature in the temperament of the predatory barbarian. It is also noticeable that a close relation subsists between the fraternities and the sporting activity of the schools. After what has already been said in an earlier chapter on the sporting and gambling habit, it is scarcely necessary further to discuss the economic value of this training in sports and in factional organization and activity.

But all these features of the scheme of life of the learned class, and of the establishments dedicated to the conservation of the higher learning, are in a great measure incidental only. They are scarcely to be accounted organic elements of the professed work of research and instruction for the ostensible pursuit of which the schools exists. But these symptomatic indications go to establish a presumption as to the character of the work performed—as seen from the economic point of view—and as to the bent which the serious work carried on under their auspices gives to the youth who resort to the schools.

The presumption raised by the considerations already offered is that in their work also, as well as in their ceremonial, the higher schools may be expected to take a conservative position; but this presumption must be checked by a comparison of the economic character of the work actually performed, and by something of a survey of the learning whose conservation is entrusted to the higher schools. On this head, it is well known that the accredited seminaries of learning have, until a recent date, held a conservative position. They have taken an attitude of depreciation towards all innovations. As a general rule a new point of view or a new formulation of knowledge have been countenanced and taken up within the schools only after these new things have made their way outside of the schools. As exceptions from this rule are chiefly to be mentioned innovations of an inconspicuous kind and departures which do not bear in any tangible way upon the conventional point of view or upon the conventional scheme of life; as, for instance, details of fact in the mathematico-physical sciences, and new readings and interpretations of the classics, especially such as have a philological or literary bearing only. Except within the domain of the "humanities," in the narrow sense, and except so far as the traditional point of view of the humanities has been left intact by the innovators, it has generally held true that the accredited learned class and the seminaries of the higher learning have looked askance at all innovation. New views, new departures in scientific theory, especially in new departures which touch the theory of human relations at any point, have found a place in the scheme of the university tardily and by a reluctant tolerance, rather than by a cordial welcome; and the men who have occupied themselves with such efforts to widen the scope of human knowledge have not commonly been well received by their learned contemporaries. The higher schools have not commonly given their countenance to a serious advance in the methods or the content of knowledge until the innovations have outlived their youth and much of their usefulness—after they have become commonplaces of the intellectual furniture of a new generation which has grown up under, and has had its habits of thought shaped by, the new, extra-scholastic body of knowledge and the new standpoint. This is true of the recent past. How far it may be true of the immediate present it would be hazardous to say, for it is impossible to see present-day facts in such perspective as to get a fair conception of their relative proportions.

So far, nothing has been said of the Maecenas function of the well-to-do, which is habitually dwelt on at some length by writers and speakers who treat of the development of culture and of social structure. This leisure-class function is not without an important bearing on the higher and on the spread of knowledge and culture. The manner and the degree in which the class furthers learning through patronage of this kind is sufficiently familiar. It has been frequently presented in affectionate and effective terms by spokesmen whose familiarity with the topic fits them to bring home to their hearers the profound significance of this cultural factor. These spokesmen, however, have presented the matter from the point of view of the cultural interest, or of the interest of reputability, rather than from that of the economic interest. As apprehended from the economic point of view, and valued for the purpose of industrial serviceability, this function of the well-to-do, as well as the intellectual attitude of members of the well-to-do class, merits some attention and will bear illustration.

By way of characterization of the Maecenas relation, it is to be noted that, considered externally, as an economic or industrial relation simply, it is a relation of status. The scholar under the patronage performs the duties of a learned life vicariously for his patron, to whom a certain repute inures after the manner of the good repute imputed to a master for whom any form of vicarious leisure is performed. It is also to be noted that, in point of historical fact, the furtherance of learning or the maintenance of scholarly activity through the Maecenas relation has most commonly been a furtherance of proficiency in classical lore or in the humanities. The knowledge tends to lower rather than to heighten the industrial efficiency of the community.

Further, as regards the direct participation of the members of the leisure class in the furtherance of knowledge, the canons of reputable living act to throw such intellectual interest as seeks expression among the class on the side of classical and formal erudition, rather than on the side of the sciences that bear some relation to the community's industrial life. The most frequent excursions into other than classical fields of knowledge on the part of members of the leisure class are made into the discipline of law and the political, and more especially the administrative, sciences. These so-called sciences are substantially bodies of maxims of expediency for guidance in the leisure-class office of government, as conducted on a proprietary basis. The interest with which this discipline is approached is therefore not commonly the intellectual or cognitive interest simply. It is largely the practical interest of the exigencies of that relation of mastery in which the members of the class are placed. In point of derivation, the office of government is a predatory function, pertaining integrally to the archaic leisure-class scheme of life. It is an exercise of control and coercion over the population from which the class draws its sustenance. This discipline, as well as the incidents of practice which give it its content, therefore has some attraction for the class apart from all questions of cognition. All this holds true wherever and so long as the governmental office continues, in form or in substance, to be a proprietary office; and it holds true beyond that limit, in so far as the tradition of the more archaic phase of governmental evolution has lasted on into the later life of those modern communities for whom proprietary government by a leisure class is now beginning to pass away.

For that field of learning within which the cognitive or intellectual interest is dominant—the sciences properly so called—the case is somewhat different, not only as regards the attitude of the leisure class, but as regards the whole drift of the pecuniary culture.

Knowledge for its own sake, the exercise of the faculty of comprehensive without ulterior purpose, should, it might be expected, be sought by men whom no urgent material interest diverts from such a quest. The sheltered industrial position of the leisure class should give free play to the cognitive interest in members of this class, and we should consequently have, as many writers confidently find that we do have, a very large proportion of scholars, scientists, savants derived from this class and deriving their incentive to scientific investigation and speculation from the discipline of a life of leisure.

Some such result is to be looked for, but there are features of the leisure-class scheme of life, already sufficiently dwelt upon, which go to divert the intellectual interest of this class to other subjects than that causal sequence in phenomena which makes the content of the sciences. The habits of thought which characterize the life of the class run on the personal relation of dominance, and on the derivative, invidious concepts of honor, worth, merit, character, and the like. The casual sequence which makes up the subject matter of science is not visible from this point of view. Neither does good repute attach to knowledge of facts that are vulgarly useful. Hence it should appear probable that the interest of the invidious comparison with respect to pecuniary or other honorific merit should occupy the attention of the leisure class, to the neglect of the cognitive interest.

Where this latter interest asserts itself it should commonly be diverted to fields of speculation or investigation which are reputable and futile, rather than to the quest of scientific knowledge. Such indeed has been the history of priestly and leisure-class learning so long as no considerable body of systematized knowledge had been intruded into the scholastic discipline from an extra-scholastic source. But since the relation of mastery and subservience is ceasing to be the dominant and formative factor in the community's life process, other features of the life process and other points of view are forcing themselves upon the scholars. The true-bred gentleman of leisure should, and does, see the world from the point of view of the personal relation; and the cognitive interest, so far as it asserts itself in him, should seek to systematize phenomena on this basis. Such indeed is the case with the gentleman of the old school, in whom the leisure-class ideals have suffered no disintegration; and such is the attitude of his latter-day descendant, in so far as he has fallen heir to the full complement of upper-class virtues. But the ways of heredity are devious, and not every gentleman's son is to the manor born.

Especially is the transmission of the habits of thought which characterize the predatory master somewhat precarious in the case of a line of descent in which but one or two of the latest steps have lain within the leisure-class discipline. The chances of occurrence of a strong congenital or acquired bent towards the exercise of the cognitive aptitudes are apparently best in those members of the leisure class who are of lower class or middle class antecedents—that is to say, those who have inherited the complement of aptitudes proper to the industrious classes, and who owe their place in the leisure class to the possession of qualities which count for more today than they did in the times when the leisure-class scheme of life took shape. But even outside the range of these later accessions to the leisure class there are an appreciable number of individuals in whom the invidious interest is not sufficiently dominant to shape their theoretical views, and in whom the proclivity to theory is sufficiently strong to lead them into the scientific quest.

The higher learning owes the intrusion of the sciences in part to these aberrant scions of the leisure class, who have come under the dominant influence of the latter-day tradition of impersonal relation and who have inherited a complement of human aptitudes differing in certain salient features from the temperament which is characteristic of the regime of status. But it owes the presence of this alien body of scientific knowledge also in part, and in a higher degree, to members of the industrious classes who have been in sufficiently easy circumstances to turn their attention to other interests than that of finding daily sustenance, and whose inherited aptitudes and anthropomorphic point of view does not dominate their intellectual processes. As between these two groups, which approximately comprise the effective force of scientific progress, it is the latter that has contributed the most. And with respect to both it seems to be true that they are not so much the source as the vehicle, or at the most they are the instrument of commutation, by which the habits of thought enforced upon the community, through contact with its environment under the exigencies of modern associated life and the mechanical industries, are turned to account for theoretical knowledge.

Science, in the sense of an articulate recognition of causal sequence in phenomena, whether physical or social, has been a feature of the Western culture only since the industrial process in the Western communities has come to be substantially a process of mechanical contrivances in which man's office is that of discrimination and valuation of material forces. Science has flourished somewhat in the same degree as the industrial life of the community has conformed to this pattern, and somewhat in the same degree as the industrial interest has dominated the community's life. And science, and scientific theory especially, has made headway in the several departments of human life and knowledge in proportion as each of these several departments has successively come into closer contact with the industrial process and the economic interest; or perhaps it is truer to say, in proportion as each of them has successively escaped from the dominance of the conceptions of personal relation or status, and of the derivative canons of anthropomorphic fitness and honorific worth.

It is only as the exigencies of modern industrial life have enforced the recognition of causal sequence in the practical contact of mankind with their environment, that men have come to systematize the phenomena of this environment and the facts of their own contact with it, in terms of causal sequence. So that while the higher learning in its best development, as the perfect flower of scholasticism and classicism, was a by-product of the priestly office and the life of leisure, so modern science may be said to be a by-product of the industrial process. Through these groups of men, then—investigators, savants, scientists, inventors, speculators—most of whom have done their most telling work outside the shelter of the schools, the habits of thought enforced by the modern industrial life have found coherent expression and elaboration as a body of theoretical science having to do with the causal sequence of phenomena. And from this extra-scholastic field of scientific speculation, changes of method and purpose have from time to time been intruded into the scholastic discipline.

In this connection it is to be remarked that there is a very perceptible difference of substance and purpose between the instruction offered in the primary and secondary schools, on the one hand, and in the higher seminaries of learning, on the other hand. The difference in point of immediate practicality of the information imparted and of the proficiency acquired may be of some consequence and may merit the attention which it has from time to time received; but there is more substantial difference in the mental and spiritual bent which is favored by the one and the other discipline. This divergent trend in discipline between the higher and the lower learning is especially noticeable as regards the primary education in its latest development in the advanced industrial communities. Here the instruction is directed chiefly to proficiency or dexterity, intellectual and manual, in the apprehension and employment of impersonal facts, in their causal rather than in their honorific incidence. It is true, under the traditions of the earlier days, when the primary education was also predominantly a leisure-class commodity, a free use is still made of emulation as a spur to diligence in the common run of primary schools; but even this use of emulation as an expedient is visibly declining in the primary grades of instruction in communities where the lower education is not under the guidance of the ecclesiastical or military tradition. All this holds true in a peculiar degree, and more especially on the spiritual side, of such portions of the educational system as have been immediately affected by kindergarten methods and ideals.

The peculiarly non-invidious trend of the kindergarten discipline, and the similar character of the kindergarten influence in primary education beyond the limits of the kindergarten proper, should be taken in connection with what has already been said of the peculiar spiritual attitude of leisure-class womankind under the circumstances of the modern economic situation. The kindergarten discipline is at its best—or at its farthest remove from ancient patriarchal and pedagogical ideals—in the advanced industrial communities, where there is a considerable body of intelligent and idle women, and where the system of status has somewhat abated in rigor under the disintegrating influence of industrial life and in the absence of a consistent body of military and ecclesiastical traditions. It is from these women in easy circumstances that it gets its moral support. The aims and methods of the kindergarten commend themselves with especial effect to this class of women who are ill at ease under the pecuniary code of reputable life. The kindergarten, and whatever the kindergarten spirit counts for in modern education, therefore, is to be set down, along with the "new-woman movement," to the account of that revulsion against futility and invidious comparison which the leisure-class life under modern circumstances induces in the women most immediately exposed to its discipline. In this way it appears that, by indirection, the institution of a leisure class here again favors the growth of a non-invidious attitude, which may, in the long run, prove a menace to the stability of the institution itself, and even to the institution of individual ownership on which it rests.

During the recent past some tangible changes have taken place in the scope of college and university teaching. These changes have in the main consisted in a partial displacement of the humanities—those branches of learning which are conceived to make for the traditional "culture," character, tastes, and ideals—by those more matter-of-fact branches which make for civic and industrial efficiency. To put the same thing in other words, those branches of knowledge which make for efficiency (ultimately productive efficiency) have gradually been gaining ground against those branches which make for a heightened consumption or a lowered industrial efficiency and for a type of character suited to the regime of status. In this adaptation of the scheme of instruction the higher schools have commonly been found on the conservative side; each step which they have taken in advance has been to some extent of the nature of a concession. The sciences have been intruded into the scholar's discipline from without, not to say from below. It is noticeable that the humanities which have so reluctantly yielded ground to the sciences are pretty uniformly adapted to shape the character of the student in accordance with a traditional self-centered scheme of consumption; a scheme of contemplation and enjoyment of the true, the beautiful, and the good, according to a conventional standard of propriety and excellence, the salient feature of which is leisure—*otium cum dignitate.* In language veiled by their own habituation to the archaic, decorous point of view, the spokesmen of the humanities have insisted upon the ideal embodied in the maxim, *fruges consumere nati.* This attitude should occasion no surprise in the case of schools which are shaped by and rest upon a leisure-class culture.

The professed grounds on which it has been sought, as far as might be, to maintain the received standards and methods of culture intact are likewise characteristic of the archaic temperament and of the leisure-class theory of life. The enjoyment and the bent derived from habitual contemplation of the life, ideals, speculations, and methods of consuming time and goods, in vogue among the leisure class of classical antiquity, for instance, is felt to be "higher," "nobler," "worthier," than what results in these respects from a like familiarity with the everyday life and the knowledge and aspirations of commonplace humanity in a modern community, that learning the content of which is an unmitigated knowledge of latter-day men and things is by comparison "lower," "base," "ignoble"—one even hears the epithet "sub-human" applied to this matter-of-fact knowledge of mankind and of everyday life.

This contention of the leisure-class spokesmen of the humanities seems to be substantially sound. In point of substantial fact, the gratification and the culture, or the spiritual attitude or habit of mind, resulting from an habitual contemplation of the anthropomorphism, clannishness, and leisurely self-complacency of the gentleman of an early day, or from a familiarity with the animistic superstitions and the exuberant truculence of the Homeric heroes, for instance, is, aesthetically considered, more legitimate than the corresponding results derived from a matter-of-fact knowledge of things and a contemplation of latter-day civic or workmanlike efficiency. There can be but little question that the first-named habits have the advantage in respect of aesthetic or honorific value, and therefore in respect of the "worth" which is made the basis of award in the comparison. The content of the canons of taste, and more particularly of the canons of honor, is in the nature of things a resultant of the past life and circumstances of the race, transmitted to the later generation by inheritance or by tradition; and the fact that the protracted dominance of a predatory, leisure-class scheme of life has profoundly shaped the habit of mind and the point of view of the race in the past, is a sufficient basis for an aesthetically legitimate dominance of such a scheme of life in very much of what concerns matters of taste in the present. For the purpose in hand, canons of taste are race habits, acquired through a more or less protracted habituation to the approval or disapproval of the kind of things upon which a favorable or unfavorable judgment of taste is passed. Other things being equal, the longer and more unbroken the habituation, the more legitimate is the canon of taste in question. All this seems to be even truer of judgments regarding worth or honor than of judgments of taste generally.

But whatever may be the aesthetic legitimacy of the derogatory judgment passed on the newer learning by the spokesmen of the humanities, and however substantial may be the merits of the contention that the classic lore is worthier and results in a more truly human culture and character, it does not concern the question in hand. The question in hand is as to how far these branches of learning, and the point of view for which they stand in the educational system, help or hinder an efficient collective life under modern industrial circumstances—how far they further a more facile adaptation to the economic situation of today. The question is an economic, not an aesthetic one; and the leisure-class standards of learning which find expression in the deprecatory attitude of the higher schools towards matter-of-fact knowledge are, for the present purpose, to be valued from this point of view only. For this purpose the use of such epithets as "noble," "base," "higher," "lower," etc., is significant only as showing the animus and the point of view of the disputants; whether they contend for the worthiness of the new or of the old. All these epithets are honorific or humilific terms; that is to say, they are terms of invidious comparison, which in the last analysis fall under the category of the reputable or the disreputable; that is, they belong within the range of ideas that characterizes the scheme of life of the regime of status; that is, they are in substance an expression of sportsmanship—of the predatory and animistic habit of mind; that is, they indicate an archaic point of view and theory of life, which may fit the predatory stage of culture and of economic organization from which they have sprung, but which are, from the point of view of economic efficiency in the broader sense, disserviceable anachronisms.

The classics, and their position of prerogative in the scheme of education to which the higher seminaries of learning cling with such a fond predilection, serve to shape the intellectual attitude and lower the economic efficiency of the new learned generation. They do this not only by holding up an archaic ideal of manhood, but also by the discrimination which they inculcate with respect to the reputable and the disreputable in knowledge. This result is accomplished in two ways: (1) by inspiring an habitual aversion to what is merely useful, as contrasted with what is merely honorific in learning, and so shaping the tastes of the novice that he comes in good faith to find gratification of his tastes solely, or almost solely, in such exercise of the intellect as normally results in no industrial or social gain; and (2) by consuming the learner's time and effort in acquiring knowledge which is of no use, except in so far as this learning has by convention become incorporated into the sum of learning required of the scholar, and has thereby affected the terminology and diction employed in the useful branches of knowledge. Except for this terminological difficulty—which is itself a consequence of the vogue of the classics of the past—a knowledge of the ancient languages, for instance, would have no practical bearing for any scientist or any scholar not engaged on work primarily of a linguistic character. Of course, all this has nothing to say as to the cultural value of the classics, nor is there any intention to disparage the discipline of the classics or the bent which their study gives to the student. That bent seems to be of an economically disserviceable kind, but this fact—somewhat notorious indeed—need disturb no one who has the good fortune to find comfort and strength in the classical lore. The fact that classical learning acts to derange the learner's workmanlike attitudes should fall lightly upon the apprehension of those who hold workmanship of small account in comparison with the cultivation of decorous ideals:

Iam fides et pax et honos pudorque Priscus et neglecta redire virtus Audet.

Owing to the circumstance that this knowledge has become part of the elementary requirements in our system of education, the ability to use and to understand certain of the dead languages of southern Europe is not only gratifying to the person who finds occasion to parade his accomplishments in this respect, but the evidence of such knowledge serves at the same time to recommend any savant to his audience, both lay and learned. It is currently expected that a certain number of years shall have been spent in acquiring this substantially useless information, and its absence creates a presumption of hasty and precarious learning, as well as of a vulgar practicality that is equally obnoxious to the conventional standards of sound scholarship and intellectual force.

The case is analogous to what happens in the purchase of any article of consumption by a purchaser who is not an expert judge of materials or of workmanship. He makes his estimate of value of the article chiefly on the ground of the apparent expensiveness of the finish of those decorative parts and features which have no immediate relation to the intrinsic usefulness of the article; the presumption being that some sort of ill-defined proportion subsists between the substantial value of an article and the expense of adornment added in order to sell it. The presumption that there can ordinarily be no sound scholarship where a knowledge of the classics and humanities is wanting leads to a conspicuous waste of time and labor on the part of the general body of students in acquiring such knowledge. The conventional insistence on a modicum of conspicuous waste as an incident of all reputable scholarship has affected our canons of taste and of serviceability in matters of scholarship in much the same way as the same principle has influenced our judgment of the serviceability of manufactured goods.

It is true, since conspicuous consumption has gained more and more on conspicuous leisure as a means of repute, the acquisition of the dead languages is no longer so imperative a requirement as it once was, and its talismanic virtue as a voucher of scholarship has suffered a concomitant impairment. But while this is true, it is also true that the classics have scarcely lost in absolute value as a voucher of scholastic respectability, since for this purpose it is only necessary that the scholar should be able to put in evidence some learning which is conventionally recognized as evidence of wasted time; and the classics lend themselves with great facility to this use. Indeed, there can be little doubt that it is their utility as evidence of wasted time and effort, and hence of the pecuniary strength necessary in order to afford this waste, that has secured to the classics their position of prerogative in the scheme of higher learning, and has led to their being esteemed the most honorific of all learning. They serve the decorative ends of leisure-class learning better than any other body of knowledge, and hence they are an effective means of reputability.

In this respect the classics have until lately had scarcely a rival. They still have no dangerous rival on the continent of Europe, but lately, since college athletics have won their way into a recognized standing as an accredited field of scholarly accomplishment, this latter branch of learning—if athletics may be freely classed as learning—has become a rival of the classics for the primacy in leisure-class education in American and English schools. Athletics have an obvious advantage over the classics for the purpose of leisure-class learning, since success as an athlete presumes, not only waste of time, but also waste of money, as well as the possession of certain highly unindustrial archaic traits of character and temperament. In the German universities the place of athletics and Greek-letter fraternities, as a leisure-class scholarly occupation, has in some measure been supplied by a skilled and graded inebriety and a perfunctory duelling.

The leisure class and its standard of virtue—archaism and waste—can scarcely have been concerned in the introduction of the classics into the scheme of the higher learning; but the tenacious retention of the classics by the higher schools, and the high degree of reputability which still attaches to them, are no doubt due to their conforming so closely to the requirements of archaism and waste.

"Classic" always carries this connotation of wasteful and archaic, whether it is used to denote the dead languages or the obsolete or obsolescent forms of thought and diction in the living language, or to denote other items of scholarly activity or apparatus to which it is applied with less aptness. So the archaic idiom of the English language is spoken of as "classic" English. Its use is imperative in all speaking and writing upon serious topics, and a facile use of it lends dignity to even the most commonplace and trivial string of talk. The newest form of English diction is of course never written; the sense of that leisure-class propriety which requires archaism in speech is present even in the most illiterate or sensational writers in sufficient force to prevent such a lapse. On the other hand, the highest and most conventionalized style of archaic diction is—quite characteristically—properly employed only in communications between an anthropomorphic divinity and his subjects. Midway between these extremes lies the everyday speech of leisure-class conversation and literature.

Elegant diction, whether in writing or speaking, is an effective means of reputability. It is of moment to know with some precision what is the degree of archaism conventionally required in speaking on any given topic. Usage differs appreciably from the pulpit to the market-place; the latter, as might be expected, admits the use of relatively new and effective words and turns of expression, even by fastidious persons. A discriminative avoidance of neologisms is honorific, not only because it argues that time has been wasted in acquiring the obsolescent habit of speech, but also as showing that the speaker has from infancy habitually associated with persons who have been familiar with the obsolescent idiom. It thereby goes to show his leisure-class antecedents. Great purity of speech is presumptive evidence of several lives spent in other than vulgarly useful occupations; although its evidence is by no means entirely conclusive to this point.

As felicitous an instance of futile classicism as can well be found, outside of the Far East, is the conventional spelling of the English language. A breach of the proprieties in spelling is extremely annoying and will discredit any writer in the eyes of all persons who are possessed of a developed sense of the true and beautiful. English orthography satisfies all the requirements of the canons of reputability under the law of conspicuous waste. It is archaic, cumbrous, and ineffective; its acquisition consumes much time and effort; failure to acquire it is easy of detection. Therefore it is the first and readiest test of reputability in learning, and conformity to its ritual is indispensable to a blameless scholastic life.

On this head of purity of speech, as at other points where a conventional usage rests on the canons of archaism and waste, the spokesmen for the usage instinctively take an apologetic attitude. It is contended, in substance, that a punctilious use of ancient and accredited locutions will serve to convey thought more adequately and more precisely than would be the straightforward use of the latest form of spoken English; whereas it is notorious that the ideas of today are effectively expressed in the slang of today. Classic speech has the honorific virtue of dignity; it commands attention and respect as being the accredited method of communication under the leisure-class scheme of life, because it carries a pointed suggestion of the industrial exemption of the speaker. The advantage of the accredited locutions lies in their reputability; they are reputable because they are cumbrous and out of date, and therefore argue waste of time and exemption from the use and the need of direct and forcible speech.

John Maynard Keynes (1883–1946)

AN INTRODUCTION TO HIS LIFE AND WORK

Charming. Daring. Brilliant. Dynamic. Controversial. Always hurling himself into the center of the most important and perilous conflicts of his day. John Maynard Keynes starred as economic theory's action-adventure hero during much of the twentieth century. Keynes provided the intellectual verve and harnessed the political and fiscal muscle to help rescue humanity from the economic super-villain that was the Great Depression and to bankroll and win a pair of World Wars, as well as the periods of peace that followed.

Like any action hero worthy of a blockbuster, Keynes had to battle curmudgeonly colleagues at the same time he was fighting off radical outsiders looking to raise the flag of some extreme new ideology over the globe. Keynes ultimately vanquished all these foes and saved the world. And, like any successful action hero, Keynes and his new Keynesian economics got rewarded with years of sequels that brought in big money until hacks misapplied his "can't miss" formula and tanked the franchise.

At least that's the heroic legend of economist John Maynard Keynes. There's a negative one, too, with Keynes as the bungling anti-hero who prolonged the Depression and acted as an unwitting undercover agent for the enemies of the Free World.

Despite years of reflection, mass application of his ideas and biographical scholarship, these legends of John Maynard Keynes can still overshadow any sober analysis of who he really was, what he actually accomplished, or even of what he actually wrote. Six decades after his death, the mere mention of his name still provokes ferocious and wildly conflicting responses.

In 2000, *Time* magazine honored Keynes as the only economist on its list of the 100 Most Important People of the Century, hailing him as the man who "probably saved capitalism from itself and surely kept latter-day Marxists at bay." Five years later, a panel of conservative scholars organized by *Human Events* magazine denounced Keynes's *General Theory of Employment, Interest and Money* as one of the Ten Most Dangerous Books of the last two hundred years, right alongside *The Communist Manifesto* and Adolph Hitler's *Mein Kampf.*

So who really was John Maynard Keynes and what did he really do? And, should he be honored or dishonored for doing it? The answers seem both terribly complicated and deceptively simple.

HIS LIFE

John Maynard Keynes was born in 1883 in Cambridge, England, into a highly educated and prestigious family. Keynes's father worked as an economics professor at Cambridge University. His mother, Florence Ada Brown, had been one of the first female students admitted to the world-renowned university, and later served as Cambridge's first female mayor.

The young Keynes attended Eton, then King's College at Cambridge, where he distinguished himself as a confident, charming, wide-ranging intellectual and a fearsome debater. During his time at Cambridge, Keynes became involved with the Bloomsbury group, an iconoclastic assortment of artistic, intellectual, and sexual adventurers that included writers Virginia Woolf and E.M. Forster, artist Vanessa Bell, and Scottish painter Duncan Grant, with whom Keynes had a long intimate relationship. Keynes became a fellow at Cambridge in 1908 and lectured on economics. He was named editor of the school's *Economic Journal* in 1911. Despite numerous other professional endeavors, he maintained both positions for most of the rest of his life.

In 1913, Keynes entered the English civil service, working first in India then in the British treasury department during World War I, figuring out ways to help finance the war. At the end of the conflict, he served as part of England's delegation for the 1919 Versailles Peace Conference. Outraged by the vindictive terms imposed on Germany at the conference, he resigned his position and published *The Economic Consequences of Peace*. In this work, Keynes correctly predicted the economic devastation that Germany would suffer as a result of the Versailles treaty and the social upheaval that would ultimately lead to the rise of Adolph Hitler.

Keynes returned to Cambridge, where he lectured throughout the 20s and published several more books on economics. He also managed to amass a small fortune through crafty investments. In 1925, he married Lydia Lopokova, a Russian dancer. With his growing reputation as an economic thinker who knew how to successfully apply theory to real-world situations, Keynes also participated vigorously in public policy debates throughout the decade.

Keynes released *The General Theory of Employment, Interest and Money*, the most influential economics book of the first half of the twentieth century, in 1936. It launched the field of macroeconomics and the Keynesian Revolution that sought to jumpstart classical free market theory and inspire government to become a more active player in economics. Many credit the book's ideas and Keynes's efforts in applying them with helping the U.S. and Europe work their way out of the Great Depression and through the fiscal hardships of World War II and beyond. Keynes's ideas continued to dominate political economic thinking and action for the next four decades.

In 1944, Keynes chaired the British delegation at the Bretton Woods conference, where the World Bank and International Monetary Fund were established to help stabilize the world economy. In rapidly deteriorating health due to a coronary condition, Keynes still brokered a huge American loan to Britain after the end of World War II that helped revive his native country's economy. He died in 1946 from heart failure.

WHEN HE DID IT

Before one can appreciate what John Maynard Keynes did, it's vital to understand when he did it. Keynes came of age professionally as civilization entered a period of deep and prolonged crisis. For three decades, world wars and economic desolation swept across much of the globe, interrupted only by a period of rash excess that helped fuel an even more devastating economic crisis.

When World War I broke out in 1914, Keynes climbed down from his comfortable economics position in the ivory tower of Cambridge University to test his mettle and his ideas in real world situations. He took a job with the British treasury department, where he excelled in finding innovative ways for England and its allies to finance the war effort.

In honor of his energy and unique understanding of international economics, Keynes was named to the British team negotiating the peace treaty in France at war's end in 1919. As the final terms of the treaty took shape, however, Keynes quit the negotiations and wrote *The Economic Consequences of Peace*, a book denouncing the proceedings for reasons that would turn out to be all too prophetic. He believed that the harsh penalties that the treaty imposed on the Germans would destroy their economy and spread woe across the rest of Europe. Germany's financial fortunes did indeed collapse, and Adolph Hitler emerged from the rubble in the 1930s.

The United States, Great Britain, and most of the rest of the world had their own economic catastrophe to attend to in the 30s: the Great Depression. It's hard for contemporaries to appreciate the level of deprivation and misery that the Great Depression forced upon so many people. Unemployment soared to record levels. Millions of people lost their homes, farms, and businesses. Hunger and homelessness grew rampant. The exact combination of causes that led to the Great Depression were the subject of much debate. Part of Keynes's genius was to mostly ignore that debate and focus on the basic dynamic of the situation and how to remedy it.

A lack of dynamics may actually be a better way to describe the economic state of affairs as the Great Depression took hold. Plummeting demand led to overstocks of supply, which led to slashed prices, which obliterated profit margins, which led to job cuts, which lowered demand even further and sent the economy around another loop in the downward spiral that no one seemed to know how to reverse. The usual method of lowering interest rates to pump more money into the economy had no effect, even when they dropped to near zero percent.

Many believed free market capitalism itself was to blame and clamored for a government takeover of business. Others thought the bust would serve as righteous medicine for the boom of the Roaring 20s. Such ideas were not just wafting in from the radical fringes, but also from the middle class and insider elites. "Liquidate labor, liquidate stocks, liquidate the farmers, liquidate real estate. . . purge the rottenness out of the system. High costs of living and high living will come down. People will work harder, live a more moral life. Values will be adjusted, and enterprising people will pick up the wrecks from less competent people." That 1930 prescription came from Andrew Mellon, Secretary of the Treasury under President Herbert Hoover.

A bigger part of John Maynard Keynes's genius was that he did see a way to get out of the mess. And, what's more, he recognized that the escape would be relatively easy, at least the mechanics of it. The biggest part of his energy and genius, however, would be dedicated to the hard part: convincing world leaders that this exercise in economic engineering was technically sound, moral, and even sane.

THE KEYNESIAN BREAKTHROUGH

Keynes recognized that the depressed economy did not require a wholesale makeover or government takeover or Mellon's baptism by liquidation. He felt the whole terrible downward death spiral of the Great Depression could be solved simply by artificially stimulating demand. Keynes theorized that increased demand would decrease supply overstocks and jumpstart production, leading to more work and more jobs and more people spending more money. This in turn would increase demand, which would diminish supplies and lead to higher prices and higher profits, which would mean increased investment and production, etc., etc. into prosperity.

Businesses and banks were unwilling and/or unable to provide the injection of cash to get the ball rolling. They had suffered great losses in the preceding years. To the ones still standing, investing in new operations seemed like throwing good money after bad debt. Everyone was hoarding cash instead. Keynes knew government was the only party able to generate the needed level of stimulation. But with drastic reductions in tax revenue, governments were broke as well.

So Keynes suggested deficit spending. The idea of deficit spending seems simple, even mundane today after decades of government budgets that casually run up deficits in the billions of dollars. But the idea sounded like anathema to economists and government officials in Keynes's day—partly because it called for government to spend vast amounts of money that it did not have, and partly because it called for government to get more involved in managing the economy. Back then, laissez-faire was the first and perhaps only commandment of political economics.

Besides, Keynes's remedy sounded ludicrous and dangerous—the fiscal equivalent of lighting a patient's bed on fire to cure his fever. How could going into debt by spending money you didn't have save an economy? Wasn't deficit spending by individuals a big part of what triggered the Depression in the first place? How could government doing it on a mass scale solve the problem?

Keynes tried unsuccessfully to persuade his fellow economists and high government officials, including Franklin Roosevelt. But, as in school—where he once failed an economics exam because his answers were too sophisticated for his teacher to understand—Keynes was too far ahead and moving too fast for anyone to see where he was going. Keynes realized that he would have to backtrack and write a book that brought everyone else up to speed.

THE GENERAL THEORY OF EMPLOYMENT, INTEREST AND MONEY

Though it is a long and at times difficult book, *The General Theory of Employment, Interest and Money* reduces itself to an idea that is relatively simple to understand, especially today after over a half-century of seeing it in wide practice. Keynes asserted that a free market economy that has lapsed into a state of low demand (and all its attending miseries) may be better served by a public sector intervention to stimulate demand through increased government spending, rather than by waiting for the economy to correct itself. In the event of a depression, such proactive measures may be essential.

Already knowing all too well how heretical such an idea seemed to his readers (whom he assumed would be mostly fellow economists), Keynes understood he would have to take them step-by-step through the long, complex thought process that he had endured to reach that conclusion. That's where *The General Theory* acquires its bulk and complexities. But Keynes also knew that to convince readers to come along on such a journey, he would first have to goose them into motion. So Keynes opens *The General Theory* with a brazen, brilliant, and seemingly outlandish assault on long-held precepts of economic thought. He dismisses traditional notions about the relationships between supply and demand, booms and busts, equilibrium and economic health, savings and investments, interests rates and economic activity, and wages and employment ,and suggests that the hoary Say's Law might have to be struck from the books. He warns readers that a failure to "escape" such limitations of classical economic thought would prove disastrous.

While it certainly gets your attention, Book I of *The General Theory* can seem disorienting and even reckless. But for Keynes, its confrontational style was a necessary risk. He knew readers would not follow him to a radical new notion of economics unless he first convinced them that the theoretical ground they had stood on for so long was unstable, dangerous, and in spots, a mirage.

Starting with Book II, Keynes takes readers by the hand and leads them step-by-step on the rest of the journey, along trails that can seem like long detours, dead ends, and freefalls into oblivion, or, more often, long, hard climbs up sheer cliffs. Reading these sections of *The General Theory* can prove difficult and, at times, even maddening. But it also serves as an essential primer on the evolution of economic thought and practice. Without this detailed tour and roadmap, it might be impossible to trace the quantum leap that economic theory seemed to take from the early part of the twentieth century to the second half, and to where it still stands today.

THE KEYNESIAN LEGACY

Debate lingers about whether Keynes's ideas were all his own (Hitler and Hoover had earlier employed some of his methods to varying degrees and levels of success). Others question whether his book and ideas emerged in time to help end the Great Depression. After all, Roosevelt didn't test deficit spending until 1938, and didn't fully embrace the practice until World War II forced his hand.

Keynes died just after the war ended, but his once radical ideas were implemented and mostly vindicated to an astonishing degree in the quarter-century that followed. *The General Theory* helped launch the field of macroeconomics and establish institutions and practices that are used to this day by governments and politicians from across the political spectrum. Keynes played a key role in the 1944 Bretton Woods Agreement, which set up an international infrastructure to regulate exchange rates and stabilize the world economy, leading to the establishment of the World Bank group and the International Monetary Fund, and steering the world away from the risk of another Great Depression. The Marshall Plan, the massive and highly successful U.S. investment in rebuilding Europe after World War II to fend off economic disaster and deter communism, can be tied to ideas Keynes put forth in *The General Theory* and his earlier *The Economic Consequences of Peace*.

Keynes still has his critics. Many blame him for leading governments into overspending the global economy into the low growth/high inflation stagflation trauma of the 1970s. They claim his ideas and practices only apply to depression scenarios and were invalidated in the 1980s by the supply side economics of Milton Friedman's disciples and the boom they helped inspire. But, whether they'd like to admit it or not, many of those same Friedmanites still rely heavily on the economic reasoning, methods, and institutions that Keynes established. Ronald Reagan was far more Keynesian than Franklin Roosevelt ever dreamed of becoming, as is George W. Bush. Richard Nixon declared himself a "Keynesian" in 1971. Even Friedman, widely regarded as Keynes's posthumous nemesis, admitted that in looking over his years working at the Treasury Department, he marveled at "how much more Keynesian I was than I thought."

The legend and reputation of John Maynard Keynes tends to distort and even invert, depending on whose eyes are beholding it. But the institutional and practical embodiments of his ideas continue to surround us, protecting and invigorating the world's economy and helping spare us the dangers that John Maynard Keynes and his contemporaries faced most of their lives.

THE GENERAL THEORY OF EMPLOYMENT, INTEREST AND MONEY BY JOHN MAYNARD KEYNES

Preface

This book is chiefly addressed to my fellow economists. I hope that it will be intelligible to others. But its main purpose is to deal with difficult questions of theory, and only in the second place with the applications of this theory to practice. For if orthodox economics is at fault, the error is to be found not in the superstructure, which has been erected with great care for logical consistency, but in a lack of clearness and of generality in the premises. Thus I cannot achieve my object of persuading economists to re-examine critically certain of their basic assumptions except by a highly abstract argument and also by much controversy. I wish there could have been less of the latter. But I have thought it important, not only to explain my own point of view, but also to show in what respects it departs from the prevailing theory. Those, who are strongly wedded to what I shall call "the classical theory", will fluctuate, I expect, between a belief that I am quite wrong and a belief that I am saying nothing new. It is for others to determine if either of these or the third alternative is right. My controversial passages are aimed at providing some material for an answer; and I must ask forgiveness if, in the pursuit of sharp distinctions, my controversy is itself too keen. I myself held with conviction for many years the theories which I now attack, and I am not, I think, ignorant of their strong points.

The matters at issue are of an importance which cannot be exaggerated. But, if my explanations are right, it is my fellow economists, not the general public, whom I must first convince. At this stage of the argument the general public, though welcome at the debate, are only eavesdroppers at an attempt by an economist to bring to an issue the deep divergences of opinion between fellow economists which have for the time being almost destroyed the practical influence of economic theory, and will, until they are resolved, continue to do so.

The relation between this book and my *Treatise on Money*, which I published five years ago, is probably clearer to myself than it will be to others; and what in my own mind is a natural evolution in a line of thought which I have been pursuing for several years, may sometimes strike the reader as a confusing change of view. This difficulty is not made less by certain changes in terminology which I have felt compelled to make. These changes of language I have pointed out in the course of the following pages; but the general relationship between the two books can be expressed briefly as follows. When I began to write my *Treatise on Money* I was still moving along the traditional lines of regarding the influence of money as something so to speak separate from the general theory of supply and demand. When I finished it, I had made some progress towards pushing monetary theory back to becoming a theory of output as a whole. But my lack of emancipation from preconceived ideas showed itself in what now seems to me to be the outstanding fault of the theoretical parts of that work (namely, Books III and IV), that I failed to deal thoroughly with the effects of *changes* in the level of output. My so-called "fundamental equations" were an instantaneous picture taken on the assumption of a given output.

They attempted to show how, assuming the given output, forces could develop which involved a profit-disequilibrium, and thus required a change in the level of output. But the dynamic development, as distinct from the instantaneous picture, was left incomplete and extremely confused. This book, on the other hand, has evolved into what is primarily a study of the forces which determine changes in the scale of output and employment as a whole; and, whilst it is found that money enters into the economic scheme in an essential and peculiar manner, technical monetary detail falls into the background. A monetary economy, we shall find, is essentially one in which changing views about the future are capable of influencing the quantity of employment and not merely its direction. But our method of analyzing the economic behavior of the present under the influence of changing ideas about the future is one which depends on the interaction of supply and demand, and is in this way linked up with our fundamental theory of value. We are thus led to a more general theory, which includes the classical theory with which we are familiar, as a special case.

The writer of a book such as this, treading along unfamiliar paths, is extremely dependent on criticism and conversation if he is to avoid an undue proportion of mistakes. It is astonishing what foolish things one can temporarily believe if one thinks too long alone, particularly in economics (along with the other moral sciences), where it is often impossible to bring one's ideas to a conclusive test either formal or experimental. In this book, even more perhaps than in writing my *Treatise on Money*, I have depended on the constant advice and constructive criticism of Mr. R. F. Kahn. There is a great deal in this book which would not have taken the shape it has except at his suggestion. I have also had much help from Mrs. Joan Robinson, Mr. R. G. Hawtrey and Mr. R. F. Harrod, who have read the whole of the proof-sheets. The index has been compiled by Mr. D. M. Bensusan-Butt of King's College, Cambridge.

The composition of this book has been for the author a long struggle of escape, and so must the reading of it be for most readers if the author's assault upon them is to be successful,—a struggle of escape from habitual modes of thought and expression. The ideas which are here expressed so laboriously are extremely simple and should be obvious. The difficulty lies, not in the new ideas, but in escaping from the old ones, which ramify, for those brought up as most of us have been, into every corner of our minds.

J. M. Keynes
December 13, 1935

Book 1

Introduction

CHAPTER 1

The General Theory

I have called this book the *General Theory of Employment, Interest and Money,* placing the emphasis on the prefix *general.* The object of such a title is to contrast the character of my arguments and conclusions with those of the *classical*[1] theory of the subject, upon which I was brought up and which dominates the economic thought, both practical and theoretical, of the governing and academic classes of this generation, as it has for a hundred years past. I shall argue that the postulates of the classical theory are applicable to a special case only and not to the general case, the situation which it assumes being a limiting point of the possible positions of equilibrium. Moreover, the characteristics of the special case assumed by the classical theory happen not to be those of the economic society in which we actually live, with the result that its teaching is misleading and disastrous if we attempt to apply it to the facts of experience.

CHAPTER 2

The Postulates of the Classic Economics

Most treatises on the theory of Value and Production are primarily concerned with the distribution of a given volume of employed resources between different uses and with the conditions which, assuming the employment of this quantity of resources, determine their relative rewards and the relative values of their products.[2]

The question, also, of the volume of the *available* resources, in the sense of the size of the employable population, the extent of natural wealth and the accumulated capital equipment, has often been treated descriptively. But the pure theory of what determines the *actual employment* of the available resources has seldom been examined in great detail. To say that it has not been examined at all would, of course, be absurd. For every discussion concerning fluctuations of employment, of which there have been many, has been concerned with it. I mean, not that the topic has been overlooked, but that the fundamental theory underlying it has been deemed so simple and obvious that it has received, at the most, a bare mention.[3]

I

The classical theory of employment—supposedly simple and obvious—has been based, I think, on two fundamental postulates, though practically without discussion, namely:

I. *The wage is equal to the marginal product of labor.*

That is to say, the wage of an employed person is equal to the value which would be lost if employment were to be reduced by one unit (after deducting any other costs which this reduction of output would avoid); subject, however, to the qualification that the equality may be disturbed, in accordance with certain principles, if competition and markets are imperfect.

II. *The utility of the wage when a given volume of labor is employed is equal to the marginal disutility of that amount of employment.*

That is to say, the real wage of an employed person is that which is just sufficient (in the estimation of the employed persons themselves) to induce the volume of labor actually employed to be forthcoming; subject to the qualification that the equality for each individual unit of labor may be disturbed by combination between employable units analogous to the imperfections of competition which qualify the first postulate. Disutility must be here understood to cover every kind of reason which might lead a man, or a body of men, to withhold their labor rather than accept a wage which had to them a utility below a certain minimum.

This postulate is compatible with what may be called "frictional" unemployment. For a realistic interpretation of it legitimately allows for various inexactnesses of adjustment which stand in the way of continuous full employment: for example, unemployment due to a temporary want of balance between the relative quantities of specialized resources as a result of miscalculation or intermittent demand; or to time-lags consequent on unforeseen changes; or to the fact that the change-over from one employment to another cannot be effected without a certain delay, so that there will always exist in a non-static society a proportion of resources unemployed "between jobs." In addition to "frictional" unemployment, the postulate is also compatible with "voluntary" unemployment due to the refusal or inability of a unit of labor, as a result of legislation or social practices or of combination for collective bargaining or of slow response to change or of mere human obstinacy, to accept a reward corresponding to the value of the product attributable to its marginal productivity. But these two categories of "frictional" unemployment and "voluntary" unemployment are comprehensive. The classical postulates do not admit of the possibility of the third category, which I shall define below as "involuntary" unemployment.

Subject to these qualifications, the volume of employed resources is duly determined, according to the classical theory, by the two postulates. The first gives us the demand schedule for employment, the second gives us the supply schedule; and the amount of employment is fixed at the point where the utility of the marginal product balances the disutility of the marginal employment.

It would follow from this that there are only four possible means of increasing employment:

(a) An improvement in organization or in foresight which diminishes "frictional" unemployment;

(b) a decrease in the marginal disutility of labor, as expressed by the real wage for which additional labor is available, so as to diminish "voluntary" unemployment;

(c) an increase in the marginal physical productivity of labor in the wage-goods industries (to use Professor Pigou's convenient term for goods upon the price of which the utility of the money-wage depends); or

(d) an increase in the price of non-wage-goods compared with the price of wage-goods, associated with a shirt in the expenditure of non-wage-earners from wage-goods to non-wage-goods.

This, to the best of my understanding, is the substance of Professor Pigou's *Theory of Unemployment*—the only detailed account of the classical theory of employment which exists.[4]

II

Is it true that the above categories are comprehensive in view of the fact that the population generally is seldom doing as much work as it would like to do on the basis of the current wage? For, admittedly, more labor would, as a rule, be forthcoming at the existing money-wage if it were demanded.[5] The classical school reconcile this phenomenon with their second postulate by arguing that, while the demand for labor at the existing money-wage may be satisfied before everyone willing to work at this wage is employed, this situation is due to an open or tacit agreement amongst workers not to work for less, and that if labor as a whole would agree to a reduction of money-wages more employ-ment would be forthcoming. If this is the case, such unemployment, though apparently involuntary, is not strictly so, and ought to be included under the above category of "vol-untary" unemployment due to the effects of collective bargaining, etc.

This calls for two observations, the first of which relates to the actual attitude of work-ers towards real wages and money-wages respectively and is not theoretically fundamen-tal, but the second of which is fundamental.

Let us assume, for the moment, that labor is not prepared to work for a lower money-wage and that a reduction in the existing level of money-wages would lead, through strikes or otherwise, to a withdrawal from the labor market of labor which is now employed. Does it follow from this that the existing level of real wages accurately measures the marginal disu-tility of labor? Not necessarily. For, although a reduction in the existing money-wage would lead to a withdrawal of labor, it does not follow that a fall in the value of the existing money-wage in terms of wage-goods would do so, if it were due to a rise in the price of the latter. In other words, it may be the case that within a certain range the demand of labor is for a minimum money-wage and not for a minimum real wage. The classical school have tac-itly assumed that this would involve no significant change in their theory. But this is not so. For if the supply of labor is not a function of real wages as its sole variable, their argu-ment breaks down entirely and leaves the question of what the actual employment will be quite indeterminate.[6] They do not seem to have realized that, unless the supply of labor is a function of real wages alone, their supply curve for labor will shift bodily with every movement of prices. Thus their method is tied up with their very special assumptions, and cannot be adapted to deal with the more general case.

Now ordinary experience tells us, beyond doubt, that a situation where labor stipulates (within limits) for a money-wage rather than a real wage, so far from being a mere possi-bility, is the normal case. Whilst workers will usually resist a reduction of money-wages, it is not their practice to withdraw their labor whenever there is a rise in the price of wage-goods. It is sometimes said that it would be illogical for labor to resist a reduction of money-wages but not to resist a reduction of real wages. For reasons given below (section III), this might not be so illogical as it appears at first; and, as we shall see later, fortunately so. But, whether logical or illogical, experience shows that this is how labor in fact behaves.

Moreover, the contention that the unemployment which characterizes a depression is due to a refusal by labor to accept a reduction of money-wages is not clearly sup-ported by the facts. It is not very plausible to assert that unemployment in the United States in 1932 was due either to labor obstinately refusing to accept a reduction of money-wages or to its obstinately demanding a real wage beyond what the productiv-ity of the economic machine was capable of furnishing. Wide variations are experi-enced in the volume of employment without any apparent change either in the minimum real demands of labor or in its productivity. Labor is not more truculent in the depression than in the boom—far from it. Nor is its physical productivity less. These facts from experience are a *prima facie* ground for questioning the adequacy of the classical analysis.

It would be interesting to see the results of a statistical enquiry into the actual relation-ship between changes in money-wages and changes in real wages. In the case of a change peculiar to a particular industry one would expect the change in real wages to be in the same direction as the change in money-wages. But in the case of changes in the general level of wages, it will be found, I think, that the change in real wages associated with a change in money-wages, so far from being usually in the same direction, is almost always in the opposite direction. When money-wages are rising, that is to say, it will be found that real wages are falling; and when money-wages are falling, real wages are rising. This is because, in the short period, falling money-wages and rising real wages are each, for independent reasons, likely to accompany decreasing employment; labor being readier to accept wage-cuts when employment is falling off, yet real wages inevitably rising in the same circumstances on account of the increasing marginal return to a given capital equipment when output is diminished.

If, indeed, it were true that the existing real wage is a minimum below which more labor than is now employed will not be forthcoming in any circumstances, involuntary unemployment, apart from frictional unemployment, would be non-existent. But to suppose that this is invariably the case would be absurd. For more labor than is at present employed is usually available at the existing money-wage, even though the price of wage-goods is rising and, consequently, the real wage falling. If this is true, the wage-goods equivalent of the existing money-wage is not an accurate indication of the marginal disutility of labor, and the second postulate does not hold good.

But there is a more fundamental objection. The second postulate flows from the idea that the real wages of labor depend on the wage bargains which labor makes with the entrepreneurs. It is admitted, of course, that the bargains are actually made in terms of money, and even that the real wages acceptable to labor are not altogether independent of what the corresponding money-wage happens to be. Nevertheless it is the money-wage thus arrived at which is held to determine the real wage. Thus the classical theory assumes that it is always open to labor to reduce its real wage by accepting a reduction in its money-wage. The postulate that there is a tendency for the real wage to come to equality with the marginal disutility of labor clearly presumes that labor itself is in a position to decide the real wage for which it works, though not the quantity of employment forthcoming at this wage.

The traditional theory maintains, in short, *that the wage bargains between the entrepreneurs and the workers determine the real wage;* so that, assuming free competition amongst employers and no restrictive combination amongst workers, the latter can, if they wish, bring their real wages into conformity with the marginal disutility of the amount of employment offered by the employers at that wage. If this is not true, then there is no longer any reason to expect a tendency towards equality between the real wage and the marginal disutility of labor.

The classical conclusions are intended, it must be remembered, to apply to the whole body of labor and do not mean merely that a single individual can get employment by accepting a cut in money-wages which his fellows refuse. They are supposed to be equally applicable to a closed system as to an open system, and are not dependent on the characteristics of an open system or on the effects of a reduction of money-wages in a single country on its foreign trade, which lie, of course, entirely outside the field of this discussion. Nor are they based on indirect effects due to a lower wages-bill in terms of money having certain reactions on the banking system and the state of credit, effects which we shall examine in detail in Chapter 19. They are based on the belief that in a closed system a reduction in the general level of money-wages will be accompanied, at any rate in the short period and subject only to minor qualifications, by some, though not always a proportionate, reduction in real wages.

Now the assumption that the general level of real wages depends on the money-wage bargains between the employers and the workers is not obviously true. Indeed it is strange that so little attempt should have been made to prove or to refute it. For it is far from being consistent with the general tenor of the classical theory, which has taught us to believe that prices are governed by marginal prime cost in terms of money and that money-wages largely govern marginal prime cost. Thus if money-wages change, one would have expected the classical school to argue that prices would change in almost the same proportion, leaving the real wage and the level of unemployment practically the same as before, any small gain or loss to labor being at the expense or profit of other elements of marginal cost which have been left unaltered.[7] They seem, however, to have been diverted from this line of thought, partly by the settled conviction that labor is in a position to determine its own real wage and partly, perhaps, by preoccupation with the idea that prices depend on the quantity of money. And the belief in the proposition that labor is always in a position to determine its own real wage, once adopted, has been maintained by its being confused with the proposition that labor is always in a position to determine what real wage shall correspond *to full* employment, i.e. the *maximum* quantity of employment which is compatible with a given real wage.

To sum up: there are two objections to the second postulate of the classical theory. The first relates to the actual behavior of labor. A fall in real wages due to a rise in prices, with money-wages unaltered, does not, as a rule, cause the supply of available labor on offer at the current wage to fall below the amount actually employed prior to the rise of prices. To suppose that it does is to suppose that all those who are now unemployed though willing to work at the current wage will withdraw the offer of their labor in the event of even a small rise in the cost of living. Yet this strange supposition apparently underlies Professor Pigou's *Theory of Unemployment,*[8] and it is what all members of the orthodox school are tacitly assuming.

But the other, more fundamental, objection, which we shall develop in the ensuing chapters, flows from our disputing the assumption that the general level of real wages is directly determined by the character of the wage bargain. In assuming that the wage bargain determines the real wage of classical school have slipped in an illicit assumption. For there may be *no* method available to labor as a whole whereby it can bring the wage-goods equivalent of the general level of money-wages into conformity with the marginal disutility of the current volume of employment. There may exist no expedient by which labor as a whole can reduce its *real* wage to a given figure by making revised *money* bargains with the entrepreneurs. This will be our contentions. We shall endeavor to show that primarily it is certain other forces which determine the general level of real wages. The attempt to elucidate this problem will be one of our main themes. We shall argue that there has been a fundamental misunderstanding of how in this respect the economy in which we live actually works.

III

Though at the struggle over money-wages between individuals and groups is often believed to determine the general level of real wages, it is, in fact, concerned with a different object. Since there is imperfect mobility of labor, and wages do not tend to an exact equality of net advantage in different occupations, any individual or group of individuals, who consent to a reduction of money-wages relatively to others, will suffer a *relative* reduction in real wages, which is a sufficient justification for them to resist it.

On the other hand it would be impracticable to resist every reduction of real wages, due to a change in the purchasing-power of money which affects all workers alike; and in fact reductions of real wages arising in this way are not, as a rule, resisted unless they proceed to an extreme degree. Moreover, a resistance to reductions in money-wages applying to particular industries does not raise the same insuperable bar to an increase in aggregate employment which would result from a similar resistance to every reduction in real wages.

In other words, the struggle about money-wages primarily affects the *distribution* of the aggregate real wage between different labor-groups, and not its average amount per unit of employment, which depends, as we shall see, on a different set of forces. The effect of combination on the part of a group of workers is to protect their *relative* real wage. The *general* level of real wages depends on the other forces of the economic system.

Thus it is fortunate that the workers, though unconsciously, are instinctively more reasonable economists than the classical school, inasmuch as they resist reductions of money-wages, which are seldom or never of an all-round character, even though the existing real equivalent of these wages exceeds the marginal disutility of the existing employment; whereas they do not resist reductions or real wages, which are associated with increases in aggregate employment and leave relative money-wages unchanged, unless the reduction proceeds so far as to threaten a reduction of the real wage below the marginal disutility of the existing volume of employment. Every trade union will put up some resistance to a cut in money-wages, however small. But since no trade union would dream of striking on every occasion of a rise in the cost of living, they do not raise the obstacle to any increase in aggregate employment which is attributed to them by the classical school.

IV

We must now define the third category of unemployment, namely "involuntary" unemployment in the strict sense, the possibility of which the classical theory does not admit.

Clearly we do not mean by "involuntary" unemployment the mere existence of an unexhausted capacity to work. An eight-hour day does not constitute unemployment because it is not beyond human capacity to work ten hours. Nor should we regard as "involuntary" unemployment the withdrawal of their labor by a body of workers because they do not choose to work for less than a certain real reward. Furthermore, it will be convenient to exclude "frictional" unemployment from our definition of "involuntary" unemployment.

My definition is, therefore, as follows: *Men are involuntarily unemployed if, in the event of a small rise in the price of wage-goods relatively to the money-wage, both the aggregate supply of labor willing to work for the current money-wage and the aggregate demand for it at that wage would be greater than the existing volume of employment.* An alternative definition, which amounts, however, to the same thing, will be given in the next chapter.

It follows from this definition that the equality of the real wage to the marginal disutility of employment presupposed by the second postulate, realistically interpreted, corresponds to the absence of "involuntary" unemployment. This state of affairs we shall describe as "full" employment, both "frictional" and "voluntary" unemployment being consistent with "full" employment thus defined. This fits in, we shall find, with other characteristics of the classical theory, which is best regarded as a theory of distribution in conditions of full employment. So long as the classical postulates hold good, unemployment, which is in the above sense involuntary, cannot occur. Apparent unemployment must, therefore, be the result either of temporary loss of work of the "between jobs" type or of intermittent demand for highly specialized resources or of the effect of a trade union "closed shop" on the employment of free labor. Thus writers in the classical tradition, overlooking the special assumption underlying their theory, have been driven inevitably to the conclusion, perfectly logical on their assumption, that apparent unemployment (apart from the admitted exceptions) must be due at bottom to a refusal by the unemployed factors to accept a reward which corresponds to their marginal productivity. A classical economist may sympathize with labor in refusing to accept a cut in its money-wage, and he will admit that it may not be wise to make it to meet conditions which are temporary; but scientific integrity forces him to declare that this refusal is, nevertheless, at the bottom of the trouble.

Obviously, however, if the classical theory is only applicable to the case of full employment, it is fallacious to apply it to the problems of involuntary unemployment—if there be such a thing (and who will deny it?). The classical theorists resemble Euclidean geometers in a non-Euclidean world who, discovering that in experience straight lines apparently parallel often meet, rebuke the lines for not keeping straight—as the only remedy for the unfortunate collisions which are occurring. Yet, in truth, there is no remedy except to throw over the axiom of parallels and to work out a non-Euclidean geometry. Something similar is required today in economics. We need to throw over the second postulate of the classical doctrine and to work out the behavior of a system in which involuntary unemployment in the strict sense is possible.

V

In emphasizing our point of departure from the classical system, we must not overlook an important point of agreement. For we shall maintain the first postulate as heretofore, subject only to the same qualifications as in the classical theory; and we must pause, for a moment, to consider what this involves.

It means that, with a given organization, equipment and technique, real wages and the volume of output (and hence of employment) are uniquely correlated, so that, in general, an increase in employment can only occur to the accompaniment of a decline in the rate of real wages. Thus I am not disputing this vital fact which the classical economists have (rightly) asserted as indefeasible. In a given state of organization, equipment and technique, the real wage earned by a unit of labor has a unique (inverse) correlation with the, volume of employment. Thus *if* employment increases, then, in the short period, the reward per unit of labor in terms of wage-goods must, in general, decline and profits increase.[9] This is simply the obverse of the familiar proposition that industry is normally working subject to decreasing returns in the short period during which equipment etc. is assumed to be constant; so that the marginal product in the wage-good industries (which governs real wages) necessarily diminishes as employment is increased. So long, indeed, as this proposition holds, *any* means of increasing employment must lead at the same time to a diminution of the marginal product and hence of the rate of wages measured in terms of this product.

But when we have thrown over the second postulate, a decline in employment, although necessarily associated with labor's receiving a wage equal in value to a larger quantity of wage-goods, is not necessarily due to labor's *demanding* a larger quantity of wage-goods; and a willingness on the part of labor to accept lower money-wages is not necessarily a remedy for unemployment. The Theory of Wages in relation to employment, to which we are here leading up, cannot be fully elucidated, however, until Chapter 19 and its appendix have been reached.

VI

From the time of Say and Ricardo the classical economists have taught that supply creates its own demand; meaning by this in some significant, but not clearly denned, sense that the whole of the costs of production must necessarily be spent in the aggregate, directly or indirectly, on purchasing the product.

In J. S. Mill's *Principles of Political Economy* the doctrine is expressly set forth:

> What constitutes the means of payment for commodities is simply commodities. Each person's means of paying for the productions of other people consist of those which he himself possesses. All sellers are inevitably, and by the meaning of the word, buyers. Could we suddenly double the productive powers of the country, we should double the supply of commodities in every market; but we should, by the same stroke, double the purchasing power. Everybody would bring a double demand as well as supply; everybody would be able to buy twice as much, because every one would have twice as much to offer in exchange.[10]

As a corollary of the same doctrine, it has been supposed that any individual act of abstaining from consumption necessarily leads to, and amounts to the same thing as, causing the labor and commodities thus released from supplying consumption to be invested in the production of capital wealth. The following passage from Marshall's *Pure Theory of Domestic Values*[11] illustrates the traditional approach:

> The whole of a man's income is expended in the purchase of services and of commodities. It is indeed commonly said that a man spends some portion of his in-

come and saves another. But it is a familiar economic axiom that a man purchases labor and commodities with that portion of his income which he saves just as much as he does with that he is said to spend. He is said to spend when he seeks to obtain present enjoyment from the services and commodities which he purchases. He is said to save when he causes the labor and the commodities which he purchases to be devoted to the production of wealth from which he expects to derive the means of enjoyment in the future.

It is true that it would not be easy to quote comparable passages from Marshall's later work[12] or from Edgeworth or Professor Pigou. The doctrine is never stated today in this crude form. Nevertheless it still underlies the whole classical theory, which would collapse without it. Contemporary economists, who might hesitate to agree with Mill, do not hesitate to accept conclusions which require Mill's doctrine as their premise. The conviction, which runs, for example, through almost all Professor Pigou's work, that money makes no real difference except frictionally and that the theory of production and employment can be worked out (like Mill's) as being based on "real" exchanges with money introduced perfunctorily in a later chapter, is the modern version of the classical tradition. Contemporary thought is still deeply steeped in the notion that if people do not spend their money in one way they will spend it in another.[13] Post-war economists seldom, indeed, succeed in maintaining this standpoint *consistently;* for their thought today is too much permeated with the contrary tendency and with facts of experience too obviously inconsistent with their former view.[14] But they have not drawn sufficiently far-reaching consequences; and have not revised their fundamental theory.

In the first instance, these conclusions may have been applied to the kind of economy in which we actually live by false analogy from some kind of non-exchange Robinson Crusoe economy, in which the income which individuals consume or retain as a result of their productive activity is, actually and exclusively, the output *in specie* of that activity. But, apart from this, the conclusion that the costs of output are always covered in the aggregate by the sale-proceeds resulting from demand, has great plausibility, because it is difficult to distinguish it from another, similar-looking proposition which is indubitable, namely that the income derived in the aggregate by all the elements in the community concerned in a productive activity necessarily has a value exactly equal to the *value* of the output.

Similarly it is natural to suppose that the act of an individual, by which he enriches himself without apparently taking anything from anyone else, must also enrich the community as a whole; so that (as in the passage just quoted from Marshall) an act of individual saving inevitably leads to a parallel act of investment. For, once more, it is indubitable that the sum of the net increments of the wealth of individuals must be exactly equal to the aggregate net increment of the wealth of the community.

Those who think in this way are deceived, nevertheless, by an optical illusion, which makes two essentially different activities appear to be the same. They are fallaciously supposing that there is a nexus which unites decisions to abstain from present consumption with decisions to provide for future consumption; whereas the motives which determine the latter are not linked in any simple way with the motives which determine the former.

It is, then, the assumption of equality between the demand price of output as a whole and its supply price which is to be regarded as the classical theory's "axiom of parallels." Granted this, all the rest follows—the social advantages of private and national thrift, the traditional attitude towards the rate of interest, the classical theory of unemployment, the quantity theory of money, the unqualified advantages of *laissez-faire* in respect of foreign trade and much else which we shall have to question.

VII

At different points in this chapter we have made the classical theory to depend in succession on the assumptions:

(1) that the real wage is equal to the marginal disutility of the existing employment;

(2) that there is no such thing as involuntary unemployment in the strict sense;

(3) that supply creates its own demand in the sense that the aggregate demand price is equal to the aggregate supply price for all levels of output and employment.

These three assumptions, however, all amount to the same thing in the sense that they all stand and fall together, anyone of them logically involving the other two.

CHAPTER 3

The Principle of Effective Demand

I

We need, to start with, a few terms which will be defined precisely later. In a given state of technique, resources and costs, the employment of a given volume of labor by an entrepreneur involves him in two kinds of expense: first of all, the amounts which he pays out to the factors of production (exclusive of other entrepreneurs) for their current services, which we shall call the *factor cost* of the employment in question; and secondly, the amounts which he pays out to other entrepreneurs for what he has to purchase from them together with the sacrifice which he incurs by employing the equipment instead of leaving it idle, which we shall call the *user cost* of the employment in question.[15] The excess of the value of the resulting output over the sum of its factor cost and its user cost is the profit or, as we shall call it, the *income* of the entrepreneur. The factor cost is, of course, the same thing, looked at from the point of view of the entrepreneur, as what the factors of production regard as their income. Thus the factor cost and the entrepreneur's profit make up, between them, what we shall define as the *total income* resulting from the employment given by the entrepreneur. The entrepreneur's profit thus defined is, as it should be, the quantity which he endeavors to maximize when he is deciding what amount of employment to offer. It is sometimes convenient, when we are looking at it from the entrepreneur's standpoint, to call the aggregate income (*i.e.* factor cost *plus* profit) resulting from a given amount of employment the *proceeds* of that employment. On the other hand, the aggregate supply price[16] of the output of a given amount of employment is the expectation of proceeds which will just make it worth the while of the entrepreneurs to give that employment.[17]

It follows that in a given situation of technique, resources and factor cost per unit of employment, the amount of employment, both in each individual firm and industry and in the aggregate, depends on the amount of the proceeds which the entrepreneurs expect to receive from the corresponding output.[18] For entrepreneurs will endeavor to fix the amount of employment at the level which they expect to maximize the excess of the proceeds over the factor cost.

Let Z be the aggregate supply price of the output from employing N men, the relationship between Z and N being written $Z = f(N)$, which can be called the *Aggregate Supply Function*.[19] Similarly, let D be the proceeds which entrepreneurs expect to receive from the employment of N men, the relationship between D and N being written $D = f(N)$, which can be called the *Aggregate Demand Function*.

Now if for a given value of N the expected proceeds are greater than the aggregate supply price, *i.e.* if D is greater than Z, there will be an incentive to entrepreneurs to increase employment beyond N and, if necessary, to raise costs by competing with one another for the factors of production, up to the value of N for which Z has become equal to D. Thus the volume of employment is given by the point of intersection between the aggregate demand function and the aggregate supply function; for it is at this point that the entrepreneurs' expectation of profits will be maximized. The value of D at the point of the aggregate demand function, where it is intersected by the aggregate supply function, will be called *the effective demand.* Since this is the substance of the General Theory of Employment, which it will be our object to expound, the succeeding chapters will be largely occupied with examining the various factors upon which these two functions depend.

The classical doctrine, on the other hand, which used to be expressed categorically in the statement that "Supply creates its own Demand" and continues to underlie all orthodox economic theory, involves a special assumption as to the relationship between these two functions. For "Supply creates its own Demand" must mean that $f(N)$ and $f(N)$ are equal for all values of N, *i.e.* for all levels of output and employment; and that when there is an increase in $Z(= f(N))$ corresponding to an increase in N, $D(= f(N))$ necessarily increases by the same amount as Z. The classical theory assumes, in other words, that the aggregate demand price (or proceeds) always accommodates itself to the aggregate supply price; so that, whatever the value of N may be, the proceeds D assume a value equal to the aggregate supply price Z which corresponds to N. That is to say, effective demand, instead of having a unique equilibrium value, is an infinite range of values all equally admissible; and the amount of employment is indeterminate except in so far as the marginal disutility of labor sets an upper limit.

If this were true, competition between entrepreneurs would always lead to an expansion of employment up to the point at which the supply of output as a whole ceases to be elastic, *i.e.* where a further increase in the value of the effective demand will no longer be accompanied by any increase in output. Evidently this amounts to the same thing as full employment. In the previous chapter we have given a definition of full employment in terms of the behavior of labor. An alternative, though equivalent, criterion is that at which we have now arrived, namely a situation in which aggregate employment is inelastic in response to an increase in the effective demand for its output. Thus Say's law, that the aggregate demand price of output as a whole is equal to its aggregate supply price for all volumes of output, is equivalent to the proposition that there is no obstacle to full employment. If, however, this is not the true law relating the aggregate demand and supply functions, there is a vitally important chapter of economic theory which remains to be written and without which all discussions concerning the volume of aggregate employment are futile.

II

A brief summary of the theory of employment to be worked out in the course of the following chapters may, perhaps, help the reader at this stage, even though it may not be fully intelligible. The terms involved will be more carefully defined in due course. In this summary we shall assume that the money-wage and other factor costs are constant per unit of labor employed. But this simplification, with which we shall dispense later, is introduced solely to facilitate the exposition. The essential character of the argument is precisely the same whether or not money-wages, etc., are liable to change.

The outline of our theory can be expressed as follows. When employment increases, aggregate real income is increased. The psychology of the community is such that when aggregate real income is increased aggregate consumption is increased, but not by so much as income. Hence employers would make a loss if the whole of the increased employment were to be devoted to satisfying the increased demand for immediate consumption. Thus, to justify any given amount of employment there must be an amount of current investment sufficient to absorb the excess of total output over what the community chooses to consume when employment is at the given level. For unless there is this amount of investment, the receipts of the entrepreneurs will be less than is required to induce them to offer the given amount of employment. It follows, therefore, that, given what we shall call the community's propensity to consume, the equilibrium level of employment, *i.e.* the level at which there is no inducement to employers as a whole either to expand or to contract employment, will depend on the amount of current investment. The amount of current investment will depend, in turn, on what we shall call the inducement to invest; and the inducement to invest will be found to depend on the relation between the schedule of the marginal efficiency of capital and the complex of rates of interest on loans of various maturities and risks.

Thus, given the propensity to consume and the rate of new investment, there will be only one level of employment consistent with equilibrium; since any other level will lead to inequality between the aggregate supply price of output as a whole and its aggregate demand price. This level cannot be *greater* than full employment, *i.e.* the real wage cannot be less than the marginal disutility of labor. But there is no reason in general for expecting it to be *equal* to full employment. The effective demand associated with full employment is a special case, only realized when the propensity to consume and the inducement to invest stand in a particular relationship to one another. This particular relationship, which corresponds to the assumptions of the classical theory, is in a sense an optimum relationship. But it can only exist when, by accident or design, current investment provides an amount of demand just equal to the excess of the aggregate supply price of the output resulting from full employment over what the community will choose to spend on consumption when it is fully employed.

This theory can be summed up in the following propositions:

(1) In a given situation of technique, resources and costs, income (both money-income and real income) depends on the volume of employment N.

(2) The relationship between the community's income and what it can be expected to spend on consumption, designated by D1, will depend on the psychological characteristic of the community, which we shall call its *propensity to consume*. That is to say, consumption will depend on the level of aggregate income and, therefore, on the level of employment N, except when there is some change in the propensity to consume.

(3) The amount of labor N which the entrepreneurs decide to employ depends on the sum (D) of *two* quantities, namely D_1 the amount which the community is expected to spend on consumption, and D_2 the amount which it is expected to devote to new investment. D is what we have called above the *effective demand*.

(4) Since $D_1 + D_2 = D = f(N)$, where f is the aggregate supply function, and since, as we have seen in (2) above, D_1 is a function of N, which we may write $x(N)$, depending on the propensity to consume, it follows that $f(N) - x(N) = D_2$.

(5) Hence the volume of employment in equilibrium depends on (i) the aggregate supply function, f, (ii) the propensity to consume, x, and (iii) the volume of investment, D_2. This is the essence of the General Theory of Employment.

(6) For every value of N there is a corresponding marginal productivity of labor in the wage-goods industries; and it is this which determines the real wage. (5) is, therefore, subject to the condition that N cannot *exceed* the value which reduces the real wage to equality with the marginal disutility of labor. This means that not all changes in D are compatible with our temporary assumption that money-wages are constant. Thus it will be essential to a full statement of our theory to dispense with this assumption.

(7) On the classical theory, according to which $D = f(N)$ for all values of N, the volume of employment is in neutral equilibrium for all values of N less than its maximum value; so that the forces of competition between entrepreneurs may be expected to push it to this maximum value. Only at this point, on the classical theory, can there be stable equilibrium.

(8) *When employment increases, D_1 will increase, but not by so much as D*; since when our income increases our consumption increases also, but not by so much. The key to our practical problem is to be found in this psychological law. For it follows from this that the greater the volume of employment the greater will be the gap between the aggregate supply price (Z) of the corresponding output and the sum (D_1) which the entrepreneurs can expect to get back out of the expenditure of consumers. Hence, if there is no change in the propensity to consume, employment cannot increase, unless at the same time D_2 is increasing so as to fill the increasing gap between Z and D_1. Thus—except on the special assumptions of the classical theory according to which there is some force in operation which, when employment increases, always causes D_2 to increase sufficiently to fill the widening gap between Z and D_1—the economic system may find itself in stable equilibrium with N at a level below full employment, namely at the level given by the intersection of the aggregate demand function with the aggregate supply function.

Thus the volume of employment is not determined by the marginal disutility of labor measured in terms of real wages, except in so far as the supply of labor available at a given real wage sets a *maximum* level to employment. The propensity to consume and the rate of new investment determine between them the volume of employment, and the volume of employment is uniquely related to a given level of real wages—not the other way round. If the propensity to consume and the rate of new investment result in a deficient effective demand, the actual level of employment will fall short of the supply of labor potentially available at the existing real wage, and the equilibrium real wage will be *greater* than the marginal disutility of the equilibrium level of employment.

This analysis supplies us with an explanation of the paradox of poverty in the midst of plenty. For the mere existence of an insufficiency of effective demand may, and often will, bring the increase of employment to a standstill *before* a level of full employment has been reached. The insufficiency of effective demand will inhibit the process of production in spite of the fact that the marginal product of labor still exceeds in value the marginal disutility of employment.

Moreover the richer the community, the wider will tend to be the gap between its actual and its potential production; and therefore the more obvious and outrageous the defects of the economic system. For a poor community will be prone to consume by far the greater part of its output, so that a very modest measure of investment will be sufficient to provide full employment; whereas a wealthy community will have to discover much ampler opportunities for investment if the saving propensities of its wealthier members are to be compatible with the employment of its poorer members. If in a potentially wealthy community the inducement to invest is weak, then, in spite of its potential wealth, the working of the principle of effective demand will compel it to reduce its actual output, until, in spite of its potential wealth, it has become so poor that its surplus over its consumption is sufficiently diminished to correspond to the weakness of the inducement to invest.

But worse still. Not only is the marginal propensity to consume[20] weaker in a wealthy community, but, owing to its accumulation of capital being already larger, the opportunities for further investment are less attractive unless the rate of interest falls at a sufficiently rapid rate; which brings us to the theory of the rate of interest and to the reasons why it does not automatically fall to the appropriate level, which will occupy Book IV.

Thus the analysis of the Propensity to Consume, the definition of the Marginal Efficiency of Capital and the theory of the Rate of Interest are the three main gaps in our existing knowledge which it will be necessary to fill. When this has been accomplished, we shall find that the Theory of Prices falls into its proper place as a matter which is subsidiary to our general theory. We shall discover, however, that Money plays an essential part in our theory of the Rate of Interest; and we shall attempt to disentangle the peculiar characteristics of Money which distinguish it from other things.

III

The idea that we can safely neglect the aggregate demand function is fundamental to the Ricardian economics, which underlie what we have been taught for more than a century. Malthus, indeed, had vehemently opposed Ricardo's doctrine that it was impossible for effective demand to be deficient; but vainly. For, since Malthus was unable to explain clearly (apart from an appeal to the facts of common observation) how and why effective demand could be deficient or excessive, he failed to furnish an alternative construction; and Ricardo conquered England as completely as the Holy Inquisition conquered Spain. Not only was his theory accepted by the city, by statesmen and by the academic world. But controversy ceased; the other point of view completely disappeared; it ceased to be discussed. The great puzzle of Effective Demand with which Malthus had wrestled vanished from economic literature. You will not find it mentioned even once in the whole works of Marshall, Edgeworth and Professor Pigou, from whose hands the classical theory has received its most mature embodiment. It could only live on furtively, below the surface, in the underworlds of Karl Marx, Silvio Gesell or Major Douglas.

The completeness of the Ricardian victory is something of a curiosity and a mystery. It must have been due to a complex of suitabilities in the doctrine to the environment into which it was projected. That it reached conclusions quite different from what the ordinary uninstructed person would expect, added, I suppose, to its intellectual prestige. That its teaching, translated into practice, was austere and often unpalatable, lent it virtue. That it was adapted to carry a vast and consistent logical superstructure, gave it beauty. That it could explain much social injustice and apparent cruelty as an inevitable incident in the scheme of progress, and the attempt to change such things as likely on the whole to do more harm than good, commended it to authority. That it afforded a measure of justification to the free activities of the individual capitalist, attracted to it the support of the dominant social force behind authority.

But although the doctrine itself has remained unquestioned by orthodox economists up to a late date, its signal failure for purposes of scientific prediction has greatly impaired, in the course of time, the prestige of its practitioners. For professional economists, after Malthus, were apparently unmoved by the lack of correspondence between the results of their theory and the facts of observation;—a discrepancy which the ordinary man has not failed to observe, with the result of his growing unwillingness to accord to economists that measure of respect which he gives to other groups of scientists whose theoretical results are confirmed by observation when they are applied to the facts.

The celebrated *optimism* of traditional economic theory, which has led to economists being looked upon as Candides, who, having left this world for the cultivation of their gardens, teach that all is for the best in the best of all possible worlds provided we will let well alone, is also to be traced, I think, to their having neglected to take account of the drag on prosperity which can be exercised by an insufficiency of effective demand. For there would obviously be a natural tendency towards the optimum employment of resources in a Society which was functioning after the manner of the classical postulates. It may well be that the classical theory represents the way in which we should like our Economy to behave. But to assume that it actually does so is to assume our difficulties away.

Book II

Definitions and Ideas

CHAPTER 4

The Choice of Units

I

In this and the next three chapters we shall be occupied with an attempt to clear up certain perplexities which have no peculiar or exclusive relevance to the problems which it is our special purpose to examine. Thus these chapters are in the nature of a digression, which will prevent us for a time from pursuing our main theme. Their subject-matter is only discussed here because it does not happen to have been already treated elsewhere in a way which I find adequate to the needs of my own particular enquiry.

The three perplexities which most impeded my progress in writing this book, so that I could not express myself conveniently until I had found some solution for them, are: firstly, the choice of the units of quantity appropriate to the problems of the economic system as a whole; secondly, the part played by expectation in economic analysis; and, thirdly, the definition of income.

II

That the units, in terms of which economists commonly work, are unsatisfactory can be illustrated by the concepts of the National Dividend, the stock of real capital and the general price-level:—

(i) The National Dividend, as defined by Marshall and Professor Pigou,[21] measures the volume of current output or real income and not the value of output or money-income.[22] Furthermore, it depends, in some sense, on *net* output;—on the net addition, that is to say, to the resources of the community available for consumption or for retention as capital stock, due to the economic activities and sacrifices of the current period, after allowing for the wastage of the stock of real capital existing at the commencement of the period. On this basis an attempt is made to erect a quantitative science. But it is a grave objection to this definition for such a purpose that the community's output of goods and services is a non-homogeneous complex which cannot be measured, strictly speaking, except in certain special cases, as for example when all the items of one output are included in the same proportions in another output.

(ii) The difficulty is even greater when, in order to calculate net output, we try to measure the net addition to capital equipment; for we have to find some basis for a quantitative comparison between the new items of equipment produced during the period and the old items which have perished by wastage. In order to arrive at the net National Dividend, Professor Pigou[23] deducts such obsolescence, etc., "as may fairly be called 'normal'; and the practical test of normality is that the depletion is sufficiently regular to be foreseen, if not in detail, at least in the large." But, since this deduction is not a deduction in terms of money, he is involved in assuming that there can be a change in physical quantity, although there has been no physical change; *i.e.* he is covertly introducing changes in *value*. Moreover, he is unable to devise any satisfactory formula[24] to evaluate new equipment against old when, owing to changes in technique, the two are not identical. I believe that the concept at which Professor Pigou is aiming is the right and appropriate concept for economic analysis. But, until a satisfactory system of units has been adopted, its precise definition is an impossible task. The problem of comparing one real output with another and of then calculating net output by setting off new items of equipment against the wastage of old items presents conundrums which permit, one can confidently say, of no solution.

(iii) Thirdly, the well-known, but unavoidable, element of vagueness which admittedly attends the concept of the general price-level makes this term very unsatisfactory for the purposes of a causal analysis, which ought to be exact.

Nevertheless these difficulties are rightly regarded as "conundrums." They are "purely theoretical" in the sense that they never perplex, or indeed enter in anyway into, business decisions and have no relevance to the causal sequence of economic events, which are clear-cut and determinate in spite of the quantitative indeterminacy of these concepts. It is natural, therefore, to conclude that they not only lack precision but are unnecessary. Obviously our quantitative analysis must be expressed without using any quantitatively vague expressions. And, indeed, as soon as one makes the attempt, it becomes clear, as I hope to show, that one can get on much better without them.

The fact that two incommensurable collections of miscellaneous objects cannot in themselves provide the material for a quantitative analysis need not, of course, prevent us from making approximate statistical comparisons, depending on some broad element of judgment rather than of strict calculation, which may possess significance and validity within certain limits. But the proper place for such things as net real output and the general level of prices lies within the field of historical and statistical description, and their purpose should be to satisfy historical or social curiosity, a purpose for which perfect precision—such as our causal analysis requires, whether or not our knowledge of the actual values of the relevant quantities is complete or exact—is neither usual nor necessary. To say that net output today is greater, but the price-level lower, than ten years ago or one year ago, is a proposition of a similar character to the statement that Queen Victoria was a better queen but not a happier woman than Queen Elizabeth—a proposition not without meaning and not without interest, but unsuitable as material for the differential calculus. Our precision will be a mock precision if we try to use such partly vague and non-quantitative concepts as the basis of a quantitative analysis.

III

On *every* particular occasion, let it be remembered, an entrepreneur is concerned with decisions as to the scale on which to work a given capital equipment; and when we say that the expectation of an increased demand, *i.e.* a raising of the aggregate demand function, will lead to an increase in aggregate output, we really mean that the firms, which own the capital equipment, will be induced to associate with it a greater aggregate employment of labor. In the case of an individual firm or industry producing a homogeneous product we can speak legitimately, if we wish, of increases or decreases of output. But when we are aggregating the activities of all firms, we cannot speak accurately except in terms of quantities of employment applied to a given equipment.

The concepts of output as a whole and its price-level are not required in this context, since we have no need of an absolute measure of current aggregate output, such as would enable us to compare its amount with the amount which would result from the association of a different capital equipment with a different quantity of employment. When, for purposes of description or rough comparison, we wish to speak of an increase of output, we must rely on the general presumption that the amount of employment associated with a given capital equipment will be a satisfactory index of the amount of resultant output;—the two being presumed to increase and decrease together, though not in a definite numerical proportion.

In dealing with the theory of employment I propose, therefore, to make use of only two fundamental units of quantity, namely, quantities of money-value and quantities of employment. The first of these is strictly homogeneous, and the second can be made so. For, in so far as different grades and kinds of labor and salaried assistance enjoy a more or less fixed relative remuneration, the quantity of employment can be sufficiently defined for our purpose by taking an hour's employment of ordinary labor as our unit and weighting an hour's employment of special labor in proportion to its remuneration; *i.e.* an hour of special labor remunerated at double ordinary rates will count as two units.

We shall call the unit in which the quantity of employment is measured the labor-unit; and the money-wage of a labor-unit we shall call the wage-unit.[25] Thus, if E is the wages (and salaries) bill, W the wage-unit, and N the quantity of employment, $E = N.W$.

This assumption of homogeneity in the supply of labor is not upset by the obvious fact of great differences in the specialized skill of individual workers and in their suitability for different occupations. For, if the remuneration of the workers is proportional to their efficiency, the differences are dealt with by our having regarded individuals as contributing to the supply of labor in proportion to their remuneration; whilst if, as output increases, a given firm has to bring in labor which is less and less efficient for its special purposes per wage-unit paid to it, this is merely one factor among others leading to a diminishing return from the capital equipment in terms of output as more labor is employed on it. We subsume, so to speak, the non-homogeneity of equally remunerated labor units in the equipment, which we regard as less and less adapted to employ the available labor units as output increases, instead of regarding the available labor units as less and less adapted to use homogeneous capital equipment. Thus if there is no surplus of specialized or practiced labor and the use of less suitable labor involves a higher labor cost per unit of output, this means that the rate at which the return from the equipment diminishes as employment increases is more rapid than it would be if there were such a surplus.[26] Even in the limiting case where different labor units were so highly specialized as to be altogether incapable of being substituted for one another, there is no awkwardness; for this merely means that the elasticity of supply of output from a particular type of capital equipment falls suddenly to zero when all the available labor specialized to its use is already employed.[27] Thus our assumption of a homogeneous unit of labor involves no difficulties unless there is great instability in the relative remuneration of different labor-units; and even this difficulty can be dealt with, if it arises, by supposing a rapid liability to change in the supply of labor and the shape of the aggregate supply function.

It is my belief that much unnecessary perplexity can be avoided if we limit ourselves strictly to the two units, money and labor, when we are dealing with the behavior of the economic system as a whole; reserving the use of units of particular outputs and equipments to the occasions when we are analyzing the output of individual firms or industries in isolation; and the use of vague concepts, such as the quantity of output as a whole, the quantity of capital equipment as a whole and the general level of prices, to the occasions when we are attempting some historical comparison which is within certain (perhaps fairly wide) limits avowedly imprecise and approximate.

It follows that we shall measure changes in current output by reference to the number of men employed (whether to satisfy consumers or to produce fresh capital equipment) on the existing capital equipment, skilled workers being weighted in proportion to their remuneration. We have no need of a quantitative comparison between this output and the output which would result from associating a different set of workers with a different capital equipment. To predict how entrepreneurs possessing a given equipment will respond to a shift in the aggregate demand function it is not necessary to know how the quantity of the resulting output, the standard of life and the general level of prices would compare with what they were at a different date or in another country.

IV

It is easily shown that the conditions of supply, such as are usually expressed in terms of the supply curve, and the elasticity of supply relating output to price, can be handled in terms of our two chosen units by means of the aggregate supply function, without reference to quantities of output, whether we are concerned with a particular firm or industry or with economic activity as a whole. For the aggregate supply function for a given firm (and similarly for a given industry or for industry as a whole) is given by

$$Z_r = f_r(N_r),$$

where Z_r is the return the expectation of which will induce a level of employment N_r. If, therefore, the relation between employment and output is such that an employment N, results in an output O_r, where $O_r = j_r(N_r)$, it follows that

$$p = Z_r/O_r = f_r(N_r)/j_r(N_r)$$

is the ordinary supply curve.

Thus in the case of each homogeneous commodity, for which $O_r = j_r(N_r)$ has a definite meaning, we can evaluate $Z_r = f_r(N_r)$ in the ordinary way; but we can then aggregate the N_r's in a way which we cannot aggregate O_r's, since SO_r is not a numerical quantity. Moreover, if we can assume that, in a given environment, a given aggregate employment will be distributed in a unique way between different industries, so that N_r is a function of N, further simplifications are possible.

CHAPTER 5

Expectation as Determining Output and Employment

I

All production is for the purpose of ultimately satisfying a consumer. Time usually elapses, however—and sometimes much time—between the incurring of costs by the producer (with the consumer in view) and the purchase of the output by the ultimate consumer. Meanwhile the entrepreneur (including both the producer and the investor in this description) has to form the best expectations[27] he can as to what the consumers will be prepared to pay when he is ready to supply them (directly or indirectly) after the elapse of what may be a lengthy period; and he has no choice but to be guided by these expectations, if he is to produce at all by processes which occupy time.

These expectations, upon which business decisions depend, fail into two groups, certain individuals or firms being specialized in the business of framing the first type of expectation and others in the business of framing the second. The first type is concerned with the price which a manufacturer can expect to get for his "finished" output at the time when he commits himself to starting the process which will produce it; output being "finished" (from the point of view of the manufacturer) when it is ready to be used or to be sold to a second party. The second type is concerned with what the entrepreneur can hope to earn in the shape of future returns if he purchases (or, perhaps, manufactures) "finished" output as an addition to his capital equipment. We may call the former *short-term expectation* and the latter *long-term expectation*.

Thus the behavior of each individual firm in deciding its daily[28] output will be determined by its *short-term expectations*—expectations as to the cost of output on various possible scales and expectations as to the sale-proceeds of this output; though, in the case of additions to capital equipment and even of sales to distributors, these short-term expectations will largely depend on the long-term (or medium-term) expectations of other parties. It is upon these various expectations that the amount of employment which the firms offer will depend. The *actually realized* results of the production and sale of output will only be relevant to employment in so far as they cause a modification of subsequent expectations. Nor, on the other hand, are the original expectations relevant, which led the firm to acquire the capital equipment and the stock of intermediate products and half-finished materials with which it finds itself at the time when it has to decide the next day's output. Thus, on each and every occasion of such a decision, the decision will be made, with reference indeed to this equipment and stock, but in the light of the *current* expectations of *prospective* costs and sale-proceeds.

Now, in general, a *change* in expectations (whether short-term or long-term) will only produce its full effect on employment over a considerable period. The change in employment due to a change in expectations will not be the same on the second day after the change as on the first, or the same on the third day as on the second, and so on, even though there be no further change in expectations. In the case of short-term expectations this is because changes in expectation are not, as a rule, sufficiently violent or rapid, when they are for the worse, to cause the abandonment of work on all the productive processes which, in the light of the revised expectation, it was a mistake to have begun; whilst, when they are for the better, some time for preparation must needs elapse before employment can reach the level at which it would have stood if the state of expectation had been revised sooner. In the case of long-term expectations, equipment which will not be replaced will continue to give employment until it is worn out; whilst when the change in long-term expectations is for the better, employment may be at a higher level at first, than it will be after there has been time to adjust the equipment to the new situation.

If we suppose a state of expectation to continue for a sufficient length of time for the effect on employment to have worked itself out so completely that there is, broadly speaking, no piece of employment going on which would not have taken place if the new state of expectation had always existed, the steady level of employment thus attained may be called the long-period employment[29] corresponding to that state of expectation. It follows that, although expectation may change so frequently that the actual level of employment has never had time to reach the long-period employment corresponding to the existing state of expectation, nevertheless every state of expectation has its definite corresponding level of long-period employment.

Let us consider, first of all, the process of transition to a long-period position due to a change in expectation, which is not confused or interrupted by any further change in expectation. We will first suppose that the change is of such a character that the new long-period employment will be greater than the old. Now, as a rule, it will only be the rate of input which will be much affected at the beginning, that is to say, the volume of work on the earlier stages of new processes of production, whilst the output of consumption-goods and the amount of employment on the later stages of processes which were started before the change will remain much the same as before. In so far as there were stocks of partly finished goods, this conclusion may be modified; though it is likely to remain true that the initial increase in employment will be modest. As, however, the days pass by, employment will gradually increase. Moreover, it is easy to conceive of conditions which will cause it to increase at some stage to a *higher* level than the new long-period employment. For the process of building up capital to satisfy the new state of expectation may lead to more employment and also to more current consumption than will occur when the long-period position has been reached. Thus the change in expectation may lead to a gradual crescendo in the level of employment, rising to a peak and then declining to the new long-period level. The same thing may occur even if the new long-period level is the *same* as the old, if the change represents a change in the direction of consumption which renders certain existing processes and their equipment obsolete. Or again, if the new long-period employment is less than the old, the level of employment during the transition may fall for a time *below* what the new long-period level is going to be. Thus a mere change in expectation is capable of producing an oscillation of the same kind of shape as a cyclical movement, in the course of working itself out. It was movements of this kind which I discussed in my *Treatise on Money* in connection with the building up or the depletion of stocks of working and liquid capital consequent on change.

An uninterrupted process of transition, such as the above, to a new long-period position can be complicated in detail. But the actual course of events is more complicated still. For the state of expectation is liable to constant change, a new expectation being superimposed long before the previous change has fully worked itself out; so that the economic machine is occupied at any given time with a number of overlapping activities, the existence of which is due to various past states of expectation.

II

This leads us to the relevance of this discussion for our present purpose. It is evident from the above that the level of employment at any time depends, in a sense, not merely on the existing state of expectation but on the states of expectation which have existed over a certain past period. Nevertheless past expectations, which have not yet worked themselves out, are embodied in the today's capital equipment with reference to which the entrepreneur has to make today's decisions, and only influence his decisions in so far as they are so embodied. It follows, therefore, that, in spite of the above, today's employment can be correctly described as being governed by today's expectations taken in conjunction with today's capital equipment.

Express reference to current long-term expectations can seldom be avoided. But it will often be safe to omit express reference to *short-term* expectation, in view of the fact that in practice the process of revision of short-term expectation is a gradual and continuous one, carried on largely in the light of realized results; so that expected and realized results run into and overlap one another in their influence. For, although output and employment are determined by the producer's short-term expectations and not by past results, the most recent results usually play a predominant part in determining what these expectations are. It would be too complicated to work out the expectations *de novo* whenever a productive process was being started; and it would, moreover, be a waste of time since a large part of the circumstances usually continue substantially unchanged from one day to the next. Accordingly it is sensible for producers to base their expectations on the assumption that the most recently realized results will continue, except in so far as there are definite reasons for expecting a change. Thus in practice there is a large overlap between the effects on employment of the realized sale-proceeds of recent output and those of the sale-proceeds expected from current input; and producers' forecasts are more often gradually modified in the light of results than in anticipation of prospective changes.[30]

Nevertheless, we must not forget that, in the case of durable goods, the producer's short-term expectations are based on the current long-term expectations of the investor; and it is of the nature of long-term expectations that they cannot be checked at short intervals in the light of realized results. Moreover, as we shall see in Chapter 12, where we shall consider long-term expectations in more detail, they are liable to sudden revision. Thus the factor of current long-term expectations cannot be even approximately eliminated or replaced by realized results.

CHAPTER 6

The Definition of Income, Saving and Investment

I. Income

During any period of time an entrepreneur will have sold finished output to consumers or to other entrepreneurs for a certain sum which we will designate as A. He will also have spent a certain sum, designated by A_1, on purchasing finished output from other entrepreneurs. And he will end up with a capital equipment, which term includes both his stocks of unfinished goods or working capital and his stocks of finished goods, having a value G.

Some part, however, of $A + G - A_1$ will be attributable, not to the activities of the period in question, but to the capital equipment which he had at the beginning of the period. We must, therefore, in order to arrive at what we mean by the *income* of the current period, deduct from $A + G - A_1$ a certain sum, to represent that part of its value which has been (in some sense) contributed by the equipment inherited from the previous period. The problem of defining income is solved as soon as we have found a satisfactory method for calculating this deduction.

There are two possible principles for calculating it, each of which has a certain significance;—one of them in connection with production, and the other in connection with consumption. Let us consider them in turn.

(i) The actual value G of the capital equipment at the end of the period is the net result of the entrepreneur, on the one hand, having maintained and improved it during the period, both by purchases from other entrepreneurs and by work done upon it by himself, and, on the other hand, having exhausted or depreciated it through using it to produce output. If he had decided not to use it to produce output, there is, nevertheless, a certain optimum sum which it would have paid him to spend on maintaining and improving it. Let us suppose that, in this event, he would have spent B' on its maintenance and improvement, and that, having had this spent on it, it would have been worth G' at the end of the period. That is to say, $G' - B'$ is the maximum net value which might have been conserved from the previous period, if it had not been used to produce A. The excess of this potential value of the equipment over $G - A_1$ is the measure of what has been sacrificed (one way or another) to produce A. Let us call this quantity, namely

$$(G' - B') - (G - A_1),$$

which measures the sacrifice of value involved in the production of A, the *user cost* of A. *User cost* will be written U.[31] The amount paid out by the entrepreneur to the other factors of production in return for their services, which from their point of view is their income, we will call the *factor cost* of A. The sum of the factor cost F and the user cost U we shall call the *prime cost* of the output A.

We can then define the *income*[32] of the entrepreneur as being the excess of the value of his finished output sold during the period over his prime cost. The entrepreneur's income, that is to say, is taken as being equal to the quantity, depending on his scale of production, which he endeavors to maximize, *i.e.* to his gross profit in the ordinary sense of this term;— which agrees with common sense. Hence, since the income of the rest of the community is equal to the entrepreneur's factor cost, aggregate income is equal to A – U.

Income, thus defined, is a completely unambiguous quantity. Moreover, since it is the entrepreneur's expectation of the excess of this quantity over his outgoings to the other factors of production which he endeavors to maximize when he decides how much employment to give to the other factors of production, it is the quantity which is causally significant for employment.

It is conceivable, of course, that $G - A_1$ may exceed $G' - B'$, so that user cost will be negative. For example, this may well be the case if we happen to choose our period in such a way that input has been increasing during the period but without there having been time for the increased output to reach the stage of being finished and sold. It will also be the case, whenever there is positive investment, if we imagine industry to be so much integrated that entrepreneurs make most of their equipment for themselves. Since, however, user cost is only negative when the entrepreneur has been increasing his capital equipment by his own labor, we can, in an economy where capital equipment is largely manufactured by different firms from those which use it, normally think of user cost as being positive. Moreover, it is difficult to conceive of a case where *marginal* user cost associated with an increase in A, *i.e.* dU/dA will be other than positive.

It may be convenient to mention here, in anticipation of the latter part of this chapter, that, for the community as a whole, the aggregate *consumption* (C) of the period is equal to $\Sigma(A - A_1)$, and the aggregate *investment* (I) is equal to $S(A_1 - U)$. Moreover, U is the individual entrepreneur's disinvestment (and –U his investment) in respect of his own equipment exclusive of what he buys from other entrepreneurs. Thus in a completely integrated system (where $A_1 = 0$) consumption is equal to A and investment to –U, *i.e.* to $G - (G' - B')$. The slight complication of the above, through the introduction of A_1, is simply due to the desirability of providing in a generalized way for the case of a non-integrated system of production.

Furthermore, the *effective demand* is simply the aggregate income (or proceeds) which the entrepreneurs expect to receive, inclusive of the incomes which they will hand on to the other factors of production, from the amount of current employment which they decide to give. The aggregate demand function relates various hypothetical quantities of employment to the proceeds which their outputs are expected to yield; and the effective demand is the point on the aggregate demand function which becomes effective because, taken in conjunction with the conditions of supply, it corresponds to the level of employment which maximizes the entrepreneur's expectation of profit.

This set of definitions also has the advantage that we can equate the marginal proceeds (or income) to the marginal factor cost; and thus arrive at the same sort of propositions relating marginal proceeds thus denned to marginal factor costs as have been stated by those economists who, by ignoring user cost or assuming it to be zero, have equated supply price[33] to marginal factor cost.[34]

(ii) We turn, next, to the second of the principles referred to above. We have dealt so far with that part of the change in the value of the capital equipment at the end of the period as compared with its value at the beginning which is due to the *voluntary* decisions of the entrepreneur in seeking to maximize his profit. But there may, in addition, be an *involuntary* loss (or gain) in the value of his capital equipment, occurring for reasons beyond his control and irrespective of his current decisions, on account of *(e.g.)* a change in market values, wastage by obsolescence or the mere passage of time, or destruction by catastrophe such as war or earthquake. Now some part of these involuntary losses, whilst they are unavoidable, are broadly speaking—not unexpected; such as losses through the lapse of time irrespective of use, and also "normal" obsolescence which, as Professor Pigou expresses it, "is sufficiently regular to be foreseen, if not in detail, at least in the large," including, we may add, those losses to the community as a whole which are sufficiently regular to be commonly regarded as "insurable risks." Let us ignore for the moment the fact that the amount of the expected loss depends on when the expectation is assumed to be framed, and let us call the depreciation of the equipment, which is involuntary but not unexpected, *i.e.* the excess of the expected depreciation over the user cost, the *supplementary cost,* which will be written V. It is, perhaps, hardly necessary to point out that this definition is not the same as Marshall's definition of supplementary cost, though the underlying idea, namely, of dealing with that part of the expected depreciation which does not enter into prime cost, is similar.

In reckoning, therefore, the *net income* and the *net profit* of the entrepreneur it is usual to deduct the estimated amount of the supplementary cost from his income and gross profit as defined above. For the psychological effect on the entrepreneur, when he is considering what he is free to spend and to save, of the supplementary cost is virtually the same as though it came off his gross profit. In his capacity as a *producer* deciding whether or not to use the equipment, prime cost and gross profit, as defined above, are the significant concepts. But in his capacity as a *consumer* the amount of the supplementary cost works on his mind in the same way as if it were a part of the prime cost. Hence we shall not only come nearest to common usage but will also arrive at a concept which is relevant to the amount of consumption, if, in defining aggregate *net* income, we deduct the supplementary cost as well as the user cost, so that aggregate *net income* is equal to A – U – V.

There remains the change in the value of the equipment, due to unforeseen changes in market values, exceptional obsolescence or destruction by catastrophe, which is both involuntary and—in a broad sense—unforeseen. The actual loss under this head, which we disregard even in reckoning net income and charge to capital account, may be called the *windfall loss.*

The *causal* significance of net income lies in the psychological influence of the magnitude of V on the amount of current consumption, since *net income* is what we suppose the ordinary man to reckon his available income to be when he is deciding how much to spend on current consumption. This is not, of course, the only factor of which he takes account when he is deciding how much to spend. It makes a considerable difference, for example, how much windfall gain or loss he is making on capital account.

But there is a difference between the supplementary cost and a windfall loss in that changes in the former are apt to affect him *in just the same way* as changes in his gross profit. It is the excess of the proceeds of the current output over the *sum* of the prime cost and the supplementary cost which is relevant to the entrepreneur's consumption; whereas, although the windfall loss (or gain) enters into his decisions, it does not enter into them on the same scale—a given windfall loss does not have the same effect as an equal supplementary cost.

We must now recur, however, to the point that the line between supplementary costs and windfall losses, *i.e.* between those unavoidable losses which we think it proper to debit to income account and those which it is reasonable to reckon as a windfall loss (or gain) on capital account, is partly a conventional or psychological one, depending on what are the commonly accepted criteria for estimating the former. For no unique principle can be established for the estimation of supplementary cost, and its amount will depend on our choice of an accounting method. The expected value of the supplementary cost, when the equipment was originally produced, is a definite quantity. But if it is re-estimated subsequently, its amount over the remainder of the life of the equipment may have changed as a result of a change in the meantime in our expectations; the windfall capital loss being the discounted value of the difference between the former and the revised expectation of the prospective series of $U + V$. It is a widely approved principle of business accounting, endorsed by the Inland Revenue authorities, to establish a figure for the sum of the supplementary cost and the user cost when the equipment is acquired and to maintain this unaltered during the life of the equipment, irrespective of subsequent changes in expectation. In this case the supplementary cost over any period must be taken as the excess of this predetermined figure over the actual user cost. This has the advantage of ensuring that the windfall gain or loss shall be zero over the life of the equipment taken as a whole. But it is also reasonable in certain circumstances to recalculate the allowance for supplementary cost on the basis of current values and expectations at an arbitrary accounting interval, *e.g.* annually. Business men in fact differ as to which course they adopt. It may be convenient to call the initial expectation of supplementary cost when the equipment is first acquired the *basic supplementary cost,* and the same quantity recalculated up to date on the basis of current values and expectations the *current supplementary cost.*

Thus we cannot get closer to a quantitative definition of supplementary cost than that it comprises those deductions from his income which a typical entrepreneur makes before reckoning what he considers his *net* income for the purpose of declaring a dividend (in the case of a corporation) or of deciding the scale of his current consumption (in the case of an individual). Since windfall charges on capital account are not going to be ruled out of the picture, it is clearly better, in case of doubt, to assign an item to capital account, and to include in supplementary cost only what rather obviously belongs there. For any overloading of the former can be corrected by allowing it more influence on the rate of current consumption than it would otherwise have had.

It will be seen that our definition of *net income* comes very close to Marshall's definition of *income*; when he decided to take refuge in the practices of the Income Tax Commissioners and—broadly speaking—to regard as income whatever they, with their experience, choose to treat as such. For the fabric of their decisions can be regarded as the result of the most careful and extensive investigation which is available, to interpret what, in practice, it is usual to treat as net income. It also corresponds to the money value of Professor Pigou's most recent definition of the National Dividend.[35]

It remains true, however, that net income, being based on an equivocal criterion which different authorities might interpret differently, is not perfectly clear-cut. Professor Hayek, for example, has suggested that an individual owner of capital goods might aim at keeping the income he derives from his possession constant, so that he would not feel himself free to spend his income on consumption until he had set aside sufficient to off-set any tendency of his investment-income to decline for whatever reason.[36] I doubt if such an individual exists; but, obviously, no theoretical objection can be raised against this deduction as providing a possible psychological criterion of net income. But when Professor Hayek infers that the concepts of saving and investment suffer from a corresponding vagueness, he is only right if he means *net saving* and *net investment*. The *saving* and the *investment*, which are relevant to the theory of employment, are clear of this defect, and are capable of objective definition, as we have shown above.

Thus it is a mistake to put all the emphasis on *net income*, which is only relevant to decisions concerning consumption, and is, moreover, only separated from various other factors affecting consumption by a narrow line; and to overlook (as has been usual) the concept of *income proper*, which is the concept relevant to decisions concerning current production and is quite unambiguous.

The above definitions of income and of net income are intended to conform as closely as possible to common usage. It is necessary, therefore, that I should at once remind the reader that in my *Treatise on Money* I defined income in a special sense. The peculiarity in my former definition related to that part of aggregate income which accrues to the entrepreneurs, since I took neither the profit (whether gross or net) actually realized from their current operations nor the profit which they expected when they decided to undertake their current operations, but in some sense (not, as I now think, sufficiently defined if we allow for the possibility of changes in the scale of output) a normal or equilibrium profit; with the result that on this definition saving exceeded investment by the amount of the excess of normal profit over the actual profit. I am afraid that this use of terms has caused considerable confusion, especially in the case of the correlative use of saving; since conclusions (relating, in particular, to the excess of saving over investment), which were only valid if the terms employed were interpreted in my special sense, have been frequently adopted in popular discussion as though the terms were being employed in their more familiar sense. For this reason, and also because I no longer require my former terms to express my ideas accurately, I have decided to discard them—with much regret for the confusion which they have caused.

II. Saving and Investment

Amidst the welter of divergent usages of terms, it is agreeable to discover one fixed point. So far as I know, everyone is agreed that *saving* means the excess of income over expenditure on consumption. Thus any doubts about the meaning of *saving* must arise from doubts about the meaning either of *income* or of *consumption*. *Income* we have defined above. Expenditure on consumption during any period must mean the value of goods sold to consumers during that period, which throws us back to the question of what is meant by a consumer-purchaser. Any reasonable definition of the line between consumer-purchasers and investor-purchasers will serve us equally well, provided that it is consistently applied. Such problem as there is, *e.g.* whether it is right to regard the purchase of a motor-car as a consumer-purchase and the purchase of a house as an investor-purchase, has been frequently discussed and I have nothing material to add to the discussion. The criterion must obviously correspond to where we draw the line between the consumer and the entrepreneur. Thus when we have defined A_1 as the value of what one entrepreneur has purchased from another, we have implicitly settled the question. It follows that expenditure on consumption can be unambiguously defined as $S(A - A_1)$, where SA is the total sales made during the period and SA_1 is the total sales made by one entrepreneur to another. In what follows it will be convenient, as a rule, to omit S and write A for the aggregate sales of all kinds, A_1 for the aggregate sales from one entrepreneur to another and U for the aggregate user costs of the entrepreneurs.

Having now defined both *income* and *consumption,* the definition of saving, which is the excess of income over consumption, naturally follows. Since income is equal to $A - U$ and consumption is equal to $A - A_1$, it follows that saving is equal to $A_1 - U$. Similarly, we have *net saving* for the excess of *net income* over consumption, equal to $A_1 - U - V$.

Our definition of income also leads at once to the definition of *current investment.* For we must mean by this the current addition to the value of the capital equipment which has resulted from the productive activity of the period. This is, clearly, equal to what we have just defined as saving. For it is that part of the income of the period which has not passed into consumption. We have seen above that as the result of the production of any period entrepreneurs end up with having sold finished output having a value A and with a capital equipment which has suffered a deterioration measured by U (or an improvement measured by –U where U is negative) as a result of having produced and parted with A, after allowing for purchases A_1 from other entrepreneurs. During the same period finished output having a value A – A1 will have passed into consumption. The excess of $A_1 - U$ over $A - A_1$, namely $A_1 - U$, is the addition to capital equipment as a result of the productive activities of the period and is, therefore, the *investment* of the period. Similarly $A_1 - U - V$, which is the *net* addition to capital equipment, after allowing for normal impairment in the value of capital apart from its being used and apart from windfall changes in the value of the equipment chargeable to capital account, is the *net investment* of the period.

Whilst, therefore, the amount of saving is an outcome of the collective behavior of individual consumers and the amount of investment of the collective behavior of individual entrepreneurs, these two amounts are necessarily equal, since each of them is equal to the excess of income over consumption. Moreover, this conclusion in no way depends on any subtleties or peculiarities in the definition of income given above. Provided it is agreed that income is equal to the value of current output, that current investment is equal to the value of that part of current output which is not consumed, and that saving is equal to the excess of income over consumption—all of which is conformable both to common sense and to the traditional usage of the great majority of economists—the equality of saving and investment necessarily follows. In short—

Income = value of output = consumption + investment.

Saving = income − consumption.

Therefore saving = investment.

Thus *any* set of definitions which satisfy the above conditions leads to the same conclusion. It is only by denying the validity of one or other of them that the conclusion can be avoided.

The equivalence between the quantity of saving and the quantity of investment emerges from the *bilateral* character of the transactions between the producer on the one hand and, on the other hand, the consumer or the purchaser of capital equipment. Income is created by the value in excess of user cost which the producer obtains for the output he has sold; but the whole of this output must obviously have been sold either to a consumer or to another entrepreneur; and each entrepreneur's current investment is equal to the excess of the equipment which he has purchased from other entrepreneurs over his own user cost. Hence, in the aggregate the excess of income over consumption, which we call saving, cannot differ from the addition to capital equipment which we call investment. And similarly with net saving and net investment. Saving, in fact, is a mere residual. The decisions to consume and the decisions to invest between them determine incomes. Assuming that the decisions to invest become effective, they must in doing so either curtail consumption or expand income. Thus the act of investment in itself cannot help causing the residual or margin, which we call saving, to increase by a corresponding amount.

It might be, of course, that individuals were so *tête montée* in their decisions as to how much they themselves would save and invest respectively, that there would be no point of price equilibrium at which transactions could take place. In this case our terms would cease to be applicable, since output would no longer have a definite market value, prices would find no resting-place between zero and infinity. Experience shows, however, that this, in fact, is not so; and that there are habits of psychological response which allow of an equilibrium being reached at which the readiness to buy is equal to the readiness to sell. That there should be such a thing as a market value for output is, at the same time, a necessary condition for money-income to possess a definite value and a sufficient condition for the aggregate amount which saving individuals decide to save to be equal to the aggregate amount which investing individuals decide to invest.

Clearness of mind on this matter is best reached, perhaps, by thinking in terms of decisions to consume (or to refrain from consuming) rather than of decisions to save. A decision to consume or not to consume truly lies within the power of the individual; so does a decision to invest or not to invest. The amounts of aggregate income and of aggregate saving are the *results* of the free choices of individuals whether or not to consume and whether or not to invest; but they are neither of them capable of assuming an independent value resulting from a separate set of decisions taken irrespective of the decisions concerning consumption and investment. In accordance with this principle, the conception of the *propensity to consume* will, in what follows, take the place of the propensity or disposition to save.

APPENDIX ON USER COST

I

User cost has, I think, an importance for the classical theory of value which has been over-looked. There is more to be said about it than would be relevant or appropriate in this place. But, as a digression, we will examine it somewhat further in this appendix.

An entrepreneur's user cost is by definition equal to

$$A_1 + (G' - B') - G,$$

where A_1 is the amount of our entrepreneur's purchases from other entrepreneurs, G the actual value of his capital equipment at the end of the period, and G' the value it might have had at the end of the period if he had refrained from using it and had spent the optimum sum B' on its maintenance and improvement. Now $G - (G' - B')$, namely the increment in the value of the entrepreneur's equipment beyond the net value which he has inherited from the previous period, represents the entrepreneur's current invest-ment in his equipment and can be written I. Thus U, the user cost of his sales-turnover A, is equal to $A_1 - I$ where A1 is what he has bought from other entrepreneurs and I is what he has currently invested in his own equipment. A little reflection will show that all this is no more than common sense. Some part of his outgoings to other entrepreneurs is balanced by the value of his current investment in his own equipment, and the rest rep-resents the sacrifice which the output he has sold must have cost him over and above the total sum which he has paid out to the factors of production. If the reader tries to express the substance of this otherwise, he will find that its advantage lies in its avoidance of in-soluble (and unnecessary) accounting problems. There is, I think, no other way of ana-lyzing the current proceeds of production unambiguously. If industry is completely integrated or if the entrepreneur has bought nothing from outside, so that $A_1 = 0$, the user cost is simply the equivalent of the current disinvestment involved in using the equipment; but we are still left with the advantage that we do not require at any stage of the analysis to allocate the factor cost between the goods which are sold and the equip-ment which is retained. Thus we can regard the employment given by a firm, whether integrated or individual, as depending on a single consolidated decision—a procedure which corresponds to the actual interlocking character of the production of what is cur-rently sold with total production.

The concept of user cost enables us, moreover, to give a clearer definition than that usu-ally adopted of the short-period supply price of a unit of a firm's saleable output. For the short-period supply price is the sum of the marginal factor cost and the marginal user cost.

Now in the modern theory of value it has been a usual practice to equate the short-pe-riod supply price to the marginal factor cost alone. It is obvious, however, that this is only legitimate if marginal user cost is zero or if supply price is specially defined so as to be net of marginal user cost, just as I have defined (Chapter 3) "proceeds" and "aggregate sup-ply price" as being net of aggregate user cost. But, whereas it may be occasionally conven-ient in dealing with *output as a whole* to deduct user cost, this procedure deprives our analysis of all reality if it is habitually (and tacitly) applied to the output of a single industry or firm, since it divorces the "supply price" of an article from any ordinary sense of its "price;" and some confusion may have resulted from the practice of doing so. It seems to have been assumed that "supply price" has an obvious meaning as applied to a unit of the saleable output of an individual firm, and the matter has not been deemed to require discussion. Yet the treatment both of what is purchased from other firms and of the wastage of the firm's own equipment as a consequence of producing the marginal output involves the whole pack of perplexities which attend the definition of income. For, even if we assume that the marginal cost of purchases from other firms involved in selling an additional unit of output has to be deducted from the sale-proceeds per unit in order to give us what we mean by our firm's supply price, we still have to allow for the marginal disinvestment in the firm's own equipment involved in producing the marginal output. Even if all production is carried on by a completely integrated firm, it is still illegitimate to suppose that the marginal user cost is zero, *i.e.* that the marginal disinvestment in equipment due to the production of the marginal output can generally be neglected.

The concepts of user cost and of supplementary cost also enable us to establish a clearer relationship between long-period supply price and short-period supply price. Long-period cost must obviously include an amount to cover the Basic supplementary cost as well as the expected prime cost appropriately averaged over the life of the equipment. That is to say, the long-period cost of the output is equal to the expected sum of the prime cost and the supplementary cost; and, furthermore, in order to yield a normal profit, the long-period supply price must exceed the long-period cost thus calculated by an amount determined by the current rate of interest on loans of comparable term and risk, reckoned as a percentage of the cost of the equipment. Or if we prefer to take a standard "pure" rate of interest, we must include in the long-period cost a third term which we might call the *risk-cost* to cover the unknown possibilities of the actual yield differing from the expected yield. Thus the long-period supply price is equal to the sum of the prime cost, the supplementary cost, the risk cost and the interest cost, into which several components it can be analyzed. The short-period supply price, on the other hand, is equal to the *marginal* prime cost. The entrepreneur must, therefore, expect, when he buys or constructs his equipment, to cover his supplementary cost, his risk cost and his interest cost out of the excess of the marginal value of the prime cost over its average value; so that in long-period equilibrium the excess of the marginal prime cost over the average prime cost is equal to the sum of the supplementary, risk and interest costs.[37]

The level of output, at which marginal prime cost is exactly equal to the sum of the average prime and supplementary costs, has a special importance, because it is the point at which the entrepreneur's trading account breaks even. It corresponds, that is to say, to the point of zero net profit; whilst with a smaller output than this he is trading at a net loss.

The extent to which the supplementary cost has to be provided for apart from the prime cost varies very much from one type of equipment to another. Two extreme cases are the following:

(i) Some part of the maintenance of the equipment must necessarily take place *pari passu* with the act of using it (*e.g.* oiling the machine). The expense of this (apart from outside purchases) is included in the factor cost. If, for physical reasons, the exact amount of the whole of the current depreciation has necessarily to be made good in this way, the amount of the user cost (apart from outside purchases) would be equal and opposite to that of the supplementary cost; and in long-period equilibrium the marginal factor cost would exceed the average factor cost by an amount equal to the risk and interest cost.

(ii) Some part of the deterioration in the value of the equipment only occurs if it is used. The cost of this is charged in user cost, in so far as it is not made good *pari passu* with the act of using it. If loss in the value of the equipment could only occur in this way, supplementary cost would be zero.

It may be worth pointing out that an entrepreneur does not use his oldest and worst equipment first, merely because its user cost is low; since its low user cost may be out-weighed by its relative inefficiency, *i.e.* by its high factor cost. Thus an entrepreneur uses by preference that part of his equipment for which the user cost plus factor cost is least per unit of output.[38] It follows that for any given volume of output of the product in question there is a corresponding user cost,[39] but that this total user cost does not bear a uniform relation to the marginal user cost, *i.e.* to the increment of user cost due to an increment in the rate of output.

II

User cost constitutes one of the links between the present and the future. For in decid-ing his scale of production an entrepreneur has to exercise a choice between using up his equipment now and preserving it to be used later on. It is the expected sacrifice of fu-ture benefit involved in present use which determines the amount of the user cost, and it is the marginal amount of this sacrifice which, together with the marginal factor cost and the expectation of the marginal proceeds, determines his stale of production. How, then, is the user cost of an act of production calculated by the entrepreneur?

We have defined the user cost as the reduction in the value of the equipment due to using it as compared with not using it, after allowing for the cost of the maintenance and improvements which it would be worth while to undertake and for purchases from other entrepreneurs. It must be arrived at, therefore, by calculating the discounted value of the additional prospective yield which would be obtained at some later date if it were not used now. Now this must be at least equal to the present value of the opportunity to post-pone replacement which will result from laying up the equipment; and it may be more.[40]

If there is no surplus or redundant stock, so that more units of similar equipment are being newly produced every year either as an addition or in replacement, it is evident that marginal user cost will be calculable by reference to the amount by which the life or effi-ciency of the equipment will be shortened if it is used, and the current replacement cost. If, however, there is redundant equipment, then the user cost will also depend on the rate of interest and the current (*i.e.* re-estimated) supplementary cost over the period of time before the redundancy is expected to be absorbed through wastage, etc. In this way inter-est cost and current supplementary cost enter indirectly into the calculation of user cost.

The calculation is exhibited in its simplest and most intelligible form when the factor cost is zero, *e.g.* in the case of a redundant stock of a raw material such as copper, on the lines which I have worked out in my *Treatise on Money,* vol. ii. chap. 29. Let us take the prospective values of copper at various future dates, a series which will be governed by the rate at which redundancy is being absorbed and gradually approaches the estimated normal cost. The present value or user cost of a ton of surplus copper will then be equal to the greatest of the values obtainable by subtracting from the estimated future value at any given date of a ton of copper the interest cost and the current supplementary cost on a ton of copper between that date and the present.

In the same way the user cost of a ship or factory or machine, when these equipments are in redundant supply, is its estimated replacement cost discounted at the percentage rate of its interest and current supplementary costs to the prospective date of absorption of the redundancy.

We have assumed above that the equipment will be replaced in due course by an identical article. If the equipment in question will not be renewed identically when it is worn out, then its user cost has to be calculated by taking a proportion of the user cost of the new equipment, which will be erected to do its work when it is discarded, given by its comparative efficiency.

III

The reader should notice that, where the equipment is not obsolescent but merely redundant for the time being, the difference between the actual user cost and its normal value (*i.e.* the value when there is no redundant equipment) varies with the interval of time which is expected to elapse before the redundancy is absorbed. Thus if the type of equipment in question is of all ages and not "bunched," so that a fair proportion is reaching the end of its life annually, the marginal user cost will not decline greatly unless the redundancy is exceptionally excessive. In the case of a general slump, marginal user cost will depend on how long entrepreneurs expect the slump to last. Thus the rise in the supply price when affairs begin to mend may be partly due to a sharp increase in marginal user cost due to a revision of their expectations.

It has sometimes been argued, contrary to the opinion of business men, that organized schemes for scrapping redundant plant cannot have the desired effect of raising prices unless they apply to the *whole* of the redundant plant. But the concept of user cost shows how the scrapping of (say) half the redundant plant may have the effect of raising prices immediately. For by bringing the date of the absorption of the redundancy nearer, this policy raises marginal user cost and consequently increases the current supply price. Thus business men would seem to have the notion of user cost implicitly in mind, though they do not formulate it distinctly.

If the supplementary cost is heavy, it follows that the marginal user cost will be low when there is surplus equipment. Moreover, when there is surplus equipment, the marginal factor and user costs are unlikely to be much in excess of their average value. If both these conditions are fulfilled, the existence of surplus equipment is likely to lead to the entrepreneur's working at a net loss, and perhaps at a heavy net loss. There will not be a sudden transition from this state of affairs to a normal profit, taking place at the moment when the redundancy is absorbed. As the redundancy becomes less, the user cost will gradually increase; and the excess of marginal over average factor and user cost may also gradually increase.

IV

In Marshall's *Principles of Economics* (6th ed. p. 360) a part of user cost is included in prime cost under the heading of "extra wear-and-tear of plant." But no guidance is given as to how this item is to be calculated or as to its importance. In his *Theory of Unemployment* (p. 42) Professor Pigou expressly assumes that the marginal disinvestment in equipment due to the marginal output can, in general, be neglected: "The differences in the quantity of wear-and-tear suffered by equipment and in the costs of non-manual labor employed, that are associated with differences in output, are ignored, as being, in general, of secondary importance."[41] Indeed, the notion that the disinvestment in equipment is zero at the margin of production runs through a good deal of recent economic theory. But the whole problem is brought to an obvious head as soon as it is thought necessary to explain exactly what is meant by the supply price of an individual firm.

It is true that the cost of maintenance of idle plant may often, for the reasons given above, reduce the magnitude of marginal user cost, especially in a slump which is expected to last a long time. Nevertheless a very low user cost at the margin is not a characteristic of the short period as such, but of particular situations and types of equipment where the cost of maintaining idle plant happens to be heavy, and of those disequilibria which are characterized by very rapid obsolescence or great redundancy, especially if it is coupled with a large proportion of comparatively new plant.

In the case of raw materials the necessity of allowing for user cost is obvious;—if a ton of copper is used up today it cannot be used tomorrow, and the value which the copper would have for the purposes of tomorrow must clearly be reckoned as a part of the marginal cost. But the fact has been overlooked that copper is only an extreme case of what occurs whenever capital equipment is used to produce. The assumption that there is a sharp division between raw materials where we must allow for the disinvestment due to using them and fixed capital where we can safely neglect it does not correspond to the facts;—especially in normal conditions where equipment is falling due for replacement every year and the use of equipment brings nearer the date at which replacement is necessary.

It is an advantage of the concepts of user cost and supplementary cost that they are as applicable to working and liquid capital as to fixed capital. The essential difference between raw materials and fixed capital lies not in their liability to user and supplementary costs, but in the fact that the return to liquid capital consists of a single term whereas in the case of fixed capital, which is durable and used up gradually, the return consists of a series of user costs and profits earned in successive periods.

CHAPTER 7

The Meaning of Saving and Investment
Further Considered

I

In the previous chapter *Saving* and *Investment* have been so defined that they are necessarily equal in amount, being, for the community as a whole, merely different aspects of the same thing. Several contemporary writers (including myself in my *Treatise on Money*) have, however, given special definitions of these terms on which they are not necessarily equal. Others have written on the assumption that they may be unequal without prefacing their discussion with any definitions at all. It will be useful, therefore, with a view to relating the foregoing to other discussions of these terms, to classify some of the various uses of them which appear to be current.

So far as I know, everyone agrees in meaning by *Saving* the excess of income over what is spent on consumption. It would certainly be very inconvenient and misleading not to mean this. Nor is there any important difference of opinion as to what is meant by expenditure on consumption. Thus the differences of usage arise either out of the definition of *Investment* or out of that of *Income*.

II

Let us take *Investment* first. In popular usage it is common to mean by this the purchase of an asset, old or new, by an individual or a corporation. Occasionally, the term might be restricted to the purchase of an asset on the Stock Exchange. But we speak just as readily of investing, for example, in a house, or in a machine, or in a stock of finished or unfinished goods; and, broadly speaking, new investment, as distinguished from reinvestment, means the purchase of a capital asset of any kind out of income. If we reckon the sale of an investment as being negative investment, *i.e.* disinvestment, my own definition is in accordance with popular usage; since exchanges of old investments necessarily cancel out. We have, indeed, to adjust for the creation and discharge of debts (including changes in the quantity of credit or money); but since for the community as a whole the increase or decrease of the aggregate creditor position is always exactly equal to the increase or decrease of the aggregate debtor position, this complication also cancels out when we are dealing with aggregate investment. Thus, assuming that income in the popular sense corresponds to my net income, aggregate investment in the popular sense coincides with my definition of net investment, namely the net addition to all kinds of capital equipment, after allowing for those changes in the value of the old capital equipment which are taken into account in reckoning net income.

Investment, thus defined, includes, therefore, the increment of capital equipment, whether it consists of fixed capital, working capital or liquid capital; and the significant differences of definition (apart from the distinction between investment and net investment) are due to the exclusion from investment of one or more of these categories.

Mr. Hawtrey, for example, who attaches great importance to changes in liquid capital, *i.e.* to undesigned increments (or decrements) in the stock of unsold goods, has suggested a possible definition of investment from which such changes are excluded. In this case an excess of saving over investment would be the same thing as an undesigned increment in the stock of unsold goods, *i.e.* as an increase of liquid capital. Mr. Hawtrey has not convinced me that this is the factor to stress; for it lays all the emphasis on the correction of changes which were in the first instance unforeseen, as compared with those which are, rightly or wrongly, anticipated. Mr. Hawtrey regards the daily decisions of entrepreneurs concerning their scale of output as being varied from the scale of the previous day by reference to the changes in their stock of unsold goods. Certainly, in the case of consumption goods, this plays an important part in their decisions. But I see no object in excluding the play of other factors on their decisions; and I prefer, therefore, to emphasize the total change of effective demand and not merely that part of the change in effective demand which reflects the increase or decrease of unsold stocks in the previous period. Moreover, in the case of fixed capital, the increase or decrease of unused capacity corresponds to the increase or decrease in unsold stocks in its effect on decisions to produce; and I do not see how Mr. Hawtrey's method can handle this at least equally important factor.

It seems probable that capital formation and capital consumption, as used by the Austrian school of economists, are not identical either with investment and disinvestment as defined above or with net investment and disinvestment. In particular, capital consumption is said to occur in circumstances where there is quite clearly no net decrease in capital equipment as defined above. I have, however, been unable to discover a reference to any passage where the meaning of these terms is clearly explained. The statement, for example, that capital formation occurs when there is a lengthening of the period of production does not much advance matters.

III

We come next to the divergences between Saving and Investment which are due to a special definition of income and hence of the excess of income over consumption. My own use of terms in my *Treatise on Money* is an example of this. For, as I have explained in Chapter 6 above, the definition of income, which I there employed, differed from my present definition by reckoning as the income of entrepreneurs not their actually realized profits but (in some sense) their "normal profit." Thus by an excess of saving over investment I meant that the scale of output was such that entrepreneurs were earning a less than normal profit from their ownership of the capital equipment; and by an increased excess of saving over investment I meant that a decline was taking place in the actual profits, so that they would be under a motive to contract output.

As I now think, the volume of employment (and consequently of output and real income) is fixed by the entrepreneur under the motive of seeking to maximize his present and prospective profits (the allowance for user cost being determined by his view as to the use of equipment which will maximize his return from it over its whole life); whilst the volume of employment which will maximize his profit depends on the aggregate demand function given by his expectations of the sum of the proceeds resulting from consumption and investment respectively on various hypotheses. In my *Treatise on Money* the concept of *changes* in the excess of investment over saving, as there defined, was a way of handling changes in profit, though I did not in that book distinguish clearly between expected and realized results,[42] I there argued that change in the excess of investment over saving was the motive force governing changes in the volume of output. Thus the new argument, though (as I now think) much more accurate and instructive, is essentially a development of the old. Expressed in the language of my *Treatise on Money,* it would run: the expectation of an increased excess of Investment over Saving, given the former volume of employment and output, will induce entrepreneurs to increase the volume of employment and output. The significance of both my present and my former arguments lies in their attempt to show that the volume of employment is determined by the estimates of effective demand made by the entrepreneurs, an expected increase of investment relatively to saving as defined in my *Treatise on Money* being a criterion of an increase in effective demand. But the exposition in my *Treatise on Money* is, of course, very confusing and incomplete in the light of the further developments here set forth.

Mr. D. H. Robertson has defined today's income as being equal to *yesterday's* consumption *plus* investment, so that today's saving, in his sense, is equal to yesterday's investment *plus* the excess of yesterday's consumption over today's consumption. On this definition saving can exceed investment, namely, by the excess of yesterday's income (in my sense) over today's income. Thus when Mr. Robertson says that there is an excess of saving over investment, he means literally the same thing as I mean when I say that income is falling, and the excess of saving in his sense is exactly equal to the decline of income in my sense. If it were true that current expectations were always determined by yesterday's realized results, today's effective demand would be equal to yesterday's income. Thus Mr. Robertson's method might be regarded as an alternative attempt to mine (being, perhaps, a first approximation to it) to make the same distinction, so vital for causal analysis, that I have tried to make by the contrast between effective demand and income.[43]

IV

We come next to the much vaguer ideas associated with the phrase "forced saving." Is any clear significance discoverable in these? In my *Treatise on Money* (vol. i. p. 171, footnote) I gave some references to earlier uses of this phrase and suggested that they bore some affinity to the difference between investment and "saving" in the sense in which I there used the latter term. I am no longer confident that there was in fact so much affinity as I then supposed. In any case, I feel sure that "forced saving" and analogous phrases employed more recently (*e.g.* by Professor Hayek or Professor Robbins) have no definite relation to the difference between investment and "saving" in the sense intended in my *Treatise on Money*. For whilst these authors have not explained exactly what they mean by this term, it is clear that "forced saving," in their sense, is a phenomenon which results directly from, and is measured by, changes in the quantity of money or bank-credit.

It is evident that a change in the volume of output and employment will, indeed, cause a change in income measured in wage-units; that a change in the wage-unit will cause both a redistribution of income between borrowers and lenders and a change in aggregate income measured in money; and that in either event there will (or may) be a change in the amount saved. Since, therefore, changes in the quantity of money may result, through their effect on the rate of interest, in a change in the volume and distribution of income (as we shall show later), such changes may involve, indirectly, a change in the amount saved. But such changes in the amounts saved are no more "forced savings" than any other changes in the amounts saved due to a change in circumstances; and there is no means of distinguishing between one case and another, unless we specify the amount saved in certain given conditions as our norm or standard. Moreover, as we shall see, the amount of the change in aggregate saving which results from a given change in the quantity of money is highly variable and depends on many other factors.

Thus "forced saving" has no meaning until we have specified some standard rate of saving. If we select (as might be reasonable) the rate of saving which corresponds to an established state of full employment, the above definition would become: "Forced saving is the excess of actual saving over what would be saved if there were full employment in a position of long-period equilibrium" This definition would make good sense, but a sense in which a forced excess of saving would be a very rare and a very unstable phenomenon, and a forced *deficiency* of saving the usual state of affairs.

Professor Hayek's interesting "Note on the Development of the Doctrine of *Forced Saving*"[44] shows that this was in fact the original meaning of the term. "Forced saving" or "forced frugality" was, in the first instance, a conception of Bentham's; and Bentham expressly stated that he had in mind the consequences of an increase in the quantity of money (relatively to the quantity of things vendible for money) in circumstances of "all hands being employed and employed in the most advantageous manner."[45] In such circumstances, Bentham points out, real income cannot be increased, and, consequently, additional investment, taking place as a result of the transition, involves forced frugality "at the expense of national comfort and national justice." All the nineteenth-century writers who dealt with this matter had virtually the same idea in mind. But an attempt to extend this perfectly clear notion to conditions of less than full employment involves difficulties. It is true, of course (owing to the fact of diminishing returns to an increase in the employment applied to a given capital equipment), that *any* increase in employment involves some sacrifice of real income to those who were already employed, but an attempt to relate this loss to the increase in investment which may accompany the increase in employment is not likely to be fruitful. At any rate I am not aware of any attempt having been made by the modern writers who are interested in "forced saving" to extend the idea to conditions where employment is increasing; and they seem, as a rule, to overlook the fact that the extension of the Benthamite concept of forced frugality to conditions of less than full employment requires some explanation or qualification.

V

The prevalence of the idea that saving and investment, taken in their straightforward sense, can differ from one another, is to be explained, I think, by an optical illusion due to regarding an individual depositor's relation to his bank as being a one-sided transaction, instead of seeing it as the two-sided transaction which it actually is. It is supposed that a depositor and his bank can somehow contrive between them to perform an operation by which savings can disappear into the banking system so that they are lost to investment, or, contrariwise, that the banking system can make it possible for investment to occur, to which no saving corresponds. But no one can save without acquiring an asset, whether it be cash or a debt or capital-goods; and no one can acquire an asset which he did not previously possess, unless *either* an asset of equal value is newly produced or someone else parts with an asset of that value which he previously had. In the first alternative there is a corresponding new investment: in the second alternative someone else must be dis-saving an equal sum. For his loss of wealth must be due to his consumption exceeding his income, and not to a loss on capital account through a change in the value of a capital-asset, since it is not a case of his suffering a loss of value which his asset formerly had; he is duly receiving the current value of his asset and yet is not retaining this value in wealth of any form, *i.e.* he must be spending it on current consumption in excess of current income. Moreover, if it is the banking system which parts with an asset, someone must be parting with cash. It follows that the aggregate saving of the first individual and of others taken together must necessarily be equal to the amount of current new investment.

The notion that the creation of credit by the banking system allows investment to take place to which "no genuine saving" corresponds can only be the result of isolating one of the consequences of the increased bank-credit to the exclusion of the others. If the grant of a bank credit to an entrepreneur additional to the credits already existing allows him to make an addition to current investment which would not have occurred otherwise, incomes will necessarily be increased and at a rate which will normally *exceed* the rate of increased investment. Moreover, except in conditions of full employment, there will be an increase of real income as well as of money-income. The public will exercise "a free choice" as to the proportion in which they divide their increase of income between saving and spending; and it is impossible that the intention of the entrepreneur who has borrowed in order to increase investment can become effective (except in substitution for investment by other entrepreneurs which would have occurred otherwise) at a faster rate than the public decide to increase their savings. Moreover, the savings which result from this decision are just as genuine as any other savings. No one can be compelled to own the additional money corresponding to the new bank-credit, unless he deliberately prefers to hold more money rather than some other form of wealth. Yet employment, incomes and prices cannot help moving in such a way that in the new situation someone does choose to hold the additional money. It is true that an unexpected increase of investment in a particular direction may cause an irregularity in the rate of aggregate saving and investment which would not have occurred if it has been sufficiently foreseen. It is also true that the grant of the bank-credit will set up three tendencies—(1) for output to increase, (2) for the marginal product to rise in value in terms of the wage-unit (which in conditions of decreasing return must necessarily accompany an increase of output), and (3) for the wage-unit to rise in terms of money (since this is a frequent concomitant of better employment); and these tendencies may affect the distribution of real income between different groups. But these tendencies are characteristic of a state of increasing output as such, and will occur just as much if the increase in output has been initiated otherwise than by an increase in bank-credit. They can only be avoided by avoiding any course of action capable of improving employment. Much of the above, however, is anticipating the result of discussions which have not yet been reached.

Thus the old-fashioned view that saving always involves investment, though incomplete and misleading, is formally sounder than the new-fangled view that there can be saving without investment or investment without "genuine" saving. The error lies in proceeding to the plausible inference that, when an individual saves, he will increase aggregate investment by an equal amount. It is true, that, when an individual saves he increases his own wealth. But the conclusion that he also increases aggregate wealth fails to allow for the possibility that an act of individual saving may react on someone else's savings and hence on someone else's wealth.

The reconciliation of the identity between saving and investment with the apparent "free-will" of the individual to save what he chooses irrespective of what he or others may be investing, essentially depends on saving being, like spending, a two-sided affair. For although the amount of his own saving is unlikely to have any significant influence on his own income, the reactions of the amount of his consumption on the incomes of others makes it impossible for all individuals simultaneously to save any given sums. Every such attempt to save more by reducing consumption will so affect incomes that the attempt necessarily defeats itself. It is, of course, just as impossible for the community as a whole to save *less* than the amount of current investment, since the attempt to do so will necessarily raise incomes to a level at which the sums which individuals choose to save add up to a figure exactly equal to the amount of investment.

The above is closely analogous with the proposition which harmonizes the liberty, which every individual possesses, to change, whenever he chooses, the amount of money he holds, with the necessity for the total amount of money, which individual balances add up to, to be exactly equal to the amount of cash which the banking system has created. In this latter case the equality is brought about by the fact that the amount of money which people choose to hold is not independent of their incomes or of the prices of the things (primarily securities), the purchase of which is the natural alternative to holding money. Thus incomes and such prices necessarily change until the aggregate of the amounts of money which individuals choose to hold at the new level of incomes and prices thus brought about has come to equality with the amount of money created by the banking system. This, indeed, is the fundamental proposition of monetary theory.

Both these propositions follow merely from the fact that there cannot be a buyer without a seller or a seller without a buyer. Though an individual whose transactions are small in relation to the market can safely neglect the fact that demand is not a one-sided transaction, it makes nonsense to neglect it when we come to aggregate demand. This is the vital difference between the theory of the economic behavior of the aggregate and the theory of the behavior of the individual unit, in which we assume that changes in the individual's own demand do not affect his income.

Book III

The Propensity to Consume

CHAPTER 8

The Propensity to Consume:
I. The Objective Factors

I

We are now in a position to return to our main theme, from which we broke off at the end of Book I in order to deal with certain general problems of method and definition. The ultimate object of our analysis is to discover what determines the volume of employment. So far we have established the preliminary conclusion that the volume of employment is determined by the point of intersection of the aggregate supply function with the aggregate demand function. The aggregate supply function, however, which depends in the main on the physical conditions of supply, involves few considerations which are not already familiar. The form may be unfamiliar but the underlying factors are not new. We shall return to the aggregate supply function in Chapter 20, where we discuss its inverse under the name of the *employment function*. But, in the main, it is the part played by the aggregate demand function which has been overlooked; and it is to the aggregate demand function that we shall devote Books III and IV.

The aggregate demand function relates any given level of employment to the "proceeds" which that level of employment is expected to realize. The "proceeds" are made up of the sum of two quantities—the sum which will be spent on consumption when employment is at the given level, and the sum which will be devoted to investment. The factors which govern these two quantities are largely distinct. In this book we shall consider the former, namely what factors determine the sum which will be spent on consumption when employment is at a given level; and in Book IV we shall proceed to the factors which determine the sum which will be devoted to investment.

Since we are here concerned in determining what sum will be spent on consumption when employment is at a given level, we should, strictly speaking, consider the function which relates the former quantity (C) to the latter (N). It is more convenient, however, to work in terms of a slightly different function, namely, the function which relates the consumption in terms of wage-units (C_w) to the income in terms of wage-units (Y_w) corresponding to a level of employment N. This suffers from the objection that Y_w is not a unique function of N, which is the same in all circumstances. For the relationship between Y_w and N may depend (though probably in a very minor degree) on the precise nature of the employment. That is to say, two different distributions of a given aggregate employment N between different employments might (owing to the different shapes of the individual employment functions—a matter to be discussed in Chapter 20 below) lead to different values of Y_w. In conceivable circumstances a special allowance might have to be made for this factor. But in general it is a good approximation to regard Y_w as uniquely determined by N. We will therefore define what we shall call the *propensity to consume* as the functional relationship x between Y_w, a given level of income in terms of wage-units, and C_w the expenditure on consumption out of that level of income, so that

$$C_w = X(Y_w) \text{ or } C = W.x(Y_w).$$

The amount that the community spends on consumption obviously depends (i) partly on the amount of its income, (ii) partly on the other objective attendant circumstances, and (iii) partly on the subjective needs and the psychological propensities and habits of the individuals composing it and the principles on which the income is divided between them (which may suffer modification as output is increased). The motives to spending interact and the attempt to classify them runs the danger of false division. Nevertheless it will clear our minds to consider them separately under two broad heads which we shall call the subjective factors and the objective factors. The subjective factors, which we shall consider in more detail in the next Chapter, include those psychological characteristics of human nature and those social practices and institutions which, though not unalterable, are unlikely to undergo a material change over a short period of time except in abnormal or revolutionary circumstances. In an historical enquiry or in comparing one social system with another of a different type, it is necessary to take account of the manner in which changes in the subjective factors may affect the propensity to consume. But, in general, we shall in what follows take the subjective factors as given; and we shall assume that the propensity to consume depends only on changes in the objective factors.

II

The principal objective factors which influence the propensity to consume appear to be the following:

(1) *A change in the wage-unit.*—Consumption (C) is obviously much more a function of (in some sense) real income than of money-income. In a given state of technique and tastes and of social conditions determining the distribution of income, a man's real income will rise and fall with the amount of his command over labor-units, *i.e.* with the amount of his income measured in wage-units; though when the aggregate volume of output changes, his real income will (owing to the operation of decreasing returns) rise less than in proportion to his income measured in wage-units. As a first approximation, therefore, we can reasonably assume that, if the wage-unit changes, the expenditure on consumption corresponding to a given level of employment will, like prices, change in

the same proportion; though in some circumstances we may have to make an allowance for the possible reactions on aggregate consumption of the change in the distribution of a given real income between entrepreneurs and renters resulting from a change in the wage-unit. Apart from this, we have already allowed for changes in the wage-unit by defining the propensity to consume in terms of income measured in terms of wage-units.

(2) *A change in the difference between income and net income.*—We have shown above that the amount of consumption depends on net income rather than on income, since it is, by definition, his net income that a man has primarily in mind when he is deciding his scale of consumption. In a given situation there may be a somewhat stable relationship between the two, in the sense that there will be a function uniquely relating different levels of income to the corresponding levels of net income. If, however, this should not be the case, such part of any change in income as is not reflected in net income must be neglected since it will have no effect on consumption; and, similarly, a change in net income, not reflected in income, must be allowed for. Save in exceptional circumstances, however, I doubt the practical importance of this factor. We will return to a fuller discussion of the effect on consumption of the difference between income and net income in the fourth section of this chapter.

(3) *Windfall changes in capital-values not allowed for in calculating net income.*—These are of much more importance in modifying the propensity to consume, since they will bear no stable or regular relationship to the amount of income. The consumption of the wealth-owning class may be extremely susceptible to unforeseen changes in the money-value of its wealth. This should be classified amongst the major factors capable of causing short-period changes in the propensity to consume.

(4) *Changes in the rate of time-discounting,* i.e. *in the ratio of exchange between present goods and future goods.*—This is not quite the same thing as the rate of interest, since it allows for future changes in the purchasing power of money in so far as these are foreseen. Account has also to be taken of all kinds of risks, such as the prospect of not living to enjoy the future goods or of confiscatory taxation. As an approximation, however, we can identify this with the rate of interest.

The influence of this factor on the rate of spending out of a given income is open to a good deal of doubt. For the classical theory of the rate of interest,[46] which was based on the idea that the rate of interest was the factor which brought the supply and demand for savings into equilibrium, it was convenient to suppose that expenditure on consumption is *cet. par.* negatively sensitive to changes in the rate of interest, so that any rise in the rate *of* interest would appreciably diminish consumption. It has long been recognized, however, that the total effect of changes in the rate of interest on the readiness to spend on present consumption is complex and uncertain, being dependent on conflicting tendencies, since some of the subjective motives towards saving will be more easily satisfied if the rate of interest rises, whilst others will be weakened. Over a long period substantial changes in the rate of interest probably tend to modify social habits considerably, thus affecting the subjective propensity to spend—though in which direction it would be hard to say, except in the light of actual experience. The usual type of short-period fluctuation in the rate of interest is not likely, however, to have much *direct* influence on spending either way.

There are not many people who will alter their way of living because the rate of interest has fallen from 5 to 4 percent, if their aggregate income is the same as before. Indirectly there may be more effects, though not all in the same direction. Perhaps the most important influence, operating through changes in the rate of interest, on the readiness to spend out of a given income, depends on the effect of these changes on the appreciation or depreciation in the price of securities and other assets. For if a man is enjoying a windfall increment in the value of his capital, it is natural that his motives towards current spending should be strengthened, even though in terms of income his capital is worth no more than before; and weakened if he is suffering capital losses. But this indirect influence we have allowed for already under (3) above. Apart from this, the main conclusion suggested by experience is, I think, that the short-period influence of the rate of interest on individual spending out of a given income is secondary and relatively unimportant, except, perhaps, where unusually large changes are in question. When the rate of interest falls very low indeed, the increase in the ratio between an annuity purchasable for a given sum and the annual interest on that sum may, however, provide an important source of negative saving by encouraging the practice of providing for old age by the purchase of an annuity.

The abnormal situation, where the propensity to consume may be sharply affected by the development of extreme uncertainty concerning the future and what it may bring forth, should also, perhaps, be classified under this heading.

(5) *Changes in fiscal policy.*—In so far as the inducement to the individual to save depends on the future return which he expects, it clearly depends not only on the rate of interest but on the fiscal policy of the Government. Income taxes, especially when they discriminate against "unearned" income, taxes on capital-profits, death-duties and the like are as relevant as the rate of interest; whilst the range of possible changes in fiscal policy may be greater, in expectation at least, than for the rate of interest itself. If fiscal policy is used as a deliberate instrument for the more equal distribution of incomes, its effect in increasing the propensity to consume is, of course, all the greater.[47]

We must also take account of the effect on the aggregate propensity to consume of Government sinking funds for the discharge of debt paid for out of ordinary taxation. For these represent a species of corporate saving, so that a policy of substantial sinking funds must be regarded in given circumstances as reducing the propensity to consume. It is for this reason that a change-over from a policy of Government borrowing to the opposite policy of providing sinking funds (or *vice versa*) is capable of causing a severe contraction (or marked expansion) of effective demand.

(6) *Changes in expectations of the relation between the present and the future level of income.*—We must catalogue this factor for the sake of formal completeness. But, whilst it may affect considerably a particular individual's propensity to consume, it is likely to average out for the community as a whole. Moreover, it is a matter about which there is, as a rule, too much uncertainty for it to exert much influence.

We are left therefore, with the conclusion that in a given situation the propensity to consume may be considered a fairly stable function, provided that we have eliminated changes in the wage-unit in terms of money. Windfall changes in capital-values will be capable of changing the propensity to consume, and substantial changes in the rate of interest and in fiscal policy may make some difference; but the other objective factors which might affect it, whilst they must not be overlooked, are not likely to be important in ordinary circumstances.

The fact that, given the general economic situation, the expenditure on consumption in terms of the wage-unit depends in the main, on the volume of output and employment is the justification for summing up the other factors in the portmanteau function "propensity to consume." For whilst the other factors are capable of varying (and this must not be forgotten), the aggregate income measured in terms of the wage-unit is, as a rule, the principal variable upon which the consumption-constituent of the aggregate demand function will depend.

III

Granted, then, that the propensity to consume is a fairly stable function so that, as a rule, the amount of aggregate consumption mainly depends on the amount of aggregate income (both measured in terms of wage-units), changes in the propensity itself being treated as a secondary influence, what is the normal shape of this function?

The fundamental psychological law, upon which we are entitled to depend with great confidence both *a priori* from our knowledge of human nature and from the detailed facts of experience, is that men are disposed, as a rule and on the average, to increase their consumption as their income increases, but not by as much as the increase in their income. That is to say, if C_w is the amount of consumption and Y_w is income (both measured in wage-units) DC_w has the same sign as DY_w but is smaller in amount, *i.e.* dC_w/dY_w is positive and less than unity.

This is especially the cue where we have short periods in view, as in the case of the so-called cyclical fluctuations of employment during which habits, as distinct from more permanent psychological propensities, are not given time enough to adapt themselves to changed objective circumstances. For a man's habitual standard of life usually has the first claim on his income, and he is apt to save the difference which discovers itself between his actual income and the expense of his habitual standard; or, if he does adjust his expenditure to changes in his income, he will over short periods do so imperfectly. Thus a rising income will often be accompanied by increased saving, and a falling income by decreased saving, on a greater scale at first than subsequently.

But, apart from short-period *changes* in the level of income, it is also obvious that a higher absolute level of income will tend, as a rule, to widen the gap between income and consumption. For the satisfaction of the immediate primary needs of a man and his family is usually a stronger motive than the motives towards accumulation, which only acquire effective sway when a margin of comfort has been attained. These reasons will lead, as a rule, to a greater *proportion* of income being saved as real income increases. But whether or not a greater proportion is saved, we take it as a fundamental psychological rule of any modern community that, when its real income is increased, it will not increase its consumption by an equal *absolute* amount, so that a greater absolute amount must be saved, unless a large and unusual change is occurring at the same time in other factors.

As we shall show subsequently,[48] the stability of the economic system essentially depends on this rule prevailing in practice. This means that if employment and hence aggregate income increase, *not all* the additional employment will be required to satisfy the needs of additional consumption.

On the other hand, a decline in income due to a decline in the level of employment, if it goes far, may even cause consumption to exceed income not only by some individuals and institutions using up the financial reserves which they have accumulated in better times, but also by the Government, which will be liable, willingly or unwillingly, to run into a budgetary deficit or will provide unemployment relief, for example, out of borrowed money. Thus, when employment falls to a low level, aggregate consumption will decline by a smaller amount than that by which real income has declined, by reason both of the habitual behavior of individuals and also of the probable policy of governments; which is the explanation why a new position of equilibrium can usually be reached within a modest range of fluctuation. Otherwise a fall in employment and income, once started, might proceed to extreme lengths.

This simple principle leads, it will be seen, to the same conclusion as before, namely, that employment can only increase *pari passu* with an increase in investment; unless, indeed, there is a change in the propensity to consume. For since consumers will spend less than the increase in aggregate supply price when employment is increased, the increased employment will prove unprofitable unless there is an increase in investment to fill the gap.

IV

We must not underestimate the importance of the fact already mentioned above that, whereas employment is a function of the expected consumption and the expected investment, consumption is, *cet. par.*, a function of *net* income, *i.e.* of *net* investment (net income being equal to consumption *plus* net investment). In other words, the larger the financial provision which it is thought necessary to make before reckoning net income, the less favorable to consumption, and therefore to employment, will a given level of investment prove to be.

When the whole of this financial provision (or supplementary cost) is in fact currently expended in the upkeep of the already existing capital equipment, this point is not likely to be overlooked. But when the financial provision *exceeds* the actual expenditure on current upkeep, the practical results of this in its *effect* on employment are not always appreciated. For the amount of this excess neither directly gives rise to current investment nor is available to pay for consumption. It has, therefore, to be balanced by new investment, the demand for which has arisen quite independently of the current wastage of old equipment against which the financial provision is being made; with the result that the new investment available to provide current income is correspondingly diminished and a more intense demand for new investment is necessary to make possible a given level of employment. Moreover, much the same considerations apply to the allowance for wastage included in user cost, in so far as the wastage is not actually made good.

Take a house which continues to be habitable until it is demolished or abandoned. If a certain sum is written off its value out of the annual rent paid by the tenants, which the landlord neither spends on upkeep nor regards as net income available for consumption, this provision, whether it is a part of U or of V, constitutes a drag on employment all through the life of the house, suddenly made good in a lump when the house has to be rebuilt.

In a stationary economy all this might not be worth mentioning, since in each year the depreciation allowances in respect of old houses would be exactly offset by the new houses built in replacement of those reaching the end of their lives in that year. But such factors may be serious in a non-static economy, especially during a period which immediately succeeds a lively burst of investment in long-lived capital. For in such circumstances a very large proportion of the new items of investment may be absorbed by the larger financial provisions made by entrepreneurs in respect of existing capital equipment, upon the repairs and renewal of which, though it is wearing out with time, the date has not yet arrived for spending anything approaching the full financial provision which is being set aside; with the result that incomes cannot rise above a level which is low enough to correspond with a low aggregate of *net* investment. Thus sinking funds, etc., are apt to withdraw spending power from the consumer long before the demand for expenditure on replacements (which such provisions are anticipating) comes into play; *i.e.* they diminish the current effective demand and only increase it in the year in which the replacement is actually made. If the effect of this is aggravated by "financial prudence," *i.e.* by its being thought advisable to "write off" the initial cost *more* rapidly than the equipment actually wears out, the cumulative result may be very serious indeed.

In the United States, for example, by 1929 the rapid capital expansion of the previous five years had led cumulatively to the setting up of sinking funds and depreciation allowances, in respect of plant which did not need replacement, on so huge a scale that an enormous volume of entirely new investment was required merely to absorb these financial provisions; and it became almost hopeless to find still more new investment on a sufficient scale to provide for such new saving as a wealthy community in full employment would be disposed to set aside. This factor alone was probably sufficient to cause a slump. And, furthermore, since "financial prudence" of this kind continued to be exercised through the slump by those great corporations which were still in a position to afford it, it offered a serious obstacle to early recovery.

Or again, in Great Britain at the present time (1935) substantial amount of housebuilding and of other new investments since the war has led to an amount of sinking funds being set up much in excess of any present requirements for expenditure on repairs and renewals, a tendency which has been accentuated, where the investment has been made by local authorities and public boards, by the principles of "sound" finance which often require sinking funds sufficient to write off the initial cost some time before replacement will actually fall due; with the result that even if private individuals were ready to spend the whole of their net incomes it would be a severe task to restore full employment in the face of this heavy volume of statutory provision by public and semi-public authorities, entirely dissociated from any corresponding new investment. The sinking funds of local authorities now stand, I think,[49] at an annual figure of more than half the amount which these authorities are spending on the whole of their new developments.[50] Yet it is not certain that the Ministry of Health are aware, when they insist on stiff sinking funds by local authorities, how much they may be aggravating the problem of unemployment. In the case of advances by Building Societies to help an individual to build his own house, the desire to be clear of debt more rapidly than the house actually deteriorates may stimulate the house-owner to save more than he otherwise would;—though this factor should be classified, perhaps, as diminishing the propensity to consume directly rather than through its effect on net income. In actual figures, repayments of mortgages advanced by Building Societies, which amounted to £24,000,000 in 1925, had risen to £68,000,000 by 1933, as compared with new advances of £103,000,000; and today the repayments are probably still higher.

That it is investment, rather than net investment, which emerges from the statistics of output, is brought out forcibly and naturally in Mr. Colin Clark's *National Income, 1924–1931*. He also shows what a large proportion depreciation, etc., normally bears to the value of investment. For example, he estimates that in Great Britain, over the years 1928–1931,[51] the investment and the net investment were as follows, though his gross investment is probably somewhat greater than my investment, inasmuch as it may include a part of user cost, and it is not clear how closely his "net investment" corresponds to my definition of this term:

(£ million)

	1928	1929	1930	1931
Gross Investment-Output	791	731	620	482
"Value of physical wasting of old capital"	433	435	437	439
Net Investment	358	296	183	43

Mr. Kuznets has arrived at much the same conclusion in compiling the statistics of the *Gross Capital Formation* (as he calls what I call investment) in the United States, 1919–1933. The physical fact, to which the statistics of output correspond, is inevitably the gross, and not the net, investment. Mr. Kuznets has also discovered the difficulties in passing from gross investment to net investment. "The difficulty," he writes, "of passing from gross to net capital formation, that is, the difficulty of correcting for the consumption of existing durable commodities, is not only in the lack of data. The very concept of annual consumption of commodities that last over a number of years suffers from ambiguity."[52] He falls back, therefore, "on the assumption that the allowance for depreciation and depletion on the books of business firms describes correctly the volume of consumption of already existing, finished durable goods used by business firms." On the other hand, he attempts no deduction at all in respect of houses and other durable commodities in the hands of individuals. His very interesting results for the United States can be summarized as follows:

(Millions of Dollars)									
	1925	1926	1927	1928	1929	1930	1931	1932	1933
Gross capital formation (after allowing for net change in business inventories)	30,706	33,571	31,157	33,934	34,491	27,538	18,721	7,780	14,879
Entrepreneurs' servicing, repairs, maintenance, depreciation and depletion	7,685	8,288	8,223	8,481	9,010	8,502	7,623	6,543	8,204
Net capital formation (on Mr. Kuznets' definition)	23,021	25,283	22,934	25,453	25,481	19,036	11,098	1,237	6,675

Several facts emerge with prominence from this table. Net capital formation was very steady over the quinquennium 1925–1929, with only a 10 percent increase in the latter part of the upward movement. The deduction for entrepreneurs' repairs, maintenance, depreciation and depletion remained at a high figure even at the bottom of the slump. But Mr. Kuznets' method must surely lead to too low an estimate of the annual increase in depreciation, etc.; for he puts the latter at less than 1 1/2 percent per annum of the new net capital formation. Above all, net capital formation suffered an appalling collapse after 1929, falling in 1932 to a figure no less than 95 percent below the *average* of the quinquennium 1925–1929.

The above is, to some extent, a digression. But it is important to emphasize the magnitude of the deduction which has to be made from the income of a society, which already possesses a large stock of capital, before we arrive at the net income which is ordinarily available for consumption. For if we overlook this, we may underestimate the heavy drag on the propensity to consume which exists even in conditions where the public is ready to consume a very large proportion of its net income.

Consumption—to repeat the obvious—is the sole end and object of all economic activity. Opportunities for employment are necessarily limited by the extent of aggregate demand. Aggregate demand can be derived only from present consumption or from present provision for future consumption. The consumption for which we can profitably provide in advance cannot be pushed indefinitely into the future. We cannot, as a community, provide for future consumption by financial expedients but only by current physical output. In so far as our social and business organization separates financial provision for the future from physical provision for the future so that efforts to secure the former do not necessarily carry the latter with them, financial prudence will be liable to diminish aggregate demand and thus impair well-being, as there are many examples to testify. The greater, moreover, the consumption for which we have provided in advance, the more difficult it is to find something further to provide for in advance, and the greater our dependence on present consumption as a source of demand. Yet the larger our incomes, the greater, unfortunately, is the margin between our incomes and our consumption. So, failing some novel expedient, there is, as we shall see, no answer to the riddle, except that there must be sufficient unemployment to keep us so poor that our consumption falls short of our income by no more than the equivalent of the physical provision for future consumption which it pays to produce today.

Or look at the matter thus. Consumption is satisfied partly by objects produced currently and partly by objects produced previously, *i.e.* by disinvestment. To the extent that consumption is satisfied by the latter, there is a contraction of current demand, since to that extent a part of current expenditure fails to find its way back as a part of net income. Contrariwise whenever an object is produced within the period with a view to satisfying consumption subsequently, an expansion of current demand is set up. Now all capital-investment is destined to result, sooner or later, in capital-disinvestment. Thus the problem of providing that new capital-investment shall always outrun capital-disinvestment sufficiently to fill the gap between net income and consumption, presents a problem which is increasingly difficult as capital increases. New capital-investment can only take place in excess of current capital-disinvestment if *future* expenditure on consumption is expected to increase. Each time we secure today's equilibrium by increased investment we are aggravating the difficulty of securing equilibrium tomorrow. A diminished propensity to consume today can only be accommodated to the public advantage if an increased propensity to consume is expected to exist some day. We are reminded of "The Fable of the Bees"—the gay of tomorrow are absolutely indispensable to provide a *raison d'être* for the grave of today.

It is a curious thing, worthy of mention, that the popular mind seems only to be aware of this ultimate perplexity where *public* investment is concerned, as in the case of road-building and house-building and the like. It is commonly urged as an objection to schemes for raising employment by investment under the auspices of public authority that it is laying up trouble for the future. "What will you do," it is asked, "when you have built all the houses and roads and town halls and electric grids and water supplies and so forth which the stationary population of the future can be expected to require?" But it is not so easily understood that the same difficulty applies to private investment and to industrial expansion; particularly to the latter, since it is much easier to see an early satiation of the demand for new factories and plant which absorb individually but little money, than of the demand for dwelling-houses.

The obstacle to a clear understanding is, in these examples, much the same as in many academic discussions of capital, namely, an inadequate appreciation of the fact that capital is not a self-subsistent entity existing apart from consumption. On the contrary, every weakening in the propensity to consume regarded as a permanent habit must weaken the demand for capital as well as the demand for consumption.

CHAPTER 9

The Propensity to Consume:
II. The Subjective Factors

I

There remains the second category of factors which affect the amount of consumption out of a given income—namely, those subjective and social incentives which determine how much is spent, given the aggregate of income in terms of wage-units and given the relevant objective factors which we have already discussed. Since, however, the analysis of these factors raises no point of novelty, it may be sufficient if we give a catalogue of the more important, without enlarging on them at any length.

There are, in general, eight main motives or objects of a subjective character which lead individuals to refrain from spending out of their incomes:

(i) To build up a reserve against unforeseen contingencies;

(ii) To provide for an anticipated future relation between the income and the needs of the individual or his family different from that which exists in the present, as, for example, in relation to old age, family education, or the maintenance of dependents;

(iii) To enjoy interest and appreciation, *i.e.* because a larger real consumption at a later date is preferred to a smaller immediate consumption;

(iv) To enjoy a gradually increasing expenditure, since it gratifies a common instinct to look forward to a gradually improving standard of life rather than the contrary, even though the capacity for enjoyment may be diminishing;

(v) To enjoy a sense of independence and the power to do things, though without a clear idea or definite intention of specific action;

(vi) To secure a *masse de manoeuvre* to carry out speculative or business projects;

(vii) To bequeath a fortune;

(viii) To satisfy pure miserliness, *i.e.* unreasonable but insistent inhibitions against acts of expenditure as such.

These eight motives might be called the motives of Precaution, Foresight, Calculation, Improvement, Independence, Enterprise, Pride and Avarice; and we could also draw up a corresponding list of motives to consumption such as Enjoyment, Shortsightedness, Generosity, Miscalculation, Ostentation and Extravagance.

Apart from the savings accumulated by individuals, there is also the large amount of income, varying perhaps from one-third to two-thirds of the total accumulation in a modern industrial community such as Great Britain or the United States, which is withheld by Central and Local Government, by Institutions and by Business Corporations—for motives largely analogous to, but not identical with, those actuating individuals, and mainly the four following:

(i) The motive of enterprise—to secure resources to carry out further capital investment without incurring debt or raising further capital on the market;

(ii) The motive of liquidity—to secure liquid resources to meet emergencies, difficulties and depressions;

(iii) The motive of improvement—to secure a gradually increasing income, which, incidentally, will protect the management from criticism, since increasing income due to accumulation is seldom distinguished from increasing income due to efficiency;

(iv) The motive of financial prudence and the anxiety to be "on the right side" by making a financial provision in excess of user and supplementary cost, so as to discharge debt and write off the cost of assets ahead of, rather than behind, the actual rate of wastage and obsolescence, the strength of this motive mainly depending on the quantity and character of the capital equipment and the rate of technical change.

Corresponding to these motives which favor the withholding of a part of income from consumption, there are also operative at times motives which lead to an excess of consumption over income. Several of the motives towards positive saving catalogued above as affecting individuals have their intended counterpart in negative saving at a later date, as, for example, with saving to provide for family needs or old age. Unemployment relief financed by borrowing is best regarded as negative saving.

Now the strength of all these motives will vary enormously according to the institutions and organization of the economic society which we presume, according to habits formed by race, education, convention, religion and current morals, according to present hopes and past experience, according to the scale and technique of capital equipment, and according to the prevailing distribution of wealth and the established standards of life. In the argument of this book, however, we shall not concern ourselves, except in occasional digressions, with the results of far-reaching social changes or with the slow effects of secular progress. We shall, that is to say, take as given the main background of subjective motives to saving and to consumption respectively. In so far as the distribution of wealth is determined by the more or less permanent social structure of the community, this also can be reckoned a factor, subject only to slow change and over a long period, which we can take as given in our present context.

II

Since, therefore, the main background of subjective and social incentives changes slowly, whilst the short-period influence of changes in the rate of interest and the other objective factors is often of secondary importance, we are left with the conclusion that short-period changes in consumption largely depend on changes in the rate at which income (measured in wage-units) is being earned and not on changes in the propensity to consume out of a given income.

We must, however, guard against a misunderstanding. The above means that the influence of moderate changes in the rate of interest on the *propensity* to consume is usually small. It does not mean that changes in the rate of interest have only a small influence on the amounts *actually* saved and consumed. Quite the contrary. The influence of changes in the rate of interest on the amount actually saved is of paramount importance, but is *in the opposite direction* to that usually supposed. For even if the attraction of the larger future income to be earned from a higher rate of interest has the effect of diminishing the propensity to consume, nevertheless we can be certain that a rise in the rate of interest will have the effect of reducing the amount actually saved. For aggregate saving is governed by aggregate investment; a rise in the rate of interest (unless it is offset by a corresponding change in the demand-schedule for investment) will diminish investment; hence a rise in the rate of interest must have the effect of reducing incomes to a level at which saving is decreased in the same measure as investment. Since incomes will decrease by a greater absolute amount than investment, it is, indeed, true that, when the rate of interest rises, the rate of consumption will decrease. But this does not mean that there will be a wider margin for saving. On the contrary, saving and spending will *both* decrease.

Thus, even if it is the case that a rise in the rate of interest would cause the community to save more *out of a given income,* we can be quite sure that a rise in the rate of interest (assuming no favorable change in the demand-schedule for investment) will decrease the actual aggregate of savings. The same line of argument can even tell us by how much a rise in the rate of interest will, *cet. par.*, decrease incomes. For incomes will have to fall (or be redistributed) by just that amount which is required, with the existing propensity to consume, to decrease savings by the same amount by which the rise in the rate of interest will, with the existing marginal efficiency of capital, decrease investment. A detailed examination of this aspect will occupy our next chapter.

The rise in the rate of Interest might induce us to save more, *if our* incomes were unchanged. But if the higher rate of interest retards investment, our incomes will not, and cannot, be unchanged. They must necessarily fall, until the declining capacity to save has sufficiently offset the stimulus to save given by the higher rate of interest. The more virtuous we are, the more determinedly thrifty, the more obstinately orthodox in our national and personal finance, the more our incomes will have to fall when interest rises relatively to the marginal efficiency of capital. Obstinacy can bring only a penalty and no reward. For the result is inevitable.

Thus, after all, the actual rates of aggregate saving and spending do not depend on Precaution, Foresight, Calculation, Improvement, Independence, Enterprise, Pride or Avarice. Virtue and vice play no part. It all depends on how far the rate of interest is favorable to investment, after taking account of the marginal efficiency of capital.[53] No, this is an overstatement. If the rate of interest were so governed as to maintain continuous full employment, Virtue would resume her sway;—the rate of capital accumulation would depend on the weakness of the propensity to consume. Thus, once again, the tribute that classical economists pay to her is due to their concealed assumption that the rate of interest always is so governed.

CHAPTER 10

The Marginal Propensity to
Consume and the Multiplier

We established in Chapter 8 that employment can only increase *pari passu* with invest-ment. We can now carry this line of thought a stage further. For in given circumstances a definite ratio, to be called the *Multiplier,* can be established between income and in-vestment and, subject to certain simplifications, between the total employment and the employment directly employed on investment (which we shall call the *primary employ-ment*). This further step is an integral part of our theory of employment, since it estab-lishes a precise relationship, given the propensity to consume, between aggregate employment and income and the rate of investment. The conception of the multiplier was first introduced into economic theory by Mr. R. F. Kahn in his article on "The Relation of Home Investment to Unemployment" (*Economic Journal,* June 1931). His argument in this article depended on the fundamental notion that, if the propensity to consume in various hypothetical circumstances is (together with certain other condi-tions) taken as given and we conceive the monetary or other public authority to take steps to stimulate or to retard investment, the change in the amount of employment will be a function of the net change in the amount of investment; and it aimed at laying down general principles by which to estimate the actual quantitative relationship be-tween an increment of net investment and the increment of aggregate employment which will be associated with it. Before coming to the multiplier, however, it will be conven-ient to introduce the conception of the *marginal propensity to consume.*

I

The fluctuations in real income under consideration in this book are those which result from applying different quantities of employment (*i.e.* of labor-units) to a given capital equipment, so that real income increases and decreases with the number of labor-units employed. If, as we assume in general, there is a decreasing return at the margin as the number of labor-units employed on the given capital equipment is increased, income measured in terms of wage-units will increase more than in proportion to the amount of employment, which, in turn, will increase more than in proportion to the amount of real income measured (if that is possible) in terms of product. Real income measured in terms of product and income measured in terms of wage-units will, however, increase and decrease together (in the short period when capital equipment is virtually unchanged). Since, therefore, real income, in terms of product, may be incapable of precise numeri-cal measurement, it is often convenient to regard income in terms of wage-units (Y_w) as an adequate working index of changes in real income. In certain contexts we must not overlook the fact that, in general, Y_w increases and decreases in a greater proportion than real income; but in other contexts the fact that they always increase and decrease together renders them virtually interchangeable.

Our normal psychological law that, when the real income of the community increases or decreases, its consumption will increase or decrease but not so fast, can, therefore, be translated—not, indeed, with absolute accuracy but subject to qualifications which are obvious and can easily be stated in a formally complete fashion—into the propositions that DC_w and DY_w have the same sign, but $DY_w > DC_w$, where C_w is the consumption in terms of wage-units. This is merely a repetition of the proposition already established in Chapter 3 above.

Let us define, then, dC_w/dY_w as the marginal propensity to consume.

This quantity is of considerable importance, because it tells us how the next increment of output will have to be divided between consumption and investment. For $DY_w = DC_w + DI_w$, where AC_w and AI_w are the increments of consumption and investment; so that we can write $DY_w = kDI_w$ where $I - I/k$ is equal to the marginal propensity to consume.

Let us call k the *investment multiplier*. It tells us that, when there is an increment of aggregate investment, income will increase by an amount which is k times the increment of investment.

II

Mr. Kahn's multiplier is a little different from this, being what we may call the *employment multiplier* designated by k', since it measures the ratio of the increment of total employment which is associated with a given increment of primary employment in the investment industries. That is to say, if the increment of investment DI_w leads to an increment of primary employment DN_2 in the investment industries, the increment of total employment $DN = kDN_2$.

There is no reason in general to suppose that $k = k'$. For there is no necessary presumption that the shapes of the relevant portions of the aggregate supply functions for different types of industry are such that the ratio of the increment of employment in the one set of industries to the increment of demand which has stimulated it will be the same as in the other set of Industries.[54] It is easy, indeed, to conceive of cases, as, for example, where the marginal propensity to consume is widely different from the average propensity, in which there would be a presumption in favor of some inequality between DY_w/DN and DI_w/DN_2, since there would be very divergent proportionate changes in the demands for consumption-goods and investment-goods respectively. If we wish to take account of such possible differences in the shapes of the relevant portions of the aggregate supply functions for the two groups of industries respectively, there is no difficulty in rewriting the following argument in the more generalized form. But to elucidate the ideas involved, it will be convenient to deal with the simplified case where $k = k'$.

It follows, therefore, that, if the consumption psychology of the community is such that they will choose to consume, *e.g.*, nine-tenths of an increment of income,[55] then the multiplier k is 10; and the total employment caused by (*e.g.*) increased public works will be ten times the primary employment provided by the public works themselves, assuming no reduction of investment in other directions. Only in the event of the community maintaining their consumption unchanged in spite of the increase in employment and hence in real income, will the increase of employment be restricted to the primary employment provided by the public works. If, on the other hand, they seek to consume the whole of any increment of income, there will be no point of stability and prices will rise without limit. With normal psychological suppositions, an increase in employment will only be associated with a decline in consumption if there is at the same time a change in the propensity to consume—as the result, for instance, of propaganda in time of war in favor of restricting individual consumption; and it is only in this event that the increased employment in investment will be associated with an unfavorable repercussion on employment in the industries producing for consumption.

This only sums up in a formula what should by now be obvious to the reader on general grounds. An increment of investment in terms of wage-units cannot occur unless the public are prepared to increase their savings in terms of wage-units. Ordinarily speaking, the public will not do this unless their aggregate income in terms of wage-units is increasing. Thus their effort to consume a part of their increased incomes will stimulate output until the new level (and distribution) of incomes provides a margin of saving sufficient to correspond to the increased investment. The multiplier tells us by how much their employment has to be increased to yield an increase in real income sufficient to induce them to do the necessary extra saving, and is a function of their psychological propensities.[56] If saving is the pill and consumption is the jam, the extra jam has to be proportioned to the size of the additional pill. Unless the psychological propensities of the public are different from what we are supposing, we have here established the law that increased employment for investment must necessarily stimulate the industries producing for consumption and thus lead to a total increase of employment which is a multiple of the primary employment required by the investment itself.

It follows from the above that, if the marginal propensity to consume is not far short of unity, small fluctuations in investment will lead to wide fluctuations in employment; but, at the same time, a comparatively small increment of investment will lead to full employment. If, on the other hand, the marginal propensity to consume is not much above zero, small fluctuations in investment will lead to correspondingly small fluctuations in employment; but, at the same time, it may require a large increment of investment to produce full employment. In the former case involuntary unemployment would be an easily remedied malady, though liable to be troublesome if it is allowed to develop. In the latter case, employment may be less variable but liable to settle down at a low level and to prove recalcitrant to any but the most drastic remedies. In actual fact the marginal propensity to consume seems to lie somewhere between these two extremes, though much nearer to unity than to zero; with the result that we have, in a sense, the worst of both worlds, fluctuations in employment being considerable and, at the same time, the increment in investment required to produce full employment being too great to be easily handled. Unfortunately the fluctuations have been sufficient to prevent the nature of the malady from being obvious, whilst its severity is such that it cannot be remedied unless its nature is understood.

When full employment is reached, any attempt to increase investment still further will set up a tendency in money-prices to rise without limit, irrespective of the marginal propensity to consume; *i.e.* we shall have reached a state of true inflation.[57] Up to this point, however, rising prices will be associated with an increasing aggregate real income.

III

We have been dealing so far with a net increment of investment. If, therefore, we wish to apply the above without qualification to the effect of (*e.g.*) increased public works, we have to assume that there is no offset through decreased investment in other directions,—and also, of course, no associated change in the propensity of the community to consume. Mr. Kahn was mainly concerned in the article referred to above in considering what offsets we ought to take into account as likely to be important, and in suggesting quantitative estimates. For in an actual case there are several factors besides some specific increase of investment of a given kind which enter into the final result. If, for example, a Government employs 100,000 additional men on public works, and if the multiplier (as defined above) is 4, it is not safe to assume that aggregate employment will increase by 400,000. For the new policy may have adverse reactions on investment in other directions.

It would seem (following Mr. Kahn) that the following are likely in a modern community to be the factors which it is most important not to overlook (though the first two will not be fully intelligible until after Book IV. has been reached):

(i) The method of financing the policy and the increased working cash, required by the increased employment and the associated rise of prices, may have the effect of increasing the rate of interest and so retarding investment in other directions, unless the monetary authority takes steps to the contrary; whilst, at the same time, the increased cost of capital goods will reduce their marginal efficiency to the private investor, and this will require an actual *fall* in the rate of interest to offset it.

(ii) With the confused psychology which often prevails, the Government program may, through its effect on "confidence," increase liquidity-preference or diminish the marginal efficiency of capital, which, again, may retard other investment unless measures are taken to offset it.

(iii) In an open system with foreign-trade relations, some part of the multiplier of the increased investment will accrue to the benefit of employment in foreign countries, since a proportion of the increased consumption will diminish our own country's favorable foreign balance; so that, if we consider only the effect on domestic employment as distinct from world employment, we must diminish the full figure of the multiplier. On the other hand our own country may recover a portion of this leakage through favorable repercussions due to the action of the multiplier in the foreign country in increasing its economic activity.

Furthermore, if we are considering changes of a substantial amount, we have to allow for a progressive change in the marginal propensity to consume, as the position of the margin is gradually shifted; and hence in the multiplier. The marginal propensity to consume is not constant for all levels of employment, and it is probable that there will be, as a rule, a tendency for it to diminish as employment increases; when real income increases, that is to say, the community will wish to consume a gradually diminishing proportion of it.

There are also other factors, over and above the operation of the general rule just mentioned, which may operate to modify the marginal propensity to consume, and hence the multiplier; and these other factors seem likely, as a rule, to accentuate the tendency of the general rule rather than to offset it. For, in the first place, the increase of employment will tend, owing to the effect of diminishing returns in the short period, to increase the proportion of aggregate income which accrues to the entrepreneurs, whose individual marginal propensity to consume is probably less than the average for the community as a whole. In the second place, unemployment is likely to be associated with negative saving in certain quarters, private or public, because the unemployed may be living either on the savings of themselves and their friends or on public relief which is partly financed out of loans; with the result that re-employment will gradually diminish these particular acts of negative saving and reduce, therefore, the marginal propensity to consume more rapidly than would have occurred from an equal increase in the community's real income accruing in different circumstances.

In any case, the multiplier is likely to be greater for a small net increment of investment than for a large increment; so that, where substantial changes are in view, we must be guided by the average value of the multiplier based on the average marginal propensity to consume over the range in question.

Mr. Kahn has examined the probable quantitative result of such factors as these in certain hypothetical special cases. But, clearly, it is not possible to carry any generalization very far. One can only say, for example, that a typical modern community would probably tend to consume not much less than 80 percent, of any increment of real income, if it were a closed system with the consumption of the unemployed paid for by transfers from the consumption of other consumers, so that the multiplier after allowing for offsets would not be much less than 5. In a country, however, where foreign trade accounts for, say, 20 percent, of consumption and where the unemployed receive out of loans or their equivalent up to, say, 50 percent, of their normal consumption when in work, the multiplier may fall as low as 2 or 3 times the employment provided by a specific new investment. Thus a given fluctuation of investment will be associated with a much less violent fluctuation of employment in a country in which foreign trade plays a large part and unemployment relief is financed on a larger scale out of borrowing (as was the case, e.g., in Great Britain in 1931), than in a country in which these factors are less important (as in the United States in 1932).[58]

It is, however, to the general principle of the multiplier to which we have to look for an explanation of how fluctuations in the amount of investment, which are a comparatively small proportion of the national income, are capable of generating fluctuations in aggregate employment and income so much greater in amplitude than themselves.

IV

The discussion has been carried on, so far, on the basis of a change in aggregate investment which has been foreseen sufficiently in advance for the consumption industries to advance *pari passu* with the capital-goods industries without more disturbance to the price of consumption-goods than is consequential, in conditions of decreasing returns, on an increase in the quantity which is produced.

In general, however, we have to take account of the case where the initiative comes from an increase in the output of the capital-goods industries which was not fully foreseen. It is obvious that an initiative of this description only produces its full effect on employment over a period of time. I have found, however, in discussion that this obvious fact often gives rise to some confusion between the logical theory of the multiplier, which holds good continuously, without time-lag, at all moments of time, and the consequences of an expansion in the capital-goods industries which take gradual effect, subject to time-lag and only after an interval.

The relationship between these two things can be cleared up by pointing out, firstly that an unforeseen, or imperfectly foreseen, expansion in the capital-goods industries does not have an instantaneous effect of equal amount on the aggregate of investment but causes a gradual increase of the latter; and, secondly, that it may cause a temporary departure of the marginal propensity to consume away from its normal value, followed, however, by a gradual return to it.

Thus an expansion in the capital-goods industries causes a series of increments in aggregate investment occurring in successive periods over an interval of time, and a series of values of the marginal propensity to consume in these successive periods which differ both from what the values would have been if the expansion had been foreseen and from what they will be when the community has settled down to a new steady level of aggregate investment. But in every interval of time the theory of the multiplier holds good in the sense that the increment of aggregate demand is equal to the increment of aggregate investment multiplied by the marginal propensity to consume.

The explanation of these two sets of facts can be seen most clearly by taking the extreme case where the expansion of employment in the capital-goods industries is so entirely unforeseen that in the first instance there is no increase whatever in the output of consumption-goods. In this event the efforts of those newly employed in the capital-goods industries to consume a proportion of their increased incomes will raise the prices of consumption-goods until a temporary equilibrium between demand and supply has been brought about partly by the high prices causing a postponement of consumption, partly by a redistribution of income in favor of the saving classes as an effect of the increased profits resulting from the higher prices, and partly by the higher prices causing a depletion of stocks. So far as the balance is restored by a postponement of consumption there is a temporary reduction of the marginal propensity to consume, i.e. of the multiplier itself, and in so far as there is a depletion of stocks, aggregate investment increases for the time being by less than the increment of investment in the capital-goods industries,—*i.e.* the thing to be multiplied does not increase by the full increment of investment in the capital-goods industries. As time goes on, however, the consumption-goods industries adjust themselves to the new demand, so that when the deferred consumption is enjoyed, the marginal propensity to consume rises temporarily above its normal level, to compensate for the extent to which it previously fell below it, and eventually returns to its normal level; whilst the restoration of stocks to their previous figure causes the increment of aggregate investment to be temporarily greater than the increment of investment in the capital-goods industries (the increment of working capital corresponding to the greater output also having temporarily the same effect).

The fact that an unforeseen change only exercises its full effect on employment over a period of time is important in certain contexts;—in particular it plays a part in the analysis of the trade cycle (on lines such as I followed in my *Treatise on Money*). But it does not in any way affect the significance of the theory of the multiplier as set forth in this chapter; nor render it inapplicable as an indicator of the total benefit to employment to be expected from an expansion in the capital-goods industries. Moreover, except in conditions where the consumption industries are already working almost at capacity so that an expansion of output requires an expansion of plant and not merely the more intensive employment of the existing plant, there is no reason to suppose that more than a brief interval of time need elapse before employment in the consumption industries is advancing *pari passu* with employment in the capital-goods industries with the multiplier operating near its normal figure.

V

We have seen above that the greater the marginal propensity to consume, the greater the multiplier, and hence the greater the disturbance to employment corresponding to a given change in investment. This might seem to lead to the paradoxical conclusion that a poor community in which saving is a very small proportion of income will be more subject to violent fluctuations than a wealthy community where saving is a larger proportion of income and the multiplier consequently smaller.

This conclusion, however, would overlook the distinction between the effects of the marginal propensity to consume and those of the average propensity to consume. For whilst a high marginal propensity to consume involves a larger *proportionate* effect from a given percentage change in investment, the *absolute* effect will, nevertheless, be small if the *average* propensity to consume is also high. This may be illustrated as follows by a numerical example.

Let us suppose that a community's propensity to consume is such that, so long as its real income does not exceed the output from employing 5,000,000 men on its existing capital equipment, it consumes the whole of its income; that of the output of the next 100,000 additional men employed it consumes 99 percent, of the next 100,000 after that 98 percent, of the third 100,000 97 percent, and so on; and that 10,000,000 men employed represents full employment. It follows from this that, when 5,000,000 + n × 100,000 men are employed, the multiplier at the margin is $100/n$, and $n(n + 1)/2.(50 + n)$ percent of the national income is invested.

Thus when 5,200,000 men are employed the multiplier is very large, namely 50, but investment is only a trifling proportion of current income, namely, 0.06 percent; with the result that if investment falls off by a large proportion, say about two-thirds, employment will only decline to 5,100,000, *i.e.* by about 2 percent. On the other hand, when 9,000,000 men are employed, the marginal multiplier is comparatively small, namely 2 1/2, but investment is now a substantial proportion of current income, namely, 9 percent; with the result that if investment falls by two-thirds, employment will decline to 6,900,000, namely, by 23 percent. In the limit where investment falls off to zero, employment will decline by about 4 percent, in the former case, whereas in the latter case it will decline by 44 percent.[59]

In the above example, the poorer of the two communities under comparison is poorer by reason of underemployment. But the same reasoning applies by easy adaptation if the poverty is due to inferior skill, technique or equipment. Thus whilst the multiplier is larger in a poor community, the effect on employment of fluctuations in investment will be much greater in a wealthy community, assuming that in the latter current investment represents a much larger proportion of current output.[60]

It is also obvious from the above that the employment of a given number of men on public works will (on the assumptions made) have a much larger effect on aggregate employment at a time when there is severe unemployment, than it will have later on when full employment is approached. In the above example, if at a time when employment has fallen to 5,200,000, an additional 100,000 men are employed on public works, total employment will rise to 6,400,000. But if employment is already 9,000,000 when the additional 100,000 men are taken on for public works, total employment will only rise to 9,200,000. Thus public works even of doubtful utility may pay for themselves over and over again at a time of severe unemployment, if only from the diminished cost of relief expenditure, provided that we can assume that a smaller proportion of income is saved when unemployment is greater; but they may become a more doubtful proposition as a state of full employment is approached. Furthermore, if our assumption is correct that the marginal propensity to consume falls off steadily as we approach full employment, it follows that it will become more and more troublesome to secure a further given increase of employment by further increasing investment.

It should not be difficult to compile a chart of the marginal propensity to consume at each stage of a trade cycle from the statistics (if they were available) of aggregate income and aggregate investment at successive dates. At present, however, our statistics are not accurate enough (or compiled sufficiently with this specific object in view) to allow us to infer more than highly approximate estimates. The best for the purpose, of which I am aware, are Mr. Kuznets' figures for the United States (already referred to in Chapter 8 above), though they are, nevertheless, very precarious. Taken in conjunction with estimates of national income these suggest, for what they are worth, both a lower figure and a more stable figure for the investment multiplier than I should have expected. If single years are taken in isolation, the results look rather wild. But if they are grouped in pairs, the multiplier seems to have been less than 3 and probably fairly stable in the neighborhood of 2.5. This suggests a marginal propensity to consume not exceeding 60 to 70 percent—a figure quite plausible for the boom, but surprisingly, and, in my judgment, improbably low for the slump. It is possible, however, that the extreme financial conservatism of corporate finance in the United States, even during the slump, may account for it. In other words, if, when investment is falling heavily through a failure to undertake repairs and replacements, financial provision is made, nevertheless, in respect of such wastage, the effect is to prevent the rise in the marginal propensity to consume which would have occurred otherwise. I suspect that this factor may have played a significant part in aggravating the degree of the recent slump in the United States. On the other hand, it is possible that the statistics somewhat overstate the decline in investment, which is alleged to have fallen off by more than 75 percent, in 1932 compared with 1929, whilst net "capital formation" declined by more than 95 percent;—a moderate change in these estimates being capable of making a substantial difference to the multiplier.

VI

When involuntary unemployment exists, the marginal disutility of labor is necessarily less than the utility of the marginal product. Indeed it may be much less. For a man who has been long unemployed some measure of labor, instead of involving disutility, may have a positive utility. If this is accepted, the above reasoning shows how "wasteful" loan expenditure[61] may nevertheless enrich the community on balance. Pyramid-building, earthquakes, even wars may serve to increase wealth, if the education of our statesmen on the principles of the classical economics stands in the way of anything better.

It is curious how common sense, wriggling for an escape from absurd conclusions, has been apt to reach a preference for *wholly* "wasteful" forms of loan expenditure rather than for *partly* wasteful forms, which, because they are not wholly wasteful, tend to be judged on strict "business" principles. For example, unemployment relief financed by loans is more readily accepted than the financing of improvements at a charge below the current rate of interest; whilst the form of digging holes in the ground known as gold-mining, which not only adds nothing whatever to the real wealth of the world but involves the disutility of labor, is the most acceptable of all solutions.

If the Treasury were to fill old bottles with banknotes, bury them at suitable depths in disused coalmines which are then filled up to the surface with town rubbish, and leave it to private enterprise on well-tried principles of *laissez-faire* to dig the notes up again (the right to do so being obtained, of course, by tendering for leases of the note-bearing territory), there need be no more unemployment and, with the help of the repercussions, the real income of the community, and its capital wealth also, would probably become a good deal greater than it actually is. It would, indeed, be more sensible to build houses and the like; but if there are political and practical difficulties in the way of this, the above would be better than nothing.

The analogy between this expedient and the goldmines of the real world is complete. At periods when gold is available at suitable depths experience shows that the real wealth of the world increases rapidly; and when but little of it is so available, our wealth surfers stagnation or decline. Thus gold-mines are of the greatest value and importance to civilization. Just as wars, have been the only form of large-scale loan expenditure which statesmen have thought justifiable, so gold-mining is the only pretext for digging holes in the ground which has recommended itself to bankers as sound finance; and each of these activities has played its part in progress—failing something better. To mention a detail, the tendency in slumps for the price of gold to rise in terms of labor and materials aids eventual recovery, because it increases the depth at which gold-digging pays, and lowers the minimum grade of ore which is payable.

In addition to the probable effect of increased supplies of gold on the rate of interest, gold-mining is for two reasons a highly practical form of investment, if we are precluded from increasing employment by means which at the same time increase our stock of useful wealth. In the first place, owing to the gambling attractions which it offers it is carried on without too close a regard to the ruling rate of interest. In the second place the result, namely, the increased stock of gold, does not, as in other cases, have the effect of diminishing its marginal utility. Since the value of a house depends on its utility, every house which is built serves to diminish the prospective rents obtainable from further house-building and therefore lessens the attraction of further similar investment unless the rate of interest is falling *pari passu*. But the fruits of gold-mining do not suffer from this disadvantage, and a check can only come through a rise of the wage-unit in terms of gold, which is not likely to occur unless and until employment is substantially better. Moreover, there is no subsequent reverse effect on account of provision for user and supplementary costs, as in the case of less durable forms of wealth.

Ancient Egypt was doubly fortunate, and doubtless owed to this its fabled wealth, in that it possessed *two* activities, namely, pyramid-building as well as the search for the precious metals, the fruits of which, since they could not serve the needs of man by being consumed, did not stale with abundance. The Middle Ages built cathedrals and sang dirges. Two pyramids, two masses for the dead, are twice as good as one; but not so two railways from London to York. Thus we are so sensible, have schooled ourselves to so close a semblance of prudent financiers, taking careful thought before we add to the "financial" burdens of posterity by building them houses to live in, that we have no such easy escape from the sufferings of unemployment. We have to accept them as an inevitable result of applying to the conduct of the State the maxims which are best calculated to "enrich" an individual by enabling him to pile up claims to enjoyment which he does not intend to exercise at any definite time.

Book IV

The Inducement to Invest

CHAPTER 11

The Marginal Efficiency of Capital

I

When a man buys an investment or capital-asset, he purchases the right to the series of prospective returns, which he expects to obtain from selling its output, after deducting the running expenses of obtaining that output, during the life of the asset. This series of annuities Q1, Q2, ... Q*n* it is convenient to call the *prospective yield* of the investment.

Over against the prospective yield of the investment we have the *supply price* of the capital-asset, meaning by this, not the market-price at which an asset of the type in question can actually be purchased in the market, but the price which would just induce a manufacturer newly to produce an additional unit of such assets, *i.e.* what is sometimes called its *replacement cost*. The relation between the prospective yield of a capital-asset and its supply price or replacement cost, *i.e.* the relation between the prospective yield of one more unit of that type of capital and the cost of producing that unit, furnishes us with the marginal efficiency of capital of that type. More precisely, I define the *marginal efficiency of capital* as being equal to that rate of discount which would make the present value of the series of annuities given by the returns expected from the capital-asset during its life just equal to its supply price. This gives us the marginal efficiencies of particular types of capital-assets. The greatest of these marginal efficiencies can then be regarded as the marginal efficiency of capital in general.

The reader should note that the marginal efficiency of capital is here defined in terms of the *expectation* of yield and of the *current* supply price of the capital-asset. It depends on the rate of return expected to be obtainable on money if it were invested in a *newly* produced asset; not on the historical result of what an investment has yielded on its original cost if we look back on its record after its life is over.

If there is an increased investment in any given type of capital during any period of time, the marginal efficiency of that type of capital will diminish as the investment in it is increased, partly because the prospective yield will fall as the supply of that type of capital is increased, and partly because, as a rule, pressure on the facilities for producing that type of capital will cause its supply price to increase; the second of these factors being usually the more important in producing equilibrium in the short run, but the longer the period in view the more does the first factor take its place. Thus for each type of capital we can build up a schedule, showing by how much investment in it will have to increase within the period, in order that its marginal efficiency should fall to any given figure. We can then aggregate these schedules for all the different types of capital, so as to provide a schedule relating the rate of aggregate investment to the corresponding marginal efficiency of capital in general which that rate of investment will establish. We shall call this the investment demand-schedule; or, alternatively, the schedule of the marginal efficiency of capital.

Now it is obvious that the actual rate of current investment will be pushed to the point where there is no longer any class of capital-asset of which the marginal efficiency exceeds the current rate of interest. In other words, the rate of investment will be pushed to the point on the investment demand-schedule where the marginal efficiency of capital in general is equal to the market rate of interest.[62]

The same thing can also be expressed as follows. If Q_r is the prospective yield from an asset at time r, and d_r is the present value of £1 deferred *r* years *at the current rate of interest*, $SQ_r d_r$ is the demand price of the investment; and investment will be carried to the point where $SQ_r d_r$ becomes equal to the supply price of the investment as defined above. If, on the other hand, $SQ_r d_r$ falls short of the supply price, there will be no current investment in the asset in question.

It follows that the inducement to invest depends partly on the investment demand-schedule and partly on the rate of interest. Only at the conclusion of Book IV will it be possible to take a comprehensive view of the factors determining the rate of investment in their actual complexity. I would, however, ask the reader to note at once that neither the knowledge of an asset's prospective yield nor the knowledge of the marginal efficiency of the asset enables us to deduce either the rate of interest or the present value of the asset. We must ascertain the rate of interest from some other source, and only then can we value the asset by "capitalizing" its prospective yield.

II

How is the above definition of the marginal efficiency of capital related to common usage? The *Marginal Productivity* or *Yield* or *Efficiency,* or *Utility* of Capital are familiar terms which we have all frequently used. But it is not easy by searching the literature of economics to find a clear statement of what economists have usually intended by these terms.

There are at least three ambiguities to clear up. There is, to begin with, the ambiguity whether we are concerned with the increment of physical product per unit of time due to the employment of one more physical unit of capital, or with the increment of value due to the employment of one more value unit of capital. The former involves difficulties as to the definition of the physical unit of capital, which I believe to be both insoluble and unnecessary. It is, of course, possible to say that ten laborers will raise more wheat from a given area when they are in a position to make use of certain additional machines; but I know no means of reducing this to an intelligible arithmetical ratio which does not bring in values. Nevertheless many discussions of this subject seem to be mainly concerned with the physical productivity of capital in some sense, though the writers fail to make themselves clear.

Secondly, there is the question whether the marginal efficiency of capital is some absolute quantity or a ratio. The contexts in which it is used and the practice of treating it as being of the same dimension as the rate of interest seem to require that it should be a ratio. Yet it is not usually made clear what the two terms of the ratio are supposed to be.

Finally, there is the distinction, the neglect of which has been the main cause of confusion and misunderstanding, between the increment of value obtainable by using an additional quantity of capital in the *existing* situation, and the series of increments which it is expected to obtain over *the whole life* of the additional capital asset;—*i.e.* the distinction between Q_1, and the complete series $Q_1, Q_2 \ldots Q_r \ldots$ This involves the whole question of the place of expectation in economic theory. Most discussions of the marginal efficiency of capital seem to pay no attention to any member of the series except Q_1. Yet this cannot be legitimate except in a static theory, for which all the Q's are equal. The ordinary theory of distribution, where it is assumed that capital is getting *now* its marginal productivity (in some sense or other), is only valid in a stationary state. The aggregate current return to capital has no direct relationship to its marginal efficiency; whilst its current return at the margin of production (*i.e.* the return to capital which enters into the supply price of output) is its marginal user cost, which also has no close connection with its marginal efficiency.

There is, as I have said above, a remarkable lack of any clear account of the matter. At the same time I believe that the definition which I have given above is fairly close to what Marshall intended to mean by the term. The phrase which Marshall himself uses is "marginal net efficiency" of a factor of production; or, alternatively, the "marginal utility of capital." The following is a summary of the most relevant passage which I can find in his *Principles* (6th ed. pp. 519–520). I have run together some non-consecutive sentences to convey the gist of what he says:

> "In a certain factory an extra £100 worth of machinery can be applied so as not to involve any other extra expense, and so as to add annually £3 worth to the net output of the factory after allowing for its own wear and tear. If the investors of capital push it into every occupation in which it seems likely to gain a high reward; and if, after this has been done and equilibrium has been found, it still pays and only just pays to employ this machinery, we can infer from this fact that the yearly rate of interest is 3 percent. But illustrations of this kind merely indicate part of the action of the great causes which govern value. They cannot be made into a theory of interest, any more than into a theory of wages, without reasoning in a circle. . . . Suppose that the rate of interest is 3 percent per annum on perfectly good security; and that the hat-making trade absorbs a capital of one million pounds. This implies that the hat-making trade can turn the whole million pounds' worth of capital to so good account that they would pay 3 percent per annum net for the use of it rather than go without any of it. There may be machinery which the

trade would have refused to dispense with if the rate of interest had been 20 percent per annum. If the rate had been 10 percent, more would have been used; if it had been 6 percent, still more; if 4 percent, still more; and finally, the rate being 3 percent, they use more still. When they have this amount, the marginal utility of the machinery, *i.e.* the utility of that machinery which it is only just worth their while to employ, is measured by 3 percent."

It is evident from the above that Marshall was well aware that we are involved in a circular argument if we try to determine along these lines what the rate of interest actually is.[63] In this passage he appears to accept the view set forth above, that the rate of interest determines the point to which new investment will be pushed, given the schedule of the marginal efficiency of capital. If the rate of interest is 3 percent, this means that no one will pay £100 for a machine unless he hopes thereby to add £3 to his annual net output after allowing for costs and depreciation. But we shall see in Chapter 14 that in other passages Marshall was less cautious—though still drawing back when his argument was leading him on to dubious ground.

Although he does not call it the "marginal efficiency of capital," Professor Irving Fisher has given in his *Theory of Interest* (1930) a definition of what he calls "the rate of return over cost" which is identical with my definition. "The rate of return over cost," he writes,[64] "is that rate which, employed in computing the present worth of all the costs and the present worth of all the returns, will make these two equal." Professor Fisher explains that the extent of investment in any direction will depend on a comparison between the rate of return over cost and the rate of interest. To induce new investment "the rate of return over cost must *exceed* the rate of interest."[65] "This new magnitude (or factor) in our study plays the central role on the investment opportunity side of interest theory."[66] Thus Professor Fisher uses his "rate of return over cost" in the same sense and for precisely the same purpose as I employ "the marginal efficiency of capital."

III

The most important confusion concerning the meaning and significance of the marginal efficiency of capital has ensued on the failure to see that it depends on the *prospective* yield of capital, and not merely on its current yield. This can be best illustrated by pointing out the effect on the marginal efficiency of capital of an expectation of changes in the prospective cost of production, whether these changes are expected to come from changes in labor cost, *i.e.* in the wage-unit, or from inventions and new technique. The output from equipment produced today will have to compete, in the course of its life, with the output from equipment produced subsequently, perhaps at a lower labor cost, perhaps by an improved technique, which is content with a lower price for its output and will be increased in quantity until the price of its output has fallen to the lower figure with which it is content. Moreover, the entrepreneur's profit (in terms of money) from equipment, old or new, will be reduced, if all output comes to be produced more cheaply. In so far as such developments are foreseen as probable, or even as possible, the marginal efficiency of capital produced today is appropriately diminished.

This is the factor through which the expectation of changes in the value of money influences the volume of current output. The expectation of a fall in the value of money stimulates investment, and hence employment generally, because it raises the schedule of the marginal efficiency of capital, *i.e.* the investment demand-schedule; and the expectation of a rise in the value of money is depressing, because it lowers the schedule of the marginal efficiency of capital.

This is the truth which lies behind Professor Irving Fisher's theory of what he originally called "Appreciation and Interest"—the distinction between the money rate of interest and the real rate of interest where the latter is equal to the former after correction for changes in the value of money. It is difficult to make sense of this theory as stated, because it is not clear whether the change in the value of money is or is not assumed to be foreseen. There is no escape from the dilemma that, if it is not foreseen, there will be no effect on current affairs; whilst, if it is foreseen, the prices of existing goods will be forthwith so adjusted that the advantages of holding money and of holding goods are again equalized, and it will be too late for holders of money to gain or to suffer a change in the rate of interest which will offset the prospective change during the period of the loan in the value of the money lent. For the dilemma is not successfully escaped by Professor Pigou's expedient of supposing that the prospective change in the value of money is foreseen by one set of people but not foreseen by another.

The mistake lies in supposing that it is the rate of interest on which prospective changes in the value of money will directly react, instead of the marginal efficiency of a given stock of capital. The prices of *existing* assets will always adjust themselves to changes in expectation concerning the prospective value of money. The significance of such changes in expectation lies in their effect on the readiness to produce *new* assets through their reaction on the marginal efficiency of capital. The stimulating effect of the expectation of higher prices is due, not to its raising the rate of interest (that would be a paradoxical way of stimulating output—in so far as the rate of interest rises, the stimulating effect is to that extent offset), but to its raising the marginal efficiency of a given stock of capital. *If the rate of interest were to rise pari passu with the marginal efficiency of capital, there would be no stimulating effect from the expectation of rising prices.* For the stimulus to output depends on the marginal efficiency of a given stock of capital rising *relatively* to the rate of interest. Indeed Professor Fisher's theory could be best re-written in terms of a "real rate of interest" defined as being the rate of interest which would have to rule, consequently on a change in the state of expectation as to the future value of money, in order that this change should have no effect on current output.[67]

It is worth noting that an expectation of a future fall in the rate of interest will have the effect of *lowering* the schedule of the marginal efficiency of capital; since it means that the output from equipment produced today will have to compete during part of its life with the output from equipment which is content with a lower return. This expectation will have no great depressing effect, since the expectations, which are held concerning the complex of rates of interest for various terms which will rule in the future, will be partially reflected in the complex of rates of interest which rule today. Nevertheless there may be some depressing effect, since the output from equipment produced today, which will emerge towards the end of the life of this equipment, may have to compete with the output of much younger equipment which is content with a lower return because of the lower rate of interest which rules for periods subsequent to the end of the life of equipment produced today.

It is important to understand the dependence of the marginal efficiency of a given stock of capital on changes in expectation, because it is chiefly this dependence which renders the marginal efficiency of capital subject to the somewhat violent fluctuations which are the explanation of the Trade Cycle. In Chapter 22 below we shall show that the succession of Boom and Slump can be described and analyzed in terms of the fluctuations of the marginal efficiency of capital relatively to the rate of interest.

IV

Two types of risk affect the volume of investment which have not commonly been distinguished, but which it is important to distinguish. The first is the entrepreneur's or borrower's risk and arises out of doubts in his own mind as to the probability of his actually earning the prospective yield for which he hopes. If a man is venturing his own money, this is the only risk which is relevant.

But where a system of borrowing and lending exists, by which I mean the granting of loans with a margin of real or personal security, a second type of risk is relevant which we may call the lender's risk. This may be due either to moral hazard, *i.e.* voluntary default or other means of escape, possibly lawful, from the fulfillment of the obligation, or to the possible insufficiency of the margin of security, *i.e.* involuntary default due to the disappointment of expectation. A third source of risk might be added, namely, a possible adverse change in the value of the monetary standard which renders a money-loan to this extent less secure than a real asset; though all or most of this should be already reflected, and therefore absorbed, in the price of durable real assets.

Now the first type of risk is, in a sense, a real social cost, though susceptible to diminution by averaging as well as by an increased accuracy of foresight. The second, however, is a pure addition to the cost of investment which would not exist if the borrower and lender were the same person. Moreover, it involves in part a duplication of a proportion of the entrepreneur's risk, which is added *twice* to the pure rate of interest to give the minimum prospective yield which will induce the investment. For if a venture is a risky one, the borrower will require a wider margin between his expectation of yield and the rate of interest at which he will think it worth his while to borrow; whilst the very same reason will lead the lender to require a wider margin between what he charges and the pure rate of interest in order to induce him to lend (except where the borrower is so strong and wealthy that he is in a position to offer an exceptional margin of security). The hope of a very favorable outcome, which may balance the risk in the mind of the borrower, is not available to solace the lender.

This duplication of allowance for a portion of the risk has not hitherto been emphasized, so far as I am aware; but it may be important in certain circumstances. During a boom the popular estimation of the magnitude of both these risks, both borrower's risk and lender's risk, is apt to become unusually and imprudently low.

V

The schedule of the marginal efficiency of capital is of fundamental importance because it is mainly through this factor (much more than through the rate of interest) that the expectation of the future influences the present. The mistake of regarding the marginal efficiency of capital primarily in terms of the *current* yield of capital equipment, which would be correct only in the static state where there is no changing future to influence the present, has had the result of breaking the theoretical link between today and tomorrow. Even the rate of interest is, virtually[68] a *current* phenomenon; and if we reduce the marginal efficiency of capital to the same status, we cut ourselves off from taking any direct account of the influence of the future in our analysis of the existing equilibrium.

The fact that the assumptions of the static state often underlie present-day economic theory, imports into it a large element of unreality. But the introduction of the concepts of user cost and of the marginal efficiency of capital, as defined above, will have the effect, I think, of bringing it back to reality, whilst reducing to a minimum the necessary degree of adaptation.

It is by reason of the existence of durable equipment that the economic future is linked to the present. It is, therefore, consonant with, and agreeable to, our broad principles of thought, that the expectation of the future should affect the present through the demand price for durable equipment.

CHAPTER 12

The State of Long-Term Expectations

I

We have seen in the previous chapter that the scale of investment depends on the relation between the rate of interest and the schedule of the marginal efficiency of capital corresponding to different scales of current investment, whilst the marginal efficiency of capital depends on the relation between the supply price of a capital-asset and its prospective yield. In this chapter we shall consider in more detail some of the factors which determine the prospective yield of an asset.

The considerations upon which expectations of prospective yields are based are partly existing facts which we can assume to be known more or less for certain, and partly future events which can only be forecasted with more or less confidence. Amongst the first may be mentioned the existing stock of various types of capital-assets and of capital-assets-in general and the strength of the existing consumers' demand for goods which require for their efficient production a relatively larger assistance from capital. Amongst the latter are future changes in the type and quantity of the stock of capital-assets and in the tastes of the consumer, the strength of effective demand from time to time during the life of the investment under consideration, and the changes in the wage-unit in terms of money which may occur during its life. We may sum up the state of psychological expectation which covers the latter as being the *state of long-term expectation;*—as distinguished from the short-term expectation upon the basis of which a producer estimates what he will get for a product when it is finished if he decides to begin producing it today with the existing plant, which we examined in Chapter 5.

II

It would be foolish, in forming our expectations, to attach great weight to matters which are very uncertain.[69] It is reasonable, therefore, to be guided to a considerable degree by the facts about which we feel somewhat confident, even though they may be less decisively relevant to the issue than other facts about which our knowledge is vague and scanty. For this reason the facts of the existing situation enter, in a sense disproportionately, into the formation of our long-term expectations; our usual practice being to take the existing situation and to project it into the future, modified only to the extent that we have more or less definite reasons for expecting a change.

The state of long-term expectation, upon which our decisions are based, does not solely depend, therefore, on the most probable forecast we can make. It also depends on the *confidence* with which we make this forecast—on how highly we rate the likelihood of our best forecast turning out quite wrong. If we expect large changes but are very uncertain as to what precise form these changes will take, then our confidence will be weak.

The *state of confidence,* as they term it, is a matter to which practical men always pay the closest and most anxious attention. But economists have not analyzed it carefully and have been content, as a rule, to discuss it in general terms. In particular it has not been made clear that its relevance to economic problems comes in through its important influence on the schedule of the marginal efficiency of capital. There are not two separate factors affecting the rate of investment, namely, the schedule of the marginal efficiency of capital and the state of confidence. The state of confidence is relevant because it is one of the major factors determining the former, which is the same thing as the investment demand-schedule.

There is, however, not much to be said about the state of confidence *a priori.* Our conclusions must mainly depend upon the actual observation of markets and business psychology. This is the reason why the ensuing digression is on a different level of abstraction from most of this book.

For convenience of exposition we shall assume in the following discussion of the state of confidence that there are no changes in the rate of interest, and we shall write, throughout the following sections, as if changes in the values of investments were solely due to changes in the expectation of their prospective yields and not at all to changes in the rate of interest at which these prospective yields are capitalized. The effect of changes in the rate of interest is, however, easily superimposed on the effect of changes in the state of confidence.

III

The outstanding fact is the extreme precariousness of the basis of knowledge on which our estimates of prospective yield have to be made. Our knowledge of the factors which will govern the yield of an investment some years hence is usually very slight and often negligible. If we speak frankly, we have to admit that our basis of knowledge for estimating the yield ten years hence of a railway, a copper mine, a textile factory, the goodwill of a patent medicine, an Atlantic liner, a building in the City of London amounts to little and sometimes to nothing; or even five years hence. In fact, those who seriously attempt to make any such estimate are often so much in the minority that their behavior does not govern the market.

In former times, when enterprises were mainly owned by those who undertook them or by their friends and associates, investment depended on a sufficient supply of individuals of sanguine temperament and constructive impulses who embarked on business as a way of life, not really relying on a precise calculation of prospective profit. The affair was partly a lottery, though with the ultimate result largely governed by whether the abilities and character of the managers were above or below the average. Some would fail and some would succeed. But even after the event no one would know whether the average results in terms of the sums invested had exceeded, equaled or fallen short of the prevailing rate of interest; though, if we exclude the exploitation of natural resources and monopolies, it is probable that the actual average results of investments, even during periods of progress and prosperity, have disappointed the hopes which prompted them. Business men play a mixed game of skill and chance, the average results of which to the players are not known by those who take a hand. If human nature felt no temptation to take a chance, no satisfaction (profit apart) in constructing a factory, a railway, a mine or a farm, there might not be much investment merely as a result of cold calculation.

Decisions to invest in private business of the old-fashioned type were, however, decisions largely irrevocable, not only for the community as a whole, but also for the individual. With the separation between ownership and management which prevails today and with the development of organized investment markets, a new factor of great importance has entered in, which sometimes facilitates investment but sometimes adds greatly to the instability of the system. In the absence of security markets, there is no object in frequently attempting to revalue an investment to which we are committed. But the Stock Exchange revalues many investments every day and the revaluations give a frequent opportunity to the individual (though not to the community as a whole) to revise his commitments. It is as though a farmer, having tapped his barometer after breakfast, could decide to remove his capital from the farming business between 10 and 11 in the morning and reconsider whether he should return to it later in the week. But the daily revaluations of the Stock Exchange, though they are primarily made to facilitate transfers of old investments between one individual and another, inevitably exert a decisive influence on the rate of current investment. For there is no sense in building up a new enterprise at a cost greater than that at which a similar existing enterprise can be purchased; whilst there is an inducement to spend on a new project what may seem an extravagant sum, if it can be floated off on the Stock Exchange at an immediate profit.[70] Thus certain classes of investment are governed by the average expectation of those who deal on the Stock Exchange as revealed in the price of shares, rather than by the genuine expectations of the professional entrepreneur.[71] How then are these highly significant daily, even hourly, revaluations of existing investments carried out in practice?

IV

In practice we have tacitly agreed, as a rule, to fall back on what is, in truth, a *convention*. The essence of this convention—though it does not, of course, work out quite so simply—lies in assuming that the existing state of affairs will continue indefinitely, except in so far as we have specific reasons to expect a change. This does not mean that we really believe that the existing state of affairs will continue indefinitely. We know from extensive experience that this is most unlikely. The actual results of an investment over a long term of years very seldom agree with the initial expectation. Nor can we rationalize our behavior by arguing that to a man in a state of ignorance errors in either direction are equally probable, so that there remains a mean actuarial expectation based on equi-probabilities. For it can easily be shown that the assumption of arithmetically equal probabilities based on a state of ignorance leads to absurdities. We are assuming, in effect, that the existing market valuation, however arrived at, is uniquely *correct* in relation to our existing knowledge of the facts which will influence the yield of the investment, and that it will only change in proportion to changes in this knowledge; though, philosophically speaking, it cannot be uniquely correct, since our existing knowledge does not provide a sufficient basis for a calculated mathematical expectation. In point of fact, all sorts of considerations enter into the market valuation which are in no way relevant to the prospective yield.

Nevertheless the above conventional method of calculation will be compatible with a considerable measure of continuity and stability in our affairs, *so long as we can rely on the maintenance of the convention.*

For if there exist organized investment markets and if we can rely on the maintenance of the convention, an investor can legitimately encourage himself with the idea that the only risk he runs is that of a genuine change in the news *over the near future,* as to the likelihood of which he can attempt to form his own judgment, and which is unlikely to be very large. For, assuming that the convention holds good, it is only these changes which can affect the value of his investment, and he need not lose his sleep merely because he has not any notion what his investment will be worth ten years hence. Thus investment becomes reasonably "safe" for the individual investor over short periods, and hence over a succession of short periods however many, if he can fairly rely on there being no breakdown in the convention and on his therefore having an opportunity to revise his judgment and change his investment, before there has been time for much to happen. Investments which are "fixed" for the community are thus made "liquid" for the individual.

It has been, I am sure, on the basis of some such procedure as this that our leading investment markets have been developed. But it is not surprising that a convention, in an absolute view of things so arbitrary, should have its weak points. It is its precariousness which creates no small part of our contemporary problem of securing sufficient investment.

V

Some of the factors which accentuate this precariousness may be briefly mentioned.

(1) As a result of the gradual increase in the proportion of the equity in the community's aggregate capital investment which is owned by persons who do not manage and have no special knowledge of the circumstances, either actual or prospective, of the business in question, the element of real knowledge in the valuation of investments by those who own them or contemplate purchasing them has seriously declined.

(2) Day-to-day fluctuations in the profits of existing investments, which are obviously of an ephemeral and non-significant character, tend to have an altogether excessive, and even an absurd, influence on the market. It is said, for example, that the shares of American companies which manufacture ice tend to sell at a higher price in summer when their profits are seasonally high than in winter when no one wants ice. The recurrence of a bank-holiday may raise the market valuation of the British railway system by several million pounds.

(3) A conventional valuation which is established as the outcome of the mass psychology of a large number of ignorant individuals is liable to change violently as the result of a sudden fluctuation of opinion due to factors which do not really make much difference to the prospective yield; since there will be no strong roots of conviction to hold it steady. In abnormal times in particular, when the hypothesis of an indefinite continuance of the existing state of affairs is less plausible than usual even though there are no express grounds to anticipate a definite change, the market will be subject to waves of optimistic and pessimistic sentiment, which are unreasoning and yet in a sense legitimate where no solid basis exists for a reasonable calculation.

(4) But there is one feature in particular which deserves our attention. It might have been supposed that competition between expert professionals, possessing judgment and knowledge beyond that of the average private investor, would correct the vagaries of the ignorant individual left to himself. It happens, however, that the energies and skill of the professional investor and speculator are mainly occupied otherwise. For most of these persons are, in fact, largely concerned, not with making superior long-term forecasts of the probable yield of an investment over its whole life, but with foreseeing changes in the conventional basis of valuation a short time ahead of the general public. They are concerned, not with what an investment is really worth to a man who buys it "for keeps," but with what the market will value it at, under the influence of mass psychology, three months or a year hence. Moreover, this behavior is not the outcome of a wrong-headed propensity. It is an inevitable result of an investment market organized along the lines described. For it is not sensible to pay 25 for an investment of which you believe the prospective yield to justify a value of 30, if you also believe that the market will value it at 20 three months hence.

Thus the professional investor is forced to concern himself with the anticipation of impending changes, in the news or in the atmosphere, of the kind by which experience shows that the mass psychology of the market is most influenced. This is the inevitable result of investment markets organized with a view to so-called "liquidity." Of the maxims of orthodox finance none, surely, is more anti-social than the fetish of liquidity, the doctrine that it is a positive virtue on the part of investment institutions to concentrate their resources upon the holding of "liquid" securities. It forgets that there is no such thing as liquidity of investment for the community as a whole. The social object of skilled investment should be to defeat the dark forces of time and ignorance which envelop our future. The actual, private object of the most skilled investment today is "to beat the gun," as the Americans so well express it, to outwit the crowd and to pass the bad, or depreciating, half-crown to the other fellow.

This battle of wits to anticipate the basis of conventional valuation a few months hence, rather than the prospective yield of an investment over a long term of years, does not even require gulls amongst the public to feed the maws of the professional;—it can be played by professionals amongst themselves. Nor is it necessary that anyone should keep his simple faith in the conventional basis of valuation having any genuine long-term validity. For it is, so to speak, a game of Snap, of Old Maid, of Musical Chairs—a pastime in which he is victor who says *Snap* neither too soon nor too late, who passes the Old Maid to his neighbor before the game is over, who secures a chair for himself when the music stops. These games can be played with zest and enjoyment, though all the players know that it is the Old Maid which is circulating, or that when the music stops some of the players will find themselves unseated.

Or, to change the metaphor slightly, professional investment may be likened to those newspaper competitions in which the competitors have to pick out the six prettiest faces from a hundred photographs, the prize being awarded to the competitor whose choice most nearly corresponds to the average preferences of the competitors as a whole; so that each competitor has to pick, not those faces which he himself finds prettiest, but those which he thinks likeliest to catch the fancy of the other competitors, all of whom are looking at the problem from the same point of view. It is not a case of choosing those which, to the best of one's judgment, are really the prettiest, nor even those which average opinion genuinely thinks the prettiest. We have reached the third degree where we devote our intelligences to anticipating what average opinion expects the average opinion to be. And there are some, I believe, who practice the fourth, fifth and higher degrees.

If the reader interjects that there must surely be large profits to be gained from the other players in the long run by a skilled individual who, unperturbed by the prevailing pastime, continues to purchase investments on the best genuine long-term expectations he can frame, he must be answered, first of all, that there are, indeed, such serious-minded individuals and that it makes a vast difference to an investment market whether or not they predominate in their influence over the game-players. But we must also add that there are several factors which jeopardize the predominance of such individuals in modern investment markets. Investment based on genuine long-term expectation is so difficult today as to be scarcely practicable. He who attempts it must surely lead much more laborious days and run greater risks than he who tries to guess better than the crowd how the crowd will behave; and, given equal intelligence, he may make more disastrous mistakes. There is no clear evidence from experience that the investment policy which is socially advantageous coincides with that which is most profitable. It needs *more* intelligence to defeat the forces of time and our ignorance of the future than to beat the gun. Moreover, life is not long enough;—human nature desires quick results, there is a peculiar zest in making money quickly, and remoter gains are discounted by the average man at a very high rate. The game of professional investment is intolerably boring and over-exacting to anyone who is entirely exempt from the gambling instinct; whilst he who has it must pay to this propensity the appropriate toll. Furthermore, an investor who proposes to ignore near-term market fluctuations needs greater resources for safety and must not operate on so large a scale, if at all, with borrowed money—a further reason for the higher return from the pastime to a given stock of intelligence and resources. Finally it is the long-term investor, he who most promotes the public interest, who will in practice come in for most criticism, wherever investment funds are managed by committees or boards or banks.[72] For it is in the essence of his behavior that he should be eccentric, unconventional and rash in the eyes of average opinion. If he is successful, that will only confirm the general belief in his rashness; and if in the short run he is unsuccessful, which is very likely, he will not receive much mercy. Worldly wisdom teaches that it is better for reputation to fail conventionally than to succeed unconventionally.

(5) So far we have had chiefly in mind the state of confidence of the speculator or speculative investor himself and may have seemed to be tacitly assuming that, if he himself is satisfied with the prospects, he has unlimited command over money at the market rate of interest. This is, of course, not the case. Thus we must also take account of the other facet of the state of confidence, namely, the confidence of the lending institutions towards those who seek to borrow from them, sometimes described as the state of credit. A collapse in the price of equities, which has had disastrous reactions on the marginal efficiency of capital, may have been due to the weakening either of speculative confidence or of the state of credit. But whereas the weakening of either is enough to cause a collapse, recovery requires the revival of *both*. For whilst the weakening of credit is sufficient to bring about a collapse, its strengthening, though a necessary condition of recovery, is not a sufficient condition.

VI

These considerations should not lie beyond the purview of the economist. But they must be relegated to their right perspective. If I may be allowed to appropriate the term *speculation* for the activity of forecasting the psychology of the market, and the term *enterprise* for the activity of forecasting the prospective yield of assets over their whole life, it is by no means always the case that speculation predominates over enterprise. As the organization of investment markets improves, the risk of the predominance of speculation does, however, increase. In one of the greatest investment markets in the world, namely, New York, the influence of speculation (in the above sense) is enormous.

Even outside the field of finance, Americans are apt to be unduly interested in discovering what average opinion believes average opinion to be; and this national weakness finds its nemesis in the stock market. It is rare, one is told, for an American to invest, as many Englishmen still do, "for income;" and he will not readily purchase an investment except in the hope of capital appreciation. This is only another way of saying that, when he purchases an investment, the American is attaching his hopes, not so much to its prospective yield, as to a favorable change in the conventional basis of valuation, *i.e.* that he is, in the above sense, a speculator. Speculators may do no harm as bubbles on a steady stream of enterprise. But the position is serious when enterprise becomes the bubble on a whirlpool of speculation. When the capital development of a country becomes a by-product of the activities of a casino, the job is likely to be ill-done. The measure of success attained by Wall Street, regarded as an institution of which the proper social purpose is to direct new investment into the most profitable channels in terms of future yield, cannot be claimed as one of the outstanding triumphs of laissez-faire capitalism—which is not surprising, if I am right in thinking that the best brains of Wall Street have been in fact directed towards a different object.

These tendencies are a scarcely avoidable outcome of our having successfully organized "liquid" investment markets. It is usually agreed that casinos should, in the public interest, be inaccessible and expensive And perhaps the same is true of Stock Exchanges.

That the sins of the London Stock Exchange are less than those of Wall Street may be due, not so much to differences in national character, as to the fact that to the average Englishman Throgmorton Street is, compared with Wall Street to the average American, inaccessible and very expensive. The jobber's "turn," the high brokerage charges and the heavy transfer tax payable to the Exchequer, which attend dealings on the London Stock Exchange, sufficiently diminish the liquidity of the market (although the practice of fortnightly accounts operates the other way) to rule out a large proportion of the transactions characteristic of Wall Street.[73] The introduction of a substantial Government transfer tax on all transactions might prove the most serviceable reform available, with a view to mitigating the predominance of speculation over enterprise in the United States.

The spectacle of modern investment markets has sometimes moved me towards the conclusion that to make the purchase of an investment permanent and indissoluble, like marriage, except by reason of death or other grave cause, might be a useful remedy for our contemporary evils. For this would force the investor to direct his mind to the long-term prospects and to those only. But a little consideration of this expedient brings us up against a dilemma, and shows us how the liquidity of investment markets often facilitates, though it sometimes impedes, the course of new investment. For the fact that each individual investor flatters himself that his commitment is "liquid" (though this cannot be true for all investors collectively) calms his nerves and makes him much more willing to run a risk. If individual purchases of investments were rendered illiquid, this might seriously impede new investment, so long as *alternative ways* in which to hold his savings are available to the individual. This is the dilemma. So long as it is open to the individual to employ his wealth in hoarding or lending *money,* the alternative of purchasing actual capital assets cannot be rendered sufficiently attractive (especially to the man who does not manage the capital assets and knows very little about them), except by organizing markets wherein these assets can be easily realized for money.

The only radical cure for the crises of confidence which afflict the economic life of the modern world would be to allow the individual no choice between consuming his income and ordering the production of the specific capital-asset which, even though it be on precarious evidence, impresses him as the most promising investment available to him. It might be that, at times when he was more than usually assailed by doubts concerning the future, he would turn in his perplexity towards more consumption and less new investment. But that would avoid the disastrous, cumulative and far-reaching repercussions of its being open to him, when thus assailed by doubts, to spend his income neither on the one nor on the other.

Those who have emphasized the social dangers of the hoarding of money have, of course, had something similar to the above in mind. But they have overlooked the possibility that the phenomenon can occur without any change, or at least any commensurate change, in the hoarding of money.

VII

Even apart from the instability due to speculation, there is the instability due to the characteristic of human nature that a large proportion of our positive activities depend on spontaneous optimism rather than on a mathematical expectation, whether moral or hedonistic or economic. Most, probably, of our decisions to do something positive, the full consequences of which will be drawn out over many days to come, can only be taken as a result of animal spirits—of a spontaneous urge to action rather than inaction, and not as the outcome of a weighted average of quantitative benefits multiplied by quantitative probabilities. Enterprise only pretends to itself to be mainly actuated by the statements in its own prospectus, however candid and sincere. Only a little more than an expedition to the South Pole, is it based on an exact calculation of benefits to come. Thus if the animal spirits are dimmed and the spontaneous optimism falters, leaving us to depend on nothing but a mathematical expectation, enterprise will fade and die;—though fears of loss may have a basis no more reasonable than hopes of profit had before.

It is safe to say that enterprise which depends on hopes stretching into the future benefits the community as a whole. But individual initiative will only be adequate when reasonable calculation is supplemented and supported by animal spirits, so that the thought of ultimate loss which often overtakes pioneers, as experience undoubtedly tells us and them, is put aside as a healthy man puts aside the expectation of death.

This means, unfortunately, not only that slumps and depressions are exaggerated in degree, but that economic prosperity is excessively dependent on a political and social atmosphere which is congenial to the average business man. If the fear of a Labor Government or a New Deal depresses enterprise, this need not be the result either of a reasonable calculation or of a plot with political intent;—it is the mere consequence of upsetting the delicate balance of spontaneous optimism. In estimating the prospects of investment, we must have regard, therefore, to the nerves and hysteria and even the digestions and reactions to the weather of those upon whose spontaneous activity it largely depends.

We should not conclude from this that everything depends on waves of irrational psychology. On the contrary, the state of long-term expectation is often steady, and, even when it is not, the other factors exert their compensating effects. We are merely reminding ourselves that human decisions affecting the future, whether personal or political or economic, cannot depend on strict mathematical expectation, since the basis for making such calculations does not exist; and that it is our innate urge to activity which makes the wheels go round, our rational selves choosing between the alternatives as best we are able, calculating where we can, but often falling back for our motive on whim or sentiment or chance.

1318 THE REAL PRICE OF EVERYTHING

VIII

There are, moreover, certain important factors which somewhat mitigate in practice the effects of our ignorance of the future. Owing to the operation of compound interest combined with the likelihood of obsolescence with the passage of time, there are many individual investments of which the prospective yield is legitimately dominated by the returns of the comparatively near future. In the case of the most important class of very long-term investments, namely buildings, the risk can be frequently transferred from the investor to the occupier, or at least shared between them, by means of long-term contracts, the risk being outweighed in the mind of the occupier by the advantages of continuity and security of tenure. In the case of another important class of long-term investments, namely public utilities, a substantial proportion of the prospective yield is practically guaranteed by monopoly privileges coupled with the right to charge such rates as will provide a certain stipulated margin. Finally there is a growing class of investments entered upon by, or at the risk of, public authorities, which are frankly influenced in making the investment by a general presumption of there being prospective social advantages from the investment, whatever its commercial yield may prove to be within a wide range, and without seeking to be satisfied that the mathematical expectation of the yield is at least equal to the current rate of interest,—though the rate which the public authority has to pay may still play a decisive part in determining the scale of investment operations which it can afford.

Thus after giving full weight to the importance of the influence of short-period changes in the state of long-term expectation as distinct from changes in the rate of interest, we are still entitled to return to the latter as exercising, at any rate, in normal circumstances, a great, though not a decisive, influence on the rate of investment. Only experience, however, can show how far management of the rate of interest is capable of continuously stimulating the appropriate volume of investment.

For my own part I am now somewhat skeptical of the success of a merely monetary policy directed towards influencing the rate of interest. I expect to see the State, which is in a position to calculate the marginal efficiency of capital goods on long views and on the basis of the general social advantage, taking an ever greater responsibility for directly organizing investment; since it seems likely that the fluctuations in the market estimation of the marginal efficiency of different types of capital, calculated on the principles I have described above, will be too great to be offset by any practicable changes in the rate of interest.

CHAPTER 13

The General Theory of the Rate of Interest

I

We have shown in Chapter 11 that, whilst there are forces causing the rate of investment to rise or fall so as to keep the marginal efficiency of capital equal to the rate of interest, yet the marginal efficiency of capital is, in itself, a different thing from the ruling rate of interest. The schedule of the marginal efficiency of capital may be said to govern the terms on which loanable funds are demanded for the purpose of new investment; whilst the rate of interest governs the terms on which funds are being currently supplied. To complete our theory, therefore, we need to know what determines the rate of interest.

In Chapter 14 and its Appendix we shall consider the answers to this question which have been given hitherto. Broadly speaking, we shall find that they make the rate of interest to depend on the interaction of the schedule of the marginal efficiency of capital with the psychological propensity to save. But the notion that the rate of interest is the balancing factor which brings the demand for saving in the shape of new investment forthcoming at a given rate of interest into equality with the supply of saving which results at that rate of interest from the community's psychological propensity to save, breaks down as soon as we perceive that it is impossible to deduce the rate of interest merely from a knowledge of these two factors.

What, then, is our own answer to this question?

II

The psychological time-preferences of an individual require two distinct sets of decisions to carry them out completely. The first is concerned with that aspect of time-preference which I have called the *propensity to consume,* which, operating under the influence of the various motives set forth in Book III., determines for each individual how much of his income he will consume and how much he will reserve in some form of command over future consumption.

But this decision having been made, there is a further decision which awaits him, namely, in *what form* he will hold the command over future consumption which he has reserved, whether out of his current income or from previous savings. Does he want to hold it in the form of immediate, liquid command (*i.e.* in money or its equivalent)? Or is he prepared to part with immediate command for a specified or indefinite period, leaving it to future market conditions to determine on what terms he can, if necessary, convert deferred command over specific goods into immediate command over goods in general? In other words, what is the degree of his *liquidity-preference*—where an individual's liquidity-preference is given by a schedule of the amounts of his resources, valued in terms of money or of wage-units, which he will wish to retain in the form of money in different sets of circumstances?

We shall find that the mistake in the accepted theories of the rate of interest lies in their attempting to derive the rate of interest from the first of these two constituents of psychological time-preference to the neglect of the second; and it is this neglect which we must endeavour to repair.

It should be obvious that the rate of interest cannot be a return to saving or waiting as such. For if a man hoards his savings in cash, he earns no interest, though he saves just as much as before. On the contrary, the mere definition of the rate of interest tells us in so many words that the rate of interest is the reward for parting with liquidity for a specified period. For the rate of interest is, in itself, nothing more than the inverse proportion between a sum of money and what can be obtained for parting with control over the money in exchange for a debt[74] for a stated period of time.[75]

Thus the rate of interest at any time, being the reward for parting with liquidity, is a measure of the unwillingness of those who possess money to part with their liquid control over it. The rate of interest is not the "price" which brings into equilibrium the demand for resources to invest with the readiness to abstain from present consumption. It is the "price" which equilibrates the desire to hold wealth in the form of cash with the available quantity of cash;—which implies that if the rate of interest were lower, *i.e.* if the reward for parting with cash were diminished, the aggregate amount of cash which the public would wish to hold would exceed the available supply, and that if the rate of interest were raised, there would be a surplus of cash which no one would be willing to hold. If this explanation is correct, the quantity of money is the other factor, which, in conjunction with liquidity-preference, determines the actual rate of interest in given circumstances. Liquidity-preference is a potentiality or functional tendency, which fixes the quantity of money which the public will hold when the rate of interest is given; so that if r is the rate of interest, M the quantity of money and L the function of liquidity-preference, we have $M - L(r)$. This is where, and how, the quantity of money enters into the economic scheme.

At this point, however, let us turn back and consider why such a thing as liquidity-preference exists. In this connection we can usefully employ the ancient distinction between the use of money for the transaction of current business and its use as a store of wealth. As regards the first of these two uses, it is obvious that up to a point it is worth while to sacrifice a certain amount of interest for the convenience of liquidity. But, given that the rate of interest is never negative, why should anyone prefer to hold his wealth in a form which yields little or no interest to holding it in a form which yields interest (assuming, of course, at this stage, that the risk of default is the same in respect of a bank balance as of a bond)? A full explanation is complex and must wait for Chapter 15. There is, however, a necessary condition failing which the existence of a liquidity-preference for money as a means of holding wealth could not exist.

This necessary condition is the existence of *uncertainty* as to the future of the rate of interest, *i.e.* as to the complex of rates of interest for varying maturities which will rule at future dates. For if the rates of interest ruling at all future times could be foreseen with certainty, all future rates of interest could be inferred from the *present* rates of interest for debts of different maturities, which would be adjusted to the knowledge of the future rates. For example, if $_1d_r$ is the value in the present year 1 of £1 deferred r years and it is known that $_nd_r$ will be the value in the year n of £ I deferred r years from that date, we have

$$_nd_r = {_1d_{n+r}}/{_1d_n};$$

whence it follows that the rate at which any debt can be turned into cash n years hence is given by two out of the complex of current rates of interest. If the current rate of interest is positive for debts of every maturity, it must always be more advantageous to purchase a debt than to hold cash as a store of wealth.

If, on the contrary, the future rate of interest is uncertain we cannot safely infer that $_nd_r$ will prove to be equal to $_1d_{n+r}/{_1d_n}$ when the time comes. Thus if a need for liquid cash may conceivably arise before the expiry of n years, there is a risk of a loss being incurred in purchasing a long-term debt and subsequently turning it into cash, as compared with holding cash. The actuarial profit or mathematical expectation of gain calculated in accordance with the existing probabilities—if it can be so calculated, which is doubtful—must be sufficient to compensate for the risk of disappointment.

There is, moreover, a further ground for liquidity-preference which results from the existence of uncertainty as to the future of the rate of interest, provided that there is an organized market for dealing in debts. For different people will estimate the prospects differently and anyone who differs from the predominant opinion as expressed in market quotations may have a good reason for keeping liquid resources in order to profit, if he is right, from its turning out in due course that the $_1d_r$'s were in a mistaken relationship to one another.[76]

This is closely analogous to what we have already discussed at some length in connection with the marginal efficiency of capital. Just as we found that the marginal efficiency of capital is fixed, not by the "best" opinion, but by the market valuation as determined by mass psychology, so also expectations as to the future of the rate of interest as fixed by mass psychology have their reactions on liquidity-preference;—but with this addition that the individual, who believes that future rates of interest will be above the rates assumed by the market, has a reason for keeping actual liquid cash,[77] whilst the individual who differs from the market in the other direction will have a motive for borrowing money for short periods in order to purchase debts of longer term. The market price will be fixed at the point at which the sales of the "bears" and the purchases of the "bulls" are balanced.

The three divisions of liquidity-preference which we have distinguished above may be defined as depending on (i) the transactions-motive, *i.e.* the need of cash for the current transaction of personal and business exchanges; (ii) the precautionary-motive, *i.e.* the desire for security as to the future cash equivalent of a certain proportion of total resources; and (iii) the speculative-motive, *i.e.* the object of securing profit from knowing better than the market what the future will bring forth. As when we were discussing the marginal efficiency of capital, the question of the desirability of having a highly organized market for dealing with debts presents us with a dilemma. For, in the absence of an

1322 THE REAL PRICE OF EVERYTHING

organized market, liquidity-preference due to the precautionary-motive would be greatly increased; whereas the existence of an organized market gives an opportunity for wide fluctuations in liquidity-preference due to the speculative-motive.

It may illustrate the argument to point out that, if the liquidity-preference due to the transactions-motive and the precautionary-motive are assumed to absorb a quantity of cash which is not very sensitive to changes in the rate of interest as such and apart from its reactions on the level of income, so that the total quantity of money, less this quantity, is available for satisfying liquidity-preferences due to the speculative-motive, the rate of interest and the price of bonds have to be fixed at the level at which the desire on the part of certain individuals to hold cash (because at that level they feel "bearish" of the future of bonds) is exactly equal to the amount of cash available for the speculative-motive.

Thus each increase in the quantity of money must raise the price of bonds sufficiently to exceed the expectations of some "bull" and so influence him to sell his bond for cash and join the "bear" brigade. If, however, there is a negligible demand for cash from the speculative-motive except for a short transitional interval, an increase in the quantity of money will have to lower the rate of interest almost forthwith, in whatever degree is necessary to raise employment and the wage-unit sufficiently to cause the additional cash to be absorbed by the transactions-motive and the precautionary-motive.

As a rule, we can suppose that the schedule of liquidity-preference relating the quantity of money to the rate of interest is given by a smooth curve which shows the rate of interest falling as the quantity of money is increased. For there are several different causes all leading towards this result.

In the first place, as the rate of interest falls, it is likely, *cet. par.,* that more money will be absorbed by liquidity-preferences due to the transactions-motive. For if the fall in the rate of interest increases the national income, the amount of money which it is convenient to keep for transactions will be increased more or less proportionately to the increase in income; whilst, at the same time, the cost of the convenience of plenty of ready cash in terms of loss of interest will be diminished. Unless we measure liquidity-preference in terms of wage-units rather than of money (which is convenient in some contexts), similar results follow if the increased employment ensuing on a fall in the rate of interest leads to an increase of wages, *i.e.* to an increase in the money value of the wage-unit. In the second place, every fall in the rate of interest may, as we have just seen, increase the quantity of cash which certain individuals will wish to hold because their views as to the future of the rate of interest differ from the market views.

Nevertheless, circumstances can develop in which even a large increase in the quantity of money may exert a comparatively small influence on the rate of interest. For a large increase in the quantity of money may cause so much uncertainty about the future that liquidity-preferences due to the security-motive may be strengthened; whilst opinion about the future of the rate of interest may be so unanimous that a small change in present rates may cause a mass movement into cash. It is interesting that the stability of the system and its sensitiveness to changes in the quantity of money should be so dependent on the existence of a *variety* of opinion about what is uncertain. Best of all that we should know the future. But if not, then, if we are to control the activity of the economic system by changing the quantity of money, it is important that opinions should differ. Thus this method of control is more precarious in the United States, where everyone tends to hold the same opinion at the same time, than in England where differences of opinion are more usual.

III

We have now introduced money into our causal nexus for the first time, and we are able to catch a first glimpse of the way in which changes in the quantity of money work their way into the economic system. If, however, we are tempted to assert that money is the drink which stimulates the system to activity, we must remind ourselves that there may be several slips between the cup and the lip. For whilst an increase in the quantity of money may be expected, *cet. par.,* to reduce the rate of interest, this will not happen if the liquidity-preferences of the public are increasing more than the quantity of money; and whilst a decline in the rate of interest may be expected, *cet. par.,* to increase the volume of investment, this will not happen if the schedule of the marginal efficiency of capital is falling more rapidly than the rate of interest; and whilst an increase in the volume of investment may be expected, *cet. par.,* to increase employment, this may not happen if the propensity to consume is falling off. Finally, if employment increases, prices will rise in a degree partly governed by the shapes of the physical supply functions, and partly by the liability of the wage-unit to rise in terms of money. And when output has increased and prices have risen, the effect of this on liquidity-preference will be to increase the quantity of money necessary to maintain a given rate of interest.

IV

Whilst liquidity-preference due to the speculative-motive corresponds to what in my *Treatise on Money* I called "the state of bearishness," it is by no means the same thing. For "bearishness" is there defined as the functional relationship, not between the rate of interest (or price of debts) and the quantity of money, but between the price of assets and debts, taken together, and the quantity of money. This treatment, however, involved a confusion between results due to a change in the rate of interest and those due to a change in the schedule of the marginal efficiency of capital, which I hope I have here avoided.

V

The concept of *Hoarding* may be regarded as a first approximation to the concept of *Liquidity-preference.* Indeed if we were to substitute "propensity to hoard" for "hoarding," it would come to substantially the same thing. But if we mean by "hoarding" an actual increase in cash-holding, it is an incomplete idea—and seriously misleading if it causes us to think of "hoarding" and "not-hoarding" as simple alternatives. For the decision to hoard is not taken absolutely or without regard to the advantages offered for parting with liquidity;—it results from a balancing of advantages, and we have, therefore, to know what lies in the other scale. Moreover it is impossible for the actual amount of hoarding to change as a result of decisions on the part of the public, so long as we mean by "hoarding" the actual holding of cash. For the amount of hoarding must be equal to the quantity of money (or—on some definitions—to the quantity of money *minus* what is required to satisfy the transactions-motive); and the quantity of money is not determined by the public. All that the propensity of the public towards hoarding can achieve is to determine the rate of interest at which the aggregate desire to hoard becomes equal to the available cash. The habit of overlooking the relation of the rate of interest to hoarding may be a part of the explanation why interest has been usually regarded as the reward of not-spending, whereas in fact it is the reward of not-hoarding.

Chapter 14

The Classical Theory of the Rate of Interest

I

What is the Classical Theory of the Rate of Interest? It is something upon which we have all been brought up and which we have accepted without much reserve until recently. Yet I find it difficult to state it precisely or to discover an explicit account of it in the leading treatises of the modern classical school.[78]

It is fairly clear, however, that this tradition has regarded the rate of interest as the factor which brings the demand for investment and the willingness to save into equilibrium with one another. Investment represents the demand for investible resources and saving represents the supply, whilst the rate of interest is the "price" of investible resources at which the two are equated. Just as the price of a commodity is necessarily fixed at that point where the demand for it is equal to the supply, so the rate of interest necessarily comes to rest under the play of market forces at the point where the amount of investment at that rate of interest is equal to the amount of saving at that rate.

The above is not to be found in Marshall's *Principles* in so many words. Yet his theory seems to be this, and it is what I myself was brought up on and what I taught for many years to others. Take, for example, the following passage from his *Principles:* "Interest, being the price paid for the use of capital in any market, tends towards an equilibrium level such that the aggregate demand for capital in that market, at that rate of interest, is equal to the aggregate stock forthcoming at that rate."[79] Or again in Professor Cassel's *Nature and Necessity of Interest* it is explained that investment constitutes the "demand for waiting" and saving the "supply of waiting," whilst interest is a "price" which serves, it is implied, to equate the two, though here again I have not found actual words to quote.

Chapter vi. of Professor Carver's *Distribution of Wealth* clearly envisages interest as the factor which brings into equilibrium the marginal disutility of waiting with the marginal productivity of capital.[80] Sir Alfred Flux (*Economic Principle*, p. 95) writes; "If there is justice in the contentions of our general discussion, it must be admitted that an automatic adjustment takes place between saving and the opportunities for employing capital profitably. . . . Saving will not have exceeded its possibilities of usefulness ... so long as the rate of net interest is in excess of zero." Professor Taussig (*Principles,* vol. ii. p. 29) draws a supply curve of saving and a demand curve representing "the diminishing productiveness of the several installments of capital," having previously stated (p. 20) that "the rate of interest settles at a point where the marginal productivity of capital suffices to bring out the marginal installment of saving."[81] Walras, in Appendix I. (III.) of his *éléments d'Economie pure,* where he deals with "l'échange d'épargnes contre capitaux neufs," argues expressly that, corresponding to each possible rate of interest, there is a sum which individuals will save and also a sum which they will invest in new capital assets, that these two aggregates tend to equality with one another, and that the rate of interest is the variable which brings them to equality; so that the rate of interest is fixed at the point where saving, which represents the supply of new capital, is equal to the demand for it. Thus he is strictly in the classical tradition.

Certainly the ordinary man—banker, civil servant or politician—brought up on the traditional theory, and the trained economist also, has carried away with him the idea that whenever an individual performs an act of saving he has done something which automatically brings down the rate of interest, that this automatically stimulates the output of capital, and that the fall in the rate of interest is just so much as is necessary to stimulate the output of capital to an extent which is equal to the increment of saving; and, further, that this is a self-regulatory process of adjustment which takes place without the necessity for any special intervention or grandmotherly care on the part of the monetary authority. Similarly—and this is an even more general belief, even today—each additional act of investment will necessarily raise the rate of interest, if it is not offset by a change in the readiness to save.

Now the analysis of the previous chapters will have made it plain that this account of the matter must be erroneous. In tracing to its source the reason for the difference of opinion, let us, however, begin with the matters which are agreed.

Unlike the neo-classical school, who believe that saving and investment can be actually unequal, the classical school proper has accepted the view that they are equal. Marshall, for example, surely believed, although he did not expressly say so, that aggregate saving and aggregate investment are necessarily equal. Indeed, most members of the classical school carried this belief much too far; since they held that every act of increased saving by an individual necessarily brings into existence a corresponding act of increased investment. Nor is there any material difference, relevant in this context, between my schedule of the marginal efficiency of capital or investment demand-schedule and the demand curve for capital contemplated by some of the classical writers who have been quoted above. When we come to the propensity to consume and its corollary the propensity to save, we are nearer to a difference of opinion, owing to the emphasis which they have placed on the influence of the rate of interest on the propensity to save. But they would, presumably, not wish to deny that the level of income also has an important influence on the amount saved; whilst I, for my part, would not deny that the race of interest may perhaps have an influence (though perhaps not of the kind which they suppose) on the amount saved *out of a given income*. All these points of agreement can be summed up in a proposition which the classical school would accept and I should not dispute; namely, that, if the level of income is assumed to be given, we can infer that the current rate of interest must lie at the point where the demand curve for capital corresponding to different rates of interest cuts the curve of the amounts saved out of the given income corresponding to different rates of interest.

But this is the point at which definite error creeps into the classical theory. If the classical school merely inferred from the above proposition that, given the demand curve for capital and the influence of changes in the rate of interest on the readiness to save out of given incomes, the level of income and the rate of interest must be uniquely correlated, there would be nothing to quarrel with. Moreover, this proposition would lead naturally to another proposition which embodies an important truth; namely, that, if the rate of interest is given as well as the demand curve for capital and the influence of the rate of interest on the readiness to save out of given levels of income, the level of income must be the factor which brings the amount saved to equality with the amount invested. But, in fact, the classical theory not merely neglects the influence of changes in the level of income, but involves formal error.

For the classical theory, as can be seen from the above quotations, assumes that it can then proceed to consider the effect on the rate of interest of (*e.g.*) a shift in the demand curve for capital, without abating or modifying its assumption as to the amount of the given income out of which the savings are to be made. The independent variables of the classical theory of the rate of interest are the demand curve for capital and the influence of the rate of interest on the amount saved out of a given income; and when (*e.g.*) the demand curve for capital shifts, the new rate of interest, according to this theory, is given by the point of intersection between the new demand curve for capital and the curve relating the rate of interest to the amounts which will be saved out of the given income. The classical theory of the rate of interest seems to suppose that, if the demand curve for capital shifts or if the curve relating the rate of interest to the amounts saved out of a given income shifts or if both these curves shift, the new rate of interest will be given by the point of intersection of the new positions of the two curves. But this is a nonsense theory. For the assumption that income is constant is inconsistent with the assumption that these two curves can shift independently of one another. If either of them shift, then, in general, income will change; with the result that the whole schematism based on the assumption of a given income breaks down. The position could only be saved by some complicated assumption providing for an automatic change in the wage-unit of an amount just sufficient in its effect on liquidity-preference to establish a rate of interest which would just offset the supposed shift, so as to leave output at the same level as before. In fact, there is no hint to be found in the above writers as to the necessity for any such assumption; at the best it would be plausible only in relation to long-period equilibrium and could not form the basis of a short-period theory; and there is no ground for supposing it to hold even in the long-period. In truth, the classical theory has not been alive to the relevance of changes in the level of income or to the possibility of the level of income being actually a function of the rate of the investment.

The above can be illustrated by a diagram[82] as follows:

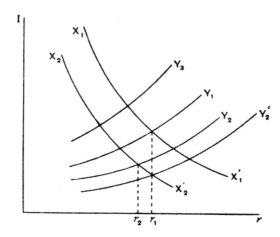

In this diagram the amount of investment (or saving) I is measured vertically, and the rate of interest r horizontally. $X_1 X_1'$ is the first position of the investment demand-schedule, and $X_2 X_2'$ is a second position of this curve. The curve Y_1 relates the amounts saved out of an income Y_1 to various levels of the rate of interest, the curves Y_2, Y_3, etc., being the corresponding curves for levels of income Y_2, Y_3, etc. Let us suppose that the curve Y_1 is the Y-curve consistent with an investment demand-schedule $X_1 X_1'$ and a rate of interest r_1. Now if the investment demand-schedule shifts from $X_1 X_1'$ to $X_2 X_2'$ income will, in general, shift also. But the above diagram does not contain enough *data* to tell us what its new value will be; and, therefore, not knowing which is the appropriate Y-curve, we do not know at what point the new investment demand-schedule will cut it. If, however, we introduce the state of liquidity-preference and the quantity of money and these between them tell us that the rate of interest is r_2, then the whole position becomes determinate. For the Y-curve which intersects $X_2 X_2'$ at the point vertically above r_2 namely, the curve Y_2, will be the appropriate curve. Thus the X-curve and the Y-curves tell us nothing about the rate of interest. They only tell us what income will be, if from some other source we can say what the rate of interest is. If nothing has happened to the state of liquidity-preference and the quantity of money, so that the rate of interest is unchanged, then the curve Y_2' which intersects the new investment demand-schedule vertically below the point where the curve Y_1 intersected the old investment demand-schedule will be the appropriate Y-curve, and Y_2' will be the new level of income.

Thus the functions used by the classical theory, namely, the response of investment and the response of the amount saved out of a given income to change in the rate of interest, do not furnish material for a theory of the rate of interest; but they could be used to tell us what the level of income will be, given (from some other source) the rate of interest; and, alternatively, what the rate of interest will have to be, if the level of income is to be maintained at a given figure (*e.g.* the level corresponding to full employment).

The mistake originates from regarding interest as the reward for waiting as such, instead of as the reward for not-hoarding; just as the rates of return on loans or investments involving different degrees of risk, are quite properly regarded as the reward, not of waiting as such, but of running the risk. There is, in truth, no sharp line between these and the so-called "pure" rate of interest, all of them being the reward for running the risk of uncertainty of one kind or another. Only in the event of money being used solely for transactions and never as a store of value, would a different theory become appropriate.[83]

There are, however, two familiar points which might, perhaps, have warned the classical school that something was wrong. In the first place, it has been agreed, at any rate since the publication of Professor Cassel's *Nature and Necessity of Interest,* that it is not certain that the sum saved out of a given income necessarily increases when the rate of interest is increased; whereas no one doubts that the investment demand-schedule falls with a rising rate of interest. But if the Y-curves and the X-curves both fall as the rate of interest rises, there is no guarantee that a given Y-curve will intersect a given X-curve anywhere at all. This suggests that it cannot be the Y-curve and the X-curve alone which determine the rate of interest.

In the second place, it has been usual to suppose that an increase in the quantity of money has a tendency to reduce the rate of interest, at any rate in the first instance and in the short period. Yet no reason has been given why a change in the quantity of money should affect either the investment demand-schedule or the readiness to save out of a given income. Thus the classical school have had quite a different theory of the rate of interest in Volume I. dealing with the theory of value from what they have had in Volume II. dealing with the theory of money. They have seemed undisturbed by the conflict and have made no attempt, so far as I know, to build a bridge between the two theories. The classical school proper, that is to say; since it is the attempt to build a bridge on the part of the neo-classical school which has led to the worst muddles of all.

For the latter have inferred that there must be *two* sources of supply to meet the investment demand-schedule; namely, savings proper, which are the savings dealt with by the classical school, *plus* the sum made available by any increase in the quantity of money (this being balanced by some species of levy on the public, called "forced saving" or the like). This leads on to the idea that there is a "natural" or "neutral"[84] or "equilibrium" rate of interest, namely, that rate of interest which equates investment to classical savings proper without any addition from "forced savings;" and finally to what, assuming they are on the right track at the start, is the most obvious solution of all, namely, that, if the quantity of money could only be kept *constant* in all circumstances, none of these complications would arise, since the evils supposed to result from the supposed excess of investment over savings proper would cease to be possible. But at this point we are in deep water. "The wild duck has dived down to the bottom—as deep as she can get—and bitten fast hold of the weed and tangle and all the rubbish that is down there, and it would need an extraordinarily clever dog to dive after and fish her up again."

Thus the traditional analysis is faulty because it has failed to isolate correctly the independent variables of the system. Saving and Investment are the determinates of the system, not the determinants. They are the twin results of the system's determinants, namely, the propensity to consume, the schedule of the marginal efficiency of capital and the rate of interest. These determinants are, indeed, themselves complex and each is capable of being affected by prospective changes in the others. But they remain independent in the sense that their values cannot be inferred from one another. The traditional analysis has been aware that saving depends on income but it has overlooked the fact that income depends on investment, in such fashion that, when investment changes, income must necessarily change in just that degree which is necessary to make the change in saving equal to the change in investment.

Nor are those theories more successful which attempt to make the rate of interest depend on "the marginal efficiency of capital." It is true that in equilibrium the rate of interest will be equal to the marginal efficiency of capital, since it will be profitable to increase (or decrease) the current scale of investment until the point of equality has been reached.

But to make this into a theory of the rate of interest or to derive the rate of interest from it involves a circular argument, as Marshall discovered after he had got half-way into giving an account of the rate of interest along these lines.[85] For the "marginal efficiency of capital" partly depends on the scale of current investment, and we must already know the rate of interest before we can calculate what this scale will be. The significant conclusion is that the output of new investment will be pushed to the point at which the marginal efficiency of capital becomes equal to the rate of interest; and what the schedule of the marginal efficiency of capital tells us, is, not what the rate of interest is, but the point to which the output of new investment will be pushed, given the rate of interest.

The reader will readily appreciate that the problem here under discussion is a matter of the most fundamental theoretical significance and of overwhelming practical importance. For the economic principle, on which the practical advice of economists has been almost invariably based, has assumed, in effect, that, *cet. par.,* a decrease in spending will tend to lower the rate of interest and an increase in investment to raise it. But if what these two quantities determine is, not the rate of interest, but the aggregate volume of employment, then our outlook on the mechanism of the economic system will be profoundly changed. A decreased readiness to spend will be looked on in quite a different light if, instead of being regarded as a factor which will, cet. par., increase investment, it is seen as a factor which will, *cet. par.,* diminish employment.

APPENDIX TO CHAPTER 14

Appendix on the Rate of Interest in Marshall's "Principles of Economics," Ricardo's "Principles of Political Economy," and Elsewhere

I

There is no consecutive discussion of the rate of interest in the works of Marshall, Edgeworth or Professor Pigou,—nothing more than a few *obiter dicta*. Apart from the passage already quoted above (Chapter 11) the only important clues to Marshall's position on the rate of interest are to be found in his *Principles of Economics* (6th edn.), Book VI. p. 534 and p. 593, the gist of which is given by the following quotations:

"Interest, being the price paid for the use of capital in any market, tends towards an equilibrium level such that the aggregate demand for capital in that market, at that rate of interest, is equal to the aggregate stock[86] forthcoming there at that rate. If the market, which we are considering, is a small one—say a single town, or a single trade in a progressive country—an increased demand for capital in it will be promptly met by an increased supply drawn from surrounding districts or trades. But if we are considering the whole world, or even the whole of a large country, as one market for capital, we cannot regard the aggregate supply of it as altered quickly and to a considerable extent by a change in the rate of interest. For the general fund of capital is the product of labor and waiting; and the extra work,[87] and the extra waiting, to which a rise in the rate of interest would act as an incentive, would not quickly amount to much, as compared with the work and waiting, of which the total existing stock of capital is the result. An extensive increase in the demand for capital in general will therefore be met for a time not so much by an increase of supply, as by a rise in the rate of interest;[88] which will cause capital to withdraw itself partially from those uses in which its marginal utility is lowest. It is only slowly and gradually that the rise in the rate of interest will increase the total stock of capital" (p. 534).

"It cannot be repeated too often that the phrase 'the rate of interest' is applicable to old investments of capital only in a very limited sense.[89] For instance, we may perhaps estimate that a trade capital of some seven thousand millions is invested in the different trades of this country at about 3 percent net interest. But such a method of speaking, though convenient and justifiable for many purposes, is not accurate. What ought to be said is that, taking the rate of net interest on the investments of new capital in each of those trades [*i.e.* on marginal investments] to be about 3 percent; then the aggregate net income rendered by the whole of the trade-capital invested in the various trades is such that, if capitalized at 33 years' purchase (that is, on the basis of interest at 3 percent), it would amount to some seven thousand million pounds. For the value of the capital already invested in improving land or erecting a building, in making a railway or a machine, is the aggregate discounted value of its estimated future net incomes [or quasi-rents]; and if its prospective income-yielding power should diminish, its value would fall accordingly and would be the capitalized value of that smaller income after allowing for depreciation" (p. 593).

In his *Economics of Welfare* (3rd edn.), p. 163, Professor Pigou writes: "The nature of the service of 'waiting' has been much misunderstood. Sometimes it has been supposed to consist in the provision of money, sometimes in the provision of time, and, on both suppositions, it has been argued that no contribution whatever is made by it to the dividend. Neither supposition is correct. 'Waiting' simply means postponing consumption which a person has power to enjoy immediately, thus allowing resources, which might have been destroyed, to assume the form of production instruments.[90] . . . The unit of 'waiting' is, therefore, the use of a given quantity of resources[91]—for example, labor or machinery—for a given time, ... In more general terms we may say that the unit of waiting is a year-value-unit, or, in the simpler, if less accurate, language of Dr. Cassel, a year-pound. . . . A caution may be added against the common view that the amount of capital accumulated in any year is necessarily equal to the amount of 'savings' made in it. This is not so, even when savings are interpreted to mean net savings, thus eliminating the savings of one man that are lent to increase the consumption of another, and when temporary accumulations of *unused* claims upon services in the form of bank-money are ignored; for many savings which are meant to become capital in fact fail of their purpose through misdirection into wasteful uses." [92]

Professor Pigou's only significant reference to what determines the rate of interest is, I think, to be found in his *Industrial fluctuations* (1st edn.), pp. 251–3, where he controverts the view that the rate of interest, being determined by the general conditions of demand and supply of real capital, lies outside the central or any other bank's control. Against this view he argues that: "When bankers create more credit for business men, they make, in their interest, subject to the explanations given in chapter xiii. of part i.,[93] a forced levy of real things from the public, thus increasing the stream of real capital available for them, and causing a fall in the real rate of interest on long and short loans alike. It is true, in short, that the bankers' rate for money is bound by a mechanical tie to the real rate of interest on long loans; but it is not true that this real rate is determined by conditions wholly outside bankers' control."

My running comments on the above have been made in the footnotes. The perplexity which I find in Marshall's account of the matter is fundamentally due, I think, to the incursion of the concept "interest," which belongs to a monetary economy, into a treatise which takes no account of money. "Interest" has really no business to turn up at all in Marshall's *Principles of Economics,*—it belongs to another branch of the subject.

Professor Pigou, conformably with his other tacit assumptions, leads us (in his *Economics of Welfare*) to infer that the unit of waiting is the same as the unit of current investment and that the reward of waiting is quasi-rent, and practically never mentions interest,—which is as it should be. Nevertheless these writers are not dealing with a non-monetary economy (if there is such a thing). They quite clearly presume that money is used and that there is a banking system. Moreover, the rate of interest scarcely plays a larger part in Professor Pigou's *Industrial Fluctuations* (which is mainly a study of fluctuations in the marginal efficiency of capital) or in his *Theory of Unemployment* (which is mainly a study of what determines changes in the volume of employment, assuming that there is no involuntary unemployment) than in his *Economics of Welfare*.

II

The following from his *Principles of Political Economy* (p. 511) puts the substance of Ricardo's theory of the Rate of Interest:

"The interest of money is not regulated by the rate at which the Bank will lend, whether it be 5, 3 or 2 percent, but by the rate of profit which can be made by the employment of capital, and which is totally independent of the quantity or of the value of money. Whether the Bank lent one million, ten millions, or a hundred millions, they would not permanently alter the market rate of interest; they would alter only the value of the money which they thus issued. In one case, ten or twenty times more money might be required to carry on the same business than what might be required in the other. The applications to the Bank for money, then, depend on the comparison between the rate of profits that may be made by the employment of it, and the rate at which they are willing to lend it. If they charge less than the market rate of interest, there is no amount of money which they might not lend;—if they charge more than that rate, none but spendthrifts and prodigals would be found to borrow of them."

This is so clear-cut that it affords a better starting-point for a discussion than the phrases of later writers who, without really departing from the essence of the Ricardian doctrine, are nevertheless sufficiently uncomfortable about it to seek refuge in haziness. The above is, of course, as always with Ricardo, to be interpreted as a long-period doctrine, with the emphasis on the word "permanently" half-way through the passage; and it is interesting to consider the assumptions required to validate it.

Once again the assumption required is the usual classical assumption, that there is always full employment; so that, assuming no change in the supply curve of labor in terms of product, there is only one possible level of employment in long-period equilibrium. On this assumption with the usual *ceteris paribus, i.e.* no change in psychological propensities and expectations other than those arising out of a change in the quantity of money, the Ricardian theory is valid, in the sense that on these suppositions there is only one rate of interest which will be compatible with full employment in the long period. Ricardo and his successors overlook the fact that even in the long period the volume of employment is not necessarily full but is capable of varying, and that to every banking policy there corresponds a different long-period level of employment; so that there are a number of positions of long-period equilibrium corresponding to different conceivable interest policies on the part of the monetary authority.

If Ricardo had been content to present his argument solely as applying to any given quantity of money created by the monetary authority, it would still have been correct on the assumption of flexible money-wages. If, that is to say, Ricardo had argued that it would make no permanent alteration to the rate of interest whether the quantity of money was fixed by the monetary authority at ten millions or at a hundred millions, his conclusion would hold. But if by the policy of the monetary authority we mean the terms on which it will increase or decrease the quantity of money, *i.e.* the rate of interest at which it will, either by a change in the volume of discounts or by open-market operations, increase or decrease its assets—which is what Ricardo expressly does mean in the above quotation—then it is not the case either that the policy of the monetary authority is nugatory or that only one policy is compatible with long-period equilibrium; though in the extreme case where money-wages are assumed to fall without limit in face of involuntary unemployment through a futile competition for employment between the unemployed laborers, there will, it is true, be only two possible long-period positions—full employment and the level of employment corresponding to the rate of interest at which liquidity-preference becomes absolute (in the event of this being less than full employment). Assuming flexible money-wages, the quantity of money as such is, indeed, nugatory in the long period; but the terms on which the monetary authority will change the quantity of money enters as a real determinant into the economic scheme.

It is worth adding that the concluding sentences of the quotation suggest that Ricardo was overlooking the possible changes in the marginal efficiency of capital according to the amount invested. But this again can be interpreted as another example of his greater internal consistency compared with his successors. For if the quantity of employment and the psychological propensities of the community are taken as given, there is in fact only one possible rate of accumulation of capital and, consequently, only one possible value for the marginal efficiency of capital. Ricardo offers us the supreme intellectual achievement, unattainable by weaker spirits, of adopting a hypothetical world remote from experience as though it were the world of experience and then living in it consistently. With most of his successors common sense cannot help breaking in—with injury to their logical consistency.

III

A peculiar theory of the rate of interest has been propounded by Professor von Mises and adopted from him by Professor Hayek and also, I think, by Professor Robbins; namely, that changes in the rate of interest can be identified with changes in the relative price levels of consumption-goods and capital-goods.[94] It is not clear how this conclusion is reached. But the argument seems to run as follows. By a somewhat drastic simplification the marginal efficiency of capital is taken as measured by the ratio of the supply price of new consumers' goods to the supply price of new producers' goods.[95] This is then identified with the rate of interest. The fact is called to notice that a fall in the rate of interest is favorable to investment. *Ergo,* a fall in the ratio of the price of consumers' goods to the price of producers' goods is favorable to investment.

By this means a link is established between increased saving by an individual and increased aggregate investment. For it is common ground that increased individual saving will cause a fall in the price of Consumers' goods, and, quite possibly, a greater fall than in the price of producers' goods; hence, according to the above reasoning, it means a reduction in the rate of interest which will stimulate investment. But, of course, a lowering of the marginal efficiency of particular capital assets, and hence a lowering of the schedule of the marginal efficiency of capital in general, has exactly the opposite effect to what the above argument assumes. For investment is stimulated either by a *raising* of the schedule of the marginal efficiency or by a *lowering* of the rate of interest. As a result of confusing the marginal efficiency of capital with the rate of interest, Professor von Mises and his disciples have got their conclusions exactly the wrong way round. A good example of a confusion along these lines is given by the following passage by Professor Alvin Hansen:[96] "It has been suggested by some economists that the net effect of reduced spending will be a lower price level of consumers' goods than would otherwise have been the case, and that, in consequence, the stimulus to investment in fixed capital would thereby tend to be minimized. This view is, however, incorrect and is based on a confusion of the effect on capital formation of (1) higher or lower prices of consumers' goods, and (2) a change in the rate of interest. It is true that inconsequence of the decreased spending and increased saving, consumers' prices would be low relative to the prices of producers' goods. But this, in effect, means a lower rate of interest, and a lower rate of interest stimulates an expansion of capital investment in fields which at higher rates would be unprofitable."

CHAPTER 15

The Psychological and Business Incentives to Liquidity

I

We must now develop in more detail the analysis of the motives to liquidity-preference which were introduced in a preliminary way in Chapter 13. The subject is substantially the same as that which has been sometimes discussed under the heading of the Demand for Money. It is also closely connected with what is called the income-velocity of money;—for the income-velocity of money merely measures what proportion of their incomes the public chooses to hold in cash, so that an increased income-velocity of money may be a symptom of a decreased liquidity-preference. It is not the same thing, however, since it is in respect of his stock of accumulated savings, rather than of his income, that the individual can exercise his choice between liquidity and illiquidity. And, anyhow, the term "income-velocity of money" carries with it the misleading suggestion of a presumption in favor of the demand for money as a whole being proportional, or having some determinate relation, to income, whereas this presumption should apply, as we shall see, only to a *portion* of the public's cash holdings; with the result that it overlooks the part played by the rate of interest.

In my *Treatise on Money* I studied the total demand for money under the headings of income-deposits, business-deposits, and savings-deposits, and I need not repeat here the analysis which I gave in Chapter 3 of that book. Money held for each of the three purposes forms, nevertheless, a single pool, which the holder is under no necessity to segregate into three water-tight compartments; for they need not be sharply divided even in his own mind, and the same sum can be held primarily for one purpose and secondarily for another. Thus we can—equally well, and, perhaps, better—consider the individual's aggregate demand for money in given circumstances as a single decision, though the composite result of a number of different motives.

In analyzing the motives, however, it is still convenient to classify them under certain headings, the first of which broadly corresponds to the former classification of income-deposits and business-deposits, and the two latter to that of savings-deposits. These I have briefly introduced in Chapter 13 under the headings of the transactions-motive, which can be further classified as the income-motive and the business-motive, the precautionary-motive and the speculative-motive.

(i) *The Income-motive.*—One reason for holding cash is to bridge the interval between the receipt of income and its disbursement. The strength of this motive in inducing a decision to hold a given aggregate of cash will chiefly depend on the amount of income and the normal length of the interval between its receipt and its disbursement. It is in this connection that the concept of the income-velocity of money is strictly appropriate.

(ii) *The Business-motive.*—Similarly, cash is held to bridge the interval between the time of incurring business costs and that of the receipt of the sale-proceeds; cash held by dealers to bridge the interval between purchase and realization being included under this heading. The strength of this demand will chiefly depend on the value of current output (and hence on current income), and on the number of hands through which output passes.

(iii) *The Precautionary-motive.*—To provide for contingencies requiring sudden expenditure and for unforeseen opportunities of advantageous purchases, and also to hold an asset of which the value is fixed in terms of money to meet a subsequent liability fixed in terms of money, are further motives for holding cash.

The strength of all these three types of motive will partly depend on the cheapness and the reliability of methods of obtaining cash, when it is required, by some form of temporary borrowing, in particular by overdraft or its equivalent. For there is no necessity to hold idle cash to bridge over intervals if it can be obtained without difficulty at the moment when it is actually required. Their strength will also depend on what we may term the relative cost of holding cash. If the cash can only be retained by forgoing the purchase of a profitable asset, this increases the cost and thus weakens the motive towards holding a given amount of cash. If deposit interest is earned or if bank charges are avoided by holding cash, this decreases the cost and strengthens the motive. It may be, however, that this is likely to be a minor factor except where large changes in the cost of holding cash are in question.

(iv) There remains the *Speculative-motive.*—This needs a more detailed examination than the others, both because it is less well understood and because it is particularly important in transmitting the effects of a *change* in the quantity of money.

In normal circumstances the amount of money required to satisfy the transactions-motive and the precautionary-motive is mainly a resultant of the general activity of the economic system and of the level of money-income. But it is by playing on the speculative-motive that monetary management (or, in the absence of management, chance changes in the quantity of money) is brought to bear on the economic system. For the demand for money to satisfy the former motives is generally irresponsive to any influence except the actual occurrence of a change in the general economic activity and the level of incomes; whereas experience indicates that the aggregate demand for money to satisfy the speculative-motive usually shows a continuous response to gradual changes in the rate of interest, *i.e.* there is a continuous curve relating changes in the demand for money to satisfy the speculative motive and changes in the rate of interest as given by changes in the prices of bonds and debts of various maturities.

Indeed, if this were not so, "open market operations" would be impracticable. I have said that experience indicates the continuous relationship stated above, because in normal circumstances the banking system is in fact always able to purchase (or sell) bonds in exchange for cash by bidding the price of bonds up (or down) in the market by a modest amount; and the larger the quantity of cash which they seek to create (or cancel) by purchasing (or selling) bonds and debts, the greater must be the fall (or rise) in the rate of interest. Where, however, (as in the United States,

1933–1934) open-market operations have been limited to the purchase of very short-dated securities, the effect may, of course, be mainly confined to the very short-term rate of interest and have but little reaction on the much more important long-term rates of interest.

In dealing with the speculative-motive it is, however, important to distinguish between the changes in the rate of interest which are due to changes in the supply of money available to satisfy the speculative-motive, without there having been any change in the liquidity function, and those which are primarily due to changes in expectation affecting the liquidity function itself. Open-market operations may, indeed, influence the rate of interest through both channels; since they may not only change the volume of money, but may also give rise to changed expectations concerning the future policy of the Central Bank or of the Government. Changes in the liquidity function itself, due to a change in the news which causes revision of expectations, will often be discontinuous, and will, therefore, give rise to a corresponding discontinuity of change in the rate of interest. Only, indeed, in so far as the change in the news is differently interpreted by different individuals or affects individual interests differently will there be room for any increased activity of dealing in the bond market. If the change in the news affects the judgment and the requirements of everyone in precisely the same way, the rate of interest (as indicated by the prices of bonds and debts) will be adjusted forthwith to the new situation without any market transactions being necessary.

Thus, in the simplest case, where everyone is similar and similarly placed, a change in circumstances or expectations will not be capable of causing any displacement of money whatever;—it will simply change the rate of interest in whatever degree is necessary to offset the desire of each individual, felt at the previous rate, to change his holding of cash in response to the new circumstances or expectations; and, since everyone will change his ideas as to the rate which would induce him to alter his holdings of cash in the same degree, no transactions will result. To each set of circumstances and expectations there will correspond an appropriate rate of interest, and there will never be any question of anyone changing his usual holdings of cash.

In general, however, a change in circumstances or expectations will cause some realignment in individual holdings of money;—since, in fact, a change will influence the ideas of different individuals differently by reason partly of differences in environment and the reason for which money is held and partly of differences in knowledge and interpretation of the new situation. Thus the new equilibrium rate of interest will be associated with a redistribution of money-holdings. Nevertheless it is the change in the rate of interest, rather than the redistribution of cash, which deserves our main attention.

The latter is incidental to individual differences, whereas the essential phenomenon is that which occurs in the simplest case. Moreover, even in the general case, the shift in the rate of interest is usually the most prominent part of the reaction to a change in the news. The movement in bond-prices is, as the newspapers are accustomed to say, "out of all proportion to the activity of dealing;"—which is as it should be, in view of individuals being much more similar than they are dissimilar in their reaction to news.

II

Whilst the amount of cash which an individual decides to hold to satisfy the transactions-motive and the precautionary-motive is not entirely independent of what he is holding to satisfy the speculative-motive, it is a safe first approximation to regard the amounts of these two sets of cash-holdings as being largely independent of one another. Let us, therefore, for the purposes of our further analysis, break up our problem in this way.

Let the amount of cash held to satisfy the transactions and precautionary-motives be M_1, and the amount held to satisfy the speculative-motive be M_2. Corresponding to these two compartments of cash, we then have two liquidity functions L_1 and L_2. L_1 mainly depends on the level of income, whilst L_2 mainly depends on the relation between the current rate of interest and the state of expectation. Thus

$$M = M_1 + M_2 = L_1 (Y) + L_2 (r),$$

where L_1 is the liquidity function corresponding to an income Y, which determines M_1, and L_2 is the liquidity function of the rate of interest r, which determines M_2. It follows that there are three matters to investigate: (i) the relation of changes in M to Y and r, (ii) what determines the shape of L_1, (iii) what determines the shape of L_2.

(i) The relation of changes in M to Y and r depends, in the first instance, on the way in which changes in M come about. Suppose that M consists of gold coins and that changes in M can only result from increased returns to the activities of gold-miners who belong to the economic system under examination. In this case changes in M are, in the first instance, directly associated with changes in Y, since the new gold accrues as someone's income. Exactly the same conditions hold if changes in M are due to the Government printing money wherewith to meet its current expenditure;—in this case also the new money accrues as someone's income. The new level of income, however, will not continue sufficiently high for the requirements of M_1 to absorb the whole of the increase in M; and some portion of the money will seek an outlet in buying securities or other assets until r has fallen so as to bring about an increase in the magnitude of M_2 and at the same time to stimulate a rise in Y to such an extent that the new money is absorbed either in M_2 or in the M_1 which corresponds to the rise in Y caused by the fall in r. Thus at one remove this case comes to the same thing as the alternative case, where the new money can only be issued in the first instance by a relaxation of the conditions of credit by the banking system, so as to induce someone to sell the banks a debt or a bond in exchange for the new cash.

It will, therefore, be safe for us to take the latter case as typical. A change in M can be assumed to operate by changing r, and a change in r will lead to a new equilibrium partly by changing M_2 and partly by changing Y and therefore M_1. The division of the increment of cash between M_1 and M_2 in the new position of equilibrium will depend on the responses of investment to a reduction in the rate of interest and of income to an increase in investment.[97] Since Y partly depends on r, it follows that a given change in M has to cause a sufficient change in r for the resultant changes in M_1 and M_2 respectively to add up to the given change in M.

(ii) It is not always made clear whether the income-velocity of money is defined as the ratio of Y to M or as the ratio of Y to M_1. I propose, however, to take it in the latter sense. Thus if V is the income-velocity of money,

$$L_1 (Y) = Y/V = M_1.$$

There is, of course, no reason for supposing that V is constant. Its value will depend on the character of banking and industrial organization, on social habits, on the distribution of income between different classes and on the effective cost of holding idle cash. Nevertheless, if we have a short period of time in view and can safely assume no material change in any of these factors, we can treat V as nearly enough constant.

(iii) Finally there is the question of the relation between M_2 and r. We have seen in Chapter 13 that *uncertainty* as to the future course of the rate of interest is the sole intelligible explanation of the type of liquidity-preference L_2 which leads to the holding of cash M_2. It follows that a given M_2 will not have a definite quantitative relation to a given rate of interest of r;—what matters is not the *absolute* level of r but the degree of its divergence from what is considered a fairly *safe* level of r, having regard to those calculations of probability which are being relied on. Nevertheless, there are two reasons for expecting that, in any given state of expectation, a fall in r will be associated with an increase in M_2. In the first place, if the general view as to what is a safe level of r is unchanged, every fall in r reduces the market rate relatively to the "safe" rate and therefore increases the risk of illiquidity; and, in the second place, every fall in r reduces the current earnings from illiquidity, which are available as a sort of insurance premium to offset the risk of loss on capital account, by an amount equal to the difference between the *squares* of the old rate of interest and the new. For example, if the rate of interest on a long-term debt is 4 percent, it is preferable to sacrifice liquidity unless on a balance of probabilities it is feared that the long-term rate of interest may rise faster than by 4 percent, of itself per annum, *i.e.* by an amount greater than 0.16 percent, per annum. If, however, the rate of interest is already as low as 2 percent, the running yield will only offset a rise in it of as little as 0.04 percent, per annum. This, indeed, is perhaps the chief obstacle to a fall in the rate of interest to a very low level. Unless reasons are believed to exist why future experience will be very different from past experience, a long-term rate of interest of (say) 2 percent leaves more to fear than to hope, and offers, at the same time, a running yield which is only sufficient to offset a very small measure of fear.

It is evident, then, that the rate of interest is a highly psychological phenomenon. We shall find, indeed, in Book V. that it cannot be in equilibrium at a level *below* the rate which corresponds to full employment; because at such a level a state of true inflation will be produced, with the result that M_1 will absorb ever-increasing quantities of cash.

But at a level *above* the rate which corresponds to full employment, the long-term market-rate of interest will depend, not only on the current policy of the monetary authority, but also on market expectations concerning its future policy. The short-term rate of interest is easily controlled by the monetary authority, both because it is not difficult to produce a conviction that its policy will not greatly change in the very near future, and also because the possible loss is small compared with the running yield (unless it is approaching vanishing point). But the long-term rate may be more recalcitrant when once it has fallen to a level which, on the basis of past experience and present expectations of *future* monetary policy, is considered "unsafe" by representative opinion. For example, in a country linked to an international gold standard, a rate of interest lower than prevails elsewhere will be viewed with a justifiable lack of confidence; yet a domestic rate of interest dragged up to a parity with the *highest* rate (highest after allowing for risk) prevailing in any country belonging to the international system may be much higher than is consistent with domestic full employment.

Thus a monetary policy which strikes public opinion as being experimental in character or easily liable to change may fail in its objective of greatly reducing the long-term rate of interest, because M_2 may tend to increase almost without limit in response to a reduction of r below a certain figure. The same policy, on the other hand, may prove easily successful if it appeals to public opinion as being reasonable and practicable and in the public interest, rooted in strong conviction, and promoted by an authority unlikely to be superseded.

It might be more accurate, perhaps, to say that the rate of interest is a highly conventional, rather than a highly psychological, phenomenon. For its actual value is largely governed by the prevailing view as to what its value is expected to be. *Any* level of interest which is accepted with sufficient conviction as *likely* to be durable *will* be durable; subject, of course, in a changing society to fluctuations for all kinds of reasons round the expected normal. In particular, when M_1 is increasing faster than M, the rate of interest will rise, and *vice versa*. But it may fluctuate for decades about a level which is chronically too high for full employment;—particularly if it is the prevailing opinion that the rate of interest is self-adjusting, so that the level established by convention is thought to be rooted in objective grounds much stronger than convention, the failure of employment to attain an optimum level being in no way associated, in the minds either of the public or of authority, with the prevalence of an inappropriate range of rates of interest.

The difficulties in the way of maintaining effective demand at a level high enough to provide full employment, which ensue from the association of a conventional and fairly stable long-term rate of interest with a fickle and highly unstable marginal efficiency of capital, should be, by now, obvious to the reader.

Such comfort as we can fairly take from more encouraging reflections must be drawn from the hope that, precisely because the convention is not rooted in secure knowledge, it will not be always unduly resistant to a modest measure of persistence and consistency of purpose by the monetary authority. Public opinion can be fairly rapidly accustomed to a modest fall in the rate of interest and the conventional expectation of the future may be modified accordingly; thus preparing the way for a further movement—up to a point. The fall in the long-term rate of interest in Great Britain after her departure from the gold standard provides an interesting example of this;—the major movements were effected by a series of discontinuous jumps, as the liquidity function of the public, having become accustomed to each successive reduction, became ready to respond to some new incentive in the news or in the policy of the authorities.

III

We can sum up the above in the proposition that in any given state of expectation there is in the minds of the public a certain potentiality towards holding cash beyond what is required by the transactions-motive or the precautionary-motive, which will realize itself in actual cash-holdings in a degree which depends on the terms on which the monetary authority is willing to create cash. It is this potentiality which is summed up in the liquidity function L_2.

Corresponding to the quantity of money created by the monetary authority, there will, therefore, be *cet. par.* a determinate rate of interest or, more strictly, a determinate complex of rates of interest for debts of different maturities. The same thing, however, would be true of any other factor in the economic system taken separately. Thus this particular analysis will only be useful and significant in so far as there is some specially direct or purposive connection between changes in the quantity of money and changes in the rate of interest. Our reason for supposing that there is such a special connection arises from the fact that, broadly speaking, the banking system and the monetary authority are dealers in money and debts and not in assets or consumables.

If the monetary authority were prepared to deal both ways on specified terms in debts of all maturities, and even more so if it were prepared to deal in debts of varying degrees of risk, the relationship between the complex of rates of interest and the quantity of money would be direct. The complex of rates of interest would simply be an expression of the terms on which the banking system is prepared to acquire or part with debts; and the quantity of money would be the amount which can find a home in the possession of individuals who—after taking account of all relevant circumstances—prefer the control of liquid cash to parting with it in exchange for a debt on the terms indicated by the market rate of interest. Perhaps a complex offer by the central bank to buy and sell at stated prices gilt-edged bonds of all maturities, in place of the single bank rate for short-term bills, is the most important practical improvement which can be made in the technique of monetary management.

Today, however, in actual practice, the extent to which the price of debts as fixed by the banking system is "effective" in the market, in the sense that it governs the actual market-price, varies in different systems. Sometimes the price is more effective in one direction than in the other; that is to say, the banking system may undertake to purchase debts at a certain price but not necessarily to sell them at a figure near enough to its buying-price to represent no more than a dealer's turn, though there is no reason why the price should not be made effective both ways with the aid of open-market operations.

There is also the more important qualification which arises out of the monetary authority not being, as a rule, an equally willing dealer in debts of all maturities. The monetary authority often tends in practice to concentrate upon short-term debts and to leave the price of long-term debts to be influenced by belated and imperfect reactions from the price of short-term debts;—though here again there is no reason why they need do so.

Where these qualifications operate, the directness of the relation between the rate of interest and the quantity of money is correspondingly modified. In Great Britain the field of deliberate control appears to be widening. But in applying this theory in any particular case allowance must be made for the special characteristics of the method actually employed by the monetary authority. If the monetary authority deals only in short-term debts, we have to consider what influence the price, actual and prospective, of short-term debts exercises on debts of longer maturity.

Thus there are certain limitations on the ability of the monetary authority to establish any given complex of rates of interest for debts of different terms and risks, which can be summed up as follows:

(1) There are those limitations which arise out of the monetary authority's own practices in limiting its willingness to deal to debts of a particular type.

(2) There is the possibility, for the reasons discussed above, that, after the rate of interest has fallen to a certain level, liquidity-preference may become virtually absolute in the sense that almost everyone prefers cash to holding a debt which yields so low a rate of interest. In this event the monetary authority would have lost effective control over the rate of interest. But whilst this limiting case might become practically important in future, I know of no example of it hitherto. Indeed, owing to the unwillingness of most monetary authorities to deal boldly in debts of long term, there has not been much opportunity for a test. Moreover, if such a situation were to arise, it would mean that the public authority itself could borrow through the banking system on an unlimited scale at a nominal rate of interest.

(3) The most striking examples of a complete breakdown of stability in the rate of interest, due to the liquidity function flattening out in one direction or the other, have occurred in very abnormal circumstances. In Russia and Central Europe after the war a currency crisis or flight from the currency was experienced, when no one could be induced to retain holdings either of money or of debts on any terms whatever, and even a high and rising rate of interest was unable to keep pace with the marginal efficiency of capital (especially of stocks of liquid goods) under the influence of the expectation of an ever greater fall in the value of money; whilst in the United States at certain dates in 1932 there was a crisis of the opposite kind—a financial crisis or crisis of liquidation, when scarcely anyone could be induced to part with holdings of money on any reasonable terms.

(4) There is, finally, the difficulty discussed in section iv of Chapter 11, in the way of bringing the effective rate of interest below a certain figure, which may prove important in an era of low interest-rates; namely the intermediate costs of bringing the borrower and the ultimate lender together, and the allowance for risk, especially for moral risk, which the lender requires over and above the pure rate of interest. As the pure rate of interest declines it does not follow that the allowances for expense and risk decline *pari passu*. Thus the rate of interest which the typical borrower has to pay may decline more slowly than the pure rate of interest, and may be incapable of being brought, by the methods of the existing banking and financial organization, below a certain minimum figure. This is particularly important if the estimation of moral risk is appreciable. For where the risk is due to doubt in the mind of the lender concerning the honesty of the borrower, there is nothing in the mind of a borrower who does not intend to be dishonest to offset the resultant higher charge. It is also important in the case of short-term loans (*e.g.* bank loans) where the expenses are heavy;—a bank may have to charge its customers 1 1/2 to 2 percent, even if the pure rate of interest to the lender is nil.

IV

At the cost of anticipating what is more properly the subject of Chapter 21 below it may be interesting briefly at this stage to indicate the relationship of the above to the Quantity Theory of Money.

In a static society or in a society in which for any other reason no one feels any uncertainty about the future rates of interest, the Liquidity Function L_2, or the propensity to hoard (as we might term it), will always be zero in equilibrium. Hence in equilibrium M_2 $=0$ and $M = M_1$; so that any change in M will cause the rate of interest to fluctuate until income reaches a level at which the change in M_1 is equal to the supposed change in M. Now $M_1 V = Y$, where V is the income-velocity of money as defined above and Y is the aggregate income. Thus if it is practicable to measure the quantity, O, and the price, P, of current output, we have $Y = OP$, and, therefore, $MV = OP$; which is much the same as the Quantity Theory of Money in its traditional form.[98]

For the purposes of the real world it is a great fault in the Quantity Theory that it does not distinguish between changes in prices which are a function of changes in output, and those which are a function of changes in the wage-unit.[99] The explanation of this omission is, perhaps, to be found in the assumptions that there is no propensity to hoard and that there is always full employment. For in this case, O being constant and M, being zero, it follows, if we can take V also as constant, that both the wage-unit and the price-level will be directly proportional to the quantity of money.

CHAPTER 16

Sundry Observations on the Nature of Capital

I

An act of individual saving means—so to speak—a decision not to have dinner today. But it does *not* necessitate a decision to have dinner or to buy a pair of boots a week hence or a year hence or to consume any specified thing at any specified date. Thus it depresses the business of preparing today's dinner without stimulating the business of making ready for some future act of consumption. It is not a substitution of future consumption-demand for present consumption-demand,—it is a net diminution of such demand. Moreover, the expectation of future consumption is so largely based on current experience of present consumption that a reduction in the latter is likely to depress the former, with the result that the act of saving will not merely depress the price of consumption-goods and leave the marginal efficiency of existing capital unaffected, but may actually tend to depress the latter also. In this event it may reduce present investment-demand as well as present consumption-demand.

If saving consisted not merely in abstaining from present consumption but in placing simultaneously a specific order for future consumption, the effect might indeed be different. For in that case the expectation of some future yield from investment would be improved, and the resources released from preparing for present consumption could be turned over to preparing for the future consumption. Not that they necessarily would be, even in this case, on a scale *equal* to the amount of resources released; since the desired interval of delay might require a method of production so inconveniently "roundabout" as to have an efficiency well below the current rate of interest, with the result that the favorable effect on employment of the forward order for consumption would eventuate not at once but at some subsequent date, so that the *immediate* effect of the saving would still be adverse to employment. In any case, however, an individual decision to save does not, in actual fact, involve the placing of any specific forward order for consumption, but merely the cancellation of a present order. Thus, since the expectation of consumption is the only *raison d'être* of employment, there should be nothing paradoxical in the conclusion that a diminished propensity to consume has *cet. par.* a depressing effect on employment.

The trouble arises, therefore, because the act of saving implies, not a substitution for present consumption of some specific additional consumption which requires for its preparation just as much immediate economic activity as would have been required by present consumption equal in value to the sum saved, but a desire for "wealth" as such, that is for a potentiality of consuming an unspecified article at an unspecified time. The absurd, though almost universal, idea that an act of individual saving is just as good for effective demand as an act of individual consumption, has been fostered by the fallacy, much more specious than the conclusion derived from it, that an increased desire to hold wealth, being much the same thing as an increased desire to hold investments, must, by increasing the demand for investments, provide a stimulus to their production; so that current investment is promoted by individual saving to the same extent as present consumption is diminished.

It is of this fallacy that it is most difficult to disabuse men's minds. It comes from believing that the owner of wealth desires a capital-asset as such, whereas what he really desires is its *prospective yield*. Now, prospective yield wholly depends on the expectation of future effective demand in relation to future conditions of supply. If, therefore, an act of saving does nothing to improve prospective yield, it does nothing to stimulate investment. Moreover, in order that an individual saver may attain his desired goal of the ownership of wealth, it is not necessary that a *new* capital-asset should be produced wherewith to satisfy him. The mere act of saving by one individual, being *two-sided* as we have shown above, forces some other individual to transfer to him some article of wealth old or new. Every act of saving involves a "forced" inevitable transfer of wealth to him who saves, though he in his turn may suffer from the saving of others. These transfers of wealth do not require the creation of new wealth—indeed, as we have seen, they may be actively inimical to it. The creation of new wealth wholly depends on the prospective yield of the new wealth reaching the standard set by the current rate of interest. The prospective yield of the marginal new investment is not increased by the fact that someone wishes to increase his wealth, since the prospective yield of the marginal new investment depends on the expectation of a demand for a specific article at a specific date.

Nor do we avoid this conclusion by arguing that what the owner of wealth desires is not a given prospective yield but the best available prospective yield, so that an increased desire to own wealth reduces the prospective yield with which the producers of new investment have to be content. For this overlooks the fact that there is always an alternative to the ownership of real capital-assets, namely the ownership of money and debts; so that the prospective yield with which the producers of new investment have to be content cannot fall below the standard set by the current rate of interest. And the current rate of interest depends, as we have seen, not on the strength of the desire to hold wealth, but on the strengths of the desires to hold it in liquid and in illiquid forms respectively, coupled with the amount of the supply of wealth in the one form relatively to the supply of it in the other. If the reader still finds himself perplexed, let him ask himself why, the quantity of money being unchanged, a fresh act of saving should diminish the sum which it is desired to keep in liquid form at the existing rate of interest.

Certain deeper perplexities, which may arise when we try to probe still further into the whys and wherefores, will be considered in the next chapter.

II

It is much preferable to speak of capital as having a yield over the course of its life in excess of its original cost, than as being *productive*. For the only reason why an asset offers a prospect of yielding during its life services having an aggregate value greater than its initial supply price is because it is scarce; and it is kept *scarce* because of the competition of the rate of interest on money. If capital becomes less scarce, the excess yield will diminish, without its having become less productive—at least in the physical sense.

I sympathize, therefore, with the pre-classical doctrine that everything is *produced* by *labor,* aided by what used to be called art and is now called technique, by natural resources which are free or cost a rent according to their scarcity or abundance, and by the results of past labor, embodied in assets, which also command a price according to their scarcity or abundance. It is preferable to regard labor, including, of course, the personal services of the entrepreneur and his assistants, as the sole factor of production, operating in a given environment of technique, natural resources, capital equipment and effective demand. This partly explains why we have been able to take the unit of labor as the sole physical unit which we require in our economic system, apart from units of money and of time.

It is true that some lengthy or roundabout processes are physically efficient. But so are some short processes. Lengthy processes are not physically efficient because they are long. Some, probably most, lengthy processes would be physically very inefficient, for there are such things as spoiling or wasting with time.[100] With a given labor force there is a definite limit to the quantity of labor embodied in roundabout processes which can be used to advantage. Apart from other considerations, there must be a due proportion between the amount of labor employed in making machines and the amount which will be employed in using them. The ultimate quantity of *value* will not increase indefinitely, relatively to the quantity of labor employed, as the processes adopted become more and more roundabout, even if their physical efficiency is still increasing. Only if the desire to postpone consumption were strong enough to produce a situation in which full employment required a volume of investment so great as to involve a negative marginal efficiency of capital, would a process become advantageous merely because it was lengthy; in which event we should employ physically *inefficient* processes, provided they were sufficiently lengthy for the gain from postponement to outweigh their inefficiency.

We should in fact have a situation in which *short* processes would have to be kept sufficiently scarce for their physical efficiency to outweigh the disadvantage of the early delivery of their product. A correct theory, therefore, must be reversible so as to be able to cover the cases of the marginal efficiency of capital corresponding either to a positive or to a negative rate of interest; and it is, I think, only the scarcity theory outlined above which is capable of this.

Moreover there are all sorts of reasons why various kinds of services and facilities are scarce and therefore expensive relatively to the quantity of labor involved. For example, smelly processes command a higher reward, because people will not undertake them otherwise. So do risky processes. But we do not devise a productivity theory of smelly or risky processes as such. In short, not all labor is accomplished in equally agreeable attendant circumstances; and conditions of equilibrium require that articles produced in less agreeable attendant circumstances (characterized by smelliness, risk or the lapse of time) must be kept sufficiently scarce to command a higher price. But if the lapse of time becomes an agreeable attendant circumstance, which is a quite possible case and already holds for many individuals, then, as I have said above, it is the short processes which must be kept sufficiently scarce.

Given the optimum amount of roundaboutness, we shall, of course, select the most efficient roundabout processes which we can find up to the required aggregate. But the optimum amount itself should be such as to provide at the appropriate dates for that part of consumers' demand which it is desired to defer. In optimum conditions, that is to say, production should be so organized as to produce in the most efficient manner compatible with delivery at the dates at which consumers' demand is expected to become effective.

It is no use to produce for delivery at a different date from this, even though the physical output could be increased by changing the date of delivery;—except in so far as the prospect of a larger meal, so to speak, induces the consumer to anticipate or postpone the hour of dinner. If, after hearing full particulars of the meals he can get by fixing dinner at different hours, the consumer is expected to decide in favor of 8 o'clock, it is the business of the cook to provide the best dinner he can for service at that hour, irrespective of whether 7.30, 8 o'clock or 8.30 is the hour which would suit him best if time counted for nothing, one way or the other, and his only task was to produce the absolutely best dinner. In some phases of society it may be that we could get physically better dinners by dining later than we do; but it is equally conceivable in other phases that we could get better dinners by dining earlier. Our theory must, as I have said above, be applicable to both contingencies.

If the rate of interest were zero, there would be an optimum interval for any given article between the average date of input and the date of consumption, for which labor cost would be a minimum;—a shorter process of production would be less efficient technically, whilst a longer process would also be less efficient by reason of storage costs and deterioration, If, however, the rate of interest exceeds zero, a new element of cost is introduced which increases with the length of the process, so that the optimum interval will be shortened, and the current input to provide for the eventual delivery of the article will have to be curtailed until the prospective price has increased sufficiently to cover the increased cost—a cost which will be increased both by the interest charges and also by the diminished efficiency of the shorter method of production. Whilst if the rate of interest falls below zero (assuming this to be technically possible), the opposite is the case. Given the prospective consumers' demand, current input today has to compete, so to speak, with the alternative of starting input at a later date; and, consequently, current input will only be worth while when the greater cheapness, by reason of greater technical efficiency or prospective price changes, of producing later on rather than now, is insufficient to offset the smaller return from negative interest. In the case of the great majority of articles it would involve great technical inefficiency to start up their input more than a very modest length of time ahead of their prospective consumption. Thus even if the rate of interest is zero, there is a strict limit to the proportion of prospective consumers' demand which it is profitable to begin providing for in advance; and, as the rate of interest rises, the proportion of the prospective consumers' demand for which it pays to produce today shrinks *pari passu*.

III

We have seen that capital has to be kept scarce enough in the long-period to have a marginal efficiency which is at least equal to the rate of interest for a period equal to the life of the capital, as determined by psychological and institutional conditions. What would this involve for a society which finds itself so well equipped with capital that its marginal efficiency is zero and would be negative with any additional investment; yet possessing a monetary system, such that money will "keep" and involves negligible costs of storage and safe custody, with the result that in practice interest cannot be negative; and, in conditions of full employment, disposed to save?

If, in such circumstances, we start from a position of full employment, entrepreneurs will necessarily make losses if they continue to offer employment on a scale which will utilize the whole of the existing stock of capital. Hence the stock of capital and the level of employment will have to shrink until the community becomes so impoverished that the aggregate of saving has become zero, the positive saving of some individuals or groups being offset by the negative saving of others. Thus for a society such as we have supposed, the position of equilibrium, under conditions of *laissez-faire*, will be one in which employment is low enough and the standard of life sufficiently miserable to bring savings to zero. More probably there will be a cyclical movement round this equilibrium position. For if there is still room for uncertainty about the future, the marginal efficiency of capital will occasionally rise above zero leading to a "boom," and in the succeeding "slump" the stock of capital may fall for a time below the level which will yield a marginal efficiency of zero in the long run. Assuming correct foresight, the equilibrium stock of capital which will have a marginal efficiency of precisely zero will, of course, be a smaller stock than would correspond to full employment of the available labor; for it will be the equipment which corresponds to that proportion of unemployment which ensures zero saving.

The only alternative position of equilibrium would be given by a situation in which a stock of capital sufficiently great to have a marginal efficiency of zero also represents an amount of wealth sufficiently great to satiate to the full the aggregate desire on the part of the public to make provision for the future, even with full employment, in circumstances where no bonus is obtainable in the form of interest. It would, however, be an unlikely coincidence that the propensity to save in conditions of full employment should become satisfied just at the point where the stock of capital reaches the level where its marginal efficiency is zero. If, therefore, this more favorable possibility comes to the rescue, it will probably take effect, not just at the point where the rate of interest is vanishing, but at some previous point during the gradual decline of the rate of interest.

We have assumed so far an institutional factor which prevents the rate of interest from being negative, in the shape of money which has negligible carrying costs. In fact, however, institutional and psychological factors are present which set a limit much above zero to the practicable decline in the rate of interest. In particular the costs of bringing borrowers and lenders together and uncertainty as to the future of the rate of interest, which we have examined above, set a lower limit, which in present circumstances may perhaps be as high as 2 or 2 1/2 percent, on long term. If this should prove correct, the awkward possibilities of an increasing stock of wealth, in conditions where the rate of interest can fall no further under *laissez-faire,* may soon be realized in actual experience. Moreover if the minimum level to which it is practicable to bring the rate of interest is appreciably above zero, there is less likelihood of the aggregate desire to accumulate wealth being satiated before the rate of interest has reached its minimum level.

The post-war experiences of Great Britain and the United States are, indeed, actual examples of how an accumulation of wealth, so large that its marginal efficiency has fallen more rapidly than the rate of interest can fall in the face of the prevailing institutional and psychological factors, can interfere, in conditions mainly of *laissez-faire,* with a reasonable level of employment and with the standard of life which the technical conditions of production are capable of furnishing.

It follows that of two equal communities, having the same technique but different stocks of capital, the community with the smaller stock of capital may be able for the time being to enjoy a higher standard of life than the community with the larger stock; though when the poorer community has caught up the rich—as, presumably, it eventually will—then both alike will suffer the fate of Midas. This disturbing conclusion depends, of course, on the assumption that the propensity to consume and the rate of investment are not deliberately controlled in the social interest but are mainly left to the influences of *laissez-faire.*

If—for whatever reason—the rate of interest cannot fall as fast as the marginal efficiency of capital would fall with a rate of accumulation corresponding to what the community would choose to save at a rate of interest equal to the marginal efficiency of capital in conditions of full employment, then even a diversion of the desire to hold wealth towards assets, which will in fact yield no economic fruits whatever, will increase economic well-being. In so far as millionaires find their satisfaction in building mighty mansions to contain their bodies when alive and pyramids to shelter them after death, or, repenting of their sins, erect cathedrals and endow monasteries or foreign missions, the day when abundance of capital will interfere with abundance of output may be postponed. "To dig holes in the ground," paid for out of savings, will increase, not only employment, but the real national dividend of useful goods and services. It is not reasonable, however, that a sensible community should be content to remain dependent on such fortuitous and often wasteful mitigations when once we understand the influences upon which effective demand depends.

IV

Let us assume that steps are taken to ensure that the rate of interest is consistent with the rate of investment which corresponds to full employment. Let us assume, further, that State action enters in as a balancing factor to provide that the growth of capital equipment shall be such as to approach saturation-point at a rate which does not put a disproportionate burden on the standard of life of the present generation.

On such assumptions I should guess that a properly run community equipped with modern technical resources, of which the population is not increasing rapidly, ought to be able to bring down the marginal efficiency of capital in equilibrium approximately to zero within a single generation; so that we should attain the conditions of a quasi-stationary community where change and progress would result only from changes in technique, taste, population and institutions, with the products of capital selling at a price proportioned to the labor, etc., embodied in them on just the same principles as govern the prices of consumption-goods into which capital-charges enter in an insignificant degree.

If I am right in supposing it to be comparatively-easy to make capital-goods so abundant that the marginal efficiency of capital is zero, this may be the most sensible way of gradually getting rid of many of the objectionable features of capitalism. For a little reflection will show what enormous social changes would result from a gradual disappearance of a rate of return on accumulated wealth. A man would still be free to accumulate his earned income with a view to spending it at a later date. But his accumulation would not grow. He would simply be in the position of Pope's father, who, when he retired from business, carried a chest of guineas with him to his villa at Twickenham and met his household expenses from it as required.

Though the rentier would disappear, there would still be room, nevertheless, for enterprise and skill in the estimation of prospective yields about which opinions could differ. For the above relates primarily to the pure rate of interest apart from any allowance for risk and the like, and not to the gross yield of assets including the return in respect of risk. Thus unless the pure rate of interest were to be held at a negative figure, there would still be a positive yield to skilled investment in individual assets having a doubtful prospective yield. Provided there was some measurable unwillingness to undertake risk, there would also be a positive net yield from the aggregate of such assets over a period of time. But it is not unlikely that, in such circumstances, the eagerness to obtain a yield from doubtful investments might be such that they would show in the aggregate a *negative* net yield.

CHAPTER 17

The Essential Properties of Interest and Money

I

It seems, then, that the *rate of interest on money* plays a peculiar part in setting a limit to the level of employment, since it sets a standard to which the marginal efficiency of a capital-asset must attain if it is to be newly produced. That this should be so, is, at first sight, most perplexing. It is natural to enquire wherein the peculiarity of money lies as distinct from other assets, whether it is only money which has a rate of interest, and what would happen in a non-monetary economy. Until we have answered these questions, the full significance of our theory will not be clear.

The money-rate of interest—we may remind the reader—is nothing more than the percentage excess of a sum of money contracted for forward delivery, *e.g.* a year hence, over what we may call the "spot" or cash price of the sum thus contracted for forward delivery. It would seem, therefore, that for every kind of capital-asset there must be an analogue of the rate of interest on money. For there is a definite quantity of (*e.g.*) wheat to be delivered a year hence which has the same exchange value today as 100 quarters of wheat for "spot" delivery. If the former quantity is 105 quarters, we may say that the wheat-rate of interest is 5 percent, per annum; and if it is 95 quarters, that it is *minus* 5 percent, per annum. Thus for every durable commodity we have a rate of interest in terms of itself,—a wheat-rate of interest, a copper-rate of interest, a house-rate of interest, even a steel-plant-rate of interest.

The difference between the "future" and "spot" contracts for a commodity, such as wheat, which are quoted in the market, bears a definite relation to the wheat-rate of interest, but, since the future contract is quoted in terms of money for forward delivery and not in terms of wheat for spot delivery, it also brings in the money-rate of interest. The exact relationship is as follows:

Let us suppose that the spot price of wheat is £100 per 100 quarters, that the price of the "future" contract for wheat for delivery a year hence is £107 per 100 quarters, and that the money-rate of interest is 5 percent; what is the wheat-rate of interest? 100 spot will buy £105 for forward delivery, and £105 for forward delivery will buy (105/107).100 (=98) quarters for forward delivery. Alternatively £100 spot will buy 100 quarters of wheat for spot delivery. Thus 100 quarters of wheat for spot delivery will buy 98 quarters for forward delivery. It follows that the wheat-rate of interest is *minus* 2 percent, per annum.[101]

It follows from this that there is no reason why their rates of interest should be the same for different commodities,—why the wheat-rate of interest should be equal to the copper-rate of interest. For the relation between the "spot" and "future" contracts, as quoted in the market, is notoriously different for different commodities. This, we shall find, will lead us to the clue we are seeking. For it may be that it is the *greatest* of the own-rates of interest (as we may call them) which rules the roost (because it is the greatest of these rates that the marginal efficiency of a capital-asset must attain if it is to be newly produced); and that there are reasons why it is the money-rate of interest which is often the greatest (because, as we shall find, certain forces, which operate to reduce the own-rates of interest of other assets, do not operate in the case of money).

It may be added that, just as there are differing commodity-rates of interest at any time, so also exchange dealers are familiar with the fact that the rate of interest is not even the same in terms of two different moneys, *e.g.* sterling and dollars. For here also the difference between the "spot" and "future" contracts for a foreign money in terms of sterling are not, as a rule, the same for different foreign moneys.

Now each of these commodity standards offers us the same facility as money for measuring the marginal efficiency of capital. For we can take any commodity we choose, *e.g.* wheat; calculate the wheat-value of the prospective yields of any capital asset; and the rate of discount which makes the present value of this series of wheat annuities equal to the present supply price of the asset in terms of wheat gives us the marginal efficiency of the asset in terms of wheat. If no change is expected in the relative value of two alternative standards, then the marginal efficiency of a capital-asset will be the same in whichever of the two standards it is measured, since the numerator and denominator of the fraction which leads up to the marginal efficiency will be changed in the same proportion. If, however, one of the alternative standards is expected to change in value in terms of the other, the marginal efficiencies of capital-assets will be changed by the same percentage, according to which standard they are measured in. To illustrate this let us take the simplest case where wheat, one of the alternative standards, is expected to appreciate at a steady rate of a percent, per annum in terms of money; the marginal efficiency of an asset, which is x percent, in terms of money, will then be x - a percent, in terms of wheat. Since the marginal efficiencies of all capital-assets will be altered by the same amount, it follows that their order of magnitude will be the same irrespective of the standard which is selected.

If there were some composite commodity which could be regarded strictly speaking as representative, we could regard the rate of interest and the marginal efficiency of capital in terms of this commodity as being, in a sense, uniquely *the* rate of interest and *the* marginal efficiency of capital. But there are, of course, the same obstacles in the way of this as there are to setting up a unique standard of value.

So far, therefore the money-rate of interest has no uniqueness compared with other rates of interest, but is on precisely the same footing. Wherein, then, lies the peculiarity of the money-rate of interest which gives it the predominating practical importance attributed to it in the preceding chapters. Why should the volume of output and employment be more intimately bound up with the money-rate of interest than with the wheat-rate of interest or the house-rate of interest?

II

Let us consider what the various commodity-rates of interest over a period of (say) a year are likely to be for different types of assets. Since we are taking each commodity in turn as the standard, the returns on each commodity must be reckoned in this context as being measured in terms of itself.

There are three attributes which different types of assets possess in different degrees; namely, as follows:

(i) Some assets produce a yield or output q, measured in terms of themselves, by assisting some process of production or supplying services to a consumer.

(ii) Most assets, except money, suffer some wastage or involve some cost through the mere passage of time (apart from any change in their relative value), irrespective of their being used to produce a yield; *i.e.* they involve a carrying cost c measured in terms of themselves. It does not matter for our present purpose exactly where we draw the line between the costs which we deduct before calculating q and those which we include in c, since in what follows we shall be exclusively concerned with $q - c$.

(iii) Finally, the power of disposal over an asset during a period may offer a potential convenience or security, which is not equal for assets of different kinds, though the assets themselves are of equal initial value. There is, so to speak, nothing to show for this at the end of the period in the shape of output; yet it is something for which people are ready to pay something. The amount (measured in terms of itself) which they are willing to pay for the potential convenience or security given by this power of disposal (exclusive of yield or carrying cost attaching to the asset), we shall call its liquidity-premium l.

It follows that the total return expected from the ownership of an asset over a period is equal to its yield *minus* its carrying cost *plus* its liquidity-premium, *i.e.* to $q - c + l$. That is to say, $q - c + l$ is the own-rate of interest of any commodity, where q, c and l are measured in terms of itself as the standard.

It is characteristic of instrumental capital (*e.g.* a machine) or of consumption capital (*e.g.* a house) which is in use, that its yield should normally exceed its carrying cost, whilst its liquidity-premium is probably negligible; of a stock of liquid goods or of surplus laid-up instrumental or consumption capital that it should incur a carrying cost in terms of itself without any yield to set off against it, the liquidity-premium in this case also being usually negligible as soon as stocks exceed a moderate level, though capable of being significant in special circumstances; and of money that its yield is *nil*, and its carrying cost negligible, but its liquidity-premium substantial. Different commodities may, indeed, have differing degrees of liquidity-premium amongst themselves, and money may incur some degree of carrying costs, *e.g.* for safe custody. But it is an essential difference between money and all (or most) other assets that in the case of money its liquidity-premium much exceeds its carrying cost, whereas in the case of other assets their carrying cost much exceeds their liquidity-premium. Let us, for purposes of illustration, assume that on houses the yield is q_1 and the carrying cost and liquidity-premium negligible; that on wheat the carrying cost is c_2 and the yield and liquidity-premium negligible; and that on money the liquidity-premium is l_3 and the yield and carrying cost negligible. That is to say, q_1 is the house-rate of interest, $-c_2$ the wheat-rate of interest, and l_3 the money-rate of interest.

To determine the relationships between the expected returns on different types of assets which are consistent with equilibrium, we must also know what the changes in relative values during the year are expected to be. Taking money (which need only be a money of account for this purpose, and we could equally well take wheat) as our standard of measurement, let the expected percentage appreciation (or depreciation) of houses be a_1 and of wheat a_2. q_1, $-c_2$ and l_3 we have called the own-rates of interest of houses, wheat and money in terms of themselves as the standard of value; *i.e.* q_1 is the house-rate of interest in terms of houses, $-c_2$ is the wheat-rate of interest in terms of wheat, and l_3 is the money-rate of interest in terms of money. It will also be useful to call $a_1 + q_1$, $a_2 - c_2$ and l_3, which stand for the same quantities reduced to money as the standard of value, the house-rate of money-interest, the wheat-rate of money-interest and the money-rate of money-interest respectively. With this notation it is easy to see that the demand of wealth-owners will be directed to houses, to wheat or to money, according as $a_1 + q_1$, or $a_2 - c_2$ or l_3 is greatest. Thus in equilibrium the demand-prices of houses and wheat in terms of money will be such that there is nothing to choose in the way of advantage between the alternatives;—*i.e.* $a_1 + q_1$, $a_2 - c_2$ and l_3 will be *equal*. The choice of the standard of value will make no difference to this result because a shift from one standard to another will change all the terms equally, *i.e.* by an amount equal to the expected rate of appreciation (or depreciation) of the new standard in terms of the old.

Now those assets of which the normal supply-price is less than the demand-price will be newly produced; and these will be those assets of which the marginal efficiency would be greater (on the basis of their normal supply-price) than the rate of interest (both being measured in the same standard of value whatever it is). As the stock of the assets, which begin by having a marginal efficiency at least equal to the rate of interest, is increased, their marginal efficiency (for reasons, sufficiently obvious, already given) tends to fall.

Thus a point will come at which it no longer pays to produce them, *unless the rate of interest falls* pari passu. When there is *no* asset of which the marginal efficiency reaches the rate of interest, the further production of capital-assets will come to a standstill.

Let us suppose (as a mere hypothesis at this stage of the argument) that there is some asset (*e.g.* money) of which the rate of interest is fixed (or declines more slowly as output increases than does any other commodity's rate of interest); how is the position adjusted? Since $a_1 + q_1$, $a_2 - c_2$ and l_3, are necessarily equal, and since l_3 by hypothesis is either fixed or falling more slowly than q_1, or $-c_2$, it follows that a1 and a_2 must be rising.

In other words, the present money-price of every commodity other than money tends to fall relatively to its expected future price. Hence, if q_1 and $-c_2$ continue to fall, a point comes at which it is not profitable to produce any of the commodities, unless the cost of production at some future date is expected to rise above the present cost by an amount which will cover the cost of carrying a stock produced now to the date of the prospective higher price.

It is now apparent that our previous statement to the effect that it is the money-rate of interest which sets a limit to the rate of output, is not strictly correct. We should have said that it is that asset's rate of interest which declines most slowly as the stock of assets in general increases, which eventually knocks out the profitable production of each of the others,—except in the contingency, just mentioned, of a special relationship between the present and prospective costs of production. As output increases, own-rates of interest decline to levels at which one asset after another falls below the standard of profitable production;—until, finally, one or more own-rates of interest remain at a level which is above that of the marginal efficiency of any asset whatever.

If by *money* we mean the standard of value, it is clear that it is not necessarily the money-rate of interest which makes the trouble. We could not get out of our difficulties (as some have supposed) merely by decreeing that wheat or houses shall be the standard of value instead of gold or sterling. For, it now appears that the same difficulties will ensue if there continues to exist *any* asset of which the own-rate of interest is reluctant to decline as output increases. It may be, for example, that gold will continue to fill this role in a country which has gone over to an inconvertible paper standard.

III

In attributing, therefore, a peculiar significance to the money-rate of interest, we have been tacitly assuming that the kind of money to which we are accustomed has some special characteristics which lead to its own-rate of interest in terms of itself as standard being more reluctant to fall as output increases than the own-rates of interest of any other assets in terms of themselves. Is this assumption justified? Reflection shows, I think, that the following peculiarities, which commonly characterize money as we know it, are capable of justifying it. To the extent that the established standard of value has these peculiarities, the summary statement, that it is the money-rate of interest which is the significant rate of interest, will hold good.

(i) The first characteristic which tends towards the above conclusion is the fact that money has, both in the long and in the short period, a zero, or at any rate a very small, elasticity of production, so far as the power of private enterprise is concerned, as distinct from the monetary authority;—elasticity of production[102] meaning, in this context, the response of the quantity of labor applied to producing it to a rise in the quantity of labor which a unit of it will command. Money, that is to say, cannot be readily produced;—labor cannot be turned on at will by entrepreneurs to produce money in increasing quantities as its price rises in terms of the wage-unit. In the case of an inconvertible managed currency this condition is strictly satisfied. But in the case of a gold-standard currency it is also approximately so, in the sense that the maximum proportional addition to the quantity of labor which can be thus employed is very small, except indeed in a country of which gold-mining is the major industry.

Now, in the case of assets having an elasticity of production, the reason why we assumed their own-rate of interest to decline was because we assumed the stock of them to increase as the result of a higher rate of output. In the case of money, however—postponing, for the moment, our consideration of the effects of reducing the wage-unit or of a deliberate increase in its supply by the monetary authority—the supply is fixed. Thus the characteristic that money cannot be readily produced by labor gives at once some *prima facie* presumption for the view that its own-rate of interest will be relatively reluctant to fall; whereas if money could be grown like a crop or manufactured like a motor-car, depressions would be avoided or mitigated because, if the price of other assets was tending to fall in terms of money, more labor would be diverted into the production of money;—as we see to be the case in gold-mining countries, though for the world as a whole the maximum diversion in this way is almost negligible.

(ii) Obviously, however, the above condition is satisfied, not only by money, but by all pure rent-factors, the production of which is completely inelastic. A second condition, therefore, is required to distinguish money from other rent elements.

The second *differentia* of money is that it has an elasticity of substitution equal, or nearly equal, to zero; which means that as the exchange value of money rises there is no tendency to substitute some other factor for it;—except, perhaps, to some trifling extent, where the money-commodity is also used in manufacture or the arts. This follows from the peculiarity of money that its utility is solely derived from its exchange-value, so that the two rise and fall *pari passu,* with the result that as the exchange value of money rises there is no motive or tendency, as in the case of rent-factors, to substitute some other factor for it.

Thus, not only is it impossible to turn more labor on to producing money when its labor-price rises, but money is a bottomless sink for purchasing power, when the demand for it increases, since there is no value for it at which demand is diverted—as in the case of other rent-factors—so as to slop over into a demand for other things.

The only qualification to this arises when the rise in the value of money leads to uncertainty as to the future maintenance of this rise; in which event, a_1 and a_2, are increased, which is tantamount to an increase in the commodity-rates of money-interest and is, therefore, stimulating to the output of other assets.

(iii) Thirdly, we must consider whether these conclusions are upset by the fact that, even though the quantity of money cannot be increased by diverting labor into producing it, nevertheless an assumption that its effective supply is rigidly fixed would be inaccurate. In particular, a reduction of the wage-unit will release cash from its other uses for the satisfaction of the liquidity-motive; whilst, in addition to this, as money-values fall, the stock of money will bear a higher proportion to the total wealth of the community.

It is not possible to dispute on purely theoretical grounds that this reaction might be capable of allowing an adequate decline in the money-rate of interest. There are, however, several reasons, which taken in combination are of compelling force, why in an economy of the type to which we are accustomed it is very probable that the money-rate of interest will often prove reluctant to decline adequately:

(a) We have to allow, first of all, for the reactions of a fall in the wage-unit on the marginal efficiencies of other assets in terms of money;—for it is the *difference* between these and the money-rate of interest with which we are concerned. If the effect of the fall in the wage-unit is to produce an expectation that it will subsequently rise again, the result will be wholly favorable. If, on the contrary, the effect is to produce an expectation of a further fall, the reaction on the marginal efficiency of capital may offset the decline in the rate of interest.[103]

(b) The fact that wages tend to be sticky in terms of money, the money-wage being more stable than the real wage, tends to limit the readiness of the wage-unit to fall in terms of money. Moreover, if this were not so, the position might be worse rather than better; because, if money-wages were to fall easily, this might often tend to create an expectation of a further fall with unfavorable reactions on the marginal efficiency of capital.

Furthermore, if wages were to be fixed in terms of some other commodity, *e.g.* wheat, it is improbable that they would continue to be sticky. It is because of money's other characteristics—those, especially, which make it *liquid*—that wages, when fixed in terms of it, tend to be sticky.[104]

(c) Thirdly, we come to what is the most fundamental consideration in this context, namely, the characteristics of money which satisfy liquidity-preference. For, in certain circumstances such as will often occur, these will cause the rate of interest to be insensitive, particularly below a certain figure,[105] even to a substantial increase in the quantity of money in proportion to other forms of wealth. In other words, beyond a certain point money's yield from liquidity does not fall in response to an increase in its quantity to anything approaching the extent to which the yield from other types of assets falls when their quantity is comparably increased.

In this connection the low (or negligible) carrying-costs of money play an essential part. For if its carrying-costs were material, they would offset the effect of expectations as to the prospective value of money at future dates. The readiness of the public to increase their stock of money in response to a comparatively small stimulus is due to the advantages of liquidity (real or supposed) having no offset to contend with in the shape of carrying-costs mounting steeply with the lapse of time. In the case of a commodity other than money a modest stock of it may offer some convenience to users of the commodity. But even though a larger stock might have some attractions as representing a store of wealth of stable value, this would be offset by its carrying-costs in the shape of storage, wastage, etc. Hence, after a certain point is reached, there is necessarily a loss in holding a greater stock.

In the case of money, however, this, as we have seen, is not so,—and for a variety of reasons, namely, those which constitute money as being, in the estimation of the public, *par excellence* "liquid." Thus those reformers, who look for a remedy by creating artificial carrying-costs for money through the device of requiring legal-tender currency to be periodically stamped at a prescribed cost in order to retain its quality as money, or in analogous ways, have been on the right track; and the practical value of their proposals deserves consideration.

The significance of the money-rate of interest arises, therefore, out of the combination of the characteristics that, through the working of the liquidity-motive, this rate of interest may be somewhat unresponsive to a change in the proportion which the quantity of money bears to other forms of wealth measured in money, and that money has (or may have) zero (or negligible) elasticities both of production and of substitution. The first condition means that demand may be predominantly directed to money, the second that when this occurs labor cannot be employed in producing more money, and the third that there is no mitigation at any point through some other factor being capable, if it is sufficiently cheap, of doing money's duty equally well. The only relief—apart from changes in the marginal efficiency of capital—can come (so long as the propensity towards liquidity is unchanged) from an increase in the quantity of money, or—which is formally the same thing—a rise in the value of money which enables a given quantity to provide increased money-services.

Thus a rise in the money-rate of interest retards the output of all the objects of which the production is elastic without being capable of stimulating the output of money (the production of which is, by hypothesis, perfectly inelastic). The money-rate of interest, by setting the pace for all the other commodity-rates of interest, holds back investment in the production of these other commodities without being capable of stimulating investment for the production of money, which by hypothesis cannot be produced.

Moreover, owing to the elasticity of demand for liquid cash in terms of debts, a small change in the conditions governing this demand may not much alter the money-rate of interest, whilst (apart from official action) it is also impracticable, owing to the inelasticity of the production of money, for natural forces to bring the money-rate of interest down by affecting the supply side. In the case of an ordinary commodity, the inelasticity of the demand for liquid stocks of it would enable small changes on the demand side to bring its rate of interest up or down with a rush, whilst the elasticity of its supply would also tend to prevent a high premium on spot over forward delivery. Thus with other commodities left to themselves, "natural forces," i.e. the ordinary forces of the market, would tend to bring their rate of interest down until the emergence of full employment had brought about for commodities generally the inelasticity of supply which we have postulated as a normal characteristic of money. Thus in the absence of money and in the absence—we must, of course, also suppose—of any other commodity with the assumed characteristics of money, the rates of interest would only reach equilibrium when there is full employment.

Unemployment develops, that is to say, because people want the moon;—men cannot be employed when the object of desire (i.e. money) is something which cannot be produced and the demand for which cannot be readily choked off. There is no remedy but to persuade the public that green cheese is practically the same thing and to have a green cheese factory (i.e. a central bank) under public control.

It is interesting to notice that the characteristic which has been traditionally supposed to render gold especially suitable for use as the standard of value, namely, its inelasticity of supply, turns out to be precisely the characteristic which is at the bottom of the trouble.

Our conclusion can be stated in the most general form (taking the propensity to consume as given) as follows. No further increase in the rate of investment is possible when the greatest amongst the own-rates of own-interest of all available assets is equal to the greatest amongst the marginal efficiencies of all assets, measured in terms of the asset whose own-rate of own-interest is greatest.

In a position of full employment this condition is necessarily satisfied. But it may also be satisfied before full employment is reached, if there exists some asset, having zero (or relatively small) elasticities of production and substitution,[106] whose rate of interest declines more slowly, as output increases, than the marginal efficiencies of capital-assets measured in terms of it.

IV

We have shown above that for a commodity to be the standard of value is not a sufficient condition for that commodity's rate of interest to be the significant rate of interest. It is, however, interesting to consider how far those characteristics of money as we know it, which make the money-rate of interest the significant rate, are bound up with money being the standard in which debts and wages are usually fixed. The matter requires consideration under two aspects.

In the first place, the fact that contracts are fixed, and wages are usually somewhat stable, in terms of money unquestionably plays a large part in attracting to money so high a liquidity-premium. The convenience of holding assets in the same standard as that in which future liabilities may fall due and in a standard in terms of which the future cost of living is expected to be relatively stable, is obvious. At the same time the expectation of relative stability in the future money-cost of output might not be entertained with much confidence if the standard of value were a commodity with a high elasticity of production. Moreover, the low carrying-costs of money as we know it play quite as large a part as a high liquidity-premium in making the money-rate of interest the significant rate. For what matters is the *difference* between the liquidity-premium and the carrying-costs; and in the case of most commodities, other than such assets as gold and silver and bank-notes, the carrying-costs are at least as high as the liquidity-premium ordinarily attaching to the standard in which contracts and wages are fixed, so that, even if the liquidity-premium now attaching to (*e.g.*) sterling-money were to be transferred to (*e.g.*) wheat, the wheat-rate of interest would still be unlikely to rise above zero. It remains the case, therefore, that, whilst the fact of contracts and wages being fixed in terms of money considerably enhances the significance of the money-rate of interest, this circumstance is, nevertheless, probably insufficient by itself to produce the observed characteristics of the money-rate of interest.

The second point to be considered is more subtle. The normal expectation that the value of output will be more stable in terms of money than in terms of any other commodity, depends of course, not on wages being arranged in terms of money, but on wages being relatively *sticky* in terms of money. What, then, would the position be if wages were expected to be more sticky (*i.e.* more stable) in terms of some one or more commodities other than money, than in terms of money itself? Such an expectation requires, not only that the costs of the commodity in question are expected to be relatively constant in terms of the wage-unit for a greater or smaller scale of output both in the short and in the long period, but also that any surplus over the current demand at cost-price can be taken into stock without cost, *i.e.* that its liquidity-premium exceeds its carrying-costs (for, otherwise, since there is no hope of profit from a higher price, the carrying of a stock must necessarily involve a loss). If a commodity can be found to satisfy these conditions, then, assuredly, it might be set up as a rival to money. Thus it is not logically impossible that there should be a commodity in terms of which the value of output is expected to be more stable than in terms of money. But it does not seem probable that any such commodity exists.

I conclude, therefore, that the commodity, in terms of which wages are expected to be most sticky, cannot be one whose elasticity of production is not least, and for which the excess of carrying-costs over liquidity-premium is not least. In other words, the expectation of a relative stickiness of wages in terms of money is a corollary of the excess of liquidity-premium over carrying-costs being greater for money than for any other asset.

Thus we see that the various characteristics, which combine to make the money-rate of interest significant, interact with one another in a cumulative fashion. The fact that money has low elasticities of production and substitution and low carrying-costs tends to raise the expectation that money-wages will be relatively stable; and this expectation enhances money's liquidity-premium and prevents the exceptional correlation between the money-rate of interest and the marginal efficiencies of other assets which might, if it could exist, rob the money-rate of interest of its sting.

Professor Pigou (with others) has been accustomed to assume that there is a presumption in favor of real wages being more stable than money-wages. But this could only be the case if there were a presumption in favor of stability of employment. Moreover, there is also the difficulty that wage-goods have a high carrying-cost. If, indeed, some attempt were made to stabilize real wages by fixing wages in terms of wage-goods, the effect could only be to cause a violent oscillation of money-prices. For every small fluctuation in the propensity to consume and the inducement to invest would cause money-prices to rush violently between zero and infinity. That money-wages should be more stable than real wages is a condition of the system possessing inherent stability.

Thus the attribution of relative stability to real wages is not merely a mistake in fact and experience. It is also a mistake in logic, if we are supposing that the system in view is stable, in the sense that small changes in the propensity to consume and the inducement to invest do not produce violent effects on prices.

V

As a footnote to the above, it may be worth emphasizing what has been already stated above, namely, that "liquidity" and "carrying-costs" are both a matter of degree;- and that it is only in having the former high relatively to the latter that the peculiarity of "money" consists.

Consider, for example, an economy in which there is no asset for which the liquidity-premium is always in excess of the carrying-costs; which is the best definition I can give of a so-called "non-monetary" economy. There exists nothing, that is to say, but particular consumables and particular capital equipments more or less differentiated according to the character of the consumables which they can yield up, or assist to yield up, over a greater or a shorter period of time; all of which, unlike cash, deteriorate or involve expense, if they are kept in stock, to a value in excess of any liquidity-premium which may attach to them.

In such an economy capital equipments will differ from one another (a) in the variety of the consumables in the production of which they are capable of assisting, (b) in the stability of value of their output (in the sense in which the value of bread is more stable through time than the value of fashionable novelties), and (c) in the rapidity with which the wealth embodied in them can become "liquid," in the sense of producing output, the proceeds of which can be re-embodied if desired in quite a different form.

The owners of wealth will then weigh the lack of "liquidity" of different capital equipments in the above sense as a medium in which to hold wealth against the best available actuarial estimate of their prospective yields after allowing for risk. The liquidity-premium, it will be observed, is partly similar to the risk-premium, but partly different;— the difference corresponding to the difference between the best estimates we can make of probabilities and the confidence with which we make them.[107] When we were dealing, in earlier chapters, with the estimation of prospective yield, we did not enter into detail as to how the estimation is made: and to avoid complicating the argument, we did not distinguish differences in liquidity from differences in risk proper. It is evident, however, that in calculating the own-rate of interest we must allow for both.

There is, clearly, no absolute standard of "liquidity" but merely a scale of liquidity— a varying premium of which account has to be taken, in addition to the yield of use and the carrying-costs, in estimating the comparative attractions of holding different forms of wealth. The conception of what contributes to "liquidity" is a partly vague one, changing from time to time and depending on social practices and institutions. The order of preference in the minds of owners of wealth in which at any given time they express their feelings about liquidity is, however, definite and is all we require for our analysis of the behavior of the economic system. It may be that in certain historic environments the possession of land has been characterized by a high liquidity-premium in the minds of owners of wealth; and since land resembles money in that its elasticities of production and substitution may be very low,[108] it is conceivable that there have been occasions in history in which the desire to hold land has played the same role in keeping up the rate of interest at too high a level which money has played in recent times. It is difficult to trace this influence quantitatively owing to the absence of a forward price for land in terms of itself which is strictly comparable with the rate of interest on a money debt. We have, however, something which has, at times, been closely analogous, in the shape of high rates of interest on mortgages.[109] The high rates of interest from mortgages on land, often exceeding the probable net yield from cultivating the land, have been a familiar feature of many agricultural economies. Usury laws have been directed primarily against encumbrances of this character. And rightly so. For in earlier social organizations where long-term bonds in the modern sense were non-existent, the competition of a high interest-rate on mortgages may well have had the same effect in retarding the growth of wealth from current investment in newly produced capital-assets, as high interest rates on long-term debts have had in more recent times.

That the world after several millennia of steady individual saving, is so poor as it is in accumulated capital-assets, is to be explained, in my opinion, neither by the improvident propensities of mankind, nor even by the destruction of war, but by the high liquidity-premiums formerly attaching to the ownership of land and now attaching to money. I differ in this from the older view as expressed by Marshall with an unusual dogmatic force in his *Principles of Economics*, p. 581:—

> Everyone is aware that the accumulation of wealth is held in check, and the rate
> of interest so far sustained, by the preference which the great mass of humanity

have for present over deferred gratifications, or, in other words, by their unwillingness to wait.

VI

In my *Treatise on Money* I defined what purported to be a unique rate of interest, which I called the *natural rate* of interest—namely, the rate of interest which, in the terminology of my *Treatise*, preserved equality between the rate of saving (as there defined) and the rate of investment. I believed this to be a development and clarification of Wicksell's "natural rate of interest," which was, according to him, the rate which would preserve the stability of some, not quite clearly specified, price-level.

I had, however, overlooked the fact that in any given society there is, on this definition, a *different* natural rate of interest for each hypothetical level of employment. And, similarly, for every rate of interest there is a level of employment for which that rate is the "natural" rate, in the sense that the system will be in equilibrium with that rate of interest and that level of employment. Thus it was a mistake to speak of the natural rate of interest or to suggest that the above definition would yield a unique value for the rate of interest irrespective of the level of employment. I had not then understood that, in certain conditions, the system could be in equilibrium with less than full employment.

I am now no longer of the opinion that the concept of a "natural" rate of interest, which previously seemed to me a most promising idea, has anything very useful or significant to contribute to our analysis. It is merely the rate of interest which will preserve the *status quo;* and, in general, we have no predominant interest in the *status quo* as such.

If there is any such rate of interest, which is unique and significant, it must be the rate which we might term the *neutral* rate of interest,[110] namely, the natural rate in the above sense which is consistent with *full* employment, given the other parameters of the system; though this rate might be better described, perhaps, as the *optimum* rate.

The neutral rate of interest can be more strictly defined as the rate of interest which prevails in equilibrium when output and employment are such that the elasticity of employment as a whole is zero.[111]

The above gives us, once again, the answer to the question as to what tacit assumption is required to make sense of the classical theory of the rate of interest. This theory assumes either that the actual rate of interest is always equal to the neutral rate of interest in the sense in which we have just defined the latter, or alternatively that the actual rate of interest is always equal to the rate of interest which will maintain employment at some specified constant level. If the traditional theory is thus interpreted, there is little or nothing in its practical conclusions to which we need take exception. The classical theory assumes that the banking authority or natural forces cause the market-rate of interest to satisfy one or other of the above conditions; and it investigates what laws will govern the application and rewards of the community's productive resources subject to this assumption. With this limitation in force, the volume of output depends solely on the assumed constant level of employment in conjunction with the current equipment and technique; and we are safely ensconced in a Ricardian world.

CHAPTER 18

The General Theory of Employment Re-Stated

I

We have now reached a point where we can gather together the threads of our argument. To begin with, it may be useful to make clear which elements in the economic system we usually take as given, which are the independent variables of our system and which are the dependent variables.

We take as given the existing skill and quantity of available labor, the existing quality and quantity of available equipment, the existing technique, the degree of competition, the tastes and habits of the consumer, the disutility of different intensities of labor and of the activities of supervision and organization, as well as the social structure including the forces, other than our variables set forth below, which determine the distribution of the national income. This does not mean that we assume these factors to be constant; but merely that, in this place and context, we are not considering or taking into account the effects and consequences of changes in them.

Our independent variables are, in the first instance, the propensity to consume, the schedule of the marginal efficiency of capital and the rate of interest, though, as we have already seen, these are capable of further analysis.

Our dependent variables are the volume of employment and the national income (or national dividend) measured in wage-units.

The factors, which we have taken as given, influence our independent variables, but do not completely determine them. For example, the schedule of the marginal efficiency of capital depends partly on the existing quantity of equipment which is one of the given factors, but partly on the state of long-term expectation which cannot be inferred from the given factors. But there are certain other elements which the given factors determine so completely that we can treat these derivatives as being themselves given. For example, the given factors allow us to infer what level of national income measured in terms of the wage-unit will correspond to any given level of employment; so that, within the economic framework which we take as given, the national income depends on the volume of employment, *i.e.* on the quantity of effort currently devoted to production, in the sense that there is a unique correlation between the two.[112] Furthermore, they allow us to infer the shape of the aggregate supply functions, which embody the *physical* conditions of supply, for different types of products;—that is to say, the quantity of employment which will be devoted to production corresponding to any given level of effective demand measured in terms of wage-units. Finally, they furnish us with the supply function of labor (or effort); so that they tell us *inter alia* at what point the employment function[113] for labor as a whole will cease to be elastic.

The schedule of the marginal efficiency of capital depends, however, partly on the given factors and partly on the prospective yield of capital-assets of different kinds; whilst the rate of interest depends partly on the state of liquidity-preference (*i.e.* on the liquidity function) and partly on the quantity of money measured in terms of wage-units. Thus we can sometimes regard our ultimate independent variables as consisting of (1) the three fundamental psychological factors, namely, the psychological propensity to consume, the psychological attitude to liquidity and the psychological expectation of future yield from capital-assets, (2) the wage-unit as determined by the bargains reached between employers and employed, and (3) the quantity of money as determined by the action of the central bank; so that, if we take as given the factors specified above, these variables determine the national income (or dividend) and the quantity of employment. But these again would be capable of being subjected to further analysis, and are not, so to speak, our ultimate atomic independent elements.

The division of the determinants of the economic system into the two groups of given factors and independent variables is, of course, quite arbitrary from any absolute standpoint. The division must be made entirely on the basis of experience, so as to correspond on the one hand to the factors in which the changes seem to be so slow or so little relevant as to have only a small and comparatively negligible short-term influence on our *quaesitum;* and on the other hand to those factors in which the changes are found in practice to exercise a dominant influence on our *quaesitum.* Our present object is to discover what determines at anytime the national income of a given economic system and (which is almost the same thing) the amount of its employment; which means in a study so complex as economics, in which we cannot hope to make completely accurate generalizations, the factors whose changes *mainly* determine our *quaesitum.* Our final task might be to select those variables which can be deliberately controlled or managed by central authority in the kind of system in which we actually live.

II

Let us now attempt to summarize the argument of the previous chapters; taking the factors in the reverse order to that in which we have introduced them.

There will be an inducement to push the rate of new investment to the point which forces the supply-price of each type of capital-asset to a figure which, taken in conjunction with its prospective yield, brings the marginal efficiency of capital in general to approximate equality with the rate of interest. That is to say, the physical conditions of supply in the capital-goods industries, the state of confidence concerning the prospective yield, the psychological attitude to liquidity and the quantity of money (preferably calculated in terms of wage-units) determine, between them, the rate of new investment.

But an increase (or decrease) in the rate of investment will have to carry with it an increase (or decrease) in the rate of consumption; because the behavior of the public is, in general, of such a character that they are only willing to widen (or narrow) the gap between their income and their consumption if their income is being increased (or diminished). That is to say, changes in the rate of consumption are, in general, *in the same direction* (though smaller in amount) as changes in the rate of income. The relation between the increment of consumption which has to accompany a given increment of saving is given by the marginal propensity to consume. The ratio, thus determined, between an increment of investment and the corresponding increment of aggregate income, both measured in wage-units, is given by the investment multiplier.

Finally, if we assume (as a first approximation) that the employment multiplier is equal to the investment multiplier, we can, by applying the multiplier to the increment (or decrement) in the rate of investment brought about by the factors first described, infer the increment of employment.

An increment (or decrement) of employment is liable, however, to raise (or lower) the schedule of liquidity-preference; there being three ways in which it will tend to increase the demand for money, in as much as the value of output will rise when employment increases even if the wage-unit and prices (in terms of the wage-unit) are unchanged, but, in addition, the wage-unit itself will tend to rise as employment improves, and the increase in output will be accompanied by a rise of prices (in terms of the wage-unit) owing to increasing cost in the short period.

Thus the position of equilibrium will be influenced by these repercussions; and there are other repercussions also. Moreover, there is not one of the above factors which is not liable to change without much warning, and sometimes substantially. Hence the extreme complexity of the actual course of events. Nevertheless, these seem to be the factors which it is useful and convenient to isolate. If we examine any actual problem along the lines of the above schematics, we shall find it more manageable; and our practical intuition (which can take account of a more detailed complex of facts than can be treated on general principles) will be offered a less intractable material upon which to work.

III

The above is a summary of the General Theory. But the actual phenomena of the economic system are also colored by certain special characteristics of the propensity to consume, the schedule of the marginal efficiency of capital and the rate of interest, about which we can safely generalize from experience, but which are not logically necessary.

In particular, it is an outstanding characteristic of the economic system in which we live that, whilst it is subject to severe fluctuations in respect of output and employment, it is not violently unstable. Indeed it seems capable of remaining in a chronic condition of sub-normal activity for a considerable period without any marked tendency either towards recovery or towards complete collapse. Moreover, the evidence indicates that full, or even approximately full, employment is of rare and short-lived occurrence.

Fluctuations may start briskly but seem to wear themselves out before they have proceeded to great extremes, and an intermediate situation which is neither desperate nor satisfactory is our normal lot. It is upon the fact that fluctuations tend to wear themselves out before proceeding to extremes and eventually to reverse themselves, that the theory of business *cycles* having a regular phase has been founded. The same thing is true of prices, which, in response to an initiating cause of disturbance, seem to be able to find a level at which they can remain, for the time being, moderately stable.

Now, since these facts of experience do not follow of logical necessity, one must suppose that the environment and the psychological propensities of the modern world must be of such a character as to produce these results. It is, therefore, useful to consider what hypothetical psychological propensities would lead to a stable system; and, then, whether these propensities can be plausibly ascribed, on our general knowledge of contemporary human nature, to the world in which we live.

The conditions of stability which the foregoing analysis suggests to us as capable of explaining the observed results are the following:

(i) The marginal propensity to consume is such that, when the output of a given community increases (or decreases) because more (or less) employment is being applied to its capital equipment, the multiplier relating the two is greater than unity but not very large.

(ii) When there is a change in the prospective yield of capital or in the rate of interest, the schedule of the marginal efficiency of capital will be such that the change in new investment will not be in great disproportion to the change in the former; *i.e.* moderate changes in the prospective yield of capital or in the rate of interest will not be associated with very great changes in the rate of investment.

(iii) When there is a change in employment, money-wages tend to change in the same direction as, but not in great disproportion to, the change in employment; *i.e.* moderate changes in employment are not associated with very great changes in money-wages. This is a condition of the stability of prices rather than of employment.

(iv) We may add a fourth condition, which provides not so much for the stability of the system as for the tendency of a fluctuation in one direction to reverse itself in due course; namely, that a rate of investment, higher (or lower) than prevailed formerly, begins to react unfavorably (or favorably) on the marginal efficiency of capital if it is continued for a period which, measured in years, is not very large.

(i) Our first condition of stability, namely, that the multiplier, whilst greater than unity, is not very great, is highly plausible as a psychological characteristic of human nature. As real income increases, both the pressure of present needs diminishes and the margin over the established standard of life is increased; and as real income diminishes the opposite is true. Thus it is natural—at any rate on the average of the community—that current consumption should be expanded when employment increases, but by less than the full increment of real income; and that it should be diminished when employment diminishes, but by less than the full decrement of real income. Moreover, what is true of the average of individuals is likely to be also true of governments, especially in an age when a progressive increase of unemployment will usually force the State to provide relief out of borrowed funds.

But whether or not this psychological law strikes the reader as plausible *a priori*, it is certain that experience would be extremely different from what it is if the law did not hold. For in that case an increase of investment, however small, would set moving a cumulative increase of effective demand until a position of full employment had been reached; while a decrease of investment would set moving a cumulative decrease of effective demand until no one at all was employed. Yet experience shows that we are generally in an intermediate position. It is not impossible that there may be a range within which instability does in fact prevail. But, if so, it is probably a narrow one, outside of which in either direction our psychological law must unquestionably hold good. Furthermore, it is also evident that the multiplier, though exceeding unity, is not, in normal circumstances, enormously large. For, if it were, a given change in the rate of investment would involve a great change (limited only by full or zero employment) in the rate of consumption.

(ii) Whilst our first condition provides that a moderate change in the rate of investment will not involve an indefinitely great change in the demand for consumption-goods our second condition provides that a moderate change in the prospective yield of capital-assets or in the rate of interest will not involve an indefinitely great change in the rate of investment. This is likely to be the case owing to the increasing cost of producing a greatly enlarged output from the existing equipment. If, indeed, we start from a position where there are very large surplus resources for the production of capital-assets, there may be considerable instability within a certain range; but this will cease to hold good as soon as the surplus is being largely utilized. Moreover, this condition sets a limit to the instability resulting from rapid changes in the prospective yield of capital-assets due to sharp fluctuations in business psychology or to epoch-making inventions—though more, perhaps, in the upward than in the downward direction.

(iii) Our third condition accords with our experience of human nature. For although the struggle for money-wages is, as we have pointed out above, essentially a struggle to maintain a high *relative* wage, this struggle is likely, as employment increases, to be intensified in each individual case both because the bargaining position of the worker is improved and because the diminished marginal utility of his wage and his improved financial margin make him readier to run risks. Yet, all the same, these motives will operate within limits, and workers will not seek a much greater money-wage when employment improves or allow a very great reduction rather than suffer any unemployment at all.

But here again, whether or not this conclusion is plausible *a priori,* experience shows that some such psychological law must actually hold. For if competition between unemployed workers always led to a very great reduction of the money-wage, there would be a violent instability in the price-level. Moreover, there might be no position of stable equilibrium except in conditions consistent with full employment; since the wage-unit might have to fall without limit until it reached a point where the effect of the abundance of money in terms of the wage-unit on the rate of interest was sufficient to restore a level of full employment. At no other point could there be a resting-place.[114]

(iv) Our fourth condition, which is a condition not so much of stability as of alternate recession and recovery, is merely based on the presumption that capital-assets are of various ages, wear out with time and are not all very long-lived; so that if the rate of investment falls below a certain minimum level, it is merely a question of time (failing large fluctuations in other factors) before the marginal efficiency of capital rises sufficiently to bring about a recovery of investment above this minimum. And similarly, of course, if investment rises to a higher figure than formerly, it is only a question of time before the marginal efficiency of capital falls sufficiently to bring about a recession unless there are compensating changes in other factors.

For this reason, even those degrees of recovery and recession, which can occur within the limitations set by our other conditions of stability, will be likely, if they persist for a sufficient length of time and are not interfered with by changes in the other factors, to cause a reverse movement in the opposite direction, until the same forces as before again reverse the direction.

Thus our four conditions together are adequate to explain the outstanding features of our actual experience;—namely, that we oscillate, avoiding the gravest extremes of fluctuation in employment and in prices in both directions, round an intermediate position appreciably below full employment and appreciably above the minimum employment a decline below which would endanger life.

But we must not conclude that the mean position thus determined by "natural" tendencies, namely, by those tendencies which are likely to persist, failing measures expressly designed to correct them, is, therefore, established by laws of necessity. The unimpeded rule of the above conditions is a fact of observation concerning the world as it is or has been, and not a necessary principle which cannot be changed.

Book V

Money-Wages and Prices

CHAPTER 19

Changes in Money-Wages

I

It would have been an advantage if the effects of a change in money-wages could have been discussed in an earlier chapter. For the Classical Theory has been accustomed to rest the supposedly self-adjusting character of the economic system on an assumed fluidity of money-wages; and, when there is rigidity, to lay on this rigidity the blame of maladjustment.

It was not possible, however, to discuss this matter fully until our own theory had been developed. For the consequences of a change in money-wages are complicated. A reduction in money-wages is quite capable in certain circumstances of affording a stimulus to output, as the classical theory supposes. My difference from this theory is primarily a difference of analysis; so that it could not be set forth clearly until the reader was acquainted with my own method.

The generally accepted explanation is, as I understand it, quite a simple one. It does not depend on roundabout repercussions, such as we shall discuss below. The argument simply is that a reduction in money-wages will *cet. par.* stimulate demand by diminishing the price of the finished product, and will therefore increase output and employment up to the point where the reduction which labor has agreed to accept in its money-wages is just offset by the diminishing marginal efficiency of labor as output (from a given equipment) is increased.

In its crudest form, this is tantamount to assuming that the reduction in money-wages will leave demand unaffected. There may be some economists who would maintain that there is no reason why demand should be affected, arguing that aggregate demand depends on the quantity of money multiplied by the income-velocity of money and that there is no obvious reason why a reduction in money-wages would reduce either the quantity of money or its income-velocity. Or they may even argue that profits will necessarily go up because wages have gone down. But it would, I think, be more usual to agree that the reduction in money-wages may have *some* effect on aggregate demand through its reducing the purchasing power of some of the workers, but that the real demand of other factors, whose money incomes have not been reduced, will be stimulated by the fall in prices, and that the aggregate demand of the workers themselves will be very likely increased as a result of the increased volume of employment, unless the elasticity of demand for labor in response to changes in money-wages is less than unity. Thus in the new equilibrium there will be more employment than there would have been otherwise except, perhaps, in some unusual limiting case which has no reality in practice.

It is from this type of analysis that I fundamentally differ; or rather from the analysis which seems to lie behind such observations as the above. For whilst the above fairly represents, I think, the way in which many economists talk and write, the underlying analysis has seldom been written down in detail.

It appears, however, that this way of thinking is probably reached as follows. In any given industry we have a demand schedule for the product relating the quantities which can be sold to the prices asked; we have a series of supply schedules relating the prices which will be asked for the sale of different quantities on various bases of cost; and these schedules between them lead up to a further schedule which, on the assumption that other costs are unchanged (except as a result of the change in output), gives us the demand schedule for labor in the industry relating the quantity of employment to different levels of wages, the shape of the curve at any point furnishing the elasticity of demand for labor. This conception is then transferred without substantial modification to industry as a whole; and it is supposed, by a parity of reasoning, that we have a demand schedule for labor in industry as a whole relating the quantity of employment to different levels of wages. It is held that it makes no material difference to this argument whether it is in terms of money-wages or of real wages. If we are thinking in terms of money-wages, we must, of course, correct for changes in the value of money; but this leaves the general tendency of the argument unchanged, since prices certainly do not change in exact proportion to changes in money-wages.

If this is the groundwork of the argument (and, if it is not, I do not know what the groundwork is), surely it is fallacious. For the demand schedules for particular industries can only be constructed on some fixed assumption as to the nature of the demand and supply schedules of other industries and as to the amount of the aggregate effective demand. It is invalid, therefore, to transfer the argument to industry as a whole unless we also transfer our assumption that the aggregate effective demand is fixed. Yet this assumption reduces the argument to an *ignoratio elenchi*. For, whilst no one would wish to deny the proposition that a reduction in money-wages *accompanied by the same aggregate effective demand as before* will be associated with an increase in employment, the precise question at issue is whether the reduction in money-wages will or will not be accompanied by the same aggregate effective demand as before measured in money, or, at any rate, by an aggregate effective demand which is not reduced in full proportion to the reduction in money-wages (*i.e.* which is somewhat greater measured in wage-units). But if the classical theory is not allowed to extend by analogy its conclusions in respect of a particular industry to industry as a whole, it is wholly unable to answer the question what effect on employment a reduction in money-wages will have. For it has no method of analysis wherewith to tackle the problem. Professor

Pigou's *Theory of Unemployment* seems to me to get out of the Classical Theory all that can be got out of it; with the result that the book becomes a striking demonstration that this theory has nothing to offer, when it is applied to the problem of what determines the volume of actual employment as a whole.[115]

II

Let us, then, apply our own method of analysis to answering the problem. It falls into two parts, (i) Does a reduction in money-wages have a direct tendency, *cet. par.,* to increase employment, *"cet. par. "* being taken to mean that the propensity to consume, the schedule of the marginal efficiency of capital and the rate of interest are the same as before for the community as a whole? And (2) does a reduction in money-wages have a certain or probable tendency to affect employment in a particular direction through its certain or probable repercussions on these three factors?

The first question we have already answered in the negative in the preceding chapters. For we have shown that the volume of employment is uniquely correlated with the volume of effective demand measured in wage-units, and that the effective demand, being the sum of the expected consumption and the expected investment, cannot change, if the propensity to consume, the schedule of marginal efficiency of capital and the rate of interest are all unchanged. If, without any change in these factors, the entrepreneurs were to increase employment as a whole, their proceeds will necessarily fall short of their supply-price.

Perhaps it will help to rebut the crude conclusion that a reduction in money-wages will increase employment "because it reduces the cost of production," if we follow up the course of events on the hypothesis most favorable to this view, namely that at the outset entrepreneurs *expect* the reduction in money-wages to have this effect. It is indeed not unlikely that the individual entrepreneur, seeing his own costs reduced, will overlook at the outset the repercussions on the demand for his product and will act on the assumption that he will be able to sell at a profit a larger output than before. If, then, entrepreneurs generally act on this expectation, will they in fact succeed in increasing their profits? Only if the community's marginal propensity to consume is equal to unity, so that there is no gap between the increment of income and the increment of consumption; or if there is an increase in investment, corresponding to the gap between the increment of income and the increment of consumption, which will only occur if the schedule of marginal efficiencies of capital has increased relatively to the rate of interest.

Thus the proceeds realized from the increased output will disappoint the entrepreneurs and employment will fall back again to its previous figure, unless the marginal propensity to consume is equal to unity or the reduction in money-wages has had the effect of increasing the schedule of marginal efficiencies of capital relatively to the rate of interest and hence the amount of investment. For if entrepreneurs offer employment on a scale which, if they could sell their output at the expected price, would provide the public with incomes out of which they would save more than the amount of current investment, entrepreneurs are bound to make a loss equal to the difference; and this will be the case absolutely irrespective of the level of money wages. At the best, the date of their disappointment can only be delayed for the interval during which their own investment in increased working capital is filling the gap.

Thus the reduction in money-wages will have no lasting tendency to increase employment except by virtue of its repercussions either on the propensity to consume for the community as a whole, or on the schedule of marginal efficiencies of capital, or on the rate of interest. There is no method of analyzing the effect of a reduction in money-wages, except by following up its possible effects on these three factors.

The most important repercussions on these factors are likely, in practice, to be the following:

(1) A reduction of money-wages will somewhat reduce prices. It will, therefore, involve some redistribution of real income (a) from wage-earners to other factors entering into marginal prime cost whose remuneration has not been reduced, and (b) from entrepreneurs to rentiers to whom a certain income fixed in terms of money has been guaranteed.

What will be the effect of this redistribution on the propensity to consume for the community as a whole? The transfer from wage-earners to other factors is likely to diminish the propensity to consume. The effect of the transfer from entrepreneurs to rentiers is more open to doubt. But if rentiers represent on the whole the richer section of the community and those whose standard of life is least flexible, then the effect of this also will be unfavorable. What the net result will be on a balance of considerations, we can only guess. Probably it is more likely to be adverse than favorable.

(2) If we are dealing with an unclosed system, and the reduction of money-wages is a *reduction relatively to money-wages abroad* when both are reduced to a common unit, it is evident that the change will be favorable to investment, since it will tend to increase the balance of trade. This assumes, of course, that the advantage is not offset by a change in tariffs, quotas, etc. The greater strength of the traditional belief in the efficacy of a reduction in money-wages as a means of increasing employment in Great Britain, as compared with the United States, is probably attributable to the latter being, comparatively with ourselves, a closed system.

(3) In the case of an unclosed system, a reduction of money-wages, though it increases the favorable balance of trade, is likely to worsen the terms of trade. Thus there will be a reduction in real incomes, except in the case of the newly employed, which may tend to increase the propensity to consume.

(4) If the reduction of money-wages is expected to be a *reduction relatively to money-wages in the future,* the change will be favorable to investment, because as we have seen above, it will increase the marginal efficiency of capital; whilst for the same reason it may be favorable to consumption. If, on the other hand, the reduction leads to the expectation, or even to the serious possibility, of a further wage-reduction in prospect, it will have precisely the opposite effect. For it will diminish the marginal efficiency of capital and will lead to the postponement both of investment and of consumption.

(5) The reduction in the wages-bill, accompanied by some reduction in prices and in money-incomes generally, will diminish the need for cash for income and business purposes; and it will therefore reduce protanto the schedule of liquidity-preference for the

community as a whole. *Cet. par.* this will reduce the rate of interest and thus prove favorable to investment. In this case, however, the effect of expectation concerning the future will be of an opposite tendency to those just considered under (4). For, if wages and prices are expected to rise again later on, the favorable reaction will be much less pronounced in the case of long- term loans than in that of short-term loans. If, moreover, the reduction in wages disturbs political confidence by causing popular discontent, the increase in liquidity-preference due to this cause may more than offset the release of cash from the active circulation.

(6) Since a special reduction of money-wages is always advantageous to an individual entrepreneur or industry, a general reduction (though its actual effects are different) may also produce an optimistic tone in the minds of entrepreneurs, which may break through a vicious circle of unduly pessimistic estimates of the marginal efficiency of capital and set things moving again on a more normal basis of expectation. On the other hand, if the workers make the same mistake as their employers about the effects of a general reduction, labor troubles may offset this favorable factor; apart from which, since there is, as a rule, no means of securing a simultaneous and equal reduction of money-wages in all industries, it is in the interest of all workers to resist a reduction in their own particular case. In fact, a movement by employers to revise money-wage bargains downward will be much more strongly resisted than a gradual and automatic lowering of real wages as a result of rising prices.

(7) On the other hand, the depressing influence on entrepreneurs of their greater burden of debt may partly offset any cheerful reactions from the reduction of wages. Indeed if the fall of wages and prices goes far, the embarrassment of those entrepreneurs who are heavily indebted may soon reach the point of insolvency,—with severely adverse effects on investment. Moreover the effect of the lower price-level on the real burden of the National Debt and hence on taxation is likely to prove very adverse to business confidence.

This is not a complete catalogue of all the possible reactions of wage reductions in the complex real world. But the above cover, I think, those which are usually the most important.

If, therefore, we restrict our argument to the case of a closed system, and assume that there is nothing to be hoped, but if anything the contrary, from the repercussions of the new distribution of real incomes on the community's propensity to spend, it follows that we must base any hopes of favorable results to employment from a reduction in money-wages mainly on an improvement in investment due either to an increased marginal efficiency of capital under (4) or a decreased rate of interest under (5). Let us consider these two possibilities in further detail.

The contingency, which is favorable to an increase in the marginal efficiency of capital, is that in which money-wages are believed to have touched bottom, so that further changes are expected to be in the upward direction. The most unfavorable contingency is that in which money-wages are slowly sagging downwards and each reduction in wages serves to diminish confidence in the prospective maintenance of wages. When we enter on a period of weakening effective demand, a sudden large reduction of money-wages to a level so low that no one believes in its indefinite continuance would be the event most favorable to a strengthening of effective demand. But this could only be accomplished by administrative decree and is scarcely practical politics under a system of free wage-bargaining. On the other hand, it would be much better that wages should be rigidly fixed and deemed incapable of material changes, than that depressions should be accompanied by a gradual downward tendency of money-wages, a further moderate wage reduction being expected to signalize each increase of, say, 1 percent, in the amount of unemployment. For example, the effect of an expectation that wages are going to sag by, say, 2 percent in the coming year will be roughly equivalent to the effect of a rise of 2 percent in the amount of interest payable for the same period. The same observations apply *mutatis mutandis* to the case of a boom.

It follows that with the actual practices and institutions of the contemporary world it is more expedient to aim at a rigid money-wage policy than at a flexible policy responding by easy stages to changes in the amount of unemployment;—so far, that is to say, as the marginal efficiency of capital is concerned. But is this conclusion upset when we turn to the rate of interest?

It is, therefore, on the effect of a falling wage- and price-level on the demand for money that those who believe in the self-adjusting quality of the economic system must rest the weight of their argument; though I am not aware that they have done so. If the quantity of money is itself a function of the wage- and price-level, there is indeed, nothing to hope in this direction. But if the quantity of money is virtually fixed, it is evident that its quantity in terms of wage-units can be indefinitely increased by a sufficient reduction in money-wages; and that its quantity in proportion to incomes generally can be largely increased, the limit to this increase depending on the proportion of wage-cost to marginal prime cost and on the response of other elements of marginal prime cost to the falling wage-unit.

We can, therefore, theoretically at least, produce precisely the same effects on the rate of interest by reducing wages, whilst leaving the quantity of money unchanged, that we can produce by increasing the quantity of money whilst leaving the level of wages unchanged. It follows that wage reductions, as a method of securing full employment, are also subject to the same limitations as the method of increasing the quantity of money. The same reasons as those mentioned above, which limit the efficacy of increases in the quantity of money as a means of increasing investment to the optimum figure, apply *mutatis mutandis* to wage reductions. Just as a moderate increase in the quantity of money may exert an inadequate influence over the long-term rate of interest, whilst an immoderate increase may offset its other advantages by its disturbing effect on confidence; so a moderate reduction in money-wages may prove inadequate, whilst an immoderate reduction might shatter confidence even if it were practicable.

There is, therefore, no ground for the belief that a flexible wage policy is capable of maintaining a state of continuous full employment;—any more than for the belief than an open-market monetary policy is capable, unaided, of achieving this result. The economic system cannot be made self-adjusting along these lines.

If, indeed, labor were always in a position to take action (and were to do so), whenever there was less than full employment, to reduce its money demands by concerted action to whatever point was required to make money so abundant relatively to the wage-unit that the rate of interest would fall to a level compatible with full employment, we should, in effect, have monetary management by the Trade Unions, aimed at full employment, instead of by the banking system.

Nevertheless while a flexible wage policy and a flexible money policy come, analytically, to the same thing, inasmuch as they are alternative means of changing the quantity of money in terms of wage-units, in other respects there is, of course, a world of difference between them. Let me briefly recall to the reader's mind the three outstanding considerations.

(i) Except in a socialized community where wage-policy is settled by decree, there is no means of securing uniform wage reductions for every class of labor. The result can only be brought about by a series of gradual, irregular changes, justifiable on no criterion of social justice or economic expediency, and probably completed only after wasteful and disastrous struggles, where those in the weakest bargaining position will suffer relatively to the rest. A change in the quantity of money, on the other hand, is already within the power of most governments by open-market policy or analogous measures. Having regard to human nature and our institutions, it can only be a foolish person who would prefer a flexible wage policy to a flexible money policy, unless he can point to advantages from the former which are not obtainable from the latter. Moreover, other things being equal, a method which it is comparatively easy to apply should be deemed preferable to a method which is probably so difficult as to be impracticable.

(ii) If money-wages are inflexible, such changes in prices as occur (*i.e.* apart from "administered" or monopoly prices which are determined by other considerations besides marginal cost) will mainly correspond to the diminishing marginal productivity of the existing equipment as the output from it is increased. Thus the greatest practicable fairness will be maintained between labor and the factors whose remuneration is contractually fixed in terms of money, in particular the rentier class and persons with fixed salaries on the permanent establishment of a firm, an institution or the State. If important classes are to have their remuneration fixed in terms of money in any case, social justice and social expediency are best served if the remunerations of all factors are somewhat inflexible in terms of money. Having regard to the large groups of incomes which are comparatively inflexible in terms of money, it can only be an unjust person who would prefer a flexible wage policy to a flexible money policy, unless he can point to advantages from the former which are not obtainable from the latter.

(iii) The method of increasing the quantity of money in terms of wage-units by decreasing the wage-unit increases proportionately the burden of debt; whereas the method of producing the same result by increasing the quantity of money whilst leaving the wage-unit unchanged has the opposite effect. Having regard to the excessive burden of many types of debt, it can only be an inexperienced person who would prefer the former.

(iv) If a sagging rate of interest has to be brought about by a sagging wage-level, there is, for the reasons given above, a double drag on the marginal efficiency of capital and a double reason for putting off investment and thus postponing recovery.

III

It follows, therefore, that if labor were to respond to conditions of gradually diminishing employment by offering its services at a gradually diminishing money-wage, this would not, as a rule, have the effect of reducing real wages and might even have the effect of increasing them, through its adverse influence on the volume of output. The chief result of this policy would be to cause a great instability of prices, so violent perhaps as to make business calculations futile in an economic society functioning after the manner of that in which we live. To suppose that a flexible wage policy is a right and proper adjunct of a system which on the whole is one of *laissez-faire,* is the opposite of the truth. It is only in a highly authoritarian society, where sudden, substantial, all-round changes could be decreed that a flexible wage-policy could function with success. One can imagine it in operation in Italy, Germany or Russia, but not in France, the United States or Great Britain.

If, as in Australia, an attempt were made to fix real wages by legislation, then there would be a certain level of employment corresponding to that level of real wages; and the actual level of employment would, in a closed system, oscillate violently between that level and no employment at all, according as the rate of investment was or was not below the rate compatible with that level; whilst prices would be in unstable equilibrium when investment was at the critical level, racing to zero whenever investment was below it, and to infinity whenever it was above it. The element of stability would have to be found, if at all, in the factors controlling the quantity of money being so determined that there always existed some level of money-wages at which the quantity of money would be such as to establish a relation between the rate of interest and the marginal efficiency of capital which would maintain investment at the critical level. In this event employment would be constant (at the level appropriate to the legal real wage) with money-wages and prices fluctuating rapidly in the degree just necessary to maintain this rate of investment at the appropriate figure. In the actual case of Australia, the escape was found, partly of course in the inevitable inefficacy of the legislation to achieve its object, and partly in Australia not being a closed system, so that the level of money-wages was itself a determinant of the level of foreign investment and hence of total investment, whilst the terms of trade were an important influence on real wages.

In the light of these considerations I am now of the opinion that the maintenance of a stable general level of money-wages is, on a balance of considerations, the most advisable policy for a closed system; whilst the same conclusion will hold good for an open system, provided that equilibrium with the rest of the world can be secured by means of fluctuating exchanges. There are advantages in some degree of flexibility in the wages of particular industries so as to expedite transfers from those which are relatively declining to those which are relatively expanding. But the money-wage level as a whole should be maintained as stable as possible, at any rate in the short period.

This policy will result in a fair degree of stability in the price-level;—greater stability, at least, than with a flexible wage policy. Apart from "administered" or monopoly prices, the price-level will only change in the short period in response to the extent that changes in the volume of employment affect marginal prime costs; whilst in the long period they will only change in response to changes in the cost of production due to new technique and new or increased equipment.

It is true that, if there are, nevertheless, large fluctuations in employment, substantial fluctuations in the price-level will accompany them. But the fluctuations will be less, as I have said above, than with a flexible wage policy.

Thus with a rigid wage policy the stability of prices will be bound up in the short period with the avoidance of fluctuations in employment. In the long period, on the other hand, we are still left with the choice between a policy of allowing prices to fall slowly with the progress of technique and equipment whilst keeping wages stable, or of allowing wages to rise slowly whilst keeping prices stable. On the whole my preference is for the latter alternative, on account of the fact that it is easier with an expectation of higher wages in future to keep the actual level of employment within a given range of full employment than with an expectation of lower wages in future, and on account also of the social advantages of gradually diminishing the burden of debt, the greater ease of adjustment from decaying to growing industries, and the psychological encouragement likely to be felt from a moderate tendency for money-wages to increase. But no essential point of principle is involved, and it would lead me beyond the scope of my present purpose to develop in detail the arguments on either side.

APPENDIX TO CHAPTER 19

Professor Pigou's "Theory of Unemployment"

Professor Pigou in his *Theory of Unemployment* makes the volume of employment to depend on two fundamental factors, namely (1) the real rates of wages for which workpeople stipulate, and (2) the shape of the Real Demand Function for Labor. The central sections of his book are concerned with determining the shape of the latter function. The fact that workpeople in fact stipulate, not for a real rate of wages, but for a money-rate, is not ignored ; but, in effect, it is assumed that the actual money-rate of wages divided by the price of wage-goods can be taken to measure the real rate demanded.

The equations which, as he says, " form the starting point of the enquiry" into the Real Demand Function for Labor are given in his *Theory of Unemployment,* p, 90. Since the tacit assumptions, which govern the application of his analysis, slip in near the outset of his argument, I will summarize his treatment up to the crucial point.

Professor Pigou divides industries into those "engaged in making wage-goods at home and in making exports the sale of which creates claims to wage-goods abroad" and the "other" industries: which it is convenient to call the wage-goods industries and the non-wage-goods industries respectively. He supposes x men to be employed in the former and y men in the latter. The output in value of wage-goods of the x men he calls $F(x)$; and the general rate of wages $F'(x)$. This, though he does not stop to mention it, is tantamount to assuming that marginal wage-cost is equal to marginal prime cost.[116] Further, he assumes that $x + y = f(x)$, *i.e.* that the number of men employed in the wage-goods industries is a function of total employment. He then shows that the elasticity of the real demand for labor in the aggregate (which gives us the shape of our *quaesitum,* namely the Real Demand Function for Labor) can be written

$$E_r = f'(x)/f(x) \cdot F'(x)/F''(x)$$

So far as notation goes, there is no significant difference between this and my own modes of expression. In so far as we can identify Professor Pigou's wage-goods with my consumption-goods, and his "other goods" with my investment-goods, it follows that his $F(x)/F'(x)$, being the value of the output of the wage-goods industries in terms of the wage-unit, is the same as my C_w. Furthermore, his function f is (subject to the identification of wage-goods with consumption-goods) a function of what I have called above the employment multiplier k'. For

$$Dx = kDy,$$

so that

$$f'(x) = I + (I/k).$$

Thus Professor Pigou's "elasticity of the real demand for labor in the aggregate" is a concoction similar to some of my own, depending partly on the physical and technical conditions in industry (as given by his function F) and partly on the propensity to consume wage-goods (as given by his function f); provided always that we are limiting ourselves to the special case where marginal labor-cost is equal to marginal prime cost.

To determine the quantity of employment, Professor Pigou then combines with his "real demand for labor," a supply function for labor. He assumes that this is a function of the real wage and of nothing else. But, as he has also assumed that the real wage is a function of the number of men x who are employed in the wage-goods industries, this amounts to assuming that the total supply of labor at the existing real wage is a function of x and of nothing else. That is to say, $n = X(x)$, where n is the supply of labor available at a real wage $F'(x)$.

Thus, cleared of all complication, Professor Pigou's analysis amounts to an attempt to discover the volume of actual employment from the equations

$$x + y = f(x)$$

and

$$n = X(x).$$

But there are here three unknowns and only two equations. It seems clear that he gets round this difficulty by taking $n = x + y$. This amounts, of course, to assuming that there is no involuntary unemployment in the strict sense, *i.e.* that all labor available at the existing real wage is in fact employed. In this case x has the value which satisfies the equation

$$f(x) = X(x);$$

and when we have thus found that the value of x is equal to (say) n_1, y must be equal to $X(n_1) - n_1$ and total employment n is equal to $X(n_1)$.

It is worth pausing for a moment to consider what this involves. It means that, if the supply function of labor changes, more labor being available at a given real wage (so that $n_1 + dn_1$ is now the value of x which satisfies the equation $f(x) = X(x)$), demand for the output of the non-wage-goods industries is such that employment in these industries is bound to increase by just the amount which will preserve equality between $f(n_1 + dn_1)$ and $X(n_1 + dn_1)$. The only other way in which it is possible for aggregate employment to change is through a modification of the propensity to purchase wage-goods and non-wage-goods respectively such that there is an increase of y accompanied by a greater decrease of x.

The assumption that $n = x + y$ means, of course, that labor is always in a position to determine its own real wage. Thus, the assumption that labor is in a position to determine its own real wage, means that the demand for the output of the non-wage-goods industries obeys the above laws. In other words, it is assumed that the rate of interest always adjusts itself to the schedule of the marginal efficiency of capital in such a way as to preserve full employment. Without this assumption Professor Pigou's analysis breaks down and provides no means of determining what the volume of employment will be. It is, indeed, strange that Professor Pigou should have supposed that he could furnish a theory of unemployment which involves no reference at all to changes in the rate of investment (*i.e.* to changes in employment in the non-wage-goods industries) due, not to a change in the supply function of labor, but to changes in (*e.g.*) either the rate of interest or the state of confidence.

His title the "Theory of Unemployment" is, therefore, something of a misnomer. His book is not really concerned with this subject. It is a discussion of how much employment there will be, given the supply function of labor, when the conditions for full employment are satisfied. The purpose of the concept of the elasticity of the real demand for labor in the aggregate is to show by how much *full* employment will rise or fall corresponding to a given shift in the supply function of labor. Or—alternatively and perhaps better—we may regard his book as a non-causative investigation into the functional relationship which determines what level of real wages will correspond to any given level of employment. But it is not capable of telling us what determines the *actual* level of employment; and on the problem of involuntary unemployment it has no direct bearing.

If Professor Pigou were to deny the possibility of involuntary unemployment in the sense in which I have defined it above, as, perhaps, he would, it is still difficult to see how his analysis could be applied. For his omission to discuss what determines the connection between x and y, *i.e.* between employment in the wage-goods and non-wage-goods industries respectively, still remains fatal.

Moreover, he agrees that within certain limits labor in fact often stipulates, not for a given real wage, but for a given money-wage. But in this case the supply function of labor is not a function of $F'(x)$ alone but also of the money-price of wage-goods;—with the result that the previous analysis breaks down and an additional factor has to be introduced, without there being an additional equation to provide for this additional unknown. The pitfalls of a pseudo-mathematical method, which can make no progress except by making everything a function of a single variable and assuming that all the partial differentials vanish, could not be better illustrated. For it is no good to admit later on that there are in fact other variables, and yet to proceed without re-writing everything that has been written up to that point. Thus if (within limits) it is a money-wage for which labor stipulates, we still have insufficient data, even if we assume that $n = x + y$, unless we know what determines the money-price of wage-goods. For, the money-price of wage-goods will depend on the aggregate amount of employment. Therefore we cannot say what aggregate employment will be, until we know the money-price of wage-goods; and we cannot know the money-price of wage-goods until we know the aggregate amount of employment. We are, as I have said, one equation short. Yet it might be a provisional assumption of a rigidity of money-wages, rather than of real wages, which would bring our theory nearest to the facts. For example, money-wages in Great Britain during the turmoil and uncertainty and wide price fluctuations of the decade 1924–1934 were stable within a range of 6 percent, whereas real wages fluctuated by more than 10 percent. A theory cannot claim to be a *general* theory, unless it is applicable to the case where (or the range within which) money-wages are fixed, just as much as to any other case. Politicians are entitled to complain that money-wages *ought* to be highly flexible; but a theorist must be prepared to deal indifferently with either state of affairs. A scientific theory cannot require the facts to conform to its own assumptions.

When Professor Pigou comes to deal expressly with the effect of a reduction of money-wages, he again, palpably (to my mind), introduces too few data to permit of any definite answer being obtainable. He begins by rejecting the argument (*op. cit.* p. 101) that, if marginal prime cost is equal to marginal wage-cost, non-wage-earners' incomes will be altered, when money-wages are reduced, in the same proportion as wage-earners', on the ground that this is only valid, *if* the quantity of employment remains unaltered—which is the very point under discussion. But he proceeds on the next page (*op. cit.* p. 102) to make the same mistake himself by taking as his assumption that "at the outset nothing has happened to non-wage-earners' money-income," which, as he has just shown, is only valid *if* the quantity of employment does not remain unaltered—which is the very point under discussion. In fact, no answer is possible, unless other factors are included in our data.

The manner in which the admission, that labor in fact stipulates for a given money-wage and not for a given real wage (provided that the real wage does not fall below a certain minimum), affects the analysis, can also be shown by pointing out that in this case the assumption that more labor is not available except at a greater real wage, which is fundamental to most of the argument, breaks down. For example, Professor Pigou rejects (*op. cit.* p. 75) the theory of the multiplier by assuming that the rate of real wages is given, *i.e.* that, there being already full employment, no additional labor is forthcoming at a lower real wage. Subject to this assumption, the argument is, of course, correct. But in this passage Professor Pigou is criticizing a proposal relating to practical policy; and it is fantastically far removed from the facts to assume, at a time when statistical unemployment in Great Britain exceeded 2,000,000 (*i.e.* when there were 2,000,000 men willing to work at the existing money-wage), that any rise in the cost of living, however moderate, relatively to the money-wage would cause the withdrawal from the labor market of more than the equivalent of all these 2,000,000 men.

It is important to emphasize that the whole of Professor Pigou's book is written on the assumption *that any rise in the cost of living, however moderate, relatively to the money-wage will cause the withdrawal from the labor market of a number of workers greater than that of all the existing unemployed.*

Moreover, Professor Pigou does not notice in this passage (*op. cit.* p. 75) that the argument, which he advances against "secondary" employment as a result of public works, is, on the same assumptions, equally fatal to increased "primary" employment from the same policy, for if the real rate of wages ruling in the wage-goods industries is given, no increased employment whatever is possible—except, indeed, as a result of non-wage-earners reducing their consumption of wage-goods. For those newly engaged in the primary employment will presumably increase their consumption of wage-goods which will reduce the real wage and hence (on his assumptions) lead to a withdrawal of labor previously employed elsewhere. Yet Professor Pigou accepts, apparently, the possibility of increased primary employment. The line between primary and secondary employment seems to be the critical psychological point at which his good common sense ceases to overbear his bad theory.

The difference in the conclusions to which the above differences in assumptions and in analysis lead can be shown by the following important passage in which Professor Pigou sums up his point of view: "With perfectly free competition among workpeople and labor perfectly mobile, the nature of the relation (*i.e.* between the real wage-rates for which people stipulate and the demand function for labor) will be very simple. There will always be at work a strong tendency for wage-rates to be so related to demand that everybody is employed. Hence, in stable conditions everyone will actually be employed. The implication is that such unemployment as exists at any time is due wholly to the fact that changes in demand conditions are continually taking place and that frictional resistances prevent the appropriate wage adjustments from being made instantaneously."[117]

He concludes (*op. cit.* p. 253) that unemployment is primarily due to a wage policy which fails to adjust itself sufficiently to changes in the real demand function for labor.

Thus Professor Pigou believes that in the long run unemployment can be cured by wage adjustments;[118] whereas I maintain that the real wage (subject only to a minimum set by the marginal disutility of employment) is not primarily determined by "wage adjustments" (though these may have repercussions) but by the other forces of the system, some of which (in particular the relation between the schedule of the marginal efficiency of capital and the rate of interest) Professor Pigou has failed, if I am right, to include in his formal scheme.

Finally, when Professor Pigou comes to the "Causation of Unemployment" he speaks, it is true, of fluctuations in the state of demand, much as I do. But he identifies the state of demand with the Real Demand Function for Labor, forgetful of how narrow a thing the latter is on his definition. For the Real Demand Function for Labor depends by definition (as we have seen above) on *nothing* but two factors, namely (1) the relationship in any given environment between the total number of men employed and the number who have to be employed in the wage-goods industries to provide them with what they consume, and (2) the state of marginal productivity in the wage-goods industries. Yet in Part V. of his *Theory of Unemployment* fluctuations in the state of "the real demand for labor" are given a position of importance. The "real demand for labor" is regarded as a factor which is susceptible of wide short-period fluctuations (*op. cit.* Part V. chaps, vi.-xii.), and the suggestion seems to be that swings in "the real demand for labor" are, in combination with the failure of wage policy to respond sensitively to such changes, largely responsible for the trade cycle. To the reader all this seems, at first, reasonable and familiar. For, unless he goes back to the definition, "fluctuations in the real demand for labor" will convey to his mind the same sort of suggestion as I mean to convey by "fluctuations in the state of aggregate demand." But if we go back to the definition of the "real demand for labor," all this loses its plausibility. For we shall find that there is nothing in the world less likely to be subject to sharp short-period swings than this factor.

Professor Pigou's "real demand for labor" depends by definition on nothing but $F(x)$, which represents the physical conditions of production in the wage-goods industries, and $f(x)$, which represents the functional relationship between employment in the wage-goods industries and total employment corresponding to any given level of the latter. It is difficult to see a reason why either of these functions should change, except gradually over a long period. Certainly there seems no reason to suppose that they are likely to fluctuate during a trade cycle. For $F(x)$ can only change slowly, and, in a technically progressive community, only in the forward direction; whilst $f(x)$ will remain stable, unless we suppose a sudden outbreak of thrift in the working classes, or, more generally, a sudden shift in the propensity to consume. I should expect, therefore, that the real demand for labor would remain virtually constant throughout a trade cycle. I repeat that Professor Pigou has altogether omitted from his analysis the unstable factor, namely fluctuations in the scale of investment, which is most often at the bottom of the phenomenon of fluctuations in employment.

I have criticized at length Professor Pigou's theory of unemployment not because he seems to me to be more open to criticism than other economists of the classical school; but because his is the only attempt with which I am acquainted to write down the classical theory of unemployment precisely. Thus it has been incumbent on me to raise my objections to this theory in the most formidable presentment in which it has been advanced.

CHAPTER 20

The Employment Function[119]

I

In Chapter 3 we have defined the aggregate supply function Z=f(N), which relates the employment N with the aggregate supply price of the corresponding output. The *employment function* only differs from the aggregate supply function in that it is, in effect, its inverse function and is defined in terms of the wage-unit; the object of the employment function being to relate the amount of the effective demand, measured in terms of the wage-unit, directed to a given firm or industry or to industry as a whole with the amount of employment, the supply price of the output of which will compare to that amount of effective demand. Thus if an amount of effective demand D_{wr}, measured in wage-units, directed to a firm or industry calls forth an amount of employment N_r in that firm or industry, the employment function is given by $N_r = F_r(D_{wr})$. Or, more generally, if we are entitled to assume that D_{wr} is a unique function of the total effective demand D_w, the employment function is given by $N_r = F_r(D_w)$. That is to say, N_r men will be employed in industry r when effective demand is D_w.

We shall develop in this chapter certain properties of the employment function. But apart from any interest which these may have, there are two reasons why the substitution of the employment function for the ordinary supply curve is consonant with the methods and objects of this book. In the first place, it expresses the relevant facts in terms of the units to which we have decided to restrict ourselves, without introducing any of the units which have a dubious quantitative character. In the second place, it lends itself to the problems of industry and output as a *whole,* as distinct from the problems of a single industry or firm in a given environment, more easily than does the ordinary supply curve—for the following reasons.

The ordinary demand curve for a particular commodity is drawn on some assumption as to the incomes of members of the public, and has to be re-drawn if the incomes change. In the same way the ordinary supply curve for a particular commodity is drawn on some assumption as to the output of industry as a whole and is liable to change if the aggregate output of industry is changed. When, therefore, we are examining the response of individual industries to changes in *aggregate* employment, we are necessarily concerned, not with a single demand curve for each industry, in conjunction with a single supply curve, but with two families of such curves corresponding to different assumptions as to the aggregate employment. In the case of the employment function, however, the task of arriving at a function for industry *as* a whole which will reflect changes in employment as a whole is more practicable.

For let us assume (to begin with) that the propensity to consume is given as well as the other factors which we have taken as given in Chapter 18 above, and that we are considering changes in employment in response to changes in the rate of investment. Subject to this assumption, for every level of effective demand in terms of wage-units there will be a corresponding aggregate employment and this effective demand will be divided in determinate proportions between consumption and investment. Moreover, each level of effective demand will correspond to a given distribution of income. It is reasonable, therefore, further to assume that corresponding to a given level of aggregate effective demand there is a unique distribution of it between different industries.

This enables us to determine what amount of employment in each industry will correspond to a given level of aggregate employment. That is to say, it gives us the amount of employment in each particular industry corresponding to each level of aggregate effective demand measured in terms of wage-units, so that the conditions are satisfied for the second form of the employment function for the industry, defined above, namely $N_r = F_r(D_w)$. Thus we have the advantage that, in these conditions, the individual employment functions are additive in the sense that the employment function for industry as a whole, corresponding to a given level of effective demand, is equal to the sum of the employment functions for each separate industry;

$$F(D_w) = N = SN_r = SF_r(D_w).$$

Next, let us define the elasticity of employment. The elasticity of employment for a given industry is

$$e_{er} = (dN_r/dD_{wr}) \cdot (D_{wr}/N_r),$$

since it measures the response of the number of labor-units employed in the industry to changes in the number of wage-units which are expected to be spent on purchasing its output. The elasticity of employment for industry as a whole we shall write

$$e_e = (dN/dD_w) \cdot (D_w/N).$$

Provided that we can find some sufficiently satisfactory method of measuring output, it is also useful to define what may be called the elasticity of output or production, which measures the rate at which output in any industry increases when more effective demand in terms of wage-units is directed towards it, namely

$$e_{or} = (dO_r/dD_{wr}) \cdot (D_{wr}/O_r),$$

Provided we can assume that the price is equal to the marginal prime cost, we then have

$$DD_{wr} = 1/(1-e_{or}) \cdot DP_r$$

where P_r is the expected profit.[120] It follows from this that if $e_{or} = 0$, *i.e.* if the output of the industry is perfectly inelastic, the whole of the increased effective demand (in terms of wage-units) is expected to accrue to the entrepreneur as profit, *i.e.* $DD_{wr} = DP_r$; whilst if $e_{or} = 1$; *i.e.* if the elasticity of output is unity, no part of the increased effective demand is expected to accrue as profit, the whole of it being absorbed by the elements entering into marginal prime cost.

Moreover, if the output of an industry is a function (N_r) of the labor employed in it, we have[121]

$$(1 - e_{or})/e_{or} = - N_r f''(N_r)/P_{wr}\{f'(N_r)\}^2$$

where p_{wr} is the expected price of a unit of output in terms of the wage-unit. Thus the condition $e_{or} = 1$ means that $f''(N_r) = 0$, *i.e.* that there are constant returns in response to increased employment.

Now, in so far as the classical theory assumes that real wages are always equal to the marginal disutility of labor and that the latter increases when employment increases, so that the labor supply will fall off, *cet. par.*, if real wages are reduced, it is assuming that in practice it is impossible to increase expenditure in terms of wage-units. If this were true, the concept of elasticity of employment would have no field of application. Moreover, it would, in this event, be impossible to increase employment by increasing expenditure in terms of money; for money-wages would rise proportionately to the increased money expenditure, so that there would be no increase of expenditure in terms of wage-units and consequently no increase in employment. But if the classical assumption does not hold good, it will be possible to increase employment by increasing expenditure in terms of money until real wages have fallen to equality with the marginal disutility of labor, at which point there will, by definition, be full employment.

Ordinarily, of course, e_{or} will have a value intermediate between zero and unity. The extent to which prices (in terms of wage-units) will rise, *i.e.* the extent to which real wages will fall, when money expenditure is increased, depends, therefore, on the elasticity of output in response to expenditure in terms of wage-units.

Let the elasticity of the expected price p_{wr} in response to changes in effective demand D_{wr} namely

$$(dp_{wr}/dD_{wr}) \cdot (D_{wr}/p_{wr}),$$

be written e'_{pr}

Since $O_r p_{wr} = D_{wr}$ we have

$$dO_r/dD_{wr} \cdot D_{wr}/O_r + dp_{wr}/dD_{wr} \cdot D_{wr}/p_{wr} = 1$$

or

$$e'_{pr} + e_{or} = 1.$$

That is to say, the sum of the elasticities of price and of output in response to changes in effective demand (measured in terms of wage-units) is equal to unity. Effective demand spends itself, partly in affecting output and partly in affecting price, according to this law.

If we are dealing with industry as a whole and are prepared to assume that we have a unit in which output as a whole can be measured, the same line of argument applies, so that $e'_p + e_0 = 1$, where the elasticities without a suffix r apply to industry as a whole.

Let us now measure values in money instead of wage-units and extend to this case our conclusions in respect of industry as a whole.

If W stands for the money-wages of a unit of labor and p for the expected price of a unit of output as a whole in terms of money, we can write

$$e_p(Ddp/pdD)$$

for the elasticity of money-prices in response to changes in effective demand measured in terms of money, and

$$e_w(DdW/WdD)$$

for the elasticity of money-wages in response to change in effective demand in terms of money. It is then easily shown that

$$e_p = 1 - e_0(1 - e_w). \text{[122]}$$

This equation is, as we shall see in the next chapter, a first step to a Generalized Quantity Theory of Money.

If eo = o or if ew = I, output will be unaltered and prices will rise in the same proportion as effective demand in terms of money. Otherwise they will rise in a smaller proportion.

II

Let us return to the employment function. We have assumed in the foregoing that to every level of aggregate effective demand there corresponds a unique distribution of effective demand between the products of each individual industry. Now, as aggregate expenditure changes, the corresponding expenditure on the products of an individual industry will not, in general, change in the same proportion;—partly because individuals will not, as their incomes rise, increase the amount of the products of each separate industry, which they purchase, in the same proportion, and partly because the prices of different commodities will respond in different degrees to increases in expenditure upon them.

It follows from this that the assumption upon which we have worked hitherto, that changes in employment depend solely on changes in aggregate effective demand (in terms of wage-units), is no better than a first approximation, if we admit that there is more than one way in which an increase of income can be spent. For the way in which we suppose the increase in aggregate demand to be distributed between different commodities may considerably influence the volume of employment. If, for example, the increased demand is largely directed towards products which have a high elasticity of employment, the aggregate increase in employment will be greater than if it is largely directed towards products which have a low elasticity of employment.

In the same way employment may fall off without there having been any change in aggregate demand, if the direction of demand is changed in favor of products having a relatively low elasticity of employment.

These considerations are particularly important if we are concerned with short-period phenomena in the sense of changes in the amount or direction of demand which are not foreseen some time ahead. Some products take time to produce, so that it is practically impossible to increase the supply of them quickly. Thus, if additional demand is directed to them without notice, they will show a low elasticity of employment; although it may be that, given sufficient notice, their elasticity of employment approaches unity.

It is in this connection that I find the principal significance of the conception of a period of production. A product, I should prefer to say,[123] has a period of production n if n time-units of notice of changes in the demand for it have to be given if it is to offer its maximum elasticity of employment. Obviously consumption-goods, taken as a whole, have in this sense the longest period of production, since of every productive process they constitute the last stage. Thus if the first impulse towards the increase in effective demand comes from an increase in consumption, the initial elasticity of employment will be further below its eventual equilibrium-level than if the impulse comes from an increase in investment. Moreover, if the increased demand is directed to products with a relatively low elasticity of employment, a larger proportion of it will go to swell the incomes of entrepreneurs and a smaller proportion to swell the incomes of wage-earners and other prime-cost factors; with the possible result that the repercussions may be somewhat less favorable to expenditure, owing to the likelihood of entrepreneurs saving more of their increment of income than wage-earners would. Nevertheless the distinction between the two cases must not be over-stated, since a large part of the reactions will be much the same in both.[124]

However long the notice given to entrepreneurs of a prospective change in demand, it is not possible for the initial elasticity of employment, in response to a given increase of investment, to be as great as its eventual equilibrium value, unless there are surplus stocks and surplus capacity at every stage of production. On the other hand, the depletion of the surplus stocks will have an offsetting effect on the amount by which investment increases. If we suppose that there are initially some surpluses at every point, the initial elasticity of employment may approximate to unity; then after the stocks have been absorbed, but before an increased supply is coming forward at an adequate rate from the earlier stages of production, the elasticity will fall away; rising again towards unity as the new position of equilibrium is approached. This is subject, however, to some qualification in so far as there are rent factors which absorb more expenditure as employment increases, or if the rate of interest increases. For these reasons perfect stability of prices is impossible in an economy subject to change—unless, indeed, there is some peculiar mechanism which ensures temporary fluctuations of just the right degree in the propensity to consume. But price-instability arising in this way does not lead to the kind of profit stimulus which is liable to bring into existence excess capacity.

For the windfall gain will wholly accrue to those entrepreneurs who happen to possess products at a relatively advanced stage of production, and there is nothing which the entrepreneur, who does not possess specialized resources of the right kind, can do to attract this gain to himself. Thus the inevitable price-instability due to change cannot affect the *actions* of entrepreneurs, but merely directs a *de facto* windfall of wealth into the laps of the lucky ones (*mutatis mutandis* when the supposed change is in the other direction). This fact has, I think, been overlooked in some contemporary discussions of a practical policy aimed at stabilizing prices. It is true that in a society liable to change such a policy cannot be perfectly successful. But it does not follow that every small temporary departure from price stability necessarily sets up a cumulative disequilibrium.

III

We have shown that when effective demand is deficient there is under-employment of labor in the sense that there are men unemployed who would be willing to work at less than the existing real wage. Consequently, as effective demand increases, employment increases, though at a real wage equal to or less than the existing one, until a point comes at which there is no surplus of labor available at the then existing real wage; *i.e.* no more men (or hours of labor) available unless money-wages rise (from this point onwards) *faster* than prices. The next problem is to consider what will happen if, when this point has been reached, expenditure still continues to increase.

Up to this point the decreasing return from applying more labor to a given capital equipment has been offset by the acquiescence of labor in a diminishing real wage. But after this point a unit of labor would require the inducement of the equivalent of an increased quantity of product, whereas the yield from applying a further unit would be a diminished quantity of product. The conditions of strict equilibrium require, therefore, that wages and prices, and consequently profits also, should all rise in the same proportion as expenditure, the "real" position, including the volume of output and employment, being left unchanged in all respects. We have reached, that is to say, a situation in which the crude quantity theory of money (interpreting "velocity" to mean "income-velocity") is fully satisfied; for output does not alter and prices rise in exact proportion to MV.

Nevertheless there are certain practical qualifications to this conclusion which must be borne in mind in applying it to an actual case.

(1) For a time at least, rising prices may delude entrepreneurs into increasing employment beyond the level which maximizes their individual profits measured in terms of the product. For they are so accustomed to regard rising sale-proceeds in terms of money as a signal for expanding production, that they may continue to do so when this policy has in fact ceased to be to their best advantage; *i.e.* they may underestimate their marginal user cost in the new price environment.

(2) Since that part of his profit which the entrepreneur has to hand on to the rentier is fixed in terms of money, rising prices, even though unaccompanied by any change in output, will re-distribute incomes to the advantage of the entrepreneur and to the disadvantage of the rentier, which may have a reaction on the propensity to consume. This, however, is not a process which will have only begun when full employment has been, attained;—it will have been making steady progress all the time that the expenditure was increasing. If the rentier is less prone to spend than the entrepreneur, the gradual withdrawal of real income from the former will mean that full employment will be reached with a smaller increase in the quantity of money and a smaller reduction in the rate of interest than will be the case if the opposite hypothesis holds. After full employment has been reached, a further rise of prices will, if the first hypothesis continues to hold, mean that the rate of interest will have to rise somewhat to prevent prices from rising indefinitely, and that the increase in the quantity of money will be less than in proportion to the increase in expenditure; whilst if the second hypothesis holds, the opposite will be the case. It may be that, as the real income of the rentier is diminished, a point will come when, as a result of his growing relative impoverishment, there will be a change-over from the first hypothesis to the second, which point may be reached either before or after full employment has been attained.

IV

There is, perhaps, something a little perplexing in the apparent asymmetry between Inflation and Deflation. For whilst a deflation of effective demand below the level required for full employment will diminish employment as well as prices, an inflation of it above this level will merely affect prices. This asymmetry is, however, merely a reflection of the fact that, whilst labor is always in a position to refuse to work on a scale involving a real wage which is less than the marginal disutility of that amount of employment, it is not in a position to insist on being offered work on a scale involving a real wage which is not greater than the marginal disutility of that amount of employment.

CHAPTER 21

The Theory of Prices

I

So long as economists are concerned with what is called the Theory of Value, they have been accustomed to teach that prices are governed by the conditions of supply and demand; and, in particular, changes in marginal cost and the elasticity of short-period supply have played a prominent part. But when they pass in volume II, or more often in a separate treatise, to the Theory of Money and Prices, we hear no more of these homely but intelligible concepts and move into a world where prices are governed by the quantity of money, by its income-velocity, by the velocity of circulation relatively to the volume of transactions, by hoarding, by forced saving, by inflation and deflation *et hoc genus omne;* and little or no attempt is made to relate these vaguer phrases to our former notions of the elasticities of supply and demand. If we reflect on what we are being taught and try to rationalize it, in the simpler discussions it seems that the elasticity of supply must have become zero and demand proportional to the quantity of money; whilst in the more sophisticated we are lost in a haze where nothing is clear and everything is possible. We have all of us become used to finding ourselves sometimes on the one side of the moon and sometimes on the other, without knowing what route or journey connects them, related, apparently, after the fashion of our waking and our dreaming lives.

One of the objects of the foregoing chapters has been to escape from this double life and to bring the theory of prices as a whole back to close contact with the theory of value. The division of Economics between the Theory of Value and Distribution on the one hand and the Theory of Money on the other hand is, I think, a false division. The right dichotomy is, I suggest, between the Theory of the Individual Industry or Firm and of the rewards and the distribution between different uses of a *given* quantity of resources on the one hand, and the Theory of Output and Employment *as a whole* on the other hand. So long as we limit ourselves to the study of the individual industry or firm on the assumption that the aggregate quantity of employed resources is constant, and, provisionally, that the conditions of other industries or firms are unchanged, it is true that we are not concerned with the significant characteristics of money. But as soon as we pass to the problem of what determines output and employment as a whole, we require the complete theory of a Monetary Economy.

Or, perhaps, we might make our line of division between the theory of stationary equilibrium and the theory of shifting equilibrium—meaning by the latter the theory of a system in which changing views about the future are capable of influencing the present situation. *For the importance of money essentially flows from its being a link between the present and the future.* We can consider what distribution of resources between different uses will be consistent with equilibrium under the influence of normal economic motives in a world in which our views concerning the future are fixed and reliable in all respects;—with a further division, perhaps, between an economy which is unchanging and one subject to change, but where all things are foreseen from the beginning. Or we can pass from this simplified propaedeutic to the problems of the real world in which our previous expectations are liable to disappointment and expectations concerning the future affect what we do today. It is when we have made this transition that the peculiar properties of money as a link between the present and the future must enter into our calculations. But, although the theory of shifting equilibrium must necessarily be pursued in terms of a monetary economy, it remains a theory of value and distribution and not a separate "theory of money." Money in its significant attributes is, above all, a subtle device for linking the present to the future; and we cannot even begin to discuss the effect of changing expectations on current activities except in monetary terms. We cannot get rid of money even by abolishing gold and silver and legal tender instruments. So long as there exists any durable asset, it is capable of possessing monetary attributes[125] and, therefore, of giving rise to the characteristic problems of a monetary economy.

II

In a single industry its particular price-level depends partly on the rate of remuneration of the factors of production which enter into its marginal cost, and partly on the scale of output. There is no reason to modify this conclusion when we pass to industry as a whole. The general price-level depends partly on the rate of remuneration of the factors of production which enter into marginal cost and partly on the scale of output as a whole, *i.e.* (taking equipment and technique as given) on the volume of employment. It is true that, when we pass to output as a whole, the costs of production in any industry partly depend on the output of other industries. But the more significant change, of which we have to take account, is the effect of changes in *demand* both on costs and on volume. It is on the side of demand that we have to introduce quite new ideas when we are dealing with demand as a whole and no longer with the demand for a single product taken in isolation, with demand as a whole assumed to be unchanged.

III

If we allow ourselves the simplification of assuming that the rates of remuneration of the different factors of production which enter into marginal cost all change in the same proportion, *i.e.* in the same proportion as the wage-unit, it follows that the general price-level (taking equipment and technique as given) depends partly on the wage-unit and partly on the volume of employment. Hence the effect of changes in the quantity of money on the price-level can be considered as being compounded of the effect on the wage-unit and the effect on employment.

To elucidate the ideas involved, let us simplify our assumptions still further, and assume (1) that all unemployed resources are homogeneous and interchangeable in their efficiency to produce what is wanted, and (2) that the factors of production entering into marginal cost are content with the same money-wage so long as there is a surplus of them unemployed. In this case we have constant returns and a rigid wage-unit, so long as there is any unemployment. It follows that an increase in the quantity of money will have no effect whatever on prices, so long as there is any unemployment, and that employment will increase in exact proportion to any increase in effective demand brought about by the increase in the quantity of money; whilst as soon as full employment is reached, it will thence-forward be the wage-unit and prices which will increase in exact proportion to the increase in effective demand. Thus if there is perfectly elastic supply so long as there is unemployment, and perfectly inelastic supply so soon as full employment is reached, and if effective demand changes in the same proportion as the quantity of money, the Quantity Theory of Money can be enunciated as follows: "So long as there is unemployment, *employment* will change in the same proportion as the quantity of money; and when there is full employment, *prices* will change in the same proportion as the quantity of money."

Having, however, satisfied tradition by introducing a sufficient number of simplifying assumptions to enable us to enunciate a Quantity Theory of Money, let us now consider the possible complications which will in fact influence events:

(1) Effective demand will not change in exact proportion to the quantity of money.

(2) Since resources are not homogeneous, there will be diminishing, and not constant, returns as employment gradually increases.

(3) Since resources are not interchangeable, some commodities will reach a condition of inelastic supply whilst there are still unemployed resources available for the production of other commodities.

(4) The wage-unit will tend to rise, before full employment has been reached.

(5) The remunerations of the factors entering into marginal cost will not all change in the same proportion.

Thus we must first consider the effect of changes in the quantity of money on the quantity of effective demand; and the increase in effective demand will, generally speaking, spend itself partly in increasing the quantity of employment and partly in raising the level of prices. Thus instead of constant prices in conditions of unemployment, and of prices rising in proportion to the quantity of money in conditions of full employment, we have in fact a condition of prices rising gradually as employment increases. The Theory of Prices, that is to say, the analysis of the relation between changes in the quantity of money and changes in the price-level with a view to determining the elasticity of prices in response to changes in the quantity of money, must, therefore, direct itself to the five complicating factors set forth above.

We will consider each of them in turn. But this procedure must not be allowed to lead us into supposing that they are, strictly speaking, independent. For example, the proportion, in which an increase in effective demand is divided in its effect between increasing output and raising prices, may affect the way in which the quantity of money is related to the quantity of effective demand. Or, again, the differences in the proportions, in which the remunerations of different factors change, may influence the relation between the quantity of money and the quantity of effective demand. The object of our analysis is, not to provide a machine, or method of blind manipulation, which will furnish an infallible answer, but to provide ourselves with an organized and orderly method of thinking out particular problems; and, after we have reached a provisional conclusion by isolating the complicating factors one by one, we then have to go back on ourselves and allow, as well as we can, for the probable interactions of the factors amongst themselves. This is the nature of economic thinking. Any other way of applying our formal principles of thought (without which, however, we shall be lost in the wood) will lead us into error.

It is a great fault of symbolic pseudo-mathematical methods of formalizing a system of economic analysis, such as we shall set down in section VI of this chapter, that they expressly assume strict independence between the factors involved and lose all their cogency and authority if this hypothesis is disallowed; whereas, in ordinary discourse, where we are not blindly manipulating but know all the time what we are doing and what the words mean, we can keep "at the back of our heads" the necessary reserves and qualifications and the adjustments which we shall have to make later on, in a way in which we cannot keep complicated partial differentials "at the back" of several pages of algebra which assume that they all vanish. Too large a proportion of recent "mathematical" economics are mere concoctions, as imprecise as the initial assumptions they rest on, which allow the author to lose sight of the complexities and interdependencies of the real world in a maze of pretentious and unhelpful symbols.

IV

(1) The primary effect of a change in the quantity of money on the quantity of effective demand is through its influence on the rate of interest. If this were the only reaction, the quantitative effect could be derived from the three elements—(a) the schedule of liquidity-preference which tells us by how much the rate of interest will have to fall in order that the new money may be absorbed by willing holders, (b) the schedule of marginal efficiencies which tells us by how much a given fall in the rate of interest will increase investment, and (c) the investment multiplier which tells us by how much a given increase in investment will increase effective demand as a whole.

But this analysis, though it is valuable in introducing order and method into our enquiry, presents a deceptive simplicity, if we forget that the three elements (a), (b) and (c) are themselves partly dependent on the complicating factors (2), (3), (4) and (5) which we have not yet considered. For the schedule of liquidity-preference itself depends on how much of the new money is absorbed into the income and industrial circulations, which depends in turn on how much effective demand increases and how the increase is divided between the rise of prices, the rise of wages, and the volume of output and employment. Furthermore, the schedule of marginal efficiencies will partly depend on the effect which the circumstances attendant on the increase in the quantity of money have on expectations of the future monetary prospects. And finally the multiplier will be influenced by the way in which the new income resulting from the increased effective demand is distributed between different classes of consumers. Nor, of course, is this list of possible interactions complete. Nevertheless, if we have all the facts before us, we shall have enough simultaneous equations to give us a determinate result. There will be a determinate amount of increase in the quantity of effective demand which, after taking everything into account, will correspond to, and be in equilibrium with, the increase in the quantity of money. Moreover, it is only in highly exceptional circumstances that an increase in the quantity of money will be associated with a *decrease* in the quantity of effective demand.

The ratio between the quantity of effective demand and the quantity of money closely corresponds to what is often called the "income-velocity of money;"—except that effective demand corresponds to the income the expectation of which has set production moving, not to the actually realized income, and to gross, not net, income. But the "income-velocity of money" is, in itself, merely a name which explains nothing. There is no reason to expect that it will be constant. For it depends, as the foregoing discussion has shown, on many complex and variable factors. The use of this term obscures, I think, the real character of the causation, and has led to nothing but confusion.

(2) As we have shown above (Chapter 4, Section III), the distinction between diminishing and constant returns partly depends on whether workers are remunerated in strict proportion to their efficiency. If so, we shall have constant labor-costs (in terms of the wage-unit) when employment increases. But if the wage of a given grade of laborers is uniform irrespective of the efficiency of the individuals, we shall have rising labor-costs, irrespective of the efficiency of the equipment. Moreover, if equipment is non-homogeneous and some part of it involves a greater prime cost per unit of output, we shall have increasing marginal prime costs over and above any increase due to increasing labor-costs.

Hence, in general, supply price will increase as output from a given equipment is increased. Thus increasing output will be associated with rising prices, apart from any change in the wage-unit.

(3) Under (2) we have been contemplating the possibility of supply being imperfectly elastic. If there is a perfect balance in the respective quantities of specialized unemployed resources, the point of full employment will be reached for all of them simultaneously. But, in general, the demand for some services and commodities will reach a level beyond which their supply is, for the time being, perfectly inelastic, whilst in other directions there is still a substantial surplus of resources without employment. Thus as output increases, a series of "bottle-necks" will be successively reached, where the supply of particular commodities ceases to be elastic and their prices have to rise to whatever level is necessary to divert demand into other directions.

It is probable that the general level of prices will not rise very much as output increases, so long as there are available efficient unemployed resources of every type. But as soon as output has increased sufficiently to begin to reach the "bottle-necks," there is likely to be a sharp rise in the prices of certain commodities.

Under this heading, however, as also under heading (2), the elasticity of supply partly depends on the elapse of time. If we assume a sufficient interval for the quantity of equipment itself to change, the elasticities of supply will be decidedly greater eventually. Thus a moderate change in effective demand, coming on a situation where there is widespread unemployment, may spend itself very little in raising prices and mainly in increasing employment; whilst a larger change, which, being unforeseen, causes some temporary "bottlenecks" to be reached, will spend itself in raising prices, as distinct from employment, to a greater extent at first than subsequently.

(4) That the wage-unit may tend to rise before full employment has been reached, requires little comment or explanation. Since each group of workers will gain, *cet. par.,* by a rise in its own wages, there is naturally for all groups a pressure in this direction, which entrepreneurs will be more ready to meet when they are doing better business. For this reason a proportion of any increase in effective demand is likely to be absorbed in satisfying the upward tendency of the wage-unit.

Thus, in addition to the final critical point of full employment at which money-wages have to rise, in response to an increasing effective demand in terms of money, fully in proportion to the rise in the prices of wage-goods, we have a succession of earlier semi-critical points at which an increasing effective demand tends to raise money-wages though not fully in proportion to the rise in the price of wage-goods; and similarly in the case of a decreasing effective demand. In actual experience the wage-unit does not change continuously in terms of money in response to every small change in effective demand; but discontinuously. These points of discontinuity are determined by the psychology of the workers and by the policies of employers and trade unions. In an open system, where they mean a change relatively to wage-costs elsewhere, and in a trade cycle, where even in a closed system they may mean a change relatively to expected wage-costs in the future, they can be of considerable practical significance. These points, where a further increase in effective demand in terms of money is liable to cause a discontinuous rise in the wage-unit, might be deemed, from a certain point of view, to be positions of semi-inflation, having some analogy (though a very imperfect one) to the absolute inflation (*cf.* Section V below) which ensues on an increase in effective demand in circumstances of full employment. They have, moreover, a good deal of historical importance. But they do not readily lend themselves to theoretical generalizations.

(5) Our first simplification consisted in assuming that the remunerations of the various factors entering into marginal cost all change in the same proportion. But in fact the rates of remuneration of different factors in terms of money will show varying degrees of rigidity and they may also have different elasticities of supply in response to changes in the money-rewards offered. If it were not for this, we could say that the price-level is compounded of two factors, the wage-unit and the quantity of employment.

Perhaps the most important element in marginal cost which is likely to change in a different proportion from the wage-unit, and also to fluctuate within much wider limits, is marginal user cost. For marginal user cost may increase sharply when employment begins to improve, if (as will probably be the case) the increasing effective demand brings a rapid change in the prevailing expectation as to the date when the replacement of equipment will be necessary.

Whilst it is for many purposes a very useful first approximation to assume that the rewards of all the factors entering into marginal prime-cost change in the same proportion as the wage-unit, it might be better, perhaps, to take a weighted average of the rewards of the factors entering into marginal prime-cost, and call this the *cost-unit*. The cost-unit, or, subject to the above approximation, the wage-unit, can thus be regarded as the essential standard of value; and the price-level, given the state of technique and equipment, will depend partly on the cost-unit and partly on the scale of output, increasing, where output increases, more than in proportion to any increase in the cost-unit, in accordance with the principle of diminishing returns in the short period. We have full employment when output has risen to a level at which the marginal return from a representative unit of the factors of production has fallen to the minimum figure at which a quantity of the factors sufficient to produce this output is available.

V

When a further increase in the quantity of effective demand produces no further increase in output and entirely spends itself on an increase in the cost-unit fully proportionate to the increase in effective demand, we have reached a condition which might be appropriately designated as one of true inflation. Up to this point the effect of monetary expansion is entirely a question of degree, and there is no previous point at which we can draw a definite line and declare that conditions of inflation have set in. Every previous increase in the quantity of money is likely, in so far as it increases effective demand, to spend itself partly in increasing the cost-unit and partly in increasing output.

It appears, therefore, that we have a sort of asymmetry on the two sides of the critical level above which true inflation sets in. For a contraction of effective demand below the critical level will reduce its amount measured in cost-units; whereas an expansion of effective demand beyond this level will not, in general, have the effect of increasing its amount in terms of cost-units. This result follows from the assumption that the factors of production, and in particular the workers, are disposed to resist a reduction in their money-rewards, and that there is no corresponding motive to resist an increase. This assumption is, however, obviously well founded in the facts, due to the circumstance that a change, which is not an all-round change, is beneficial to the special factors affected when it is upward and harmful when it is downward.

If, on the contrary, money-wages were to fall without limit whenever there was a tendency for less than full employment, the asymmetry would, indeed, disappear. But in that case there would be no resting-place below full employment until either the rate of interest was incapable of falling further or wages were zero. In fact we must have some factor, the value of which in terms of money is, if not fixed, at least sticky, to give us any stability of values in a monetary system.

The view that any increase in the quantity of money is inflationary (unless we mean by *inflationary* merely that prices are rising) is bound up with the underlying assumption or the classical theory that we are always in a condition where a reduction in the real rewards of the factors of production will lead to a curtailment in their supply.

VI

With the aid of the notation introduced in Chapter 20 we can, if we wish, express the substance of the above in symbolic form.

Let us write MV = D where M is the quantity of money, V its income-velocity (this definition differing in the minor respects indicated above from the usual definition) and D the effective demand. If, then, V is constant, prices will change in the same proportion as the quantity of money provided that

$$e_p(= Ddp/pdD)$$

is unity.

This condition is satisfied (see Chapter 20 above) if $e_o = 0$ or if $e_w = 1$. The condition $e_w = 1$ means that the wage-unit in terms of money rises in the same proportion as the effective demand, since

$$e_w(= DdW/WdD);$$

and the condition $e_o = 0$ means that output no longer shows any response to a further increase in effective demand, since

$$e_o(= DdO/OdD).$$

Output in either case will be unaltered.

Next, we can deal with the case where income-velocity is not constant, by introducing yet a further elasticity, namely the elasticity of effective demand in response to changes in the quantity of money,

$$e_d = MdD/DdM.$$

This gives us

$$Mdp/pdM = e_p \cdot e_d \text{ where } e_p = 1 - e_p \cdot e_o (1 - e_w);$$

so that

$$e = e_d - (1 - e_w) e_d \cdot e_e \cdot e_o$$
$$= e_d (1 - e_e \cdot e_o + e_e \cdot e_o \cdot e_w)$$

where e without suffix (=Mdp/pdM) stands for the apex of this pyramid and measures the response of money-prices to changes in the quantity of money.

Since this last expression gives us the proportionate change in prices in response to a change in the quantity of money, it can be regarded as a generalized statement of the Quantity Theory of Money. I do not myself attach much value to manipulations of this kind; and I would repeat the warning, which I have given above, that they involve just as much tacit assumption as to what variables are taken as independent (partial differentials being ignored throughout) as does ordinary discourse, whilst 1 doubt if they carry us any further than ordinary discourse can. Perhaps the best purpose served by writing them down is to exhibit the extreme complexity of the relationship between prices and the quantity of money, when we attempt to express it in a formal manner. It is, however, worth pointing out that, of the four terms e_d, e_w, e_e, and e0 upon which the effect on prices of changes in the quantity of money depends, e_d stands for the liquidity factors which determine the demand for money in each situation, e_w for the labor factors (or, more strictly, the factors entering into prime-cost) which determine the extent to which money-wages are raised as employment increases, and e_e and e_o for the physical factors which determine the rate of decreasing returns as more employment is applied to the existing equipment.

If the public hold a constant proportion of their income in money, $e_d = 1$; if money-wages are fixed, $e_w = 0$; if there are constant returns throughout so that marginal return equals average return, $e_e e_o = 1$; and if there is full employment either of labor or of equipment, $e_e e_o = 0$.

Now $e = 1$, if $e_d = 1$ and $e_w = 1$; or if $e_d = 1$, $e_w = 0$ and $e_e e_o = 1$; or if $e_d = 1$ and $e_o = 0$. And obviously there is a variety of other special cases in which $e = 1$. But in general e is not unity; and it is, perhaps, safe to make the generalization that on plausible assumptions relating to the real world, and excluding the case of a "flight from the currency" in which e_d and e_w become large, e is, as a rule, less than unity.

VII

So far, we have been primarily concerned with the way in which changes in the quantity of money affect prices in the short period. But in the long run is there not some simpler relationship?

This is a question for historical generalization rather than for pure theory. If there is some tendency to a measure of long-run uniformity in the state of liquidity-preference, there may well be some sort of rough relationship between the national income and the quantity of money required to satisfy liquidity-preference, taken as a mean over periods of pessimism and optimism together. There may be, for example, some fairly stable proportion of the national income more than which people will not readily keep in the shape of idle balances for long periods together, provided the rate of interest exceeds a certain psychological minimum; so that if the quantity of money beyond what is required in the active circulation is in excess of this proportion of the national income, there will be a tendency sooner or later for the rate of interest to fall to the neighborhood of this minimum. The falling rate of interest will then, *cet. par.,* increase effective demand, and the increasing effective demand will reach one or more of the semi-critical points at which the wage-unit will tend to show a discontinuous rise, with a corresponding effect on prices. The opposite tendencies will set in if the quantity of surplus money is an abnormally low proportion of the national income. Thus the net effect of fluctuations over a period of time will be to establish a mean figure in conformity with the stable proportion between the national income and the quantity of money to which the psychology of the public tends sooner or later to revert.

These tendencies will probably work with less friction in the upward than in the downward direction. But if the quantity of money remains very deficient for a long time, the escape will be normally found in changing the monetary standard or the monetary system so as to raise the quantity of money, rather than in forcing down the wage-unit and thereby increasing the burden of debt. Thus the very long-run course of prices has almost always been upward. For when money is relatively abundant, the wage-unit rises; and when money is relatively scarce, some means is found to increase the effective quantity of money.

During the nineteenth century, the growth of population and of invention, the opening-up of new lands, the state of confidence and the frequency of war over the average of (say) each decade seem to have been sufficient, taken in conjunction with the propensity to consume, to establish a schedule of the marginal efficiency of capital which allowed a reasonably satisfactory average level of employment to be compatible with a rate of interest high enough to be psychologically acceptable to wealth-owners. There is evidence that for a period of almost one hundred and fifty years the long-run typical rate of interest in the leading financial centers was about 5 percent, and the gilt-edged rate between 3 and 3 1/2 percent; and that these rates of interest were modest enough to encourage a rate of investment consistent with an average of employment which was not intolerably low. Sometimes the wage-unit, but more often the monetary standard or the monetary system (in particular through the development of bank-money), would be adjusted so as to ensure that the quantity of money in terms of wage-units was sufficient to satisfy normal liquidity-preference at rates of interest which were seldom much below the standard rates indicated above. The tendency of the wage-unit was, as usual, steadily upwards on the whole, but the efficiency of labor was also increasing. Thus the balance of forces was such as to allow a fair measure of stability of prices;—the highest quinquennial average for Sauerbeck's index number between 1820 and 1914 was only 50 percent above the lowest. This was not accidental. It is rightly described as due to a balance of forces in an age when individual groups of employers were strong enough to prevent the wage-unit from rising much faster than the efficiency of production, and when monetary systems were at the same time sufficiently fluid and sufficiently conservative to provide an average supply of money in terms of wage-units which allowed to prevail the lowest average rate of interest readily acceptable by wealth-owners under the influence of their liquidity-preferences. The average level of employment was, of course, substantially below full employment, but not so intolerably below it as to provoke revolutionary changes.

Today and presumably for the future the schedule of the marginal efficiency of capital is, for a variety of reasons, much lower than it was in the nineteenth century. The acuteness and the peculiarity of our contemporary problem arises, therefore, out of the possibility that the average rate of interest which will allow a reasonable average level of employment is one so unacceptable to wealth-owners that it cannot be readily established merely by manipulating the quantity of money. So long as a tolerable level of employment could be attained on the average of one or two or three decades merely by assuring an adequate supply of money in terms of wage-units, even the nineteenth century could find a way. If this was our only problem now—if a sufficient degree of devaluation is all we need—we, today, would certainly find a way.

But the most stable, and the least easily shifted, element in our contemporary economy has been hitherto, and may prove to be in future, the minimum rate of interest acceptable to the generality of wealth-owners.[126] If a tolerable level of employment requires a rate of interest much below the average rates which ruled in the nineteenth century, it is most doubtful whether it can be achieved merely by manipulating the quantity of money. From the percentage gain, which the schedule of marginal efficiency of capital allows the borrower to expect to earn, there has to be deducted (1) the cost of bringing borrowers and lenders together, (2) income and surtaxes and (3) the allowance which the lender requires to cover his risk and uncertainty, before we arrive at the net yield available to tempt the wealth-owner to sacrifice his liquidity. If, in conditions of tolerable average employment, this net yield turns out to be infinitesimal, time-honored methods may prove unavailing.

To return to our immediate subject, the long-run relationship between the national income and the quantity of money will depend on liquidity-preferences. And the long-run stability or instability of prices will depend on the strength of the upward trend of the wage-unit (or, more precisely, of the cost-unit) compared with the rate of increase in the efficiency of the productive system.

Book VI

Short Notes Suggested by the General Theory

CHAPTER 22

Notes on the Trade Cycle

Since we claim to have shown in the preceding chapters what determines the volume of employment at any time, it follows, if we are right, that our theory must be capable of explaining the phenomena of the Trade Cycle.

If we examine the details of any actual instance of the Trade Cycle, we shall find that it is highly complex and that every element in our analysis will be required for its complete explanation. In particular we shall find that fluctuations in the propensity to consume, in the state of liquidity-preference, and in the marginal efficiency of capital have all played a part. But I suggest that the essential character of the Trade Cycle and, especially, the regularity of time-sequence and of duration which justifies us in calling it a *cycle,* is mainly due to the way in which the marginal efficiency of capital fluctuates. The Trade Cycle is best regarded, I think, as being occasioned by a cyclical change in the marginal efficiency of capital, though complicated and often aggravated by associated changes in the other significant short-period variables of the economic system. To develop this thesis would occupy a book rather than a chapter, and would require a close examination of facts. But the following short notes will be sufficient to indicate the line of investigation which our preceding theory suggests.

I

By a *cyclical* movement we mean that as the system progresses in, *e.g.,* the upward direction, the forces propelling it upwards at first gather force and have a cumulative effect on one another but gradually lose their strength until at a certain point they tend to be replaced by forces operating in the opposite direction; which in turn gather force for a time and accentuate one another, until they too, having reached their maximum development, wane and give place to their opposite. We do not, however, merely mean by a *cyclical* movement that upward and downward tendencies, once started, do not persist forever in the same direction but are ultimately reversed. We mean also that there is some recognizable degree of regularity in the time-sequence and duration of the upward and downward movements.

There is, however, another characteristic of what we call the Trade Cycle which our explanation must cover if it is to be adequate; namely, the phenomenon of the *crisis*—the fact that the substitution of a downward for an upward tendency often takes place suddenly and violently, whereas there is, as a rule, no such sharp turning-point when an upward is substituted for a downward tendency.

Any fluctuation in investment not offset by a corresponding change in the propensity to consume will, of course, result in a fluctuation in employment. Since, therefore, the volume of investment is subject to highly complex influences, it is highly improbable that all fluctuations either in investment itself or in the marginal efficiency of capital will be of a cyclical character. One special case, in particular, namely, that which is associated with agricultural fluctuations, will be separately considered in a later section of this chapter. I suggest, however, that there are certain definite reasons why, in the case of a typical industrial trade cycle in the nineteenth-century environment, fluctuations in the marginal efficiency of capital should have had cyclical characteristics. These reasons are by no means unfamiliar either in themselves or as explanations of the trade cycle. My only purpose here is to link them up with the preceding theory.

II

I can best introduce what I have to say by beginning with the later stages of the boom and the onset of the "crisis."

We have seen above that the marginal efficiency of capital[127] depends, not only on the existing abundance or scarcity of capital-goods and the current cost of production of capital-goods, but also on current expectations as to the future yield of capital-goods. In the case of durable assets it is, therefore, natural and reasonable that expectations of the future should play a dominant part in determining the scale on which new investment is deemed advisable. But, as we have seen, the basis for such expectations is very precarious. Being based on shifting and unreliable evidence, they are subject to sudden and violent changes.

Now, we have been accustomed in explaining the "crisis" to lay stress on the rising tendency of the rate of interest under the influence of the increased demand for money both for trade and speculative purposes. At times this factor may certainly play an aggravating and, occasionally perhaps, an initiating part. But I suggest that a more typical, and often the predominant, explanation of the crisis is, not primarily a rise in the rate of interest, but a sudden collapse in the marginal efficiency of capital.

The later stages of the boom are characterized by optimistic expectations as to the future yield of capital-goods sufficiently strong to offset their growing abundance and their rising costs of production and, probably, a rise in the rate of interest also. It is of the nature of organized investment markets, under the influence of purchasers largely ignorant of what they are buying and of speculators who are more concerned with forecasting the next shift of market sentiment than with a reasonable estimate of the future yield of capital-assets, that, when disillusion falls upon an over-optimistic and over-bought market, it should fall with sudden and even catastrophic force.[128] Moreover, the dismay and uncertainty as to the future which accompanies a collapse in the marginal efficiency of capital naturally precipitates a sharp increase in liquidity-preference—and hence a rise in the rate of interest. Thus the fact that a collapse in the marginal efficiency of capital tends to be associated with a rise in the rate of interest may seriously aggravate the decline in investment. But the essence of the situation is to be found, nevertheless, in the collapse in the marginal efficiency of capital, particularly in the case of those types of capital which have been contributing most to the previous phase of heavy new investment. Liquidity-preference, except those manifestations of it which are associated with increasing trade and speculation, does not increase until *after* the collapse in the marginal efficiency of capital.

It is this, indeed, which renders the slump so intractable. Later on, a decline in the rate of interest will be a great aid to recovery and, probably, a necessary condition of it. But, for the moment, the collapse in the marginal efficiency of capital may be so complete that no practicable reduction in the rate of interest will be enough. If a reduction in the rate of interest was capable of proving an effective remedy by itself, it might be possible to achieve a recovery without the elapse of any considerable interval of time and by means more or less directly under the control of the monetary authority. But, in fact, this is not usually the case; and it is not so easy to revive the marginal efficiency of capital, determined, as it is, by the uncontrollable and disobedient psychology of the business world. It is the return of confidence, to speak in ordinary language, which is so insusceptible to control in an economy of individualistic capitalism. This is the aspect of the slump which bankers and business men have been right in emphasizing, and which the economists who have put their faith in a "purely monetary" remedy have underestimated.

This brings me to my point. The explanation of the *time-element* in the trade cycle, of the fact that an interval of time of a particular order of magnitude must usually elapse before recovery begins, is to be sought in the influences which govern the recovery of the marginal efficiency of capital. There are reasons, given firstly by the length of life of durable assets in relation to the normal rate of growth in a given epoch, and secondly by the carrying-costs of surplus stocks, why the duration of the downward movement should have an order of magnitude which is not fortuitous, which does not fluctuate between, say, one year this time and ten years next time, but which shows some regularity of habit between, let us say, three and five years.

Let us recur to what happens at the crisis. So long as the boom was continuing, much of the new investment showed a not unsatisfactory current yield. The disillusion comes because doubts suddenly arise concerning the reliability of the prospective yield, perhaps because the current yield shows signs of falling off, as the stock of newly produced durable goods steadily increases. If current costs of production are thought to be higher than they will be later on, that will be a further reason for a fall in the marginal efficiency of capital. Once doubt begins it spreads rapidly. Thus at the outset of the slump there is probably much capital of which the marginal efficiency has become negligible or even negative. But the interval of time, which will have to elapse before the shortage of capital through use, decay and obsolescence causes a sufficiently obvious scarcity to increase the marginal efficiency, may be a somewhat stable function of the average durability of capital in a given epoch. If the characteristics of the epoch shift, the standard time-interval will change. If, for example, we pass from a period of increasing population into one of declining population, the characteristic phase of the cycle will be lengthened. But we have in the above a substantial reason why the duration of the slump should have a definite relationship to the length of life of durable assets and to the normal rate of growth in a given epoch.

The second stable time-factor is due to the carrying-costs of surplus stocks which force their absorption within a certain period, neither very short nor very long. The sudden cessation of new investment after the crisis will probably lead to an accumulation of surplus stocks of unfinished goods. The carrying-costs of these stocks will seldom be less than 10 percent per annum. Thus the fall in their price needs to be sufficient to bring about a restriction which provides for their absorption within a period of, say, three to five years at the outside. Now the process of absorbing the stocks represents negative investment, which is a further deterrent to employment; and, when it is over, a manifest relief will be experienced.

Moreover, the reduction in working capital, which is necessarily attendant on the decline in output on the downward phase, represents a further element of disinvestment, which may be large; and, once the recession has begun, this exerts a strong cumulative influence in the downward direction. In the earliest phase of a typical slump there will probably be an investment in increasing stocks which helps to offset disinvestment in working-capital; in the next phase there may be a short period of disinvestment both in stocks and in working-capital; after the lowest point has been passed there is likely to be a further disinvestment in stocks which partially offsets reinvestment in working-capital; and, finally, after the recovery is well on its way, both factors will be simultaneously favorable to investment. It is against this background that the additional and superimposed effects of fluctuations of investment in durable goods must be examined. When a decline in this type of investment has set a cyclical fluctuation in motion there will be little encouragement to a recovery in such investment until the cycle has partly run its course.[129]

Unfortunately a serious fall in the marginal efficiency of capital also tends to affect adversely the propensity to consume. For it involves a severe decline in the market value of Stock Exchange equities. Now, on the class who take an active interest in their Stock Exchange investments, especially if they are employing borrowed funds, this naturally exerts a very depressing influence. These people are, perhaps, even more influenced in their readiness to spend by rises and falls in the value of their investments than by the state of their income. With a "stock-minded" public, as in the United States today, a rising stock-market may be an almost essential condition of a satisfactory propensity to consume; and this circumstance, generally overlooked until lately, obviously serves to aggravate still further the depressing effect of a decline in the marginal efficiency of capital.

When once the recovery has been started, the manner in which it feeds on itself and cumulates is obvious. But during the downward phase, when both fixed capital and stocks of materials are for the time being redundant and working-capital is being reduced, the schedule of the marginal efficiency of capital may fall so low that it can scarcely be corrected, so as to secure a satisfactory rate of new investment, by any practicable reduction in the rate of interest. Thus with markets organized and influenced as they are at present, the market estimation of the marginal efficiency of capital may suffer such enormously wide fluctuations that it cannot be sufficiently offset by corresponding fluctuations in the rate of interest. Moreover, the corresponding movements in the stock-market may, as we have seen above, depress the propensity to consume just when it is most needed. In conditions of *laissez-faire* the avoidance of wide fluctuations in employment may, therefore, prove impossible without a far-reaching change in the psychology of investment markets such as there is no reason to expect. I conclude that the duty of ordering the current volume of investment cannot safely be left in private hands.

III

The preceding analysis may appear to be in conformity with the view of those who hold that over investment is the characteristic of the boom, that the avoidance of this over-investment is the only possible remedy for the ensuing slump, and that, whilst for the reasons given above, the slump cannot be prevented by a low rate of interest, nevertheless the boom can be avoided by a high rate of interest. There is, indeed, force in the argument that a high rate of interest is much more effective against a boom than a low rate of interest against a slump.

To infer these conclusions from the above would, however, misinterpret my analysis; and would, according to my way of thinking, involve serious error. For the term over-investment is ambiguous. It may refer to investments which are destined to disappoint the expectations which prompted them or for which there is no use in conditions of severe unemployment, or it may indicate a state of affairs where every kind of capital-goods is so abundant that there is no new investment which is expected, even in conditions of full employment, to earn in the course of its life more than its replacement cost. It is only the latter state of affairs which is one of over-investment, strictly speaking, in the sense that any further investment would be a sheer waste of resources.[130] Moreover, even if over-investment in this sense was a normal characteristic of the boom, the remedy would not lie in clapping on a high rate of interest which would probably deter some useful investments and might further diminish the propensity to consume, but in taking drastic steps, by redistributing incomes or otherwise, to stimulate the propensity to consume.

According to my analysis, however, it is only in the former sense that the boom can be said to be characterized by over-investment. The situation, which I am indicating as typical, is not one in which capital is so abundant that the community as a whole has no reasonable use for any more, but where investment is being made in conditions which are unstable and cannot endure, because it is prompted by expectations which are destined to disappointment.

It may, of course, be the case—indeed it is likely to be—that the illusions of the boom cause particular types of capital-assets to be produced in such excessive abundance that some part of the output is, on any criterion, a waste of resources;—which sometimes happens, we may add, even when there is no boom. It leads, that is to say, to *misdirected* investment. But over and above this it is an essential characteristic of the boom that investments which will in fact yield, say, 2 percent, in conditions of full employment are made in the expectation of a yield of, say, 6 percent, and are valued accordingly. When the disillusion comes, this expectation is replaced by a contrary "error of pessimism," with the result that the investments, which would in fact yield 2 percent, in conditions of full employment, are expected to yield less than nothing; and the resulting collapse of new investment then leads to a state of unemployment in which the investments, which would have yielded 2 percent, in conditions of full employment, in fact yield less than nothing. We reach a condition where there is a shortage of houses, but where nevertheless no one can afford to live in the houses that there are.

Thus the remedy for the boom is not a higher rate of interest but a lower rate of interest![131] For that may enable the so-called boom to last. The right remedy for the trade cycle is not to be found in abolishing booms and thus keeping us permanently in a semi-slump; but in abolishing slumps and thus keeping us permanently in a quasi-boom.

The boom which is destined to end in a slump is caused, therefore, by the combination of a rate of interest, which in a correct state of expectation would be too high for full employment, with a misguided state of expectation which, so long as it lasts, prevents this rate of interest from being in fact deterrent. A boom is a situation in which over-optimism triumphs over a rate of interest which, in a cooler light, would be seen to be excessive.

Except during the war, I doubt if we have any recent experience of a boom so strong that it led to full employment. In the United States employment was very satisfactory in 1928–29 on normal standards; but I have seen no evidence of a shortage of labor, except, perhaps, in the case of a few groups of highly specialized workers. Some "bottle-necks" were reached, but output as a whole was still capable of further expansion. Nor was there over-investment in the sense that the standard and equipment of housing was so high that everyone, assuming full employment, had all he wanted at a rate which would no more than cover the replacement cost, without any allowance for interest, over the life of the house; and that transport, public services and agricultural improvement had been carried to a point where further additions could not reasonably be expected to yield even their replacement cost. Quite the contrary. It would be absurd to assert of the United States in 1929 the existence of over-investment in the strict sense. The true state of affairs was of a different character. New investment during the previous five years had been, indeed, on so enormous a scale in the aggregate that the prospective yield of further additions was, coolly considered, falling rapidly. Correct foresight would have brought down the marginal efficiency of capital to an unprecedentedly low figure; so that the "boom" could not have continued on a sound basis except with a very low long-term rate of interest, and an avoidance of misdirected investment in the particular directions which were in danger of being over-exploited. In fact, the rate of interest was high enough to deter new investment except in those particular directions which were under the influence of speculative excitement and, therefore, in special danger of being over-exploited; and a rate of interest, high enough to overcome the speculative excitement, would have checked, at the same time, every kind of reasonable new investment. Thus an increase in the rate of interest, as a remedy for the state of affairs arising out of a prolonged period of abnormally heavy new investment, belongs to the species of remedy which cures the disease by killing the patient.

It is, indeed, very possible that the prolongation of approximately full employment over a period of years would be associated in countries so wealthy as Great Britain or the United States with a volume of new investment, assuming the existing propensity to consume, so great that it would eventually lead to a state of full investment in the sense that an aggregate gross yield in excess of replacement cost could no longer be expected on a reasonable calculation from a further increment of durable goods of any type whatever. Moreover, this situation might be reached comparatively soon—say within twenty-five years or less. I must not be taken to deny this, because I assert that a state of full investment in the strict sense has never yet occurred, not even momentarily.

Furthermore, even if we were to suppose that contemporary booms are apt to be associated with a momentary condition of full investment or over-investment in the strict sense, it would still be absurd to regard a higher rate of interest as the appropriate remedy. For in this event the case of those who attribute the disease to under-consumption would be wholly established. The remedy would lie in various measures designed to increase the propensity to consume by the redistribution of incomes or otherwise; so that a given level of employment would require a smaller volume of current investment to support it.

IV

It may be convenient at this point to say a word about the important schools of thought which maintain, from various points of view, that the chronic tendency of contemporary societies to under-employment is to be traced to under-consumption;—that is to say, to social practices and to a distribution of wealth which result in a propensity to consume which is unduly low.

In existing conditions—or, at least, in the conditions which existed until lately—where the volume of investment is unplanned and uncontrolled, subject to the vagaries of the marginal efficiency of capital as determined by the private judgment of individuals ignorant or speculative, and to a long-term rate of interest which seldom or never falls below a conventional level, these schools of thought are, as guides to practical policy, undoubtedly in the right. For in such conditions there is no other means of raising the average level of employment to a more satisfactory level. If it is impracticable materially to increase investment, obviously there is no means of securing a higher level of employment except by increasing consumption.

Practically I only differ from these schools of thought in thinking that they may lay a little too much emphasis on increased consumption at a time when there is still much social advantage to be obtained from increased investment. Theoretically, however, they are open to the criticism of neglecting the fact that there are two ways to expand output. Even if we were to decide that it would be better to increase capital more slowly and to concentrate effort on increasing consumption, we must decide this with open eyes after well considering the alternative. I am myself impressed by the great social advantages of increasing the stock of capital until it ceases to be scarce. But this is a practical judgment, not a theoretical imperative.

Moreover, I should readily concede that the wisest course is to advance on both fronts at once. Whilst aiming at a socially controlled rate of investment with a view to a progressive decline in the marginal efficiency of capital, I should support at the same time all sorts of policies for increasing the propensity to consume. For it is unlikely that full employment can be maintained, whatever we may do about investment, with the existing propensity to consume. There is room, therefore, for both policies to operate together;—to promote investment and, at the same time, to promote consumption, not merely to the level which with the existing propensity to consume would correspond to the increased investment, but to a higher level still.

If—to take round figures for the purpose of illustration—the average level of output of today is 15 percent, below what it would be with continuous full employment, and if 10 percent, of this output represents net investment and 90 percent, of it consumption—if, furthermore, net investment would have to rise 50 percent, in order to secure full employment with the existing propensity to consume, so that with full employment output would rise from 100 to 115, consumption from 90 to 100 and net investment from 10 to 15:—then we might aim, perhaps, at so modifying the propensity to consume that with full employment consumption would rise from 90 to 103 and net investment from 10 to 12.

V

Another school of thought finds the solution of the trade cycle, not in increasing either consumption or investment, but in diminishing the supply of labor seeking employment; *i.e.* by redistributing the existing volume of employment without increasing employment or output.

This seems to me to be a premature policy—much more clearly so than the plan of increasing consumption. A point comes where every individual weighs the advantages of increased leisure against increased income. But at present the evidence is, I think, strong that the great majority of individuals would prefer increased income to increased leisure; and I see no sufficient reason for compelling those who would prefer more income to enjoy more leisure.

VI

It may appear extraordinary that a school of thought should exist which finds the solution for the trade cycle in checking the boom in its early stages by a higher rate of interest. The only line of argument, along which any justification for this policy can be discovered, is that put forward by Mr. D. H. Robertson, who assumes, in effect, that full employment is an impracticable ideal and that the best that we can hope for is a level of employment much more stable than at present and averaging, perhaps, a little higher.

If we rule out major changes of policy affecting either the control of investment or the propensity to consume, and assume, broadly speaking, a continuance of the existing state of affairs, it is, I think, arguable that a more advantageous average state of expectation might result from a banking policy which always nipped in the bud an incipient boom by a rate of interest high enough to deter even the most misguided optimists. The disappointment of expectation, characteristic of the slump, may lead to so much loss and waste that the average level of useful investment might be higher if a deterrent is applied. It is difficult to be sure whether or not this is correct on its own assumptions; it is a matter for practical judgment where detailed evidence is wanting. It may be that it overlooks the social advantage which accrues from the increased consumption which attends even on investment which proves to have been totally misdirected, so that even such investment may be more beneficial than no investment at all. Nevertheless, the most enlightened monetary control might find itself in difficulties, faced with a boom of the 1929 type in America, and armed with no other weapons than those possessed at that time by the Federal Reserve System; and none of the alternatives within its power might make much difference to the result. However this may be, such an outlook seems to me to be dangerously and unnecessarily defeatist. It recommends, or at least assumes, for permanent acceptance too much that is defective in our existing economic scheme.

The austere view, which would employ a high rate of interest to check at once any tendency in the level of employment to rise appreciably above the average of, say, the previous decade, is, however, more usually supported by arguments which have no foundation at all apart from confusion of mind. It flows, in some cases, from the belief that in a boom investment tends to outrun saving, and that a higher rate of interest will restore equilibrium by checking investment on the one hand and stimulating savings on the other. This implies that saving and investment can be unequal, and has, therefore, no meaning until these terms have been defined in some special sense. Or it is sometimes suggested that the increased saving which accompanies increased investment is undesirable and unjust because it is, as a rule, also associated with rising prices. But if this were so, any upward change in the existing level of output and employment is to be deprecated. For the rise in prices is not essentially due to the increase in investment;—it is due to the fact that in the short period supply price usually increases with increasing output, on account either of the physical fact of diminishing return or of the tendency of the cost-unit to rise in terms of money when output increases. If the conditions were those of constant supply-price, there would, of course, be no rise of prices; yet, all the same, increased saving would accompany increased investment. It is the increased output which produces the increased saving; and the rise of prices is merely a by-product of the increased output, which will occur equally if there is no increased saving but, instead, an increased propensity to consume. No one has a legitimate vested interest in being able to buy at prices which are only low because output is low.

Or, again, the evil is supposed to creep in if the increased investment has been promoted by a fall in the rate of interest engineered by an increase in the quantity of money. Yet there is no special virtue in the pre-existing rate of interest, and the new money is not "forced" on anyone;—it is created in order to satisfy the increased liquidity-preference which corresponds to the lower rate of interest or the increased volume of transactions, and it is held by those individuals who *prefer* to hold money rather than to lend it at the lower rate of interest. Or, once more, it is suggested that a boom is characterized by "capital consumption," which presumably means negative net investment, *i.e.* by an excessive propensity to consume. Unless the phenomena of the trade cycle have been confused with those of a flight from the currency such as occurred during the post-war European currency collapses, the evidence is wholly to the contrary. Moreover, even if it were so, a reduction in the rate of interest would be a more plausible remedy than a rise in the rate of interest for conditions of under-investment. I can make no sense at all of these schools of thought; except, perhaps, by supplying a tacit assumption that aggregate output is incapable of change. But a theory which assumes constant output is obviously not very serviceable for explaining the trade cycle.

VII

In the earlier studies of the trade cycle, notably by Jevons, an explanation was found in agricultural fluctuations due to the seasons, rather than in the phenomena of industry. In the light of the above theory this appears as an extremely plausible approach to the problem. For even today fluctuation in the stocks of agricultural products as between one year and another is one of the largest individual items amongst the causes of changes in the rate of current investment; whilst at the time when Jevons wrote—and more particularly over the period to which most of his statistics applied—this factor must have far outweighed all others.

Jevons's theory, that the trade cycle was primarily due to the fluctuations in the bounty of the harvest, can be re-stated as follows. When an exceptionally large harvest is gathered in, an important addition is usually made to the quantity carried over into later years. The proceeds of this addition are added to the current incomes of the farmers and are treated by them as income; whereas the increased carry-over involves no drain on the income-expenditure of other sections of the community but is financed out of savings. That is to say, the addition to the carry-over is an addition to current investment. This conclusion is not invalidated even if prices fall sharply. Similarly when there is a poor harvest, the carry-over is drawn upon for current consumption, so that a corresponding part of the income-expenditure of the consumers creates no current income for the farmers. That is to say, what is taken from the carry-over involves a corresponding reduction in current investment. Thus, if investment in other directions is taken to be constant, the difference in aggregate investment between a year in which there is a substantial addition to the carry-over and a year in which there is a substantial subtraction from it may be large; and in a community where agriculture is the predominant industry it will be overwhelmingly large compared with any other usual cause of investment fluctuations. Thus it is natural that we should find the upward turning-point to be marked by bountiful harvests and the downward turning-point by deficient harvests. The further theory, that there are physical causes for a regular cycle of good and bad harvests, is, of course, a different matter with which we are not concerned here.

More recently, the theory has been advanced that it is bad harvests, not good harvests, which are good for trade, either because bad harvests make the population ready to work for a smaller real reward or because the resulting redistribution of purchasing-power is held to be favorable to consumption. Needless to say, it is not these theories which I have in mind in the above description of harvest phenomena as an explanation of the trade cycle.

The agricultural causes of fluctuation are, however, much less important in the modern world for two reasons. In the first place agricultural output is a much smaller proportion of total output. And in the second place the development of a world market for most agricultural products, drawing upon both hemispheres, leads to an averaging out of the effects of good and bad seasons, the percentage fluctuation in the amount of the world harvest being far less than the percentage fluctuations in the harvests of individual countries. But in old days, when a country was mainly dependent on its own harvest, it is difficult to see any possible cause of fluctuations in investment, except war, which was in any way comparable in magnitude with changes in the carry-over of agricultural products.

Even today it is important to pay close attention to the part played by changes in the stocks of raw materials, both agricultural and mineral, in the determination of the rate of current investment. I should attribute the slow rate of recovery from a slump, after the turning-point has been reached, mainly to the deflationary effect of the reduction of redundant stocks to a normal level. At first the accumulation of stocks, which occurs after the boom has broken, moderates the rate of the collapse; but we have to pay for this relief later on in the damping-down of the subsequent rate of recovery. Sometimes, indeed, the reduction of stocks may have to be virtually completed before any measurable degree of recovery can be detected. For a rate of investment in other directions, which is sufficient to produce an upward movement when there is no current disinvestment in stocks to set off against it, may be quite inadequate so long as such disinvestment is still proceeding.

We have seen, I think, a signal example of this in the earlier phases of America's "New Deal." When President Roosevelt's substantial loan expenditure began, stocks of all kinds—and particularly of agricultural products—still stood at a very high level. The "New Deal" partly consisted in a strenuous attempt to reduce these stocks—by curtailment of current output and in all sorts of ways. The reduction of stocks to a normal level was a necessary process—a phase which had to be endured. But so long as it lasted, namely, about two years, it constituted a substantial offset to the loan expenditure which was being incurred in other directions. Only when it had been completed was the way prepared for substantial recovery.

Recent American experience has also afforded good examples of the part played by fluctuations in the stocks of finished and unfinished goods—"inventories" as it is becoming usual to call them—in causing the minor oscillations within the main movement of the Trade Cycle. Manufacturers, setting industry in motion to provide for a scale of consumption which is expected to prevail some months later, are apt to make minor miscalculations, generally in the direction of running a little ahead of the facts. When they discover their mistake they have to contract for a short time to a level below that of current consumption so as to allow for the absorption of the excess inventories; and the difference of pace between running a little ahead and dropping back again has proved sufficient in its effect on the current rate of investment to display itself quite clearly against the background of the excellently complete statistics now available in the United States.

CHAPTER 23

Notes on Mercantilism, the Usury Laws, Stamped Money and Theories of Under-Consumption

I

For some two hundred years both economic theorists and practical men did not doubt that there is a peculiar advantage to a country in a favorable balance of trade, and grave danger in an unfavorable balance, particularly if it results in an efflux of the precious metals. But for the past one hundred years there has been a remarkable divergence of opinion. The majority of statesmen and practical men in most countries, and nearly half of them even in Great Britain, the home of the opposite view, have remained faithful to the ancient doctrine ; whereas almost all economic theorists have held that anxiety concerning such matters is absolutely groundless except on a very short view, since the mechanism of foreign trade is self-adjusting and attempts to interfere with it are not only futile, but greatly impoverish those who practice them because they forfeit the advantages of the international division of labor. It will be convenient, in accordance with tradition, to designate the older opinion as *Mercantilism* and the newer as *Free Trade*, though these terms, since each of them has both a broader and a narrower signification, must be interpreted with reference to the context.

Generally speaking, modern economists have maintained not merely that there is, as a rule, a balance of gain from the international division of labor sufficient to outweigh such advantages as mercantilist practice can fairly claim, but that the mercantilist argument is based, from start to finish, on an intellectual confusion.

Marshall,[132] for example, although his references to Mercantilism are not altogether unsympathetic, had no regard for their central theory as such and does not even mention those elements of truth in their contentions which I shall examine below.[133] In the same way, the theoretical concessions which free-trade economists have been ready to make in contemporary controversies, relating, for example, to the encouragement of infant industries or to the improvement of the terms of trade, are not concerned with the real substance of the mercantilist case. During the fiscal controversy of the first quarter of the present century I do not remember that any concession was ever allowed by economists to the claim that Protection might increase domestic employment. It will be fairest, perhaps, to quote, as an example, what I wrote myself. So lately as 1923, as a faithful pupil of the classical school who did not at that time doubt what he had been taught and entertained on this matter no reserves at all, I wrote: "If there is one thing that Protection can *not* do, it is to cure Unemployment. . . . There are some arguments for Protection, based upon its securing possible but improbable advantages, to which there is no simple answer. But the claim to cure Unemployment involves the Protectionist fallacy in its grossest and crudest form."[134] As for earlier mercantilist theory, no intelligible account was available; and we were brought up to believe that it was little better than nonsense. So absolutely overwhelming and complete has been the domination of the classical school.

II

Let me first state in my own terms what now seems to me to be the element of scientific truth in mercantilist doctrine. We will then compare this with the actual arguments of the mercantilists. It should be understood that the advantages claimed are avowedly national advantages and are unlikely to benefit the world as a whole.

When a country is growing in wealth somewhat rapidly, the further progress of this happy state of affairs is liable to be interrupted, in conditions of *laissez-faire,* by the insufficiency of the inducements to new investment. Given the social and political environment and the national characteristics which determine the propensity to consume, the well-being of a progressive state essentially depends, for the reasons we have already explained, on the sufficiency of such inducements. They may be found either in home investment or in foreign investment (including in the latter the accumulation of the precious metals), which, between them, make up aggregate investment. In conditions in which the quantity of aggregate investment is determined by the profit motive alone, the opportunities for home investment will be governed, in the long run, by the domestic rate of interest; whilst the volume of foreign investment is necessarily determined by the size of the favorable balance of trade. Thus, in a society where there is no question of direct investment under the aegis of public authority, the economic objects, with which it is reasonable for the government to be preoccupied, are the domestic rate of interest and the balance of foreign trade.

Now, if the wage-unit is somewhat stable and not liable to spontaneous changes of significant magnitude (a condition which is almost always satisfied), if the state of liquidity-preference is somewhat stable, taken as an average of its short-period fluctuations, and if banking conventions are also stable, the rate of interest will tend to be governed by the quantity of the precious metals, measured in terms of the wage-unit, available to satisfy the community's desire for liquidity. At the same time, in an age in which substantial foreign loans and the outright ownership of wealth located abroad are scarcely practicable, increases and decreases in the quantity of the precious metals will largely depend on whether the balance of trade is favorable or unfavorable.

Thus, as it happens, a preoccupation on the part of the authorities with a favorable balance of trade served *both* purposes; and was, furthermore, the only available means of promoting them. At a time when the authorities had no direct control over the domestic rate of interest or the other inducements to home investment, measures to increase the favorable balance of trade were the only *direct* means at their disposal for increasing foreign investment; and, at the same time, the effect of a favorable balance of trade on the influx of the precious metals was their only *indirect* means of reducing the domestic rate of interest and so increasing the inducement to home investment.

There are, however, two limitations on the success of this policy which must not be overlooked. If the domestic rate of interest falls so low that the volume of investment is sufficiently stimulated to raise employment to a level which breaks through some of the critical points at which the wage-unit rises, the increase in the domestic level of costs will begin to react unfavorably on the balance of foreign trade, so that the effort to increase the latter will have overreached and defeated itself. Again, if the domestic rate of interest falls so low relatively to rates of interest elsewhere as to stimulate a volume of foreign lending which is disproportionate to the favorable balance, there may ensue an efflux of the precious metals sufficient to reverse the advantages previously obtained.

The risk of one or other of these limitations becoming operative is increased in the case of a country which is large and internationally important by the fact that, in conditions where the current output of the precious metals from the mines is on a relatively small scale, an influx of money into one country means an efflux from another; so that the adverse effects of rising costs and falling rates of interest at home may be accentuated (if the mercantilist policy is pushed too far) by falling costs and rising rates of interest abroad.

The economic history of Spain in the latter part of the fifteenth and in the sixteenth centuries provides an example of a country whose foreign trade was destroyed by the effect on the wage-unit of an excessive abundance of the precious metals. Great Britain in the pre-war years of the twentieth century provides an example of a country in which the excessive facilities for foreign lending and the purchase of properties abroad frequently stood in the way of the decline in the domestic rate of interest which was required to ensure full employment at home. The history of India at all times has provided an example of a country impoverished by a preference for liquidity amounting to so strong a passion that even an enormous and chronic influx of the precious metals has been insufficient to bring down the rate of interest to a level which was compatible with the growth of real wealth.

Nevertheless, if we contemplate a society with a somewhat stable wage-unit, with national characteristics which determine the propensity to consume and the preference for liquidity, and with a monetary system which rigidly links the quantity of money to the stock of the precious metals, it will be essential for the maintenance of prosperity that the authorities should pay close attention to the state of the balance of trade. For a favorable balance, provided it is not too large, will prove extremely stimulating; whilst an unfavorable balance may soon produce a state of persistent depression.

It does not follow from this that the maximum degree of restriction of imports will promote the maximum favorable balance of trade. The earlier mercantilists laid great emphasis on this and were often to be found opposing trade restrictions because on a long view they were liable to operate adversely to a favorable balance. It is, indeed, arguable that in the special circumstances of mid-nineteenth-century Great Britain an almost complete freedom of trade was the policy most conducive to the development of a favorable balance. Contemporary experience of trade restrictions in post-war Europe offers manifold examples of ill-conceived impediments on freedom which, designed to improve the favorable balance, had in fact a contrary tendency.

For this and other reasons the reader must not reach a premature conclusion as to the *practical* policy to which our argument leads up. There are strong presumptions of a general character against trade restrictions unless they can be justified on special grounds.

The advantages of the international division of labor are real and substantial, even though the classical school greatly overstressed them. The fact that the advantage which our own country gains from a favorable balance is liable to involve an equal disadvantage to some other country (a point to which the mercantilists were fully alive) means not only that great moderation is necessary, so that a country secures for itself no larger a share of the stock of the precious metals than is fair and reasonable, but also that an immoderate policy may lead to a senseless international competition for a favorable balance which injures all alike.[135] And finally, a policy of trade restrictions is a treacherous instrument even for the attainment of its ostensible object, since private interest, administrative incompetence and the intrinsic difficulty of the task may divert it into producing results directly opposite to those intended.

Thus, the weight of my criticism is directed against the inadequacy of the *theoretical* foundations of the *laissez-faire* doctrine upon which I was brought up and which for many years I taught;—against the notion that the rate of interest and the volume of investment are self-adjusting at the optimum level, so that preoccupation with the balance of trade is a waste of time. For we, the faculty of economists, prove to have been guilty of presumptuous error in treating as a puerile obsession what for centuries has been a prime object of practical statecraft.

Under the influence of this faulty theory the City of London gradually devised the most dangerous technique for the maintenance of equilibrium which can possibly be imagined, namely, the technique of bank rate coupled with a rigid parity of the foreign exchanges. For this meant that the objective of maintaining a domestic rate of interest consistent with full employment was wholly ruled out. Since, in practice, it is impossible to neglect the balance of payments, a means of controlling it was evolved which, instead of protecting the domestic rate of interest, sacrificed it to the operation of blind forces. Recently, practical bankers in London have learnt much, and one can almost hope that in Great Britain the technique of bank rate will never be used again to protect the foreign balance in conditions in which it is likely to cause unemployment at home.

Regarded as the theory of the individual firm and of the distribution of the product resulting from the employment of a given quantity of resources, the classical theory has made a contribution to economic thinking which cannot be impugned. It is impossible to think clearly on the subject without this theory as a part of one's apparatus of thought. I must not be supposed to question this in calling attention to their neglect of what was valuable in their predecessors. Nevertheless, as a contribution to statecraft, which is concerned with the economic system as a whole and with securing the optimum employment of the system's entire resources, the methods of the early pioneers of economic thinking in the sixteenth and seventeenth centuries may have attained to fragments of practical wisdom which the unrealistic abstractions of Ricardo first forgot and then obliterated. There was wisdom in their intense preoccupation with keeping down the rate of interest by means of usury laws (to which we will return later in this chapter), by maintaining the domestic stock of money and by discouraging rises in the wage-unit; and in their readiness in the last resort to restore the stock of money by devaluation, if it had become plainly deficient through an unavoidable foreign drain, a rise in the wage-unit[136], or any other cause.

III

The early pioneers of economic thinking may have hit upon their maxims of practical wisdom without having had much cognizance of the underlying theoretical grounds. Let us, therefore, examine briefly the reasons they gave as well as what they recommended. This is made easy by reference to Professor Heckscher's great work on *Mercantilism*, in which the essential characteristics of economic thought over a period of two centuries are made available for the first time to the general economic reader. The quotations which follow are mainly taken from his pages.[137]

(1) Mercantilist thought never supposed that there was a self-adjusting tendency by which the rate of interest would be established at the appropriate level. On the contrary they were emphatic that an unduly high rate of interest was the main obstacle to the growth of wealth; and they were even aware that the rate of interest depended on liquidity-preference and the quantity of money. They were concerned both with diminishing liquidity-preference and with increasing the quantity of money, and several of them made it clear that their preoccupation with increasing the quantity of money was due to their desire to diminish the rate of interest. Professor Heckscher sums up this aspect of their theory as follows:

> The position of the more perspicacious mercantilists was in this respect, as in many others, perfectly clear within certain limits. For them, money was—to use the terminology of today—a factor of production, on the same footing as land, sometimes regarded as "artificial" wealth as distinct from the "natural" wealth; interest on capital was the payment for the renting of money similar to rent for land. In so far as mercantilists sought to discover objective reasons for the height of the rate of interest—and they did so more and more during this period—they found such reasons in the total quantity of money. From the abundant material available, only the most typical examples will be selected, so as to demonstrate first and foremost how lasting this notion was, how deep-rooted and independent of practical considerations.

Both of the protagonists in the struggle over monetary policy and the East India trade in the early 1620's in England were in entire agreement on this point. Gerard Malynes stated, giving detailed reason for his assertion, that "Plenty of money decreaseth usury in price or rate" (*Lex Mercatoria and Maintenance of Free Trade*, 1622). His truculent and rather unscrupulous adversary, Edward Misselden, replied that "The remedy for Usury may be plenty of money" (*Free Trade or the Meanes to make Trade Florish*, same year). Of the leading writers of half a century later, Child, the omnipotent leader of the East India Company and its most skilful advocate, discussed (1668) the question of how far the legal maximum rate of interest, which he emphatically demanded, would result in drawing "the money" of the Dutch away, from England. He found a remedy for this dreaded disadvantage in the easier transference of bills of debt, if these were used as currency, for this, he said, "will certainly supply the defect of at least one-half of all the ready money we have in use in the nation." Petty, the other writer, who was entirely unaffected by the clash of interests, was in agreement with the rest when he explained the "natural" fall in the rate of interest from 10 percent to 6 percent by the increase in the amount of money (*Political Arithmetick,* 1676), and advised lending at interest as an appropriate remedy for a country with too much "Coin" (*Quantulum-cunque concerning Money,* 1682).

This reasoning, naturally enough, was by no means confined to England. Several years later (1701 and 1706), for example, French merchants and statesmen complained of the prevailing scarcity of coin (*disette des espéces*) as the cause of the high interest rates, and they were anxious to lower the rate of usury by increasing the circulation of money.[138]

The great Locke was, perhaps, the first to express in abstract terms the relationship between the rate of interest and the quantity of money in his controversy with Petty.[139] He was opposing Petty's proposal of a maximum rate of interest on the ground that it was as impracticable as to fix a maximum rent for land, since "the natural Value of Money, as it is apt to yield such an yearly Income by Interest, depends on the whole quantity of the then passing Money of the Kingdom, in proportion to the whole Trade of the Kingdom (*i.e.* the general Vent of all the commodities)."[140] Locke explains that Money has two values: (1) its value in use which is given by the rate of interest "and in this it has the Nature of Land, the Income of one being called Rent, of the other, Use[141], and (2) its value in exchange "and in this it has the Nature of a Commodity," its value in exchange "depending only on the Plenty or Scarcity of Money in proportion to the Plenty or Scarcity of those things and not on what Interest shall be." Thus Locke was the parent of twin quantity theories. In the first place he held that the rate of interest depended on the proportion of the quantity of money (allowing for the velocity of circulation) to the total value of trade. In the second place he held that the value of money in exchange depended on the proportion of the quantity of money to the total volume of goods in the market. But—standing with one foot in the mercantilist world and with one foot in the classical world[142]—he was confused concerning the relation between these two proportions, and he overlooked altogether the possibility of *fluctuations* in liquidity-preference. He was, however, eager to explain that a reduction in the rate of interest has no *direct* effect on the price-level and affects prices "only as the Change of Interest in Trade conduces to the bringing in or carrying out Money or Commodity, and so in time varying their Proportion here in England from what it was before," *i.e.* if the reduction in the rate of interest leads to the export of cash or an increase in output. But he never, I think, proceeds to a genuine synthesis.[143]

How easily the mercantilist mind distinguished between the rate of interest and the marginal efficiency of capital is illustrated by a passage (printed in 1621) which Locke quotes from *A Letter to a Friend concerning Usury:* "High Interest decays Trade. The advantage from Interest is greater than the Profit from Trade, which makes the rich Merchants give over, and put out their Stock to Interest, and the lesser Merchants Break." Fortrey (*England's Interest and Improvement,* 1663) affords another example of the stress laid on a low rate of interest as a means of increasing wealth.

The mercantilists did not overlook the point that, if an excessive liquidity-preference were to withdraw the influx of precious metals into hoards, the advantage to the rate of interest would be lost. In some cases (e.g. Mun) the object of enhancing the power of the

State led them, nevertheless, to advocate the accumulation of state treasure. But others frankly opposed this policy:

> Schrötter, for instance, employed the usual mercantilist arguments in drawing a lurid picture of how the circulation in the country would be robbed of all its money through a greatly increasing state treasury . . . he, too, drew a perfectly logical parallel between the accumulation of treasure by the monasteries and the export surplus of precious metals, which, to him, was indeed the worst possible thing which he could think of. Davenant explained the extreme poverty of many Eastern nations—who were believed to have more gold and silver than any other countries in the world—by the fact that treasure is suffered to stagnate "In the Princes' Coffers." . . . If hoarding by the state was considered, at best, a doubtful boon, and often a great danger, it goes without saying that private hoarding was to be shunned like the pest. It was one of the tendencies against which innumerable mercantilist writers thundered, and I do not think it would be possible to find a single dissentient voice.[144]

(2) The mercantilists were aware of the fallacy of cheapness and the danger that excessive competition may turn the terms of trade against a country. Thus Malynes wrote in his *Lex Mercatoria* (1622): "Strive not to undersell others to the hurt of the Commonwealth, under color to increase trade: for trade doth not increase when commodities are good cheap, because the cheapness proceedeth of the small request and scarcity of money, which maketh things cheap; so that the contrary augmenteth trade, when there is plenty of money, and commodities become dearer being in request."[145] Professor Heckscher sums up as follows this strand in mercantilist thought:

> In the course of a century and a half this standpoint was formulated again and again in this way, that a country with relatively less money than other countries must "sell cheap and buy dear. . . ."
>
> Even in the original edition of the *Discount of the Common Weal,* that is in the middle of the 16th century, this attitude was already manifested. Hales said, in fact, "And yet if strangers should be content to take but our wares for theirs, what should let them to advance the price of other things (meaning: among others, such as we buy from them), though ours were good cheap unto them? And then shall we be still losers, and they at the winning hand with us, while they sell dear and yet buy ours good cheap, and consequently enrich themselves and impoverish us. Yet had I rather advance our wares in price, as they advance theirs, as we now do; though some be losers thereby, and yet not so many as should be the other way." On this point he had the unqualified approval of his editor several decades later (1581). In the 17th century, this attitude recurred again without any fundamental change in significance. Thus, Malynes believed this unfortunate position to be the result of what he dreaded above all things, *i.e.* a foreign under-valuation of the English exchange. . . . The same conception then recurred continually. In his *Verbum Sapienti* (written 1665, published 1691), Petty believed that the violent efforts to increase the quantity of money could only cease "when we have certainly more money than any of our Neighbor States (though never so little), both in Arithmetical and Geometrical proportion." During the period be-

tween the writing and the publication of this work, Coke declared, "If our Treasure were more than our Neighboring Nations, I did not care whether we had one fifth part of the Treasure we now have" (1675).[146]

(3) The mercantilists were the originals of "the fear of goods" and the scarcity of money as causes of unemployment which the classicals were to denounce two centuries later as an absurdity:

One of the earliest instances of the application of the unemployment argument as a reason for the prohibition of imports is to be found in Florence in the year 1426. . . . The English legislation on the matter goes back to at least 1455. . . . An almost contemporary French decree of 1466, forming the basis of the silk industry of Lyons, later to become so famous, was less interesting in so far as it was not actually directed against foreign goods. But it, too, mentioned the possibility of giving work to tens of thousands of unemployed men and women. It is seen how very much this argument was in the air at the time. . . .

The first great discussion of this matter, as of nearly all social and economic problems, occurred in England in the middle of the 16th century or rather earlier, during the reigns of Henry VIII and Edward VI. In this connection we cannot but mention a series of writings, written apparently at the latest in the 1530's, two of which at any rate are believed to have been by Clement Armstrong. . . . He formulates it, for example, in the following terms: "By reason of great abundance of strange merchandises and wares brought yearly into England hath not only caused scarcity of money, but hath destroyed all handicrafts, whereby great number of common people should have works to get money to pay for their meat and drink, which of very necessity must live idly and beg and steal."[147]

The best instance to my knowledge of a typically mercantilist discussion of a state of affairs of this kind is the debates in the English House of Commons concerning the scarcity of money, which occurred in 1621, when a serious depression had set in, particularly in the cloth export. The conditions were described very clearly by one of the most influential members of parliament, Sir Edwin Sandys. He stated that the farmer and the artificer had to suffer almost everywhere, that looms were standing idle for want of money in the country, and that peasants were forced to repudiate their contracts, "not (thanks be to God) for want of fruits of the earth, but for want of money." The situation led to detailed enquiries into where the money could have got to, the want of which was felt so bitterly. Numerous attacks were directed against all persons who were supposed to have contributed either to an export (export surplus) of precious metals, or to their disappearance on account of corresponding activities within the country.[148]

Mercantilists were conscious that their policy, as Professor Heckscher puts it, "killed two birds with one stone." "On the one hand the country was rid of an unwelcome surplus of goods, which was believed to result in unemployment, while on the other the total stock of money in the country was increased",[149] with the resulting advantages of a fall in the rate of interest.

It is impossible to study the notions to which the mercantilists were led by their actual experiences, without perceiving that there has been a chronic tendency throughout human history for the propensity to save to be stronger than the inducement to invest. The weakness of the inducement to invest has been at all times the key to the economic problem. Today the explanation of the weakness of this inducement may chiefly lie in the extent of existing accumulations; whereas, formerly, risks and hazards of all kinds may have played a larger part. But the result is the same. The desire of the individual to augment his personal wealth by abstaining from consumption has usually been stronger than the inducement to the entrepreneur to augment the national wealth by employing labor on the construction of durable assets.

(4) The mercantilists were under no illusions as to the nationalistic character of their policies and their tendency to promote war. It was *national* advantage and *relative* strength at which they were admittedly aiming.[150]

We may criticize them for the apparent indifference with which they accepted this inevitable consequence of an international monetary system. But intellectually their realism is much preferable to the confused thinking of contemporary advocates of an international fixed gold standard and *laissez-faire* in international lending, who believe that it is precisely these policies which will best promote peace.

For in an economy subject to money contracts and customs more or less fixed over an appreciable period of time, where the quantity of the domestic circulation and the domestic rate of interest are primarily determined by the balance of payments, as they were in Great Britain before the war, there is no orthodox means open to the authorities for countering unemployment at home except by struggling for an export surplus and an import of the monetary metal at the expense of their neighbors. Never in history was there a method devised of such efficacy for setting each country's advantage at variance with its neighbors' as the international gold (or, formerly, silver) standard. For it made domestic prosperity directly dependent on a competitive pursuit of markets and a competitive appetite for the precious metals. When by happy accident the new supplies of gold and silver were comparatively abundant, the struggle might be somewhat abated.

But with the growth of wealth and the diminishing marginal propensity to consume, it has tended to become increasingly internecine. The part played by orthodox economists, whose common sense has been insufficient to check their faulty logic, has been disastrous to the latest act. For when in their blind struggle for an escape, some countries have thrown off the obligations which had previously rendered impossible an autonomous rate of interest, these economists have taught that a restoration of the former shackles is a necessary first step to a general recovery.

In truth the opposite holds good. It is the policy of an autonomous rate of interest, unimpeded by international preoccupations, and of a national investment program directed to an optimum level of domestic employment which is twice blessed in the sense that it helps ourselves and our neighbors at the same time. And it is the simultaneous pursuit of these policies by all countries together which is capable of restoring economic health and strength internationally, whether we measure it by the level of domestic employment or by the volume of international trade.[151]

IV

The mercantilists perceived the existence of the problem without being able to push their analysis to the point of solving it. But the classical school ignored the problem, as a consequence of introducing into their premises conditions which involved its non-existence; with the result of creating a cleavage between the conclusions of economic theory and those of common sense. The extraordinary achievement of the classical theory was to overcome the beliefs of the "natural man" and, at the same time, to be wrong. As Professor Heckscher expresses it:

> If, then, the underlying attitude towards money and the material from which money was created did not alter in the period between the Crusades and the 18th century, it follows that we are dealing with deep-rooted notions. Perhaps the same notions have persisted even beyond the 500 years included in that period, even though not nearly to the same degree as the "fear of goods." . . . With the exception of the period of *laissez-faire,* no age has been free from these ideas. It was only the unique intellectual tenacity of *laissez-faire* that for a time overcame the beliefs of the "natural man" on this point.[152]
>
> It required the unqualified faith of doctrinaire *laissez-faire* to wipe out the "fear of goods" . . . [which] is the most natural attitude of the "natural man" in a money economy. Free Trade denied the existence of factors which appeared to be obvious, and was doomed to be discredited in the eyes of the man in the street as soon as *laissez-faire* could no longer hold the minds of men enchained in its ideology.[153]

I remember Bonar Law's mingled rage and perplexity in face of the economists, because they were denying what was obvious. He was deeply troubled for an explanation. One recurs to the analogy between the sway of the classical school of economic theory and that of certain religions. For it is a far greater exercise of the potency of an idea to exorcise the obvious than to introduce into men's common notions the recondite and the remote.

V

There remains an allied, but distinct, matter where for centuries, indeed for several millenniums, enlightened opinion held for certain and obvious a doctrine which the classical school has repudiated as childish, but which deserves rehabilitation and honor. I mean the doctrine that the rate of interest is not self-adjusting at a level best suited to the social advantage but constantly tends to rise too high, so that a wise Government is concerned to curb it by statute and custom and even by invoking the sanctions of the moral law.

Provisions against usury are amongst the most ancient economic practices of which we have record. The destruction of the inducement to invest by an excessive liquidity-preference was the outstanding evil, the prime impediment to the growth of wealth, in the ancient and medieval worlds. And naturally so, since certain of the risks and hazards of economic life diminish the marginal efficiency of capital whilst others serve to increase the preference for liquidity. In a world, therefore, which no one reckoned to be safe, it was almost inevitable that the rate of interest, unless it was curbed by every instrument at the disposal of society, would rise too high to permit of an adequate inducement to invest.

I was brought up to believe that the attitude of the Medieval Church to the rate of interest was inherently absurd, and that the subtle discussions aimed at distinguishing the return on money-loans from the return to active investment were merely jesuitical attempts to find a practical escape from a foolish theory. But I now read these discussions as an honest intellectual effort to keep separate what the classical theory has inextricably confused together, namely, the rate of interest and the marginal efficiency of capital. For it now seems clear that the disquisitions of the schoolmen were directed towards the elucidation of a formula which should allow the schedule of the marginal efficiency of capital to be high, whilst using rule and custom and the moral law to keep down the rate of interest.

Even Adam Smith was extremely moderate in his attitude to the usury laws, For he was well aware that individual savings may be absorbed either by investment or by debts, and that there is no security that they will find an outlet in the former. Furthermore, he favored a low rate of interest as increasing the chance of savings finding their outlet in new investment rather than in debts; and for this reason, in a passage for which he was severely taken to task by Bentham,[154] he defended a moderate application of the usury laws.[155] Moreover, Bentham's criticisms were mainly on the ground that Adam Smith's Scotch caution was too severe on "projectors" and that a maximum rate of interest would leave too little margin for the reward of legitimate and socially advisable risks. For Bentham understood by *projectors* "all such persons, as, in the pursuit of wealth, or even of any other object, endeavor, by the assistance of wealth, to strike into any channel of invention . . . upon all such persons as, in the line of any of their pursuits, aim at anything that can be called *improvement.* ... It falls, in short, upon every application of the human powers, in which ingenuity stands in need of wealth for its assistance." Of course Bentham is right in protesting against laws which stand in the way of taking legitimate risks. "A prudent man," Bentham continues, "will not, in these circumstances, pick out the good projects from the bad, for he will not meddle with projects at all."[156]

It may be doubted, perhaps, whether the above is just what Adam Smith intended by his term. Or is it that we are hearing in Bentham (though writing in March 1787 from "Crichoff in White Russia") the voice of nineteenth-century England speaking to the eighteenth? For nothing short of the exuberance of the greatest age of the inducement to investment could have made it possible to lose sight of the theoretical possibility of its insufficiency.

VI

It is convenient to mention at this point the strange, unduly neglected prophet Silvio Gesell (1862–1930), whose work contains flashes of deep insight and who only just failed to reach down to the essence of the matter. In the post-war years his devotees bombarded me with copies of his works; yet, owing to certain palpable defects in the argument, I entirely failed to discover their merit. As is often the case with imperfectly analyzed intuitions, their significance only became apparent after I had reached my own conclusions in my own way. Meanwhile, like other academic economists, I treated his profoundly original strivings as being no better than those of a crank. Since few of the readers of this book are likely to be well acquainted with the significance of Gesell, I will give to him what would be otherwise a disproportionate space.

Gesell was a successful German[157] merchant in Buenos Aires who was led to the study of monetary problems by the crisis of the late 'eighties, which was especially violent in the Argentine, his first work, *Die Reformation im Munzwesen als Brüke zum socialen Staat,* being published in Buenos Aires in 1891. His fundamental ideas on money were published in Buenos Aires in the same year under the title *Nervus rerum,* and many books and pamphlets followed until he retired to Switzerland in 1906 as a man of some means, able to devote the last decades of his life to the two most delightful occupations open to those who do not have to earn their living, authorship and experimental farming.

The first section of his standard work was published in 1906 at Les Hauts Geneveys, Switzerland, under the title *Die Verwirklichung des Rechtes auf dem vollen Arbeitsertrag,* and the second section in 1911 at Berlin under the title *Die neue Lehre vom Zins.* The two together were published in Berlin and in Switzerland during the war (1916) and reached a sixth edition during his lifetime under the title *Die natürliche Wirt-schafsordnung durch Freiland und Freigeld,* the English version (translated by Mr. Philip Pye) being called *The Natural Economic Order.* In April 1919 Gesell joined the short-lived Soviet cabinet of Bavaria as their Minister of Finance, being subsequently tried by court-martial. The last decade of his life was spent in Berlin and Switzerland and devoted to propaganda. Gesell, drawing to himself the semi-religious fervor which had formerly centered round Henry George, became the revered prophet of a cult with many thousand disciples throughout the world. The first international convention of the Swiss and German Freiland-Freigeld Bund and similar organizations from many countries was held in Basle in 1923. Since his death in 1930 much of the peculiar type of fervor which doctrines such as his are capable of exciting has been diverted to other (in my opinion less eminent) prophets. Dr. Buchi is the leader of the movement in England, but its literature seems to be distributed from San Antonio, Texas, its main strength lying today in the United States, where Professor Irving Fisher, alone amongst academic economists, has recognized its significance.

In spite of the prophetic trappings with which his devotees have decorated him, Gesell's main book is written in cool, scientific language; though it is suffused throughout by a more passionate, a more emotional devotion to social justice than some think decent in a scientist. The part which derives from Henry George,[158] though doubtless an important source of the movement's strength, is of altogether secondary interest. The purpose of the book as a whole may be described as the establishment of an anti-Marxian socialism, a reaction against *laissez-faire* built on theoretical foundations totally unlike those of Marx in being based on a repudiation instead of on an acceptance of the classical hypotheses, and on an unfettering of competition instead of its abolition. I believe that the future will learn more from the spirit of Gesell than from that of Marx. The preface to *The Natural Economic Order* will indicate to the reader, if he will refer to it, the moral quality of Gesell. The answer to Marxism is, I think, to be found along the lines of this preface.

Gesell's specific contribution to the theory of money and interest is as follows. In the first place, he distinguishes clearly between the rate of interest and the marginal efficiency of capital, and he argues that it is the rate of interest which sets a limit to the rate of growth of real capital. Next, he points out that the rate of interest is a purely monetary phenomenon and that the peculiarity of money, from which flows the significance of the money rate of interest, lies in the fact that its ownership as a means of storing wealth involves the holder in negligible carrying charges, and that forms of wealth, such as stocks of commodities which do involve carrying charges, in fact yield a return because of the standard set by money. He cites the comparative stability of the rate of interest throughout the ages as evidence that it cannot depend on purely physical characters, inasmuch as the variation of the latter from one epoch to another must have been incalculably greater than the observed changes in the rate of interest; *i.e.* (in my terminology) the rate of interest, which depends on constant psychological characters, has remained stable, whilst the widely fluctuating characters, which primarily determine the schedule of the marginal efficiency of capital, have determined not the rate of interest but the rate at which the (more or less) given rate of interest allows the stock of real capital to grow.

But there is a great defect in Gesell's theory. He shows how it is only the existence of a rate of money interest which allows a yield to be obtained from lending out stocks of commodities. His dialogue between Robinson Crusoe and a stranger[159] is a most excellent economic parable—as good as anything of the kind that has been written—to demonstrate this point. But, having given the reason why the money-rate of interest unlike most commodity rates of interest cannot be negative, he altogether overlooks the need of an explanation why the money-rate of interest is positive, and he fails to explain why the money-rate of interest is not governed (as the classical school maintains) by the standard set by the yield on productive capital. This is because the notion of liquidity-preference had escaped him. He has constructed only half a theory of the rate of interest.

The incompleteness of his theory is doubtless the explanation of his work having suffered neglect at the hands of the academic world. Nevertheless he had carried his theory far enough to lead him to a practical recommendation, which may carry with it the essence of what is needed, though it is not feasible in the form in which he proposed it. He argues that the growth of real capital is held back by the money-rate of interest, and that if this brake were removed the growth of real capital would be, in the modern world, so rapid that a zero money-rate of interest would probably be justified, not indeed forthwith, but within a comparatively short period of time. Thus the prime necessity is to reduce the money-rate of interest, and this, he pointed out, can be effected by causing money to incur carrying-costs just like other stocks of barren goods. This led him to the famous prescription of "stamped" money, with which his name is chiefly associated and which has received the blessing of Professor Irving Fisher. According to this proposal currency notes (though it would clearly need to apply as well to some forms at least of bank-money) would only retain their value by being stamped each month, like an insurance card, with stamps purchased at a post office. The cost of the stamps could, of course, be fixed at any appropriate figure. According to my theory it should be roughly equal to the excess of the money-rate of interest (apart from the stamps) over the marginal efficiency of capital corresponding to a rate of new investment compatible with full employment.

The actual charge suggested by Gesell was 1 per mil. per month, equivalent to 5.4 percent per annum. This would be too high in existing conditions, but the correct figure, which would have to be changed from time to time, could only be reached by trial and error.

The idea behind stamped money is sound. It is, indeed, possible that means might be found to apply it in practice on a modest scale. But there are many difficulties which Gesell did not face. In particular, he was unaware that money was not unique in having a liquidity-premium attached to it, but differed only in degree from many other articles, deriving its importance from having a *greater* liquidity-premium than any other article. Thus if currency notes were to be deprived of their liquidity-premium by the stamping system, a long series of substitutes would step into their shoes—bank-money, debts at call, foreign money, jewelry and the precious metals generally, and so forth. As I have mentioned above, there have been times when it was probably the craving for the ownership of land, independently of its yield, which served to keep up the rate of interest;—though under Gesell's system this possibility would have been eliminated by land nationalization.

VII

The theories which we have examined above are directed, in substance, to the constituent of effective demand which depends on the sufficiency of the inducement to invest. It is no new thing, however, to ascribe the evils of unemployment to the insufficiency of the other constituent, namely, the insufficiency of the propensity to consume. But this alternative explanation of the economic evils of the day—equally unpopular with the classical economists—played a much smaller part in sixteenth-and seventeenth-century thinking and has only gathered force in comparatively recent times.

Though complaints of under-consumption were a very subsidiary aspect of mercantilist thought, Professor Heckscher quotes a number of examples of what he calls "the deep-rooted belief in the utility of luxury and the evil of thrift. Thrift, in fact, was regarded as the cause of unemployment, and for two reasons: in the first place, because real income was believed to diminish by the amount of money which did not enter into exchange, and secondly, because saving was believed to withdraw money from circulation."[160] In 1598 Laffemas (*Les Trésors et richesses pour mettre l'Estat en Splendeur*) denounced the objectors to the use of French silks on the ground that all purchasers of French luxury goods created a livelihood for the poor, whereas the miser caused them to die in distress.[161] In 1662 Petty justified "entertainments, magnificent shows, triumphal arches, etc.," on the ground that their costs flowed back into the pockets of brewers, bakers, tailors, shoemakers and so forth. Fortrey justified "excess of apparel." Von Schrotter (1686) deprecated sumptuary regulations and declared that he would wish that display in clothing and the like were even greater. Barbon (1690) wrote that "Prodigality is a vice that is prejudicial to the Man, but not to trade. . . . Covetousness is a Vice, prejudicial both to Man and Trade."[162] "In 1695 Cary argued that if everybody spent more, all would obtain larger incomes "and might then live more plentifully."[163]

But it was by Bernard Mandeville's *Fable of the Bees* that Barbon's opinion was mainly popularized, a book convicted as a nuisance by the grand jury of Middlesex in 1723, which stands out in the history of the moral sciences for its scandalous reputation. Only one man is recorded as having spoken a good word for it, namely Dr. Johnson, who declared that it did not puzzle him, but "opened his eyes into real life very much." The nature of the book's wickedness can be best conveyed by Leslie Stephen's summary in the *Dictionary of National Biography*:

> Mandeville gave great offence by this book, in which a cynical system of morality was made attractive by ingenious paradoxes. . . . His doctrine that prosperity was increased by expenditure rather than by saving fell in with many current economic fallacies not yet extinct.[164] Assuming with the ascetics that human desires were essentially evil and therefore produced "private vices" and assuming with the common view that wealth was a "public benefit," he easily showed that all civilization implied the development of vicious propensities. . . .

The text of the *Fable of the Bees* is an allegorical poem—"The Grumbling Hive, or Knaves turned honest," in which is set forth the appalling plight of a prosperous community in which all the citizens suddenly take it into their heads to abandon luxurious living, and the State to cut down armaments, in the interests of Saving:

> No Honour now could be content,
> To live and owe for what was spent,
> Liv'ries in Broker's shops are hung;
> They part with Coaches for a song;
> Sell stately Horses by whole sets;
> And Country-Houses to pay debts.
> Vain cost is shunn'd as moral Fraud;
> They have no Forces kept Abroad;
> Laugh at th' Esteem of Foreigners,
> And empty Glory got by Wars;
> They fight, but for their Country's sake,
> When Right or Liberty's at Stake.
> The haughty Chloe
> Contracts th' expensive Bill of Fare,
> And wears her strong Suit a whole Year.
> And what is the result?—
> Now mind the glorious Hive, and see
> How Honesty and Trade agree:
> The Shew is gone, it thins apace;
> And looks with quite another Face,
> For 'twas not only they that went,
> By whom vast sums were yearly spent;
> But Multitudes that lived on them,
> Were daily forc'd to do the same.
> In vain to other Trades they'd fly;
> All were o'er-stocked accordingly.
> The price of Land and Houses falls;
> Mirac'lous Palaces whose Walls,

Like those of Thebes, were rais'd by Play,
Are to be let . . .
The Building Trade is quite destroy'd,
Artificers are not employ'd;
No limner for his Art is fam'd,
Stone-cutters, Carvers are not nam'd.
So "The Moral" is:
Bare Virtue can't make Nations live
It Splendour. They that would revive
A Golden Age, must be as free,
For Acorns as for Honesty.

Two extracts from the commentary which follows the allegory will show that the above was not without a theoretical basis:

> As this prudent economy, which some people call Saving, is in private families the most certain method to increase an estate, so some imagine that, whether a country be barren or fruitful, the same method if generally pursued (which they think practicable) will have the same effect upon a whole nation, and that, for example, the English might be much richer than they are, if they would be as frugal as some of their neighbors. This, I think, is an error.[165]

On the contrary, Mandeville concludes:

> The great art to make a nation happy, and what we call flourishing, consists in giving everybody an opportunity of being employed; which to compass, let a Government's first care be to promote as great a variety of Manufactures, Arts and Handicrafts as human wit can invent; and the second to encourage Agriculture and Fishery in all their branches, that the whole Earth may be forced to exert itself as well as Man. It is from this Policy and not from the trifling regulations of Lavishness and Frugality that the greatness and felicity of Nations must be expected; for let the value of Gold and Sliver rise or fall, the enjoyment of all Societies will ever depend upon the Fruits of the Earth and the Labor of the People; both which joined together are a more certain, a more inexhaustible and a more real Treasure than the Gold of Brazil or the Silver of Potosi.

No wonder that such wicked sentiments called down the opprobrium of two centuries of moralists and economists who felt much more virtuous in possession of their austere doctrine that no sound remedy was discoverable except in the utmost of thrift and economy both by the individual and by the state. Petty's "entertainments, magnificent shews, triumphal arches, etc." gave place to the penny-wisdom of Gladstonian finance and to a state system which "could not afford" hospitals, open spaces, noble buildings, even the preservation of its ancient monuments, far less the splendors of music and the drama, all of which were consigned to the private charity or magnanimity of improvident individuals.

The doctrine did not reappear in respectable circles for another century, until in the later phase of Malthus the notion of the insufficiency of effective demand takes a definite place as a scientific explanation of unemployment. Since I have already dealt with this somewhat fully in my essay on Malthus[166] it will be sufficient if I repeat here one or two characteristic passages which I have already quoted in my essay:

We see in almost every part of the world vast powers of production which are not put into action, and I explain this phenomenon by saying that from the want of a proper distribution of the actual produce adequate motives are not furnished to continued production. . . . I distinctly maintain that an attempt to accumulate very rapidly, which necessarily implies a considerable diminution of unproductive consumption, by greatly impairing the usual motives to production must prematurely check the progress of wealth. . . . But if it be true that an attempt to accumulate very rapidly will occasion such a division between labor and profits as almost to destroy both the motive and the power of future accumulation and consequently the power of maintaining and employing an increasing population, must it not be acknowledged that such an attempt to accumulate, or that saving too much, may be really prejudicial to a country?[167]

The question is whether this stagnation of capital, and subsequent stagnation in the demand for labor arising from increased production without an adequate proportion of unproductive consumption on the part of the landlords and capitalists, could take place without prejudice to the country, without occasioning a less degree both of happiness and wealth than would have occurred if the unproductive consumption of the landlords and capitalists had been so proportioned to the natural surplus of the society as to have continued uninterrupted the motives to production, and prevented first an unnatural demand for labor and then a necessary and sudden diminution of such demand. But if this be so, how can it be said with truth that parsimony, though it may be prejudicial to the producers, cannot be prejudicial to the state; or that an increase of unproductive consumption among landlords and capitalists may not sometimes be the proper remedy for a state of things in which the motives to production fail?[168]

Adam Smith has stated that capitals are increased by parsimony, that every frugal man is a public benefactor, and that the increase of wealth depends upon the balance of produce above consumption. That these propositions are true to a great extent is perfectly unquestionable. . . . But it is quite obvious that they are not true to an indefinite extent, and that the principles of saving, pushed to excess, would destroy the motive to production. If every person were satisfied with the simplest food, the poorest clothing, and the meanest houses, it is certain that no other sort of food, clothing, and lodging would be in existence. . . . The two extremes are obvious; and it follows that there must be some intermediate point, though the resources of political economy may not be able to ascertain it, where, taking into consideration both the power to produce and the will to consume, the encouragement to the increase of wealth is the greatest.[169]

Of all the opinions advanced by able and ingenious men, which I have ever met with, the opinion of M. Say, which states that, *un produit consommé ou détruit est un débouché fermé* (I. i. ch. 15), appears to me to be the most directly opposed to just theory, and the most uniformly contradicted by experience. Yet it directly follows from the new doctrine, that commodities are to be considered only in their relation to each other,—not to the consumers. What, I would ask, would become of the demand for commodities, if all consumption except bread and water were suspended for the next half-year? What an accumulation of commodities! *Quels débouchés!* What a prodigious market would this event occasion![170]

Ricardo, however, was stone-deaf to what Malthus was saying. The last echo of the controversy is to be found in John Stuart Mill's discussion of his Wages-Fund Theory[171] which in his own mind played a vital part in his rejection of the later phase of Malthus, amidst the discussions of which he had, of course, been brought up. Mill's successors rejected his Wages-Fund Theory but overlooked the fact that Mill's refutation of Malthus depended on it. Their method was to dismiss the problem from the corpus of Economics not by solving it but by not mentioning it. It altogether disappeared from controversy. Mr. Cairncross, searching recently for traces of it amongst the minor Victorians,[172] has found even less, perhaps, than might have been expected.[173] Theories of under-consumption hibernated until the appearance in 1889 of *The Physiology of Industry*, by J. A. Hobson and A. F. Mummery, the first and most significant of many volumes in which for nearly fifty years Mr. Hobson has flung himself with unflagging, but almost unavailing, ardor and courage against the ranks of orthodoxy. Though it is so completely forgotten today, the publication of this book marks, in a sense, an epoch in economic thought.[174]

The Physiology of Industry was written in collaboration with A. F. Mummery. Mr. Hobson has told how the book came to be written as follows:[175]

It was not until the middle 'eighties that my economic heterodoxy began to take shape. Though the Henry George campaign against land values and the early agitation of various socialist groups against the visible oppression of the working classes, coupled with the revelations of the two Booths regarding the poverty of London, made a Jeep impression on my feelings, they did not destroy my faith in Political Economy. That came from what may be called an accidental contact. While teaching at a school in Exeter I came into personal relations with a business man named Mummery, known then and afterwards as a great mountaineer who had discovered another way up the Matterhorn and who, in 1895, was killed in an attempt to climb the famous Himalayan mountain Nanga Parbat. My intercourse with him, I need hardly say, did not lie on this physical plane. But he was a mental climber as well, with a natural eye for a path of his own finding and a sublime disregard of intellectual authority. This man entangled me in a controversy about excessive saving, which he regarded as responsible for the underemployment of capital and labor in periods of bad trade. For a long time I sought to counter his arguments by the use of the orthodox economic weapons. But at length he convinced me and I went in with him to elaborate the over-saving argument in a book entitled *The Physiology of Industry*, which was published in 1889. This was the first open step in my heretical career, and I did not in the least realize its momentous consequences. For just at that time I had given up my scholastic post and was opening a new line of work as University Extension Lecturer in Economics and Literature. The first shock came in a refusal of the London Extension Board to allow me to offer courses of Political Economy. This was due, I learned, to the intervention of an Economic Professor who had read my book and considered it as equivalent in rationality to an attempt to prove the flatness of the earth. How could there be any limit to the amount of useful saving when every item of saving went to increase the capital structure and the fund for paying wages? Sound economists could not fail to view with horror an argument which sought to check the source of all industrial progress.[176] Another interesting personal experience helped to bring home to me the sense of my iniquity. Though prevented from lecturing on economics in London, I had been allowed by the greater liberality of the Oxford University Extension Movement to address audiences in the Provinces, confining myself to practical issues relating to working-class life. Now it happened at this time that the Charity Organization Society was planning a lecture campaign upon economic subjects and invited me to prepare a course. I had expressed my willingness to undertake this new lecture work, when suddenly, without explanation, the invitation was withdrawn. Even then I hardly realized that in appearing to question the virtue of unlimited thrift I had committed the unpardonable sin.

In this early work Mr. Hobson with his collaborator expressed himself with more direct reference to the classical economics (in which he had been brought up) than in his later writings; and for this reason, as well as because it is the first expression of his theory, I will quote from it to show how significant and well-founded were the authors' criticisms and intuitions. They point out in their preface as follows the nature of the conclusions which they attack:

Saving enriches and spending impoverishes the community along with the individual, and it may be generally defined as an assertion that the effective love of money is the root of all economic good. Not merely does it enrich the thrifty individual himself, but it raises wages, gives work to the unemployed, and scatters blessings on every side. From the daily papers to the latest economic treatise, from the pulpit to the House of Commons, this conclusion is reiterated and re-stated till it appears positively impious to question it. Yet the educated world, supported by the majority of economic thinkers, up to the publication of Ricardo's work strenuously denied this doctrine: and its ultimate acceptance was exclusively due to their inability to meet the now exploded wages-fund doctrine. That the conclusion should have survived the argument on which it logically stood, can be explained on no other hypothesis than the commanding authority of the great men who asserted it. Economic critics have ventured to attack the theory in detail, but they have shrunk appalled from touching its main conclusions. Our purpose is to show that these conclusions are not tenable, that an undue exercise of the habit of saving is possible, and that such undue exercise impoverishes the Community, throws laborers out of work, drives down wages, and spreads that gloom and prostration through the commercial world which is known as Depression in Trade. . . .

The object of production is to provide "utilities and conveniences" for consumers, and the process is a continuous one from the first handling of the raw material to the moment when it is finally consumed as a utility or a convenience. The only use of Capital being to aid the production of these utilities and conveniences, the total used will necessarily vary with the total of utilities and conveniences daily or weekly consumed. Now saving, while it increases the existing aggregate of Capital, simultaneously reduces the quantity of utilities and conveniences consumed;

any undue exercise of this habit must, therefore, cause an accumulation of Capital in excess of that which is required for use, and this excess will exist in the form of general over-production.[177]

In the last sentence of this passage there appears the root of Hobson's mistake, namely, his supposing that it is a case of excessive saving causing the *actual* accumulation of capital in excess of what is required, which is, in fact, a secondary evil which only occurs through mistakes of foresight; whereas the primary evil is a propensity to save in conditions of full employment more than the equivalent of the capital which is required, thus preventing full employment except when there is a mistake of foresight. A page or two later, however, he puts one half of the matter, as it seems to me, with absolute precision, though still overlooking the possible role of changes in the rate of interest and in the state of business confidence, factors which he presumably takes as given:

We are thus brought to the conclusion that the basis on which all economic teaching since Adam Smith has stood, viz. that the quantity annually produced is determined by the aggregates of Natural Agents, Capital, and Labour available, is erroneous, and that, on the contrary, the quantity produced, while it can never exceed the limits imposed by these aggregates, may be, and actually is, reduced far below this maximum by the check that undue saving and the consequent accumulation of over-supply exerts on production; *i.e.* that in the normal state of modern industrial Communities, consumption limits production and not production consumption.[178]

Finally he notices the bearing of his theory on the validity of the orthodox Free Trade arguments:

We also note that the charge of commercial imbecility, so freely launched by orthodox economists against our American cousins and other Protectionist Communities, can no longer be maintained by any of the Free Trade arguments hitherto adduced, since all these are based on the assumption that oversupply is impossible.[179]

The subsequent argument is, admittedly, incomplete. But it is the first explicit statement of the fact that capital is brought into existence not by the propensity to save but in response to the demand resulting from actual and prospective consumption. The following portmanteau quotation indicates the line of thought:

It should be clear that the capital of a community cannot be advantageously increased without a subsequent increase in consumption of commodities. . . . Every increase in saving and in capital requires, in order to be effectual, a corresponding increase in immediately future consumption.[180] . . . And when we say future consumption, we do not refer to a future often, twenty, or fifty years hence, but to a future that is but little removed from the present. . . . If increased thrift or caution induces people to save more in the present, they must consent to consume more in the future.[181] . . .

No more capital can economically exist at any point in the productive process than is required to furnish commodities for the current rate of consumption.[182]. . . It is clear that my thrift in no wise affects the total economic thrift of the community, but only determines whether a particular portion of the total thrift shall have been exercised by myself or by somebody else. We shall show how the thrift of one part of the community has power to force another part to live beyond their income.[183] . . . Most modern economists deny that consumption could by any possibility be insufficient. Can we find any economic force at work which might incite a community to this excess, and if there be any such forces are there not efficient checks provided by the mechanism of commerce? It will be shown, firstly, that in every highly organized industrial society there is constantly at work a force which naturally operates to induce excess of thrift; secondly, that the checks alleged to be provided by the mechanism of commerce are either wholly inoperative or are inadequate to prevent grave commercial evil.[184] . . . The brief answer which Ricardo gave to the contentions of Malthus and Chalmers seems to have been accepted as sufficient by most later economists. "Productions are always bought by productions or by services; money is only the medium by which the exchange is effected. Hence the increased production being always accompanied by a correspondingly increased ability to get and consume, there is no possibility of Overproduction" (Ricardo, *Prin. of Pal. Econ.* p. 362).[185]

Hobson and Mummery were aware that interest was nothing whatever except payment for the use of money.[186] They also knew well enough that their opponents would claim that there would be "such a fall in the rate of interest (or profit) as will act as a check upon Saving, and restore the proper relation between production and consumption."[187] They point out in reply that "if a fall of Profit is to induce people to save less, it must operate in one of two ways, either by inducing them to spend more or by inducing them to produce less."[188] As regards the former they argue that when profits fall the aggregate income of the community is reduced, and "we cannot suppose that when the average rate of incomes is falling, individuals will be induced to increase their rate of consumption by the fact that the premium upon thrift is correspondingly diminished;" whilst as for the second alternative, "it is so far from being our intention to deny that a fall of profit, due to over-supply, will check production, that the admission of the operation of this check forms the very centre of our argument."[189] Nevertheless, their theory failed of completeness, essentially on account of their having no independent theory of the rate of interest; with the result that Mr. Hobson laid too much emphasis (especially In his later books) on under-consumption leading to over-investment, in the sense of unprofitable investment, instead of explaining that a relatively weak propensity to consume helps to cause unemployment by requiring and *not* receiving the accompaniment of a compensating volume of new investment, which, even if it may sometimes occur temporarily through errors of optimism, is in general prevented from happening at all by the prospective profit falling below the standard set by the rate of interest.

Since the war there has been a spate of heretical theories of under-consumption, of which those of Major Douglas are the most famous. The strength of Major Douglas's advocacy has, of course, largely depended on orthodoxy having no valid reply to much of his destructive criticism. On the other hand, the detail of his diagnosis, in particular the so-called A + B theorem, includes much mere mystification. If Major Douglas had limited his B-items to the financial provisions made by entrepreneurs to which no current expenditure on replacements and renewals corresponds, he would be nearer the truth. But even in that case it is necessary to allow for the possibility of these provisions being off-set by new investment in other directions as well as by increased expenditure on consumption. Major Douglas is entitled to claim, as against some of his orthodox adversaries, that he at least has not been wholly oblivious of the outstanding problem of our economic system. Yet he has scarcely established an equal claim to rank—a private, perhaps, but not a major in the brave army of heretics—with Mandeville, Malthus, Gesell and Hobson, who, following their intuitions, have preferred to see the truth obscurely and imperfectly rather than to maintain error, reached indeed with clearness and consistency and by easy logic, but on hypotheses inappropriate to the facts.

CHAPTER 24

Concluding Notes on the Social Philosophy Towards Which the General Theory Might Lead

I

The outstanding faults of the economic society in which we live are its failure to provide for full employment and its arbitrary and inequitable distribution of wealth and incomes. The bearing of the foregoing theory on the first of these is obvious. But there are also two important respects in which it is relevant to the second.

Since the end of the nineteenth century significant progress towards the removal of very great disparities of wealth and income has been achieved through the instrument of direct taxation—income tax and surtax and death duties—especially in Great Britain. Many people would wish to see this process carried much further, but they are deterred by two considerations; partly by the fear of making skilful evasions too much worth while and also of diminishing unduly the motive towards risk-taking, but mainly, I think, by the belief that the growth of capital depends upon the strength of the motive towards individual saving and that for a large proportion of this growth we are dependent on the savings of the rich out of their superfluity. Our argument does not affect the first of these considerations. But it may considerably modify our attitude towards the second. For we have seen that, up to the point where full employment prevails, the growth of capital depends not at all on a low propensity to consume but is, on the contrary, held back by it; and only in conditions of full employment is a low propensity to consume conducive to the growth of capital. Moreover, experience suggests that in existing conditions saving by institutions and through sinking funds is more than adequate, and that measures for the redistribution of incomes in a way likely to raise the propensity to consume may prove positively favorable to the growth of capital.

The existing confusion of the public mind on the matter is well illustrated by the very common belief that the death duties are responsible for a reduction in the capital wealth of the country. Assuming that the State applies the proceeds of these duties to its ordinary outgoings so that taxes on incomes and consumption are correspondingly reduced or avoided, it is, of course, true that a fiscal policy of heavy death duties has the effect of increasing the community's propensity to consume. But inasmuch as an increase in the habitual propensity to consume will in general (*i.e.,* except in conditions of full employment) serve to increase at the same time the inducement to invest, the inference commonly drawn is the exact opposite of the truth.

Thus our argument leads towards the conclusion that in contemporary conditions the growth of wealth, so far from being dependent on the abstinence of the rich, as is commonly supposed, is more likely to be impeded by it. One of the chief social justifications of great inequality of wealth is, therefore, removed. I am not saying that there are no other reasons, unaffected by our theory, capable of justifying some measure of inequality in some circumstances. But it does dispose of the most important of the reasons why hitherto we have thought it prudent to move carefully. This particularly affects our attitude towards death duties; for there are certain justifications for inequality of incomes which do not apply equally to inequality of inheritances.

For my own part, I believe that there is social and psychological justification for significant inequalities of incomes and wealth, but not for such large disparities as exist today. There are valuable human activities which require the motive of money-making and the environment of private wealth-ownership for their full fruition. Moreover, dangerous human proclivities can be canalized into comparatively harmless channels by the existence of opportunities for money-making and private wealth, which, if they cannot be satisfied in this way, may find their outlet in cruelty, the reckless pursuit of personal power and authority, and other forms of self-aggrandizement. It is better that a man should tyrannize over his bank balance than over his fellow-citizens; and whilst the former is sometimes denounced as being but a means to the tatter, sometimes at least it is an alternative. But it is not necessary for the stimulation of these activities and the satisfaction of these proclivities that the game should be played for such high stakes as at present. Much lower stakes will serve the purpose equally well, as soon as the players are accustomed to them. The task of transmuting human nature must not be confused with the task of managing it. Though in the ideal commonwealth men may have been taught or inspired or bred to take no interest in the stakes, it may still be wise and prudent statesmanship to allow the game to be played, subject to rules and limitations, so long as the average man, or even a significant section of the community, is in fact strongly addicted to the money-making passion.

II

There is, however, a second, much more fundamental inference from our argument which has a bearing on the future of inequalities of wealth; namely, our theory of the rate of interest. The justification for a moderately high rate of interest has been found hitherto in the necessity of providing a sufficient inducement to save. But we have shown that the extent of effective saving is necessarily determined by the scale of investment and that the scale of investment is promoted by a *low* rate of interest, provided that we do not attempt to stimulate it in this way beyond the point which corresponds to full employment. Thus it is to our best advantage to reduce the rate of interest to that point relatively to the schedule of the marginal efficiency of capital at which there is full employment.

There can be no doubt that this criterion will lead to a much lower rate of interest than has ruled hitherto; and, so far as one can guess at the schedules of the marginal efficiency of capital corresponding to increasing amounts of capital, the rate of interest is likely to fall steadily, it should be practicable to maintain conditions of more or less continuous full employment—unless, indeed, there is an excessive change in the aggregate propensity to consume (including the State).

I feel sure that the demand for capital is strictly limited in the sense that it would not be difficult to increase the stock of capital up to a point where its marginal efficiency had fallen to a very low figure. This would not mean that the use of capital instruments would cost almost nothing, but only that the return from them would have to cover little more than their exhaustion by wastage and obsolescence together with some margin to cover risk and the exercise of skill and judgment. In short, the aggregate return from durable goods in the course of their life would, as in the case of short-lived goods, just cover their labor-costs of production *plus* an allowance for risk and the costs of skill and supervision.

Now, though this state of affairs would be quite compatible with some measure of individualism, yet it would mean the euthanasia of the rentier, and, consequently, the euthanasia of the cumulative oppressive power of the capitalist to exploit the scarcity-value of capital. Interest today rewards no genuine sacrifice, any more than does the rent of land. The owner of capital can obtain interest because capital is scarce, just as the owner of land can obtain rent because land is scarce. But whilst there may be intrinsic reasons for the scarcity of land, there are no intrinsic reasons for the scarcity of capital.

An intrinsic reason for such scarcity, in the sense of a genuine sacrifice which could only be called forth by the offer of a reward in the shape of interest, would not exist, in the long run, except in the event of the individual propensity to consume proving to be of such a character that net saving in conditions of full employment comes to an end before capital has become sufficiently abundant. But even so, it will still be possible for communal saving through the agency of the State to be maintained at a level which will allow the growth of capital up to the point where it ceases to be scarce.

I see, therefore, the rentier aspect of capitalism as a transitional phase which will disappear when it has done its work. And with the disappearance of its rentier aspect much else in it besides will suffer a sea-change. It will be, moreover, a great advantage of the order of events which I am advocating, that the euthanasia of the rentier, of the functionless investor, will be nothing sudden, merely a gradual but prolonged continuance of what we have seen recently in Great Britain, and will need no revolution.

Thus we might aim in practice (there being nothing in this which is unattainable) at an increase in the volume of capital until it ceases to be scarce, so that the functionless investor will no longer receive a bonus; and at a scheme of direct taxation which allows the intelligence and determination and executive skill of the financier, the entrepreneur *et hoc genus omne* (who are certainly so fond of their craft that their labor could be obtained much cheaper than at present), to be harnessed to the service of the community on reasonable terms of reward. At the same time we must recognize that only experience can show how far the common will, embodied in the policy of the State, ought to be directed to increasing and supplementing the inducement to invest; and how far it is safe to stimulate the average propensity to consume, without forgoing our aim of depriving capital of its scarcity-value within one or two generations. It may turn out that the propensity to consume will be so easily strengthened by the effects of a falling rate of interest, that full employment can be reached with a rate of accumulation little greater than at present. In this event a scheme for the higher taxation of large incomes and inheritances might be open to the objection that it would lead to full employment with a rate of accumulation which was reduced considerably below the current level, I must not be supposed to deny the possibility, or even the probability, of this outcome. For in such matters it is rash to predict how the average man will react to a changed environment. If, however, it should prove easy to secure an approximation to full employment with a rate of accumulation not much greater than at present, an outstanding problem will at least have been solved. And it would remain for separate decision on what scale and by what means it is right and reasonable to call on the living generation to restrict their consumption, so as to establish, in course of time, a state of full investment for their successors.

III

In some other respects the foregoing theory is moderately conservative in its implications. For whilst it indicates the vital importance of establishing certain central controls in matters which are now left in the main to individual initiative, there are wide fields of activity which are unaffected. The State will have to exercise a guiding influence on the propensity to consume partly through its scheme of taxation, partly by fixing the rate of interest, and partly, perhaps, in other ways. Furthermore, it seems unlikely that the influence of banking policy on the rate of interest will be sufficient by itself to determine an optimum rate of investment. I conceive, therefore, that a somewhat comprehensive socialization of investment will prove the only means of securing an approximation to full employment; though this need not exclude all manner of compromises and of devices by which public authority will co-operate with private initiative. But beyond this no obvious case is made out for a system of State Socialism which would embrace most of the economic life of the community. It is not the ownership of the instruments of production which it is important for the State to assume. If the State is able to determine the aggregate amount of resources devoted to augmenting the instruments and the basic rate of reward to those who own them, it will have accomplished all that is necessary. Moreover, the necessary measures of socialization can be introduced gradually and without a break in the general traditions of society.

Our criticism of the accepted classical theory of economics has consisted not so much in finding logical flaws in its analysis as in pointing out that its tacit assumptions are seldom or never satisfied, with the result that it cannot solve the economic problems of the actual world. But if our central controls succeed in establishing an aggregate volume of output corresponding to full employment as nearly as is practicable, the classical theory comes into its own again from this point onwards. If we suppose the volume of output to be given, i.e. to be determined by forces outside the classical scheme of thought, then there is no objection to be raised against the classical analysis of the manner in which private self-interest will determine what in particular is produced, in what proportions the factors of production will be combined to produce it, and how the value of the final product will be distributed between them. Again, if we have dealt otherwise with the problem of thrift, there is no objection to be raised against the modern classical theory as to the degree of consilience between private and public advantage in conditions of perfect and imperfect competition respectively. Thus, apart from the necessity of central controls to bring about an adjustment between the propensity to consume and the inducement to invest, there is no more reason to socialize economic life than there was before.

To put the point concretely, I see no reason to suppose that the existing system seriously misemploys the factors of production which are in use. There are, of course, errors of foresight; but these would not be avoided by centralizing decisions. When 9,000,000 men are employed out of 10,000,000 willing and able to work, there is no evidence that the labor of these 9,000,000 men is misdirected. The complaint against the present system is not that these 9,000,000 men ought to be employed on different tasks, but that tasks should be available for the remaining 1,000,000 men. It is in determining the volume, not the direction, of actual employment that the existing system has broken down.

Thus I agree with Gesell that the result of filling in the gaps in the classical theory is not to dispose of the "Manchester System," but to indicate the nature of the environment which the free play of economic forces requires if it is to realize the full potentialities of production. The central controls necessary to ensure full employment will, of course, involve a large extension of the traditional functions of government. Furthermore, the modern classical theory has itself called attention to various conditions in which the free play of economic forces may need to be curbed or guided. But there will still remain a wide field for the exercise of private initiative and responsibility. Within this field the traditional advantages of individualism will still hold good.

Let us stop for a moment to remind ourselves what these advantages are. They are partly advantages of efficiency—the advantages of decentralization and of the play of self-interest. The advantage to efficiency of the decentralization of decisions and of individual responsibility is even greater, perhaps, than the nineteenth century supposed; and the reaction against the appeal to self-interest may have gone too far. But, above all, individualism, if it can be purged of its defects and its abuses, is the best safeguard of personal liberty in the sense that, compared with any other system, it greatly widens the field for the exercise of personal choice. It is also the best safeguard of the variety of life, which emerges precisely from this extended field of personal choice, and the loss of which is the greatest of all the losses of the homogeneous or totalitarian state. For this variety preserves the traditions which embody the most secure and successful choices of former generations; it colors the present with the diversification of its fancy; and, being the handmaid of experiment as well as of tradition and of fancy, it is the most powerful instrument to better the future.

Whilst, therefore, the enlargement of the functions of government, involved in the task of adjusting to one another the propensity to consume and the inducement to invest, would seem to a nineteenth-century publicist or to a contemporary American financier to be a terrific encroachment on individualism, I defend it, on the contrary, both as the only practicable means of avoiding the destruction of existing economic forms in their entirety and as the condition of the successful functioning of individual initiative.

For if effective demand is deficient, not only is the public scandal of wasted resources intolerable, but the individual enterpriser who seeks to bring these resources into action is operating with the odds loaded against him. The game of hazard which he plays is furnished with many zeros, so that the players *as a whole* will lose if they have the energy and hope to deal all the cards. Hitherto the increment of the world's wealth has fallen short of the aggregate of positive individual savings; and the difference has been made up by the losses of those whose courage and initiative have not been supplemented by exceptional skill or unusual good fortune. But if effective demand is adequate, average skill and average good fortune will be enough.

The authoritarian state systems of today seem to solve the problem of unemployment at the expense of efficiency and of freedom. It is certain that the world will not much longer tolerate the unemployment which, apart from brief intervals of excitement, is associated—and, in my opinion, inevitably associated—with present-day capitalistic individualism. But it may be possible by a right analysis of the problem to cure the disease whilst preserving efficiency and freedom.

IV

I have mentioned in passing that the new system might be more favorable to peace than the old has been. It is worth while to repeat and emphasize that aspect.

War has several causes. Dictators and others such, to whom war offers, in expectation at least, a pleasurable excitement, find it easy to work on the natural bellicosity of their peoples. But, over and above this, facilitating their task of fanning the popular flame, are the economic causes of war, namely, the pressure of population and the competitive struggle for markets. It is the second factor, which probably played a pre-dominant part in the nineteenth century, and might again, that is germane to this discussion.

I have pointed out in the preceding chapter that, under the system of domestic *laissez-faire* and an international gold standard such as was orthodox in the latter half of the nineteenth century, there was no means open to a government whereby to mitigate economic distress at home except through the competitive struggle for markets. For all measures helpful to a state of chronic or intermittent under-employment were ruled out, except measures to improve the balance of trade on income account.

Thus, whilst economists were accustomed to applaud the prevailing international system as furnishing the fruits of the international division of labor and harmonizing at the same time the interests of different nations, there lay concealed a less benign influence; and those statesmen were moved by common sense and a correct apprehension of the true course of events, who believed that if a rich, old country were to neglect the struggle for markets its prosperity would droop and fail. But if nations can learn to provide themselves with full employment by their domestic policy (and, we must add, if they can also attain equilibrium in the trend of their population), there need be no important economic forces calculated to set the interest of one country against that of its neighbors. There would still be room for the international division of labor and for international lending in appropriate conditions. But there would no longer be a pressing motive why one country need force its wares on another or repulse the offerings of its neighbor, not because this was necessary to enable it to pay for what it wished to purchase, but with the express object of upsetting the equilibrium of payments so as to develop a balance of

1442 THE REAL PRICE OF EVERYTHING

trade in its own favor. International trade would cease to be what it is, namely, a desperate expedient to maintain employment home by forcing sales on foreign markets and restricting purchases, which, if successful, will merely shift the problem of unemployment to the neighbor which is worsted in the struggle, but a willing and unimpeded exchange of goods and services in conditions of mutual advantage.

V

Is the fulfillment of these ideas a visionary hope? Have they insufficient roots in the motives which govern the evolution of political society? Are the interests which they will thwart stronger and more obvious than those which they will serve?

I do not attempt an answer in this place. It would need a volume of a different character from this one to indicate even in outline the practical measures in which they might be gradually clothed. But if the ideas are correct—a hypothesis on which the author himself must necessarily base what he writes—it would be a mistake, I predict, to dispute their potency over a period of time. At the present moment people are unusually expectant of a more fundamental diagnosis; more particularly ready to receive it; eager to try it out, if it should be even plausible. But apart from this contemporary mood, the ideas of economists and political philosophers, both when they are right and when they are wrong, are more powerful than is commonly understood. Indeed the world is ruled by little else. Practical men, who believe themselves to be quite exempt from any intellectual influences, are usually the slaves of some defunct economist. Madmen in authority, who hear voices in the air, are distilling their frenzy from some academic scribbler of a few years back. I am sure that the power of vested interests is vastly exaggerated compared with the gradual encroachment of ideas. Not, indeed, immediately, but after a certain interval; for in the field of economic and political philosophy there are not many who are influenced by new theories after they are twenty-five or thirty years of age, so that the ideas which civil servants and politicians and even agitators apply to current events are not likely to be the newest. But, soon or late, it is ideas, not vested interests, which are dangerous for good or evil.

ENDNOTES

1 "The classical economists" was a name invented by Marx to cover Ricardo and James Mill and their *predecessors,* that is to say for the founders of the theory which culminated in the Ricardian economics. I have become accustomed, perhaps perpetrating a solecism, to include in "the classical school" *followers* of Ricardo, those, that is to say, who adopted and perfected the theory of the Ricardian economics, including (for example) J. S. Mill, Marshall, Edgeworth and Prof. Pigou.

2 This is in the Ricardian tradition. For Ricardo expressly repudiated any interest in the *amount* of the national dividend, as distinct from its distribution. In this he was assessing correctly the character of his own theory. But his successors, less clear-sighted, have used the classical theory in discussions concerning the causes of wealth. *Vide* Ricardo's letter to Malthus of October 9, 1820: "Political Economy you think is an enquiry into the nature and causes of wealth—I think it should be called an enquiry into the laws which determine the division of the produce of industry amongst the classes who concur in its formation. No law can be laid down respecting quantity, but a tolerably correct one can be laid down respecting proportions. Every day I am more satisfied that the former enquiry is vain and delusive, and the latter only the true objects of the science."

3 For example. Prof. Pigou in the *Economics of Welfare* (4th ed. p. 127) writes (my italics): "Throughout this discussion, except when the contrary is expressly stated, the fact that some resources are generally unemployed against the will of the owners is ignored. *This does not affect the substance of the argument,* while it simplifies its exposition." Thus, whilst Ricardo expressly disclaimed any attempt to deal with the amount of the national dividend as a whole, Prof. Pigou, in a book which is specifically directed to the problem of the national dividend, maintains that the same theory holds good when there is some involuntary unemployment as in the *case* of full employment.

4 Prof. Pigou's *Theory of Unemployment* is examined in more detail in the Appendix to Chapter 19 below.

5 *Cf.* the quotation from Prof. Pigou above, p. 5, footnote.

6 This point is dealt with in detail in the Appendix to Chapter 19 below.

7 This argument would, indeed, contain, to my thinking, a large element of truth, though the complete results of a change in money-wages are more complex, as we shall show in Chapter 19 below.

8 Cf. Chapter 19, Appendix.

9 The argument runs as follows : *n* men are employed, the *n*th man adds a bushel a day to the harvest, and wages have a buying power of a bushel a day. The *n* + 1th man, however, would only add 9 bushels a day, and employment cannot, therefore, rise to *n* + 1 men unless the price of corn rises relatively to wages until daily wages have a buying power of 9 bushels. Aggregate wages would then amount to ((set equation)) 9/10 . (*n* + 1) bushels as compared with *n* bushels previously. Thus the employment of an additional man will, if it occurs, necessarily involve a transfer of income from those previously in work to the entrepreneurs.

10 *Principles of Political Economy,* Book III. Chap. xiv. §2.

11 P. 34.

12 Mr. J. A. Hobson, after quoting in his *Physiology of Industry* (p. 102) the above passage from Mill, points out that Marshall commented as follows on this passage as early as his *Economics of Industry,* p. 154. "But though men have the power to purchase, they may not choose to use it." "But," Mr Hobson continues, "he fails to grasp the critical importance of this fact, and appears to limit its action to periods of 'crisis.'" This has remained fair comment, I think, in the light of Marshall's later work.

13 *Cf.* Alfred and Mary Marshall, *Economics of Industry,* p. 17: "It is not good for trade to have dresses made of material which wears out quickly. For if people did not spend their means on buying new dresses they would spend them on giving employment to labor in some other way." The reader will notice that I am again quoting from the earlier Marshall. The Marshall of the *Principles* had become sufficiently doubtful to be very cautious and evasive. But the old ideas were never repudiated or rooted out of the basic assumptions of his thought.

14 It is the distinction of Prof. Robbins that he, almost alone, continues to maintain a consistent scheme of thought, his practical recommendations belonging to the same system as his theory.

15 A precise definition of *user cost* will be given in Chapter 6.

16 Not to be confused *(vide infra)* with the supply price of a unit of output in the ordinary sense of this term.

17 The reader will observe that I am deducting the user cost both from the *proceeds* and from the *aggregate supply price* of a given volume of output, so that both these terms are to be interpreted net of user cost; whereas the aggregate sums paid by the purchasers are, of course, *gross* of user cost. The reasons why this is convenient will be given in Chapter 6. The essential point is that the aggregate proceeds and aggregate supply price net of user cost can be defined uniquely and unambiguously; whereas, since user cost is obviously dependent both on the degree of integration of industry and on the extent to which entrepreneurs buy from one another, there can be no definition of the aggregate sums paid by purchasers, *inclusive* of user cost, which is independent of these factors. There is a similar difficulty even in defining supply price in the ordinary sense for an individual producer; and in the case of the aggregate supply price of *output as a whole* serious difficulties of duplication are involves, which have not always been faced. If the term is to be interpreted gross of user cost, they can only be overcome by making special assumptions relating to the integration of entrepreneurs in groups according as they produce consumption-goods or capital-goods, which are obscure and complicated in themselves and do not correspond to the facts. If, however, aggregate supply price is defined as above *net* of user cost, these difficulties do not arise. The reader is advised, however, to await the fuller discussion in Chapter 6 and its appendix.

18 An entrepreneur, who has to reach a practical decision as to his scale of production, does not, of count, entertain a single undoubting expectation of what the sale-proceeds of a given output will be, but several hypothetical expectations held with varying degrees of probability and definiteness. By expectation of proceeds I mean, therefore, that expectation of proceeds which, if it were held with certainty, would lead to the same behavior as does the bundle of vague and more various possibilities which actually makes up his state of expectation when he reaches his decision.

19 In Chapter 20 a function closely related to the above will be called the employment function.

20 Defined in Chapter 10, below.

21 *Vide* Pigou, *Economics of Welfare, passim,* and particularly Part I. chap. iii.

22 Though, as a convenient compromise, the real income, which is taken to constitute the National Dividend, is usually limited to those goods and services which can be bought for money.

23 *Economics of Welfare.,* Part 1. chap, v., on "What is meant by maintaining Capital intact"; as amended by a recent article in the *Economic Journal,* June 1935, p. 225.

24 Cf. Prof. Hayek's criticisms, *Economica,* Aug. 1935, p. 247.

25 If X stands for any quantity measured in terms of money, it will often be convenient to write X_w for the same quantity measured in terms of the wage-unit.

26 This is the main reason why the supply price of output rises with increasing demand even when there is still a surplus of equipment identical in type with the equipment in use. If we suppose that the surplus supply of labor forms a pool equally available to all entrepreneurs and that labor employed for a given purpose is rewarded, in part at least, per unit of effort and not with strict regard to its efficiency in its actual particular employment (which is in most cases the realistic assumption to make), the diminishing efficiency of the labor employed is an outstanding example of rising supply price with increasing output, not due to internal diseconomies.

27 How the supply curve in ordinary use is supposed to deal with the above difficulty I cannot say, since those who use this curve have not made their assumptions very clear. Probably they are assuming that labor employed for a given purpose is always rewarded with strict regard to its efficiency for that purpose. But this is unrealistic. Perhaps the essential reason for treating the varying efficiency of labor as though it belonged to the equipment lies in the fact that the increasing surpluses, which emerge as output is increased, accrue in practice mainly to the owners of the equipment and not to the more efficient workers (though these may get an advantage through being employed more regularly and by receiving earlier promotion); that is to say, men of differing efficiency working at the same job are seldom paid at rates closely proportional to their efficiencies. Where, however, increased pay for higher efficiency occurs, and in so far as it occurs, my method takes account of it; since in calculating the number of labor units employed, the individual workers are weighted in proportion to their

remuneration. On my assumptions interesting complications obviously arise where we are dealing with particular supply curves since their shape will depend on the demand for suitable labor in other directions. To ignore these complications would, as I have said, be unrealistic. But we need not consider them when we are dealing with employment as a whole, provided we assume that a given volume of effective demand has a particular distribution of this demand between different products uniquely associated with it. It may be, however, that this would not hold good irrespective of the particular cause of the change in demand. *E.g.* an increase in effective demand due to an increased propensity to consume might find itself faced by a different aggregate supply function from that which would face an equal increase in demand due to an increased inducement to invest. All this, however, belong to the detailed analysis of the general ideas here set forth, which it is no part of my immediate purpose to pursue.

27 For the method of arriving at an equivalent of these expectations in terms of sale-proceeds see footnote (3) to p. 14 above.

28 *Daily* here stands for the shortest interval after which the firm is free to revise its decision as to how much employment to offer. It is, so to speak, the minimum effective unit of economic time.

29 It is not necessary that the level of long-period employment should be *constant, i.e.* long-period conditions are not necessarily static. For example, a steady increase in wealth or population may constitute a part of the unchanging expectation. The only condition is that the existing expectations should have been foreseen sufficiently far ahead.

30 This emphasis on the expectation entertained when the decision to produce is taken, meets, I think, Mr. Hawtrey's point that input and employment are influenced by the accumulation of stocks *before* prices have fallen or disappointment in respect of output is reflected in a realized loss relatively to expectation. For the accumulation of unsold stocks (or decline of forward orders) is precisely the kind of event which is most likely to cause input to differ from what the mere statistics of the sale-proceeds of previous output would indicate if they were to be projected without criticism into the next period.

31 Some further observations on user cost are given in an appendix to this chapter.

32 As distinguished from his *net income* which we shall define below.

33 *Supply price* is, I think, an incompletely defined term, if the problem of defining user cost has been ignored. The matter is further discussed in the appendix to this chapter, where I argue that the exclusion of user cost from supply price, whilst sometimes appropriate in the case of aggregate supply price, is inappropriate to the problems of the supply price of a unit of output for an individual firm.

34 For example, let us take $Z_w = f(N)$, or alternatively $Z = W \cdot f(N)$ as the aggregate supply function (where W is the wage-unit and $W. Z_w = Z$). Then, since the proceeds of the marginal product is equal to the marginal factor-cost at every point on the aggregate supply curve, we have

$$DN = DA_w - DU_w = DZ_w = D f(N),$$

that is to say $f'(N) = 1$; provided that factor cost bears a constant ratio to wage cost, and that the aggregate supply function for each firm (the number of which is assumed to be constant) is independent of the number of men employed in other industries, so that the terms of the above equation, which hold good for each individual entrepreneur, can be summed for the entrepreneurs as a whole. This means that, if wages are constant and other factor costs are a constant proportion of the wages-bill, the aggregate supply function is linear with a slope given by the reciprocal of the money-wage.

35 *Economic Journal,* June 1935, P. 235.

36 "The Maintenance of Capital," *Economica,* August 1935, p. 241 *et seq.*

37 This way of putting it depends on the convenient assumption that the marginal prime cost curve is continuous throughout its length for changes in output. In fact, this assumption is often unrealistic, and there may be one or more point: of discontinuity, especially when we reach an output corresponding to the technical full capacity of the equipment. In this case the marginal analysis partially breaks down; and the price may *exceed* the marginal prime cost, where the latter is reckoned in respect of a small *decrease* of output. (Similarly there may often be a discontinuity in the downward direction, *i.e.* for a reduction in output *below* a certain point.) This is important when

we are considering the short-period supply price in long-period equilibrium, since in that case any discontinuities, which may exist corresponding to a point of technical full capacity, must be supposed to be in operation. Thus the short-period supply price in long-period equilibrium may have to exceed the marginal prime cost (reckoned in terms of a small *decrease* of output).

38 Since user cost partly depends on expectations as to the future level of wages, a reduction in the wage-unit which is expected to be short-lived will cause factor cost and user cost to move in different proportions and so affect what equipment is used, and, conceivably, the level of effective demand, since factor cost may enter into the determination of effective demand in a different way from user cost.

39 The user cost of the equipment which is first brought into use is not necessarily independent of the total volume of output (see below); *i.e.* the user cost may be affected all along the line when the total volume of output is changed.

40 It will be more when it is expected that a more than normal yield can be obtained at some later date, which, however, is not expected to last long enough to justify (or give time for) the production of new equipment. Today's user cost is equal to the maximum of the discounted values of the potential expected yield of all the tomorrows.

41 Mr. Hawtrey (*Economica*, May 1934, p. 145) has called attention to Prof. Pigou's identification of supply price with marginal labor cost, and has contended that Prof. Pigou's argument is thereby seriously vitiated.

42 My method there was to regard the current realized profit as determining the current expectation of profit.

43 *Vide Mr.* Robertson's article "Saving and Hoarding" (*Economic Journal,* September 1933, p. 399) and the discussion between Mr. Robertson, Mr, Hawtrey and myself (*Economic Journal,* December 1933, p. 658).

44 *Quarterly Journal of Economics,* Nov. 1932, p. 123.

45 *Loc. Cit.* p. 125.

46 *Cf.* Chapter 14 below.

47 It may be mentioned, in passing, that the effect of fiscal policy on the growth of wealth has been the subject of an important misunderstanding which, however, we cannot discuss adequately without the assistance of the theory of the rate of interest to be given in Book IV.

48 *Cf.* p. 251 below.

49 The actual figures are deemed of so little interest that they are only published two years or more in arrear.

50 In the year ending March 31, 1930, local authorities spent £87,000,000 on capital account, of which £37,000,000 was provided by sinking funds, etc., in respect of previous capital expenditure; in the year ending March 31, 1933, the figures were £81,000,000 and £46,000,000.

51 *Op. cit.* pp. 117 and 138.

52 These references are taken from a Bulletin (No. 52) of the National Bureau of Economic Research, giving preliminary results of Mr. Kuznets' forthcoming book.

53 In some passages of this section we have tacitly anticipated ideas which will be introduced in Book IV.

54 More precisely, if e, and e', are the elasticities of employment in industry as a whole and in the investment industries respectively, and if N and N_2 are the numbers of men employed in industry as a whole and in the investment industries, we have

$$DY_w = Y_w/e_e.N \cdot DN$$

and

$$DI_w = I_w/e'_e.N_2 \cdot DN_2,$$

so that

$$DN_w = e_e/e'_e - I_w/N_2 - N/Y_w \cdot k .DN_2,$$

i.e.,

$$k' = I_w/e'_e N_2 \cdot e_e N/Y_w \cdot k.$$

If, however, there is no reason to expect any material relevant difference in the shapes of the aggregate supply functions for industry as a whole and for the investment industries respectively, so that $I_w/e'_e N_2 = Y_w/e_e.N$, then it follows that $DY_w/DN = DI_w/DN2$ and, therefore, that $k = k'$.

55 Our quantities are measured throughout in terms of wage-units.

56 Though in the more generalized case it is also a function of the physical conditions of production in the investment and consumption Industries respectively.

57 *Cf.* Chapter 21, p. 303, below.

58 *Cf.*, however, below, p. 128, for an American estimate.

59 Quantity of investment is measured, above, by the number of men employed in producing it. Thus if there are diminishing returns per unit of employment as employment increases, what is double the quantity of investment on the above scale will be less than double on a physical scale (if such a scale is available).

60 More generally, the ratio of the proportional change in total demand to the proportional change in investment

= DY/Y / DI/I = DY/Y . (Y-C)/(DY – DC) = (I – C/Y)/(I – dC/dY)

As wealth increases dC/dY diminishes, but C/Y also diminishes. Thus the fraction increases or diminishes according as consumption increases or diminishes in a smaller or greater proportion than income.

61 It is often convenient to use the term "loan expenditure" to include both public investment financed by borrowing from individuals and also any other current public expenditure which is so financed. Strictly speaking, the latter should be reckoned as negative saving, but official action of this kind is not influenced by the same sort of psychological motives as those which govern private saving. Thus "loan expenditure" is a convenient expression for the net borrowings of public authorities on all accounts, whether on capital account or to meet a budgetary deficit. The one form of loan expenditure operates by increasing investment and the other by increasing the propensity to consume.

62 For the sake of simplicity of statement I have slurred the point that we are dealing with complexes of rates of interest and discount corresponding to the different lengths of time which will elapse before the various prospective returns from the asset are realized. But it is not difficult to re-state the argument so as to cover this point.

63 But was he not wrong in supposing that the marginal productivity theory of wage: is equally circular?

64 *Of. cit.* p. 168

65 *Op. cit.* p. 159.

66 *Op, cit.* p, 155.

67 *Cf.* Mr. Robertson's article on "Industrial Fluctuations and the Natural Rate of Interest," *Economic Journal,* December 1934.

68 Not completely; for its value partly reflects the *uncertainty* of the future. Moreover, the relation between rates of interest for different terms depends on expectations.

69 By "very uncertain" I do not mean the same thing as "very improbable." *Cf.* my *Treatise on Probability,* chap. 6, on "The Weight of Arguments".

70 In my *Treatise on Money* (vol. ii. p. 195) I pointed out that when a company's shares are quoted very high so that it can raise more capital by issuing more shares on favorable terms, this has the same effect as if it could borrow at a low rate of interest. I should now describe this by saying that a high quotation for existing equities involves an increase in the marginal efficiency of the corresponding type of capital and therefore has the same effect (since investment depends on a comparison between the marginal efficiency of capital and the rate of interest) as a fall in the rate of interest.

71 This does not apply, of course, to classes of enterprise which are not readily marketable or to which no negotiable instrument closely corresponds. The categories falling within this exception were formerly extensive. But measured as a proportion of the total value of new investment they are rapidly declining in importance.

72 The practice, usually considered prudent, by which an investment trust or an insurance office frequently calculates not only the income from its investment portfolio but also its capital valuation in the market, may also tend to direct too much attention to Short-term fluctuations in the latter.

73 It is said that, when Wall Street is active, at least a half of the purchases or sales of investments are entered upon with an intention on the part of the speculator to reverse them the *same day.* This is often true of the commodity exchanges also.

74 Without disturbance to this definition, we can draw the line between "money" and "debts" at whatever point

is most convenient for handling a particular problem. For example, we can treat as *money* any command over general purchasing power which the owner has not parted with for a period in excess of three months, and as *debt* what cannot be recovered for a longer period than this; or we can substitute for "three months" one month or three days or three hours or any other period; or we can exclude from *money* whatever is not legal tender on the spot. It is often convenient in practice to include in *money* time-deposits with banks and, occasionally, even such instruments as (*e.g.*) treasury bills. As a rule, I shall, as in my *Treatise on Money*, assume that money is co-extensive with bank deposits.

75 In general discussion, as distinct from specific problems where the period of the debt is expressly specified, it is convenient to mean by the rate of interest the complex of the various rates of interest current for different periods of time. *i.e.* for debts of different, maturities.

76 This is the same point as I discussed in my *Treatise on Money* under the designation of the two views and the "bull-bear" position.

77 It might be thought that, in the same way, an individual, who believed that the prospective yield of investments will be below what the market is expecting, will have a sufficient reason for holding liquid cash. But this is not the case. He has a sufficient reason for holding cash or debts in preference to equities; but the purchase of debts will be a preferable alternative to holding cash, unless he also believes that the future rate of interest will prove to be higher than the market is supposing.

78 *See* the Appendix to this Chapter for an abstract of what I have been able to find.

79 *Cf.* p, 186 below for a further discussion of this passage.

80 Prof. Carver's discussion of Interest is difficult to follow (1) through his inconsistency as to whether he means by "marginal productivity of capital" quantity of marginal product or value of marginal product, and (2) through his making no attempt to define quantity of capital.

81 In a very recent discussion of these problems ("Capital, Time and the Interest Rate," by Prof. F. H. Knight, *Economica*, August 1932), a discussion which contains many interesting and profound observations on the nature of capital, and confirms the soundness of the Marshallian tradition as to the uselessness of the Bohm-Bawerkian analysis, the theory of interest is given precisely in the traditional, classical mould. Equilibrium in the field of capital production means, according to Prof. Knight, "such a rate of interest that savings flow into the market at precisely the same time-rate or speed as they flow into investment producing the same net rate of return as that which is paid savers for their use".

82 This diagram was suggested to me by Mr. R. F. Harrod. Cf. also a partly similar schematism by Mr D. H. Robertson, *Economic Journal*, December 1934, p. 652.

83 *Cf.* Chapter 17 below.

84 The "neutral" rate of interest of contemporary economists is different both from the "natural" rate of Bohm-Bawerk and from the "natural" rate of Wicksell.

85 See the Appendix to this Chapter.

86 It is to be noticed that Marshall uses the word "capital" not "money" and the word "stock" not "loans"; yet interest is a payment for borrowing *money*, and "demand for capital" in this context should mean "demand for loans of money for the purpose of buying a stock of capital-goods." But the equality between the stock of capital-goods offered and the stock demanded will be brought about by the *prices* of capital-goods, not by the rate of interest. It is equality between the demand and supply of loans of money, *i.e.* of debts, which is brought about by the rate of interest.

87 This assumes that income is *not* constant. But it is not obvious in what way a rise in the rate of interest will lead to "extra work." Is the suggestion that a rise in the rate of interest is to be regarded, by reason of its increasing the attractiveness of working in order to save, as constituting a sort of increase in real wages which will induce the factors of production to work for a lower wage? This is, I think, in Mr. D. H. Robertson's mind in a similar context. Certainly this "would not quickly amount to much"; and an attempt to explain the actual fluctuations in the amount of investment by means of this factor would be most implausible, indeed absurd. My rewriting of the latter half of this sentence would be: "and if an extensive increase in the demand for capital in general, due to an

increase in the schedule of the marginal efficiency of capital, is *not* offset by a rise in the rate of interest, the extra employment and the higher level of income, which will ensue as a result of the increased production of capital-goods, will lead to an amount of extra waiting which in terms of money will be exactly equal to the value of the current increment of capital-goods and will, therefore, precisely provide for it."

88 Why not by a rise in the supply price of capital-goods? Suppose, for example, that the "extensive increase in the demand for capital in general" is due to a *fall* in the rate of interest. I would suggest that the sentence should be rewritten: "In so far, therefore, as the extensive increase in the demand for capital-goods cannot be immediately met by an increase in the total stock, it will have to be held in check for the time being by a rise in the supply price of capital-goods sufficient to keep the marginal efficiency of capital in equilibrium with the rate of interest without there being any material change in the scale of investment; meanwhile (as always) the factors of production adapted for the output of capital-goods will be used in producing those capital-goods of which the marginal efficiency is greatest in the new conditions."

89 In fact we cannot speak of it at all. We can only properly speak of the rate of interest on *money* borrowed for the purpose of purchasing investments of capital, new or old (or for any other purpose).

90 Here the wording is ambiguous as to whether we are to infer that the postponement of consumption *necessarily* has this effect, or whether it merely releases resources which are then either unemployed or used for investment according to circumstances.

91 Not, be it noted, the amount of money which the recipient of income might, but does not, spend on consumption; so that the reward of waiting is not interest but quasi-rent. This sentence seems to imply that the released resources are necessarily *used*. For what is the reward of waiting if the released resources are left unemployed?

92 We are not told in this passage whether net savings would or would not be equal to the increment of capital, if we were to ignore misdirected investment but were to take account of "temporary accumulations of *unused* claims upon services in the form of bank-money." But in *Industrial Fluctuations* (p. 22) Prof. Pigou makes it clear that such accumulations have no effect on what he calls "real savings".

93 This reference (*op. cit.* pp. 129-134) contains Prof. Pigou's view as to the amount by which a new credit creation by the banks increases the stream of real capital available for entrepreneurs. In effect he attempts to deduct "from the floating credit handed over to business men through credit creations the floating capital which would have been contributed in other ways if the banks had not been there." After these deductions have been made, the argument is one of deep obscurity. To begin with, the rentiers have an income of 1500, of which they consume 500 and save 1000; the act of credit creation reduces their income to 1500, of which they consume 500 - x and save 800 + x; and x, Prof. Pigou concludes, represents the net increase of capital made available by the act of credit creation. Is the entrepreneurs' *income* supposed to be swollen by the amount which they *borrow* from the banks (after making the above deductions)? Or is it swollen by the amount, *i.e.* 200, by which the rentiers' income is reduced? In either case, are they supposed to save the whole of it? Is the increased investment equal to the credit creations *minus* the deductions? Or is it equal to x? The argument seems to stop just where it should begin.

94 *The Theory of Money and Credit,* p. 339 *et passim,* particularly p, 363.

95 If we are in long-period equilibrium, special assumptions might be devised on which this could be justified. But when the prices in question are the prices prevailing in slump conditions, the simplification of supposing that the entrepreneur will, in forming his expectations, assume these prices to be permanent, is certain to be misleading. Moreover, if he does, the prices of the existing stock of producers' goods will fall in the same proportion as the prices of consumers' goods.

96 Economic Reconstruction, p. 233.

97 We must postpone to Book V. the question of what will determine the character of the new equilibrium.

98 If we had defined V, not as equal to Y/M_1 but as equal to Y/M, then, of course, the Quantity Theory is a truism which holds in all circumstances, though without significance.

99 This point will be further developed in Chapter 21 below.

100 *Cf.* Marshall's note on Böhm-Bawerk, *Principles,* p. 583.

101 This relationship was first pointed out by Mr. Sraffa, *Economic Journal,* March 1932, p. 50.

102 See Chapter 20.

103 This is a matter which will be examined in greater detail in Chapter 19 below.

104 If wages (and contracts) were fixed in terms of wheat, it might be that wheat would acquire some of money's liquidity-premium;—we will return to this question in (iv) below.

105 See p. 172 above.

106 A zero elasticity is a more stringent condition than is necessarily required.

107 *Cf.* the footnote to p. 148 above.

108 The attribute of "liquidity" is by no means independent of the presence of these two characteristics. For it is unlikely that an asset, of which the supply can be easily increased or the desire for which can be easily diverted by a change in relative price, will possess the attribute of "liquidity" in the minds of owners of wealth. Money itself rapidly loses the attribute of "liquidity" if its future supply is expected to undergo sharp changes.

109 A mortgage and the interest thereon are, indeed, fixed in terms of money. But the fact that the mortgagor has the option to deliver the land itself in discharge of the debt—and must so deliver it if he cannot find the money on demand—has sometimes made the mortgage system approximate to a contract of land for future delivery against land for spot delivery. There have been sales of lands to tenants against mortgages effected by them, which, in fact, came very near to being transactions of this character.

110 This definition does not correspond to any of the various definitions of *neutral money* given by recent writers; though it may, perhaps, have some relation to the objective which these writers have had in mind.

111 *Cf.* Chapter 20 below.

112 We are ignoring at this stage certain complications which arise when the employment functions of different products have different curvatures within the relevant range of employment. See Chapter 20 below.

113 Defined in Chapter 20 below.

114 The effects of changes in the wage-unit will be considered in detail in Chapter 19.

115 In an appendix to this chapter Professor Pigou's *Theory of Unemployment* is criticized in detail.

116 The source of the fallacious practice of equating marginal wage-cost to marginal prime-cost may, perhaps, be found in an ambiguity in the meaning of *marginal wage-cost*. We might mean by it the cost of an additional unit of output if no additional cost is incurred except additional wage-cost; or we might mean the additional wage-cost involved in producing an additional unit of output in the most economical way with the help of the existing equipment and other unemployed factors. In the former case we are precluded from combining with the additional labor any additional entrepreneurship or working capital or anything else other than labor which would add to the cost; and we are even precluded from allowing the additional labor to wear out the equipment any faster than the smaller labor force would have done. Since in the former *case* we have forbidden any element of cost other than labor cost to enter into marginal prime-cost, it does, of course, follow that marginal wage-cost and marginal prime-cost are equal. But the results of an analysis conducted on this premises have almost no application, since the assumption on which it is based is very seldom realized in practice. For we are not so foolish in practice as to refuse to associate with additional labor appropriate additions of other factors, in so far as they are available, and the assumption will therefore, only apply if we assume that all the factors, other than labor, are already being employed to the utmost.

117 *Op. cit.* p. 252.

118 There is no hint or suggestion that this comes about through reactions on the rate of interest.

119 Those who (rightly) dislike algebra will lose little by omitting the first section of this chapter.

120 For, if p_{wr} is the expected price of a unit of output in terms of the wage-unit,

$$DD_{wr} = D(P_{wr}O_r) = P_{wr}DO_r + O_rDP_{wr}$$
$$= D_{wr}/O_r \cdot DO_r + O_r \cdot DP_{wr}$$

so that

$$O_rDP_{wr} + DD_{wr}(I - e_{or})$$

or

$$DD_{wr} = O_r \cdot DP_{wr}/(I - e_{or})$$

But

$$O_r DP_{wr} = DD_{wr} - P_{wr} DO_r$$
$$= DD_{wr} - \text{(marginal prime cost)} \, DO_r$$
$$= DP.$$

Hence

$$DDwr = I/(I - e_{or}) \cdot DP_r$$

121 For, since $D_{wr} = P_{wr} O_r$, we have

$$I = P_{wr} \cdot dO_r/dD_{wr} + O_r \cdot dPwr/dD_{wr}$$
$$= e_{or} - N_r f''(N_r) e_{or}/\{f'(N_r)\}^2 P_{wr}$$

122 For, since $P = P_w$. W and $D = D_w$. W, we have

$$DP = W.DP_w + P/W \cdot DW$$
$$= W.e'_D \cdot P_w/D_w \cdot DD_w + P/W \cdot DW$$
$$= e'_D \cdot P/D \cdot DD \, (DD - D/W \cdot DW) + P/W \cdot DD$$
$$= e'_p \cdot P/D \cdot DD + DW \cdot P/W \cdot (I - e'_p),$$

so that

$$e_p = DDP/PDD = e'_p + D/PDD \cdot VW.P/W \cdot (I - e'_r)$$
$$= É'_p + E_W (I - É'_V)$$
$$= I - E_O (I - E_W).$$

123 This is not identical with the usual definition, but it seems to me to embody what is significant in the idea.

124 Some further discussion of the above topic is to be found in my *Treatise on Money,* Book IV.

125 *Cf.* Chapter 17 above.

126 *Cf.* the nineteenth-century saying, quoted by Bagehot, that "John Bull can stand many things, but he cannot stand 2 percent."

127 It is often convenient in contexts where there is no room for misunderstanding to write "the marginal efficiency of capital," where "the schedule of the marginal efficiency of capital" is meant.

128 I have shown above (Chapter 12) that, although the private investor is seldom himself directly responsible for new investment, nevertheless the entrepreneurs, who are directly responsible, will find it financially advantageous, and often unavoidable, to fall in with the ideas of the market, even though they themselves are better instructed.

129 Some part of the discussion in my *Treatise on Money,* Book IV, bears upon the above.

130 On certain assumptions, however, as the distribution of the propensity to consume through time, investment which yielded a negative return might be advantageous in the sense that, for the community as a whole, it would maximize satisfaction.

131 See below (p. 327) for some arguments which can be urged on the other side. For, if we are precluded from making large changes in our present methods, I should agree that to raise the rate of interest during a boom may be, in conceivable circumstances, the lesser evil.

132 *Vide* his *Industry and Trade,* Appendix D; *Money, Credit and Commerce,* p. 130; and *Principles of Economics,* Appendix 1.

133 His view of them is well summed up in a footnote to the first edition of his *Principles,* p. 51: "Much study has been given both in England and Germany to medieval opinions as to the relation of money to national wealth. On the whole they are to be regarded as confused through want of a clear understanding of the functions of money, rather than as *wrong* in consequence of a deliberate assumption that the increase in the net wealth of a nation can be effected only by an increase of the stores of the precious metals in her."

134 *The Nation and the Athenaeum,* November 24, 1923.

135 The remedy of an elastic wage-unit, so that a depression is met by a reduction of wages, is liable, for the same reason, to be a means of benefiting ourselves at the expense of our neighbors.

136 Experience since the age of Solon at least, and probably, if we had the statistics, for many centuries before that, indicates what a knowledge of human nature would lead us to expect, namely, that there is a steady tendency for the wage-unit to rise over long periods of time and that it can be reduced only amidst the decay and dissolution

of economic society. Thus, apart altogether from progress and increasing population, a gradually increasing stock of money has proved imperative.

137 They are the more suitable for my purpose because Prof. Heckscher is himself an adherent, on the whole, of the classical theory and much less sympathetic to the mercantilist theories than I am. Thus there is no risk that his choice of quotations has been biased in any way by a desire to illustrate their wisdom.

138 Heckscher, *Mercantilism,* vol. ii. pp. 200, 201, very slightly abridged.

139*Some Considerations of the Consequences of the Lowering of Interest and Raising the Value of Money,* 1692, but written some years previously.

140 He adds: "not barely on the quantity of money but the quickness of its circulation".

141 "Use" being, of course, old-fashioned English for "interest".

142 Hume a little later had a foot and a half in the classical world. For Hume began the practice amongst economists of stressing the importance of the equilibrium position as compared with the ever-shifting transition towards it, though he was still enough of a mercantilist not to overlook the fact that it is in the transition that we actually have our being: "It is only in this interval or intermediate situation, between the acquisition of money and a rise of prices, that the increasing quantity of gold and silver is favorable to industry.... It is of no manner of consequence, with regard to the domestic happiness of a state, whether money be in a greater or less quantity. The good policy of the magistrate consists only in keeping it, if possible, still increasing; because by that means he keeps alive a spirit of industry in the nation, and increases the state of labor in which consists all real power and riches. A nation, whose money decreases, is actually, at that time, weaker and more miserable than another nation, which possesses no more money but is on the increasing trend," (Essay *On Money,* 1752).

143 It illustrates the completeness with which the mercantilist view, that interest means interest on money (the view which is, as it now seems to me, indubitably correct), has dropt out, that Prof. Heckscher, as a good classical economist, sums up his account of Locke's theory with the comment—"Locke's argument would be irrefutable. . . if interest really were synonymous with the price for the loan of money; as this is not so, it is entirely irrelevant" (*op. cit.* vol. ii. p. 204).

144 Heckscher, *op. cit.* vol. ii. pp. 210, 211.

145 Heckscher, *op. cit.* vol. ii. p. 228.

146 Heckscher, *op. cit.* vol. ii. p. 235.

147 Heckscher, *op. cit.* vol. ii. p. 122.

148 Heckscher, *op. cit.* vol. ii. p. 223.

149 Heckscher, *op. cit.* vol. ii. p. 178.

150 "*Within* the state, mercantilism pursued thoroughgoing dynamic ends. But the important thing is that this was bound up with a static conception of the total economic resources in the world; for this it was that created that fundamental disharmony which sustained the endless commercial wars. . . . This was the tragedy of mercantilism. Both the Middle Ages with their universal static ideal and *laissez-faire* with its universal dynamic ideal avoided this consequence" (Heckscher, *op. cit.* vol. ii. pp. 25, 26).

151 The consistent appreciation of this truth by the International Labor Office, first under Albert Thomas and subsequently under Mr. H. B. Butler, has stood out conspicuously amongst the pronouncements of the numerous post-war international bodies.

152 Heckscher, *op. cit.* vol. ii. p. 176-7.

153 *op. cit.* vol. ii. p. 335.

154 *In his Letter to Adam Smith appended to his Defence of Usury.*

155 *Wealth of Nations, Book II, chap. 4.*

156 Having started to quote Bentham in this contest, I must remind the reader of his finest passage: "The career of art, the great road which receives the footsteps of projectors, may be considered as a vast, and perhaps unbounded, plain, bestrewed with gulphs, such as Curtius was swallowed up in. Each requires a human victim to fall into it ere it can close, but when it once closes, it closes to open no more, and so much of the path is safe to those who follow,"

157 Born near the Luxembourg frontier of a German father and a French mother.

158 Gesell differed from George in recommending the payment of compensation when the land is nationalized.

159 *The Natural Economic Order*, pp. 297 *et seq.*

160 Heckscher, *op. cit.* vol. ii. p. 208.

161- *Op. cit.* vol. ii. p. 290.

162 *Op. cit.* vol. ii. p. 291.

163 *Op. cit.* vol. ii. p. 209.

164 In his *History of English Thought in the Eighteenth Century* Stephen wrote (p. 197) in speaking of "the fallacy made celebrated by Mandeville" that "the complete confutation of it lies in the doctrine—so rarely understood that its complete apprehension is, perhaps, the best test of an economist—that demand for commodities is not demand for labor".

165 Compare Adam Smith, the forerunner of the classical school, who wrote, "What is prudence in the conduct of every private family can scarce be folly in that of a great Kingdom"—probably with reference to the above passage from Mandeville.

166 *Essays in Biography*, pp. 139-47.

167 A letter from Malthus to Ricardo, dated July 7, 1821.

168 A letter from Malthus to Ricardo, dated July 16, 1821.

169 Preface to Malthus's *Principles of Political Economy*, pp. 8, 9.

170 Malthus's *Principles of Political Economy*, p. 363, footnote.

171 J. S. Mill, *Political Economy*, Book I. chapter v. There is a most important and penetrating discussion of this aspect of Mill's theory in Mummery and Hobson's *Physiology of Industry*, pp. 38 *et seq.*, and, in particular, of his doctrine (which Marshall, in his very unsatisfactory discussion of the Wages-Fund Theory, endeavored to explain away) that "a demand for commodities is not a demand for labor".

172 "The Victorians and Investment," *Economic History*, 1936.

173 Fullarton's tract *On the Regulation of Currencies* (1844) is the most interesting of his references.

174 J. M. Robertson's *The Fallacy of Saving*, published in 1892, supported the heresy of Mummery and Hobson. But it is not a book of much value or significance, being entirely lacking in the penetrating intuitions of *The Physiology of Industry*.

175 In an address called "Confessions of an Economic Heretic," delivered before the London Ethical Society at Conway Hall on Sunday, July 14, 1935. I reproduce it here by Mr. Hobson's permission.

176 *Hobson had written disrespectfully in The Physiology of Industry*, p. 26: "Thrift is the source of national wealth, and the more thrifty a nation is the more wealthy it becomes. Such is the common teaching of almost all economists; many of them assume a tone of ethical dignity a) they plead the infinite value of thrift; this note alone in all their dreary song has caught the favor of the public ear."

177 Hobson and Mummery, *Physiology of Industry*, pp. iii-v.

178 Hobson and Mummery, *Physiology of Industry*, p. vi.

179 *Op. cit.* p. ix.

180 *Op. cit.* p. 27.

181 *Op. cit.* pp. 50, 51.

182 *Op. cit.* p. 69.

183 *Op. cit.* p. 113.

184 *Op. cit.* p. 100.

185 *Op. cit.* p. 101.

186 *Op. cit.* p. 79.

187 *Op. cit.* p. 117.

188 *Op. cit.* p. 130.

189 Hobson and Mummery, *Physiology of Industry*, p. 131.

A Chronological Listing of Recommended Texts

David Hume, *An Enquiry Regarding the Principle of Morals* (1751)

Adam Smith, *The Theory of Moral Sentiments* (1759)

Jeremy Bentham, *A Defense of Usury* (1787)

Jean-Baptiste Say, *A Treatie on Political Economy* (1803)

Robert Owen, *Observations on the Effect of the Manufacturing System* (1815)

Jane Haldimand Marcet, *Conversations on Political Economy, In Which the Elements of the Science Are Familiarly Explained* (1816)

Harriet Martineau, *Illustrations of Political Economy, Taxation, Poor Laws and Paupers* (1834)

Thomas Tooke, *A History of Prices* (1840)

John Stuart Mill, *Principles of Political Economy* (1848)

Claude Frederic Bastiat, *The Law* (1850)

Karl Marx, *Capital* (1864)

William Stanley Jevons, *Theory of Political Economy* (1871)

J. E. Cairnes, *Some Leading Principles of Political Economy Newly Expounded* (1874)

Henry George, *Progress and Poverty* (1879)

Francis Beaufort (Ysidro) Edgeworth, *Mathematical Psychics* (1881)

Alfred Marshall, *Principles of Economics* (1890)

Joseph Schumpeter, *Theory of Economic Development: An Inquiry into Profits, Capital, Credit, Interest and the Business Cycle* (1911)

John Hobson, *Work and Wealth: A Human Valuation* (1914)

Adolph Lowe, *Economics and Sociology* (1935)

F.A. Hayek, *The Road to Serfdom* (1944)

Ludwig von Mises, *Human Action* (1949)

Robert L. Heilbroner, *The Worldly Philosophers* (1953)

John Kenneth Galbraith, *The Affluent Society* (1958)

Jane Jacobs, *Death and Life of Great American Cities* (1961)

Milton Friedman, *Capitalism and Freedom* (1962)

E.F. Schumacher, *Small Is Beautiful* (1974)

Jude Thaddeus Wanniski, *The Way the World Works* (1978)

Arthur Laffer, *Supply Side Economics: Financial Decision-Making for the 80s* (1983)

Murray Rothbard, *Man, Economy and State* (1993)

Jean-Jacques Laffont and David Martimort, *The Theory of Incentives: The Principal-Agent Model (2001)*

Joseph E. Stiglitz, *Globalization and Its Discontents* (2002)

INDEX

A

B

C

F

Fable of the Bees, 1427-1429
factor cost, 1247, 1261
family, 65, 666, 675-676
famine, 8, 654, 656-658, 674, 686, 693
fashion, 1122-1131
Fisher, Irving, 1305-1306, 1425
fluctuations, 1366-1367, 1403, 1406
food, 118, 131, 158, 663
   price of, 655-656, 678, 739
   production of, 8, 72-73, 118, 654, 659, 662-663, 664-665, 679, 706-707
Franklin, Benjamin, 654
free trade. See trade, free.
Friedman, Milton, 1047, 1233
furniture, 1106

G

gentility, 1071-1072, 1081-1082
Gesell, Silvio, 1424-1427
Godwin, William, 654, 659, 662, 703-735
gold, 42, 43, 149, 161-165, 295-308, 932-934, 1300-1301, 1359, 1422
Good Time Coming, The (song), 976
goods, 1058-1061, 1104-1121
governments, 243, 1289, 1367
   assistance to the poor, 656
   expenses of, 475-558
   interventions and spending of, 9, 11-12, 244-245, 899, 1229, 1230, 1232, 1282, 1284, 1285-1286, 1288, 1292, 1294, 1300-1301, 1318, 1326, 1406, 1410, 1413, 1423, 1437, 1439-1442
   regulation by, 114-115, 312-317
   revenue of, 559-652
   See also taxes and taxation.
Grant, Duncan, 1229
Great Depression, 1228, 1230-1231, 1232, 1239, 1285-1286
greed, 21
green revolution, 657-658

H

habits, 1094-1098, 1099
Hayek, F. A., 1265, 1334
Heckscher, Eli F., 1418, 1420,
Hitler, Adolph, 1229, 1230
Hobson, J. A., 1431-1435

O

output,1234-1235, 1237, 1249, 1255
  See also labor; production.
ownership, individual, 1057-1060, 1053-1054, 1070-1071, 1099-1100, 1141

P

parks, 1107-1109
peace, effect on economy, 884-886, 1441
pecuniary emulation. See emulation, pecuniary.
penalties, 1100
philanthropy, 1152
philosophy, moral, 17, 18, 19
Physiology of Industry, The, 1431-1434
Pierce, Charles Sanders, 1044
Pigou, A. C., 1241, 1245, 1253-1254
Pitt, William, 657, 682, 692
political economy, 294
Political Economy Club, 654, 760
Poor Laws (England), 656, 677-683, 692, 803-804
population, 8, 15, 66-67, 73, 130, 653, 654-656, 659, 663, 664, 665, 669, 673-676, 684-686, 687-693, 746-752
post offices, 560
potatoes, 693
poverty, 1250, 1298-1299
priests. See clergy.
primogeniture, 269-270
Principles of Economics, 1331-1333
Principles of Political Economy, 1333-1334
printers, 1087-1088
privacy, 1097
production, 896, 941, 1261-1262
  See also labor; output.
profit, 55, 83, 805-814, 896, 898
public works and institutions, 496-519, 1299

R

religion, 1100-1102, 1180-1196
  instruction, 538-556
rent, 44, 53, 59, 63, 116-139, 187, 784-791, 839-840, 843-847, 912-917, 949-962, 1437-1439
reproduction, 9
resources, raw, 21, 830-838, 1413
  See also agriculture; commodities.
returns, law of diminishing, 760
revenue. See income and revenue.